Proceedings

Sixteenth National Conference on
Artificial Intelligence (AAAI-99)

Eleventh Innovative Applications of
Artificial Intelligence Conference (IAAI-99)

Yaxin Liu

AAAI PRESS/THE MIT PRESS

MENLO PARK, CALIFORNIA • CAMBRIDGE, MASSACHUSETTS • LONDON, ENGLAND

Distributed by The MIT Press, Massachusetts Institute of Technology, Cambridge, Massachusetts and London, England.

ISBN 0-262-51106-1

Printed on acid-free paper in the United States of America

Contents

AAAI-99 Technical Papers

Agents

AI & the World Wide Web

Cognitive Systems

Constraint Satisfaction Problems

Hybrid Methods

Knowledge Acquisition

Knowledge Representation

Learning

Model-Based Reasoning

Natural Language and Information Retrieval

Planning

Robotics

Satisfiability

Innovative Applications of Artificial Intelligence Papers

Deployed Applications

Emerging Applications

AAAI-99 Intelligent Systems Demos

Robot Competition and Exhibition

1999 SIGART/AAAI Doctoral Consortium

Student Abstracts

Invited Talk

AAAI Organization

Officers

AAAI President
David L. Waltz, *NEC Research Institute, Inc.*

AAAI President-Elect
Bruce G. Buchanan, *University of Pittsburgh*

Past President
Randall Davis, *Massachusetts Institute of Technology*

Secretary-Treasurer
Norman R. Nielsen, *SRI International*

Councilors

(through 1999):
Jon Doyle, *Massachusetts Institute of Technology*
Leslie Pack Kaelbling, *Brown University*
Mel Montemerlo, *NASA*
Edwina Rissland, *University of Massachusetts*

(through 2000):
Jan Aikins, *Sun Microsystems*
Bonnie Dorr, *University of Maryland*
Eric Horvitz, *Microsoft Corporation*
Stuart Russell, *University of California, Berkeley*

(through 2001):
Henry Kautz, *AT&T Labs–Research*
David McAllester, *AT&T Labs –Research*
Johanna Moore, *University of Pittsburgh*
Michael P. Wellman, *University of Michigan*

Standing Committees

Conference Chair
Paul Rosenbloom, *University of Southern California*

Fellows/Nominating Chair
Randall Davis, *Massachusetts Institute of Technology*

Finance Chair
Norman R. Nielsen, *SRI International*

Publications Chair
Kenneth Ford, *University of West Florida and NASA Ames Research Center*

Scholarship Chair
Katia Sycara, *Carnegie Mellon University*

Symposium Chair
Ian Horswill, *Northwestern University*

Symposium Cochair
Daniel Clancy, *NASA Ames Research Center*

Symposium Associate Chair
Leslie Pack Kaelbling, *Brown University*

Workshop Grants Chair
Jan Aikins, *Sun Microsystems*

AI Magazine

Editor
David Leake, *Indiana University*

Editor Emeritus
Robert Engelmore, *Stanford University*

Associate Editor, Workshop Reports
Peter Patel-Schneider, *Bell Labs Research*

AAAI Press

Editor-in-Chief,
Kenneth Ford, *University of West Florida and NASA Ames Research Center*

Management Board
Kenneth Ford, *University of West Florida*
Robert Prior, Liaison, *The MIT Press*
Carol McKenna Hamilton, *Executive Director, AAAI*

Editorial Board
Kenneth Ford, *University of West Florida and NASA Ames Research Center*
Ken Forbus, *Northwestern University*
Pat Hayes, *University of West Florida*
Janet Kolodner, *Georgia Institute of Technology*
George Luger, *University of New Mexico*
Robert Morris, *Florida Institute of Technology*
Alain Rappaport, *Neuron Data*
Brian Williams, *NASA Ames Research Center*

AAAI & IAAI Conference Program Committees

Conference Chairs

AAAI-99 Program Cochairs
Jim Hendler, *University of Maryland & DARPA/ISO*
Devika Subramanian, *Rice University*

AAAI-99 Associate Program Cochairs
Henry Kautz, *AT&T Labs –Research*
Bruce Porter, *University of Texas, Austin*

AAAI-99 Assistant Program Chair
Vibhu Mittal, *Just Research & Carnegie Mellon University*

IAAI-99 Chair
Ramasamy Uthurusamy, *General Motors Research*

IAAI-99 Cochair
Barbara Hayes-Roth, *Extempo Systems, Inc.*

Intelligent Systems Demonstrations Chair
George Ferguson, *University of Rochester*

Mobile Robot Competition and Exhibition Chair
Alan C. Schultz, *Naval Research Lab*

Robot Contest Subchair
Lisa Meeden, *Swarthmore College*

Robot Exhibit Subchairs
Karen Zita Haigh, *Honeywell Technology Center*
Marc Böhlen, *Carnegie Mellon University*

Robot Challenge Subchair
Tucker Balch, *Carnegie Mellon University*

Robot Building Laboratory Chair
David Miller, *KISS Institute for Practical Robotics*

SIGART/AAAI-99 Doctoral Consortium Chair
Janyce Wiebe, *New Mexico State University*

Student Abstract and Poster Chair
Sven Koenig, *Georgia Institute of Technology*

Student Volunteer Coordinator
Thomas Haynes, *Wichita State University*

Tutorial Chair
Bart Selman, *Cornell University*

Workshop Chair and Cochair
David Leake, *Indiana University*
Marie desJardins, *SRI International*

AAAI-99 Senior Program Committee

Craig Boutilier, *University of British Columbia*
James Crawford, *i2 Technologies*
Ken Forbus, *Northwestern University*
Lee Giles, *NEC Research Institute*
Russell Greiner, *University of Alberta*
Julia Hirschberg, *AT&T Labs –Research*
Leslie Kaelbling, *Brown University*
Henry Kautz, *AT&T Labs*
Daphne Koller, *Stanford University*
Kurt Konolige, *SRI International*
David McAllester, *AT&T Labs –Research*
Vibhu Mittal, *Just Research & Carnegie Mellon University*
Leora Morgenstern, *IBM T.J. Watson Research Center*
Pandurang Nayak, *RIACS/NASA Ames Research Center*
Gregory Piatetsky-Shapiro, *Knowledge Stream Partners*
Bruce Porter, *University of Texas*
Lee Spector, *Hampshire College*
Lynn Andrea Stein, *Massachusetts Institute of Technology*
Ron Sun, *NEC Research Institute and University of Alabama*
Milind Tambe, *University of Southern California*
Sebastian Thrun, *Carnegie Mellon University*
Manuela Veloso, *Carnegie Mellon University*
Daniel Weld, *University of Washington*

AAAI-99 Program Committee

Fahiem Bacchus, *University of Waterloo*
Tucker Balch, *Carnegie Mellon University*
Chitta Baral, *University of Texas at El Paso*
Rachel Ben-Eliyahu-Zohary, *Ben-Gurion University*
Hamid Berenji, *IIS Corp/NASA Ames Research Center*
Gautam Biswas, *Stanford University*
Avrim Blum, *Carnegie Mellon University*
Mark Boddy, *Honeywell Technology Center*
Daniel Borrajo, *Universidad Carlos III de Madrid*
Ronen Brafman, *Ben-Gurion University*
Eric Brill, *Johns Hopkins University*
Carla Brodley, *Purdue University*

Wolfram Burgard, *University of Bonn*
Marco Cadoli, *Universitá di Roma*
Jennifer Chu-Carroll, *Lucent Technologies Bell Labs*
Dan Clancy, *NASA Ames Research Center*
Christian Darken, *Siemens Corporate Research*
Adnan Darwiche, *Rockwell Science Center*
Ernie Davis, *New York University*
Johan de Kleer, *Xerox PARC*
Kenneth DeJong, *George Mason University*
Pedro Domingos, *Instituto Superior Tecnico*
Denise Draper, *Harlequin, Inc.*
Oskar Dressler
Didier Dubois, *IRIT-CNRS, Toulouse*
Gregory Dudek, *McGill University*
Charles Elkan, *Harvard University*
Matt Evett, *Florida Atlantic University*
Adam Farquhar, *Schlumberger*
Tom Fawcett, *Bell Atlantic Science and Technology*
Claude Fennema, *Mount Holyoke College*
Dieter Fox, *Carnegie Mellon University*
Nir Friedman, *Hebrew University of Jerusalem*
Hector Geffner, *Universidad Simon Bolivar*
Bob Givan, *Purdue University*
Keith Golden, *NASA Ames Research Center*
Robert Goldman, *Honeywell Technology Center*
Marco Gori, *Universita di Siena*
Benjamin Grosof, *IBM T.J. Watson Research Center*
Andrew Haas, *State University of New York, Albany*
Peter Haddawy, *University of Wisconsin, Milwaukee*
Karen Haigh, *Honeywell Technology Center*
Milos Hauskrecht, *Brown University*
Robert Holte, *University of Ottawa*
Vasant Honavar, *Iowa State University*
Ian Horswill, *Northwestern University*
Adele Howe, *Colorado State University*
Charles Isbell, *AT&T Labs –Research*
Tommi Jaakkola, *Massachusetts Institute of Technology*
David Jensen, *University of Massachusetts, Amherst*
Froudald Kabanza, *Universite de Sherbrooke*
Hiroaki Kitano, *Sony Computer Science Laboratory*
Kenneth Koedinger, *Carnegie Mellon University*
David Kortenkamp, *Metrica Inc.*
Deepak Kumar, *Bryn Mawr College*
Nicholas Kushmerick, *University College Dublin*
John Lafferty, *Carnegie Mellon University*
Yann LeCun, *AT&T Labs - Research*
Alon Levy, *University of Washington*
Diane Litman, *AT&T Labs –Research*
Michael Littman, *Duke University*
Ron Loui, *Washington University*
Maja Mataric, *University of Southern California*
Sheila McIlraith, *Stanford University*
Lisa Meeden, *Swarthmore College*
Christopher Meek, *Microsoft Research*
Nicolas Meuleau, *Brown University*
Risto Miikkulainen, *The University of Texas at Austin*
Hector Munoz-Avila, *University of Maryland*
Robin Murphy, *University of South Florida*

Tom Murray, *University of Massachusetts and Hampshire College, Amherst*
Nicola Muscettola, *RECOM Technologies/NASA Ames Research Center*
Dana Nau, *University of Maryland*
David Page, *University of Louisville*
Andrew Parkes, *University of Oregon*
Ronald Parr, *Stanford University*
Mark Peot, *Rockwell Science Center and Duke University*
Avi Pfeffer, *Stanford University*
Rosalind Picard, *Massachusetts Institute of Technology*
David Poole, *University of British Columbia*
Greg Provan, *Rockwell Science Center*
Foster Provost, *Bell Atlantic Science and Technology*
Tuomas Sandholm, *Washington University*
Jonathan Schaeffer, *University of Alberta*
Torsten Schaub, *University of Potsdam*
Hinrich Schuetze, *Xerox Corporation*
Alan Schultz, *Naval Research Laboratory*
Dale Schuurmans, *University of Waterloo*
Bart Selman, *Cornell University*
Sandip Sen, *University of Tulsa*
Moninder Singh, *IBM Thomas J. Watson Research Center*
David E. Smith, *NASA Ames Research Center*
Stephen Smith, *Carnegie Mellon University*
Reinhard Stolle, *Stanford University*
Dan Suthers, *University of Hawaii*
Rich Sutton, *AT&T Labs–Research*
Katia Sycara, *Carnegie Mellon University*
Rich Thomason, *University of Michigan*
Peter van Beek, *University of Alberta*
Pascal Van Hentenryck, *Université Catholique de Louvain*
K. Vijay-Shanker, *University of Delaware*
Darrell Whitley, *Colorado State University*
Mary-Anne Williams, *Newcastle University*
M. J. Wooldridge, *Queen Mary & Westfield College*
Ronald Yager, *Iona College*
Nevin Zhang, *Hong Kong University of Science & Technology*
Shlomo Zilberstein, *University of Massachusetts*
Jan Zytkow, *UNC Charlotte*

1999 Auxiliary Reviewers

Steven Abney
Srinivas Bangalore
Chumki Basu
Yngvi Bjornsson
Sviatoslav Brainov
Bob Carpenter
Jennifer Casper
Anna Helena Reali Costa
Goksel Dedeoglu
Frank Dellaert
Thuong Doan
Oskar Dressler
Mark Flick
Lenny Foner
Jeremy Frank

Marc Friedman
Aaron Gage
Christopher Geib
Brian Gerkey
Dani Goldberg
Vu Ha
Eric Hansen
Andreas Herzig
Haym Hirsh
Rune Jensen
Andreas Junghanns
John Langford
Stan Matwin
Kathleen McCoy
Laurent Michel
Tom Minka
Abdel-Illah Mouaddib
Todd Neller
Hien Nguyen
Monica Nicolescu
Rachel Pottinger
Owen Rambow
Marie-Christine Rousset
Nicholas Roy
Erik Selberg
Eyal Solomon Shimony
Amit Singhal
Ellen Spertus
Deborah Strahman
Will Uther
Thomas Wagner
Barry Werger

IAAI-99 Program Committee

Bruce G. Buchanan, *University of Pittsburgh*
Robert S. Engelmore, *Stanford University*
Barbara Hayes-Roth, *Extempo Systems Inc.*
Philip Klahr, *TriVida Corporation*
Alain Rappaport
Charles Rosenberg, *Carnegie Mellon University*
Ted Senator, *National Association of Securities Dealers*
Howard E. Shrobe, *Massachusetts Institute of Technology*
Reid Smith, *Schlumberger Limited*
Ramasamy Uthurusamy, *General Motors Research*
Marilyn Walker, *AT&T Labs–Research*

AAAI–99 Outstanding Paper Award

This year, AAAI's National Conference on Artificial Intelligence honors one paper that exemplifies the highest standards in technical contribution and exposition. During the blind review process, members of the Program Committee recommended papers to consider for the Outstanding Paper Award. A subset of the Senior Program Committee, carefully chosen to avoid conflicts of interest, reviewed all these papers and selected the winning paper:

PROVERB: The Probabilistic Cruciverbalist

Greg A. Keim, Noam M. Shazeer, Michael L. Littman, Sushant Agarwal,
Catherine M. Cheves, Joseph Fitzgerald, Jason Grosland, Fan Jiang,
Shannon Pollard and Karl Weinmeister
Duke University

AAAI–99 Sponsoring Organizations

American Association for Artificial Intelligence

ACM/SIGART

Defense Advance Research Projects Agency

Microsoft Corporation

Naval Research Laboratory

Office of Naval Research

NASA Ames Research Center

National Science Foundation

Rent-a-Computer

Preface

AAAI–99

The National Conference on Artificial Intelligence is the pre-eminent American AI conference. It provides a unique forum for timely interaction and communication among researchers and practitioners from *all* areas of AI. As in previous years, the papers chosen for inclusion reflect the best of our field and provide a unique snapshot of the exciting new areas and maturing sub-disciplines of our young field. In this short introduction, we will point out key trends in this, the last year of this century.

Based on the papers submitted, we see that the most active areas of our field include topics that have been around since the early days, and others that are newly emerging. The former category includes some of the key AI subdisciplines, particularly knowledge representation, machine learning, and planning. Newer areas generating many submissions included multi-agent systems and reasoning under uncertainty. In addition, we have seen an increase in the number of submissions from the mobile robotics and statistical natural language processing communities.

To combat the perceived balkanization of the different sub-areas in AI over the last few years, we made a very special effort to attract top-notch, task-oriented research that crossed traditional subarea boundaries, and that addressed issues in the design of integrated intelligences. We are delighted to highlight *Proverb: The Probabilistic Cruciverbalist* by Michael Littman and his students at Duke University, which was unanimously chosen by the best paper committee as this year's outstanding paper winner. Proverb, a system that solves New York *Times* style crossword puzzles at the level of a good human is a *tour-de-force* integration of the best ideas in constraint solving, machine learning, uncertain reasoning, and information retrieval.

The 109 papers in this volume were selected out of 400 submissions by a rigorous double-blind review process. Each paper was carefully assigned to a supervising member of the Senior Program Committee and to three members of the AAAI-99 Program Committee. Selecting the best reviewers for each paper is the key to obtaining high-quality reviews and accepting the best submissions, and Vibhu Mittal and Ramesh Patil deserve special credit for developing software to make this monumental task manageable. In addition, Henry Kautz and Bruce Porter, cochairs of AAAI-2000, provided invaluable assistance in the paper sorting and reviewer assignment process. Carol Hamilton and the entire AAAI staff (especially Mary Beth Jensen, Rick Skalsky and the proceedings staff, Mike Hamilton, Daphne Black-Sdun, and Jhossy Quezada), deserve special appreciation from the AI community for meeting a grueling schedule and managing huge volumes of papers, reports and requests.

We are excited by the excellence of the papers in this volume. These papers contribute immensely to our understanding of how we can imbue computers with ever increasingly complex behaviors. As chairs, we feel most strongly that Artificial Intelligence has been, and will continue to be, one of the most exciting areas of pursuit in modern science. We thank the community for giving us this opportunity to help contribute to the growth of this important field.

James Hendler & Devika Subramanian

IAAI–99

The Eleventh Annual Conference on Innovative Applications of Artificial Intelligence (IAAI-99) continues the IAAI tradition of case studies of deployed applications with measurable benefits whose value depends on the use of AI technology. In addition, IAAI-99 augments these case studies with papers and invited talks that address emerging areas of AI technology or applications. IAAI is organized as an independent program within the National Conference, with schedules coordinated to allow attendees to move freely between IAAI and National Conference sessions. IAAI and the National Conference are jointly sponsoring several invited talks that fit the theme of both programs.

AI applications developers benefit from learning about new AI techniques that will enable the next generation of applications. Basic AI research will benefit by learning about challenges of real-world domains and difficulties and successes in applying AI techniques to real business problems. IAAI-99 will address the full range of AI techniques including knowledge-based systems, natural language, and vision.

IAAI-99 showcases the deployed applications on the first day. The papers are case studies that provide a valuable guide to designing, building, managing, and deploying systems incorporating AI technologies. These applications provide clear evidence of the impact and value that AI technology has in today's world.

Papers in the Emerging Applications and Technologies track describe efforts whose goal is the engineering of AI applications. They inform AI researchers about the utility of specific AI techniques for applications domains and also inform applications developers about tools and techniques that will enable the next generation of new and more powerful applications.

This year's papers address applications in education, the military, networking, spacecraft, medicine, games, the stock market, and more. AI techniques include, among others, planning, natural language processing, diagnostic reasoning, and cognitive simulation.

Ramasamy Uthurusamy & Barbara Hayes-Roth

Invited Talks

IT**2: Information Technology Initiative for the Twenty-First Century

Ruzena Bajcsy, Assistant Director of CISE, National Science Foundation

This presentation has two parts: The first part explains what this Initiative is all about. We will describe the history, how it evolved, what are the supporting arguments and what are its goals. The second part presents the NSF specific plan for this Initiative. We shall elaborate on the scientific content of this program, pose some open questions and outline the path of how we plan to achieve the goals. We shall discuss the identity of Computer Science as a scientific discipline and the consequences for funding. Finally, we shall speculate about the future of our discipline and the challenges stemming from it.

Game Playing: The Next Moves

Susan L. Epstein, Hunter College and The Graduate School of The City University of New York
(An extended abstract of this talk is included at the end of this Proceedings.)

As people do it, game playing addresses critical AI issues: learning, planning, resource allocation, and the integration of multiple streams of knowledge. Epstein highlights recent developments in game playing, describes some cognitively-oriented work, and poses three new challenge problems for the AI community.

Thinking on our Feet: Wearable Computing and Artificial Intelligence

Steven K. Feiner, Columbia University

As computers decrease in size and increase in power, they are beginning to move off our desks and onto our bodies to become wearable. Wearability implies a host of important properties that distinguish wearable computing from desktop and laptop computing (S. Mann, Smart Clothing: The Wearable Computer and Wearcam, *Personal Technologies,* 1(1), March 1997, 21-27; B. Rhodes, The Wearable Remembrance Agent: A System for Augmented Memory, *Personal Technologies,* 1(4), December 1997, 218-224; T. Starner, Wearable Computing and Contextual Awareness, Ph.D dissertation, Program in Media Arts and Sciences, Massachusetts Institute of Technology, Cambridge, Mass., June 1999). These include mobility, which ideally allows the wearer to use the system both indoors and outdoors; intimacy, which makes it possible to sense the wearer's body and present information privately; context sensitivity, which takes into account the continually changing environment experienced as the wearer moves about; and constancy, which encourages the permeation of the user interface into much of the wearer's activities, even when she is not actively "computing."

I will describe research in developing wearable user interfaces that mix different displays and interaction devices, and will discuss some of the ways that these user interfaces can exploit AI techniques. Our approach to wearability is based on *augmented reality,* in which a synthesized virtual world is overlaid on and registered with the surrounding real world. Our audiovisual augmented reality is presented using a see-through head-worn display and earphones whose position and orientation are tracked. In our outdoor augmented reality testbed (S. Feiner, B. MacIntyre, T. Hoellerer, and A. Webster, A Touring Machine: Prototyping 3D Mobile Augmented Reality Systems for Exploring the Urban Environment, *Personal Technologies,* 1(4), December 1997, 208–217), we use real-time kinematic differential GPS for position tracking, and inertial and magnetometer trackers for orientation tracking. A hand-held display with stylus input complements the head-worn display. Opportunities for applying AI techniques in such systems include hybrid tracking, fusing vision with other sensors; user and context modeling, perceptual user interfaces, and location-aware user interfaces, to adapt the system to the wearer and context; multimodal input and output, coordinating the use of speech, graphics, sound, gesture, and haptics; and knowledge representation and reasoning strategies that address the rich set of available sensory data. The goal is to create user interfaces that meet the changing needs of the wearer, without continually requiring the undivided attention and low-level interaction demanded by conventional desktop applications.

How Common Sense Might Work

Kenneth D. Forbus, Northwestern University

This talk describes how a combination of analogical and first-principles reasoning, relying heavily on qualitative representations, might provide a computational model of common sense reasoning. Forbus discusses the psychological and computational support for this approach, and illustrates how it can be used in building new kinds of multimodal interfaces and educational software.

AI and Space Exploration: Where No Machine Has Gone Before

Kenneth M. Ford, Institute for Human and Machine Cognition, University of West Florida, and NASA Ames Research Center

Humans are quintessentially explorers and makers of things. These traits, which identify us as a species and account for our survival, are reflected with particular clarity in the mission and methods of space exploration. The romance associated with the Apollo project is being replaced with a different vision, one where we make tools to do our exploring for us. We are building computational machines that will carry our curiosity and intelligence with them as they extend the human exploration of the universe.

In order to succeed in places where humans could not possibly survive, these "remote agents" must take something of us with them. They must be self-reliant, smart, adaptable and curious. Our mechanical explorers cannot be merely passive observers or puppets dancing on tenuous radio tethers from earth. They simply will not have time to ask us what to do: the twin constraints of distance and light-speed would render them helpless while waiting for our instructions, even if we knew what to tell them. AI plays a central role in space exploration because there is, literally, no other way to make it work. Our bodies cannot fly in the tenuous Martian atmosphere, endure Jupiter's gravity or the electromagnetic turbulence of Saturn's rings; but our machines can, and we can send them there. Once at distant worlds, however, they must deal with the details themselves. The only thing we can do is to make them smart enough to cope with the tactics of survival.

How clever will these agents of human exploration need to be? Certainly, cleverer then we can currently make them. It will not be enough to be situated and autonomous: they will need to be intelligent and inquisitive and thoughtful and quick. NASA is committed to integrating intelligent systems into the very center of our long-range strategy to explore the universe.

In this talk, I will describe the current and future research directions of NASA's expanding information technology effort with a particular emphasis on intelligent systems.

Real-time Applications of Computer Vision: Computer Assisted Neurosurgery and Visual Monitoring of Activities

W. Eric L. Grimson, Artificial Intelligence Laboratory, Massachusetts Institute of Technology

Recent advances in computational power, coupled with constraints enforced by real-world applications, have led to two real-time vision systems: an image-guided neurosurgical system, now in daily use; and a monitoring system that learns common activity patterns by visual observation over extended periods, and automatically detects unusual events.

Decrypting the Human Genome

Jill P. Mesirov, Whitehead Institute / MIT Center for Genome Research

There has been a recent explosion in the need for computational support in molecular biology. This has been driven by new laboratory technologies which generate biological data at a more rapid pace than ever before. The exploitation of this large amount of data by biologists and medical scientists requires contributions from many areas of computer science. Mesirov will present a few key examples where computing has made a major impact in today's genomic research, and also point out some interesting opportunities for the future. The examples will be drawn both from structural genomics (determining the actual sequence of the genome) as well as functional genomics (decoding the sequence to understand gene function).

AI Rising

Nils J. Nilsson, Robotics Laboratory, Stanford University

Serious work toward artificial intelligence (AI) began about fifty years ago. In this talk I review what I think are the major milestones of our first half-century and make some guesses about what might lie ahead. In the spirit of millennial appraisals, I will survey what I think are the most important things we have learned about AI in the last fifty years. Are these lessons sufficient to produce human-level artificial intelligence within the next fifty?

Quantum Computation and AI

Lee Spector, Howard Barnum, Herbert J. Bernstein, and Nikhil Swamy, Hampshire College

Computational complexity theory underpins current discussions across the cognitive sciences in general and artificial intelligence in particular. But classical computational complexity theory does not hold for the best computational devices allowed by modern physics. According to current quantum theory, computers that are designed to exploit atomic-scale dynamics—so-called quantum computers—can compute significantly more efficiently than one would expect from classical computational complexity theory. A few examples of dramatic quantum speedups are already known.

Two of the questions driving a wave of new work in this area are, "How much more efficiently can quantum computers compute?" and "Can we really build quantum computers?"

This talk will briefly survey current thinking on these questions and then move on to a longer discussion about the relations between quantum computing and AI.

The questions on which we will focus are, "How can AI technologies advance the study of quantum computation?" and "How can quantum computers, if built, advance AI?" On the first of these there are already concrete results, and we will look in detail at one example, the use of genetic programming to find new better-than-classical quantum algorithms. Our answers to the second question are more speculative, but the possibilities—for example a quantum logic machine that could answer Prolog queries in better-than-classical time—are enticing.

Why I Am Optimistic

Patrick Henry Winston, Artificial Intelligence Laboratory, Massachusetts Institute of Technology

From the engineering perspective, artificial intelligence is a grand success. Today, most big systems are built with elements that are readily traced to research done by the field's practitioners. From the scientific perspective, however, achievements have been small, and the goal of understanding human intelligence, from a computational point of view, remains elusive.

Nevertheless, to an optimist, the current state of artificial intelligence seems analogous to that of biology in 1950: on the engineering side, antibiotics had been discovered, developed, and applauded; on the science side, many prominent biologists said the field was dead, and little more of value could be done. But then, along came Watson and Crick, and their discovery of DNA's structure launched a fifty-year period of fantastic progress.

Is artificial intelligence ready for its own analog to the discovery of DNA? Have we been looking under the wrong lamp posts? Is there a new paradigm that will revitalize the field? Or must we resign ourselves to 300 years of slow progress?

It is time to rekindle the original enthusiasm that actuated the pioneers. We should squarely, bravely, and optimistically confront the problems that block our understanding of human intelligence and prevent our construction of programs with human-level intelligence and beyond.

This time, however, we must exploit an abundance of neglected clues accumulating not only in artificial intelligence, but also in allied fields, such as systems neuroscience and developmental psychology. These clues will help us to unlock the secrets of intelligence, and likely lead to the conclusion that our sophisticated vision and language faculties are not mere I/O channels. Instead, our vision and language faculties embody powerful computational and engineering ideas that account for much of our intelligence.

AAAI–99 Technical Papers

Agents

Time-Quality Tradeoffs in Reallocative Negotiation with Combinatorial Contract Types

Martin Andersson and Tuomas Sandholm*
{mra, sandholm}@cs.wustl.edu
Department of Computer Science
Washington University
St. Louis, MO 63130-4899

Abstract

The capability to reallocate items—*e.g.* tasks, securities, bandwidth slices, Mega Watt hours of electricity, and collectibles—is a key feature in automated negotiation. Especially when agents have preferences over combinations of items, this is highly nontrivial. Marginal cost based reallocation leads to an anytime algorithm where every agent's payoff increases monotonically over time. Different contract types head toward different locally optimal allocations of items, and OCSM-contracts head toward the global optimum. Reaching it can take impractically long, so it is important to trade off solution quality against negotiation time. To construct negotiation protocols that lead to good allocations quickly, we evaluated original (O), cluster (C), swap (S), and multiagent (M) contracts experimentally. O-contracts led to the highest social welfare when the ratio of agents to tasks was large, and C-contract were best when that ratio was small. O-contracts led to the largest number of contracts made. M-contracts were slower per contract, and required a significantly larger number of contracts to be tried to verify that a local optimum had been reached. S-contracts were not competitive because they restrict the search space by keeping the number of items per agent invariant. O-contracts spread the items across agents while C-contracts and M-contracts concentrated them on a few agents.

Introduction

The importance of automated negotiation systems is increasing as a consequence of the development of technology as well as increased application pull, *e.g.*, electronic commerce (Kalakota & Whinston 1996), electricity markets (Sandholm & Ygge 1997), and transportation exchanges (Sandholm 1993). A central part of such systems is the ability to (re)allocate tasks (or analogously, other types of items, *e.g.* securities, bandwidth slices, Mega Watt hours of electricity, or collectibles) among the agents. Generally, the tasks have a dependency upon each other, as well as upon the agents. That is, some of the tasks are synergistic and preferably handled by the same agent, whereas others interact negatively and are better handled by different agents.

The agents can also have different resources that lead to different costs for handling the various tasks.[1] Furthermore, an agent may not be capable of handling all combinations of the tasks. We analyze task allocation (or, analogously, the allocation of other types of items) under the following model which captures these considerations.

Definition. 1 *Our task allocation problem is a set of tasks T, a set of agents A, a cost function $c_i : 2^T \to \Re \cup \{\infty\}$ (which states the cost that agent i incurs by handling a particular subset of tasks), and the initial allocation of tasks among agents $\langle T_1^{init}, ..., T_{|A|}^{init} \rangle$, where $\bigcup_{i \in A} T_i^{init} = T$, and $T_i^{init} \cap T_j^{init} = \emptyset$ for all $i \neq j$.[2]*

In the case where agent i cannot handle a specific set of tasks, T_i, the cost function $c_i(T_i) = \infty$. In our example problem domain the agents incur different costs for handling tasks but each agent has the capability to handle any tasks.

In task allocation, the agents try to minimize the cost functions. The same would hold for reallocation of any types of undesirable items. To model settings where the items are desirable, such as bandwidth slices, the cost functions can be interpreted as value functions which the agents attempt to maximize.

Combinatorial auctions, i.e. auctions where the bidders can bid on combinations of items, have recently received a lot of interest because they often lead to better allocations than traditional auctions in settings where the items' valuations are not additive (Rothkopf, Pekeč, & Harstad 1998; Rassenti, Smith, & Bulfin 1982). Combinatorial auctions are a special case of our setting, where one agent has all the tasks initially, and allocates them to the other agents. Unlike combinatorial auctions which are one-to-many, our setting allows many-to-many markets. This is needed in settings where there are inherently many buyers and many sellers. Our approach can also be used as a reallocative market to

---

[1] Dependencies between tasks in human negotiations are discussed e.g. in (Raiffa 1982). The concepts of linkage and log-rolling are also presented, which are similar to swapping tasks and clustering tasks.

[2] This definition generalizes the "Task Oriented Domain" presented by (Rosenschein & Zlotkin 1994). Particularly asymmetric cost functions among agents are allowed, as well as the possibility that some agents may be unable to handle some tasks. In that case the cost of handling the task will be infinite.

correct inefficient allocations after some one-to-many auction has been held. In other words, some of the bidders may not have received the (combinations of) items that they want, and may have received (combinations of) items that they do not want. The bidders can then participate in our reallocative many-to-many aftermarket to improve the overall allocation of items.

The agents can change the task allocation by reallocating tasks among themselves by contracting. The agents can also recontract out tasks that they contracted in earlier. We study agents that are *self-interested* and *myopically individually rational*. This means that an agent agrees to a contract if and only if the contract increases the agent's immediate payoff. An agent's payoff consists of the payments received from others for handling their tasks minus the current value of the cost function, c_i, minus payments sent to others for them to handle some of the former agent's tasks.

This paper experimentally studies task reallocation among such agents using combinatorial contract types that were recently introduced (Sandholm 1993; 1996; 1998) to be used in contract nets (Smith 1980). The next section presents the application domain of the experiments. The different contract types and their use is described in the following section. Then evaluation criteria are discussed and the results are presented. The final section concludes the paper.

Example problem: Multiagent TSP

We study contracting in a particular task allocation problem, the *multiagent Traveling Salesman Problem (TSP)*. This domain is used as an example because it is structurally simple—providing repeatability and easy presentability—yet it captures the essence of the difficulties in reallocative negotiation. The TSP is NP-complete and the space of task allocations contains many local optima when using hill-climbing-based contracting algorithms (Sandholm 1993; 1998).

The multiagent TSP is defined as follows (Andersson & Sandholm 1998a; 1998b). Several salesmen are going to visit several cities in a world that consists of a unit square, see Figure 1. Each city must be visited by exactly one salesman, and each salesman must return to his starting location after visiting the cities assigned to him. A salesman can visit the cities assigned to him in any order. The locations of the cities and the starting points of the salesmen are randomly chosen as is each salesman's initial assignment of cities to visit.

Agents' objectives

From this initial assignment, the salesmen can exchange cities, *i.e.* tasks, with each other. Each salesman, i.e. agent, tries to maximize his immediate payoff. The payoff of salesman i consists of the payments received from others for handling their cities, minus his distance traveled, c_i, minus payments sent to others for them to handle some of the former agent's cities.

The cost of travel between any two locations, q and r, is the Euclidean distance: $c_{qr} =$

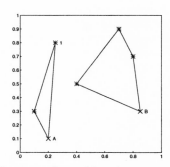

Figure 1: *An example problem instance of a multiagent TSP consisting of five cities (*) and two salesmen (X). If salesman A contracts out city 1 to salesman B, the social welfare will increase due to less travel, i.e., lower costs.*

$\sqrt{(x_q - x_r)^2 + (y_q - y_r)^2}$. The cost that salesman i incurs when visiting his cities is the sum of the costs along his tour:

$$c_i = \sum_{q,r \in \text{ tour of salesman } i} c_{qr}$$

Solution quality, social welfare, is the sum of the distances traveled by the salesmen:

$$Social\ welfare = -\sum_{i=1}^{|A|} c_i$$

The side payments do not affect social welfare because they just redistribute wealth among the agents. Since the salesmen are individually rational in giving and taking tasks and side payments, each agent's payoff improves monotonically during the negotiation. It follows that social welfare improves monotonically.

In our experiments the negotiation occurs before the salesmen are dispatched. The contracting scheme can also directly be used in dynamic settings where new tasks arrive and are handled during the negotiation. Each new domain event simply changes the cost function, c_i, of the corresponding agent.

Summary of contract types

The contracts most commonly used in multiagent contracting systems only allow for one task to move from one agent to another at a time (Smith 1980; Sen 1993). We will refer to this type as an *original (O) contract*. In settings where an agent's cost (or even feasibility) of handling a task depends on what other tasks the agent has, O-contracts often reach local optima where no agreeable contract exists—*i.e.* a contract that improves social welfare so that it could be made profitable for both parties using a side payment—but a globally optimal allocation has not been reached (Sandholm 1998). To address this problem, new types of contracts were recently introduced (Sandholm 1993; Sandholm & Lesser 1995; Sandholm 1996; 1998): *cluster (C), swap (S),* and *multiagent (M) contracts*, as well as all the above, including the original contracts, combined (*OCSM-contracts*). These new contract types allow more than one task to be transferred between the agents participating in the contract. C-contracts transfer two or more tasks from one agent to another. S-contracts let two agents swap tasks with each other: one task is transferred from each agent to the other. M-contracts allow atomic transfers of tasks among more than two agents. We now present these contract types in more detail.

Original contracts (O-contracts)

The most common contracts used in contract net implementations and analysis of contracting games are ones in which one task is transferred from one agent to another. A side payment can also be transferred between the agents to compensate the party that is worse off after the transfer of the tasks, i.e., the agent taking on the task will be paid to do so. Due to this, any social welfare improving contract can be made beneficial to both parties. Formally:

Definition. 2 *An O-contract is a pair* $\langle T_{i,j}, \rho_{i,j} \rangle$, *where* $|T_{i,j}| = 1$. $T_{i,j}$ *is the task set (including one task) that agent* i *gives to agent* j, *and* $\rho_{i,j}$ *is the contract price that* i *pays to* j *for handling the task set.*

If the agents carried out a full lookahead, i.e., completely searched the tree of all possible future contracts, O-contracts would suffice to reach the globally optimal task allocation (Sandholm 1998). However, this generally cannot be accomplished, except for small problem instances, due to the complexity of searching the tree. The global optimum is not necessarily reached if the agents are myopically individually rational when contracting. Such agents may get stuck in a local optimum since they will not accept a temporary decrease of payoff, which may be necessary to reach the global optimum. Individually rational contracting can be seen as hill-climbing in the task allocation space, where there is a risk of being trapped in a local optimum instead of reaching the globally optimal task allocation.

Cluster contracts (C-contracts)

Cluster contracts allow the agents to exchange more than one task in each contract, together with a side payment (Sandholm 1993; 1998):

Definition. 3 *(Sandholm 1997; 1998) A cluster contract (C-contract) is a pair* $\langle T_{i,j}, \rho_{i,j} \rangle$, *where* $|T_{i,j}| > 1$. $T_{i,j}$ *is the task set that agent* i *gives to agent* j, *and* $\rho_{i,j}$ *is the contract price that* i *pays to* j *for handling the task set.*

Swap contracts (S-contracts)

Even when both O-contracts and C-contracts are used, local optima exist. For example, even if there is no profitable O- or C-contract, there may be beneficial swaps of tasks to be made between two agents. In a swap contract (Sandholm 1998), one agent gives a task to another agent and receives another task from the latter agent. A side payment may also be paid between the agents to compensate for any value difference between the tasks. Formally:

Definition. 4 *(Sandholm 1997; 1998) A swap contract (S-contract) is a 4-tuple* $\langle T_{i,j}, T_{j,i}, \rho_{i,j}, \rho_{j,i} \rangle$, *where* $|T_{i,j}| = |T_{j,i}| = 1$. $T_{i,j}$ *is the task set (including one task) that agent* i *gives to agent* j. $T_{j,i}$ *is the task set (including one task) that agent* j *gives to agent* i. $\rho_{i,j}$ *is the amount that* i *pays to* j, *and* $\rho_{j,i}$ *is the amount that* j *pays to* i.

Multiagent contracts (M-contracts)

Even when all three of the contracts described above (O, C, and S) are used, the global optimum may still not be reached if the agents are myopically individually rational when contracting. To avoid some of the remaining local optima, M-contracts were introduced (Sandholm 1998):[3]

Definition. 5 *(Sandholm 1997; 1998) A multiagent contract (M-contract) is a pair* $\langle \mathbf{T}, \rho \rangle$ *of* $|A| \times |A|$ *matrices, where at least three elements of* $\mathbf{T}$ *are non-empty (otherwise this would be just a 2-agent contract), and for all* i *and* j, $|T_{i,j}| \leq 1$. *An element* $T_{i,j}$ *is the set of tasks that agent* i *gives to agent* j, *and an element* $\rho_{i,j}$ *is the amount that* i *pays to* j.

OCSM-contracts

OCSM-contracts are defined as contracts that merge the characteristic of all the contract types discussed so far. That is, any number of tasks can be transferred from and to any agent or between many agents in one single contract:

Definition. 6 *An OCSM-contract is a pair* $\langle \mathbf{T}, \rho \rangle$ *of* $|A| \times |A|$ *matrices. An element* $T_{i,j}$ *is the set of tasks that agent* i *gives to agent* j, *and an element* $\rho_{i,j}$ *is the amount that* i *pays to* j.

OCSM-contracts are necessary and sufficient for reaching a globally optimal allocation (Sandholm 1996; 1997; 1998). A global optimum will be reached in a finite number of contracts using any hill-climbing algorithm, i.e. via any sequence of individually rational contracts. So, from a social welfare perspective, the agents need not look ahead in the tree of possible future contracts. They do not have to take unprofitable contracts in anticipation of synergic ones later on that would make the combination profitable. Furthermore, when accepting a profitable contract, an agent does not need to worry that it will preclude other profitable contracts later on. This is a powerful result for small problem instances, but for large ones the number of contracts made before the global optimum is reached may be prohibitively large. Also, identifying profitable OCSM-contracts can be difficult in the large. Therefore, in large-scale problem instances it is important to be able trade off solution quality against negotiation time. For example, the agents may want to find the best solution that is obtainable in a given amount

---

[3] Sathi and Fox (1989) (Sathi & Fox 1989) studied a simpler version of multiagent contracts where bids were grouped into cascades.

of time. This paper studies how the different contract types affect that tradeoff.

Contracting system

In principle our contracting system implementation can be used to solve reallocation problems with any number of agents and items. The simulations of this paper focus on the multiagent TSP domain with up to 8 agents and 8 tasks per problem instance. For all combinations of numbers of agents between 2 and 8, and numbers of tasks between 2 and 8, 1000 TSP instances were randomly generated.

Each problem instance was solved five times, four of which used myopically individually rational (i.e. hillclimbing) contracting. In the first run, O-contracts were used until a local optimum was found. In the second, C-contracts were used until a local optimum was found. In the third, S-contracts were used until a local optimum was found. In the fourth, M-contracts were used until a local optimum was found. In addition, an exhaustive enumeration of task allocations was conducted in order to find the globally optimal allocation. This corresponds to the outcome that would be reached via myopically individually rational contracting using OCSM-contracts.

In the experiments, each problem instance was tackled in two phases. First, all possible TSPs were solved (for each salesman, there is one TSP corresponding to each subset of cities).[4] Second, the four contracting runs and the exhaustive enumeration of task allocations were conducted.

Contract sequencing

During the contracting run, contracts of the particular type (O, C, S, or M) were applied repeatedly. The algorithm knows that a local optimum has been reached when all possible contracts of the type have been tried but none have been performed. The next subsections discuss the order of trying different contracts within each contract type. The agents are numbered from 1 to $|A|$, and each agent's tasks from 1 to $|T_i|$.

Sequencing of original contracts An O-contract allows one agent to move one task to one other agent. The former agent pays the latter for accepting the contract at least as much as it costs the latter agent to handle the task, and at most as much as it costs the former agent to handle it. In our experiments, O-contracts were sequenced as follows. First, agent 1's tasks are attempted to be moved, one at a time, to agent 2. If any

[4]The IDA* search algorithm (Korf 1985) was used to solve the TSPs. To ensure that the optimal solution was reached an admissible $\hat{h}$-function was used. It was constructed by underestimating the cost function of the remaining nodes by the minimum spanning tree (Cormen, Leiserson, & Rivest 1990) of those nodes (that is, of nodes not yet on that path of the search tree, the last city of that path of the search tree, and the finish (=start) location of the salesman).

contract (move of a task) is profitable, it is performed and the next contract is tried. After having tried to move all tasks one at a time from agent 1 to 2, agent 1 tries to move its tasks to agent 3. This continues until agent 1 has attempted to move all its tasks to all the other agents. Then the procedure continues with agent 2, which tries to move its tasks to agent 1, followed by all the other agents in increasing order. When agent $|A|$ has attempted to move all its tasks to all the other agents, each O-contract has been tried. However, the process repeats because some O-contracts may have made other O-contracts profitable that were not profitable before. The process stops when no O-contracts have been made during one of these loops were all of them are tried.

Sequencing of cluster contracts In a C-contract one agent moves at least two tasks to another agent, and a side payment is used as with O-contracts. C-contracts were sequenced as follows. We start by trying out all combinations of two tasks followed by all combinations of three tasks, and so on. The order in which the tasks are tried to be moved is: $(1,2)$, $(1,3)$, ..., $(1, |T_1|)$, $(2,3)$, $(2,4)$, ..., $(|T_1|-1, |T_1|)$, $(1,2,3)$, $(1,2,4)$, ... If any contract is profitable, it is performed and the next contract is tried. After having tried to move all tasks (one at a time) from agent 1 to 2, agent 1 tries to move its tasks to agent 3. This continues until agent 1 has attempted to move all its tasks to all the other agents. Then the procedure continues with agent 2, which tries to move its tasks to agent 1, followed by all the other agents in increasing order. When agent $|A|$ has attempted to move its tasks to all other agents, each C-contract has been tried. However, the process repeats because some C-contracts may have made other C-contracts profitable that were not profitable before. The process stops when no C-contracts have been made during one of these loops were all of them are tried.

Sequencing of swap contracts In an S-contract, one agent transfers one task to another agent and it also receives one task from that agent. If the S-contract is acceptable, i.e., social welfare improving, a side payment can be used so that each one of the two agents is better off than before the contract. S-contracts were sequenced as follows. One at a time, agent 1 tries to move its tasks to agent 2, and in exchange agent 2 tries to move one task to agent 1. For every task agent 1 tries to move, agent 2 tries to move all its tasks to agent 1 one at a time before agent 1 continues with its next task. If any contract is profitable, it is performed and the next contract is tried. When all contracts that include agent 1 and agent 2 have been attempted, all possible contracts including agent 1 and agent 3 are tried according to the procedure above. When agent 1 has attempted all contracts with all the other agents, agent 2 tries all contracts, according to the procedure above, with agent 1 followed by the other agents in increasing order. When agent $|A|$ has attempted to exchange tasks with all other agents, each S-contract has been tried. However, the process repeats because some S-contracts may have made other S-contracts profitable that were not profitable before. The process stops when no S-contracts have been made during one of these loops were all of them are tried.

Sequencing of multiagent contracts In an M-contract tasks are being moved between at least three agents. Each agent can transfer at most one task to each other agent. If an M-contract increases social welfare, side payments can be used so that each contract party is better off than before the contract.

First, all combinations where only agent $|A|$ transfers tasks to 3 other agents are tried. The combinations of agents receiving tasks are in order: $(1,2,3)$, $(1,2,4)$, ..., $(1,2,|A|-1)$, $(1,3,2)$, $(1,3,4)$, ..., $(|A|-1,|A|-2,|A|-3)$. For each of these combinations all possible tasks transfers are tried. For agent combination $(1,2,3)$ that is (from agent $|A|$ to agent 1, from agent $|A|$ to agent 2, from agent $|A|$ to agent 3): $(1,2,3)$, $(1,2,4)$, ..., $(|T|_{|A|},|T|_{|A|}-1,|T|_{|A|}-2)$. Then, all combinations where only agent $|A|-1$ transfers 3 tasks to other agents are tried in the same manner as above.

After that, contracts where agent $|A|$ transfers tasks to 4 other agents are tried. After that agent $|A|-1$ tries to transfer tasks to 4 other agents, *etc.* After that, the loop is repeated with giving tasks to 5 other agents, then 6, *etc.*

After individual agents have tried to move their tasks, all combinations of two agents try to move their tasks. First agents $|A|$ and $|A|-1$ try to transfer their tasks (all combinations of their tasks are tried) to all combinations of agents. The order of all agents that will try to transfer their tasks is: $(|A|)$, ..., (1), $(|A|,|A|-1)$, ..., $(1,2)$, $(|A|,|A|-1,|A|-2)$, ... If one of the agents does not have the task needed, that combination is skipped.

As soon as a contract is performed, the scheme starts over from the beginning. The process stops when no M-contracts have been made during one loop were all of them are tried.

Results

To compare the solution quality obtained by the different contract types, the *ratio bound* was used. Let x_j^l denote the social welfare of the task allocation achieved by protocol $l \in \{O,C,S,M\}$ on problem instance j, $j \in \{1,\ldots,1000\}$. Let x_j^G denote the social welfare of the global optimum (or equivalently OCSM-contracts). The ratio bound, r_j^l, is the optimal welfare divided by the welfare obtained by a given protocol: $r_j^l = \frac{x_j^G}{x_j^l}$. The average ratio bound is

$$\bar{r}^l = \frac{1}{1000} \sum_{j=1}^{1000} r_j^l$$

This average ratio bound was calculated for all possible combinations of numbers of agents and numbers of tasks.

The differences of the ratio bounds between the contract types were also calculated for statistical significance testing. The difference in ratio bounds between two different contract types, k and l, applied to the same problem instance j, is

$$r_j^{kl} = r_j^k - r_j^l$$

The mean difference between the contract types is

$$\bar{r}^{kl} = \frac{1}{n} \sum_{j=1}^{n} r_j^{kl}$$

Comparison of social welfare

Compared to the other contract types, the mean ratio bound for O-contracts, $\bar{r}^O$, does not vary as much in the number of agents or tasks. The ratio bound increases slightly with both the numbers of agents (Figure 2) and the number of tasks (Figure 3). The ratio bound for O-contracts varies between 1.1 and 1.2, which means that the social welfare using O-contracts is 10% - 20% from optimal.

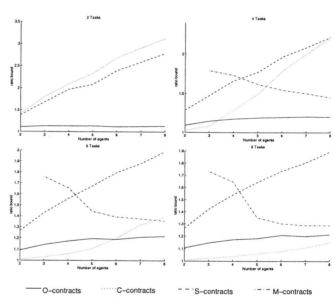

Figure 2: *Ratio bound as a function of the number of agents. The graphs for M-contracts do not include any values for two agents or two tasks since at least three agents and three tasks are needed in an M-contract.*

As the number of tasks increases, the mean ratio bound, $\bar{r}^C$, for C-contracts decreases (Figure 3), *i.e.*, using C-contracts leads to local optima that are closer to the global optimum when the number of tasks is large. While the decrease is monotonic, it is greatest for small numbers of tasks. The ratio bound increases as the number of agents increases (Figure 2). This is especially noticeable in the cases with few tasks (2-5). For greater numbers of tasks, the increase in the ratio bound is smaller (Figure 2, bottom left).

The mean ratio bound, $\bar{r}^S$, for S-contracts also decreases with the number of tasks, and increases with

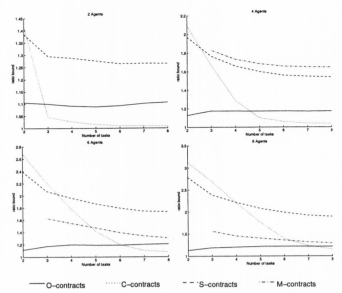

Figure 3: *Ratio bound as a function of the number of tasks.*

the number of agents. However, for S-contracts the increase in the ratio bound is considerable even for large numbers of tasks.

As expected, M-contracts perform better both when the number of agents increases (Figure 2) and when the number of tasks increases (Figure 3). In other words, the mean ratio bound, $\overline{r}^M$, decreases with the number of tasks and agents. This is obvious in the bottom right graph in Figure 3. Extrapolating from these results suggests that M-contracts could reach a lower ratio bound than any of the other contract types for much greater numbers of agents and tasks than eight.

Figure 4 shows that O-contracts always perform better than S- and M-contracts. C-contracts provide a lower ratio bound than O-contracts when the number of tasks is greater than the number of agents. For those numbers of agents and tasks, C-contracts are the best contract type also when compared to S- and M- contracts. So, the top left graph in Figure 4 summarizes which contract types are best for which numbers of agents and tasks.[5]

Computational aspects

The number of contracts that has to be tried before reaching a local optimum varies considerably across the contract types, as does the number of contracts that is needed to verify that a local optimum has been reached, Figure 5. As expected, the number of contracts made

---

[5]The black and white areas represent results that are significant at the 0.05 confidence level of the mean difference ratio bounds in a paired t-test. The gray areas represent results that are not significant at the 0.05 level, yet one of the contracts is better. In the dark gray areas the latter contract is better while in the lighter gray areas the former is better. While the paired t-test formally assumes normal distributions, we use it because it has been shown to be very robust against distributional variations (Cohen 1995).

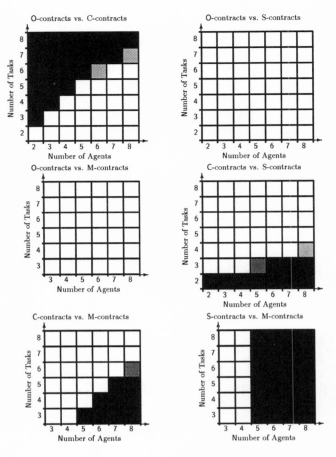

Figure 4: *Pairwise comparison of the differences in ratio bounds $\overline{r}^{kl}$ for O-, C-, S-, and M-contracts. Above each graph the two contract types under comparison are stated. The darker the color in a square is, the better the latter contract type.*

and tried before reaching a local optimum, and the number of contracts needed to verify the local optimum increase with the number of tasks. These numbers are polynomial in tasks for all contract types (the curves are sublinear on a logarithmic scale). Similarly, the numbers are polynomial in agents—these curves are omitted for brevity.

O-contracts perform on average the largest number of contracts before reaching a local optimum, followed by C-contracts, S-contracts, and M-contracts. The fact that O-contracts only move one task in each contract is likely to contribute to this result. This result is interesting since O-contracts are desirable because they require the smallest number of contracts to *verify* that a local optimum has been reached. On the other hand, O- and C-contracts need to try a larger number of contracts before reaching a local optimum than S- and M-contracts do. In the case of six agents and six tasks, O-contracts and C-contracts still need less than 100 contracts to reach a local optimum—except in a small number of cases. With the exclusion of some exceptional cases where several thousand contracts are needed, M-contracts find local optima after a small number of con-

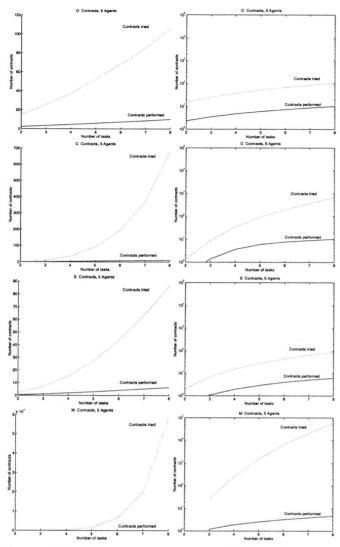

Figure 5: *Number of contracts tried (including those to verify the local optimum) before the system reached a local optimum (dotted line), and number of contracts performed before reaching the local optimum (solid line). Left graphs have linear scales. The scales on the value axes differ between the graphs. The value axes of the graphs on the right have logarithmic scales.*

tracts have been tried. This may be affected by the specific order of trying M-contracts. Note that the discussion until now concerns the number of contracts needed to reach a local optimum, not the number needed to verify that one has been reached. M-contracts need by far the greatest number of contracts to verify that the solution is a local optimum. Then, in order, C-contracts, S-contracts, and O-contracts follow.

The CPU-time used for negotiation is proportional to the number of contracts tried, but the constant of proportionality varies greatly between the contract types: it is much greater for M-contracts than O-, C-, and S-contracts. This is because M-contracts are more complicated than the other contract types, and because

many contracts need to be checked to verify that a local optimum has been reached.

Dynamics of contracting

The typical final task allocations are very different between the contract types. C-contracts tend to concentrate the tasks to one agent or a few of them. O-contracts tend to spread the contracts to all the agents. Due to the sequencing of M-contracts, the tasks tend to be allocated too often to agent 1. One could avoid such anomalies by randomly picking M-contracts to try. However, a systematic scheme is necessary to verify that a local optimum has been reached. The number of tasks per agent cannot change at all when S-contracts are used, which contributes to their poor performance. As is desired from an anytime contracting perspective, contracts performed earlier often improved the social welfare more than later contracts.

Conclusions

The capability to profitably reallocate items is a key feature in automated negotiation. Currently, the most widely used contract type allows for only one task at a time to be moved from one agent to another (O-contracts). New contract types (cluster (C), swap (S), multiagent (M), and OCSM-contracts) were recently introduced to avoid some of the local optima in which O-contracts can get stuck when used by myopic self-interested agents. They are all based on moving several tasks in a single contract. This reduces the number of local optima in the search space of task allocations for hill-climbing-based contracting algorithms.

OCSM-contracts guarantee that a global optimum is reached in a finite number of contracts independent of the order of the contracts. Although this is a powerful result for small problem instances, in large-scale problems the number of steps needed to reach the global optimum may be impractically large. In such problems it is better to accept the best achievable solution in a limited amount of time than to strive for the global optimum. Marginal cost based contracting allows this because it is an anytime algorithm: each agent's payoff increases monotonically in time. However, the rate of increase depends on which contract types are used. To determine how best to increase social welfare quickly in time, we compared the five contract types on an example problem called the multiagent TSP.

The results regarding the social welfare of the local optima of the different contract types provide guidelines to system builders regarding what contract types to use in different environments when computation is limited. We also presented timing results which can be used in the choice of contract type if there is not enough time to even reach a local optimum. In addition, our results help in the choice of contract type when certain properties of the final outcome are desired, *e.g.*, that tasks are distributed among multiple agents or concentrated to just a small number of agents. For six agents and six tasks, a local optimum was reached within the first 100 contracts tried, with the exclusion of some exceptional cases. This is important since several hundred - sometimes several thousand - contracts were often tried before it could be verified that a local optimum had been reached. M-contracts reached a local optimum faster (when measured in the number of contracts tried or in the number of contracts performed before the optimum was reached) than the other contract types. However, M-contracts require more CPU-time per contract than O-, C-, or S-contracts. They also require a significantly larger number of contracts to be tried in order to verify that a local optimum has been reached.

For these relatively small problem instances, O- and C-contracts led to better local optima than S- and M-contracts. C-contracts performed best when the number of tasks was greater than the number of agents; otherwise O-contracts were best. Extrapolating to problems containing more agents and tasks, M-contracts may reach the best local optima. Despite the fact that O- and C-contracts lead to similar social welfare values, the typical task allocations are very different: O-contracts tend to spread the tasks among all agents while C-contracts tend to concentrate the tasks to only one agent or a few agents.

Sequencing of contracts within a particular contract type influences the results. Analyzing this effect further is part of our future research. Also, to improve the social welfare, more than one contract type can be used during contracting (Andersson & Sandholm 1998c). Further research is required to determine the optimal way to sequence the different contract types in order to obtain satisfactory social welfare with bounded negotiation time. There are several possible approaches: change the contract type for every single contract, apply many possible contracts (maybe all) of one contract type before changing the type, or find a local optimum using one contract type before changing to another contract type. There is also the question of which of the contract types should be interleaved with each other. Yet another interesting area for future work is combining the different contract types, thus forming atomic contracts having characteristics of more than one of the O-, C-, S-, and M-contracts, but not all of them (unlike OCSM-contracts). These composite contract types would not guarantee that myopic individually rational agents will reach the globally optimal allocation, but they would lead to a local optimum faster than OCSM-contracts, and to higher average social welfares than O-, C-, S-, or M-contracts individually.

References

Andersson, M. R., and Sandholm, T. W. 1998a. Contract types for satisficing task allocation: II experimental results. In *AAAI Spring Symposium Series: Satisficing Models*, 1–7.

Andersson, M. R., and Sandholm, T. W. 1998b. Leveled commitment contracting among myopic individually rational agents. In *ICMAS*, 26–33.

Andersson, M. R., and Sandholm, T. W. 1998c. Sequencing of contract types for anytime task reallocation. In *Agents-98 Workshop on Agent-Mediated Electronic Trading (AMET)*. Reprinted in Springer Verlag LNAI 1571, pp. 54–69, 1999.

Cohen, P. R. 1995. *Empirical Methods for Artificial Intelligence*. MIT Press.

Cormen, T. H.; Leiserson, C. E.; and Rivest, R. L. 1990. *Introduction to Algorithms*. MIT Press.

Kalakota, R., and Whinston, A. B. 1996. *Frontiers of Electronic Commerce*. Addison-Wesley.

Korf, R. E. 1985. Depth-first iterative-deepening: An optimal admissible tree search. *Artificial Intelligence* 27(1):97–109.

Raiffa, H. 1982. *The Art and Science of Negotiation*. Cambridge, Mass.: Harvard Univ. Press.

Rassenti, S. J.; Smith, V. L.; and Bulfin, R. L. 1982. A combinatorial auction mechanism for airport time slot allocation. *Bell J. of Economics* 13:402–417.

Rosenschein, J. S., and Zlotkin, G. 1994. *Rules of Encounter*. MIT Press.

Rothkopf, M. H.; Pekeč, A.; and Harstad, R. M. 1998. Computationally manageable combinatorial auctions. *Management Science* 44(8):1131–1147.

Sandholm, T. W., and Lesser, V. R. 1995. Issues in automated negotiation and electronic commerce: Extending the contract net framework. In *ICMAS*, 328–335. Reprinted in *Readings in Agents*, Huhns and Singh, eds., pp. 66–73, 1997.

Sandholm, T. W., and Ygge, F. 1997. On the gains and losses of speculation in equilibrium markets. In *IJCAI*, 632–638.

Sandholm, T. W. 1993. An implementation of the contract net protocol based on marginal cost calculations. In *AAAI*, 256–262.

Sandholm, T. W. 1996. *Negotiation among Self-Interested Computationally Limited Agents*. Ph.D. Dissertation, University of Massachusetts, Amherst. At www.cs.wustl.edu/~sandholm/dissertation.ps.

Sandholm, T. W. 1997. Contract types for optimal task allocation: I theoretical results. WUCS-97-35, Washington University, Dept. of Computer Science.

Sandholm, T. W. 1998. Contract types for satisficing task allocation: I theoretical results. In *AAAI Spring Symposium Series: Satisficing Models*, 68–75.

Sathi, A., and Fox, M. 1989. Constraint-directed negotiation of resource reallocations. In Huhns, M. N., and Gasser, L., eds., *Distributed Artificial Intelligence*, volume 2, Pitman, chapter 8, 163–193.

Sen, S. 1993. *Tradeoffs in Contract-Based Distributed Scheduling*. Ph.D. Dissertation, Univ. of Michigan.

Smith, R. G. 1980. The contract net protocol: High-level communication and control in a distributed problem solver. *IEEE Transactions on Computers* C-29(12):1104–1113.

Power, Dependence and Stability in Multiagent Plans

Sviatoslav Brainov and Tuomas Sandholm

Washington University
Department of Computer Science
St. Louis, MO 63130
{brainov, sandholm}@cs.wustl.edu

Abstract

In this paper we present a decision-theoretic model of social power and social dependence that accounts for origins of different choices available in different situations. According to the model almost every group activity, whether it is cooperation or exploitation, has its origins in resolving some dependence or power relation. The model is intended for self-interested agents and explains power and dependence in terms of relations between agents' plans. It is a generalization of the dependence network model and accounts for situations of group dependence, i.e., situations in which an agent depends on a group or a group depends on an agent. The model is applied to the analysis of stability of multiagent plans. Stable dependence structures of multiagent plans are identified. Necessary and sufficient conditions for stability of joint plans are provided.

Introduction

Social relations between autonomous agents have been a subject of continuous interest in both multiagent systems and distributed AI (Castelfranchi 1990; Sichman et al. 1994; d'Iverno and Luck 1997). The set of all social relations between agents defines the social structure of society. Reasoning about the social structure enables agents to make consistent decisions about when and with whom to interact.

Since interaction is a distinctive feature of multiagent activity, agents need to know how to avoid accidental and harmful interactions and how to take advantage of beneficial interactions. Therefore, agents need a model of how to influence other agents' behavior. The ability of an agent to exert influence over another agent is captured by the notion of power. Almost every multiagent interaction has its origins in resolving some power relation. Power relations become relevant in both conflict and cooperative situations. In a situation where two or more agents have conflicting interests a decision has to be made as to whose interest shall prevail. In a cooperative situation, in order to achieve his goal, an agent relies on the power of another

agent or a group of agents. A special kind of power situation is a dependence situation. In a dependence situation an agent submits himself to the power of another agent.

Social power and social dependence play a central role in game theory (Harsanyi 1962) and sociology (Coleman 1973). The notion of social power was introduced in AI in (Castelfranchi 1990). Later, this notion was employed in the definition of the social dependence network model and the implementation of different social reasoning mechanisms (Sichman et al. 1994). It was proved that the problem of determining whether cooperation is possible in a given social structure is NP-complete (d'Iverno, Luck and Wooldridge 1997).

Prior research on social dependence does not, however, exhibit credible causal mechanisms for dependence resolution or submission to someone's power. Usually social dependence is explained in terms of the theory of joint intentions and joint actions (Cohen and Levesque 1990; Levesque, Cohen and Nunes 1990). The theory of Cohen and Levesque is not intended for self-interested agents and, therefore, does not provide sufficient grounds for explaining self-motivated behavior. The notions of joint persistent goal and joint persistent action usually presuppose altruistic behavior (Brainov 1996). Achieving persistent and stable behavior of self-interested agents is a difficult task. Considerable research in multiagent systems has already focused on stability of multiagent agreements (Brainov 1994; Sandholm and Lesser 1995).

Another limitation of social dependence theory is that it accounts only for bilateral dependence situations, i.e., for situations involving two agents. In many situations of practical interest an agent might depend on another agent as well as on a group of agents.

In this paper we propose a decision-theoretic model for explaining social power and social dependence in multiagent plans. The model is intended for self-interested agents and explains power relations in terms of individual interest. It is a generalization of the dependence network model and accounts for situations of group dependence, i.e., situations in which an agent depends on a group or a group depends on an agent.

The model is applied to the analysis of stability of multiagent plans. It is shown that in order to be stable a joint plan has to balance the power of different agents.

This material is based upon work supported by the National Science Foundation under CAREER Award IRI-9703122, Grant IRI-9610122, and Grant IIS-9800994.

The paper is organized as follows. First, the notion of dependence is introduced and generalized to the case of more than two agents. Next, the resolution of dependence relations is discussed. Finally, the notion of dependence is applied in the analysis of stability of multiagent plans. The paper concludes by summarizing the results and providing directions for future research.

Unilateral Dependence

Let the set of all agents be denoted by N, $N=\{1,2,\ldots,n\}$. The n-tuple $(p_1,p_2,\ldots,p_n)$ is used to denote a joint plan of all agents for moving the world from the initial state s^1 to some final state s^r. Here p_i stands for the individual subplan of agent i. Each agent's subplan can be viewed as a sequence of actions: $p_i=(a_i^1,\ldots,a_i^{r-1})$ such that every n-tuple $[a_1^k,\ldots,a_n^k]$, possibly with some precedence constraints between pairs (a_i^k,a_j^k), moves the world from a state s^k to the state s^{k+1}. As usual, agents are utility maximizers and each agent i, $i\in N$, attempts to maximize his utility U_i in the final state. Let p_{N-i} denote the plan of the group of agents $N-\{i\}$. In this notation we can write the plan $(p_1,p_2,\ldots,p_n)$ as (p_{N-i}, p_i).

The following definition introduces the notion of individual dependence, i.e., an agent's dependence on another agent in some joint plan.

Definition 1. In a joint plan (p_{N-j},p_j) agent i *depends* on agent j if there exists plan p^*_j such that for every plan p'_{N-j} of the other agents:

$$U_i(p'_{N-j},p^*_j) < U_i(p_{N-j},p_j), \tag{1}$$
$$U_j(p_{N-j},p^*_j) \geq U_j(p_{N-j},p_j). \tag{2}$$

The plan p^*_j is said to be gainful for agent j at the expense of agent i. To indicate that the gainful plan depends on the initial plan (p_{N-j},p_j), we denote it by $p_j^{gain}(i,p_{N-j},p_j)$.

Condition (1) says that by implementing his plan p^*_j, agent j lowers the utility of agent i. According to Condition (2) the plan p^*_j is at least as beneficial to agent j as the original plan p_j, provided that the other agents do not change their plans. The situation described by Definition 1 can be classified as one where agent j has social power (Harsanyi 1962). The plan p^*_j serves as the *means of power*, i.e., those specific actions by which agent j can influence agent i's behavior. According to Condition (2) the *cost of power* is zero or negative. That is, agent j does not incur any additional costs in order to exert any influence over agent i. Therefore, with each unilateral power situation we can associate two features: the means of power and the cost of power. The means of power is the particular plan by which the powerful agent can exert his power over the dependent agent. The cost of power is the cost of applying the means of power.

Condition (1) of Definition 1 holds for every plan p'_{N-j} of the other agents. That is, no matter how other agents will help agent i, they cannot prevent agent j from harming agent i. Therefore, the power of agent j with respect to agent i is unconditional and does not depend on other agents. The notion of dependence introduced in Definition 1 generalizes traditional concepts of resource and action dependence (Sichman et al. 1994). Consider the following example. Agent i needs a resource r_j for achieving his goal, i.e., without r_j agent i is either incapable of achieving his goal or the achievement is too costly. The only agent who controls resource r_j is agent j. Suppose that agent j has committed himself to give r_j to agent i at some stage of the joint plan (p_{N-j},p_j). If the commitment is not binding, agent j can deviate from the plan (p_{N-j},p_j) by withholding r_j to himself. By so doing, agent j gains at the expense of agent i. Therefore, agent i depends on agent j. Thus, the notion of resource dependence is a special case of dependence. It is worth noting that the other agents in the environment cannot oppose agent j. Eventually, they could punish agent j for his behavior, but they cannot provide agent i with a resource equivalent or better than r_j.

The traditional notion of resource (action) dependence does not account for the case when a resource (action) can be provided by several agents. Suppose that in the previous example resource r_j can be provided by agent j or agent k. According to the traditional notion of resource dependence agent i depends on agent j for r_j. If agent j deviates from the plan (p_{N-j},p_j) by withholding r_j to himself, agent i can still receive the resource from agent k. Therefore, in accordance with Definition 1, in this case agent i does not depend on agent j. Later we will classify this situation as conditional dependence of agent i on agent j with the tacit consent of agent k. That is, agent i might depend on agent j if agent k is backing up agent j.

Group Dependence

In this section the notion of dependence is generalized to the case where there are more than two agents. The existence of other agents in an environment gives rise to different types of group dependence. The next definition introduces the transitive closure of a dependence relation.

Definition 2. In a joint plan $p=(p_1,\ldots,p_n)$ agent i, $i\in N$, *depends transitively* on agent j, $j\in N$, if
(i)   agent i depends on agent j, or
(ii)   there exists agent k, $k\in N$, such that agent i depends on agent k and agent k depends transitively on agent j.

With the help of transitive dependence we are now in a position to define reciprocal dependence, i.e., a situation in which everybody depends on everybody directly or indirectly.

Definition 3. A joint plan $p=(p_1,\ldots,p_n)$ is based on *reciprocal dependence* if for every two agents i and j, $i,j\in N$, $j\neq j$, agent i depends transitively on agent j in the plan p.

Dependence structure of a joint plan can be represented by a dependence graph (Brainov 1994; Sichman et al. 1994). The dependence graph is constructed in the following way. The agents are represented by nodes and if I and J are two nodes corresponding to agents i and j respectively, these two nodes are joined by an arc pointing toward J if and only if agent i depends on agent j. It is evident that a joint plan is based on reciprocal dependence if and only if the dependence graph associated with it is strongly connected.

The following definition introduces the notion of group dependence. In this paper we consider two types of group dependence. The first type refers to the case where a group of agents depends on a single agent. The second type occurs when an agent depends on a group

Definition 4. In a joint plan $(p_{N\text{-}j}, p_j)$ a group of agents S, $S \subseteq N\text{-}j$, *depends* on agent j if there exists a plan p^*_j such that for every plan $p'_{N\text{-}j}$ of the other agents:

$$U_k(p'_{N\text{-}j}, p^*_j) < U_k(p_{N\text{-}j}, p_j) \quad \text{for every } k \in S$$
$$U_j(p_{N\text{-}j}, p^*_j) \geq U_j(p_{N\text{-}j}, p_j).$$

The plan p^*_j is said to be gainful for agent j at the expense of group S. To indicate that the gainful plan depends on the initial plan $(p_{N\text{-}j}, p_j)$, we denote it by $p_j^{gain}(S, p_{N\text{-}j}, p_j)$.

Definition 4 requires that plan p^*_j be common for all agents of the group S. If every agent in S depended on j for a different plan, then he would be able to resolve his dependence separately and without the help of the other members of the group. In this case there would not be sufficient grounds to regard agents in S as a group. Therefore, if every agent in the set of agents S depends on agent j, we cannot conclude that S depends on j. That is, individual dependence does not imply group dependence. The opposite statement, however, is true.

Proposition 1. If in a joint plan $(p_{N\text{-}j}, p_j)$ a group of agents S, $S \subseteq N\text{-}j$, depends on agent j, then every member of the group depends on agent j.

Since the proofs of most of the propositions require considerable technical preparation and space, in this version of the paper the proofs are omitted. The complete proofs are provided in (Brainov, 1998).

The notion of dependence formalizes power situations in which the ability of an agent to influence other agents is unconditional and does not depend on the will or abilities of third parties. Many situations of practical importance, however, exhibit constrained power. In such situations several agents have power over an agent or group of agents. That is, the power of each powerful agent is constrained by the other powerful agents. Since the actions of the powerful agents interfere, the final effect on the dependent agent is determined by a strategic interaction between the powerful agents.

The next definition introduces the notion of conditional dependence. In a situation of conditional dependence, a powerful agent needs the consent of all other powerful agents in order to influence the dependent agent.

Definition 5. In a joint plan $(p_{N\text{-}S\text{-}j}, p_S, p_j)$ agent i *depends conditionally* on agent j with the *tacit consent* of a group S, $i \notin S$, if there exists p^*_j such that for every $p'_{N\text{-}S\text{-}j}$:

$$U_i(p'_{N\text{-}S\text{-}j}, p_S, p^*_j) < U_i(p_{N\text{-}S\text{-}j}, p_S, p_j)$$
$$U_j(p_{N\text{-}S\text{-}j}, p_S, p^*_j) \geq U_j(p_{N\text{-}S\text{-}j}, p_S, p_j).$$

The plan p^*_j is called conditionally gainful for agent j and is denoted by $p_j^{gain}(i, p_{N\text{-}S\text{-}j}, p_S, p_j/p_S)$.

In Definition 5 the powerful agents are agent j and the group S. Agent j can gain at the expense of agent i if the group S adheres to the plan p_S. By adhering to p_S the group S does not oppose agent j. Definition 5 says that if we disregard the existence of group S, agent i depends on agent j. Therefore, the notion of conditional dependence is more general and subsumes the notion of dependence.

Consider the previous example where the resource r_j needed by agent i can be provided by agent j or agent k. In this case, in order to apply their power, agents j and k depend on each other. If agent j withholds his resource r_j, then agent k can provide agent i with the same resource. Therefore, in order to harm agent i, agent j needs the consent of agent k.

Proposition 2. If in a joint plan $(p_{N\text{-}j}, p_j)$ agent i depends on agent j, then agent i depends conditionally on agent j with the tacit consent of every group S, $S \subseteq N\text{-}i\text{-}j$.

Proposition 2 is in accordance with the intuition that if an agent has unconstrained power over another agent, then the consent of the other agents in the environment is unnecessary.

Definition 6. Agent j can *gain without harming* agent i in the plan $(p_{N\text{-}j}, p_j)$ if there exist p^*_j and p^*_i such that for every $p'_{N\text{-}i\text{-}j}$:

$$U_i(p'_{N\text{-}i\text{-}j}, p^*_i, p^*_j) \geq U_i(p_{N\text{-}j}, p_j)$$
$$U_j(p'_{N\text{-}i\text{-}j}, p^*_i, p^*_j) > U_j(p_{N\text{-}j}, p_j).$$

According to this definition agent i has a reply to the plan p^*_j of agent j. Therefore, after agent j has changed his plan, agent i needs only to adjust his activity in accordance with the change. For this adjustment, agent i does not rely on the other agents in the environment. It is evident that if a joint plan is Pareto optimal, then no agent can gain without harming the other agents. The opposite statement is not true. That is, a joint plan might not be Pareto optimal even if no agent can gain without harming the other agents. A joint plan is Pareto optimal if there does not exist another plan which is as good or better for all the agents and strictly better for at least one agent.

The following definition introduces a second type of group dependence, viz., the case when an agent depends on a group of agents.

Definition 7. In a joint plan $(p_{N\text{-}j}, p_j)$ agent i *depends on a group* of agents S, $i \notin S$, if

(i)   (group requirement) agent i depends conditionally on every agent k, $k \in S$, with the tacit consent of the group S-k;

(ii)   (minimality requirement) for every agent k, $k \in S$, every conditionally gainful plan $p_k^{gain}(i, p_{N\text{-}S}, p_{S\text{-}k}, p_k/p_{S\text{-}k})$ and every plan $p'_{N\text{-}S}$, it holds that every agent m, $m \in S\text{-}k$, can gain without harming agent i in the plan $(p'_{N\text{-}S}, p_{S\text{-}k}, p_k^{gain}(i, p_{N\text{-}S}, p_{S\text{-}k}, p_k/p_{S\text{-}k}))$

Definition 7 is justified by the intuition that only by acting together can members of the group S help or harm agent i. Every member of the group acting separately cannot exert any power over agent i. The first condition of

Definition 7 says that agent k needs the tacit consent of the rest of the group S in order to gain at the expense of agent i. The second condition states that the group S is the minimal group (in the sense of set theoretic inclusion) that has any power over agent i. That is, every member of S contributes to the power of the group, i.e., there are no dummy members.

The following example helps to clarify Definition 7. Suppose that there are three agents i, j, and k operating in the blocks world. The goal of agent i is to move block A from Position 1 to Position 2. Block A is heavy and only agents j and k acting together can pick it up. Suppose further that in the joint plan (p_i, p_j, p_k) agents j and k have committed unilaterally to move block A from Position 1 to Position 2. It is clear that in the plan (p_i, p_j, p_k) agent i depends on the group of agents j and k. Both j and k, however, can deviate unilaterally and gain at the expense of agent i. Suppose that agent j has already deviated from his commitment. Since block A will not be moved to Position 2, damage has been inflicted upon agent i. After the deviation of agent j, it does not matter to agent i whether agent k continues to adhere to his commitment. Since agent j has already deviated, agent k can also deviate from his commitment and gain without harming agent i. Thus, in the case of group dependence the first deviating agent can inflict damage upon the dependent agent. Agents deviating afterwards can gain without harming the dependent agent.

After the deviation of agent j, agent i might still depend on agent k for things other than moving block A. That is, agent k can still gain at the expense of agent i, but this gain has nothing to do with the group activity and particularly with agent j.

The following proposition follows immediately from Definition 7.

Proposition 3. If in a joint plan (p_{N-i}, p_i) agent i depends on the group of agents S, $i \notin S$, then agent i conditionally depends on every member of the group S with the tacit consent of the rest of the group.

Proposition 3 can be regarded as the inverse of Proposition 1. In general, it is not true that if agent i depends on a group S, then agent i depends on every member of the group. In this case, one can only conclude that agent i depends *conditionally* on every member of the group.

If agent i depends on every member of a group, Definition 7 does not allow us to conclude that agent i depends on the group of these agents. Thus, we cannot mechanically group agents on account of their relationship to agent i. Agent i can depend on different agents for different purposes and these agents can even conflict with one another. To summarize, according to Definition 7, group activity is a necessary requirement for group formation.

Consider again the example with the three agents i, j and k operating in the blocks world. Suppose now that the goal of agent i is to move blocks B and C. Block B can be moved only by agent j and block C only by agent k. In this case agent i depends on agent j as well as on agent k. However, agent i does not depend on the group of agents j and k.

Resolution of Dependence

Definition 1 accounts for the case when a powerful agent can benefit by harming another agent. In many situations an agent can still have power over another agent but at some cost. The following definition formalizes the case when the power is associated with a cost.

Definition 8. In a joint plan (p_i, p_j) agent j has *power* over agent i if there exists plan p^*_j such that for every plan p'_i of the other agents:

$$U_i(p'_i, p^*_j) < U_i(p_i, p_j)$$

The cost of power $c_j^{power}(i, p_i, p_j)$ is defined by:

$$c_j^{power}(i, p_i, p_j) = U_j(p_i, p_j) - U_j(p_i, p^*_j).$$

The damage $d_i^{depend}(j, p_i, p_j)$ of agent i and is defined by:

$$d_i^{depend}(j, p_i, p_j) = U_i(p_i, p_j) - U_i(p_i, p^*_j),$$

Definition 8 is a generalization of Definition 1. That is, if agent i depends on agent j, then agent j has power over agent i. In Definition 8 we do not require the plan p^*_j be gainful for agent j. It is sufficient that agent j can harm agent i and thereby can influence his behavior. Consider the following example. Agent m, $m \in N$, is executing his plan and according to it he is going to use some resource r_s. The resource r_s is shared between him and agent n, $n \in N$. Agent n is idle. He anticipates that agent m will use r_s and occupies it before agent m accomplishes his current task. By doing so agent n bears some negligible costs c_n. Suppose that the resource r_s can be used only by one agent at a time and by occupying it, agent n does not deplete it. If the goal of agent m is valuable enough to him, agent m will be willing to pay agent n some compensation for the right to use the resource first. If the compensation exceeds the cost c_n, agent n will benefit from occupying the resource r_s. In this example agent n exerts some power over agent m. The source of the power is agent n's ability to use the resource r_s at any time.

Since self-interested agents are utility maximizers they should try to resolve each power relation. That is, the powerful agent should attempt to receive some compensation for not exerting his power and the dependent agent should be willing to offer compensation to avoid harm. The amount and the form of compensation should be determined e.g. by a negotiation between the powerful and the dependent agent.

Consider the unilateral power situation when agent j has power over agent i in the joint plan (p_i, p_j). Such a power situation can be resolved if:

$$c_j^{power}(i, p_i, p_j) < d_i^{depend}(j, p_i, p_j) \qquad (3)$$

That is, the situation can be resolved, if the cost of damaging is less than the damage. Agent i is willing to pay agent j at most $d_i^{depend}(j, p_i, p_j)$ and agent j is willing to receive at least $c_j^{power}(i, p_i, p_j)$. Therefore, if inequality (3) holds, then a mutually acceptable side payment exists.

Definition 9. The *amount of power* $A_{ji}(p_i,p_j)$ of agent j over agent i in a joint plan (p_i,p_j) is defined by:

$$A_{ji}(p_i,p_j) = d_i^{depend}(j,p_i,p_j) - c_j^{power}(i,p_i,p_j).$$

That is, the amount of power that agent j wields is the difference between the damage and the cost of power. It follows from (3) that a unilateral power situation can be resolved if the amount of power is strictly positive.

Consider the bilateral power situation where in the joint plan (p_i,p_j) agent i has power over agent j and agent j has power over agent i. If

$$A_{ji}(p_i,p_j) \neq A_{ij}(p_i,p_j),$$

than the power is balanced, so no side payment is necessary. Otherwise, the situation can be resolved by having the less powerful agent pay the more powerful agent some compensation.

Throughout this paper we assume that every dependence can be resolved permanently. More formally, if agent i depends on agent j in the joint plan (p_{N-j},p_j) and $p_j^{gain}(i,p_{N-j},p_j)$ is a gainful plan for agent j, then in every joint plan $(p'_{N-j}, p_j^{gain}(i,p_{N-j},p_j))$ agent i does not depend any more on agent j. Thus, we eliminate the case of total dependence. Total dependence occurs when, after resolving a particular dependence, the dependent agent or group of agents find themselves in the same dependent position. Suppose that agent i depends on agent j in the joint plan (p_{N-j},p_j). Agent j can apply his gainful plan $p_j^{gain}(i,p_{N-j},p_j)$ thereby harming agent i. Let $p*_{N-j}$ be the reaction of all other agents to the plan $p_j^{gain}(i,p_{N-j},p_j)$. That is, agents arrive at the plan $(p*_{N-j}, p_j^{gain}(i,p_{N-j},p_j))$. If in this plan agent i depends again on agent j, then there exists a second gainful plan for agent j: $p_j^{gain}(i,p*_{N-j}, p_j^{gain}(i,p_{N-j},p_j))$. After agent j has applied the new gainful plan, agent i finds himself again dependent on agent j, etc., ad infinitum. Thus, we obtain a sequence of gainful plans for agent j: $p_1,p_2,p_3,\ldots$. Each plan in this sequence results from applying the previous one and gives rise to the next one. Therefore, the power of agent j over agent i is total. Dependence based on total power cannot always be resolved. It can be proved, however, that if for every sequence of gainful plans $p_1,p_2,p_3,\ldots$, the sequence of losses incurred by agent i is convergent and its limit belongs to some set bounded from above, then the total dependence can be resolved (Brainov 1998).

Stability of Multiagent Plans

In this section we move to the case where agents cannot make side payments. Therefore, the only way for a dependent agent to resolve a dependence relation is by changing his plan. One agent's change of plan (even before execution) can cause other agents to change their plans which induces further changes by others, etc. Therefore, the question of stability of a multiagent plan becomes crucial.

In this section we analyze the dependence structure of multiagent plans and provide necessary and sufficient conditions for stability. In order to approach the problem of stability of multiagent plans we need some preliminary notions, in particular the notions of individual and coalitional stability. A joint plan is individually stable if every agent's plan is a best response to the plans of other agents. Formally,

Definition 10. A joint plan (p_{N-i},p_i) is *individually stable* if there exists no agent i, $i \in N$, and a plan $p*_i$ such that:

$$U_i(p_{N-i},p*_i) > U_i(p_{N-i},p_i).$$

Thus individual stability eliminates incentives for unilateral deviations. Group deviations are captured by the notion of coalitional stability. A joint plan is coalitionally stable if no coalition, taking the actions of all other agents as fixed, can deviate in a way that benefits all its members.

Definition 11. (Aumann 1959) A joint plan $p*$ is *coalitionally stable* if for every group of agents S, $S \subseteq N$, and every plan p_S of the group S there exists an agent i, $i \in S$, such that:

$$U_i(p*) > U_i(p_S,p*_{N-S}).$$

That is, every attempt to deviate is opposed by at least one member of the deviating group. This definition of coalitional stability is known as Strong Nash equilibrium.

Hereafter we assume that agents are able to revise their plans dynamically based on the actions of the other agents. We suppose that the actions of all agents are observable. We also assume that the cost of achieving agents' goals increases with the time when replanning occurs. In the context of this paper replanning is usually a result of other agents' actions. The later an agent realizes that the other agents will not help him or will obstruct his current plan, the greater is the number of his previous actions that usually become obsolete. That is, the later an agent replans, the higher are his costs.

The following proposition provides necessary conditions for stability of 2-agent plans.

Proposition 4. If a plan (p_i,p_j) is Pareto optimal, agent i depends on agent j, and agent j depends on agent i, then the plan (p_i,p_j) is individually and coalitionally stable.

Proposition 4 says that if in a bilateral power situation the power of the agents is balanced, no agent or group of agents is willing to change its current plan. If a bilateral situation has only one powerful agent, it might be unstable. In such a situation the powerful agent might gain at the expense of the dependent agent. According to the next proposition, if a bilateral situation does not have powerful agents, it is stable.

Proposition 5. If a plan (p_i,p_j) is Pareto optimal, agent i does not depend on agent j, and agent j does not depend on agent i, then the plan (p_i,p_j) is individually and coalitionally stable.

Proposition 4 can be generalized to the case of more than two agents. In this case, the reciprocal dependence is a balanced power structure. In such a structure everybody depends on everybody directly or transitively. Therefore, every attempt to gain at the expense of somebody else will be opposed by the rest of the agents.

Proposition 6. Every Pareto optimal joint plan which is based on reciprocal dependence is individually and coalitionally stable.

The next definition accounts for multiagent plans that contain at least one dependence relation. Special attention has to be given to such plans, since the existence of dependence is a potential source of instability.

Definition 12. A joint plan $(p_1,...,p_n)$ is *based on dependence* if there exist agents i and j, such that agent i depends on agent j.

Proposition 7 provides necessary and sufficient conditions for individual stability of a multiagent plan based on dependence. Surprisingly, the only dependence structure that can guarantee individual stability is reciprocal dependence.

Proposition 7. Every joint plan $(p_1,...,p_n)$ which is based on dependence is individually stable if and only if it is based on reciprocal dependence.

Propositions 8 and 9 refer to the case of group dependence. According to Proposition 8, if in a joint plan an agent depends on a stable group and the group depends on that agent, then the plan is stable.

Proposition 8. If in a Pareto optimal joint plan (p_s,p_j):
(i) p_s is based on reciprocal dependence,
(ii) group S depends on agent j,
(iii) agent j depends on the group S,
then the plan (p_s,p_j) is individually and coalitionally stable.

The dependence between agent j and the group S can be thought of as a reciprocal dependence between an agent and a group of agents. Proposition 9 provides a stronger result than Proposition 8. In Proposition 9 the dependence of agent j on the group S is replaced by an ordinary dependence.

Proposition 9. If in a Pareto optimal joint plan (p_s,p_j):
(i) p_s is based on reciprocal dependence,
(ii) group S depends on agent j,
(iii) agent j depends on some agent i, $i \in S$,
then the plan (p_s,p_j) is individually and coalitionally stable.

Proposition 9 says that if power is well balanced in every group of agents and between groups, then the joint plan is stable.

Conclusions

In this paper a decision-theoretic model of social dependence and social power was presented. The model enables self-interested agents to recognize the means and the amount of their power and to influence other agents' behavior. The model was applied to the analysis of stability of multiagent plans. It was shown how dependence can guarantee stability.

In contrast to game theory and sociology where power is defined as general ability to influence someone's behavior, in our approach power is related to a particular multiagent plan. Thus, the notion of dependence captures all the possibilities for strategic interaction available in a particular environment. In addition, we differentiate between the notion of power potential and the exercising of power.

The model proposed in the paper forms a basis for agents to perform deliberative actions in order to increase the amount and to enlarge the means of their power. That is, to transform their power potential into existing power.

Acknowledgements

The authors would like to thank Prof. V. Khoroshevsky from the Computer Center of Russian Academy of Sciences for his supervision of the research reported in this paper.

References

Aumann, R. 1959. Acceptable Points in General Cooperative N-persons Games. In *Contributions to the Theory of Games IV*. Princeton University Press.

Brainov, S. B. 1994. Deviation-Proof Plans in Open Multiagent Environments. In *Proceedings of the European Conference on Artificial Intelligence*, 274-278.

Brainov, S. B. 1996. Altruistic Cooperation Between Self-Interested Agents. In *Proceedings of the European Conference on Artificial Intelligence*, 519-523.

Brainov, S. B. 1998. Models of Stable Cooperation in Multiagent Systems. Ph.D. diss., Computer Center of Russian Academy of Sciences, Moscow.

Castelfranchi, C. 1990. Social Power. In Demazeau Y. and Muller J.-P. eds. *Decentralized AI,* 49-62. Elsevier.

Cohen, P. R., Levesque, H. J. 1990. Intention is Choice with Commitment. *Artificial Intelligence*, 42:213-261.

Coleman, J. 1973. *The Mathematics of Collective Action.* Aldine Publishing Company.

D'Iverno, M., Luck, M., Wooldridge, M. 1997. Cooperation Structures. In *Proceedings of the International Joint Conference on Artificial Intelligence*, 600-605.

Harsanyi, J. 1962. Measurement of Social Power, Opportunity Costs, and the Theory of Two-Person Bargaining Games. *Behavioral Science* 7:67-80.

Levesque, H. J., Cohen, P. R., Nunes, J. H. T. 1990. On Acting Together. In *Proceedings of the Eighth National Conference on Artificial Intelligence,* 94-99. AAAI Press.

Sandholm, T. W., Lesser, V. R. 1995. Equilibrium Analysis of the Possibilities of Unenforced Exchange in Multiagent Systems. In *Proceedings of the International Joint Conference on Artificial Intelligence*, 694-701.

Sichman, J., Demazeau, Y., Conte, R., Castelfranchi, C. 1994. A Social Reasoning Mechanism Based on Dependence Networks, In *Proceedings of the European Conference on Artificial Intelligence*, 274-278. John Wiley&Sons.

Combatting Maelstroms in Networks of Communicating Agents

James E. Hanson and **Jeffrey O. Kephart**
IBM Thomas J. Watson Research Center
P.O. Box 704
Yorktown Heights, NY 10598
{hanson,kephart}@watson.ibm.com

Abstract

Multi-agent systems in which agents can respond to messages by automatically generating and multicasting other messages are inherently vulnerable to a phenomenon that we call a *maelstrom*. We define a maelstrom to be a self-sustaining chain reaction in which a single message can unintentionally trigger the generation of a rapidly growing, potentially infinite number of messages, quickly incapacitating the communications network. There is reason to fear that modest advances in agent technology and usability could lead to spontaneous maelstroms on the Internet in the near future, particularly in the realm of electronic mail. In this article we describe various classes of maelstroms that may arise due to automated forwarding of messages and propose a novel and practical means of combatting them.

Introduction

The rapidly growing literature on multi-agent systems (e.g., [Demazeau, 1998]) is largely concerned with the design or behavioral study of systems that have been engineered from a global or systemic standpoint. By this we mean that, in addition to defining the individual agent behaviors, the system designers carefully specify the agents' roles in the collective and choreograph the sequences of interaction among them. Often, the agents are endowed with an intimate understanding of other agents that may be present in the system. The focus is typically on demonstrating that the individual agents and the multi-agent system as a whole behave as intended by the designer.

Much less well investigated, however, are what might be called *emergent* multi-agent systems, which arise through the haphazard aggregation of individual agents that can communicate, even if only marginally, with one another. By definition, the agents in such a system were designed separately, in a variety of ways, to pursue a variety of goals. Furthermore, the set of agents and agent types typically changes over time as existing agents become inactive and new agents become active.

No designer can have knowledge of all the agent types that might interact with his agent, let alone the power to modify the other agents individually or in aggregate.

The Internet appears to be a conducive environment for the development of this more informal type of multi-agent system. Apart from the underlying protocols that make communication possible, the information content, usage patterns, computational properties, and goals and intentions of agents on the Web are unconstrained and, in practice, unknowable. This is especially true in the context of electronic commerce, where organizational boundaries act as barriers to the gathering of information and the imposition of global controls.

To the extent that agent technology comes into common usage, the number, variety, and sophistication of agents on the Internet will continue to grow. Inseparable from this development is a correspondingly growing potential—which is both threat and promise—for the emergence of novel and unforseen collective behaviors in the population of agents. Even in engineered systems, designing against destructive collective behaviors can be a subtle and difficult task; but at least in principle, it can be done through sufficiently careful adjustment of the agents' individual behaviors, of their interactions, or both. This kind of global legislation is simply impossible in an emergent system. Therefore it is vitally important to understand any collective modes of behavior that may arise in such systems, and to develop methods whereby an individual agent may, so far as is possible, exploit those which are favorable and combat those which are unfavorable.

In this paper we describe one potentially disastrous class of collective behavior that may arise in a multi-agent milieu of the sort just described, and propose a method whereby individual agents may combat it. For definiteness, we model an agent as an information processing system that receives messages from other agents, processes them in some way, and possibly sends messages to other agents as a result. In a population of such agents, it is natural to suppose that a single message could trigger a chain reaction of messages, and that, under certain circumstances, this chain reaction might be self-sustaining. Manber [Manber, 1990] has reviewed a number of real-world chain reactions of this type, which range from the Internet worm of 1988 to infinite loops of low-level error messages in a local area network, to the cycling of e-mail messages among a user's multiple accounts. In all the examples he gives, the chain reaction was due to some hardware or software failure at one or more of the workstations involved, or to an unnoticed flaw in one of the protocols used. With the advent of user-programmable intelligent agents, however, comes the possibility of a new type of chain reaction, in which the actions of any individual agent, considered in isolation, are entirely useful, intentional and benign. We will refer to self-sustaining chain reactions in networks of agents, whether due to a failure or a supposedly innocent action, as *maelstroms*.

The rest of the paper is organized as follows. A scenario for how a maelstrom of electronic mail messages might develop is given in section 2, followed by a partial taxonomy of maelstrom types. Previous methods for preventing maelstroms are critiqued in section 3. In section 4, we describe a novel anti-maelstrom technique that has several advantages. The performance of an implementation of the algorithm is evaluated in section 5, and simulation studies are used in section 6 to demonstrate that sufficient deployment within the agent population will successfully prevent maelstroms. We close with a summary and discussion of future work.

Maelstroms

One type of user-programmable agent that already exists in widely-used commercial electronic mail software packages is a mail forwarding agent. The forwarding agent scans the header and body of an incoming mail message for specified keywords. If the right combination of keywords is found, the agent automatically forwards the message to a designated set of recipients.

Now consider the following scenario: A typical computer user ("Fred") is one of a small group of friends who exchange jokes with one another via e-mail. He decides to automate distribution of jokes. He instructs his mail agent to forward any incoming mail with the word "Joke" in the subject line to his friends.[1] Over time, this idea occurs independently to more and more users. Jokes start getting forwarded several times, from mailing list to mailing list. One day, the social network of automated forwarders closes upon itself, and one of the jokes that Fred's agent had forwarded is sent back to Fred. It is of course automatically forwarded, and begins the second of an endless succession of trips around the cycle. Every time it goes around, everyone who originally got the joke gets it again, and forwards it again. Furthermore, because both the original message and each copy are forwarded independently, the number of copies of the message grows rapidly with time. Before long, the network used for e-mail delivery is swamped, and can't be used to transmit useful infor-

---

[1] It took us 25 seconds to program an agent in Microsoft Outlook Express to perform exactly this operation. Similar functionality is available in Lotus Notes.

mation to Fred or anyone else—even those not involved in the mail loop.

The above is an example of a *simple maelstrom*, in which messages are forwarded verbatim. We may identify other specialized types of maelstrom as follows:

Additive maelstroms. This is automatic message forwarding in which additional information is added to the message before it is sent. The additional information may be of any nature from the most insignificant, such as an extra blank line added to the bottom of the original message, to the most important, such as a complete disavowal of the original by its author.

Combinatorial maelstroms. This involves forwarding in which several messages or parts of messages are combined to form a single new message prior to forwarding. An example of such a message is an automatically generated personalized newspaper that can be received by another agent and in turn used by it as fodder for its own automatically generated newspaper.

Maelstroms with finitary transformation. As the message is forwarded from agent to agent, it is transformed into a succession of variations of which there is a finite (usually small) number of types. Simple examples include conversion of the message to all capital letters or all lower case letters, adding or removing whitespace characters, or applying simple character encodings.

Previous ID-based solutions

Previous approaches to preventing chain reactions in networks have centered on inserting identifiers into header fields of messages. One such approach was proposed by Manber [Manber, 1990]. The key concept is to assign a unique ID to each newly generated message in the network, and to insert this ID into the header of the message prior to forwarding. At each forwarding step, each outgoing message, however transformed, is given the same ID as the message that triggered it. All agents maintain a list of all IDs of messages sent, against which every incoming message is checked. If the ID of an incoming message is found in the list, it is not forwarded. When this prescription is strictly adhered to, no message is forwarded twice by any agent. No maelstrom occurs.

A second approach was proposed by Spagna specifically for e-mail messages [Spagna, 1997]. In this case, instead of assigning a unique ID to each message, each agent inserts its own unique ID into the header of each message that it sends. When it receives a message, the agent searches the header message for its own ID. If the ID is found, then it does not forward the message. This prescription also prevents maelstroms, and it has the advantage of reducing the amount of data each agent must store in order to recognize messages. It is slightly less powerful than Manber's approach because it fails to detect multiple copies of a single message that have reached an agent for the first time along distinct paths. The agent is incapable of recognizing that the incoming messages are duplicates, so it forwards both copies.

While ID-based approaches such as these can work in certain contexts, there are several important situations in which the general concept of deliberately inserting a unique identifier of some sort into a message is either inappropriate or ineffective:

1. If the agent doing the forwarding is written as an add-on to an existing system. In this case, the agent may not have write access to the message header, in which case it can't insert or manipulate IDs.

2. If the message is transmitted to other domains that employ protocols other than the one used to encode identifiers. In such situations the message header containing the inserted ID may get lost in the translation. When the message is re-injected into the system that checks for the identifiers, it is treated as new, reinitiating the maelstrom.

3. If the agent modifies the message in a way that is important to some of the other agents in the network, but unimportant to others. In this case, only those agents to whom the modification is important should resend the modified version. The identifier method prevents this, or at best severely limits it.

4. If an agent wishes to ignore some types of modification and pay attention to others when it decides whether to forward a modified version of a message. As in the previous case, the identifier method prevents or severely limits this.

The last two cases above illustrate a *semantic* drawback to ID-based methods: they effectively prescribe a fixed convention to be applied to all messages modified in any way by any agent. The decision of "same" or "different", which determines whether the original ID is preserved or a new one is generated, is made once and for all by the originating agent prior to transmission. This prevents exactly the sort of contextual, individualized decision-making that is one of the central benefits of using intelligent agents in the first place. For example, Manber's scheme requires that the forwarded message, however modified, have the same identifier as the original—or at minimum as one of a predefined, strictly limited set of variants of it. One consequence of this (pointed out by Manber) is that it severely constrains extensive interagent "conversations" (i.e., series of automatically generated messages passing between two agents). Spagna's scheme, on the other hand, requires that the modified message always be treated as new. This prevents the agents from ignoring trivial changes in a message already encountered.

Signature-based maelstrom solution

We propose a maelstrom prevention method that is based directly on the contents of the message itself, rather than a message or agent ID imbedded in the header. The content-based solution avoids the cited drawbacks of the ID-based methods. It requires no manipulation of the message header, and does not rely on the header remaining inviolate. It gives individual

agents the freedom to make their own decisions about whether a new message is sufficiently distinct from a previous one to warrant forwarding.

In order to explain the content-based solution, we now follow the sequence of events that ensues when a new message M is received by the agent.

1. **Determine eligibility.** First, M is examined to determine whether it is eligible for forwarding. If M does not meet the forwarding criteria, no further processing is necessary. It may be desirable to filter out incoming duplicate messages even if they are not going to be forwarded by the agent, in which case control passes to the signature extraction step below.

2. **Match text.** If M is eligible for forwarding, a text matching algorithm that employs signature scanning is used to locate any previously forwarded messages or significant portions thereof that M may contain.

3. **Generate summary.** A *summary* of M is created from the matches located in the previous step. The summary expresses M as a combination of one or more previously forwarded messages (or portions thereof), plus any text that is unique to M.

4. **Heuristically evaluate summary.** A heuristic procedure is applied to M's summary to determine whether forwarding is warranted, and if so the forwarding takes place automatically.

5. **Extract signature, update database.** M's status as a new or previously forwarded message is reflected by updating the signature database. This may involve the automatic extraction of one or more signatures and auxiliary information from M or perhaps just the previously unencountered portions of M.

The remainder of this section is devoted to more detailed descriptions of text matching, summary generation, heuristic evaluation, and signature extraction and updates to the signature database.

Text matching

The text matching procedure attempts to locate previously forwarded messages (or portions thereof) within M. In order to reduce sensitivity to common insignificant textual transformations that occur when mail is forwarded, such as the addition of right angle brackets to indicate quoting, extra blank lines, etc., M's text is first filtered. In a current implementation, the filtering entails removing header data, replacing multiple consecutive whitespace characters with a single whitespace, removing (most) non-alphanumeric characters, and mapping all characters to lower case. In what follows, this transformed text shall be referred to as M'.

Next, M' is to be matched against similarly transformed versions of all previously forwarded messages. The naive approach of applying something like the Unix diff operation sequentially to M' and each of the hundreds or even thousands of previously forwarded messages P is clearly much too inefficient. Instead, a highly efficient signature scanning procedure originally developed for detecting computer viruses is used to scan M'. The relatively slow text matching procedure only needs to be invoked for those messages P that are associated with signatures located within M. If the signatures (which consist of sequences of s characters occurring in the transformed version of a given message) are selected carefully, they will hardly ever be found by chance, so that if M' contains entirely new material it is likely that no signatures will be located, and expensive matching will be avoided altogether. The careful selection of signatures is performed by an automated signature extraction technique described more fully below.

A potential problem arises when a signature for P has been located within M', but P itself has been deleted. In such a case, it is still possible to determine the location and approximate extent of the match between P and M'. The trick is to extract a small amount of extra information from P before deleting P. In a current implementation, we extract 4-byte checksums for a series of roughly concentric regions of text centered around each signature in P. Associated with each checksum is an offset of the signature from the beginning of the region and the number of characters in the region; this information constitutes a "textblock triple". Each region is roughly twice the size of the previous one, up to and including the entire message. Thus, if the transformed version of a message is 580 characters in length and the signature length is $s = 20$, there will be 5 checksummed regions with lengths of 40, 80, 160, 320, and 580 bytes.

If a signature for P has been located within M', then each textblock triple is tested against the M' to identify the longest matching region, and this information is passed to the summary generation step. If there are no matching triples, then the length of the partial match is taken to be the signature length. Note that some loss of information is expected because the length of the matching region will be underestimated consistently.

Summary generation

The list of matching regions generated in the previous step is used to construct a summary that replaces each matching block of text with a short identifier that refers to the original message in which that text occurred. A sample message and message summary are shown in Fig. 1. If there are multiple possible matches for a given region of M', preference is given to the longest match that contains that region.

Heuristic evaluation

The generated message summary is used by a heuristic that decides whether to permit M to be forwarded. [2] One can contemplate a range of possible heuristics that vary widely in computational feasibility and effectiveness. One simple heuristic would forbid the forwarding

---

[2] If automatic forwarding of M is prevented, a user interface could still offer the option of manual forwarding.

	Message Summary	ID
a	Meeting today, 3pm	1426
b	FYI: *[copy of message 1426]*	1465
c	CANCELLED: *[copy of message 1426]*	1466

Figure 1: Schematic depiction of message summaries. The original message (a) is not summarizable. Messages (b) and (c) are forwarded versions of (a) with some prepended text.

of M solely on the basis of the form of the message summary, not its textual content. For example, the heuristic could forbid forwarding only if M exactly contains in full a previously encountered message P, and contains no more than 10 additional characters.

More sophisticated heuristics would take into account both the form of the summary and any block of text that is unique to M. Plausible heuristics might search for the presence of keywords in the non-matching text regions, or alternatively apply a text classifier to the non-matching text regions and map the result of the classifier into a yes/no forwarding decision. As an example of the first approach, a keyword-based algorithm might decide against forwarding message (b) in Fig. 1 because the additional text consists of a recognizably unimportant word "FYI", but it would permit message (c) to be forwarded because of the recognizably important keyword "CANCELLED".

The heuristic could be adjusted or trained to the tastes of the individual user. As with any heuristic, there will be false positives and false negatives; the effects of false negatives will be investigated below.

Signature extraction and updating

The scanner uses a database that contains signatures and their associated textblock triples, pointers to messages containing the signatures, a TimeLastSeen field, whose purpose will be discussed below, and possibly other relevant information.

If M is a new message with no relationship to a previously encountered message, then one or more signatures for M are extracted and added to the database. As has been discussed, it is important to select signatures that are unlikely to appear at random in ordinary messages, so that the expensive matching operation between M and a previously forwarded message P is only called upon when there is a very strong likelihood that M and P have a significant block of text in common.

We have adapted an automatic signature extraction procedure described in [Kephart & Arnold, 1994], originally developed for computer virus signatures. At infrequent intervals (perhaps once per year), a large corpus of mail messages (for example, those stored in the user's mail archive or database) is filtered as described above. The number of occurrences of each unigram a, bigram ab, and trigram abc in the filtered database is tallied and recorded in tables as $t(a)$, $t(ab)$, and $t(abc)$, respectively, along with the corpus size Z. For English and several other languages, there are at most 128 different ASCII characters that occur in text, so this requires storage of 2^{21} 4-byte integers for the trigram table, or about 8 megabytes; the sizes of the bigram and unigram tables are relatively insignificant.

When M is submitted to the signature extraction procedure, it is first filtered to obtain M'. Next, all s-byte sequences in M are considered as candidate signatures. (Typically, s is set to approximately 20.) For each candidate signature, the tallied n-gram statistics are used to estimate the likelihood for that s-byte sequence to appear by chance in an ordinary (filtered) mail message. In our implementation, we ignore possible correlations that span more than 3 characters, allowing us to estimate the likelihood of the sequence $c_1 c_2 \ldots c_s$ as

$$p(c_1 c_2 \ldots c_s) \approx \frac{t(c_1 c_2 c_3) \ldots t(c_{s_2} c_{s-1} c_s)}{Z t(c_2 c_3) \ldots t(c_{s-2} c_{s-1})}, \quad (1)$$

If any trigram frequencies are zero, they are replaced with estimated trigram frequencies based on bigram and unigram frequencies.

Finally, the candidate signature or signatures that minimize $p(c_1 c_2 \ldots c_s)$ are selected and recorded in the database, and the TimeLastSeen field is initialized to the time at which M was received. If more than one signature is chosen, the selection criterion is modified slightly to encourage the selected signatures to be as far apart as possible. For each selected signature, a textblock triple is also computed as described above, although this step may be deferred until M is deleted.

If M is not entirely original, but is still regarded as sufficiently distinct from its ancestors, then it is desirable to reduce the potential for confusion during the scanning phase by extracting a signature that distinguishes M from its ancestors. In this case, signature extraction proceeds as described above, except that the candidate signatures are drawn only from the non-matching text regions in M's message summary.

In cases where M is identical or nearly identical to a previously encountered message P, it may not be worthwhile to extract a new signature for it. The signature database is simply updated by recording the current time in the TimeLastSeen field of each signature located within M. This keeps track of how "current" the signatures are. In order to bound the growth of the database, signatures and associated data that are deemed sufficiently old may be purged from the database.

Standalone Performance

For a single agent, the essential performance measures of the anti-maelstrom method are the storage requirements and processing time. To estimate these, we describe the application of the method to a fixed corpus of over 10,000 e-mail messages consisting of several years' mail received by one of us.

In two experiments conducted on a model F50 RISC System 6000 workstation with a 166 MHz processor,

we generated two signatures per message, each $s = 20$ bytes in length. For each signature, the storage requirement was 20 bytes for the signature, a 4-byte pointer to the original message, a 4-byte LastTimeSeen field, and a number of 12-byte textblock triples (4 bytes each for the checksum, signature offset, and length) that depended on the size of the message.

In a first experiment involving 3569 messages, 6889 signatures were extracted; there were some failures due to short messages. The number of textblock triples was 39,393. Thus the total storage required was $(20 + 4 + 4) * 6889 + 12 * 39,393 = 665,608$ bytes, or less than 100 bytes per signature. If messages are purged from the database after a year of inactivity, a user receiving 5,000 messages per year requires just a one-megabyte signature database.

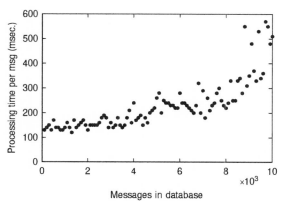

Figure 2: Processing time vs. number of scanned files when signatures are simultaneously being extracted.

In a second experiment, we built a signature database from scratch by running through 10,000 mail messages. Each message was scanned using the current signature database, and whenever a signature was found the appropriate full-text match was carried out and a message summary was generated. Then, two signatures and their textblock triples were extracted for the message, the database was updated, and the next message was processed. The amount of time required to process each message (averaged in blocks of 100 messages) is plotted in Fig. 2. Early on, the processing time per message is somewhat less than 150 msec. Practically all of this time is taken by signature extraction. As the number of messages database grows in size towards a few thousand, the processing time per message grows noticeably because the scan starts to become slower; at 5,000 messages, it takes 200 to 250 msec per message. This would be the asymptotic performance for a database that is kept pruned to this size. Especially when one considers that no algorithmic tuning has been done, this suggests that the method is entirely practical, and would have very little impact on storage or CPU usage.

Performance in a Network

The second test of an anti-maelstrom method is in its performance as deployed across a network. In the context of an emergent multi-agent system, we cannot hope to universally suppress redundant messages. At best, a "successful" solution is one which reduces the number of undesirable messages to a level sustainable by the network and by the agents themselves. Here, we can only present the beginnings of such an evaluation pending more detailed investigation. We will present preliminary results on the behavior of maelstroms as a function of two separate parameters: (i) the rate of misidentifications induced by the anti-maelstrom method; and (ii) the fraction of agents employing it.

As noted, the anti-maelstrom method will induce a certain degree of error due to misclassification of messages by the AI heuristic. These will take the form of *false positives*, in which a message that is not part of a maelstrom is misclassified as being one that is, and *false negatives* in which a "bad" message is misclassified as "good". Obviously the actual false positive and false negative rates will depend sensitively on the nature of the transformations of the messages being sent and on the actual heuristics in use. In practice, the transformations will be the forcing function that drives the evolution of the heuristic. Here, we do not speculate on the form they will take, but rather show the behavior of the system as a function of the error rates, however they may come about.

For the simulations presented here, we generated a random digraph with $n = 1000$ nodes and $k = 4000$ edges, in which each edge's source and destination were selected at random, but in which loops (self-edges) were not permitted. Then we removed all nodes and edges outside the giant strongly connected component, which resulted in a graph with $n = 969$ nodes and $k = 3878$ edges in which a communication path existed between each pair of nodes. At each time step, all nodes were updated synchronously. When updated, a node processed all incoming messages, determining whether each was new or whether it had been received already. If classified as new, the message was forwarded verbatim to each of the node's downstream neighbors (but not back to the sender); if not, the message was not forwarded. The network was seeded with a single outgoing message from a randomly selected node.

To measure the behavior under imperfect classification, the classifier was set to randomly misidentify messages with false negative rate r_N. Then the number of messages extant in the system was measured as a function of time. Figure 3 shows the number of messages plotted vs. time for $r_N = 0.0$ to $r_N = 1.0$ in increments of 0.1, plus $r_N = 0.25$. Most notable is the qualitative change in behavior at $R_N \approx 0.25$. For values of r_N greater than this critical false negative rate, the number of messages grew without bound. (In practice, the number of messages is bounded by the maximum carrying capacity of the network.) For $r_N < R_N$, after an initial period of exponential growth, the number of

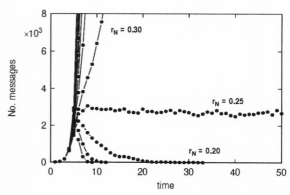

Figure 3: Number of messages vs. time for different false negative error rates.

messages eventually fell back to 0. At $r_N = 0.25$, the system reached a steady state in which the maelstrom persisted indefinitely but the number of messages did not grow. Because the average outdegree of each agent is approximately 4, at $r_N = 0.25$, each agent sends about as many messages as it receives.

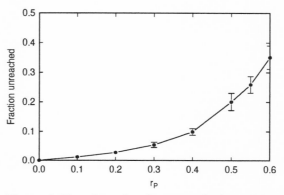

Figure 4: Fraction of nodes unreached vs. false positive error rate.

The effect of false positives is summarized in fig. 4, which shows the fraction of nodes that failed to receive even one copy of the message as a function of the false positive rate r_P. The data were averaged over 10 trials using different random number seeds. The mean values at each r_P are plotted, bracketed by error bars showing the standard deviations. Beyond $r_P = 0.6$, the fraction of unreached nodes quickly approached 1.0.

When both r_N and r_P are nonzero, the redundant messages generated by positive r_N and the unsent messages due to positive r_P tend to counteract each other, but only partially. For example, when $r_N = 0.10$, the fraction of unreached nodes at various r_P is typically reduced by approximately one half. But the critical false negative rate R_N remains at approximately 0.25 for values of r_P up to about 0.25.

To measure the behavior for different heterogeneous populations, we disabled the anti-maelstrom solution in a randomly selected fraction f_B of nodes ("bozos"), by

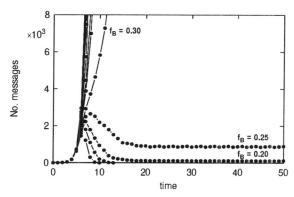

Figure 5: Number of messages vs. time for different fractions of "bozo" agents.

setting $r_N = 1$ and $r_P = 0$; the rest of the nodes had $r_N = r_P = 0$. Figure 5 shows the number of messages extant at a given time, plotted vs. time for $f_B = 0.0$ to $f_B = 1.0$ in increments of 0.1, plus $f_B = 0.25$. One notable finding is the similarity, both qualitative and quantitative, with the data of Fig. 3. For f_B below a critical value $F_B \approx 0.25$, the maelstrom was eventually quenched. For $f_B > F_B$, the number of messages increased exponentially. At $f_B = F_B$, the maelstrom persisted, but the number of messages reached an equilibrium value. Note that at $f_B = 0.25$, each agent—and in particular, each bozo—has on average one bozo for a downstream neighbor.

Obviously, more investigation is needed to verify these findings and to interpret them. Of particular interest are the apparent relationships between the critical values R_N and F_B and the average outdegree, as observed in this data.

Conclusion

In this paper, we have taken notice of a new type of emergent phenomenon that is likely to arise in networks of message-passing agents, with potentially disastrous results. We have presented a solution that hinges on the recognition of similarities in message texts. We have evaluated that solution, both in isolation and, by simulation, in the context of a randomly connected network of mail-forwarding agents.

In isolation, the anti-maelstrom solution was seen to have minimal impact on storage or CPU usage. When deployed among agents in a random network, we found that when the rate at which redundant messages were incorrectly identified was below a threshold value, the maelstrom was eventually quenched. Similarly, when the fraction of agents refusing to adopt the anti-maelstrom method was less than a threshold, the maelstrom was reduced to manageable proportions. Both of these thresholds were linked to topological properties of the network. Even for false positive rates as high as 10%, the fraction of agents in the network that failed to receive the message was negligible. In addition, a nonzero false negative rate was found to

mitigate the effect of false positives.

Plans for future work include more detailed numerical experiments on the performance of the solution we proposed, particularly under different network topologies. The connection between collective dynamics and network topology has been investigated in a number of different contexts (see, for example, [Kephart, 1994], [Watts & Strogatz, 1998]); some of those methods and results may be applied or adapted to maelstrom dynamics.

We have barely touched on the heuristic classification methods used by the agents in distinguishing, for example, important variations in a message from unimportant ones. In any practical implementation, of course, a viable heuristic is essential. But for the purpose of understanding collective behavior in a network, it is reasonable to approximate any such heuristic by false positive and false negative error rates. Studies of the sort presented here, if conducted on sufficiently realistic network topologies, are an essential tool in establishing the relation between the "microscopic" observables of a heuristic—e.g., its error rates—and the induced "macroscopic" behavior of the network—such as delivery failures and flooding. Since notions of acceptable behavior are likely to be expressed in terms of macroscopic properties, this relation will help heuristic designers to achieve a reasonable tradeoff between false negative and false positive rates.

Perhaps more important than the details of the particular phenomenon we have studied, however, is the example it provides of a danger innate to emergent multi-agent systems: Agents may easily be programmed to perform actions which, considered in isolation, are perfectly innocent, benign, and well-behaved—yet when deployed in a network, wreak collective havoc. Without due attention, this danger could prove to be a significant barrier to the widespread, continued use of agent technology on the Internet.

References

Demazeau, Y., ed. 1998. *Proceedings of the Third International Conference on Multi-Agent Systems*. IEEE Computer Society.

Kephart, J. O., and Arnold, W. C. 1994. Automatic extraction of computer virus signatures. In Duffield, P., ed., *Proceedings of the Fourth International Virus Bulletin Conference*, 179–194. Abingdon, England: Virus Bulletin Limited.

Kephart, J. O. 1994. How topology affects population dynamics. In Langton, C. G., ed., *Artificial Life III*, 447–464. Reading, MA: Addison Wesley.

Manber, U. 1990. Chain reactions in networks. *Computer* 57–63.

Spagna, R. 1997. A method and system for preventing routing maelstrom loops of automatically routed electronic mail. Patent application.

Watts, D. J., and Strogatz, S. H. 1998. Collective dynamics of 'small-world' networks. *Nature* 393:440.

Learning Quantitative Knowledge for Multiagent Coordination

David Jensen, Michael Atighetchi, Régis Vincent, Victor Lesser
Computer Science Department
University of Massachusetts at Amherst
Amherst, MA 01003
{jensen,adi,vincent,lesser}@cs.umass.edu

Abstract

A central challenge of multiagent coordination is reasoning about how the actions of one agent affect the actions of another. Knowledge of these interrelationships can help coordinate agents — preventing conflicts and exploiting beneficial relationships among actions. We explore three interlocking methods that learn quantitative knowledge of such non-local effects in TÆMS, a well-developed framework for multiagent coordination. The surprising simplicity and effectiveness of these methods demonstrates how agents can learn domain-specific knowledge quickly, extending the utility of coordination frameworks that explicitly represent coordination knowledge.

Introduction

A major challenge of designing effective multiagent systems is managing non-local effects — situations where the actions of one agent impact the performance of other agents' actions. For example, one agent's action can enable, disable, facilitate, or hinder the actions of other agents. Poor accounting for these non-local effects (NLEs) can cause multiagent activities to deadlock or waste resources, so representing and reasoning about NLEs is a central feature of frameworks for multiagent coordination (Decker and Lesser 1995; Barbuceanu and Fox 1995).

Multiagent coordination frameworks often assume that agents possess accurate knowledge of the relationships among actions and the basic performance characteristics of those actions (e.g., cost and duration). Such knowledge allows agents to schedule activities in ways that exploit beneficial relationships, and avoid pathological ones. Unfortunately, accurate knowledge of NLEs is difficult to maintain in heterogeneous and open systems. Agent designers may not know the future operating environment for their agents, the complete set of actions open to other agents, and the effects those actions have on their own agents. For all of these reasons, the ability for multiagent systems to autonomously learn coordination knowledge appears critical for next-generation coordination frameworks (Sugawara and Lesser 1998).

We investigated and implemented techniques to learn the statistical knowledge about NLEs represented in one well-established framework for multiagent coordination (TÆMS). We found that a combination of three simple learning techniques can be surprisingly effective. The learned knowledge can be used to accurately predict the performance of a particular action, given its context within a set of actions executed by the same agent or other agents. The success of these methods demonstrates how coordination knowledge can be learned explicitly, as opposed to learning coordination policies that implicitly represent knowledge of agents, environments, and their association.

Context

Learning for multiagent coordination has become a popular topic in the past several years. Much of the existing work aims to equip agents with effective policies — functions that map environmental conditions directly to coordinated actions. For example, Weiß (Weiß 1998) investigates reinforcement learning (RL) techniques to improve the coordinated performance of *reactive* agents. Similarly, Tan (Tan 1998) investigates how to extend RL to create coordinated multiagent policies.

In contrast, we explore learning explicit quantitative knowledge needed by *deliberative* agents — agents that explicitly plan sequences of actions and that can trace the assumptions embedded in those plans. We assume that the coordination framework (TÆMS in this case) encodes all relevant characteristics of the environment needed to guide coordination and that agents can use this knowledge to devise coordinated actions. Separating knowledge from coordination mechanisms provides opportunities (e.g., the coordination strategy can be changed without altering the knowledge), as well as costs (e.g., using the knowledge requires explicit reasoning).

Another theme of learning for multiagent coordination has been learning to predict the future actions of other agents. Such predictions can help produce coordinated actions even without explicit communication among agents. Hu and Wellman (Hu and Wellman 1998) study this type of learning in the context of a simulated double auction. Similarly, Zeng and Sycara (Zeng and Sycara 1997) study learning to predict agent actions in the context of sequential negotiation. In contrast, we focus on learning how agent actions affect each other. While some of this knowledge could be used to predict the reasoning of other agents, it does not directly predict their actions.

Some of the work closest to our own focuses on learning the effects of environmental context on the outcomes of agent actions. For example, Schmill, Rosenstein, Cohen, and Utgoff (Schmill *et al.* 1998) use decision trees to learn the environmental states and actions that produce changes in particular sensor values of a mobile robot. Similarly, Haigh and Veloso (Haigh and Veloso 1998) learn situation-dependent costs of actions from execution traces of robot navigation. This work and other similar work focuses on the relationships among actions and outcomes, a notion closely allied with our focus on actions and their non-local effects (NLEs) in a multiagent context. However, the "environment" in our work consists almost entirely of the actions of other agents, and the desired knowledge concerns how to coordinate the actions of multiple agents.

Tasks

We investigated learning techniques for TÆMS, an existing framework for multiagent coordination. TÆMS (Decker and Lesser 1993) represents quantitative information about agent activities, including candidate actions and how those actions can combine to achieve high-level tasks. TÆMS represents a task as a tree whose root is the overall task and whose leaves are primitive actions referred to as *methods*. Internal nodes represent subtasks composed of other tasks and methods. Internal nodes also specify how the constituent methods and tasks combine for successful execution (e.g., all must execute successfully, or only a single alternative must execute successfully). In addition to this structural information about tasks and methods, TÆMS represents two types of statistical information — 1) probability distributions that describe the possible values of performance parameters of a method (e.g., the quality of a method's result, the cost of the method, and its duration); and 2) non-local effects (NLEs) of one method on another (e.g., enables, disables, facilitates, and hinders).

Reasoners can use the knowledge represented in TÆMS (Wagner *et al.* 1998a) to evaluate the quality, cost, and duration of possible courses of action and their effects on other agent's actions. Using this information, reasoners can select the one that best[1] meets the current

---

[1] The general action selection problem in TÆMS is exponential and reasoners generally use a real-time, satisficing, goal-directed, approximation strategy (Wagner *et al.* 1998a). Thus, "best" in this case does not necessarily denote optimal.

constraints and environmental conditions. For example, in a time-constrained situation, an agent may sacrifice solution quality, and pay a larger fee, to produce a result within the specified deadline. Detailed discussions of TÆMS are provided elsewhere (Decker and Lesser 1993; Wagner *et al.* 1998b).

For example, consider how TÆMS could be used to coordinate the tasks assigned to different departments in a hospital. The departments need to coordinate the execution of these tasks to produce maximum medical benefit to patients under time and cost constraints. For a given patient, the radiology department may wish to schedule an x-ray, the nursing staff may wish to draw blood for diagnostic tests, and the cafeteria may wish to provide breakfast for the patient. The existence of NLEs among the methods needed to complete these tasks implies a specific order of execution. For example, eating breakfast may disable some diagnostic tests and the radioactive elements ingested for some x-rays may hinder obtaining accurate results from blood tests. These constraints imply a schedule with the order: blood tests, x-rays, and breakfast.

To be more specific, Figure 1 shows a partial TÆMS task structure for the hospital agents (Decker and Li 1998) coordinating their services for a single patient. Radiology has the task of taking an x-ray of the patient. This task requires execution of three methods: providing a barium solution for the patient to ingest, producing an exposure of the patient, and interpreting the exposure. The barium solution enables the interpretation (without it the interpretation would always have zero quality) and the exposure enables the interpretation. Similarly, the nursing staff wish to conduct tests on the patient's blood. The first method of this activity, drawing blood, enables the two tests. One of the tests is hindered if the patient has ingested a barium solution. Finally, hospital policy requires that blood be drawn and barium solutions be administered when the patient has an empty stomach.

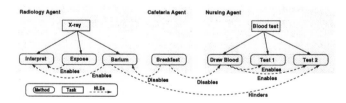

Figure 1: TÆMS Task Structure for hospital patient services.

This paper focuses on learning the statistical knowledge encoded in TÆMS about distributions and NLEs (distributions were left off figure 1 for simplicity). In particular, we focus on learning four of the most common NLEs – enables, disables, facilitates, and hinders. Each NLE defines a relation between one task or method (A) and another task or method (B). For clarity and brevity, only effects on quality are discussed; effects on duration and cost can be inferred from context. Similarly, the term "precede" is used to mean that a method successfully completes execution prior the the beginning of execution for another method.

- *Enables* — If A does not precede B, then B fails, achieving a quality $q(B) = 0$. If multiple methods or tasks enable B, then *all* must precede B in order for B to be enabled.

- *Disables* — The complement of *enables*. If A precedes B, then B fails, achieving a quality $q(B) = 0$. If multiple methods or tasks disable B, then B will fail if *any* of them precede B.

- *Facilitates* — If A precedes B, then the quality of B is multiplied by a given power factor ϕ, where $\phi > 1$. That is, $q(B|A) = \phi_{AB}q(B|\overline{A})$. *Facilitates* can modify one or more performance characteristics of B. Multiple facilitating methods are multiplicative in their effects. That is, if A and B both facilitate C, and precede C in a schedule, then $q(C|AB) = \phi_{AC}\phi_{BC}q(C|\overline{AB})$.

- *Hinders* — The complement of *facilitates*. If A precedes B, then the quality of B is multiplied by a given power factor ϕ, where $\phi < 1$.

Learning Methods

Our work focuses on learning accurate knowledge of distributions and NLEs. We assume that agents already know what methods are available to be executed, and how to use TÆMS knowledge to produce effective schedules.

To learn distributions and NLEs, agents monitor the performance of schedules — finite sets of methods with at least a partial order. Each learning instance consists of the performance characteristics of a given method in the schedule (e.g., quality, duration, and cost) and the set of all methods in the schedule that successfully completed execution prior to the given method.[2] We assume that all methods in a schedule are either executed directly by the learning agent, or that the learning agent is informed of their execution. Agents are not required to infer the existence of hidden methods. Further, we assume that each schedule execution is independent; methods executed in one schedule do not affect methods executed in another schedule. This limits the scope of NLEs to methods in the schedule, consistent with the original assumptions of TÆMS.

The goal is to use learning instances to infer distributions of unaffected performance characteristics (quality, duration, and cost) for each method and to infer the existence of all NLEs and their associated power factors (ϕ). To acquire this knowledge, we built the TÆMS

---

[2]From this point forward, we refer only to methods, not the more general term "methods and tasks."

Learning System (TLS). TLS uses three relatively simple learning methods: 1) empirical frequency distributions; 2) deterministic properties of schedules; and 3) linear regression. Below, we discuss each method individually and discuss the interactions among the methods that allow them to be effective.

Empirical frequency distributions are used to estimate distributions of performance parameters such as quality, duration, and cost. The frequency distribution for a given method and performance parameter is derived from a moving window of k instances of the execution of that method. Our goal is to estimate the distribution when *unaffected* by NLEs (i.e., the quality of method C may be affected by methods A and B that *facilitate* its execution). As a result, nearly all values are assumed to be affected by NLEs, and they are divided by the current estimates of the relevant power factors to render an estimate of the *unaffected* quality. For example, if A and B were the only methods currently thought to affect C, then $q(C|\overline{NLE}) = q(C)/(\phi_{AC}\phi_{BC})$.

An alternative approach is to learn from only those results of method executions that are guaranteed to be unaffected (e.g., the results of methods executed at the start of each schedule). In empirical tests, this approach proved far slower than the methods reported here. Figure 2 shows the results of one experiment. The top line shows the error associated with learning from only quality values guaranteed to be unaffected. The bottom line shows the error associated with learning from all values, when whose values are corrected based on estimated power factors.

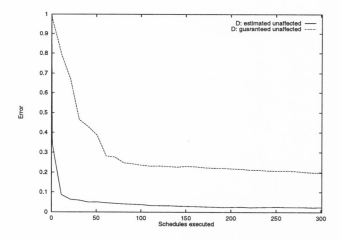

Figure 2: Error of two different methods for estimating distributions.

Deterministic properties of schedules are used to learn "hard" NLEs such as *enables* and *disables*. Although we derived a total of six such properties, two proved particularly useful in the experiments reported here. The first, *enables exclusion* states that successful execution of method A at any point in a schedule excludes all methods that did not precede A as possible enabling conditions (TÆMS requires that *all* enabling methods precede a given method for it to execute successfully). The second, *disables exclusion* states that successful execution of method A at any point in a schedule excludes all methods that precede A as possible disabling conditions (TÆMS specifies that *any* disabling method preceding a given method will disable it).

Linear regression is used to infer the existence of "soft" NLEs and to estimate their associated power factors (ϕ). Recall the TÆMS specification of how *facilitates* and *hinders* affect the performance characteristics of methods. For example, the quality of a given method m_0 is determined by its unaffected quality ($q(m_0|\overline{NLE})$) and the power factors of methods that facilitate or hinder it (e.g., m_1, m_2, and m_3). Given these NLEs, TÆMS specifies that:

$$q(m_0) = \phi_1{}^{x_1} \phi_2{}^{x_2} \phi_3{}^{x_3} q(m_0|\overline{NLE})$$

where $x_n = 1$ when m_n precedes m_0 and $x_n = 0$ otherwise. Taking the log of both sides:

$$\begin{aligned} log(q(m_0)) = {} & log(\phi_1)x_1 + log(\phi_2)x_2 + \\ & log(\phi_3)x_3 + log(q(m_0|\overline{NLE})) \end{aligned}$$

This equation is in the classic form of a linear regression equation: $y = \beta_1 x_1 + \beta_2 x_2 + \beta_3 x_3 + \beta_0 + \epsilon$, where y corresponds to the log of the affected quality and β_1, β_2, and β_3 correspond to the logs of the respective power factors. β_0 and ϵ combine to correspond to the unaffected quality distribution, where β_0 is the distribution's mean and ϵ corresponds to the random deviations of its values from that mean.

To find NLEs affecting each method, we search for equations containing power factors ϕ that are significantly different than one (represented by regression coefficients β significantly different from zero). We conduct this search using a standard statistical method, stepwise linear regression (Draper and Smith 1981; J. Neter 1990). Stepwise regression conducts a simple local search over possible regression equations, starting with an equation containing only β_0 and ending with an equation containing at most k terms, where k is the number of methods available in each schedule. Terms are added to the equation if their coefficients are significantly different than one, and are removed if their coefficients are not significantly different than one (coefficients of existing terms in an equation can change when new terms are added).

Three assumptions of linear regression create potential problems for applying the technique to learn power factors for soft NLEs. Under the first assumption, independence of the variables x_n, knowing a value of one x should tell us nothing about the value of any other x. Unfortunately, hard NLEs can cause successful execution of some methods to be dependent on the successful execution of others, introducing dependence among the variables x_n. The NLE A *enables* B introduces

a positive correlation between x_A and x_B; A *disables* B introduces a negative correlation. Regression is robust against moderate violations of this assumption, but strong violations can greatly increase the variance of estimated coefficients of the regression equation (in our case, causing the estimates of power factors to be extremely inflated or deflated). TLS addresses this problem in two ways. First, it checks for strong violations of this assumption (often referred to as perfect multicollinearity), and doesn't alter the current state of knowledge in such cases. In our experiments, such violations typically occurred only in very small datasets. Second, TLS uses *stepwise* regression which greatly reduces the total number of variables in regression equations, thus reducing the probability that two or more of them will be dependent.

Under the second assumption, normally-distributed errors, the distribution of the error term in the regression equation should be normal. In our case, the error term represents the log of the unaffected quality distribution $log(q(m_0|\overline{NLE}))$ (shifted so its mean is zero). To match this assumption, the distribution itself should be log-normal. While this is one reasonable quality distribution, it is not the only reasonable one. We experiment with an alternative distribution to indicate how linear regression is robust to moderate violations of this assumption.

The third assumption affects how we test statistical significance. Such tests are run to determine which coefficients β differ significantly from zero. The stringency of any one test is determined by α_1, which indicates the probability of a Type I error (incorrectly rejecting the null hypothesis that a single coefficient is zero). However, for a single performance parameter (e.g., quality) and k methods in a schedule, $k(k-1)$ possible NLEs exist. TLS tests whether each of these NLEs exists. Under these conditions, the probability of TLS making at least one Type I error is much larger than α_1. If the NLEs are independent, the probability is:

$$\alpha_{\text{TLS}} = 1 - (1 - \alpha_1)^{k(k-1)}$$

For example, for the overall probability of error α_{TLS} to be small (e.g., 0.10) in our base case experiment, the probability of error on any one test α_1 must be much smaller (0.000012). This process is called *Bonferroni adjustment*. Some such adjustment is important in any context where many explicit or implicit hypothesis tests are made (Jensen and Cohen 1999). TLS uses Bonferroni adjustment to set appropriate values of α_1 so that α_{TLS} is small.

Experiments

We measure the effectiveness of TLS with metrics that directly measure the quality of the learned knowledge, rather than indirectly measuring its effect on agent coordination. This approach focuses evaluation on TLS and avoids confounding TLS' performance with the performance of other system components for scheduling and coordination (Wagner *et al.* 1997). However, it could also inappropriately credit or penalize TLS for learning knowledge that is unimportant or infrequently used, respectively. To guard against this latter error, we review the utility of the learned knowledge at the the next section and show that the most useful knowledge is generally learned most quickly.

In each experiment, agents create learning data by generating and executing schedules. In all experiments reported here, agents operate in an exploration mode, executing randomly-generated schedules, rather than attempting to use already learned knowledge to generate maximally effective schedules. In practice, agents are likely to mix exploration and exploitation of learned knowledge, and even to use directed exploration. These options will be explored in later work.

Agents have access to performance parameters of executed schedules — values of quality, duration, and cost for each method in a schedule — that are affected by an initially unknown set of NLEs. The actual unaffected distributions and NLEs are hidden from agents, but they determine the values of performance parameters observed by agents.

Consistent with other projects using TÆMS, we use discrete probability distributions. However, our methods for learning hard and soft NLEs apply equally well to cases with continuous probability distributions, and a method such as kernel density estimators (John and Langley 1995) could be used to estimate continuous probability distributions from empirical data.

The experiments were conducted in two phases. First, a base case was run with settings corresponding to the assumptions of the learning techniques, particularly linear regression. Second, those settings were systematically altered to test the effects of violations of those assumptions. For the base case, schedules contain 30 unique methods, executed in a random order. Method performance is controlled by a TÆMS task structure containing 15 NLEs (three disables, four enables, four facilitates, and four hinders). In addition, the task structure avoids cases where a single method is affected by more than one NLE. Values of ϕ for the soft NLEs deviate moderately from unity (3.0 for facilitate and 0.5 for hinders). The discrete probability distributions for performance parameters of methods (e.g., quality) are approximately log-normal. To learn empirical frequency distributions, TLS uses a window size of 100, and to learn soft NLEs, it uses $\alpha_{\text{TLS}} = 0.10$. In the next section, we show results for this base case, and results for dependent NLEs, log-uniform quality distributions, soft NLEs with small deviations from unity, and a larger number of soft NLEs.

To measure learning in TLS, we use four error metrics, each of which applies to one of the three pairs of learning methods and learned knowledge. TLS' error in learning distributions with empirical frequencies is measured by the mean difference in areas ($\overline{D}$) between the cumulative probability plots of the actual and learned distributions. For example, figure 3 shows how D is calculated for a method in a particularly simple case. D is normalized by dividing by the total range of the quality ($q_{max} - q_{min}$) so that it varies between 0 and 1. The mean of D, $\overline{D}$, measures the average D across all methods.

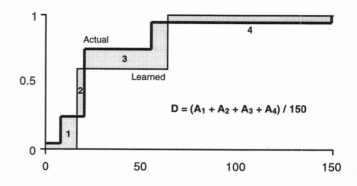

Figure 3: Difference in cumulative probability between learned and actual distributions

TLS' error in learning hard NLEs with deterministic properties is measured by the proportion of misclassified hard NLEs (H). All experiments reported in this paper begin with the assumption that all possible hard NLEs exist — a total of $k(k-1)$ possible hard NLEs among k methods. Deterministic properties are then used to eliminate hard NLEs until only true ones remain. The deterministic properties used by TLS are guaranteed to preserve actual hard NLEs, thus H always measures the extra NLEs that the system was unable to eliminate from consideration.

TLS' error in learning soft NLEs with stepwise linear regression is measured by two different metrics. The first measures the errors in TLS' inferences about *which* soft NLEs exist; the second measures the errors in TLS' estimates of the *power factors* for inferred NLEs. The first metric, S, is the proportion of all true soft NLEs that are learned correctly (*number of soft NLEs learned / number of true soft NLEs*). In the base case used in the experiments, there are eight soft NLEs. The second metric, $\overline{\delta}$, is the average difference between the actual power factor and the learned power factor. For a given soft NLE i, $\delta = |\phi_{i_{actual}} - \phi_{i_{learned}}|$). The mean difference, $\overline{\delta}$, measures the average δ across all possible soft NLEs.

Results

Figure 5a shows the values of the first three error metrics (excluding $\overline{\delta}$) for the base conditions (the settings outlined above). In fewer than 100 schedules, the distributions and hard NLEs are learned with low error. TLS continues to reduce the number of spurious hard NLEs, reaching one by the time 300 schedules are executed. The existence of all soft NLEs is not correctly inferred until more than 240 schedules have been executed, although all but one is inferred in less than 150 schedules.

To explore the robustness of TLS, we tested four alternatives to the base conditions: 1) dependent NLEs rather than independent NLEs; 2) log-uniform quality distributions rather than log-normal; 3) $\phi_{facilitates} = 1.5$ and $\phi_{hinders} = 0.75$ rather than $\phi_{facilitates} = 3.0$ and $\phi_{hinders} = 0.5$; and 4) 15 soft NLEs rather than 8 soft and 7 hard.

Figure 5b shows the sum of the errors in the power factors, δ, for the base conditions and all four alternative conditions. All tend toward zero as the number of schedule executions increases, but the base conditions cause the fastest convergence. Decreasing the deviations of the power factors from one causes a long plateau before sufficient data accumulate to begin learning these small deviations. Similarly, dependence among the NLEs also causes a plateau, because the hard NLEs prevent some methods from executing, depriving the regression of the data needed to infer soft NLEs. A log-uniform distribution causes larger errors in power factors.

One result that figures 5a and b do not convey clearly is the degree to which distributions are learned correctly. Figure 4 shows a cumulative probability plot comparing an actual distribution and a learned distribution for a method affected by a single *hinders* under the base conditions. The plot shows the distribution after 300 schedules. The learned distribution closely approximates the actual distribution.

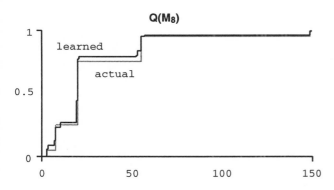

Figure 4: Cumulative probability plot of actual and learned distributions of quality

Figures 5c-f show the same content as figure 5a, but for the four alternative conditions outlined above. In these alternative conditions, distributions and hard NLEs are still learned very rapidly, but the speed with which soft NLEs can be inferred is generally reduced.

The experiments revealed some unexpected difficulties in learning. For example, the overall low error rate for NLEs masks some subtle limitations that prevents TLS from accurately learning all NLEs when such relationships are dependent (e.g., Figure 5c). The situation shown in figure 6 demonstrates three cases of such limitations. The *disables* between M_1 and M_3 is spu-

rious, but cannot be eliminated. For any schedule in which M_1 precedes M_3, M_3 will be disabled because of the valid hard NLEs connecting M_1, M_2, and M_3, thus simulating a *disables* between M_1 and M_3. For the same reason, the *hinders* between M_1 and M_3 cannot be learned. Finally, the spurious *disables* between M_1 and M_2 cannot be eliminated because the valid *enables* NLE between the two methods prevents M_1 from every preceding M_2. Fortunately, much of the knowledge made inaccessible by these limitations concerns "impossible schedules" — schedules that could never be executed in practice. However, future versions of TLS will account for this minor pathology.

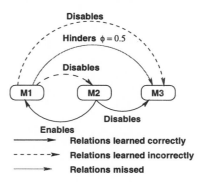

Figure 6: Dependent NLEs that prevent learning

The error graphs in figure 5 also indicate how the most important coordination knowledge is often learned most quickly. For example, TLS learns large power factors more quickly than small factors, and it learns hard NLEs (e.g., *enables* and *disables*) much more quickly than soft NLEs. Though not shown in experiments, empirical probability distributions learn the probabilities of the most frequent values of distributions most rapidly.

Conclusions

Our results indicate that TLS is relatively robust and can learn hard NLEs and method distributions from a small number of schedule executions, often less than 50 schedules. TLS can infer the existence of soft NLEs and their associated power factors, although this requires a moderately larger number of schedules.

These learned NLEs may act among the local methods of one agent, or methods in several different agents (as indicated in the hospital scheduling example). Although we experiment with a single agent learning quantitative coordination knowledge, TLS is fully able to learn NLEs across multiple agents if each agent has access to the schedule and execution characteristics of methods. We have already designed a distributed version of TLS, where each agent exchanges executed schedules for learning. In this design, we can have several agents using TLS to learn only those NLEs that affect their own methods or one dedicated learning agent that learns for the whole community.

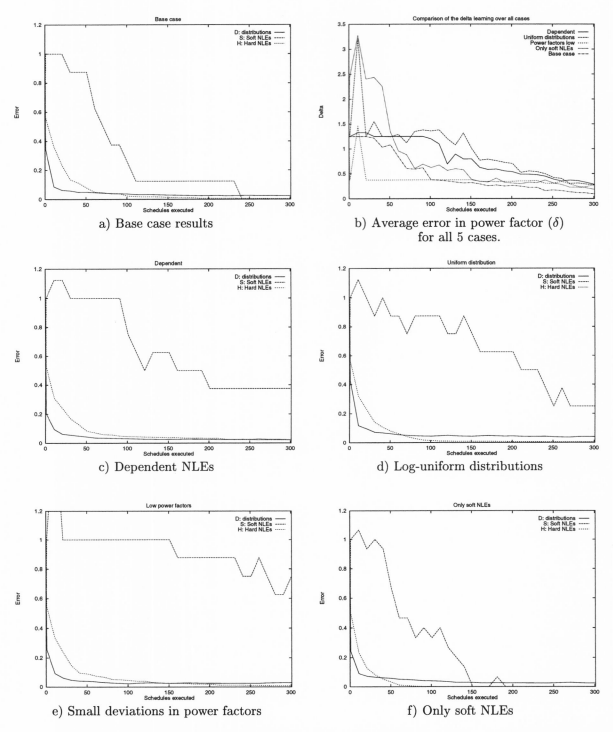

Figure 5: Errors for learning hard NLEs, soft NLEs, and method distributions under different conditions

Acknowledgment

Effort partially sponsored by the Defense Advanced Research Projects Agency (DARPA) and Air Force Research Laboratory Air Force Materiel Command, USAF, under agreement number F30602-97-1-0249. The U.S. Government is authorized to reproduce and distribute reprints for Governmental purposes notwithstanding any copyright annotation thereon.This material is based upon work supported by the National Science Foundation under Grant No.IIS-9812755. Disclaimer: The views and conclusions contained herein are those of the authors and should not be interpreted as necessarily representing the official policies or endorsements, either expressed or implied, of the Defense Advanced Research Projects Agency (DARPA), Air Force Research Laboratory, National Science Foundation, or the U.S. Government.

References

Mihai Barbuceanu and Mark S. Fox. COOL: A language for describing coordination in multi agent systems. In *Proceedings of the First International Conference on Multi-Agent Systems (ICMAS95)*, pages 17–25, 1995.

Keith S. Decker and Victor R. Lesser. Quantitative modeling of complex environments. *International Journal of Intelligent Systems in Accounting, Finance, and Management*, 2(4):215–234, December 1993. Special issue on "Mathematical and Computational Models of Organizations: Models and Characteristics of Agent Behavior".

Keith S. Decker and Victor R. Lesser. Designing a family of coordination algorithms. In *Proceedings of the First International Conference on Multi-Agent Systems*, pages 73–80, San Francisco, June 1995. AAAI Press. Longer version available as UMass CS-TR 94–14.

Keith Decker and Jinjiang Li. Coordinated hospital patient scheduling. In *Proceedings of the Third International Conference on Multi-Agent Systems (ICMAS98)*, pages 104–111, 1998.

N.R. Draper and H. Smith. *Applied Regression Analysis, 2nd edition*. Whiley Series in Probability and Mathematical Statistics. "John Wiley & Sons", 1981.

K.Z. Haigh and M.M. Veloso. Learning situation-dependent costs: Improving planning from probabilistic robot execution. In *Proceedings of the Second International Conference on Autonomous Agents*, pages 231–238, 1998.

J. Hu and M. Wellman. Online learning about other agents in a dynamic multiagent system. In *Proceedings of the Second International Conference on Autonomous Agents*, pages 239–246, 1998.

M. Kutner J. Neter, W Wasserman. *Applied Linear Statistical Models*. Irwin, 1990.

David Jensen and Paul R. Cohen. Multiple comparisons in induction algorithms. *Machine Learning*, 1999. Forthcoming.

George John and Pat Langley. Estimating continuous distributions in bayesian classifiers. In *Proceedings of the Eleventh Conference on Uncertainty in Artificial Intelligence*, pages 338–345, 1995.

M.D. Schmill, M.T. Rosenstein, P.R. Cohen, and P. Utgoff. Learning what is relevant to the effects of actions for a mobile robot. In *Proceedings of the Second International Conference on Autonomous Agents*, pages 247–253, 1998.

Toshi Sugawara and Victor R. Lesser. Learning to improve coordinated actions in cooperative distributed problem-solving environments. *Machine Learning*, 33, Nov./Dec. 1998.

M. Tan. Multi-agent reinforcement learning: Independent vs. cooperative agents. In M.P. Singh M.N. Huhns, editor, *Readings in Agents*, chapter 4.5 Adaptive Agency, pages 487–494. Morgan Kaufmann, 1998.

Thomas Wagner, Alan Garvey, and Victor Lesser. Complex Goal Criteria and Its Application in Design-to-Criteria Scheduling. In *Proceedings of the Fourteenth National Conference on Artificial Intelligence*, pages 294–301, July 1997. Also available as UMASS CS TR-1997-10.

Thomas Wagner, Alan Garvey, and Victor Lesser. Criteria-Directed Heuristic Task Scheduling. *International Journal of Approximate Reasoning, Special Issue on Scheduling*, 19:91–118, 1998. A version also available as UMASS CS TR-97-59.

Thomas Wagner, Victor Lesser, Brett Benyo, Anita Raja, Ping Xuan, and Shelly XQ Zhang. $GPGP^2$: Supporting Situation Specific Protocols in Multi-Agent Coordination. Computer Science Technical Report TR-98-05, University of Massachusetts at Amherst, October 1998.

G. Weiß. Learning to coordinate actions in multi-agent systems. In M.P. Singh M.N. Huhns, editor, *Readings in Agents*, chapter 4.5 Adaptive Agency, pages 481–486. Morgan Kaufmann, 1998.

D. Zeng and K. Sycara. Benefits of learning in negotiation. In *Proceedings of the Fourteenth National Conference on Artificial Intelligence*, pages 36–41, 1997.

Distributed Games: From Mechanisms to Protocols

Dov Monderer and Moshe Tennenholtz

Faculty of Industrial Engineering and Management
Technion – Israel Institute of Technology
Haifa 32000, Israel

Abstract

The theory of mechanism design in economics/game theory deals with a center who wishes to maximize an objective function which depends on a vector of information variables. The value of each variable is known only to a selfish agent, which is not controlled by the center. In order to obtain its objective the center constructs a game, in which every agent participates and reveals its information, because these actions maximize its utility. However, several crucial new issues arise when one tries to transform existing economic mechanisms into protocols to be used in computational environments. In this paper we deal with two such issues: 1. The communication structure, and 2. the representation (syntax) of the agents' information. The existing literature on mechanism design implicitly assumes that these two features are not relevant. In particular, it assumes a communication structure in which every agent is directly connected to the center. We present new protocols that can be implemented in a large variety of communication structures, and discuss the sensitivity of these protocols to the way in which information is presented.

Introduction

Work in mechanisms design deals with the design of multi-agent interactions of rational agents. This work is fundamental to Economics (Kreps 1990), as well as to the attempt to design protocols for non-cooperative computational environments (Boutilier, Shoham, & Wellman 1997; Rosenschein & Zlotkin 1994; Bond & Gasser 1988; Durfee 1992). The importance of the latter has increased dramatically due to the desire to design economic interactions in the Internet setup. In such a context, the fact we have different human users in a distributed system, suggests we can not rely on standard protocol design; we have to design protocols that are incentive-compatible. In order to handle the above problem the theory of mechanism design has to be adapted to computational environments, i.e. to the context of distributed computing.

In a typical mechanism design setup (Fudenberg & Tirole 1991; Kreps 1990; Monderer & Tennenholtz 1998), a center

attempts to perform some task, or to arrive at some decision, based on information available to a set of agents. The major problem is that the agents might not supply the desired information to the center, and might cheat the center in order to increase their individual payoffs. The central problem is to design a mechanism that when the agents interact rationally through that mechanism, the center will be able to obtain its objective. For example, the center may wish to sell a particular good while obtaining maximal profit, or to distribute goods among the agents in a way that maximizes social welfare. In order to do so, a mechanism has to be designed; typically, this mechanism determines actions to be taken by the center as a function of messages sent to it by the agents; the agents' strategies correspond to the messages they send to the center as a function of the private information they have. Such interaction is modeled by a Bayesian game. The aim is to design a mechanism that when the agents behave rationally (i.e. according to an equilibrium of the corresponding game), a desired behavior is obtained.

The design of mechanisms is the part of economics that is the most relevant to Artificial Intelligence and computer science. At first glance it may seem that mechanism design is in fact a different terminology for protocol design, when it is applied to non-cooperative environments. Although this claim is basically correct, researchers have noticed that in order to design protocols for non-cooperative computational environments, various modifications to the mechanism design theory are needed. In particular, researchers have been concerned with the fact that agents are resource bounded (Linial 1992; Sandholm & Lesser 1997; Kraus & Wilkenfeld 1991). However, except for the important issue of bounded resources there are several other issues that may make a difference when one tries to adapt the game theoretical approach to mechanism design in computational settings. These issues arise from the fact that the players in such a mechanism are part of a distributed system. So, what we need is a model for dealing with the classical and newer problems in distributed systems within the framework of game theory. Such a model is naturally titled a *distributed game*. Hence, a distributed game is a model for dealing with the most general multi-agent interactions in distributed systems. As such, its definition is quite complex and requires the description of many features which are crucial in some of these interactions. A particular type of a distributed game is presented in (Monderer & Tennenholtz 1999). The complete definition of distributed games is given in the full paper. In the current report we concentrate on two aspects of distributed games that are essential to the design of protocols for non-cooperative computational environments, and have been ignored by the mechanism design literature:

1. In a computational environment protocols are run by agents/processors that are connected by a *communication network*. However, the theory of mechanism design ignores this aspect, and in fact implicitly assumes a very concrete communication network, where each agent is directly connected to the center. This assumption, which is not realistic in most computational settings, is crucial for the mechanism design literature; as it turns out, its adaptation to general computational settings is non-trivial.

2. The theory of mechanism design ignores the actual way the information available to the agents is represented, as well as the (bit) structure of the messages. As it turns out, and as we later show, the design of the representation language takes a significant role in the adaptation of economic mechanisms to computational environments.

This paper presents several basic results with regard to the transition from mechanisms to protocols in communication networks. We take each node in the network to be associated with a different player (i.e. each node can be viewed as an agent of a different player). A basic observation is that when we try to implement a mechanism in a communication network, a new game-theoretic feature arises: an agent may have the ability to modify the messages sent by other agents to the center. We need therefore to make such malicious behavior irrational for the agents.

We start by presenting a general model for *distributed protocols* in a game-theoretic setting. Distributed protocols extend the concept of standard (economic) mechanisms to the context of computational environments. The two added features of distributed protocols is that they run in a communication network (which is in general different from the one that is implicitly assumed in the game-theory literature), and that they have to be explicit about the syntactic representation of the agents' information and messages. The main problem we face is the need to transform a mechanism that implements some desired behavior into a distributed protocol that obtains that behavior.

Our first result deals with distributed protocols, such that a unilateral deviation of an agent from them is not beneficial for it, when we assume that the agents' private information is selected from a given set with a uniform distribution. We show that given any 2-connected communication network L, any desired behavior which is implementable by a standard mechanism is also implementable by a distributed protocol executed in L. As it turns out, the corresponding implementation technique is not satisfactory for non-uniform distribution functions. In order to handle the more general case, we present improved protocols, which make use of a more complicated representation (syntax) of the agents' information and messages. This enables to implement any de-

sired behavior, that is implementable by a standard mechanism, by a distributed protocol executed in the communication graph L. Together, these results show that economic mechanisms can be constructively transformed into working protocols, and emphasize the crucial role played by the communication network and the syntactic representation of the agents' information and messages. Finally, we introduce the notion of strong implementation by mechanisms and distributed protocols. This notion refers to the concept of strong equilibrium, and requires the protocols to be stable against deviations by any subset of the agents. We show that any desired behavior that is strongly implementable by a standard mechanism is also strongly implementable by a distributed protocol in a communication network with a ring topology.

Distributed Protocols

Consider a set of agents, $N = \{1, \ldots, n\}$, and a *center* denoted by 0. Each agent i is associated with a type $v_i \in W$, where W is a finite set. The interpretation of a type is context dependent. For example, v_i may be the maximal willingness of agent i to pay for a good or for a service. The type of an agent is known only to this agent. It is assumed that for each agent i there exists a random variable $\tilde{v}_i$ that determines its type. We assume that these random variables are independent and identically distributed, with the distribution function f. That is, $Prob(\tilde{v}_i = x) = f(x)$ for every $x \in W$. The center is associated with a set of possible actions A. Each $a \in A$ is also called an *outcome*[1]. We assume that A contains a distinguished action, Λ, which stands for *no action*. In addition there is a utility function $u : A \times W \to R_+$, where R_+ denotes the set of nonnegative real numbers. The utility of agent i with type v_i from the action $a \in A$ is $u(a, v_i)$. We assume the normalization $u(\Lambda, v_i) = 0$ for every $v_i \in W$. The tuple $E = (N, A, u, W, f)$ is called an *environment*.

The center has some objective function which depends on the types of the agents and on the action it chooses. For example, the center may wish to maximize social welfare or to maximize its own profit. The exact nature of this objective function is irrelevant to this paper. In order to achieve its goal, and since it does not know the types of the players, the center uses a mechanism. A *mechanism* is a pair $H = (M, h)$, where M is a set of messages and $h : M^n \to A$. Each agent is asked to send a message, and the center commits itself to the action $h(m) = h(m_1, m_2, \ldots, m_n)$, if it receives the message m_i from agent i for every $i \in N$. We assume that M contains a distinguished null message e which stands for "no message", that $h(\bar{e}) = \Lambda$, where $\bar{e}$ is the vector of null messages. The environment E and the mechanism H generates a Bayesian game $B = (E, H)$. In this game, agent i sends a message m_i, and receives the utility $u(h(m), v_i)$[2]. In the mechanism

---

[1] In some applications it is useful to distinguish between the notions of action and outcome. In such cases there is also a set of outcomes and a mapping which assign outcomes to actions.

[2] In some applications it is useful to allow probabilistic mecha-

design theory it has been assumed that agent i has a strategy $b_i : W \to M$, where $b_i(v_i)$ is the message sent to the center by i when its type is v_i[3]. Let $b = (b_1, b_2, \ldots, b_n)$ be a vector of strategies that are used by the agents. If the vector of types drawn by Nature is $v = (v_1, v_2, \ldots, v_n)$, then the vector of messages that are sent to the center is $m = b(v) = (b_1(v_1), b_2(v_2), \ldots, b_n(v_n))$, and the center chooses the action $h(b(v))$. Therefore the utility of agent i is $u(h(b(v)), v_i)$. Note that the utility of agent i depends on the messages sent by the other agents as well as on its own message. However, agent i does not know the types or the strategies of the other agents.

The basic question in game theory and economics is how do agents choose their strategies given their ignorance about the other agents' strategies and types? The economics literature assumes that the vector of strategies $b = (b_1, b_2, \ldots, b_n)$ chosen by rational agents is in equilibrium. That is, for every player i and for every type v_i, the maximal expected utility of i given $\tilde{v}_i = v_i$, and given that each agent j, $j \neq i$ is using b_j, is obtained in choosing $m_i = b_i(v_i)$. This definition of rationality in multi-agent interactions is the most common in economics in the last four decades. It was introduced by (Nash 1950). It is based on the idea that every agent is a utility maximizer, and that every agent believes that all other agents use their equilibrium strategies. However, there is no good explanation to the question of how do agents form their beliefs about the strategies played by the other agents. One of the stories that usually comes in economics as a justification for this equilibrium assumption (i.e., that people behavior is in equilibrium) refers to an implicit dynamics, that after a while converges to a stable behavior. The equilibrium assumption is in particular problematic in a mechanism that has more than one equilibrium. To slightly resolve this difficulty we assume in this paper that the center, except for publishing the rules of the mechanism also recommends a particular behavior to the agents, which is an equilibrium vector of strategies b. Hence, agent i uses b_i because it knows that every other agent j is recommended to use b_j, and for every possible type v_i, sending the message $b_i(v_i)$ maximizes $i's$ utility under the assumption that every agent j uses b_j. The fact that the center recommends b makes b a correlated equilibrium in the sense of (Aumann 1974). The concept of correlated equilibrium is more general, but we do not discuss this novel concept in this paper.

Suppose that the environment E is fixed. Given a pair (H, b) of a mechanism H and an equilibrium vector of strategies b, we define $g : W^n \to A$ by $g(v) = h(b(v))$. That is, g is an outcome-valued random variable that determines the outcome as a function of Nature's draw. g is called the outcome function of (H, b), and we say that (H, b) implements g. When the mechanism H has a unique equilibrium, or when the equilibrium under discussion is clear from the context, we say that H implements g.

A mechanism $H = (M, h)$ is a *direct mechanism* if $M = W \cup \{e\}$. A direct mechanism is *truth revealing* if the vector of strategies t in which every agent reveals its true type is in equilibrium, that is $t_i(v_i) = v_i$ for every $i \in N$ and for every $v_i \in W$. The revelation principle (see e.g., (Myerson 1991)) implies that if (H, b) implements g, then there exists a direct mechanism H' such that (H', t) implements g. Hence, we we can restrict our attention to direct mechanisms where agents send their actual types as their messages.

Assume now that a certain outcome function g can be implemented in an environment E. That is, there exists a mechanism that implements g. However, we assume the existence of a communication network in which the center and the agents are operating. This network is described by a *communication graph L* as follows: Let $L = (V, E, \psi)$ be an undirected graph, where $V = N \cup \{0\}$ is the set of nodes, E is the set of edges, and ψ is the incidence function, which associates with every edge e an unordered pair of nodes. For every $i \in V$ let $D(i)$ be the set of all nodes j for which there exists an edge e that joins i and j, that is $\psi(e) = ij$. We assume that there are no loops. That is, for every i, $i \notin D(i)$. So, $D(i)$ denotes the set of agents (including the center) with which i has a direct communication line. We assume that for every agent i there exists a path that connects it to the center. We call the pair (E, L) a *distributed environment*.

Let (H, b) be a mechanism that implements g in the environment E. If the center attempts to use this mechanism in the distributed environment, it may fail to implement g because the incorporation of the new environment enriches the set of strategies of the agents. For example, if the path that joins the center to agent j goes through agent i, then i may read the message sent by j, and it may also change this message or destroy it. For example, in auction mechanisms (Milgrom 1987; Wilson 1992), if agent j sends its bid via a path that goes through i, then i can change the bid of j to the minimal possible bid. In fact, it may be able to do so even if the message is encrypted by some standard cryptographic technique. If the communication graph L has the property that every agent is directly connected to the center, that is, $D(0) = N$, then the distributed environment (E, L) is equivalent to the environment E, and every outcome function which is implementable in E is also implementable in (E, L) by the same mechanism. However, implementation in non-degenerate distributed environments requires a new definition of mechanisms (and strategies).

A mechanism in a distributed environment is called a *center's protocol*. Every such protocol induces a game which we refer to as a *distributed game*. A strategy of an agent in a distributed game is called an *agent's protocol*, and an $(n + 1)^{th}$ tuple of a center's protocol and an equilibrium vector of agents' protocols, together with some additional necessary parameters is called a *distributed protocol*. We now describe more specifically the notion of distributed protocols: Let (E, L) be a distributed environment. Every message m is assumed to be a string of bits, that is $m \in \{0, 1\}^*$.

---

nisms in which $h(m)$ is a probability distribution over outcomes. In such a case $u(h(m), v_i)$ is the expected utility of agent i.

[3] In more general applications it is assumed that an agent can use a *behavioral strategy*, which is a function that maps types to probability distributions on M.

The first parameter in a distributed protocol is a positive integer k determining the length of a legal message. That is, the set of messages is $M_k = \{0,1\}^k \cup \{e\}$. The second parameter describes the language. It is given by an interpretation function $I : \{0,1\}^k \to W$. We assume that for every $w \in W$ there exists $x \in \{0,1\}^k$ with $I(x) = w$. Actually, every message has two parts, the actual content, and the header with the sender name, the name of the agent to whom the message is addressed, and ordered location stamps, from the locations at which this message passed. An agent may change the header, the content and both. For the ease of exposition we assume in this paper that the agents cannot interfere with the headers of the messages. The distributed protocols that we give in this paper work also in an environment in which this assumption does not hold.

We assume a synchronous system: time is discrete, and at each round (i.e. time unit) each agent recalls all messages received by it in the previous rounds, as well as all messages sent by it, and can send messages to other agents through its neighbors (Tanenbaum 1988). These messages are to be received by the neighbors after at most q rounds, where q is some given constant. Hence, the system is fair, in the sense that any message is received after no more than q rounds. In general, there also exists a probability distribution from which the arrival time of messages is drawn, but this probability distribution will not play a role in our analysis, and therefore it will be ignored. We further assume that there is a (big) number Q such that at each round an agent can send at most Q messages. Let H_i^t, $0 \leq i \leq n$, be the set of all possible histories that may be observed by agent i at stage t, $t \geq 1$. So, $H_1^i = \{\phi\}$– the empty history, and for $t \geq 1$, a typical member of H_i^t has the form $h_i^t = (d^{s,1}, d^{s,2})_{s=1}^{t-1}$, where $d^{s,1}$ is the set of all messages received by i at stage s, and $d^{s,2}$ is the set of all messages sent by i at stage s. A protocol for agent $i \in N$ is a sequence of functions $((f_{ijq}^t)_{j \in (N-\{i\}) \cup \{0\}, q \in D(i)})_{t \geq 1}$, where $f_{ijq}^t : H_i^t \to M_k$ determines the message sent to j at round t, through q. That is $f_{ijq}^t(h_i^t)$ is the message sent by i to q, intended to be received by j. The center protocol is similar to an agent protocol, alongside two sequence of functions $(\delta_1^t)_{t>1}$ and $(\delta_2^t)_{t \geq 1}$, where $\delta_1^t : H_0^t \to \{HALT, COTINUE\}$, and $\delta_2^t : \bar{H}_o^t \to A$. These functions determine the action selected by the center at each round, and the termination of the process. It is assumed that $\delta_2^t = \Lambda$ if $\delta_1^t = CONTINUE$. We assume that there exists a time T_e such that for every sequence of histories $(h_0^t)_{t=1}^{\infty}$ that can be generated by the agents, there exists $1 \leq T \leq T_e$ such that $\delta(h_0^t) = CONTINUE$ for every $t < T$ and $\delta(h_o^T) = HALT$. In particular, the distributed protocol terminates after a finite number of stages, whether the agents obey it or not (it is obviously assumed that the center obeys its protocol).

As we said, the basic question we tackle is whether an outcome function that is implementable by a standard mechanism in an environment E, is also implementable by a distributed protocol in a given distributed environment (E, L).

In the sequel, we will restrict our attention to 2-connected graphs. This assumption is appropriate for most classical communication networks (e.g. ring, hypercube), and it is essential if we wish the system to be immuned at least against one machine failure (Dwork & Moses 1990).

Implementation by distributed protocols: the uniform distribution case

Consider a fixed environment E, an outcome function g and a truth revealing direct mechanism $H = (W \cup \{e\}, h)$ that implements g. Without loss of generality we assume that the number of types (i.e., the cardinality of W) is 2^k for some positive integer k, and that the distribution function f is the uniform distribution. That is, $f(x) = \frac{1}{2^k}$ for every $x \in W$. The latter assumption will be relaxed in the next section. Let L be a 2-connected communication graph L as described in the previous section. We present a distributed protocol that implements g in the distributed environment (E, L). The length of a legal message content in this protocol is k, and the interpretation function is any 1-1 function $I : M_k \to W$. To simplify the notations we can assume without loss of generality that $W = M_k$. We give a shortened description of the distributed protocol. The full description can be easily derived from this shorter version. In order to describe the protocol, we specify for every agent i an ordered pair of node-disjoint paths, (Γ_i^1, Γ_i^2) to the center. This is possible since the graph is 2-connected.

The protocol of agent i with type v_i (sketch):

1. Use the uniform distribution on W to generate a random bit string, y_1 of k bits.
2. Let y_2 be the bit-by-bit exclusive or (XOR) of y_1 and v_i.
3. Send y_1 and y_2 to the center through your neighbors determined by Γ_i^1 and Γ_i^2, respectively.
4. If you receive a message with a header in which the original sender is j, send it without any change to the next node in the designated path of j.

If every agent uses the above protocol then for every vector of types $v \in W^n$ there exists a stage $T(v)$ such that at least one of the agents may be active (in particular, one of its messages may not arrive yet) at every stage $t < T(v)$, and all agents are not active from this stage on. Let T^* be the maximal value of $T(v)$ over $v \in W^n$.

The description of the center's protocol:

1. The center receives messages and execute "CONTINUE" until stage T^*.
2. If the sequence of messages received by the center up to stage T^* can be generated by the agents' protocols, then it does as follows:
   - It takes the XOR of the y_1 and y_2 it received from each agent and treats it as this agent's type. Let $v = (v_1, v_2, \ldots, v_n)$ be the vector of types obtained in this way.
   - It runs the truth revealing mechanism that implements g. That is, it executes the action $h(v) \in A$ and halts.

3. If the sequence of messages received by the center is not consistent with any vector of types, then it executes Λ and halts.

Note that we do not deal with efficiency issues in this paper. E.g., it is obvious that in many cases the center can detect deviations of the agents from their protocol, and halt before stage T^*.

The above distributed protocol is the main tool in proving the following theorem:

Theorem 1 *Let E be an environment, in which the type of each agent is selected according to the uniform probability function on the set of types, and let L be a 2-connected graph. If an outcome function is implementable by a mechanism in E, then it is implementable by a distributed protocol executed in (E, L).*

The proof of the above theorem, as well as the proofs of the other theorems presented in this paper are omitted from this report. The first step of the proof is to use the revelation principle in order to get an implementation of g with a truth revealing mechanism. We then define a distributed protocol as described above and show that the agents' protocols are in equilibrium. That is, an agent does not gain by deviating from its protocol assuming the others stick to their protocols. Consider agent i with type v_i. Let a_i be the expected payoff of i, if all agents (including itself) obey their designated protocols. Recall that $a_i \geq 0$. If this agent deviates and generates an history which is not consistent with any vector of types, it receives 0, because $u(\Lambda, v_i) = 0$. Agent i can also deviate in a way that generates a consistent history. It can do it by not sending its true type and/or by changing the content of some of the messages of the other agents. However, it can be shown that all such changes do not change the distribution of types faced by it (here the uniform distribution assumption is used), and keep its expected payoff at the level of a_i. Hence, such deviations are not profitable.

Implementation by distributed protocols: the general case

In the previous section we proved that if the types of each agent are uniformly distributed, then every outcome function that can be implemented by a mechanism can also be implemented by a distributed protocol executed in a 2-connected communication network. In this section we generalize this result to the case of arbitrary probability functions on the agents' types.

In order to see the problematic issue which one faces in this case, assume an environment in which the set of types is $W = \{x_0, x_1\}$, where $0 < x_0 < x_1$, and $f(x_0) = \frac{1}{4}$ and $f(x_1) = \frac{3}{4}$.

Now, assume that the outcome function we wish to implement in a given communication graph L, is the one which is implemented in a standard second-price auction (Vickrey 1961). In a second-price auction each agent submits a

bid for a good held by the center. The good is sold to the agent who has made the highest bid in a price that equals the second-highest bid; in a case of a tie we use a random unbiased coin flipping. It is well known that a second-price auction is a truth revealing mechanism. We take x_0 and x_1 to be the valuations (i.e. maximal willingness to pay) of an agent. Let $M_1 = \{0, 1\}$ and let $I : M_1 \to W$ be the natural interpretation function, that is $I(0) = x_0$ and $I(1) = x_1$. If the center uses the distributed protocol described in the previous section, it becomes worthwhile for an agent to change the content of another agent's message by replacing it with a random bit, where each value of this bit is chosen with probability 0.5. Such a change will decrease the probability that the bid of the other agent is high. However, by using another language, i.e., by using a set of messages with a bigger cardinality and an appropriate interpretation function, we can show the following generalization of Theorem 1.

Theorem 2 *Let E be an environment, and let L be a 2-connected graph. If an outcome function is implementable by a mechanism in E, then it is implementable by a distributed protocol executed in (E, L).*

We now illustrate the ideas of the proof in the framework of the above example. We consider encodings of the two possible types by strings of two bits. There are 4 such strings, and we associate three of them (e.g., 11, 01, 10) with x_1 and only one string (e.g., 00) is associated with x_0. That is, the set of messages is M_2, $I(11) = I(01) = I(10) = x_1$, and $I(00) = x_0$. We modify the protocols given in the proof of Theorem 1 in the following way: The agent selects y_1 as a random 2-bit string (with the uniform probability), and y_2 is defined to be the XOR of y_1 with a random representation of x_i (i.e. 00 if the type is x_0, and either 11, 01, or 10, with equal probability to each one of them, if the type is x_1). It follows that both y_1 and y_2 are selected uniformly from the set of 2-bit strings. The rest of the proof is similar to the analogous proof in Theorem 1. In general, we represent each type with a set of bit strings such that the sizes of these representing sets are proportional to the probabilities of the types. The novel idea of this representation technique is that it enables us to view the agents' types *as if* they are selected from a uniform distribution. This in turn enables us to apply the techniques of proof used in Theorem 1.

Strong Implementation

The general techniques we have introduced in the previous sections enable to implement outcome functions that are implementable by standard mechanisms, by protocols in communication networks. Our work relies on the game theoretic notion of equilibrium; that is, we are interested in protocols, in which it is irrational for an agent to deviate from its protocol, assuming the other agents stick to their protocol. More generally one may replace the concept of equilibrium with the concept of *strong equilibrium* (Aumann 1959). In a strong equilibrium, there does not exist a group (coalition) of agents such that a joint deviation of this group can benefit each of its members. If an outcome function g is implemented by a mechanism and by an equilibrium profile b, which is also a strong equilibrium, we say that the mechanism *strongly implements g*. We similarly define strong implementation by a distributed protocol in a communication graph. It can be easily shown that the revelation principle holds with "strong equilibrium" replacing "equilibrium". We prove:

Theorem 3 *Let E be an environment, and let L be a ring. If an outcome function g is strongly implementable by a mechanism in E, then it is strongly implementable by a distributed protocol executed in (E, L).*

For ease of exposition, we sketch the proof of this result for the case in which the types of an agent are uniformly distributed. The proof of the general case can be derived from this proof analogously to the way in which the proof of Theorem 2 is derived from the proof of Theorem 1, that is by an appropriate change of language. We describe the dynamics generated by the distributed protocol when all agents obey their protocols. In game theoretic language, we describe the equilibrium path. If the center observes a deviation from the equilibrium path of any group of agents, it punishes all agents by an appropriate chosen payments (in the full paper we present elaborated protocols, where there are no monetary punishments). If an agent observes a deviation which will not be necessarily observed by the center, it deviates from the equilibrium path in a way that is observed by the center. We assume that the order of the agents in the clockwise direction of the ring is $1, 2, \ldots, n$. The types of the agents are represented by k bit strings, where 2^k is the cardinality of W. Without loss of generality we assume that $W = M_k$. At stage 0 the center makes n independent uniformly distributed draws $z_1, z_2, \ldots, z_n$ of k bit strings, which will be used as keys. At stage $2j - 1, 1 \le j \le n$, the center sends the key z_j to agent j through the path starting at agent n. Agent j computes the XOR, y_j of z_j with the representation of its type, $v_j \in \{0, 1\}^k$. At stage $2j$, agent j sends y_j to the center through the path that goes through agent 1. At stage $2n + j$ agent j sends z_j to the center through the path that goes through agent 1. The center computes the type v_j of j by XORing y_j with z_j. If, at end, the center receives the z_j's back from the agents, it applies the mechanism that strongly implements g to the resulting vector of types.

Given the above protocols it is easy to see that if all agents obey them then the true types will arrive at the center. In order to get the strong implementation result we should show that agents in $N - \{i\}$ can do nothing about agent i-th or their submissions that will increase their payoff. The full proof is omitted from this report. However, the reader should notice that the technique which is used here differs from the techniques we introduced previously. The idea here is that the center distributes a key, z_i, with which agent i's type announcement will be encrypted. By receiving the key back at end, the center will know that no agent has modified it.

References

Aumann, R. 1959. Acceptable points in general cooperative n-person games. In Tucker, A., and Luce, R., eds., *Contribution to the Thoery of Games, Vol. IV (Annals of Mathematics Studies, 40)*. 287–324.

Aumann, R. 1974. Subjectivity and correlation in randomized strategies. *Journal of Mathematical Economics* 1:67–96.

Bond, A. H., and Gasser, L. 1988. *Readings in Distributed Artificial Intelligence*. Ablex Publishing Corporation.

Boutilier, C.; Shoham, Y.; and Wellman, M. 1997. Special issue on economic principles of multi-agent systems. *Artificial Intelligence* 94.

Durfee, E. 1992. What your computer really needs to know, you learned in kindergarten. In *10th National Conference on Artificial Intelligence*, 858–864.

Dwork, C., and Moses, Y. 1990. Knowledge and Common Knowledge in a Byzantine Environment: Crash Failures. *Information and Computation* 88(2):156–186.

Fudenberg, D., and Tirole, J. 1991. *Game Theory*. MIT Press.

Kraus, S., and Wilkenfeld, J. 1991. The Function of Time in Cooperative Negotiations. In *Proc. of AAAI-91*, 179–184.

Kreps, D. 1990. *A Course in Microeconomic Theory*. Princeton University Press.

Linial, N. 1992. Games Computers Play: Game-Theoretic Aspects of Computing. Technical Report 92–5, CS Department, Hebrew University, Israel.

Milgrom, P. 1987. Auction theory. In Bewly, T., ed., *Advances in Economic Theory: Fifth World Congress*. Cambridge University Press.

Monderer, D., and Tennenholtz, M. 1998. Optimal Auctions Revisited. In *Proceedings of AAAI-98*.

Monderer, D., and Tennenholtz, M. 1999. Distributed Games. to apear in Games and Economic Behavior.

Myerson, R. B. 1991. *Game Theory*. Harvard University Press.

Nash, J. 1950. Equilibrium points in n-person games. *Proceedings of the National Academy of Sciences of the United States of America* 36:48–49.

Rosenschein, J. S., and Zlotkin, G. 1994. *Rules of Encounter*. MIT Press.

Sandholm, T. W., and Lesser, V. R. 1997. Coalitions Among Rationally Bounded Agents. *Artificial Intelligence* 94(1):99–137.

Tanenbaum, A. 1988. *Computer Networks*. Prentice Hall.

Vickrey, W. 1961. Counterspeculations, auctions, and competitive sealed tenders. *Journal of Finance* 16:15–27.

Wilson, R. 1992. Strategic analysis of auctions. In Aumann, R., and Hart, S., eds., *Handbook of Game Theory*, volume 1. Elsevier Science Publisher.

Evolutionary Economic Agents

Fergus Nolan, Jarek Wilkiewicz, Dipankar Dasgupta, Stan Franklin

The University of Memphis
758 North McLean Boulevard
Memphis TN 38107 USA.
fergus@fnolan.com, jwilkiewicz@acm.org, dasgupta@msci.memphis.edu, stan.franklin@memphis.edu

Abstract

An empirical work is described which compares the optimization levels produced by a group of economic agents versus those of a similar group of economic agents which additionally employ a genetic algorithm (GA) to attain a higher level of optimization. The problem domain is multimodal. It incorporates multiple hard and soft constraints and dynamical behaviors. It also has areas of infeasibility and non-linear behaviors. The simulated model environment provides several types of sensors, actuators and opportunities for inter-agent resource mediation. Evidence is offered to support the theory that multiple weak methods operating in concert, on a shared problem, can produce better results than the individual weak methods acting alone. The problem area is resistant to the use of strong methods.

Introduction

Many real-world domains require the ability to deal with environments and problems which include multimodal features, non-linear functions, environmental interactions, feasibility constraints both hard and soft, and often, dynamical elements.

An example of one of these problems is natural language understanding. An interpretation of human natural language understanding proposed by cognitive science researchers (Bates and Goodman, 1997, Tomasello, 1998) could suggest that the human natural language process possesses many or all of these real-world features.

Such systems are referred to as complex systems, following nomenclature established by the researchers at the Santa Fe institute (Holland and Mimnaugh 1996, Kauffman 1993).

The initial idea for this study is from Holland and Mimnaugh, where they suggest that Genetic Algorithms could be combined with an economic agent (Wellman 1996, Mullen and Wellman 1996) to solve complex systems problems. However, the Echo agent discussed in Holland and Mimnaugh's work lacks essential elements of the Wellman economic agent model, and Holland never followed up on his idea. This paper is an attempt to do some work in this area.

The essential enhancement obtained by adding the economic agent capability to the hybrid agent/GA architecture

exemplified in Holland's Echo is the market-based ordering behavior of the economic agent model. A market is a mechanism used by agents to mediate the distribution of constrained resources. In complex systems terms, a market allows Pareto optimization in the presence of hard constraints (quality requirements applied by a consumer prior to acceptance of a good or service) and soft constraints (a preference of a consumer to accept the less expensive of two goods which both meet hard constraints).

Using Luc Steels (1990) example of agents operating locally using weak methods, and adding the enhancement of a market for resource conflict mediation, yields the idea of economic agents. As a group, they can achieve a stable state of equilibrium which, according to General Equilibrium Theory, has the properties of Pareto Optimality and Pareto Quality. This implies that a stable solution meets all hard and soft constraints, and that the fitness or welfare of one agent cannot be improved without worsening the condition of at least one other agent. The emergent effect of the economic agent community is to provide a satisficing solution to a complex optimization problem. Economic agents are weak methods because the summation of their fitness or welfare values is not guaranteed to be optimal.

Genetic Algorithms are best at optimization of general functions using an exploratory approach. They become more complex and lose generality when faced with constrained problems or multi-modal problems. They are also weak methods, but they can produce satisficing optimization.

Holland's suggestion of combining GA with Economic Agent processing has several interesting potential features, when combined with Franklin (1995, 1997). Agents are autonomous, they have goals and drives, they can sense their environment and change it. Economic agents additionally obey hard and soft constraints and allocate resources efficiently. A group of economic agents can obtain a globally feasible solution to a multi-modal problem with a good degree of global optimization. Evolutionary economic agents can breed better agents that can improve the overall global level of optimization. This is group-level learning.

The question to be addressed by this study is: Does the addition of an evolutionary process to a community of economic agents improve the overall level of optimization?

We note that the existing mathematical models used for GAs cannot be relied on, as the assumption of a stable environment is violated. In addition, we cannot rely on General Equilibrium Theory for this system, as equilibrium might never be achieved in a non-static environment. The complex systems mathematical analysis (Kauffman, 1993) addresses mainly inter-species genetic interactions, such as herbivore kills by predators, and does not easily look extendable to economic analysis. Issues of computability are likely to arise. As a practical matter, experimentation offers a promising opportunity to explore these techniques.

Related Work

There is a large literature on hybrid genetic algorithms. Hybrid schemes are available with neural networks (Genetica, NeuroForecaster, Moriarty and Miikkullainen, 1998), cellular automata (Dolan 1997-1999, Agre and Chapman 1990, Holland 1996), subsumption or simulated subsumption, case-based reasoning, hillclimbing (Lobo and Goldberg 1996), and fuzzy systems (Wilson 1994) as the lower layer.

The complex system nature of economies is discussed persuasively (Anderson, Arrow and Pines, 1988, Arthur, Durlauf and Lane, 1997, Kollman and Miller, 1996 and Krugman, 1996). These works focus on modeling real economies, which provides useful techniques and modeling prototypes. It should be noted that this empirical study uses an economic simulation mainly as a metaphor and that modeling real economies is not our objective.

Memetic Algorithms use a population-based approach with local heuristic search in optimization problems, and is described with examples at www.densis.fee.unicamp.br/~moscato/memetic_home.html, the Memetic Algorithms Home Page (accessed on 12/06/1998).

Pure genetic algorithms exist which deal with multi-modal problems and seek to achieve Pareto optimality within the GA (Horn, Nafpliotis and Goldberg 1994). This type of problem typically involves multiple constraints. The solution space in these problems therefore contains infeasible areas. The GA may generate infeasible points in the optimization process. The technique is successful in allocating the population over multiple modes and in sharing fitness over the modes, but can be difficult.

Parallel GAs are an alternative technique (Cantu-Paz 1998, Cantu-Paz 1997) with application to multi-modal problems. Motivated by a need to distribute processing over multiple nodes in a parallel computer, this technique maintains parallel populations and introduces interplay between the populations using new genetic operators like migration.

There is no evidence that the combination of Economic Agents and GA has been tried before.

Simulation Objective

After the example of Echo (Holland and Mimnaugh 1996), and with respectful gestures to Animat (Wilson 1994), a simple simulation of a complex system was chosen as a test case for the theory.

A community of agents is proposed which inhabit an environment, which they can sense to some extent and which they can change by their actions. They produce commodities and trade them in an effort to survive, to consume and to create wealth. The wealth of each agent is used as a fitness value for the GA.

Each agent has a set of 10 chromosomes. The GA acts on these chromosomes to simulate breeding between agents and the selection of agents for replacement (or death). The fitness value being optimized by the GA is the wealth measure produced by the economy.

The chromosomes influence the decisions of the agents, as does the market prices and other information from the environment, and fuzzy logic adds an explorarory, stochiastic factor.

The GA rates for selection, crossover and mutation are controlled by parameter. These parameters can be set to zero to prevent GA processing.

The objective is to measure the wealth summations produced by several runs of the model with GA active and compare with similar measures produced by a community of economic agents without evolutionary capability.

Model Description

This section describes the environment, the products, the economic agents (producer, consumer and auctioneer), the GA, and the evaluation cycle of the model. The metaphor of a simplified primitive human economy is used, as this is a complex system whose workings are familiar to most.

Environment

Figure 1 is an edited screen shot of the simulated agent envronment. It shows an overall wealth indicator as a bar on the left, and a 10 X 10 grid representing a 100 square mile area. There is a town near the center shown as a black square. It is the location of the annual market and the auctioneer is based there.

The four shaded areas represent farmland and the two farmer groups live there. The farmland can produce food, clothing and beer when worked by a farmer. The remaining 95 white areas are forest, which has two populations of animals, herbivores and predators. The forest localities object maintains the two animal populations in a simple cycle which is deterministic except for the actions of the hunters.

Figure 1 also shows the four groups of economic agents, as small pie charts. F1 and F2 are the farmers and H1 and H2 are the hunters.

The Products in the Economy

Wellman's economic agent model defines the resources in the system as products or goods.

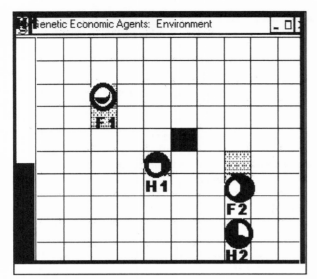

Figure 1. The simulated agent environment

The simulated products in the economy are food, clothing and beer, and these are generic commodities. They are accounted in arbitrary units, where one unit of clothing is the equivalent of a large outer garment, a unit of food supports an agent for six weeks, and the unit of beer is a keg.

Farmers can produce all products, a total of about 10 to 20 units per year. The amount produced per farmer is a function of genetic factors, the farmer's production decisions, environmental factors, group size, crop specialization and a large measure of fuzziness. The farmer decides what to grow at the beginning of the season based on the latest available prices which he evaluates as market-follower or contra, depending on his genetic disposition. He can raise or lower the percentage of a given crop 10% in any year.

Hunters try to fuzzily sense their environment for presence of other groups and animal population levels. They sense all squares contiguous to their current position, with an error level based on their genetic ability for hunting and sensing, and decide fuzzily where to move. They try to hunt where their activities will affect animal population sizes beneficially, in accordance with the predator/prey population cycle status at that locality. They hunt all year as a group, then divide the food and clothing produced by a tournament process in which a pecking order is established based on random factors and genetic aggression and hunting ability.

Each agent is endowed initially with an arbitrary number of gold pieces, and it is the universal medium of exchange, one of the items exchanged in each transaction. Unlike the other commodities, negative gold levels may be carried by agents. This is done because a fixed gold standard appears to suppress economic activity and we are not interested right now in simulating monetary effects. This can and does mean that individual agents can end up with big negative balances, and even inherit them from an agent replaced in a genetic

operation. These individuals are at increased risk of selection for death each round, but the issue seems not to effect the model. To ameliorate the problem, we added a solvency drive to the agents. The behavior appears to favor the non-GA simulations slightly, as the GA tends to thresh in the presence of large negative wealth balances.

The Economic Agents

The producers are the only true agents in the system. They are autonomous, they sense their environment and global price data, they change their environment, including their peers, by taking resources, killing animals and helping set market prices. They have drives (eat, be warm, drink beer, breed). They have goals (survive, accumulate wealth). They decide what to do, based on their sensor data, on their genetic dispositions, on their goals and drives and in a fuzzy manner. They participate in a market for all goods. They offer their goods to the market and bid on goods available.

A limitation of the model is that the population, number and size of groups are fixed during a run. There are two groups of farmers and two of hunters, of equal size. The overall size of population is set by parameter, and fixed during a simulation. Populations of 80 were used in this study.

The Consumer

Wellman specifies the consumer as an agent. In this model, there is one consumer per producer, and it is implemented as a simple, deterministic method in the Producer agent bean. Each year it accesses the producer's storehouse and consumes some amount of goods. It then awards a fitness score to the agent, which is a scaled measure of wealth incorporating some constraints.

The wealth score of 1 denotes the basic survival level. It is currently set at 8 units of food and 2 of clothing. The consumer sets a score of less than 1 if the basic survival level is not met, based on the proportion of the survival quota the agent has. This reduces the agent's chances of survival.

If the (hard) survival constraint is met, the consumer then assesses an additional amount of beer and clothing to consume. If the agent has this quantity, it is consumed and the agent's score increases according to the value of goods and gold he owns, expressed as a multiple of the survival quota.

The fitness score therefore incorporates wealth, the hard survival constraint and the additional wealth-accumulation and consumption objectives, which are soft constraints.

The Auctioneer

An economic agent in the Wellman scheme, the auctioneer is a simple, deterministic mechanism in this model. It collects bids and offers, compares them, sets the price which will allow maximum sales, then performs the transactions implied by the offers less or equal to the price, and the bids greater than or equal to the price.

There is a simple, iterative process of auction rounds with an arbitrary deadline. The auctioneer also supplies agents with current global commodity prices on demand.

The Genetic Algorithm

We use a simple steady state GA, which is invoked once per economic agent year. There is a parameter to control the percentage of the population selected for breeding. Agents are selected one at a time until this quota is met, with probability equal to their wealth. The selected agents are paired randomly and crossed over at a random bit in the gene. Mutation is them performed on each bit with a probability determined by parameter. Selection rates of 0.25 and mutation of 0.001 were used in the GA version of the test runs. During testing, higher levels of crossover were very disruptive.

A group is selected for replacement by using a weighted probability equal to the highest wealth minus the agent's wealth. This results in the wealthiest agent always surviving until the next year, while the least successful agents are more likely to be selected for the replacement group.

The offspring is assessed for farmer and hunter genetic aptitudes and matched with a replacement in a corresponding occupational group. The offspring then replaces the culled individual, inheriting his (probably meager) wealth, and receives one third each from the parents accumulated goods and gold. The splitting of parental wealth in this way is arbitrary and is intended to reflect the economic costs of child rearing while keeping the goods in the system constant. We found during testing that improved genes produced late in the run had little effect on the overall results unless they were given some initial wealth, and this allocation results in the offspring having the mean wealth of the parents.

This keeps the population constant, which is the result of a technical limitation, not an objective of the model.

There are 10 genes, each of which occupies 2 bits. The allele values, from 00 to 11, are Low, Medium, High and eXtra. Each gene controls an attribute and contributes to economic agent's performance at various sensory, productive and decision-making tasks. The genes helpful to farmers are: Defense, Focus, Physical Strength, Work Ethic. Hunters are helped by Aggression, Swiftness, Tool Use and Wanderlust. Both groups are helped by Cunning and Explore. The chromosome has ten genes occupying a 20-bit string.

The Yearly Processing Cycle.

The number of processing cycles in a model run is determined by parameter, typically 30. Each cycle corresponds to a calendar year in the model. See figure 2 for an outline of the processing.

In the production part of the cycle, different processing is provided for farmers and hunters. Farmers decide what to grow based on what was grown last year, current produce

prices and various technical points. The growth is based on farmer genetics, farmers preferences, group factors, crop specialization, and a major random component. Hunting genes are a negative to a farmer as he wants to go hunting during the growing season.

All hunting activities and decisions are done as a group. There are arbitrarily 140 hunting days per year. At the beginning of the season the hunters decide what to hunt based on market prices and preferences based on their genetics. Each day of hunting, the hunter group collectively estimates the predator/prey populations in all adjacent squares, with accuracy based on genetic and random factors. They then decide which adjoining locality to move to, based on an estimation of the potential bag in adjoining localities, the product preference they decided at the beginning of the season and genetic factors including wanderlust. The hunters then perform hunt-

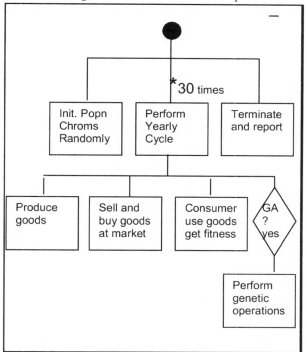

Figure 2: Outline of Agent Processing Cycle.

ing. The day's bag is determined by genetic factors relating to hunting ability, randomness and the numbers of predator and prey in the location. The long-term well-being of the hunters depends on their innate hunting ability and the accuracy at which they estimate the predator/prey positions on their characteristic population cycle. If the hunters choose well, they tend to act as a dynamical element in the animal population cycles, reducing the fluctuations and optimizing the potential bag in the future. If they exacerbate the natural predator/prey cycles, they can crash all animal populations in a location, thus making famine more likely in the future.

One wonders at our forebears expertise in these complex life-and-death decisions, and wishes that more of this expertise had survived the scientific era.

At year end, the bag is divided among the hunter group. Each gets a survival ration, if possible, and the rest is fought over in a random tournament, weighted by individuals hunting aptitudes and aggression gene level.

Implementation Details

The implementation uses Java on Intel equipment, Windows 98 and Windows NT 4.0, Borland Jbuilder 2 and a package entitled GA Playground (Dolan 1997-1999).

Additional beans were written to implement the Agent processing and the Agent Environment GUI, and these were combined with minor changes in the GA Playground source, as kindly provided by the author. See (Dolan 1997-1999) for details of additional freely-distributed class libraries used by the GA Playground.

The simplest possible technical approach was taken to the agent processing, implying that concurrency issues, reusability and performance opportunities were avoided.

Basic reporting tools, including a GUI, ASCII diagnostics and a report file in spreadsheet format are provided.

Empirical Results

Two series of tests were run and statistics gathered for comparison. Each series was 30 runs of the model. Each run simulated 30 years in the agent environment. The test population was 80. Endowment was 100 gold pieces. The chromosomes for all agents were generated randomly and an assessment of hunting versus farming capability was used to assign individuals to the groups.

The only difference between the two series was that no GA was employed in the second series. This was done by setting the parameters for selection, crossover and mutation to zero. For the with-GA series, selection for crossover was 0.25 and mutation 0.001. In the with-GA tests, each year, from the population of 80, 20 become parents, 10 die, 10 offspring are born and 70 individual economic agents survive into the next year. This is a steady-state GA.

Figures 3 and 4 show the results of both test series. The minimum value for charting purposes was forced to 2 to allow for the logarithmic axis in the charts, as there was a small number of negative wealth values caused by major price fluctuations and 'recession'.

The graphs show a clear superiority in the version with GA, although this requires fairly close study. The maxima and end points for the GA run dominate the upper reaches, for example, with 8 runs versus 5 for the no-GA series ending up in the 100k-1M band. The average maximum wealth over the 30 runs for the no-GA scenario was 732,992 versus 1,174,727 for the with-GA run, an improvement of 60%. The variation between individual runs is large, and it is unlikely

that the current data establishes a statistically significant result. The inherent instability of the model precludes reliability in results from one run to the next, and it is clear that the model has enough random factors in it. It is also apparent that the type of dynamic factor that Wellman noted in the operation of the speculator/arbitrageur agents is badly needed.

The model does not converge in the 30 annual cycles used in the experiment. We would expect more consistent results if that occurred. However, the chaotic and emergent nature of the model would not guarantee that a convergent run would not contain large deviances also.

Several epiphenomena were noted: cycles of recession (or famine), inflation, individual agent insolvency and animal population crashes, as well as the emergence of tycoons. Many of these are predicted by Wellman or by general economic theory. The emergence of super-performing individuals was interesting. These individuals typically gained wealth of 100 times the population average. We would be interested

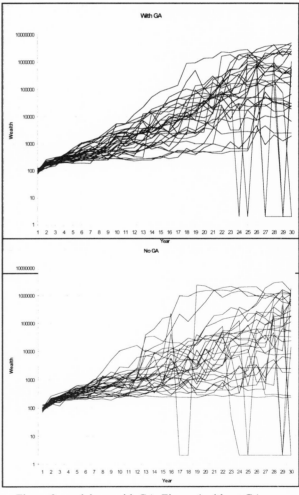

Figure 3, model run with GA, Figure 4 without GA.

in formulating future problems in such a way that they would represent outstanding solutions to the problem or search at hand. The typical execution of the model for 30 cycles took one and a half minutes on a 300MHz Pentium II.

Future Work

Although the initial results, given the crudeness of the model, are encouraging, this work raises more issues than it answers. We need better design techniques for emergent systems, a fuller economic agent implementation, a real-world environment to work with, and an interesting problem to solve.

One of the most critical issues during development was the lack of a comprehensive, easy-to-use set of monitoring and visualization tools. Time spent developing these at the outset of an emergent system development will be saved many times over later in the project.

Acknowledgments

The authors acknowledge the kindness and expertise of Ariel Dolan (Dolan 1997-1999), who shared the unpublished Java source code for his software, GA Playground (Dolan 1997-1999), and who helped with guidance and support. We recommend his example and his web page.

References

Agre, Philip E. and Chapman, David. "What Are Plans For?". Designing Autonomous Agents, Maes, Pattie, ed. Amsterdam, Elsevier Science Publishers, 1990. 17-34.

Anderson, Philip W.; Arrow, Kenneth J. and Pines, David (ed). The Economy as an Evolving Complex System. Proceedings Volume XXVII, Santa Fe Institute. Reading, Mass: Perseus Books 1997.

Arthur, W. Brian; Durlauf, Steven N. and Lane, David A. (ed). The Economy as an Evolving Complex System II. Proceedings of the Evolutionary Paths of the Global Economy Workshop, 1987. Reading, Mass: Perseus Books 1988.

Baars, Bernard J. A Cognitive Theory of Consciousness. Cambridge: Cambridge Press, (reprinted) 1990.

Baars, Bernard J. In the Theatre of Consciousness. Oxford: Oxford Press, 1997.

Bates, Elizabeth and Goodman, Judith. 1997. On the inseparability if grammar and the lexicon: evidence from acquisition, aphasia and real-time processing. In proceedings, Language and Cognitive Processes, 12(5/6), 507-584.

Cantu-Paz, Erick. Designing Scalable Multi-Population Parallel Genetic Algorithms. IlliGAL Report No. 98009. May 1998. http://www-illigal.ge.uiuc.edu

Cantu-Paz, Erick. A Survey of Parallel Genetic Algorithms. University of Illinois, 1997. http://www-illigal.ge.uiuc.edu

Dolan, Ariel. GA Playground. http://www.aridolan.com. Java code and HTML document, 1997-1999.

Franklin, Stan. 1995. Artificial Minds. Cambridge Mass. MIT Press.

Franklin, Stan. Graesser, Art. 1997. Is it an Agent, or just a Program? : A Taxonomy for Autonomous Agents. In proceedings of Third International Workshop on Agent Theories, Architectures and Languages. Intelligent Agents III. Berlin. Springer-Verlag. 21-35.

Genetica. commercial GA software by NIBS Inc. at http://sunflower.singnet.com.sg/~midaz/Nfga611.htm, viewed 11/1/1998.

Holland , John H., Mimnaugh , Heather. 1996 Hidden Order : How Adaptation Builds Complexity. Reading MA. Perseus Press.

Horn, Jeffrey; Nafpliotis, Nicholas and Goldberg, David E. A Niched Pareto Genetic Algorithm for Multiobjective Optimization. In Proceedings IEEE-ICEC 1994.

Kauffman, Stuart. The Origins of Order: Self Organization and Selection in Evolution. Oxford: Oxford University Press, 1993.

Kollman, Ken and Miller, John H. Computational Political Economy. Santa Fe: Santa Fe Institute, 1996.

Krugman, Paul. The Self-Organizing Economy. Malden: Blackwell Publishers, 1996.

Lobo, Fernando G., and Goldberg, David E. Decision making in a hybrid genetic algorithm. IlliGAL Report No. 96009, September 1996. http://www-illigal.ge.uiuc.edu

Moriarty, David E. and Miikkulainen, Risto. Forming Neural Networks through Efficient and Adaptive Coevlution. Evolutionary Computation, 5(4), 1998.

Mullen, Tracy and Wellman, Michael P. Some Issues in the Design of Market-Oriented Agents. In M. Wooldridge, J. Mueller, and M. Tambe (eds.), Intelligent Agents II: Agent Theories, Architectures, and Languages, Berlin Springer-Verlag, 1996.

NeuroForecaster. software by NIBS Inc. Website at http://sunflower.singnet.com.sg/~midaz/Nfga611.htm viewed 11/1/98.

Steels, Luc, Exploiting Analogical Representations, Designing Autonomous Agents, (ed) Maes, Pattie. Amsterdam, Elsevier Science Publishers, 1990. 71:88.

Tomasello, Michael (ed). 1998. The New Psychology of Lantuage: Cognitive and Functional Approaches to Language Structure. Mahwah, NJ. Lawrence Erlbaum Associates.

Wellman, Michael P, Market-Oriented Programming: Some Early Lessons. In Market-Based Control: A Paradigm for distributed Resource Allocation, (ed) Scott H. Clearwater. Singapore: World Scientific, 1996. 74-95.

Wilson, Stewart W. ZCS: A Zeroth Level Classifier System. 1994.

Bargaining with Deadlines

Tuomas Sandholm[*]
sandholm@cs.wustl.edu
Department of Computer Science
Washington University
One Brookings Drive
St. Louis, MO 63130-4899

Nir Vulkan[†]
n.vulkan@bristol.ac.uk
Department of Economics
University of Bristol
8 Woodland Road
Bristol BS8 1TN, England

Abstract

This paper analyzes automated distributive negotiation where agents have firm deadlines that are private information. The agents are allowed to make and accept offers in any order in continuous time. We show that the only sequential equilibrium outcome is one where the agents wait until the first deadline, at which point that agent concedes everything to the other. This holds for pure and mixed strategies. So, interestingly, rational agents can never agree to a nontrivial split because offers signal enough weakness of bargaining power (early deadline) so that the recipient should never accept. Similarly, the offerer knows that it offered too much if the offer gets accepted: the offerer could have done better by out-waiting the opponent. In most cases, the deadline effect completely overrides time discounting and risk aversion: an agent's payoff does not change with its discount factor or risk attitude. Several implications for the design of negotiating agents are discussed. We also present an effective protocol that implements the equilibrium outcome in dominant strategies.

1 Introduction

Multiagent systems for automated negotiation between self-interested agents are becoming increasingly important due to both technology push and application pull. For many-to-many negotiation settings, market mechanisms are often used, and for one-to-many negotiation, auctions are often appropriate. The competitive pressure on the side with many agents often reduces undesirable strategic effects. On the other hand, market mechanisms often have difficulty in "scaling down" to small numbers of agents (Osborne & Rubinstein 1990). In the limit of one-to-one negotiation, strategic considerations become prevalent. At the same time, one-to-one negotiation settings that crave software agents are ubiquitous. Consider, for example, two scheduling agents negotiating meeting times on behalf of their users, or any e-commerce application where agents negotiate the final price of a good, or a scenario where agents representing different departments bargain over the details of a service which they provide jointly.

One-to-one negotiation generally involves both integrative and distributive bargaining. In integrative bargaining the agents search for *Pareto efficient* agreements, i.e. deals such that no other deal exists for making one agent better off without making the other worse off. Intuitively, integrative bargaining is the process of making the joint cake as large as possible. Enumerating and evaluating the Pareto efficient deals can be difficult especially in combinatorially complex settings. Automated negotiating agents hold significant promise in this arena due to their computational speed (Sandholm 1993).

In distributive bargaining, the focus of this paper, the agents negotiate on how to split the surplus provided by the deal, i.e. how to divide the cake. A continuum of splits is possible at least if the agents can exchange sidepayments. We call any split where each agent gets a nonnegative benefit from the deal *individually rational*, i.e. each agent would rather accept the deal than no deal. Splitting the gains of an optimal contract in an individually rational way can be modeled generically as follows. Without loss of generality, the surplus provided by the contract is normalized to 1, and each agent's fallback payoff that would occur if no contract is made is normalized to 0. Then, distributive bargaining can be studied as the process of "splitting-a-dollar". This paper focuses on designing software agents that optimally negotiate on the user's behalf in distributive bargaining.

The designer of a multiagent system can construct the interaction *protocol* (aka. mechanism) which determines the legal actions that agents can take at any point in time. Violating the protocol can sometimes be made technically impossible—e.g. disallowing a bidder from submitting multiple bids in an auction—or illegal actions can be penalized e.g. via the regular legal system. To maximize global good, the protocol needs to be designed carefully taking into account that each self-interested agent will take actions so as to maximize its own utility regardless of the global good. In other words, the protocol has to provide the right incentives for the agents. In the extreme, the protocol could specify everything, i.e. give every agent at most one action to choose from at any point. However, in most negotiation settings, the agents can choose whether to participate or not. So, to have the protocol used, the designer has to provide incentives for participation as well. We will return to this question in Section 8.

The most famous model of strategic bargaining is the infinite horizon alternating offers game (Rubinstein 1982). Since it has a unique solution where agents agree on a split immediately, it seems attractive for automated negotiation, see e.g. (Kraus, Wilkenfeld, &

---

[*]Copyright ©, American Association for Artificial Intelligence (www.aaai.org). All rights reserved. This material is based upon work supported by the National Science Foundation under CAREER Award IRI-9703122, Grant IRI-9610122, and Grant IIS-9800994.

[†]Supported by the EPSRC Award GR M07052.

Zlotkin 1995). However, the model has some weaknesses. The infinite horizon assumption is often not realistic. Moreover, the results change considerably if there is a known last period, or even if the distribution from which the number of negotiation rounds is drawn is known and has a finite support. Also, the predictions of the model are specific to exponential time discounting and to the assumption that the dollar is infinitely divisible. For example, under linear time discounting— i.e. a fixed bargaining cost per round of offers—the results change dramatically. The first mover either gets the whole surplus or most of it depending on the ratio of the fixed costs of the two agents. The assumption of perfect information is also of limited use to designers of agents and negotiation protocols. In practice, agents have private information. In such settings, the alternating offers model leads to multiple equilibria, including some where the true types are revealed after long delays, or never. The length of the delay depends on the number of types. See e.g. (Fudenberg & Tirole 1983), (Fudenberg, Levine, & Tirole 1985), and (Rubinstein 1988). The usefulness of the model as a blueprint for designing agents and protocols is questionable when it allows for such qualitatively different outcomes.

Still, the tools of game theory and mechanism design can be used to study new types of bargaining models, inspired by the various applications of automated negotiation. In fact, game theory and mechanism design theory are more suitable for software agents than for humans because agents can be designed off-line to act rationally even if determining rational strategies is complex (Rosenschein & Zlotkin 1994). Also, computational agents do not suffer from emotional irrationality. Finally, the bounded rationality of computational agents can be more systematically characterized than that of humans (Sandholm & Lesser 1997).

In our model, agents face firm deadlines in their bargaining. This is an appealing assumption from a practical perspective since users easily understand deadlines and can trivially communicate them to software agents. Since each agent's deadline is private information, there is a disadvantage in making offers. Any offer—with the exception of demanding everything for oneself— reveals some information about the proposer's deadline, namely that it cannot be very long. If it were, the proposer would stand a good chance of being able to out-wait the opponent, and therefore would ask for a bigger portion of the surplus than it did. Similarly, the offerer knows that it offered too much if the offer gets accepted: the offerer could have done better by out-waiting the opponent. To model real world automated negotiation, we replace the temporal monopoly assumption of alternating offers at fixed intervals, which underlies Rubinstein's model, by a protocol where each agent can make and accept offers in continuous time. However, our results go through even if time is discrete.

Our model resembles war of attrition games where two agents compete for an object and winner-takes-all when one concedes. Those games exhibit multiplicity of equilibria. If the value of the object is common knowledge, there is a symmetric equilibrium where one agent concedes immediately. There is also a symmetric equilibrium where agents concede at a rate which depends on the value of the object. (Hendricks, Weiss, & Wilson 1988) study the general class of war of attrition games with perfect information. (Hendricks & Wilson 1989) study the case of incomplete information, normally about the object's value, see also (Riley 1980). The game was introduced by (Smith 1974) in a biological context and has been applied in industrial economics (Fudenberg et al. 1983), (Kreps & Wilson 1982)).

Our model differs from the war of attrition. Agents are allowed to split the dollar instead of winner-takes-all. One would expect that to enlarge the set of equilibria and equilibrium outcomes. This intuition turns out to be false. We show that the only equilibrium outcome is one where agreement is delayed until one of the deadlines is reached, and then one agent gets the entire surplus.

We show that there exists a sequential equilibrium where agents do not agree to a split until the first deadline, at which time the agent with the later deadline receives the whole surplus. Conversely, we show that there do not exist any other Bayes-Nash equilibria where agents agree to any other split at any other time. Therefore both our positive and negative results are strong with respect to the degree of sequential rationality agents are assumed to have. Intuitively speaking, in these equilibria the agents update their beliefs rationally, and neither agent is motivated to change its strategy at any point of the game given that the other agent does not change its strategy.

Our results are robust in other ways as well. First, there does not exist even a mixed strategy equilibrium where an agent concedes at any rate before its deadline. This, again, is in contrast with the usual equilibrium analysis of war of attrition games. Second, the results hold even if the agents discount time in addition to having deadlines. Third, even if agents have different risk attitudes, they will not agree to any split before their deadline. That is, even risk averse agents will refuse safe and generous offers and will instead prefer to continue to the risky "waiting game".

The rest of the paper is organized as follows. Section 2 describes our formal model of bargaining with deadlines. Section 3 presents our main results for pure-strategy equilibria. Section 4 extends them to mixed strategies. Sections 5 and 6 present the results with time discounting and with agents with risk attitudes. Section 7 describes the entailed insights for designing automated negotiating agents. Section 8 discusses implications for the design of interaction protocols. Finally, Section 9 concludes.

2 Our model of bargaining under deadlines

Our bargaining game, $\Gamma(a, b)$, has two agents, 1 and 2. The type of agent 1 is its deadline d_1. The type of agent 2 is its deadline d_2. The types are private information: each agent only knows its own type. The type d_1 is drawn from a distribution $a(d_1)$, and d_2 is independently drawn from a distribution $b(d_2)$, where a and b are common knowledge. Without loss of generality we scale the time axis so that

$$\min(\min(d_1), \min(d_2)) = 0, \text{ and} \quad (1)$$

$$\max(\max(d_1), \max(d_2)) = 1 \quad (2)$$

That is, $d_1, d_2 \in (0, 1)$.

A history $\langle H(t) \rangle$ is a (possibly empty) list of all unaccepted offers up to time t. An *action* at time t describes the threshold of what offers are acceptable to the agent from then on, and what offer the agent has outstanding from then on. We do not assume that the agents have to improve their offers over time. They can even offer less than they offered earlier. Each agent also has a belief updating rule. Finally, each agent chooses a strategy for the game. A *pure strategy* is an agent's deterministic mapping from her history to action, i.e. it defines what offers the agent would accept and make as a function of what offers and rejections/acceptances the other agent has made so far. A *mixed strategy* is an agent's probability mixture over pure strategies, i.e. the agent can secretly throw a (possibly biased) dice to choose up front which pure strategy to use.

The agents can agree to any split $(x, 1 - x)$ where $x \in [0, 1]$. The payoffs from an agreement $(x, 1 - x)$ at time $t < d_1, d_2$ are x and $1 - x$ for agents 1 and 2 respectively.[1] The payoff for an agent from any agreement which takes place after her deadline is 0. We assume that an agent strictly prefers to hand over the whole surplus than to miss her deadline. In other words, if the agent will get zero payoff anyway, it will rather give the surplus to the other agent than not.[2]

We use two standard game-theoretic solution concepts to model how rational agents would play the game: Bayes-Nash equilibrium and sequential equilibrium. In brief, a strategy-profile (s_1, s_2) is a *Bayes-Nash equilibrium* if s_1 is best response to s_2 in every information set, s_2 is best response to s_1 in every information set, and each agent updates her beliefs based on the strategies and the observed history using Bayes rule (Mas-Colell, Whinston, & Green 1995).

A *sequential equilibrium* is a refinement of Bayes-Nash equilibrium which places the further requirement that agents act rationally also in zero probability information sets. Intuitively speaking, agents must not

---

[1] Payoffs could be defined in several ways. One approach, by Smith (1997), is to define payoffs in terms of aspiration levels, or acceptance thresholds. However, it turns out to be sufficient for the results of this paper to express payoffs not in terms of strategies, but in the traditional way of stating them in terms of preferences over final agreements.

[2] Our results still hold if this assumption is removed, but an additional set of equilibria appears where agents miss their deadline with probability 1. Still, our assumption can be defended on the grounds that there is usually a small (possibly infinitesimally small), but positive utility associated with reaching an agreement.

use threats that are not credible. Formally, a strategy-profile (s_1, s_2) is a sequential equilibrium if (s_1, s_2) is a Bayes-Nash equilibrium and there exists a sequence (s_1^n, s_2^n) such that (i) for any n, s_1^n and s_2^n consist of beliefs which are fully mixed, i.e. beliefs which attach positive probability to every information set, and (ii) (s_1^n, s_2^n) converges to (s_1, s_2) (Mas-Colell, Whinston, & Green 1995).

3 Pure strategy equilibria

It turns out that a "sit-and-wait" way of playing the game is one rational way for agents to behave:

Proposition 3.1 *There exists a sequential equilibrium of $\Gamma(a, b)$, where the agent with the latest deadline receives the whole surplus exactly at the earlier deadline.*

Proof. Consider the following (symmetric) strategies: $s_i(d_i)$: demand $x = 1$ (everything) at any time $t < d_i$. At $t = d_i$ accept any offer. At any time $t < d_i$, reject offers $x_i \geq d_i$. Update beliefs according to Bayes rule, putting all the weight of the posterior distribution over the values of the opponent's deadline, d_{-i}, over the interval $(1 - x_i, 1)$. At any time $t < d_i$, reject offers $x_i < d_i$. Update beliefs in the following way. If $1 - x_i$ is already in the prior of d_{-i} then the posterior is simply equal to the prior. If $1 - x_i$ is not in the prior of d_{-i} then add the point $1 - x_i$ and update according to Bayes rule.

We first show that the beliefs specified above are consistent: Let s_i^ϵ (for $i = 1, 2$) assign probability $1 - \epsilon$ to the above specified posterior beliefs, and probability ϵ to the rest of the support of d_{-i}. As $\epsilon \to 0$ the fully mixed strategy pair converges to (s_1, s_2), while the beliefs generated by the fully mixed strategy pair converge to the beliefs described above. It is now easy to see that, given these beliefs, actions are sequentially rational. Along the equilibrium path agents will always demand the full surplus and therefore no agreement will be achieved before the fist deadline. At the first deadline, the agent with the later deadline will receive the whole surplus. □

The equilibrium described above is clearly also an equilibrium of any subgame beginning at time t onwards regardless of the history, $\langle H(t) \rangle$. That is, at any stage of the game each agent can move to this waiting game, and the other agent's best response is to do the same. We use this property in the proof of our main result which states that, surprisingly, the "sit-and-wait" way of playing the game is the only rational one. We could prove this impossibility result using sequential equilibrium. However, we prove the stronger claim that there is no equilibrium even using a weaker definition of equilibrium, the Bayes-Nash equilibrium. It follows that no sequential equilibrium exists either. For pedagogical reasons we present the result for pure strategies first. We generalize it to mixed strategies in Section 4.

Theorem 3.1 *If $d_1 > 0$ or $d_2 > 0$, there does not exist a pure strategy Bayes-Nash equilibrium of $\Gamma(a, b)$, where agents agree to a split other than $(1, 0)$ or $(0, 1)$.*

Proof. Assume, for contradiction, that there exist types $d_1 > 0$ and $d_2 > 0$ and a pure strategy Bayes-Nash equilibrium (s_1, s_2) where the agents agree to a split $(\pi_1, \pi_2) = (x, 1 - x)$, where $x \in (0, 1)$ at time $t \geq 0$. We assume, without loss of generality, that agent 1 receives at least one half, i.e. $x \geq \frac{1}{2}$. We can therefore write $x = \frac{1}{2} + \epsilon$, where $\frac{1}{2} > \epsilon \geq 0$.

Let $g_0(d_2)$ denote agent 1's beliefs about d_2 at time t. Similarly, let $f_0(d_1)$ denote agent 2's beliefs about d_1 at time t. Denote by $G(d_2) \equiv \int_t^1 g_0(d_2) dd_2$ the cumulative distribution of g_0, and by $F(d_1) \equiv \int_t^1 f_0(d_1) dd_1$ the cumulative distribution of f_0.

In equilibrium, agent 2 will accept $1 - x$ only if she does not expect to receive more by unilaterally moving to the waiting game. The expected payoff from the waiting game is simply agent 2's subjective probability that $d_2 < d_1$. Hence agent 2 would accept only if

$$\frac{1}{2} - \epsilon \geq \int_t^{d_2} f_0(d_1) dd_1 = F(d_2) - F(t) = F(d_2) \quad (3)$$

In other words, agent 2's type, d_2, must not be too high. Let $\alpha(y) \equiv \inf[d_2 \mid y \geq F(d_2)]$. With this notation, (3) can be rewritten as $d_2 \leq \alpha(\frac{1}{2} - \epsilon)$.

Now, agent 1 will only accept this offer if it will give her an expected payoff at least as large as that of the waiting game, which equals her subjective probability of winning the waiting game. There are two cases. First, if $d_1 > \alpha(\frac{1}{2} - \epsilon)$, agent 1 knows that she will win the waiting game with probability one, so the split $(x, 1-x)$ could not occur in equilibrium. The second case occurs when $d_1 \leq \alpha(\frac{1}{2} - \epsilon)$. Agent 1 can use the fact that $d_2 \leq \alpha(\frac{1}{2} - \epsilon)$ to update her beliefs about agent 2's deadline as follows:

$$g_1(d_2) = 0 \quad \text{if } d_2 > \alpha\left(\frac{1}{2} - \epsilon\right). \text{ Otherwise,}$$

$$g_1(d_2) = g_0(d_2) \frac{\int_t^1 g_0(d_2)}{\int_t^{\alpha(\frac{1}{2}-\epsilon)} g_0(d_2)}$$

$$= g_0(d_2) \underbrace{\left[1 + \frac{\int_{\alpha(\frac{1}{2}-\epsilon)}^1 g_0(d_2)}{\int_t^{\alpha(\frac{1}{2}-\epsilon)} g_0(d_2))}\right]}_{\geq 2 \text{ because } \alpha(\frac{1}{2}-\epsilon) \leq \text{median}(g_0)} \quad (4)$$

Based on these updated beliefs, agent 1 would accept only if

$$\frac{1}{2} + \epsilon \geq \int_t^{d_1} g_1(d_2) dd_2 \geq 2[G(d_1) - G(t)] = 2G(d_1) \quad (5)$$

In other words, agent 1's type, d_1, must also not be too high. Let $\beta(y) \equiv \inf[d_1 \mid y \geq G(d_1)]$. With this notation, (5) can be rewritten as $d_1 \leq \beta(\frac{\frac{1}{2}+\epsilon}{2})$.

In equilibrium, agent 2 only accepts if it gives her an expected payoff at least as large as that of the waiting game, which equals her subjective probability of winning the waiting game. There are two cases. First, if $d_2 > \beta(\frac{\frac{1}{2}+\epsilon}{2})$, agent 2 knows that she will

win the waiting game with probability one, so the split $(x, 1 - x)$ could not occur. The second case occurs when $d_2 \leq \beta(\frac{\frac{1}{2}+\epsilon}{2})$. Agent 2 can use the fact that $d_1 \leq \beta(\frac{\frac{1}{2}+\epsilon}{2})$ to update her beliefs about agent 1's deadline as follows:

$$f_1(d_1) = 0 \quad \text{if } d_1 > \beta\left(\frac{\frac{1}{2}+\epsilon}{2}\right). \text{ Otherwise,}$$

$$f_1(d_1) = f_0(d_1) \frac{\int_t^1 f_0(d_1)}{\int_t^{\beta(\frac{\frac{1}{2}+\epsilon}{2})} f_0(d_1)}$$

$$= f_0(d_1) \underbrace{\left[1 + \frac{\int_{\beta(\frac{\frac{1}{2}+\epsilon}{2})}^1 f_0(d_1)}{\int_t^{\beta(\frac{\frac{1}{2}+\epsilon}{2})} f_0(d_1))}\right]}_{\geq 2 \text{ because } \beta(\frac{\frac{1}{2}+\epsilon}{2}) \leq \text{median}(f_0)} \quad (6)$$

Based on these updated beliefs, agent 2 would accept only if

$$\frac{1}{2} - \epsilon \geq \int_t^{d_2} f_1(d_1) dd_1 \geq 2[F(d_2) - F(t)] = 2F(d_2) \quad (7)$$

i.e. $d_2 \leq \alpha(\frac{\frac{1}{2}-\epsilon}{2}))$.

This process of belief update and acceptance threshold resetting continues to alternate between agents. After r rounds of this alternation, all types have been eliminated except those that satisfy $d_1 \leq \beta(\frac{\frac{1}{2}-\epsilon}{2^r})$ and $d_2 \leq \alpha(\frac{\frac{1}{2}+\epsilon}{2^r})$. This process can continue for an unlimited number of steps, r, so the upper bounds approach zero. Therefore the equilibrium cannot exist if $d_1 > 0$ or $d_2 > 0$. Contradiction. $\square$

4 Mixed strategy equilibria

We now strengthen our impossibility result by showing that it holds for mixed strategies as well, i.e. that there is no other rational way of playing the game than "sit-and-wait" even if randomization is possible. This is yet another difference between our setting and war of attrition games. In the latter, mixed strategies play an important role: typically the unique symmetric equilibrium has concession rates that are mixed strategies.

Theorem 4.1 *If $d_1 > 0$ or $d_2 > 0$, there does not exist a mixed strategy Bayes-Nash equilibrium of $\Gamma(a, b)$, where the agents agree to a split other than $(1, 0)$ or $(0, 1)$ with positive probability.*

Proof. Assume, for contradiction, that there exist types $d_1 > 0$ and $d_2 > 0$ and a mixed strategy Bayes-Nash equilibrium where there is positive probability of an agreement other than $(1, 0)$ or $(0, 1)$. Now there has to exist at least one point in time, t, where there is positive probability of an agreement other than $(1, 0)$ or $(0, 1)$. We analyze the equilibrium at such a time t. Recall f, g, F, G, α, and β from the proof of Thrm. 3.1.

Agent 1 will accept an agreement if she gets a share $x \geq a_1$, where a_1 is her acceptance threshold. That threshold depends on her type. Since we are analyzing a mixed strategy equilibrium, the threshold can also depend on randomization. We therefore say that a_1 is randomly chosen for time t from a probability density function $m(a_1)$. Similarly, agent 2 will accept an agreement if she has to offer 1 a share of $x \leq a_2$ where a_2 is agent 2's offering threshold. We say that a_2 is chosen for time t from a probability density function $n(a_2)$.

Without loss of generality, we assume that there is positive probability that the agreement is made in the range $x \geq \frac{1}{2}$. This implies that there is positive probability that $a_2 \geq \frac{1}{2}$.

Let $\underline{a_1}$ be the smallest a_1 in the support of m (alternatively let $\underline{a_1}$ be the infimum of m). The assumption that there is positive probability of an agreement other than $(1,0)$ or $(0,1)$ means that $\underline{a_1} = 1 - \epsilon$ for some $\epsilon > 0$.

Because the strategies are in equilibrium, m and n must be best responses to each other. For n to be a best response, each threshold, a_2, in the support of n has to give agent 2 at least the same payoff as she would get by going to the waiting game. Focusing on those a_2 for which $a_2 \geq \frac{1}{2}$ this means

$$\frac{1}{2} \geq E[\pi_2^{wait}] = \int_t^{d_2} f_0(d_1) dd_1 = F(d_2) - F(t) = F(d_2) \tag{8}$$

So, $d_2 \leq \alpha(\frac{1}{2})$.

Now, in equilibrium, every strategy in the support of m has to give agent 1 at least the same payoff that she would get by going to the waiting game. There are two cases. First, if $d_1 > \alpha(\frac{1}{2})$, agent 1 knows that she will win the waiting game with probability one, so the split $(x, 1-x)$ could not occur in equilibrium. The second case occurs when $d_1 \leq \alpha(\frac{1}{2})$. Agent 1 can use the fact that $d_2 \leq \alpha(\frac{1}{2})$ to update her beliefs about agent 2's deadline:

$$g_1(d_2) = 0 \quad \text{if } d_2 > \alpha\left(\frac{1}{2}\right). \text{ Otherwise,}$$

$$g_1(d_2) = g_0(d_2) \frac{\int_t^1 g_0(d_2)}{\int_t^{\alpha(\frac{1}{2})} g_0(d_2)}$$

$$= g_0(d_2) \underbrace{\left[1 + \frac{\int_{\alpha(\frac{1}{2})}^1 g_0(d_2)}{\int_t^{\alpha(\frac{1}{2})} g_0(d_2))}\right]}_{\geq 2 \text{ because } \alpha(\frac{1}{2}) \leq \text{ median}(g_0)} \tag{9}$$

Based on these updated beliefs, the support of m can include $\underline{a_1}$ only if

$$\underline{a_1} = 1 - \epsilon \geq \int_t^{d_1} g_1(d_2) dd_2 \geq 2[G(d_1) - G(t)] = 2G(d_1) \tag{10}$$

In other words, agent 1's type, d_1, cannot be too high. Specifically, this can be written as $d_1 \leq \beta(\frac{1-\epsilon}{2})$.

In equilibrium, every strategy in the support of n has to give agent 2 at least the same payoff that she would get by going to the waiting game, which equals her subjective probability of winning the waiting game. There are two cases. First, if $d_2 > \beta(\frac{1-\epsilon}{2})$, agent 2 knows that she will win the waiting game with probability one, so the split $(x, 1-x)$ could not occur. The second case occurs when $d_2 \leq \beta(\frac{1-\epsilon}{2})$. Agent 2 can use the fact that $d_1 \leq \beta(\frac{1-\epsilon}{2})$ to update her beliefs about agent 1's deadline:

$$f_1(d_1) = 0 \quad \text{if } d_1 > \beta\left(\frac{1-\epsilon}{2}\right). \text{ Otherwise,}$$

$$f_1(d_1) = f_0(d_1) \frac{\int_t^1 f_0(d_1)}{\int_t^{\beta(\frac{1-\epsilon}{2})} f_0(d_1)}$$

$$= f_0(d_1) \underbrace{\left[1 + \frac{\int_{\beta(\frac{1-\epsilon}{2})}^1 f_0(d_1)}{\int_t^{\beta(\frac{1-\epsilon}{2})} f_0(d_1))}\right]}_{\geq 2 \text{ because } \beta(\frac{1-\epsilon}{2}) \leq \text{ median}(f_0)} \tag{11}$$

Based on these updated beliefs, and focusing on those a_2 for which $a_2 \geq \frac{1}{2}$ we can rule out high values of d_2 (otherwise agent 2 would be better off by waiting):

$$\frac{1}{2} \geq E[\pi_2^{wait}] = \int_t^{d_2} f_1(d_1) dd_1 \geq 2F(d_2) \tag{12}$$

i.e. $d_2 \leq \alpha(\frac{1}{4})$).

This process of belief update and acceptance threshold resetting continues to alternate between agents. After r rounds of this alternation, all types have been eliminated except those that satisfy $d_1 \leq \beta(\frac{1-\epsilon}{2^{r+1}})$ and $d_2 \leq \alpha(\frac{1}{2^{r+1}})$. This process can continue for an unlimited number of steps, r, so the upper bounds approach zero. Therefore the equilibrium cannot exist if $d_1 > 0$ or $d_2 > 0$. Contradiction. $\square$

5 Incorporating discounting

Time discounting is a standard way of modeling settings where the value of the good decreases over time, e.g. due to inflation or due to perishing. In the previous sections we assumed that agents do not discount time. However, we now show that our results are robust to the case where agents do discount time in addition to having firm deadlines. Let δ_1 be the discount factor of agent 1, and δ_2 be the discount factor of agent 2. The utility of agent i from an agreement where he receives a share x at time $t < d_i$ is then $\delta_i^t x$. We denote by $\Gamma(a, b, \delta_1, \delta_2)$ the bargaining game where a, b, δ_1, and δ_2 are common knowledge. We now prove that our previous result for $\Gamma(a, b)$ holds also for a large range of parameters in $\Gamma(a, b, \delta_1, \delta_2)$. So, interestingly, the bargaining power of an agent does not change with her discount factor, in contrast to the results of most other bargaining games. In other words, the deadline effect completely suppresses the discounting effect. This crisp result is important in its own right for the design of automated negotiating agents, and it also motivates the study of deadline-based models as opposed to focusing only on discounting-based ones.

Proposition 5.1 *For any $\delta_1, \delta_2, 0 < \delta_1 \leq 1, 0 < \delta_2 \leq 1$, there exists a sequential equilibrium of $\Gamma(a, b, \delta_1, \delta_2)$ where the agent with the latest deadline receives the whole surplus exactly at the earlier deadline.*

Proof. The equilibrium strategies and proof of sequential equilibrium are identical to those in the proof of Proposition 3.1 with the difference that the threshold is no longer d_i but $\delta_i^t d_i$. Also the posteriors are now defined only until δ_i^t and not 1. □

Theorem 5.1 *If $\delta_1 \delta_2 > \frac{1}{2}$, there does not exist a Bayes-Nash equilibrium of $\Gamma(a, b, \delta_1, \delta_2)$, (in pure or mixed strategies) where agents agree to a split other than $(1, 0)$ or $(0, 1)$.*

Proof. We prove the case for pure strategy equilibrium. The extension for mixed strategy equilibrium is identical to that in Theorem 4.1. The proof is a variant of the proof in Theorem 3.1, and we keep the notation from there.

Assume, for contradiction, that there exist types $d_1 > 0$ and $d_2 > 0$ and a pure strategy Bayes-Nash equilibrium (s_1, s_2) where the agents agree to a split of the total surplus available at time t, according to proportions $(\pi_1, \pi_2) = (x, 1 - x)$, where $x \in (0, 1)$ at time $t \geq 0$. We assume, without loss of generality, that agent 1 receives at least one half, i.e. $x \geq \frac{1}{2}$. We can therefore write $x = \frac{1}{2} + \epsilon$, where $\frac{1}{2} > \epsilon \geq 0$.

In equilibrium, agent 2 will accept $1 - x$ only if she does not expect to receive more by unilaterally moving to the waiting game. The expected payoff from the waiting game is now agent 2's subjective probability that $d_2 < d_1$, multiplied by the discounted value of winning. Hence agent 2 would accept only if

$$\delta_2^t \left(\frac{1}{2} - \epsilon \right) \geq \int_t^{d_2} \delta_2^{d_1} f_0(d_1) dd_1 \geq \delta_2 \int_t^{d_2} f_0(d_1) dd_1 \quad (13)$$

Dividing both sides by δ_2^t, we get:

$$\frac{1}{2} - \epsilon \geq \delta_2^{1-t} \int_t^{d_2} f_0(d_1) dd_1 = \delta_2^{1-t} F(d_2) \geq \delta_2 F(d_2) \quad (14)$$

In other words: $d_2 \leq \alpha \frac{(\frac{1}{2} - \epsilon)}{\delta_2}$.

Now, agent 1 can use this to update her beliefs about agent 2's deadline in the same way as in equation (4), with the difference that now $g_1 \geq 2\delta_2 g_0$. Since $\delta_2 > 0.5$ (by the assumption that $\delta_1 \delta_2 > 0.5$), we know that $g_1 > g_0$ (when g_1 is not zero).

Based on these updated beliefs, agent 1 would accept only if

$$\delta_1^t \left(\frac{1}{2} + \epsilon \right) \geq \int_t^{d_1} \delta_1^{d_2} g_1(d_2) dd_2 \geq \delta_1 \int_t^{d_1} g_1(d_2) dd_2 \quad (15)$$

Dividing both sides by δ_1^t and using the updated beliefs, g_1, we can now rule out "high" types of agent 1. Formally, $d_1 \leq \beta \left(\frac{\frac{1}{2} + \epsilon}{2\delta_2 \delta_1} \right)$.

Once more, belief updating by agent 2 (in the same way as in (6)) yields $f_1 \geq 2\delta_2 \delta_1 f_0$. Since $\delta_1 \delta_2 > 0.5$ we get that $f_1 > f_0$ (when it is not zero). Based on these updated beliefs, agent 2 would accept only if

$$\delta_2^t \left(\frac{1}{2} - \epsilon \right) \geq \int_t^{d_2} \delta_2^{d_1} f_1(d_1) dd_1 \geq \delta_2 \int_t^{d_2} f_0(d_1) dd_1 \quad (16)$$

Dividing by δ_2^t and using the updated beliefs, f_1 we can rule out the following types: $d_2 \leq \alpha \left(\frac{\frac{1}{2} - \epsilon}{2\delta_2^2 \delta_1} \right) < \alpha \left(\frac{\frac{1}{2} - \epsilon}{2\delta_2} \right)$. This process of belief update and acceptance threshold resetting continues to alternate between agents. After r rounds of this alternation, all types have been eliminated except those that satisfy $d_1 \leq \beta \left(\frac{\frac{1}{2} - \epsilon}{(2\delta_1)^r} \right)$ and $d_2 \leq \alpha \left(\frac{\frac{1}{2} + \epsilon}{(2\delta_2)^r} \right)$. This process can continue for an unlimited number of steps, r, so the upper bounds approach zero. Therefore the equilibrium cannot exist if $d_1 > 0$ or $d_2 > 0$. Contradiction. □

For example, if the annual interest rate is 10%, the discount factor would be $\delta = \frac{1}{1+0.1} \approx 0.909$ per year. For the conditions of Theorem 5.1 to be violated, at least one agent's discount factor would have to be $\delta_i \leq \frac{1}{2}$. This would mean that the unit of time from which its deadline is drawn would have to be no shorter than 7 years because $\frac{1}{2} < (\frac{1}{1+0.1})^7$. Since most deadline bargaining situations will certainly have shorter deadlines than 7 years, Theorem 5.1 shows that "sit-and-wait" is the only rational strategy. So, in practice, the effect of deadlines suppresses that of discount factors. This is even more commonly true in automated negotiation because that is most likely going to be used mainly for fast negotiation at the operative decision making level instead of strategic long-term negotiation.

6 Robustness to risk attitudes

We now generalize our results to agents that are not necessarily risk neutral. Usually in bargaining games the equilibrium split of the surplus depends on the agents' risk attitudes. However, we show that this does not happen in our setting. This is surprising at first since a risk averse agent generally prefers a smaller but safe share to the risky option of the waiting game even if she expects to win it with high probability. However, we show that the type-elimination effect described in the theorems so far is still present and dominates any concessions which may be consistent with risk aversion.

Let the agents' risk attitudes be captured by utility functions, u_i where $i = 1, 2$. Without loss of generality we let $u_i(0) = 0$ and $u_i(1) = 1$ for both agents.

Proposition 6.1 *There exists a sequential equilibrium of $\Gamma(a, b, u_1, u_2)$, where the agent with the latest deadline receives the whole surplus exactly at the earlier deadline.*

Proof. The equilibrium strategies and proof of sequential equilibrium are identical to those in the proof of Proposition 3.1 with the difference that the threshold is no longer d_i but $u_i(d_i)$. □

The following definition is used to state our main result for the case of different risk attitudes.

Definition. 6.1 *The* maximum risk aversion *of agent i is*

$$\rho_i \equiv \max_x \frac{u_i(x)}{x} \qquad (17)$$

We can now show that our impossibility result applies to a large range of risk attitudes of the agents:

Theorem 6.1 *If $\rho_1\rho_2 < 2$, there does not exist a Bayes-Nash equilibrium (pure or mixed) of $\Gamma(a, b, u_1, u_2)$, where agents agree to a split other than $(1, 0)$ or $(0, 1)$.*

Proof. We prove the case for pure strategy equilibrium. The extension to mixed strategies is identical to that in Theorem 4.1. We keep the notations from Theorem 3.1. Assume, for contradiction, that there exist types $d_1 > 0$ and $d_2 > 0$ and a pure strategy Bayes-Nash equilibrium (s_1, s_2) where the agents agree to a split $(\pi_1, \pi_2) = (x, 1-x)$, where $x \in (0, 1)$ at time $t \geq 0$. Assume, without loss of generality, that agent 1 receives at least half, i.e. $x \geq \frac{1}{2}$. Thus we can write $x = \frac{1}{2} + \epsilon$, where $\frac{1}{2} > \epsilon \geq 0$. In equilibrium, agent 2 accepts $1 - x$ only if she does not expect to receive more by unilaterally moving to the waiting game. The expected payoff from the waiting game is agent 2's subjective probability that $d_2 < d_1$. So, agent 2 would accept only if

$$\rho_2(\frac{1}{2} - \epsilon) \geq u_2(\frac{1}{2} - \epsilon) \geq \int_t^{d_2} f_0(d_1) dd_1 = F(d_2) \quad (18)$$

In other words, $d_2 \leq \alpha(\rho_2(\frac{1}{2} - \epsilon))$. Now, agent 1 can use this to update her beliefs about agent 2's deadline in the same way as in equation (4), with the difference that now $g_1 \geq \frac{2}{\rho_2} g_0$. Since (by assumption) $\rho_2 < 2$, then $g_1 > g_0$ (when g_1 is not zero). Based on these updated beliefs, agent 1 would accept only if:

$$u_1(\frac{1}{2} + \epsilon) \geq \int_t^{d_1} g_1(d_2) dd_2 \qquad (19)$$

Using ρ_1 and the updated beliefs, g_1, we can rule out "high" types of agent 1. Formally, $d_1 \leq \beta(\rho_2\rho_1(\frac{1}{2} + \epsilon))$.

Once more, belief updating by agent 2 (in the same way as in (6)) yields $f_1 \geq \frac{2}{\rho_2\rho_1} f_0$. Since $\rho_2\rho_1 < 2$ we get $f_1 > f_0$ (when f_1 is not zero). Based on these updated beliefs, agent 2 would accept only if

$$u_2(\frac{1}{2} - \epsilon) \geq \int_t^{d_2} f_1(d_1) dd_1 \qquad (20)$$

Using ρ_2 and the updated beliefs, f_1, we can rule out the following types: $d_2 \leq \alpha(\rho_2^2\rho_1(\frac{1}{2}-\epsilon)) < \alpha(\rho_2(\frac{1}{2}-\epsilon))$. This process of belief update and acceptance threshold resetting continues to alternate between agents. After r rounds of this alternation, all types have been eliminated except those that satisfy $d_1 \leq \beta(\rho_1^r(\frac{1}{2} - \epsilon))$ and $d_2 \leq \alpha(\rho_2^r(\frac{1}{2} - \epsilon))$. This process can continue for an unlimited number of steps, r, so the upper bounds approach zero. Therefore the equilibrium cannot exist if $d_1 > 0$ or $d_2 > 0$. Contradiction. $\square$

7 Designing bargaining agents

Our motivation for studying bargaining with deadlines stems from our desire to construct software agents that will optimally negotiate on behalf of the real world parties that they represent. That will put experienced and poor human negotiators on an equal footing, and save human negotiation effort.

Deadlines are widely advocated and used in automated electronic commerce to capture time preference. For example when a user delegates priceline.com to find an inexpensive airline flight on the web, the user gives it one hour to complete (while priceline.com uses an agent with a deadline, the setting is a form of auction, not bargaining). Users easily understand deadlines, and it is simple to specify a deadline to an agent.

Our results show that in distributive bargaining settings with two agents with deadlines, it is not rational for either agent to make or accept offers. But what if a rational software agent receives an offer from the other party? This means that the other party is irrational, and could perhaps be exploited. However, the type-elimination argument from the proofs above applies here too, and it is not rational for the software agent to accept the offer, no matter how good it is. To exploit the other party, the agent would have to have an opponent model to model the other party's irrationality. While game theory allows us to give precise prescriptions for rational play, it is mostly silent about irrationality, and how to exploit it.

Another classic motivation for automated negotiation is that computerized agents can negotiate faster. However, in distributive bargaining settings where the agents have deadlines, this argument does not hold because in such settings, rational software agents would sit-and-wait until one of the deadlines is reached. From an implementation perspective this suggests the use of daemons that trigger right before the deadline instead of agents that use computation before the deadline.

Finally, our results suggest that a user will be in a much stronger bargaining position by inputting time preferences to her agent in terms of a time discount function instead of a deadline, even if the discounting is significant. To facilitate this, software agent vendors should provide user interfaces to their agents that allow easy human-understandable specification of time discounting functions instead of inputting a deadline.

8 Designing bargaining protocols

The following mechanism implements, in dominant strategies, the equilibrium of the deadline bargaining game described above. First, agents report their deadlines, $\tilde{d}_i$, to the protocol—possibly insincerely ($\tilde{d}_i \neq d_i$). The protocol then assigns the whole dollar to the agent with the highest $\tilde{d}_i$, but this only takes place at time $t = \tilde{d}_{-i}$, i.e. at the earlier reported deadline. Truthtelling is a dominant strategy in this mechanism. By reporting $\tilde{d}_i < d_i$ agent i's probability of winning is reduced. By reporting $\tilde{d}_i > d_i$, agent i increase its probability of winning, but only in cases where $\tilde{d}_{-i} > d_i$, i.e. when i misses its deadline. Therefore, reporting $\tilde{d}_i = d_i$ is a dominant strategy.

This mechanism is efficient in several ways. First, it minimizes counterspeculation. In equilibria that are based on refinements of the Nash equilibrium—such as Bayes-Nash or sequential equilibrium—an agent's best strategy depends on what others will do. This requires speculation about the others' strategies, which can be speculated by considering the others' types, their rationality, what they think of the former agent, what they think the former agent thinks about them, *etc. ad infinitum*. On the other hand, in a dominant strategy mechanism an agent's strategy is optimal no matter what others do. Therefore, counterspeculation is not useful. The agent need not waste time in counterspeculation which can be intractable or even noncomputable. In addition, it is easier to program an agent that executes a given dominant strategy than an agent that counterspeculates. Second, dominant strategy mechanisms are robust against irrational agents since their actions do not affect how others should behave. Finally, the mechanism minimizes communication: each agent only sends one message.

However, the mechanism is not Pareto efficient if time is being discounted, because the agreement is delayed as it was in the original free-form bargaining game. In such settings, any mechanism that results in an immediate agreement is Pareto efficient, e.g. a protocol that forces a 50:50 split up front. This protocol is efficient in all respects discussed above. It might seem like a good solution to the problem raised by our impossibility results. However, agents in e-commerce applications usually can choose whether to use a protocol or not. If agents know their types before they choose the protocol they want to use, an adverse selection problem arises. To see why, assume that types are normally distributed. This is assumed for simplicity of presentation and is not crucial. Agents with deadlines above $1/2$ will not participate in such a protocol because they can expect to do better in a free-form bargaining setting. But if only agents with deadlines below $1/2$ participate, agents with deadlines between $1/4$ and $1/2$ should not participate. Next, agents with deadlines between $1/8$ and $1/4$ would not participate, and so on. In equilibrium, no agent would participate. This argument does not rely on a 50:50 split. The adverse selection problem will affect any protocol that does not implement Nash (or stronger) equilibrium outcomes.

9 Conclusions

Automated agents have been suggested as a way to facilitate increasingly efficient negotiation. In settings where the bargaining set, i.e. set of individually rational Pareto efficient deals, is difficult to construct for example due to a combinatorial number of possible deals (Sandholm 1993) or the computational complexity of evaluating any given deal (Sandholm & Lesser 1997), the computational speed of automated agents can sig-

nificantly enhance negotiation. Additional efficiency can stem from the fact that computational agents can negotiate with large numbers of other agents quickly and virtually with no negotiation overhead. However, this paper showed that in one-to-one negotiation where the optimal deal in the bargaining set has been identified and evaluated, and distributing the profits is the issue, an agent's power does not stem from speed, but on the contrary, from the ability to wait.

We showed that in one-to-one bargaining with deadlines, the only sequential equilibrium is one where the agents wait until the first deadline is reached. This is in line with some human experiments where adding deadlines introduced significant delays in reaching agreement (Roth, Murnighan, & Schoumaker 1988). We also showed that deadline effects almost always completely suppress time discounting effects. Impossibility of an interim agreement also applies to most types of risk attitudes of the agents. The results show that for deadline bargaining settings it is trivial to design the optimal agent: it should simply wait until it reaches its deadline or the other party concedes. On the other hand, a user is better off by giving her agent a time discount function instead of a deadline since a deadline puts her agent in a weak bargaining position. Finally, we discussed mechanism design, and presented an effective protocol that implements the outcome of the free-form bargaining game in dominant strategy equilibrium.

References

Fudenberg, D., and Tirole, J. 1983. Sequential bargaining with incomplete information. *Review of Economic Studies* 50:221–247.

Fudenberg, D.; Glibert, R.; Stiglitz, J.; and Tirole, J. 1983. Preemption, leapfrogging, and competition in patent races. *European Economic Review* 22:3–31.

Fudenberg, D.; Levine, D.; and Tirole, J. 1985. Infinite-horizon models of bargaining with one-sided incomplete information. In Roth, ed., *Game-Theoretic Models of Bargaining*. Cambridge U. Press. 73–98.

Hendricks, K., and Wilson, C. 1989. The war of attrition in discrete time. Technical report, State University of New York, Stony Brook. Mimeo.

Hendricks, K.; Weiss, A.; and Wilson, C. 1988. The war of attrition in continuous time with complete information. *Internat. Economic Review* 29:663–680.

Kraus, S.; Wilkenfeld, J.; and Zlotkin, G. 1995. Multiagent negotiation under time constraints. *Artificial Intelligence* 75:297–345.

Kreps, E., and Wilson, R. 1982. Reputation and imperfect information. *J. of Economic Theory* 27:253–279.

Mas-Colell, A.; Whinston, M.; and Green, J. R. 1995. *Microeconomic Theory*. Oxford University Press.

Osborne, M. J., and Rubinstein, A. 1990. *Bargaining and Markets*. Academic Press, Inc.

Riley, J. 1980. Strong evolutionary equilibrium and the war of attrition. *J. of Theoretical Biology* 82:383–400.

Rosenschein, J. S., and Zlotkin, G. 1994. *Rules of Encounter*. MIT Press.

Roth, A.; Murnighan, J.; and Schoumaker, F. 1988. The deadline effect in bargaining: some experimental evidence. *American Economic Review* 78:806–823.

Rubinstein, A. 1982. Perfect equilibrium in a bargaining model. *Econometrica* 50.

Rubinstein, A. 1988. A bargaining model with incomplete information about time preferences. *Econometrica* 53:1151–1172.

Sandholm, T. W., and Lesser, V. R. 1997. Coalitions among computationally bounded agents. *Artificial Intelligence* 94(1):99–137. Special issue on Economic Principles of Multiagent Systems.

Sandholm, T. W. 1993. An implementation of the contract net protocol based on marginal cost calculations. In *AAAI*, 256–262.

Smith, J. 1974. The theory of games and evolution in animal conflict. *J. of Theoretical Biology* 47:209–221.

Verifying that Agents Implement a Communication Language

Michael Wooldridge

Queen Mary & Westfield College
Department of Electronic Engineering
London E1 4NS, United Kingdom
M.J.Wooldridge@qmw.ac.uk

Abstract

In recent years, a number of attempts have been made to develop standardized agent communication languages. A key issue in such languages is that of conformance testing. That is, given a program which claims to semantically conform to some agent communication standard, how can we determine whether or not it does indeed conform to it? In this article, we present an expressive agent communication language, and give a semantics for this language in such a way that verifying semantic conformance becomes a realistic possibility. The techniques we develop draw upon those used to give a semantics to reactive systems in theoretical computer science. To illustrate the approach, we give an example of a simple agent system, and show that it does indeed respect the semantics.

Introduction

Perhaps the biggest single obstacle that stands in the way of the wider industrial take-up of agent technology is the issue of interoperability. That is, it must be possible for agents built by different organisations, using different hardware and software platforms, to communicate, cooperate, and negotiate using commonly agreed communication languages and protocols. This concern has lead to the development of several standardized agent communication languages (ACLs), including KQML (Patil et al., 1992) and FIPA's communication language (FIPA, 1997).

As part of these standardisation initiatives, attempts have been made to give a precise formal semantics to these ACLs (e.g., (Labrou and Finin, 1997)). Typically, these formal semantics have been developed using techniques adapted from speech act theory (Cohen and Perrault, 1979; Cohen and Levesque, 1990). If these ACL standardisation initiatives are to succeed, then the issue of *semantic conformance testing* must be successfully addressed. The conformance testing problem can be summarised as follows (Wooldridge, 1998): We are given program π_i, and an agent communication language $\mathcal{L}_C$ with the semantics $[\![\ldots]\!]_C$. The aim is to determine whether or not π_i respects the semantics $[\![\ldots]\!]_C$ whenever it communicates using $\mathcal{L}_C$. We say a program *implements* a communication language $\mathcal{L}_C$ if it respects its semantics. (Syntactic conformance testing is of course trivial.)

The importance of conformance testing *has* been recognised by the ACL community (FIPA, 1997, p1). However, to date, little research has been carried out either on how verifiable communication languages might be developed, or on how existing ACLs might be verified. One exception is (Wooldridge, 1998), where the issue of conformance testing is discussed from a formal point of view. (Wooldridge, 1998) points out that ACL semantics are generally developed in such as way as to express *constraints* on the senders of messages. For example, the semantics for an "inform φ" message in some ACL might state that the sender of the message is respecting the semantics of the language if it truly believes φ. This constraint — that the sender believes the message content — can be viewed as a *specification*. Verifying that an agent respects the semantics of the ACL then reduces to a conventional program verification problem: show that the agent sending the message satisfies the specification given by the ACL semantics.

(Wooldridge, 1998) notes that this poses the following problem for ACL conformance testing. The formalisms used to give a semantics to ACLs are typically quantified multimodal logics, with modalities for referring to the "mental state" of agents. In the FIPA case, this mental state consists of beliefs, intentions, and the like. However, we do not currently understand how to attribute FIPA-like mental states to programs, and so we cannot verify whether or not such programs implement "mentalistic" semantics.

In this paper, we present an expressive ACL that overcomes this problem. The language, (which is intended as a proof of concept for the basic approach to ACL semantics, rather than as a serious ACL proposal), contains performatives similar to those of both KQML and FIPA. In addition, the language has a rigorous formal semantics, which superficially resemble those of (Cohen and Levesque, 1990; Labrou and Finin, 1997; FIPA, 1997). However, the language semantics are based on the semantics of concurrent systems from theoretical computer science (Manna and Pnueli, 1992; Manna and Pnueli, 1995; Fagin et al., 1995). Specifically, the semantics are given in terms of a quantified epistemic temporal logic, (QUETL). The paper begins in the next section by fully defining QUETL. We subsequently define our ACL, which we shall call $\mathcal{L}_C$. We then present a general computational model of multi-agent systems, and use QUETL to give a semantics to this model of multi-agent systems and our agent communication framework. To illustrate the approach, we present an agent program that respects the semantics we give. Finally, note that this paper is *not* concerned with giving a semantics to *human* speech acts. We are only concerned with *software* agents.

A Quantified Epistemic Temporal Logic

In this section, we define a quantified epistemic temporal logic (QUETL). This logic is essentially classical first-order logic augmented by a set of modal connectives for representing the *temporal ordering* of events and an indexed set of unary modal connectives for representing the *knowledge* possessed by agents in a system. QUETL is thus a quantified version of the epistemic temporal logics studied in (Halpern and Vardi, 1989; Fagin et al., 1995).

QUETL provides the following temporal connectives:

- the nullary temporal operator "**start**" is satisfied only at the beginning of time;

- $\bigcirc \varphi$ is satisfied now if φ is satisfied at the next moment;

- $\Diamond \varphi$ is satisfied now if φ is satisfied either now or at some future moment;

- $\Box \varphi$ is satisfied now if φ is satisfied now and at all future moments;

- $\varphi \, \mathcal{U} \, \psi$ is satisfied now if ψ is satisfied at some future moment, and φ is satisfied until then — $\mathcal{W}$ is a binary connective similar to $\mathcal{U}$, allowing for the possibility that the second argument might never be satisfied.

To express the knowledge possessed by each agent i, QUETL contains a unary modal operator $\mathcal{K}_i$. The intended reading of a formula $\mathcal{K}_i \varphi$ is "agent i knows φ" (Fagin et al., 1995).

In addition to these temporal and epistemic operators, QUETL contains the usual truth-functional connectives of classical logic, and the usual apparatus of first-order quantification.

Syntax

Formulae of QUETL are constructed from the (denumerable) sets *Pred* (predicate symbols), *Const* (individual constants), and *Var* (logical variables). In addition, QUETL contains the truth constant "**true**", the binary connective "$\lor$" (or), unary connective "$\neg$" (not), equality symbol "$=$", universal quantifier "$\forall$", and punctuation symbols ")", and "(", and ".". In addition, QUETL contains the unary modal epistemic connective "$\mathcal{K}$" (knows), a denumerable set $Ag = \{1, \ldots, n\}$ of *agent identifiers*, (used to index epistemic connectives), the binary temporal connective "$\mathcal{U}$" (until), unary temporal connective "$\bigcirc$", and nullary temporal connective **start**. The syntax of QUETL is defined by the grammar in Figure 1.

In the interests of simplicity, we assume QUETL contains no functional terms other than individual constants. Let $Term = Var \cup Const$ be the set of all terms. We use τ (with decorations: $\tau', \tau_1, \ldots$) to stand for arbitrary terms. We assume each predicate symbol is associated with a natural number called its arity, which determines the number of arguments it takes — it is assumed that predicate symbols are only applied to the appropriate number of arguments.

$\langle const \rangle$	$::=$	any element of *Const*
$\langle var \rangle$	$::=$	any element of *Var*
$\langle term \rangle$	$::=$	$\langle const \rangle \mid \langle var \rangle$
$\langle pred \rangle$	$::=$	any element of *Pred*
$\langle ag\text{-}id \rangle$	$::=$	any element of *Ag*
$\langle wff \rangle$	$::=$	**true** $\mid$ **start**
	$\mid$	$\langle pred \rangle (\langle term \rangle, \ldots, \langle term \rangle)$
	$\mid$	$\mathcal{K}_{\langle ag\text{-}id \rangle} \langle wff \rangle$
	$\mid$	$(\langle term \rangle = \langle term \rangle)$
	$\mid$	$\neg \langle wff \rangle \mid \langle wff \rangle \lor \langle wff \rangle$
	$\mid$	$\forall \langle var \rangle \cdot \langle wff \rangle$
	$\mid$	$\bigcirc \langle wff \rangle \mid \langle wff \rangle \, \mathcal{U} \, \langle wff \rangle$

Figure 1: Syntax of QUETL

Semantics

The temporal model that underpins QUETL is $(I\!N, \leq)$, i.e., the natural numbers ordered by the usual "less than" relation. This model is widely used in theoretical computer science for representing the semantics of concurrent and distributed systems (Manna and Pnueli, 1992; Manna and Pnueli, 1995).

A *domain*, D, is a non-empty set. If D is a domain and $u \in I\!N$, then by D^u we mean the set of u-tuples over D. In order to interpret QUETL, we need various functions that associate symbols of the language with semantic objects. The first of these is an *interpretation for predicates*

$$\Phi : Pred \times I\!N \to \wp\left(\bigcup_{u \in I\!N} D^u \right)$$

which for every predicate P at every time n determines a set of tuples over D denoting the extension of P at n. (We assume Φ respects the arity of its arguments.) An *interpretation for constants* is a function $I : Const \times I\!N \to D$ which gives the denotation of a constant at some time. Note that constants are *not* assumed to be rigid designators: they may have different denotations at different times. A *variable assignment* is a function $V : Var \to D$, which gives the semantic value of every variable. We introduce a derived function $[\![\ldots]\!]_{V,I}$, which gives the denotation of an arbitrary term with respect to a particular interpretation for constants, variable assignment, and time:

$$[\![\tau]\!]_{V,I}^u \; \hat{=} \; \begin{cases} I(\tau, u) & \text{if } \tau \in Const \\ V(\tau) & \text{if } \tau \in Var. \end{cases}$$

As V and I will generally be understood, reference to them will usually be suppressed.

Finally, in order to give a semantics to epistemic connectives, we require an indexed set of binary equivalence relations, $\sim_i \subseteq I\!N \times I\!N$, one for each $i \in Ag$ (Fagin et al., 1995).

Models for QUETL are $(n+3)$-tuples of the form

$$M = \langle D, \sim_1, \ldots, \sim_n, I, \Phi \rangle$$

where:

- D is a domain;

$$
\begin{array}{lll}
\langle M, V, u \rangle \models \mathbf{true} & & \\
\langle M, V, u \rangle \models \mathbf{start} & \text{iff } u = 0 & \\
\langle M, V, u \rangle \models P(\tau_1, \ldots, \tau_n) & \text{iff } \langle [\![\tau_1]\!]^u, \ldots, [\![\tau_n]\!]^u \rangle \in \Phi(P, u) & \\
\langle M, V, u \rangle \models \mathcal{K}_i \varphi & \text{iff } \langle M, V, v \rangle \models \varphi \text{ for all } v \in I\!N \text{ such that } u \sim_i v & \\
\langle M, V, u \rangle \models (\tau = \tau') & \text{iff } [\![\tau]\!]^u = [\![\tau']\!]^u & \\
\langle M, V, u \rangle \models \neg \varphi & \text{iff } \langle M, V, u \rangle \not\models \varphi & \\
\langle M, V, u \rangle \models \varphi \vee \psi & \text{iff } \langle M, V, u \rangle \models \varphi \text{ or } \langle M, V, u \rangle \models \psi & \\
\langle M, V, u \rangle \models \forall x \cdot \varphi & \text{iff } \langle M, V \dagger \{x \mapsto d\}, u \rangle \models \varphi \text{ for all } d \in D & \\
\langle M, V, u \rangle \models \bigcirc \varphi & \text{iff } \langle M, V, u + 1 \rangle \models \varphi & \\
\langle M, V, u \rangle \models \varphi \mathcal{U} \psi & \text{iff } \exists v \in I\!N \text{ such that } (v \geq u) \text{ and } \langle M, V, v \rangle \models \psi, & \\
& \quad \text{and } \forall w \in I\!N, \text{ if } (u \leq w < v) \text{ then } \langle M, V, w \rangle \models \varphi &
\end{array}
$$

Figure 2: Semantics of QUETL

- $\sim_i \subseteq I\!N \times I\!N$ is a knowledge accessibility relation, one for each agent $i \in Ag$;

- $I : Const \times I\!N \to D$ interprets constants; and

- $\Phi : Pred \times I\!N \to \wp(\bigcup_{n \in I\!N} D^n)$ interprets predicates.

As usual, we define the semantics of the language via the satisfaction relation, "$\models$". For QUETL, this relation holds between triples of the form $\langle M, V, u \rangle$, (where M is a model, V is a variable assignment, and $u \in I\!N$ is a temporal index into M), and QUETL-formulae. The rules defining the satisfaction relation are given in Figure 2 (note that if f is a function, then $f \dagger \{x \mapsto d\}$ denotes the same function as f except that x maps to d). Satisfiability and validity for QUETL are defined in the standard way.

The remaining temporal connectives of QUETL are introduced as abbreviations:

$$
\begin{array}{lll}
\diamondsuit \varphi & \hat{=} & \mathbf{true} \, \mathcal{U} \, \varphi \\
\square \varphi & \hat{=} & \neg \diamondsuit \neg \varphi \\
\varphi \mathcal{W} \psi & \hat{=} & \varphi \mathcal{U} \psi \vee \square \varphi
\end{array}
$$

It should be clear that QUETL inherits the expected proof theoretic properties of its temporal, epistemic, and first-order fragments.

An Agent Communication Language

We now define our agent communication language, $\mathcal{L}_C$. Like KQML and the FIPA ACL, this language has two main parts:

- An "outer" language, which defines a number of *performatives* such as "inform". In speech act terminology, the outer language is used to define the illocutionary force of a message (Searle, 1969). The performative of a message defines how the content of the message should be interpreted. In addition to the performative, the outer language contains some "housekeeping" information such as the sender and recipient of the message.

- A *content language*, which is used to define the actual content of the message. In $\mathcal{L}_C$, the content language is actually QUETL itself. QUETL is a powerful, highly expressive language, which will afford agents much greater expressive power than (for example) first-order logic.

In addition, we will assume that, (unlike KQML and FIPA) our language is *synchronous*, in the sense of Hoare's Communicating Sequential Processes (CSPs) (Hoare, 1978). Intuitively, this means that whenever an agent i attempts to execute one of the $\mathcal{L}_C$ performatives by sending a message to some other agent, the intended recipient of the message must execute a "receive message" action. To represent this, every agent is assumed to be able to perform a special action "recv", indicating that it has received a message. When an agent attempts to execute a performative, it will block (i.e., suspend its activities) until the recipient executes a recv action.

In general, a message in $\mathcal{L}_C$ has the form $p_{i,j}(\varphi)$, where p is the performative, $i \in Ag$ is the sender of the message (i.e., the agent that performs the communicative act), $j \in Ag$ is the intended recipient, and φ is the message content, expressed as a formula of the content language, i.e., QUETL. $\mathcal{L}_C$ provides four performatives: see Table 1.

The "inform" performative is the basic mechanism through which agents communicate information. The intuitive semantics of the inform performative are identical to that of the FIPA inform (FIPA, 1997, p25). Thus an agent will use inform to communicate information to another agent. More formally, an agent i that sends the message $\text{inform}_{i,j}(\varphi)$ must *carry the information* φ in order to satisfy the semantics of $\mathcal{L}_C$. That is not to say that φ must be present in an internal database, or that i has some variable called φ. Rather, we mean that i must *know* φ in the sense of knowledge theory (Fagin et al., 1995).

Note that the semantics of inform refer to the *knowledge* of the agent sending the message. Although this is a kind of "mentalistic" terminology, it should be understood that knowledge theory provides us with a precise way of attributing knowledge to arbitrary programs (Fagin et al., 1995). Unlike the mentalistic terminology of, (for example), the FIPA ACL semantics, our semantics are clearly *grounded* in the sense that they have a well-defined interpretation in terms of the states of programs. We see how this grounding works in the following section.

The "ask-whether" performative is the question-asking performative of $\mathcal{L}_C$. The intuitive semantics of ask-whether are the same as the semantics of the FIPA "query-if" performative (FIPA, 1997, p30): an

Performative	Informal meaning	Classification
$\text{inform}_{i,j}(\varphi)$	i informs j of φ	information passing
$\text{ask-whether}_{i,j}(\varphi)$	i asks j whether φ	information passing
$\text{commit}_{i,j}(\alpha, \varphi)$	i commits to performing action α before φ	action performing/commissive
$\text{refrain}_{i,j}(\alpha, \varphi)$	i will refrain from α while φ	action performing/commissive

Table 1: Summary of Performatives

agent i executes the performative $\text{ask-whether}_{i,j}(\varphi)$ in an attempt to find out from j whether or not φ is true. More formally, an agent i executing the performative $\text{ask-whether}_{i,j}(\varphi)$ will respect the semantics of $\mathcal{L}_C$ if it does not currently carry the information that φ, and it does not currently carry the information that $\neg\varphi$.

Neither the original KQML language nor the FIPA ACL provide *commissive* performatives, which commit an agent to a course of action (Searle, 1969). It has been argued that the provision of such performatives is essential to the process of coordination in many multi-agent systems (Cohen and Levesque, 1995). $\mathcal{L}_C$ provides two commissives, called "commit" and "refrain" respectively.

An agent i will execute the performative $\text{commit}_{i,j}(\alpha, \varphi)$ in order to assert to agent j that it guarantees to perform the action denoted by α before the condition φ is true. (This *does not* assert that eventually φ *will* be true.) The sender i will be respecting the semantics of $\mathcal{L}_C$ if it carries the information that before φ becomes true, it will perform α.

The "refrain" performative provides agents with a way of committing never to perform some action. Thus if i executes $\text{refrain}_{i,j}(\alpha, \varphi)$, then i will be respecting the semantics of $\mathcal{L}_C$ if it carries the information that it will not perform α until after the condition φ becomes true. Notice that there is a kind of duality between commit and refrain.

Our next step is to define a model of multi-agent systems that is in some sense generic, and to show how agents modeled in this framework can be seen to satisfy the informal semantics discussed above.

A Model of Multi-Agent Systems

In this section, we develop a formal model of multi-agent systems that, we claim, is sufficiently general, intuitive, and powerful that it can be considered as a model for multi-agent systems implemented in most programming languages. The formal model is based upon a model of concurrent systems from theoretical computer science, which has been widely studied for several decades (Manna and Pnueli, 1992).

Formally, a multi-agent system will be considered to be the parallel composition of n programs $\pi_1, \ldots, \pi_n$. We model each program π_i as a labelled multi-graph (i.e., a graph that can have more than one arc connecting two nodes). Nodes in the graph correspond to *control points*. Let Lab_i be the set of control points for agent i, and let $Lab = \bigcup_{i \in Ag} Lab_i$ be the set of all labels. Arcs in a program correspond to the execution of actions by agents. Actions are assumed to be atomic. The paradigm example of an action would be an assignment statement. However, the performatives discussed above are also actions. Thus $\text{inform}_{i,j}(\varphi)$

would be one of agent i's actions. Let Ac_i be the actions that agent i can perform, and let $Ac = \bigcup_{i \in Ag} Ac_i$ be the set of all actions.

The *memory* of a program π_i is defined by a finite set of program variables, $Pvar_i$, each of which is associated with a domain (type) from which it can take a value. For simplicity, we assume that the type of every program variable is $I\!N$. Let $Pvar = \bigcup_{i \in Ag} Pvar_i$ be the set of all program variables. Formally, the memory state of an agent i at any instant is defined by a total function $ms_i : Pvar_i \rightarrow I\!N$. Let $MS_i = Pvar_i \rightarrow I\!N$ be the set of all memory states for agent i.

The effect of an action is to modify the memory state of the program that executes it. Thus an action $\alpha \in Ac_i$ can be viewed as a function $\alpha : MS_i \rightarrow MS_i$.

A *program statement* for an agent $i \in Ag$ is a four tuple: (ℓ, C, α, ℓ'). Here, $\ell \in Lab_i$ is a control point that marks the starting point of the statement, $\ell' \in Lab_i$ is the end point, C is a predicate over ms_i known as the *guard* of the statement, and α is the *action* of the statement. Following the usual convention, we write the statement (ℓ, C, α, ℓ') as $(\ell, C \longrightarrow \alpha, \ell')$. We let $Stmt$ be the set of all such statements.

Collecting these components together, a program is a structure $\pi_i = (Lab_i, Ac_i, Pvar_i, \ell_i^0, ms_i^0, Stmt_i)$ where Lab_i is the set of control points of the program, Ac_i is the set of actions that the program can perform, $Pvar_i$ is the set of program variables, $\ell_i^0 \in Lab_i$ is a distinguished member of Lab_i that marks the point at which the program starts executing, ms_i^0 is the initial memory state of the program, and finally, $Stmt_i \subseteq Stmt$ are agent i's actual program statements.

The *local state* of a program π_i at any instant is uniquely determined by a pair (ℓ_i, ms_i), where $\ell_i \in Lab_i$ is a control point (i.e., a node in the program's graph, which intuitively corresponds to a program counter), and $ms_i \in MS_i$ is a memory state. The set of all such local states for an agent i is denoted S_i, i.e., $S_i = Lab_i \times MS_i$.

The set G of all *global states* of a multi-agent system $\pi_1, \ldots, \pi_n$ is the cross product of all local states: $G = S_1 \times \cdots \times S_n$. We use $g, g', \ldots$ to stand for members of G. If g is a local state, then we write $\ell_i(g)$ to denote agent i's control point in g, and $ms_i(g)$ to denote i's memory state in g.

Now, suppose the system $\pi_1, \ldots, \pi_n$ is in state $g = (s_1, \ldots, s_n)$. Then a state $g' = (s'_1, \ldots, s'_n)$ will represent an acceptable transition from g iff some agent $i \in Ag$ has a statement $(\ell, C \longrightarrow \alpha, \ell')$ such that

1. $C(ms_i(g))$ (the guard is satisfied);

2. $\ell = \ell_i(g)$ and $\ell' = \ell_i(g')$;

3. $\ell_j(g) = \ell_j(g')$ for all $j \neq i$;

4. $ms_i(g') = \alpha(ms_i(g))$;

5. $ms_j(g') = ms_j(g)$ for all $j \neq i$.

We write $g \rightsquigarrow g'$ to denote the fact that g' is an acceptable transition from g. A run, or computation of a multi-agent system $\pi_1, \ldots, \pi_n$ is then an infinite sequence of global states

$$g_0 \xrightarrow{\alpha_0} g_1 \xrightarrow{\alpha_1} g_2 \xrightarrow{\alpha_2} \cdots$$

such that g_0 is the initial state of the system, and for all $u \in I\!N$ we have $g_u \rightsquigarrow g_{u+1}$.

Before leaving the model of multi-agent systems, we introduce an indexed set of binary relations over global states. If $g = (s_1, \ldots, s_n)$ and $g' = (s'_1, \ldots, s'_n)$ are global states, then we write $g \sim_i g'$ if $s_i = s'_i$ (Fagin et al., 1995). We will refer to $\sim_i$ as a *knowledge accessibility relation* for agent i. Intuitively, if $g \sim_i g'$, then states g and g' are indistinguishable to agent i, as it has exactly the same information in both. These relations are the mechanism through which we can attribute knowledge to programs.

Semantics for Multi-Agent Systems

Models for QUETL and runs of multi-agent systems are very closely related: both are infinite sequences of states, isomorphic to the natural numbers. This is the key to the use of temporal logic for reasoning about non-terminating programs (Manna and Pnueli, 1992). The idea is that, given a multi-agent system $\pi_1, \ldots, \pi_n$, we can systematically derive a QUETL formula $\mathcal{M}(\pi_1, \ldots, \pi_n)$, which characterizes the behaviour of the system, in the sense that every QUETL model which validates $\mathcal{M}(\pi_1, \ldots, \pi_n)$ corresponds to one of the possible runs of $\pi_1, \ldots, \pi_n$. The formula $\mathcal{M}(\pi_1, \ldots, \pi_n)$ is known as the *theory* of the system $\pi_1, \ldots, \pi_n$. In order to demonstrate that $\pi_1, \ldots, \pi_n$ satisfies specification φ, it suffices to show that $\mathcal{M}(\pi_1, \ldots, \pi_n) \vdash \varphi$, i.e., that φ is a theorem of the theory $\mathcal{M}(\pi_1, \ldots, \pi_n)$. Formally, the semantic function $\mathcal{M}$ can be understood as a mapping

$$\mathcal{M} : \text{Multi-agent system} \rightarrow \text{QUETL-formula}.$$

The procedure for generating the temporal semantics of a multi-agent system is well-documented, see e.g., (Manna and Pnueli, 1992). Here, we will simply sketch out the key aspects of the process.

The basic idea is to use two domain predicates, $at_i(\ldots)$ and $do_i(\ldots)$. The predicate $at_i(\ell)$ is used to indicate that agent i is currently at location $\ell \in Lab_i$. The predicate $do_i(\alpha)$ is used to indicate that agent i now performs the action $\alpha \in Ac_i$. Formally, let

$$g_0 \xrightarrow{\alpha_0} g_1 \xrightarrow{\alpha_1} g_2 \xrightarrow{\alpha_2} \cdots$$

be a computation of the system $\pi_1, \ldots, \pi_n$, and let M be a QUETL model. Then:

$$\langle M, V, u \rangle \models at_i(\ell) \quad \text{iff} \quad \ell_i(g_u) = \ell$$
$$\langle M, V, u \rangle \models do_i(\alpha) \quad \text{iff} \quad \alpha = \alpha_u \text{ and } \alpha \in Ac_i$$

We also require that the $\sim_i$ relations in M correspond to those obtained from the run using the techniques described earlier.

It is convenient to introduce a proposition $next_i$ which expresses the fact that agent i is the next one to act.

$$next_i \hat{=} \exists \alpha \cdot do_i(\alpha)$$

Semantics for Agent Communication

Our task is now to give a semantics for the agent communication framework introduced above. First, we must ensure that communication is truly synchronous: every message send action is matched on the recipient's part by a corresponding receive action, and that between the message send and the message receive, the sender executes no other actions. Formally, we have

$$do_i(\alpha) \Rightarrow (\neg next_i) \, \mathcal{U} \, do_j(\texttt{rcv}) \qquad (1)$$

where α is one of the performative actions introduced above, of which i is the sender and j is the recipient. Note that (1) is a *liveness property* (Manna and Pnueli, 1992).

Corresponding to this liveness property, we have a *safety property* which states that an agent cannot execute a `recv` instruction unless it is preceded by a corresponding message send operation:

$$(\neg do_j(\texttt{recv})) \Rightarrow (\neg do_j(\texttt{recv})) \, \mathcal{U} \, do_i(\alpha) \qquad (2)$$

where α is once again a performative in which i is the sender and j is the recipient.

We now move on to the performatives proper. First, we give a semantics for the `inform` performative. Recall that an agent executing $\texttt{inform}_{i,j}(\varphi)$ must know φ.

$$do_i(\texttt{inform}_{i,j}(\varphi)) \Rightarrow \mathcal{K}_i(\varphi) \qquad (3)$$

(Strictly speaking, this axiom is a cheat, since the argument to the $do_i(\ldots)$ predicate contains a formula of QUETL. However, as long as we are careful not to quantify over such nested formula, it will cause no problems — the argument to $do_i(\ldots)$ can simply be understood as a QUETL constant that denotes an action.)

Corresponding to this constraint on the sender of the `inform`, we have a "rational effect" constraint, which specifies the behaviour of the system if the communicative act is successful (FIPA, 1997). Note that the recipient of a message is *not* required to respect the rational effect condition; instead, it is merely intended to characterise an "ideal" situation.

$$do_i(\texttt{inform}_{i,j}(\varphi)) \Rightarrow \Diamond \mathcal{K}_j \varphi \qquad (4)$$

If successful, therefore, an inform message will lead to the recipient of the message knowing the content.

An agent executing $\texttt{ask-whether}_{i,j}(\varphi))$ must not know whether φ or $\neg \varphi$.

$$do_i(\texttt{ask-whether}_{i,j}(\varphi)) \Rightarrow \neg(\mathcal{K}_i \varphi \vee \mathcal{K}_i \neg \varphi) \qquad (5)$$

The rational effect of a message $\texttt{ask-whether}_{i,j}(\varphi)$ will lead to j informing i either that φ, or that $\neg \varphi$, or that it does not know either φ or $\neg \varphi$.

$$do_i(\texttt{ask-whether}_{i,j}(\varphi)) \Rightarrow \Diamond do_j(\texttt{inform}_{j,i}(\psi)) \qquad (6)$$

where $\psi = \varphi$, or $\psi = \neg \varphi$, or $\psi = \neg(\mathcal{K}_j \varphi \vee \mathcal{K}_j \neg \varphi)$.

An agent executing $\texttt{commit}_{i,j}(\alpha, \varphi)$ must know that it will perform α before condition φ is true.

$$do_i(\text{commit}_{i,j}(\alpha, \varphi)) \Rightarrow \mathcal{K}_i \neg ((\neg do_i(\alpha)) \, \mathcal{W} \, \varphi) \quad (7)$$

Note that the use of $\mathcal{W}$ allows for the possibility that φ is *never* satisfied, and hence that α is never executed. The rational effect of commit is simply to make the recipient aware of the commitment.

$$do_i(\text{commit}_{i,j}(\alpha, \varphi)) \Rightarrow \Diamond \mathcal{K}_j \neg ((\neg do_i(\alpha)) \, \mathcal{W} \, \varphi) \quad (8)$$

Finally, an agent performing $\text{refrain}_{i,j}(\alpha, \varphi)$ must know that it will not do α until φ becomes true.

$$do_i(\text{refrain}_{i,j}(\alpha, \varphi)) \Rightarrow \mathcal{K}_i(\neg do_i(\alpha) \, \mathcal{W} \, \varphi) \quad (9)$$

As with commit, the rational effect is to make the recipient aware of the commitment.

$$do_i(\text{refrain}_{i,j}(\alpha, \varphi)) \Rightarrow \Diamond \mathcal{K}_j(\neg do_i(\alpha) \, \mathcal{W} \, \varphi) \quad (10)$$

An Example

To illustrate the communication language and its semantics, we present a small example. Consider the following program (it is straightforward to derive the formal program from the text given below):

```
0 :   x := 5
1 :   if x = 5 then goto 3
2 :   inform_{i,j}(x ≠ 5)
3 :   refrain_{i,j}(inform_{i,j}(x > 6), (x = 7))
4 :   if x > 6 then goto 7
5 :   x := x + 1
6 :   goto 4
7 :   inform_{i,j}(x > 6)
```

We claim that this program respects the semantics defined above. The proof is straightforward, although somewhat lengthy. The basic idea is to use temporal reasoning to derive the theory of the program, using conventional techniques (Manna and Pnueli, 1992). We then use some simple epistemic rules, such as

$$(\mathsf{x}_i = n) \Rightarrow \mathcal{K}_i(\mathsf{x}_i = n)$$

(if x_i is one of i's program variables, then i knows the value of x_i), to derive an epistemic temporal theory of the program. Verifying conformance involves proving that the axioms defining the semantics of the performatives follow from this theory. The proof is done using the proof theory of QUETL, which combines that of linear discrete temporal logic, epistemic logic, and first-order logic.

Conclusions

Conformance testing is a critical issue for agent communication languages that aspire to status as international standards. If there is no practical method via which the conformance (or otherwise) to a particular ACL may be verified, then this ACL is unlikely to be accepted into the international software engineering community. Despite this, comparatively

little attention has been paid to this problem. In this paper, we have demonstrated that semantic conformance testing for an ACL is possible, if the semantics of that language have a computational interpretation. We have presented a simple but, we argue, useful ACL, containing several performatives whose intuitive interpretation closely resembles that of their FIPA counterparts. In addition, we have defined the semantics of this ACL using a quantified epistemic temporal logic QUETL, demonstrated how this logic can be used to reason about multi-agent systems, and finally, given a simple agent system that respects the semantics of our language.

References

Cohen, P. R. and Levesque, H. J. (1990). Rational interaction as the basis for communication. In Cohen, P. R., Morgan, J., and Pollack, M. E., editors, *Intentions in Communication*, pages 221–256. The MIT Press: Cambridge, MA.

Cohen, P. R. and Levesque, H. J. (1995). Communicative actions for artificial agents. In *Proceedings of the First International Conference on Multi-Agent Systems (ICMAS-95)*, pages 65–72, San Francisco, CA.

Cohen, P. R. and Perrault, C. R. (1979). Elements of a plan based theory of speech acts. *Cognitive Science*, 3:177–212.

Fagin, R., Halpern, J. Y., Moses, Y., and Vardi, M. Y. (1995). *Reasoning About Knowledge*. The MIT Press: Cambridge, MA.

FIPA (1997). Specification part 2 — Agent communication language. The text refers to the specification dated 23 October 1997.

Halpern, J. Y. and Vardi, M. Y. (1989). The complexity of reasoning about knowledge and time. I. Lower bounds. *Journal of Computer and System Sciences*, 38:195–237.

Hoare, C. A. R. (1978). Communicating sequential processes. *Communications of the ACM*, 21:666–677.

Labrou, Y. and Finin, T. (1997). Semantics and conversations for an agent communication language. In *Proceedings of the Fifteenth International Joint Conference on Artificial Intelligence (IJCAI-97)*, pages 584–591, Nagoya, Japan.

Manna, Z. and Pnueli, A. (1992). *The Temporal Logic of Reactive and Concurrent Systems*. Springer-Verlag: Berlin, Germany.

Manna, Z. and Pnueli, A. (1995). *Temporal Verification of Reactive Systems — Safety*. Springer-Verlag: Berlin, Germany.

Patil, R. S., Fikes, R. E., Patel-Schneider, P. F., McKay, D., Finin, T., Gruber, T., and Neches, R. (1992). The DARPA knowledge sharing effort: Progress report. In Rich, C., Swartout, W., and Nebel, B., editors, *Proceedings of Knowledge Representation and Reasoning (KR&R-92)*, pages 777–788.

Searle, J. R. (1969). *Speech Acts: An Essay in the Philosophy of Language*. Cambridge University Press: Cambridge, England.

Wooldridge, M. (1998). Verifiable semantics for agent communication languages. In *Proceedings of the Third International Conference on Multi-Agent Systems (ICMAS-98)*, pages 349–365, Paris, France.

Artificial Intelligence &
the World Wide Web

Recognizing Structure in Web Pages using Similarity Queries

William W. Cohen

AT&T Labs–Research Shannon Laboratory
180 Park Avenue Florham Park, NJ 07932
wcohen@research.att.com

Abstract

We present general-purpose methods for recognizing certain types of structure in HTML documents. The methods are implemented using WHIRL, a "soft" logic that incorporates a notion of textual similarity developed in the information retrieval community. In an experimental evaluation on 82 Web pages, the structure ranked first by our method is "meaningful"—*i.e.*, a structure that was used in a hand-coded "wrapper", or extraction program, for the page—nearly 70% of the time. This improves on a value of 50% obtained by an earlier method. With appropriate background information, the structure-recognition methods we describe can also be used to learn a wrapper from examples, or for maintaining a wrapper as a Web page changes format. In these settings, the top-ranked structure is meaningful nearly 85% of the time.

Introduction

Web-based information integration systems allow a user to query structured information that has been extracted from the Web (Levy, Rajaraman, & Ordille 1996; Garcia-Molina *et al.* 1995; Knoblock *et al.* 1998; Genesereth, Keller, & Dushka 1997; Lacroix, Sahuguet, & Chandrasekar 1998; Mecca *et al.* 1998; Tomasic *et al.* 1997). In most such systems, a different *wrapper* must be written for each Web site that is accessed. A *wrapper* is a special-purpose program that extracts information from Web pages written in a specific format. Because data can be presented in many different formats, and because Web pages frequently change, building and maintaining wrappers is time-consuming and tedious. To reduce the cost of building wrappers, some researchers have proposed special languages for writing wrappers (Hammer *et al.* 1997; Cohen 1998b), or semi-automated tools for wrapper construction (Ashish & Knoblock 1997). Others have implemented systems that allow wrappers to be trained from examples (Kushmerick, Weld, & Doorenbos 1997; Hsu 1998; Muslea, Minton, & Knoblock 1998). Data exchange standards like XML have also been proposed, although as yet none are in widespread use.

Here, we explore another approach to this problem: developing general-purpose methods for automatically

Exploding porpoises, over four score and seven, well before configuration.

- *Department of Computer and Information Sciences, University of New Jersey.* Citrus flavorings: green, marine, clean and under lien.
- *Computer Engineering Center, Lough Polytechnical Institute.* This, that page extensionally left to rights of manatees.
- *Electrical Engineering and Computer Science Dept, Bismark State College.* Tertiary; where cola substitutes are frequently underutilized.

This page under construction. (Last update: 9/23/98.)

Figure 1: Nonsense text with a meaningful structure.

recognizing structure in HTML documents. Our ultimate goal is to extract structured information from Web pages without any page-specific programming or training.

To motivate this approach, consider Figure 1. To a human reader, this text is perceived as containing a list of three items, each containing the italized name of a university department, with the university name underlined. This apparently meaningful structure is recognized without previous knowledge or training, even though the text is ungrammatical nonsense and the university names are imaginary. This suggests that people employ general-purpose, page-independent strategies for recognizing structure in documents. Incorporating similar strategies into a system that automatically (or semi-automatically) constructs wrappers would clearly be valuable.

Below we show that effective structure recognition methods for certain restricted types of list structures can be encoded compactly and naturally, given appropriate tools. In particular, we will present several methods that can be concisely implemented in WHIRL (Cohen 1998a), a "soft" logic that includes both "soft" universal quantification, and a notion of textual similarity developed in the information retrieval (IR) community. The structure-recognition methods we present are based on natural heuristics, such as detecting repetition of sequences of markup commands, and detecting repeated patterns of "familiar-looking" strings.

The methods can be used in a page-independent manner: given an HTML page, but no additional information about it, the methods produce a ranked list of pro-

HTML source for a simple list:
```
<html><head>...</head>
<body>
<h1>Editorial Board Members</h1>
<table> <tr>
    <td>G. R. Emlin, Lucent</td>
    <td>Harry Q. Bovik, Cranberry U</td></tr>
  <tr>
    <td>Bat Gangley, UC/Bovine</td>
    <td>Pheobe L. Mind, Lough Tech</td>
...
```
Extracted data:

G. R. Emlin, Lucent
Harry Q. Bovik, Cranberry U
...

HTML source for a simple hotlist:
```
<html><head>...</head>
<body><h1>Publications for Pheobe Mind</h1>
<ul>
<li>Optimization of fuzzy neural networks using
distributed parallel case-based genetic knowledge discovery
  (<a href="buzz.pdf">PDF</a>)</li>
<li>A linear-time version of GSAT
  (<a href="peqnp.ps">postscript</a>)</li>
...
```
Extracted data:

Optimization ... (PDF)	buzz.pdf
A linear-time version of ...	peqnp.ps
...	...

Figure 2: A simple list, a simple hotlist, and the data that would be extracted from each.

posed "structures" found in the page. This ranking is generally quite useful: in an experimental evaluation on 82 Web pages associated with real extraction problems, the top-ranked structure is "meaningful" (as defined below) nearly 70% of the time. This improves on an earlier method (Cohen & Fan 1999), which proposes meaningful structures about 50% of the time on the same data.

By providing different types of additional information, about a page, the same methods can also be used for page-specific wrapper learning as proposed by Kushmeric *et al* (1997), or for updating a wrapper after the format of a wrapped page has changed. When used for page-specific learning or wrapper update, the top-ranked structure is meaningful nearly 85% of the time.

Background

Benchmark problems

We begin by clarifying the structure-recognition problem, with the aim of stating a task precise enough to allow quantitative evaluation of performance. Deferring for now the question of what a "structure" is, we propose to rate the "structures" identified by our methods as either *meaningful* or *not meaningful*. Ideally, a structure in a Web page would be rated as *meaningful* iff it contains structured information that could plausibly be extracted from the page. Concretely, in our experiments, we will use pages that were actually wrapped by an information integration system, and consider a structure as meaningful iff it corresponds to information actually extracted by an existing, hand-coded wrapper for that page.

In this paper, we will restrict ourselves to wrappers in two narrow classes (and therefore, to a narrow class of potential structures). We call these wrapper classes *simple lists* and *simple hotlists*. In a page containing a *simple list*, the information extracted is a one-column relation containing a set of strings $s_1, \ldots, s_N$, and each s_i is all the text that falls below some node n_i in the HTML parse tree for the page. In a *simple hotlist*, the extracted information is a two-column relation, containing a set of pairs $\langle s_1, u_1 \rangle, \ldots, \langle s_n, u_N \rangle$; each s_i is all the text that falls below some node n_i in the HTML parse tree; and each u_i is a URL that is associated with some HTML anchor element a_i that appears somewhere inside n_i. Figure 2 shows the HTML source for a simple list and a simple hotlist, and the data that is extracted from each.

This restriction is based on our experience with a working information integration system (Cohen 1998b). Of 111 different wrapper programs written for this system, 82 (or nearly 75%) were based on simple lists or simple hotlists, as defined above.[1] We will use this corpus of problems in the experiments described below.

The vector space representation for text

Our ability to perceive structure in the text of Figure 1 is arguably enhanced by the regular appearance of substrings that are recognizable as (fictitious) university names. These strings are recognizable because they "look like" the names of real universities. Implementing such heuristics requires a precise notion of similarity for text, and one such notion is provided by the *vector space* model of text.

In the vector space model, a piece of text is represented as a *document vector* (Salton 1989). We assume a vocabulary T of *terms*; in this paper, terms are word stems produced by the Porter stemming algorithm (Porter 1980). A *document vector* is a vector of real numbers $\vec{v} \in \mathcal{R}^{|T|}$, each component of which corresponds to a term $t \in T$. We will denote the component of $\vec{v}$ which corresponds to $t \in T$ by v_t, and employ the TF-IDF weighting scheme (Salton 1989): for a document vector $\vec{v}$ appearing in a collection C, we let v_t be zero if the term t does not occur in text represented by $\vec{v}$, and otherwise let $v_t = (\log(TF_{\vec{v},t}) + 1) \cdot \log(IDF_t)$. In this formula, $TF_{\vec{v},t}$ is the number of times that

---

[1]We say "based on" because some lists also included preprocessing or filtering steps. We note also that the relative simplicity of wrappers is due in part to special properties of the information integration system. Further discussion of this dataset can be found elsewhere (Cohen & Fan 1999).

term t occurs in the document represented by $\vec{v}$, and $IDF_t = \frac{|C|}{|C_t|}$, where C_t is the set of documents in C that contain t.

In the vector space model, the *similarity* of two document vectors $\vec{v}$ and $\vec{w}$ is given by the formula $SIM(\vec{v}, \vec{w}) = \sum_{t \in T} \frac{v_t \cdot w_t}{||\vec{v}|| \cdot ||\vec{w}||}$. Notice that $SIM(\vec{v}, \vec{w})$ is always between zero and one, and that similarity is large only when the two vectors share many "important" (highly weighted) terms.

The WHIRL logic

Overview. WHIRL is a logic in which the fundamental items that are manipulated are not atomic values, but entities that correspond to fragments of text. Each fragment is represented internally as a document vector, as defined above; this means the similarity between any two items can be computed. In brief, WHIRL is nonrecursive, function-free Prolog, with the addition of a built-in similarity predicate; rather than being true or false, a similarity literal is associated with a real-valued "score" between 0 and 1; and scores are combined as if they were independent probabilities.

As an example of a WHIRL query, let us suppose that the information extracted from the simple list of Figure 2 is stored as a predicate *ed_board(X)*. Suppose also that the information extracted from the hotlist of Figure 2, together with a number of similar bibliography hotlists, has been stored in a predicate *paper(Y,Z,U)*, where Y is an author name, Z a paper title, and U a paper URL. For instance, the following facts may have been extracted and stored: *ed_board("Pheobe L. Mind, Lough Tech")*, and *paper("Pheobe Mind", "A linear-time version of GSAT", "http://.../peqnp.ps")*. Using WHIRL's similarity predicate "$\sim$", the following query might be used to find papers written by editorial board members:

$\leftarrow$ *ed_board(X)* $\land$ *paper(Y,Z,U)* $\land$ $X \sim Y$

The answer to this query would be a list of substitutions θ, each with an associated score. Substitutions that bind X and Y to similar documents would be scored higher. One high-scoring substitution might bind X to "Pheobe L. Mind, Lough Tech" and Y to "Pheobe Mind".

Below we will give a formal summary of WHIRL. A complete description is given elsewhere (Cohen 1998a).

WHIRL semantics. Like a conventional deductive database (DDB) program, a WHIRL program consists of two parts: an *extensional database* (EDB), and an *intensional database* (IDB). The IDB is a non-recursive set of function-free definite clauses. The EDB is a collection of ground atomic facts, each associated with a numeric *score* in the range $(0, 1]$. In addition to the types of literals normally allowed in a DDB, clauses in the IDB can also contain *similarity literals* of the form $X \sim Y$, where X and Y are variables. A WHIRL predicate definition is called a *view*. We will assume below views are *flat*—that is, that each clause body in the view contains only literals associated with predicates defined in the EDB. Since WHIRL does not support recursion, views that are not flat can be "flattened" (unfolded) by repeated resolution.

In a conventional DDB, the answer to a conjunctive query would be the set of ground substitutions that make the query true. In WHIRL, the notion of provability will be replaced with a "soft" notion of *score*, which we will now define. Let θ be a ground substitution for B. If $B = p(X_1, \ldots, X_a)$ corresponds to a predicate defined in the EDB, then $SCORE(B, \theta) = s$ if $B\theta$ is a fact in the EDB with score s, and $SCORE(B, \theta) = 0$ otherwise. If B is a similarity literal $X \sim Y$, then $SCORE(B, \theta) = SIM(\vec{x}, \vec{y})$, where $\vec{x} = X\theta$ and $\vec{y} = Y\theta$. If $B = B_1 \land \ldots \land B_k$ is a conjunction of literals, then $SCORE(B, \theta) = \prod_{i=1}^{k} SCORE(B_i, \theta)$. Finally, consider a WHIRL view, defined as a set of clauses of the form $A_i \leftarrow Body_i$. For a ground atom a that is an instance of one or more A_i's, we define the *support* of a, $SUPPORT(a)$, to be the set of all pairs $\langle \sigma, Body_i \rangle$ such that $A_i\sigma = a$, $Body_i\sigma$ is ground, and $SCORE(Body_i, \sigma) > 0$. We define the score of an atom a (for this view) to be

$$1 - \prod_{\langle \sigma, Body_i \rangle \in SUPPORT(a)} (1 - SCORE(Body_i, \sigma))$$

This definition follows from the usual semantics of logic programs, together with the observation that if e_1 and e_2 are independent events, then $\text{Prob}(e_1 \lor e_2) = 1 - (1 - \text{Prob}(e_1))(1 - \text{Prob}(e_2))$.

The operations most commonly performed in WHIRL are to define and *materialize* views. To materialize a view, WHIRL finds a set of ground atoms a with non-zero score s_a for that view, and adds them to the EDB. Since in most cases, only high-scoring answers will be of interest, the materialization operator takes two parameters: r, an upper bound on the number of answers that are generated, and ϵ, a lower bound on the score of answers that are generated.

Although the procedure used for combining scores in WHIRL is naive, inference in WHIRL can be implemented quite efficiently. This is particularly true if ϵ is large or r is small, and if certain approximations are allowed (Cohen 1998a).

The "many" construct. The structure-recognition methods we will present require a recent extension to the WHIRL logic: a "soft" version of universal quantification. This operator is written $many(Template, Test)$ where the *Test* is an ordinary conjunction of literals, and the *Template* is a single literal of the form $p(Y_1, \ldots, Y_n)$, where p is an EDB predicate and the Y_i's are all distinct; also, the Y_i's may appear only in *Test*. The score of a "many" clause is the weighted average score of the *Test* conjunction on items that match the *Template*. More formally, for a substitution θ and a conjunction W,

$$SCORE(many(p(Y_1, \ldots, Y_k), Test), \theta) =$$

$$\sum_{\langle s,a_1,\ldots,a_k\rangle \in P} \frac{s}{S} \cdot SCORE(\mathit{Test}, (\theta \circ \{Y_i = a_i\}_i))$$

where P is the set of all tuples $\langle s, a_1, \ldots, a_k \rangle$ such that $p(a_1, \ldots, a_k)$ is a fact in the EDB with score s; S is the sum of all such scores s; and $\{Y_i = a_i\}_i$ denotes the substitution $\{Y_1 = a_1, \ldots, Y_k = a_k\}$.

As an example, the following WHIRL query is a request for editorial board members that have written "many" papers on neural networks.

$q(X) \leftarrow ed\_board(X) \wedge$
  $many(papers(Y, Z, W),$
    $(X \sim Y \wedge Z \sim \text{``neural networks''})).$

Recognizing structure with WHIRL

Encoding HTML pages and wrappers

We will now give a detailed description of how structure-recognition methods can be encoded in WHIRL. We begin with a description of the encoding used for an HTML page.

To encode an HTML page in WHIRL, the page is first parsed. The HTML parse tree is then represented with the following EDB predicates.

- *elt(Id, Tag, Text, Position)* is true if *Id* is the identifier for a parse tree node, n, *Tag* is the HTML tag associated with n, *Text* is all of the text appearing in the subtree rooted at n, and *Position* is the sequence of tags encountered in traversing the path from the root to n. The value of *Position* is encoded as a a document containing a single term t_{pos}, which represents the sequence, *e.g.*, $t_{pos} = \text{``html\_body\_ul\_li''}$.

- *attr(Id, AName, AValue)* is true if *Id* is the identifier for node n, *AName* is the name of an HTML attribute associated with n, and *AValue* is the value of that attribute.

- *path(FromId, ToId, Tags)* is true if *Tags* is the sequence of HTML tags encountered on the path between nodes *FromId* and *ToId*. This path includes both endpoints, and is defined if *FromId=ToId*.

As an example, wrappers for the pages in Figure 2 can be written using these predicates as follows.

page1(NameAffil) $\leftarrow$
  elt(_, _, NameAffil, "html_body_table_tr_td").
page2(Title, Url) $\leftarrow$
  elt(ContextElt, _, Title, "html_body_ul_li")
  $\wedge$ *path(ContextElt, AnchorElt, "li_a")*
  $\wedge$ *attr(AnchorElt, "href", Url)*.

Next, we need to introduce an appropriate encoding of "structures" (and in so doing, make this notion precise.) Most simple lists and hotlists in our benchmark collection can be wrapped with some variant of either the *page1* or *page2* view, in which the constant strings (*e.g.*, "html_body_ul_li" and "li_a") are replaced with different values. Many of the remaining pages can be wrapped by views consisting of a disjunction of such clauses.

We thus introduce a new construct to formally represent the informal idea of a "structure" in a structured document: a *wrapper piece*. In the most general setting, a *wrapper piece* consists of a *clause template* (*e.g.*, a generic version of *page2* above), and a set of *template parameters* (*e.g.*, the pair of constants "html_body_ul_li" and "li_a"). In the experiments below, we consider only two clause templates—the ones suggested by the examples above—and also assume that the recognizer knows, for each page, if it should look for list structures or hotlist structures. In this case, the clause template need not be explicitly represented; a wrapper piece for a *page2* variant can be represented simply as a pair of constants (*e.g.*, "html_body_ul_li" and "li_a"), and a wrapper piece for a *page1* variant can be represented as a single constant (*e.g.*, html_body_table_tr_td).

For brevity, we will confine the discussion below to methods that recognize simple hotlist structures analogous to *page2*, and will assume that structures are encoded by a pair of constants *Path1* and *Path2*. However, most of the methods we will present have direct analogs that recognize simple lists.

Enumerating and ranking wrappers

We will now describe three structure-recognition methods based on these encodings. We begin with some basic building blocks. Assuming that some page of interest has been encoded in WHIRL's EDB, materializing the WHIRL view *possible_piece*, shown in Figure 3, will generate all wrapper pieces that would extract at least one item from the page. The *extracted_by* view determines which items are extracted by each wrapper piece, and hence acts as an interpreter for wrapper pieces.

Using these views in conjunction with WHIRL's soft universal quantification, one can compactly state a number of plausible recognition heuristics. One heuristic is to prefer wrapper pieces that extract many items; this trivial but useful heuristic is encoded in the *fruitful_piece* view. Recall that materializing a WHIRL view results in a set of new atoms, each with an associated score. The *fruitful_piece* view can thus be used to generate a ranked list of proposed "structures" by simply presenting all *fruitful_piece* facts to the user in decreasing order by score.

Another structure-recognition method is suggested by the observation that in most hotlists, the text associated with the anchor is a good description of the associated object. This suggests the *anchorlike_piece* view, which adds to the *fruitful_piece* view an additional "soft" requirement that the text *Text1* extracted by the wrapper piece be similar to the text *Text2* associated with the anchor element.

A final structure-recognition method is shown in the Figure as the *R_like_piece* view. This view is a copy of *fruitful_piece* in which the requirement that many items are extracted is replaced by a requirement that many "*R* like" items are extracted, where an item is "*R* like" if it is similar to some second item X that is stored in the EDB relation R. The "soft" semantics of the *many*

$$fruitful\_piece(Path1,Path2) \leftarrow$$
$$\quad possible\_piece(Path1,Path2) \wedge$$
$$\quad many(\ extracted\_by(Path1a,Path2a,\_,\_),$$
$$\quad\quad (Path1a=Path1 \wedge Path2a=Path2)\ ).$$
$$possible\_piece(Path1,Path2) \leftarrow$$
$$\quad elt(TextElt,\ \_,\ \_,\ Path1)$$
$$\quad \wedge\ elt(AnchorElt,\ \_,\ "a",\ \_)$$
$$\quad \wedge\ attr(AnchorElt,\ "href",\ \_)$$
$$\quad \wedge\ path(TextElt,\ AnchorElt,\ Path2).$$
$$extracted\_by(Path1,Path2,TextElt,AnchorElt) \leftarrow$$
$$\quad elt(TextElt,\ \_,\ \_,\ Path1)$$
$$\quad \wedge\ path(TextElt,\ AnchorElt,\ Path2).$$

$$anchorlike\_piece(Path1,Path2) \leftarrow$$
$$\quad possible\_piece(Path1,Path2) \wedge$$
$$\quad many(\ extracted\_by(Path1a,Path2a,TElt,AElt),$$
$$\quad\quad (Path1a=Path1 \wedge Path2a=Path2$$
$$\quad\quad \wedge\ elt(TElt,\_,Text1,\_) \wedge elt(AElt,\_,Text2,\_) \wedge Text1{\sim}Text2\ ).$$
$$R\_like\_piece(Path1,Path2) \leftarrow$$
$$\quad possible\_piece(Path1,Path2) \wedge$$
$$\quad many(\ R\_extracted\_by(Path1a,Path2a,\_,\_),$$
$$\quad\quad (Path1a=Path1 \wedge Path2a=Path2)\ ).$$
$$R\_extracted\_by(Path1,Path2,TextElt,AnchorElt) \leftarrow$$
$$\quad elt(TextElt,\ \_,\ Text,\ Path1)$$
$$\quad \wedge\ path(TextElt,\ AnchorElt,\ Path2)$$
$$\quad \wedge\ R(X) \wedge Text{\sim}X.$$

Figure 3: WHIRL programs for recognizing plausible structures in an HTML page. (See text for explanation.)

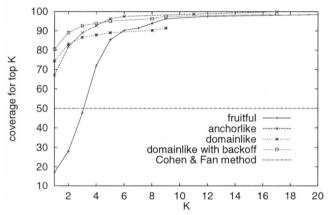

Figure 4: Performance of ranking heuristics that use little or no page-specific information.

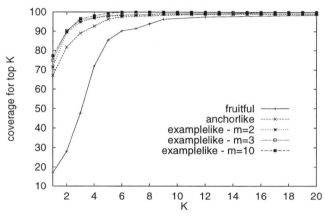

Figure 5: Performance of ranking heuristics that use page-specific training examples.

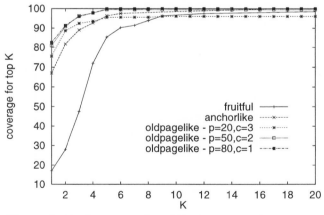

Figure 6: Performance of ranking heuristics that use text extracted from an previous version of the page.

construct imply that more credit is given to extracting items that match an item in R closely, and less credit is given for weaker matches. As an example, suppose that R contains a list of all accredited universities in the US. In this case, the R_like_piece would prefer wrapper pieces that extract many items that are similar to some known university name; this might be useful in processing pages like the one shown in Figure 1.

Experiments

Ranking programs with (almost) no page-specific information

We will now evaluate the three structure-recognition methods shown in Figure 3. We took the set of 82 hand-coded list and hotlist wrappers described above, and paired each hand-coded wrapper with a single Web page that was correctly wrapped. We then analyzed the hand-coded wrapper programs, and determined which wrapper pieces they contained. The result of this pre-processing was a list of 82 Web pages, each of which is associated with a set of "meaningful" wrapper pieces. To evaluate a method, we materialize the appropriate

view,[2] thus generating a ranked list of proposed struc-

[2]Thresholds of $\epsilon = 0.5$ and $r = 100,000$ were used in materializing the view $R\_extracted\_by$, and thresholds of $\epsilon = 0$ and $r = 100,000$ were used elsewhere. We also assume that the system "knows" whether a list or a hotlist is to be extracted from each page: $i.e.$, we apply to each hotlist page

tures. A good method is one that ranks meaningful structures ahead of non-meaningful structures.

To obtain useful aggregate measures of performance, it is useful to consider how a structure-recognition method might be used. One possibility is *interactive use:* given a page to wrap, the method proposes wrapper pieces to a human user, who then examines them in order, and manually selects pieces to include in a wrapper for the page. To evaluate performance, we vary K and record for each K the *coverage* at rank K—that is, the percentage of the 82 problems that can be wrapped using pieces ranked in the top K. The resulting "coverage curve" can be plotted. We also compute a measure we call the *average number of skips*: the average number of non-meaningful pieces that are ranked ahead of some meaningful piece; or, equivalently, the average number of wrapper pieces that would be unnecessarily examined (skipped over) by the user.

Another possibility use for the system is *batch use:* given a page, the method proposes a single structure, which is then used by a calling program without any filtering. For batch use, a natural measure of performance is the percentage of the time that the top-ranked structure is meaningful. Below, we call this measure *accuracy at rank 1*, and define *error rate at rank 1* analogously.[3]

Figure 4 shows the coverage curves obtained from methods that require no page-specific information. For comparison, we also show the performance of a earlier structure-recognition method (Cohen & Fan 1999). (To summarize this method briefly, structure recognition is reduced to the problem of classifying nodes in an HTML parse tree as to whether or not they are contained in some meaningful structure. The node-classification problem can then be solved by off-the-shelf inductive learning methods such as CART (Brieman *et al.* 1984) or RIPPER (Cohen 1995).) This method produces a single wrapper program (which may correspond to multiple wrapper pieces), rather than a ranked list of wrapper pieces. On the data used here, the wrapper proposed coincides with the true wrapper, or some close approximation of it, on exactly half the cases.

The *anchorlike* method[4] performs quite well, obtaining accuracy at rank 1 of nearly 70%, and an average of 0.9 skips. (These numbers are summarized in Table 1). Even the strawman *fruitful* method works surprisingly well in interactive use, obtaining an average number of skips of only 3.3; however, for batch use, its accuracy

at rank 1 is less than 20%.

The third curve shown in Figure 4, labeled *domainlike*, is an instance of the *R_like_piece* method in which R contains a large list of items in the same domain as the items to be extracted. (For instance, if the data to be extracted is a list of universities, then R would be a second list of universities.) We consider this structure-recognition method in this section because, although it does require some page-specific information, the information required is quite easy to obtain.[5] The average skip rate and error at rank 1 for the *domainlike* method are roughly half that of *anchorlike*. However, this method does not obtain 100% coverage, as in some fraction of the problems, the secondary relation R is either unavailable or misleading.

The final curve in Figure 4, labeled "domainlike with backoff", is a simple combination of the *domainlike* and *anchorlike* strategies. In this method, one first materializes the view *R_extracted_by*. If it is non-empty, then the *R_like_piece* view is materialized, and otherwise, *anchorlike_piece* is materialized. This method does as well in a batch setting as *domainlike*. In an interactive setting, it achieves a final coverage of nearly 100% with a skip rate somewhat lower than *anchorlike*.

Ranking structures with training data

Several previous researchers have considered the problem of learning wrappers from examples (Kushmerick, Weld, & Doorenbos 1997; Hsu 1998; Muslea, Minton, & Knoblock 1998). In these systems, the user provides examples of the items that should be extracted from a sample Web page, and the system induces a general procedure for extracting data from that page. If page-specific training examples are available, they can be used by storing them in a relation R, and then applying the *R_like* method. This use of structure-recognition methods is quite similar to previous wrapper-learning systems; one major difference, however is that no negative examples need be provided, either explicitly or implicitly.

To evaluate this wrapper-learning technique, we ran the target wrappers on each page in order to build a list of page-specific training examples. We then fixed a number of training examples m, and for each Web page, stored m randomly chosen page-specific examples in the relation R, and applied the *R_like* structure-recognition method. We call this the *examplelike* method. This process was repeated 10 times for each value of m, and the results were averaged.

The results from this experiment are shown in Figure 5. Even two or three labeled examples perform

---

only structure-recognition views that recognize hotlists, and apply to each list page only views that recognize lists.

[3]Note that accuracy at rank 1 is not identical to coverage at $K = 1$; the former records the number of times the top-ranked wrapper piece is part of the target wrapper, and the later records number of times the top-ranked wrapper piece is the *only* piece in the target wrapper.

[4]Recall that the *anchorlike* can only be applied to hotlists. In the curve labeled *anchorlike*, we used the *fruitful* method for simple list wrappers, and the *anchorlike* method for simple hotlist wrappers.

---

[5]It seems reasonable to assume that the user (or calling program) has general knowledge about the type of the items that will be extracted. In the experiments, the items in R were always obtained from a second Web page containing items of the same type as the page being wrapped; again, it seems plausible to assume that this sort of information will be available.

	Average # Skips	Accuracy at Rank 1	Coverage at $K = \infty$
fruitful	3.3	18.3	100.0
anchorlike	0.9	69.5	100.0
domainlike	0.4	84.0	91.5
with backoff	0.6	84.0	98.8
examplelike			
$m = 2$	0.3	77.8	99.0
$m = 3$	0.3	79.3	99.3
$m = 10$	0.3	84.2	100.0
oldpagelike			
$p = 20, c = 3$	0.3	85.0	96.1
$p = 50, c = 2$	0.3	82.9	99.5
$p = 80, c = 1$	0.3	85.4	100.0

Table 1: Summary of results

somewhat better than the *anchorlike* and *fruitful* methods, and unlike the *domainlike* method, achieve complete (or nearly complete) coverage. However, the average accuracy at rank 1 is not as high as for the *domainlike* method, unless many examples are used.

These results show an advantage to presenting the user with a ranked list of wrapper pieces, as in general, coverage is improved much more by increasing K than by increasing m. For example, if the user labels two examples, then 58.6% of the pages are wrapped correctly using the top-ranked wrapper piece alone. Providing eight more examples increases coverage of the top-wranked piece to only 63.3%; however, if the user labels no additional examples, but instead considers the top *two* wrapper pieces, coverage jumps to 89.4%.

Maintaining a wrapper

Because Web pages frequently change, maintaining existing wrappers is a time-consuming process. In this section, we consider the problem of updating an existing wrapper for a Web page that has changed. Here a new source of information is potentially available: one could retain, for each wrapper, the data that was extracted from the previous version of the page. If the format of the page has been changed, but not its content, then the previously-extracted data can be used as page-specific training examples for the new page format, and the *examplelike* method of the previous section can be used to derive a new wrapper. If the format and content both change, then the data extracted from the old version of the page could still be used; however, it would be only an approximation to the examples that a user would provide. Using such "approximate examples" will presumably make structure-recognition more difficult; on the other hand, there will typically be many more examples than a user would provide.

Motivated by these observations, we evaluated the *R_like* structure-recognition method when R contains a large number of entries, each of which is a *corrupted* version of a data item that should be extracted from the page. Specifically, we began with a list of all data items that are extracted by the target wrapper, and

Oklahoma	dietitians
Yukon	Yukon codpiece
Vermont	Vermont
British Columbia	British Columbia Talmudizations
Oklahoma	Oklahoma
Wisconsin	Wisconsin
New Jersey	New Jersey incorrigible blubber
Alaska	Alaska
New Brunswick	
New Mexico	New Mexico cryptogram

Table 2: Ten US States and Canadian Provinces, before and after corruption with $c = 1$.

then corrupted this list as follows. First, we discarded all but randomly-chosen percentage p of the items.[6] We next perform $c \cdot n$ random edit operations, where n is the number of retained examples. Each edit operation randomly selects one of the n items, and then either deletes a randomly chosen word from the item; or else adds a word chosen uniformly at random from */usr/dict/words*.

Figure 6 shows the results of performing this experiment (again averaged over 10 runs) with values of p ranging from 80% to 20%, and values of c ranging from 1 to 3. We call this structure-recognition method the *oldpagelike* method. With moderately corrupted example sets, the method performs very well: even with a corruption level of $p = 50\%$ and $c = 2$ it performs better on average than the *anchorlike* method.

It must be noted, however, that the corrupted examples used in this experiment are not very representative of the way a real Web page would be changed. As an illustration, Table 2 shows one list of familiar items before and after corruption with $c = 1$ (really!). It remains to be seen if more typical modifications are harder or easier to recover from.

Conclusions

In this paper, we considered the problem of recognizing "structure" in HTML pages. As formulated here, structure recognition is closely related to the task of automatically constructing wrappers: in our experiments, a "structure" is equated with a component of a wrapper, and a recognized structure is considered "meaningful" if it is part of an existing wrapper for that page. We used WHIRL, a "soft" logic that incorporates a notion of textual similarity developed in the information retrieval community, to implement several heuristic methods for recognizing structures from a narrow but useful class. Implementing these methods also required an extension to WHIRL—a "soft" version of bounded universal quantification.

Experimentally, we showed that one proposed structure-recognition method, the *anchorlike* method, performs quite well: the top-ranked structure is meaningful about 70% of the time, substantially improving

---

[6]Note that typically, Web pages change by having new items added, and we are trying to simulate text that would have been extracted from an old version of the page.

on simpler ranking schemes for structures, and also improving on an earlier result of ours which used more conventional methods for recognizing structure. This method is completely general, and requires no page-specific information. A second structure-recognition method, the *R_like* method, was also described, which can make use of information of many different kinds: examples of correctly-extracted text; an out-of-date version of the wrapper, together with a cached version of the last Web page that this out-of-date version correctly wrapped; or a list of objects of the same type as those that will be extracted from the Web page. In each of these cases, performance can be improved beyond that obtained by the *anchorlike* method.

References

Ashish, N., and Knoblock, C. 1997. Wrapper generation for semistructured Internet sources. In Suciu, D., ed., *Proceedings of the Workshop on Management of Semistructured Data.* Tucson, Arizona: Available on-line from http://www.research.att.com/~suciu/workshop-papers.html.

Brieman, L.; Friedman, J. H.; Olshen, R.; and Stone, C. J. 1984. *Classification and Regression Trees.* Belmon, CA: Wadsworth.

Cohen, W. W., and Fan, W. 1999. Learning page-independent heuristics for extracting data from web pages. In *Proceedings of the 1998 AAAI Spring Symposium on Intelligent Agents in Cyberspace.*

Cohen, W. W. 1995. Fast effective rule induction. In *Machine Learning: Proceedings of the Twelfth International Conference.* Lake Tahoe, California: Morgan Kaufmann.

Cohen, W. W. 1998a. Integration of heterogeneous databases without common domains using queries based on textual similarity. In *Proceedings of ACM SIGMOD-98.*

Cohen, W. W. 1998b. A Web-based information system that reasons with structured collections of text. In *Proceedings of Autonomous Agents-98.*

Garcia-Molina, H.; Papakonstantinou, Y.; Quass, D.; Rajaraman, A.; Sagiv, Y.; Ullman, J.; and Widom, J. 1995. The TSIMMIS approach to mediation: Data models and languages (extended abstract). In *Next Generation Information Technologies and Systems (NGITS-95).*

Genesereth, M.; Keller, A.; and Dushka, O. 1997. Infomaster: an information integration system. In *Proceedings of the 1997 ACM SIGMOD.*

Hammer, J.; Garcia-Molina, H.; Cho, J.; and Crespo, A. 1997. Extracting semistructured information from the Web. In Suciu, D., ed., *Proceedings of the Workshop on Management of Semistructured Data.* Tucson, Arizona: Available on-line from http://www.research.att.com/~suciu/workshop-papers.html.

Hsu, C.-N. 1998. Initial results on wrapping semistructured web pages with finite-state transducers and contextual rules. In *Papers from the 1998 Workshop on AI and Information Integration.* Madison, WI: AAAI Press.

Knoblock, C. A.; Minton, S.; Ambite, J. L.; Ashish, N.; Modi, P. J.; Muslea, I.; Philpot, A. G.; and Tejada, S. 1998. Modeling web sources for information integration. In *Proceedings of the Fifteenth National Conference on Artificial Intelligence (AAAI-98).*

Kushmerick, N.; Weld, D. S.; and Doorenbos, R. 1997. Wrapper induction for information extraction. In *Proceedings of the 15th International Joint Conference on Artificial Intelligence.*

Lacroix, Z.; Sahuguet, A.; and Chandrasekar, R. 1998. User-oriented smart-cache for the web: what you seek is what you get. In *Proceedings of the 1998 ACM SIGMOD.*

Levy, A. Y.; Rajaraman, A.; and Ordille, J. J. 1996. Querying heterogeneous information sources using source descriptions. In *Proceedings of the 22nd International Conference on Very Large Databases (VLDB-96).*

Mecca, G.; Atzeni, P.; Masci, A.; Merialdo, P.; and Sindoni, G. 1998. The ARANEUS web-base management system. In *Proceedings of the 1998 ACM SIGMOD.*

Muslea, I.; Minton, S.; and Knoblock, C. 1998. Wrapper induction for semistructured, web-based information sources. In *Proceedings of the Conference on Automated Learning and Discovery (CONALD).*

Porter, M. F. 1980. An algorithm for suffix stripping. *Program* 14(3):130–137.

Salton, G., ed. 1989. *Automatic Text Processing.* Reading, Massachusetts: Addison Welsley.

Tomasic, A.; Amouroux, R.; Bonnet, P.; and Kapitskaia, O. 1997. The distributed information search component (Disco) and the World Wide Web. In *Proceedings of the 1997 ACM SIGMOD.*

Navigational Plans For Data Integration

Marc Friedman
University of Washington
friedman@cs.washington.edu

Alon Levy
University of Washington
alon@cs.washington.edu

Todd Millstein
University of Washington
todd@cs.washington.edu

Abstract

We consider the problem of building data integration systems when the data sources are webs of data, rather than sets of relations. Previous approaches to modeling data sources are inappropriate in this context because they do not capture the relationships between linked data and the need to navigate through paths in the data source in order to obtain the data. We describe a language for modeling data sources in this new context. We show that our language has the required expressive power, and that minor extensions to it would make query answering intractable. We provide a sound and complete algorithm for reformulating a user query into a query over the data sources, and we show how to create query execution plans that both query and navigate the data sources.

Introduction

The purpose of data integration is to provide a *uniform* interface to a multitude of data sources. Data integration applications arise frequently as corporations attempt to provide their customers and employees with a consistent view of the data associated with their enterprise. Furthermore, the emergence of XML as a format for data transfer over the world-wide web is making data integration of autonomous, widely distributed sources an imminent reality. A data integration system frees its users from having to *locate* the sources relevant to their query, *interact* with each source in isolation, and manually *combine* the data from the different sources. The problem of data integration has already fueled significant research in both the AI and Database communities, e.g., (Ives *et al.* 1999; Cohen 1998b; Knoblock *et al.* 1998; Beeri *et al.* 1998; Friedman & Weld 1997; Duschka, Genesereth, & Levy 1999; Garcia-Molina *et al.* 1997; Haas *et al.* 1997; Levy, Rajaraman, & Ordille 1996; Florescu, Raschid, & Valduriez 1996; Adali *et al.* 1996), as well as several industrial solutions.

Data integration systems are usually built according to the following architecture. Each data source is modeled as a relation (or a set of relations). The user poses

queries in terms of the relations and attributes of a *mediated database schema* as opposed to the schemas of the individual sources. The relations in the mediated schema are *virtual* in the sense that their extensions (i.e., the tuples of the relations) are not actually stored anywhere. The mediated schema is manually designed for a particular data integration application, and is intended to capture the aspects of the domain of interest to the users of the application. In addition to the mediated schema, the system has a set of *source descriptions* that specify the semantic mapping between the mediated schema and the source schemas. The data integration system uses these source descriptions to reformulate a user query into a query over the source schemas.

Two of the main approaches for specifying source descriptions use restricted forms of first-order logic sentences. In the *global-as-view* (GAV) approach (Garcia-Molina *et al.* 1997; Adali *et al.* 1996) Horn rules define the relations in the mediated schema in terms of the source relations. The *local-as-view* (LAV) approach (Levy, Rajaraman, & Ordille 1996; Friedman & Weld 1997; Duschka, Genesereth, & Levy 1999) is the opposite: the source relations are defined as expressions over the relations in the mediated schema.

Our first observation is that modeling web sites requires the expressive power of GAV and LAV combined. Furthermore, as the WWW expands and sites become more complex, we observe a growing number of sources that can no longer be modeled as sets of relations, but rather as *webs* of data with a set of entry points. There are two main characteristics distinguishing data webs from collections of relations: (1) linked pairs of pages contain related data, and (2) obtaining the data from the site may require navigation through a particular path in the site. These properties render previous formalisms inappropriate for incorporating data webs as sources in a data integration system. Previous works that considered such sources (e.g., the ARIADNE System (Knoblock *et al.* 1998)) modeled each page as a separate data source and assumed each page was an entry point.

This paper describes a formalism for modeling data webs, a formalism for incorporating them into a data integration system, and an algorithm for reformulating user queries into execution plans that both *query* and *navigate* the data sources. Our solution combines the following contributions.

First, we describe a formalism for modeling data webs. The formalism captures the contents of each page in the data web, the relationships between linked pages, and the constraints on the possible paths through the web.

Second, we describe GLAV, a language for source descriptions that is more expressive than GAV and LAV combined. We describe a query reformulation algorithm for sources described in GLAV and show that query answering for GLAV sources is no harder than it is for LAV sources. Furthermore, we show that in some sense, GLAV reaches the limits on the expressive power of a data source description language. Slight additions to the expressive power of GLAV would make query answering co-NP-hard in the size of the data in the sources. It should be noted that GLAV is also of interest for data integration independent of data webs, because of the flexibility it provides in integrating diverse sources.

Finally, we show how to reformulate user queries into execution plans over the data sources. The reformulation consists of two parts. First we use our GLAV reformulation algorithm to obtain a query over the relations in the data webs. Then we augment the resulting query over the sources with the navigational instructions needed to interact with the data webs.

Incorporating Data Webs

In this section we describe how we represent data webs and incorporate them into a data integration system. We begin by recalling some basic terminology. Then we explain how we model a data web by a web schema, and finally we explain how to specify the relationship between the relations in web schemas and the mediated schema.

Preliminaries

In our discussion variables are denoted by capital letters and constants by lowercase letters. Overscores denote tuples of zero or more variables and constants (e.g., $\bar{X}$). An atom consists of a predicate symbol p followed by an argument list $(\bar{X})$. A Horn rule is a logical sentence of the form $r_1(\bar{X}_1) \wedge \ldots \wedge r_k(\bar{X}_k) \Rightarrow r(\bar{X})$, where $\bar{X} \subseteq \bigcup_i \bar{X}_i$. The variables in $\bar{X}$ are universally quantified, and all other variables are existentially quantified. Given the extensions of the relations appearing in the antecedent, a Horn rule defines a unique extension for the relation in the consequent. It should be noted that there is a direct correspondence between single Horn rules and select-project-join queries in relational databases (often called *conjunctive queries*).

Datalog programs are sets of Horn rules, in which the predicate symbols appearing in the consequents, called the intensional database (IDB) predicates, may also appear in any antecedents. A datalog program defines a unique extension for the IDB relations given the extensions of the other relations, called the extensional

database (EDB) relations, as follows. We begin with empty extensions for the IDB relations and apply the rules, deriving new facts for the IDB relations, until no new facts can be derived.[1] We often distinguish one IDB predicate as the query predicate. The result of applying a datalog program to a database is the set of tuples computed for the query predicate.

Data Webs

A data web consists of pages and the links between them. In this paper we are concerned with the logical modeling of data webs. In practice, one also needs to address the problem of actually extracting structured data from an HTML page. Several researchers have considered the construction of *wrappers* for this purpose (Cohen 1998a; Kushmerick, Doorenbos, & Weld 1997; Ashish & Knoblock 1997).

In order to model a data web we need to represent the set of pages and links in the web, the data available at every page, whether each link is a hyperlink or a search form, and which pages can be accessed directly by name. We represent the structure of a data web with a *web schema*, a directed graph G with nodes representing sets of pages and directed edges representing sets of directed links between them. For example, Figure 1 shows web schemas for three different university webs. Nodes in G are annotated with:

- the node's name and unique id
- a parameter (a variable or constant)
- an *entry point* flag (an asterisk)
- a list of contents

Every node name defines a unary function symbol. For example, consider node 1 in Figure 1, representing the home page of university u_1. Its name is *Univ*, with parameter u_1, a constant. $Univ(u_1)$ denotes the home page object of university u_1. Every web site has a set of entry points, *i.e.*, nodes that the integration system can access directly by URL. We indicate them with an asterisk. For example, node 1 is an entry point to university u_1's data web.

There are three kinds of logical information stored on a page $N(X)$. These correspond to ordinary contents of the page, outgoing edges from the page, and search forms on the page. (1) Tuples of a predicate p are listed as atoms of the form $p(Y_1, \ldots, Y_k)$ in the contents of $N(X)$. For instance, node 7, a department page, contains the source relation $chair(D, P)$, indicating that department pages list their department chairs. Typically X will appear as one of the Y_i's, but in general it may not. (2) Edges from a page are often labelled with an identifier of the target page. For instance, the $Univ(u_2)$ page (node 5) lists each college G satisfying source relation $univcollege(u_2, G)$, with a link to that college's page. We indicate this by the expression

---

[1]This unique model is known as the least fixed-point model of the Horn rules. Since our discussion only considers the derivation of positive atoms, the difference between the least fixed-point semantics and the classical first-order semantics is immaterial.

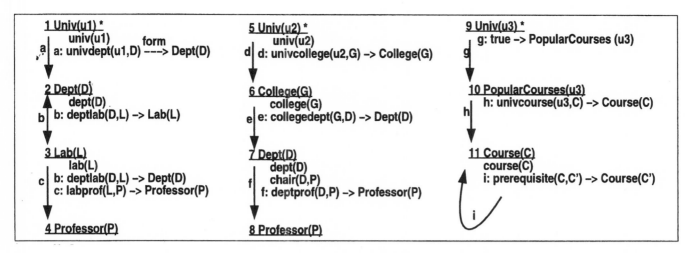

Figure 1: Three university web schemas.

$p(X, Y) \longrightarrow M(Y)$. (3) Search forms, much like links, map from binary relations to other pages, but the value of the target page parameter Y must be provided before accessing the link. We denote this by

$$p(X, Y) \xrightarrow{form} M(Y).$$

Note that in this case the value of Y is not available on the page $N(X)$. For instance, node 1 has a search form in which the user enters a department name, and the home page of that department is returned.

Mediated Schemas

A set of relations known as a mediated schema serves as a uniform query interface for all the sources. It is designed to represent the attributes of the domain relevant to the integration application, and does not necessarily represent all of the attributes available in all of the sources. In our university domain, we use the following mediated schema.

$$collegeOf(College, University)$$
$$deptOf(Department, College)$$
$$profOf(Professor, Department)$$
$$courseOf(Course, Department)$$
$$chairOf(Professor, Department)$$
$$prereqOf(Course, Course)$$

As data webs are added, they need only be 'hooked' to the mediated schema, without reference to the other data webs. This is done via a *source description* language, which relates the source relations to the mediated schema relations.

GLAV Source Descriptions

Source description languages are necessary because the mediated schema relations do not match the source relations in a one-to-one fashion. There are two reasons for the mismatch. First, the source schemas often contain differing levels of *detail* from each other, and from the mediated schema. In Figure 1, university u_2 identifies the colleges in a university, a distinction that does

source description	#
u_1 :	
$univdept(u_1, D) \Rightarrow deptOf(D, G),$	1
$\qquad\qquad\qquad collegeOf(G, u_1).$	
$deptlab(D, L), labprof(L, P) \Rightarrow profOf(D, P).$	2
u_2 :	
$univcollege(u_2, G) \Rightarrow collegeOf(G, u_2).$	3
$collegedept(G, D) \Rightarrow deptOf(D, G).$	4
$deptprof(D, P) \Rightarrow profOf(P, D).$	5
$chair(D, P) \Rightarrow chairOf(P, D)$	6
u_3 :	
$prereq(C, C') :\text{-} prerequisite(C, C').$	7
$prereq(C, C') :\text{-} prereq(C, C''), prereq(C'', C').$	
$prereq(C, C') \Rightarrow prereqOf(C', C).$	

Figure 2: Sample source descriptions.

not exist in university u_1. On the other hand, u_1 identifies laboratories within departments, a detail not in the mediated schema or in u_2.

The second reason is that even if the different schemas model the same information, they may split attributes into relations in different ways (in database terms, this corresponds to different normalizations of a database schema). For example, one schema may choose to store all the attributes of a person in a single relation, while another may decide to have a separate relation for every attribute.

The LAV and GAV source description languages only partially address these problems. LAV source descriptions have the form

$$v(\bar{X}) \Rightarrow r_1(\bar{X}_1, \bar{Z}_1) \wedge \ldots \wedge r_k(\bar{X}_k, \bar{Z}_k)$$

where v is a source relation, the r_i's are mediated schema relations, and $\bar{X} = \bigcup_i \bar{X}_i$. LAV descriptions handle the case in which the mediated schema contains details that are not present in every source, such as colleges. Statement 1 in Figure 2 is an example of a LAV source description.

The GAV language deals with the converse case,

when the source contains details not present in the mediated schema. Descriptions in GAV have the form

$$v_1(\bar{X}_1, \bar{Y}_1) \land \ldots \land v_j(\bar{X}_j, \bar{Y}_j) \Rightarrow r(\bar{X}).$$

Statement 2 in Figure 2 is an example of a GAV source description.

Using either pure LAV or pure GAV source descriptions has undesirable consequences. In LAV, the mediated schema must mention all attributes shared by multiple source relations, whether or not they are of interest in the integration application. In our example, the lab name L is such an attribute. To make matters worse, some sites use shared attributes that are only meaningful internally, such as URLs of intermediate pages or local record ids. In GAV, on the other hand, the mediated schema relations must all be relations present in the sources, or conjunctive queries over them, making the mediated schema contingent on which source relations are available.

Hence, we propose the GLAV language that combines the expressive power of both LAV and GAV, allowing flexible schema definitions independent of the particular details of the sources. Formally, a statement in GLAV is of the form

$$V(\bar{X}, \bar{Y}) \Rightarrow r_1(\bar{X}_1, \bar{Z}_1) \land \ldots \land r_k(\bar{X}_k, \bar{Z}_k). \quad (1)$$

where $V(\bar{X}, \bar{Y})$ is either a conjunction of source relations, or the distinguished query predicate of a datalog query over source relations.[2] GLAV source descriptions for the university example are in Figure 2. GLAV combines the expressive power of GAV and LAV and allows source descriptions that contain recursive queries over sources. Recursion is useful when retrieving the desired information requires navigating arbitrarily long paths. University u_3 contains such a situation: in order to obtain the prerequisites of a given course, it may be necessary to traverse the prerequisite edge (which represents direct prerequisites) arbitrarily many times before finding them all. The multi-line Statement 7 illustrates this example in GLAV, where $prereq$ is a new relation defined by a datalog program over the source relations.

Data Integration Domains

In summary, a set of web schemas and a set of source descriptions in GLAV form a *data integration domain*. Formally, a data integration domain D is a triple $\langle \mathcal{R}, \{G_i\}, \mathcal{SD} \rangle$, consisting of the set of mediated schema relations $\mathcal{R}$, web schemas G_i, and source descriptions $\mathcal{SD}$.

Planning to Answer a Query

A user of a data integration system poses a query over the mediated schema relations, which the system answers using a query processor. We consider conjunctive queries in which the consequent is the new predicate

---

[2]We further stipulate that $\cup_i \bar{Z}_i \bigcap \bar{Y} = \emptyset$.

symbol q, and the antecedents are mediated schema relations. For instance, to retrieve all chairs of history departments, a user could pose the query:

$$chairOf(Person, history) \Rightarrow q(Person). \quad (2)$$

To collect the answers to the query automatically, the integration system must translate this into a low-level procedural program, called an *execution plan*. For a relational query processor, this program is expressed in annotated relational algebra, which has operators to fetch relations and do basic relational operations such as project, select, join, and union. The annotations indicate operator implementations, memory allocations, and scheduling. In this work we augment relational algebra with an operation that traverses sets of links.

This section describes how to reformulate a query into an execution plan. We generate plans at progressively more detailed levels. First we construct a *logical plan* by reformulating the user's query into a query over the source relations in the data webs. Then we augment the logical plan with navigational information to describe how to locate the desired relations in the data webs, forming a *navigational plan*. Converting a navigational plan into an efficient execution plan is beyond the scope of this paper. See (Ives *et al.* 1999) for work on optimization of data integration queries. A non-recursive navigational plan can be converted straightforwardly into an execution plan in augmented relational algebra, though we do not provide the details here.

Logical Plans

A logical plan is a datalog program whose EDB relations are the source relations and whose answer predicate is q. The soundness and completeness of a logical plan can be defined in terms of logical entailment with respect to the source descriptions and contents of the data webs. Specifically, let T be the knowledge base containing the sentences in the source descriptions $\mathcal{SD}$, the ground atoms representing the extensions $\mathcal{I}$ of the source relations, and the query Q. Let P be the logical plan constructed for $\mathcal{SD}$ and Q, and let $P(\mathcal{I})$ be the set of facts derived by applying P to the database $\mathcal{I}$. The logical plan P is sound (resp. complete) if for every ground atom $q(\bar{a})$, $q(\bar{a}) \in P(\mathcal{I}) \implies T \models q(\bar{a})$ (resp. $T \models q(\bar{a}) \implies q(\bar{a}) \in P(\mathcal{I})$).

Given a conjunctive query Q over the mediated schema relations, we construct a sound and complete logical plan for the query using the inverse rules algorithm for GLAV, which we call GlavInverse(Figure 3). The key insight is that although the source descriptions are written in GLAV, an extension of the inverse rule method for LAV (Duschka, Genesereth, & Levy 1999) correctly produces the desired set of rules. Moreover, the low polynomial complexity of the inverse rules method is unchanged.

The algorithm converts the theory T into a datalog program. The theory T differs from an ordinary datalog program in two ways. (1) Not all of the rules in T are Horn rules, since the source descriptions may have

```
Given source descriptions $\mathcal{SD}$ and query $Q$,
$\Delta = \{Q\}$.
for each source description $s \in \mathcal{SD}$,
    let $s$ be $V(\bar{X}, \bar{Y}) \Rightarrow r_1(\bar{X}_1, \bar{Z}_1) \ldots r_k(\bar{X}_k, \bar{Z}_k)$.
    $\Delta \mathrel{+}= V(\bar{X}, \bar{Y}) \Rightarrow u_s(\bar{X})$,
        where $u_s$ is a new predicate symbol.
    let $\bar{Z} = \bigcup_i(\bar{Z}_i) = \{Z_1, \ldots, Z_m\}$.
    for each $Z_i$ in $\bar{Z}$,
        let $f_i^s$ be a new function symbol
        corresponding to $Z_i$.
    for $l = 1$ to $k$,
        let $\bar{f}_l$ represent the vector of $f$'s
        corresponding to elements of $\bar{Z}_l$.
        $\Delta \mathrel{+}= u_s(\bar{X}) \Rightarrow r_l(\bar{X}_l, \bar{f}_l(\bar{X}))$.
return $\Delta$.
```

Figure 3: Algorithm GlavInverse

```
Given logical plan $\Delta$ and web schemas $\{G_i\}$,
$\Delta' = \{\}$.
for each source atom $A = v(X_1, \ldots, X_k)$ in $\Delta$,
construct $Replacements_A$, as follows:
    $Replacements_A \mathrel{+}= [Location_v()] : A$.
    for $i = 1$ to $k$,
        $Replacements_A \mathrel{+}= [Location_{v,i}(X_i)] : A$.
for each rule $r \in \Delta$
    add to $\Delta'$ all rules formed by replacing each atom
    $A$ in the body of $r$ with an atom in $Replacements_A$.
for each source relation $v(X_1, \ldots, X_k)$,
    for each node $N(Z)$ it appears on,
        if $Z$ is $X_i$, $\Delta' \mathrel{+}= [N(Z)] \Rightarrow [Location_{v,i}(Z)]$
        else $\Delta' \mathrel{+}= [N(Z)] \Rightarrow [Location_v()]$.
for each edge $e$ from $N(X)$ to $M(Y)$,
    $\Delta' \mathrel{+}= [N(X) \overset{e}{\to} M(Y)] \Rightarrow [M(Y)]$.
for each entry point $N(X)$,
    $\Delta' \mathrel{+}= [N(X)]$.
return $\Delta'$.
```

Figure 4: Algorithm NavigationalPlan

a conjunction of atoms in the consequent. The algorithm converts each such source description into several Horn rules whose conjunction is equivalent to the original rule. (2) Source descriptions may have existential variables in the consequent. The algorithm converts these variables into terms containing function symbols. Although the resulting logical plan contains function symbols, their form is limited in such a way that naive datalog evaluation of the plan on a database will terminate (Duschka, Genesereth, & Levy 1999).

Theorem 1 *Let $D = \langle \mathcal{R}, \{G_i\}, \mathcal{SD} \rangle$ be an information integration domain. Let Q be a conjunctive query. Then the logical plan Δ returned by GlavInverse is sound and complete.*

Proof Sketch: Let $\mathcal{I}$ be the extensions of the source relations in D, and $T = \mathcal{SD} + Q + \mathcal{I}$. It suffices to show that any ground fact $q(\bar{X})$ entailed by T is a result of evaluating Δ on database $\mathcal{I}$, and vice versa. **(1)** u **predicates:** It is easy to see that $\Delta + \mathcal{I}$ entails any consequence of T, since you can apply modus ponens to Δ to generate any single rule in T. Since all facts in T are positive, and all rules have non-null consequent, T entails no negative facts. A sufficient deduction rule to nondeterministically obtain all *consequences* of T is to apply modus ponens on any rule and any facts. Consider a proof tree of a fact x from T. A proof tree for Δ can be constructed by splicing in nodes for the u predicates. **(2) function symbols:** Function symbols are usually manipulated as constants. Since we don't consider a fact containing a function symbol an answer to a query, however, function symbols behave exactly like variables. Since there is one for each existential variable, the conversion to function symbols is just a renaming of variables, which has only a superficial effect on the proof trees.

Navigational Plans

Logical plans by themselves cannot be executed, since they do not explain how to populate the source relations from the data webs. (Friedman & Weld 1997;

Lambrecht & Kambhampati 1998) explore how to optimize and execute logical plans when the source relations are directly accessible. For source relations stored in data webs, we must extend the logical plans to navigational plans. Navigational plans are augmented datalog programs. Their atoms may be relational atoms, paths, or *navigational terms*. Navigational terms specify both the location and the logical content of the relation being accessed. A navigational term is of the form $P{:}v(\bar{X})$, where P is a *path* and v is a source relation. A path denotes a connected sequence of directed edges in a web schema, with variable bindings. A path P starts at $source(P)$, and ends at $target(P)$. We define paths recursively as follows:

- **trivial paths:** $P = [N(X)]$ is a path, if N names a node and X is a variable or constant. $source(P) = target(P) = N(X)$.
- **compound paths:** $P' = [P \overset{e}{\to} M(Y)]$ is a path, if P is a path with $target(P) = N(X)$, Y is a variable or constant, and there is an edge e from node $N(X)$ to node $M(Y)$. $source(P') = source(P)$ and $target(P') = M(Y)$.

For instance,

$$[Univ(u_2) \overset{d}{\to} College(G) \overset{e}{\to} Dept(D)]$$

is a path, with edges elided for clarity, while

$$[Univ(u_2) \overset{d}{\to} College(G) \overset{e}{\to} Dept(D)] : chair(D, P) \quad (3)$$

is a navigational term. A navigational term is *executable* if it corresponds to some valid sequence of instructions for a navigational query processor. In particular, $P{:}v(\bar{X})$ is executable whenever:

- $source(P)$ is an entry point,
- $v(\bar{X})$ matches one of the contents of $target(P)$,

A	$[Univ(u_2)]$.
B	$[Univ(u_2) \overset{d}{\to} College(G)] \Rightarrow [College(G)]$.
C	$[College(G) \overset{e}{\to} Dept(D)] \Rightarrow [Dept(D)]$.
D	$[Dept(D)] \Rightarrow [Location_{chair}(D)]$.
E	$[Location_{chair}(D)] : chair(D,P) \Rightarrow chairOf(P,D)$.
F	$chairOf(history, P) \Rightarrow q(P)$.

Figure 5: Plan to find history department chairs

- if P contains an edge $X \overset{e}{\to} Y$, and edge e represents a search form, then Y is bound.

An *executable rule* is a rule whose antecedent contains only executable terms and whose consequent is $q(\bar{X})$.

The soundness and completeness of a navigational plan Δ' can be defined in terms of executable rules. The colon symbol (:) in a navigational term can be interpreted as conjunction for the purposes of deduction. Consider each executable rule R deducible from Δ' using modus ponens, whose antecedent contains only executable terms and whose consequent is $q(\bar{X})$. Let $\mathcal{J}$ be a set of data webs consistent with the web schemas, and let $\mathcal{I}$ be the extension of the source relations. Let Δ be the underlying logical plan of Δ', which can be recovered from Δ' by removing all paths and throwing away trivial rules. Navigational plan Δ' is sound whenever Δ is sound, and for each executable rule R deducible from Δ', for any $\mathcal{J}$, $R(\mathcal{J}) \subseteq \Delta(\mathcal{I})$. Δ' is complete whenever Δ is complete, and every sound executable rule is deducible from Δ.

Algorithm NavigationalPlan in Figure 4 produces a navigational plan Δ' given a logical plan Δ and the web schemas. It first annotates each source atom in the logical plan with a new symbol associated with its location. It then produces rules associating the locations of individual relations with the pages on which they appear. For example, relation $chair(D,P)$ becomes

$$[Location_{chair}(D)] : chair(D,P).$$

chair appears on only one page, so we add the single rule

$$[Dept(D)] \Rightarrow [Location_{chair}(D)].$$

Next we add *path rules* to Δ, indicating how one reaches each node $N(X)$. For instance, the rule

$$[College(G) \overset{e}{\to} Dept(D)] \Rightarrow [Dept(D)]$$

indicates that we can reach node $Dept(D)$ if we are at node $College(G)$ and follow edge e. The rule $[Univ(u_2)]$ indicates that we can always reach entry point $Univ(u_2)$. Figure 5 shows all of the relevant parts of the navigational plan to find history department chairs.

Theorem 2 *The navigational plan Δ' produced by* NavigationalPlan *is sound and complete.*

Optimization

In principle, it is straightforward to give navigational plans operational semantics and to execute them with an interpreter. However in a traditional database system, logical plans are converted into trees of relational algebra expressions, optimized, and executed by a query processor. Navigational plans can be compiled into expressions in relational algebra augmented with the operator *traverse(Source, Edge, Target)*, which returns the target pages given a source page and edge. The query optimization methods discussed in (Florescu *et al.* 1999; Mecca, Mendelzon, & Merialdo 1998) can be applied in this context as well.

The Complexity of GLAV

In this section we show that GLAV reaches the limits of the tradeoff between expressive power and tractability of query answering in data integration systems. Two measures of complexity are used for query processing problems: query complexity and data complexity. The query complexity measures the query answering time in terms of the size of the query Q, holding the other inputs fixed. High query complexity (NP-complete or worse), which is quite common for practical database languages, is not considered a serious impediment to implementation, because queries are generally considered to be very small compared with the size of the data. Data complexity measures the running time in terms of the size of the data. Since the data (data webs in this case) can be quite large, data complexity is by far the more important measure. In our discussion we model accessing a page, fetching a tuple of a relation, and traversing a link as unit-time operations.

Our first result shows that the data complexity of answering queries in GLAV is no harder than in LAV, extending the results of (Duschka, Genesereth, & Levy 1999; Levy, Rajaraman, & Ordille 1996):

Theorem 3 *Given data integration domain D with GLAV source descriptions, conjunctive query Q, and extensions $\mathcal{I}$ of the source relations, (i) the query complexity of generating navigational plans is polynomial, and (ii) the data complexity of answering queries is polynomial.*

The data complexity reduces to the polynomial problem of applying a datalog program to a set of facts. (Abiteboul & Duschka 1998) show that the data complexity of answering a query becomes co-NP-hard if the query contains atoms of the form $X \neq Y$. The following theorems strengthen their results by showing that restricting the equality and comparison predicates does not necessarily reduce the data complexity. This is interesting because such restrictions (known as local inequalities) do reduce the data complexity of query answering to polynomial in other contexts (van der Meyden 1992). It should be noted that Theorem 5 holds also when using $<$ instead of $\neq$.

Theorem 4 *For conjunctive queries with constraints of the form $(X \neq c)$ and LAV source descriptions, the data complexity of answering queries is co-$\mathcal{NP}$-hard, even when queries have just one relational conjunct.*

Theorem 5 *For conjunctive queries with constraints of the form* $(X \neq Y)$ *and LAV source descriptions, the data complexity of answering queries is co-$\mathcal{NP}$-hard, even when queries have just one relational conjunct and no constants.*

Finally, the following theorem considers one of the most common uses of interpreted predicates and shows that it remains tractable for GLAV.

Theorem 6 *For conjunctive queries with semi-interval constraints of the form* $(X < c)$ *and GLAV source descriptions, the data complexity of answering queries is polynomial.*

Conclusions

We have shown how to extend data integration systems to incorporate data webs. We define a formalism for modeling data webs and a language for source descriptions (GLAV) that make querying multiple web-structured sources possible. In addition, GLAV pushes the envelope of expressive power with efficient reasoning. We present an algorithm for answering queries using GLAV source descriptions that can be used independently of data webs.

For future work, we are considering the extension of our query answering algorithm (and the associated complexity results) when additional constraints are stated on the mediated schema using description logics, using techniques described in (Calvanese, Giacomo, & Lenzerini 1998).

References

Abiteboul, S., and Duschka, O. 1998. Complexity of answering queries using materialized views. In *Proc. of the ACM SIGACT-SIGMOD-SIGART Symposium on Principles of Database Systems (PODS)*.

Adali, S.; Candan, K.; Papakonstantinou, Y.; and Subrahmanian, V. 1996. Query caching and optimization in distributed mediator systems. In *Proc. of ACM SIGMOD Conf. on Management of Data*.

Ashish, N., and Knoblock, C. A. 1997. Wrapper generation for semi-structured internet sources. *SIGMOD Record* 26(4):8–15.

Beeri, C.; Elber, G.; Milo, T.; Sagiv, Y.; O.Shmueli; N.Tishby; Y.Kogan; D.Konopnicki; Mogilevski, P.; and N.Slonim. 1998. Websuite-a tool suite for harnessing web data. In *Proceedings of the International Workshop on the Web and Databases*.

Calvanese, D.; Giacomo, G. D.; and Lenzerini, M. 1998. On the decidability of query containment under constraints. In *Proc. of the ACM SIGACT-SIGMOD-SIGART Symposium on Principles of Database Systems (PODS)*.

Cohen, W. 1998a. A web-based information system that reasons with structured collections of text. In *Proc. Second Intl. Conf. Autonomous Agents*, 400–407.

Cohen, W. 1998b. Integration of heterogeneous databases without common domains using queries based on textual similarity. In *Proc. of ACM SIGMOD Conf. on Management of Data*.

Duschka, O.; Genesereth, M.; and Levy, A. 1999. Recursive query plans for data integration. *To appear in Journal of Logic Programming, special issue on Logic Based Heterogeneous Information Systems*.

Florescu, D.; Levy, A.; Manolescu, I.; and Suciu, D. 1999. Query optimization in the presence of limited access patterns. In *Proc. of ACM SIGMOD Conf. on Management of Data*.

Florescu, D.; Raschid, L.; and Valduriez, P. 1996. A methodology for query reformulation in CIS using semantic knowledge. *Int. Journal of Intelligent & Cooperative Information Systems, special issue on Formal Methods in Cooperative Information Systems* 5(4).

Friedman, M., and Weld, D. 1997. Efficient execution of information gathering plans. In *Proceedings of the International Joint Conference on Artificial Intelligence*.

Garcia-Molina, H.; Papakonstantinou, Y.; Quass, D.; Rajaraman, A.; Sagiv, Y.; Ullman, J.; and Widom, J. 1997. The TSIMMIS project: Integration of heterogeneous information sources. *Journal of Intelligent Information Systems* 8(2):117–132.

Haas, L.; Kossmann, D.; Wimmers, E.; and Yang, J. 1997. Optimizing queries across diverse data sources. In *Proc. of the Int. Conf. on Very Large Data Bases (VLDB)*.

Ives, Z.; Florescu, D.; Friedman, M.; Levy, A.; and Weld, D. 1999. An adaptive query execution system for data integration. In *Proc. of ACM SIGMOD Conf. on Management of Data*.

Knoblock, C. A.; Minton, S.; Ambite, J. L.; Ashish, N.; Modi, P. J.; Muslea, I.; Philpot, A. G.; and Tejada, S. 1998. Modeling web sources for information integration. In *Proceedings of the 15th National Conference on Artificial Intelligence*.

Kushmerick, N.; Doorenbos, R.; and Weld, D. 1997. Wrapper induction for information extraction. In *Proceedings of the 15th International Joint Conference on Artificial Intelligence*.

Lambrecht, E., and Kambhampati, S. 1998. Optimization strategies for information gathering plans. TR 98-018, Arizona State University Department of Computer Science.

Levy, A. Y.; Rajaraman, A.; and Ordille, J. J. 1996. Query answering algorithms for information agents. In *Proceedings of AAAI*.

Mecca, G.; Mendelzon, A. O.; and Merialdo, P. 1998. Efficient queries over web views. In *Proc. of the Conf. on Extending Database Technology (EDBT)*.

van der Meyden, R. 1992. The complexity of querying indefinite data about linearly ordered domains. In *Proc. of the ACM SIGACT-SIGMOD-SIGART Symposium on Principles of Database Systems (PODS)*, 331–345.

Regression testing for wrapper maintenance

Nicholas Kushmerick

Department of Computer Science, University College Dublin, Dublin 4, Ireland

nick@ucd.ie

Abstract

Recent work on Internet information integration assumes a library of *wrappers*, specialized information extraction procedures. Maintaining wrappers is difficult, because the formatting regularities on which they rely often change. The *wrapper verification* problem is to determine whether a wrapper is correct. Standard regression testing approaches are inappropriate, because both the formatting regularities and a site's underlying content may change. We introduce RAPTURE, a fully-implemented, domain-independent verification algorithm. RAPTURE uses well-motivated heuristics to compute the similarity between a wrapper's expected and observed output. Experiments with 27 actual Internet sites show a substantial performance improvement over standard regression testing.

Introduction

Systems that integrate heterogeneous information sources have recently received substantial research attention (*e.g.* (Wiederhold 1996; Knoblock *et al.* 1998; Levy *et al.* 1998)). A 'movie information' integrator, for example, might provide a single interface to the review, cast list, and schedule information available from dozens of Internet sites.

Such systems rely on a library of *wrappers*, specialized procedures for extracting the content from a particular site. For example, the site in Fig. 1 lists countries and their telephone country codes. The information extraction task is to identify the ⟨county, code⟩ pairs in this site's pages. The ccwrap wrapper does so by scanning for the delimiters <B>···</B> and <I>···</I>, which works because of a formatting regularity: **countries** are bold and *codes* are italic.

Scalability is the main challenge to building wrappers. While they are usually rather short programs, writing wrappers by hand is tedious and error-prone. Recently, there has been substantial progress on *wrapper induction*, techniques for automatically generating wrappers (Kushmerick, Weld, & Doorenbos 1997; Kushmerick 1997; Muslea, Minton, & Knoblock 1998; Hsu & Dung 1998).

However, this work ignores an important complication. Suppose the owners decide to 'remodel' the country/code site, so that pages look like p_d instead of p_a–p_c. The ccwrap wrapper fails for p_d, because the formatting regularities ccwrap exploits no longer hold.

Wrapper maintenance is the task of repairing a broken wrapper. For example, given p_d, a wrapper maintenance system would modify ccwrap to expect italic *countries* and bold **codes**.

Wrapper maintenance is our ultimate goal. In this paper, we define an important subproblem, the *wrapper verification* problem, and present RAPTURE, a fully-implemented, domain-independent, heuristic algorithm for solving this problem.

Wrapper verification involves determining whether a wrapper correctly processes a given page. Our approach is based on the black-box or *regression testing* paradigm (*e.g.* (Beizer 1995)): we give the wrapper a page for which the correct output is known, and check that the wrapper in fact generates this output.

The simplest such regression tester is STRAWMAN. To verify a wrapper, STRAWMAN invokes it on the page returned in response to a given query, and also on an earlier page for the same query when the wrapper was known to be correct. STRAWMAN declares the wrapper verified if the two outputs are identical.

While STRAWMAN works for some Internet sites, it fails for most. STRAWMAN assumes that sites always return the same information for a fixed query. This assumption sometimes holds (*e.g.* a list of *historical* commodity prices), but is often violated (*e.g.* a site serving *today's* prices). Wrapper verification is thus complicated by two moving targets: the formatting regularities of the pages, and the site's underlying content.

In the remainder of this paper, we formalize the wrapper verification problem, describe RAPTURE, and empirically compare RAPTURE's performance to STRAWMAN.

Problem statement

Our work is based on an a simple yet generic information extraction task: a *site* accepts a *query*, returning a *page* in response. In our implementation, sites are HTTP servers, queries are CGI form values, and pages are HTML text. (While the our examples are posed in

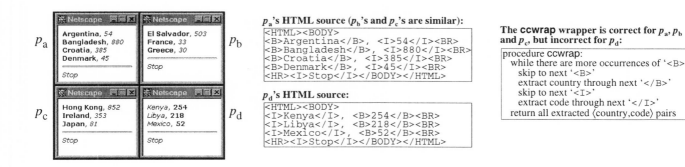

pₐ's HTML source (pᵦ's and pᵧ's are similar):

```
<HTML><BODY>
<B>Argentina</B>, <I>54</I><BR>
<B>Bangladesh</B>, <I>880</I><BR>
<B>Croatia</B>, <I>385</I><BR>
<B>Denmark</B>, <I>45</I><BR>
<HR><I>Stop</I></BODY></HTML>
```

p_d's HTML source:

```
<HTML><BODY>
<I>Kenya</I>, <B>254</B><BR>
<I>Libya</I>, <B>218</B><BR>
<I>Mexico</I>, <B>52</B><BR>
<HR><I>Stop</I></BODY></HTML>
```

The ccwrap wrapper is correct for pₐ, pᵦ and pᵧ, but incorrect for p_d:

```
procedure ccwrap:
    while there are more occurrences of '<B>'
        skip to next '<B>'
        extract country through next '</B>'
        skip to next '<I>'
        extract code through next '</I>'
    return all extracted ⟨country,code⟩ pairs
```

Figure 1: An example Internet site listing countries and their telephone country codes, and the ccwrap wrapper.

terms of HTML, this is for simplicity only. Our techniques do not assume that pages are HTML.)

A *wrapper* is an information extraction procedure tailored to a particular site. A wrapper takes as input a page, and outputs a *label*, a representation of the page's content. We assume a standard *relational* data model: a page's label is a set of *tuples*, each a vector of K *attributes*. For example, $K = 2$ for page p_a, and its label is $\ell_a = \{\langle\texttt{Argentina}, 54\rangle, \langle\texttt{Bangladesh}, 880\rangle, \langle\texttt{Croatia}, 385\rangle, \langle\texttt{Denmark}, 45\rangle\}$.

For wrapper w and page p, we write $w(p) = \ell$ to indicate that w returns label ℓ when invoked on p.

As we are concerned with cases in which a wrapper's output is wrong, we say that a w is *correct* for p iff p's label is in fact $w(p)$. Thus, ccwrap is incorrect for p_d, because $\texttt{ccwrap}(p_d) = \{\langle 254, \texttt{Libya}\rangle, \langle 218, \texttt{Mexico}\rangle, \langle 52, \texttt{Stop}\rangle\}$ instead of $\{\langle\texttt{Hong Kong}, 254\rangle, \langle\texttt{Libya}, 218\rangle, \langle\texttt{Mexico}, 52\rangle\}$.

Wrapper verification is the problem of determining whether a wrapper is correct. We assume access to a collection of previously verified pages for which the wrapper is known to be correct. We also assume that we know the query used to generate each verified page.

The *wrapper verification problem* is the following. The input is a wrapper w, page p, query q, sequence $L = \{\ell_1, \ldots, \ell_M\}$ of labels, and sequence $Q = \{q_1, \ldots, q_M\}$ of queries. The output should be TRUE if w is correct for p and FALSE otherwise.

The intent is that page p was retrieved using query q, L contains the verified labels, and the page to which label $\ell_i \in L$ corresponds was retrieved with $q_i \in Q$. While queries can be structured objects, RAPTURE treats them "atomically", only checking whether two queries are equal.

The RAPTURE algorithm

RAPTURE is a domain-independent, heuristic algoraithm for solving the wrapper verification problem. RAPTURE compares the verified labels with the label output by the wrapper being verified.

Specifically, RAPTURE compares the value of various numeric features of the strings comprising the label output by the wrapper. For example, the **word count** feature is 2 for **Great Britain**, and 1 for **Iraq**. RAPTURE

computes the values of such features for each extracted attribute.[1]

These values are compared with those for the verified label attributes. The mean feature values are calculated, and then the probabilities that each extracted attribute's feature values agree with these values are calculated. Each such probability captures the strength of the evidence provided by a particular feature that a specific attribute was correctly extracted. Finally, the individual probabilities are combined, producing an overall probability that the wrapper is correct for the page.

We use upper-case letters (*e.g.* R) for random variables and lower-case (*e.g.* r) for values of such variables. μ_R is R's mean, and σ_R is R's standard deviation. Let R be normally distributed with parameters μ_R and σ_R; $\mathrm{P}[r; \mu_R; \sigma_R]$ is the probability that R equals r, and $\mathrm{P}[\leq r; \mu_R; \sigma_R]$ is the probability that R does not exceed r. These probabilities are taken to be the probability and cumulative density functions of the normal distribution: $\mathrm{P}[r; \mu_R; \sigma_R] = \frac{1}{\sigma_R\sqrt{2\pi}}e^{-\frac{1}{2}\left(\frac{r-\mu_R}{\sigma_R}\right)^2}$ and $\mathrm{P}[\leq r; \mu_R; \sigma_R] = \int_{-\infty}^{r}\mathrm{P}[r'; \mu_R; \sigma_R]\mathrm{d}r'$.

Example

We begin by demonstrating RAPTURE on the country/code example. Suppose ccwrap has been verified for pages p_a and p_b, and we want to verify ccwrap for pages p_c and p_d. Since ccwrap is in fact correct for p_c, RAPTURE$(p_c, \texttt{ccwrap}, \{\ell_a, \ell_b\})$ should return TRUE; in contrast, RAPTURE$(p_d, \texttt{ccwrap}, \{\ell_a, \ell_b\})$ should return FALSE. (We temporarily ignore the q and Q inputs to RAPTURE; we extend the algorithm below.)

Step 1: Number-of-tuple distribution parameters. RAPTURE assumes that the number of tuples in a label is described by the normally distributed random variable N. RAPTURE computes the distribution parameters μ_N and σ_N by treating the number of tuples n in p_a and p_b as samples of N (column 2 will be

---

[1] A wrapper's execution can be undefined. For example, ccwrap fails if it sees a <B> with no subsequent </B>, <I> or </I>. For simplicity, we do not discuss this scenario further, though our implementations of STRAWMAN and RAPTURE immediately reject failed wrappers.

explained in Step 5):

	n	$P[n; \mu_N; \sigma_N]$
p_a	4	0.44
p_b	3	0.44

$$\mu_N = 3.5$$
$$\sigma_N = 0.71$$

Step 2: Feature value distribution parameters. RAPTURE examines the text fragments extracted from p_a and p_b, and computes the values of a set of features. These values are assumed to be normally distributed for each feature/attribute combination.

In this example, we consider two features: word count, and mean word length. For example, El Salvador has 2 words and mean word length 6. RAPTURE reasons about a unique random variable for each feature/attribute combination: C_1 is the word count of the first attribute (country), C_2 is the word count of the second attribute (code), U_1 is the country's mean word length, and U_2 is the code's mean word length.

RAPTURE uses p_a and p_b to estimate the 8 distribution parameters. For example, $\mu_{C_1} = 1.1$ indicates that country names usually contain a single word, while $\sigma_{U_2} = 0.52$ indicates that the mean word length of codes have relatively low variance (columns 3 and 5 will be explained in Step 5):

	country	c	$P[c; \mu_{C_1}; \sigma_{C_1}]$	u	$P[u; \mu_{U_1}; \sigma_{U_1}]$
p_a	Argentina	1	0.98	9	0.12
	Bangladesh	1	0.98	10	0.057
	China	1	0.98	5	0.12
	Denmark	1	0.98	7	0.22
p_b	El Salvador	2	0.081	6	0.19
	France	1	0.98	6	0.19
	Greece	1	0.98	6	0.19

$$\mu_{C_1} = 1.1 \qquad \mu_{U_1} = 7.0$$
$$\sigma_{C_1} = 0.38 \qquad \sigma_{U_1} = 1.8$$

	code	c	$P[c; \mu_{C_2}; \sigma_{C_2}]$	u	$P[u; \mu_{U_2}; \sigma_{U_2}]$
p_a	54	1	1.0	2	0.54
	880	1	1.0	3	0.42
	385	1	1.0	3	0.42
	32	1	1.0	2	0.54
p_b	503	1	1.0	3	0.42
	33	1	1.0	2	0.54
	30	1	1.0	2	0.54

$$\mu_{C_2} = 1.0 \qquad \mu_{U_2} = 2.4$$
$$\sigma_{C_2} = 0.0 \qquad \sigma_{U_2} = 0.53$$

Step 3: Feature probabilities. RAPTURE uses the distribution parameters from Steps 1–2 to compare ccwrap's labels for p_a and p_b, with those for p_c and p_d. Recall that ccwrap is correct for p_c but incorrect for p_d.

RAPTURE begins by examining the number of tuples extracted by ccwrap: $n = 3$ for both pages. In Step 1, we estimated N's distribution parameters $\mu_N = 3.5$ and $\sigma_N = 0.71$. We can thus compute the probability of the observed number of tuples n for each page:

	n	$P[n; \mu_N; \sigma_N]$
p_c	3	0.44
p_d	3	0.44

RAPTURE then computes the feature values for the extracted fragments. Using the distribution parameters from Step 2, we compute the probability of each

observed feature value. In the example, we compute 12 probabilities each for p_c and p_d: 1 per feature, for each of the 3 extracted fragments, for each of the 2 attributes. For example, $P[2; \mu_{C_1}; \sigma_{C_1}] = 0.081$ indicates that a country name is somewhat unlikely to contain 2 words, while $P[4; \mu_{U_2}; \sigma_{U_2}] = 9.9 \times 10^{-4}$ indicates that the mean word length of a code is rarely 4.

	country	c	$P[c; \mu_{C_1}; \sigma_{C_1}]$	u	$P[u; \mu_{U_1}; \sigma_{U_1}]$
p_c	Hong Kong	2	0.081	4	0.057
	Ireland	1	0.98	7	0.22
	Japan	1	0.98	5	0.12
p_d	254	1	0.98	3	0.020
	218	1	0.98	3	0.020
	52	1	0.98	2	5.1×10^{-3}

	code	c	$P[c; \mu_{C_2}; \sigma_{C_2}]$	u	$P[u; \mu_{U_2}; \sigma_{U_2}]$
p_c	852	1	1.0	3	0.42
	353	1	1.0	3	0.42
	81	1	1.0	2	0.54
p_d	Libya	1	1.0	5	7.0×10^{-6}
	Mexico	1	1.0	6	1.5×10^{-10}
	Stop	1	1.0	4	9.9×10^{-4}

Step 4: Verification probability. Each probability in Step 3 represents the evidence from one feature that a particular text fragment is correct. RAPTURE now combines this evidence conjunctively, deriving an overall *verification probability* that ccwrap is correct. RAPTURE assumes independence, and derives the verification probability by multiplying the conjuncts' probabilities. (Our experiments consider other assumptions.) The following table shows the verification probability v for each page (column 3 will be explained in Step 5):

	probabilities from Step 3	v	$P[\leq v; \mu_V; \sigma_V]$
p_c	.44, .081, .98, .98, .057, .22, .12, 1, 1, 1, .42, .42, .54	4.9×10^{-6}	0.26
p_d	.44, .98, .98, .98, .020, .020, 5.1×10^{-3}, 1, 1, 1, 7.0×10^{-6}, 1.5×10^{-10}, 9.9×10^{-4}	8.8×10^{-25}	0.18

Note that p_d has a low v because the mean word length of the countries is so small, and so large for the codes.

Step 5: Evaluating verification probability. As expected, ccwrap is much more likely to be correct for p_a than for p_d. To complete our analysis, we could simply compare such probabilities to a fixed threshold. However, since we assumed independence and normality, the calculated verification probabilities may deviate greatly from their 'true' values.

To address this problem, we treat each verification probability v as a sample of a normal random variable V. To calculate μ_V and σ_V, we repeat Step 4 for p_a and p_b:

	probabilities from Steps 1–2	v
p_a	.44, .98, .98, .98, .98, .12, .057, .12, .22, 1, 1, 1, 1, .54, .42, .42, .54	3.8×10^{-6}
p_b	.44, .081, .98, .98, .19, .19, .19, 1, 1, 1, .42, .54, .54	2.9×10^{-5}

$$\mu_V = 1.6 \times 10^{-5}$$
$$\sigma_V = 1.8 \times 10^{-5}$$

At this point, RAPTURE can compare the verification probabilities with those of p_c or p_d. The simplest approach is to return FALSE if $v < \mu_V$. However, we would

```
function RAPTURE(wrapper w, page p, label set L)
    if LABELPR(w(p), L) < τ return FALSE else return TRUE
function LABELPR(label ℓ, label set L)
    ⟨μ_V, σ_V⟩ ← VERIFPRPARAMS(L)
    return P[≤VERIFPR(ℓ, L); μ_V; σ_V]
function VERIFPRPARAMS(label set L)
    probs ← {VERIFPR(ℓ, L) | ℓ ∈ L}
    compute μ_V and σ_V from probs
    return ⟨μ_V, σ_V⟩
function VERIFPR(label ℓ, label set L)
    ⟨μ_N, σ_N⟩, {..., ⟨μ_{F_{i,k}}, σ_{F_{i,k}}⟩, ...} ← FEAPARAMS(L)
    q ← P[|ℓ|; μ_N; σ_N]
    probs ← {q} [a]
    for each feature f_i ∈ F
        for each attribute 1 ≤ k ≤ K
            for each tuple ⟨..., s_k, ...⟩ ∈ ℓ
                q ← P[f_i(s_k); μ_{F_{i,k}}; σ_{F_{i,k}}]
                probs ← probs ∪ {q}
    return A(probs) [b]
function FEAPARAMS(label set L)
    values ← {|ℓ| | ℓ ∈ L} [c]
    compute μ_N and σ_N from values
    for each feature f_i ∈ F
        for each attribute 1 ≤ k ≤ K
            values ← {f_i(s) | s in column k of a label in L}
            compute μ_{F_{i,k}} and σ_{F_{i,k}} from values
    return ⟨μ_N, σ_N⟩, {..., ⟨μ_{F_{i,k}}, σ_{F_{i,k}}⟩, ...}
```

Figure 2: The RAPTURE algorithm.

like to be able to adjust RAPTURE's 'pessimism', making it more or less likely to declare a wrapper correct. We thus use the cumulative normal density function to evaluate v. Specifically, the third column in Step 4 lists the probabilities that $V < v$, for p_c and p_d. RAPTURE then compares this probability to a threshold τ. For example, if $\tau = \frac{1}{4}$, RAPTURE returns TRUE for p_c and FALSE for p_d. Note that $\tau = \frac{1}{2}$ corresponds to the simple approach of returning FALSE if $v < \mu_V$.

Details

With the ideas underlying RAPTURE now in place, we list the RAPTURE algorithm in detail; see Fig. 2. The main subroutine is VERIFPR, which computes a label's verification probability v.

RAPTURE refers to three parameters: a **threshold** τ against which verification probabilities are compared; a **feature set** $\mathcal{F}$, where each feature is function from a string to a number; and a **dependency assumption** $\mathcal{A}$, a function from a set of numbers to a number.

Feature set $\mathcal{F}$

RAPTURE is parameterized by a *feature set* $\mathcal{F} = \{..., f_i, ...\}$. Each feature f_i is a function from a string to a number. Ideally, features can be rapidly computed (so RAPTURE runs quickly) and are not domain specific (so RAPTURE can be applied without modification to new sites).

We used the following nine features in our experiments (numbers in parentheses are values for the string '20 Maple St.'): **digit density:** fraction of numeric characters ($\frac{2}{12} = 0.167$); **letter density**, fraction of letters ($\frac{7}{12} = 0.583$); **upper-case density**, fraction of upper-case letters ($\frac{2}{12} = 0.167$); **lower-case density** ($\frac{5}{12} = 0.417$); **punctuation density**, ($\frac{1}{12} = 0.083$); **HTML density**, fraction of < and > characters ($\frac{0}{12} = 0$); **length** (12); **word count** (3); and **mean word length** ($\frac{2+5+2}{3} = 3$).

Dependency assumption $\mathcal{A}$

Abstractly, RAPTURE reasons about E events $e_1, ..., e_E$. e_{27} might represent the event 'the number of words in the third extracted country is consistent with the countries extracted from the verified pages'. The algorithm has derived $P[e_1], ..., P[e_E]$, and must compute the probability that all feature values are consistent with the verified labels, $P[\wedge_i e_i]$. RAPTURE uses the dependency assumption $\mathcal{A}$ to compute this probability; see Step 4 above and line [b] in Fig. 2.

Computing $P[\wedge_i e_i]$ exactly requires knowledge of the dependencies between the e_i. In principle, this information could be derived for our domain, resulting in a set of conditional probabilities for exactly calculating $P[\wedge_i e_i] = P[e_1]P[e_2|e_1] \cdots P[e_E|e_{E-1}, ..., e_1]$. But as this analysis would be extremely cumbersome, we instead simply make assumptions about the dependencies of the domain. While the resulting probability can be inaccurate, our experiments demonstrate that these assumptions yield reasonable performance.

We have investigated three specific assumptions: the *independence*, *entailment*, and *equivalence* assumptions. Each corresponds to a particular function for computing $P[\wedge_i e_i]$ from $P[e_1], ..., P[e_E]$.

Independence assumption: If the e_i are independent, then $\mathbf{P}[\wedge_i e_i] = \prod_i \mathbf{P}[e_i]$.

Entailment assumption: If there exists an $1 \leq I \leq E$ such that e_I logically entails every other e_i, then $\mathbf{P}[\wedge_i e_i] = \min_i \mathbf{P}[e_i]$. The entailment assumption presumes that one piece of evidence (e.g., perhaps the number of extracted tuples) completely determines the rest.

Equivalence assumption: If the e_i are all logically equivalent, then $\mathbf{P}[\wedge_i e_i] = \mathbf{P}[e_1] = \cdots = \mathbf{P}[e_E]$. Under the equivalence assumption, any piece of evidence is as reliable as any other. This assumption can not be invoked directly, because the $P[e_i]$ are often unequal. RAPTURE treats the $P[e_i]$ as noisy samples of the 'true' value, which is estimated as the sample's geometric mean: $\mathbf{P}[\wedge_i e_i] = (\prod_i \mathbf{P}[e_i])^{1/E}$.

Using q and Q

In the presentation so far, we have ignored RAPTURE's q and Q inputs. Recall that Q is the sequence of queries used to generated the verified labels L, and q is the query from which input page p was generated.

RAPTURE uses Q and q to improve verification in a relatively simple manner. The intuition is that the number of tuples in p's label often depends on q. If the site lists people, for example, queries for Jones return more hits than for Jablonsky. If this dependency is ignored, RAPTURE will assess the evidence provided by the number of tuples ($\mathrm{P}[n; \mu_N, \sigma_N]$) incorrectly.

Extending RAPTURE to make use of this information is straightforward. Arguments Q and q are added to every function, and then line [c] in Fig. 2 is changed so that only verified labels with query q are used to estimate μ_N and σ_N: 'values $\leftarrow \{|\ell_i| \mid \ell_i \in L \wedge q_i = q\}$'.

Evaluation

Methodology. We tested RAPTURE on 27 actual Internet sites. We systematically varied $\mathcal{F}$, $\mathcal{A}$ and τ, and compared RAPTURE's performance with the STRAWMAN algorithm described earlier. Our experiment was designed to model the scenario in which the goal is to continually monitor whether a site's wrapper has changed.

The sites were chosen to be representative of the sort that the information integration community wants to wrap.[2] Fifteen queries were selected for each site. Each query is a keyword appropriate to the site. For example, ALTA's queries included frog, dog, happy, apple and tomato. While many sites allow complex queries, we do not think that focusing on keyword queries invalidates our verification results.

As shown in Fig. 3, the 27×15 queries were issued approximately every 3 days over 6 months (5–10/1998); in total, 23,416 pages were gathered.

We then generated a wrapper for every page using semi-automated techniques, extracting between $K = 2$ and $K = 8$ attributes. Like ccwrap in Fig. 1, the wrappers are instances of the LR wrapper classes (Kushmerick 1997). However, since we examine only the output of the wrappers, the choices of wrappers is immaterial.

These wrappers provide the 'gold standard' against which STRAWMAN's and RAPTURE's performance were judged. For a fixed site, call the sequence of P gathered pages $p_1, p_2, \ldots, p_P$. For each p_i, we stored the query q_i from which p_i was generated, and a wrapper w_i that is correct for p_i. We then invoked RAPTURE for each page in turn, using the previous page's wrapper: RAPTURE$(p_i, w_{i-1}, q_i, \{w_j(p_j)\}_{j=1}^P, \{q_j\}_{j=1}^P)$.

Performance metrics. RAPTURE should return TRUE iff the site's wrapper does not changes at p_i— ie. if $w_i = w_{i-1}$. We measure performance in terms of 2×2 matrix of integers:

[2]AltaVista (ALTA), Bible (BIBL), CD-Plus, Computer ESP, Cinemachine, Cost-of-living calculator (COLC), Corel stock photographs, Expedia currency calculator, Fortune-500 list (FOR5), Internet address finder, Irish Times, Lycos, Metacrawler, Monster Job Search, NewJour, CNET News, Rain or Shine, Shops.net, Time, Thrive, US Constitution (USCO), US News & World Report, US Patents, US Income Tax code (USTX), Virtual Garden, Webcrawler, and Yahoo people search.

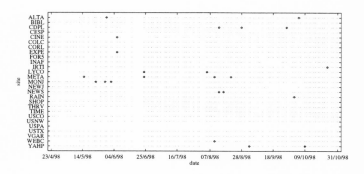

Figure 3: The experimental data: dots are fetched pages (15 per site), and diamonds are wrapper changes.

	$w_i = w_{i-1}$	$w_i \neq w_{i-1}$
predict TRUE	n_1	n_2
predict FALSE	n_3	n_4

Perfect performance yields $n_2 = n_3 = 0$. Several performance metrics are derived from this matrix (higher values indicate better performance): **accuracy** $= \frac{n_1 + n_4}{n_1 + n_2 + n_3 + n_4}$ measures overall performance; **precision** $= \frac{n_1}{n_1 + n_2}$ is the fraction of correct TRUE responses; **recall** $= \frac{n_1}{n_1 + n_3}$ is the fraction of unchanged wrappers for which the system responds TRUE; and **F** $= \frac{2 \cdot \text{recall} \cdot \text{precision}}{\text{recall} + \text{precision}}$ combines precision and recall into a single metric.

Results. The wrappers for many sites (56%) did not change at all; see Fig. 3. A total of 23 wrapper changes were seen over the 6 months, for an average of 0.85 per site. For the 44% of sites with at least one wrapper change, the average number of changes was 1.9, and the maximum was 4.

STRAWMAN performs perfectly for only 19% of the sites (BIBL, COLC, FOR5, USCO and USTX). Thus 81% of the sites can not be handled by standard regression testing. Note that STRAWMAN's overall accuracy is rather high (64%) because so few wrappers changed; indeed, a verifier that always returns TRUE has accuracy exceeding 99% (though it will have $F = 0$).

Fig. 4 shows RAPTURE's performance for $\tau = \frac{1}{2}$, and for 22 settings for $\mathcal{F}$ and $\mathcal{A}$. RAPTURE outperforms STRAWMAN for every parameter setting, with an average gain of 30% in accuracy and 16% in F.

Settings (1–3) compare the three dependency assumptions. Since **equivalence** generally performs best, setting (4–21) use **equivalence** as well.

Settings (4–12) examine the importance of each feature: each setting uses just a single feature. **HTML density** appears to significantly outperforms the others, because the attributes extracted by an incorrect wrapper are likely to contain HTML tags.

Settings (13–21) examine whether any feature harms performance: each setting uses all *except* a particular feature. None of the features stands out as being particularly damaging. (4–12) generally outperform (1–3) and (13–21), suggesting that fewer features are better.

	assumption $\mathcal{A}$	digit density feature	letter density feature	UC density feature	LC density feature	punc density feature	HTML density feature	length feature	word count feature	mean word len feature	Accuracy × 100	F × 100	
1	equiv	√	√	√	√	√	√	√	√	√	82	90	
2	entail	√	√	√	√	√	√	√	√	√	79	88	
3	indep	√	√	√	√	√	√	√	√	√	65	79	
4	equiv	√	×	×	×	×	×	×	×	×	89	94	
5	equiv	×	√	×	×	×	×	×	×	×	87	93	
6	equiv	×	×	√	×	×	×	×	×	×	85	92	
7	equiv	×	×	×	√	×	×	×	×	×	84	91	
8	equiv	×	×	×	×	√	×	×	×	×	86	93	
9	equiv	×	×	×	×	×	√	×	×	×	97	98	
10	equiv	×	×	×	×	×	×	√	×	×	79	88	
11	equiv	×	×	×	×	×	×	×	√	×	81	90	
12	equiv	×	×	×	×	×	×	×	×	√	80	89	
13	equiv	×	√	√	√	√	√	√	√	√	81	90	
14	equiv	√	×	√	√	√	√	√	√	√	81	90	
15	equiv	√	√	×	√	√	√	√	√	√	81	90	
16	equiv	√	√	√	×	√	√	√	√	√	81	90	
17	equiv	√	√	√	√	×	√	√	√	√	81	90	
18	equiv	√	√	√	√	√	×	√	√	√	81	90	
19	equiv	√	√	√	√	√	√	×	√	√	84	91	
20	equiv	√	√	√	√	√	√	√	×	√	81	89	
21	equiv	√	√	√	√	√	√	√	√	×	81	90	
22	indep	×	×	×	×	√	×	×	×	×	>99	>99	*
	STRAWMAN										64	78	

Figure 4: RAPTURE's performance for several settings of $\mathcal{F}$ and $\mathcal{A}$, and $\tau = \frac{1}{2}$.

Setting (22) shows the best performing parameters: the **independence** assumption, and just the **HTML density** feature. (22) is marked '*' to stress two additional changes to RAPTURE: the number-of-tuples information is ignored (line [a] in Fig. 2 is skipped); and FEAPARAMS calculates the probability of the mean feature value across all tuples for each attribute (instead of a separate probability for each tuple).

While these modifications are not well motivated, the results are impressive: this modified version of RAPTURE performs nearly perfectly, with just 3 mistakes over 23,416 predictions, and gains over STRAWMAN of 56% in accuracy and 28% in F. Furthermore, performance according to two additional metrics—$\frac{n_4}{n_4+n_3}$, the fraction of correct FALSE responses, and $\frac{n_4}{n_4+n_2}$, the fraction of noticed wrapper changes—is 344-fold better than STRAWMAN.

Finally, we can change RAPTURE's "pessimism" by varying τ. For example, in setting (1), varying τ from 1 to 0 decreases recall from 1 to 0.003, while precision (always very high) increases from 0.999 to 1.

Conclusions

We are motivated by the task of Internet information extraction, which is relevant to a wide variety of information-management applications. Data-exchange standards such as XML will simplify this process, but they are not widely used. Furthermore, they do not entirely solve the problem, since they force the data consumer to accept the producer's ontological decisions. We conclude that the thorny problems of wrapper construction and maintenance will remain for some time.

We have introduced the wrapper verification problem, and presented RAPTURE, a fully-implemented, domain-independent, heuristic solution. Verification is difficult because at many Internet sites, both the formatting regularities used by wrappers, and the underlying content, can change. Standard regression testing approaches (*e.g.* see (Beizer 1995)) are inapplicable, as they assume the underlying content is static.

RAPTURE uses a set of syntactic features to compute the similarity between a wrapper's output and the output for pages for which the wrapper is known to be correct. RAPTURE combines the similarities to derive an overall probability that the wrapper is correct. Our experiments demonstrate significant performance improvements over standard regression testing.

We are currently exploring several extensions to our techniques. First, the features were selected in an *ad-hoc* manner; we are investigating additional features. Second, we are identifying additional probabilistic assumptions; while they were effective, the three assumptions examined here are intuitively unsatisfactory. Third, we assumed normal distributions throughout, but have not verified this assumption, and some of the statistical computations are not well founded; while the normality assumption delivers reasonable performance, we are exploring alternatives, such as the Gamma distribution, which may model our data more accurately. Finally, we are generalizing our techniques to object-oriented, semi-structured, and other non-relational data models.

References

Beizer, B. 1995. *Black-Box Testing*. John Wiley & Sons.

Hsu, C., and Dung, M. 1998. Generating finite-state transducers for semistructured data extraction from the web. *J. Information Systems* 23(8).

Knoblock, A.; Levy, A.; Duschka, O.; Florescu, D.; and Kushmerick, N., eds. 1998. *Proc. 1998 Workshop on AI and Information Integration*. AAAI Press.

Kushmerick, N.; Weld, D.; and Doorenbos, R. 1997. Wrapper Induction for Information Extraction. In *Proc. 15th Int. Joint Conf. AI*, 729–35.

Kushmerick, N. 1997. *Wrapper Induction for Information Extraction*. Ph.D. Dissertation, Univ. of Washington.

Levy, A.; Knoblock, C.; Minton, S.; and Cohen, W. 1998. Trends and controversies: Information integration. *IEEE Intelligent Systems* 13(5).

Muslea, I.; Minton, S.; and Knoblock, C. 1998. Wrapper Induction for Semi-structured, Web-based Information Sources. In *Proc. Conf. Automatic Learning & Discovery*.

Wiederhold, G. 1996. *Intelligent Information Integration*. Kluwer.

A Knowledge-Based Approach to Organizing Retrieved Documents

Wanda Pratt
Information & Computer Science
University of California, Irvine
Irvine, CA 92697-3425
pratt@ics.uci.edu

Marti A. Hearst
School of Information Management & Systems
UC Berkeley, 102 South Hall
Berkeley, CA 94720-4600
hearst@sims.berkeley.edu

Lawrence M. Fagan
Stanford Medical Informatics
Stanford University
Stanford, CA 94305-5479
fagan@smi.stanford.edu

Abstract

When people use computer-based tools to find answers to general questions, they often are faced with a daunting list of search results or "hits" returned by the search engine. Many search tools address this problem by helping users to make their searches more specific. However, when dozens or hundreds of documents are relevant to their question, users need tools that help them to explore and to understand their search results, rather than ones that eliminate a portion of those results. In this paper, we present DynaCat, a tool that dynamically categorizes search results into a hierarchical organization by using knowledge of important kinds of queries and a model of the domain terminology. Results from our evaluation show that DynaCat helps users find answers to those important types of questions more quickly and easily than when they use a relevance-ranking system or a clustering system.

Introduction

Current information-retrieval tools usually return results that consist of a simple list of documents. Such long, undifferentiated lists can overwhelm people and cause them to abandon their search before they assess the available information.

Most search tools assist in solving the problem of too many search results by helping the user reformulate her query into a more specific one. However, even if a user could express her information need perfectly to the search engine, and even if the search engine found only documents that were relevant to the query, the user might still be confronted with a very long list of documents, and would need tools to help her understand those documents. By focusing on query formulation, the search-tool developers assume that relevant documents are few. However, the user may have a broad information need, or the document collection being searched may contain many documents covering the user's information need. If the user provides a more specific query, she may miss valuable, relevant documents.

We have created an approach that addresses this problem by dynamically categorizing search results into meaningful groups that correspond to the user's query. Our approach uses knowledge of important kinds of queries and a model of the domain terminology to create the

hierarchical categorization of search results. We have implemented this approach in a tool called **DynaCat** for the domain of medicine, where the amount of information in the primary medical literature alone is overwhelming. For example, **MEDLINE**, an on-line repository of medical abstracts, contains more than 9.2 million bibliographic entries from over 3800 biomedical journals; it adds 31,000 new entries each month (NLM 1998). Our approach summarizes the information returned from a search by placing the retrieved documents into useful categories, thus helping users to gain quick and easy access to important information.

Search Scenario

The amount of medical literature continues to grow and specialize. At the same time, many patients and their families are becoming more proactive in searching the medical literature for information regarding their medical problems, despite the fact that medical journal articles can be intimidating to read for lay people.

Consider a woman whose mother was diagnosed recently with breast cancer. She is worried about her own chances of developing breast cancer and wants to know what she can do to prevent breast cancer. She has read a few options in patient information pamphlets, but she wants to see more detailed and recent information available in medical journal articles.

She could choose to search the primary medical literature using PubMed, the free, web-based MEDLINE search tool. If she searches for documents in the previous year that use the keywords *breast neoplasms* (a more general medical term for breast cancer) and *prevention*, PubMed returns the titles of over 400 documents displayed as a long list. If the user notices a document title that she finds interesting, she can find related documents using the *See Related Articles* link, but she cannot see a summary of the information contained in those search results. If she wants to form an accurate model of all possible preventive measures, she must examine all 472 documents. Even if she spends only 30 seconds examining each document, it will take her nearly 4 hours to browse the entire list of search results.

In contrast, if she were to use DynaCat, she could see the search results organized by the preventive actions found in those documents. Figure 1 shows the interface

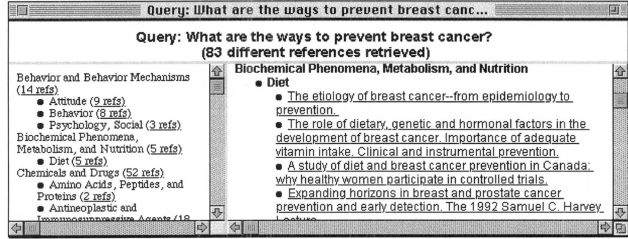

Figure 1. DynaCat's interface. The interface is broken into three frames, or window panes. The top window pane displays the user's query and the number of documents found. The left pane shows the categories in the first two levels of the hierarchy. This pane provides a table-of-contents view of the organization of search results. The right pane displays all the categories in the hierarchy and the titles of the documents that belong in those categories.

generated by DynaCat for a search on the CancerLit database using the keywords *breast neoplasms* and *prevention*.

By organizing the documents into a hierarchy of categories that represent the preventive actions discussed, this interface helps the user to learn about the various preventive measures that are discussed in the literature. For example, she can determine immediately that five documents discuss diet as a preventive measure. This organization of results also helps her to find information about specific preventive measures quickly and easily.

Other Approaches

Automatic approaches to organizing search results include relevance ranking and clustering. These techniques typically represent each document as a vector of all words that appear in the document.

Relevance-ranking systems create an ordered list of search results (Harman 1992). The order of the documents is based on a measure of how likely it is that the document is relevant to the query. Even if the documents are ranked by relevance criteria, an ordered list does not give the user much information on the similarities or differences in the contents of the documents. For example, the user would not be able to determine that 30 different preventive measures were discussed in the retrieved documents or that 10 documents discussed the same method.

Document-clustering systems create groups of documents based on the associations among the documents (Allen, Obry et al. 1993; Hearst and Pedersen 1996) (Sahami, Yusufali et al. 1998). To determine the degree of association among documents, clustering systems require a similarity metric, such as the number of words that the documents have in common. The systems then label each

group (or cluster) with that group's commonly occurring word or words. Unfortunately, the similarities found by clustering may not correspond to a grouping that is meaningful to the user. Even if the grouping is meaningful to the user, it may not correspond well to the user's query because clustering algorithms usually do not use information about the user's query in forming the clusters. The document groups are labeled by words extracted from the clusters, usually chosen by an information-theoretic measure. Lists of words of this sort may be understandable if the contents of the cluster are cohesive, but a list of words is not as inviting to the general user as a well-selected category label.

A Knowledge-Based Method

To retrieve textual information, most information retrieval systems use statistical, word-based approaches. Knowledge-based techniques are seen as untenable because of the time and work required to create and maintain the necessary models for each domain. Our approach is domain-specific, but it takes advantage of an existing model for much of the knowledge, rather than requiring the developer to create and maintain a large, new model. It requires two types of models: a small query model that must be created by the developer, and a large domain-specific terminology model that should already exist. For the medical domain, DynaCat uses the terminology model created by the National Library of Medicine (NLM), the Unified Medical Language System (UMLS), which provides information on over 500,000 biomedical terms. Figure 2 illustrates how DynaCat extends the standard search process.

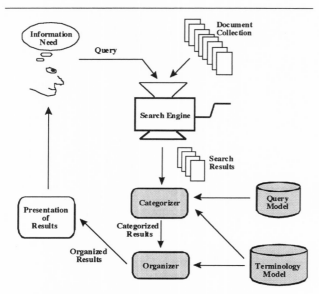

Figure 2. The search process using DynaCat. The components in light grey are the components that DynaCat adds to the traditional search process. These components do not influence which documents are retrieved, rather they determine how the search results are organized and displayed to the user.

Query Model

To organize the documents into categories that correspond to the user's query, the system needs knowledge about what kinds of queries users make in that domain, and how search results from those queries should be categorized. The **query model** provides this information through query types, and category types.

It would be impossible to generate a comprehensive list of all the questions that people may want to ask, even if the question topics were limited to a specific domain such as medicine. However, it is possible to create an abstraction of the typical kinds of queries that people make. We created such an abstraction, called **query types**, for the domain of medicine. Query types, such as *treatment—problems* or *problem—preventive-actions*, are generalizations of common, specific queries, such as *What are the complications of a mastectomy?* or *What actions can I take to prevent breast cancer?* Because the query types are abstractions and thus are independent of specific medical terms, a small number of query types can cover many specific questions that user might ask. For example, both specific questions *What are the complications of a mastectomy?* and *What are the side effects of taking the drug aspirin?* have the same *treatment—problems* query type, even though the questions refer to different treatments (e.g., the surgical procedure *mastectomy*, and the drug *aspirin*).

For DynaCat's medical query model (see Table 1), we created nine query types that correspond to questions that patients ask when they look for information in medical journal articles. We based this abstraction on a list of frequently-asked questions from a breast-cancer clinic. These query types may not provide comprehensive coverage of all questions that patients have, but the query types do cover many possible queries. For example, there are over 30,000 concepts in the medical terminology model that could be considered problems. Since the query model contains seven problem-oriented query types, the model covers at least 210,000 specific, problem-oriented queries.

Other researchers have used similar abstractions of medical queries with clinicians as the targeted user group. The *clinical queries* component of PubMed provides canned MEDLINE queries that return information about diagnosis, prognosis, etiology, or therapy of a clinician-selected medical problem. Researchers from McMaster University created the search expressions that correspond to those clinical queries (Haynes, Wilczynski et al. 1994). Researchers from Columbia University created a similar query abstraction called *generic queries* (Cimino, et al. 1993). Although none of these researchers have used their query abstractions to organize search results, their query abstractions are similar to those that we defined.

Table 1. Medical query types and their typical forms

Query Type	Form of Question
Prevention	
problem—preventive actions	What can be done to prevent <problem>?
problem—risk-factors	What are the risk factors for <problem>?
Diagnosis	
problem—tests	What are the diagnostic tests for <problem>?
problem—symptoms	What are the warning signs and symptoms for <problem>?
symptoms—diagnoses	What are the possible diagnoses for <symptoms>?
Treatment	
problem—treatments	What are the treatments for <problem>?
treatment—problems	What are the adverse effects of <treatment>?
Prognosis	
Problem—prognostic-indicators	What are the factors that influence the prognosis for <problem>?
problem—prognoses	What is the prognosis for <problem>?

For each query type, the system also needs an abstraction for the topics or categories that are appropriate for groups of search results. We call this abstraction **category types**. For example, when the user asks about the side effects of some drug, the types of categories that make

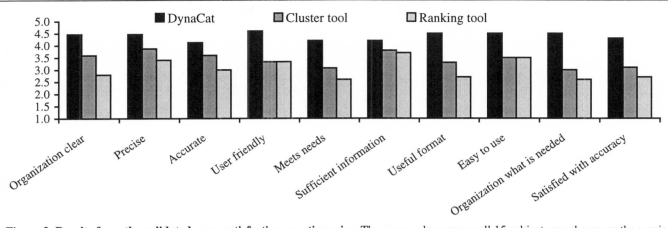

Figure 3. Results from the validated, user-satisfaction questionnaire. The mean values across all 15 subjects are shown on the y axis. The x axis shows a brief summary of the questions asked. Subjects answered the questions using a scale from 1 to 5, where 1 meant *almost never* and 5 meant *almost always* (the ideal answer). The difference between DynaCat and the cluster tool was statistically significant ($p < 0.05$) for all questions, as was that between DynaCat and the ranking tool, with the exception of the question about sufficient information where $p = 0.11$.

sense are those that indicate the various side effects or problems that can arise when a person takes that drug.

The medical query model for DynaCat contains nine category types: *problems, symptoms, preventive-actions, risk-factors, diagnoses, tests, treatments, prognoses,* and *prognostic-indicators.* As indicated by these names, each query type in the query model is linked to a category type, which determines the kinds of categories that DynaCat will generate whenever the user issues a query of that type.

By representing the category types separately from the query types, the system can link the multiple query types to the same category type, although currently the mapping is one-to-one. More important, this representation decision allows the system to provide a categorization option for queries that do not fit one of the predefined query types. Users could issue a normal search (without specifying a query type), and choose one of the category types as the way to categorize their search results.

Terminology Model

To determine appropriate category labels for the document groups, the system needs to know which category labels are valid for the given category type. The **terminology model** provides this information by connecting individual **terms** (i.e., single words, abbreviations, acronyms, or multiword phrases) to their corresponding general concept, called a **semantic type**. The UMLS medical terminology model links every term to at least one semantic type in a semantic network. For example, the term *penicillin* has a semantic type of *pharmacologic substance.* Individual, specific terms may become category labels if their semantic type is connected to the desired category type. For example, terms such as *AIDS, depression,* or *headache* could be category labels when the

search results are organized by the category type *problems,* because their semantic types (*disease or syndrome, mental or behavioral dysfunction, sign or symptom*) correspond to the category type *problems.*

The query model does not contain references to specific terms in the terminology model; it only lists the appropriate semantic types for each category type. This representation isolates the query model from many changes that could occur in a terminology model. For example, if the NLM added a new drug to their terminology model and linked the new drug to its appropriate semantic type (*pharmacologic substance*), we would not need to modify the query model. If DynaCat were organizing the search results by the category type *treatments* and one of the retrieved documents uses the new drug as a keyword, that keyword would become a category label automatically.

Categorizer

Many published documents contain keywords that authors or indexers have selected to describe the documents' content. The **categorizer** takes advantage of this information to determine which categories to select and which documents to assign to those categories.

Because many of a document's keywords do not correspond to the user's query, the categorizer must prune the irrelevant keywords from the list of potential categories. To accomplish this task, the categorizer retrieves the categorization criteria for the corresponding query type, and examines each document in the set of results individually. For each document, the categorizer examines each keyword. It looks up the keyword's semantic type in the terminology model, and compares that type to the list of acceptable semantic types from the categorization criteria. When a keyword satisfies all the categorization criteria, the categorizer adds the document to the category labeled with that keyword. If it has not created such a category already, it makes a new category labeled by that keyword. The categorizer checks every keyword in a document against the categorization criteria; thus, it may categorize each document under as many labels as is appropriate for the given query type.

Organizer

After a set of documents have been retrieved and assigned to categories, the categorizer then passes this information to the **organizer**, which arranges the categories into a hierarchy. The goal of the category organizer is to create a hierarchical organization of the categories that is neither too broad nor too deep, as defined by set thresholds. It produces the final categorization hierarchy based on the distribution of documents from the search results. When the number of categories at one level in the hierarchy exceeds a predefined threshold, the categories are grouped under a more general label. DynaCat generates the more general label by traversing up the terminology model's hierarchy to find a term that is a parent to several document categories.

DynaCat is implemented in Common LISP, and makes use of the search engine developed by Lexical Technology, Inc. (Tuttle, et al. 1996). For more information on the system and algorithms see (Pratt 1997; Pratt 1999).

Evaluation

We performed a user study to assess the usefulness of the DynaCat approach. Our hypothesis is that the dynamic categorization of search results is more useful to users who have general questions than are the two other dominant dynamic approaches to organizing search results: ranked lists and clusters. We define a useful system as one that helps users to

- learn about the kinds of information that are available to answer their question
- find answers to their question efficiently and easily
- feel satisfied with their search experience

We recruited 15 breast-cancer patients and their family members for this evaluation. Every subject used all three organizational tools: (1) DynaCat, (2) a tool that clusters the search results, and (3) a tool that ranks the search results according to relevance criteria. For the clustering tool, we used SONIA (Sahami, et al. 1998). It creates clusters by using group-average hierarchical, agglomerative clustering to form the initial set of clusters, and then refines them with an iterative method. For the relevance ranking, we used a standard algorithm recommended by Salton for situations in which the queries are short and the vocabulary is technical (Salton and Buckley 1988). Each subject used all three different queries: *What are the ways to prevent breast cancer?* (83 documents retrieved), *What*

are the prognostic factors for breast cancer? (81 documents retrieved*)*, and *What are the treatments for breast cancer?* (78 documents retrieved), but we randomized the query used with each tool and the order in which the subjects used the tools.

To measure the amount of information that the subjects learned using the tools, we asked each subject to list answers to the three queries before she used any tool, and to answer the same queries after she had used all the tools. For each tool, the amount learned was the number of new answers that the subject provided on the final answer list. The mean number of new answers was greater when subjects used DynaCat than when they used the cluster tool or the ranking tool; however, this difference was not significant. The tool used may have had an influence on the amount learned, but the number of new answers was correlated more strongly with how recently the subjects used a tool to find answers to that question, rather than which tool they used.

All subjects completed two types of timed tasks to determine how quickly they could find information related to the query. For the first type of timed task, subjects found as many answers as possible to the general question (e.g., *What are the preventive actions for breast cancer?*) in a 4-minute time limit. When the subjects used DynaCat, they found more answers than they did with the other two tools. The mean number of answers found for DynaCat was 7.80, for the cluster tool was 4.53, and for ranking tool was 5.60. This difference was significant ($p < 0.05$).

For the second type of timed task, we measured the time that it took the subjects to find answers to two specific questions (e.g., *Can diet be used in the prevention of breast cancer?*) that related to the original, general query. We found no significant difference among the tools. The time that it took subjects to read and understand the abstract, rather than the time that it took them to find a document among the search results, most heavily influenced the time for them to find an answer.

We used a 26-question, user-satisfaction questionnaire to assess several aspects of the user's experience. The first 10 questions were adapted from a validated satisfaction questionnaire (Doll and Torkzadeh 1988). Figure 3 illustrates the results for that portion of the questionnaire. On all the questions that requested quantitative answers, the satisfaction scores for DynaCat were much higher than they were with either for the ranking tool or for the cluster tool. On 13 of the 14 questions, this difference was statistically significant ($p < 0.05$). For the yes—no questions, all 15 users affirmed that DynaCat makes sense, is helpful, is useful, and has clear labels. All 15 also said that they would use DynaCat again for another search. In comparison, for the cluster tool, the number of subjects that responded positively ranged between only 5 and 10. For the ranking tool, the number of positive responses ranged from 6 to 9. When asked if they were frustrated, one user said she was frustrated and another was somewhat frustrated when she used DynaCat. In contrast, 9 subjects were frustrated using the cluster tool, and 8 subjects were frustrated using the ranking tool. On the final subjective assessment, no subjects chose DynaCat as the worst tool, and most of the subjects (70 percent) chose DynaCat as the best tool.

In summary, the results showed that DynaCat is a more useful organization tool than the cluster tool or the ranking tool. DynaCat was significantly better than the other two tools in terms of the number of answers that users found in a fixed amount of time and of user satisfaction. The objective results for the amount learned were inconclusive; however, most subjects (87 percent) thought that DynaCat helped them to learn about the topic of the query, compared to only 47 percent for the cluster tool and only 60 percent for the ranking tool.

Conclusions and Contributions

In summary, we have presented a new, knowledge-based method for dynamically categorizing search results. We have explained how this method provides information about (1) what kinds of information are represented in (or are absent from) the search results, by hierarchically organizing the document categories and by providing meaningful labels for each category; (2) how the documents relate to the query, by making the categorization structure dependent on the type of query; and (3) how the documents relate to one another, by grouping ones that cover the same topic into the same category.

Although we created DynaCat exclusively for the domain of medicine, the approach should be extensible to other domains that have large terminology models. Many terminology models for other domains exist and may be useful for this technique (Rowley 1996). For example, the Association for Computing Machinery uses a taxonomy of computing terms (Coulter, et al. 1998), and Mathematical Review sponsors a similar taxonomy of mathematics terminology (Review 1991).

We have demonstrated a successful application of AI technology for the field of medicine. Our evaluation suggests that DynaCat helps users find answers to certain types of questions more efficiently and easily than the common statistical approaches. Since the study involved a small number of queries, more evaluation is needed to allow for larger claims. Nevertheless, these initial results suggest that if we use knowledge about users' queries, and the kinds of organizations that are useful for those queries, we can provide users with helpful and satisfying search experiences. By providing a useful organization of medical search results, DynaCat can help lay people, patients and their families, explore the medical literature, and become informed about their own medical care. Health-care professionals who have used this system have also expressed enthusiasm for using it in their work.

Acknowledgements

This work was conducted with the support of NLM grant LM-07033 and NCI contract N44-CO-61025.

References

Allen, R. B.; Obry, P. and Littman, M. 1993. An interface for navigating clustered document sets returned by queries. In Proceedings of the ACM SIGOIS: Conference on Organizational Computing Systems (COOCS). Milpitas, CA, 166-171.

Cimino, J. J., et al. 1993. Generic queries for meeting clinical information needs. *Bulletin of the Medical Library Association.* 81(2): 195-206.

Coulter, N., French et al. 1998. Computing Classification System 1998: Current Status and Future Maintenance. Report of the CCS Update Committee, ACM Computing Reviews.

Doll, W. and Torkzadeh, F. 1988. The measurement of end-user computing satisfaction. *MIS Quarterly.* 12: p. 259-274.

Harman, D. 1992. Ranking Algorithms. *Information Retrieval Data Structures & Algorithms.* R. B.-Y. William B. Frakes, Prentice Hall.

Haynes, R., et al. 1994. Developing optimal search strategies for detecting clinically sound studies in MEDLINE. *Journal of the American Medical Informatics Association.* 1(6): p. 447-458.

Hearst, M. A. and Pedersen, J. O. 1996. Reexamining the cluster hypothesis: Scatter/Gather on retrieval results. In Proceedings of the ACM Conference on Research and Development in Information Retrieval: SIGIR '96, p. 76-84.

NLM. 1998. NLM Online Databases and Databanks. http://wwwindex.nlm.nih.gov/pubs/factsheets/online_databases.html.

Pratt, W. 1997. Dynamic organization of search results using the UMLS. In Proceedings of the American Medical Informatics Association (AMIA) Annual Fall Symposium, 480-4.

Pratt, W. 1999. Dynamic Categorization: A Method for Decreasing Information Overload. Medical Information Sciences. Stanford, Stanford University.

Review,. Mathematical Review 1991 Subject Classification. http://www.ma.hw.ac.uk/~chris/MR/MR.html.

Rowley, J. E. 1996. *Organizing Knowledge: an introduction to information retrieval.* Aldershot, England, Gower.

Sahami, M.; Yusufali, S. and Baldonado, M. Q. W. 1998. SONIA: A Service for Organizing Network Information Autonomously. In Proceedings of the Digital Libraries 98. Pittsburgh, PA, USA.

Salton, G. and Buckley, C. 1988. Term-Weighting Approaches in Automatic Text Retrieval. *Information Processing and Management.* 24(5): 513-23.

Tuttle, M. S., et al. 1996. Toward reusable software components at the point of care. In Proceedings of the American Medical Informatics Association (AMIA) Annual Fall Symposium, 150-4.

A Limitation of the Generalized Vickrey Auction in Electronic Commerce : Robustness against False-name Bids

Yuko Sakurai and **Makoto Yokoo** and **Shigeo Matsubara**

NTT Communication Science Laboratories

2-4 Hikaridai, Seika-cho

Soraku-gun, Kyoto 619-0237 Japan

email: {yuko, yokoo, matsubara}@cslab.kecl.ntt.co.jp

url: http://www.kecl.ntt.co.jp/csl/ccrg/members/{yuko, yokoo, matubara}

Abstract

Electronic Commerce (EC) has rapidly grown with the expansion of the Internet. Among these activities, auctions have recently achieved huge popularity, and have become a promising field for applying agent and Artificial Intelligence technologies. Although the Internet provides an infrastructure for much cheaper auctioning with many more sellers and buyers, we must consider the possibility of a new type of cheating, i.e., an agent tries to get some profit by submitting several bids under fictitious names (false-name bids). Although false-name bids are easier to execute than forming collusion, the vulnerability of auction protocols to false-name bids has not been discussed before.

In this paper, we examine the robustness of the generalized Vickrey auction (G.V.A.) against false-name bids. The G.V.A. has the best theoretical background among various auction mechanisms, i.e., it has proved to be incentive compatible and be able to achieve a Pareto efficient allocation. We show that false-name bids may be effective, i.e., the G.V.A. loses incentive compatibility under the possibility of false-name bids, when the marginal utility of an item increases or goods are complementary. Moreover, we prove that there exists no single-round sealed-bid auction protocol that simultaneously satisfies individual rationality, Pareto efficiency, and incentive compatibility in all cases if agents can submit false-name bids.

Introduction

Electronic commerce (EC) has made rapid progress in recent years. Internet auctions have become especially popular in EC. Commercial auction sites such as eBay (http://www.ebay.com/) and Onsale (http://www.onsale.com/) have been very successful and continue to expand. Computational agents are expected to work on behalf of humans in Internet auctions, e.g., to seek sellers or buyers and to negotiate the prices (Guttman, Moukas, & Maes 1998). Various theoretical and practical studies on Internet auctions have already been conducted. Sandholm pointed out several problems in applying tradi-

tional auction protocols to computational agent auctions (Sandholm 1996). Monderer presented a theoretical analysis of an upper bound on the seller's revenue (Monderer & Tennenholtz 1998). AuctionBot (http://auction.eecs.umich.edu/) is a configurable auction server that provides a tool for exploring auction mechanism designs (Wurman, Walsh, & Wellman 1998; Wurman, Wellman, & Walsh 1998). Moreover, auctions with multiple items or multiple units have been studied. Ausubel & Cramton investigated the effect of demand reduction lies on multiple unit auctions (Ausubel & Cramton 1998). Sandholm developed the *eMediator* prototype to support a variety of combinational auctions (Sandholm 1999). Auction techniques have also been applied to various fields, such as air conditioning control in building environments (Huberman & Clearwater 1995).

The Internet provides an excellent infrastructure for executing much cheaper auctions with many more sellers and buyers from all over the world. However, we must consider the possibility of new types of cheating. For example, an agent may try to profit by submitting a false bid under a fictitious name. Such an action is very difficult to detect since identifying each participant on the Internet is virtually impossible. We call a bid under a fictitious name a *false-name bid*.

As far as the authors know, the problem of false-name bids has not been previously addressed. On the other hand, the problems resulting from collusion have been discussed by many researchers (Milgrom 1998; Rasmusen 1989; Sandholm 1996). Compared with collusion, a false-name bid is easier to execute since it can be done alone, while a bidder has to seek out and persuade other bidders to join collusion.

In this paper, we examine the robustness of the Generalized Vickrey Auction (G.V.A.) against false-name bids. The G.V.A. is one instance of the Clarke-Groves mechanism (Mas-Colell, Whinston, & Green 1995; Varian 1995), and it is a generalized version of the well-known, widely advocated Vickrey auction (Vickrey 1961). The G.V.A. has proved to be incentive compatible, namely, the dominant strategies is for a bidder to bid his/her true valuation. In addition, the G.V.A.

achieves a Pareto efficient allocation. These characteristics are advantages of the G.V.A. compared to other auction mechanisms such as the simultaneous multiple round auction used in the FCC auction (McAfee & McMillan 1996; Milgrom 1998), where the free rider problem may cause inefficient allocations.

In this paper, we first introduce some preliminaries, and describe the G.V.A. in detail. Next, we first show simple cases where the G.V.A. is robust against false-name bids, and examine more general settings where the G.V.A. is vulnerable to false-name bids. Furthermore, we prove that there exists no single-round sealed-bid auction protocol that simultaneously satisfies individual rationality, Pareto efficiency, and incentive compatibility in all cases if agents can submit false-name bids.

Preliminaries

Auction protocol properties depend on each agent's utility structure. Auction protocols are divided into three classes according to the value of goods: private value auctions, common value auctions, and correlated value auctions (Rasmusen 1989). In this paper, we concentrate on private value auctions. Although an agent's valuation may be correlated with other agents' valuations, this restriction is reasonable for making a tractable analysis. In private value auctions, each agent knows its own preference, and its valuation is independent of the other agents' valuations. For example, an auction of antiques that will not be resold can be considered to be a private value auction. Furthermore, we assume that the value of goods is equivalent to their monetary value. We define an agent's utility as the difference between the true value of the allocated goods and the payment for the allocated goods. Each agent tries to maximize its own utility.

Different auction protocols have different properties. Although they are evaluated from various viewpoints, we primarily judge auction protocols by whether these protocols fulfill the three properties: incentive compatibility, Pareto efficiency, and individual rationality.

Incentive compatibility: An auction protocol is incentive compatible, if, for each agent, bidding its true private value is the best way to maximize its utility, i.e., lying does not benefit the agent. In computational settings, agents can deal with enormous amounts of data and infer other agents' preferences from the results of their bids. If knowing other agents' preferences is profitable, each agent tends to waste its resources in order to keep its preference secret and obtain the preferences of others. This situation can be avoided if bidding a true valuation becomes the dominant strategy.

Pareto efficiency: A Pareto efficient allocation means that the goods are allocated to bidders whose valuations are the highest, and that the sum of all participants' utilities (including the seller), namely,

the social welfare, is maximized. In a more general setting, Pareto efficiency does not necessarily mean maximizing the social welfare. In an auction setting, since agents can transfer money among themselves, the sum of the utilities is always maximized in a Pareto efficient allocation.

Individual rationality: An auction protocol is individually rational if each auction participant does not suffer any loss, in other words, the payment never exceeds the valuation of the obtained goods. If an auction protocol is not individually rational, then some agents do not want to participate in the auction.

We say that auction protocols are robust against false-name bids, if each agent cannot obtain additional profit by submitting a false bid under a fictitious name. If the robustness is not satisfied, the auction mechanism loses incentive compatibility, in other words, participants try to manipulate the auction by submitting false-name bids. This may result in inefficient allocations.

The Generalized Vickrey Auction

Protocol

The generalized Vickrey auction is based on the Clarke-Groves mechanism (Milgrom 1998; Wurman, Walsh, & Wellman 1998). The Clarke-Groves mechanism is a mechanism that induces each agent to tell the true value of public goods (Clarke 1971; Groves & Loeb 1975; Vickrey 1961). The G.V.A. protocol can be applied to various auctions, including auctions for multiple items with interdependent values. Auction protocols that can deal with interdependent value goods are useful for auctions among computational agents (Sandholm 1996).

In addition to its wide applicability, the G.V.A. satisfies individual rationality, Pareto efficiency, and incentive compatibility. Furthermore, the required time for the G.V.A. is shorter than the simultaneous multiple round auction, which requires multiple rounds.

The G.V.A. protocol: Let G denote one possible allocation of goods.

1. Each agent declares a valuation function[1]. Let $v_i(G)$ denote agent i's valuation function for the allocation G.

2. The G.V.A. chooses the optimal allocation G^* that maximizes the sum of all the agents' declared valuations.

3. The G.V.A. announces winners and their payment p_i:

$$p_i = \sum_{j \neq i} v_j(G^*_{\sim i}) - \sum_{j \neq i} v_j(G^*). \quad (1)$$

---

[1]The reported valuation function may or may not be the truth.

Here, $G_{\sim i}^*$ is the allocation that maximizes the sum of all agents' valuations except agent i's valuation.

Agent i's utility after the payment is given by the following formula. Let $u_i(G^*)$ denote agent i's true valuation function for G^*.

$$u_i(G^*) - p_i = u_i(G^*) + \sum_{j \neq i} v_j(G^*) - \sum_{j \neq i} v_j(G_{\sim i}^*). \quad (2)$$

The reason why the G.V.A. is incentive compatible is as follows. The third term in formula (2), $(\sum_{j \neq i} v_j(G_{\sim i}^*))$, is independent of agent i's declaration. The optimal allocation G^* is chosen so that the sum of the agents' declared valuations are maximized, i.e.,

$$G^* = \arg\max_G (v_i(G) + \sum_{j \neq i} v_j(G)). \quad (3)$$

Agent i wants to maximize its utility represented as formula (2). Therefore, agent i can maximize its utility by submitting the true valuation, i.e., by setting $v_i(G) = u_i(G)$.

The Vickrey auction (second-price sealed-bid auction) is a well-known auction protocol (Vickrey 1961). The G.V.A. for a single item and a single unit is reduced to the Vickrey auction, where the highest bidder wins and pays the second highest bid.

The G.V.A. for multiple units of a single item, where each agent needs only a single unit, is reduced to the first rejected bid auction $((M+1)$th-price auction) (Wurman, Wellman, & Walsh 1998). In the first rejected bid auction for M units ($M \geq 1$), winners are the highest bidders from the first to the Mth highest bid, and they pay a uniform price, the $(M+1)$th highest bid.

Example of the G.V.A.

We show how the G.V.A works with a simple example. Suppose that two agents denoted by agent 1 and agent 2 are bidding in the G.V.A. with two different items denoted by g_1 and g_2. An agent's bid is denoted by using a tuple: (a bid for g_1, a bid for g_2, a bid for a set $\{g_1, g_2\}$).

Suppose each agent bids as follows.

- agent 1's bid: ($20, $5, $25)

- agent 2's bid: ($10, $15, $30)

The G.V.A. allocates item g_1 to agent 1 and item g_2 to agent 2, respectively, since the allocation maximizes the sum of all agents' valuations. Agent 1's payment is calculated as follows. When agent 1 does not bid, both g_1 and g_2 are allocated to agent 2, and the valuation is $30. When g_1 is allocated to agent 1 and g_2 is allocated to agent 2, agent 2's valuation of g_2 is $15. Therefore, agent 1's payment is calculated as $30 - $15 = $15 and its utility becomes $20 - $15 = $5. Agent 2's payment is calculated as $25 - $20 = $5 and its utility becomes $15 - $5 = $10.

Features of the G.V.A.

Since the G.V.A. is an incentive compatible mechanism, it is robust against the free rider problem (Mas-Colell, Whinston, & Green 1995). In general, the free rider problem is that an agent makes unfair profit without paying the cost. The free rider problem can occur in other protocols, such as the simultaneous multiple round auction (McAfee & McMillan 1996; Milgrom 1998). This auction is designed to assign radio spectrum licenses, and it is currently used by the FCC (http://www.fcc.gov/wtb/auctions/).

The Simultaneous Multiple Round Auction:
In the simultaneous multiple round auction, each agent submits one sealed-bid for the combination of items that it wants. Bidding occurs over rounds. The round result is announced before the next round starts. The auction is closed when no agent is willing to bid up from the previous round. The highest bidder for each item gets at the price of his/her bid. The agent has to pay a penalty to withdraw a bid.

We illustrate the free rider problem in the simultaneous multiple round auction. Suppose that agent 1, agent 2, and agent 3 are bidding for two different goods denoted by g_1 and g_2. Agent 1 bids $5 for g_1 (where the true valuation is $7), agent 2 bids $5 for g_2 (where the true valuation is $7), and agent 3 bids $11 for a set of g_1 and g_2 (where the true valuation is $11). After the first round, they learn each other's bid. In the second round, both agent 1 and agent 2 have to make the decision whether to raise the bid or not. Each agent hopes that the other agent raises the bid, so it can get the good without increasing the payment, i.e., it can get a free ride. If neither agent raises the bid (hoping to get a free ride), a Pareto efficient allocation cannot be achieved.

Although the G.V.A. is not widely used, it has the potential to be used in the Internet auctions aided by agents since it is theoretically well-founded as described so far.

Robustness of the G.V.A. in Simple Situations

First, we show the cases where the G.V.A. is robust against false-name bids in simple auction settings.

In an auction of a single item and a single unit, the G.V.A. is reduced to the normal Vickrey auction. It is robust against false-name bids for the following reason. If an agent can win the auction without a false-name bid, submitting a false-name bid only results in increasing its payment. If the agent cannot win the auction without a false-name bid, although the agent may win the auction by submitting a false-name bid, it has to pay more than its true valuation. As a result, submitting a false-name bid does not increase its utility in the Vickrey auction.

In an auction of a single item with multiple units, where each bidder needs only a single item, the G.V.A.

is reduced to the first rejected bid auction. The first rejected bid auction is robust against false-name bids. The reason for this is similar to that in the Vickrey auction.

In the following, we examine the robustness of the G.V.A. in more general settings.

Robustness of the G.V.A. in Single Item, Multiple Unit, Multiple Requirement Auctions

This section discusses the G.V.A. in an auction of a single item with multiple units, where each bidder may desire multiple units. In this situation, the key to deciding whether the G.V.A is robust/vulnerable is the agents' marginal utilities. First, we examine the robustness using some examples.

Example

Example 1 [vulnerable] Suppose that two agents denoted by agent 1 and agent 2 are bidding for a single item with two units.

- agent 1's bid: ($6, $6)
  Agent 1 bids $6 for the first unit and $6 for the second unit, a total of $12 for both units.

- agent 2's bid: ($3, $5)
  Agent 2 bids $3 for the first unit and $5 for the second unit, a total of $8 for both units.

The G.V.A. allocates the two units to agent 1. Agent 1 pays $8 and its utility is $12 − $8 = $4.

Now, suppose that instead of bidding ($6, $6), agent 1 submits a bid ($6, $0), and then submits a false-name bid ($6, $0) using the identity of agent 3.

- agent 1's bid: ($6, $0)
- agent 2's bid: ($3, $5)
- agent 3's bid: ($6, $0)

The G.V.A. allocates a single unit to agent 1 and a single unit to agent 3. Agent 1's payment is $9 − $6 = $3 and agent 3's payment is $9 − $6 = $3. It turns out that agent 1 can get both units and its utility is $12 − $6 = $6, since agent 3 is a fictitious name of agent 1.

The difference between agent 1's utility with a false-name bid and the truthful bid is $6 − $4 = $2. Therefore, submitting a false-bid is profitable for agent 1.

Example 2 [robust] Let us assume that two agents denoted by agent 1 and agent 2 are bidding for two units of a single item.

- agent 1's bid: ($5, $5)
  agent 1 bids $5 for the first unit, and $5 for the second unit, a total of $10 for both units.

- agent 2's bid: ($4, $2)

The G.V.A. allocates the two units to agent 1. The payment is $6 − $0 = $6 and the utility is $10 − $6 = $4.

In this case, if agent 1 submits a false-name bid using the identity of agent 3, agent 1's utility does not increase. Suppose that agent 1 submits a false-name bid (using the identity of agent 3) by separating its original bid.

- agent 1's bid: ($5, $0)
- agent 2's bid: ($4, $2)
- agent 3's bid: ($5, $0)

The G.V.A. allocates a single unit to agent 1 and a single unit to agent 3, respectively. Agent 1's payment is $9 − $5 = $4 and agent 3's payment is $9 − $5 = $4. As a result, agent 1's utility is $10 − $8 = $2. Submitting a false-name bid is not profitable for agent 1.

Marginal utility

As we have seen in the previous subsection, the G.V.A. is robust in some situations, and vulnerable in other situations. We find that the robustness of the G.V.A. for a single item with multiple units depends on the marginal utility of a single item. The marginal utility of an item means an increase in the agent's utility as a result of obtaining one additional unit. For example, when we buy a CD or a book, the marginal utility usually diminishes, since having a CD or a book is enough, multiple units of the same CD or book are wasteful. One example where the marginal utility increases is an all-or-nothing situation, where an agent needs a certain number of units, otherwise the good is useless (one sock, glove, etc.).

The following theorem shows one sufficient condition where the G.V.A. is robust against false-name bids.

Theorem 1 *The G.V.A. is robust, i.e., submitting false-name bids is not profitable, if the declared marginal utility of each agent is constant/diminishes*[2].

Proof: Let us assume that an agent is submitting false-name bids, i.e., submitting bids using multiple identities. We show that if the agent merges these bids under a single identity, the same allocation as in the original case is attained, and the payment of the agent never increases.

Suppose that there are n units of a single item. Let A denote the set of all buyer agents, and $b_{i,j}$ denote agent i's bid for jth units of the item. Next, let $B(A)$ denote the set of bids $\{b_{i,j} \mid i \in A, 1 \leq j \leq n\}$, $nth(1, B(A))$ denote the largest bid in $B(A)$, $nth(2, B(A))$ denote the second largest bid in $B(A)$, and so on.

The inequality $b_{i,j} \geq b_{i,j+1}$ holds for all i, j according to the assumption that the declared marginal utility is constant/diminishes. In this case, the sum of the declared valuations is maximized by allocating units for the bids $nth(1, B(A))$, $nth(2, B(A)), \ldots,$

---

[2]Even if the true marginal utility of each agent is constant/diminishes, there is a chance that an agent exists whose declared marginal utility increases, i.e., the agent declares a false valuation. In such a case, submitting false-name bids might be profitable.

$nth(n, B(A))$. If the declared marginal utility increases, this property cannot be satisfied.

Suppose that agent x submits false-name bids using two identities, agent y and agent z, and obtains l items under the identity y, and m items under the identity z (where $l + m = k$). For simplicity, let us assume that $b_{y,j} = 0$ for $l < j \leq n$ and $b_{z,j} = 0$ for $m < j \leq n$ [3].

Agent y's payment P_y is represented by the sum of the bids $nth(n+1, B(A)), nth(n+2, B(A)), \ldots, nth(n+l, B(A))$ [4]. Similarly, agent z's payment P_z is also calculated by the sum of the bids $nth(n + 1, B(A)), \ldots, nth(n + m, B(A))$.

Then, let us assume that agent x merges these bids and submits them under a single identity x. For simplicity, let us assume $b_{x,j} = 0$ for $k < j \leq n$. This assumption does not affect the allocation result and x's payment. By submitting these bids, agent x can still obtain k units, and its payment P_x becomes equal to the sum of the bids $nth(n+1, B(A)), nth(n+2, B(A)), \ldots, nth(n+k, B(A))$.

From these facts, it is obvious that $P_y + P_z \geq P_x$ holds. In other words, the payment of an agent becomes smaller (or equal) when the agent merges the false-name bids and submits them using a single identity. Therefore, the G.V.A. is robust against false-name bids, as long as the declared marginal utility of each agent is constant/diminishes. $\square$

In Example 1, agent 2's marginal utility increases. On the other hand, the marginal utility of each agent is constant/diminishes in Example 2.

Robustness of the G.V.A. in Multiple Item Auctions

This section discusses the robustness of the G.V.A. in multiple item auctions. In this situation, the key to decide whether the G.V.A is robust/vulnerable is the utility structure of an agent. The structure is represented by introducing economic notions, i.e., substitutional/complementary.

Example We present an example where the G.V.A. is vulnerable to false-name bids. Suppose that there are different items denoted by g_1 and g_2 and two agents denoted by agent 1 and agent 2. We denote an agent's bid using a tuple: (a bid for g_1, a bid for g_2, a bid for set$\{g_1, g_2\}$).

- agent 1's bid: ($25, $5, $30)
- agent 2's bid: ($0, $0, $40)

Agent 2 wins a set $\{g_1, g_2\}$ at $30 and its utility is $10, while agent 1's utility is $0.

Next, we suppose agent 1 submits a false-name bid under the identity of agent 3.

- agent 1's bid: ($25, $5, $30)
- agent 2's bid: ($0, $0, $40)
- agent 3's bid: ($0, $30, $30)

The item g_1 goes to agent 1 and g_2 goes to agent 3. The payment for agent 1 is $40 - $30 = $10 and the payment for agent 3 is $40 - $25 = $15. Namely, agent 1 can obtain the two items with $25, so its utility is $30 - $25 = $5. This means a false-name bid is effective.

Substitutional/Complementary

Since the robustness of the G.V.A. for a single item with multiple units depends on the agents' marginal utilities, we find that the robustness of the G.V.A. with multiple items depends on whether the goods are complementary/substitutional [5].

Suppose that there are two different items denoted by A and B. We define A and B are complementary, if the sum of the utility of only having A and the utility of only having B is lower than the sum of the utility of simultaneously having A and B, i.e.,

$$u_i(A) + u_i(B) < u_i(\{A, B\}).$$

Here, let u_i denote a valuation function of an item or a set of items for an agent i.

We define A and B are substitutional, if the sum of the utility of only having A and the utility of only having B is higher than (or equal to) the utility of simultaneously having A and B, i.e.,

$$u_i(A) + u_i(B) \geq u_i(\{A, B\}).$$

For example, we can consider tea and sugar to be complementary and tea and coffee to be substitutional.

The following theorem shows one sufficient condition where the G.V.A. is robust against false-name bids.

Theorem 2 *The G.V.A. is robust, i.e., submitting false-name bids is not profitable, if all items are substitutional for all agents according to the declared valuations of agents.*

The proof can be given in a way similar to that of Theorem 1.

In the previous example, the items are complementary for agent 2. Therefore, there is a chance that submitting a false-name can be profitable.

Table 1 summarizes the obtained results.

---

[3]Without this assumption, the payments could be larger, since agent z's bids $\{b_{z,j} \mid m < j \leq n\}$ might be used to calculate the payment of agent y.

[4]In general, P_y is calculated by the sum of the bids $nth(n - l + 1, B(A - \{y\})), nth(n - l + 2, B(A - \{y\})), \ldots, nth(n, B(A - \{y\}))$. We can obtain the above result since the set $\{b_{y,j} \mid 1 \leq j \leq l\}$ is included in the winning bids, and $b_{y,j} = 0$ for $l < j \leq n$.

[5]In microeconomic studies, the definition that item A and item B are complementary is as follows: if the price of item B increases, the demand of item A decreases, and vice versa. This definition is more strict than our definition.

Table 1: Robustness against false-name bids

number of items	number of units	number of requirements	property	robustness
single	single	single		○
single	multiple	single		○
single	multiple	multiple	marginal utility is constant/diminishes	○
			marginal utility increases	×
multiple	multiple	multiple	substitutional	○
			complementary	×

Non-Existence of Desirable Protocols

So far, we have investigated the robustness of the G.V.A., and clarified the circumstances where submitting a false-name bid is effective in the G.V.A. The next question is whether any auction protocol exists that is robust against false-name bids or not. In this section, we show a negative result, i.e., we show proof that there exists no single-round sealed-bid auction protocol that simultaneously satisfies individual rationality, Pareto efficiency, and incentive compatibility in all cases if agents can submit false-name bids.

Theorem 3 *In auctions for multiple units of a single item and multiple requirements of agents, there exists no single-round sealed-bid auction protocol that simultaneously satisfies individual rationality, Pareto efficiency, and incentive compatibility in all cases if agents can submit false-name bids.*

Proof: It is sufficient to show one instance where no auction protocol satisfies the prerequisites.

Let us assume that there are two units of a single item, and three agents denoted by agent 1, agent 2, and agent 3.

- agent 1's bid: $(a, 0)$
  agent 1 bids a for the first unit and 0 for the second unit, total of a for both units.

- agent 2's bid: (b, a)

- agent 3's bid: $(a, 0)$

Let us assume $a > b$. According to Pareto efficiency, agent 1 and agent 3 get one unit. Let P_a denote the payment of agent 1.

When agent 2 and agent 3 reveal their true valuations, if agent 1 submits a bid, $a' = b + \epsilon$, the allocation does not change. Let $P_{a'}$ denote agent 1's payment in this situation. According to individual rationality, the inequality $P_{a'} \leq a'$ should hold. Furthermore, according to incentive compatibility, $P_a \leq P_{a'}$ should hold. These assumptions lead to $P_a \leq b + \epsilon$. The condition for agent 3's payment is identical to that for agent 1's payment.

Next, we assume another case with two agents denoted by agent 1 and agent 2.

- agent 1's bid: (a, a)

- agent 2's bid: (b, a)

According to Pareto efficiency, the two units go to agent 1. Let us denote the payment of agent 1 $P_{(a,a)}$. If agent 1 submits a false-name bid using the identity of agent 3, the same result as in the previous case can be obtained. According to incentive compatibility, the following inequality must hold, otherwise, agent 1 can profit by submitting a false-name bid: $P_{(a,a)} \leq 2 \times P_a \leq 2b + 2\epsilon$.

On the other hand, let us consider the case when there are two agents.

- agent 1's bid: (c, c)

- agent 2's bid: (b, a)

Let us assume $b + \epsilon < c < a$, and $a + b > 2c$. According to Pareto efficiency, the two units go to agent 2. So, agent 1 cannot gain any utility. However, if agent 1 replaces the bid (c, c) with (a, a), both units go to agent 1 and the payment is $P_{(a,a)} \leq 2b + 2\epsilon$, which is smaller than $2c$, i.e., agent 1's true value of these two units. Therefore, agent 1 can increase the utility by submitting a false bid (over-bidding its true valuation).

Thus, in auctions for multiple units of a single item and multiple requirements of agents, there exists no auction protocol that simultaneously satisfies individual rationality, Pareto efficiency, and incentive compatibility in all cases if agents can submit false-name bids. □

Theorem 4 *In auctions with multiple items, there exists no single-round sealed-bid auction protocol that simultaneously satisfies individual rationality, Pareto efficiency, and incentive compatibility in all cases if agents can submit false-name bids.*

The proof can be given in a way similar to that of Theorem 3.

Conclusions

We have discussed the robustness of the generalized Vickrey auction (G.V.A.) against false-name bids. Although, to our knowledge, this problem has not been previously addressed, it can be a serious problem in Internet auctions. We have clarified the circumstances where submitting false-name bids is profitable. More specifically, we have shown that the robustness of the G.V.A. depends on the utility structure of each agent. Moreover, we have proved that there exists no single-round sealed-bid auction protocol that simultaneously satisfies individual rationality, Pareto efficiency, and incentive compatibility in all cases if agents can submit false-name bids.

We obtained a rather negative result in the problem of false-name bids. However, there are many situations where obtaining the optimal allocation is not necessary. In such a situation, it is enough to design an auction mechanism simultaneously satisfying individual rationality and incentive compatibility. Our future goal is to find an auction mechanism that can obtain reasonably good (but not Pareto efficient) allocations.

Acknowledgments

The initial idea of this work originated during a summer seminar on Market-Based Computing in Ishida Laboratory, Kyoto University. The authors would like to thank the participants of the seminar, Toru Ishida, Katsumi Tanaka, Hiroshi Yamaki, and Hideki Fujiyama.

References

Ausubel, L., and Cramton, P. 1998. Demand reduction and inefficiency in multi-unit auctions. http://www.market-design.com/library.html.

Clarke, E. 1971. Multipart pricing of public goods. *Public Choice* 2:19–33.

Groves, T., and Loeb, M. 1975. Incentives and public inputs. *Journal of Public Economics* 4:311–326.

Guttman, R.; Moukas, A.; and Maes, P. 1998. Agent-mediated electronic commerce: A survey. *The Knowledge Engineering Review* 13(2):147–159.

Huberman, B., and Clearwater, S. 1995. A multiagent system for controlling building environments. In *Proceedings of the First International Conference on Multiagent Systems*, 171–176.

Mas-Colell, A.; Whinston, M.; and Green, J. 1995. *Microeconomic Theory*. Oxford University Press.

McAfee, P., and McMillan, J. 1996. Analyzing the airwaves auction. *Journal of Economic Perspectives* 10(1):159–175.

Milgrom, P. 1998. Putting auction theory to work: The simultaneous ascending auction. http://www.cramton.umd.edu/conference/Auction-Conference.html.

Monderer, D., and Tennenholtz, M. 1998. Optimal auctions revisited. In *Proceedings of 15th National Conference on Artificial Intelligence*, 32–37.

Rasmusen, E. 1989. *Games and Information*. Basil Blackwell.

Sandholm, T. 1996. Limitations of the Vickrey auction in computational multiagent systems. In *Proceedings of the Second International Conference on Multiagent Systems*, 299–306.

Sandholm, T. 1999. *eMediator* : A next generation electronic commerce server. Working paper, Washington University, Department of Computer Science. http://siesta.cs.wustl.edu/~sandholm/.

Varian, H. 1995. Economic mechanism design for computerized agents. In *First Usenix Workshop on Electronic Commerce*.

Vickrey, W. 1961. Counter speculation, auctions, and competitive sealed tenders. *Journal of Finance* 16:8–37.

Wurman, P.; Walsh, W.; and Wellman, M. 1998. Flexible double auctions for electronic commerce: Theory and implementation. *Decision Support Systems* 24:17–27.

Wurman, P.; Wellman, M.; and Walsh, W. 1998. The Michigan Internet AuctionBot: A configurable auction server for human and software agents. In *Proceedings of the Second International Conference on Autonomous Agents*, 301–308.

Hybrid Neural Plausibility Networks for News Agents

Stefan Wermter, Christo Panchev and **Garen Arevian**
The Informatics Center
School of Computing, Engineering & Technology
University of Sunderland
St. Peter's Way, Sunderland SR6 0DD, United Kingdom
Email: stefan.wermter@sunderland.ac.uk

Abstract

This paper describes a learning news agent HyNeT which uses hybrid neural network techniques for classifying news titles as they appear on an internet newswire. Recurrent plausibility networks with local memory are developed and examined for learning robust text routing. HyNeT is described for the first time in this paper. We show that a careful hybrid integration of techniques from neural network architectures, learning and information retrieval can reach consistent recall and precision rates of more than 92% on an 82 000 word corpus; this is demonstrated for 10 000 unknown news titles from the Reuters newswire. This new synthesis of neural networks, learning and information retrieval techniques allows us to scale up to a real-world task and demonstrates a lot of potential for hybrid plausibility networks for semantic text routing agents on the internet.

Introduction

In the last decade, a lot of work on neural networks in artificial intelligence has focused on fundamental issues of connectionist representations (Hendler 1991; Miikkulainen 1993; Giles & Omlin 1993; Sun 1994; Honavar 1995). Recently, there has been a new focus on neural network learning techniques and text processing-such as for newswires and world wide web documents (Papka, Callan, & Barto 1997; Lawrence & Giles 1998; Craven *et al.* 1998; Joachims 1998).

However, it has been an open research question (Wermter & Sun 1998) as to whether hybrid neural architectures will be able to learn large-scale real-world tasks, such as learning the classification of noisy newswire titles. Neural networks with their properties of robustness, learning and adaptiveness are good candidates for weighted rankings and weighted routing of ambiguous or corrupted messages, in addition to well-established techniques from information retrieval, symbolic processing, and statistics (Lewis 1994).

In this paper, we develop and examine new **Hy**brid **Ne**ural/symbolic agents for **T**ext routing on the internet (HyNeT). We integrate different preprocessing

strategies based on information retrieval with recurrent neural network architectures, including variable-length short-term memories. In particular, we explore simple recurrent networks and new more sophisticated recurrent plausibility networks. Recurrent plausibility networks are extended with a dynamic short-term memory which allows the processing of sequences in a robust manner. As a real-world testbed, we describe extensive experiments with learning news agents.

Recurrent Plausibility Networks

Recurrent neural networks introduce previous states and extend feedforward networks with short-term incremental memories. In fully recurrent networks, all the information is processed and fed back into one single layer. Partially recurrent networks, such as simple recurrent networks, have recurrent connections between the hidden layer and context layer (Elman 1990) or Jordan networks have connections between the output and context layer (Jordan 1986).

In other research (Wermter 1995), different decay memories were introduced by using distributed recurrent delays over the separate context layers representing the contexts at different time steps. At a given time step, the network with n hidden layers processes the current input as well as the incremental contexts from the $n-1$ previous time steps.

Figure 1 shows the general structure of our recurrent plausibility network. It combines the features of recurrent networks with distributed context layers and self-recurrent connections of the context layers. The input to a hidden layer L_n is constrained by the underlying layer L_{n-1} as well as the incremental context layer C_n. The activation of a unit $L_{ni}(t)$ at time t is computed on the basis of the weighted activation of the units in the previous layer $L_{(n-1)i}(t)$ and the units in the current context of this layer $C_{ni}(t)$ limited by the logistic function f.

$$L_{ni}(t) = f(\sum_k w_{ki} L_{(n-1)i}(t) + \sum_l w_{li} C_{ni}(t))$$

The units in the context layers perform a time-averaging of the information using the equation

$$C_{ni}(t) = (1 - \varphi_n) L_{ni}(t-1) + \varphi_n C_{ni}(t-1)$$

where $C_{ni}(t)$ is the activation of a unit in the context layer at time t. We represent the self-recurrent connections using the hysteresis value φ_n. The hysteresis value of the context layer C_{n-1} is lower than the hysteresis value of the next context layer C_n. This ensures that the context layers closer to the input layer will perform as memory that represents a more dynamic context. Having higher hysteresis values, the context layers closer to the output layer will incrementally build more stable sequential memory. Therefore the larger context is built on the more recent, dynamic one.

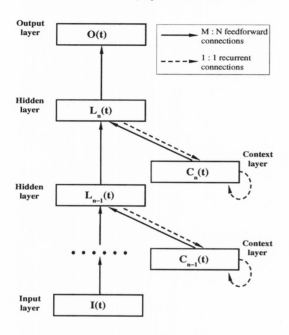

Figure 1: Recurrent plausibility network.

The Reuters News Corpus

For learning the subtask of text routing, we used the Reuters text categorization test collection (Lewis 1997). This corpus contains documents which appeared on the Reuters newswire. All news titles in the Reuters corpus belong to one or more of eight main categories[1]: Money/Foreign Exchange (**money-fx, MF**), Shipping (**ship, SH**), Interest Rates (**interest, IN**), Economic Indicators (**economic, EC**), Currency (**currency, CR**), Corporate (**corporate, CO**), Commodity (**commodity, CM**), Energy (**energy, EN**).

Examples of typical titles from these categories are shown in Table 1. As we can see, there are abbreviated phrases or sentences, specific characters, and terms which would make it difficult to manually encode a tra-

---

[1]There is also a second level categorization into 135 specific categories, but since we wanted to study the learning of difficult and possibly ambiguous classifications, we used the 8 main categories from the first level.

ditional semantic grammar. We can find incompleteness or ambiguity in the category assignments. For example, the title "U.K. money market offered early assistance" occurs six times in the corpus belonging to different semantic categories. Three times it is classified into the "money-fx" category, and three times into both "money-fx" and "interest" categories. Therefore there is an inherent ambiguity in the corpus and such examples pose challenges to learning algorithms and necessarily increase the classification error, since there is no perfect unambiguous category assignment in such cases. However, since we wanted to study hybrid neural agents under hard, real-world conditions, we did not perform any cleaning up of the underlying corpus data.

We use exactly all 10 733 titles of the so-called Mod-Apte split whose documents have a title and at least one topic. The total number of words is 82 339 and the number of different words in the titles is 11 104. For our training set, we use 1 040 news titles, the first 130 of each of the 8 categories. All the other 9 693 news titles are used for testing the generalization to new and unseen examples. The description of this corpus is shown in Table 2. Since categories may overlap, i.e. one news title can be in exactly one or several semantic categories, the actual distribution of the titles over the training set is not even.

Category	Training titles		Test titles	
	Number	Average length	Number	Average length
money-fx	286	8.26	427	8.13
ship	139	7.04	139	7.32
interest	188	8.79	288	8.50
economic	198	8.43	1 099	8.50
currency	203	8.54	92	8.42
corporate	144	7.10	6 163	7.43
commodity	321	7.35	2 815	7.54
energy	176	7.80	645	8.08
All titles	1 040	7.96	9 693	7.64

Table 2: The distribution of the titles from the Reuters news corpus over the semantic categories. Note that since one title can be classified in more than one semantic category, 1 040 titles represent the total number of 1 655 category occurrences for the training set and 9 693 titles represent the total number of 11 668 category occurrences in the test set.

Hybrid Neural News Routing

In this section, we will describe different architectures for learning news title classification. Each news title is presented to the network as a sequence of word input representations and category output representations, one such pair for each word. At the beginning of a news title, the context layers are initialized with 0 values. Each unit in the output layer corresponds to a particular semantic category. Those output units (one

Semantic Category	Title
money-fx	Bankers trust issuing STG/DLR currency warrants
ship	U.S. cargo preference squabble continues
interest	Volcker says FED policy not responsible for prime rate rise
economic	German net currency reserves rise 400 mln marks to 87.0 billion - Bundesbank
currency	Stoltenberg not surprised by dollar reaction
corporate	First Granite Bancorp Inc agrees to be acquired by Magna Group Inc for stock
commodity	Indonesian coffee production may fall this year
energy	U.S. oil dependency seen rising to record level
ship&energy	Kuwait may re-register gulf tankers - Newspaper
money-fx&interest&currency	J.P. Morgan <JPM> says DLR may prevent FED easing

Table 1: Example titles from the corpus.

or more) which represent the desired semantic categories are set to 1. All other output units are set to 0. We define a news title as *classified* to a particular semantic category if at the end of the sequence the value of the output unit for the desired category is higher than 0.5. Using this output classification, we compute the recall and precision values for each title. These values are used to compute the average recall and precision rates for each semantic category, as well as for the overall training and test sets, which all determine the network performance.

Supervised learning techniques based on plausibility networks were used for the training (Rumelhart *et al.* 1995). The training regime forces the recurrent plausibility network to assign the desired category, starting from the beginning of the news title as early as possible. Supervised training is continued until the error over the training set stops decreasing. Typically, between 700 and 900 epochs through the training set were necessary. In one epoch, we present all titles from the training set. Weights were adjusted at the end of each title.

Complete Titles and Significance Vectors

In our first set of experiments, we use significance vectors as the basis for representing words for semantic category routing. Significance vectors are determined based on the frequency of a word in different semantic categories. Each word w is represented with a *vector* $(c_1 c_2 \cdots c_n)$, where c_i represents a certain semantic category. A *value* $v(w, c_i)$ is computed for each dimension of the vector as the frequency of occurrences of word w in semantic category c_i (the category frequency), divided by the frequency of occurrences of word w in the corpus (the corpus frequency). That is:

$$v(w, c_i) = \frac{Frequency\ of\ w\ in\ c_i}{\sum_j Frequency\ for\ w\ in\ c_j}\ for\ j \in \{1, \cdots n\}$$

The same significance vector can represent two different words if they actually occur with the same frequency across all semantic categories in the whole corpus. However, a news title will be represented by a sequence of significance vectors so that phrases with the same sequence of significance vectors are less likely. Figure 2 shows the significance vectors of words from the lexicon. As we can see, words like "mortgage", "bureau" or "parker" have clear semantic preferences for specific semantic categories, while domain-independent words like "a", "of", "and" have more distributed preferences.

Word	MF	SH	IN	EC	CR	CO	CM	EN
a	.07	.02	.04	.17	.04	.28	.27	.10
and	.06	.02	.03	.15	.03	.25	.34	.09
bureau	.02	.00	.00	.38	.02	.02	.56	.01
mortgage	.01	.00	.30	.18	.00	.51	.00	.00
of	.07	.02	.03	.14	.03	.28	.31	.09
parker	.13	.00	.00	.00	.13	.73	.00	.00
the	.09	.03	.05	.18	.05	.20	.31	.09

Figure 2: Examples of significance vectors.

Simple recurrent networks were trained using significance vector representations as the input word representation of the input layer. The performance of the best trained network in terms of recall and precision is shown in Table 3. The table contains detailed results for each semantic category as well as for the whole training and test sets. The two categories "money-fx" and "economic" are fairly common, which explains their lower recall and precision rates, but in general, 91.23% recall and 90.73% precision are reached for the 9 693 unknown test titles.

Complete Titles and Semantic Vectors

In our second set of experiments, we use a different semantic vector representation of the words in the lexicon. These vectors mainly represent the plausibility of a particular word occurring in a semantic category and they are independent of the number of examples observed in each category. A *value* $v(w, c_i)$ is computed for each element of the semantic vector as the *normalized* frequency of occurrences of word w in semantic category c_i (the normalized category frequency), divided by the

Category	Training set		Test set	
	recall	precision	recall	precision
money-fx	84.36	84.62	84.74	69.56
ship	81.06	93.17	77.34	94.96
interest	77.93	82.71	85.42	83.45
economic	71.70	80.79	74.74	77.82
currency	85.75	91.46	85.36	87.16
corporate	88.81	92.31	94.87	95.10
commodity	86.27	94.77	86.47	88.31
energy	81.88	92.26	85.22	91.65
Total	85.15	86.99	**91.23**	**90.73**

Table 3: Results using significance vectors

normalized frequency of occurrences of word w in the corpus (the normalized corpus frequency). That is:

$$v(w, c_i) = \frac{Norm.\ freq.\ of\ w\ in\ c_i}{\sum_j Norm.\ freq.\ for\ w\ in\ c_j}, \ j \in \{1, \cdots n\}$$

where:

$$Norm.\ freq.\ of\ w\ in\ c_i = \frac{Freq.\ of\ w\ in\ c_i}{Number\ of\ titles\ in\ c_i}$$

Some examples of semantic vectors are shown in Figure 3. As we can see, the domain-independent words like "a", "of", "and" have fairly even distributions, while the domain-dependent words "bureau", "parker" have more specific preferences. An example of the difference between the two types of representation is the word "mortgage". Compared to the significance representation, here the preference entirely changes from the category "corporate" to the category "interest".

Word	MF	SH	IN	EC	CR	CO	CM	EN
a	.13	.12	.11	.16	.16	.06	.11	.15
and	.12	.12	.09	.16	.14	.05	.15	.15
bureau	.00	.00	.00	.50	.11	.00	.32	.01
mortgage	.02	.00	.72	.15	.02	.09	.00	.00
of	.13	.11	.11	.15	.15	.06	.14	.14
parker	.25	.00	.00	.00	.56	.17	.00	.00
the	.15	.13	.12	.15	.18	.04	.11	.12

Figure 3: Examples of semantic vectors

Simple recurrent networks were trained using the same training parameters and network architecture as in the previous experiment, but the titles were processed using the semantic vector representations. The performance of the trained network in terms of recall and precision is shown in Table 4. Using the semantic vectors rather than the significance vectors, we improved the test recall and precision rates to 92.47% and 91.61% respectively.

News Titles without Insignificant Words

So far we have examined complete phrases in a simple recurrent network. However, a symbolic preprocessing

Category	Training set		Test set	
	recall	precision	recall	precision
money-fx	87.78	88.60	84.07	69.59
ship	81.65	88.13	82.73	93.88
interest	85.33	86.97	88.25	88.19
economic	76.22	83.54	78.36	80.30
currency	87.76	92.59	89.64	89.86
corporate	89.16	91.96	95.90	95.98
commodity	86.27	90.52	86.20	87.22
energy	89.19	95.48	86.58	91.56
Total	88.57	88.59	**92.47**	**91.61**

Table 4: Results using semantic vectors

strategy from information retrieval could be useful, one that emphasizes significant domain-dependent words. To investigate such a strategy from information retrieval, we removed insignificant words (sometimes also called "stop words") from the unrestricted title phrases. We defined the set of *insignificant words* as equally frequent, domain-independent words that belong to any of the following syntactic categories: determiners, prepositions and conjunctions. Using the semantic vector representation, we extracted a set of 19 insignificant words of which the difference between the highest and lowest values in their vector was less than 0.2. For instance, examples of these words are: *a, an, and, as, at, but, by, for, from*. These words occur 7 094 times in the training and test corpus. After removing these words, the average length of a title in the training set is 7.11 and average length of a title in the test set is 7.00.

The experiment was conducted with the same learning conditions as for the complete unrestricted titles. The test results are shown in Table 5. We can see that the removal of insignificant words improves the recall and precision rates slightly over the last two experiments, but the improvement is small. However, by removing the insignificant stop words, we have also deleted some domain-independent words; hence this experiment also suggests that noisy corrupted titles can also be processed.

Category	Training set		Test set	
	recall	precision	recall	precision
money-fx	87.40	89.12	84.97	69.36
ship	79.14	88.85	78.42	93.53
interest	86.61	93.09	88.89	88.77
economic	79.12	87.80	79.28	82.64
currency	85.55	92.59	87.39	87.16
corporate	89.51	93.71	96.47	96.48
commodity	87.25	91.18	86.74	86.51
energy	85.32	94.19	83.86	90.54
Total	88.47	90.05	**92.88**	**91.92**

Table 5: Results without insignificant words

Complete Titles with Plausibility Networks

In this experiment, we use the recurrent plausibility network described in Figure 1 with two hidden and two context layers. Different networks have been trained using different combinations of the hysteresis value for the first and second context layers. The best results were achieved with the network having a hysteresis value of 0.2 for the first context layer, and 0.8 for the second. In order to be able to compare the results of this architecture with the previous ones, the rest of the training and testing environment parameters were set to be the same as in the experiment of the complete titles with the semantic vector representation of the words. Table 6 shows the recall and precision rates obtained with the recurrent plausibility network. There was an improvement in the classification, especially for the longer titles, as the two context layers and recurrent hysteresis connections support a larger and dynamic short-term memory.

Category	Training set		Test set	
	recall	precision	recall	precision
money-fx	87.34	89.47	86.03	76.70
ship	84.65	89.21	82.37	90.29
interest	85.24	87.77	88.19	86.05
economic	90.24	91.77	81.89	83.80
currency	88.89	91.36	89.64	89.86
corporate	92.31	92.66	95.55	95.43
commodity	92.81	93.14	88.84	90.29
energy	85.27	87.74	87.69	92.95
Total	89.05	90.24	**93.05**	**92.29**

Table 6: Results using recurrent plausibility network with semantic vectors

Examples of the Network Output

Figure 4 presents the output representations after processing three unknown example titles from the test corpus with the recurrent plausibility network from the last experiment. Here we show a representative behavior of the network, and in all these examples, the computed final categories are correct. The first two examples start with the same word sequence "Bank of Japan", but later, when a sequence of more domain-dependent words has been processed, the network changes its output preference according to the semantic meaning of the different input sequences: "intervenes shortly after Tokyo opens" provides a "money-fx" and "currency" category assignment, while "easy money policy" leads to an "interest" category assignment. Both these assignments are correct according to the Reuters classification.

In the third example in Figure 4, we illustrate how the network, based on the incrementally built context, can turn the strong output preference from the category "ship" to "energy". The network starts with preference for the "ship" and "energy" categories because, according to all news documents from the corpus, "Iran"

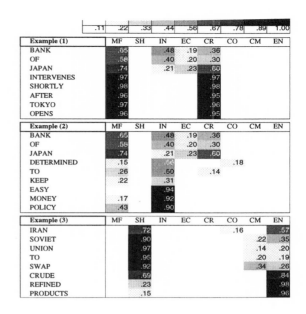

Figure 4: Examples and their category preferences

is associated with oil shipping. A recognizable number of news titles in the corpus are about the Soviet Union commodity crisis and are classified in the "shipping" and "commodity" categories. In the middle of the title however, when "crude" is processed as a significant term for the "energy" category, the output preference is changed to this category and subsequent words confirm this category assignment.

Discussion

We have described several hybrid neural architectures for classifying news headlines. In general, the recall and precision rates for simple recurrent networks and recurrent plausibility networks were fairly high given the degree of ambiguity of title/category and word/category assignments (for instance, see Table 1). The generalization performance for new and unseen news titles has been even better than the performance on the training data (for instance, see experiment 1). This is a very desirable effect and demonstrates that overfitting on the training set does not exist.

In other related work on text classification, whole documents rather than titles are often used to classify a news story. Obviously whole documents contain more information than titles, but we wanted to examine how far we can get in terms of classification based only on the title. However, since a news title contains on average around 8 words, it is unlikely that most of the words in the sequence are ambiguous and that they would lead to an incorrect category. Our good recall and precision results of at least 92% confirm that the influence of misleading word representations is limited.

Other related work on a different book title classification task using neural networks (Wermter 1995) has reached 95% recall and precision, but the library titles are much less ambiguous and only 1 000 test titles have been used in that approach while we used 10 000 corrupted and ambiguous titles. Also, the titles in our task are about 25% longer and more difficult to classify.

Our integration of new variations of the vector space model (significance vectors, semantic vectors) with nonlinear incremental classification from neural networks was shown as a viable new way for classification and routing tasks. The removal of insignificant stop words was shown to provide better results in the simple recurrent network as well. Best results were obtained with a plausibility network with two hidden layers, two context layers and recurrent connections for the context layer. Although the performance was in general fairly high for different architectures, an additional 2% improvement in the test set would mean another 200 correctly classified titles. The architecture with plausibility network has more possibilities to encode the preceding context and reaches at least 92% minimum value for recall and precision.

There has been interesting related work on text categorization on the Reuters corpus using whole documents (Joachims 1998). For the ten most frequently occurring categories, the recall/precision breakeven point was 86% for a Support Vector Machine, 82% for k-Nearest Neighbor, 72% for Naive Bayes. However, a different set of categories and whole documents rather than titles are used and therefore the results are not directly comparable to ours. Nevertheless, they give some indication of document classification performance on this corpus. In particular, for medium text data sets or when only titles are available, our approach produces very good performance.

Conclusions

We have described and analyzed HyNeT, a novel news agent for real-world headline routing which learns to classify news titles. A neural network architecture with several context layers and recurrent hysteresis connections is proposed which particularly supports a larger and dynamic short-term memory. Different from most related approaches for language processing, we have used hybrid neural learning techniques.

HyNeT is robust, classifies noisy arbitrary real-world titles, processes titles incrementally from left to right, and shows better classification reliability towards the ends of titles. This synthesis of techniques and constraints from plausibility neural network architectures, information retrieval and learning holds a lot of potential for building robust hybrid neural architectures of semantic text routing agents for the internet in the future.

References

Craven, M.; DiPasquo, D.; Freitag, D.; McCallum, A.; Mitchell, T.; Nigam, K.; and Slattery, S. 1998. Learning to extract symbolic knowledge from the world wide web. In *Proceedings of the 15th National Conference on Artificial Intelligence*.

Elman, J. L. 1990. Finding structure in time. *Cognitive Science* 14:179–211.

Giles, C. L., and Omlin, C. W. 1993. Extraction, insertion and refinement of symbolic rules in dynamically driven recurrent neural networks. *Connection Science* 5:307–337.

Hendler, J. 1991. Developing hybrid symbolic/connectionist models. In Barnden, J. A., and Pollack, J. B., eds., *Advances in Connectionist and Neural Computation Theory, Vol.1: High Level Connectionist Models*. Norwood, NJ: Ablex Publishing Corporation. 165–179.

Honavar, V. 1995. Symbolic artificial intelligence and numeric artificial neural networks: towards a resolution of the dichotomy. In Sun, R., and Bookman, L. A., eds., *Computational Architectures integrating Neural and Symbolic Processes*. Boston: Kluwer. 351–388.

Joachims, T. 1998. Text categorization with support vector machines: learning with many relevant features. In *Proceedings of the European Conference on Machine Learning*.

Jordan, M. I. 1986. Attractor dynamics and parallelism in a connectionist sequential machine. In *Proceedings of the Eighth Conference of the Cognitive Science Society*, 531–546.

Lawrence, S., and Giles, C. L. 1998. Searching the world wide web. *Science* 280.

Lewis, D. D. 1994. A sequential algorithm for training text classifiers. In *Proceedings of the Seventeenth Annual SIGIR Conference on Research and Development in Information Retrieval*.

Lewis, D. D. 1997. Reuters-21578 text categorization test collection, http://www.research.att.com/ lewis.

Miikkulainen, R. 1993. *Subsymbolic Natural Language Processing*. Cambridge, MA: MIT Press.

Papka, R.; Callan, J. P.; and Barto, A. G. 1997. Text-based information retrieval using exponentiated gradient descent. In Mozer, M. C.; Jordan, M. I.; and Petsche, T., eds., *Advances in Neural Information Processing Systems*, volume 9, 3. The MIT Press.

Rumelhart, D. E.; Durbin, R.; Golden, R.; and Chauvin, Y. 1995. Backpropagation: the basic theory. In Chauvin, Y., and Rumelhart, D. E., eds., *Backpropagation: theory, architectures and applications*. Hillsdale, NJ: Lawrence Erlbaum Associates. 1–34.

Sun, R. 1994. *Integrating Rules and Connectionism for Robust Commonsense Reasoning*. New York: Wiley.

Wermter, S., and Sun, R. 1998. *Nips Workshop on Hybrid Neural Symbolic Integration*. Breckenridge, CO: Nips.

Wermter, S. 1995. *Hybrid Connectionist Natural Language Processing*. London, UK: Chapman and Hall, Thomson International.

Cognitive Systems

Cognitive Classification

Janet Aisbett and Greg Gibbon

School of Information Technology
The University of Newcastle, University Drive, Callaghan 2308 AUSTRALIA
{mgjea, mgggg}@cc.newcastle.edu.au

Abstract

Classification assigns an entity to a category on the basis of feature values encoded from a stimulus. Provided they are presented with sufficient training data, inductive classifier builders such as C4.5 are limited by encoding deficiencies and noise in the data, rather than by the method of deciding the category. However, such classification techniques do not perform well on the small, dirty /or and dynamic data sets which are all that are available in many decision making domains. Moreover, their computational overhead may not be justified. This paper draws on conjectures about human categorization processes to design a frugal algorithm for use with such data. On presentation of an observation, case-specific rules are derived from a small subset of the stored examples, where the subset is selected on the basis of similarity to the encoded stimulus. Attention is focused on those features that appear to be most useful for distinguishing categories of observations *similar to the current one*. A measure of logical semantic information value is used to discriminate between categories that remain plausible after this. The new classifier is demonstrated against neural net and decision tree classifiers on some standard UCI data sets and shown to perform well.

Introduction

Classification/categorization can be seen as a special case of commonsense or hypothetical reasoning, in which the competing hypotheses are the various possible assignments, and the observations are sets of feature-value pairs, or some other representation of data, relevant to the stimuli. Any classifier requires prior knowledge as to the relationship between the possible categories and the patterns of observational stimuli that will be encountered. The learning phase of classification is concerned with assembling this knowledge, that is, with building a classifier.

Categorization processes divide between those that induce rules from training data or cases, and then apply them to observations, and those which determine the similarity of an observation to stored exemplars of a category and then invoke a probabilistic decision function.

Classification techniques also divide into those which build a fixed classifier, and those that support change. Classifiers may change incrementally upon receipt of new data which relate feature values to categories, or may be recompiled for each observational stimulus, for example by using only those features deemed relevant to the current situation (Shepherd 1961)

The performance of inductive classifier builders developed in machine learning has for some time been limited more by encoding deficiencies and noise than by the method of making the categorization decision. To average out data anomalies, recent work has concentrated on pooling results from classifiers developed using single or multiple base learning algorithms, applied to different subsets of the data set and/or with different learning parameters (Dietterech 1997). As well as this trend toward more complex computational machinery, a popular research area is the analysis of massive data sets: massive in number of attributes, size of fields, and/or number of records. Finally there is renewed interest in defining and computing what is desirable in classification performance (eg. Cameron – Jones and Richards 1998)

Frugal data and frugal processes

In contrast to the categorization problems receiving most attention in machine learning, real-world decision making often involves classification performed on small, incomplete, dynamic data sets, for which there may be little opportunity to review performance. It may not be cost effective to collect the data needed to make accurate categorizations or evaluations, or the data are not available. In such situations, the contribution of the encoding of the stimulus to categorization errors overwhelms the contribution of the method of making the categorization decision. This paper is targeted at this type of classification decision where frugal approaches to processing are appropriate. Examples abound, and many are commercially and/or socially important. They involve rare events (diagnosing an uncommon disease), sparse data (categorising an individual consumer's purchase decisions within a business transaction database), noisy data (predicting how senators will vote on a non-standard matter) and dynamic data (categorising teenage fashion items) as well as situations in which detailed decision making is not warranted (selecting which apples to buy for lunch).

Our method seeks to mimic human categorization processes. It is quite general and quite simple. A frugal set of rules is recompiled on presentation of each stimulus. The rules are formulated from examples retrieved from long-term memory on the basis of their similarity to the stimulus. Attention is then focussed on those features, or more generally, on those parts of the description of the entities in memory, that are expected to convey most information about the categories in this data set. Here, information is calculated as difference in entropy. Generalization of the truncated exemplars provides a rule set. The size of the rule set is further reduced using a logical semantic information measure (Lozinskii 1994), the use of which is motivated by our desire to mimic conscious deductive human reasoning at this stage. The entity is assigned to the category about which there is most logical information brought by the knowledge base consisting of the encoded stimulus together with any other prior knowledge about the entity, and the frugal rule set. If required, ties between categories are broken by acquiring more information from long term memory, in the first instance through looking at further features. This step is again motivated by human reasoning processes.

Unlike conventional commonsense reasoning that starts with a set of (possibly conflicting) rules and facts, we start with a set of facts and derive rules from these in order to answer a question about an entity. Unlike common machine learning algorithms, we design a new classifier for each stimulus, and combine rule and exemplar based approaches. Moreover, the method naturally accommodates prior knowledge in forms other than attribute value pairs, to make it more "commonsense".

The remainder of this paper is organised as follows. The next section looks at work in cognitive science that suggests how human categorization might be performed. This is used in section 3 to develop an algorithm to perform frugal categorization. The algorithm is described in general terms, to allow it to be applied to categorization decisions in which both prior knowledge and observations are presented as logical formulae. Section 4 applies the new cognitively-inspired classifier to some standard data sets from the UCI repository. The method is seen to outperform standard decision tree and neural net classifiers when the training sets are small. Surprisingly, the method performs as well on the difficult UCI data set Cleveland Heart on a training set of 20 as conventional packages which have used more than five times as many training examples. The final section reviews our contribution and flags further work.

Background

Some version of a *principle of frugality* is recognised in any automatic computational area that involves complex computations on noisy data. Thus, in statistical data classification, data are routinely reduced through principal component analysis. Such algorithms rely either upon redundancy in the original data, or on more active search for new data to compensate for limited "memory" (eg Havens 1997). However, the main driver for frugal approaches is the fact that data often cannot support more sophisticated processing. This was the argument put in (Gigerenzer and Goldstein 1996). The authors presented various strategies for problem solving which were frugal in their processing and data requirements compared with conventional approaches such as linear models and multiple regression, and showed that these performed comparably on the types of data sets that would be encountered in real world decision making.

In our setting, the key issue surrounding data encoded from a stimulus is that these may not have the power to fully explain the categorization. Thus, a data set puts an associated "ceiling" on the classification accuracy of any classifier. On the simplest level, this may be due to missing values or to noise on the encoded values. It may also be due to significant interactions between features that have been encoded and features that have not. There may be instability in the underlying relationship between observational stimuli and the categories of the stimuli eg. as in credit application data where different decision makers may employ different rules and where all the knowledge used in the decision making may not be encoded. Stimuli may be encoded using different representation for different classes, unlike the fixed representation used in machine learning data sets. (For example humans appear to use different representations of facial features for different races (Levin 1996).)

Because data collection and storage are expensive, a complete data record may also not be encoded for each and every stimuli even if the data are available. Thus, humans are thought to encode feature data with exemplars of common categories containing the most typical features, and exemplars of rare categories containing the most distinctive features (Krushke 1996). In this particular case common categories may appear to have missing the very data that would enable them to be distinguished. So it is not just redundant information about a class that is dropped.

We want to develop a classification algorithm that can deal with such domains, so will draw on methods inspired by human processing. Part of our algorithm will mimic unconscious processes and will involve data reduction from recalled exemplars, and part will mimic conscious deductive reasoning on a frugal rule set derived from the examples. Unfortunately, the nature of the interaction between exemplar and rule based approaches remains an open question in the cognitive science literature. Rules derived from small data sets are often claimed to be unstable and likely to be invalid. On the other hand, the performance of exemplar based methods relies on the richness of the example space, and they do not deal well with extrapolation compared with rule or model based methods.

Smith, Patalano and Jonides (1998) showed that the results of many experimental studies could be explained by assuming either a rule based or exemplar based approach, by varying other under-specified elements of the experimental situation (eg. difference in instructions). However, they say cognitive neuroscience research suggests that there exist separate neural circuits for categorising an observation using similarity to exemplars, and using rules. Shanks (1997) claims that categorization is mediated by references to remembered instances represented in a multidimensional psychological space, and supports the view that neural net type models are good descriptions of the process by which instances are encoded. On the other hand, conceptual knowledge is mediated by rules derived from the known members of the conceptual grouping.

If both exemplars and rules are used, then it is plausible that rules are derived as generalizations of at least some of the examples. The connectionist retrieval from memory of exemplars will be mediated by some measure of similarity between the observation and the stored exemplars of competing categories. Different measures may be invoked depending on the context. Nosofsky's Generalise Context Model (McKinley and Nofosky 1996) allows for an *attention weight* on features to model selective attention.

Exemplar and rule based categorization processes have been modeled with triggers for switching between the two (eg, Kalish and Kruschke 1997, Erickson and Kruschke 1998). Such models involve parameters that are fitted through typical feedback techniques which involve probabilities estimated using frequencies of occurrence. While we are going to develop a categorization process which derives rules from examples and does not switch between the two, we will need some notion of probability.

It has been widely held that humans do not reason in accord with a calculus of probability, and famous work has been done in this area by the "heuristics and biases" school of Amos Tversky. This has recently been revisited. A reinterpretation of probability in terms of observed frequencies of occurrence removes much of the evidence about neglect of base rates and other indicators of illogical reasoning (eg. Cosmides and Tooby 1996, Gigerenzer and Hoffrage 1995). The probabilistic model can be replaced by an experiential model where probability reflects the observed proportion, or the recalled proportion of observations. Base rates are less likely to be neglected when learned from experience (Kruschke 1996). It is still not clear to cognitive researchers when or whether probabilities are hard-coded through learning, rather than computed when needed through inquiry of stored instances (Jonides and Jones 1992).

We will in fact use two different notions of probability, one that is assumed to be computed on-the-fly on the basis of frequency, and the other that reflects the language of description of the problem. This is detailed in the next section. We will also invoke the phenomenon of anchoring. The tendency of humans to modify probability in order to anchor on prior beliefs about frequency has been recorded in many laboratory and real world situations. People tend to disregard data that are disconfirming of previously formed opinions, and tend to seek confirming evidence (eg. Garb 1996, Hogarth 1980). Thus, new data that increase the objective probability of an interest have a different impact to data that decrease its probability (Spies 1995). Subjects are also likely to be more confident of their judgement about events which they believe to be either very likely or very unlikely (eg. Lichenstein reported in Kleindorfer et al. 1993, Pulford and Colma 1996) than about those which they are uncertain. The tendency to anchor will be least when prior probability is around one half.

A Frugal Classification Algorithm

This section develops the frugal classification algorithm inspired by possible cognitive categorization processes. The presentation is very general, so some of the equations look reasonably cumbersome. However, the underlying algorithm is straightforward and natural. The design choices available are illustrated throughout by the choices made in the implementation used in section 4. The implementation introduces just two parameters.

Consider a decision maker tasked to assign a category to an observation about an entity y. The decision maker has access to a knowledge base M in which knowledge is encoded as formulae ϑ, which, for representational purposes in this paper, we write as statements in a typed first order language L. The language has two distinguished types: the type of the category labels, and the type of the labels identifying the entities. The identifier label is often implicit in machine learning data sets.

On presentation of the observational stimulus, the decision maker encodes the new information as a formula φ. The decision maker also formulates an hypothesis set $\Phi(y) = \{\phi_i : C(y, c_i)\}$ where each hypothesis assigns y to a possible category. The encoded stimulus φ is used along with M to select between the hypotheses in $\Phi(y)$. In general, though not in the standard machine learning scenarios, M may contain formulae that directly refer to the entity y and which may be brought to bear in the decision making. Such prior knowledge is important in human categorization eg (Heit 1998).

(In the standard machine learning classification scenario, observational stimuli are encoded using typed binary predicates $A_j(u, v)$ where without loss of generality the first variable identifies the entity and second variable specifies the jth. feature value. The observation φ is then representable as a conjunction of instantiations of some or all of the feature predicates, $\wedge_j A_j(y, b_j)$. The knowledge base M is a set of exemplars $\vartheta = \mathcal{H}(x)$, each stored as the conjunction of its instantiation of the category and of some or all of the feature predicates, viz. $\vartheta = C(x, c_i) \wedge_j A_j(x, a_{j,k})$. In general $A_j(x, a)$ does not imply $\neg A_j(x, b)$ for $a \neq b$: that is, a feature may take multiple values, because of uncertainty or non-exclusivity.)

Stage 1. Filtering

In deriving case-specific rules from the data in memory M, we model subconscious recall using two types of filters on M. The filters are orthogonal in the sense that one decreases the number of formulae to be considered and one restricts the size of each formula. When M is a conventional table of attribute-values, the filters are respectively a *select* and a *project* operation.

The first filter selects those exemplars that are in some sense "similar enough" to the encoded stimulus. In the following, this is defined in terms of syntactic similarity, on the basis that this type of measure appears to be used in low level recall processes in humans.

The second filter acts to focus attention on those parts of the exemplars that appear to be most relevant to the task of distinguishing between the hypotheses in $\Phi(y)$. Focussing is done in two ways. Firstly, the set of feature values (constants in the language) is reduced. If a car that is to be categorized as a sports car or some other type of car is blue, then the color of other remembered cars is not going to help this categorization unless they too are blue. Because of this, and in the spirit of frugality, we might suppose that the decision maker uses the observation to focus only on the terms that appear in φ. However, a remembered case should not be excluded because it refers to red cars, because there is a chance that the case conclusions may generalize to blue cars. Thus the filtered version of the language will have predicates typed to feature domains with up to two elements, as in "blue" and "a color other than blue" if such is known to exist. This filtering operation is formalized below. The second way that attention is focussed is by reducing the number of predicates under consideration. The method of selecting which predicates to retain will be discussed below.

The following definitions formally present the filtering operations:

Definitions

(i) The *recall triggered by* φ is the set $R_\varphi(M) = \{\vartheta \in M: Sim(\varphi, \vartheta) > threshold\}$ where $Sim(-, -)$ is a measure of similarity between formulae.

In the next section, $Sim(\varphi, \vartheta)$ is defined to be the count of common constants. That is, $Sim(\varphi, \vartheta) = |Const(\varphi) \cap Const(\vartheta)|$ where $Const(\Omega)$ is the set of constants appearing in the formulation of Ω.

(ii) The *focus set triggered by* φ, $T_{\varphi, \Phi}(M) = \{\vartheta_{/L}: \vartheta \in M\}$, is obtained by restricting formulae in M to the sublanguage L' of L defined as follows:

(a) The constants in L' are either entity identifiers, categories, constants that appear in φ, or constants that represent the "other values" of a type set that do not appear in φ. Formally, for each type predicate $Type$ in L other than the distinguished types, $Type \cap L' = \{c, c''\}$ where $c \in Const(\varphi)$ and c'' is some arbitrarily-chosen representative element of $Type \cap L \setminus Const(\varphi)$.

(b) The predicates in L' are those that convey highest relative information about φ. That is, there is a function $Ivalue_\Phi(-)$ from the predicates in L to the real numbers, together with a selection criterion, and $P \in L'$ if and only if $P \in L$ and $Ivalue_\Phi(P)$ satisfies the selection criterion (an example of this is given below).

Typically, $Ivalue$ would be the expected relative entropy; this is the definition we use in the next section. Computing entropy requires a definition of probability, or at least, a frequency of occurrence. Given a set of formulae S, the frequentist probability $p_S(\gamma)$ of any formula γ is the proportion of formulae in S which prove γ. Then the relative entropy of γ given η is $-p_S(\gamma \wedge \eta) \log p_S(\gamma \wedge \eta) + p_S(\eta) \log p_S(\eta)$.

The expected relative entropy brought by a predicate P for a given hypothesis is obtained by summing over all the possible instantiations of P for fixed entity y, weighting each contribution to entropy with the proportion of formulae in S which prove the instantiation. The weighted sum over all hypotheses gives the expected total entropy, where the weight on the summand contributed by a hypothesis ϕ is the proportion of formulae in S which prove ϕ. The relevant set S here is $R_\varphi(M)$. Formally, we are suggesting:

Definition

$$Ivalue_\Phi(P) = \sum_v \sum_\phi \{p_{R_\varphi(M)}(\phi) \{ p_{R_\varphi(M)}(P(v))(p_{R_\varphi(M)}(\phi \wedge P(v)) \log p_{R_\varphi(M)}(\phi \wedge P(v)) - p_{R_\varphi(M)}(\phi) \log p_{R_\varphi(M)}(\phi)) : v \in Domain\ P \cap \{y\}\}, \phi \in \Phi(y)\}$$

The selection criterion that we have used along with $Ivalue_\Phi$ is to take five predicates P such that no predicate that has not been selected has a higher $Ivalue_\Phi$ than a selected predicate. Ties are broken on a first-come-first-in basis. An alternative strategy would be to threshold on $Ivalue_\Phi$.

The enumeration of categories used in forming the hypothesis set is obtained from the categories instantiated in the exemplars recalled, that is, in $R_\varphi(M)$.

The next step is to form rules as generalizations of the formulae in $T_{\varphi, \varPhi} R_{\varphi}(M)$. A generalization of a formula is obtained by replacing any identifiers with variables. Thus the exemplar $\vartheta = C(x, c_i) \wedge_j A_j(x, a_{j,k})$ generalizes to the rule $\forall x \wedge_j A_j(x, a_{j,k}) \Rightarrow C(x, c_i)$, $j = 1, \ldots n$.

In memory M there may be duplicate exemplars, and the likelihood of this increases in $T_{\varphi, \varPhi} R_{\varphi}(M)$ because of the reduced language of description. It is reasonable to suppose that when duplicate formulae are encountered, their generalization is given more weight in the decision maker's mind. The strength of a formula is therefore important.

Definitions

Retain multiple occurrences of a formula $\varOmega$ in both $R_{\varphi}(M)$ and $T_{\varphi, \varPhi}(M)$, and say that $\varOmega$ has *strength* h if there are h occurrences of the formulae in the focussed recall set $T_{\varphi, \varPhi} R_{\varphi}(M)$.

$GT_{\varphi, \varPhi} R_{\varphi}(M)$, the generalization of $T_{\varphi, \varPhi} R_{\varphi}(M)$, is the set of ordered pairs $(\gamma, h(\gamma))$, where γ is the generalization of a formula in $T_{\varphi, \varPhi} R_{\varphi}(M)$ in the sense described above, and $h(\gamma)$ is its strength.

Stage 2. Deductive Reasoning

Up to now we have been mimicking subconscious recall and focussing. Now we want to bring information in to the "conscious memory", that is, the working knowledge base. There are too many formulae in $GT_{\varphi, \varPhi} R_{\varphi}(M)$ to keep in the working memory of a frugal decision maker at the one time, if we are to keep within the limits of the "magic number 7" long postulated to constrain human reasoning (Miller 1956). A further cull of the set makes sense in any case as the set will be in general inconsistent with the observation φ which, as "prior knowledge", is already in the working knowledge base.

The decision maker should aim to bring into the working knowledge base those rules that carry most information about the hypotheses (that is, about the categories to which y could be assigned) relative to the prior knowledge. Usually, prior knowledge is taken just to be the encoded stimulus φ. It is possible that M contains other knowledge pertaining to the category of the entity to be classified, and in a general system this could be assembled before the task was attempted. However, here we assume that prior knowledge is just φ.

How should the information that a rule brings about a hypothesis given the observation be measured? It will need to be defined in terms of some difference in relative information (see for example (Blachman 1968)). Restated, it is a measure of how much knowing the rule and the observation reduce the surprise value on learning that the hypothesis is true, compared with the surprise value of finding the hypothesis is true when all you have is the observation.

We claim that the information intrinsic in measuring surprise should not be based on a frequentist view of probability, because humans do not normally consciously count up occurrences. Rather, here it is more appropriate to take a logical semantic definition of probability, as defined for example in (Lozinskii 1994). The logical semantic probability of a formula γ expressed in a language L is the proportion of models of the language that are models of γ. We employ a modified definition of semantic probability that takes account of anchoring. We suppose that in the face of disconfirming data the decision maker anchors on prior belief in whether the categorization is likely or not, with anchoring proportionate to that estimate. Specifically, if $p^*(\phi|\gamma)$ is the logical semantic posterior probability, our posterior probability $p(\phi|\gamma)$ is given by $(1 - p(\phi))p^*(\phi|\gamma) + p(\phi)p(\phi))$ if $p(\phi) \geq \frac{1}{2}$, and by $p(\phi)p^*(\phi|\gamma) + (1 - p(\phi))p(\phi)$ otherwise. Logical semantic information in a formula γ is then as usual given by $-\log p(\gamma)$. Relative information $I(\phi|\gamma)$ is $-\log(p(\phi|\gamma)/p(\phi))$.

The value of information about a hypothesis ϕ brought by γ given the observation φ is defined to be the difference of relative information values $I(\phi | \gamma \wedge \varphi) - I(\phi | \varphi)$. The total information brought by γ can be defined to be the sum of the information brought by each of the hypotheses, multiplied by the strength of γ. That is, the information brought by γ given the observation φ is $h(\gamma) \sum_i I(\phi_i | \gamma \wedge \varphi) - I(\phi_i | \varphi)$. For a similar formulation, see (Aisbett and Gibbon 1998).

This computation is not complicated in practice, and in most cases reduces to choosing the rules that have most terms in common with the observation. (Remember that while the initial filtering operation chose exemplars with a high degree of commonality, the orthogonal second filtering operation may have left exemplars with little or nothing in common with the observation).

Given a ranking of rules based on the value of information brought by each rule, a strategy is needed to determine which rules to actually bring in to the working knowledge base. For example, a strategy might be to bring in any rule which exceeds a threshold information value, or the J most informative rules for some given $J > 0$, or, most frugally, only those rules which maximise the information value. We adopted this last strategy in deriving the results presented in the next section. Only one or two rules are normally in this set, and refer to only a small number of feature values and one or two categories. This corresponds to a human using only a few key features to determine between a few of the most salient categories.

The final step is to determine which category the instance y belongs to on the basis of the information set consisting of the observation φ and the rule set $\varDelta$ which maximises Equation (1). This is achieved by selecting the hypothesis that is most supported, that is: assign the entity to the category i for which the hypothesis ϕ_i has maximal logical semantic information relative to $\{\varphi\} \cup \varDelta$. If there is more than one such i then more features will have to be considered. This corresponds to a human reasoner seeking more clues about the classification. Features will be considered in order corresponding to their predicate ranking in the second filtering step. In the runs reported, if this procedure did not break the tie, then the first rule encountered would be given higher priority. More sophisticated tie breaking could be implemented, eg. picking the most probable category, where probability is assessed from the set $T_{\varphi, \phi}$ $R_\varphi(M)$.

Table 1: Average fractional misclassification rates

	Notes about runs	Mushroom (2 categories)	Cleveland Heart (5 categories)	German Credit (2 categories)
Cognitive classifier	**20 training observations, 5 runs**	**0.08**	**0.47**	**0.34**
CART	20 training observations unless otherwise stated, 5 runs	0.17	0.66 0.47 (100 training observations)	0.38
NeuroShell	20 training observations, 5 runs	0.19	0.53	0.36
1 - Probability of most common class	Calculated on full data set; see text	0.48	0.46	0.30
C4.5	Trained on 200 for Mushrooms, 500 for Heart and Credit, average of 50 runs	0.01	0.48	0.29

Results

The data sets used in initial testing of the cognitively-inspired classifier are from the UCI Repository of Machine Learning Databases (Blake, Keogh, & Merz 1998). These results are presented as indicative of performance, and not as a rigorous comparison between classifiers which are designed to operate in different conditions (Salzberg, 1997). Of the UCI data sets, the Mushroom set was chosen because conventional techniques perform very well on it, whereas the German credit is moderately difficult and the Cleveland Heart produces high fractional error rates.

All data sets were converted to categorical, with any field taking more than 20 values converted to 5 values by simple linear transformation between the minimum and maximum. Five runs were used on each set. Twenty training and 100 test samples were randomly selected for each run. Other runs were done to ensure that 100 tests were sufficient for asymptotic error rates to have been achieved. The recall parameter for the cognitive classifier was fixed so that all 20 training samples were considered, and the focus parameter was fixed to focus on 5 attributes out of the available 13 (Heart) to 24 (German credit). These settings were designed to be cognitively realistic; no other parameter settings were investigated and so there has been no tuning to suit these data sets.

The new classifier was tested against a binary recursive partitioning tree building method, and a neural net. CART was selected as the decision tree builder in part because of its good handling of missing data (Steinberg and Colla 1995). A Probabilistic Neural Network implemented in NeuroShell2 package was selected because of its performance on sparse data sets (Burrascano 1991). Missing data were replaced by average field values when required by these classifiers. For CART, training data had to be enlarged in some of the Heart runs to ensure all categories had at least one representative.

As well, C4.5 error rates are reported, taken from Table 2 of Cameron-Jones and Richards. These rates are for classifiers trained on sets of between 200 and 500 items, so can be taken as representative of good classifier performance on typical machine learning data sets. (Note the Mushroom training set is still smaller than in most experiments reported in the literature -- the classification accuracy is also less than the almost-perfect scores achievable when 8000 or so records are used). One minus the probability of the most common class is the misclassification rate that would be achieved if a "dumb" decision maker always chose the most common category. These probabilities (which were reported by Cameron-Jones) are calculated over the full data sets, and so represent prior information unavailable to the frugal reasoner who only has 20 observations to hand.

Convergence characteristics depend heavily on the characteristics of the data set. On a set like the German Credit in which there are only 2 classes and the attributes do not explain the categorisations well, the cognitive classifier can perform adequately (though not as well as the "dumb" decision maker picking the most common class) even on 5 training/recall samples. Performance improves steadily with size of the recall set. When a recall set pegged to 20 exemplars could be selected from a larger set of exemplars in "long term memory", then improvement was only marginal for this type of data set. On very small training sets, CART will not build a tree, in which case the default is to become a "dumb" decision maker -- on a difficult dataset like German credit this means CART actually improves its performance, as measured by misclassification rate, over its performance when more training data are available.

In contrast, on databases like the UCI dermatology whose 34 attributes can explain all the six classes, having more exemplars in long term memory allows the cognitive classifier to perform better when recalling the most similar 20 exemplars to an observation than it can when it has only limited experience.

Discussion and further work

We have described and implemented a classifier that is frugal in a number of senses. Firstly, it builds a new but simple classifier for each observation, which is frugal behaviour for one-off classification tasks, or for classification using unstable data when the overhead of building a classifier is not justified. Our classifier is also frugal in the sense that it requires little training data to provide reasonable results. It is also frugal in the processing sense that it uses elementary filters to reduce the data. It is frugal in that it uses only a very small data set after the filters are applied. And finally, it is frugal in having few free parameters.

We showed that this classifier performed surprisingly well both on the sort of data sets for which it was designed, and for cleaner data. Thus, on a training set of 20 examples chosen at random from some of the standard UCI machine learning data sets, the frugal classifier outperforms some standard classifiers, and actually has performance comparable with classifiers trained on hundreds of training samples.

It is important to note that the UCI data sets were used to give a comparative feel for the performance of the new classifier, and should not be taken as suggesting that it is "just-another-classifier" in an already crowded field. We reiterate that our classifier is unique in being designed to cope with small training sets.

The classifier needs to be extensively tested on three different types of data. Firstly, it needs to be tested against the sort of data for which it is designed, to ensure that results are accurate enough to be useable in actual applications. Secondly, it needs to be comprehensively comparatively

tested on the standard machine learning data sets, to gauge its performance as an all-round classifier. Thirdly, it needs to be tested on more complex data that include first order formulae.

When dealing with larger data sets, a design decision arises as to whether the decision maker should be modelled as retaining a perfect memory of all cases in long term memory. If not, and it is assumed that the decision maker retains the most recently experienced samples in memory, then the classifier will be able to cope with change but may be locally sensitive. If memory retains only the first samples encountered, then the classifier may have anchored on the past and may not be able to cope with change. A sensible and cognitively-supported scheme would be for the decision maker to retain a library of "good" exemplars for each category. This may affect base rate estimations.

Developments of the algorithm include modelling the formation of rules from exemplars, and using weights to focus attention on some attributes. Attributes encode stimuli in quite different ways, and Krushke (1996) suggested humans go further in treating different categories differently, encoding typical features for some categories, and distinguishing features for others. Treating all attributes equally, as our algorithm has done, is not cognitively supported. Alternative possibilities to having the system learn weights through training are to investigate differential encoding or, more generally, to allow users to weight features for their applications (eg. Minka & Picard 1997).

Other research underway is examining the impact on classification performance of some of the more complicating parts of the algorithm, such as anchoring.

References

Aisbett, J. and Gibbon, G. 1999. A practical measure of the information in a logical theory *Journal of Experimental and Theoretical AI.* 11 (1): +1-17.

Blachman, N. 1968. A mathematical theory of communication, *IEEE Transactions on Information Theory* IT-14: 27-31.

Blake, C., Keogh, E. and Merz, C. 1998. *UCI Repository of machine learning databases* Irvine, CA: Uni of California, Dept Information & Comp. Sc. http://www.ics.uci.edu/~mlearn/MLRepository.html

Burrascano, P. 1991. Learning Vector Quantization for the Probabilistic Neural Network. *IEEE Transactions on Neural Networks* 2: 458-461.

Cosmides, L. and Tooby, J. 1996. Are humans good intuitive statisticians after all? *Cognition* 58: 1-73.

Dietterich, T. 1997. Machine learning research. *AI Magazine.* 18: 97-136.

Cameron-Jones, M. and Richards, L. 1998. Repechage bootstrap aggregating for misclassification cost reduction. In *Proceedings of the 5th Pacific Rim Conference on Artificial Intelligence,* ed. H-Y Lee and H. Motoda, *Lecture Notes in Artificial Intelligence* 1531 1-11.: Springer.

Erickson, M. and Kruschke, J. 1998. Rules and exemplars in category learning. *Journal of Experimental Psychology: General* 127(2): 107-140.

Garb, H. 1994. Cognitive heuristics and biases in personality assessment. In Heath, L., Tindale, L, Edwards, J. et al (ed.) *Applications of heuristics and biases to social issues,* Plenum Press.

Hogarth, R. 1980. *Judgement and Choice,* John Wiley and Sons.

Gigerenzer, G. and Goldstein, D. 1996. Reasoning the fast and frugal way: Models of bounded rationality. *Psychological Review* 103 (4): 650-669.

Gigerenzer, G. and Hoffrage, U. 1995. How to improve Bayesian reasoning without instruction: frequency formats. *Psychological Review* 102 (4): 684-704.

Havens, W. 1997. Extending dynamic backtracking for distributed constraint satisfaction problems. In, *Proc 10th Aust. Joint Conf. on Artificial Intelligence, AI'97,* ed. A. Sattar, *Lecture Notes in Artificial Intelligence* 1342. 37-46.: Springer.

Heit, E. 1998. Influences of prior knowledge on selective weighting of category members. *Journal of Experimental Psychology: Learning, Memory and Cognition* 24(3): 712-731.

Jonides, J. and Jones, C. 199. Direct coding of frequency of occurrence. *Journal of Experimental Psychology: Learning, Memory and Cognition* 18(2): 368-378.

Kleindorfer, P., Kunreuther, H. and Schoemaker, P. 1993. *Decision Sciences: An Integrative Perspective.:* Cambridge University Press.

Kalish, M. and Kruschke, J. 1997. Decision boundaries in one dimensional categorization. *Journal of Experimental Psychology: Learning, Memory and Cognition* 23(6) :1362-1377.

Kruschke, J. 1996. Base rates in category learning. *Journal of Experimental Psychology: Learning, Memory and Cognition* 22(1): 3-26.

Lassaline, M. 1996. Structural alignments in induction and similarity. *Journal of Experimental Psychology: Learning, Memory and Cognition* 22(3): 754-770.

Levin, D. 1996. Classifying faces by race: the structure of face categories. *Journal of Experimental Psychology: Learning, Memory and Cognition* 22(6): 1364-1382.

Lozinskii, E. 1994. Information and evidence in logic systems. *Journal of Experimental and Theoretical Artificial Intelligence* 6: 163-193.

McKinley, S. and Nosofsky, R. 1996. Selective attention and the formation of linear decision boundaries. *Journal of Experimental Psychology: Human perception and performance.* 22(2): 294-317.

Miller, G. 1956. The magical number seven plus or minus two: some limits on our capacity for processing information. *Psychological Review* 101: 343-352 (1994) (reprinted from *Psychological Review* 63: 81-97).

Minka, T. and Picard, R. 1997. Interactive learning with a 'society of models'. *Pattern Recognition* 30 (4): 565-581.

Pulford, B. and Colman, A. 1996. Overconfidence, base rates and outcome positivity/negativity of predicted events *British J. of Psychology* 87(3): 431-447.

Salzberg, S. 1997. On Comparing Classifiers: Pitfalls to avoid and a recommended approach. *Data Mining and Knowledge Discovery* 1: 317-327.

Shanks, D. 1997. Representation of categories and concepts in memory. In *Cognitive models of memory. Studies in cognition.* Ed. Conway, M. et al. The MIT Press. Cambridge :111-146.

Shepherd, R. and Chang, J. 1961. Stimulus generalization in the learning of classifications. *Journal of Experimental Psychology* 65: 94-102.

Smith, E. Patalano, A. and Jonides, J. 1998. Alternative strategies of categorization. *Cognition* 65(2-3):167-196.

Spies, M. 1995. Uncertainty and Decision Making. In *Contributions to Decision Making* ed. Caverni, J., Bar-Hillel, M. et al, North Holland 51-83.

Steinberg, D. and Colla, P. 1995. CART: Tree-structured non-parametric data analysis. San Diego: Salford Systems.

What are contentful mental states?
Dretske's theory of mental content viewed in the light of
robot learning and planning algorithms

Paul Cohen

Department of Computer Science, Lederle GRC, University of Massachusetts, Amherst MA 01003
Phone: 413 545 3638; fax: 413 545 1249

Mary Litch

Department of Philosophy, University of Alabama, 414A Humanities Building, Birmingham, AL 35294-1260
Phone: 205-934-8907; fax: 205-975-6639

Abstract

One concern of philosophy of mind is how sensorimotor agents such as human infants can develop contentful mental states. This paper discusses Fred Dretske's theory of mental content in the context of results from our work with mobile robots. We argue that Dretske's theory, while attractive in many ways, relies on a distinction between kinds of representations that cannot be practically maintained when the subject of one's study is robotic agents. In addition, Dretske fails to distinguish classes of representations that carry different kinds of mental content. We conclude with directions for a theory of mental content that maintains the strengths of Dretske's theory.

Introduction

An empirical philosophy of mind might tackle the question, "How do sensorimotor agents develop contentful mental states," by building a sensorimotor agent and, constrained by certain ground rules, trying to have it develop contentful mental states. Our sensorimotor agent is a Pioneer 1 mobile robot, which roams around our lab and records its experiences through roughly forty sensors, controlled by a remote computer via radio modem. The ground rules for the project are designed to counteract the tendency in Good Old Fashioned AI to build systems that do exactly what *we* want them to do: First, while prior or innate structure is necessary, it should be minimized, and the robot should learn most of what it knows. Only when learning proves intractable will we consider adding some prior structure to facilitate the learning. Second, the learning should be unsupervised. Specifically, our learning algorithms either require no training signal, or the signal is

endogenous to the robot (e.g., a pain sensor). We will not argue that what the robot learns is completely independent of us, but we do strive to have the robot learn what the environment affords, rather than what we want it to learn.

Constrained by these ground rules, the robot has learned quite a lot. We will argue in this paper that the robot's mental states are representational and contentful. This conclusion presents some difficulties for an account of content ascription due to the philosopher Fred Dretske [4]. One difficulty is that an essential distinction in Dretske's theory between two kinds of representation is not practical; the authorship of mental states, on which Dretske's distinction depends, is ambiguous in learning robots, as Dennett has noted [3]. Second, and more importantly, the class of representations that figures in Dretske's theory of content ascription includes many subclasses, some more "contentful" than others.

The Robot and Some of What It Learns

The Pioneer 1 robot has two independent drive wheels, a trailing caster, a two degree of freedom gripper, and roughly forty sensors including five forward-pointing sonars, two side-pointing sonars, a rudimentary vision system, bump and stall sensors, and sensors that report the state of the gripper. The robot is controlled by a remote computer, connected by radio modem.

The robot has learned numerous contingencies [5,7,8,9,12,13,14], including dependencies between its actions, the world state, and changes in the world state. More accurately, several algorithms have learned these contingencies by processing data gathered by the robot as it roams around our laboratory. In this section we will focus on one learning method, *clustering by dynamics*, and a primitive ontology of actions that it learned without supervision.

The robot's state is polled every 100msec., so a vector of 40 sensed values is collected ten times each second. These vectors are ordered by time to yield a multivariate time series. Figure 1 shows four seconds of data from just four of the Pioneer's forty sensed values. Given a little practice, one can see that this short time series represents (in a sense we will explain later) the robot moving past an object. Prior to moving, the robot establishes a coordinate frame with an x axis perpendicular to its heading and a y axis parallel to its heading. As it begins to move, the robot measures its location in this coordinate frame. Note that the ROBOT-X line is almost constant. This means that the robot did not change its location on a line perpendicular to its heading, that is, it did not change its heading, during its move. In contrast, the ROBOT-Y line increases, indicating that the robot does increase its distance along a line parallel to its original heading. Note especially the VIS-A-X and VIS-A-Y lines, which represent the horizontal and vertical locations, respectively, of the centroid of a patch of light on the robot's "retina," a CCD camera. VIS-A-X decreases, meaning that the object drifts to the left on the retina, while VIS-A-Y increases, meaning the object moves toward the top of the retina. Simultaneously, both series jump to constant values. These values are returned by the vision system when nothing is in the field of view. In sum, the four-variable time series in Figure 1 represents the robot moving in a straight line past an object on its left, which is visible for roughly 1.8 seconds and then disappears from the visual field.

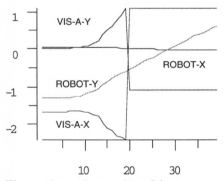

Figure 1. A time series of four sensors that represents the robot moving past an object on its left.

Every time series that corresponds to moving past an object has qualitatively the same structure as the one in Figure 1, namely, ROBOT-Y increases; VIS-A-Y increases to a maximum then takes a constant value; and VIS-A-X either increases or decreases to a maximum or minimum depending on whether the object is on the robot's left or right, then takes a constant value. ROBOT-X might change or not, depending on whether the robot changes its heading or not.

It follows that if we had a statistical technique to group the

robot's experiences by the characteristic patterns in time series, then this technique would in effect learn a taxonomy of the robot's experiences. *Clustering by dynamics* is such a technique. The version we describe here was developed by Tim Oates [7], similar methods are described in [5,8,9]. First, one divides a long time series into segments, each of which represents an *episode* such as moving toward an object, avoiding an object, crashing into an object, and so on. Episode boundaries can be inserted by humans or by a simple algorithm that looks for simultaneous changes in multiple state variables. Obviously we prefer the latter technique (and apply it in [14]) because it minimizes human involvement in the learning process; however, for the experiment described here, episode boundaries were marked by us. We did *not* label the episodes in any way. Second, a dynamic time warping algorithm compares every pair of episodes and returns a number that represents the degree of similarity of the time series in the pair. Dynamic time warping is a technique for "morphing" one multivariate time series into another by stretching and compressing the horizontal (temporal) axis of one series relative to the other [11]. If two multivariate series are very similar, relatively little stretching and compressing is required to warp one series into the other. A number that indicates the amount of stretching and compressing is thus a proxy for the similarity of two series. Third, having found this similarity number for the series that correspond to every pair of episodes, it is straightforward to cluster episodes by their similarity. Agglomerative clustering is a method to group episodes by similarity such that the within-cluster similarity among episodes is high and the between-cluster similarity is low. Fourth, another algorithm finds the "central member" of each cluster, which we call the cluster *prototype* following Rosch [10].

In a recent experiment, this procedure produced prototypes corresponding to passing an object on the left, passing an object on the right, driving toward an object, bumping into an object, and backing away from an object [7].

We claim that these prototypes were learned largely without supervision and constitute a primitive ontology of activities – the robot learned some of the things it can do. What supervision or help did we provide? We wrote the programs that controlled the robot and made it do things. We divided the time series into episodes (although this can be done automatically). We limited the number of variables that the dynamic time warping code had to deal with, as it cannot efficiently handle multivariate series of forty state variables. We did not label the episodes to tell the learning algorithm which clusters of activities it should consider. In fact, the only guidance we provided to the formation of clusters was a threshold statistic for adding an episode to a cluster. To reiterate, we did not anticipate, hope for, or otherwise coerce the algorithms to learn *particular* clusters and prototypes. Thus we claim that the robot's ontology of activities is its own.

Recently we have been trying to "close the loop" and have the robot learn enough about the preconditions and effects of its actions that it can plan to accomplish a goal. For instance, suppose the robot wants to drive the state of the bump sensor from low to high (i.e., it wants to bump into something); what should it do?[1] [12,13] discusses how the robot learns models of single actions from its prototypes. But planning is more than just executing single actions. Planning means reasoning about the effects of sequences of actions to achieve a goal state. To plan, the robot needs to transform prototypes into planning operators that specify the preconditions and effects of actions. Actually, prototypes already specify the effects of actions because they are multivariate time series, and the effects of actions are just the values of state variables over time. The tricky thing is to learn preconditions. First, each episode is labeled with the cluster to which it belongs. Next, the first 1000 msec. time series of each state variable in each episode is replaced by its mean value. These are the "initial conditions," the average values of state variables at the beginning (i.e., the first 1000 msec.) of each episode. Initial conditions are not the same as preconditions. To qualify as a precondition in an episode, an initial condition must at least make good predictions about how the episode will unfold. That is, an initial condition cannot be a precondition for a prototype if it is uncorrelated with that prototype across episodes. We have a batch of episodes, and each is labeled with its cluster membership, and each has a list of initial conditions, so it is a simple matter to run these data through a decision tree induction algorithm to find those initial conditions that best predict the cluster membership of the episodes. Since each cluster is represented by exactly one prototype, these predictive initial conditions are interpreted as preconditions for the prototypes.

Representational States in the Robot

We claim that our robot possesses contentful mental states. More precisely, we claim that, after the learning process, our robot possesses perceptually-based beliefs (a sub-type of mental states). This section is concerned with arguing for that thesis. Recall that the last stage of the learning process involves transforming the prototypes into planning operators that specify the preconditions and effects of actions. A single set of preconditions (one set for each prototype) is the vector of average sensor values that accurately predicts the future series of sensor values when a particular operator is applied. After learning, the robot will perform the operation specified by a prototype whenever both (i) its most recent time series of sensor state values matches the set of preconditions for that prototype,

and (ii) it currently has a want that is satisfied by an effect of the operator. We shall henceforth use the term "preconditions satisfier" (abbreviated "PS") to refer to the data structure encoding the time series of sensor state values, *when that time series matches any of the sets of learned preconditions*. (This term is applicable to the sensor state data structure only when a match occurs.)

Note that a preconditions satisfier has several interesting properties. First, PSs are caused by things going on in the environment external to the robot. (This causal relation is indirect and is mediated by the analog to digital converter associated with each sensor.) Second, a PS, when instantiated, causes the robot to act in a way that is appropriate, given the robot's other mental states (in particular, given the robot's wants). ("Appropriate" here means "tends to bring about satisfaction of a want".) A third property of PSs to note is that they are doubly the result of learning. We (i.e., the designers of the robot's controller) do not stipulate which sensor time series states are the preconditions for actions, nor do we preordain which set of preconditions will ultimately be associated with which action. (Indeed, the action types are themselves the result of learning.) Both the actual preconditions and the causal role played by the PSs are determined during the learning process. Notice that the above-mentioned properties are nothing other than the properties associated with perceptually-based beliefs in general: (a) they are caused by something external to the individual, (b) they cause the individual to act in appropriate ways, given the individual's other mental states, and (c) they are the result of learning in the individual's past. (Note that properties (a) and (b) are just the functionalist interpretation of perceptually-based beliefs.) Therefore, we feel justified in saying that PSs are perceptually-based beliefs. Some philosophers of mind [6] have added an additional condition: the web of beliefs and desires must attain some critical level of complexity; thus, punctate minds (e.g., minds containing only one belief) are impossible. We reject this complexity condition. Our reason is simple: the model of a cognitive agent that we have uppermost is not an adult human (for whom the complexity condition is appropriate), but an infant. We are trying to understand how mental content can be bootstrapped, given a small primitive set of wants and action types. A major goal of our project is to show how this bootstrapping is possible with limited innate structure. Thus, our rejection of the complexity condition is justified.

Some may object to our argument that PSs are perceptually-based beliefs as follows: we set the terms (by providing the definition of "perceptually-based belief"), so it should come as no surprise that PSs are perceptually-based beliefs. A more legitimate approach would be for us to have used some independent theory of mental states and to have argued that, *according to that analysis*, PSs are mental states. So, let's begin again.

---

[1] The robot's "wants" are implemented by a trivial algorithm that selects a sensor and tries to change the sensor's current value. Obviously, most human wants are more sophisticated, yet we think our simple algorithm is a primitive model of exploratory motor behavior in infants.

We adopt the analysis provided by Dretske in *Explaining Behavior* [4]. In that work, he provides and motivates a taxonomy of representational states and argues that mental states are one subclass within that taxonomy (a subclass which he names "Type III learned representational states"). The taxonomy is part of a larger project that includes an analysis of mental content in naturalistic terms and a defense of the view that mental content has an explanatory role to play in the behavior of humans and other minded individuals. Space considerations prevent us from a review of the wider project – all we shall focus on here is the claim that PSs are Type III learned representational states (henceforth, "Type III states"). Dretske sets out very clear criteria for being a Type III state. (We first give the criteria in Dretske's terminology, then unpack them in subsequent discussion.) In order to fit the bill for Type III status, PSs must: *indicate* some external condition, have the *function* of indicating that condition, and have this function assigned as the result of a *learning* process. According to Dretske, one physical state *indicates* some external condition when the first state is a state in a larger system, and the larger system goes into that state when and only when the external condition happens. So, the physical states of a standard thermometer (in particular, the level of mercury) indicate the ambient temperature. Likewise, the states of the data structure encoding the time series of sensor state values indicate certain states of affairs involving the position of the robot relative to objects in the world. Indicators can acquire the *function* of indicating in one of two ways according to Dretske, either by having an outside agent stipulate what an indicator indicates, or as a result of learning. If the function of an indicator is assigned by an exogenous agent, the indicator is not a Type III representation – Dretske calls it a representation of Type II – and it doesn't qualify as a contentful mental state. Only learned indicator functions – Type III representations – qualify.

We shall argue that PSs acquire their indicator functions through learning; although, as we discuss in the next section, there are problems in applying the learning criterion from Drestke's theory to our robot. PSs in the post-learning robot cause the robot to take specific actions to satisfy its wants. PSs have been given this control duty because of what they indicate about the state of the world (namely, that the state of the world is such that execution of these actions is likely to bring about the desired result). The specific control duty assigned to a PS is determined by a learning process. – namely, by the learning algorithm that runs on top of the controller. Thus, PSs are Type III states. Attaching the above argument to Dretske's overall theory, we reach our ultimate conclusion: PSs are mental states.

Difficulties with Dretske

In the above argument, we showed that PSs are Type III states; however, there were a couple of places where the fit wasn't exact (i.e., where the distinctions made within Dretske's theory didn't exactly match the distinctions we want to make in describing the actual robot). The first point of mismatch involves Dretske's understanding of the sort of learning necessary to achieve Type III status. We are certainly not the first to question this aspect of Dretske's theory [1,2,3]; however, our take on the issue differs from that taken by others and is based, not on "philosophical" concerns, but on concerns relating to the application of the theory to a concrete system.

We have tried to avoid "reverse engineering" the robot or the robot's environment so as to coerce the end product we are looking for. (The charge of "reverse engineering" arises in both the traditional AI and connectionist approach; the "tweaking" of network parameters that goes on in connectionist research is not qualitatively difference from the "reverse engineering" in traditional AI learning systems.) Even though we have minimized task-specific innate structure, we cannot avoid playing a significant role in the design of the robot's control algorithms and learning algorithms. That said, does our role invalidate the learning achieved by the robot, such that it is not really a Type III representational system? If so, we must ask which if any choices we are allowed to make and still claim Type III status for the robot's representations. If the answer is "none," then according to Dretske's theory our robot will never have contentful mental states; but if the answer is "some," then we face the impossible task of teasing apart the design choices that do and do not prevent our robot's mental states from being contentful.

To illustrate, although we didn't mention this earlier, the prototypes for moving toward and past objects were learned from trials that we set up. We varied the placement of objects relative to the robot and instructed the robot to move. Even so, we had no idea whether the robot's learning algorithm would produce prototypes, we did not anticipate the prototypes it produced, and we were pleasantly surprised that the prototypes made sense to us. So who is the author of the prototypes? Dretske might take a hard line and say that the robot did not develop its prototypes all by itself, so they are not Type III representations, but then he would also have to rule out concepts in a curriculum learned by human schoolchildren. In fact, curricular concepts are even more suspect than our robot's prototypes, because teachers intend their students to believe something while our placement of objects around the robot was not intended to "teach" the robot any particular prototype. On the other hand, if our contribution to what the robot learned does not disqualify its prototypes as Type III representations, then what other help are we allowed to provide? Suppose we classify prototypes as good and bad, and make the robot learn our classification rule. The fact that a learning algorithm does the work of inserting the rule into the robot's knowledge hardly qualifies the rule as a Type III representation, because the rule is entirely conventional and could just as well have been inserted by a programmer – it is *our* rule. We must also consider "in-between" cases like those in reinforcement learning, where a system learns *our* rule by seeking to maximize a reinforcement signal that may well be endogenous; for example, when I reward a child for saying "please," she undoubtedly learns, mediated by her unique reinforcement function, but she is learning *my* rule. In short, the fact that a system learns *p* does not mean that *p* is not conventional, nor does the fact that someone helps a system to learn *p* mean *p* is conventional. Dretske wishes to distinguish types of representations based on whether they are learned, but as he points out himself, learning is not well-defined. Dennett [3] accuses Dretske of wanting "do it yourself understanding," in which the authorship of concepts belongs entirely to the individual. Among our robots, at least, there are no such individuals and they have no such concepts. The distinction between Type II representations, in which the functions of indicators are assigned, and Type III representations, in which the functions are learned, is not practical.

Even if it were a practical distinction, we find that not all kinds of Type III representations are equally contentful. At a minimum, contentful means "being about something," so when you think of a good bottle of wine, your mental state has content by merit of "being about" the wine. We have learned that the robot's mental states can be in several different relations to the world. Consider again the sensory prototype illustrated in Figure 1. This prototype is "about" passing an object on the left, as it is evoked when the robot starts to pass an object on the left and it makes accurate predictions about the robot's sensory experience during this activity. The prototype in Figure 1 *represents* the robot passing an object on the left (and as a learned prototype, it qualifies as a Type III representation in Dretske's taxonomy) but what does it represent, exactly, what is its *content*? Suppose we told the robot, "Turn to the object on your left," would it understand? No, because although the prototype represents passing an object on the left, it does not *denote* the object, the robot, or the spatial relationships between them. The object, the robot and the spatial relationship between them are not part of the content of the robot's prototype. Prototypes represent the *sensory* experience of activities, they do not denote the roles of participants in the activities. If our robot had prototypes that denote the roles of participants in its activities, these prototypes would be more contentful than the robot's sensory prototypes, though both would be equally Type III representations.

Toward an Explanation of Mental Content

Perhaps there is a better way to explain the content of mental states than Dretske's theory. The problem of naturalizing content – explaining how mental states come to be about something – is not completely solved unless one can explain how we come to have representations that denote the roles of participants in activities, not just simple

sensory prototypes. Dretske's taxonomy does not differentiate these types of representation, so his theory cannot naturalize content. We agree with Dretske that learning is an important component of a theory of content, but we disagree with Dretske's use of learning as a criterion for whether mental states are genuinely contentful. The content of a state – what it is about, what reasoning it supports – is orthogonal to whether the state is learned. But Dretske is forced to make learning a criterion for genuine content to *divorce* mental states from any possible causes of those states exogenous to the learner. After all, if mental states are caused by something else, then Dretske hasn't explained them until he has explained their cause. Learning serves Dretske as an insulator of mental states from other causes. Yet the fact remains that states can be contentful even if they aren't learned – the only problem is that their content isn't explained. Rather than making learning a criterion for *whether* states have content, we think it should be part of the explanation of *how* states have content. In particular, a theory of the content of mental states would explain how humans make the transition from sensorimotor representations very much like our robot's sensory prototypes, to representations of the roles of participants in activities – representations that support classification of things by their roles, and thus the development of ontologies, and support mental activities that depend on representations of roles, such as language.

References

1. Davidson, D. 1987. Knowing One's Own Mind. *Proceedings and Addresses of the American Philosophical Association*, pp. 441-458.
2. Dennett, D. 1991. Ways of Establishing Harmony in B. McLaughlin's (editor) *Dretske and His Critics*, Basil Blackwell. Cambridge, MA. 1991.
3. Dennett, D. 1992. Do-It-Yourself Understanding. Reprinted in D. Dennett's *Brainchildren*. MIT Press. Cambridge, MA. 1998.
4. Dretske, F. 1988. *Explaining Behavior*. MIT Press. Cambridge, MA.
5. Firoiu, Laura and Paul R. Cohen, 1999. Abstracting from Robot Sensor Data using Hidden Markov Models. To appear at The Sixteenth International Conference on Machine Learning.
6. Fodor, J. and LePore, E. (editors) 1992. *Holism: A Shopper's Guide*. Basil Blackwell. Cambridge, MA.
7. Oates, Tim, Matthew D. Schmill and Paul R. Cohen. 1999. Identifying Qualitatively Different Experiences: Experiments with a Mobile Robot. To appear at The Sixteenth International Joint Conference on Artificial Intelligence.
8. Rosenstein, M. and Cohen, P. 1998a. Concepts from time series. In *Proceedings of the Fifteenth National Conference on Artificial Intelligence*. AAAI Press, pp. 739-745.
9. Rosenstein, Michael T. and Paul R. Cohen. 1999.

Continuous Categories for a Mobile Robot. To be presented at The Sixteenth National Conference on Artificial Intelligence.

10. E. Rosch and C. B. Mervis. Family resemblances: Studies in the internal structure of categories. Cognitive Psychology, 7:573--605, 1975.

11. David Sankoff and Joseph B. Kruskal (Eds.) Time Warps, String Edits, and Macromolecules: Theory and Practice of Sequence Comparisons. Addison-Wesley. Reading, MA. 1983

12. Schmill, Matthew D, Tim Oates and Paul R. Cohen. 1998. Learned Models for Continuous Planning. Presented as a poster at Uncertainty '99: The Seventh Internatinal Workshop on Artificial Intelligence and Statistics.

13. Schmill, Matthew D., Michael T. Rosenstein, Paul R. Cohen, and Paul Utgoff. 1998. Learning What is Relevant to the Effects of Actions for a Mobile Robot.© Copyright, 1998 ACM, Inc. In Proceedings of the Second International Conference on Autonomous Agents. Pp. 247-253

14. Sebastiani, Paola, Marco Ramoni, Paul R. Cohen, John Warwick and James Davis. 1999. Discovering Dynamics using Bayesian Clustering. Submitted to The Third Symposium on Intelligent Data Analysis.

Student-Sensitive Multimodal Explanation Generation for 3D Learning Environments*

Brent H. Daniel
Multimedia Laboratory
Department of Computer Science
North Carolina State University
Raleigh, NC 27695-8206

William H. Bares
Center for Advanced Computer Studies
University of Southwestern Louisiana
PO Box 44330
Lafayette, LA 70504-4330

Charles B. Callaway
Multimedia Laboratory
Department of Computer Science
North Carolina State University
Raleigh, NC 27695-8206

James C. Lester
Multimedia Laboratory
Department of Computer Science
North Carolina State University
Raleigh, NC 27695-8206

Abstract

Intelligent multimedia systems hold great promise for knowledge-based learning environments. Because of recent advances in our understanding of how to dynamically generate multimodal explanations and the rapid growth in the performance of 3D graphics technologies, it is becoming feasible to create multimodal explanation generators that operate in realtime. Perhaps most compelling about these developments is the prospect of enabling generators to create explanations that are customized to the ongoing "dialogue" in which they occur. To address these issues, we have developed a student-sensitive multimodal explanation generation framework that exploits a discourse history to automatically create explanations whose content, cinematography, and accompanying natural language utterances are customized to the dialogue context. By these means, they create integrative explanations that actively promote knowledge integration. This framework has been implemented in CINESPEAK, a student-sensitive multimodal explanation generator.

Introduction

Intelligent multimedia systems hold great promise for knowledge-based learning environments. Recent years have witnessed significant strides in techniques for automatically creating 2D graphics (Green *et al.* 1998; McKeown *et al.* 1992; Mittal *et al.* 1995; Wahlster *et al.* 1993), constructing static 3D illustrations (Seligmann & Feiner 1993), and generating 3D animations (Bares & Lester 1997; Butz 1997; Christianson *et al.* 1996; Karp & Feiner 1993; Seligmann & Feiner 1993; Towns, Callaway, & Lester 1998). Because of the central role that communication plays in learning, as graphics capabilities grow in sophistication, knowledge-based learning environments will significantly benefit from full-scale multimodal explanation generation.

Because of recent advances in our understanding of how to dynamically generate multimodal explanations and the rapid growth in the performance of 3D graphics technologies, it is becoming feasible to create multimodal explanation generators that operate in realtime with the compute power available in classrooms. Students will soon be able to pose questions to 3D learning environments depicting complex physical systems such as biological organisms or electro-mechanical devices. These environments will be able to dynamically create explanations by selecting content, constructing rhetorical structures, synthesizing animations, planning cinematic organizations, and generating natural language. As a result, students in the not-too-distant future may be able to interactively explore the physical systems found in science and engineering disciplines in a manner almost unimaginable a decade ago.

Perhaps most compelling about these developments is the prospect of enabling students to have interactions that are customized to the ongoing "dialogue" in which they participate. Multimodal explanation systems for learning environments should be able to dynamically create explanations whose content, rhetorical structure, cinematic organization, and natural language are highly sensitive to the multimodal discourse in which they are constructed. However, previous models of multimodal explanation generation have not focused on taking multimodal discourse context into account.

To address these problems, we propose the *multimodal discourse generation* framework for automatically creating customized explanations whose animation and natural language are tailored to the discourse

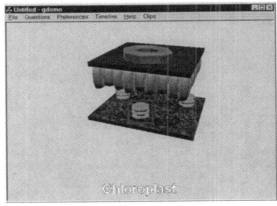 

(a) Shot of the chloroplast   (b) Food sugars traveling down the phloem

Figure 1: The CineSpeak multimodal generator in the PlantWorld learning environment

in which they occur. In particular, this framework is designed to produce *integrative multimodal explanations* whose content and form are optimized for enabling students to integrate new knowledge into their current knowledge of the domain. By exploiting a discourse history of recently generated multimodal explanations and employing integrative multimodal explanation planning strategies, the framework dynamically produces extended animations whose content, cinematography, and accompanying natural language utterances are customized to the context in which they are generated. It has been implemented in CineSpeak, a student-sensitive multimodal explanation system consisting of a media-independent explanation planner, a visuo-linguistic mediator, a 3D animation planner, and a realtime natural language generator with a speech synthesizer. CineSpeak has been used in conjunction with PlantWorld (Figure 1), a prototype 3D learning environment for the domain of botany, to generate realtime multimodal explanations.

Integrative Multimodal Explanations

The context in which multimodal explanation generators for learning environments will operate consists of a complex matrix of knowledge activated by student-system exchanges. Multimodal explanation systems should therefore exploit this context to assist students in incorporating new knowledge into their existing set of beliefs about the domain. In their landmark work on reading comprehension, Adams and Bruce set forth rhetorical requirements for authors who wish to clearly communicate with their readers (Adams & Bruce 1982).

The task of constructing an effective linguistic message consists of (1) correctly guessing what sorts of related knowledge the intended readers already have, (2) producing expressions that will evoke appropriate subsets of that knowledge, and (3) presenting those expressions in a way that will induce readers to interrelate the evoked knowledge into a structure that most nearly captures the meaning intended. (Adams & Bruce 1982)

Analogously, multimodal explanation systems should construct *integrative* explanations whose content, rhetorical structure, cinematography, and natural language promote knowledge integration. They should follow what have been termed *epistemological gradients*, which are "relations between the to-be-communicated and whatever guesses are available about the hearer's knowledge state" (Suthers 1993). Computationalizing such integrative desiderata entails providing solutions to each of the following problems:

- *Integrative Content and Structure:* The knowledge selected for presentation must not be determined in a vacuum but rather must take into account the discourse in which it will be presented (Moore 1995).

- *Integrative Animation Synthesis:* The visual elements of animations must be selected so that students can make visual connections between the imagery associated with currently understood concepts and new ones. Optimizing for knowledge integration can be significantly aided by showing new objects/processes in the physical context of familiar ones and by transitioning from known to new concepts.

- *Integrative Natural Language Generation:* Each of the traditional tasks of generating natural language, e.g., sentence planning and surface generation, must be performed in such a manner that the conceptual relations between familiar concepts and new concepts are communicated verbally.

Planning Customized Explanations

Generating integrative multimodal explanations hinges on dynamically performing each of the tasks above in a manner that takes into account the student's evolving

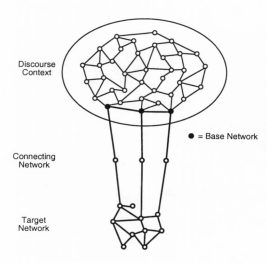

Figure 2: Integrative Explanation

interests and knowledge of the domain. To do so, explanation systems must be able to (1) recognize opportunities in the discourse for generating integrative explanations and (2) construct explanations' content and organization (including rhetorical, visual, and linguistic structure) in such a manner that they provide multiple links in multiple modalities from familiar concepts to new concepts. We formalize this notion of multimodal integrative explanations in a graph-theoretic manner. This framework defines three networks of relevant concepts and relations for integrative multimodal explanation generation (Figure 2). The *target* network is the set of concepts and relations that an explanation generator seeks to communicate to respond to the student's question. The *base* network is the set of concepts and relations that model what the student already understands and are relevant in some way to the target. The *connecting* network is the set of concepts and relations that relate the target to the base.

Identifying Target and Base Networks

The integrative framework identifies the target and base networks in different ways. Employing traditional content determination techniques, e.g., (Moore 1995; Suthers 1993), target networks are selected based on the the student's question type and the concept of interest. To illustrate, when requested to explain a process, the explanation system inspects the knowledge base to obtain the `location`, principle `actors`, and `sub-events` of the specified process. In contrast to target networks, which are determined by "context-insensitive" strategies, base networks must be cognizant of the ongoing discourse and students' interests. This knowledge is provided by two knowledge sources:

- **Multimodal Discourse History:** The explanation system will ultimately construct explanation trees whose leaves are annotated with media realization specifications (animation and/or natural language) for each proposition to be communicated. To track

the ongoing explanation session, it maintains the sequence of trees for the past n explanations it has generated. This provides a rich, structured representation of (1) concepts the student has expressed interest in, (2) the communication strategies that have been employed to explain these concepts, and (3) the order in which the explanation session has unfolded.

- **Conceptual Centrality Specification:** The explanation system also maintains a *centrality concept* that indicates which concept the student would most benefit from new knowledge being "integrated into." For example, a high school student studying a curricular unit on food production in the domain of botanical anatomy and physiology might wish to have new information related to photosynthesis.

Creating Connecting Networks

For a given concept in the target network, the explanation system must obtain the concepts in the connecting and base networks that are appropriate for the student's current knowledge state. Typically, for a concept in the target network, there are a plethora of connections to other concepts. Moreover, many subsets of concepts in a knowledge base may be known to a given student at a particular juncture in a learning session. Hence, there may be many connections between concepts in the target network and concepts that are familiar to the student. Presenting arbitrary connections between new concepts and familiar concepts would result in confusing explanations that meander aimlessly. To combat this, the explanation system finds the connecting network by searching for the following categories of connections between (1) concepts T in the target network and *historical* concepts H in the base network or (2) concepts T in the target network and central concepts C in the base network.

- **Base Super-Structure**
  - *Triggering Connection:* Some H or C is a super-structure of some concept T.
  - *Integrative Visual/verbal Specifications:* ((Show H/C), (Say H/C super-structural-relationship T)).
  - *Sequencing:* Integrative $\rightarrow$ Target
  - *Example:* To generate an explanation of xylem, the system will note that the tree, a superstructure, has recently been discussed. It will therefore show the tree and say that the xylem is part of the tree.

- **Base Sub-Structure**
  - *Triggering Connection:* Some H or C is a substructure of some concept T.
  - *Integrative Visual/verbal Specifications:* ((Show T), (Say H/C sub-structural-relationship T)).
  - *Sequencing:* Integrative $\rightarrow$ Target
  - *Example:* To generate an explanation of a leaf, the system will note that the stomata, a part of the the leaf, is of central interest to the student. It

will therefore show the leaf and say that the leaf contains the stomata.

- **Base Categorical**
  - *Triggering Connection:* Either some H has the same superstructure as T, or some C has the same superstructure as T.
  - *Integrative Visual/verbal Specifications:* ((Show super-structure H/C T), (Say H/C categorical-relationship T)).
  - *Sequencing:* Integrative → Target
  - *Example:* To generate an explanation of a chloroplast, the system will note that the stomata, which is also a part of the leaf, has recently been discussed. It therefore shows the leaf and then says, "Like the stomata, the chloroplasts are located in the leaf."

- **Recent Pre-Temporal**
  - *Triggering Connection:* H and T are involved in the same process and the role of T in the process occurs immediately before the role of H in the process.
  - *Integrative Visual/verbal Specifications:* ((Show (Role-Of T wrt P)) (Say Temporal-Relation (Role-Of T wrt P) (Role-Of H wrt P))), where P is the process involved in the roles of H and T.
  - *Sequencing:* Target → Integrative
  - *Example:* To generate an explanation of chloroplasts, if the system has recently explained the role of phloem, it will first explain the basics of the role chloroplasts perform and then, to preserve appropriate temporal ordering, turn to the integrative knowledge. The latter will be communicated by showing the role of the chloroplasts and verbally explaining that the role of phloem (food sugar distribution) occurs directly after the role of the chloroplast (food sugar production) by generating the sentence, "After the chloroplasts produce food sugars, the food sugars are distributed by the phloem."

- **Recent Post-Temporal**
  - *Triggering Connection:* H and T are involved in the same process and the role of T in the process occurs immediately after the role of H in the process.
  - *Integrative Visual/verbal Specifications:* ((Show (Role-Of T wrt P)) (Say Temporal-Relation (Role-Of T wrt P) (Role-Of H wrt P))), where P is the process involved in the roles of H and T.
  - *Sequencing:* Integrative → Target
  - *Example:* To generate an explanation of xylem, if the system has recently explained the role of the chloroplast, it will show the role of the xylem and verbally explain that the role of the xylem (water and mineral transport) occurs directly before the role of the chloroplast (food sugar synthesis)

by generating the sentence, "Before the chloroplast can produce food sugars, water and minerals must enter the chloroplast from the xylem."

- **Recurring Target**
  - *Triggering Connection:* H and T are identical (H was discussed initially in low detail.)
  - *Integrative Visual/verbal Specifications:* ((Show T) (Say T :higher-detail))
  - *Sequencing:* Increased detail.
  - *Example:* If the chloroplast was recently discussed and the student asks about it again, the system will generate a more detailed explanation that describes more specific layers in the process structure. In this case, it will include animated behaviors and utterances communicating the details of glucose production while relating them to the previous explanation, including narration such as, "As you saw earlier, chloroplasts produce food sugars for the plant."

- **Central Super-Process**
  - *Triggering Connection:* C is a super-process of T, i.e., T is a "step" of C.
  - *Integrative Visual/verbal Specifications:* ((Show (location C)) (Say Super-Process-Relationship C T))
  - *Sequencing:* Integrative → Target
  - *Example:* If the student (or the learning environment) has noted that photosynthesis is currently of central interest to the student and the student asks about the light reactions, the system will show the location of photosynthesis (the leaf) and say that the light reactions are a step of photosynthesis.

- **Central Sub-Process**
  - *Triggering Connection:* C is a sub-process of T, i.e., C is one of the "steps" of T.
  - *Integrative Visual/verbal Specifications:* ((Show (location T)) (Say Sub-Process-Relationship C T))
  - *Sequencing:* Integrative → Target
  - *Example:* If the learning environment asserts that in the current unit on the Calvin Cycle, new information should be explained in relation to the dark reactions, when the student asks about photosynthesis, the explanation system shows the location of photosynthesis (the leaf) while it explains that the dark reactions are a step of photosynthesis.

Student-Sensitive Multimodal Explanation Architecture

In the multimodal discourse generation framework (Figure 3), explanation construction begins when a student poses a question about a particular concept in the domain. For example, while perusing a 3D visualization of the leaf, the student might become curious about the chloroplast and ask about its physiological role. When

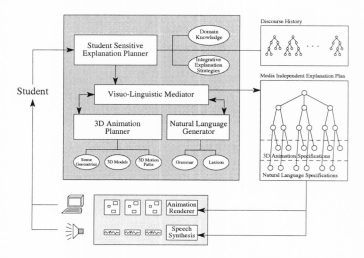

Figure 3: The student-sensitive multimodal explanation architecture

she poses a question, the student-sensitive explanation generator operates in three interleaved phases to construct an integrative multimodal explanation:

1. **Integrative Explanation Planning:** By inspecting the discourse context, which is represented by the discourse history and the current centrality concept, it selects the student-sensitive content, i.e., the propositions in the target, base, and connecting networks, and rhetorically organizes them.

2. **Integrative Animation Planning:** To visually communicate the selected integrative content, the animation planner directs the student's attention along Suthers' "epistemological gradients" by (a) selecting relevant 3D models, (b) selecting relevant 3D motion paths, and (c) issuing camera directives to the virtual camera.

3. **Integrative Natural Language Generation:** To verbally communicate the selected integrative content, the natural language generator (a) sends the propositions to a sentence planner that creates full sentential specifications, and (b) sends the resulting sentential specifications to a unification-based systemic-functional surface generator.

To construct explanation plans, the system consults the discourse history, extracts relevant propositions from the knowledge base, and organizes them into an explanation tree. The discourse history is represented as a sequence of the n previously generated explanation plans; centrality concepts simply specify a particular concept. The planner first selects the concepts for the target network as described above. Next, it consults the discourse history and the current centrality concept. Together, these are used to identify candidate concepts for the base network. It then inspects the triggering connections to identify the most useful connective relations between concepts in the discourse history and concepts in the target network. The net result of this

phase is a media-independent explanation plan.

Finally, the 3D animation specifications and the natural language specifications of the explanation plans are passed to the media realization engines. The 3D animation specifications are passed to the animation renderer (Bares & Lester 1997; Towns, Callaway, & Lester 1998), while the linguistic specifications are passed to the natural language generator's sentence planner (Callaway & Lester 1995) and surface generator (Elhadad 1992). The text constructed by the latter is passed to a speech synthesizer. Visualizations and speech are synchronized in an incremental fashion and presented in atomic presentation units as dictated by the structure of the initial media-independent plan. Both are presented in realtime within the 3D learning environment. The discourse history is then updated to include the newly constructed explanation plan. Both the animation planner and the natural language generation system are products of long-term research in our laboratory. Below we briefly overview their operation.

Integrative Animation Planning

Given a set of `show` communicative goals in an explanation plan, the animation planner must construct an animation that visually presents the propositions in the target, base, and connecting networks. Planning animated explanations is a synthetic process of selecting and organizing 3D models, the 3D behaviors they will exhibit, and the camera planning directives that will be used to plan the movements of the virtual camera that films the action. All of these decisions must take into account the content and organization decisions made during the integrative explanation planning phase:

1. *3D Model and Behavior Selection:* Given a query which specifies a question type, e.g., (`explain-role ?T`), and a target concept, e.g., `stomata`, the animation planner uses the ontological indices of the knowledge base to retrieve the relevant *concept suite*. Indicating the most relevant visual elements, a concept suite is defined by a sequence of concepts, each of which is either an object, e.g., `Chloroplast` or a process, e.g., `Photosynthesis`, annotated with their associated 3D models and 3D behaviors. 3D models indicate the geometric properties of the objects, and also contain annotations indicating texture maps. Behavior models specify the motion paths that objects can follow in a scene relative to other objects.

2. *Designing Focus Effects:* Enabling a student to focus her attention on the most salient characteristics of the new knowledge presented in an animation is essential for pedagogical reasons. This central feature of integrative explanations is provided by the animation planner's ability to introduce two categories of *visual markers*: (1) it highlights objects depicting new concepts, and (2) it introduces onscreen labels to indicate the nomenclature.

3. *Cinematography Planning:* Through judicious camera shot selection, explanations can direct students'

attention to the most important aspects of a scene. For example, while high and far shots present more information, close-up shots are useful for centering on a single subject (Mascelli 1965). To provide visual context, it initially selects far shots for unfamiliar objects, unfamiliar processes, and tracking moving objects. It selects close-ups for presenting the details of familiar objects.

Integrative Natural Language Generation

To ensure that natural language expressions clearly communicate the integrative content specified for the narration, the natural language generator uses specifications issued in the **say** nodes of explanation plans. The propositions selected for generation include concepts and relations in the target, base, and connecting networks, which are then used to construct sentential specifications by the sentence planner (Callaway & Lester 1995). Because lexical choice has been performed by this point, sentential specifications include all of the open class lexemes and their linguistic roles. After the sentence planner constructs functional descriptions, it passes them to a unification-based surface generator (Elhadad 1992) to yield the surface strings, which are then passed to a speech synthesizer. and delivered in synchronization with the actions of the associated 3D visualization.

The Implemented Generator

The student-sensitive multimodal discourse generation framework has been implemented in CINESPEAK, a generator that constructs integrative explanations with 3D animations and speech.[1] Given queries about physical phenomena, CINESPEAK consults the discourse history, invokes a library of integrative multimodal explanation strategies, and creates animated explanations with accompanying natural language. The integrative multimodal explanation strategies, the media-independent explanation planner, and visuo-linguistic mediator were implemented in the CLIPS production system. The 3D animation planner was implemented in C++. The natural language generator was implemented in Harlequin Lispworks and employs the FUF surface generator and SURGE (Elhadad 1992), a comprehensive unification-based English grammar. The animation renderer was created with the OpenGL rendering library, and the speech synthesis module employs the Microsoft speech synthesizer. CINESPEAK operates in realtime.[2]

---

[1]CINESPEAK is implemented in a networked computing environment consisting of two PentiumPro 300s communicating via TCP/IP socket protocols over an Ethernet. It's various modules consists of more than 60,000 lines of Lisp, CLIPS, and C++.

[2]Typical explanations last approximately 30 seconds. To construct a typical explanation, CINESPEAK (1) exhibits an initial latency of less than 1 second, (2) conducts animation planning, rendering, natural language generation, and speech synthesis in parallel with explanation delivery,

The PLANTWORLD Testbed

To investigate CINESPEAK's behavior, it has been incorporated into PLANTWORLD, a prototype 3D learning environment for the domain of botanical anatomy and physiology. This domain is challenging to explanation generators because it requires well constructed scenes and camera planning, as well as clear natural language expressions, to communicate the complexities of plants' structure and function. Its knowledge base represents objects (such as stomata, chloroplasts, and xylem), and resources (such as oxygen and water molecules), all of which have corresponding 3D models. It represents processes (such as photosynthesis, water transport, and oxygen efflux), all of which have associated 3D motion paths. Students interact with CINESPEAK by posing questions with a menu-based question construction interface.

To illustrate CINESPEAK's behavior, suppose a student initially sets the centrality concept to be **light reactions** and then asks, "What is the role of photosynthesis?" Because photosynthesis is a superprocess of the light reactions, it begins by noting this relationship. It opens with a shot of the chloroplast and explains, "The photosynthetic light reactions are a step of photosynthesis." It then cuts to an interior shot of the leaf and says, "Photosynthesis produces food sugars for the plant." Next, the student asks about the role of the dark reactions. The system determines that the dark reactions are related to the light reactions by category, i.e., they are siblings, so the explanation begins by noting that both are steps in photosynthesis. With a shot of the chloroplast in full view, the system says, "Like the photosynthetic light reactions, the dark reactions are part of photosynthesis." It then cuts to a shot of a sugar molecule exiting from the chloroplast and says, "During the dark reactions, carbon dioxide and hydrogen are converted into glucose by the chloroplast."

Next, the student indicates that she no longer wishes the light reactions to be a central concept. She then asks what the role of the chloroplast is, and the system constructs a low detail explanation that shows it and briefly overviews its role. She then asks again what the role of the chloroplast is, and the system responds with a detailed explanation as shown in (Figure 1). First, it opens with a shot of the chloroplast and says, "Let's take a look at the chloroplast in more detail. As you saw earlier, the chloroplasts produce food sugars for the plant. Glucose production occurs within the chloroplast." Cutting to a shot of water entering the chloroplast, it says, "Water in the chloroplast is converted into hydrogen and oxygen. Carbon dioxide, hydrogen, minerals and sunlight are converted into food sugars." It transitions then to a shot of a sugar molecule traveling through the phloem and explains, "Food sugars are used throughout the plant for energy."

---

(3) completes all media independent planning and animation planning in under 1 second, and (4) completes all natural language generation activities after roughly 8 seconds.

Finally, the student asks about the role of the xylem. Because the xylem has a role (`xylem-distribution`) that occurs immediately before a role of the chloroplast (`oxygen-production`), the system constructs an explanation that makes the connection between the two processes, and then gives the role of the xylem. With a shot of minerals traveling up the xylem, it says, "Before the chloroplasts can produce food sugars, water and minerals must enter the chloroplast from xylem." It concludes by explaining, "Water and minerals are carried by xylem to the leaf."

Conclusions and Future Work

Dynamically generating rich multimodal explanations holds significant promise for learning environments. Because of the communicative power of engaging 3D animations coupled with well-crafted natural language, multimodal explanations offer the potential of facilitating effective learning experiences. By exploiting a discourse history to determine the content, rhetorical organization, cinematic structure, and spoken natural language narration in a manner that makes explicit connections between new and familiar concepts, multimodal student-sensitive explanation generators can construct explanations that actively promote knowledge integration.

This work is designed for rapid deployment into the classroom. Hence, a critical next step in its evolution is to empirically investigate the efficacy of the integrative explanation generation methods in full-scale learning environments with actual students. The prototype systems on which this work is based have all been subjected to such studies and revealed the strong need for the customization capabilities provided by the strategies proposed here. While we have experimented extensively with the integrative strategies in the implemented prototype learning environment, studying them under controlled conditions in the classroom is sure to yield significant insights. We will be exploring these issues in our future research.

Acknowledgements

The authors gratefully acknowledge the following individuals' assistance: Stuart Towns, for his work on early versions of CINESPEAK; Bradford Mott, for his assistance in preparing the manuscript and for comments on earlier drafts of this paper; and Dr. Loren Winters of the North Carolina School of Science and Mathematics for collaboration on PHYSVIZ, the second learning environment in which components of CINESPEAK are being studied. Support for this work was provided by a grant from the NSF (Career Award IRI-9701503), the IntelliMedia Initiative of North Carolina State University, the William R. Kenan Institute for Engineering, Technology and Science, and a gift from Novell, Inc.

References

Adams, M., and Bruce, B. 1982. Background knowledge and reading comprehension. In Langer, J. A., and Smith-Burke, M. T., eds., *Reader Meets Author / Bridging the Gap: A Psycholinguistic and Sociolinguistic Perspective.* Newark, DE: International Reading Association. 2–25.

Bares, W., and Lester, J. 1997. Realtime generation of customized 3D animated explanations for knowledge-based learning environments. In *Proceedings of the Fourteenth National Conference on Artificial Intelligence,* 347–354.

Butz, A. 1997. Anymation with CATHI. In *Proceedings of the Ninth Innovative Applications of Artificial Intelligence Conference,* 957–62.

Callaway, C., and Lester, J. 1995. Robust natural language generation from large-scale knowledge bases. In *Proceedings of the Fourth Bar-Ilan Symposium on the Foundations of Artificial Intelligence,* 96–105.

Christianson, D.; Anderson, S.; He, L.-W.; Salesin, D.; Weld, D.; and Cohen, M. 1996. Declarative camera control for automatic cinematography. In *Proceedings of the Thirteenth National Conference on Artificial Intelligence,* 148–155.

Elhadad, M. 1992. *Using Argumentation to Control Lexical Choice: A Functional Unification Implementation.* Ph.D. Dissertation, Columbia University.

Green, N.; Kerpedjiev, S.; Roth, S.; Carenini, G.; and Moore, J. 1998. Generating visual arguments: a media-independent approach. In *Proceedings of the AAAI-98 Workshop on Representations for Multi-modal Human-Computer Interaction.*

Karp, P., and Feiner, S. 1993. Automated presentation planning of animation using task decomposition with heuristic reasoning. In *Proceedings of Graphics Interface '93,* 118–127.

Mascelli, J. 1965. *The Five C's of Cinematography.* Cine/Grafic Publications, Hollywood.

McKeown, K. R.; Feiner, S. K.; Robin, J.; Seligmann, D.; and Tanenblatt, M. 1992. Generating cross-references for multimedia explanation. In *Proceedings of the Tenth National Conference on Artificial Intelligence,* 9–15.

Mittal, V.; Roth, S.; Moore, J. D.; Mattis, J.; and Carenini, G. 1995. Generating explanatory captions for information graphics. In *Proceedings of the International Joint Conference on Artificial Intelligence,* 1276–1283.

Moore, J. D. 1995. *Participating in Explanatory Dialogues.* MIT Press.

Seligmann, D. D., and Feiner, S. 1993. Supporting interactivity in automated 3D illustrations. In *Proceedings of Intelligent User Interfaces '93,* 37–44.

Suthers, D. D. 1993. *An Analysis of Explanation and Its Implications for the Design of Explanation Planners.* Ph.D. Dissertation, University of MA.

Towns, S.; Callaway, C.; and Lester, J. 1998. Generating coordinated natural language and 3D animations for complex spatial explanations. In *Proceedings of the Fifteenth National Conference on Artificial Intelligence,* 112–119.

Wahlster, W.; André, E.; Finkler, W.; Profitlich, H.-J.; and Rist, T. 1993. Plan-based integration of natural language and graphics generation. *Artificial Intelligence* 63:387–427.

Moving Right Along: A Computational Model of Metaphoric Reasoning about Events

Srinivas Narayanan
snarayan@icsi.berkeley.edu
International Computer Science Institute and University of California, Berkeley
1947 Center Street Suite 600, Berkeley CA 94704 USA

Abstract

This paper describes the results of an implemented computational model that cashes out the belief that reasoning about abstract events and actions relies on metaphoric projections of embodied primitives. The specific task addressed is the interpretation of simple causal narratives taken from newspaper articles in the domains of Politics and Economics. When presented with a surface-parsed version of these narratives as input, the system described is able to generate commonsense inferences consistent with the input.

Introduction

Work in Cognitive Semantics (Talmy 1987; Johnson 1987; Langacker 1987; Lakoff 1994) suggests that the structure of abstract actions (such as states, causes, purposes, means) are characterized cognitively in terms of *image schemas* which are *schematized* recurring patterns from the embodied domains of force, motion, and space. However, so far the work in Cognitive Semantics has lacked a computational model for such theories, and consequently these ideas cannot currently be used in natural language understanding or problem solving systems.

We have implemented a computational model that suggests that a key reason for using words and phrases from the domain of spatial motion is that it allows for the deep semantics of causal narratives to be *dynamic* and arise from a *continuous interaction* between input and memory. Since knowledge of moving around or manipulating objects is essential for survival, it has to be highly compiled and readily accessible knowledge. Representations meeting these criteria must be context sensitive and allow changing input context to dramatically affect the correlation between input and memory and thereby the set of possible expectations, goals, and inferences. Speakers are able to felicitously exploit this context-sensitivity in specifying important information about abstract actions and plans that take place in complex, uncertain and dynamically changing environments. This paper reports on the results of applying our model to metaphoric reasoning about events in narrative understanding. (Narayanan, 1999) shows how the basic architecture provides cognitively motivated solutions to well

known problems in representing and reasoning about actions.

Motivation

Consider the following narrative about India's march toward liberalized economics.[1]

Example 1 In 1991, in response to World Bank pressure, India boldly set out on a path of liberalization. The government loosened its strangle-hold on business, and removed obstacles to international trade. While great strides were made in the first few years, the Government is currently stumbling in its efforts to implement the liberalization plan. ∎

In Example 1, note that institutions are conceptualized as causal agents, causes as forces, actions as motions, and goals as states in a spatial terrain. These mappings are part of a crosslinguistic metaphor system called the Event Structure Metaphor (Lakoff 1994) which is the general name for projections from the concrete experiential domain of forces and spatial motion (source domain) to the abstract domain of causes, actions, and events (target domain). Following from the fact that institutions are conceptualized as agents, specific causal events are attributed as effected by or affecting the institution; such as apply pressure, respond to pressure, loosen strangle-hold, remove obstacles, stride, and stumble. Commonsense inferences that are required for interpreting the article often *rely* on our experience of force dynamics and motion in space. For instance, the inference that stumbling *leads to* falling can felicitously be transferred to the abstract domain of economic policy through a conventionalized metaphor that *falling* ↦ *failure*. This enables the interpreter to conclude that the government is likely to fail in its liberalization plan. Many other inferences rely on the source domain (consider the implications of strangle-hold).

While source domain inferences contribute significantly to interpretation, they are asymmetric, context-sensitive and may be overridden by target domain knowl-

---

[1] While this story appeared in the New York Times in 1995, the reader is invited to convince herself of the ubiquity of the mappings discussed (albeit at the risk of severely impaired newspaper reading pleasure).

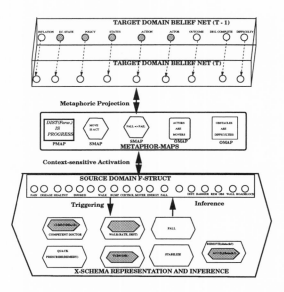

Figure 1: Metaphors capture systematic correlations between features of different domains.

edge. For instance, stumble ⇒ fall (and the corresponding metaphoric inference of plan failure) is only a default causal inference that is made in the absence of information to the contrary. Such an inference may be non-monotonically disabled in the face of target domain evidence that the liberalization plan is succeeding.

In summary, we note that a large proportion of commonplace descriptions of abstract events seem to project embodied, familiar, concepts onto more abstract domains such as economics and politics. This allows non-experts to comprehend and reason about such abstract policies and actions in terms of more familiar and universal embodied concepts. The fact that the metaphoric inferences are context-sensitive, immediate, and defeasible set up fairly strong representational requirements for a metaphor interpretation system.

Model

The specific hypothesis pursued here is that the meaning of motion and manipulation terms is grounded in patterns generated by our sensory and motor systems as we interact in the world. Systematic metaphors project these features onto abstract domains such as Economics enabling linguistic devices to use motion terms to describe abstract actions and processes. Figure 1 shows the basic computational architecture of the implemented system. As shown in the figure the system has three main components, namely the **source domain**, the **target domain** and the **metaphor maps**. These components are discussed below.

The source domain

We hypothesize that the causal theory of the familiar and essential domain of embodied motion is encoded as

highly accessible *compiled* knowledge used both for action monitoring and failure recovery and for fast, parallel, real-time reflexive inference in interpretation. We refer to this fine-grained, executing model of events as **x-schemas**. The model is based on results in sensory-motor control (Pearson 1993) and linguistic research in Cognitive Semantics. Formally, the computational model is an extension to Stochastic Petri Nets (Murata 1989). A Petri net is a bipartite graph containing *places* (drawn as circles) and *transitions* (rectangles). Places hold *tokens* and represent predicates about the world state or internal state. Transitions are the active component. When all of the places pointing into a transition contain an adequate number of tokens (usually 1) the transition is *enabled* and may *fire*, removing its input tokens and depositing a new set of tokens in its output places. The most relevant features of Petri nets for our purposes are their ability to model events and states in a distributed system and cleanly capture sequentiality, concurrency and event-based asynchronous control. Our extensions to the basic Petri net formalism include *typed arcs, hierarchical control, durative transitions, parameterization, typed (individual) tokens* and *stochasticity*. For this paper, the crucial fact about our representation is that it is *active* with a well specified real-time execution semantics that can be used for acting and reacting in dynamic environments or for context sensitive simulative inference in language understanding.

The central idea behind our model is that the reader interpreting a phrase that corresponds to a motion term is in fact performing a mental simulation of the entailed event in the current context. The basic idea is simple. We assume that people can execute x-schemas with respect to structures that are not linked to the body, the here and the now. In this case, x-schema actions are not carried out directly, but instead trigger simulations of what they would do in the imagined situation. We model the physical world as other x-schemas that have i/o links to the x-schema representing the planned action.

In our implementation, source domain structure is encoded as connected x-schemas. Our model of the source domain is a dynamic system based on inter-x-schema *activation, inhibition* and *interruption*. In the simulation framework, whenever an executing x-schema makes a control transition, it potentially modifies state, leading to asynchronous and parallel triggering or inhibition of other x-schemas. The notion of state as a graph marking is inherently distributed over the network, so the working memory of an x-schema-based inference system is distributed over the entire set of x-schemas and source domain f-structs (see Figure 1). Of course, this is intended to model the massively parallel computation of the brain.

Figure 2 depicts a simplified x-schema model of walk-

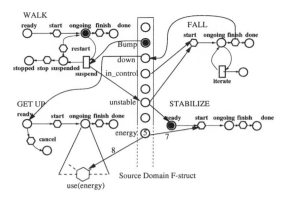

Figure 2: Source Domain is a x-schema simulation environment used for inference.

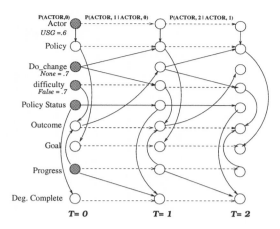

Figure 3: Target Domain is a temporally extended Belief net.

ing and reacting to obstacles. For instance, during a walk (specified by a token in the *ongoing* phase of the WALK x-schema) encountering an unanticipated **bump**, you become *unstable*. [2] This *may lead* to a FALL unless you are able to simultaneously *expend energy* and STABILIZE, in which case you may *resume* the *interrupted* walk. If you are unable to STABILIZE, and thus FALL, you will be **down** and **hurt**. In order to *start walking* again you will have to GET UP and be standing and in control again.

An important and novel aspect of our source domain representation is that the same system is able to respond to either direct sensory-motor input **or** other ways of setting the agent state (such as linguistic devices). This allows for the same mechanism to perform simulative reasoning and generate inferences from linguistic input as well as be used for high-level control and reactive planning. There is some biological evidence to support this view (Rizzolatti et al 1996; Tanji & Shima 1994) that planning, recognition and imagination share a common representational substrate.

Target domain representation

The structure of the abstract domain (the domain of international economic policies) encodes knowledge about Economic Policies. We require that our representation be capable of a) representing background knowledge (such as US is a market economy), b) modeling inherent target domain structure and constraints (high-growth may result in higher inflation), and c) be capable of computing the impact of new observations which may from direct input ("US economy is experiencing high-growth"), or from metaphoric (or other) inferences ("Economy stumbling"). Furthermore, these different sources of evidence have different degrees of believability, and the representation must provide a framework for their combination. For all these reasons, we chose to

represent the target domain as a Belief network (Jensen 1996). Belief networks are the dominant methodology for reasoning with uncertain knowledge sources. They provide a principled and coherent semantics based on probability theory, which allows us to study the joint impact of metaphoric inference, background knowledge and inherent target structure using well understood, off-the-shelf algorithms.

Our model of the target domain consists of multiple copies (up to 4) of a temporally extended Belief net (Dean & Wellman 1991), representing different time slices. The structure of the target domain for three temporal slices of the Belief network is shown in Figure 3. Within a single temporal slice, the nodes of the network correspond to economic variables which can take on different values. For instance, in Figure 1, we have a node corresponding the the economic actor which can be instantiated to be the US government, IMF, Indian Government, etc. Links within a single time slice model the probabilistic dependence between variables. For instance, there is a link between the actor variable and the policy variable, which models the fact that if we knew the actor in question (US Government) we would have a good idea of the policy (free-market economy). The strength of this belief is quantified as the conditional probability table $P(Policy|Actor)$. Links between nodes at different time slices encode the conditional probability of a variable's value at time t, given its value at $t-1$. For instance, the link $P((Actor, 1)|(Actor, 0))$ (ref. to the top of Figure 3) results in the conditional probability table (CPT) that corresponds to the probability of a specific actor being instantiated at time $t = 1$, given the value of the actor at time $t = 0$. These values are default values and are often overridden by specific assertions as we will soon see in detail in the next section. From such local conditional probability tables, BELIEF PROPAGA-

---

[2]In fact, the simulation is of finer granularity in that it is during an ongoing STEP (subschema of WALK), that the interruption occurs. This is not shown to simplify exposition.

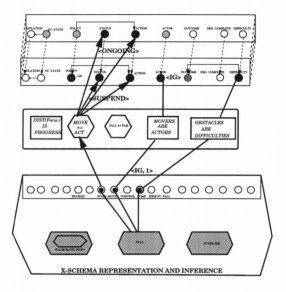

Figure 4: Metaphor maps project source f-struct values as target domain evidence on one or more slice of the target domain Belief net.

TION algorithms (Jensen 1996) compute the global posterior probabilities for the entire network propagating influences backward and forward in time.

Metaphor maps

In our model, metaphor maps connect the x-schema based representations to the belief network representing knowledge about international economics. Such maps project specific results of x-schema executions by projecting specific source domain f–struct values to the target domain by asserting new *evidence* at one or more time slices of the temporally extended Belief net. Figure 4 shows the projection of "stumbling" onto the target domain. We will return to this example in the next section.

Our model currently includes three different types of embodied maps. One type of map corresponds to **ontological** maps (Lakoff 1994) which map entities and objects between embodied and abstract domains. Such maps are called OMAPS. One central function of OMAPS is to map the fillers of various case-roles of an *event phrase* across domains. A second type of map projects *events*, *actions*, and *processes* from embodied to abstract domains. In keeping with our representation, we will call such maps Schema maps or SMAPS. An important function of SMAP projection is to **invariantly** map the *aspect* of the embodied domain event onto the target domain. A third type of map projects x-schema parameters from source to target domains. Such maps are called x-schema parameter maps (PMAPS). Examples include maps that project velocities onto the abstract domain as the rate of progress made; or distance traveled onto the abstract

domain as degree of completion of a plan.

I/O behavior

In this model, a story represents the specification of a *partial* trajectory over epistemic states. This is done by clamping some of the Belief network nodes to specific values. The remaining features are estimated using known target domain inter-feature correlations as well as from metaphoric projections from the highly compiled embodied domain knowledge (x-schemas). Metaphoric projections of x-schema executions may clamp target features to specific values (by creating new *evidence* on the target domain belief net shown in Figure 3).

Table 1 and Table 2 illustrate the I/0 behavior of the implemented system interpreting the newspaper headline *Liberalization plan stumbling*. The input to the system is a set of feature-value pairs (called "F-structs") resulting from a partial parse.

Table 1: Input is a set of F-structs

Feature	Value
Event	stumble
Domain	Ec. Policy
Ec. Policy	Liberalization
Aspect	Present-Prog

Comprehending a story corresponds to finding the set of trajectories that satisfy the constraints of the story and are consistent with the domain knowledge. This may involve *filling in* missing values or creating new evidence on the Belief network. Features with highly selective posterior distributions are likely to be present in the recall of the story.

Table 2: Output is a new set of F-structs

Feature	Value
Event	stumble
Domain	Ec. Policy
Ec. Policy	Liberalization
Aspect	Present-Prog
Context	**ongoing-plan ∧ difficulty**
Status	**suspended (.8)**
Outcome	**fail (.7)**
Goal	free-trade ∧ deregulation

The result of processing the input in Table 1 is a set of new bindings asserted in the target domain resulting in an updated posterior for other variables. This is the situation shown in Table 2. **Bold** entries correspond to cases where the change from the prior is a result of metaphoric inference. Of particular interest is the *context setting inference* which projects the embodied knowledge that stumbling occurs as a result of an obstacle while executing a step (causing an interruption to forward motion) to the target as plan difficulty (causing a temporary suspension).

Of course, many possible x-schema bindings, especially those that don't activate any conventional metaphor are invalid and thus have no impact on the agent's epistemic state (for example the source inference stumble $\Rightarrow$ losing balance). Thus the inferences that are actually made are context-sensitive and depend on the target domain and the associated set of metaphoric maps.

The resultant target network state shown in Table 2 is now a prior for processing the next input at stage $t = 2$. Background knowledge is encoded as the network state at $t = 0$. Potentially target inferences can go forward and backward in time in the estimation of the most probable explanation of the input story.

Results

Currently our embodied domain theory has about 100 linked x-schemas, while the abstract domain theory is relatively sparse with a belief net of about 20 multi-valued variables with at most 4 temporal stages. We have also encoded about 50 metaphor maps from the domains of *health* and *spatial motion*. These were developed using a database of 30 $2-3$ phrase fragments from newspaper stories all of which have been successfully interpreted by the program. All the examples in this section have been taken from our database.

X-schema parameters

Distances, *speeds*, *force-values*, *sizes* and *energy-levels* are obviously important perceptual and motor control parameters, but with PMAP projections, they become important descriptive features of events in abstract domains including impacting early parsing decisions of inferring semantic role assignments.

In our examples, we were able to use PMAPs to map size parameters like *giant steps*, *large step*, *small steps*, *great leap forward* (including the Chinese Economic Reform); speed parameters in expressions like *slow progress*, *slowed down*, *sprint*, *jog*, and *long, painful slide into recession*; rate and manner parameters in *crawl*, *leap*, *trod*, *plod*, *slog*, *lurch* and *slither*; distance related parameters in expressions like *almost there*, *long way to go*, *halfway there*, and *a little further*. Force magnitudes and durations were also routinely projected as in *grip,tear down hold back*.

Aspectual inferences

(Narayanan, 1997) previously described an x-schema based model of of *aspect* (the internal temporal structure of events) which is able to detect and model subtle interactions between grammatical devices (such as morphological modifiers like *be + V-ing* (progressive aspect)

versus *has V-ed* (perfect aspect)) and the inherent aspect of events (such as the inherent iterativity of *tap* or *rub*, or the punctuality of *cough* or *hit*). In examining our metaphor database, we found aspectual distinctions to be *invariantly projected* across domains.

In addition to the *stumbling* example described earlier, our system could interpret cases which used the *perfect* aspect to signal focus on the *consequent* state of the described event as in *have robbed, has been lurching forward, has sidestepped*. We could also nicely model several other high frequency aspectual expressions such as *start to pullout, on the verge of, still trying to climb out of recession* and metaphoric expressions of aspect such as *set out, remain stuck in recession, on-track*, and the interesting phrase *back-on-track*. In summary, almost every event description had an aspectual component, and so we believe attention to the details of the semantics of verbal aspect is essential even to interpret the simplest of event phrases and distinctions. We believe our model is unique in integrating the semantics of aspect with metaphoric interpretation.

Goals, resources

It is well known that narratives are generally about *goals* (their accomplishment, abandonment, etc.) and *resources* (their presence, absence, levels, etc.) (Wilensky 1983; Schank & Abelson 1977; Carbonell 1982). However, in our experiments, we found that embodied motion and manipulation terms may in fact be *compactly coding* for these features as well. Narratives are able to exploit the dynamic and context-sensitive nature of x-schema representations to assert changing goals and resources. Amount of *energy* usually maps to *resource* levels as in *slog, anemic, sluggish* or *bruised and bloodied*, or *stagger to their feet*. Similarly *tearing barriers* or *lightening burdens* are able to assert conditions where an impediment to goal achievement has now been removed. Compare this to the expression *go around* or *sidestep* where the strategy is one of avoidance rather than direct confrontation. Similarly *slippery slopes, slipperiest stones, slide into recessions*, get projected through SMAPS as the possible thwarting of goals due to unanticipated circumstances. *Falling* is interesting in this regard in that in all the cases where a country was described as *falling* into recession, we never saw a case in which the country's administration was directly blamed as being able to control the downturn, a fact directly projectable from the fact that falling is not controllable (an obvious and easy inference about fall). No such inference is intended or available from processing *Germany has walked into recession*.

Multiple source domains

Multiple source domains pose no problem for the system, as long as they are interpretable and coherent in the *target*. For instance, in the input *Stocks were down*, but recovered, *Stocks down* activates the *Less IS Down* metaphor, while the second input *recover* activates the *More IS Healthy* metaphor leading to the inference of increasing stocks.

Novel expressions

As (Lakoff 1994; Gibbs 1994) and other researchers point out, a variety of novel expressions in ordinary discourse as well as in poetry make use of highly conventionalized mappings such as the ones described here. In fact, the implemented system is able to interpret novel expressions which it has never seen in the context of abstract actions and plans. For example, the concrete domain meaning of *crossroads* (multiple possible paths) and the event structure metaphor maps allow the system to interpret the previously unseen expression in the domain of abstract actions as a choice point for the planner with multiple possible plan continuations.

Other examples of novel expressions (in our database) correctly interpreted by our program include *roadblocks*, *anemic recovery*, *lurching forward*, *long, painful slide*, *treading on toes*, and the beautiful *stumble over rocky relationship*.

Agent attitudes and affects

We found agent attitudes to be essential ways of encoding anticipatory conditions, motivation and determination of agents involved. We have implemented some of this in the prototype system. For instance *bold* (Example 1) encodes determination in the face of anticipated obstacles/counterforces ahead. In the current model this is directly encoded as the semantics of *bold* in the context of the embodied domain (anticipating some counterforces at future time steps). As in the case of stumbling, obstacle at the next time step gets translated to anticipated difficulty at the $t + 1$ temporal slice. Determination to keep on the path gets translated as a reduced *prior* chance of policy change. The point to note here is that the embodied term *bold* codes for possible future obstacles, and the readiness to deal with them. [3]

Communicative intent and metaphor

One of the important aspects of communication involves specifying evaluative judgments of situations to communicate speaker intentions and attitudes. We hypothesize that the cross-linguistic prevalence of the use of embodied notions of force and motion to communicate aspects of situations and events is linked to the ease with which evaluative aspects can be communicated in experiential terms. To study this phenomenon, we enhanced the target domain Belief network (see Figure 3) to include information about the interpreter's bias toward specific actors

_____
[3] Another example where linguistic devices are able to exploit the distinctions between READY and START, a fine-grained control distinction that is useful for motor control but proving quite indispensable for language.

and policies. We can now set the interpreter to be biased favorably toward a specific actor (like World Bank) or a specific policy (liberalization). This directly influences both conditional belief of some outcome variables (so a free-market biased interpreter would consider tariff reduction as a successful policy) or could result in different source domain inferences as in the example below.

With these additions, our implemented system was able to distinguish between the following sentences (second is from Example 1).

`Government deregulated business.`
`Government loosened strangle-hold on business.`

Both sentences communicate the same fact in the domain of economics, namely the the situation corresponding to business deregulation. But the source domain inference of "stranglehold" is able to assert the detrimental nature of Government control leading to the possible eventual "demise" of business.

In another example, we tested the program with the example "World Bank prescribed Structural Adjustment Program (SAP) bleeding Indian Economy" under different prior speaker attitudes toward World Bank. In the three cases, we set the prior belief of the speaker to be positive, neutral or negative with respect to the World Bank. In the positive case, the prior belief of the interpreter activates the CURE x-schema. Here, the target domain inferences is one of *ongoing therapy*. In the negative case, the prior belief of the interpreter activates the HARMER schema. where the source domain inferences is one of systemic harm and eventual death. In the neutral case, the prior of the interpreter activates the TREAT x-schema. Here, there is a conflict between CURE and MISTAKEN THERAPY, where the cure is not working.

One crucial difference in the three cases is in the positive case, the the outcome of a *cure* is asserted as succeeding for India, in the negative case the outcome of the policy is asserted as *unsuccessful* for India, while in the neutral case it is *ambiguous*. Thus in the three cases, we are able to model how changes in prior evaluation of a situation can be used to compute what the *meaning* of an utterance is. Crucially, the difference seems to be in which **source domain** schema gets invoked, and the resulting inferences. We know of no other implemented model of metaphor understanding that can reason about these phenomena.

Discussion

It is now generally accepted that metaphor interpretation requires the ability to explicitly represent the source and target domains as well as the metaphor maps themselves. Metaphoric reasoning with knowledge-rich sources and targets and explicit maps have been the primary method of choice for several implemented metaphor interpretation systems (Martin 1990; Barnden *et al.* 1994; Carbonell 1982; Indurkhya 1992; Sun 1995).

These approaches share many goals and bear some similarities with the work described here. However, there are some crucial differences as well.

First, our representation of actions and events with durations is more fine-grained than other systems we are aware of. Specifically, we believe our system to be novel in being able to model rich temporal and aspectual inferences across domains. Such fine-grained semantic distinctions are routinely exploited by metaphors found in ordinary discourse. Second, our use of a temporally extended Belief network to represent target domain knowledge allows us to uniformly combine direct linguistic input and background knowledge with results of metaphoric projections in a single normative framework. It allows us to study the evidential interaction of these different sources in interpretation, while previous efforts have focussed on isolating one or more of these components. Third, while most approaches require extra resources to process novel expressions, our approach explains why *some* novel expressions can be processed with no additional resources (consistent with psychological observations (Gibbs 1994)). Fourth, our approach is quite unique in being able to exploit **implicit** *evaluative* information and speaker *intent* which we believe is often the reason to choose embodied expressions in the first place. Finally, evidence from a recent study by Joe Grady (Grady 1997), suggests that complex metaphoric maps are composed from simple experiential correlations, consistent with the work reported here.

Conclusion

This paper outlined an implemented computational model for interpreting simple narratives such as newspaper story fragments and headlines involving political or economic causation. The central novel ideas investigated are a) a model of narrative understanding by metaphoric mapping from abstract domains to concrete and embodied domains and b) the grounding of the deep semantics of the abstract causal terms in body-based *active* models. It is somewhat interesting that even our prototype model is able to detect rather subtle differences in speaker intent and communicative goals. We believe the choice of the motion term is often a compact and efficient way to encode such information. Conversely, the unconscious choice by a speaker of an embodied term can give the hearer significant clues as to the prior belief and intent of the speaker, something that we are currently exploring.

Acknowledgements

Thanks to J. Feldman, G. Lakoff and the NTL group at UC Berkeley and ICSI.

References

Barnden, J. et al (1994). An integrated implementation of simulative, uncertain, and metaphorical reasoning about mental states. *Proceedings of the Fourth Priniciples of KR and Reasoning Conference* Bonn, Germany, 24-27 May 1994, San Mateo, CA: Morgan Kaufmann.

Carbonell, J. (1982) Metaphor Comprehension. *Strategies for Natural Language Processing*, 413–433, Lawrence Earlbaum, 1982.

Dean, Tom and Wellman, Michael, (1991). *Planning and Control.* Morgan Kaufman Series in Representation and Reasoning, 1991.

Gibbs, R. Jr. (1994). *The Poetics Of Mind.* Cambridge University Press, 1994.

Grady J. (1997). *Foundations of meaning: Primary metaphors and primary scenes.* UC Berkeley Dissertation, Dept. of Linguistics, Fall 1997.

Indurkhya, B. (1992). *Metaphor and Cognition.* Kluwer Academic Publishers.

Jensen, F. (1996). *An Introduction to Bayesian Networks.* Springer-Verlag ISBN 0-387-91502-8.

Johnson, M. (1987). *The Body In The Mind: The Bodily Basis of Meaning, Imagination, and Reason.* University Of Chicago Press, ISBN 0-226-40318-1.

Langacker, R. (1987). *Foundations of Cognitive Grammar I: Theoretical Prerequisites.* Stanford University Press, Stanford.

Lakoff, G. (1994). What is Metaphor?. *Advances in Connectionist Theory. V3 : Analogical Connections*, V3,1994.

Martin, J. (1990). *A Computational Model of Metaphor Interpretation.* Academic Press, NY, 1990.

Murata, T. (1989). Petri Nets: Properties, Analysis, and Applications. In *Proc. IEEE–89, V77, Number 4, April 1989, pp. 541-576.*

Narayanan, S. (1999). Reasoning about Actions in Narrative Understanding. *Proceedings of the IJCAI 99* (to appear) Stockholm, August 1-6, 1999.

Narayanan, S. (1997). *Knowledge-based Action Representations for Metaphor and Aspect (KARMA).* PhD thesis, Computer Science Division, EECS Department, University of California at Berkeley.

Pearson K.G. (1993). Common Principles of Motor Control in Vertebrates and Invertebrates. *Ann. Review Of Neuroscience*, 1993, 16:265-97.

Rizzolatti, et al. (1996). Premotor Cortex and the recognition of motor actions. *Cognitive Brain Research*, 3 (1996) 131-141.

Schank, R.C. & and Abelson, R.P. (1977). *Scripts, Plans, Goals, and Understanding: An inquiry into human knowledge structures.* Hillsdale, NJ:Erlbaum 1977.

Sun, R. (1995). A Microfeature Based Approach to Metaphor Interpretation. *Proceedings of the IJCAI 95.* 424-429, San Mateo, CA: Morgan Kaufmann.

Talmy, L. (1987). Force Dynamics in Language. Tech Report. Institute For Cognitive Science, UC Berkeley, 1987.

Tanji J. and Shima S. (1994). The supplementary motor area in the cerebral cortex. *Nature*, vol. 371, issue 6496, (SEP 29, 1994) : pp. 413-416.

Wilensky, R. (1983). *Planning and Natural Language Understanding.* Addison Wesley, 1983.

Delivering Hints in a Dialogue-Based Intelligent Tutoring System

Yujian Zhou[1], Reva Freedman[2], Michael Glass[1],
Joel A. Michael[3], Allen A. Rovick[3], Martha W. Evens[1]

[1]Department of CSAM	[2]LRDC #819	[3]Department of Physiology
Illinois Inst. of Technology	University of Pittsburgh	Rush Medical College
10 W. 31st Street 236–SB	3939 O'Hara Street	1750 W. Harrison Street
Chicago, IL 60616	Pittsburgh, PA 15260	Chicago, IL 60612

zhouyuj@charlie.iit.edu, freedrk+@pitt.edu, glass@steve.iit.edu,
{jmichael, arovick}@rush.edu, csevens@minna.cns.iit.edu
http://www.csam.iit.edu/~circsim

Abstract

Hinting is an important tutoring tactic in one-on-one tutoring, used when the tutor needs to respond to an unexpected answer from the student. To issue a follow-up hint that is pedagogically helpful and conversationally smooth, the tutor needs to suit the hinting strategy to the student's need while making the strategy fit the high level tutoring plan and the tutoring context. This paper describes a study of the hinting strategies in a corpus of human tutoring transcripts and the implementation of these strategies in a dialogue-based intelligent tutoring system, CIRCSIM-Tutor v. 2. We isolated a set of hinting strategies from human tutoring transcripts. We describe our analysis of these strategies and a model for choosing among them based on domain knowledge, the type of error made by the student, the focus of the tutor's question, and the conversational history. We have tested our model with two classes totaling 74 medical students. Use of this extended model of hinting increases the percentage of questions that students are able to answer for themselves rather than needing to be told.

Introduction

Hinting is a general and effective tutoring tactic in one-on-one tutoring when the student has trouble solving a problem or answering a question. In many student-oriented tutoring systems, the machine tutor will give hints when the student asks for help, e.g. Andes (Gertner et al., 1998). In this tutoring setup, the central issue of hinting is to help the student recall the related domain rules or facts that the student may have trouble with. In a system where the tutor has control over the conversation and asks the questions, hinting is also a good strategy to help the student find the expected answer when the student gives an unexpected one. But in this tutoring setup, not only the student's possible weakness but also the tutor's plan and the tutoring context are important for issuing hints. Since there may be more than one pedagogical plan for tutoring a domain concept, the hinting strategy is closely related to the tutoring method or tutoring plan, although the detailed content of each hint is closely related to the domain concept. So how to issue a follow-up hint which is helpful to the student, coordinated with the tutoring plan, and coherent in the dialogue context is an important issue in this tutoring setup.

In this paper we will address how to deliver hints by considering all of these factors in CIRCSIM-Tutor, a conversational intelligent tutoring system (ITS) which uses free-text input and output as its dialogue interface. To do so, we will first study human tutors' hinting strategies. Then we describe our attempts to implement these strategies in CIRCSIM-Tutor in order to dynamically deliver versatile hints in the tutoring dialogue.

Another purpose of this work is to find out how far the tutoring system can go and how effective it will be by depending mainly on hinting to help students find the expected answer after they have given an unexpected one. Other approaches to the problem of unexpected answers have been proposed. For example, the model used by Freedman and Evens (1996) and Kim et al. (1998) is based on schemata, and allows unlimited nested plans and plan updating during execution. This is a more sophisticated model but it cannot be implemented in the current version of CIRCSIM-Tutor, as the current planner does not support unlimited nested plans. The work described here will allow us to gain experience in hinting.

Background

The CIRCSIM-Tutor Project

CIRCSIM-Tutor is an intelligent tutoring system designed to help medical students understand the negative feedback system that controls blood pressure. CIRCSIM-Tutor tutors by having students solve problems. The system presents the student with a description of a physiological change and asks for predictions about the effect of that change on

This work was supported by the Cognitive Science Program, Office of Naval Research under Grant No. N00014-94-1-0338, to Illinois Institute of Technology. The content does not reflect the position or policy of the government and no official endorsement should be inferred.

seven important physiological parameters. Then it conducts a dialogue with the student to correct the errors in the predictions.

The current working version is a revised version of CIRCSIM-Tutor v. 2, developed in Lisp by Woo and others (Woo et al., 1991). It has seven modules: instructional planner, student modeler, input understander, text generator, screen manager, problem solver, and knowledge base. The instructional planner includes two levels of planners, a lesson planner and a discourse planner. The lesson planner generates lesson goals and decomposes them into discourse tasks. The discourse planner is responsible for controlling interactions between the tutor and the student. Most discourse tasks are executed as questions. When the student gives an unexpected answer to a question, the planner adds tasks to the agenda to complete the original goal by other means—giving the answer or giving a hint.

Earlier Work on Hints in CIRCSIM-Tutor

Hume et al. (1996) studied the use of hints by experienced tutors in the hope of formulating a strategy for using hints in an ITS. They observed that human tutors frequently use hints as a pedagogical tactic. However, the theory of hints in their framework is too broad, as they identify most tutoring moves as hints in some contexts. Furthermore, these hints were defined without reference to the structure required by the CIRCSIM-Tutor planner.

The original CIRCSIM-Tutor v. 2 produced very general hints to ask about physiological variables missed by the student. But it failed to tailor the content to the student's previous answer, as it issued only fixed hints such as "Think about the value of <the desired physiological variable>." To improve the hinting capability in CIRCSIM-Tutor, we started by adding hints, tailored to the student answer, which were given in response to a partially correct answer (this is the main situation in which the tutor gives hints in the original CIRCSIM-Tutor). This improved version was used by 24 students from Rush Medical College in April 1998. After reading the log files from this experiment, we found that the new hints were effective but there were other kinds of student answers that the system failed to respond to with follow-up hints.

For this reason we broadened the hinting ability in CIRCSIM-Tutor to include responses to other categories of student answers. This new version was used by 50 students from Rush Medical College in November 1998. We will discuss the experimental results later in this paper. This improved version, which also has a new input understander (Glass, 1999), is robust and useful enough that our expert tutors from Rush Medical College believe that it can be used without supervision by medical students as a regular part of the curriculum.

Interviewing Human Tutors

In an interview with our expert tutors they identified two rules for how they give hints:

First give evoking terms or synonyms.
Otherwise try to give an intermediate step.

These two rules indicate that human tutors are trying to help the students think actively (by giving more evocative language) and also trying to help them think along the right chain of causal relationships by giving a small step along the causal path.

These two rules cover many of the cases of the human tutors' usage of hints, but they are too general and abstract to actually implement hinting in CIRCSIM-Tutor. So we analyzed transcripts of human-to-human tutoring sessions conducted by the expert tutors in order to identify the types of hints used in different situations and identify more specific strategies that could actually be used to build an ITS.

Hinting Strategies in Human Tutoring

Hints occur in many different surface forms. To implement them in a principled and useful way in a real ITS, we need to identify the underlying principles in order to avoid just giving canned hints in each situation. So we want to isolate hinting strategies that are not dependent on specific domain facts or rules.

The following strategies are some examples of hinting strategies frequently used in our human tutoring transcripts.

Strategy: Give an Intermediate Causal Link

This is one of the rules indicated by our human tutors. It actually has three sub-rules, each related to a different tutoring plan. Suppose there are several causally related physiological variables A affects X affects B, where the tutor usually teaches the relationship between A and B, ignoring intermediate steps like X.

- If the tutor asked which variable is affected by a change in A, then mentioning the link from A to X can be an effective hint toward the answer B.
- If the tutor asked which variables cause a change in B, then mentioning the link from X to B can be an effective hint backward toward the answer A.
- If the tutor asked how A and B are related, then mentioning either of the relationships from A to X or from X to B can be a hint.

By giving hints like this, the tutor offers a small piece of information relating the variable in question to the desired answer. The pedagogical expectation is that the student will think along these lines and find the desired answer.

Strategy: Refer to an Anatomy Object

Although our tutors prefer to focus on the physiology, they

occasionally point to an anatomy object to help the student concentrate on the right part of the cardiovascular system if the student can not answer a question. This kind of hint is especially useful when the student has trouble finding the first variable affected by a physiological change. For example:

T: What is the first variable affected by the alpha agonist?
S: I don't know.
T: Where in the CV [cardiovascular] system are alpha receptors found?

Strategy: Point Out the Laws of Physics Involved

Although our domain is physiology, it is occasionally useful for the tutor to point to some physics rules to help the student visualize why the causal relation should be the way it is. For example:

T: When MAP [mean arterial pressure] increases, what will that affect?
S: (incorrect answer)
T: When MAP increases, it's harder for the ventricle to pump blood.

Strategy: Give Evoking Terms or Synonyms

While most of the time our tutors use a specific set of physiology terms in order to encourage students to use the same terms, they sometimes choose more evocative phrases. For example, in certain contexts they often use "afterload" as a synonym for "mean arterial pressure," evoking images of the pressure the heart is pumping against. This strategy is used mostly when the tutor is tutoring the causal relationship from mean arterial pressure to stroke volume after an incorrect student answer.

Strategy: Linguistic Hint

Since our human tutors use natural language (just as our tutoring system does), they sometimes give subtle linguistic hints which include very little domain information. These hints are intended to help the student to think more actively.

A typical example occurs when the tutor is expecting several parameters from the student and the student gives only some of them. The tutor may simply reply with "And?" to indicate that more is expected.

Other Strategies

The above strategies are the most frequently used. There are also some other strategies that are used infrequently or are used only in special tutoring situations. These include pointing out the function of a drug, using capital letters to indicate a core variable, giving a definition, pointing out the problem-solving context, and referring to an equation.

Implementing Hinting in CIRCSIM-Tutor

Now that we have analyzed the hinting strategies of human tutors, we will discuss our implementation of these strategies in a running intelligent tutoring system—CIRCSIM-Tutor. Although there may be some deeper cognitive reasoning behind the human tutors' hinting strategy, we do not model such reasoning in the tutoring system. First, we lack a sufficiently comprehensive cognitive theory of hinting. Second, from a practical point of view, our analysis of human tutors' hinting strategies demonstrates that we can generate precise hints without invoking such a theory. The following algorithms describe our simulation of human tutors' hinting behavior.

Factors Determining the Hinting Strategies

There are several factors that may affect the choice of a specific hint: tutoring topic, tutoring context, tutoring history, student's answer, and so on. From the interview with human tutors and the study of their tutoring transcripts we find several factors to be particularly relevant.

First, to be pedagogically useful, a hint has to be related to the tutoring topic and be useful in helping the student find the expected answer. So the tutoring topic is important.

Second, the student's answer is important since hints are intended to help the student figure out the expected answer from what he or she has already said.

Third, the specific question used by the tutor, which is a reflection of the high level tutorial plan, is important because there may be several questions available for tutoring the same concept. Different kinds of tutor questions may indicate a different conversational context or focus.

Finally, the tutoring history is also important, especially for the second or third hint in a row. The tutor needs to base further hints on earlier ones for two reasons. From a discourse point of view, it increases the coherence of the conversation. From a pedagogical point of view, it makes the tutoring logic stand out more clearly.

A Classification Model for Student Answers

We added a classification module to categorize student answers. Below are the categories that we use to classify students' answers:

1. Correct
2. Partially correct answer, i.e. some part of the answer is correct and the rest is incorrect
3. Near miss answer, which is pedagogically useful but not the desired answer (Glass, 1997)
4. "I don't know" answer
5. "Grain of truth" answer, where the student gives an incorrect answer, but also indicates a partially correct understanding of the problem (Woolf, 1984)

6. Misconception, a common confusion or piece of false knowledge about the concept being tutored
7. Other incorrect answers
8. Mixed answers, i.e. a combination of answers from other categories

These categories, which were abstracted from our analysis of human tutoring transcripts, are one of the features used to decide which hint to give. The more information the tutor can find in the student's answer, the more specific the hint can be. Although the categorization is based on the domain model, it is important to recognize that it is largely a pragmatic categorization, i.e. a correct answer is one which our human tutors do not feel the need to correct or augment.

Use of a Simple Quantitative Student Model

Hume et al. (1996) observed that human tutors maintain a rough assessment of the student's performance. They argued that when and how to give hints is based on that measurement of student performance. Although our definition of hint is narrower than theirs, we still feel that student performance is a good criterion for deciding when to deliver hints rather than giving the answer. Thus we added a student performance module to CIRCSIM-Tutor's original student model. It includes four levels of measurement: global assessment (total measurement of the student so far), procedure-level assessment (measurement for each problem the student is asked to solve), stage assessment (measurement for each of the three physiological stages in a problem), and the local assessment attached to each variable that has been tutored. The local assessment is updated after each tutoring interaction and other assessments are calculated from the local assessment. If the student's performance is too low, the tutor gives the answer instead of issuing a hint.

This assessment model is based on intuitive rules and is still being refined. From experiments with medical students, we have found that we need other history data along with the assessment of the student for deciding between giving a hint and giving the answer, especially when the student gives the same wrong answer twice in a row.

Identifying the Possible Hinting Strategies

From our analysis of human tutoring transcripts, we abstracted a set of hinting strategies, detailed below. We then built a hinting algorithm for each category of student answer. Each answer category is associated with a predefined list of strategies. Some of the algorithms are quite simple. For example, if the student gives a near miss answer, the tutor responds with a leading question that points to an intermediate link from the near miss to the correct answer. Some of the algorithms are more complex. For example, if the student's answer is incorrect, there are several strategies available. If the tutor is tutoring a causal link in the forward direction, the hinting strategies mostly prefer to give evoking terms related to the variable already mentioned or to give an intermediate link in the forward direction.

Using Heuristic Rules to Rank the Strategies

If the tutor still has several strategies to choose among, the tutor ranks the possible hints using heuristic rules which attempt to generate more specific hints first. We consider hints in the following order:

1. Hints that are specifically related to the student's answer
2. Hints involving equations
3. Hints involving evocative synonyms
4. Hints involving a related anatomical object
5. Hints that give an intermediate logical step
6. Others

Locating Appropriate Content

The result of this procedure is a list of hint types only. To decide the details of the content in a hint, the tutor searches the domain knowledge base for each of the available hinting strategies. For the first hinting strategy, it looks to see if the knowledge base has an entry for the concept currently being tutored. If the domain knowledge has an entry, then the search terminates; if not, the algorithm tries the remaining hinting strategies in sequence. If no entry is available for any of the possible strategies, the tutor gives a default hint.

To support the hinting strategies that we identified from the human tutoring sessions, we are in the process of extending our domain knowledge base with additional evocative terms, related anatomical objects, and related physics rules.

Using Templates to Deliver Hints

We use hint templates determined by the content selection algorithms discussed above to deliver the hints. For example:

> Like <the related variable in the student's answer>, the other determinant is also related to <the anatomy object>.

> But what I am asking is <definition of the tutored variable>.

> Do you remember an equation written as: <the variable been tutored> =...?

The Model in Practice

Derivation of a Hint

The following example illustrates how the machine tutor

determines the follow-up hint step by step after the student gives an unexpected answer. Suppose the recent dialogue is:

T: What determines CVP [central venous pressure]?
S: I don't know.

Here the category of the student's answer is "I don't know." If the tutor decides to give hints, the hint algorithm related to the "I don't know" answer will be evoked. Since there are several strategies available, the algorithm will first check the tutoring plan. Here it is trying to tutor a causal relation backward. So the possible hinting strategies reduce to:

- Find equations related to the dependent variable.
- Point to a feature of an anatomy object related to the dependent variable.
- Give an intermediate step backward from the dependent variable.

Using the heuristic rules above, this list is the final list after ranking the preferences. Then the tutor checks the domain knowledge base and finds that the second strategy has suitable content available. Finally the tutor will find the related hint template and deliver the hint as:

T: Remember the CVC [central venous compartment] is very compliant. So what determines CVP?

If the student still can not get the correct answer, the tutor could issue a further hint giving an intermediate step between CVC and CVP. But if the student gives a near miss answer, e.g. CBV (central blood volume) instead, the tutor could use the near miss as a basis for issuing a follow-up hint instead. That hint might be expressed as a question pointing to an intermediate link between the near miss and the desired answer:

S: How about CBV?
T: What determines CBV?

Influence of the Tutoring Question

The wording or intent of the tutor's questions is not an issue in systems where the student asks the questions. But the opposite is true in CIRCSIM-Tutor, particularly when the question indicates the direction the tutor is following along a causal link. When the tutor is teaching the relationship between A and B, different questions can address the same causal link in different directions. In response to an incorrect answer, each question might benefit from a different hint. In Dialogue 1 below, the tutor tries to teach about the link from cardiac output to central venous pressure, working backward from CVP. In Dialogue 2, the tutor works forward from CO. Although the student gives an incorrect response in both cases, the resulting hint is different.

Dialogue 1:
T: What determines CVP?
S: (Incorrect answer.)

T: Remember the CVC is very compliant. (Looks backwards from CVP to the volume of blood in the CVC.)

Dialogue 2:
T: When Cardiac Output decreased, how would that affects the value of Central Venous Pressure?
S: Decrease. (Incorrect answer.)
T: No. When CO decreases, think about what will happen to the volume of blood in the central venous compartment. (Gives a forward hint from CO to the volume of blood in the CVC.)

Influence of Tutoring History

The tutor keeps a tutoring history to avoid repeating the same hint and to make sure that the hints do not return to a causal relationship that was already tutored if there are several hints in a row.

T: What are the determinants of Stroke Volume?
S: It is RAP [right atrial pressure]. (Near miss.)
T: And what determines RAP? (Hint based on the near miss.)
S: EDP [end diastolic pressure]. (A near miss, but further from the correct answer than RAP.)
T: EDP comes from RAP. Think again, what parameter in the prediction table determines RAP? (Point out the relation between RAP and EDP, then give further hint based on RAP.)

If we did not keep a dialogue history, the tutor could ask "And what determines EDP?" In that case the tutor would be following the student's lead away from the right answer.

Sample Output

Although our model of hinting is based on a number of simple algorithms, it can generate a variety of hints that allow the students to answer for themselves rather than being told. Below is an example produced by CIRCSIM-Tutor using our model.

T: What are the determinants of Stroke Volume?
S: Heart Rate and Cardiac Output. ("Grain of truth" answer, i.e. wrong but pedagogically useful.)
T: Well, it is true that CO = SV * HR. But what I was asking is what determines how much blood is ejected from the heart each time it beats (the SV)? (Hinting strategy: give definition.)
S: Preload. (Near miss.)
T: Right. And what represents preload in the prediction table? (Hinting strategy: point to the intermediate link from the near miss. Note that the tutor gave a positive acknowledgment ("right") to the near miss, showing that there is not always a one-to-one relationship between student evaluation and the correct discourse move.)
S: Central Venous Pressure. (Correct, but still missing one determinant for the original question, so we

categorize it as a partial answer.)

T: Right. Central Venous Pressure determines SV. The other determinant of SV is neurally controlled. What is the other determinant of SV? *(Hinting strategy: point to the domain type of the missing variable.)*

S: It is Inotropic State. *(Correct.)*

T: Right. Inotropic State is the other determinant of SV. SV is determined by Central Venous Pressure and Inotropic State. *(The goal of the original question has been satisfied without telling the student the correct answer. The tutor can move to the next item on the agenda now.)*

Comparison to Related Work

There are several tutoring systems that use hints as a tutoring tactic. Andes (Gertner et al., 1998) generates individual hints. It uses a Bayesian-network based student model to tailor its follow-up hints to the student's knowledge, and delivers them by using an associated sequence of hint templates for each goal and fact in its knowledge base. The Lisp tutor (Anderson et al., 1995) also generates hints from a sequence of hint templates. It uses model tracing techniques to detect that the student is not following the correct solution path. Sherlock II (Lesgold et al., 1992) generates a paragraph after the conclusion of the tutoring session.

In CIRCSIM-Tutor, we use heuristic rules to choose a hinting strategy based on the category of the student's answer, the tutorial plan, and the tutoring history. We then decide the content by searching the domain knowledge base to instantiate the strategy. So our hints are focused on both the student's needs and the current tutorial plan. By considering the current tutorial plan, the tutor can make sure the hints are coordinated with the tutorial plan and ensure conversational coherence while at the same time tailoring the content of the hint to the student's needs.

Merrill et al. (1992) compared the effectiveness of human tutors and intelligent tutoring systems. Their study indicated that a major reason that human tutors are more effective is that they let the students do most of the work in overcoming impasses, while at the same time providing as much assistance as necessary. Although in CIRCSIM-Tutor the tutor mainly leads the students in correcting the errors they have made in the prediction table, it is also important to let the student do as much as possible. By giving follow-up hints tailored to the student's answer rather than giving the correct answer, the tutor provides necessary guidance to the student while promoting a more active style of learning.

In CIRCSIM-Tutor sometimes the student model can recognize the specific confusion of the student through its categorization of the student's answer. In that case, the hint is specifically related to the student's knowledge state. But even if the student model can not infer a deep understanding of the student's mental model, hinting is still more useful than just giving the answer for two reasons. In addition to giving the student a second chance to correct the error, the content of the hint may offer the student useful information for understanding the material.

Evaluation

An earlier version of CIRCSIM-Tutor which implemented a portion of the hinting model described above was used by 50 first-year students from Rush Medical College in November 1998. All of the students had already completed the regular lectures. They used the program for one hour. Twenty-four students worked in pairs at a computer and 26 students worked alone. We obtained a log file from each student or pair of students, giving a total of 38 log files.

The tables below describe our initial formative evaluation of this portion of the hinting model. In this experiment, CIRCSIM-Tutor asked approximately 1700 questions. In the course of tutoring 565 student errors, it generated 97 hints. Table 1 shows the effectiveness of hints for different student answer categories and Table 2 shows the effectiveness of each hinting strategy.

Category of answer	No. of hints	No. of correct answers	% of correct ans.
Partially correct	55	41	75%
Near miss	12	9	75%
Incorrect	14	14	100%
Mixed	16	14	88%

Table 1: Hints used by answer category

Category of hinting strategy	No. of hints	No. of correct ans.	% of correct ans.
Involving equations	2	2	100%
Evocative language	17	10	59%
Point to anatomical object	4	3	75%
Intermediate step	19	16	84%
Point to variable type	31	25	81%
Others	24	22	92%

Table 2: Effectiveness of hints by strategy

In evaluating this performance it must be noted that in this experiment CIRCSIM-Tutor did not have a hint to give in all situations. In particular, hints for the incorrect answer category tended to occur on questions which had only a few possible answers, such as yes/no questions. Additionally, we believe that these questions were among the easier ones. As a result these hints tended to produce good results. Hints for the near miss and partially correct answers were more likely to come from questions with a larger range of possible responses.

We have now implemented most of the possible hinting strategies for each answer category, and we hope to evaluate these hints in a later experiment. We are also looking forward to comparing the learning results between students who use the system with hints and without. Additionally, we are in the process of analyzing experimental data that will allow us to do a detailed analysis of student learning by comparing pretest and posttest results.

Another possible method for evaluating hints would be to let our human tutors compare the hints generated by CIRCSIM-Tutor to what they would like to say in the same situation. This method was used during the initial development of the system. We believe that this method of evaluation is important since the goal of this project is to simulate human tutoring behavior as closely as possible. Currently one of our expert tutors is working with the latest version of CIRCSIM-Tutor with this goal in mind.

The students were also positive about the quality of the hints and explanations (1.90 on a scale from 1= definitely YES to 5 = definitely NO, computed from the experiment survey form).

Conclusions and Future Work

In this paper we addressed how to systematically deliver pedagogically sound and conversationally coherent hints in a dialogue-based ITS, CIRCSIM-Tutor. Our strategy involved categorizing student answers, and considering both tutoring plan and dialogue history. We first studied human tutoring transcripts to identify human tutors' hinting strategies and factors that might affect their choice of a hinting strategy. We then implemented these strategies in a real tutoring system as much as possible.

During the spring semester of 1999, CIRCSIM-Tutor will be installed as a standard program at Rush Medical College to be used by any student who wants. We plan to analyze the log files to see how effective the new hints are. We will also analyze the inappropriate hints and discuss with our expert tutors how to fix them.

It is worthwhile to note that we are also planning to replace CIRCSIM-Tutor v. 2 by a completely rewritten v. 3 based on the work of Freedman and Evens (1996). That project, currently in progress, will allow us to add more complex kinds of remediation since we will be able to use nested plans and delete agenda items that have become irrelevant. We are looking forward to identifying uses for these new features. However, since the hinting algorithms described here are based on an actual corpus of tutoring transcripts, they will remain pedagogically valid and we intend to re-implement them in the new system.

Since most of the strategies isolated from the tutoring

transcripts are not related to specific domain knowledge, we also expect them to generalize to other causal domains.

References

Anderson, J., Corbett, A., Koedinger, K., and Pelletier, R. (1995). Cognitive Tutors: Lessons Learned. *Journal of the Learning Sciences* 4(2): 167–207.

Freedman, R. and Evens, M. (1996). Generating and Revising Hierarchical Multi-turn Text Plans in an ITS. *Intelligent Tutoring Systems: Third International Conference (ITS '96)*, Montreal, 632–640. (Springer-Verlag Lecture Notes in Computer Science, 1086.) Berlin: Springer.

Gertner, A., Conati, C., and VanLehn, K. (1998). Procedural Help in Andes: Generating Hints using a Bayesian Network Student Model. *Proceedings of the Fifteenth National Conference on Artificial Intelligence*, Madison, 106–111. Menlo Park: AAAI Press.

Glass, M. (1997). Some Phenomena Handled by the CIRCSIM-Tutor Version 3 Input Understander. Proceedings of the Tenth Florida Artificial Intelligence Research Symposium, Daytona Beach, 21–25.

Glass, M. (1999). Broadening Input Understanding in an Intelligent Tutoring System. Ph.D. diss., Dept. of CSAM, Illinois Institute of Technology.

Hume, G., Michael, J., Rovick, A., and Evens, M. (1996). Hinting as a Tactic in One-on-One Tutoring. *Journal of the Learning Sciences* 5(1): 32–47.

Kim, J., Freedman, R., and Evens, M. (1998). Responding to Unexpected Student Utterances in CIRCSIM-Tutor v. 3: Analysis of Transcripts. *Proceedings of the Eleventh Florida Artificial Intelligence Research Symposium (FLAIRS '98)*, Sanibel Island, 153–157. Menlo Park: AAAI Press.

Lesgold, A., Katz, S., Greenberg, L., Hughes, E., and Eggan, G. (1992). Extensions of Intelligent Tutoring Paradigms to Support Collaborative Learning. In Dijkstra, S., Krammer, H., and van Merrienboer, J., eds., *Instructional Models in Computer-based Learning Environments*, 291–311. (NATO ASI Series, series F: Computer and System Sciences, 104.) Berlin: Springer.

Merrill, D., Reiser, B., Ranney, M., and Trafton, J. (1992). Effective Tutoring Techniques: A Comparison of Human Tutors and Intelligent Tutoring Systems. *Journal of the Learning Sciences* 2(3): 277–305.

Woo, C., Evens, M., Michael, J., Rovick, A. (1991). Dynamic Instructional Planning for an Intelligent Physiology Tutoring System. *Proceedings of the Fourth Annual IEEE Computer-Based Medical Systems Symposium*, Baltimore, 226–233. Los Alamitos: IEEE Computer Society Press.

Woolf, B. (1984). Context-Dependent Planning in a Machine Tutor. Ph.D. diss., Dept. of Computer and Information Science, University of Massachusetts at Amherst. COINS Technical Report 84–21.

Constraint Satisfaction Problems

On Integrating Constraint Propagation and Linear Programming for Combinatorial Optimization

John N. Hooker,[†] **Greger Ottosson,**[‡] **Erlendur S. Thorsteinsson**[†] and **Hak-Jin Kim**[†]

† Graduate School of Industrial Administration
Carnegie Mellon University, Pittsburgh, PA 15213, U.S.A.
‡ Computing Science Dept., Uppsala University
PO Box 311, S-751 05 Uppsala, Sweden

Abstract

Linear programming and constraint propagation are complementary techniques with the potential for integration to benefit the solution of combinatorial optimization problems. Attempts to combine them have mainly focused on incorporating either technique into the framework of the other — traditional models have been left intact. We argue that a rethinking of our modeling traditions is necessary to achieve the greatest benefit of such an integration. We propose a declarative modeling framework in which the structure of the constraints indicates how LP and CP can interact to solve the problem.

Introduction

Linear programming (LP) and constraint propagation (CP) are techniques from different fields that tend to be used separately in integer programming (IP) and constraint (logic) programming (CLP), respectively. They have the potential for integration to benefit the solution of combinatorial optimization problems. Yet only recently have attempts been made at combining them.

IP has been successfully applied to a wide range of problems, such as capital budgeting, bin packing, crew scheduling and traveling salesman problems. CLP has in the last decade been shown to be a flexible, efficient and commercially successful technique for scheduling, planning and allocation. These problems usually involve permutations, discretization or symmetries that may result in large and intractable IP models.

Both CLP and IP rely on branching to enumerate regions of the search space. But within this framework they use dual approaches to problem solving: inference and search. CLP emphasizes inference in the form of constraint propagation, which removes infeasible values from the variable domains. It is not a search method, i.e., an algorithm that examines a series of complete labellings until it finds a solution. IP, by contrast, does exactly this. It obtains complete labellings by solving linear programming relaxations of the problem in the branching tree.

IP has the advantage that it can generate cutting planes (inequalities implied by the constraint set) that strengthen the linear relaxation. This can be a powerful technique when the problem is amenable to polyhedral analysis. But IP has the disadvantage that its constraints must be expressed as inequalities (or equations) involving integer-valued variables. Otherwise the linear programming relaxation is not available. This places a severe restriction on IP's modeling language.

In this paper we argue that the key to effective integration of CP and LP lies in the design of the modeling language. We propose a language in which conditional constraints indicate how CP and LP can work together to solve the problem.

We begin, however, by reviewing efforts that have hitherto been made toward integration.

Previous Work

Several articles compare CLP and IP (Smith *et al.* 1995; Darby-Dowman & Little 1998). They report experimental results that illustrate some key properties of the techniques: IP is very efficient for problems with good relaxations, but it suffers when the relaxation is weak or when its restricted modeling framework results in large models. CLP, with its more expressive constraints, has smaller models that are closer to the problem description and behaves well for highly constrained problems, but it lacks the "global perspective" of relaxations.

Some attempts have been made at integration. Early out was (Beringer & Backer 1995) in which the idea is explored of coupling CP and LP solvers with bounds propagation and fixed variables. In (Rodosek, Wallace, & Hajian 1997), CP is used along with LP relaxations in a single search tree to prune domains and establish bounds. A node can fail either because propagation produces an empty domain, or the LP relaxation is infeasible or has an optimal value that is worse than the value of the optimal solution (discussed below). A systematic procedure is used to create a "shadow" MIP model for the original CLP model. It includes reified arithmetic constraints (which produce big-M constraints, illustrated below) and `alldifferent` constraints. The modeler may annotate constraints to indicate which solver should handle them — CP, LP or both.

Some research has been aimed at incorporating better support for symbolic constraints in IP. (Hajian, Rodosek, & Richards 1996; Hajian 1996) show how disequalities ($X_i \neq X_j$) can be handled (more) efficiently in IP solvers. Further, they give a linear modeling of the `alldifferent` constraint.

Bockmayr and Kasper propose an interesting framework in (Bockmayr & Kasper 1998) for combining CLP and IP, in which several approaches to integration or synergy are possible. They investigate how symbolic constraints can be incorporated into IP much as cutting planes are. They also show how a linear system of inequalities can be used in CLP by incorporating it as a symbolic constraint. They also discuss a closer integration in which both linear inequalities and domains appear in the same constraint store.

Characterization

We start with a basic characterization of CLP and IP.

Constraint (Logic) Programming

In Finite Domain CLP each integer variable x_i has an associated *domain* D_i, which is the set of possible values this variable can take on in the (optimal) solution. The cartesian product of the domains, $D_1 \times \ldots \times D_n$, forms the solution space of the problem. This space is finite and can be searched exhaustively for a feasible or optimal solution, but to limit this search CP is used to infer infeasible solutions and prune the corresponding domains. From this viewpoint, CP operates on the set of possible solutions and narrows it down.

Integer Programming

In contrast to CLP, IP does not maintain and reduce a set of solutions defined by variable domains. It generates a series of complete labellings, each obtained at a node of the branching tree by solving a relaxation of the problem at that node. The relaxation is usually constructed by dropping some of the constraints, notably the integrality constraints on the variables, and perhaps by adding valid constraints (cutting planes) that make the relaxation tighter. In a typical application the relaxation is rapidly solved to optimality with a linear programming algorithm.

If the aim is to find a feasible solution, branching continues until the solution of the relaxation happens to be feasible in the original problem (in particular, until it is integral). Relaxations therefore provide a heuristic method for identifying solutions. In an optimization problem, relaxation also provides bounds for a branch-and-bound search. At each node of the branching tree, one can check whether the optimal value of the relaxation is better than the value of the best feasible found so far. If not, there is no need to branch further at that node.

The dual of the LP relaxation can also provide useful information, perhaps by fixing some integer variables or generating additional constraints (nogoods) in the form of "Benders cuts." (Benders 1962; Geoffrion 1974). We will see how the latter can be exploited in an integrated framework.

Comparison of CP and LP

CP can accelerate the search for a solution by

- reducing variable domains (and in particular by proving infeasibility),

- tightening the linear relaxation by adding bounds and cuts in addition to classical cutting planes, and

- eliminating search of symmetric solutions, which are often more easily excluded by using symbolic constraints.

LP can enhance the solver by

- finding feasible solutions early in the search by "global reasoning," i.e., solution of an LP relaxation,

- similarly providing stronger bounds that accelerate the proof of optimality, and

- providing reasons for failure or a poor solution, so as to produce nogoods.

Modeling for Hybrid Solvers

The approaches taken so far to integration of CP and LP are (a) to use both models in parallel, and (b) to try to incorporate one within the other. The more fundamental question of whether a *new* modeling framework should be used has not yet been explored in any depth. The success of (a) depends on the strength of the links between the models and to what degree the overhead of having two models can be avoided. Option (b) is limited in what it can achieve. The high-level symbolic constraints of CLP cannot directly be applied in an IP model, and the same holds for attempts to use IP's cutting planes and relaxations in CLP.

We will use a simple multiple-machine scheduling problem to illustrate the advantages of a new modeling framework. Assume that we wish to schedule n tasks for processing on as many as n machines. Each machine m runs at speed r_m. The objective is to minimize the total fixed cost of the machines we use. Let R_j be the release time, P_j the processing time for speed $r_m = 1$ and D_j the deadline for task j. Let C_m be the fixed cost of using machine m and t_j the start time of task j.

We first state an IP model, which uses 0–1 variables x_{ij} to indicate the sequence in which the jobs are processed. Let $x_{ij} = 1$ if task i precedes task j, $i \neq j$, on the same machine, with $x_{ij} = 0$ otherwise. Also let 0–1 variable $y_{mj} = 1$ if task j is assigned to machine m, and 0–1 variable $z_m = 1$ if machine m is used. Then an IP formulation of this problem is,

$$\min \quad \sum_m C_m z_m$$

$$\text{s.t.} \quad z_m \geq y_{mj}, \qquad\qquad \forall m, j, \qquad (1)$$

$$\sum_m y_{mj} = 1, \qquad\qquad \forall j, \qquad (2)$$

$$t_j + \sum_m \frac{P_j}{r_m} y_{mj} \leq D_j, \qquad \forall j,$$

$$R_j \leq t_j, \qquad\qquad \forall j,$$

$$t_i + \sum_m \frac{P_i}{r_m} y_{mi} \leq t_j + M(1 - x_{ij}), \quad \forall i \neq j, \qquad (3)$$

$$x_{ij} + x_{ji} \geq y_{mi} + y_{mj} - 1, \qquad \forall m, i < j, \quad (4)$$

$$z_m, y_{mj}, x_{ij} \in \{0, 1\}, \ t_j \geq 0, \qquad \forall m, i, j.$$

Constraint (3) is a "big-M" constraint. If M is a sufficiently large number, the constraint forces task i to precede task j if $x_{ij} = 1$ and has no effect otherwise.

A CLP model for the same problem is

$$\min \quad \sum_m C_m z_m$$

s.t.   if $m_i = m_j$ then

$$\left(t_i + \frac{P_i}{r_{m_i}} \leq t_j\right) \vee \left(t_j + \frac{P_j}{r_{m_j}} \leq t_i\right), \quad \forall i, j, \quad (5)$$

$$t_j + \frac{P_j}{r_{m_j}} \leq D_j, \qquad\qquad \forall j,$$

$$R_j \leq t_j, \qquad\qquad \forall j,$$

if $\mathtt{atleast}(m, [m_1, \ldots, m_n], 1)$

then $z_m = 1$ else $z_m = 0$, $\forall m$,   (6)

$$m, m_j \in \{1, \ldots, n\}, \ t_j \geq 0, \qquad \forall j,$$

where m_j is the machine assigned to task j. The CLP model has the advantage of dispensing with the doubly-subscripted 0–1 variables x_{ij} and y_{mi}, which are necessary in IP to represent permutations and assignments. This advantage can be pronounced in larger problems. A notorious example is the progressive party problem (Smith et al., 1995), whose IP model requires an enormous number of multiply-subscripted variables.

The IP model has the advantage of a useful linear programming relaxation, consisting of the objective function, constraints (1)–(2), and bounds $0 \leq y_{mj} \leq 1$. The 0–1 variables y_{mj} enlarge the model but compensate by making this relaxation possible. However, the IP constraints involving the permutation variables x_{ij} yield a very weak relaxation and needlessly enlarge the LP relaxation.

Somehow we must combine the succinctness of the CLP model with an ability to create a relaxation from that portion of the IP model that has a useful relaxation. To do this we propose taking a step back to investigate how one can design a model to suit the solvers rather than adjust the solvers to suit the traditional models.

Mixed Logical/Linear Programming

We begin with the framework of Mixed Logical/Linear Programming (MLLP) proposed in (Hooker 1994; Hooker & Osorio 1997; Hooker, Kim, & Ottosson 1998). It writes constraints in the form of conditionals that link the discrete and continuous elements of the problem. A model has the form

$$\min \quad cx \qquad\qquad (7)$$

s.t. $h_i(y) \to A^i x \geq b^i, \ i \in I,$

       $x \in R^n, y \in D,$

where y is a vector of discrete variables and x a vector of continuous variables. The antecedents $h_i(y)$ of the conditionals are constraints that can be treated with CP techniques. The consequents are linear inequality systems that can be inserted into an LP relaxation.

A linear constraint set $Ax \geq b$ which is enforced unconditionally may be so written for convenience, with the understanding that it can always be put in the conditional form

$(0 = 0) \to Ax \geq b$. Similarly, an unconditional discrete constraint h can be formally represented with the conditional $\neg h \to (1 = 0)$.

The absence of discrete variables from the objective function will be useful algorithmically. Costs that depend on discrete variables can be represented with conditional constraints. For example, the objective function $\sum_j c_j x_j$, where $x_j \in \{0, 1\}$, can be written $\sum_j z_j$ with constraints $(x_j = 1) \to (z_j = c_j)$ and $z_j \geq 0$ for all j.

A useful modeling device is a *variable subscript*, i.e., a subscript that contains one or more discrete variables. For example, if c_{jk} is the cost of assigning worker k to job j, the total cost of an assignment can be written $\sum_j c_{jy_j}$, where y_j is a discrete variable that indicates the worker assigned job j. The value of c_{jy_j} is in effect a function of $y = (y_1, \ldots, y_n)$ and can be written $g_j(y)$, where function g_j happens to depend only on y_j. The MLLP model can incorporate this device as follows:

$$\min \quad cx$$

s.t. $h_i(y) \to L_i(x, y), \ i \in I,$

       $x \in R^n, y \in D,$

where

$$L_i(x, y) = \sum_{k \in K_i(y)} a_{ik}(y) x_{j_{ik}(y)} \geq b_i(y).$$

Note that the model also allows for a summation taken over a *variable index set* $K_i(y)$, which is a set-valued function of y, as well as real-valued "variable constants" $b_i(y)$.

Models of this sort can in principle be written in the more primitive form (7) by adding sufficiently many conditional constraints. For example, the constraint $z \geq \sum_j c_{jy_j}$ can be written $z \geq \sum_j z_j$, if the following constraints are added to the model

$$(y_j = k) \to (z_j = c_{jk}), \quad \text{all } j, k \in \{1, \ldots n\},$$

where each $y_j \in \{1, \ldots, n\}$. It is preferable, however, for the solver to process variables subscripts and index sets directly.

The Solution Algorithm

An MLLP problem is solved by branching on the discrete variables. The conditionals assign roles to CP and LP: CP is applied to the discrete constraints to reduce the search and help determine when partial assignments satisfy the antecedents. At each node of the branching tree, an LP solver minimizes cx subject to the inequalities $A^i x \geq b^i$ for which $h_i(y)$ is determined to be true. This delayed posting of inequalities leads to small and lean LP problems that can be solved efficiently. A feasible solution is obtained when the truth value of every antecedent is determined, and the LP solver finds an optimal solution subject to the enforced inequalities.

Computational tests reported in (Hooker & Osorio 1997) suggest that an MLLP framework not only has modeling advantages but can often permit more rapid solution of the problem than traditional MILP solvers. However, a number of issues are not addressed in this work, including: (a) systematic implementation of variable subscripts and index sets, (b) taking full advantage of the LP solution at each node, and (c) branching on continuous variables and propagation of continuous constraints.

An Example

We can now formulate the multiple machine scheduling problem discussed earlier in an MLLP framework. Let k index a sequence of *events*, each of which is the start of some task. In the following model we will focus on the events, using mappings from events to tasks and events to machines, respectively.

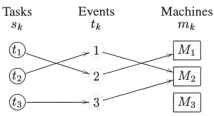

Variable t_k will now be the start time of event k, s_k the task that starts, and m_k the machine to which it is assigned. The formal MLLP model is,

$$\min \quad \sum_m f_m$$

$$\text{s.t.} \quad (m_k = m_l) \rightarrow (t_k + \frac{P_{s_k}}{r_{m_k}} \leq t_l), \ \forall k < l,$$

$$t_k + \frac{P_{s_k}}{r_{m_k}} \leq D_{s_k}, \qquad \forall k,$$

$$R_{s_k} \leq t_k, \qquad \forall k,$$

$$\texttt{alldifferent}\{s_1, \ldots, s_n\},$$

$$f_{m_k} = C_{m_k}, \ f_m \geq 0, \qquad \forall k, m.$$

The model shares CLP's succinctness by dispensing with doubly-subscripted variables. To obtain the relaxation afforded by IP, we can simply add the objective function and constraints (1)–(2) to the model, and link the variables y_{mi} to the other variables logically in (10).

$$\min \quad \sum_m C_m z_m$$

$$\text{s.t.} \quad (m_k = m_l) \rightarrow (t_k + \frac{P_{s_k}}{r_{m_k}} \leq t_l), \ \forall k < l,$$

$$t_k + \frac{P_{s_k}}{r_{m_k}} \leq D_{s_k}, \qquad \forall k,$$

$$R_{s_k} \leq t_k, \qquad \forall k,$$

$$\texttt{alldifferent}\{s_1, \ldots, s_n\},$$

$$z_m \geq y_{mj}, \qquad \forall m, j, \qquad (8)$$

$$\sum_m y_{mj} = 1, \qquad \forall j, \qquad (9)$$

$$y_{m_k s_k} = 1, \qquad \forall k. \qquad (10)$$

The relaxation now minimizes $\sum_m C_m z_m$ subject to (8), (9), $0 \leq y_{mj} \leq 1$, and $y_{mj} = 1$ for all y_{mj} fixed to 1 by (10). One can also add a number of additional valid constraints involving the y_{mj}'s and the t_k's.

A Perspective on MLLP

The framework for integration described in (Bockmayr & Kasper 1998) provides an interesting perspective on MLLP. The CLP literature distinguishes between *primitive* and *nonprimitive* constraints. Primitive constraints are "easy" constraints for which there are efficient (polynomial) satisfaction and optimization procedures. They are maintained in a *constraint store*, which in finite-domain CLP consists simply of variable domains. Propagation algorithms for nonprimitive constraints retrieve current domains from the store and add the resulting smaller domains to the store.

In IP, linear inequalities over continuous variables are primitive because they can be solved by linear programming. The integrality conditions are (the only) nonprimitive constraints.

Bockmayr and Kasper propose two ways of integrating LP and CP. The first is to incorporate the LP part of the problem into a CLP framework as a nonprimitive constraint. Thus LP becomes a constraint propagation technique. It accesses domains in the form of bounds from the constraint store and add new bounds obtained by minimizing and maximizing single variable.

A second approach is to make linear inequalities primitive constraints. The constraint store contains continuous inequality relaxations of the constraints but excludes integrality conditions. For example, discrete constraints $x_1 \vee x_2$ and $\neg x_1 \vee x_2$ could be represented in the constraint store as inequalities $x_1 + x_2 \geq 1$ and $(1 - x_1) + x_2 \geq 1$ and bounds $0 \leq x_j \leq 1$. If constraint propagation deduced that x_2 is true, the inequality $x_2 \geq 1$ would be added to the store. This is an instance of what has long been known as "preprocessing" in MILP, which can therefore be viewed as a special case of this second kind of integration.

MLLP is a third type of integration in which two constraint stores are maintained (see Figure 1). A classical fi-

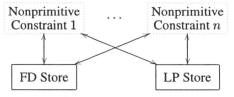

Figure 1: Constraint stores and nonprimitive constraints in MLLP

nite domain constraint store, S_{FD}, contains domains, and the LP constraint store, S_{LP}, contains linear inequalities and bounds. The nonprimitive constraints can access and add to both constraint stores. Since only domain constraints $x_i \in D_i$ exist in the FD store, integrality constraints can remain therein as primitive constraints. There are no continuous variables in the CP store and no discrete variables in the LP store. The conditional constraints of MLLP act as the prime inference agents connecting the two stores, reading domains of the CP store and adding inequalities to the LP store (Figure 2).

In the original MLLP scheme, the conditionals are unidirectional, in the sense that they infer from S_{FD} and post to S_{LP} and not vice-versa. This is because the solution algorithm branches on discrete variables. As the discrete domains are reduced by branching, the truth value of more antecedents is inferred by constraint propagation, and more inequality constraints are posted. However, conditionals in the opposite direction could also be used if one branched on continuous variables by splitting intervals. The antecedents would contain continuous numerical constraints (not necessarily linear inequalities), and the consequents would contain primitive discrete constraints, i.e., restrictions on discrete variable domains. The truth value of the antecedents might be inferred using interval propagation.

We will next give two more examples of nonprimitive constraints in MLLP; a generalized version of the element constraint for handling variable subscripts, and a constraint which derives nogoods from S_{LP}.

Variable Subscripts

As seen before, MLLP provides variable subscripts as a modeling component, but an expansion to conditional constraints is in most cases not tractable. Instead a nonprimitive constraint, or inference agent, can be designed to handle variable subscripts more efficiently.

There are basically two cases in which a variable subscript can occur — in a discrete constraint or in a continuous inequality. In the former case it can either be a vector of constants or a vector of discrete variables; both of these correspond to the traditional use of the element/3 (Marriott & Stuckey 1998) constraint found in all major CP systems and libraries (e.g. (Dincbas *et al.* 1988; Carlsson 1995)). This constraint takes the form $\text{element}_{FD}(I, [X_1, \dots, X_n], Y)$, where I is an integer variable with domain $D_I = \{1, \dots, n\}$, indexing the list, and $Y = X_I$.

Here we will consider the second case, $\text{element}_{LP}(I, [X_1, \dots, X_n], Y)$, where I is still a discrete, indexing variable, but x_i and Y are *continuous* variables or constants. Propagating this constraint can be done almost as before. Let the interval $[\min(x_i), \max(x_i)]$ be the domain of x_i. Then upon change of the domain of I, we can compute

$$\min = \{\min(x_i) | i \in D_I\}$$
$$\max = \{\max(x_i) | i \in D_I\}$$

reading D_I from the S_{CP} and the adding new bounds

$$\min \leq Y \leq \max$$

to S_{LP}. Similarly, bounds of Y can be used to prune D_I. (Stronger bounds for variables in LP can be obtained by minimizing and maximizing the variable subject to the linear inequalities in S_{LP}, which for some cases might be beneficial.)

The important point here is not the details of how we can propagate this constraint, but rather to exemplify how an inference agent can naturally access both constraint stores.

Infeasible LP

When the LP is infeasible, any dual solution specifies an infeasible linear combination of the constraint set. For each conditional constraint $y_i \rightarrow A^i x \geq b^i, i \in I$ where some

$ax \geq b \in A^i x \geq b^i$ has a corresponding nonzero dual multiplier, we can form the logical constraint

$$\bigvee_{i \in I} \neg y_i$$

This nogood (Tsang 1993) must be satisfied by any solution of the problem, because its corresponding set of linear inequalities forms an infeasible combination. This scheme can naturally be encapsulated within a nonprimitive constraint, nogood, reading from S_{LP} and writing to S_{FD}. This agent can collect, merge and maintain no-goods for any combination of nonzero dual values in any infeasible LP node, and can infer primitive and nonprimitive constraints which will strengthen S_{FD}. A related use of the infeasible combination has previously been explored in the context of intelligent backtracking (De Backer & Beringer 1991). Figure 2 shows our nogood constraint and the other basic nonprimitive constraints of MLLP.

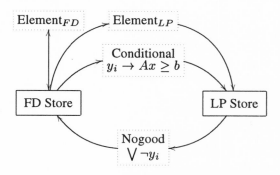

Figure 2: Nonprimitive constraints in MLLP

Feasible LP

In IP, the solution of the relaxation provides a complete labelling of the variables. This sort of labelling is not immediately available in MLLP, because the relaxation involves only continuous variables. However, the solution $\bar{x}$ of a feasible relaxation can be heuristically extended to a complete labelling $(\bar{x}, \bar{y})$ that may satisfy the constraints. (Because y does not occur in the objective function, its value will not affect the optimal value of the problem.) Given any conditional $h_i(y) \rightarrow A^i x \geq b^i$, $h_i(\bar{y})$ must be false if $A^i \bar{x} \not\geq b^i$, but it can be true or false if $A^i \bar{x} \geq b^i$. One can therefore employ a heuristic (or even an exhaustive search) that tries to assign values $\bar{y}_j$ to the y_j's from their current domains so as to falsify the antecedents that must be false.

Conclusion

LP and CP have long been used separately, but they have the potential to be integrated as complementary techniques in future optimization frameworks. To do this fully and in general, the modeling traditions of mathematical programming and constraint programming also must be integrated. We propose a unifying modeling and solution framework that aims to do so. Continuous and discrete constraints are naturally combined using conditional constraints, allowing a clean separation and a natural link between constraints amenable to CP and continuous inequalities efficiently handled by LP.

References

Benders, J. F. 1962. Partitioning procedures for solving mixed-variables programming problems. *Numer. Math.* 4:238–252.

Beringer, H., and Backer, B. D. 1995. Combinatorial problem solving in constraint logic programming with cooperating solvers. In Beierle, C., and Plümer, L., eds., *Logic Programming: Formal Methods and Practical Applications*, Studies in Computer Science and Artificial Intelligence. Elsevier. chapter 8, 245–272.

Bockmayr, A., and Kasper, T. 1998. Branch-and-infer: A unifying framework for integer and finite domain constraint programming. *INFORMS J. Computing* 10(3):287–300.

Carlsson, M. 1995. SICStus Prolog User's Manual. SICS research report, Swedish Institute of Computer Science. URL: http://www.sics.se/isl/sicstus.html.

Darby-Dowman, K., and Little, J. 1998. Properties of some combinatorial optimization problems and their effect on the performance of integer programming and constraint logic programming. *INFORMS Journal on Computing* 10(3):276–286.

De Backer, B., and Beringer, H. 1991. Intelligent backtracking for CLP languages: An application to CLP(R). In Saraswat, V., and Ueda, K., eds., *Logic Programming, Proceedings of the 1991 International Symposium*, 405–419. San Diego, USA: The MIT Press.

Dincbas, M.; Van Hentenryck, P.; Simonis, H.; Aggoun, A.; Graf, T.; and Berthier, F. 1988. The Constraint Logic Programming Language CHIP. In *FGCS-88: Proceedings International Conference on Fifth Generation Computer Systems*, 693–702. Tokyo: ICOT.

Geoffrion, A. 1974. Lagrangian relaxation for integer programming. *Mathematical Programming Study* 2:82–114.

Hajian, M.; Rodosek, R.; and Richards, B. 1996. Introduction of a new class of variables to discrete and integer programming problems. *Baltzer Journals*.

Hajian, M. T. 1996. Dis-equality constraints in linear/integer programming. Technical report, IC-Parc.

Hooker, J. N., and Osorio, M. A. 1997. Mixed logical/linear programming. *Discrete Applied Mathematics, to appear*.

Hooker, J. N.; Kim, H.-J.; and Ottosson, G. 1998. A declarative modeling framework that integrates solution methods. *Annals of Operations Research, Special Issue on Modeling Languages and Approaches, to appear*.

Hooker, J. N. 1994. Logic-based methods for optimization. In Borning, A., ed., *Principles and Practice of Constraint Programming*, volume 874 of *Lecture Notes in Computer Science*, 336–349.

Marriott, K., and Stuckey, P. J. 1998. *Programming with Constraints: An Introduction*. MIT Press.

Rodosek, R.; Wallace, M.; and Hajian, M. 1997. A new approach to integrating mixed integer programming and constraint logic programming. *Baltzer Journals*.

Smith, B.; Brailsford, S.; Hubbard, P.; and Williams, H. P. 1995. The Progressive Party Problem: Integer Linear Programming and Constraint Programming Compared. In *CP95: Proceedings 1st International Conference on Principles and Practice of Constraint Programming)*.

Tsang, E. 1993. *Foundations of Constraint Satisfaction*. Academic Press.

Hierarchical Constraint Satisfaction in Spatial Databases

Dimitris Papadias, Panos Kalnis, Nikos Mamoulis

Department of Computer Science
Hong Kong University of Science and Technology
Clear Water Bay, Hong Kong
http://www.cs.ust.hk/{~dimitris, ~kalnis, ~mamoulis}

Abstract

Several content-based queries in spatial databases and geographic information systems (GISs) can be modelled and processed as constraint satisfaction problems (CSPs). Regular CSP algorithms, however, work for main memory retrieval without utilizing indices to prune the search space. This paper shows how systematic and local search techniques can take advantage of the hierarchical decomposition of space, preserved by spatial data structures, to efficiently guide search. We study the conditions under which hierarchical constraint satisfaction outperforms traditional methods with extensive experimentation.

Introduction

Consider that a user is searching for a triplet (v_1, v_2, v_3) of a residential area, a commercial center and a park, such that v_1 covers v_2 and v_2 meets v_3. The query can be modeled as a CSP where: i) each query object corresponds to a CSP variable ii) a pair of variables is related by the respective query constraints (e.g., covers(v_1, v_2)) iii) the domain of each variable consists of the corresponding objects in the database (e.g., the domain of v_1 is the set of all stored residential areas). As opposed to other CSP applications, here the number of variables is relatively small (usually less than ten), while the domains are very large (geographic maps may contain more than 100,000 objects).

Because of the large amount of data involved, spatial databases and GIS employ indexing for efficient retrieval. The R-tree (Guttman 1984) and its variations is the most popular multi-dimensional access method, currently used in many commercial GISs and DBMS (e.g., Informix, Illustra, MapInfo). R-trees have been applied for a variety of queries including spatial selections, nearest neighbors, and spatial joins. This paper illustrates how the hierarchical decomposition of space, preserved by R-trees, can be utilized by CSP algorithms to accelerate search.

In order to provide a general framework of retrieval we use the 9-intersection model (Egenhofer 1991) as the basis for defining spatial constraints. This model, which is becoming a standard in commercial systems (e.g., Intergraph and Oracle spatial products), describes eight mutually exclusive topological relations between planar regions (Figure 1) using intersections of object interiors and boundaries. The same set of relations, called RCC-8 (region connection calculus) in AI literature, was defined independently in (Randell, Cui, and

Cohn 1992). Alternatively, depending on the application needs, the proposed techniques could be used with other types of spatial constraints such as directions (e.g., *north*) and distances.

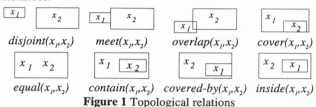

$disjoint(x_1, x_2)$ $meet(x_1, x_2)$ $overlap(x_1, x_2)$ $cover(x_1, x_2)$

$equal(x_1, x_2)$ $contain(x_1, x_2)$ $covered\text{-}by(x_1, x_2)$ $inside(x_1, x_2)$

Figure 1 Topological relations

The rest of the paper is organized as follows: Section 2 describes R-trees and spatial query processing techniques. Section 3 defines hierarchical constraint satisfaction based on indexing and outlines pre-processing techniques. Section 4 experimentally evaluates the performance gain of hierarchical constraint satisfaction for systematic search and local search techniques. Finally, Section 5 concludes the paper.

Background

The R-tree data structure is a height-balanced tree that consists of intermediate and leaf nodes corresponding to disk pages in secondary memory (R-trees are extensions of B+-trees to many dimensions). The root is at level $h-1$, where h is the height of the tree, and the leaf nodes at level 0. The minimum bounding rectangles (MBR) of the actual data objects are stored in the leaf nodes, and intermediate nodes are built by grouping rectangles at the lower level. Notice, that each object has a distinct identity and location in space. Furthermore, in most applications there is a separate R-tree for every type of object (e.g., residential areas, parks).

Figure 2 illustrates R-trees that index three sets of objects covering the same area. For this example we assume that the maximum node capacity C is 3 rectangles (in real 2D applications C is normally 50-400 depending on the page size). MBRs a_1, a_2 and a_3 of the first R-tree are grouped together in an intermediate node A_1, which is contained in the root. In the rest of the paper, we make the distinction between an R-tree node X_i and its *entries* $X_{i,1}, .., X_{i,C_i}$ (where $C_i \leq C$ is the capacity of X_i) which correspond to MBRs included in X_i. $X_{i,k}.ref$ points to the corresponding node X_k at the next (lower) level. For instance, at level 1 of the first tree, the entries of the root are A_1 and A_2, which point to nodes at level 0. An entry of a leaf node X_i is an object MBR $x_{i,k}$.

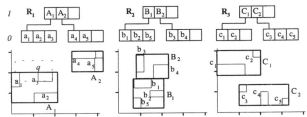

Figure 2 A set of objects and the corresponding R-tree

Traditionally, R-trees have been used for *window queries* which ask for a set of objects that *intersect*[1] a window *q*. The processing of a window query in R-trees involves the following procedures: Starting from the top node, exclude the entries that are *disjoint* with *q*, and recursively search the remaining ones. Among the entries of the leaf nodes retrieved, select the ones that are *non-disjoint* with *q*. For instance when searching for objects sharing common points with the dotted window in the first tree, we need not access A_2 since it cannot contain qualifying objects.

When two MBRs are *disjoint,* the objects that they approximate are also *disjoint*. If the MBRs however share common points, no conclusion can be drawn about the relation between the actual objects. For this reason, spatial queries involve the following two step strategy: (i) a *filter step*, in which the tree is used to retrieve a set of candidates that includes all the results and possibly some *false hits*, and (ii) a *refinement step* where each candidate is examined and false hits are eliminated. Here, as in most related literature, we will only consider MBRs, avoiding the refinement step (which is based on computational geometry techniques and is outside the scope of this paper).

The above method can be extended for the retrieval of the topological relations of Figure 1. In contrast to window queries where the retrieval condition is *non-disjoint* for all levels of the tree, in order to retrieve topological relations using R-trees one needs to define conditions for the intermediate nodes. For instance, A_1 encloses a_3 which is *covered-by* *q*, but the relation between A_1 and *q* is *overlap*. Table 1 presents, for each relation, the condition between an intermediate node *X* and *q*, so that *X* may contain qualifying objects *x*.

Relation (*x,q*)	Condition for intermediate nodes (*X,q*)
equal	equal ∨ cover ∨ contain
contain	contain
inside	overlap∨covered-by∨inside∨equal∨cover∨contain
cover	cover ∨ contain
covered-by	overlap∨ covered-by ∨ equal ∨ cover ∨ contain
disjoint	disjoint∨ meet∨ overlap∨ cover∨ contain
meet	meet∨ overlap ∨ cover ∨contain
overlap	overlap ∨ cover ∨ contain

Table 1 Conditions for intermediate nodes (window queries)

R-trees can also effectively support *intersection joins*, i.e., queries that select from two object sets, the pairs that satisfy some spatial predicate, usually *intersect* (e.g., "find all land parcels intersecting some forest area"). The most influential

---

[1] *Intersect* (or *non-disjoint*) is the complementary relation of *disjoint*.

algorithm for processing intersection joins using R-trees, is *R-tree join* (*RTJ*) proposed in (Brinkhoff, Kriegel, and Seeger 1993). It is based on the *enclosure property* of R-trees: if two intermediate nodes X_i and Y_j (possibly belonging to different trees) are *disjoint*, then all pairs $(X_{i,k}, Y_{j,l})$ of their entries are also *disjoint*. *RTJ* starts from the roots of the two trees to be joined (e.g., R_1 and R_2) and finds all pairs of *non-disjoint* entries inside them (e.g., (A_1, B_1) and (A_1, B_2)). These are the only pairs that may lead to solutions; for instance, there can be no pair (a_i, b_j) $a_i \in A_2$ and $b_j \in B_1$ such that (a_i, b_j) is a solution, since A_2 is *disjoint* with B_1. For each *non-disjoint* pair of entries, the algorithm is recursively called until the leaf levels where intersecting pairs constitute solutions.

Like window queries, in order to process arbitrary topological relations using *RTJ*, we need to define the conditions between intermediate nodes X_i and Y_j that could enclose (at any level below) objects x_k and y_l satisfying the join predicate. Table 2 contains the allowed relations between X_i and Y_j, so that they could contain qualifying pairs (x_k, y_l).

Relation (x_k, y_l)	Condition for intermediate nodes (X_i, Y_j)
equal, contain, inside, overlap, cover, covered-by	overlap ∨ covered-by ∨ inside ∨ equal ∨ cover ∨ contain
disjoint	disjoint ∨ meet ∨ overlap ∨ covered-by ∨ inside∨ equal∨ cover ∨ contain
meet	meet ∨ overlap∨ covered-by ∨ inside∨ equal ∨ cover ∨ contain

Table 2 Conditions for intermediate nodes (spatial joins)

Consider again the query given in the introduction: "find a triplet of objects (v_1, v_2, v_3) such that v_1 *covers* v_2 and v_2 *meets* v_3". This can be viewed as a *multi-way* spatial join and processed by computing the result of one pairwise join (e.g., v_1 *covers* v_2) using *RTJ*; then joining the results with v_3 by some spatial hash algorithm applicable when only one R-tree is available (since the results of the first join are not indexed). This approach is described in detail in (Mamoulis and Papadias 1999a). Alternatively, as shown in (Papadias, Mamoulis, and Delis 1998), the query could be processed as a CSP, where the query objects (variables) can take values from the corresponding domains.

The hierarchical structure of R-trees can be used to decompose the initial problem (with size $n \cdot log_2(m)$, where m is the cardinality of the datasets) to smaller sub-problems (with size $n \cdot log_2(C)$, where C is the node capacity) at each tree level. A solution of a sub-problem at an intermediate level is an instantiation of variables to entries that may contain objects satisfying the query constraints. Similarly to *RTJ*, the nodes pointed by these entries constitute the domains of the variables at the next (lower) level. In the sequel we describe hierarchical constraint satisfaction using R-trees, and evaluate its performance with systematic and local search.

Hierarchical CSPs using R-trees

Content-based queries like the previous one are transformed to two types of CSPs: one for the intermediate levels and one for the leafs. Formally, a hierarchical CSP using R-trees can be defined by:

- A set of n variables, $v_1, v_2, .., v_n$.
- For each variable v_i a domain D_i which i] for level 0, consists of the entries $\{x_{i,1}, .., x_{i,C_i}\}$ of a leaf node X_i, and ii] for levels 1 to h-1, of the entries $\{X_{i,1}, .., X_{i,C_i}\}$ of an intermediate node X_i.
- For each pair of variables (v_i, v_j) a binary constraint: i] for level 0, c_{ij} is a disjunction of topological relations restricting the relative positions of v_i and v_j as specified by the query ii] for levels 1 to h-1, C_{ij} is derived by replacing each relation in c_{ij} by the corresponding condition for intermediate nodes in Table 2.

Consider again the example query: the CSP for the top level of the tree in Figure 2 has three variables which can be instantiated to entries of the roots ($D_1 = \{A_1, A_2\}$, $D_2 = \{B_1, B_2\}$, $D_3 = \{C_1, C_2\}$). C_{12} is the entry of Table 2 that corresponds to relation *cover* (i.e., *overlap* ∨ *covered-by* ∨ *inside* ∨ *equal* ∨ *cover* ∨ *contain*), while C_{23} is the entry that corresponds to *meet*. Out of the 8 possible combinations of root entries (e.g., (A_1, B_1, C_1), (A_1, B_1, C_2), .., (A_2, B_2, C_2)), only (A_1, B_1, C_2) and (A_1, B_2, C_1) may lead to actual solutions. The triplet (A_1, B_1, C_2) constitutes a solution at the root since *overlap*(A_1, B_1) and *overlap*(B_1, C_2) satisfy the intermediate level constraints. Then the algorithm will proceed to level 0 with $D_1 = \{a_1, a_2, a_3\}$, $D_2 = \{b_1, b_2, b_5\}$ and $D_3 = \{c_3, c_4, c_5\}$. The constraints now become $c_{12} =$ *cover* and $c_{23} =$ *meet*. The only leaf level (i.e., actual) solution (a_2, b_2, c_4) is found. On the other hand, the root solution (A_1, B_2, C_1) does not lead to an actual one, i.e., it is a false hit. Figure 3 illustrates the above example, giving the domains, constraints and solutions at each level.

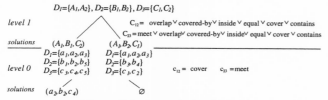

Figure 3 Path to solution (a_2, b_2, c_4)

Space-restriction (Brinkhoff, Kriegel, and Seeger 1993) is a pre-processing heuristic (employed before the application of the CSP algorithm at each level) that scans the domains of all variables, removing the entries that cannot satisfy the query constraints given their positions with respect to the other nodes. If an entry $X_{i,k} \in X_i$ is *disjoint* with Y_j, then it is *disjoint* with all entries contained in Y_j. In order to apply *space-restriction* for topological relations, Table 1 is used for entries at level 0, and Table 2 for the rest. In the example query, when the solution (A_1, B_1, C_2) is found at the top, entry a_1 can be safely pruned from D_1 at the next level since it is *disjoint* with node B_1, therefore it cannot *cover* any entry inside B_1.

Another type of pre-preprocessing is path consistency, which can be employed as a form of semantic query optimization to discard inconsistent queries. For instance, the query $c_{12} =$ *cover*, $c_{23} =$ *cover* and $c_{13} =$ *disjoint* cannot have any solutions. For the detection of such inconsistencies prior to search, we use the composition table for topological relations in (Egenhofer 1991) and the algorithm in (Allen 1983), which does not check value consistency, but *constraint graph con-*

sistency, and its complexity is, therefore, independent from the domain sizes. Note that the algorithm is not complete, i.e., depending on the query, it may not detect all inconsistencies.

Hierarchical constraint satisfaction can be applied with a variety of heuristics. In the next section we measure its performance using representative systematic and local search algorithms for the following three cases:

i] Hierarchical systematic search - Systematic search is applied at every level. This results in an exhaustive depth-first search of the trees.

ii] Hierarchical local search - Local search is used at every level. Once a solution is found at level l the algorithm locally searches the references to l-1.

iii] Hierarchical local/systematic search - Local search is applied for the intermediate levels where there exist numerous solutions due to the non-restrictive constraints and the large areas of intermediate nodes. Systematic search is employed at the leafs.

Experiments

The problems were randomly generated by modifying the parameters $<n, m, p_1, p_2>$ (Dechter and Meiri 1994), where p_1 is the probability that a random pair of variables is constrained (*network density*), and p_2 the probability that a random assignment for a constrained pair is inconsistent (*constraint tightness*). The usual methodology for generating random CSPs is to specify each binary constraint as a subset of the domains' Cartesian product. In this case the same tightness for all constraints is achieved by filtering out $p_2 \cdot m^2$ value pairs for every constraint. In the current problem, where constraints are disjunctions of relations, this method cannot be applied.

In order to generate various values of tightness we created uniform datasets with different density values. The density D of a set of rectangles is the average number of rectangles that contain a given point in the workspace. Equivalently, D can be expressed as the ratio of the sum of the areas of all rectangles over the area of the workspace. Figure 4 shows one dataset with $m = 10^4$ uniformly distributed rectangles where the average rectangle side in each dimension is $|x| = 0.0045$, resulting in $D \approx 0.2$ (assuming a $[0,1) \times [0,1)$ (unit) workspace, the density is defined as $D = m \cdot |x|^2$). It also illustrates the probability with which a random pair satisfies each topological relation. For uniform datasets, D is the single factor determining relation probabilities, which can be calculated by analytical models (Theodoridis and Sellis, 1996). Sampling and statistical information can be used for real data. Like Figure 4, in most real-life situations *disjoint* is satisfied by the vast majority of object pairs (D=0.2 is a typical value for real datasets). The tightness of a constraint, i.e. the probability that a random pair of variable assignments will violate it, can be calculated from the probabilities of the relations it consists of. For instance, the tightness of a constraint {*meet* ∨ *contain*} is 1-(*Prob(meet)* + *Prob(contain)*). Since in most problems, each constraint has a different tightness, we use the average tightness of all constraints to define p_2.

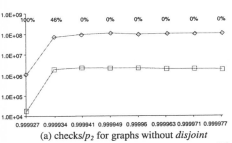

Figure 4 A sample dataset used in the experiments

Relation	probability
disjoint	$9.999182 \cdot 10^{-1}$
meets	$3.760376 \cdot 10^{-6}$
equal	$2.000200 \cdot 10^{-8}$
inside	$2.280228 \cdot 10^{-6}$
covered by	$2.500250 \cdot 10^{-7}$
contains	$2.280228 \cdot 10^{-6}$
covers	$2.500250 \cdot 10^{-7}$
overlap	$7.298730 \cdot 10^{-5}$

The datasets were organized in R*-trees (Beckmann et al. 1990) with height $h=3$ and node capacity $C=50-200$ (depending on cardinality). Performance is measured in terms of consistency checks, i.e., number of object pairs checked for the satisfaction of a topological constraint. In case of hierarchical CSPs, comparisons involving intermediate nodes are also counted as consistency checks.

Hierarchical Systematic Search

We first compare hierarchical and flat versions of systematic search through the whole solution space. In the following experiments we use forward checking (*FC*) with the *fail first* dynamic variable ordering heuristic (Haralick and Elliott 1980), because of its efficiency and relatively simple implementation.

For the first experiment, a series of problem ensembles was generated. An ensemble contains 50 random problems with complete constraint graphs (cliques), i.e., $p_1=1$, and the same average constraint tightness. The number of variables in all problems is $n=5$, $m=10^4$ and $D \approx 0.2$. Figure 5a shows the performance of *FC* and hierarchical *FC* (with *space-restriction*) for problems where none of the constraints contain *disjoint* (since *disjoint* is very loose, its existence in a binary constraint is almost equivalent to the absence of the corresponding constraint edge from the graph). The x-axis corresponds to the value of p_2 for each ensemble, and the y-axis shows the mean consistency checks of the algorithms. The number over each ensemble presents the percentage of problems that were soluble.

As a general observation, in the current experimental settings, *H-FC* outperforms *FC* by two orders of magnitude.

Observe that in the first ensemble all problems are easy and soluble. This is due to the fact that all constraints contain the relation *overlap*, which is also relaxed compared to the others. The rest of the ensembles were harder and only the second contained soluble problems. This is because the third, and subsequent ensembles involve two or more constraints with *contain*, *inside*, *cover*, *covered-by* or *equal* (but without *disjoint* or *overlap*). The low probability of these relations renders the existence of object pairs (in the same neighborhood) satisfying the two constraints highly unlikely.

The performance of *FC* and *H-FC* was also tested for graphs containing constraints with *disjoint*. Figure 5b illustrates the consistency checks of the two algorithms for a series of problem ensembles in this category. As expected, ensembles with smaller constraint tightness (i.e., many *disjoint* constraints) contain more soluble problems than "dense" ones. For dense graphs the difference is again about two orders of magnitude, but as the tightness decreases the performance of the algorithms converges. This happens because the large number of *disjoint* constraints results in numerous solutions at the intermediate levels, many of which do not lead to actual solutions.

Observe that, due to the special nature of *disjoint*, the problem does not have the *easy-hard-easy* behaviour with respect to the value of p_2, usually observed in other CSPs (Prosser 1996). Rather, both hierarchical and plain systematic search appear to have two distinct behaviors depending on the existence of *disjoint*.

The next experiment tests the effect of the number of variables, when the number of solutions remains constant. We use datasets of 10^4 objects and clique graphs where all constraints are *non-disjoint*. In order to keep the number of solutions stable, the density of the datasets has to be modified for each value of n. According to the analysis in (Papadias, Mamoulis, and Theodoridis 1999), the expected number of solutions for a 2-dimensional problem with a clique constraint graph where all constraints are *non-disjoint*, is given by the following formula:

$$Sol = \prod_{i=1}^{n} m_i \cdot \left(\sum_{i=1}^{n} \cdot \prod_{j=1, j \neq i}^{n} |x_i| \right)^2 \quad (1)$$

where $|x_i|$ is the average MBR extent in each dimension for dataset i. Assuming that all datasets have the same cardinality m and extent $|x|$, eq. 1 can be re-written as:

$$Sol = m^n \cdot n^2 \cdot |x|^{2 \cdot (n-1)} \quad (2)$$

$\diamond$— FC $\square$— H-FC

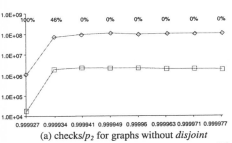
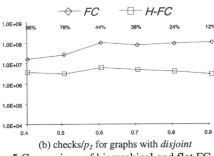
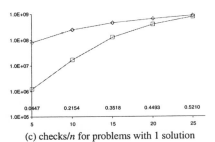

(a) checks/p_2 for graphs without *disjoint*   (b) checks/p_2 for graphs with *disjoint*   (c) checks/n for problems with 1 solution

Figure 5 Comparison of hierarchical and flat FC

Finally, after replacing |x| by the density using $D = m \cdot |x|^2$, eq.2 becomes:

$$Sol = m \cdot n^2 \cdot D^{n-1} \qquad (3)$$

Solving eq. 3 with respect to D, one can create synthetic variable domains such that the number of solutions can be controlled. Figure 5c illustrates the consistency checks for FC and H-FC, as a function of the number of variables for problems that have one solution (such problems usually belong to the hard region). Density is set according to:

$$D = 1 / \sqrt[n-1]{m \cdot n^2} \qquad (4)$$

and its value for each experiment appears on top of n. The performance of the algorithms converges as the number of variables increases. For $n > 25$, FC outperforms H-FC.

As the number of variables increases, the performance of FC does not deteriorate significantly because most inconsistent instantiations are detected during the early check-forwards. On the other hand, as shown in Table 3, the number of intermediate level solutions explodes with n. In general, the percentage of combinations that constitute solutions increases as we go up the levels of the trees because of the large node extents. Since a part of node area corresponds to "dead space" (space not covered by object MBRs) most high level solutions (in this case all but one) are false hits.

#solutions at $l=2$	159	1559	13567	27331	128781
#solutions at $l=1$	6430	49670	340480	2314492	15166017
#solutions at $l=0$	1	1	1	1	1
#variables n	5	10	15	20	25

Table 3 Number of solutions as a function of n

Similar behaviour is expected for other CSP algorithms including backtracking-based and hybrid algorithms. As a conclusion, hierarchical systematic search significantly outperforms flat search when the domains are large and the number of variables is small (as in most spatial database applications). Some preliminary experiments indicate that H-FC also outperforms methods based on pairwise join algorithms (Mamoulis and Papadias 1999a) for finding all solutions of multi-way intersection joins involving dense queries and datasets. The performance gain is higher when only a small subset of the solutions is required. In the next section we apply hierarchical constraint satisfaction with local search.

Hierarchical Local Search

For local search we used hill-climbing with the *min-conflicts* (*MC*) heuristic (Minton et al. 1992; Sosic and Gu 1994). *MC* starts with a random initial assignment for all variables. At each step, it chooses a variable that is currently in conflict and reassigns its value so that the number of conflicts is minimized. This step is repeated until a solution is found or until a deadlock is met, i.e. a local minimum where the number of conflicts can not be further minimized. In this case, the algorithm is restarted.

The hierarchical version of *MC* applies this procedure for each level of the tree. Since a deadlock in the current level may occur because of a false hit at a previous level, the algo-

rithm will backtrack to a higher lever after a number of restarts. In our experiments, this number was proportional to the depth and the size of the problem, i.e., the number of restarts at level l was set to: $(h-l) \cdot n \cdot log_2(C)$ (in other words, the number of restarts decreases for the upper levels in order to avoid searching false hits). We experimented with the following variations of local search:

a] Flat *MC*: *MC* is applied directly at the leaf level without using the trees.

b] Hierarchical uninformed *MC* (*HU-MC*): *MC* is used at every level. Once a solution is found at level l the algorithm follows the references to l-1. If no solution can be found at l-1, it will backtrack to l, attempting to find another solution and repeat the same process.

c] Hierarchical informed *MC* (*HI-MC*): this is similar to b] but the algorithm keeps a memory of already visited solutions, so when it backtracks from l-1, it will avoid retrieving a solution already found at l.

d] Hierarchical root *MC* (*HR-MC*): *MC* is used for every level but when a solution cannot be found at l-1, the algorithm re-starts again directly from the root.

e] Hierarchical root *MC/FC* (*HR-MC/FC*): this is similar to d] but *FC* is used for systematic search at the leaf level.

We experimented with three domain sizes of 10^3, 10^4 and 10^5 objects. In all experiments, the clique query graph contains five variables ($n=5$) related by *non-disjoint* constraints. The expected number of solutions for each domain size ranges from 1 to 10^5. In order to generate problems with a desired number of solutions we used eq. 3, varying the value of D. All algorithms were executed 10 times for every setting; their execution was terminated if a solution could not be found after 10^9 checks.

Figure 6 shows the mean consistency checks as a function of the number of solutions. Among the pure hierarchical local search techniques (b], c] and d]), HR-MC performs best in most cases. Recall that HR-MC restarts directly from the root when a deadlock occurs, so it can explore the whole domain more extensively. On the other hand, HU-MC has the worst behavior because it consumes a considerable amount of time at the lower levels, misled by false hits. In some cases HU-MC is at least one order of magnitude slower that HR-MC. HI-MC's performance lies between the previous mentioned algorithms. HI-MC searches the domain in the same way as HU-MC but, since it keeps a history of the already visited nodes at each level, it avoids entering the same combination of sub-trees more than once.

The comparison of hierarchical local search versus flat search indicates that for small domains ($m=10^3$), *MC* performs almost one order of magnitude better that the hierarchical algorithms. This happens because flat *MC* avoids the overhead of searching false hits; in addition, it can easily escape from a local minimum since it focuses on the whole domain. This situation changes when dealing with larger domains. For $m=10^4$, *MC*'s performance is very similar to HR-MC. For $m=10^5$, *MC* is outperformed by HR-MC by one order of magnitude because the overhead imposed by the hierarchical structure is less than the effort required for searching in a large unstructured domain.

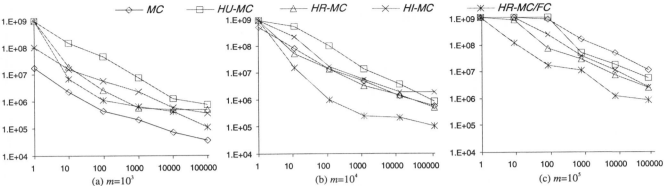

Figure 6 Performance of local search algorithms (consistency checks/number of solutions)

Due to the large number of solutions at the upper tree levels, hierarchical local search succeeds fast, but spends more time trying to find a solution at the leaf level. This motivated the replacement of *MC* at leaf levels with *FC*. For a small domain, *HR-MC/FC* achieves only a marginal performance gain with respect to *HR-MC*, while for larger domains it is almost an order of magnitude faster.

Conclusion

This paper describes a methodology for hierarchical constraint satisfaction in spatial databases using R-trees. Instead of processing content-based queries as flat CSPs, computation can be decomposed in smaller problems at each tree level. The experimental evaluation suggests that systematic search is significantly faster in the case of hierarchical CSPs for typical conditions ($m \geq 10^4$ and $n \leq 10$). On the other hand, hierarchical local search pays-off only for very large domains ($m \approx 10^5$).

Although we experimented with two representative algorithms (*FC*, *MC*), hierarchical constraint satisfaction can be used with a variety of systematic and local search techniques. Several heuristics, like plain sweep, can take advantage of the inherent order of domains to restrict search. Furthermore, these methods can be applied with other spatial access methods based on the hierarchical decomposition of space.

An alternative approach for solving spatial CSPs, is to exploit the data structure in order to avoid exhaustive search of domains while assigning or pruning values. Going back to the example query, once v_1 is instantiated to some MBR x_1, x_1 becomes the query window for retrieval of all objects satisfying $cover(x_1, v_2)$. In this way linear scan of domains at each instantiation is replaced by window queries which are very cheap operations in R-trees. An application of this technique with forward checking and backtracking in the context of temporal CSPs can be found in (Mamoulis and Papadias 1999b). Furthermore, this method can be combined with hierarchical constraint satisfaction, e.g., for the example query we could use hierarchical search to retrieve qualifying pairs of values for (v_1, v_2), and for each such pair apply window queries to retrieve consistent values for v_3. The optimal combination can be based on cost models and appropriate analytical formulae (Papadias, Mamoulis, and Theodoridis 1999) for the expected number of solutions.

Acknowledgements

This work was supported by grant HKUST 6151/98E from Hong Kong RGC and grant DAG97/ 98.EG02. We would like to thank Kostas Stergiou and Marios Mantzourogiannis for their comments.

References

Allen, J.F. Maintaining Knowledge about Temporal Intervals. *CACM 26* (11), 832-843, 1983.

Beckmann, N., Kriegel, H.P. Schneider, R., Seeger, B. "The R*-tree: an Efficient and Robust Access Method for Points and Rectangles". *ACM SIGMOD*, 1990.

Brinkhoff, T., Kriegel, H. Seeger, B. Efficient Processing of Spatial Joins Using R-trees. *ACM SIGMOD*, 1993.

Dechter, R., Meiri, I. Experimental Evaluation of preprocessing algorithms for constraint satisfaction problems. *Artificial Intelligence* 68(2): 211-241, 1994.

Egenhofer, M. Reasoning about Binary Topological Relations. In Günther, O. and Schek, H.J. (eds.) *Advances in Spatial Databases*. Springer Verlag LNCS, 1991.

Guttman, A. R-trees: A Dynamic Index Structure for Spatial Searching. *ACM SIGMOD*, 1984.

Haralick, R., Elliott, G. Increasing tree search efficiency for constraint satisfaction problems. *Artificial Intelligence* 14(3): 263-313, 1980.

Minton, S., Johnston, M., Philips, A., Laird, P. Minimizing Conflicts: A Heuristic Method for Constraint-Satisfaction and Scheduling Problems. *Artificial Intelligence* 58, 161-205, 1992.

Mamoulis, N., Papadias, D. Integration of Spatial Join Algorithms for Processing Multiple Inputs. *ACM SIGMOD*, 1999a.

Mamoulis, N., Papadias, D. Improving Search Using Indexing: a Study with Temporal CSPs. *IJCAI*, 1999b.

Papadias, D., Mamoulis, N., Delis, V. Querying by Spatial Structure. *VLDB*, 1998.

Papadias, D., Mamoulis, N., Theodoridis, Y., Processing and Optimization of Multi-way Spatial Joins Using R-trees. *ACM PODS*, 1999.

Prosser, P. An Empirical Study of Phase Transitions in Binary Constraint Satisfaction Problems. *Artificial Intelligence*, 81 (1-2), 1996.

Randell, D., Cui, Z., Cohn., A. A Spatial Logic Based on Regions and Connection. *Knowledge Representation and Reasoning*, 1992.

Sosic, R., Gu, J. Efficient Local Search with Conflict minimization: A Case Study of the n-Queens Problem. *IEEE Transactions on Knowledge and Data Engineering*, 6(5): 661-668, 1994.

Theodoridis, Y., Sellis, T. A Model for the Prediction of R-tree Performance. *ACM PODS*, 1996.

A Constraint-Based Model for Cooperative Response Generation in Information Dialogues

Yan Qu
CLARITECH Corporation
5301 Fifth Avenue
Pittsburgh, PA 15232
yqu@claritech.com

Steve Beale
Computing Research Laboratory
New Mexico State University
Box 30001, Las Cruces, NM 88003-0001
sb@crl.nmsu.edu

Abstract

This paper presents a constraint-based model for cooperative response generation for information systems dialogues, with an emphasis on detecting and resolving situations in which the user's information needs have been over-constrained. Our model integrates and extends the AI techniques of constraint satisfaction, solution synthesis and constraint hierarchy to provide an incremental computational mechanism for constructing and maintaining partial parallel solutions. Such a mechanism supports immediate detection of over-constrained situations. In addition, we explore using the knowledge in the solution synthesis network to support different relaxation strategies.

Introduction

In typical human-computer information-seeking dialogues, the user and the system do not have perfect and detailed models of each other. Over-constrained situations occur when the preferences and restrictions in the user's information needs cannot all be satisfied. Generation of cooperative response in over-constrained situations has been addressed in many human-computer dialogue systems, e.g., (Kaplan 1979; Abella, Brown, & Buntschuh 1996; Pieraccini, Levin, & Eckert 1997; Litman, Pan, & Walker 1998). In identifying relaxation candidates, however, existing systems often employ heuristics (e.g., relaxation based on constraint weights (Abella, Brown, & Buntschuh 1996; Pieraccini, Levin, & Eckert 1997)) which do not take into account the interaction effects of constraints and lack a principled and efficient way to explore the interaction effects in arriving at relaxation candidates. In our work, we implement a constraint satisfaction-based model by integrating various AI techniques such as constraint satisfaction, solution synthesis (Tsang & Foster 1990; Beale 1997) and constraint hierarchy. Solution synthesis, when integrated with constraint satisfaction and constraint hierarchy, provides a mechanism

where the effects of constraint interaction are maintained as partial solutions. These effects can be exploited as a system's knowledge sources for diagnosing and resolving over-constrained situations.

Our constraint-based model supports the framework of incremental problem formulation and solution construction and refinement, consisting of *cycles of constraint acquisition, solution construction, solution evaluation, and solution modification*. The stage of constraint acquisition relies on interaction with the user. The stages of solution construction, solution evaluation and solution modification are conducted by the constraint-based problem solver. Through solution evaluation, over-constrained situations can be evaluated immediately. Through solution modification, the system can use its knowledge about the solution states to guide the adoption of cooperative strategies for resolving over-constrained situations. Repeating the cycles allows the system to help users with their problem formulation until a satisfying solution is found.

The next sections detail our constraint-based model for cooperative response generation. First, we present some terminology related to constraint satisfaction problems. Then we present in detail how the user's information needs and solutions are incrementally formulated and refined. We then illustrate how the use of knowledge sources in the constraint-based problem solver supports generation of cooperative responses in over-constrained situations. Finally, we discuss related work and summarize the paper.

Definitions

A *constraint satisfaction problem (CSP)* is typically defined as the problem of finding consistent assignment of values to a fixed set of variables given some constraints over these variables. In modeling human-computer interaction in information systems, a user's information request can be readily modeled as a CSP, with the set of attributes that constitutes a user's information need as the variables in a CSP, and the user's preferences and restrictions over these attributes as constraints. For instance, in the travel domain, attributes such as `arrival-city, departure-city,` date, carrier, time are treated as variables. The domains for these variables are legal values found in the database (e.g., carrier can be {UA,AA,USAIR,...}). The variables are constrained by domain relations in the database and by user preferences and restrictions on these variables.

In information domains, the user's preferences and restrictions may be of different strengths. For example, in the travel domain, the departure city and the arrival city are usually *required* to be satisfied, while the airline carrier is *preferred* but not required. We introduce *labeled constraints*, constraints which are labeled with their respective strengths. There can be an arbitrary number of strengths reflecting varying degrees of preferences. Constraints and their strengths constitute a *constraint hierarchy*. In information domains, the task of the system is to provide users with information satisfying their information needs as much as possible. In over-constrained situations, constraints with weaker strengths should be relaxed before constraints with higher strengths. The constraint strengths used for describing examples in our system include required, strong, weak, and weakest.

We use the labeled constraint formalism to represent various types of relationships found in the information domain. *Database constraints* reflect the functional dependencies between attributes in a database (assuming a relational one in this work). Such dependencies are usually represented as tuples. Database constraints have the default strength required. *Domain constraints* record attributes and their importance in solving stereotypical domain problems. *User constraints* represent the restrictions and preferences in the user's information needs. User constraints are usually domain reduction constraints for variables. *User profiles* record general constraints for a certain types of users or idiosyncratic constraints for individual users.

In CSPs, the variables, domains and constraints are fixed and known beforehand. In many problems, the set of variables and the set of constraints can change in the problem solving process. Such problems are modeled as *dynamic constraint satisfaction problems* (DSCPs). A dynamic CSP can be considered as a sequence of static CSPs each resulting from a change in the preceding one, representing new facts about the environment being modeled. As a result of such an incremental change, the set of solutions of the CSP may potentially decrease (i.e., a **restriction**) or increase (i.e., a **relaxation**). In information-seeking applications, the set of variables that are relevant to a user's information need and the values that can be assigned to them change dynamically in response to user input and the negotiation between the user and the system during the course of interaction. Therefore, information-seeking human-computer dialogues is a dynamic CSP.

Dynamic CSP-based Problem Solving

In this section, we present in detail each phase in the cycles of constraint-based constraint acquisition and solution construction/refinement model of information dialogues: constraint acquisition, solution construction, solution evaluation, and solution modification.

Constraint Acquisition

In the constraint acquisition phase, the system acquires constraints to update the problem definition which is modeled as a CSP. The system gathers constraints through (1) recognition of constraints from user input, (2) requesting constraints from the user, or (3) proposing constraints for user to confirm. Constraints gathered from (1) are user-initiated constraints. Constraints gathered through (2) and (3) are system-initiated constraints. The system's requests and proposals are initiated based on the recommended strategies from the solution modification phase, incorporating its knowledge of the solution status, domain-specific task solving knowledge sources, and user profiles. The user's answer to the system-initiated requests results in new constraints being added. As a cooperative agent, system-initiated proposals need to be negotiated with the user before they are finalized in the problem definition. In contrast, user-initiated constraints are generally incorporated into the current CSP the moment they are recognized without negotiation.

Currently, the strengths of the acquired constraints are deduced based on the linguistic cues in the user's utterances. From a corpus analysis of naturally occurring dialogues (Transcripts 1992), we classify linguistic cues into three strengths, required, strong, and weak. For example, we assign a required strength to constraints expressed through *I need to*, a strong strength to *it'd better be*, and a weak strength to *maybe* or *it could be*. When no linguistic cues are available, constraints get default strengths from user profiles, which are calculated based on corpus analysis of distributions of attributes and distributions of relaxed or modified attribute-value pairs in the corpus. The current constraint strength recognition mechanism could be extended by taking into account conversation circumstances and endorsing confidence measures as discussed in (Elzer, Chu, & Carberry 1994).

Solution Construction

We use solution synthesis techniques (Tsang & Foster 1990; Beale 1997) to generate all solutions to a CSP by iteratively combining partial answers to arrive at a complete list of all correct answers. In solution synthesis, the variables in a CSP are represented as the base level nodes in a graph (SS-graph). Subsets of base level nodes are combined yielding higher level nodes which represent legal compound labels satisfying k-variable constraints. Partial solutions for a subset of constraints are represented by the legal compound labels at the highest nodes covering the participating variables. The arcs represent the combination method used for combining lower level nodes into higher level nodes. Through solution synthesis, all assignments of values to variables that satisfy the problem's constraints are produced. Often, this list is then rated according to some separate criteria in order to pick the most suitable answer. Solution synthesis is applicable for problems when all possible solutions are required and for optimization problems.

We extend the solution synthesis technique in two ways: (1) we adapt the technique to dynamic CSPs, and (2) we integrate solution synthesis with constraint hierarchy.

Dynamic solution synthesis Applications that utilize solution synthesis are typically static CSPs (Tsang & Foster 1990; Beale 1997). A constraint-based model of interaction, however, is a DCSP: constraints and variables are dynamically added or removed during interaction in forming the problem definition and constructing a solution. Figure 1 demonstrates how solution synthesis is used and dynamically updated for constructing partial parallel solutions based on incrementally acquired constraints from dialogue excerpt 1 where the user specifies his or her constraints for a flight:

Dialogue excerpt 1:
User:
(U1) I need to reserve a flight to Dallas.
(U2) Maybe American Airlines.
(U3) It'd better be a night flight.
System:
(S1) American Airlines do not have any night flights to Dallas.

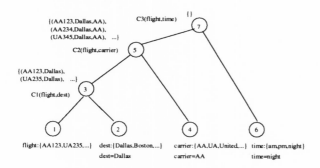

Figure 1: Solution synthesis

Through constraint acquisition, the system acquires new variables and constraints from utterances U1 to U3. The variables acquired include **flight, dest, carrier**, and **time**. The user constraints acquired include (1) the **dest** being Dallas with a **required** strength, (2) the **carrier** being American Airlines with a **weak** strength, and (3) the travel **time** being night with a **strong** strength. For utterance U1, the variables **flight** and **dest** are posted to the solution

space. Their initial domains are shown at nodes 1 and 2. The constraint that the flight have a destination of Dallas reduces the domain at node 2, with the synthesized solutions shown at node 3 containing all flights with a destination of Dallas as constrained by the database constraint $C_1(flight, dest)$[1][2], which specifies the functional dependency relation between **flight** and **dest** in the database. For utterance U2, the variable **carrier** is posted to the solution space (node 4). The constraint that the carrier be American Airlines reduces its domain. This can then be synthesized with node 3 to produce a set of answers at node 5 which include all American Airlines flights to Dallas, constrained by the database constraint $C_2(flight, carrier)$. Similarly, the variable travel **time** is posted to the solution space (node 6). After domain reduction, it is synthesized with node 5 to produce a set of answers at node 7 which include all American Airlines flights to Dallas departing at night, constrained by the database constraint $C_3(flight, time)$. In this dialogue, the final set of flights is empty.

In the above example, solution synthesis is extended by incrementally adding variables and constraints. Partial solutions are constructed and maintained in the dynamically updated SS-graph as new variables and constraints are introduced. In general, solution synthesis can be extended for DCSPs through operations for adding/removing variables and adding/removing/modifying constraints (Tsang & Foster 1990).

Adding or removing variables affects the structure of the SS-graph. In our system, added variables are simply appended to the tail of the ordered nodes at the base level, but synthesized with the top level nodes of the current SS-graph. Adding one variable in this way to an existing N-variable SS-graph involves constructing two extra nodes, one at the base level for the new variable, and the other at level $N + 1$ for the top level node. Removing variables from a SS-graph is in general complicated. Basically, when a node which represents the domain of the deleted variable is removed, all the nodes which are ancestors to the node must be either deleted or re-constructed. In our model of problem solving for the information domain, however, a variable is added into the solution space as a result of the negotiation process between the system and the user; variables never are deleted.

Adding, relaxing or modifying a constraint affects the size of nodes in the solution synthesis graph. Adding or tightening a constraint involves possible deletion of elements in some nodes. Relaxing con-

---

[1]Constraints C_1, C_2 and C_3 are simplified database constraints for illustration purposes. Actual database constraints can be n-ary rather than binary as in our illustration.

[2]This is where the constraint-based problem solver would normally interact with the back-end database.

straints involves possible addition of elements in some nodes. (Qu Forthcoming) gives the details on operations for updating the sets of variables and constraints and their complexity analysis.

Solution synthesis with constraint hierarchy The information of the preferential choices specified by a constraint hierarchy can be encoded in a graph such as an SS-graph with an incrementally maintained value called the *walkabout strength* (Maloney 1991). Specifically, every node in the SS-graph is annotated with a walkabout strength, which indicates the strength of the weakest constraint in the current graph that could be removed from the graph to allow some other constraints to be enforced by changing that node. The walkabout strength of a node may reflect the existence of a constraint quite far away in the SS-graph. Thus, the walkabout strengths encapsulate information for updating the SS-graph, which would otherwise have to be acquired by traversing the graph.

Walkabout strengths of nodes in an SS-graph are calculated by looking at the strengths of constraints in which the nodes participates, and the strengths of all the input nodes. The walkabout strength of a node in an SS-graph is defined as follows:

- if a node N is a base level node representing a variable without any constraint over it, then it gets a system-supplied walkabout strength **required**. This technicality simply means that once a variable is added to the graph, it stays there and never gets removed.

- if a node N is a base level node representing a variable, and a domain constraint C constrains the size of the node, then its walkabout strength is the weaker of C's strength and the node's **required** walkabout strength supplied by the system.

- if a node N is not a base level node, and a constraint C constrains the size of the node, then its walkabout strength is the weaker of C's strength and the weakest walkabout strengths among all the input nodes that participate in generating N.

Walkabout strength annotation can be straightforwardly incorporated into the dynamic solution synthesis procedures by annotating each node with its walkabout strength when the node is being constructed or when the node is being updated as a result of constraint update, yielding an SS-graph annotated with walkabout strengths.

For instance, suppose the constraints participating in solution synthesis have the following strengths (S) for the CSP of dialogue excerpt 1[3]:

---

[3] It is important to note the difference between walkabout strengths for variables (base level nodes in an SS-graph) and the strengths for user constraints. Walkabout strengths assigned to variables such as **dest** and **carrier** are based on the definition of walkabout strength for an SS-graph. The system-supplied **required** walkabout

strengths for user constraints:
$S(dest = Dallas) = $ **required**
$S(carrier = AA) = $ **weak**
$S(time = night) = $ **strong**
strengths for database constraints:
$S(C_1(flight, dest)) = $ **required**
$S(C_2(flight, carrier)) = $ **required**
$S(C_3(flight, time)) = $ **required**

According to the walkabout strength definition, the walkabout strengths (WS) of the nodes in the SS-graph for the CSP in Figure 2 are calculated as follows:

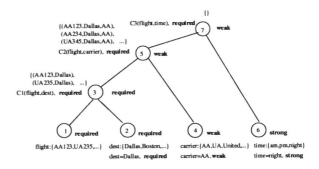

Figure 2: Solution synthesis with walkabout strengths

$WS_{Node1} = $ **required**
$WS_{Node2} = min\{$**required**$, S(dest = Dallas)\}$
$= $ **required**
$WS_{Node3} = min\{WS_{Node1}, WS_{Node2}, S(C_1)\}$
$= $ **required**
$WS_{Node4} = min\{$**required**$, S(carrier = AA)\}$
$= $ **weak**
$WS_{Node5} = min\{WS_{Node3}, WS_{Node4}, S(C_2)\}$
$= $ **weak**
$WS_{Node6} = min\{$**required**$, S(time = night)\}$
$= $ **strong**
$WS_{Node7} = min\{WS_{Node5}, WS_{Node6}, S(C_3)\}$
$= $ **weak**

Solution Evaluation

Solution evaluation characterizes the solution space into different solution situations. We use an evaluation function to characterize the solution space. Specifically, the evaluation function evaluates the top level node of the SS-graph, which records all the partial solutions obtained so far, to three possible values. If the top node evaluates to **NIL**, then an over-constrained

strength reflects the claim in our model that once an attribute is introduced as a variable into the problem definition, the attribute (variable) itself never gets dropped from the problem definition (SS-graph), even though the constraints over the variable may get modified. The fact that the destination city being a certain city is usually required for the information task while the carrier constraint can be optional is reflected by the strengths assigned to user constraints, e.g., $S(dest = Dallas) = $required, and $S(carrier = AA) = $**weak**.

```
1 PROCEDURE LocateRelaxCandidate (NodesOfSS)
2 RelaxCandidate < - NIL;
3 TopNode < - top level node from NodesOfSS
4 while RelaxCandidate not found,
(4.a) if walkabout strength of TopNode resulted
from a constraint C,
then RelaxCandidate < - constraint C;
(4.b) else if walkabout strength resulted from
an InputNode, then TopNode < - InputNode;
(4.c) else if there is a tie between the candidate
InputNodes or constraints,
then TopNode < - a randomly selected InputNode;
5 return RelaxCandidate;
```

Figure 3: Use of walkabout strengths for relaxation

situation is detected, which suggests that some constraints need to be relaxed to get a solution. If the top node evaluates to a set whose number of solutions exceeds a pre-defined threshold k (e.g., $k = 5$ is a good heuristic number), then the problem is under-constrained, which suggests that a cooperative system should employ initiative taking strategies to help the user deal with the under-constrained situations. If the top node evaluates to a set whose number of solutions is within a pre-defined threshold k, then the solution set is small enough, and the system can decide to present the solutions to the user at this point.

Consider again Figure 2 for dialogue excerpt 1. The constraints from utterance U2 are incorporated into the SS-graph resulting in a new top level node 7, which evaluates to **NIL**. This signals an over-constrained situation.

Solution Modification

When no solutions can be found to satisfy the user's information needs, a cooperative system need to provide relaxed solutions in addition to informing the user of the over-constrained situation. The solution modification module is invoked when over-constrained situations are detected. Its task is to support strategies for relaxation in over-constrained situations to help the user with the problem definition. Efficient instantiation of the parameters in these strategies are made possible by exploiting knowledge sources recorded in the solution synthesis graph, and by interacting with domain knowledge sources and user models. Our model recognizes the fact that over-constrained situations result from *interactions* between constraints, e.g. between user constraints and database constraints, and that the partial solutions in an SS-graph encode the effects of such interactions.

Knowledge sources for constraint relaxation
The knowledge sources we explore for resolving over-constrained situations include the walkabout strengths and node density ratios.
Constraint hierarchy and walkabout strengths

We use the constraint hierarchy as a systematic way of ordering the importance of the constraints. As we mentioned earlier, such preferential information can be encoded as walkabout strengths of the nodes in an SS-graph, while the partial solutions are computed. The walkabout strength of a node indicates the strength of the weakest constraint in the current solution graph that could be removed or modified from the solution graph to allow some other constraints to be enforced by changing that node. When an over-constrained situation is detected, the system tries to satisfy the constraints with higher strengths in the constraint hierarchy, while relaxing constraints with lower strengths first. Figure 3 describes the procedure for locating the constraint with the weakest walkabout strength as the relaxation candidate. The incremental running time of this algorithm grows linearly with the number of variables in the CSP.

Solution synthesis network structure The sizes of the nodes in the solution synthesis network, which encode partial solutions, yield another source of information that we can exploit. For example, relaxation of constraints is typically most advantageous at a point where a solution synthesis node yields a partial solution that is relatively small compared to its inputs. This indicates that some constraint has removed many possible solutions. We introduce the notion of *node density* with respect to its input nodes to record the number of compound labels satisfying participating constraints at this node over the number of possible compound labels as a result of product combination of the values from its input nodes. The node density ratio reflects the combined efforts of all the constraints effective over the compound labels of a node. The smaller the node density ratio, the more constraining the participating constraints. The node density information can be combined with the walkabout strengths in identifying candidates for relaxation. We give priority to the walkabout strengths over node density ratios, and use the latter only for breaking the ties among candidates. In Figure 3, we use a simple tie-breaking heuristic in preferring input nodes over constraints with the same strength. This heuristic reflects an artifact of our domain where the user constraints are usually domain reduction constraints represented at the base level of the SS-graph, while domain and database constraints are usually exerted at higher level nodes to reduce the set of possible solutions. Since domain and database constraints usually have **required** strengths, the relaxation is likely to happen with the user constraints over base level nodes. Using the combined knowledge sources, we introduce another heuristic to break the tie between candidate nodes. The revised tie-breaking act becomes:
(4.c') if there is a tie between the candidate
InputNodes or constraints,
then TopNode < - InputNode with the lowest
node density ratio;

Relaxation example Relaxation candidates can be identified based on the knowledge sources we just discussed.

Relaxation using walkabout strengths Consider again the SS-graph for dialogue excerpt 1 repeated here in Figure 4. When an over-constrained situation is detected, solution modification is evoked to identify the candidate constraint for relaxation. The traversal starts from the top node 7. Since the **weak** walkabout strength of node 7 results from the walkabout strength of node 5, node 5 is chosen as the candidate node. This process repeats recursively until node 4 is identified as a candidate node. Since the **weak** walkabout strength of node 4 results from the user constraint carrier being American Airlines, this constraint is identified as the constraint for relaxation.

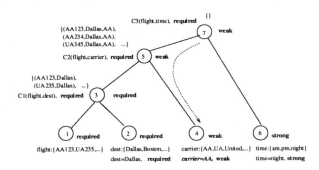

Figure 4: Relaxation based on walkabout strengths

Relaxation based on solution synthesis network structure and walkabout strength Suppose in dialogue excerpt 1, instead of saying in U3 *"It'd better be a night flight"*, the user said *"I could take a night flight"*, then during constraint acquisition, the strength of the constraint travel time being night would be recognized as **weak** as illustrated in Figure 5 instead of **strong** (in Figure 4). Consequently, the walkabout strength for node 6 is **weak** instead of **strong**. Also suppose that as a result of the constraint $C_1(flight, dest)$, the number of legal solution tuples at node 3 is 100. Since the number of possible solution tuples at node 4 is 1 due to the constraint $carrier = AA$, the number of possible compound labels at node 5 as a result of product combination of its input nodes (nodes 3 and 4) is 100. Suppose after satisfying the constraint $C_2(flight, carrier)$, only 87 tuples remain at node 5, then node 5 has a node density ratio (ND) of 87/100. At node 6, the constraint $time = night$ results in a ND ratio of 1/3. Now when traversal starts from the top node 7, both node 5 and node 6 are tied as relaxation candidates based on walkabout strengths. Our revised tie-breaking rule (4.c') chooses node 6, as the constraints at node 6 more tightly constrain the solution tuples at that node. As the **weak** walkabout strength of node 6 results from the user constraint travel time being night, this constraint is identified as the constraint for relaxation.

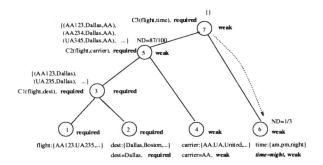

Figure 5: Relaxation based on walkabout strengths and node density ratios with walkabout strength of node 6 changed to **weak**

Evaluation of relaxation candidates Simply identifying a constraint for relaxation does not guarantee that a solution will be found. As a cooperative agent who has access to the back-end databases to evaluate the relaxation candidates, the system should make sure that relaxation of the candidate constraint will lead to a solution. In our system, when a user constraint is chosen for relaxation, the user constraint $v_i = val$ is replaced by assigning all the possible domain values to v_i, with the strength **required**, as no further relaxation is possible when all domain values are considered. Then all the ancestor nodes to the current node are re-computed, yielding a new solution synthesis graph. If a solution is found at the top node, then such a relaxation is valid; the system can in turn initiate appropriate dialogue acts to inform the user of such relaxation proposal. If however, after such a relaxation, the relaxed problem is still over-constrained, a new relaxation candidate is further identified by repeating the procedure in Figure 3 until a solution is found.

Before a solution is found, a set of constraints may have been relaxed. If there exists a solution for all the **required** constraints of the CSP, our procedure is guaranteed to find that solution by incrementally relaxing constraints of weaker strengths. We define solution optimality for a relaxed CSP as (1) satisfying the constraints with higher strengths first, and (2) satisfying as many original constraints as possible[4]. The incremental relaxation procedure guarantees the first condition of optimality. The second condition of optimality is satisfied by ranking all solution tuples based on the order of maximally satisfying (a) the original set of user constraints, (b) the constraints in user models, and (c) the constraints in domain knowledge. The solution satisfying more constraints in a set is ranked higher than other solutions. Such an ordering could be further augmented by introducing metrics

---

[4]Note that in over-constrained situations, solution ordering only becomes meaningful when the system has the turn.

such as closeness of the matched values (Elzer, Chu, & Carberry 1994) and semantic distances between solutions (Pieraccini, Levin, & Eckert 1997).

Cooperative Response Generation

The focus of solution modification for over-constrained problems is to identify the candidate constraints for relaxation that will yield solutions to resolve the over-constrained situations. The system will be considered uncooperative, however, if it modifies the problem definition without the user's consent. Thus cooperative principles require that the proposed modifications by the system be accepted by the user. This requirement causes the system to go back to the constraint acquisition phase to interact with the user by generating natural language utterances to negotiate the changes in the problem definition. The selection of a particular dialogue act should be based on the system's existing knowledge of the solution status and the degrees of system initiative. We conducted corpus analysis of naturally occurring information dialogues (Transcripts 1992) to identify problem solving initiative-taking dialogue acts for various dialogue situations. Detailed enumeration of these dialogue acts and the criteria under which they occur are discussed in (Qu Forthcoming). Three dialogue acts, presented in an increasing degree of system initiative, could be selected to resolve the over-constrained situations.

Dialogue act 1: Request a new value for a variable. The system takes the initiative in indicating the constraint that requires relaxation. An example NL utterance for this dialogue act is: ***Does any other airline work for you?*** in which the system proposes replacing the previous constraint $carrier = AA$ with some new constraint. Specific airline values provided by the user or simple positive answer to this request will result in an update in the problem definition and in new solutions in the solution construction phase.

Dialogue act 2: Propose a new value for a variable. The system takes the initiative in proposing a new constraint to replace an existing one. The proposed instantiation of the variable is obtained from the optimal solution obtained during solution modification. Being a cooperative agent, the system needs to obtain the user's acceptance first before the constraint can be finalized into the SS-graph. An example NL utterance for this act is: ***Does United Airlines work for you?*** in which the system proposes replacing the previous constraint $carrier = AA$ with the new constraint $carrier = United$. Acceptance of this utterance by the user will result in an update in the problem definition and in new solutions in the solution construction phase.

Dialogue act 3: Propose a new value for an attribute and inform user of solutions. The system takes the problem solving initiative one step further than that in act 2, in also informing the optimal solutions resulted from such proposed modification. An

example NL utterance for this act is ***United Airlines has one leaving at 8:45pm.*** in which the system proposes replacing the previous constraint $carrier = AA$ with the new constraint $carrier = United$, and informs the user that once such constraint modification is made, solution is possible.

A possible future extension is to generate reasons to support the above relaxation dialogue acts, e.g., ***Does United Airlines work for you? Since no other airlines have such flights.*** Such supporting rationales could be generated in our framework by comparing the attribute values between different solutions.

Related Work

Generation of cooperative response in over-constrained situations has been addressed in many human-computer dialogue systems, e.g., (Kaplan 1979; Abella, Brown, & Buntschuh 1996; Pieraccini, Levin, & Eckert 1997; Litman, Pan, & Walker 1998). Our work is similar to many of these systems in (1) using solution evaluation in identifying over-constrained situations, and (2) interleaving information gathering and solution update. In identifying relaxation candidates, however, existing systems employ heuristics (e.g., relaxation based on constraint weights (Abella, Brown, & Buntschuh 1996; Pieraccini, Levin, & Eckert 1997)) which do not take into account the interaction effects of constraints and lack a principled way to explore the interaction effects in arriving at relaxation candidates. The solution synthesis-based problem solver in our model provides a mechanism where the effects of constraint interaction are maintained as partial solutions, which can be exploited as the system's knowledge sources when over-constrained situations occur. The use of walkabout strengths provides a principled way to explore the SS-graph for relaxation candidates in linear running time. In addition, the SS-graph supports re-use of many partial solutions in constructing or modifying solutions.

Relaxing over-constrained queries and possibly proposing relaxation modification is also analogous to previous work on detecting invalid beliefs/plans and suggesting possible alternative solutions, e.g., (Joshi, Webber, & Weischedel 1984; van Beek 1987; Chu-Carroll & Carberry 1994). In particular, the cycles in the framework of incremental constraint acquisition and solution construction/refinement are similar to the *Propose-Evaluation-Modify* cycle for collaborative response generation in (Chu-Carroll & Carberry 1994). However, the above work addresses cooperative response generation based on modeling of plans and beliefs, while our work focuses on using CSP-based models for problem solving. The CSP-based problem solver could be incorporated with other aspects of dialogue processing, such as belief and plan modeling, to formulate different types of cooperative responses.

Constraint computation has been used for modeling the dynamic nature of discourse in (Donaldson & Cohen 1997). The focus of their work, however, is to use local repair techniques to generate solutions in managing turn-taking goals.

Conclusions and Future Work

In this paper, we presented a novel way to integrate and extend the AI techniques of constraint satisfaction, solution synthesis and constraint hierarchy for the problem of cooperative response generation. We illustrated that the knowledge sources in an SS-graph can be exploited in a principled and efficient way for suggesting relaxation candidates in over-constrained situations.

Our ongoing work addresses several open issues of the CSP model. The current framework for incremental problem definition and solution construction requires database retrieval whenever database constraints are encountered, e.g., constraints C_1-C_3. Access to back-end databases incur communication cost and retrieval cost, which can be expensive in excess. In many tasks, it is reasonable to assume that an information need is not over-constrained without actually accessing the database (e.g., at the beginning of a dialogue when few constraints are introduced) by specifying a minimal set of constraints for each particular topic before database retrieval occurs. In fact, such an assumption has been generally followed in most existing information systems, in which the systems collect user constraints to a certain set before interacting with the back-end databases. However, the drawbacks of such an assumption are (1) that identification of over-constrained situations may be delayed, and (2) that partial solutions will not be available to support identification of relaxation candidates in an efficient and principled manner. Our proposal is to use a caching mechanism to store portions of retrieved results, and to access this cache to reduce communication and retrieval costs while building an SS-graph. The trade-off between space demand and cost reduction of utilizing the caching mechanism requires further investigation.

Adoption of different dialogue acts can affect the dialogue efficiency and effectiveness of human-computer dialogue. For example, we hypothesize that dialogue act 1 is less efficient than dialogue acts 2 and 3 because new user constraints obtained from a user's response to dialogue act 1 may again lead to an over-constrained situation. Our ongoing work focuses on evaluating the effectiveness and efficiency of the dialogue acts with respect to factors such as problem structure, solution structure, user profiles, and constraints in domain data.

Acknowledgments

The work reported here is based on the first author's dissertation research at Language Technologies Institute, Carnegie Mellon University. We thank Nancy Green, Jaime Carbonell, Barbara Di Eugenio and three anonymous reviewers for their comments on earlier versions of this paper.

References

Abella, A.; Brown, M. K.; and Buntschuh, B. 1996. Development principles for dialogue-based interfaces. In *Proceedings of ECAI'96 Workshop on Dialogue Processing in Spoken Language Systems*, 1–7.

Beale, S. 1997. *HUNTER-GATHERER: Applying Constraint Satisfaction, Branch-and-Bound and Solution Synthesis to Computational Semantics*. Ph.D. Dissertation, School of Computer Science, Carnegie Mellon University.

Chu-Carroll, J., and Carberry, S. 1994. A plan-based model for response generation in collaborative task-oriented dialogues. In *Proceedings of the AAAI-94*, 799–805.

Donaldson, T., and Cohen, R. 1997. A constraint satisfaction framework for managing mixed-initiative discouse. In *Proceedings of 1997 AAAI Spring Symposium on Mixed-Initiative Interaction*.

Elzer, S.; Chu, J.; and Carberry, S. 1994. Recognizing and utilizing user preferences in collaborative consulation dialogues. In *User Modeling Conference*.

Joshi, A.; Webber, B.; and Weischedel, R. M. 1984. Living up to expectations: computing expert responses. In *Proceedings of the AAAI-84*, 169–175.

Kaplan, S. J. 1979. *Cooperative responses from a portable natural language data base query system*. Ph.D. Dissertation, School of Computer and Information Science, University of Pennsylvania.

Litman, D. J.; Pan, S.; and Walker, M. A. 1998. Evaluating response strategies in a web-based spoken dialogue agent. In *COLING/ACL-98*, 780–786.

Maloney, J. H. 1991. *Using Constraints for User Interface Construction*. Ph.D. Dissertation, Department of Computer Science and Engineering, University of Washington.

Pieraccini, R.; Levin, E.; and Eckert, W. 1997. *AMICA*: the *at & t* mixed initiative conversational architecture. In *Proceedings of EUROSPEECH 97*.

Qu, Y. Forthcoming. A constraint-based model of cooperative response generation in spoken information systems.

Transcripts, S. 1992. Transcripts derived from audiotape conversations made at SRI International, Menlo Park, CA. Prepared by Jacqueline Kowtko under the direction of Patti Price.

Tsang, E., and Foster, N. 1990. Solution synthesis in the constraint satisfaction problem. Technical Report Technical Report CSM-142, Department of Computer Science, University of Essex.

van Beek, P. 1987. A model for generating better explanations. In *Proceedings of the ACL*, 215–220.

Solving Crossword Puzzles as Probabilistic Constraint Satisfaction

Noam M. Shazeer, Michael L. Littman, Greg A. Keim
Department of Computer Science
Duke University, Durham, NC 27708-0129
{noam,mlittman,keim}@cs.duke.edu

Abstract

Crossword puzzle solving is a classic constraint satisfaction problem, but, when solving a real puzzle, the mapping from clues to variable domains is not perfectly crisp. At best, clues induce a probability distribution over viable targets, which must somehow be respected along with the constraints of the puzzle. Motivated by this type of problem, we describe a formal model of constraint satisfaction with probabilistic preferences on variable values. Two natural optimization problems are defined for this model: maximizing the probability of a correct solution, and maximizing the number of correct words (variable values) in the solution. To the latter, we apply an efficient iterative approximation equivalent to turbo decoding and present results on a collection of real and artificial crossword puzzles.

Introduction

Constraint satisfaction is a powerful and general formalism. Crossword puzzles are frequently used as examples of constraint satisfaction problems (CSPs), and search can be used to great effect in crossword-puzzle creation (Ginsberg *et al.* 1990). However, we are not aware of any attempts to apply CSPs to the problem of solving a crossword puzzle from a set of clues. This is due, in part, to the fact that traditional CSPs have no notion of "better" or "worse" solutions, making it difficult to express the fact that we prefer solutions that fill the grid and match the clues to ones that simply fill the grid.

To address this problem, this paper describes a probabilistic extension to CSPs that induces probability distributions over solutions. We study two optimization problems for this model. The maximum probability solution corresponds to maximizing the probability of a correct solution, while the maximum expected overlap solution corresponds to maximizing the number of correct variable values in the solution. The former can be solved using standard constrained-optimization techniques. The latter is closely related to belief network inference, and we apply an efficient iterative approximation equivalent to Pearl's belief propagation algorithm (Pearl 1988) on a multiply connected network.

We describe how the two optimization problems and the approximation result in different solutions on a collection of artificial puzzles. We then describe an extension to our solver that has been applied to a collection of real New York Times crossword puzzles. Our system achieves a score of 89.5% words correct on average, up from 51.8% for a more naive approximation.

Constraint Satisfaction Problems

We define a (Boolean) constraint satisfaction problem (Mackworth 1977), or CSP, as a set of variables and constraints on the values of these variables. For example, consider the crossword puzzle in Figure 1. Here, variables, or slots, are the places words can be written. The binary constraints on variable instantiations are that across and down words mesh. The domain of a variable, listed beneath the puzzles, is the set of values the variable can take on; for example, variable 3A (3 across) can take on values FUN or TAD. A solution to a CSP is an instantiation (assignment of values to the variables) such that each variable is assigned a value in its domain and no constraint is violated. The crossword CSP in Figure 1 has four solutions, which are labeled **A** through **D** in the figure. (The probability values in the figure will be explained next.)

Although CSPs can be applied to many real-world problems, some problems do not fit naturally into this framework. The example we consider in this paper is the problem of solving a crossword puzzle from its clues. The slots of the puzzle are nicely captured by CSP variables, and the grid by CSP constraints, but how do we transform the clues into domain values for the variables? A natural approach is to take a clue like "Small amount [3]" and generate a small set of candidate answers of the appropriate length to be the domain: TAD, JOT, DAB, BIT, for example.

This approach has several shortcomings. First, because of the flexibility of natural language, almost any word can be the answer to almost any clue; limiting domains to small sets will likely exclude critical candidates. Second, even with a direct clue, imperfections in automated natural language processing may cause a

	A	B	C	D
P :	0.350	0.250	0.267	0.133
Q :	2.367	2.833	3.233	2.866
Q^{∞}:	2.214	2.793	3.529	3.074

slot 1A				slot 1D			
v	p	q	$q^{(\infty)}$	v	p	q	$q^{(\infty)}$
AS	.5	.250	.190	IT	.4	.400	.496
IN	.3	.617	.645	IF	.3	.350	.314
IS	.2	.133	.165	AT	.3	.250	.190

slot 3A				slot 2D			
v	p	q	$q^{(\infty)}$	v	p	q	$q^{(\infty)}$
FUN	.7	.350	.314	NAG	.4	.267	.331
TAD	.3	.650	.686	SAG	.3	.383	.355
				NUT	.3	.350	.314

slot 5A				slot 4D			
v	p	q	$q^{(\infty)}$	v	p	q	$q^{(\infty)}$
GO	.7	.650	.686	NO	.7	.350	.314
TO	.3	.350	.314	DO	.3	.650	.686

Figure 1: This crossword puzzle with probabilistic preferences (p) on the candidate words (v) has four possible solutions, varying in probability (P) and expected overlap (Q). Posteriors (q) and their approximations ($q^{(\infty)}$) are described in the text.

reasonable candidate to be excluded. To avoid these difficulties, we might be tempted to over-generate our candidate lists. Of course, this has the new shortcoming that spurious solutions will result.

This is a familiar problem in the design of grammars for natural language parsing: "Either the grammar assigns too many structures ... or it incorrectly predicts that examples...have no well-formed structure" (Abney 1996). A solution in the natural language domain is to annotate grammar rules with probabilities, so that uncommon rules can be included (for coverage) but marked as less desirable than more common rules (for correctness). Then, no grammatical structure is deemed impossible, but better structures are assigned higher probability.

Following this line of thought for the crossword puzzle CSP, we annotate the domain of each variable with preferences in the form of probabilities. This gives a solver a way to distinguish better and worse solutions to the CSP with respect to goodness of fit to the clues.

Formally, we begin with a CSP specified as a set of n variables $X = \{x_1, \dots, x_n\}$ with domain D_i for each $x_i \in X$. The variables are coupled through a constraint relation match, defined on pairs of variables and values: if x_i, x_j are variables and v, w are values, the proposition $\text{match}_{x_i, x_j}(v, w)$ is true if and only if the partial instantiation $\{x_i = v, x_j = w\}$ does not violate any constraints. The match relation can be represented as a set

of constraint tables, one for each pair of variables in X. The variables, values, and constraints are jointly called a *constraint network*. We then add preference information to the constraint network in the form of probability distributions over domains: $p_{x_i}(v)$ is the probability that we take $v \in D_i$ to be the value of variable x_i. Since p_{x_i} is a probability distribution, we insist that for all $1 \le i \le n$, $\sum_{v \in D_i} p_{x_i}(v) = 1$ and for all $v \in D_i$, $p_{x_i}(v) \ge 0$. This is a special case of probabilistic CSPs (Schiex, Fargier, & Verfaillie 1995). An opportunity for future work is to extend the algorithms described here to general probabilistic CSPs.

In the crossword example, probabilities can be chosen by a statistical analysis of the relation between the clue and the candidate; we have adopted a particular approach to this problem, which we sketch in a later section. Extending the running example, we can annotate the domain of each variable with probabilities, as shown in Figure 1 in the columns marked "p". (We have no idea what clues would produce these candidate lists and probabilities; they are intended for illustration only.) For example, the figure lists $p_{2D}(\text{NUT}) = 0.3$.

We next need to describe how preferences on values can be used to induce preferences over complete solutions. We consider the following probability model. Imagine that solutions are "generated" by independently selecting a value for each variable according to its probability distribution p, then, if the resulting instantiation satisfies all constraints, we "keep" it, otherwise we discard it and draw again. This induces a probability distribution over solutions to the CSP in which the probability of a solution is proportional to the product of the probabilities of each of the values of the variables in the solution. The resulting solution probabilities for our example CSP are given in Figure 1 in the row marked P.

The solution probabilities come from taking the product of the value probabilities and then normalizing by the total probability assigned to all valid solutions ($\Pr(\text{match})$). For example, the probability assigned to solution **C** is computed as:

$$
\begin{aligned}
P(\mathbf{C}) &= p_{1A}(\text{IN}) \cdot p_{3A}(\text{TAD}) \cdot p_{5A}(\text{GO}) \cdot p_{1D}(\text{IT}) \\
&\quad \cdot p_{2D}(\text{NAG}) \cdot p_{4D}(\text{DO}) / \Pr(\text{match}) \\
&= (0.3)(0.3)(0.7)(0.4)(0.4)(0.3) / \Pr(\text{match}) \\
&= 0.00302/0.01134 = 0.26667.
\end{aligned}
$$

In the next section, we discuss how these values can be used to guide the selection of a solution.

Optimization Problems

We can use the probability distribution over solutions, as defined above, to select a "best" solution to the CSP. There are many possible notions of a best solution, each with its own optimization algorithms. In this paper, we consider two optimization problems on CSPs with probabilistic preferences: maximum probability solution and maximum expected overlap solution.

The *maximum probability* solution is an instantiation of the CSP that satisfies the constraints and has the largest probability of all such instantiations (solution **A** with $P(\mathbf{A}) = 0.350$ from Figure 1). It can be found by computing

$$\underset{\text{soln:}v_1,\ldots,v_n}{\text{argmax}} \quad P(v_1,\ldots,v_n)$$

$$= \underset{\text{soln:}v_1,\ldots,v_n}{\text{argmax}} \prod_{i=1}^{n} p_{x_i}(v_i)/\Pr(\text{match})$$

$$= \underset{\text{soln:}v_1,\ldots,v_n}{\text{argmax}} \prod_{i=1}^{n} p_{x_i}(v_i). \qquad (1)$$

That is, we just need to search for the solution that maximizes the product of the preferences p. This is an NP-complete problem (Garey & Johnson 1979), but it can be attacked by any of a number of standard search procedures: A*, branch and bound, integer linear programming, weighted Boolean satisfiability, etc.

Another way of viewing the maximum probability solution is as follows. Imagine we are playing a game against Nature. Nature selects a solution at random according to the probability distribution described in the previous section, and keeps its selection hidden. We must now propose a solution for ourselves. If our solution matches the one selected by Nature, we win one dollar. If not, we win nothing. If we want to select the solution that maximizes our expected winnings (the probability of being completely correct), then clearly the maximum probability solution is the best choice.

The *maximum expected overlap* solution is a more complicated solution concept and is specific to our probabilistic interpretation of preferences. It is motivated by the crossword puzzle scoring procedure used in the yearly human championship known as the American Crossword Puzzle Tournament (Shortz 1990). The idea is that we can receive partial credit for a proposed solution to a crossword puzzle by counting the number of words it has in common with the true solution.

In a probabilistic setting, we can view the problem as another game against Nature. Once again, Nature selects a solution at random weighted by the P distribution and we propose a solution for ourselves. For every word (variable-value pair) in common between the two solutions (i.e., the overlap), we win one dollar. Again, we wish to select the solution that maximizes our expected winnings (the number of correct words).

In practice, the maximum expected overlap solution is often highly correlated with the maximum probability solution. However, they are not always the same. The expected overlap Q for each the four solutions in figure 1 is listed in the table; the maximum expected overlap solution is **C**, with $Q(\mathbf{C}) = 3.233$ whereas the maximum probability solution is **A**. Thus, if we choose **A** as our solution, we'd expect to have 2.367 out of six words correct, whereas solution **C** scores almost a full word higher, on average.

To compute the expected overlap, we use a new set of probabilities: $q_x(v)$ is the probability that variable x has value v in a solution. It is defined as the sum of the probabilities of all solutions that assign v to x. Whereas $p_x(v)$ is a prior probability on setting variable x to value v, $q_x(v)$ is a posterior probability. Note that for some slots, like 3A, the prior p and posterior q of the values differ substantially.

As a concrete example of where the q values come from, consider $q_{2D}(\text{SAG}) = \Pr(\mathbf{B}) + \Pr(\mathbf{D}) = 0.250 + 0.133 = 0.383$. For the expected overlap Q, we have

$$\begin{aligned} Q(\mathbf{D}) &= q_{1A}(\text{IS}) + q_{3A}(\text{TAD}) + q_{5A}(\text{GO}) + \\ &\quad q_{1D}(\text{IT}) + q_{2D}(\text{SAG}) + q_{4D}(\text{DO}) \\ &= 0.133 + 0.650 + 0.650 + 0.400 + \\ &\quad 0.383 + 0.650 = 2.867 \end{aligned}$$

By the linearity of expectation,

$$\underset{\text{soln:}v_1,\ldots,v_n}{\text{argmax}} \quad Q(v_1,\ldots,v_n)$$

$$= \underset{\text{soln:}v_1,\ldots,v_n}{\text{argmax}} \sum_{i=1}^{n} q_{x_i}(v_i), \qquad (2)$$

thus, computing the maximum expected overlap solution is a matter of finding the solution that maximizes the sum of a set of weights, q. The weights are very hard to compute in the worst case because they involve a sum over all solutions. The complexity is #P-complete, like belief network inference (Roth 1996).

In the next section, we develop a procedure for efficiently approximating q. We will then give results on the use of the resulting approximations for solving artificial and real crossword puzzles.

Estimating the Posteriors

Constraint satisfaction problems with probabilistic preferences have elements in common with both constraint networks and belief networks (Pearl 1988). So, it is not surprising that, although computing posterior probabilities in general CSPs with probabilistic preferences is intractable, when the constraint relations form a tree (no loops), computing posterior probabilities is easy.

Given a constraint network N with cycles, a variable x with domain D, and value $v \in D$, we want to approximate the posterior probability $q_x(v)$ that variable x gets value v in a complete solution. We develop a series of approximations of N around x described next.

Let the "unwrapped network" $U_x^{(d)}$ be the breadth-first search tree of depth d around x where revisitation of variables is allowed, but immediate backtracking is not. For example, Figure 2(a) gives the constraint network form of the crossword puzzle from Figure 1. Figures 2(b)–(f) give a sequence of breadth-first search trees $U_{3A}^{(d)}$ of differing depths around 3A. The graph $U_x^{(d)}$ is acyclic for all d. The limiting case $U_x^{(\infty)}$, is a possibly infinite acyclic network locally similar to N in the sense that the labels on neighbors in the infinite tree match

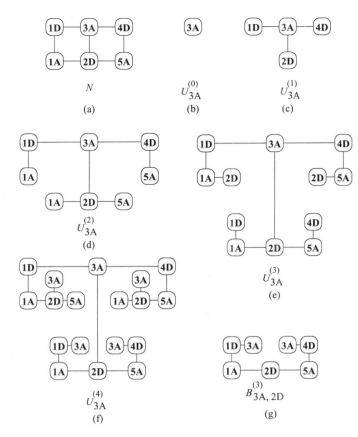

Figure 2: A cyclic constraint network can be approximated by tractable tree-structured constraint networks.

those in the cyclic network. This construction parallels the notion of a universal covering space from topology theory (Munkres 1975).

We consider $U_x^{(d)}$ as a constraint network. We give each variable an independent prior distribution equal to that of the variable in N with the same label.

Let $q_x^{(d)}(v)$ be the posterior probability that x takes value v in the network $U_x^{(d)}$. As d increases, we'd expect $q_x^{(d)}(v)$ to become a better estimate of $q_x(v)$ since the structure of $U^{(d)}$ becomes more similar to N. (In fact, there is no guarantee this will be the case, but it is true in the examples we've studied.)

Computing the posteriors on unwrapped networks has been shown equivalent to Pearl's belief propagation algorithm (Weiss 1997), which is exact on singly connected networks but only approximate on loopy ones (Pearl 1988).

We will now derive efficient iterative equations for $q_x^{(d)}(v)$. Consider a variable x with neighbors $y_1, \ldots, y_m$. We define $B_{x,y_i}^{(d)}$ as the y_i-branch of $U_x^{(d+1)}$, or equivalently, $U_{y_i}^{(d)}$ with the x-branch removed (see Figure 2(g)). Let $b_{x,y_i}^{(d)}(w)$ be the posterior probability that y_i takes value w in the network $B_{x,y_i}^{(d)}$. Note

that $U_x^{(0)}$ and $B_{x,y_i}^{(0)}$ contain the single variables x and y_i respectively. Thus,

$$q_x^{(0)}(v) = p_x(v) \quad \text{and} \quad b_{x,y_i}^{(0)}(w) = p_{y_i}(w).$$

For positive d, we view $U_x^{(d)}$ as a tree with root x and branches $B_{x,y_i}^{(d-1)}$. According to our model, a solution on $U_x^{(d)}$ is generated by independently instantiating all variables according to their priors, and discarding the solution if constraints are violated. This is equivalent to first instantiating all of the branches and checking for violations, then instantiating x and checking for violations. Furthermore, since the branches are disjoint, they can each be instantiated separately. After instantiating and checking the branches, the neighbors y_1 through y_m are independent and y_i has probability distribution $b_{x,y_i}^{(d-1)}$. The posterior probability $q_x^{(d)}(v)$ that x takes the value v is then proportional to the probability $p_x(v)$ that v is chosen multiplied by the probability that $x = v$ does not violate a constraint between x and one of its neighbors. We get

$$q_x^{(d)}(v) = k_x^{(d)} p_x(v) \cdot \prod_{i=1}^{m} \sum_{w | \text{match}_{y_i,x}(w,v)} b_{x,y_i}^{(d-1)}(w),$$

where $k_x^{(d)}$ is the normalization constant necessary to make the probabilities sum to one. Since $B_{y_i,x}^{(d)}$ is simply $U_x^{(d)}$ with one branch removed[1], the equation for $b_{y_i,x}^{(d)}(v)$ is very similar to the one for $q_x^{(d)}(v)$:

$$b_{y_i,x}^{(d)}(v) = k_{y_i,x}^{(d)} p_x(v) \cdot \prod_{j=1..m, j \neq i} \sum_{w | \text{match}_{y_j,x}(w,v)} b_{x,y_j}^{(d-1)}(w).$$

Note that, as long as the constraint network N is 2-consistent, the candidate lists are non-empty and the normalization factors are non-zero.

The sequence $\{q_x^{(d)}(v)\}$ does not always converge. However, it converges in all of our artificial experiments. If it converges, we call its limit $q_x^{(\infty)}(v)$.

In the case in which N is a tree of maximum depth k, $U_x^{(d)} = U_x^{(\infty)} = N$ for all $d \geq k$. Thus, $q_x^{(\infty)}(v) = q_x(v)$, the true posterior probability. However, in the general case in which N contains cycles, $U_x^{(\infty)}$ is infinite. We hope that its local similarity to N makes $q_x^{(\infty)}(v)$ a good estimator of $q_x(v)$.

The running time of the calculation of $q^{(d)}$ is polynomial. If there are n variables, each of which is constrained by at most μ other variables, and the maximum size of any of the constraint tables is s, then $\{b^{(d)}\}$ and $\{q^{(d)}\}$ can be computed from $b^{(d-1)}$ in $O(n\mu^2 s)$ time. In our crossword solver, the candidate lists are very large, so s is enormous. To reduce the value of s, we inserted

---

[1] We reversed subscripts in $B^{(d)}$ to maintain parallelism.

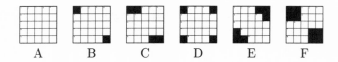

Figure 3: After symmetries have been removed, there are six tournament-legal 5×5 crossword grids.

Maximized Qty.	P	Q	$\frac{P}{P(maxP)}$	$\frac{Q}{Q(maxQ)}$
$P \propto \prod p$	.0552	3.433	1.00	.943
$Q = \sum q$	.0476	3.639	.862	1.00
$Q^{(100)} = \sum q^{(100)}$	.0453	3.613	.820	.993

Table 1: The solution with maximum $\prod p$ is most likely, while the solution with maximum $\sum q$ has the most in common on average with a randomly generated solution. Averages are taken over the 600 randomly generated puzzles.

an extra variable for each square of the puzzle. These letter variables can only take on twenty-six values and are assigned equal prior probabilities. Each of the constraints in the revised network relates a letter variable and a word variable. Thus, s is only linear in the length of the candidate lists, instead of quadratic.

Crossword Results

We applied the iterative approximation method to optimize the expected overlap of a set of artificial and real crossword puzzles.

Artificial Puzzles

To explore how the expected overlap and solution probability relate, and how the iterative estimate compares to these, we randomly generated 100 puzzles for each of the six possible 5×5 crossword grids[2], as shown in Figure 3. Candidates were random binary strings. Each slot was assigned a random 50% of the possible strings of the right length. The prior probabilities were picked uniformly at random from the interval $[0, 1]$, then normalized to sum to 1. We discarded puzzles with no solution; this only happened twice, both times on grid F.

For each puzzle, we computed the complete set of solutions and their probabilities (average number of solutions are shown in Table 2), from which we derived the exact posteriors q on each slot. We also used the iterative approximation to compute approximate posteriors $q^{(0)}, \ldots, q^{(100)}$. We found the solutions with maximum probability $(maxP)$, maximum expected overlap $(maxQ)$, and maximum approximate expected overlap $(maxQ^{(0)} \ldots maxQ^{(100)})$. For each of these solu-

---

[2]By convention, all slots in American crossword puzzles must have at least three letters, and all grid cells must participate in an across and down slot. We fold out reflections and rotations because candidates are randomly created and are thus symmetric on average.

#solns	$P(maxP)$	$Q(maxQ)$	$\frac{Q(maxP)}{Q(maxQ)}$	$\frac{Q(maxQ^{(100)})}{Q(maxQ)}$
A: 32846	.004	1.815	.854	.994
B: 7930.8	.014	2.555	.921	.991
C: 2110.2	.033	3.459	.925	.992
D: 2025.4	.034	3.546	.940	.994
E: 520.9	.079	4.567	.961	.992
F: 131.1	.167	5.894	.980	.993

Table 2: Different grid patterns generated different numbers of solutions. The probability and expected overlap of solutions varied with grid pattern. All numbers in the table are averages over 100 random puzzles.

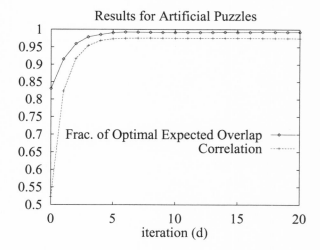

Figure 4: Successive iterations yield better approximations of the posteriors.

tions, we calculated its probability (P), expected overlap (Q), and the percent of optimum achieved. The results, given in Table 1, confirm the difference between the maximum probability solution and the maximum expected overlap solution. The solution obtained by maximizing the approximate expected overlap $(Q^{(100)})$ scored an expected overlap 5% higher than the maximum probability solution, less than 1% below optimum.

Over the six grids, the final approximation $(maxQ^{(100)})$ consistently achieved an expected overlap of between 99.1% and 99.4% of the optimal expected overlap $Q(maxQ)$ (see Table 2). The expected overlap of the maximum probability solution $Q(maxP)$ fell from 98.0% to 85.4% of optimal expected overlap as puzzles became less constrained (F to A). One possible explanation is that puzzles with fewer solutions tend to have one "best" solution, which is both most likely and has a high expected overlap with random solutions.

The approximation tended to improve with iteration. The lower curve of Figure 4 shows the correlation of the approximate posterior $q^{(d)}$ with the true posterior q. The upper curve shows the expected overlap of the solution that maximizes $Q^{(d)}$ $(maxQ^{(d)})$ divided by that of the maximum expected overlap solution. The approxi-

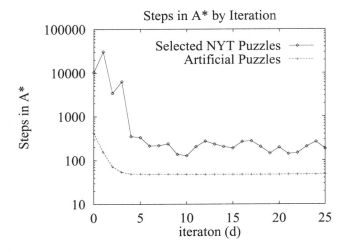

Figure 5: Maximizing the approximate expected overlap with A* tended to get faster with successive iterations of our approximation.

mate posteriors $q^{(d)}$ seemed to converge in all cases, and for all of the 600 test puzzles, the maximum expected overlap solution was constant after iteration 38.

Computing the maximum probability solution and the maximum approximate expected overlap solution both involve finding an instantiation that maximizes the sum of a set of weights. In the first case, our weights are $\log(p_x(v))$ and, in the second case, they are $q_x^{(d)}(v)$. This is an NP-complete problem, and in both cases, we solve it with an A* search. Our heuristic estimate of the value of a state is the sum of the weights of the values of all of its assigned variables and of the maximum weight of the not-yet-considered values of the unassigned variables.

In our set of artificial puzzles, this A* search is much faster when maximizing $\sum q^{(100)}$ than when maximizing $\prod p$. The former took an average of 47.3 steps, and the latter 247.6 steps. Maximizing $\sum q^{(d)}$ got faster for successive iterations d as shown in Figure 5.

We believe that optimizing $\sum q^{(d)}$ is faster because the top candidates have already shown themselves to fit well into a similar network ($U^{(d)}$), and therefore are more likely to fit with each other in the puzzle grid.

Real Puzzles

We adapted our approach to solve published crossword puzzles. Candidate lists are generated by a set of thirty expert modules using a variety of databases and techniques for information retrieval (Keim *et al.* 1999). Each module returns a weighted list of candidates, and these lists are combined according to a set of parameters trained to optimize the mean log probability assigned to the correct target.

Without returning all possible letter combinations, it is impossible for our expert modules to always return the correct target in their candidate lists; in fact, they

miss it about 2.1% of the time. To ensure that solutions exist and that the correct solution is assigned a positive probability, we implicitly represent the probability distribution over all letter strings according to a letter-bigram model. The total probability assigned to this model is learned along with the weights on the expert modules. Because of its simple form, the system is able to manipulate this distribution efficiently to calculate $b^{(d)}$ and $q^{(d)}$ correctly on the explicit candidates. The full solver includes a combination of several of these "implicit distribution modules."

Note that, because of the implicit bigram distribution, all possible patterns of letters have non-zero probability of being a solution. As noted in Table 2, the maximum probability solution tends to give a poor approximation of the maximum overlap solution when there are many solutions; thus, the iterative approximation plays an important role in this type of puzzle.

The solver itself used an implementation of A* to find the solution that maximizes the approximate expected overlap score $Q^{(d)}$ for each iteration d from 0 to 25. In a small number of instances, however, A* required too much memory to complete, and we switched to a heuristic estimate that was slightly inadmissible (admissible plus a small amount) to ensure that some solution was found. Maximizing $Q^{(d)}$ tended to be easier for greater d. The inadmissible heuristic was required in 47 of 70 test puzzles in maximizing $Q^{(1)}$ but only once in maximizing $Q^{(25)}$. Figure 5 plots the number of steps required by A* for each iteration, averaged over the 23 puzzles where the inadmissible heuristic was unused.

Because of some of the broad-coverage expert modules, candidate lists are extremely long (often over 10^5 candidates), which makes the calculation of our approximate posteriors $q^{(d)}$ expensive. To save time, we compute $b^{(d)}$ using *truncated* candidate lists. To begin, these lists contain the candidates with the greatest priors: We remove all candidates with prior probability less than 10^{-3} of the greatest prior from the list. Doing this usually throws out some of the correct targets, but makes the lists shorter. To bring back a possibly correct target once the approximation has improved, at every iteration we "refresh" the candidate lists: We compute $q^{(d)}$ for all candidates in the full list (based on $b^{(d-1)}$ of only the truncated list). We discard our old abbreviated list and replace it with the list of candidates with the greatest $q^{(d)}$ values (at least 10^{-3} of the maximum). The missing probability mass is distributed among candidates in the implicit bigram-letter model. (In a faster version of the solver we only refresh the candidate lists once every seven iterations. This does not appear to affect accuracy.)

Figure 6 shows the fraction of words correct for the solutions that maximized $Q^{(0)}$ through $Q^{(25)}$. Performance increased substantially, from 51.8% words correct at iteration zero to 89.5% before iteration 25. Figure 6 also shows the fraction of slots for which the candidate with the maximum $q^{(d)}$ is the correct target. This

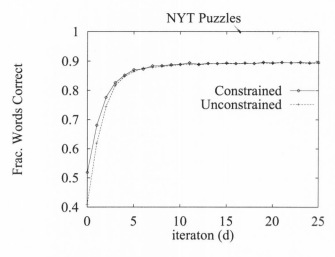

Figure 6: Average number of words correct on a sample of 70 New York Times puzzles increases with the number of iterations. This graph shows two measures, one for solutions constrained to fit the grid, and one unconstrained.

would be our score if our solution did not need to satisfy the constraints. Note that the same candidate lists are used throughout—the improvement in performance is due to better grid filling and not to improved clue solving. We have also run the solver on puzzles less challenging than those published in the New York Times and achieved even better results; the average score on 50 LA Times puzzles, was 98.0% words correct.

Relationship to Turbo Codes

To perform our approximate inference, we use Pearl's belief propagation algorithm on loopy networks. This approximation is best known for its success in decoding turbo codes (McEliece, MacKay, & Cheng 1998), achieving error correcting code performance near the theoretical limit. In retrospect it is not surprising that the same approximation should yield such positive results in both cases. Both problems involve reconstructing data based on multiple noisy encodings. Both networks contain many cycles, and both are bipartite, so all cycles have length at least four.

Conclusions

Faced with the problem of solving real crossword puzzles, we applied an extension of CSPs that includes probabilistic preferences on variable values. The problem of maximizing the number of correct words in a puzzle was formalized as the problem of finding the maximum expected overlap in the CSP. We applied an iterative approximation algorithm for this problem and showed that it is accurate on a collection of artificial puzzles. As a happy side effect, the proposed iterative approximation algorithm speeds optimization. After extending the resulting algorithm to handle real puzzles with implicitly defined candidate lists, the solver

scored 89.5% words correct on a sample of challenging New York Times crossword puzzles.

Having identified the importance of maximum overlap score in the crossword domain, we believe that this measure could be useful in other problems. For example, in machine vision, we might be interested in a consistent interpretation for a scene that is expected to have as much in common with the true scene as possible; this could be formalized in a manner similar to our crossword puzzle problem.

All in all, this work suggests that combinations of probability theory and constraint satisfaction hold promise for attacking a wide array of problems.

Acknowledgments. Thanks to Rina Dechter, Moises Goldszmidt, Martin Mundhenk, Mark Peot, Will Shortz, and Yair Weiss for feedback and suggestions.

References

Abney, S. 1996. Statistical methods and linguistics. In Klavans, J., and Resnik, P., eds., *The Balancing Act.* Cambridge, MA: The MIT Press. chapter 1, 2–26.

Garey, M. R., and Johnson, D. S. 1979. *Computers and Intractability: A Guide to the Theory of NP-completeness.* San Francisco, CA: Freeman.

Ginsberg, M. L.; Frank, M.; Halpin, M. P.; and Torrance, M. C. 1990. Search lessons learned from crossword puzzles. In *Proceedings of the Eighth National Conference on Artificial Intelligence*, 210–215.

Keim, G. A.; Shazeer, N.; Littman, M. L.; Agarwal, S.; Cheves, C. M.; Fitzgerald, J.; Grosland, J.; Jiang, F.; Pollard, S.; and Weinmeister, K. 1999. Proverb: The probabilistic cruciverbalist. In *Proceedings of the Sixteenth National Conference on Artificial Intelligence.*

Mackworth, A. K. 1977. Consistency in networks of relations. *Artificial Intelligence* 8(1):99–118.

McEliece, R.; MacKay, D.; and Cheng, J. 1998. Turbo decoding as an instance of Pearl's 'belief propagation' algorithm. *IEEE Journal on Selected Areas in Communication* 16(2):140–152.

Munkres, J. R. 1975. *Topology, A First Course.* Englewood Cliffs, New Jersey: Prentice-Hall, Inc.

Pearl, J. 1988. *Probabilistic Reasoning in Intelligent Systems.* San Mateo, CA: Morgan Kaufmann, 2nd edition.

Roth, D. 1996. On the hardness of approximate reasoning. *Artificial Intelligence* 82(1–2):273–302.

Schiex, T.; Fargier, H.; and Verfaillie, G. 1995. Valued constraint satisfaction problems: Hard and easy problems. In *Proceedings of the 14th International Joint Conference on Artificial Intelligence (IJCAI-95)*, 631–637.

Shortz, W., ed. 1990. *American Championship Crosswords.* Fawcett Columbine.

Weiss, Y. 1997. Belief propagation and revision in networks with loops. Technical Report Technical Report 1616, MIT AI lab.

Encodings of Non-Binary Constraint Satisfaction Problems

Kostas Stergiou and **Toby Walsh**

Department of Computer Science
University of Strathclyde
Glasgow G1 1XL
Scotland
{ks,tw}@cs.strath.ac.uk

Abstract

We perform a detailed theoretical and empirical comparison of the dual and hidden variable encodings of non-binary constraint satisfaction problems. We identify a simple relationship between the two encodings by showing how we can translate between the two by composing or decomposing relations. This translation suggests that we will tend to achieve more pruning in the dual than in the hidden variable encoding. We prove that achieving arc-consistency on the dual encoding is strictly stronger than achieving arc-consistency on the hidden variable, and this itself is equivalent to achieving generalized arc-consistency on the original (non-binary) problem. We also prove that, as a consequence of the unusual topology of the constraint graph in the hidden variable encoding, inverse consistencies like neighborhood inverse consistency and path inverse consistency collapse down onto arc-consistency. Finally, we propose the "double encoding", which combines together both the dual and the hidden variable encodings.

Introduction

Many constraint satisfaction problems (CSPs) can be compactly formulated using non-binary relations. We can solve a non-binary CSP either by using one of the algorithms like forward checking (FC) which have been generalized to non-binary constraints or by translating it into a binary CSP. There exist two well known methods for translating non-binary CSPs into binary CSPs: the dual encoding (sometimes call the "dual graph method") and the hidden variable encoding. Recently, Bacchus and van Beek have started to compare how backtracking algorithms like FC perform on the two encodings and on the original non-binary problem (Bacchus & van Beek 1998). Their ultimate aim is to provide guidance on when to translate. We continue this research programme, focusing on higher levels of consistency like arc-consistency (AC) and on the comparison of the two encodings. Bacchus and van Beek remark "...An important question that we have not addressed here is the relationship between the two binary translations.

When is the dual representation to be preferred to the hidden representation and vice versa? Are there any theoretical results that can be proved about their relative behaviour? ..." p.317-8 of (Bacchus & van Beek 1998). In this paper, we provide answers to many of these questions. In addition, we propose a new encoding which combines together both the dual and the hidden variable encodings.

Formal background

A constraint satisfaction problem (CSP) is a triple (X, D, C). X is a set of variables. For each $x_i \in X$, D_i is the domain of the variable. Each k-ary constraint $c \in C$ is defined over a set of variables $(x_1, \ldots x_k)$ by the subset of the cartesian product $D_1 \times \ldots D_k$ which are consistent values. A solution is an assignment of values to variables that is consistent with all constraints. Many lesser levels of consistency have been defined for binary constraint satisfaction problems (see (Debruyne & Bessiere 1997) for references). A problem is (i, j)-consistent iff it has non-empty domains and any consistent instantiation of i variables can be extended to a consistent instantiation involving j additional variables. A problem is arc-consistent (AC) iff it is $(1, 1)$-consistent. A problem is path-consistent (PC) iff it is $(2, 1)$-consistent. A problem is strong path-consistent iff it is $(j, 1)$-consistent for $j \leq 2$. A problem is path inverse consistent (PIC) iff it is $(1, 2)$-consistent. A problem is neighborhood inverse consistent (NIC) iff any value for a variable can be extended to a consistent instantiation for its immediate neighborhood. A problem is restricted path-consistent (RPC) iff it is arc-consistent and if a variable assigned to a value is consistent with just a single value for an adjoining variable then for any other variable there exists a value compatible with these instantiations. A problem is singleton arc-consistent (SAC) iff it has non-empty domains and for any instantiation of a variable, the problem can be made arc-consistent.

Many of these definitions can be extended to non-binary constraints. For example, a (non-binary) CSP is generalized arc-consistent (GAC) iff for any variable in a constraint and value that it is assigned, there exist compatible values for all the other variables in the constraint (Mohr & Masini 1988). We can also maintain a level of consistency at every node in a search tree. For example, the MAC algorithms for binary CSPs maintains arc-consistency at each node in the search tree (Gaschnig 1979). As a second example, the forward checking algorithm (FC) maintains a restricted form of arc-consistency that ensures that the most recently instantiated variable and those that are uninstantiated are arc-consistent.

Following (Debruyne & Bessiere 1997), we call a consistency property A stronger than B ($A \geq B$) iff in any problem in which A holds then B holds, and strictly stronger ($A > B$) iff it is stronger and there is at least one problem in which B holds but A does not. We call a local consistency property A incomparable with B ($A \sim B$) iff A is not stronger than B nor vice versa. Finally, we call a local consistency property A equivalent to B iff A implies B and vice versa. The following identities summarize results from (Debruyne & Bessiere 1997) and elsewhere: strong PC > SAC > PIC > RPC > AC, NIC > PIC, NIC $\sim$ SAC, and NIC $\sim$ strong PC.

Encodings of non-binary problems

Dual encoding

The dual encoding simply swaps the variables for constraints and vice versa. There is a dual variable v_c for each k-ary constraint c. Its domain is the set of consistent tuples for that constraint. For each pair of constraints c and c' in the original problem with variables in common, we introduce a compatibility constraint between the dual variables v_c and v_c'. This constraint restricts the dual variables to tuples in which the variables that are shared take the same value.

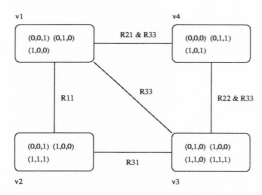

Fig. 1. Dual encoding of a non-binary CSP. Rij is the binary relation on a pair of tuples that is true iff the ith element of the 1st tuple equals the jth element of the 2nd tuple.

Consider an example with six 0-1 variables, and four arithmetic constraints: $x_1 + x_2 + x_6 = 1$, $x_1 - x_3 + x_4 = 1$, $x_4 + x_5 - x_6 \geq 1$, and $x_2 + x_5 - x_6 = 0$. The dual en-

coding represents this problem with 4 dual variables, one for each constraint. The domains of these dual variables are the tuples that satisfy the respective constraint. For example, the dual variable associated with the third constraint v_3 has the domain $\{(0, 1, 0), (1, 0, 0), (1, 1, 0), (1, 1, 1)\}$ as these are the tuples of values for (x_4, x_5, x_6) which satisfy $x_4 + x_5 - x_6 \geq 1$. The dual encoding of the problem is shown in Figure 1.

Hidden variable encoding

The hidden variable encoding also introduces a dual variable v_c for each (nonbinary) constraint c. Its domain is again the set of consistent tuples for the variables in the constraint c. For each tuple in the domain of the dual variable v_c, we introduce compatibility constraints between v_c and each variable x_i in the constraint c. Each constraint specifies that the tuple assigned to v_c is consistent with the value assigned to x_i. Consider again the example with four arithmetic constraints. There are, in addition to the original six 0-1 variables, four dual variables with the same domains as in the dual encoding. For example, the dual variable associated with the third constraint v_3 again has the domain $\{(0, 1, 0), (1, 0, 0), (1, 1, 0), (1, 1, 1)\}$. There are now compatibility constraints between v_3 and x_2, between v_3 and x_5 and between v_3 and x_6, as these are the variables mentioned in the third constraint. For example, the compatibility constraint between v_3 and x_2 is the relation that is true iff the first element in the tuple assigned to v_3 equals the value of x_2. The hidden variable encoding is shown in Figure 2.

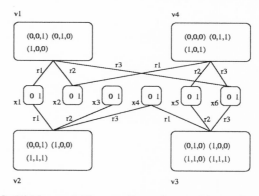

Fig. 2. Hidden variable encoding of a non-binary CSP. The binary relation ri applies to a tuple and a value and is true iff the ith element of the tuple equals the value.

Mapping between the encodings

We can construct the dual encoding by performing a (solution preserving) simplification of the hidden variable encoding. This mapping compiles out the role of the original variables by composing binary relations. Given the constraint graph of a hidden variable encoding, we collect the set of paths of length 2 between each pair of dual variables, v_c and v'_c. We delete these paths and replace them with a single constraint formed from the composition of the relations on the deleted paths. When any of the original variables becomes isolated from the rest of the constraint graph, or connected just to a single dual variable, we can safely delete it. Applying these simplifying transformations to every pair of dual variables transforms the hidden variable encoding into the dual.

As an example, consider the hidden variable encoding in Figure 2. We take a pair of dual variables, v_1 and v_2. The variable x_1 lies on the only path of length 2 between v_1 and v_2. We delete the two $r1$ constraints on this path and add a new relation $R11$ that is the composition of the two $r1$ relations. As x_1 is now isolated from the rest of the constraint graph, we can safely delete it. We then take another pair of dual variables, say v_1 and v_4. There are two paths of length 2 between v_1 and v_4. We delete both of these paths. The path between v_1 and v_4 via x_2 had $r2$ and $r1$ constraints on it so induces a constraint $R21$ between v_1 and v_4. Similarly, the path between v_1 and v_4 via x_6 had two $r3$ constraints on it so induces a constraint $R33$ between v_1 and v_4. We therefore add their union $R21 \& R33$ as the new induced constraint between v_1 and v_4. We can now delete x_2 and x_3 as they are isolated from the rest of the problem. The intermediate CSP constructed at this point is shown in Figure 3. If we continue this simplification on the remaining pairs of dual variables, we construct the dual encoding shown in Figure 1.

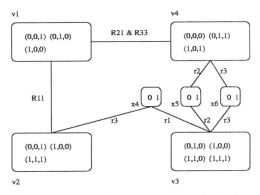

Fig. 3. An intermediate point in the transformation of the hidden variable encoding into the dual variable encoding.

The transformation of the hidden variable encoding into the dual can easily be reversed. We simply take constraints between pairs of dual variables and decompose them into paths of constraints which take in the original variables. Note that, at any point in the transformation, we still have a binary CSP. It is therefore possible to have "hybrid" encodings, in which some parts of the problem are represented by a dual encoding and others by a hidden variable encoding.

It is also possible to construct a "double" encoding in which both the dual and the hidden variable encoding are present in their entirety. In the double encoding, we have both the original variables and the dual variables. We also have both the constraints between dual variables (as in the dual encoding), and the constraints between dual variables and the original variables (as in the hidden variable encoding). In the double encoding, we will have the extra pruning achievable in the dual encoding. We will also be able to branch on the original variables as in the hidden variable encoding; branching heuristics may be able to perform better on these than on the dual variables with their potentially large domains.

We believe that this may be the first time this close relationship between the hidden variable and the dual encoding has been identified. This observation has several practical and theoretical consequences. For example, our ability to propagate efficiently and effectively through the compatibility constraints in the hidden variable encoding is likely to be a major cause of difference between the dual and the hidden variable encodings. As a second example, enforcing the same level of consistency in the two encodings will inevitably do more pruning in the dual than in the hidden variable encoding.

Theoretical comparison

To compare constraint propagation in a non-binary problem and its encoding, we must tackle a variety of problems.

First, a static analysis in which we simply compare the levels of consistency in a problem and in its encoding is not very informative. The problem is that the translation into the encoding builds in a significant level of consistency. For example, the dual variables only have consistent tuples in their domains. Hence, by construction, the dual encoding has a level of consistency at least equal to GAC in the original problem. A solution to this problem is to perform a more dynamic analysis in which we compare the levels of consistency *achieved* by constraint propagation during search.

Second, constraint propagation may infer nogoods involving the dual variables, and these cannot be directly compared with nogoods inferred in the original problem. A solution to this problem is simply to translate nogoods involving dual variables into nogoods involving the original variables and values. For example, if we prune a k-ary tuple from the domain of a dual variable, we translate this into a k-ary nogood on the original variables.

Third, if we prune values or instantiate variables in the original problem, we cannot perform the same simplification on the dual encoding as the original variables have been discarded. Any solution to this problem should ensure that, when all the variables in a constraint c have been instantiated, the dual variable v_c is reduced to an unitary domain. The solution we adopt is to remove any tuples from the domains of dual variables that contain the value pruned or that are not consistent with the variable instantiation in the original problem. Note that the reverse direction is not problematic. For instance, if we instantiate a dual variable v_c, we can simply instantiate all variables x_i in the original problem which appear in c.

Fourth, constraint propagation in the dual encoding will infer nogoods which, when translated back into the original problem, have a large arity. Constraint propagation in the original problem may infer much fewer but much smaller nogoods which can be derived from these larger arity nogoods. For example, constraint propagation in the dual encoding may remove all tuples from a dual variable which assign the value a_i to a variable x_i. ¿From this, we can derive an unitary nogood that removes a_i from the domain of x_i. A solution to this problem is to compare the nogoods that can be derived from the translated nogoods with those that can be derived in the original problem.

We will therefore call achieving a consistency property A stronger than achieving B iff the nogoods identified when achieving B are derivable from those identified when achieving A, and strictly stronger if it is stronger and there exists at least one problem on which one nogood identified when achieving A is not derivable from those identified when achieving B.

Hidden variable encoding

If we ignore pruning of values in the dual variables, enforcing AC on the hidden variable encoding is equivalent to enforcing GAC on the original problem.

Theorem 1 *Achieving AC on the hidden variable encoding is equivalent to achieving GAC on the variables in the original problem.*

Proof: Assume that, after removing some values from the domains of variables in the original problem, we make the problem GAC and this prunes the value a_i from a variable x_i. Then there exists some constraint c mentioning x_i and the assignment of a_i to x_i cannot be consistently extended to the other variables in c. In the hidden variable encoding, enforcing AC between these variables and v_c will remove all tuples that assign a_i to x_i. Hence, considering the arc between x_i and v_c, if we assign a_i to x_i, there are no tuples in the domain of v_c that are consistent. Hence, achieving AC on the hidden variable encoding will prune a_i from the domain of x_i.

Assume that we make the problem AC and this prunes the value a_i from a variable x_i. Then there exists a dual variable v_c in the hidden variable encoding where c mentions x_i and none of the tuples left in the domain of v_c assigns a_i to x_i. Hence, in the original representation of the problem, the assignment of a_i to x_i cannot be consistently

extended to the other variables in c. We will therefore prune a_i from the domain of x_i. □

This theorem shows that we can achieve GAC by means of a simple AC algorithm and the hidden variable encoding. Whether this is computationally effective will depend on the tightness and arity of the non-binary constraint. The best AC algorithm has worst-case time complexity of $O(d^2)$ where d is the domain size. For the hidden variable encoding of very loose k-ary constraints, this may be $O(m^{2k})$ where m is the domain size in the original problem. By comparison, we may be able to achieve GAC at much less cost. For example, GAC on all different constraints takes just $O(m^2k^2)$ worst-case time (Régin 1994).

In practive, we may see different results with a hidden variable encoding as we can now branch on the hidden variables and reason explicitly about the valid tuples in their domains. For example, consider a parity constraint $even(x_1 + x_2 + x_3)$ on three 0-1 variables. If we remove 1 from the domain of x_1 then the problem remains GAC, and we do will not *explicitly* perform any pruning. However, in the hidden variable encoding, achieving AC will prune two of the four values from the dual variable leaving just the tuples, $(0, 0, 0)$ and $(0, 1, 1)$. In other words, in the hidden variable encoding, we identify the additional constraint that $x_2 = x_3$.

The constraint graph of a hidden variable encoding has a star-shaped topology in which constraints "radiate" out from the original variables. Because of this topology, certain consistency techniques fail to achieve any additional pruning over AC. In particular, NIC collapses down onto AC. Other lesser levels of consistency between NIC and AC (like PIC and RPC) therefore collapse down onto AC. Note that, as we are comparing levels of consistency in the hidden variable encoding, stronger than or equal to AC, we can perform a static analysis that does not worry about the level of consistency built into the encoding.

Theorem 2 *On a hidden variable encoding, NIC is equivalent to AC.*

Proof: Consider a hidden variable encoding that is AC. The proof divides into two cases. In the first case, consider a hidden variable and its immediate neighborhood. As the problem is AC, the hidden variable has a non-empty domain. Take any tuple in this domain, say $a_0 \times \ldots \times a_k$. Then the neighboring (non-hidden) variables, x_0 to x_k can consistently take the values a_0 to a_k. In the second case, consider a non-hidden variable x_0 and its immediate neighborhood. Pick any value a_0 from the domain of x_0. Now, as the problem is AC, we can pick values for any of the neighboring hidden variables. As these are not connected directly to each other, these values are consistent with each other. Hence the problem is NIC. □

Whilst we do not get any more pruning over AC by enforcing inverse consistencies like NIC and PIC, there are levels of consistency stronger than AC that it can be useful to enforce.

Theorem 3 *On a hidden variable encoding, strong PC is strictly stronger than SAC, which itself is strictly stronger than AC.*

Proof: Consider a problem with a single parity constraint, $even(x_1 + x_2 + x_3)$ with variable x_1 set to 0, and variables x_2 and x_3 having 0-1 domains. The hidden variable encoding of this problem is SAC but enforcing strong PC adds the additional constraint that $x_2 = x_3$.

Consider a problem with three parity constraints: $even(x_1 + x_2 + x_3)$, $even(x_1 + x_3 + x_4)$, and $even(x_1 + x_4 + x_2)$. If x_1 is assigned to 1, and every other variable has a 0-1 domain then the hidden variable encoding is AC but it is not SAC. Enforcing SAC will show that the problem is insoluble. □

Dual encoding

The dual encoding binds together the (non-binary) constraints much more tightly than the hidden variable encoding. As a consequence, constraint propagation in the dual can achieve high levels of consistency in the original (non-binary) problem.

Theorem 4 *Achieving AC on the dual encoding is strictly stronger than achieving GAC on the original problem.*

Proof: Assume that, after removing some values from domains of variables in the original problem, we make the problem GAC and this prunes the value a_i from variable x_i. Then there exists some constraint c mentioning x_i and the assignment of a_i to x_i cannot be consistently extended to the other variables in c. In the dual encoding, we remove tuples from the domains of the dual variables that assign values to variables in the original problem that have been removed. This will remove all tuples in v_c that assign a_i to x_i. Hence, we can derive the nogood that a_i cannot be assigned to x_i. To show strictness, consider two parity constraints, $even(x_1 + x_2 + x_3)$ and $even(x_2 + x_3 + x_4)$ with x_1 assigned to 1, x_4 assigned to 0, and all other variables having 0-1 domains. Each constraint is GAC. However, achieving AC on the dual encoding will prove that the problem is insoluble since $x_2 + x_3$ cannot be both even and odd. □

This extra pruning may come at computational cost if the non-binary constraints have a large arity and are loose. As predicted earlier, AC on the dual encoding is more pruningful than AC on the hidden variable encoding.

Theorem 5 *Achieving AC on the dual encoding is strictly stronger than achieving AC on the hidden variable encoding.*

Proof: The proof follows from Theorems 1 and 4. □

These results can be extended to rank algorithms that maintain AC and GAC during search, using arguments similar to (Kondrak & van Beek 1997). For example, under a

suitable static variable and value ordering, MAC on the dual encoding strictly dominates MAC on the hidden variable encoding, which itself will be equivalent to an algorithm that maintains GAC on the non-binary representation.

Experimental results

To support our theoretical results, we experimented with two domains that involve non-binary constraints: Golomb rulers and crossword puzzle generation.

Table 1 compares three encodings of some standard crossword puzzles. The worst-time complexity of GAC on the non-binary encoding of the puzzles is in the order of $O(m^k)$, where m is the number of letters in the alphabet and k is the length of the words. In the puzzles we generated, k was up to 10. This obviously makes the non-binary encoding completely impractical, so we did not consider it in the experiments. The small domain size of the original variables compared to the dual variables makes the hidden representation better. Note, that because of the large size of the dual variables, AC is expensive and it may be the case that forward checking is enough to solve these problems in reasonable time.

Size	Dual	Hidden	Double
n - m	Br.-CPU	Br.-CPU	Br.-CPU
68 - 135	18 - 488.75	2 - 53.85	2 - 552.66
88 - 180	11 - 550.4	0 - 78.15	0 - 632.03
86 - 177	50 - 451	5 - 73.52	5 - 564.88
80 - 187	34 - 900.95	19 - 93	19 - 1272
64 - 128	3 - 298.5	11 - 53.4	11 - 309.24
12 - 36	346 - 901.16	138 - 60.88	138 - 485.18

Table 1: Branches and CPU time when generating crossword puzzles. Fail First was used for variable ordering. n is the number of variables and m is the number of constraints.

A *Golomb Ruler* can be represented by a set of n variables of domain size m, such that $x_1 < x_2 < \ldots < x_n$, $x_1 = 0$, and the $n(n-1)/2$ differences $x_j - x_i, 1 \le i < j \le n$, are distinct. Such a ruler has n marks and is of length m. The constraints can be encoded by adding an auxiliary variable x_{ji} for each difference $x_j - x_i$, such that $x_j - x_i = x_{ji}$, and then constraining all of the auxiliary variables to be distinct. This gives $n(n-1)/2$ ternary constraints and a clique of binary `not equals' constraints. Table 2 compares MGAC on the ternary representation to MAC on the hidden and double representations. As Theorem 1 predicted, MGAC in the non-binary encoding explores the same number of branches as MAC in the hidden. The extra filtering in the double encoding reduces the number of branches. In terms of CPU time, though, the non-binary encoding is the clear winner with the double performing poorly. The dual encoding for this problem is impractical because of the large domain size ($O(m^4)$) of the dual variables needed to represent the not-equals constraints. Such constraints are redundant in the double so they can be ignored.

Ruler n-m	Ternary Branches	Ternary CPU	Hidden CPU	Double Branches	Double CPU
7-25	12	0.2	0.45	12	2.42
7-24	436	1.36	3.37	382	9.03
8-34	35	0.7	1.75	35	14.84
8-33	2585	12.82	31.3	2139	94.06
9-44	283	4.26	9.71	257	80.09
9-43	15315	111.97	261.68	11170	824.17
10-55	1786	27.63	60.24	1455	444.66
10-54	73956	862.56	1861.93	*	*

Table 2: Branches explored and CPU time (seconds) used to find an optimal golomb ruler or prove that none exists. The variables were ordered lexicographically. The numbers of branches in the hidden representation are not given because they are always equal to the corresponding numbers in the non-binary representation. A * means that there was a cut off after 1 hour of CPU.

Related work

Bacchus and van Beek present one of the first detailed experimental and theoretical studies of the hidden variable and dual encodings (Bacchus & van Beek 1998). However, their analysis is restricted to the FC algorithms (and a simple extension called FC+). Our analysis identifies the benefits of enforcing higher levels of consistency. Such analysis is valuable as toolkits like ILOG's Solver enforce these higher levels of consistency during search. Bacchus and van Beek also do not study the relationship between the two encodings. Our results identify a simple mapping between the two. This mapping motivates many of our theoretical results.

Dechter has studied the trade-off between the number of hidden variables and their domain size (Dechter 1990). She shows that any n-ary constraint R can be represented by $(|R| - 2)/(k - 2)$ hidden variables of domain size k where $|R|$ is the number of allowed tuples in the constraint. As required, when $k = |R|$, this degenerates to a single hidden variable for each n-ary constraint.

Conclusions

We have performed a detailed theoretical and empirical comparison of the dual and hidden variable encodings of non-binary constraint satisfaction problems. We have shown how the hidden variable encoding can be transformed into the dual encoding by composing relations. Motivated by this observation, we proved that achieving arc-consistency on the dual encoding is strictly stronger than achieving arc-consistency on the hidden variable, and this itself is equivalent to achieving generalized arc-consistency on the original (non-binary) problem. We also proved that, as a consequence of the unusual topology of the constraint graph in the hidden variable encoding, inverse consistencies like neighborhood inverse consistency and path inverse consistency collapse down onto arc-consistency. Finally, we proposed the double encoding, which combines together both the dual and the hidden variable encodings.

What general lessons can be learnt from this study? First, there is a simple relationship between the dual and the hidden variable encoding based on the composition and decomposition of the binary relations. Second, this relationship suggests that enforcing the same level of consistency in the two encodings will do more pruning in the dual. We were able to prove this conjecture theoretically. Third, it may pay to encode a non-binary constraint satisfaction problem into a binary form. We can, for instance, achieve generalized arc-consistency on a non-binary problem by enforcing arc-consistency on the hidden variable encoding. It remains to be seen if these lessons can be translated back into the solution of non-binary problems without the overhead of encoding.

References

Bacchus, F., and van Beek, P. 1998. On the conversion between non-binary and binary constraint satisfaction problems. In *Proceedings of 15th National Conference on Artificial Intelligence*, 311–318. AAAI Press/The MIT Press.

Debruyne, R., and Bessiere, C. 1997. Some practicable filtering techniques for the constraint satisfaction problem. In *Proceedings of the 15th IJCAI*, 412–417. International Joint Conference on Artificial Intelligence.

Dechter, R. 1990. On the expressiveness of networks with hidden variables. In *Proceedings of the 8th National Conference on AI*, 555–562. American Association for Artificial Intelligence.

Gaschnig, J. 1979. Performance measurement and analysis of certain search algorithms. Technical report CMU-CS-79-124, Carnegie-Mellon University. PhD thesis.

Kondrak, G., and van Beek, P. 1997. A theoretical evaluation of selected backtracking algorithms. *Artificial Intelligence* 89:365–387.

Mohr, R., and Masini, G. 1988. Good old discrete relaxation. In *Proceedings of the European Conference on Artificial Intelligence (ECAI-88)*, 651–656.

Régin, J.-C. 1994. A filtering algorithm for constraints of difference in CSPs. In *Proceedings of the 12th National Conference on AI*, 362–367. American Association for Artificial Intelligence.

A Generic Customizable Framework for Inverse Local Consistency

Gérard Verfaillie and **David Martinez**
ONERA-CERT
2 av. Edouard Belin, BP 4025
31055 Toulouse Cedex 4, France
{verfaillie,martinez}@cert.fr

Christian Bessière
LIRMM-CNRS (UMR 5506)
161 rue Ada
34392 Montpellier Cedex 5, France
bessiere@lirmm.fr

Abstract

Local consistency enforcing is at the core of *CSP* (*Constraint Satisfaction Problem*) solving. Although *arc consistency* is still the most widely used level of local consistency, researchers are going on investigating more powerful levels, such as *path consistency*, *k-consistency*, *(i,j)-consistency*. Recently, more attention has been turned to *inverse local consistency* levels, such as *path inverse consistency*, *k-inverse consistency*, *neighborhood inverse consistency*, which do not suffer from the drawbacks of the other local consistency levels (changes in the constraint definitions and in the constraint graph, prohibitive memory requirements).

In this paper, we propose a *generic framework* for inverse local consistency, which includes most of the previously defined levels and allows a rich set of new levels to be defined. The first benefit of such a generic framework is to allow a user to define and test many different inverse local consistency levels, in accordance with the problem or even the instance he/she has to solve. The second benefit is to allow a *generic algorithm* to be defined. This algorithm, which is parameterized by the chosen inverse local consistency level, generalizes the *AC7* algorithm used for *arc consistency*, and produces from any instance its locally consistent closure at the chosen level.

Motivations

Local consistency enforcing techniques are at the core of the *CSP* (*Constraint Satisfaction Problem* (Mackworth 1992)) solving techniques and are probably the main ingredients of their success. Thanks to local reasoning, they allow any instance P to be simplified, by eliminating values or combinations of values that cannot be involved in any solution of P. More precisely, from any instance P, they produce a new instance $\widehat{P}$, with the following properties:

(1) when compared with P, $\widehat{P}$ is simplified: some values have been removed from the variable domains of P, some tuples of values have been removed from the constraint relations of P;

(2) P and $\widehat{P}$ are equivalent: they have the same set of solutions;

(3) $\widehat{P}$ is locally consistent at the specified level.

$\widehat{P}$ is often referred to as the locally consistent closure of P at the specified level of consistency. Always thanks to local reasoning, local consistency enforcing may allow global inconsistency to be detected, when a variable domain or a constraint relation becomes empty.

Used in a preprocessing step, they allow either a search for a solution to be started with a simplified instance, or sometimes any search to be avoided in case of inconsistency detection. Used at each node of a search tree, they allow branches that do not lead to any solution to be cut earlier. Lastly, used in the framework of an interactive solving, they allow consequences of the user's choices (variable assignment, variable domain reduction, constraint adding) to be explicited.

After this picture, it may seem strange that the most widely used local consistency level is one of the simplest: *arc consistency* whose enforcing removes from the domain of a variable v the values that cannot be consistently extended to another variable v'. Although various extensions of *arc consistency* have been proposed (*path consistency*, *k-consistency*, *(i,j)-consistency* (Freuder 1978; 1985)), it remains that they are not often used. There are three reasons for that:

(a) a worst case time complexity of the associated algorithms, which grows quickly (for example, exponentially as a function of k with *k-consistency* (Cooper 1989));

(b) a worst case space complexity, which grows the same way (for example, also exponentially as a function of k with *k-consistency*);

(c) the recording of forbidden tuples, which implies either to create new extensionally defined constraints (changes in the constraint network), or to add an extensional definition to existing possibly intensionally defined constraints (changes in the constraint definitions).

Starting from these observations, more attention has been recently turned to inverse local consistency levels, such as *path inverse consistency*, *k-inverse consistency*, *neighborhood inverse consistency*, *restricted path consistency*, *max restricted path consistency* or *singleton arc consistency* (Freuder & Elfe 1996; Debruyne & Bessière 1997a), which do not suffer from all the drawbacks of the previous local consistency levels.

Informally speaking, for all these levels but the last three, inverse local consistency enforcing removes from the domain of a variable v the values that cannot be consistently extended to some additional variables. *Arc consistency*, whose enforcing removes values that cannot be consistently extended to any other variable, is the simplest level of inverse local consistency. *Path inverse consistency* enforcing removes values that cannot be consistently extended to any set of two other variables. *k-inverse consistency* enforcing removes values that cannot be consistently extended to any set of $k-1$ other variables. *Neighborhood inverse consistency* enforcing removes values that cannot be consistently extended to the set of variables directly linked to v.

Since inverse local consistency enforcing never removes combinations of values, and then does not create new constraints and does not modify existing constraint definitions, it does not suffer from the drawbacks (b) and (c) listed above[1]:

(b') the memory that is necessary for recording the removed values is $O(nd)$, if n is the number of variables and d the maximum size of the variable domains;

(c') there is no change, neither in the constraint graph, nor in the constraint definitions.

It can be observed that most of the defined inverse local consistency levels consider the ability to extend the assignment of a variable v with a value val to some sub-instances, involving v and some additional variables, and that they *differ from each other only in the definition of the considered sub-instances*. This observation paves the way for a generic definition of inverse local consistency. In this paper, we propose such a definition. Its advantages are multiple:

- it allows most of the inverse local consistency levels, separately and differently presented in the literature, to be brought together;

- doing that, it makes their theoretical comparison easier, for example, in terms of filtering power and worst case complexity of the associated algorithms;

- it paves the way for the definition of many new levels, either generic, or specifically defined for an instance or a kind of instance;

- it allows a generic algorithm for inverse local consistency enforcing, parameterized by the chosen level, to be defined; in this paper, we propose an algorithm that generalizes the *AC7* algorithm used for *arc consistency*;

- doing that, it saves a lot of time that otherwise would be wasted, for each new level, in algorithm definition, implementation and debugging tasks;

- it allows a user to define and test easily many levels of inverse local consistency and to build the level that is the

---

[1]Note that the drawback (a) does not disappear: as we will see in the next section, the worst case time complexity of the associated algorithms grows exponentially as a function of the number of additional variables.

most suited to the instance or kind of instance he/she has to solve.

A generic framework for inverse local consistency

A generic definition of inverse local consistency

The generic definition of inverse local consistency we propose is naturally based on the notion of *viability* of a value in a sub-instance:

Definition 1 *Let $P = (V, C)$ be an instance, defined by a set V of variables (a finite domain $d(v)$ being associated with each variable $v \in V$) and a set C of constraints. A sub-instance of P is an instance $P' = (V', C')$, where $C' \subseteq C$ and V' is the set of the variables in V that are linked by the constraints in C'.*

Definition 2 *Let $P = (V, C)$ be an instance and $P' = (V', C')$ be a sub-instance of P. Let $v \in V'$ and $val \in d(v)$. The value (v, val) is said to be viable in P' iff the sub-instance P' restricted by the assignment $v \leftarrow val$ is consistent, i.e. has at least one solution.*

If a value (v, val) is not viable in a sub-instance P', then it is not involved in any solution of P', and thus not involved in any solution of P. It can be removed from the domain of v without losing any solution.

We can easily extend this notion of viability to variables and *(sub-instance, set of variables)* pairs:

Definition 3 *Let $P = (V, C)$ be an instance and $P' = (V', C')$ be a sub-instance of P. Let $v \in V'$. The variable v is said to be viable in P' iff all the values in $d(v)$ are viable in P'. Let $V'' \subseteq V'$. The pair (P', V'') is said to be viable iff P' is consistent and all the variables in V'' are viable in P'.*

In the latter definition, the condition enforcing the consistency of P' may seem useless. It has been added to take into account pairs (P', V'') where $V'' = \varnothing$.

The idea is to define an inverse local consistency level ilc by a function $\mathbf{def}_{ilc}$, which associates with any instance P a set $\mathbf{def}_{ilc}(P)$ of *(sub-instance, set of variables)* pairs whose viability has to hold. Then, we can define the inverse local consistency of an instance P at the level ilc (denoted as *ilc-consistency*) as follows:

Definition 4 *Let $P = (V, C)$ be an instance. Let ilc be a local consistency level and $\mathbf{def}_{ilc}$ be the associated function. P is said to be ilc-consistent iff all the pairs of (sub-instance, set of variables) in $\mathbf{def}_{ilc}(P)$ are viable.*

According to this definition, specifying a function $\mathbf{def}_{ilc}$ is sufficient to specify an inverse local consistency level ilc. In the next subsection, we define the function $\mathbf{def}$ associated with some well known inverse local consistency levels. In the subsection after, we point out how this definition can be used to specify new inverse local consistency levels, either generic or specific.

Already known inverse local consistency levels

In the general framework of binary or non-binary CSPs, the functions **def** associated with *arc consistency*, *neighborhood inverse consistency* and *global consistency* can be defined as follows:

- For each constraint $c \in C$, *arc consistency* (*ac*) (Mackworth 1977) considers the sub-instance P' involving the set $v(c)$ of variables linked by c and the constraint c itself; it requires that each variable in $v(c)$ be viable in P'; then, $\mathbf{def}_{ac}((V,C)) = \{((v(c), \{c\}), v(c))/c \in C\}$;

- For each variable $v \in V$, *neighborhood inverse consistency* (*nic*) (Freuder & Elfe 1996) considers the sub-instance P' involving the set $lv(v)$ of variables directly linked to v and the set $clv(v)$ of constraints linking these variables[2]; it requires that v be viable in P'; then, $\mathbf{def}_{nic}((V,C)) = \{(((lv(v), clv(v))), \{v\})/v \in V\}$;

- *Global consistency* (*gc*) (Freuder 1991; Dechter 1992)[3] is the highest inverse local consistency level; it requires that each variable in V be viable in P, then, $\mathbf{def}_{gc}((V,C)) = \{((V,C), V)\}$.

Other known inverse local consistency levels like, for example, *path inverse consistency* or *k-inverse consistency* (Freuder & Elfe 1996) can be easily expressed in this framework.

New inverse local consistency levels

In addition to these levels, the framework we defined paves the way for the definition of multiple new inverse local consistency levels, as limitless as the number of functions **def** we can imagine. Here are some examples:

- *k-length neighborhood inverse consistency* (*k-lnic*) is a generalization of *nic*, which considers, for each variable v, the sub-instance involving all the variables that are linked to v using a path whose length is less than or equal to k; for example, *nic* is equivalent to 1-*lnic*;

- *k-neighborhood inverse consistency* (*k-nic*) is a restriction of *nic*, which considers only sub-instances involving a number of variables less than or equal to k; there are several ways to enforce this limitation; we can consider only the variables whose number of linked variables is less than or equal to k; we can also consider all the variables, but, for each variable, consider only k linked variables (or several sets of k linked variables), chosen according to any criterion: domain size, arity and tightness of the involved constraints, etc

- all the previously defined inverse local consistency levels (in this subsection and in the previous one) can be restricted by considering only the constraints whose tightness is greater than or equal to a given threshold or whose arity

is smaller than or equal to another threshold; as in the example of *k-nic*, they can also be restricted by considering only sub-instances whose size (number of variables and domain sizes) is less than or equal to a given threshold.

Using prior knowledge on the structure of the instance or of the kind of instance he/she has to solve, the user can define and test suited inverse local consistency levels. To do that, he/she only needs to define the associated functions **def**. Note that specifying functions **def** such that $\forall (P', V'') \in \mathbf{def}(P), V'' = \varnothing$ allows him/her to define local consistency levels that enforce only sub-instance consistency, without any value removal.

A generic algorithm for inverse local consistency enforcing

General description

The generic algorithm we propose is an extension of the *AC7* algorithm (Bessière, Freuder, & Régin 1999), which is currently considered as one of the most efficient algorithms for *arc consistency* enforcing. It is widely drawn from (Bessière & Régin 1997) and (Bessière & Régin 1998). As in (Bessière, Freuder, & Régin 1999), it is based on the notion of *supporting assignment*:

Definition 5 *Let $P = (V,C)$ be an instance and $P' = (V', C')$ be a sub-instance of P. Let $v \in V'$ and $val \in d(v)$. The assignment SA of the variables in V' is a supporting assignment for the value (v, val) in the sub-instance P' iff $SA[v] = val$ [4] and SA is solution of P'.*

According to Definitions 2 and 5, a value is viable in a sub-instance iff it has a supporting assignment in this sub-instance. If not, it is not viable and can be removed, without losing any solution.

As a result, for each triple (v, val, P') it has to check, the algorithm searches for a supporting assignment of (v, val) in P'. If such an assignment SA is found, (v, val) is recorded as supported by SA and for all the values $(v', val') \in SA$, SA is recorded as supported by (v', val') in P'. If such an assignment is not found, the value val is removed from the domain of v and all the values supported by an assignment that is itself supported by (v, val) in any sub-instance P', have to search for a new supporting assignment in P'.

Data structure

The data structure we use has six main components:

(CL) a list CL (for *Checking List*) of *(sub-instance, set of variables)* pairs (P', V'') whose viability has to be checked; this list is initialized by a call to the function $\mathbf{def}_{ilc}$ associated with the considered inverse local consistency level;

(SIL) for each variable v, a static list $SIL(v)$ (for *Sub Instance List*) of sub-instances $P' = (V', C')$ that have to be checked again when a value val is removed from the domain of v;

---

[2]Two variables are said to be directly linked iff they are involved in the same constraint. Given a set V' of variables, a constraint c is said to link these variables iff $v(c) \subseteq V'$.

[3](Freuder 1991) speaks of *completable* values and (Dechter 1992) of *globally consistent* variables. If n is the number of variables, one refers also to *global consistency* as *(1,n-1)-consistency* or *n-inverse consistency*.

[4]$SA[v]$ denotes the value of the variable v in the assignment SA.

(SSL) a list SSL (for *Seeking Support List*) of *(variable, value, sub-instance)* triples (v, val, P'), associated with the values (v, val) that are searching for a supporting assignment in the sub-instance P';

(SVL) for each supporting assignment SA, a list $SVL(SA)$ (for *Supported Value List*) of values that are supported by SA;

(SAL) for each triple (v, val, P'), a list $SAL(v, val, P')$ (for *Supported Assignment List*) of supporting assignments that are themselves supported by (v, val) in P';

(MSA) for each triple (v, val, P'), an assignment $MSA(v, val, P')$ (for *Minimum-Supporting Assignment*), such that no supporting assignment exists before $MSA(v, val, P')$ for (v, val) in P', according to the lexicographic ordering of the assignments of P' defined by the static orderings chosen for variables and values;

Figure 1 gives a graphical representation of the supporting links between values and assignments and between assignments and values (data structures SAL and SVL).

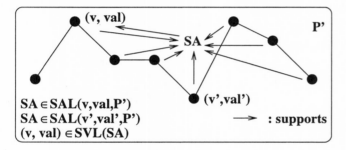

$SA \in SAL(v, val, P')$
$SA \in SAL(v', val', P')$
$(v, val) \in SVL(SA)$
$\longrightarrow$: supports

Figure 1: Graphical representation of the supporting links.

Algorithm

The high level pseudo-code of the generic algorithm is shown in Figures 2 to 7.

The principal novelty with respect to $AC7$ lies in the use of the function **search** called by the function **seek-next-support**. This function searches for a new supporting assignment of a value (v, val) in a sub-instance P'. The method used for searching for such an assignment depends on the size of the sub-instance:

- if P' contains only one constraint, as with ac, the search is a simple enumeration;

- if it contains more than one constraint, as with nic, k-nic, k-$lnic$, gc or any other inverse local consistency level, a tree search is performed.

Any of the techniques that have been developed for *CSP* solving can be selected for this search. The SAL structure avoids searching if a supporting assignment can be directly inferred: if a value supports an assignment, this value is also supported by this assignment. The MSA structure avoids exploring parts of the search space that have been previously explored, but imposes static variable and value

```
function local-consistency-enforcing(P, ilc)
CL ← init-cl(P, ilc);
while CL ≠ ∅
        (P', V") ← pick-and-remove(CL);
        if V" = ∅
        then if not consistent(P')
                then return false;
        else SSL ← init-ssl(P', V");
                if not seek-supports(SSL, ilc)
                then return false;
return true;
```

Figure 2: Inverse local consistency enforcing of an instance P at the level ilc.

```
function seek-supports(SSL, ilc)
while SSL ≠ ∅
        (v, val, P') ← pick-and-remove(SSL);
        if not removed(val, domain(v))
        then if not seek-inferred-support(v, val, P')
                then if not seek-next-support
                                (v, val, P', MSA(v, val, P'))
                        then remove(val, domain(v));
                                if domain(v) = ∅
                                then return false;
                                SSL ← add-ssl(SSL, v, val);
return true;
```

Figure 3: Searching for supporting assignments for a list SSL of *(variable, value, sub-instance)* triples.

```
function seek-inferred-support(v, val, P')
if SAL(v, val, P') ≠ ∅
then SA ← pick-not-remove(SAL(v, val, P'));
        add((v, val), SVL(SA));
        return true;
return false;
```

Figure 4: Searching for an inferred supporting assignment for a value (v, val) in a sub-instance P'.

```
function seek-next-support(v, val, P', MSA)
SA ← search(v, val, P', MSA);
if SA ≠ ∅
then forall (v', val') ∈ SA
                add(SA, SAL(v', val', P'));
        SVL(SA) ← {(v, val)};
        MSA(v, val, P') ← SA;
        return true;
return false;
```

Figure 5: Searching for a supporting assignment for a value (v, val) in a sub-instance P', starting from MSA.

```
function init-cl(P, ilc)
init-sil(P)
CL ← def_ilc(P);
init-sil-sal (CL);
return CL;


function init-sil(P)
forall v ∈ variables(P)
        SIL(v) ← ∅;


function init-sil-sal(CL)
forall (P',V") ∈ CL
      forall v ∈ variables(P')
            add(P', SIL(v));
            forall val ∈ d(v)
                  SAL(v, val, P') ← ∅;


function init-ssl(P',V")
SSL ← ∅;
forall v ∈ V"
      forall val ∈ d(v)
            SSL ← add((v, val, P'), SSL);
            MSA(v, val, P') ← ∅;
return SSL;
```

Figure 6: Initialization of the data structures.

```
function add-ssl(SSL, v, val)
forall P' ∈ SIL(v)
      forall SA ∈ SAL(v, val,P')
            forall (v', val') ∈ SA
                  remove(SA, SAL(v', val', P'));
            forall (v",val") ∈ SVL(SA)
                  add((v",val",P'), SSL);
            remove(SA);
```

Figure 7: Update of the data structure SSL.

the end of the algorithm, all the remaining values are viable in all the associated sub-instances.

Its time and space complexity can be easily obtained by generalizing the reasoning used for *AC7*. Let p be the number of *(sub-instance, set of variables)* pairs ($P' = (V', C'), V"$) to consider, n' be the maximum number of variables in V', $n"$ be the maximum number of variables in $V"$, and d be the maximum domain size. Time and space complexities are respectively $O(p.dn".d^{n'-1})$ and $O(p.dn".n')$.

Extending definitions and algorithms

As explained in the previous section, as soon as the number of constraints involved in the sub-instance to consider is greater than 1, a tree search is performed in order to prove the viability or the non-viability of a value. But other less expensive methods could be considered.

First of all, any limited local search can be used to establish viability; if it succeeds, viability is proven. If not, a systematic tree search is needed.

Second, inverse local consistency enforcing can be used to prove non-viability. This implies an extension of the notions of viability and inverse local consistency previously introduced. Definitions 2 and 4 can be replaced by the following recursive definitions:

Definition 6 *Let $P = (V, C)$ be an instance and $P' = (V', C')$ be a sub-instance of P. Let ilc_2 be an inverse local consistency level. Let $v \in V'$ and $val \in d(v)$. The value (v, val) is said to be ilc_2-viable in P' iff the sub-instance P' restricted by the assignment $v \leftarrow val$ is ilc_2-consistent.*

Definition 7 *Let $P = (V, C)$ be an instance. Let ilc_1 and ilc_2 be two inverse local consistency levels and $\mathbf{def}_{ilc_1}$ be the function associated with ilc_1. P is said to be ilc_1-ilc_2-consistent iff all the pairs in $\mathbf{def}_{ilc_1}(P)$ are ilc_2-viable.*

Note that recursivity stops when ilc_2 equals *consistency*. This extension allows other levels, previously known or not, to be included. For example:

- *singleton arc consistency* (Debruyne & Bessière 1997b) could be defined as *gc-ac* ($ilc_1 = gc$, $ilc_2 = ac$); *singleton neighborhood inverse consistency* could be defined as *gc-nic*; more generally, *singleton ilc* could be defined as *gc-ilc*;

orderings. If one wants to use dynamic orderings or, more generally, if one wants to derive more benefit from the previous searches for a supporting assignment of any value in the same sub-instance, any of the techniques of solution or reasoning reuse that have been developed for *dynamic CSPs* (Verfaillie & Schiex 1994b; Schiex & Verfaillie 1994; Verfaillie & Schiex 1994a), can be considered. Moreover, any level of inverse local consistency can be maintained during this search: *forward checking, arc consistency*, etc. Our current implementation (Martinez 1998) uses *forward checking* and static variable and value orderings.

It is easy to show informally that such an algorithm turns any instance P into an instance $\widehat{P}$, which is simplified, equivalent and locally consistent at the specified level:

(1) $\widehat{P}$ is simplified because some values involved in P have been removed;

(2) it is equivalent because all the instances successively generated during algorithm execution are equivalent to P: let $\widehat{P}_c$ be the current instance resulting from the removal of some values; initially, $\widehat{P}_c = P$; let us assume that, at a given step of the execution, $\widehat{P}_c$ is equivalent to P; if a value is removed, it is not viable in a sub-instance $\widehat{P}'_c$ of $\widehat{P}_c$, and thus not involved in any solution of $\widehat{P}_c$; the resulting new current instance is consequently equivalent to the previous one, and thus equivalent to P;

(3) it is locally consistent at the specified level, because, at

- *nic-ac* would be an interesting trade-off between *neighborhood inverse consistency* and *arc consistency*: for each variable v, one considers the sub-instance P' involving all the variables that are directed linked to v and all the constraints that link these variables; but for each value val of v, only *arc consistency* of P' restricted by the assignment $v \leftarrow val$ is required.

Conclusion and perspectives

As a conclusion, we have defined a generic customizable framework for inverse local consistency, which includes most of the previously defined levels and allows as many new levels as we can imagine to be built, according to the instance or kind of instance we have to solve. Let us point out that this framework does not include specific inverse local consistency levels, such as *restricted path consistency* and *max restricted path consistency*: their inclusion would have implied important changes in the proposed framework and a loss in terms of simplicity and clarity.

Associated with this framework, we have defined a generic algorithm, parameterized by the chosen level. This algorithm has been implemented in the frame of an interactive tool for CSP solving. No comparison in terms of efficiency has been carried out between this generic algorithm and other algorithms dedicated to a given level. Genericity may induce a loss of efficiency. But one can argue that a generic carefully implemented algorithm is often more efficient than a specific rapidly implemented algorithm.

Always associated with this framework, it would be worth developing a small language, allowing the user to express easily any level he/she wants. Finally, two remarks:

- the current constraint programming tools do not specify the levels of local consistency they use; "opening the box" and offering at least an advanced user the means of defining this level may allow him/her, on the one hand, to understand better how local consistency enforcing works and, on the other hand, to tune it according to the instance or kind of instance he/she has to solve;

- the generic framework we defined reverses the "landscape" of CSP solving: whereas local consistency enforcing is most of the time presented as a subroutine for tree search, tree search is presented here as a subroutine for local consistency enforcing; but nothing prevents us from defining a tree search, which calls local consistency enforcing, which in turn calls another tree search, etc.

Acknowledgements

We would like to thank the anonymous reviewers for their comments and Bertrand Cabon, Simon de Givry, Michel Lemaitre, Lionel Lobjois and Thomas Schiex for stimulating discussions about this work.

References

Bessière, C., and Régin, J. 1997. Arc Consistency for General Constraint Networks: Preliminary Results. In *Proc. of the 15th International Joint Conference on Artificial Intelligence (IJCAI-97)*, 398–404.

Bessière, C., and Régin, J. 1998. Local Consistency on Conjunctions of Constraints. In *Proc. of the ECAI-98 Workshop on "Non-Binary Constraints"*, 53–59.

Bessière, C.; Freuder, E.; and Régin, J. 1999. Using Inference to Reduce Arc Consistency Computation. *Artificial Intelligence* 107:125–148.

Cooper, M. 1989. An Optimal k-Consistency algorithm. *Artificial Intelligence* 41:89–95.

Debruyne, R., and Bessière, C. 1997a. From Restricted Path Consistency to Max-Restricted Path Consistency. In *Proc. of the 3rd International Conference on Principles and Practice of Constraint Programming (CP-97)*, 312–326.

Debruyne, R., and Bessière, C. 1997b. Some Practical Filtering Techniques for the Constraint Satisfaction Problem. In *Proc. of the 15th International Joint Conference on Artificial Intelligence (IJCAI-97)*, 412–417.

Dechter, R. 1992. From Local to Global Consistency. *Artificial Intelligence* 55:87–107.

Freuder, E., and Elfe, C. 1996. Neighborhood Inverse Consistency Preprocessing. In *Proc. of the 13th National Conference on Artificial Intelligence (AAAI-96)*, 202–208.

Freuder, E. 1978. Synthesizing Constraint Expressions. *Communications of the ACM* 21(11):958–966.

Freuder, E. 1985. A Sufficient Condition for Backtrack-Bounded Search. *Journal of the ACM* 32(4):755–761.

Freuder, E. 1991. Completable Representations of Constraint Satisfaction Problems. In *Proc. of the 1st International Conference on the Principles of Knowledge Representation and Reasoning (KR-91)*, 186–195.

Mackworth, A. 1977. Consistency in Networks of Relations. *Artificial Intelligence* 8(1):99–118.

Mackworth, A. 1992. Constraint Satisfaction. In Shapiro, S., ed., *Encyclopedia of Artificial Intelligence*. John Wiley & Sons. 285–293.

Martinez, D. 1998. *Résolution Interactive de Problèmes de Satisfaction de Contraintes*. Thèse de doctorat, ENSAE, Toulouse, France.

Schiex, T., and Verfaillie, G. 1994. Nogood Recording for Static and Dynamic Constraint Satisfaction Problems. *International Journal of Artificial Intelligence Tools* 3(2):187–207.

Verfaillie, G., and Schiex, T. 1994a. Dynamic Backtracking for Dynamic Constraint Satisfaction Problems. In *Proc. of the ECAI-94 Workshop on "Constraint Satisfaction Issues Raised by Practical Applications"*.

Verfaillie, G., and Schiex, T. 1994b. Solution Reuse in Dynamic Constraint Satisfaction Problems. In *Proc. of the 12th National Conference on Artificial Intelligence (AAAI-94)*, 307–312.

Functional Elimination and 0/1/All Constraints

Yuanlin Zhang, Roland H.C. Yap and Joxan Jaffar

School of Computing
National University of Singapore
Lower Kent Ridge Road, Singapore 119260, Republic of Singapore
{zhangyl, ryap, joxan}@comp.nus.edu.sg

Abstract

We present new complexity results on the class of 0/1/All constraints. The central idea involves functional elimination, a general method of elimination whose focus is on the subclass of functional constraints. One result is that for the subclass of "All" constraints, strong n-consistency and minimality is achievable in $\mathcal{O}(en)$ time, where e, n are the number of constraints and variables. The main result is that we can solve 0/1/All constraints in $\mathcal{O}(e(d + n))$ time, where d is the domain size. This is an improvement over known results, which are $\mathcal{O}(ed(d + n))$. Furthermore, our algorithm also achieves strong n-consistency and minimality.

1. Introduction

Constraint Satisfaction Problem(s) (CSP) are known to be NP-complete in general (Mackworth 1977). There are two approaches for attacking the computational intractability. One way is to identify those tractable class of problems by suitable restrictions so that it can be solved in polynomial time. A restriction is on the topological structure of the CSP constraint network, one example is (Freuder 1982). Another restriction is to exploit semantic properties of special classes of constraints, examples of this approach are (Dechter 1992; Van Beek and Dechter 1995; Cooper et al. 1994). (Van Beek and Dechter 1995) introduces the class of row-convex constraints which under some conditions can be solved in polynomial time. (Cooper et al. 1994) identifies a class of 0/1/All constraints, a special case of row-convex constraints, and proves that the class of problems generated by any set of constraints not contained in that class is NP-complete.

A different approach is to improve the efficiency of the basic step in searching the solution space of a CSP. Consistency techniques, especially arc-consistency, have been the method of choice for solving finite domain problems (Van Hentenryck 1989). Much effort has been made to find fast algorithms for arc-consistency. For a general CSP, we have AC-3 (Mackworth 1977), AC-4 (Mohr and Henderson 1986) which has an optimal

worst-case time complexity $\mathcal{O}(ed^2)$, and AC-6 which provides a better space complexity and average time complexity while giving the optimal worst-case time complexity, where e is the number of constraints and d the size of the largest domain. In addition, many arc-consistency algorithms have been proposed for dealing with CSPs with special properties. The algorithms of interest here are: (Van Hentenryck et al. 1992) gives an arc-consistency algorithm for special constraints such as functional constraints and monotone constraints in time $\mathcal{O}(ed)$, and (Liu 1995) gives another algorithm to deal with increasing functional constraint where each functional constraint is only checked once. (Affane and Bennaceur 1996) and (Zhang 1998) also study functional constraints in CSP.

In this paper we investigate the class of 0/1/All constraints. These 0/1/All constraints, also called *implicational* constraints, represent a significant class of scene labeling problems (Kirousis 1993). The class of functional constraints, which arises frequently in practice (Van Hentenryck et al. 1992), is in fact a subclass of 0/1/All constraints. Using a central idea of functional elimination, which is a general method of elimination on functional constraints, we obtain new complexity results for 0/1/All constraints. First, we prove that for the subclass of "All" constraints, strong n-consistency and minimality is achievable in $\mathcal{O}(en)$ time, where e, n are the number of constraints and variables. The main result is that we can solve 0/1/All constraints in $\mathcal{O}(e(d+n))$ time, where d is the domain size. This is an improvement over known results, which are $\mathcal{O}(ed(d+n))$. Furthermore, our algorithm also achieves strong n-consistency and minimality.

The paper is organized as follows. We start with background material on consistency techniques. Next, we investigate the properties of functional constraints (section 3) and two-fan constraints (section 4). Section 5, gives the elimination method and an algorithm for solving mixed 0/1/All CSPs. We conclude with a discussion on related work and the application of elimination method in general CSP.

2. Preliminaries

Definitions on general CSP follow (Montanari 1974; Mackworth 1977; Freuder 1978; Freuder 1982).

Definition 1 *A* Constraint Satisfaction Problem *(N, D, C) consists of a finite set of variables* $N = \{1, \cdots, n\}$, *a set of domains* $D = \{D_1, \cdots, D_n\}$, *where* $i \in D_i$, *and a set of constraints* $C = \{c_{ij} \mid i, j \in N\}$, *where each constraint* c_{ij} *is a binary relation between variables* i *and* j. *For the problem of interest here, we require that* $(x, y) \in c_{ij}$ *if and only if* $(y, x) \in c_{ji}$. *There is always a graph* $G = (V, E)$ *associated with the CSP where* $V = N$ *and* $E = \{(i, j) \mid \exists c_{ij} \in C\}$. *A solution to a constraint satisfaction problem is an instantiation of the variables which satisfies all the constraints in the problem.*

Throughout this paper, we will use n to represent the number of variables, d the size of the largest domain, C the set of constraints of the CSP, and e the number of constraints in C.

Definition 2 *A CSP is k-consistent if and only if given any instantiation of any* $k - 1$ *variables satisfying all of the constraints among those variables, there exists an instantiation of any kth variable such that the k values taken together satisfy all of the relations among the k variables. A CSP is strongly k consistent if and only if it is i-consistent for all* $i \leq k$. *A CSP is minimal if each pair of values allowed by each of the constraints is a part of a solution of the CSP.*

Well known consistency techniques like arc and path consistency correspond to strong two and three-consistency.

We now recall definitions of constraints with some special properties.

Definition 3 *(Cooper et al. 1994) A constraint,* c_{ij}, *is a directed 0/1/All constraint if for each value* $x \in D_i$, c_{ij} *satisfies the following:*

1. *for any value* $y \in D_j$, $(x, y) \notin c_{ij}$, *or*
2. *for any value* $y \in D_j$, $(x, y) \in c_{ij}$, *or*
3. *there is a unique value* $y \in D_j$, $(x, y) \in c_{ij}$.

A constraint is called functional *if either condition 1 or condition 3 is satisfied. A two-fan constraint, also called an "All" constraint,* c_{ij} *is a constraint where there exists* $x \in D_i$ *and* $y \in D_j$ *such that* $c_{ij} = (x \times D_j) \cup (y \times D_i)$. *A fan-out constraint is a constraint* c_{ij} *such that* $\exists x \in D_i$ *and* $\forall y$ $(x, y) \in c_{ij}$.

Property 1 *(Cooper et al. 1994) After enforcing arc-consistency on 0/1/All constraints, any 0/1/All constraint is either a trivial relation, a bijective function or a two-fan constraint. A trivial relation* c_{ij} *is either empty or* $D_i \times D_j$.

An example of two-fan (left) and fan-out (right) constraints are illustrated as follows:

Property 2 *(Cooper et al. 1994) The set of 0/1/All constraints is closed under the operations involved in path consistency:*

1. *Intersection of constraints.*
2. *Composition,* $\circ$, *where* $c_{ij} \circ c_{jk} = \{(p, q) \mid \exists r \in D_j, \text{such that } (p, r) \in c_{ij} \wedge (r, q) \in c_{jk}\}$.

Definition 4 *(Van Beek and Dechter 1995) A binary relation* c_{ij} *represented as a* $(0, 1)$*-matrix is* row convex *if and only if in each row all of the ones are consecutive; that is, no two ones within a single row are separated by a zero in that same row.*

Both functional and 0/1/All constraints are row convex. For row convex constraints there is the result:

Theorem 1 *(Van Beek and Dechter 1995) For a path-consistent CSP, if there exists an ordering of the domains* $D_1, \cdots, D_n$ *such that all constraints are row convex, the CSP is minimal and strongly n-consistent.*

It is obvious that a path consistency enforcing algorithm will make the 0/1/All constraint system minimal by theorem 1 and property 1 and 2, and thus the problem is solved. However, the complexity of a typical path algorithm is high, such as $\mathcal{O}(n^3 d^3)$ in (Mohr and Henderson 1986) and $\mathcal{O}(n^3 d^2)$ in (Devile et al. 1997). In this paper, we obtain more efficient algorithms.

3. The O (one) algorithm

We first present an algorithm for a CSP (N, D, C) which contains only functional constraints (functional CSP for short) and then give the analysis of certain properties of these constraints.

For the sake of simplicity and clarity, we assume the graph of the CSP is connected without loss of generality.

The algorithms are shown in figure 1 and figure 2.

```
Algorithm O((N, D, C)) {
    ∀i∀x,  x ∈ Dᵢ x.touched ← false;
    Select any variable i ∈ N
    for each value x of i {
        x.touched ← true;
        x.delete ← false;
        if not Propagate(x, i) then x.delete ← true;
    }
    ∀i∀x, x ∈ Dᵢ
        if (not x.touched) or (x.coordinate).delete
            then
            remove x from i;
}
```

Figure 1: *O*-algorithm for functional CSP

The *O*-algorithm uses an adaptation of brute force searching (Garey and Johnson 1979; Cooper et al. 1994) which takes advantage of the properties of functional constraints. In contrast, other known algorithms (Van Hentenryck et al. 1992) etc. are based on arc consistency where the emphasis is on finding those values which can be immediately removed by checking only a single constraint. The direct brute force searching

```
Function Propagate (in x, i) {
    L ← {(x, i)};
    for each j ∈ N x_j ← null;
    x_i ← x;
    repeat
        Delete first element (y, j) from L;
        for each c_jk
            if ∃z such that (y, z) ∈ c_jk then
                if x_k = null then {
                    z.coordinate ← x;
                    z.touched ← true;
                    x_k ← z;
                    L ← L ∪ {(z, k)};
                } end else if x_k ≠ z then return false;
    until (L = ∅);
    return true;
}
```

Figure 2: Propagate algorithm for functional CSP

method here gives a simpler algorithm. The intuition behind the O-algorithm is that if at some point in the search we cannot continue because of inconsistency, we simply restart at the initial starting point since the path propagated between the starting point and the current failure point is unique in a functional CSP.

Definition 5 *Given a CSP (N, D, C), its value graph is $G = (V, E)$ where $V = \{(D_i, x) : x \in D_i, i \in N\}$ and $E = \{((D_i, x), (D_j, y)) \mid \exists i, j \text{ such that } (x, y) \in c_{ij}\}$. An instantiation tree of G wrt. (D_i, x) is a maximal sub-graph $\bar{G}$ satisfying:*
1. $(D_i, x) \in \bar{G}$,
2. $\bar{G}$ *is a tree, and*
3. $(D_j, y) \in \bar{G}$ *and* $(D_j, z) \in \bar{G}$ *implies* $y = z$.
The candidate set wrt. (D_i, x) is the set of vertices of $\bar{G}$. A value graph G is stable wrt. (D_i, x) if all the instantiation trees wrt. (D_i, x) have the same candidate set. A candidate set wrt. (D_i, x) is unique if the graph G is stable wrt. each of the vertices in the candidate set. Finally, a candidate set is complete if it has n vertices.

Property 3 *In a functional CSP, $x \in D_i$ is a part of a solution if and only if the candidate set wrt. (D_i, x) is unique and complete.*

Proof. Obviously, if a candidate set is not complete, then x cannot be extended to a solution of the functional CSP. The proof of uniqueness is by contradiction. Assume that for some vertex (D_k, u) in the candidate set of (D_i, x), there are two instantiation trees G' and G'' which cover different sets of vertices. Then, $\exists (D_j, y) \in G'$ and $(D_j, z) \in G''$ where $y \neq z$. Hence when variable k takes x, variable j takes both y and z, which is a contradiction. □

It is easy to see that if a candidate set of $x \in D_i$ is not complete, or if it is not unique, then all values in the possible candidate sets wrt. (D_i, x) will be invalid. The value x here is called the *coordinate* of all other nodes

in the candidate set and i (the variable) is called the *origin*. In the O-algorithm, we associate the following attributes to any value $y \in D_j$:

- $y.touched$ indicates if this value has been tried;
- $y.delete$ indicates if the value should be removed;
- $y.coordinate$ is the coordinate of y with regard to an origin i.

Theorem 2 *Given a functional CSP, the O-algorithm is correct and enforces the CSP to be minimal and strongly n-consistent. The complexity of O-algorithm is $\mathcal{O}(ed)$.*

Proof.
(1) The purpose of Propagate is to identify whether a candidate set wrt. $x \in D_i$ is complete and also unique. The **repeat** loop is to find an instantiation tree wrt. (D_i, x). The condition statement is to check the uniqueness of the candidate set. The Propagate function can detect only one instantiation tree wrt. (D_i, x). Suppose the candidate set is not complete or not unique, the question is how to delete all the nodes of the other candidate sets? We use the property that either all vertices of other candidate sets will never be visited again; or if it is visited, its coordinate will be labeled as deleted. This property is implemented by the attribute $x.touched$.
(2) The minimal and strong n-consistency is immediate by the above proof.
(3) It is straightforward to show that the complexity of O-algorithm is $\mathcal{O}(ed)$. □

4. The A ("All") algorithm

In this section, we analyse two-fan constraints (also called "All" constraints) and give an algorithm for this class. Without loss of generality, we will assume that the CSP only contains "All" constraints.

For the ease of presentation, we introduce the following notations:

Definition 6 *Given a two-fan constraint c_{ij}, a pivot of c_{ij} with respect to i, is denoted by the notation p_i^{ij}. The pivot p_i^{ij} is defined to be the value $x \in D_i$ such that $\forall y \in D_j$ $(x, y) \in c_{ij}$. The coordinate of p_j^{ij} with respect to D_i is defined to be p_i^{ij}.*

A two-fan constraint c_{ij} can be simply represented by the two pivots (p_i^{ij}, p_j^{ij}). The use of coordinate here is analogous to its use in functional constraints. In the A-algorithm (fig 3) the coordinate is the only value in D_i such that j can take any value; and furthermore for values other than the coordinate there is a unique choice in j. Thus, the role of coordinates in the A-algorithm is an adaptation of that in the O-algorithm.

Like the O-algorithm, the A-algorithm is also based on a search procedure. Before we present the algorithm, we will first highlight some important properties of two-fan constraints. We begin by recalling an important observation mentioned in (Cooper et al. 1994). Here we formalize it to emphasize its importance.

Definition 7 *Given a CSP (N, D, C), an instantiation of a set of variables $S \subseteq N$ is separable, if it satisfies all constraints among S, and any constraint $c_{ij} \in C$ between variables $i \in S$ and $j \in N - S$ allows j to take any value under the current instantiation of i.*

For a single two-fan constraint c_{ij}, it is immediate that the instantiation of i by the pivot p_i^{ij} is separable.

Proposition 1 *Given any CSP (N, D, C) and a separable instantiation of a set of variables. If the CSP has a solution, then the instantiation is part of some solution.*

The correctness of the above proposition is immediate. The usefulness of this proposition, is that after a separable instantiation is found, we can subtract out those variables and all constraints involved in at least one of those variables. and thus we get a smaller problem to work on (search). By continuing in this fashion, at the end, the combination of all the separable instantiations is a solution to the original problem. One task of the A-algorithm is to identify some set of variables whose instantiation is separable since the two-fan constraint gives a strong hint on how to achieve that goal.

The rationale for identifying the separable instantiations, by using some special properties of two-fan functions, is that a faster algorithm can be achieved. The identification step is achieved using the A-propagate procedure in a similar fashion to Propagate in the O-algorithm. It works as follows. First, select a starting variable and instantiate it to a value x. The next step is to try to instantiate its uninstantiated neighbor variables. For any uninstantiated k such that there exists $c_{ik} \in C$, we have two choices. In one case, we have that x is p_i^{ik}, and this stops the identification procedure along direction of c_{ik}. In the other case, by definition, we have a unique choice in D_k and thus we need repeat the propagation above to deal with the neighbors of k because in the direction of c_{ik} the instantiation has not yet been found to be separable. Finally we get a set of variables whose instantiation is separable. A trivial case is that the set of variables is N itself. One problem in the procedure is that the instantiation step for a variable may fail. Fortunately, this failure case only occurs when the instantiation step tries to set a variable to two different values which is a contradiction. In (Cooper et al. 1994), they simply return to the starting variable and select the next value available. However, there is a better and faster way for resolving the failure because of the following properties.

The values of D_i fall into two classes. One, called the *pivot class P*, contains all the pivots while the other, called the *nonpivot class NP*, contains all the other values.

Definition 8 *Given a two-fan CSP, a value $x \in i$ is valid if x is part of a solution of the CSP.*

Property 4 *Given a two-fan CSP and a variable i with domain D_i, we have for the*

- *NP class of D_i: if two of the values are valid, then any value will also be valid;*
- *P class of D_i: if three of the values are valid, then any value will also be valid.*

Proposition 2 *In the procedure of identifying the set of variables with separable instantiations, if there is a contradiction, then for the starting variable there are at most two valid values from the P class and no value from the NP class.*

Proof. It is obvious for NP class. For P class, only coordinates of the two contradicted values are possible. For all other values, contradiction still remains. $\square$

The A algorithm is given in figures 3 and 4.

Algorithm A (**in** (N, D, C)) {
Select any value $x \in D_i$ for any variable $i \in N$
A-Propagate($x, i, N, M, consistent, p_1, p_2$);
if not *consistent* **then** {
A-Propagate($x, p_1, N, M, consistent, -, -$);
if not *consistent* **then**
A-Propagate($x, p_2, N, M, consistent, -, -$);
}
if *consistent* **then** {
$N \leftarrow N - M$;
if $N \neq \emptyset$ **then** A((N, D, C));
} **else** report no solution for (N, D, C)
}

Figure 3: Algorithm for Two-fan Constraints

Theorem 3 *Given a two-fan CSP, there exists an algorithm such that strong n-consistency can be enforced in time complexity $\mathcal{O}(en)$.*

Proof. The A-algorithm is correct according to proposition 1 and 2. The complexity of A-Propagate is at most e and it is called at most n times. The A-algorithm finds one solution to the CSP. To achieve the strong n-consistency and minimality, it can be slightly modified using property 4 to check each variable rather than a set of variables in the main loop. The time complexity is still $\mathcal{O}(en)$, the same as in the A-algorithm. $\square$

5. The OA algorithm

Now we are in a position to deal with a CSP with 0/1/All constraints. First we simplify the CSP by removing those values not allowed by any complete or two-fan constraint. Secondly, we remove those complete constraints and trivial two-fan functions. The above procedure will take no more than $\mathcal{O}(ed)$ time. Now, the new CSP, called a mixed 1/All CSP, contains only functional and two-fan constraints. While it may be possible to directly use O- and A-algorithms to design

```
Proc A-Propagate(in x, i, N, out M, con, p₁, p₂) {
    L ← ∅;
    for each j ∈ N    x_j ← null;
    con ← true;
    for each j such that c_{ij} ∈ C {
        p_j^{ij}.coordinate = p_i^{ij};
        L ← L ∪ {(p_j^{ij}, j)};
    }
    repeat {
        Delete first element (y, j) from L
        for each c_{jk}
            if there is only one z such that
                    (y, z) ∈ c_{jk} then
                if x_k = null then {
                    L ← L ∪ {(z, k)};
                    x_k ← z;
                    z.coordinate ← y.coordinate;
                } else if x_k ≠ z then {
                    con ← false;
                    p₁ = y.coordinate;
                    p₂ = z.coordinate;
                    M ← all the other uninstantiated
                            variables
                }
    } until (L = ∅) or (not con);
}
```

Figure 4: A-Propagate for two-fan CSP

```
Proc Eliminate (inout (N, D, C), out consistent) {
    consistent ← true;
    Let i ∈ FV, L ← {j | ∃c_{ij} ∈ FC}
    repeat {
        Select and delete j ∈ L
        for each c_{jk} ∈ C {
            c'_{ik} ← c_{ij} ∘ c_{jk};
            if ∃c_{ik} ∈ C c'_{ik} then ← c'_{ik} ∩ c_{ik};
            switch (c'_{ik}) {
                case ∅ : consistency ← false;
                    return;
                case functional: L ← L ∪ {k};
                    c_{ik} ← c'_{ik};
                case fan-out:
                    if the pivot appears in D_i, remove the
                        other values, and vice versa;
                    C ← C − {c_{ik}};
                case two-fan: c_{ik} ← c'_{ik};
            }
        }
    } until L = ∅;
}
```

Figure 5: Elimination algorithm for functional Constraints

```
Algorithm OA-algorithm {
    Eliminate ((N, D, C), consistent);
    if consistent then A((N, D, C))
    else report inconsistency
}
```

Figure 6: Algorithm for mixed CSP

an algorithm for the mixed system, we however use an integrated approach using following theorem.

Theorem 4 *Given a CSP, two variables i and j with c_{ij} being functional, we can eliminate one of variable i or j, to give a new CSP which leaves the solution of the original CSP unchanged.*

The motivation of this theorem comes from the O-algorithm. If there is a functional constraint between i and j, we can eliminate variable j and redirect all constraints involving j to i. We remark that other elimination methods in symbolic computation, eg. Gaussian elimination, can also be thought of as a specialization of the this elimination idea.

The Eliminate algorithm given in figure 5 uses the result of theorem 4 but specialized to the context of 0/1/All constraints. In figure 5, $FC = \{c_{ij} \mid c_{ij} \in C$ is functional$\}$ and $FV = \{i, j \mid \exists c_{ij} \in FC\}$. The algorithm for solving the mixed CSP is shown in figure 6.

Theorem 5 *Given a mixed CSP, the OA-algorithm has a time complexity of $\mathcal{O}(ed + en)$ and enforces the CSP to be minimal and strongly n-consistent.*

Proof. Without loss of generality, in this proof we assume all the functional constraints are connected. After the elimination procedure, there are only two-fan functions. So, the algorithm is correct and the resulted CSP

is minimal and strongly n-consistent. For the elimination procedure, each **for** loop takes at most $d * d_i$ times where d_i is the degree of node i because all operations on constraint manipulation can be done in d time. Altogether, we have at most n nodes to deal with and thus the complexity is $\mathcal{O}(ed)$. □

6. Related Work and Discussion

The directly related works on 0/1/All constraints are (Cooper et al. 1994) and (Kirousis 1993), both of which give a sequential algorithm with time complexity of $\mathcal{O}(ed(n + d))$ to find one solution. Note that the n-ary 0/1/All constraints system defined in (Kirousis 1993) is actually a binary constraint system.

In this paper, we obtain better results with a time complexity of $\mathcal{O}(en)$ for a CSP with only "All" constraints and $\mathcal{O}(e(d + n))$ for CSPs with mixed 0/1/All constraints. In both cases, this time complexity obtains a solution to the CSP as well as enforcing strong n-consistency and minimality. Thus, a higher degree of consistency is obtained compared to (Cooper et al. 1994; Kirousis 1993) with more efficient algorithms.

The other related works (Van Hentenryck et al. 1992; Liu 1995; Affane and Bennaceur 1996; Zhang 1998) are done mainly in the context of arc consistency. Those works consider only functional constraints. Here we give simpler algorithms and an explicit analysis which fully reflects the global property of functional constraints. More specifically, (Van Hentenryck et al. 1992) do not consider finding the global solution, (Liu 1995) only deals with giving a more efficient algorithm for dealing with increasing functional constraints. (Affane and Bennaceur 1996) introduces a new kind of consistency, label-arc consistency, and show that the pure functional constraints with limited extensions to other constraints can be solved, but no detailed analysis of their algorithms is given. (Zhang 1998) embeds the techniques dealing with functional constraint in arc-consistency algorithms in a similar way to (Liu 1995) and proposes the problem of *conflict of orienting* from which all the above mentioned algorithms (except (Van Hentenryck et al. 1992)) suffer.

One result, which we obtain for the class of functional or "1" constraints, is a new algorithm for functional constraints with time complexity $\mathcal{O}(ed)$. In terms of time complexity, it is the same as existing results. However, an advantage of the algorithm here is its conceptual simplicity and ability to achieve minimality. The development of the O-algorithm clarifies how functional elimination can be applied in general, resulting in its use in the OA-algorithm and the special form of propagation in the A-algorithm. In addition, both the O and OA algorithms avoid the problem of conflict of orienting for CSPs which are known in advance.

An important consequence of the techniques developed here for functional elimination is that functional elimination is of broad applicability in the more general context of arbitrary CSP problems. It is possible to show that the elimination method for functional constraints here, for general CSP problems, will be at most $\mathcal{O}(ed^2)$ time. This means that, it can be incorporated into general arc-consistency algorithms without any increase in time complexity, while at the same time obtaining more consistency. Other results with elimination methods on linear equations, (Harvey and Stuckey 1998; Zhang 1998), also suggest the efficacy of such elimination approaches.

7. Conclusion

The 0/1/All constraints play an important role both theoretically (Cooper et al. 1994) and in practice (Van Hentenryck 1989; Kirousis 1993). This paper gives fast algorithms and analyses for functional, two-fan, and mixed CSPs. The elimination method used in solving the mixed CSPs is of broader applicability in a more general CSP setting. In addition, its incremental nature makes it suitable in a solver engine of a constraint logic programming language (Jaffar and Maher 1994).

References

M. S. Affane and H. Bennaceur 1996. A Labelling Arc Consistency Method for Functional Constraints, *Proceedings of CP96*, Cambridge, MA, USA: Springer.

P. van Beek and R. Dechter 1995., Minimality and Global Consistency of Constraint Networks, *Journal of ACM*, Vol 42(3):543-561.

M. C. Cooper, D. A. Cohen and P. G. Jeavons 1994., Characterizing Tractable Constraints, *Artificial Intelligence* 65:347-361.

R. Dechter 1992., From Local to Global Consistency, *Artificial Intelligence* 34:1-38 .

Y. Deville, O. Barette and P. van Hentenryk 1997., Connected Row Convex Constraints, *Proceedings of IJCAI-97*, 405-410. Nagoya, Japan: IJCAI Inc.

E. C. Freuder 1982., Synthesizing Constraint Expressions, *Communications of the ACM*, Vol 21(11):958-966.

E. C. Freuder 1982., A sufficient condition for backtrack-free search , *Journal of ACM*, Vol 29(1):24-32 .

M.R. Garey and D.S. Johnson 1979., *Computers and Intractability: A Guide to NP-Completeness*. San Francisco, CA: Freeman.

W. Harvey and P.J. Stuckey 1998., Constraint Representation for Propagation, *Proceedings CP98*, Pisa,Italy: Springer.

J. Jaffar and M.J. Maher 1994., Constraint Logic Programming, *Journal of Logic Programming* 19/20:503-581.

L. M. Kirousis 1993., Fast Parallel Constraint Satisfaction, *Artificial Intelligence* 64:147-160.

B. Liu 1995., Increasing Functional Constraints Need to be checked only once, *Proceedings of IJCAI-95*, 586-591.Montreal, Canada: IJCAI Inc.

A. K. Mackworth 1977., Consistency in Networks of Relations,, *Artificial Intelligence* 8(1):118-126.

R. Mohr and T. C. Henderson 1986., Arc and Path Consistency Revisited, *Artificial Intelligence* 28:225-233.

U. Montanari 1974, Networks of Constraints: Fundamental Properties and Applications, *Information Science* 7(2):95-132.

P. van Hentenryk 1989., *Constraint Satisfaction and Logic Programming*. Cambridge, Mass.: MIT Press.

P. van Hentenryk, Y. Deville, and C. M. Teng 1992., A Generic Arc-Consistency Algorithm and its Specializations, *Artif. Int.* 58:291-321.

Y. Zhang 1998., Consistency Techniques for Linear Arithmetic and Functional Constraints. *MSc. Thesis*, Dept. of Compter Science, Natl. Univ. of Singapore.

Y. Zhang and H. Wu 1998, Bound Consistency on Linear Constraints in Finite Domain Constraint Programming, *Proceedings of ECAI98*, Brighton, UK: John Wiley & Sons, Ltd.

Hybrid Methods

An Evolvable Hardware Chip and Its Application as a Multi-Function Prosthetic Hand Controller

Isamu Kajitani and **Tsutomu Hoshino**
University of Tsukuba
1-1-1 Tennou-dai, Tsukuba, Ibaraki, 305-8573, JAPAN
i_kajita@etl.go.jp

Nobuki Kajihara
Adaptive Devices NEC Laboratory, RWCP

Masaya Iwata and **Tetsuya Higuchi**
Electrotechnical Laboratory

Abstract

This paper describes the application of genetic algorithms to the biomedical engineering problem of a multi-function myoelectric prosthetic hand controller. This is achieved by an innovative LSI chip (EHW chip), i.e., a VLSI implementation of Evolvable Hardware (EHW), which can adapt its own circuit structure to its environment autonomously and quickly by using genetic algorithms. Usually, a long training period (almost one month) is required before multi-function myoelectric prosthetic hands can be controlled, however, the EHW chip controller developed here can reduce this period and it has been designed for easy implementation within a prosthetic hand. There are plans to commercialize the prosthetic hand with the EHW chip, and the medical department of Hokkaido University has already decided to adopt this for clinical treatment.

Introduction

In contrast to conventional hardware, where the structure is irreversibly fixed in the design process, Evolvable Hardware (EHW) (Higuchi *et al.* 1993) is designed to adapt to changes in task requirements or changes in the environment, through its ability to reconfigure its own hardware structure dynamically and autonomously. This capacity for adaptation, achieved by employing efficient search algorithms known as genetic algorithms (GAs)(Goldberg 1989), has great potential for the development of innovative industrial applications.

Although most works on EHW citeYao98 have been done with software simulations, this paper presents a VLSI implementation of EHW (EHW chip) and its application to the biomedical engineering problem of a multi-function myoelectric prosthetic hand controller.

In designing this EHW chip, we have modified the genetic operations used in (Kajitani *et al.* 1998) to include a gene replacement operation to accelerate the

adaptation speed of the EHW chip, which we refer to as Gene Replacement Genetic Algorithm (GRGA).

The myoelectric prosthetic hand is operated by the signals generated in muscular movement (electromyography, EMG). However, it takes a long time, usually almost one month, before a disabled person is able to control a multi-function prosthetic hand freely (Uchida, H, & Ninomija 1993). During this period, the disabled person has to undertake training to adapt to the myoelectric hand. We hope to reverse this situation, by having the myoelectric hand adapt itself to the disabled person.

Although, work is being done on applying neural networks for adaptable prosthetic hand controllers, this approach is not very promising due to implementation problems, because systems using neural networks are large and thus difficult to implement within a prosthetic hand.

In contrast, the system using the EHW chip is suitable for this kind of application, because of its compactness and high-speed adaptability, and, in this paper, we show that the EHW chip controller is a viable alternative to neural network controllers.

There are plans to commercialize the prosthetic hand with the EHW chip, and the medical department of Hokkaido University has already decided to adopt this for clinical treatment.

This paper is organized as follows. Section 2 provides some background to this research. In Section 3, the basic idea of EHW is explained. Section 4 introduces the EHW chip, and its application to the controller for a prosthetic artificial limb, which is presented in Section 5.

Background

EHW is based on the idea of combining a reconfigurable hardware device with GAs to execute reconfiguration autonomously (Higuchi *et al.* 1993).

In conventional works on EHW (Yao & Higuchi 1998), genetic operations are carried out with software on personal computers (PCs) or workstations (WSs). This makes it difficult to use EHW in situations that need circuits to be as small and light as possible. For

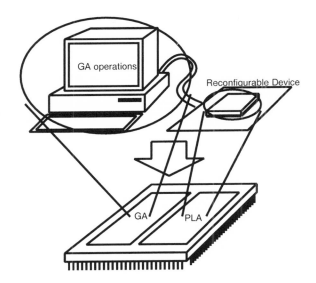

Figure 1: The basic idea of the EHW chip

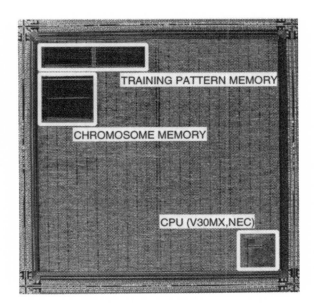

Figure 2: The earlier version of the EHW chip.(Kajitani *et al.* 1998).

example, a myoelectric prosthetic hand should be the same size as a human hand and weight less than 700 gram.

One solution to this is to incorporate the hardware that carries out the GA operations together with the reconfigurable hardware logic within a single LSI chip, as shown in Figure 1. Such compact and quickly reconfigurable EHW chips can serve as off-the-shelf devices for practical applications that require on-line hardware reconfiguration.

This paper describes the EHW chip, which is actually an improved version of the chip developed in (Kajitani *et al.* 1998)(Figure 2). The two improvements to this EHW chip are: 1. Speed of adaptation. 2. *On-line* circuit synthesis.

(Kajitani *et al.* 1998) demonstrated the possibility of employing an EHW chip as the pattern classification circuit for EMG signals in a multi-function myoelectric prosthetic hand controller.

In that application, the pattern classification circuit was synthesized *off-line*, in two distinct phases (i.e. "input-output pattern training sample phase" and "circuit synthesis with GA phase"). Although this *off-line* approach is used in most adaptable prosthetic hand applications of neural network controllers (such as (Kelly, Parker, & Scott 1990)), this approach is often ineffective due to changes in EMG signal features after construction of a training sample (Ito *et al.* 1991) (Fujii, Nishikawa, & Yokoi 1998).

To overcome this problem, we apply an *on-line* approach to the EHW chip prosthetic hand controller.

The Basic Idea of EHW

The basic idea of EHW is the combination of a reconfigurable hardware device and GAs (Higuchi *et al.* 1993).

PLA (Programmable Logic Array, Figure 3) is most commonly used as the reconfigurable hardware device *. A PLA consists of an AND-array and an OR-array as shown in Figure 3. In Figure 3, the black and white circles indicate switches, which determine the interconnections between the inputs and outputs (the black circles indicate connections). The row lines (product term lines) in the AND-array form logical products of connected inputs, and the column lines in the OR-array form logical sums of the connected row lines of the AND-array (i.e. product term lines). We can specify these switch settings by using a configuration bit string as shown in Figure 3.

The basic concept behind the combination of GAs and the PLA in EHW is to regard the configuration bit strings for the PLA as chromosomes for the GAs (Figure 4). If a fitness function is properly designed for a task, then the GAs can autonomously find the best hardware configuration in terms of the chromosomes (i.e. configuration bits).

Usually, a training sample of input-output patterns (e.g. Table 1) is used to evaluate chromosomes (Higuchi *et al.* 1993). In this case, the fitness value for a chromosome (i.e. circuit candidate) is the output pattern rate, that is, the rate at which actual output corresponds to the expected output pattern for a given training input pattern.

The EHW Chip.

The improvements to this EHW chip are in "Speed of adaptation" and "*On-line* circuit synthesis." These

---

*Other EHW works use special hardware, in which the circuit structure can be changed by arithmetic functional blocks or analogue circuit components.

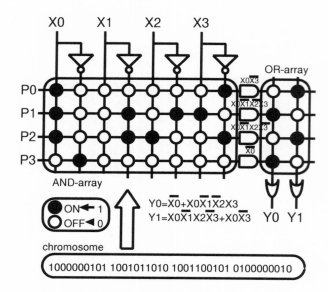

$$Y0 = \overline{X0} + X0\overline{X1}X2X3$$
$$Y1 = X0\overline{X1}X2X3 + X0\overline{X3}$$

Figure 3: The basic structure of the PLA.

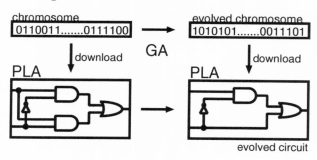

Figure 4: The basic idea of EHW.

improvements are achieved through two modifications; firstly, by employing GRGA (Gene Replacement Genetic Algorithm), and secondly, by adding an extra *"on-line* training pattern memory edit" mode, which is indispensable for an application such as the prosthetic hand controller.

Architecuture and Workflow of The EHW Chip.

The EHW chip consists of the following six functional blocks, shown in Figure 5.

- GA UNIT : This is the hardware that carries out the GA operations.
- CHROMOSOME MEMORY, TRAINING PATTERN MEMORY and MEMORY for FITNESS VALUE: These are the memories for the chromosomes, the training samples and the fitness values of each chromosome, respectively.
- PLA UNIT (2 arrays): Two PLAs are for parallel evaluation of two circuits.
- 16 bit CPU (8086 compatible, V30MX(NEC)): This is used as the interface between outside and inside

Table 1: Training input-output patterns and an example of fitness value.

training pattern		output pattern of the circuit in Figure 3. $Y0Y1$
input pattern $X0X1X2X3$	output pattern	
1001	10	10
0001	10	10
0101	10	10
1100	01	01
0011	10	10
0000	00	$\underline{10}$
0100	10	$\underline{10}$
0010	10	10
1010	00	$\underline{01}$
1110	01	$\underline{01}$
fitness value		0.8

the chip. It can be used to calculate fitness values for each circuit without using training patterns.

The adaptation of the EHW chip is carried out in the following way.

1. The GA UNIT reads two chromosomes from the CHROMOSOME MEMORY in units of 32 bits, and applies genetic operations on them to make two segments (32 bits) from the chromosomes.

2. These two segments are written to the PLA UNIT and are used to implement a circuit on both of the two PLAs. The two circuits are then evaluated.

3. Evaluations of the circuits on the PLAs are carried out by using the training samples, which are read from the TRAINING PATTERN MEMORY, and the fitness values are written to the MEMORY for FITNESS VALUE.

GRGA (Gene Replacement Genetic Algorithm)

The basic idea of GRGA is to accelerate the genetic search by replacing a part of a chromosome with a bit string, referred to as the "chromosome candidate segment." In this application, the chromosome candidate segment is generated from a training input-output pattern used for the evaluation of circuit candidates, as shown in Figure 6.

To implement this replacement operation on the EHW chip, we combined this operation with the ER (Elitist Recombination)(Thierens & Goldberg 1994) and the UC (Uniform Crossover) operations used in the earlier version of the EHW chip (Kajitani *et al.* 1998) and have named this combination of genetic operations GRGA. This replacement operation is carried out when the output pattern for a training input pattern does not match the expected training output pattern, with the replacement of the chromosome candidate segment being carried out with a fixed probability.

For example, generation of a chromosome candidate segment, in the case of the first training pattern in Table 1 (expected output pattern for the input pattern "1001" is "10"), would proceed as follows.

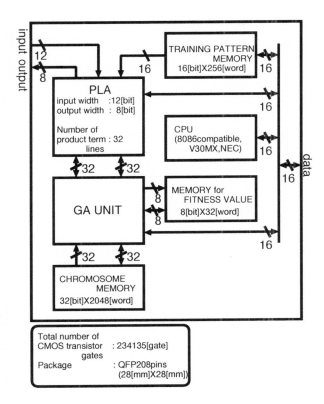

Figure 5: Block diagram of the EHW chip.

When the switches of a product term line in the PLA are set as they are in line P1 in Figure 3, the output pattern for the input pattern "1001" is "10," and the output patterns for all the other input patterns are "00". These switches can be set with the bit string "1001011010", which is treated as a chromosome candidate segment.

We present the results from simulations carried out to evaluate the adaptability of the GRGA. These simulated the number of evaluations required to synthesize a basic combination circuit for both the GRGA and for the combination of the ER and the UC operations. The three bit comparator circuit (six input bits and one output bit) was used as the target circuit in the simulations, because this circuit requires a long time to be synthesized by GAs (Higuchi *et al.* 1995) (Kajitani *et al.* 1996).

The result was that the combination of the ER and the UC operations took about 61874 evaluations (averaged ten times), and the GRGA took about 9710 evaluations (averaged ten times) to synthesize the circuit. This indicates that the evaluation time for the combination of the ER and the UC operations is over sixth times longer than that required with the GRGA.

On-line Training Pattern Memory Edit Mode.

In the earlier EHW chip, the TRAINING PATTERN MEMORY could not be edited after the GA UNIT had

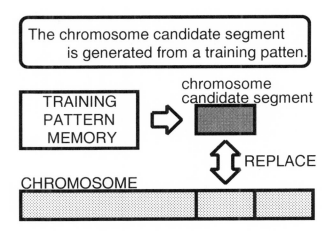

Figure 6: The basic idea of the GRGA.

begun to operate. Therefore, training sample patterns had to be made *off-line*(Kajitani *et al.* 1998).

To overcome this problem, we have incorporated an "*On-line* training patter n edit mode" within the chip. This allows us to terminate the genetic operation s when necessary, so that the TRAINING PATTERN MEMORY can be edited *on-line* , The ability to edit the TRAINING PATTERN MEMORY *on-line* helps to ensur e a smooth adaptation process for the prosthetic hand controller.

Prosthetic Hand Control By The EHW Chip

EMG Pattern Classification with The EHW Chip

The purpose of the EHW controller in the prosthetic hand is to synthesize pattern classification hardware to map input patterns (i.e. feature vectors of the two channel EMG signals, which are detected by two sensors (Kajitani *et al.* 1998), to desired actions of the hand (i.e. one of six actions in Figure 7). However, because EMG signals vary greatly between individuals, it is impossible to design in advance such a control (classification) circuit. Furthermore, even for a particular person, feature vectors of the EMG signals sometimes change even over short periods (Ito *et al.* 1991) (Fujii, Nishikawa, & Yokoi 1998). Therefore, the control hardware circuit must be synthesized adaptively.

Problems With Conventional Works

In conventional work on adaptable prosthetic hands, there are two problems.

1. Inefficiency of *off-line* construction of training sample patterns.

2. Computational overheads of preprocessing EMG signals.

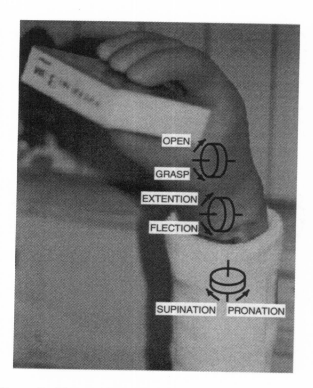

Figure 7: The artificial prosthesis used in our experiments.

Inefficiency of *Off-line* Construction of Training Sample Patterns. Although most adaptable prosthetic hand controllers using either neural networks (such as (Kelly, Parker, & Scott 1990)(Hudgins, Parker, & Scott 1993)) or the EHW chip (Kajitani *et al.* 1998) have taken an *off-line* approach to training, this is often ineffective due to changes in EMG signal features after construction of training sample patterns (Ito *et al.* 1991) (Fujii, Nishikawa, & Yokoi 1998).

To overcome this problem, an *on-line* approach has been applied to neural network controllers (Ito *et al.* 1991)(Fujii, Nishikawa, & Yokoi 1998), and, in this paper, we also adopt this *on-line* approach to the prosthetic hand controller using the EHW chip.

If the prosthetic hand fails to function as the user intends, it may be due to changes in EMG signal features. With this *on-line* approach, we can supplement the set of training samples with new patterns and can reconfigure the pattern classification circuit accordingly.

Computational Overheads of Preprocessing EMG Signals. In (Fujii, Nishikawa, & Yokoi 1998)(Kajitani *et al.* 1998), the frequency spectrum power of the detected EMG signals was used as the feature vectors of the EMG signals. Usually, the frequency spectrum powers are calculated using FFT (Fast Fourier Transform) that needs a high performance CPU (e.g. Pentium) or a DSP (Digital Signal Processor) to carry out calculations quickly. However,

in general, systems using high performance CPUs or DSPs become large, and this makes it difficult to implement them within the prosthetic hand.

Therefore, we have decided to use integrated EMG(IEMG) signals (Ito *et al.* 1991), which are calculated by integrating the absolute value of a EMG signal for each channel within a fixed period (one second, in this paper), as the feature vectors of the EMG signals, in this prosthetic hand controller. These IEMGs are converted into four bit binary numbers to be input signals to the PLAs in the EHW chip.

Experiments

Overview This section explains some experiments on the synthesis of a pattern classification circuit for the EMG feature vectors. In this experiment, because the EHW chip introduced in this paper is still in debugging stage, its simulator on a PC (Pentium Pro, 200MHz) was used.

This experiment consisted of the following six stages.

1. Construction of a training sample of input-output patterns (sixty patterns; 10[pattern]X6[action]).

2. Circuit synthesis with GRGA for five minutes.

3. Test of the synthesized circuit.

4. Construction of additional training sample patterns (thirty patterns; 10[pattern]X3[action]).

5. Reconfiguration of the circuit with GRGA for five minutes.

6. Test of the reconfigured circuit.

Training Pattern Construction. A training sample of input-output patterns consists of the input patterns, i.e., binary expressions of the amplitude of the EMG signals, and the expected output patterns, which determine the action of the prosthetic hand (one of six actions). Training patterns were generated in the following way for each of the six prosthetic hand actions.

1. Envisage one of the prosthetic hand actions, and contract remnant muscles.

2. Enter key corresponding to the action. This operation generates ten training sample patterns.

The pattern classification circuit is synthesized using these training sample patterns (10[pattern] X 6[action] = 60[pattern]).

Test of The Synthesized Circuit. The synthesized circuit was tested in the following way.

1. Envisage one of the prosthetic hand actions, and contract remnant muscles.

2. Enter key corresponding to the action. This operation calculates the output pattern rate for the synthesized circuit, which is the same as the expected output pattern for an intended action, during ten seconds.

Table 2: Output pattern rates of synthesized circuit, which correspond to expected output patterns (averaged for three people).

	before training pattern addition (%)	after training pattern addtion (%)
SUPINATION	66	74
PRONATION	49	72
FLECTION	67	88
EXTENSION	84	95
GRASP	38	75
OPEN	36	84
AVERAGE	57	81

The results of this test are shown in Table 2 (middle column).

Then, ten additional training sample patterns are generated for the three actions with the lowest output pattern rates for the synthesized circuit. The circuit on the PLA is reconfigured using these training sample patterns (60[pattern] + 10[pattern] X 3[action] = 90[pattern]), and the reconfigured circuit is tested again. The results of this test are shown in Table 2 (right column).

Results The averaged output pattern rate (Table 2) for the EHW chip controller is 81.0[%]. In contrast, the averaged output pattern rate for neural network controllers, which are learned with training samples generated by an *on-line* approach (Fujii, Nishikawa, & Yokoi 1998), is 81.5[%]. These results indicate that the EMG pattern classification with the EHW chip is a viable alternative to neural networks.

Conclusion

This paper has described the EHW chip and its application as a myoelectric prosthetic hand controller. Recent improvements to the EHW chip in terms of both increased adaptation speeds and the addition of an *on-line* edit mode have greatly enhanced the performance of the EHW chip controller. Our software simulations show that this is a viable alternative to neural network controllers, and that prosthetic hands with the EHW chip can adapt to users in a short period (about ten minutes).

The EHW chip can adapt its circuit structure autonomously and quickly, and therefore, represents a breakthrough for applications that require compact implementation and high-speed adaptation (such as autonomous mobile vehicles (Keymeulen *et al.* 1998)).

Acknowledgments

This work is supported by MITI Real World Computing Project.We thank Dr. Otsu and Dr. Ohmaki at Electrotechnical Laboratory and Dr. Shimada of RWCP for their supports.

References

Fujii, S.; Nishikawa, D.; and Yokoi, H. 1998. Development of prosthetic hand using adaptable control method for human characteristics. In *IAS-5*, 360–367.

Goldberg, D. E. 1989. *Genetic Algorithms in Search, Optimization, and Machine Learning*. Addison-Wesley.

Higuchi, T.; Niwa, T.; Tanaka, T.; Iba, H.; de Garis, H.; and Furuya, T. 1993. Evolvable hardware with genetic learning: A first step towards building a darwin machine. In *Proceedings of 2nd International Conference on the Simulation of Adaptive Behavior*, 417–424. MIT Press.

Higuchi, T.; Iwata, M.; Kajitani, I.; Iba, H.; Hirao, Y.; Furuya, T.; and Manderick, B. 1995. Evolvable hardware and its applications to pattern recognition and fault-tolerant systems. In Sanchez, E., and Tomassini, M., eds., *Towards Evolvable Hardware*. Springer.

Hudgins, B.; Parker, P.; and Scott, R. N. 1993. A new strategy for multifunction myoelectric control. *IEEE Transaction on Biomedical Engineering* 40(1):82–94.

Ito, K.; Tsuji, T.; Kato, A.; and Ito, M. 1991. Limb-function discrimination using emg signals by neural network and application to prosthetic forearm control. In *Proceedings of the IJCNN91*, 1214–1219.

Kajitani, I.; Hoshino, T.; Iwata, M.; and Higuchi, T. 1996. Variable length chromosome ga for evolvable hardware. In *Proceedings of ICEC96*.

Kajitani, I.; Hoshino, T.; Nishikawa, D.; Yokoi, H.; Nakaya, S.; Yamauchi, T.; Inuo, T.; Kajiwara, N.; Keymeulen, D.; Iwata, M.; and Higuchi, T. 1998. A gate-level ehw chip; implementing ga operations and reconfigurable hard ware on a single lsi. In *Evolvable Systems: From Biology to Hardware, Lecture Notes in Computer Science 1478, Springer Verlag*, 1–12.

Kelly, M. F.; Parker, P. A.; and Scott, R. N. 1990. The application of neural networks to myoelectric signal analysis: Preliminary study. *IEEE Transaction on Biomedical Engineering* 37(3):221–230.

Keymeulen, D.; Konaka, K.; Iwata, M.; Kuniyoshi, Y.; ; and Higuchi, T. 1998. Robot learning using gate-level evolvable hardware. In *Sixth European Workshop on Learning Robots (EWLR-6)*.

Thierens, D., and Goldberg, D. 1994. Elitist recombination: an integrated selection recombination ga. In *Proceedings of First IEEE conference on Evolutionary Computation*, 508–512.

Uchida, M.; H, I.; and Ninomija, S. P. 1993. Control of a robot arm by myoelectric potential. In *Journal of Robotics and Mechatronics vol.5 no.3*, 259–265.

Yao, X., and Higuchi, T. 1998. Promises and challenges of evolvable hardware. *IEEE Transaction on Systems, Man, and Cybernetics, Part C* 28(4).

Initializing RBF-Networks with Small Subsets of Training Examples

Miroslav Kubat and Martin Cooperson, Jr.
Center for Advanced Computer Studies
University of Southwestern Louisiana, Lafayette, LA 70504-4330
{mkubat,mxc6421}@cacs.usl.edu

Abstract

An important research issue in RBF networks is how to determine the gaussian centers of the radial-basis functions. We investigate a technique that identifies these centers with carefully selected training examples, with the objective to minimize the network's size. The essence is to select three very small subsets rather than one larger subset whose size would exceed the size of the three small subsets unified. The subsets complement each other in the sense that when used by a nearest-neighbor classifier, each of them incurs errors in a different part of the instance space. The paper describes the example-selection algorithm and shows, experimentally, its merits in the design of RBF networks.

Introduction

Radial-basis-function (RBF) networks, such as the one depicted in Figure 1, are used to approximate functions $f : R^m \to R^p$ by appropriate adjustments of the parameters in the formula $f_j(\mathbf{x}) = \Sigma_{ij} w_i \varphi_i(\mathbf{x})$, where $\mathbf{x} = (x_1, \ldots, x_n)$ is an input vector and each $\varphi_i(\mathbf{x}) = \exp{-\frac{\|\boldsymbol{x} - \boldsymbol{\mu_i}\|^2}{2\sigma_i^2}}$ is an RBF function. The parameters to be determined by learning are the gaussian centers $\boldsymbol{\mu_i}$, the variances σ_i^2, and the weights w_i. Since the weights are easy to determine (e.g. by linear regression) and the variances do not pose any major challenge, the main difficulty is presented by the centers $\boldsymbol{\mu_i}$. Existing methods associate these vectors with the gravity centers of data clusters (Moody and Darken, 1989; Musavi et al., 1992), with hyperrectangles defined on the instance space by decision-tree induction (Kubat, 1998), or with vectors determined by AI search techniques (Chen, Cowan, and Grant, 1991; Cheng and Lin, 1994). A method that adds one neuron at a time with subsequent tuning of the centers was developed by Fritzke (1993, 1994). Techniques to adjust the centers by learning have been studied also by Wettschereck and Dietterich (1992).

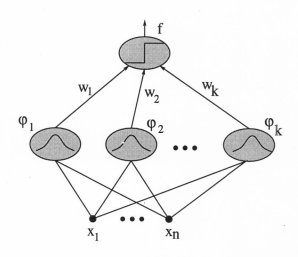

Figure 1: A Radial Basis Function Network

In this paper we focus on *2-class pattern-recognition* in which the network's output is reduced to a boolean variable, $f : R^n \to [-1, 1]$, and we explore the approach that associates each $\boldsymbol{\mu_i}$ with one training example (Poggio and Girosi, 1990). Since turning *all* training examples into gaussian centers would create an unnecessarily large network, Lowe (1989) and Lee (1991) recommend selecting only a random subset. This is still unsatisfactory in applications where many examples are noisy, redundant, or non-representative. We surmise that choosing only those examples that have particular merit will make it possible to model the given pattern with a *smaller* network.

The search for representative examples has received attention among researchers that study *edited nearest-neighbor* classifiers, notably Hart (1968), Gates (1972), Wilson (1972), Ritter et al. (1975), Tomek (1976), and, more recently, Cortez and Vapnik (1995), and Wilson and Martinez (1997). Their algorithms can remove many noisy and redundant examples at the price of high computational costs—typically at least $O(mn^2)$, where m is the number of attributes and n is the number of examples. Moreover, these authors primarily concentrate on how to find "consistent" subsets that, when used by a nearest-neighbor rule, give the same classifications as the original set. In the search for gaussian centers for RBF networks, consistency is not requried because the weights and non-linearities can make up for imperfections of the selected examples.

We suggest a novel technique that, at costs $O(mn)$, sorts out just a few representative training examples. The idea is that, rather than a single subset with N examples, we create three small subsets, S_1, S_2, and S_3, such that $|S_1 \cup S_2 \cup S_3| < N$. These subsets complement each other in the sense that, when employed by a 1-nearest-neighbor classifier, each of them tends to err in a different part of the instance space so that occasional mistakes of one classifier can be outvoted by the others.

When S_i's satisfying the complementarity condition have been found, their examples are pooled, $S = S_1 \cup S_2 \cup S_3$, and the elements of S are used as the gaussian centers μ_i's. We hypothesize that the complementary behavior of S_i's ensures that the resulting RBF network will have favorable classification accuracy despite its small size. Whether this expectation is realistic will be examined by a series of simple experiments with synthetic as well as benchmark data. Prior to that, however, the next section explains the details of the example-selection algorithm.

Description of the Algorithm

The gaussian centers μ_i are identified with carefully selected training examples in the subsets S_1, S_2, and S_3. Each S_i, when used by a 1-nearest-neighbor algorithm, defines a subclassifier C_i. The subsets S_i's are to be selected in a manner that ensures that each C_i will be prone to err on different examples. Here, our inspiration comes from the recent work on combining expert decisions (Vovk 1990; Breiman 1996) and, indirectly, from the essence of the boosting algorithm (Schapire, 1990).

Each S_i contains only very few training examples (say 2 or 3), and care is taken that both classes (positive and negative) are represented in each S_i. Applying C_i's to example $\mathbf{x}$ results in three class labels, and the final decision is achieved by *voting* of the triplet of C_i's. This will correctly classify any example that has been correctly classified by C_1 *and* C_2. Conversely, any example that has been misclassified by both C_1 and C_2 will be misclassified by the voting triplet regardless of the behavior of C_3. Therefore, C_3 should maximize its performance on those examples where C_1 and C_2 disagree. Let the error rates of C_1, C_2, and C_3 be denoted ε_1, ε_2, and ε_3, and let ε_k denote the percentage of examples misclassified by both C_1 and C_2. (Remember that the error rates of C_1 and C_2 will be measured on the entire training set, but ε_3 will be measured on those examples where C_1 and C_2 disagree.)

Figure 2 clarifies the notation and illustrates the fact that the error rate (P_E) of voting consists of ε_k, increased by the percentage of those examples on which C_3 is wrong while C_1 and C_2 disagree ($\varepsilon_1 + \varepsilon_2 - 2\varepsilon_k$):

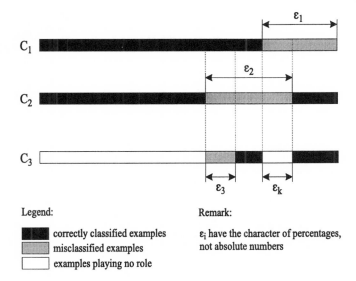

Figure 2: The behavior of the three classifiers

$$P_E = \varepsilon_k + \varepsilon_3(\varepsilon_1 + \varepsilon_2 - 2\varepsilon_k) \qquad (1)$$

In the event of $\varepsilon_1 = \varepsilon_2 = \varepsilon_3 = \varepsilon$, Equation 1 degenerates into $P_E = \varepsilon_k + \varepsilon(\varepsilon + \varepsilon - 2\varepsilon_k) = \varepsilon_k(1 - 2\varepsilon) + 2\varepsilon^2$. Then, $P_E \leq \varepsilon$ for any $\varepsilon_k < \varepsilon$, and the voting is guaranteed to outperform any C_i. The expression turns into $P_E = 2\varepsilon^2$ for $\varepsilon_k = 0$, and it turns into $P_E = \varepsilon$ for $\varepsilon_k = \varepsilon$. The best accuracy for $\varepsilon_1 = \varepsilon_2 = \varepsilon_3 = \varepsilon$ is therefore achieved when C_1 and C_2 never misclassify the same example ($\varepsilon_k = 0$). Conversely, P_E reaches its maximum when $\varepsilon_k = \varepsilon$.

In realistic applications, $\varepsilon_k = 0$ is hard to achieve if $\varepsilon_1 = \varepsilon_2$. In the search for the most appropriate C_2, the condition $\varepsilon_k = 0$ can often be satisfied only at the price of significantly increased ε_2, which means that the trade-off between ε_2 and ε_k has to be considered. Suppose the learner has chosen some C_1, and then succeeded in finding C_2 such that ε_k is low, while ε_2 is high. What if another classifier, C_2', can be found such that $\varepsilon_2' < \varepsilon_2$, and $\varepsilon_k' > \varepsilon_k$? How to decide whether the improvement in ε_2 outweighs the loss in ε_k? A guideline is offered by the following lemma:

Lemma 1. *Given fixed ε_1 and ε_3, assume two candidates for the second classifier, C_2 and C_2', such that $\varepsilon_2' = \varepsilon_2 + \Delta\varepsilon_2$ and $\varepsilon_k' = \varepsilon_k + \Delta\varepsilon_k$. Define $\alpha = \frac{1-2\varepsilon_3}{\varepsilon_3}$. For the error rates, P_E and P_E', of C_2 and C_2', the following equivalence holds:*

$$P_E' < P_E \iff \Delta\varepsilon_2 < -\alpha\Delta\varepsilon_k$$

Proof. Equation 1 establishes for the overall error rate:

Table 1: The algorithm for the selection of example subsets, S_1, S_2 and S_3, that complement each other when used by a nearest-neighbor classifier.

---

1. Make K_1 choices of S_1, and then select the one that minimizes ε_1.
2. Select randomly S_2 and S_3 and establish the initial value of α.
3. Make K_2 choices of an alternative for S_2. Whenever $\Delta\varepsilon_2 < -\alpha\Delta\varepsilon_k$ is satisfied, replace S_2 with this new candidate.
4. Make K_3 choices of S_3, and select the one that minimizes ε_3. Unless a stopping criterion is satisfied, update $\alpha = (1 - 2\varepsilon_3)/\varepsilon_3$, and return to step 3.

$$
\begin{aligned}
P'_E &= \varepsilon'_k + \varepsilon_3(\varepsilon_1 + \varepsilon'_2 - 2\varepsilon'_k) \\
&= \varepsilon_k + \Delta\varepsilon_k + \varepsilon_3(\varepsilon_1 + \varepsilon_2 + \Delta\varepsilon_2 - 2\varepsilon_k - 2\Delta\varepsilon_k) \\
&= P_E + \Delta\varepsilon_k + \varepsilon_3(\Delta\varepsilon_2 - 2\varepsilon_k)
\end{aligned}
$$

From here, $P'_E < P_E$ iff $\Delta\varepsilon_k + \varepsilon_3(\Delta\varepsilon_2 - 2\Delta\varepsilon_k) < 0$. This inequality is satisfied whenever $\varepsilon_2 < -\Delta\varepsilon_k \frac{1-2\varepsilon_3}{\varepsilon_3} = -\alpha\Delta\varepsilon_k$.

Q.E.D.

For illustration, suppose that some initial choice for C_2 implies $\varepsilon_k = 0.05$ and $\varepsilon_2 = 0.35$, and let $\alpha = 3$. This gives $P_E = \alpha\varepsilon_k + \varepsilon_2 = 0.15 + 0.35 = 0.50$. Then, another classifier, C'_2, is found, entailing error rates $\varepsilon'_2 = 0.18$ and $\varepsilon'_k = 0.10$. According to the previous lemma, this new classifier is better ($P'_E < P_E$) because $\Delta\varepsilon_2 = -0.17$, which is less than $-\alpha\Delta\varepsilon_k = -3 \cdot 0.05 = -0.15$. Indeed, it is easy to verify that $P'_E = \alpha\varepsilon'_k + \varepsilon'_2 = 3 \cdot 0.10 + 0.18 = 0.48 < P_E$.

Suppose that C_1 and C_2 have been chosen. Then, C_3 is selected and the values of ε_3 and α determined. The learner will search for some C'_2 that satisfies the condition $\Delta\varepsilon_2 < -\alpha\Delta\varepsilon_k$. Lemma 1 guarantees that the replacement of C_2 by C'_2 reduces P_E. The search is repeated, with the error rate P_E gradually decreasing, until no C'_2 satisfying the condition of Lemma 1 can be found. The learner will then find a C_3 that minimizes ε_3. As a result, ε_3 might depart from its initial value, which chanes α. The program will return to the previous step to further adjust C_2, and the procedure is repeated several times, terminating when no reasonable improvement of P_E is observed.

The algorithm that employs this analysis for the choice of complementary instance-based classifiers is summarized in Table 1. The precise values of the K_i values were: $K_1 = 10, K_2 = 5$, and $K_3 = 10$. This means that in the first step, 10 different (random) subsets S_1 are considered, and the one with lowest ϵ_1 value

is chosen. The program generates the initial S_2 and S_3 subsets (so as to calculate the initial value of α), and then cycles through steps 3 and 4 until some termination criterion is reached. In our experiments, we simply stopped the program after 5 visits at steps 3 and 4. In each of these visits, $K_2 = 5$ random candidate S_2 subsets were generated. Whenever the condition $\Delta\varepsilon_2 < -\alpha\Delta\varepsilon_k$, the current S_2 is replaced with the new candidate. The program then generates $K_3 = 10$ random candidates for S_3 and chooses the one that has the lowest ϵ_3.

The number of subsets considered by this algorithm is $K_1 + 5(K_2 + K_3) = 10 + 5(5 + 10) = 85$ which, together with the initial choices of S_2 and S_3, gives 87. Evaluation of each subset on the training set is linear in the number of examples. More precisely, if each S_i contains three examples, then the overall computational costs are upper bounded by $87 \times 3 \times n$, where n is the number of training examples. The real costs are somewhat lower because S_3 is evaluated only on those examples where the first two subclassifiers disagree.

Experiments

Our objective is to select a compact subset of the training examples that will be identified with the gaussian centers, $\boldsymbol{\mu}_i$, of a radial-basis function network. In our experiments, the weight vector $\mathbf{w}$ was obtained using the statistical linear-regression technique of pseudoinverse matrices (see, e.g., Duda and Hart 1973). More specifically, if $\mathbf{X}$ is a matrix whose each row contains the outputs of the RBF units, and $\mathbf{b}$ is the classification vector whose elements are 1 for positive examples and -1 for negative examples, then $\mathbf{w} = \mathbf{X^P b}$ where $\mathbf{X^P}$ is a pseudoinverse matrix of $\mathbf{X}$. The variance, σ_i^2, of the i-th RBF is set to $\sigma_i^2 = \sqrt{d}$ where d is the Euclidean distance of the center that is closest to $\boldsymbol{\mu}_i$.

Our question is whether our example-selection method can really lead to smaller RBF networks with still high classification accuracy. In the search for an answer, we experimented with simple synthetic data with known characteristics, and then proceeded to experiments with more realistic benchmark domains.

In the sequel, an RBF network that has been created from randomly selected examples will be referred to by the acronym RANDEX. A RBF network that has been created from examples selected by the algorithm described in the previous section will be referred to by the acronym SELEX.

Synthetic Data

To develop initial insight into the behavior of SELEX, we experimented with synthetic data in which the decision surface between positive and negative examples is known. We worked with three noise-free artificial domains, created as follows:

1. *Hyperbola*. Examples are generated as pairs, (x, y), of uniformly distributed numbers. All points satis-

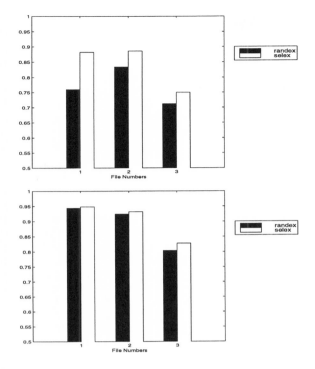

Figure 3: Classification accuracies in synthetic domains. Left to right: hyperbola, hypercubes, hyperspheres. Top: 6 gaussian centers. Bottom: 15 centers.

fying $3x^2 - 3y^2 < 1$ are positive; all other points are negative.

2. *Hypercubes.* Examples are 5-tuples of uniformly distributed numbers. Three 5-dimensional hypercubes are created. All points inside any hypercube are positive; all other points are negative.

3. *Hyperspheres.* Examples are 5-tuples of uniformly distributed numbers. Three 5-dimensional hyperspheres are created. All points inside any hypersphere are positive, all other points are negative.

In all these three domains, care is taken that the positive and negative examples are equally represented in the data.

One of the advantages of experiments with synthetic data is that arbitrarily large sets of examples can be generated to warrant statistical significance of the results. In the experiments reported below, we always used 500 training examples and 500 testing examples. Given the relative simplicity of the decision surfaces (and the fact that the examples are noise-free), these numbers appear to be sufficient for good estimates of classification performance.

We carried out two sets of experiments with SELEX, differing in the sizes of the subsets S_i. In the first series, we required that $|S_i| = 2$, which led to RBF networks with $3 \times 2 = 6$ gaussian centers. In the second series, we

required that $|S_i| = 5$ which led to RBF networks with $3 \times 5 = 15$ gaussian centers. By way of reference, we organized the experiments with RANDEX as follows: for each training set, we conducted 5 separate runs, each with a different set of randomly selected examples (6 or 15 examples), and averaged the results.

The results are graphically displayed in Figure 3. The bars show the classification accuracies observed on testing examples (classification acccuracy being defined as the percentage of correctly classified examples among all examples).

Expectedly, an increased number of gaussian centers (from $3 \times 2 = 6$ to $3 \times 5 = 15$ vectors) means higher classification accuracy in RANDEX as well as in SELEX. Also expectedly, SELEX outperformed RANDEX in all experimental domains. What is more important, however, is the fact that the margin is more clearly pronounced in the case of 6 centers than in the case of 15 centers (reaching 13% in the domain *hyperbola*). This observation corroborates the intuitive expectation that the example-selecting algorithm described in the previous section improves classification accuracy especially in very small RBF networks. When the number of centers is high, even random selection will be sufficiently representative, and the advantage of SELEX dissipates.

Note that the domain *hyperspheres* was especially difficult for the RBF network. Many more gaussian centers would be necessary if the network were to achieve satisfactory performance. For this reason, SELEX in this domain clearly outperformed RANDEX, even in the case of 15 centers.

Benchmark Data

To make sure that our conjectures extend also to real-world domains, we experimented with the benchmark data files from the Machine Learning Database Repository of the University of California, Irvine (Blake, Keogh, and Merz, 1998). The particular choice of testbeds was constrained by our focus on two-class problems and by the requirement that the examples be described mainly by numeric attributes. Occasional boolean attributes were treated as numeric attributes, acquiring value 1 for *true* and 0 for *false*. The upper part of Figure 4 summarizes the experimental data files by providing information about the size of each file, the number of attributes, and the percentage of examples that are labeled by the majority class (the right-most column).

The first seven datasets have two classes. The last three domains (*balance, glass,* and *wine*) originally involved more than two classes, but we turned them into two-class problems. Specifically, the classes in the *balance* domain say whether the balance is tilted left, right, or whether there is no tilt at all. We combined `tilt-right` and `tilt-left` into one class. We aggregated the 7 classes in the *glass* domain into into `windows` (the first four classes) versus `non-windows`. In the *wine* domain, the second class and the third class were combined into one.

	Dataset	#ex.	# att.	majority
1	Hepatitis	80	19	83.75
2	B. Cancer WI 1	683	9	65.01
3	B. Cancer WI 2	569	30	62.74
4	Pima	768	8	65.10
5	Ion	351	34	64.10
6	Balance	625	4	92.16
7	Echocardiogram	61	12	72.13
8	Glass	214	9	76.17
9	Liver	345	6	57.97
10	Wine	178	12	68.85

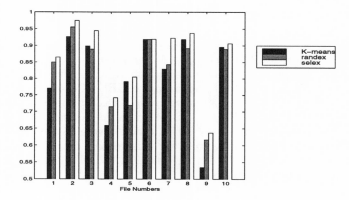

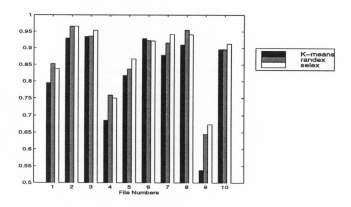

Figure 4: Classification accuracies observed in benchmark domains. Upper graph: 6 gaussian centers. Lower graph: 15 gaussian centers. For comparison, the results of initialization by k-means ($k = 6$ and $k = 15$) are shown.

These data files are not large enough to warrant statistically safe estimates of classification accuracies. Since the popular t-tests are unreliable in random subsampling of data files of this size, and since N-fold cross-validation on some of the smaller domains would entail very high standard errors, we opted for a compromise: we used 10-fold cross-validation, repeated 5 times, each time for a different partitioning of the data, and then averaged the accuracies measured in different runs. In each experiment, 90% of the examples were used for training, and the remaining 10% for testing. The variances then became reasonably small. In view of the fact that we are interested only in general tendencies, the chosen experimental methodology is sufficiently sound.

The SELEX and RANDEX experiments were organized analogically as in the case of synthetic data. This means that in SELEX, the sizes of the individual subsets were $|S_i| = 2$ or $|S_i| = 5$, meaning that the resulting RBF network would contain 6 and 15 units, respectively. The RANDEX results are averages from 5 random runs, each time with 6 (or 15) randomly selected examples used for μ_i.

For reference, the graphs in Figure 4 show also the performance of RBF networks that have been initialized by clustering techniques (each μ_i is identified with the center of gravity of a cluster found by the k-means algorithm)[1] where, again, $k = 6$ or $k = 15$. The reader can see that in most domains the clustering-based initialization is a clear loser among the three techniques. From the results, one can therefore conclude that to identify μ_i's with selected training examples is a more promising approach.

Further on, our example-selecting mechanism gives in nearly all domains better results than random selection of examples (the only exception being *balance*). Again, the margin is reduced when the number of centers increases to 15.

Conclusions

One of the main issues in RBF networks is how to define the gaussian centers of the individual radial-basis functions. One of the possibilities is to identify these centers with representative training examples. A natural requirement is that the ensuing network should be as small as possible to prevent overfitting and to minimize classification costs.

Our solution is based on a simple heuristic that says that rather than a single subset containing N examples, one should search for three smaller subsets, S_1, S_2, and S_3, such that $|S_1 \cup S_2 \cup S_3| < N$. The sets should complement each other in the sense that, when employed by a 1-nearest-neighbor classifier, each would lead to errors in a different part of the instance space.

This approach turned out to outperform random selection of examples. Another observation is that (at

[1]Clustering techniques did not make much sense in the synthetic data because the examples were uniformly distributed.

least in the benchmark domains we used) initialization by selected training examples gave better results than the more expensive clustering technique suggested by Moody and Darken, (1989) and Musavi et al. (1992).

On the other hand, the achieved performance does not seem to reach the classification accuracies reported by Kubat (1998) for his decision-tree based initialization. However, a great advantage of SELEX is the compactness of the resulting network. In the decision-tree based approach, a typical network contained dozens of neurons.

The encouraging results suggest that example-selecting techniques (used in RBF initialization) deserve further attention. We recommend that instead of just triplets of subsets, one should study the behavior of the more general K-tuples ($K > 3$). This will lead to more general version of Equation 1 and of Lemma 1.

Although not included in our results, preliminary experiments showed that if the size of the S_i's was two, the classifier accuracy sometimes suffered. Increasing the size from three to five did not significantly improve the results with other datasets. We therefore left the size of the S_i's at three because this seemed optimal for the majority of datasets involved. Additionally, similar preliminary experiments suggested the number of randomly generated candidates used in choosing the S_1, S_2 and S_3 subsets were optimal for the given benchmark datasets.

Apart from that, we observed that different domains called for different sizes of S_i's. This means that one should look for heuristics that would suggest the ideal size for the given problem. Flexibility can be further enhanced by allowing that each S_i has a different size.

References

Blake, C., Keogh, E., and Merz, C.J. (1998). UCI Repository of machine learning databases [www.ics.uci.edu/ mlearn/MLRepository.html]. Irvine, CA: University of California, Department of Information and Computer Science.

Breiman, L. (1996). Bagging Predictors. *Machine Learning*, 24, pp. 123–140.

Broomhead, D.S. and Lowe D.(1988). Multivariable Functional Interpolation and Adaptive Networks. *Complex Systems*, 2, 321–355.

Chen, S., Cowan, C.F.N., and Grant, P.M. (1991). Orthogonal Least Squares Learning Algorithm for Radial Basis Function Networks. *IEEE Transactions on Neural Networks*, 2, 302–309.

Cheng, Y.-H. and Lin, C.-S. (1994). A Learning Algorithm for Radial Basis Function Networks: with the Capability of Adding and Pruning Neurons. *Proceedings of the IEEE*, 797–801.

Cortes, C. and Vapnik, V. (1995). Support Vector Networks. *Machine Learning*, 20, 273–279.

Duda R.O. and Hart, P.E. (1973). *Pattern Classification and Scene Analysis*. John Wiley & Sons, New York.

Fritzke, B. (1993). Supervised Learning with Growing Cell Structures. In *Advances in Neural Information Processing Systems 6*, J. Cowan, G. Tesauro, and J. Alspector (eds.), San Mateo, CA: Morgan Kaufmann, pp.255–262

Fritzke, B. (1994). Fast Learning with Incremental RBF Networks. *Neural Processing Letters*, 1 ,2–5

Gates, G.W. (1972). The Reduced Nearest-Neighbor Rule. *IEEE Transactions on Information Theory*, IT-18, pp.431–433.

Hart, P.E. (1968). The Condensed Nearest-Neighbor Rule. *IEEE Transactions on Information Theory*, IT-14, pp. 515–516.

Kubat, M. (1998). Decision Trees Can Initialize Radial-Basis Function Networks. *IEEE Transactions on Neural Networks*, 9, pp. 813–821.

Moody, J.E. (1989). Fast Learning in Multi-Resolution Hierarchies. *Advances in Neural Information Processing Systems*, vol. 1 (pp. 29–39), Morgan Kaufmann, San Francisco, CA.

Musavi, M.T., W. Ahmed, K.H. Chan, K.B. Faris, and D.M. Hummels (1992). On the Training of Radial Basis Function Classifiers. *Neural Networks*, 5, 595–603.

Ritter, G.L., Woodruff, H.B., Lowdry, S.R., and Isenhour, T.L. (1975). An Algorithm for a Selective Nearest-Neighbor Decision Rule. *IEEE Transactions on Information Theory*, IT-21, pp. 665–669.

Schapire, R.E. (1990). The Strength of Weak Learnability. *Machine Learning*, 5,197–227.

Tomek I. (1976). Two Modifications of CNN. *IEEE Transactions on Systems, Man and Communications*, SMC-6, 769–772.

Vovk V. G. (1990). Aggregating Strategies. In *Proceedings of the Third Annual Workshop on Computational Learning Theory*, pp. 371-383.

Wettschereck D. and Dietterich T.G. (1992). Improving the Performance of Radial Basis Function Networks by Learning Center Locations. *Advances in Neural Information Processing Systems 4*, (J.E. Moody, S.J. Hanson, and R.P. Lippmann, eds.), 1133–1140. San Mateo, CA: Morgan Kaufmann

Wilson, D.L. (1972). Asymptotic Properties of Neraest Neighbor Rules Using Edited Data. *IEEE Transactions on Systems, Man, and Cybernetics*, 2, pp.408–421.

Wilson, D.R. and Martinez, T.R. (1997). Instance Pruning Techniques. *Proceedings of the 14th International Conference on Machine Learning*. Morgan Kaufmann.

A Neural Network Model of Dynamically Fluctuating Perception of Necker Cube as well as Dot Patterns

Hiroaki Kudo†, Tsuyoshi Yamamura††, Noboru Ohnishi†, Shin Kobayashi‡, and Noboru Sugie‡

†Graduate School of Engineering, Nagoya University, Nagoya 464-8603, Japan
††Faculty of Information Science and Technology, Aichi Prefectural University, Aichi 480-1198, Japan
‡Faculty of Science and Technology, Meijo University, Nagoya 468-8502, Japan
kudo@nuie.nagoya-u.ac.jp, yamamura@ist.aichi-pu.ac.jp, sugie@meijo-u.ac.jp

Abstract

The mechanism underlying perceptual grouping of visual stimuli is not static, but dynamic. In this paper, the dynamical grouping process is implemented with a neural network model consisting of an array of (hyper)columns suggested by Hubel & Wiesel, where intracolumnar inhibition and intercolumnar facilitation are incorporated. The model was applied successfully to figures consisting of a set of dots yielding either of two ways of groupings from time to time due to neural fluctuations and fatigue. Then the model was extended to introduce dependency on fixation points as well as neural fluctuations and fatigue. Then, it was applied to the Necker Cube. The model output from time to time either of two ways of 3D interpretations depending on the fixation points.

Introduction

Perceptual grouping plays an essential role in segmenting objects in the scene and recognizing each of them. Gestalt psychologists have proposed that there are several factors underlying the grouping: they are factor of proximity, factor of similarity, factor of smooth continuation, and so on. Recently, computer implementations of the grouping processes have been reported (Stevens 1978; Hiratsuka, Ohnishi, and Sugie 1992). However, the mechanism underlying perceptual grouping of visual stimuli is not static; but dynamic as in Marroquin pattern (**Fig.1**) (Marr 1982). The dynamical aspect of grouping seems to reflect the flexible nature of human visual information processing to deal with ambiguous patterns. However, it has not been studied seriously. In this paper, the dynamical grouping process is implemented with a neural network model consisting of a 2D array of hypercolumns suggested by Hubel & Wiesel (1977), where intracolumnar inhibition and intercolumnar facilitation are incorporated. The model was applied successfully to figures which consist of a set of dots yielding either of two ways

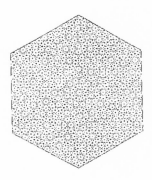

Figure 1: Marroquin pattern.

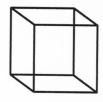

Figure 2: Necker Cube.

of groupings from time to time due to neural fluctuations and fatigue. Moreover, the model was able to interpret line drawings, a grouping at a higher level; it was applied to the Necker cube (**Fig.2**). It also exhibited dependence on fixation points about the Necker cube. The model output either of two 3D interpretations reflecting fixation point dependence as reported by Kawabata *et al.* (1978).

Neural Network Model

This model is based on the neural network model consisting of hypercolumnar structure. It has been used to explain the early visual process such as retinal rivalry (Sugie 1982). We extend it to deal with highly ambiguous figures of more than two interpretations.

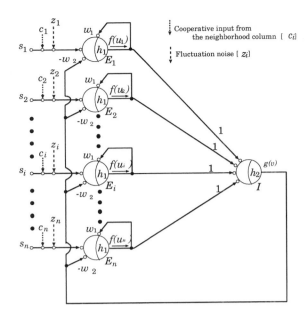

Figure 3: Generalized flip-flop.

Basic Structure – hypercolumn –

In the human visual system, visual stimuli are received first by the retina. Then, outputs of retinal ganglion cells are sent to the V1 of the cerebral visual cortex via the lateral geniculate body. The V1 consists of a 2D array of hypercolumns, each of which corresponds to a specific local visual area preserving the topological relationship in the retina.

This columnar structure is modeled with network structure which has intracolumnar inhibitory as well as intercolumnar facilitator connection. **Fig.3** shows the network structure of one column. The units of $E_1, E_2, \cdots, E_i, \cdots, E_n$ correspond to neurons, each of which is selective to specific stimulus orientation of its own. Each neural output $f(u_i)$ is weighted (w_1) and feedback to itself, directly. It is also fed to an inhibitory neuron I with a unit weight, whereas the output of neuron I is fed to each of E_i's with weight w_2. These two inputs ensure that at the steady state only one of E_i's becomes activated or the winner depending on the inputs s_i's, c_i's, and z_i's (Amari 1978). Thus, we call the network shown in Fig.3 as generalized flip-flop. Now three kinds of inputs to each of E_i's are explained.

1. visual stimulus via the retina and the lateral geniculate body $\cdots$ [s_i]

2. an inhibitory input from I summing up all the outputs of E_i's $\cdots$ [$g(v)$]

3. a facilitator input from the orientation sensitive unit in the neighboring hypercolumn (intercolumnar facilitation) $\cdots$ [c_i]

This element of columnar structure (or, network) (Fig.3) is corresponding to the structure which locates at one point on visual cortex. As shown in **Fig.4**, a

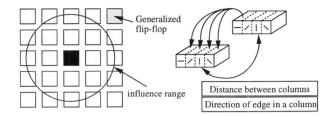

Figure 4: Intercolumnar facilitation network.

2D array of generalized flip-flops are arranged so that each of which corresponds to its own specific local visual field preserving the topological relation. Further, neighboring generalized flip-flops are facilitatively interconnected via c_i as described in 3 above. c_i is dependent on both the mutual distance and mutual difference in orientations between each pair of generalized flip-flops. In Fig.3, h_1 and h_2 are the thresholds of the corresponding units. u_i's and v are the inner potentials of the corresponding units. Here the inner potential means the total sum of weighted inputs and threshold. Thus u_i and v satisfy the following differential equations (1) and (2), respectively. The time constant for u_i is 1, and that for v is τ.

$$\dot{u}_i = -u_i + w_1 f(u_i) - w_2 g(v) - h_1 + s_i \quad (1)$$

$$\tau \dot{v} = -v + \sum_{i=1}^{n} f(u_i) - h_2 \quad (2)$$

As already mentioned, $f(u_i)$ and $g(v)$ are the excitatory and inhibitory outputs of E_i and I, respectively. Each E_i has its own excitatory feedback collateral with weight w_1, which plays the role of keeping its activity high once it is excited. The inhibitory unit I serves for keeping E_i's from saturation as well as for deciding the winner among E_i's. We define $f(u_i)$ and $g(v)$ as equations (3) and (4), respectively.

$$f(u) = \begin{cases} 1 & (u > 0) \\ 0 & (u \leq 0) \end{cases} \quad (3)$$

$$g(v) = \begin{cases} v & (v > 0) \\ 0 & (v \leq 0) \end{cases} \quad (4)$$

Further, we assume that $0 \leq s_i \leq s_{max}$.

As analyzed by Amari (1978), the generalized flip-flops behaves as follows:

1. When all the inputs s_i's do not attain the level of s_{min}, none of E_i's are excited.

2. When there are plural s_i's exceeding s_{min}, E_i corresponding to the maximal s_i becomes excited or the winner, while the others are suppressed and are not excited at the steady state.

3. Once one E_i becomes the winner, it remains excited even after the input s_i is set to 0. Only by resetting the whole system E_i is set to off.

In the model shown in Fig.4, certain orientation selective units corresponding to the positions where visual stimuli do exist will be excited. Moreover due to intercolumnar facilitation, some other units may be excited as well even if there is not any corresponding visual stimuli. This facilitative effect may reflect the factor of smooth continuation complementing gaps along a smooth line. The winner-take-all nature of the model may correspond to only one interpretation of a stimulus figure at one time.

This kind of intercolumnar and intracolumnar interaction scheme has been proposed for the elucidation of self-organization mechanism of binocular stereopsis (Sawada and Sugie 1982). The generalized flip-flop is based on the system of winner-take-all. So, it is an appropriate model of binocular rivalry (Sugie 1982).

Extension to Deal with Dynamical Grouping

In the situation of dynamical grouping, humans do not always have a single stable percept, but have one of plural percepts competing one another from time to time. For example, when we look at **Fig.5**(a), the percepts alternate between (b) and (c). To deal with such phenomena, we introduce the following three factors into the model.

fluctuation of neural activities (z_i) As each neuron is under the influence of noises contained in the external stimulus as well as intrinsic fluctuations in cellular activities, the neural activities fluctuate from time to time. Therefore, only one neuron becomes the winner at the steady state, even if each input s_i to E_i is one and the same. z_i represents such noises.

neural fatigue Once a unit E_i continues to fire, the threshold h_1 of which becomes higher resulting in difficulty in firing on. This is the neural fatigue, which may cause the change in the winner unit. The detail of fatigue process will be described later.

fixation point When we look at stimulus figures, we usually change the fixation point from time to time, which causes the change in the retinal image.

Considering these factors, the processing in the model proceeds as shown in **Fig.6**.

First a fixation point is decided. Then the retinal image is formed accordingly. Next, at the stage of feature extraction, the position, and allowable orientations formed by grouping neighboring dots in the stim-

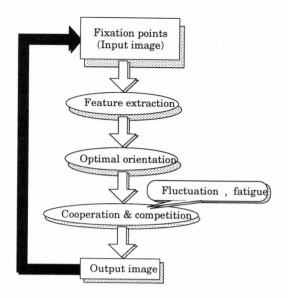

Figure 6: Model of dynamical grouping process.

ulus figure at each local region are extracted. Then at the stage of determining the optimal orientation, the inputs to each E_i is determined, which reflect the factors of perceptual grouping (proximity or mutual distance, similarity in shape or orientation , and smooth continuation).

At the stage of cooperation and competition, the proposed neural network decides the winner among orientation selective E_i's in each hypercolumn. In order to realize the neural fluctuations, we introduce one noise-generating neuron corresponding to each E_i. The output of the noise-generating neuron represents z_i. As for the neural fatigue, it is realized through the change in h_1 as already stated, the detail of which will be described in the next section.

At the stage of output image, the simulated percept at each instant is displayed, where E_i yielding the maximal output among other E_i's at each location at each instant is assumed to correspond to the perceived grouping (connection) between the dot of concern and one of the neighboring dots. Since the percepts may change from time to time except at the equilibrium state, the output images are generated and displayed at each instant.

As for the factor of change in fixation points, we assume the factor as restarting of the whole process. Thus the factor is introduced at the first of all the stages.

Simulation Studies

We implemented and simulated the proposed scheme. For simplicity, we assume the processes from the fixation point through the optimal orientation as a preprocessing prepared beforehand. The results of the preprocessing are given as inputs to the succeeding process of cooperation and competition shown in Figs.3

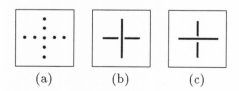

Figure 5: Example of dynamical grouping.

Figure 7: Variations of connection between elements.

and 4. One general flip-flop is assigned to each dot in the stimulus figure. Each of E_i's corresponds to a connection between the dot of concern and one of neighboring dots with the orientation specific to E_i. We assume the following three types of connections for each dot of concern as shown in **Fig.7**, where the filled circle represents the dot of concern and open circles represent neighboring dots.

1. the case with two connected neighbors, where the distances to them are $d1$ and $d2$ and the angle formed by two line segments are θ.

2. the case with one connected neighbor, the distance to which is d.

3. the case without any connection.

We set the initial value s_i for E_i considering perceptual grouping factors. That is, in the first case above, we assign the value is larger for smaller distance ($d1$ and $d2$) and for θ closer to 180 degrees. In the second case, the initial value is larger for smaller d, while in the third case the initial value is set to zero.

For those inputs described above, each generalized flip-flop outputs such a connection corresponding to E_i with the highest activity among others.

As for the neural fatigue, we changed the threshold h_1 of each E_i according to Eqs.(5) and (6) below. The changing profiles of h_1 with respect to time are shown in **Figs.8** and **9**. The former corresponds to the case where the inner potential is positive and the unit is firing, while the latter is applied in the case where the inner potential is negative and the unit not active.

$$h_1 = h_{1\_min} + \frac{1}{1 + \exp \frac{-(t-h_\tau)}{T}} \cdot (h_{1\_max} - h_{1\_min}) \quad (5)$$

where $t, h_\tau, T, h_{1\_min}, h_{1\_max}$ designate the time, the time constant, the increase rate of threshold, the minimum value of the threshold, and the maximum value of the threshold, respectively.

$$h_1 = h_{1\_min} + \exp(-at) \cdot (h_{1\_max} - h_{1\_min}) \quad (6)$$

where a means the time constant.

In **Fig10**, we show two sample visual stimuli for simulation studies. Since these stimuli are simple figures, we experimented without considering the factor of change in fixation points. As a measure of processing time unit, we introduce a prescribed time unit. It is the time to obtain one output image after giving the inputs to generalized flip-flops. We observed output

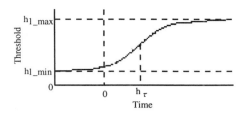

Figure 8: Change in threshold [1] due to fatigue.

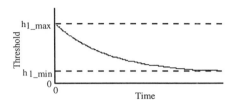

Figure 9: Recovery of threshold [2] from fatigue.

images during 6,000 time units (Fig.10(a)) and 3,000 time units (Fig.10(b)), respectively.

In **Fig.11**, we show the outputs of the neural network for the visual stimulus, Fig.10(a), in the course of the time after the stimulus presentation. We can see that at $t = 500$ a complete vertical line is perceived, while the horizontal line is interrupted in the middle. At $t = 3000$, however, the percept is just in the contrary. The horizontal line is complete, while the vertical line is interrupted in the middle. At $t = 1000, 2000, 3500,$ and 5000, some of the dots are left alone without forming any connection with other dots. Such fluctuating percepts similar to human perception are caused primarily by the neural fluctuations and fatigue.

In **Fig.12**, we show the outputs of the neural network in the course of time after the presentation of the visual stimulus, Fig.10(b). When humans observe the stimulus, humans perceive in the course of the time either fragments of circles of various radii (arcs), or line segments of various orientations and lengths at various positions. The outputs shown in Fig.12 may be considered as simulating and the fluctuating human perception stated above. The simulated percepts in Fig.12 are mostly fragmentary circles or short lines. However, human percepts tend to prefer more complete circles or lines. This difference should be studied further by taking into consideration of more global measure of 'Gestaltian Praegnanz'.

Applying to Ambiguous Figures

When humans observe the figure shown in Fig.2 (Necker cube), human percepts alternate from time to time between either of two 3D interpretations shown in **Fig.13**(a) and (b), where hidden (only partly) lines are removed for convenience. Note that only one of the two interpretations are exclusively perceived at each in-

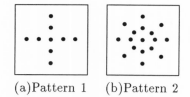

(a)Pattern 1   (b)Pattern 2

Figure 10: Sample stimulus 1,2.

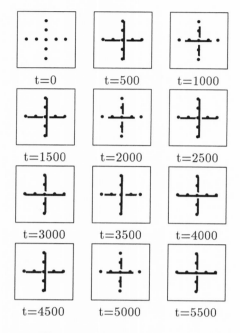

Figure 11: Time course of perception (pattern 1).

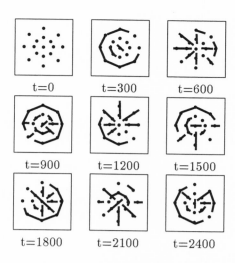

Figure 12: Time course of perception (pattern 2).

stant. We consider this kind of higher visual processes can be realized using the scheme of 2D array of generalized flip-flops shown in Figs.3 and 4. Each vertex of the visual stimulus in Fig.2 corresponds to one generalized flip-flop. Each E_i corresponds to one of the two interpretations at the assigned vertex. Facilitative intercolumnar interactions are introduced between a pair of E_i's with the same interpretation in generalized flip-flops for each pair of adjacent vertices.

According to Kawabata *et al.*, which of the two interpretations are preferred is remarkably dependent on which vertex the subjects look at (Kawabata, Yamagami, and Noaki 1978). It is reported that when the fixation point is around A in **Fig.14**, the subjects tend to perceive the interpretation 1 more often. When the fixation point is around A', however, the subjects tend to perceive the interpretation 2 more often. So we set s_i's dependent on the fixation point as follows, where let s_1 stands for the interpretation 1 and s_2 the interpretation 2. Let Pi denote a fixation point. Then s_1 is set to be proportional to the distance between A and A' divided by that between Pi and A plus α, where α is a positive constant to keep the value from diverging

for Pi very close to A. Similar s_2 is set to be proportional to the distance between A and A' divided by that between Pi and A' plus α. Thus at $P1$, $P2$, $P3$, and $P4$, the ratios between s_1 and s_2 were set to 5:1, 2:1, 1:2, and 1:5, respectively.

The simulation studies were conducted while the fixation points were shifted from $P1$ through $P4$ successively. At each Pi, the duration of fixation was 1,500 time units. As an example of the inner potential change, the result on the vertex A is shown in **Fig.15**. In **Fig.16** are shown some of the snapshot percepts of the model. The duration ratios between the interpretation 1 and 2 are summarized in **Table 1**. It is obvious that the percepts fluctuate from time to time. We can see that at $P1$ the interpretation 1 is overwhelmingly dominant. As the fixation points were shifted towards $P4$, the interpretation 2 becomes dominant gradually. However, even at $P4$, the dominance of interpretation 2 over 1 is not so overwhelming as that of 1 over 2 at $P1$. Thus as a whole the duration ratio of interpretation 1 and 2 during 0 — 6,000 time units is 53.4 : 46.6 preferring the interpretation 1. To see the hysteresis effects due to the shifts in fixation points, we carried out simulation studies for the cases of no shifts in fixation points. Each fixation started from the same initial condition. The result is shown in **Table 2**. The change in interpretations ($P1$ versus $P4$, and $P2$ versus $P3$) is almost symmetrical with respect to two interpretations. Thus the results in Table 1 can be understood as reflecting the hysteresis effects. These behaviors of the model coincides well with the findings by Kawabata *et al.*

Concluding Remarks

Grouping process is dynamic in nature. However, in most cases only one kind of grouping is possible. Therefore the perception is stable and grouping seems static only apparently. In some pathological cases, the

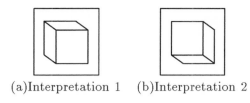

(a)Interpretation 1   (b)Interpretation 2

Figure 13: 3D interpretation of Necker cube.

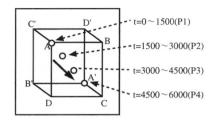

Figure 14: Movement of fixation points.

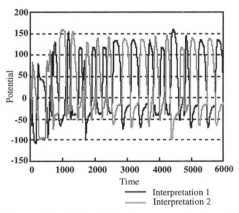

Figure 15: Potential change on vertex A.

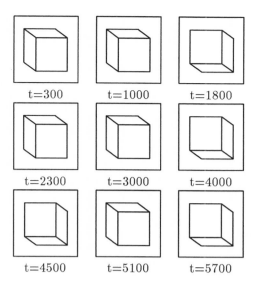

Figure 16: Time course of 3D interpretation.

Table 1: Duration ratio of two 3D interpretations, where movements of fixation points exist.

t [time unit]	Interpretation 1 [%]	Interpretation 2 [%]
0~1500	97.8	2.1
1500~3000	42.3	57.7
3000~4500	51.6	48.4
4500~6000	33.9	66.1
0~6000	53.4	46.6

Table 2: Duration ratio of two 3D interpretations, where there was no movements of fixation points.

fixation point	Duration ratio [%]			
	P1	P2	P3	P4
interpretation 1	98.7	51.7	44.9	5.4
interpretation 2	1.3	48.3	55.1	94.6

dynamical aspect of grouping shows up. The present article may be the first serious attempt to simulate some of the typical phenomena, related to figures which consist of dots and the Necker cube. The Gestalt concept of similarity should be extended to include 3D interpretations as in the Necker cube.

Acknowledgements

The research was supported in part by the Grant-in-aid of the Ministry of Education for "Quantum Information Theoretical Approach to Life Science".

References

Stevens, K. A. 1978. Computation of Locally Parallel Structure. *Biol. Cybernetics* 29:19–28.

Hiratsuka, S., Ohnishi, N. and Sugie, N. 1992. Extracting Global Structures Using Perceptual Grouping.*IEICE Trans. D-II* J76-D-II:74–83. (in Japanese)

Marr, D. 1982. *Vision.* New York.: W.H.Freeman

Hubel, D. H., Wiesel, T. H. 1977, Functional Architecture of Macaque Monkey Visual Cortex, Proc. Roy. Soc. Lond. B. 198. 1–59

Kawabata, N.; Yamagami, K.; and Noaki, M. 1978. Visual Fixation Points and Depth Perception. *Vision Research* 18.:853–854

Sugie, N. 1982. Neural Model of Brightness Perception and Retinal Rivalry in Binocular Vision. *Biol. Cybernetics* 43.:13–21

Amari, S. 1978. *Mathematical Principles of Neural Networks.* Tokyo. :Sangyo Tosho (in Japanese)

Sawada, R. and Sugie, N. (Amari, S., and Arbib, M. A. eds.) 1982. Self-organization of Neural Nets with Competitive and Cooperative Interaction. *Lecture Notes in Biomathematics 45, Competition and Cooperation in Neural Nets.* :238–247

What's in a Fuzzy Set?

Marco Piastra

Dipartimento di Informatica e Sistemistica
Università degli Studi di Pavia
Via Ferrata, 1, I-27100 Pavia, Italy
pmarco@vision.unipv.it

Abstract

A modified version of the first-order logic of probability presented in (Halpern 1990) – with probability on possible worlds – makes it possible to formulate an alternative characterisation of fuzzy sets. In this approach, fuzzy sets are no longer seen as primitive entities with an intuitive justification, but rather as structured entities emerging in a suitable logical framework. Some fuzzy techniques of practical relevance are shown to be encodable in this way. In addition, the resulting approach leads to a clearer epistemological analysis in that it clarifies the purposive nature of the kind of uncertainty that can be modelled by fuzziness.

1. Introduction

A fairly common characterisation of fuzzy sets in the literature is as a primitive notion – usually but not necessarily related with uncertainty – which is given intuitive justification in terms of similarity with classical sets. Typically, a textbook on the topic will start by describing the real-valued generalisation of classical characteristic functions and will then discuss a few examples of fuzzy set modelling applied to everyday knowledge immediately after.

From an epistemological standpoint, this attitude would appear to assume an incremental modelling strategy for the notion itself. One disadvantage, deriving from the rather weak premises, is that further formal and informal elements have to be introduced at all subsequent stages of theoretical development. For instance, a viable mathematical definition for the fundamental set-theoretic operators – i.e. conjunction, disjunction and complement – is typically achieved by positing an ensemble of natural axioms (e.g. continuity, commutativity, monotonicity, etc.). However sensible, these axioms are restricted to each group of items to be defined and are grounded on pragmatic intuition alone. Not surprisingly, as the formal apparatus grows, the method becomes less and less effective.

The problem is particularly noticeable with the closely-related field of fuzzy logic. Paris (1994) for instance gives a set of natural axioms for negation, conjunction and disjunction and then skates over the detailed assessment of an implication-like connective, as "it seems far less clear what axioms should hold for this function". Clearly, the situation

does not improve when defining a fuzzy-logical consequence relation.

The central claim of this paper is that fuzzy sets could be characterised in a different way, namely as a derivative notion in a suitable logical framework. More precisely, fuzzy sets may be made to emerge from a logical 'deep structure' which governs their 'surface' behaviour. Although the modal probabilistic framework that has to be adopted is somewhat elaborate, the resulting characterisation leads to clearer epistemological analysis. In addition, the approach would appear to preserve the qualitative flavour of the original setting. At the very least, it can be shown that some well-known fuzzy techniques can be encoded in the proposed framework.

The paper first describes the modal probabilistic logical framework and subsequently provides a tentative definition of fuzzy sets with respect to this framework. The possible encoding for existing fuzzy techniques is then discussed in some detail. In so doing, the informal notion of fuzziness is reconsidered again and the relationship with Gärdenfors' notion of *conceptual spaces* (1992) is discussed in detail.

The ideas presented here owe much to the influence of a number of other studies. As already stated, the logical apparatus is derived from (Halpern 1990). The construction of a possible world semantics for fuzzy logic was first explored in (Ruspini 1991), whereas the characterisation of fuzzy sets given here has some similarity with that developed by Gerla (1994), who instead adopts probability on formulas, and in (Wang and Tan 1997). To a large extent, the treatment of compositionality follows the line presented in (Dubois and Prade 1994).

2. A Modal Probabilistic Framework

The logical framework we are seeking in this section has the two main goals of providing:

- a language for expressing statements about fuzzy sets;
- a clearly-defined consequence relation.

Sometimes, fuzzy logic is investigated by assuming a many-valued propositional logic as a basis and by establishing a relation with fuzzy set theory. Here we follow a different path. We shall start by constructing a logic of fuzzy sets, whereas the relationship with many-valued logics will be discussed in a subsequent section. Note that the achievement of an axiomatisation is not assumed as a goal in this context. One significant reason is that, as we shall see below, this goal cannot be achieved at all. Another reason is that most fuzzy logic techniques are applied in practice as numerical techniques. Hence the informal goal in this paper is not to develop a form of automated reasoning as a replacement, but rather a suitable formal encoding that allows us to assess the soundness of the techniques in question.

As mentioned above, the construction of the framework is based on the first order logic of probability on possible worlds developed by Halpern (1990). At the outset, we have a first order language Φ with equality containing predicate and function symbols of various arities, together with a family of *object constants* and *object variables*. Terms of this first sort are to be interpreted, as usual, in a domain of objects D. It is further assumed that the language Φ includes a name for every object in D.

In order to simplify the exposition that follows, we adopt a modal translation of Halpern's original language following the approach described in (Voorbraak 1993). This translation makes use of the two special modal symbols $\Box$ and $\Box_p$, where p is real number in $[1, 0]$. Informally, the meaning of a formula $\Box \varphi$ is that φ is true in every possible world (see below), whereas $\Box_p \varphi$ means that φ is true with a probability at least equal to p.

Define a probability structure M as a tuple (D, W, π, S, μ), where D is a domain of objects, W is a set of possible worlds, π is a binary function assigning the proper meaning in each world $w \in W$ to the symbols in Φ. Define also a valuation function v assigning an element of D to each *object term* in Φ. To keep things manageable, we assume that v does not vary across W, i.e. that all terms are *rigid*. Note however that this does not say anything about the extensions of predicate symbols, which are in fact allowed to vary. Semantic rules for $(M, v, w) \models \varphi$ are defined as usual in first order logic, i.e. by induction over the structure of φ, with the sole exception that a reference to the world w is kept as required by the function π. The function μ is a countably additive probability measure over the algebra of sets $\{w : (M, w) \models \varphi\}$ generated by the sentences φ in Φ. The set S is defined as follows:

$$S = \{w : \forall \varphi, \ \mu(\varphi) = 1 \Rightarrow (M, w) \models \varphi\}$$

in other words, S is the subset containing *random worlds* (see Gaifman and Snir 1982); i.e. worlds that do not satisfy any sentence with a zero probability of being true. The semantic rules for the two modal symbols are:

- $(M, v) \models \Box \varphi$ iff $\forall w \in S, \ w \models \varphi$
- $(M, v) \models \Box_p \varphi$ iff $\mu(\{w \in W : w \models \varphi\}) \geq p$

which yield the expected meaning. Note that both definitions are given w.r.t. to S and this validates the identity:

$$\Box \varphi \equiv \Box_1 \varphi.$$

We also introduce two derivative modal symbols $\Diamond_p$ and P_p defined as follows:

$$\Diamond_p \varphi \equiv \neg \Box_{1-p} \neg \varphi$$
$$P_p \varphi \equiv (\Box_p \varphi \ \wedge \ \neg \Diamond_p \varphi).$$

The modal operator P_p expresses a point-valued probability constraint. Note that, syntactically, modal operators might be nested. Voorbraak (1993) proves that in a setting of this kind – which is of modality KD45 – any nested formula has a non-nested equivalent.

We assume that any formula ϕ in the final language of the framework is a composition:

$$\lambda \ : \ \psi$$

where ψ is a formula in the first order language with modal extensions. The *label* λ contains symbols from the first order language Φ plus symbols from a language of a second sort, namely the language of real closed fields. The latter includes the binary predicates $>$ and $=$, the binary functions $+$ and $\times$, the three constants -1, 0 and 1 plus *field functions* and *field variables*. The interpretation of this second sort of symbols is given as usual, i.e. with respect to the set of real numbers $\mathbf{R}$. In addition, λ may also contain *measuring functions* (Bacchus 1990), i.e. functions mapping object terms to field terms. Finally, we allow *field variables* to appear in ψ as indexes to the modal operators $\Box_p$. As a convention, we shall use the letters x, y, z for object variables and p, q, r, for field variables.

Informally, the label λ acts as a *generalised quantifier* binding both sorts of variables in ψ. From a formal standpoint, however, the labelled notation is a mere notational facility for preserving a clear separation between the algebraic part and the logical part of each formula. The semantics of labelled formulas is given in terms of a translation rule. Let:

$$Q_1 v_1 \ldots Q_n v_n \lambda^*$$

be the prenex form of λ, where each $Q_i v_i$ represents a quantifier Q_i applied to a variable v_i of either kind. Hence, by definition, a labelled formula $\lambda : \psi$ is a shorthand notation for:

$$\forall v_{n+1} \ldots \forall v_m \ Q_1 v_1 \ldots Q_n v_n \ (\lambda^* \rightarrow \psi)$$

where $v_{n+1} \ldots v_m$ are variables of either kind occurring free in λ^*. The semantic rule for labelled formulas $\phi = \lambda : \psi$ is defined with respect to a class of extended structures M' where v' is an extended valuation function assigning a real value to field terms as well. We write $M' \models \phi$ iff for every valuation v', $(M', v') \models \phi$. The consequence relation is defined in the usual way – i.e. given a set of labelled formulas Σ, we write $\Sigma \models \phi$ iff every structure M' satisfying the formulas in the set Σ also satisfies ϕ.

A first example of a labelled formula is:

$$p \ : \ \forall x \ (\Box_p A(x) \rightarrow \Box_p B(x)).$$

By convention, the term p in the label λ is taken here as the abbreviation of $p = p$, which is satisfied by any valuation. Hence in the above formula p is universally quantified; the formula states that, for any object in D, the probability of its being B is at least equal to that of its being A. A more interesting example of labelled notation relates to the definition of conditional formulas:

$$(q = 0 \wedge p = 0) \vee (q \geq 0 \wedge r = p \times q) :$$
$$(P_q \beta \wedge P_r(\alpha \wedge \beta)) \rightarrow P_p (\alpha \mid \beta)$$

which is the axiom given in (Bacchus 1990). A ternary modality of conditional independence can be defined as:

$p = q \times r$:
$$(\alpha, \beta \perp \gamma) \equiv ((\boldsymbol{P}_q(\alpha \mid \gamma) \wedge \boldsymbol{P}_r(\beta \mid \gamma)) \to \boldsymbol{P}_p(\alpha \wedge \beta \mid \gamma)).$$

The analysis of finitary properties, however, reveals that the framework is intractable. One of the proofs contained in (Halpern 1990) can be adapted to show that any formula in his setting, with probability on possible worlds, can be translated into a labelled formula of the above kind. Hence the proofs contained in (Abadi and Halpern 1991) also demonstrate that the framework presented is hopelessly non axiomatisable. Nevertheless, the two above goals have been achieved, as we shall see.

3. A Tentative Definition of Fuzzy Sets

We start by describing the characterisation in question with a rather informal observation. Consider an open formula $\varphi(x)$ in Φ, i.e. a formula with no modal extensions, where x occurs as the sole free variable. With respect to a probability structure M, each valuation v turns $\varphi(x)$ into the analogue of a binary *random variable*. In fact, given the assumptions made, any value assignment to x causes $\varphi(x)$ to have a clearly-defined probability of being true. When we consider a *set* of valuations, we obtain something similar to a binary *random field*. In our characterisation, fuzzy sets are assumed to coincide precisely with these entities.

For simplicity, we will restrict our attention to monadic open formulas from this point onwards. The extension to polyadic formulas should be obvious in most cases. The machinery of generalised quantifiers enables us to express statements about fuzzy sets. For instance:

$$(x = \text{Jane} \wedge p = 0) \vee (x = \text{John} \wedge p = 0.3) \vee$$
$$(x = \text{Jill} \wedge p = 0.8) \vee (x = \text{Jack} \wedge p = 1) : \boldsymbol{P}_p \, \text{Old}(x)$$

Note that the free variables x and p in ψ are bound in λ. Basically, the formula expresses a constraint about the fuzzy set corresponding to the (open) formula "Old(x)". This constraint is partial, in that it relates only to a few objects which are explicitly mentioned. Another example is:

$$p = \chi_{\text{Old}}(\text{age}(x)) : \boldsymbol{P}_p \, \text{Old}(x)$$

Here, age( ) is a *measuring function* assigning an age to the objects in D, while χ_{Old} may be any suitable function that can be either encoded or approximated in the language of real closed fields. Note that we have assumed that all terms are rigid, so both functions do not depend on the world of reference. The function χ_{Old} acts as the membership function in a 'classical' fuzzy set, as shown in the following figure.

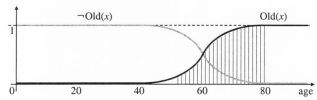

The function χ_{Old} defines a global constraint over the set of binary random variables, shown as vertical bars, corresponding to the valuations of x. Note that χ_{Old} is solely re-

quired to have $[0, 1]$ as its domain; since it models a binary random field and not a probability distribution, such a function may consistently assign the value 1 to two or more distinct instantiations of Old(x).

Clearly, in this scenario, fuzzy sets are given an entirely probabilistic 'deep structure'. Such a probabilistic characterisation is not new (Zimmerman 1991). The main difference, however, is that here the probabilistic trait is structurally related to a logical framework. Regarding this point, let us also observe that probability plays a role in the definition of the consequence relation only. This can also be regarded as a pragmatic advantage, as probability measures are the most constraining in the family of fuzzy measures (Klir and Yuan 1995). In other words, in the framework presented, probability leads to a stronger consequence relation.

4. Fuzzy Logic

In this section we will consider the most common algebraic rules for fuzzy logic from the perspective of the proposed logical framework.

Proposition 4.1 – These three formulas are equivalent:

$p = \min(q, r)$:
$$\forall x \, ((\boldsymbol{P}_q \, \varphi(x) \wedge \boldsymbol{P}_r \, \psi(x)) \to \boldsymbol{P}_p \, (\varphi(x) \wedge \psi(x)))$$

$p = \max(q, r)$:
$$\forall x \, ((\boldsymbol{P}_q \, \varphi(x) \wedge \boldsymbol{P}_r \, \psi(x)) \to \boldsymbol{P}_p \, (\varphi(x) \vee \psi(x)))$$

$p = \min(1 - q + r)$:
$$\forall x \, ((\boldsymbol{P}_q \, \varphi(x) \wedge \boldsymbol{P}_r \, \psi(x)) \to \boldsymbol{P}_p \, (\varphi(x) \to \psi(x))).$$

Furthermore, any of the above is equivalent to:

$$\forall x \, (\square \, (\varphi(x) \to \psi(x)) \vee \square \, (\psi(x) \to \varphi(x))).$$

Proposition 4.2 – These three formulas are equivalent:

$p = \max(q + r - 1, 0)$:
$$\forall x \, ((\boldsymbol{P}_q \, \varphi(x) \wedge \boldsymbol{P}_r \, \psi(x)) \to \boldsymbol{P}_p \, (\varphi(x) \wedge \psi(x)))$$

$p = \min(p + q, 1)$:
$$\forall x \, ((\boldsymbol{P}_q \, \varphi(x) \wedge \boldsymbol{P}_r \, \psi(x)) \to \boldsymbol{P}_p \, (\varphi(x) \vee \psi(x)))$$

$p = \max(1 - q, r)$:
$$\forall x \, ((\boldsymbol{P}_q \, \varphi(x) \wedge \boldsymbol{P}_r \, \psi(x)) \to \boldsymbol{P}_p \, (\varphi(x) \to \psi(x))).$$

Furthermore, any of the above is equivalent to:

$$\forall x \, (\square \, (\varphi(x) \to \neg\psi(x)) \vee \square \, (\neg\psi(x) \to \varphi(x))).$$

Clearly, the propositional versions of these properties also hold true. Nevertheless, the quantified sentences presented are richer in meaning due to the existing relationship between modal formulas and the sets representing the extensions of formulas in each possible world.

Definition 4.3 – The extension in a world of an open formula $\varphi(x)$, x being the only free variable in φ, is defined as:

$$\text{Ext}(w, \varphi(x)) = \{d \in D : \, (M, v[x/d], w) \models \varphi(x)\}.$$

In the light of the above definition, from a purely mathematical standpoint, every unary open formula can be taken to correspond to the analogue of a *random set*. Furthermore, all random sets of this kind share a common indexing, namely the set of possible worlds.

Proposition 4.4 – The formula:

$$\forall x \, (\square \, (\varphi(x) \to \psi(x)) \lor \square \, (\psi \, (x) \to \varphi(x)))$$

corresponds to a semantic condition of *nesting*:

$$\forall \, (w, w') \in S, w \neq w' \Rightarrow$$
$$(\mathrm{Ext}(w, \varphi(x) \land \psi(x)) \subseteq \mathrm{Ext}(w', \varphi(x) \land \psi(x))) \text{ OR}$$
$$(\mathrm{Ext}(w, \varphi(x) \land \psi(x)) \supseteq \mathrm{Ext}(w', \varphi(x) \land \psi(x))).$$

Proposition 4.5 – The formula:

$$\forall x \, (\square \, (\varphi(x) \to \neg\psi(x)) \lor \square \, (\neg\psi(x) \to \varphi(x)))$$

corresponds to the semantic condition of *nesting* in Proposition 4.4 for the open formula $(\varphi(x) \land \neg\psi(x))$.

Proposition 4.6 – The formula:

$$\forall x \, \forall y \, (\square \, (\varphi(x) \to \varphi(y)) \lor \square \, (\varphi(y) \to \varphi(x)))$$

corresponds to the semantic condition of *nesting* in Proposition 4.4 for the open formula $\varphi(x)$.

In keeping with (Shafer 1976), the property described in Proposition 4.4 is called *joint consonance* here, whereas the property in Proposition 4.5 is called *joint dissonance*. For completeness, we also define the property in Proposition 4.6 as *consonance*.

Proposition 4.7 – These three formulas are equivalent:

$p = q \times r :$
$$\forall x \, ((P_q \, \varphi(x) \land P_r \, \psi(x)) \to P_p \, (\varphi(x) \land \psi(x)))$$
$p = q + r - (q \times r):$
$$\forall x \, ((P_q \, \varphi(x) \land P_r \, \psi(x)) \to P_p \, (\varphi(x) \lor \psi(x)))$$
$p = 1 - (1 - q) \times r :$
$$\forall x \, ((P_q \, \varphi(x) \land P_r \, \psi(x)) \to P_p \, (\varphi(x) \to \psi(x))).$$

Furthermore, any of the above is equivalent to:

$$\forall x \, (\varphi(x) \perp \psi(x)).$$

The latter is an abbreviation for $(\varphi(x), \psi(x) \perp true)$. Regarding conditional forms, we have:

Proposition 4.8 – The formula:

$(q = 0 \land p = 0) \lor (q \geq 0 \land p = \min(1, r / q)) :$
$$\forall x \, ((P_q \, \varphi(x) \land P_r \, \psi(x)) \to P_p \, (\varphi(x) \, | \, \psi(x)))$$
is equivalent to:
$$\forall x \, (\square \, (\varphi(x) \to \psi(x)) \lor \square \, (\psi \, (x) \to \varphi(x))).$$

Proposition 4.9 – The formula:

$(q = 0 \land p = 0) \lor (q \geq 0 \land p = \max(q + r - 1, 0) / q) :$
$$\forall x \, ((P_q \, \varphi(x) \land P_r \, \psi(x)) \to P_p \, (\varphi(x) \, | \, \psi(x)))$$
is equivalent to:
$$\forall x \, (\square \, (\varphi(x) \to \neg\psi(x)) \lor \square \, (\neg\psi(x) \to \varphi(x))).$$

The ratio symbol '/' has been used for the sake of brevity.

Obviously, none of the properties presented above is a new finding. See for instance (Sales 1996) for a thorough investigation of the relationship between logic and probability. The main difference between the above algebraic rules and many-valued logics, is that the latter are taken to be fully compositional, whereas the probabilistic rules can be applied only in particular cases, i.e. when the equivalent modal conditions hold. Hájek, Godo and Esteva (1995) suggest that this difference is precisely what distinguishes the two realms; i.e. fuzzy logic is seen as a compositional theory for *degrees of truth* whereas probability is seen as a non-compositional theory of *uncertainty*. Intuitively though, the similarities between the two domains seems worth commenting on further. From a mathematical standpoint, for instance, Paris (1994) proves that the algebraic rules presented above, in a certain sense, contain all the possible definitions for many-valued logics. More precisely, he shows that any T-norm is isomorphic to either of the algebraic rules for conjunction in Propositions 4.7 and 4.2; analogously, any T-conorm is isomorphic to either of the algebraic rules for disjunction in the same propositions.

On the other hand, these algebraic rules for implication admit a further degree of freedom, depending on whether this is informally interpreted, as Lukasiewicz did (Rescher 1969), in terms of strict implication or, alternatively, as a conditional form. Note that the equivalent modal formulas are the same in both cases. Indeed, the most common choices for many-valued implications happen to fall among those described above (see Hájek and Godo 1997). Having observed that many compositional fuzzy techniques applied in practice are intentionally of a *local* nature – i.e. they are not related to a broader logical system – we come up against the suspicion that these techniques may, in fact, fall into one of the classes where compositional rules apply. In passing, Dubois and Prade (1994) are more cautious about compositionality, admitting that fuzzy sets may also be used to deal with uncertainty in a non-compositional setting, as happens in possibility theory. Nevertheless, they suggest that the formalism for degrees of truth is appropriate to fuzzy inference systems. In the next sections, we will show that these techniques may instead involve fuzzy sets of the uncertainty-based kind.

5. Fuzzy Inference Systems

Fuzzy inference systems are mostly, but not exclusively, used in fuzzy control systems. A comprehensive and up-to-date introduction is given in (Jang et al. 1997).

Basically, these techniques are designed to approximate a real-valued function $u = f(z)$, where z is a finite vector of real-valued parameters z_i. For instance, the function may describe a control signal for a system with state variables z_i. For simplicity, let us use a binary target function, whereby $z = [z_1 \, z_2]^\mathrm{T}$. A Mamdani-type inference system is a set of rules of the kind

if z_1 **is** $\mathbf{A}_k$ **and** z_2 **is** $\mathbf{B}_k$ **then** u **is** $\mathbf{C}_k$

where $\mathbf{A}_k$, $\mathbf{B}_k$ and $\mathbf{C}_k$ are fuzzy subsets of the real axis in rule k.

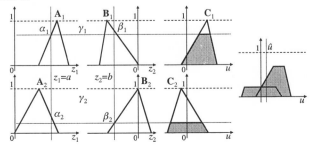

The inference method for two such rules is visually described in the above figure. The vertical bars correspond to the two values a and b for the parameters z_1 and z_2 respectively. These values are intersected with the fuzzy sets; the intersection values α_k and β_k are then combined through a T-norm (e.g. min) to obtain the values γ_k. The latter are used as thresholds to 'cut' the fuzzy sets C_k; 'cut' sets originating from different rules are combined through a T-conorm (e.g. max) to yield a final fuzzy set. The estimated value $\hat{u}$ is finally obtained through a *defuzzification* method; typically through an average-like operation.

In a Sugeno-type inference system, fuzzy rules are of a slightly different kind:

if z_1 is $\mathbf{A}_k$ **and** z_2 is $\mathbf{B}_k$ **then** u is $f_k(z_1, z_2)$.

Each f_k is intended to be a local approximation to the function f. The values γ_k are computed in the same way as with Mamdani-type rules. The main difference resides in how the estimated value $\hat{u}$ is computed, typically as the 'average' of the contributions given by the f_k:

$$\hat{u} \ = \ \gamma_1 f_1(a, b) + \gamma_2 f_2(a, b) + \ldots + \gamma_n f_n(a, b).$$

It can be proven that both inference systems, under certain conditions, are universal approximators; i.e. the value $\hat{u}$ can be made arbitrarily close to any continuous target function (Buckley, 1995). In the field of practical applications, fuzzy approximation techniques are particularly appreciated when the target function is either unknown or unobservable, as they apparently relate more directly to human knowledge.

The logical encoding of the above techniques can be made clearer by establishing an informal relation with a possibly more familiar probabilistic model. Assuming that the target function is unobservable, we may model the variable u and the parameters z_i as random variables on a suitable sample space Ω. The conditional density $P(u \mid z)$ would then describe the probability for u to be the 'true' value of the function, given the parameter vector z. In the logical encoding we assume a bijective correspondence in meaning between the objects $d \in D$ and the sample points $\omega \in \Omega$. For instance, if the target function describes a control strategy, each object/point represents a possible state of the physical system being controlled.

The encoding of the fuzzy sets which occur in the rules is exemplified as follows:

$$p = \chi_{A_k}(z_1(x)) \ : \ \boldsymbol{P}_p A_k(x)$$
$$p = \chi_{B_k}(z_2(x)) \ : \ \boldsymbol{P}_p B_k(x)$$
$$p = \chi_{C_k}(u(x)) \ : \ \boldsymbol{P}_p C_k(x).$$

Here, z_1, z_2 and u are encoded as *measuring functions* assigning a real value to the objects in D. In passing, measuring functions are used in (Bacchus 1990) to represent the analogue of random variables. The analogy does not hold here since there is no 'randomness' on the variable x, i.e. probability distributes on W rather than on D. Mamdani-type rules are encoded as strict implications:

$$\forall x \ \Box \ ((A_k(x) \land B_k(x)) \to C_k(x)).$$

An entire rule base is encoded as the overall disjunction of the above rules. Any specific value assignment to the parameters z_1 and z_2 can be expressed through a restriction:

$$(z_1(x) = a) \land (z_2(x) = b)$$

which circumscribes the relevant objects in D. There is a crucial analogy here between the latter circumscription and the *conditional* update of a probability space. In a probability space, the acquisition of new facts causes the elimination of the sample points in Ω which have become irrelevant. This forces the updating of $P(\ )$ into the conditional form $P(\ \mid z_1 = a, z_2 = b)$. Similarly, the above circumscription corresponds to the elimination of the irrelevant objects from D. Nevertheless, the measure μ on possible worlds and hence the probability operators are unaffected since no worlds are ruled out.

The intersection values α_k and β_k are algebraically computed from the conjunctions:

$$p = \chi_{A_k}(z_1(x)) \land (z_1(x) = a) \ : \ \boldsymbol{P}_p A_k(x)$$
$$p = \chi_{B_k}(z_2(x)) \land (z_2(x) = b) \ : \ \boldsymbol{P}_p B_k(x).$$

The min operator is a sound choice in this case, as it represents the 'erosion' of irrelevant objects from the original fuzzy sets. A quite different matter is the combination of α_k and β_k to obtain γ_k. Observe that the min operator – i.e. the most popular choice – is only applicable when the modal condition in Proposition 4.1 holds between $A_k(x)$ and $B_k(x)$. This also means that the two fuzzy sets would have to be jointly consonant. Let us provisionally assume that this is true of all pairs A_k and B_k; the implication of this will be discussed shortly. It can be proved that:

$$p \ : \ \forall x \ (\Box \ (\varphi(x) \to \psi(x)) \to (\Box_p \varphi(x) \to \Box_p \psi(x)))$$
$$p = \max(q, r) :$$
$$\forall x \ ((\Box_q \varphi(x) \land \Box_r \psi(x)) \to \Box_p (\varphi(x) \lor \psi(x)))$$

are valid formulas. The first makes it possible to derive the formula describing the 'cut' fuzzy sets:

$$(p = \max(\chi_{C_k}(u(x)), \gamma_k)) \land (z_1(x) = a) \land (z_2(x) = b) :$$
$$\Box_p C_k(x)$$

i.e. a lower bound on probabilities. The second valid formula makes it possible to combine the 'cut' fuzzy sets arising from different rules through the max operator, thus obtaining the final fuzzy set; i.e. a cumulative lower bound.

In this light, the identification of $\hat{u}$ through an 'averaging' operation is vaguely reminiscent of the calculation of an expected value. However, the fuzzy set in question is not a probability distribution, nor even a lower one, so this choice seems difficult to justify.

Sugeno-type rules are encoded in the following way:

$$V_k(x) \equiv \text{Approx}f(u(x), f_k(z_1(x), z_2(x))) :$$
$$\forall x \ \Box \ ((A_k(x) \land B_k(x)) \to V_k(x))$$

where V_k is an auxiliary predicate and Approx$f$ describes a viable approximation to f. When applied to input values, each of these rules yields a point-wise estimate of $\hat{u}$, thus the final 'expected value' can be obtained directly. One critical point in Sugeno's technique, however, is precisely this 'expected value'. In a certain sense, $\{\gamma_k\}$ appears to be quite similar to a conditional, discrete probability distribution over the possible values of $\hat{u}$. If this is the case, the expectation operator would be appropriate. This point leads us to discussing a fundamental aspect of informal interpretation.

6. A Short Epistemological Interlude

Intuitively, the techniques in the previous section require proper coverage of the domain of the target function through fuzzy sets such as A_k and B_k. In passing, the notion of a fuzzy partition is usually defined in the literature by a set of natural axioms accounting for what in this respect is proper coverage. From another point of view, Definition 4.3 says that fuzzy sets such as A_k and B_k have a 'deep structure' in terms of random sets. Technical details apart, the main question here regards the informal rationale for uncertainty in a structure of related predicate extensions.

A few helpful ideas for providing an answer have been formulated by P. Gärdenfors. In (1997, 1992), with the support of some psychological experiments, he theorises an intermediate level of information representation between the 'symbolic' level – namely the level of predicates – and what he calls the 'sub-conceptual' level, i.e. the kind of associative, intrinsic representation proper to neural networks. This kind of 'missing link', called the 'conceptual' level, is designed to explain how concept formation may take place. A *conceptual space* is a number of *quality dimensions*. For instance, dimensions of these kinds may be closely related to human sensory receptors, such as spatial dimensions, temperature, colours, etc. The term 'dimension' is to be understood in its proper mathematical sense; conceptual spaces are taken as being endowed with a geometric or topological structure. In this abstraction, properties are regions, possibly convex; concepts – corresponding to predicates – are either a property or a set of properties defined on different dimensions.

Gärdenfors also adopts a theory of *prototypes*, i.e. highly representative points acting as attractors in a conceptual space, around which concepts are potentially formed. As one formal pattern for concept formation, he considers a variation of Voronoï tessellations called *power diagrams* (Aurenhammer 1991). An example of a power diagram is given in the figure:

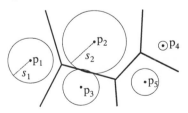

A Voronoï tessellation is a topological abstraction based on the notion of distance, which applies to many natural phenomena, such as crystal growth. Given a metric space and a set of characteristic points – e.g. the prototypes in this case – the Voronoï cell around each characteristic point is defined as the region closer to it than to any other characteristic point. With power cells, every characteristic

point is also endowed with its own *strength*, as represented by the radius of a hypersphere centred in it. Formally, the boundary equation between two contiguous cells is:

$$(x - \mathrm{p}_i)^{\mathrm{T}}(x - \mathrm{p}_i) - s_i^2 = (x - \mathrm{p}_j)^{\mathrm{T}}(x - \mathrm{p}_j) - s_j^2$$

where s_i is the strength of point p_i. Voronoï tessellations correspond to the case when all strengths s_i are zero. In all other cases, distances are measured from the borders of the power hypersphere rather than from the points themselves. In passing, both Voronoï and power cells are always convex and divided by straight lines. Of course, shapes other than a sphere might be considered for further generality.

In such a scenario, we propose that uncertainty could be construed as yet another dimension relating to the relative strengths of prototypes. In other words, a symbolic system in a conceptual space might conveniently be modelled as a family of 'possible tessellations' where the prototypes are fixed and their relative strengths vary. In turn, the addition of (subjective) probability makes the symbolic system to correspond to a random tessellation where each concept is represented by a random set.

The proposal can be further clarified by relating it to our main topic. Let us consider a Sugeno-type inference system with a set of k prototypical points in the domain of the target function f for which suitable approximations f_k are known. For instance, f could again describe the control signal for a physical system, with each f_k being a local control strategy whose effectiveness has been experimentally assessed. In the logical encoding, the 'concepts' – i.e. the extension of predicates V_k – are simply the regions where the corresponding approximation applies. In this respect, the adoption of just one such tessellation is very committing from an informal standpoint and leads to technical difficulties. On the other hand, fuzzy inference systems may be taken as proving that an effective approximation technique with a low computational cost can be achieved by adopting random tessellations.

In this light, uncertainty may be held to add flexibility to a conceptual space in that it improves the pragmatic applicability of a symbolic system defined in it. It is crucial to observe, however, that uncertainty comes into play when a *purpose* is attached to a conceptual tessellation, or, to put the matter differently, when the symbols associated to the concepts are inserted into the dynamics of a reasoning process, such as that of identifying a purposeful approximation to an unknown function. Informally, this is quite different from uncertainty about actual facts, as for instance in the random model of a noisy sensor. In the latter case, randomness stems from the sum of the erratic effects in the sensing system, whereas randomness in a conceptual space is taken to be due to the purposeful application of a complex of symbols in a reasoning process.

Inter alia, this also explains why the actual modelling of fuzzy sets is commonly reported to be so strongly dependent on context. The shape of a fuzzy set such as $\mathrm{Old}(x)$ depends on what is taken to be entailed from accepting that a an object is 'Old' in a reasoning context. Likewise, fully-shaped fuzzy sets can hardly make sense outside the reasoning system in which they are originated. The main advantage of a logical framework for this analysis is to make this systemic nature of fuzzy sets much more evident.

7. Fuzzy Partitions, Topological Reasoning

We can now turn to the logical encoding of fuzzy partitions by discussing the use of random tessellations for the underlying 'deep structure'. Let V_k denote a finite set of n predicates describing a random tessellation. Two main axiom schema apply:

a) $\forall x \; \Box \; (V_1(x) \lor \ldots \lor V_n(x))$
b) $\forall x \; \Box \; (V_i(x) \rightarrow \neg V_j(x)), \quad \forall i,j \in [1..n], \; i \neq j$.

These axioms mean that each possible world in S contains the complete description of a tessellation of D.

In the light of the previous section, we may further assume that a conceptual space is encoded by a suitable set of measuring functions corresponding to each dimension. The idea of concepts as convex regions is straightforwardly extensible to the random dimension by adopting random power tessellations. Two more properties derive from this:

c) $\exists x \; \Box \; V_i(x)$
d) $\forall x \forall y \; (\Box \; (V_i(x) \rightarrow V_i(y)) \lor \Box \; (V_i(y) \rightarrow V_i(x)))$

which hold for any $i \in [1..n]$. Property c) states that each 'concept' V_k has at least one prototype, which also means that fuzzy sets V_k are normal – i.e. their membership functions reaches unity for some objects. Property d) states that fuzzy sets V_k are *consonant*.

For obvious computational reasons, fuzzy partitions are often taken in practice to be decomposable, i.e. to be expressible as the combination of fuzzy partitions on each dimension. For instance, a monodimensional fuzzy partition may have the following shape:

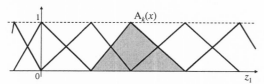

As already stated, the min T-norm can be consistently applied to combinations of fuzzy sets which are jointly consonant. At first sight, this seems to support an informal 'psychological' preference for convex tessellating elements. In the case of the example in Section 5, decomposability plus joint consonance would entail that

$$p = \min(q, r) : \forall x \; ((P_q \, A_k(x) \land P_r \, B_k(x)) \rightarrow P_p \, V_k(x)).$$

as we provisionally assumed in Section 5.

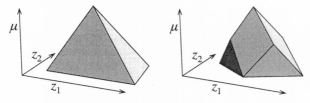

However, this is incompatible with a random tessellation. In fact, when the two dimensions are orthogonal and

A_k and B_k are triangularly shaped, the tessellating element for the three-dimensional space – z_1 and z_2 plus the 'random' axis – is a kind of pyramid, as in the left part of the above figure. Clearly, such a pyramid is not a tessellating element for the three-dimensional space in question. Accordingly, it is easily proved that no random power tessellation exists where rectangles are the only possible shapes. Hence complete coverage with nested rectangles of varying dimensions can only be achieved by allowing the cells to overlap in some worlds, thus violating axiom b) above. This situation is represented in the left hand part of the following figure:

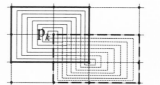 

Consequently, the set of values γ_k defined in Section 5 is not a discrete probability distribution since, due to the overlapping of rectangles, the sum will generally exceed one. Nevertheless, the use of max is always sound in Mamdani-type rules if lower probability limits are intended; the price to pay, however, is that it is not possible to infer point-valued constraints. A similar line of reasoning applies to the product T-norm as well – i.e. the second most popular choice – with the further problem that not even convexity is preserved. In turn this makes it difficult to justify informally why the prototypical elements, i.e. the vertices of triangles, are still there.

Interestingly, the same reasoning can be used to find a random power tessellation – based on a generalised distance – admitting a simple algebraic rule for conjunction. Without going into details, the random tessellation in question is represented on the right hand side of the figure above. In this case, the varying rectangles are allowed to mutate into more complex shapes to avoid overlapping. The tessellating element for the three-dimensional space is given above, on the right hand side of the pyramid. In this case, the monodimensional fuzzy sets are construed as the projections of the random tessellation onto each axis. The corresponding compositional rule is:

$$((\delta_k(x) = 1) \land (p = \min(q, r)) \lor ((\delta_k(x) = 0) \land (p = 0) :$$
$$\forall x \; ((P_q \, A_k(x) \land P_r \, B_k(x)) \rightarrow P_p \, V_k(x))$$

where δ_k is the characteristic function of the bounding 'diamond' for V_k. Note that in general this is not a T-norm, unless the diamond is a square. However, the net advantage is that the set of values γ_k computed with the above rule is now a conditional, discrete distribution over the possible estimates for $\hat{u}$.

As we have seen, analysis of the 'deep structure' of a fuzzy partition throws a different light on the meaning of algebraic rules. Note also that these aspects are totally invisible when the very same algebraic rules are studied in isolation. Instead, the adoption of a structured characterisation for fuzzy sets brings to light an underlying 'deep' level of topological reasoning that also emerges with Gär-denfors' conceptual spaces.

8.   Conclusions and Future Work

One aspect which has not been discussed in this paper is how the uncertainty model for fuzzy sets presented ties up with other uncertainty models regarding factual phenomena, e.g. the random model of a noisy sensor. Models of the latter kind, from the standpoint of the logical framework, involve randomness over the object domain D and hence require the introduction of a second probability measure on D. Thus, the fuzzy inference systems discussed in Section 5 could be extended to embrace the case where the parameter values are described by a probability density.

The extension of the formalism to include a second probability measure has already been contemplated in (Halpern 1990) and formally studied in a number of subsequent works. In these studies, however, the informal objective is somewhat different from what we are proposing here. In keeping with a long-standing tradition dating back to Carnap, the two measures are held to represent two different kinds of probability, namely statistical probability – i.e. on D – and degrees of belief – i.e. on W. In our line of thinking, a slightly different direction seems appropriate, namely conceiving a unique probability space where the two forms of uncertainty, one relating to factual phenomena and the other intrinsic to the purposive use of a symbolic system, are brought together. It might be assumed that the unique probability space is decomposable into the two independent measures mentioned above. However, in our understanding, the assumption that the learning of new facts does not in any way alter a systemic fuzzy set model cannot be taken for granted. Hopefully, the assessment of the interactions may instead help to achieve a formal account for more complex, 'gestalt'-like phenomena.

As we have seen, the logical framework presented may provide a valuable formal tool for investigating fuzzy models in terms of their 'deep structures'. Maybe this will provide a safer bridge over the gap between the realm of fuzziness and that of probability.

Acknowledgements. Thanks are due to Didier Dubois, Université Paul Sabatier, Toulouse, and Rosella Gennari, University of Amsterdam, for their precious advice and suggestions.

References

Abadi, M., Halpern, J. Y., 1994, Decidability and expressiveness for first-order logics of probability, *Information and Computation*, 112 (1), 1-36.

Aurenhammer, F., 1991, Voronoi diagrams: A survey of a fundamental geometric data structure, *ACM Computing Surveys*, 23, 345-405.

Bacchus, F., 1990, *Representing and Reasoning with Probabilistic Knowledge*, Cambridge, MA: The MIT Press.

Buckley, J. J., 1995, System Stability and the Fuzzy Controller, in Nguyen, H. T. et al. (eds.), *Theoretical Aspects of Fuzzy Control*, New York: John Wiley & Sons.

Dubois, D., Prade, H., 1994, Can We Enforce Full Compositionality in Uncertainty Calculi? In *Proceedings of the 12th National Conference on Artificial Intelligence*, Vol. 1, 149-154, Menlo Park, CA: AAAI Press.

Gaifman, H., Snir, M., 1982, Probabilities over rich languages, testing and randomness, *The Journal of Symbolic Logic*, 47 (3), 495-548.

Gärdenfors, P., 1992, A geometric model of concept formation, in S. Ohsuga et al. (eds.), *Information Modelling and Knowledge Bases III*, 1-16, Amsterdam: IOS Press.

Gärdenfors, P., 1997, Symbolic, conceptual and subconceptual representations, in Cantoni, V., et al. (eds.), *Human and Machine Perception: Information Fusion*, 255-270, New York: Plenum Press.

Gerla, G., 1994, Inferences in probability logic, *Artificial Intelligence*, 70, 33-52.

Hájek, P., Godo, L., 1997, Deductive systems of fuzzy logic – a tutorial, Technical Report no. 707, Inst. of Computer Science, Academy of Sciences of the Czech Republic.

Hájek, P., Godo, L., Esteva, F., 1995, Fuzzy Logic and Probability, *Proceedings of the 11th Annual Conference on Uncertainty in Artificial Intelligence*, San Francisco, CA: Morgan Kaufmann Publishers.

Halpern, J. Y., 1990, An analysis of first-order logics of probability, *Artificial Intelligence* 46, 1990, 311-350.

Jang, J. S. R., Sun, C. T., Mizutani, E., 1997, *Neuro-Fuzzy and Soft Computing*, Upper Saddle River, NJ: Prentice Hall.

Klir, G. J., Yuan, B., 1995, *Fuzzy Sets and Fuzzy Logic*, Upper Saddle River, NJ: Prentice Hall.

Paris, J. B., 1994, *The Uncertain Reasoner's Companion*, Cambridge, UK: Cambridge University Press.

Rescher, N., 1969, *Many-Valued Logics*, New York: Mc Graw-Hill.

Ruspini, E. H., 1991, On the Semantics of Fuzzy Logic, *International Journal of Approximate Reasoning*, 5, 45-88.

Sales, T., 1996, Logic as General Rationality: A Survey, in Gabbay, D., Guenthner, F. (eds.), *Handbook of Philosophical Logic, 2nd ed.*, Forthcoming.

Shafer, G., 1976, *A mathematical theory of evidence*, Princeton, NJ : Princeton University Press.

Voorbraak, F. 1993. As Far as I Know, Ph.D. diss., Dept. of Philosophy, Utrecht Univ.

Wang, P., Tan, S., 1997, *Soft Computing and Fuzzy Logic*, Soft Computing, 1, 35-41.

Zadeh, L.A., 1965, Fuzzy sets. *Information and Control*, 8, 338-353.

Zadeh, L.A., 1978, Fuzzy sets as a basis for a theory of possibility. *Fuzzy Sets and Systems*, 1, 3-28.

Zimmerman, H. J., 1991, *Fuzzy Set Theory and Its Applications, 2nd ed.*, Boston, MA: Kluwer Academic Publishers.

ARGUS: An Automated Multi-Agent Visitor Identification System

Rahul Sukthankar[*†] and **Robert G. Stockton**[*]

*Just Research
4616 Henry Street
Pittsburgh, PA 15213

†The Robotics Institute
Carnegie Mellon Univ.
Pittsburgh, PA 15213

{rahuls,rgs}@justresearch.com

Abstract

ARGUS is a multi-agent visitor identification system distributed over several workstations. Human faces are extracted from security camera images by a neural-network-based face detector, and identified as frequent visitors by ARENA, a memory-based face recognition system. ARGUS then uses a messaging system to notify hosts that their guests have arrived. An interface agent enables users to submit feedback, which is immediately incorporated by ARENA to improve its face recognition performance. The ARGUS components were rapidly developed using JGram, an agent framework that is also detailed in this paper. JGram automatically converts high-level agent specifications into Java source code, and assembles complex tasks by composing individual agent services into a JGram pipeline. ARGUS has been operating successfully in an outdoor environment for several months.

Introduction

Consider the following scenario. Visitors to large apartment complexes are typically screened by a security guard in the lobby before being allowed to enter. Over time, guards learn to associate frequent visitors with the tenants whom they plan to visit, and are able to immediately notify the visitor's host of the guest's arrival over the building intercom. This paper presents an automated version of such a security guard: a multi-agent system for visitor identification, named ARGUS (after the vigilant watchman from Greek mythology).

At a high-level, ARGUS's operation consists of the following steps, each of which is managed by one or more JGram (Sukthankar, Brusseau, & Pelletier 1998) agents. A security camera photographs the building entrance every two seconds, and a motion detection algorithm identifies potential scenes containing visitors. Faces from these images are extracted using a neural-network-based face detector (Rowley, Baluja, & Kanade 1998). ARENA (Sim *et al.* 1999), a memory-based face recognition system, examines these face images and attempts to find visually similar matches in its stored

database of visitors. Users interested in receiving notification of visitors may run a JGram agent which will automatically be informed when the relevant visitors are identified. This agent also allows users to provide ARGUS with immediate corrections for identification errors. Since ARENA is capable of online learning, this feedback can be immediately incorporated into the recognition dataset.

ARGUS is implemented as a collection of agents in a multi-agent system (Sycara 1998) for several reasons. First, the components require different platforms: for instance, the camera interface is limited to Windows, while the face recognition system prefers Linux. Similarly, ARGUS users, distributed over an intranet, require notification on their individual workstations. (Some run Linux and others run Windows.) JGram agents, which use Java RMI for communication, are well suited for this scenario. Second, the computational load imposed by some of the image processing routines is severe enough to merit splitting the task over multiple machines. Third, a multi-agent architecture offers a high degree of modularity, allowing ARGUS agents to be dynamically added or removed from the system. For instance, interface agents can be created and killed as users arrive and leave without affecting the rest of the ARGUS system. Similarly, monitoring agents can be inserted to diagnose problems without disrupting service, and different face recognition algorithms can be seamlessly tested.

The remainder of this paper is organized as follows. First, the JGram agent framework is described. Next, the architecture of the ARGUS system is detailed, with an emphasis on the ARENA face recognizer. In the following section, ARGUS is evaluated in three experiments. The discussion explores strategies for improving visitor identification accuracy. The paper concludes by presenting promising directions for future research.

The JGram Agent Framework

The JGram agent framework was designed to simplify agent development in Java by providing strong support in three areas: (1) automatic generation of low-level agent code from high-level agent service specifications; (2) dynamic composition of agent services; (3) an in-

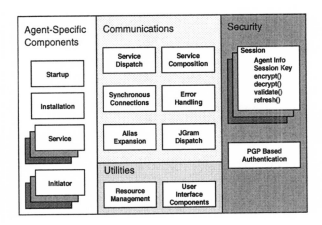

Figure 1: An overview of the internals of a JGram agent (See the text for details).

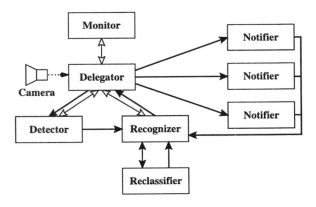

Figure 2: This diagram shows an overview of the ARGUS architecture, where each box depicts a JGram agent. The heavier lines show the major data pathways and the light lines show monitoring information. A line with a double arrows represents a synchronous exchange while one with a single arrow indicates asynchronous dataflow. (See the text for details.)

telligent scheme for handling errors (exceptions) across agents.

All inter-agent communications in the JGram framework is performed using an object known as a "slate": essentially a small and self-contained blackboard that is passed from agent to agent, containing named objects that can be read, added or removed. By sending parameters to services as slates, JGram is able to multiplex multiple remote communications through a single remote method interface. All JGram agents can therefore provide reconfigurable agent interfaces while sharing a single, static, RMI stub file. Details are available in (Sukthankar, Brusseau, & Pelletier 1998).

Figure 1 shows the internals of a JGram agent. The JGram framework concentrates on providing general low-level aspects of agent communication. For instance, agent services can easily be executed in parallel, and can be invoked either synchronously (function call semantics) or asynchronously (message semantics). The JGram framework can also provide transparent support for secure interactions between agents: in the initial exchange, agents use public-key authentication and create a fast symmetric session-key for further communications. Note that the JGram framework is largely independent of higher-level issues such as agent communication languages or specific agent architectures. Rapid development of complex agent systems is possible because most of the components in the *Communications*, *Security* and *Utilities* sections (see Figure 1) are provided and Java source skeletons for the *Agent-Specific Components* are automatically generated from the high-level agent specification file. The JGram framework also provides a name server for alias expansion, managing lists of agents and public key dissemination.

A variety of Java-based agent frameworks have recently become available (Jeon 1998; Chauhan & Baker 1998). JGram differs from these in that it does not provide agent templates nor support for specific agent methodologies. Instead, JGram enables rapid development of communities where the agent interactions can be modeled as service requests. Additionally, JGram provides a novel, cross-agent generalization of pipes and exceptions that significantly simplifies development of certain complex applications. See (Sukthankar, Brusseau, & Pelletier 1998) for details.

An Overview of ARGUS Components

This section presents an overview of the ARGUS system architecture (see Figure 2) and details the important agents and their interactions. ARGUS' three tasks may be summarized as: (1) visitor identification and notification; (2) interactive labelling of unknown visitors; (3) evaluation of face detection and face recognition algorithms. Since these tasks occur in parallel, most ARGUS agents perform several roles simultaneously.

In the primary task, visitor identification, the *delegator* agent collects images from the camera hardware (every 2 seconds), performs image differencing (Ballard & Brown 1982) on successive images, and sends those images that contain motion through a JGram pipeline to the *detector* and *recognizer* agents. In the event of a positive visitor identification, the *delegator* broadcasts messages to all *notifier* agents that are interested in this visitor's arrival. User feedback acquired from the *notifier* agents is used by the *recognizer* to update its face database.

The secondary task, labelling unknown visitors, is performed every few days by ARGUS administrators, through the *reclassifier* interface agent. The *reclassifier* requests a list of unlabelled faces from the *recognizer* and allows the administrator to add them as training examples. The *reclassifier* agent is also used to correct

Figure 3: The ARGUS notifier displays an image captured by the security camera along with a box surrounding the face of the visitor and a tentative identification. User feedback is used to improve face recognition. (The window size was reduced for publication.)

errors in the face database, and to dynamically create new visitor classes. In the current implementation, the *recognizer* does not require offline training, so the updates are immediately available for the primary task.

ARGUS' final task is supported by the *monitor* agent that allows users to interactively query evaluation metrics collected by all of the other ARGUS agents. This is particularly useful when the *recognizer* agent is evaluating experimental algorithms in addition to using an established algorithm for the primary task. In addition, the *monitor* simplifies remote administration of the visitor identification system by verifying that all agents are operating normally.

Since we cannot present all of these agents in detail due to space limitations, we restrict ourselves to a brief discussion of the highlights. The *delegator*, in addition to its image processing responsibilities, also operates as a facilitator for the agent community, forwarding messages between different agents. The *detector* uses the neural-network-based face finder described in (Rowley, Baluja, & Kanade 1998). Its primary limitation, that it can only reliably detect upright, frontal faces, is not a major problem for ARGUS, since visitors typically face forward as they walk through the building entrance. The neural network weights were trained to locate faces

from web photographs and are not specialized for the visitor identification task. Since the face detector locates very tightly cropped faces (typically without hair and ears), ARGUS enlarges the recommended region by 140% in each dimension before extracting the face image. A *notifier* agent runs on each ARGUS user's personal workstation and pops up a window with an image of the visitor (as shown in Figure 3). The user may restrict notification to a subset of visitors, and *notifier* agents may join and leave the ARGUS community at any time. The *recognizer* employs a novel algorithm and is fully described below.

Face Recognition

The visitor identification problem is well served by a memory-based face recognition algorithm for the following reasons. First, since the set of visitors is not known *a priori*, the algorithm should be able to accommodate such changes easily. Memory-based algorithms (Atkeson, Moore, & Schaal 1997) do not have an explicit training phase and are ideally suited for incremental training. Second, the training data should be acquired without asking the visitors to pose for photographs under controlled conditions. A collection of several images per visitor, spanning a variety of illumination conditions can be used instead. Fortunately, non-parametric approaches, such as nearest-neighbor matching, may perform well even if these images do not form a single cluster in feature space. Finally, since the face recognition is used only for notification rather than access control, the cost for mis-identification is not severe. Thus, poor initial accuracy on a new visitor may be tolerated by users since recognition accuracy improves as feedback is provided.

The current ARGUS *recognizer* agent uses ARENA, a view-based face recognition system. The training phase is summarized as follows: (1) Minimize illumination variations using histogram equalization (Ballard & Brown 1982); (2) From each training image, generate 10 additional synthetic training images by making small, random perturbations to the original (rotation upto $\pm 5°$, scale upto $\pm 5\%$, and translation upto ± 2 pixels in each direction). (3) Create reduced-resolution (16×16) versions of these images (using simple averaging over rectangular regions) and store them into the face database. Our experiments (see below) indicate that classification speed may be increased by a factor of 11, in exchange for a 5% drop in accuracy, by omitting step (2) when the database contains a large selection of images for each visitor.

The classification phase is similarly straightforward: (1) Pre-process the input image using histogram equalization; (2) Create a reduced-resolution image as discussed above; (3) Return the label of the single nearest-neighbor to the input image, among the stored low-resolution images, using the $L_{0.5}$ metric.[1] (As shown

---

[1] $L_{0.5}(\vec{a} - \vec{b}) \equiv \left(\sum \sqrt{|a_i - b_i|} \right)^2$.

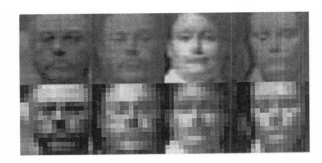

Figure 4: Top row: Sample images of two people, as extracted by the face detector. The image quality is poor due to lighting and camera placement. Also note the variation in appearance due to differences in illumination, pose and facial expression. Bottom row: the corresponding ARENA reduced-resolution images (16×16) pixels.

in (Sim *et al.* 1999), the Euclidean metric, L_2, does not perform as well.) Figure 4 shows sample faces extracted from images by the face detector, along with the corresponding (enlarged) ARENA reduced-resolution images.

Although face recognition is an old problem, it has received much attention in the last few years (Chellappa, Wilson, & Sirohey 1995; Fromherz 1998). The research effort has largely focused on the subproblem of frontal face recognition, and in this domain, techniques based on Principal Components Analysis, popularly termed *eigenfaces* (Turk & Pentland 1991; Pentland, Moghaddam, & Starner 1994) have demonstrated good performance. Most published results report experiments on standard datasets such as ORL (Samaria & Harter 1994) or FERET (Phillips *et al.* 1997).

Our extensive experiments with ARENA and PCA-based methods on both FERET and ORL datasets appear in (Sim *et al.* 1999). Here, we present only the results of one such test: Table 1 summarizes a direct comparison of ARENA with the best published face recognition results (Lawrence *et al.* 1996) on the ORL database. The ORL database contains 10 frontal images of each of 40 people taken under consistent conditions. The three columns in the table indicate how many of these images were placed in the training set (the rest were used for testing). "CN" and "SOM" refer to convolutional neural network and self-organizing map respectively; see (Lawrence *et al.* 1996) for details. One could reasonably argue that a simple system like ARENA achieved this accuracy solely by exploiting the relatively uniform illumination and background conditions present in the standard datasets. Thus, one of our primary motivations for integrating ARENA in ARGUS was to evaluate its accuracy in a more challenging, real-world setting.

Images per person	1	3	5
Eigenface avg per class	61.4%	71.1%	74.0%
Eigenface one per img	61.4%	81.8%	89.5%
PCA+CN	65.8%	76.8%	92.5%
SOM+CN	70.0%	88.2%	96.5%
ARENA $L_{0.5}$	**76.2%**	**92.7%**	**97.4%**

Table 1: Comparison of ARENA with results reported in (Lawrence *et al.* 1996) on the ORL dataset.

Experiments in Visitor Identification

This section summarizes three experiments that evaluate ARGUS on the task of visitor identification. In accordance with the terminology used in the FERET (Phillips *et al.* 1997) test, the set of labeled training images is termed the *gallery* and a test face (which must not appear in the gallery) is termed a *probe*. All of the experiments reported here used face images collected by ARGUS between January and March 1999. Compared to the standard datasets used in the face recognition community, these are very challenging photographs for the following reasons: The images were taken by an outdoor camera in a variety of lighting conditions, at different times during the day, and in very different weather conditions (including snow and rain). Since visitors were not instructed to pose for the camera, their head orientations varied significantly, and many of the individuals were wearing accessories such as hats, hoods or sunglasses. Several of the night images resulted from internal reflections of individuals as they approached the glass doors from the interior of the building. The extracted face image sizes ranged from 33×33 to 100×100 pixels, with a median face image size of 47×47.

Leave-One-Out Tests

In the Leave-One-Out (LOO) tests, each of the faces in the gallery was used as a probe image. The probe and its synthesized images were temporarily removed from the gallery, and ARGUS was asked to identify the individual in the probe. The fraction of probes that were correctly classified is reported as the accuracy. Two versions of this experiment were conducted: one with almost all of the stored faces (973 images from 44 individuals), and the second restricted to photographs of the most common visitors (881 images from 23 individuals). On the first version, ARGUS achieved an overall classification accuracy of 64.1% (60.4% without synthetic images). The second version of this test focused on the task of identifying regular visitors. ARGUS correctly identified 69.7% of probes in this test (65.2% without synthetic images). Two individuals (shown in Figure 4), each with approximately 100 images in the gallery, were correctly identified approximately 90% of the time.

Online Training

The LOO tests described above model the visitor identification task inaccurately in one important respect:

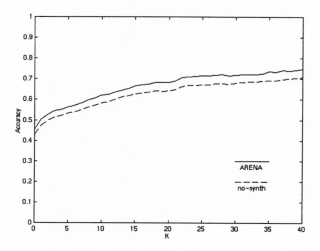

Figure 5: This graph illustrates the variation in face recognition accuracy with respect to k, the minimum number of raw training images per individual present in the database. The dashed line shows accuracy for the version of ARENA without synthesized training data.

when multiple images of a person, all taken within a short span of time, are present in the gallery, a probe selected from this subset is likely to be very similar to a labeled image in the gallery. However, in a real visitor identification task, all of these images would have appeared together as probes and none of the probe images would be eligible to match the other (visually similar) images in its batch. The Online Training experiment addressed this potential criticism by more faithfully simulating the sequence of online training that occurs in ARGUS.

The gallery was initialized to be the empty set. The stored images were successively fed (as probes) to ARGUS in time-stamp order. During the face recognition step, the matching was restricted to images that had been acquired at least five minutes earlier than the probe image's timestamp. This prevented ARENA from exploiting any image similarity that may have existed among images taken at approximately the same time.

The Online Training experiment explored how recognition accuracy varies with k, the minimum number of raw training images (per individual) present in the database (see Figure 5). For example, when $k = 20$, only the 11 most common visitors (each with at least 20 images in the database) are retained in the gallery. Recognition accuracy improves as k increases, showing that ARGUS is fairly accurate over a limited subset of visitors. The second line shows that, without synthetic images, recognition accuracy lags by 3%–5%.

Robustness Tests

ARGUS has been operational at Just Research for the last two months. To increase speed, we have eliminated the synthesized images from the ARENA training set. The current system is quite responsive: the *notifier* typically displays a window within seconds of a visitor's arrival, and occasionally before the visitor has even pressed the doorbell.

The observed recognition accuracy for common visitors (individuals with 10 or more training images) was 53.9%. For the full case, even including visitors for which no training data exists, the observed accuracy was 43.4%.

To explore ARGUS' resilience to distractors, approximately 1500 spurious images of faces collected by a web spider (all labeled as "stranger"), were added to the database of 750 actual camera images. This change only reduced the observed accuracy by 3.1%. Although new visitors and infrequent visitors, with few examples in the database were often misclassified as "stranger", the distractors had surprisingly little detrimental impact on the regular visitor (or overall) recognition accuracy. This strengthens the hypothesis that ARENA's simple view-based nearest-neighbor classification scheme may be more robust than anticipated.

Discussion

Although ARENA achieves excellent results on the standard datasets, its performance on the ARGUS data shows that there is clearly room for improvement. Strategies for improving accuracy can be divided into three classes: higher-quality input data; combining multiple classifiers; and better face recognition techniques.

The current security camera images used for ARGUS (See Figures 3 and 4) are fairly poor-quality for several reasons. First, the visitor only occupies a small area in a wide field of view. Second, during daylight hours, images tends to be severely back-lit because the camera is looking from relative darkness, through a glass door, into direct sunlight. At night, the tinted glass acts as a (partial) mirror, causing reflections of the building interior to appear over visitors' faces. Third, since visitors are not asked to pose for the camera, they may appear anywhere in the image, with their faces oriented suboptimally. In fact, many of the images are of partially-illuminated faces that are difficult for humans to identify.[2] Thus, improving camera position, installing controlled lighting and asking visitors to pose would all improve ARGUS' recognition accuracy (and make the problem less interesting from a research standpoint).

Accuracy could also be improved by combining the outputs from multiple, independent face recognition algorithms using voting. Alternatively, ARGUS could

---

[2]Although they have difficulty identifying the visitor from the face alone, humans are able to make intelligent guesses based on clothing, overall size and time of day.

wait for consistent classification of several successive images before issuing a notification. Either of these schemes offer potential for user customization.

We have also experimented with several variants of ARENA that show promising performance on this task. These include: (1) better preprocessing of input images to compensate for lighting conditions; (2) simple feature extraction using wavelet decomposition; and (3) incorporating texture information using Gabor filters. The ARGUS architecture enables us to evaluate several recognition algorithms in parallel and transparently upgrade the visitor identification system without interruption of service.

Conclusions and Future Work

ARGUS solves a real-world application by combining image processing, machine learning and messaging technologies in a multi-agent framework. However there is still work to be done:

- While we have evaluated the individual components in ARGUS, we plan to get a better idea of the overall system's performance by getting feedback from a larger population of users. We are also interested in observing how the performance of a memory-based face recognizer scales with large populations of visitors.

- Since it is collecting a large dataset of labeled human faces, with multiple images taken over a period of time, ARGUS enables us to easily test different face recognition systems in real-world situations. This dataset may be valuable to others in the face recognition community, and we hope to make it publicly available over the web.

- The ARGUS implementation easily accommodates the addition of new types of agents. For instance, the visitor could be automatically notified if his/her host were unavailable, by an interface agent at the building entrance.

Acknowledgments

The JGram agent system was developed in collaboration with Antoine Brusseau and Ray Pelletier. The ARENA face recognition system was developed in collaboration with Terence Sim, Shumeet Baluja and Matt Mullin. The face detection software was provided by Henry Rowley. Thanks to Gita Sukthankar and Martha Underwood for their valuable feedback on this paper.

References

Atkeson, C.; Moore, W.; and Schaal, S. 1997. Locally weighted learning. *AI Review* 11.

Ballard, D., and Brown, C. 1982. *Computer Vision.* Prentice-Hall.

Chauhan, D., and Baker, A. 1998. JAFMAS: A multi-agent application development system. In *Proceedings of Autonomous Agents.*

Chellappa, R.; Wilson, C.; and Sirohey, S. 1995. Human and machine recognition of faces: A survey. *Proceedings of the IEEE* 83(5).

Fromherz, T. 1998. Face recognition: A summary of 1995–1997. Technical Report ICSI TR-98-027, International Computer Science Institute, Berkeley.

Jeon, H. 1998. An introduction to JATLite. Technical report, CDR, Stanford University. `<http://-java.stanford.edu/java_agent/html/>`.

Lawrence, S.; Giles, C.; Tsoi, A.; and Back, A. 1996. Face recognition: A hybrid neural network approach. Technical Report UMIACS-TR-96-16, University of Maryland.

Pentland, A.; Moghaddam, B.; and Starner, T. 1994. View-based and modular eigenspaces for face recognition. In *Proceedings of Computer Vision and Pattern Recognition.*

Phillips, P.; Moon, H.; Rauss, P.; and Rizvi, S. 1997. The FERET september 1996 database and evaluation procedure. In *Proceedings of Audio and Video-based Biometric Person Authentication.*

Rowley, H.; Baluja, S.; and Kanade, T. 1998. Neural network-based face detection. *IEEE Transactions on Pattern Analysis and Machine Intelligence* 20(1).

Samaria, F., and Harter, A. 1994. Parametrisation of a stochastic model for human face identification. In *Proceedings of IEEE Workshop on Applications on Computer Vision.* ORL database is available at: `<www.cam-orl.co.uk/facedatabase.html>`.

Sim, T.; Sukthankar, R.; Mullin, M.; and Baluja, S. 1999. High-performance memory-based face recognition for visitor identification. Submitted to ICCV-99. An expanded version is available as Just Research TR-1999-001-1.

Sukthankar, R.; Brusseau, A.; and Pelletier, R. 1998. A gentle introduction to developing *JGram* agents. Technical Report JPRC-TR-1998-001-2, Just Research.

Sycara, K. 1998. Multiagent systems. *AAAI AI Magazine* 19(2).

Turk, M., and Pentland, A. 1991. Eigenfaces for recognition. *Journal of Cognitive Neuroscience* 3(1).

Implicative and conjunctive fuzzy rules –
A tool for reasoning from knowledge and examples

Laurent UGHETTO*, Didier DUBOIS** and Henri PRADE**

* IRISA, IUT de Lannion, rue Edouard Branly, BP 150, 22302 LANNION Cedex, FRANCE
e-mail: Laurent.Ughetto@iut-lannion.fr
** IRIT – CNRS, UPS, 118 route de Narbonne, 31062 TOULOUSE Cedex 4, FRANCE
e-mail: {dubois,prade}@irit.fr

Abstract

Fuzzy rule-based systems have been mainly used as a convenient tool for synthesizing control laws from data. Recently, in a knowledge representation-oriented perspective, a typology of fuzzy rules has been laid bare, by emphasizing the distinction between implicative and conjunctive fuzzy rules. The former describe pieces of generic knowledge either tainted with uncertainty or tolerant to similarity, while the latter encode examples-originated information expressing either mere possibilities or how typical situations can be extrapolated.

The different types of fuzzy rules are first contrasted, and their representation discussed in the framework of possibility theory. Then, the paper studies the conjoint use of fuzzy rules expressing knowledge (as fuzzy constraints which restrict the possible states of the world), or gathering examples (which testify the possibility of appearance of some states). Coherence and inference issues are briefly addressed.

Introduction

Fuzzy rules of the form "if X is A, then Y is B", where A and/or B are fuzzy sets, are often advocated as the basic unit used in fuzzy logic-based systems for expressing pieces of knowledge (Zadeh 1992), or modeling data. Although expressiveness is increased by the introduction of fuzzy sets in if-then rules, and by the existence of a wide panoply of possible operators for connecting the membership functions of A and B in the representation of the rules (e.g., (Dubois & Prade 1996)), little attention has been paid to the possible intended semantics of fuzzy rules. Indeed, researchers involved in fuzzy modeling use sets of fuzzy rules as black box tools for the approximation of control laws. In this type of works, the intended meaning of the fuzzy rules as a summary of data meaningful for a human operator is not a major concern. Besides, works more oriented towards knowledge engineering have mainly focused on the study of the properties of the generalized modus ponens, introduced by (Zadeh 1979), which extends inference to fuzzy rules.

However, a formal study (Dubois & Prade 1996) has pointed out that there exist different types of fuzzy rules with very different intended semantics. A first dichotomy must be made between implicative and conjunctive rules. The former, whose representation is of the form $\mu_A \to \mu_B$ (where

$\to$ is a multiple-valued implication operator), express a more or less strict *constraint* on the values allowed for Y, conditioned by the value taken by X. The latter, whose representation is of the form $\mu_A \wedge \mu_B$ (where $\wedge$ denotes a, maybe non-symmetric, conjunction), gather sets of pairs of values which are *known as* (more or less) *feasible* for (X, Y). Thus, given the value for X, implicative (resp. conjunctive) rules *forbid* (resp. *guarantee possible*) values for Y.

This basic distinction is important since expert knowledge can be composed of both restrictions or constraints on the possible values on the one hand (e.g., induced by general laws), and of examples of possible values on the other hand (e.g., induced by observations). In this case, using simultaneously implicative and conjunctive rules allows to represent these two kinds of knowledge in the same rule base. These two types of information may also reveal some incoherence, when a constraint forbids values which are assessed as possible by an example.

Moreover, reasoning in AI is usually driven either from generic knowledge, expressed by, maybe fuzzy, expert rules (e.g., (Ruspini, Bonissone, & Pedrycz 1998), (Ayoun & Grabisch 1997)), or from data or examples, as in Case-Based Reasoning (e.g., (Bonissone & Cheetham 1997) in the fuzzy case), or in KDD which aims at extracting rules from data. In this perspective, distinguishing between the two kinds of rules or, even better, using them simultaneously is also of interest when rules are induced from both positive and negative examples of a concept. Indeed, these examples can lead to conjunctive and implicative rules respectively.

Besides, the choice between several types of fuzzy implication or conjunction operators leads to a more accurate representation of knowledge, where we can further distinguish between rules involving uncertainty in their conclusions, and rules which take benefit of fuzzy sets for expressing tolerance to similarity (without genuine uncertainty).

First, the semantics of the four main kinds of fuzzy rules is presented, emphasizing the difference between implication-based and conjunction-based rules. Then, the conjoint use of these two kinds of rules is studied. Knowledge representation, inference and coherence issues are addressed.

Different fuzzy rules for different information

In possibility theory, the available information is represented by means of possibility distributions which rank-order the possible values in a given referential set or attribute domain. A piece of information "X is (in) A_i", where X is a variable ranging on a domain U, and A_i is a subset of U (maybe fuzzy), is represented by the constraint:

$$\forall u \in U, \ \pi_X(u) \leq \mu_{A_i}(u), \tag{1}$$

where π_X is a possibility distribution restricting the values of X. Several such pieces of information are naturally aggregated conjunctively into:

$$\forall u \in U, \ \pi_X(u) \leq \min_i \mu_{A_i}(u). \tag{2}$$

Then, once all the constraints are taken into account, a minimal specificity principle is applied, which allocates to each value (or state of the world) the greatest possibility degree in agreement with the constraints. It leads to the equality:

$$\forall u \in U, \ \pi_X(u) = \min_i \mu_{A_i}(u). \tag{3}$$

Observation-based information corresponds to the converse inequalities. Let A_i be a subset of values testified as possible for X since all the values in A_i have been observed as possible for X by a source i (A_i may be a fuzzy set if some values are less guaranteed as possible for X). Then, the feasible values for X are restricted by the constraint:

$$\forall u \in U, \ \delta_X(u) \geq \mu_{A_i}(u). \tag{4}$$

If several sources provide examples of possible values for X, all this information is aggregated disjunctively into:

$$\forall u \in U, \ \delta_X(u) \geq \max_i \mu_{A_i}(u). \tag{5}$$

A converse principle, of maximal specificity, expressing that nothing can be guaranteed if it has not been observed, leads to limit the set of feasible values for X to:

$$\forall u \in U, \ \delta_X(u) = \max_i \mu_{A_i}(u). \tag{6}$$

This two-sided approach is applied to possibility distributions representing fuzzy rules in the following.

The semantics of the four main kinds of fuzzy rules, of the form "if X is A_i, then Y is B_i" is now detailed. The difference between implication-based and conjunction-based models is particularly addressed, emphasizing ideas first introduced in (Dubois & Prade 1996) or (Weisbrod 1996).

Implicative rules: restrictions of possible values

In the possibilistic framework (e.g.,(Dubois & Prade 1996)), each piece of knowledge is represented by a possibility distribution π^i on the Cartesian product of the domains of the involved variables, which expresses a (fuzzy) restriction on the possible values of these variables. Thus, considering a knowledge base $\mathcal{K} = \{A_i \rightarrow B_i, \ i = 1, \ldots, n\}$, made of n parallel fuzzy rules (i.e., rules with the same input space U and output space V), each rule "if X is A_i, then Y is B_i" (denoted $A_i \rightarrow B_i$) is represented by a conditional possibility distribution $\pi^i_{Y|X} = \mu_{A_i \rightarrow B_i}$ (the membership function of $A_i \rightarrow B_i$), which is determined according to the semantics of the rule. X is the tuple of input variables (on which information can be obtained) and Y the tuple of non-input variables (on which we try to deduce information). According to (2), the possibility distribution $\pi^\mathcal{K}$ representing the base $\mathcal{K}$ is obtained as the (min-based) conjunction of the $\pi^i_{Y|X}$'s:

$$\pi^\mathcal{K} = \min_{i=1,\ldots,n} \pi^i_{Y|X}. \tag{7}$$

This equation shows that rules are viewed as (fuzzy) constraints since the more rules, the more constraints, the smaller the number of values that satisfy them, and the smaller the levels of possibility. $\pi^\mathcal{K}$ is then an upper bound of possible values.

In order to compute the restriction induced on the values of Y, given a possibility distribution π'_X restricting the values of input variable(s) X, π'_X is combined conjunctively with $\pi^\mathcal{K}$ and then projected on V, the domain of Y:

$$\pi_Y(v) = \sup_{u \in U} \min(\pi^\mathcal{K}(u,v), \pi'_X(u)). \tag{8}$$

This combination-projection is known as *sup-min* composition and often denoted $\circ$. Then, given a set of rules $\mathcal{K}$ and an input A', one can deduce the output B' given by:

$$B' = A' \circ \bigcap_{i=1}^{n} A_i \rightarrow B_i = A' \circ R^\mathcal{K}, \tag{9}$$

with $\mu_{R^\mathcal{K}} = \pi^\mathcal{K}$. The obtained fuzzy set B' is then an upper bound of the possible values for the output variable Y.

If, for a given precise input $A' = \{u^0\}$, the rule $A_i \rightarrow B_i$ does not apply, i.e., $\mu_{A_i}(u^0) = 0$, the *sup-min* composition yields the conclusion $B' = V$, the entire output space. This conclusion is in accordance with the conjunctive combination of the rules. Indeed, when a rule does not apply, it is not supposed to modify the conclusion B' given by the other rules. Thus V plays the role of the neutral element for the aggregation operator. This is why implicative rules are combined conjunctively.

Moreover, this conjunctive combination implies that some output values, which are possible according to some rules, can be forbidden by other ones. Then, the possibility degree $\pi^\mathcal{K}(u,v) = 0$ means that if $X = u$, then v is an impossible value for Y; (u,v) is an impossible pair of input/output values. By contrast, $\pi^\mathcal{K}(u,v) = 1$ denotes ignorance. It means that for the input value $X = u$, no rule in $\mathcal{K}$ forbids the value v for the output variable Y. However, the addition of a new rule to $\mathcal{K}$ (expressing a new piece of knowledge) can lead to forbid this value. A possibility degree $\pi^\mathcal{K}(u,v) > 0$ means that the pair (u,v) is not known as totally impossible, with respect to the current knowledge.

As a consequence, the conclusion $B' = V$, obtained for a given precise input $A' = \{u^0\}$, should not be understood as "each output value is possible (for sure)" but rather as "the knowledge base gives no information, then it leads to no restriction on the values of the output variable", i.e., this case of total ignorance leads to an uncertainty level uniformly equal to 1. In conclusion, a membership degree 0 to B' means impossibility, while a degree 1 represents ignorance.

According to the typology of fuzzy rules proposed in (Dubois & Prade 1996), there are two main kinds of implicative rules, whose prototypes are *certainty* and *gradual* rules.

Certainty rules are of the form "The more X is A, the more certainly Y lies in B", as in "The younger a man, the more certainly he is single", or "The more crowded is the cafeteria in the morning, the more certainly it is about ten o'clock". This statement corresponds to the following conditional possibility distribution modeling the rule:

$$\forall(u,v), \ \pi_{Y|X}(v,u) \leq \max(\mu_B(v), 1 - \mu_A(u)). \tag{10}$$

Clearly, A and B are combined with Kleene-Dienes implication: $a \to b = \max(1 - a, b)$. For a precise input $A' = \{u^0\}$, $\forall v \in V$, $\mu_{B'}(v) \geq 1 - \mu_A(u^0)$ holds, i.e., a uniform level of uncertainty $1 - \mu_A(u^0)$ appears in B' (see Figure 1.a). Then, "Y is B" is certain only to the degree $\mu_A(u^0)$, since values outside B are possible to the complementary degree. A similar behavior is obtained with the implication $a \to b = 1 - a \star (1 - b)$, where $\star$ is the product instead of min.

Gradual rules are of the form "The more X is A, the more Y is B", as in "The redder the tomato, the riper it is". This statement corresponds to the constraint:

$$\forall u \in U, \ \mu_A(u) \star \pi_{Y|X}(v, u) \leq \mu_B(v), \qquad (11)$$

where $\star$ is a conjunction operation. The greatest solution for $\pi_{Y|X}(v, u)$ in (11) (according to the minimal specificity principle which calls for the greatest permitted degrees of possibility) corresponds to the residuated implication:

$$\mu_{A \to B}(u, v) = \sup\{\beta \in [0, 1], \ \mu_A(u) \star \beta \leq \mu_B(v)\} \quad (12)$$

When $\star$ is min, equation (12) corresponds to Gödel implication: $a \to b = 1$ if $a \leq b$, and b if $a > b$.

If only a crisp relation between X and Y is supposed to underlie the rule, it can be modeled by Rescher-Gaines implication: $a \to b = 1$ if $a \leq b$, and 0 if $a > b$.

Applying (9) with one rule, the core of B' is enlarged w.r.t. B (see Figure 1.c), i.e., the less X satisfies A, the larger the set of values in the support of B which are completely possible for Y. This embodies a tolerance to similarity: if the value of X is close to the core of A, then Y is close to the core of B.

Conjunctive rules: guaranteed possible values

In the fuzzy control tradition, rule-based systems are often made of conjunction-based rules, as Mamdani-rules for instance. These rules, denoted $A_i \wedge B_i$, can no more be viewed as constraints, but rather as pieces of data, i.e., as couples of conjointly possible input/output (fuzzy) values. Each rule is then represented by a conjoint possibility distribution:

$$\delta^i_{X,Y} = \mu_{A_i \wedge B_i}.$$

A first justification of this interpretation comes directly from the semantics of the conjunction. Moreover, given a precise input $A' = \{u^0\}$, and a conjunctive rule $A_i \wedge B_i$, if the rule does not apply (i.e., $\mu_{A_i}(u^0) = 0$), then the *sup-min* composition leads to the conclusion $B' = \emptyset$. This implies a disjunctive combination of the conjunctive rules, which appropriately corresponds to an accumulation of data and leads to a set of values whose possibility/feasibility is guaranteed to some minimal degree. Equation (7) is then turned into:

$$\delta_{\mathcal{K}} = \max_{i=1,\dots,n} \delta^i_{X,Y}. \qquad (13)$$

The distribution $\delta_{\mathcal{K}}$ is then a lower bound of possible values.

From a set of conjunctive rules $\mathcal{K}$ and an input A', the *sup-min* composition leads to an output B' given by:

$$B' = A' \circ \bigcup_{i=1}^{n} A_i \wedge B_i = A' \circ R_{\mathcal{K}}. \qquad (14)$$

Thus, a possibility degree $\delta_{\mathcal{K}}(u, v) = 1$ means that if $X = u$, then v is a totally possible value for Y. This is a guaranteed possibility degree. By contrast, $\delta_{\mathcal{K}}(u, v) = 0$

only means that if $X = u$, no rule can guarantee that v is a possible value for Y. By default, v is considered as not possible (since possibility cannot be guaranteed). A membership degree 0 to B' represents ignorance, while a degree 1 means a guaranteed possibility. Thus, a conclusion $B' = \emptyset$ should not be understood as "all the output values are impossible", but as "no output value can be guaranteed".

As for implicative rules, there are two main kinds of conjunctive rules, called *possibility* and *antigradual* rules.

Possibility rules are of the form "the more X is A, the more possible Y lies in B", as in "the more cloudy the sky, the more possible it will rain soon". It corresponds to the following possibility distribution modeling the rule:

$$\forall (u, v), \ \min(\mu_A(u), \mu_B(v)) \leq \delta_{X,Y}(u, v). \qquad (15)$$

These rules, modeled with the conjunction *min*, correspond to the ones introduced by Mamdani and Assilian in 1975.

For an input value u^0 such that $\mu_A(u^0) = \alpha$, a possibility rule expresses that when $\alpha = 1$, B is a set of possible values for Y (to different degrees if B is fuzzy). When $\alpha < 1$, values in B are still possible, but they are guaranteed possible only up to the degree α. To obtain B', the set B is then truncated as shown on Figure 1.b. Finally, if $\alpha = 0$, the rule does not apply, and $B' = \emptyset$ as already said.

Antigradual rules have been obtained by symmetry relations between (10), (11) and (15) (see (Dubois & Prade 1996) for details). They correspond to the inequality:

$$\forall (u, v), \ \mu_A(u) \star (1 - \delta_{X,Y}(u, v)) \geq 1 - \mu_B(v), \quad (16)$$

which can also be written, when the conjunction $\star$ is min:

$$\forall (u, v), \ \mu_A(u) \wedge \mu_B(v) \leq \delta_{X,Y}(u, v), \qquad (17)$$

where $\wedge$ is the non-commutative multiple-valued conjunction: $a \wedge b = b$ if $a + b > 1$ and 0 otherwise.

Such a rule expresses that "the more X is A, the larger the set of possible values for Y is, around the core of B", as in "the more experienced a manager, the wider the set of situations he can manage". For a given input value $A' = \{u^0\}$, this rule means that if $\mu_A(u^0) = 1$, all the values in B are possible for Y ($B' = B$). If $\mu_A(u^0) = \alpha < 1$, the values in B such that $\mu_B(v) < \alpha$, cannot be guaranteed, as shown on Figure 1.d. Such a rule expresses how values which are guaranteed possible can be extrapolated on a closeness basis.

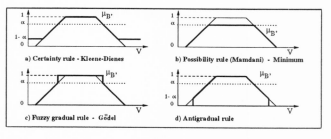

Figure 1: Inference with different kinds of fuzzy rules, and a precise input value $A' = \{u^0\}$ such that $\mu_A(u^0) = \alpha$.

Choosing between different types of rules

Given a fuzzy rule and a precise input $A' = \{u^0\}$, the conclusions B' obtained for each of the four kinds of fuzzy rules presented in the previous sections are depicted on Figure 1. Clearly, the B'''s are obtained from B by applying four different thresholding functions: horizontal ones for certainty and possibility rules (low degrees of possibility are increased, and high degrees are decreased respectively), and vertical ones for gradual and antigradual rules (enlargement of the core, and squeezing of the support respectively). Thus, these four kinds of fuzzy rules can be considered as the basic ones, in particular if the considered triple (conjunction, disjunction, negation) is (min, max, 1-.).

For the valuation scale, only a complete order on the membership degrees is assumed when using *min*, *max*, and the order reversing operation $1 - (.)$. They can belong to a discrete, linearly ordered scale of membership degrees. Then, $1 - (.)$ is just the order reversing map of the scale. When the continuous $[0, 1]$ scale is used as a ratio scale, the *product* can be used instead of *min* for the conjunction. In this case, the behavior of the four kinds of rules can be made continuous, with a similar semantics. Thus, the triple of operators (conjunction, disjunction, negation), has to be chosen depending on the scale of the membership degrees. Besides, the particular case of Lukasiewicz implication $a \rightarrow b = \min(1, 1 - a + b)$ is worth noticing. Indeed, it combines the effects of both certainty and gradual rules (addition of an uncertainty level, and enlargement of the core of the output). Similarly, the bounded sum $a \wedge b = \min(a+b, 1)$ combines the effects of the two conjunctive rules.

It is important to use the right kind of rule for the representation of each piece of knowledge. First, the choice has to be made between implicative and conjunctive models.

For if-then rules expressing constraints, as for instance "if the speed of a car is highly too fast, then the driver must brake strongly", or "if a vegetable is big and orange, then it is a pumpkin", the problem is to determine if it corresponds to certainty or gradual rules. Consider an input $A' = \{u^0\}$ such that $\mu_A(u^0) = \alpha$, with a partial membership degree to the condition part of the rule ($0 < \alpha < 1$). The answer depends on the effect of α on B', as shown on Figure 1.

If the rule expresses typicality, a partial membership degree leads to an uncertainty level on the conclusion, and it is a *certainty rule*. It is the case with the second rule: being big and orange is typical of a pumpkin, if the vegetable is not really big, it can be a pumpkin, but it is not certain. Then the rule expresses "The more a vegetable is big and orange, the more certainly it is a pumpkin". A certainty rule is a rule which holds in normal cases; counter-examples should correspond to rather exceptional situations.

If by contrast the rule expresses a closeness relation, or a gradual evolution of a variable with respect to another, a partial membership degree leads to a less precise conclusion, and it is a *gradual rule*. It is the case for the first rule which expresses that the strength of the braking must be proportional to the speed of the car, and which writes "the higher the over-speed of a car, the stronger the driver must brake".

For rules expressing examples of possible values, as for instance "if someone is very rich, then this person can access to numerous means of transport, including the least common (and most expensive) ones", or "if a city is big, then its shops are open in the evening", the problem is to determine if they correspond to possibility or to antigradual rules. As for implicative rules, the answer depends on the effect of α on B'.

If the rule expresses that the whole conclusion is more or less possible, α leads to a bounding of the possibility degrees of the values in B. It is then a *possibility rule*, as in the second example which expresses the level of possibility that shops are open at "evening" time. It then writes "the bigger a city, the more possible its shops are open in the evening".

By contrast, if the rule only gives a set of more or less possible values, and α leads to the deletion of the less possible values, it is then an *antigradual rule*. It is the case in the first example, which means that the less common means of transport (supposed here to be the most expensive ones) cannot be guaranteed as possible ones for not very rich people. The rule is understood as "the richer someone, the more numerous the means of transport this person can access to".

Sometimes, certainty and possibility rules can be contrasted according to counter-examples. Indeed, the rule "the younger someone, the more it is certain that s/he is single" should be a certainty rule since counter-examples are rather exceptional. By contrast, the rule "the older someone, the more it is possible s/he has been married" is a possibility rule since even if non-married old persons are less numerous than married ones, they are not exceptional at all.

Joint use of implicative and conjunctive rules

Usually, fuzzy rule-based systems are made of parallel rules of the same kind. This section shows the interest of using several kinds of rules in the same rule base, and in particular one kind of implicative with one kind of conjunctive rules.

Thus, the considered knowledge base $\mathcal{K} = \mathcal{K}_{\rightarrow} \cup \mathcal{K}_{\wedge}$ is composed of a set $\mathcal{K}_{\rightarrow} = \{A_i \rightarrow B_i, \ i = 1, \ldots, n\}$ of implicative rules and a set $\mathcal{K}_{\wedge} = \{A_j \wedge B_j, \ j = 1, \ldots, m\}$ of conjunctive rules, where $\rightarrow$ and $\wedge$ are multiple-valued implication and conjunction operators.

Dealing with both fuzzy constraints and examples

Information pertaining to a domain can be composed of both examples of possible values, and of constraints expressing sets of impossible values. To accurately represent this information, examples and constraints must be distinguished, using conjunctive and implicative rules together.

For instance, consider an expert system for assessing the buying price of a one-roomed flat in a big city. The considered input variables are the surface (Size, in m^2), the proximity to the university (Puni) and to the town center (Pcen, in minutes). The output variable is the price (Pr × 1000 dollars). An expert salesman can give the following rules (which are very sketchy, and then not very realistic, for the sake of simplicity).

- the more Puni is (12,15,20,23), the more certainly Pr is (30,35,60,65),
- the more Puni is (12,15,20,23) and the more Pcen is (7,10,20,23), the more certainly Pr is (40,45,55,60),
- the more Puni is (12,15,20,23) and the more Pcen is (20,23,30,33), the more certainly Pr is (30,35,50,55),

where (a,b,c,d) is a trapezoïdal shaped fuzzy set whose support is $]a, d[$, and core $[b, c]$. For instance, (12,15,20,23) means "approximately [15, 20]" (the interval]12, 23[expressing what is meant by approximately) and could be given a linguistic label, as "not too far".

Certainty rules have been chosen here since the given prices are considered as boundaries. The upper bound is the maximal price a buyer would pay for the flat, and the lower bound the minimal price the seller would accept. However, gradual rules, which encode the notion of proximity or resemblance, are also of interest in this context, and particularly if knowledge about "reference flats" is available, as it seems natural to assess: "the more similar two flats, the more similar their prices should be" (see (Dubois *et al.* 1998)).

In this kind of application, another important source of knowledge is the database of recently sold flats. This is also the case in many engineering sciences which are data-driven rather than knowledge-driven. The available information is often under the form of data, each piece of data corresponding to an actually observed situation. By contrast, each model of a knowledge base expressing constraints represents a potentially observable situation only. For instance, consider the following entries of a database:

Size (m^2)	Puni (mn)	Pr (dollars)
30	18	43,000
29	15	47,000
35	13	52,000
32	20	45,000

These data can be summarized by a conjunctive rule, like:

- the more `Size` is (28,30,32,36) and the more `Puni` is (12,15,20,23), the more possibly `Pr` is (40,43,50,55).

This extraction can be done either by a human expert, or an adequate KDD process. It is not discussed here. The membership grades should reflect the typicality of the examples.

Usually, fuzzy rules extracted from rough data are conjunctive ones, since they seem more natural to produce from a (generally incomplete) set of examples. However, data can be composed of both positive and negative examples, and the latter could lead to implicative rules, since they express impossible values. Depending on the applications, negative examples may be rather difficult to find, as in the flat pricing problem, where impossible values are more naturally assessed through constraints provided by experts.

This example shows that both implicative and conjunctive rules are required in order to accurately represent all the available knowledge.

Inference mechanisms

The considered rule base $\mathcal{K}$ contains two kinds of knowledge, represented in $\mathcal{K}_\rightarrow$ and $\mathcal{K}_\wedge$, whose representations $\pi^{\mathcal{K}_\rightarrow}$ and $\delta^{\mathcal{K}_\wedge}$ express an upper and a lower bound of possible values respectively. This is why the fuzzy inference mechanism (the Generalized Modus Ponens) should not be applied directly on $\mathcal{K}$, but separately on $\mathcal{K}_\rightarrow$ and $\mathcal{K}_\wedge$. Then, with only one kind of implicative and one kind of conjunctive rules, no special inference mechanisms is required. The methods consists in partitioning $\mathcal{K}$ into $\mathcal{K}_\rightarrow$ and $\mathcal{K}_\wedge$, and applying the usual algorithms.

With conjunctive rules, it is possible to apply the usual rule by rule inference technique of classical expert systems. Indeed, in equation (14), $\bigcup$ and $\circ$ commute, and then:

$$B'_\wedge = A' \circ \left(\bigcup_{j=1}^m A_j \wedge B_j \right) = \bigcup_{j=1}^m \left(A' \circ A_j \wedge B_j \right).$$

With implicative rules, this approach (called FITA, for first infer then aggregate) should not be applied as soon as the input A' is fuzzy. Only a global inference (called FATI for first aggregate then infer) has to be used, since only the following inclusion generally holds:

$$B'_\rightarrow = A' \circ \left(\bigcap_{i=1}^n A_i \rightarrow B_i \right) \subseteq \bigcap_{i=1}^n \left(A' \circ A_i \rightarrow B_i \right).$$

However, for certainty rules, the addition of well-chosen redundant rules allow to design a rule by rule inference method (Ughetto, Dubois, & Prade 1997) and, for gradual rules, specific inference techniques have been proposed.

For a (maybe fuzzy) input A', the rule base $\mathcal{K}$ leads to a double information: an upper bound $B'_\rightarrow$ and a lower bound $B'_\wedge$ of the possible values for the variable Y. With these two bounds, usual *defuzzification* methods are no longer appropriate when a precise output is required. An intuitive method consists in choosing one of the values v which maximize both $\mu_{B'_\rightarrow}(v)$ and $\mu_{B'_\wedge}(v)$. Otherwise, the two bounds provide an accurate view of the possible range of values for Y.

If this choice involves an optimization criterion, the output value can be chosen according to a notion of higher order uncertainty. In our example, if a flat sizing 31 m^2 and at 18 mn from university is to be sold, the previous rules give the range of prices depicted on Figure 2. It means that we are sure to sell it between 43 and 50. It is also possible, but not certain, to sell it between 55 and 60, and one cannot expect more than 65. In order to sell the flat very rapidly, the price can range in [35, 40]. If only money (and not time) is involved, the price can be then around 60.

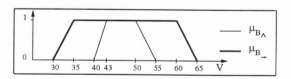

Figure 2: Possible prices for a flat (thousand dollars)

The inference mechanism becomes less simple when the input A' is also ill-known, and only bounded by $A'_\rightarrow$ and $A'_\wedge$. This is the case in particular when rules have to be chained. Here again, the natural approach consists in using $A'_\rightarrow$ with $\mathcal{K}_\rightarrow$ for obtaining $B'_\rightarrow$, and $A'_\wedge$ with $\mathcal{K}_\wedge$ for obtaining $B'_\wedge$.

Accurate representation of what is known

If the boundaries of the conclusion, namely $\{B'_\rightarrow, B'_\wedge\}$ are more difficult to handle than a usual fuzzy set B', they allow for an accurate representation of what is known about the possible values of Y. With only one kind of fuzzy rules, the membership degree of an output value v to the conclusion B' can be interpreted as follows. For implicative rules:

- $\mu_{B'}(v) = 0$ means that v is impossible,

- $\mu_{B'}(v) = 1$ means ignorance, as no rule forbids v. By default, v is considered possible.

For conjunctive rules:

- $\mu_{B'}(v) = 1$ means that v is guaranteed to be possible,
- $\mu_{B'}(v) = 0$ means ignorance, as no rule can guarantee v. By default, v is considered not possible.

Now, for sets containing both implicative and conjunctive rules, the case of ignorance is no more ambiguous since:

- $\mu_{B'_{\rightarrow}}(v) = 1$ and $\mu_{B'_{\wedge}}(v) = 1$ means that v is guaranteed to be completely possible (certainly possible),
- $\mu_{B'_{\rightarrow}}(v) = 1$ and $\mu_{B'_{\wedge}}(v) = 0$ means ignorance on v which is neither guaranteed, nor forbidden,
- $\mu_{B'_{\rightarrow}}(v) = 0$ and $\mu_{B'_{\wedge}}(v) = 0$ means that v is certainly impossible.

Absence of information is no more interpreted *by default* as possibility or impossibility, but expresses ignorance only.

Coherence checking

Validation is an important issue for rule-based systems, in order to avoid inconsistent conclusions especially. In the possibilistic framework, a set of rules is said to be coherent if for all (allowed) input variable, there is at least one output value totally compatible with the input value and the rules:

The rule base $\mathcal{K} = \{A_i \rightarrow B_i, i = 1, \dots, n\}$ is coherent if $\forall u \in U$, $\sup_{v \in V} \pi^{\mathcal{K}}(u, v) = 1$.

According to this definition, it is easy to show that only implicative rules can be incoherent. Indeed, conjunctive rules represent only a lower bound of the possibility distribution $\delta^{\mathcal{K}}$. Thus, it is not possible to prove that $\delta^{\mathcal{K}}(u, v) < 1$, and the rule base $\mathcal{K}_{\wedge}$ is always coherent. Examples cannot be incoherent, while constraints can be. Far from being a drawback, it can be considered as a good property of implicative rules. Since coherence checking algorithms have been designed (see for instance (Dubois, Prade, & Ughetto 1997)), potential incoherence can be detected and removed.

However, checking the coherence of $\mathcal{K}_{\rightarrow}$ is not sufficient to ensure the coherence of $\mathcal{K}$. Indeed, for a given precise input, an output value can be guaranteed possible by a conjunctive rule and forbidden by an implicative rule. It is then necessary to check the coherence of $\mathcal{K}_{\wedge}$ with respect to $\mathcal{K}_{\rightarrow}$.

A set of rules $\mathcal{K} = \mathcal{K}_{\rightarrow} \cup \mathcal{K}_{\wedge}$ is said to be coherence if $\mathcal{K}_{\rightarrow}$ is coherent and if $\mathcal{K}_{\wedge}$ is coherent w.r.t. $\mathcal{K}_{\rightarrow}$, i.e., if:

$$\begin{cases} \forall u \in U, \exists v \in V \text{ such that } \pi^{\mathcal{K}_{\rightarrow}}(u, v) = 1, \\ and \quad \forall (u, v) \in U \times V, \pi^{\mathcal{K}_{\rightarrow}}(u, v) \geq \delta^{\mathcal{K}_{\wedge}}(u, v). \end{cases}$$

Efficient coherence checking algorithms for sets of parallel certainty or gradual rules have been proposed in (Dubois, Prade, & Ughetto 1997). They can be used to validate $\mathcal{K}_{\rightarrow}$.

The coherence of $\mathcal{K}_{\wedge}$ w.r.t. $\mathcal{K}_{\rightarrow}$ is rather simple to check. Indeed, according to the following propositions, it comes down to check the coherence of each rule $A_j \wedge B_j$ in $\mathcal{K}_{\wedge}$ w.r.t. each rule $A_i \rightarrow B_i$ in $\mathcal{K}_{\rightarrow}$ such that $A_i \cap A_j \neq \emptyset$:

- *A set of conjunctive rules $\mathcal{K}_{\wedge} = \{A_j \wedge B_j, j = 1, \dots, m\}$ is coherent with respect to a set of implicative rules $\mathcal{K}_{\rightarrow} = \{A_i \rightarrow B_i, i = 1, \dots, n\}$ if and only if each rule in $\mathcal{K}_{\wedge}$ is coherent w.r.t. each rule in $\mathcal{K}_{\rightarrow}$.*

- *A conjunctive rule $A_j \wedge B_j$ and an implicative rule $A_i \rightarrow B_i$ are always coherent if $A_i \cap A_j = \emptyset$.*

Coherence conditions can be defined for the different pairs of rules (see (Ughetto 1997)).

Conclusion

This paper has advocated the interest of distinguishing between different kinds of rules for representing data and knowledge, which can be appropriately modeled in the fuzzy sets and possibility theory framework. It has been also shown how to check the coherence of sets of different types of rules and how to use them in inference. The differences between the various kinds of fuzzy rules are meaningful from a cognitive modeling point of view. Each kind, either constraint-based or example-based, requires a separate processing, leading to two conclusions which can be then fused, and whose coherence can be discussed. The typology of fuzzy rules should be also relevant when trying to extract rules from data in learning. The distinction between data and knowledge is discussed in a more general logical setting by (Dubois, Hajek, & Prade 1997).

References

Ayoun, A., and Grabisch, M. 1997. Tracks real-time classification based on fuzzy rules. *Int J of Int Syst* 12:865–876.

Bonissone, P., and Cheetham, W. 1997. Financial application of fuzzy case-based reasoning to residential property valuation. In *Proc. of the 6th IEEE Int. Conf. on Fuzzy Syst. (FUZZ-IEEE'97)*, 37–44.

Dubois, D., and Prade, H. 1996. What are fuzzy rules and how to use them. *Fuzzy Sets and Syst.* 84(2):169–186.

Dubois, D.; Esteva, F.; Garcia, P.; Godo, L.; de Mantaras, R. L.; and Prade, H. 1998. Fuzzy sets in case-based reasoning. *Int. J. of Int. Syst.* 13:345–373.

Dubois, D.; Hajek, P.; and Prade, H. 1997. Knowledge-driven versus data-driven logics. Technical Report 97-46R, IRIT. To appear in *J. of Logic, Language and Information*.

Dubois, D.; Prade, H.; and Ughetto, L. 1997. Checking the coherence and redundancy of fuzzy knowledge bases. *IEEE Trans. on Fuzzy Syst.* 5(3):398–417.

Ruspini, E.; Bonissone, P.; and Pedrycz, W., eds. 1998. *Hanbook of fuzzy computation*. Institute of Physics Publ.

Ughetto, L.; Dubois, D.; and Prade, H. 1997. Efficient inference algorithms with fuzzy inputs. In *Proc. of the 6th IEEE Int. Conf. on Fuzzy Syst. (FUZZ-IEEE'97)*, 567–572.

Ughetto, L. 1997. Utilisations conjointes de différents types de règles floues. In *Proc. 7⁰ Renc. Franc. sur la Log. Floue et Appl. (LFA'97)*, 269–276. Cépaduès, Toulouse.

Weisbrod, J. 1996. A combined approach to fuzzy reasoning. In *Proc. of the 4th Europ. Conf. on Intel. Tech. and Soft Comp. (EUFIT'96)*, 554–557.

Zadeh, L. 1979. A theory of approximate reasoning. In J.E. Hayes, D. M., and Mikulich, L., eds., *Machine Intell.* NY, USA: Elsevier. 149–194.

Zadeh, L. 1992. The calculus of fuzzy if-then rules. *AI Expert* 7(3):23–27.

Knowledge Acquisition

Does Prior Knowledge Facilitate the Development of Knowledge-based Systems?

Paul Cohen

Cohen@cs.umass.edu

U. of Massachusetts

Vinay Chaudhri

chaudhri@ai.sri.com

SRI International

Adam Pease

apease@teknowledge.com

Teknowledge

Robert Schrag

schrag@dc.iet.com

IET Inc.

Abstract

One factor that affects the rate of knowledge base construction is the availability and reuse of *prior knowledge* in ontologies and domain-specific knowledge bases. This paper reports an empirical study of reuse performed in the first year of the High Performance Knowledge Bases (HPKB) initiative. The study shows that some kinds of prior knowledge help more than others, and that several factors affect how much use is made of the knowledge.

Introduction

One hypothesis of recent knowledge sharing efforts has been that significant productivity gains can be realized by reusing prior knowledge in ontologies and domain-specific knowledge bases (Patil et al. 1992). Until now, there have been no systematic studies of knowledge reuse. This paper reports an empirical study performed in the first year of the High Performance Knowledge Bases (HPKB) initiative sponsored by the Defense Advanced Research Projects Agency (Cohen et al., 1998)[1]. By comparing the efforts of two HPKB groups under different conditions, we find that prior knowledge in the form of ontologies does help, though many factors affect how much it helps. This work also introduces metrics and methods for evaluating the contribution of prior knowledge to knowledge-based systems.

By *prior knowledge* we mean the knowledge one has available in an ontology or knowledge base prior to developing a knowledge-based system. Several large ontologies have been developed including Cyc (Lenat,1995), Sensus (Knight, 1994), Ontolingua (Farquhar, 1996). All these systems contain hierarchies of knowledge. At the upper levels, one finds knowledge that

is general to many applications, such as knowledge about movement, animate agents, space, causality, mental states, and so on. The lower levels contain knowledge specific to domains; for example, rules for inferring the effects of tactical military operations. Bridging general and specific knowledge, one finds middle-level knowledge (Lenat and Guha, 1990); collections of terms and axioms about phenomena such as human physiology, more general than a particular medical expert system but less general than, say, knowledge about physical systems. In addition to hierarchies of terms, all the ontologies cited above contain *axioms* or *rules*, for instance, "if x is an educational institution then x pays no taxes"; and inference methods such as resolution or more specialized forms of theorem-proving. Axioms and rules confer a functional kind of *meaning* on the terms they contain, that is, the meaning of a term is the things one can legitimately say (infer) about it.

One claim of ontologists is that it is easier to build a domain-specific knowledge base **KB** inside an ontology **O**, or informed by **O**, than without **O**. Some of the ways that **O** can help are illustrated in Figure 1. First, a term **p** that you wish to add to **KB** might already exist in **O**, saving you the trouble of adding it. Second, axioms or rules relating to **p** might already exist in **O**, saving you the trouble of thinking of them and encoding them. Third, within **O**, **p** might be a subclass of **v**, so you also have the benefit of axioms about **v** inherited through **p**.

Now suppose you want to add a concept **p'** to **KB**, and **p'** is not exactly **p**, but is similar in some respects. For instance, **p** might be part of a microtheory about economics, and **p'** might belong to a microtheory about fluid flows, but both **p** and **p'** represent the concept "source." More generally, suppose the *structure* of the theory of economics in **O** parallels the structure of the theory of fluids that you are trying to build in **KB**. Thus, a fourth way that **O** can help you to build **KB** is to help you structure the theory in **KB**. Designing the structure of microtheories is very time consuming, so this kind of help may be the most important of all.

[1] See http://www.teknowledge.com/HPKB for a collection of documents about HPKB including the Challenge Problem specifications.

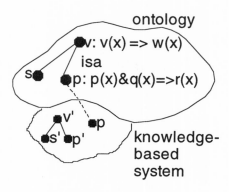

ontology

isa

knowledge-based system

Figure 1. Some ways an ontology O can help one build a knowledge base KB.

Unfortunately it is difficult to assess experimentally how the structure of **O** helps one build **KB**s with similar structure, so we focus here on the first three ways that **O** can help one build **KB**.

A Metric

Suppose one wishes to add an axiom, "If x is a nation then x maintains an army," to **KB**. This axiom contains three terms, **nation**, **maintains**, and **army**. Suppose the first two terms already exist in **O** but **army** does not. As two thirds of the terms required to add the axiom to **KB** exist in **O**, we say the *support* provided by **O** in this case is 2/3. In general, every item i one wishes to add to **KB** contains n(i) terms, k(i) of which are already in **O**, and support is $s(i)=k(i)/n(i)$. Of course, adding **army** to **O** changes **O**, and the support offered by **O** for future axioms might be higher because **army** was added. Thus, support is indexed by versions of the ontology: $s(i,j)=k(i,j)/n(i)$ is the support provided by version **O**j of the ontology for concept i.

Experiment Design

We evaluated the support provided by ontologies during a month-long process called the *Crisis Management Challenge Problem* (CMCP). The CMCP was designed by a team led by IET, Inc. and PSR Corp. Two integrated knowledge-based systems were developed to answer questions about international crises, such as, "What will the US response be if Iran closes the Strait of Hormuz?" (Cohen et al., 1998). The systems were developed by teams led by Teknowledge and SAIC. The CMCP had several phases:

1. Some months before any testing began, *a crisis scenario* was released. The scenario bounded the domain and thus the scope of the problems to be solved by the Teknowledge and SAIC systems.
2. Several weeks before testing, a batch of sample questions (SQs) was released.
3. On the first day of the evaluation, a batch of 110 test questions, TQA, was released, and the Teknowledge

and SAIC systems were immediately tested. After four days for improvements, the systems were re-tested on TQA.
4. Batch TQB was released at the time of the retest. The purpose of TQB, which contained questions similar to those in TQA, was to check the generality of the improvements made to the systems.
5. After a brief respite, a change was made to the crisis scenario, increasing the scope of the problems that the Teknowledge and SAIC systems would have to solve. Several days were allowed for knowledge entry prior to the release of a new batch of questions, TQC, reflecting the new scope. The systems were tested immediately.
6. Four days were allowed to extend the systems to the new crisis scenario, then the systems were re-tested on TQC. To check the generality of these extensions, the systems were also tested on batch TQD, which was similar to TQC.

One of the methodological innovations of this experiment was to generate all the batches of questions from a *question grammar* – a set of parameterized questions, or PQs – which had been made available to the participants in the experiment several months before testing began. Batches SQ, TQA and TQB were generated by one grammar. The grammar was extended to reflect the change in the crisis scenario and used to generate batches TQC and TQD. Figure 2 shows one of the parameterized questions (PQ53) from the grammar. Many billions of questions could be generated by the question grammar, so it would not have made sense to develop systems to solve particular questions; however, by getting the PQs early, the system developers could limit the scope of their systems to the subjects mentioned in the PQs (e.g., terrorist attacks, EconomicSector, etc.)

PQ53 [During/After <TimeInterval>,] what {risks, rewards} would <InternationalAgent> face in <InternationalActionType>?
    <InternationalActionType> =
        {[exposure of its] {supporting, sponsoring} <InternationalAgentType in <InternationalAgent2>, successful terrorist attacks against <InternationalAgent2>'s <EconomicSector>, <InternationalActionType>, taking hostage citizens of <InternationalAgent2>, attacking targets <SpatialRelationship> <InternationalAgent2> with <Force>}
    <InternationalAgentType> =
        {terrorist group, dissident group, political party, humanitarian organization}

Figure 2. A parameterized question suitable for generating sample questions and test questions.

In the following section we analyze how prior ontology – what was available before SQs, TQA and TQC were released – supported the development of the Teknowledge and SAIC systems. The former system was based on Cyc, and much of its development was done at Cycorp, so we call it Cyc/Tek here. The SAIC system was a collection of component systems, none of which answered all the questions in any test batch. The one we analyze here, developed by SRI International, answered roughly 40 of the 110 questions in each batch; we lack data for the other components of the SAIC system. To compare the Cyc/Tek and SRI systems properly we will report two sets of results for Cyc/Tek, one for all the test questions and another for the subset of questions answered by the SRI system.

The Cyc/Tek and SRI systems also differed in the prior ontologies available to them. Long before testing began, Cycorp, the developers of Cyc, released their *upper ontology* (UO), which contains very general class names; subclass relationships; instance-type relationships; relation names and their argument types; function names, their argument types, and the types of value they return; as well as English documentation of every class, function and relation; and a mapping to terms in the Sensus ontology developed by ISI. Whereas the SRI team had access to the UO, only, Cyc/Tek had access to all of Cyc.

Results

The performance of the Teknowledge and SAIC integrated systems is analyzed in (Cohen et al., 1998). Performance is not the focus of this paper – support provided by ontologies is – but two performance results set some context for the following discussion of support and reuse: Both systems performed better on the sample questions (SQs) than on TQA, and both performed better when re-tested on TQA and TQC than on the corresponding tests performed four days earlier. In the four days between test and retest, significant improvements were made to the systems. The question is, how much did the prior ontologies help in making these improvements?

We present results for two kinds of knowledge development. One is the development of knowledge sufficient to encode in a formal language the test questions in each batch, the other is the development of knowledge to answer the test questions. Results for the former are summarized in Table 1. The columns of the table represent the SRI system, which was tested on roughly 40 questions in each batch of 110; the Cyc/Tek system tested on the same questions as the SRI system; and the Cyc/Tek system tested on all 110 questions in each batch. Three numbers are reported for each system: n is the number of terms needed to encode all the questions attempted (i.e., roughly 40 or 110); k is the number of terms available in a prior ontology; and s is the ratio of k to n. The rows of Table 1

represent the batches of questions and the help provided by different prior ontologies.

For example, SQ | UO means "the help provided by the upper ontology (UO) in encoding the sample questions (SQ)." One can see in this row that SRI needed 104 terms to encode roughly 40 of the sample questions, and 22 of these terms were found in the UO, so the help provided by the UO is 22/104 =.21. Encoding the questions in SQ required a number of terms to be added to the ontologies, and these terms were available to help encode questions in TQA and TQC. The notation TQA | UO denotes the help provided by the UO *only*, whereas TQA | SQ denotes the help provided by *everything encoded up through* SQ. Similarly, TQC | TQA denotes the help provided in encoding the questions in TQC by the terms in the ontology including those defined for SQ and TQA. For the Cyc/Tek system, our data support only a simpler distinction, between UO terms and non-UO terms, the latter category including the entire Cyc ontology and all terms defined while encoding the test questions. The category of non-UO terms is reported in rows labeled "Cyc" in Table 1. For instance, 292 terms were required by Cyc/Tek to encode the 110 questions in TQA, 289 of them were available in Cyc, including some defined when the sample questions SQ were added. Note that SRI used only the public release of the upper ontology, so all rows in which questions were encoded with the help of Cyc are marked n/a for SRI.

		SRI			Cyc/Tek(40)			Cyc/Tek(110)		
		n	k	s	n	k	s	n	k	s
SQ	UO	10	22	.2	14	60	.4	24	97	..
SQ	Cyc	n/	n/	n/	14	10	.7	24	18	.7
TQA	UO	10	20	.1	15	67	.4	29	11	.4
TQA	SQ	10	81	.7	n/	n/	n/	n/	n/	n/
TQA	Cyc	n/	n/	n/	15	15	1.	29	28	.9
TQC	UO	10	16	.1	15	71	.4	30	11	.3
TQC	TQ	10	82	.7	n/	n/	n/	n/	n/	n/
TQC	Cyc	n/	n/	n/	15	15	1.	30	39	.9

Table 1. Support (s) provided by ontologies for the task of encoding test questions.

The six reuse rates from Table 1 are presented graphically in Figure 3. Reuse from the UO on all test question batches clusters in the lower half of the graph. The highest levels of reuse from the UO are achieved by Cyc/Tek on the roughly 40 test questions encoded by SRI. The upper half of the graph represents reuse from the UO *and* all of Cyc in the Cyc/Tek conditions; and reuse of terms defined for earlier test question batches, in the SRI condition.

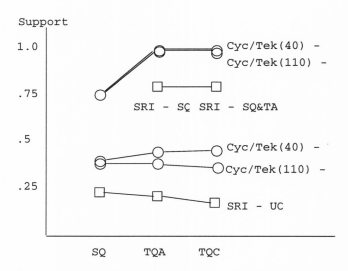

Figure 3. Support rates for SRI and Cyc/Tek. Lines denoted "UO" represent reuse of terms from the upper ontology. SRI-SQ denotes SRI's reuse of terms from the UO and the SQ-encoding effort; SRI-SQ&TA adds in terms defined during the TA-encoding effort. Cyc/Tek(40)-all and Cyc/Tek(110)-all denote reuse of terms from all of Cyc.

Cyc/Tek had higher support numbers in all conditions than SRI, meaning they reused more terms in their prior ontologies than SRI did. However, we have broken the data into support provided to Cyc/Tek by *all* of Cyc vs. support provided by just the upper ontology, which SRI had. For example, the first row of Table 1 shows that to encode roughly 40 sample questions, SRI required 104 terms of which it found 22 in the UO; whereas Cyc/Tek required 143 terms to encode the *same* questions, and found 60 in the UO. Similarly, Cyc/Tek required 246 terms to encode all 110 sample questions, and found 97 in the UO.

Cyc/Tek required slightly more terms to encode test questions (2.86 terms/question) than SRI (2.62 terms/question), and got more support from prior ontologies. For example, for Cyc/Tek to encode the roughly 40 questions in the TQA batch that SRI encoded, they required 150 terms, all of which existed in the Cyc ontology.

In one respect, the SRI and Cyc/Tek results are very similar. The reuse rate of terms *not* in the upper ontology – terms in Cyc or terms developed for earlier batches of test questions – was 55%-60% for both SRI and Cyc/Tek, across question batches TQA and TQC. This result is shown in Table 2. The columns in this table represent the number of terms needed to encode a test batch, N; the number found in the upper ontology, K(UO); the number found elsewhere, K(other); and the ratios of K(UO) and K(other) to N. That is, the support provided by terms in the upper ontology is s(UO)=K(UO)/N, while the support provided by other prior ontology is s(other)=K(other)/N.

Note that s(other) ranges from .54 to .62 for test batches TQA and TQC. (Cyc/Tek also found support for coding up the SQ questions from parts of Cyc other than UO; these support figures are .31 and .40 for the 40 and 110 test questions, respectively.) For TQA and TQC, the overall rates of reuse of non-UO terms for Cyc/Tek and SRI were .58 and .60, respectively; whereas the overall reuse of UO terms for Cyc/Tek and SRI was .41 and .17, respectively. Thus, much of the difference in reuse statistics between SRI and Cyc/Tek is due to their exploitation of the upper ontology. Said differently, 22% of the terms SRI reused came from the upper ontology while the figure was 42% for Cyc/Tek.

	N	K(UO)	K(other)	S(UO)	S(other)
SRI TQA	104	20	61	.19	.59
SRI TQC	106	16	66	.15	.62
CycTek SQ(40)	143	60	45	.42	.31
CycTek TQA(40)	150	67	83	.45	.55
CycTek TQC(40)	153	71	82	..46	.54
CycTek SQ(110)	246	97	85	.39	.40
CycTek TQA(11	292	118	171	.40	..58
CycTek TQA(11	304	117	185	.38	.60

Table 2. Support provided by terms in UO and terms from other prior knowledge bases and ontologies for the task of encoding test questions.

In addition to encoding test questions, Cyc/Tek and SRI developed knowledge to answer the questions. This knowledge, called *axioms* generically, is composed of terms, so we can ask how prior ontologies helped the development of axioms. As before the relevant metric is s(i,j)=k(i,j)/n(i), only here, n(i) denotes the number of terms required to encode the ith axiom.

SRI provided data on how ontologies supported writing axioms. The rows of Table 3 represent the phases of the experiment and the source of prior ontology. The first row, SQ I UO shows that 1703 axioms were encoded to solve the sample questions SQ, and these axioms required 461 terms, of which 51 were in the upper ontology, UO, for a support value of 0.11. The second row shows that in the four days between the test and retest on batch TQA, 123 axioms were encoded, requiring 195 terms. 30 of these terms were found in the UO. The third row shows that 109 of the 195 terms were found in *all* the ontology developed prior to the test on TQA, namely UO *and* SQ. A comparison of the second and third rows shows that 109–30=79 reused terms came from SQ. The same pattern repeats in the two remaining phases of the experiment: After the scenario modification but before TQC, 1485 axioms were added to the SRI system. These required 583 terms of which 40 existed in the UO and 254 were found in the UO, SQ, and TQA prior ontologies. Similarly, between the test and retest on TQC, 215 terms were required for 304 axioms; only 24 of these existed in the UO, and 100 more were found in the ontologies developed after the UO.

It is unclear why prior ontologies provided significantly less support for encoding axioms than for encoding test questions. In both cases the support came in the form of terms, but why are the terms required to define axioms less likely to be in a prior ontology than the terms needed for test questions? One possibility is that test questions include fewer terms that represent *individuals* (e.g., #$HassiMessaoud-Refinery) than do axioms, so terms in test questions are less specific and more likely to exist in a prior ontology than terms in axioms. We will be looking at our data more closely to see whether this is the case.

	SRI			
	Axiom	n	k	s
SQ | UO	1703	461	51	.1
From TQA to TQA retest	UO3	195	30	.1
From TQA to TQA retest	SQ3	195	109	.5
From TQA retest to TQC	1485	583	40	.0
From TQA retest to TQC	TQA5	583	254	.4
From TQC to TQC retest	304	215	24	.1
From TQC to TQC retest	TQC	215	124	.5

Table 3: SRI measured the number of terms required to add problem-solving axioms to their system, and the reuse of terms from the UO and subsequent ontology efforts.

Discussion

Does prior knowledge in ontologies and domain-specific knowledge bases facilitate the development of knowledge-based systems? Our results suggest that the answer depends on the kind of prior knowledge, who is using it, and what it is used for. The HPKB upper ontology, 3000 very general concepts, was less useful than other ontologies, including Cyc and ontologies developed specifically for the crisis management domain. This said, Cyc/Tek made more effective use of the upper ontology: 42% of the terms it reused came from there whereas 22% of the terms SRI reused came from the upper ontology. Why is this? One reason is probably that Cycorp developed the upper ontology and was more familiar with it than SRI. Knowledge engineers tend to define terms for themselves if they cannot quickly find the terms in an available ontology. Once this happens – once a term is defined anew instead of reused – the knowledge base starts to diverge from the available ontology, because the new definition will rarely be identical with the prior one. Another reason for disparity in reuse of the upper ontology is that SRI preferred their own definitions of concepts to the available ones.

As to the uses of prior knowledge, our data hint at the possibility that prior knowledge is less useful for encoding axioms than it is for encoding test questions.

Whereas reuse of the upper ontology depends on who is using it, other ontologies seem to account for a roughly constant (60%) rate of reuse, irrespective of who developed these ontologies. For SRI, these ontologies were just those developed for batches of questions SQ, TQA, TQB, TQC and TQD. To be concrete, 62% of the terms required for TQC were defined while encoding SQ, TQA and TQB. The picture is a bit cloudier for Cyc/Tek because they had the Cyc ontology throughout, and we have not yet analyzed whether the overall 60% non-UO reuse came from terms defined for previous batches or from Cyc.

Despite this ambiguity we speculate that in the process of building a domain-specific knowledge-based system, the rate of reuse of terms defined earlier in the process is roughly 60%. Although the rate of reuse of terms from very general ontologies may be significantly lower (e.g., 20%–40%), the real advantage of these ontologies probably comes from helping knowledge engineers organize their knowledge bases along sound ontological lines. It is essential for the ontology community to collect data on this use of general ontologies.

Conclusion

Although the idea of knowledge sharing has been in the literature for many years (e.g., Patil et al. 1992), the current paper presents the first empirical results quantifying ontology reuse. Many questions remain. Our data are crude summaries of reuse of terms, they do not tell us much about the work that knowledge engineers do when they build domain-specific knowledge bases. How long will a knowledge engineer hunt for a relevant term or axiom in a prior ontology? How rapidly do knowledge bases diverge from available ontologies if knowledge engineers don't find the terms they need in the ontologies? By what process does a knowledge engineer reuse not an individual term but a larger fragment of an ontology, including axioms? How does a very general ontology inform the design of knowledge bases, and what factors affect whether knowledge engineers take advantage of the ontology? Why do prior ontologies apparently provide less support for encoding axioms than for encoding test questions? Finally, will the results we report here generalize to domains other than crisis management and research groups other than SRI and Cyc/Tek? We expect to answer some of these questions retrospectively by analyzing other data from the first year of the HPKB program and prospectively by designing experiments for the second year.

Acknowledgments

Doug Lenat and Cycorp shared the Cyc upper ontology, and provided data, advice, expertise and encouragement during all phases of the work reported here. SAIC provided support for SRI's effort. SRI, Teknowledge, IET and the University of Massachusetts were supported by the DARPA High Performance Knowledge Bases project, managed by David Gunning and Murray Burke.

References

Paul Cohen, Robert Schrag, Eric Jones, Adam Pease, Albert Lin, Barbara Starr, David Gunning, and Murray Burke. The DARPA High Performance Knowledge Bases Project. AI Magazine, Winter, 1998. pp. 25-49

Farquhar, A. Fikes, R., Rice, J. 1997. A collaborative tool for ontology contruction. International Journal of Human Computer Studies. Vol. 46. pp 707 - 727

Knight, K., and Luk, S. 1994. Building a large-scale knowledge base for machine translation. AAAI-94.

Lenat D. 1995. Artificial Intelligence. Scientific American. September.

Lenat D. and Guha R. 1990. Building Large Knowledge based system. Reading MA Addison Wesley.

Patil, R., Fikes, R., Patel-Schneider, P., Mackay, D., Finin, T., Gruber, T., and Neches, R. 1992. The DARPA Knowledge Sharing Effort: Progress Report. In KRR-92. pp 777 – 788.

Representing Problem-Solving for Knowledge Refinement

Susan Craw and Robin Boswell

School of Computer and Mathematical Sciences
The Robert Gordon University
Aberdeen AB25 1HG, UK
Email: s.craw,rab@scms.rgu.ac.uk

Abstract

Knowledge refinement tools seek to correct faulty knowledge based systems (KBSs) by identifying and repairing potentially faulty rules. The goal of the KRUSTWorks project is to provide a source of refinement components from which specialised refinement tools tailored to the needs of a range of KBSs are built. A core refinement algorithm reasons about the knowledge that has been applied, but this approach demands general knowledge structures to represent the reasoning of a particular problem solving episode. This paper investigates some complex forms of rule interaction and defines a knowledge structure encompassing these. The approach has been applied to KBSs built in four shells and is demonstrated on a small example that incorporates some of the complexity found in real applications.

Introduction

Knowledge refinement tools support the development and maintenance of knowledge-based decision-support systems by assisting with the debugging of faulty knowledge based systems (KBSs) and the updating of KBSs whose application environment is gradually changing, so that the knowledge they contain remains effective and current.

Many knowledge acquisition and refinement systems have been developed for particular expert system shells (Murphy & Pazzani 1994) or logic programming languages (Richards & Mooney 1995; Ourston & Mooney 1994), or even specific applications. In contrast, we aim to develop a refinement framework that defines a set of generic KBS concepts and refinement steps. We are also implementing an extensible toolkit that provides refinement components to achieve these steps. To this end we are designing an internal knowledge structure that will allow the core knowledge refinement algorithm to reason about the problem-solving in the actual KBS.

We have found that, although knowledge refinement alters the knowledge content of the KBS, the knowledge refinement process must also take account of the KBS's

problem-solving; i.e. refinement is concerned with the inferences of the KBS as well as its static knowledge. In this paper we focus on the knowledge structure that represents individual problem-solving events. To achieve our goal of generality, the structure we propose must be sufficiently expressive and flexible to cover the different inference mechanisms found in a variety of KBSs.

We first describe the KRUSTWorks framework and the requirements of the refinement tools it creates. We then explore the effects on inference of chaining direction and conflict resolution, in order to justify our claim that refinement tools must alter their process depending on the inferencing that the KBS applies. This investigation highlights the key features that must be incorporated in the generalised reasoning knowledge structure. Finally we describe the problem graph, the way it is created from a problem solving episode, and how it provides the knowledge about the reasoning that is necessary to suggest useful refinements.

A Generic Refinement Framework

The goal of the KRUSTWorks framework is to provide facilities to allow the construction of a specialised refinement tool, a KRUSTTool, tailored to suit the particular KBS being refined. Central to our approach is the idea that refinement is achieved by selecting appropriate refinement operators from a repository and applying them with a core refinement algorithm to internal representations of the KBS to be refined (Figure 1). The core refinement algorithm is abstracted from experience with specific KRUSTTools applied to KBSs on various platforms (Craw & Hutton 1995; Craw, Boswell, & Rowe 1997): Prolog applies backward chaining, both Clips and Logica's PFES use exclusively forward-chaining rules, and IntelliCorp's PowerModel permits both forward and backward chaining.

KRUSTTools apply the standard refinement steps of allocating blame to potentially faulty rules and then proposing repairs to rules that prevent this faulty behaviour. But KRUSTTools are unusual in generating many refinements, and postponing the selection of which repair to choose until the refined KBSs have been evaluated by executing in the original KBS format on further examples. Figure 2 illustrates the compo-

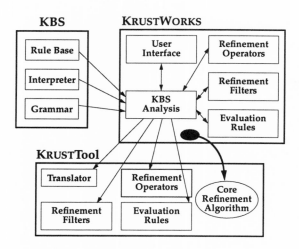

Figure 1: Creating a KRUSTTool from KRUSTWorks

nents of a KRUSTTool, in particular the two key generic knowledge structures, the knowledge skeleton and problem graph, that are central to this approach.

The *knowledge skeleton* is an internal representation of the rules in the KBS. It contains the essential features of the knowledge content; i.e. the KBS' knowledge that is relevant to the refinement process. During translation, each knowledge element is classified within a knowledge hierarchy and this classification is used to reference suitable refinement operators. Details of the knowledge skeleton and its use appear in (Boswell & Craw 1999).

The *problem graph* is the focus of this paper. It captures the problem-solving for the refinement case and allows the KRUSTTool to reason about the fault that is being demonstrated. We investigate a range of KBS inference mechanisms in order to define the problem graph, a general knowledge structure that effectively represents the way rules interact. Minor deficiencies of the problem graph do not cause serious problems for the refinement generation process, given the KRUSTTool's approach of generating large numbers of refinements.

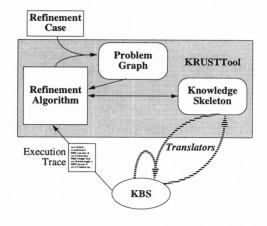

Figure 2: The KRUSTTool and KBS Processes

Reasoning in KBSs

Many refinement systems assume that the KBS employs an exhaustive, monotonic reasoning (Richards & Mooney 1995; Ourston & Mooney 1994). However, real-life KBSs frequently employ non-logical features to restrict the search and exploit non-monotonic reasoning. Since our goal is to refine a wide range of KBSs, we are concerned with the effects of different forms of reasoning on refinement.

A General View of Inference

We start by adopting a simple iterative algorithm (Fensel 1997) as the basis for inference:

1. Initialise the current state of the problem solving

2. Repeat until the termination condition is achieved:

   (a) form the conflict set: match the current state of the problem-solving with rules in the KBS

   (b) apply the conflict resolution strategy: select the rule in the conflict set that should be used

   (c) fire the rule: apply the selected rule to update the current state of the problem-solving.

The initialisation step (1) sets the context of the new problem-solving by representing the features of the new problem and possibly indicating the goal to be achieved. Therefore knowledge refinement is not concerned with this problem initialisation step.

In contrast, the iterative loop (2) determines the reasoning, and knowledge refinement seeks to alter the knowledge that is applied here. Identifying the conflict set (2a) is a purely logical step and so refinement involves altering the knowledge in rules that are, or should be, in the conflict set. All refinement systems apply this type of change.

However, many refinement systems assume an exhaustive backward chaining approach in which conflict resolution (2b) is simply a search ordering mechanism and has no ultimate effect on the solutions proposed by the KBS. This assumption is appropriate for Prolog-like applications with no non-logical features, but is not true for real-life applications that commonly employ mechanisms, such as rule priority and conflict resolution, to restrict the search for a solution. This is particularly true when the reasoning is forward chaining, and is relevant if the termination condition determines that the reasoning halts as soon as the goal is proved.

Firing the selected rule (2c) can be achieved in different ways. Monotonic systems add the new knowledge irrespective of the existing knowledge already inferred. However many systems are non-monotonic in that knowledge can be overwritten (e.g. the field of an object) or the old fact is retracted and a new one asserted. Such behaviour is unusual in Prolog applications but common with Clips facts, or PowerModel objects. These effects are considered in the next section.

In our diagrams that illustrate reasoning we adopt the convention that leaf nodes at the bottom of the graph are observable facts, nodes at the top of the graph are the goals of the reasoning process, and rules at the top of the graph are called *end-rules*. We shall also be concerned with the order of rule firings; this is shown in a left to right ordering of branches from a rule node.

When Chaining Direction Matters

In KBSs which exhaustively find all solutions and are monotonic, backward and forward chaining find exactly the same rule chains and so refinement of each system is equivalent. We now investigate how selection and non-monotonicity complicate forward chaining and the circumstances in which chaining direction affects the conclusion of the KBS.

Selection from the conflict set alters the order in which inferences are made. Although on many occasions this is used simply to guide the reasoning towards more efficient routes and so has no effect on the ultimate solutions, under some circumstances, such as early termination, the order in which solutions appear is important because some are ignored.

A simple example when backward and forward chaining differ occurs when the KBS's inference terminates as soon as the first end-rule fires. Figure 3 contains a small example. The rule priority is shown in square brackets and rules with higher priority are fired first. If we assume P and Q are true, under forward chaining, R2 fires first, then R4, and the conclusion is X=on. In contrast, under backward chaining, R3 fires first, then R1, and the conclusion is X=off.

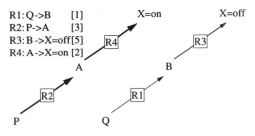

Figure 3: Inference stops when an end-rule fires

Thus, when the relative priority of rules differs between layers of the inference, the priority of the first layer to fire takes precedence; i.e. the leaf rules for forward chaining, and the end-rules for backward chaining. This effect also occurs when there are several *potentially clashing* rules that infer different values for the same attribute without demanding the rules are end-rules, as happened in Figure 3. Examples include Clips rules asserting new ordered terms with the same first element, Prolog clauses having heads that unify, Clips rules updating multi-valued fields, and PFES rules adding to PFES agendas[1]. In this case, conflict resolution in later cycles is affected by the order in which the various instantiations from previous cycles are retrieved.

---

[1] A PFES agenda is a stack or queue of potential formulation components. This should not be confused with the Clips execution agenda; i.e. the ordered conflict set.

Non-Monotonicity is introduced when knowledge is retracted or overwritten during problem solving. Explicit retraction can occur in backward and forward chaining. Forward chaining systems may also update objects, so that each rule in turn overwrites the value written by the previous rule. Again sets of potentially clashing rules are important.

Figure 4 contains another small rule-set where now suppose Temp is an overwriting property. Under forward chaining when P and Q are true, R1 fires first, R2 fires next overwriting Temp=60 with 50 (shown as a dotted arrow), then R4 fires concluding X=off. R3 is not able to fire since R2 fires first, thereby making its antecedent false; this is shown as a shaded area.

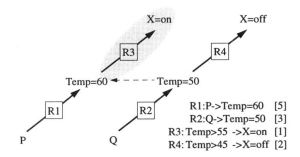

Figure 4: Chaining with Overwriting Rules

Thus, for clashing rules with overwriting conclusions under forward chaining, the lowest priority satisfied path in the graph leads to the eventual solution. The priority of each path is determined by the priority of the leaf node rules. Under backward chaining, exactly the reverse is true; the first rule to fire is the end-rule with the highest priority, here R4 which then chains back to R1 concluding X=off, but this is overwritten with X=on when R3 fires.

This example also demonstrates that the effect of rule priority is not just to choose between the potentially clashing rules R1 and R2 but it also encompasses the rules with which they chain. Thus, rule priority has an influence in a vertical direction, not just horizontally.

Self-Disabling Rules These rules contain exception conditions that ensure only the first from a set of rules fire. They are a specialised form of non-monotonicity since later rules are in effect retracted, and the result is to select only the *highest* priority rules in the direction of chaining. Self-disabling rules constitute a special case of negation and occur frequently in PFES KBSs; e.g. choosing a binder in the tablet formulation application (Craw, Boswell, & Rowe 1997) where the exception checks whether the value of binder has already been set:

```
IF in-agenda stability-agenda
      ?stability after gelatin
AND ?stability greater 90 AND ...
THEN refine-attribute binder gelatin
UNLESS attribute-has-value binder ?any
```

Self-disabling also occurs in backward chaining systems, as with Prolog's cut (!) for commitment; e.g.

```
temp(40) :- p, !.     x :- temp(T), T > 45.
temp(50) :- q.
```

where the first temp rule firing precludes the later temp rule and so the rule for x would not fire.

Conflict Resolution Strategies

We have consistently referred to rule priority and implied that we are restricted to a Clips-like salience attached to static rules. However, Clips uses rule priority only as the first criterion for choosing which rule from the conflict set should fire. Where rule priorities are equal, a variety of further strategies are available; other shells often offer a subset of those available in Clips. The effects of selection and non-monotonicity apply equally to other conflict resolution strategies such as recency, specificity, LEX and MEA[2].

Representing Reasoning

We have seen that the behaviour of forward-chaining rules can be different from that of backward-chaining ones. Therefore, refinement systems need to alter their process depending on the chaining direction of the KBS. We have also seen that the behaviour of forward-chaining rules is often more complex than that of backward-chaining ones, so that if a common procedure is to be adopted for handling both, its form will probably depend largely on the requirements of forward-chaining rules. The comparison of forward and backward chaining identifies the areas of difference and provides a foundation for the generalised mechanism that we propose for both forward and backward chaining KBSs.

Refinement consists of determining what happened, then trying to change it. There are two ways of determining what happened: querying the KBS and then reasoning about rule priorities and conflict resolution in order to *infer* what happened (i.e. running a partial simulation), or else looking at the execution trace to find out what *actually* happened. We have found the retrospective approach works well for backward chaining rules (Craw & Hutton 1995), but the preceding examples suggest that accurately simulating forward-chaining rules is likely to be difficult, so we propose an approach based on traces.

The Problem Graph

We define a knowledge structure that represents the reasoning by capturing both the rules that fired for a given problem-solving activity and the knowledge that might have been applied at each stage in the process. The knowledge is acquired directly from the execution trace and by reasoning about the contents of the trace.

---

[2]LEX and MEA extend recency by considering the relative assertion times of facts satisfying individual antecedents.

Its content informs the blame allocation and refinement generation stages in the KRUSTTool's cycle.

Previously, with backward chaining systems, navigating a simple virtual structure worked well, so we are now extending this approach to forward chaining systems, but here we have found it helpful to create the structure explicitly. We have seen that the ordering of the rules in the conflict set has an effect only when the rules are clashing and so involve some form of negation, retraction, or overwriting. From the point of view of refinement it does not matter why they clash provided we know how to re-order the firing agenda. The problem graph contains a history of the firing agenda and its effects. It links the knowledge that was applied to the knowledge that was inferred, represents relative timings of these events, and identifies knowledge that might have been applied. The problem graph in Figure 5 is applied in a later example.

The *positive* part of the problem graph is extracted directly from the execution trace and contains the knowledge that has been applied. *Rule activation nodes* maintain logical knowledge such as the variable bindings associated with this activation, and timing information about when the rule was activated, when it was fired, and when it was retracted, if appropriate. Similarly, a *fact assertion node* stores the time of assertion and the time of retraction if appropriate. The arcs in the graph link rule activations to the facts they conclude, and fact assertions to the rule activations whose antecedents they match. When an antecedent does not involve another rule (e.g. an inequality check), the structure records the test's truth as T or *NIL*.

We have been discussing rule activations and fact assertions that actually took place when the KBS was run on the refinement example, but this is not enough. A problem graph also has a *negative* part consisting of rules activations and facts which did not appear during the run, but which could contribute to the desired behaviour of the system. We refer to these as non-activations and non-facts. Some of a non-activation's antecedents may actually be satisfied; these are connected to facts as in the positive part. Those that fail are recorded as *failure links* connecting each antecedent to matching non-facts.

The problem graph representation also applies to *negated* antecedents; we assume negation as failure in a closed world. For negated knowledge components, we must decide how to link facts and non-facts. If not(Goal) is satisfied then there is a link to T. Conversely, if not(Goal) fails then there is a failure link from the offending fact, Goal. When the negated antecedent does not involve other rules, then the truth of the antecedent as a whole is recorded; e.g. if the antecedent not(X < 42) fails, then *NIL* is recorded.

Building the Problem Graph

The positive part of the problem graph is derived directly from the KBS's execution trace by extracting information about rule firings and their associated variable bindings, and when facts were asserted and retracted. The negative part of the problem graph is formed by exhaustively exploring backwards from the desired conclusion to identify potential routes through the knowledge. When the KBS itself is backward chaining then both steps can be naturally combined. This may explain why most current work on refinement has dealt only with backward-chaining rules. Refining forward chaining rules is more complicated since they execute in the opposite direction to the refinement process, and so the KRUSTTool must find a way to ensure that the chosen route found by backward chaining is actually executed under the KBS's forward chaining control.

A two-stage translation process creates the positive part of the problem graph from the trace. This is needed since there is not a 1-1 relationship between nodes in the problem-graph and lines in the original trace. For example, separate rule activation and rule firing statements in the Clips trace contribute to the same rule activation node in the problem graph. Conversely, a rule firing in the trace may contribute information to both a rule activation node and a fact node. The translation is therefore most conveniently done by first creating an internal representation of the trace, and then manipulating this internal trace to construct the positive part of the problem graph.

Furthermore, representing rule firings themselves is not sufficient. We also need to know the content of working memory before any rule firing, to determine whether a rule failed to fire because its antecedents were not satisfied, or because its priority was too low. Many KBSs have tracing facilities that provide all this information; e.g. for a Clips trace we elect to watch rules, facts and activations, with PowerModel we select the highest level of verbosity. Otherwise, it is often possible to deduce a snapshot of working memory from previous rule firings; we use this with PFES.

The negative part of the problem graph is constructed by backward chaining from the desired conclusion in the knowledge skeleton. First, the desired conclusion is created as a non-fact. Then rule non-activations are created for all the rules that could conclude this fact, with appropriate bindings. The algorithm then proceeds recursively: for each rule antecedent in a non-activation, if the antecedent is not satisfied by an existing fact, then a matching non-fact is created. The procedure terminates when it reaches non-facts that do not match the conclusion of any rule (observables).

If a rule's antecedents are matched by multiple facts or non-facts, then non-activations are created for all the possible combinations, provided that the variable bindings are compatible; for example, if one antecedent is matched by one fact and one non-fact, and another by two non-facts, then up to four rule non-activations will be created.

Problem Graphs in Practice

We have built problem graphs from Clips, PowerModel and PFES KBSs and their traces. Both stages of the translation from trace to positive problem graph, together with the first internal representation of the trace, are specific to the particular KBS. The form of the problem graph itself is generic. Consequently, the creation of the negative part of the problem graph is independent of the KBS.

Rather than demonstrating the approach using a complex KBS, we have chosen to illustrate the process on a very simple Clips KBS:

Initial Facts: (c), (a), (b)

Rules with Salience 5   Rules with Salience 10
rule1: (a)   rule4: (not (result ?)), (p), (r)
    $\Rightarrow$ (assert (p)) $\Rightarrow$ (assert (result x))
rule2: (b)   rule5: (not (result ?)), (q), (r)
    $\Rightarrow$ (assert (q)) $\Rightarrow$ (assert (result y))
rule3: (c)
    $\Rightarrow$ (assert (r))

Suppose also Clips applies the LEX conflict resolution strategy when rule salience does not distinguish a single rule on the activation agenda. This generates the Clips trace showing the facts being asserted one at a time, each followed by a Clips activation when the rule it satisfies is placed in the conflict set:

```
==> f-1      (c)
==> Activation 10      rule3: f-1
==> f-2      (a)
==> Activation 10      rule1: f-2
==> f-3      (b)
==> Activation 10      rule2: f-3
FIRE    1 rule2: f-3
==> f-4      (q)
FIRE    2 rule1: f-2
==> f-5      (p)
FIRE    3 rule3: f-1
==> f-6      (r)
==> Activation 5       rule5: ,,f-4,f-6
==> Activation 5       rule4: ,,f-5,f-6
FIRE    4 rule4: ,,f-5,f-6
==> f-7      (result x)
<== Activation 5       rule5: ,,f-4,f-6
```

LEX fires the rules as rule2, rule1, rule3, since the most recently asserted fact is used first. To discriminate between rule4 and rule5, since they are both activated simultaneously (when fact r was asserted), LEX uses the next most recent pairs of antecedents, p and q. p was asserted more recently, so rule4 fires. But when rule4 fires this removes rule5 from the conflict set (indicated by <==) and so Clips's solution is result(x). Notice that negation is not explicitly mentioned in the trace but the knowledge skeleton provides the information.

Suppose in this example that the "correct" solution is known to be result(y). Figure 5 shows the problem graph that is constructed. Rule activations are rectangular nodes, fact assertions are oval nodes, and dashed outlines indicate non-facts and non-activations. Arcs indicate the various links; conjunctive antecedents are shown circled, arrows point towards conclusions, failure links are shown dashed, and negations are indicated with a ⋈ through the link.

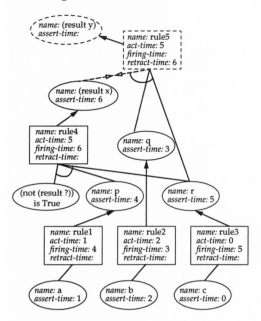

Figure 5: A Sample Problem Graph

One of the many features of PowerModel and PFES which makes the construction of the problem graph more difficult is the phenomenon of backtracking: whenever a rule is executed, the interpreter forces the generation of all possible variable instantiations, rather as if a Prolog goal were followed by a `fail` statement. Consequently, each successful rule firing requires the creation of a separate rule activation node, and determining the variable bindings for each rule firing may require some searching forwards and backwards through the trace.

Refinement Generation

Blame allocation and refinement generation seek to disable a faulty proof and to identify and enable a correct proof in the rules. The problem graph contains the faulty proof and potential proofs together with the information that is required for the KRUSTTool to find a way to ensure that the chosen route is actually executed.

The most common type of refinement operators found in refinement systems are those that alter the logical content of the rule and so affect whether the rule is added to the conflict set. However, we believe there is another important class of refinements: those that alter the way the rule is handled by the conflict resolution strategy and so affect whether the rule is selected to fire or not. This is particularly relevant for forward chaining rules where selection plays a larger role.

To correct the behaviour of the KBS, it may be necessary to make several changes at the same time. For example, if the KRUSTTool wants a rule to fire, but

two of its antecedents are currently unsatisfied, the KRUSTTool will probably have to make at least two changes somewhere in the rules. We describe all the individual changes required to fix a particular fault as a refinement. The output from the algorithm is a series of refinements, each of which individually is designed to correct the behaviour of the KBS.

Logical Refinements

This type of refinement is common to all refinement systems, although the changes that achieve the refinement can vary. Here we describe how a KRUSTTool generates these from the problem graph.

To *enable a desired conclusion* the KRUSTTool enables any one rule which matches that conclusion. Such rules may be read from the problem graph, where the desired fact is linked to one or more rule non-activations. To enable a rule, for each failed antecedent in the associated non-activation, the KRUSTTool either weakens that antecedent so that it is satisfied for the refinement case, or else applies the algorithm recursively, by enabling a non-fact linked to the failed antecedent.

To *prevent an undesired conclusion* the KRUSTTool disables all rules that fired and match that conclusion. To disable a rule, the KRUSTTool disables any one of its antecedents, or deletes the rule. It disables an antecedent either by strengthening it, or by disabling all the rules linked to the fact that caused the antecedent to be satisfied.

The presence of negation requires the following extensions to the above basic algorithms. To *enable a failed negation*, the KRUSTTool identifies the matching fact in the problem graph, and disables all the rule activations that concluded that fact, using the algorithm above. Conversely, to *disable a negation*, the KRUSTTool identifies the matching non-fact, and enables any one of the rule non-activations which conclude that fact.

Conflict Resolution Refinements

It is always possible to generate only logical refinements but in certain circumstances it is appropriate to also generate refinements based on the conflict resolution strategy. Conflict Resolution is used as a basis for refinement in two situations: when a rule is activated but then de-activated before firing, and when a group of potentially clashing rules fires in the wrong order, so that, for example, the desired conclusion is overwritten by a later conclusion. Multiple potentially clashing rules on an agenda would most naturally arise in the case of a group of self-disabling rules.

For the purposes of refinement, the two situations are handled in the same way: we observe that rule R1, say, fires before R2, and we wish to ensure that R2 fires before R1. One way to achieve this is by applying a logical refinement to disable rule R1. However, when the KRUSTTool determines from the problem graph that R1 and R2 are on the rule execution agenda at the same time then an alternative refinement modifies the priority of R2 so that it is higher than R1. To determine the required priority change, it is also necessary to identify any other rules present on the agenda at the same time which would also prevent R2 from firing.

These refinements have assumed a conflict resolution strategy based on rule priority, but other strategies are possible. In Clips, any conflict resolution refinement can be applied as a salience change, because Clips uses other strategies only when rule priorities are tied. However, in some situations rule priority changes might be too radical and this might prevent the KRUSTTool from finding a satisfactory refinement. We now consider which conflict strategy refinements should be adopted. Firstly, the KRUSTTool should *not* refine the strategy itself, on the grounds that such a global change would be non-conservative, and would have unpredictable side-effects. Secondly, the KRUSTTool does *not* propose to add or delete antecedents *simply* in order to modify the effects of a specificity/generality strategy, again because of undesired side-effects. The remaining strategies are based on the order of fact assertions, and it is possible to take these into account when generating refinements. The task of altering the firing order of rules at one level can be carried out by a recursive procedure which alters priorities either at that level, or at lower levels. Sucn lower level refinements affect the order of fact assertions, and and hence of rule firings, at higher levels. The example in the next section illustrates this.

Refinement Using a Problem Graph

We have applied KRUSTTools to a range of KBSs, and the problem graph is simply a common format in which to represent the various reasoning mechanisms that can happen in KBSs. The ability of the core refinement algorithm to generate useful refinements has been demonstrated elsewhere: a KRUSTTool achieves competitive results with other refiners when applied to a benchmark backward-chaining Prolog KBS (Craw & Hutton 1995); a PFES KRUSTTool debugs an early version of Zeneca's Tablet Formulation System, implemented in forward-chaining PFES, (Craw, Boswell, & Rowe 1997).

Our problem graph approach works well for larger KBSs but these are difficult to illustrate. Instead, we revert to the simple problem graph in Figure 5 as our example and illustrate the problem graph's use when refining this KBS. The refinements are described below but are highlighted by shading in Figure 6 where disabled rules are shown with "X"s and the changed priorities are shown with lightly shaded arrows.

Three Logical Refinements:

- disable rule1, rule3 or rule4

Disabling rule3 does not actually repair the rules, as it prevents rule5 from firing as well as rule4, but this is an unpredictable side-effect and is identified by the KRUSTTool when it tests its proposed refinements. In practice each disabling can be implemented in many different ways by disabling any one of the antecedents or deleting the rule.

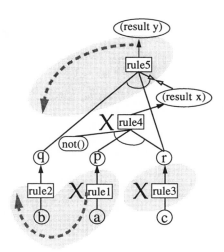

Figure 6: Generated Refinements

Two Conflict Resolution Refinements:

- increase the priority of rule5 above rule4 by setting its salience to 11
- increase the priority of rule1 above rule2 by setting its salience to 6.

Increasing the priority of rule1 has the effect that rule2's conclusion is asserted later and so LEX will fire rule5 before rule4. The KRUSTTool could in principle recurse a further level when generating these refinements, and change the fact order.

Even this very simple example demonstrates the variety of refinements and the interactions that can occur.

Comparison with Other Approaches

The problem graph we have defined is the basis of a common representation for reasoning. Fensel *et al.* (1997) also seek to define problem solving methods (PSMs) in a task-independent way so that they can re-use the PSMs by tailoring them to a specific task. Fensel *et al.*'s goal and approach is thus similar to KRUSTWorks'. Their adapter selects a PSM whose abilities partially match the task's requirements and specialises the PSM for the task. Similarly, our KRUSTWorks framework allows the use of generic components which then act on a particular KBS

Both Etzioni (1993) and Smith & Peot (1996) create structures similar to our negative problem graph. Since their domain is planning, the nodes correspond to operators and pre-conditions rather than rules and conditions. Their graphs are constructed in a similar way to ours, by backward chaining from the final goal, and are used for reasoning about potential interactions between operators. In both cases, the graph is created before the planner is run, so no structure corresponding to our positive problem graph is created. The purpose of the graphs is to improve the subsequent performance of the planners. Smith & Peot's *operator graph* determines which rule conditions have the potential to lead to recursion; knowing this, they can prevent the planner from entering an infinite loop. Etzioni uses the *problem space graph* to learn control rules to guide operator application, rejecting inappropriate operators and ordering appropriate ones.

CLIPS-R (Murphy & Pazzani 1994) refines Clips KBSs, and is the only other refinement system for forward-chaining rules. CLIPS-R shares KRUSTWorks' aim of applying knowledge refinement to real-world expert systems, and thus takes account of non-logical features such as rule priority. Instead of using the trace from a single example, CLIPS-R combines the traces of all examples into a trie-structure, grouping together those examples which have a common initial sequence of rule firings. CLIPS-R chooses to refine first the group that exhibits the greatest proportion of errors. The trie-structure is not used directly for refinement, in the way that a KRUSTTool's problem graph is, but CLIPS-R does backward chain from failed goals; it just does not build an explicit structure like KRUSTTools.

Conclusions

Many refinement tools assume an exhaustive backward chaining control and therefore restrict attention to logical refinements. We have found that additional refinements may be relevant; these alter the knowledge content so that the rule is handled differently by the conflict resolution strategy. An exploration of this behaviour showed that backward and forward chaining could produce different answers when the problem-solving terminated prematurely (e.g. as soon as a solution was found) or non-monotonicity was introduced. These are common features of industrial KBSs where default reasoning is standard practice to achieve efficiency.

The blame allocation phase of knowledge refinement naturally reasons backwards from the desired solution. Therefore, forward chaining and mixed chaining KBSs pose some problems. The proposed refinement must ensure that the solution path found by backward chaining is actually executed, and so blame allocation involves more complex reasoning about what will happen.

We defined a knowledge structure that captures the reasoning: what happened and what might have happened. This knowledge does not need to faithfully simulate the reasoning since the KRUSTTool does not rely on it exclusively for generating refinements. Instead, it forms a basis for the reasoning about refinements, but all refinements are checked by executing the refined KBS on its native platform. We have noted that the knowledge cannot be extracted entirely from the execution trace, but requires additional reasoning about the static knowledge.

The approach has been evaluated with forward or backward chaining systems in Prolog, Clips and PFES, and the mixed chaining of PowerModel. Experience with these KBSs has shown that the problem graph contains the reasoning information that allows a KRUSTTool to identify what may have gone wrong and to suggest possible repairs.

Acknowledgements

Susan Craw is currently on sabbatical at the University of California, Irvine. The work described in this paper is supported by EPSRC grant GR/L38387, awarded to Susan Craw. We also thank IntelliCorp Ltd and Zeneca Pharmaceuticals for their contributions to the project and the anonymous reviewer who highlighted the related work from planning.

References

Boswell, R., and Craw, S. 1999. Knowledge Modelling for a Generic Refinement Framework. *Knowledge Based Systems* (in press). Also appears in Proceedings of the BCS Expert Systems Conference, 58–74, Springer, 1998.

Craw, S., and Hutton, P. 1995. Protein folding: Symbolic refinement competes with neural networks. In Prieditis, A., and Russell, S., eds., *Machine Learning: Proceedings of the Twelfth International Conference*, 133–141. Tahoe City, CA: Morgan Kaufmann.

Craw, S.; Boswell, R.; and Rowe, R. 1997. Knowledge refinement to debug and maintain a tablet formulation system. In *Proceedings of the 9TH IEEE International Conference on Tools with Artificial Intelligence (TAI'97)*, 446–453. Newport Beach, CA: IEEE Press.

Etzioni, O. 1993. Acquiring search-control knowledge via static analysis. *Artificial Intelligence* 62:255–301.

Fensel, D.; Motta, E.; Decker, S.; and Zdrahal, Z. 1997. Using ontologies for defining tasks, problem-solving methods and their mappings. In Plaza, E., and Benjamins, R., eds., *Knowledge Acquisition, Modeling and Management, Proceedings of the 10th European Workshop (EKAW97)*, 113–128. Sant Feliu de Guixols, Spain: Springer.

Fensel, D. 1997. The tower-of-adapters method for developing and reusing problem-solving methods. In Plaza, E., and Benjamins, R., eds., *Knowledge Acquisition, Modeling and Management, Proceedings of the 10th European Workshop (EKAW97)*, 97–112. Sant Feliu de Guixols, Spain: Springer.

Murphy, P. M., and Pazzani, M. J. 1994. Revision of production system rule-bases. In Cohen, W. W., and Hirsh, H., eds., *Machine Learning: Proceedings of the 11th International Conference*, 199–207. New Brunswick, NJ: Morgan Kaufmann.

Ourston, D., and Mooney, R. 1994. Theory refinement combining analytical and empirical methods. *Artificial Intelligence* 66:273–309.

Richards, B. L., and Mooney, R. J. 1995. Refinement of first-order horn-clause domain theories. *Machine Learning* 19(2):95–131.

Smith, D. E., and Peot, M. A. 1996. Suspending recursion in causal-link planning. In *Proceedings of the Third International Conference on AI Planning Systems*. Edinburgh, Scotland: AAAI press.

Deriving Expectations to Guide Knowledge Base Creation

Jihie Kim and Yolanda Gil
Information Sciences Institute and Computer Science Department
University of Southern California
4676 Admiralty Way
Marina del Rey, CA 90292, U.S.A.
jihie@isi.edu, gil@isi.edu

Abstract

Successful approaches to developing knowledge acquisition tools use expectations of what the user has to add or may want to add, based on how new knowledge fits within a knowledge base that already exists. When a knowledge base is first created or undergoes significant extensions and changes, these tools cannot provide much support. This paper presents an approach to creating expectations when a new knowledge base is built, and describes a knowledge acquisition tool that we implemented using this approach that supports users in creating problem-solving knowledge. As the knowledge base grows, the knowledge acquisition tool derives more frequent and more reliable expectations that result from enforcing constraints in the knowledge representation system, looking for missing pieces of knowledge in the knowledge base, and working out incrementally the inter-dependencies among the different components of the knowledge base. Our preliminary evaluations show a thirty percent time savings during knowledge acquisition. Moreover, by providing tools to support the initial phases of knowledge base development, many mistakes are detected early on and even avoided altogether. We believe that our approach contributes to improving the quality of the knowledge acquisition process and of the resulting knowledge-based systems as well.

Introduction

Knowledge acquisition (KA) is recognized as an important research area for making knowledge-based AI succeed in practice (Feigenbaum 1993). An approach that has been very effective to develop tools that acquire knowledge from users is to use *expectations* of what users have to add or may want to add next (Eriksson *et al.* 1995; Birmingham & Klinker 1993; Marcus & McDermott 1989; Davis 1979). Most of these expectations are derived from the *inter-dependencies* among the components in a knowledge-base system (KBS). EXPECT (Gil & Melz 1996; Swartout & Gil 1995) and Protégé-II (Eriksson *et al.* 1995) use dependencies between factual knowledge and problem-solving methods to find related pieces of knowledge in their KBS and create expectations from them. To give an example of these expectations, suppose that the user is building a KBS for a configuration task that finds constraint violations and then applies fixes to them. When

the user defines a new constraint, the KA tool has the expectation that the user should specify possible fixes for cases where the constraint is violated, and helps the user do so. These tools can successfully build expectations because there is already a body of knowledge where the new knowledge added by the user must fit in. In the configuration example, there would be problem solving knowledge about how to solve configuration tasks (how to describe a configuration, what is a constraint, what is the relation between a constraint and a fix, how to apply a fix, etc.) However, when a new knowledge base (KB) is created (or when an existing one is significantly extended) there is little or no pre-existing knowledge in the system to draw from. How can a KA tool support the user in creating a large body of new knowledge? Are there any sources of expectations that the KA tool can exploit?

This paper describes our approach to developing KA tools that derive expectations from the KB in order to guide users during KB creation. Through an analysis of the KB creation task, we were able to detect several sources for such expectations. The expectations result from enforcing constraints in the knowledge representation system, looking for missing pieces of knowledge in the KB, and working out incrementally the inter-dependencies among the different components of the KB. As the user defines new *KB elements* (i.e., new concepts, new relations, new problem-solving knowledge), the KA tool can form increasingly more frequent and more reliable expectations. We implemented a KA tool called EMeD that uses these sources of expectations to support users in adding problem-solving knowledge. Our preliminary evaluation shows an *average time savings of 30%* to enter the new knowledge. We believe it will be even higher for users who are not experienced knowledge engineers.

The paper begins by describing why KB creation is hard. Then we present our approach, and describe the KA tool that we implemented. Finally, we show the results from our experiments with several subjects, and discuss our conclusions and directions for future work.

Creating Knowledge Bases

There are several reasons why creating a knowledge base is hard:

- **Developers have to design and create a large number of KB elements.** KB developers have to turn models and abstractions about a task domain into individual KB elements. When they are creating an individual KB element, it is hard to remember the details of all the definitions that have already been created. It is also hard to anticipate all the details of the definitions that remain to be worked out and implemented. As a result, many of these KB elements are not completely flawless from the beginning, and they tend to generate lots of errors that have unforeseen side effects. Also, until a KB element is debugged and freed from these errors, the expectations created from it may not be very reliable.

- **There are many missing pieces of knowledge at a given time.** Even if the developers understand the domain very well, it is hard to picture how all the knowledge should be expressed correctly. As some part of the knowledge is represented, there will be many missing pieces that should be completed. It is hard for KB developers to keep track of what pieces are still missing, and to take them into account as they are creating new elements.

- **It is hard to predict what pieces of knowledge are related and how.** Since there is not a working system yet, many of the relationships between the individual pieces are in the mind of the KB developer and have not been captured or correctly expressed in the KB.

- **There can be many inconsistencies among related KB elements that are newly defined.** It is hard for KB developers to detect all the possible conflicts among the definitions that they create. Often times they are detected through the painful process of trying to run the system and watching it not work at all. The debugging is done through an iterative process of running the system, failing, staring at various traces to see what is happening, and finally finding the cause for the problem.

As intelligent systems operate in real-world, large-scale knowledge intensive domains, these problems are compounded. As new technology enables the creation of knowledge bases with thousands and millions of axioms, KB developers will be faced an increasingly more unmanageable and perhaps impossible task. Consider an example from our experience with a Workarounds domain selected by DARPA as one of the challenge problems of the High-Performance Knowledge Bases program that investigates the development of large-scale knowledge based systems. The task is to estimate the delay caused to enemy forces when an obstacle is targeted by reasoning about how they could bypass, breach or improve the obstacle. After several large ontologies of terms relevant to battlespace reasoning were built (military units, engineering assets, transport vehicles, etc.), we faced the task of creating the problem solving knowledge base that used all those terms and facts to actually estimate the workaround time. We built eighty-four problem-solving methods from scratch on top of several thousand defined concepts, and it took two intense months to put together all the pieces. Figure 1 shows some examples of our methods. Each method has a *capability* that describes what goals it

```
(define-method M1
(documentation "In order to estimate the time that it takes to narrow
a gap with a bulldozer, combine the total dirt volume to be moved
and the standard earthmoving rate.")

(capability (estimate (obj (?t is (spec-of time)))
                      (for (?s is (inst-of narrow-gap)))))
 (result-type (inst-of number))
 (body (divide (obj (find (obj (spec-of dirt-volume))
                          (for ?s)))
               (by (find (obj (spec-of standard-bulldozing-rate))
                         (for ?s))))))

(define-method M2
(documentation "The amount of dirt that needs to be moved in any
workaround step that involves moving dirt (such as narrowing a gap
with a bulldozer) is the value of the role earth-volume for that step.")

(capability (find (obj (?v is (spec-of dirt-volume)))
                  (for (?s is (inst-of move-earth)))))
 (result-type (inst-of number))
 (body (earth-volume ?s)))

(define-method M3
(documentation "The standard bulldozing rate for a workaround step
that involves earthmoving is the combined bulldozing rate of the doz-
ers specified as dozer-of of the step.")

(capability (find (obj (?r is (spec-of standard-bulldozing-rate)))
                  (for (?s is (inst-of bulldoze-region)))))
 (result-type (inst-of number))
 (body (find (obj (spec-of standard-bulldozing-rate))
             (of (dozer-of ?s)))))
```

Figure 1: Methods in a simplified workaround generation domain.

can achieve, a *method body* that specifies the procedure to achieve that capability (including invoking subgoals to be resolved with other methods, retrieving values of roles, and combining results through control constructs such as conditional expressions), and a *result type* that specifies the kind of result that the body is expected to return (more details of their syntax are discussed below). Creating each method so that it would use appropriate terms from ontologies was our first challenge. Once created, it was hard to understand how the methods were related to each other, especially when these interdependencies result from the definitions in the ontologies. Despite the modular, hierarchical design of our system, small errors and local inconsistencies tend to blend together to produce inexplicable results making it very hard to find and to fix the source of the problems. Although some portions of the knowledge base could be examined locally by testing subproblems, we often found ourselves working all the way back to our own documentation and notes to understand what was happening in the system.

In summary, it is hard for KB developers to keep in mind all the definitions that they create and to work out their interdependencies correctly. KB developers generate and resolve many errors while they build a large body of knowledge. Our goal is to develop KA tools that help users resolve these errors and, more importantly, help them avoid making the errors in the first place.

Approach

We identified several sources of expectations that KA tools can exploit in order to guide users in creating a new knowledge base. We explain our approach in terms of the problems and examples described in the previous section.

- *Difficulty in designing and creating many KB elements* ⇒ *Guide the users to avoid errors and look up related KB elements.*

First, each time a KB element is created by a user, we can check the dependencies within the element and find any potential errors based on the given representation language. For example, when undefined variables are used in method body, this will create an expectation that the user needs to define them in the method.

In our example, Method M1 has two variables, ?t and ?s, defined in its capability, and if the method body uses a different variable, the system can send a warning message to the user. Likewise, if a concept definition says that a role can have at most one value but also at least two values, then this local inconsistency can be brought up. By isolating these local errors and filtering them out earlier in the KB development process, we can prevent them from propagating to other elements in the system.

However small the current KB is, if there are KB elements that *could be* similar to the one being built, then they can be looked up to develop expectations on the form of new KB element. For example, developers may want to find existing KB elements that are related with particular terms or concepts based on the underlying ontology. If there is a concept hierarchy, it will be possible to retrieve KB elements that refer to superconcepts, subconcepts, or given concepts and let the user develop expectations on the current KB element based on related KB elements. For example, if a developer wants to find all the methods related to moving earth, the system can find the above methods, because narrow-gap and bulldoze-region are subtypes of move-earth. When the user adds a new method about moving earth to fill a crater, then it may be useful to take them into account. Specifically, M1 can generate expectations on how a method for estimating time to fill a crater should be built.

- *Many pieces of knowledge are missing at a given time:* ⇒ *Compute surface relationships among KB elements to find incomplete pieces and create expectations from them*

The KA tool can predict relationships among the methods based on what the capability of a method can achieve and the subgoals in the bodies of other methods. For example, given the three methods in Figure 1, method M1 can use M2 and M3 for its two subgoals — find dirt volume and find bulldozing rate. These relationships can create method-submethod trees that are useful to predict how methods will be used in problem solving. In the process of building this kind of structure, the system can expose missing pieces in putting the methods together. For example, *unmatched subgoals* can be listed by collecting all the subgoals in a method that cannot be achieved by any of the already defined methods. The user will be reminded to define the missing methods and shown the subgoals that they are supposed to match. In Figure 1, if a method for the subgoal of method M3 to find the standard bulldozing rate of given dozer is not defined yet, the user is asked to define one and may create one that only works for military dozer or any dozer in general.

Similarly, if a concept is used in a KB element definition but not defined yet, then the system will detect the *undefined concept*. Instead of simply rejecting such definition, if the developer still wants to use the term, the KA tool can collect undefined concepts and create an expectation that the developer (or other KB developers) will define the term later.

- *Difficulty in predicting what pieces of knowledge are related and how* ⇒ *Use surface relationships to find unused KB elements and propose potential uses of the elements*

The above surface relationships among KB elements, such as method-submethod relationship can also help detect unused KB elements. If a method is not used by any other methods, then it can be collected into an *unused method list*. In addition to finding such unused methods, the KA tool can propose potential uses of it. For example, if the capability of a method is similar to one of the unmatched subgoals (e.g., same goal name and similar parameter types), then a potential user of the method will be the method that has the unmatched goal.

In the same way, concepts created but not referred to in any other definitions can be collected into an *unused concept list*. The KA tool can develop expectations of KB elements that will use the definitions or perhaps even deleting these concepts if they end up being unnecessary.

- *Inconsistencies among newly defined KB elements* ⇒ *Help users find them early and propose fixes*

The KA tool can check if the user-defined result type of a method is inconsistent with what the method body returns based on the results of the subgoals. If there are inconsistent definitions, the system will develop an expectation that user has to modify either the current method or the methods that achieve the subgoals.

Also, for concept definitions, there can be cases where a user wants to retrieve a role value of a concept, but the role is not defined for the concept. In addition to simply detecting such a problem, the system may propose to define the role for the concept or to change the method to refer to a different but related concept that does have that role.

Finally, once the KA tool indicates that there are no errors, inconsistencies, or missing knowledge, the user can run the inference engine, exposing additional errors in solving a given problem or subproblems. The errors are caused by particular interdependencies among KB elements that arise in specific contexts. If most of the errors are detected by the above analyses, users should see significantly fewer errors at this stage.

Notice that as the KB is more complete and more error-free it becomes a stronger basis for the KA tool in creating

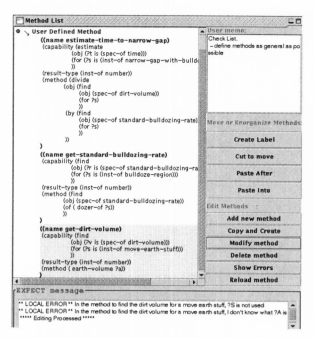

Figure 2: EMeD Interface (Editor).

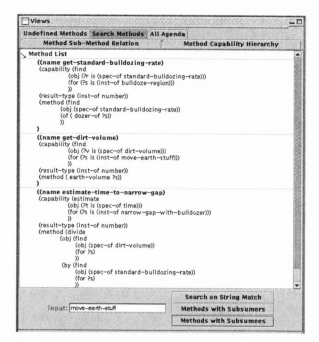

Figure 3: Search Methods in EMeD.

expectations to guide the user.

EMeD: Expect Method Developer

We have concentrated our initial effort in developing a KA tool that uses these kinds of expectations to support users to develop problem solving methods. We built a KA tool called *EMeD* (EXPECT Method Developer) for the EXPECT framework for knowledge-based systems (Gil & Melz 1996; Gil 1994; Swartout & Gil 1995).

An EXPECT knowledge base is composed of factual knowledge and of problem-solving knowledge. The factual knowledge includes concepts, relations, and instances in Loom (Macgregor 1990), a knowledge representation system of the KL-one family. The problem-solving knowledge is represented as a set of problem-solving methods such as those shown in Figure 1. As described earlier, each method has a capability, a result type, and a method body. Within the capability and body sections, each goal is expressed as a goal name followed by a set of parameters. Also, each parameter consists of a parameter name and a type.

Figure 2 shows the method editor in the EMeD user interface. There is a list of current methods and buttons for editing methods. Users can add, delete, or modify the methods using these buttons. (Other buttons and windows will be explained later.) Users often create new methods that are similar to existing ones so the tool has a copy/edit facility.

Every time a new method is defined, the method is checked for possible parsing errors based on the method representation language. If there are interdependencies among the subparts of a method, they are also used in detecting errors. For example, if a variable is used but not defined for the method, the same variable is defined more than once, or

there are unused variables, the system will produce warning messages. Also, if there were terms (concepts, relations, or instances) used in a method but not defined in the KB yet, error messages will be sent to the developer. When the term definition is obvious, as the verbs used in capabilities, a definition will be proposed by the tool. In Figure 2, the small panel in the bottom left corner with the label "EXPECT message" displays these errors. Using this method definition checker, users can detect the local errors earlier, separating them from other types of errors.

Users can find existing methods related with particular terms in concepts, relations or instances through the Loom ontology. The KA tool can retrieve methods that refer to subconcepts, superconcepts, or a given concept and let the user create new methods based on related methods. Figure 3 shows the result from retrieving methods about moving earth. The system was able to find all the methods in Figure 1, because narrow-gap and bulldoze-region are subconcepts of move-earth.

Figure 4 shows relationships among methods based on how the subgoals of a method can be achieved by other methods. The trees built from this are called *method sub-method relation trees*. There can be multiple trees growing in the process of building a number of methods when they are not fully connected. These method-relation trees are incomplete problem-solving trees to achieve some intermediate subgoal. The (sub)trees should be eventually put together to build a problem-solving tree for the whole problem. For example, given these three methods, the system can build a method-relation tree, as shown in Figure 4.

Method sub-method relation trees can be used to detect *undefined methods* based on the subgoals in a method that

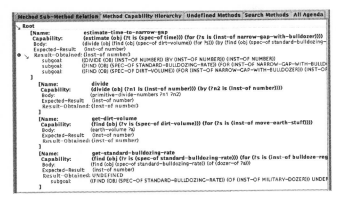

Figure 4: A Method Sub-method Relation Tree.

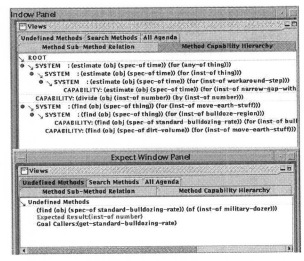

Figure 5: A Capability Tree and Undefined Methods.

are not achieved by any existing methods. These can be collected and users can be informed of them. If there are constraints imposed on the methods to be built, such as the expectations coming from the methods that invoke them, then these can be also incorporated. For example, the method to find the standard bulldozing rate of a step calls a subgoal to find the standard bulldozing rate of a given dozer, which is undefined yet. Since the result type of the given method is a number, the system can expect (through an interdependency analysis) the same result type for the undefined method. Figure 5 (bottom window) shows the capability that the tool proposes for the currently undefined method — a method to find standard bulldozing rate of a given military dozer.

In the process of building this method-relation tree, there can be subgoals whose parameters are not fully specified because their arguments are subgoals that are not achieved by any of existing methods. For example, given the method to estimate the time to narrow gap (the first method in Figure 1) only (i.e., if M2 and M3 were missing), its subgoal 'divide' has two parameters with parameter names 'obj' and 'by'. Because the arguments to divide are the subgoals 'find dirt-volume of the step' and 'find standard-bulldozing-rate for the step' whose methods would be undefined, the tool could not fully state the goal. This would be represented as 'divide (obj UNDEFINED) (by UNDEFINED)'. However, one of the built-in methods in EXPECT has capability of 'divide (obj Number) (by Number)', and the tool creates a link between this and the subgoal as a *potential interdependency*. Users can use this hint to make the potential interdependency a real one or create other appropriate methods.

There are other relationships among problem-solving methods based on their capabilities that the KA tool can exploit. For example, a hierarchy of the goals based on the subsumption relations of their goal names and their arguments can be created. In the hierarchy, if a goal is to build a military bridge, and another goal is to build a kind of military bridge, such as an AVLB, then the former subsumes the latter. This dependency among the goal descriptions of the methods (called *capability tree*) is useful in that it allows

the user to understand the kinds of sub-problems the current set of methods can solve. To make their relationships more understandable, EMeD also computes potential capabilities. For example if there are super-concepts defined for the parameters of a capability, a capability with these concepts is created as a parent of the capability. The capability tree for the given example methods is in Figure 5 (top window).

Finally, there are user-expected dependencies among the problem-solving methods, which are usually represented in comments or by grouping of methods in the files where they are built. They do not directly affect the system, but they often become the user's own instrument to understand the structure of what they are building. Also, it can be the user's own interpretation of additional interdependencies among methods. EMeD provides a way of organizing methods into hierarchies and groups, and allows users to provide documentation for the methods. In Figure 2, the "Move or Organize Methods" buttons support these functions.

In addition, EMeD can use the expectations derived from running the problem solver, detecting problems that arise while attempting to build a complete problem-solving tree.

Preliminary Evaluations

We performed a preliminary evaluation of our approach by comparing the performance of four subjects in two different KA tasks from a Workarounds domain. Each subject did one of the tasks with EMeD and the other task using a version of EMeD that only allowed them to edit methods (the buttons to add, delete, or modify methods), but did not have any additional support from EMeD. Before the experiment, each subject was given a tutorial of the tools with simpler scenarios. The scenarios and tools were used in different orders to reduce the influences from familiarity with tools or fatigue. Each experiment took several hours, including the tutorial, and we took detailed transcripts to record actions performed by the subjects. The subjects had some previous experience in building EXPECT knowledge

Results	Total Time(min)	Number of Methods Added	Time/Method (min)
Without EMeD	218	25	8.72
With EMeD	153	24	6.38

Average time savings: 30 %

Table 1: Results from experiments with subjects.

Functionality	Number of Times Used
Undefined Methods	23
Editor Error Message	17
Method Sub-method Relation Tree	7
Capability Tree	10
Search Methods	1
Method Organizer	2
Problem Solving Agenda	5

Table 2: Number of times that the different components of EMeD were used.

bases, but not with EMeD.

In Table 1, the total time is computed by summing the times with each subject for each tool. The time for each subject is the time to complete the given task (by creating a successful problem-solving tree and eliminating errors). EMeD was able to **reduce the development time to 70%** of the time that users needed without it. Subjects built a comparable number of methods with the different tools. Note that the subjects were not exposed to the EMeD environment before, but were very familiar with the EXPECT framework. The time savings may be more if the subjects had more familiarity with EMeD. We had multiple trial experiments with one of the subjects, with slightly different tasks, and the subject had become more and more skillful, reducing the time per each action. For these reasons, we expect that the time reduction with EMeD will be larger in practice. Also note that there is a practical limit to the amount of time saved using any KA tool. There is a significant amount of time that users spend doing tasks such as thinking and typing, where a machine can provide little help. We would like to measure the improvement over the time actually doing knowledge input, instead of the time to complete a KA task.

We counted the number of times each component of EMeD was used during the experiments, as shown in Table 2. The list of undefined methods was most useful (used 23 times to build 24 methods) during the experiment, and the subjects checked it almost every time they created a new method. The subjects seemed to be comparing what they expected with the list created by the KA tool, and built new methods using the suggestions proposed by the system. The error messages showed after editing each individual method effectively detected the errors within a method definition, and was used every time there were local errors in the definition.

Users looked at the Method Sub-method Relation Tree

but not as many times as what we expected. The subjects felt the tree was useful but there were too many items shown for each node, making it hard to read. We are planning to display items selectively, showing the details only when they are needed. The Capability Tree was often used to find some capability description of another method needed while defining a method body. However, the hierarchical structure was not so meaningful to the subjects, since sometimes people choose arbitrary concepts (compute, estimate, etc.) to describe their capabilities. We are planning to develop a better way of organizing the methods based on what tasks they can achieve.

Search Methods and Method Organizer were used very little during the experiment. Since the size of the KB was relatively small (about 3 methods were given in the beginning and 6 methods were built for each task), the subjects were able to see them easily in the editor window. However, during real KB development, the size of the KB is usually much larger, and we expect that they will be more useful in real settings.

With EMeD, the subjects run the problem solver mostly to check if they had finished their tasks. EMeD was able to find errors earlier and provide guidance on how they may fix the problem, filtering out most of the errors. Without EMeD, the subjects run the problem solver to detect errors, and ended up spending more time to find the sources of errors and fix them.

Related Work

There are other KA tools that take advantage of relationships among KB elements to derive expectations. Teireisias (Davis 1979) uses *rule models* to capture relationships among the rules based on their general structure and guide the user in following that general structure when a new rule is added that fits a model. Some of the capabilities of EMeD are similar in spirit to the rule model (e.g., the method capability tree), and are also used in EMeD to help developers understand potential dependencies among the KB elements. Other KA tools (Eriksson *et al.* 1995; Birmingham & Klinker 1993; Marcus & McDermott 1989) also use dependencies between factual knowledge and problem-solving methods to guide users during knowledge acquisition. These tools help users to populate and extend a system that already has a significant body of knowledge, but they are not designed to help users in the initial stages of KB development. More importantly, these tools are built to acquire factual domain knowledge and assume that users cannot change or add problem-solving knowledge. In this sense, EMeD is unique because it guides users in adding new problem-solving methods.

In the field of software engineering, it has been recognized that it is generally better to focus on improving the process of software development rather than on the output program itself (Dunn 1994). Our approach embraces this view and tries to improve the initial phases of KB development. Some previous work on using formal languages to specify knowledge bases (Fensel, Angele, & Studer 1998) is inspired by software engineering approaches. This work provides a framework for users to model and capture the initial requirements of the system, and require that users are experienced with formal logic. Our approach is complementary in that it addresses the stage of implementing the knowledge-based system, and we believe that our formalism is more accessible to users that have no formal training. Other approaches (Wielinga, Schreiber, & Breuker 1992; Gaines & Shaw 1993) support users in the initial stages of development by providing a methodology that can be followed systematically to elicit knowledge from experts and to design the new system. These methodologies can be used in combination with our approach.

There is also related research in developing tools to help users build ontologies (Fikes, Farquhar, & Rice 1997; Terveen & Wroblewski 1990; Clark & Porter 1997). Unlike our work, these tools do not tackle the issue of using these ontologies within a problem-solving context. Many of the research contributions in these tools concern the reuse of ontologies for new problems, collaborative issues in developing knowledge bases, and the visualization of large ontologies. We believe that integrating our approach with these capabilities will result in improved environments to support KB creation.

Conclusion

We analyzed the process of KB development to support KB creation and KB extension, and found a set of expectations to help KA tools guide users during the development process. We have classified the sources of errors in the KB development process based on their characteristics, and found ways to prevent, detect, and fix errors earlier. These expectations were derived from the dependencies among KB elements. Although EMeD aims to provide support for KB creation, its functionality is also useful for modifying existing knowledge or populating a KB with instances.

We are now extending the EMeD framework to be able to derive expectations in solving particular problems. Currently EMeD computes relationship among the KB components regardless of the context. Depending on what problem episode we are solving, the relationships may show different patterns, since the problem-solving methods may become specialized.

In our initial evaluations, EMeD was able to provide useful guidance to users reducing KB development time by 30%. We expect that EMeD will be even more beneficial for domain experts who don't have much KA experience. EMeD also opens the door to collaborative tools for knowledge acquisition, because it captures what KA tasks remain to be done and that may be done by other users.

Acknowledgments

We gratefully acknowledge the support of DARPA with grant F30602-97-1-0195 as part of the DARPA High Performance Knowledge Bases Program and with contract DABT63-95-C-0059 as part of the DARPA/Rome Laboratory Planning Initiative. We would like to thank the members of the EXPECT project, Andre Valente, Jim Blythe, Marcelo Tallis, Surya Ramachandran, and Bill Swartout for their thoughtful input on this work. We also would like to thank Kevin Knight for the helpful comments on earlier drafts.

References

Birmingham, W., and Klinker, G. 1993. Knowledge-acquisition tools with explicit problem-solving methods. *The Knowledge Engineering Review* 8(1):5–25.

Clark, P., and Porter, B. 1997. Building concept representations from reusable components. In *Proceedings of the Fourteenth National Conference on Artificial Intelligence*, 369–376.

Davis, R. 1979. Interactive transfer of expertise: Acquisition of new inference rules. *Artificial Intelligence* 12:121–157.

Dunn, R. H. 1994. Quality assurance, Encyclopedia of software engineering. 2.

Eriksson, H.; Shahar, Y.; Tu, S. W.; Puerta, A. R.; and Musen, M. 1995. Task modeling with reusable problem-solving methods. *Artificial Intelligence* 79:293–326.

Feigenbaum, E. 1993. The tiger in the cage. A Plenary Talk in Fifth Innovative Applications of AI Conference.

Fensel, D.; Angele, J.; and Studer, R. 1998. The knowledge acquisition and representation language KARL. *IEEE Transactions on Knowledge and Data Engineering* 10(4):527–550.

Fikes, R.; Farquhar, A.; and Rice, J. 1997. Tools for assembling modular ontologies in ontolingua. In *Proceedings of the Fourteenth National Conference on Artificial Intelligence*, 436–441.

Gaines, B. R., and Shaw, M. 1993. Knowledge acquisition tools based on personal construct psychology. *The Knowledge Engineering Review* 8(1):49–85.

Gil, Y., and Melz, E. 1996. Explicit representations of problem-solving strategies to support knowledge acquisition. In *Proceedings of the Thirteenth National Conference on Artificial Intelligence*.

Gil, Y. 1994. Knowledge refinement in a reflective architecture. In *Proceedings of the Twelfth National Conference on Artificial Intelligence*.

Marcus, S., and McDermott, J. 1989. SALT: A knowledge acquisition language for propose-and-revise systems. *Artificial Intelligence* 39(1):1–37.

Swartout, W., and Gil, Y. 1995. EXPECT: Explicit representations for flexible acquisition. In *Proceedings of the Ninth Knowledge-Acquisition for Knowledge-Based Systems Workshop*.

Terveen, L. G., and Wroblewski, D. 1990. A collaborative interface for editing large knowledge bases. In *Proceedings of the Eighth National Conference on Artificial Intelligence*, 491–496.

Wielinga, B. J.; Schreiber, A. T.; and Breuker, A. 1992. KADS: a modelling approach to knowledge acquisition. *Knowledge Acquisition* 4(1):5–54.

Designing Scripts to Guide Users in Modifying Knowledge-based Systems

Marcelo Tallis and Yolanda Gil

Information Sciences Institute
University of Southern California
Marina del Rey, CA 90292
tallis@isi.edu, gil@isi.edu

Abstract

Knowledge Acquisition (KA) Scripts capture typical modification sequences that users follow when they modify knowledge bases. KA tools can use these Scripts to guide users in making these modifications, ensuring that they follow all the ramifications of the change until it is completed. This paper describes our approach to design, develop, and organize a library of KA Scripts. We report the results of three different analysis to develop this library, including a detailed study of actual modification scenarios in two knowledge bases. In addition to identifying a good number of KA Scripts, we found a set of useful attributes to describe and organize the KA Scripts. These attributes allow us to analyze the size of the library and generate new KA Scripts in a systematic way. We have implemented a portion of this library and conducted two different studies to evaluate it. The result of this evaluation showed a 15 to 52 percent time savings in modifying knowledge bases and that the library included relevant and useful KA Scripts to assist users in realistic settings.

Introduction

Developing Knowledge Acquisition (KA) tools that help users create and maintain knowledge bases (KBs) is an important research issue for AI. Once a prototype knowledge base is initially developed, users would like to maintain and extend it throughout its lifetime. Users need KA tools to guide them make these changes, because it is hard for them to foresee and follow up on all the effects and implications of each individual modification that they make. Script-based KA tools (Gil & Tallis 1997) help users follow typical modification procedures (*KA Scripts*), ensuring that they follow up the effects of each individual change and complete the overall modification. This kind of approach has also been shown to be useful for developing software (Waters 1985; Johnson & Feather 1991; Johnson, Feather, & Harris 1992), and for developing intelligent assistants for common tasks (e.g., the wizards that are now a part of many commercial tools).

Previous work has showed promising results with a scripts-based tool that contained a limited set of KA Scripts (Gil & Tallis 1997). We set out to scale up this approach and develop a library of KA Scripts that would provide a more extensive coverage of situations when users modify knowledge bases. We found that there are many ways to define these Scripts, that it is hard to find the appropriate level of generality, and that it is challenging to generate KA Scripts systematically to ensure good coverage. This paper reports our findings in all these areas. The paper also describes three different analyses that we conducted, each unveiling different insights about how to populate a KA Script library.

First, we carried out an analysis of the follow-up procedures for every possible syntactic modification to the elements of a knowledge-based systems (KBSs). The result was a set of KA scripts that has proven to be complete in its coverage but too general to provide useful guidance to users.

Second, we carried out a detailed analysis of KBS modification scenarios. The results obtained from this analysis were the reverse of those from the prior analysis, which was not satisfactory either. Using this method we obtained KA Scripts that proved to be very useful to users. Unfortunately, this method cannot produce a complete set of KA Scripts. There are few other reports in the literature of what kinds of modifications are made to knowledge bases, and they are often anecdotal. We report the results of this analysis in detail, so other researchers can benefit from this empirical perspective on what are typical knowledge acquisition tasks.

Finally, we combined both analyses to conceive a method that turned to be satisfactory in both, coverage as well as user support. The problem with our first analysis was that an indication of a syntactic change to a KBS element was too general to determine an operative procedure for following up that change. We needed a more specific description of the change as well as of the situation in which that change was performed and the strategy chosen to follow up that change. These more specific descriptions could be generated by combining all possible values for a set of defining attributes of a KA Script. A set of attributes was determined by analyzing KBS modification scenarios.

We used this set of attributes to generate systematically a subset of the KA Scripts library, which we implemented. Our preliminary tests with subjects show a 15 to 52 percent improvement in terms of time to complete a modification. We also conducted an experiment in a realistic setting, using five modification scenarios to a knowledge base that were proposed by a third party. Our Script-Based KA tool found relevant scripts to guide the user in most situations.

The rest of the paper is organized as follows. First we introduce some background on script-based knowledge acquisition and our framework for representing knowledge. Following that, we discuss some important considerations for developing a KA script library. Then we describe each one of the analyses that we have carried out and report on their results. Finally we describe our implementation of a SBKA tool and present some results from its evaluation.

Background: Script-based Knowledge Acquisition

The script-based knowledge acquisition (SBKA) approach (Gil & Tallis 1997) was conceived to support users in completing a KBS modification. KBS modifications usually require changing several related parts of a system. Identifying all of the related portions of the system that need to be changed and determining how to change them is hard for users to figure out. Furthermore, if the modification is not completed, the KBS will be left inconsistent.

To assist users in performing all of the required changes, a KA tool needs to understand how changes in different parts of the system are related. In script-based knowledge-acquisition this is achieved by incorporating a library of *knowledge-acquisition scripts*, which represent prototypical procedures for modifying knowledge-based systems. KA scripts provide a context for relating individual changes of different parts of a KBS, and hence enabling the analysis of each change from the perspective of the overall modification.

Figure 1 shows an example of a typical procedure for modifying a KBS. In our knowledge representation framework which is EXPECT (Gil & Melz 1996; Swartout & Gil 1995; Gil 1994), a knowledge-based system includes a model of the domain and problem-solving methods for achieving goals in that domain. The domain model describes concepts, relations, and their instances. A problem solving method (or *method* for short) consist of a *capability description* that indicates the goals that the method is able to achieve, and a *body* that describes a procedure for achieving those goals. The body procedure can include *subgoal expressions* that have to be solved by other methods whose capability subsumes the posted subgoal. The method's body can also include *relational expressions* that make reference to other elements of the domain.

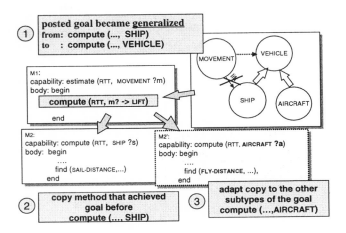

Figure 1: A typical KBS modification procedure

The domain model of Figure 1 describes two kind of VEHICLES: SHIPS and AIRCRAFT, and TRANSPORTATION MOVEMENTS with LIFTS consisting of SHIPS (crossed over). The figure also shows two problem-solving methods. Method M1 for *estimating the round-trip time (RTT) of a movement* posts a subgoal for *computing the RTT of the lift of the movement*. Because the lift of a movement consist of ships, this goal could be achieved by method M2 which *computes the RTT of ships*.

Suppose now that the LIFT relation is changed to include any kind of vehicle in its range. This change will cause the goal COMPUTE, posted by M1, to compute the RTT for both ships and aircraft. At this state, the KBS contains an error because the system will not be able to achieve the goal *compute RTT of vehicle* with any available problem-solving method. Hence, additional changes are needed to complete the modification and leave the KBS in a coherent state.

The example also describes a typical procedure for following up these kinds of changes. The procedure indicates that:

if 1) a) a posted goal is made more general (e.g., the goal *compute the round trip time of a ship* is changed to *compute the round trip time of a vehicle*) and
   b) the generalized goal can now be decomposed into two disjunct subcases (e.g, the goal *compute the round trip time of a vehicle* can be decomposed into one case for **ship** and another case for **aircraft**), and
   c) one of these subcases is equivalent to the goal before being generalized
then 2) copy the method that achieved the goal before being changed (this method can still achieve one of the subcases), and
   3) adapt this copy to the other subcase (e.g., copy the method for **ships** and adapt it to **aircraft**). This way, the two methods combined would achieve the modified goal.

The following sections discuss the methods used to develop a library of KA scripts.

Developing a Library of Knowledge Acquisition Scripts

A KA scripts library is the core of a script-based knowledge-acquisition (SBKA) tool. To maximize its utility, this library should not merely be a repository of isolated KA scripts. Rather, this library should combine KA Scripts such that as a whole it covers most possible situations with minimum overlap. This section discusses some important considerations for a KA script library.

Which Procedures

One important aspect is what kind of procedures would be represented. It is useful to distinguish the following types of procedures:

1. *Macros.* Procedures for automating common sequences of changes in a knowledge-based system. The purpose of these procedures is to simplify and speed-up modifications to a KBS. An example of a procedure of this type might be a macro for splitting a problem-solving method. This would be useful, for example, when a method is too complex or when one wants to reuse a portion of it. This procedure substitutes a fragment of the original method by an invocation to a new method, and creates a new method that corresponds to the substituted code.

2. *Methods for fixing errors.* Procedures that implement common remedies to known errors types in the KB. The purpose of these procedures is to assist a naive user in fixing the error. An example might be a procedure that, to remedy the absence of a method for achieving a goal, adapts another method to that purpose. This procedure would guide a user in choosing and adapting an existing method to solve the unachieved goal.

3. *Procedures for following up changes.* Procedures for propagating the changes performed to one KB element into other related elements in the KB. The purpose of these procedures is to help a user to deal with the complexity of the interactions among elements of a KBS. An example of a procedure of this type might be a procedure that modifies a goal statement to conform to a change of the capability of the method that achieves it.

These categories are not mutually exclusive. Some KB modification procedures may belong to more than one of these classes. For example, a macro can be used to fix an error, and this fix might consist in following up a previous change. We decided to focus on the procedures for following up changes because they are more directly related to the issue of assisting users in performing all required changes of a KBS modification.

What changes

Changes can be described at different levels, from a purely syntactical level (e.g., change a goal argument from X to Y) to a knowledge level (e.g., modify a problem-solving method so instead of considering trips exclusively with ships, it now considers aircraft too).

While a low-level description would make it easier to describe and formulate changes, it fails to capture the intention behind each change, and KA Scripts for following them up end up being so general that they are typically not very useful. For example, consider a KA Script that propagates a change in a goal argument to the method that is supposed to achieve that goal. This KA script cannot provide too much guidance in modifying that method because this modification would be very different depending on the specifics of the change in the goal (e.g., whether the goal was made more general or more specific). Another drawback of using low level descriptions is that descriptions at this level might constitute only a small fraction of the change that has to be followed up. For example, a goal expression might have changed several parameters, and it would be better to follow this whole change at once and not each change to a parameter in isolation.

Therefore, we believe it is more useful to describe changes at a more conceptual level. However, we have found difficulty in systematically enumerating changes at this higher level, while enumerating syntactic changes is a relatively easy task.

We have found that the procedures for following changes are more dependent on the effect of the changes than on the change itself. First, because changes to KB elements have different effects depending on how these elements interact with each other. For example, a change to generalize the range of a relation will have different effects whether the elements in this range were used as arguments of a goal or as a domain for a relational expression. In the case of the goal, this change will cause a generalization of the goal. In the case of the relational expression, this change will cause a generalization of the domain of the relational expression. Depending on the case, this change should have to be followed up differently. In the goal case, the continuation might change the method that used to achieve that goal, while in the case of the relational expression the continuation might change the definition of the relation. Another reason to follow effects instead of changes is that different changes may produce the same effect and this effect is followed up independently of its cause (i.e., the original change). Therefore, our KA scripts were designed to follow up possible effects of changes rather than the performed changes. The following sections describe the analyses that we carried out in order to develop a KA script library.

Analysis of Syntactic Changes

Our first analysis looked at the kinds of syntactic changes that can be done to a knowledge-based system, their possible consequences, and the successive changes that could follow up on those consequences. For example, we analyzed different types of changes to goals (e.g., modify one parameter), their possible consequences (it might not be possible to match that goal to a method), and their follow-up changes (e.g., change that same parameter in the method that achieved that goal before, and then change the body of that method accordingly). The set of all possible changes was generated from the grammar of the language used to describe the knowledge bases.

The result of this analysis was a complete set of KA scripts for following up all possible changes. These KA Scripts cover all the situations in which a user can get when modifying a knowledge base. However, tests with our initial implementation showed that the guidance they provide to users was too general to be very useful. The main problem was that they do not make good use of the context available, like more specific characteristics of the change (e.g., the parameter was changed to a more general type), existing knowledge (e.g., the modified goal can be decomposed into two subcases), or the changes performed to other parts of the knowledge base (e.g., a similar change was performed to a related element).

Another problem of this approach was that it produced somewhat cumbersome and redundant KA scripts. As we explained in the previous section, changes to KBS elements have different effects depending on how these elements interact with each other, and we have found that the procedures for following changes are more dependent on the effect of the changes than on the change itself. Especially because different changes can produce the same effect and this effect is followed up independently of its cause. By structuring KA Scripts around the type of change to be followed up, each KA script had to include provisions for every possible consequence that the change to be followed up can have. However, because these consequences are independent of the change itself, these same provisions have to be repeated in every related KA script.

Nevertheless, this analysis allowed us to follow a systematic procedure for enumerating KA Scripts and generate a complete set.

Analysis of KBS modification scenarios

This analysis was aimed to generate KA Scripts that were less general (and thus more helpful) than those generated in our previous analysis. Our hypothesis was that a detailed analysis of KBS modification scenarios would allow us to identify patterns of related changes more specific to the context in which those changes were performed. For this analysis, we compared a number of subsequent versions of KBSs that were saved by users as they were developing them. Another possibility for doing this analysis is to record the changes while users are editing the KB. The problem with that approach is that the analysis would include changes that are later undone by users, or partially undone and then completed in a way that has more of an error recovery flavor and where it would be best if the user went back to the original KBS and started the change again. We generated our data by comparing different versions of KBSs and reconstructed the changes done across versions.

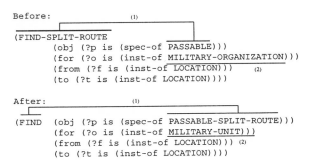

Figure 2: Two independent clusters of related changes between two versions of a method capability description. Cluster 1) corresponds to a *rephrasing of a capability* to enhance readability, while cluster 2) corresponds to a *specialization of a capability* (military-unit is a subtype of military-organization)

To reconstruct the changes performed between versions A and B of the same KBS and to identify KA scripts, we followed the following procedure:

1. **Correlating KB versions:** Build the trees of method invocation for A and B and correlate their nodes. The correlation between nodes helps in recognizing methods that have changed their names or capability descriptions between versions, and also new methods that are similar to others that existed before.

2. **Comparing versions:** For each method in the KB, find the differences between the two versions of the KBS.

3. **Identifying conceptual changes:** Not all changes performed in a method share their purpose. For each method in the KB, hypothesize the purpose of each observed change and then cluster the changes with related purposes. Figure 2 shows an example of clusters. Each cluster would constitute a *conceptual change*.

4. **Relating conceptual changes:** Find sets of related conceptual changes. One way to accomplish this is by hypothesizing what changes should have been necessary to follow up an observed conceptual change and then trying to locate them. Use the tree of method invocation to find out relations among methods.

5. **Generalizing sequences of conceptual changes:** Generalize the observed sequences of changes and determine the features from the scenario that would make these sequences possible and meaningful.

6. **Proposing other sequences:** Propose other sequences of changes by permuting the order of the changes in the sequence.

We carried out this analysis based on the following input data:

- Case Study I: 4 successive versions of a *trafficability* KBS where the user was developing an initial prototype.

- Case Study II: 6 successive versions of an *air campaign plan evaluation* KBS where the user was extending an already implemented prototype.

Case study I: Initial prototype implementation

In this scenario we identified 41 conceptual changes. The following is a list of the different conceptual changes observed and the number of times that they occurred.

1. **rephrase method capability.** The capability of a method has been rephrased by renaming, adding or deleting constant terms, usually to enhance readability. However, the method's procedure remains the same. (13 occurrences)

2. **rephrase goal.** Like the previous conceptual change but with goals (13 occurrences)

3. **restrict applicability of a method.** A method capability is specialized but the method's procedure is not changed. (9 occurrences)

4. **add exception.** A fragment of the method's procedure is embedded inside the *then* (or *else*) clause of an *If* statement. (1 occurrence)

5. **restrict result type.** Specialize result type declaration. (1 occurrence)

6. **pass an additional argument in a method invocation.** (1 occurrence)

7. **require an additional parameter in a method capability.** (1 occurrence)

8. **split a method.** Extract a fragment from a method into a newly created method. (1 occurrence)

9. **reorganize access path to domain elements.** Reorganize the sequence of domain relations used to retrieve domain elements from the KB (probably because the domain model has been reorganized too). (1 occurrence)

The following relations between conceptual changes were observed:

1. rephrase goal / rephrase capability of invoked method

2. rephrase capability / rephrase internal goals that refer to the changed capability parameters

3. restrict applicability of a method / restrict result type of method

4. restrict applicability of a method / restrict applicability of the methods invoked by internal goals that refer to the specialized parameter (i.e., propagates capability restrictions to other methods)

5. rename concept in domain model / rename concept reference in methods

6. reorganize domain model / reorganize access path to domain elements

7. rephrase goal / rephrase similar goals in same method

8. change body expression / replicate change in similar expressions in same method

9. pass an additional argument in a method invocation / require an additional parameter in a method capability

Case study II: Extending implemented prototype

In this scenario we identified 25 conceptual changes. The following is a list of the kinds of conceptual changes observed and the number of times that they occurred.

1. **rename a relational expression.** Rename a relational expression because the referred relation was also renamed in the domain model. (1 occurrence)

2. **add goal to a set of goals.** The analyzed KBS used to generate a set of goals corresponding to a set of instances. After adding an instance to the set, a new goal was automatically generated and added to the initial set of goals. (1 occurrence)

3. **create a method to achieve a new goal added to a set.** (1 occurrence)

4. **create method to achieve a new goal added to a method procedure.** (3 occurrences)

5. **reduce the number of elements from a set to be processed.** Filter the elements of a set before processing them. (1 occurrence)

6. **remove an *append* operand.** (1 occurrence)

7. **remove an unused method.** (3 occurrences).

8. **collapse two methods into one.** (2 occurrences)

9. **remove unused goal argument.** (2 occurrences).

10. **remove unused capability argument.** (2 occurrences).

11. **rephrase goal.** (2 occurrences)

12. **rephrase capability.** (2 occurrences)

13. **split a method.** (2 occurrences).

14. **regroup operations performed by a set of methods into a different set of methods.** The operations performed by a chain of methods invocations is regrouped into a different set of methods to enhance method reusability. (2 occurrences)

The following relations between conceptual changes were observed:

1. rename relation in domain model / rename relational expression

2. add goal to the set of goals / create a method to achieve a new goal added to a set

3. add goal expression to method procedure / create method to achieve new goal added to a method

4. remove goal expression from method procedure / remove unused method

5. remove unused goal argument / remove unused capability argument

6. regroup operations from a chain of methods invocations into a different set of methods / repeat the same changes for a parallel branch of method invocations.

7. rephrase goal / rephrase capability of invoked method

This scenario analysis permitted us to recognize a number of additional interesting characteristics of KBS modifications and KA scripts:

- **Conceptual changes:** Conceptual changes describe changes at a level that captures the user's intention behind the changes. For example, generalizing the type of a goal parameter conceptually correspond to *generalizing a goal*. Note that a conceptual change has several realizations. For example, another way of generalizing a goal is by generalizing its verb or by eliminating a goal parameter.

  Referring to changes at a conceptual level has the following advantages:

  - Enhance user comprehension of the KA script procedure because it is closer to the level in which users reason about changes.

  - Develop a KA Scripts library at an appropriate level of abstraction.

  - Factorize KA Scripts because referring to a conceptual change is equivalent to referring to all possible realizations of it.

  - Design a KA Script library that is not so specific to any particular knowledge-representation language because most conceptual changes have corresponding changes in other KB frameworks.

  Referring to changes at a conceptual level has the problem that it is more difficult to systematically enumerate all possible types of changes.

- **Interdependencies between KBS elements:** The observed sequences of changes allowed us to infer *Interdependencies* between elements of a KBS. For example, from two related conceptual changes, one in a method capability and the other in a method subgoal that shared the type of one of their parameters, we inferred a possible interdependency between elements of this kind. Determining the possible types of interdependencies between elements of a KBS would help us to identify new KA Scripts by analyzing how the interdependent elements should be modified in coordination. It was not possible to establish the necessary conditions for all observed interdependencies between KBS elements. Hence, some identified KA Scripts were based on the hypothetical existence of such interactions.

- **Recurrent KA scripts:** Several detected KA Scripts were observed repeatedly in different parts and in different KBSs. Whether the generation of

KA scripts based on specific scenarios would produce KA scripts general enough to be reused was an issue that had concerned us before carrying out this analysis.

Although the analysis of KBS modification scenarios allowed us to identify KA Scripts that were more specific to their context, it did not help in generating a comprehensive library of KA scripts. Nevertheless, this analysis permitted us to identify important attributes of the KA Scripts that constitute the base for the third and last analysis.

Analysis of Attributes of Knowledge Acquisition Scripts

In this analysis we extended the method used in the first analysis to a full set of attributes. Starting from this set of attributes together with an enumeration of their range values, we can develop a comprehensive KA script library by defining a KA script for any feasible combination of attribute values. The attributes that we considered were as follows:

1. **Change to follow up:** We designed a typology of *conceptual changes* based on.

   (a) changed element. A KB element (or a subelement) that describes a conceptual unit (e.g., goal expression, method capability).

   (b) type of change. Whether the change created, modified, copied, or deleted an element.

   (c) transformation. The relationship between the changed element before and after the change (e.g., generalization, addition of an argument).

2. **Interdependency:** We listed all possible KB elements that could be interdependent with the changed element referred in 1 (e.g., goal / method for achieving it). A KA Script procedure would be concerned with propagating the change performed in 1 to the KB element indicated by this attribute.

3. **Strategy:** This dimension enumerates some general strategies for propagating the change indicated in 1 along the interdependency indicated in 2. For example, a strategy for propagating the addition of a new posted goal to the method that will achieve it is to generalize an existing problem-solving method that achieves a goal similar to the one recently added, so that it is applicable to both goals. We have included several strategies that either modify existing KB elements or create new KB elements based on an existing one to make it easier for users to perform the modification and to encourage knowledge reuse. The indication of which existing element should be used as a basis is the purpose of the next attribute.

4. **Base element:** This attribute enumerates good candidates to be used as a basis for strategies that modify an existing element or create a new one based on an existing one (e.g., the method that used to achieve a changed goal before starting the modification, a

method used for achieving a similar goal posted in an analogous method)

Using a set of KA script attributes to generate a KA Script library offered us some additional benefits. It allowed us to describe the content of the library by indicating the range of attribute values covered by the KA scripts in the library. It also permitted us to estimate the size of the whole library before completing its development.

An implemented KA Script Library

We have implemented a KA script library to be used with ETM (Gil & Tallis 1997), a script-based knowledge-acquisition tool that supports modifications of EXPECT knowledge-based systems (Gil & Melz 1996; Swartout & Gil 1995; Gil 1994). The following are the regions of the KA script library that we have implemented:

1. KA Scripts to follow any type of **change to a goal expressions**, that take care of its **interdependency with the problem-solving method** that achieves that goal. We considered all the strategies that consisted in creating or modifying problem-solving methods. Other possible strategies, not considered in our current implementation, include modifying the changed goal expression further to match an existing problem-solving methods in its current state.

2. KA Scripts to follow **changes to a method capability**, that take care of its **interdependency with goal expressions** to be solved by it. We considered all types of changes to method capabilities, and all strategies that consisted in creating or changing goal expressions. Other possible strategies, not considered in our current implementation, include creating or modifying further the same or other problem-solving methods to match the existing goal expressions.

These two regions of the KA Scripts space were chosen because they address the interdependencies between goal and method capability, which are in our experience one of the most prevalent and harder to solve problems that arise during knowledge-based system modifications. These two regions contain up to 100 KA Scripts altogether, from which we have implemented 37.

We were able to identify a few general operators that could be used to implement steps of the KA scripts (e.g., generalize a method, create analogous method to achieve similar goal). These operators could be reused to implement most of the steps in our KA Scripts library. For example, the operator to *Generalize a method* was used by a KA Script that in order to achieve a new goal generalizes the problem-solving method that achieves an existing goal similar to the one just added, and was also used by a KA script that, in order to achieve a goal that was generalized, generalizes the method that used to achieve that goal before being modified.

KA scripts at work

We have carried out two different studies to evaluate our KA scripts library. In the first one we conducted a series of *controlled experiments* to measure the comparative performance of subjects in modifying KBSs with and without ETM. In our second study we conducted an empirical analysis of subjects using ETM in *realistic domains and scenarios* previously unseen by the developers of ETM.

Controlled Experiments

These experiments compared the performance in modifying KBSs for subjects using ETM vs. subjects using EXPECT only. Each subject had to solve two scenarios, one of them using EXPECT and the other using ETM. One of the scenarios was slightly more complex than the other one. All of our subjects were familiar with EXPECT (but not with ETM), and had some previous exposure to the domain.

We conducted this experiment twice. The first time we only had implemented a subset of the KA script library (7 KA scripts). To put subjects in a context in which the KA scripts in the library were applicable, we indicated the first change that had to be performed for each scenario. Four subjects participated this first time. The results obtained showed that the time needed to complete the scenarios could be reduced 15% for the simpler scenario and 52% for the more complex one (Gil & Tallis 1997). Notice that the subjects were familiar with EXPECT but not with ETM. We expect the difference to be much larger in our future tests with users who are not familiar with EXPECT.

We have repeated the experiment with a more complete set of KA scripts (37 KA scripts) and with no restrictions for the initial changes to the scenarios. In this occasion the time needed to complete the scenario was reduced between a 15% and a 52%. Besides, the experiment was important in that it showed that scaling up the KA scripts library did not degrade the performance of the subjects. An issue that had also concerned us.

Realistic and Unseen Scenarios

For this study we used the knowledge-bases and scenarios of the *Challenge Problems* from the *High Performance Knowledge Bases* (HPKB) DARPA project (Cohen *et al.* 1998). These problems were developed independently and with the specific purpose of testing the technologies being developed within the project. In particular, both, the domain and the modification scenarios were unknown to the designers of the KA script library before this experiment. The modification scenarios consisted in performing five extensions to a large KBS concerned with evaluating enemy workarounds for a targeted obstacle and containing 62 problem-solving methods. Each extension required creating and modifying several problem-solving methods.

In this experiment, a subject used ETM to implement the KBS extensions requested by the scenarios.

Our subject was one of the developers of the KBS who had also performed these same modifications months before the experiment without ETM. During this experiment, the subject was allowed to consult the KBS that has resulted from that previous episode, and to copy and paste fragments of that KBS in order to speed-up typing. However, we asked the subject to follow the guidance of ETM if appropriate.

We expected that our library would cover all the situations in which methods should be created or modified to follow up additions or modifications of goals. Therefore, the following analysis concentrates on those situations.

The complete modification of the KBS required the creation and modification of 16 methods. From this total, 14 were achieved with the guidance of ETM through the application of 12 KA Scripts. Most of these method modifications (12) were new methods added to the KBS, which our KA scripts helped to achieve by creating and then modifying copies of existing methods. It is interesting to note that when the subject wrongly thought that the modification was complete, ETM detected the need to perform additional changes. These changes were omitted the first time that the subject had made these modifications. KA scripts are useful not only to make changes faster but also as checklists to ensure that the changes are completed well.

Related Work

Some knowledge-based software engineering (KBSE) tools have incorporated a concept similar to our KA Scripts. KBEmacs (Waters 1985) is a knowledge-based program editor that permits the construction of a program by combining algorithmic fragments (called *cliches*) from a library. KBEmacs cliches are equivalent to KA Scripts except that cliches are algorithmic fragments that are used to *generate* programs while our KA Scripts are procedures that are used to *modify* knowledge-based systems. The developers of KBEmacs have concentrated on the design of cliches and on the overall architecture to handle them, but did not directly addressed the issue of developing a library of cliches.

The Knowledge-based Software Assistant (KBSA) and its successor ARIES are other related KBSE tools (Johnson & Feather 1991; Johnson, Feather, & Harris 1992). The purpose of these tools is to provide integrated support for requirements analysis and specifications development. They provide a library of *evolution transformations* that a user can apply to make consistency-preserving modifications to the description of a software system. These evolution transformations are similar in spirit to our KA Scripts. Their main distinction lies in that evolution transformations are used to manipulate a semi-formal description of a system, while our KA scripts modified the actual implementation of a system. In developing a library of evolution transformations, the authors of these systems have followed a similar analysis to those performed by ourselves, including a detailed analysis of one scenario and

an analysis of the different *semantic dimensions* embodied in software specifications. Like our KA scripts attributes, their dimensions are also independent of the notation used to describe specifications and hence can be applied to others systems too.

Conclusions

KA Scripts are a useful mechanism to guide users in modifying knowledge bases. This paper presents a number of useful insights for developing libraries of KA Scripts that are based on different kinds of analysis of modification scenarios. One of the results reported is a characterization of the modifications made to two real knowledge bases. We also describe a set of attributes that we found very useful to characterize and to systematically generate a KA Scripts library. Our initial evaluations show that our library contains KA Scripts that can be applied to most situations in real modification tasks, and that subjects spend 15 to 52 percent less time modifying knowledge bases.

Acknowledgments

We would like to thank Jose Luis Ambite, Kevin Knight, and the past and present members of the EX-PECT research group. We gratefully acknowledge the support of DARPA with contract DABT63-95-C-0059 as part of the DARPA/Rome Laboratory Planning Initiative and with grant F30602-97-1-0195 as part of the DARPA High Performance Knowledge Bases Program.

References

Cohen, P.; Schrag, R.; Jones, E.; Pease, A.; Lin, A.; Starr, B.; Gunning, D.; and Burke, M. 1998. The Darpa High-Performance Knowledge Bases Project. *AI Magazine* 19(4).

Gil, Y., and Melz, E. 1996. Explicit Representations of Problem-solving Strategies to Support Knowledge Acquisition. In *Proceedings of the Thirteenth National Conference on Artificial Intelligence*.

Gil, Y., and Tallis, M. 1997. A Script-based Approach to Modifying Knowledge-based Systems. In *Proceedings of the Fourteenth National Conference on Artificial Intelligence*.

Gil, Y. 1994. Knowledge Refinement in a Reflective Architecture. In *Proceedings of the Twelfth National Conference on Artificial Intelligence*.

Johnson, W. L., and Feather, M. S. 1991. Using Evolution Transformations to Construct Specifications. In *Automating Software Design*. AAAI Press. 65–92.

Johnson, W. L.; Feather, M. S.; and Harris, D. R. 1992. Representation and Presentation of Requirements Knowledge. *IEEE Transactions on Software Engineering* 18(10):853–869.

Swartout, B., and Gil, Y. 1995. EXPECT: Explicit Representations for Flexible Acquisition. In *Proceedings of the Ninth Knowledge-Acquisition for Knowledge-Based Systems Workshop*.

Waters, R. 1985. The Programmer's Apprentice: A session with Kbemacs. *IEEE Transactions on Software Engineering* 11(11):1296–1320.

An Integrated Shell and Methodology
for Rapid Development of Knowledge-Based Agents

Gheorghe Tecuci, Mihai Boicu, Kathryn Wright, Seok Won Lee, Dorin Marcu, and Michael Bowman

Learning Agents Laboratory, Department of Computer Science, MSN 4A5, George Mason University, Fairfax, VA 22030
{tecuci, mboicu, kwright, swlee, dmarcu, mbowman3}@gmu.edu

Abstract

This paper introduces the concept of *learning agent shell* as a new class of tools for rapid development of practical end-to-end knowledge-based agents, by domain experts, with limited assistance from knowledge engineers. A learning agent shell consists of a learning and knowledge acquisition engine as well as an inference engine and supports building an agent with a knowledge base consisting of an ontology and a set of problem solving rules. The paper describes a specific learning agent shell and its associated agent building methodology. The process of developing an agent relies on importing ontologies from existing repositories of knowledge, and on teaching the agent how to perform various tasks, in a way that resembles how an expert would teach a human apprentice when solving problems in cooperation. The shell and methodology represent a practical integration of knowledge representation, knowledge acquisition, learning and problem solving. This work is illustrated with an example of developing a hierarchical non-linear planning agent.

Introduction

This paper describes recent progress in developing an integrated shell and methodology for rapid development of practical end-to-end knowledge-based agents, by domain experts, with limited assistance from knowledge engineers.

We use the term "knowledge-based agent" to broadly denote a knowledge based system that interacts with a subject matter expert (SME) to learn from the expert how to assist him or her with various tasks.

Our work advances the efforts of developing methods, tools, and methodologies for more rapidly building knowledge-based systems. One of the early major accomplishments of these efforts was the concept of expert system shell (Clancey 1984). An expert system shell consists of a general inference engine for a given expertise domain (such as diagnosis, design, monitoring, or interpretation), and a representation formalism for encoding the knowledge base for a particular application in that domain.

The idea of the expert system shell emerged from the architectural separation between the general inference engine and the application-specific knowledge base, and the goal of reusing the inference engine for a new system.

Currently, we witness a similar separation at the level of the knowledge base, which is more and more regarded as consisting of two main components: an ontology that defines the concepts from the application domain, and a set of problem solving rules (methods) expressed in terms of these concepts.

While an ontology is characteristic to a certain domain (such as an ontology of military units, or an ontology of military equipment), the rules are much more specific, corresponding to a certain type of application in that domain (e.g. rules for an agent that assists a military commander in critiquing courses of action, or rules for an agent that assists in planning the repair of damaged bridges or roads).

The emergence of domain ontologies is primarily a result of terminological standardization in more and more domains to facilitate automatic processing of information, particularly information retrieval. Some of existing ontologies are UMLS (UMLS 1998), CYC (Lenat 1995), and WordNet (Fellbaum 1998).

The availability of domain ontologies raises the prospects of sharing and reusing them when building a new system. However, sharing and reusing the components of different knowledge representation systems are hard research problems because of the incompatibilities in their implicit knowledge models. Recently, the Open Knowledge Base Connectivity (OKBC) protocol has been developed as a standard for accessing knowledge bases stored in different frame representation systems (Chaudhri et al. 1998). OKBC provides a set of operations for a generic interface to such systems. There is also an ongoing effort of developing OKBC servers for various systems, such as Ontolingua (Farquhar et al. 1996) and Loom (MacGregor 1991). These servers are becoming repositories of reusable ontologies and domain theories, and can be accessed using the OKBC protocol.

The existence of domain ontologies facilitates the process of building the knowledge base, which may reduce to one of reusing an existing ontology and defining the application specific problem solving rules. This effort, however, should not be underestimated. Several decades of knowledge engineering attests that the traditional process by which a knowledge engineer interacts with a domain expert to manually encode his or her knowledge into rules is long, difficult and error-prone. Also, automatic learning of rules from data does not yet provide a practical solution to this problem. An alternative approach to acquiring problem solving rules is presented in (Tecuci 1998). In this approach an expert interacts directly with the agent to teach it how to perform domain specific tasks. This teaching of the agent is done in much the same way as teaching a student or apprentice, by giving the agent examples and explanations, as well as supervising and correcting its behavior. During the interaction with the expert the agent learns problem solving rules by integrating a wide range of knowledge acquisition and machine learning techniques, such as apprenticeship learning, empirical inductive learning from examples and explanations, analogical learning and others.

Based on these developments and observations, we propose the concept of "learning agent shell" as a tool for building intelligent agents by domain experts, with limited assistance from knowledge engineers. A learning agent shell consists of a learning and knowledge acquisition engine and an inference engine that support building an agent with a knowledge base composed of an ontology and a set of problem solving rules.

In this paper we present the Disciple Learning Agent Shell (Disciple-LAS) and its methodology for rapid development of knowledge based agents, which relies upon importing ontologies from existing repositories using the OKBC protocol and on teaching the agents to perform various tasks through cooperative problem solving and apprenticeship multistrategy learning. Among the major developments of Disciple-LAS with respect to previous versions of Disciple, we could mention:

- the adoption of the OKBC knowledge model as the basic representation of Disciple's ontology and the extension of the Disciple's apprenticeship multistrategy learning methods to deal with this more powerful knowledge model. These methods have become more knowledge-intensive and less dependent on expert's help, especially through the use of more powerful forms of analogical reasoning. The primary motivation of this extension was to facilitate the ontology import process.
- the development and integration into Disciple of a general purpose cooperative problem solver, based on task reduction. It can run both in a step by step mode and in autonomous mode.
- the development of an integrated methodology for building end-to-end agents.

With respect to the Disciple-LAS shell and methodology we formulate the following three claims:

- they enable rapid acquisition of relevant problem solving knowledge from subject matter experts, with limited assistance from knowledge engineers;
- the acquired problem solving knowledge is of a good enough quality to assure a high degree of correctness of the solutions generated by the agent;
- the acquired problem solving knowledge assures a high performance of the problem solver.

The rest of the paper is organized as follows. We first introduce the Disciple modeling of an application domain. Then we present the architecture of Disciple-LAS, the specification of an agent built with Disciple, and the agent building methodology. We present experimental results of building the specified agent, and we conclude the paper.

Domain Modeling for Integrated Knowledge Acquisition, Learning and Problem Solving

We claim that the Disciple modeling of an application domain provides a natural way to integrate knowledge representation, knowledge acquisition, learning and problem solving, into an end-to-end shell for building practical knowledge-based agents.

As problem solving approach we have adopted the classical task reduction paradigm. In this paradigm, a task to be accomplished by the agent is successively reduced to simpler tasks until the initial task is reduced to a set of elementary tasks that can be immediately performed.

Within this paradigm, an application domain is modeled based on six types of knowledge elements:

1. Objects that represent either specific individuals or sets of individuals in the application domain. The objects are hierarchically organized according to the generalization relation.

2. Features and sets of features that are used to further describe objects, other features and tasks. Two important features of any feature are its domain (the set of objects that could have this feature) and its range (the set of possible values of the feature). The features may also specify functions for computing their values, and are also hierarchically organized.

3. Tasks and sets of tasks that are hierarchically organized. A task is a representation of anything that the agent may be asked to accomplish.

The objects, features and tasks are represented as frames, according to the OKBC knowledge model, with some extensions.

4. Examples of task reductions, such as:

TR: If the task to accomplish is T_1
then accomplish the tasks $T_{11}, \ldots, T_{1n}$

A task may be reduced to one simpler task, or to a (partially ordered) set of tasks. Correct task reductions are called positive examples and incorrect ones are called negative examples.

5. Explanations of task reduction examples. An explanation is an expression of objects and features that indicates why a task reduction is correct (or why it is incorrect). It corresponds to the justification given by a domain expert to a specific task reduction:

the task reduction TR is correct because E

One could more formally represent the relationship between TR and E as follows:

$E \rightarrow TR$, or $E \rightarrow$ (accomplish(T_1) $\rightarrow$ accomplish($T_{11}, \ldots, T_{1n}$))

This interpretation is useful in a knowledge acquisition and learning context where the agent tries to learn from a domain expert how to accomplish a task and why the solution is correct.

However, the example and its explanation can also be represented in the equivalent form:

((accomplish(T_1) & E) $\rightarrow$ accomplish($T_{11}, \ldots, T_{1n}$))

which, in a problem solving context, is interpreted as:

If   the task to accomplish is T_1 (1)
and E holds
then accomplish the tasks $T_{11}, \ldots, T_{1n}$

6. Rules. The rules are generalizations of specific reductions, such as (1), and are learned by the agent through an interaction with the domain expert, as described in (Tecuci, 1998):

If   the task to accomplish is T_{1g} and   (2)
E_h holds
then accomplish the tasks $T_{11g}, \ldots, T_{1ng}$

In addition to the rule's condition that needs to hold in order for the rule to be applicable, the rule may also have several "except-when" conditions that should not hold, in order for the rule to be applicable. An except-when condition is a generalization of the explanation of why a negative example of a rule does not represent a correct task reduction. Finally, the rule may also have "except-for" conditions (that specify instances that are negative exceptions of the rule) and "for" conditions (that specify positive exceptions).

The ontology of objects, features and tasks serves as the generalization hierarchy for Disciple-LAS. An example is basically generalized by replacing its objects with more general objects from the ontology. In the current version of Disciple-LAS the features and the tasks are not generalized, but they are used for analogical reasoning and learning.

Another important aspect of Disciple is that the ontology is itself evolving during knowledge acquisition and learning. This distinguishes Disciple from most of the other learning agents that make the less realistic assumption that the representation language for learning is completely defined before any learning could take place.

Because the Disciple agent is an incremental learner, most often its rules are only partially learned. A partially learned rule has two conditions, a plausible upper bound (PUB) condition E_g which, as an approximation, is more general than the exact condition E_h, and a plausible lower bound (PLB) condition E_s which, as an approximation, is less general than E_h:

If   the task to accomplish is T_{1g} and   (3)
      PUB: E_g holds
      PLB: E_s holds
then accomplish the tasks $T_{11g}, ... , T_{1ng}$

We will refer to such a rule as a plausible version space rule, or PVS rule. Plausible version space rules are used in problem solving to generate task reductions with different degrees of plausibility, depending on which of its conditions are satisfied. If the PLB condition is satisfied, then the reduction is very likely to be correct. If PLB is not satisfied, but PUB is satisfied, then the solution is considered only plausible. The same rule could potentially be applied for tasks that are similar to T_{1g}. In such a case the reductions would be considered even less plausible.

Any application of a PVS rule however, either successful or not, provides an additional (positive or negative) example, and possibly an additional explanation, that are used by the agent to further improve the rule.

Architecture of the Disciple-LAS

The architecture of Disciple-LAS is presented in Figure 1. It includes seven main components, shown in the light gray area, which are domain independent:

- a knowledge acquisition and learning component for developing and improving the KB. It contains several modules for rule learning, rule refinement, and exception handling, and a set of browsers and editors, each specialized for one type of knowledge (objects, features, tasks, examples, explanations and rules).

- a domain-independent problem solving engine based on task reduction. It supports both interactive (step by step) problem solving and autonomous problem solving.

- a knowledge import/export component for accessing remote ontologies located on OKBC servers, or for importing knowledge from KIF files (Genesereth and Fikes, 1992).

- a knowledge base manager which controls access and updates to the knowledge base. Each module of Disciple can access the knowledge base only through the functions of the KB manager.

- an OKBC layer which assures a uniform management of all the elements of the knowledge base, according to the OKBC knowledge model. It also allows future integration with Disciple of efficient memory management systems, such as PARKA (Stoffel et al. 1997).

- an initial domain-independent knowledge base to be developed for the specific application domain. This knowledge base contains the elements that will be part of each knowledge base built with Disciple, such as an upper-level ontology.

- a window-based, domain-independent, graphical user interface, intended to be used primarily by the knowledge engineer.

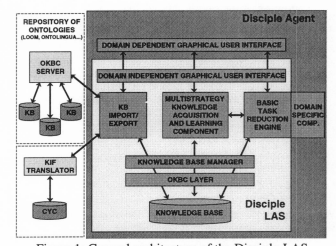

Figure 1: General architecture of the Disciple-LAS

The two components in the dark gray area are the domain dependent components that need to be developed and integrated with the Disciple-LAS shell to form a customized agent for a specific application. They are:

- a domain-dependent graphical user interface which is built for the specific agent to allow the domain experts to communicate with the agent as close as possible to the way they communicate in their environment.

- a domain-specific problem solving component that extends the basic task-reduction engine in order to satisfy the specific problem solving requirements of the application domain.

Disciple-LAS is implemented in JAVA and LISP, in a client-server architecture that assures portability, multi-user development of agents, and fast (socket) connection.

Rapid Development of a Workaround Agent

The integrated Disciple-LAS and methodology were developed as part of the DARPA's High Performance Knowledge Bases Program (Cohen et al. 1998), and were applied to rapidly build a planning agent for solving the workaround challenge problem. We will use this problem to illustrate the Disciple methodology. The problem consisted of assessing how rapidly and by what method a military unit can reconstitute or bypass damage to an infrastructure, such as a damaged bridge or a cratered road (Alphatech 1998).

The input to the agent includes two elements: (1) a description of the damage (e.g. a span of the bridge is dropped and the area is mined), and of the terrain (e.g. the soil type, the slopes of the river's banks, the river's speed, depth and width), (2) a detailed description of the resources in the area that could be used to repair the damage. This includes a description of the engineering assets of the military unit that has to workaround the damage, as well as the descriptions of other military units in the area that could provide additional resources.

The output of the agent consists of the most likely repair strategies, each described in terms of three elements: (1) a reconstitution schedule, giving the transportation capacity of the damaged link (bridge, road or tunnel), as a function of time, including both a minimum time and an expected time; (2) a partially ordered plan of engineering actions to perform the repair, and the minimum as well as the expected time that each of these actions require; and (3) a set of required resources for the entire plan and for each action.

Workaround generation requires detailed knowledge about the capabilities of various types of engineering equipment and about their use. For example, repairing damage to a bridge typically involves different types of mobile bridging equipment and earth moving equipment. Each kind of mobile bridge takes a characteristic amount of time to deploy, requires different kinds of bank preparation, and is owned by different echelons in the military hierarchy. This information was acquired from military experts and Army field manuals.

The Methodology for Building Agents

In this section we will briefly present the main steps of the integrated Disciple-LAS methodology for building end-to-end agents, stressing the characteristic features of this methodology and illustrating them with informal intuitive examples from its application to the development of the workaround agent described above. The steps are to be executed in sequence but at each step one could return to any of the previous steps to fix any discovered problem.

1. Specification of the problem

The SME and the knowledge engineer generally accomplish this step. In the HPKB program, the workaround challenge problem was defined in a 161-page report created by Alphatech (1998). This report already identified many concepts needed to be represented in agent's ontology, such as military units, engineering equipment, types of damage, and geographical features of interest. Therefore, it provided a significant input to the ontology building process.

2. Modeling the problem solving process as task reduction

Once the problem is specified, the expert and the knowledge engineer have to model the problem solving process as task reduction, because this is the problem solving approach currently supported by the Disciple shell. However, the knowledge acquisition and learning methods of Disciple are general, and they could be applied in conjunction with other types of problem solvers, this being one of our future research directions.

In the case of the workaround challenge problem, task reduction proved to actually be a very natural way to model it, the problem solver being a hierarchical non-linear planner.

During the modeling process, the domain is partitioned into classes of typical problem solving scenarios, and for each such scenario, an informal task reduction tree is defined. Examples of problem solving scenarios for the workaround domain are: workaround a damaged bridge by performing minor preparation to install a fixed bridge over the river, workaround a damaged bridge by performing gap reduction to install a fixed bridge, workaround a damaged bridge through fording, workaround a gap in the bridge by using a fixed bridge, workaround a damaged bridge by installing a ribbon bridge, etc.

There are several important results of the modeling process: (1) an informal description of the agent's tasks is produced, (2) additional necessary concepts and features are identified, (3) conceptual task reduction trees are produced that will guide the training of the agent by the domain expert.

3. Developing the customized agent

For the workaround domain, the task reduction engine had to be customized by including a component for ordering the generated plans based on the minimum time needed to execute them, and by generating a summary description of each plan. Also, an interface for displaying maps with the damaged area was integrated into the agent architecture.

4. Importing concepts and features from other ontologies

As a result of the first two steps of the methodology, a significant number of necessary concepts and features have been identified. Interacting with the Knowledge Import/Export Module, the domain expert and the knowledge engineer attempt to import the descriptions of these concepts from an OKBC server. The expert can select a concept or its entire sub-hierarchy and the knowledge import module will automatically introduce this new knowledge into Disciple's knowledge base. This process involves various kinds of verifications to maintain the consistency of Disciple's knowledge.

In the case of the HPKB experiment, we imported from the LOOM server (MacGregor, 1991) elements of the military unit ontology, as well as various characteristics of military equipment (such as their tracked and wheeled military load classes). The extent of knowledge import was more limited than it could have been because the LOOM's ontology was developed at the same time as that of Disciple, and we had to define concepts that have later been also defined in LOOM and could have been imported.

In any case, importing those concepts proved to be very helpful, and has demonstrated the ability to reuse previously developed knowledge.

5. Extending the ontology

The Disciple shell contains specialized browsing and editing tools for each type of knowledge element. It contains an object editor, a feature editor, a task editor, an example editor, a rule editor, a hierarchy browser and an association browser. We have defined a specialized editor for each type of knowledge element to facilitate the interaction with the domain expert.

Using these tools, the domain expert and the knowledge engineer will define the rest of the concepts and features identified in steps 1 and 2 (that could not be imported), as well as the tasks informally specified in step 3. New tasks, objects and features, could also be defined during the next step of training the agent.

6. Training the agent for its domain-specific tasks

While the previous steps are more or less standard in any agent building methodology (with the possible exception of the agent customization step and the ontology importing step), the training of the agent is a characteristic step of the Disciple agent building methodology.

The main result of this step is a set of problem solving rules. Defining correct problem solving rules in a traditional knowledge engineering approach is known to be very difficult. The process implemented in Disciple is based on the following assumptions:

- it is easier for an SME to provide specific examples of problem solving episodes than general rules;
- it is easier for an SME to understand a phrase in agent's language (such as an example or an explanation) than to create it;
- it is easier for an SME to specify hints on how to solve a problem than to give detailed explanations;
- it is easier for the agent to assist the SME in the knowledge acquisition process if the agent has more knowledge.

As a consequence, Disciple incorporates a suite of methods that reduce knowledge acquisition and learning from an SME to the above simpler operations, and are based on increasing assistance from the agent. These methods include:

- methods to facilitate the definition of examples of task reductions;
- heuristic, hint-based and analogy-based methods to generate the explanations of a task reduction;
- analogy-based method to generalize examples to rules;
- methods to generate relevant examples to refine the reduction rules, etc.

During this step, the expert teaches Disciple to solve problems in a cooperative, step by step, problem solving scenario. The expert selects or defines an initial task and asks the agent to reduce it.

The agent will try different methods to reduce the current task. First it will try to apply the rules with their exact or plausible lower bound conditions, because these are most likely to produce correct results. If no reduction is found, then it will try to use the rules considering their plausible upper bound conditions. If again none of these rules apply, then the agent may attempt to use rules corresponding to tasks known to be similar with the one to be reduced. For instance, to reduce the task "Workaround a destroyed bridge using a floating bridge with slope reduction", the agent may consider the reduction rules corresponding to the similar task "Workaround a destroyed bridge using a fixed bridge with slope reduction."

If the solution was defined or modified by the expert, then it represents an initial example for learning a new reduction rule. To learn the rule, the agent will first try to find an explanation of why the reduction is correct. Then the example and the explanation are generalized to a

plausible version space rule. The agent will attempt various strategies to propose plausible explanations from which the user will choose the correct ones. The strategies are based on an ordered set of heuristics. For instance, the agent will consider the rules that reduce the same task into different subtasks, and will use the explanations corresponding to these rules to propose explanations for the current reduction. This heuristic is based on the observation that the explanations of the alternative reductions of a task tend to have similar structures. The same factors are considered, but the relationships between them are different. For instance, if the task is to workaround a damaged bridge using a fixed bridge over the river gap, then the decision of whether to employ (or, equivalently, the explanation of why to employ) an installation of the bridge with minor preparation of the area, or with gap reduction, or with slope reduction, depends upon the specific relationships between the dimensions of the bridge and the dimensions of the river gap. The goal is to have the agent propose explanations ordered by their plausibility and the expert to choose the right ones, rather than requiring the explanations from the expert.

This above strategy works well when the agent already has a significant amount of knowledge related to the current reduction. In the situations when this is not true the agent has to acquire the explanations from the expert. However, even in such cases, the expert need not provide explanations, but only hints that may have various degrees of detail. Let us consider, for instance, the reduction of the task "Workaround damaged bridge using an AVLB70 bridge over the river gap", to the task "Install AVLB70 with gap reduction over the river gap". The expert can give the agent a very general hint, such as, "Look for correlations between the river gap and AVLB70." A more specific hint would be "Look for correlations between the length of the river gap and the lengths of the gaps breachable with AVLB70." Such hints will guide the agent in proposing the correct explanation: "The length of the river gap is greater than the length of AVLB70, but less than the maximum gap that can be reduced in order to use AVLB70".

The goal is to allow the expert to provide hints or incomplete explanations rather than detailed explanations.

The above situations occur when the expert provides the reduction of the current task and will ultimately result in learning a new task reduction rule.

We will now briefly consider some of the other possible cases, where the agent proposes reductions based on the existing rules. If the reduction was accepted by the expert and it was obtained by applying the plausible upper bound condition of a rule, then the plausible lower bound condition of the rule is generalized to cover this reduction.

If the reduction is rejected by the expert, then the agent will attempt to find an explanation of why the reduction is not correct, as described above. This explanation will be used to refine rule's conditions. When no such failure explanation is found, the agent may simply specialize the rule, to uncover the negative example. When this is not possible, the rule will be augmented with an except-for condition.

In a given situation, the agent may propose more than one solution. Each may be characterized separately as good or bad, and treated accordingly. Learning may also be postponed for some of these examples.

This training scenario encourages and facilitates knowledge reuse between different parts of the problem space, as has been experienced in the workaround domain. For instance, many of the rules corresponding to the AVLB bridges have been either generalized to apply to the bridges of types MGB and Bailey, or have been used to guide the learning of new rules for MGB and Bailey. These rules have in turn facilitated the learning of new rules for floating bridges. The rules for floating bridges have facilitated the learning of the rules for ribbon rafts, and so on.

7. Testing and using the agent

During this phase the agent is tested with additional problems, the problem solver being used in autonomous mode to provide complete solutions without the expert's interaction. If any solution is not the expected one, then the expert enters the interactive mode to identify the error and to help the agent to fix it, as described before.

The developed agent can be used by a non-expert user. More interesting is, however, the case where the agent continues to act as an assistant to the expert, solving problems in cooperation, continuously learning from the expert, and becoming more and more useful.

In the case of the workaround domain, the evaluator provided a set of 20 testing problems, each with up to 9 different types of relevant solutions. These examples were used to train and test the agent.

As has been shown above, the Disciple-LAS shell and methodology provide solutions to some of the issues that have been found to be limiting factors in developing knowledge-based agents:

- limited ability to reuse previously developed knowledge;
- the knowledge acquisition bottleneck;
- the knowledge adaptation bottleneck;
- the scalability of the agent building process;
- finding the right balance between using general tools and developing domain specific modules;
- the portability of the agent building tools and of the developed agents.

Experimental Evaluation

The Disciple methodology and workaround agent were tested together with three other systems in a two week intensive study, in June 1998, as part of DARPA's annual HPKB program evaluation (Cohen et al. 1998). The evaluation consisted of two phases, each comprising a test and a re-test. In the first phase, the systems were tested on 20 problems that were similar with those used for systems development. Then the solutions were provided and the developers had one week to improve their systems, which were tested again on the same problems. In the second phase, the systems were tested on five new problems, partially or completely out of the scope of the systems. For instance, they specified a new type of damage (cratered roads), or required the use of new types of engineering equipment (TMM bridges, ribbon rafts and M4T6 rafts). Then again the correct solutions were provided and the developers had one week to improve and develop their systems, which were tested again on the same five problems and five new ones. Solutions were scored along five equally weighted dimensions: (1) generation of the

best workaround solutions for all the viable options, (2) correctness of the overall time estimate for each workaround solution, (3) correctness of each solution step, (4) correctness of temporal constraints among these steps, and (5) appropriateness of engineering resources used. Scores were assigned by comparing the systems' answers with those of Alphatech's human expert. Bonus points were awarded when systems gave better answers than the expert and these answers were used as standard for the next phase of the evaluation.

The participating teams were not uniform in terms of prior system development and human resources. Consequently, only one of them succeeded to enter the evaluation with a system that had a fully developed KB. The other three teams entered the evaluation with systems that had incompletely developed knowledge bases. Figure 2 shows a plot of the overall coverage of each system against the overall correctness of that system, for each of the two phases of the evaluation.

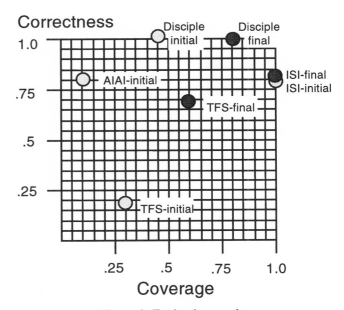

Figure 2: Evaluation results.

We entered the evaluation with a workaround agent the knowledge base of which was covering only about 40% of the workaround domain (11841 binary predicates). The coverage of our agent was declared prior to each release of the testing problems and all the problems falling within its scope were attempted and scored. During the evaluation period we continued to extend the knowledge base to cover more of the initially specified domain, in addition to the developments required by the modification phase. At the end of the two weeks of evaluation, the knowledge base of our agent grew to cover about 80% of the domain (20324 binary predicates). This corresponds to a rate of knowledge acquisition of approximately 787 binary predicates/day, as indicated in Figure 3. This result supports the claim that the Disciple approach enables rapid acquisition of relevant problem solving knowledge from subject matter experts.

With respect to the quality of the generated solutions, within its scope, the Disciple agent performed at the level of the human expert. There were several cases during the evaluation period when the Disciple workaround agent generated more correct or more complete solutions than those of the human expert. There were also cases when the agent generated new solutions that the human expert did not initially consider. For instance, it generated solutions to work around a cratered road by emplacing a fixed bridge over the crater in a similar way with emplacing a fixed bridge over a river gap. Or, in the case of several craters, it generated solutions where some of the craters were filled while on others fixed bridges were emplaced. These solutions were adopted by the expert and used as standard for improving all the systems. For this reason, although the agent also made some mistakes, the overall correctness of its solutions was practically as high as that of the expert's solutions. This result supports the second claim that the acquired problem solving knowledge is of a good enough quality to assure a high degree of correctness of the solutions generated by the agent.

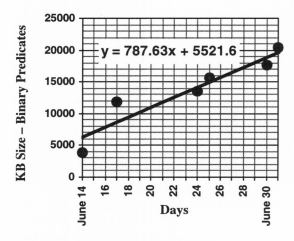

Figure 3: KB Development time.

Finally, our workaround generator had also a very good performance, being able to generate a solution in about 0.3 seconds, on a medium power PC. This supports the third claim that the acquired problem solving knowledge assures a high performance of the problem solver.

Based on the evaluation results, the agent developed with Disciple-LAS was selected by DARPA and Alphatech to be further extended and was integrated by Alphatech into a larger system that supports air campaign planning by the JFACC and his/her staff. The integrated system was one of the systems selected to be demonstrated at EFX'98, the Air Force's annual show case of the promising new technologies.

Related Work

From the point of view of the methods and techniques employed, this work is mostly related to the work on apprenticeship learning that has produced experimental agents that assimilate new knowledge by observing and analyzing the problem solving steps contributed by their expert users through their normal use of the agents (Mahadevan et al. 1993, Wilkins 1993). Disciple-LAS is different from these agents in terms of the types of learning employed. Also it has been scaled up and developed into a general integrated shell and methodology for building practical end-to-end agents.

Disciple-LAS is also related to the tools for building knowledge-based systems. Many of these tools provide an inference engine, a representation formalism in which the KB could be encoded, and mechanisms for acquiring, verifying or revising knowledge expressed in that formalism. These tools trade power (i.e., the assistance given to the expert) against generality (i.e., their domain of applicability), covering a large spectrum. At the power end of the spectrum there are tools customized to a problem-solving method and a particular domain (Musen and Tu, 1993). At the generality end are the tools applicable to a wide range of tasks or domains, such as CLIPS (Giarratano and Riley, 1994). In between are tools that are method-specific and domain independent (Chandrasekaran and Johnson, 1993).

With respect to the power-generality trade-off, Disciple-LAS takes a different approach. It provides a set of general and powerful modules for knowledge acquisition and learning that are domain-independent and are incorporated as such in a developed agent. However, for the interface and the problem solver, the Disciple shell contains a generic graphical-user interface and a problem solver based on task-reduction. Therefore, for a given application domain, one has to develop additional, domain-specific interfaces and to further develop the problem solver, in order to create an easy to train and a useful agent. In spite of its generality, and due to its powerful learning capabilities, Disciple's support in knowledge acquisition is similar to that of the specific tools. Moreover, it provides support in all the stages of knowledge base construction, both ontology and rules creation, and their refinement. Many of the other systems stress either initial knowledge creation, or its refinement. Finally, most of the other tools are intended for the knowledge engineer, while Disciple-LAS is oriented toward direct knowledge acquisition from a human expert, attempting to limit as much as possible the assistance needed from the knowledge engineer.

As compared with Disciple-LAS, the other tools used in the HPKB project to solve the workaround challenge problem reflect a different approach and philosophy to rapid development of knowledge-based systems.

ISI's development environment consists of two domain-independent tools, the LOOM ontology server (MacGregor 1991), and the EXPECT system for knowledge base refinement (Gil 1994), both being tools designed to assist the knowledge engineer, rather than the domain expert. Also, the focus is on assisting the refinement of the knowledge base rather than its initial creation.

The approach taken by both Teknowledge (TFS) and the University of Edinburgh (AIAI) is based on Cyc (Lenat 1995) and emphasizes rapid development of knowledge-based systems through the reuse of the previously developed Cyc ontology. A main difference from our approach is that Cyc is based on a very carefully engineered general ontology, that is to be reused for different applications, while in our case we take the position that the imported ontology should be customized for the current domain. Also, Cyc's concepts and axioms are manually defined, while in Disciple the rules are learned and refined by the system through an interaction with the user.

Conclusion and Future Research

The main result of this paper is an integration of knowledge representation, knowledge acquisition, learning and problem solving into an agent shell and methodology for efficient development of practical end-to-end knowledge-based agents, by domain experts, with limited assistance from knowledge engineers. This approach is based on the reuse and adaptation of previously developed knowledge, and on a natural interaction with the domain expert which are achieved through the use of synergism at several levels. First, there is the synergism between different learning methods employed by the agent. By integrating complementary learning methods (such as inductive learning from examples, explanation-based learning, learning by analogy, learning by experimentation) in a dynamic way, the agent is able to learn from the human expert in situations in which no single strategy learning method would be sufficient. Second, there is the synergism between teaching (of the agent by the expert) and learning (from the expert by the agent). For instance, the expert may select representative examples to teach the agent, may provide explanations, and may answer agent's questions. The agent, on the other hand, will learn general rules that are difficult to be defined by the expert, and will consistently integrate them into its knowledge base. Finally, there is the synergism between the expert and the agent in solving a problem, where the agent solves the more routine parts of the problem and the expert solves the more creative parts. In the process, the agent learns from the expert, gradually evolving toward an intelligent agent.

There are, however, several weaknesses of this approach that we plan to address in the future. For instance, the initial modeling of the domain, which is critical to the successful development of the agent, is not yet supported by the shell. We therefore plan to develop a modeling tool that will use abstract descriptions of tasks and objects in a scenario similar to that used in teaching the agent. Also, importing concepts and features from previously developed ontologies, although very appealing is actually quite hard to accomplish. We are therefore planning to develop methods where the modeling process and the agent provide more guidance in identifying the knowledge pieces to import. We also need to develop a more powerful and natural approach to hint specification by the expert. The current types of allowable hints do not constrain enough the search for explanations. Also, some of them are not very intuitive for the expert. Finally, we are investigating how the learning methods of the agent could become even more knowledge intensive, primarily through the use of more powerful methods of analogical reasoning.

Acknowledgments. This research was supported by the AFOSR grant F49620-97-1-0188, as part of the DARPA's High Performance Knowledge Bases Program. Andrei Zaharescu has contributed to Disciple-LAS.

References

Alphatech, Inc. 1998. *HPKB Year 1 End-to-End Battlespace Challenge Problem Specification*, Burlington, MA.

Chandrasekaran, B., and Johnson, T. R. 1993. Generic Tasks and Task Structures: History, Critique and New Directions, In David, J.M., Krivine, J.P., and Simmons, R. eds. *Second Generation Expert Systems,* pp.239-280. Springer-Verlag.

Chaudhri, V. K., Farquhar, A., Fikes, R., Park, P. D., and Rice, J. P. 1998. OKBC: A Programmatic Foundation for Knowledge Base Interoperability. In *Proc. AAAI-98*, pp. 600 – 607, Menlo Park, CA: AAAI Press.

Clancey, W. J. 1984. NEOMYCIN: Reconfiguring a rule-based system with application to teaching. In Clancey W. J. and Shortliffe, E. H., eds. *Readings in Medical Artificial Intelligence*, pp.361-381. Reading, MA: Addison-Wesley.

Cohen P., Schrag R., Jones E., Pease A., Lin A., Starr B., Gunning D., and Burke M. 1998. The DARPA High-Performance Knowledge Bases Project, *AI Magazine*, 19(4),25-49.

Farquhar, A., Fikes, R., and Rice, J. 1996. The Ontolingua Server: a Tool for Collaborative Ontology Construction. In *Proceedings of the Knowledge Acquisition for Knowledge-Based Systems Workshop*, Banff, Alberta, Canada.

Fellbaum, C. ed. 1998. *WordNet: An Electronic Lexical Database* , MIT Press.

Genesereth M.R. and Fikes R.E. 1992. Knowledge Interchange Format, Version 3.0 Reference Manual. KSL-92-86, Knowledge Systems Laboratory. Stanford University.

Giarratano, J., and Riley, G. 1994. *Expert Systems: Principles and Programming*, Boston, PWS Publ. Comp.

Gil, Y. 1994. Knowledge Refinement in a Reflective Architecture. In *Proc. AAAI-94,* Seattle, WA.

Lenat, D. B. 1995. CYC: A Large-scale investment in knowledge infrastructure *Comm of the ACM* 38(11):33-38.

MacGregor R. 1991. The Evolving Technology of Classification-Based Knowledge Representation Systems. In Sowa, J. ed. *Principles of Semantic Networks: Explorations in the Representations of Knowledge*, pp. 385-400. San Francisco, CA: Morgan Kaufmann.

Mahadevan, S., Mitchell, T., Mostow, J., Steinberg, L., and Tadepalli, P. 1993. An Apprentice Based Approach to Knowledge Acquisition, *Artificial Intelligence*, 64(1):1-52.

Musen, M.A. and Tu S.W. 1993. Problem-solving models for generation of task-specific knowledge acquisition tools. In Cuena J. ed. *Knowledge-Oriented Software Design*, Elsevier, Amsterdam.

Stoffel, K., Taylor, M., and Hendler, J. 1997. Efficient Management of Very Large Ontologies. In *Proc. AAAI-97,* Menlo Park, Calif.: AAAI Press.

Tecuci, G. 1998. *Building Intelligent Agents: An Apprenticeship Multistrategy Learning Theory, Methodology, Tool and Case Studies.* London, England: Academic Press.

UMLS 1998. *Unified Medical Language System*, UMLS Knowledge Sources 9th Edition, National Library of Medicine. (http://www.nlm.nih.gov/research/umls/)

Wilkins, D. 1993. Knowledge base refinement as improving an incomplete and incorrect domain theory. In Buchanan, B. and Wilkins, D. eds. *Readings in Knowledge Acquisition and Learning*, San Mateo, CA: Morgan Kaufmann.

Knowledge Representation

A New Method for Consequence Finding and Compilation in Restricted Languages

Alvaro del Val

Departamento de Ingeniería Informática
Universidad Autónoma de Madrid
28049 Madrid, Spain
delval@ii.uam.es
http://www.ii.uam.es/~delval

Abstract

SFK (skip-filtered, kernel) resolution is a new method for finding "interesting" consequences of a first order clausal theory Σ, namely those in some restricted target language $\mathcal{L}_T$. In its more restrictive form, SFK resolution corresponds to a relatively efficient SAT method, directional resolution; in its more general form, to a full prime implicate algorithm, namely Tison's. It generalizes both of them by offering much more flexible search, first order completeness, and a much wider range of inferential capabilities.

SFK resolution has many applications: computing "characteristic" clauses for task-specific languages in abduction, explanation and non-monotonic reasoning (Inoue 1992); obtaining LUB approximations of the input theory (Selman and Kautz 1996) which are of polynomial size; incremental and lazy exact knowledge compilation (del Val 1994); and compilation into a tractable form for restricted target languages, *independently* of the tractability of inference in the given target language.

Introduction

We introduce kernel deductions, which in the propositional case can be succintly described as the set of resolution proofs explored by Tison's method for computing the prime implicates of a propositional theory (Tison 1967). Kernel resolution, which resembles somewhat ordered resolution, is complete for first-order consequence finding. Skip-filtered kernel resolution (SFK for short) provides a very general way of restricting kernel resolution to make it complete for all consequences in some restricted target language.

A first order clausal theory Σ is written over some clausal language $\mathcal{L}$, consisting of all clauses that can be constructed using terms and predicates occurring in Σ. Among the implicates or clausal consequences of Σ (clauses $C \in \mathcal{L}$ such that $\Sigma \models C$), we might be interested in all of them, or only in those that belong to some target language $\mathcal{L}_T \subseteq \mathcal{L}$. These are the $\mathcal{L}_T$-implicates (clauses $C \in \mathcal{L}_T$ such that $\Sigma \models C$). Let $PI_{\mathcal{L}_T}(\Sigma)$ be the set of prime $\mathcal{L}_T$-implicates of Σ, i.e. $\mathcal{L}_T$-implicates not properly (θ-)subsumed by any other $\mathcal{L}_T$-implicate of Σ. Then the restricted task of $\mathcal{L}_T$-

consequence finding is (mainly) finding all clauses in $PI_{\mathcal{L}_T}(\Sigma)$.

Consequence finding (as opposed to refutation finding) has received relatively little attention in the theorem proving literature. However, and as convincingly argued by (Inoue 1992), this relative disregard is no longer justified, as consequence-finding has multiple applications. Inoue discusses finding the set of prime $\mathcal{L}_T$-implicates (what he calls "characteristic clauses") for certain task-specific languages $\mathcal{L}_T$ (e.g. involving only certain predicates), and its application to explanation, abduction, diagnosis, and non-monotonic reasoning. SFK resolution can be used for all of them.

A second set of more recent applications of consequence-finding arise from *knowledge compilation* (KC) (see (Cadoli and Donini 1997) for a review), where the knowledge base is preprocessed in an "off-line phase," so as to make "online" query answering tractable. In *exact* KC, all queries can be answered tractably after compilation; (del Val 1994, Marquis 1995) are examples of exact KC using full full consequence finding. In the main version of *approximate* KC (Selman and Kautz 1991, Selman and Kautz 1996), on the other hand, the theory is approximated by a theory formulated in some target sublanguage $\mathcal{L}_T$. This approximation is equivalent to the set of all $\mathcal{L}_T$-consequences of the input theory, so *provided* inference in $\mathcal{L}_T$ is tractable, all queries in $\mathcal{L}_T$ can be answered tractably.

Our contribution to KC is threefold. We show how to systematically obtain polynomial size approximations (e.g. obtain all implicates smaller than some constant), thus repairing a weak spot of Selman and Kautz's LUB framework. Second, we define an incremental version of the exact KC algorithm of (del Val 1994) using kernel resolution, with support for lazy and query-directed compilation. Finally, by combining our exact KC algorithm with SFK resolution, we provide a way to ensure tractable answers for any target language $\mathcal{L}_T$, *independently of whether inference in $\mathcal{L}_T$ is tractable*.

The structure of this paper is as follows. In section 1 we introduce kernel and SFK resolution, and prove them sound and complete for ($\mathcal{L}_T$)-implicate finding in predicate calculus. Section 2 discusses propositional search strategies, in particular "bucket elimination" and incremental saturation, suitable for any form of SFK resolution. Section 3 introduces various applications of SFK-resolution: computing characteristic clauses and LUB approximations, polynomial size approximations, exact KC, and compilation for restricted target languages.

Kernel resolution

Kernel resolution generalizes Tison's (1967) well-known algorithm for computing prime implicates. Tison's algorithm processes propositional variables in order, and is based on the idea that once all resolvents on a given literal have been computed, no further resolutions on that literal are needed.

Procedure Tison-PI(Σ)
$PI := \Sigma$;
for each variable x_i in $[x_1..x_n]$ **do**
    for each pair of clauses $x_i C, \overline{x_i} D \in PI$ **do**
        if their resolvent $E = C \cup D$ is not a tautology **and**
          E is not subsumed by any clause of PI
        then remove from PI any clause F subsumed by E
          $PI := PI \cup \{E\}$
return PI

We can view Tison's algorithm as engaged in an implicit proof enumeration task. For each clause C it generates, we can trace back the deduction of C through its parent and ancestor clauses, obtaining the usual resolution tree for C. Seeing the method in this way allows us to separate the proof finding task from the particular enumeration technique implicit in Tison's method.

Specifically, in Tison's method a clause C can be resolved exactly upon literals which are later in the ordering ("larger") than the literal resolved upon to obtain C (or upon any literal if C is an input clause). We call this "usable" set of literals, the *kernel* of C, which we denote $k(C)$. The remaining literals (those smaller than the literal resolved upon) we call the *skip*, denoted $s(C)$, because neither they nor any of their descendants will be resolved upon. We write a clause C as an ordered pair $A[B]$ where $C = A \cup B$, $s(C) = A$ and $k(C) = B$.

As an example, with the obvious ordering, if $x_1 \overline{x_2}$ and $x_2 x_3$ are clauses in the input then we would obtain the clause $x_1 x_3$. Because x_1 has already been processed by Tison method when the clauses are resolved upon x_2 and $\overline{x_2}$, we know that $x_1 x_3$ will never be resolved upon x_1, and may be resolved upon x_3. We record this information by writing the clause as $x_1[x_3]$.

Kernel resolution deductions are simply resolution deductions in which every literal resolved upon is in its clause's kernel, just as in Tison's method. We extend this definition slightly to deal with the first order case directly. Formally:

Definition 1 *Let $p_1, \ldots, p_n$ be an ordering of the predicate symbols. We say that p_i has ordinal i. Let l_i and l_j literals with predicate symbols p_i and p_j respectively. We say that l_j is larger or equal than l_i iff $i \leq j$.*

Definition 2 *A kernel deduction of a clause C from a set of clauses Σ is a sequence of clauses of the form $S_1[K_1], \ldots, S_n[K_n]$ such that:*

1. $C = S_n \cup K_n$
2. *For every k, $S_k \cup K_k$ is not a tautology.*
3. *For every k, either:*
  (a) *$K_k \in \Sigma$ and $S_k = \emptyset$ (input clause); or*
  (b) *$S_k[K_k]$ is a factor of $S_j[K_j]$, $j < k$;[1] or*
  (c) *$S_k \cup K_k$ is a resolvent of two clauses $S_i \cup K_i$ and $S_j \cup K_j$ ($i, j < k$) such that:*
    i. *the literals resolved upon to obtain $S_k \cup K_k$ are in, respectively, K_i and K_j; and*
    ii. *K_k is the set of all literals of $S_k \cup K_k$ which are larger or equal than the literals resolved upon, according to the given ordering, and S_k is the set of smaller literals.*

The kernel index of $S_k[K_k]$ is the ordinal i of the predicate p_i resolved upon to obtain $S_k[K_k]$ (or 0 if $S_k[K_k]$ is an input clause). The kernel depth of the deduction is the kernel index of its conclusion C.

The "clausal meaning" of a kernel clause $S_k[K_k]$ is simply given by $S_k \cup K_k$; the crucial aspect is that resolutions are only permitted upon kernel literals, condition 3.b.ii, and that the literal resolved upon partitions the literals of the resolvent into those smaller (the skip) and those larger or equal (the kernel) than the literal resolved upon, condition 3.b.iii. The same partition can be induced from the kernel index.

Definition 3 *A clause D θ-subsumes a clause C just in case there exists a substitution σ such that $D\sigma \subseteq C$ and D has no more literals than C.*

Definition 4 *We write $\Sigma \vdash_k C$ iff there exists a kernel deduction of a clause D that θ-subsumes C from Σ.*

Example 1 Suppose $\Sigma_1 = \{C_1, C_2, C_3, C_4\}$ is as depicted below. The left column shows the computation of Tison–PI(Σ_1) under the natural ordering, with each step explained in the middle column.

$$
\begin{array}{l}
C_1 = x_1 x_2 \\
C_2 = \overline{x_2} x_3 \\
C_3 = \overline{x_1} x_4 \\
C_4 = \overline{x_3} x_4
\end{array} \left.\begin{array}{l} \\ \\ \\ \\ \end{array}\right\} \quad \begin{array}{c} \text{input} \\ \Sigma_1 \end{array} \quad \left\{\begin{array}{l}
C_1' = [x_1 x_2]_{(0)} \\
C_2' = [\overline{x_2} x_3]_{(0)} \\
C_3' = [\overline{x_1} x_4]_{(0)} \\
C_4' = [\overline{x_3} x_4]_{(0)}
\end{array}\right.
$$

$C_5 = x_2 x_4$	Resolve(C_1, C_3, x_1)	$C_5' = [x_2 x_4]_{(1)}$
$C_6 = x_1 x_3$	Resolve(C_1, C_2, x_2)	$C_6' = x_1[x_3]_{(2)}$
$C_7 = x_3 x_4$	Resolve(C_2, C_5, x_2)	$C_7' = [x_3 x_4]_{(2)}$
$C_8 = \overline{x_2} x_4$	Resolve(C_2, C_4, x_3)	$C_8' = \overline{x_2}[x_4]_{(3)}$
$C_9 = x_1 x_4$	Resolve(C_4, C_6, x_3)	$C_9' = x_1[x_4]_{(3)}$
$C_{10} = x_4$	Resolve(C_4, C_7, x_3)	$C_{10}' = [x_4]_{(3)}$

After obtaining C_{10}, all clauses containing x_4 are deleted, since they are now subsumed. The resulting

---

[1] There cannot be two literals with the same predicate symbol one of which is in S_j and the other in K_j. Thus there is no possible ambiguity in defining the factoring operation.

set of prime implicates is $\{C_1, C_2, C_6, C_{10}\}$. We can describe this process as computing kernel deductions, as shown in the right column, where the rightmost numbers are kernel indexes. ■

Proposition 1 *Every resolution deduction carried out by Tison's method from a set of ground clauses Σ can be written as a kernel deduction from Σ.*

Thus, using the completeness of Tison's method for computing prime implicates, we immediately obtain:

Corollary 2 (Ground soundness/completeness)
Ground kernel deductions are sound and complete for consequence-finding, that is, for any ground clause C and set of ground clauses Σ, $\Sigma \models C$ iff $\Sigma \vdash_k C$.

Using standard lifting techniques from (Slagle *et al.* 1969, Minicozzi and Reiter 1972) we can show:

Theorem 3 (FOL soundness/completeness) *Let Σ be a set of clauses, C a clause. $\Sigma \models C$ iff $\Sigma \vdash_k C$.*

In addition, first order kernel resolution satisfies:

Proposition 4

1. *Every descendant D of a clause C is such that $[s(C)]\sigma \subseteq s(D)$ for some substitution σ.*

2. *Descendants of skipped literals are never resolved upon.*

Property 4.1 is crucial to SFK-resolution, the generalization of kernel resolution to focus on restricted target languages which is discussed next. As a special case, ground skipped literals of a clause stay in all its descendants. Property 4.2 is crucial for applications in knowledge compilation.

Skip-filtered kernel resolution

As already suggested, we are often interested in finding only the consequences of the input theory in some restricted "target language" $\mathcal{L}_T$, rather than all consequences. Skip–filtered kernel resolution, or SFK resolution for short, is a restriction of kernel resolution which achieves exactly this.

Definition 5 *An $\mathcal{L}_T$-SFK resolution deduction of C from Σ is a kernel deduction of C from Σ satisfying the following additional restriction:*

4. *For every k: S_k or some factor of S_k is in $\mathcal{L}_T$ (in which case we say that $S_k[K_k]$ is $\mathcal{L}_T$-acceptable).*

We write $\Sigma \vdash_k^{\mathcal{L}_T} C$ when there is a $\mathcal{L}_T$-SFK resolution deduction from Σ of some D which θ-subsumes C.

We will consider only target languages which are *closed under θ-subsumption (c.u.s.)*, i.e. such that for any $C \in \mathcal{L}_T$, if D θ-subsumes C then $D \in \mathcal{L}_T$. If a language $\mathcal{L}_S$ is not c.u.s, one can always *close it off*, by defining the language $cus(\mathcal{L}_S) = \{D \in \mathcal{L} \mid \exists C \in \mathcal{L}_S : D \theta\text{-subsumes } C\}$.

There are many languages which are c.u.s, e.g. the set of Horn clauses, sets of clauses which use only some subset of the predicates, the set of clauses with less than k literals. For many others, closing off is a useful operation; e.g. consider $cus(\{C\})$, where C is a single clause, or $cus(\mathcal{L}_S)$ when $\mathcal{L}_S$ is some subset of ground clauses of $\mathcal{L}$.

Theorem 5 (FOL soundness/completeness for $\mathcal{L}_T$)
Suppose $\mathcal{L}_T$ is c.u.s. $\forall C \in \mathcal{L}_T$: $\Sigma \models C$ iff $\Sigma \vdash_k^{\mathcal{L}_T} C$.

Corollary 6 *Let $SFK_{\mathcal{L}_T}(\Sigma)$ be the set of unsubsumed clauses generated by any exhaustive form of SFK resolution. $PI_{\mathcal{L}_T}(\Sigma) = SFK_{\mathcal{L}_T}(\Sigma) \cap \mathcal{L}_T$.*

Note that c.u.s. implies that the empty clause $\square$ is in $\mathcal{L}_T$. There are therefore two extreme special cases of this theorem. If $\mathcal{L}_T = \mathcal{L}$ is the full language, then SFK-resolution is complete for consequence finding; and if $\mathcal{L}_T = \mathcal{L}_\square = \{\square\}$ then SFK resolution is a satisfiability method, where the only "interesting" potential implicate of Σ is the empty clause.

Subsumption

Deletion of subsumed clauses is a very powerful pruning technique for any search strategy. SFK-resolution remains complete under the following *replacement policy*: if C θ-subsumes D, then delete D, and update C's kernel index to be the minimum of the indexes of C and D; semantically, this amounts to possibly enlarging the kernel of the subsumer, adding literals that were already skipped. For certain search strategies (see BE below), we can use a stronger *deletion policy*, by which we just delete clauses as soon as they become subsumed (as usual, checking for forward subsumption before backward subsumption); but this policy destroys completeness in other cases (e.g. IS below).

Propositional search strategies

Kernel resolution differs from other consequence finding procedures in that it does not prejudge the search strategy. Any exhaustive search of the space of SFK deductions will do, including standard saturation methods (Chang and Lee 1973) and lazy evaluation strategies. We introduce in this section two propositional exhaustive search procedures: "Bucket elimination," a generalization for SFK resolution of the methods of (Dechter 1998); and an alternative method of "incremental saturation" which processes input clauses incrementally, and is specially suited for situations where the input is initially only partially specified.

All the results in this section assume $\mathcal{L}_T$ is c.u.s. (without loss of generality, as seen above), and apply only to the ground case. The reason for the latter restriction is that in FOL both methods fail to guarantee *fairness*, i.e. that every derivable clause is eventually derived, and are therefore incomplete for FOL.

Indexing functions

Before we present both methods, we will discuss the basic data structures we use. Consider an ordered array of buckets $b[x_i]$, one for each propositional variable

$x_1, \ldots, x_n$. Each bucket $b[x_i]$ contains clauses containing occurrences of x_i, according to some *indexing function* $I_{\mathcal{L}_T}$. $I_{\mathcal{L}_T}$ is a function that maps each clause into a subset of the clause's variables; it determines which clauses go to which buckets by the rule $C \in b[x_i]$ iff $x_i \in I_{\mathcal{L}_T}(C)$.

Definition 6 ($\mathcal{L}_T$-acceptable indexing) *An indexing function $I_{\mathcal{L}_T}$ is $\mathcal{L}_T$-acceptable iff $x_i \in I_{\mathcal{L}_T}(C)$ whenever resolving C on x_i can generate some $\mathcal{L}_T$-acceptable resolvent as a child.*

The long version of this paper discusses indexing functions in more detail, as the complexity of search is a direct function of bucket size. For any $\mathcal{L}_T$, we will use the $\mathcal{L}_T$-acceptable function $I_{\mathcal{L}_T}^o(C) = \{$kernel variables of the largest prefix $l_1 \ldots l_k$ of C s.t. $l_1 l_2 \ldots l_{k-1} \in \mathcal{L}_T \}$, where C is assumed sorted in ascending kernel order.

Bucket elimination

Bucket elimination (BE) processes buckets $b[x_1]$, $b[x_2]$, $\ldots$, in order. It computes in step i all resolvents on x_i obtained from clauses in $b[x_i]$; among these, it selects the $\mathcal{L}_T$-acceptable resolvents, and adds them to their "corresponding" buckets by calling $I_{\mathcal{L}_T}$. Variable x_i is "eliminated" when finished with its bucket, in the sense that it will never be revisited: no further resolutions upon x_i are needed.

BE exhaustively explores the space of SFK deductions in breadth-first search relative to the *kernel depth* of SFK-derivations (see Def. 2). This allows us to show:

Theorem 7 (Ground completeness of BE)
Ground bucket elimination with any $\mathcal{L}_T$-acceptable indexing function $I_{\mathcal{L}_T}$ is a terminating and exhaustive search strategy for SFK resolution and therefore for propositional $\mathcal{L}_T$-consequence finding.

Furthermore, ground BE remain complete under the deletion policy *for subsumed clauses.*

Consider now the two extreme cases of theorem 5 under the light of theorem 7. First, when $\mathcal{L}_T = \mathcal{L}$ then every possible resolvent is $\mathcal{L}$-acceptable, which suggests the implementation $I_{\mathcal{L}_T}(C) = I_{\mathcal{L}}(C) = k(C)$. The resulting bucket elimination procedure corresponds exactly to Tison-PI, where clauses can be resolved upon any of their kernel literals. On the other hand, if $\mathcal{L}_T = \mathcal{L}_\square = \{\square\}$ then $I_{\mathcal{L}_T}(C) = I_{\mathcal{L}_\square}(C) = \{$smallest kernel variable of $C\}$, since resolving on any other kernel variable cannot yield any $\mathcal{L}_\square$-acceptable resolvents. Bucket elimination with this indexing function is identical to *directional resolution* (DR), Dechter and Rish's (1994) version of the original Davis-Putnam (1960) satisfiability procedure Because DR is a relatively efficient satisfiability method for semi-structured problems, it is encouraging that it is at the same time the simplest form of SFK resolution. In the long paper we'll reinforce this point by providing a wide class of *realistic* problems for which DR is tractable.

Example 2 Let $\Sigma_2 = \{x_1 x_2 x_3, x_1 x_2 \overline{x_3}, x_1 \overline{x_2} x_3, x_1 \overline{x_2 x_3}\}$, with the natural ordering. Satisfiability of Σ_2 can be

determined without computing a single resolvent by DR, i.e. by $\mathcal{L}_\square$-BE, as $I_{\mathcal{L}_\square}$ leaves all buckets empty except $b[x_1]$, which does not generate any resolvent.

Note that the unit implicate x_1 is not in the output $DR(\Sigma_2)$ of DR. Furthermore, the obvious attempt to obtain a *tractable* answer to the query whether $\Sigma \models x_1$ fails, as $DR(\Sigma_2) \cup \{\overline{x_1}\}$ is not unit refutable.

Let now $\mathcal{L}_T = \mathcal{L}_1$ consist of all clauses with at most one literal. The indexing function $I_{\mathcal{L}_1}^o(C)$ selects the kernel variables among the first two literals of C. In this case, initially $b[x_1] = b[x_2] = \Sigma_2$. $\mathcal{L}_1$-BE yields the clauses $x_1[x_3]$ and $x_1[\overline{x_3}]$ when processing $b[x_2]$. Both clauses are indexed in $b[x_3]$, so when processing x_3 we obtain $x_1[\ ]$, the only $\mathcal{L}_1$-implicate of Σ_2. ∎

Incremental saturation

A different kind of strategy is "incremental saturation," where each input clause C is processed in turn, until the store of clauses is "saturated" under $\mathcal{L}_T$-SFK resolution, that is, until no unsubsumed $\mathcal{L}_T$-acceptable resolvents can be generated from the available clauses.

Incremental saturation (IS) adds a new input clause C to a $\mathcal{L}_T$-saturated set of clauses Σ as follows. We use a set of parallel buckets $bn[x_i]$ for each x_i, to index the newly generated clauses separately. Begin by indexing C with $I_{\mathcal{L}_T}$ in the bn buckets. Then process buckets one by one, starting from the bucket $bn[x_j]$ of the smallest $x_j \in I_{\mathcal{L}_T}(C)$. For each variable $x_k \geq x_j$, compute all resolvents that can be obtained by resolving clauses of $bn[x_k]$ with clauses of $bn[x_k]$ and $b[x_k]$, and index the $\mathcal{L}_T$-acceptable resolvents among them in the bn buckets.

The procedure is thus driven by the parallel buckets; we never resolve together two clauses in $b[x_i]$, i.e. two "old" clauses. When finished, the parallel buckets should be emptied into the original buckets, to prepare the mechanism for receiving more clauses.

IS can be generalized to add a set of clauses Γ by indexing all clauses of Γ in the bn array, and starting with the smallest variable x_j with non-empty $bn[x_j]$.

Theorem 8 (Ground completeness of IS)
Ground incremental saturation with any $\mathcal{L}_T$-acceptable indexing function $I_{\mathcal{L}_T}$ is a terminating and exhaustive search strategy for SFK resolution and therefore for propositional $\mathcal{L}_T$-consequence finding.

IS comes with two important benefits over BE. First, IS can incrementally compute $\mathcal{L}_T$-implicates, as new input clauses are received. There is no need to recompute everything anew if the input grows. Second, IS supports queries about the *new $\mathcal{L}_T$-implicates* of a theory after adding a clause (set). To show this, define the set of *new prime $\mathcal{L}_T$-implicates induced by adding Γ to Σ* as:

$$nPI_{\mathcal{L}_T}(\Sigma, \Gamma) = PI_{\mathcal{L}_T}(\Sigma \cup \Gamma) \setminus PI_{\mathcal{L}_T}(\Sigma).$$

Thus, if Σ is $\mathcal{L}_T$-saturated, adding Γ to Σ with IS yields $nPI_{\mathcal{L}_T}(\Sigma, \Gamma)$, by simply intersecting the (unsubsumed) newly generated clauses with $\mathcal{L}_T$.

But IS also has its drawbacks with respect to BE. First, IS must use a weaker subsumption policy than

BE, namely *replacement* instead of deletion. Second, IS, unlike BE, is limited in its ability to dynamically order variables and to use global information about the structure of the theory in deciding an ordering.

It is not difficult to provide examples where IS requires exponentially more time and space than BE, and conversely, depending on the strategy used by each.

Applications

We discuss very briefly in this section some of the applications of SFK resolution.

1. Task-specific languages. There are many AI tasks, e.g. abduction, diagnosis, reason-maintenance, and non-monotonic reasoning, which can be cast in terms of restricted sets of consequences of the input theory. Let V be any set of literals (typically closed under instantiation), and consider the language $\mathcal{L}_V = \{C \in \mathcal{L} \mid C \subseteq V\}$. (Inoue 1992) discusses multiple applications of the sets $PI_{\mathcal{L}_V}$ and $nPI_{\mathcal{L}_V}$ in these areas. For example, abduction can be captured in terms of clauses which contain only "assumables;" circumscription in terms of clauses which involve only "fixed" predicates and positive "minimized" literals; diagnosis, in terms of clauses containing positive "abnormality" literals.

2. LUB approximations. For a given target language $\mathcal{L}_T$, the $\mathcal{L}_T$-LUB (lowest upper bound) approximation of a first order theory Σ is the strongest theory $\Sigma_{lub} \subseteq \mathcal{L}_T$ entailed by Σ (Selman and Kautz 1991, Selman and Kautz 1996). Σ_{lub} is unique modulo logical equivalence, and equivalent to $PI_{\mathcal{L}_T}(\Sigma)$ (see (del Val 1995, del Val 1996) for the general case). Thus, SFK-resolution can be used to generate LUB approximations.

SFK-resolution, however, does not compute very concise LUBs. For vocabulary-based languages we can do better. Specifically, suppose that we put all symbols in V last in the ordering, and that we allow all literals whose symbol is in V. We can modify BE so that it stops after processing all symbols preceding the first symbol from V. Until then, every resolvent with a non-empty skip is discarded (since it would contain symbols not in V), i.e. the algorithm works essentially as DR. The set of $\mathcal{L}_T$-clauses obtained by this procedure can be shown to be equivalent to the $\mathcal{L}_V$-LUB. The analogous procedure for other search strategies (including FOL) is straightforward: resolve only on the first literal of each clause, provided it's symbol is not in V.

3. Polynomial size approximations. In computing LUB approximations, it is important that Σ_{lub} has polynomial size. This can be achieved, in the propositional case, by further restricting the clauses of our target language to have no more than k-literals, for a fixed k; in FOL one also needs to bound the complexity of terms. Let $\mathcal{L}_k$ be any such language. The algorithm available for this task, GLUB-1 (Selman and Kautz 1996, del Val 1996) is quite unsatisfactory, as it only forbids resolutions among pairs of clauses both of which are in $\mathcal{L}_k$. Thus e.g. for $\mathcal{L}_1$ only resolutions

among pairs of unit clauses are forbidden, and thus for satisfiable theories it is equivalent to resolution closure. SFK resolution is clearly much better.

4. Exact knowledge compilation. The task of exact knowledge compilation (del Val 1994) is to preprocess an input knowledge base Σ so that after the "off-line" compilation is completed, every query can be answered in polynomial time with respect to the size of the compiled knowledge base. The idea is that the cost of compilation can be amortized over many queries.

We present here a version of the (ground) KC algorithm FPI_1 (del Val 1994). $FPI_1(\Sigma)$ computes $PI(\Sigma)$ with Tison's method, storing in the compiled theory only some of these implicates, specifically the kernel merge resolvents. A merge resolvent is a resolvent such that some of its literals, called the merge literals, occur in both parent clauses (and must therefore be "merged" in the resolvent). When some merge literals are in the resolvent's kernel, we speak of a *kernel merge resolvent*.

The procedure IFPIA (Incremental Filtered Prime Implicates Algorithm), given below, differs from FPI_1 only in the use of kernel deductions instead of Tison's method. IFPIA is compatible with any incremental search strategy for kernel deductions, or with forms of lazy evaluation. In particular, Σ *need to be given in its entirety before beginning execution.* If new clauses are added, they can be processed just as with kernel deductions, with whichever strategy we are using.

Procedure IFPIA(Σ)

1. Compute the closure under kernel resolution of Σ.
2. Return the unsubsumed clauses which are either: input clauses, or kernel merge resolvents, of subsumers of either.

Let $IFPIA(\Sigma)$ be the output of the algorithm. Using theorem 1 from (del Val 1994), and proposition 4.2 above, we can easily obtain:

Theorem 9 $IFPIA(\Sigma)$ *is logically equivalent to* Σ, *and unit refutation complete. That is, for any clause* C, $\Sigma \models C$ *iff* $IFPIA(\Sigma) \models C$ *iff there exists a unit resolution refutation of* $IFPIA(\Sigma) \cup \neg C$.

5. KC for restricted languages. The completeness of IFPIA depends only on the completeness of the underlying consequence finding method, namely kernel resolution. Accordingly, if we replace kernel resolution by $\mathcal{L}_T$–SFK resolution, we can ensure tractability just for the queries in $\mathcal{L}_T$. Formally, let $\mathcal{L}_T$–IFPIA be as IFPIA but with $\mathcal{L}_T$–SFK resolution, and let $IFPIA(\Sigma, \mathcal{L}_T)$ be its output.

Theorem 10 $IFPIA(\Sigma, \mathcal{L}_T)$ *is unit refutation complete with respect to* $\mathcal{L}_T$ *queries. That is, for any clause* $C \in \mathcal{L}_T$, $\Sigma \models C$ *iff* $IFPIA(\Sigma \mathcal{L}_T) \models C$ *iff there exists a unit resolution refutation of* $IFPIA(\Sigma) \cup \neg C$.

Note that the approach here is quite different from that of LUB approximations, in the sense that $IFPIA(\Sigma, \mathcal{L}_T)$ need not be a subset of $\mathcal{L}_T$, nor be equivalent to the $\mathcal{L}_T$-LUB. And, most crucially, tractability of answers to $\mathcal{L}_T$-queries does no longer depend on the tractability of inference in $\mathcal{L}_T$.

Related work in consequence-finding

We have already mentioned directional resolution and Tison-PI as instances of SFK-BE. Bucket elimination is introduced in (Dechter 1998) as a uniform framework for dealing with a wide variety of inference problems. We extend BE for the special case of resolution on logical clauses by treating the indexing function and $\mathcal{L}_T$-acceptability criterion as parameters. Incremental saturation, in turn, is motivated in part by IPIA, an alternative incremental version of Tison-PI introduced by (Kean and Tsiknis 1990). Neither IPIA nor most other propositional consequence finding methods have anywhere near the inferential and compilation capabilities of SFK resolution.

In contrast to the propositional case, relatively few first order methods are known which are complete for consequence-finding. The ones known to us include: unrestricted resolution (Lee 1967); m.s.l. (merge, subsumption, linear) resolution (Minicozzi and Reiter 1972); and SOL (skip, ordered, linear) resolution (Inoue 1992). Other methods are complete only for finding the consequences in some restricted language; for example, positive hyperresolution finds all positive clauses entailed by the input theory (Slagle *et al.* 1969). Of more direct relevance to this paper is SOL resolution, which is also complete for restricted $\mathcal{L}_T$ languages.

We do not know of any implementation of SOL resolution for full consequence finding, whereas Tison's method, $\mathcal{L}$-BE, is well regarded in practice for this task (de Kleer 1992, Forbus and de Kleer 1993). The goal-directedness and low memory usage of linear resolution are advantageous for theorem proving, but this is not so clear for consequence finding, where the computed clauses are typically not discarded.[2]

Kernel resolution resembles ordered resolution (Basin and Ganzinger 1996) in the use of an ordering of atoms or A-ordering. Ordered resolution can be seen as a sophisticated first order version of directional resolution, or more exactly of $\mathcal{L}_\square - SFK$ resolution. Kernel resolution generalizes directional resolution for consequence finding, while ordered resolution generalizes DR to use much more sophisticated ground orderings. Presumably both aspects are quite compatible, so it should be possible to merge these two generalizations.

Discussion

We have introduced kernel resolution, as a flexible method to compute consequences in restricted sublanguages, and discussed some of its applications. In subsequent work, we will show that it provides a theoretical

---

[2]SOL resolution involves a large amount of redundancy for consequence-finding: a) every input clause has to be considered as a top clause, which leads to many essentially identical proofs; b) all possible orderings of non-top clauses have to be considered; c) very limited deletion of subsumed clauses in linear resolution (Stickel 1992), which has a much larger potential impact in consequence-finding applications.

framework that allows for orders of magnitude improvements in some exact knowledge compilation approaches, and to allow the latter to be applied to compilation for restricted languages.

References

David Basin and Harald Ganzinger. Complexity analysis based on ordered resolution. In *LCS'96*, 1996.

Marco Cadoli and Francesco M. Donini. A survey on knowledge compilation. *AI Communications*, 10:137–150, 1997. Printed in 1998.

Chin-Liang Chang and Richard Char-Tung Lee. *Symbolic Logic and Mechanical Theorem Proving*. Academic Press, 1973.

M. Davis and H. Putnam. A computing procedure for quantification theory. *J. of the ACM*, 7(3):201–215, 1960.

Johan de Kleer. An improved incremental algorithm for generating prime implicates. In *AAAI'92*, 1992.

Rina Dechter. Bucket elimination: A unifying framework for structure-driven inference. In *Learning and Inference in Graphical Models*. 1998.

Alvaro del Val. Tractable databases: How to make propositional unit resolution complete through compilation. In *KR'94*, 1994.

Alvaro del Val. An analysis of approximate knowledge compilation. In *IJCAI'95*, 1995.

Alvaro del Val. Approximate knowledge compilation: The first order case. In *AAAI'96*, 1996.

Ken Forbus and Johan de Kleer. *Building Problem Solvers*. The MIT Press, 1993.

Katsumi Inoue. Linear resolution for consequence-finding. *Artificial Intelligence*, 56:301–353, 1992.

Alex Kean and George Tsiknis. An incremental method for generating prime implicants/implicates. *Journal of Symbolic Computation*, 9:185–206, 1990.

R.C.T. Lee. *A Completeness Theorem and a Computer Program for Finding Theorems Derivable from Given Axioms*. PhD thesis, UC Berkeley, 1967.

Pierre Marquis. Knowledge compilation using theory prime implicates. In *IJCAI'95*, 1995.

Eliana Minicozzi and Raymond Reiter. A note on linear resolution strategies in consequence-finding. *Artificial Intelligence*, 3:175–180, 1972.

Bart Selman and Henry Kautz. Knowledge compilation using Horn approximations. In *AAAI'91*, 1991.

Bart Selman and Henry Kautz. Knowledge compilation and theory approximation. *Journal of the ACM*, 43(2):193–224, March 1996.

J. R. Slagle, C. L. Chang, and R. C. T. Lee. Completeness theorems for semantic resolution in consequence finding. In *IJCAI'69*, 1969.

Mark E. Stickel. A Prolog technology theorem prover: Implementation by an extended Prolog compiler. *Journal of Theoretical Computer Science*, 104:109–128, 1992.

P. Tison. Generalized consensus theory and application to the minimization of boolean circuits. *IEEE Transactions on Computers*, EC-16:446–456, 1967.

Constraint-based integrity checking in abductive and non-monotonic extensions of constraint logic programming

Aditya K. Ghose
Department of Business Systems
University of Wollongong,
NSW 2522 Australia
aditya@uow.edu.au

Srinivas Padmanabhuni
Department of Computing Science
University of Alberta, Edmonton
Alberta, Canada, T6G 2H1
srinivas@cs.ualberta.ca

Abstract

Recent research on the integration of the abductive and constraint logic programming paradigms has led to systems which are both expressive and computationally efficient. This paper investigates the role of constraints in integrity checking in the context of such systems. Providing support for constraints in this role leads to a framework that is significantly more expressive, without significant loss in efficiency. We augment the Abductive Constraint Logic Programming framework with *assumed constraints* and provide model- and proof-theoretic accounts of two variants: one which involves *commitment* to such assumptions, and one which does not. We also show that such accounts extend easily to a constraint logic programming framework which supports both negation and assumed constraints. The gains in expressivity in these frameworks turn out to be particularly useful in a variety of application domains, including scheduling and constraint database updates.

Introduction

Recent research on the integration of the abductive and constraint logic programming paradigms has led to systems which are both expressive and computationally efficient. The Abductive Constraint Logic Programming (ACLP) paradigm (Kakas & Michael 1995) involves the cooperation of abductive and constraint solvers in efficiently generating solutions to complex problems represented in an expressive, high-level language. This paper seeks to enhance the expressive power of frameworks such as ACLP by augmenting the representation language with constraints whose sole purpose is integrity checking. Equivalently, this may be thought of as the extension of the representation language with *assumed constraints*. Our intent is to develop more robust and expressive representational frameworks without sacrificing computational efficiency.

Integrity constraints play a key role in a variety of abductive and nonmonotonic reasoning systems. Reiter has convincingly argued in (Reiter 1988) that integrity constraints are best viewed as meta-theoretic assertions concerning the content of a knowledge base as opposed to object-level assertions in the knowledge base. To our knowledge, there has been no previous work on the use of constraints for integrity checking,

either in the context of pure constraint-based reasoning, or hybrid frameworks such as constraint logic programming (CLP) (Jaffar & M.J.Maher 1994) or ACLP which integrate constraints with other reasoning systems (however, default reasoning notions have been considered in the context of concurrent constraint programming in (Saraswat, Jagadeesan, & Gupta 1996)). Yet, the question is a non-trivial one, since constraints used for integrity checking must meta-theoretically restrict the set of consequences of a knowledge base without restricting the values that solution variables may take. The following example clarifies the point. Let $\{x < 10, x > 5, y = 1, x + y < 9\}$ be a given set of constraints on the domain of integers. One may then specify $x \geq 8$ as an integrity constraint with the intention of ensuring that every set of constraints used to obtain a solution is consistent with it. The initial set of constraints is not consistent with this integrity constraint, but the following two subsets are:

- $\{x < 10, x > 5, y = 1\}$
- $\{x < 10, x > 5, x + y < 9\}$

Notice that both of these sets of constraints, while being consistent with $x \geq 8$, admit solutions which violate it (e.g., $x = 7, y = 1$ for the first set). Here the integrity constraint has been used to restrict the subproblem that is solved, without being enforced on the values that output variables may take in solutions. Thus, the integrity constraint plays precisely the same role as integrity constraints in abductive systems such as THEORIST (Poole, Goebel, & Aleliunas 1987). A THEORIST system with a and $a \rightarrow b$ as hypotheses and $\neg b$ as an integrity constraint admits two distinct maximal scenarios, containing a and $a \rightarrow b$ respectively. Notice that $\neg b$ is used to restrict what may appear in a maximal scenario, but does not itself appear in one. We argue that several classes of applications require that constraints predicates play such a role. No existing system supports this. For instance, constraint predicates that appear in the integrity constraints of ACLP are actually enforced on the output values that variables may take.

An alternative view of constraints in integrity checking roles treats them as *assumptions*, in the same sense as the justifications of default rules in default logic (Reiter 1980) (which are used as assumptions concerning the content of extensions with the consistency of such assumptions sanctioning the application of a default rule). Our intent is to explore how *assumed constraints* might play a role similar to default justifications in hybrid frameworks such as ACLP and CLP by serving as filters that must be checked to determine the applicability of a program clause. Once again, constraint assumptions restrict the set of valid conclusions but are not themselves derivable as conclusions. In the context of systems such as ACLP and CLP, we distinguish between two classes of constraints: *enforced constraints* (which constrain the values that output variables may take) and *assumed constraints* in the sense just discussed.

Constraints as assumptions are useful in variety of domains including planning, scheduling and configuration. The following is a typical rule that one might need to encode in a scheduling application:

> *If it is consistent to assume that a given order is ready to be shipped and that the order arrives at the loading dock at time t1 and that truck A may be loaded at time t2, then conclude that truck A must be loaded at time t2, provided the constraint t2=t1+5 is satisfiable.*

Notice that $t2 = t1+5$ is not an *enforced constraint* since the values of $t1$ and $t2$ are independently determined. It is an *assumed constraint* which, if violated, blocks the applicability of the corresponding rule.

Constraints used for integrity checking find useful application in enforcing constraint database updates. Returning to our initial example involving a set of constraints on the domain of integers, the retraction of the constraint $x < 8$ from a database given by $\{x < 10, x > 5, y = 1, x + y < 9\}$ is achieved simply by asserting $x \geq 8$ as an integrity constraint. Similarly, one might wish to specify constraints which determine valid updates of the values of certain variables, without enforcing them on the values of output variables in solutions. In a companion paper, we describe how constraint predicates in integrity checking roles may be used to define a meaningful notion of *minimal specialization* in formalizations of incremental learning of constraint-based representations. One such account of incremental learning is being trialed in a system for automatically acquiring scheduling knowledge. Constraints in integrity checking roles may be used for enforcing the mutual exclusivity of constraints. Thus, the mutual exclusivity of constraints c_1 and c_2 may be enforced by asserting $\neg(c_1 \wedge c_2)$ as an integrity constraint without requiring that the resulting constraint be enforced on solutions. Constraint assumptions may be used to implement a weak notion of conditional constraints (e.g., *enforce c_1 if it is consistent to assume c_2*).

We discuss two variants of the ACLP framework in detail in this paper. Both involve augmenting the basic ACLP representational framework by permitting the specification of *assumed constraints* in both the program clauses and the integrity constraints. In the first variant, which we shall call the *Extended ACLP (E-ACLP) framework*, assumed constraints in program clauses are tested for consistency against a *constraint store* consisting of the current set of accumulated enforced constraints to determine whether the corresponding clause is applicable. The second variant, which we shall call the *EC-ACLP framework*, involves *committing to assumptions* in a manner analogous to what Rational Default Logic (Mikitiuk & Truszczynski 1993) and Constrained Default Logic (Delgrande, Schaub, & Jackson 1994) achieve in the context of default reasoning. The intent is to ensure that contradictory constraint assumptions are not made; this is achieved by maintaining a separate store which accumulates all assumed constraints in addition to the enforced ones. We present a model theory and proof theory for each variant. We then show how these semantics and proof procedures extend to the case of CLP with default negation (applicable to non-constraint predicates) and assumed constraints.

Extending ACLP with constraints for integrity checking

In this section we shall define the syntax and present the model theory of the E-ACLP and EC-ACLP frameworks. As with CLP, we shall assume that both these frameworks are parameterized by a choice of constraint domain $\mathcal{D}$. We shall use the standard notions of *entailment* in constraint domain, and *valuations* as defined in (Jaffar & M.J.Maher 1994). In the following, B_P refers to the Herbrand base of P.

Extended ACLP

Definition 1 [Extended ACLP Framework] *An Extended ACLP($\mathcal{D}$) framework is a triple (P, A, IC) where:*

- *P is a collection of clauses of the form:*

  $p \leftarrow q_1, \ldots, q_m [] c_1, \ldots, c_n : d_1, \ldots, d_r$

  where $p, q_1, \ldots, q_m$ are non-constraint predicate symbols while $c_1, \ldots, c_n$ and $d_1, \ldots, d_r$ are constraint predicates defined on $\mathcal{D}$.

- *A is a distinguished subset of the set of non-constraint predicates called* abducibles.

- *IC, the set of integrity constraints is a collection of clauses of the form:*

  $\perp \leftarrow q_1, \ldots, q_m [] c_1, \ldots, c_n : d_1, \ldots, d_r$

  where $q_1, \ldots, q_m$ are non-constraint predicate symbols while $c_1, \ldots, c_n$ and $d_1, \ldots, d_r$ are constraint predicates defined on $\mathcal{D}$.

Program clauses of the form $p \leftarrow q_1, \ldots, q_m [] c_1, \ldots, c_n : d_1, \ldots, d_r$ read as follows: *if $q_1, \ldots, q_m$ have been established and the set of all enforced constraints c_i together with all assumed* constraints d_i are consistent with the current constraint store of accumulated enforced constraints, conclude p and add each c_i to the constraint store. An integrity constraint of the form $\bot \leftarrow q_1, \ldots, q_m [] c_1, \ldots, c_n : d_1, \ldots, d_r$ ensures that the following are not simultaneously true: $q_1, \ldots, q_m$ are simultaneously derivable, each enforced constraint c_i is entailed by the constraint store and the constraint store is consistent with the assumed constraints d_i.

Definition 2 *Let P be an E-ACLP program. For any pair (R, T) where $R \subseteq B_P$ and T is any set of constraint predicates on the domain $\mathcal{D}$, let $\Gamma(R, T) = (R', T')$ where R' and T' are the smallest sets such that:*

- $R' \subseteq B_P$
- *T' is a set of constraint predicates defined on $\mathcal{D}$.*
- *for any clause $p \leftarrow q_1, \ldots, q_m [] c_1, \ldots, c_n : d_1, \ldots, d_r \in P$, if there exist valuations v and v' such that $v(q_1), \ldots, v(q_m) \in R$, $\mathcal{D} \models v(c_1) \wedge \ldots \wedge v(c_n) \wedge v(T)$ and $\mathcal{D} \models v'(c_1) \wedge \ldots \wedge v'(c_n) \wedge v'(d_1) \wedge \ldots \wedge v'(d_r) \wedge v'(T)$, then $v(p) \in R'$, $\{c_1, \ldots, c_n\} \subseteq T'$*

A pair (M, S), where $M \subseteq B_P$ and S is a set of constraints defined on $\mathcal{D}$, is a model of P iff $\Gamma(M, S) = (M, S)$ and $\bot \notin M$.

Definition 3 [E-ACLP Abductive Explanations]
Given an E-ACLP framework (P, A, IC), an explanation of a goal of the form:

$$q_1, \ldots, q_m [] c_1, \ldots, c_n : d_1, \ldots, d_r$$

is a set Δ of clauses of the form:

$$a \leftarrow e_1, \ldots, e_s$$

where a is an atom whose predicate symbol belongs to A and each e_i is a constraint predicate defined on $\mathcal{D}$, such that there exists a model (M, S) of $P \cup \Delta \cup IC$ such that $S \cup \{c_1, \ldots, c_n\} \cup \{d_1, \ldots, d_r\}$ is solvable and for every valuation v where $\mathcal{D} \models v(S \cup \{c_1, \ldots, c_n\})$, $\{v(q_1), \ldots, v(q_m)\} \subseteq M$.

Adding commitment to assumptions in extended ACLP

Syntactically, EC-ACLP frameworks are identical to E-ACLP frameworks. However, the notions of model and abductive explanation differ. EC-ACLP models augment E-ACLP models by explicitly recording every constraint assumption made (in addition to all enforced constraint) in a separate store. This store thus enables explicit commitment to assumptions. For a program clause to be applicable, its assumed constraints and its enforced constraints must be jointly consistent with this store. If a program clause is deemed to be applicable, all assumed and enforced constraints contained in the clause are added to this store (in addition to the enforced constraints being added to the set of accumulated enforced constraints). Each integrity constraint involves a similar consistency check with this additional constraint store.

Definition 4 *Let P be an EC-ACLP program. For any triple (R, S, T) where $R \subseteq B_P$ while S and T are sets of constraint predicates on the domain $\mathcal{D}$, let $\Gamma(R, S, T) = (R', S', T')$ be the smallest set R', S' and T' such that:*

- $R' \subseteq B_P$
- *S' and T' are constraint predicates defined on $\mathcal{D}$.*
- *for any clause $p \leftarrow q_1, \ldots, q_m [] c_1, \ldots, c_n : d_1, \ldots, d_r \in P$, if there exist valuations v and v' such that $v(q_1), \ldots, v(q_m) \in R$, $\mathcal{D} \models v(c_1) \wedge \ldots \wedge v(c_n) \wedge v(T)$ and $\mathcal{D} \models v'(c_1) \wedge \ldots \wedge v'(c_n) \wedge v'(d_1) \wedge \ldots \wedge v'(d_r) \wedge v'(S)$, then $v(p) \in R'$, $\{c_1, \ldots, c_n\} \subseteq T'$ and $\{c_1, \ldots, c_n\} \cup \{d_1, \ldots, d_r\} \subseteq S'$.*

A triple (M, C, S), where $M \subseteq B_P$ and C and S are constraints defined on $\mathcal{D}$, is a model of P iff $\Gamma(M, C, S) = (M, C, S)$ and $\bot \notin M$.

Definition 5 [EC-ACLP Abductive Explanations] *Given an EC-ACLP framework (P, A, IC), an explanation of a goal of the form:*

$$q_1, \ldots, q_m [] c_1, \ldots, c_n : d_1, \ldots, d_r$$

is a set Δ of clauses of the form:

$$a \leftarrow e_1, \ldots, e_s$$

where a is an atom whose predicate symbol belongs to A and each e_i is a constraint predicate defined on $\mathcal{D}$, such that there exists a model (M, C, S) of $P \cup \Delta \cup IC$ such that $S \cup \{c_1, \ldots, c_n\} \cup \{d_1, \ldots, d_r\}$ is solvable and for every valuation v where $\mathcal{D} \models v(C \cup \{c_1, \ldots, c_n\})$, $\{v(q_1), \ldots, v(q_m)\} \subseteq M$.

Observation: The E-ACLP and EC-ACLP frameworks without assumed constraints in the program clauses and integrity constraints coincide with the ACLP framework.

Proof Procedure for EC-ACLP

In this section, we present a proof procedure for EC-ACLP which builds on the abductive proof procedure defined in (Kakas & Michael 1995). For convenience let us denote a clause R_j of the above form by the short form $p \leftarrow Q_j [] C_j : D_j$ where C_j denotes the set of *enforced* constraints in the clause and D_j denotes the set of *assumed* constraints in the clause and Q_j represents the predicate literals in the clause R_j. A solution to the set of clauses of the above form are of the form $\exists x(a(x), C(x))$ where C(x) is a set of *enforced* constraints on the variables in the vector x in the abducible predicate. The framework is a direct generalization of the concept of clauses in CLP(R). The only additional feature in the clauses of EC-ACLP$(\mathcal{D})$ is the presence of the *assumed* constraints. The *assumed* constraints of the form d_i are responsible for constraining the solution space of the solutions to the constraint logic program. Without loss of generality we shall assume any goal clause to be of the form $\leftarrow L_1, L_2, \ldots, L_n [] c_1, \ldots, c_m$, because corresponding to any generic goal of the form $\leftarrow L_1, L_2, \ldots, L_n [] c_1, c_2, c_3, \ldots, c_m : d_1, d_2, \ldots, d_k$, we can add the integrity constraint $\leftarrow L_1, L_2, \ldots, L_n [] \phi :$

$d_1, d_2, \ldots, d_k$ to set of integrity constraints IC, and pass the initial goal $\leftarrow L_1, L_2, \ldots, L_n[]c_1, c_2, c_3, \ldots, c_m$ as the initial goal G_1 to the abductive proof procedure, still preserving the semantics.

Abductive Derivation: An abductive derivation from $(G_1, \delta_1, \delta_1^*, J_1)$ to $(G_k, \delta_k, \delta_k^*, J_k)$ in $< P, A, IC >$ is a sequence $(G_1, \delta_1, \delta_1^*, J_1), (G_2, \delta_2, \delta_2^*, J_2), \ldots ,(G_k, \delta_k, \delta_k^*, J_k)$ such that for each i, G_i has the form $\leftarrow L_1, L_2, \ldots, L_n[]C$, C being a set of *enforced* constraints(could be empty), L_j is a selected atom, each δ_j is a set of ground abducibles over the domain of R extended by the skolem constants, each δ_j^* is a set of goals , J_i is a set of *enforced* and *assumed* constraint terms denoting the set of constraints of both kind encountered in the present goal G_i and $(G_{i+1}, \delta_{i+1}, \delta_{i+1}^*, J_{i+1})$ is derived according to the following rules:

A1) If L_i is not an abducible then $G_{i+1} = S, \delta_{i+1} = \delta_i$, $J_{i+1}=J_i \cup C_j \cup D_j$ and $\delta_{i+1}^* = \delta_i^*$ where S is the set of *enforced* constraints and literals in the CLP resolvent of some clause R_j of the form $p(u) \leftarrow Q_j[]C_j : D_j$ in P with G_i on L_j and the set of constraints J_{i+1} is solvable.

A2) If L_j is an atom with an abducible predicate and L_j unifies with a member of δ_i returning the constraints C_θ and $J_i \cup C_\theta$ is solvable then $G_{i+1} =\leftarrow, \ldots, L_{j-1}, L_{j+1}, \ldots, L_n[]C \cup C_\theta$, $\delta_{i+1} = \delta_i$ and $\delta_{i+1}^* = \delta_i^*$, $J_{i+1} = J_i \cup C_\theta$.

A3) If L_j is an atom with an abducible predicate and $L_j \notin \delta_i$, let $Sk(L_j) = L_j\theta = L_j'$ and $C'' = C \cup \{x = t \mid x \in var(L_j), t = x\theta\}$. $J'' = J_i \cup \{x = t \mid x \in var(L_j), t = x\theta\}$. Then there exists a consistency derivation from $(\{L_j'\}, C'', \delta_i \cup \{L_j'\}, \delta_i^*, J'')$ to $(\{\}, C', \delta', \delta^{*'}, J')$ then $G_{i+1} =\leftarrow L_1, \ldots, L_3, L_4, \ldots, L_n[]C'$. $\delta_{i+1} = \delta'$ and $\delta_{i+1}^* = \delta^{*'}$ and $J_{i+1} = J'$.

Consistency derivation A consistency derivation for an abducible atom L, from $(L, C_1, \delta_1, \delta_1^*, J_1)$ to $(F_m, C_m, \delta_m, \delta_m^*, J_m)$ in $< P, A, IC >$ is a sequence $(L, C_1, \delta_1, \delta_1^*, J_1), (F_1, C_1, \delta_1, \delta_1^*, J_1), (F_2, C_2, \delta_2, \delta_2^*, J_2),$ $\ldots, (F_m, C_m, \delta_m, \delta_m^*, J_m)$ where:

i) F_1 is the set of resolvents of the form G_{11}, G_{12} etc. where all goals G_{1k} are of the form $\leftarrow L_1, \ldots, L_n[]C_{di} : D_{di}$ obtained by resolving the abducible L with the denials in IC and δ_1^*. All the constraints C_{di} here involved in any goal are *enforced* constraints, and D_{di} contain only *assumed* constraints.

ii) For each $i > 1$, F_i has the form $\{\leftarrow L_1, \ldots, L_n[]C_{di} : D_{di}\} \cup F_i'$, L_j or C_{di} or D_{di} is selected and $(F_{i+1}, C_{i+1}, \delta_{i+1}, \delta_{i+1}^*, J_{i+1})$ is obtained according to the following rules:

C1) If L_j is not an abducible, let R be the set of all r_i where r_i is a resolvent of $\leftarrow L_1, \ldots, L_n[]C_{di} : D_{di}$ with clauses in P on L_j and J_{ij} is the set of *enforced*

as well as *assumed* constraints in the resolvent in conjunction with J_i, and J_{ij} is solvable. $F_{i+1} = R \cup F_i'$ $C_{i+1} = C_i$ $\delta_{i+1}^* = \delta_i^*$ $\delta_{i+1} = \delta_i$. and $J_{i+1} = J_i$.

(C2) If L_j is an abducible predicate atom, let R be the set of all r_i where r_i is a resolvent of $\leftarrow L_1, \ldots, L_n[]C_{di} : D_{di}$ with atoms in δ_i on L_j and J_{ij} is the set of *enforced* as well as *assumed* constraints in the resolvent in conjunction with J_i, and J_{ij} is solvable. $F_{i+1} = R \cup F_i'$ $C_{i+1} = C_i$ $\delta_{i+1}^* = \delta_i^* \cup \{\leftarrow L_1, \ldots, L_n[]C_{di} : D_{di}\}$ $\delta_{i+1} = \delta_i$ and $J_{i+1} = J_i$.

C3) if C_{di} is selected then $F_{i+1} = F_i'$, $C_{i+1} = C_i \cup C'$, $\delta_{i+1}^* = \delta_i^*$ and $\delta_{i+1} = \delta_i$ and $J_{i+1} = J_i \cup C'$. Here C' is such that $J_i \cup C'$ is solvable but $C_{di} \cup C'$ is not solvable.

C4) if D_{di} is selected then $F_{i+1} = F_i'$, $C_{i+1} = C_i$ $\delta_{i+1}^* = \delta_i^*$ and $\delta_{i+1} = \delta_i$ and $J_{i+1} = J_i \cup D'$. Here D' is such that $J_i \cup D'$ is solvable but $D_{di} \cup D'$ is not solvable.

The difference from the treatment of D_{di} from C_{di} is that the constraint D' is only added to the justifications and not to the actual solution to enforce consistency, while in C_{di} C' is used to constrain the solution set of constraints in C_i.

Theorem 1 *If $< P, A, IC >$ is an EC-ACLP program, and $(\leftarrow G, \{\}, \{\}, \{\}), \ldots, (\leftarrow \phi[]C, \delta, \delta^*, J)$ is an abductive derivation, it is termed as an abductive refutation. If $\delta_{sol} = Rs(\delta \cup \exists xC)$ where x is the vector of free variables in the constraint store C, and Rs stands for the reverse skolemisation function, then δ_{sol} is an abductive explanation for the goal G.*

Example 1 Consider the ACLP with *assumed* constraints in the following set of EC-ACLP clauses.

$C1 : s(X, Y) \leftarrow r(X), p(Y)[]X + Y < 9.$
$C2 : s(X, Y) \leftarrow r(X)[]X + Y > 8$
$C3 : p(Y) \leftarrow []Y = 1.$
$C4 : r(X) \leftarrow q(X), a(X), []X > 5, X < 10.$
$C5 : q(X) \leftarrow [] : X \geq 8.$

We have an integrity constraint IC1 as $\leftarrow a(X)[]X \leq 3$. It has no *assumed* constraint in the global IC. Consider the query $\leftarrow s(X, Y)[]\phi : \phi$. In the absence of any *assumed* or *enforced* constraint, we start with $G_1 =\leftarrow s(X, Y)[]\phi$. At the outset, we resolve this with the clause C1. The CLP resolvent is $\leftarrow r(X), p(X)$ and constraint store C= $\{X + Y < 9\}$, and J = $\{X + Y < 9\}$. On further resolving this with the clause C3, we get new goal as $\leftarrow r(X)$, with the constraint store C= $\{Y = 1, X + Y < 9\}$ and J = $\{Y = 1, X + Y < 9\}$. Now r(X) can be resolved with clause C4, to get $\leftarrow q(X), a(X)$ with the constraint store C and J both as $\{X > 5, X < 10, Y = 1, X + Y < 9\}$. Next q(X) can be resolved with the clause C5, and here the *assumed* constraint $X \geq 8 \cup J$ is not solvable, hence this path of finding a solution stops. Retracting the path, we now try to resolve the goal $\leftarrow s(X,Y)$ with the clause C2. The CLP resolvent is $\leftarrow r(X)$, with the constraint store C $= \{X + Y > 8\}$, and J $= \{X + Y > 8\}$. On further resolving this with the clause C4, we get the new goal as $\leftarrow q(X), a(X)$, with C $= \{X > 5, X < 10, X + Y > 8\}$ and J $=$ C. Next when we resolve q(X) with C5, we get the *assumed* constraint $X \geq 8$. This constraint is solvable in conjunction with J. So we can carry out the resolution and now J $= \{X > 5, X < 10, X + Y > 8, X \geq 8\}$. C still remains the same. Now since we only have the abducible a(X), we skolemise a(X), to a(t), t being a skolem constant. We add the substitution X=t to J as well as C. Now we need to obtain a consistency derivation for a(t), with $J_1 = \{X > 5, X < 10, X + Y > 8, X \geq 8, X = t\}$, $\delta_1 = \{a(t)\} C_1 = \{X > 5, X < 10, X + Y > 8, X = t\}$ $\delta_1^* = \{\}$.

The only integrity constraint against which a(t) can be resolved is the integrity constraint IC1. On resolving $\leftarrow a(t)$, against IC1, we get the resolvent $\leftarrow Y \leq 3, Y = t$ All others remain the same. Now to get the consistency derivation we note that there are no abducibles in this resolvent. Thus by selecting rule C3, we select $t > 3$ as the constraint C' such that $J_i = \{X > 5, X < 10, X + Y > 8, X \geq 8, X = t\} \cup C'$ is solvable but $C' \cup \{Y = t, Y \leq 3\}$ is not satisfiable. So we end the consistency derivation with $F_m = , C_m = \{X > 5, X < 10, X + Y > 8, X = t, t > 3\}$, $\delta_m = \{a(t)$ and $\delta_m^* = \{\}$ and $J_m = \{X > 5, X < 10, X + Y > 8, X \geq 8, X = t, t > 3\}$.

So coming back to the abductive derivation, we get $G_{i+1} = \leftarrow X > 5, X < 10, X + Y > 8, X = t, t > 3$, where we have no more abducibles left. Hence the resulting solution for the query $\leftarrow s(X,Y)$ is the set of constraints $\{X > 5, X < 10, X + Y > 8, X = t, t > 3\}$, which when condensed along with δ_i and reverse skolemised gives $\leftarrow a(X)[]X > 5, X < 10, X + Y > 8$ as the solution.

Proof Procedure for E-ACLP

In the previous section, the detailed proof procedure for the EC-ACLP with commitment to assumptions was explored in detail. The semantics of E-ACLP without commitment to assumptions offers a more general view of obtaining solution explanations than the rigid framework offered by the commitment to assumptions. A simple modification of the procedure defined for the semantics in the previous section is sufficient to capture the notion of solution in this semantics. As already explained in the case of EC-ACLP, the *assumed* constraints can be presumed absent in the goal clause, without loss of generality.

Changes The following changes in the abductive and consistency derivations of the proof procedure shall achieve the required result.

1. In all the steps, whether the consistency derivation or the abductive derivation, the set of justifications J_i is no longer required.

2. In any step where the solvability of J_i is seen in conjunction with the set of *enforced* as well as *assumed* constraints in the resolvent, the new form requires solvability of the existing constraint store C_i of *enforced* constraints, in conjunction with the set of both *enforced* as well as the *assumed* constraints in the resolvent. The rules which are affected in this change are A1,A2 and C1,C2,C3 and C4.

3. In case, the set of constraints in C_i, is solvable in conjunction with the constraints of both types in the resolvent, add the *enforced* constraints in the resolvent to the constraint store, in rules A1 and A2.

4. The entire consistency derivation has no use of J_i in the steps. In step C3, only C_i is modified by addition of such a C'. In step C4, do no changes to anything but only look for the existence of a D' such that D' is solvable in conjunction with C_i but not solvable with D_{di}.

Example of commitment-free E-ACLP Consider Example 1 in the previous section for the goal $\leftarrow s(X,Y)$ for the same set of clauses and integrity constraints. We start by resolving this with the clause C1. The CLP resolvent is $\leftarrow r(X), p(X)$ and constraint store C$= \{X + Y < 9\}$, and J $= \{X + Y < 9\}$. On further resolving this with the clause C3, we get new goal as $\leftarrow r(X)$, with the constraint store C$=\{Y = 1, X + Y < 9\}$. r(X) can be resolved with clause C4, to get $\leftarrow q(X), a(X)$ with the constraint store C as $\{X > 5, X < 10, Y = 1, X + Y < 9\}$ and Next the q(X) can be resolved with the clause C5, and here the *assumed* constraint $X \geq 8 \cup$ C is not solvable, hence this path of finding a solution stops. Retracting the path, we now try to resolve the goal $\leftarrow s(X,Y)$ with the clause C2. The CLP resolvent is $\leftarrow r(X)$, with the constraint store C $= \{X + Y > 8\}$, On further resolving this with the clause C4, we get the new goal as $\leftarrow q(X), a(X)$ with C$= \{X > 5, X < 10, X + Y > 8\}$. Next when we resolve q(X) with C5, we get the *assumed* constraint $X \geq 8$. This constraint is solvable in conjunction with C. So we can carry out the resolution and C still remains the same. Now since we only have the abducible a(X), we skolemise a(X), to say a(t). We add the substitution X=t to C. Now we need to obtain a consistency derivation for a(t), with $\delta_1 = \{a(t)\} C_1 = \{X > 5, X < 10, X + Y > 8, X = t\}$. $\delta_1^* = \{\}$ The only integrity constraint against which a(t) can be resolved is the integrity constraint IC1. On resolving $\leftarrow a(t)$, against IC1, we get the resolvent $\leftarrow Y \leq 3, Y = t$ All others remain the same. Now to get the consistency derivation we note that there are no abducibles in this resolvent. Thus by selecting rule C3, we select $t > 3$ as the constraint C' such that $C_i = \{X > 5, X < 10, X + Y > 8, X = t\} \cup C'$ is solvable but $C' \cup \{Y = t, Y \leq 3\}$ is not satisfiable. So we end the consistency derivation with $F_m =$

$, C_m = \{X > 5, X < 10, X + Y > 8, X = t, t > 3\}$, $\delta_m = \{a(t)$ and $\delta_m^* = \{\}$. The final constraint set is $\leftarrow X > 5, X < 10, X + Y > 8, X = t, t > 3$ giving the final solution as $\leftarrow a(X)[] X > 5, X < 10, X + Y > 8$.

CLP extensions

In this section, we shall provide some comments on the semantics and proof procedures required for CLP programs with default negation (applicable to non-constraint predicates) and assumed constraints. We shall refer to these as CLPNC programs. The syntax of such programs is similar to that of program clauses in E-ACLP and EC-ACLP, except that each q_i is now additionally permitted to be of the form $notq(x_1, \ldots, x_k)$ as well. The model theory relies on the Gelfond-Lifschitz transform that forms the basis of stable model semantics (Gelfond & Lifschitz 1990). Let $M' \subseteq B_P$ for a CLPNC program P. Let P' represent the program obtained by applying every possible valid grounding to clauses in P. Let P'' be the program obtained by applying the Gelfond-Lifschitz transform to P', ignoring both enforced and assumed constraints. To obtain semantics similar to those for E-ACLP (i.e., without commitment to assumptions), we compute the model (M, S) obtained by treating P'' as an E-ACLP program. Then (M, S) is treated as the model of the original program P iff M coincides with M'. To obtain semantics similar to those for EC-ACLP (i.e., with commitment to assumptions), we compute the model (M, C, S) obtained by treating P'' as an EC-ACLP program. Then (M, C, S) is treated as the model of the original program P iff M coincides with M'.

In contrast to the model-theoretic semantics which computes total extensions in the form of stable models, the proof procedures involved in logic programs with negation formulate a top-down query answering procedure for a target goal. The Eshghi-Kowalski procedure (Eshghi & Kowalski 1989) has been modified for use in logic programming with negation by Dung (Dung 1995) by considering negation as failure as a kind of abduction. The scenarios(models) generated by this top down procedure have been related to stable models and other models of logic programs with negation in (Dung 1995). There have been specific versions of the Eshghi-Kowalski procedure proposed by Dung for negation as failure in (Dung 1995), with minor variations to take care of the specific integrity constraints present in case of negation by failure as the only rule of abduction.

Here too the only difference from the EC-ACLP framework above is the formulation of integrity constraints. The only integrity constraints IC in the CLPNC framework are of the form $\forall(t_i)p_i(t_i) \lor notp_i(t_i)$ and $\forall(t_i)\neg(p_i(t_i) \land notp_i(t_i))$. This pair of constraints holds for all predicates p_i and its corresponding abducible predicate $notp_i$. Here t_i's are vectors of variables contained in p_i. The only abducibles are the those of type $notp_i$.

Conclusions

We have examined in this paper a set of related frameworks which implement the notion of constraint assumptions, or constraints in integrity checking roles, motivated by the need to represent complex problems drawn from a broad range of application domains, including planning, scheduling and configuration. We have presented the model-theoretic and proof-theoretic bases for two distinct extensions of the ACLP framework. We have also outlined how these, coupled with intuitions from the stable model semantics of logic programs with negation, might be used to define a model theory and proof theory for CLP programs with default negation and assumed constraints. We believe these are important advances, yielding more robust and expressive systems without sacrificing computational efficiency.

References

Delgrande, J. P.; Schaub, T.; and Jackson, W. K. 1994. Alternative approach to default logic. *Artificial Intelligence* 70:167–237.

Dung, P. 1995. An argumentation theoretic foundation for logic programming. *J. Logic Programming* 22:151–177.

Eshghi, K., and Kowalski, R. 1989. Abduction compared with negation by failure. In *Proc. 6th ICLP*, 234–254. MIT Press.

Gelfond, M., and Lifschitz, V. 1990. Logical programs with classical negation. In *Proc. 7th ICLP*, 579–597. MIT Press.

Jaffar, J., and M.J.Maher. 1994. Constraint logic programming: a survey. *Journal of Logic Programming* 503–581.

Kakas, A., and Michael, A. 1995. Integrating abductive and constraint logic programming. In *Proc. 12th ICLP*, 399–413.

Mikitiuk, A., and Truszcynski, M. 1993. Rational default logic and disjunctive logic programming. In *Logic programming and nonmonotonic reasoning*. MIT Press.

Poole, D.; Goebel, R.; and Aleliunas, R. 1987. Theorist: A logical system for defaults and diagnosis. In Cercone, N., and McCalla, G., eds., *The Knowledge Frontier*. Springer. 331–352.

Reiter, R. 1980. A logic for default reasoning. *Artificial Intelligence* 13:81–132.

Reiter, R. 1988. On integrity constraints. In *Proc. of TARK-88*, 97–112.

Saraswat, V.; Jagadeesan, R.; and Gupta, V. 1996. Timed default concurrent constraint programming. *Journal of Symbolic Computation* 22(5-6):475–520.

Thomas Eiter, J. L., and Subrahmanian, V. 1997. Computing non-ground representations of stable models. In *Proc of 4th LPNMR*, 198–217. Springer-Verlag.

Partonomic Reasoning as Taxonomic Reasoning in Medicine

Udo Hahn [a]   Stefan Schulz [a,b]   Martin Romacker [a,b]

[a] (CLIF) Text Knowledge Engineering Lab, Freiburg University (`http://www.coling.uni-freiburg.de`)
[b] Department of Medical Informatics, Freiburg University Hospital (`http://www.imbi.uni-freiburg.de/medinf`)

Abstract

Taxonomic anatomical knowledge, a major portion of medical ontologies, is fundamentally characterized by is-a and part-whole relations between concepts. While taxonomic reasoning in generalization hierarchies is well-understood, no fully conclusive mechanism as yet exists for partonomic reasoning. We here propose a new representation construct for part-whole relations, based on the formal framework of description logics, that allows us to fully reduce partonomic reasoning to classification-based taxonomic reasoning.

Introduction

In the fields of health sciences and health care, broad-coverage terminologies have evolved over the years. A prime terminology source is the Unified Medical Language System (UMLS) metathesaurus (NLM 1998). It combines 53 heterogeneous conceptual systems, composed of a hierarchy totaling 476,313 concepts (updated on a yearly basis). From a knowledge representation perspective, UMLS can be viewed as a huge semantic network. Unfortunately, it shares all the drawbacks pointed out in the seminal paper by Brachman (1979). Hence, given its size, evolutionary diversity and long-lasting maintenance history, the apparent lack of a formal semantic foundation leads to inconsistencies, circular definitions, etc. (Cimino 1998).

Taxonomic anatomical knowledge, a major portion of these ontologies, is fundamentally characterized by is-a and part-whole relationships between concepts. As a matter of fact then a frequent mixture of generalization (IS-A) and partitive (PART-OF) relations occur at the same hierarchical level. For instance, "blood" subsumes "blood plasma" (partitive), as well as "fetal blood" (generalization).

The Common Reference Model for medical terminology, developed within the GALEN and GALEN-IN-USE projects (Rector et al. 1995) marks, for the time being, one of the few attempts to construct a large-scale medical ontology in a formally founded way. In

this context, GRAIL, a KL-ONE-like knowledge representation language, has been developed and, by design, specifically adapted to the requirements of the medical domain (Rector et al. 1997). GRAIL, unlike most description logics, has a built-in mechanism that explicitly targets at part-whole reasoning, an extension that reflects the outstanding importance of this reasoning pattern in the medical domain.

In our research, the necessity to account for medical knowledge in a principled way arose from the need to make deductive reasoning capabilities available to MEDSYNDIKATE, a text understanding system that processes pathology reports (Hahn, Schulz, & Romacker 1999). To supply MEDSYNDIKATE with the enormous amount of medical knowledge already specified in the UMLS metathesaurus, we transfer UMLS specifications to the more rigorous framework of description logics.

Hence, generalization hierarchies (via IS-A and INSTANCE-OF relations), as well as PART-OF relations have to be accounted for in a systematic way. In the course of many ontology engineering cycles we recognized some problems that challenged conventional wisdom in medical knowledge representation. In particular, we encountered many exceptions to the rule of transitivity of PART-OF and the way it effects specialization of associated concepts.

We here abandon the notion of "flat" concept nodes and rather replace them by a tripartite concept encoding that fully incorporates part-whole knowledge. Since we embed our approach into the framework of KL-ONE-style description logics (Woods & Schmolze 1992), we subsequently rely upon the standard terminological classifier for partonomic reasoning along PART-OF relations, basically, in the same way as for taxonomic reasoning along generalization (IS-A) hierarchies.

Part-Whole Reasoning Problems

Two aspects of reasoning on part-whole relations have received special attention — whether transitivity can be considered a general property and how partonomic reasoning relates to taxonomic reasoning, i.e., whether specialization relations can be inferred from part-whole relations in related parts of a knowledge base.

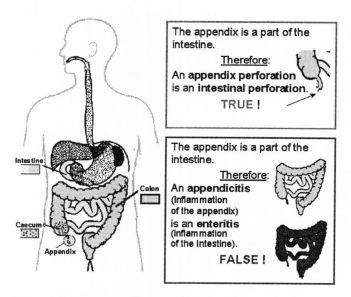

Figure 1: Digestive Tract and its Parts
Left: Position of the Appendix within the Digestive Tract.
Right: Disease Concepts Related to *Appendix* and to *Intestine*, with and without Concept Specialization

Transitivity. The importance of transitivity of the PART-OF relation for adequate reasoning has largely been discussed in the literature (cf. the overview in Artale *et al.* (1996)). Winston, Chaffin, & Herrmann (1987) argue that part-whole relations can be considered transitive as long as "a single sense of part" is kept. This means that the general PART-OF relation is not transitive, whereas *each* distinct subrelation of PART-OF is transitive. As soon as more than one single-sense PART-OF subrelation is involved in a relation chain, transitivity no longer holds, in general. For instance, a FINGER is a PHYSICAL-PART-OF an ARM which is a PHYSICAL-PART-OF a MUSICIAN; a MUSICIAN is a MEMBER-OF an ORCHESTRA. Because FINGER and MUSICIAN are related by the same PART-OF subrelation (viz. PHYSICAL-PART-OF) we conclude that a FINGER is a PHYSICAL-PART-OF a MUSICIAN, whereas it is not a PART-OF an ORCHESTRA, since a second kind of a PART-OF (viz. MEMBER-OF) relation comes into play.

The transitivity property is widely acknowledged in the domain of medical anatomy, too. If an anatomical object is PART-OF another one, which itself is included in a larger structure, the first one is also a PART-OF the larger structure. For instance, the APPENDIX is a PART-OF the CAECUM, the CAECUM is a PART-OF the COLON, and the COLON is a PART-OF the INTESTINE. Hence, the APPENDIX is also a PART-OF the INTESTINE (cf. Fig. 1, left side). Since we have encountered many instances of subrelations of the anatomical PART-OF relation, for which the transitivity assumption is questionable or may even be rejected (cf. our discussion of the phenomena illustrated in Fig. 5), we consider it as a decision at the level of ontology engineering — for each and every PART-OF relation — whether transitiv-

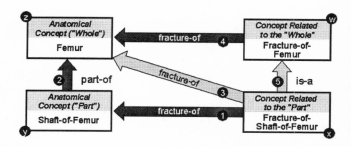

Figure 2: Taxonomic Reasoning in Partonomies

ity must be granted or not. In particular, it turns out that this problem cannot be solved at the level of the axiomatic definition of knowledge representation languages and the operators they supply.

Taxonomic reasoning in partonomies. Rector *et al.* (1997) discuss two taxonomic reasoning patterns that crucially depend on part-whole relations. The first one accounts for **role propagation** in partonomies, i.e., the portion of a knowledge base that is linked via PART-OF relations. Consider, e.g., Fig. 2, where a concept x (FRACTURE-OF-SHAFT-OF-FEMUR) is related to a "part" concept y (SHAFT-OF-FEMUR) via some relation $\mathbf{R}$ (FRACTURE-OF ❶). The "part" concept y is an anatomical PART-OF (❷) a "whole" z (FEMUR). Given that a concept from the range of the relation FRACTURE-OF (y) is in the domain of a PART-OF relation whose range concept is z, the relation $\mathbf{R}$ (FRACTURE-OF) can also be propagated to z (❸). More generally, when two relations, $\mathbf{R}$ and $\mathbf{S}$, are given, $\mathbf{S}$ being a subrelation of PART-OF, the following implication holds:

$$x\mathbf{R}y \wedge y\mathbf{S}z \Rightarrow x\mathbf{R}z \qquad (1)$$

Second, the above framework also allows for **concept specialization** in partonomies. As an example (cf. Fig. 2), we assume the relation FRACTURE-OF to link x (FRACTURE-OF-SHAFT-OF-FEMUR) and y (SHAFT-OF-FEMUR) (❶), as well as w (FRACTURE-OF-FEMUR) and z (FEMUR) (❹). Given the PART-OF relation between y and z (❷), we conclude that x (FRACTURE-OF-SHAFT-OF-FEMUR) specializes w (FRACTURE-OF-FEMUR) (❺), hence x IS-A w. The general reasoning pattern can be phrased as follows for two relations, $\mathbf{R}$ and $\mathbf{S}$, $\mathbf{S}$ being a subrelation of PART-OF:

$$x\mathbf{R}y \wedge w\mathbf{R}z \wedge y\mathbf{S}z \Rightarrow x\mathrm{ISA}w \qquad (2)$$

Obviously, the reasoning pattern (2) is a special form of (1). Along the lines of these two schemes, dedicated knowledge representation languages, such as GRAIL (Rector *et al.* 1997), have been developed. In this framework, taxonomic reasoning in partonomies can be defined as a property of a conceptual relation by an axiom in the form $\mathbf{R}$ *specializedBy* $\mathbf{S}$, iff $\mathbf{S} \sqsubseteq$ PART-OF. This implies that the relation $\mathbf{R}$ is *always* propagated along hierarchies based on $\mathbf{S}$, i.e., the inheritance mechanism is invariably associated with the relation $\mathbf{S}$, and that concept specialization is deduced on the basis of PART-OF relations (hence, *"part-whole" specialization*).

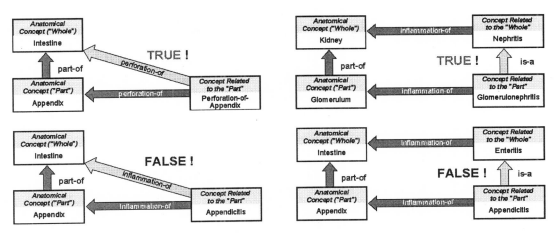

Figure 3: Regular and Irregular Reasoning Patterns (Upper vs. Lower Part) for Role Propagation and Concept Specialization (Left vs. Right Part)

This way, partonomic reasoning is dealt with at the axiomatic language definition level. We have, however, collected empirical evidence at the ontology engineering level that such an axiomatic approach might be fundamentally inadequate. We make the following claims:

1. Role propagation in partonomies does *not generally* hold. Consider Fig. 3 (left side), where a PERFORATION-OF the APPENDIX (PERFORATION-OF-APPENDIX) implies a PERFORATION-OF the INTESTINE, whereas an INFLAMMATION-OF the APPENDIX (APPENDICITIS) does not imply an INFLAMMATION-OF the INTESTINE, given that AP-PENDIX is an ANATOMICAL-PART-OF the INTESTINE.

2. Also concept specialization in partonomies does *not generally* hold for certain concepts related to a partonomy by the *same* relation. For instance, given that GLOMERULUM and KIDNEY are related by an ANATOMICAL-PART-OF relation just like APPENDIX and INTESTINE, we observe another clash of inference results (cf. Fig. 3 right side). For example, in contradistinction to the fact that a GLOMERU-LONEPHRITIS (an INFLAMMATION-OF the GLOMERU-LUM) specializes a NEPHRITIS (an INFLAMMATION-OF the KIDNEY), an APPENDICITIS (INFLAMMATION-OF the APPENDIX) does not specialize the concept EN-TERITIS (INFLAMMATION-OF the INTESTINE).

Both reasoning patterns interact. Concept specialization requires the role propagation pattern to be true. Vice versa, if the role propagation pattern is false, consequently also concept specialization cannot hold (cf. Fig. 3, left and right side, lower example).

Currently, neither established large-scale terminologies nor dedicated medical knowledge representation languages are able to properly account for the above-mentioned, regular as well as irregular, phenomena typical of part-whole hierarchies. The solution we propose rests on the assumption that the generality of the reasoning patterns (1) and (2) have to be restricted. Instead of giving them the status of generally valid axioms or devise (costly) language built-ins such as transitive closure or part-of operators, we reduce partonomic reasoning entirely into standard classification-based taxonomic reasoning. In order to circumvent many of the contradictions we have pointed out we introduce tripartite concept descriptions that already incorporate part-whole relations. This allows us to assign the decision as to whether transitivity or specialization actually hold down to the ontology engineering level where medical expertise becomes decisive.

Partonomic Reasoning Goes Taxonomic

We now turn to the special properties of partonomic reasoning by reducing it to taxonomic reasoning. The crucial point about the feasibility of this reduction lies in the provision of a tripartite concept encoding, so-called SEP triplets, to which we turn first. Following on that, we exploit the generalization hierarchy to enable useful inferences that are typical of transitive relations and show, moreover, how the same formalism allows conditioned taxonomic reasoning on partonomies.

SEP-Triplets. In our domain model, the relation ANATOMICAL-PART-OF describes the partitive relation between physical parts of an organism and is embedded in a specific triplet structure by which anatomical concepts are modeled (cf. Fig. 4). The restriction to a single tree of subrelations of PART-OF is sufficient for the logical deductions we encounter in the medical domain. A triplet consists, first of all, of a composite "structure" concept, the so-called **S-node** (e.g. INTESTINE-STRUC-TURE). Each "structure" concept subsumes both an anatomical *entity* and each of the anatomical *parts* of this entity. Unlike entities and their parts, "structures"

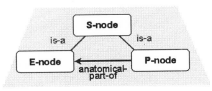

Figure 4: Structure of SEP-Triplets

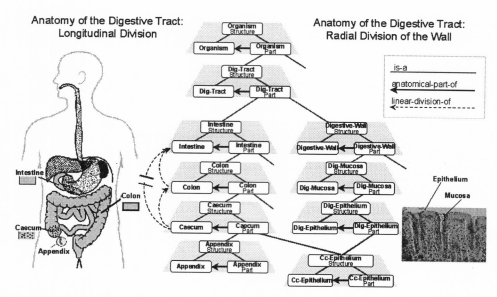

Figure 5: Segment of the Part-Whole Taxonomy of the Gastrointestinal Tract in SEP-Triplet Encoding

have no correlate in the real world — they constitute a representational artifact required for the formal reconstruction of the patterns of part-whole reasoning we have already discussed.

The two direct subsumees of an S-node are called **E-node** ("entity") and **P-node** ("part"), e.g., INTESTINE and INTESTINE-PART, respectively. Unlike an **S-node**, these nodes refer to specific ontological objects. The E-node denotes the *whole* anatomical entity to be modeled, whereas the P-node is the common subsumer of any of the parts of the E-node. Hence, for every P-node there exists a corresponding E-node for the role ANATOMICAL-PART-OF. Fig. 5 illustrates the model of a segment of the gastro-intestinal anatomy subdomain. Note that the formalism supports the definition of concepts as conjunctions of more than one P-node concept, as illustrated by the concept Cc-EPITHELIUM.

Transitivity via Inheritance of SEP-Triplets. Let C and D be E-nodes (e.g., the organs CAECUM and APPENDIX), and $AStr$ be the top-level structure concept of a domain subgraph (e.g., ORGANISM-STRUCTURE). $CStr$ and $DStr$ (e.g., CAECUM-STRUCTURE and APPENDIX-STRUCTURE), are then the S-nodes that subsume C and D, respectively, just as $CPart$ and $DPart$, e.g., CAECUM-PART and APPENDIX-PART, are the P-nodes related to C and D, respectively, via the role ANATOMICAL-PART-OF. All these concepts are embedded in a generalization hierarchy such that

$$D \sqsubseteq DStr \sqsubseteq CPart \sqsubseteq CStr \sqsubseteq .. \sqsubseteq APart \sqsubseteq AStr \quad (3)$$

$$C \sqsubseteq CStr \sqsubseteq .. \sqsubseteq APart \sqsubseteq AStr \quad (4)$$

The P-node for $CPart$ is defined as follows:

$$CPart \doteq CStr \sqcap \exists \text{ANATOMICAL-PART-OF}.C \quad (5)$$

Since D is subsumed by $CPart$ (3), we infer that D is an ANATOMICAL-PART-OF the organ C :

$$D \sqsubseteq \exists \text{ANATOMICAL-PART-OF}.C \quad (6)$$

Clearly, this pattern of *part-of inheritance* holds at every level of the part-whole hierarchy. In our example (cf. Fig. 5), the subsumption relation expressed in (3) may be illustrated by identifying the concept D with APPENDIX that is a subconcept of APPENDIX-STRUCTURE, CAECUM-PART, CAECUM-STRUCTURE etc. up to ORGANISM-PART and ORGANISM-STRUCTURE. In the same way, C is identified with CAECUM which is a subconcept of CAECUM-STRUCTURE, etc. (4). Between CAECUM-PART and CAECUM, there exists an ANATOMICAL-PART-OF relation (5). We conclude that a relation ANATOMICAL-PART-OF also holds between APPENDIX and CAECUM (6), but also between APPENDIX and COLON, APPENDIX and INTESTINE, COLON and INTESTINE, etc.

Analyzing the ontological structure of the medical domain reveals an interesting observation. Various specializations of ANATOMICAL-PART-OF are not transitive, although transitivity seems to hold for the general ANATOMICAL-PART-OF relation. The PART-OF inheritance mechanism is able to cope with this exception phenomenon. This feature is illustrated by the dotted arrows in Fig. 5 (left side). PART-OF inheritance can be selectively obviated in case of certain subrelations of ANATOMICAL-PART-OF, such as LINEAR-DIVISION-OF. This is achieved by linking the LINEAR-DIVISION-OF relation to the entity nodes rather than to the structure nodes of the concepts involved. We then describe COLON as a LINEAR-DIVISION-OF INTESTINE, CAECUM as a LINEAR-DIVISION-OF COLON, but CAECUM cannot be described as a LINEAR-DIVISION-OF INTESTINE.

Thus, SEP-triplets provide a flexible and powerful ontology engineering methodology which embeds reasoning about partonomies simply into Is-A taxonomies. Their characteristic properties, viz. *transitivity* and *antisymmetry*, by which acyclicity is guaranteed, apply directly to the way we model partonomic relations.

Concept specialization on partonomies is based on the transitivity of the PART-OF relation and the spezialization axiom (3). Provided our triplet structures consisting of E-nodes, P-nodes and S-nodes, we can flexibly enable or suppress concept specialization on partonomies, i.e., the inference of a subsumption relation between concepts that are related to partonomies. The decision whether the switch is set to "on" or "off" has to be made by the medical expert. Whenever, e.g., a disease concept is related to an anatomical concept, the knowledge engineer must explicitly determine whether it effects concept specialization or not (see the ENTERITIS/NEPHRITIS example from Fig. 3, right part). Just as with transitivity, concept specialization on partonomies is enabled when a disease concept is attached to an S-node, while it is disabled when the concept is linked to an E-node. Why this is the case can be shown by looking at the same taxonomy as described in the terminological statements (3) to (6). Let R and S be relations that link the disease concepts W, X, Y, Z to the anatomical hierarchy. From

$$W \doteq \exists S.CStr \qquad (7)$$
$$X \doteq \exists S.DStr \qquad (8)$$
$$DStr \sqsubseteq CStr \qquad (9)$$

we conclude that

$$X \sqsubseteq W \qquad (10)$$

While the "S-node pattern", (7) to (10), allows concept specialization in partonomies, the following "E-node pattern" does not:

$$Y \doteq \exists R.C \qquad (11)$$
$$Z \doteq \exists R.D \qquad (12)$$

The conclusion

$$Z \sqsubseteq Y \qquad (13)$$

cannot be drawn, since the extension of D is not a subset of the extension of C.

In our example (cf. Fig. 6: top, right side), (7) and (8) can be interpreted as follows: INTESTINAL-PERFORATION is a PERFORATION-OF an INTESTINE-STRUCTURE and PERFORATION-OF-APPENDIX is a PERFORATION-OF an APPENDIX-STRUCTURE. Since APPENDIX-STRUCTURE is subsumed by INTESTINE-STRUCTURE (9), it follows by the **S-node** pattern that a PERFORATION-OF-APPENDIX specializes INTESTINAL-PERFORATION (10).

Considering an alternative encoding in Fig. 6 (top, left side), the concept ENTERITIS is not linked to the S-node INTESTINE-STRUCTURE by the role INFLAMMATION-OF, but to the **E-node** INTESTINE instead (11), just as APPENDICITIS is linked to the E-node APPENDIX (12). As INTESTINE does not subsume APPENDIX, according to the **E-node** pattern *no* specialization relation (13) between APPENDICITIS (= Z) and ENTERITIS (= Y) can be inferred.

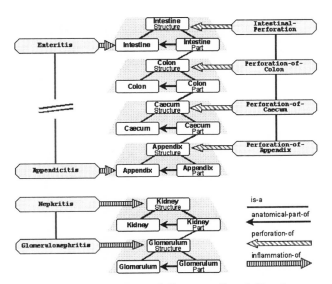

Figure 6: Conditioned Concept Specialization

It is therefore only the difference in the concept linkage patterns (linkage to S-nodes vs. linkage to E-nodes) that liberates or obviates concept specialization on partonomies. If $R = S$, the same relation is used for concept specialization in one case, though not in the other. Therefore, concept specialization on partonomies is not a property of the relation itself, but derives from the parametrization of SEP-triplets.

We may illustrate this case with the relation INFLAMMATION-OF, by comparing its use in two subgraphs. In the lower part of Fig. 6, the S-node pattern (expressions (7) to (10)) is applied to the KIDNEY subgraph in order to define the concepts NEPHRITIS and GLOMERULONEPHRITIS, whereas in the upper part the definition of ENTERITIS and APPENDICITIS obeys the E-node pattern in the INTESTINE subgraph. This example shows clearly how the same relation (INFLAMMATION-OF) supports concept specialization on partonomies in one case (KIDNEY), while in the other (INTESTINE) it does not. Thus, our methodology allows for conditioned enabling or disabling of concept specialization for concepts related to partonomies.

With these examples we may challenge the validity of the inference rule (2) in two ways. First, we have determined subrelations of **S** (e.g., LINEAR-DIVISION-OF), for which transitivity does not hold. Second, we may even claim that, depending on the choice of the domain/range concepts, a particular relation **S** allows transitivity, while in other cases it prohibits transitivity.

Role propagation on partonomies follows when specialization is given between the concepts related to a partonomy by the same relation. In Fig. 6 (right side), the deduction that a PERFORATION-OF an APPENDIX-STRUCTURE is also a PERFORATION-OF an INTESTINE-STRUCTURE clearly results from the fact that APPENDIX-STRUCTURE is subsumed by INTESTINE-STRUCTURE. The mapping of partonomies to generalization (IS-A) hierarchies provides the representational mechanisms for appropriate reasoning.

Related Work

For the medical domain, Haimowitz, Patil, & Szolovits (1988) first requested a representation formalism for *part-whole* relations and corresponding reasoning capabilities as an extension to terminological logics. As a response, three basic approaches can be distinguished.

In the first, part-whole reasoning is dealt with by extending a knowledge representation language by new operators dedicated to partonomic reasoning. Such a proposal, a transitive closure operator for roles, has been elaborated by Baader (1991), who also discusses the computational costs implied, viz. intractability of the resulting terminological system. In a similar vein, the GRAIL language constitutes an extension of terminological logics adapted to the part-whole reasoning patterns in the medical domain (Rector *et al.* 1997). However, role propagation and concept specialization are hard-wired to role definitions and, therefore, fail to match empirical data from anatomical ontologies.

In the second approach, reasoning patterns are adapted to particular (sub)relations (Cohen & Loiselle 1988). Since the concept nodes to which these relations are linked cannot be constrained, this approach fails when the same relation allows and prohibits, e.g., transitivity. The same counterargument hits proposals in which subrelations of PART-OF are declared to be transitive, in general (Hahn, Markert, & Strube 1996).

The third approach tries to preserve standard language definitions for reasons of simplicity and parsimony. Along this line, Schmolze & Marks (1991) proposed a solution similar to ours using subsumption to obtain inferences resembling those of transitive roles or transitive closure of roles. Artale *et al.* (1996) criticize this proposal for the "proliferation of (artificial) concepts" involved. We argue, on the contrary, that these additional concepts are necessary from an ontological point of view, as the distinct mechanisms for conditioned specialization modeling reveal (cf. Fig. 6).

It remains to be seen, however, whether conservative structural extensions of a stable language platform are able to carry over to the many varieties of partonomic reasoning and different part-whole relations (discussed in a survey by Sattler (1995)), or whether newly designed operators or other fundamental language extensions are needed. In the medical domain, at least, where the restriction to one subrelation of PART-OF, viz. ANATOMICAL-PART-OF, is sufficient, a relatively simple "data structure" extension like the SEP triplets yields already adequate results, without the necessity to resort to profound extensions of the terminological language.

Conclusion

In this paper, we have argued against two commonly shared opinions about partonomic reasoning. First, that part-whole relations are transitive and transitivity can be considered an inherent property of the relation itself; second, that subsumption relations invariably hold within partonomies.

Our alternative focuses on a tripartite encoding schema for concepts that incorporates part-whole specifications. Embedding the corresponding SEP-triplets into an inheritance hierarchy allows us to use standard terminological classifiers of description logics systems for partonomic reasoning in the same way they are used for taxonomic reasoning. The SEP-triplets provide the flexibility required for an ontology engineer to decide whether transitivity should hold or not.

This approach might generalize to other domains as well. Consider the following commonsense scenario. The car-body is clearly a part of the car. From the car-body's color we may infer the color of the car. So are the seats part of a car. The color of the car, however, would not be inferred from that of the seats.

Acknowledgements. We would like to thank Katja Markert for valuable suggestions. M. Romacker and St. Schulz are supported by a grant from DFG (Ha 2097/5-1).

References

Artale, A.; Franconi, E.; Guarino, N.; and Pazzi, L. 1996. Part-whole relations in object-centered systems: an overview. *Data and Knowledge Engineering* 20(3):347–383.

Baader, F. 1991. Augmenting concept languages by transitive closure of roles: an alternative to terminological cycles. In *Proc. of the IJCAI'91*, 446–451. Morgan Kaufmann.

Brachman, R. 1979. On the epistemological status of semantic networks. In Findler, N., ed., *Associative Networks*. Academic Press. 3–50.

Cimino, J. 1998. Auditing the Unified Medical Language System with semantic methods. *Journal of the American Medical Informatics Association* 5(1):41–51.

Cohen, P., and Loiselle, C. 1988. Beyond ISA: structures for plausible inference in semantic networks. In *Proc. of the AAAI'88*, 415–420. Morgan Kaufmann.

Hahn, U.; Markert, K.; and Strube, M. 1996. A conceptual reasoning approach to textual ellipsis. In *Proc. of the ECAI'96*, 572–576. John Wiley.

Hahn, U.; Schulz, S.; and Romacker, M. 1999. How knowledge drives understanding. Matching medical ontologies with the needs of medical language processing. *Artificial Intelligence in Medicine* 15(1):25–51.

Haimowitz, I.; Patil, R.; and Szolovits, P. 1988. Representing medical knowledge in a terminological language is difficult. In *Proc. of the SCAMC'88*, 101–105. IEEE.

NLM. 1998. *Unified Medical Language System*. Bethesda, MD: National Library of Medicine.

Rector, A.; Solomon, W.; Nowlan, W.; and Rush, T. 1995. A terminology server for medical information systems. *Methods of Information in Medicine* 34(2):147–157.

Rector, A.; Bechhofer, S.; Goble, C.; Horrocks, I.; and Nowlan, W. 1997. The GRAIL concept modelling language for medical terminology. *Art. Int. in Medicine* 9:139–171.

Sattler, U. 1995. A concept language for an engineering application with part-whole relations. In *DL'95 – Proc. of the Intl. Workshop on Description Logics*, 119–123.

Schmolze, J., and Marks, W. 1991. The NIKL experience. *Computational Intelligence* 6:48–69.

Winston, M.; Chaffin, R.; and Herrmann, D. 1987. A taxonomy of part-whole relationships. *Cognitive Science* 11:417–444.

Woods, W., and Schmolze, J. 1992. The KL-ONE family. *Computers & Math. with Applications* 23(2/5):133–177.

Verbalization of High-Level Formal Proofs

Amanda M. Holland-Minkley
Department of Computer Science
Cornell University
Ithaca, NY 14853
hollandm@cs.cornell.edu

Regina Barzilay
Department of Computer Science
Columbia University
New York, NY 10027
regina@cs.columbia.edu

Robert L. Constable
Department of Computer Science
Cornell University
Ithaca, NY 14853
rc@cs.cornell.edu

Abstract

We propose a new approach to text generation from formal proofs that exploits the high-level and interactive features of a tactic-style theorem prover. The design of our system is based on communication conventions identified in a corpus of texts. We show how to use dialogue with the theorem prover to obtain information that is required for communication but is not explicitly used in reasoning.

Introduction

The problem of generating text from formal proofs has become more important as use of theorem provers in hardware and software verification creates a large body of formal mathematics (O'Leary *et al.* 1994; Rushby 1997; Gordon & Melham 1993). There is also independent interest in the subject of *formalized mathematics* for its own sake (Cederquist, Coquand, & Negri 1997; Jackson 1995). Some automated reasoning groups are putting their formal mathematics on the web but it cannot be searched in its current form by standard web tools. This kind of material may also play a role in mathematics education. In each case, there is interest in making the formal mathematics produced accessible to an audience that is untrained in the formalism's specialized language.

At least two of the theorem provers generating this large body of mathematics, Coq (Paulin-Mohring & Werner 1993) and Nuprl, are used to create formal proofs that are intended to be readable. However, even these readable formal proofs require training to understand. Consequently, the massive amounts of material that experts can create with these theorem provers remains less accessible than it should be. While natural language proofs would increase accessibility, the texts produced must be faithful to the essential reasoning behind these proofs.

In this paper we describe an approach to providing faithful natural language proofs where the high-level nature of the formalism is used to guide the generation process. The high-level proof representation is an accessible source of the information needed in content planning and sentence construction. We also demonstrate the usefulness of allowing the generation tool to query the prover in order to acquire this type of information.

The specific technical question that we consider here is how to generate text from tactic-style formal proofs created by the Nuprl system. A tactic can be thought of as a large inference step that is assembled from many small primitive ones. The Nuprl tactic system was designed to mimic human reasoning. A sample of a formal Nuprl proof is given in Figure 1. We will give evidence that tactic steps correspond approximately with human inference steps. This property of tactic-style proofs will make the structure of the proof easily accessible.

The tactic proof by itself does not necessarily contain all of the information needed to generate good proof text. Some proof content is captured within the general mathematical knowledge of the reasoner and is not included in specific proofs. In addition, there is a gap between the information that is needed by the reasoner to determine that an inference is correct and the information that is needed to communicate to a person why that inference is correct. We will show that if the theorem prover makes available the primitive proof that lies beneath the tactic proof and allows queries from the generation system, we can obtain this additional semantic information.

Based on these new methods, we generated natural texts from a collection of tactic-based proofs. We used the high-level proof structure for discourse planning and used the mathematics communication conventions that we identified from the corpus to determine sentence content in the context of the discourse. Furthermore, we began to identify knowledge needed for natural language communication that is not present in the formal proof and explored how to use the theorem prover's reasoning capabilities to obtain it. The texts we produced show that these methods are effective, at least in the chosen domain of elementary arithmetic.

Previous Work

Previous work on the task of generating text from formal proofs has focused on translating from low-level

Nuprl Proof

```
*T ndiff_ndiff
⊢ ∀a,b:ℤ.∀c:ℕ.(a -- b) -- c = a -- (b + c)
|
BY (UnivCD ...a) THEN Unfold 'ndiff' 0
|
1. a: ℤ
2. b: ℤ
3. c: ℕ
⊢ imax(imax(a - b;0) - c;0) =
| imax(a - (b + c);0)
|
BY (ArithSimp 0 ...a)
|
⊢ imax(-c + imax(a + -b;0);0) =
| imax(a + -b + -c;0)
|
BY RWN 1 (LemmaC 'add_com') 0 THEMM
|  RWH (LemmaC 'imax_add_r') 0 THENA Auto
|
⊢ imax(imax((a + -b) + -c;0 + -c);0) =
| imax(a + -b + -c;0)
|
BY RWH (RevLemmaC 'imax_assoc') 0 THENA Auto
|
⊢ imax((a + -b) + -c;imax(0 + -c;0)) =
| imax(a + -b + -c;0)
|
BY RWN 2 (UnfoldTopC 'imax') 0
|  THEN SplitOnConclITE THENA Auto'
|\
| 4. 0 + -c ≤ 0
| ⊢ imax((a + -b) + -c;0) =
| imax(a + -b + -c;0)
| |
1 BY Auto
 \
  4. 0 < 0 + -c
  ⊢ imax((a + -b) + -c;0 + -c) =
  | imax(a + -b + -c;0)
  |
  BY Assert ⌈c = 0⌉ THENA Auto'
  |
  5. c = 0
  |
  BY HypSubst 5 0  THEN Auto'
```

Definitions

```
*A ndiff     a -- b ==  imax(a - b;0)

*T imax_add_r
⊢ ∀a,b,c:ℤ.imax(a;b) + c = imax(a + c;b + c)

*T imax_assoc
⊢ ∀a,b,c:ℤ.imax(a;imax(b;c)) =
  imax(imax(a;b);c)
```

Figure 1: A sample Nuprl proof

Theorem: For integers a and b and natural number c, $(a - -b) - -c = a - -(b + c)$.

Consider that a and b are integers and c is a natural number. Now, the original expression can be transformed to $\mathrm{imax}(\mathrm{imax}(a - b; 0) - c; 0) = \mathrm{imax}(a - (b + c); 0)$. From the add_com lemma, we conclude $\mathrm{imax}(-c + \mathrm{imax}(a + -b; 0); 0) = \mathrm{imax}(a + -b + -c; 0)$. From the imax_assoc lemma, the goal becomes $\mathrm{imax}(\mathrm{imax}((a + -b) + -c; 0 + -c); 0) = \mathrm{imax}(a + -b + -c; 0)$. There are 2 possible cases. The case $0 + -c \leq 0$ is trivial. Consider $0 < 0 + -c$. Now, the original expression can be transformed to $\mathrm{imax}((a + -b) + -c; 0 + -c) = \mathrm{imax}(a + -b + -c; 0)$. Equivalently, the original expression can be rewritten as $\mathrm{imax}((a + -b) + -c) = \mathrm{imax}(a + -b + -c; 0)$. This proves the theorem.

Figure 2: Automatically generated text; associated Nuprl proof and relevant definitions shown in Figure 1

formal languages, particularly from natural deduction style formal proofs *without tactics*. In some cases generation was based on a low-level proof even when a corresponding high-level proof was available (Coscoy, Kahn, & Théry 1995). The high-level proof was avoided because each reasoning step in a high-level proof could incorporate trial-and-error techniques or show facts that may not be necessary in the final proof. There was also concern that the set of available tactics varies between theorem proving systems and may change within a system as it is improved. Though the former is a concern for us, the latter does not seem to be a problem to us because we believe that a theorem proving system and its generation component must work together. Furthermore, it was conceded that the higher-level proof encompassed information about the reasoning process that was quite valuable for communication.

When generating text from a low-level formal proof, two major problems arise. The first problem is that if every low-level step is expressed, the text will be too verbose and contain many unnecessary or "obvious" steps. To give an idea of the magnitude of this problem, in the Nuprl system the low-level primitive proof underlying the example shown in Figure 1 has 674 steps in it. The EXPOUND system (Chester 1976) addresses this problem of verboseness by omitting certain specific low-level inference steps whenever they are encountered or indicating their presence while suppressing the details. The generation system for the Coq theorem prover takes the approach of generating text for every step but aggregating the text for multiple proofs steps into a single sentence when the steps are of the same logical form and occur adjacent in the proof (Coscoy 1997). In general, though, each low-level step produces a sentence in the output proof. In the PROVERB system (Huang 1994b), before generation is performed the input natural deduction proof is translated to an intermediate form that combines several low-level inference steps into one larger high-level step that is intended to reflect a human reasoning step. Generation then proceeds using this new representation. This is a time-consuming process that often requires heuristics to determine what information will be omitted.

The second major problem with low-level proofs is determining the order in which to express the steps of the proof (discourse planning). In a low-level proof format, proof steps can be listed in an almost arbitrary order so long as a step that establishes a precondition of another step in the proof occurs before that step in the proof order. Chester (1976) defines a partial order on steps of a natural deduction proof such that a graph can be drawn showing these dependencies between proof steps. From this graph a coherent linear ordering is given to the proof steps. PROVERB gets its proof step ordering by organizing its assertion-level steps into a dependency tree and then using a notion of local focus to determine a path through the tree (Huang 1994b). In both cases, the system has to create a tree structure in order to determine the text's discourse structure.

We find that by using high-level tactic-style formal proofs as input both of the above problems can be solved easily. First, a Nuprl proof is a tree, and it can be traversed in a depth-first manner to obtain an appropriate linear ordering on the proof steps. Also, we will show that each proof step is already of approximately the same size as a human reasoning step; the proof already resembles the assertion level proof that Huang claims is necessary for generating a good text version of a proof.

The Nuprl Theorem Prover

Since 1983, the Nuprl proof development system (Constable *et al.* 1986; Constable 1997; Jackson 1995) has been used to help people interactively create formal proofs in a theory considered adequate as a foundation for all mathematics, including computational mathematics and programming. The system has been used to produce thousands of proofs. Most of these have been by-products of verifying that hardware and software systems meet formal specifications.

Nuprl was designed to support the kinds of reasoning seen in rigorous mathematical writings in nearly all mathematical fields, especially computer science. So its formal proofs tend to resemble nonformal but rigorous ones, and when users are creating them they are able to imitate what they would produce in less formal contexts.

The Nuprl logic has two separable components, an *assertion language* (sometimes called the logical theory) and a *proof language* (a deductive mechanism). The proof language includes a procedural language for building primitive proofs. The programs for building proofs are called tactics. They can be written as justifications in proofs. The resulting data structure is a *tactic tree*, a sequent proof that allow tactics as justifications (Allen *et al.* 1990). Tactic-style proofs can be

represented as a proof tree where each node in the tree represents a current goal and the children of a node are the new subgoals remaining after application of a tactic. Some tactics are programs that assemble a large inference step from many small primitive ones, such as `SplitOnConclITE` in Figure 1. However, some tactics are programs that search for proofs using heuristics. We will see the impact of these search tactics later. The proofs that users see are in this high-level tactic proof language, as in Figure 1.

Building and Evaluating the Corpus

In choosing to generate texts from tactic-style proofs, we act on the intuition that these proofs are closer to ones that humans create than are low-level proofs. By this, we mean that each tactic step corresponds approximately to an inference that a person would take when proving the same theorem. The steps are at the same level of granularity as human proof steps. The size of a proof step is an intuitive notion that indicates how much reasoning is happening within that step or how much closer to the goal that step takes the proof.

Among practicing mathematicians it is commonly accepted that there are a variety of general proof strategies to which specific steps in proofs correspond. There have been efforts to define and describe these types of proof steps in order to establish principles for creating proofs and writing them effectively (Solow 1982; deBruijn 1994; Constable, Knoblock, & Bates 1984). We pursue a parallel effort and define categories of proof steps that are not only part of the same strategy but are also communicated in the same manner. We call these categories Mathematics Communication Conventions (MCCs). If our claim that tactic steps approximate human proof steps holds, we can associate a single MCC with each step in a formal proof.

In order to verify our intuition that tactic proof steps closely resemble the proof steps which people would use to explain a proof, we followed the traditional generation methodology (McKeown 1985; Lester 1994) and built a corpus of texts generated by people from formal proofs produced by Nuprl. This corpus is based on fourteen formal proofs, all of which prove basic facts about integer arithmetic. We chose to use proofs from a library that was created with readability in mind. The proofs are all simple enough that the mathematics presented was straightforward for the participants to understand. Study participants were asked to read these proofs and then write translations of them into English. The participants ranged from being experts in the Nuprl system to having never used the system or seen its formal language before. However, all participants had at least a basic familiarity with formal languages in general.

A brief tutorial on how to read Nuprl proofs and a guide to the meaning of terms in the proof was available for novice participants to consult while performing the translations. The study was administered electronically on the web with the proofs given in their HTML format

Type of mapping	# occurrences	% occurrences
1-1	180	64%
1-2	52	19%
1-3	12	4%
2-1	23	8%
3-1, 4-1	8	3%
1-0	4	1%
0-1	1	<1%
1-1, 1-2, 2-1	255	91%
1-1, case split, or analogy	232	83%

Figure 3: Number and percentage of occurrences of types of mappings from Nuprl proofs to English sentences in corpus; percentage taken out of 280 total mappings

and participants performed the tasks at their own pace. They were not required to translate all of the proofs. In all, there were nine participants in the study; the resulting corpus has 52 translated proofs in it.

Our corpus afforded us the observations we needed to verify our intuition that Nuprl's proof steps closely approximate human reasoning steps in written proofs. The first hypothesis we wanted to check was that Nuprl proof steps and English text proof steps are approximately the same size. To verify this, we compared the English proofs collected in our study with the Nuprl proofs on which they were based. Specifically, we noted whether a single step in the Nuprl proof was reflected in the corresponding English proofs by a single sentence or multiple sentences, or whether it and one or more other Nuprl proof steps were described together in a single sentence.

In our corpus, there were a total of 352 English sentences, and 280 matchings between Nuprl proof steps and English sentences. The statistics we collected on the frequency with which mappings from Nuprl proof steps to English sentences were one-to-one or of another type are shown in Figure 3. We also consider how many of the mappings that are not one-to-one involve a case split or analogous reasoning occurring in the proof. Case splits often involve "set-up" sentences in English texts to indicate what parameter of splitting was used, or to show that a case was finished and the next is being considered. When cases are analogous in a proof, the Nuprl steps in the analogous case are omitted form the English proof.

In summary, we observed that 64% of the proof steps map to exactly one English sentence and that 91% of the sentences either map one Nuprl proof step to one or two English sentences or map two Nuprl proof steps to one English sentence. Furthermore, in looking at the mappings which are not one-to-one, 52% of these are due to a case split or an analogy is occurring in the proof (45% due to case splits, 7% due to analogy).

From these observations we conclude that Nuprl

proof steps are approximately the same size as human inference steps. Most of the departures from the one-to-one mapping between Nuprl steps and English sentences are due to case splits in the proof. We conclude that it is practical for a generation system, using a Nuprl formal proof that was built with readability in mind as input, to plan what content to include in each sentence on a node-by-node basis. Given the ease with which case splits can be identified in a proof, it is straightforward to identify cases in which it might be suitable to generate multiple sentences.

Having verified that we can treat tactic steps as approximating human reasoning steps, we would like to define a set of MCCs such that all proof steps whose communication involves the same information presented in the same general structure are grouped together. We did this by first reading the English proofs and collecting together all of the sentences that had the same general content or role in the proof. Having done this, we looked at the Nuprl proof steps that corresponded to these sentences and observed that the reasoning being done was also similar. By using these observations we were able to define a set of ten MCCs (shown in Figure 4) that group together Nuprl proof steps that can be articulated by similar utterances communicating the same content.

In most cases, there was substantial similarity between all but a small number of the English sentences in an MCC. For some MCCs, the similarity among its corresponding sentences in the corpus was so strong that we were able to write a regular expression that generated every one of those English sentences. Therefore, once one identifies an MCC that covers a given proof step, one knows what type of sentence should be generated.

Overview of the System

Using the information that we collected from the corpus, we have built a simple natural language generation system in order to determine if it is feasible to use the patterns we discerned as the basis for such a system and to identify areas where more sophisticated techniques would be required. Our system is based on the traditional language generation system architecture (McKeown 1985; Hovy 1988). A typical language generator consists of two main components: a content planner, which selects the information from the knowledge base that should be included in the generated text, and a linguistic component, which maps concepts to words and builds an English sentence from them. The linguistic component follows the standard structure:

- a lexical chooser, which determines the syntactic structure of the sentence and the words to realize each semantic role; and

- a sentence generator, here FUF, which builds a syntactic tree, chooses closed class words, and linearizes the tree as a sentence.

Statement of Goal — communicates the theorem to be proved — *"Show for $x, y : Z. |x| = |y|$ iff $x = \pm y$."*

Variable Declaration — communicates the names of any variables introduced in the proof and possibly their types — *"Consider any two integers a and b."*

Case Statement — communicates that proof will proceed by argument by cases — *"It is either the case that $a * b = 0$ or it isn't."*

Case Consideration — introduces one of the cases in an argument by cases, possibly stating the assumption made in that case — *"In the first case, assume that $0 + -c$ is less than or equal to 0."*

Trivial Case Consideration — introduces a case which can be proved trivially in an argument by cases — *"If $a * b \neq 0$ the result follows immediately."*

Contradiction — communicates that the conclusion is proved by virtue of a contradiction being reached — *"We conclude that $a = 0$ and $b = 0$, which contradicts our initial assumptions."*

Analogy — indicates that two or more cases from a case statement are proved by the same reasoning — *"The second case is symmetric."*

Inference Step — communicates that the reasoning proceeds by an inference on the conclusion or one of the hypotheses, a generic type of reasoning not covered by one of the previous categories — *"By the lemma, either $a = 0$ or $b = 0$."*

Transformation — communicates a chain of reasoning steps, usually from the inference step category — *"By lemmas minus_imin and add_com this reduces to $imax(-a, -b) + -c = imax(-(a + c), -(b + c))$."*

Trivial Step — an inference step which is either omitted entirely or where "math" or "obviousness" are given as justification — *"It is trivial to see that both sides are equal."*

Statement of Conclusion — communicates that the conclusion has been proved, possibly with a restatement of that conclusion — *"Therefore it must be that $a * b$ is not zero."*

Figure 4: Mathematics Communication Conventions, with sample sentences from corpus

The lexical chooser is implemented in FUF and represents the lexicon as a grammar following (Elhadad 1993). The main work in this part was building the *domain vocabulary*, which maps concepts in the mathematics domain to words according to the context. The FUF sentence generator, which uses SURGE as its English grammar, was unchanged.

The major effort in the development of the system was the construction of the *content planner*. The content planner determines what information from the Nuprl proof tree should be included in the proof text. Each node in the proof tree represents one step of reasoning. A proof node contains the list of assumptions that are currently active, the conclusion that node is trying to draw, what tactic is applied at that step and the set of children of that proof node. It also contains information that is relevant only for the theorem prover, such as well-formedness information for each expression and information needed to transform proofs into executable code.

However, as we have noted, there is information that is needed for communication that is not stored in the proof tree, either because it is part of the background mathematics knowledge assumed in the system or because it was determined by the proof agent in a manner that did not produce a suitable proof object. This is the information that we must determine by appealing to the theorem prover. Adding this capability to the generation system results in turning the communication between the content planner and the Nuprl system into a dialogue, rather than one-directional communication as is standard in natural language generation systems.

In this section we will show our solutions to two problems that arose while constructing the system. One problem was made easy to solve by having high-level proofs. The other problem was made more complicated because of Nuprl's rich type system. We will point out specific places where dialogue with the theorem prover can help the generation process and describe the type of querying that might take place.

The first of these two problems is how to map the tree structure of Nuprl proofs to a linear structure that approximates human-written proofs. As we described before, the step size and ordering of proof steps are very similar between Nuprl proofs and the human-written versions in our corpus. Taking advantage of this, we traverse the tree in a depth-first manner and translating each proof node to a single sentence (or two sentences, at the start of a case consideration). The major issue to address, then, is how to determine which MCC from Figure 4 covers the step, since the Nuprl proof does not include this information. The MCC will completely define what information should be selected from the Nuprl node for that reasoning step. We discuss MCC identification further below.

The second problem we address on the content planner level is what representation of an object in the proof is most suitable for the current context. Since Nuprl is system with rich type hierarchy, the type of a variable may be a subtype of many other types in the system. As a simple example, a variable x that is a natural number can be thought of as an integer with the restriction on it that $x \geq 0$. We found from our corpus and mathematical literature that the choice of which type to use is highly determined by the context. So given our variable $x \in \mathbb{N}$ we might choose to refer to it as a natural number or as an integer in the text, depending on how it is being used and its surrounding context. This issue will be mentioned again later.

A sample of the output that our system generates is shown in Figure 2. It should be noted that, for technical reasons, the generation system is as of yet unable to import the Nuprl formula display forms and lemma names and these need to be added by hand, though the generation system does indicate where this information should be given. We use the lemma names as they are given in the Nuprl system in order to be consistent with the library structure that already exists and with which the users are familiar.

MCC Identification

We have developed a set of rules derived from the corpus that identify the MCC of Nuprl reference steps. For each of an MCC's occurrences in the corpus, we analyzed the node structure, its level in the tree, and the node's neighbors in the tree. We found that in some cases a node's local information completely determines its MCC. For example, every node that has more than one child falls in the **case statement** MCC, or one of the two subtypes of this MCC: **contradiction** and **analogy**. Other MCCs require looking at which tactic is applied. For example, to determine if a lemma application has occurred it must be checked whether one of a set of lemma-application tactics were used.

Generally, more analysis than this is required. A step falls in the **contradiction** MCC if after a case split one of the two cases is proved by obtaining false as a hypothesis. For us, this is not information that is necessarily available in the tactic-tree representation of the proof. However, Nuprl also stores a second, low-level representation of the proof: the primitive proof tree. This representation is not generally accessible by Nuprl users. Contradictions can be identified by retrieving the primitive proof tree associated with a leaf of the tactic-proof tree and checking this piece of the primitive proof tree for an occurrence of false as a hypothesis. Because our planning is initiated at the tactic-level, we only have to examine part of the primitive proof tree, thus saving time.

All of the cases described above can be accurately identified by examining features of the Nuprl output. A more difficult MCC to identify is **trivial case**. In general, this is a highly subjective judgement that humans do not agree on. We do not attempt to answer the most general question here of what does and does not qualify as being a trivial reasoning step; this is a significant and difficult open area of research. Instead, we say that a reasoning step is trivial if it follows from the Nuprl tactic Auto. This tactic applies simple automated proof search; it is an example of a heuristic. In practice, Nuprl users invoke this tactic to finish off lines of reasoning when the result has become obvious. Because we are dealing with Nuprl proofs designed to be readable we make the justifiable assumption that Auto

will have been invoked by the Nuprl user only in cases they deemed obvious themselves.

One of the MCCs whose identification requires a more semantic understanding of the proof tree is **analogy**. This occurs when the reasoning used to prove each of the subproofs of a case split is similar, or analogous. What it means for two cases to be analogous is not well defined; again, this is a subjective notion. The naive approach of comparing cases by checking if the same tactics were used in each reasoning step can result in wrong predictions. In some instances a tactic, such as Auto, may have a variety of primitive proof trees it can generate. It cannot be determined from the tactic level tree which of the alternatives has been generated. This means that two instances of the same tactic do not need to result in the same reasoning, hence leading to non-analogous cases. Therefore, solely syntactic features of the subtrees are not sufficient to find similarity between trees, and the whole problem requires a solution on the semantic level.

We have developed a method by which Nuprl can be used to solve this problem. Given two trees, the Analogy tactic, which runs in the Nuprl system, identifies whether the reasoning method used in the first tree can be "re-run" on the second tree to prove its result. Tactic application of this type is expensive, since Analogy tries to repeat the whole proof, and therefore it is unreasonable to invoke this tactic for every proof step. It is necessary for the content planner to examine the syntactic context and only apply the tactic if it is likely that the cases are analogous.

According to an analysis of Nuprl proofs, we find that there is reason to suspect that the Analogy tactic will apply if, for each of the first few steps in the two tactic trees, the set of tactics applied are the same and, when one of those tactics is a lemma or definition application, the same argument is given to the tactic in both cases. By varying how many proof steps need to match before running the Analogy tactic, the number of times that the tactic is run and the precision with which the analogy MCC is detected would vary. The fewer steps that are compared, the more often the Analogy tactic is run and the more instances of analogy would be detected. This is because our technique for saying that two tactic trees are not similar enough occasionally discards trees that would be judged analogous. However, by being conservative in this way we only end up omitting a simplification to the proof; we never add any inaccuracy. When we do claim that two proof trees followed by analogous reasoning, we are certain that this was the case because the line of reasoning from one proof tree was explicitly re-run on the other proof tree. Determining this requires a dialogue between Nuprl and the generation system.

Variable Type Representation

Consider a proof that introduces three variables x, y and z, where x is a natural number and y and z are integers. According to our corpus, people often prefer to introduce these variables in the text by saying "Let x, y and z be integers where x ≥ 0." Also, if one knows that a natural number variable is introduced in order to be used in a lemma that takes integers as input, it is clearer to state initially that the variable is an integer. In order to solve this problem, one must know about the subtype relations in the system. If one has a static hierarchy of types it is straightforward to check for any such relations. However, Nuprl does not store a type hierarchy and because its type system is dynamic and constantly growing it is not possible to build such a hierarchy outside of the system. This makes the problem of describing the type of a variable more difficult when using output from Nuprl.

Our solution is to start another dialogue with Nuprl to determine whether two types are in a subtype relation with each other. We have designed a tactic for Nuprl which allows us to check this. This tactic allows us to determine for any two variables whether one is a subtype of the other and, if it is, what additional conditions hold for the variable with the more restrictive type that do not hold for the other variable. With this information we can create alterative references for variables that make our text more concise.

This problem becomes much more serious in more complicated domains such as algebra and automata theory where the type hierarchy will have many levels. In these domains, this is an important problem to solve. Because we solve this problem by appealing to the theorem prover, which has a deeper understanding of the type system than our content planner can, we will be able to apply our solution to types of any complexity.

Discussion

In this paper, we have presented a simple system which uses the structure of a tactic-style formal proof and the Mathematics Communication Conventions defined for such proofs to guide the generation process. We implemented and tested our generation system using a pre-existing Nuprl library about integer mathematics. We ran our generator on 37 proofs and obtained an accurate and readable version of the proof in each case. An example of our output is in Figure 2. More examples of our output can be seen on the web at www.cs.cornell.edu/home/hollandm/res3_99.html.

We found that the structure and content of high-level tactic-style proofs offers a useful starting knowledge representation for use in generation. This representation already contains much of the information needed for the generation process. We have been able to identify some of the additional knowledge that is not necessary for the reasoning process, and hence not included in the formal proof, but that is critical for communication. We have shown how this information can be extracted from the proof. As McAllester and Givan (1992) noted, this information affects the ease of understanding mathematical arguments. We intend to explore the question of what additional information is needed for understanding further.

We identified that the advantages obtained by using a tactic-style theorem prover are balanced by some disadvantages not faced when using low-level input proofs. The dynamic nature of the Nuprl type theory led to difficulties in identifying what type reference to use for variables. In addition, because tactics are high-level abstractions of reasoning there is occasionally low-level information that is lost and has to be obtained through the methods we have described here. In some instances the best solution will be to alter the Nuprl system to add the information to the formal proof.

We also observed that sometimes the communication knowledge we need requires mathematical information that is not present in the proof. We suggest that the solution to this problem is to directly use the reasoning capabilities of the theorem prover. This requires an adjustment to the standard generation architecture to allow for interaction between the theorem prover and the generation system. In this way, the content planner does not have to make semantic decisions about the proof. These semantic issues are passed off to the theorem prover, which is better suited to handle them, and heuristics are avoided in resolving these questions. Avoiding heuristics allows our solutions to be fairly domain independent and should be able to apply them as we extend the system.

Our accomplishments here have also helped us verify that the Nuprl developers were successful in their goal to create a theorem prover that reflects the reasoning processes of people.

Future Work

This work has shown that high-level formal proofs are suitable and even have special advantages as input to a generation system. Having located some of the places where the information in high-level formal proofs is not sufficient for the generation task, and identified the potential for using dialogue between the generation system and the theorem prover to acquire this information, we want to incorporate this dialogue into our system and continue to explore its use in supplying communication information.

One problem that we will focus on is refining our notion of trivial proof to more closely approximate the notion of trivial used by people when they write proofs. We would also like a method for identifying analogous cases in proofs which relies more on determining whether the differences between the cases would seem significant to a reader or not. We believe that solving these problems will require adding a *user model* to our generation system, in order to have a specific type of reader against which our judgements of what type of reasoning is obvious or significant can be compared.

We also want to approach the problem of determining the best form for expressions when logically equivalent options are available; for example, chosing between the statement that "A implies that B implies C" and "A and B implies C". This will require the ability to determine which form is most useful to the reader given subsequent uses of the expression (McAllester & Givan 1992). It will also require the ability to create alternate forms of expressions in general cases, something we would be able to do by querying the theorem prover.

Additionally, we want to verify that our approach affords easy extension to generation from proofs in other domains of mathematics. Specifically, we want to focus on Nuprl's growing library of automata theory. This library is used in a joint project with the Ensemble system for verifying code (Hickey, Lynch, & Renesse 1999). The text generated from these proofs could be used as code explanations.

Acknowledgments

We would like to thank Yael Dahan-Netzer and Michael Elhadad for their assistance with FUF/SURGE and Michael Elhadad, Lillian Lee, Kathy McKeown, James Shaw, and the anonymous referees for their comments on this paper. We would also like to thank the participants in our study for their part in generating our corpus. This work was funded by NSF grant DGE-9454149 and DARPA grant F30602-95-1-0047.

References

Allen, S. F.; Constable, R. L.; Howe, D. J.; and Aitken, W. 1990. The semantics of reflected proof. In *Proceedings of the Fifth Symposium on Logic in Computer Science*, 95–197. IEEE.

Cederquist, J.; Coquand, T.; and Negri, S. 1997. The Hahn-Banach theorem in type theory. In Sambin, G., and Smith, J., eds., *Proceedings of Twenty-Five Years of Constructive Type Theory*. Oxford University Press. To appear.

Chester, D. 1976. The translation of formal proofs into English. *Artificial Intelligence* 7:261–278.

Constable, R.; Allen, S.; Bromley, H.; Cleaveland, W.; Cremer, J.; Harper, R.; Howe, D.; Knoblock, T.; Mendler, N.; Panangaden, P.; Sasaki, J.; and Smith, S. 1986. *Implementing Mathematics with the Nuprl Development System*. Prentice-Hall.

Constable, R. L.; Knoblock, T.; and Bates, J. 1984. Writing programs that construct proofs. *J. Automated Reasoning* 1(3):285–326.

Constable, R. L. 1997. The structure of Nuprl's type theory. In Schwichtenberg, H., ed., *Logic of Computation*. Springer. 123–156.

Coscoy, Y.; Kahn, G.; and Théry, L. 1995. Extracting text from proofs. *Lecture Notes in Computer Science* 902:109–123.

Coscoy, Y. 1997. A natural language explanation for formal proofs. In Retoré, C., ed., *Proceedings of the 1st International Conference on Logical Aspects of Computational Linguistics (LACL-96)*, volume 1328 of *LNAI*, 149–167. Berlin: Springer.

deBruijn, N. G. 1994. The mathematical vernacular, a language for mathematics with typed sets. In Nederpelt, R. P.; Geuvers, J. H.; and Vrijer, R. C. D., eds.,

Selected Papers in Automath, volume 133 of *Studies in Logic and the Foundations of Mathematics*. Amsterdam: Elsevier. 865–935.

Elhadad, M. 1993. FUF: the Universal Unifier. User Manual Version 5.2. Technical Report CUCS-038-91, University of Columbia.

Gordon, M., and Melham, T. 1993. *Introduction to HOL: A Theorem Proving Environment for Higher-Oder Logic*. University Press, Cambridge.

Hickey, J.; Lynch, N.; and Renesse, R. V. 1999. Specifications and proofs for ensemble layers. In *Fifth International Conference on Tools and Algorithms for the Construction and Analysis of Systems*. Springer.

Hovy, E. H. 1988. Planning coherent multisentential text. In *Proceedings of the 26th Annual Meeting of the Association for Computational Linguistics*. Buffalo, N.Y.: Association for Computational Linguistics.

Huang, X. 1994a. *Human Oriented Proof Presentation: A Reconstructive Approach*. Ph.D. Dissertation, Fachbereich Informatik, Universität des Saarlandes, Saarbrücken, Germany.

Huang, X. 1994b. PROVERB: A system explaining machine-found proofs. In Ram, A., and Eiselt, K., eds., *Proceedings of 16th Annual Conference of the Cognitive Science Society*, 427–432. Atlanta, USA: Lawrence Erlbaum Associates.

Jackson, P. B. 1995. *Enhancing the Nuprl Proof Development System and Applying it to Computational Abstract Algebra*. Ph.D. Dissertation, Cornell University, Ithaca, NY.

Lester, J. 1994. *Generating Natural Language Explanations from Large-Scale Knowledge Bases*. Ph.D. Dissertation, Department of Computer Science, University of Texas at Austin, Austin, TX.

McAllester, D. A., and Givan, R. 1992. Natural language syntax and first-order inference. *Artificial Intelligence* 56(1):1–20.

McKeown, K. R. 1985. *Text Generation: using Discource Strategies and Focus constraints to Generate Natural Language Text*. Cambridge, England: Cambridge University Press.

O'Leary, J.; Leeser, M.; Hickey, J.; and Aagaard, M. 1994. Non-restoring integer square root: A case study in design by principled optimization. In *International Conference on Theorem Proving & Circuit Design*.

Paulin-Mohring, C., and Werner, B. 1993. Synthesis of ML programs in the system Coq. *Journal of Symbolic Computations* 15:607–640.

Rushby, J. 1997. Systematic formal verification for fault-tolerant time-triggered algorithms. In Meadows, C., and Sanders, W., eds., *Dependable Computing for Critical Applications: 6*. Garmisch-Partenkirchen, Germany: IEEE Computer Society. 191–210.

Solow, D. 1982. *How to Read and Do Proofs: An Introduction to Mathematical Thought Process*. John Wiley & Sons.

On Criteria for Formal Theory Building:
Applying Logic and Automated Reasoning Tools to the Social Sciences

Jaap Kamps
Applied Logic Laboratory
Institute for Logic, Language and Computation
University of Amsterdam
Sarphatistraat 143, 1018 GD Amsterdam, the Netherlands
kamps@ccsom.uva.nl

Abstract

This paper provides practical operationalizations of criteria for evaluating scientific theories, such as the consistency and falsifiability of theories and the soundness of inferences, that take into account definitions. The precise formulation of these criteria is tailored to the use of automated theorem provers and automated model generators—generic tools from the field of automated reasoning. The use of these criteria is illustrated by applying them to a first order logic representation of a classic organization theory, Thompson's Organizations in Action.

Introduction

Philosophy of science's classical conception of scientific theories is based on the axiomatization of theories in (first order) logic. In such an axiomatization, the theory's predictions can be derived as theorems by the inference rules of the logic. In practice, only very few theories from the empirical sciences have been formalized in first order logic. One of the reasons is that the calculations involved in formalizing scientific theories quickly defy manual processing. The availability of automated reasoning tools allows us to transcend these limitations. In the social sciences, this has led to renewed interest in the axiomatization of scientific theories (Péli *et al.* 1994; Péli & Masuch 1997; Péli 1997; Bruggeman 1997; Hannan 1998; Kamps & Pólos 1999). These authors present first order logic versions of heretofore non-formal scientific theories.

The social sciences are renowned for the richness of their vocabulary (one of the most noticeable differences with theories in other sciences). Social science theories are usually stated using many related concepts that have subtle differences in meaning. As a result, a formal rendition of a social science theory will use a large vocabulary. We recently started to experiment with the use of definitions as a means to combine a rich vocabulary with a small number of primitive terms.

> Now definitions are unlike theorems and unlike axioms. Unlike theorems, definitions are not things we prove. We just declare them by fiat. But unlike axioms, we do not expect definitions to add substantive information. A definition is expected to add to our convenience, not to our knowledge. (Enderton 1972, p.154)

If dependencies between different concepts are made explicit, we may be able to define some concepts in terms of other concepts, or in terms of a smaller number of primitive concepts. If the theory contains definitions, the defined concepts can be eliminated from the theory by expanding the definitions. Eliminating the defined concepts does not affect the theory, in the sense that the models and theorems of the theory remain the same.

This paper provides practical operationalizations of criteria for evaluating scientific theories, such as the consistency and falsifiability of theories and the soundness of inferences. In earlier discussion of the criteria for evaluating theories, we did not distinguish between different types of premises (Kamps 1998). In this paper, we will provide practical operationalizations of these criteria that take definitions into account, and illustrate their use on a formal fragment of organization theory.

Logical formalization

Most social science theories are stated in ordinary language (except, of course, for mathematical theories in economics). The main obstacle for the formalization of such a discursive theory is their rational reconstruction: interpreting the text, distinguishing important claims and argumentation from other parts of the text, and reconstructing the argumentation. This reconstruction is seldom a straightforward process, although there are some useful guidelines (Fisher 1988). When the theoretical statements are singled-out, they can be formulated in first order logic. The main benefit of the formalization of theories in logic is that it provides clarity by providing an unambiguous exposition of the theory (Suppes 1968). Moreover, the fields of logic and philosophy of science have provided a number of criteria for evaluating formal theories, such as the consistency and falsifiability of theories and the soundness of inferences. Our aim is to develop support for the axiomatization of theories in first order logic by giving specific operationalizations of these criteria. These specific formulations are chosen such that the criteria can be established in practice with relative ease, i.e., such that existing automated reasoning tools can be used for this purpose.[1]

---

[1] Of course, we hope that this will be regarded as an original contribution, but the claim to originality is a difficult one to establish. The novelty is in the combination of ideas from various fields and our debts to the fields of logic and philosophy of science fan out much further than specific citations indicate.

Criteria for Evaluating Theories

We will use the following notation. Let Σ denote the set of premises of a theory. A formula φ is a theorem of this theory if and only if it is a logical consequence, i.e., if and only if $\Sigma \models \varphi$. The theory itself is the set of all theorems, in symbols, $\{\varphi \mid \Sigma \models \varphi\}$.

Consistency The first and foremost criterion is *consistency*: we can tell whether a theory in logic is contradiction-free. If a theory is inconsistent, it cannot correspond to its intended domain of application. Therefore, empirical testing should focus on identifying those premises that do not hold in its domain. The formal theory can suggest which assumptions are problematic by identifying (minimal) inconsistent subsets of the premises.

The theory is *consistent* if we can find a model $\mathcal{A}$ such that the premises are satisfied: $\mathcal{A} \models \Sigma$. A theory is *inconsistent* if we can derive a contradiction, $\bot$, from the premises: $\Sigma \vdash \bot$.

Soundness Another criterion is *soundness* of arguments: we can tell whether a claim undeniably follows from the given premises. If the derivation of a claim is unsound, empirical testing of the premises does not provide conclusive support for the claim. Conversely, empirically refuting the claim may have no further consequences for the theory. Many of our basic propositions are inaccessible for direct empirical testing. Such propositions can be indirectly tested by their testable implications (Hempel 1966). In case of unsound argumentation, examining the counterexamples provides useful guidance for revision of the theory.

A theorem φ is *sound* if it can be derived from the premises $\Sigma \vdash \varphi$. A theorem φ is *unsound* (i.e., φ is no theorem) if we can construct a counterexample, that is, a model $\mathcal{A}$ in which the premises hold, and the theorem is false: $\mathcal{A} \models \Sigma$ and $\mathcal{A} \not\models \varphi$.

Falsifiability Falsifiability of a theorem means that it is possible to refute the theorem. Self-contained or tautological statements are unfalsifiable—their truth does not depend on the empirical assumptions of the theory. Falsifiability is an essential property of scientific theories (Popper 1959). If no state of affairs can falsify a theory, empirical testing can only reassert its trivial validity. A theory is falsifiable if it contains at least one falsifiable theorem.

An initial operationalization of falsifiability is: a theorem φ is *unfalsifiable* if it can be derived from an empty set of premises: $\vdash \varphi$ and *falsifiable* if we can construct a model $\mathcal{A}$ (of the language) in which the theorem is false: $\mathcal{A} \not\models \varphi$. Note that we cannot require this model to be a model of the theory. A theorem is necessarily true in all models of the theory (otherwise it would not be a theorem). We should therefore ignore the axioms of the theory, and consider arbitrary models of the language. This initial formulation works for some unfalsifiable statements like tautologies, but may fail in the context of definitions. Consider the following simple example: a theory that contains a definition of a Bachelor predicate.

$$\forall x \, [\text{Bachelor}(x) \, \leftrightarrow \, \text{Man}(x) \wedge \text{Unmarried}(x)]$$

In such a theory, we will have a the following theorem.

$$\forall x \, [\text{Bachelor}(x) \, \rightarrow \, \text{Man}(x)]$$

Using falsifiability as formulated above, we would conclude that this statement is falsifiable. It is easy to construct models (of the language) in which the theorem is false, that is, models in which an object a occurs such that $\text{Bachelor}(a)$ is assigned *true* and $\text{Man}(a)$ is *false*. However, if we expand the definition, then the theorem becomes

$$\forall x \, [\text{Man}(x) \wedge \text{Unmarried}(x) \, \rightarrow \, \text{Man}(x)]$$

This expanded theorem is tautologically true and therefore unfalsifiable by the above formulation. This is problematic, since "we do not expect definitions to add substantive information" (Enderton 1972, see the above quotation). Therefore, the elimination of defined concepts should also not affect any of the criteria for evaluating theories. Although we have to ignore the axioms, we must take the definitions into account when establishing falsifiability.

In the context of definitions $\Sigma_{\text{def}} \subseteq \Sigma$, a theorem φ is *falsifiable* if there exists a model $\mathcal{A}$ in which the definitions hold, and the theorem is false: $\mathcal{A} \models \Sigma_{\text{def}}$ and $\mathcal{A} \not\models \varphi$. A theorem φ is *unfalsifiable* if the theorem can be derived from only the set of definitions: $\Sigma_{\text{def}} \vdash \varphi$.

Satisfiability Satisfiability is the counterpart of falsifiability. Satisfiability of a theorem ensures that it can be fulfilled. Self-contradictory statements are unsatisfiable. It makes no sense to subject an unsatisfiable theorem to empirical testing, since it is impossible to find instances that corroborate the theorem.

In the context of definitions $\Sigma_{\text{def}} \subseteq \Sigma$, a theorem φ is *satisfiable* if there exists a model $\mathcal{A}$ in which the definitions hold, and the theorem is true: $\mathcal{A} \models \Sigma_{\text{def}}$ and $\mathcal{A} \models \varphi$. A theorem φ is *unsatisfiable* if we can derive a contradiction from only the set of definitions and the theorem: $\Sigma_{\text{def}} \cup \{\varphi\} \vdash \bot$.

Contingency Theorems that can both be fulfilled and refuted are called *contingent*—their validity strictly depends on the axioms, they are neither tautologically true, nor self-contradictory. The empirical investigation of non-contingent theorems does not make any sense because the outcome is predetermined.

A theorem is *contingent* if it is both satisfiable and falsifiable. A theorem is *non-contingent* if it is unsatisfiable or unfalsifiable (or both).

Further advantages Making the inference structure of a theory explicit will make it possible to assess the theory's *explanatory and predictive power* (by looking at the set of theorems because these are the predictions of the theory, and the proofs give explanations for them); its *domain* or scope (by investigating the models of the theory); its *coherence* (for example, a theory may turn out to have unrelated or independent parts); its *parsimony* (for example, it may turn out that some assumptions are not necessary, or can be relaxed); and other properties.

Computational tools

The above operationalizations require particular proof or model searches for establishing the criteria. The field of automated reasoning has provided us with automated theorem provers and model generators—generic tools that can directly be used for computational testing of the criteria. Automated theorem provers, such as OTTER (McCune 1994b), are programs that are designed to find proofs of theorems. Typical theorem provers use *reductio ad absurdum*, that is, the program attempts to derive a contradiction from the premises and the negation of the theorem. A theorem prover can also be used to prove that a theory is inconsistent if it can derive a contradiction from the set of premises of the theory. Automated model generators, such as MACE (McCune 1994a), are programs that can find (small) models of sets of sentences. A model generator can prove the consistency of a theory, if it can generate a model of the premises. It can also be used to prove underivability of a conjecture, by attempting to generate a model of the premises in which the conjecture is false. Table 1 summarizes how to test for the criteria.[2]

CRITERION	OTTER	MACE
Consistency		$(\exists \mathcal{A})\mathcal{A} \models \Sigma$
Inconsistency	$\Sigma \vdash \bot$	
Soundness	$\Sigma \cup \{\neg\varphi\} \vdash \bot$	
Unsoundness		$(\exists \mathcal{A})\mathcal{A} \models \Sigma \cup \{\neg\varphi\}$
Falsifiability		$(\exists \mathcal{A})\mathcal{A} \models \Sigma_{\mathsf{def}} \cup \{\neg\varphi\}$
Unfalsifiability	$\Sigma_{\mathsf{def}} \cup \{\neg\varphi\} \vdash \bot$	
Satisfiability		$(\exists \mathcal{A})\mathcal{A} \models \Sigma_{\mathsf{def}} \cup \{\varphi\}$
Unsatisfiability	$\Sigma_{\mathsf{def}} \cup \{\varphi\} \vdash \bot$	

Note: Σ denotes a premise set, with Σ_{def} the definitions in this set, and φ a conjecture or theorem.

Table 1: Criteria and Automated Reasoning Tools.

The decision to use either automated theorem provers or model generators is not an arbitrary one. Although (syntactic) proof-theoretic and (semantic) model-theoretical characterizations are logically equivalent, determining the criteria is a different matter. First, there is a fundamental restriction on what we can hope to achieve because first order logic is undecidable. Although undecidable, first-order logic is semi-decidable—we can prove $\Sigma \vdash \bot$ if it is true. We suggest the use of theorem provers only for cases in which a contradiction can be derived. The other cases are, in general, undecidable (causing theorem provers to run on for ever). However, finding finite models is, again, decidable—we can find a finite model $\mathcal{A}$ such that $\mathcal{A} \models \Sigma$ if there exists such a finite model. Current model generators can only find finite models—even only models of small cardinalities. We have no solution for those cases in which only infinite models exist (or only models that are too large for current programs). Second, the tests we suggest to evaluate the criteria do not only prove a criterion, but also present a specific proof or model that is available for further inspection. In simple cases theorem provers may terminate after exhausting their search space without finding a contradiction, proving indirectly that the problem set is consistent, or that a conjecture is not derivable. Even in these cases a direct proof is far more informative, for example, if we can find specific counterexamples to a conjecture, it is immediately clear why our proof attempt has failed.

---

[2] OTTER and MACE are companion programs that can read the same input format. This facilitates switching between theorem proving and model searching, depending on which type of tool is most suitable for the specific proof or disproof attempt at hand. Kamps (1998) discusses the use of these tools for formal theory building in detail.

Case Study: A Formal Theory of Organizations in Action

We will illustrate the criteria outlined above by applying them to the formal theory of Organizations in Action (Kamps & Pólos 1999), a formal rendition of (Thompson 1967). Thompson (1967) is one of the classic contributions to organization theory: it provides a framework that unifies the perspective treating organizations as closed systems, with the perspective that focuses on the dependencies between organizations and their environment. This framework has influenced much of the subsequent research in organization theory. Thompson (1967) is a ordinary language text, in which only the main propositions are clearly outlined. Kamps and Pólos (1999) provide a formal rendition of the first chapters of the book, by reconstructing the argumentation used in the text.

PREDICATES	
Primitive:	
$O(o)$	o is an organization
$SO(o, so)$	so is a suborganization of o
$TC(o, tc)$	tc is the technical core of o
$REVA(o, tc)$	tc is rationally evaluated by o
$UC(o, u)$	o has uncertainty u
$RED(o, i, tc)$	o attempts to reduce i for tc
$FL(tc, f, o)$	tc is exposed to a fluctuation f from o
$CS(tc, c, o)$	tc is exposed to a constraint c from o
$C(i, u)$	i causes u
$HC(o, i)$	o has control over i
Defined:	
$CO(o)$	o is a complex organization
$ENVI(tc, i, o)$	tc is exposed to an influence i from o
$SEFF(o, i, tc)$	o seals off tc from i
$ATO(o)$	o is an atomic organization
$BUF(o, f, tc)$	o buffers f for tc
$ANA(o, c, tc)$	o anticipates and adapts to c for tc
$CEE(o_1, o_2)$	o_2 is in o_1's controlled environment
$SM(o, f, tc)$	o smoothes f for tc
$NEG(o, c, tc)$	o negotiates c for tc

Table 2: Predicates (Kamps & Pólos 1999).

The formal theory uses the predicate symbols reprinted in table 2. Although the text of (Thompson 1967) does not contain explicit definitions, the use of terminology in the text strongly suggests strict dependencies between several important concepts. This allowed for the definition of these concepts in terms of a small number of primitive notions of organization theory. Table 3 lists the premises (both definitions and assumptions) and theorems of the formal theory. In the formal theory, the key propositions of (Thompson 1967) can be derived as theorems (theorem 3, corollaries 8, 9, and 11). The proofs of these theorems are based on a reconstruction of the argumentation in the text (assumptions 1–8). Additionally, the formal theory explains why the theory is restricted to a particular type of organizations (theorem 6). Moreover, it derives a heretofore unknown implication of the theory (corollary 12) that relates Thompson's theory to recent empirical findings and current developments in organization theory. For detailed discussion we refer the reader to (Kamps & Pólos 1999).

The criteria of the previous section played an important

Premises:		
Def.1	$\forall x\ [CO(x) \leftrightarrow O(x) \land \exists y\ [SO(x,y) \land TC(x,y)]]$	
Def.2	$\forall x,y,z\ [ENVI(x,y,z) \leftrightarrow FL(x,y,z) \lor CS(x,y,z)]$	
Def.3	$\forall x,y,z\ [SEFF(x,y,z) \leftrightarrow SO(x,z) \land \exists v,w\ [ENVI(z,y,v) \land UC(z,w) \land C(y,w) \land RED(x,w,z)]]$	
Def.4	$\forall x\ [ATO(x) \leftrightarrow O(x) \land \neg CO(x)]$	
Def.5	$\forall x,y,z\ [BUF(x,y,z) \leftrightarrow SO(x,z) \land FL(z,y,x) \land RED(x,y,z)]$	
Def.6	$\forall x,y,z\ [ANA(x,y,z) \leftrightarrow SO(x,z) \land CS(z,y,x) \land RED(x,y,z)]$	
Def.7	$\forall x,y\ [CEE(x,y) \leftrightarrow O(x) \land \forall z\ [ENVI(x,z,y) \rightarrow HC(x,z)]]$	
Def.8	$\forall x,y,z\ [SM(x,y,z) \leftrightarrow SO(x,z) \land \exists v\ [FL(x,y,v) \land RED(x,y,z)]]$	
Def.9	$\forall x,y,z\ [NEG(x,y,z) \leftrightarrow SO(x,z) \land \exists v\ [CS(x,y,v) \land RED(x,y,z)]]$	
Ass.1	$\forall x,y,z\ [TC(x,y) \land TC(x,z) \rightarrow y = z]$	
Ass.2	$\forall x,y\ [TC(x,y) \rightarrow REVA(x,y)]$	
Ass.3	$\forall x,y,z\ [SO(x,y) \land REVA(x,y) \land UC(y,z) \rightarrow RED(x,z,y)]$	
Ass.4	$\forall x,y,z\ [ENVI(x,y,z) \rightarrow \exists v\ [UC(x,v) \land C(y,v)]]$	
Ass.5	$\forall x,y\ [O(x) \land TC(x,y) \land \neg SO(x,y) \rightarrow x = y]$	
Ass.6	$\forall x,y,z,v,w\ [ENVI(x,y,z) \land UC(x,v) \land C(y,v) \land UC(x,w) \land C(y,w) \rightarrow v = w]$	
Ass.7	$\forall x,y,z,v\ [O(x) \land SO(x,y) \land ENVI(y,z,v) \rightarrow HC(x,z)]$	
Ass.8	$\forall x,y,z,v\ [RED(x,y,z) \land C(v,y) \land HC(x,v) \rightarrow RED(x,v,z)]$	
Theorems:		
Lem.1	$\forall x,y\ [CO(x) \land TC(x,y) \rightarrow SO(x,y)]$	
Lem.2	$\forall x,y,z\ [CO(x) \land TC(x,y) \land UC(y,z) \rightarrow RED(x,z,y)]$	
Thm.3	$\forall x,y,z,v\ [CO(x) \land TC(x,y) \land ENVI(y,z,v) \rightarrow SEFF(x,z,y)]$	
Lem.4	$\forall x\ [ATO(x) \leftrightarrow O(x) \land \neg \exists y\ [SO(x,y) \land TC(x,y)]]$	
Lem.5	$\forall x,y\ [ATO(x) \land TC(x,y) \rightarrow x = y]$	
Thm.6	$\forall x,y,z,v,w\ [ATO(x) \land TC(x,y) \land ENVI(y,v,z) \land UC(y,w) \land C(v,w) \rightarrow \exists u\ [UC(x,u) \land C(v,u) \land w = u]]$	
Thm.7	$\forall x,y,z,v\ [CO(x) \land TC(x,y) \land ENVI(y,z,v) \rightarrow RED(x,z,y)]$	
Cor.8	$\forall x,y,z\ [CO(x) \land TC(x,y) \land FL(y,z,x) \rightarrow BUF(x,z,y)]$	
Cor.9	$\forall x,y,z\ [CO(x) \land TC(x,y) \land CS(y,z,x) \rightarrow ANA(x,z,y)]$	
Thm.10	$\forall x,y,z,v,w\ [CO(x) \land TC(x,y) \land ENVI(y,z,x) \land CEE(x,v) \land ENVI(x,w,v) \land C(w,z) \rightarrow RED(x,w,y)]$	
Cor.11	$\forall x,y,z,v,w\ [CO(x) \land TC(x,y) \land FL(y,z,x) \land CEE(x,v) \land FL(x,w,v) \land C(w,z) \rightarrow SM(x,w,y)]$	
Cor.12	$\forall x,y,z,v,w\ [CO(x) \land TC(x,y) \land CS(y,z,x) \land CEE(x,v) \land CS(x,w,v) \land C(w,z) \rightarrow NEG(x,w,y)]$	

Table 3: A Formal Theory of Organizations in Action (Kamps & Pólos 1999).

	Lem.1	Lem.2	Thm.3	Lem.4	Lem.5	Thm.6	Thm.7	Cor.8	Cor.9	Thm.10	Cor.11	Cor.12
Consistent						yes						
Sound	yes	yes	yes	yes	yes	yes	yes	yes	yes	yes	yes	yes
Falsifiable	yes	yes	yes	no	yes	yes	yes	yes	yes	yes	yes	yes
Satisfiable	yes	yes	yes	yes	yes	yes	yes	yes	yes	yes	yes	yes
Contingent	yes	yes	yes	no	yes	yes	yes	yes	yes	yes	yes	yes

Table 4: Evaluating the Theory.

role during the construction of the formal theory. Table 4 give an assessment of the final version of the theory in terms of the criteria.

Consistency Using an automated model generator it is easy to find models of the theory. MACE produced a model of cardinality 4 within a second (a model having universe $\{0, 1, 2, 3\}$, reprinted in tables 5 and 6). This is a prototypical model of the theory corresponding to the claims of theorem 3, theorem 7, and corollary 8. It represents an organization that seals its core technologies off from environmental fluctuations, by the use of buffering (for example the stockpiling of materials and supplies). It is easy to verify that all premises (and theorems) hold in the model—the model proves that the theory is consistent.

Finding any arbitrary model of the theory is, formally speaking, sufficient to prove its consistency. We can find models on smaller cardinalities. For example, on cardinality 1 there exists a trivial model that assigns *false* to all predicates. In practice, we try to find more natural models of the theory. That is, we can examine the models and see if

they conform to our mental models of the theory. This is an easy safeguard against hidden inconsistencies—theories that are only consistent because background knowledge has remained implicit.[3] We can look for prototypical models of the theory directly by adding premises that express appropriate initial conditions (typically existential statements). If we find a model of this enlarged set of premises, it is obviously

---

[3] Consider the following simple example:

$$\forall x\ [Dog(x) \rightarrow Bark(x)]$$
$$Rottweiler(Johnny)$$
$$\neg Bark(Johnny)$$

Can we find a model of this theory? Yes, although inspection of the models will reveal that in every model of the theory, Johnny the rottweiler is not a dog. These models are nonintended models because of the (implicit) background knowledge that rottweilers are a particular breed of dogs.

$$\forall x\ [Rottweiler(x) \rightarrow Dog(x)]$$

Adding this assumption to the theory will make it inconsistent, that is, we can then derive a contradiction from it.

O	
0	T
1	F
2	F
3	F

SO	0	1	2	3
0	F	T	F	F
1	F	F	F	F
2	F	F	F	F
3	F	F	F	F

TC	0	1	2	3
0	F	T	F	F
1	F	F	F	F
2	F	F	F	F
3	F	F	F	F

REVA	0	1	2	3
0	F	T	F	F
1	F	F	F	F
2	F	F	F	F
3	F	F	F	F

UC	0	1	2	3
0	F	F	F	F
1	F	F	F	T
2	F	F	F	F
3	F	F	F	F

$RED(0,3,1) = T$ and
$RED(0,2,1) = T$ and
$RED(x,y,z) = F$ otherwise.

$FL(1,2,0) = T$ and
$FL(x,y,z) = F$ otherwise.

$CS(x,y,z) = F$ for all x,y,z in $\{0,1,2,3\}$.

C	0	1	2	3
0	F	F	F	F
1	F	F	F	F
2	F	F	F	T
3	F	F	F	F

HC	0	1	2	3
0	F	F	T	F
1	F	F	F	F
2	F	F	F	F
3	F	F	F	F

Table 5: A Model of the Theory (only primitives).

CO	
0	T
1	F
2	F
3	F

$ENVI(1,2,0) = T$ and
$ENVI(x,y,z) = F$ otherwise.

$SEFF(0,2,1) = T$ and
$SEFF(x,y,z) = F$ otherwise.

$BUFF(0,2,1) = T$ and
$BUFF(x,y,z) = F$ otherwise.

Table 6: Selected Defined Predicates (extending Tab.5).

also a model of the theory.

Soundness In the final formal theory (as reprinted in table 3), all theorems are derivable. Figure 1 shows the inference structure of the formal theory. None of the proofs is very complex (the automated theorem prover OTTER required only 12 seconds for the longest proof).

The original text of the theory presupposes common background knowledge—assumptions taken for granted in the substantive field. In order for the theorems to be deductively derivable, several implicit assumptions had to be added to the theory (notably assumptions 1, 6 and 7). Which precise background assumptions to add is one of the thorniest problems in the formalization of a theory, requiring a deep understanding of the substantive field under consideration. Fortunately, the formal tools can help: suppose we cannot derive a theorem due to a missing background assumption. We can prove that the theorem is underivable by generating counterexamples, that is, models of the premises in which the theorem is false. If the unsoundness of the theorem is due to missing background knowledge, inspection of the counterexamples will reveal that they are nonintended models—models that violate our common sense, or implicit back-

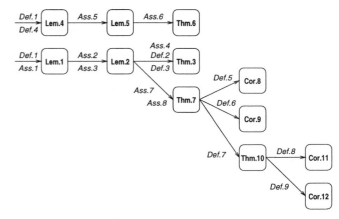

Figure 1: Inferences in the Formal Theory

ground assumptions from the substantive domain. For example, we found models of organizations having more than one operational core (conflicting with assumption 1, which is implicit in the original text). We can make the theorem derivable if we add sufficient assumptions to exclude these nonintended models from the theory.

Falsifiability We tried to prove the falsifiability of the theorems as discussed above: by finding a model in which the definitions hold and the theorem is false. We failed to find such a model for lemma 4. As it turns out, lemma 4 can be derived from just definitions 1 and 4—proving that this lemma is unfalsifiable. Lemma 4 is true by definition, and therefore does not make an empirical claim. If we would subject lemma 4 to empirical testing, we will be unable to refute it, but can at best reassert the trivial validity of the statement.

Fortunately, the other theorems of the formal theory are falsifiable. For each of these theorems, we can find models of the definitions in which the theorem is false (not reproduced here). MACE generated these models in a matter of seconds.

Satisfiability/Contingency For proving the satisfiability of the theorems, we need to find models that make both the definitions and the theorem true. The model of tables 5 and 6 also proves the satisfiability of all theorems. As a result, we can conclude that only lemma 4 is non-contingent—it is not an empirical statement, but its truth is determined by virtue of the definitions only. The other theorems make empirical claims that can, in principle, be corroborated or refuted by empirical testing.

Conclusions and Discussion

This paper discussed the axiomatization of scientific theories in first order logic. We provided practical operationalizations of criteria for evaluating scientific theories, such as the consistency and falsifiability of theories and the soundness of inferences. The precise formulation of these criteria is tailored to the use of computational support. The tests for the criteria, in practice amounting to particular proof or model searches, can be directly performed by existing automated reasoning tools.

The efficient treatment of definitions is one of the basic research problems in automated reasoning (Wos 1988, Problem 30). A naive approach is to eliminate all defined predicates and functions from the problem set by expanding the definitions. This, however, also eliminates useful ways chunking information and as a result it "increases the likelihood that a program will get lost" (Wos 1988, p.62).[4] Since only few problems are provable without expanding (some of) the definitions, dealing with definitions is a difficult challenge for automated reasoning tools. As a result, most automated theorem provers treat definitions and axioms alike (a notable exception is (Giunchiglia & Walsh 1989)). Interestingly, the above argument does not seem to apply to automated model generators.[5] The search space of automated model generators is the set of all possible models, i.e., all possible interpretation functions of the logical vocabulary. Reducing the vocabulary of the formal language by eliminating the defined concepts will proportionally reduce this search space. Moreover, after eliminating the defined concepts, the definitions themselves can be removed from the problem set, which reduces the number of "constraints" that need to be taken into account when deciding whether a particular interpretation is a model of the problem set.

We used the criteria to evaluate a formal rendition of a classic organization theory (Kamps & Pólos 1999). Assessing the criteria allows for an exact evaluation of the merits of a theory. In some cases, this may reveal important facts about the theory, for example, the case study showed that one of the derived statements is unfalsifiable—empirical investigation of it is futile. However, we do not view the criteria as rigid, final tests. Quite the opposite, in our experience the criteria are especially useful during the process of formalizing a theory. During the construction of a formal theory, the criteria can provide useful feedback on how to revise the theory in case of a deficiency. For example, examining counterexamples can reveal which implicit (background) assumptions need to be added to the theory. There are, of course, important principled and practical limitations to the axiomatization of theories in first order logic: the undecidability of first order logic, the scientific knowledge available in the substantive domains, or the availability of resources like processor power, memory, and time. There is yet no equivocal answer to the question whether it is possible, or even desirable, to axiomatize large parts of substantive domains. Axiomatization is often viewed as the ultimate step in the lifetime of a scientific theory—the axioms are frozen in their final form, and active research moves on to areas where still progress can be made. The main motivation for the research reported in this paper is that the formalization of theories can play a broader role: it need not end the life of a theory, but rather contribute to its further development.

Acknowledgments Thanks to Michael Masuch, László Pólos, Ivar Vermeulen, and the *AAAI* reviewers for discussion and insightful comments, and to Mary Beth Jenssen without whom this paper would not have been possible.

References

Bruggeman, J. 1997. Niche width theory reappraised. *Journal of Mathematical Sociology* 22(2):201–220.

Enderton, H. B. 1972. *A Mathematical Introduction to Logic*. Academic Press, New York.

Fisher, A. 1988. *The logic of real arguments*. Cambridge University Press, Cambridge UK.

Giunchiglia, F., and Walsh, T. 1989. Theorem proving with definitions. In Cohn, A., and Dennison, J., eds., *AISB-89: Proceedings of the seventh conference of Artificial Intelligence and the Simulation of Behaviour*, 175–183. Pitman, London.

Hannan, M. T. 1998. Rethinking age dependence in organizational mortality: Logical formalizations. *American Journal of Sociology* 104:126–164.

Hempel, C. G. 1966. *Philosophy of Natural Science*. Foundations of Philosophy Series. Prentice-Hall, Englewood Cliffs NJ.

Kamps, J., and Pólos, L. 1999. Reducing uncertainty: A formal theory of *Organizations in Action*. *American Journal of Sociology* 104(6):1774–1810.

Kamps, J. 1998. Formal theory building using automated reasoning tools. In Cohn, A. G.; Schubert, L. K.; and Shapiro, S. C., eds., *Principles of Knowledge Representation and Reasoning: Proceedings of the Sixth International Conference (KR'98)*, 478–487. Morgan Kaufmann Publishers, San Francisco CA.

McCune, W. 1994a. A Davis-Putnam program and its application to finite first-order model search: Quasigroup existence problems. Technical report, Argonne National Laboratory, Argonne IL. DRAFT.

McCune, W. 1994b. OTTER: Reference manual and guide. Technical Report ANL-94/6, Argonne National Laboratory, Argonne IL.

Péli, G., and Masuch, M. 1997. The logic of propagation strategies: Axiomatizing a fragment of organizational ecology in first-order logic. *Organization Science* 8:310–331.

Péli, G.; Bruggeman, J.; Masuch, M.; and Ó Nualláin, B. 1994. A logical approach to formalizing organizational ecology. *American Sociological Review* 59:571–593.

Péli, G. 1997. The niche hiker's guide to population ecology: A logical reconstruction of organizational ecology's niche theory. In Raftery, A. E., ed., *Sociological Methodology 1997*, 1–46. Blackwell, Oxford UK.

Popper, K. R. 1959. *The Logic of Scientific Discovery*. Hutchinson, London.

Suppes, P. 1968. The desirability of formalization in science. *Journal of Philosophy* LXV(20):651–664.

Thompson, J. D. 1967. *Organizations in Action: Social Science Bases of Administrative Theory*. McGraw-Hill, New York.

Wos, L. 1988. *Automated Reasoning, 33 Basic Research Problems*. Prentice Hall, Englewood Cliffs, New Jersey.

---

[4]This is substantiated by the theory in our case study: after eliminating all defined predicates, OTTER proved several theorems slightly faster, but some others slower. These are preliminary observations without taking into account the time needed expand the definitions (a preprocessing step that is done once for any number of queries). This expansion was done manually but is of no great complexity: since definitions are not allowed to be circular, we only need to expand each definition once.

[5]For the theory in our case study, eliminating defined concepts gave significantly better performance on all model searches (roughly halving MACE's processor and memory usage). Again, these are preliminary observations that do not consider the preprocessing of definitions.

A Policy Description Language

Jorge Lobo   Randeep Bhatia   Shamim Naqvi

Network Computing Research Department
Bell Labs
600 Mountain Av, Murray Hill, NJ 07974
{jlobo,randeep,shamim}@research.bell-labs.com

Abstract

A policy describes principles or strategies for a plan of action designed to achieve a particular set of goals. We define a policy as a function that maps a series of events into a set of actions. In this paper we introduce $\mathcal{PDL}$, a simple but expressive language to specify policies. The design of the language has been strongly influenced by the action languages of Geffner and Bonet (Geffner & Bonet 1998) and Gelfond and Lifschitz (Gelfond & Lifschitz 1993) and the composite temporal event language of Motakis and Zaniolo (Motakis & Zaniolo 1997). The semantics is founded on recent results on formal descriptions of action theories based on automata and their application to active databases. We summarize some complexity results on the hardness of evaluating polices and briefly describe the implementation of a policy server being used to provide centralized administration of a soft switch in a communication network.

Introduction

In AI, a policy is usually defined as a complete mapping from states (of the world) to actions (Russell & Norvig 1995). In system management, a policy describes principles or strategies for a plan of action designed to achieve a particular set of goals identified by the managers of the system. This high level description of management applies to very general situations such as establishing policies to increase inter-departmental interactions in a company to more technical situations such as defining traffic policies to reduce overload in a computer network. Policies can be specified at different levels of abstraction. At a very elementary level we find policies specified using production rules as in the standard AI definition. At a very high level we can find policies specified using natural language. In this document we are interested in some intermediate point for which we still have an effective computational model.

We define a policy as a function that maps a series of events into a set of actions. In contrast to the standard AI definition of policies, we assume that there is an intermediate service (with sensors) between the policy server and the environment that continuously polls the environment and communicates to the policy server only the changes in the environment (events) that may require the enforcement of a policy. This concept is not new, and it has been informally used in network management. Network management requires the definition of policies to specify configuration parameters, to handle faults, to ensure certain level of performance, to handle security and accounting. As the examples in the paper will show, this model highly simplifies the description of policies.

Below we describe $\mathcal{PDL}$, a simple but expressive language to specify policies. The design of the language has been strongly influenced by the *state language* of actions of Geffner and Bonet (Geffner & Bonet 1998), the action description language $\mathcal{A}$ of Gelfond and Lifschitz (Gelfond & Lifschitz 1993) and the composite temporal event language of Motakis and Zaniolo (Motakis & Zaniolo 1997). It uses the *event-condition-action* rule paradigm of active databases (Widom & Ceri 1995), a successor of the production rule paradigm of languages such as OPS5 (Brownston *et al.* 1985). In fact, *our language can be described as a real-time specialized production rule system to define policies.*

An *event-condition-action* rule is triggered when the event occurs, and if the condition is true the action is executed. In general, besides the informal definition of an active rule, there is no consensus about the definition of events, how to process rules when several of them are triggered simultaneously, and how to characterize the set of possible actions. There is a tendency to consider events modifications or access to the database, conditions to be queries to the database, and actions either modifications to the database or remote procedure calls. The operational semantics is informally described with wide variations from system to system and it is tightly coupled to the concept of transaction, making the database semantics the central point for the interpretation of rules. In contrast, we have developed a domain-independent semantics of our rules by making the events, conditions and actions parameters of the language. We have also concentrated in a precise description of the execution since we are interested in predicting the efficiency of the implementation of policies.

We envision a system manager defining a policy in two steps. First, the manager will consult a policy server to obtain: 1) the set of events that the system is able to monitor (e.g. a router went down), 2) the set of actions that can be invoked by a policy (e.g. send e-mail to a user) and 3) the set of functions that system supports to evaluate the status of the environment (e.g. disk is 90% full). Then the manager will write policies (i.e. write a set of rules) by combining events, actions and functions from these sets. The policy server will take this policy and implement it in the system.

The most salient feature of the language is its declarative semantics. In our approach, a policy description defines a transition function that maps a series of events into a set of actions to be executed by the policy enforcer. This function is implementation-independent. The semantics is founded on recent results on formal descriptions of action theories based on automata (Baral, Gelfond, & Provetti 1997; Gelfond & Lifschitz 1993) and their application to active databases (Baral, Lobo, & Trajcevski 1997). In the next section we describe the syntax of the language. Next, we present a series of examples to informally describe the semantics of the language. Then we present the formal semantics in terms of transition functions and briefly describe how the semantics can be casted in terms of logic programs. The next section describes complexity issues associated with the implementation of a policy server. We currently have an implementation of a server that supports a sub-set of the language. The server is being used to monitor software switches for telephone communication. Most of the examples in the paper have been inspired by the application. Some concluding remarks are found in the last section.

The syntax

$\mathcal{PDL}$ consists of three basic classes of symbols: *primitive event* symbols, *action* symbols and *function* symbols. The primitive event symbols are partitioned into two sets, the set of *system defined* primitive event symbols and the set of *policy defined* primitive event symbols. Action and function symbols and system defined symbols are pre-defined and are given to the user that defines the policies. Policy defined primitive event symbols will be defined by the user. There is also a set of standard domains and types such as integers, floats, string of characters, etc. and possibly complex types such as stacks, queues, etc. depending on the domain of application.

Action and function symbols are of different arities. There might be symbols of arity 0. Each action symbol of arity n denotes the name of a procedure that takes n arguments (also called parameters) each of a particular type. A function symbol of arity n denotes a function that takes n arguments of a particular type and returns the value of another type. If $n = 0$, the function symbol represents a constant from one of the given domains. The type of a function is the type of the value returned by the function.

Policies are described by a collection of propositions of of two types, policy rule propositions and policy defined event propositions. *Policy rule* propositions are expressions of the form:

event **causes** *action* **if** *condition*

The intuitive reading of this proposition is: if the *event* occurs in a situation where the *condition* is true then the *action* will be executed.

As an example, suppose we have a pool of modems to provide two customers access to Internet services. We have assigned the number 5559991 to Customer1 and the number 5559992 to Customer2. We have 20 modems in our pool. There can be simultaneous connections from the same customer to the pool. All modems in the pool are shared by both customers but the server can be configured to limit the connections per number. We would like to allow a maximum of 15 connections to Customer1 during the day and 5 to Customer2. During the night we will allow a maximum of 10 to each customer.

The event to monitor is time. We will have a symbol associated with this event, say $CoarseTimeEvent$. This symbol represents a class of events for which instances occur four times a day, at 6:00am, 12:00pm, 6:00pm and 00:00am. In the *condition* part of the propositions describing the policy we will need to check when an instance of the *event* occurs to take the appropriate action. Thus, we will extend the $CoarseTimeEvent$ with an attribute named $Time$. In general, events will have a set of attribute names associated with them, each one having an associated type. For our example, the type of $Time$ will be the enumerated type {"morning", "noon", "evening", "midnight"}. We will use the standard dot "." notation to refer to the attributes of an event. An *instance* of an event is given by a complete denotation of its attributes. We will use one action in the example, $ModemPoolAssigment$. The signature of this action is Telephone_Numbers$\times\{1, 2, \ldots, 20\}$. When this action is executed the configuration of the pool is changed to limit the maximum number of connections of the telephone number given in the first argument to be the number given in the second argument.

The following two propositions cover the actions required in the morning:

1) $CoarseTimeEvent$
   causes $ModemPoolAssigment(5559991, 15)$
   if $(CoarseTimeEvent.Time = "morning")$.
2) $CoarseTimeEvent$
   causes $ModemPoolAssigment(5559992, 5)$
   if $(CoarseTimeEvent.Time = "morning")$.

Similarly, there will be two more rules in the policy that will set the number of modems to 10 for both customers in the evening. The four propositions together define the policy.

Before we introduce policy defined event propositions we need to take a closer look at the notion of event. Policies may depend on several events or the lack of certain events happening, or even on events happening in the past. We can have the following situations:

1. A policy must be enforced if two events e_1 and e_2 occur simultaneously.

2. A policy must be enforced if an event e does not occur.

3. A policy must be enforced if an event e_2 immediately follows an event e_1.

4. A policy must be enforced if an event e_2 occurs after an event e_1 occurs.

Thus, policy decisions are made after a pre-determined stream of primitive event instances is observed by the policy service running the policy. We will call the streams of event instances *event histories*. There may be several instances of one or more primitive events occurring at the same time. Each set of primitive event instances occurring simultaneously in a stream is called an *epoch*. An *event literal* is an event symbol e or an event symbol preceded by !. The event literal !e occurs in an epoch if there are no instances of the event e in the epoch.

Definition 1 *A basic event is an expression of the form*

1. $e_1 \& \ldots \& e_n$ *representing the occurrence of instances of e_1 through e_n in the current epoch (i.e. the simultaneous occurrence of the n events) where each e_i is an event literal, or*

2. $e_1 | \ldots | e_n$ *representing the occurrence of an instance of one of the e_is in the current epoch. Each e_i is an event literal.*

Basic events only refer to instances of events that occur in a single epoch, but we could have composite events that refer to several epochs simultaneously. For example, the sequence $loginFail, loginFail, loginFail$ may represent the event: "three consecutive attempts to login that result in failure." In general $e_1, \ldots, e_{n-1}, e_n$ may represent the moment when an instance of the basic event e_n occurred in the current epoch, immediately preceded by an instance of the basic event e_{n-1} (i.e. an instance of e_{n-1} occurred in the previous epoch), ..., with an instance of the basic event e_1 occurring $n-1$ epochs ago.

We can describe many classes of sequences if we borrow the notion of a sequence of zero or more events from regular expressions. We will denote zero or more occurrences of an event E by "$\hat{} E$". Formally,

Definition 2 *An event is either* **(a)** *a basic event,* **(b)** *$group(E)$ where E is a basic event, or* **(c)** *an expression that can be formed by a finite number of applications of the following rules:*

1. *If E_1 through E_n are events then $E_1, \ldots, E_n$ is a (complex) event representing the sequence: event E_1, immediately followed by E_2, ..., immediately followed by E_n.*

2. *If E is an event then $\hat{} E$ is a (complex) event representing the sequence of zero or more occurrences of the event E.*

3. *If E is an event then (E) is a (complex) event.*

To motivate the meaning of *group* note that if we have a history where there are n instances of event e_2 in the current epoch and m instances of event e_1 in the previous epoch, there will be a total of $n \times m$ instances of the event (e_1, e_2) in the history. There are situations in which we are not interested in single instances of a basic event but on a global property of all the instances in a epoch. For example, we can describe "a network failure (nf) followed by at least one disc crash (dc)" with $(nf, group(dc))$. In this case if we have m occurrences of nf and n of dc there will be only m occurrences of the complex event. If we have $(group(nf), group(dc))$ then there will be only one occurrence of the event. We will see examples of the "$\hat{}$" and *group* operators in the next section.

The last class of events we will consider are *policy defined* primitive events. So far, an event is defined as a combination of primitive events that have occurred in an event history. Policy defined primitive events allow us to mark incoming epochs with new event instances that we can later use as a component of a complex event. They provide a policy with a limited amount of memory. To define an event we will use policy defined event propositions, but we need to define terms first. Recall that it was assumed that there is set of types known by the user.

Definition 3 *A term is either*

1. *A constant from one of the known types, or*

2. *An expression of the form $f(t_1, \ldots, t_n)$, where f is a function symbol of arity n and each t_i is a term of the appropriate type, or*

3. *An expression of the form $e[k].m$, where e is a primitive event, k is positive integer, m is an attribute associated with e.*

The index in the event term is to distinguish different occurrences of the same primitive event symbol in a complex event expression. The index is assigned left to right in increasing order. If there is no ambiguity in the reference the index can be omitted. The denotation of a term of the form $f(t_1, \ldots, t_n)$ is the result of calling a function (or script) that will be associated with the function symbol f with the values that the internal terms denote as parameters. We will use infix notation for function symbols with well-understood meanings such as $+$, $*$, etc. We will also assume a cast system translation from types such as the one in C or Java.

A *policy defined event* proposition is an expression of the form:

$$event \quad \textbf{triggers} \quad pde(m_1 = t_1, \ldots, m_k = t_k)$$
$$\textbf{if} \quad condition$$

pde is a policy defined primitive event symbol. m_1 through m_k are the attributes associated with the defined event symbol *pde* and each t_i is a term of the appropriate type. The intuitive reading of this expression is: If the *event* occurs in a situation where the *condition* is true, an instance of the primitive event *pde* will occur in the immediately following epoch with the valuation of each t_i as the value assigned to each attribute m_i of *pde*.

Complex events in policy propositions can include policy defined or a system defined primitive events.

With the definition of terms we can also give a precise characterization of actions and conditions.

Definition 4 *An* action *is an expression of the form* $a(t_1, \ldots, t_n)$, *where a is action symbol of n arguments and each t_i is a term of the appropriate type.*

A condition *is a expression of the from* $p_1, \ldots, p_n$, *where each p_i is a predicate of the form $t_1 \theta t_2$, θ is a relation operator from the set $\{=, \neq, <, \leq, >, \geq\}$ and t_1 and t_2 are terms of the same type.*

Examples

Soft switch overload control: Suppose we characterize overload as an excessive number of signaling network time-outs over calls made, let say at a ratio of t. If an overload occurs some call requests must be rejected until the time-out rate goes down to a reasonable number, say t'. We can define this policy as follows.

Events:

    normal_mode : policy defined event.
    restricted_mode : policy defined event.
    call_made
    time_out

The events do not have attributes.

Actions: *restrict_calls, accept_all_calls*

Policy description:

1)   *normal_mode,* ^*(call_made|time_out)*
      triggers *restricted_mode*
      if $Count(time\_out) > t * Count(call\_made)$.
2)   *restricted_mode* **causes** *restrict_calls*.
3)   *restricted_mode,* ^*(call_made|time_out)*
      triggers *normal_mode*
      if $Count(time\_out) < t' * Count(call\_made)$.
4)   *normal_mode* **causes** *accept_all_calls*.

We assume that when the system starts the primitive event *normal_mode* is triggered. This can be accomplished by adding the event proposition "*power_on* **triggers** *normal_mode*" to the policy description. The complex event triggering the first policy defined event proposition occurs in an event history in which there is an epoch with an instance of the *normal_mode* event, followed by a sequence of epochs where there is an instance of either the event *call_made* or *time_out* in each epoch in the sequence. The *restricted_mode* event will be triggered the <u>first</u> time that the condition in the event definition is true.

Note that as far as this policy is concerned there are only four types of events.

There is a special function symbol in the conditions of the policy description: "*Count*". This function symbol is a *temporal aggregate* that evaluates over the sequence of primitive event occurrences that form the complex event. In the example, the aggregate is used to count the number of occurrences of the events *time_out* and *call_made* in the sequence. In general, a temporal aggregate has the structure of a function call with a primitive event symbol or an attribute of a primitive event symbol as its argument. Typical temporal aggregates are *Sum, Avg, Min, Max*, etc. The condition in the first policy defined event proposition is true as soon as in the instance of the complex event the number of *time_out* events is larger than the number of *call_made* events times t.

The example above assumes that there can only be one *call_made* event or *time_out* event in each epoch. If several calls or time outs happen simultaneously there will be several instances of the complex event in the history. For example, in the history with the sequence of epochs

    {normal_mode},   *{call_made}*,
    {time_out, call_made, call_made},
    {call_made, call_made}

there are six instances of the complex event *normal_mode,* ^*(call_made|time_out)* occurring at the last epoch of the history.[1] The intention of the policy is to group these instances into a single instance and count the timeouts and the calls made in the whole group. This is captured if the policy is defined in terms of the *group* operator as followed:

   normal_mode, group(^*(call_made|time_out))*
      triggers *restricted_mode*
      if $Count(time\_out)/Count(call\_made) > t$.
   restricted_mode **causes** *restrict_calls*.
   restricted_mode, group(^*(call_made|time_out))*
      triggers *normal_mode*
      if $Count(time\_out)/count(call\_made) < t'$.
   normal_mode **causes** *accept_all_calls*.

We use the notation $group(E)$, for a complex event E, as the shorthand of the event that results after replacing any basic event e in E with $group(e)$.

Routing: Suppose that in a communication network if the average gapping of a trunk group is larger than a given threshold (say g) in the last five hours re-route calls to a different trunk. Gapping is the interval necessary between requests sent to a telephone switch service control point (SCP) in order to process the requests on time.

Events:

    *window*5 : policy defined event { *Start* : Date }

---

[1]There are three instances of the event *(call_made|time_out)* in the epoch *{time_out, call_made, call_made}*, and two in *{call_made, call_made}*.

hour :{ *Time* : Date }

Instances of *hour* will occur every hour on the hour. The attribute *Time* is set with the time when the event occurred. We are assuming the existence of a standard type "Date". Instances of the *window*5 event will be triggered by the policy every hour (after the first four hours since the policy was enabled in the system). This event will mark the end of a 5 hour sliding window. *Start* is set to the time when the window begins.

Actions: *reroute* : Trunk Name.

When this action is executed the configuration of the server is changed to limit the calls that go through the trunk that is passed as argument of the action.

Policy description:

> *hour,* ˜*hour, hour*
> **triggers** *window*5(*Start = hour*[1].*Time*)
> **if** *hour*[3].*Time − hour*[1].*Time* = 5.
> *hour,* ˜(*call_gapping_t*1), *window*5
> **causes** *reroute*(*trunk*1)
> **if** *ave*(*call_gapping_t*1.*gap*) > *g*,
> *window*5.*Start = hour.Time*.

The expression ˜*e* denotes a sequence of zero or more events ending in the basic event *e*. This is a shorthand for the complex event ^(^!*e, e*).[2] The event *hour* occurs on the hour. The complex event *hour,* ˜*hour* occurs in a history any time an instance of the *hour* event has occurred in previous epoch and another instance of *hour* has occurred in the current epoch. The *window*5 event is triggered the first time the second *hour* event instance occurs five hours apart from the first *hour* event. *call_gapping* occurs when this message is sent from an off the SCP to a soft switch.

The semantics

Policies are interpreted over *event histories*. An event history is a sequence of zero or more epochs. An *epoch* is a set of primitive event instances. The instance of a primitive event is a denotation for all attributes of the primitive event. There may be zero, one or more instances of a primitive event in a given epoch. Every epoch, in addition to the denotation of the attributes of each primitive event occurring in the epoch, will also have a denotation for all function symbols in the language. We will denote an epoch by a pair (S, D), with S the set of instances and D the denotation of function symbols. We denote the empty history by ϵ and assume there are no primitive event instances in ϵ.

An event history $\mathcal{H} = I_1 \ldots, I_n, 0 \le n$, is a *minimal history* of an event E iff one of the following conditions holds:

1. E is a primitive event, $n = 1$ (i.e. the history is just an epoch) and there is an instance i of E in $I_1 = (S, D)$. $((\{i\}, D), E)$ is called a *trace* of E in $\mathcal{H}$.

2. $E = !e$, $n = 1$ and there are no instances of e in $\mathcal{H}$. $(\mathcal{H}, E)$ is the (only) *trace* of E in $\mathcal{H}$.

3. $E = e_1 \& \ldots \& e_m$, $n = 1$ (i.e. the history is just an epoch), each e_j is an event literal, and there is a trace $((S_j, D), e_j)$ of e_j in $I_1 = (S, D)$ for every j, $1 \le j \le m$. $((\bigcup_{l=1}^{m} S_l, D), E)$ is a *trace* of E in $\mathcal{H}$.

4. $E = e_1 | \ldots | e_m$, $n = 1$ (i.e. the history is just an epoch), each e_j is an event literal, and there is an instance of e_j in I_1 for some j, $1 \le j \le m$. T is a *trace* of E in I_1 if T is a trace of e_j in I_1.

5. $E = group(E')$, E' is a basic event, $n = 1$, $\mathcal{H}$ is a minimal history of E', and the (only) trace of E in $\mathcal{H}$ is $((\cup\{S : (S, D)$ is a trace of E' in $I_1\}, D), group(E'))$.

6. $E = E_1, \ldots, E_m$, and there exists a minimal history $\mathcal{H}_i$ for each E_i such that $\mathcal{H} = \mathcal{H}_1, \ldots, \mathcal{H}_m$. If T_1 is a trace of E_1 in $\mathcal{H}_1, \ldots, T_m$ is a trace of E_m in $\mathcal{H}_m$, then $\mathcal{T} = T_1, \ldots, T_m$ is a *trace* of E in $\mathcal{H}$.

7. $E = {}^\wedge E'$ and either $\mathcal{H} = \epsilon$ and $(\mathcal{H}, null)$ is a *trace* of E in $\mathcal{H}$, or $\mathcal{H}$ is a minimal history of E', E and any trace of E', E in $\mathcal{H}$ is a *trace* of E in $\mathcal{H}$.

8. $E = (E')$ and $\mathcal{H}$ is a minimal history of E'. Any trace of E' in $\mathcal{H}$ is a *trace* of E in $\mathcal{H}$.

Before we define the satisfaction of a condition in a policy proposition we need to precisely define the denotation of terms. Since terms involve attributes of primitive events the denotation of a term will also involve traces of events. To simplify the presentation we will assume for the rest of this section that there is at most one occurrence of a primitive event symbol in a complex event.[3] We will describe the denotation of two aggregate functions, *Count* and *Avg*. Other aggregate functions can be defined similarly.

Definition 5 *Let $\mathcal{T}$ be a trace of an event in an event history. If $\mathcal{T} = ((S_1, D_1), e_1)), \ldots, ((S_n, D_n), e_n)$, and $e_n \ne null$, the denotation $t^\mathcal{T}$ of any term t in $\mathcal{T}$ is:*

1. *t, if t is a constant from one of the known types.*

2. *$f^{D_n}(t_1^\mathcal{T}, \ldots, t_k^\mathcal{T})$, if $t = f(t_1, \ldots, t_k)$ and f is a function symbol of arity k and f^{D_n} is the denotation of f in D_n.*

3. *$e.m^s$, if $t = e.m$ and m is an attribute associated with the event symbol e, there exists a unique j, $1 \le j \le n$ such that $e_j = e$, and s is the only instance of e in S_j. If there is no j such that $e_j = e$ in $\mathcal{T}$, or if there is more than one instance of e in S_j, the denotation of t is undefined.*

4. *The number of instances of e in $S_1, \ldots, S_n$, if $t = Count(e)$, and e is a event symbol, otherwise the denotation of t is undefined.*

5. *the average of $e.x^s$ for every instance s of e in $S_1, \ldots, S_n$, if $t = Ave(e.x)$ and $e.x$ is an integer attribute associated with e and the number of instances of e in $S_1, \ldots, S_n$ is $\ne 0$; otherwise the denotation of t is undefined.*

---

[2]If *e* is a non-primitive event, !*e* can be transformed into a basic event by repeated applications of De Morgan rules and a rule that cancels two consecutive !.

[3]Multiple occurrences can be handled by renaming or indexing the events (see the definition of terms).

If $e_n = null$ and $n > 1$, the denotation of t in $\mathcal{T}$ is the same as the denotation of t in $((S,D_1),e_1)),\ldots,((S_{n-1},D_{n-1}),e_{n-1})$; otherwise $t^{\mathcal{T}}$ is undefined.

Truth values of predicates are obtained using the standard definition of the comparison operators. The only special consideration is when the denotation of a term that appears in a predicate is undefined. In that case the predicate will be undefined. A condition is true if every predicate in the condition is true; it is unknown if at least one predicate is unknown; otherwise is false. However, we will limit any reference made in a condition of a primitive event that occurs under the scope of a caret $\char94$, or a *group* operator, or as part of a basic event of the form "$e_1|\ldots|e_n$" with $n > 0$, to only appear as an argument of an aggregate operator. It is easy to see that under this restriction a condition will never be undefined because of references to terms with undefined denotation. This restriction can be enforced syntactically. We will assume all policy descriptions obey the restriction.

Let $\mathcal{H} = I_1,\ldots,I_n$, be an event history. A policy defined event proposition "E **triggers** e **if** c" is *satisfied* in $\mathcal{H}$ iff the following conditions hold:

1. There exists an i such that $I_i,\ldots,I_n$ is a minimal history of E, and a trace $\mathcal{T}$, of E in this minimal history.

2. The denotation of c in $\mathcal{T}$, $c^{\mathcal{T}}$, is true.

3. There is no trace $\mathcal{T}'$ of E in $I_i,\ldots,I_k$ such that $\mathcal{T} = \mathcal{T}',\mathcal{T}''$ (i.e. $\mathcal{T}'$ a prefix of $\mathcal{T}$), and the denotation of c in $\mathcal{T}'$, $c^{\mathcal{T}'}$, is true.

$\mathcal{T}$ is called a satisfying *trace* of the event definition in $\mathcal{H}$. We can similarly define when a history satisfies a policy proposition of the form "E **causes** a **if** c". The third condition on the definition ensures that once a trace of an event satisfies a proposition, extensions of the same trace, due to the occurrence of a caret "$\char94$", do not satisfy the same proposition or event definition. For example, take the following history with four epochs, $(\{e_1\},D_1),(\{e_2\},D_2),(\{e_1\},D_3),(\{e_2\},D_4)$.
Assume that the condition c is satisfied in the prefix $(\{e_1\},D_1)$, $(\{e_2\},D_2)$, in the suffix $(\{e_1\},D_3)$, $(\{e_2\},D_4)$ and in the whole history $(\{e_1\},D_1)$, $(\{e_2\},D_2)$, $(\{e_1\},D_3)$, $(\{e_2\},D_4)$. The proposition "$\char94(e_1,e_2)$ **causes** $a(x)$ **if** c" is satisfied once by this history. The minimal history satisfying the proposition is the second pair $(\{e_1\},D_3)$, $(\{e_2\},D_4)$. Although the whole history is a minimal history of $\char94(e_1,e_2)$, it will not satisfy the proposition since a prefix of the history has already "consumed" the beginning of the event.

A history $\mathcal{H}$ is *plausible* for a policy description P iff either $\mathcal{H}$ is empty or $\mathcal{H} = I_1,\ldots,I_n$ and for every sub-history $\mathcal{H}_j = I_1,\ldots,I_j, 1 \le j < n$, of $\mathcal{H}$, and every policy defined event e, the following holds:

$\mathcal{H}_j$ satisfies event definition "E **triggers** $e(m_1 = t_1,\ldots,m_k = t_k)$ **if** c" in P iff there is an instance

of e in I_{j+1} for each satisfying trace $\mathcal{T}$ of E in $\mathcal{H}_j$ with the denotation of $e.m_i$ in I_{j+1} is $t_i^{\mathcal{T}}$.

The underlying idea behind plausible histories is twofold: 1) it ensures that an instance of a policy defined primitive event occurs in an event history only if it is triggered by the satisfaction of a policy event definition and 2) it ensures that the instance is not spontaneously generated (i.e. it is only generated by a triggering event).

A policy description P defines a partial mapping π_P from event histories to sets of action symbols.

Definition 6 *Let P be a policy description. $\pi_P : Histories \longrightarrow 2^{Actions}$ is the policy defined by P iff* **(a)** *for every plausible event history $\mathcal{H}$ the following conditions hold:*

1. *For any satisfying trace $\mathcal{T}$ of a proposition of the form*

$$E \text{ causes } a(t_1,\ldots,t_n) \text{ if } c$$

in P, $a(t_1^{\mathcal{T}},\ldots,t_n^{\mathcal{T}}) \in \pi_P(\mathcal{H})$.

2. *Nothing else is in $\pi_P(\mathcal{H})$.*

(b) *If $\mathcal{H}$ is not plausible, $\pi_P(\mathcal{H})$ is undefined.*

A logic program for π_P

The following is a fragment of a logic program LP that implements the transition function π_P for any policy P. To save space we restrict the definitions to the main predicates. We use the standard PROLOG list notation to represent histories and epochs. A list representing a history stores the epochs in reverse order, most recent epochs are at the beginning, old epochs are at the end. Policy rules of the form "E **causes** A **if** C" are assumed to be added to the program as facts of the form `policyrule(E causes A if P)`. Rules of the form "E **triggers** E' **if** C" are stored as facts of the form `trigger(E triggers E' if C)`. We do not specify how to represent instances of primitive events and the denotations of functions but this is not important for understating the program. Note that the logic program is hierarchical (Shepherdson 1997). Thus, Clark completion gives us an equivalent first order logic definition of π_P and PROLOG with negation as failure a correct implementation.

```
exec(History,A) <-
     plausible(History),
     policyrule(E causes A if C),
     fired(E causes A if C, History).

plausible([]).
plausible([(Epoch,D)]).
plausible([(Epoch,D)|History]) <-
     NOT ignoredtrigger(Epoch,History),
     plausible(History).

ignoredtrigger(Epoch,History) <-
     trigger(E triggers E' if C),
     fired(E triggers E' if C,History),
```

```
          Not member(E',Epoch).

fired(E causes A if C,History) <-
      holds(E,History,Trace),holds(C,Trace),
      noHoldsInPrefix(E,C,Trace).

noHoldsInPrefix(Event,C,[]).
noHoldsInPrefix(Event,C,Trace) <-
      holds(Event,Trace,Trace),
      NOT holds(C,Trace),Trace = [E|Trace'],
      noHoldsInPrefix(Event,C,Trace').
noHoldsInPrefix(Event,C,Trace) <-
      NOT holds(Event,Trace,Trace),
      Trace = [E|Trace'],
      noHoldsInPrefix(Event,C,Trace').

holds(E,[(Epoch,Denotation)|H]),
      [(Inst,Denotation)]) <-
      instance(E,Epoch,Inst).
holds((E1,E2),History,Trace) <-
      append(H1,H2,History),
      holds(E1,H1,T1),holds(E2,H2,T2),
      append(Trace,T1,T2).
holds(^E,_,[]).
holds(^E,History,Trace) <-
      holds((E,^E),History,Trace).
```

holds(C,Trace) evaluates the condition C (attribute comparisons of the events in Trace and function denotations) in the most recent state.

```
instance(E,Epoch,[E]) <- member(E,Epoch).
instance(!E,Epoch,Epoch) <-
      Not member(E,Epoch).
instance(E1&E2,Epoch,Inst) <-
      instance(E1,Epoch,Inst1),
      instance(E2,Epoch,Inst2),
      union(Inst1,Inst2,Inst).
instance(E1|E2,Epoch,Inst) <-
      instance(E1,Epoch,Inst).
instance(E1|E2,Epoch,Inst) <-
      instance(E2,Epoch,Inst).
instance(group(E),Epoch,S) <-
      getinstances(E,epoch,S).
```

getinstances(E,Epoch,S) gets from the Epoch all the occurrences of the event E.

Proposition 1 *Given a policy P and a history $\mathcal{H}$ = (Ep1,D1),...,(Epm,Dm); $A \in \pi_P(\mathcal{H})$ iff LP$\models$* exec([(Epm,Dm),...,(Ep1,D1)],A).

Complexity and algorithm

This section discusses the complexity of the policy evaluation problem. We show that even restricted instances are quite intractable. These hardness results provide us with insights that help us design an efficient algorithm for evaluating policies under very realistic assumptions. A full paper describing these results is under preparation.

The algorithm is implemented as the engine of a *policy server*, in the PacketStar IP Services Platform software developed at Bell Labs. The policy server is being used to provide centralized administration in circuit and packet telephony networks. It has been used to implement policies for detecting alarm conditions, fail-overs, device configuration and provisioning, service class configuration, congestion control etc.

We have established the hardness of the easier decision version of the problem: given a policy P of description size n and an action A and history $\mathcal{H}$ of length h, is action A caused by policy P in any of the epochs of $\mathcal{H}$ (i.e. $A \in \pi_P(\mathcal{H})$)?

Theorem 1 *The decision version of the policy evaluation problem is NP-Hard for any of the following restricted class of policies:*

- *Policies with one rule in which* **event** $= e_1, e_2 \ldots e_h$, *at most two primitive events per epoch in the history* $\mathcal{H}$, *no policy defined primitive events and n a polynomial in h.*
- *Policies with one rule in which* **event** *is a sequence of h $\hat{\ }e$-s for a system defined primitive event e, at most one primitive event per epoch in the history $\mathcal{H}$, no policy defined primitive events and n a polynomial in h.*
- *Policies for which the description size n is a bounded constant but we allow policy rules using policy defined primitive events.*
- *Policies for which the description size n is a bounded constant, we do not allow policy defined primitive events, however the* **event** *in the policy rules may use "double non-determinism" (e.g.* **event** $= \hat{\ }(\hat{\ }e_1, \hat{\ }e_2)$).*

Policy evaluation algorithm: Although very restricted instances of the policy evaluation problem are hard to solve, the hard cases seem to arise only for contrived instances of the problem, i.e. policies used in practice do not belong to the restricted classes of policies for which Theorem 1 holds. For example policy rules tend to have small size descriptions (n is a bounded constant). We are able to design an efficient algorithm for evaluating such practical policies. The policy evaluation algorithm **PE** has two phases:

(1) Initialization phase This phase involves, among other things, the construction of a non-deterministic finite automata (NDFA) for the complex event E in the rule. The algorithm simulates the transitions in the NDFA in the real-time evaluation phase.

(2) Real-time evaluation phase At any epoch t the algorithm maintains the set $R(t)$ of all possible distinct partial traces for event E in the event history. A partial trace is defined to be a prefix of a trace. That is a partial trace at epoch t may after appending a trace from epochs $t + 1, t + 2 \ldots$ be converted into a trace for event E. We refer to these distinct partial traces as *active threads*. An active thread at epoch t is maintained as a path A_1 in the NDFA for E that starts from the initial state and a sequence A_2 of "sub-epochs" of a suffix of the history at epoch t. In other words A_2

is a partial trace at epoch t for event E in the event history, such that the epochs over which A_2 is defined form a suffix of the epochs of the history at epoch t. An active thread also carries with it the partial information (attribute values, aggregated values etc) that can be obtained from the partial trace A_2 to evaluate the condition, the arguments of the action or the triggered event in the proposition.

The algorithm **PE** works as follows. Let us say the algorithm has just seen the events in epoch t. By our assumption the algorithm has the set of active threads $R(t-1)$. Let $A(t-1) \in R(t-1)$ be an active thread. Let s be the last state of the NDFA, in the path A_1 for $A(t-1)$. We will say that the active thread $R(t-1)$ is in state s of the NDFA. Let (s, s') be a transition in the NDFA which is labeled with an event $E(i)_{(s,s')}$. Note that $E(i)_{(s,s')}$ is of the form e or $!e$ or $e_1 \& e_2 \& \dots$ or $e_1 | e_2 | \dots$, where each e, e_i is a basic event. Let I be the set of instances of $E(i)_{(s,s')}$ in epoch t. For each instance $k \in I$ a new active thread is computed, which has $A_1 = append(A_1 \text{ of } A(t-1), s')$, $A_2 = append(A_2 \text{ of } A(t-1), k)$ and the additional information obtained for evaluating the policy rule from the instance k. At this point it is checked if this new active thread is in a final state of the NDFA and it has all the information required to evaluate the policy rule. If it is then the policy rule is evaluated in this active thread. Otherwise the active thread is added to the set $R(t)$. This procedure is carried out for every active thread in $R(t-1)$. In addition a new active thread $\omega(0)$ is added to $R(t)$ with $A_1 =$ the initial state of the NDFA, an empty trace and no information to compute the policy rule.

In the current implementation of the policy server, a policy registers with network devices the system defined primitive events that it is interested in. Whenever such a registered event happens at a device, a java object for the event is streamed to the policy. This may cause actions by the policy at network devices. An action is streamed to the network device as a java object whose methods are evaluated at the device server leading to device specific commands sent to the device.

Final remarks

Formal descriptions of general polices is a challenging problem for the KR community. We probably need a fairly sophisticated language if we intent to cover all classes of polices. For example, Subrahmanian and some of his collaborators at the University of Maryland use a deontic logic based language to describe policies in the IMPACT project, a platform for agent collaboration (Subrahmanian *et al.* 1998) to express very complex policies. Our approach to the design of the language has been guided by two principles: 1) We would like policy specifications that can be (efficiently) implemented and 2) We would like succinct representations of policies. This is our initial proposal but we expect the language to evolve.

There is a direction of research orthogonal to the design of the language. Once polices are written one needs to reason about them. We would like to prevent a policy from executing conflicting actions, i.e. we would like consistent policies. We will also need to reason about inter-policy interactions. Take the rules:

$FaxArrive$ **causes** $DeliverFaxMainFloor$
 if $FaxArrive.Size > \kappa$
$FaxArrive$ **causes** $DeliverFaxHome$
 if $FaxArrive.Time > 5:00p.m.$

These rules may be considered to be in conflict since there are situations where a single fax is delivered to two different places. For conflict verification it is essential to have languages with precise semantics. Much of the work on policy languages in network management lacks any type of formal semantics (see for example (Moffett & Sloman 1993; Wies 1994)). We are preparing a paper addressing some of the consistency issues.

References

Baral, C.; Gelfond, M.; and Provetti, A. 1997. Representing Actions: Laws, Observations and Hypothesis. *Journal of Logic Programming* 31(1-3):201–244.

Baral, C.; Lobo, J.; and Trajcevski, G. 1997. Formal characterizations of active databases: II. In *Proc. of the International Conference on DOOD*.

Brownston, L.; Farell, R.; Kant, E.; and Martin, N. 1985. *Programming Expert Systems in OPS5: An Introduction to Rule-Based Programming*. Addison-Wesley.

Geffner, H., and Bonet, B. 1998. High-level planning and control with incomplete information using POMDP's. In *working notes of the AAAI fall symposium on Cognitive Robotics*.

Gelfond, M., and Lifschitz, V. 1993. Representing action and change by logic programs. *JLP* 17:301–321.

Moffett, J., and Sloman, M. 1993. Policy hierarchies for distributed system management. *IEEE JSAC* 11(9).

Motakis, I., and Zaniolo, C. 1997. Temporal aggregation in active database rules. In *Proc. of SIGMOD*.

Russell, S., and Norvig, P. 1995. *Artificial Intelligence - A Modern Approach*. Prentice Hall.

Shepherdson, J. C. 1997. Negation as failure, completion and stratification. In D. M. Gabbay, and Robinson, J. A., eds., *Handbook of Logic in Artificial Intelligence and Logic Programming*, volume 5. London: Oxford Science Publications. 356–420.

Subrahmanian, V. S.; Bonatti, P.; Eiter, T.; Dix, J.; and Kraus, S. 1998. IMPACT: Interactive Maryland Platform for Agents aCting Together. URL: http://www.cs.umd.edu/~vs/agent/impact.html.

Widom, J., and Ceri, S. 1995. *Active Database Systems*. Morgan-Kaufmann.

Wies, R. 1994. Policies in network and system management - formal definition and architecture. *Journal of Network and System Management* 2(1):63–83.

A Semantic Decomposition of Defeasible Logics

M.J. Maher and G. Governatori

School of Computing and Information Technology, Griffith University
Nathan, QLD 4111, Australia
{mjm,guido}@cit.gu.edu.au

Abstract

We investigate defeasible logics using a technique which decomposes the semantics of such logics into two parts: a specification of the structure of defeasible reasoning and a semantics for the meta-language in which the specification is written. We show that Nute's Defeasible Logic corresponds to Kunen's semantics, and develop a defeasible logic from the well-founded semantics of Van Gelder, Ross and Schlipf. We also obtain a new defeasible logic which extends an existing language by modifying the specification of Defeasible Logic. Thus our approach is productive in analysing, comparing and designing defeasible logics.

Introduction

In this paper we start from Nute's Defeasible Logic (Nute, 1987; Nute 1994). This logic has an expressive syntax, a strongly skeptical semantics and a tractable computational behavior. Our interest, in this paper, is to decompose Defeasible Logic into parts, for the analysis of the logic, and also to reassemble it with different parts to create new and different logics.

We show that one component of Defeasible Logic is Kunen's semantics for logic programs (Kunen, 1987). As a consequence of this link, inference in predicate Defeasible Logic (where arbitrary function symbols are allowed) is computable, and inference in propositional Defeasible Logic is polynomial.

The technique that we use – meta-programming – allows us to provide several different semantics to the syntactic elements of Defeasible Logic without violating the underlying intuitive meaning of the syntax. Thus we can create several different defeasible logics, all adhering to the defeasible structure underlying Defeasible Logic. (Of course, the computational complexity of such logics varies with the semantics.) In particular, we show that a defeasible logic developed using unfounded sets corresponds exactly to the use of the well-founded semantics of logic programs (Van Gelder et al., 1991).

The paper is organized as follows. The next section introduces Defeasible Logic and its proof theory. We establish a bottom-up characterization of the consequences of a defeasible theory that serves as our semantics for Defeasible Logic. We also define Well-Founded Defeasible Logic and show that it is coherent and consistent.

In the third section we present the metaprogram that encodes the basic behavior of the Defeasible Logic syntactic constructs. We outline Kunen's semantics and the well-founded semantics of logic programs, and show that the composition of these semantics with the metaprogram produces, respectively, Defeasible Logic and Well-Founded Defeasible Logic. We also show, using the metaprogram, that explicit failure operators can be added to defeasible logics in a conservative way. Finally, we present some future work and conclusions.

Defeasible Logic

Outline of Defeasible Logic

A *rule r* consists of its *antecedent* $A(r)$ (written on the left; $A(r)$ may be omitted if it is the empty set) which is a finite set of literals, an arrow, and its *consequent* $C(r)$ which is a literal. In writing rules we omit set notation for antecedents.

There are three kinds of rules: *Strict rules* are denoted by $A \rightarrow p$, and are interpreted in the classical sense: whenever the premises are indisputable (e.g. facts) then so is the conclusion. An example of a strict rule is "Emus are birds". Written formally: $emu(X) \rightarrow bird(X)$. Inference from facts and strict rules only is called *definite inference*.

Defeasible rules are denoted by $A \Rightarrow p$, and can be defeated by contrary evidence. An example of such a rule is $bird(X) \Rightarrow flies(X)$, which reads as follows: "Birds typically fly".

Defeaters are denoted by $A \rightsquigarrow p$ and are used to prevent some conclusions. In other words, they are used to defeat some defeasible rules by producing evidence to the contrary. An example is the rule $heavy(X) \rightsquigarrow \neg flies(X)$, which reads as follows: "If an animal is heavy then it may not be able to fly". The main point is that the information that an animal is heavy is not sufficient evidence to conclude that it doesn't fly. It is only evidence that the animal *may* not be able to fly.

A *superiority relation on R* is a relation $>$ on R (that is, the transitive closure of $>$ is irreflexive). When $r_1 > r_2$, then r_1 is called *superior* to r_2, and r_2 *inferior* to r_1. This expresses that r_1 may override r_2. For example, given the defeasible rules

$$r : \qquad\qquad bird(X) \quad \Rightarrow flies(X)$$
$$r' : \quad brokenWing(X) \quad \Rightarrow \neg flies(X)$$

which contradict one another, no conclusive decision can be made about whether a bird with a broken wing can fly. But if we introduce a superiority relation $>$ with $r' > r$, then we can indeed conclude that it cannot fly.

A defeasible theory consists of a set of facts, a set of rules, and a superiority relation. A *conclusion* of a defeasible theory D is a tagged literal and can have one of the following four forms:

- $+\Delta q$, which is intended to mean that q is definitely provable in D.

- $-\Delta q$, which is intended to mean that we have proved that q is not definitely provable in D.

- $+\partial q$, which is intended to mean that q is defeasibly provable in D.

- $-\partial q$ which is intended to mean that we have proved that q is not defeasibly provable in D.

Definite provability involves only strict rules and facts.

Proof Theory

In this presentation we use the formulation of Defeasible Logic given in (Billington 1993). A *defeasible theory* D is a triple $(F, R, >)$ where F is a set of literals (called *facts*), R a finite set of rules, and $>$ a superiority relation on R. In expressing the proof theory we consider only propositional rules. Rules such as the previous examples are interpreted as the set of their variable-free instances.

Given a set R of rules, we denote the set of all strict rules in R by R_s, the set of strict and defeasible rules in R by R_{sd}, the set of defeasible rules in R by R_d, and the set of defeaters in R by R_{dft}. $R[q]$ denotes the set of rules in R with consequent q. In the following $\sim p$ denotes the complement of p, that is, $\sim p$ is $\neg p$ if p is an atom, and $\sim p$ is q if p is $\neg q$.

Provability is defined below. It is based on the concept of a *derivation* (or *proof*) in $D = (F, R, >)$. A derivation is a finite sequence $P = (P(1), \dots P(n))$ of tagged literals satisfying the following conditions ($P(1..i)$ denotes the initial part of the sequence P of length i):

$+\Delta$: If $P(i + 1) = +\Delta q$ then either
$\qquad q \in F$ or
$\qquad \exists r \in R_s[q] \ \forall a \in A(r) : +\Delta a \in P(1..i)$

That means, to prove $+\Delta q$ we need to establish a proof for q using facts and strict rules only. This is a deduction in the classical sense – no proofs for the negation of q need to be considered (in contrast to defeasible provability below, where opposing chains of reasoning must be taken into account, too).

$-\Delta$: If $P(i + 1) = -\Delta q$ then
$\qquad q \notin F$ and
$\qquad \forall r \in R_s[q] \ \exists a \in A(r) : -\Delta a \in P(1..i)$

To prove $-\Delta q$, i.e. that q is not definitely provable, q must not be a fact. In addition, we need to establish that every strict rule with head q is *known to be* inapplicable. Thus for every such rule r there must be at least one antecedent a for which we have established that a is not definitely provable $(-\Delta a)$.

$+\partial$: If $P(i + 1) = +\partial q$ then either
$\qquad$ (1) $+\Delta q \in P(1..i)$ or
$\qquad$ (2) $\quad$ (2.1) $\exists r \in R_{sd}[q] \forall a \in A(r) : +\partial a \in P(1..i)$ and
$\qquad\qquad$ (2.2) $-\Delta \sim q \in P(1..i)$ and
$\qquad\qquad$ (2.3) $\forall s \in R[\sim q]$ either
$\qquad\qquad\qquad$ (2.3.1) $\exists a \in A(s) : -\partial a \in P(1..i)$ or
$\qquad\qquad\qquad$ (2.3.2) $\exists t \in R_{sd}[q]$ such that
$\qquad\qquad\qquad\qquad \forall a \in A(t) : +\partial a \in P(1..i)$ and $t > s$

Let us illustrate this definition. To show that q is provable defeasibly we have two choices: (1) We show that q is already definitely provable; or (2) we need to argue using the defeasible part of D as well. In particular, we require that there must be a strict or defeasible rule with head q which can be applied (2.1). But now we need to consider possible "counterattacks", that is, reasoning chains in support of $\sim q$. To be more specific: to prove q defeasibly we must show that $\sim q$ is not definitely provable (2.2). Also (2.3) we must consider the set of all rules which are not known to be inapplicable and which have head $\sim q$ (note that here we consider defeaters, too, whereas they could not be used to support the conclusion q; this is in line with the motivation of defeaters given above). Essentially each such rule s attacks the conclusion q. For q to be provable, each such rule s must be counterattacked by a rule t with head q with the following properties: (i) t must be applicable at this point, and (ii) t must be stronger than (i.e. superior to) s. Thus each attack on the conclusion q must be counterattacked by a stronger rule.

The definition of the proof theory of defeasible logic is completed by the condition $-\partial$. It is nothing more than a strong negation of the condition $+\partial$.

$-\partial$: If $P(i + 1) = -\partial q$ then
$\qquad$ (1) $-\Delta q \in P(1..i)$ and
$\qquad$ (2) $\quad$ (2.1) $\forall r \in R_{sd}[q] \ \exists a \in A(r) : -\partial a \in P(1..i)$ or
$\qquad\qquad$ (2.2) $+\Delta \sim q \in P(1..i)$ or
$\qquad\qquad$ (2.3) $\exists s \in R[\sim q]$ such that
$\qquad\qquad\qquad$ (2.3.1) $\forall a \in A(s) : +\partial a \in P(1..i)$ and
$\qquad\qquad\qquad$ (2.3.2) $\forall t \in R_{sd}[q]$ either
$\qquad\qquad\qquad\qquad \exists a \in A(t) : -\partial a \in P(1..i)$ or $t \not> s$

To prove that q is not defeasibly provable, we must first establish that it is not definitely provable. Then we must establish that it cannot be proven using the defeasible part of the theory. There are three possibilities to achieve this: either we have established that none of the (strict and defeasible) rules with head q can be applied (2.1); or $\sim q$ is definitely provable (2.2); or there must be an applicable rule s with head $\sim q$ such that no applicable rule t with head q is superior to s.

The elements of a derivation are called *lines* of the derivation. We say that a tagged literal L is *provable* in $D =$

$(F, R, >)$, denoted $D \vdash L$, iff there is a derivation in D such that L is a line of P.

Under some assumptions, the logic and conditions concerning defeasible provability can be simplified (Antoniou et al., 1998) but we do not need those assumptions here.

A Bottom-Up Characterization of Defeasible Logic

The proof theory provides the basis for a top-down (backward-chaining) implementation of the logic. However, there are advantages to a bottom-up (forward-chaining) implementation. Furthermore, a bottom-up definition of the logic provides a bridge to the logics we will define later. For these reasons we now provide a bottom-up definition of Defeasible Logic.

We associate with D an operator $\mathcal{T}_D$ which works on 4-tuples of sets of literals. We call such 4-tuples an *extension*.

$$\mathcal{T}_D(+\Delta, -\Delta, +\partial, -\partial) = (+\Delta', -\Delta', +\partial', -\partial') \text{ where}$$

$$+\Delta' = F \cup \{q \mid \exists r \in R_s[q]\ A(r) \subseteq +\Delta\}$$

$$-\Delta' = -\Delta \cup (\{q \mid \forall r \in R_s[q]\ A(r) \cap -\Delta \neq \emptyset\} - F)$$

$$+\partial' = +\Delta \cup \{q \mid \exists r \in R_{sd}[q]\ A(r) \subseteq +\partial,$$
$$\sim q \in -\Delta, \text{ and}$$
$$\forall s \in R[\sim q] \text{ either}$$
$$A(s) \cap -\partial \neq \emptyset, \text{ or}$$
$$\exists t \in R[q] \text{ such that}$$
$$A(t) \subseteq +\partial \text{ and } t > s\}$$

$$-\partial' = \{q \in -\Delta \mid \forall r \in R_{sd}[q]\ A(r) \cap -\partial \neq \emptyset, \text{ or}$$
$$\sim q \in +\Delta, \text{ or}$$
$$\exists s \in R[\sim q] \text{ such that } A(s) \subseteq +\partial \text{ and}$$
$$\forall t \in R[q] \text{ either}$$
$$A(t) \cap -\partial \neq \emptyset, \text{ or}$$
$$t \not> s\}$$

The set of extensions forms a complete lattice under the pointwise containment ordering[1], with $\bot = (\emptyset, \emptyset, \emptyset, \emptyset)$ as its least element. The least upper bound operation is the pointwise union, which is represented by $\cup$. It can be shown that $\mathcal{T}_D$ is monotonic and the Kleene sequence from $\bot$ is increasing. Thus the limit $F = (+\Delta_F, -\Delta_F, +\partial_F, -\partial_F)$ of all finite elements in the sequence exists, and $\mathcal{T}_D$ has a least fixpoint $L = (+\Delta_L, -\Delta_L, +\partial_L, -\partial_L)$. When D is a finite propositional defeasible theory $F = L$.

The extension F captures exactly the inferences described in the proof theory.

Theorem 1 *Let D be a finite propositional defeasible theory and q a literal.*

- $D \vdash +\Delta q$ *iff* $q \in +\Delta_F$
- $D \vdash -\Delta q$ *iff* $q \in -\Delta_F$
- $D \vdash +\partial q$ *iff* $q \in +\partial_F$
- $D \vdash -\partial q$ *iff* $q \in -\partial_F$

[1] $(a_1, a_2, a_3, a_4) \leq (b_1, b_2, b_3, b_4)$ iff $a_i \subseteq b_i$ for $i = 1, 2, 3, 4$.

The restriction of Theorem 1 to finite propositional theories derives from the formulation of the proof theory; proofs are guaranteed to be finite under this restriction. However, the bottom-up semantics and the following work do not need this restriction, and so apply to predicate defeasible logic rules that represent infinitely many propositional rules. Indeed, for the remainder of this paper we will take the bottom-up semantics F as representative of Defeasible Logic in this wider sense. We will write $D \vdash +\Delta q$ to express $q \in +\Delta_F$, and similarly with other conclusions.

The analysis of the proof theory of Defeasible Logic in (Maher et al., 1998) was based on a 4-tuple defined purely in terms of the (top-down) proof theory. By Theorem 1, that 4-tuple is precisely F.

An extension $(+\Delta, -\Delta, +\partial, -\partial)$ is *coherent* if $+\Delta \cap -\Delta = \emptyset$ and $+\partial \cap -\partial = \emptyset$. An extension is *consistent* if whenever $p \in +\partial$ and $\sim p \in +\partial$, for some p, then also $p \in +\Delta$ and $\sim p \in +\Delta$. Intuitively, coherence says that no literal is simultaneously provable and unprovable. Consistency says that a literal and its negation can both be defeasibly provable only when it and its negation are definitely provable; hence defeasible inference does not introduce inconsistency. A logic is coherent (consistent) if the meaning of each theory of the logic, when expressed as an extension, is coherent (consistent).

The following result was shown in (Billington, 1993).

Proposition 2 *Defeasible Logic is coherent and consistent.*

Well-Founded Defeasible Logic

It follows from the above definitions that defeasible theories such as

$$r : \quad p \Rightarrow p$$

conclude neither $+\partial p$ nor $-\partial p$. In some contexts it is desirable for a logic to recognize such "loops" and to conclude $-\partial p$. Building on the bottom-up definition of the previous subsection, and inspired by the work of (Van Gelder et al., 1991), we define a well-founded defeasible logic which draws such conclusions.

The central definition required is that of an unfounded set. Since defeasible logic involves both definite and defeasible inference, we need two definitions. A set S of literals is unfounded with respect to an extension E and definite inference (or Δ-*unfounded*) if: For every literal s in S, and for every strict rule $B \rightarrow s$ either

- $B \cap -\Delta_E \neq \emptyset$, or
- $B \cap S \neq \emptyset$

This definition is very similar to the definition of unfounded set in (Van Gelder et al., 1991). The main differences are that the basic elements of S are literals (and negation is classical negation) and "negation as failure" is not present in the bodies of rules.

The corresponding definition for defeasible inference is more complex, since there are more factors that influence defeasible inference. Nevertheless, the basic idea is the same.

We use $\hookrightarrow$ to denote that the arrow of a rule is not specified. That is, $B \hookrightarrow s$ refers to a rule that might be strict, defeasible, or a defeater.

A set S of literals is unfounded with respect to an extension E and defeasible inference (or ∂-*unfounded*) if: For every literal s in S, and for every strict or defeasible rule $r_1 : A(r_1) \hookrightarrow s$ in D either

- $A(r_1) \cap -\partial_E \neq \emptyset$, or
- $A(r_1) \cap S \neq \emptyset$, or
- there is a rule $r_2 : A(r_2) \hookrightarrow \sim s$ in D such that $A(r_2) \subseteq +\partial_E$ and for every rule $r_3 : A(r_3) \hookrightarrow s$ in D either
  - $A(r_3) \cap -\partial_E \neq \emptyset$, or
  - $r_3 \not\succ r_2$.

Clearly the classes of Δ-unfounded and ∂-unfounded sets are both closed under unions. Hence there is a greatest Δ-unfounded set wrt E (denoted by $U_D^{\Delta}(E)$), and a greatest ∂-unfounded set wrt E (denoted by $U_D^{\partial}(E)$). Let $\mathcal{U}_D(E) = (\emptyset, U_D^{\Delta}(E), \emptyset, U_D^{\partial}(E))$.

We define $\mathcal{W}_D(E) = \mathcal{T}_D(E) \cup \mathcal{U}_D(E)$.

Let I_α be the elements of the (possibly transfinite) Kleene sequence starting from $\bot = (\emptyset, \emptyset, \emptyset, \emptyset)$. $\{I_\alpha \mid \alpha \geq 0\}$ is an increasing sequence and thus has a limit.

Let $WF = (+\Delta_{WF}, -\Delta_{WF}, +\partial_{WF}, -\partial_{WF})$ be the limit of this sequence. Then WF defines the conclusions of Well-Founded Defeasible Logic. If a literal $q \in +\Delta_{WF}$ we write $D \vdash_{WF} +\Delta q$, and similarly with the three other sets in WF.

We can verify that the resulting logic is sensible in the following sense.

Proposition 3 *Well-Founded Defeasible Logic is coherent and consistent.*

To illustrate the definitions, consider the following Well-Founded Defeasible Logic theory.

$$
\begin{array}{rrcl}
r_1 : & b & \Rightarrow & a \\
r_2 : & \neg c & \Rightarrow & a \\
r_3 : & d & \Rightarrow & a \\
r_4 : & a & \Rightarrow & \neg c \\
r_5 : & true & \Rightarrow & d \\
r_6 : & true & \Rightarrow & \neg d
\end{array}
$$

With respect to the extension E where $-\partial \neg a, -\partial b$ and $-\partial c$ hold, an unfounded set is $U = \{a, \neg c, d, \neg d\}$. Well-Founded Defeasible Logic will conclude $-\partial a, -\partial \neg c, -\partial d$ and $-\partial \neg d$, whereas conventional Defeasible Logic will conclude only $-\partial d$ and $-\partial \neg d$.

Decomposition of Defeasible Logics

In this section we show how a defeasible logic can be decomposed into a metaprogram specifying the structure of defeasible reasoning, and a semantics for the meta-language (logic programming). We first introduce the metaprogram, then the two semantics that, when composed with the metaprogram, produce the two logics defined previously. Finally we discuss an example where the metaprogram is modified.

The Defeasible Logic Metaprogram

In this section we introduce a metaprogram $\mathcal{M}$ in a logic programming form that expresses the essence of the defeasible reasoning embedded in the proof theory. The metaprogram assumes that the following predicates, which are used to represent a defeasible theory, are defined.

- `fact`($Head$),
- `strict`($Name, Head, Body$),
- `defeasible`($Name, Head, Body$),
- `defeater`($Name, Head, Body$), and
- `sup`($Rule1, Rule2$),

$\mathcal{M}$ consists of the following clauses. We first introduce the predicates defining classes of rules, namely

```
supportive_rule(Name, Head, Body):-
    strict(Name, Head, Body).

supportive_rule(Name, Head, Body):-
    defeasible(Name, Head, Body).

rule(Name, Head, Body):-
    supportive_rule(Name, Head, Body).

rule(Name, Head, Body):-
    defeater(Name, Head, Body).
```

We introduce now the clauses defining the predicates corresponding to $+\Delta$, $-\Delta$, $+\partial$, and $-\partial$. These clauses specify the structure of defeasible reasoning in Defeasible Logic. Arguably they convey the conceptual simplicity of Defeasible Logic more clearly than does the proof theory.

$c1$
```
definitely(X):-
    fact(X).
```

$c2$
```
definitely(X):-
    strict(R, X, [Y_1, ..., Y_n]),
    definitely(Y_1),...,definitely(Y_n).
```

$c3$
```
not_definitely(X):-
    not definitely(X).
```

$c4$
```
defeasibly(X):-
    definitely(X).
```

$c5$
```
defeasibly(X):-
    not definitely(~ X),
    supportive_rule(R, X, [Y_1, ..., Y_n]),
    defeasibly(Y_1),...,defeasibly(Y_n),
    not overruled(S, R, X).
```

$c6$
```
overruled(S, R, X):-
    sup(S, R),
    rule(S, ~ X, [U_1, ..., U_n]),
    defeasibly(U_1),...,defeasibly(U_n),
    not defeated(T, S, ~ X).
```

$c7$
```
defeated(T, S, ~ X):-
    sup(T, S),
    supportive_rule(T, X, [V_1, ..., V_n]),
    defeasibly(V_1),...,defeasibly(V_n).
```

$c8$ `not_defeasibly(`X`):-`
      `not defeasibly(`X`).`

The first three clauses address definite provability, while the remainder address defeasible provability. The clauses specify if and how a rule in Defeasible Logic can be overridden by another, and which rules can be used to defeat an over-riding rule, among other aspects of the structure of defeasible reasoning.

We have permitted ourselves some syntactic flexibility in presenting the metaprogram. However, there is no technical difficulty in using conventional logic programming syntax to represent this program.

This metaprogram is similar to – though briefer and more intelligible than – the meta-interpreter d-Prolog for Defeasible Logic defined in (Covington et al., 1997). The d-Prolog meta-interpreter was designed for execution by Prolog, with the Prolog implementation of negation-as-failure. It contains many complications due to this intended use.

Given a defeasible theory $D = (F, R, >)$, the corresponding program $\mathcal{D}$ is obtained from $\mathcal{M}$ by adding facts according to the following guidelines:

1. `fact(`p`).`   for each $p \in F$;

2. `strict(`$r_i, p, [q_1, \ldots, q_n]$`).`
      for each rule $r_i : q_1, \ldots, q_n \rightarrow p \in R$;

3. `defeasible(`$r_i, p, [q_1, \ldots, q_n]$`).`
      for each rule $r_i : q_1, \ldots, q_n \Rightarrow p \in R$;

4. `defeater(`$r_i, p, [q_1, \ldots, q_n]$`).`
      for each rule $r_i : q_1, \ldots, q_n \rightsquigarrow p \in R$;

5. `sup(`r_i, r_j`).`
      for each pair of rules such that $r_i > r_j$.

Kunen Semantics

Kunen's semantics (Kunen, 1987) is a 3-valued semantics for logic programs. A *partial interpretation* is a mapping from ground atoms to one of three truth values: **t** (true), **f** (false), and **u** (unknown). This mapping can be extended to all formulas using Kleene's 3-valued logic.

Kleene's truth tables can be summarized as follows. If ϕ is a boolean combination of the atoms **t**, **f**, and **u**, its truth value is **t** iff all the possible ways of putting in **t** or **f** for the various occurrences of **u** lead to a value **t** being computed in ordinary 2-valued logic: ϕ gets the value **f** iff $\neg\phi$ gets the value **f**, and ϕ gets the value **u** otherwise. These truth values can be extended in the obvious way to predicate logic, thinking of the quantifiers as infinite disjunction or conjunction.

The Kunen semantics of a program $\mathcal{P}$ is obtained from a sequence $\{I_n\}$ of partial interpretations, defined as follows.

1. $I_0(\alpha) = \mathbf{u}$ for every atom α

2. $I_{n+1}(\alpha) = \mathbf{t}$ iff for some clause

$$\beta\text{:-}\phi$$

in the program, $\alpha = \beta\sigma$ for some ground substitution σ such that
$$I_n(\phi\sigma) = \mathbf{t}\ .$$

3. $I_{n+1}(\alpha) = \mathbf{f}$ iff for all the clauses

$$\beta\text{:-}\phi$$

in the program, and all ground substitution σ, if $\alpha = \beta\sigma$, then
$$I_n(\phi\sigma) = \mathbf{f}\ .$$

4. $I_{n+1}(\alpha) = \mathbf{u}$ otherwise.

We shall say that the Kunen semantics of $\mathcal{P}$ supports α iff there is an interpretation I_n, for some finite n, such that $I_n(\alpha) = \mathbf{t}$. This semantics has an equivalent characterization in terms of 3-valued logical consequence. We refer the reader to (Kunen, 1987) for more details.

We use $\mathcal{P} \models_K \alpha$ to denote that the Kunen semantics for the program $\mathcal{P}$ supports α.

We can now relate the bottom-up characterization of a defeasible theory D with the Kunen semantics for the corresponding program $\mathcal{D}$.

Theorem 4 *Let D be a defeasible theory and $\mathcal{D}$ denote its metaprogram counterpart.*

For each literal p,

1. *$D \vdash +\Delta p$ iff $\mathcal{D} \models_K$ `definitely(`p`)`;*

2. *$D \vdash -\Delta p$ iff $\mathcal{D} \models_K$ `not_definitely(`p`)`;*

3. *$D \vdash +\partial p$ iff $\mathcal{D} \models_K$ `defeasibly(`p`)`;*

4. *$D \vdash -\partial p$ iff $\mathcal{D} \models_K$ `not_defeasibly(`p`)`;*

Thus Kunen's semantics of $\mathcal{D}$ characterizes the consequences of Defeasible Logic. Defeasible Logic can be decomposed into $\mathcal{M}$ and Kunen's semantics.

This has a further interesting implication: The consequences of predicate Defeasible Logic are computable. That is, if we permit predicates and uninterpreted function symbols of arbitrary arity, then the four sets of consequences are recursively enumerable. This follows from the fact that Kunen's semantics is recursively enumerable (Kunen, 1989). It contrasts with most nonmonotonic logics, in which the consequence relation is not computable.

For propositional Defeasible Logic, we can use the relationship with Kunen's semantics to establish a polynomial bound on the cost of computing consequences. In unpublished work we have a more precise bound.

Well-Founded Semantics

The presentation of the well-founded semantics in this section is based on (Van Gelder et al., 1991).

The notion of *unfounded sets* is the cornerstone of well-founded semantics. These sets provide the basis to derive negative conclusions in the well-founded semantics.

Definition 5 *Given a program $\mathcal{P}$, its Herbrand base H, and a partial interpretation I, a set $A \subseteq H$ is an unfounded set with respect to I iff each atom $\alpha \in A$ satisfies the following condition: For each instantiated rule R of $\mathcal{P}$ whose head is α, (at least) one of the following holds:*

1. *Some subgoal of the body is false in I.*

2. *Some positive subgoal of the body occurs in A*

The *greatest unfounded set* of $\mathcal{P}$ with respect to I ($U_{\mathcal{P}}(I)$) is the union of all the unfounded sets with respect to I.

Definition 6 *The transformations $T_{\mathcal{P}}(I)$, $U_{\mathcal{P}}(I)$, and $W_{\mathcal{P}}(I)$ are defined as follows:*

- $\alpha \in T_{\mathcal{P}}$ *iff there is some instantiated rule R of $\mathcal{P}$ such that α is the head of R, and each subgoal of R is true in I.*

- $U_{\mathcal{P}}(I)$ *is the greatest unfounded set with respect to I.*

- $W_{\mathcal{P}} = T_{\mathcal{P}} \cup \neg U_{\mathcal{P}}(I)$, *where $\neg U_{\mathcal{P}}(I)$ denotes the set obtained from $U_{\mathcal{P}}(I)$ by taking the complement of each atom in $U_{\mathcal{P}}(I)$.*

We are now able to introduce the notion of *well-founded semantics*. The well-founded semantics of a program $\mathcal{P}$ is represented by the least fixpoint of $W_{\mathcal{P}}$.

We write $\mathcal{P} \models_{WF} \alpha$ to mean that α receives the value **t** in the well-founded semantics of $\mathcal{P}$.

The following theorem establishes a correspondence between Well-Founded Defeasible Logic and the well-founded semantics of $\mathcal{D}$.

Theorem 7 *Let D be a defeasible theory and $\mathcal{D}$ denote its metaprogram counterpart.*

For each ground literal p

1. $D \vdash_{WF} +\Delta p$ *iff* $\mathcal{D} \models_{WF} \texttt{definitely}(p)$;

2. $D \vdash_{WF} -\Delta p$ *iff* $\mathcal{D} \models_{WF} \texttt{not\_definitely}(p)$;

3. $D \vdash_{WF} +\partial p$ *iff* $\mathcal{D} \models_{WF} \texttt{defeasibly}(p)$;

4. $D \vdash_{WF} -\partial p$ *iff* $\mathcal{D} \models_{WF} \texttt{not\_defeasibly}(p)$;

Thus Well-Founded Defeasible Logic can be decomposed into $\mathcal{M}$ and the well-founded semantics.

As a result, the consequences of a propositional Well-Founded Defeasible Logic theory can be computed in time polynomial in the size of the theory, using the fact that the well-founded semantics of propositional logic programs can be computed in polynomial time (Van Gelder et al., 1991). However, predicate Well-Founded Defeasible Logic is not computable, in contrast with predicate Defeasible Logic, which is computable.

Through the relationship between Kunen's semantics and the well-founded semantics of logic programs we can establish the relationship between Defeasible Logic and Well-Founded Defeasible Logic. The latter is an extension of Defeasible Logic in the sense that it respects the conclusions that are drawn by Defeasible Logic but generally draws more conclusions from the same syntactic theory.

Theorem 8 *Let D be a defeasible theory. For every conclusion C,*
if $D \vdash C$ then $D \vdash_{WF} C$

Defeasible Logic with Explicit Failure

Although the meaning of conclusions $-\partial p$ and $-\Delta p$ is expressed in terms of failure-to-prove, there is not a way to express directly within the above defeasible logics that a literal should fail to be proved; tagged literals are not permitted in rules. In contrast, most logic programming-based formalisms employ "negation as failure" to express directly that a literal should fail.

The characterization of defeasible logics by a metaprogram and a semantics for logic programs provides a way for these logics to be extended with explicit failure without modifying their underlying semantics (i.e. a conservative extension). We introduce two operators on literals: $fail\Delta\ q$ which expresses that it should be proved that the literal q cannot be proven definitely, and $fail\partial\ q$ which expresses that it should be proved that q cannot be proven defeasibly. (Some syntactic restrictions must apply: classical negation ($\neg$) and the operators must not be applied to an operator expression, and $fail\partial$ is not permitted in strict rules.)

The meaning of such expressions can be given by appropriately modifying clauses $c2$, $c5$, $c6$ and $c7$ of the metaprogram. If an element Y_i of the body of a rule has the form $fail\partial\ Z_i$ then the body of $c5$ (say) should contain $\texttt{not defeasibly}(Z_i)$ in place of $\texttt{defeasibly}(Y_i)$. The resulting metaprogram is more general in that it defines a more expressive language but it has no different effect on theories that do not use the failure operators. Defeasible logic rules that do not involve explicit failure retain the same interpretation that they had before.

The resulting language, when we use the Kunen semantics, generalizes both Defeasible Logic and Courteous Logic Programs (Grosof, 1997). Indeed, it was already shown in (Antoniou et al., 1998) that Courteous Logic Programs can be expressed by Defeasible Logic theories, by encoding uses of the $fail$ operator with defeasible rules. With the explicit failure operators we can express $fail$ directly. Thus Courteous Logic Programs are essentially a syntactic subset of (with the same semantics as) the extended Defeasible Logic.

Future Work

This work opens up several variations of Defeasible Logic, in addition to the ones we have presented. The many different semantics for negation in logic programs have corresponding different semantics for the defeasible logic syntax. For example, the composition of stable model semantics (Gelfond and Lifschitz, 1988) with the metaprogram might produce a credulous version of defeasible logic.

Equally, we can vary the fundamental defeasible structure by modifying the metaprogram. Such changes will generally not alter the computational complexity, since it is the semantics of the meta-language which has the dominant effect on complexity.

The results also open up alternative implementations of defeasible logics. One possibility is to execute the metaprogram and data in a logic programming system with the appropriate semantics. The connection between Defeasible Logic and Kunen's semantics suggests an implementation incorporating constructive negation (Stuckey, 1995).

Conclusion

We have provided a semantic decomposition of defeasible logics into two parts: a metaprogram which specifies the fundamental defeasible structure of the logic (e.g. when a rule can be defeated by another), and a semantics which determines how the meta-language is interpreted.

We showed that Nute's Defeasible Logic is characterized by Kunen's semantics and that Well-Founded Defeasible Logic is characterized by the well-founded semantics. We also briefly developed a variant of Defeasible Logic with explicit failure by modifying the metaprogram. Thus different defeasible logics can be obtained by varying either the metaprogram or the semantics of the meta-language.

Decomposition is a useful tool for the analysis and comparison of logics. It provided a straightforward way to compare Defeasible Logic and Well-Founded Defeasible Logic. Equally, the reverse process of composition can be useful to design a logic with specific characteristics.

Acknowledgements

We thank Grigoris Antoniou and David Billington for discussions and comments on defeasible logic. This research was supported by the Australia Research Council under Large Grant No. A49803544.

References

G. Antoniou, D. Billington and M.J. Maher. Normal Forms for Defeasible Logic. In *Proc. Joint International Conference and Symposium on Logic Programming*, J. Jaffar (Ed.), 160–174. MIT Press, 1998.

D. Billington, K. de Coster and D. Nute. A Modular Translation from Defeasible Nets to Defeasible Logic. *Journal of Experimental and Theoretical Artificial Intelligence* 2 (1990): 151–177.

D. Billington. Defeasible Logic is Stable. *Journal of Logic and Computation* 3 (1993): 370–400.

M.A. Covington, D. Nute and A. Vellino. *Prolog Programming in Depth*. Prentice Hall 1997.

M. Gelfond and V. Lifschitz. The Stable Model Semantics for Logic Programming. In *Proc. Joint International Conference and Symposium on Logic Programming*, 1070–1080, MIT Press, 1988.

B.N. Grosof. Prioritized Conflict Handling for Logic Programs. In *Proc. Int. Logic Programming Symposium*, J. Maluszynski (Ed.), 197–211. MIT Press, 1997.

J.F. Horty, R.H. Thomason and D. Touretzky. A Skeptical Theory of Inheritance in Nonmonotonic Semantic Networks. In *Proc. AAAI-87*, 358–363.

K. Kunen. Negation in Logic Programming. *Journal of Logic Programming* 4 (1987): 289–308.

M. Maher, G. Antoniou and D. Billington. A Study of Provability in Defeasible Logic. In *Proc. Australian Joint Conference on Artificial Intelligence*, 215–226, LNAI 1502, Springer, 1998.

D. Nute. Defeasible Reasoning. In *Proc. 20th Hawaii International Conference on Systems Science*, IEEE Press 1987, 470–477.

D. Nute. Defeasible Logic. In D.M. Gabbay, C.J. Hogger and J.A. Robinson (eds.): *Handbook of Logic in Artificial Intelligence and Logic Programming Vol. 3*, Oxford University Press 1994, 353–395.

P.J. Stuckey. Negation and Constraint Logic Programming. *Information and Computation* 118 (1995): 12–33.

A. Van Gelder, K. Ross and J.S. Schlipf. Unfounded Sets and Well-Founded Semantics for General Logic Programs. *Journal of the ACM* 38 (1991): 620–650.

$\mathcal{S}acre$: a Constraint Satisfaction Problem Based Theorem Prover

Jean-Michel Richer **Jean-Jacques Chabrier**
LIRSIA, Université de Bourgogne
9 Avenue Alain Savary, BP 47870, 21078 Dijon cedex, France
{richer,chabrier}@crid.u-bourgogne.fr

Abstract

The purpose of this paper is to present a new approach for solving first-order predicate logic problems stated in conjunctive normal form. We propose to combine resolution with the Constraint Satisfaction Problem (CSP) paradigm to prove the inconsistency and find a model of a problem. The resulting method benefits from resolution and constraint satisfaction techniques and seems very efficient when confronted to some problems of the CADE-13 competition.

Introduction

From a general point of view we can classify methods for solving first-order predicate calculus problems stated in conjunctive normal form, into two categories. The first one is *consistency searching* or *proof searching* and is syntax-oriented. It consists of raising a contradiction from a set of clauses by applying inference rules. For example, the theorem prover Otter (McCune 1994) uses *resolution, unit-resolution, hyperresolution*, while Setheo (Bayerl & Letz 1987) is based on *model elimination* (Loveland 1978).

The second one, *satisfiability checking*, also called *model finding*, is related to semantics and tries to find a model or a counterexample of a problem. In this last category we can draw a distinction between *saturation* and *extension* approaches. In the former case, we iteratively generate ground instantiations of the problem and test ground clause sets for unsatisfiability with a propositional calculus prover (Chu & Plaisted 1997). In the latter case, we try to build a model of the problem by assuming new ground facts. One of the first satisfiability approaches was the saturation approach of Gilmore (Gilmore 1960) which proved to be very inefficient. We believe it is because this kind of approach has to tackle with the whole Herbrand base while only a part of it is necessary.

Another kind of approach is the combined approach implemented in the theorem prover Satchmo (Manthey & Bry 1988) which uses syntactic and semantic features to solve problems. It can be qualified as an extension approach. However Satchmo is based on the *model generation* reasoning paradigm (Bry & Yahya 1996). Satchmo suffers from certain drawbacks. The first one is *range restriction* requiring that each head variable must occur in the body of a clause. The second drawback is the fact that Satchmo can sometimes choose a clause irrelevant to the current goal to be solved and thus causes unnecessary model candidate extensions. This may result in a potential explosion of the search space. Nevertheless, some improvements can be made, such as *relevancy testing* (Loveland, Reed, & Wilson 1995) to avoid unnecessary case splittings.

Apart from those semantic approaches, Finder (Slaney 1995) searches for finite models of first order theories presented as sets of clauses. Falcon (Zhang 1996), for which model generation is viewed as constraint satisfaction, constructs finite algebras from given equational axioms. Finite models are able to provide some kind of semantic guidance that helps refutation-based theorem provers find proofs more quickly (Slaney, Lusk, & McCune 1994).

It is also possible to combine *resolution* with rewrite techniques so as to guide the search and design more efficient inference rules, such as the *problem reduction format* (Loveland 1978) or the *simplified problem reduction format* (Plaisted 1982), that permits the deletion of unachievable subgoals, or its extension the *modified problem reduction format* (Plaisted 1988).

The key novelty introduced in this paper is the combination of *resolution* with the *Constraint Satisfaction Problem* (CSP) paradigm, so as to solve first-order predicate calculus problems, stated in conjunctive normal form. This combination is not fortuitous. First, consistency searching and model finding are both common problems related to logic and CSPs. Second, the CSP techniques have proved to be very powerful to solve large combinatorial problems by applying strategies and heuristics that help guide the search and improve the resolution process by efficiently pruning the search space. The resulting method, called $\mathcal{S}acre$[1] is based

---

[1]for SAtisfaction de Contraintes et REsolution - Constraint satisfaction and resolution

on a unique forward chaining rule and combines constraint satisfaction heuristics and techniques together with theorem-proving techniques and is able to prove the inconsistency or find a model of a problem. It is, to our knowledge, the first attempt of this kind ever tried in this direction.

The paper is organized as follows : in section 2, we will set forth some basic definitions of constraint satisfaction problems. The next section is devoted to the use of CSPs in propositional calculus. Section 4 presents the *Sacre* approach. The last section exhibits some results for some of the problems of the CADE-13 competition.

Constraint satisfaction problems

The past 10 years have witnessed the development of efficient algorithms for solving Constraint Satisfaction Problems (CSPs). Examples of CSPs include propositional theorem proving, map coloring, planning and scheduling problems.

Definition 1 - CSP - : *A CSP (Montanari 1974) is traditionally defined by a set of variables $X = \{x_1, \ldots, x_n\}$ ranging over a finite set of domains $D = \{d_1, \ldots, d_n\}$ that need to satisfy a set of constraints $C = \{c_1, \ldots, c_m\}$ between variables.*

A constraint is *satisfied* if there exists an assignment of its variables such that the relationship between the variables holds. A CSP is *consistent* if there exists an assignment of $\mathcal{X}$ such that all the constraints of $\mathcal{C}$ are satisfied. Given a CSP we can check if there exists a solution (consistency checking), find a solution or all the solutions (model finding) or find an optimal solution for a given criterion (optimization problem).

Example 1- Consider the following CSP :

$$(CSP_1) \begin{cases} \mathcal{X} = & \{x_1, x_2, x_3\}, \\ \mathcal{D} = & \{d_1, d_2, d_3\}, \text{ with} \\ & d_1 = d_2 = d_3 = \{0, 1, 2\} \\ \mathcal{C} = & \{x_1 + x_2 = x_3\}, \end{cases}$$

This CSP is consistent and its solutions are :

$$S_1 = \{(0,0,0), (0,1,1), (1,0,1), \\ (1,1,2), (0,2,2), (2,0,2)\}$$

Propositional calculus and CSPs

The satisfiability problem (SAT) in propositional calculus consists in determining whether there exists an assignment of the propositional variables of a set of clauses that renders the set satisfiable. The translation of a set of propositional clauses into a CSP is quite obvious. Propositional variables become the variables of the CSP and range over the boolean domain. Clauses of the form $p_1 \vee \ldots \vee p_k$ (where the p_is are literals) are translated into cardinality constraints (Van-Hentenryck & Deville 1991) $\#\langle \alpha, \beta, p_1, \ldots, p_k \rangle$ which state that at least α and at most β propositional variables must be instantiated to true. Not only does the cardinality constraint model more concisely problems but it also improve the efficiency of the resolution process (Chabrier, Juliard, & Chabrier 1995). For example, the following set of clauses :
$\{p \vee q \vee r, \neg p \vee \neg q, \neg p \vee \neg r, \neg q \vee \neg r\}$ can be represented by $\#\langle 1, 1, p, q, r \rangle$. Among the algorithms developed to solve the satisfiability problem, the methods relying on CSP techniques have proved to be far more efficient than the basic Davis and Putnam procedure (Davis & Putnam 1960). We can draw a distinction (Chabrier, Juliard, & Chabrier 1995) between systematic approaches like C-SAT (Dubois *et al.* 1993), non-systematic approaches such as GSAT (Selman, Levesque, & Mitchell 1991) and hybrid approaches like *Score* (Chabrier, Juliard, & Chabrier 1995).

Systematic approaches are complete. They rely on a backtrack algorithm that tries to find a solution by successively instantiating variables while constraints are satisfied. Non-systematic approaches start from an initial instantiation (also called a configuration) of the variables and try to make local changes to the configuration until a solution is found following heuristic criteria. This kind of approach is incomplete, for heuristics may cause the algorithm to be stuck in a local optimum, but tends to be more efficient than systematic approaches because they correspond to a more focused search. Finally, hybrid approaches start from an initial configuration of the variables generated for example by a Min-Conflict algorithm (Minton *et al.* 1992) and try to repair it using a backtrack algorithm to avoid testing the same configuration twice.

The *Sacre* approach

Score, that has proved to be fairly efficient for random SAT problems (3-SAT) and structured problems (Ramsey, Pigeon-hole) (Chabrier 1997), led us naturally therefore to venture out beyond the limits of propositional calculus. To some extent, *Sacre* can be considered as an attempt at extending *Score* to first-order logic.

A new original approach to theorem proving for first-order logic based on a constraint representation of predicate calculus problems was defined in (Richer & Chabrier 1997).

This approach originates from the observation that a logic problem in conjunctive normal form is able to be expressed as a special case of a CSP, that we call CSP^T,

Definition 2 - CSP^T - *A CSP^T is a kind of CSP defined to represent the set of terms T of a problem in logic expressed in conjunctive normal form.*

The main idea of our work was to transform a predicate calculus problem into a CSP^T and solve it using heuristic techniques related to the resolution of Constraint Satisfaction Problems and thus take advantage of the efficiency of CSP techniques.

The major stumbling block in trying to translate a set of clauses of the predicate calculus into a CSP concerns the representation of literals as variables ranging over sets of terms. To take into account the characteristic of CSP^T, we introduce the notations of Ψ-domain and Ψ-variable to help represent respectively the domains and variables of CSP^T. These notations rely on a membership interpretation of literals. For example, when we write $man(socrate)$ we mean that $socrate$ is a member of the set of men. In the same way, $\neg man(tweety)$ means that $tweety$ does not belong to the set of men but that the concept of man applies to $tweety$. We can then think of the concept of man in terms of two separate and complementary subsets (or Ψ-subdomains) that capture the notion of a boolean interpretation. A Ψ-domain is then the set composed of these two subsets (see fig. 1).

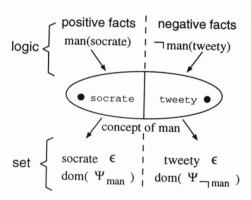

Figure 1: Notion of Ψ-domain

Furthermore, any element of a Ψ-domain can not belong to both subsets without raising an inconsistency. More precisely, if p is a predicate symbol we will note $dom(\Psi_p)$ and $dom(\Psi_{\neg p})$ the subsets (or Ψ-subdomains) respectively related to literals p and $\neg p$. The Ψ-domain of p is noted $dom(\Psi_{p,\neg p})$ and is such that

$$dom(\Psi_{p,\neg p}) = \; < dom(\Psi_p), dom(\Psi_{\neg p}) >$$
$$with \quad dom(\Psi_p) \cap dom(\Psi_{\neg p}) \; = \emptyset$$

where the notation $E = < A, B >$ expresses the fact that the set E is composed of two disjoint subsets A and B.

The notion and notation of Ψ-variable is then straightforward. A Ψ-variable represents the translation of a literal into a variable. Each literal p (resp. $\neg p$) is associated to a Ψ-variable, noted Ψ_p (resp. $\Psi_{\neg p}$) ranging over $dom(\Psi_{p,\neg p})$. Any literal $p(t)$ where t is a list of terms represents an occurrence of the variable Ψ_p for which the values that Ψ_p can be assigned to are restricted to values of $dom(\Psi_{p,\neg p})$ that unify with t and is noted $\Psi_p^{[t]}$. Provided with this formalism we can describe a linear time transformation of a predicate calculus problem stated in conjunctive normal form into a CSP^T for which unit clauses will form the Ψ-domains of the CSP and non-unit clauses will be transformed into cardinality constraints so as to turn clauses into constraints.

Definition 3 - Transformation into a CSP^T - *A first-order predicate calculus problem P stated in conjunctive normal form can be transformed into a CSP over the set of terms T of P (noted CSP^T), by applying the following rules :*

- *for each predicate p of P :*
  - *$\mathcal{X}$ is made up of the variables Ψ_p and $\Psi_{\neg p}$ that take their values in $dom(\Psi_{p,\neg p})$ and related to literals of the form $p(t)$ and $\neg p(t)$.*
  - *$\mathcal{D}$ is made up of the domains $dom(\Psi_{p,\neg p})$ defined over T; each $dom(\Psi_{p,\neg p})$ is separated into two subdomains $dom(\Psi_{p,\neg p}) = dom(\Psi_p) \cup dom(\Psi_{\neg p})$ such that $dom(\Psi_p) \cap dom(\Psi_{\neg p}) = \emptyset$,*
    - *$dom(\Psi_p) = \{t, \; such \; that \; p(t)\}$, represents the set of terms that are true under a partial interpretation of P,*
    - *$dom(\Psi_{\neg p}) = \{t, \; such \; that \; \neg p(t)\}$, represents the set of terms that are false under a partial interpretation of P,*
  - *$\mathcal{C}$ initially contains the consistency constraints of the form $\#\langle 1, 1, \Psi_p, \Psi_{\neg p}\rangle$, that maintain consistency at the logical level;*

- *unit clauses of P initially define the domains :*
  - *$dom(\Psi_p) = \{t_0\}$, for each unit clause $p(t_0)$ of P,*
  - *$dom(\Psi_{\neg p}) = \{t_0\}$, for each unit clause $\neg p(t_0)$ of P,*

- *non-unit clauses are transformed into cardinality constraints. A clause $p_1(t_1) \vee \cdots \vee p_k(t_k)$ is transformed into $\#\langle 1, n, \Psi_{p_1}^{[t_1]}, \ldots, \Psi_{p_k}^{[t_k]}\rangle$ thus following the Ψ-variable notation.*

We give here a simple example of the representation of a logic problem P as a CSP^T :

(P)
$$\begin{cases} p(a) \\ \neg p(X) \vee q(f(X)) \\ \neg q(f(f(X))) \end{cases}$$

(CSP^T)
$$\begin{cases} \mathcal{X} = \{ \Psi_p, \Psi_{\neg p}, \Psi_q, \Psi_{\neg q} \}; \\ \mathcal{D} = \begin{cases} dom(\Psi_{p,\neg p}) = \{a\} \cup \{\} \\ dom(\Psi_{q,\neg q}) = \{\} \cup \{f(f(X))\} \end{cases} \\ \mathcal{C} = \{ \#\langle 1, 2, \Psi_{\neg p}^{[X]}, \Psi_q^{[f(X)]}\rangle \} \end{cases}$$

Resolution

In (Richer 1999) it was clearly underlined that the resolution of CSP^T was not compatible with the standard resolution approach of CSPs which considers that domains are finite and not extendable. The resolution of CSP^T relies on a domain extension that compels the introduction of the notion of an extended CSP.

Definition 4 - Extended CSP - *An extended CSP, noted CSP_{ext}, has the ability to extend its domains through constraint satisfaction.*

For example, the assignment $(x_1 = 1, x_2 = 2, x_3 = 3)$ for (CSP_1) is not valid for a standard approach because

3 does not belong to d_3 but is acceptable for an *extended* approach and the value 3 is added to domain d_3. In the remainder of this paper we will only consider CSP^T_{ext}.

The principle of the general algorithm designed to solve the CSP^T_{ext} is to build a partial interpretation by iteratively satisfying constraints. The partial interpretation may be viewed as an attempt at constructing a counterexample for refuting the given hypothesis. Constraint satisfaction leads to the production of new values that do not appear in their related Ψ-domains. Following an extended approach, new values are added to their related domains to perform further deductions and increase the partial interpretation. The unsatisfiability of a CSP arises from the discovery of a value μ belonging to both Ψ-subdomains ($\mu \in dom(\Psi_p) \wedge \mu \in dom(\Psi_{\neg p})$) of a Ψ-domain $dom(\Psi_{p,\neg p})$. From a logic view point this is equivalent to generating two resolvents $p(t_1)$ and $\neg p(t_2)$ such that there exists a most general unifier σ of t_1 and t_2 ($\sigma(t_1) = \sigma(t_2)$).

function $Solve(\mathcal{P} : CSP^T_{ext}) : boolean$
input   a $CSP^T_{ext} = \{\mathcal{X}, \mathcal{D}, \mathcal{C}\}$
output $\mathcal{P}$ with extended domains
return   true if the problem $\mathcal{P}$ is consistent,
         false otherwise.
begin
    $V = \{\Psi_p \in \mathcal{V}, dom(\Psi_p) \neq \emptyset\}$
    $consistency = true$
    while $V \neq \emptyset$ **and** $consistency$ **do**
       choose $\Psi_v \in V$
       $V = V/\{\Psi_v\}$
       $C(x_v) = \{\#\langle 1, n, \Psi_{p_1}^{[t_1]}, \ldots, \Psi_{p_{n-1}}^{[t_{n-1}]}, \Psi_v^{[t_v]}\rangle\}$
       while $C(\Psi_v) \neq \emptyset$ **and** $consistency$ **do**
          choose $c \in C(\Psi_v)$
          $C(\Psi_v) = C(\Psi_v)/\{c\}$
          $consistency = propagate(V, c, \Psi_v)$
       end
    end
    return $consistency$
end

Figure 2: Resolution of a CSP^T_{ext}

The interesting point is that we do not confine ourselves to ground atoms. For example, we can add the term X to the Ψ-subdomain of a unary predicate p. This prevents us from enumerating the whole Herbrand universe by using subsumption.

The resolution procedure underlying the implementation of *Sacre*, based on constraint satisfaction, has been identified as a forward chaining rule applied to a set of contrapositives. To give the reader a yet clearer view of the resolution procedure, we shall refer to figures 2 and 3. The role of the *propagate* function is to determine the domains that are extended by the satisfaction of constraint c that contains the Ψ-variable Ψ_v.

function $propagate(V, c, \Psi_v) : boolean$
input/output V a set of Ψ-variables
input c a constraint $\#\langle 1, n, \Psi_{p_1}^{[t_1]}, \ldots, \Psi_{p_{n-1}}^{[t_{n-1}]}, \Psi_v^{[t_v]}\rangle$
input Ψ_v a Ψ-variable
return   true if the satisfaction of constraint c did
         not lead to an inconsitency.
begin
    foreach $\mu \in dom(\Psi_{\neg v})$ **do**
       if the satisfaction of c where $\Psi_v^{[t_v]} = \mu$
          leads to the extension of $dom(\Psi_q)$ **then**
          if μ *already* $\in dom(\Psi_{\neg q})$ **then**
             return false   // inconsistency
          else
             extend $dom(\Psi_q)$
             $V = V \cup \{\Psi_q\}$
          end
       end
    end
    return true
end

Figure 3: Satisfaction of a constraint with domain extension

Heuristic and strategy tuning

The major point in *Sacre* is that it is possible to combine several heuristics and restriction techniques issuing from theorem proving (such as weighting) or constraint satisfaction (like forward-checking). These heuristics help improve the efficiency of the resolution of the CSP^T_{ext}. For example, when choosing a variable it is possible to select a min-domain (choose the variable with the minimum number of values in its domain), max-domain, min-constraint or max-constraint heuristic. New values can be rejected if their weight exceeds an upper bound or, the satisfaction of a constraint can be ended if a maximum number of values has been reached. The major difficulty is to combine these heuristics together so as to sufficiently decrease the search space without restricting it to a space hiding the solution. It is also worth mentioning that it is possible to choose between a depth-first, breadth-first or depth-first iterative deepening search (Korf 1985).

Other features

Sacre also applies to problems written in first-order logic with equality. Demodulation with Lex Recursive Path Ordering (Dershowitz 1987) has been implemented. Further versions will probably integrate paramodulation. One main feature of *Sacre* is the possibility to *direct* the search by orientating cardinality constraints. This ability, as in Prolog, is intended to compute a solution with very little searching and has the potential of being quite efficient compared to a non-directed approach. For example, problem NUM084.010 (evaluation of 10!) could not be solved in less than one second without taking this feature into account (see table 1).

Soundness and completeness

Unfortunately *Sacre* is incomplete, but a lack of completeness can generally lead to more efficiency. This seems to be the case considering the results obtained table 1.

Incompleteness is due to cardinality constraints that act as the *unit-resulting resolution* inference rule (or a forward chaining algorithm) which is sound but incomplete. Efficiency also stems from the lack of a *case splitting rule*. It is possible to design a case splitting rule that ensures completeness but causes a loss of efficiency (Richer 1999). This rule is not yet implemented in the current version of our solver.

Results

The *Sacre* method was implemented in C under Unix. In order to point out the real interest of our approach and the efficiency of our solver, we decided to tackle to some problems of the CADE-13 Automated Theorem Proving System competition (Suttner & Sutcliffe 1997).

Problem	Otter	Setheo	Sacre
BOO006-1	3	0	0
BOO012-1	8	0	0
BOO016-1	2	11	1
LCL196-1	7	6	23
LCL210-1	4	7	3
NUM003-1	0	0	0
NUM009-1	8	152	0
NUM284-1	0		0
PLA011-2		0	
PLA014-1		0	
RNG005-1	1	199	0
RNG038-2	0	94	8
RNG040-1	0	0	0
SET008-1	0	0	0
SET061-6	16		1
SET063-6	6		1
SET075-6	42		2
SET080-6	0	3	0
SET083-6	76		1
SET101-6	0	0	6
SET232-6		21	1
SYN200-1	0	0	0
SYN202-1	1	0	0
SYN271-1	0	0	1
Group	0	0	0
coloring	0	0	0

Table 1: Comparison between Otter, *Sacre* and Setheo.

We present in this section some comparatives results between *Sacre* and two other theorem provers Otter and Setheo. Otter (McCune 1994) is one of the most complete and efficient theorem prover using inference rules based on *resolution* (unit resolution, binary resolution, hyperresolution). Setheo (Bayerl & Letz 1987) uses *model elimination*. Otter and Setheo were chosen for comparison because they took part in the CADE-13 competition and obtained the best results.

Table 1 shows the results for some problems. Times are given in seconds. A resolution time of 0 second means that it took less than one second to prove inconsistency. Blanks mean that the problem could not be solved within 300 seconds. The tests were run on a Sun Sparc Ultra 1 workstation. The columns Otter and Setho respectively provide the results of Otter 3.0.4. in auto mode, and the best results of Setheo 3.3. with the "-dr" or "-wdr" option.

Sacre performs well on some kind of problems but there remains some problems out of *Sacre*'s scope. The problems PLA004-1 and PLA011-2 can not be solved by *Sacre* and Otter.

Conclusion and future work

In this paper we have shown that there exists a certain correspondence between first-order calculus problems in conjunctive normal form and constraint satisfaction problems. A new species of solvers can be built on this paradigm. Not only did we prove the validity of our approach but also its effectiveness with the *Sacre* prover. Improvements are still possible, and much work is under completion. We think it is possible to implement an oracle, like the autonomous mode of Otter(McCune 1994), able to determine the best strategies and heuristics for solving a given problem. The introduction of a *case splitting rule* that ensures completeness would probably be more efficient than the Satchmo case splitting rule because we are not forced to work with ground terms. In the case of predicate calculus problems with non-recursive clauses and non-extended domains (as it is the case for the Map Coloring problem), we are confronted to *standard* CSP. Moreover, the specification of the domains of predicates, instead of their computation, combined with a non-domain extension, can greatly reduce the search space. Further experimentation and improvements will determine how worthwhile are approcah is.

References

Bayerl, S., and Letz, R. 1987. Setheo : A sequential theorem prover for first-order logic. In *Esprit'87 - Achievements and Impacts, part 1*, 721–735. North-Holland.

Bry, F., and Yahya, A. 1996. Minimal model generation with positive unit hyper-resolution tableaux. In *Proceedings of the 5th Workshop on Theorem Proving with Tableaux and Related Methods*, Lectures Notes in Artificial Intelligence 1071, 143–159. New York: Springer-Verlag.

Chabrier, J.; Juliard, V.; and Chabrier, J.-J. 1995. SCORE(FD/B) : an efficient complete local-based search method for satisfiability problems. In *CP'95 Workshop - Studying and solving hard problems.*

Chabrier, J. 1997. *Programmation par contraintes : langages méthodes et applications sur les domaines booléens et entiers.* In *HDR.* Ph.D. Dissertation, LIRSIA, Université de Bourgogne.

Chu, H., and Plaisted, D. A. 1997. Clin-s. *Journal of Automated Reasoning* 18(2):183–188.

Davis, M., and Putnam, H. 1960. A computing procedure for quantification theory. *Journal of the ACM* 7:201–215.

Dershowitz, N. 1987. Termination of rewriting. *Journal of Symbolic Computation* 3:69–116.

Dubois, O.; André, P.; Boufkhad, Y.; and Carlier, J. 1993. Sat versus unsat. *In Second DIMACS Challenge.*

Gilmore, P. C. 1960. A proof method for quantification theory : its justification and realization. *IBM JRD* 28–35.

Korf, K. E. 1985. Depth-first iterative deepening : an optimal admissible tree search. *Artificial Intelligence* 27:97–109.

Loveland, D. W.; Reed, D. W.; and Wilson, D. S. 1995. Satchmore : Satchmo with relevancy. *Journal of Automated Reasoning* 14:325–351.

Loveland, D. W. 1978. *Automated Theorem Proving : A Logical Basis.* New York: North-Holland.

Manthey, R., and Bry, F. 1988. Satchmo : A theorem prover implemented in prolog. In *Proceedings of the 9th International Conference on Automated Deduction,* LNCS 310, 415–434. New York: Springer-Verlag.

McCune, W. W. 1994. *Otter 3.0 Reference Manual and Guide.*

Minton, S.; Johnston, M.; Philips, A.; and Laird, P. 1992. Minimizing conflicts : a heuristic repair method for constraint satisfaction and scheduling problems. *Artificial Intelligence* 58:161–205.

Montanari, U. 1974. Networks of constraints : Fundamental properties and applications to picture processing. *Information Science* 7:95–132.

Plaisted, D. A. 1982. A simplified problem reduction format. *Artificial Intelligence* 18:227–261.

Plaisted, D. A. 1988. Non-horn clause logic programming without contrapositives. *JAR* 4:287–325.

Richer, J.-M., and Chabrier, J.-J. 1997. Une approche de résolution de problèmes en logique basée sur des techniques de satisfaction de contraintes. In *JFPLC'97.*

Richer, J.-M. 1999. *Sacre : une approche de résolution en logique fondée sur des techniques de satisfaction de contraintes.* Ph.D. Dissertation, LIRSIA - Université de Bourgogne.

Selman, B.; Levesque, H.; and Mitchell, D. 1991. A new method for solving hard satisfiability problems. *In 10th NCAI* 440–446.

Slaney, J.; Lusk, E.; and McCune, W. 1994. Scott : Semantically constrained otter - system description. Technical Report TR-ARP-3-94, Centre for Information Science Research, Australian National University.

Slaney, J. 1995. *FINDER - Finite Domain Enumerator, Version 3.0 - Notes and Guide.*

Suttner, C., and Sutcliffe, G. 1997. The design of the CADE-13 atp system competition. *Journal of Automated Reasoning* 18(2):139–162.

Van-Hentenryck, P., and Deville, Y. 1991. The cardinality operator : A new logical connective for constraint logic programming. In Furukawa, K., ed., *Proceedings of the 8th ICLP, Paris, France 24-28 June 1991,* 745–759.

Zhang, J. 1996. Constructing finite algebras with falcon. *Journal of Automated Readoning* 17:1–22.

Learning

Exploiting the Architecture of Dynamic Systems

Xavier Boyen
Computer Science Department
Stanford University
xb@cs.stanford.edu

Daphne Koller
Computer Science Department
Stanford University
koller@cs.stanford.edu

Abstract

Consider the problem of monitoring the state of a complex dynamic system, and predicting its future evolution. Exact algorithms for this task typically maintain a *belief state*, or distribution over the states at some point in time. Unfortunately, these algorithms fail when applied to complex processes such as those represented as dynamic Bayesian networks (DBNs), as the representation of the belief state grows exponentially with the size of the process. In (Boyen & Koller 1998), we recently proposed an efficient approximate tracking algorithm that maintains an *approximate* belief state that has a compact representation as a set of independent factors. Its performance depends on the error introduced by approximating a belief state of this process by a factored one. We informally argued that this error is low if the interaction between variables in the processes is "weak". In this paper, we give formal information-theoretic definitions for notions such as weak interaction and sparse interaction of processes. We use these notions to analyze the conditions under which the error induced by this type of approximation is small. We demonstrate several cases where our results formally support intuitions about strength of interaction.

Introduction

Consider an intelligent agent whose task is to monitor a complex dynamic system such as a freeway system with multiple vehicles (Forbes *et al.* 1995). Tracking the state of such systems is a difficult task: their dynamics are noisy and unpredictable, and their state is only partially observable. Stochastic processes provide a coherent framework for modeling such systems. In many cases, the state of the system is represented using a set of *state variables*, where individual state are assignments of values to these variables. *Dynamic Bayesian networks (DBNs)* (Dean & Kanazawa 1989) allow complex systems to be represented compactly by exploiting the fact that each variable typically interacts only with few others.

Unfortunately, although this type of limited interaction helps us achieve a compact representation, it does not support effective inference. Consider the task of maintaining a *belief state* — a distribution over the current process

state (Aström 1965). A naive representation of such a distribution is exponential in the number of state variables. Unfortunately, it can be shown that, unless the system is completely decoupled (i.e., composed of non-interacting subprocesses), any two variables will have some common influence in the past and will thus be correlated. The belief state therefore has no structure, and can only be represented as an explicit joint distribution over the system variables. This limitation renders algorithms that try to track the system exactly (Kjærulff 1992) impractical for complex problems.

However, one has a strong intuition that keeping track of these correlations is often unnecessary. While the variables might be correlated, this correlation is often very weak. In Herbert Simon's words, these are "nearly decomposable systems, in which the interactions among the subsystems are weak but not negligible" (Simon 1962). Simon argues that these "nearly decomposable systems are far from rare. On the contrary, systems in which each variable is linked with almost equal strength with almost all other parts of the system are far rarer and less typical."

In (Boyen & Koller 1998) — hereafter, BK — we propose an algorithm that exploits this idea of weak interaction by momentarily ignoring the weak correlations between the states of different system components. More precisely, the BK algorithm represents the belief state over the entire system as a set of localized beliefs about its parts. For example, it might represent the beliefs about the freeway as a set of independent beliefs about the state of the individual vehicles; or, more appropriately, the states of the vehicles might be represented as conditionally independent given the overall traffic load. The algorithm chooses a restricted class of factored belief states. Given a time t belief state in this class, it propagates it to time $t + 1$; this step typically has the effect of inducing correlations between the subsystems. The algorithm projects the resulting distribution back into the restricted space. Note that the correlations between subsystems are not eliminated; they are merely "summarized" at every point in time by the projection step.

The analysis in BK shows that the stochasticity of the process prevents the repeated errors resulting from the projection steps at every time t from accumulating unboundedly. However, the amount of error resulting from the approximation is not quantified. Rather, the justification is based on the intuition that, if the processes interact only weakly, the error cannot be too large. In order to make this intuition precise, we must formally define what it means for processes to interact weakly, and show that weak interaction does allow us to bound the error introduced by this approximation.

We provide a formal information-theoretic notion of interaction, that corresponds to the amount of correlation between subsystems that is generated in a single step of the process. We then use this idea to provide a quantitative measure for the strength of interaction between systems. We also analyze the case of two processes whose correlation is largely mediated by a third; we show that such processes can be approximated as conditionally independent given the third if the latter evolves more slowly than they do, and thereby "remembers" its state. These notions allow us to determine the error induced by a decoupled approximation to the belief state.

We also analyze a new notion of *sparse interaction*, where subprocesses mostly interact only weakly, but have an occasional strong interaction. Indeed, this type of interaction might be more accurate as a fine-grained traffic model, as individual cars do occasionally have a very strong interaction (e.g., when one makes an emergency stop directly in front of another). In this case, the weak interaction assumption is warranted only part of the time. We extend the BK algorithm to settings such as this. The algorithm tailors the approximation it uses to the circumstances; after a strong interaction between two subsystems takes place, it stops decoupling their states. Thus, it temporarily resorts to a different approximation structure. If the strong interaction is momentary, then the processes go back to their usual mode of weak interaction. Hence, after some amount of time, the correlation attenuates. At that point, we can go back to decoupling the subprocess states. Our analysis shows how long this coupling needs to last in order to guarantee that we incur only small error by decoupling the processes.

Our results show how the architecture of a dynamic system can be exploited to provide an effective algorithm for reasoning about it. The system structure can be used to select an approximation scheme appropriate to it, and to adapt it as the system evolves. Our analysis provides error bounds, allowing a tradeoff between accuracy and computation.

Approximate inference in DBNs

In this section, we review the basic definitions of dynamic systems represented compactly as *dynamic Bayesian networks*. We also review the approximate inference of the BK algorithm, which is the starting point for our analysis.

A stochastic dynamic system is defined via a set of states, and a *transition model* that represents the way in which one state leads to the next. In complex systems, a state is best described using a set of *random variables* $A_1, \ldots, A_n$. We use U, V, W, X, Y, Z to denote sets of random variables, and their lower case version to denote instantiations of values for the variables in the set. The transition model is described via a directed acyclic graph $\mathcal{B}$. The network contains nodes $A_1, \ldots, A_n$ reprsenting the current state, and $A'_1, \ldots, A'_n$

representing the next state. Each node A'_i has a set of parents $\mathrm{Pa}(A'_i)$; nodes A_i have no parents. The network represents the qualitative structure of the transition model — the variables that directly influence the new value of each variable A'_i. The transition model is made quantitative by associating with each variable A'_i a conditional probability table $\boldsymbol{P}[A'_i \mid \mathrm{Pa}(A'_i)]$.

Our goal in many dynamic systems is *monitoring*: keeping track of the state of the system as it evolves. In general, we do not have access to the full state of the system. Rather, we get to observe only some subset of the state variables. Thus, the best we can do is to maintain a *belief state* — a probability distribution $\mu^{(t)}$ over the possible states at the current time t. In principle, the process of maintaining a belief state is straightforward. Having computed $\mu^{(t)}$, we propagate it forward using the transition model to obtain the expected next belief state $\mu^{(\bullet t+1)}$; we then condition $\mu^{(\bullet t+1)}$ on our time $t + 1$ evidence to get $\mu^{(t+1)}$.

In practice, however, this process can be very computationally intensive. The problem is that $\mu^{(t)}$ is a distribution over all possible assignments of values to $A_1, \ldots, A_n$, i.e., an exponentially sized space. One might hope that this belief state can be represented compactly. After all, the transition model is structured; perhaps that also induces structure on the belief state, allowing a compact representation. Unfortunately, despite the limited interaction that the transition model induces between the variables, they all become correlated. Intuitively, unless the system is completely decoupled into noninteracting subprocesses, any two variables $A_i^{(t)}$ and $A_j^{(t)}$ will eventually be influenced by a common cause, somewhere in the history of the process. Regardless of how long ago that was, and how weak the correlation currently is, the variables are qualitatively correlated. As any decomposition of a distribution rests on some form of conditional independence structure, no factored representation of the belief state is possible.

In BK, we propose an approach for circumventing this problem. Our algorithm maintains an *approximate* belief state that admits a factored representation. Specifically, we consider belief states that fall into some restricted family of distributions Σ, e.g., ones where certain sets of variables are marginally independent. Let $\tilde{\mu}^{(t)} \in \Sigma$ be our current approximate to the belief state. When we transition it to the next time slice, the result is a distribution $\varphi^{(t+1)}$ which is usually not in Σ. We must therefore project it back into Σ. We now make this algorithm more precise.

Definition 1 A *cluster forest* (Jensen, Lauritzen, & Olesen 1990) $\mathcal{F}$ is an undirected forest whose nodes are *clusters* $F_1, \ldots, F_m \subset \{A_1, \ldots, A_n\}$ and whose edges are $E = \{(i, j)\}$. The forest has the *running intersection property* — if F_i and F_j are clusters such that $A_k \in F_i$ and $A_k \in F_j$, then every cluster on the path between F_i and F_j also contains A_k.

Definition 2 We say that a distribution ψ is *representable* over $\mathcal{F}$ if it is represented as a set of marginals ψ_i over the clusters F_i, which are *calibrated*, i.e., $\psi_i[F_i \cap F_j] =$

$\psi_j[F_i \cap F_j]$ for any i, j. The distribution ψ is defined as:

$$\psi(A_1, \ldots, A_n) = \frac{\prod_{i=1}^m \psi[F_i]}{\prod_{(i,j) \in E} \psi_i[F_i \cap F_j]}.$$

We define $\Sigma[\mathcal{F}]$ to be the set of distributions ψ that are representable over $\mathcal{F}$.

The BK algorithm takes the approximate belief state $\tilde{\mu}^{(t)}$ in $\Sigma[\mathcal{F}]$, and generates the approximate belief state $\tilde{\mu}^{(t+1)}$ in $\Sigma[\mathcal{F}]$, as follows. In the first phase, the algorithm propagates $\tilde{\mu}^{(t)}$ to $\varphi^{(t+1)}$ using the transition model. It then projects $\varphi^{(t+1)}$ into $\Sigma[\mathcal{F}]$, generating $\psi^{(t+1)}$. Finally, it conditions on the time $t + 1$ evidence, resulting in $\tilde{\mu}^{(t+1)}$.

In order for this process to be performed correctly, we require that, if $A'_k \in \text{Pa}(A'_l)$, i.e., A_l has a parent A_k in its own time slice, then there must be some cluster F_i such that A_k and A_l are both in F_i. That is, all intra-time-slice edges must be contained in some cluster. This assumption allows us to focus attention on inter-time-slice influences. We therefore define $\text{Pa}^-(A'_l)$ to be $\text{Pa}(A'_l) \cap \{A_1, \ldots, A_n\}$, and $\text{Pa}^-(Y')$ for a set of variables Y' analogously.

The potential problem with this approach is that the repeated approximation at every time slice t could accumulate unboundedly, resulting in a meaningless approximation. In BK, we analyze this algorithm, and provide conditions under which the error remains bounded. The first condition is that the process is somewhat stochastic, so that errors from the past are "forgotten." The second is that each approximation step does not introduce too much error.

Definition 3 Let Y' be a cluster at time $t + 1$, and X be $\text{Pa}^-(Y')$. We define the *mixing rate* of the generalized transition $X \rightarrow Y'$ as

$$\gamma[X \rightarrow Y'] \triangleq \min_{x_1, x_2} \sum_y \min[\boldsymbol{P}[y \mid x_1], \boldsymbol{P}[y \mid x_2]].$$

If $X = V \cup W$, we also define the *mixing rate* of the conditional transition $V \rightarrow Y'$ as the minimal mixing rate obtained over all possible values of W;

$$\gamma[V \rightarrow Y' \mid W]$$
$$\triangleq \min_w \min_{v_1, v_2} \left[\sum_y \min[\boldsymbol{P}[y \mid v_1, w], \boldsymbol{P}[y \mid v_2, w]] \right].$$

Intuitively, the mixing rate is the minimal amount of mass that two distributions over Y' are guaranteed to have in common: one is the distribution we would get starting at x_1 and the other the one starting at x_2. The minimal mixing rate in the conditional transition is similar, except that we now restrict to starting points that agree about the variables in W. From here on, we will often drop the explicit reference to W in the notation for mixing rate, as W is defined implicitly to be $\text{Pa}^-(Y') \setminus V$.

The mixing rate can be used to bound the rate at which errors arising from approximations in the past are "forgotten." Let $\mathcal{Q} = \{Q_1, \ldots, Q_k\}$ be the finest disjoint partition of $A_1, \ldots, A_n$, such that each cluster F_i is contained in some Q_j; i.e., each Q_j is one of the connected components — or *trees* — in the forest defined by $\mathcal{F}$. Let r be the maximum *inward connectivity* of the process relative to $\mathcal{Q}$, i.e., an upper bound, over all partitions Q'_j, on the number of partitions Q_i such that there is an edge from (a variable in) Q_i to (a variable in) Q'_j. Similarly, let q be the maximum *outward connnectivity* of the process relative to $\mathcal{Q}$, i.e., an upper bound, over all Q_i, on the number of Q'_j such that there is an edge from Q_i to Q'_j. We define:

$$\gamma^* \triangleq \left(\frac{1}{r} \min_l \gamma[Q_l \rightarrow Q'_l] \right)^q.$$

Based on this definition, we prove that the stochastic transition decreases the error between the two distributions, measured as their Kullback-Leibler divergence. The *KL divergence* (*relative entropy*) (Cover & Thomas 1991) between a reference distribution μ and another $\tilde{\mu}$ is:

$$\boldsymbol{D}[\mu \| \tilde{\mu}] \triangleq \boldsymbol{E}_\mu \left[\ln \frac{\mu(s)}{\tilde{\mu}(s)} \right] = \sum_s \mu(s) \cdot \ln \frac{\mu(s)}{\tilde{\mu}(s)}.$$

Theorem 1 (Boyen & Koller 1998)
$$\boldsymbol{D}[\mu^{(t+1)} \| \varphi^{(t+1)}] \leq (1 - \gamma^*) \cdot \boldsymbol{D}[\mu^{(t)} \| \tilde{\mu}^{(t)}].$$

Of course, the time $t + 1$ approximation step — going from $\varphi^{(t+1)}$ to $\psi^{(t+1)}$ — introduces a new error into our approximate belief state. We can show that if this error is bounded, then the overall error in our approximation also remains bounded.

Definition 4 The *implicit projection error* of approximating φ by ψ with respect to a "true" distribution μ, as

$$\varepsilon_\mu(\varphi \mapsto \psi) \triangleq \boldsymbol{E}_\mu \left[\ln \frac{\varphi(s)}{\psi(s)} \right].$$

Theorem 2 (Boyen & Koller 1998) *Let ε^* be a bound on $\varepsilon_{\mu^{(\bullet t)}}(\varphi^{(t)} \mapsto \psi^{(t)})$ for all t. Then, on expectation over the sequence of observations, for all t:*

$$\boldsymbol{E}\, \boldsymbol{D}[\mu^{(t)} \| \tilde{\mu}^{(t)}] \leq \varepsilon^*/\gamma^*.$$

Note that, since $\varphi^{(t)}$ and $\psi^{(t)}$ are distributions prior to conditioning on the time t observation, the implicit projection error should be taken relative to $\mu^{(\bullet t)}$ — the true time t belief state prior to the conditioning step.

Measuring interaction

In BK, we provide an analysis for the contraction rate γ^*, allowing it to be bounded in terms of parameters of the dynamic system. We do not provide a similar analysis for ε^*. Rather, we argue that, if the processes do not interact very strongly, such an approximation does not incur too large an error. Indeed, our experimental results support this prediction. Our goal in this paper is to try to analyze this error and to relate it to the structure of the process.

The problem with analyzing the implicit error is that it is, as its name suggests, implicit. As we do not have access to the true distribution $\mu^{(\bullet t)}$, we cannot measure the error incurred by the projection. Instead, we will analyze a closely related quantity — the KL divergence from φ to ψ. Then, we show how this projection error can be analyzed in terms of the architecture of the system and its dynamics.

Definition 5 We define the *projection error* of approximating φ by ψ as

$$\varepsilon(\varphi \mapsto \psi) \triangleq \boldsymbol{D}[\varphi \,\|\, \psi] = \boldsymbol{E}_\varphi \left[ln \, \frac{\varphi(s)}{\psi(s)} \right].$$

Although the projection error is not precisely the quantity that appears in the analysis of the BK algorithm, there are good reasons for believing it to be close. In particular, if our current approximation $\tilde{\mu}^{(t)}$ is fairly close to the true distribution $\mu^{(t)}$, then our estimate of the projection error relative to $\varphi^{(t)}$ is close to the implicit approximation error relative to $\mu^{(t)}$. In this case, if we guarantee that the projection error is small, we can show that $\tilde{\mu}^{(t+1)}$ remains close to $\mu^{(t+1)}$. We are currently working on formalizing this intuition. For now, we will analyze the projection error.

The key aspect of this analysis is based on a close relation between the projection error and mutual information between clusters in the cluster forest $\mathcal{F}$.

The *mutual information* between two (sets of) variables X and Y given Z, is defined as (Cover & Thomas 1991):

$$\boldsymbol{I}[X; Y \mid Z] \triangleq \boldsymbol{E}_Z \boldsymbol{D}[\boldsymbol{P}[X, Y \mid Z] \,\|\, \boldsymbol{P}[X \mid Z] \otimes \boldsymbol{P}[Y \mid Z]],$$

where $\otimes$ is the outer product.

We now show that the projection error ε can be decomposed according to our clustering. In fact, the decomposition is done on a related structure, which is a hierarchical grouping of the clusters of $\mathcal{F}$.

Definition 6 We define a *cluster hierarchy* $\mathcal{G}$ as a binary tree whose leaves are the clusters $F_1, \ldots, F_m$, such that, for every pair of sibling subtrees, there is at most one edge in the cluster forest between those clusters at the leaves of one sibling and those at the leaves of the other. Each interior node is associated with a *(cluster) group* G_i, which is the union of the clusters F_k at its leaves. We say that the groups G_i and G_j for sibling subtrees are *sibling groups*, and use R to denote the set of the $m - 1$ pairs (i, j) such that G_i and G_j are siblings. For $(i, j) \in R$, we denote by M_{ij} the intersection $G_i \cap G_j$, and by $G_{i \setminus j}$ the difference $G_i \setminus M_{ij}$.

Intuitively, $\mathcal{G}$ is a recursive partition of $\mathcal{F}$, where each split divides up the clusters of a group G_k into a pair of "reciprocal" sub-groups G_i, G_j, so that no more than one edge of $\mathcal{F}$ is broken by the partition (in which case G_i and G_j will share the variables shared by the clusters on the broken edge). The following picture shows one possible cluster hierarchy (dotted lines) for a given cluster forest (solid lines).

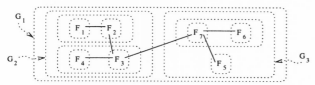

It is important to emphasize the distinction between the cluster forest $\mathcal{F}$ and the group hierarchy $\mathcal{G}$. The former has a material effect, as it defines the approximation scheme used by the inference algorithm. On the other hand, the group hierarchy $\mathcal{G}$ is merely used for the purpose of analysis, and

can be chosen freely once $\mathcal{F}$ is fixed. The nature of $\mathcal{F}$ and $\mathcal{G}$ is also different: the clusters in $\mathcal{F}$ may or may not be overlapping, and if they are, they must satisfy the running intersection property; in contrast, some groups in $\mathcal{G}$ are necessarily overlapping, since each group is a proper subset of its parent in the hierarchy. The key insight is that the approximation error for using the clusters in $\mathcal{F}$ decomposes nicely according to the structure of $\mathcal{G}$, as we now show.

Theorem 3 *Let φ be a distribution and ψ its projection on the cluster forest $\mathcal{F}$. Then the projection error*

$$\varepsilon(\varphi \mapsto \psi) = \sum_{(i,j) \in R} \boldsymbol{I}[G_i; G_j \mid M_{ij}],$$

where the mutual informations are computed with respect to the distribution φ.

Proof sketch We use an induction argument. Let G_k be any interior node, and G_i, G_j the children of G_k. Since M_{ij} is fully contained in some cluster F_l, we have $\psi[M_{ij}] = \varphi[M_{ij}]$. Therefore,

$$
\begin{aligned}
&\boldsymbol{D}[\varphi[G_k] \,\|\, \psi[G_k]] \\
&= \boldsymbol{E}_{\varphi(G_k)}[ln\,(\varphi(G_k)/\varphi(M_{ij})\varphi(G_i \mid M_{ij})\varphi(G_j \mid M_{ij})) \\
&\quad + ln\,(\varphi(M_{ij})\varphi(G_i \mid M_{ij})/\psi(M_{ij})\psi(G_i \mid M_{ij})) \\
&\quad + ln\,(\varphi(M_{ij})\varphi(G_j \mid M_{ij})/\psi(M_{ij})\psi(G_j \mid M_{ij}))] \\
&= \boldsymbol{I}[G_i; G_j \mid M_{ij}] \\
&\quad + \boldsymbol{D}[\varphi(G_i) \,\|\, \psi(G_i)] + \boldsymbol{D}[\varphi(G_j) \,\|\, \psi(G_j)].
\end{aligned}
$$

The claim follows by recursion on the last two terms, noticing that for any cluster F_l, $\boldsymbol{D}[\varphi(F_l) \,\|\, \psi(F_l)] = 0$. ∎

The key to exploiting this decomposition is the following. Recall that $\varphi^{(t+1)}$ is obtained from propagating a distribution $\psi^{(t)}$. The distribution $\psi^{(t)}$ is in the restricted space $\Sigma[\mathcal{F}]$, i.e., it satisfies the independence assumptions defined by $\mathcal{F}$. Intuitively, there is a limit to the amount of dependencies introduced by a factored stochastic transition on a factored distribution. This should result in bounds on each of the mutual information terms that appear in the theorem. Our analysis will make this idea formal.

It turns out that the notion of mixing rate, which captures the extent to which information is retained from a set of variables X to a set of variables Y', can also be viewed as representing the extent to which a set of variables influences another. In particular, we are interested in the extent to which one group G_i at time t influences another group G_j at time t. We therefore define

$$\gamma_{ij} \triangleq \gamma[(G_i \setminus M_{ij}) \to (G'_j \setminus M'_{ij})].$$

(As usual, the dependence on other parents of G'_j is implicit.)

Theorem 3 shows that the projection error is decomposed as a sum of conditional mutual informations — one term for each pair of siblings G_i, G_j. In the rest of the paper, we shall derive bounds on those mutual information terms.

Weak interaction

We begin with analyzing the error for two groups that our approximation takes to be completely independent, i.e., groups contained in different connected components of the cluster forest. Intuitively, we would expect the error in this case to depend on the extent to which these two groups interact. In other words, if our system is such that the variables in these two groups interact only weakly, the error incurred by assuming them to be independent is small.

We first state a central lemma for this kind of analysis.

Lemma 4 *Let U, V, W, X, Y, Z be sets of random variables with the following dependency structure:*

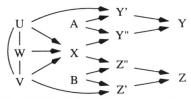

Then, writing γ_{UY} for $\gamma[U \to Y]$, etc.,

$$
\begin{aligned}
\boldsymbol{I}[Y; Z \mid W] &\leq (1 - \gamma_{UY}) \cdot (1 - \gamma_{VZ}) \cdot \boldsymbol{I}[U; V \mid W] \\
&\quad + 3 \cdot \ln |\mathrm{dom}\, X| \cdot (1 - \min[\gamma_{XY}, \gamma_{XZ}])
\end{aligned}
$$

Proof sketch We pose $\gamma_Y = \gamma[(U, X) \to Y]$ and $\gamma_Z = \gamma[(V, X) \to Z]$.

To start with, we observe that we can decompose the given system as

Each of Y' and Y'' either copies the value of its parent, or enters a special "contraction state" c, depending on the value of A. The domain of A has four values, respectively triggering the contraction for Y', Y'', both, or none. These values are distributed with probabilities $(\gamma_{UY} - \gamma_Y), (\gamma_{XY} - \gamma_Y), \gamma_Y, (1 - \gamma_{UY} - \gamma_{XY} + \gamma_Y)$ respectively. We can show that all of these quantities are non-negative, so that they form a well-defined distribution.

It suffices to show that: (i) One can construct the conditional probabilities of Y and Z in the new network so as to emulate the joint distribution specified by the original network. (ii) The mutual information $\boldsymbol{I}[Y; Z \mid W]$ computed in the new network is bounded as claimed. We defer details to a longer version of this paper. ∎

We are now ready to prove our theorem.

Theorem 5 *Let $\mathcal{F}$ and $\mathcal{G}$ be a cluster forest and group hierarchy, and G_i and G_j two siblings contained in different connected components of $\mathcal{F}$. Let $\bar{\mu}$ be a distribution factored according to $\mathcal{F}$. Let φ be obtained from $\bar{\mu}$ by propagation through the given transition model. Then, with respect to φ,*

$$
\boldsymbol{I}[G_i'; G_j'] \leq 3 \cdot \ln |\mathrm{dom}\, (G_i \cup G_j)| \cdot (1 - \min[\gamma_{ij}, \gamma_{ji}]).
$$

Proof sketch We consider the transition model involving G_i and G_j at t and $t + 1$. The idea is to transform it into an equivalent model by introducing a "mediator" variable X through which the cross-interaction between G_i and G_j is funneled.

Specifically, X simply copies the values of G_i and G_j, and the new edges from X to G_i' and G_j' reproduce the previous cross-dependences $G_i \to G_j'$ and $G_j \to G_i'$. Notice that γ_{Xi} and γ_{Xj} in the new model are respectively equal to γ_{ji} and γ_{ij} in the original one. Then, an application of Lemma 4 to the new structure gives

$$
\begin{aligned}
\boldsymbol{I}[G_i'&; G_j'] \\
&\leq 3 \cdot (1 - \min[\gamma_{Xi}, \gamma_{Xj}]) \cdot \ln |\mathrm{dom}\, X| + c \cdot \boldsymbol{I}[G_i; G_j] \\
&= 3 \cdot (1 - \min[\gamma_{Xi}, \gamma_{Xj}]) \cdot \ln |\mathrm{dom}\, (G_i \cup G_j)|,
\end{aligned}
$$

where we have used the fact that $\boldsymbol{I}[G_i; G_j] = 0$ since G_i and G_j are independent in the belief state representation at time t. ∎

Note that, as G_i and G_j are disjoint, we have $M_{ij} = \emptyset$. Thus, the term $\boldsymbol{I}[G_i'; G_j']$ bounded in this theorem is precisely the term $\boldsymbol{I}[G_i; G_j \mid M_{ij}]$ that appears in Theorem 3. In other words, Theorem 5 gives us a bound on the error introduced by two specific groups G_i', G_j'. To get the overall bound on the error, we simply add the contributions of all pairs of siblings.

The bound for G_i' and G_j' closely matches our intuition regarding their "strength of interaction." To understand this, consider the term γ_{YX} for two groups X and Y that are "weakly interacting". In this case, we believe that Y is not a strong influence on X, i.e., $\boldsymbol{P}[X' \mid x, y_1]$ is close to $\boldsymbol{P}[X' \mid x, y_2]$ for any x, y_1, and y_2. But in this case, $\sum_{x'} \min[\boldsymbol{P}[x' \mid x, y_1], \boldsymbol{P}[x' \mid x, y_2]]$ is close to one for all x, y_1, y_2, and hence so is γ_{YX}. If both γ_{ij} and γ_{ji} are close to one, the error bound in our analysis will be close to zero.

To illustrate, consider the process composed of a number of cars on a highway. In normal circumstances, the cars interact weakly with each other, so we want to place each car in a separate cluster F_i in our belief state representation. We can use the above theorem to justify this, as the weak interaction between the cars will ensure that each $\gamma_{ij} \simeq 1$ in any group hierarchy $\mathcal{G}$ that we choose. In fact, since the choice of $\mathcal{G}$ is arbitrary given a clustering $\mathcal{F}$, we can choose $\mathcal{G}$ to maximize the various γ_{ij}. In our highway example, it is reasonable to assume that only neighboring cars may experience any kind of (weak) interaction. We can maximize γ_{ij} by minimizing the number of neighboring cars belonging to any two siblings G_i and G_j. This is very intuitive: we simply group cars according to their proximity.

Conditional weak interaction

The previous section analyzed the error of approximating clusters of variables as completely independent. However, as we show experimentally in BK, we can sometimes obtain much lower errors by approximating distributions (or parts of them) as *conditionally independent*. For example, it may be much more reasonable to have an approximate belief states where the states of individual cars are conditionally independent given the overall traffic on the road. In this case, our cluster forest would contain a cluster for each vehicle, which also contains the *Traffic* random variable. In this case, the clusters are overlapping, which will cause some siblings to overlap in $\mathcal{G}$. We therefore analyze the error bound for two groups that need not be disjoint.

The *conditional entropy* of X given Y, denoted $H[X \mid Y]$, is defined as

$$H[X \mid Y] \triangleq E_Y E_{X|Y} \left[\ln \frac{1}{P[X \mid Y]} \right].$$

Lemma 6 *Let W, X, Y, Z four sets of random variables with an arbitrary dependency structure. Then,*

$$|I[Y; Z \mid X] - I[Y; Z \mid W]| \le H[X \mid W] + H[W \mid X].$$

Theorem 7 *Let $\mathcal{F}$ be a cluster forest, $\mathcal{G}$ a cluster hierarchy, and G_i and G_j two siblings in $\mathcal{G}$. Let $\bar{\mu}$ and φ be defined as in Theorem 5. Then, with respect to φ, we have*

$$
\begin{aligned}
& I[G_i'; G_j' \mid M_{ij}'] \\
& \le \ 3 \cdot \ln |\text{dom} \left(G_{i \setminus j} \cup G_{j \setminus i} \right)| \cdot (1 - \min[\gamma_{ij}, \gamma_{ji}]) \\
& \quad + H[M_{ij} \mid M_{ij}'] + H[M_{ij}' \mid M_{ij}].
\end{aligned}
$$

Proof sketch The proof is based on a similar construction as in Theorem 5, introducing a mediator variable X to capture the cross-interactions between $G_{i \setminus j}$ and $G_{j \setminus i}$. Using Lemma 4, we obtain

$$
\begin{aligned}
& I[G_i'; G_j' \mid M_{ij}] \\
& \le \ 3 \cdot \ln |\text{dom} \left(G_{i \setminus j} \cup G_{j \setminus i} \right)| \cdot (1 - \min[\gamma_{ij}, \gamma_{ji}]).
\end{aligned}
$$

Applying Lemma 6, we get

$$
\begin{aligned}
I[G_i'; G_j' \mid M_{ij}'] \ \le \ & I[G_i'; G_j' \mid M_{ij}] \\
& + H[M_{ij} \mid M_{ij}'] + H[M_{ij}' \mid M_{ij}],
\end{aligned}
$$

so the claim follows. ∎

Let us examine the result of the theorem from an intuitive standpoint. The first term was already present in Theorem 5 and represents the amount of correlation introduced by the weak interaction. The second term is new: it represents the amount by which conditioning on M_{ij}' instead of M_{ij} might change the mutual information. Intuitively, if M_{ij}' is a faithful (deterministic) copy of M_{ij}, then conditioning on one or the other should not make any difference. In this case, indeed, we would have both conditional entropies equal to zero. This behavior generalizes to more realistic situations, where M_{ij} does evolve over time, but more slowly than the

two clusters it separates. More precisely, let us assume that G_i and G_j interact only through M_{ij}, and that M_{ij} tends to preserve its value from one step to the next. (In particular, this implies that all external influences on M_{ij} are weak.)

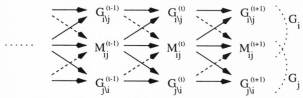

The processes G_i and G_j are conditionally independent given the entire sequence $M_{ij}^{(\cdot)}$. Assuming that $G_{i \setminus j}$ and $G_{j \setminus i}$ are mixing fast enough, $G_i^{(t)}$ and $G_j^{(t)}$ will be approximately independent given the values of $M_{ij}^{(\cdot)}$ in a vincinity of t. If M_{ij} evolves slowly (implying $H[M_{ij} \mid M_{ij}'] \simeq 0$, $H[M_{ij}' \mid M_{ij}] \simeq 0$), these values of $M_{ij}^{(\cdot)}$ will be approximately determined by the knowledge of $M_{ij}^{(t)}$, so that $G_i^{(t)}$ and $G_j^{(t)}$ are approximately independent given the single point $M_{ij}^{(t)}$. The same analysis holds if $G_{i \setminus j}$ and $G_{j \setminus i}$ do interact directly, but only weakly.

In the real world, we find many examples of processes whose primary interaction is via some more slowly evolving process. Our freeway example is a typical one: we can refine the model of the previous section if we consider external influences that affect some or all cars in mostly the same way, such as road work or the weather. Different stocks on the stock market is another: the price trend of different stocks is clearly correlated, but they are reasonably modeled as conditionally independent given the current market trends. In both cases, the conditioning variables fluctuate more slowly than the dependent subprocesses. In these examples, our model will contain a number of clusters $F_1, \ldots, F_k$ that all contain some variable W, which will therefore appear in the M_{ij} at one or more levels in the group hierarchy.

Sparse interaction

As we have argued, many systems are composed of interacting processes. However, the assumption of weak interaction throughout the entire lifetime of the system is an idealization. In many domains, we may have processes that interact weakly (if at all) most of the time, but may have an occasional strong interaction. In our example of cars on a freeway, the interaction of one car with another is very weak most of the time. However, there are momentary situations when the interaction becomes quite strong, e.g., if one car gets too close to another, or if one wants to change lanes into a position occupied by the other.

The interaction structure of the system is very different in these two situations. So long as the processes interact weakly, an approximation of the belief state as independent components is a very reasonable one. However, when a strong interaction occurs, this approximation incurs a large error. A naive solution would have us correlate the belief states of any two processes that can interact strongly. Unfortunately, in many systems, this solution greatly reduces our ability to select clusters of small sizes and achieve computational efficiency.

An alternative solution is to target our approximation to the context. When two processes have a momentary strong interaction, we should avoid decoupling them in the belief state. In fact, we must take care. The strong correlation between the two processes usually lasts for more than one time slice. But as the system evolves, and the two processes return to their standard weak interaction, the correlation decays. After some amount of time, we will be able to return to an approximation that decouples the states of these two processes.

We now proceed to extend both the inference algorithm and the analysis to account for this type of *sparse interaction*. First, we define the notion of sparse interaction. The idea is to consider two separate transition models, which will be applicable respectively in the standard and exceptional mode of interaction. Concretely, if X and Y interact sparsely, we define a binary random variable B_{XY} which will be a parent of both X' and Y', and will select their mode of interaction. We will speak of the *weak interaction model* and the *strong interaction model* to designate the portions of the conditional probability distributions of X' and Y' that are relevant to either value of B_{XY}.

The extended algorithm uses a different cluster forest $\mathcal{F}^{(t)}$ at each time slice t. If at time t the algorithm detects a strong interaction between the variables in two clusters, it couples them for some length of time. In fact, it couples all the variables in the two siblings which contained either of the two clusters. More precisely, at each time t, we maintain a set $C^{(t)} \subseteq R$ of *couplings* — pairs (i, j) of siblings. At time t, we define a new cluster forest $\mathcal{F}^{(t)}$, derived from the basic cluster forest $\mathcal{F}$. Each cluster $F_k^{(t)}$ in $\mathcal{F}^{(t)}$ is either a cluster of $\mathcal{F}$, or obtained by merging two siblings G_i, G_j. In other terms, each cluster F_l in $\mathcal{F}$ is assigned to some cluster $F_k^{(t)}$, in which case $F_l \subseteq F_k^{(t)}$. We require that if F_l is assigned to $F_k^{(t)}$, $F_l \subseteq G_i$, and $(i, j) \in C^{(t)}$, then $G_i \cup G_j \subseteq F_k^{(t)}$.

Note that, in general, the algorithm might not be able to observe directly the existence of a strong correlation. In some circumstances, there may be certain tests that are reliable indicators of such an event, e.g., a sensor detecting a car signalling a lane change with its blinkers. In other domains, the strong interaction may be due to an action taken by the agent tracking the system; in this case, correlations can be predicted. One general (but expensive) approach for discovering strong interactions is by evaluating the error that would be incurred by taking two clusters to be independent. Here, to simplify the analysis, we assume that strong interactions can be detected. When one occurs, the algorithm couples the two sibling groups involved. If no strong interaction occurs for some number of time slices d, the algorithm decouples them back.

We begin by analyzing the error of this algorithm in the case the groups are disjoint. Let G_i and G_j be two siblings

decoupled at time $t + 1$. What do these groups contribute to the error at time $t + 1$? There are two cases. If G_i and G_j were decoupled at time t, then we assume that their most recent interaction was weak. In this case, the analysis reduces to that of Theorem 5. Otherwise, the groups were coupled at t, and we have chosen this time slice to decouple them. In this case, we have assumed that, for some number of time slices d, these groups have been coupled. For that period of time, no error has been incurred by this pair. We therefore need to estimate the extent to which the strong correlation that occurred d time slices ago has attenuated. Let $\gamma_{ij}^w = \gamma[G_i^{(t)} \to G_j^{(t+1)}]$ be the mixing rate using the conditional probabilities of the weak interaction model.

Theorem 8 *Let G_i and G_j be two disjoint reciprocal groups of clusters in $\mathcal{G}$, and assume that no strong interaction has occured between them since time slice $t - d$.*

1. If G_i and G_j were decoupled at time t, then

$$\boldsymbol{I}[G_i^{(t+1)}; G_j^{(t+1)}] \leq$$
$$3 \cdot \ln |\text{dom}\, (G_i \cup G_j)| \cdot (1 - \min[\gamma_{ij}^w, \gamma_{ji}^w]).$$

2. If G_i and G_j were coupled at time t and have just been decoupled, then

$$\boldsymbol{I}[G_i^{(t+1)}; G_j^{(t+1)}] \leq \ln |\text{dom}\, (G_i \cup G_j)| \cdot$$
$$\left((1 - \gamma_{ii}^w)^d \cdot (1 - \gamma_{jj}^w)^d + \frac{3 \cdot (1 - \min[\gamma_{ij}^w, \gamma_{ji}^w])}{\gamma_{ii}^w + \gamma_{jj}^w - \gamma_{ii}^w \cdot \gamma_{jj}^w} \right).$$

Proof sketch The first case follows from Theorem 5. The general case is obtained by applying Lemma 4 d times, giving

$$\boldsymbol{I}[G_i^{(t+1)}; G_j^{(t+1)}] \leq$$
$$(1 - \gamma_{ii}^w)^d \cdot (1 - \gamma_{jj}^w)^d \cdot \boldsymbol{I}[G_i^{(t-d)}; G_j^{(t-d)}]$$
$$+ 3 \cdot \ln |\text{dom}\, (G_i \cup G_j)| \cdot (1 - \min[\gamma_{ij}^w, \gamma_{ji}^w]) \cdot$$
$$\sum_{k=0}^{d-1} (1 - \gamma_{ii}^w)^k \cdot (1 - \gamma_{jj}^w)^k$$

Note that all the γ's are for the weak interaction model, since no strong interaction has occured since epoch $t - d$. Then, the claim follows from the fact that $\boldsymbol{I}[G_i^{(t-d)}; G_j^{(t-d)}] \leq \ln |\text{dom}\, (G_i \cup G_j)|$ and $\sum_{k=0}^{d-1} x^d \leq 1/(1 - x)$. ∎

Thus, the error induced by decoupling two groups d time slices after a strong correlation decreases exponentially with d. The analysis also tells us how long we need to couple two groups in order to guarantee a bound on the error.

To see how this theorem can be used, let us go back to our highway example, and assume that we observe a strong interaction between two vehicles (such as one cutting in front of the other). Our algorithm would then "couple" the reciprocal groups G_i and G_j to which these vehicles belong, which results in the merging of G_i and G_j (and all their subgroups) for a certain number of time slices, until the correlation induced by the strong correlation has sufficiently decayed that the groups can be decoupled without incurring too much error. Our theorem guarantees that this eventually happens, and gives us an upper bound on the time it takes.

We finally put all of our results together, and state the theorem for models that involve both sparse interactions and overlapping clusters.

Theorem 9 *Let G_i and G_j be two reciprocal groups of clusters in $\mathcal{G}$, and M_{ij} their intersection. Assume that no strong interaction has occured between them since time slice $t - d$. Then*

1. If G_i and G_j were decoupled at time t, then

$$
\boldsymbol{I}[G_i^{(t+1)}; G_j^{(t+1)} \mid M_{ij}^{(t+1)}] \leq
$$
$$
3 \cdot \ln |\text{dom}\,(G_i \cup G_j)| \cdot (1 - \min[\gamma_{ij}^w, \gamma_{ji}^w])
$$
$$
+ \boldsymbol{H}[M_{ij}^{(t)} \mid M_{ij}^{(t+1)}] + \boldsymbol{H}[M_{ij}^{(t+1)} \mid M_{ij}^{(t)}].
$$

2. If G_i and G_j were coupled at time t and have just been decoupled, then $\boldsymbol{I}[G_i^{(t+1)}; G_j^{(t+1)} \mid M_{ij}^{(t+1)}] \leq$

$$
\ln |\text{dom}\,(G_{i\backslash j} \cup G_{j\backslash i})| \cdot (1 - \gamma_{ii}^w)^d \cdot (1 - \gamma_{jj}^w)^d
$$
$$
+ \sum_{k=0}^{d-1} (1 - \gamma_{ii}^w)^k \cdot (1 - \gamma_{jj}^w)^k
$$
$$
\cdot \left(\begin{array}{l} 3 \cdot (1 - \min[\gamma_{ij}^w, \gamma_{ji}^w]) \cdot \ln |\text{dom}\,(G_{i\backslash j} \cup G_{j\backslash i})| \\ + \boldsymbol{H}[M_{ij}^{(t-k)} \mid M_{ij}^{(t-k+1)}] + \boldsymbol{H}[M_{ij}^{(t-k+1)} \mid M_{ij}^{(t-k)}] \end{array} \right)
$$

Discussion and conclusions

Our results show how various system properties, such as weak interaction, conditional weak interaction, and sparse interaction, can be exploited by our inference algorithm. We argue that these properties appear in many real-world systems. Complex systems are almost always hierarchically structured out of subsystems. For example, a freeway system is made up of individual roads, which are composed of many road segments; each segment has several vehicles on it. A computer network has multiple subnets, each with multiple devices, each in turn has several users, running many processes. From a different perspective, one could argue that, regardless of whether complex systems are actually hierarchical, people can deal with them only by decomposing their description into more manageable chunks.

Hierarchical dynamical systems, such as those investigated in (Friedman, Koller, & Pfeffer 1998), are ideally suited for the kind of decomposition provided by the algorithm. Let us consider the interaction structure of such a system. Most of the interaction in the system occurs within subsystems. The lower-level the system, the more tightly it is coupled. Besides this internal interaction, a subsystem usually interacts primarily with its enclosing system. Our results apply exactly to situations such as this. As our results demonstrate, if the interaction between subsystems in a level is weak (or sparse), the correlation it induces can (mostly) be ignored. The correlation induced by the enclosing system is often stronger. However, as Simon states, "the higher-frequency dynamics are associated with the subsystems, the lower-frequency dynamics with the larger systems." This

is precisely the case to which our results for conditionally independent clusters apply. Thus, we can model the variables in the subsystems as conditionally independent given the state of the enclosing system. This decomposition can be extended to lower levels of a hierarchy, resulting in a hierarchical decomposition of the belief state analogous to that of the system.

Finally, in many settings, there may be an occasional strong interaction that crosses tradional boundaries. Our extended algorithm and analysis for sparse interactions are precisely designed to handle such situations.

Our results can also help guide the construction of models that will support effective approximation. For example, the decomposition described above relies on the existence of a slowly-evolving enclosing system that renders its subsystems almost independent. We may therefore wish to introduce such a component deliberately into our model, enabling such a decomposition. For example, we can introduce a variable that corresponds to aggregate properties of the system as a whole, e.g., the amount of overall traffic on the road, or stock market indicators. Such aggregate variables typically evolve very slowly, making them suitable to the type of analysis described above.

In summary, the results we have presented allow us to exploit the architecture of a dynamic system for efficient and accurate approximate inference. They also allow us to design the architecture of the system so as to support such an approximation. We therefore hope that they will help us to reason effectively about the very large complex systems that we encounter in the real world.

Acknowledgements This research was supported by ARO under the MURI program "Integrated Approach to Intelligent Systems", grant number DAAH04-96-1-0341, by DARPA contract DACA76-93-C-0025 under subcontract to Information Extraction and Transport, Inc., and through the generosity of the Powell Foundation and the Sloan Foundation.

References

Aström, K. 1965. Optimal control of Markov decision processes with incomplete state estimation. *J. Math. Anal. Applic.* 10.

Boyen, X., and Koller, D. 1998. Tractable inference for complex stochastic processes. In *Proc. UAI.*

Cover, T., and Thomas, J. 1991. *Elements of Information Theory.* Wiley.

Dean, T., and Kanazawa, K. 1989. A model for reasoning about persistence and causation. *Comp. Int.* 5(3).

Forbes, J.; Huang, T.; Kanazawa, K.; and Russell, S. 1995. The BATmobile: Towards a Bayesian automated taxi. In *Proc. IJCAI.*

Friedman, N.; Koller, D.; and Pfeffer, A. 1998. Structured representation of complex stochastic systems. In *Proc. AAAI.*

Jensen, F.; Lauritzen, S.; and Olesen, K. 1990. Bayesian updating in recursive graphical models by local computations. *Computational Statistical Quarterly* 4.

Kjærulff, U. 1992. A computational scheme for reasoning in dynamic probabilistic networks. In *Proc. UAI.*

Simon, H. 1962. The architecture of complexity. *Proc. Am. Phil. Soc.* 106:467–482.

Estimating Generalization Error Using Out-of-Bag Estimates

Tom Bylander and Dennis Hanzlik

Division of Computer Science
University of Texas at San Antonio
San Antonio, Texas 78249-0667
bylander@cs.utsa.edu

Abstract

We provide a method for estimating the generalization error of a bag using out-of-bag estimates. In bagging, each predictor (single hypothesis) is learned from a bootstrap sample of the training examples; the output of a bag (a set of predictors) on an example is determined by voting. The out-of-bag estimate is based on recording the votes of each predictor on those training examples omitted from its bootstrap sample. Because no additional predictors are generated, the out-of-bag estimate requires considerably less time than 10-fold cross-validation. We address the question of how to use the out-of-bag estimate to estimate generalization error. Our experiments on several datasets show that the out-of-bag estimate and 10-fold cross-validation have very inaccurate (much too optimistic) confidence levels. We can improve the out-of-bag estimate by incorporating a correction.

Introduction

Supervised learning involves finding a hypothesis to correctly classify examples in a domain. If, for example, we wanted to classify mushrooms as edible or poisonous based on relevant characteristics such as color, smell, habitat, etc., we could learn a hypothesis by using mushrooms whose characteristics and classifications are known.

Much work has been done in supervised learning in developing learning algorithms for decision trees, neural networks, Bayesian networks, and other hypothesis spaces. As an improvement on these learning algorithms, work has recently been done using algorithms that combine several "single hypotheses" (called "predictors" from this point onward) into one "aggregate hypothesis." One such algorithm is bagging (bootstrap aggregating) (Breiman 1996a). Bagging involves repeated sampling with replacement to form several bootstrap training sets from the original dataset. Bagging should not be viewed as a competitor to other aggregation algorithms (such as boosting) because bagging can use any learning algorithm to generate predictors.

Over many types of predictor algorithms, bagging has been shown to improve on the accuracy of a single predictor (Breiman 1996a; Dietterich 1998b; Freund & Schapire 1996; Maclin & Opitz 1997; Quinlan 1996). An important issue is determining the generalization error of

a bag (a bagging aggregate hypothesis). Usually, generalization error is estimated by k-fold cross-validation over the dataset (Michie, Spiegelhalter, & Taylor 1994; Weiss & Kulikowski 1991).

There are two potential problems with the cross-validation estimate (Wolpert & Macready 1996). One is the additional computation time. If there are B predictors in the bag, then $10B$ additional predictors must be generated for 10-fold cross-validation. This becomes a serious issue if significant time is needed to generate each predictor, e.g., as in neural networks.

The other is that the cross-validation estimate does not directly evaluate the aggregate hypothesis. None of the $10B$ predictors generated during 10-fold cross-validation become part of the bag (except by coincidence). It is an assumption that the performance of the hypotheses learned from the cross-validation folds will be similar to the performance of the hypothesis learned using the whole dataset (Kearns & Ron 1997).

One solution is to use the predictors in the bag to estimate generalization error (Breiman 1996b; Wolpert & Macready 1996; Tibshirani 1996). Each predictor is generated from a bootstrap sample, which typically omits about 37% of the examples. The *out-of-bag estimate* records the votes of each predictor over the examples omitted from its corresponding bootstrap sample. The aggregation of the votes followed by plurality voting for each example results in an estimate of generalization error.

We performed experiments on 10 two-class datasets. We used ID3 (Quinlan 1986) and C4.5 (Quinlan 1993) to generate predictors. Generalization error is represented by the empirical error of the bag on a separate test set.

In these experiments, the out-of-bag estimate slightly overestimates generalization error on average. 10-fold cross-validation has similar behavior. A two-sample t test (the two samples are the training examples and test examples), for both the out-of-bag estimate and 10-fold cross-validation, has very inaccurate (much too optimistic) confidence levels. In several cases, a supposedly 95% confidence interval corresponds to less than 90% empirically; in one case, less than 75%.

Previous research (Kohavi 1995) has shown that 10-fold cross-validation tends to have a pessimistic bias, i.e., the estimated error rate tends to have a higher expected value than the true error rate. Besides duplicating this finding in the context of bagging, our methodology uses a better statistical test and also studies the confidence intervals of the estimates.

We can improve the out-of-bag estimate by incorporating a correction. If there are B predictors in the bag, then there are B votes for each test example compared to about $0.37B$ out-of-bag votes on average for each training example. We propose two corrections by taking this factor into account.

One correction is based on the voting patterns in the test examples, where a voting pattern is specified by the number of votes for each class, e.g., 29 votes for class A and 21 votes for class B. This correction is not practical for estimating generalization error because the test-example voting-patterns are unknown if all available examples are used for training. However, we gain an understanding of what is needed to calculate a correction.

For a given test example, we can simulate out-of-bag voting by drawing a subsample of the votes on the test examples, i.e., each vote is selected with probability $1/e$. For two-class datasets, we can directly compute two values: the expected value and the variance of the difference between the simulated out-of-bag voting and test error. Using these statistics and an appropriate t test, we obtain acceptable confidence intervals in our experiments.

Our second correction tries to reverse this process. It uses the out-of-bag voting patterns on the training examples to estimate the distribution of B-vote patterns. Based on this estimated distribution, we compute the expected value and variance of the difference between the out-of-bag estimate and B-vote voting. This second correction has a heuristic component because it (roughly) assumes that the B-vote distribution is selected from a a uniform distribution of B-vote distributions. Perhaps for this reason, the second estimate often leads to optimistic confidence levels, though they are better than the uncorrected out-of-bag estimate.

The remainder of this paper is organized as follows. First, we describe the experimental procedure. Next, we provide the results of the experiments and their implications. Finally, we conclude with a summary and future research issues.

Experimental Procedure

We selected a number of two-class datasets from the UCI repository and the C4.5 distribution (certain quantities are easier to compute precisely with two-class datasets). Several of these datasets were used extensively to develop the generalization error estimates. The other datasets (see the Appendix) were used for the experiments presented in this paper.

We used two learning algorithms. One algorithm was C4.5 using default parameters (Quinlan 1993). We also used the ID3 decision-tree learning algorithm with no pruning (Quinlan 1986). In our version of ID3, missing values are handled by creating an extra branch from each internal node to represent the case of a missing value. If there are no examples for a leaf node, it is given a classification equal to the most common class of its parent.

For this paper, the following procedure for experimenting with the bagging method was used:

1. The data set is randomly divided in half to create a training set S and a test set T.

2. A bootstrap sample S_1^* is selected from S and a predictor is created from S_1^* using a learning algorithm. This is repeated B times to create B predictors, $h_1, \ldots, h_B$, from the B bootstrap samples $S_1^*, \ldots, S_B^*$.

3. The out-of-bag estimate is determined from the training set S by allowing each predictor h_i to vote only on the examples $S - S_i^*$, i.e., the training examples omitted from the ith bootstrap sample. Then the predicted class of each example is determined by a plurality vote with ties broken in favor of the most common class in S. On average, about 37% of the examples are excluded from each bootstrap sample, so on average, about 37% of the predictors vote on each training example.

4. Test error is determined from the test set T by a plurality vote on each example over the B predictors. Ties are broken in favor of the most common class in S. Test error is considered to be an accurate estimate of generalization error.[1]

5. The above steps 1–4 are repeated 1000 times for each data set, learning algorithm, and value for B (we used $B = 50$). Averages and standard deviations for the out-of-bag estimate, test error, and the paired difference were computed. 1000 trials were used for two reasons. Any substantial difference in the averages ought to become statistically significant after 1000 trials. Also, we performed a two-sample t test on each trial with the anticipation of falling within the calculated 95% confidence interval at least 95% of the time, i.e., to determine if the confidence level of the test can be trusted.

Other Generalization Error Estimates

Besides the out-of-bag estimate, we also evaluated 10-fold cross-validation and two different corrections to the out-of-bag estimate.

10-Fold Cross-Validation For $B = 50$, we computed a 10-fold cross-validation estimate of generalization error. Cross validation has been widely accepted as a reliable method for calculating generalization accuracy (Michie, Spiegelhalter, & Taylor 1994; Weiss & Kulikowski 1991), and experiments have shown that cross validation is relatively unbiased (less biased than bootstrap sampling) (Efron & Tibshirani 1993). However, there is some evidence that 10-fold cross-validation has high type I error for comparing learning algorithms (Dietterich 1998a).

In order to compute the cross-validation estimate, a step is inserted between steps 4 and 5 in the procedure described

---

[1]This assumes that the examples in the dataset are independently drawn from some probability distribution, and that the probability mass of the training set S is near 0%. These assumptions are not true for at least the monks datasets. In this case, the generalization error estimates can be treated as estimates of error on examples outside of the training set.

above. In this new step, the training set S is partitioned into 10 cross-validation sets or folds of nearly equal size. Then for each cross-validation fold F_i, the examples $S - F_i$ are used with bagging to form B predictors. The resulting bag is used to classify the examples in F_i and produce an error measure. The average and variance are computed from the 10 iterations.

Test Error Correction In the out-of-bag estimate, there are about $0.37B$ out-of-bag votes on average for each training example. The test error is determined from B votes for each test example, so it might be expected that the out-of-bag voting would be inaccurate.

A "test error correction" is determined as follows. Given the voting patterns on the test examples, we can simulate out-of-bag voting by choosing each vote with probability $1/e$. This is expected to be a good simulation of the out-of-bag estimate because test examples and training examples should be interchangeable as far as out-of-bag voting is concerned. We did not perform the simulation, but instead directly computed the expected value of the out-of-bag simulation, using this value as the sample mean in statistical tests. For sample variance, we treated the mean as if it was the result of n Bernoulli trials, where n is the number of test examples. The second appendix describes the calculations in more detail.

Out-of-Bag Correction A serious disadvantage of the test error correction is its dependence on the voting on the test examples. We would like to estimate generalization error purely from the training examples so that all available examples can be used for training. So one might alternatively compute an "out-of-bag correction" based on the out-of-bag voting patterns by simulating B-vote patterns from the out-of-bag voting patterns. The difficulty here is that determining $P(E_B \mid E_O)$, where E_B and E_O are respectively events of some B-vote pattern and out-of-bag voting pattern, depends on the distribution of B-vote patterns.

We heuristically guess the distribution of B-vote patterns as follows. Two different distributions are calculated for the two classes. Consider one of the classes and the training examples with that class as their label. Let $\mathcal{U}$ be a probability distribution in which all B-vote patterns are equally likely, e.g., the pattern of 30 votes for class A and 20 votes for class B is as likely as 15 votes for class A and 35 votes for class B. We determine $P_{\mathcal{U}}(E_B \mid E_O)$ for each training example, sum up the probabilities for each B-vote pattern, and normalize them so they sum to 1; these are used to define a probability distribution $\mathcal{D}$ over the B-vote patterns. This distribution is adjusted to better account for the number of out-of-bag errors. Then we determine $P_{\mathcal{D}}(E_B \mid E_O)$ for each training example and compute the expected value of the simulated test error.

The two expected values from the two different distributions are combined and used as sample mean in statistical tests. For sample variance, we treated the mean as if it was the result of n Bernoulli trials, where n is the number of training examples. The second appendix describes the calculations in more detail.

Statistical Tests

The following statistical tests were employed to compare the results of different experiments over the 1000 trials. In our notation, μ_i, $\overline{X_i}$, and s_i^2 are respectively the expected value, the sample average, and sample variance over n_i samples.

A paired difference t test (paired comparison of means) was performed over 1000 pairs to compare the four different estimates of generalization error with test error. This test evaluates the hypothesis that the average estimate of generalization error has the same expected value as the average test error. To pass this test with a 5% significance level, the magnitude of the t value should be no more than 1.962. t is computed by:

$$t = \frac{\overline{X_1}}{\sqrt{s_1^2/n_1}} \tag{1}$$

where $n_1 = 1000$ in our experiments

Two different t tests (unpaired comparison of means) was performed on each trial to determine whether the generalization error estimate on that trial was significantly different (5% level) from the test error on that trial. That is, for each trial, we evaluate the hypothesis that the generalization error estimate has the same expected value as the test error. Because this hypothesis is tested for each of 1000 trials, we can count the number of trials that fail the test and see if the number of failures is about 5% (or less). This would imply that a 95% confidence interval according to the test appears to correspond to a 95% confidence interval in reality. For a binomial distribution with probability of success $p = .95$, the probability of 939 successes or more (61 failures or less) is about 95%.

The number of failures should be interpreted cautiously in our experiments. Simply splitting the file into a training set and test set generally results in a negative correlation between the error estimates and the test error. This appears to be because the "bad" examples might not be proportionally distributed between the two sets, which causes the error estimate and the test error to go in opposite directions.

For the out-of-bag estimate, the test correction, and the out-of-bag correction, we used the standard two-sample t test assuming equal variances (Cohen 1995; Snedecor & Cochran 1980). To test the hypothesis $\mu_1 = \mu_2$, we compute

$$s_{pooled}^2 = \frac{(n_1 - 1)s_1^2 + (n_2 - 1)s_2^2}{n_1 + n_2 - 2} \tag{2}$$

$$t = \frac{\overline{X_1} - \overline{X_2}}{\sqrt{s_{pooled}^2(1/n_1 + 1/n_2)}} \tag{3}$$

and compare t against the critical value for $n_1 + n_2 - 2$ degrees of freedom. Here, n_1 and n_2 are the number of examples in the training set and test set, respectively.

For 10-fold cross-validation, we used a two-sample t test allowing for unequal variances (Snedecor & Cochran 1980). This is because the variance over $n_1 = 10$ folds will be much different from the variance over n_2 test examples. To test the hypothesis $\mu_1 = \mu_2$, we compute

$$a_i = \frac{s_i^2}{n_i}, \qquad v_i = n_i - 1 \qquad (4)$$

$$t = \frac{\overline{X_1} - \overline{X_2}}{\sqrt{a_1 + a_2}} \qquad (5)$$

$$v = \frac{(a_1 + a_2)^2}{a_1^2/v_1 + a_2^2/v_2} \qquad (6)$$

and compare t against the critical value for $\lfloor v \rfloor$ degrees of freedom. Here, n_1 and n_2 are the number of examples in the training set and test set, respectively.

Justification for The Two-Sample t Tests

An informal survey of several statistics texts indicated a variety of ways to estimate the degrees of freedom v for a two-sample t test with unequal variances. A common, but cautious, approach is to set v to the minimum of v_1 and v_2. However, this would put the uncorrected out-of-bag estimate at a disadvantage because it uses the more stringent two-sample t test assuming equal variances. The calculation of v by Equation (6) appears to have some acceptance as a better approximation.

It is unclear what sample variance should be used for the test correction and out-of-bag correction. Our choice is in some sense "fair" because it ensures that the size of the confidence interval will be similar to that used to the out-of-bag estimate. However, one might derive a sample variance for the test correction from the probabilities derived for each test example (likewise for the out-of-bag correction and each training example). We tried this, but it fails badly empirically because it leads to an artificially small variance. We believe the reason is that incorporating the corrections corresponds to adding more variance rather than reducing variance. In particular, our results suggest that additional variance should be added for the out-of-bag correction, but this would give the correction an apparently "unfair" advantage.

Results

Bagging Estimate

Table 1 shows the statistics that were collected for the 10 data sets using $B = 50$ predictors. The first column gives the abbreviations for the datasets (see the Appendix), and the second column gives the test error percentage. The next three columns compares the out-of-bag estimate to test error: the percent difference between the averages, the t value from the paired-difference t test over 1000 pairs, and the number of failures for 1000 applications of the two-sample t test at 5% significance. The last three columns provide the same information comparing 10-fold cross-validation with the out-of-bag estimate.

The table shows that both the out-of-bag estimate and 10-fold cross-validation can be expected to slightly overestimate test error. On average, the out-of-bag estimate differed from test error by 0.52% on average, and 10-fold

Data	Test	OOB − Test Error			CV − Test Error		
Set	Error	Diff.	t	Fails	Diff.	t	Fails
BA	27.55	0.88	6.20	111	0.31	1.99	112
CR	16.24	0.43	4.33	72	0.27	2.76	77
FL	20.52	0.07	0.85	78	0.15	1.69	82
IO	8.18	0.46	4.59	61	0.26	2.60	68
M1	1.77	0.78	13.03	231	1.02	15.28	115
M2	51.93	−0.90	−5.40	79	−1.39	−8.42	93
M3	0.00	0.004	2.31	0	0.014	3.77	0
PI	24.74	0.71	6.96	57	0.22	2.15	72
PR	17.84	1.70	5.59	119	1.01	3.31	111
SO	22.81	1.05	5.17	82	0.64	3.21	63
Average		0.52	4.36	89	0.25	2.83	79

Table 1: Results for ID3, $B = 50$: Out-of-Bag Estimate and 10-Fold Cross-Validation

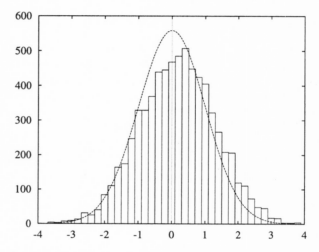

Figure 1: Histogram of t Values Comparing the Out-of-Bag Estimate to Test Error

cross-validation differed by 0.25%. The paired-difference t test showed a significant difference (5% level, $|t| > 1.962$) between the generalization error estimates and test error for all the datasets except FL.

The results of the two-sample t test also show that the out-of-bag estimate and 10-fold cross-validation yield similar performance. For most of the datasets, the two-sample t test has an overoptimistic confidence level (more than 61 failures). That is, a 95% confidence interval according to the test does not correspond to a 95% confidence interval for either the out-of-bag estimate or 10-fold cross-validation. On average, around 8% to 9% of the trials fail the test, with especially poor performance on the BA, M1, and PR datasets (over 100 fails each).

Figure 1 displays a histogram of the t values for 7 of the datasets (excluding M1, M2, and M3 because of extreme error rates). The normal density function is superimposed. It can be seen that the histogram has a normal-like shape, but flatter and skewed to the right (corresponding to where test error is overestimated).

Data Set	OOB − Test Error − Test Error Corr.			OOB − Test Error − OOB Correction		
	Diff.	t	Fails	Diff.	t	Fails
BA	−0.02	−0.14	57	−0.19	−1.34	97
CR	0.06	0.59	61	−0.05	−0.55	71
FL	0.02	0.19	63	−0.04	−0.46	85
IO	0.05	0.57	43	−0.01	−0.13	54
M1	0.07	1.21	52	0.05	0.80	115
M2	−0.05	−0.31	75	−0.24	−1.38	91
M3	0.003	1.81	0	0.003	2.39	0
PI	0.16	1.64	42	−0.06	−0.61	50
PR	0.06	0.23	61	0.10	0.32	113
SO	0.05	0.27	46	−0.32	−1.62	73
Avg.	0.04	0.61	50	−0.08	−0.26	75

Table 2: Results for ID3, $B = 50$: Corrections to the Out-of-Bag Estimate

Corrections to the Out-of-Bag Estimate

Table 2 shows the statistics that were collected for the 10 data sets using the corrections to the out-of-bag estimate. The first column gives the abbreviations for the datasets (see the Appendix). The next three columns compare the out-of-bag estimate to the test error and the test error correction: the percent difference between the averages, the t value from the paired-difference t test over 1000 pairs, and the number of passes for 1000 applications of a multiple-sample t test at 5% significance. The last three columns provide the same information comparing the out-of-bag estimate to the test error and the out-of-bag correction.

Table 2 shows that both corrections lead to better estimates of generalization error. The test error correction differed from by 0.04% on average, and so, comes very close to an unbiased estimate of generalization error. The paired-difference t test shows no significant difference (5% level, $|t| > 1.962$) on any of the datasets, though the test error is still overestimated on 8 of the 10 datasets. The out-of-bag correction is almost as good according to the paired-difference t test, with an average difference of −0.08% and with a significant difference on only one of the 10 datasets, but is better than the uncorrected out-of-bag estimate and 10-fold cross-validation (Table 1).

The results of the two-sample t test also show that the test error correction has excellent performance and is better than the out-of-bag correction, which in turn is slightly better than the uncorrected out-of-bag estimate and 10-fold cross-validation. This t test with the test error correction empirically provides a much more acceptable confidence level; there were more than 61 failures only 2 of the datasets. The t test with the out-of-bag correction is less acceptable with more than 61 failures on 7 of the 10 datasets. The slightly lower average compared to the out-of-bag and 10-fold cross-validation estimates is encouraging, but not statistically significant.

	OOB	10CV	TEC	OOBC
Rejections Paired t	7	6	0	2
Avg. Number of Fails	110	96	55	99

Table 3: Results for C4.5, $B = 50$: Generalization Error Estimates

Additional Results

For C4.5 and $B = 50$, we obtained results for all four generalization error estimates, summarized in Table 3. The columns correspond to the difference estimates (out-of-bag estimate, 10-fold cross-validation, test error correction, out-of-bag correction). The first row shows the number of datasets in which the paired difference t shows that the generalization error estimate is biased, i.e., rejects the hypothesis that the average estimate of generalization error has the same expected value as the average test error. The second row shows the average number of failures using the two-sample t test. Failure means rejecting the hypothesis that the generalization error estimate has the same expected value as test error on that trial.

It can be seen that the test correction again clearly outperforms the other estimates. Compared to the out-of-bag and 10-fold cross-validation estimates, the out-of-bag correction again has less bias based on the number of paired-t rejections, but has similar performance on the 2-sample t test. In the detailed results (not shown), by far the worse performance was by the out-of-bag estimate, 10-fold cross-validation, and out-of-bag correction on the M1 dataset (292, 273, and 202 fails, respectively). The out-of-bag correction also performed badly on the M1 and PR datasets (147 and 151 fails, respectively, but still better than OOB and 10CV). The test error correction had 61 or fewer failures on 8 of the datasets, with the worse performance on the PR dataset (93 fails).

Conclusion

With the use of any learning algorithm, it is important to use as many examples as possible for training the hypothesis (or hypotheses) from a dataset. It is also important to determine a good estimate of generalization error so that we can have confidence that a good hypothesis has been learned. Our methodology statistically compares an estimate of generalization error determined from a training set to the empirical error on a separate test set.

Cross-validation is one way of estimating generalization error, while using all of the examples for training, but our experiments have shown that it is biased and can provide inaccurate confidence interval estimates of generalization error. When bagging is used, the out-of-bag estimate can be to estimate generalization error, and it also uses all examples that are available. Unfortunately, the out-of-bag estimate is also biased and leads to similarly inaccurate confidence intervals.

We have developed corrections that improve the out-of-bag estimate and outperform 10-fold cross-validation. A test error correction, i.e., based on the voting patterns on the test examples, empirically provides a nearly unbiased estimate of generalization error and leads to good confidence intervals. However, this correction is not practical because it cannot be applied until the bag is evaluated on examples outside of the training set.

We also developed an out-of-bag correction, i.e., based on the voting patterns on the training examples. This correction makes an assumption about the distribution of domains, and so, must be regarded as heuristic. Perhaps as a result, this correction is not as good as the previous correction. The out-of-bag correction is relatively unbiased compared to 10-fold cross-validation and an uncorrected out-of-bag estimate, but does not significantly improve the accuracy of the confidence intervals.

We conclude that 10-fold cross-validation and the uncorrected out-of-bag estimate should be cautiously used for generalization error estimates because they can result in confidence levels that are much too high. We recommend the out-of-bag estimate with a correction based on the voting patterns on the training examples. The corrected out-of-bag estimate uses all the data, is unbiased, and avoids the additional time needed for 10-fold cross-validation; however, it still often leads to inflated confidence levels. Further research is needed to develop generalization error estimates with confidence intervals that can be fully trusted.

Acknowledgments

This research was funded in part by Texas Higher Education Coordinating Board grant ARP-225. We thank the anonymous reviewers for their comments.

Appendix: Datasets

For each dataset, we list our abbreviation, the number of examples, the number of attributes, and a brief description. The datasets come from the Irvine dataset (Blake, Keogh, & Merz 1998) or the C4.5 distribution (Quinlan 1993). We did not consider larger datasets because of the time required to perform bagging and 10-fold classification multiple times.

BA, 550, 35. The UCI cylinder bands dataset.

CR, 690, 15. The C4.5 credit card applications dataset.

FL, 1066, 10. The UCI solar flare dataset. This was changed to a two-class dataset: any flare activity vs. no flare activity.

IO, 351, 34. The UCI ionosphere dataset.

M1, 432, 6. The C4.5 monk 1 dataset.

M2, 432, 6. The C4.5 monk 2 dataset.

M3, 432, 6. The C4.5 monk 3 dataset. The dataset in the C4.5 distribution has no classification noise.

PI, 768, 8. The UCI Pima Indians diabetes dataset.

PR, 106, 57. The UCI promoter gene sequence dataset.

SO, 208, 60. The UCI sonar signals dataset.

Appendix: Deriving the Corrections

For a given trial with a two-class dataset, designate one class to be the majority class, and let the other class be the minority class. The majority class is determined using the training set. Assume that B predictors are in the bag.

For a given example, let $E_B(x, y)$ be the event of x votes for the majority class and y votes for the minority class, where $x + y = B$. Let $E_O(u, v)$ be the event of u votes for the majority class and v votes for the minority class, where the votes are a subsample of the B votes, where each vote is independently selected to be in the subsample with probability $1/e$. That is, we treat out-of-bag voting as if we were taking a subsample of B votes on that example. We call this "out-of-bag sampling." A probability distribution is specified by assigned priors to $P(E_B(x, y))$.

We note that:

$$P(E_O(u, v) \mid E_B(x, y))$$
$$= \quad b(u, x, 1/e) b(v, y, 1/e) \qquad (7)$$

where $b(k, n, p)$ is the probability of k successes in n i.i.d. Bernouilli trials, each with probability of success $1/e$. That is, $E_O(u, v)$ means that u of the x votes for the majority class were chosen, and v of the y votes for the minority class were chosen.

Test Error Correction

For test example i, let x be the number of votes for the majority class, let y be the number of votes for the minority class, and let $l(i)$ be the example's label, with a label of 1 corresponding to the majority class. Here, $x + y = B$.

We can then determine the probability that out-of-bag sampling favors the majority class or the minority class:

$$p_1(i) = \sum_{u \geq v} P(E_O(u, v) \mid E_B(x, y))$$

$$p_0(i) = \sum_{u < v} P(E_O(u, v) \mid E_B(x, y))$$

and the expected error by out-of-bag sampling from the B votes.

$$\mu(i) = \begin{cases} p_1(i) & \text{if } x < y \wedge l(i) = 0 \\ 1 - p_1(i) & \text{if } x < y \wedge l(i) = 1 \\ p_0(i) & \text{if } x \geq y \wedge l(i) = 1 \\ 1 - p_0(i) & \text{if } x \geq y \wedge l(i) = 0 \end{cases}$$

Over n test examples, we obtain a sample mean and sample variance:

$$\mu = \frac{\sum_{i=1}^{n} \mu(i)}{n}$$

$$s^2 = \frac{n(\mu - \mu^2)}{n - 1}$$

μ and s^2 are the values used in our two-sample t test. The sample variance is based on treating μ as the sample mean of n Bernoulli trials.

Out-of-Bag Correction

For training example i, let u be the number of votes for the majority class, and let v be the number of votes for the minority class. Here, $u + v$ on average will be about B/e. The out-of-bag correction is based on estimating the distribution of $E_B(x, y)$ based on the out-of-bag votes. This is done by pretending that the out-of-bag voting was really out-of-bag sampling from B votes and assuming that each $E_B(x,y)$ is equally likely. We actually estimate two different distributions: one for when the label is the majority class, and the other for the minority class. Consider, then, those n training examples that have a majority class label.

Define $P_\mathcal{U}(E_B(x,y)) = 1/(B+1)$ for $x \in \{0,1,\ldots,B\}$ and $y = B - x$. We can then derive:

$$P_\mathcal{U}(E_B(x,y) \mid E_O(u,v))$$
$$= \frac{P_\mathcal{U}(E_O(u,v) \mid E_B(x,y)) P_\mathcal{U}(E_B(x,y))}{P_\mathcal{U}(E_O(u,v))}$$
$$\sim P_\mathcal{U}(E_O(u,v) \mid E_B(x,y))$$

because $P_\mathcal{U}(E_B(x,y))$ is a constant and the denominator is a normalizing term. Equation (7) gives the calculations.

We define an intermediate probability distribution $\mathcal{I}$:

$$P_\mathcal{I}(E_B(x,y)) = \theta \sum_{i=1}^{n} P_\mathcal{U}(E_B(x,y) \mid E_O(u,v))$$

setting θ so that $1 = \sum_{j=0}^{B} P_\mathcal{I}(E_B(j, B-j))$.

This probability distribution implies the probability that out-of-bag voting will result in predicting the majority class and minority class.

$$c_1 = \sum_{u >= v} P_\mathcal{I}(E_O(u,v))$$

Let $c_0 = 1 - c_1$. Let d_1 be the percentage of training examples that favor the majority class in out-of-bag voting. Let $d_0 = 1 - d_1$.

We obtain the probability distribution $\mathcal{D}$ by:

$$P_\mathcal{D}(E_B(x,y)) \sim \begin{cases} d_1 P_\mathcal{I}(E_B(x,y))/c_1 & \text{if } x >= y \\ d_0 P_\mathcal{I}(E_B(x,y))/c_0 & \text{if } x < y \end{cases}$$

These probabilities are normalized so they sum to 1. This mostly, but not completely, adjusts the probabilities so that the distribution of majority/minority class predictions corresponds to the out-of-bag voting.

Assuming this probability distribution, we estimate the B-vote predictions based on the out-of-bag voting by calculating $P_\mathcal{D}(E_B(x,y) \mid E_O(u,v))$. For training example i, we can determine the probability that B-vote voting favors the majority class ($x \geq y$) and the minority class ($x < y$). By adding the probabilities over all the examples, we estimate the number of majority and minority class predictions. If we are considering the training examples with a majority (minority) class label, then the number of minority (majority) class predictions is the estimated number of test errors.

Let μ be the estimated percentage of test errors by combining the results from the two distributions. Let n now be the total number of training examples. Then we use

$$s^2 = \frac{n(\mu - \mu^2)}{n-1}$$

The sample variance is based on treating μ as the sample mean of n Bernoulli trials.

References

Blake, C.; Keogh, E.; and Merz, C. J. 1998. UCI repository of machine learning databases.

Breiman, L. 1996a. Bagging predictors. *Machine Learning* 24:123–140.

Breiman, L. 1996b. Out-of-bag estimation. Technical report, Dept. of Statistics, Univ. of Calif., Berkeley. ftp://ftp.stat.berkeley.edu/pub/users/breiman/OOBestimation.ps.Z.

Cohen, P. R. 1995. *Empirical Methods for Artificial Intelligence*. Cambridge, MA: MIT Press.

Dietterich, T. G. 1998a. Approximate statistical tests for comparing supervised classification algorithms. *Neural Computation* 10:1895–1924.

Dietterich, T. G. 1998b. An experimental comparison of three methods for constructing ensembles of decision trees: Bagging, boosting, and randomization. Technical report, Dept. of Computer Science, Oregon State Univ. ftp://ftp.cs.orst.edu/pub/tgd/papers/tr-randomized-c4.ps.gz.

Efron, B., and Tibshirani, R. J. 1993. *An Introduction to the Bootstrap*. New York: Chapman and Hall.

Freund, Y., and Schapire, R. E. 1996. Experiments with a new boosting algorithm. In *ICML-96*, 148–156.

Kearns, M. J., and Ron, D. 1997. Algorithmic stability and sanity-check bounds for leave-one-out cross-validation. In *Proc. Tenth Annual Conf. on Computational Learning Theory*, 152–162.

Kohavi, R. 1995. A study of cross-validation and bootstrap for accuracy estimation and model selection. In *IJCAI-95*, 1137–1143.

Maclin, R., and Opitz, D. 1997. An empirical evaluation of bagging and boosting. In *AAAI-97*, 546–551.

Michie, D.; Spiegelhalter, D. J.; and Taylor, C. C. 1994. *Machine Learning, Neural and Statistical Classification*. Englewood Cliffs, NJ: Prentice Hall.

Quinlan, J. R. 1986. Induction of decision trees. *Machine Learning* 1:81–106.

Quinlan, J. R. 1993. *C4.5: Programs for Machine Learning*. San Mateo, CA: Morgan Kaufmann.

Quinlan, J. R. 1996. Bagging, boosting, and C4.5. In *AAAI-96*, 725–730.

Snedecor, G. W., and Cochran, W. G. 1980. *Statistical Methods*. Ames, IA: Iowa State Univ. Press.

Tibshirani, R. 1996. Bias, variance and prediction error for classication rules. Technical report, Department of Statistics, University of Toronto. http://www-stat.stanford.edu/~tibs/ftp/biasvar.ps.

Weiss, S. M., and Kulikowski, C. A., eds. 1991. *Computer Systems That Learn: Classification and Prediction Methods from Statistics, Neural Nets, Machine Learning, and Expert Systems*. San Mateo, CA: Morgan Kaufmann.

Wolpert, D. H., and Macready, W. G. 1996. An efficient method to estimate bagging's generalization error. Technical report, Santa Fe Institute. http://www.santafe.edu/sfi/publications/WorkingPapers/96-06-038.ps.

Relational Learning of Pattern-Match Rules for Information Extraction

Mary Elaine Califf
Applied Computer Science Department
Illinois State University
Normal, IL 61790
mecalif@ilstu.edu

Raymond J. Mooney
Department of Computer Sciences
University of Texas at Austin
Austin, TX 78712
mooney@cs.utexas.edu

Abstract

Information extraction is a form of shallow text processing that locates a specified set of relevant items in a natural-language document. Systems for this task require significant domain-specific knowledge and are time-consuming and difficult to build by hand, making them a good application for machine learning. We present a system, RAPIER, that uses pairs of sample documents and filled templates to induce pattern-match rules that directly extract fillers for the slots in the template. RAPIER employs a bottom-up learning algorithm which incorporates techniques from several inductive logic programming systems and acquires unbounded patterns that include constraints on the words, part-of-speech tags, and semantic classes present in the filler and the surrounding text. We present encouraging experimental results on two domains.

Introduction

As the amount of information available in the form of electronic documents increases, so does the need to intelligently process such texts. Of particular importance is information extraction (IE), the task of locating specific pieces of data from a natural language document, allowing one to obtain useful structured information from unstructured text. In recognition of their significance, IE systems have been the focus of DARPA's MUC program (DARPA 1995). Unfortunately, IE systems, although they do not attempt full text understanding, are still time-consuming to build and generally contain highly domain-specific components, making them difficult to port to new applications.

Thus, IE systems are an attractive application for machine learning. Several researchers have begun to use learning methods to aid the construction of IE systems (Soderland *et al.* 1995; Riloff 1993;

Kim & Moldovan 1995; Huffman 1996). However, in these systems, learning is used for part of a larger IE system. Our system, RAPIER (Robust Automated Production of IE Rules), was one of the first systems to learn rules for the complete IE task. The resulting rules extract the desired items directly from documents without parsing or subsequent processing. Simultaneous with RAPIER's development, other learning systems have recently been developed for this task (Freitag 1999; Soderland 1999). Using a corpus of documents paired with filled templates, RAPIER learns unbounded patterns that use limited syntactic information, such as the output of a part-of-speech (POS) tagger, and semantic class information, such as that provided by WordNet (Miller *et al.* 1993).

The remainder of the paper is organized as follows. Section 2 presents background material on IE and relational learning. Section 3 describes RAPIER's rule representation and learning algorithm. Section 4 presents and analyzes results obtained on two domains and compares RAPIER's performance to a simple Bayesian learner and two relational learners. Section 5 discusses related work in applying learning to IE and Section 6 presents our conclusions.

Background

Information Extraction

Our system addresses the type of IE problem in which strings directly lifted from a document are used to fill slots in a specified template. Figure 1 shows part of a job posting and the corresponding slots of the filled computer-science job template.

IE can be useful in a variety of domains. The various MUC's have focused on domains such as Latin American terrorism, joint ventures, microelectronics, and company management changes. Others have used IE to track medical patient records (Soderland *et al.* 1995) or company mergers (Huffman 1996). A general task considered in this paper is extracting information from postings to

Posting from Newsgroup

```
Telecommunications. SOLARIS Systems
Administrator. 38-44K. Immediate need
```

```
Leading telecommunications firm in need
of an energetic individual to fill the
following position in the Atlanta
office:
```

```
    SOLARIS SYSTEMS ADMINISTRATOR
    Salary: 38-44K with full benefits
    Location: Atlanta Georgia, no
         relocation assistance provided
```

Filled Template

```
computer_science_job
title: SOLARIS Systems Administrator
salary: 38-44K
state: Georgia
city: Atlanta
platform: SOLARIS
area: telecommunications
```

Figure 1: Sample Message and Filled Template

USENET newsgroups, such as job announcements.

Relational Learning

Most empirical natural-language research has employed statistical techniques that base decisions on very short fixed-length contexts, or symbolic techniques such as *decision trees* that require the developer to specify a manageable, finite set of features for use in making decisions. Inductive Logic Programming (ILP) and other *relational learning* methods allow induction over *structured* examples that can include first-order logical representations and unbounded data structures such as lists, strings, and trees. Experimental comparisons of ILP and feature-based induction have demonstrated the advantages of relational representations in two language related tasks, text categorization (Cohen 1995) and generating the past tense of English verbs (Mooney & Califf 1995). While RAPIER is not strictly an ILP system, its learning algorithm was inspired by ideas from three ILP systems.

GOLEM (Muggleton & Feng 1992) employs a bottom-up algorithm based on the construction of relative least-general generalizations, *rlggs*. Rules are created by computing the *rlggs* of randomly selected positive examples. CHILLIN (Zelle & Mooney 1994) combines bottom-up and top-down techniques. The algorithm starts with a most specific definition (the set of positive examples) and introduces generalizations that compress the definition. The third system, PROGOL (Muggleton 1995), also combines bottom-up and top-down search. It constructs a most specific clause for a random seed ex-

Pre-filler:	Filler:	Post-filler:
1) tag: {nn,nnp}	1) word: undisclosed	1) sem: price
2) list: length 2	tag: jj	

Figure 2: Sample Rule Learned by RAPIER

ample and employs a A* search to find the simplest consistent generalization.

The RAPIER System

Rule Representation

RAPIER's rule representation uses patterns that can make use of limited syntactic and semantic information. The extraction rules are indexed by template name and slot name and consist of three parts: 1) a pre-filler pattern that matches text immediately preceding the filler, 2) a pattern that matches the actual slot filler, and 3) a post-filler pattern that matches the text immediately following the filler. Each pattern is a sequence of pattern elements of one of two types: *pattern items* and *pattern lists*. A pattern item matches exactly one word that satisfies its constraints. A pattern list has a maximum length N and matches 0 to N words, each satisfying a set of constraints. RAPIER uses three kinds of constraints: on the specific word, on its assigned part-of-speech, and on its semantic class. The constraints are disjunctive lists of one or more words, tags, or semantic classes.

Figure 2 shows a rule constructed by RAPIER for extracting the transaction amount from a newswire concerning a corporate acquisition. This rule extracts the value "undisclosed" from phrases such as "sold to the bank for an undisclosed amount" or "paid Honeywell an undisclosed price". The pre-filler pattern consists of two pattern elements: 1) a word whose POS is noun or proper noun, and 2) a list of at most two unconstrained words. The filler pattern requires the word "undisclosed" tagged as an adjective. The post-filler pattern requires a word in the WordNet semantic category "price".

The Learning Algorithm

RAPIER's learning algorithm is compression-based and primarily consists of a specific to general search. We chose a bottom-up approach in order to limit search without imposing artificial limits on the constants to be considered, and in order to prefer high precision (by preferring more specific rules), which we believe is relatively more important in many IE tasks.

Like CHILLIN, RAPIER begins with a most specific definition and compresses it by replacing sets of rules with more general ones. To construct the initial definition, most-specific patterns for each slot are created for each example, specifying words and tags for the filler and its complete context. Thus, the pre-filler pattern contains an item for each word from the beginning of the document to the word immediately preceding the filler with constraints listing the specific word and its POS tag. Likewise, the filler pattern has one item from each word in the filler, and the post-filler pattern has one item for each word from the end of the filler to the end of the document.

Given this maximally specific rule-base, RAPIER attempts to compress the rules for each slot. New rules are created by selecting pairs of existing rules and creating generalizations (like GOLEM). The aim is to make small generalization steps so a standard approach is to generate the least general generalization (LGG) of each pair of rules. However, since our pattern language allows for unconstrained disjunction, the LGG may be overly specific. Therefore, in cases where the LGG of two constraints is a disjunction, we create two alternative generalizations: 1) the disjunction and 2) the removal of the constraint. Since patterns consist of a sequence of items, this results in a combinatorial number of potential generalizations, and it is intractable to compute complete generalizations of two initial rules.

Although we do not want to arbitrarily limit the length of a pre-filler or post-filler pattern, it is likely that the important parts of the pattern will be close to the filler. Therefore, RAPIER starts with rules containing only generalizations of the filler patterns and performs a kind of top-down beam search to efficiently specialize the pre and post fillers. It maintains a priority queue of the best k rules and repeatedly specializes them by adding pieces of the generalizations of the pre and post-filler patterns of the seed rules, working outward from the fillers. The rules are ordered using an information gain metric (Quinlan 1990) weighted by the size of the rule (preferring smaller rules). When the best rule in the queue produces no spurious fillers when matched against the training texts, specialization ceases and it is added to the final rule base, replacing any more specific rules it renders superfluous. Specialization is abandoned if the value of the best rule does not improve across k specialization iterations. Compression of the rule base for each slot is abandoned when the number of successive iterations of the compression algorithm that fail to produce a compressing rule exceed a pre-defined limit. Figure 3 gives psuedocode for the basic algorithm. *SpecializePreFiller* and *SpecializePostFiller* create specializations of *CurRule* using the n items from the context preceding or following the filler.

As an example of the creation of a new rule, consider generalizing the rules based on the phrases "located in Atlanta, Georgia." and "offices in

For each slot, S in the template being learned
   SlotRules = most specific rules for S from examples
   while compression has failed fewer than *CLim* times
      RuleList = an empty priority queue of length k
      randomly select M pairs of rules from *SlotRules*
      find the set L of generalizations of the fillers of
         each rule pair
      for each pattern P in L
         create a rule *NewRule* with filler P and empty
            pre and post-fillers
         evaluate *NewRule* and add *NewRule* to *RuleList*
      let $n = 0$
      loop
         increment n
         for each rule, *CurRule*, in *RuleList*
            NewRL = SpecializePreFiller(*CurRule,n*)
            evaluate rules in *NewRL* and add to *RuleList*
         for each rule, *CurRule*, in *RuleList*
            NewRL = SpecializePostFiller(*CurRule,n*)
            evaluate rules in *NewRL* and add to *RuleList*
      until best rule in *RuleList* produces only valid fillers
         or the value of the best rule in *RuleList* has
         failed to improve over the last *Lim* iterations
   if best rule in *RuleList* covers no more than an
      allowable percentage of spurious fillers
      add to *SlotRules*, removing empirically
         subsumed rules

Figure 3: RAPIER Algorithm

Kansas City, Missouri." These phrases are sufficient to demonstrate the process. The initial, specific rules created from these phrases for the city slot for a job template would be

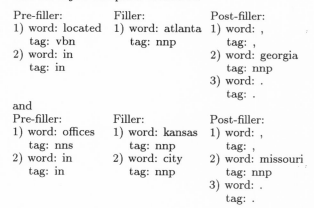

and

For the purposes of this example, we assume that there is a semantic class for states, but not one for cities. The fillers are generalized to produce two possible rules with empty pre and post-filler patterns. Because one filler has two items and the other only one, they generalize to a list of no more than two words. The word constraints generalize to either a disjunction of all the words or no constraint. The tag constraints on all of the items are the same, so the generalized rule's tag constraints are also the same. Since the three words do not belong to a single semantic class in the lexicon, the semantics remain unconstrained. The fillers produced are:

```
Pre-filler:     Filler:                    Post-filler:
                1) list: max length: 2
                   word: {atlanta, kansas, city}
                   tag: nnp
and
Pre-filler:     Filler:                    Post-filler:
                1) list: max length: 2
                   tag: nnp
```

Either of these rules is likely to cover spurious examples, so we add pre-filler and post-filler generalizations. At the first iteration of specialization, the algorithm considers the first pattern item to either side of the filler. The items produced from the "in"'s and commas are identical and, therefore, unchanged. Continuing the specialization, the algorithm considers the second to last elements in the pre-filler pattern. The generalization of these elements produce several possible specializations for each of the rules in the current beam, but none is likely to improve the rule, so specialization proceeds to the second elements of the post-fillers. Generalizing the state names produces a 'state' semantic tag and a 'nnp' (proper noun) POS tag, creating the final best rule:

```
Pre-filler:    Filler:                      Post-filler:
1) word: in    1) list: max length: 2       1) word: ,
   tag: in        tag: nnp                      tag: ,
                                             2) tag: nnp
                                                semantic: state
```

Experimental Evaluation

RAPIER has been tested on two data sets: a set of 300 computer-related job postings from austin.jobs and a set of 485 seminar announcements from CMU.[1] In order to analyze the effect of different types of knowledge sources on the results, three different versions of RAPIER were tested. The full representation used words, POS tags as assigned by Brill's tagger (Brill 1994), and semantic classes taken from WordNet. The other two versions are ablations, one using words and tags (labeled RAPIER-WT in tables), the other words only (labeled RAPIER-W).

We also present results from three other learning IE systems. One is a Naive Bayes system which uses words in a fixed-length window to locate slot fillers (Freitag 1998). Very recently, two other systems have been developed with goals very similar to RAPIER's. These are both relational learning systems which do not depend on syntactic analysis. Their representations and algorithms; however, differ significantly from each other and from RAPIER. SRV (Freitag 1999) employs a top-down,

set-covering rule learner similar to FOIL (Quinlan 1990). It uses four pre-determined predicates which allow it to express information about the length of a fragment, the position of a particular token, the relative positions of two tokens, and various user-defined token features (e.g. capitalization, digits, word length). The second system is WHISK (Soderland 1999) which like RAPIER uses pattern-matching, employing a restricted form of regular expressions. It can also make use of semantic classes and the results of syntactic analysis, but does not require them. The learning algorithm is a covering algorithm, and rule creation begins by selection of a single seed example and creates rules top-down, restricting the choice of terms to be added to a rule to those appearing in the seed example (similar to PROGOL).

Computer-Related Jobs

The first task is extracting information from computer-related job postings that could be used to create a database of available jobs. The computer job template contains 17 slots, including information about the employer, the location, the salary, and job requirements. Several of the slots, such as the languages and platforms used, can take multiple values. We performed ten-fold cross-validation on 300 examples, and also trained on smaller subsets of the training examples for each test set in order to produce learning curves. We present two measures: precision, the percentage of slot fillers produced which are correct, and recall, the percentage of slot fillers in the correct templates which are produced by the system. Statistical significance was evaluated using a two-tailed paired t-test.

Figure 4 shows the learning curves for precision and recall. Clearly, the Naive Bayes system does not perform well on this task, although it has been shown to be fairly competitive in other domains, as will be seen below. It performs well on some slots but quite poorly on many others, especially those which usually have multiple fillers. In order to compare at reasonably similar levels of recall (although Naive Bayes' recall is still considerably less than Rapier's), Naive Bayes' threshold was set low, accounting for the low precision. Of course, setting the threshold to obtain high precision results in even lower recall. These results clearly indicate the advantage of relational learning since a simpler fixed-context representation such as that used by Naive Bayes appears insufficient to produce a useful system.

By contrast, RAPIER's precision is quite high, over 89% for words only and for words with POS tags. This fact is not surprising, since the bias of the bottom-up algorithm is for specific rules. High precision is important for such tasks, where

---

[1] The seminar dataset was annotated by Dayne Freitag, who graciously provided the data.

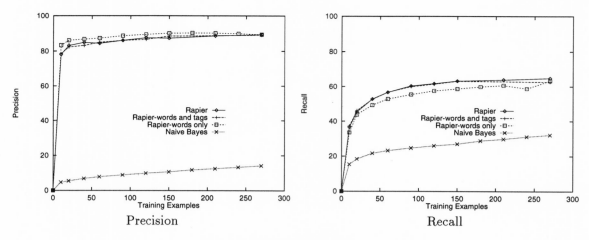

Figure 4: Performance on job postings

having correct information in the database is generally more important than extracting a greater amount of less-reliable information. Also, the learning curve is quite steep. The RAPIER algorithm is apparently quite effective at making maximal use of a small number of examples. The precision curve flattens out quite a bit as the number of examples increases; however, recall is still rising, though slowly, at 270 examples. The use of *active learning* to intelligently select training examples can improve the rate of learning even further (Califf 1998). Overall, the results are very encouraging.

In looking at the performance of the three versions of RAPIER, an obvious conclusion is that word constraints provide most of the power. Although POS and semantics can provide useful classes that capture important generalities, with sufficient examples, these relevant classes can be implicitly learned from the words alone. The addition of POS tags does improve performance at lower number of examples. The recall of the version with tag constraints is significantly better at least at the 0.05 level for each point on the training curve up to 120 examples. Apparently, by 270 examples, the word constraints are capable of representing the concepts provided by the POS tags, and any differences are not statistically significant. WordNet's semantic classes provided no significant performance increase over words and POS tags only.

One other learning system, WHISK (Soderland 1999), has been applied to this data set. In a 10-fold cross-validation over 100 documents randomly selected from the data set, WHISK achieved a precision of 85% and recall of 55%. This is slightly worse than RAPIER's performance at 90 examples with part-of-speech tags with precision of 86% and recall of 60%.

Seminar Announcements

For the seminar announcements domain, we ran experiments with the three versions of RAPIER, and we report those results along with previous results on this data using the same 10 data splits with the Naive Bayes system and SRV (Freitag 1999). The dataset consists of 485 documents, and this was randomly split approximately in half for each of the 10 runs. Thus training and testing sets were approximately 240 examples each. The results for the other systems are reported by individual slots only. We also report results for WHISK. These results are from a 10-fold cross-validation using only 100 documents randomly selected from the training set. Soderland presents results with and without post-pruning of the rule set. Table 1 shows results for the six systems on the four slots for the seminar announcement task. The line labeled WHISK gives the results for unpruned rules; that labeled WH-PR gives the results for post-pruned rules.

All of the systems perform very well on the start time and end time slots, although RAPIER with semantic classes performs significantly worse on start time than the other systems. These two slots are very predictable, both in contents and in context, so the high performance is not surprising. Start time is always present, while end time is not, and this difference in distribution is the reason for the difference in performance by Naive Bayes on the two slots. The difference also seems to impact SRV's performance, but RAPIER performs comparably on the two, resulting in better performance on the end time slot than the two CMU systems. WHISK also performs very well on the start time task with post-pruning, but also performs less well on the end time task.

Location is a somewhat more difficult field and one for which POS tags seem to help quite a bit. This is not surprising, since locations typically con-

System	stime		etime		loc		speaker	
	Prec	Rec	Prec	Rec	Prec	Rec	Prec	Rec
RAPIER	93.9	92.9	95.8	94.6	91.0	60.5	80.9	39.4
RAP-WT	96.5	95.3	94.9	94.4	91.0	61.5	79.0	40.0
RAP-W	96.5	95.9	96.8	96.6	90.0	54.8	76.9	29.1
NAIBAY	98.2	98.2	49.5	95.7	57.3	58.8	34.5	25.6
SRV	98.6	98.4	67.3	92.6	74.5	70.1	54.4	58.4
WHISK	86.2	100.0	85.0	87.2	83.6	55.4	52.6	11.1
WH-PR	96.2	100.0	89.5	87.2	93.8	36.1	0.0	0.0

Table 1: Results for seminar announcements task

sist of a sequence of cardinal numbers and proper nouns, and the POS tags can recognize both of those consistently. SRV has higher recall that RAPIER, but substantially lower precision. It is clear that all of the relational systems are better than Naive Bayes on this slot, despite the fact that building names recur often in the data and thus the words are very informative.

The most difficult slot in this extraction task is the speaker. This is a slot on which Naive Bayes, WHISK, and RAPIER with words only perform quite poorly, because speaker names seldom recur through the dataset and all of these systems are using word occurrence information and have no reference to the kind of orthographic features which SRV uses or to POS tags, which can provide the information that the speaker names are proper nouns. RAPIER with POS tags performs quite well on this task, with worse recall than SRV, but better precision.

In general, in this domain semantic classes had very little impact on RAPIER's performance. Semantic constraints are used in the rules, but apparently without any positive or negative effect on the utility of the rules, except on the start time slot, where the use of semantic classes may have discouraged the system from learning the precise contextual rules that are most appropriate for that slot. POS tags help on the location and speaker slots, where the ability to identify proper nouns and numbers is important.

Discussion

The results above show that relational methods can learn useful rules for IE, and that they are more effective than a propositional system such as Naive Bayes. Differences between the various relational systems are probably due to two factors. First, the three systems have quite different learning algorithms, whose biases may be more or less appropriate for particular extraction tasks. Second, the three systems use different representations and features. All use word occurrence and are capable of representing constraints on unbounded ordered sequences. However, RAPIER and SRV are capable of explicitly constraining the lengths of fillers

(and, in RAPIER's case, sequences in the pre and post fillers), and WHISK cannot. RAPIER makes use of POS tags, and the others do not (but could presumably be modified to do so). SRV uses orthographic features, and neither of the other systems have access to this information (though in some cases POS tags provide similar information: capitalized words are usually tagged as proper nouns; numbers are tagged as cardinal numbers). Many of the features used in SRV seem quite specific to the seminar announcements domain. Since all of the systems are fairly easily extended to include the lexical features used by the others, it would be useful to examine the effect of various features, seeing how much of the differences in performance depends upon them versus basic representational and algorithmic biases.

Related Work

Some of the work closest to RAPIER was discussed in the previous section. In this section, we briefly mention some other related systems. Previous researchers have generally applied machine learning only to parts of the IE task and have required more human interaction than providing texts with filled templates. CRYSTAL uses a form of clustering to create a dictionary of extraction patterns by generalizing patterns identified in the text by an expert (Soderland et al. 1995). AUTOSLOG creates a dictionary of extraction patterns by specializing a set of general syntactic patterns (Riloff 1993), and assumes that an expert will later filter the patterns it produces. PALKA learns extraction patterns relying on a concept hierarchy to guide generalization and specialization (Kim & Moldovan 1995). These systems all rely on prior detailed sentence analysis to identify syntactic elements and their relationships, and their output requires further processing to produce the final filled templates. LIEP also learns IE patterns (Huffman 1996), but also requires a a sentence analyzer to identify noun groups, verbs, subjects, etc. and assumes that all relevant information is between two entities it identifies as "interesting." Finally, ROBOTAG uses decision trees to learn the locations of slot-fillers in a document (Bennett, Aone, & Lovell 1997). The features available to the decision trees are the result of pre-processing the text and are based on a fixed context. ROBO-TAG learns trees to identify possible start and end tokens for slot-fillers and then uses a matching algorithm to pair up start and end tokens to identify actual slot-fillers.

Conclusion

The ability to extract desired pieces of information from natural language texts is an important task with a growing number of potential applications. Tasks requiring locating specific data in newsgroup messages or web pages are particularly promising applications. Manually constructing such IE systems is a laborious task; however, learning methods have the potential to help automate the development process. The RAPIER system described in this paper uses relational learning to construct unbounded pattern-match rules for IE given only a database of texts and filled templates. The learned patterns employ limited syntactic and semantic information to identify potential slot fillers and their surrounding context. Results from two realistic applications demonstrate that fairly accurate rules can be learned from relatively small sets of examples, and that its results are superior to a probabilistic method applied to a fixed-length context.

Acknowledgements

Thanks to Dayne Freitag for supplying his seminar announcements data. This research was supported by a fellowship from AT&T awarded to the first author and by the National Science Foundation under grant IRI-9704943.

References

Bennett, S. W.; Aone, C.; and Lovell, C. 1997. Learning to tag multilingual texts through observation. In *Proceedings of the Second Conference on Empirical Methods in Natural Language Processing*, 109–116.

Brill, E. 1994. Some advances in rule-based part of speech tagging. In *Proceedings of the Twelfth National Conference on Artificial Intelligence*, 722–727.

Califf, M. E. 1998. *Relational Learning Techniques for Natural Language Information Extraction*. Ph.D. Dissertation, Department of Computer Sciences, University of Texas, Austin, TX. Available from http://www.cs.utexas.edu./users/ai-lab.

Cohen, W. W. 1995. Text categorization and relational learning. In *Proceedings of the Twelfth International Conference on Machine Learning*, 124–132. San Francisco, CA: Morgan Kaufman.

DARPA., ed. 1995. *Proceedings of the 6th Message Understanding Conference*. San Mateo, CA: Morgan Kaufman.

Freitag, D. 1998. Multi-strategy learning for information extraction. In *Proceedings of the Fifteenth International Conference on Machine Learning*, 161–169.

Freitag, D. 1999. Machine learning for information extraction in informal domains. *Machine Learning* in press.

Huffman, S. B. 1996. Learning information extraction patterns from examples. In Wermter, S.; Riloff, E.; and Scheler, G., eds., *Connectionist, Statistical, and Symbolic Approaches to Learning for Natural Language Processing*. Berlin: Springer. 246–260.

Kim, J.-T., and Moldovan, D. I. 1995. Acquisition of linguistic patterns for knowledge-based information extraction. *IEEE Transactions on Knowledge and Data Engineering* 7(5):713–724.

Miller, G.; Beckwith, R.; Fellbaum, C.; Gross, D.; and Miller, K. 1993. Introduction to WordNet: An on-line lexical database. Available by ftp to clarity.princeton.edu.

Mooney, R. J., and Califf, M. E. 1995. Induction of first-order decision lists: Results on learning the past tense of English verbs. *Journal of Artificial Intelligence Research* 3:1–24.

Muggleton, S., and Feng, C. 1992. Efficient induction of logic programs. In Muggleton, S., ed., *Inductive Logic Programming*. New York: Academic Press. 281–297.

Muggleton, S. 1995. Inverse entailment and Progol. *New Generation Computing Journal* 13:245–286.

Quinlan, J. 1990. Learning logical definitions from relations. *Machine Learning* 5(3):239–266.

Riloff, E. 1993. Automatically constructing a dictionary for information extraction tasks. In *Proceedings of the Eleventh National Conference on Artificial Intelligence*, 811–816.

Soderland, S.; Fisher, D.; Aseltine, J.; and Lehnert, W. 1995. Crystal: Inducing a conceptual dictionary. In *Proceedings of the Fourteenth International Joint Conference on Artificial Intelligence*, 1314–1319.

Soderland, S. 1999. Learning information extraction rules for semi-structured and free text. *Machine Learning* 34.

Zelle, J. M., and Mooney, R. J. 1994. Combining top-down and bottom-up methods in inductive logic programming. In *Proceedings of the Eleventh International Conference on Machine Learning*, 343–351.

A Simple, Fast, and Effective Rule Learner

William W. Cohen   **Yoram Singer**
AT&T Labs–Research Shannon Laboratory
180 Park Avenue
Florham Park, NJ 07932-0971 USA
{wcohen,singer}@research.att.com

Abstract

We describe SLIPPER, a new rule learner that generates rulesets by repeatedly boosting a simple, greedy, rule-builder. Like the rulesets built by other rule learners, the ensemble of rules created by SLIPPER is compact and comprehensible. This is made possible by imposing appropriate constraints on the rule-builder, and by use of a recently-proposed generalization of Adaboost called confidence-rated boosting. In spite of its relative simplicity, SLIPPER is highly scalable, and an effective learner. Experimentally, SLIPPER scales no worse than $O(n \log n)$, where n is the number of examples, and on a set of 32 benchmark problems, SLIPPER achieves lower error rates than RIPPER 20 times, and lower error rates than C4.5rules 22 times.

Introduction

Boosting (Schapire 1990; Freund 1995; Freund & Schapire 1997) is usually used to create ensemble classifiers. It is popular because it is simple, easy to implement, well-understood formally, and effective at improving accuracy. One disadvantage of boosting is that improvements in accuracy are often obtained at the expense of comprehensibility. If comprehensibility is important, it is more appropriate to use some learner that produces a compact, understandable hypothesis—for instance, a rule learning system like CN2 (Clark & Niblett 1989), RIPPER (Cohen 1995), or C4.5rules (Quinlan 1994). However, the rule learning systems that perform best experimentally have the disadvantage of being complex, hard to implement, and not well-understood formally.

Here, we describe a new rule learning algorithm called SLIPPER (for Simple Learner with Iterative Pruning to Produce Error Reduction). SLIPPER generates rulesets by repeatedly boosting a simple, greedy, rule-builder. SLIPPER's rule-builder is much like the inner loops of RIPPER (Cohen 1995) and IREP (Fürnkranz & Widmer 1994). However, SLIPPER does not employ the "set-covering" process used by conventional rule learners—rather than removing examples covered by a new rule, SLIPPER uses boosting to reduce the weight of these examples.

Like the rulesets constructed by RIPPER and other rule learners, SLIPPER's rulesets have the desirable property that the label assigned to an instance depends only on the rules that "fire" for that instance. This property is not shared by earlier applications of boosting to rule learning (see for instance (Freund & Schapire 1996)), in which the behavior of the entire ensemble of rules can affect an instance's classification. This property makes classifications made by the rulesets easier to understand, and is made possible by imposing appropriate constraints on the base learner, and use of a recently-proposed generalization of AdaBoost (Schapire & Singer 1998).

SLIPPER is simpler and better-understood formally than other state-of-the-art rule learners. In spite of this, SLIPPER scales well on large datasets, and is an extremely effective learner. Experimentally, SLIPPER's run-time on large real-world datasets scales no worse than $O(n \log n)$, where n is the number of examples. On a set of 32 benchmark problems, SLIPPER achieves lower error rates than RIPPER 20 times, and lower error rates than C4.5rules 22 times. The rulesets produced by SLIPPER are also comparable in size to those produced by C4.5rules.

The SLIPPER Algorithm

SLIPPER uses boosting to create an ensemble of rules. The weak learner that is boosted finds a single rule, using essentially the same process as used in the inner loops of IREP (Fürnkranz & Widmer 1994) and RIPPER (Cohen 1995). Specifically, the weak learner splits the training data, grows a single rule using one subset of the data, and then prunes the rule using the other subset. In SLIPPER, the *ad hoc* metrics used to guide the growing and pruning of rules are replaced with metrics based on the formal analysis of boosting algorithms. The specific boosting algorithm used is a generalization of Freund and Schapire's AdaBoost (Freund & Schapire 1997) that employs confidence-rated predictions (Schapire & Singer 1998). This generalization allows the rules generated by the weak learner to "abstain" (vote with confidence zero) on examples not covered by the rule, and vote with an appropriate non-zero confidence on covered examples.

The current implementation of SLIPPER only handles two-class classification problems. The output of SLIPPER is a weighted ruleset, in which each rule R is associated with a confidence C_R. To classify an instance x, one computes the sum of the confidences of all rules that cover x, then predicts according to the sign of this sum: if the sum is greater than zero, one predicts the positive class. In order to make the ruleset more comprehensible, we further constrain SLIPPER to generate only rules that are associated with a positive confidence rating—that is, all rules predict membership in the positive class. The only rule with a negative confidence rating (*i.e.*, that predicts membership in the negative class) is a single default rule. This representation is a generalization of propositional DNF, and is similar to that used by many other rule learners: for most rule learners the classifier is a set of rules, often with some associated numerical confidence measure, and often with some sort of voting scheme for resolving possible conflicts in the predictions.

Below, we describe the SLIPPER algorithm in detail.

Boosting Confidence-rated Rules

The first boosting algorithms (Schapire 1990; Freund 1995) were developed for theoretical reasons—to answer certain fundamental questions about pac-learnability (Kearns & Valiant 1994). While mathematically beautiful, these two algorithms were rather impractical. Later, Freund and Schapire (1997) developed the Ada-Boost algorithm, which proved to be a practically useful meta-learning algorithm. AdaBoost works by making repeated calls to a *weak learner*. On each call the weak learner generates a single *weak hypothesis*, after which the examples are re-weighted. The weak hypotheses are combined into an ensemble called a *strong hypothesis*.

Recently, Schapire and Singer (1998) studied a generalization of AdaBoost, in which a weak-hypothesis can assign a real-valued *confidence* to each prediction. The weak-hypothesis can assign different confidences to different instances, and in particular, it can "abstain" on some instances by making a prediction with zero confidence. The ability to abstain is important for our purposes. We now give a brief overview of this extended boosting framework and describe how it is used for constructing weighted rulesets. Since we have thus far implemented only a two-class version of SLIPPER, we will focus on the two-class case; however, the theory extends nicely to multiple classes.

Assume that we are given a set of examples $\langle(x_1, y_1), \ldots, (x_m, y_m)\rangle$ where each instance x_i belongs to a domain $\mathcal{X}$ and each label y_i is in $\{-1, +1\}$. Assume also that we have access to a *weak learning* algorithm, which accepts as input the training examples along with a distribution over the instances (initially uniform). In the generalized boosting setting, the weak learner computes a weak hypothesis h of the form $h : \mathcal{X} \rightarrow \mathbb{R}$, where

Given: $(x_1, y_1), \ldots, (x_m, y_m)$; $x_i \in \mathcal{X}, y_i \in \{-1, +1\}$
Initialize $D_1(i) = 1/m$.
For $t = 1, \ldots, T$:
- Train weak learner using distribution D_t.
- Get weak hypothesis $h_t : \mathcal{X} \rightarrow \mathbb{R}$.
- Choose $\alpha_t \in \mathbb{R}$.
- Update: $D_{t+1}(i) = D_t(i) \exp(-\alpha_t y_i h_t(x_i))/Z_t$

Output final hypothesis: $H(x) = \text{sign}\left(\sum_{t=1}^{T} \alpha_t h_t(x)\right)$

Figure 1: A generalized version of AdaBoost with real valued predictions (Schapire & Singer 1998).

---

the sign of $h(x)$ is interpreted as the predicted label and the magnitude $|h(x)|$ as the confidence in the prediction: large numbers for $|h(x)|$ indicate high confidence in the prediction, and numbers close to zero indicate low confidence. The weak hypothesis can abstain from predicting the label of an instance x by setting $h(x) = 0$. Pseudo-code describing the generalized boosting algorithm is given in Figure 1; here Z_t is a normalization constant that ensures the distribution D_{t+1} sums to 1, and α_t depends on the weak-learner.

The weak-hypotheses that we use here are *rules*. In SLIPPER, rules are conjunctions of primitive conditions. As used by the boosting algorithm, however, a rule R can be any hypothesis that partitions the set of instances $\mathcal{X}$ into two subsets: the set of instances which satisfy (are covered by) the rule, and those which do not satisfied the rule. If x satisfies R, we will write $x \in R$.

In order to make the strong-hypothesis similar to a conventional ruleset, we will force the weak-hypothesis based on a rule R to abstain on all instances unsatisfied by R, by setting the prediction $h(x)$ for $x \notin R$ to 0. We will also force the rules to to predict with the same confidence C_R on every $x \in R$; in other words, for the t-th rule R_t generated by the weak learner, we will require that $\forall x \in R_t, \alpha_t h_t(x) = C_{R_t}$. Thus, to classify an instance x with the strong-hypothesis, one simply adds up the confidence C_{R_t} for each rule R_t that is satisfied by x, and predicts according to the sign of this sum. As a final constraint, we will require each rule R to be in one of two forms: either R is a "default rule" (i.e., $x \in \mathcal{X} \Rightarrow x \in R$) or else R is such that C_R is positive. Thus each non-default rule R is associated with a single real-valued confidence C_R, and can be interpreted as follows: if R is satisfied then predict class "positive" with confidence C_R, and otherwise abstain.

In Figure 1, Z_t is a real value used to normalize the distribution: $Z_t = \sum_i D_t(i) \exp(-\alpha_t y_i h_t(x_i))$. Thus Z_t depends on both h_t and α_t. Schapire and Singer (1998) showed that to minimize training error, the weak-learning algorithm should pick, on each round of boosting, the weak hypothesis h_t and weight α_t which lead to the smallest value of Z_t. Assume that a rule R has been generated by the weak learner. We will now show how the confidence value C_R for rule R can be set to minimize Z_t. Omitting the dependency on t, Z can rewritten in our case as

$$Z = \sum_{x_i \notin R} D(i) + \sum_{x_i \in R} D(i) \exp(-y_i C_R), \quad (1)$$

where $C_R = \alpha h(x)$. Let $W_0 = \sum_{x_i \notin R} D(i)$, $W_+ = \sum_{x_i \in R:y_i=+1} D(i)$, and $W_- = \sum_{x_i \in R:y_i=-1} D(i)$. We can now further simplify Equ. (1) and rewrite Z as

$$Z = W_0 + W_+ \exp(-C_R) + W_- \exp(+C_R) . \quad (2)$$

Following Schapire and Singer (1998), to find C_R we need to solve the equation $\frac{dZ}{dC_R} = 0$, which implies that Z is minimized by setting

$$C_R = \tfrac{1}{2} \ln\left(\frac{W_+}{W_-}\right) . \quad (3)$$

Since a rule may cover only a few examples, W_- can be equal to 0, leading to extreme confidence values: to prevent this, in practice, we "smooth" the confidence by adding $\frac{1}{2n}$ to both W_+ and W_-:

$$\hat{C}_R = \tfrac{1}{2} \ln\left(\frac{W_+ + 1/(2n)}{W_- + 1/(2n)}\right) \quad (4)$$

The smoothed confidence value of any rule R is therefore bounded from above by $\frac{1}{2}\ln(2n)$.

The analysis of Singer and Schapire also suggests an objective function to be used by the weak-learner which constructs rules. Plugging the value of C_R into Equ. (2) we get that

$$\begin{aligned} Z &= W_0 + 2\sqrt{W_+ W_-} \\ &= 1 - \left(W_+ - 2\sqrt{W_+ W_-} + W_-\right) \\ &= 1 - \left(\sqrt{W_+} - \sqrt{W_-}\right)^2 . \end{aligned} \quad (5)$$

Thus, a rule R minimizes Z iff it maximizes $|\sqrt{W_+} - \sqrt{W_-}|$. Note that a rule which minimizes Z by maximizing $\sqrt{W_-} - \sqrt{W_+}$ may be negatively correlated with the positive class, and hence its confidence value C_R is negative. As described earlier, in SLIPPER we restrict ourselves to positively correlated rules, hence the objective function we attempt to maximize when searching for a good rule is

$$\tilde{Z} = \sqrt{W_+} - \sqrt{W_-} . \quad (6)$$

In summary, this use of boosting corresponds roughly to the outer "set-covering" loop found in many rule learners (Pagallo & Haussler 1990; Quinlan 1990; Brunk & Pazzani 1991; Fürnkranz & Widmer 1994; Cohen 1995). The major difference is that examples covered by a rule are not immediately removed from the training set. Instead, covered examples are given lower weights; further, the degree to which an example's weight is reduced depends on the accuracy of the new rule. The formal analysis of boosting given by Schapire and Singer also suggests a new quality metric for rules:

Given: $(x_1, y_1), \ldots, (x_m, y_m)$; $x_i \in \mathcal{X}, y_i \in \{-1, +1\}$
Initialize $D(i) = 1/m$.
For $t = 1, \ldots, T$:

1. *Train the weak-learner using current distribution D:*
   (a) Split data into GrowSet and PruneSet.
   (b) GrowRule: starting with empty rule, greedily add conditions to maximize Equ. (6).
   (c) PruneRule: starting with the output of GrowRule, delete some final sequence of conditions to minimize Equ. (7), where $\hat{C}_{R'}$ is computed using Equ. (4) and GrowSet.
   (d) Return as R_t either the output of PruneRule, or the default rule, whichever minimizes Equ. (5).

2. *Construct $h_t : \mathcal{X} \to \mathbb{R}$:*
   Let $\hat{C}_{R_t}$ be given by Equ. (4) (evaluated on the entire dataset). Then

   $$h_t(x) = \begin{cases} \hat{C}_{R_t} & \text{if } x \in R_t \\ 0 & \text{otherwise} \end{cases}$$

3. *Update:*
   (a) For each $x_i \in R_t$, set $D(i) \leftarrow D(i)/\exp(y_i \cdot \hat{C}_{R_t})$
   (b) Let $Z_t = \sum_{i=1}^{m} D(i)$.
   (c) For each x_i, set $D(i) \leftarrow D(i)/Z_t$.

Output final hypothesis: $H(x) = \text{sign}\left(\sum_{R_t:x \in R_t} \hat{C}_{R_t}\right)$

Figure 2: The SLIPPER algorithm

---

notice that $\tilde{Z}$ encompassed a natural trade-off between *accuracy* (the proportion of the positive examples satisfied by a rule to the total number of examples that the rule satisfies) and *coverage* (the fraction of examples that satisfy the rule).

Below, we will discuss how to construct rules based on the objective function $\tilde{Z}$ as given by Equ. (6).

Rule growing and pruning

We will now describe the weak-learner which generates individual rules. This procedure is similar to the heuristic rule-building procedure used in RIPPER (Cohen 1995) and IREP (Fürnkranz & Widmer 1994).

The rule-builder begins by randomly splitting the dataset into two disjoint subsets, GrowSet and PruneSet. The split is constrained so that the total weight of examples in GrowSet is about 2/3.

The rule-builder then invokes the GrowRule routine. GrowRule begins with an empty conjunction of conditions, and considers adding to this conjunction any condition in one of the following forms: $A_n = v$, where A_n is a nominal attribute and v is a legal value for A_n; or $A_c \leq \theta$ or $A_c \geq \theta$, where A_c is a continuous variable and θ is some value for A_c that occurs in the training data. GrowRule then adds the condition that attains the maximal value for $\tilde{Z}_t$ on GrowSet. This process is repeated until the rule covers no negative examples from GrowSet, or no further refinement improves $\tilde{Z}_t$.

This rule is often too specific, and "overfits" the training data; thus the resulting rule is immediately pruned using the PruneRule routine. PruneRule considers deleting any final sequence of conditions from the rule. Each sequence of deletions defines a new rule whose goodness is evaluated on PruneSet. As before, each candidate rule R' partitions the PruneSet into two subsets, depending on whether or not R' is satisfied. Similar to the definition of W_+ and W_-, let V_+ (respectively V_-) be the total weight of the examples in PruneSet that are covered by R' and labeled $+1$ (respectively -1). Denote by $\hat{C}_{R'}$ the (smoothed) prediction confidence obtained by evaluating Equ. (4) on the W_+, W_- associated with GrowSet. PruneRule minimizes the formula

$$(1 - V_+ - V_-) + V_+ \exp\left(-\hat{C}_{R'}\right) + V_- \exp\left(+\hat{C}_{R'}\right) . \quad (7)$$

This can be interpreted as the loss (as defined by Singer and Schapire) of the rule R', with associated confidence $\hat{C}_{R'}$, as estimated on the examples in PruneSet.

Subject to the limitations of this greedy, incomplete search procedure, this rule will have a low Z score. It is also guaranteed to be positively correlated with the positive class. We also allow a default rule (a rule that is satisfied for all examples) to be used in a hypothesis—indeed, without such a rule, it would be impossible for the strong-hypothesis to classify any instances as negative. The rule-builder will thus return to the booster either the output of PruneRule, or the default rule—whichever rule has the lowest Z value, as determined by Equ. (5). (This behavior is different from other rule-learners, which typically add a single default rule after all other rules have been learned.)

Note that the value of Equ. (7) and the confidence value $\hat{C}_{R'}$ which was calculated on GrowSet is used only in the weak-learner search for a good rule—the booster will assign a confidence using Equ. (4) on the entire dataset.

Pseudo-code for SLIPPER is given in Figure 2.

Other details

It is possible for the weak-learner to generate the same rule several times—for instance, the default rule is often generated many times during boosting. Therefore, after the last round of boosting, the final strong-hypothesis is "compressed" by removing duplicate rules. Specifically, if the strong-hypothesis contains a set of identical rules $R_1, \ldots, R_k$, these are replaced by a single rule R' with confidence $C_{R'} = \sum_{i=1}^k C_{R_i}$. This step reduces the size of the strong-hypothesis, thus reducing classification time and improving comprehensibility.[1]

---

[1]Note that this step does not alter the actual predictions of the learned ruleset. Other approaches that perform "lossy" compaction of the strong hypothesis by, for instance, deleting rules associated with low confidence values,

As described above, SLIPPER has one free parameter—the number of rounds of boosting T. Although there are theoretical analyses of the number of rounds needed for boosting (Freund & Schapire 1997; Schapire *et al.* 1997), these tend not to give practically useful bounds. Therefore, we use internal five-fold cross-validation (on the training set) to fix T. Five training/holdout divisions of the data are created in the usual way, and the algorithm of Figure 2 is run five times for T_{max} rounds on each training sets (where T_{max} is an upper bound set by the user). The number of rounds T^* which produces the lowest average error on the holdout data is then determined, breaking ties in favor of smaller values of T^*, and the algorithm is finally run again for T^* rounds on the entire dataset. In the experiments below, we always used a value of $T_{max} = 100$.

Experiments

To evaluate SLIPPER, we used two sets of benchmark problems, each containing 16 two-class classification problems. The first set, the *development set*, was used in debugging SLIPPER and evaluating certain variations of it. The second set, the *prospective set*, was used as a secondary evaluation of the SLIPPER algorithm, after development was complete. This two-stage procedure was intended as a guard against the possibility of "overfitting" the benchmark problems themselves; however, since the experimental results are qualitatively similar on both the development and prospective sets, we will focus on results across all 32 benchmark problems in the discussion below. These results are summarized in Table 2 and Figure 3, and presented in more detail in Table 1.

The benchmark problems are summarized in Table 1. The problems from the development set are discussed elsewhere (Cohen 1995). The problems in the prospective set are taken without modification from the UC/Irvine repository (Blake, Keogh, & Merz 1989), with these exceptions: the hypothyroid and splice-junction problems were artificially made two-class problems—in each case, the goal is to separate most frequent class from the remaining classes; for adult, we used a 5000-element subsample of the designated training set; and market1 and market2 are real-world customer modeling problems provided by AT&T. To measure generalization error, we used a designated test set, when available; a single random partition of the training set, for the larger problems; and stratified 10-fold cross-validation otherwise, as indicated.

We compared SLIPPER's performance to RIPPER (Cohen 1995), with and without its "optimization" step; the C4.5 decision-tree learner (Quinlan 1994), with pruning, and the C4.5rules rule learner (hence-

---

might lead to better generalization error (see for instance (Margineantu & Dietterich 1997)) but are beyond the scope of this this paper.

Percent Error on Test Data

Problem Name	Source	#Train	#Test	#Feat	RIPPER		C4.5		C5.0	SLIPPER
					−opt	+opt	Trees	Rules	Rules	
Prospective:										
adult	uci	5000	16281	14	17.2	16.0	16.0	15.0	15.1	14.7
blackjack	att	5000	10000	4	29.1	29.1	27.9	28.0	27.8	27.9
market2	att	5000	6000	68	43.1	41.3	45.5	43.1	41.4	42.6
market3	att	5000	15000	4	9.1	8.6	9.5	9.3	8.6	8.9
splice-junction	uci	2190	1000	60	6.5	5.9	4.3	4.8	4.5	5.9
hypothyroid	uci	2514	1258	29	1.0	0.9	0.4	0.4	0.4	0.7
breast-wisc	uci	699	10CV	9	3.7	4.6	6.6	5.2	5.0	4.2
bands	uci	540	10CV	39	28.3	27.0	30.0	30.0	30.2	22.8
crx	uci	690	10CV	15	15.5	15.2	14.2	15.5	14.0	15.7
echocardiogram	uci	74	10CV	12	2.9	5.5	5.5	6.8	4.3	4.3
german	uci	1000	10CV	20	28.6	28.7	27.5	27.0	28.3	27.2
hepatitis	uci	155	10CV	19	20.7	23.2	18.8	18.8	21.8	17.4
heart-hungarian	uci	294	10CV	13	19.7	20.1	20.8	20.0	21.8	19.4
ionosphere	uci	351	10CV	34	10.3	10.0	10.3	10.3	12.3	7.7
liver	uci	345	10CV	6	32.7	31.3	37.7	37.5	31.9	32.2
horse-colic	uci	300	10CV	23	17.0	16.3	16.3	16.0	15.3	15.0
Development:										
mushroom	uci	3988	4136	22	0.2	0.0	0.2	0.2	0.7	0.2
vote	uci	300	135	16	3.7	3.0	3.0	5.2	3.0	3.0
move	att	1483	1546	10	35.1	29.3	27.8	25.3	26.8	23.9
network1	att	2500	1077	30	25.0	25.7	28.4	26.6	26.3	25.1
network2	att	2600	1226	35	21.7	21.3	23.3	22.3	22.9	26.6
market1	att	1565	1616	10	23.4	22.3	21.8	20.5	21.2	20.1
weather	att	1000	4597	35	28.5	28.9	31.3	28.7	29.2	28.7
coding	uci	5000	15000	15	34.3	32.8	34.1	32.6	32.4	30.2
ocr	att	1318	1370	576	3.0	3.4	3.6	3.6	4.7	2.0
labor	uci	57	10CV	16	18.0	18.0	14.7	14.7	18.4	12.3
bridges	uci	102	10CV	7	13.7	13.7	15.7	17.5	15.7	13.7
promoters	uci	106	10CV	57	18.1	19.0	22.7	18.1	22.7	18.9
sonar	uci	208	10CV	60	29.8	24.2	30.3	29.8	28.3	25.5
ticket1	att	556	10CV	78	1.8	1.6	1.6	1.6	1.6	2.7
ticket2	att	556	10CV	53	6.3	4.7	4.2	4.9	4.2	4.5
ticket3	att	556	10CV	61	4.5	3.2	2.9	3.4	2.9	4.3
Average: Prospective Set					17.83	17.75	18.20	17.97	17.55	16.65
Average: Development Set					16.70	15.70	16.60	15.93	16.31	15.11
Average: All Problems					17.26	16.72	17.40	16.95	16.93	15.88
Average Rank: All Problems					4.05	3.36	4.06	3.59	3.41	2.53
#Lowest Error Rates: All Problems					6	9	6	3	8	13

Table 1: Summary of the datasets used, and error rates for SLIPPER, four alternative rule learners (RIPPER with and without optimization, C4rules, and C5rules), and the C4.5 decision tree learner.

forth, C4rules); and the C5.0 rule learner[2] (henceforth, C5rules), a proprietary, unpublished descendent of C4rules. RIPPER without optimization is included as a relatively simple separate-and-conquer variant; this algorithm has been evaluated elsewhere under the names IREP* (Cohen 1995) and IRIP (Fürnkranz 1998).

The results are shown in detail in Table 1. SLIPPER obtains the average lowest error rate for both sets of

benchmarks; also, among the rule learners SLIPPER, RIPPER, C4rules, and C5rules, SLIPPER obtains the lowest error rate 17 times, C5rules 10 times, RIPPER 9 times, and C4rules 5 times. Also among these rule learners, the average rank of SLIPPER is 2.0, compared to 2.6 for RIPPER and C5rules, and 2.8 for C4rules.[3]

Summaries of the experimental results are given in Figure 3 and Table 2. In the scatterplot of Figure 3,

[3]The corresponding figures across all learning algorithms compared are given in the table.

[2]That is, C5.0 run with the -r option.

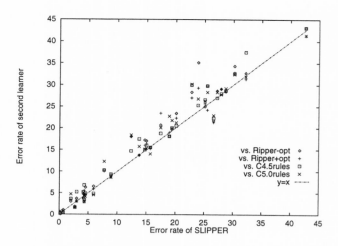

Figure 3: Summary of experimental results. Points above the lines $y = x$ correspond to datasets for which SLIPPER performs better than some second learner.

	RIPPER	C4rules	C5rules	SLIPPER
RIPPER		1.023	0.993	0.961
C4rules	14-17-1		1.066	0.971
C5rules	14-15-3	16-14-2		0.977
SLIPPER	<u>20-9-3</u>	**22-8-2**	19-11-2	
SLIPPER	11-4-1	<u>12-4-0</u>	8-7-1	(Prosp.)
	9-5-2	10-4-2	11-4-1	(Devel.)

Table 2: Summary of experimental results. If L_R and L_C are the learners corresponding to a row and column, respectively, the upper triangle entries are the average of $\text{error}(L_C)/\text{error}(L_R)$. The lower triangle entries are the won-loss-tied record of learner L_R versus L_C, a "win" indicating L_R achieved a lower error rate.

each point compares SLIPPER to some second learning system L on a single dataset: the x-axis position of the point is the error rate of SLIPPER, and the y-axis position is the error rate of L. Thus, points above the lines $y = x$ correspond to datasets for which SLIPPER performs better than some second learner. Visual inspection confirms that SLIPPER often substantially outperforms each of the other rule learners, and that its performance is almost always close to the best of the other rule learners.[4]

In Table 2, let L_R be the learner corresponding to a row of the table, and let L_C correspond to a column. The upper triangle entries are the average, across all benchmarks, of the quantity $\text{error}(L_C)/\text{error}(L_R)$; for instance, the entries of the fourth column indicate that SLIPPER's error rate is, on average, about 2% to 4% lower than the other rule learners. The lower triangle entries are the won-loss-tied record of learner L_R versus L_C, a "win" indicating L_R achieved a lower error rate. A record is underlined if it is statistically significant at the 90% level, and bold-faced if it is statistically significant at the 95% level.[5] For instance, the first entry of the fourth row indicates that SLIPPER achieves a lower error rate than RIPPER 20 times, a higher error rate 9 times, and the same error rate 3 times. SLIPPER's records versus C4rules and C5rules are similar. The last two lines of the table give SLIPPER's won-loss-tied records for the development set and prospective set only, indicating that these results are generally comparable across both test sets. (An exception is SLIPPER's performance versus C5rules: it appears to be superior on the development set, but only comparable on the prospective set.)

We also measured the size of the rulesets produced

by the different algorithms.[6] The most compact rule-sets are produced by RIPPER: the average size of RIPPER's rulesets is 6.0 rules (or 8.1 without optimization), and RIPPER virtually always produces the smallest ruleset.[7] The remaining three learners produce similar sized rulesets, with SLIPPER tending to produce somewhat smaller rulesets than the other two. The average size rulesets for C4rules, C5rules, and SLIPPER are 22.1 rules, 30.7 rules, and 17.8 rules, respectively, and the respective average ranks among these three are 1.8, 2.3, and 1.9. The largest ruleset produced by SLIPPER is 49 rules (for `coding`).

Finally, we evaluated the scalability of the rule learners on several large datasets. We used `adult`; `blackjack`, with the addition of 20 irrelevant noise variables; and `market3`, for which many examples were available. C4rules was not run, since it is known to have scalability problems (Cohen 1995). The results are shown in the log-log plots of Figure 4.[8] The fastest rule learner for these datasets is usually C5rules, followed by the RIPPER variants. SLIPPER (at least in the current implementation) is much slower than either C5rules or RIPPER; however, it scales very well with increasing amounts of data. In absolute terms, SLIPPER's performance is still quite reasonable: SLIPPER needs 1-2 hours to process 100,000 examples of the `blackjack+` and `market3` datasets, and 30 minutes to process the 30,000 training examples from the `adult` dataset.

To summarize, SLIPPER obtains the lowest error rates on average. SLIPPER also scales well to large datasets, although it is somewhat less efficient than C5rules and RIPPER. SLIPPER's rulesets are comparable in size to those of C4rules and C5rules, although somewhat larger than RIPPER's.

---

[4]The sole exception to this is `network2`, on which SLIPPER performs noticeably worse than the other methods.

[5]That is, if one can reject the null hypothesis that the probability of a win is 0.50, given there is no tie, with a

two-tailed binomial test.

[6]In the 10-CV experiments, we looked at the size of the ruleset generated by running on all the data, not the average of the cross-validation runs.

[7]However, it has been argued that RIPPER over-prunes on the sort of the smaller problems that predominate in the UC/Irvine repository (Frank & Witten 1998).

[8]Timing results are given in CPU seconds on a MIPS Irix 6.3 with 200 MHz R10000 processors.

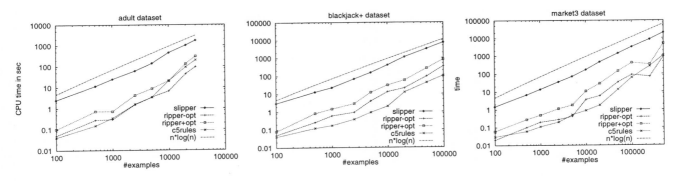

Figure 4: Run-time performance of SLIPPER, RIPPER, and C5rules on large datasets.

Concluding remarks

We have described SLIPPER, a new rule learning algorithm which uses confidence-rated boosting to learn an ensemble of rules. Although the SLIPPER algorithm is relatively simple, SLIPPER performs well on a set of 32 benchmark problems: relative to RIPPER, SLIPPER achieves lower error rates 20 times, and the same error rate 3 times; relative to C4.5rules, SLIPPER achieves lower error rates 22 times, and the same rate 2 times; and relative to C5.0rules, SLIPPER achieves lower error rates 19 times, and the same rate 2 times. Using a two-tailed sign test, these differences between RIPPER, C4.5rules, and C5.0rules are significant at 94%, 98%, and 80% levels respectively. SLIPPER also performs best among these three systems according to several measures of aggregate performance, such as average rank. SLIPPER's rulesets are of moderate size—comparable to those produced by C4.5rules and C5.0rules—and the algorithm also scales well on large datasets.

As noted above, SLIPPER is based on two lines of research. The first line of research is on scalable, noise-tolerant separate-and-conquer rule learning algorithms (Pagallo & Haussler 1990; Quinlan 1990), such as reduced error pruning (REP) for rules (Brunk & Pazzani 1991), IREP (Fürnkranz & Widmer 1994), and RIPPER (Cohen 1995). The second line of research is on boosting (Schapire 1990; Freund 1995), in particular the AdaBoost algorithm (Freund & Schapire 1997), and its recent successor developed by Schapire and Singer (1998).

SLIPPER is similar to an earlier application of boosting to rule learning (Freund & Schapire 1996), in which AdaBoost was used to boost a rule-builder called **FindDecRule**. In contrast to SLIPPER, Freund and Schapire used a heuristic based on an information gain criterion that has no formal guarantees. SLIPPER also places a greater emphasis on generating comprehensible rulesets; in particular, SLIPPER generates relatively compact rulesets, and SLIPPER's use of confidence-rated boosting allows it to construct rules that "abstain" on instances that are not covered by a rule; thus the label assigned to an instance depends only on the rules that "fire" for that instance. In Freund and Schapire's rule boosting algorithm, in contrast, the label for an instance always depends on all the rules in the ensemble. The algorithm also always generates a ruleset of fixed size (in their experiments, 100 rules).

SLIPPER's use of boosting is a departure from the separate-and-conquer approach used by many earlier rule learners. Another alternative is the RISE algorithm (Domingos 1996), which combines rule learning and nearest-neighbour classification using a bottom-up "conquering without separating" control structure. However, the ruleset constructed by RISE is somewhat more difficult to interpret, since the label assigned to an instance depends not on the rules that cover it, but on the rule that is "nearest".

More recently, Hsu, Etzioni, and Soderland (1998) described an experimental rule learner called DAIRY which extends the set-covering approach of traditional rule learners by "recycling" examples—that is, by reducing the weight of examples that have been "covered" by previous rules, rather than removing these examples. DAIRY's recycling method was shown experimentally to improve performance on a number of text classification problems. SLIPPER's combination of boosting and rule-building is similar to recycling, and could be viewed as a formally justified variant of it.

We note that there are important practical advantages to using learning methods that are formally well understood. For instance, existing formal analysis (Schapire & Singer 1998) generalizes the boosting method used here to multi-class learning problems, and also to a setting in which misclassification costs are unequal. In further work, we plan to implement a multi-class version of SLIPPER, and an extension of SLIPPER for minimizing an arbitrary cost matrix, which maps each pair of (predicted label,correct label) to an associated cost. We also plan to evaluate SLIPPER on text classification benchmarks: the current implementation of SLIPPER, which is based on code used in RIPPER, inherits from RIPPER the ability to handle text efficiently.

Acknowledgments

We would like to thank Rob Schapire for helpful discussions, and Haym Hirsh for comments on a draft of this paper.

References

Blake, C.; Keogh, E.; and Merz, C. J. 1989. UCI repository of machine learning databases [www.ics.uci.edu/~mlearn/MLRepository.html]. Irvine, CA: University of California, Department of Information and Computer Science.

Brunk, C., and Pazzani, M. 1991. Noise-tolerant relational concept learning algorithms. In *Proceedings of the Eighth International Workshop on Machine Learning*. Ithaca, New York: Morgan Kaufmann.

Clark, P., and Niblett, T. 1989. The CN2 induction algorithm. *Machine Learning* 3(1).

Cohen, W. W. 1995. Fast effective rule induction. In *Machine Learning: Proceedings of the Twelfth International Conference*. Lake Tahoe, California: Morgan Kaufmann.

Domingos, P. 1996. Unifying instance-based and rule-based induction. *Machine Learning* 24(2):141–168.

Frank, E., and Witten, I. 1998. Generating accurate rule sets without global optimization. In *Machine Learning: Proceedings of the Fifteenth International Conference*.

Freund, Y., and Schapire, R. E. 1996. Experiments with a new boosting algorithm. In *Machine Learning: Proceedings of the Thirteenth International Conference*, 148–156.

Freund, Y., and Schapire, R. E. 1997. A decision-theoretic generalization of on-line learning and an application to boosting. *Journal of Computer and System Sciences* 55(1):119–139.

Freund, Y. 1995. Boosting a weak learning algorithm by majority. *Information and Computation* 121(2):256–285.

Fürnkranz, J., and Widmer, G. 1994. Incremental reduced error pruning. In *Machine Learning: Proceedings of the Eleventh Annual Conference*. New Brunswick, New Jersey: Morgan Kaufmann.

Fürnkranz, J. 1998. Integrative windowing. *Journal of Artificial Intelligence Research* 8:129–164.

Hsu, D.; Etzioni, O.; and Soderland, S. 1998. A redundant covering algorithm applied to text classification. In *AAAI Workshop on Learning for Text Categorization*.

Kearns, M., and Valiant, L. G. 1994. Cryptographic limitations on learning Boolean formulae and finite automata. *Journal of the Association for Computing Machinery* 41(1):67–95.

Margineantu, D. D., and Dietterich, T. G. 1997. Pruning adaptive boosting. In *Machine Learning: Proceedings of the Fourteenth International Conference*, 211–218.

Pagallo, G., and Haussler, D. 1990. Boolean feature discovery in empirical learning. *Machine Learning* 5(1).

Quinlan, J. R. 1990. Learning logical definitions from relations. *Machine Learning* 5(3).

Quinlan, J. R. 1994. *C4.5: programs for machine learning*. Morgan Kaufmann.

Schapire, R. E., and Singer, Y. 1998. Improved boosting algorithms using confidence-rated predictions. In *Proceedings of the Eleventh Annual Conference on Computational Learning Theory*, 80–91.

Schapire, R. E.; Freund, Y.; Bartlett, P.; and Lee, W. S. 1997. Boosting the margin: A new explanation for the effectiveness of voting methods. In *Machine Learning: Proceedings of the Fourteenth International Conference*.

Schapire, R. E. 1990. The strength of weak learnability. *Machine Learning* 5(2):197–227.

Monte Carlo Localization: Efficient Position Estimation for Mobile Robots

Dieter Fox, Wolfram Burgard[†], Frank Dellaert, Sebastian Thrun

School of Computer Science
Carnegie Mellon University
Pittsburgh, PA

[†]Computer Science Department III
University of Bonn
Bonn, Germany

Abstract

This paper presents a new algorithm for mobile robot localization, called Monte Carlo Localization (MCL). MCL is a version of Markov localization, a family of probabilistic approaches that have recently been applied with great practical success. However, previous approaches were either computationally cumbersome (such as grid-based approaches that represent the state space by high-resolution 3D grids), or had to resort to extremely coarse-grained resolutions. Our approach is computationally efficient while retaining the ability to represent (almost) arbitrary distributions. MCL applies sampling-based methods for approximating probability distributions, in a way that places computation "where needed." The number of samples is adapted on-line, thereby invoking large sample sets only when necessary. Empirical results illustrate that MCL yields improved accuracy while requiring an order of magnitude less computation when compared to previous approaches. It is also much easier to implement.

Introduction

Throughout the last decade, sensor-based localization has been recognized as a key problem in mobile robotics (Cox 1991; Borenstein, Everett, & Feng 1996). Localization is a version of on-line temporal state estimation, where a mobile robot seeks to estimate its position in a global coordinate frame. The localization problem comes in two flavors: *global localization* and *position tracking*. The second is by far the most-studied problem; here a robot knows its initial position and "only" has to accommodate small errors in its odometry as it moves. The global localization problem involves a robot which is not told its initial position; hence, it has to solve a much more difficult localization problem, that of estimating its position from scratch (this is sometimes referred to as the *hijacked robot problem* (Engelson 1994)). The ability to localize itself—both locally and globally—played an important role in a collection of recent mobile robot applications (Burgard *et al.* 1998a; Endres, Feiten, & Lawitzky 1998; Kortenkamp, Bonasso, & Murphy 1997).

While the majority of early work focused on the tracking problem, recently several researchers have developed what is now a highly successful family of approaches capable of solving both localization problems: *Markov localization* (Nourbakhsh, Powers, & Birchfield 1995; Simmons & Koenig 1995; Kaelbling, Cassandra, & Kurien 1996; Burgard *et al.* 1996). The central idea of Markov localization is to represent the robot's belief by a probability distribution over possible positions, and use Bayes rule and convolution to update the belief whenever the robot senses or moves. The idea of probabilistic state estimation goes back to Kalman filters (Gelb 1974; Smith, Self, & Cheeseman 1990), which use multivariate Gaussians to represent the robot's belief. Because of the restrictive nature of Gaussians (they can basically represent one hypothesis only annotated by its uncertainty) Kalman-filters usually are only applied to position tracking. Markov localization employs discrete, but *multi-modal* representations for representing the robot's belief, hence can solve the global localization problem. Because of the real-valued and multi-dimensional nature of kinematic state spaces these approaches can only *approximate* the belief, and accurate approximation usually requires prohibitive amounts of computation and memory.

In particular, *grid-based* methods have been developed that approximate the kinematic state space by fine-grained piecewise constant functions (Burgard *et al.* 1996). For reasonably-sized environments, these approaches often require memory in the excess of 100MB, and high-performance computing. At the other extreme, various researchers have resorted to coarse-grained *topological* representations, whose granularity is often an order of magnitude lower than that of the grid-based approach. When high resolution is needed (see e.g., (Fox *et al.* 1998), who uses localization to avoid collisions with static obstacles that cannot be detected by sensors), such approaches are inapplicable.

In this paper we present **M**onte **C**arlo **L**ocalization (in short: MCL). Monte Carlo methods were introduced in the Seventies (Handschin 1970), and recently rediscovered independently in the target-tracking (Gordon, Salmond, & Smith 1993), statistical (Kitagawa 1996) and computer vision literature (Isard & Blake 1998), and they have also be applied in dynamic probabilistic networks (Kanazawa, Koller, & Russell 1995). MCL uses fast sampling techniques to represent the robot's belief. When the robot moves or senses, importance re-sampling (Rubin 1988) is applied to estimate the posterior distribution. An adaptive sampling scheme (Koller & Fratkina 1998), which determines the number of samples on-the-fly, is employed to trade-off computation and accuracy. As a result, MCL uses many samples during global localization when they are most needed, whereas the sample set size is small during tracking, when the position of the robot is approximately known.

By using a sampling-based representation, MCL has several key advantages over earlier work in the field:

1. In contrast to existing Kalman filtering based techniques, it is able to represent multi-modal distributions and thus can *globally* localize a robot.

2. It drastically reduces the amount of memory required compared to grid-based Markov localization and can integrate measurements at a considerably higher frequency.

3. It is more *accurate* than Markov localization with a fixed cell size, as the state represented in the samples is not discretized.

4. It is much easier to implement.

Markov Localization

This section briefly outlines the basic Markov localization algorithm upon which our approach is based. The key idea of Markov localization—which has recently been applied with great success at various sites (Nourbakhsh, Powers, & Birchfield 1995; Simmons & Koenig 1995; Kaelbling, Cassandra, & Kurien 1996; Burgard *et al.* 1996; Fox 1998)—is to compute a probability distribution over all possible positions in the environment. Let $l = \langle x, y, \theta \rangle$ denote a position in the state space of the robot, where x and y are the robot's coordinates in a world-centered Cartesian reference frame, and θ is the robot's orientation. The distribution $Bel(l)$ expresses the robot's belief for being at position l. Initially, $Bel(l)$ reflects the initial state of knowledge: if the robot knows its initial position, $Bel(l)$ is centered on the correct position; if the robot does not know its initial position, $Bel(l)$ is uniformly distributed to reflect the global uncertainty of the robot. As the robot operates, $Bel(l)$ is incrementally refined.

Markov localization applies two different probabilistic models to update $Bel(l)$, an action model to incorporate movements of the robot into $Bel(l)$ and a perception model to update the belief upon sensory input:

Robot motion is modeled by a conditional probability $P(l \mid l', a)$ (a kernel), specifying the probability that a measured movement action a, when executed at l', carries the robot to l. $Bel(l)$ is then updated according to the following general formula, commonly used in Markov chains (Chung 1960):

$$Bel(l) \quad \longleftarrow \quad \int P(l \mid l', a) \, Bel(l') \, dl' \qquad (1)$$

The term $P(l \mid l', a)$ represents a model of the robot's kinematics, whose probabilistic component accounts for errors in odometry. Following (Burgard *et al.* 1996), we assume odometry errors to be distributed normally.

Sensor readings are integrated with Bayes rule. Let s denote a sensor reading and $P(s \mid l)$ the likelihood of perceiving s given that the robot is at position l, then $Bel(l)$ is updated according to the following rule:

$$Bel(l) \quad \longleftarrow \quad \alpha \, P(s \mid l) \, Bel(l) \qquad (2)$$

Here α is a normalizer, which ensures that $Bel(l)$ integrates to 1.

Strictly speaking, both update steps are only applicable if the environment is *Markovian*, that is, if past sensor readings are conditionally independent of future readings given the true position of the robot. Recent extensions to non-Markovian environments (Fox *et al.* 1998) can easily be stipulated to the MCL approach; hence, throughout this paper will assume that the environment is Markovian and will not pay further attention to this issue.

Prior Work

Existing approaches to mobile robot localization can be distinguished by the way they represent the state space of the robot.

Kalman filter-based techniques. Most of the earlier approaches to robot localization apply Kalman filters (Kalman 1960). The vast majority of these approaches is based on the assumption that the uncertainty in the robot's position can be represented by a unimodal Gaussian distribution. Sensor readings, too, are assumed to map to Gaussian-shaped distributions over the robot's position. For these assumptions, Kalman filters provide extremely efficient update rules that can be shown to be optimal (relative to the assumptions) (Maybeck 1979). Kalman filter-based techniques (Leonard & Durrant-Whyte 1992; Schiele & Crowley 1994; Gutmann & Schlegel 1996) have proven to be robust and accurate for keeping track of the robot's position. However, since these techniques do not represent multi-modal probability distributions, which frequently occur during global localization. In practice, localization approaches using Kalman filters typically require that the starting position of the robot is known. In addition, Kalman filters rely on sensor models that generate estimates with Gaussian uncertainty—which is often unrealistic.

Topological Markov localization. To overcome these limitations, different approaches have used increasingly richer schemes to represent uncertainty, moving beyond the Gaussian density assumption inherent in the vanilla Kalman filter. These different methods can be roughly distinguished by the type of discretization used for the representation of the state space. In (Nourbakhsh, Powers, & Birchfield 1995; Simmons & Koenig 1995; Kaelbling, Cassandra, & Kurien 1996), Markov localization is used for landmark-based corridor navigation and the state space is organized according to the coarse, topological structure of the environment. The coarse resolution of the state representation limits the accuracy of the position estimates. Topological approaches typically give only a rough sense as to where the robot is.

Grid-based Markov localization. To deal with multimodal and non-Gaussian densities at a fine resolution (as opposed to the coarser discretization in the above methods), grid-based approaches perform numerical integration over an evenly spaced grid of points (Burgard *et al.* 1996; 1998b; Fox 1998). This involves discretizing the interesting part of the state space, and use it as the basis for an approximation of the state space density, e.g. by a piece-wise constant function. Grid-based methods are powerful, but suffer from excessive computational overhead and *a priori* commitment to the size and resolution of the state space. In addition, the resolution and thereby also the precision at which they can represent the state has to be fixed beforehand. The computational requirements have an effect on accuracy as well, as not all measurements can be processed in real-time, and valuable information about the state is thereby discarded. Recent work (Burgard *et al.* 1998b) has begun to address some of these problems, using *oct-trees* to obtain a variable resolution representation of the state space. This has the advantage of concentrating the computation and memory usage where needed, and addresses the limitations arising from fixed resolutions.

Monte Carlo Localization
Sample-Based Density Approximation

MCL is a version of sampling/importance re-sampling (SIR) (Rubin 1988). It is known alternatively as the bootstrap filter (Gordon, Salmond, & Smith 1993), the Monte-Carlo filter (Kitagawa 1996), the Condensation algorithm (Isard & Blake 1998), or the survival of the fittest algorithm (Kanazawa, Koller, & Russell 1995). All these methods are generically known as *particle filters*, and a discussion of their properties can be found in (Doucet 1998).

The key idea underlying all this work is to represent the posterior belief $Bel(l)$ by a set of N weighted, random samples or *particles* $S = \{s_i \mid i = 1..N\}$. A sample set constitutes a discrete approximation of a probability distribution. Samples in MCL are of the type

$$\langle \langle x, y, \theta \rangle, p \rangle \tag{3}$$

where $\langle x, y, \theta \rangle$ denote a robot position, and $p \geq 0$ is a numerical weighting factor, analogous to a discrete probability. For consistency, we assume $\sum_{n=1}^{N} p_n = 1$.

In analogy with the general Markov localization approach outlined in the previous section, MCL proceeds in two phases:

Robot motion. When the robot moves, MCL generates N new samples that approximate the robot's position after the motion command. Each sample is generated by *randomly* drawing a sample from the previously computed sample set,

with likelihood determined by their p-values. Let l' denote the position of this sample. The new sample's l is then generated by generating a single, random sample from $P(l \mid l', a)$, using the action a as observed. The p-value of the new sample is N^{-1}.

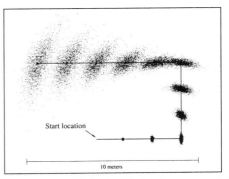

Fig. 1: Sampling-based approximation of the position belief for a non-sensing robot.

Figure 1 shows the effect of this sampling technique, starting at an initial known position (bottom center) and executing actions as indicated by the solid line. As can be seen there, the sample sets approximate distributions with increasing uncertainty, representing the gradual loss of position information due to slippage and drift.

Sensor readings are incorporated by re-weighting the sample set, in a way that implements Bayes rule in Markov localization. More specifically, let $\langle l, p \rangle$ be a sample. Then

$$p \longleftarrow \alpha P(s \mid l) \tag{4}$$

where s is the sensor measurement, and α is a normalization constant that enforces $\sum_{n=1}^{N} p_n = 1$. The incorporation of sensor readings is typically performed in two phases, one in which p is multiplied by $P(s \mid l)$, and one in which the various p-values are normalized. An algorithm to perform this re-sampling process efficiently in O(N) time is given in (Carpenter, Clifford, & Fernhead 1997).

In practice, we have found it useful to add a small number of uniformly distributed, random samples after each estimation step. Formally, this is legitimate because the SIR methodology (Rubin 1988) can accommodate arbitrary distributions for sampling as long as samples are weighted appropriately (using the factor p), and as long as the distribution from which samples are generated is non-zero at places where the distribution that is being approximated is non-zero—which is actually the case for MCL. The added samples are essential for relocalization in the rare event that the robot loses track of its position. Since MCL uses finite sample sets, it may happen that no sample is generated close to the correct robot position. In such cases, MCL would be unable to re-localize the robot. By adding a small number of random samples, however, MCL can effectively re-localize the robot, as documented in the experimental results section of this paper.

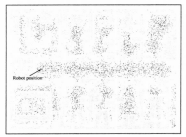
Fig. 2: Global localization: Initialization.

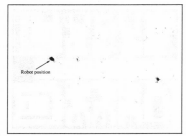
Fig. 3: Ambiguity due to symmetry.

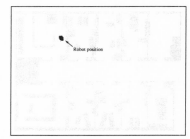
Fig. 4: Successful localization.

Properties of MCL

A nice property of the MCL algorithm is that it can universally approximate arbitrary probability distributions. As shown in (Tanner 1993), the variance of the importance sampler converges to zero at a rate of $1/\sqrt{N}$ (under conditions that are true for MCL). The sample set size naturally trades off accuracy and computational load. The true advantage, however, lies in the way MCL places computational resources. By sampling in proportion to likelihood, MCL focuses its computational resources on regions with high likelihood, where things really matter.

MCL is an online algorithm. It lends itself nicely to an any-time implementation (Dean & Boddy 1988; Zilberstein & Russell 1995). Any-time algorithms can generate an answer at *any* time; however, the quality of the solution increases over time. The sampling step in MCL can be terminated at any time. Thus, when a sensor reading arrives, or an action is executed, sampling is terminated and the resulting sample set is used for the next operation.

Adaptive Sample Set Sizes

In practice, the number of samples required to achieve a certain level of accuracy varies drastically. During global localization, the robot is completely ignorant as to where it is; hence, it's belief uniformly covers its full three-dimensional state space. During position tracking, on the other hand, the uncertainty is typically small and often focused on lower-dimensional manifolds. Thus, many more samples are needed during global localization to accurately approximate the true density, than are needed for position tracking.

MCL determines the sample set size on-the-fly. As in (Koller & Fratkina 1998), the idea is to use the divergence of $P(l)$ and $P(l \mid s)$, the belief *before* and *after* sensing, to determine the sample sets. More specifically, both motion data and sensor data is incorporated in a single step, and sampling is stopped whenever the sum of weights p (before normalization!) exceeds a threshold η. If the position predicted by odometry is well in tune with the sensor reading, each individual p is large and the sample set remains small. If, however, the sensor reading carries a lot of surprise, as is typically the case when the robot is globally uncertain or when it lost track of its position, the individual p-values are small and the sample set is large.

Our approach directly relates to the well-known property that the variance of the importance sampler is a function of the mismatch of the sampling distribution (in our case $P(l)$) and the distribution that is being approximated with the weighted sample (in our case $P(l \mid s)$) (Tanner 1993). The less these distributions agree, the larger the variance (approximation error). The idea is here to compensate such error by larger sample set sizes, to obtain approximately uniform error.

A Graphical Example

Figures 2 to 4 illustrate MCL in practice. Shown there is a series of sample sets (projected into 2D) generated during global localization of our robot RHINO (Figure 5), as it operates in an office building. In Figure 2, the robot is globally uncertain; hence the samples are spread uniformly through the free-space. Figure 3 shows the sample set after approximately 1 meter of robot motion, at which point MCL has disambiguated the robot's position up to a single symmetry. Finally, after another 2 meters of robot motion, the ambiguity is resolved, the robot knows where it is. The majority of samples is now centered tightly around the correct position, as shown in Figure 4.

Experimental Results

To evaluate the utility of sampling in localization, we thoroughly tested MCL in a range of real-world environments, applying it to three different types of sensors (cameras, sonar, and laser proximity data). The two primary results are:

1. MCL yields significantly more accurate localization results than the most accurate previous Markov localization algorithm, while consuming an order of magnitude less memory and computational resources. In some cases, MCL reliably localizes the robot whereas previous methods fail.

2. By and large, adaptive sampling performs equally well as MCL with fixed sample sets. In scenarios involving a large range of different uncertainties (global vs. local), however, adaptive sampling is superior to fixed sample sizes.

Our experiments have been carried out using several B21, B18, and Pioneer robots manufactured by ISR/RWI, shown in Figure 5. These robots are equipped with arrays of sonar sensors (from 7 to 24), one or two laser range finders, and

Fig. 5: Four of the robots used for testing: Rhino, Minerva, Robin, and Marian.

in the case of Minerva, shown in Figure 5, a B/W camera pointed at the ceiling. Even though all experimental results discussed here use pre-recorded data sets (to facilitate the analysis), all evaluations have been performed strictly under run-time conditions (unless explicitly noted). In fact, we have routinely ran cooperative teams of mobile robots using MCL for localization (Fox *et al.* 1999).

Comparison to Grid-Based Localization

The first series of experiments illustrates different capabilities of MCL and compares it to grid-based Markov localization, which presumably is the most accurate Markov localization technique to date (Burgard *et al.* 1996; 1998b; Fox 1998).

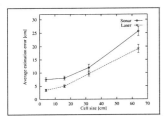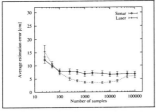

Fig. 6: Accuracy of (a) grid-based Markov localization using different spatial resolutions and (b) MCL for different numbers of samples (log scale).

Figure 6 (a) plots the localization accuracy for grid-based localization as a function of the grid resolution. These results were obtained using data recorded in the environment shown in Figure 2. They are nicely suited for our experiments because the exact same data has already been used to compare different localization approaches, including grid-based Markov localization (which was the only one that solved the global localization problem) (Gutmann *et al.* 1998). *Notice that the results for grid-based localization shown in Figure 6 were not generated in real-time.* As shown there, the accuracy increases with the resolution of the grid, both for sonar (solid line) and for laser data (dashed line). However, grid sizes below 8 cm do not permit updating in real-time, even when highly efficient, selective update schemes are used (Fox, Burgard, & Thrun 1999). Results for MCL with fixed sample set sizes are shown in Figure 6 (b). These results have been generated using real-

time conditions. Here very small sample sets are disadvantageous, since they infer too large an error in the approximation. Large sample sets are also disadvantageous, since processing them requires too much time and fewer sensor items can be processed in real-time. The "optimal" sample set size, according to Figure 6 (b), is somewhere between 1,000 and 5,000 samples. Grid-based localization, to reach the same level of accuracy, has to use grids with 4cm resolution—which is infeasible given even our best computers.

In comparison, the grid-based approach, with a resolution of 20 cm, requires almost exactly ten times as much memory when compared to MCL with 5,000 samples. During global localization, integrating a single sensor scan requires up to 120 seconds using the grid-based approach, whereas MCL consumes consistently less than 3 seconds under otherwise equal conditions. Once the robot has been localized globally, however, grid-based localization updates grid-cells *selectively* as described in (Burgard *et al.* 1998b; Fox 1998), and both approaches are about equally fast.

Vision-based Localization

To test MCL in extreme situations, we evaluated it in a populated public place. During a two-week exhibition, our robot Minerva was employed as a tour-guide in the Smithsonian's Museum of Natural History (Thrun *et al.* 1999). To aid localization, Minerva is equipped with a camera pointed towards the ceiling. Figure 7 shows a mosaic of the museum's ceiling, constructed using a method described in (Thrun *et al.* 1999). The data used here is the most difficult data set in our possession, as the robot traveled with speeds of up to 163 cm/sec. Whenever it entered or left the carpeted area in the center of the museum, it crossed a 2cm bump which introduced significant errors in the robot's odometry. Figure 8 shows the path measured by Minerva's odometry.

When *only* using vision information, grid-based localization fails to track the robot accurately. This is because the computational overhead makes it impossible to incorporate sufficiently many images. MCL, however, succeeded in globally localizing the robot, and tracking the robot's position (see also (Dellaert *et al.* 1999a)). Figure 9 shows the path estimated by our MCL technique. Although the localization error is sometimes above 1 meter, the system is able to keep track of multiple hypotheses and thus to recover from localization errors. The grid-based Markov localization system, however, was not able to track the whole 700m long path of the trajectory. In all our experiments, which were carried out under real-time conditions, the grid-based technique quickly lost track of the robot's position (which, as was verified, would not be the case if the grid-based approach was given unlimited computational power). These results document that MCL is clearly superior to our previous grid-based approach.

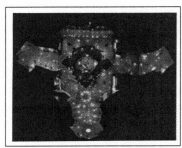

Fig. 7: Ceiling map of the NMAH

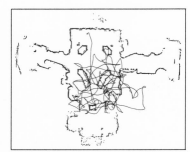

Fig. 8: Odometry information recorded by Minerva on a 700 m long trajectory

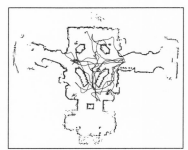

Fig. 9: Trajectory estimated given the ceiling map and the center pixels of on-line images.

Adaptive Sampling

Finally, we evaluated the utility of MCL's *adaptive* approach to sampling. In particular, were were interested in determining the relative merit of the adaptive sampling scheme, if any, over a fixed, static sample set (as used in some of the experiments above and in an earlier version of MCL (Dellaert *et al.* 1999b)). In a final series of experiments, we applied MCL with adaptive and fixed sample set sizes using data recorded with Minerva in the Smithsonian museum. Here we use the laser range data instead of the vision data, to illustrate that MCL also works well with laser range data in environments as challenging as the one studied here.

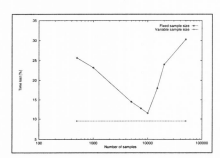

Fig. 10: Localization error for MCL with fixed sample set sizes (top figure) and adaptive sampling (bottom line)

In the first set of experiments we tested the ability of MCL to track the robot as it moved through the museum. In this case it turned out that adaptive sampling has no significant impact on the tracking ability of the Monte Carlo Localization. This result is not surprising since during tracking the position of the robot is concentrated on a small area.

We then evaluated the influence of adapting the sample size on the ability to *globally* localize the robot, and to recover from extreme localization failure. For the latter, we manually introduced severe errors into the data, to test the robustness of MCL in the extreme. In our experiments we "tele-ported" the robot at random points in time to other locations. Technically, this was done by changing the robot's orientation by 180 ± 90 degrees and shifting it by ± 200 cm, without letting the robot know. These perturbations were introduced randomly, with a probability of 0.01 per meter of robot motion. Obviously, such incidents make the robot lose its position, and therefore are well suited to test localization

under extreme situations.

Here we found adaptive sampling to be superior to MCL with fixed sample sets. Figure 10 shows the comparison. The top curve depicts the frequency with which the error was larger than 1 meter (our tolerance threshold), for different sample set sizes. The bottom line gives the same result for the adaptive sampling approach. As is easy to be seen, adaptive sampling yields smaller error than the best MCL with fixed sample set sizes. Our results have been obtained by averaging data collected along 700 meters of high-speed robot motion.

Conclusion and Future Work

This paper presented Monte Carlo Localization (MCL), a sample-based algorithm for mobile robot localization. MCL differs from previous approaches in that it uses randomized samples (particles) to represent the robot's belief. This leads to a variety of advantages over previous approaches: A significant reduction in computation and memory consumption, which leads to a higher frequency at which the robot can incorporate sensor data, which in turn implies much higher accuracy. MCL is also much easier to implement than previous Markov localization approaches. Instead of having to reason about entire probability distributions, MCL randomly *guesses* possible positions, in a way that favors likely positions over unlikely ones. An adaptive sampling scheme was proposed that enables MCL to adjust the number of samples in proportion to the amount of surprise in the sensor data. Consequently, MCL uses few samples when tracking the robot's position, but increases the sample set size when the robot loses track of its position, or otherwise is forced to globally localize the robot.

MCL has been tested thoroughly in practice. As our empirical results suggest, MCL beats previous Markov localization methods by an order of magnitude in memory and computation requirements, while yielding significantly more accurate results. In some cases, MCL succeeds where grid-based Markov localization fails.

In future work, the increased efficiency of our sample-based localization will be applied to multi robot scenarios, where the sample sets of the different robots can be synchronized whenever one robot detects another. First experiments conducted with two robots show that the robots are able to localize themselves much faster when combining their sample sets (Fox *et al.* 1999). Here, the robots were equipped with laser range-finders and cameras to detect each other. We also plan to apply Monte Carlo methods to the problem of map acquisition, where recent work has led to new statistical frameworks that have been successfull applied to large, cyclic environments using grid representations (Thrun, Fox, & Burgard 1998).

Acknowledgment

This research is sponsored in part by NSF, DARPA via TACOM (contract number DAAE07-98-C-L032) and Rome Labs (contract number F30602-98-2-0137), and also by the EC (contract number ERBFMRX-CT96-0049) under the TMR programme.

References

Borenstein, J.; Everett, B.; and Feng, L. 1996. *Navigating Mobile Robots: Systems and Techniques.* A. K. Peters, Ltd..

Burgard, W.; Fox, D.; Hennig, D.; and Schmidt, T. 1996. Estimating the absolute position of a mobile robot using position probability grids. Proc. of AAAI-96.

Burgard, W.; Cremers, A.; Fox, D.; Hähnel, D.; Lakemeyer, G.; Schulz, D.; Steiner, W.; and Thrun, S. 1998a. The Interactive Museum Tour-Guide Robot. Proc. of AAAI-98.

Burgard, W.; Derr, A.; Fox, D.; and Cremers, A. 1998b. Integrating global position estimation and position tracking for mobile robots: the Dynamic Markov Localization approach. Proc. of IROS-98.

Carpenter, J.; Clifford, P.; and Fernhead, P. 1997. An improved particle filter for non-linear problems. TR, Dept. of Statistics, Univ. of Oxford.

Chung, K. 1960. *Markov chains with stationary transition probabilities.* Springer.

Cox, I. 1991. Blanche—an experiment in guidance and navigation of an autonomous robot vehicle. *IEEE Transactions on Robotics and Automation* 7(2).

Dean, T. L., and Boddy, M. 1988. An analysis of time-dependent planning. Proc. of AAAI-92.

Dellaert, F.; Burgard, W.; Fox, D.; and Thrun, S. 1999a. Using the condensation algorithm for robust, vision-based mobile robot localization. Proc. of CVPR-99.

Dellaert, F.; Fox, D.; Burgard, W.; and Thrun, S. 1999b. Monte Carlo localization for mobile robots. Proc. of ICRA-99.

Doucet, A. 1998. On sequential simulation-based methods for Bayesian filtering. TR CUED/F-INFENG/TR.310, Dept. of Engineering, Univ. of Cambridge.

Endres, H.; Feiten, W.; and Lawitzky, G. 1998. Field test of a navigation system: Autonomous cleaning in supermarkets. Proc. of ICRA-98.

Engelson, S. 1994. *Passive Map Learning and Visual Place Recognition.* Ph.D. Diss., Dept. of Computer Science, Yale University.

Fox, D.; Burgard, W.; Thrun, S.; and Cremers, A. 1998. Position estimation for mobile robots in dynamic environments. Proc. of AAAI-98.

Fox, D.; Burgard, W.; Kruppa, H.; and Thrun, S. 1999. A monte carlo algorithm for multi-robot localization. TR CMU-CS-99-120, Carnegie Mellon University.

Fox, D.; Burgard, W.; and Thrun, S. 1998. Active markov localization for mobile robots. *Robotics and Autonomous Systems* 25:3-4.

Fox, D. 1998. *Markov Localization: A Probabilistic Framework for Mobile Robot Localization and Naviagation.* Ph.D. Diss, University of Bonn, Germany.

Gelb, A. 1974. *Applied Optimal Estimation.* MIT Press.

Gordon, N.; Salmond, D.; and Smith, A. 1993. Novel approach to nonlinear/non-Gaussian Bayesian state estimation. *IEE Procedings F* 140(2).

Gutmann, J.-S., and Schlegel, C. 1996. AMOS: Comparison of scan matching approaches for self-localizati on in indoor environments. Proc. of Euromicro. IEEE Computer Society Press.

Gutmann, J.-S.; Burgard, W.; Fox, D.; and Konolige, K. 1998. An experimental comparison of localization methods. Proc. of IROS-98.

Handschin, J. 1970. Monte Carlo techniques for prediction and filtering of non-linear stochastic processes. *Automatica* 6.

Isard, M., and Blake, A. 1998. Condensation—conditional density propagation for visual tracking. *International Journal of Computer Vision* 29(1).

Kaelbling, L.; Cassandra, A.; and Kurien, J. 1996. Acting under uncertainty: Discrete bayesian models for mobile-robot navigation. Proc. of IROS-96.

Kalman, R. 1960. A new approach to linear filtering and prediction problems. *Tansaction of the ASME–Journal of basic engineering* 35–45.

Kanazawa, K.; Koller, D.; and Russell, S. 1995. Stochastic simulation algorithms for dynamic probabilistic networks. Proc. of UAI-95.

Kitagawa, G. 1996. Monte carlo filter and smoother for non-gaussian nonlinear state space models. *Journal of Computational and Graphical Statistics* 5(1).

Koller, D., and Fratkina, R. 1998. Using learning for approximation in stochastic processes. Proc. of ICML-98.

Kortenkamp, D.; Bonasso, R.; and Murphy, R., eds. 1997. *AI-based Mobile Robots: Case studies of successful robot systems.* MIT Press.

Leonard, J., and Durrant-Whyte, H. 1992. *Directed Sonar Sensing for Mobile Robot Navigation.* Kluwer Academic.

Maybeck, P. 1979. *Stochastic Models, Estimation and Control,* Vol. 1. Academic Press.

Nourbakhsh, I.; Powers, R.; and Birchfield, S. 1995. DERVISH an office-navigating robot. *AI Magazine* 16(2).

Rubin, D. 1988. Using the SIR algorithm to simulate posterior distributions. *Bayesian Statistics 3.* Oxford University Press.

Schiele, B., and Crowley, J. 1994. A comparison of position estimation techniques using occupancy grids. Proc. of ICRA-94.

Simmons, R., and Koenig, S. 1995. Probabilistic robot navigation in partially observable environments. Proc. of ICML-95.

Smith, R.; Self, M.; and Cheeseman, P. 1990. Estimating uncertain spatial relationships in robotics. Cox, I., and Wilfong, G., eds., *Autonomous Robot Vehicles.* Springer.

Tanner, M. 1993. *Tools for Statistical Inference.* Springer.

Thrun, S.; Bennewitz, M.; Burgard, W.; Cremers, A.; Dellaert, F.; Fox, D.; Hähnel, D.; Rosenberg, C.; Roy, N.; Schulte, J.; and Schulz, D. 1999. MINERVA: A second generation mobile tour-guide robot. Proc. of ICRA-99.

Thrun, S.; Fox, D.; and Burgard, W. 1998. A probabilistic approach to concurrent mapping and localization for mobile robots. *Machine Learning* 31.

Zilberstein, S., and Russell, S. 1995. Approximate reasoning using anytime algorithms. *Imprecise and Approximate Computation.* Kluwer.

Detecting Feature Interactions from Accuracies of Random Feature Subsets*

Thomas R. Ioerger
Department of Computer Science
Texas A&M University
ioerger@cs.tamu.edu

Abstract

Interaction among features notoriously causes difficulty for machine learning algorithms because the relevance of one feature for predicting the target class can depend on the values of other features. In this paper, we introduce a new method for detecting feature interactions by evaluating the accuracies of a learning algorithm on random subsets of features. We give an operational definition for feature interactions based on when a set of features allows a learning algorithm to achieve higher than expected accuracy, assuming independence. Then we show how to adjust the sampling of random subsets in a way that is fair and balanced, given a limited amount of time. Finally, we show how decision trees built from sets of interacting features can be converted into DNF expressions to form constructed features. We demonstrate the effectiveness of the method empirically by showing that it can improve the accuracy of the C4.5 decision-tree algorithm on several benchmark databases.

Introduction

One of the most challenging aspects of applying machine learning algorithms to difficult real-world problems is choosing an appropriate representation for examples. The choice of features often has a significant impact on the accuracy of many learning algorithms. Most learning algorithms are effective only when there exist some attributes that are fairly directly relevant to (or correlated with) the target concept. Numerous anecdotal examples have been reported where shifting the representation of examples has been the key to increasing accuracy, in domains from chess (Flann & Dietterich 1986) to splice junctions in DNA (Hirsh & Japkowicz 1994), for example.

The initial selection of features is often done with the assistance of a domain expert, and there are usually many options for smoothing, quantizing, normalizing, or otherwise transforming the raw data. This process is often called "feature engineering." To facilitate decision-making, it would be convenient to have

an automated way of quantifying the *utility* of features. Unfortunately, this has proven to be a tricky task. Some approaches, called "wrapper" methods, evaluate features by running the learning algorithm itself on subsets of features and examining the marginal impact on accuracy of adding or dropping features (John, Kohavi, & Pfleger 1994). However, highly relevant features can mask the utility of less relevant or correlated features, which might otherwise have information to contribute. Other approaches, called "filter" methods, attempt to evaluate the relationship between features and the target class using an independent measure, such as conditional entropy, or class-similarity between nearest neighbors along each dimension (Kira & Rendell 1992). In either approach, the utility of an individual feature is often not apparent on its own, but only in combination with just the right other features.

The root of these difficulties lies in a larger issue - *feature interaction* - which is one of the central problems facing machine learning today. Feature interaction is informally defined as when the relationship between one feature and the target class depends on another. As a result, the utility of a feature might not be recognizable on its own, but only when combined with certain other ones, which are needed to form a context in order to reveal its relationship to the target concept. Feature interaction often disperses positive examples in instance space, making learning more difficult, as exemplified by *parity* functions. In fact, feature interaction causes problems for almost all standard learning algorithms (Rendell & Seshu 1990), from decision-trees to perceptrons, which tend to make greedy decisions about one attribute at a time. Feature interaction is also related to lack of conditional independence among features, which violates a basic assumption of the Naive Bayes algorithm, but can be addressed by searching for a Bayesian network with a specific structure that captures any dependencies via restricted joint probability distribution tables at each node (Singh & Provan 1996).

If the interacting features were known, then feature construction techniques could be used to augment the initial representation in such a way as to circumvent the interaction by forcing the features to combine together. This change of representation effectively merges instances back together in instance space and allows greedy algorithms to make more complex and informed decisions. A wide variety of feature construction techniques have been proposed (for a survey, see (Matheus 1989)). In many cases, the operators available for constructing features are limited, and the main difficulty lies in determining which features to combine. Previous feature construction algorithms each use a different approach to avoiding a combinatorial search (such as FRINGE exploiting the replication problem in decision trees, or LFC using lookahead). However, the complexity of feature construction in general remains a challenge.

In this paper, we describe a new approach to detecting feature interactions. Our main idea is to use random sampling to select subsets of features, and then to evaluate whether these features produce higher than expected accuracy when used during learning. The key technical details are: a) how to define the expected accuracy for comparison, and b) how to organize the sampling to provide a fair and balanced search for interacting features within a limited amount of time. Then we describe a simple method for constructing new features from sets of interacting features discovered during the search. Finally, we demonstrate the effectiveness of this approach by showing that it can improve the accuracy of C4.5 on three benchmark databases.

Defining Interactions

We start by developing an operational definition for feature interactions. Informally, a set of features is said to interact if their utility for classifying the target concept is only apparent when they are all combined together. We take an empirical approach to capturing this idea formally: we run the underlying learner on some representative examples using various sets of features, and observe the average accuracy of the constructed decision trees by cross-validation. While this should work for any learner, we focus on decision-tree algorithms in this paper. We define a (positive) interaction among a set of features as when the observed accuracy for all the features taken together is larger than expected, based on the accuracies of trees built using any known subsets of those features.

Definition 1 *A set of features constitutes an* interaction *when the observed accuracy of the underlying learning algorithm with all of the features is higher than "expected."*

At the very least, we can try to estimate what the accuracy of the subset will be based on the performance of the individual features (i.e. one-level decision trees). However, the estimates will clearly be more accurate if we have some information about the performance of various combinations of features.

Bayesian Expectations for Accuracies

The key to this definition is determining what a reasonable expectation is for the accuracy of the whole combination, since interactions are defined in contrast to this (i.e. when the observed accuracy differs from it). One might expect that the accuracy of decision trees built from a set of features would be at least be equal to the maximum for any subset, since the same features are available and presumably could be used to reconstruct the tree. However, it is in general hard to predict how new features will interleave with other ones in being selected for splits, which could improve the accuracy, or possibly even decrease it.

We can use a simple Bayesian analysis to provide a reasonable estimate of the accuracy of a combination of features. To simplify, assume we have two disjoint sets of features, F and G, and we are interested in predicting the accuracy of trees built from the union $F \cup G$. We do not know the exact structure of the trees built from each set of features; they can change with each run of cross-validation. However we can treat the trees built by the decision-tree algorithm with each set of features as a black box, and combine them as independent learners. Call trees built with the first set of features L_F and trees built with the second set of features L_G. To classify a new example with a hypothetical composite learner, we would get the predicted class for the example by running it through L_F, get the class predicted by L_G, and then make the optimal decision based on the probabilities of mis-classification for each of the learners.

For example, if the class predicted by L_F is c_1 and the class predicted by L_G is c_2, then the Bayes-optimal decision would be to output the class that is most likely, given these states of the component learners: $argmax_{c_i} \; Prob[c(x) = c_i \mid L_F(x) = c_1, L_G(x) = c_2]$. The estimated accuracy of this approach would be equal to the probability of the chosen class, which is simply the max. This is summed over all combinations of class labels that could be output by L_F and L_G, weighted by the probabilities of these cases:

$$P[L_{F \cup G}(x) = c(x)] = \sum_{c_j, c_k} P[L_F(x) = c_j, L_G(x) = c_k] \times$$

$$max_{c_i} \; P[c(x) = c_i \mid L_F(x) = c_j, L_G(x) = c_k]$$

Next, re-write the conditional probability using Bayes Rule and cancel the denominators with the weights:

$$P[L_{F \cup G}(x) = c(x)] = \sum_{c_j, c_k} P[L_F(x) = c_j, L_G(x) = c_k] \times$$

$$max_{c_i} \frac{P[L_F(x) = c_j, L_G(x) = c_k | c(x) = c_i] \; P[c(x) = c_i]}{P[L_F(x) = c_j, L_G(x) = c_k]}$$

$$= \sum_{c_j, c_k} (\; max_{c_i} \; P[L_F(x) = c_j, L_G(x) = c_k \mid c(x) = c_i]$$

$$\times P[c(x) = c_i] \;)$$

Finally, invoke the Independence Assumption to break apart the conditional probabilities into values that are easy to determine experimentally:

$$P[L_{F \cup G}(x) = c(x)] =$$

$$\sum_{c_j, c_k} (\; max_{c_i} \; P[L_F(x) = c_j \mid c(x) = c_i] \times$$

$$P[L_G(x) = c_k \mid c(x) = c_i] \cdot P[c(x) = c_i] \;)$$

The values required for this computation can be derived directly from the average rates of true and false positives and negatives for trees built from each subset of features (along with prior class probabilities). Specifically, they can be extracted from the confusion matrix averaged over multiple runs of cross-validation. This approach can easily be extended to predicting the accuracy for partitions with more than two subsets of features. We note that this method of calculating expected accuracies often produces the maximum of the accuracies of the combined subsets, consistent with what is often observed in decision trees, though the expected accuracy can also be higher than the maximum for synergistic combinations.

So this Bayesian approach provides reasonable estimates of the performance of decision trees built from a combination of features, based on the performance of subsets. An important consequence of this approach is that it essentially equates feature interactions with *non-independence*. If the whole combination of features produces an accuracy higher than expected, then the Bayesian explanation for this would be that the probabilities used in the calculation were not in fact independent. The observed accuracy can also be *lower* than expected, which we call a *negative* interaction. This can happen in cases where features interfere with each other in terms of selection of splits in trees.

Apical Interactions

This definition for interactions so far is awkward because the appropriate partition to base the calculation on is undefined, and essentially, the more subsets whose performance we know, the better the estimate will become. However, we can make a pragmatic improvement by restricting the definition to a special class of features interactions. We note that, since the accuracy produced by a subset of features is usually at least as great as the accuracy of the best feature by itself (in the subset), interactions among lesser features will often be masked. Therefore, any observed interaction will typically involve the most accurate individual feature in the subset, which we call an *apical* interaction.

Definition 2 *An apical interaction is an interaction among a set of features such that the most accurate feature by itself is required for the interaction.*

Of course, any feature can participate in an apical interaction with features of lower accuracy than it.

Detecting these types of interactions is much easier. Suppose $F_1 ... F_m$ is a set of features sorted in increasing order such that F_m has the highest accuracy by itself. Consider the partition $\{\{F_1 ... F_{m-1}\}\{F_m\}\}$. Empirically determining the accuracy of the combination of the first $m - 1$ features would reveal the utility of almost all of them together, including possible interactions among lesser features. This can be combined with the accuracy of the single most accurate feature to produce a reasonable Bayesian expectation for the whole set. And yet, this calculation will probably underestimate the true accuracy for apical interactions, since it does not include the added boost in accuracy that occurs only when F_m is combined with the others.

Searching for Interactions

Now that we have an operational definition for feature interactions, we need to determine a way of finding them efficiently. To establish a frame of reference, we start by considering the amount of work it takes to do an exhaustive search. Suppose we have a total of n features and we are looking for interactions of order b (i.e. a set of b features constituting an apical interaction). To determine whether such an interaction exists, and if so to identify it, we would have to run the learning algorithm on all possible combinations of n features taken b at a time. This gives the observed accuracy for each of the combinations, but we have to compare it to the expected accuracy. To compute the expected accuracy, we would have to evaluate the accuracy of all but the highest feature ($b - 1$ total) and then calculate the expected value of the full combination using the Bayesian formula. Apical interactions would thus be detected in cases where the observed accuracy is higher than this expected value.

To fairly account for the work required, we need to consider how the underlying algorithm itself is affected by the number of features involved. In practice, decision-tree algorithms typically have run-time roughly linear in the number of features (though theoretically they could be quadratic in the worst case, since they depend on the size of the trees) (Quinlan 1986). Therefore, to a first approximation, we can treat the run-time as a constant times the number of features being evaluated. The constant can be determined empirically by running the decision-tree algorithm on various randomly chosen sets of features, using the actual number of examples and cross-validation procedure that will be used throughout the experiment. We call this constant u, and hereafter concern ourselves only with units of work based on numbers of features evaluated.

Hence, the work for exhaustive search requires $_nC_b$ runs of the algorithm on b features at a time (b units of work) plus $_nC_{b-1}$ runs of the algorithm on $b - 1$ features at a time ($b - 1$ units of work), or:

$$work_{exh} = b \cdot {_nC_b} + (b-1) \cdot {_nC_{b-1}}$$

This work scales up badly as n increases, and very badly as b increases. It is usually only feasible to exhaustively search for at most binary interactions in real-world datasets.

Random Sampling

To reduce the complexity of the search, we propose sampling subsets larger than the postulated interaction. The idea is that, if we are looking for an interaction of size 3, for example, then instead of testing them all, which is essentially exponential, we can try randomly evaluating subsets of size 6, for example. The probability of combining the right 3 features is higher because the larger subsets each contain multiple triples which are being evaluated simultaneously.

Of course, not all of these triples are easily identifiable as interactions in the set of 6 features. We discuss this in more detail below. But for now, it is useful to point out in general that the probability of selecting the right b features of an interaction in a subset of size $k > b$ is:

$$p(n,k,b) = \frac{{}_{n-b}C_{k-b}}{{}_{n}C_k} = \frac{k(k-1)...(k-b+1)}{n(n-1)...(n-b+1)}$$

where the numerator represents the number of ways that the remaining $k-b$ features can be chosen out of $n - b$ total if the b interacting ones are forced to be included, and the denominator represents all possible combinations of n things taken k at a time.

Since we are generating subsets by random sampling rather than exhaustive search, we cannot guarantee that we will observe an arbitrary interaction of size b. However, if we repeat this process some number of times, eventually the probability becomes quite high. For example, if we repeat the sampling of subsets of size k for r times, the chances that we will observe an arbitrary combination of b features (the postulated interacting ones) becomes:

$$p(n,k,b,r) = 1 - (1 - p(n,k,b))^r$$

In the approach we will be describing, we will allow the user to specify the minimum acceptable probability, such as $p > 0.95$, to set the level of completeness required in the search. For a given value of k, determined by our approach, we can then solve for the smallest number of repetitions of sampling required to meet the requirement specified by p. Generally, as k grows, many fewer repetitions are required.

To use this idea of sampling to search for interactions requires a bit more sophistication. First, even if a given set of features contains a subset of interacting features, it might be masked by other features with higher accuracies. Also, we must consider that sampling larger sets of features costs more. Therefore, we break up the search into sub-searches for specific apical interactions. Apical interactions are easy to identify since they necessarily involve the top feature in the subset. Such an interaction will generally not be affected by the inclusion of additional (non-interacting) features of lower accuracy, and the only penalty is that we have to repeat these tests for each feature as the candidate apical feature.

In detail, we sort all of the features by their individual accuracies (assume w.l.o.g. that $F_1...F_n$ are in sorted order). Starting with $m = b$, we look for apical interactions of F_b with the $b - 1$ features below it. Then we increment m to search for apical interactions where F_{b+1} is the top feature, and so on, up to F_n.

If we were to structure the exhaustive search in levels like this, it would require ${}_{m-1}C_{b-1}$ subsets to be evaluated (running the decision-tree algorithm) with and without F_m, for each m from b up to n. However, at each level m, we can use our idea of sampling subsets larger than $b - 1$ to reduce the amount of work. What size subsets should be sampled, and how many should we generate? Since the number of features to choose from grows with m, we suggest increasing the size of the sampled subsets linearly. The growth rate γ can be anything between 0 and 1. For example, using $\gamma = 1/2$, finding apical interactions with the 12th (least accurate) feature F_{12} would involve evaluating combinations of 6 features at a time including F_{12} (or F_{12} combined with 5 of the 11 lesser features). In any case, if $m \cdot \gamma < b$, we always evaluate subsets of size at least b (exhaustive for small cases). When $\gamma = 1$, this is essentially equivalent to asking for each feature: when combined with all the features with lower accuracy than it, is there an interaction? However, the problem with this extreme case is that it risks confusion if multiple sets of interacting features are mixed together. We would prefer to make γ as small as possible, so that the subsets of features provide an isolated context and hence the best chance to identify a given interaction, with as little distraction from additional features as possible.

Making γ smaller means we have to repeat the sampling at each level a greater number of times to achieve the desired probability p. However, evaluating smaller subsets for apical interactions requires less time in running the decision-tree algorithm. Although it is not immediately obvious, it turns out that as γ decreases, the overall cost (summed over all levels m) increases, taking into account both the number and size of samples required. For a given value of γ, the cost of evaluating each sample to identify apical interactions for each feature F_m is approximately: $m \cdot \gamma + (m \cdot \gamma - 1) = 2m\gamma - 1$ (for running the cross-validation once with $m \cdot \gamma$ features and once without F_m). This has to be repeated enough times to ensure with probability $> p$ that an interaction among b arbitrary features will be observed. So we compute the minimum number of repetitions r_m required by increasing r until $p(m-1, m \cdot \gamma, b-1, r) > p$, since we have $m - 1$ features to choose from, we are sampling subsets of a fraction γ of that size, and we are trying to identify the right $b - 1$ features that complete the apical interaction. Hence the total cost for determining whether F_m is involved in an apical interaction is $r_m \cdot (2m\gamma - 1)$. This is summed up for all levels m:

$$Work_{sampling} = \sum_{m=b}^{n} r_m \cdot (2m\gamma - 1)$$

This cost estimate is used to determine the optimal value for γ. Suppose we have a fixed amount of time t (in units of work, or $t \cdot u$ seconds) to devote to searching for interactions. Our approach involves determining the minimum value for γ such that the overall cost of the experiments does not exceed t. This is done by estimating the cost for various values of γ distributed uniformly between 0 and 1, and selecting the smallest value of γ that allows the total work to be completed within t.

Example

Table 1 shows an example that gives the schedules for several values of γ (0.2, 0.4, 0.6, and 0.8), designed to identify interactions up to order $b = 4$ among $n = 20$ features. Each column gives a prescription for testing features (in increasing order of accuracy) for apical interactions. Each entry shows the size of the random subsets to generate and combine with the corresponding apical feature for the evaluation, along with the number of repetitions required to guarantee with at least 95% confidence that a hypothetical interaction will be contained in at least one of the subsets. For example, in the row for $m = 8$ and the column $\gamma = 0.2$, we see that 104 random subsets of size 3 among the 7 features with lower accuracy than F_8 would have to be generated. Each of these would be tested for apical interactions with F_8 by calculating the cross-validated accuracy of the decision tree algorithm on the random set of features with and without F_8, and comparing to the expected accuracy from the Bayesian analysis of confusion matrices. As γ increases across a row, proportionally larger subsets of lesser features must be sampled (e.g. for F_{16}: 3/15, 6/15, 9/15, and 12/15).

In the table, we also indicate the work (units of runtime) estimated for evaluating each feature for apical interactions. These are shown at the bottom. Note how the total work required drastically decreases as γ increases. Figure 1 gives a better picture of how the work decreases for increasing values of γ. For comparison, the amount of computation required for an exhaustive search of all four-way interactions among 20 features would be 22,800 units of time. Therefore, if one did not have enough time to do an exhaustive search, one could use random sampling with a value for γ that requires less time (e.g. $>\sim 0.3$ in this case).

To use this analysis to generate a search schedule for a specific time bound, we could compute the work required for a uniform distribution of values of γ, such as in increments of 0.05, and take the lowest one that meets the time bound. For example, suppose we only wanted to allot 5,000 units of time for the search for interactions. Based on the above graph, $\gamma = 0.55$ would

Table 1: Example schedule for searching for interactions of order 4 among 20 features. W=work.

m	$\gamma = 0.2$ Sz	$\gamma = 0.2$ Rp	$\gamma = 0.4$ Sz	$\gamma = 0.4$ Rp	$\gamma = 0.6$ Sz	$\gamma = 0.6$ Rp	$\gamma = 0.8$ Sz	$\gamma = 0.8$ Rp
4	3	1	3	1	3	1	3	1
5	3	11	3	11	3	11	4	1
6	3	29	3	29	3	29	4	6
7	3	59	3	59	4	14	5	5
8	3	104	3	104	4	25	6	4
9	3	167	3	167	5	16	7	4
10	3	251	4	62	6	12	8	3
11	3	358	4	89	6	17	8	5
12	3	493	4	123	7	13	9	5
13	3	658	5	65	7	18	10	4
14	3	856	5	85	8	14	11	4
15	3	1089	6	54	9	12	12	4
16	3	1362	6	67	9	15	12	4
17	3	1677	6	83	10	13	13	5
18	3	2036	7	57	10	16	14	4
19	3	2444	7	69	11	14	15	4
20	4	725	8	51	12	12	16	4
W		87690		12122		3638		1376

suffice. In fact, by sampling for apical interactions using 55% of the features with accuracy less than each one being tested for apical interactions, the work can be accomplished in 4991 units of time.

Feature Construction

Once we have discovered a feature interaction, we would like to take advantage of this knowledge to construct a new feature based on it, hopefully to improve the overall accuracy of the learning algorithm. If the features interact, then there must be something about the way that they combine together in a decision tree that produces a higher accuracy than expected based on a simple Bayesian analysis. If this is the case, then we would like to create a new feature that instanta-

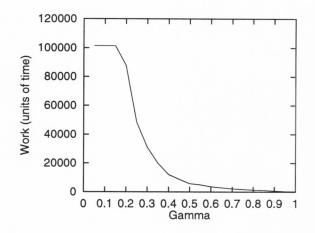

Figure 1: Work (in units of time) required to search for interactions using different values of γ.

neously captures the information in this complex decision, effectively allowing the splitting algorithm to realize the benefit (information gain) of several tests in one step and avoid the pitfalls of making greedy, less informed decisions based on one attribute at a time.

The method we propose for constructing the new feature is to build a decision tree using the interacting features and then extract a DNF expression that represents a grouping of the positive leaves. Let $T(S)$ be a tree built from a subset $S \subset \mathcal{F}$ of the initial features. Let $L_1...L_n$ be the leaf nodes of $T(S)$. Each leaf node can be expressed as a conjunction of attribute tests $(a_1 = v_1) \wedge (a_2 = v_2) \wedge ...$ on the path from the root to that node in the tree. Now, we could construct a DNF expression $L_{i_1} \vee L_{i_2} \vee ...L_{i_d}$ for the d leaf nodes L_i that are positive $(P[c(x) = + \mid L_i] > 0.5$, assuming a two-class model). However, this does not necessarily guarantee to form a new feature with maximum information gain. It is possible that it might be better to group some positive leaves with negative leaves to avoid diluting the impact of a few very pure leaves.

Therefore, the algorithm we use is to sort the leaves according to their purity (100% to 0% positive), and incrementally try shifting the proportion p^* that separates the two groups. For each division, we form the DNF expression of the group of more positive leaves and evaluate the information gain (Quinlan 1986) of this new candidate feature. Call the leaves in sorted order $L_{s_1}...L_{s_n}$, such that the fraction of positives decreases monotonically $p(L_{s_1}) \geq p(L_{s_2}) \geq ...$. We begin by separating out the most positive leaf and calculating the information gain of the partition: $\{\{L_{s_1}\}\{L_{s_2} \vee ...L_{s_n}\}\}$. Then we shift the next most positive leaf over: $\{\{L_{s_1} \vee L_{s_2}\}\{L_{s_3} \vee ...L_{s_n}\}\}$, recalculate the information gain, and so on. Finally, we return the disjunction $L_{s_1} \vee L_{s_2} \vee ...L_{s_q}$ that produces the maximum information gain. The value of this new feature is calculated for each example and appended to its attribute vector.

Experiments

In this section, we describe the results of some experiments with this approach for discovering interactions and constructing new features from them, using C4.5 (Quinlan 1993) as the underlying learning system. We applied our approach to three databases from the UC Irvine repository: *congressional-voting* (with **physician-fee-freeze** feature removed), *census*, and *heart-disease*. In each of the databases, we were able to discover interactions among features that, when used in feature construction, boosted the accuracy of C4.5 by $3 - 8\%$ using cross-validation.

The general course of the experiments is as follows:

1. First, the database is randomly divided into three equal subsets, which we call the "training," "pruning," and "testing" sets, respectively.

2. Next a schedule is generated that is estimated to take about $10 - 15$ minutes on a typical workstation. (This may require some preliminary tests to evaluate how long it takes to run C4.5 with cross-validation on various numbers of features.)

3. Then this schedule is followed to test random subsets of features for apical interactions using the training examples. A given subset with its apical feature are evaluated for interaction by determining the accuracy of C4.5 on the set of features with and without the apical feature, and comparing the observed accuracy to that expected by a Bayesian analysis.

4. When an interacting subset is discovered, a decision tree based on the features is built by C4.5 using all of the training data, and is pruned with the pruning set using *reduced-error pruning* (Quinlan 1987).

5. This pruned tree is used to construct a new feature by converting its paths into a DNF expression and finding the subset of disjuncts (in linear order) that produces the highest entropy reduction.

6. Finally, the new feature is added to the original features in the database, and the change in accuracy is determined over the testing examples using a paired T-test (i.e. running cross-validation within the testing examples to see if the new feature leads C4.5 to generate more accurate trees).

It is important to note that the accuracies we report are slightly lower (but not much) than have been reported by others in the literature, but this is because we are evaluating the utility of constructed features by running C4.5 on only one-third of the data.

Voting Database

The *Voting* database contains the voting records for 435 US Congresspersons during 1984 on 15 key bills. The attributes are all discrete, consisting of three possible votes. The goal is to learn to how to discriminate between Democrats and Republicans. In the original database, one feature, **physician-fee-freeze**, could be used to achieve 95% classification accuracy on its own. We removed this feature, which make the problem a little more challenging; C4.5 can usually only get $85 - 90\%$ accuracy using the remaining features.

Table 2 shows the 15 features, their individual accuracies cross-validated within the training set, and a schedule established for searching for interactions. This schedule was designed for searching for interactions of up to third order within 3000 units of time.

During the search, a total of 389 subsets with three to six features were evaluated for apical interactions. 108 subsets exhibited some degree of interaction, where the accuracy when the most accurate feature was added to the rest was higher than expected, by a difference ranging from just over 0 up to 8.0% (note: we do not require the increase to be statistically significant at this stage). Each of these was used to construct a new feature by building a decision tree, pruning it, converting to a DNF expression, and finding a set of disjuncts

Table 2: Features, accuracies, and sampling schedule for the Voting database. 'Sz' means how many of the features with lower accuracy should be selected in random subsets and tested for apical interactions, and 'Rp' means how many times this should be repeated.

num	feature	acc	Sz	Rp
F1	Religious-Groups-In-Schools	0.589		
F2	Synfuels-Corporation-Cutback	0.605		
F3	Water-Projects-Cost-Sharing	0.642	2	1
F4	Immigration	0.648	2	8
F5	Exports-To-South-Africa-Act	0.704	2	17
F6	Handicapped-Infants	0.707	2	29
F7	Duty-Free-Exports	0.710	2	44
F8	Superfund-Right-To-Sue	0.729	2	62
F9	Crime	0.753	3	27
F10	Anti-Satellite-Test-Ban	0.774	3	35
F11	Aid-To-Nicaraguan-Contras	0.796	3	44
F12	MX-Missle-Program	0.831	4	26
F13	Education-Spending	0.843	4	32
F14	El-Salvador-Aid	0.860	4	38
F15	Adoption-Of-The-Budget-Res	0.863	5	26

with maximal entropy reduction. Many of these new features, when added to the original 15 attributes, did not produce a measurable increase in the performance of C4.5. Often this was because interactions were detected among less relevant features, the combinations of which were masked by the performance of better features in the decision trees anyway.

However, there were several interactions that produced feature constructions that improved the accuracy of C4.5 over the testing set. One example involved an interaction between EL-SALVADOR-AID (F14) and SYNFUELS-CORP-CUTBACK (F2). This was discovered when evaluating a subset of features including these two plus HANDICAPPED-INFANTS (F6), IMMIGRATION (F4), and EXPORTS-SOUTH-AFRICA (F5). On the training data, the accuracy of F14 was highest (86.3%), and the accuracy of the others combined (F2, F4, F5, and F6) was 81.6%. Based on the Bayesian analysis of confusion matrices, the accuracy for all five features together was expected to be 89.6%, but when the accuracy of C4.5 on all five features was determined by cross-validation on the training set, the accuracy was observed to be 91.2%, which was 1.7% higher than expected. Hence this is assumed to be an apical interaction.

A decision tree was constructed with these five features using the training examples, and was then pruned using the pruning examples. Here is the pruned tree:

```
EL-SALVADOR=N : DEMOCRAT
EL-SALVADOR=? : DEMOCRAT
EL-SALVADOR=Y :
|    SYNFUELS-CORP-CUTBACK=Y : DEMOCRAT
|    SYNFUELS-CORP-CUTBACK=N : REPUBLICAN
|    SYNFUELS-CORP-CUTBACK=? : REPUBLICAN
```

The pruned tree was used to construct the follow-

Table 3: Results on the Voting database. The features constructed from some detected interactions are shown. The 'acc w/o' column represents the accuracy of C4.5 on the original features, using cross-validation on the set of testing examples, while the 'acc with' column shows the accuracy when the constructed feature is added. The last two columns show the difference and the Z-score, which is the test statistic for a paired T-test; $Z > 1.83$ is significant for $p < 0.05$.

acc w/o	acc with	diff	Z
(EL-SALVADOR=?) or (EL-SALVADOR=N) or ((EL-SALVADOR=Y) and (SYNFUELS=Y))			
81.7%	87.1%	5.4%	4.91
(MX-MISSLE=Y) or (MX-MISSLE=?) or ((MX-MISSLE=N) and (SYNFUELS=Y))			
80.8%	84.6%	3.8%	3.29
(EL-SALVADOR=?) or (EL-SALVADOR=N) or ((EL-SALVADOR=Y) and (BUDGET=Y or ?))			
80.2%	86.2%	6.0%	3.26

ing feature (DNF expression), which covered mostly Democrats:

```
(EL-SALVADOR=N) or (EL-SALVADOR=?) or
((EL-SALVADOR=Y) and (SYNFUELS-CORP-CUTBACK=Y))
```

When this constructed feature was added to the original 15 features, the cross-validated accuracy of C4.5 on the *testing* examples rose from 81.7% to 87.1%, and the increase of 5.4% in accuracy was significant based on a paired T-test ($Z = 4.91$, $p < 0.05$). Table 3 shows several other features, constructed from interactions, that were found to improve the accuracy of C4.5 on the testing set. It should be noted that these types of paired T-tests have been shown to occasionally lead to high type I error (Dietterich 1998), and more robust methods are being explored to assess the significance of the constructed features more accurately.

Census Database

The *Census* database consists of thousands of records of people taken during a recent census. For each individual, a total of 14 attributes, including both discrete and continuous ones, are given, such as age, sex, education, type of occupation, marital status, etc. The goal is to predict from these attributes whether the annual income of an individual is > or ≤ $50,000. We used a subset of 1000 randomly selected examples in our experiment. A schedule similar to the one for the Voting database was developed for searching for interactions.

A total of 681 feature subsets were evaluated, and of these, 54 were found to have apical interactions; the accuracies of these subsets were greater than expected by up to 3.8%. Table 4 shows some features that were constructed from these detected interactions which produced significant gains in the accuracy of C4.5 (each by around 3.5%) for predicting income levels on the set of testing examples (about 300 examples)

Table 4: Results on the Census database.

acc w/o	acc with	diff	Z
(RELATIONSHIP≠Husband) or ((RELATIONSHIP=Husband) and (YEARS-EDUCATION≤9))			
75.2%	78.4%	3.2%	2.23
(MARITAL-STAT≠MarriedToCivilian) or ((MARITAL-STAT=MarriedToCivilian) and (YEARS-EDUCATION≤9))			
76.6%	80.3%	3.7%	2.50
(CAPITAL-GAIN≤5013) and (CAPITAL-LOSS≤1741)			
76.9%	80.4%	3.5%	5.4

Table 5: Results on the Heart Disease database.

acc w/o	acc with	diff	Z
(NUM-COLOR-VESSELS=0) or ((NUM-COLOR-VESSELS=1) and (SEX=Fem))			
70.4%	78.8%	8.4%	4.25
((EX-ANGINA=T) and (CHEST-PAIN=None or Asymp)) or ((EX-ANGINA=F) and (COLORED-VESSELS≤1))			
69.7%	74.8%	5.1%	2.13

Heart Disease Database

The *Heart* database consists of medical records taken from approximately 300 patients in a clinic in Cleveland. It contains 13 attributes, both continuous and discrete, on personal history and various test results. The state of health for each of the patients is given as a number from 0 to 4 indicating level of heart disease, with 0 representing absence and 4 being worst. For this experiment, we grouped all of the levels from 1 to 4 together, making the goal to distinguish between health and sickness. A schedule similar to the one for the Voting database was developed for searching for interactions by sampling random subsets and evaluating their accuracy with and without the apical feature. Out of 422 feature subsets evaluated, 27 revealed apical interactions, with accuracies that were greater than expected by up to 5.8%. Table 5 shows two of the features that were constructed from detected interactions which produced significant gains (5.1% and 8.4%) in the accuracy of C4.5 on the set of testing examples.

Conclusion

We have shown that feature interactions can be effectively discovered by random sampling. We introduced the notion of an apical interaction, in which the accuracy a learning algorithm can achieve with a given subset of features is higher than the expected accuracy from a Bayesian combination of the most accurate feature with a hypothesis learned from the rest of the features. This definition essentially equates interactions with feature non-independence. An important consequence of defining interactions this way is that they are dependent on the learning algorithm being used. Thus an interaction discovered with a decision-tree algorithm might not necessarily interact in a neural network, for example. We also provided a method for adjusting the sampling for a limited amount of CPU time so that testing for interactions remains fair and balanced. Exhaustive testing for interactions is generally infeasible. By randomly selecting slightly larger subsets to test for apical interactions, we can increase the probability of observing an interaction with less work. We provide a prescription for determining the optimal size of subsets to sample, and how many, to make a probabilistic guarantee of adequate search within resource bounds. Finally, we describe a method for converting observed interactions into new features by extracting DNF expressions from pruned decision trees built with the interacting features. The resulting constructed features combine multiple attribute tests that allow the learning algorithm to make more complex and informed decisions with each test, which can potentially overcome the greediness of many learning algorithms.

References

Dietterich, T. 1998. Approximate statistical tests for comparing supervised classification learning algorithms. *Neural Computation* 10:1895–1924.

Flann, N., and Dietterich, T. 1986. Selecting appropriate representations for learning from examples. In *Proceedings of the Fifth National Conference on Artificial Intelligence*, 460–466.

Hirsh, H., and Japkowicz, N. 1994. Bootstrapping training-data representations for inductive learning. In *Proc. AAAI*, 639–644.

John, G.; Kohavi, R.; and Pfleger, K. 1994. Irrelevant features and the subset selection problem. In *Eleventh International Conf. on Machine Learning*, 121–129.

Kira, K., and Rendell, L. 1992. A practical approach to feature selection. In *Proceedings of the Ninth International Workshop on Machine Learning*, 249–256.

Matheus, C. 1989. *Feature Construction: An Analytic Framework and an Application to Decision Trees*. Ph.D. Dissertation, University of Illinois, Department of Computer Science.

Quinlan, J. 1986. Induction of decision trees. *Machine Learning* 1:81–106.

Quinlan, J. 1987. Simplifying decision trees. *International Journal of Man-Machine Studies* 27:221–234.

Quinlan, J. 1993. *C4.5: Programs for Machine Learning*. Morgan Kaufmann: Palo Alto, CA.

Rendell, L., and Seshu, R. 1990. Learning hard concepts through constructive induction: Framework and rationale. *Computational Intelligence* 6:247–270.

Singh, M., and Provan, G. 1996. Efficient learning of selective bayesian network classifiers. In *Thirteenth International Conf. on Machine Learning*, 453–461.

Simulation-based inference for plan monitoring

Neal Lesh[1], James Allen[2]

lesh@merl.com, james@cs.rochester.edu

[1] MERL - A Mitsubishi Electric Research Laboratory, 201 Broadway, Cambridge, MA 02139
[2] University of Rochester, Rochester, NY 14627

Abstract

The dynamic execution of plans in uncertain domains requires the ability to infer likely current and future world states from past observations. We cast this task as inference on Dynamic Belief Networks (DBNs) but the resulting networks are difficult to solve with exact methods. We investigate and extend simulation algorithms for approximate inference on Bayesian networks and propose a new algorithm, called Rewind/Replay, for generating a set of simulations weighted by their likelihood given past observations. We validate our algorithm on a DBN containing thousands of variables, which models the spread of wildfire.

Introduction

In domains that contain uncertainty, evidential reasoning can play an important role in plan execution. For example, suppose we are executing an evacuation plan and have received the following messages:

Bus_1: Arrived in Abyss, loading 5 passengers.
Exodus weather: Storm clouds are forming to the east.
Bus_2: Engine overheated on the way to Delta.
Bus_1: Got a flat tire on the way to Barnacle.
Bus_2: Loading 9 passengers.
Bus_1: It is starting to snow in Barnacle.

Given the messages received so far, we might ask questions such as what is the probability that a severe storm will hit Barnacle? Or what is the probability that Bus_1 will get another flat tire? Answers to these questions can be used to improve the plan. We might send storm supplies to Barnacle or send Bus_1 on a longer but better paved road. We might also ask about the likely outcomes of various actions. For example, given the evidence received so far, will the plan be more likely to succeed if we send a helicopter to evacuate the people in Exodus or use Bus_3, as originally planned?

We cast plan monitoring as inference on Bayesian networks, but are interested in planning domains for which the resulting networks are difficult to solve with exact methods. In this paper, we explore the use of

stochastic sampling methods for performing plan monitoring. Our objective is an algorithm for quickly generating a set of weighted simulations, where the weight indicates the probability of the simulation given observations made during the partial execution of a plan. We show that a set of weighted simulations can be used to estimate the probability of events and also as a basis for planning future actions based on past evidence.

There are several simulation-based inference algorithms for Bayesian networks, including: likelihood weighting (Shachter and Peot 1989; Fung and Chang 1989), arc reversal (Shachter 1986; Fung and Chang 1989), and Survival Of The Fittest (SOF) (Kanazawa et al. 1995). Below, we consider these algorithms and find that none are especially well suited for, or were designed for, plan monitoring. We describe a modification to SOF that improves its performance and introduce a new algorithm, Rewind/Replay (RR). We show that RR performs significantly better than the other algorithms on a large DBN which models the spread of wildfire.

The rest of this paper is organized as follows. We first formulate our task and then discuss previous algorithms and analyze them on two example networks. We then present RR and a generalization of SOF. Finally, we describe our experiments and then discuss related and future work.

Problem formulation

Previous work has shown how to encode probabilistic processes and plans as Bayesian networks (e.g., (Dean and Kanazawa 1989; Hanks et al. 1995)). Here, we formulate our task as inference on Bayesian networks.

A Bayesian network describes the joint distribution over a finite set of discrete random variables $\mathcal{X}$. Each variable $X_i \in \mathcal{X}$ can take on any value from a finite domain $val(X_i)$. A *variable assignment* is an expression of the form $X_i = x_j$ indicating that X_i has value x_j. We use capital letters (e.g., X, Y, Z) for variables and lowercase letters (e.g., x, y, z) for values of variables.

A Bayesian network is a directed, acyclic graph in which nodes correspond to variables and arcs to direct probabilistic dependence relations among variables. A network is defined by a variable set $\mathcal{X}$, a parent function Π, and a conditional probability table CPT. The Π function maps X_i to X_i's parents. The CPT function maps X_i and a variable assignment for each parent of X_i to a probability distribution over $val(X_i)$. Variable X_i can be *sampled* by randomly drawing one value from the probability distribution returned by CPT. An entire network can be sampled by sampling the variables in an order such that each variable is sampled after its parents are sampled. See (Pearl 1988) for a more thorough description.

We are especially interested in *Dynamic belief networks* (DBNs) also called temporal belief networks (e.g., (Kjaerulff 1992)). DBNs are Bayesian networks used to model temporal processes. A DBN can be divided into subsections, called *time slices*, that correspond to snapshots of the state of the world. Typically, certain variables are designated as observation variables.

Figure 1 shows a simple DBN. The state variables Pos_i and Dir_i represent a person's position and direction, respectively, at time i. The person's direction influences their position and direction in the following time slice. The variable Obs_i represents some possibly noisy observation on Dir_i, such as the output of a compass or the observed person announcing their direction. Note that we can infer a probability distribution over the position of the person given a set of observations, even though the position is never directly observed.

We now define the *simulated inference task*. The inputs are a Bayesian network B and a set of assignments $\mathcal{O} = \{O_1 = o_1, ..., O_n = o_n\}$, which give the observed values for some of the observation variables in B, such as $\{Obs_1 = west, Obs_2 = east\}$. The output is a set of positively weighted samples of B, where each sample s_i is weighted by an estimate of the probability $\mathbf{P}(s_i|\mathcal{O})$.

Inference on Bayesian networks is more typically formulated as determining the probability of a query expression given the evidence. We chose our formulation because it offers a wide range of reasoning for plan monitoring. Suppose we are projecting from past observations to find the safest escape route in some hazardous environment. We might enumerate each possible path and query a probabilistic reasoner to infer the probability that it is safe. A more tractable alternative, however, is to apply path-following algorithms to a set of weighted simulations and let each simulation "vote" its weight as to what is the safest path. We give an example of this approach in our experiments.

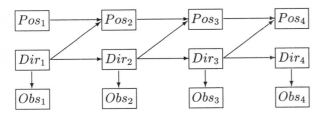

Figure 1: Example DBN

Previous algorithms

We now discuss previous simulation methods.

Logical sampling

A simple approach, called *logical sampling* (LS) (Henrion 1988), is to repeatedly sample the network and discard samples in which $O_i \neq o_i$ for any $O_i = o_i \in \mathcal{O}$. LS assigns the same weight to each retained simulation. Given a query Ω, LS estimates the probability of Ω as the percentage of retained samples in which Ω holds. Logical sampling is an *unbiased* technique: as the number of simulations approaches infinity, the estimate of Ω approaches the true probability of Ω.

The probability of retaining a simulation, however, is exponentially low in the number of observations, assuming some independence among the observations. In many examples we consider, LS can run for hours without retaining a single sample.

Likelihood weighting

The most commonly implemented simulation technique, called *likelihood weighting* (LW), is a variation on logical sampling which can converge much faster in some cases (Shachter and Peot 1989; Fung and Chang 1989; Dagum and Pradhan 1996).

LW also samples the network repeatedly but weights each instantiation by the probability it could have produced the observations. Consider a simple case in which there is a single observation node O_1 with observed value o_1. Logical sampling would repeatedly simulate the network and discard any samples in which $O_1 \neq o_1$. LW, however, weights each sample by the probability that O_1 would be assigned o_1 under the network's CPT function given the values of O_1's parents in the sample.[1] For example, if O_1 had a .08 probability of being assigned o_1 in a sample then LW would weight the sample .08, regardless of what value O_1 was actually assigned.

In the more general case, LW weights each sample s as the Likelihood$(\mathcal{O}|s)$, where **Likelihood**$(\mathcal{O}|s)$ denotes the product of the individual conditional probabilities for the evidence in $\mathcal{O}$ given the sampled values for their parents in s.

LW is also unbiased and has been shown to be effective on many problems. However, as demonstrated in (Kanazawa *et al.* 1995), LW does not work well on DBNs. When the network models a temporal process with an exponential number of possible execution paths, the vast majority of random samples can have a likelihood of, or near, zero.

SOF

Of the algorithms we investigated, the *Survival Of The Fittest* (SOF) algorithm is the best suited for plan monitoring. SOF uses the evidence to guide the simulation, rather than simply to weight it afterwards (Kanazawa *et al.* 1995). We now provide an informal description

---

[1] We assume observation variables have no children. Thus, their values do not effect the value of other variables.

of the SOF algorithm. Figure 5 contains pseudo-code for a slight generalization.

SOF was designed specifically for DBNs. The idea is to seed the next round of simulations, at each time point, with the samples that best matched the evidence in the previous round. SOF maintains a fixed number of possible world states, but re-generates a sample population of world states for each time t by a weighted random selection from the world states at time $t-1$ where the weight for a world state is given by the likelihood of the observations at time t in that world state.

Initially, SOF generates a fixed number, say 100, of samples of the state variables in the first time slice. The weight, w_i, of the ith sample, s_i, is the likelihood of the observed evidence for time 1 in sample s_i. SOF now generates a new set of 100 samples by randomly selecting from samples $s_1, ..., s_{100}$ using weights $w_1, ..., w_{100}$. Some samples may be chosen (and copied) multiple times and others may not be chosen at all. SOF next samples the state variables in the second slice in each of its 100 samples. SOF then weights each sample by the likelihood of the evidence at time 2 and re-populates its samples by random selection using these weights. SOF repeats this process for all time slices.

Investigation of SOF

We now describe two DBN's designed to expose potential problems with using SOF for plan monitoring.

Discarding plausible hypotheses

Consider the following thought experiment. Suppose you put 1,000 distinct names in a hat and repeatedly draw a name from the hat, write it down, and return the name to the hat. If you repeat the process 1,000 times you will have, on average, about 632 distinct names.[2] SOF can discard hypotheses by random chance in a similar manner. Even though the evidence favors selecting the most likely hypotheses, SOF can lose plausible hypothesis if there are hidden state variables whose value becomes apparent only by integrating information over time from a series of reports.

We designed the following network to demonstrate this problem. The network contains one state and one sensor node for each time slice. At time 1, the state node is assigned an integer value between 1 and 50 from a uniform distribution. For $t > 1$, the state simply inherits its value from the state node at time $t-1$. At each time step $t \geq 1$, if the state node's value is evenly divisible by t then the sensor returns *Yes* with .9 probability or *No* with .1 probability and otherwise returns *Yes* with .1 probability or *No* with .9 probability. If, for example, we observe *Yes, Yes, Yes, No, Yes*, then there is a 22.5% chance that the state's value is 30.

The goal is to guess the state node's value. This seems like an easy problem for SOF to solve with, say, 1000 samples. There are only 50 distinct hypotheses, and thus SOF initially has several copies of each of

---
[2]Each name has a 1 - .999^{1000} chance of being selected.

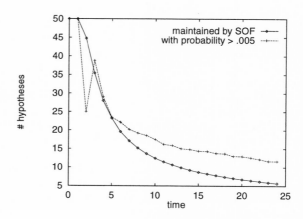

Figure 2: Number of hypotheses maintained by SOF compared to the number of hypotheses with probability greater than .005 on the NumberNet DBN.

them. As time progresses, the more likely hypotheses should be steadily re-enforced by the evidence. We tested SOF by summing the weights associated with each hypothesis, and seeing if the one with the highest weight is, in fact, one of the most likely hypotheses.[3] Based on 1,000 trials, however, SOF with $N = 1000$ achieves only an 81% accuracy on this problem. Even with $N = 2000$, SOF achieves only 92% accuracy.

The graph in figure 2 shows the average number of distinct hypotheses that SOF maintains, with $N = 1000$, after t time steps for $0 \leq t \leq 25$ as well as the average number of hypotheses that have a .005 or greater probability of being true given the evidence at time t.[4] We counted the hypotheses maintained by SOF by counting the number of distinct values for the state node contained in the 1000 samples maintained by SOF. As the graph shows, the number of hypotheses that SOF maintains is noticeably lower than the number of plausible hypotheses.

Premature variable assignment

We designed the following problem to reduce the usefulness of SOF's re-population strategy. We consider a case in which the state variables are assigned values several time steps before they are observed. We believe this represents an important aspect of plan monitoring. Probabilistic planners (e.g. (Kushmerick *et al.* 1995)) take as input a probability distribution over initial states. The value of conditions in the initial state are decided before they are observed, but may be crucial to the success of a plan. For example, in evacuation plans, there might be uncertainty about whether a certain bridge is usable, and the first report on its condition may come when a vehicle encounters the bridge during plan execution.

---
[3]We can easily compute the exact probability of each hypothesis given the evidence, but there may be ties.

[4]The set of hypotheses with probability $\geq$ .005 can grow as evidence favors some hypotheses and eliminates others.

Consider a simple DBN in which there are K fair coins, all flipped at time 1. The ith coin is reported with 95% accuracy at times $i + 1$ and $K + i + 1$. The network for this DBN contains a state node c_i for each coin and a single sensor node. Initially all the coins are given a random value from $\{Heads, Tails\}$. For all times $j > 1$ the coin c_i simply inherits its value at time $j - 1$. At time $j + 1$ the sensor outputs the value of coin c_j at time $j + 1$, with .95 accuracy. Similarly, at time $K + j + 1$ the sensor outputs the value of coin c_j at time $K + j + 1$, with .95 accuracy.[5]

The goal is to compute the probability that coin $c_i = Heads$ for each coin, given all $2K$ observations. To evaluate SOF, we compare the actual probability of $c_i = Heads$ with the estimate computed from the simulations returned by SOF. We compute the estimate from SOF by dividing the sum of the weights of the simulations in which $c_i = Heads$ by the sum of the weights of all simulations.

The graph in figure 3 shows the average error rate on a problem with 15 coins for SOF with $N = 1000$ samples. The graph reports the absolute error between the actual probability of $c_i = Heads$ given the evidence and the weighted estimate from SOF. The graph shows both that the errors are high (the average error is .24) and that the error is worse for the higher number coins. Our explanation is as follows. At time 1, SOF picks 1000 of the possible 2^{15} combinations of $Heads$ or $Tails$ for the coins. At time 2, SOF re-populates its samples based on the first report on coin 1. At time 3, SOF does the same for coin 2. As SOF gets to the higher number coins, its sample population becomes more and more skewed as it generates more copies of the combinations of coin flips that match the lower number coins.

Figure 3 also shows the performance of a modified version of SOF, called SOF-Bayes, which we describe below. As shown in the graph, SOF-Bayes performs much better on this problem.

New algorithms

We now present new methods.

Rewind/replay algorithm

We now introduce the *Rewind/Replay* (RR) algorithm, which is closely related to the sampling method called sequential imputation (discussed below).

We first describe RR informally in terms of solving a DBN. RR samples each time slice of the network a fixed number of times, and then randomly chooses one sample from those that contain the observations for that time slice. It discards all the other samples of the current time slice and simulates forward from the chosen sample into the next time slice. If the observed evidence does not arise in any of the samples of a time slice, then

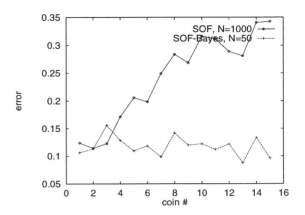

Figure 3: Error for SOF with $N = 1000$ and SOF-Bayes with $N = 50$ on the CoinNet problem. Results averaged from 200 trials.

RR abandons the current instantiation of the DBN it is constructing, and begins again from the first time slice.

The number of times RR samples each time slice is an input integer, R_{max}, to the RR algorithm. Each time RR makes it through all the time slices it generates a single sample of the entire network that matches all the evidence. RR assigns the sample a weight of $F_1 \times F_2 \times ... \times F_n$ where F_i is the fraction of samples of time slice i that matched the observations for time i. The justification for this weighting method is that the probability of the sample given the evidence is $\mathbf{P}(E_1 \mid S_1) \times \mathbf{P}(E_2 \mid S_2) \times ... \times \mathbf{P}(E_n \mid S_n)$, where $\mathbf{P}(E_i \mid S_i)$ is the probability of the evidence at time i given the state at time i and is approximated by F_i.

An optimization in our implementation of RR is to proceed to the next time slice as soon as the evidence arises in any sample. This is as random as choosing from the samples that matched the evidence after R_{max} tries, since the trials are independent. If RR manages to fully instantiate the network, it computes the weight for the network by returning to each time slice j and sampling it $R_{max} - k_j$ times, where k_j is the number of samples already performed on the jth time slice. This optimization reduces the computation expended in RR's failed attempts to sample the network.

The intuition behind RR can be explained in terms of the task of flipping twenty coins until all of them are heads. The logical sampling approach is to flip all twenty coins, and if they do not all come up heads, flip them all again. This is expected to succeed in 1 out of 2^{20} trials. The Rewind/Replay approach is to flip each coin until it is heads and then move on to the next coin. For $R_{max} = 5$, RR should succeed with $1 - (\frac{2^5-1}{2^5})^{20}$ probability, or about 1 in 2 times. With $R_{max} = 10$, RR will succeed with over .99 probability.

We now describe RR in terms of an arbitrary Bayesian network. To do so, we need to distribute the input observations $\mathcal{O} = \{O_1 = o_1, ..., O_n = o_n\}$ into a sequence of sets of observations $\mathcal{E}_1, \mathcal{E}_2, ... \mathcal{E}_m$ such that

---

[5]Note that not all time slices are identical in this DBN, because different state nodes are connected to the observation node in different time slices.

procedure: RR($B, \mathcal{E} = \{\mathcal{E}_1...\mathcal{E}_m\}, N, R_{max}$)
$\mathcal{SIMS} \leftarrow \emptyset$
for $i = 1$ to N
   $s_i \leftarrow \emptyset; w_i \leftarrow 1; step \leftarrow 0$
   while ($step \leq m$ **and** $w_i > 0$)
      $nodes \leftarrow \text{ANC}(\mathcal{E}_{step}, \mathcal{E}, B)$
      $\mathcal{M} \leftarrow \emptyset$
      for $l = 1$ **to** R_{max}
         add a sample of $nodes$ to s_i
         if $\text{HOLDS}(\mathcal{E}_{step}, s_i)$
            then add copy of s_i to $\mathcal{M}$
         remove sampled values of $nodes$ from s_i
      $w_i \leftarrow w_i \times \frac{|\mathcal{M}|}{R_{max}}$
      if $|\mathcal{M}| > 0$
         then $s_i \leftarrow$ random selection from $\mathcal{M}$
      $step \leftarrow step + 1$
   if $w_i > 0$,
      then add $\langle s_i, w_i \rangle$ to $\mathcal{SIMS}$
return $\mathcal{SIMS}$

function: $\text{ANC}(\mathcal{E}_i, \{\mathcal{E}_1...\mathcal{E}_m\}, B)$
   Return set of all variables V_i in B from which
   there is a directed path in B from V_i to a
   variable in $\mathcal{E}_j$ but not a directed path to
   any variable $e_j \in \mathcal{E}_1 \cup \mathcal{E}_2 \cup ... \cup \mathcal{E}_{j-1}$.

Figure 4: The Rewind/Replay algorithm.

each observation goes into exactly one evidence set. Although it will not effect correctness, the distribution of the evidence can have a significant impact on the performance of RR. For example, if all the evidence is put into a single set, i.e., $\mathcal{E}_1 = \{\mathcal{O}\}$, then RR is equivalent to LS. Unless otherwise stated, we will assume the opposite extreme of putting each observation in its own set, i.e, for $1 \leq i \leq n$, $\mathcal{E}_i = \{O_i = o_i\}$.

RR needs to determine which nodes influence the observations in each set $\mathcal{E}_j$. When sampling a Bayesian network, the only nodes which can influence the probability distribution over the value of some node O_i when O_i is sampled are the ancestors of O_i (i.e., the parents of O_i, the parents of the parents O_i, and so on). As we process each evidence set $\mathcal{E}_j$, we want to sample only the variables which are ancestors of $\mathcal{E}_j$ and that we have not already sampled, i.e., that are not ancestors of any observation in $\mathcal{E}_1, ..., \mathcal{E}_{j-1}$. This set is determined by the function ANC, defined in figure 4.

The pseudo code for RR is shown in figure 4. For each simulation, RR iterates through the evidence sets $\mathcal{E}_1, ..., \mathcal{E}_m$. For each $\mathcal{E}_j$, RR samples the unsampled ancestors of $\mathcal{E}_j$ a total of R_{max} times and selects one of the samples that satisfies every variable assignment in $\mathcal{E}_j$. The weight for each returned sample is $\frac{M_1}{R_{max}} \times \frac{M_2}{R_{max}} \times ... \times \frac{M_m}{R_{max}}$, where M_i is the number of samples that matched evidence set $\mathcal{E}_i$.

RR uses the evidence to guide the simulations, but can avoid the problems caused by SOF's re-population phase. With $R_{max} = 10$ and $N = 500$, RR achieved .96 accuracy on the number guessing problem described

procedure: SOF-Bayes ($B, \mathcal{E} = \{\mathcal{E}_1...\mathcal{E}_m\}, N$)
for $i = 1$ to N
   $s_{1,i} \leftarrow \emptyset; w_i \leftarrow 1$
for $j = 1$ to m
   $X_j \leftarrow \text{ANC}(\mathcal{E}_j, \mathcal{E}, B)$
   for $i = 1$ to N
      $s_{j,i} \leftarrow$ randomized selection from $s_{j-1,1}, ..., s_{j-1,N}$
         weighted by $w_1, ..., w_N$.
      add a sample of X_j to $s_{j,i}$
      $w_i \leftarrow \text{LIKELIHOOD}(E_j | s_i)$
for $i = 1$ to N
   sample of any unsampled nodes in $s_{m,i}$
return $\langle s_{m,1}, w_1 \rangle ... \langle s_{m,N}, w_N \rangle$

Figure 5: The Survival-of-the-fittest algorithm for an arbitrary Bayesian network

above, on 1000 random trials. In the worst case, RR might effectively sample the network $10 \times 500 = 5000$ times, but in practice RR samples it much less frequently and, on average, only generates 69.4 complete instantiations of the network per 500 attempts. The other 430.6 attempts to instantiate the network require many fewer than 5000 samples of the network. In our Lisp implementations, RR required 3.3 CPU seconds to complete its inference, which is comparable to the 4.8 CPU seconds for SOF with $N = 1000$ to achieve an accuracy of .82. Additionally, RR achieved .09 error on the CoinNet problem, with $R_{max} = 10$ and $N = 1,000$.

The RR algorithm is closely related to the statistical sampling technique called sequential imputation (Kong *et al.* 1994; Liu 1996). Sequential imputation is a Monte Carlo technique for solving nonparametric Bayes models given some data $d_1, ..., d_i$ by incrementally sampling from the probability distribution $\mathbf{P}(d_i \mid d_1, ..., d_{i-1})$ for increasing values of i. RR is perhaps best viewed as one of many possible instantiations of sequential imputation for the task of inference on Bayesian networks.

SOF-Bayes

Figure 5 shows pseudo code for a variation of SOF that works on arbitrary Bayesian networks (SOF was designed for DBNs). Like RR, SOF-Bayes requires that the evidence be distributed into evidence sets $\mathcal{E}_1, ..., \mathcal{E}_m$. Like SOF, SOF-Bayes incrementally instantiates a set of N samples of the given network in parallel. However, while SOF samples the nodes time slice by time slice, SOF-Bayes first samples the ancestors of $\mathcal{E}_1$, then the (unsampled) ancestors of $\mathcal{E}_2$, and so on until all the evidence is accounted for. As a final step, SOF-Bayes samples any nodes which are not ancestors of any of the evidence variables.

There are two advantages of SOF-Bayes over SOF even for solving DBNs, both of which are also enjoyed by RR. First, SOF-Bayes lazily samples the network, only assigning values to variables when necessary for determining the likelihood of the evidence currently being used to re-populate the samples. Note that in any

DBN, a state variable in time slice i is only observed in time slice i if it is directly connected to an observation variable. In the CoinNet problem, for example, SOF-Bayes generates N independent samples of a coin just before the evidence re-enforces the most likely value of that coin. In contrast, SOF samples all the coins at time 0. By the time a coin's value is observed, SOF may have copied and re-populated the samples so many times that only a few independent samples of the coin remain, copied hundreds of times each.

A second advantage, somewhat conflated with the first advantage in the CoinNet problem, is that SOF-Bayes does not have to sample an entire time slice of nodes at once. Suppose K coins are flipped at time 1 and then all are reported with 100% accuracy at time 2. For SOF, only one of out 2^K samples will likely match the evidence. SOF-Bayes can work on each coin flip independently and thus will very likely match all the evidence with as few as $N = 10$ samples.

Experiments

We now describe our experiments. Our goal was to generate a large, non-trivial DBN in order to demonstrate the potential value of simulation-based reasoning for plan monitoring in uncertain domains.

We constructed a simple forest-fire domain based loosely on the Phoenix fire simulator (Hart and Cohen 1992).We use a grid representation of the terrain. During the course of the simulation, each cell is either burning or not. At each time step, the probability that a cell will be burning is computed (by a function not described here) based on the status of that cell and that cell's neighbors at the previous time slice.

There are ten noisy fire sensors, each of which reports on a 3×3 block of grid cells. The sensor can output *Low*, *Med*, or *High*, indicating that 0, 1–3, or 4–9 of the cells are on fire, respectively (with 10% noise added in). Additionally, each sensor has a solar battery with a 75% chance of being charged in each time slice. If the battery is not charged at time t then the sensor outputs *Recharging* at time $t + 1$.

A fire fighter is initially situated in the middle of the grid. The fire fighter monitors the fire sensors in order to decide whether to flee to one of four helipads situated on the edges of the grid. Each helipad, however, has only a .65 chance of being functional. The fire fighter receives reports of varying reliability about the condition of four helipads.

In these experiments, we used a 10×10 grid, and created a DBN with 30 identical time slices, resulting in a network with 3660 nodes. Most nodes in the network have nine parents. There are a total of 14 observations per time slice: 10 fire sensors and 4 helipad reports.[6] Figure 6 contains an ASCII representation of several time slices from one execution trace.

---

[6]A complete description of the domain is available at http://www.merl.com/projects/sim-inference/.

	LW	SOF $N = 1000$	SOF-Bayes $N = 1000$	RR $R_{max} = 50$
CPU seconds	181	235	168	128
Acc. on fire	–	.64	.83	.82
Acc. on helipad	–	.53	.66	.94

Table 1: Accuracy at predicting if a cell will contain fire and the condition of the helipads. Numbers averaged over 100 trial runs.

	LW	SOF $N = 1000$	SOF-Bayes $N = 1000$	RR $R_{max} = 75$
Survival rate	–	.61	.75	.95

Table 2: Survival rate of simulated fire fighter. Numbers averaged over 25 trial runs.

Results

The first set of experiments measured how accurately the algorithms could predict aspects of the world state from past observations. The results in table 1 were produced as follows. First we generated a sample of the network, s_r. We then set $\mathcal{O}_r$ to be the variable assignments for all the sensor nodes in s_r in the first 6 time steps. We then called LW, SOF, SOF-Bayes, and RR with observations $\mathcal{O}_r$. The algorithms ran until they produced at least 50 sample simulations or a 3 minute time limit elapsed. If the algorithm was still running after 3 minutes, we allowed it to finish its current run and included the simulations it returned (note that some of the reported times exceed 3 minutes). The SOF and SOF-Bayes algorithms require more time per run because they compute N simulations in parallel.

We then evaluated the sample simulations returned by the inference algorithms against the sample s_r. For each grid cell, we compared the status (*Burning* or *Safe*) of the cell at time 10 with the weighted estimate of the returned cell. We credit the algorithm with a correct prediction if the weighted estimate of the cell being *Safe* was greater than .5 and the cell's status in s_r is *Safe* or if the weighted estimate is less than .5 and the cell's status is *Burning*. Similarly, for each helipad, we compared the value of the helipad in s_r (either *Usable* or *Unusable*) with the weighted estimate of the returned distributions. If no distributions were returned, we counted this as guessing that all cells are *Safe* and all helipads *Usable*. As shown in table 1, RR performs best, and SOF-Bayes performed better than SOF. LW never generated any matches, primarily because it never matched all the *Recharging* signals, and thus we did not list any accuracies for LW.

In the second set of experiments, we used the weighted simulations to control the movements of the fire fighter and then compared the survival rate with the different inference algorithms. In each iteration the fire fighter can stay in its current cell or move to one of the eight adjacent cells. The procedure for decid-

State Variables

```
......h...    ......h...    ......h...    ......h...    ......h...    ......h...    .+....+...    .++++++++.
..........    ..........    ..........    ..........    ..........    .........++.   ..++..++++.   ++++++++++
..........    ..........    ..........    ..........    ..........    .........++   +++..+.+++    ++++++++++
H.........    H.........    H...f.....    H.f.......    f.....++++    +.....++++    ++++..++++    ++++++++++
..xx..f...    ..xx..f...    ..xx......    .+xx....++    ..xx.++.++    ++xx.+++++    ++xx+++++     ++xx++++++
..xx......    ..xx......    ..xx+..+..    .+xx+++++.    ++xx++++++    ++xx++++++    ++xx++++++    ++xx++++++
.........H    ...++....H    +..+++++.H    ++.+++++.+    ++++++++++    ++++++++++    ++++++++++    ++++++++++
....++....    ....++++..    .+..+++++.    ++.++++++.    ++++++++++    ++++++++++    ++++++++++    ++++++++++
....H+....    ...+++++..    ..+++++++.    ++++++++++.   +++++++++.    ++++++++++    ++++++++++    ++++++++++

time: 1       time: 4       time: 7       time: 10      time: 13      time: 16      time: 19      time: 23
```

```
..........    ..........    ..........    ..........    ..........    ..........    ..........    ..........
...-.-.-..    ...-.0.0..    ...2.0.0..    ...0.2.-..    ...0.0.1..    ...-.1.-..    ...-.2.2..    ....1.2.1..
.0......0.    .0......0.    .0......0.    .-......0.    .-......2     .-......-.    .-......2.    .-......-.
..........    ..........    ..........    ..........    ..........    ..........    ..........    ..........
.........-.   .........0.   .........1.   .........2.   .........-.   .........-.   .........2.   .........0.
.0........    .0........    .1........    .2........    .-........    .-........    .-........    .-........
....1.1...    ....2.0...    ....-.2...    ....2.2...    ....-.2...    ....-.-...    ....-.2...    ....2.2...
..........    ..........    ..........    ..........    ..........    ..........    ..........    ..........
```

Sensor Variables

Figure 6: ASCII representation of several time slices of an example simulation of the fire world domain. A '+' indicates fire, an 'H' indicates a working helipad, an 'h' indicates a non-working 'helipad', an 'x' indicates an impassable terrain. The fire fighter is denoted by an 'f'. In the sensor readings, a 0 indicates a low reading, a 1 indicates a medium reading, a 2 indicates a high reading, and a '-' indicates that the sensor is recharging. The messages indicating the condition of the helipads are not shown here.

ing where to go computes, for each weighted simulation and each cell, whether there is a path to safety from the cell. Based on the weights of the simulations, the procedure then moves to one of the cells with the highest probability of being safe, with a preference for remaining in the same cell. To speed the experiments, we only re-computed the weighted simulations given the observations at time 6, 8, and 10. As shown in table 2, the fire fighter survives much more often when using the Rewind/Replay algorithm than the other algorithms.

Discussion- plan monitoring

Although the above domain contains very little planning, recall that our initial motivation was to monitor and improve plans during their execution in dynamic domains. We now discuss how simulation-based inference can be applied to the task of plan monitoring.

Due to space limitations we will not describe in detail how a probabilistic plan and domain can be encoded as a DBN. Roughly speaking, however, the known information about possible initial states must be encoded into the first time slice of the network. The model of how actions effect the world must be encoded into all subsequent time slices. Additionally, the plan being executed must be incorporated into the network in order to indicate which actions will be executed in each time step.

We now briefly discuss how the simulation-based inference algorithms can be used to evaluate a possible modification to the plan. We assume that some of the actions in the plan will generate observable results.

Thus, at any point during plan execution there will be observed values for some of the variables in the DBN. These values can be input to RR or SOF-Bayes which will return weighted instantiations, or samples, of the DBN. For each returned instantiation, we can extract the time slice corresponding to the current state of the world. We now have a set of world states, each weighted by the probability that it is the current world state. In order to evaluate a potential modification to the plan, we can simulate the execution of the remaining steps of the original plan from each of the returned states, and do the same for the modified plan. These simulations will give us an estimate of the probability that the plan will succeed with and without the proposed modification. The more simulations we perform, the better our estimates will be.

Related and future work

One previous technique we have not yet mentioned is arc reversal (Shachter 1986; Fung and Chang 1989), which has been applied to DBNs (Cheuk and Boutilier 1997). Arc reversal involves reversing the arcs that point to the evidence nodes. This technique essentially uses the information in the CPT of the Bayesian network to perform reverse simulation from the observed evidence. Arc reversal can increase the size of the network exponentially and would do so on our networks. When reversing an arc from node n_1 to node n_2, all parents of n_1 and n_2 become parents to both nodes. Reversing a single arc in the fire network can increase the number of parents of a node from 9 to 17. This increases the size of the CPT for that node from 2^9 to 2^{17}. Furthermore, in our algorithm the original CPT is encoded compactly as a function, but would have to be expanded out into a table in order to reverse an arc.

There have been many other approaches to approximate inference on Bayesian networks (e.g., (Dechter and Rish 1997)) though most have not been specifically evaluated on complex temporal processes. (Boyen and Koller 1998) propose a method for approximating the belief state for DBNs and prove that, under certain assumptions, the error in the belief state can be bounded over time. Additionally, this approach allows for continuous monitoring of a system while RR, as presented here, requires an initial starting time. Prior work has suggested the use of sequential imputation for solving Bayes nets (Hanks *et al.* 1995), but did not propose our specific implementation of this idea or compare RR to SOF.

In this paper we have investigated simulation techniques for plan monitoring and have shown that some techniques have significant advantages over others. We have extended existing simulation algorithms by generalizing SOF to arbitrary Bayesian networks and introducing the Rewind/Replay algorithm.

Our plans for future work include determining whether RR is unbiased, substituting in LW rather than LS on the sampling step for RR, and developing strategies for distributing the evidence into evidence sets and for choosing the value for R_{max}. Additionally, we would like to compare RR and SOF-Bayes both with each other and previous methods on the task of solving arbitrary Bayesian networks.

Acknowledgments

Many thanks to Andy Golding and the AAAI reviewers for their comments on earlier drafts of this paper. This material is based upon work supported by ARPA under Grant number F30602-95-1-0025

References

X. Boyen and D. Koller. Tractable inference for complex stochastic processes. In *UAI'98*, pages 33–42, 1998.

A. Y.W Cheuk and C. Boutilier. Structured arc reversal and simulation of dynamic probabilistic networks. In *UAI'97*, pages 72–79, 1997.

P. Dagum and M. Pradhan. Optimal Monte Carlo Estimation Of Belief Network Inference. In *UAI'96*, pages 446–453, 1996.

Thomas Dean and Keiji Kanazawa. A model for reasoning about persistence and causation. *Computational Intelligence*, 5:142–150, 1989.

R. Dechter and I. Rish. A scheme for approximating probabilistic inference. In *UAI'97*, 1997.

R. Fung and K. Chang. Weighing and integrating evidence for stochastic simulation in Bayesian networks. In *UAI'89*, pages 209–219, 1989.

S. Hanks, D. Madigan, and J. Gavrin. Probabilistic temporal reasoning with endogenous change. In *UAI'95*, pages 245–254, 1995.

D.M Hart and P.R Cohen. Predicting and explaining success and task duration in the phoenix planner. In *Proceedings of the First International Conference on AI Planning Systems*, pages 106–115, 1992.

M. Henrion. Propagation of uncertainty in Bayesian networks by probabilistic logic sampling. In *Uncertainty in Artificial Intelligence 2*, pages 149–163, 1988.

K. Kanazawa, Koller D., and S. Russell. Stochastic simulation algorithms for dynamic probabilistic networks. In *UAI'95*, pages 346–351, 1995.

U. Kjaerulff. A computational scheme for reasoning in dynamic probabilistic networks. In *UAI'92*, pages 121–129, July 1992.

A. Kong, J.S. Liu, and W.H. Wong. Sequential imputation and Bayesian missing data problems. *J. Americian Statistical Association*, pages 278–288, 1994.

N. Kushmerick, S. Hanks, and D. Weld. An Algorithm for Probabilistic Planning. *J. Artificial Intelligence*, 76:239–286, 1995.

J.S. Liu. Nonparametric hierarchical bayes via sequential imputation. *Ann. Statist.*, pages 910–930, 1996.

J. Pearl. *Probablistic Reasoning in Intelligent Systems*. Morgan Kaufmann, San Mateo, CA, 1988.

R.D. Shachter and M. A. Peot. Simulation approaches to general probabilistic inference on belief networks. In *UAI'89*, 1989.

R.D. Shachter. Evaluating influence diagrams. *Operations Research*, 33(6):871–882, 1986.

Selective Sampling for Nearest Neighbor Classifiers

Michael Lindenbaum
mic@cs.technion.ac.il

Shaul Markovich
shaulm@cs.technion.ac.il

Dmitry Rusakov
rusakov@cs.technion.ac.il

Computer Science Department,
Technion - Israel Institute of Technology,
32000, Haifa, Israel

Abstract

In the *passive*, traditional, approach to learning, the information available to the learner is a set of classified examples, which are randomly drawn from the instance space. In many applications, however, the initial classification of the training set is a costly process, and an intelligently selection of training examples from unlabeled data is done by an *active* learner.

This paper proposes a lookahead algorithm for example selection and addresses the problem of active learning in the context of nearest neighbor classifiers. The proposed approach relies on using a *random field* model for the example labeling, which implies a dynamic change of the label estimates during the sampling process.

The proposed selective sampling algorithm was evaluated empirically on artificial and real data sets. The experiments show that the proposed method outperforms other methods in most cases.

Introduction

In many real-world domains it is expensive to label a large number of examples for training, and the problem of reducing training set size, while maintaining the quality of the resulting classifier, arises. A possible solution to this problem is to give the learning algorithm some control over the inputs on which it trains.

This paradigm is called *active learning*, and is roughly divided into two major subfields: learning with *membership queries* and *selective sampling*. In learning with membership queries (Angluin 1988) the learner is allowed to construct artificial examples, while selective sampling deals with selection of informative examples from a large set of unclassified data.

Selective sampling methods have been developed for various classification learning algorithms: for neural networks (Davis & Hwang 1992; Cohn, Atlas, & Lander 1994), for the $C4.5$ rule-induction algorithm (Lewis & Catlett 1994) and for HMM (Dagan & Engelson 1995).

The goal of the research described in this paper is to develop a selective sampling methodology for nearest neighbor classification learning algorithms. The

nearest neighbor (Cover & Hart 1967; Aha, Kibler, & Albert 1991) algorithm is a non-parametric classification method, useful especially when little information is known about the structure of the distribution, implying that parametric classifiers are harder to construct. The problem of active learning for nearest neighbor classifiers was considered by Hasenjager and Ritter (1998). They proposed querying in points which are the farthest from previously sampled examples, i.e. in the vertices of Voronoi diagram of the points labeled so far. This method, however, falls under the membership queries paradigm and is not suitable for selective sampling.

Most existing selective sampling algorithms focus on choosing examples from regions of uncertainty. One approach to define uncertainty is to specify a committee (Seung, Opper, & Sompolinsky 1992) or an ensemble (Krogh & Vedelsby 1994) of hypotheses consistent with the sampled data and then to choose an example on which the committee members most disagree. *Query By Committee* is an active research topic, and strong theoretical results (Freund *et al.* 1997) along with practical justifications (Dagan & Engelson 1995; Hasenjager & Ritter 1996; RayChaudhuri & Hamey 1995) were achieved. It is not clear, however, how to apply this method to nearest-neighbor classification.

This paper introduces a lookahead approach to selective sampling that is suitable for nearest neighbor classification. We start by formalizing the problem of selective sampling and continue with a lookahead based framework which chooses the next example (or sequence of examples) in order to maximize the expected utility (*goodness*) of the resulting classifier. The major components needed to apply this framework are an utility function for appraising classifiers and a posteriori class probability estimates for points in the instance space. We propose a *random field* model for the feature space classification structure. This model serves as the basis for a class probability estimation. The merit of our approach is empirically demonstrated on artificial and real problems.

The Selective Sampling Process

We consider here the following selective sampling paradigm. Let $\mathcal{X}$ be a set of objects. Let f be a *teacher* (also called an oracle or an expert) which labels instances by 0 or 1, $f : \mathcal{X} \to \{0, 1\}$. A *learning algorithm* takes a set of *classified examples*, $\{\langle x_1, f(x_1) \rangle, \ldots, \langle x_n, f(x_n) \rangle\}$, and returns a *hypothesis* h, $h : \mathcal{X} \to \{0, 1\}$. Throughout this paper we assume that $\mathcal{X} = \mathbb{R}^d$.

Let X be an *instance space* - a set of objects drawn randomly from $\mathcal{X}$ according to distribution p. Let $D \subset X$ be a finite set of classified examples. A *selective sampling algorithm* S_L with respect to learning algorithm L takes X and D, and returns an unclassified element of X. An *active learning* process can be described as follows:

1. $D \leftarrow \emptyset$

2. $h \leftarrow L(\emptyset)$

3. While stop-criterion is not satisfied do:

   (a) Apply S_L and get the next example, $x \leftarrow S_L(X, D)$.

   (b) Ask the teacher to label x, $\omega \leftarrow f(x)$

   (c) Update the labeled examples set, $D \leftarrow D \bigcup \{\langle x, \omega \rangle\}$

   (d) Update the classifier, $h \leftarrow L(D)$

4. Return classifier h

The stop criterion may be a limit M on the number of examples that the teacher is willing to classify or a lower bound on the classifier accuracy. We will assume here the first case. The goal of the selective sampling algorithm is to produce a sequence of length M which leads to a best classifier according to some given criterion.

Lookahead Algorithms for Selective Sampling

Knowing that we are allowed to ask for exactly M labels allows, in principle, to consider all object sequences of length M. Not knowing the labeling of these objects, however, prevents us from evaluating the resulting classifiers directly. One way to overcome this difficulty is to consider the selective sampling process as an interaction between the learner and the teacher. At each stage the learner must select an object from the set of unclassified instances and the teacher assigns one of the possible labels to the selected object. This interaction can be represented by a "game tree" of $2M$ levels such as the one illustrated Figure 1.

We can use such a tree representation to develop a lookahead algorithm for selective sampling. Let $U_L(D)$ be a *utility evaluation function* that is capable of appraising a set D as examples for a learning algorithm L. Let us define a k-deep lookahead algorithm for selective sampling with respect to learning algorithm L as illustrated on Figure 2.

Note that this algorithm is a specific case of a decision theoretic agent, and that, while it is specified for maximizing the expected utility, one can be, for exam-

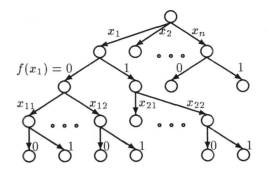

Figure 1: Selective sampling as a game.

$\mathbf{S_L^k(X, D)}$:
Select $x' \in X$ with maximal expected utility:

$$x' = \arg\max_{x \in X} E_\omega[U_L^*(X, D \cup \{\langle x, \omega \rangle\}, k - 1)]$$

where $U_L^*(X, D, k)$ is a recursive utility propagation function:

$$U_L^*(X, D, k) = \begin{cases} U_L(D) & k = 0 \\ \max_x E_\omega[U_L^*(X, D', k - 1)] & k > 0 \end{cases}$$

where $D' = D \cup \{\langle x, \omega \rangle\}$ and the expected value $E_\omega[\cdot]$ is taken according to conditional probabilities for classification of x given D, $P(f(x) = \omega | D)$.

Figure 2: Lookahead algorithm for selective sampling.

ple, pessimistic and consider a *minimax* approach. In our implementation we use a simplified one-step lookahead algorithm:

$\mathbf{S_L^*(X, D)}$:
Select $x \in X$ with maximal expected utility, $E_{\omega \in \{0, 1\}}[U_L(D \cup \{\langle x, \omega \rangle\})]$, which is equal to:

$$P(f(x) = 0 | D) \cdot U_L(D \cup \{\langle x, 0 \rangle\}) +$$
$$P(f(x) = 1 | D) \cdot U_L(D \cup \{\langle x, 1 \rangle\})$$

The actual use of the lookahead example selection scheme relies on two choices:

- The utility function $U_L(D)$.

- The method for estimating $P(f(x) = 0 | D)$ (and $P(f(x) = 1 | D)$).

Two particular choices are considered in the next sections.

The Classifier Accuracy Utility Function

Taking a Bayesian approach, we specify the utility of the classifier as its expected accuracy relative to the distribution of consistent target functions. First, consider a specific target f. Let $I_{f,h}$ be a binary indicator function, where $I_{f,h}(x) = 1$ iff $f(x) = h(x)$, and let $\alpha_f(h)$ denote the accuracy of hypothesis h relative to f: $\alpha_f(h) = f \cap h = \int_{x \in \mathbb{R}^d} I_{f,h}(x)\mathfrak{p}(x)dx$. Recall that $\mathfrak{p}(x)$ is the probability density function specifying the instance distribution over $\mathbb{R}^d$. Let $\mathcal{A}_L(D)$ denote the expected accuracy of a hypothesis produced by learning algorithm L:

$$
\begin{aligned}
\mathcal{A}_L(D) = \ & E_{f|D}[\alpha_f(h = L(D))] = \\
& E_{f|D}[\int_{x \in \mathbb{R}^d} I_{f,h}(x)\mathfrak{p}(x)dx] = \\
& \int_{x \in \mathbb{R}^d} P(f(x) = h(x)|D)\mathfrak{p}(x)dx
\end{aligned} \tag{1}
$$

where $P(f(x) = h(x)|D)$ is the probability that a random target function f consistent with D will be equal to h in the point x, i.e $P(f(x) = h(x)|D) = E_{f|D}[f(x) = h(x)]$.

Note that $P(f(x) = h(x)|D)$ is the probability that a particular point x gets the correct classification. Therefore, for every given hypothesis h, estimating the class probabilities $P(f(x) = 0|D), P(f(x) = 1|D)$, gives also the accuracy estimate (from Equation 1):

$$
\mathcal{A}_L(D) \approx \sum_{x \in X} P(f(x) = h(x)|D)/|X|. \tag{2}
$$

(The number of examples in X is assumed to be finite). Thus the problem of evaluating the utility measure as the classifier accuracy is translated into the problem of estimating the class probabilities. Assuming that the probability computation model is correct, the optimal selective sampling strategy is one that uses $U_L^*(D) \triangleq \mathcal{A}_L(D)$ as the utility function.

Random Field Model for Feature Space Classification

Feature vectors from the same class tend to cluster in the feature space (though sometimes the clusters are quite complex). Therefore close feature vectors share the same label more often than not. This intuitive observation, which is the rationale for the nearest neighbor classification approach, is used here to estimate the classes of unlabeled feature points and their uncertainties.

Mathematically, this observation is described by assuming that the label of every point is a random variable, and that these random variables are mutually dependent. Such dependencies are usually described (in a higher than 1-dimensional space) by *random field models*. In the probabilistic setting, estimating the classification of unlabeled vectors and their uncertainties is equivalent to calculating the conditional class probabilities from the labeled data, relying on the random field model. In the full version of the paper (Lindenbaum, Markovich, & Rusakov 1999), we consider several options for such estimates. This shorter version focuses on one particular model.

Thus, we assume that the classification of an instance space is a *sample function* of a binary valued *homogeneous isotropic random field* (Wong & Hajek 1985) characterized by a *covariance* function decreasing with a distance. (see (Eldar *et al.* 1997) where a similar method was used for progressive image sampling.) That is: let x_0, x_1 be points in X and let θ_0, θ_1 be their classifications, i.e. random variables that can have values of 0 or 1. The homogeneity and isotropy properties imply that the expected values of θ_0 and θ_1 are equal, i.e. $E[\theta_0] = E[\theta_1] = \bar{\theta}$, and the covariance between θ_0 and θ_1 is specified only by the distance between x_0 and x_1:

$$
C[\theta_0, \theta_1] = E[(\theta_0 - \bar{\theta})(\theta_1 - \bar{\theta})] \triangleq \gamma(d(x_0, x_1)) \tag{3}
$$

where $\gamma : \mathbb{R}^+ \to (-1, 1)$ is a covariance function with $\gamma(0) = Var[\theta] = E[(\theta - \bar{\theta})^2] = P_0 P_1$, where P_0, $P_1 = 1 - P_0$ are the a priori class probabilities. Usually we will assume that γ is decreasing with the distance and that $\lim_{r \to \infty} \gamma(r) = 0$. Note that the random field model specifies (indirectly) a distribution of target functions.

In estimation, one tries to find the value of some unobserved random variable, from observed values of other, related, random variables, and prior knowledge about their joint statistics.

The class probabilities associated with some feature vector are uniquely specified by the conditional mean of its associated random variable (r.v.) This conditional mean is also the best estimator for the r.v. value in the least squares sense (Papoulis 1991). Therefore, the widely available methods for *mean square error* (MSE) estimation can be used for estimating the class probabilities.

We choose a linear estimator, for which a closed form solution, described below, is available. Let θ be the binary r.v. associated with some unlabeled feature vector, x_0, and let $\theta_1, \ldots, \theta_n$ be the known labels r.v. associated with the feature vectors, $x_1, \ldots, x_n$, that were already sampled. Now let

$$
\hat{\theta} = \alpha_0 + \sum_{i=1}^{n} \alpha_i \theta_i \tag{4}
$$

be the estimate of the unknown label. The estimate uses the known labels and relies on unknown coefficients which should be set so that the MSE, $\epsilon_{mse} = E[(\hat{\theta} - \theta_0)^2]$ is minimized.

The optimal linear approximation in the MS sense (Papoulis 1991) is described by:

$$
\hat{\theta} = E[\theta_0] + \vec{\mathbf{a}} \cdot (\vec{\theta} - E[\vec{\theta}])^t \tag{5}
$$

where $\vec{\mathbf{a}}$ is an n-dimensional vector specified by the covariance values:

$$
\begin{aligned}
& \vec{\mathbf{a}} = \mathbf{R}^{-1} \cdot \vec{\mathbf{r}}, \\
& R_{ij} = E[(\theta_i - E[\theta])(\theta_j - E[\theta])], \\
& r_i = E[(\theta_0 - E[\theta])(\theta_j - E[\theta])].
\end{aligned} \tag{6}
$$

($\mathbf{R}$ is an $n \times n$ matrix, and $\vec{\mathbf{a}}, \vec{\mathbf{r}}$ are n-dimensional vectors). The values of $\mathbf{R}$ and $\vec{\mathbf{r}}$ are specified by the random field model:

$$
\begin{aligned}
& R_{ij} = \gamma(d(x_i, x_j)), \\
& r_i = \gamma(d(x_0, x_i)).
\end{aligned} \tag{7}
$$

See the experimental part for an evaluation of some covariance function and for their use in estimating the parameters. With this method, every sampled point influences the estimated probability. In practice, such long range influence is non-intuitive and is also computationally expensive. Therefore, in practice, we neglect the influence of all except the two closest neighbors. This choice gives a higher probability to the nearest neighbor class and is therefore consistent with 1-NN classification. One deficiency of this estimation process is that the estimated probabilities are not guaranteed to lie in the required $[0, 1]$ range. When such overflows indeed happen (very rarely), we correct them by clipping the estimate. This deficiency is corrected in more complex estimation procedures, described in the full version (Lindenbaum, Markovich, & Rusakov 1999). (The framework we use is similar to *Bayesian Classification* via *Gaussian Process Modeling* (MacKay 1998; Williams & Barber 1998)

Experimental Evaluation

We have implemented our random-field based lookahead algorithm and tested it on several problems, comparing its performance with several other selective sampling methods.

Experimental Methodology

The algorithm described in the previous sections allows us to heuristically choose the covariance function, $\gamma(d)$. In the experiments described here, every class contained a nearly equal number of examples and therefore we assume that the a priori class probabilities are equal. This implies that $\gamma(0) = 0.25$. We choose an exponentially decreasing covariance function (common in image processing) $\gamma(d) = 0.25e^{-d/\sigma}$. We tested the effect of a range of σ values on the performance of the algorithm and found that changing σ had almost no effect (these results are included in the full version (Lindenbaum, Markovich, & Rusakov 1999)

The lookahead algorithm was compared with the following three selective sampling algorithms, which represent the most common choices (see introduction):

- *Random sampling:* The algorithm randomly selects the next example. While this method looks unsophisticated, it has the advantage of yielding a uniform exploration of the instance space. This method actually corresponds to a *passive* learning model.

- *Uncertainty sampling:* The method selects the example which the current classifier is most uncertain about. The uncertainty for each example depends on the ratio between the distances to the closest labeled neighbors of different classes This method tends to sample on the existing border, and while for some decision boundaries that may be beneficial, for others it may be a source for serious failure (as will be shown in the following subsections).

- *Maximal distance:* An adaptation of the method described by Hasenjager and Ritter (1998). This method selects the example from the set of all unlabeled points that have different labels among their three nearest classified neighbors. The example selected is the one which is most distant from its closest labeled neighbor.

The basic measurement used for the experiments is the expected error rate. For each selective sampling method and for each dataset the following procedure was applied:

1. 1000 examples from the dataset were drawn randomly - this is a set used for selective sampling and learning ,X, the rest 19000 examples (all datasets included 20000 examples) were used *only* for the evaluation of error rates of the resulting classifiers.

2. The selective sampling algorithm was applied to the chosen set, X. After selection of each example, the error rate of the current hypothesis, h (which is the nearest neighbor classifier), was calculated using the test set of 19000 examples put aside.

3. Steps 1, 2 were performed 100 times and the average error rate was calculated.

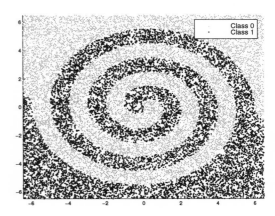

Figure 3: The feature space of the "two spirals" data.

The 'Two Spirals' Problem

The *two spirals* problem was studied by a number of researchers (Lang & Witbrock 1988; Hasenjager & Ritter 1998). This is an artificial problem where the task is to distinguish between two spirals of uniform density in XY-plane, as shown in Figure 3. (The code for generating these spirals was based on (Lang & Witbrock 1988)) The Bayes error of such classification is zero since the classes are perfectly separable. The learning rate of the various selective sampling methods is shown in Figure 4. All three non-random methods demonstrated comparable performance, better than random sampling. In the next experiment we will show that other methods lack one of the basic properties required from selective sampling algorithms - exploration - and fail in the datasets consisting of separated regions of the same classification.

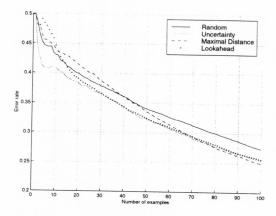

Figure 4: Learning rate graphs for various selective sampling methods applied to the "two spirals" data.

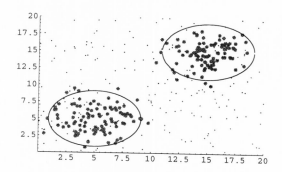

Figure 5: A feature space with bayes decision boundaries (only 400 points are shown) for "two gaussians" data.

'Two Gaussians' Data

The test set of "two gaussians" consists of two dimensional vectors belonging to two classes with equal a priori probability (0.5). The distribution of class 1 is uniform over the region $[0, 20] \times [0, 20]$ and the distribution of class 0 consists of two symmetric gaussians, with means in points $(5, 5)$ and $(15, 15)$ and covariance matrix $\Sigma = 2^2 I$, illustrated in Figure 5. The bayes error is 0.18207.

The learning rate of the various selective sampling methods is shown in Figure 6. We can see that apparently the uncertainty and maximal distance selective sampling methods fail to detect one of the gaussians, resulting in higher error rates. This is due to fact that these methods consider sampling only at the existing boundary.

Letters Data

The *letter recognition database* (contributed to UCI Machine learning repository (Blake, Keogh, & Merz 1998) by Frey and Slate (1991) consists of 20000 feature vectors belonging to 26 classes that represent capital letters of Latin alphabet. Since our current implementation works only with binary classification, we converted the database to such by changing all letters from 'a' to 'm'

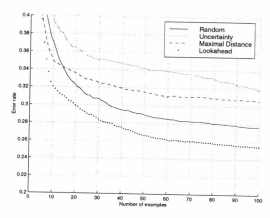

Figure 6: Learning rate graphs for various selective sampling methods applied to the "two gaussians" data.

to 0 and all the letters from 'n' to 'z' to 1. The learning rate of the various selective sampling methods is shown in Figure 7. The lookahead selective sampling algorithm outperforms other selective sampling methods in this particularly hard domain, where every class consists of many different (associated with the different letters).

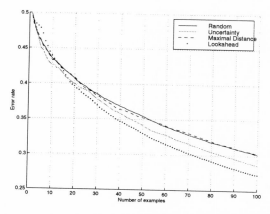

Figure 7: Learning rate graphs for various selective sampling methods applied to the letters dataset.

Discussion

Nearest neighbor classifiers are often used when little or no information is available about the instance space structure. There, the loose, minimalistic specification of the instance space labeling structure, which is implied by the distance based random field model, seems to be adequate. We also observe that large changes in the covariance function had no significant effect on the classification performance.

The experiments show that lookahead sampling method performs better or comparatively to other selective sampling algorithms on both artificial and real domains. It is especially strong when the instance space

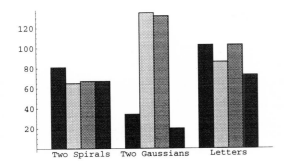

Figure 8: Number of examples needed for average error to reach 0.3. From left to right: random, uncertainty, maximal distance and lookahead sampling methods.

contains more than one region of some class. Then, the selective sampling algorithm must consider not only the examples from the hypothesis boundary, but must also explore large unsampled regions. The lack of 'exploration' element in 'uncertainty' and 'maximal distance' sampling methods often results in a failure in such cases. The benefit of a lookahead selective sampling method can be seen by comparing the number of examples needed to reach some pre-defined accuracy, Figure 8.

Counting the classification of one point (including finding 1 or 2 labeled neighbors) as a basic operation, the uncertainty and maximal distance methods have time complexity of $O(|X|)$ while the straightforward implementation of lookahead selective sampling has a time complexity of $O(|X|^2)$ (we need to compute class probabilities for all points in the instance space after each lookahead hypothesis). This higher complexity, however, is well justified for a natural setup, where we are ready to invest computational resources to save time for a human expert whose role is to label an examples.

References

Aha, D. W.; Kibler, D.; and Albert, M. K. 1991. Instance-based learning algorithms. *Machine Learning* 6(1):37–66.

Angluin, D. 1988. Queries and concept learning. *Machine Learning* 2(3):319–42.

Blake, C.; Keogh, E.; and Merz, C. 1998. UCI repository of machine learning databases [http://www.ics.uci.edu/~mlearn/MLRepository.html] University of California, Irvine, Dept. of Information and Computer Sciences.

Cohn, D. A.; Atlas, L.; and Lander, R. 1994. Improving generalization with active learning. *Machine Learning* 15(2):201–21.

Cover, T. M., and Hart, P. E. 1967. Nearest neighbor pattern classification. *IEEE Transactions on Information Theory* 13(1):21–27.

Dagan, I., and Engelson, S. P. 1995. Committee-based sampling for training probabilistic classifiers. In *Ma-chine Learning - International Workshop then Conference - 1995; conf 12*, 150–157. Morgan Kaufmann.

Davis, D. T., and Hwang, J.-N. 1992. Attentional focus training by boundary region data selection. In *IJCNN*, volume 1, 676–81. IEEE.

Eldar, Y.; Lindenbaum, M.; Porat, M.; and Zeevi, Y. Y. 1997. The farthest point strategy for progressive image sampling. *IEEE Transactions on Image Processing* 6(9):1305–15.

Freund, Y.; Seung, H. S.; Shamir, E.; and Tishbi, N. 1997. Selective sampling using the query by committee algorithm. *Machine Learning* 28(2-3):133–68.

Frey, P. W., and Slate, D. J. 1991. Letter recognition using holland-style adaptive classifiers. *Machine Learning* 6(2):161–82.

Hasenjager, M., and Ritter, H. 1996. Active learning of the generalized high-low-game. In *ICANN*, xxv+922, 501–6. Springer-Verlag.

Hasenjager, M., and Ritter, H. 1998. Active learning with local models. *Neural Processing Letters* 7(2):107–17.

Krogh, A., and Vedelsby, J. 1994. Neural network ensembles, cross validation, and active learning. In *NIPS*, volume 7, 231–8. MIT Press.

Lang, K. J., and Witbrock, M. J. 1988. Learning to tell two spirals apart. In *Proceedings of the Connectionist Models Summer School*, 52–59. Morgan Kaufmann.

Lewis, D. D., and Catlett, J. 1994. Heterogeneous uncertainty sampling for supervised learning. In *Machine Learning - International Workshop then Conference - 1994; conf 11*, 148–156.

Lindenbaum, M.; Markovich, S.; and Rusakov, D. 1999. Selective sampling by random field modelling. Technical Report CIS9906, Technion - Israel Institute of Technology.

MacKay, D. J. 1998. Introduction to gaussian processes. *NATO ASI series. Series F, Computer and system sciences.* 168:133.

Papoulis, A. 1991. *Probability, Random Variables, and Stohastic Processes.* McGraw-Hill series in electrical engineering, Communications and signal processing. McGraw-Hill, Inc., 3rd edition.

RayChaudhuri, T., and Hamey, L. 1995. Minimisation of data collection by active learning. In *IEEE ICNN*, volume 3, 6 vol. l+3219, 1338–41. IEEE.

Seung, H. S.; Opper, M.; and Sompolinsky, H. 1992. Query by committee. In *Proceedings of the Fifth Annual ACM Workshop on Computational Learning Theory*, v+452, 287–94. ACM; New York, NY, USA.

Williams, C. K. I., and Barber, D. 1998. Bayesian classification with gaussian processes. *IEEE PAMI* 20(12):1342.

Wong, E., and Hajek, B. 1985. *Stohastic Processes in Engineering Systems.* Springer-Verlag.

Toward a Theoretical Understanding of Why and When Decision Tree Pruning Algorithms Fail

Tim Oates and David Jensen
Experimental Knowledge Systems Laboratory
Department of Computer Science
Box 34610 LGRC
University of Massachusetts
Amherst, MA 01003-4610
{oates, jensen}@cs.umass.edu

Abstract

Recent empirical studies revealed two surprising pathologies of several common decision tree pruning algorithms. First, tree size is often a linear function of training set size, even when additional tree structure yields no increase in accuracy. Second, building trees with data in which the class label and the attributes are independent often results in large trees. In both cases, the pruning algorithms fail to control tree growth as one would expect them to. We explore this behavior theoretically by constructing a statistical model of reduced error pruning. The model explains why and when the pathologies occur, and makes predictions about how to lessen their effects. The predictions are operationalized in a variant of reduced error pruning that is shown to control tree growth far better than the original algorithm.

Introduction

Despite more than three decades of intense research on decision trees, arguably the most commonly used learning mechanism in implemented AI systems, existing characterizations of their behavior are overwhelmingly empirical rather than theoretical. There is currently a large gap between the algorithms and representations that appear to be amenable to theoretical analysis on the one hand, and decision trees on the other. Empirical studies have identified solutions to various parts of the overall process of building decision trees that work well in a broad set of circumstances. However, making precise statements about when and, perhaps more importantly, why those solutions are either appropriate or inappropriate remains difficult.

This paper attempts to narrow the gap between theory and practice by presenting a statistical model that explains one particularly surprising pathology of several common pruning algorithms that occurs with data devoid of structure. The pathology is illustrated in Figure 1, which plots tree size as a function of dataset size for three common pruning techniques – error-based (EBP) (Quinlan 1993), reduced error (REP) (Quinlan

1987), and minimum description length (MDL) (Quinlan & Rivest 1989).[1] All trees were built with C4.5. The datasets contained 30 binary attributes and a binary class label, all with values assigned randomly from a uniform distribution. There was no relationship between the attributes and the class label. Given such datasets, one would expect pruning algorithms to emit trees with a single node – a leaf labeled with the majority class. This does not happen. Trees built with these data exhibit an almost perfectly linear relationship between the amount of structureless data used to build the tree and the size of the final pruned tree.

Although the phenomenon depicted in Figure 1 is most clearly demonstrated with structureless artificial data, it occurs in a broad range of real world datasets (Oates & Jensen 1997; 1998) because they contain subsets of instances with no structure (or structure that cannot be identified by tree growing algorithms). Decision tree growing algorithms typically do not stop splitting the data precisely when all of the structure in the data has been captured. Instead, they push past that point, splitting subsets of the data wherein the attributes and the class label are either totally or nearly independent, leaving it to the pruning phase to find the "correct" tree. The result is that some number of subtrees in the unpruned tree are constructed through recursive invocations of the tree growing algorithm on structureless data, such as that used in Figure 1. The question that remains to be answered is why trees (and subtrees) built from such data escape pruning.

To better understand why several well-studied pruning algorithms leave large amounts of excess structure in trees, we developed a statistical model of one particular algorithm – REP. Analysis of the model provides insights into why and under what conditions REP fails to control tree growth as it should. For example, we identify two properties that hold for almost every deci-

---

[1] The horizontal axis is the total number of instances available to the tree building process. Each point in the plot reflects the result of 10-fold cross validation, so the actual number of instances used to build the trees is 9/10 of the corresponding position on the horizontal axis. In addition, REP further split the data into a growing set (2/3 of the data) and a pruning set (1/3 of the data).

sion node rooting a subtree that fits noise. They are:

- The probability of pruning such nodes *prior to pruning beneath them* is close to 1. That is especially true for large pruning sets.

- Pruning that occurs beneath such nodes often has the counterintuitive effect of reducing the probability that they will be pruned to be close to 0.

Insights gleaned from the model led to the development of a novel variant of REP that yields significantly smaller trees with accuracies that are comparable to those of trees pruned by the original algorithm. Rather than considering all of the available pruning data when making pruning decisions, the new algorithm selects a randomly sampled subset of that data prior to making each decision. The degree of overlap between samples is a user controlled parameter, with 100% overlap corresponding to standard REP, and 0% overlap (which is feasible when large amounts of data are available) virtually eliminating the effect shown in Figure 1. Other degrees of overlap can be chosen depending on the amount of data available.

The remainder of the paper is organized as follows. The next section presents the statistical model of REP, and the following section discusses implications of the model, including an explanation for the behavior shown in Figure 1. We then present the variant of REP based on the theoretical model. The final section concludes and points to future work.

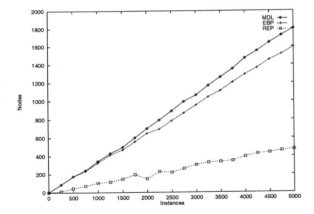

Figure 1: Tree size as a function of dataset size for three common pruning techniques when the class labels are independent of the attributes.

A Statistical Model of Reduced Error Pruning

This section presents a statistical model of REP. The goal is to model pruning decisions at nodes for which the class label and the attribute values of instances are independent, i.e. where there is no structure in the data that, if found, would make it possible to predict the class label better than always guessing the majority

class. Independence holds at node N when all of the attributes with any utility in predicting the class label have already been used to split the data on the path from the root of the tree to N. Ideally, such nodes will always be pruned, but as we saw in the previous section, that is often not the case. The model will make it possible to make probabilistic statements about the likelihood of pruning under various conditions.

REP was chosen for analysis primarily because of its simplicity. The algorithm takes as input an unpruned tree and a set of instances, called the pruning set, drawn from the same population as the set of instances used to build the tree, but disjoint from that set. To begin, the unpruned tree is used to classify all of the instances in the pruning set. Let D_N be the subset of the pruning instances that pass through decision node N on their way to leaf nodes. The subtree rooted at N, denoted T_N, commits some number of errors on the instances in D_N. Let that number be r_T. If T_N is pruned back to a leaf and assigned as a class label the majority class in D_N, then, assuming a binary class label, it will commit a number of errors equal to the number of instances in the minority class.[2] Let that number be r_L. In a bottom-up manner, r_T and r_L are computed for each decision node, and T_N is pruned when the number of errors committed by the tree is greater than or equal to the number of errors committed by the leaf, i.e. when $r_T \geq r_L$.

The intuition behind REP is appealing. The number of errors that a subtree commits on the training data is clearly biased downward because the tree was constructed to minimize errors on this set, but the number of errors committed on an independent sample of data, the pruning set, is unbiased. Where the unpruned tree fits noise in the training data (i.e. is overfitting those data) the tree should perform poorly on the pruning set, making it likely that pruning will occur. (We will prove this assertion in the following section.) Where the tree is fitting structure in the data, pruning back to a leaf should result in more errors than retaining the subtree. Given unbiased error estimates, the behavior shown in Figure 1 seems inexplicable.

To model pruning decisions, and thus to explain Fig-

---

[2] The original formulation of REP as described in (Quinlan 1987) uses the majority class in the training set rather than the pruning set to assign class labels when pruning. The analysis in the remainder of the paper makes the simplifying assumption that the pruning set is used to assign class labels. In practice, there is very little difference between the two approaches. To verify that assertion, we took 19 different datasets (the same ones used in (Oates & Jensen 1998)) and built trees on 10 different splits of the data, with 2/3 of the data being used to build the tree and 1/3 used to prune the tree. For every one of those 190 trees, we counted the number of nodes for which the class label assigned by the training set was the same as the label assigned by the pruning set. To avoid spurious differences near the leaves of the trees, nodes with fewer than 10 pruning set instances were ignored. Over those 19 datasets, 94% of the nodes were labeled identically by the training and pruning sets.

ure 1, we must characterize r_T and r_L because they are the only quantities that enter into pruning decisions. Given D_N, determining the value of r_L is straightforward. Let $n = |D_N|$ be the number of pruning set instances that arrive at N. Assuming a binary class label, which will be the case for the remainder of the paper, let p_C be the probability that an instance in D_N is labeled with class '+'. (That probability is simply the number of instances in D_N labeled '+' divided by n.) Then the value of r_L is given by the following equation:

$$r_L = n \min(p_C, 1 - p_C)$$

If $p_C < 1 - p_C$ the majority class in D_N is '-'. Pruning T_N will result in a leaf labeled '-', and all of the np_C instances in D_N labeled '+' will be misclassified. If $1 - p_C < p_C$ the majority class in D_N is '+', and after pruning all of the $n(1 - p_C)$ instances in D_N labeled '-' will be misclassified.

Characterization of r_T is more difficult because its value depends on the tree structure beneath N. Without exact knowledge of the instances in D_N and of T_N, the exact value of r_T cannot be determined. However, the distribution of values from which r_T is drawn can be characterized. Let R_T be a random variable that represents the number of errors committed by T_N on D_N. Let the probability that a randomly selected instance in D_N will arrive at a leaf labeled '+' be p_L.[3] The probability that the subtree will misclassify an instance in D_N, which we will denote $p_{C \neq L}$, is the probability that an instance labeled '+' will arrive at a leaf labeled '-' plus the probability that an instance labeled '-' will arrive at a leaf labeled '+'. Because the class label and attribute values are independent, that quantity is given by the following equation:

$$\begin{aligned} p_{C \neq L} &= p_C(1 - p_L) + (1 - p_C)p_L \\ &= p_C + p_L - 2p_C p_L \end{aligned}$$

We can think of assigning a class label to an instance in D_N as a Bernoulli trial in which the two outcomes are an incorrect classification (which occurs with probability $p_{C \neq L}$) and a correct classification (which occurs with probability $1 - p_{C \neq L}$). Therefore, the number of errors committed by T_N on D_N has a binomial distribution with mean $\mu_T = np_{C \neq L}$ and standard deviation $\sigma_T = \sqrt{np_{C \neq L}(1 - p_{C \neq L})}$ which, for large n, can be approximated by a normal distribution. There is no way to precisely specify when n is large enough to use the normal approximation, but one commonly used rule of thumb is that it can be used when both $np_{C \neq L}$ and $n(1 - p_{C \neq L})$ are greater than five (Olson 1987).

The model is shown graphically in Figure 2. Given n, p_C and p_L, an exact value of r_L can be determined. However, we can only say that r_T is drawn from a normal distribution with known mean and standard deviation. The node will be pruned if the value drawn from that distribution is greater than or equal to r_L.

---

[3]Although p_L depends on T_N and D_N just as r_T does, we will see later that the actual value of p_L has little qualitative effect on the predictions of the model.

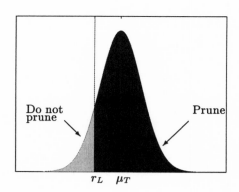

Figure 2: Given n, p_C and p_L, an exact value for r_L can be determined, and r_T is drawn from a normal distribution with know mean and standard deviation. The node will be pruned if $r_T \geq r_L$.

Implications of the Model

This section uses the model just presented to derive several results that provide insight into the behavior of REP. At a high level, there are two important conclusions, both concerning decision nodes rooting subtrees that fit noise. First, the probability of pruning such nodes *prior to pruning beneath them* is close to 1. Second, pruning that occurs beneath such nodes often has the counterintuitive effect of reducing the probability that they will be pruned to be close to 0.

The Probability of Pruning a Node Prior to Pruning Beneath It

It is easy to show that the expected number of errors committed by subtree T_N on D_N is greater than the number of errors committed by the leaf that results from pruning T_N. The expected number of errors for the subtree is $E(R_T)$, which is simply μ_T. In terms of Figure 2, the fact that $E(R_T) > r_L$ means that r_L is always to the left of the mean of the distribution.

Theorem 1 *For* $p_C \neq 0.5$, $E(R_T) > r_L$.

Proof: There are two cases to consider. Either $1/2 > p_C$ or $1/2 < p_C$.

Case 1:

$$\begin{aligned} 1/2 &> p_C \\ 1 &> 2p_C \\ p_L &> 2p_C p_L \\ p_L - 2p_C p_L &> 0 \\ p_C + p_L - 2p_C p_L &> p_C \\ n(p_C + p_L - 2p_C p_L) &> np_C \\ np_{C \neq L} &> np_C \\ \mu_T &> np_C \\ E(R_T) &> r_L \end{aligned}$$

Case 2:

$$p_C > 1/2$$
$$2p_C > 1$$
$$2p_C(1 - p_L) > 1 - p_L$$
$$2p_C - 2p_Cp_L > 1 - p_L$$
$$2p_C + p_L - 2p_Cp_L - 1 > 0$$
$$2p_C + p_L - 2p_Cp_L > 1$$
$$p_C + p_L - 2p_Cp_L > 1 - p_C$$
$$n(p_C + p_L - 2p_Cp_L) > n(1 - p_C)$$
$$np_{C \neq L} > n(1 - p_C)$$
$$\mu_T > n(1 - p_C)$$
$$E(R_T) > r_L$$

∎

Deriving an expression for the probability that T_N will be pruned is straightforward as well. It is simply the probability that $r_T \geq r_L$, which is the area under the normal distribution to the right of r_L in Figure 2. Let $\Phi(\mu, \sigma, x)$ be the cumulative density up to x of the normal distribution with mean μ and standard deviation σ. $\Phi(\mu_T, \sigma_T, r_L)$ is the area to the left of r_L in Figure 2, so the area to the right of that point is:

$$p_{T \rightarrow L} = 1 - \Phi(\mu_T, \sigma_T, r_L) \quad (1)$$

Figure 3 shows plots of $p_{T \rightarrow L}$ for all possible values of p_C and p_L at various levels of n. When the class labels of instances in D_N are distributed evenly ($p_C = 0.5$) the probability of pruning is 0.5 ($p_{T \rightarrow L} = 0.5$) regardless of the value of p_L. However, that probability rapidly approaches 1 as you move away from the $p_C = 0.5$ line, with the steepness of the rise increasing with n. That is, for all values of p_C and p_L, you are more likely to prune a subtree that fits noise the more pruning instances are available. For example, numerical integration of the curves in Figure 3 shows that the average of $p_{T \rightarrow L}$ when $n = 100$ is 0.926. That number is 0.970 when $n = 1000$ and 0.988 when $n = 10,000$. Unless p_C is very close to 0.5, pruning of subtrees that fit noise in the data is virtually assured *given that no pruning has occurred beneath them*. Note that most decision tree splitting criteria either explicitly or implicitly choose the split that maximizes purity of the data. Said differently, they attempt to move p_C as far away from 0.5 as possible.

The intuition that $p_{T \rightarrow L}$ increases with n, all other things being equal, is now made rigorous. Let $p_{T \rightarrow L}(p_C, p_L, n)$ be the probability of pruning given the specified values of p_C, p_L and n.

Theorem 2 *For $p_C \neq 0.5$ and $\delta > 0$, it holds that $p_{T \rightarrow L}(p_C, p_L, n) < p_{T \rightarrow L}(p_C, p_L, n + \delta)$.*

Proof: First, we manipulate Equation 1 so that Φ refers to the standard normal:

$$\begin{aligned} p_{T \rightarrow L} &= 1 - \Phi(\mu_T, \sigma_T, r_L) \\ &= 1 - \Phi(0, 1, \frac{r_L - \mu_t}{\sigma_T}) \\ &= 1 - \Phi(0, 1, z) \end{aligned}$$

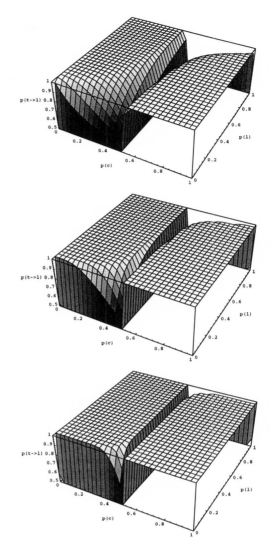

Figure 3: Plots of $p_{T \rightarrow L}$ for p_C and p_L ranging from 0 to 1 and $n = 100$ (the top graph), $n = 1000$ (the middle graph), and $n = 10,000$ (the bottom graph).

Φ increases monotonically as z increases, so $p_{T \rightarrow L}$ decreases monotonically as z increases. That is, the probability of pruning is inversely related to z. The question then becomes, what is the effect of changing n on z?

$$\begin{aligned} z &= \frac{r_L - \mu_t}{\sigma_T} \\ &= \frac{n \min(p_C, 1 - p_C) - np_{C \neq L}}{\sqrt{np_{C \neq L}(1 - p_{C \neq L})}} \\ &= \sqrt{n} \frac{(\min(p_C, 1 - p_C) - p_{C \neq L})}{\sqrt{p_{C \neq L}(1 - p_{C \neq L})}} \\ &= \sqrt{n}K \end{aligned}$$

Because $r_L < \mu_T$ (see Theorem 1) and σ_T is non-negative (from the definition of the standard deviation), the quantity $(r_L - \mu_t)/\sigma_T$ is always negative.

It follows that K is always negative as well. Because K does not depend on n, $\sqrt{(n+\delta)}K < \sqrt{n}K$. Coupling that fact with the previous observation that $p_{T \to L}$ increases monotonically with decreasing z, we conclude that $p_{T \to L}(p_C, p_L, n) < p_{T \to L}(p_C, p_L, n + \delta)$. ∎

The Probability of Pruning a Node After Pruning Beneath It

How does pruning that occurs beneath a decision node affect the probability that the node itself will ultimately be pruned? Recall that the number of errors committed by T_N is defined recursively to be the sum of the errors committed by N's children. Because pruning occurs when the leaf commits the same number or fewer errors than the subtree, if any of the descendants of N are pruned, r_T (the number of errors committed by T_N) must either stay the same or decrease. In effect, there are two values of r_T in which we are interested. There is the value that exists prior to pruning beneath N, and there is that value that exists when all of the descendants of N have been visited by the pruning procedure and a decision is about to be made concerning N. Denote the latter value r'_T.

Let r_{Ndi} be the number of errors committed by the ith descendant of N at depth d after a pruning decision has been made concerning that descendant. If no leaf nodes occur in T_N until depth $d + 1$, then r'_T is simply $\sum_i r_{Ndi}$. Assume that N and all of its descendants at depth d share the same values of p_C and p_L.[4] If each of the subtrees rooted at those descendants is pruned, then r'_T becomes the following:

$$
\begin{aligned}
r'_T &= \sum_i r_{Ndi} \\
&= \sum_i n_i \min(p_C, 1 - p_C) \\
&= n \min(p_C, 1 - p_C) \\
&= r_L
\end{aligned}
$$

That is, the number of errors committed by the subtree rooted at N will be the same as the number of errors committed when that subtree is pruned back to a leaf, and so the subtree will be pruned.

Now consider what happens if just one of the descendants at depth d is not pruned. If descendant k is not pruned, then $r_{Ndk} < n_k \min(p_C, 1 - p_C)$, so the sum above becomes:

$$
\begin{aligned}
r'_T &= \sum_{i \neq k} r_{Ndi} + r_{Ndk} \\
&= \sum_{i \neq k} n_i \min(p_C, 1 - p_C) + r_{Ndk} \\
&= (n - n_k) \min(p_C, 1 - p_C) + r_{Ndk}
\end{aligned}
$$

$$
\begin{aligned}
&< (n - n_k) \min(p_C, 1 - p_C) + n_k \min(p_C, 1 - p_C) \\
&< n \min(p_C, 1 - p_C) \\
&< r_L
\end{aligned}
$$

If just one of the descendants of N at depth d is not pruned, T_N will be retained. If more than one descendant is not pruned, T_N will still be retained as that can only decrease r'_T. Said differently, N will be pruned only if all of its descendants at depth d are pruned.

We can now derive an expression for the probability of pruning a subtree given that pruning has occurred beneath it. Let $p'_{T \to L}$ denote that probability. (As with r_T and r'_T, the prime indicates the value of the variable at the time that a pruning decision is to be made for the node.) Let the number of descendants at depth d be m, and let p_i be the probability that the ith descendant will be pruned. Then the following holds:

$$
p'_{T \to L} = \prod_{i=1}^{m} p_i
$$

The value of d has two effects on $p'_{T \to L}$ that may not be immediately obvious. First, as d increases, m increases exponentially, leading to an exponential decrease in $p'_{T \to L}$. Second, as d increases, the number of pruning set instances that reach each of the descendants decreases exponentially. As Theorem 2 makes clear, that decrease leads to a decrease in the value of p_i, and thus to a dramatic decrease in $p'_{T \to L}$.

Figure 4 shows plots of $p'_{T \to L}$ for all possible values of p_C and p_L. The top graph assumes a subtree rooted at a node with 10 descendants, the middle graph assumes 20 descendants, and the bottom graph assumes 50 descendant. All three graphs assume that each descendant has 5 pruning instances. In each case, there are large regions in which the probability of pruning is virtually zero. Only when p_C and p_L are very different (i.e. where $|p_C - p_L| \approx 1$) is the probability of pruning close to one. Numerical integration of the curves in Figure 4 shows that the average value of $p'_{T \to L}$ is 0.33 when the number of descendants is 10. The average is 0.25 and 0.18 when the number of descendants is 20 and 50 respectively. As the number of descendants of a node increases, the probability of pruning that node decreases.

There are two important observations to make about Figure 4. First, as a practical matter, combinations of p_C and p_L yielding a value of $|p_C - p_L|$ close to one are rare. Such a combination would indicate that the class distributions in the training and pruning sets are vastly different, and should not be the case when the two samples are drawn from the same population. The implication is that the effective probability of pruning in any scenario that is likely to occur is much lower than the averages mentioned above. Second, Figure 4 involves exactly the same quantities as Figure 3, only the latter is plotted prior to pruning beneath a node and the former is plotted after pruning beneath a node.

[4]To a first approximation, that is a good assumption when there is no structure in the data and n is large.

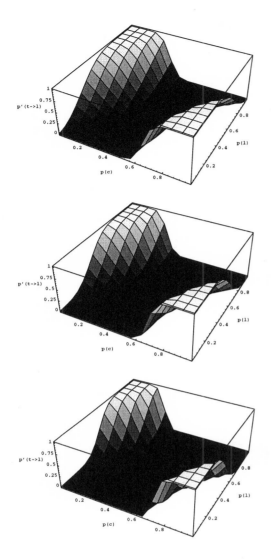

Figure 4: Plots of $p'_{T \to L}$ for p_C and p_L ranging from 0 to 1, where N has 10 descendants (top), 20 descendants (middle) and 50 descendants (bottom).

An Improved REP Algorithm

As demonstrated in the previous section, the probabilities of pruning node N before and after pruning has occurred beneath it are often quite different (i.e. $p_{T \to L} \gg p'_{T \to L}$). This phenomenon exists because pruning decisions are made so as to minimize errors on the pruning set, and the number of errors committed by the subtree rooted at N is a sum of the errors committed by N's descendants at any given depth (assuming no leaf nodes exist above that depth). This observation suggests that excess tree structure might be avoided if a pruning set different from the one used to prune N's descendants was available to prune N itself. The reason is that although N's descendants were pruned so as to minimize errors on the original pruning set, that has no effect on whether N will be pruned when a new

pruning set is obtained just for N.

The above intuition was tested on three artificial datasets: the `rand` structureless dataset that was used to create Figure 1, and the `led-24` and `waveform-40` datasets taken from the UC Irvine repository. Figure 5 shows tree size and accuracy as a function of training set size given that a *completely new pruning set* is generated prior to making each pruning decision. Creating new pruning sets is possible with these particular artificial datasets, and may be possible with very large real-world datasets as are common in the KDD community. Note that over all training set sizes, the trees pruned with non-overlapping pruning sets are smaller and just as accurate (determined by a t-test at the 0.05 significant level) as the trees pruned with a single pruning set.

Generating completely new pruning sets for each node is often impractical. However, it is possible that part of the benefit of totally independent pruning sets can be obtained by drawing a random sample of the available pruning instances for each node. Specifically, given m pruning instances, a random sample of size αm where $0 < \alpha \leq 1$ can be drawn. Note that $\alpha = 1$ corresponds to standard REP; the same pruning set (the full pruning set) is used at each node. Smaller values of α lead to less overlap in the pruning sets used at each node and make those pruning sets smaller.

We ran this variant of REP with $\alpha = 0.5$ on the 19 datasets used in (Oates & Jensen 1998) and found that sampling led to significantly smaller trees in 16 cases, and in only one of those cases was accuracy significantly less. (Significance was measured by a t-test comparing means of 10-fold cross-validated tree sizes and accuracies with a significance level of 0.05.) Accuracy was lower on the `tic-tac-toe` dataset because it is noise-free and all of the attributes are relevant (much like the parity problem). Pruning trees built on that dataset almost invariably leads to lower accuracy, with more aggressive pruning leading to additional losses.

Discussion and Future Work

Despite the use of pruning algorithms to control tree growth, increasing the amount of data used to build a decision tree, even when there is no structure in the data, often yields a larger tree that is no more accurate than a tree built with fewer data. A statistical model of REP led to a theoretical understanding of why this behavior occurs, and to a variant of REP that results in significantly smaller trees with the same accuracies as trees pruned with the standard REP algorithm.

Future work will include generalizing the results in this paper to other pruning algorithms, such as MDL and EBP (Oates & Jensen 1997), and to further exploration of the idea of using partially overlapping samples of pruning sets to minimize excess structure in trees.

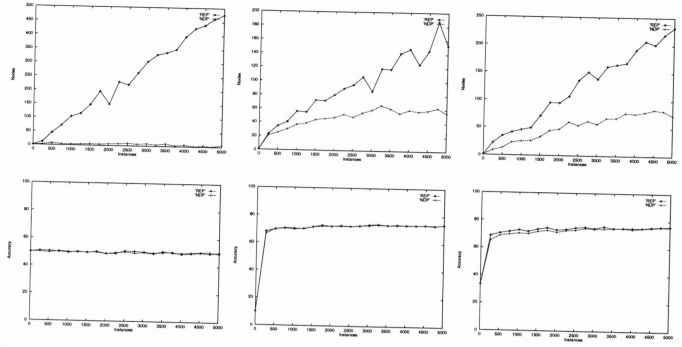

Figure 5: Tree size (top row) and accuracy (bottom row) as a function of training set size for the following datasets: rand (first column), led-24 (middle column) and waveform-40 (last column). In each plot, the REP curve corresponds to standard REP, and the NDP curves refers to a variant of the algorithm in which a completely new pruning set is generated and classified by the tree prior to making each pruning decision.

Acknowledgments

This research is supported by DARPA/AFOSR under contract number F49620-97-1-0485. The U.S. Government is authorized to reproduce and distribute reprints for governmental purposes notwithstanding any copyright notation hereon. The views and conclusions contained herein are those of the authors and should not be interpreted as necessarily representing the official policies or endorsements, either expressed or implied, of the Defense Advanced Research Projects Agency, Air Force Office of Scientific Research or the U.S. Government.

References

Oates, T., and Jensen, D. 1997. The effects of training set size on decision tree complexity. In *Proceedings of The Fourteenth International Conference on Machine Learning*, 254–262.

Oates, T., and Jensen, D. 1998. Large datasets lead to overly complex models: an explanation and a solution. In *Proceedings of the Fourth International Conference on Knowledge Discovery and Data Mining*, 294–298.

Olson, C. 1987. *Statistics: Making Sense of Data*. Allyn and Bacon.

Quinlan, J. R., and Rivest, R. 1989. Inferring decision trees using the minimum description length principle. *Information and Computation* 80:227–248.

Quinlan, J. R. 1987. Simplifying decision trees. *International Journal of Man-Machine Studies* 27:221–234.

Quinlan, J. R. 1993. *C4.5: Programs for Machine Learning*. Morgan Kaufmann.

Feature Selection for Ensembles

David W. Opitz

Computer Science Department
University of Montana
Missoula, MT 59812
opitz@cs.umt.edu

Abstract

The traditional motivation behind feature selection algorithms is to find the best subset of features for a task using one particular learning algorithm. Given the recent success of ensembles, however, we investigate the notion of *ensemble feature selection* in this paper. This task is harder than traditional feature selection in that one not only needs to find features germane to the learning task and learning algorithm, but one also needs to find a set of feature subsets that will promote disagreement among the ensemble's classifiers. In this paper, we present an ensemble feature selection approach that is based on genetic algorithms. Our algorithm shows improved performance over the popular and powerful ensemble approaches of AdaBoost and Bagging and demonstrates the utility of ensemble feature selection.

Introduction

Feature selection algorithms attempt to find and remove the features which are unhelpful or destructive to learning (Almuallim & Dietterich 1994; Cherkauer & Shavlik 1996; Kohavi & John 1997). Previous work on feature selection has focused on finding the appropriate subset of relevant features to be used in constructing *one* inference model; however, recent "ensemble" work has shown that combining the output of a *set* of models that are generated from separately trained inductive learning algorithms can greatly improve generalization accuracy (Breiman 1996; Maclin & Opitz 1997; Shapire *et al.* 1997). This paper argues for the importance of and presents an approach to the task of *feature selection for ensembles*.

Research has shown that an effective ensemble should consist of a set of models that are not only highly correct, but ones that make their errors on different parts of the input space as well (Hansen & Salamon 1990; Krogh & Vedelsby 1995; Opitz & Shavlik

1996). Varying the feature subsets used by each member of the ensemble should help promote this necessary diversity. Thus, while traditional feature-selection algorithms have the goal of finding the best feature subset that is germane to both the learning task and the selected inductive-learning algorithm, the task of ensemble feature selection has the additional goal of finding a *set* of features subsets that will promote disagreement among the component members of the ensemble. This search space is enormous for any non-trivial problem.

In this paper, we present a genetic algorithm (GA) approach for searching for an appropriate set of feature subsets for ensembles. GAs are a logical choice since they have been shown to be effective global optimization techniques (Holland 1975; Mitchell 1996). Our approach works by first creating an initial population of classifiers where each classifier is generated by randomly selecting a different subset of features. We then continually produce new candidate classifiers by using the genetic operators of crossover and mutation on the feature subsets. Our algorithm defines the overall fitness of an individual to be a combination of accuracy and diversity. The most fit individuals make up the population which in turn comprise the ensemble. Using neural networks as our classifier, results on 21 datasets show that our simple and straight-forward algorithm for creating the initial population produces better ensembles on average than the popular and powerful ensemble approaches of Bagging and Boosting. Results also show that further running the algorithm with the genetic operators improves performance.

Review of Ensembles

Figure 1 illustrates the basic framework of a predictor ensemble. Each predictor in the ensemble (predictor 1 through predictor N in this case) is first trained using the training instances. Then, for each example, the predicted output of each of these predictors (o_i in Figure 1) is combined to produce the output of the ensem-

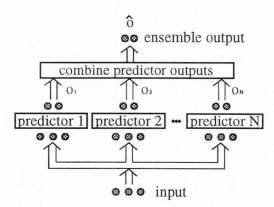

Figure 1: A predictor ensemble.

ble ($\hat{o}$ in Figure 1). Many researchers (Breiman 1996; Hansen & Salamon 1990; Opitz & Shavlik 1997) have demonstrated the effectiveness of combining schemes that are simply the weighted average of the predictors (i.e., $\hat{o} = \sum_{i \in N} w_i \cdot o_i$ and $\sum_{i \in N} w_i = 1$); this is the type of ensemble on which we focus in this paper.

Combining the output of several predictors is useful only if there is disagreement on some inputs. Obviously, combining several identical predictors produces no gain. Hansen and Salamon 1990 proved that for an ensemble, if the average error rate for an example is less than 50% and the predictors in the ensemble are independent in the production of their errors, the expected error for that example can be reduced to zero as the number of predictors combined goes to infinity; however, such assumptions rarely hold in practice. Krogh and Vedelsby 1995 later proved that the ensemble error can be divided into a term measuring the average generalization error of each individual classifier and a term measuring the disagreement among the classifiers. What they formally showed was that an ideal ensemble consists of highly correct classifiers that disagree as much as possible. Numerous authors have empirically verified that such ensembles generalize well (e.g., Opitz & Shavlik 1996; Breiman 1996a; Freund 1996).

As a result, methods for creating ensembles center around producing predictors that disagree on their predictions. Generally, these methods focus on altering the training process in the hope that the resulting predictors will produce different predictions. For example, neural network techniques that have been employed include methods for training with different topologies, different initial weights, different parameters, and training only on a portion of the training set (Breiman 1996; Freund & Schapire 1996; Hansen & Salamon 1990). *Varying the feature subsets to create a diverse set of accurate predictors is the focus of this article.*

Numerous techniques try to generate disagreement

among the classifiers by altering the training set each classifier sees. The two most popular techniques are Bagging (Breiman 1996) and Boosting (particularly AdaBoost; Freund & Schapire 1996). Bagging is a bootstrap ensemble method that trains each predictor in the ensemble with a different partition of the training set. It generates each partition by randomly drawing, with replacement, N examples from the training set, where N is the size of the training set. Breiman 1996 showed that Bagging is effective on "unstable" learning algorithms (such as neural network) where small changes in the training set result in large changes in predictions. As with Bagging, AdaBoost also chooses a training set of size N and initially sets the probability of picking each example to be $1/N$. After the first predictor, however, these probabilities change as follows. Let ϵ_k be the sum of the misclassified instance probabilities of the currently trained classifier C_k. AdaBoost generates probabilities for the next trial by multiplying the probabilities of C_k's incorrectly classified instances by the factor $\beta_k = (1 - \epsilon_k)/\epsilon_k$ and then re-normalizing these probabilities so that their sum equals 1. AdaBoost then combines the classifiers $C_1, \ldots, C_k$ using weighted voting where C_k has weight $\log(\beta_k)$. Numerous empirical studies have shown that Bagging and Boosting are highly successful methods that usually generalize better than their base predictors (Bauer & Kohavi 1998; Maclin & Opitz 1997; Quinlan 1996); thus, we include these two methods as baselines for our study.

Ensemble Feature Selection

Kohavi & John 1997 showed that the efficacy of a set of features to learning depends on the learning algorithm itself; that is, the appropriate feature subset for one learning algorithm may not be the appropriate feature subset for another learner. Kohavi & John's 1997 wrapper approach works by conducting a search through the space of possible feature subsets, explicitly testing the accuracy of the learning algorithm on each search node's feature subset. The search space of feature subsets is enormous and quickly becomes impractical to do hill-climbing searches (the traditional wrapper search technique) with slow-training learners such as neural networks; this search space is even larger when considering an appropriate set of feature subsets for ensembles. This is why we consider a global search technique (GAs) in this paper.

The notion of feature selection for ensembles is new. Other researchers have investigated using GAs for feature selection (e.g., Cherkauer & Shavlik 1996; Guo & Uhrig 1992); however, they have only looked at it from the aspect of traditional feature selection – finding one appropriate set for learning – rather than from the ensemble perspective.

The GEFS Algorithm

Table 1 summarizes our algorithm (called GEFS for Genetic Ensemble Feature Selection) that uses GAs to generate a set of classifiers that are accurate and diverse in their predictions. (We focus on neural networks in this paper; however, GEFS can be easily extended to other learning algorithms as well.) GEFS starts by creating and training its initial population of networks. The representation of each individual of our population is simply a dynamic length string of integers, where each integer indexes a particular feature. We create networks from these strings by first having the input nodes match the string of integers, then creating a standard single-hidden-layer, fully connected neural network. Our algorithm then creates new networks by using the genetic operators of crossover and mutation.

GEFS trains these new individuals using backpropogation. It adds new networks to the population and then scores each population member with respect to its prediction accuracy and diversity. GEFS normalizes these scores, then defines the fitness of each population member (i) to be:

$$Fitness_i = Accuracy_i + \lambda\ Diversity_i \qquad (1)$$

where λ defines the tradeoff between accuracy and diversity. Finally, GEFS prunes the population to the N most-fit members, then repeats this process. At every point in time, the current ensemble consists of simply averaging (with equal weight) the predictions of the output of each member of the current population. Thus as the population evolves, so does the ensemble.

We define accuracy to be network i's training-set accuracy. (One may use a validation-set if there are enough training instances). We define diversity to be the average difference between the prediction of our component classifier and the ensemble. We then separately normalize both terms so that the values range from 0 to 1. Normalizing both terms allows λ to have the same meaning across domains.

It is not always clear at what value one should set λ; therefore, we automatically adjust λ based on the discrete derivatives of the ensemble error $\hat{E}$, the average population error $\bar{E}$, and the average diversity $\bar{D}$ within the ensemble. First, we never change λ if $\hat{E}$ is decreasing; otherwise we (a) increase λ if $\bar{E}$ is not increasing and the population diversity $\bar{D}$ is decreasing; or (b) decrease λ if $\bar{E}$ is increasing and $\bar{D}$ is not decreasing. We started λ at 1.0 for the experiments in this article. The amount λ changes is 10% of its current value.

Table 1: The GEFS algorithm.

GOAL: Find a set of input subsets to create an accurate and diverse classifier ensemble.

1. Using varying inputs, create and train the initial population of classifiers.

2. Until a stopping criterion is reached:

   (a) Use genetic operators to create new networks.
   (b) Measure the diversity of each network with respect to the current population.
   (c) Normalize the accuracy scores and the diversity scores of the individual networks.
   (d) Calculate the fitness of each population member.
   (e) Prune the population to the N fittest networks.
   (f) Adjust λ.
   (g) The current population composes the ensemble.

We create the initial population by first randomly choosing the number of features to include in each feature subset. For classifier i, the size of each feature subset (N_i) is independently chosen from a uniform distribution between 1 and twice the number of original features in the dataset. We then randomly pick, with replacement, N_i features to include in classifier i's training set. Note that some features may be picked multiple times while other may not be picked at all; replicating inputs for a neural network may give the network a better chance to utilize that feature during training. Also, replicating a feature in a genome encoding allows that feature to better survive to future generations.

Our crossover operator uses dynamic-length, uniform crossover. In this case, we chose the feature subsets of two individuals in the current population proportional to fitness. Each feature in both parent's subset is independently considered and randomly placed in the feature set of one of the two children. Thus it is possible to have a feature set that is larger (or smaller) than the largest (or smallest) of either parent's feature subset. Our mutation operator works much like traditional genetic algorithms; we randomly replace a small percentage of a parent's feature subset with new features. With both operators, the network is trained from scratch using the new feature subset; thus no internal structure of the parents are saved during the crossover.

Since GEFS continually considers new networks to include in its ensemble, it can be viewed as an "anytime" learning algorithm. Such a learning algorithm

Table 2: Summary of the data sets used in this paper. Shown are the number of examples in the data set; the number of output classes; the number of continuous and discrete input features; the number of input, output, and hidden units used in the neural networks tested; and how many epochs each neural network was trained.

| Dataset | Cases | Classes | Features | | Neural Network | | | |
			Continuous	Discrete	Inputs	Outputs	Hiddens	Epochs
credit-a	690	2	6	9	47	1	10	35
credit-g	1000	2	7	13	63	1	10	30
diabetes	768	2	9	-	8	1	5	30
glass	214	6	9	-	9	6	10	80
heart-cleveland	303	2	8	5	13	1	5	40
hepatitis	155	2	6	13	32	1	10	60
house-votes-84	435	2	-	16	16	1	5	40
hypo	3772	5	7	22	55	5	15	40
ionosphere	351	2	34	-	34	1	10	40
iris	159	3	4	-	4	3	5	80
kr-vs-kp	3196	2	-	36	74	1	15	20
labor	57	2	8	8	29	1	10	80
letter	20000	26	16	-	16	26	40	30
promoters-936	936	2	-	57	228	1	20	30
ribosome-bind	1877	2	-	49	196	1	20	35
satellite	6435	6	36	-	36	6	15	30
segmentation	2310	7	19	-	19	7	15	20
sick	3772	2	7	22	55	1	10	40
sonar	208	2	60	-	60	1	10	60
soybean	683	19	-	35	134	19	25	40
vehicle	846	4	18	-	18	4	10	40

should produce a good concept quickly, then continue to search concept space, reporting the new "best" concept whenever one is found (Opitz & Shavlik 1997). This is important since, for most domains, an expert is willing to wait for weeks, or even months, if a learning system can produce an improved concept.

GEFS is inspired by our previous approach of applying GAs to ensembles called ADDEMUP (Opitz & Shavlik 1996); however, the algorithms are quite different. ADDEMUP is far more complex, does not vary its inputs, and its genetic operators were designed explicitly for hidden nodes in *knowledge-based* neural networks; in fact ADDEMUP does not work well with problems lacking prior knowledge.

Results

To evaluate the performance of GEFS, we obtained a number of data sets from the University of Wisconsin Machine Learning repository as well as the UCI data set repository (Murphy & Aha 1994). These data sets were hand selected such that they (a) came from real-world problems, (b) varied in characteristics, and (c) were deemed useful by previous researchers. Table 2 gives the characteristics of our data sets. The data sets chosen vary across a number of dimensions

including: the type of the features in the data set (i.e., continuous, discrete, or a mix of the two); the number of output classes; and the number of examples in the data set. Table 2 also shows the architecture and training parameters used with our neural networks.

All results are averaged over five standard 10-fold cross validation experiments. For each 10-fold cross validation the data set is first partitioned into 10 equal-sized sets, then each set is in turn used as the test set while the classifier trains on the other nine sets. For each fold an ensemble of 20 networks is created (for a total of 200 networks for each 10-fold cross validation). We trained the neural networks using standard backpropagation learning. Parameter settings for the neural networks include a learning rate of 0.15, a momentum term of 0.9, and weights are initialized randomly to be between 0.5 and -0.5. Table 2 also shows the architecture and training parameters used in our neural networks experiments. We chose the number of hidden units based on the number of input and output units. This choice was based on the criteria of having at least one hidden unit per output, at least one hidden unit for every ten inputs, and five hidden units being a minimum. Parameter settings for the GA portion of GEFS includes a mutation rate of 50%, a population

Table 3: Test set error rates for the data sets using (1) a single neural network classifier; (2) the Bagging ensemble method, (3) the AdaBoost ensemble method; (4) the ensemble of GEFS's initial population, and (5) GEFS run to consider 250 networks. The bottom of the table contains a win-loss-tie comparison between the learning algorithms on the datasets.

Dataset	Traditional			GEFS	
	Single Net	Bagging	AdaBoost	Initial Pop	100 networks
credit-a	14.8	13.8	15.7	13.6	13.1
credit-g	27.9	24.2	25.3	23.9	24.8
diabetes	23.9	22.8	23.3	24.5	23.0
glass	38.6	33.1	31.1	30.8	30.4
heart-cleveland	18.6	17.0	21.1	16.8	16.1
hepatitis	20.1	17.8	19.7	15.5	16.7
house-votes-84	4.9	4.1	5.3	3.9	4.4
hypo	6.4	6.2	6.2	7.5	5.9
ionosphere	9.7	9.2	8.3	6.3	5.4
iris	4.3	4.0	3.9	4.0	3.3
kr-vs-kp	2.3	0.8	0.3	3.0	0.7
labor	6.1	4.2	3.2	3.5	3.5
letter	18.0	10.5	4.6	10.3	9.5
promoters-936	5.3	4.0	4.6	4.9	4.3
ribosome-bind	9.3	8.4	8.2	7.9	7.8
satellite	13.0	10.6	10.0	14.2	11.2
segmentation	6.6	5.4	3.3	5.2	3.6
sick	5.9	5.7	4.5	6.1	3.5
sonar	16.6	16.8	13.0	17.3	17.8
soybean	9.2	6.9	6.3	6.0	5.9
vehicle	24.9	20.7	19.7	22.2	19.0
Single Net		**20-1-0**	**18-3-0**	**15-6-0**	**20-1-0**
Bagging			13-7-1	13-7-1	**15-6-0**
AdaBoost				9-12-0	14-7-0
Initial Pop					**16-4-1**

size of 20, a $\lambda = 1.0$, and a search length of 250 networks (note this is not 250 generations). While the mutation rate may seem high as compared with traditional GAs, certain aspects of our approach call for a higher mutation rate (such as the goal of generating a population that cooperates as well as our emphasis on diversity); other mutation values were tried during our pilot studies.

Table 3 shows the error rates for the algorithms on all the datasets. As points of comparison, we include the results of running the *Bagging* and *AdaBoost* algorithms. (We described these algorithms in the second section.) Two results are presented for the GEFS algorithm: (1) accuracy after the initial population was created (the population size was 20), and (2) accuracy after 250 trained networks are considered during the search (20 for the initial population plus 230 with our genetic operators). For the convenience of the reader, the bottom of the Table 3 contains a win-loss-tie comparison between the learning algorithms on the

datasets. A comparison in bold means the difference in performance between the algorithms is statistically significant at the 95% confidence level when using the one-tailed sign test.

Discussion and Future Work

First, our results confirm earlier findings (Maclin & Opitz 1997; Quinlan 1996) that Bagging almost always produces a better classifier than a single neural network and that the AdaBoost method is a powerful technique that can usually produce better ensembles than Bagging; however, it is more susceptible to noise and can quickly overfit a data set.

We draw two main conclusions with our new algorithm's performance. First, GEFS can produce a good initial population and the algorithm for producing this population is both simple and fast. The fact that the initial population is competitive with both Bagging and AdaBoost is somewhat surprising. This shows that in many cases more diversity is created among the predictors by varying our feature set in this manner than is lost in individual predictor accuracy by not using the whole feature set.

The second conclusion we draw is that running GEFS longer usually increases performance. This is desirable since it allows the user to fully utilize available computer cycles to generate an improved model. Running AdaBoost and Bagging longer does not appreciably increase performance since previous results have shown their performance nearly fully asymptotes at around 20 networks; thus they do not appear to have the same ability to get better over time.

While GEFS's results are already impressive, we view this as just the first step toward ensemble feature selection. An important contribution of this paper is simply the demonstration of the utility for creating ensemble feature selection algorithms. Many improvements are possible and need to be explored. One area of future research is combining GEFS with AdaBoost's approach of emphasizing examples not correctly classified by the current ensemble. We also plan a further investigation of tuning parameters, such as the maximum size of the feature subsets in the initial population (results of such experiments are not presented in this paper due to limited space). Finally, we plan to investigate applying GEFS to other inductive learning algorithms such as decision trees and Bayesian Learning.

Conclusions

In this paper we have argued for the importance of feature detection for ensembles and presented such an algorithm, GEFS, that is based on genetic algorithms. Our ensemble feature selection approach is straightforward, simple, generates good results quickly, and has the ability to further increase its performance if allowed to run longer. Our results show that GEFS compared favorably with the two powerful ensemble techniques of AdaBoost and Bagging. Thus, this paper shows the utility of feature selection for ensembles and provides an important and effective first step in this direction.

Acknowledgments

This work was partially supported by National Science Foundation grant IRI-9734419 and a University of Montana MONTS grant.

References

Almuallim, H., and Dietterich, T. 1994. Learning Boolean concepts in the presence of many irrelevant features. *Artificial Intelligence* 69(1):279–305.

Bauer, E., and Kohavi, R. 1998. An empirical comparison of voting classification algorithms: Bagging, boosting, and variants. *Machine Learning*.

Breiman, L. 1996. Bagging predictors. *Machine Learning* 24(2):123–140.

Cherkauer, K., and Shavlik, J. 1996. Growing simpler decision trees to facilitate knowledge discovery. In *The Second International Conference on Knowledge Discovery and Data Mining*, 315–318. AAAI/MIT Press.

Freund, Y., and Schapire, R. 1996. Experiments with a new boosting algorithm. In *Proceedings of the Thirteenth International Conference on Machine Learning*, 148–156. Morgan Kaufmann.

Guo, Z., and Uhrig, R. 1992. Using genetic algorithms to select inputs for neural networks. In *Int. Conf. on Genetic Algorithms and Neural Networks*, 223–234.

Hansen, L., and Salamon, P. 1990. Neural network ensembles. *IEEE Transactions on Pattern Analysis and Machine Intelligence* 12:993–1001.

Holland, J. 1975. *Adaptation in Natural and Artificial Systems*. Ann Arbor, MI: Univ of Michigan Press.

Kohavi, F., and John, G. 1997. Wrappers for feature subset selection. *Artificial Intelligence* 97(1):273–324.

Krogh, A., and Vedelsby, J. 1995. Neural network ensembles, cross validation, and active learning. In *Advances in Neural Information Processing Systems*, volume 7, 231–238. Cambridge, MA: MIT Press.

Maclin, R., and Opitz, D. 1997. An empirical evaluation of bagging and boosting. In *Proceedings of the Fourteenth National Conference on Artificial Intelligence*, 546–551. Providence, RI: AAAI/MIT Press.

Mitchell, M. 1996. *An Introduction to Genetic Algorithms*. MIT Press.

Murphy, P. M., and Aha, D. W. 1994. UCI repository of machine learning databases (machine-readable data repository). University of California-Irvine, Department of Information and Computer Science.

Opitz, D., and Shavlik, J. 1996. Actively searching for an effective neural-network ensemble. *Connection Science* 8(3/4):337–353.

Opitz, D., and Shavlik, J. 1997. Connectionist theory refinement: Searching for good network topologies. *Journal of Artificial Intelligence Research* 6:177–209.

Quinlan, J. R. 1996. Bagging, boosting, and c4.5. In *Proceedings of the Thirteenth National Conference on Artificial Intelligence*, 725–730. AAAI/MIT Press.

Shapire, R.; Freund, Y.; Bartlett, P.; and Lee, W. 1997. Boosting the margin: A new explanation for the effectiveness of voting methods. In *Proceedings of the Fourteenth International Conference on Machine Learning*, 322–330. Morgan Kaufmann.

Efficient exploration for optimizing immediate reward

Dale Schuurmans
Department of Computer Science
University of Waterloo
Waterloo, ON N2L 3G1, Canada
dale@cs.uwaterloo.ca

Lloyd Greenwald
Department of Mathematics and Computer Science
Drexel University
Philadelphia, PA 19104-2875, USA
lgreenwald@mcs.drexel.edu

Abstract

We consider the problem of learning an effective behavior strategy from reward. Although much studied, the issue of how to use prior knowledge to scale optimal behavior learning up to real-world problems remains an important open issue.

We investigate the inherent data-complexity of behavior-learning when the goal is simply to optimize immediate reward. Although easier than reinforcement learning, where one must also cope with state dynamics, immediate reward learning is still a common problem and is fundamentally harder than supervised learning.

For optimizing immediate reward, prior knowledge can be expressed either as a bias on the space of possible reward models, or a bias on the space of possible controllers. We investigate the two paradigmatic learning approaches of *indirect* (reward-model) learning and *direct*-control learning, and show that neither uniformly dominates the other in general. Model-based learning has the advantage of generalizing reward experiences across states and actions, but direct-control learning has the advantage of focusing only on potentially optimal actions and avoiding learning irrelevant world details. Both strategies can be strongly advantageous in different circumstances. We introduce hybrid learning strategies that combine the benefits of both approaches, and uniformly improve their learning efficiency.

Introduction

Reinforcement learning and control learning are significant subareas of machine learning and neural network research. Although a lot of effort has gone into studying these problems, it is fair to say that our current understanding of reinforcement and control learning problems still lags behind our comprehensive understanding of supervised learning. One of the main issues in reinforcement and control learning is *scaling up*. Although several "general purpose" learning algorithms such as Q-learning (Watkins 1989; Watkins & Dayan 1992) have been developed for reinforcement learning problems, and recent variants have

been proved to learn "efficiently" in some sense (Kearns & Singh 1998), getting these algorithms to solve significant real world problems ultimately requires the use of prior knowledge and domain constraints, just as in supervised learning. However, the issue of how to effectively exploit domain knowledge in reinforcement learning is still an open research issue—if not the central one in this area (Mahadevan & Kaelbling 1996; Sutton & Barto 1998).

In this paper we consider a simplified version of reinforcement learning and focus on learning to optimize *immediate* rewards. In standard (full) reinforcement learning the agent's actions affect not only its immediate rewards but also its future states, and therefore the agent must *tradeoff* any immediate gains against the long term payoffs it might receive by following certain paths (Sutton & Barto 1998). Here we consider a simpler interaction where the agent's actions determine its immediate reward, but do not affect its future states. That is, the agent interacts with the environment by receiving a current state s, chosing an action a, and then receiving an immediate reward r; but the next world state is then chosen *obliviously* to the agent's action. (For example, we can assume that the environment choses states independently from a stationary random source.) The goal of the agent, then, is to learn a behavior map $c : S \rightarrow A$ that optimizes its expected (immediate) reward.

Although simpler than full reinforcement learning, immediate reward learning has often been studied in the literature under the name of "associative reinforcement learning" (Kaelbling, Littman, & Moore 1996; Barto & Anandan 1985; Ackley & Littman 1990) and "associative search" (Sutton & Barto 1998). Examples of this problem include skill acquisition from "episodic" training and learning from repeated "attempts," where the agent must experiment with its actions in order to achieve a desired outcome. Some interesting case studies that have appeared in the literature are: learning the inverse kinematics of a robot manipulator (*i.e.*, learning which joint angle settings will place a robot's hand at a desired location in its workspace) (Jordan & Rumelhart 1992; DeMers & Kreutz-Delgado 1997), learning to volley a ping pong ball to a desired location (Moore

1990), learning to sink billiard balls in designated pockets (Moore 1990), learning to deflect an air hockey puck towards a goal (Brodie & DeJong 1998), learning "hit/no-hit" strategies for blackjack (Sutton & Barto 1998), learning to shoot baskets (illustrative example from (Jordan & Rumelhart 1992)), learning to putt a golf ball into a hole (illustrative example from (Sutton & Barto 1998)), learning to behave optimally with limited resources (Russell, Subramanian, & Parr 1993), neural networks for learning "one shot set-point" control (Miller, Sutton, & Werbos 1990), and learning the inverse of functions with neural networks (Bishop 1995; Kindermann & Linden 1990). In each of these cases, the environment presents a problem to the agent, the agent acts to achieve the desired goal, and the environment immediately responds with an indication of success/failure; then the cycle repeats *independently* of the previous events.

Note that, even though this problem is simpler than the full reinforcement learning problem, associative reward learning is still fundamentally harder than standard supervised learning. This is because in reward learning we only receive *partial* evaluation feedback from the environment. That is, in supervised learning, every training instance $\langle x, y \rangle$ evaluates *every* candidate function $f : X \to Y$ via the prediction error $loss(f(x), y)$. In a reward learning problem, by contrast, each training instance $\langle s, a, r \rangle$ evaluates only a *subset* of the candidate control functions $c : S \to A$; namely, those that would have taken action a in state s (Barto & Anandan 1985; Kaelbling, Littman, & Moore 1996). The reward r says nothing *directly* about what would have been obtained if a controller took a different action a' in situation s.

One key observation is that this type of partial feedback automatically creates a distinction between two types of prior knowledge/constraints that does not exist in complete-feedback learning: prior knowledge could be about the set of possible reward models one might face in the world, or it could specify a restricted class of controllers one might be limited to considering. This distinction is mirrored in two fundamental learning approaches that one might consider for this problem:

Model-based learning: Do we learn a model of the total reward function, and then infer the best candidate controller?

Direct-control learning: Do we restrict attention to a set of possible controllers, and attempt to identify a good one directly?

Note that this distinction is independent of temporal credit assignment and exploration/exploitation trade-off issues. Thus, we can investigate the issue of model-based versus direct-control learning in a very simple setting. In fact, in this paper we will consider the problem of *batch* learning a good controller from a stationary distribution of training instances. The simplicity of this framework allows us to make some straightforward yet telling observations about the relative benefits of the two learning approaches. Here we can clearly determine when one is advantageous over the other, and devise hybrid learning strategies that dominate the performance of both.

We begin the investigation by formalizing our model and drawing the major distinctions we wish to make. We then briefly investigate each of the two fundamental learning approaches—model-based and direct-control learning—and present learning strategies and data-complexity results for each. The paper then brings these two investigations together and asks which learning strategy is best. We show that in fact neither approach dominates the other in general: for some classes of reward models it is best to learn the model first and then infer the optimal controller, but for other classes it is best to ignore the models entirely and just focus on the corresponding class of potentially optimal controllers. This distinction is made strictly in terms of the *data-complexity* of learning, and is not necessarily tied to the issue of computational efficiency (as is sometimes suggested, for example in (Wyatt 1997)).

Finally, we consider whether there are hybrid learning strategies that are neither purely model-based nor controller-based, but that can strictly dominate the performance of both. We demonstrate that such learning strategies do indeed exist.

Formulation

The learner interacts with the world according to a protocol where the world chooses a state $s \in S$, the learner responds with an action $a \in A$, and the world returns a scalar reward $r \in \mathbb{R}$; and the cycle repeats. The reward process could be stochastic (or even nonstationary) in general, but for simplicity we will find it convenient to think of the rewards as being generated from a deterministic function $m_w : S \times A \to \mathbb{R}$, which we refer to as the (true) reward model.

The direct goal of reward learning is not to identify the underlying reward model *per se*, but rather identify a good behavior strategy $c : S \to A$. Of course, this might be achieved indirectly, by first approximating the reward model and then inferring a good controller. (But whether one would actually want to learn a controller this way is exactly the point of this investigation.) Notice that attempting to identify a good control function directly from training data introduces the problem of incomplete feedback: each training instance $\langle s, a, r \rangle$ evaluates only a *subset* of possible controllers—namely, those controllers c such that $c(s) = a$—but does not directly inform us about the rewards that other controllers might have obtained in this state. Therefore, given an accumulated sequence of training instances $\langle s_1, a_1, r_1 \rangle, ..., \langle s_t, a_t, r_t \rangle$ we can estimate the expected rewards of a set of controllers in the usual way, but the effective sample size of these estimates will *vary* from controller to controller; *i.e.*, some will have been "tried" more than others. (This is unlike standard supervised learning where each candidate prediction function f can be evaluated by *every* training example $\langle x, y \rangle$, and thus the effective sample size is always uniform among the candidates.) So there is an inherent exploratory aspect to the learning problem here—the learner must choose actions that evaluate different parts of the controller space (at different rates) to build up enough evidence to reliably distinguish good candidates from bad.

Formally, we assume successive states are drawn independently according to some stationary distribution P_s, and therefore characterize the world by a state distribution P_s and the reward model m_w. For each state $s \in S$ a controller c picks an action $c(s) \in A$ and receives reward $m_w(s, c(s)) \in \mathbb{R}$. Since successive states are independent of a controller's actions, we can characterize the expected reward of a controller simply in terms of its expected *immediate* reward

$$ER(c) = \int m_w(s, c(s)) \, dP_s.$$

In this paper we also focus on a *batch* learning protocol where the learner is free to choose actions to gain information in an initial training phase, but then settles on a fixed controller in the subsequent test phase. The significance of this assumption is that the need for *exploitation* is completely eliminated from the training phase, and the learner can concentrate solely on gaining information. That is, the problem is entirely *exploration*. (We therefore do not address the exploration/exploitation tradeoff directly in this paper. The benefit of focusing on the batch paradigm instead of the customary on-line model is that we can still formulate the distinction between model-based and direct-control learning, but compare them in a much simpler setting that permits provable separations between the two approaches and clear suggestions for new learning strategies.)

We now describe the two approaches to learning that we will be considering. The key distinction is how we express our prior knowledge/constraints on the learning problem.

The first approach, embodied by direct-control learning, is just to directly consider a restricted class of control functions C. In this case, C expresses any prior constraints we have about the solutions to the learning task, but does not express direct knowledge about the reward model m_w. In this situation the learner is forced to learn from partial evaluations, since any action it chooses can only return information about a *subset* of C. Learning strategies in this situation therefore amount to strategies for deciding which subsets of C to examine in order to accumulate evidence about which controllers are best and which are suboptimal.

The second approach we consider is to directly learn the reward model $m_w : S \times A \to \mathbb{R}$ and then, once an accurate reward model has been acquired, using it to deduce a good controller. In this situation prior knowledge is not expressed as a restricted class of controllers, but rather as a restricted class of possible reward models M. This type of learning seems advantageous since it is just a *supervised* learning task; that is, each training instance $\langle s, a, r \rangle$ evaluates *every* possible model m

in M. (This is a slightly novel supervised learning problem however, in that it has both passive and active elements—the world chooses the state s but the learner chooses the action a.)

On the face of it, the model-based approach seems superior to direct-control learning, since supervised learning is intuitively easier than partial feedback learning. However, to properly compare the two approaches, we need to adequately control for their different forms of prior knowledge. Note that there is a natural relation between reward models and controllers: for any reward model $m : S \times A \to \mathbb{R}$ there is a controller $c_m : S \to A$ that is optimal for m (perhaps more than one). Thus (since states are independent of actions) we can characterize the optimal controller c_m as the one which takes the immediately optimal action in each state:

$$c_m(s) = \underset{a \in A}{\operatorname{argmax}} \, m(s, a).$$

Therefore from a class M of possible reward models, we obtain a corresponding induced class C_M of potentially optimal controllers. From this correspondence we can formulate a direct comparison between the two learning approaches: Given a class of reward models M and implied class of controllers C_M, how do direct-control learning and model-based learning compare in terms of inherent data-efficiency? Below we show that neither approach dominates the other in general. However we then show that there is a hybrid learning strategy which dominates both.

Direct-control learning

We first consider the direct-control approach to learning. Here prior knowledge is expressed as a restricted class of control functions $C = \{c : S \to A\}$ which we assume contains a good candidate. Notice that this says nothing directly about the reward model m_w (except perhaps that one of the candidate controllers is optimal) so in principle we have no way of generalizing the outcome $\langle s, a, r \rangle$ of a particular action a to other actions a'. As noted above, direct-control methods have to accumulate evidence for the quality of each controller in a "differential" fashion: each training instance evaluates only a subset of the controllers, therefore some controllers will have been "tried" more often than others and consequently have a higher quality estimate of their true performance. So direct-control learning methods need to decide which actions (controllers) to focus their attention on at each stage.

Direct-control learning methods were the focus of much early research on associative reward learning (Kaelbling, Littman, & Moore 1996; Kaelbling 1994; Ackley & Littman 1990; Barto & Anandan 1985; Williams 1988; 1992), learning in behavior based robotics (Maes & Brooks 1990), neural networks for learning direct inverse control (Brodie & DeJong 1998; DeMers & Kreutz-Delgado 1997; Mel 1989), and neural nets for learning the inverse of functions (Bishop 1995; Kindermann & Linden 1990). There is a large and interesting literature on this approach (even though most recent research has focused on the model-based approaches considered below).

To gain a concrete understanding of this problem, we will investigate a simple version where we assume rewards are 0-1 valued and that there exists a perfect controller in C (i.e., a controller $c \in C$ that always receives reward 1). This allows us to formulate a very simple "PAC learning" version of the task.

Problem: Batch DC-Learning. Given a class of controllers C, an approximation parameter ϵ, and a reliability parameter δ; with probability at least $1 - \delta$ return a controller c whose expected reward is at least $1 - \epsilon$, for any distribution P_s and reward model m_w.

The benefit of this formalization is that we can now ask concrete questions and prepare for future comparisons: What are good learning strategies for batch DC-learning, and how can we measure the "complexity" of C so as to quantify the inherent data-complexity of the task? (That is, how can we quantify the "strength" of the prior knowledge encoded by C?)

To measure the complexity of C we note that in the two action case it suffices to use the standard notion of VC-dimension.[1] (For the multi-action case we need to resort to the generalized notions of VC-dimension developed by (Ben-David *et al.* 1995; Natarajan 1991).) We observe that, as in standard PAC learning, there is a simple generic learning strategy that achieves near optimal data-efficiency.

Procedure: DC-Learn. Proceed in a series of rounds. For each round, observe random states $s \in S$ and take uniform random actions $a \in A$ until every controller $c \in C$ has been "tried" at least once; that is, for every $c \in C$ there exists an example $\langle s_i, a_i, r_i \rangle$ such that $c(s_i) = a_i$. (Below we note that this occurs within a reasonable number of examples for most C.) Repeat for a number of rounds that is sufficient to obtain uniform ϵ-accurate estimates of the expected reward of every controller in C with probability at least $1 - \delta$ (using the standard PAC bounds from VC-theory, and its generalizations (Blumer *et al.* 1989; Ben-David *et al.* 1995)). Return any controller that has always been successful every time it has been "tried".

The idea here is simply to accumulate evidence across the entire space of possible controllers to reliably distinguish the good candidates from bad. As simple-minded

---

[1] It is often claimed that the two action case reduces to standard supervised learning—by making the hypothesis that $\langle s, a, r \rangle$ implies $\langle s, \neg a, \neg r \rangle$. But this cannot work in general (Sutton & Barto 1998). If the actions are not randomly sampled with a *uniform* distribution, then an inferior action can accidentally demonstrate a higher expected reward. Barto and Anandan (Barto & Anandan 1985) reduce the two-action case to supervised learning by making the *assumption* that $m(s, \neg a) = 1 - m(s, a)$. But this just amounts to making explicit assumptions about the reward model. We address such a model-based approach to learning in the next section.

as this procedure seems, it turns out that it is impossible to dramatically improve its data-efficiency in terms of scaling in ϵ, δ and the VC-dimension of C.

Proposition 1. For any $\epsilon > 0$, $\delta > 0$ and class C with VC-dimension d, procedure DC-learn correctly solves the batch DC-learning problem and halts with an expected sample size of $O\left(\frac{1}{\epsilon}\left((d^2 \ln d)(\ln \frac{1}{\epsilon}) + \ln \frac{1}{\delta}\right)\right)$.

(Proof idea) The key step is showing that each round of DC-learn halts within a reasonable number of training examples. This is proved by observing that the only way a controller can be completely avoided is by always matching the actions of its "negation". But the class of negated control functions also has small VC-dimension, and the probability of staying in this class by choosing random actions becomes vanishingly small as the sample size increases. This leads to an $O(d \ln d)$ expected stopping time for each round.

The next proposition shows that it is impossible to improve on the performance of DC-learn beyond a $(d \ln d)(\ln \frac{1}{\epsilon})$ factor.

Proposition 2. It is impossible to solve the batch DC-learning problem with an expected sample size that is less than $\Omega\left(\frac{1}{\epsilon}(d + \ln \frac{1}{\delta})\right)$.

(Proof idea) The idea is simply to fix a set of shattered states $s_1, ..., s_d$ and choose a difficult distribution such that every state must be seen to guarantee a good controller, and yet one state is left out with significant probability if the expected sample size is too small (Schuurmans & Greiner 1995).

Although the generic direct-control learning procedure DC-learn does not seem very refined, it has some interesting advantages over well-known learning algorithms in the literature: For example, consider the IEKDNF algorithm from (Kaelbling 1994), which learns controllers $c: \{0,1\}^n \to \{0,1\}$ that can be expressed as k-DNF formulae. The class of k-DNF controllers clearly has finite VC-dimension, so the procedure DC-learn is guaranteed to reliably learn a near-optimal controller using a reasonable sample size. However the IEKDNF procedure presented in (Kaelbling 1994) is not! In fact, there are simple cases where IEKDNF is guaranteed to converge to a bad controller, even when a perfect controller exists in the assumed class C_{k-DNF}.

(To see this, consider a state space described by two bits $s = \langle x_1, x_2 \rangle$ and concentrate on the class of pure disjunctive controllers C_{1-DNF}. Assume the distribution P_s puts probability $1/3$ on state $\langle 0, 1 \rangle$ and $2/3$ on $\langle 1, 0 \rangle$, and the reward model is such that $m_w(s, 1) = 1$ and $m_w(s, 0) = 0$ for all states s. Then, using the notation of (Kaelbling 1994), we let $er(x_i, a)$ denote the expected reward of a specific controller c which takes actions $c(\langle x_1, x_2 \rangle) = a$ if $x_i = 1$ and $\neg a$ if $x_i = 0$. In this case we have $er(x_1, 0) = 1/3$, $er(x_1, 1) = 2/3$, $er(x_2, 0) = 2/3$, and $er(x_2, 1) = 1/3$. So here IEKDNF will converge to the controller $c(\langle x_1, x_2 \rangle) \equiv x_1$ with probability 1, and this controller has expected reward

2/3. However, the optimal controller in C_{1-DNF}, $c(\langle x_1, x_2 \rangle) \equiv x_1 \vee x_2$, actually has expected reward 1; and *this* is the controller that will be discovered by DC-learn with probability at least $1 - \delta$ for reasonable ϵ.)

Given that the IEKDNF algorithm was actually designed to cope with the exploration/exploitation trade-off this might not seem like an appropriate comparison. However, notice that convergence to a suboptimal controller means that IEKDNF could not compete with DC-learn after the batch training phase is complete, even in an on-line evaluation. That is, convergence to a sub-optimal controller is an undesirable property whether one is using a batch or an on-line assessment. This example demonstrates the benefit of our analysis: carefully evaluating the data-complexity of learning led us to uncover a weakness in an existing learning procedure that had not been previously observed.

Model-based learning

We now consider the alternative model-based approach to learning. Here we consider prior knowledge that is expressed in a rather different form: we assume the world's reward model m_w belongs to some restricted class of models M. Learning a good reward model $m : S \times A \to \mathbb{R}$ from training examples $\langle s, a, r \rangle$ is a standard supervised learning problem, so it seems like it should be easier than direct-control learning. Once an adequate model $m \in M$ has been identified, we can simply infer a corresponding optimal controller c_m and return this as the final hypothesis for the test phase.

This model-based approach to learning control has been commonly pursued in the literature on associative reinforcement learning (Munroe 1987; Kaelbling, Littman, & Moore 1996), particularly under the guise of learning "forward models" for control (Moore 1990; 1992; Jordan & Rumelhart 1992).[2]

As in the previous section, to develop a concrete understanding of this problem and to facilitate comparisons with the direct-control approach, we consider a simple version of the learning task where we assume that the rewards are 0-1 valued, and that the class of reward models M always contains the true model m_w.

Problem: Batch MB-Learning. Given a class of reward models M, an approximation parameter ϵ, and a reliability parameter δ; with probability at least $1 - \delta$ return a reward model m that agrees with the true reward model m_w on every action for at least $1 - \epsilon$ of the states, for any state distribution P_s and any true reward model $m_w \in M$.

[2]Note that Moore (Moore 1990; 1992) does not consider a restricted class of models per se, but his work makes a strong model-based assumption that similar actions in similar states will yield similar outcomes. We view this as relying on the true reward model to be sufficiently well-behaved so that one can generalize across states and actions. Generalizing in this way is what we are characterizing as a model-based approach to learning.

Clearly, identifying an accurate model of the pay-off function to this extent is sufficient to infer a near optimal controller: If successful, we can correctly deduce the optimal action for at least $1 - \epsilon$ of the states and therefore return a controller that achieves expected reward at least $1 - \epsilon$. Note that this is a slightly unorthodox supervised learning problem in that the states are observed passively but the actions chosen actively, and both are inputs to the target function m_w. Moreover, we have to *identify* the marginal reward map $A \to \mathbb{R}$ exactly for most states $s \in S$, so our success criterion is harder than standard PAC learning. This forces us to define a measure of complexity for M that combines the notion of the VC-dimension of the class M on its domain $S \times A$, with a measure of how hard it is to exactly identify the marginal reward map $A \to \mathbb{R}$ for each state. We do this by appealing to the notion of "universal identification sequence" developed in (Goldman & Kearns 1991; Goldman, Kearns, & Schapire 1990) which measures the difficulty of identifying an arbitrary boolean function from a given class of functions. (A universal identification sequence is a set of points that is labeled uniquely by each function in the class.)

As is typical for batch learning tasks, we find that a very simple learning procedure can achieve near optimal performance in terms of scaling in ϵ, δ and the complexity of M.

Procedure: MB-learn. For each state $s \in S$ identify off-line a shortest universal identification sequence $\langle s, a_{i_1} \rangle, ..., \langle s, a_{i_k} \rangle$ for the class of maps $A \to \mathbb{R}$ that M induces from s. Proceed in a series of rounds. Given a random state s, choose an action a_{i_j} uniformly at random from the universal identification sequence for s. Repeat until a sufficient number of training examples have been observed. Take any model m that is consistent with every training example and return a corresponding optimal controller c_m. (Note that this procedure is not limited to a finite state or action space, so long as there is a finite bound on the lengths of the universal identification sequences.)

Proposition 3. For any $\epsilon > 0$, $\delta > 0$ and class M with VC-dimension d over the joint space $S \times A$, procedure MB-learn correctly solves the batch MB-learning problem and halts with an expected sample size of $O\left(\frac{t}{\epsilon}(d \ln \frac{1}{\epsilon} + \ln \frac{1}{\delta})\right)$; where t is the length of the longest universal identification sequence over all $s \in S$.

(Proof idea) The only minor trick is to observe that learning a global approximation with error less than ϵ/t on the induced joint distribution over $S \times A$ means that the model could make a mistake on one action for at most ϵ of the states (since each action is observed with conditional probability at least $1/t$ in any state).

Proposition 4. *Any* learning procedure requires at least $\Omega\left(\frac{1}{\epsilon}(d + \ln \frac{1}{\delta})\right)$ training examples to correctly solve the batch MB-learning problem. (Follows from (Ehrenfeucht *et al.* 1989).)

These definitions formalize our intuition about what it means to follow a strictly model-based approach (that is, where we attempt to identify the true payoff structure of the world). Having completed this formalization, we are now in a position to rigorously compare the model-based approach in its simple form against the simple form of direct-control learning described in the previous section.

Comparison

We can now compare the two basic learning approaches considered so far, and examine the presumption that model-based learning is always more efficient than direct-control learning, given that model-based learning apparently receives more feedback from each training example. However, we will see immediately that this fact does not always help. (Note that we draw our distinctions based strictly on the exploration costs of learning and not on issues of computational complexity.)

To conduct the comparison, recall that for any class of reward models $M = \{m : S \times A \to I\!R\}$ there exists a corresponding class of potentially optimal controllers $C_M = \{c : S \to A\}$. The basis of the comparison is: given a class M and corresponding class C_M, how does the data-efficiency of model-based learning on M compare to that of direct-control learning on C_M?

To best illustrate the fundamental differences, we first consider a simple setting where the world has just one state but there are several possible actions. In this case we can represent a class of reward models M as a matrix whose rows correspond to actions and whose columns represent the individual 0-1-valued reward models $m \in M$.

(A)	m_1	m_2
a_1	0	1
a_2	0	1
a_3	0	1
$\vdots$	0	1
a_n	1	0

First, consider the question of when model-based learning is more data-efficient than direct-control learning. The intuition is clearly that model-based learning should obtain its greatest advantage when the class of reward models allows us to *generalize* the outcome of a single training instance $\langle a, r \rangle$ across a *set* of actions a'. Matrix A demonstrates this in its most extreme form. Here, observing any single action a will allow us to exactly identify the true reward model over the entire action space. Model-based learning in this case will be able to return a successful action after just one training example. On the other hand, direct-control learning needs to examine all n actions (in the worst case) before it could be guaranteed to find a successful one. (This is because a direct-control learner is oblivious to any

restrictions on the payoff model, and therefore must follow a fixed exploration strategy through the action space. For any deterministic strategy the rows of the matrix can be permuted and a column selected so that the successful action is the *last* one visited. Similarly, a random (uniform) search strategy takes $|A|$ trials in expectation to find a single successful action.)

(B)	m_1	m_2	m_3	$\cdots$	m_n	m_{n+1}
a_1	0	1	1	1	1	1
a_2	1	0	1	1	1	1
a_3	1	1	0	1	1	1
$\vdots$	1	1	1	0	1	1
a_n	1	1	1	1	0	1

However, this situation could easily go the other way. The problem with naively attempting to identify the reward model is that one could spend significant effort learning details about the model that are simply not relevant for achieving optimal control. For instance, consider Matrix B. Here, any direct-control learning technique needs to examine at most two distinct actions before it is guaranteed to find a successful one. Model-based learning, on the other hand, would need to examine at least $n - 1$ actions in this situation before it is guaranteed to identify the true reward model in the worst case. (This is because the data-complexity of identifying the reward model is lower bounded by the "teaching dimension" of the class of models M (Goldman & Kearns 1991). So, for example, the teaching dimension of the last column in Matrix B is $n - 1$ (easily determined using the technique of (Goldman & Kearns 1991)). This is a lower bound on the smallest number of actions that can guarantee that this column is distinguished from all others in the matrix.)

Thus, we see that there is no strict domination either way. Of course, these examples might seem trivial in that, once represented this way, it is *obvious* that naive model-based or naive direct-control learning are not sensible approaches to this problem. But that is exactly our point! By conducting a careful evaluation of the data-complexity of learning optimal controllers we have been led to uncover a specific tradeoff that has not always been carefully described. Neither of these two extreme forms of learning can be the proper way to approach associative reward learning problems in general.

These observations easily generalize to the case of stochastic rewards and multi-state problems. For stochastic rewards the learner must repeatedly sample actions to get reliable estimates of their expected reward, but must still identify near-optimal actions with high probability in order to succeed. In this case, constructions very similar to those above can be used to demonstrate the same advantages and disadvantages of the two approaches.

Thus, in general, investigating these two extreme forms of learning highlights the dangers of single-mindedly pursuing either approach, and clarifies the tradeoffs between the two. With this new understanding, we can turn to the question of deriving more refined learning strategies that combine the benefits of both approaches.

Hybrid learning

Given a class of reward models M, it seems sensible to consider a learning approach that exploits this prior knowledge but pays attention to the fact that we are only trying to derive a good controller, and not necessarily learn all the details about the reward model.

(C)	m_1	m_2	m_3	$\cdots$	m_n
a_1	1	0	0	0	0
a_2	0	1	0	0	0
a_3	0	0	1	0	0
$\vdots$	0	0	0	1	0
a_n	1	1	1	1	1

Continuing in the simple setting discussed above, it is actually easy to see what a good hybrid learning strategy might look like. Consider matrix C. In this case the worst case exploration costs of model-based and direct-control learning are $n-1$ and n respectively. However, no exploration is required at all in this case! In this matrix there is a single action, a_n, that is successful in every reward model, and therefore a_n could be immediately returned as the optimal controller without examining a single point. From this simple observation we can derive an optimal learning procedure for the single state task.

Optimal procedure. Given a matrix of possible reward models M, choose a subset of actions $\{a_{i_1}, ..., a_{i_k}\}$ that is a *minimal cover* of the columns of M (where each action "covers" those columns in which it receives reward 1). Explore these actions in any fixed order until either a successful action is found or only one action remains. Return this as the final hypothesis.

Note that this procedure is neither model-based nor direct-control based in the sense discussed above, but it necessarily dominates the data-efficiency of both:

Proposition 5 (Optimality). The size of the minimal cover (minus one) determines the worst case data-efficiency of the optimal procedure. Moreover, the size of this minimal cover (minus one) is also a *lower bound* on the worst case exploration cost of *any* procedure.

(Proof idea) The upper bound is immediate. The lower bound follows because any smaller set of actions must leave some world "uncovered," which permits an adversary to choose a reward model under which every chosen action fails.

It is not hard to scale this basic exploration procedure up to handle multiple states and stochastic rewards. The multi-state case can be handled by considering a minimal cover of the potentially successful actions for each state s, and then follow a strategy that only considers actions that fall within these covers. In fact, we can use this method to construct examples of reward learning problems with boolean controllers $c : \{0,1\}^n \to \{0,1\}^k$ and reward models $m : \{0,1\}^{n+k} \to \{0,1\}$ where our hybrid approach requires $O(1)$ observations to identify a successful controller, but naive model-based and direct-control learning both require $\Omega(k2^n)$ observations in the worst case. (The construction just multiplies a representation of Matrix C across the set of states, $\{0,1\}^n$.)

To handle stochastic rewards, one converts each stochastic reward model $m : s \times a \mapsto$ "expected reward" to a 0-1 reward model m', where $m'(s,a) = 1$ if the conditional expected reward of action a given state s is within $\epsilon/2$ of the best conditional expected reward for state s, and $m'(s,a) = 0$ otherwise. Then one can apply the minimal set cover approach on each conditional reward map $A \to \{0,1\}$, as outlined above, and combine this with repeatedly sampling chosen actions for each state to obtain $\epsilon/2$-accurate estimates of their true conditional expected rewards. This leads to a provably correct procedure that has near optimal data-efficiency (as in propositions 1 and 3).

We are currently extending our hybrid learning approach to apply to robot learning problems, and in particular to learning the inverse kinematics for robot manipulators. Here we hope to gain advantages over current approaches in two ways. First, robotic manipulators often have excess degrees of freedom which allow them to place their end-effectors at targets using several different arm configurations. This means that the set of possible control maps $c :$ "goal position" $\to$ "arm configuration" might contain several optimal solutions. By ignoring the reward models, direct-control learning cannot automatically infer that these distinct controllers are equally effective, and therefore can waste significant training data in detecting their equivalence (or worse, we might accidentally average distinct solutions together to obtain an inferior controller (Bishop 1995, Chapter 6)). On the other hand, a hybrid learning method can exploit the possible error models $m :$ "target position" $\times$ "arm configuration" $\to$ "sensed position error" to determine when two controllers are equally effective and thereby avoid this inefficiency.

Second, sensors must be used to measure the positioning error, and models of these sensors must often be *learned* before one can predict the configurations to use on novel targets. (That is, the robot must learn the error map m.) Although the characteristics of these sensors can vary greatly, which makes the problem of learning the error map quite difficult, most sensors operate in a way that the reported errors are monotonic functions of the true error, and small errors are reported near optimal solutions. Therefore, rather than learn every detail of the error map (which is characteristic of naive model-based learning), we can use the hybrid learning approach to focus on learning an accurate model of the map only in regions that are close to zero-error configurations, and ignore the remaining details of the map that are irrelevant for achieving optimal control.

Conclusions

We considered the two fundamental approaches to associative reward learning, compared their advantages, and proposed a notion for hybrid learning which dominates the performance of both. The key insight is that naively following a strictly model-based or direct-control approach is generally not the most effective way to learn a good controller. Although it is important to exploit prior knowledge that encodes information about the reward models—this can yield tremendous benefits and is essential to scaling up to real-world tasks—careful attention must be paid to the fact that this knowledge will ultimately be used to derive a good controller, and that not every detail about the reward model is needed to accomplish this. The notions for hybrid learning strategies proposed here, we feel, are a first step towards understanding how prior domain knowledge might be concretely exploited to achieve systematic benefits in reward learning tasks.

Future work. Obviously these are preliminary theoretical steps, and there is a long way to go before significant contributions to reward and reinforcement learning practice can be made. Some immediate directions are to (1) pursue application studies of these techniques and compare their performance on real tasks, for example, on the problem of learning the inverse kinematics of a robot manipulator, (2) extend the theoretical model to stochastic rewards, and most importantly (3) to introduce dependence between actions and states and extend our learning strategies and theoretical analysis to deal with state-transition dynamics and temporal credit assignment issues (Kearns & Singh 1998).

References

Ackley, D., and Littman, M. 1990. Generalization and scaling in reinforcement learning. In *NIPS-2*, 550–557.

Barto, A., and Anandan, P. 1985. Pattern-recognizing stochastic learning automata. *IEEE Trans. Sys. Man Cyb.* 15(3):360–375.

Ben-David, S.; Cesa-Bianchi, N.; Haussler, D.; and Long, P. 1995. Characterizations of learnability for classes of $\{0,..,n\}$-valued functions. *J. Comput. Sys. Sci.* 50:74–86.

Bishop, C. 1995. *Neural Networks for Pattern Recognition.* Oxford: Clarendon Press.

Blumer, A.; Ehrenfeucht, A.; Haussler, D.; and Warmuth, M. K. 1989. Learnability and the Vapnik-Chervonenkis dimension. *Journal of the ACM* 36(4):929–965.

Brodie, M., and DeJong, G. 1998. Iterated phantom induction: A little knowledge can go a long way. In *AAAI-98*, 665–670.

DeMers, D., and Kreutz-Delgado, K. 1997. Inverse kinematics of dextrous manipulators. In Omidvar, O., and van der Smagt, P., eds., *Neural Systems for Robotics.* Academic Press.

Ehrenfeucht, A.; Haussler, D.; Kearns, M. J.; and Valiant, L. 1989. A general lower bound on the number of examples needed for learning. *Information and Computation* 82:247–261.

Goldman, S., and Kearns, M. 1991. On the complexity of teaching. In *COLT-91*, 303–314.

Goldman, S.; Kearns, M.; and Schapire, R. 1990. Exact identification of circuits using fixed points of amplification functions. In *FOCS-90*, 193–202.

Jordan, M., and Rumelhart, D. 1992. Forward models: Supervised learning with a distal teacher. *Cognitive Science* 16(3):307–354.

Kaelbling, L.; Littman, M.; and Moore, A. 1996. Reinforcement learning: A survey. *Journal of Artificial Intelligence Research* 4:237–285.

Kaelbling, L. 1994. Associative reinforcement learning: Functions in k-DNF. *Machine Learning* 15:279–299.

Kearns, M., and Singh, S. 1998. Near-optimal reinforcement learning in polynomial time. In *ICML-98*, 260–268.

Kindermann, J., and Linden, A. 1990. Inversion of neural networks by gradient descent. *Parallel Comput.* 14:277–286.

Maes, P., and Brooks, R. 1990. Learning to coordinate behaviors. In *AAAI-90*, 796–802.

Mahadevan, S., and Kaelbling, L. 1996. The NSF workshop on reinforcement learning: Summary and observations. *AI Magazine* 17.

Mel, B. 1989. Further explorations in visually guided reaching: Making MURPHY smarter. In *NIPS-1*, 348–355.

Miller, W.; Sutton, R.; and Werbos, P., eds. 1990. *Neural Networks for Control.* MIT Press.

Moore, A. 1990. Acquisition of dynamic control knowledge for a robotic manipulator. In *ICML-90*, 244–252.

Moore, A. 1992. Fast, robust adaptive control by learning only forward models. In *NIPS-4*, 571–578.

Munroe, P. 1987. A dual back-propagation scheme for scalar reward learning. In *COGSCI-87*, 165–176.

Natarajan, B. 1991. Probably approximate learning of sets and functions. *SIAM J. Comput.* 20(2):328–351.

Russell, S.; Subramanian, D.; and Parr, R. 1993. Provably bounded optimal agents. In *IJCAI-93*, 338–344.

Schuurmans, D., and Greiner, R. 1995. Sequential PAC learning. In *COLT-95*, 377–384.

Sutton, R., and Barto, A. 1998. *Reinforcement Learning: An Introduction.* MIT Press.

Watkins, C., and Dayan, P. 1992. Q-learning. *Machine Learning* 8(3/4).

Watkins, C. 1989. *Models of Delayed Reinforcement Learning.* Ph.D. Dissertation, Psychology Department, Cambridge University.

Williams, R. 1988. On the use of backpropagation in associative reinforcement learning. In *ICNN-88*, 263–270.

Williams, R. 1992. Simple statistical gradient-following algorithms for connectionist reinforcement learning. *Machine Learning* 8(3/4):229–256.

Wyatt, J. 1997. *Exploration and inference in learning from reinforcement.* Ph.D. Dissertation, Artificial Intelligence Department, University of Edinburgh.

Model-Based Reasoning

Towards Diagram Processing:
A Diagrammatic Information System

Michael Anderson

Department of Computer Science
University of Hartford
West Hartford, CT 06117
anderson@hartford.edu

Abstract

We advocate the development of an agent capable of processing diagrammatic information directly in all its forms. In the same way that we will require intelligent agents to be conversant with natural language, we will expect them to be fluent with diagrammatic information and its processing. We present a methodology to this end, detail a *diagrammatic information system* that shows the merit of this line of research, and evaluate this system to motivate its future extensions.

Introduction

Of the set of behaviors that will be required of an artificially intelligent agent, a somewhat neglected member has been the ability to deal with diagrammatic information. Much attention has been paid to machine synthesis, recognition and understanding of natural language in both textual and audio forms. The understanding has been that such capabilities are required of an agent if it is expected to fully communicate with human beings and function in human environments. Much less attention has been given to machine understanding of diagrammatic information, an equally important mode of human communication. Effective capabilities in this mode will be crucial to an agent intended as a full partner in human discourse and activity. In the same way that we will require such agents to be conversant with natural language, we will expect them to be fluent with diagrammatic information and its processing. Ultimately, a machine with such capabilities will interact with a real world environment, rife with diagrammatic information, with a higher degree of autonomy than those without such capabilities.

The main thrust of diagrammatic reasoning research to date (from an artificial intelligence perspective) has been a search for computational efficiency gains through representations, and related inference mechanisms, that analogously model a problem domain. As this has been the aim of much of the seminal work in the field (e.g. Gelernter 1959; Larkin and Simon 1987), it is understandable that much effort has been expended in this direction. Although it is arguable that some progress has been made through this line of research, we believe that the field's most important contribution will be the development of an agent that is capable of dealing directly with diagrammatic information in all its forms.

We envision a system that takes diagrams as input, processes these diagrams, abstracting information and drawing inferences from them alone and in concert with other forms of knowledge representation, and expresses this newly gained knowledge as output in the form of text, new diagrams, actions, etc. Although the approach taken by this system will not necessarily claim cognitive plausibility, the fact that human beings do these things as a matter of course will stand as proof by existence that such a system has been fashioned.

This *diagram processing system* will be comprised of a number of important components. It will require a means to input diagrams such as a vision component. It will require a way to internally represent diagrams. The diagrammatic representations so acquired will require storage, as will knowledge needed to deal with these representations, necessitating some storage management component. A processing component will be required that synthesizes and abstracts new knowledge from combinations of diagrammatic and other forms of knowledge representations. Various components will be required to use the new knowledge to produce desired output in a variety of situations.

Reflection on the design of these components raises a number of questions: What constitutes a diagram? In what form will diagrams be accepted as input by the system? How will diagrams be internally represented? How will knowledge be gleaned from diagrams? What is the nature and content of *a priori* knowledge that will be required? How will other forms of representation and inference be integrated with diagrammatic representations and inference? What is nature of the desired output? How will this output be produced? Etc. These are hard questions with a multiplicity of answers that in themselves generate more questions. They form the parameters of the problem. Our intent is to build a test bed in which various values for these parameters can be tested, compared and contrasted, and ultimately forged into a single general purpose diagram processing system.

Following the methodology advocated in (Allen 1998), we 1) identify the particular intelligence we seek to study, 2) define a set of telescoping restricted tasks, 3) define evaluation criteria, 4) develop a model and system for our most restricted domain, and 5) evaluate this model and system for the next level of complexity.

Topic of Study

As we have stated, we are ultimately interested in developing an agent with full diagrammatic reasoning capabilities on par with human beings. If a picture is worth a thousand words, we would like to obviate the need for this text by being able to communicate with an agent directly via pictures or diagrams. An agent should be able to accept and understand such diagrammatic input from us and our environment as well as being able to produce such diagrams in its attempt to communicate diagrammatically representable notions to us.

Restricted Tasks Set

As this ultimate system is clearly beyond the grasp of current theory and technology, we refine it into a nested group of successively simpler tasks. Each nested level is a subset of all levels it is nested within and, further, a simplification of these containing levels. At the simplest level, we attempt to prove the merit of this line of research by developing a system that realizes the goal of this level. As we succeed at one level, we will attempt to build upon this success by applying what we have learned to the next less simplified level, expanding our solution to cover new problems it entails.

Given, as the outer most level, a system with *full diagrammatic reasoning capabilities*, we define as a simpler subset of this ultimate system a system that has *diagrammatic reasoning capabilities in some arbitrary task*. Examples of such systems are map understanding robots, scientific diagram abstracting agents, diagram generation systems, etc.

We choose, as the next level of simplification, to focus on *diagrammatic reasoning capabilities in one particular task* namely what we term *diagrammatic information systems*— systems that allow users to pose queries concerning diagrams, seeking responses that require the system to infer information from diagrams. As a final level of simplification we constrain any given instantiation of this diagrammatic information system to be knowledgeable about *particular* diagram types in a *particular* domain.

That said, we strive to develop a core of this diagrammatic information system that remains diagram type and domain independent, capable of accepting domain dependent diagrammatic and non-diagrammatic knowledge. In this way, each body of knowledge produces a new instantiation of the diagrammatic information system knowledgeable in the particular domain and diagram types represented by this knowledge.

Evaluation Criteria

To evaluate systems at all levels of nesting, we compare its understanding of diagrammatic information with the understanding that a human being exhibits with the same information. In this manner, we evaluate an instantiation of a diagrammatic information system in a particular domain by the number of diagram types it can handle, the variety of queries it can respond to, and the quality of responses it gives to these queries. The level of success of such a system is measured by how it approaches, matches, or exceeds the performance of a human being reasonably capable within the chosen domain.

Model and System

As the first task we have set for ourselves is an implementation of a *diagrammatic information system*, we choose one possible set of values to the parameters of this problem.

We define a *diagram* to be a *tessellation* (tiling) of a planar area such that it is completely covered by atomic two dimensional regions or *tesserae* (tiles). Such a definition is broad enough to include arbitrarily small tesserae (points, at the limit), pixels, and, at the other end of the spectrum, domain-specific entities such as countries, regions, blocks, etc. Further, as this definition is not tied to any particular semantics, it is general enough to encompass all diagrams. Given the wide variety of semantic mappings employed by diagrams, a general definition that makes no semantic commitment is useful.

We sidestep a vision component by accepting bitmaps depicting diagrams as input to our system. As this is a likely output of a vision component, such a component can be appended later.

Our currently chosen approach gleans knowledge from diagrams by directly manipulating spatial representations of them. This approach is motivated by noting that, given diagrams directly input as bitmaps, any translation into another representation will require some form of direct manipulation of these bitmaps. In many cases, this translation is superfluous. Given this approach, we store input bitmaps directly with no further abstraction. This strategy not only allows us to manipulate spatial representations directly but, should the need arise, it will

Figure 1: Vegetation in the United States

Figure 2: Response to query: "Which states have grassland?"

allow us to translate to any other representations as required.

We use, as a basis for this direct manipulation of diagrams, the theory of *inter-diagrammatic reasoning* (IDR) (Anderson and McCartney 1995, 1996). IDR leverages the spatial and temporal coherence often exhibited by groups of related diagrams for computational purposes. Using concepts from set theory, image processing theory, color theory, and others, like diagrams are combined in ways that produce new like diagrams that infer information implicit in the original diagrams.

Knowledge required to process diagrams is likely to be both domain and diagram specific. Facts and rules pertinent to targeted domains are necessary as is information germane to processing diagram types represented. We represent this knowledge both diagrammatically and non-diagrammatically, as appropriate, constraining both domains and diagram types as necessary. We achieve integration of diagrammatic and non-diagrammatic knowledge and inferencing by providing an inter-lingua abstraction that furnishes a homogeneous interface to various modes of representation and inferencing, permitting inferences to be made with heterogeneously represented knowledge.

Our output is both diagrammatic and textual, meant for direct human consumption. Although we skirt other forms of output such as action or intermediate output intended for use by some other system, there is nothing in the nature of the processing that precludes use of its product in such ways.

Our first instantiation of a diagrammatic information system is informed about *cartograms* (maps representing information as grayscale or color shaded areas) of the United States.

An Example

As an example, consider the diagram in Figure 1. This is a cartogram that depicts in three levels of gray where each of the major vegetation types are situated in the United States. The darkest gray represents *forest*, medium gray represents *grassland*, and the lightest gray represents *desert*. Given this diagram as input to the system, as well as the semantics of the gray levels in this particular diagram, posing the query "Which states have grassland?" elicits the diagram in Figure 2 as a response from the system. In this diagrammatic response, each state in which grassland exists is represented by its shape in black positioned where the state lies within the United States. We use this example to examine the implementation of this instantiation of a diagrammatic information system in further detail.

Figure 1 is input to the system as a bitmap and is stored as such with no further manipulation. The system is supplied with the semantic mapping of the gray levels of the diagram to the vegetation types present. The input diagram is then parsed into three diagrams, each comprised of a single gray level. Each of these diagrams represents, then, the location of a particular vegetation type within the United States. Figure 3, for example, shows the diagram resulting from this parsing that represents the locations of grassland in the United States.

A priori diagrammatic knowledge required to respond to this query is comprised of a set of diagrams that represent the locations of each state within the United States. Figure 4 is an example of such a diagram which shows the location of the state of Nevada within the United States by marking its area on the map in black. There are fifty such state diagrams.

The response to the query "Which states have grassland?" is generated by comparing each of these state diagrams with the diagram representing grassland. When a

Figure 3: Location of grassland in the United States

Figure 4: Location of Nevada in the United States

state diagram intersects the grassland diagram (both diagrams without the United States outline), the semantics of the domain dictate that that state contains grassland. All such states are then accumulated on a single diagram (with the United States outline) and presented to the user as the response to the query.

In this manner, diagrammatic responses can be generated for a wide variety of queries concerning vegetation in the United States including "Which states do not have forest?", "How many states have desert?" (Simply return a count of the state diagrams that intersect the desert diagram.), "Does Rhode Island have desert?" (Simply return true if the state diagram for Rhode Island intersects the desert diagram.), "Which vegetation type covers the most states?", "Do any states have both grassland and desert?", "Which states have either desert or forest?", "Do more states have grassland than desert?", "Which states have forest but not grassland?", etc.

An overview of the formalism we use to generate responses to these queries, the theory of inter-diagrammatic reasoning, follows.

Inter-Diagrammatic Reasoning

The theory of inter-diagrammatic reasoning (Anderson and McCartney 1995, 1996; Anderson and Armen 1998) defines diagrams as tessellations. Tesserae take their values from an I, J, K valued subtractive CMY color scale. Intuitively, these CMY (Cyan, Magenta, Yellow) color scale values (denoted $v_{i, j, k}$) correspond to a discrete set of transparent color filters where i is the cyan contribution to a filter's color, j is the magenta contribution, and k is the yellow contribution. When overlaid, these filters combine to create other color filters from a minimum of WHITE ($v_{0,0,0}$) to a maximum of BLACK ($v_{I-1, J-1, K-1}$). In the current work, i, j, and k are always equal, providing grayscale values from WHITE to BLACK only. The following unary operators, binary operators, and functions provide a set of basic tools to facilitate the process of inter-diagrammatic reasoning.

Binary operators each take two diagrams, d_1 and d_2, of equal dimension and tessellation and each return a new diagram where each tessera has a value v that is some function of the values of the two corresponding tesserae, $v_{i1, j1, k1}$ and $v_{i2, j2, k2}$, in the operands.

- *OR,* denoted $d_1 \lor d_2$, returns the *maximum* of each pair of tesserae where the maximum of two corresponding tesserae is defined as $v_{max(i1,i2),\ max(j1, j2),\ max(k1,k2)}$.

- *AND,* denoted $d_1 \land d_2$, returns the *minimum* of each pair of tesserae where the minimum of two corresponding tesserae is defined as $v_{min(i1,i2),\ min(j1, j2),\ min(k1,k2)}$.

- *OVERLAY,* denoted $d_1 + d_2$, returns the *sum* of each pair of tesserae where the sum of values of

corresponding tesserae is defined as $v_{min(i1+i2,\ I-1),\ min(j1+j2,\ J-1),\ min(k1+k2,\ K-1)}$.

- *PEEL,* denoted $d_1 - d_2$, returns the *difference* of each pair of tesserae the difference of values of corresponding tesserae is defined as $v_{max(i1-i2,\ 0),\ max(j1-j2,\ 0),\ max(k1-k2,\ 0)}$.

- *NONNULL (NULL),* denoted NONNULL(d), (NULL(d)) is a one place Boolean function taking a single diagram that returns TRUE if d contains any non-WHITE (all WHITE) tesserae else it returns FALSE.

- *ACCUMULATE,* denoted $\alpha(d, ds, o)$, is a three place function taking an initial diagram, d, a set of diagrams of equal dimension and tessellation, ds, and the name of a binary diagrammatic operator, o, that returns a new diagram which is the accumulation of the results of successively applying o to d and each diagram in ds.

- *MAP,* denoted $\mu(f, ds)$, is a two place function taking a function f and a set of diagrams of equal dimension and tessellation, ds, that returns a new set of diagrams comprised of all diagrams resulting from application of f to each diagram in ds.

- *FILTER,* denoted $\phi(f, ds)$, is a two place function taking a Boolean function, f and a set of diagrams of equal dimension and tessellation, ds, that returns a new set of diagrams comprised of all diagrams in ds for which f returns TRUE.

Given these inter-diagrammatic operations, the vegetation and state maps as previously described, and a null diagram (denoted $\emptyset$) standing for a diagram with all tesserae WHITE-valued, the following more formally specifies the generation of a diagrammatic response to the query "Which states have grassland?":

$$\alpha(\emptyset, \phi(\lambda(x)\ \text{NONNULL(Grassland} \land x), \text{State}), +).$$

This 1) defines a lambda function that ANDs its parameter with the grassland diagram and returns true if the result is not null, 2) filters out diagrams from the set of state diagrams for which this lambda function does not return true (these are the state diagrams that do not intersect the grassland diagram), and 3) overlays the remaining state diagrams onto the null diagram giving the desired result. Figure 5 details this example.

Responses to all of the queries suggested previously can be generated via IDR operators. As in the example, those queries requiring a diagrammatic response produce an appropriate set of diagrams which are OVERLAYed together. Those queries requiring a numeric response produce an appropriate set of diagrams and return the cardinality of it. For instance, the number of states that have grassland can be returned by taking the cardinality of the set returned by the filtering operation instead of accumulating that set upon the null diagram as is done in the example. Those queries requiring a Boolean response

[ACCUMULATE State diagrams that give NONNULL result]

Figure 5: Generation of response to query "Which states have grassland?" via inter-diagrammatic reasoning operators

return the value of the **NONNULL** function applied to an appropriately derived diagram. For instance, a response to the query "Are there any states that have grassland?" will derive a diagram as in the example and return the result of applying the **NONNULL** function to it. Responses to queries seeking negative information can be derived by using the **NULL** function to produce an appropriate set of diagrams. For instance, a response to the query "Which states do not have grassland?" can be generated by simply replacing the **NONNULL** function with the **NULL** function. Queries seeking responses to conjunctions or disjunctions need to use set intersection and set union (respectively) to produce the appropriate sets of diagrams. Responses to relational ($<,>,<=,>=,<>,=$) queries need to compare the cardinality of each set of diagrams produced for each subquery involved.

Although IDR operators can produce responses to this wide variety of queries in this domain, it is by no means intuitive *how* they should be used to do so. In the following, we introduce a higher level query language that permits a user to query diagrams more intuitively, specifying *what* they wish to know more than *how* it should be generated.

Diagrammatic SQL

Diagrammatic SQL (DSQL) is an extension of Structured Query Language (SQL) (Date 1989) that supports querying

of diagrammatic information. Just as SQL permits users to query information in a relational database, DSQL permits a user to query information in diagrams.

We have chosen to extend SQL for use as our query language for a number of reasons. As we will show, SQL has a remarkable fit to the uses we wish to make of it. It is a reasonably intuitive language that allows specification of what data you want without having to specify exactly how to get it. It is a well-developed prepackaged technology whose use allows us to focus on more pressing system issues. SQL's large installed base of users provides a ready and able audience for a fully developed version of the system. The availability of immediate and imbedded modes provide means to use the system for both direct human consumption and further machine processing. The availability of natural language interfaces to SQL will allow the system to provide an even more intuitive interface for its users.

Besides providing a basis for a diagrammatic query language, a relational database that stores image data can be used by the system as a storage management component. Further, as relational databases already manage other types of data, use of one as a storage management component with a diagrammatic extension to its SQL gives the system a means to query both diagrammatic and non-diagrammatic data simultaneously. This provides a linkage between heterogeneous data

a. CREATE SCHEMA;
   CREATE TABLE US (State, Vegetation);
   INSERT INTO US (State)
   VALUES (Alabama, Arizona, ...);
   INSERT INTO US (Vegetation)
   VALUES (Grassland, Desert, Forest);

b. SELECT State
   FROM   US
   WHERE Vegetation = Grassland
              AND
              Vegetation IN State;

c. SELECT State
   FROM   US
   WHERE Vegetation = Forest
              AND
              Vegetation NOT IN State;

d. SELECT COUNT(State)
   FROM   US
   WHERE Vegetation = Desert
              AND
              Vegetation IN State;

e. EXISTS
   ((SELECT State
     FROM   US
     WHERE Vegetation = Grassland
                AND
                Vegetation IN State)
   INTERSECT
   (SELECT State
     FROM   US
     WHERE Vegetation = Desert
                AND
                Vegetation IN State));

f. (SELECT State
    FROM   US
    WHERE Vegetation = Desert
               AND
               Vegetation IN State)
   UNION
   (SELECT State
    FROM   US
    WHERE Vegetation = Forest
               AND
               Vegetation IN State));

g. (SELECT State
    FROM   US
    WHERE Vegetation = Forest
               AND
               Vegetation IN State)
   EXCEPT
   (SELECT State
    FROM   US
    WHERE Vegetation = Grassland
               AND
               Vegetation IN State);

Figure 6: DSQL data definition and example queries

allowing whole new classes of queries, for example, "What is the total population of states having desert?", "Which of the states having forest has the highest per capita income?", "What vegetation is contained by the state with the highest annual rainfall?", etc.

We have developed a grammar for a subset of DSQL that allows it to handle queries of the types previously discussed. Where SQL queries return relations, DSQL queries return sets of diagrams. These diagram sets can have their members OVERLAYed upon a null diagram for diagrammatic results or counted to return numeric results. Further, these sets can be tested for emptiness to return Boolean results or used as operands in set operations such as union, intersection, and difference. Examples of DSQL syntax and semantics follow.

DSQL Example. Figure 6 shows an example data definition and sample queries in DSQL. Figure 6a uses DSQL to define a schema for the diagrammatic information required by the examples presented previously. It creates a table named US that contains two diagram sets named State and Vegetation. In the current Lisp implementation, as no connection has yet been established to a relational database management system, a table is simply a list of related diagram sets. Each diagram set has inserted into it a number of diagrams appropriate to the set. In the current Lisp implementation, these are actually symbols that evaluate to diagrams.

Figure 6b is a DSQL query that represents the example query "Which states have grassland?". It has the same SELECT FROM WHERE clauses that SQL queries have

and these share similar semantics with their SQL counterparts. Most often, the SQL SELECT clause specifies what attribute(s) will have values in the resulting relation. In DSQL, the SELECT clause specifies what diagram set(s) will have values returned from the query. The SQL FROM clause specifies which table(s) are involved in the query. In DSQL, the FROM clause specifies which list(s) of diagram sets are involved in the query. The SQL WHERE clause specifies which condition(s) have to be satisfied by values returned by the query. This is the same use that a WHERE clause is put to in DSQL.

The DSQL query in Figure 6b states that the set of diagrams from the diagram set State of the diagram set list US that conform to the constraints specified will be returned. The WHERE clause specifies 1) that the Vegetation diagram set of the diagram set list US is restricted to the Grassland diagram only and 2) that the diagram in the Vegetation diagram set must intersect given State diagrams. In one context, the SQL IN Boolean operator returns true if and only if the value on the left hand side is a value in the attribute on the right hand side. In DSQL, IN is a Boolean operator that returns true if and only if the diagrams involved intersect. When sets of diagrams are involved, as in this and following examples, the semantics of a DSQL query dictate that this intersection be tested for each member of each set. In this case, the Grassland diagram will be tested for intersection with each member of the State diagram set, in turn, allowing the query to return only those states that contain grassland. As previously detailed, the response to this query is achieved by IDR operators as:

$a(\emptyset, \phi(\lambda(x) \text{ NONNULL(Grassland} \wedge x), \text{State}),+).$

Figure 6c is a DSQL query that seeks a response to the question "Which states do not have forest?". The semantics of this query is much like the previous example. In this example, though, the **Vegetation** diagram set is restricted to the **Forest** diagram and this diagram must *not* intersect with a state diagram for it to be included as part of the result. The response to this query is achieved by IDR operators as:

$a(\emptyset, \phi(\lambda(x) \text{ NULL(Forest} \wedge x), \text{State}),+).$

Figure 6d is a DSQL query that seeks a response to the question "How many states have desert?". This change in mode from a diagrammatic response to a numeric response is signaled by the application of the **COUNT** function to the diagram set in the **SELECT** clause. It is realized by the following IDR formulation where *cardinality* is a function returning the number of members in a set:

$cardinality(\phi(\lambda(x) \text{ NONNULL(Desert} \wedge x), \text{State})).$

Figure 6e is a DSQL query that asks "Are there any states that have both grassland and desert?". The fact that a Boolean response is required is signaled by the use of the **EXISTS** function. In SQL, the **EXISTS** function tests for an empty (single attributed) relation resulting from a subquery. In DSQL, it is used to test for an empty set of diagrams resulting from any query. To produce the set to be tested using IDR operations, the set of state diagrams that have grassland is intersected ($\cap$) with the set of state diagrams that have desert. If this resulting set is *not empty* ($\neg empty$), return true else return false. Following is the IDR realization of this query:

$\neg empty(\phi(\lambda(x) \text{ NONNULL(Grassland} \wedge x), \text{State})$
$\cap$
$\phi(\lambda(x) \text{ NONNULL(Desert} \wedge x), \text{State})).$

Figure 6f is a DSQL query that seeks a diagrammatic response to the question "Which states have either desert or forest. This response is generated by taking the union ($\cup$) of the set of states that have desert and the set of states that have forest and, then, **OVERLAY**ing them onto the null diagram. Expressed as IDR operations:

$a(\emptyset, \phi(\lambda(x) \text{ NONNULL(Desert} \wedge x), \text{State})$
$\cup$
$\phi(\lambda(x) \text{ NONNULL(Forest} \wedge x), \text{State}),+).$

In a similar vein, Figure 6g is a DSQL query that seeks a diagrammatic response to the question "Which states have forest but not grassland?". This response is generated by taking the difference (-) of the set of states that have forest and the set of states that have grassland and, then, **OVERLAY**ing them onto the null diagram. Expressed as IDR operations:

$a(\emptyset, \phi(\lambda(x) \text{ NONNULL(Forest} \wedge x), \text{State})$

$\phi(\lambda(x) \text{ NONNULL(Grassland} \wedge x), \text{State}),+).$

Evaluation of Model and System

To reiterate, our current goal is to develop an instantiation of a diagrammatic information system knowledgeable about a particular diagram type (cartograms) in a particular domain (United States) that produces quality responses to the full range of queries that would be expected of a reasonably capable human being given the same knowledge.

A subset of a DSQL grammar required to handle the range of queries exemplified in this work has been developed, a rudimentary compiler that translates this range of DSQL queries into their IDR formulations has been constructed, and the IDR operations that produce the desired output have been realized in Common Lisp. The current instantiation of the diagrammatic information system responds to an interesting range of queries posed against cartograms of the United States. This range of queries can be characterized as those whose responses are generated by various combinations of input diagrams and *a priori* diagrams. It is arguable that, within this range, the quality of responses equals or exceeds human capabilities with the same diagrammatic information. These are indicators of a promising line of research.

That said, there is much work yet to accomplish to realize fully the goal of even this relatively simple level. For example, not all queries that a human would be expected to answer in the example domain can be handled currently by the system. These include, for instance, queries that seek information about area or neighborhood relations. Further, only cartograms of the same size and orientation as the *a priori* diagrammatic knowledge can be handled by the system. Clearly, humans are capable of handling such variations. Noise and uncertainty concerns present in real world data have also been avoided. For instance, textual annotations on a cartogram, although helpful to a human, are noise to the current system. Ready recognition of these limitations is the product of a clearly delineated task and well-defined goal. These limitations, then, provide the focus for future work.

Queries that seek information about area provide an opportunity to integrate IDR with another theory of diagrammatic reasoning. Furnas' *BITPICT theory* (Furnas 1992) postulates a logic that deals with diagrams via BITPICT rule mappings that can be used to transform one diagram into another and, therefore, allow reasoning from diagrams to diagrams. A BITPICT rule is meant to convey that all instances in a diagram of the bit pattern on the left hand side of a rule are replaced with the bit pattern on the right hand side of that rule. As interesting as this theory is, it can be subsumed by IDR by using appropriate sets of diagrams representing the universal instantiation of BITPICT rules. With this theory irregular shapes can be normalized, allowing comparison of their relative areas. Queries such as "Does California have more desert than grassland?" can then be handled. Further, domains that seem less amenable to IDR techniques (for instance, line graphs) can be made more manageable by use of this theory (for instance, by shading the area under a curve).

Queries that seek information about neighborhoods provide an opportunity to integrate IDR with an image processing theory. *Mathematical morphology* (Serra 1982; Serra 1988) is a image processing technique based on shape that is used to simplify, enhance, extract or describe image data. Sets of pixels describe an *image object*. Information about the geometric structure of image objects is extracted via use of other objects called *structural elements*. Information pertaining to the size, spatial distribution, shape, connectivity, convexity, smoothness, and orientation can be obtained by transforming the original image object by various structural elements. As primitive mathematical morphological operators can be modeled by IDR operators, IDR subsumes this theory as well. One such primitive operator, *dilation*, can be intuitively viewed as an operation that adds layers to the border of a two-dimensional object. Adding a sufficiently wide layer to a state diagram, for instance, allows this modified diagram to be tested for intersection with the other state diagrams. This can produce the set of state diagrams that neighbor the original state. In combination with area querying capabilities introduced previously, new classes of interesting queries can be handled. For example, "Which of the states surrounding Nevada have the greatest amount of forest?" is one such query that could then be handled.

Problems with real world data can be approached using geometrical transformations. Orientation and size of cartograms can be normalized by combinations of rotation and scaling operations. The search for the required combination and parameters of operations could be guided by the user. These operations, themselves, are implementable within the theory of IDR.

In addition to the above extensions, we are developing a full DSQL grammar, a complete interpreter and compiler to translate DSQL to IDR, and support for both immediate and imbedded modes of operation. We also are planning a relational database implementation with an exploration of the heterogeneous data inference that such an implementation will allow. We are also interested in investigating the extension to DSQL of natural language interfaces for SQL. Finally, when we have satisfactorily accomplished the stated goals for this level, we will then lift constraints and focus on the set of problems introduced by exploring new diagrams types in new domains.

Acknowledgments

We thank Dr. Chris Armen for his insightful comments and encouragement throughout the duration of this project. This research is supported by a grant from the National Science Foundation.

References

Allen, J. 1998. AI Growing Up: The Changes and Opportunities. *AI Magazine* 19(4):13-23.

Anderson, M. and Armen, C. 1998. Diagrammatic Reasoning and Color. In Proceedings of the AAAI Fall Symposium on Formalization of Reasoning with Visual and Diagrammatic Representations, Orlando, Florida. October.

Anderson, M. and McCartney, R. 1995. Inter-diagrammatic Reasoning. In Proceedings of the 14th International Joint Conference on Artificial Intelligence, Montreal, Canada. August.

Anderson, M. and McCartney, R. 1996. Diagrammatic Reasoning and Cases. In Proceedings of the 13th National Conference on Artificial Intelligence, Portland, Oregon. August.

Date, C. 1989. *A Guide to the SQL Standard, Second Edition*. Addison-Wesley.

Feigenbaum, E. A. and Feldman, J., eds. 1963. *Computers and Thought*, McGraw-Hill.

Furnas, G. 1992. Reasoning with Diagrams Only. In (Narayanan 1992).

Gelernter, H. 1959. Realization of a Geometry Theorem Proving Machine. In Proceedings of an International Conference on Information Processing, 273-282. UNESCO House. (also in [Feigenbaum & Feldman 1963]).

Larkin, J. and Simon, H. 1987. Why a Diagram is (Sometimes) Worth Ten Thousand Words. *Cognitive Science* 11, 65-99.

Narayanan, N. editor 1992. Working Notes of AAAI Spring Symposium on Reasoning with Diagrammatic Representations.

Serra, J. 1982. *Image analysis and Mathematical Morphology*, Vol. 1. Academic Press.

Serra, J. 1988. *Image analysis and Mathematical Morphology*, Vol. 2. Academic Press.

Influence-Based Model Decomposition *

Christopher Bailey-Kellogg
Dartmouth College
6211 Sudikoff Laboratory
Hanover, NH 03755
cbk@cs.dartmouth.edu

Feng Zhao
Xerox Palo Alto Research Center
3333 Coyote Hill Road
Palo Alto, CA 94304
zhao@parc.xerox.com

Abstract

Recent rapid advances in MEMS and information processing technology have enabled a new generation of AI robotic systems — so-called Smart Matter systems — that are sensor rich and physically embedded. These systems range from decentralized control systems that regulate building temperature (smart buildings) to vehicle on-board diagnostic and control systems that interrogate large amounts of sensor data. One of the core tasks in the construction and operation of these Smart Matter systems is to synthesize optimal control policies using data rich models for the systems and environment. Unfortunately, these models may contain thousands of coupled real-valued variables and are prohibitively expensive to reason about using traditional optimization techniques such as neural nets and genetic algorithms. This paper introduces a general mechanism for automatically decomposing a large model into smaller subparts so that these subparts can be separately optimized and then combined. The mechanism decomposes a model using an influence graph that records the coupling strengths among constituents of the model. This paper demonstrates the mechanism in an application of decentralized optimization for a temperature regulation problem. Performance data has shown that the approach is much more efficient than the standard discrete optimization algorithms and achieves comparable accuracy.

Introduction

The new-generation sensor-rich AI robotic systems present a number of challenges. First, these systems must reason about large amounts of sensor data in real time. Second, they must construct and reason about large models of themselves and the environment in order to rapidly determine optimal control response (Williams & Nayak 1996). This paper describes an efficient computational mechanism to automate one of the major tasks in reasoning about distributed physical systems: decomposition of large models for these systems into a set of submodels that can be separately optimized and then combined.

This paper makes important contributions to qualitative and model-based reasoning in two ways. (1) The paper introduces a novel graph formalization for a model decomposition problem upon which powerful graph partitioning algorithms can be brought to bear. The graph formalism is applicable to a large number of problems where the dependency information in a model of a distributed system can be either derived from numerical trial data or reconstructed from analytic descriptions commonly used in science and engineering. (2) The paper develops two efficient partitioning algorithms to decompose a large model into submodels. The first algorithm employs spectral partitioning to maximize intra-component dependencies (called the influences) while minimizing inter-component dependencies. The second algorithm determines weakly coupled groups of model components by systematically and efficiently examining the structural similarities exhibited by trial partitions. To illustrate the utility of these algorithms, this paper applies the decomposition algorithms to a distributed thermal control problem. Performance data has confirmed that the model decomposition algorithms have yielded an efficient control optimization algorithm that outperforms standard optimization algorithms such as genetic algorithms and simulated annealing. Our optimization algorithm exploits the locality in the decomposition to attain efficiency and is able to generate solutions that are interpretable in terms of problem structures. These contributions significantly extend our previous work (Bailey-Kellogg & Zhao 1998) on qualitative models and parametric optimization for large distributed physical systems.

Other researchers in qualitative reasoning, Bayesian nets, and image processing have also investigated the problem of using decomposition to efficiently model complex physical systems. Williams and Millar developed a decomposition algorithm for parameter estimation that determines for each unknown variable in a model a minimally overdetermined subset of constraints (Williams & Millar 1996). The algorithms of this paper identify similar dependencies among nodes of a net either from a constraint net or directly from numerical data, and then partition the dependency graph into nearly decoupled subsets. Clancy introduced an

Rings of Lamps
(viewed from the wafer looking up)

Figure 1: Rapid thermal processing for semiconductor manufacturing maintains a uniform temperature profile by independent control to separate rings of heat lamps.

algorithm for generating an envisionment of a model expressed as a qualitative differential equation, once a partition of the model is given by the modeler (Clancy 1997). Our influence-based decomposition algorithms can produce the model partitions required by Clancy's algorithm. Recent work in image segmentation has introduced measures of dissimilarity to decompose images, based on pixel intensity differences (Shi & Malik 1997; Felzenszwalb & Huttenlocher 1998). Friedman et al. in probabilistic reasoning have introduced a method to decompose a large Bayesian belief net into weakly-interacting components by examining the dependency structure in the net (Friedman, Koller, & Pfeffer 1998).

Many scientific and engineering applications have exploited similar insights in order to divide and conquer large computational problems. In the well-studied N-body problem, the interactions among particles are classified into near and far field so that they can be decomposed into a hierarchy of local interactions to achieve a linear-time speed-up (Zhao 1987). In engineering computation, domain decomposition techniques (Chan & Mathew 1994) have been developed to separately simulate submodels of large models, based on *connectivity* in the models. This paper utilizes a similar insight to formalize the task of model decomposition based on *influences* in the models. Furthermore, our approach explicitly represents the physical knowledge and structures that it exploits, so that higher-level reasoning mechanisms have an explainable basis for their decisions.

Problem Description

We develop the influence-based decomposition mechanism for large models typically arising from distributed sensing and control problems. For example, consider a distributed thermal regulation system for rapid thermal processing in semiconductor curing, where a uniform temperature profile must be maintained to avoid defects (Figure 1). The control strategy is decentralized, providing separate power zones for three rings of heat lamps (Kailath & others 1996). As a similar example, rapid prototyping in thermal fabrication can employ moving plasma-arc heat sources to control the temperature of parts to be joined (Doumanidis 1997).

Abstracting these real-world applications, this paper adopts as a running example the generic problem of

decentralized temperature regulation for a piece of material. The temperature distribution over the material must be regulated to some desired profile by a set of individually controlled point heat sources. Many sensor-rich systems employ such decentralized control that accomplishes global objectives through local actions in order to ensure adaptivity, robustness, and scalability. For example, a smart building regulates its temperature using a network of sensors and actuators; decentralized control allows the network to overcome failures in individual control elements and to scale up without incurring exponential complexity. Rapid synthesis of optimal control policies for these distributed systems requires efficient methods for reasoning about large coupled models.

In particular, we focus on the control placement design task: to determine the number and location of heat sources, subject to a variety of structural constraints (e.g. geometry, material properties, and boundary conditions) and performance constraints (e.g. maximum output and maximum allowed error). While we only consider the placement design here, we have also studied the parametric optimization (in this example, the actual heat output) and reported it elsewhere. The engineering community has applied various discrete optimization techniques (e.g. genetic algorithms in (Dhingra & Lee 1994) and simulated annealing in (Chen, Bruno, & Salama 1995)) to the control placement design problem. In contrast to these techniques, we seek to use domain knowledge to extract and exploit qualitative structural descriptions of physical phenomena in the design process. This yields a principled method for reasoning about designs and design trade-offs, based on an encapsulation of deep knowledge in structures uncovered for a particular problem. This in turn supports reasoning about and explanation of the design decisions.

The control placement design task will be used as a specific example illustrating our general mechanism for partitioning distributed models; the discussion section further discusses the generality of our approach. The goal here will be to design a placement that aids parametric optimization, by placing controls so that they minimally interfere with each other. This is particularly appropriate for applications where the placement design is performed once, and the parametric design is performed repeatedly (e.g. for various desired temperature profiles). The design approach taken here is to decompose a problem domain into a set of *decoupled, atomic* subregions, and then independently design controls for the separate subregions. Regions are considered decoupled if the exact control design in one region is fairly independent of the exact control design in another. A region is considered atomic if it needs no further decomposition — control design for the region yields adequate control of the region. Influence-based model decomposition provides a powerful high-level mechanism for achieving such designs.

Figure 2: Thermal hill for a heat source.

Influence Graph

In order to design decentralized controls for a physical field, it is necessary to reason about the effects of the controls on the field. We previously introduced the *influence graph* (Bailey-Kellogg & Zhao 1998) to represent such dependencies. Figure 2 shows an example of influences in a temperature domain — a "thermal hill," with temperatures decaying away from the location of a heat source. When multiple sources affect a thermal field, their influences interact, yielding multiple peaks and valleys.

The influences in this example obey the locality principle: a heat source strongly affects nearby field nodes and only weakly affects further away field nodes, depending on the conduction properties of the material. In addition, despite nonlinearities in the spatial variables (e.g. non-uniform conduction characteristics or irregular geometry), influences from multiple heat sources can be linearly superposed to find joint influences. These properties are characteristic of a variety of physical phenomena. In order to take advantage of these and other properties, influence graphs serve as an abstract, domain-independent representation of this knowledge. The definition of influence graph assumes a discretized model, as in (Bailey-Kellogg & Zhao 1998), and as is common to standard engineering methods.

Definition 1 (Influence Graph) *An influence graph is a tuple (F, C, E, w) where*

- *F is a set of field nodes.*
- *C is a set of control nodes.*
- *$E = C \times F$ is a set of edges from control nodes to field nodes.*
- *$w : E \to \mathcal{R}$ is an edge weight function with $w((c, f))$ the field value at f given a unit control value at c.*

Hence, the graph edges record a normalized influence from each control node to each field node. A thermal hill (e.g. Figure 2) is a pictorial representations of the edge weights for an influence graph from one heat source to the nodes of a temperature field.

An influence graph is constructed by placing a control with unit value at each control location of interest, one at a time, and evaluating the field at field node locations of interest. The method of evaluation is problem-specific. For example, it could be found by numerical simulation, experimental data, or even explicit inversion of a capacitance matrix. An influence graph then serves as a high-level interface caching the dependency information. The following two sections use this dependency information in order to decompose models based on influences between their parts.

Graph Decomposition

As discussed in the introduction, many applications require decomposing models into smaller pieces, in order to reason more tractably with the components or to divide-and-conquer a problem. Many models can be formalized in terms of graphs describing the structural dependencies of components. Decomposing a model is then equivalent to partitioning the corresponding graph. Given a graph, a decomposition identifies subsets of vertices so that a metric such as the number of edges or total edge weight between vertices in different subsets is minimized. In particular, the decomposition of an influence graph partitions a model so that the connected components maximize internal influence and minimize external influence. For the running example of decentralized heat control, this decomposes a thermal field so that controls in one part are maximally independent from those in other parts.

The numerical analysis and computational geometry communities have developed a number of methods for partitioning graphs; these methods have varying costs and varying effectiveness. In particular, we concentrate here on spectral partitioning (Simon 1991), which examines the structure of a graph's *Laplacian matrix* encoding the connectivity between points. Specifically, entry (i, j) in the Laplacian matrix has value -1 if and only if there is an edge from node i to node j in the graph; entry (i, i) has value equal to the total number of edges from node i. It turns out that a good approximation to the optimal partitioning (minimum number of cut edges) can be achieved by separating nodes according to the corresponding values in the eigenvector for the first non-trivial eigenvalue of this matrix (the *Fiedler vector*). Intuitively, in a one-dimensional domain, this is similar to partitioning the domain by looking at the sign of a sine wave stretched over it. This technique can be extended to minimize the total weight of edges cut, and normalization of edge weights allows simultaneous optimization of both inter-partition dissimilarity and intra-partition similarity. Shi and Malik showed, in the context of image segmentation, that this approach yields a good estimate of the optimal decomposition (Shi & Malik 1997).

This novel formalization of control placement design in terms of influence graph partitioning provides a graph-based framework in which to develop design algorithms. The spectral partitioning algorithm serves as one instantiation of this framework, based on an all-to-all influence graph. The next section introduces an alternative approach that uses a less detailed model, decomposing a model using an influence graph from a set of representative nodes to all the other nodes.

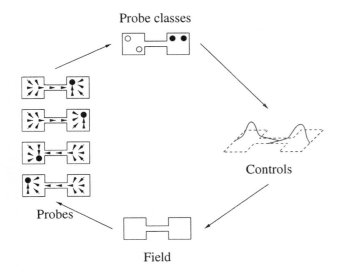

Figure 3: Overview of influence-based decentralized control design for thermal regulation.

Equivalence Class Partitioning

The equivalence class partitioning mechanism decomposes a model based on structural similarities exhibited in a field in response to the actions of sample control probes. Figure 3 overviews the mechanism. In the example shown, the geometric constraint imposed by the narrow channel in the dumbbell-shaped piece of material results in similar field responses to the two probes in the left half of the dumbbell and similar responses to the two probes in the right half of the dumbbell. Based on the resulting classes, the field is decomposed into regions to be separately controlled. In this case, the left half of the dumbbell is decomposed from the right half.

The following subsections detail the components of this mechanism.

Control Probes

For a temperature field to exhibit structures, heat sources must be applied; then an influence graph can be constructed. For example, Figure 4 shows the iso-influences resulting from two different heat source placements; in both cases, the structure of the contours indicates the constraint on heat flow due to the narrow channel. The control placement design algorithm is based on the response of temperature fields to such *control probes*. The number and placement of control probes affects the structures uncovered in a temperature field, and thus the quality of the resulting control design. Possible probe placement strategies include random, evenly-spaced, or dynamically-placed (e.g. in inadequately explored regions or to disambiguate inconsistent interpretations). Experimental results presented later in this paper illustrate the trade-off between number of probes and result quality, using the simple random probe placement strategy.

Figure 4: Temperature fields exhibit structures in response to heat source probes.

Probes serve as representatives for the effects of arbitrarily-placed controls. In particular, the probes that most strongly affect a location (e.g. influence greater than average or a fixed threshold) serve to approximate the effects that would be produced by a control placed at that location. The quality of the approximation of controls at arbitrary locations by representative probes depends on the effects of geometry and material properties. Since the influence graph encapsulates these effects, it provides a natural mechanism for reasoning about approximation quality.

Using control probes as representatives of control placement effects supports reformulation of the decomposition problem into that of partitioning probes into equivalence classes. Each equivalence class of probes serves as a representatives for a region of strongly-affected potential control locations, as discussed above. A good decomposition produces probe classes with regions decoupled from the regions of other classes, and which have no acceptable subclasses.

Evaluating Control Decoupling

The first criterion for evaluating a decomposition is that each region be *decoupled* from other regions; that is, that controls in one region have little effect on nodes in the other, and vice-versa. In terms of control probe equivalence classes, decoupling will be evaluated by considering independence of both control placement and control parameters.

To evaluate independence of control placement, consider the influence gradient vectors induced by a set of probes; Figure 5 shows a simple example for two probes.[1] While the flows are different near the locations of the two probes, they are quite similar far away from the probe locations. This similarity is due to constraints imposed by geometry and material properties; in this case, the narrow channel of the material effectively decouples the left and right halves. A numerical measure for the similarity is implemented, for example, by averaging the angular difference between gradient vectors produced by different probes. This measure evaluates the indistinguishability of control placement within the set of probe locations, and thus is correlated with a good decomposition into decoupled regions.

To evaluate independence of control parameters, we distinguish between nodes strongly and weakly influenced by a control (the *near field* and the *far field*, re-

---

[1] Recall that an influence graph is constructed from field values for unit controls. By influence gradient vectors, we mean vectors in the gradient field for a control — rate and direction of steepest change in field value.

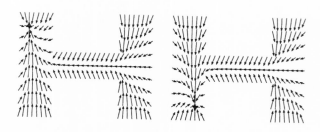

Figure 5: Similarity of flows due to control probes suggests indistinguishability of control placement.

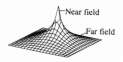

Figure 6: An influence hill partitions a field into near and far fields relative to a control.

```
Given probes P = {p_1, p_2, ..., p_n}.

Form classes C = {{p_1}, {p_2}, ..., {p_n}}.

Repeat until stable
    For each neighboring c_i, c_j ∈ C
        If  Forall k with k ≠ i and k ≠ j
                decoupling of c_i and c_k and
                decoupling of c_j and c_k are better than
                decoupling of c_i and c_j
            And c_i ∪ c_j is atomic
        Then replace c_i and c_j in C with c_i ∪ c_j
```

Table 1: Probe clustering algorithm.

spectively), due to locality in the domain (Figure 6). Possible near/far distinctions include a fixed influence threshold, a threshold proportional to the peak of the hill, or a threshold based on the "knee" of the hill. A probe only weakly affects its far field, and thus can be effectively decomposed from it. Alternatively, probes that have significant overlap in their near fields can be reasonably grouped together.

In addition to independence from any single control, a well-decoupled region must be independent from the combined effects of other controls. That is, for a set of probes, the *total* influence on its controlled region from controls for other probe sets must be sufficiently small.

Evaluating Region Atomicity

The second criterion for evaluating a decomposition is that each region be decomposed far enough. A region is considered *atomic* if none of its subregions are adequately decoupled from each other. For example, in Figure 7 a partition $\{\{A, B, C, D\}, \{E, F, G\}\}$ achieves good decoupling, since the probes in the first class are relatively independent from those in the second class. However, it is not atomic, since $\{A, B, C, D\}$ can be further decomposed into $\{\{A, B\}, \{C, D\}\}$.

One approach to ensuring atomicity of the classes of a decomposition is to recursively test subsets of probes to see if they result in valid decompositions. For example, by testing partitions of the class $\{A, B, C, D\}$ for independence, the partition $\{\{A, B\}, \{C, D\}\}$ would be

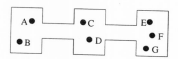

Figure 7: Control probe placement with potential non-atomic decomposition.

uncovered. The test can use heuristics to avoid testing all possible subclasses. For example, just by examining overlap in influences in the class $\{A, B, C, D\}$, the partition $\{\{A, B\}, \{C, D\}\}$ can be generated as a counterexample to the atomicity of $\{A, B, C, D\}$. If a class is already small, out-of-class probes can be used in such a test, and, if necessary, new probes can be introduced. For example, in an atomicity test for $\{A, B\}$, checking independence of $\{A, C\}$ from $\{B, D\}$ would show that $\{A, B\}$ is indeed atomic. An inexpensive and empirically effective method is to allow grouping of pairs of probes only if their near fields sufficiently overlap.

Probe Clustering Algorithm

Based on these criteria, control probes can be clustered into decoupled, atomic equivalence classes. One effective clustering method is greedily merging neighboring probe classes based on similarity. Start with each probe in its own class, and form a graph of classes based on proximity (e.g. Delaunay triangulation or nearness neighborhood). Then greedily merge neighboring pairs of classes that are most similar, as long as a region is strongly influenced by other regions, and until a merger would result in a non-atomic class. Table 1 provides pseudocode for this algorithm. Figure 8 illustrates a sample probe neighborhood graph, Figure 9 depicts some influence gradients for sample probes, and Figure 10 shows the controlled regions for equivalence classes of probes after the merging process. While more sophisticated clustering mechanisms could be applied, the results in the next section show this algorithm to be empirically effective on a set of example problems.

Implementation Results

The influence-based decomposition algorithms have proved effective in designing control placements for decentralized thermal regulation. The performance has been measured in two ways: quality of the decomposition, and ability of the resulting control design to achieve an objective.

Data for three sample problems are given here: a

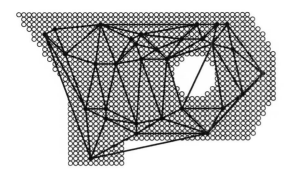

Figure 8: Probe clustering example: probe neighborhood graph.

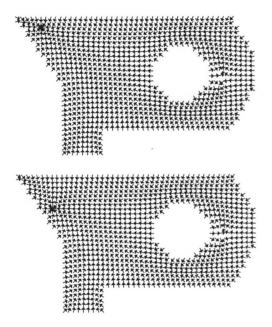

Figure 9: Probe clustering example: influence gradient vectors from two probes.

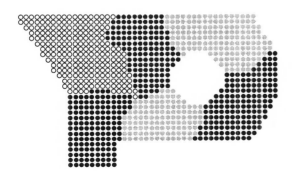

Figure 10: Probe clustering example: region decomposition after merging.

plus-shaped piece of material, a P-shaped piece of material, and an anisotropic (non-uniform conduction coefficient) bar. These problems illustrate different geometries, topologies (the P-shaped material has a hole), and material properties. Other problems have also been tested; the results are similar.

The decomposition algorithm forms groups of control probes with similar effects on the field. This requires that probes be dense enough, relative to conditions imposed by geometry and material properties, so that groups of probes with similar effects can be uncovered. Otherwise, each probe ends up in its own class, and the decomposition is too dependent on probe placement. To study the impact of the number of control probes on the effectiveness of the resulting design, different numbers of probes (4, 8, 16, and 32) were placed at random in a given domain, and results were averaged over a number of trial runs. While smarter probe placement techniques might yield more consistently effective designs, this approach provides a baseline and illustrates the trade-off between number of probes and error/variance. The probe clustering algorithm used a Delaunay triangulation probe neighborhood graph, a near field based on influence of at least 10 percent of peak, and a similarity measure based on flow vector direction. For comparison, merging was performed until four classes remained.

Decomposition Quality

The goal of a decomposition algorithm is to partition a domain into regions such that source placement and parametric optimization in each region is relatively independent of that in other regions (decomposed) and has no internally independent regions (atomic). The estimate of the quality of a decomposition used here is based on a corresponding formalization for image segmentation by Shi and Malik (Shi & Malik 1997): compare the total influence from each control location on locations in other regions (decomposed), and the amount of influence from that location on locations in its own region (atomic). To be more specific, define the decomposition quality q ($0 \leq q \leq 1$) for a partition P of a set of nodes S as follows (i is the influence):

$$q = \prod_{R \in P} \sum_{c \in R} \frac{\sum_{r \in R} i(c, r)}{\sum_{s \in S} i(c, s)}$$

For each control node, divide its influence on nodes in its own region by its total influence. Summing that over each region yields an estimate of the fraction of control output of any control location in the region that is used to control the other locations in that region. The quality measure is combined over all regions by taking the product of each region's quality.

Figure 11 compares the performance of the equivalence class partitioning mechanism with that of the spectral partitioning mechanism. It provides the average error and standard deviation in error over a number of trial runs, with respect to different numbers of control

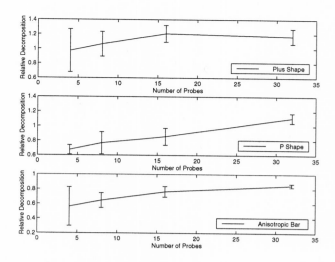

Figure 11: Performance data indicate that the probe clustering algorithm supports trading decomposition quality for computation. Results are relative to spectral partitioning.

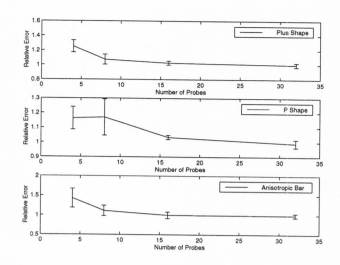

Figure 12: Performance data indicate that equivalence class-based control placement design supports trading control quality for computation. Results are relative to simulated annealing.

probes. For all three problems, the average quality for the equivalence class partitioning mechanism naturally decreases as the number of probes decreases. (There is a slight taper in the performance for the plus shape, due to statistical sampling.) Furthermore, the standard deviation of quality tends to increase as the number of probes decreases, since the partition is more sensitive to specific probe placements. The curve indicates a trade-off between amount of computation and resulting decomposition quality. With enough probes, the quality is commensurate with that of spectral partitioning.

Control Placement Quality

The ultimate measure of the control design algorithm is how well a design based on a decomposition can achieve a control objective. This section evaluates the ability of decomposition-based control designs to achieve a uniform temperature profile. This profile is better than other, non-uniform profiles at indicating the performance of a decomposition, since it does not depend as much on local placement adjustment and parametric optimization. Intuitively, if a decomposition clumps together sources, then some other region will not get enough heat and thus will have a large error.

Simulated annealing (Metropolis *et al.* 1953) serves as a baseline comparison for error; an optimizer was run for 100 steps. The decomposition-based control design used a simple approach: for each region of a decomposition, place controls in the "center of influence" (like the center of mass, but weighted with total influence from the probes, rather than mass, at each point). In both cases, only the global control placement was designed; local adjustment could somewhat reduce the error.

Figure 12 illustrates average error and standard de-

viation in error over a set of trial runs. The equivalence class algorithm was tested with different numbers of control probes; as shown above, the spectral partitioning algorithm would yield similar results. The error here is the sum of squared difference between actual temperature profile and desired temperature profile. As with decomposition quality, the average and standard deviation of control quality tend to improve with the number of probes; enough probes yields quality commensurate with that of simulated annealing.

Run-Time Performance

There are two implementation strategies to consider in terms of run-time performance. The *centralized* approach explicitly inverts the capacitance matrix describing the system (e.g. from a finite-element mesh), yielding influences from every potential control node to every field node. The matrix inversion constitutes the bulk of the run time. Spectral partitioning then performs an eigenvalue computation. Simulated annealing examines some number of configurations (in the tests above, 100) with respect to the effects encoded in this matrix. Our approach does simple comparisons between fields due to different probe locations.

The *decentralized* approach treats the system as a black box function to be computed for each configuration; the run time primarily depends on the number of function evaluations. The spectral method is not directly amenable to this approach. Simulated annealing requires the function to be evaluated for each configuration (in the tests above, 100). Our apprach requires the function to be evaluated for each probe (in the tests above, 4, 8, 16, or 32 times).

Discussion

This paper has developed mechanisms for automatically decomposing large models, based on structural representations of influences. This formalization in terms of influences differs from the formalisms in related engineering work, which typically use topology and geometry, and related AI work, which typically use constraint nets. Redescribing a model decomposition problem as an influence graph partitioning problem allows application of powerful, general algorithms.

We first introduced the influence graph mechanism in (Bailey-Kellogg & Zhao 1998) as a generic basis for representing and manipulating dependency information between control nodes and field nodes. The properties of physical fields that it encapsulates (locality, linear dependence, etc.) are exhibited by a variety of physical phenomena, from electrostatics to incompressible fluid flow. Note that these phenomena are all governed by diffusion processes; it remains future work to develop similar mechanisms for wave processes. Since they are based on influence graphs, the model decomposition formalism and algorithms developed here are applicable to this wide variety of models.

The influence graph provides a common interface to the model of a distributed physical system, whether it is derived from partial differential equations, simulation data, or actual physical measurements. In the case of physical measurements, sensor outliers can be detected by comparing the data with the expected value based on nearby points. Additionally, since the algorithms reason about the qualitative structures of influences, they are less sensitive to individual sensor errors.

The decomposition-based control design algorithms search a design space in a much different manner from that of other combinatorial optimization algorithms, such as genetic algorithms (Holland 1975) and simulated annealing (Metropolis *et al.* 1953). Rather than (perhaps implicitly) searching the space of all possible combinations of source locations, the influence-based decomposition approach divides and conquers a problem, breaking a model into submodels based on influences. This approach explicitly forms equivalence classes and structures in the domain, rather than implicitly representing them in terms of, for example, increased membership of highly-fit members in a population. Since design decisions are based on the influence structure of the field, this approach supports higher-level reasoning about and explanation of its results; for example, a design decision could be explained in terms of constrained influence flows through a field.

Conclusion

This paper has developed efficient influence-based model decomposition algorithms for optimization problems for large distributed models. Model decomposition is formalized as a graph partitioning problem for an influence graph representing node dependencies. The first algorithm applies spectral partitioning to an influence graph. The second algorithm decomposes a graph using structural similarities among representative control probes. Both algorithms reason about the structure of a problem using influences derived from either a constraint net or numerical data. Computational experiments show that the algorithms compare favorably with more exhaustive methods such as simulated annealing in both solution quality and computational cost.

Acknowledgments

The work is supported in part by ONR YI grant N00014-97-1-0599, NSF NYI grant CCR-9457802, and a Xerox grant to the Ohio State University.

References

Bailey-Kellogg, C., and Zhao, F. 1998. Qualitative analysis of distributed physical systems with applications to control synthesis. In *Proceedings of AAAI*.

Chan, T., and Mathew, T. 1994. *Domain Decomposition Algorithms*, volume 3 of *Acta Numerica*. Cambridge University Press. 61–143.

Chen, G.-S.; Bruno, R.; and Salama, M. 1995. Optimal placement of active / passive members in truss structure using simulated annealing. *AIAA Journal* 29.

Clancy, D. 1997. Model decomposition and simulation: a component based qualitative simulation algorithm. In *Proceedings of AAAI*.

Dhingra, A., and Lee, B. 1994. Optimal placement of actuators in actively controlled structures. *Engineering Optimization* 23:99–118.

Doumanidis, C. 1997. In-process control in thermal rapid prototyping. *IEEE Control Systems*.

Felzenszwalb, P., and Huttenlocher, D. 1998. Image segmentation using local variation. In *Proceedings of CVPR*.

Friedman, N.; Koller, D.; and Pfeffer, A. 1998. Structured represenation of complex stochastic systems. In *Proceedings of AAAI*.

Holland, J. 1975. *Adaptation in Natural and Artificial Systems*. The University of Michigan Press.

Kailath, T., et al. 1996. Control for advanced semiconductor device manufacturing: A case history. In Levine, W., ed., *The Control Handbook*. CRC Press.

Metropolis, N.; Rosenbluth, A.; Rosenbluth, M.; Teller, A.; and Teller, E. 1953. Equation of state calculations by fast computing machines. *Journal of Chemical Physics* 21:1087–1092.

Shi, J., and Malik, J. 1997. Normalized cuts and image segmentation. In *Proceedings of CVPR*.

Simon, H. 1991. Partitioning of unstructured problems for parallel processing. *Computing Systems in Engineering* 2:135–148.

Williams, B., and Millar, B. 1996. Automated decomposition of model-based learning problems. In *Proceedings of 10th International Workshop on Qualitative Reasoning*.

Williams, B., and Nayak, P. 1996. Immobile robots: AI in the new millenium. *AI Magazine* 17(3).

Zhao, F. 1987. An O(N) algorithm for three-dimensional n-body simulations. Technical Report AI-TR-995, MIT AI Lab.

Model-based Support for Mutable Parametric Design Optimization

Ravi Kapadia and **Gautam Biswas**
Computer Science Department
Vanderbilt University
Nashville, TN 37235
email: ravi, biswas@vuse.vanderbilt.edu

Abstract

Traditional methods for parametric design optimization assume that the relations between performance criteria and design variables are known algebraic functions with fixed coefficients. However, the relations may be *mutable*, i.e., the functions and/or coefficients may not be known explicitly because they depend on input parameters and vary in different parts of the design space. We present a model-based reasoning methodology to support parametric, mutable, design optimization. First, we derive *event models* to represent the effects of the system's parameters on the material that flows through it. Next, we use these models to discover mutable relations between the system's design variables and its optimization criteria. We then present an algorithm that searches for "optimal" designs by employing sensitivity analysis techniques on the derived relations.

Introduction

Traditional methods for parametric multicriteria design optimization in Operations Research, e.g., (Steuer 1986) and Artificial Intelligence (see examples in (Tong & Sriram 1992)) assume that the relations between performance criteria and design variables are known algebraic functions with fixed coefficients. However, in many real world applications, the relations may be *mutable*, i.e., the functions and/or coefficients may not be known explicitly because they depend on input parameters and vary in different parts of the design space.

We employ *model-based reasoning* techniques to develop a framework for parametric, mutable design optimization. Given a configuration of the system, we are interested in tuning its design variables to optimize desired objectives while meeting specified constraints. We describe techniques that start from a valid design solution and generate better solutions for the required artifact. Our methodology first develops *event models* that capture the effects of the system's parameters on the material that flows through it. Next, we use these models to discover mutable relations between the system's design variables and its optimization objectives.

Then, we employ sensitivity analysis based heuristic techniques to determine directions and magnitudes of change of design variables to generate better design solutions.

Mutable design optimization

A parametric design optimization problem contains the following elements. *Optimization objectives*, $y_1, \ldots, y_m$, represent behavior and performance parameters that must be optimized, e.g., speed of execution and manufacturing cost. *Design variables*, $v_1, \ldots, v_n$, represent system parameters that can be changed by the designer to affect system performance and attain optimization objectives. *Design constraints*, $C_1, \ldots, C_p$, on design variables and system behavior arise from domain principles and serve to define valid designs. *Optimization relations* describe how changes in design variables cause changes in optimization criteria. In general, the relation between each optimization objective y_i and the design variables $v_1, \ldots, v_n$, for a given input task I is defined as: $y_i \bowtie F_i(I, v_1, \ldots, v_n)$, where the relation operator $\bowtie \in \{=, \leq, \geq, <, >, \propto\}$.

The relation between y_i and the design variables $v_1, \ldots, v_n$, is *invariant* if $F_i(I, v_1, \ldots, v_n) = \sum_{j=1}^{n} c_j * v_j$, and each c_j is a constant. We refer to y_i as an *invariant* optimization objective (Steuer 1986; Tong & Sriram 1992). When $F_i(I, v_1, ..., v_n) = \sum_{j=1}^{n} f_{ij}(I, v_1, \ldots, v_n) * v_j$, the relation between y_i and $v_1, \ldots, v_n$, is *mutable* since the coefficient of v_j is dependent on I and $v_1, \ldots, v_n$. We refer to y_i as a *mutable* optimization objective.

In this paper, we consider real world design problems which combine both invariant and mutable optimization objectives. In our applications, $f_{ij}(I, v_1, \ldots, v_n)$ is not a continuous function over the design space, i.e., it varies at different points in the design space. Due to the complex nature of the system, it is not practical to express the function in the form of an analytic expression. Typically, it is possible to determine the function's value at a particular point in the design space through simulation. We use model-based reasoning techniques to determine each $f_{ij}(I, v_1, \ldots, v_n)$ for a specified input task I and a given design solution.

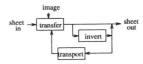

Figure 1: Reprographic machine

Reprographic machine

As a test bed for our design optimization methodology, we use a digital reprographic machine (e.g., printer, photocopier), which is a computer-controlled electromechanical system that produces documents by manipulating images and sheets of paper. Given a configuration for this system, we are interested in tuning its parameters so that the designed machine optimizes job completion times and manufacturing cost, while meeting specified design constraints.

In the simplified form of Fig. 1, the system prints simplex (one-sided) and duplex (two-sided) sheets. A sheet enters the machine through an input port. An image is transferred (or printed) to the sheet as it passes through the *transfer* component. A simplex sheet passes through without inversion (i.e., it bypasses inversion) on its way to the output port. A duplex sheet is inverted, routed to the *duplex transport* along the duplex loop, an image is transferred on the back side of the sheet (*transfer*), and the sheet is inverted again (*inverter*), before it is sent to the output port. Parameters that affect desired optimization criteria include the transit times of the components, and the capacity of buffers at the input and output ports (Kapadia & Fromherz 1997). To generate a document or job (i.e., an ordered sequence of simplex and duplex sheets), the transportation and printing of sheets must satisfy behavior constraints, for example, sheets must be manipulated such that they are available at the output in the specified order, and they must not collide with each other anywhere in the paper path.

State-of-the-art reprographic machines are equipped with control software that determines optimal times to schedule its operations (Kapadia & Fromherz 1997). Table 1 shows an optimal schedule for the document consisting of one simplex sheet followed by two duplex sheets, and then a simplex sheet (i.e., s_1, d_2, d_3, s_4) which is completed in 12 time units. While generating this schedule, we assumed the following parameter values: printing an image on to a sheet requires 1 unit of time, inverting a sheet takes 2 units, transporting a sheet along the duplex loop requires 3 units, and bypassing inversion takes 1 unit. The job completion time is a function of the system parameters and the schedule for the job. For example, the arrival time of s_4 at the output in Table 1 is a function of component transit times and the sequence of events that preceded it. There is no predefined optimization function that applies to all jobs; the function may be different for each new job. Furthermore, with a different set of design pa-

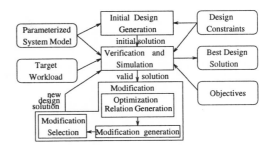

Figure 2: Design optimization methodology

rameters, different schedules are possible for the same job description. For example, if inverting a sheet takes 1 time unit, and bypassing inversion takes 3 units, the optimal schedule for s_1, d_2, d_3, s_4 introduces sheet d_2 at time 0, d_3 at time 1, s_1 at time 2, and s_4 at time 7, which generates the complete job in 11 time units. Thus, optimizing the behavior of the reprographic machine system comprises a mutable optimization problem.

Design optimization methodology

Fig. 2 shows the architecture of our design optimization methodology. Using *design constraints*, *initial design generation* produces a valid, though usually not optimal, initial solution (typically, one that has worked in similar cases in the past). *Simulation* uses the *system model* to generate system behavior for a given design solution and specified input tasks chosen from the *target workload*. *Verification* checks that the solution and its behavior satisfy specified *design constraints*. *Modification* encompasses multiple tasks. *Optimization relation generation* maps each mutable *optimization objective* to system design variables for a particular design solution. *Modification generation* identifies a set of modifications to a design solution that improve desired objectives. *Modification selection* compares different modifications and picks the most promising one to generate the next design solution. Our methodology iterates through these tasks until it finds the *best design solution*.

Parameterized system model. Component parameters model attributes of the system components that affect the behaviors of interest. Consider a representative set of parameters for the reprographic machine system shown in Fig. 1. k_1 is the transit time of the transfer component, k_2 is the transit time for inversion of a duplex sheet, k_3 is the transit time for bypassing inversion, and k_4 is the transit time for transporting a duplex sheet for a second printing. Our test bed is best modeled as a discrete event system with discrete valued parameters. In (Kapadia, Biswas, & Fromherz 1997) we adapted the Environment Relationship (ER) net framework of (Ghezzi *et al.* 1991) (an extension of basic Petri nets, that incorporates time modeling) to represent our system model. Tokens represent material (e.g., sheets) and their attributes capture the material's properties. A component is a collection of places and tran-

Component	Place in ER net	\multicolumn Time 0–12												
		0	1	2	3	4	5	6	7	8	9	10	11	12
Input	p_1	d_2		d_3		s_1		d_2		d_3		s_4		
Transfer	p_2		d_2		d_3		s_1		d_2		d_3		s_4	
Inverter	p_3				d_2	d_3	s_1			d_2		d_3	s_4	
Transport	p_4				d_2	d_3								
Output	p_5						s_1			d_2		d_3	s_4	

Table 1: Optimal printing sequence for document s_1, d_2, d_3, s_4

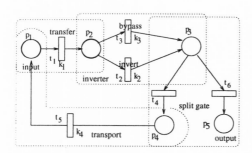

Figure 3: Reprographic machine model with ER nets

sitions. Places correspond to input and output ports. Transitions correspond to functions that the component performs and associated actions describe its behavior, i.e., how the function transforms the material flowing through the component. Component parameters are properties associated with transitions and places in an ER Net. For example, in Fig. 3 which shows a system level model for the reprographic machine of Fig. 1, the inverter component is modeled by transitions t_2 and t_3, places p_2 and p_3, and k_2 and k_3 represent the transit times for the invert and bypass operations, respectively. The ER net model is used to simulate the behavior of the system as shown in Table 1 and to develop parameterized optimization relations between design variables and optimization objectives.

Design constraints. In this paper, we present two classes of design constraints. *Domain constraints* define valid designs by constraining the domains of design variables. *Cost constraints* capture our intuition that associated with each decision is a price that must be paid to implement that decision. Other classes of constraints, including *behavior* and *performance* constraints, are covered in (Kapadia 1999). We present examples of domain and cost constraints later in the paper.

Objectives. A system should be designed and evaluated with respect to its expected use. For instance, a printer used mainly for books and magazines will require a different set of parameters from another used for printing short reports and office memos. We assume that a *target workload*, $J = \{J_1, J_2, \ldots, J_j\}$, which is composed of a finite set of the most likely jobs in the user's workplace, captures the intended user's workload characteristics. An objective is to develop a design solution that optimizes the performance of the system with respect to this workload, where the performance of a design solution on a job is measured in terms of the job completion time (*jct*). In the examples that follow, we assume $J = \{\{s_1, d_2, d_3, s_4\}, \{s_1, d_2, d_3, s_4, d_5, d_6\}\}$[1], and our objective is to *minimize job completion time* for each job in J. Simultaneously, the designer may choose to *minimize manufacturing cost* (*Cost*).

Design solution. A *design solution* is an assignment of values to design variables. A *valid* design solution is one that meets design constraints, while an *optimal* design solution is a valid solution which optimizes desired objectives. However, a design solution that optimizes one set of jobs may not produce good solutions for others, and the objectives of minimizing cost and maximizing performance are often in conflict with each other. Thus, there may be no single design solution that optimizes all objectives. A *non-inferior* design solution is a valid solution with the property that there is no other known valid solution that will yield an improvement in one criterion without causing a degradation in at least one other criterion. Our methodology develops non-inferior design solutions which are accepted or rejected based on the designer's preferences. We allow designers to articulate their preferences either prior to the generation of design solutions, after the generation of design solutions, or progressively, i.e., during the optimization process (similar to (Mollaghasemi & Evans 1994)).

Design optimization algorithm. Our design optimization methodology is implemented as a hill climbing algorithm as follows.

1. Generate mutable optimization relations for a given design solution from the ER net model and input task descriptions. This may require simulation of system behavior one or more times, e.g., for each job in the target workload:
   (a) simulate its behavior;
   (b) generate a relation between the job's completion time and the system's design variables.
2. Generate a set of modifications that lead to better performance on the objectives.
3. If there is no valid modification, stop.
4. Otherwise, select the "best" modification and apply it to the existing solution.

---

[1]A simplifying assumption in this paper is that each job in the target workload has equal priority. (Kapadia & Fromherz 1997), describe techniques for dealing with jobs with different priorities.

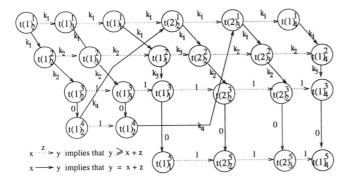

$x \xrightarrow{z} y$ implies that $y \geqslant x + z$

$x \longrightarrow y$ implies that $y = x + z$

Figure 4: Event model for Table 1

5. Modifying the parameters of a design solution changes the mutable optimization relations. Determining a new relation may require simulation, which is computationally expensive and we want to avoid it unless it is necessary. Thus, repeat steps 1 to 4 with the following changes.

   (a) Before step 1(a) check if simulation is required to generate the new relation. If yes, perform 1(a), otherwise skip it for that objective.

   (b) Before step 2, check if the new design solution is inferior to the *best known solution*. If yes, stop. Otherwise, make it the best known solution.

In this paper, we focus on steps 1 and 2 of this algorithm.

Generating optimization relations

The relationship between a mutable optimization objective y_i, the input task I, and the design variables $v_1, \ldots, v_n$, is: $y_i \bowtie \sum_{j=1}^{n} f_{ij}(I, v_1, \ldots, v_n) * v_j$. Generating a mutable optimization relation requires building an *event model* (that reflects the mutability of f_{ij}) from an ER net behavior simulation for a given design solution and document description (as shown in Table 1). An event model is a directed acyclic graph where each vertex represents an event (informally, an event is the arrival of a token in a place in the ER net system model) and a directed edge between two vertices represents a precedence relation between the corresponding events.

Fig. 4 shows the event model for the events depicted in Table 1. Formally, $t(r)_i^j$ denotes the event that the ith token (i.e., sheet) arrives in place j on its rth pass through the machine. Edges in the event model correspond to temporal constraints among events in the ER net model of Fig. 3 as explained below (see (Kapadia 1999) for details).

• There is an edge for every firing of a transition in the generation of the system's behavior. The transit time associated with the transition is represented by the weight along the corresponding edge in the event model, e.g., Fig. 4 shows an edge $t(1)_2^1 \rightarrow t(1)_2^2$ with weight k_1 which represents transition t_1 which prints an image to a sheet (where $t(1)_2^1$ is the event that en-

ables t_1 and $t(1)_2^2$ is the result of firing t_1).

• Sheets arrive at the output (p_5) in the specified order, e.g., s_1 must arrive before d_2 at the output. Thus, we have the following *order* constraints: $\forall i = 1, \ldots, n, r = 1, 2 : t(r)_i^5 < t(r)_{i+1}^5$. Each order constraint is represented by a dotted edge with a weight of 1 (since there must be a separation of at least one unit of time between the arrival of two successive sheets at the output).

• There must be no collisions in any place in the machine, so two or more sheets cannot be present in the same place at the same time. Thus, we have the following *resource allocation* constraints: $\forall x, y = 1, \ldots, n, p, q = 1, 2 : $ if $x \neq y$, $t(p)_x^j \neq t(q)_y^j$. In a known, valid sequence of events, $t(p)_i^j > (<) t(q)_k^j$. The dotted edge $t(p)_i^j \rightarrow t(q)_k^j$ indicates that event $t(p)_i^j$ precedes $t(q)_k^j$. The weight of the edge is the largest transit time (w) of all the transitions for which place j is an input, since tokens must arrive at least w units apart in j to avoid a collision after the firing of any transition enabled by the tokens in j.

We get relations between design variables and optimization criteria as follows. First, we substitute parameter values for the edges in the event model. Then, we use a topological sort to get the *critical path* which establishes a lower bound on the time that must be spent to execute the job. For the example of Fig. 4, we get: $t(1)_2^1 \rightarrow t(1)_2^2 \rightarrow t(1)_2^3 \rightarrow t(1)_2^4 \rightarrow t(2)_2^1 \rightarrow t(2)_2^2 \rightarrow t(2)_2^3 \rightarrow t(2)_3^3 \rightarrow t(2)_3^5 \rightarrow t(1)_4^5$. Finally, we find the *lower bound* on the job completion time by symbolically summing the parameters along the critical path, e.g., job completion time for J_1, $jct_1 \geq 2 * k_1 + 3 * k_2 + k_4$. To extract better performance from the system, we must direct our efforts at "minimizing" this relation.

Each job's event model may have a different structure and, therefore, it may have a different critical path leading to a different optimization relation. For example, job $J_2 = s_1, d_2, d_3, s_4, d_5, d_6$, which is completed in 21 time units has the optimization relation: $jct_2 \geq 3 * k_1 + 6 * k_2 + 2 * k_4$.

When the designer modifies the parameters of a design solution, event models (and their optimization relations) may change, as stated in step 5 of our design optimization algorithm. If the structure of an event model remains the same (i.e., the set of vertices and edges is identical, but only some weights on the edges are changed) it requires updating the weights of the edges and then performing a topological sort to discover a new optimization relation. Otherwise, it is necessary to derive a new event model by simulating system behavior. (Kapadia 1999) describes the use of strong domain knowledge to predict when the structure of an event model may change with alterations to a design solution necessitating the simulation of system behavior.

Modification generation

Given a design solution, modification generation identifies a set of variables that must be changed and the direction and magnitude of change for each variable in this set to bring about desired improvement in the optimization objectives. We use the sensitivity of an optimization objective's lower bound to changes in design variables (e.g., incrementing k_4 by 1 increases the lower bound for jct_2 by 1, but incrementing k_2 by 1 increases it by 6) to determine suitable parameter modifications.

The following example illustrates our approach. We assume that the initial design solution is $k_1 = 1$, $k_2 = 2$, $k_3 = 1$, and $k_4 = 3$. We have the following mutable optimization relations: $jct_1 \geq 2 * k_1 + 3 * k_2 + k_4$, and $jct_2 \geq 3 * k_1 + 6 * k_2 + 2 * k_4$. The following invariant relation: $Cost = 65 - 5 * k_1 - 3 * k_2 - 3 * k_3 - 2 * k_4$, indicates that lowering transit times increases manufacturing cost and that the cost is more sensitive to changes in some design variables than others. The constant 65 represents fixed manufacturing costs. We assume the following domain constraints: $k_1 \in \{1, 2\}$, $k_2 \in \{1, 2, 3\}$, $k_3 \in \{1, 2, 3\}$, and $k_4 \in \{2, 3, 4, 5\}$. (See (Kapadia 1999) for details on cost and domain constraints.)

We extend the sensitivity analysis method of (Biswas, Kapadia, & Yu 1997) for qualitative, steady state diagnosis to identify parameter modifications for design optimization. Let $Y = \{y_1, y_2, \ldots, y_m\}$ be the set of optimization criteria and $V = \{v_1, v_2, \ldots, v_n\}$ be the set of design variables. We have optimization relations between V and Y. A high level description for our modification generation algorithm is presented below.
(1) Establish a qualitative $(+, -, 0)$ relationship between each optimization criterion (y_i) and each design variable (v_j) by determining the sensitivity of y_i with respect to v_j. This is obtained by taking the partial derivative $\partial y_i / \partial v_j, \forall i, j$, e.g., $\partial jct_1 / \partial k_2 = 3$. The relationship is $+$ $(-)$ if an increase in v_j causes an increase (decrease) in y_i and 0 if v_j has no effect on y_i.
(2) Choose an appropriate direction of change for each y_i. If y_i is to be maximized (minimized), increase y_i, i.e., y_i+ (decrease y_i, i.e., y_i-).
(3) Express the relation between y_i and V as a Conjunctive Normal Form (CNF) expression, e.g., (a) $Cost- \leftarrow (k_1+) \vee (k_2+) \vee (k_3+) \vee (k_4+)$, (b) $jct_1- \leftarrow (k_1-) \vee (k_2-) \vee (k_4-)$, and (c) $jct_2- \leftarrow (k_1-) \vee (k_2-) \vee (k_4-)$. The logical formulas represent cause-effect relations between optimization criteria and design variables, e.g., from relation (a) we see that decreasing k_1, k_2, or k_4 reduces jct_1.
(4) Find a satisfying assignment to the CNF formula $y_1 \wedge y_2 \wedge \ldots \wedge y_m$. While this problem is inherently exponential, CNF satisfiability algorithms like GSAT (Russell & Norvig, 1995) have been reported to solve large problems in reasonable times. In our example, the following satisfying assignments form a set of qualitative modifications: $(k_1+) \wedge (k_2-)$, $(k_1+) \wedge (k_4-)$, $(k_1-) \wedge (k_2+)$, $(k_1-) \wedge (k_3+)$, $(k_1-) \wedge (k_4+)$, $(k_2+) \wedge (k_4-)$, $(k_2-) \wedge (k_3+)$, $(k_2-) \wedge (k_4+)$, $(k_3+) \wedge (k_4-)$.
(5) Assign magnitudes to the design variables in the set of qualitative modifications that satisfy the following difference relations:
$\Delta y_1 = \Delta v_1 * \frac{\partial y_1}{\partial v_1} + \Delta v_2 * \frac{\partial y_1}{\partial v_2} + \ldots \Delta v_n * \frac{\partial y_1}{\partial v_n}$,

$\Delta y_2 = \Delta v_1 * \frac{\partial y_2}{\partial v_1} + \Delta v_2 * \frac{\partial y_2}{\partial v_2} + \ldots \Delta v_n * \frac{\partial y_2}{\partial v_n}, \ldots,$
$\Delta y_m = \Delta v_1 * \frac{\partial y_m}{\partial v_1} + \Delta v_2 * \frac{\partial y_m}{\partial v_2} + \ldots \Delta v_n * \frac{\partial y_m}{\partial v_n}$.
In our example, we have the following relations:
$\Delta Cost = -5 * \Delta k_1 - 3 * \Delta k_2 - 3 * \Delta k_3 - 2 * \Delta k_4$,
$\Delta jct_1 = \Delta k_1 + 3 * \Delta k_2 + 1 * \Delta k_4$,
$\Delta jct_2 = 3 * \Delta k_1 + 6 * \Delta k_2 + 2 * \Delta k_4$.
In general, we cannot directly solve these equations to generate magnitudes for design variable modifications because we do not know values of Δy_i ($\forall i = 1, \ldots, m$) and there may be no closed-form solution to this system of equations. Instead, we analyze each candidate to determine the magnitudes of modification for its variables as follows. A variable in a modification is labeled *free* if there is no optimization criterion which is adversely affected by its direction of change, otherwise it is *bound*. Then, we use the following heuristics to determine optimal parameter magnitude changes. To each free element, greedily assign the largest magnitude of change consistent with domain constraints to maximize its beneficial effects on optimization criteria. To each bound element, assign the smallest incremental change consistent with its constraints. This minimizes its adverse effects on the optimization objectives. For example, in modification candidate $(k_2-) \wedge (k_3+)$, k_2 is bound (since k_2- increases $Cost$) so we assign it the smallest increment, i.e., $\Delta k_2 = -1$, while k_3 is free, so we assign it the largest increment, i.e., $\Delta k_3 = 2$.
(6) If the modification pushes a variable outside its range as defined by its domain constraint, the resulting design solution is invalid. Eliminate any modifications that result in invalid solutions by checking domain constraints.
(7) Finally, eliminate inferior modifications. For example, $(k_3+) \wedge (k_4-)$ with $\Delta k_3 = 2, \Delta k_4 = -1$ has the following effect on optimization objectives: $\Delta Cost = -4, \Delta jct_1 = -1, \Delta jct_2 = -2$ while $(k_2+) \wedge (k_4-)$ with $\Delta k_2 = 1, \Delta k_4 = -1$ affects the optimization criteria as follows: $\Delta Cost = -1, \Delta jct_1 = 1, \Delta jct_2 = 4$. Since $(k_3+) \wedge (k_4-)$ is better than $(k_2+) \wedge (k_4-)$ for *every* criterion, the latter is an inferior modification and can be eliminated. We are developing strategies that incorporate designer's preferences to discriminate among multiple non-inferior modifications.

Interactive design navigation

We have built a modeling and design optimization prototype tool in the language CLP(fd) (a constraint logic programming language over finite domains) to model systems using ER Nets, and generate and optimize their designs. The designer and our tool may collaborate to exploit their different strengths. The user provides the system with an initial design solution which is valid but non-optimal. The design tool simulates system behavior for this solution, discovers mutable optimization relations, and applies sensitivity analysis techniques to identify suitable modifications. The user may guide the tool to explore the more promising regions of the design solution space by choosing which modifications

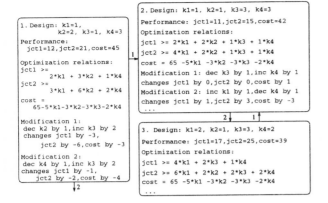

```
1. Design: k1=1,
          k2=2, k3=1, k4=3

Performance:
  jct1=12,jct2=21,cost=45

Optimization relations:
jct1 >=
        2*k1 + 3*k2 + 1*k4
jct2 >=
        3*k1 + 6*k2 + 2*k4
cost =
    65-5*k1-3*k2-3*k3-2*k4

Modification 1:
dec k2 by 1,inc k3 by 2
changes jct1 by -3,
        jct2 by -6,cost by -3

Modification 2:
dec k4 by 1,inc k3 by 2
changes jct1 by -1,
        jct2 by -2,cost by -4
```

```
2. Design: k1=1, k2=1, k3=3, k4=3

Performance: jct1=11,jct2=15,cost=42

Optimization relations:
jct1 >= 2*k1 + 2*k2 + 1*k3 + 1*k4
jct2 >= 4*k1 + 2*k2 + 1*k3 + 1*k4
cost = 65 -5*k1 -3*k2 -3*k3 -2*k4
Modification 1: dec k3 by 1,inc k4 by 1
changes jct1 by 0,jct2 by 0,cost by 1
Modification 2: inc k1 by 1,dec k4 by 1
changes jct1 by 1,jct2 by 3,cost by -3
...
```

```
3. Design: k1=2, k2=1, k3=3, k4=2

Performance: jct1=17,jct2=25,cost=39

Optimization relations:
jct1 >= 4*k1 + 2*k3 + 1*k4
jct2 >= 6*k1 + 2*k2 + 2*k3 + 2*k4
cost = 65 -5*k1 -3*k2 -3*k3 -2*k4
...
```

Figure 5: Interactively navigating the design space

to apply and which performance criteria to optimize. A trace of the tool's navigation of the design space is shown in Fig. 5. In the initial solution state, the user chooses modification 1 to generate the second solution. Next, he chooses modification 2 to generate the third solution. Having examined three states the user may choose solution 2, i.e., $k_1 = 1, k_2 = 1, k_3 = 3, k_4 = 3$ with performance $jct_1 = 11, jct_2 = 15, cost = 42$ which is non-inferior in the space of known design solutions (but not necessarily non-inferior in the context of all solutions).

Discussion

This paper presents a mutable optimization problem and describes model-based reasoning techniques to address different aspects of this problem. We present a model-based reasoning approach to discover mutable optimization relations and a sensitivity analysis algorithm that uses the mutable relations to optimize multiple conflicting performance objectives. We apply our methods to optimize a real system's dynamic performance parameters. The techniques described in this paper are part of an overall methodology to address system-level design optimization where the components of the system may belong to different domains (Kapadia 1999).

(Kapadia & Fromherz 1997) address dynamic design optimization using constraint satisfaction techniques but their search process is only slightly better than exhaustive search. Our heuristic modification generation algorithm explores fewer solutions in the design space. (Goel & Chandrasekaran 1989), have also used model-based reasoning to effectively navigate the design space. They represent interactions in the form of directed, acyclic causal graphs that are created a priori by system designers. Our event models, which are generated dynamically, are more similar to the work of (Williams 1990), who develops a network of interactions by envisioning the behavior of the system from a model of its components and their interconnections.

Representing an event model as a graph structure

will allow us to apply a number of well known algorithms for analyzing system behavior (e.g., maximum flow, shortest path) which may support other forms of optimization (e.g., capacity optimization). Our design optimization algorithm is sensitive to the initial solution: if the initial solution is in a good region of the design space, optimal or near optimal solutions will be found; otherwise, it is likely to get trapped in a local optimum. We must formalize our techniques for detecting changes to optimization relations with alterations in design solutions without resorting to simulation. Preliminary results for our methodology are promising but extensive testing and empirical evaluation is required. We will study scalability issues by considering a larger and more diverse target workload and a larger set of component parameters. We anticipate that some form of problem decomposition may be required to overcome the increase in time complexity as the number of optimization criteria rise for a larger workload.

Acknowledgements. We thank Markus Fromherz for helping us refine the ideas presented in this paper.

References

Biswas, G.; Kapadia, R.; and Yu, X. 1997. Combined qualitative-quantitative diagnosis of continuous valued systems. *IEEE Trans. on Systems, Man, and Cybernetics* 167–185.

Ghezzi, C.; Mandrioli, D.; Morasca, S.; and Pezze, M. 1991. A unified high-level petri net formalism for time critical systems. *IEEE Trans. on Software Engg.* 160–172.

Goel, A., and Chandrasekaran, B. 1989. Functional representation of designs and redesign problem solving. In *Proc. of AAAI-89*, 1388–1394.

Kapadia, R., and Fromherz, M. 1997. Design optimization with uncertain application knowledge. In *Proc. of the Tenth Intl. Conf. IEA/AIE-97*, 421–430.

Kapadia, R.; Biswas, G.; and Fromherz, M. 1997. Hybrid modeling for smart system design. In *Proc. Tenth Intl. FLAIRS*, 111–115.

Kapadia, R. 1999. Model-based support for system-level mutable parametric design optimization. Technical Report TR-99-02, CS Dept. Vanderbilt University, Nashville TN 37235.

Mollaghasemi, M., and Evans, G. 1994. A unified high-level petri net formalism for time critical systems. *IEEE Trans. on Systems, Man, and Cybernetics.* 1407–1411.

Steuer, R. 1986. *Multiple Criteria Optimization: Theory, Computation, and Application.* John Wiley & Sons.

Tong, C., and Sriram, D. 1992. *Artificial Intelligence in Engg. Design. Vol. I.* Academic Press Inc.

Williams, B. 1990. Interaction-based invention: Designing novel devices from first principles. In *Proc. AAAI-90*, 349–356.

Qualifying the Expressivity/Efficiency Tradeoff: Reformation-Based Diagnosis

Helmut Prendinger and **Mitsuru Ishizuka**
Department of Information and Communication Engineering
School of Engineering, University of Tokyo
7-3-1, Hongo, Bunkyo-ku, Tokyo 113-8656, Japan
E-mail: {helmut,ishizuka}@miv.t.u-tokyo.ac.jp

Abstract

This paper presents an approach to model-based diagnosis that first compiles a first-order system description to a propositional representation, and then solves the diagnostic problem as a linear programming instance. Relevance reasoning is employed to isolate parts of the system that are related to certain observation types and to economically instantiate the theory, while methods from operations research offer promising results to generate near-optimal diagnoses efficiently.

Introduction and Motivation

A central problem of model-based diagnosis is the computational complexity of the underlying diagnostic reasoning task (see, e.g. Eiter and Gottlob (1995)). Therefore, several researchers have proposed to preprocess a given system description, mostly a propositional theory, such that the 'compiled' form can be processed more efficiently (Williams & Nayak 1996; Darwiche 1998). In many cases, however, it is more natural to describe systems in a more expressive language, such as *first-order logic*. In this paper, we will consider the case where the system description is given as a first-order Horn theory (without function symbols), and compile this description to a propositional one. Techniques from relevance reasoning (Levy, Fikes, & Sagiv 1997; Schurz 1999) will be employed to keep the resulting propositional theory within manageable size. More specifically, relevance reasoning is used to filter out the part of the system that is 'relevant' for certain observation types, and to economically instantiate variables by appropriate constants (usually denoting values of system attributes). In this way, we may preserve the compactness of first-order descriptions, and allow for processing an efficient propositional theory. Thus we qualify the notorious expressivity/efficiency tradeoff.

Given a propositional system description, we will use the Networked Bubble Propagation (NBP) mechanism (Ohsawa & Ishizuka 1997), a high-speed hypothetical ('abductive') reasoner, as the diagnostic engine. Focusing on most-probable (least-expensive) diagnoses is

realized by assigning a numerical weight to each hypothesis (possible system fault). The NBP mechanism tries to find an optimal solution, i.e., a diagnosis with a minimal sum of individual faults' weights, and actually generates a near-optimal solution in polynomial time of approximately $\mathcal{O}(n^{1.4})$, where n the number of hypotheses in the problem formulation. The efficiency of the NBP mechanism relies on methods from the area of 0-1 integer linear programming.

Following a comprehensive step-by-step approach, we show how a general definition of model-based diagnosis can be translated to a integer linear programming problem. Although the possibility of such a translation is not completely surprising, we are not aware of any previous attempts in the literature. In the planning field, however, Bylander (1997) shows how to translate propositional STRIPS planning instances to linear programming instances, and Williams and Nayak (1996) recast their model-based configuration manager as a combinatorial optimization problem.

The main contribution of this paper can be seen as bringing together methods from the fields of deductive databases and operations research. In particular, relevance reasoning is employed to preprocess a given behavioral model encoded in first-order Horn logic, and operations research methods allow to efficiently solve diagnosis problems.

The rest of the paper is organized as follows. In the following section, we explain some notions related to model-based diagnosis. Then we introduce a general framework for extracting information relevant to finding diagnoses, relative to certain observation types and the structure of the system. Moreover, we discuss a sophisticated instantiation method based on relevance reasoning. Next, we explain how hypothetical reasoning problems (corresponding to diagnostic problems) can be recast as problems of integer linear programming. We also report on some preliminary experimental results obtained in testing our approach. Finally, we discuss related work and draw some conclusions.

Model-based Diagnosis

A *diagnostic problem* is characterized by a set of observations to be explained, given a behavioral model of some system (device). The behavioral model of a system describes its normal and/or faulty behavior. A solution to a diagnostic problem (a *diagnosis* for short) is a set of hypotheses which, if assumed, would 'explain' the observations. We adopt the general definition of a diagnostic problem proposed by Console and Torasso (1991), which subsumes both abductive and consistency-based definitions of diagnosis.

Definition 1 *A diagnostic problem DP is a quadruple* $DP = \langle T, I, CXT, OBS \rangle$, *such that*

(1) T is a behavioral model, *i.e., a set of Horn clauses of the form* "$p(\bar{X}_{n+1}) \leftarrow q_1(\bar{X}_1) \wedge \ldots \wedge q_n(\bar{X}_n)$" *where* $p(\bar{X}_{n+1}), q_1(\bar{X}_1), \ldots, q_n(\bar{X}_n)$ *are atomic formulas, and* $\bar{X}_i$ *denotes the sequence of variables* $X_{i,1}, \ldots, X_{i,m_i}$. *Each* q_i *in the body (the RHS of the clause) denotes either (i) a state that can be assumed as a hypothesis (an* abducible*), or (ii) context conditions on which the behavior of the system depends, such as 'inputs' to a device, or (iii) a state that can neither be observed nor assumed (internal state). The atom p in the head (the LHS of the clause) denotes either a state that can be observed or measured and for which we want to find an explanation, or an internal state.*

(2) I is a set of inconsistency constraints, *i.e., a set of Horn clauses of the form* "$\perp \leftarrow q_1(\bar{X}_1) \wedge \ldots \wedge q_n(\bar{X}_n)$" *where each* q_i *denotes a context condition or a hypothesis, and the symbol* $\perp$ *denotes the logical constant falsum.*

(3) CXT is a set of variable-free (ground) atoms that denote context conditions (inputs).

(4) OBS is a set atoms that denote observations.

We require that T contains no cycles, i.e., a state must not be a direct or indirect cause of itself. The class of acyclic theories properly contains the class of so-called 'tree-structured' theories (Stumptner & Wotawa 1997) where each state can cause at most one other state.

The notion of 'diagnosis' will be explained by giving a definition of a *solution* to a diagnostic problem. A *diagnostic procedure* allows to generate a solution to a diagnostic problem automatically. Since the diagnostic procedure will be implemented as a hypothetical reasoning mechanism, we first reformulate a diagnostic problem as a problem of hypothetical reasoning. We borrow the reformulation suggested by Console and Torasso (1991).

Definition 2 *Let* $DP = \langle T, I, CXT, OBS \rangle$ *be a diagnostic problem. A hypothetical reasoning problem HRP corresponding to DP is a quadruple* $HRP = \langle T, I, CXT, \langle \mathcal{O}^+, \mathcal{O}^- \rangle \rangle$, *such that*

- $\mathcal{O}^+ \subseteq OBS$;
- $\mathcal{O}^- = \{\neg m(v_i) : m(v_j) \in OBS$, *for each value* v_i *of* m *different from* $v_j\}$.

Here, $\mathcal{O}^+$ denotes the set of observations that have to be covered by the solution; $\mathcal{O}^-$ is the set of observations that 'contradict' (or 'conflict with') the observations.

The following definition of a *solution* for a HRP problem is an extension of the definition given by Console and Torasso (1991).

Definition 3 *Let* $HRP = \langle T, I, CXT, \langle \mathcal{O}^+, \mathcal{O}^- \rangle \rangle$ *be a hypothetical reasoning problem, and* $\mathcal{H}$ *a set of abducibles. A set* $H \subseteq \mathcal{H}$ *is a* solution hypotheses set *for HRP if and only if*

- *for each* $m \in \mathcal{O}^+$: $T \cup CXT \cup H \vdash m$;
- $T \cup CXT \cup H \cup \mathcal{O}^- \nvdash \perp$;
- $I \cup CXT \cup H \nvdash \perp$.

For convenience, we will sometimes call a solution hypotheses set simply a *solution* or *explanation*. The second condition in the definition is called *consistency constraint* in (Console & Torasso 1991). We also account for the case where certain solution sets are not admissible, by means of so-called *inconsistency constraints* (third condition). This condition is not present in (Console & Torasso 1991).

Reformation by Relevance Reasoning

In the off-line reformation (or compilation) phase, the first-order system description is first partitioned into subtheories, possibly indexed with an observation type. Next, clauses that cannot contribute to the solution of any query, also called *strongly irrelevant* clauses, are removed from the subtheory (Schurz 1999). Finally, the *query-tree* idea is employed to obtain exactly the set of ground clauses relevant to a query type (Levy, Fikes, & Sagiv 1997).

Theory Factorizing

For the case of *tree-structured* systems, the idea of theory factorizing is to split a theory T into disjoint subtheories $T_1, \ldots, T_n$ such that no clause C in a given subtheory T_i resolves with some clause D from a different subtheory T_j. This means that the search space for a given atomic query type $p(\bar{X})$ can be restricted to a single subtheory T_i. The theory factorizing algorithm is described in (Prendinger & Ishizuka 1999) and can be summarized as follows: (i) if a clause C does not resolve with any independent subset of the already generated partition, then $\{C\}$ is added as a new element of the partition; (ii) if C resolves with independent subsets $\mathcal{D}_1, \ldots, \mathcal{D}_k$ in the partition, then those subsets and C form a new element of the partition while the old elements $\mathcal{D}_1, \ldots, \mathcal{D}_k$ get cancelled. Theory factorizing has to be applied only once, and can be done in polynomial time. Note that factorizing is an application of the formal notion of *independence* (Lang & Marquis 1998).

In the more general case of *acyclic* theories, factorizing is performed by means of an algorithm that computes all clauses that are 'reachable' from a query type. Informally, a clause C is *reachable* from a query type $p(\bar{X})$ if there exists some path from $p(\bar{X})$ to the head of C. The set of clauses reachable from $p(\bar{X})$ is denoted by T_p. It is important to note that in either case, factorizing can be done by only considering the query *types* such as $p(\bar{X})$, i.e., independent of particular instantiations such as $p(a)$ or $p(b)$.

Theory Simplification

A given (independent) theory may still contain strongly irrelevant clauses. This is the case when a clause C contains an atom in $bd(C)$ that does not resolve with the head of any other clause. C is called a *failing* clause. Theory simplification removes failing clauses from the initial theory T, obtaining the simplified theory T'. The simplification process is repeated until no failing clauses are detected. Note that clauses having hypotheses $h \in \mathcal{H}$ in their body are *not* deleted, since hypotheses *may* contribute to a proof (if they are assumed). In addition to remove strongly irrelevant clauses, theory simplification can be utilized to detect unspecified context conditions in a behavioral model. A situation where a subquery does not resolve with a fact indicates that some input to a device has not been declared in the model.

Theory Instantiation

In the last phase of the reformation process, the theory is actually instantiated. By employing the query-tree idea (Levy, Fikes, & Sagiv 1997), we obtain exactly the set of ground clauses relevant to a query type, together with all instantiations of the query type that have a solution w.r.t. the theory. A *query-tree* is a compact representation of a search tree for first-order Horn theories and has the form of an AND-OR tree with goal-nodes and rule-nodes (Levy, Fikes, & Sagiv 1997). Since we do not allow for recursion in clauses, our construction of the query tree is simpler than the original one in (Levy, Fikes, & Sagiv 1997). On the other hand, we allow that some leaves of the query-tree are uninstantiated. Those typically denote hypotheses (abducibles).

Example 1 *Consider the following theory T where the atom with predicate h denotes a hypothesis.*

(r_1) $p(X,Y) \leftarrow q1(X,Y) \wedge q2(X,Y).$
(r_2) $q1(X,Y) \leftarrow r1(X,Y) \wedge h(X,Y).$
(r_3) $q2(X,Y) \leftarrow r2(X,Y).$
(r_4) $q2(X,Y) \leftarrow r3(X,Y).$
(f_1) $r1(a,b).$ (f_2) $r1(a,c).$
(f_3) $r2(a,b).$ (f_4) $r2(c,d).$ (f_5) $r3(b,d).$

The query tree algorithm consists of two phases (a more detailed description is given in (Levy, Fikes, & Sagiv 1997)). In the *bottom-up* phase, a set of *adorned* predicates and rules is generated. An adorned predicate p^c is a predicate p with constraint c on its arguments. The adorned rules are the rules of the theory with predicates replaced by adorned predicates. We start with the base predicates of the theory, i.e., the predicates of facts and hypotheses. For instance, the adorned predicate $r1^c$ is obtained by completion: $r1(X,Y) \leftrightarrow (X = a \wedge Y = b) \vee (X = a \wedge Y = c)$. For convenience, the adornment of $r1$ is written as $c(X,Y) = \{\langle a, b \rangle, \langle a, c \rangle\}$. Let U be the set of all constants appearing in the theory. Then the adornment of the (uninstantiated) hypothesis h is $\{\langle X, Y \rangle : \langle X, Y \rangle \in U^2\}$. The adornments of predicates in head atoms of rules are generated by projecting the adornments of predicates in body atoms onto the

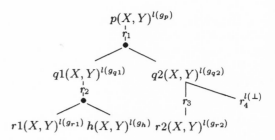

Figure 1: Query-tree for Example 1. The label for each goal-node g is $l(g) = \{\langle a, b \rangle\}$. For simplicity, labels of rule nodes are omitted. Note that expanding node $q2(X,Y)$ with rule r_4 would result in an inconsistent label.

head variables. For instance, the adornment of $q1$ is $\{\langle a, b \rangle, \langle a, c \rangle\}$. The bottom-up phase terminates when no new adornments are generated. In Example 1, the following further predicate adornments are generated: $\{\langle a, b \rangle, \langle c, d \rangle\}$ for $r2$, $\{\langle b, d \rangle\}$ for $r3$, $\{\langle a, b \rangle, \langle c, d \rangle, \langle b, d \rangle\}$ for $q2$, and $\{\langle a, b \rangle\}$ for p.

In the *top-down* phase, the predicate adornment of the query type is 'pushed down' to the base predicates. Starting with the node of the adorned query type q^c, we construct the query-tree such that each node g of a predicate p has a *label* $l(g)$. Initially the goal-node $l(g) = q^c$ is created (see Fig. 1). A goal-node g for a predicate q^{ch} can be unified with adorned rules r of the form $q^{ch}(\bar{X}_{n+1}) \leftarrow c \wedge p_1^{c_1}(\bar{X}_1) \wedge ... \wedge p_n^{c_n}(\bar{X}_n)$. If $l(g) \wedge c$ is satisfiable, a rule-node g_r is created as a child of g, with $l(g_r) = l(g) \wedge c$ as its label. For every body atom $p_i^{c_i}$ in r, the rule-node $l(g_r)$ has a child goal-node whose label is the projection of $l(g_r)$ onto $\bar{X}_i$. The top-down construction halts, since nodes of base predicates and nodes with unsatisfiable label, denoted by $l(\perp)$, are not expanded. As shown in (Levy, Fikes, & Sagiv 1997), the complexity of building the query-tree is linear in the number of rules and possibly exponential in the arity of predicates.

Interestingly, *instantiation* of the theory is simply a by-product of the top-down construction of the query-tree: if $l(g_r)$ is the label of a rule r in the query-tree, the propositional version of r is obtained by performing all unifications appearing $l(g_r)$. As a result, the following propositional KB is obtained for Example 1.

(r_1') $p(a,b) \leftarrow q1(a,b) \wedge q2(a,b).$
(r_2') $q1(a,b) \leftarrow r1(a,b) \wedge h(a,b).$
(r_3') $q2(a,b) \leftarrow r2(a,b).$
(f_1') $r1(a,b).$ (f_3') $r2(a,b).$

It is a consequence of the construction of the query-tree that $p(a,b)$ is the only instance of the query type $p(X,Y)$ with a solution (given that $h(a,b)$ is assumed).

As output of the reformation process, we obtain either independent propositional theories (tree-structured systems), or propositional theories indexed with query types (acyclic systems). It is important to note that rather than creating specialized theories for specific observations, we extract the relevant part for a set of observations (denoted by query types).

Diagnosis as Linear Programming

In this section, we show how hypothetical reasoning problems (HRPs) corresponding to diagnostic problems (DPs) can be solved by integer linear programming problems (LPPs). First, we describe the translation from HRP to a problem of integer linear programming. Next, the notion of 'best explanation' is explicated within the framework of linear programming. Finally, we briefly describe the mechanism of Networked Bubble Propagation (NBP), an efficient hypothetical reasoning method for computing near-optimal solutions.

From Diagnosis to Integer Linear Programming

An *integer linear programming problem (LPP)* is defined by a set of variables, a set of linear constraints, and an objective function. The set of linear constraints consists of linear inequalities and equalities, and the objective function is a linear function on the variables. A solution for LPP is called *feasible* if it satisfies the constraints, and it is called *optimal* if it is feasible and maximizes (or minimizes) the objective function.

Let V denote the union of the set of all propositional variables occurring in $T \cup I \cup CXT$ and $\{\perp\}$. Then $\mathcal{V}$ is the set of variables indexed by V, i.e., $\mathcal{V} = \{x_p : p \in V\}$. The set $\mathcal{V}$ has the following distinguished subsets: (i) $\mathcal{V}_{\mathcal{O}+} \subset \mathcal{V}$ is the set of variables denoting symptoms; (ii) $\mathcal{V}_{\mathcal{O}-} \subset \mathcal{V}$ is the set of variables denoting observations that conflict with symptoms; (iii) $\mathcal{V}_{\mathcal{H}} \subset \mathcal{V}$ is the set of hypothesis variables; (iv) $\mathcal{V}_{CXT} \subset \mathcal{V}$ is the set of variables denoting context conditions; and (v) $x_{\perp} \in \mathcal{V}$ is the variable associated with $\perp$.

Clauses in the behavioral model T are assumed to have one of the following forms, depending on whether the bodies of clauses in T are AND-related or OR-related. The heads of clauses with AND-related and OR-related bodies are called AND-nodes and OR-nodes, respectively: (AND) $p \leftarrow q_1 \wedge ... \wedge q_n$, or (OR) $p \leftarrow q_1, ..., p \leftarrow q_m$. If the body of an OR-node p is a conjunction of propositional variables $q_{k,1} \wedge ... \wedge q_{k,n_k}$, an auxiliary propositional variable $q_{k,0}$ is invented such that $p \leftarrow q_{k,0}$ and $q_{k,0} \leftarrow q_{k,1} \wedge ... \wedge q_{k,n_k}$. For convenience, we define a successor set S_p for each $p \in V$ as follows: $S_p = \{q : q$ occurs in an AND-related or OR-related body in clauses with head $p\}$. $|S_p|$ is the cardinality of S_p.

The following translation is similar to the one given by Santos (1994).

Definition 4 *Let $HRP = \langle T, I, CXT, \langle \mathcal{O}^+, \mathcal{O}^- \rangle \rangle$ be a hypothetical reasoning problem. An integer linear programming problem (LPP) corresponding to HRP is a pair $LPP = \langle \mathcal{V}, \mathcal{I} \rangle$, where $\mathcal{V}$ is a set of variables and $\mathcal{I}$ is a finite set of linear inequalities and equalities on $\mathcal{V}$.*
(1) Clauses with AND-related and OR-related bodies are translated to linear inequalities as follows:

- *Let p be an AND-node with successor set S_p.*

$$x_p \leq x_q \ (q \in S_p), \quad \sum_{q \in S_p} x_q - |S_p| + 1 \leq x_p$$

- *Let p be an OR-node with successor set S_p.*

$$\sum_{q \in S_p} x_q \geq x_p, \quad x_p \geq x_q \ (q \in S_p)$$

(2) Inconsistency constraints $ic \in I$ of the form "$\perp \leftarrow p_1 \wedge ... \wedge p_n$" are a special cases of clauses with AND-related body because their head is the constant $\perp$, where $x_{\perp} = 0$. Therefore, we only need a single linear inequality

$$\sum_{p \in S_{\perp}} x_p - |S_{\perp}| + 1 \leq 0$$

(3) In general, for each $x_p \in \mathcal{V}$, x_p is either 0 or 1. In particular, (i) for each $x_p \in \mathcal{V}_{\mathcal{O}+}$, we add the equation $x_p = 1$, i.e., a given observation p must be assigned the value true; (ii) for each $x_p \in \mathcal{V}_{\mathcal{O}-}$, we add the equation $x_p = 0$, thereby assigning observations that contradict symptoms the value false; (iii) for each $x_q \in \mathcal{V}_{CXT}$, the variable associated with a context atom q, we add the equation $x_q = 1$, saying that the conditions expressed by contextual data hold.

By way of example, we show how the second condition guarantees that the inconsistency constraints are satisfied. Since $\perp$ is (always) assigned *false*, some p in $S_{\perp}$ must be false. Take the $ic \ \perp \leftarrow h_1 \wedge h_2 \wedge h_3$ and assume that each of the hypothesis is assigned the value *true* (each of the hypothesis is assumed). Then we have $1 + 1 + 1 - 3 + 1 \leq 0$, i.e., $1 \leq 0$, which violates the constraint.

Definition 5 *A variable assignment for $LPP = \langle \mathcal{V}, \mathcal{I} \rangle$ is a function ϕ from $\mathcal{V}$ to $\{0, 1\}$. ϕ is a 0-1 solution for LPP if ϕ satisfies all the constraints in $\mathcal{I}$. A 0-1 solution hypotheses set H_{0-1} for LPP consists of all $x_p \in \mathcal{V}_{\mathcal{H}}$ which are assigned 1 in the 0-1 solution for LPP.*

Not surprisingly, the following theorem of Santos (1994) can be extended to problems including inconsistency constraints.

Theorem 1 *H is a solution hypotheses set for HRP if and only if H_{0-1} is a 0-1 solution hypotheses set for LPP.*

Optimal 0-1 Solutions

In *cost-based* hypothetical reasoning, each hypothesis has an associated numerical weight, and the weight of an solution hypotheses set is simply the sum of the weights associated with hypotheses in the set (Santos 1994; Ohsawa & Ishizuka 1997). A solution hypotheses set is optimal if the sum is minimal.

In diagnostic reasoning, it is often desirable to obtain an optimal solution or best explanation; a fault can be said to have low weight if the fault is easy to repair, or even, a fault with low weight is more probable (de Kleer 1991). The idea to concentrate on the preferred (more probable, less expensive) diagnoses is also known as *focusing* (e.g. Freitag and Friedrich (1992)). To capture the notion of optimal solution (or best explanation) formally, we define a function w from $\mathcal{H}$ to the set of natural numbers. Given an integer linear programming problem, the *objective function* being minimized is as follows:

$$\Psi_{LPP} = \sum_{h \in \mathcal{V}_{\mathcal{H}}} x_h w(h)$$

Definition 6 *An optimal 0-1 solution hypotheses set for LPP is a 0-1 solution hypotheses set (for LPP) that minimizes Ψ_{LPP}.*

The cost-based variant of hypothetical reasoning has great potential for incorporating notions of uncertain reasoning such as probability. In the case where all hypotheses are uniformly assigned a default weight, an optimal solution corresponds to a *minimal* diagnosis.

Networked Bubble Propagation (NBP)

In practice, it is more advantageous (in terms of efficiency) to search for a *near-optimal* solution rather than for the optimal one. NBP is a method for cost-based hypothetical reasoning that can be used to compute near-optimal diagnoses (Ohsawa & Ishizuka 1997). The search mechanism draws inspiration from 0-1 linear integer programming and improves the behavior of the so-called 'pivot and complement' method, which is known to find a near-optimal solution close to the optimal solution in polynomial time. NBP can find a near-optimal solution in polynomial time of approximately $\mathcal{O}(n^{1.4})$, where n is the number of hypotheses in the problem formulation (for details, see (Ohsawa & Ishizuka 1997)).

Preliminary Empirical Evaluation

The reformation methods are implemented in Sicstus Prolog, the NBP method is implemented in C. For the experiments we use a Sun Ultra 2 workstation with 320 MB memory. Running times exclude the time needed for reformation. For example, the relevant part of a theory consisting of 1000 clauses can be extracted in about 4 seconds. Our results should be seen as preliminary, more experiments are planned.

Acyclic first-order Horn theories. In the first experiment we show the efficiency gain of relevance reasoning (factorizing and simplification[1]). It involves first-order Horn theories from 40 up to 1000 rules with a fixed percentage of hypotheses (about 30%) and integrity constraints (about 20%) and few facts. The theory of Ex. # 1 is systematically expanded to theories of larger size. Fig. 2 shows the inference time as a function of the number of hypotheses before and after reformation by relevance reasoning. In both cases, the same solution sets H are generated, each corresponding to a minimal explanation. Results are obtained by averaging over three different query types. The results show

---

[1]The speedup effect of the instantiation technique has not been tested in our experiments (see Levy *et al.* (1997) for a related empirical evaluation).

Ex. #	# hypotheses		time (sec)	
	before ref.	after ref.	before ref.	after ref.
1	13	6	0.02	0.01
2	39	17	0.08	0.04
3	78	33	0.21	0.07
4	156	67	0.63	0.16
5	312	129	2.14	0.46

Figure 2: Comparision for first-order Horn theories.

that the reformed theories can be processed more efficiently, usually in excess of a factor of 3. The best speedup factor was 196, for a query type where 98% of the hypotheses are irrelevant.

Medical diagnosis. The second experiment is intended to show the efficiency of the NBP method as a diagnostic procedure. It involves a propositional theory from the medical domain and real-world patient cases, first used by Ng and Mooney (1992) to validate their abductive system ACCEL. The behavioral model consists of 648 rules of the form "$e \leftarrow c$", where e a symptom type and c refers to one of 25 damaged brain areas. Ng and Mooney (1992) consider 50 patient cases of an average of 8.56 symptoms, where ACCEL computed all minimal diagnoses in an average of 2.4 seconds per case (with an average of 4.6 diagnoses per case). We consider the first 25 cases (average of 8.64 symptoms). The NBP method finds a near-optimal diagnosis in an average of 0.06 seconds per case, where the near-optimal diagnosis corresponds to one of the minimal diagnoses. When using the factorized model, we could not measure any speedup effect, although on average, 83% of the rules were strongly irrelevant to the query types. This can be explained by the fact that the number of hypotheses is only slightly decreased. Note that simplification does not apply here since all leaves are hypotheses.

Discussion and Conclusion

In this paper, we describe a new approach for generating diagnoses for observations. The diagnostic task is performed in two successive phases: in the off-line phase a first-order behavioral model is compiled to a propositional representation, in the on-line phase integer linear programming is employed to generate a near-optimal solution to the diagnostic problem. Note that our reformation procedures are equivalence-preserving w.r.t. query types. The procedures are guaranteed not to slow down inference and preserve all solutions.

Our notion of 'reformation' differs from other compilation methods found in the diagnosis literature. For instance, Williams and Nayak (1996) generate all prime implicants of (propositional) transition models; Darwiche (1998) compiles a propositional system description into a sentence called *consequence* that has good computational properties. By contrast, we introduce an effective way to produce a compact propositional theory from a given *first-order* model. In this respect, our approach shares intuitions with the 'first-order planning as (propositional) satisfiability' framework of Kautz and Selman (1996).

Similar to the work of de Kleer (1991), *focusing* is integrated to the diagnostic engine (the NBP mechanism), by associating costs to individual hypotheses, and not part of the compilation (Darwiche 1998). Freitag and Friedrich (1992) discuss an approach to focusing that confines search to the smallest submodel which is independent of the remaining behavioral model. For the class of tree-structured systems, their notion of smallest independent submodel corresponds to the subtheories listed in the partition of a factorized model.

Recently, there is growing interest in developing diagnosing systems that deal with behavioral models exhibiting a particular *structure*, such as tree-structured systems (Stumptner & Wotawa 1997; Darwiche 1998). It is shown both theoretically (Darwiche 1998) and experimentally (Stumptner & Wotawa 1997) that tree-structured systems allow for significantly faster inference than acyclic systems. The experiments in (Ohsawa & Ishizuka 1997) re-enforce those findings with the NBP method. We have shown that structure is also important from a reformation point of view. Factorizing tree-structured systems has to be done only once, whereas for acyclic systems, the relevant part has to be determined for each (combination of) query type(s).

This paper is part of ongoing work on reformation-based diagnosis. In the near future, we want to test our approach on more diverse first-order Horn theories, and compare our results to competing approaches (e.g., de Kleer (1991), Darwiche (1998)). We try to provide formal guarantees on performance.

A major problem of current NBP is that it does not scale well if the width of OR-related nodes is high. Hence we plan to employ another hypothetical reasoner which scales better than the NBP method. Ishizuka and Matsuo (1998) developed the so-called 'slide-down and lift-up' (SL) method that employs both linear and non-linear programming techniques to solve hypothetical reasoning problems. Although the SL method is slightly slower than the NBP method, it is attractive in terms of memory requirements and scalability.

In any case, reformation methods seem to be prime candidates for improving scalability. In (Prendinger & Ishizuka 1999) we describe further reformation methods that allow to 'shrink' the propositional theory by orders-of-magnitude. So-called *variable elimination* procedures allow to reduce the number of different variables in a clause, which becomes crucial when the clause is to be instantiated by constants. The methods developed in that paper also allow to handle (certain forms of) *recursive* Horn theories.

Acknowledgments

We would like to thank the anonymous referees for their very valuable comments. The first author was supported by a fellowship from the Japan Society for the Promotion of Science (JSPS).

References

Bylander, T. 1997. A linear programming heuristic for optimal planning. In *Proceedings 14th National Conference on Artificial Intelligence (AAAI-97)*, 694–699.

Console, L., and Torasso, P. 1991. A spectrum of logical definitions of model-based diagnosis. *Computational Intelligence* 7(3):133–141.

Darwiche, A. 1998. Compiling devices: a structure-based approach. In *Proceedings 6th International Conference on Knowledge Representation and Reasoning (KR-98)*, 156–166.

de Kleer, J. 1991. Focusing on probable diagnosis. In *Proceedings 9th National Conference on Artificial Intelligence (AAAI-91)*, 842–848.

Eiter, T., and Gottlob, G. 1995. The complexity of logic-based abduction. *Journal of the ACM* 42(1–2):3–42.

Freitag, H., and Friedrich, G. 1992. Focusing on independent diagnosis problems. In *Proceedings 3rd International Conference on Knowledge Representation and Reasoning (KR-92)*, 521–531.

Ishizuka, M., and Matsuo, Y. 1998. SL method for computing a near-optimal solution using linear and non-linear programming in cost-based hypothetical reasoning. In *Proceedings 5th Pacific Rim Conference on Artificial Intelligence (PRICAI-98)*, 611–625.

Kautz, H., and Selman, B. 1996. Pushing the envelope: Planning, propositional logic, and stochastic search. In *Proceedings 13th National Conference on Artificial Intelligence (AAAI-96)*.

Lang, J., and Marquis, P. 1998. Complexity results for independence and definability in propositional logic. In *Proceedings 6th International Conference on Knowledge Representation and Reasoning (KR-98)*, 356–367.

Levy, A. Y.; Fikes, R. E.; and Sagiv, Y. 1997. Speeding up inferences using relevance reasoning: a formalism and algorithms. *Artificial Intelligence* 97:83–136.

Ng, H. T., and Mooney, R. J. 1992. Abductive plan recognition and diagnosis: A comprehensive empirical evaluation. In *Proceedings 3rd International Conference on Knowledge Representation and Reasoning (KR-92)*, 499–508.

Ohsawa, Y., and Ishizuka, M. 1997. Networked bubble propagation: a polynomial-time hypothetical reasoning method for computing near-optimal solutions. *Artificial Intelligence* 91:131–154.

Prendinger, H., and Ishizuka, M. 1999. Preparing a first-order knowledge base for fast inference. In *Proceedings 12th International FLAIRS Conference (FLAIRS-99)*. To appear.

Santos, E. 1994. A linear constraint satisfaction approach to cost-based abduction. *Artificial Intelligence* 65:1–27.

Schurz, G. 1999. Relevance in deductive reasoning: A critical overview. In Schurz, G., and Ursic, M., eds., *Beyond Classical Logic*. St. Augustin: Academia Press.

Stumptner, M., and Wotawa, F. 1997. Diagnosing tree structured systems. In *Proceedings 15th International Conference on Artificial Intelligence (IJCAI-97)*, 440–445.

Williams, B. C., and Nayak, P. P. 1996. A model-based approach to reactive self-configuring systems. In *Proceedings 13th National Conference on Artificial Intelligence (AAAI-96)*, 971–978.

Natural Language &
Information Retrieval

The Role of Lexicalization and Pruning for Base Noun Phrase Grammars

Claire Cardie and **David Pierce**
Department of Computer Science
Cornell University
Ithaca, NY 14853
cardie, pierce@cs.cornell.edu

Abstract

This paper explores the role of lexicalization and pruning of grammars for base noun phrase identification. We modify our original framework (Cardie & Pierce 1998) to extract lexicalized treebank grammars that assign a score to each potential noun phrase based upon both the part-of-speech tag sequence and the word sequence of the phrase. We evaluate the modified framework on the "simple" and "complex" base NP corpora of the original study. As expected, we find that lexicalization dramatically improves the performance of the unpruned treebank grammars; however, for the simple base noun phrase data set, the lexicalized grammar performs below the corresponding unlexicalized but pruned grammar, suggesting that lexicalization is not critical for recognizing very simple, relatively unambiguous constituents. Somewhat surprisingly, we also find that error-driven pruning improves the performance of the probabilistic, lexicalized base noun phrase grammars by up to 1.0% recall and 0.4% precision, and does so even using the original pruning strategy that fails to distinguish the effects of lexicalization. This result may have implications for many probabilistic grammar-based approaches to problems in natural language processing: error-driven pruning is a remarkably robust method for improving the performance of probabilistic and non-probabilistic grammars alike.

Introduction

Base noun phrase identification (see Figure 1) is a critical component in many large-scale natural language processing (NLP) applications: it is among the first steps for many partial parsers; information retrieval systems rely on base noun phrases as a primary source of linguistic phrases for indexing; base noun phrases support information extraction, a variety of text-mining operations, and distributional clustering techniques that attempt to relieve sparse data problems. As a result, a number of researchers have targeted the problem of base noun phrase recognition (Church 1988; Bourigault 1992; Voutilainen 1993; Justeson & Katz 1995).

[The survival] of [spinoff Cray Computer Corp.] as [a fledgling] in [the supercomputer business] appears to depend heavily on [the creativity] — and [longevity] — of [its chairman] and [chief designer], [Seymour Cray].

Base noun phrases: simple, nonrecursive noun phrases — noun phrases that do not contain other noun phrase descendants.

Figure 1: Base NP Examples

Only recently, however, have efforts in this area attempted the automatic acquisition of base noun phrase (base NP) parsers and their automatic evaluation on the same large test corpus: Ramshaw & Marcus (1998) applied transformation-based learning (Brill 1995); Argamon, Dagan, & Krymolowski (1998) devised a memory-based sequence learning (MBSL) method; previously we introduced error-driven pruning of treebank grammars (Cardie & Pierce 1998). All three methods for base NP recognition have been evaluated using part-of-speech tagged and base NP annotated corpora derived from the Penn Treebank (Marcus, Marcinkiewicz, & Santorini 1993), thus offering opportunity for more direct comparison than algorithms that have been evaluated by hand.

Ramshaw & Marcus's noun phrase bracketer learns a set of transformation rules. Each transformation locally updates the noun phrase bracketing associated with a single word based on nearby features, such as neighboring words, part-of-speech tags, and bracket boundaries. After the training phase, the learned transformations are applied, in order, to each novel text to identify base NPs. Argamon *et al.* develop a variation of memory-based learning (Stanfill & Waltz 1986) for base NP recognition. During training, their MBSL algorithm saves the entire raw training corpus. Generalization of the implicit noun phrase rules in the training corpus occurs at application time — MBSL searches the novel text for tag sequences or combinations of tag subsequences (tiles) that occurred during training in a similar context.

Our corpus-based algorithm for noun phrase recognition uses a simpler representation for the base NP grammar, namely part-of-speech tag sequences. It extracts the tag sequence grammar from the treebank training corpus, then prunes it using an error-based benefit metric. To identify a base NP in a novel sentence, a simple longest-match bracketer scans input text from left to right, at each point selecting the longest sequence of tags matching a grammar rule (if any) to form a base NP. The approach has a number of attractive features: both the training and the bracketer are very simple; the bracketer is very fast; the learned grammar can be easily modified. Nonetheless, while the accuracy of the treebank approach is very good for applications that require or prefer fairly simple base NPs, it lags the alternative approaches when identifying more complex noun phrases. This can be explained in part by examining the sources of knowledge employed by each method: The treebank approach uses neither lexical (i.e. word-based) information nor context; MBSL captures context in its tiles, but uses no lexical information; the transformation-based learner uses both lexical information and the surrounding context to make decisions about bracket boundary placement. Context and lexicalization have been shown to be important across a variety of natural language learning tasks; as a result, we might expect the treebank approach to improve with the addition of either. However, lexicalization and its accompanying transition to a probabilistic grammar has at least one goal similar to that of pruning: to reduce the effect of "noisy" rules in the grammar. Therefore, it is not clear that lexicalization alone will improve the error-driven pruning treebank approach to base noun phrase recognition.

This paper explores the role of lexicalization and pruning of base noun phrase grammars. More specifically, we modify our original framework to extract lexicalized treebank grammars that assign a score to each potential noun phrase based upon both the tag sequence and the word sequence of the phrase. In addition, we extend the noun phrase bracketer to select the combination of brackets with the highest score. We evaluate the modified framework on the "simple" and "complex" base NP corpora of the original study.

As expected, we find that lexicalization dramatically improves the performance of the unpruned treebank grammars, with an increase in precision and recall of approximately 70% and 50%, respectively. However, for the simple base NP data set, the lexicalized grammar still performs below the unlexicalized, but pruned, grammar of the original base NP study, suggesting that lexicalization is not critical for recognizing very simple, relatively unambiguous constituents. For the simple base NP task, pruning serves much the same function as lexicalization in that both suppress the application of bad rules. Pruning, however, allows the simplicity of the grammar and bracketing procedure to remain intact. In contrast, for more complex base NPs, the lexicalized grammar performs comparably to the pruned unlexicalized grammar of the original study.

Thus, the importance of lexical information appears to increase with the complexity of the linguistic task: more than just the tag sequence is needed to determine the quality of a candidate phrase when the targets are more ambiguous. For many applications, however, the added complexity of the lexicalized approach may not be worth the slight increase in performance.

There were a couple of surprises in our results: both the longest-match heuristic of the original bracketer and the original error-driven pruning strategy improved the performance of the lexicalized base NP grammars. First, the longest-match heuristic proved to be more useful than lexical information for the unpruned grammar on both corpora. Second, we found that pruning improves bracketing by up to 1.0% recall and 0.4% precision, and does so even using the original strategy that fails to distinguish the effects of lexicalized rules. This result may have implications for many probabilistic grammar-based approaches to problems in natural language processing: error-driven pruning is a remarkably robust method for improving the performance of probabilistic and non-probabilistic grammars alike.

The next section of this paper defines base noun phrases and reviews the basic framework used to extract, prune, and apply grammars using a treebank base NP corpus. The following section extends the framework to include lexicalized grammars. We then evaluate the modified framework and conclude with a discussion and comparison of approaches to base noun phrase identification.

The Treebank Approach to Base Noun Phrase Identification

In this work we define *base NPs* to be simple, non-recursive noun phrases — noun phrases that do not contain other noun phrase descendants. The bracketed portions of Figure 1, for example, show the base NPs in one sentence from the Penn Treebank Wall Street Journal corpus. Thus, the string *the survival of spinoff Cray Computer Corp. as a fledgling in the supercomputer business* is too complex to be a base NP; instead, it contains four simpler noun phrases, each of which is considered a base NP: *the survival, spinoff Cray Computer Corp., a fledgling,* and *the supercomputer business.* This section reviews the treebank approach to base noun phrase identification depicted in Figure 2. For more detail, see Cardie & Pierce (1998).

Grammar Extraction

Grammar extraction requires a corpus that has been annotated with base NPs. More specifically, we assume that the training corpus is a sequence of words $w_1, w_2, \ldots$, along with a set of base NP annotations $b_{(i_1,j_1)}, b_{(i_2,j_2)}, \ldots$, where $b_{(i,j)}$ indicates that the noun phrase includes words i through j: $[_{NP}\ w_i, \ldots, w_j]$. The goal of the training phase is to create a base NP grammar from this training corpus:

Grammar Extraction

Base Noun Phrase Identification

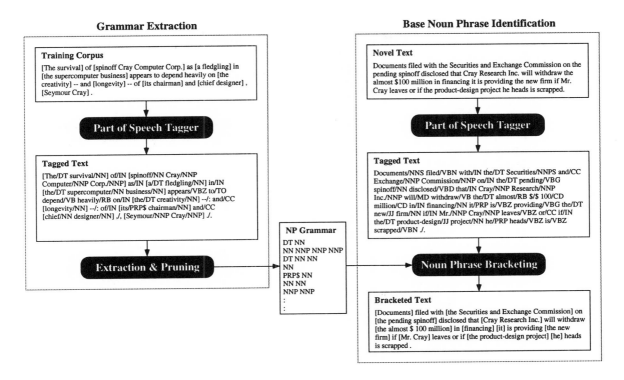

Figure 2: The Treebank Approach to Base NP Identification

1. Using any available part-of-speech tagger, assign a part-of-speech tag t_i to each word w_i in the training corpus.

2. Extract from each base noun phrase $b_{(i,j)}$ in the training corpus its sequence of part-of-speech tags $t_i, \ldots, t_j$ to form base NP rules, one rule per base NP.

3. Remove any duplicate rules.

The resulting grammar can then be used to identify base NPs in a novel text using a "longest-match" heuristic:

1. Assign part-of-speech tags $t_1, t_2, \ldots$ to the input words $w_1, w_2, \ldots$

2. Proceed through the tagged text from left to right, at each point matching the NP rules against the remaining part-of-speech tags $t_i, t_{i+1}, \ldots$ in the text.

3. If there are multiple rules that match beginning at t_i, use the longest matching rule R. Add the new base noun phrase $b_{(i,i+|R|-1)}$ to the set of base NPs. Continue matching at $t_{i+|R|}$.

Unfortunately, these extracted grammars pick up many "bad" rules due to noise in the training data (including annotation errors, part-of-speech tagging errors, and genuine ambiguities). The framework therefore includes a pruning phase whose goal is to eliminate bad rules from the grammar.

Error-Driven Pruning

At a high level, the pruning phase estimates the accuracy of each rule in the grammar using an unseen base NP corpus (the *pruning corpus*); it then eliminates rules with unacceptable performance. This process is illustrated in Figure 3. Like the training corpus, the pruning corpus is annotated with base noun phrases. Initially ignoring the NP annotations, the pruning algorithm first applies the bracketing procedure to the pruning corpus to identify its NPs. The proposed NPs are then compared to the original NPs. Performance of the rule set is measured in terms of labeled precision (P):

$$P = \frac{\text{\# of correct proposed NPs}}{\text{\# of proposed NPs}}$$

We then assign to each rule a score that denotes the "net benefit" achieved by the rule during parsing of the pruning corpus. The benefit of rule r is given by

$$B_r = C_r - E_r$$

where C_r is the number of NPs correctly identified by r, and E_r is the number of precision errors for which r is responsible. This benefit measure is identical to that used in transformation-based learning (Brill 1995) to select an ordered set of useful transformations. The benefit scores from evaluation on the pruning corpus are used to rank the rules in the grammar. With such a ranking, we can improve the rule set by discarding the worst rules. The pruning procedure is then repeated on the resulting rule set.

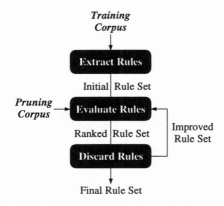

Figure 3: Pruning the Base NP Grammar

We have investigated two iterative approaches for discarding rules, a *thresholding* approach and an *incremental* approach. At each pruning iteration, thresholding discards rules whose score is less than a predefined threshold T. For all of our experiments, we set $T = 1$ to select rules that propose more correct bracketings than incorrect. Threshold pruning repeats until no rules have a score less than T. For our evaluation, this typically requires only four to five iterations. Incremental pruning is a more fine-grained method of discarding rules. At each iteration, incremental pruning discards the N worst rules. In all of our experiments, we set $N = 10$. Incremental pruning repeats until it finds the rule set that maximizes precision on the pruning corpus.

Lexicalization

As noted in the introduction, lexicalized representations have been shown to uniformly increase the accuracy of automated approaches to a variety of natural language learning tasks including syntactic parsing (e.g. Collins (1996), Charniak (1997)), part-of-speech tagging (e.g. Brill (1995)), named entity identification (e.g. Bikel *et al.* (1997)), and word-sense disambiguation (e.g. Ng & Lee (1996)). Ramshaw & Marcus (1998), for example, find that lexicalization accounts for a 2.7% increase in recall and precision for base noun phrase identification. As a result, we believe that lexicalization will also improve the accuracy of the base NP bracketer described above. This section describes lexicalization of the treebank approach to base noun phrase identification.

At a high level, lexicalization uses information about the words in each potential noun phrase bracket to decide how reasonable the bracket is. In our framework, the most straightforward means for incorporating lexical information is to extract a word-based grammar from the training corpus rather than a tag-based grammar. The word-level rules, however, exhibit severe sparse data problems: matching on an exact sequence of words is too strict. Instead, we propose to first find potential brackets using the tag-based grammar, and then use lexical information to further inform the final bracket choices.

More specifically, the goal of the lexicalized bracketer is to use lexical information to assign to each candidate NP bracket b a score $S(b)$, meant to loosely indicate the bracket's likelihood of occurrence.[1] The set of candidate brackets with their scores can be viewed as a weighted graph. Figure 4 shows such a graph (but without arc weights) for the short sentence *Stock prices increased 5 percent yesterday morning.*

- Vertices denote inter-word boundaries. Since the sentence contains seven words, the graph contains eight vertices.

- Weighted "bracket" arcs denote potential NP brackets. For example, *stock* is contained in two bracket arcs: one for the bracket [*stock*] from vertex 0 to 1 and another for [*stock prices*] from 0 to 2.

- Weighted "nonbracket" arcs denote individual words that are not part of any noun phrase bracket. For example, the word *stock* also has a nonbracket arc *stock/NN* from 0 to 1. This allows for the possibility that the word is better off in no NP bracket at all.

In this bracket graph, any path from the source to the sink represents a base NP bracketing of the sentence. For the best combination of brackets, we find the path having the maximum product of arc weights.

Note that the role of pruning for the lexicalized grammars is unclear: both pruning and lexicalization are attempts to increase the performance of a tag sequence grammar. The addition of probabilities to rules — the norm for most lexicalized grammars — is generally believed to preclude the need for pruning rules from the grammar. We investigate the role of pruning for the lexicalized grammars in the Evaluation section.

In the paragraphs below, we provide the remaining details for lexicalizing the treebank approach to base noun phrase identification: the scoring functions used to weight bracket and non-bracket arcs; parameter selection for the lexicalization scoring; and the algorithm for finding the best path through the graph.

Computing a Score for Base NP Bracket Arcs.
To score a potential base NP bracket, we consider both the tag sequence r (the rule), and the word sequence p (the phrase), that comprise the bracket. Further, we assume that the first and last words, u and v, of a bracketed phrase are the most informative; thus we drop other words and use (u, v) to approximate p.[2] The score $S(b)$ of a bracket is then a linear combination of several scoring functions that employ frequencies derived from the training corpus. First, there is a score

---

[1]In future work it may be appropriate to formulate a true probabilistic model of the likelihood that a candidate b is or is not an actual NP; in this work we consider only the much simpler scoring function presented here.

[2]In fact, this simplified instance representation $b = (r, u, v)$ performs comparably to one that considers all the words in a phrase as a set of modifiers M with head h.

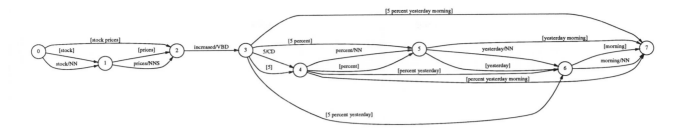

Figure 4: Possible Bracketings of *Stock prices increased 5 percent yesterday morning*

for the rule r.

$$S(r) = \frac{\text{\# of base NPs with tag sequence } r}{\text{\# of occurrences of tag sequence } r}$$

Second, there is a score for the words u, v.

$$S_r(u, v) = \frac{\substack{\text{\# of base NPs with tag sequence } r, \\ \text{first word } u, \text{ and second word } v}}{\text{\# of base NPs with tag sequence } r}$$

Since there are not very many training occurrences of brackets with the same rule, first, and last words, we combine $S_r(u, v)$ with similarly computed scores $S_r(u)$ and $S_r(v)$, considering u and v each with r individually.

Last, motivated by the surprising success of the longest-match heuristic, we add a length score $|r|/R$, where R is the maximum rule length. The complete score function is as follows.

$$S(b) = \lambda_r S(r) + \lambda_p [S_r(u, v) + S_r(u) + S_r(v)] + \lambda_l \frac{|r|}{R}$$

Note that the three parameters allow us to determine the right contribution for each source of information. The parameters are constrained to sum to 1.

Computing a Score for Non-Bracket Arcs. The score of a nonbracket arc n is a similar combination of scores for the arc's tag t and word w.

$$S(n) = \lambda_t S(t) + \lambda_w S_t(w)$$

where the tag and word scores are as follows.

$$S(t) = \frac{\substack{\text{\# of times tag } t \text{ appears} \\ \text{outside of a base NP}}}{\text{\# of occurrences of tag } t}$$

$$S_t(w) = \frac{\substack{\text{\# of times tag } t \text{ and word } w \\ \text{appear outside of a base NP}}}{\substack{\text{\# of times tag } t \text{ appears} \\ \text{outside of a base NP}}}$$

Parameter Selection. The values for λ_r, λ_p, λ_l, λ_t, and λ_w were selected automatically by comparing the performance of 44 selected combinations of parameter settings on the pruning corpus. The following combinations of bracket parameters (11) and nonbracket parameters (4) considered.

λ_r	0.8	0.1	0.1	0.6	0.5	0.5	0.3	0.4	0.5	0.4	0.33
λ_p	0.1	0.8	0.1	0.2	0.3	0.2	0.2	0.2	0.1	0.1	0.33
λ_l	0.1	0.1	0.8	0.2	0.2	0.3	0.5	0.4	0.4	0.5	0.33
λ_t	0.25	0.50	0.75	0.85							
λ_w	0.75	0.50	0.25	0.15							

Finding the Best Base NP Bracketing. We find the best path through the bracket graph using standard dynamic programming techniques. However, since different paths in the graph have different lengths (measured in number of arcs), each bracket arc score is first normalized for length: $\sqrt[|r|]{S(b)}$. This essentially makes a bracket that contains five words look like five single word arcs; thus it can be fairly compared to paths containing more but shorter arcs.

Compared to the quick linear time longest-match bracketer, the lexicalized bracketer is theoretically slower, since it compares multiple bracketings of the sentence. In practice, however, the number of alternative bracketings at any point is quite small and the lexicalized bracketer is only two or three times slower than the longest-match version.

Evaluation

We evaluated the lexicalized treebank grammars using the base NP corpora from our original study. The "Complex" corpus attempts to duplicate the base NPs used in the Ramshaw & Marcus study. The "Simple" corpus contains slightly less complicated base NPs — ones that may be better suited for use in some NLP applications, e.g., information extraction and information retrieval. In short, each Complex base NP corresponds to a non-recursive noun phrase in the Treebank parse. The Simple corpus further simplifies some of the Treebank base NPs by removing ambiguities that other components of the NLP system can be expected to handle: base NPs that contain conjunctions, prepositions, and leading or trailing adverbs and verbs are simplified.

The training, pruning, and testing sets are derived from the 25 sections of Wall Street Journal distributed with the Penn Treebank II. All experiments employ 5-fold cross validation. More specifically, the 25 sections are divided into five folds (sections 00–04, 05–09, and so on). In each of five runs, a different fold is used for testing the final, pruned rule set; three of the remaining

Corpus	Lexicalized Unpruned	Unlexicalized Unpruned	Pruned
Complex	88.7P/90.1R	18.3P/35.3R	88.7P/90.4R
Simple	91.5P/92.6R	22.1P/45.7R	92.1P/93.1R

Table 1: Performance of the Initial Lexicalized Grammar

Corpus	Lexicalized Unpruned	Threshold	Incremental	Baseline	Unlexicalized Incremental
Complex	88.7P/90.1R	87.4P/90.5R	89.0P/90.9R	88.4P/90.5R	88.7P/90.4R
Simple	91.5P/92.6R	90.8P/93.2R	91.9P/93.6R	91.4P/93.1R	92.1P/93.1R

Table 2: The Effect of Pruning on the Lexicalized Grammar

folds comprise the training corpus (to create the initial rule set); and the fifth fold is the pruning corpus (which is also used for parameter selection). All results are averages across the five runs. Performance is measured in terms of precision and recall. Precision was described earlier — it is a standard measure of accuracy. Recall, on the other hand, is an attempt to measure coverage:

$$P = \frac{\# \text{ of correct proposed NPs}}{\# \text{ of proposed NPs}}$$

$$R = \frac{\# \text{ of correct proposed NPs}}{\# \text{ of NPs in the annotated text}}$$

We first evaluate the performance of the initial (i.e. unpruned) lexicalized grammars in Table 1. Not surprisingly, the lexicalized grammar (first column of results) is much more accurate than the initial unlexicalized grammar (column two) for both base NP data sets. When compared to the much simpler, unlexicalized grammars that were pruned using the incremental method (column three), however, we see slightly different results from the two corpora. For the Simple corpus, the lexicalized grammar performs somewhat below (−0.6P/−0.5R) the unlexicalized, but pruned, grammar of the original base NP study.[3] For the Complex corpus, the lexicalized grammar performs just comparably (+0.0P/−0.3R) to the unlexicalized pruned grammar. In general, these results suggest that lexicalization is not critical for recognizing very simple, relatively unambiguous constituents: For the simple base NP task, pruning appears to serve much the same function as lexicalization, in that both suppress the application of bad rules. Pruning, however, preserves the simplicity of the grammar and bracketing procedure. But as the complexity of the linguistic task increases, the importance of lexical information increases as well.

Given the strong performance of the initial lexicalized grammar, it is especially unclear whether pruning will have any effect for the lexicalized grammars. No existing statistical parsers for probabilistic context-free grammars, for example, include a grammar pruning

---

[3]The results in the second and third columns of Table 1 differ slightly from those given in Cardie & Pierce (1998), due to changes in the training data.

step: it is assumed that the rule and lexical probabilities will effectively ignore "bad" rules. Table 2 shows our results for pruned lexicalized grammars. First, we see that the coarser threshold pruning (column two of results) performs worse than incremental pruning (column three) for both corpora. Not surprisingly, we originally showed that this result also holds for the unlexicalized grammars. When compared to the unpruned grammar (column one), threshold pruning lowers precision (−1.0) but raises recall (+0.5) for both corpora. Incremental pruning, on the other hand, increases both precision and recall (up to +0.4P/+1.0R) for both corpora, making the lexicalized grammar slightly better (for Complex) or just below (for Simple) the unlexicalized grammar (column five). Finally, incremental pruning yields better grammars than a baseline pruning strategy (column four) that discards all rules occurring only once during training as Charniak (1996) does.

That pruning can improve lexicalized grammars was unexpected: pruning considers each rule as an atomic source of errors — it does not prune the lexicalized versions of each rule independently. We believed that this might ultimately harm overall performance since lexicalized rules may vary in accuracy depending on the lexical content of the candidate bracket. Indeed, the more coarse-grained threshold pruning caused a drop in precision, while the finer-grained incremental pruning ultimately yielded an increase in performance. This suggests that a still more fine-grained pruning strategy — one that distinguishes the effects of the lexical content of candidate phrases — could be successfully employed with the lexicalized grammars.

The results in Table 2 were obtained using the parameter settings automatically selected on the pruning corpus. The final settings for all folds and for both corpora were $\lambda_r = 0.5, \lambda_p = 0.1, \lambda_l = 0.4, \lambda_t = 0.75, \lambda_w = 0.25$. Note that the value for λ_p — the lexical weight — is surprisingly low. In particular, λ_r indicates that the tag sequence rule scores are more important than the lexical information; while λ_l suggests that the "common-wisdom" heuristic of longest-match is actually quite relevant for this task. Accordingly, we evaluate the overall contribution of different sources of information in Ta-

Corpus	Rule Score + Length Score + Word Score	Rule Score + Length Score	Rule Score Only
Complex	88.7P/90.1R	88.2P/89.8R	84.7P/88.7R
Simple	91.5P/92.6R	91.6P/92.7R	88.5P/91.5R

Table 3: The Contribution of Sources of Information to a Lexicalized Base NP Grammar

		No	Yes
Context	Yes	Memory-Based 91.6P/91.6R	Transformation-Based 93.1P/93.5R
	No	Treebank-LM 88.7P/90.4R	Treebank-Lex 89.0P/90.9R

Lexical Information

Table 4: Comparison of error-driven pruning of treebank grammars, transformation-based learning, and memory-based learning in terms of available knowledge sources for local context and lexical information

ble 3. The first column repeats the unpruned lexicalized grammar results. The second column shows results for the grammar without lexical information ($\lambda_p = \lambda_t = 0$). Then in the third column, the length term is also removed ($\lambda_l = 0$), leaving just the rule scores. The table shows that the longest-match heuristic contributes more to performance (more than 3.1P/1.1R) than lexical information (up to 0.5P/0.3R) for both corpora.

We conclude this section with examples from the Complex corpus that indicate the qualitative difference in performance between the unlexicalized (U) and lexicalized (L) versions of the base NP bracketer. The correct bracketing (C) is shown first for each example. In particular, note that the lexicalized bracketer correctly handles ambiguities that fool the original bracketer, such as some gerunds and conjunctions. And in cases where both bracketers err, the lexicalized one may produce more reasonable brackets.

C: *representing [general and administrative expenses]*
U: *[representing general and administrative expenses]*
L: *representing [general and administrative expenses]*

C: *[his previous real-estate investment and asset-management duties]*
U: *[his previous real-estate investment] and [asset-management duties]*
L: *[his previous real-estate investment and asset-management duties]*

C: *[president] and [chief operating officer]*
U: *[president and chief] operating [officer]*
L: *[president and chief operating officer]*

Comparison with Competing Approaches and Conclusions

To our knowledge, four different approaches to base noun phrase recognition have now been evaluated with respect to similar base NP corpora derived from the Penn Treebank — Ramshaw & Mar-

cus's transformation-based bracketer, Argamon *et al.*'s MBSL, and the original and lexicalized versions of the treebank approach. As a result, we are now able to compare more or less directly a collection of trainable, corpus-based bracketing algorithms. In general, each method relies on slightly different information from the training corpus as depicted in Table 4. The Transformation-Based learner uses both lexical information and the surrounding context to make decisions about bracket boundary placement. MBSL's Memory-Based approach captures context in its tiles, but uses no lexical information. Our new lexicalized treebank grammar (Treebank-Lex) uses lexical information to score potential brackets, but no context. Finally, the simplest longest-match bracketer (Treebank-LM) uses neither lexical information nor context.

The results in Table 4 were not obtained on the same breakdown of training and test data; nevertheless, we can still attempt to glean from the table the role of context and lexicalization for base noun phrase identification. As we might expect, methods that employ lexical information perform better than those that do not; and methods that employ contextual information perform better than those that do not. The Transformation-Based bracketer, employing both, performs best in this group of algorithms. Comparing MBSL with Treebank-Lex, we might conclude that contextual information is more important than lexical information for base NP identification. However, MBSL has the added advantage of its ability to generalize its training data at recognition time.

In addition to performance differences, the four methods also vary in practical ways. For example, the Transformation-Based bracketer requires the most training time, with one pass through the training data for each candidate template for each new transformation. The Treebank methods need only a handful to a few hundred passes for pruning, while MBSL trains in a single pass over the training data. Regarding runtime speed, the Treebank-LM bracketer is the fastest, using a quick linear time algorithm. The Transformation-Based bracketer can be equally fast, provided that the transformation rules are precompiled into a single finite-state transducer (Roche & Schabes 1997). The Treebank-Lex bracketer is theoretically much slower than Treebank-LM due to its strategy of comparing multiple bracketings; but in practice it is only two to three times as slow. We believe MBSL to be the slowest bracketer, comparing multiple tiling covers to score each potential NP. In addition, the runtime space burden for MBSL is very large because the memory-base stores the entire training corpus. In contrast, the Transformation-Based and Treebank bracketers store only a few thousand transformation or grammar rules at runtime. Finally, in terms of portability, the two Treebank approaches are the only ones of the four that construct a grammar that may be modified for new genres of text without retraining.

In conclusion, we began with a simple and practical approach — treebank-derived tag-sequence grammars — for identifying simple syntactic phrases such as base noun phrases. We adapted this approach to incorporate lexical information into the selection of NP brackets, demonstrating its effectiveness for improving the accuracy of such grammars. We also showed that grammar pruning independently fulfills much the same function as lexicalization, reducing the impact of the noisiness of the training corpus, and in some cases proving to be more useful than lexical preferences. Somewhat surprisingly, we found that lexicalization and pruning can even be applied together with slightly increased performance over using them separately. Finally, we investigated the contributions of knowledge sources for the base noun phrase recognition task. For simple phrases, lexical information plays less of a role than expected; for complex phrases, lexicalization is more important; and the longest-match heuristic is quite useful for both simple and complex noun phrases. Although we focused only on base noun phrase recognition, we believe our results have implications for other probabilistic grammar-based approaches to natural language processing.

Acknowledgments. This work was supported in part by NSF Grants IRI–9624639 and GER–9454149. We thank Mitre for providing their part-of-speech tagger.

References

Argamon, S.; Dagan, I.; and Krymolowski, Y. 1998. A Memory-Based Approach to Learning Shallow Natural Language Patterns. In *Proceedings of the 36th Annual Meeting of the ACL and COLING-98*, 67–73. Association for Computational Linguistics.

Bikel, D.; Miller, S.; Schwartz, R.; and Weischedel, R. 1997. Nymble: A High-Performance Learning Name-Finder. In *Proceedings of the Fifth Conference on Applied Natural Language Processing*, 194–201. San Francisco, CA: Morgan Kaufmann.

Bourigault, D. 1992. Surface Grammatical Analysis for the Extraction of Terminological Noun Phrases. In *Proceedings, COLING-92*, 977–981.

Brill, E. 1995. Transformation-Based Error-Driven Learning and Natural Language Processing: A Case Study in Part-of-Speech Tagging. *Computational Linguistics* 21(4):543–565.

Cardie, C., and Pierce, D. 1998. Error-Driven Pruning of Treebank Grammars for Base Noun Phrase Identification. In *Proceedings of the 36th Annual Meeting of the ACL and COLING-98*, 218–224. Association for Computational Linguistics.

Charniak, E. 1996. Treebank Grammars. In *Proceedings of the Thirteenth National Conference on Artificial Intelligence*, 1031–1036. Portland, OR: AAAI Press / MIT Press.

Charniak, E. 1997. Statistical Parsing with a Context-free Grammar and Word Statistics. In *Proceedings of the Fourteenth National Conference on Artificial Intelligence*, 598–603. American Association for Artificial Intelligence.

Church, K. 1988. A Stochastic Parts Program and Noun Phrase Parser for Unrestricted Text. In *Proceedings of the Second Conference on Applied Natural Language Processing*, 136–143. Association for Computational Linguistics.

Collins, M. 1996. A New Statistical Parser Based on Bigram Lexical Dependencies. In *Proceedings of the 34th Annual Meeting of the ACL*, 184–191. Association for Computational Linguistics.

Justeson, J. S., and Katz, S. M. 1995. Technical Terminology: Some Linguistic Properties and an Algorithm for Identification in Text. *Natural Language Engineering* 1:9–27.

Marcus, M.; Marcinkiewicz, M.; and Santorini, B. 1993. Building a Large Annotated Corpus of English: The Penn Treebank. *Computational Linguistics* 19(2):313–330.

Ng, H., and Lee, H. 1996. Integrating Multiple Knowledge Sources to Disambiguate Word Sense: An Examplar-Based Approach. In *Proceedings of the 34th Annual Meeting of the ACL*, 40–47. Association for Computational Linguistics.

Ramshaw, L. A., and Marcus, M. P. 1998. Text chunking using transformation-based learning. In *Natural Language Processing Using Very Large Corpora*. Kluwer. Originally appeared in WVLC95, 82–94.

Roche, E., and Schabes, Y. 1997. Deterministic Part-of-Speech Tagging with Finite-State Transducers. In *Finite-State Language Processing*. The MIT Press. 205–239.

Stanfill, C., and Waltz, D. 1986. Toward Memory-based Reasoning. *Communications of the ACM* 29:1213–1228.

Voutilainen, A. 1993. NPTool, A Detector of English Noun Phrases. In *Proceedings of the Workshop on Very Large Corpora*, 48–57. Association for Computational Linguistics.

Two Dimensional Generalization in Information Extraction

Joyce Yue Chai
30 Saw Mill River Rd.
IBM T. J. Watson Research Center
Hawthorne, NY 10532
jchai@us.ibm.com

Alan W. Biermann
Computer Science Department
Duke University,
Durham, NC 27708
awb@cs.duke.edu

Curry I. Guinn
3400 Cornwallis Rd.
Research Triangle Institute
RTP, NC 27709
cig@rti.org

Abstract

In a user-trained information extraction system, the cost of creating the rules for information extraction can be greatly reduced by maximizing the effectiveness of user inputs. If the user specifies one example of a desired extraction, our system automatically tries a variety of generalizations of this rule including generalizations of the terms and permutations of the ordering of significant words. Where modifications of the rules are successful, those rules are incorporated into the extraction set. The theory of such generalizations and a measure of their usefulness is described.

Introduction

Information extraction (IE) has become a promising area since the advent of the DARPA Message Understanding Conferences (Cowie & Lehnert 1996). Given the vast amount of information available today, successful extraction of useful information has become increasingly important. Most IE systems (MUC6 1995) have used hand-crafted semantic resources for each application domain. However, generation of this domain specific knowledge (i.e., customization) unfortunately requires highly expert computational linguists or developers and is also difficult, time consuming, and prone to error. To address this problem, some researchers have looked at techniques for automatically or semi-automatically constructing lexicons or extraction rules of annotated texts in the domain (Riloff 1993) (Riloff 1996) (Califf & Mooney 1997) (Soderland 1999). Most of these techniques have applied machine learning approaches to learn rules based on texts with filled templates. Either pre-annotation of text is done by a human expert, or the rules are post-processed by a human expert. To keep up with the vast amount of information available for casual users, techniques oriented toward non-experts are desired. By providing an easy training environment to the casual user and by learning rules from the user's input instead of pre-annotated texts, the cost of adapting a system to different domains can be reduced.

In this paper, a new trainable information extraction system is described (Chai 1998). In the new scenario, any user, based on his or her interests, can train the system on different domains. The system learns from the training and automatically outputs the structure target information. A major issue in learning rules concerns the tradeoff between specific, unambiguous extraction rules and the need for general rules that can be applied widely. The balance between those twin goals is essential for good performance.

In building a trainable information extraction system, the cost of creating the rules for information extraction can be greatly reduced by maximizing the effectiveness of user inputs. If the user specifies one example of a desired extraction, our system automatically tries a variety of generalizations of this rule including generalizations of the terms and permutations of the ordering of significant words. Where modifications of the rules are successful, those rules are incorporated into the extraction set. The theory of such generalizations and a measure of their usefulness is given in this paper.

System Overview

Our *T*rainable *Infor*M*ation* *E*xtraction *S*ystem (TIMES) includes four major subprocesses: Tokenization, Lexical Processing, Partial Parsing, and Rule Learning and Generalization (Bagga, Chai, & Biermann 1997). The general structure of TIMES is shown in Figure 1. The first stage of processing is carried out by the Tokenizer which segments the input text into sentences and words. Next, the Lexical Process acquires lexical syntactic/semantic information for the words. To achieve this, a Preprocessor is used for semantic classification. The Preprocessor can identify special semantic categories such as email and web addresses, file and directory names, dates, times, and dollar amounts, telephone numbers, zip codes, cities, states, countries, names of companies, and many others. The syntactic information is retrieved from the CELEX database[1] and the semantic information is from WordNet (Miller

---

[1] CELEX was developed by several universities and institutions in the Netherlands, and is distributed by the Linguistic Data Consortium.

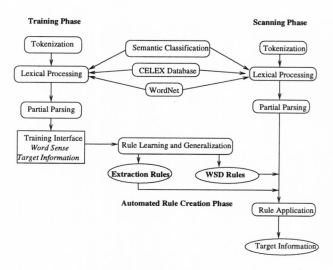

Training Phase

Tokenization

Lexical Processing

Partial Parsing

Training Interface
Word Sense
Target Information

Scanning Phase

Tokenization

Lexical Processing

Partial Parsing

Semantic Classification

CELEX Database

WordNet

Rule Learning and Generalization

Extraction Rules   WSD Rules

Automated Rule Creation Phase

Rule Application

Target Information

Figure 1: System Overview

1990). Following the Lexical Processing, a Partial Parser, which is based on a set of finite-state rules, is applied to produce a sequence of non-overlapping phrases as output. It identifies noun phrases (NG), verb phrases(VG) and prepositions (PG). The last word of each phrase is identified as its headword. The phrases, together with their syntactic and semantic information are used in Rule Learning and Generalization. Based on the training examples, the system automatically acquires and generalizes a set of rules for future use.

The system has three running modes which implement training, automated rule creation, and scanning, respectively. In the training phase, the user is required to train the system on sample documents based on his/her interests. That is, the user specifically points out the desired information in the text. Because the WordNet hierarchy depends on word senses, in the training phase, the system also requires some semantic tagging by the user. This phase tends to use minimum linguistic and domain knowledge so that it can be used by the casual user. The rule creation phase builds a set of useful rules, including both extraction rules for information of interest and word sense disambiguation (WSD) rules for sense identification. The scanning phase applies the learned rules to any new body of text in the domain.

The Training Phase TIMES provides a convenient training interface for the user. Through this interface, the user identifies the information of interest (i.e., the target information). One issue in training is the trade-off between the user's effort and the system's learning cost. TIMES requires some minimum training from the user. This training identifies the target information for the training articles and assigns the correct sense to the words if their senses are not used as sense one in WordNet. (Sense one is the most frequently used sense in WordNet. The training interface provides sense definitions so that the user would know which sense to

choose.) By default, the system will assign sense one to the headwords if no other specific sense is given by the user. If the user performs the minimum training, then the system will learn the rules based on every phrase in the training sentences, and the resulting learning cost will be relatively high. If besides the minimum training, the user decides to select the important phrases from the training examples, then the rules can be learned based only on the important phrases. Thus the training effort is increased, and the system learning cost is reduced. Furthermore, if the user has sufficient expertise and decides to create rules for the system (the rules could be generated from the training articles or from the user's own knowledge), then more training effort is required and the system learning cost is further reduced. In general, to make the system easily and quickly adapted to a new domain, computational linguists and domain experts can apply their expertise if they prefer; casual users can provide the minimum training and rely on the system learning ability.

For example, suppose the training sentence is "The National Technology Group has a need for qualified Inventory Specialists to work at an RTP client site for one month." The user of our system will employ the interface to indicate the key target information in this sentence which is to be extracted. The target information is: companies which have job openings (use *COMPANY* to represent this target), positions available (*POSITION*), locations of those positions (*LOCATION*). Based on the user's input, the system internally generates a record as shown in Table 1. In this table, the first column lists seven important phrases from the sentence; the second column is the target information specified by the user. If a phrase is identified as a type of target information, then this phrase is called *target phrase*. For example, "The National Technology Group," "qualified Inventory Specialist" and "an RTP client site" are three target phrases. The third column lists the specific semantic types classified by the Preprocessor for each important phrase. The fourth column lists the headwords for the important phrases. If a phrase can be identified as a special semantic type, then the headword is the name for that semantic type; otherwise, the headword is the last word in the phrase. The fifth column lists the syntactic categories identified by the Partial Parser. The last column is the sense number for the headwords. From the information in Table 1, the system will create an initial template rule as shown in Figure 2 for doing extraction.

Specific Rules In general, rules in the system are pattern-action rules. The pattern, defined by the left hand side (LHS) of a rule, is a conjunction (expressed by $\wedge$) of *subsumption functions* $S(X, \alpha, target(\alpha))$. X is instantiated by a new phrase when the rule is applied; α is the concept corresponding to the headword of an important phrase in the training sentence; and $target(\alpha)$ is the type of target information identified for α. The action in the right hand side (RHS) of a

important phrases	target	semantic type	headword	syntactic category	sense
The National Technology Group	COMPANY	company_type	company	NG	1
has	none	none	has	VG	1
a need	none	none	need	NG	1
for	none	none	for	PG	1
qualified Inventory Specialists	POSITION	none	specialist	NG	1
at	none	none	at	PG	1
an RTP client site	LOCATION	none	site	NG	1

Table 1: Internal Structure for a Training Example. NG represents noun phrases; VG represents verb phrases and PG represents Prepositions

$$S(X_1, \{company\}, COMPANY) \wedge S(X_2, \{has\}, none) \wedge S(X_3, \{need\}, none) \wedge S(X_4, \{for\}, none)$$
$$\wedge S(X_5, \{specialist\}, POSITION) \wedge S(X_6, \{at\}, none) \wedge S(X_7, \{site\}, LOCATION)$$
$$\longrightarrow FS(X_1, COMPANY), FS(X_5, POSITION), FS(X_7, LOCATION)$$

Figure 2: Initial Template Rule /Most Specific Rule

rule, $FS(X, target(\alpha))$ fills a template slot, or in other words, assigns the type of target information $target(\alpha)$ to the phrase X.

The subsumption function $S(X, \alpha, target(\alpha))$ essentially looks for subsumption of concepts. It returns true if the headword of X is subsumed to the concept α. If all subsumption functions return true, then the RHS actions will take place to extract X as a type $target(\alpha)$. In the following sections, the subsumption function will be referred to as a *rule entity*.

For example, the initial template rule (i.e., the most specific rule) in Figure 2 says that if a pattern of phrases $X_1, X_2, ..., X_7$ is found in a sentence such that the headword of X_1 is subsumed by (or equal to) *company*, the headword of the second phrase X_2 is subsumed by *has*, and so on, then one has found the useful fact that X_1 is a *COMPANY*, X_5 is a *POSITION* and X_7 is a *LOCATION*. (In the most specific rule, the headwords of important phrases are used directly as α in subsumption functions. They are referred to as specific concepts.) Apparently, the initial template rule is very specific and has tremendous limitations. Since the occurrence of the exact same pattern rarely happens in the unseen data, the initial template rule is not very useful. We need to generalize these specific rules.

Rule Generalization

The above sections have shown how the initial template rule is created from a user input. Now we address the issue of how such rules are generalized. In fact, they are generalized by a two dimensional model which is a combination of syntactic (horizontal) and semantic (vertical) generalization.

Syntactic Generalization

From our early experiments, we noticed that the optimum number of entities required in the rules varied for different types of target information. In the job advertisement domain, when a token is classified as the dollar amount semantic type, it is the target salary information 95% of the time. A rule with one rule entity suffices. Rules with more entities are too specific and will lower the performance. For example, in Figure 2, by removing the second, the fourth, the sixth, and the seventh entity, the most specific rule becomes two rules with three entities in Figure 3. Since two target phrases remain and in our convention, each generalized rule only corresponds to one target phrase, two rules are necessary to capture two types of target information. When these two rules are applied for unseen data, the first one will extract the target information *COMPANY* and the second one will extract *POSITION*. On the other hand, since the number of constraints on the LHS are reduced, more target information will be identified. By this observation, removing entities from specific rules results in syntactically generalized rules.

Furthermore, syntactic generalization is also aimed at tackling paraphrase problems. For example, by reordering entities in the rule generated from the training sentence "Fox head Joe Smith ...", it can further process new sentence portions such as "Joe Smith, the head of Fox, ...", "The head of Fox, Joe Smith,...", "Joe Smith, Fox head,..." etc. This type of syntactic generalization is optional in the system. This technique is especially useful when the original specific rules are generated from the user's knowledge.

Therefore, syntactic generalization is designed to learn the appropriate number of entities, and the order of entities in a rule. By reordering and removing rule entities, syntactic generalization is achieved. More precisely, syntactic generalization is attained by a combination function and a permutation function. The combination function selects a subset of rule entities in the most specific rule to form new rules. The permutation function re-orders rule entities to form new rules.

Combination Function If a training sentence has n important phrases, then there are n corresponding

1. $S(X_1, \{company\}, COMPANY) \wedge S(X_2, \{need\}, none) \wedge S(X_3, \{specialist\}, POSITION)$
   $\longrightarrow FS(X_1, COMPANY)$
2. $S(X_1, \{company\}, COMPANY) \wedge S(X_2, \{need\}, none) \wedge S(X_3, \{specialist\}, POSITION)$
   $\longrightarrow FS(X_3, POSITION)$

Figure 3: An Example of Syntactically Generalized Rules

1. $S(X_1, \{need\}, none) \wedge S(X_2, \{specialist\}, POSITION) \wedge S(X_3, \{company\}, COMPANY)$
   $\longrightarrow FS(X_3, COMPANY)$
2. $S(X_1, \{need\}, none) \wedge S(X_2, \{specialist\}, POSITION) \wedge S(X_3, \{company\}, COMPANY)$
   $\longrightarrow FS(X_2, POSITION)$

Figure 4: An Example of Permutation Rules

rule entities, $e_1, ..., e_n$ (each e_i is a subsumption function). The combination function selects k rule entities and form the LHS of the rule as $e_{i_1} \wedge e_{i_2} .. \wedge e_{i_k}$ (the order of the entities is the same as the order of the corresponding phrases in the training sentences). At least one of k entities corresponds to a target phrase. If i ($1 < i \leq k$) entities are created from i target phrases, then i rules will be generated. These rules have the same LHS and different RHS, with each corresponding to one type of target information. Rules created by the combination function are named *combination rules*. For example, in Figure 3, $k = 3$ and $i = 2$, therefore, two rules are necessary to identify two different types of target information.

Permutation Function The permutation function generates new rules by permuting rule entities in the combination rules. This function creates rules for processing paraphrases. Rules created by the permutation function are named *permutation rules*. For example, the permutation function can generate rules in Figure 4 by re-ordering rule entities in Figure 3. While rules in Figure 3 are created based on the sentence "The National Technology Group has a need for qualified Inventory Specialist", the permutation rules can process a paraphrased sentence such as "There is a need for a Inventory Specialist at the National Technology Group."

Semantic Generalization

Syntactic generalization deals with the number and the order of the rule entities. However, each rule entity is still very specific. For a rule entity $S(X, \alpha, target(\alpha))$, semantic generalization is designed to replace α with a more general concept. Thus it will cover more semantically related instances. We use a generic lexical semantic resource, WordNet, for lexical semantic information (Chai & Biermann 1997b).

Concepts in WordNet A concept is defined in WordNet as a set of synonyms (synset). For a word w, the corresponding concept in WordNet is represented by $\{w, w_1, ..., w_n\}$, where each w_i is a synonym of w. Given a word w, its part-of-speech, and sense number,

the system can locate a unique corresponding concept in the WordNet hierarchy if w exists in WordNet. For a word, especially a proper noun, if the Preprocessor can identify it as a special semantic type expressed in a concept in WordNet, then a virtual link is created to make the concept of this special noun as the hyponym of that semantic type. For example, "IBM" is not in WordNet, however, it is categorized as a kind of $\{company\}$. The system first creates the concept of "IBM" as $\{IBM\}$, then creates a virtual link between $\{IBM\}$ and $\{company\}$. For any other word w, if it is not in WordNet, and it is not identified as any semantic type, then the concept of w is $\{w\}$ and is virtually put into WordNet, with no hierarchical structure. Therefore, every headword of an important phrase should have a corresponding concept in WordNet.

Let α be a concept in WordNet. The hypernym hierarchical structure provides a path for locating the superordinate concept of α, and it eventually leads to the most general concept above α. (WordNet is an acyclic structure, which suggests that a synset might have more than one hypernym. However, this situation doesn't happen often. In case it happens, the system selects the first hypernym path.)

Therefore, semantic generalization acquires the generalization for each rule entity by replacing the specific concept with a WordNet concept (Chai & Biermann 1997a). For example, rules in Figure 3 could be generalized to rules in Figure 5.

Two Dimensional Generalization

The two-dimensional generalization model is a combination of semantic (vertical) generalization and syntactic (horizontal) generalization. Our method applies a brute force algorithm, which performs semantic generalization on top of syntactically generalized rules generated from the training set, then apply those rules on the training set again. Based on the training examples and a threshold, the system selects useful rules.

The *relevancy_rate* $rel(r_i)$ for rule r_i is defined as the percentage of the correct information extracted by the r_i. A threshold is predefined to control the process. If

1. $S(X_1, \{group, ...\}, COMPANY) \land S(X_2, \{need, ...\}, none) \land S(X_3, \{professional, ...\}, POSITION)$
$\longrightarrow FS(X_1, COMPANY)$
2. $S(X_1, \{organization, ...\}, COMPANY) \land S(X_2, \{need, ...\}, none) \land S(X_3, \{engineer, ...\}, POSITION)$
$\longrightarrow FS(X_3, POSITION)$

Figure 5: An Example of Semantically Generalized Rules

$rel(r_i)$ is greater or equal to the threshold, then r_i will be put in the rule base for future use.

The procedure of generating generalized rules is the following:

- Predefine N, the maximum number of entities allowed in the rule.

- For each target phrase in the training sentence, based on the important phrases in the sentence, generate all combinations rules with number of entities from one to N, as well as their permutation rules.

- For every rule, generate all possible semantically generalized rules by replacing each entity with a more general entity with different degree of generalization.

- Apply all rules to the training set. Based on the training examples, compute relevancy_rate for each rule.

- Select rules with relevancy_rate above the defined threshold. If two rules r_1 and r_2 both have n entities, and if each entity of r_1 corresponds to a more general or the same concept as that of r_2, then the system will choose r_1 for future use if $rel(r_1)$ is greater than or equal to the threshold and eliminate r_2.

- Sort the rules with the same number of entities to avoid rule repetition.

By following this procedure, the system will generate a set of useful rules that are both syntactically and semantically generalized. Those rules will be applied to unseen documents. First, the system applies rules with N number of entities to the unseen sentence. If some matches are found, the system identifies the target information as that which is extracted by the most rules and then processes the next sentence. If there is no match, the system applies rules with fewer entities until either there are some matches or all the rules (including those with one entity) have been applied. By doing so, the system will first achieve the highest precision and then gradually increase recall without too much cost in precision. (Precision is the percentage of target information extracted by the system which is correct; recall is the percentage of target information from the text which is correctly extracted by the system.)

Experiments

Our experiments were conducted based on the domain of *triangle.jobs* newsgroup. Eight types of target information were extracted.

- COMPANY (COM.): The name of the company which has job openings.

- POSITION (POS.): The name of the available position.

- SALARY (SAL.): The salary, stipend, compensation information.

- LOCATION (LOC.): The state/city where the job is located.

- EXPERIENCE (EXP.): Years of experience.

- CONTACT (CON.): The phone number or email address for contact.

- SKILLS (SKI.): The specific skills required, such as programming languages, operating systems, etc.

- BENEFITS (BEN.): The benefits provided by the company, such as health, dental insurance,.. etc.

There were 24 articles for training and 40 articles for testing. These 64 articles were randomly selected. Training articles were grouped to three training sets. The first training set contained 8 articles; the second contained 16 articles including ones in the first set; the third training set consisted of all 24 articles. In all of the experiments, the relevancy_rate threshold was set to 0.8 unless specified otherwise. In addition to precision and recall, the F-measure was also computed, which is a combination of precision and recall (Sundheim 1992).

Syntactic Generalization

The first experiment tested the impact of pure syntactic generalization. The system only generated combination rules and permutation rules without semantic generalization. Table 2 shows that rules with pure syntactic generalization (represented by "*all*") achieve better performance (in terms of F-measure) than those rules with one, two or three fixed number of entities.

	one ent.	two ent.	three ent.	all
precision	80.0%	67.4%	67.8%	66.3%
recall	39.8%	54.2%	30.9%	63.9%
F-meas.	53.2%	60.1%	42.5%	65.1%

Table 2: Effect of Rules on All Target Information from Syntactic Generalization

In particular, different types of target information require different numbers of entities in the rules. As shown in Table 3, for the both target information COMPANY and EXPERIENCE, no rule with one entity was learned from the training set. For the target information *SALARY*, the rules with one entity performed much better (in terms of F-measure) than those with

h_{max}	0	1	2	3	4	5	no bound
precision	97.3%	96.5%	96.6%	96.3%	94.0%	92.7%	92.7%
recall	76.8%	77.1%	78.3%	79.2%	80.7%	81.3%	81.3%
F-measure	85.8%	85.7%	86.5%	86.9%	86.8%	86.8%	86.6%

Table 4: Training Set Performance with Respect to Limit of Semantic Generalization

h_{max}	0	1	2	3	4	5	no bound
precision	76.0%	71.0%	59.7%	52.9%	47.1%	44.2%	42.2%
recall	64.6%	67.5%	71.8%	73.3%	74.0%	74.3%	75.8%
F-measure	69.8%	69.2%	65.2%	61.4%	57.6%	55.4%	54.2%

Table 5: Testing Set Performance with Respect to Limit of Semantic Generalization

Fact	meas.	one entity	two entities	three entities	all
COM.	P	0%	76.5%	75.0%	65.9%
	R	0%	68.4%	71.1%	76.3%
	F	0%	72.2%	73.0%	70.7%
POS.	P	94.3%	71.9%	64.3%	76.4%
	R	51.6%	35.9%	14.1%	60.9%
	F	66.7%	47.9%	23.1%	67.8%
SAL.	P	91.7%	84.6%	100%	88.9%
	R	68.8%	34.4%	12.5%	75.0%
	F	78.6%	48.9%	28.1%	81.4%
LOC.	P	16.7%	33.7%	37.2%	32.0%
	R	2.7%	41.1%	21.9%	42.5%
	F	4.6%	37.0%	27.6%	36.5%
EXP.	P	0%	54.8%	53.6%	48.6%
	R	0%	54.8%	48.4%	54.8%
	F	0%	54.8%	50.9%	51.5%
CON.	P	97.6%	87.3%	91.7%	88.4%
	R	51.9%	71.4%	14.3%	79.2%
	F	67.8%	78.6%	24.7%	83.7%
SKI.	P	74.1%	75.0%	76.4%	71.7%
	R	61.3%	64.4%	41.7%	70.0%
	F	67.1%	69.3%	54.0%	70.8%
BEN.	P	90.0%	93.3%	100%	94.1%
	R	22.5%	35.0%	25.0%	40.0%
	F	36.0%	50.9%	40.0%	56.1%

Table 3: Effect of Rules on Target Information from Syntactic Generalization, where P is precision, R is recall, and F is F-measure.

two entities or three entities. For the target information *LOCATION*, the rules with two entities performed better than those of one entity and three entities. For the target information *COMPANY*, the rules with three entities perform the best. Thus, for different types of information, the best extraction requires different numbers of entities in the rules. However, the appropriate number of entities for each type of information is not known in advance. If applying rules with the fixed number of entities, a less than optimal number of entities will cause a significant loss in the performance. By ap-

plying our approach, for each type of information, the performance is either better (as in the SALARY row), or slightly worse (as in the COMPANY row). The overall performance of the application algorithm is better than that achieved by the rules with the fixed number of entities.

Two Dimensional Generalization

When the semantic generalization is added to the model, the evaluation of the effectiveness of WordNet becomes important. In this experiment, the system generated rules both syntactically and semantically. In those rules, some entities were only generalized to include the synonyms of the specific concept from the training sentence; some were generalized to direct hypernyms (one level above the specific concept in the conceptual hierarchy), and some were generalized to various higher degrees. The question is, even though the rules have been learned from the training examples, are they reliable? Do we need to put some upper bound on the generalization degree for the entities in order to achieve good performance? To answer that, we used h_{max} as the limit for the degree of generalization for each entity. We modified the rules to only generalize each entity to h_{max} level above the specific concept in WordNet hierarchy. We applied those rules (the threshold was 1.0) with different limitations on semantic generalization to the 24 training documents and 40 testing documents.

As in Table 4, for the training set, with no upper bound on semantic generalization degree in the rules, the system had an overall 86.6% F-measure, with very high (92.7%) precision. When the various limits on the generalization degree were applied, the performance was still about the same. This indicated that the rules were indeed learned from the training examples, and these rules sufficiently represented the training examples.

We then applied the same set of rules on the testing data. As shown in Table 5, without an upper bound on the semantic generalization, the system only achieved an F-measure of 54.2%. However, when the upper bound on the degree of generalization was $h_{max} = 0$, which only generalized the entities to include the synonyms of the specific concepts, the overall performance was about 70%. The results indicated further restriction on the semantic generalization degree could enhance the performance. WordNet hypernyms are useful in achieving high recall, but with a high cost in precision. WordNet synonyms and direct hypernyms are particularly useful in balancing the tradeoff between precision and recall and thus improving the overall performance.

training articles	8	16	24
precision	61.5%	66.7%	66.3%
recall	48.8%	61.8%	63.9%
F-measure	54.4%	64.2%	65.1%

Table 6: Performance vs. Training Effort from Syntactic Generalization

training articles	8	16	24
precision	68.8%	70.2%	71.0%
recall	59.8%	65.2%	67.5%
F-measure	64.0%	68.0%	69.2%

Table 7: Performance vs. Training Effort from Two Dimensional Generalization

We compared the experimental results from rules with pure syntactic generalization and the rules with two dimensional generalization (with a limit of $h_{max} = 1$ on the semantic generalization). As shown in Table 6 and Table 7, when the training set is small, the semantic generalization can be particularly helpful. The F-measure increased about 10% when the training set only had eight articles. The F-measure for training 16 articles is about the same as that from training 24 articles. Thus no more training is necessary. This result implies that for the two-dimensional rule generalization approach, there is a performance upper bound in this domain. If we would like to break this upper bound, generalizing only concepts and orders of the rules may not be enough. We should approach other strategies for generalization. For example, verb forms could be generalized to verb nominalization forms.

The semantic generalization can be particularly effective for extracting certain types of information. Comparing Table 3 and Table 8, we can see that the semantic generalization is especially useful for extracting both LOCATION and BENEFITS facts. The performance was improved about 30% in F-measure for those two facts.

Discussion

Automated rule learning from examples can also be found in other systems such as AutoSlog (Riloff 1993), PALKA (Kim & Moldovan 1993), RAPIER (Califf & Mooney 1997) and WHISK (Soderland 1999). AutoSlog

Fact	meas.	one entity	two entity	three entity	all
COM.	P	0%	71.8%	71.4%	67.4%
	R	0%	75.7%	81.1%	83.8%
	F	0%	73.7%	75.9%	74.7%
POS.	P	94.3%	69.8%	57.1%	72.3%
	R	51.6%	46.9%	25.0%	53.1%
	F	66.7%	56.1%	34.8%	61.2%
SAL.	P	92.0%	84.6%	100%	88.5%
	R	71.9%	34.4%	12.5%	71.9%
	F	80.7%	48.9%	22.2%	80.2%
LOC.	P	25.0%	63.3%	66.7%	59.4%
	R	1.4%	78.1%	63.0%	78.1%
	F	2.7%	69.9%	64.8%	67.5%
EXP.	P	0%	42.9%	51.4%	40.4%
	R	0%	54.5%	57.6%	57.6%
	F	0%	48.0%	54.3%	47.5%
CON.	P	83.3%	86.4%	78.6%	81.8%
	R	51.9%	74.0%	14.3%	81.8%
	F	64.0%	79.7%	27.1%	81.8%
SKI.	P	33.3%	66.9%	67.9%	63.0%
	R	1.9%	71.4%	57.8%	70.8%
	F	3.59%	69.1%	62.4%	66.7%
BEN.	P	95.8%	95.7%	100%	96.8%
	R	57.5%	55.0%	42.5%	75.0%
	F	71.9%	69.9%	60.0%	84.5%

Table 8: Effect of Rules on Target Information from Two Dimensional Generalization

uses heuristics to create rules from the examples and then requires the human expert to accept or reject the rules. PALKA applies a conceptual hierarchy to control the generalization or specification of the target slot. RAPIER uses inductive logic programming to learn the patterns that characterizes slot-fillers and their context. WHISK learns the rules by starting with a seed example and then selectively adding terms that appear in the seed example to a rule.

TIMES differentiates itself in the sense that it learns rules by interleaving syntactic generalization and semantic generalization. It automatically decides the number, the order and the generalization/specification of constraints. It learns these three aspects in each rule while other systems concentrate on one or two aspects. Furthermore, most of those systems focus on the improvement of performance by refining learning techniques in an environment of large databases of examples. TIMES is designed to provide a paradigm where rule learning makes it possible to build an IE system based on minimum training by a casual user. Indeed, TIMES emphasizes the usability to the casual user. When a large amount of pre-annotated information is not available and when the user is not experienced enough to tag the information, how does one make an IE system effective based on minimum training? In our experiments, we intentionally chose a small training set since for a casual user, large amount of training is difficult. The experimental results suggest that the two dimensional generalization obtains reasonable performance while the effort and time involved in the training is dramatically reduced.

Most information extraction systems are created based on hand-crafted domain specific knowledge. This is because the lexical semantic definitions given by the generic resources sometimes cannot meet the actual needs of the specific domain. No use is made of existing general lexical semantic resources by any of the MUC systems. NYU's MUC-4 system (Grishman, Macleod, & Sterling 1992) made some attempt at using WordNet for semantic classification. However, they ran into the problem of automated sense disambiguation because the WordNet hierarchy is sense dependent. As a result, they gave up using WordNet. TIMES attempts to integrate WordNet with WSD techniques (Chai & Biermann 1999). The use of WordNet hypernyms in the two-dimensional generalization could raise the recall performance from 65% to 76% (see Table 5) at the cost of precision. However, we found that the WordNet synonyms and the direct hypernyms are particularly useful in balancing the tradeoff between the precision and recall. The use of WordNet enhanced overall performance by 5%. Despite the typographical errors, incorrect grammars and rare abbreviations in the free text collection which make information extraction more difficult, in this domain, the two-dimensional generalization model based on both syntactic generalization and semantic generalization achieved about 69% (see Table 7) F-measure in overall performance.

Conclusion

This paper presents the basic machinery for creating an efficient synthesizer of information extraction systems. The user can start with a basic system and an extraction problem in mind and create the rules necessary to do the extraction from hand-entered examples. If the problem is no more difficult than the domain described here, then only eight to sixteen example articles must be hand-processed to obtain F-measure in the 60-70 percent range. With a well designed GUI, these examples can be done in just a few minutes each, and the total user investment will be approximately two hours. The result will be a set of rules that have numbers of entities, orderings of the entities, and levels of generalization automatically specialized to optimally extract each fact of interest from a large database.

Acknowledgements

We would like to thank Amit Bagga for developing Tokenizer and Preprocessor. We would also like to thank Jerry Hobbs for providing us with the finite state rules for the Partial Parser. This work was supported in part by an IBM Fellowship.

References

Bagga, A.; Chai, J.; and Biermann, A. 1997. The role of WordNet in the creation of a trainable message understanding system. *Proceedings of Ninth Conference on Innovative Applications of Artificial Intelligence (IAAI-97)*.

Califf, M., and Mooney, R. 1997. Relational learning of pattern-match rules for information extraction. *Proceedings of Computational Language Learning'97*.

Chai, J., and Biermann, A. 1997a. Corpus based statistical generalization tree in rule optimization. *Proceedings of Fifth Workshop on Very Large Corpora (WVLC-5)*.

Chai, J., and Biermann, A. 1997b. A WordNet based rule generalization engine for meaning extraction. *Lecture Notes in Artificial Intelligence (1325): Foundations of Intelligent Systems*.

Chai, J., and Biermann, A. 1999. The use of word sense disambiguation in an information extraction system. *Proceedings of Eleventh Conference on Innovative Applications of Artificial Intelligence (IAAI-99)*.

Chai, J. 1998. *Learning and Generalization in the Creation of Information Extraction Systems*. Ph.D. Dissertation, Department of Computer Science, Duke University.

Cowie, J., and Lehnert, W. 1996. Information extraction. *Communications of ACM*.

Grishman, R.; Macleod, C.; and Sterling, J. 1992. New York University Proteus System: MUC-4 test results and analysis. *Proceedings of the Fourth Message Understanding Conference*.

Kim, J., and Moldovan, D. 1993. Acquisition of semantic patterns for information extraction from corpora. *Proceedings of the Ninth IEEE Conference on Artificial Intelligence for Applications*.

Miller, G. 1990. WordNet: An on-line lexical database. *International Journal of Lexicography*.

MUC6. 1995. *Proceedings of the Sixth Message Understanding Conference*.

Riloff, E. 1993. Automatically constructing a dictionary for information extraction tasks. *Proceedings of the Eleventh National Conference on Artificial Intelligence*.

Riloff, E. 1996. An empirical study of automated dictionary construction for information extraction in three domains. *AI Journal*.

Soderland, S. 1999. Learning information extraction rules for semi-structured and free text. *Machine Learning Journal Special Issues on Natural Language Learning*.

Sundheim, B. 1992. Overview of the fourth message understanding evaluation and conference. *Proceedings of Fourth Message Understanding Conference (MUC-4)*.

Combining Collaborative Filtering with Personal Agents for Better Recommendations

Nathaniel Good, J. Ben Schafer, Joseph A. Konstan, Al Borchers,
Badrul Sarwar, Jon Herlocker, and John Riedl

GroupLens Research Project
Department of Computer Science and Engineering
University of Minnesota
Minneapolis, MN 55455
http://www.grouplens.org/

Abstract

Information filtering agents and collaborative filtering both attempt to alleviate information overload by identifying which items a user will find worthwhile. Information filtering (IF) focuses on the analysis of item content and the development of a personal user interest profile. Collaborative filtering (CF) focuses on identification of other users with similar tastes and the use of their opinions to recommend items. Each technique has advantages and limitations that suggest that the two could be beneficially combined.

This paper shows that a CF framework can be used to combine personal IF agents and the opinions of a community of users to produce better recommendations than either agents or users can produce alone. It also shows that using CF to create a personal combination of a set of agents produces better results than either individual agents or other combination mechanisms. One key implication of these results is that users can avoid having to select among agents; they can use them all and let the CF framework select the best ones for them.

Introduction

Recommender systems help individuals and communities address the challenges of information overload. Information filtering recommenders look at the syntactic and semantic content of items to determine which are likely to be of interest or value to a user. Collaborative filtering recommenders use the opinions of other users to predict the value of items for each user in the community. For example, in the domain of movie selection, content filtering would allow recommendation based on the movie genre (horror, comedy, romance, etc.) and cast/credits (Woody Allen, Steven Spielberg, Bette Midler). Collaborative filtering, by contrast, might be completely unaware of genre and cast, but would know

that a group of like-minded people recommends "Hoop Dreams" and suggests avoiding "Dumb and Dumber."

In this work, we examine collaborative filtering, personal information filtering agents, and mechanisms for combining them to produce a better recommender system. The next section reviews existing approaches to alleviating information overload, including a variety of content-based and collaborative approaches, and presents our model for how these approaches can be more effective when combined. The following sections present our experimental design and results. We conclude with observations about the implications of these results.

Information Overload: Problem and Approaches

Each day, more and more books, journal articles, web pages, and movies are created. As each new piece of information competes for our attention, we quickly become overwhelmed and seek assistance in identifying the most interesting, worthwhile, valuable, or entertaining items on which we should expend our scarce money and time. Historically, humans have adapted well to gluts of information. Our senses are tuned to notice change and the unusual. Our ability to communicate allows us to collaboratively address large problems. And, we have developed an astonishingly good ability to make quick judgements—indeed, we often *can* judge a book by its cover, an article by its title or abstract, or a movie by its trailer or advertisement. Today we are also finding that it is becoming easier and easier to produce and publish content. As computers, communication, and the Internet make it easier for anyone and everyone to speak to a large audience, we find that even our well-developed filtering skills may be inadequate.

In response to the challenge of information overload, we have sought to develop useful recommender systems—systems that people can use to quickly identify content that will likely interest them. This project draws from work in creating recommender systems for movies – film fans tell the MovieLens system (movielens.umn.edu) how much they like or dislike movies they've already seen, and MovieLens recommends other movies they would likely enjoy.

There are three different technologies that are commonly used to address information overload challenges. Each technology focuses primarily on a particular set of tasks or questions. *Information retrieval* focuses on tasks involving fulfilling ephemeral interest queries such as finding the movies directed by Woody Allen. *Information filtering* focuses on tasks involving classifying streams of new content into categories, such as finding any newly released movies directed by Steven Spielberg (to consider watching) or any newly released movies without an English-language soundtrack or subtitles (to reject). *Collaborative filtering* focuses on answering two questions:

- *Which items (overall or from a set) should I view?*
- *How much will I like these particular items?*

Each of these technologies has a role in producing an effective recommender system.

Information retrieval (IR) systems focus on allowing users to express queries to select items that match a topic of interest to fulfill a particular information need. They may index a collection of documents using either the full text of the document or document abstracts. For non-textual items such as movies, IR systems index genres, keywords, actors, directors, etc. IR systems are generally optimized for ephemeral interest queries, such as looking up a topic in the library. (Belkin and Croft 1992) Internet search engines are popular IR systems, and the Internet Movie Database (www.imdb.com) provides extensive support for IR queries on movies.

An IR front-end is useful in a recommender system both as a mechanism for users to identify specific movies about which they would like to express an opinion and for narrowing the scope of recommendation. For example, MovieLens allows users to specifically request recommendations for newer movies, for movies released in particular time periods, for particular movie genres such as comedy and documentary, and for various combinations of movie. Information retrieval techniques are less valuable in the actual recommendation process, since they capture no information about user preferences other than the specific query. For that reason, we do not consider IR further in this paper.

Information filtering (IF) systems require a profile of user needs or preferences. The simplest systems require the user to create this profile manually or with limited assistance. Examples of these systems include: "kill files" that are used to filter out advertising, e-mail filtering software that sorts e-mail into categories based on the sender, and new-product notification services that request notification when a new book or album by a favorite author or artist is released. More advanced IF systems may build a profile by learning the user's preferences. A wide range of agents including Maes' agents for e-mail and Usenet news filtering (Maes 1995) and Lieberman's Letizia (Lieberman 1997) employ learning techniques to classify, dispose of, or recommend documents based on the user's prior actions. Similarly, Cohen's Ripper system has been used to classify e-mail (Cohen 1996); alternative approaches use other learning techniques and term frequency (Boone 1998)

Information filtering techniques have a central role in recommender systems. IF techniques build a profile of user preferences that is particularly valuable when a user encounters new content that has not been rated before. An avid Woody Allen fan doesn't need to wait for reviews to decide to see a new Woody Allen film, and a person who hates horror films can as quickly dismiss a new horror film without regret. IF techniques also have an important property that they do not depend on having other users in the system, let alone users with similar tastes. IF techniques can be effective, as we shall see, but they suffer certain drawbacks, including requiring a source of content information, and not providing much in the way of serendipitous discovery; indeed, a Woody Allen-seeking agent would likely never discover a non-Woody Allen drama that just happens to appeal greatly to most Woody Allen fans.

Collaborative filtering (CF) systems build a database of user opinions of available items. They use the database to find users whose opinions are similar (i.e., those that are highly correlated) and make predictions of user opinion on an item by combining the opinions of other like-minded individuals. For example, if Sue and Jerry have liked many of the same movies, and Sue liked *Titanic,* which Jerry hasn't seen yet, then the system may recommend *Titanic* to Jerry. While Tapestry (Goldberg et al. 1992), the earliest CF system, required explicit user action to retrieve and evaluate ratings, automatic CF systems such as GroupLens (Resnick et al. 1994) (Konstan et al. 1997) provide predictions with little or no user effort. Later systems such as Ringo (Shardanand and Maes 1995) and Bellcore's Video Recommender (Hill et al. 1995) became widely used sources of advice on music and movies respectively. More recently, a number of systems have begun to use observational ratings; the system infers user preferences from actions rather than requiring the user to explicitly rate an item (Terveen et al. 1997). In the past year, a wide range of web sites have begun to use CF recommendations in a diverse set of domains including books, grocery products, art, entertainment, and information.

Collaborative filtering techniques can be an important part of a recommender system. One key advantage of CF is that it *does not* consider the content of the items being recommended. Rather than map users to items through "content attributes" or "demographics," CF treats each item and user individually. Accordingly, it becomes possible to discover new items of interest simply because other people liked them; it is also easier to provide good recommendations even when the attributes of greatest interest to users are unknown or hidden. For example, many movie viewers may not want to see a particular actor or genre so much as "a movie that makes me feel good" or "a smart, funny movie." At the same time, CF's dependence on human ratings can be a significant drawback. For a CF system to work well, several users must evaluate each item; even then, new items cannot be recommended until some users have taken the time to evaluate them. These limitations, often referred to as the *sparsity* and *first-rater problems*, cause trouble for users seeking obscure movies (since nobody may have rated them) or advice on movies about to be released (since nobody has had a chance to evaluate them).

Hybrid Recommender Systems

Several systems have tried to combine information filtering and collaborative filtering techniques in an effort to overcome the limitations of each. Fab (Balabanovic and Shoham 1997) maintains user profiles of interest in web pages using information filtering techniques, but uses collaborative filtering techniques to identify profiles with similar tastes. It then can recommend documents across user profiles. (Basu, Hirsh, and Cohen 1998) trained the Ripper machine learning system with a combination of content data and training data in an effort to produce better recommendations. Researchers working in collaborative filtering have proposed techniques for using IF profiles as a fall-back, e.g., by requesting predictions for a director or actor when there is no information on the specific movie, or by having dual systems and using the IF profile when the CF system cannot produce a high-quality recommendation.

In earlier work, Sarwar, et al. (1998) showed that a simple but consistent rating agent, such as one that assesses the quality of spelling in a Usenet news article, could be a valuable participant in a collaborative filtering community. In that work, they showed how these *filterbots*—ratings robots that participate as members of a collaborative filtering system – helped users who agreed with them by providing more ratings upon which recommendations could be made. For users who did not agree with the filterbot, the CF framework would notice a low preference correlation and not make use of its ratings.

This work extends the filterbot concept in three key ways. First, we use a more intelligent set of filterbots, including learning agents that are personalized to an individual user. Second, we apply this work to small communities, including using CF to serve a single human user. Third, we evaluate the simultaneous use of multiple filterbots. In addition, we explore other combination mechanisms as alternatives to CF. We demonstrate that CF is a useful framework both for integrating agents and for combining agents and humans.

Hypotheses and Experimental Design

In this paper, we systematically explore the value of collaborative filtering, information filtering, and different combinations of these techniques for creating an effective personal recommendation system. Specifically, we look at four key models as shown in figure 1:

- Pure collaborative filtering using the opinions of other community members
- A single personalized "agent" – a machine learning or syntactic filter
- A combination of many "agents"
- A combination of multiple agents and community member opinions

The experimental design uses two tiers. First, where there are several implementations for a particular model, we evaluate them to find the model that provides the best filtering. Second, we compare the best implementation

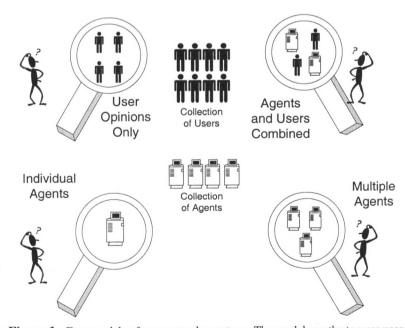

Figure 1. Four models of recommender system. The models on the top use user opinions while the models on the bottom use only IF agents. The models on the right use multiple IF agents while the ones on the left use at most one agent. In each case, the user receives personal recommendations.

from each model with the other implementations. These are operationalized as four primary hypotheses below.

H1. The opinions of a community of users provide better recommendations than a single personalized agent.

H2. A personalized combination of several agents provides better recommendations than a single personalized agent.

H3. The opinions of a community of users provides better recommendations than a personalized combination of several agents.

H4. A personalized combination of several agents and community opinions provides better recommendations than either agents or user opinions alone.

The context in which these hypotheses are tested is a small, anonymous community of movie fans. The combination of small size and non-textual content cause disadvantages for both collaborative filtering and information filtering; it provides a middle-ground between the common contexts for collaborative filtering (many users, little content information) and information filtering (one user, much content information).

Data Set

The user ratings for this experiment were drawn from the MovieLens system (http://movielens.umn.edu) which has more than 3 million ratings from over 80,000 users. Fifty users were selected at random from the set of users with more than 120 movie ratings. For each user, three sets of movies/ratings were selected at random without replacement. The first set of 50 ratings, termed the **training set**, was set aside for use in training the personalized information filtering agents. The second set of 50 ratings, termed the **correlation set** was used when combining users, agents, or both together. The final set of 20 ratings served as the **test set**. In each experiment, the test ratings of the target user were withheld and compared against the recommendation value produced by the system.

Metrics

Recommender systems researchers use several different measures for the quality of recommendations produced.

Coverage metrics evaluate the number of items for which the system could provide recommendations. In many systems, coverage decreases as a function of accuracy—the system can produce fewer accurate recommendations or more inaccurate ones. Because our information filtering systems provide total coverage, we do not report coverage except as part of the analysis of the standard CF system.

Statistical accuracy metrics evaluate the accuracy of a filtering system by comparing the numerical prediction values against user ratings for the items that have both predictions and ratings. (Shardanand and Maes, 1995) and (Sarwar et al, 1998) have both used mean absolute error (MAE) to measure the performance of a prediction engine. Other metrics used include root mean squared error (Sarwar et al. 1998) and correlation between ratings and predictions (Hill et al. 1995) (Konstan et al. 1997) (Sarwar et al. 1998). Our experience has shown that these metrics typically track each other closely. We have chosen to report mean absolute error, therefore, because it is the most commonly used and the easiest to interpret directly.

Decision-support accuracy metrics evaluate how effective a prediction engine is at helping a user select high-quality items from the item set. These metrics are based on the observation that, for the majority of users, filtering is a binary operation – they will either view the item, or they will not. If this is true, then whether an item has a rating of 1.5 or 2.5 on a five-point scale is irrelevant if the user only views items with a rating of 4 or higher. The most common decision-support accuracy measures are reversal rate, weighted errors, and ROC sensitivity. *Reversal rate* is the frequency with which the system makes recommendations that are extremely wrong. On a five point scale, it is commonly defined as the percentage of recommendations where the recommendation was off by 3 points or more. Weighted error metrics give extra weight to large errors that occur when the user has a strong opinion about the item. For example, errors might count double or more when the user considers the item a favorite (5 out of 5). *ROC sensitivity* is a signal processing measure of the decision making power of a filtering system. Operationally, it is the area under the receiver operating characteristic curve (ROC) – a curve that plots the *sensitivity* vs. *1 - specificity* of the test (Swets 1988). Sensitivity refers to the probability of a randomly selected good item being accepted by the filter. Specificity is the probability of a randomly selected bad item being rejected by the filter. Points on the ROC curve represent trade-offs supported by the filter. A good filter might allow the user to choose between receiving 90% of the good items while accepting only 10% of the bad ones, or receiving 95% of the good ones with 20% of the bad ones. A random filter always accepts the same percentage of the good and the bad items. The ROC sensitivity ranges from 0 to 1 where 1 is perfect and 0.5 is random.

We use ROC sensitivity as our decision support accuracy measure. To operationalize ROC, we must determine which items are "good" and which are "bad." We use the user's own rating, with a mapping that 4 and 5 are good and 1,2, and 3 are bad. Our experience has shown that this reflects user behavior on MovieLens. We found that one user had no movies rated below 4; we eliminated that user from the statistics compiled for each experiment.

Evaluating the hypotheses in the face of multiple metrics can be a challenge. We considered it important to consider both statistical and decision-support accuracy in evaluating different recommender systems. When several agents, for example, provide different but incomparable trade-offs among the two metrics, we consider each one to be a possible "best agent" and compare each of them against the alternative recommender. We consider one alternative to dominate another, however, if there is a significant improvement in one metric and no significant difference in the other.

Statistical significance is assessed for mean absolute errors using the Wilcoxan test on paired errors. Differences reported as significant are based on a significance level of *p<0.05*. Statistical significance assessment for ROC sensitivity is less clear;[*] from experience we therefore assert that changes of 0.01 or more are "meaningful" and smaller differences are "not meaningful."

Experimental Components

Our hypotheses are based on four models of recommender system:

- user opinions only,
- individual IF agents,
- combinations of IF agents, and
- combinations of IF agents and user opinions.

In this section, we describe the variety of implementations of these models with an overview of how we constructed each implementation. The effectiveness of each implementation is reported in the results section.

User Opinions Only. Extensive research has already been performed on the problem of generating recommendations from a set of user opinions. Nearest-neighbor collaborative filtering is already generally accepted to be the most effective mechanism for performing this task, and we therefore use it (Breese, 1998). In particular, we use the DBLens research collaborative filtering engine developed by the GroupLens Research project for exploration of collaborative filtering algorithms. DBLens allows experimenters to control several parameters that trade among performance, coverage, and accuracy. For our experiments, we set each of these to prefer maximum coverage and to use all data regardless of performance.

The CF result set was computed for each user by loading the correlation data set (50 ratings per user) into the engine, then loading the test set (20 ratings per user) for each user, and requesting a prediction for each test set

movie for each user. DBLens has a control that allows us to ignore a user's rating when making a prediction for that user. The resulting 20 predictions per user were compared against that user's ratings to produce error and ROC statistics.

Individual IF Agents. Three types of IF agents, or filterbots, were created and studied in this project: DGBots, RipperBot, and a set of GenreBots.

Doppelganger Bots (DGBots) are personalized bots that create profiles of user preferences and generate predictions using IR/IF techniques (specifically, a modified TFIDF, (Salton and Buckley 1987) based upon the content features of each movie. We created three DGBots, one that used only cast data, one that used only descriptive keywords, and one that used both. These data were found at the Internet Movie Database (http://www.imdb.com/). Each DGBot was implemented similarly, so we will describe the keyword DGBot here.

To produce personal recommendations for movies, the keyword DGBot followed five steps:

1. Create an IDF vector that represents the relative scarcity of each keyword in the movie set.
2. Create a term frequency vector for each movie indicating which keywords occur.
3. Build a user profile of weights associated with each term
4. Produce a score for each movie based on the user weights.
5. Rank order the movies and divide into recommendation bands.

The IDF vector is created using the following formula for the value associated with each keyword:

$$idf = \log_2\left(\frac{N}{O}\right)$$

N is the total number of movies and O is the number of movies for which that keyword is used.

We modified traditional TFIDF by counting each keyword as either occurring (1) or not occurring (0) in any given movie. Accordingly, the TF vector for a movie is produced by inserting a 1 for each keyword and 0 elsewhere.

Building the user profile requires a balanced set of user ratings, so we subtract 3 from each rating to transform them to a -2 to +2 scale. For each movie in the 50-rating training set, we produce a keyword preference vector that is the product of the transformed rating, the movie's TF vector, and the IDF vector. We then normalize the keyword preference vector to length 1. The mean of the user's 50 keyword preference vectors is the user profile.

The DGBot produces ratings for all movies at once. For each movie, it computes the dot product of the user

---

[*]There are statistical measures to compare ROC curves themselves, but the measures that we have found for comparing areas under the curve appear to overstate statistical significance.

profile vector and the TF vector. Those scores are then ranked and broken into rating levels with a distribution matching the MovieLens overall rating distribution. The top 21% of movies received a rating of 5, the next 34% a rating of 4, the next 28% a 3, the next 12% a 2, and the bottom 5% a 1. While each user has a separate user profile vector and set of recommendations, the TF and IDF vectors could be re-used from user to user.

RipperBot was created using Ripper, an inductive logic program created by William Cohen (Cohen, 1995). We found that Ripper performed best when trained on a set of data limited to genre identifiers and the 200 most frequent keywords. Ripper also works best when asked to make binary decisions, so for each user we trained four Ripper instances, tuned to distinguish between 5/4321, 54/321, 543/21, and 5432/1 respectively. Each instance was trained on the 50-rating training set along with the identifiers and keywords for those 50 movies. After training, we asked each instance to classify the entire set of movies and summed the number of Ripper instances that indicated the higher value and added one to create a recommendation value.

Ripper requires substantial tuning; we experimented with several parameters and also relied on advice from (Basu Hirsh and Cohen, 1998). In particular, we adjusted default settings to *allow negative tests in set value attributes* and experimented by varying the *loss ratio*. We found a loss ration of 1.9 to give us the best results.

The GenreBots consisted of 19 simple bots that rated each movie a 5 if the movie matched the bot's genre and a 3 otherwise. For example, *Toy Story*, which is a children's animated comedy would receive a 5 from the ChildrensBot, the AnimatedBot and the ComedyBot, and a 3 from each of the remaining bots. Genre data was obtained from IMDB.

A Mega-GenreBot was created for each user. This was done by using linear regression and training the bot on each user's training set. A user's known rating was treated as a dependent variable of the 19 individual GenreBots. The regression coefficients formed an equation that could then be used to generate predictions for each other movie from the genre identifiers.

Combinations of IF Agents. We identified four different strategies for combining agents: selecting one agent for each person, averaging the agents together, using regression to create a personal combination, and using CF to create a personal combination. For all but the first of these, we found it valuable to create two combinations: one that used all 19 GenreBots and one that used the Mega-GenreBot. Adding the 3 DGBots and RipperBot, we refer to these as 23-agent and 5-agent versions, respectively.

BestBot. The best agent per user was selected by testing each bot on the correlation data set (50 ratings) and selecting the bot with the lowest MAE. BestBot then used the ratings generated by that bot for the test data set to produce statistics for evaluation.

Agent Average. The average combination was produced by taking the arithmetic mean of the 5 or 23 agent recommendations, respectively.

Regression. We used linear regression to produce a "best fit" combination for a given user. To do this we used the predictions on the correlation sets for the 23 and 5 agents respectively as the independent variables and the known user's rating as the dependent variable. Using the resultant weights, we could generate predictions for the movies in the test sets by creating linear combinations of the agents' recommendations.

CF Combination. We used the DBLens CF engine to create a CF combination of agents. For this purpose, we loaded all ratings from the 5 or 23 agents into the engine, along with the user's 50 ratings from the correlation set. We generated predictions for the user's 20 test movies. The ratings database was cleared after each user. The parameters used were the same as for the simple CF case.

Combination of Users and IF Agents. Because user ratings were incomplete, and because CF with 23 agents proved to be the most effective combination of IF agents, we used CF to combine the 23 agents and all 50 users. The method is identical to the CF combination of agents except that we also loaded the ratings for the other 49 users. Again, the database was cleared after each user.

Results

✗ H1: Collaborative Filtering better than Single Agents
We hypothesized that collaborative filtering using the opinions of the 50-user community would provide better results than any individual agent. To compare these, we first identified the best individual agent. We evaluated the three DGBots, RipperBot, the 19 individual genreBots, and the personalized Mega-GenreBot (see table 1). Of these, only RipperBot, Mega-GenreBot, and the DGBot that used both cast and keywords were not dominated by other agents. RipperBot had the highest accuracy (lowest MAE) by far, but low ROC sensitivity (poor decision support). The combined DGBot has the

Bot or Method	MAE	ROC	Bot or Method	MAE	ROC
ActionBot	1.0755	0.4925	RomanceBot	1.0897	0.4931
AdventureBot	1.0653	0.5148	Sci-FiBot	1.0714	0.5026
AnimationBot	1.0612	0.5017	ThrillerBot	1.0897	0.4815
ChildrensBot	1.0346	0.5155	UnknownBot	1.0816	0.4922
ComedyBot	1.2652	0.4767	WarBot	1.0428	0.5187
CrimeBot	1.1000	0.5006	WesternBot	1.0673	0.5078
DocumntryBot	1.0918	0.4927	DGBot Cast	1.2775	0.5673
DramaBot	1.0591	0.5151	DGBot Kwd	1.1397	0.5706
FamilyBot	1.0489	0.5161	DGBot Comb.	1.1428	0.5771
Film-NoirBot	1.0959	0.4924	MegaGnrBot	0.9578	0.5742
HorrorBot	1.0632	0.5066	RipperBot	0.8336	0.5236
MusicalBot	1.0673	0.5182	CF of Users	0.9354	0.5788
MysteryBot	1.0734	0.5114			

Table 1. Individual Bots vs. CF of Users

highest ROC sensitivity, but relatively low accuracy. The Mega-GenreBot has the second-best accuracy and second-best decision-support. We compare these three against the results of collaborative filtering using user opinions.

Collaborative filtering is significantly less accurate than RipperBot, but has a meaningfully higher ROC sensitivity value. In effect, while RipperBot avoids making large errors, it performs little better than random at helping people find good movies and avoid bad ones. If accuracy were paramount, H1 would be rejected.

Collaborative filtering is significantly more accurate than the combined DGBot and has comparable ROC sensitivity. While both approaches provide comparable support for decision-making, on average the DGBot is more than 20% less accurate. If decision-support were paramount, H1 would be accepted.

The Mega-GenreBot is slightly worse than collaborative filtering of user opinions on both MAE and ROC, but the differences were not statistically significant. We would consider Mega-GenreBot to be a good pragmatic substitute for user-based collaborative filtering for a small community. Furthermore, the collaborative filtering result was only able to provide coverage of 83% (other desired recommendations could not be made due to a lack of ratings for those movies).

Accordingly, overall we reject H1. A more accurate alternative exists (RipperBot), and comparably accurate and valuable alternatives exist without the problem of reduced coverage.

✔ **H2: Many Agents better than Just One**
We hypothesized that combining several agents would yield better results than any single personalized agent. In testing H1, we found that for single agents, RipperBot had the best accuracy value (MAE), DGBot Combo had the best decision support value (ROC) and the Mega-GenreBot was competitive with both values. In table 2 we compare these values to those obtained from the seven methods of combining the agents – regression, agent average, collaborative filtering of a single user and its bots, and manually selecting the "best bot."

Bot or Method	MAE	ROC	Bot or Method	MAE	ROC
5 agent regress	0.8610	0.6030	RipperBot	0.8336	0.5236
23 agent regress	0.9729	0.5676	MegaGenreBot	0.9578	0.5742
5 agent avg.	0.8990	0.6114	DG Combo Bot	1.1428	0.5771
23 agent avg.	0.9579	0.5760	CF 1 usr, 5 bots	0.9682	0.6071
Best Bot	0.8714	0.5173	CF 1 usr, 23 bts	0.8343	0.6118

Table 2. Individual Bots vs. Combined Bots

Collaborative filtering using all 23 (CF23) agents is clearly the best combination method, with a significant accuracy advantage over all of the other combinations and similar or better ROC values. CF23 provides both MAE and ROC advantages over both the Mega-GenreBot and the DGBot Combo.

The remaining interesting comparison is between CF23 and RipperBot. We conclude that CF23 is better because

there was no significant difference in MAE, and the ROC value for CF23 was dramatically better than for RipperBot. Accordingly we accept H2. We also observe that H2 depended on using collaborative filtering technology; no other combination method was close to dominating RipperBot's accuracy.

✘ **H3: CF of Users better than Combination of Agents**
At this stage, it is clear that we must reject H3. Table 3 summarizes the results, but we recognize that collaborative filtering with a group of 50 users is indeed not as accurate or valuable as we had hypothesized.

Bot or Method	MAE	ROC	Bot or Method	MAE	ROC
CF (users only)	0.9354	0.5788	CF 1 usr, 23 bts	0.8343	0.6118

Table 3. CF of Users vs. Combined Bots

✔ **H4: Agents and Users Together is best overall**
We hypothesized that the combination of the opinions of a community of users and the personalized agents for a given user will provide that user with better results than either users alone or agents alone. From both H2 and H3 we found that collaborative filtering of a single user and that user's 23 agents provides the best accuracy and decision support of all agent-only or user-only methods tested. Table 4 shows a small, but statistically significant improvement in accuracy resulting from including the other users in the collaborative filtering mix. ROC also improves, but not by a meaningful amount.

Bot or Method	MAE	ROC	Bot or Method	MAE	ROC
CF 50 usr, 23 bt	0.8303	0.6168	CF 1 usr, 23 bts	0.8343	0.6118

Table 4. CF of Users and Bots vs. Combined Bots

Accordingly, we accept H4 and find that a mixed collaborative filtering solution that uses users and agents does indeed provide the best overall results.

Discussion

The most important results we found were the value of combining agents with CF and of combining agents and users with CF. In essence, these results suggest that an effective mechanism for producing high-quality recommendations is to throw in any available data and allow the CF engine to sort out which information is useful to each user. In effect, it becomes less important to invent a brilliant agent, instead we can simply invent a collection of useful ones. We should point out that these experiments tested the quality of the resulting recommender system, not the performance or economics of such a system. Current CF recommendation engines cannot efficiently handle "users" who rate all items and re-rate them frequently as they "learn." To take advantage of learning agents, these engines must be redesigned to accommodate "users" with dynamic rating habits. We are examining several different CF engine designs that could efficiently use filterbots.

We were also pleased, though somewhat surprised, to find that CF outperformed linear regression as a combining mechanism for agents. While linear regression should provide an optimal linear fit, it appears that CF's non-optimal mechanism actually does a better job avoiding overfitting the data when the number of columns approaches the number of rows. CF also has the advantage of functioning on incomplete (and indeed very sparse) data sets, suggesting that it retains its value as a useful combination tool whenever human or agents are unlikely to rate each item.

We were surprised by several of the results that we'd found, and sought to explain them. Foremost, we clearly overestimated the value of collaborative filtering for a small community of 50 users. In retrospect, our expectations may have been built from our own positive experiences when starting CF systems with a small group of researchers and friends. Those successes may have been due in part to close ties among the users; we often had seen the same movies and many had similar tastes. Using real users resulted in real diversity which may explain the lower, and more realistic, value. Future work should both incorporate larger user sets (other experiments have consistently shown MAE values in the range of 0.71-0.73 and ROC sensitivity values near 0.72 for MovieLens communities with thousands of users) and look explicitly at closer-knit communities to see whether a smaller but more homogeneous community would have greater benefits from collaborative filtering.

We also were surprised by the results we achieved using Ripper. We were impressed by its accuracy, after extensive tuning, but dismayed by how close to random it was in distinguishing good from bad movies. We are still uncertain as to why RipperBot performs as it does, and believe further work is needed to understand why it behaves as it does and whether it would be possible to train it to perform differently.

In the future, we plan to examine further combinations of users and agents in recommender systems. In particular, we are interested in developing a combined community where large numbers of users and agents co-exist. One question we hope to answer is whether users who agree with each other would also benefit from the opinions of each other's trained agents.

Acknowledgements

Funding for this research was provided by the National Science Foundation under grants IIS 9613960, IIS 9734442, and DGE 9554517. Support was also provided by Net Perceptions Inc. We would also like to thank members of the GroupLens research team, especially Hannu Huhdanpaa for developing the initial testbed.

References

Balabanovic, M., and Shoham, Y. 1997. Fab: Content-Based, Collaborative Recommendation. *Communications of the ACM* 40(3):66-72.

Basu C., Hirsh H., and Cohen, W.W. 1998. Using Social and Content-Based Information in Recommendation. In *Proceedings of the AAAI-98,*:AAAI Press.

Belkin, N., and Croft, B.W. 1992. Information Filtering and Information Retrieval: Two Sides of the Same Coin?. *Communications of the ACM* 35(12):29-38.

Boone, G. 1998. Concept Features in Re:Agent, an Intelligent Email Agent. In *The Second International Conference on Autonomous Agents*, 141-148, Minneapolis/St. Paul, MN:ACM.

Breese, J. Heckerman, D., and Kadie, C. 1998. Empirical Analysis of Predictive Algorithms for Collaborative Filtering. In *Proceedings of the Fourteenth Conference on Uncertainty in Artificial Intelligence*, Madison, WI.

Cohen, W.W. 1996. Learning Rules that Classify E-mail. In *Proceeding of the AAAI Spring Symposium on Machine Learning in Information Access,*: AAAI Press.

Cohen, W.W. 1995. Fast Effective Rule Induction. In *Proceedings of the Twelfth International Conference on Machine Learning*, Lake Tahoe, CA.:AAAI Press.

Goldberg, D., Nichols, D., Oki, B.M. and Terry, D. 1992. Using Collaborative Filtering to Weave an Information Tapestry. *Communications of the ACM* 35(12):61-70.

Hill, W., Stead, L., Rosenstein, M., and Furnas, G., 1995. Recommending and Evaluating Choices in a Virtual Community of Use. In *Proceedings of ACM CHI'95*, 194-201. Denver, CO.: ACM.

Konstan, J.A., Miller, B.N., Maltz, D., Herlocker, J.L., Gordon, L.R., and Riedl, J. 1997Applying Collaborative Filtering to Usenet News. *Communications of the ACM* 40(3):77-87.

Lieberman, H., 1997. Autonomous Interface Agents. In *Proceedings of ACM CHI 97,*67-74,:ACM

Maes, P. 1995. Agents that Reduce Work and Information Overload. In *Readings in Human-Computer Interaction, Toward the Year 2000*, :Morgan Kauffman.

Resnick, P., Iacovou, N., Suchak, M., Bergstrom, P. and Riedl, J. 1994. GroupLens: An Open Architecture for Collaborative Filtering of Netnews. In Proceedings of 1994 Conference on Computer Supported Collaborative Work, 175-186.: ACM.

Salton, G., Buckley, C. 1987. Term Weighting Approaches in Automatic Text Retrieval., Technical Report, Dept. of Computer Science, Cornell Univ.

Sarwar, B.M., Konstan, J.A., Borchers, A., Herlocker, J.L., Miller, B.N., and Riedl, J. 1998. Using Filtering Agents to Improve Prediction Quality in the Grouplens Research Collaborative Filtering System. In *Proceedings of CSCW '98*, Seattle, WA.: ACM.

Shardanand, U., and Maes, P. 1995. Social Information Filtering: Algorithms for Automating "Word of Mouth". In *Proceedings of ACM CHI '95,*. Denver, CO.: ACM.

Swets, J.A. 1988. Measuring the Accuracy of Diagnostic Systems. *Science* 240:1285-1289.

Terveen, L., Hill, W., Amento, B., McDonald, D., Creter J. 1997. PHOAKS: A System for Sharing Recommendations. Communications of the ACM 40(3):59-62.

Application-Embedded Retrieval from Distributed Free-Text Collections

Vladimir A. Kulyukin

School of Computer Science, Telecommunications,
and Information Systems
DePaul University
243 South Wabash Avenue
Chicago, IL 60604
vkulyukin@cs.depaul.edu

Abstract

A framework is presented for application-embedded information retrieval from distributed free-text collections. An application's usage is sampled by an embedded information retrieval system. Samples are converted into queries to distributed collections. Retrieval is adjusted through sample size and structure, anydata indexing, and dual space feedback. The framework is investigated with a retrieval system embedded in a text processor.

The Problem

The integration of query generation and feedback challenges information retrieval (IR) technologies. Relevance feedback (Aalbersberg 1992; Robertson and Walker 1997), while useful to information science professionals (Spink and Saracevic 1997), is frequently inappropriate for lay users. Many users are unable to adequately state their information needs in queries (Burke, Hammond, and Young 1996). The constant, explicit solicitation of relevance judgments interferes with many users' information-seeking behaviors (Kulyukin 1998c). Feedback utilization in the query space alone prohibits retrieval adjustments over multiple interactions (Kulyukin 1998a; Kulyukin, Hammond, and Burke 1998). The focus on maximizing the number of relevant documents in every retrieval is inconsistent with many users' information needs (Jansen et al. 1998).

The approach to the integration of query generation and feedback henceforth presented is called *application-embedded distributed IR*. The approach is implemented in an embedded IR (EMIR) system for text processors. The objective is a technology for building non-intrusive, feedback-sensitive IR tools that users embed into their applications to tap into and monitor information sources, while engaged in routine usages of those applications. The technology is motivated by a growing number of sources with a wealth of data, but few tools to timely put it to use.

A Solution

An application-embedded IR system is deployed through *resource subscription* and *mode selection*. During resource subscription, the user specifies distributed resources from which information is retrieved. During mode selection, the user specifies how the application is used. For example, EMIR has a LaTeX mode in which the text processor is used for typesetting LaTeX documents. As the user typesets a document, EMIR takes background text samples and converts them into queries to the subscribed collections. The retrievals are examined by the user at the user's convenience. The following techniques form the system's core:

- **Background Sampling**: Two types of sampling are distinguished: *random* and *structured*. In random sampling, the entire sample is chosen randomly. In structured sampling, samples are components of known templates, e.g., abstracts and references of LaTeX papers. Structured sampling is based on the assumption that some document components carry more information than others (Bradshaw 1998; Kulyukin, Hammond, and Burke 1996). Query generation from background sampling does not disrupt the user.

- **Anydata Indexing**: The vector space retrieval model is used (Salton and McGill 1983). A document is a vector of its terms' weights. A document collection is a vector space whose dimensions are the documents' terms. In smaller collections, a term's rarity is its main distinguishing property. In larger collections, the term's pattern of occurrences in the documents prevails. Since indexing is adjusted to the currently available data, it is called *anydata*.

- **Dual Space Feedback**: Document space relevance feedback modifies term weights in the document vectors from relevance judgments (Brauen 1971). Over long periods, some terms acquire negative weights, which adversely affect performance (Robertson and Walker 1997). Since only the dimensions' weights are modified, query terms that are not dimensions have no impact (Kulyukin 1998c). Dual space feedback addresses both problems with two vector spaces, *positive* and *negative*, both of which represent the same document collection. When a document is relevant to a query, the weights are adjusted in the positive space (p-space). When a document is nonrelevant, the same adjustments are made in the negative space (n-space).

- **Distributed Indexing**: The Common Object Request Broker Architecture (http://www.omg.org) (CORBA) connects the system to distributed resources. Interobject communication occurs through Object Request Brokers (ORB's) via the Internet Inter-ORB Protocol (IIOP). A resource is a server offering a set of indexing and retrieval services. Collection indexing and maintenance are delegated to the servers.

Details

Terms

The terms are computed from queries, i.e., background free-text samples of LATEX papers, and the documents in each collection. The Xerox Part-of-Speech tagger (ftp://parcftp.xerox.com/pub/tagger/) assigns each term stochastically determined parts of speech (stpos) (Cutting et al. 1992). The tagged text is stoplisted with an extended version of the Brown Corpus stoplist (Francis and Kucera 1982). Terms are normalized through a greedy morphological analysis (Kulyukin 1998c). A list of rules for the term's tag is searched. Each rule has the form {`match`, `add`, `id`}, where `match` and `add` are strings, and `id` is an integer. A rule applies when `match` and the term's suffix match, whereupon the suffix is removed, and `add` is added. When no rules apply, the term is left as is. The normalization procedure is implemented on top of the morphological kernel of WordNet^{TM} (Miller 1995) (ftp://ftp.cogsci.princeton.edu/pub/wordnet/).

Term weights

A term's weight combines its semantic and statistical weights. The semantic weight is intrinsic. The statistical weight depends on the collection's size and the term's distribution in the documents. The semantic weight of a term t_i, $\omega_{sm}(i)$, is inverse to its polysemy and proportional to its stpos: $\omega_{sm}(i) = \pi(i)^{-1}\rho(i)$, where $\pi(i)$ is t_i's polysemy in WordNet, and $\rho(i)$ is its stpos weight. Nouns are valued at 1.0, verbs and adjectives at .5, and adverbs at .25.

The statistical weight unifies two approaches: *inverse document frequency* (IDF) (Salton and McGill 1983) and *condensation clustering* (CC) (Bookstein, Klein, and Raita 1998; Kulyukin, Hammond, and Burke 1998). IDF values a term's rarity in the collection; CC values terms' nonrandom distribution patterns over the collection's documents.

Let D be the total number of documents. Define $f(i,j)$ to be t_i's frequency in the j-th document d_j. Put $\tilde{n}_j = 1$ if $f(i,j) > 0$, and 0, otherwise. Put $D_i = \sum_{i=1}^{D} \tilde{n}_i$. For t_i's IDF-weight, put $\omega_{idf}(i) =$

$A_{idf} + log(D/D_i)$, with A_{idf} a constant. For t_i's *tfidf* weight in d_j, put $\omega_{tfidf}(i,j) = f(i,j)(A_{idf} + log(D/D_i))$. The CC-weight of t_i is the ratio of the actual number of documents containing at least one occurrence of t_i over the expected number of such documents: $\omega_{cc}(i) = A_{cc} + log(E(\tilde{D}_i)/D_i)$, where A_{cc} is a constant and $\tilde{D}_i$ is a random variable assuming D_i's values. Put $T_i = \sum_{j=1}^{D} f(i,j)$. Since $\tilde{n}_i$ assumes 1 and 0 with the respective probabilities of p_i and $q_i = 1 - p_i$, $E(\tilde{n}_i) = p_i = 1 - (1 - 1/D)^{T_i}$. Since $\tilde{D}_i = \sum_{i=1}^{D} \tilde{n}_i$, $E(\tilde{D}_i) = Dp_i$. For t_i's *tfcc* weight in d_j, put $\omega_{tfcc}(i,j) = f(i,j)\omega_{cc}(i)$. Let $A_{cc} = A_{idf}$. By definition, $\omega_{cc}(i) = \omega_{idf}(i) + logp_i$. Hence, the lemma: If $A_{cc} = A_{idf}$, $\omega_{cc}(i) = \omega_{idf}(i) + \log p_i$.

The lemma brings a closure to the discussion of the relationship between IDF and CC (Bookstein, Klein, and Raita 1998; Kulyukin, Hammond, and Burke 1998). A class of metrics obtains, unifying IDF and CC: $\omega_{idfcc}(i) = A + B\omega_{idf}(i) + Clogp_i$, where A, B, and C are constants. If $A = A_{idf}$, $B = 1$, and $C = 0$, $\omega_{idfcc} = \omega_{idf}$; if $A = A_{cc}$, $B = 1$, and $C = 1$, $\omega_{idfcc} = \omega_{cc}$. Since $f(i,j)$ approximates the importance of t_i in d_j, t_i's weight in d_j is given by $\omega_{tfidfcc}(i,j) = f(i,j)\omega_{idfcc}(i)$. Combining t_i's semantic and statistical weights gives t_i's weight in d_j: $\omega_{cw}(i,j) = \omega_{sm}(i)^{\alpha_1}\omega_{tfidfcc}(i,j)^{\alpha_2}$, where α's reflect the component weights' importance.

Feedback

A collection is represented by two vectors: the p-space centroid (p-centroid) and the n-space centroid (n-centroid). Centroid weights are the average weights of the space's dimensions. Two vector spaces are stored locally: one of p-centroids and one of n-centroids. A query is turned into a term vector (q-vector). The similarity is the cosine of the angle between the q-vector and a centroid. The similarity between the q-vector and a p-centroid is *positive*. The similarity between the q-vector and an n-centroid is *negative*. A collection is relevant if the difference between its positive and negative similarities exceeds a threshold. When the collection is relevant, the query is marshalled to its server. The retrievals are sorted locally by their similarity to the query. Relevance judgments cause adjustments in the appropriate space. When a document is relevant, the adjustments are made in the p-space; otherwise, they are made in the n-space. The adjustment procedure is the same for both spaces: the similarities are rewarded, the differences are punished, and the new terms are added to the vectors to encourage or discourage future retrievals. This approach to feedback utilization is similar to negative evidence acquisition (Kulyukin, Hammond, and Burke 1998), a technique for adjusting content representations in response to feedback. However, it stays within one model, precludes negative weights, and avoids the proliferation of ad hoc representations.

slen vs. qsize	10	20	30
$avslen_1$	10.1	7.5	6.4
$avslen_2$	12.4	8.9	7.7
$avslen_3$	15.7	11.3	8.3

slen vs. part	abst			intro			refs		
$avslen_1$	8.5	5.1	3.2	8.1	4.7	3.4	14.4	11.1	8.7
$avslen_2$	8.9	7.3	3.7	9.2	7.5	7.1	15.7	14.5	12.3
$avslen_3$	11.1	8.1	4.7	11.9	7.9	8.5	18.2	18.1	15.4

Figure 1: Random vs. structured queries with dual space feedback

Evaluation

The experimental data were taken from the collection of requests for comments (rfc's) maintained by the Internet Engineering Task Force (ftp://ftp.isi.edu/in-notes/). 1423 rfc's were manually partitioned into three topics: data transport protocols, applications protocols, and data content. Each topic constituted a collection. Each collection was managed by a CORBA server on a separate CPU. EMIR was implemented as a CORBA client. Each server published its services through the Interface Definition Language (http://www.omg.org). The services included indexing a collection, retrieving top n matches under a given similarity metric, retrieving all matches above a threshold, computing centroids, adjusting term weights, adding new terms, retrieving rfc texts, and several other operations. The inputs were 20 papers randomly selected from a pool of 100 LaTeX papers on network protocols. In each experiment, the following mode was used. A subject with a background in network protocols was asked to typeset each paper as if it were his own. The subject would, at his convenience, inspect the retrieval folder and volunteer relevance judgments on retrieved rfc's. Two options, relevant and nonrelevant, were available. To keep the feedback solicitation nonintrusive, the subject was not obligated to render judgment on every retrieved rfc. To preclude the fatigue factor, each paper was typeset on a different day.

Metric

The evaluation metric used in all experiments was the average search length, $avslen_n$, i.e., the number of nonrelevant rfc's before the n-th relevant one. For example, if $n = 1$, the numbers of nonrelevant rfc's before the first relevant one in all retrieved sets are added and divided by the number of submitted queries. The two standard evaluation metrics, *precision* and *recall* (Harman 1996; Salton and McGill 1983), were not used. Recall was not used, because its assumption that *all* relevant documents are known for *every* query is not realistic for large, dynamic collections. A growing body of experimental evidence (Burke et al. 1997; Jansen et al. 1998; Kulyukin 1998c) suggests that most users (80-90%) examine only the top 2-4% of retrievals. Consequently, little benefit is gained from retrieving all relevant documents, if none of them makes it to the top. Precision was not used, because, while it does consider relevant documents with respect to the actual retrievals, it fails to consider *where* in the retrieved set the relevant documents are. A retrieved set of 20 documents with the relevant documents in the last two positions has the same precision as a set of 20 documents with the relevant documents in the first two positions. In EMIR, empty retrieved sets are probable. If precision is used, such sets must be treated as special cases inasmuch as precision is undefined if nothing is retrieved.

Results

The first experiment tested the differences between random and structured sampling. In random sampling, queries were computed from random term samples of sizes 10, 20, and 30. The system did the greedy morphological analysis of the paper's text typeset to this point, ignoring the LaTeX commands, and randomly selected the required number of terms. In structured sampling, queries were computed from samples taken from specific parts of the paper: abstract, introduction, and references. To compute a sample of size n from a part P, the system parsed the text for P, computed the total number of terms (T) in it, chose a random position i, $0 \leq i \leq T - n - 1$, took n consecutive terms beginning at i, and applied the greedy morphological analysis to the selection. The sizes for structured samples were the same as for random samples. When sampling from references, the terms were taken from titles. The top 20 rfc's were retrieved in response to every query. Three metrics, $avslen_1, avslen_2$, and $avslen_3$, were computed. A retrieved set with at least one relevant rfc had a minimum search length of 0 and a maximum search length of 19. Sets with no relevant rfc's had the search length of 20. For each of the 20 test papers, 20 queries (10 random and 10 structured) were computed for each query size (qsize). The term weight metric was $\omega_{cw}(i,j) = \omega_{sm}(i)^{\alpha_1} \omega_{tfidfcc}(i,j)^{\alpha_2}$, where $\alpha_1 = \alpha_2 = 1$. The experiment's results are presented in Figure 1. The top table gives the random queries' avslen's. The bottom table gives the structured queries' avslen's for the three document parts. Thus, the values in the $avslen_1$ row under *abst*, i.e., 8.5, 5.1, and 3.2, are the $avslen_1$'s for the qsizes 10, 20, and 30, respectively,

slen vs. qsize	10	20	30
$avslen_1$	11.4	8.5	7.0
$avslen_2$	12.7	10.7	7.9
$avslen_3$	17.7	15.4	10.3

slen vs. part	abst			intro			refs		
$avslen_1$	10.1	6.2	4.2	8.9	5.2	4.2	14.7	11.3	8.7
$avslen_2$	10.7	7.9	5.8	10.1	8.4	7.8	15.9	14.7	12.5
$avslen_3$	14.3	9.4	7.7	13.0	10.7	9.3	18.6	18.4	15.7

Figure 2: Random vs. structured queries without dual space feedback

computed from the abstracts. The top table suggests that the avslen improves as the random queries' sizes increase. Thus, random queries may be a viable backup when no structure is available because of the nature of the data or parsing failures. The bottom table suggests that the introduction of structure into sampling makes a difference. The avslen's for the queries computed from abstracts and introductions are lower than their random counterparts. No significant difference was found between the abstract and introduction queries. A closer analysis revealed that many papers had an overlap between the terms in the abstract and introduction. Ideas were stated in short sentences in the abstract and repeated or expanded with the same terms in the introduction. The reference queries performed worse than their structured and random counterparts. One explanation is that the titles may not provide sufficient descriptions of the papers' content. Another explanation is that authors may cite each other for political reasons, e.g., to promote a research agenda, for which EMIR cannot account.

The second experiment tested the dual space feedback. Using the queries and relevance judgments from the first experiments, the avslen's were recomputed with the dual space feedback disabled. As the tables in Figure 2 show, feedback disablement had a negative impact on avslen's. The change was pronounced with abstract and introduction queries. It was less noticeable with random and reference queries. A closer analysis indicated that the dual space feedback prevented non-relevant rfc's from moving ahead of the relevant ones.

The third experiment tested anydata indexing. The experiment's objective was to find evidence to support the hypothesis that in larger collections, both homogeneous and heterogeneous, a term's tendency to condense in documents is a better predictor of relevance than its rarity. Two document collections, homogeneous and heterogeneous, were used. The homogeneous collection included 432 rfc's on TCP, UDP, and IP. The heterogeneous collection included the homogeneous collection plus 510 rfc's on Mail and Usenet message formats. The similarity metric, queries, and relevance judgments were the same as in the first two experiments. The performance metric was $avslen_3$. For each collection, the values of A and C ran between -30 and

30 in steps of .25; B was set to 1. Fixing B at 1 and varying A and C were aimed at testing the effects of the constant and the correction on IDF. If the best performance were to be found at $C = 0$, it would indicate that the tendency to condense is not as good a content predictor as rarity. In the first collection, the best $avslen_3$ was 9.21, when $A = -1$ and $C = -1.2$; the best value of $avslen_3$ for IDF, i.e., $A = B = 1$, and $C = 0$, was 12.74. In the second collection, the best $avslen_3$ was 8.2 when $A = -1.25$ and $C = -20$; the best value of $avslen_3$ for IDF was 15.25. Thus, in the larger heterogeneous collection, CC performed better than IDF. In both collections, the correction's effect was greater than the effect of the constant. The effect was more pronounced in the larger heterogeneous collection. One explanation is that a larger collection is likely to cover different topics. If terms are valued by their tendency to condense in the documents pertinent to their topics, content-bearing terms have a better chance to deviate from being randomly distributed over the documents.

Discussion

The integration of query generation and feedback continues to attract the attention of AI and IR researchers (Burke, Hammond, and Young 1996; Fitzgerald 1995; Kulyukin, Hammond, and Burke 1998). The presented approach shares with this research the intuition that better integrations are achieved in task-embedded systems. However, application-embedded IR differs from its counterparts in several respects.

First, since indexing is distributed, there is no central content repository that is either static (Burke, Hammond, and Young 1996; Fitzgerald 1995), or must be periodically maintained with expensive reindexing operations (Burke et al. 1997; Kulyukin 1998b; Kulyukin 1998c). Information sources maintain themselves and offer an IR system a set of services agreed upon in advance. To index a source is not to build and maintain an adequate representation of its content, but to know what services the source offers and when to use them.

Second, no explicit query generation is required of the user. Since many lay users find it hard to put their information needs into queries, let alone into formalisms of modern IR systems, queries are automatically generated by the system from sampling the application's usage. In this respect, EMIR is similar to example-based knowledge navigation systems, such as FindMe systems (Burke, Hammond, and Young 1996), which monitor how users navigate in information spaces. However, EMIR differs from FindMe systems, because query generation occurs in the background, while in FindMe systems it depends on the user explicitly critiquing multiple examples before the right one is found.

Third, feedback solicitation is nonintrusive. Such feedback solicitation is consistent with the empirical evidence that, unlike information science professionals, lay users almost never give feedback when it is solicited explicitly (Jansen et al. 1998; Spink and Saracevic 1997).

Fourth, feedback utilization is persistent. Unlike many other IR systems that use relevance feedback in the query space alone (Aalbersberg 1992; Harman 1996), EMIR uses feedback to modify its representations in the document space. The user is assumed to be consistent in his or her relevance judgments over a long period of time. The assumption is valid, because EMIR targets one user, whereas similar systems target large and heterogeneous user groups that are unlikely to be consistent in their judgments.

Conclusion

A framework for application-embedded retrieval from distributed free-text collections was developed and illustrated with EMIR, an IR system embedded in a text processor. Queries are generated from background samples of free-text papers and used in retrievals from distributed collections. Feedback is never solicited explicitly, and is utilized persistently only when volunteered. A family of term weight metrics was presented, unifying IDF and CC. It was shown how retrieval can be adjusted through background sampling, anydata indexing, and dual space feedback.

Acknowledgments

I would like to thank the reviewers for their insightful and constructive comments. Alain Roy showed me the rfc repository and partitioned it into topics. Shannon Bradshaw gave me permission to use the collection of technical papers he had gathered for his Rosetta project. This paper benefited from my discussions with Clark Elliott, Kurt Fenstermacher, Steve Lytinen, Bomshad Mobasher, Amber Settle, and Noriko Tomuro. I am grateful to Deborah Kulyukin for editorial work.

References

Aalbersberg, I. J. 1992. Incremental Relevance Feedback. In Proceedings of the 15th Annual International SIGIR Conference, 11-21.

Bookstein, A.; Klein, S. T.; and Raita, T. 1998. Clumping Properties of Content-Bearing Words. *Journal of the American Society for Information Science* 49(2):102-114.

Bradshaw, S. G. 1998. Reference Directed Indexing: Attention to Descriptions People Use for Information. M.S. thesis, Dept. of Computer Science, The University of Chicago.

Brauen, T. L. 1971. Document Vector Modification. In G. Salton, ed. *The SMART Retrieval System: Experiments in Automatic Document Processing*, 456-484. Englewood Cliffs, NJ: Prentice-Hall, Inc.

Burke, R. D.; Hammond, K. J.; Kulyukin, V.; Lytinen, S. L.; Tomuro, N.; and Schoenberg, S. 1997. Question Answering from Frequently Asked Question Files: Experiences with the FAQ Finder System. *AI Magazine* 18(2):57-66.

Burke, R. D.; Hammond, K. J.; and Young, B. C. 1996. Knowledge-based Navigation of Complex Information Spaces. In Proceedings of AAAI-96.

Cutting, D.; Kupiec, J.; Pederson, J.; and Sibun, P. 1992. A Practical Part-of-Speech Tagger. In Proceedings of the Third Conference on Applied Natural Language Processing. Trentano, Italy: Association of Computational Linguistics.

Fitzgerald, W. 1995. Building Embedded Conceptual Parsers. Ph.D. diss., Dept. of Computer Science, Northwestern University.

Francis, W., and Kucera, H. 1982. *Frequency Analysis of English Usage*. New York: Houghton Mufflin.

Harman, D. 1996. Overview of the Fourth Text REtrieval Conference. In Proceedings of the Fourth Text REtrieval Conference (TREC-4).

Jansen, B. J.; Spink, A.; Bateman, J.; and Saracevic, T. 1998. Real Life Information Retrieval: A Study of User Queries on the Web. *SIGIR Forum* 32(1):5-18.

Kulyukin, V. 1998a. FAQ Finder: A Gateway to Newsgroups' Expertise. In Proceedings of the 40th Conference of Lisp Users.

Kulyukin, V. 1998b. An Interactive and Collaborative Approach to Answering Questions for an Organization. In Proceedings of the ASIS-98 Mid Year Conference.

Kulyukin, V. 1998c. Question-Driven Information Retrieval Systems. Ph.D. diss., Dept. of Computer Science, The University of Chicago.

Kulyukin, V.; Hammond, K.; and Burke, R. 1996. Automated Analysis of Structured Online Documents. In Proceedings of the AAAI-96 Workshop on Internet-Based Information Systems.

Kulyukin, V.; Hammond, K.; and Burke, R. 1998. Answering Questions for an Organization Online. In Proceedings of AAAI-98.

Miller, G. A. 1995. WordNet: A Lexical Database for English. *Communications of the ACM* 38(11):39-41.

Robertson, S., and Walker, S. 1997. On Relevance Weights with Little Relevance Information. In Proceedings of ACM SIGIR.

Salton, G., and McGill, M. 1983. *Introduction to Modern Information Retrieval.* New York: McGraw-Hill.

Spink, A., and Saracevic, T. 1997. Interactive Information Retrieval: Sources and Effectiveness of Search Terms During Mediated Online Searching. *Journal of the American Society for Information Science* 48(8):741-761.

Towards Multidocument Summarization by Reformulation:
Progress and Prospects

Kathleen R. McKeown, Judith L. Klavans, Vasileios Hatzivassiloglou,
Regina Barzilay and **Eleazar Eskin**

Department of Computer Science
Columbia University
1214 Amsterdam Avenue
New York, NY 10027

{kathy, klavans, vh, regina, eeskin}@cs.columbia.edu

Abstract

By synthesizing information common to retrieved documents, multi-document summarization can help users of information retrieval systems to find relevant documents with a minimal amount of reading. We are developing a multi-document summarization system to automatically generate a concise summary by identifying and synthesizing similarities across a set of related documents. Our approach is unique in its integration of machine learning and statistical techniques to identify similar paragraphs, intersection of similar phrases within paragraphs, and language generation to reformulate the wording of the summary. Our evaluation of system components shows that learning over multiple extracted linguistic features is more effective than information retrieval approaches at identifying similar text units for summarization and that it is possible to generate a fluent summary that conveys similarities among documents even when full semantic interpretations of the input text are not available.

Introduction

Currently, most approaches to single document summarization involve extracting key sentences to form the summary (e.g., [Paice 1990; Kupiec *et al.* 1995; Marcu 1998]). Yet, given the multitude of sources that describe the same event in a similar manner (e.g., on-line news sources), it would be helpful to the end-user to have a summary of multiple related documents. Multiple document summarization could be useful, for example, in the context of large information retrieval systems to help determine which documents are relevant. Such summaries can cut down on the amount of reading by synthesizing information common among all retrieved documents and by explicitly highlighting distinctions. In contrast, with single document summarization, users would have to read numerous individual summaries, one for each of the top retrieved documents and infer similarities.

While sentence extraction may be adequate for single document summarization, it will not work effectively for multiple document summarization. Any individual document does not contain explicit comparisons with all other documents which can be extracted; alternatively, if all sentences

A federal office building was devastated by a car bomb in Oklahoma City on April 19th 1995. Around 250 people are still unaccounted for. More than 80 victims were killed in the explosion. The Oklahoma blast was the biggest act of suspected terror in U.S. history, overtaking the 1993 bombing of the World Trade Center in New York which killed six and injured 1,000 others.

President Clinton vowed to capture the bombers and brought them to a swift justice.

On 04/21 Reuters reported Federal agents have arrested a suspect in the Oklahoma City bombing. Timothy James McVeigh, 27, was formally charged on Friday with the bombing. Brothers James and Terry Nichols, known friends of McVeigh and reported to share his extreme right-wing views, have been held since last week as material witnesses to the Oklahoma bombing.

Figure 1: Summary produced by our system using 24 news articles as input.

containing similar information are extracted (Mani and Bloedorn, 1997; Yang *et al.* 1998), this would make for lengthy and repetitive reading.

We are developing a multi-document summarization system to automatically generate a concise summary by identifying similarities and differences across a set of related documents. Input to the system is a set of related documents, such as those retrieved by a standard search engine in response to a particular query. Our work to date has focused on generating similarities across documents. Our approach uses machine learning over linguistic features extracted from the input documents to identify several groups of paragraph-sized text units which all convey approximately the same information. Syntactic linguistic analysis and comparison between phrases of these units is used to select the phrases that can adequately convey the similar information. This task is performed by the content planner of the language generation component and results in the determination of the summary content. Sentence planning and generation are then used to combine the phrases together to form a coherent whole. An example summary produced by the system is shown in Figure 1; this is a summary of 24 news articles on the Oklahoma

> Timothy James McVeigh, 27, was formally charged on Friday with the bombing of a federal building on Oklahoma City which killed at least 65 people, the Justice Department said.

> Timothy James McVeigh, 27, was formally charged on Friday with the bombing of a federal building on Oklahoma City which killed at least 65 people, the Justice Department said.

> The first suspect, Gulf War veteran Timothy McVeigh, 27, was charged with the bombing Friday after being arrested for a traffic violation shortly after Wednesday's blast.

> Federal agents have arrested suspect in the Oklahoma City bombing Timothy James McVeigh, 27. McVeigh was formally charged on Friday with the bombing.

> Timothy McVeigh, the man charged in the Oklahoma City bombing, had correspondence in his car vowing revenge for the 1993 federal raid on the Branch Davidian compound in Waco, Texas, the Dallas Morning News said Monday.

Figure 2: A collection of similar paragraphs (part of a *theme*) from the Oklahoma bombing event.

City bombing.

The key features of our work are:

1. **Identifying themes.** Given the 24 input articles, how can we identify the similar paragraphs shown in Figure 2? We term each set of similar paragraphs (or generally, text units) a *theme* of the input articles. There may be many themes for a set of articles; for these 24 articles, there are 9 themes. Unlike most systems that compute a measure of similarity over text, our features extend beyond simple word matching and include entire noun phrases, proper nouns, and semantic senses; we also utilize positional and relational information between pairs of words. We ran a series of experiments that compared the use of different features and the baseline provided by standard information retrieval matching techniques, establishing that targeted selection of linguistic features is indeed beneficial for this task.

2. **Information fusion.** Given the subset of one theme extracted from the articles, shown in Figure 2, how can we determine that only the phrases resulting in the sentence "Timothy James McVeigh, 27, was formally charged on Friday with the bombing." should be represented in the summary? We have developed and implemented a novel algorithm for this task which analyzes grammatical structure extracted from each theme with off-the-shelf tools. Our information fusion algorithm compares predicate argument structures of the phrases within each theme to determine which are repeated often enough to be included in the summary. This process yields an average accuracy of 79% when tested on a collection of text units from multiple documents already clustered into themes by hand.

3. **Text reformulation.** Once the content of the summary has been determined, how can we fluently use the similar phrases in novel contexts? Simply stringing the phrases

together can produce ungrammatical results because phrases are placed in new syntactic contexts. We have developed an algorithm that maps the predicate argument structure of input document phrases to arguments expected by FUF/SURGE [Elhadad 1993; Robin 1994], a robust language generation system. This has required developing new techniques for identifying constraints on realization choice (e.g., on the order of circumstantial roles such as time, location, instrument, etc.), using surface features in place of the semantic or pragmatic ones typically used in language generation.

Related Work

To allow summarization in arbitrary domains, most current systems use sentence extraction, identifying and extracting key sentences from an input article using a variety of different criteria. These approaches have all been developed to produce a summary of a single input document. One recent statistical approach [Kupiec *et al.* 1995] uses a corpus of articles with summaries for training to identify the features of sentences that are typically included in abstracts. Other recent approaches use lexical chains [Barzilay and Elhadad 1997], sentence position [Lin and Hovy 1997], discourse structure [Marcu 1997; Marcu 1998], and user features from the query [Strzalkowski *et al.* 1998] to find key sentences.

While most work to date focuses on summarization of single articles, early work is emerging on summarization across multiple documents. Radev and McKeown [1998] use a symbolic approach, pairing information extraction systems with language generation. The result is a domain dependent system for summarization of multiple news articles on the same event, highlighting how perspective of the event has changed over time. In ongoing work at Carnegie Mellon, Yang et al. [1998] are developing statistical techniques to identify similar sentences and phrases across articles. While they have developed a novel statistical approach to identify similar sentences, their system simply lists all extracted similar sentences as the summary. Mani and Bloedorn [1997] use spreading activation and graph matching to compute similarities and differences between the salient topics of two articles. Output is presented as a set of paragraphs which contain similar and distinguishing words, emphasized in different fonts. The problem is a redundant summary since no synthesis of results through generation is attempted.

System Architecture

Our system follows a pipeline architecture, shown in Figure 3. Input to the system is a set of related documents, such as those retrieved by a standard search engine. The analysis component of the system breaks documents into smaller text units and then computes a similarity metric across text units, regardless of the source document. Once similar paragraphs are identified, they are passed to the generation component which further identifies and selects information to be reformulated as coherent text.

The analysis, or similarity computation component takes as input a set of articles that have been previously identified as being on the same topic. In building our system, we used

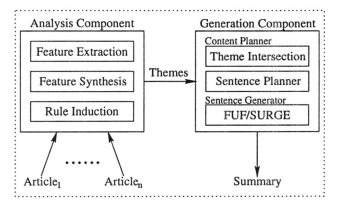

Figure 3: System architecture.

articles from the pilot Topic Detection and Tracking (TDT) corpus [Allan *et al.* 1998] for training and testing. The analysis component breaks the article into paragraph-sized units for comparison, and then extracts a set of linguistic and positional features for input into the similarity algorithm. We construct a vector for each pair of paragraphs, representing matches on each of the different features. These vectors are passed to a machine learning algorithm [Cohen 1996] which combines these features into a classifier using the most discriminating ones to judge similarity. Output is a listing of binary decisions on paragraph pairs, with each pair classified as containing similar or dissimilar text units. The similarity decisions drive a subsequent clustering algorithm, which places the most related paragraphs in the same group, and thus identifies themes.

The generation component consists of a content planner, sentence planner, and a sentence generator. Since input is full text, the process of selecting and ordering content is quite different from typical language generators. For each theme, the content planner identifies phrases within the paragraphs of a theme that are close enough to other phrases in the theme that they can be included in the summary. It does this by producing a predicate-argument structure for each sentence in each input paragraph, comparing arguments to select phrases that are similar. The sentence planner then determines which phrases should be combined into a single, more complex sentence, looking again at constraints from the input document as well as common references between phrases. Finally, the constituent structure produced by these two stages is mapped to the functional representation required as input by FUF/SURGE [Elhadad 1993; Robin 1994].

Document Analysis

Our definition of similarity is different than the one adopted in most text matching tasks (such as information retrieval) because of two factors: first, the size of the unit of text affects what is similar; documents have a lot of information, so even a modest amount of common elements can make two documents similar. Second, our goal is different. We are looking for text units that are quite close in meaning, not just for topical similarity.[1]

We thus consider two textual units similar if they both refer to the same object and that object performs the same action in both textual units, or the object is described in the same way in both of them. Such a common description must be more than just a single modifier. For example, the following two sentences satisfy our criteria for similarity,

> Britain Thursday sent back to the United States a possible suspect in the Oklahoma bomb blast, the interior ministry said.

> "A possible suspect connected with the Oklahoma bomb has been returned to the United States by the U.K. immigration service," a ministry statement said.

because they both refer to a common event (the returning of the suspect to the United States). On the other hand, the following sentence

> Federal agents have arrested a suspect in the Oklahoma City bombing and U.S. television networks reported he was a member of a paramilitary group called the Michigan Militia.

is not similar to the above, as it focuses on a different suspect and his paramilitary connections. Existing methods based on shared words are likely to identify all these sentences as related, since they all contain key words such as "suspect", "Oklahoma", and "bomb".

Traditional metrics for determining similarity among textual units compare term occurrence vectors using frequencies modified by the rarity of each term (the TF*IDF approach) [Salton and Buckley 1988]. Terms are single words, occasionally with simple transformations such as stemming, although sometimes multi-word units and collocations have been used [Smeaton 1992]. Since we are aiming for a different, more fine-grained notion of similarity and operate on much shorter texts than information retrieval does, we explored a number of alternative features. Our features draw on a number of linguistic approaches to text analysis, and are based on both single words and simplex noun phrases (sequences of adjectives and nouns with no embedded recursion). We thus consider the following potential matches between text units:

- **Word co-occurrence**, i.e., sharing of a single word between text units. Variations of this feature restrict matching to cases where the parts of speech of the words also match, or relax it to cases where the stems of the two words are identical.

- **Matching noun phrases**. We use the LinkIt tool [Wacholder 1998] to identify simplex noun phrases and match those that share the same head.

- **WordNet synonyms**. The WordNet semantic database [Miller *et al.* 1990] provides sense information, placing words in sets of synonyms (*synsets*). We match as synonyms words that appear in the same synset.

- **Common semantic classes for verbs**. Levin's [1993] semantic classes for verbs have been found to be useful for determining document type and text similarity [Klavans

---

[1]Note that we start with a set of documents about the same topic, which is the usual goal of information retrieval systems.

and Kan 1998]. We match two verbs that share the same semantic class in this classification.

In addition to the above *primitive* features that all compare single items from each text unit, we use *composite* features that combine pairs of primitive features. Our composite features impose particular constraints on the order of the two elements in the pair, on the maximum distance between the two elements, and on the syntactic classes that the two elements come from. They can vary from a simple combination (e.g., "two text units must share two words to be similar") to complex cases with many conditions (e.g., "two text units must have matching noun phrases that appear in the same order and with relative difference in position no more than five"). In this manner, we capture information on how similarly related elements are spaced out in the two text units, as well as syntactic information on word combinations. Matches on composite features indicate combined evidence for the similarity of the two units.

To determine whether the units match overall, we employ a machine learning algorithm [Cohen 1996] that induces decision rules using the features that really make a difference. A set of pairs of units already marked as similar or not by a human is used for training the classifier. We have manually marked a set of 8,225 paragraph comparisons from the TDT corpus for training and evaluating our similarity classifier.

For comparison, we also use an implementation of the TF*IDF method which is standard for matching texts in information retrieval. We compute the total frequency (TF) of words in each text unit and the number of units in our training set each word appears in (DF, or document frequency). Then each text unit is represented as a vector of TF*IDF scores, calculated as

$$TF(\text{word}_i) \cdot \log \frac{\text{Total number of units}}{DF(\text{word}_i)}$$

Similarity between text units is measured by the cosine of the angle between the corresponding two vectors (i.e., the normalized inner product of the two vectors), and the optimal value of a threshold for judging two units as similar is computed from the training set.

After all pairwise similarities between text units have been calculated, we utilize a clustering algorithm to identify themes. As a paragraph may belong to multiple themes, most standard clustering algorithms, which partition their input set, are not suitable for our task. We use a greedy, one-pass algorithm that first constructs groups from the most similar paragraphs, seeding the groups with the fully connected subcomponents of the graph that the similarity relationship induces over the set of paragraphs, and then places additional paragraphs within a group if the fraction of the members of the group they are similar to exceeds a preset threshold.

Language Generation

Given a group of similar paragraphs—a theme—the problem is to create a concise and fluent fusion of information in this theme, reflecting facts common to all paragraphs. A straightforward method would be to pick a representative

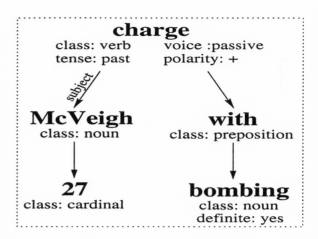

Figure 4: Dependency grammar representation of the sentence "McVeigh, 27, was charged with the bombing".

sentence that meets some criteria (e.g., a threshold number of common content words). In practice, however, any representative sentence will usually include embedded phrase(s) containing information that is *not* common to all sentences in the theme. Furthermore, other sentences in the theme often contain *additional* information not presented in the representative sentence. Our approach, therefore, uses intersection among theme sentences to identify phrases common to most paragraphs and then generates a new sentence from identified phrases.

Intersection among Theme Sentences

Intersection is carried out in the content planner, which uses a parser for interpreting the input sentences, with our new work focusing on the comparison of phrases. Theme sentences are first run through a statistical parser [Collins 1996] and then, in order to identify functional roles (e.g., subject, object), are converted to a dependency grammar representation [Kittredge and Mel'čuk 1983], which makes predicate-argument structure explicit.

We developed a rule-based component to produce functional roles, which transforms the phrase-structure output of Collins' parser to dependency grammar; function words (determiners and auxiliaries) are eliminated from the tree and corresponding syntactic features are updated. An example of a theme sentence and its dependency grammar representation are shown in Figure 4. Each non-auxiliary word in the sentence has a node in the representation, and this node is connected to its direct dependents.

The comparison algorithm starts with all subtrees rooted at verbs from the input dependency structure, and traverses them recursively: if two nodes are identical, they are added to the output tree, and their children are compared. Once a full phrase (verb with at least two constituents) has been found, it is confirmed for inclusion in the summary.

Difficulties arise when two nodes are not identical, but are similar. Such phrases may be paraphrases of each other and still convey essentially the same information. Since theme sentences are *a priori* close semantically, this significantly constrains the kind of paraphrasing we need to check for. We verified this assumption by analyzing paraphrasing patterns through themes of our training corpus, drawn from the TDT (see the Evaluation section). We found that that a high percentage of paraphrasing is at the "surface" level, using semantically related words and syntactic transformations.

When similar nodes are detected, the algorithm tries to apply an appropriate paraphrasing rule, drawn from the corpus analysis. For example, if the phrases "group of students" and "students" are compared, then the *omit empty head* rule is applicable, since "group" is an empty noun and can be dropped from the comparison, leaving two identical words, "students". In the case that a matching paraphrase rule cannot be found, the comparison is finished and the phrase is dropped. Other examples of paraphrase include ordering of syntactic components in the sentence (e.g., inversion of subject and object because of passive), realization of the predicate in a main clause versus a relative clause, and use of synonyms based on WordNet.

For the theme in Figure 2, intersection results in the clause "McVeigh was formally charged on Friday with the bombing" and the description "Timothy James McVeigh, 27".

Sentence Generation Component

The primary task of this component is to construct the summary text from phrases selected from the theme. During this process, the system orders phrases based on their time sequence of appearance, adds additional information needed for clarification (e.g., entity descriptions, temporal references, and newswire source references) that appeared in the full articles but not in the theme [Barzilay *et al.* 1999], and maps the dependency representations to an English sentence. Output of this component is the full summary, such as the one shown in Figure 1.

Ordering of phrases within the summary is based on chronological order inferred from their appearance in the original text. To do this, for each theme, we record a date that is the earliest date on which any of its sentences were published. We sort extracted phrases according to these dates.

Sentence realization is done by mapping the dependency structure to the input required by FUF/SURGE [Elhadad 1993; Robin 1994]. The use of a language generator, with full grammar, means that the system can combine phrases together in ways that did not occur in the input text. A phrase that occurred as the main clause in an input text, for example, may be realized in the summary as a subordinate clause. The grammar is used to determine inflections, subject-verb agreement, and word orderings. This gives us the ability to generate coherent, fluent text as opposed to rigidly using extracted sentences in the same ways they were used in the input.

Sentence generators such as FUF/SURGE, however, typically require a set of sentential semantic roles as input. They were developed for use within a system that builds a semantic sentence representation from data. However, in our case, we have no access to semantic information; all that we have are syntactic roles, derived from the parse tree for the sentence. In many cases, this simply means less work

for FUF/SURGE. Processing starts using roles such as subject, object, and main verb instead of deriving these syntactic roles from roles such as agent, goal, and predicate. However, in other cases, it means producing a sentence with only vague knowledge of the function of a particular constituent. For example, for circumstantials such as time, location, or manner, the summarizer can only determine from the input that it is a circumstantial and cannot determine its type. The specific function determines the options for paraphrasing (e.g., whether it appears at the beginning or end of the sentence, or next to some other constituent). We use the ordering derived from the input to constrain these options and leave the specific function unspecified. We will continue to look at cases where different kinds of syntactic constraints on paraphrasing can be derived from the input in place of semantic or pragmatic constraints.

System Status

We have an initial system prototype which includes implementation of system components and integration of components for a number of examples. More work needs to be done to tune output of the theme identifier to produce better input for the generation component. Our experiments show that high recall and low precision in finding themes is better for the generator than low recall and high precision. This is because the content planner, which performs information fusion, makes a more thorough analysis and weeds out sentences that are not similar when comparing phrases. Thus, it can handle errors in its input, but it cannot handle missing input. As the noise in its input increases, the size of the intersection decreases. In such cases, the output summary will be short, but the system will never generate nonsensical output.

Given noisy input (i.e., dissimilar articles), the system components degrade in different ways. Given poor input, the theme identification component may produce low-quality themes. But, as noted above, the intersection component will weed out these errors and produce an empty, or small intersection, and a short summary. Also, we are focusing on articles that have already been judged similar by some means (e.g., by an information retrieval engine), so it is unlikely that our system will receive markedly different documents as input.

Evaluation

Given that our implementation of components is complete, but full integration of components is still underway, our evaluation at this stage focuses on quantifying results for each of the system components separately. Following the division in our system architecture, we identify three separate questions to which results can be produced independently and to which the system's answers can be evaluated. We elaborate on these three questions and on how we quantitatively measure performance on them in the first subsection, and then present the results of the evaluation on specific data collections.

Identifying Themes

The first question we address is how good our system is in identifying themes, or similar paragraphs. We quantify the answer to this question by presenting to the system a list of pairs of paragraphs (all extracted from documents on the same topic) and measuring how many correct decisions the system makes on characterizing the paragraphs in each pair as similar or dissimilar.

Since placing incoming documents into topical clusters is a non-trivial task for large document collections, we use as input a set of articles already classified according to subject matter, the pilot Topic Detection and Tracking (TDT) corpus. The TDT effort, sponsored by DARPA and NIST, aims to promote new research on document classification and clustering; as a necessary step towards comparing different systems on these tasks, a corpus of articles from written and broadcast news sources (Reuters and CNN) is marked with subject categories that correspond to our criteria for selecting similar documents (e.g., "Oklahoma City bombing" or "Pentium chip flaw"). We are using the Reuters part of the first such collection made available in early 1998 (the TDT pilot corpus), which contains 16,000 articles (see `http://morph.ldc.upenn.edu/ Catalog/ LDC98T25. html` for more details).

We selected 6 of the 25 topical categories in the pilot TDT corpus, favoring categories that had a significant number of member documents. For each such category, we selected articles from randomly chosen days, for a total of 30 articles.

Documents in each topical category are broken into paragraphs, and paragraphs from different documents in the same theme are compared using the various alternatives described in our document analysis section. For example, our first category about two Americans lost in Iraq has 61 paragraphs across 8 selected articles, and $61 \cdot 60 / 2 = 1,830$ comparisons are made between those 61 paragraphs. All the selected categories have 264 paragraphs and 8,225 comparisons between paragraphs, calculated as

$$\sum_{i=1}^{6} \binom{N_i}{2}$$

where N_i is the number of paragraphs in category i. We randomly divided these pairs of paragraphs into a training set (6,225 pairs) and a testing set (2,000 pairs). These 8,225 pairs were manually compared independently by two evaluators (who subsequently met and reconciled differences), and classified as either similar or dissimilar.

We extracted the primitive features discussed in the document analysis section, calculated our composite features, and trained both the machine learning model that uses these features and the TF*IDF classifier on the training set. Our feature-based approach was able to recover 39.7% of the similar pairs of paragraphs with 60% precision and had an overall accuracy over both similar and dissimilar pairs of 97%, while the corresponding numbers for the TF*IDF method were 31.4% recall of similar paragraphs, 41.8% precision and 96.5% overall accuracy.

Note that since we have a fine-grained model of similarity, most paragraphs are dissimilar to most other paragraphs.

As a result, the baseline method of always guessing "dissimilar" will have a very high accuracy (percentage of total correct answers), 97% in our experiments. However, as in comparable information retrieval tasks with no pre-constructed, balanced evaluation document sets, it is important to focus primarily on evaluation results for the rarer similar pairs (respectively, on the documents relevant to a particular query), rather than all pairs (or documents) in the collection. Our results indicate that our approach outperforms traditional text matching techniques, especially on the harder-to-find similar paragraphs.

Information Fusion

The second evaluation question addresses the performance of our content planner, measuring how well we identify phrases that are repeated throughout the multiple paragraphs within a theme. We present the system with several manually constructed themes and compare the system-produced collection of phrases to manually identified common phrases. Manually constructed themes allow us to obtain an independent view of the content planner's performance, without including any misclassifications that the first stage of the system makes. Then standard measures such as precision and recall can be used to quantitatively compare the system's results to the reference list.

To carry out this evaluation, we constructed five themes each containing 3.8 paragraphs on average. To do this, we used themes automatically constructed by the first stage of the system and edited errors by hand. Repeated information was manually extracted from each theme, producing seven sentence-level predicate-argument structures corresponding to phrases that should be included in the summary. Then we applied our intersection algorithm which proposed six predicate-argument structures for the summary and was able to correctly identify 81% of the subjects, 85% of the main verbs, and 72% of the other constituents in our list of model predicate-argument structures.

Generating Sentences

The final evaluation task is to assess how well our surface generation component performs on the task of putting together the extracted phrases in coherent sentences. We evaluate performance on this task by asking humans to rate each produced sentence in terms of fluency, but not in terms of content. In fact, the evaluators do not see the original documents, and thus base their judgements only on the quality of the produced sentences in isolation.

This is an important first step in evaluation; given that we are taking apart sentences and putting them together in novel ways, we need to measure how well we do at producing fluent and grammatical sentences. While this is not an issue for extraction-based summarization systems, robustness at the sentence generation level is critical to success in our approach. We are also looking at alternative methods for rating sentences on fluency. A logical next step will be to evaluate sentences in context, measuring overall coherence. In addition, the grades that people assign to sentences are subjective; an alternative is to ask evaluators to order sentences

The defense department said an OH-58 military U.S. scout helicopter made an emergency landing in the North Korea friday.   Score: 95
North Korea said it shot the helicopter down over the its territory.   Score: 80
Richardson cancelled other discussions that it was taken place on the recent nuclear U.S.-NORTH KOREA agreement.   Score: 50

Figure 5: Three of the sentences automatically generated by our system and the fluency scores assigned to them.

on the basis of fluency, presenting them with the system's output together with sentences written by humans.

We evaluated the fluency of our sentence generator by having it generate 31 sentences from the correct list of predicate argument structures used in the second evaluation experiment. Each of these sentences was read by an independent evaluator, who graded it on fluency with a numeric score between 0 and 100. This process resulted in an average score of 79.5, with 15 of the 31 sentences scored at 90 or more. Figure 5 shows three of the generated sentences and their assigned scores.

Conclusions and Future Work

This paper presents a novel architecture for accomplishing summarization of multiple documents in any domain. In order to achieve this, our work builds on existing tools, such as a parser and generator, as a springboard to take us further than would otherwise be possible. This has allowed us to address key higher-level issues including the development of a paragraph similarity module using learning over a set of linguistic features, an algorithm for identifying similar clauses within the resulting themes, and sentence generation techniques to combine clauses in novel ways within new contexts. These new features enable the development of a multi-document summarizer that uses reformulation to produce natural and fluent text. Unlike sentence extraction techniques which present a concatenated list of sentences or phrases picked on the basis of statistical or locational criteria, our system presents a synthesized summary, created using both statistical and linguistic techniques.

In the future, we plan to experiment with an alternative evaluation approach that rates the produced summary as a whole. We are in contact with professional journalists who perform the task of synthesizing an article from multiple news sources. One possibility is to ask them to evaluate the summaries directly; another is to identify through user analysis other measures that they internally use to arrive at "good" articles and try to apply them to the summarization task.

Acknowledgments

This material is based upon work supported by the National Science Foundation under grant No. IRI-96-1879. Any opinions, findings, and conclusions or recommendations expressed in this material are those of the authors and do not necessarily reflect the views of the National Science Foundation.

References

[Allan *et al.* 1998] James Allan, Jaime Carbonell, George Doddington, Jon Yamron, and Y. Yang. Topic Detection and Tracking Pilot Study: Final Report. In *Proceedings of the Broadcast News Understanding and Transcription Workshop*, pages 194–218, 1998.

[Barzilay and Elhadad 1997] Regina Barzilay and Michael Elhadad. Using Lexical Chains for Text Summarization. In *Proceedings of the ACL Workshop on Intelligent Scalable Text Summarization*, pages 10–17, Madrid, Spain, August 1997. Association for Computational Linguistics.

[Barzilay *et al.* 1999] Regina Barzilay, Kathleen R. McKeown, and Michael Elhadad. Information Fusion in the Context of Multi-Document Summarization. In *Proceedings of the 37th Annual Meeting of the ACL*, College Park, Maryland, June 1999. Association for Computational Linguistics.

[Cohen 1996] William Cohen. Learning Trees and Rules with Set-Valued Features. In *Proceedings of the Fourteenth National Conference on Artificial Intelligence (AAAI-96)*. American Association for Artificial Intelligence, 1996.

[Collins 1996] Michael Collins. A New Statistical Parser Based on Bigram Lexical Dependencies. In *Proceedings of the 35th Annual Meeting of the Association for Computational Linguistics*, Santa Cruz, California, 1996.

[Elhadad 1993] Michael Elhadad. *Using Argumentation to Control Lexical Choice: A Functional Unification Implementation*. PhD thesis, Department of Computer Science, Columbia University, New York, 1993.

[Kittredge and Mel'čuk 1983] Richard Kittredge and Igor A. Mel'čuk. Towards a Computable Model of Meaning-Text Relations Within a Natural Sublanguage. In *Proceedings of the Eighth International Joint Conference on Artificial Intelligence (IJCAI-83)*, pages 657–659, Karlsruhe, West Germany, August 1983.

[Klavans and Kan 1998] Judith Klavans and Min-Yen Kan. The Role of Verbs in Document Access. In *Proceedings of the 36th Annual Meeting of the Association for Computational Linguistics and the 17th International Conference on Computational Linguistics (ACL/COLING-98)*, Montreal, Canada, 1998.

[Kupiec *et al.* 1995] Julian M. Kupiec, Jan Pedersen, and Francine Chen. A Trainable Document Summarizer. In Edward A. Fox, Peter Ingwersen, and Raya Fidel, editors, *Proceedings of the 18th Annual International ACM SIGIR Conference on Research and Development in Information Retrieval*, pages 68–73, Seattle, Washington, July 1995.

[Levin 1993] Beth Levin. *English Verb Classes and Alternations: A Preliminary Investigation*. University of Chicago Press, Chicago, Illinois, 1993.

[Lin and Hovy 1997] Chin-Yew Lin and Eduard Hovy. Identifying Topics by Position. In *Proceedings of the 5th ACL Conference on Applied Natural Language Processing*, pages 283–290, Washington, D.C., April 1997.

[Mani and Bloedorn 1997] Inderjeet Mani and Eric Bloedorn. Multi-document Summarization by Graph Search and Matching. In *Proceedings of the Fifteenth National Conference on Artificial Intelligence (AAAI-97)*, pages 622–628, Providence, Rhode Island, 1997. American Association for Artificial Intelligence.

[Marcu 1997] Daniel Marcu. From Discourse Structures to Text Summaries. In *Proceedings of the ACL Workshop on Intelligent Scalable Text Summarization*, pages 82–88, Madrid, Spain, August 1997. Association for Computational Linguistics.

[Marcu 1998] Daniel Marcu. To Build Text Summaries of High Quality, Nuclearity is not Sufficient. In *Proceedings of the AAAI Symposium on Intelligent Text Summarization*, pages 1–8, Stanford University, Stanford, California, March 1998. American Association for Artificial Intelligence.

[Miller *et al.* 1990] George A. Miller, Richard Beckwith, Christiane Fellbaum, Derek Gross, and Katherine J. Miller. Introduction to WordNet: An On-Line Lexical Database. *International Journal of Lexicography*, 3(4):235–312, 1990.

[Paice 1990] Chris D. Paice. Constructing Literature Abstracts by Computer: Techniques and Prospects. *Information Processing and Management*, 26:171–186, 1990.

[Radev and McKeown 1998] Dragomir R. Radev and Kathleen R. McKeown. Generating Natural Language Summaries from Multiple On-Line Sources. *Computational Linguistics*, 24(3):469–500, September 1998.

[Robin 1994] Jacques Robin. *Revision-Based Generation of Natural Language Summaries Providing Historical Background: Corpus-Based Analysis, Design, Implementation, and Evaluation*. PhD thesis, Department of Computer Science, Columbia University, New York, 1994. Also Columbia University Technical Report CU-CS-034-94.

[Salton and Buckley 1988] G. Salton and C. Buckley. Term Weighting Approaches in Automatic Text Retrieval. *Information Processing and Management*, 25(5):513–523, 1988.

[Smeaton 1992] Alan F. Smeaton. Progress in the Application of Natural Language Processing to Information Retrieval Tasks. *The Computer Journal*, 35(3):268–278, 1992.

[Strzalkowski *et al.* 1998] Tomek Strzalkowski, Jin Wang, and Bowden Wise. A Robust Practical Text Summarization. In *Proceedings of the AAAI Symposium on Intelligent Text Summarization*, pages 26–33, Stanford University, Stanford, California, March 1998. American Association for Artificial Intelligence.

[Wacholder 1998] Nina Wacholder. Simplex NPs Clustered by Head: A Method For Identifying Significant Topics in a Document. In *Proceedings of the Workshop on the Computational Treatment of Nominals*, pages 70–79, Montreal, Canada, October 1998. COLING-ACL.

[Yang *et al.* 1998] Yiming Yang, Tom Pierce, and Jaime Carbonell. A Study on Retrospective and On-Line Event Detection. In *Proceedings of the 21st Annual International ACM SIGIR Conference on Research and Development in Information Retrieval*, Melbourne, Australia, August 1998.

An Automatic Method for Generating Sense Tagged Corpora

Rada Mihalcea and Dan I. Moldovan
Department of Computer Science and Engineering
Southern Methodist University
Dallas, Texas, 75275-0122
{rada, moldovan}@seas.smu.edu

Abstract

The unavailability of very large corpora with semantically disambiguated words is a major limitation in text processing research. For example,
statistical methods for word sense disambiguation
of free text are known to achieve high accuracy results when large corpora are available to develop
context rules, to train and test them.

This paper presents a novel approach to automatically generate arbitrarily large corpora for word
senses. The method is based on (1) the information provided in WordNet, used to formulate
queries consisting of synonyms or definitions of
word senses, and (2) the information gathered
from Internet using existing search engines. The
method was tested on 120 word senses and a precision of 91% was observed.

Introduction

Word Sense Disambiguation (WSD) is an open problem
in Natural Language Processing. Its solution impacts
other tasks such as discourse, reference resolution, coherence, inference and others.

Thus far, statistical methods have been considered
the best techniques in WSD. They produce high accuracy results for a small number of preselected words;
the disambiguation process is based on the probability
of occurrence of a particular sense in a given context
The context is determined by the part of speech of surrounding words, keywords, syntactic relations, collocations.

Statistical methods for WSD consist usually of two
phases:

1. a training phase, in which rules are acquired using
various algorithms

2. a testing phase in which the rules gathered in the first
step are used to determine the most probable sense
for a particular word.

The weakness of these methods is the lack of widely
available semantically tagged corpora.

The disambiguation accuracy is strongly affected by
the size of the corpora used in the disambiguation process. A larger corpora will enable the acquisition of
a larger set of rules during the training phase, thus a
higher accuracy.

Typically, 1000-2500 occurrences of each word are
manually tagged in order to create a corpus. From this,
about 75% of the occurrences are used for the training
phase and the remaining 25% are used for testing. Although high accuracy can be achieved with these approaches, a huge amount of work is necessary to manually tag words to be disambiguated.

For the disambiguation of the noun *interest* with an
accuracy of 78%, as reported in (Bruce and Wiebe,
1994), 2,476 usages of *interest* were manually assigned
with sense tags from the Longman Dictionary of Contemporary English (LDOCE).

For the LEXAS system, described in (Ng and Lee,
1996), the high accuracy is due in part to the use of
a large corpora. For this system, 192,800 word occurrences have been manually tagged with senses from
WordNet; the set consists of the 191 most frequently
occurring nouns and verbs. As specified in their paper, approximatively one man-year of effort was spent
in tagging the data set.

Thus, the sense tagging is done manually and creates
serious impediments in applying statistic methods to
word sense disambiguation.

In this paper, we present an automatic method for
the *acquisition of sense tagged corpora*. It is based on
(1) the information provided in WordNet, particularly
the word definitions found within the glosses, and (2)
information gathered from the Internet using existing
search engines. The information from WordNet is used
to formulate a query consisting of synonyms or definitions of a word sense, while the Internet search engine
extracts texts relevant to such queries.

Given a word for which corpora is to be acquired, we
first determine the possible senses that the word might
have based on the WordNet dictionary. Then, for each
possible sense, we either determine the monosemous
synonyms from the word synset, if such synonyms exist,
or if not use the information provided by the gloss of
that word sense. Each gloss contains a definition, which

can be used as a more detailed explanation for each particular sense of the word we consider. The monosemous synonyms or the definitions constitute the basis for creating a query which will be used for searching on Internet. From the texts we gather, only those sentences containing the searching phrase will be selected. Further, the searching phrase will be replaced by the original word. In this way, we create example sentences for the usage of each sense of the word.

Background on resources.

The following resources have been used in developing and testing our method.

WordNet [1] is a Machine Readable Dictionary developed at Princeton University by a group led by George Miller (Miller 1995), (Fellbaum 1998). WordNet covers the vast majority of nouns, verbs, adjectives and adverbs from the English language. It has a large network of 129,509 words, organized in 99,643 synonym sets, called *synsets*. There is a rich set of 299,711 relation links among words, between words and synsets, and between synsets.

WordNet glosses The synsets of WordNet have defining glosses. A gloss consists of a definition, comments and examples. For example, the gloss of the synset {interest, interestingness} is (the power of attracting or holding one's interest (because it is unusual or exciting etc.); ''they said nothing of great interest''; ''primary colors can add interest to a room''). It has a definition ''the power of attracting or holding one's interest'', a comment ''because it is unusual or exciting'' and two examples: ''they said nothing of great interest'' and ''primary colors can add interest to a room''.
Some glosses contain multiple definitions or multiple comments.

AltaVista (AltaVista) is a search engine developed in 1995 by the Digital Equipment Corporation in its Palo Alto research labs. In choosing AltaVista for use in our system, we based our decision on the size of the Internet information that can be accessed through AltaVista (it has a growing index of over 160,000,000 unique World Wide Web pages) and on the possibility to create complex search queries using boolean operators (*AND*, *OR*, *NOT* and *NEAR*). This makes this search engine suitable for the development of software around it, with the goal of increasing the quality of the information retrieved.

Automatic acquisition of corpora

The method described in this paper enables the automatic acquisition of sentences as possible examples in which a particular sense of a word might occur; the word will be sense tagged in all these examples.

---

[1] WordNet 1.6 has been used in our method.

The basic idea is to determine a lexical phrase, formed by one or several words, which uniquely identifies the meaning of the word, and then finds examples including this lexical phrase. Such a lexical phrase can be created either using monosemous synonyms of the word considered, or using the definition provided within the gloss attached to the WordNet synset in which the word occurs.

The idea of using the definitions is based on the fact that, in order to identify possible examples in which a word with a given sense might occur, we need to locate that particular meaning of the word within some text. The definitions provided in WordNet are specific enough to uniquely determine each sense of the word, thus searching for these definitions will enable us to find concrete examples.

To our knowledge, the only semantically tagged corpora with senses from WordNet is SemCor (Miller et al. 1994), which consists of files taken from the Brown corpus. In SemCor, all the nouns, verbs, adjectives and adverbs defined in WordNet are sense tagged. Although SemCor is a large collection of tagged data, the information provided by SemCor is not sufficient for the purpose of disambiguating words with statistical methods.

Consider, for example, the noun *interest*, which has 7 senses defined in WordNet. The number of occurrences of the senses of *interest* in SemCor is shown in Table 1

Sense number	No.of occurrences		Total occurrences	Automatic acquisition
	brown1	brown2		
1	33	25	58	246
2	15	6	21	545
3	7	25	32	895
4	5	9	14	1000
5	1	2	3	1000
6	0	7	7	718
7	0	4	4	1000
Total	61	78	139	5404

Table 1: The number of occurrences of each sense of the noun *interest* in brown1 and brown2 concordance files from SemCor

The total of 139 occurrences of the noun *interest* is by far insufficient for creating rules leading to high accuracy disambiguation results.

To augment the data provided by SemCor, researchers have manually tagged other publicly available corpora, like for example The Wall Street Journal. We are proposing here a method for automatic acquisition of sense tagged corpora; even though this might be noisy, still it is much easier and less time consuming to check already tagged data then to start tagging from scratch. For the noun *interest*, a total of 5404 occurrences have been found using our method, thus significantly more than the 139 occurrences found in SemCor for the same word. The number of examples acquired for each of the senses of this noun are shown in Table 1 in the last column. Only a maximum of 1,000 examples can be acquired for each search phrase, due to a limitation imposed by the DEC-AltaVista that allows only the first 1,000 hits resulting from a search to be accessed.

The algorithm

The acquisition of sense tagged corpora for a particular word W, using our method, involves three main steps.

1. Preprocessing phase. For each sense $\#i$ of a word W, determine the synset from WordNet in which $W\#i$ is included. For each such synset:

   - Determine all the monosemous words included in the synset. A word is *monosemous* if it has exactly one sense defined in WordNet; a word having multiple senses is said to be *polysemous*.
   - Parse the gloss attached to the synset. This involves: (1) the separation of the gloss into its component parts (definitions, explanations, examples), (2) part of speech tagging and (3) syntactic tagging of the gloss definitions.

2. Search phase. For each sense $\#i$ of the word W, (1) form search phrases SP using, in ascending order of preference, one of the procedures 1 through 4, described below; then (2) search on Internet using the search phrases previously determined and gather documents; and (3) extract from these documents the sentences containing the search phrases.

3. Postprocessing phase. The sentences gathered during phase 2 will become examples for the usage of the original word $W\#i$. For this: (1) the part of speech of the search phrase SP within these examples is checked to be the same as the part of speech for $W\#i$; (2) the sentences in which SP has the same part of speech as $W\#i$ become valid examples by replacing SP with $W\#i$; the examples in which the part of speech of SP is different with respect to $W\#i$ are eliminated.

<u>PREPROCESSING.</u> During this phase: (1) For each sense $\#i$ of a word W, its monosemous synonyms are determined. For example, the adjective *large#3* belongs to the synset {macroscopic, macroscopical, large}. Both *macroscopic* and *macroscopical* have only one sense defined in WordNet, thus they will be picked as monosemous synonyms of *large#3*; (2) The gloss from the synset of $W\#i$ is parsed.

The input to the parser is the gloss attached to the word synset. The output is a set of definitions, part of speech and syntactically tagged. Six steps are performed in order to parse the gloss.

Step 1. From each gloss, extract the definition part.

Step 2. Eliminate the explanatory part of the definition, such as words included in brackets, or phrases starting with *as of, of, as in, as for* etc.

Step 3. Part of speech tag the definition using Brill's tagger (Brill 1992).

Step 4. If the definition includes several phrases or sentences separated by semicolon, then each of these phrases can be considered as an independent definition.

Step 5. Syntactically parse the definitions, i.e. detect the noun phrases, verb phrases, preposition attachments (Srinivas 1997).

Step 6. Based on the parsing from the previous step and the position of the *or* conjunction, create definitions with maximum one verb phrase and one noun phrase. For example, the definition for better#1 ``to make better in quality or more valuable'' will be separated into two definitions ``to make better in quality'' and ``to make more valuable''

<u>SEARCH.</u> In order to determine one or more search phrases for a sense $\#i$ of a word W, denoted as $W\#i$, one of the following procedures will be applied, in ascending order. If a search on the Internet using the search phrases from *Procedure i* does not provide any hits, then *Procedure i+1* will be applied.

<u>Procedure 1.</u> Determine a monosemous synonym, from the $W\#i$ synset. If such a synonym exists, this will constitute the search phrase.

Rationale. The context of a word is determined by the sense of that word. In the case of monosemous words, the context does not depend anymore on the sense of the word and is determined only by the word as a lexical string.

We performed several tests by considering also the direct hyponyms and direct hypernyms as possible relatives; the examples we gathered using such words proved to give less representative examples then using the definition from the glosses (*Procedure 2.*). Based on these empirical observations, we restricted the patterns for *Procedure 1* to synonymy relations.

Example. The noun *remember#1* has *recollect* as a monosemous synonym. Thus the search phrase for this word will be *recollect*.

<u>Procedure 2.</u> Parse the gloss, as explained above in this section. After the parse phase, we are left with a set of definitions, each of them constituting a search phrase.

Rationale. The role of a dictionary is to give definitions which uniquely identify the meaning of the words. Thus, the definition is specific enough to determine the context in which a particular word could appear.

Example. The verb *produce#5* has the definition (bring onto the market or release, as of an intellectual creation). The search phrase will be *bring onto the market* (the other possible definition *release* is eliminated, as being an ambiguous word).

<u>Procedure 3.</u> Parse the gloss. Replace the stop-words with the NEAR search-operator. The query will be strengthened by concatenating the words from the current synset, using the AND search-operator.

Rationale. Using a query formed with the NEAR operator increases the number of hits but reduces the precision of the search; for this, we reinforce the query with words from the synset. This is based on the idea of one sense per collocation, as presented in (Yarowsky 1993).

Example. The synset of *produce#6* is {grow, raise, farm, produce} and it has the definition (cultivate by growing). This will result in the following search phrase: *cultivate NEAR growing AND (grow OR raise OR farm OR produce)*.

Procedure 4. Parse the gloss. Keep only the head phrase, combined with the words from the synset using the AND operator, as in (*Procedure 3.*).

Rationale. If the search phrase determined during the previous procedure does not give any hits, the query can be relaxed by replacing the NEAR operator with the AND operator. Again, a reinforcement is achieved by appending to the query the words from the synset.

Example. The synset of *company#5* is {party, company}, and the definition is (band of people associated temporarily in some activity). The search phrase for this noun will be: *band of people AND (party OR company)*.

Searching on Internet with the queries from *Procedures 1-4*, several documents will be found. From these texts, only those sentences containing the search phrases SP, formed by monosemous synonyms or definitions of *W#i*, will be extracted.

POSTPROCESSING. The examples gathered during the search phase contain SP phrases, which have to have the same part of speech functionality as the original word *W*. If SP consists of a single word, then part of speech tagging (Brill 1992) will be enough to check if SP has the same functionality as the original word *W*. If SP consists of a phrase, then a further syntactic parsing is needed to determine if SP is a noun, verb, adjective or adverb phrase and whether or not it has the same functionality as *W*. Those examples containing SP with a different part of speech / syntactic tag with respect to the original word will be eliminated. In the remaining collection of examples, SP will be replaced with the original word, labeled with the appropriate sense number, i.e. *W#i*.

An example

Let us consider the acquisition of sentences for the different meanings of the noun *interest*. As defined in WordNet 1.6, *interest* is a common word, with a polysemy count of 7. The synset and the associated gloss for each sense of *interest* are presented in Figure 1.

In Table 2, we present the search phrases created for each of the senses of the noun *interest*, by applying one of the *Procedures 1-4*.

Sense #	Search phrase
1	sense of concern AND (interest OR involvement)
2	interestingness
3	reason for wanting AND (interest OR sake)
4	fixed charge AND interest
	percentage of amount AND interest
5	pastime
6	right share AND (interest OR stake)
	legal share AND (interest OR stake)
	financial involvement AND (interest OR stake)
7	interest group

Table 2: Search phrases for each sense of the noun *interest*

1. {interest#1, involvement} - (a sense of concern with and curiosity about someone or something; "an interest in music")
2. {interest#2, interestingness} - (the power of attracting or holding one's interest (because it is unusual or exciting etc.); "they said nothing of great interest"; "primary colors can add interest to a room")
3. {sake, interest#3} - (a reason for wanting something done); "for your sake"; "died for the sake of this country"; "in the interest of safety"; "in the common interest"
4. {interest#4} - (a fixed charge for borrowing money; usually a percentage of the amount borrowed; "how much interest do you pay on your mortgage?")
5. {pastime, interest#5} - (a subject or pursuit that occupies one's time and thoughts (usually pleasantly): "sailing is her favorite pastime"; his main pastime is gambling"; "he counts reading among his interests"; "they criticized the boy for his limited interests")
6. {interest#6, stake} - (a right or legal share of something; a financial involvement with something; "they have interests all over the world"; "a stake in the company's future")
7. {interest#7, interest group} - ((usually plural) a social group whose members control some field of activity and who have common aims; "the iron interests stepped up production")

Figure 1: Synsets and associated glosses of the different senses of the noun *interest*

Using the (AltaVista) search-engine, 5404 sentences have been extracted for the various senses of the noun *interest*, using the search phrases from Table 2. From these, 70 examples were manually checked, out of which 67 were considered correct based on human judgment, thus an accuracy of 95.7% with respect to manually tagged data. Some of these examples are presented in Figure 2.

1. I appreciate the genuine interest#1 which motivated you to write your message
2. The webmaster of this site warrants neither accuracy nor interest#2.
3. He forgives us not only for our interest#3, but for his own!
4. Interest coverage was 4.6x, and interest#4 coverage, including rents, was 3.6x.
5. As an interest#5, she enjoyed gardening and taking part in church activities.
6. Voted on issues, when they should have abstained because of direct and indirect personal interests#6 in the matters at hand.
7. The Adam Smith Society is a new interest#7 organized within the American Philosophical Association.

Figure 2: Context examples for various senses of the noun *interest*

Results

The algorithm presented here was tested on 20 polysemous words. The set consists of 7 nouns: *interest, report, company, school, problem, pressure, mind*; 7 verbs: *produce, remember, write, speak, indicate, believe, happen*; 3 adjectives: *small, large, partial* and 3 adverbs: *clearly, mostly, presently*. Overall, the 20 words have 120 word senses. The algorithm was applied to each of these senses and example contexts were acquired. Since experiments were performed for the purpose of testing the efficiency of our method, rather then for acquiring large corpora, we retained only a maximum of 10 examples for each sense of a word, from the top ranked documents. The correctness of the results was checked manually.

Table 3 presents the polysemy of each word, the total number of examples found in the SemCor corpus, the total number of examples acquired using our method, the number of examples that were manually checked and the number of examples which were considered to be correct, based on human judgment.

Word	Poly-semy count	Examples in SemCor	Total # examples acquired	Examples manually checked	Correct examples
interest	7	139	5404	70	67
report	7	71	4196	70	63
company	9	90	6292	80	77
school	7	146	2490	59	54
problem	3	199	710	23	23
pressure	5	101	2067	50	45
mind	7	113	7000	70	56
produce	7	148	4982	67	60
remember	8	166	3573	67	57
write	8	285	2914	69	67
speak	4	147	4279	40	39
indicate	5	183	4135	50	47
believe	5	215	3009	36	33
happen	5	189	5000	50	46
small	14	192	10954	107	92
large	8	129	5107	80	66
partial	3	1	598	23	18
clearly	4	48	4031	29	28
mostly	2	12	2000	20	20
presently	2	8	2000	20	20
Total	120	2582	80741	1080	978

Table 3: Results obtained for example contexts gathered for 20 words

As it results from this table, for the 120 different meanings considered, a total of 1081 examples have been automatically acquired and then manually checked. Out of these 1081 examples, 981 proved to be correct, leading to an accuracy of 91% such as the tag assigned with our method was the same as the tag assigned by human judgment.

Using this method, very large corpora can be generated. For the total of 20 words, 80,741 examples have been acquired using this method, over thirty times more than the 2,582 examples found in SemCor for these words. Even though the corpora might be noisy, still it is much easier and less time consuming to check for correctness an already existing tagged corpora, then to start tagging free text from scratch.

Discussion. In almost all the cases considered, a large number of example sentences were found as a result of the Internet search. For some cases, though, only a few sentences have been retrieved. For example, the word *believe#5* belongs to the synset {believe} and it has the definition (credit with veracity). Searching on the Internet with the query created based on our method, i.e. *credit with veracity*, or with a variant of this query *credit NEAR veracity AND believe*, resulted in only 4 hits. For such cases, a refinement of our method is needed, which considers also the hypernyms and hyponyms of a synset, together with their gloss definitions.

An important observation is that the number of examples obtained does not always correlate with the frequency of senses, thus classifiers using such a corpora will have to establish prior probabilities.

Related work

Several approaches have been proposed so far for the automatic acquisition of training and testing materials. In (Gale, Church et al., 1992), a bilingual French-English corpus is used. For an English word, the classification of contexts in which various senses of that word appear is done based on the different translations in French for the different word meanings. The problem with this approach is that aligned bilingual corpora is very rare; also, different senses of many polysemous words in English often translate to the same word in French, for such words being impossible to acquire examples with this method.

Another approach for creating training and testing materials is presented in (Yarowsky 1992). He is using Roget's categories to collect sentences from a corpus. For example, for the noun *crane* which appears in both Roget's categories *animal* and *tool*, he uses words in each category to extract contexts from *Grolier's Encyclopedia*. (Yarowsky 1995) proposes the automatic augmentation of a small set of seed collocations to a larger set of training materials. He locates examples containing the seeds in the corpus and analyzes these to find new patterns; then, he retrieves examples containing these patterns. WordNet is suggested as a source for seed collocations. Given an ambiguous word W, with its different meanings W#i, the algorithm presented in (Yarowsky 1995) identifies example sentences for W#i based on the words occurring in its context; the set of words likely to appear in W#i context is built iteratively. On the other hand, our method tries to locate example sentences for W#i by identifying words or expressions similar in meaning with W#i and which uniquely identify the sense #i of the word W.

In (Leacock, Chodorow et al., 1998) a method based on the monosemous words from WordNet is presented. For a given word, its monosemous lexical relatives provide a key for finding relevant training sentences in a corpus. An example given in their paper is the noun *suit* which is a polysemous word, but one sense of it has *business suit* as monosemous hyponym, and another has *legal proceeding* as a hypernym. By collecting examples containing *business suit* and *legal proceeding*, two sets of contexts for the senses of *suit* are built. Even this method exhibits high accuracy results for WSD with respect to manually tagged materials, its applicability for a particular word W is limited by the existence of monosemous "relatives" (i.e. words semantically related to the word W) for the different senses of W and by the number of appearances of these monosemous "relatives" in the corpora. Restricting the semantic relations to synonyms, direct hyponyms and direct hypernyms, they found that about 64% of the words in WordNet have monosemous "relatives" in the 30-million-word corpus of the *San Jose Mercury News*.

Our approach tries to overcome these limitations (1) by using other useful information in WordNet for a particular word, i.e. the word definitions provided by glosses and (2) by using a very large corpora, consisting of texts electronically stored on the Internet. The unique identification of a word is provided either by its monosemous relatives, as they are defined in (Leacock, Chodorow et al., 1998), or by its definition.

Conclusion and further work

In this paper we presented a method which enables the automatic acquisition of sense tagged corpora, based on the information found in WordNet and on the very large collection of texts available on the World Wide Web. The system has been tested on a total of 120 different word meanings and 80,741 context examples for these words have been acquired. Out of these, 1,081 examples were checked against human judgment which resulted in a 91% accuracy.

There is no basic limitation on the size of the corpus acquired for each word, other than the need to check the results of the Internet search, and filter out the inappropriate texts. Further work is needed to automate this verification. We plan to use this method for automatic acquisition of very large corpora which will be used to test word sense disambiguation accuracy.

References

Digital Equipment Corporation. AltaVista Home Page. URL:*http://www.altavista.com.*

Brill, E. 1992, A simple rule-based part of speech tagger, *Proc. 3rd Conference on Applied Natural Language Conference*, ACL, Trento, Italy 1992.

Bruce, R. and Wiebe, J. 1994 Word Sense Disambiguation using Decomposable Models, *Proceedings of the 32nd Annual Meeting of the Association for Computational Linguistics* (ACL-94), LasCruces, June 1994.

Fellbaum, C. 1998, *WordNet, An Electronic Lexical Database.* The MIT Press.

Gale, W.; Church, K. and Yarowsky, D. 1992, One Sense per Discourse, *Proceedings of the DARPA Speech and Natural Language Workshop*, New York, 1992.

Leacock, C.; Chodorow, M. and Miller, G.A. 1998, Using Corpus Statistics and WordNet Relations for Sense Identification, *Computational Linguistics*, March 1998.

Miller, G.A.; Chodorow, M.; Landes, S.; Leacock, C. and Thomas, R.G. 1994, Using a semantic concordance for sense identification. *Proceedings of the ARPA Human Language Technology Workshop*, 240-243, 1994.

Miller, G.A. 1995, WordNet: A Lexical Database, *Communication of the ACM*, vol 38: No11, November 1995.

Ng, H.T. and Lee, H.B. 1996, Integrating Multiple Knowledge Sources to Disambiguate Word Sense: An Examplar-Based Approach, *Proceedings of the 34th Annual Meeting of the Association for Computational Linguistics* (ACL-96), Santa Cruz, 1996.

Srinivas, B. 1997, Performance Evaluation of Supertagging for Partial Parsing, *Proceedings of Fifth International Workshop on Parsing Technology*, Boston, USA, September 1997.

Yarowsky, D. 1992, Word-sense disambiguation using statistical models of Roget's categories trained on large corpora, *Proceedings of COLING-92*, Nantes, France, 1992.

Yarowsky, D. 1993, One sense per collocation, *Proceedings of ARPA Human Language Technology*, Princeton, 1993

Yarowsky, D. 1995, Unsupervised Word Sense Disambiguation rivaling Supervised Methods, Proceedings of the 33rd Association of Computational Linguistics, 1995.

Selecting Text Spans for Document Summaries: Heuristics and Metrics

Vibhu Mittal*   **Mark Kantrowitz***   **Jade Goldstein†**   **Jaime Carbonell†**

*Just Research
4616 Henry Street
Pittsburgh, PA 15213
U.S.A.

†Language Technologies Institute
Carnegie Mellon University
Pittsburgh, PA 15213
U.S.A.

Abstract

Human-quality text summarization systems are difficult to design, and even more difficult to evaluate, in part because documents can differ along several dimensions, such as length, writing style and lexical usage. Nevertheless, certain cues can often help suggest the selection of sentences for inclusion in a summary. This paper presents an analysis of news-article summaries generated by sentence extraction. Sentences are ranked for potential inclusion in the summary using a weighted combination of linguistic features – derived from an analysis of news-wire summaries. This paper evaluates the relative effectiveness of these features. In order to do so, we discuss the construction of a large corpus of extraction-based summaries, and characterize the underlying degree of difficulty of summarization at different compression levels on articles in this corpus. Results on our feature set are presented after normalization by this degree of difficulty.

Introduction

Summarization is a particularly difficult task for computers because it requires natural language understanding, abstraction and generation. Effective summarization, like effective writing, is neither easy and nor innate; rather, it is a skill that is developed through instruction and practice. Writing a summary requires the summarizer to *select, evaluate, order* and *aggregate* items of information according to their relevance to a particular subject or purpose.

Most of the previous work in summarization has focused on a related, but simpler, problem: *text-span deletion*. In text-span deletion – also referred to as text-span extraction – the system attempts to delete "less important" spans of text from the original document; the text that remains can be deemed a summary of the original document. Most of the previous work on extraction-based summarization is based on the use of statistical techniques such as frequency or variance analysis applied to linguistic units such as tokens, names, anaphoric or co-reference information (e.g., (Baldwin & Morton 1998; Boguraev & Kennedy 1997; Aone *et al.* 1997; Carbonell & Goldstein 1998; Hovy & Lin 1997; Mitra, Singhal, & Buckley 1997)). More involved approaches have attempted to use discourse

structure (Marcu 1997), combinations of information extraction and language generation (Klavans & Shaw 1995; McKeown, Robin, & Kukich 1995), and the use of machine learning to find patterns in text (Teufel & Moens 1997; Barzilay & Elhadad 1997; Strzalkowski, Wang, & Wise 1998). However, it is difficult to compare the relative merits of these various approaches because most of the evaluations reported were conducted on different corpora, of varying sizes at varying levels of compression, and were often informal and subjective.

This paper discusses summarization by sentence extraction and makes the following contributions: (1) based on a corpus of approximately 25,000 news stories, we identified several syntactic and linguistic features for ranking sentences, (2) we evaluated these features – on a held-out test set that was not used for the analysis – at different levels of compression, and (3) finally, we discuss the degree of difficulty inherent in the corpus being used for the task evaluation in an effort to normalize scores obtained across different corpora.

Ranking Text Spans for Selection

The text-span selection paradigm transforms the problem of *summarization*, which in the most general case requires the ability to understand, interpret, abstract and generate a new document, into a different problem: *ranking sentences* from the original document according to their salience (or likelihood of being part of a summary). This kind of summarization is closely related to the more general problem of information retrieval, where documents from a document set (rather than sentences from a document) are ranked, in order to retrieve the most relevant documents.

Ranking text-spans for importance requires defining at least two parameters: (i) the granularity of the text-spans, and (ii) metrics for ranking span salience. While there are several advantages of using *paragraphs* as the minimal unit of span extraction, we shall conform to the vast majority of previous work and use the *sentence* as our level of choice. However, documents to be summarized can be analyzed at varying levels of detail, and in this paper, each sentence can be ranked by considering the following three levels:

- *Sub-document Level:* Different regions in a document often have very different levels of significance for summarization. These sub-documents become especially important for text genres that contain either (i) articles on multiple, equally important topics, or (ii) multiple sub-sections, as often occurs in longer, scientific articles, and books. All sentences within a sub-document are assigned an initial score based on the whole sub-document. Sub-document scores depend both on various properties independent of the content in the sub-document (e.g., length and position), as well as the lexical and syntactic relations that hold between the sub-documents (e.g., discourse relations, co-references, etc.).

- *Sentence Level:* Within a sub-document, individual sentences can be ranked by using both features that are independent of the actual content, such as the length and position, as well as content specific features that are based on number of anaphoric references, function words, punctuation, named-entities, etc.

- *Phrase/Word Level:* Within a sentence, phrases or words can be ranked by using features such as length, focus information, part of speech (POS), co-reference information, definiteness, tense, commonality, etc.

Some of these features are harder, or costlier, to compute than others. By analyzing their relative utility for a particular task, users can make informed decisions on the cost-benefit ratios of various combinations in different contexts without having to first build a system with which to experiment. Section lists the features we evaluated and discusses our results in detail.

Data Sets: Properties and Features

A corpus of documents and corresponding summaries at various levels of compression are required for experimenting with various summarization methods because summarizer performance can vary significantly at different compression levels. In our experiments, different algorithms for summarization performed best at different levels of compression. This suggests that experiments evaluating summarizers should be conducted at a variety of compression levels, and should be reported in a manner similar to the 11-point precision-recall scores that are used in information retrieval (Salton & McGill 1983). To conduct our experiments, we collected three corpora. The first data set, *Model Summaries*, was created from four data sets supplied as part of the Tipster (Tipster 1998) evaluation: the training set for the Question and Answer task and three other data sets used in the formal evaluation. This data set is relatively small: it consists of 138 documents and "model" summaries. Each "model" summary contains sentences extracted from the document that answer possible questions for the given document. Because of concerns about the small size of the first data set (and its uniformity of summary compression ratios), we acquired two additional, larger data sets consisting of news-wire summaries from Reuters and the Los Angeles Times. Our analysis covered approximately 24,000 summaries over a six-month period in 1997–1998 on a variety of news topics (international, political, sports, business, health and entertainment news articles). Statistics about the average length of stories and summaries from randomly chosen subsets of all three of these data-sets are shown in Table 1.

However, the summaries in the latter two datasets could not be used directly by us, because these were *not* generated by sentence extraction. Therefore, we first converted the hand-written summaries into their corresponding extracted summaries to conduct an analysis of their discourse, syntactic and lexical properties. This conversion – from hand-written to extracted – was done by matching each sentence in the hand-written summary with the smallest subset of sentences in the full-length story that contained all of the key concepts mentioned in that sentence. Initially, this was done manually, but we were able to automate the matching process by defining a threshold value (typically 0.85) for the minimum number of concepts (keywords and noun phrases, especially named entities) that were required to match between the two. Detailed inspections of the two sets of sentences indicate that the transformations are highly accurate, especially in this document genre of news-wire articles. This approach is a simplified version of the text alignment problem used to align different languages. The success of this technique depends on consistent vocabulary usage between the articles and the summaries, which, fortunately for us, is true for news-wire articles. Application of this technique to other document genres will depend upon the lexical distribution patterns between summaries and the articles; it may require knowledge of synonyms and hypernyms, such as those provided by WordNet. More details on this work can be found in (Banko *et al.* 1999). This transformation resulted in a 20% increase in summary length on average, probably because hand-written summaries often employ complex syntactic sentential patterns with multiple clauses. Several story sentences were sometimes necessary to cover a single summary-sentence.

Evaluation Metrics

There have been several recent attempts to define evaluation criteria for summarizers, the most extensive being the one organized by the Tipster (Tipster 1998) program. Tipster was motivated partly by the difficulty of evaluating the relative merits of two summarization systems unless their performance was measured on the same task: summaries generated from identical documents at identical character compression levels. This evaluation recognized the fact that different corpora can yield different results because of the inherent properties of the documents contained in them. For instance, some types of documents can be very structured or focused on the main topic. Extraction of sentences from such a document, even at random, is more likely to form a reasonable summary, than random extraction of sentences from a document that is long and rambling with many digressions. Thus, to be able to compare the performance of a particular heuristic or algorithm for summarization on a corpus, it becomes essential to first understand the underlying degree of difficulty of that corpus. Consider, for instance, the performance of random sentence selection on three randomly selected subsets of approximately 1000 articles each from Reuters, The Los Angeles Times and the Christian Science Monitor: at a 20% compression level, the "score" for the same summarizer was 0.263, 0.202 and 0.353 respectively. If these scores were reported separately, as three dif-

Property	Model Summaries	Reuters Summaries	Los Angeles Times Summaries
task	Q and A	generic summaries	generic summaries
source	Tipster	human $\Rightarrow$ extracted	human $\Rightarrow$ extracted
number of docs	48	1000	1250
average no. of sent. per doc	22.6	23.10	27.9
median sentences per doc	19	22	26
maximum sentences per doc	51	89	87
minimum sentences per doc	11	5	3
summary as % of doc length	19.4%	20.1%	20.0%
summary includes 1st sentence	72%	70.5%	68.3%
average summary size (sent)	4.3	4.3	3.7
median summary size (sent)	4	4	4
typical summary length (75% of docs)	–	3–6	3–5

Table 1: Characteristics of data sets used in the summarization experiments

ferent experiments, one might wrongly infer that the 'different' algorithms varied widely in performance Thus, even when testing and evaluation is done on the same document genre, it is important to clearly state the baseline performance expected from that corpus.

The second issue, directly related to the previous one, is the desired compression level. Clearly, generating summaries at a 50% compression level should be much easier than generating summaries at a 10% compression level.

Current methods of evaluating summarizers often measure summary properties on absolute scales, such as precision, recall, and F_1 (Salton & McGill 1983). Although such measures can be used to compare summarization performance on a common corpus, they do not indicate whether the improvement of one summarizer over another is significant or not. One possible solution to this problem is to derive a relative measure of summarization quality by comparing the absolute performance measures to a theoretical baseline of summarization performance. Adjusted performance values are obtained by normalizing the change in performance relative to the baseline against the best possible improvement relative to the baseline. Given a baseline value b and a performance value p, the adjusted performance value is calculated as

$$p' = \frac{(p - b)}{(1 - b)} \qquad (1)$$

For the purpose of this analysis, the baseline is defined to be an "average" of all possible summaries. This is equivalent to the absolute performance of a summarization algorithm that randomly selected sentences for the summary. It measures the expected amount of overlap between a machine-generated and a "target" summary.

If D_t is the total number of sentences in a document, D_r the number of summary-relevant sentences in the document, and S_r the target number of sentences to be selected for inclusion in the summary, then let $P_i(D_t, D_r, S_r)$ denote the probability of selecting S_r sentences such that i of them are from the set of D_r relevant sentences. Then $P_i(D_t, D_r, S_r)$

is the product of the number of ways to select i sentences from the D_r relevant sentences, multiplied by the number of ways to select the remaining $S_r - i$ sentences from the $D_t - D_r$ non-relevant sentences, and divided by the number of ways to select S_r sentences from the D_t sentences in the document. Thus

$$P_i(D_t, D_r, S_r) = \frac{\left(\begin{array}{c} D_r \\ i \end{array} \right) \left(\begin{array}{c} D_t - D_r \\ S_r - i \end{array} \right)}{\left(\begin{array}{c} D_t \\ S_r \end{array} \right)} \qquad (2)$$

Let $E(D_t, D_r, S_r)$ be the expected number of relevant sentences. Then

$$E(D_t, D_r, S_r) \;\; = \;\; \sum_{i=0}^{D_r} i \cdot P_i(D_t, D_r, S_r) \;\; = \;\; \frac{D_r \cdot S_r}{D_t}$$

From this it can be derived that

$$F_1 = \frac{2 \cdot D_r \cdot S_r}{D_t \cdot (D_r + S_r)} \qquad (3)$$

This formula relates F_1, D_t, D_r, and S_r. Given three of the values, the fourth can be easily calculated. In particular, the value of a baseline F_1 can be calculated once the average corpus statistics are known (lengths of an average document and summary and the number of relevant sentences per document). For instance, for the Reuters articles in our case, the values of the relevant parameters D_t, D_r and S_r are 23.10, 10, 4.3. This yields a baseline F_1 score of approximately 0.260 at a compression level of 20%. In similar fashion, one can compute the baseline F_1 scores for any desired compression level (or vice versa).

Experiments

Summary lengths in our corpus seemed to be mostly independent of document length; they were narrowly distributed around 85–90 words, or approximately five sentences. Thus, compression ratios decrease with document length. This

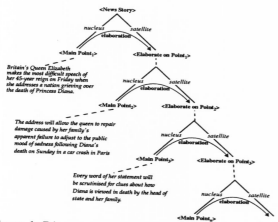

Figure 1: Discourse structure of a stereotypical news story

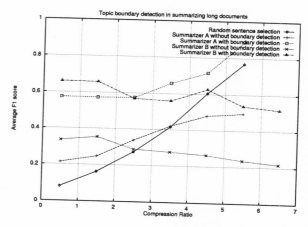

Figure 2: Effect of topic detection.

suggests that the common practice of using a fixed compression ratio in evaluation may not be appropriate, and that using a genre-specific constant summary length may be more natural.

Our experiments to evaluate features were conducted as follows: first, we identified article-summary pairs at various levels of compression ranging from 0–10%, 10–20% ... 40-50%. Our dataset contained summaries upto seven-tenths of the length of the original article, but at these relatively large ratios, the summaries begin approaching the original article, so we restricted the comparison to summaries that were at most half the length of the original article. For each of these compression ratios, we randomly selected 3000 of these article-summary pairs. These 15,000 pairs were then split up into 10,000 training articles for analysis and 5000 were held out for testing. During testing, the summarizers were invoked for each article with a parameter specifying the length of the summary to be generated. This length, in sentences, was also the length of the original summary for that article. The overlap between the generated summary and the original summary was then measured using the well-known F_1 measure from information retrieval. This enabled us to measure the summarizer performance at various levels of compression. To reduce the five values to one number for reporting purposes, we computed the average F_1 score for all five intervals. Some of the tables towards the end of this section contain this "five point average" score.

The rest of this section discusses some of the features we looked at, starting from the largest granularity level (the document structure) and moving to the smallest (individual words).

Document Level Features in Summarization

It has been argued previously that discourse structure can be a very useful source of information for summarization (Marcu 1997; Sparck-Jones 1993). This argument is based on theories of discourse which recursively indicate "core" and "contributor" spans of text in the document (Mann & Thompson 1988). The problem of summarizing a document can be addressed by selecting the most

abstract "core" spans until the desired summary length is reached. The utility of this approach is very effectively illustrated in the news-wire document genre, where selecting the first few sentences of the story results in better-than-average summaries (Brandow, Mitze, & Rau 1995). This is because news-wire stories are written with a rigid, right-branching discourse structure. (This stereotypical structure is partly due to the fact that the page and column layouts of the newspaper are not known at the time the article is written; thus, the article can be chopped off at any point, and must still be comprehensible.) (Figure 1 shows one of these structures.) Thus selecting the first n sentences of a news-wire story approximates the selection of the top "core" spans in the text. (This approach is not perfect because news-wire stories do not always employ a perfectly right-branching discourse structure.)

Unfortunately, finding the underlying discourse structure is almost as difficult as generating a good summary (Marcu 1997). In this paper, we considered a simpler version of the problem: rather than finding the underlying discourse structure, we segmented the text into sub-documents according to topic boundaries using the TextTiling system (Hearst 1994). (Our experiments with other segmentation systems resulted approximately equivalent bopundaries.) The segmentation represents an approximation to the top level discourse structure, minus knowledge of the relations between nodes, which represent the sub-documents. Note that in theory, sub-document segmentation can be carried out recursively, yielding approximate boundaries for a hierarchical approximation to the discourse structure. At this point, information at the sub-document level, such as the position and length of a sub-document relative to other sub-documents, can be used to augment information available at finer levels of detail. Segmentation becomes increasingly important as documents grow in length and complexity. For instance, the average conference paper at 5,000 words is over 10 times longer than the average news-wire article in the Reuters corpus. In such cases, making use of information at this level can yield significant advantages.

To evaluate the cost-benefit tradeoff of pre-processing

documents to find topic boundaries, we created a synthetic data-set for our experiments. This is because, there does not yet exist a corpus of longer documents with "gold standard summaries" to test on.[1] We created composite documents by concatenating several news-wire articles of various lengths. The number of such sub-documents in a larger document was normally distributed between 2 and 14. The summary for this composite document was assumed to be the collection of sentences in the summaries for the individual sub-documents. Our experiments found that in all cases, pre-processing for topic boundaries can significantly improve the quality of a summarization system, often by a factor of 2. (This factor is based on average 5-point F_1 score averaged across compression levels and normalized with the random-sentence-selection baseline. The actual improvement will depend on the length and complexity of the original document and the summarization algorithm being used. Clearly this approach has maximum utility when a sentence-position based approach is used for selecting sentences.) This approach is analogous to related work on summarization aimed at reducing redundancy (Carbonell & Goldstein 1998). As in this case, that approach attempts to select summary sentences from different topic areas in the document, but without any explicit topic segmentation steps. Figure 2 shows the effectiveness of being able to identify topic boundaries on two different summarization algorithms. (Algorithm-A was based on a TF·IDF approach to ranking sentences; Algorithm-B was based on a combination of syntactic complexity and named-entity relationships between sentences in the document; neither of the two used positional information.)

Sentence Level Patterns in Summary Sentences

Most of the heuristics that have been used in selecting text-spans for summarization have been at the sentence level. These include sentence-level features such as the length of the span, its complexity, the presence of certain punctuation, thematic phrases, anaphora/co-occurrence density, etc. It is essential to understand the relative advantages of these features over one another for a specific corpus, especially since these features vary widely in computational cost and some of them subsume one another. We looked at the following sentence level characteristics as possible cues for summary selection:

- *Syntactic Complexity:* Our analysis of summary sentences found that sentences included in summaries differed from non-summary sentences in several characteristics related to complexity. Two of these are:

  - NP Complexity: We found that the average length of complex noun phrases in summary sentences was more

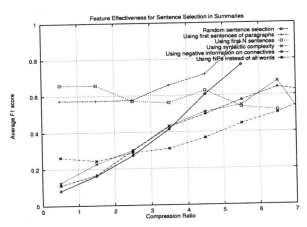

Figure 3: Feature effectiveness for Reuters dataset.

than twice as long than those in non-summary sentences.

  - Coordinate Conjunctions: On the negative side, our dataset possessed a higher density of coordinate conjunctions in story sentences than summary sentences.

- *Density of Named-Entities:* Named entities represented 16.3% of the words in summaries, compared to 11.4% of the words in non-summary sentences, an increase of 43%. 71% of summaries had a greater named-entity density than the non-summary sentences.

  For sentences with 5 to 35 words, the average number of proper nouns per sentence was 3.29 for summary sentences and 1.73 for document sentences, an increase of 90.2%. The average density of proper nouns (the number of proper nouns divided by the number of words in the sentence) was 16.60% for summary sentences, compared with 7.58% for document sentences, an increase of 119%. Summary sentences had an average of 20.13 words, compared with 20.64 words for document sentences. Thus the summary sentences had a much greater proportion of proper nouns than the document and non-summary sentences.

- *Punctuation:* Punctuation symbols (not counting periods) tend to also appear more frequently in story sentences as compared to summary sentences.

- *Given vs. New Information:* In a simplified analysis of "given" vs. "new" information (Werth 1984), as indicated by the presence of the definite or indefinite articles, we found that summaries included new information more frequently than the non-summary sentences. Summary sentences also tended to start with an article more frequently than non-summary sentences. In particular, Table 2 shows that the token "A" appeared 62% more frequently in the summaries.

- *Pronominal References:* Anaphoric references at sentence beginnings, such as "these", "this", "those", etc. are a good source of negative evidence, possibly because such sentences cannot introduce a topic. Personal pronouns such as "us", "our" and "we" are also a good source of

---

[1] Some researchers have reported experiments using conference papers from the CMP-LG archive, but there are two problems with that approach: (i) abstracts in scientific papers are not generic summaries, and (ii) scientific papers and their abstracts are written by technical people who are not necessarily skilled abstractors. We have conducted experiments with non-synthetic datasets, but we do not have sufficiently large numbers of such documents at various compression levels for us to be able to report on them here.

Table 2: A comparison of word occurrences in summary sentences to non-summary sentences. Calculated by taking the ratio of the two, subtracting 1, and representing as a percent.

Article	Reuters	LA Times
the	-5.5%	0.9%
The	7.5%	10.7%
a	6.2%	7.1%
A	62.0%	62.2%
an	15.2%	11.7%
An	29.6%	38.3%

Table 3: Effectiveness of sentence level heuristics by raw score and normalized score (Equation 1).

Feature Set	Reuters		LA Times	
	Raw	$p'_{0.26}$	Raw	$p'_{0.20}$
synt. complexity	0.32	0.08	0.24	0.05
named-entity density	0.30	0.05	0.26	0.07
synonym density	0.31	0.07	0.25	0.06
first n (FN)	0.61	0.47	0.58	0.47
FN + syntax	0.61	0.47	0.61	0.51
FN + named-entity	0.65	0.53	0.64	0.55
FN + given/new	0.67	0.55	0.64	0.55
FN + SD	0.64	0.51	0.62	0.52
ALL (weighted comb.)	0.82	0.75	0.72	0.65

negative evidence for summary sentences, perhaps because they frequently occur in quoted statements.

- *Density of Related Words:* Words that have multiple related terms in the document – synonyms, hypernyms and antonyms – are much more likely to be in the summary than not.

Figure 3 illustrates the effectiveness of some these features at different compression levels from the Reuters data-set.[2] Note that some of the features may not appear as important as others in the 5-point average scheme used here because these features, such as for instance, named-entities, may not occur in more than a small percentage of the sentences. As the summaries get larger, their individual effect on the summary decreases. Table 3 shows the average performance of various features for summarization. Since this was a news-wire corpus, where the selection of the first n sentences has been shown to be a very effective heuristic, the table also includes, for illustration, the performance of the summarizers when other features are combined with the heuristic. The tables indicate both the raw scores, as well as normalized scores. While the raw scores between the two datasets vary widely in some cases, the normalized scores are much closer and are a better reflection on the effective-

ness of the features being used.

Phrase/Word Level Patterns in Summary Sentences

In addition to features at the document and sentence level, there are certain characteristics at the phrase/word level that can be used to rank sentences as well. These include:

- *Word Length:* 63% of the Reuters summaries and 66% of the Los Angeles Times summaries had a greater average word length than the average word length of the article's non-summary sentences.

- *Communicative Actions:* Words and phrases common in direct or indirect quotations also suggest non-summary sentences. Examples of words occurring at least 75% more frequently in non-summary sentences include "according", "adding", "said", and other verbs (and their variants) related to communication.

- *Thematic Phrases:* Phrases such as "finally," "in conclusion," etc. also occur more frequently in summary sentences. We found a total of 22 such terms in our data-set that occur at least 75% more frequently in summary sentences than non-summary sentences.

- *Miscellaneous:* Furthermore, informal or imprecise terms such as "got", "really" and "use" also appear significantly more frequently in non-summary sentences. Other sources of negative lexical significance we found are:
  - Honorifics: Honorifics such as "Dr.", "Mr.", and "Mrs.", are also negatively indicated. This may be due to the fact that news articles often introduce people by name, (e.g., "John Smith") and subsequently refer to them either formally (e.g., "Mr. Smith") or pronominally.
  - Auxillary verbs: such as "was", "could", "did", etc.
  - Negations: such as "no", "don't", "never", etc.
  - Integers, whether written using digits (e.g., 1, 2) or words (e.g., "one", "two").
  - Evaluative and qualifying words, such as "often", "about", "significant", "lot", "some" and "several".
  - Prepositions, such as "at", "by", "for" "of", "in", "to", and "with".

Our analysis found that each of these features, individually, can be helpful as a cue in selecting summary sentences. Figure 3 shows the effectiveness of some of these features in relationship to the random baseline. At very small summary lengths, all of these features are better than the baseline. As summaries get longer, the effectiveness of an individual feature starts to fall. This is understandable, since features such as anaphoric references or dangling connectives are unlikely to occur in more than a small percentage of the sentences. The outstanding line in this case is the positional feature, which, as discussed earlier, implicitly takes advantage of the underlying discourse structure of the news story. As discussed earlier, it is essential to clearly understand the relative costs and benefits of each of these features. It is also important to understand the relative effects of using *combinations* of these features. Results based on combinations of

---

[2]Note that we did not include *punctuation* or *pronominal information* information for our table, since these features are mostly used diminish the likelihood of summary selection; thus these features are best used in combination with other positive features. Similarly, in Table 4, certain features have been left off.

Table 4: Effectiveness of word level heuristics.

Feature Set	Reuters		LA Times	
	Raw	$p'_{0.26}$	Raw	$p'_{0.20}$
Phrase Complexity	0.28	0.03	0.22	0.04
thematic phrases	0.29	0.04	0.25	0.06
misc ftrs	0.25	-0.01	0.19	-0.01

features can be useful for inferences about the orthogonality and the interdependence between these features. The space in which a hill-climbing technique must search for appropriate weights in a linear combination of these features is quite large; experiments to understand these approaches are currently under way.

Conclusions and Future Work

Human-quality text summarization systems are difficult to design, and even more difficult to evaluate; results reported by different research projects are also difficult to compare because the reported results often do not discuss the characteristics of the corpora on which the experiments were conducted – specifically, characteristics such as redundancy, which can have significant effects on any evaluation measures. We have argued that for specific datasets, characterizing (1) sentence redundancy, and (2) results at a variety of compression levels, are necessary if these results are to be useful to other researchers.

This paper has presented a discussion of sentence selection heuristics at three different granularity levels. We conducted experiments to evaluate the effectiveness of these heuristics on the largest corpus of news-article summaries reported so far. Our experiments emphasized the need for sub-document segmentation on longer, more complex documents. This paper also shows that there are significant advantages in using fine grained lexical features for ranking sentences. Results in our work are reported using a new metric that combines scores at various compression levels taking into account the corpus difficulty on the task.

In future work, we plan to characterize different document genres, and attempt to achieve a better understanding of why certain phenomena play a greater/lesser role for sentence selection in those genres – phenomena such as the role of co-reference chains, the given/new distinction and others.

References

Aone, C.; Okurowski, M. E.; Gorlinsky, J.; and Larsen, B. 1997. A scalable summarization system using robust NLP. In Mani and Maybury (1997), 66–73.

Baldwin, B., and Morton, T. S. 1998. Dynamic coreference-based summarization. In *Proceedings of EMNLP-3 Conference.*

Banko, M.; Mittal, V.; Kantrowitz, M.; and Goldstein, J. 1999. Generating Extraction-Based Summaries from Hand-Written One by Text Alignment. In *Submitted to the 1999 Pac. Rim Conf. on Comp. Linguistics.*

Barzilay, R., and Elhadad, M. 1997. Using lexical chains for text summarization. In Mani and Maybury (1997), 10–17.

Boguraev, B., and Kennedy, C. 1997. Salience based content characterization of text documents. In Mani and Maybury (1997), 2–9.

Brandow, R.; Mitze, K.; and Rau, L. F. 1995. Automatic condensation of electronic publications by sentence selection. *Info. Proc. and Management* 31(5):675–685.

Carbonell, J. G., and Goldstein, J. 1998. The use of MMR, diversity-based reranking for reordering documents and producing summaries. In *Proceedings of SIGIR-98.*

Hearst, M. A. 1994. Multi-paragraph segmentation of expository text. In *Proceedings of the 32nd Annual Meeting of the ACL.*

Hovy, E., and Lin, C.-Y. 1997. Automated text summarization in SUMMARIST. In Mani and Maybury (1997), 18–24.

Klavans, J. L., and Shaw, J. 1995. Lexical semantics in summarization. In *Proceedings of the First Annual Workshop of the IFIP Working Group FOR NLP and KR.*

Mani, I., and Maybury, M., eds. 1997. *Proceedings of the ACL'97/EACL'97 Workshop on Intelligent Scalable Text Summarization.*

Mann, W. C., and Thompson, S. 1988. Rhetorical Structure Theory: toward a functional theory of text organization. *Text* 8(3):243–281.

Marcu, D. 1997. From discourse structures to text summaries. In Mani and Maybury (1997), 82–88.

McKeown, K.; Robin, J.; and Kukich, K. 1995. Designing and evaluating a new revision-based model for summary generation. *Info. Proc. and Management* 31(5).

Mitra, M.; Singhal, A.; and Buckley, C. 1997. Automatic text summarization by paragraph extraction. In Mani and Maybury (1997), 31–36.

Salton, G., and McGill, M. J. 1983. *Introduction to Modern Information Retrieval.* McGraw-Hill Computer Science Series. New York: McGraw-Hill.

Sparck-Jones, K. 1993. Discourse modelling for automatic summarising. Technical report, Cambridge University, Cambridge, England.

Strzalkowski, T.; Wang, J.; and Wise, B. 1998. A robust practical text summarization system. In *AAAI Intell. Text Summarization Wkshp*, 26–30.

Teufel, S., and Moens, M. 1997. Sentence extraction as a classification task. In Mani and Maybury (1997), 58–65.

Tipster. 1998. Tipster text phase III 18-month workshop notes. Fairfax, VA.

Werth, P. 1984. *Focus, Coherence and Emphasis.* London, England: Croom Helm.

Learning Dictionaries for Information Extraction by Multi-Level Bootstrapping

Ellen Riloff
Department of Computer Science
University of Utah
Salt Lake City, UT 84112
riloff@cs.utah.edu

Rosie Jones
School of Computer Science
Carnegie Mellon University
Pittsburgh, PA 15213
rosie@cs.cmu.edu

Abstract

Information extraction systems usually require two dictionaries: a semantic lexicon and a dictionary of extraction patterns for the domain. We present a multi-level bootstrapping algorithm that generates both the semantic lexicon and extraction patterns simultaneously. As input, our technique requires only unannotated training texts and a handful of seed words for a category. We use a *mutual bootstrapping* technique to alternately select the best extraction pattern for the category and bootstrap its extractions into the semantic lexicon, which is the basis for selecting the next extraction pattern. To make this approach more robust, we add a second level of bootstrapping (*metabootstrapping*) that retains only the most reliable lexicon entries produced by mutual bootstrapping and then restarts the process. We evaluated this multilevel bootstrapping technique on a collection of corporate web pages and a corpus of terrorism news articles. The algorithm produced high-quality dictionaries for several semantic categories.

Introduction

The purpose of *information extraction* (IE) systems is to extract domain-specific information from natural language text. IE systems typically rely on two domain-specific resources: a dictionary of extraction patterns and a semantic lexicon. The extraction patterns may be constructed by hand or may be generated automatically using one of several techniques. Most systems that generate extraction patterns automatically use special training resources, such as texts annotated with domain-specific tags (e.g., AutoSlog (Riloff 1993; 1996a), CRYSTAL (Soderland *et al.* 1995), RAPIER (Califf 1998), SRV (Freitag 1998), WHISK (Soderland 1999)) or manually defined keywords, frames, or object recognizers (e.g., PALKA (Kim & Moldovan 1993) and LIEP (Huffman 1996)). AutoSlog-TS (Riloff 1996b) takes a different approach by using a preclassified training corpus in which texts only need to be labeled as relevant

or irrelevant to the domain. Semantic lexicons[1] for information extraction are almost always constructed by hand because general-purpose resources, such as WordNet (Miller 1990), do not contain the necessary domain-specific vocabulary. However there have been recent efforts to automate the construction of domain-specific semantic lexicons as well (Riloff & Shepherd 1997; Roark & Charniak 1998).

We explore the idea of learning both a dictionary of extraction patterns and a domain-specific semantic lexicon simultaneously. Furthermore, our technique requires no special training resources. The input to our algorithm is a set of unannotated training texts and a handful of "seed" words for the semantic category of interest. The heart of our approach is a *mutual bootstrapping* technique that learns extraction patterns from the seed words and then exploits the learned extraction patterns to identify more words that belong to the semantic category. We also introduce a second level of bootstrapping that retains only the most reliable lexicon entries from the results of mutual bootstrapping and restarts the process with the enhanced semantic lexicon. This two-tiered bootstrapping process is less sensitive to noise than a single level of bootstrapping and produces highly-quality dictionaries.

In this paper, we first describe the mutual bootstrapping algorithm that generates both a semantic lexicon and extraction patterns simultaneously. In the second section, we describe how the mutual bootstrapping process is itself bootstrapped to produce more accurate dictionaries at each iteration. In the third section, we present the results from experiments with two text collections: a set of corporate web pages, and a corpus of terrorism newswire articles.

Mutual Bootstrapping

Information extraction (IE) systems are designed to extract specific types of information from text. The categories of interest are defined in advance and usually require the extraction of noun phrases (NPs), such as the names of people, companies, or locations. For

---

[1]For our purposes, a semantic lexicon just refers to a dictionary of words with semantic category labels.

some IE tasks, the set of possible extractions is finite. For example, extracting country names from text is straightforward because it is easy to define a list of all countries. However, most IE tasks require the extraction of a potentially open-ended set of phrases. For example, it is impossible to enumerate all noun phrases that might describe a person, company, or location.

Most IE systems use both a semantic lexicon of known phrases and a dictionary of extraction patterns to recognize relevant noun phrases. For example, an IE system to identify locations might use a semantic lexicon that lists country names and the 50 U.S. states, and then rely on extraction patterns to recognize other location phrases such as cities, neighborhoods, and general descriptions like "downtown" or "northwest region". The semantic lexicon can also support the use of semantic constraints in the extraction patterns.

Our goal is to automate the construction of both a lexicon and extraction patterns for a semantic category using bootstrapping. The heart of our approach is based on the observation that extraction patterns can generate new examples of a semantic category, which in turn can be used to identify new extraction patterns. We will refer to this process as *mutual bootstrapping*.

The mutual bootstrapping process begins with a text corpus and a handful of predefined *seed words* for a semantic category. Before bootstrapping begins, the text corpus is used to generate a set of candidate extraction patterns. We used AutoSlog (Riloff 1993; 1996a) in an exhaustive fashion to generate extraction patterns for every noun phrase in the corpus. Given a noun phrase to extract, AutoSlog uses heuristics to generate a linguistic expression that represents relevant context for extracting the NP. This linguistic expression should be general enough to extract other relevant noun phrases as well. Because we applied AutoSlog exhaustively, the complete set of extraction patterns that it produced is capable of extracting every noun phrase in the training corpus. We then applied the extraction patterns to the corpus and recorded their extractions.

Using this data, the mutual bootstrapping procedure identifies the extraction pattern that is most useful for extracting known category members. This extraction pattern is then used to propose new phrases that belong in the semantic lexicon. Figure 1 outlines the mutual bootstrapping algorithm. At each iteration, the algorithm saves the best extraction pattern for the category to a list (*Cat_EPlist*). All of its extractions are assumed to be category members and are added to the semantic lexicon (*SemLex*). Then the next best extraction pattern is identified, based on both the original seed words plus the new words that were just added to the lexicon, and the process repeats. Since the semantic lexicon is constantly growing, the extraction patterns need to be rescored after each iteration. An important question is how long to run the bootstrapping loop. The simplest approach is to use a threshold cutoff, but we will discuss this issue more in the evaluation section.

The scoring heuristic is based on how many different lexicon entries a pattern extracts. This scoring metric rewards generality; a pattern that extracts a variety of category members will be scored higher than a pattern that extracts only one or two different category members, no matter how often. Scoring is also based on a "head phrase" matching scheme instead of requiring an exact match. Head phrase matching means that X matches Y if X is the rightmost substring of Y. For example, "New Zealand" will match any phrase that ends with "New Zealand", such as "eastern New Zealand" or "the modern day New Zealand". It would not match "the New Zealand coast" or just "Zealand". Head phrase matching is important for generality because any noun phrase can be preceded by an arbitrary number of modifiers.

Generate all candidate extraction patterns from the training corpus using AutoSlog.

Apply the candidate extraction patterns to the training corpus and save the patterns with their extractions to *EPdata*

SemLex = {seed_words}

Cat_EPlist = {}

MUTUAL BOOTSTRAPPING LOOP

1. Score all extraction patterns in *EPdata*.
2. *best_EP* = the highest scoring extraction pattern not already in *Cat_EPlist*
3. Add *best_EP* to *Cat_EPlist*
4. Add *best_EP*'s extractions to *SemLex*.
5. Go to step 1

Figure 1: Mutual Bootstrapping Algorithm

Each NP was stripped of leading articles, common adjectives (e.g., "his", "its", "other"), and numbers before being matched and saved to the lexicon. We used a small stopword list[2] and a number recognizer to discard overly general words such as pronouns and numbers. Using these criteria, we scored each extraction pattern using the *RlogF* metric used previously by AutoSlog-TS (Riloff 1996b). The score for extraction pattern i is computed as:

$$score(pattern_i) = R_i * log_2(F_i)$$

where F_i is the number of unique lexicon entries among the extractions produced by $pattern_i$, N_i is the total number of unique NPs that $pattern_i$ extracted, and $R_i = \frac{F_i}{N_i}$. This metric was designed for information extraction tasks, where it is important to identify not

---

[2]Most information retrieval systems use a *stopword list* to prevent extremely common words from being used for retrieval purposes. Our stopword list contained 35 words, mainly pronouns, determiners, and quantifiers.

only the most reliable extraction patterns but also patterns that will frequently extract relevant information (even if irrelevant information will also be extracted). For example, the pattern "kidnapped in <x>" will extract locations but it will also extract many dates (e.g., "kidnapped in January"). Even if it extracts dates and locations equally often, the fact that it frequently extracts locations makes it essential to have in the dictionary or many locations will be missed. Intuitively, the *RlogF* metric tries to strike a balance between reliability and frequency. The R value is high when the pattern's extractions are highly correlated with the semantic category, and the F value is high when the pattern extracts a large number of category members.

Figure 2 shows the results of the first five iterations of mutual bootstrapping to build location dictionaries from a terrorism corpus. Ten seed words were used: *bolivia, city, colombia, district, guatemala, honduras, neighborhood, nicaragua, region, town*. An asterisk after a noun phrase means that the noun phrase was acquired as a category member through bootstrapping. The F and N values for each pattern are shown in parentheses. Note that because of head phrase matching, "chapare region" will match the seed word "region" and be counted as a location when scoring the extraction pattern. But since that exact phrase was not in the lexicon before, it is considered to be a new location and added to it.

Best pattern	"headquartered in <x>" (F=3,N=4)		
Known locations	*nicaragua*		
New locations	*san miguel, chapare region, san miguel city*		
Best pattern	"gripped <x>" (F=2,N=2)		
Known locations	*colombia, guatemala*		
New locations	none		
Best pattern	"downed in <x>" (F=3,N=6)		
Known locations	*nicaragua, san miguel*, city*		
New locations	*area, usulutan region, soyapango*		
Best pattern	"to occupy <x>" (F=4,N=6)		
Known locations	*nicaragua, town*		
New locations	*small country, this northern area, san sebastian neighborhood, private property*		
Best pattern	"shot in <x>" (F=5,N=12)		
Known locations	*city, soyapango**		
New locations	*jauja, central square, head, clash, back, central mountain region, air, villa el_salvador district, northwestern guatemala, left side*		

Figure 2: Five iterations of mutual bootstrapping

Figure 2 shows both the strengths and weaknesses of the mutual bootstrapping approach. The extraction patterns are indicative of locations and have identified several new location phrases (e.g., *jauja, san miguel, soyapango*, and *this northern area*). But several non-location phrases have also been generated (e.g., *private property, head, clash, back, air, left side*). Most of these

mistakes came from the pattern "shot in <x>", because this expression can refer to non-location phrases such as body parts. Also, most of these extraction patterns occur infrequently in the corpus. Although "headquartered in <x>" and "gripped <x>" are good location extractors, together they appeared only seven times in the 1500 training texts. As we will show in the next section, there are many other location patterns that occur much more frequently and are therefore more important to have in the dictionary.

Multi-level Bootstrapping

The mutual bootstrapping algorithm works well but its performance can deteriorate rapidly when non-category words enter the semantic lexicon. Once an extraction pattern is chosen for the dictionary, all of its extractions are immediately added to the lexicon and a few bad entries can quickly infect the dictionary. For example, if a pattern extracts dates as well as locations, then the dates are added to the lexicon and subsequent patterns are rewarded for extracting them.

To make the algorithm more robust, we introduced a second level of bootstrapping. The outer bootstrapping mechanism, which we call *meta-bootstrapping*, compiles the results from the inner (mutual) bootstrapping process and identifies the five most reliable lexicon entries. These five NPs are retained for the permanent semantic lexicon and the rest of the mutual bootstrapping process is discarded. The entire mutual bootstrapping process is then restarted from scratch. The meta-bootstrapping process is illustrated in Figure 3.

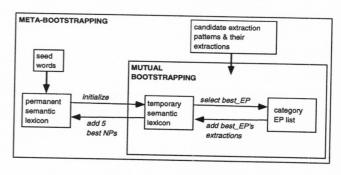

Figure 3: The Meta-Bootstrapping Process

To determine which NPs are most "reliable", we score each NP based on the number of different category patterns (members of *Cat_EPlist*) that extracted it. This criteria is based on the intuition that a noun phrase extracted by three different category patterns is more likely to belong to the category than a noun phrase extracted by only one pattern. We also add in a small factor to account for the strength of the patterns that extracted it. This is used mainly for tie-breaking purposes. The scoring formula is shown below, where N_i is the number of different category patterns that extracted NP_i.

Web Location Patterns	Web Title Patterns	Web Company Patterns	Terrorism Location Patterns	Terrorism Weapon Patterns
offices in <x>	served as <x>	owned by <x>	living in <x>	<x> exploded
facilities in <x>	became <x>	both as <x>	traveled to <x>	threw <x>
operations in <x>	company as <x>	<x> employed	become in <x>	bringing <x>
loans in <x>	to become <x>	<x> is distributor	sought in <x>	seized <x>
operates in <x>	experience as <x>	<x> positioning	presidents of <x>	quantity of <x>
locations in <x>	q. is <x>	marks of <x>	parts of <x>	surrender <x>
producer in <x>	appointed as <x>	motivated <x>	to enter <x>	search for <x>
states of <x>	to serve as <x>	<x> trust company	condemned in <x>	rocket <x>
seminars in <x>	elects <x>	sold to <x>	relations between <x>	<x> parked
activities in <x>	<x> capitalize	devoted to <x>	ministers of <x>	hurled <x>
consulting in <x>	williams is <x>	<x> consolidated stmts.	part in <x>	clips for <x>
countries of <x>	position of <x>	<x> thrive	taken in <x>	defused <x>
rep. of <x>	retired <x>	message to <x>	returned to <x>	million in <x>
outlets in <x>	expectations of <x>	<x> is obligations	process in <x>	confiscated <x>
consulting in <x>	promotion to <x>	<x> request information	involvement in <x>	<x> was hurled
customers in <x>	founded as <x>	<x> is foundation	intervention in <x>	placed <x>
diensten in <x>	established as <x>	<x> has positions	linked in <x>	rounds for <x>
distributors in <x>	assistant to <x>	incorporated as <x>	operates in <x>	consisted of <x>
services in <x>	meyerson is <x>	offices of <x>	kidnapped in <x>	firing <x>
expanded into <x>	<x> seated	<x> required to meet	refuge in <x>	explosion of <x>

Figure 4: Top 20 extraction patterns for 4 categories

$$score(NP_i) = \sum_{k=1}^{N_i} 1 + (.01 * score(pattern_k))$$

The main advantage of meta-bootstrapping comes from re-evaluating the extraction patterns after each mutual bootstrapping process. For example, after the first mutual bootstrapping run, five new words are added to the permanent semantic lexicon. Then mutual bootstrapping is restarted from scratch with the original seed words plus these five new words. Now, the best pattern selected by mutual bootstrapping might be different from the best pattern selected last time. This produces a snowball effect because its extractions are added to the temporary semantic lexicon which is the basis for choosing the next extraction pattern. In practice, what happens is that the ordering of the patterns changes (sometimes dramatically) between subsequent runs of mutual bootstrapping. In particular, more general patterns seem to float to the top as the permanent semantic lexicon grows.

Figure 4 shows the top 20 extraction patterns produced for several categories after 50 iterations of meta-bootstrapping. Note that the top five terrorism location patterns are different from the top five terrorism location patterns generated by mutual bootstrapping alone (shown in Figure 2). The top five patterns produced by meta-bootstrapping are much more common, extracting a total of 79 unique NPs, while the top five patterns produced by mutual bootstrapping extracted only 30 unique NPs.

Evaluation

To evaluate the meta-bootstrapping algorithm, we performed experiments with two text collections:

corporate web pages collected for the WebKB project (Craven *et al.* 1998) and terrorism news articles from the MUC-4 corpus (MUC-4 Proceedings 1992). For training, we used 4160 of the web pages and 1500 of the terrorism texts. We preprocessed the web pages first by removing html tags and adding periods to separate independent phrases.[3] AutoSlog generated 19,690 candidate extraction patterns from the web page training set, and 14,064 candidate extraction patterns from the terrorism training set.[4] Then we ran the meta-bootstrapping algorithm on three semantic categories for the web pages (locations, person titles, and companies), and two semantic categories for the terrorism articles (locations and weapons). We used the seed word lists shown in Figure 5. We used different location seeds for the two text collections because the terrorism articles were mainly from Latin America while the web pages were much more international.

We ran the meta-bootstrapping algorithm (outer bootstrapping) for 50 iterations. The extraction patterns produced by the last iteration were the output of the system, along with the permanent semantic lexicon. For each meta-bootstrapping iteration, we ran the mutual bootstrapping procedure (inner bootstrapping) until it produced 10 patterns that extracted at least one new NP (i.e., not currently in the semantic

---

[3]Web pages pose a problem for NLP systems because separate lines do not always end with a period (e.g., list items and headers). We used several heuristics to insert periods whenever an independent line or phrase was suspected.

[4]AutoSlog actually generated many more extraction patterns, but for practical reasons we only used the patterns that appeared with frequency ≥ 2.

	Iter 1	Iter 10	Iter 20	Iter 30	Iter 40	Iter 50
Web Company	5/5 (1)	25/32 (.78)	52/65 (.80)	72/113 (.64)	86/163 (.53)	95/206 (.46)
Web Location	5/5 (1)	46/50 (.92)	88/100 (.88)	129/150 (.86)	163/200 (.82)	191/250 (.76)
Web Title	0/1 (0)	22/31 (.71)	63/81 (.78)	86/131 (.66)	101/181 (.56)	107/231 (.46)
Terr. Location	5/5 (1)	32/50 (.64)	66/100 (.66)	100/150 (.67)	127/200 (.64)	158/250 (.63)
Terr. Weapon	4/4 (1)	31/44 (.70)	68/94 (.72)	85/144 (.59)	101/194 (.52)	124/244 (.51)

Table 1: Accuracy of the Semantic Lexicons

Web Company:	co. company corp. corporation inc. incorporated limited ltd. plc
Web Location:	australia canada china england france germany japan mexico switzerland united_states
Web Title:	ceo cfo president vice-president vp
Terr. Location:	bolivia city colombia district guatemala honduras neighborhood nicaragua region town
Terr. Weapon:	bomb bombs dynamite explosive explosives gun guns rifle rifles tnt

Figure 5: Seed Word Lists

lexicon). But there were two exceptions: (1) if the best pattern had score < 0.7 then mutual bootstrapping stopped, or (2) if the best pattern had score > 1.8 then mutual bootstrapping continued. Intuitively, mutual bootstrapping stops when the best pattern looks especially dubious (its extractions would be risky to add to the lexicon) or keeps going if it is still generating strong extraction patterns. This scheme allows mutual bootstrapping to produce a variable number of extraction patterns, depending on how reliable it believes them to be. These criteria worked well empirically on the categories that we tested, but a more formal strategy is a worthwhile avenue for future research.

First, we evaluated the semantic lexicons in isolation by manually inspecting each word. We judged a word to belong to the category if it was a specific category member (e.g., "IBM" is a specific company) or a general referent for the category (e.g., "the company" is a referent for companies). Although referents are meaningless in isolation, they are useful for information extraction tasks because a coreference resolver should be able to find their antecedent. The referents were also very useful during bootstrapping because a pattern that extracts "the company" will probably also extract specific company names.

Table 1 shows the accuracy of the semantic lexicon after the 1st iteration of meta-bootstrapping and after each 10th iteration. Each cell shows the number of true category members among the entries generated thus far. For example, 32 phrases were added to company semantic lexicon after the tenth iteration and 25 of those (78%) were true company phrases. Table 1 shows that our algorithm found about 100-200 new phrases for all of the categories, and the density of

good phrases was high. To put our results in perspective, other researchers have generated a semantic lexicon for the terrorism weapon category and achieved accuracy rates of 34/200 (17%) (Riloff & Shepherd 1997) and 93/257 (36%) (Roark & Charniak 1998). So our results are significantly better than those reported previously for this category. To our knowledge, no one has reported results for the other categories that we tested.

We also wanted to verify that the phrases in the semantic lexicon would be likely to appear in new texts. So we created a test set by manually tagging all noun phrases that were legitimate extractions for each category in 233 new web pages.[5] Table 2 shows the recall and precision scores on the test set for three experiments. In the first experiment (Baseline), we generated a baseline by extracting all noun phrases in the test set that contained one of the original seed words. In the second experiment (Lexicon), we manually filtered the semantic lexicon to remove incorrect entries and then extracted every noun phrase in the test set that contained a lexicon entry. In the third experiment (Union), we extracted all noun phrases in the test set that either contained a lexicon entry or were extracted by an extraction pattern generated for the category.

Recall/Precision (%)	Baseline	Lexicon	Union
Web Company	10/32	18/47	18/45
Web Location	11/98	51/77	54/74
Web Title	6/100	46/66	47/62

Table 2: Recall/Precision (%) Results on Web Test Set

Table 2 shows that the seed words by themselves achieved high precision for locations and titles but low recall. The low precision for companies is mainly due to the presence of "company" in the seed word list, which is extremely common but extracts mostly referents and not specific company names. We did not count referents as legitimate extractions in these experiments.

The second column (Lexicon) shows that the semantic lexicons were useful for extracting information from new web pages. The lexicon achieved about 50% recall with 66-77% precision for locations and titles. The results for companies were substantially lower, but still above the baseline. We hypothesize that the set of possible company names is much larger than the set of

---

[5]Due to time constraints, we only hand-labeled the noun phrases that were extracted by at least one of the 19,690 candidate patterns produced by AutoSlog.

locations and titles in corporate web pages, so we probably need to generate a much larger lexicon of company names to achieve good results for this category.

The third column (*Union*) shows that using the lexicon and the extraction patterns to identify new information slightly increases recall for locations and titles, but also slightly decreased precision. In retrospect, we realized that we probably need to use more extraction patterns. For this experiment, we only used patterns with a score > 0.7, which produced only 63 title extraction patterns and 87 company extraction patterns. Since the patterns represent very specific linguistic expressions, we probably need to lower that threshold. We also plan to consider schemes for allowing both the semantic lexicon and the extraction patterns to vote on possible extractions.

Conclusions

Bootstrapping is a powerful technique for leveraging small amounts of knowledge to acquire more domain knowledge automatically. An important aspect of our bootstrapping mechanism is that it generates domain-specific dictionaries. For example, the location dictionary generated from the web pages contained mainly country names and U.S. cities while the location dictionary generated from the terrorism articles contained mostly cities and towns in Latin America. Generating domain-specific dictionaries is a strength because the dictionaries are tailored for the domain of interest. But some categories may behave strangely if one does not anticipate their role in the domain. For example, we tried using this bootstrapping technique for the semantic category "vehicle" using the terrorism corpus, but the resulting dictionaries looked remarkably similar to the weapon dictionaries. In retrospect, we realized that vehicles are often weapons in the terrorism texts, either as car bombs or fighter planes. So in this domain, considering vehicles to be weapons usually makes sense.

In summary, we have shown that multi-level bootstrapping can produce high-quality dictionaries for a variety of categories. Our bootstrapping method has two advantages over previous techniques for learning information extraction dictionaries: both a semantic lexicon and a dictionary of extraction patterns are acquired simultaneously, and no special training resources are needed. Our algorithm needs only a corpus of (unannotated) training texts and a small set of seed words as input. The resulting semantic lexicon does need to be manually inspected to get rid of bad entries, but this can be done in a few minutes. Multi-level bootstrapping appears to be a promising approach for acquiring domain knowledge automatically, and we hope to apply this technique to other knowledge acquisition tasks as well.

Acknowledgments

This research is supported in part by the National Science Foundation under grants IRI-9509820, IRI-9704240, and SBR-9720374, and the DARPA HPKB program under contract F30602-97-1-0215.

References

Califf, M. E. 1998. *Relational Learning Techniques for Natural Language Information Extraction.* Ph.D. Dissertation, Tech. Rept. AI98-276, Artificial Intelligence Laboratory, The University of Texas at Austin.

Craven, M.; DiPasquo, D.; Freitag, D.; McCallum, A.; Mitchell, T.; Nigam, K.; and Slattery, S. 1998. Learning to Extract Symbolic Knowledge from the World Wide Web. In *Proceedings of the Fifteenth National Conference on Artificial Intelligence.*

Freitag, D. 1998. Toward General-Purpose Learning for Information Extraction. In *Proceedings of the 36th Annual Meeting of the Association for Computational Linguistics.*

Huffman, S. 1996. Learning information extraction patterns from examples. In Wermter, S.; Riloff, E.; and Scheler, G., eds., *Connectionist, Statistical, and Symbolic Approaches to Learning for Natural Language Processing.* Springer-Verlag, Berlin. 246–260.

Kim, J., and Moldovan, D. 1993. Acquisition of Semantic Patterns for Information Extraction from Corpora. In *Proceedings of the Ninth IEEE Conference on Artificial Intelligence for Applications*, 171–176. Los Alamitos, CA: IEEE Computer Society Press.

Miller, G. 1990. Wordnet: An On-line Lexical Database. *International Journal of Lexicography* 3(4).

MUC-4 Proceedings. 1992. *Proceedings of the Fourth Message Understanding Conference (MUC-4).* San Mateo, CA: Morgan Kaufmann.

Riloff, E., and Shepherd, J. 1997. A Corpus-Based Approach for Building Semantic Lexicons. In *Proceedings of the Second Conference on Empirical Methods in Natural Language Processing*, 117–124.

Riloff, E. 1993. Automatically Constructing a Dictionary for Information Extraction Tasks. In *Proceedings of the Eleventh National Conference on Artificial Intelligence*, 811–816. AAAI Press/The MIT Press.

Riloff, E. 1996a. An Empirical Study of Automated Dictionary Construction for Information Extraction in Three Domains. *Artificial Intelligence* 85:101–134.

Riloff, E. 1996b. Automatically Generating Extraction Patterns from Untagged Text. In *Proceedings of the Thirteenth National Conference on Artificial Intelligence*, 1044–1049. The AAAI Press/MIT Press.

Roark, B., and Charniak, E. 1998. Noun-phrase Co-occurrence Statistics for Semi-automatic Semantic Lexicon Construction. In *Proceedings of the 36th Annual Meeting of the Association for Computational Linguistics*, 1110–1116.

Soderland, S.; Fisher, D.; Aseltine, J.; and Lehnert, W. 1995. CRYSTAL: Inducing a conceptual dictionary. In *Proceedings of the Fourteenth International Joint Conference on Artificial Intelligence*, 1314–1319.

Soderland, S. 1999. Learning Information Extraction Rules for Semi-structured and Free Text. *Machine Learning.* (to appear).

Feature Selection in SVM Text Categorization

Hirotoshi Taira
NTT Communication Science Labs.
2-4 Hikaridai Seika-cho Soraku-gun
Kyoto 619-0237 Japan
taira@cslab.kecl.ntt.co.jp

Masahiko Haruno
ATR Human Information Processing Research Labs.
2-2 Hikaridai Seika-cho Soraku-gun
Kyoto 619-0231 Japan
mharuno@hip.atr.co.jp

Abstract

This paper investigates the effect of prior feature selection in Support Vector Machine (SVM) text categorization. The input space was gradually increased by using mutual information (MI) filtering and part-of-speech (POS) filtering, which determine the portion of words that are appropriate for learning from the information-theoretic and the linguistic perspectives, respectively. We tested the two filtering methods on SVMs as well as a decision tree algorithm C4.5. The SVMs' results common to both filtering are that 1) the optimal number of features differed completely across categories, and 2) the average performance for all categories was best when all of the words were used. In addition, a comparison of the two filtering methods clarified that POS filtering on SVMs consistently outperformed MI filtering, which indicates that SVMs cannot find irrelevant parts of speech. These results suggest a simple strategy for the SVM text categorization: use a full number of words found through a rough filtering technique like part-of-speech tagging.

Introduction

With the rapid growth of the Internet and online information, automatic text categorization has attracted much attention among researchers and companies. Some machine learning methods have been applied to text categorization, which include, for example, k-nearest-neighbor (Yang 1994), decision trees (Lewis & Ringuette 1994) and Naive-Bayes (Lewis & Ringuette 1994). The huge number of words in these data, which can potentially contribute to the overall task, challenges machine learning approaches. More specifically, the difficulties in handling the large input space are twofold: the learning machine used and the portion of words effective for the classification depend on each other (Yang & Pederson 1997). We have to find learning machines with a feature selection criteria because the best set of words greatly differs with the learning machine used (Lewis & Ringuette 1994).

Support Vector Machines (SVMs) (Vapnik 1995; Cortes & Vapnik 1995) construct the optimal hyperplane that separates a set of positive examples from a set of negative examples with a maximum margin [1]. SVMs have been shown to yield good generalization performances on a wide variety of classification problems that require large-scale input space, such as handwritten character recognition (Vapnik 1995) and face detection (Osuna, Freund, & Girosi 1998) problems.

Recently, two groups have explored the use of SVMs for text categorization (Joachims 1998; Dumais *et al.* 1998). Although they both achieved promising performances, they used completely different feature (word) selection strategies. In (Joachims 1998), words are considered features only if they occur in the training data at least three times and if they are not stop words such as 'and' and 'or.' Then the inverse document frequency (IDF) (Salton & Buckley 1988) is employed as a value for each feature. In contrast, (Dumais *et al.* 1998) considers only 300 words for each category, which are handled by a threshold for high mutual information (Cover & Thomas 1991). The feature value in this case is assigned as a binary to indicate whether a word appears in a text. A natural question about SVM text categorization occurs to us: how much influence do different feature selection strategies have? Does there exist one best strategy for choosing appropriate words?

Feature selection becomes especially delicate in agglutinative languages such as Japanese and Chinese because in these languages, word identification itself is not a straight-forward task. Unknown words output by word-segmentation and part-of-speech tagging systems contain both important keywords (like personal and company names) and useless portions of words. The selection of these unknown words is crucial to these languages.

To address these questions, this paper investigates the effect of prior feature selection in SVM text categorization by using Japanese newspaper articles. In our experiments, the number of input spaces was gradually increased by two distinct criteria: mutual informa-

---

[1] A margin is intuitively the distance from a data point to the classification boundary.

tion (MI) filtering and part-of-speech (POS) filtering. MI selects discriminating words for a particular category from an information-theoretical viewpoint. Words with higher mutual information are more highly representative in a specific text category. In contrast, POS filtering constructs word input space based on part of speech.

Our first experiment addresses how many words are appropriate for each category and to what extent the numbers differ between categories in SVM text categorization. The results are: 1) the optimal number of features differed completely across categories, and 2) the average performance for all categories was best when all of the words were used. The additional comparison between SVMs and a decision tree induction algorithm C4.5 (Quinlan 1993) clarifies that C4.5 achieves the best performance for each category at much smaller number of words, and the SVMs significantly outperforms C4.5. These results indicate that SVMs are more appropriate to make the best use of the huge number of input words.

Our second experiment changes input space in the following order without further thresholding: 1) common nouns, 2) step1+proper nouns, 3) step2+verbal nouns, 4) step3+unknown words, 5) step4+verbs. This experiment aims to investigate general tendencies in increasing the number of input spaces and the effect of each part-of-speech on SVM text categorizations. The result was similar to that was seen in the first experiment.

A comparison of the two experiments clarified that POS filtering consistently outperformed MI filtering, which indicates that SVMs cannot find irrelevant parts of speech. These results suggest a simple strategy in SVM text categorization: use a full number of words found through a rough filtering technique like part-of-speech tagging.

The rest of the paper is organized as follows. The next section introduces SVMs and gives a rough theoretical sketch of why SVMs can avoid overfitting even if the input space is sufficiently large. We then report our experimental results on MI filtering and POS filtering. The last section discusses the results of the two filtering methods and concludes the paper.

Support Vector Machines

SVMs are based on *Structural Risk Minimization* (Vapnik 1995). The idea of structural risk minimization is to find a hypothesis h for which we can guarantee the lowest generalization error. The following upper bound (1) connects $error_g(h)$, the generalization error of a hypothesis h with the error of h on the training set $error_t(h)$ and the complexity of h (Vapnik 1995). This bound holds with a probability of at least $1 - \eta$. In the second term on the right hand side, n denotes the number of training examples and λ is the *VC dimension*, which is a property of the hypothesis space and indicates its complexity.

$$error_g(h) \leq error_t(h) + 2\sqrt{\frac{\lambda(\ln\frac{2n}{\lambda} + 1) - \ln\frac{\eta}{4}}{n}} \quad (1)$$

Equation (1) reflects the well-known trade-off between the training error and the complexity of the hypothesis space. A simple hypothesis (small λ) would probably not contain good approximating functions and would lead to a high training (and true) error. On the other hand, a too-rich hypothesis space (high λ) would lead to a small training error, but the second term on the right hand side of (1) will be large (overfitting). The right complexity is crucial to achieving good generalization. In the following, we assume that the linear threshold functions represent a hypothesis space in which w and b are parameters of a hyperplane and x is an input vector:

$$h(\boldsymbol{x}) = sign\{\boldsymbol{w} \cdot \boldsymbol{x} + b\} = \begin{cases} +1, & \text{if } \boldsymbol{w} \cdot \boldsymbol{x} + b > 0 \\ -1, & \text{else.} \end{cases}$$

Lemma 1 sheds light on the relationship between the dimension of the input space x of a set of hyperplanes and its VC dimension λ.

Lemma 1 (Vapnik) *Consider hyperplanes* $h(\boldsymbol{x}) = sign\{\boldsymbol{w} \cdot \boldsymbol{x} + b\}$ *as a hypothesis. If all example vectors* x_i *are contained in a ball of radius R and the following is required such that for all examples x_i:*

$$|\boldsymbol{w} \cdot \boldsymbol{x} + b| \geq 1, \quad with \quad ||\boldsymbol{w}|| = A,$$

then this set of hyperplanes has a VC dimension λ bounded by

$$\lambda \leq min([R^2A^2], n) + 1. \quad (2)$$

Note here that the VC dimension of these hyperplanes does not always depend on the number of input features. Instead, the VC dimension depends on the Euclidean length $||\boldsymbol{w}||$ of the weight vector $\boldsymbol{w}$. Equation (2) supports the possibility that SVM text categorization achieves good generalization even if a huge number of words are given as an input space. Further experimental evaluations are required because Equations (1) and (2) both give us only a loose bound.

Basically, SVM finds the hyperplane that separates the training data with the shortest weight vector (i.e., $min||\boldsymbol{w}||$). The hyperplane maximizes the margin between the positive and negative samples. Since the optimization problem is difficult to handle numerically, Lagrange multipliers are introduced to translate the problem into an equivalent quadratic optimization problem. For this kind of optimization problem, efficient algorithms exist that are guaranteed to find the global optimum. The result of the optimization process is a set of coefficients α_i^* for which (3) is minimum. These coefficients can be used to construct the hyperplane satisfying the maximum margin requirement.

$$Minimize: \quad -\sum_{i=1}^{n}\alpha_i + \frac{1}{2}\sum_{i,j=1}^{n}\alpha_i\alpha_j y_i y_j \mathrm{x} \cdot \mathrm{x} \quad (3)$$

$$so \quad that: \sum_{i=1}^{n} \alpha_i y_i = 0 \quad \forall i : \alpha_i \geq 0.$$

SVMs can handle nonlinear hypotheses by simply substituting every occurrence of the inner product in equation (3) with any Kernel function $K(x_1, x_2)$ [2]. Among the many types of Kernel functions available, we will focus on the dth polynomial functions (Equation (4)):

$$K_{poly}(x_1, x_2) = (x_1 \cdot x_2 + 1)^d. \quad (4)$$

Experimental Results

This section describes our experimental results for two feature selection methods in SVM text categorization: mutual information filtering and part-of-speech filtering. For comparison, we also tested a decision tree induction algorithm C4.5 (Quinlan 1993) with default parameters. Before going into the details of the results, we first explain the experimental setting.

Experimental Setting

Table 1: RWCP corpus for training and test.

Category	training sets	test sets
sports	161	147
criminal law	156	148
government	135	142
educational system	110	124
traffic	112	103
military affairs	110	118
international relations	96	97
communications	76	83
theater	86	95
agriculture	78	72

We performed our experiments using the RWCP corpus (Toyoura *et al.* 1996), which contains 30,207 newspaper articles taken from the Mainichi Shinbun Newspaper published in 1994 (Mainichi 1995). Each article was assigned multiple UDC codes, each of which represented a category of texts. In the rest of this paper, we will focus on the ten categories that appeared most often in the corpus [3]: sports, criminal law, government, education, traffic, military affairs, international relations, communications, theater and agriculture. The total number of articles used for both training and test were 1,000. Table 1 summarizes the number of training and test articles in each category.

---

[2]More precisely, the Mercer's condition (Vapnik 1995) should be satisfied.

[3]The results for other categories were very similar to these 10 categories.

These articles were word-segmented and POS tagged by the Japanese morphological analyzing system Chasen (Matsumoto *et al.* 1997). The process generated 20,490 different words. We used all types of parts of speech in the mutual information filtering and used only common nouns, proper nouns, verbal nouns, unknown words and verbs (total number of subset words was 18,111) in the part-of-speech filtering. Throughout our experiments, various subsets of these extracted words were used as input feature spaces, and the value for each feature was a binary value that indicated whether a word appeared in a document or not. A binary value was adopted to study the pure effects of each word.

Mutual Information Filtering

The mutual information (MI) between a word t_i and a category c is defined in equation (5). MI becomes large when the occurrence of t_i is biased to one side between a category c and other categories. Consequently, it can be expected that the words with high mutual information in category c are keywords in the category. The question we would like to discuss here is whether words with a fixed number of high mutual information can achieve a good generalization over all text categories.

$$MI(t_i, c) = \sum_{t_i \in \{0,1\}} \sum_{c \in \{+,-\}} P(t_i, c) \log \frac{P(t_i, c)}{P(t_i)P(c)}. \quad (5)$$

Table 2 shows the words at the points of the 300th, 500th, 1,000th, 5,000th and 10,000th mutual information in each category. In general, up to the 500th or 1,000th term, the words were specific to each category. For example, 'screwball' and 'golfer,' 'peace' and 'Moscow' are specific to sports and military, respectively. It is also interesting to note that 'Kazakhstan' is an unknown word that plays an important role in the category of military affairs. In contrast, after the 1,000th term, words do not seem to be specialized to any specific category.

Table 3 and 4 show the average of the recall and precision on SVMs and C4.5, respectively, when the number of words is changed with various MI thresholds. The order of polynomial d (See Equation (4)) used is 1 and 2. The boldface values in the tables represent the best performance for each category. It is easily understood that the best number of words differs greatly from category to category in SVMs, while the best performance in C4.5 is achieved at much smaller number of words. The average performance is best for SVM when the number of words is 15,000; it improves continuously although in C4.5 abrupt drop is seen at 500 words. It is also notable that in average SVMs significantly outperform C4.5, which indicates that SVMs are more appropriate to make the best use of the huge number of input words.

Let us now look more closely at the recall and precision on SVMs for the same data. Figure 1 plots the

Table 2: Words selected with MI.

Feature	words				
	300th	500th	1000th	5000th	10000th
sports	変化球 (screwball)	応援 (cheering)	ゴルファー (golfer)	アンケート (questionnaire)	目安 (standard)
criminal law	疑惑 (suspicion)	送検 (commit for trial)	地下 (underground)	売る (sell)	増進 (increase)
government	藏会 (parliament)	運輸省 (The Ministry of Transport)	約束 (promise)	根幹 (basis)	さえぎる (interrupt)
education	塾 (cram school)	文相 (Minister of Education)	理想的だ (ideal)	涙 (tear)	即 (immediately)
traffic	大型車 (large-size car)	配達 (delivery)	速さ (speed)	双方向 (bi-direction)
military	平和 (peace)	モスクワ (Moscow)	カザフスタン (Kazakhstan)	実際 (practical)	降下 (descend)
international	有事 (emergency)	各国 (countries)	大筋 (outline)	年内 (within the year)	裁く (judge)
communications	会議 (meeting)	衛星通信 (satellite communications)	伝送 (transmission)	正常 (normal)	慎重 (careful)
theater	台本 (play script)	終演 (the end of a show)	賞 (prize)	要素 (element)	ロイ (Roy)
agriculture	イモ (potato)	砂糖 (sugar)	飼料 (livestock feed)	改善 (improvement)	変貌 (look different)

Table 3: Average of recall and precision with MI on SVMs.

Feature	poly degree $d = 1/d = 2$					
	300	500	1000	5000	10000	15000
sports	**91.9**/**91.9**	89.5/89.5	90.9/90.9	90.8/90.0	90.0/89.6	90.4/89.6
criminal law	71.5/70.7	69.2/71.0	68.2/70.3	72.2/73.0	74.3/74.1	75.5/**76.4**
government	66.6/66.1	68.4/68.2	74.4/76.4	79.3/79.0	76.8/78.0	78.2/**79.8**
education	68.4/68.2	69.1/69.7	71.7/73.5	78.1/77.8	80.0/79.8	**80.1**/79.6
traffic	66.6/66.6	70.5/71.6	**72.1**/71.8	70.7/68.3	71.0/69.1	71.0/71.1
military affairs	66.3/68.3	71.3/71.9	74.5/75.7	74.6/74.7	75.6/75.9	**77.1**/76.3
international relations	54.3/56.9	60.1/61.9	62.9/**63.5**	61.6/60.4	61.0/59.2	57.1/58.9
communications	64.0/64.9	65.7/**66.6**	59.3/59.3	55.7/53.3	53.6/50.0	58.2/50.0
theater	83.9/84.0	**88.7**/83.9	86.2/88.2	83.6/86.2	83.8/82.2	83.8/82.4
agriculture	85.9/85.2	**87.5**/86.6	85.7/85.7	85.0/83.2	85.9/85.0	84.1/84.1
avg.	71.9/72.2	74.0/74.0	74.5/75.5	75.1/74.5	75.2/74.2	**75.5**/74.8

recall and precision of $d = 1$. Overall, recall tends to improve as the number of words increase except for the 'international relations' category, which monotonically decreases. Thus, we can safely say that increasing the number of words improves recall.

In contrast to recall, the change in precision is more complicated. For the five categories with the highest precision, the curves decline continuously but only slightly. This is a reasonable phenomenon because the excessive amount of key words may extract irrelevant documents. The other five categories with middle precision differ greatly. Two curves increase monotonically and two others drift, while the remaining one has a peak at 10,000 features. The point here is that the increase in features does not involve a large decrease in precision. In other words, the feature selection ability inherent in SVM can prevent precision from dropping abruptly with an increase in feature space. These results show that good generalization performance with a large number of features (15,000) depends on achieving good precision.

Part-of-Speech Filtering

We tested the following five feature sets. The number of different words in each part of speech is summarized in Table 5. The total number of different words of these parts of speech is 18,111.

1. common nouns

2. 1 + proper nouns

3. 2 + verbal nouns

4. 3 + unknown words

5. 4 + verbs

Table 6 and 7 show the averages of recall and precision on SVMs and C4.5, respectively, when each of the above five features are used. Boldface numbers represent the best value in each category. It is clear that the best feature set greatly differs from category to category in both cases. The best average performance is achieved in SVMs when all of the words are used (Feature Set 5).

What are the contributions of each part of speech in SVM text categorization? In Table 6, common nouns are so powerful that near-optimal performance can be achieved only with one part of speech. Proper nouns, verbal nouns and verbs improve results in more than half of the categories, while unknown words contribute to only three categories. This is probably because the unknown words contain irrelevant portions of a word as well as important keywords for a category. Note that there is no abrupt drop in performance as a result of incrementally adding any parts of speech.

Table 4: Average of recall and precision with MI on C4.5.

Feature	300	500	1000	5000	10000	15000
sports	**87.5**	86.2	85.2	83.6	83.6	83.6
criminal law	67.9	**70.8**	68.9	68.8	68.8	68.8
government	**65.5**	63.0	58.0	57.9	57.9	57.9
education	**72.0**	69.2	70.1	70.1	70.1	70.1
traffic	**63.0**	61.0	61.0	61.0	61.0	61.0
military affairs	**75.9**	73.3	69.1	68.8	68.8	68.8
international relations	**50.0**	45.6	42.4	42.4	42.4	42.4
communications	**52.7**	50.3	50.3	50.3	50.3	50.3
theater	**80.9**	80.9	79.5	79.5	79.5	79.5
agriculture	**84.4**	84.4	84.4	83.8	83.8	83.8
avg.	**70.0**	68.5	66.9	66.6	66.6	66.6

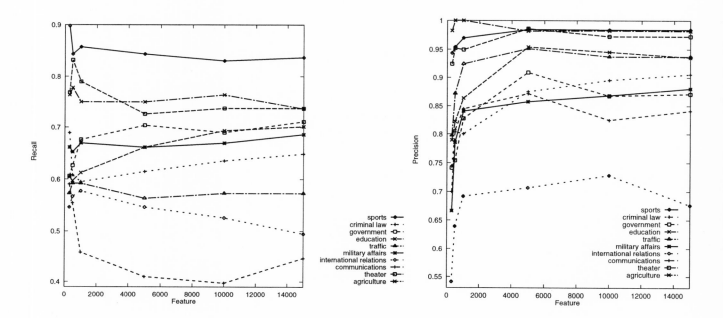

Figure 1: Recall and precision with MI features on SVMs.

Let us now consider the recall and precision results for the same data. Figures 2 plots the recall and precision on SVMs. The situation looks completely different from that of the MI filtering experiment because the number of Feature Set 1 (common nouns) reaches 8,629. Looking at Figures 1, only after 10,000 features, do we notice that POS filtering and MI filtering have the same tendencies: precision curves increase monotonically while recall curves differ among categories. This monotonic increase in the precision curve shows that every part of speech contains powerful keywords specific to one category. The recall curve shows that the increase in features above 10,000 words does not always improve recall but also that the drop in recall is not serious.

Discussion

We have described the feature selection in SVM text categorization by focusing on two distinct experiments: MI filtering and POS filtering. The results on SVMs for each filtering technique can be summarized as follows and coincide on two points: One, the best feature set for categories changes and two, the best average performance is achieved when all of the features are given to SVMs. These are distinct characteristics of SVMs when compared with a decision tree learning algorithm C4.5.

MI filtering : The best number of words selected differs greatly among categories and is difficult to be determined a priori. The average performance is best when all of the words are used.

POS filtering The best feature set changes depending

Table 5: POS distribution of training data.

	POS (part of speech)				
	common noun	proper noun	verbal noun	unknown	verb
Number of words	8629	2725	2829	1634	2294
Percentage (%)	47.6	15.0	16.0	7.4	12.7

Table 6: Average of recall and precision with POS filtering on SVMs.

	poly degree $d = 1/d = 2$				
Feature	1	2	3	4	5
sports	92.2/91.4	**93.2**/92.4	92.9/92.4	92.0/92.0	90.5/90.8
criminal law	74.0/73.0	73.3/73.6	72.5/73.3	73.0/73.3	**75.2**/74.9
government	76.9/76.7	78.4/78.7	79.3/79.0	78.9/78.2	**79.6**/79.2
education	81.4/81.4	80.8/80.3	81.4/80.9	81.4/**81.8**	81.2/80.3
traffic	72.8/72.0	76.0/74.5	74.8/**76.0**	74.8/75.2	73.0/72.2
military affairs	80.1/77.3	76.1/76.1	78.8/76.2	77.0/77.0	**80.1**/77.9
international relations	54.5/54.6	59.2/60.2	60.7/61.4	61.2/62.2	**64.0**/64.0
communications	65.7/67.6	63.8/62.3	**69.3**/68.0	68.9/67.1	65.7/63.2
theater	83.8/83.8	82.4/82.4	85.2/85.2	85.2/85.2	**87.0**/85.0
agriculture	87.5/87.5	**88.3**/88.3	87.5/86.6	86.6/86.6	85.0/84.8
avg.	76.9/76.5	77.5/77.2	78.0/77.9	77.9/77.8	**78.1**/77.2

on the category. The best average performance is achieved when all of the words are used. Each part of speech makes a contribution but differs in influence among categories.

It is also important to note that POS filtering consistently outperforms MI filtering on SVMs (see 15,000 words in Table 3 and Feature Set 5 in Table 6). In MI filtering, every part of speech is adopted, including postpositional particles, conjunctions, etc. POS filtering on the other hand, selects only five parts of speech by using a natural language processing (NLP) technology (POS tagger). These include common nouns, proper nouns, verbal nouns, unknown words and verbs. The less crucial parts of speech are expected to be harmful to MI filtering. This comparison clearly shows that SVM text categorization has a limitation on its feature selection ability: it cannot detect irrelevant parts of speech.

Finally, we will briefly refer to the kernel functions we used. Changing the polynomial orders 1 and 2 makes no distinct difference in performance, although more significant influence was seen in lower level tasks like image processing (Cortes & Vapnik 1995).

Conclusion

This paper has described various aspects of feature selection in SVM text categorization. Our experimental results clearly show that SVM text categorization handles large-scale word vectors well but is a limited in finding irrelevant parts of speech. This suggests a simple and strongly practical strategy for organizing a large

number of words found through a rough filtering technique like part-of-speech tagging. SVMs and other large margin classifiers should play more important roles in handling complex and real-world NLP tasks (Haruno, Shirai, & Ooyama 1999).

References

Cortes, C., and Vapnik, V. 1995. Support vector networks. *Machine Learning* 20:273–297.

Cover, T., and Thomas, J. 1991. *Elements of Information Theory*. John Wiley & Sons.

Dumais, S.; Platt, J.; Heckerman, D.; and Sahami, M. 1998. Inductive learning algorithms and representations for text categorization. In *Proc. of 7th International Conference on Information and Knowledge Management*.

Haruno, M.; Shirai, S.; and Ooyama, Y. 1999. Using decision trees to construct a practical parser. *Machine Learning* 131–150. Special Issue on Natural Language Learning.

Joachims, T. 1998. Text categorization with support vector machines. In *Proc. of European Conference on Machine Learning(ECML)*.

Lewis, D., and Ringuette, M. 1994. A comparison of two learning algorithms for text categorization. In *Proc. of Third Annual Symposium on Document Analysis and Information Retrieval*, 81–93.

Mainichi. 1995. *CD Mainichi Shinbun 94*. Nichigai Associates Co.

Table 7: Average of recall and precision with POS filtering on C4.5.

Feature	1	2	3	4	5
sports	**84.7**	82.9	83.4	83.0	83.4
criminal law	61.5	59.3	**71.3**	71.3	71.3
government	58.0	**62.8**	62.7	62.7	60.4
education	60.2	63.5	62.8	**70.2**	70.2
traffic	58.2	56.4	58.1	58.1	**59.4**
military affairs	**75.5**	71.8	71.8	71.8	71.8
international relations	**49.3**	44.1	48.9	46.4	46.4
communications	49.6	48.5	**51.0**	44.6	44.6
theater	**79.7**	71.3	79.2	79.2	79.2
agriculture	81.2	**81.4**	81.4	81.4	81.4
avg.	65.8	63.9	**67.1**	66.9	66.8

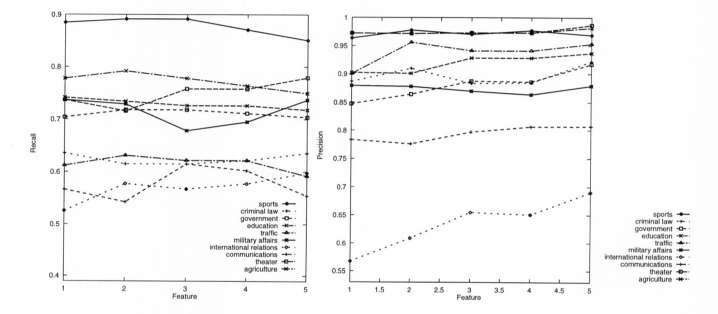

Figure 2: Recall and precision with POS features on SVMs.

Matsumoto, Y.; Kitauchi, A.; Yamashita, T.; Hirano, Y.; Imaichi, O.; and Imamura, T. 1997. *Japanese Morphological Analysis System Chasen Manual.* NAIST Technical Report NAIST-IS-TR97007.

Osuna, E.; Freund, R.; and Girosi, F. 1998. Training support vector machines: An application to face detection. In *Proc. of Computer Vision and Pattern Recognition '97*, 130–136.

Quinlan, J. 1993. *C4.5: Programs for Machine Learning.* Morgan Kaufmann.

Salton, G., and Buckley, C. 1988. Term weighting approaches in automatic text retrieval. *Information Proceedings and Management* 24(5):513–523.

Toyoura, J.; Tokunaga, T.; Isahara, H.; and Oka, R. 1996. Development of a RWC text database tagged with classification code(in Japanese). In *NLC96-13.* *IEICE*, 89–96.

Vapnik, V. 1995. *The Nature of Statistical Learning Theory.* New York: Springer-Verlag.

Yang, Y., and Pederson, J. 1997. A comparative study on feature selection in text categorization. In *Machine Learning: Proc. of the 14th International Conference (ICML'97)*, 412–420.

Yang, Y. 1994. Expert network: Effective and efficient learning from human decisions in text categorization and retrieval. In *Proc. of the 17th Annual International ACM SIGIR Conference on Research and Development in Information Retrieval*, 13–22.

Automatic Construction of Semantic Lexicons for Learning Natural Language Interfaces

Cynthia A. Thompson
Center for the Study of Language and Information
Stanford University
Stanford, CA 94305-4115
cthomp@csli.stanford.edu

Raymond J. Mooney
Department of Computer Sciences
University of Texas
Austin, TX 78712
mooney@cs.utexas.edu

Abstract

This paper describes a system, WOLFIE (WOrd Learning From Interpreted Examples), that acquires a semantic lexicon from a corpus of sentences paired with semantic representations. The lexicon learned consists of words paired with meaning representations. WOLFIE is part of an integrated system that learns to parse novel sentences into semantic representations, such as logical database queries. Experimental results are presented demonstrating WOLFIE's ability to learn useful lexicons for a database interface in four different natural languages. The lexicons learned by WOLFIE are compared to those acquired by a similar system developed by Siskind (1996).

Introduction & Overview

The application of learning methods to natural-language processing (NLP) has drawn increasing attention in recent years. Using machine learning to help automate the construction of NLP systems can eliminate much of the difficulty of manual construction. The semantic lexicon, or the mapping from words to meanings, is one component that is typically challenging and time consuming to construct and update by hand. This paper describes a system, WOLFIE (WOrd Learning From Interpreted Examples), that acquires a semantic lexicon of word/meaning pairs from a corpus of sentences paired with semantic representations. The goal of this research is to automate lexicon construction for an integrated NLP system that acquires both semantic lexicons and parsers for natural-language interfaces from a single training set of annotated sentences.

Although a few others (Siskind 1996; Hastings & Lytinen 1994; Brent 1991) have presented systems for learning information about lexical semantics, this work is unique in combining several features. First, interaction with a system, CHILL (Zelle & Mooney 1996), that learns to parse sentences into semantic representations is demonstrated. Second, it uses a fairly straightforward batch, greedy learning algorithm that is fast and accurate. Third, it is easily extendible to new representation formalisms. Fourth, no prior knowledge is

required although it can exploit an initial lexicon if provided.

We tested WOLFIE's ability to acquire a semantic lexicon for an interface to a geographical database using a corpus of queries collected from human subjects and annotated with their logical form. In this test, WOLFIE was integrated with CHILL, which learns parsers but requires a semantic lexicon (previously built manually). The results demonstrate that the final acquired parser performs nearly as accurately at answering novel questions when using a learned lexicon as when using a hand-built lexicon. WOLFIE is also compared to an alternative lexicon acquisition system developed by Siskind (1996), demonstrating superior performance on this task. Finally, the corpus was translated into Spanish, Japanese, and Turkish and experiments conducted demonstrating an ability to learn successful lexicons and parsers for a variety of languages. Overall, the results demonstrate a robust ability to acquire accurate lexicons directly usable for semantic parsing. With such an integrated system, the task of building a semantic parser for a new domain is simplified. A single representative corpus of sentence/representation pairs allows the acquisition of both a semantic lexicon and parser that generalizes well to novel sentences.

Background

CHILL uses *inductive logic programming* (Muggleton 1992; Lavrač & Džeroski 1994) to learn a deterministic shift-reduce parser written in Prolog. The input to CHILL is a corpus of sentences paired with semantic representations, the same input required by WOLFIE. The parser learned is capable of mapping the sentences into their correct representations, as well as generalizing well to novel sentences. In this paper, we limit our discussion to acquiring parsers that map natural-language questions directly into Prolog queries that can be executed to produce an answer (Zelle & Mooney 1996). Following are two sample queries for a database on U.S. geography, paired with their corresponding Prolog query:

What is the capital of the state with the biggest population?
`answer(C, (capital(S,C), largest(P,`

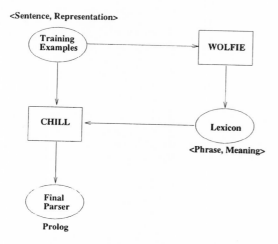

<Sentence, Representation>

<Phrase, Meaning>

Prolog

Figure 1: The Integrated System

```
(state(S), population(S,P))))).
```
What state is Texarkana located in?
```
answer(S, (state(S),
    eq(C,cityid(texarkana,_)), loc(C,S))).
```

CHILL treats parser induction as a problem of learning rules to control the actions of a shift-reduce parser. During parsing, the current context is maintained in a stack and a buffer containing the remaining input. When parsing is complete, the stack contains the representation of the input sentence. There are three types of operators used to construct logical queries. One is the introduction onto the stack of a predicate needed in the sentence representation due to the appearance of a phrase at the front of the input buffer. A second type of operator unifies variables appearing in stack items. Finally, a stack item may be embedded as an argument of another stack item. The introduction operators require a semantic lexicon as background knowledge. By using WOLFIE, the lexicon can be provided automatically. Figure 1 illustrates the complete system.

Problem Definition

A semantic lexicon learner is presented with a set of sentences, each consisting of an ordered list of words and annotated with a semantic representation in the form of a labeled tree; the goal is to find a semantic lexicon consistent with this data. Such a lexicon consists of *(phrase, meaning)* pairs (e.g., ([**biggest**], largest(_,_))), where the phrases and their meanings are extracted from the input sentences and their representations, respectively, such that each sentence's representation can be composed from a set of components each chosen from the possible meanings of a phrase appearing in the sentence. Such a lexicon is said to *cover* the corpus. We will also refer to the coverage of components of a representation (or sentence/representation pair) by a lexicon entry. Ideally, the goal is to minimize the ambiguity

For each phrase, *p* (of at most two words):
    1.1) Collect the training examples in which *p* appears
    1.2) Calculate LICS from (sampled) pairs of these examples' representations
    1.3) For each *l* in the LICS, add (*p*, *l*) to the set of candidate lexicon entries
Until the input representations are covered, or there are no remaining candidate lexicon entries do:
    2.1) Add the best (phrase, meaning) pair to the lexicon
    2.2) Update candidate meanings of phrases occurring in the same sentences as the phrase just learned
Return the lexicon of learned (phrase, meaning) pairs.

Figure 2: WOLFIE Algorithm Overview

and size of the learned lexicon, since this should improve accuracy and ease parser acquisition. Note that this notion of semantic lexicon acquisition is distinct from learning selectional restrictions (Manning 1993; Brent 1991) or clusters of semantically similar words (Riloff & Sheperd 1997).

Note that we allow phrases to have multiple meanings (homonymy) and multiple phrases to have the same meaning (synonymy). Also, some phrases may have a null meaning. We make only a few fairly straightforward assumptions. First is *compositionality*: the meaning of a sentence is composed from the meanings of phrases in that sentence. Since we allow multi-word phrases in the lexicon (e.g., ([**kick the bucket**], die(_))), this assumption seems fairly unproblematic. Second, we assume each component of the representation is due to the meaning of exactly one word or phrase in the sentence, and not more than one or to an external source such as noise. Third, we assume the meaning for each word in a sentence appears at most once in the sentence's representation. Finally, we assume that a phrase's meaning is a connected subgraph of a sentence's representation, not a more distributed representation. The second and third assumptions are preliminary, and we are exploring methods for relaxing them. If any of these assumptions are violated, WOLFIE may not learn a covering lexicon; however, the system can still be run and produce a potentially useful result.

The WOLFIE Algorithm and an Example

The WOLFIE algorithm outlined in Figure 2 has been implemented to handle two kinds of semantic representations: a case-role form based on *conceptual dependency* (Schank 1975) and a logical query language illustrated above. The current paper will focus on the latter; the changes required for the former are minimal. In order to limit search, a form of greedy set covering is used to find a covering lexicon. The first step is to derive an initial set of candidate meanings for each possible phrase. The current implementation is limited to one and two word phrases, but easily extended to longer phrases with a linear increase in complexity. For example, consider the following corpus:

1. What is the capital of the state with the biggest population?

```
answer(C, (capital(S,C),
    largest(P, (state(S), population(S,P)))))).
```

2. What is the highest point of the state with the biggest area?
```
answer(P, (high_point(S,P),
    largest(A, (state(S), area(S,A)))))).
```

3. What state is Texarkana located in?
```
answer(S, (state(S), eq(C,cityid(texarkana,_)),
    loc(C,S))).
```

4. What capital is the biggest?
```
answer(A, largest(A, capital(A))).
```

5. What is the area of the United States?
```
answer(A, (area(C,A), eq(C,countryid(usa)))).
```

6. What is the population of a state bordering Minnesota?
```
answer(P, (population(S,P), state(S),
    next_to(S,M), eq(M,stateid(minnesota)))).
```

7. What is the highest point in the state with the capital Madison?
```
answer(C, (high_point(B,C), loc(C,B), state(B),
    capital(B,A), eq(A,cityid(madison,_)))).
```

Although not required, for simplification, assume sentences are stripped of phrases that we know have empty meanings ([what], [is], [with], [the]) and that it is known that some phrases refer directly to given database constants (e.g., location names).

Initial candidate meanings are produced by computing the common substructures between pairs of representations of sentences that contain a given phrase. This is performed by computing their Largest Isomorphic Connected Subgraphs (LICS), taking labels into account in the isomorphism. The Largest Common Subgraph problem is solvable in polynomial time if, as we assume, both inputs are trees (Garey & Johnson 1979). The exact algorithm is complicated a bit by variables and conjunction. Therefore, we use LICS with an addition similar to computing the Least General Generalization (LGG) of first-order clauses (Plotkin 1970), i.e., the most specific clause subsuming two given clauses. Specifically, we find the LICS between two trees and then compute the LGG of the resulting subexpressions. The sets of initial candidate meanings for some of the phrases in the sample corpus (after removing the mandatory answer predicate) are:

Phrase	LICS	From Sent's
[capital]:	largest(_,_)	1,4
	(capital(A,_), state(A))	1,7
[biggest]:	largest(_,state(_))	1,2
	largest(_,_)	1,4;2,4
[state]:	largest(_,state(_))	1,2
	state(_)	1,3;2,3
	(capital(A,_), state(A))	1,7
	(high_point(B,_), state(B))	2,7
	(state(S),loc(_,S))	3,7
[highest point]:	(high_point(B,_), state(B))	2,7
[located]:	(state(S), loc(_,S))	3
[in]:	(state(S), loc(_,S))	3,7

Note that [state] has five candidate meanings, each generated from a different pair of representations of sentences in which it appears. For phrases appearing in only one sentence (e.g., [located]), the entire sentence representation is used as an initial candidate meaning. Such candidates are typically generalized in step 2.2 to only the correct portion of the representation before they are added to the lexicon.

After deriving initial candidates, the greedy search begins. The heuristic used to evaluate candidates is the sum of two weighted components, where p is the phrase and m its candidate meaning:

1. $P(m|p) \times P(p|m) \times P(m) = P(p) \times P(m|p)^2$

2. The generality of m

The first component is analogous the the cluster evaluation heuristic used by COBWEB (Fisher 1987). The goal is to maximize the probability of predicting the correct meaning for a randomly sampled phrase. The equality holds by Bayes Theorem. Looking at the right side, $P(m|p)^2$ is the expected probability that meaning m is correctly guessed for a given phrase, p. This assumes a strategy of probability matching, in which a a meaning m is chosen for p with probability $P(m|p)$ and correct with the same probability. The other term, $P(p)$, biases the component by how common the phrase is. Interpreting the left side of the equation, the first term biases towards lexicons with low ambiguity, the second towards low synonymy, and the third towards frequent meanings. The probabilities are estimated from the training data and then updated as learning progresses to account for phrases and meanings already covered.

The second component, *generality*, is computed as the negation of the number of nodes in the meaning's tree structure, and helps prefer smaller, more general meanings. In this example and all experiments, we use a weight of 10 for the first component of the heuristic, and a weight of 1 for the second. The first component has smaller absolute values and is therefore given a higher weight. Results are not overly-sensitive to the weights and automatically setting them using cross-validation on the training set (Kohavi & John 1995) had little effect on overall performance. To break ties, less ambiguous (those with currently fewer meanings) and shorter phrases are preferred. Below we illustrate the calculation of the heuristic measure for some of the above twelve pairs, and the resulting value for all.

([capital], largest(_,_)): $10(2^2/3) + 1(-1) = 12.33$,

([capital], (capital(A,_), state(A))): 11.33

([biggest], largest(_,_)): 29,

([biggest], largest(_,state(_))): 11.3,

([state], largest(_,state(_))): 8,

([state], state(_)): $10(4^2/4) + 1(-1) = 39$,

([state], (capital(A,_), state(A))): 8,

([state], (high_point(B,_), state(B))): 8,

([state], (state(S), loc(_,S))): 8

([highest point], (high_point(B,_), state(B))):
    $10(2^2/2) + 1(-2) = 18$,

([located], (state(S), loc(_,S))):
    $10(1^2/1) + 1(-2) = 8$,

([in], (state(S), loc(_,S))): 18.
The highest scoring pair is ([state], state(_)), so it is added to the lexicon.

Next is the candidate generalization phase (step 2.2). One of the key ideas of the algorithm is that each (phrase, meaning) choice can constrain the candidate meanings of phrases yet to be learned. Given the assumption that each portion of the representation is due to at most one phrase in the sentence, once part of a representation is covered, no other phrase in the sentence can be paired with that meaning (at least for that sentence). Therefore, in this step the meaning of a new lexicon entry is potentially removed from the candidate meanings of other words occurring in the same sentences. In our example, the learned pair covers all occurrences of [state], so remaining meanings for it are removed from the candidate set. However, now that state(_) is covered, the candidates for several other words are generalized. For example, the meaning (capital(A,_), state(A)) for [capital], is generalized to capital(_,_), with a new heuristic value of $10(2^2/3) + 1(-1) = 12.3$. Subsequently, the greedy search continues until the resulting lexicon covers the training corpus, or until no candidate phrase meanings remain.

Experimental Results

This section describes results on a database query application. The first corpus discussed contains 250 questions about U.S. geography. This domain was originally chosen due to the availability of a hand-built natural language interface, *Geobase*, to a database containing about 800 facts. It was supplied with Turbo Prolog 2.0 (Borland International 1988), and designed specifically for this domain. The corpus was assembled by asking undergraduate students to generate English questions for this database. To broaden the test, we had the same 250 sentences translated into Spanish, Turkish, and Japanese. The Japanese translations are in word-segmented Roman orthography.

To evaluate the learned lexicons, we measured their utility as background knowledge for CHILL. This is performed by choosing a random set of 25 test examples and then creating lexicons and parsers using increasingly larger subsets of the remaining 225 examples. The test examples are parsed using the learned parser, the resulting queries submitted to the database, the answers compared to those generated by submitting the correct representation, and the percentage of correct answers recorded. By using the difficult "gold standard" of retrieving a correct answer, we avoid measures of partial accuracy which we believe do not adequately measure final utility. We repeated this process for ten different random training and test sets and evaluate performance differences using a two-tailed, paired t-test with a significance level of $p \leq 0.05$.

We compared our system to an incremental (on-line) lexicon learner developed by Siskind (1996), originally

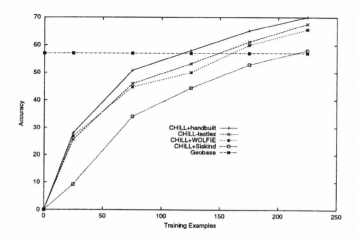

Figure 3: Accuracy on English Geography Corpus

evaluated only on artificial data. To make a more equitable comparison to our batch algorithm, we ran his in a "simulated" batch mode, by repeatedly presenting the corpus 500 times, analogous to running 500 epochs to train a neural network. We also removed WOLFIE's ability to learn phrases of more than one word, since the current version of Siskind's system does not have this ability. We also made comparisons to the parsers learned by CHILL when using a hand-coded lexicon as background knowledge.

In this and similar applications, there are many terms, such as state and city names, whose meanings can be automatically extracted from the database. Therefore, all tests below were run with such names given to the learner as an initial lexicon; this is helpful but not required.

The first experiment was a comparison of the two systems on the original English corpus. Figure 3 shows learning curves for CHILL when using the lexicons learned by WOLFIE (CHILL+WOLFIE) and by Siskind's system (CHILL+Siskind). The uppermost curve (CHILL+handbuilt) shows CHILL's performance when given the hand-built lexicon. CHILL-testlex shows the performance when words that never appear in the training data are deleted from the hand-built lexicon (since a learning algorithm has no chance of getting these). Finally, the horizontal line shows the performance of the *Geobase* benchmark.

The results show that a lexicon learned by WOLFIE led to parsers that were almost as accurate as those generated using a hand-built lexicon. The best accuracy is achieved by the hand-built lexicon, followed by the hand-built lexicon with words only in the test set removed, followed by WOLFIE, followed by Siskind's system. All the systems do as well or better than *Geobase* by 225 training examples. The differences between WOLFIE and Siskind's system are statistically significant at all training example sizes except 125. These results show that WOLFIE can learn lexicons that lead

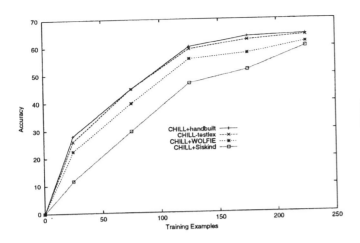

Figure 4: Accuracy on Spanish

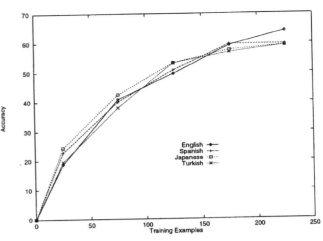

Figure 5: Accuracy on All Four Languages

to successful parsers, and that are better from this perspective than those learned by a competing system. Also, comparing to the CHILL-testlex curve, we see that most of the drop in accuracy from a hand-built lexicon is due to words in the test set that the system has not seen during training.

One of the implicit hypotheses of our problem definition is that coverage of the training data implies a good lexicon. The results show a coverage of 100% of the 225 training examples for WOLFIE versus 94.4% for Siskind. In addition, the lexicons learned by Siskind's system were more ambiguous and larger than those learned by WOLFIE. WOLFIE's lexicons had an average of 1.1 meanings per word, and an average size of 56.5 words (after 225 training examples) versus 1.7 meanings per word and 154.8 entries in Siskind's lexicons. For comparison, the hand-built lexicon had 88 entries and 1.2 meanings per word on average. These differences undoubtedly contribute to the final performance differences.

Figure 4 shows the results on the Spanish version of the corpus. In these tests, we gave closed class words to the lexicon learners as background knowledge since a similar addition for English improved performance slightly. Though the performance compared to a hand-built lexicon is not quite as close as in English, the accuracy of the parser using the learned lexicon is very similar.

Figure 5 shows the results for all four languages without any information about closed-class words. The performance differences among the four languages are quite small, demonstrating that our methods are not language dependent.

Finally, we present results on a larger, more diverse corpus from the geography domain, where the additional sentences were collected from computer science undergraduates in an introductory AI course. The set of questions in the previous experiments was collected from students in a German class, with no special in-

structions on the complexity of queries desired. The AI students tended to ask more complex queries: their task was to give 5 sentences and the associated logical query representation for a homework assignment. They were requested to give at least one sentence whose representation included a predicate containing embedded predicates, for example largest(S, state(S)), and we asked for variety in their sentences. There were 221 new sentences, for a total of 471 (including the original 250 sentences).

For these experiments, we split the data into 425 training sentences and 46 test sentences, for 10 random splits, then trained WOLFIE and then CHILL as before. Our goal was to see whether WOLFIE was still effective for this more difficult corpus, since there were approximately 40 novel words in the new sentences. Therefore, we tested against the performance of CHILL with an extended hand-built lexicon. For this test, we gave the system access to background knowledge about closed class words. We did not use phrases of more than one word, since these do not seem to make a significant difference in this domain.

Figure 6 shows the resulting learning curves. None of the differences between CHILL and WOLFIE are statistically significant, probably because the difficulty of parsing overshadows errors in word learning. Also, the improvement of machine learning methods over the Geobase hand-built interface is much more dramatic for this corpus.

Related Work

Work on automated lexicon and language acquisition dates back to Siklossy (1972), who demonstrated a system that learned transformation patterns from logic back to natural language. More recently, Pedersen & Chen (1995) describe a method for acquiring syntactic and semantic features of an unknown word, assuming access to an initial concept hierarchy, but they give no experimental results. Manning (1993)

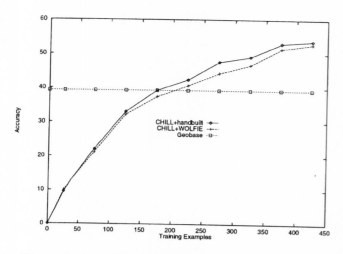

Figure 6: Accuracy on the Larger Geography Corpus

and Brent (1991) acquire subcategorization information for verbs, which is different from the information required for mapping to semantic representation. Several systems (Knight 1996; Hastings & Lytinen 1994; Russell 1993) learn new words from context, assuming that a large initial lexicon and parsing system are already available. Tishby and Gorin (1994) learn associations between words and actions (as meanings of those words). Their system was tested on a corpus of sentences paired with representations but they do not demonstrate the integration of learning a semantic parser using the learned lexicon.

The aforementioned work by Siskind is the closest. His approach is somewhat more general in that it handles noise and referential uncertainty (multiple possible meanings for a sentence), while ours is specialized for applications where a single meaning is available. The experimental results in the previous section demonstrate the advantage of our method for such an application. His system does not currently handle multiple-word phrases. Also, his system operates in an incremental or on-line fashion, discarding each sentence as it processes it, while ours is batch. While he argues for psychological plausibility, we do not. In addition, his search for word meanings is most analogous to a version space search, while ours is a greedy search. Finally, his system does not compute statistical correlations between words and their possible meanings, while ours does.

His system proceeds in two stages, first learning what *symbols* are part of a word's meaning, and then learning the structure of those symbols. For example, it might first learn that `capital` is part of the meaning of **capital**, then in the second stage learn that `capital` can have either one or two arguments. By using common substructures, we can combine these two stages in WOLFIE.

This work also has ties to the work on automatic construction of translation lexicons (Wu & Xia 1995;

Melamed 1995; Kumano & Hirakawa 1994; Catizone, Russell, & Warwick 1993; Gale & Church 1991). While most of these methods also compute association scores between pairs (in their case, word/word pairs) and use a greedy algorithm to choose the best translation(s) for each word, they do not take advantage of the constraints between pairs. One exception is Melamed (1996); however, his approach does not allow for phrases in the lexicon or for synonymy within one text segment, while ours does.

Future Work

Although the current greedy search method has performed quite well, a better search heuristic or alternative search strategy could result in improvements. A more important issue is lessening the burden of building a large annotated training corpus. We are exploring two options in this regard. One is to use *active learning* (Cohn, Atlas, & Ladner 1994) in which the system chooses which examples are most usefully annotated from a larger corpus of unannotated data. This approach can dramatically reduce the amount of annotated data required to achieve a desired accuracy (Engelson & Dagan 1996). Initial promising results for semantic parser acquisition are given in Thompson (1998).

A second avenue of exploration is to apply our approach to learning to parse into more popular SQL database queries. Such corpora should be easily constructible by recording queries submitted to existing SQL applications along with their original English forms, or translating existing lists of SQL queries into English (presumably an easier direction to translate). The fact that the same training data can be used to learn both a semantic lexicon and a parser also helps limit the overall burden of constructing a complete natural language interface.

Conclusions

Acquiring a semantic lexicon from a corpus of sentences labeled with representations of their meaning is an important problem that has not been widely studied. WOLFIE demonstrates that a fairly simple greedy symbolic learning algorithm performs fairly well on this task and obtains performance superior to a previous lexicon acquisition system on a corpus of geography queries. Our results also demonstrate that our methods extend to a variety of natural languages besides English.

Most experiments in corpus-based natural language have presented results on some subtask of natural language, and there are few results on whether the learned subsystems can be successfully integrated to build a complete NLP system. The experiments presented in this paper demonstrated how two learning systems, WOLFIE and CHILL were successfully integrated to learn a complete NLP system for parsing database queries into executable logical form given only a single corpus of annotated queries.

Acknowledgements

We would like to thank Jeff Siskind for providing us with his software, and for all his help in adapting it for use with our corpus. Thanks also to Agapito Sustaita, Esra Erdem, and Marshall Mayberry for their translation efforts. This research was supported by the National Science Foundation under grants IRI-9310819 and IRI-9704943.

References

Borland International. 1988. *Turbo Prolog 2.0 Reference Guide.* Scotts Valley, CA: Borland International.

Brent, M. 1991. Automatic acquisition of subcategorization frames from untagged text. In *Proceedings of the 29th Annual Meeting of the Association for Computational Linguistics*, 209–214.

Catizone, R.; Russell, G.; and Warwick, S. 1993. Deriving translation data from bilingual texts. In *Proceedings of the First International Lexical Acquisition Workshop.*

Cohn, D.; Atlas, L.; and Ladner, R. 1994. Improving generalization with active learning. *Machine Learning* 15(2):201–221.

Engelson, S., and Dagan, I. 1996. Minimizing manual annotation cost in supervised training from corpora. In *Proceedings of the 34th Annual Meeting of the Association for Computational Linguistics.*

Fisher, D. H. 1987. Knowledge acquisition via incremental conceptual clustering. *Machine Learning* 2:139–172.

Gale, W., and Church, K. 1991. Identifying word correspondences in parallel texts. In *Proceedings of the Fourth DARPA Speech and Natural Language Workshop.*

Garey, M., and Johnson, D. 1979. *Computers and Intractability: A Guide to the Theory of NP-Completeness.* New York, NY: Freeman.

Hastings, P., and Lytinen, S. 1994. The ups and downs of lexical acquisition. In *Proceedings of the Twelfth National Conference on Artificial Intelligence*, 754–759.

Knight, K. 1996. Learning word meanings by instruction. In *Proceedings of the Thirteenth National Conference on Artificial Intelligence*, 447–454.

Kohavi, R., and John, G. 1995. Automatic parameter selection by minimizing estimated error. In *Proceedings of the Twelfth International Conference on Machine Learning*, 304–312.

Kumano, A., and Hirakawa, H. 1994. Building an MT dictionary from parallel texts based on linguistic and statistical information. In *Proceedings of the Fifteenth International Conference on Computational Linguistics.*

Lavrač, N., and Džeroski, S. 1994. *Inductive Logic Programming: Techniques and Applications.* Ellis Horwood.

Manning, C. D. 1993. Automatic acquisition of a large subcategorization dictionary from corpora. In *Proceedings of the 31st Annual Meeting of the Association for Computational Linguistics*, 235–242.

Melamed, I. 1995. Automatic evaluation and uniform filter cascades for inducing n-best translation lexicons. In *Proceedings of the Third Workshop on Very Large Corpora.*

Melamed, I. 1996. Automatic construction of clean broad-coverage translation lexicons. In *Second Conference of the Association for Machine Translation in the Americas.*

Muggleton, S. H., ed. 1992. *Inductive Logic Programming.* New York, NY: Academic Press.

Pedersen, T., and Chen, W. 1995. Lexical acquisition via constraint solving. In *Papers from the 1995 AAAI Symposium on the Representation and Acquisition of Lexical Knowledge: Polysemy, Ambiguity, and Generativity*, 118–122.

Plotkin, G. D. 1970. A note on inductive generalization. In Meltzer, B., and Michie, D., eds., *Machine Intelligence (Vol. 5).* New York: Elsevier North-Holland.

Riloff, E., and Sheperd, K. 1997. A corpus-based approach for building semantic lexicons. In *Proceedings of the Second Conference on Empirical Methods in Natural Language Processing*, 117–124.

Russell, D. 1993. *Language Acquisition in a Unification-Based Grammar Processing System Using a Real World Knowledge Base.* Ph.D. Dissertation, University of Illinois, Urbana, IL.

Schank, R. C. 1975. *Conceptual Information Processing.* Oxford: North-Holland.

Siklossy, L. 1972. Natural language learning by computer. In Simon, H. A., and Siklossy, L., eds., *Representation and meaning: Experiments with Information Processsing Systems.* Englewood Cliffs, NJ: Prentice Hall.

Siskind, J. M. 1996. A computational study of cross-situational techniques for learning word-to-meaning mappings. *Cognition* 61(1):39–91.

Thompson, C. A. 1998. *Semantic Lexicon Acquisition for Learning Natural Language Interfaces.* Ph.D. Dissertation, Department of Computer Sciences, University of Texas, Austin, TX. Also appears as Artificial Intelligence Laboratory Technical Report AI 99-278 (see http://www.cs.utexas.edu/users/ai-lab).

Tishby, N., and Gorin, A. 1994. Algebraic learning of statistical associations for language acquisition. *Computer Speech and Language* 8:51–78.

Wu, D., and Xia, X. 1995. Large-scale automatic extraction of an English-Chinese translation lexicon. *Machine Translation* 9(3-4):285–313.

Zelle, J. M., and Mooney, R. J. 1996. Learning to parse database queries using inductive logic programming. In *Proceedings of the Thirteenth National Conference on Artificial Intelligence.*

Planning

Theory for Coordinating Concurrent Hierarchical Planning Agents Using Summary Information

Bradley J. Clement and **Edmund H. Durfee**
University of Michigan
Ann Arbor, MI 48109
{bradc, durfee}@umich.edu

Abstract

Interacting agents that interleave planning, plan coordination, and plan execution for hierarchical plans (e.g. HTNs or procedures for PRS) should reason about abstract plans and their concurrent execution before they are fully refined. Poor decisions made at abstract levels can lead to costly backtracking or even failure. We claim that better decisions require information at abstract levels that summarizes the preconditions and effects that must or may apply when a plan is refined. Here we formally characterize concurrent hierarchical plans and a method for deriving summary information for them, and we illustrate how summary conditions can be used to coordinate the concurrent interactions of plans at different levels of abstraction. The properties of summary conditions and rules determining what interactions can or might hold among asynchronously executing plans are proven to support the construction of sound and complete coordination mechanisms for concurrent hierarchical planning agents.

Introduction

The study of concurrent action in relation to planning (Georgeff 1984) has improved our understanding of how agents can reason about their interactions in order to avoid conflicts during concurrent plan execution. Conflicts can be avoided by reducing or eliminating interactions by localizing plan effects to particular agents (Lansky 1990), and by merging the individual plans of agents by introducing synchronization actions (Georgeff 1983). In fact, planning and merging can be interleaved, such that agents can propose next-step extensions to their current plans and reconcile conflicts before considering extensions for subsequent steps. By formulating extensions in terms of constraints rather than specific actions, a "least commitment" policy can be retained (Ephrati & Rosenschein 1994).

For many applications, planning efficiency can be enhanced by exploiting the hierarchical structure of

Copyright ©1999, American Association for Artificial Intelligence (www.aaai.org). All rights reserved.
    This work was supported in part by NSF (IRI-9158473) and DARPA (F30602-98-2-0142).

planning operations. Rather than building a plan from the beginning forward (or end backward), hierarchical planners identify promising classes of long-term activities (abstract plans), and incrementally refine these to eventually converge on specific actions. Planners such as NOAH (Sacerdoti 1977) and NONLIN (Tate 1977) have this character, and are often considered instances of a class of planners called Hierarchical Task Network (HTN) planners. By exploiting the hierarchical task structure to focus search, HTN planners often converge much more quickly to effective plans. They are also becoming increasingly well understood (Erol, Hendler, & Nau 1994).

Using HTN planning for concurrently-executing agents is less well understood, however. If several HTN planning agents are each generating their own plans, how and when should these be merged? Certainly, merging could wait until the plans were fully refined, and techniques like those of Georgeff (mentioned previously) would work. But interleaving planning and merging holds greater promise for identifying and resolving key conflicts as early in the process as possible to try to avoid backtracking or failure. Such interleaving, however, requires the ability to identify potential conflicts among abstract plans.

Corkill (Corkill 1979) studied interleaved planning and merging in a distributed version of the NOAH planner. He recognized that, while most of the conditions affected by an abstract plan operator might be unknown until further refinement, those that deal with the overall effects and preconditions that hold no matter how the operator is refined can be captured and used to identify and resolve some conflicts. He recognized that further choices of refinement or synchronization choices at more abstract levels could lead to unresolvable conflicts at deeper levels, and backtracking could be necessary. Our work is directed toward avoiding such backtracking by improving how an abstract plan operator represents all of the potential needs and effects of all of its potential refinements.

Our motivation for doing this is not simply to make interleaved planning and merging with HTNs more efficient, but also to support another crucial use of HTN concepts–specifically, flexible plan execution systems such as PRS (Georgeff & Lansky 1986), RAPS

(Firby 1989), etc., that similarly exploit hierarchical plan spaces. Rather than refine abstract plan operators into a detailed end-to-end plan, however, these systems interleave refinement with execution. By postponing refinement until absolutely necessary, such systems leave themselves flexibility to choose refinements that best match current circumstances. However, this means that refinement decisions at abstract levels are made and acted upon before all of the detailed refinements need be made. If such refinements at abstract levels introduce unresolvable conflicts at detailed levels, the system ultimately gets stuck part way through a plan that cannot be completed. While backtracking is possible for HTN planning (since no actions are taken until plans are completely formed), it might not be possible when some (irreversible) plan steps have already been taken. It is therefore critical that the specifications of abstract plan operators be rich enough to summarize all of the relevant refinements to anticipate and avoid such conflicts. In this paper, we formally characterize methods for deriving and exploiting such rich summaries to support interleaved local planning, coordination (plan merging), and execution.

Simple Example

This example illustrates the use of summary information, explains some terminology, and further motivates the formalism of a theory for concurrent hierarchical plans (CHiPs) and summary information.

Suppose that two agents wish to go through a doorway to another location, (*row, column*), as shown in Figure 1. Agent A has a hierarchical plan, p, to move from $(0,0)$ to $(0,4)$, and B also has a plan, q, to move from $(2,0)$ to $(2,4)$, but they need to coordinate their plans to avoid collision. Agent A could have preprocessed plan p to derive its summary information. The set of *summary preconditions* of p includes all its preconditions and those of its subplans that must be met external to p in order for p to execute successfully: $\{At(A,0,0), \neg At(B,0,1), \neg At(B,1,0), \ldots, \neg At(B,0,4)\}$. The proposition $At(A,0,0)$ is a *must* condition because no matter how p is executed, the condition must hold. $\neg At(B,1,0)$ is *may* because it may be required depending on the path A takes. Likewise, the *summary postconditions* of p are its effects and those of its subplans that are seen externally: $\{At(A,2,0), \neg At(A,0,0), \neg At(A,1,0), \ldots\}$. The *summary incondITIONS* are any conditions that must hold within the interval of time that the plan is executing and can be *must* or *may* and *always* or *sometimes*. An *always* condition is required to hold throughout the duration of any execution of the plan. For example, a *must, always* incondition of p could be $PowerOn(A)$ – the power must always be on. $At(A,1,0)$ is a *may, sometimes* incondition of p because A *may* choose that path and would only be there at *some time*. These conditions and descriptors, such as *must* and *always*, provide the necessary information to reason about what

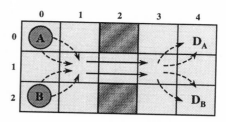

Figure 1: Agents A and B go through a doorway.

conditions must or may be achieved or clobbered when ordering a set of plan executions.

Now suppose A sends B p_{sum}, the summary information for p. Agent B can now reason about the interactions of their plans based on their combined summary information. For instance, based only on the summary information, B can determine that if p is restricted to execute before q, then the plans *can* be executed (refined) in *any way*, or $CanAnyWay(b,p_{sum},q_{sum})$.[1] So, B could tell A to go ahead and start execution and to send back a message when p is finished executing. However, B may instead wish to overlap their plan executions for better efficiency. Although $CanAnyWay(o,p_{sum},q_{sum})$ is not true, B could use the summary conditions to determine that there *might* be *some way* to overlap them, or $MightSomeWay(o,p_{sum},q_{sum})$. Then, B could ask A for the summary information of each of p's subplans, reason about the interactions of lower level actions in the same way, and find a way to synchronize the subplans for a more fine-grained solution.

Consider another case where A and B plan to move to the spot directly between them, $(1,0)$, and can choose from different routes. $MightSomeWay(b, p_{sum}, q_{sum})$ would be false since the postconditions of p must always clobber the preconditions of q. If we wanted to describe a rule for determining whether two actions can or might overlap, it is not obvious how this should be done. The difficulty of composing such rules stems from an imprecise specification of concurrent plan execution and the large space of potential plans that have the same summary information. If the $MightSomeWay(o, p_{sum}, q_{sum})$ rule is not specified in a complete way, the agent may not determine that the *overlaps* relation cannot hold until it has exhaustively checked all synchronizations of p and q's primitive subplans. As the number of subplans grows, this becomes an intractable procedure (Vilain & Kautz 1986). Even worse would be if, for the sake of trying to be complete, a rule is specified in an unsound way leading to a synchronization choice that causes failure. We give an example of this in (Clement & Durfee 1999b), where we also implement a hierarchical plan coordi-

---

[1] We will often abbreviate Allen's thirteen temporal relations (Allen 1983). Here, "b" is for the *before* relation. "o" is for *overlaps*.

nation algorithm that uses summary information in the manner described above. Our evaluations show that coordinating at different levels of abstraction for different cost scenarios results in better performance. Thus, formalizing concurrent hierarchical plans, their execution, and the derivation of summary conditions is necessary to avoid costly, irreversible decisions made during planning, plan execution, and coordination.

Overview

In the next section we describe the semantics of hierarchical plans and their concurrent execution to ground our theory. The simple theory of action consistently describes all temporal interactions among primitive or hierarchical plans. We basically add a set of *inconditions* to popular STRIPS-style plan representations to reason about concurrent plan execution. In addition, we formalize traditional planning concepts, such as *clobbers* and *achieves*, and reintroduce *external conditions* (Tsuneto, Hendler, & Nau 1998) for reasoning about CHiPs. We then describe the semantics of plan summary information and a correct method for deriving it efficiently. This, in turn, is used to describe the construction of sound and complete rules for determining how plans can definitely or might possibly be temporally related. The result is a theory for proving correct coordination and planning mechanisms.

A Model of Hierarchical Plans and their Concurrent Execution

The original purpose of developing the following theory was to provide, as simply as possible, a consistent model of execution to generally reason about the concurrent interaction of hierarchical plans. However, we also wanted the model to share important aspects of plans used by PRSs, HTNs, Allen's temporal plans, and many STRIPS-style plan representations. As such, this theory of action tries to distill appropriate aspects of other theories, including (Allen & Koomen 1983), (Georgeff 1984), and (Fagin *et al.* 1995).

CHiPs

A concurrent hierarchical plan p is a tuple $\langle pre, in, post, type, subplans, order \rangle$. $pre(p)$, $in(p)$, and $post(p)$ are sets of literals (v or $\neg v$ for some propositional variable v) representing the preconditions, inconditions, and postconditions defined for plan p.[2] The *type* of plan p, $type(p)$, has a value of either *primitive*, *and*, or *or*. An *and* plan is a non-primitive plan that is accomplished by carrying out all of its subplans. An *or* plan is a non-primitive plan that is accomplished by carrying out one of its subplans. So, *subplans* is a set of plans, and a *primitive* plan's *subplans* is the empty set. $order(p)$ is only defined for an *and* plan

---

[2]Functions such as $pre(p)$ are used for referential convenience throughout this paper. Here, pre and $pre(p)$ are the same, and $pre(p)$ is read as "the preconditions of p."

p and is a set of temporal relations (Allen 1983) over pairs of subplans that together are consistent; for example, $before(p_i, p_j)$ and $before(p_j, p_i)$ could not both be in *order*. Plans left unordered with respect to each other are interpreted to potentially execute in concurrently. For the example in Figure 1, A's highest level plan p is the tuple $\langle \{\}, \{\}, \{\}, and, \{m_1, m_2, m_3\}, \{before(m_1, m_2), before(m_2, m_3)\} \rangle$. Here, m_1, m_2, and m_3 correspond to p's subplans for moving to $(1,1)$, $(1,3)$, and $(0,4)$ respectively. There are no conditions defined because p can rely on the conditions defined for the primitive plans for moving between grid locations. The primitive plan for moving agent A from $(1,3)$ to $(0,3)$ is the tuple $\langle \{At(A,1,3)\}, \{At(A,1,3), \neg At(B,1,3), \neg At(B,0,3)\}, \{At(A,0,3), \neg At(A,1,3), \neg At(B,0,3), \neg At(B,1,3)\}, primitive, \{\}, \{\} \rangle$.

We also require postconditions to specify whether the inconditions change or not. This helps simplify the notion of inconditions as conditions that hold only *during* plan execution whether because they are *caused* by the action or because they are *necessary conditions* for successful execution. If a plan's postconditions did not specify the truth values of the inconditions' variables at the end of execution, then it is not intuitive how those values should be determined in the presence of concurrently executing plans. By requiring postconditions to specify such values, we resolve all ambiguity and simplify state transitions (described in the section below on Histories and Runs).

The decomposition of a CHiP is in the same style as that of an HTN as described by Erol *et al.* (Erol, Hendler, & Nau 1994). An *and* plan is a task network, and an *or* plan is an extra construct representing a set of all tasks that accomplish the same goal or compound task. Tasks in a network are subplans of the plan corresponding to the network. High-level effects (Erol, Hendler, & Nau 1994) are simply the postconditions of a non-primitive CHiP. CHiPs can also represent a variety of interesting procedures executable by PRSs.

Executions

We recursively describe an execution of a plan as an instance of a decomposition and ordering of its subplans' executions. This helps us reason about the outcomes of different ways to execute a group of plans, describe state transitions, and formalize other terms.

The possible executions of a plan p is the set $\mathcal{E}(p)$. An *execution* of p, $e \in \mathcal{E}(p)$, is a triple $\langle d, t_s, t_f \rangle$. $t_s(e)$ and $t_f(e)$ are positive, non-zero real numbers representing the start and finish times of execution e, and $t_s < t_f$. $d(e)$ is a set of subplan executions representing the decomposition of plan p under this execution e. Specifically, if p is an *and* plan, then it contains one execution from each of the subplans; if it is an *or* plan, then it contains only one execution of one of the subplans; and it is empty if it is *primitive*. In addition, for all subplan executions, $e' \in d$, $t_s(e')$ and $t_f(e')$ must be consistent with the relations specified in $order(p)$. Also, the first subplan(s) to start must start at the same time as p, $t_s(e') = t_s(e)$; and the last subplan(s) to finish must finish at the same time as the p, $t_f(e') = t_f(e)$. An execution for agent A's top-level plan p (described previously in the section on CHiPs) would be some $e \in \mathcal{E}(p)$. e might be $\langle\{e_1, e_2, e_3\}, 4.0, 10.0\rangle$ where $e_1 \in \mathcal{E}(m_1)$, $e_2 \in \mathcal{E}(m_2)$, $e_3 \in \mathcal{E}(m_3)$, and e begins at time 4.0 and ends at time 10.0. e_1 also starts at 4.0, and e_3 ends at 10.0.

The *subexecutions* of an execution e, sometimes referred to as $subex(e)$, is defined recursively as the set of subplan executions in e's decomposition unioned with their subexecutions. For agent A, $subex(e) = \{e_1, e_2, e_3\} \cup subex(e_1) \cup subex(e_2) \cup subex(e_3)$. For convenience, we say that a condition of a plan with an execution in the set containing e and e's subexecutions is a *condition of* e. So, if A executes its top-level plan, since $\neg At(B, 1, 2)$ is an incondition of the primitive for A to move from $(1,1)$ to $(1,2)$, it is also an incondition of the primitive's execution, e_2, and e.

Histories and Runs

We describe hypothetical possible worlds, called histories, so that we can determine what happens in all worlds, some, or none. We then can describe how the state transforms according to a particular history. A state of the world, s, is a truth assignment to a set of propositions, each representing an aspect of the environment. We treat a state as the set of true propositional variables.

A *history*, h, is a tuple $\langle E, s_I \rangle$. E is a set of plan executions including those of all plans and subplans executed by all agents, and s_I is the initial state of the world before any plan is begun. So, a history h is a hypothetical world that begins with s_I as the initial state and where only executions in $E(h)$ occur.

A *run*, r, is a function mapping time to states. It gives a complete description of how the state of the world evolves over time. We take time to range over the positive real numbers. $r(t)$ denotes the state of the world at time t in run r. So, a condition is *met* at time t if the condition is a non-negated propositional variable v, and $v \in r(t)$ or if the condition is a negated propositional variable $\neg v$, and $v \notin r(t)$.

For each history h there is exactly one run, $r(h)^3$, that specifies the state transitions *caused* by the plan executions in $E(h)$. The interpretation of a history by its run is defined as follows. The world is in the initial state at time zero: $r(h)(0) = s_I(h)$. In the smallest interval after any point where one or more executions start and before any other start or end of an execution, the state is updated by adding all non-negated inconditions of the plans and then removing all negated inconditions. Similarly, at the point where one or more executions finish, the state is updated by adding all

non-negated postconditions of the plans and then removing all negated postconditions. Lastly, if no execution of a plan begins or ends between two points in time, then the state must be the same at those points. First order logic sentences for these axioms are specified in a larger report (Clement & Durfee 1999a).

Now we can define what it means for a plan to execute successfully. An execution $e = \langle d, t_s, t_f \rangle$ *succeeds in* h if and only if the plan's preconditions are met at t_s; the inconditions are met throughout the interval (t_s, t_f); the postconditions are met at t_f; and all executions in e's decomposition are in $E(h)$ and succeed. Otherwise, e *fails*. So, in a history h where agent A successfully executes a plan (as described previously in the section on Executions) to traverse the room, $E(h) = \{e\} \cup subex(e)$, and all conditions of all plans with executions in $E(h)$ are met at the appropriate times. Given the example primitive conditions in the section on CHiPs and the axioms just described for state transitions, if agent B happened to start moving into A's target location, $(0,4)$, at the same time as A, then either A's primitive plan execution e_A finishes before B's and the $\neg At(A, 0, 4)$ incondition of B's primitive execution e_B is not met (clobbered) at $t_f(e_A)$; e_B finishes before e_A and similarly clobbers e_A's incondition; or they both finish simultaneously clobbering each others' $At(A/B, 0, 4)$ postconditions. If e_A fails, then e_3 and the top-level execution e must also fail.

Asserting, Clobbering, and Achieving

In conventional planning, we often speak of *clobbering* and *achieving* preconditions of plans (Weld 1994). In CHiPs, these notions are slightly different since inconditions can clobber and be clobbered, as seen in the previous section. Formalizing these concepts helps prove properties of summary conditions. However, it will be convenient to define first what it means to *assert* a condition.

An execution e of plan p is said to *assert* a condition ℓ at time t in a history h if and only if ℓ is an incondition of p, t is in the smallest interval beginning after $t_s(e)$ and ending before a following start or finish time of any execution in $E(h)$, and ℓ is satisfied by $r(h)(t)$; or ℓ is a postcondition of p, $t = t_f(e)$, and ℓ is satisfied by $r(t)$. So, asserting a condition only *causes* it to hold if the condition was not previously met. Otherwise, the condition was already satisfied and the action requiring it did not really *cause* it.

A *precondition* ℓ of plan p_1 is [*clobbered, achieved*][4] in e_1 (an execution of p_1) by e_2 (an execution of plan p_2) at time t if and only if e_2 asserts [ℓ', ℓ] at t; $\ell \Leftrightarrow \neg\ell'$; and e_2 is the last execution to assert ℓ or ℓ' before or at $t_s(e_1)$. An [*incondition, postcondition*] ℓ of plan p_1 is *clobbered* in e_1 by e_2 at time t if and only if e_2 asserts ℓ' at t; $\ell \Leftrightarrow \neg\ell'$; and [$t_s(e_1) < t < t_f(e_1)$,

---

[3] For convenience, we now treat r as a function mapping histories to runs, so $r(h)(t)$ is a mapping of a history and a time to a state.

[4] We use braces [ ] as a shorthand when defining similar terms and procedures. For example, saying "[a, b] implies [c, d]" means a implies c, and b implies d.

$t = t_f(e_1)]$. Achieving inconditions and postconditions does not make sense for this formalism, so it is not defined. In the previous section when e_A finished first and asserted $At(A, 0, 4)$, it clobbered the incondition $\neg At(A, 0, 4)$ of B's primitive plan in e_B at $t_f(e_A)$.

External Conditions

As recognized in (Tsuneto, Hendler, & Nau 1998), external conditions are important for reasoning about potential refinements of abstract plans. Although the basic idea is the same, we define them a little differently and call them *external preconditions* to differentiate them from other conditions we call *external postconditions*. Intuitively, an external precondition of a group of partially ordered plans is a precondition of one of the plans that is not achieved by another in the group and must be met external to the group. External postconditions, similarly, are those that are not undone by plans in the group and are net effects of the group.

Formally, an *external precondition* ℓ of an *interval* (t_1, t_2) in history h is a precondition of a plan p with some execution $e \in E(h)$ for which $t_1 \le t_s(e) < t_2$, and ℓ is neither achieved nor clobbered by an execution at a time t where $t_1 \le t \le t_s(e)$. An *external precondition* of an *execution* $e = \langle d, t_s, t_f \rangle$ is an external precondition of an interval (t_1, t_2) in some history where $t_1 \le t_s$; $t_f \le t_2$; and there are no other plan executions other than the subexecutions of e. An *external precondition* of a *plan* p is an external precondition of any of p's executions. It is called a *must* precondition if it is an external precondition of all executions; otherwise it is called a *may* precondition. $At(A, 0, 0)$ is an external precondition of agent A's top-level plan p (Figure 1) since no subplan in p's hierarchy achieves $At(A, 0, 0)$. $At(A, 1, 1)$ is not an external precondition of p because it is achieved internally by the execution of subplan m_1 (described in the section on CHiPs).

Similarly, an *external postcondition* ℓ of an *interval* (t_1, t_2) in h is a postcondition of a plan p with some execution $e \in E(h)$ for which $t_1 \le t_f(e) \le t_2$; ℓ is asserted by e; and ℓ is not clobbered by any execution at a time t where $t_f(e) < t \le t_2$. External postconditions of executions and plans can be defined in the same way as external preconditions. $At(A, 0, 4)$ is an external postcondition of agent A's top-level plan p since no subplan in p's hierarchy cancels the effect. $At(A, 1, 3)$, an external postcondition of m_2 is not an external postcondition of p because it is cancelled internally by the execution of subplan m_3 when it later asserts $\neg At(A, 1, 3)$.

Plan Summary Information

With the previous formalisms, we can now define summary information and describe a method for computing it for non-primitive plans. The *summary information* for a plan p is p_{sum}. Its syntax is given as a tuple $\langle pre_{sum}, in_{sum}, post_{sum} \rangle$, whose members are sets of *summary conditions*. The *summary [pre, post]*

conditions of p, $[pre_{sum}(p), post_{sum}(p)]$, contain the external [pre, post] conditions of p. The *summary inconditions* of p, $in_{sum}(p)$, contain all conditions that must hold within some execution of p for it to be successful. A condition c in one of these sets is a tuple $\langle \ell, existence, timing \rangle$. $\ell(c)$ is a literal. The *existence* of c can be *must* or *may*. If $existence(c) = must$, then c is called a *must* condition because ℓ holds for every successful plan execution (ℓ *must* hold). For convenience we usually write $must(c)$. c is a *may* condition ($may(c)$ is *true*) if there is at least one plan execution where $\ell(c)$ must hold. The *timing* of c can take the values *always*, *sometimes*, *first*, *last*. $timing(c)$ is *always* for $c \in in_{sum}$ if $\ell(c)$ is an in-condition that must hold throughout the execution of p (ℓ holds *always*); otherwise, $timing(c) = sometimes$ meaning $\ell(c)$ holds at one point, at least, within an execution of p. The *timing* is *first* for $c \in pre_{sum}$ if $\ell(c)$ holds at the beginning of an execution of p; otherwise, $timing = sometimes$. Similarly, $timing$ is *last* for $c \in post_{sum}$ if $\ell(c)$ holds at the end of an execution of p; otherwise, it is *sometimes*. Although *existence* and *timing* syntactically only take one value, semantically $must(c) \Rightarrow may(c)$, and $always(c) \Rightarrow sometimes(c)$. See the Introduction for an example of summary conditions derived for an abstract plan.

Deriving Summary Conditions

The method for deriving the summary conditions of a plan p is recursive. First, summary information must be derived for each of p's subplans, and then the following procedure derives p's summary conditions from those of its subplans and its own sets of conditions. This procedure only apply to plans whose expansion is finite and which have the downward solution property. This is the property where every *or* plan in the hierarchy can be refined successfully through one or more of its subplans.

Summary conditions for primitives and non-primitives

- First, for each literal ℓ in $pre(p)$, $in(p)$, and $post(p)$, add a condition c with literal ℓ to the respective set of summary conditions for plan p. $existence(c)$ is *must*, and $timing(c)$ is *first*, *always*, or *last* if ℓ is a pre-, in-, or postcondition respectively.

Summary [pre, post] conditions for *and* plan

- Add a condition c to the summary [pre, post] conditions of *and* plan p for each summary [pre, post] condition c' of p's subplans that is not [*must-achieved*, *must-undone*][5] by another of p's subplans, setting $\ell(c) = \ell(c')$.[6]
- Set $existence(c) = must$ if $\ell(c)$ is a [pre, post] condition of p or is the literal of a *must* summary [pre, post]

---

[5] See (Clement & Durfee 1999a) and the proof ending this section about how to determine *must-achieved*, *may-achieved*, *must-undone*, and *may-undone*.

[6] To resolve ambiguity with set membership, we say that any two summary conditions, c and c' are equal if $\ell(c) = \ell(c')$ and they belong to the same set of summary conditions for some plan.

condition in a subplan of p that is not [may-achieved, may-undone] by any other subplans. Otherwise, set $existence(c) = may$.

- Set $timing(c) = [first, last]$ if $\ell(c)$ is a [pre, post] condition of p or the literal of a [first, last] summary [pre, post] condition of a [least, greatest] temporally ordered subplan (i.e. no others are constrained by $order(p)$ to [begin before, end after] it). Otherwise, set $timing(c) = sometimes$.

Summary [pre, post] conditions for *or* plan

- Add a condition c to the summary [pre, post] conditions of *or* plan p for each summary [pre, post] condition c' in p's subplans, setting $\ell(c) = \ell(c')$.
- Set $existence(c) = must$ if $\ell(c)$ is a [pre, post] condition of p or a *must* summary [pre, post] condition of all of p's subplans. Otherwise, set $existence(c) = may$.
- Set $timing(c) = [first, last]$ if $\ell(c)$ is a [pre, post] condition of p or the literal of a [first, last] summary [pre, post] condition in a subplan. Otherwise, set $timing(c) = sometimes$.

Summary inconditions for *and* plan

- Add a condition c to the summary inconditions of *and* plan p for each c' in C defined as the set of summary inconditions of p's subplans unioned with the set of summary preconditions of the subplans that are not *first* in a least temporally ordered subplan and with the set of summary postconditions of the subplans that are not *last* in a greatest temporally ordered subplan, and set $\ell(c) = \ell(c')$.
- Set $existence(c) = must$ if $\ell(c)$ is an incondition of p or a literal of a *must* summary condition $c' \in C$, as defined above. Otherwise, set $existence(c) = may$.
- Set $timing(c) = always$ if $\ell(c)$ is an incondition of p or a literal in an *always* summary incondition in every subplan of p. Otherwise, set $timing(c) = sometimes$.

Summary inconditions for *or* plan

- Add a condition c to the summary inconditions of *or* plan p for for each summary incondition c' in p's subplans, setting $\ell(c) = \ell(c')$.
- Set $existence(c) = must$ if $\ell(c)$ is an incondition of p or a *must* summary incondition of all of p's subplans. Otherwise, set $existence(c) = may$.
- Set $timing(c) = always$ if $\ell(c)$ is an incondition of p or an *always* summary incondition of all of p's subplans. Otherwise, set $timing(c) = sometimes$.

Consider deriving the summary conditions of m_2 from its two primitive subplans (as introduced in the section on CHiPs). Suppose p_1 is the primitive subplan for moving agent A from (1,1) to (1,2), and p_2 moves A from (1,2) to (1,3). First, the summary conditions of the primitives must be derived. These are simply the conditions already defined for the primitives according to the first step of the procedure. m_2 has no conditions defined for itself, so all will come from p_1 and p_2. Since m_2 is an *and* plan, its only summary precondition is $At(A, 1, 1)$ from p_1 because p_1 *must* achieve p_2's only precondition $At(A, 1, 2)$. $At(A, 1, 1)$ is a *must* summary condition because it is a *must* summary precondition in p_1, and no other subplan (p_2) *may* achieve $At(A, 1, 1)$. $At(A, 1, 1)$ is also *first* because it is a *first* summary precondition of p_1, and p_1 precedes p_2.

The procedure above ensures that external conditions are captured by summary conditions and *must*, *always*, *first*, and *last* have their intended meanings. The actual proof of these properties is all-inclusive since the truth of each property depends on those of others. However, we give a proof of one (assuming the others) to illustrate how we verify these properties using the language developed in this paper. The full proof is given in an extended report (Clement & Durfee 1999a). These results ease the proofs of soundness and completeness for inference rules determining how CHiPs can definitely or potentially interact so that good planning and coordination decisions can be made at various levels within and among plan hierarchies.

Theorem The set of external preconditions for a plan is equivalent to the set of all literals in the plan's summary preconditions.

Proof by induction over the maximum subplan depth. The base case is a primitive plan p (subplan depth zero). The summary preconditions include a condition for every precondition of p, which must be an external precondition of p, so this case is satisfied. Assume that the theorem is true for all plans of maximum depth $\leq k$. Any plan p of maximum depth $k + 1$ must have subplans with maximum depths $\leq k$. It is not difficult to show that the external preconditions of p must be the preconditions of p and those external preconditions (call them pre_x) of p's subplans that are not *must-achieved* (achieved in all executions) by another subplan of p.

By the inductive hypothesis, the external conditions of the subplans are captured in their summary conditions, and the *existence* and *timing* information together with the *order* of p's subplans can be used to determine whether some external precondition of a subplan is *must-achieved*. Table 1 shows this by describing for all cases the constraints on $order(p)$ where $\ell(c')$ of p' is *must-achieved* by p''. If we did not assume the downward solution property, then we would additionally need to make sure that no other plan could clobber $\ell(c')$ after p'' asserts the condition. Hence, the external preconditions in pre_x that are not *must-achieved* are exactly those determined in the rule for determining the summary preconditions of an *and* plan. Therefore, the external conditions of p are exactly those described as the summary preconditions of p in the procedure described above. $\square$

Complexity

The procedure for deriving summary conditions works by basically propagating the conditions from the primitives up the hierarchy to the most abstract plans. Because the conditions of any non-primitive plan depend only on those of its immediate subplans, deriving summary conditions can be done quickly. Given that an agent has an instantiated plan hierarchy with n non-primitive plans, each of which have b subplans and c conditions in each of their summary pre-, in-, and

$c'' \in$ $post_{sum}(p'')$		$c' \in$ $pre_{sum}(p')$		p'' $must\text{-}achieve$ c' $\forall e' \in \mathcal{E}(p')$, $e'' \in \mathcal{E}(p'')$
$must$	$last$	$must$	$first$	
F	?	?	?	$false$
T	?	?	?	$t_f(e'') \leq t_s(e')$
$c'' \in in_{sum}(p'')$				
$must$	$always$	$must$	$first$	
F	?	?	?	$false$
?	F	?	?	$false$
T	T	?	F	$t_s(e'') \leq t_s(e') \wedge$ $t_f(e') \leq t_f(e'')$
		?	T	$t_s(e'') < t_s(e') < t_f(e'')$

Table 1: Ordering constraints necessary for subplan p'' to $must\text{-}achieve$ $c' \in pre_{sum}$ of subplan p'. "?" means that the constraints hold for both truth values. $false$ means that there are no ordering constraints guaranteeing that p' is achieved by p''.

postconditions, deriving the summary conditions of the non-primitive plans can be bounded by $O(nb^2c^2)$ operations. This comes from the worst case in which all plans are and plans requiring the procedure to test each of c conditions in each of b subplans to see if they are achieved/clobbered by any those same conditions in any of the same subplans for each of the n and plans. However, $n = O(b^d)$ for hierarchies of depth d, so the complexity of the procedure for deriving summary conditions is more simply $O(n(log^2n)c^2)$.

Soundness and Completeness of Determining Temporal Relations

With the properties of summary information proven, we can safely reason about the interactions of plans without information about their subplans. Based on the *existence* and *timing* information carried by summary conditions, we can determine what relations can or might hold between CHiPs without searching their subplans. In many coordination tasks, if it could be determined that certain temporal relations can hold among plans no matter how they are decomposed ($CanAnyWay$) or that certain relations cannot hold for any decomposition ($\neg MightSomeWay$), then coordination decisions can be made at abstract levels without entering a potentially costly search for valid plan merges. Here we prove the soundness and completeness of rules determining $CanAnyWay$ and $MightSomeWay$ relations based on summary information. The use of these rules is illustrated in the Introduction and explored further in (Clement & Durfee 1999b). For convenience, we will abbreviate Can to C, Any to A, Way to W, and so on.

Informally, [$CAW(rel,\ p_{sum},\ q_{sum})$, $MSW(rel,$ $p_{sum}, q_{sum})$] says that the temporal relation rel [can, might] hold for any CHiPs p and q whose summary information is p_{sum} and q_{sum} for [any way, some way] that p and q may be executed. We formally describe these relations by explaining what soundness and completeness mean for rules to determine them.

Let us define $AW(P, s_I)$ to mean that in any history h with initial conditions s_I and where $E(h)$ includes an execution of each plan in set P as well as its subexecutions, all executions succeed. Also, let [$AW(rel,$ $p, q)$, $SW(rel, p, q)$] be true iff for [any, some] history h where $AW(\{p\}, s_I(h))$ and $AW(\{q\}, s_I(h))$ are true, and $E(h)$ includes executions of p and q and their subexecutions satisfying relation rel, all executions succeed. So, a rule for determining [$CAW(rel,$ $p_{sum}, q_{sum})$, $MSW(rel, p_{sum}, q_{sum})$] is sound if whenever the rule returns $true$, [$AW(rel, p, q)$, $SW(rel,$ $p, q)$] is true for [all pairs, some pair] of plans whose summary information is p_{sum} and q_{sum}. The rule is complete if whenever [$AW(rel, p, q)$, $SW(rel, p, q)$] is true for [all, some pair of] plans p and q with summary conditions p_{sum} and q_{sum}, the rule also returns $true$.

Now we state the rules for determining $overlaps$. $CAW(\text{o}, p_{sum}, q_{sum})$ returns $true$ iff there is no c_p and c_q such that $\ell(c_p) \Leftrightarrow \neg\ell(c_q)$ and either $c_p \in in_{sum}(p)$ and $c_q \in pre_{sum}(q) \cup in_{sum}(q)$ or $c_p \in post_{sum}(p)$ and $c_q \in in_{sum}(q)$. $MSW(\text{o}, p_{sum}, q_{sum})$ returns $true$ iff there is no c_p and c_q such that $\ell(c_p) \Leftrightarrow \neg\ell(c_q)$; $must(c_p)$ and $must(c_q)$ is true; the $timing$ of c_p and c_q is either $first$, $always$, or $last$; and either $c_p \in in_{sum}(p)$ and $c_q \in pre_{sum}(q) \cup in_{sum}(q)$ or $c_p \in post_{sum}(p)$ and $c_q \in in_{sum}(q)$. Note that for n conditions in each of the pre-, in-, and postconditions of p and q, in the worst case each condition in one plan must be compared with each in another plan, so the complexity of determining CAW and MSW is $O(n^2)$. Now we will show that the above rules are both sound and complete. The proofs of rules for other temporal relations are no more difficult than this one and can be done constructively in the same style.

Theorem $CAW(\text{o}, p_{sum}, q_{sum})$ and $MSW(\text{o}, p_{sum}, q_{sum})$ are sound and complete.

Proof Since we assume $AW(\{p\}, s_I)$ and $AW(\{q\}, s_I)$, the only way executions of p or q could fail is if a condition in one is clobbered by the other. However, a condition is clobbered only by the assertion of the negation of its literal. Thus, the presence of conditions involving the propositional variable v cannot clobber or achieve conditions involving the propositional variable v' if $v \neq v'$. In addition, all cases of execution failure can be broken down into inconditions of some execution e clobbering conditions that must be met in the interval $(t_s(e), t_f(e))$ and postconditions of some execution e clobbering conditions at or after $t_f(e)$. With this established it is not difficult to show that the only pairs of interacting sets where clobbering occurs for the $overlaps$ relation include $(in_{sum}(p), pre_{sum}(q))$, $(in_{sum}(p),$ $in_{sum}(q))$, and $(post_{sum}(p), in_{sum}(q))$. And, because the clobbering of a single literal causes execution failure, we can describe all histories in terms of the presence and absence of summary conditions based on a single propositional variable.

This is done for the $overlaps$ relation in Table 2. Here, we give all instances of these interacting sets and claim that the listed truth values for CAW and MSW

	A	B	$A = in_{sum}(p)$ $B = pre_{sum}(q)$		$A = in_{sum}(p)$ $B = in_{sum}(q)$		$A = post_{sum}(p)$ $B = in_{sum}(q)$	
			CAW	MSW	CAW	MSW	CAW	MSW
1	-	?	T	T	T	T	T	T
	?	-	T	T	T	T	T	T
2	ℓ	ℓ	T	T	T	T	T	T
3	ℓ	$\neg\ell$						
	m	a/l	m	f/a				
a	T T T T		F	F	F	F	F	F
b	F ? ? ?		F	T	F	T	F	T
c	? F ? ?		F	T	F	T	F	T
d	? ? F ?		F	T	F	T	F	T
e	? ? ? F		F	T	F	T	F	T
4	$\ell,\neg\ell$	ℓ	F	T	F	T	F	T
5	ℓ	$\ell,\neg\ell$	F	T	F	T	F	T
6	$\ell,\neg\ell$	$\ell,\neg\ell$	F	T	F	T	F	T

Table 2: Truth values of $CanAnyWay(o, p, q)$ and $MightSomeWay(o, p, q)$ for all interactions of conditions. ℓ and $\neg\ell$ are literals of summary conditions in sets A and B. The condition is *must* if $m = $ T, *first* for $f = $ T, *last* for $l = $ T, and *always* for $a = $ T.

are correct for the space of plan pairs (p, q) that elicit the instances represented by each row. The literal ℓ in the first two columns represents any literal that appears in any condition of the set in whose column it appears. For example, row 4 for the interaction of $(in_{sum}(p), pre_{sum}(q))$ is interpreted as the case where there is a literal that appears in both sets, and its negation also appears in just $in_{sum}(p)$. [F, T] in the [CAW, MSW] column means that [*not all* histories, there is at least one history] with only the executions and subexecutions of [any, some] pair of plans whose summary conditions have literals appearing this way are such that all executions succeed. Thus, [CAW(o, p_{sum}, q_{sum}), MSW(o, p_{sum}, q_{sum})] is true iff there are no summary conditions matching cases in the table where there is an F entry in a [CAW, MSW] column.

The validity of most entries in Table 2 is simple to verify. In row 1 either there is no condition to be clobbered or no condition to clobber it, so all executions must succeed. In row 3 unless the conditions are all *must* and either *first*, *always*, or *last* (row 3a), there is always a history containing the executions of some plans where the two conflicting conditions are not required to be met at the same time, and MSW is true. Because rules defined for CAW(o, p_{sum}, q_{sum}) and MSW(o, p_{sum}, q_{sum}) return *true* whenever the table has a T entry, they are complete. And because the table has a T entry for every case in which the rules return *true*, the rules are sound. □

Conclusions and Future Work

Coordination and planning for hierarchical plans often involve the refinement of abstract plans into more detail. However, the cost of backtracking or making irreversible commitments makes it critical that the specification of abstract plan operators be rich enough to anticipate and avoid costly planning/execution decisions. We have addressed this directly by offering a formalism for describing concurrent hierarchical plan

execution and methods for deriving summary conditions and determining legal plan interactions in a sound and complete fashion. This provides a foundation upon which provably correct coordination and planning mechanisms can be built. In prior work that motivates and validates this formalism, we describe a general algorithm for merging hierarchical plans using summary information, a specific implementation, and a preliminary evaluation of the approach (Clement & Durfee 1999b). Future work includes relaxing assumptions, such as the downward solution property, investigating other types of plan summary information, and constructing sound and complete algorithms for concurrent hierarchical planning and for interleaving planning, plan coordination, and plan execution.

References

Allen, J. F., and Koomen, J. A. 1983. Planning using a temporal world model. In *Proc. IJCAI*, 741–747.

Allen, J. F. 1983. Maintaining knowledge about temporal intervals. *Communications of the ACM* 26(11):832–843.

Clement, B., and Durfee, E. 1999a. Theory for coordinating concurrent hierarchical planning agents. http://www.eecs.umich.edu/~bradc/papers/aaai99.

Clement, B., and Durfee, E. 1999b. Top-down search for coordinating the hierarchical plans of multiple agents. In *Proc. Intl. Conf. Autonomous Agents*.

Corkill, D. 1979. Heirarchical planning in a distributed environment. In *Proc. IJCAI*, 168–175.

Ephrati, E., and Rosenschein, J. 1994. Divide and conquer in multi-agent planning. In *Proc. AAAI*, 375–380.

Erol, K.; Hendler, J.; and Nau, D. 1994. Semantics for hierarchical task-network planning. Technical Report CS-TR-3239, University of Maryland.

Fagin, R.; Halpern, J.; Moses, Y.; and Vardi, M. 1995. *Reasoning about knowledge*. MIT Press.

Firby, J. 1989. *Adaptive Execution in Complex Dynamic Domains*. Ph.D. Dissertation, Yale University.

Georgeff, M. P., and Lansky, A. 1986. Procedural knowledge. *Proc. IEEE* 74(10):1383–1398.

Georgeff, M. P. 1983. Communication and interaction in multiagent planning. In *Proc. AAAI*, 125–129.

Georgeff, M. P. 1984. A theory of action for multiagent planning. In *Proc. AAAI*, 121–125.

Lansky, A. 1990. Localized search for controlling automated reasoning. In *Proc. DARPA Workshop on Innov. Approaches to Planning, Scheduling and Control*, 115–125.

Sacerdoti, E. D. 1977. *A structure for plans and behavior*. Elsevier-North Holland.

Tate, A. 1977. Generating project networks. In *Proc. IJCAI*, 888–893.

Tsuneto, R.; Hendler, J.; and Nau, D. 1998. Analyzing external conditions to improve the efficiency of htn planning. In *Proc. AAAI*, 913–920.

Vilain, and Kautz, H. 1986. Constraint propagation algorithms for temporal reasoning. In *Proc. AAAI*, 377–382.

Weld, D. 1994. An introduction to least commitment planning. *AI Magazine* 15(4):27–61.

Fast Planning through Greedy Action Graphs *

Alfonso Gerevini and Ivan Serina

Dipartimento di Elettronica per l'Automazione
Universitá di Brescia, via Branze 38, 25123 Brescia, Italy
{gerevini,serina}@ing.unibs.it

Abstract

Domain-independent planning is a notoriously hard search problem. Several systematic search techniques have been proposed in the context of various formalisms. However, despite their theoretical completeness, in practice these algorithms are incomplete because for many problems the search space is too large to be (even partially) explored.

In this paper we propose a new search method in the context of Blum and Furst's planning graph approach, which is based on local search. Local search techniques are incomplete, but in practice they can efficiently solve problems that are unsolvable for current systematic search methods. We introduce three heuristics to guide the local search (Walkplan, Tabuplan and T-Walkplan), and we propose two methods for combining local and systematic search.

Our techniques are implemented in a system called GPG, which can be used for both plan-generation and plan-adaptation tasks. Experimental results show that GPG can efficiently solve problems that are very hard for current planners based on planning graphs.

Introduction

Domain-independent planning is a notoriously very hard search problem. The large majority of the search control techniques that have been proposed in the recent literature rely on a systematic method that in principle can examine the complete search space. However, despite their theoretical completeness, in practice these search algorithms are incomplete because for many planning problems the search space is too large to be (even partially) explored, and a plan cannot be found in reasonable time (if one exists).

Here we are concerned with an alternative search method which is based on a local search scheme. This method is formally incomplete, but in practice it can efficiently solve problems that are very hard to solve by more traditional systematic methods.[1]

Though local search techniques have been applied with success to many combinatorial problems, they

[1]Local search methods are incomplete in the sense that they cannot detect that a search problem has *no* solution.

have only recently been applied to planning (Ambite & Knoblock 1997; Kautz & Selman 1998; 1996; Serina & Gerevini 1998). In particular, Kautz and Selman experimented the use of a stochastic local search algorithm (Walksat) in the context of their "planning as satisfiability" framework, showing that Walksat outperforms more traditional systematic methods on several problems (Kautz & Selman 1996).

In the first part of this paper we propose a new method for local search in the context of the "planning through planning graph analysis" approach (Blum & Furst 1995). We formulate the problem of generating a plan as a search problem, where the elements of the search space are particular subgraphs of the planning graph representing partial plans. The operators for moving from one search state to the next one are particular graph modification operations, corresponding to adding (deleting) some actions to (from) the current partial plan. The general search scheme is based on an iterative improvement process, which, starting from an initial subgraph of the planning graph, greedily improves the "quality" of the current plan according to some evaluation functions. Such functions measure the cost of the graph modifications that are possible at any step of the search. A final state of the search process is any subgraph representing a valid complete plan.

We introduce three heuristics: *Walkplan, Tabuplan,* and *T-Walkplan.* The first is inspired by the stochastic local search techniques used by Walksat (Selman, Kautz & Cohen 1994), while the second and the third are based on different ways of using a tabu list storing the most recent graph modifications performed.

In the second part of the paper we propose two methods for combining local and systematic search for planning graphs. The first is similar to the method used in Kautz and Selman's Blackbox for combining different search algorithms, except that in our case we use the same representation of the problem, while Blackbox uses completely different representations. The second method is based on the following idea. We use local search for efficiently producing a plan which is *almost* a solution, i.e., that possibly contains only a few flaws (unsatisfied preconditions or exclusion relations involving actions in the plan), and then we use a particular systematic search to "repair" such a plan and produce a valid solution.

Our techniques are implemented in a system called GPG (Greedy Planning Graph). Experimental results show that GPG can efficiently solve problems that are hard for IPP (Koehler *et al.* 1997), Graphplan (Blum & Furst 1995) and Blackbox (Kautz & Selman 1999).

Although this paper focuses on plan-generation, we also give some preliminary experimental results showing that our approach can be very efficient for solving plan-adaptation tasks as well. Fast plan-adaptation is important, for example, during plan execution, when the failure of some planned action, or the acquisition of new information affecting the world description or the goals of the plan, can make the current plan invalid.

In the rest of the paper, we first briefly introduce the planning graph approach; then we present our local search techniques and the methods for combining systematic and local search; finally, we present experimental results and give our conclusions.

Planning Graphs

A planning graph is a directed acyclic levelled graph with two kinds of nodes and three kinds of edges. The levels alternate between a fact level, containing fact nodes, and an action level containing action nodes. A fact node represents a proposition corresponding to a precondition of one or more operators instantiated at time step t (actions at time step t), or to an effect of one or more actions at time step $t-1$. The fact nodes of level 0 represents the positive facts of the initial state of the planning problem.[2] The last level is a proposition level containing the fact nodes corresponding to the goals of the planning problem.

In the following we indicate with $[u]$ the proposition (action) represented by the fact node (action node) u. The edges in a planning graph connect action nodes and fact nodes. In particular, an action node a of level i is connected by:

- *precondition edges* to the fact nodes of level i representing the preconditions of $[a]$,
- *add-edges* to the fact nodes of level $i+1$ representing the positive effects of $[a]$,
- *delete-edges* to the fact nodes of level $i+1$ representing the negative effects of $[a]$.

Two action nodes of a certain level are *mutually exclusive* if no valid plan can contain both the corresponding actions. Similarly, two fact nodes are mutually exclusive if no valid plan can make both the corresponding propositions true.

Two proposition nodes p and q in a proposition level are marked as exclusive if each action node a having

---

[2]Planning graphs adopt the closed world assumption.

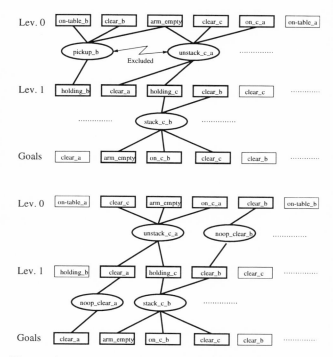

Figure 1: An action subgraph (bold nodes and edges) and a solution subgraph of a planning graph. The problem goals are clear_a, arm_empty, on_c_b and clear_c.

an add-edge to p is marked as exclusive of each action node b having an add-edge to q. In the last level of a planning graph there is no pair of mutually exclusive nodes representing goals.

An action node a of level i can be in a "valid subgraph" of the planning graph (a subgraph representing a valid plan) only if all its precondition nodes are *supported*, and a is not involved in any mutual exclusion relation with other action nodes of the subgraph. We say that a fact node q of level i representing a proposition $[q]$ is supported in a subgraph $\mathcal{G}'$ of a planning graph $\mathcal{G}$ if either (a) in $\mathcal{G}'$ there is an action node at level $i-1$ representing an action with (positive) effect $[q]$, or (b) $i=0$ (i.e., $[q]$ is in the initial state).

Given a planning problem $\mathcal{P}$ and a planning graph $\mathcal{G}$, a *solution* (plan) for $\mathcal{P}$ is a subgraph $\mathcal{G}'$ of $\mathcal{G}$ such that (1) all the precondition nodes of actions in $\mathcal{G}'$ are supported, (2) every goal node is supported, and (3) there are no mutual exclusion relations between action nodes of $\mathcal{G}'$.

Local Search for Planning Graphs

Our local search method for a planning graph $\mathcal{G}$ of a given problem $\mathcal{P}$ is a process that, starting from an initial subgraph $\mathcal{G}'$ of $\mathcal{G}$ (a partial plan for $\mathcal{P}$), transforms $\mathcal{G}'$ into a solution of $\mathcal{P}$ through the iterative application of some graph modifications that greedily improve the "quality" of the current partial plan. Each modification is either an extension of the subgraph to include a new action node of $\mathcal{G}$, or a reduction of the subgraph to remove an action node (and the relevant edges).

Adding an action node to the subgraph corresponds to adding an action to the partial plan represented by the subgraph (analogously for removing an action node). At any step of the search process the set of actions that can be added or removed is determined by the *constraint violations* that are present in the current subgraph of $\mathcal{G}$. Such violations correspond to

- mutual exclusion relations involving action nodes in the current subgraph;
- unsupported facts, which are either preconditions of actions in the current partial plan, or goal nodes in the last level of the graph.

More precisely, the search space is formed by the *action subgraphs* of the planning graph $\mathcal{G}$, where an action subgraph of $\mathcal{G}$ is defined in the following way:

Definition 1 *An **action subgraph** $\mathcal{A}$ of a planning graph $\mathcal{G}$ is a subgraph of $\mathcal{G}$ such that if a is an action node of $\mathcal{G}$ in $\mathcal{A}$, then the fact nodes of $\mathcal{G}$ corresponding to the preconditions and positive effects of [a] are also in $\mathcal{A}$, together with the edges of $\mathcal{G}$ connecting them to a.*

A *solution subgraph* (a final state of the search space) is defined in the following way:

Definition 2 *A **solution subgraph** of a planning graph $\mathcal{G}$ is an action subgraph $\mathcal{A}_s$ containing the goal nodes of $\mathcal{G}$ and such that*

- *all the goal nodes and fact nodes corresponding to preconditions of actions in $\mathcal{A}_s$ are supported;*
- *there is no mutual exclusion relation between action nodes.*

The first part of Figure 1 shows a simple example of an action subgraph $\mathcal{A}$. The actions pickup_b and unstack_c_a of level 0 are mutually exclusive, and therefore they can not be both present in any solution subgraph. Note that the goal node clear_a is not supported in $\mathcal{A}$ and does not belong to $\mathcal{A}$, even though it must belong to all solution subgraphs. The second part of Figure 1 gives a solution subgraph.

Our general scheme for searching a solution graph consists of two main steps. The first step is an initialization of the search in which we construct an initial action subgraph. The second step is a local search process in the space of all the action subgraphs, starting from the initial action subgraph. In the context of local search for CSP, the initialization phase is an important step which can significantly affect the performance of the search phase (Minton *et al.* 1992). In our context we can generate an initial action subgraph in several ways. Two possibilities that we have considered in our experiments are: (1) a randomly generated action-subgraph; (2) an action-subgraph where all precondition facts and goal facts are supported (but in

which there may be some violated mutual exclusion relations). These kinds of initialization can be performed in linear time in the size of the graph $\mathcal{G}$.

The search phase is performed in the following way. A constraint violation in the current action subgraph is randomly chosen. If it is an unsupported fact node, then in order to eliminate this constraint violation, we can either add an action node that supports it, or we can remove an action node which is connected to that fact node by a precondition edge. If the constraint chosen is an exclusion relation, then we can remove one of the action nodes of the exclusion relation. Note that the elimination of an action node can remove several constraint violations (i.e., all those corresponding to the set of exclusion relations involving the action node eliminated). On the other hand, the addition of an action node can introduce several new constraint violations. Also, when we add (remove) an action node to satisfy a constraint, we also add (remove) all the edges connecting the action node with the corresponding precondition and effect nodes in the planning graph – this ensures that each change to the current action subgraph is another action subgraph.

The decision of how to deal with a constraint violation can be guided by a *general objective function*, which is defined in the following way:

Definition 3 *Given the partial plan π represented by an action subgraph $\mathcal{A}$, the **general objective function** $f(\pi)$ of π is defined as:*

$$f(\pi) = g(\mathcal{A}) + \sum_{a \in \mathcal{A}} me(a, \mathcal{A}) + p(a, \mathcal{A})$$

where a is an action in $\mathcal{A}$, $me(a, \mathcal{A})$ is the number of action nodes in $\mathcal{A}$ which are mutually exclusive with a, $p(a, \mathcal{A})$ is the number of precondition facts of a which are not supported, and $g(\mathcal{A})$ is the number of goal nodes in $\mathcal{A}$ which are not supported.

It is easy to see that the value of this objective function is zero for any valid plan of a given planning problem. This function can be used in the search process at each search step to discriminate between different possible graph modifications, and to choose one which minimizes the objective function.

Local search heuristics

The use of the general objective function to guide the local search might be effective for some planning problems, but it has the drawback that it can lead to local minima from which the search can not escape. For this reason, instead of using the general objective function we use an *action cost function F*. This function defines the cost of inserting (F^i) and of removing (F^r) an action [a] in the partial plan π represented by the current action subgraph $\mathcal{A}$. $F([a], \pi)$ is defined in the following way:

$$\begin{cases} F([a],\pi)^i = \alpha^i \cdot p(a,\mathcal{A}) + \beta^i \cdot me(a,\mathcal{A}) + \gamma^i \cdot unsup(a,\mathcal{A}) \\ F([a],\pi)^r = \alpha^r \cdot p(a,\mathcal{A}) + \beta^r \cdot me(a,\mathcal{A}) + \gamma^r \cdot sup(a,\mathcal{A)}, \end{cases}$$

where $me(a,\mathcal{A})$ and $p(a,\mathcal{A})$ are defined as in Definition 3, $unsup(a,\mathcal{A})$ is the number of unsupported precondition facts in $\mathcal{A}$ that become supported by adding a to $\mathcal{A}$, and $sup(a,\mathcal{A})$ is the number of supported precondition facts in $\mathcal{A}$ that become unsupported by removing a from $\mathcal{A}$.

By appropriately setting the values of the coefficients α, β and γ we can implement various heuristic methods aimed at making the search less susceptible to local minima by being "less committed" to following the gradient of the general objective function. Their values have to satisfy the following constraints:

$$\alpha^i > 0, \ \beta^i > 0, \ \gamma^i \leq 0, \ \alpha^r \leq 0, \ \beta^r \leq 0, \ \gamma^r > 0.$$

Note that the positive coefficients of F (α^i, β^i and γ^r) determine an increment in F which is related to an increment of the number of constraint violations. Analogously, the non-positive coefficients of F (α^r, β^r and γ^i) determine a decrement in F which is related to a decrement of the number of constraint violations.

In the following we describe three simple search heuristics, and in the last part of the paper we will present some preliminary experimental results obtained by using these heuristics. The general search procedure at each step randomly picks a constraint violation s and considers the costs of the action deletions/insertions which resolve s. The action subgraphs that can be obtained by performing the modifications corresponding to such action deletions/insertions constitute the neighborhood $N(s,\mathcal{A})$ of s, where $\mathcal{A}$ is the current action subgraph. The following heuristics can be used to choose the next action subgraph among those in $N(s,\mathcal{A})$.

Walkplan

Walkplan uses a random walk strategy similar to the strategy used in Walksat (Selman, Kautz & Cohen 1994). Given a constraint violation s, in order to decide which of the action subgraphs in $N(s,\mathcal{A})$ to choose, Walkplan uses a greedy bias that tends to minimize the number of new constraint violations that are introduced by the graph modification. Since this bias can easily lead the algorithm to local minima from which the search cannot escape, it is not always applied.

In particular, if there is a modification that does not introduce new constraint violations, then the corresponding action subgraph in $N(s,\mathcal{A})$ is chosen as the next action subgraph. Otherwise, with probability p one of the subgraphs in $N(s,\mathcal{A})$ is chosen randomly, and with probability $1-p$ the next action subgraph is chosen according to minimum value of the action cost function.

Walkplan can be implemented by setting the α, β and γ coefficients to values satisfying the following con-

straints: $\alpha^i, \beta^i > 0, \gamma^i = 0$ and $\alpha^r, \beta^r = 0, \gamma^r > 0$.

Tabuplan

Tabuplan uses a tabu list (Glover & Laguna 1993; Glover, Taillard, & de Werra 1993) which is a special short term memory of actions inserted or removed. A simple strategy of using the tabu list that we have tested in our experiments consists of preventing the deletion (insertion) of an action just introduced (removed) for the next k search steps, where k is the length of the tabu list.

At each step of the search, from the current action subgraph Tabuplan chooses as next subgraph the "best" subgraph in $N(s,\mathcal{A})$ which can be generated by adding or removing an action that is *not* in the tabu list. The length k of the tabu list is a parameter that is set at the beginning of the search, but that could also be dynamically modified during the search (Glover & Laguna 1993).

T-Walkplan

This heuristic uses a tabu list simply for *increasing the cost* of certain graph modifications, instead of preventing them as in Tabuplan. More precisely, when we evaluate the cost of adding or removing an action $[a]$ which is in the tabu list, the action cost $F([a],\pi)$ is incremented by $\delta \cdot (k-j)$, where δ is a small quantity (e.g. 0.1), k is the length of the tabu list, and j is the position of $[a]$ in the tabu list.[3]

Combining local and systematic search

As the experimental results presented in the next section show, local search techniques can efficiently solve several problems that are very hard to solve for IPP or Graphplan. On the other hand, as general planning algorithms they have the drawback that they cannot detect when a valid plan does *not* exist in a planning graph with a predefined number of levels. (Hence they cannot determine when the planning graph should be extended.) Furthermore, we observed that some problems that are very easy to solve for the systematic search as implemented in IPP, are harder for our local search techniques (though they are still solvable in a few seconds, and our main interest concerns problems that are very hard for current planners based on planning graphs).

Motivated by these considerations, we have developed a simple method for automatically increasing the size of a planning graph, as well as two methods for

---

[3]We assume that the tabu list is managed according to a first-in-first-out discipline.

[4]In our current implementation the search from goal-level to init-level at step 5 is initially restricted by limiting the possible number of levels in the (re)planning graph to 3. This number is automatically increased by 2 each time the replanning window is increased by 1 level.

ADJUST-PLAN
Input: A plan $\mathcal{P}$ containing some flaws and a CPU-time limit `max-adjust-time`.
Output: Either a correct plan or `fail`.

1. Identify the set `F` of levels in $\mathcal{P}$ containing a flaw; If `F` is empty, then return $\mathcal{P}$;

2. Let `i` be a level in `F` and remove `i` from `F`;

3. If `i` is the last level of $\mathcal{P}$, then set `init-level` to `i − 1` and `goal-level` to `i`, otherwise set `init-level` to `i` and `goal-level` to `i + 1`;

4. While CPU-time $\leq$ `max-adjust-time`

5. Systematically replan using as initial facts $F(\texttt{init-level})$ and as goals $G(\texttt{goal-level})$, where $F(\texttt{init-level})$ is the set of facts that are true at level `init-level`, and $G(\texttt{goal-level})$ is the set of preconditions of the actions in $\mathcal{P}$ at level `goal-level` (including the no-ops);

6. If there is no plan from $F(\texttt{init-level})$ to $G(\texttt{goal-level})$, or a search limit is exceeded, then decrease `init-level` or increase `goal-level` (i.e., we enlarge the replanning window), otherwise insert the (sub)plan found into $\mathcal{P}$ and goto 1.[4]

7. Return fail.

Figure 2: Description of the algorithm used by GPG for adjusting a plan generated by the local search.

combining our local search techniques with IPP's systematic search. These methods are implemented in a planner called GPG (Greedy Planning Graph).[5]

Like IPP, GPG starts searching when the construction of the planning graph has reached a level in which all the fact goals of the problem are present and are not mutually exclusive. When used in a purely local-search mode, if after a certain number of search steps a solution has not been found, GPG extends the planning graph by adding a level to it, and a new search on the extended graph is performed.[6]

The first method for combining local and systematic search borrows from Kautz and Selman's Blackbox the idea of combining different search algorithms in a serial way. In particular, we alternate systematic and local search in the following way. First we search the planning graph using a systematic method as in Graphplan or IPP until either (a) a solution is found, (b) the problem is proved to be unsolvable, or (c) a predefined CPU time limit is exceeded (this limit can be modified by the user). If the CPU-time has been exceeded, then we activate a local search on the planning graph using our local search techniques, which has the same termination conditions as the systematic search, except that the problem cannot be proved to be unsolvable.

If the local search also does not find a solution within a certain CPU-time limit, then we extend the planning graph by adding a new level to it, and we repeat the process.

The second method exploits the fact that often when the local search does not find a solution in a reasonable amount of time, it comes "very close" to it, producing action subgraphs representing plans that are *quasi*-solutions, and that can be adjusted to become a solution by making a limited number of changes to them. A *quasi*-solution is an *almost correct* plan, i.e., a plan $\mathcal{P}$ which contains a few unsatisfied preconditions or exclusion relations involving actions in the plan.

This method consists of two phases. In the first phase we search for a *quasi*-solution of the planning problem using local search (the number of levels in the graph is automatically increased after a certain number of search steps). The second phase identifies the flaws that are present in $\mathcal{P}$, and tries to "repair" them by running ADJUST-PLAN, an algorithm performing systematic search (see Figure 2).

ADJUST-PLAN first identifies the levels of $\mathcal{P}$ which contain a pair of mutually exclusive actions or an action with some unachieved precondition(s). Then it processes these levels in the following way. If level `i` contains a flaw, then it tries to repair it by replanning from time level `i` to level `i + 1` using systematic search. If there exists no plan or a certain search limit is exceeded, then the replanning window is enlarged (e.g., we replan from `i - 1` to `i + 1`).[4] The process is iterated until a (sub)plan is found, or the search has reached a predefined CPU-time limit (`max-adjust-time`). The idea is that if $\mathcal{P}$ contains some flaw that cannot be repaired by limited (systematic) replanning, then ADJUST-PLAN returns fail, and the local search is executed again to provide another plan that may be easier to repair.[7] When a subplan is found, it is appropriately inserted into $\mathcal{P}$.

At step 6 of ADJUST-PLAN the replanning window can be increased going either backward in time (i.e., `init-level` is decreased), forward in time (i.e., `goal-level` is increased), or both.[8] The introduction of any subplan found at step 5 does not invalidate the

---

[5]GPG is written in C and it uses IPP's data structures. IPP is available at http://www.informatik.uni-freiburg/~koehler/ipp.html.

[6]GPG has a default value for this search limit, which is increased each time the graph is extended. The user can change its value, as well as its increment when the graph is extended.

[7]GPG has a default `max-adjust-time` that can be modified by the user. In principle, if `max-adjust-time` were set to sufficiently high values, then ADJUST-PLAN could increase the replanning window to reach the original initial and goal levels of the planning graph. This would determine a complete systematic search, that however we would like to avoid. Also, note that in our current implementation of ADJUST-PLAN, during replanning the actions of $\mathcal{P}$ that are present in the replanning window are ignored (a new local planning graph is constructed).

[8]Note that when the replanning window is increased by moving the goal state forward, keeping the same initial state, we can use the memoization of unachieved subgoals to prune the search as indicated in (Blum & Furst 1995; Koehler *et al.* 1997).

rest of the plan. On the contrary, such a subplan may be useful for achieving unachieved preconditions that are present at levels later than the level that started the process at step 2. Note also that since we are currently considering STRIPS-like domains, step 1 can be accomplished in polynomial time by doing a simulation of $\mathcal{P}$. Similarly, the facts that are (necessarily) true at any level can be determined in polynomial time.

As the experimental results presented in the next section show, this method often leads to a solution very efficiently. However, such a solution is not guaranteed to be optimal with respect to the number of time steps that are present in the solution. For this reason, when ADJUST-PLAN finds a solution, we attempt to optimize the adjusted plan, trying to produce a more compact plan (however, for lack of space we omit the description of this process).

On the other hand, it should be noticed that the plans obtained by IPP or Graphplan from a planning graph with the minimum number of levels are *not* guaranteed to be optimal in terms of the number of *actions* involved, which is an important feature of the quality of a plan. The experimental results in the next section show that GPG can generate plans with a lower number of actions than the number of actions in plans generated by IPP. Thus, in this sense, in general the quality of the plans obtained with our method is no worse than the quality of the plans obtained with IPP or Graphplan.

Finally, note that the two methods for combining local and systematic search can be merged into a single method, which iteratively performs systematic search, local search and plan-adjustment.

Experimental results

In order to test the effectiveness of local search techniques, we have been conducting three kind of experiments. The first is aimed at testing the efficiency of local search in a planning graph with the (predetermined) minimum number of levels that are sufficient to solve the problem. The second is aimed at testing the combination of local search and plan-adjustment described in the previous section, in which the number of levels in the planning graph is not predetermined. The third concerns the use of our techniques for the task of repairing a precomputed plan in order to cope with some changes in the initial state or in the goal state. Preliminary results from these experiments concern the following domains: Rocket, Logistics, Gripper, Blocks-world, Tyre-world, TSP, Fridge-world and Monkey-world.[9]

---

[9]The formalization of these domains and of the relative problems is available as part of the IPP package. For the blocks world we used the formalization with four operator: `pick_up`, `put_down`, `stack` and `unstack`.

Table I gives the results of the first kind of experiments, which was conducted on a Sun Ultra 1 with 128 Mbytes. The CPU-times for the local search techniques are averages over 20 runs. The table includes the CPU-time required by IPP and by Blackbox (using only Walksat for the search) for solving each of the problems considered. Each run of our methods consists of 10 tries, and each try consists of (a) an initialization phase, in which an initial action subgraph is generated; (b) a search phase with a default search limit of 500,000 steps (graph modifications).[10]

The first part of the table concerns some problems that are hard to solve for IPP, but that can be efficiently solved using local search methods. In particular, our techniques were very efficient for Rocket and Logistics, where the local search methods were up to more than four orders of magnitude faster than the systematic search of IPP.

The second half of Table I gives the results for some problems that are easy to solve for the systematic search of IPP. Here our local search techniques also performed relatively well. Some of the problems were solved more efficiently with a local search and some others with a systematic search, but in all cases the search required at most a few seconds.

Compared to Blackbox, in general, in this experiment the performance improvement of our search methods was less significant, except for bw_large_a where they were significantly faster than Walksat.

Table II gives results concerning the second kind of experiment, where GPG uses local search for a fast computation of a *quasi*-solution, which is then processed by ADJUST-PLAN. This experiment was conducted on a Sun Ultra 60 with 512 Mbytes. As local search heuristic in every run we used Walkplan with noise equal to either 0.3, 0.4 or 0.5 (lower noise for harder problems, higher noise for easier problems).[11] In all the tests `max-adjust-time` was set to 180 seconds and the number of flaws admitted in a quasi-solution was limited to either 2, 4 or 6.

Compared to IPP, GPG found a solution very efficiently. In particular, on average GPG required less than a minute (and 6.3 seconds in the fastest run) to solve Logistics-d, a test problem introduced in (Kautz & Selman 1996) containing 10^{16} possible states. More-

---

[10]It should be noted that the results of this experiment were obtained by setting the parameters of our heuristics and of Walksat to particular values, that were empirically chosen as the best over many values tested.

[11]However, we observed that the combination of local search and plan-adjustment in GPG does not seem to be significantly sensitive to the values of the parameters of the heuristics, and we expect that the use of default values for all the runs would give similar results. Probably the major reason of this is that here local search is not used to find a solution, but to find a *quasi*-solution. Further experiments for confirming this observation are in progress.

Problem	graph levels	graph creation	Walkplan	Tabuplan	T-Walkplan	IPP	Blackbox (Walksat)
Rocket_a	7	0.46	48.57 (2)	1.16	0.5	126.67	5.77
Rocket_b	7	0.49	6.5	1.4	2.78	334.51	8.23
Logistics_a	11	1.58	2.5	1.77	1.04	2329.06	4.0
Logistics_b	13	1.15	19.9	85.43 (3)	5.25	1033.75	12.83
Logistics_c	13	2.22	19.4	37.63	7.05	> 24 hours	20.91
Bw_large_a	12	0.3	4.04	123 (8)	13.1	0.38	705 (4)
Blocks-suss	6	0.04	0.01	0.01	0.02	0.01	0.139
Tyre-fixit	12	0.08	0.09	0.2	0.077	0.05	0.273
Rocket-10	3	0.1	0.006	0.003	0.005	0.005	0.083
Monkey-2	8	0.2	5.49	6.9	0.68	0.04	3.882
TSP-complete	9	0.28	1.26	0.99	0.59	1.65	0.833
Fridge-2	6	0.88	0.056	0.063	0.09	0.06	0.243
Logistics-4	9	0.37	0.01	0.007	0.01	0.01	0.041
Logistics-4pp	9	0.34	0.007	0.005	0.008	0.005	0.079
Logistics-6h	11	0.48	0.33	2.01	0.15	2.82	0.156
Logistics-8	9	0.65	0.17	0.18	0.05	0.01	0.147

Table I: CPU seconds required by our local search heuristics, by IPP (v. 3.3) and by Blackbox (v. 3.4) for solving some hard problems (first part of the table) and some easy problems (second part). The numbers into brackets indicate the number of runs in which a solution was not found (if this is not indicated, then a solution was found in all the runs.)

Problem	GPG					IPP			Blackbox	
	total time mean(min)	local time	repair time	levels mean (min)	actions mean (min)	total time	num. levels	num. actions	Graphplan + Satz	Graphplan + Walksat
Bw_large_a	1.6(0.8)	0.35	1.25	13.6 (12)	13.6 (12)	0.31	12	12	1.24	1.24
Bw_large_b	27.3(2.3)	3.5	23.8	20.6 (18)	20.6 (18)	7.75	18	18	109.88	3291
Rocket_a	1.1(0.5)	0.8	0.28	9.2 (7)	33 (30)	53.5	7	34	59.7	60.86
Rocket_b	1.3(0.4)	1.0	0.3	9.4 (7)	32.4 (30)	146.7	7	30	65.64	60.58
Logistics_a	3.9(0.8)	0.36	3.5	13.6 (11)	63.3 (56)	956	11	64	70.34	76.34
Logistics_b	3.9(1.4)	0.9	3.0	15.6 (13)	58 (52)	423	13	45	112.05	302
Logistics_c	2.42(2.15)	1.66	0.76	15.6 (14)	70.8 (69)	> 24 h.	–	–	162.4	539
Logistics_d	57(6.3)	5.6	50.7	20.5 (17)	94.5 (84)	> 24 h.	–	–	132.2	912
Gripper-10	51.2(15.4)	46.8	4.3	26.7 (19)	35.16 (29)	126.47	19	29	2607.8	2467
Gripper-12	320(63.8)	71.4	248.7	29 (29)	38.4 (35)	1368.5	23	35	> 9070	> 8432

Table II: Performance of GPG using Walkplan and ADJUST-PLAN compared to IPP 3.3 and Blackbox 3.4. The 2nd column gives the average (minimum) CPU-seconds required by GPG to find a solution over 5 runs. The 3rd gives the average time spent by the local search, and the 4th the time for adjusting the plan. The 5th column gives the average (minimum) number of levels that were required to find a solution by GPG. The 6th column gives the average (minimum) number of actions in a solution found by GPG. The 7–9th columns give CPU-seconds, number of levels and actions required by IPP. The 10–11th columns give the average CPU-seconds required by Blackbox over 5 runs.

over, in terms of the number of actions, the plans generated by GPG on average are not significantly worse than the plans generated by IPP. On the contrary, in some cases GPG found plans involving a number of actions lower than in the plans found by IPP. For example, for Rocket_a GPG found plans involving a minimum of 30 actions and on average of 33 actions, while the plan generated by IPP contains 34 actions.

Concerning the problems in the blocks world (bw_large-a e bw_large-b), on average GPG did not perform as well as IPP (though these problems are still solvable in seconds). In these problems the local search can take a relatively high amount of time for generating quasi-solutions, which can be expensive to repair. The reasons for this are not completely clear yet, but we believe that they partly depend on the fact that in planning graphs with a limited number of levels these problems have only a few solutions and quasi-solutions (Clark *et al.* 1997).

In general, GPG was significantly faster than Blackbox (last columns of Table II) regardless the SAT-solver that we used (either Satz or Walksat).[12]

Table III shows preliminary results of testing the use of local search for the task of plan adaptation, where in the input we have a valid plan (solution) for a problem P, and a set of changes to the initial state or the goal state of P. The plan for P is used as initial subgraph of the planning graph for the revised problem P', that is greedily modified to derive a new plan for P'.

In particular, the table gives the plan-adaptation and plan-generation times for some variants of Logistics_a, where in general the local search performed much more efficiently than a complete replanning using IPP (up to five orders of magnitude faster).[13]

I_1-5 correspond to five modifications of the problem obtained by changing a fact in the initial state that affects the applicability of some planned action. G_1-11 are modifications corresponding to some (significant) changes to the goals in the last level of the planning graph. Every change considered in this ex-

---

[12] Graphplan plus Satz was run using the default settings of Blackbox for all the problems, except for Gripper-10/12 in which we used the settings suggested in (Kautz & Selman

1999) for hard logistics problems. Graphplan plus Walksat iteratively performed a graph search for 30 seconds, and then ran Walksat using the same settings used for Table I, except for Gripper-10/12 and bw_large_b where we used cutoff 3000000, 10 restarts and noise 0.2 (for Gripper-12 we tested cutoff 30000000 as well, but this did not help Blackbox, which did not find a solution.)

[13] These tests were performed on a Sun Ultra 10, 64Mb.

Log_a	W	T	T-W	ADJUST	IPP
I_1	0.008	0.009	0.019	0.1	1742
I_2	0.32	30.3	0.264	0.73	236
I_3	0.117	29.7	0.214	0.93	1198
I_4	0.318	141.9	0.231	1.9	1186
I_5	0.008	0.005	0.006	0.31	3047
G_1	0.502	162.1	0.31	0.88	69.6
G_2	0.008	0.007	0.008	0.32	864
G_3	0.066	142	0.03	0.22	3456
G_4	0.111	15.19	0.194	0.77	2846.6
G_5	0.009	0.389	0.005	0.37	266.3
G_6	0.006	0.196	0.005	0.09	459.5
G_7	0.005	0.034	0.006	0.23	491
G_8	0.006	0.006	0.005	0.04	520
G_9	0.102	0.464	0.068	0.77	663
G_10	0.162	22.145	0.034	0.78	445
G_11	0.121	160.8	0.284	0.77	1023

Table III: Plan-adaptation CPU-seconds required on average by the local search methods (20 runs), by ADJUST-PLAN and by IPP for some modifications of Logistics_a. W indicates Walkplan, T Tabuplan and T-W T-walkplan.

periment admits a plan with the same number of time steps as in the input plan. Some additional results for this experiment are given in (Gerevini & Serina 1999).

Further experimental results concern the use of ADJUST-PLAN for solving plan-modification problems. In particular, the fifth column of the Table III gives the CPU-time for 16 modifications of Logistics_a. These results together with others concerning 44 modifications of Logistics_b (Gerevini & Serina 1999), Rocket_a and Rocket_b indicate that adjusting a plan using ADJUST-PLAN is much more efficient than a complete replanning with IPP (up to three orders of magnitude faster).

Finally, we are currently testing a method for solving plan-adaptation problems based on a combination of local search and ADJUST-PLAN. The general idea is that we first try to adapt the plan using local search and without increasing the number of time steps in the plan. Then, if the local search was not able to efficiently adapt the plan and this contains only a few flaws, we try to repair it using ADJUST-PLAN, otherwise we use GPG with the combination of local and systematic search described in the previous section. Preliminary results in the Logistics and Rocket domains indicate that the approach is very efficient.

Conclusions

We have presented a new framework for planning through local search in the context of planning graph, as well as methods for combining local and systematic search techniques, that can be used for both plan-generation and plan-adaptation tasks.

Experimental results show that our methods can be much more efficient than the search methods currently used by planners based on the planning graph approach. Current work includes further experimental analysis and the study of further heuristics for the local search and the plan-adjustment phases of GPG.

Our search techniques for plan-generation have some

similarities with Blackbox. A major difference is that, while Blackbox (Walksat) performs the local search on a CNF-translation of the graph, GPG performs the search directly on the graph structure. This gives the possibility of specifying further heuristics and types of search steps exploiting the semantics of the graph, which in Blackbox's translation is lost. For example, if an action node that was inserted to support a fact f violates some exclusion constraint c, then we could replace it with another action node, which still supports f and does not violate c. This kind of replacement operators are less natural to specify and more difficult to implement using a SAT-encoding of the planning problem.

Another significant difference is the use of local search for computing a quasi-solution, instead of a complete solution, which is then repaired by a plan-adjustment algorithm.

Acknowledgments

This research was supported in part by CNR project SCI*SIA. We thank Yannis Dimopoulos, Len Schubert and the anonymous referees for their helpful comments.

References

Ambite, J. L., and Knoblock, C. A. 1997. Planning by rewriting: Efficiently generating high-quality plans. In *Proc. of AAAI-97*, 706–713. AAAI/MIT Press.

Blum, A., and Furst, M. 1995. Fast planning through planning graph analysis. In *Proc. of IJCAI-95*, 1636–1642.

Clark, D. A.; Frank, J.; Gent, I. P.; MacIntyre, E.; Tomov, N.; and Walsh, T. 1997. Local search and the number of solutions. In *Proc. of CP-97*, 119–133. Springer Verlag.

Gerevini, A., and Serina, I. 1999. Fast Planning through Greedy Action Graphs. Tech. Rep. 710, Computer Science Dept., Univ. of Rochester, Rochester (NY), USA.

Glover, F., and Laguna, M. 1993. Tabu search. In Reeves, C. R., ed., *Modern heuristics for combinatorial problems*. Oxford, GB: Blackwell Scientific.

Glover, F.; Taillard, E.; and de Werra, D. 1993. A user's guide to tabu search. *Annals of Oper. Research*. 41:3–28.

Kautz, H., and Selman, B. 1996. Pushing the envelope: Planning, propositional logic, and stochastic search. In *Proc. of AAAI-96*, 1194–1201.

Kautz, H., and Selman, B. 1998. The role of domain-specific knowledge in the planning as satisfiability framework. In *Proc. of AIPS-98*.

Kautz, H., and Selman, B. 1999. Blackbox (version 3.4). http://www.research.att.com/~kautz/blackbox.

Koehler, J.; Nebel, B.; Hoffman, J.; and Dimopoulos, Y. 1997. Extending planning graphs to an ADL subset. In *Proc. of ECP'97*. Springer Verlag.

Minton, S.; Johonson, M.; Philips, A.; and Laird, P. 1992. Minimizing conflicts: A heuristic repair method for constraint satisfaction and scheduling problems. *Artificial Intelligence* 58:161–205.

Selman, B., and Kautz, H. 1994. Noise Strategies for Improving Local Search. In *Proc. of AAAI-94*, 337–343.

Serina, I., and Gerevini, A. 1998. Local search techniques for planning graph. In *Proc. of the 17th UK Planning and Scheduling SIG Workshop*.

Control Knowledge in Planning: Benefits and Tradeoffs

Yi-Cheng Huang
Department of Computer Science
Cornell University
ychuang@cs.cornell.edu

Bart Selman
Department of Computer Science
Cornell University
selman@cs.cornell.edu

Henry Kautz
Shannon Laboratory
AT&T Labs – Research
kautz@research.att.com

Abstract

Recent new planning paradigms, such as Graphplan and Satplan, have been shown to outperform more traditional domain-independent planners. An interesting aspect of these planners is that they do not incorporate domain specific control knowledge, but instead rely on efficient graph-based or propositional representations and advanced search techniques. An alternative approach has been proposed in the TLPlan system. TLPlan is an example of a powerful planner incorporating declarative control specified in temporal logic formulas. We show how these control rules can be parsed into Satplan. Our empirical results show up to an order of magnitude speed up. We also provide a detailed comparison with TLPlan, and show how the search strategies in TLPlan lead to efficient plans in terms of the number of actions but with little or no parallelism. The Satplan and Graphplan formalisms on the other hand do find highly parallel plans, but are less effective in sequential domains. Our results enhance our understanding of the various tradeoffs in planning technology, and extend earlier work on control knowledge in the Satplan framework by Ernst *et al.* (1997) and Kautz and Selman (1998).

Introduction

In recent years, there has been a burst of activity in the planning community with the introduction of a new generation of constraint and graph-based methods, such as graphplan and satplan (Blum and Furst 1995; Kautz and Selman 1996; Kambhampati 1997; Weld 1999). These planners are domain-independent and outperform more traditional planners on a range of benchmark problems. The surprising effectiveness of these planners represents a departure from the long held believe that the use of domain-specific planning control knowledge is unavoidable during plan search. Nevertheless, control knowledge has the potential to significantly increase the performance of the new planners. In fact the constraint-based framework behind graphplan and satplan allows one, at least in principle, to incorporate

control knowledge in a purely declarative manner by encoding the control as additional constraints.

A recent example of the effectiveness of declarative control knowledge is the TLPlan system by Bacchus and Kabanza (1996; 1998). In the TLPlan system, control knowledge is represented by formulas in temporal logic. For example, the "next" operator from temporal logic allows one to specify what can and cannot happen at the next time step. The control knowledge is used to steer a forward chaining planner. One of the surprises of this system is that, despite the rather basic search method, with the right control knowledge, the system is highly efficient on a range of benchmark problems, often outperforming Graphplan and Blackbox (Blackbox is the latest version of the Satplan system (Kautz and Selman 1999); Bacchus and Kabanza 1998). Of course, in this comparison Graphplan and Blackbox ran without any control; in addition, developing the right control formulas for TLPlan is a non-trivial task.

As Bacchus and Kabanza point out, the forward chaining approach is a good match with the declarative control specification. At each node in the search tree, the control formula is evaluated to determine what new nodes are reachable from the current state. With good control knowledge, many nodes are pruned and the search is "pushed" towards the goal state. To give some intuition as to how this is achieved, note that the control rules can encode information about the difference between the current state and the goal state by using a predicate that states, for example, "package currently not at goal location."

One interesting research question is whether the same level of control can be effectively incorporated into the Graphplan or Blackbox style planner. This is a non-trivial question because TLPlan's efficiency stems from the tight coupling between the pruning rules and the forward chaining search strategy. In addition, TLPlan allows for almost arbitrary complex control formulas that can generally be evaluated efficiently at each node (the process is in general intractable but in practice it appears efficient for control information Bacchus and Kabanza 1998). In the Graphplan or Blackbox framework the search proceeds very differently. The planning task is captured as a set of constraints mapped out over a fixed number of time steps. In Graphplan, the constraints are captured in a planning graph, which is subsequently searched for a valid plan. In Blackbox, the constraints are translated into a propositional formula (CNF), which can be searched with a satisfibility tester of the user's choice. In any case, in both Graphplan and Blackbox, the search does not proceed through a set of well-defined world states. In fact, the search may even involve as intermediate states states that are unreachable from the initial state or even physically impossible. Especially in Satplan the search is difficult to characterize, because the problem is reduced to a generic propositional representation, without an explicit link to the original planning problem. The SAT solvers proceed in finding a truth assignment for the encoding (corresponding to a valid plan) without taking into account the fact that the encoding represents a planning problem (Baioletti *et al.* 1998; Ernst *et al.* 1997; Kautz and Selman 1998).

One way to incorporate the control knowledge from TLPlan into a Satplan encoding is by specifying additional constraints. We have extended the PDDL planning input language (McDermott 1998) of the Blackbox planner to allow for plan control as specified in temporal logic formulas.[1] The control knowledge is automatically translated into a class of additional propositinal clauses, which are added to the planning formula. We will discuss below the kinds of control that can be efficiently translated into a set of constraints, as well as the rules that cannot be captured efficiently.

Using a detailed experimental evaluation, we will show that control knowledge can indeed speed up the plan search significantly in the Blackbox framework. We also provide a detailed comparison with TLPlan. As we will see, our planner becomes competitive with the TLPlan performance. Initially, this was somewhat of a disappointment to us because we assumed that the Blackbox framework with control should be able to outperform TLPlan with the same control. However, a closer inspection of the results clarified the difference in approaches.

TLPlan is good at finding plans with a relatively few actions but it does not do well in domains that allow for parallel actions. In particular, we studied the logistics planning domain. This domain involves the task of delivering a set of packages to a number of different locations using one or more planes and vehicles. When several planes are available, one can find parallel plans, where different packages are moved using different planes simultaneously, allowing one to minimize the overall time span of the plan. Much of the combinatorics of the domain arises from the problem of finding good ways to interleave the movements of packages and planes. The sophisticated control in TLPlan will dramatically narrow the search. However, combined with the depth-first forward chaining strategy, the planner generates highly sequential plans. In fact, on the larger

---

[1]Source code and data available from the first author.

problems, the plan will use a single plane to deliver all packages. (Such plans can actually be found in polynomial time.) Blackbox, on the other hand, naturally searches for the shortest parallel plan because it operates by searching plans that fit within a certain number of time steps. So, although both planners with control find plans in comparable amounts time, Blackbox produces plans that have a much higher level of parallelism, thereby tackling the true combinatorial nature of the underlying planning problem. It is not clear how TLPlan can be made to generate more parallel plans. (We decribe several attempts to increase TLPlan's parallelism below.) Which planner should be preferred will depend on one's application and the level of inherent parallelism in the domain.

We believe our analysis provides new insights into the relative performance of different state-of-the-art planning methods. We hope that our findings can be used to further enhance these methods, and in general deepen our understanding of the design space of planning systems (Kambhampati 1997).

Temporal Logic for Control

In TLPlan the control knowledge is encoded in temporal logic formulas (Bacchus and Kabanza 1996; 1998). The best way to introduce this approach is by considering an example control formula:

$$\Box\, (\forall\, [p : airplane(p)]\exists\, [l : at(p, l)]$$
$$\forall\, [o : in\_wrong\_city(o, l)] \quad in(o, p) \Rightarrow \bigcirc in(o, p))$$

In temporal logic, $\Box f$ means f is true in all states from the current state on and $\bigcirc f$ means f is true in the next state. Therefore, the above formula can be read as "If a package o is in airplane p, p is at location l, and l is not in o's goal city, then package o should stay in airplane p in the *next* time step", and the above sentence should "always" hold. Predicate in_wrong_city is defined as follows:

$$in\_wrong\_city(o, l) \equiv$$
$$\exists\, [g{:}\text{GOAL}(at(o, g))]\, \exists\, [c : in\text{-}city(l, c)]\, \neg in\text{-}city(g, c)$$

After careful review of the control rules used by Bacchus and Kabanza, we found that the rules can be classified into the following categories:

I Control that involves only static information derivable from the initial state and goal state;

II Control that depends on the current state and can be captured using only static user-defined predicates;

III Control that depends on the current state and requires dynamic user-defined predicates.

The meaning of these categories may not be immediately obvious. Hopefully, the detailed examples below will clarify the distinctions. We will focus on two different ways of incoporating control: by pruning the planning graph (rules from category I), and and by adding additional propositional clauses to the planning formula (rules from categories I and II). The rules in catergory III cannot be captured compactly.

Control by Pruning the Planning Graph

Graphplan constructs a special graph structure, called the planning graph, from the initial plan specification. Graphplan uses this graph to search for a plan leading from the intial state to the goal state. Blackbox translates the graph into a propositional encoding and then uses various SAT solution methods to search for a satisfying assignment, which corresponds to a plan. (This strategy closely mimics the original Satplan approach using linear encodings generated directly from a set of logical axiom schemas.) The planning graph contains two types of nodes, proposition nodes ("facts") and action nodes, arranged into levels indexed by time.

We can use a control formula to directly prune nodes in this planning graph. Consider the following control rule (category I) in the logistics domain.

Rule 1 Do not unload an object from an airplane unless the object is at its goal destination.

To illustrate this rule, suppose object `obj-1` is initially located in city `A` and its destination location is in city `C`. Once `obj-1` is loaded into an airplane `plane-1`, it is not necessary to unload `obj-1` at the airports in cities other than `C`. In other words, action (UNLOAD-AIRPLANE `obj-1` `plane-1` `B-airport`) can be removed from the planning graph at all levels (provided that B is another city). After pruning these nodes, one can also prune, facts nodes (`at obj-1 B-airport`), since this cannot be achieved by any other action except for the one we just pruned.

In constructing the planning graph, the planner can be instructed to prune action nodes in the plan-graph as implied by the category I rules. In our implementation, rule #1 is captured by augmenting the original PDDL (Mcdermott 1998) planning language as follows:

```
(:action UNLOAD-AIRPLANE
  :parameters (?obj ?airplane ?loc)
  :precondition
    (and (obj ?obj) (airplane ?airplane)
         (location ?loc) (in ?obj ?airplane)
         (at ?airplane ?loc))
  :effect
    (and (not (in ?obj ?airplane))
         (at ?obj ?loc)))

(:defpredicate in_wrong_city
 :parameters (?obj ?loc)
 (exists (?goal_loc)
   (goal (at ?obj ?goal_loc))
     (exists (?city) (in-city ?loc ?city)
       (not (in-city ?goal_loc ?city)))))

(:action UNLOAD-AIRPLANE
 :exclude (in_wrong_city ?obj ?loc))
```

The user-defined predicate `in_wrong_city` is used to determine whether a location is the goal location for an object. It is worth noting that the value for predicate `in_wrong_city` can be decided purely based on the information in the goal state. The instantiated action UNLOAD-AIRPLANE will not be added to the planning graph when the predicate (`in_wrong_city ?obj ?loc`) is true. (Note the "exclude" condition in the UNLOAD-AIRPLANE rule.) The `in_wrong_city` predicate is purely an auxiliary predicate, it is not incorporated in the final planning graph.

Before an instantiated action is added into the graph, it will be checked against all exclude conditions for that action; if any of them holds, the action will be pruned and the effects introduced by that action at the next proposition node level may be pruned as well.

Table 1 shows the planning graph size before and after pruning. We see that, in the logistics domain, when applying the category I control rules from TLPlan, the number of nodes is reduced by $\approx 40\%$.

problem	length	#nodes orig.	#nodes w. pruning
log-a	11	4246	2825
log-b	13	5177	3437
log-c	13	6321	3815
log-d	14	9842	5135

Table 1: The effect of graph pruning (category I rules).

This approach can be easily applied to the descendants of Graphplan and Blackbox. However, pruning of the planning graph does require that the rules rely solely on information of the goal state and possibly the initial state. Adding new propositional clauses provides a more powerful mechanism for adding control.

Control by Adding Constraints

For some domain-specific knowledge, which cannot be captured via pruning of the planning graph, we can often add additional clauses to the propositional plan formulation as used in Blackbox to capture the control information. Consider the following control rule (category II):

Rule 2 Do not move an airplane if there is an object in the airplane that needs to be unloaded at that location.

First note that this rule cannot be captured using graph pruning. For example, consider removing the node (FlY-AIRPLANE `plane-1` `city1` `city2`) node in layer i (*i.e.*, time i). Whether this can be done would depend on the truth value of the predicates that indicate what is in `plane-1` at time t, but of course, those truth values are not known in advance and are actually different for different plans. Therefore the node cannot be removed from the graph without the risk of losing certain plans. What we need to do is add clauses to the formula that in effect capture the rule but depend also on truth values of the propositions that indicate what is in the plane.

Logically, the rule can be illustrated as follows:

$$\forall \, pln, loc \, \forall[obj : (\texttt{not (in\_wrong\_city}(obj, loc)))]$$
$$(at(pln, loc, i) \land in(obj, pln, i)) \Rightarrow at(pln, loc, i+1)$$

The following shows how to translate the above rule in our implementation:

```
(:wffctrl w3
 :scope
   (forall (?pln) (airplane ?pln)
     (forall (?loc) (airport ?loc)
       (forall (?obj) (obj ?obj)
         (not (in_wrong_city ?obj ?loc))
 )))
 :precondition
   (and (at ?pln ?loc) (in ?obj ?pln))
 :effect (next (at ?pln ?loc)))
```

The :scope field defines the domain where the rule applies, while :precondition and :effect fields represent the antecedent and consequent for the implication expression which will be added to the propositional formula. As mentioned earlier, predicate in_wrong_city is only used by the system and it will not be added into the formula.

Similary, we can also translate rule #1 into propositional form:

```
(:wffctrl wg6
 :scope
   (forall (?pln) (airplane ?pln)
     (forall (?obj) (obj ?obj)
       (forall (?loc) (airport ?loc)
         (in_wrong_city ?obj ?loc)
 )))
 :precondition
   (and (at ?pln ?loc) (in ?obj ?pln))
 :effect (next (in ?obj ?pln)))
```

Problem	length	before simpl.		after simpl.	
		pruning	prop.	pruning	prop.
		#vars	#vars	#vars	#vars
rocket-a	7	1004	1337	826	826
rocket-a	7	1028	1413	868	868
log-a	11	2175	2709	1505	1511
log-b	13	2657	3287	2182	2182
log-c	13	3109	4197	2582	2590
log-d	14	4241	6151	3547	3551
log-e	15	5159	7818	4285	4285

Table 2: Comparison between planning graph pruning and propositional control of category I control rules.

One important observation about the application of the above rule is that the predicate in_wrong_city does not need to be added to the formula. It simply functions as a filter (indicated by the "scope" keyword) for adding the clauses defined by :precondition and :effect part. By doing so we do not lose any information because the in_wrong_city is static (independent of current state) and completely defined by the goal state. For example, if the goal destination of package1

is in city A, it follows that (in_wrong_city package1 B) is true, independent of the current state. Below, we will see that category III rules involve defined predicates that do not have this property.

One reasonable question to consider is how adding rules of category I using additional clauses compares to the graph pruning approach discussed earlier. In the table 2, we consider the planning formulas as created from the planning graph. (We used the 6 category I control rules from TLPlan.) The first two columns give the number of variables for the two different strategies. As might be expected, planning graph pruning strategy gives the smallest number of variables. However, we also included the result of running a polynomial time simplification procedure (Crawford 1994). As can be seen from the last two columns, the remaining numbers of variables are identical for most formulas, with only some small differences for certain instances. When we checked into the remaining differences, we found that those result from some specialized additional pruning Blackbox does specifically for the final layer of the planning graph. Overall, table 2 shows that direct graph pruning or a coding via additional clauses leads to formulas on essentially the same set of variables. (We also verified that the variables actually refer to the same planning propositions in terms of the original planning problem.) As a result, the two mechanisms are essentially equivalent, although they do capture the planning problem using a different clause set. Below we will compare the computational properties of these two approaches.

Rules With No Compact Encoding

We now consider the category III rules. Although these rules can be translated into additional propositional constraints in principle, they do lead to an impractical number of large clauses to be added to the formula. Consider the following rule from TLPlan:

Rule 3 Do not move a vehicle to a location unless, (1) the location is where we want the vehicle to be in the goal, (2) there is an object at that location that needs to be picked up, or (3) there is an object in the vehicle that needs to be unloaded at that location.

The main purpose of rule #3 is to avoid unnecessary move of vehicles. First of all, the rule requires current state information, and therefore cannot be handled by graph pruning. Secondly, in order to translate the rule into propositional constraints, we need to introduce extra predicates to represent the idea that there is an object in the destination location that needs to be loaded or unloaded by the vehicle. For example, in order to avoid unnecessary move of airplanes (a form of vehicle), one way to to encode it is to define predicate *need_to_move_by_airplane* for each airport first:

$$\forall apt \, \forall[obj : \texttt{in\_wrong\_city}(obj, \texttt{apt})]$$
$$at(obj, apt, i) \Rightarrow need\_to\_move\_by\_airplane(apt, i)$$

$$\forall apt \, need\_to\_move\_by\_airplane(apt, i) \Rightarrow$$
$$\exists[obj : \texttt{in\_wrong\_city}(obj, \texttt{apt})] \, at(obj, apt, i)$$

Problem	length	blackbox time	blackbox(I_a) time	blackbox(I_b) time	blackbox(II) time	blackbox(I_a&II) time	blackbox(I_b&II) time
rocket-a	7	2.06	4.20	3.41	2.10	3.92	3.82
rocket-b	7	2.87	2.09	2.46	3.26	1.85	2.49
logistics-a	11	3.80	2.78	3.64	3.74	2.78	3.63
logistics-b	13	4.83	3.46	4.56	4.75	3.41	4.66
logistics-c	13	6.75	3.89	5.64	6.71	3.94	5.81
logistics-d	14	15.85	7.29	10.4	15.69	6.82	10.23
logistics-e	15	3522	151	201	2553	60	148
logistics-1	9	4.80	3.68	4.97	4.83	3.70	4.98
logistics-2	11	406	>7200	270	360	130	141
tire-a	12	1.37	1.34	1.35	1.36	1.33	1.34
tire-b	30	114	93	72	55	21	23

Table 3: Blackbox with control knowledge. Experiments were run on a 300Mhz Sparc Ultra. Times are given in cpu seconds.

I_a: Category I control knowledge used for pruning planning graph.
I_b: Category I control knowledge added in propositional form.
II: Category II control knowledge added in propositional form.

Similarly, we can also define an extra predicate *need_to_unload_by_airplane*. And finally, we will need the following to translate the rule:

$\forall pln \, \forall [apt1, apt2, (not \, (= apt1 \, apt2))]$
$(at(pln, apt1, i) \land$
$\neg need\_to\_unload\_by\_airplane(apt2, i) \land$
$\neg need\_to\_move\_by\_airplane(apt2, i))$
$\Rightarrow \neg at(pln, apt2, i+1)$

Suppose there are n objects, m cities, and k airplanes. The encoding will introduce $O(mn)$ predicates and $O(mn + km^2)$ propositional clauses in each time step. Furthermore, some of them are lengthy clauses, containing up to mn number of literals. We explored adding this kind of control information to our formulas but, except for the smallest planning problems, the formulas become too large for our SAT solvers. The key difference with a category II rule (such as rule #2) is that in this case we also need to add clauses that capture our defined predicates, such as *need_to_move_by_airplane*. This is in contrast with the encoding of, *e.g.*, rule #2, where, because of the static nature of the defined predicates, they can simply be used as a filter when adding clauses (see discussion on :scope above). This cannot be done for our *need_to_move_by_airplane* because its truth value depends on where a package is at the current time. As a consequence, the category III rules are examples of rules that cannot effectively be captured into a constraint-based planner, such as Blackbox. Fortunately, as we will see below, in terms of computational efficiency the category I and II rules appear to do most of the work, at least in the domains we considered. An interesting research question is whether there is a more effective way to encode rules such as rule #3.

Empirical Evaluation

The testbed used in this paper is a series of problems from the logistics planning domain and the rocket domain (Veloso 1992; Blum and Furst 1995; Kautz and Selman 1996; Mcdermott 1998), and the tire-world domain from the TLPlan distribution (Bacchus and Kabanza 1998). In addition, we created two new problem instances: logistics-1 and logistics-2, which can be solved with highly parallel plans (up to 20 actions in parallel).

Table 3 gives the result of Blackbox running on problems with different levels of domain knowledge. The column labeled "Blackbox" gives the runtime without any control knowledge. Subsequent columns give results for the different control strategies. (Results of randomized solvers were averaged over 10 runs. We used 6 category I rules and 5 category II rules.) As a general observation, we note that the effect of control knowledge becomes more apparent for the larger problem instances. For example, on our hardest problem, "logistics-e", basic Blackbox takes almost one hour, but with control (catergory Ia & II) it only takes 60 seconds. The results on the larger instances are more significant than those for the smaller problems, because the solution times on the smaller instances are often dominated by basic I/O operations such as reading the formula from disk, as opposed to the actual compute time for solving the formulas.

Based on the table, we can make the following observations:

- Control information does reduce the solution time, especially on the harder problem instances. Consider the data on logistics-e, logistics-2, and tire-b.

- Control category I rules, encoded via graph pruning and as additional clauses (columns Ia &Ib) lead to roughly the same speedup on the larger problems. One notable exception is the logistics-2 problem, where the solution time actually goes up for strategy Ia. This is most likely a consequence of the fact that clauses are eliminated by the pruning, lead-

problem	tlplan-dfs			blackbox(I_a&II)			tlplan-rand-dfs		
	length	#action	time	length	#action	time	length	#action	time
logistics-a	13	51	0.49	11	72	2.78	15	57	0.66
logistics-b	15	42	0.4	13	71	3.41	15	46	0.43
logistics-c	17	51	0.64	13	83	3.94	15	55	0.72
logistics-d	26	70	2.13	14	104	6.82	18	75	2.43
logistics-e	24	89	4.27	15	107	60	23	96	4.57
logistics-1	15	44	0.9	9	77	3.70	15	49	1.01
logistics-2	29	93	33.16	11	147	130	16	100	34.52

Table 4: Comparison between TLPlan and Blackbox.

ing to less propagation in the SAT solver. We do not see this problem when the knowledge is added via additional clauses (Ib), which therefore appears to be a more robust strategy. The smaller problems instances are already solved within a few seconds by basic Blackbox: not much can be gained from control (again, partly because I/O dominates the overall times).

- Category I rules are most effective on problems from the logistics domain; category II rules are more effective in the tireworld. One interesting research issues is whether one can identify in advance which kinds of rules are most effective. (Measurements such as clause-to-variable ratios and degree of unit propagation may be useful here.)

- The effect of control is largely cumulative. Our category I rules combined with category II lead to the best overall performance (see columns Ia&II and Ib&II).

Next, we compare the performance of TLPlan and Blackbox. Table 4 gives our results. We note that, in general, TLPlan is still somewhat faster than Blackbox with similar control. Note that both planners now use the same control information except for some category III rules in TLPlan. However, the differences are much smaller than with the original Blackbox without control (Table 3 and Bacchus and Kabanza 1998). We believe these results demonstrate that we can meet the challenge, proposed by Bacchus and Kabanza, to effectively incorporate declarative control as used in TLPlan into a constraint-based planner. Nevertheless, as noted in the introduction, we were somewhat disappointed that Blackbox with control was not faster than the TLPlan approach, given the more sophisticated search of the SAT solvers. In order to get a better understanding of the issues involved, we consider the plan quality of the genrated plans.

Table 4 gives plan length in terms of number of actions and parallel time steps for the logistics domain. Note that the logistics domain allows for a substantial amount of parallelism because several planes can fly simultaneously. We see that TLPlan often finds plans with fewer actions; however, in term of parallel lengths the plans are much longer than those found by Blackbox. In fact, Blackbox because of its plan represen-

tation can often find the minimal length parallel plan. Especially on the larger problems, we observe a substantial difference. For example, on logistics-e, TLPlan requires 24 time steps versus 15 for Blackbox. After a closer look at the plans generated by TLPlan, we found plans that only use a single plane to transport the packages. Such plans can be found very fast (polynomial time) but ignore much of the inherent combinatorics of the domain. The reason TLPlan finds such plans is a consequence of its control rules and the depth-first search strategy.

It is not clear how one can improve the (parallel) quality of the plans generated by TLPlan. Part of the difficulty lies in the fact that the control knowledge is taylored towards more sequential plans. For example, rules that keep a plane from flying if there are still packages to be picked up at a location. (This prevents a plan where another plane picks up the package later.) In addition, the depth-first style search also tends to steer the planner towards more sequential plans (e.g., always picking plane-1 to move). We experimented with several different search strategies to try to improve the plans generated by TLPlan. First, we checked wether the parallel quality of plans obtained with breadth first search was better. This does not appear to be the case. (We could only check this on very small instances, because the search quickly runs out of memory.) An approach that does lead to some improvement is to randomize the depth-first search. Table 4 shows some improvement in parallel length but still not close to the minimal possible. The reason for the improvement is that TLPlan now can pick different planes more easily in its branching. (The deterministic depth-first search repeatedly selects planes in the same order.) It is an interesting question how TLPlan can be made to find more parallel plans and how this would affect its performance.

Conclusions

Intuitively speaking, the control in TLPlan attempts to push the planning problem into a polynomial solvable problem. This is along the lines of the general focus in planning on eliminating or avoiding search as much as possible.[2] TLPlan achieves its objective in a very elegant manner because the control rules are quite intuitive and purely declarative. In combination with the forward chaining planner, the rules do lead to polynomial scaling in a number of interesting domains. Our analysis shows that there is a price to be paid for this gain in efficiency, which is the loss of much of the parallel nature of many planning tasks.[3]

We have shown that one can obtain the benefits of the control rules in terms of efficiency, without paying the price of reduced parallelism, by incorporating the control rules in the Blackbox planner. In a sense, the SAT solvers in Blackbox still tackle the combinatorial aspect of the task but the extra constraints provide substantial additional pruning of the search space.

We implemented the system by enhancing the Blackbox planner with a parser for temporal logic control rules, which are translated in additional propositional clauses. We also showed that a subset of the control (category I rules) can also be handled by direct pruning of the planning graph. Our experimental results show a speedup due to the search control of up to order of magnitude on our problem domains. Given the effectiveness of the control, it would be interesting to add further constraints, such as state invariants (Fox and Long 1998; Gerevini and Schubert 1998; Kautz and Selman 1998).

We believe our work demonstrates that declarative control knowledge can be used effectively in constraint-planners without loss of (parallel) plan quality. Compared to TLPlan, which is a highly efficient planner in and of itself, the main advantage of our approach is that we maintain parallel plan quality. Overall, incorporating declarative control in constraint-based planning appears to be a promising research direction. With more sophisticated control, another order of magnitude speedup may be achievable.

Another fascinating direction for future research is the possible use of rule-based learning techniques for acquiring control knowledge automatically by "training" the planner on a sequence of smaller problems. Learning of control knowledge has been explored previously for other, more procedural, planners. See, for example, Etzioni (1993), Knoblock (1994), Minton (1988), and Veloso (1992). We are currently exploring forms of control rule learning in our declarative constraint-based framework.

Acknowledgements

We thank Fahiem Bacchus, Carla Gomes, Dana Nau, and Dan Weld for many useful comments and suggestions. The second author received support from by an NSF Career grant and a Sloan Fellowship.

---

[2] Austin Tate is said to have said "If you need to search, you're dead."

[3] Given that these planning problems are NP-complete, it is clear that something will be lost by solving them in polynomial time.

References

Bacchus, F. and Kabanza, F. (1996). Using temporal logic to control search in a forward-chaining planner. In *New Dir. in Planning*, M. Ghallab and A. Milani (Eds.), IOS Press.

Bacchus, F. and Kabanza, F. (1998). Using Temporal Logics to Express Search Control Knowledge for Planning. See http://www.lpaig.uwaterloo.ca/~fbacchus/online.html.

Baioletti, M. , Marcugini, S., and Milani, A. (1998). C-SATPlan: a SATPlan-based tool for planning with constraints. AIPS-98 Wrks. on Planning as Combinatorial Search, Pittsburgh, PA.

Blum, A. and Furst, M.L. (1995). Fast planning through planning graph analysis. *Proc. IJCAI-95*, Canada.

Crawford, C. (1984). Compact: A fast simplifier of Boolean formulas. Available via Crawford's web page.

Ernst, M.D., Millstein, T.D., and Weld, D.S. (1997). Automatic SAT-compilation of planning problems. *Proc. IJCAI-97*, Nagoya, Japan.

Etzioni, Oren (1993). Acquiring search-control knowledge via static analysis. *Artificial Intelligence*, 62(2), 255–302.

Fikes, R. E., and Nilsson, N. 1971. STRIPS: A New Approach to the Application of Theorem Proving to Problem Solving. *Artificial Intelligence* 5(2): 189-208.

Fox, M., and Long, D. 1998. The automatic inference of state invariants in TIM. Forthcoming.

Geffner, H. (1998). HSP: Heuristic Search Planner, Working notes of the Workshop on Planning as Combinatorial Search, Pittsburgh, PA, 1998.

Gerevini, A. and Schubert, L. 1998. Inferring state constraints for domain-independent planning. *Proc AAAI-98*, Madison, WI.

Kambhampati, S. (1997). Challenges in bridging plan synthesis paradigms. *Proc. IJCAI-97*, Nagoya, Japan.

Kautz, H. and Selman, B. (1992). Planning as satisfiability. *Proc. ECAI-92*, Vienna, Austria, 359–363.

Kautz, H. and Selman, B. (1996). Pushing the envelope: planning, propositional logic, and stochastic search. *Proc. AAAI-1996*, Portand, OR.

Kautz, H. and Selman, B. (1998). The role of domain-specific axioms in the planning as satisfiability framework. *Proc. AIPS-98*, Pittsburgh, PA.

Kautz, H. and Selman, B. (1999). Unifying SAT-based and Graph-based planning. *Proc. IJCAI-99*, to appear.

Knoblock, C. (1994). Automatically generating abstractions for planning. *Artificial Intelligence* 68(2).

Koehler, J., Nebel, B., Hoffmann, J., and Dimopoulos, Y. (1997). Extending planning graphs to an ADL subset. *Proc. 4th European Conf. on Planning*, S. Steel, ed., vol. 1248 of *LNAI*, Springer.

McDermott, D., *et al.* (1998). PDDL — the planning domain definition language. Draft.

Minton, S. (1988). Quantitative results concerning the utility of explanation-based learning. *Proc. AAAI-88*, St. Paul, MN, 564–569.

Veloso, M. (1992). Learning by analogical reasoning in general problem solving. Ph.D. Thesis, CMU, CS Techn. Report CMU-CS-92-174.

Weld, D. *et al.* (1999). Recent advances in AI planning. AI Magazine (to appear). Available from author's web site.

A Framework for Recognizing Multi-Agent Action
from Visual Evidence

Stephen S. Intille   Aaron F. Bobick

Perceptual Computing Group
MIT Media Laboratory
Cambridge, Massachusetts, MA 02139
`intille | bobick @media.mit.edu`

Abstract

A probabilistic framework for representing and visually recognizing complex multi-agent action is presented. Motivated by work in model-based object recognition and designed for the recognition of action from *visual evidence*, the representation has three components: (1) temporal structure descriptions representing the temporal relationships between agent goals, (2) belief networks for probabilistically representing and recognizing individual agent goals from visual evidence, and (3) belief networks automatically generated from the temporal structure descriptions that support the recognition of the complex action. We describe our current work on recognizing American football plays from noisy trajectory data.[1]

Keywords: action recognition, plan recognition, representing visual uncertainty

Introduction

Evaluating whether an observed set of visual phenomena constitute a particular dynamic event requires representation and recognition of temporal relationships and uncertain information. The goal of this paper is to present a new approach to the representation and recognition of complex multi-agent probabilistic actions. By *complex* we simply mean that the action contains many components that occur in, typically, a partially ordered temporal relation to one another, subject to certain logical constraints (e.g. A happens `before` B, B is `before` C or D, but only one of C or D can occur). These relations generally reflect causal connections or influences between components. The actions we are considering are *multi-agent*, resulting in parallel event streams that interact in interesting temporal (typically causal) ways.

By *probabilistic* we refer to the uncertain nature of both the model and the data. The action description itself is typically probabilistic: e.g. B follows A, but only 80% of the time. This uncertainty results from complex actions defined

---
[1]This research was funded by Office of Research and Development (ORD) contracts 94-F133400-000 and 97-F157800-000.

by typical components that are only sometimes observed due to uncertainty in the world. Another source of uncertainty is the fuzziness of attributes used to describe agent interaction (e.g. `obj1` is `near` `obj2`). Finally, the design of the representation is intended to support recognition and we therefore need to consider real sensing capabilities, which are probabilistic at best. Often, perceptual evidence can be either missed or hallucinated.

There are numerous domains that contain interesting, complex, probabilistic actions. Examples include sporting events, military and security surveillance, traffic monitoring, and robotic collaboration. The task and domain developed here is recognizing American football plays. It has the necessary attributes of containing complex actions (plays) performed by a multi-agent system (the offense) in which there is great uncertainty and unpredictability (the defense). Methods exist for tracking football players from video (Intille & Bobick 1995). For the recognition task, we presume tracked data that provides the location and rough orientation of each player at each time during the play. Our current system uses a database of 29 manually, though noisily, tracked plays. Figure 1 shows 3 "chalkboard" image examples of 3 different observations of a "p51curl" play.

An analogy to object recognition

At the heart of our approach to complex action recognition is an idea developed within the context of model-based object recognition. The task there is to match a given object model to an image from which edge elements have been extracted. One of the more successful approaches to this problem is that of using feature-model interpretation matching trees, where the visual features are edge segments (Grimson & Lozano-Pérez 1987). Each layer of the tree represents a given model edge. The fanouts of each node span the potential image edge fragments that might match the given model edge of the given layer. A *hypothesis* is a path from the root to the leaves that specifies the match of each model edge to specific image features.

The goal, of course, is to find the correct hypotheses. However the number of edges make exhaustive search computationally prohibitive. Rather, the approach is to find a *consistent* hypothesis, and assume that consistency implies correctness. As developed in (Grimson & Lozano-Pérez

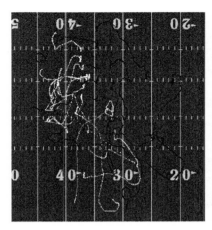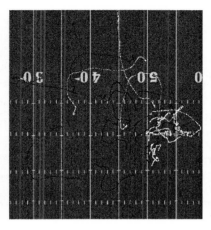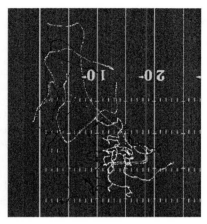

Figure 1: Three examples of a p51curl play. The lighter trajectories are the offensive players. The data provided to the system consists of trajectories for all the objects including the ball, the approximate orientation of each object at each point along its trajectory, and a position label for each trajectory.

1987) the *order of the consistency* can be varied depending upon computational resources and accuracy requirements. For example, if we restrict our attention to two-dimensional objects, a unary consistency check simply requires that each model edge is at least as long as the proposed matching image edge. A binary consistency check verifies not only the unary relations but also all pairwise relationships, namely the angle and bounded distance between edges.

Grimson and Lozano-Pérez (Grimson & Lozano-Pérez 1987) note that although it is mathematically possible for an incorrect interpretation to satisfy the binary relations but not higher order relations, the probability of an object doing so falls precipitously as object complexity increases. This allows them to construct heuristic pruning methods that search for the correct interpretation by only maintaining binary consistency. It is this idea, *that massive low order consistency typically implies correctness,* that drives our approach to recognizing complex actions.

Our approach

The approach we have developed consists of the following representational elements:

- We first define a *temporal structure description* of the global behavior, in this case a football play. The basic elements of this structure represent individual, local goals or events that must be detected. The relations coded in the structure are temporal constraints to be verified.

- For each basic element of the temporal structure, we define a *visual network* that detects the occurrence of the individual goal or event at a given time accounting for uncertain information.

- Temporal analysis functions are defined which evaluate the validity of a particular temporal relationships, such as `before`.

- A large multi-agent belief network is automatically constructed reflecting the temporal structure of the action.

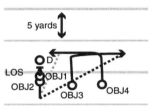

Figure 2: An football play diagramming the s51 example play. The play consists of 4 offensive agents and a ball. Also marked is the line-of-scrimmage (LOS) and some 5-yard marker yardlines. The heavy dotted line indicates the most typical path for the ball when it is thrown by OBJ2 after the ball is handed to OBJ2 from OBJ1. The lighter dotted line indicates a secondary pass option. Implicit is that OBJ3 and OBJ4 turn at the same time.

This network, similar in structure to a naive Bayesian classifier, represents a particular play using *only* beliefs and evidence about the expected temporal relationships between agent goals.

The likelihood that a particular play has been observed is computed by evaluating the appropriate belief networks.

s51 play example

The task for a recognition system is to recognize whether a given set of trajectory inputs like those illustrated by Figure 1 corresponds to a particular type of play, such as the p51curl. Normally plays consist of 11 offensive players. A simplified example of a p51curl play, called the "s51," containing only 4 offensive players and a reduced number of actions per player will be used for illustration in this paper. The s51 chalkboard diagram is shown in Figure 2.

The input to the system consists of trajectories given by (x,y,orientation,label) tuples as a function of the frame number, i.e. time. Here, *orientation* denotes the approximate upper-body orientation of the player and *label* is the name of the player's starting position.

Prior work

Prior multi-agent plan recognition work can be roughly divided into two methods. Some approaches have an explicit representation for group intentionality (e.g. (Grosz & Kraus 1996)), typically using modal logics. Other approaches "compile down" intentional reasoning into procedural components, trading off the ability to reason about complex intentional interaction for computational tractability in domains with noisy evidence detectors. Our hypothesis is that for some useful recognition tasks visually-detected agent-based goals can be "compiled" into efficient and powerful classifier networks using binary temporal relationships between detected goals.

Promising work on recognizing single-agent action from trajectory information using transition diagrams and fuzzy reasoning (Nagel *et al.* 1995) led us to investigate the use of belief networks for multi-agent action recognition, which more explicitly represent knowledge dependencies and are computationally well-understood. Bayesian networks have been used to relax the strict assumptions of plan hierarchy models such as (Kautz & Allen 1986). For example, networks can represent multiple top-level goals where probabilistic priors can be used to rank two equally possible but not equally likely plans (Charniak & Goldman 1993). Further, they have been used to integrate "action patterns" and beliefs about an agent's mental state (Pynadath & Wellman 1995). Previous work in traffic understanding has used an agent-based belief network and agent-centered features for recognition of driving activity from simulated (Forbes *et al.* 1995) and real data (Buxton & Gong 1995; Huang *et al.* 1994). Unlike that work our task requires that the system must also represent the logical and temporal relationships between multiple agents. Remagnino, Tan, and Baker (Remagnino, Tan, & Baker 1998) recently described a pedestrian and car tracking and surveillance system that models the interaction between any two agents using a small belief network. Dynamic belief networks (DBNs) and hidden Markov models (HMMs) have been used with some success but have not been demonstrated to be appropriate for domains in which multi-agent relationships result in large feature spaces and in which large and complete data sets for training are unavailable.

Although some search-based systems for recognizing multi-agent goals and actions have been proposed (Retz-Schmidt 1988; Azarewicz, Fala, & Heithecker 1989; Tambe 1996), noisy visual data requires a representation that can handle uncertainty. (Devaney & Ram 1998) have demonstrated that pairwise comparison of features between trajectories can be used to recognize some group military behaviors for large numbers of agents.

Huber has shown that simple goal recognition belief networks can be constructed automatically from representations of action used for a plan generation system and then used by a planning agent in a multi-object scene (Huber 1996). Our approach builds on Huber's work of automatic

```
(goalTeam s51
 "Team goal for simple-p51curl (s51) play."

  (agentGoal obj1
    (agent (obj1 (C))) ; Obj1 is always the Center (C)
    (goal obj1_act1 "snapToQB (obj1)")
    (goal obj2_act2 "blockQBPass (obj1)")
    (before obj1_act1 obj1_act2))

  (agentGoal obj2
    (agent (obj2 (QB))) ;Obj2 is always the Quarterback (QB)
    (goal obj1_act1 "dropback (obj2 5)")
    (goal obj2_act2 "throwPass (obj2)")
    (before obj2_act1 obj2_act2))

  (agentGoal obj3 ;The Right Wing Back (RWB)
    (agent (obj3 (RWB RTE RHB HB FB TB LWB LSB)))
    (goal obj3_act1 "passPatStreaking
                      (obj3 4 45 defReg nearRightSidelineReg 0)")
    (goal obj3_act2 "passPatCutting (obj3 70 offSidelineRightReg
                                      freeBlockingZoneReg)")
    (goal obj3_act3 "runbehind (obj3 obj4)")
    (goal obj3_act4 "passPatParaLos
                      (obj3 3 defReg offSidelineRightReg 4)")
    (goal obj3_act5 "catchPass (obj3)")
    (before obj3_act1 obj3_act2)
    (before obj3_act2 obj3_act4))

  (agentGoal obj4 ;The Right Flanker (RFL)
    (agent (obj4 (RFL RWB RSB LFL LSB LWB)))
    (goal obj4_act1 "passPatStreaking
                      (obj4 4 50 defReg offEndZoneReg 0)")
    (goal obj4_act2 "passPatCutting (obj4 70 offSidelineLeftReg
                                      freeBlockingZoneReg)")
    (goal obj4_act3 "passPatParaLos
                      (obj4 3 defReg offCenterLineReg 4)")
    (goal obj4_act4 "catchPass (obj4)")
    (before obj4_act1 obj4_act2)
    (before obj4_act2 obj4_act3))

  (around obj3_act2 obj4_act2)
  (xor obj3_act5 obj4_act4))
```

Figure 3: A temporal structure description for the *s51* play example with only some actions and temporal relationships specified.

construction of networks.

The remaining sections of this paper describe each component of our representation and some recognition results.

Temporal structure description

The temporal structure description represents the prototypical scenario of the described action. It is comprised of fundamental behavior elements connected by temporal constraints. We assume that the complex actions we wish to recognize have such a prototype and that they can be expressed with this language.

Individual goals and behaviors

We use individual agent *goals* as the basis for the descriptive structure and view complex actions as a partially ordered set of goal directed behaviors on the part of interacting agents. We *define* goals by their (probabilistic) characteristic behaviors, building on work in probabilistic plan recognition (Charniak & Goldman 1993). To evaluate whether an agent has a particular goal at a particular time we will evaluate the perceptual evidence.

For example, the halfback can have the goal of running between the tackle and the guard. To determine if indeed he has such a goal a recognition system must evaluate the visual evidence, particularly the position of the tackle and the guard and the direction of motion of the halfback. The interaction of multiple agents and the reaction of agents to the movement of other agents can lead to large variations in some movement, as indicated by the examples in Figure 1. However, at any given time, evidence detected in a local space-time window can indicate that an agent has a particular goal. Later we will more fully detail the construction of belief networks that serve as the definition of the individual agent goals.

Goal action components

Figure 3 shows a simplified temporal structure description for the s51 example in Figure 2. The description contains four agents: obj1, obj2, obj3, and obj4. Each object in the temporal structure graph has a set of goal action components. The example indicates that in an s51 play, obj1 should have a goal to snapToQB (snap (or hand) the ball to the quarterback) and blockQBPass (block for the QB as the QB passes the ball). Each goal has a label, such as obj1_act1 (short for object1's action1). The s51 example has been limited to just six goal types: snapToQB, blockQBPass, passPatStreaking, passPatCutting, passPatParaLos, and catchPass. The detector for each goal type receives a list of parameters.[2]

Object assignment

The trajectories in our dataset are labeled using standard football position notations (e.g. QB, C, HB). However, since all football plays can be run from several different starting formations (so that the defense cannot determine the play from the starting formation of the offense), the temporal structure description must indicate the valid position types for each object. In the example description in Figure 3, the agent slot of the agentGoal obj3 description indicates that object obj3 can possibly match with a trajectory if the trajectory has one of labels (RWB RTE RHB HB FB TB LWB LSB). This list is a preference ordering. obj3 will most often be the RFL, then the RWB, and so on. Given the preference orders for all objects, a *consistent* assignment of trajectory data to the play description must be made. Here our system finds the single most consistent interpretation using preference assignments, the constraint that all trajectories must be assigned to an object in the temporal structure description, and a heuristic scoring function. Due to space limitations this matching process is not discussed further.

Temporal constraints

The remaining slots in the the temporal structure description indicate the temporal and logical relationships between agent goals. Two temporal primitives are available: *before* and *around*. For example, "(before obj1_act1 obj1_act2)" indicates that goal obj1_act1 occurs before obj1_act2, where

obj1_act1 is the label for "snapToQB (obj1)" and obj2_act2 is the label for "blockQBPass (obj1)". Similarly, "(around obj3_act2 obj4_act2)" indicates that object3's passPatCutting goal occurs around the same time as object4's passPatCutting goal. The meanings of "before" and "around" will be defined shortly. Finally, "(xor obj3_act5 obj4_act4)" indicates that object3's catchPass goal xor object4's catchPass goal should be observed.

By assumption, the goals of an agent are active during temporal intervals of finite duration; they are not instantaneous events. As such, Allen's interval algebra (Allen 1983) applies and there are potentially 7 possible temporal relations (not counting inverses). However, that algebra requires precise definition of the endpoints of the intervals. Our ability to assign goals to agents based upon perceptual evidence will be fuzzy, allowing us only to assign a graded value that varies over time. In the ideal case there would be a nice peak or plateau in the probability a goal is active during a temporal window, but real data is rarely ideal.

Note that our temporal constraints do not support most temporal implications. For example, the temporal relation of simultaneity is expressed as around which can be interpreted as "about the same time as." Clearly such a 'fuzzy' relation is not transitive and we cannot apply transitive closure to the temporal relations. Rather, we only exploit those relations manually constructed by the knowledge engineer designing the action description.

Visual nets and temporal functions

Previous work has shown that agent goals can be represented in a probabilistic framework using Bayesian belief networks (Charniak & Goldman 1993; Huber 1996; Pynadath & Wellman 1995). We also use belief networks based on visual evidence, or *visual networks*, that offer a rich representation designed to handle uncertainty in evidence, goal models, spatial reasoning, and temporal reasoning. Further, the networks can be used as building blocks for recognizing multi-agent activity.

Network structure and evaluation

A single belief network represents each goal or event and can be instantiated at any time during a play. The networks typically contain between 15 and 25 nodes with a relatively tree-like link complexity and therefore exact propagation algorithms can be used to compute the probabilities of each node state (Pearl 1988). The structure of each network is manually specified. Currently the priors are also manually assigned, however some priors can be obtained from analyzing the evidence and the performance of particular feature detectors.

Figure 4 shows one such network, catchPass. The network consists of two types of nodes: unobservable belief and observable evidence.

Unobservable belief nodes A belief node has two states, *true* and *false*, and represents an internal state of the agent or some external state in the world at the time when the network is evaluated. Each visual network has a designated *main goal node* (e.g. catchPass).

---

[2]For example, passPatCutting takes parameters (obj a toReg inReg). The network encodes detects the following: *Obj*, which must be an eligible receiver, runs a pass pattern segment making a sharp (e.g. about *a* degrees) change in motion in *inReg* after which *obj* is moving in towards the *toReg*.

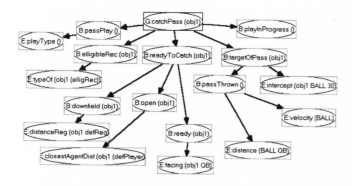

Figure 4: The catchPass goal network.

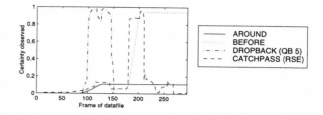

Figure 5: Goal likelihood curves returned by the networks "dropback (QB 5)" and "catchPass (RSE)" superimposed with the corresponding temporal curves for "dropback (QB 5) before catchPass (RSE)" and "dropback (QB 5) around catchPass (RSE)".

Observable evidence nodes An evidence node's states and state values are directly dependent upon the data. Some nodes are binary (e.g. *observed, notObserved*), most are trinary, (e.g. *observed, maybeObserved, notObserved*), and the remainder have specialized states that quantize a particular feature detector output (e.g. the result of the distance detector is quantized into states *inContact, nextTo, near, inVicinity, far, distant*). To maintain continuous valued information, whenever possible evidence is entered as "virtual" likelihood evidence.[3]

The main belief node of each network can accept parameters set by the caller of the network at run-time. For example, goal node catchPass (obj1) accepts one argument, a specific agent. Each network is designed so that it can be applied to any world object and return a reasonable result.

Locality in space-time

Visual networks can be applied to any agent at any time. As much as possible, visual goal networks are designed to use evidence observed locally in space and time. Further, evidence features are typically deictic, or agent centered. For example, networks sometimes compute the distance between the current agent and the *closest agent*.

Because goal networks can make use of dynamic state variables (e.g. snapTime) and the output of other goal networks (e.g. catchPass uses the result of the playInProgress network), the networks are not entirely "closed." Incorporating input from other networks or dynamic state variables violates the belief network assumption that all variable dependencies are modeled via explicit conditional probabilities. We accept this approximation, noting that the networks themselves are simplified approximations to the actual dependency structure and that partitioning actions into small networks simplifies and makes manageable the job of the knowledge engineer.

---

[3] So-called "virtual" evidence, or the relative likelihood of each of the discrete states, is entered into a network to use continuous-valued evidence in a node with discrete evidence states (see (Pearl 1988)). The likelihood is obtained using the relative activation levels of each discrete state which are computed with piecewise linear functions.

We incorporate evidence from an external network, such as the playInProgress evidence node, into a network such as catchPass (obj1) as follows. If the playInProgress network cannot evaluate and returns NIL, no evidence is entered for the node. If the playInProgress network returns a high likelihood of a particular state that exceeds a predetermined threshold for playInProgress, evidence is entered directly into the catchPass network (e.g. if *observed* = .99 and *notObserved* = .01 and threshold(playInProgress) = .85 then *observed* = 1.0 is entered into catchPass). Finally, if playInProgress evaluates below the threshold, the beliefs are treated as direct evidence and the probabilities are converted to likelihood evidence (Pearl 1988) (e.g. if *observed* = .8 and *notObserved* = .2 and threshold(playInProgress) = .85 then the evidence that *observed* is 4 times more likely than *notObserved* will be entered into the catchPass network).

Temporal analysis functions

The output of a visual goal network at each frame for a given object results in a likelihood curve over time. Temporal relationship evidence detectors use these curves as input. The functions compute a certainty value for the *observed*, *before*, and *around* tests at each time frame using heuristic functions that compare the activation levels of each goal over time, characteristics of each input curve, the temporal distance between features of the curves, the amount of overlap between the curves, and a minimal activation time for each goal. The functions are designed to preserve the uncertainty in the output of the visual goal networks and to avoid hard thresholding. Two curves returned by the networks "dropback (QB 5)" and "catchPass (RSE)" are shown in Figure 5 overlaid with the likelihood values for the *before* and *around* detectors corresponding to "dropback (QB 5) before catchPass (RSE)" and "dropback (QB 5) around catchPass (RSE)".

Multi-agent networks

Multi-agent action is recognized using a multi-agent belief network. At each time, the network integrates the likelihood values returned by temporal analysis functions at that time and returns a likelihood that a given play has been observed.

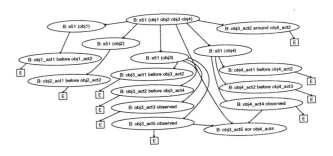

Figure 6: The s51 multi-agent recognition network.

Figure 6 shows an example of a multi-agent network for the s51 play. The network structure is generated *automatically* from the temporal structure description. In the system discussed in this paper, a two-level naive Bayesian classifier network structure is generated that encodes the temporal structure of a play. All nodes in the multi-agent networks represent beliefs or evidence observed over all the play data seen from the start of the play until the current time. The state characterization of all nodes comprises the values (*observed*, *notObserved*). The main node in the example is *B: s51 (obj1 obj2 obj3 obj4)*. Linked to that node is one node for each agent – for example *B: s51 (obj1)* – representing the belief that the agent's goals for the s51 have been observed. Below these nodes are nodes representing:

- Binary temporal relationships between goals (e.g. *B: obj1_act1 before obj1_act2*). These nodes represent the belief that a particular temporal ordering has been *observed* or *notObserved* at some point during the action sequence.

- Evidence for binary temporal relationships (e.g *E: obj1_act1 before obj1_act2*). There is a conditional link from the temporal relation belief node to the evidence. The evidence values are computed by the temporal analysis functions. To avoid cluttering the figure, these nodes are represented with a boxed "E" node.

Temporal relationships between agents are linked directly to the top-level belief node (e.g. see *B: obj3_act2 around obj4_act2*). Additional links can be added for logical relationships, which conditionally link the two related goal observations.

A detector such as *E:obj3_act1 before obj3_act2* implicitly encodes the observation *E:obj3_act1 observed* and *E:obj3_act2*. Therefore, when an agent goal node is temporally compared to some other agent goal node, only the temporal comparison belief node is incorporated into the network. However, some goal actions are not included in any temporal comparisons in the temporal action description. In these cases, the network includes an *observed* belief and evidence node (e.g. *B:obj3_act3 observed*).

Conditional and prior probabilities for the network are determined automatically using heuristics matching table templates to specific node-link combinations, similar to the method used by Huber (Huber 1996). The structure of the

network for the s51 shown in Figure 6 essentially implements a weighted voting scheme between observed goals and temporal relationships between goals.

Experimental evaluation has demonstrated that naive Bayesian networks are surprisingly good classifiers, despite making strict independence assumptions between attributes and the class. Moreover, recent work has shown that augmenting such networks with additional binary conditional dependencies improves classification performance so that it is often better and otherwise comparable to more complex representations, including more highly-connected learned network structures (Friedman & Goldszmidt 1996). Our multi-agent networks are naive classifiers where binary temporal relations between goals have been encoded *within* nodes, not in links between nodes.

The network shown in Figure 6 is only for a play with four agents where the number of actions for each agent is restricted to just a few examples. For a play with 11 agents, the networks typically contain *at least* 50 belief nodes and 40 evidence nodes and often twice that number. Network propagation by exact algorithms is feasible, however, because the network has a shallow tree linking structure and consists of binary internal belief nodes. The temporal analysis functions return continuous valued likelihood information. This information is entered into the multi-play network as continuous evidence, avoiding unnecessary thresholding of uncertain information.

Results

We are using the representation described in this paper in a football play recognition system. The system has knowledge of about 40 region definitions (e.g. line-of-scrimmage), 60 player types (e.g. quarterback, receiver), and ISA relationships between player types (wide-receiver ISA receiver). We have constructed approximately 60 evidence detectors (e.g. distance(closestAgent)) that are applied to the trajectory data and produce probabilistic quantized outputs (e.g. *inContact* = 0.3, *nextTo* = 0.7). We estimate 70 robust visual networks will ultimately be required for recognition of most of the plays in our database, and about 50 of those have been constructed.

We have evaluated our system on 29 tracked plays using a database of 10 temporal play descriptions. Figure 7 shows the likelihood value obtained by evaluating the multi-agent network at each frame for 7 play models on a datafile for a t39 play. Here the desired behavior is achieved: uncertain evidence of temporal relationships between goals is sufficient to cause the t39 play detector's likelihood value to quickly rise above the other plays shortly after the play action begins at frame 90.[4]

Figure 8 is a confusion matrix showing the final likelihood value obtained for each temporal play description when run on 29 example plays. A "-" value indicates a

---

[4] The system requires approximately 1 second of computation per frame per tested play on a 500 MHz Digital Alphastation and could be highly parallelized.

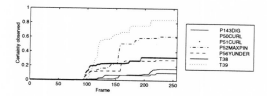

Figure 7: Result of running 7 play detectors on a t39 play example. Shown is the likelihood of each play having been observed at frame t considering all evidence from frames $0 - t$.

play where no good object-to-trajectory consistency match could be found.[5] The examples below the line (i.e. p58 through s35) do not yet have fully implemented temporal play descriptions. The highest likelihood value obtained on each data file (each row) is marked in bold.

Considering only the top portion of the table, the maximum likelihood value along each row selects the correct play for 21 of the 25 play instances. 3 of the 4 errors are caused by p56yunder examples being misclassified as p52maxpin plays. Figure 9, which shows the diagrams for those two plays with a misclassified example approximately overlaid on top demonstrates why the system has difficulty classifying the example. The diagram shows that both plays, when executed perfectly, are similar when the "optional action" is not taken into account. The only large observed difference between the plays is for the rightmost player, who follows a trajectory different from both the p56yunder and the p52maxpin. Our models currently do not include the optional actions, which would contribute evidence to the desired p56yunder classification. We are currently extending the multi-agent networks so they can encode optional compound goals.

The bottom section of the table are the probabilities produced when applying the system to instances of plays for which there is (as yet) no action network. The discouraging result here is that false positives have values comparable to the correct positives above. That is, while our current system is capable of selecting the correct play description, it cannot yet determine when a play does not belong to one of its known categories. One reason for this is that we have not yet completed constructing all the visual networks necessary to provide rich descriptions of the plays. The weaker the model, the more easily it is matched by some incorrect instance. More detailed models will improve the ability of the system to determine that a play is "none of the above."

Overall the results are promising, especially considering the complexity and variation of the input data. We have data to evaluate additional play descriptions but must first complete coding the additional goal networks. Further, the multi-agent belief networks need to be extended to handle compound groups of actions

---

[5]Prior to evaluating a particular multi-agent network, a consistent match between the labeled trajectories and the object label preference orderings must be found. This component of the system is not discussed in this paper.

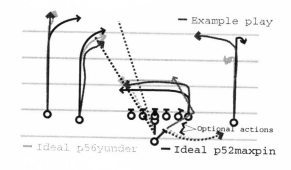

Figure 9: P56yunder and p52maxpin play diagrams with one p56under example play approximately overlaid. The system returned likelihoods of .64 for p56yunder and .76 for p52maxin.

(e.g. player performs `(XOR (goal-a and goal-b) (goal-c and goal-d))` before we can completely characterize the competence of the representation.

Final remarks

We have proposed a representation – motivated by findings in the computer vision object recognition literature and the power of augmented naive Bayesian classifiers – that represents complex, multi-agent action using low-order temporal graphs. The primitives in these graphs are agent-based belief networks that can recognize agent goals by probabilistic integration of visual evidence. Networks with a structure similar to naive classifiers are automatically generated from a simple description of a team play. These networks contain nodes that encode binary spatial and temporal relationships and are small and therefore computationally manageable. We have demonstrated that these networks can recognize multi-agent action for a real domain with noisy input trajectory data. Studying the representational, recognition, and computational properties of the multi-agent networks is the focus of our current work.

References

Allen, J. 1983. Maintaining knowledge about temporal intervals. *Communications of the ACM* 26(11):832–843.

Azarewicz, J.; Fala, G.; and Heithecker, C. 1989. Template-based multi-agent plan recognition for tactical situation assessment. In *Proc. of the Sixth Conference on Artificial Intelligence Applications*, 248–254.

Buxton, H., and Gong, S. 1995. Advanced visual surveillance using Bayesian networks. In *Proc. of the Workshop on Context-Based Vision*, 111–123. Cambridge, MA: IEEE Computer Society Press.

Charniak, E., and Goldman, R. P. 1993. A Bayesian model of plan recognition. *Artificial Intelligence* 64:53–79.

Devaney, M., and Ram, A. 1998. Needles in a haystack: Plan recognition in large spatial domains involving multiple agents. In *Proc. Fifteenth Nat. Conf. on Artificial Intelligence*, 942–947.

Name	p143dig	p50curl	p51curl	p52maxpin	p54maxcross	p56yunder	p63up	p63upa	t38	t39
p143dig (file aa00185)	**.75**	.49	-	-	.37	.33	-	.24	.53	-
p143dig (file aa00412)	**.98**	.63	-	-	.75	.71	-	.57	.65	-
p143dig (file aa00606)	**.93**	.45	-	-	.57	.63	-	.32	.39	-
p143dig (file aa00847)	**.87**	.35	-	-	.53	.49	-	.27	.30	-
p143dig (file aa01032)	**.91**	.42	-	-	.50	.36	-	.60	.41	-
p143dig (file aa02128)	**.86**	.42	-	-	.43	.41	-	.70	.43	-
p143dig (file aa02329)	**.98**	.58	-	-	.85	.65	-	.57	.36	-
p50curl (file aa06046)	.19	**.87**	-	-	-	.44	-	.62	.58	.27
p51curl (file aa10542)	-	.21	**.69**	-	-	.27	.35	.34	-	.58
p51curl (file aa10736)	-	.54	**.95**	-	-	-	-	.55	-	.66
p51curl (file aa11033)	-	-	**.98**	-	-	-	-	.82	.09	.68
p52maxpin (file aa14122)	-	-	.37	**.93**	-	.66	.88	-	-	-
p54maxcross (file aa19487)	.55	.55	.37	.57	**.97**	.48	-	.77	-	-
p56yunder (file aa28294)	-	-	.47	-	-	**.63**	-	-	-	-
p56yunder (file aa29325)	-	-	.24	.51	-	**.69**	.39	-	-	-
p56yunder (file aa29486)	-	-	.75	.88	-	**.83**	.72	-	-	-
p56yunder (file aa30045)	.61	.26	-	-	-	**.80**	-	.73	.41	.47
p56yunder (file aa30560)	.38	-	.38	.78	-	**.62**	.57	-	-	-
p56yunder (file aa30761)	-	-	.54	.76	-	**.64**	.34	-	-	-
p63up (file ab00958)	-	.41	.56	-	-	-	**.87**	-	-	-
p63up (file ab01196)	-	.61	.79	-	-	-	**.95**	-	-	-
p63up (file ab01570)	-	.35	.43	-	-	-	**.89**	-	-	-
p63upa (file ab00636)	-	-	.52	-	-	-	-	.73	.12	**.76**
t38 (file bb23079)	-	-	-	-	-	-	-	.27	**.83**	.51
t39 (file bb31597)	-	.25	.39	-	-	.27	.55	.30	-	**.83**
p58 (file aa36188)	-	-	-	.30	-	-	.57	-	-	-
r34wham (file ba28768)	.35	.62	-	-	.42	.43	-	**.65**	.56	-
s14wham (file ba45295)	-	-	-	-	-	.27	-	.57	**.72**	.53
s35 (file bb05291)	.16	.45	.22	**.64**	-	.31	.40	-	-	-

Figure 8: Likelihood values when the recognition system is run for each of 10 play models over a dataset of 29 examples.

Forbes, J.; Huang, T.; Kanazawa, K.; and Russell, S. 1995. The BATmobile: towards a Bayesian automated taxi. In *Int'l Joint Conf. on Artificial Intelligence*, volume 14, 1878–1885.

Friedman, N., and Goldszmidt, M. 1996. Building classifers using Bayesian networks. In *Proc. Nat. Conf. on Artificial Intelligence*, 1277–1284. AAAI Press.

Grimson, W., and Lozano-Pérez, T. 1987. Localizing overlapping parts by searching the interpretation tree. *IEEE Trans. Pattern Analysis and Machine Intelligence* 9(4):469–482.

Grosz, B., and Kraus, S. 1996. Collaborative plans for complex group action. *Artificial Intelligence* 86(2):269–357.

Huang, T.; Koller, D.; Malik, J.; Ogasawara, G.; Rao, B.; Russell, S.; and Weber, J. 1994. Automatic symbolic traffic scene analysis using belief networks. In *Proc. Nat. Conf. on Artificial Intelligence*, 966–972. AAAI Press.

Huber, M. 1996. *Plan-Based Plan Recognition Models for the Effective Coordination of Agents Through Observation*. Ph.D. Dissertation, University of Michigan.

Intille, S., and Bobick, A. 1995. Closed-world tracking. In *Proceedings of the Fifth International Conference on Computer Vision*, 672–678.

Kautz, H., and Allen, J. 1986. Generalized plan recognition. In *Proc. Nat. Conf. on Artificial Intelligence*, 32–37.

Nagel, H.-H.; Kollnig, H.; Haag, M.; and Damm, H. 1995. Association of situation graphs with temporal variations in image sequences. In *Computational Models for Integrating Language and Vision*, 1–8.

Pearl, J. 1988. *Probabilistic Reasoning in Intelligent Systems : Networks of Plausible Inference*. San Mateo, CA: Morgan Kaufmann Publishers.

Pynadath, D., and Wellman, M. 1995. Accounting for context in plan recognition, with application to traffic monitoring. In Besnard, P., and Hanks, S., eds., *Int'l Conference on Uncertainty in Artificial Intelligence*, volume 11.

Remagnino, P.; Tan, T.; and Baker, K. 1998. Agent orientated annotation in model based visual surveillance. In *Proc. Int'l Conf. Computer Vision*, volume 6. IEEE Computer Society.

Retz-Schmidt, G. 1988. A REPLAI of SOCCER: recognizing intentions in the domain of soccer games. In *Proc. European Conf. AI*, volume 8, 455–457.

Tambe, M. 1996. Tracking dynamic team activity. In *Proc. Nat. Conf. on Artificial Intelligence*, 80–87.

State-space Planning by Integer Optimization

Henry Kautz
AT&T Shannon Labs
180 Park Avenue
Florham Park, NJ 07932, USA
kautz@research.att.com

Joachim P. Walser[1]
i2 Technologies
Airway Park, Lozenberg 23
B-1932 St. Stevens Woluwe, Belgium
walser@i2.com

Abstract

This paper describes ILP-PLAN, a framework for solving AI planning problems represented as integer linear programs. ILP-PLAN extends the planning as satisfiability framework to handle plans with resources, action costs, and complex objective functions. We show that challenging planning problems can be effectively solved using both traditional branch-and-bound IP solvers and efficient new integer local search algorithms. ILP-PLAN can find better quality solutions for a set of hard benchmark logistics planning problems than had been found by any earlier system.

1 Introduction

In recent years the AI community witnessed the unexpected success of satisfiability testing as a method for solving state-space planning problems (Weld 1999). Kautz and Selman (1996) demonstrated that in certain computationally challenging domains, the approach of axiomatizing problems in propositional logic and solving them with general randomized SAT algorithms (SATPLAN) was competitive with or superior to the best specialized planning systems. The framework has been shown to be quite broad, for example encompassing both action-centered and fluent-centered representations of change, conditional and maintenance goals, causal planning (Kautz, McAllester, & Selman 1996), automatic generation of axioms from STRIPS operators (Ernst, Millstein, & Weld 1997; Kautz & Selman 1999), hierarchical task networks (Mali & Kambhampati 1998), and domain-specific knowledge (Kautz & Selman 1998b).

Despite this generality, certain limitations in the framework still prevent it from being used for many practical, real-world domains. One problem is the difficulty in dealing with resources and the associated numeric constraints. For example, you might wish to assert that a "drive" action consumes 3 units of fuel, and that a "refuel" action resets the vehicle's tank to 15 units. Numeric variables that have a very small range can be represented by a set of Boolean

variables, one for each possible value, but in general this introduces too many variables. In theory one could adopt a binary encoding of numeric quantities, but this would only keep the number of variables small by introducing a huge number of clauses to encode binary arithmetic.

Perhaps a more important limitation from an applications standpoint is that the notion of optimality inherent in the SATPLAN framework may be too weak. SATPLAN allows one to minimize the *parallel length* of a solution, where several *non-interfering* actions may occur at each time step. This notion of optimality, which is also shared by the popular Graphplan system and its descendents (Blum & Furst 1995; Koehler *et al.* 1997), is an advance over planning frameworks that treat all feasible solutions indifferently: for many popular test domains finding a shortest solution is at least NP-hard, while finding a feasible solution can be done in linear time (Bylander 1991). However, real world planning problems usually have more complex optimality criteria, that take into account *e.g.* different costs for different types of actions, minimization of resource usage, and so forth. Furthermore, even if all actions have the same cost, one may wish to minimize the number of *actions* in a solution, that is, the *sequential length* rather than the parallel length: or, more generally, some function of both the parallel and sequential length. The two notions of length may actually be in conflict: for example, in the logistics domain that we consider in detail below, one can construct examples where the solution with the lowest sequential length has a greater than minimum parallel length.

It is desirable, therefore, to enrich the underlying language of the SATPLAN framework while retaining its computational advantages. This paper introduces an approach to AI planning based on *integer optimization* of integer linear programs (ILP), which we call ILP-PLAN. An ILP contains both Boolean (0/1) and integer valued variables, and represents both constraints and optimization functions as linear inequalities. ILP generalizes SAT because any clause can be written as a linear inequality over 0/1 variables (*e.g.*, $(p \lor \neg q)$ becomes $p + (1 - q) \geq 1$ (Hooker 1988)). ILP is a standard tool for Operations Research, but has been

---

[1]This work was carried out during a visit of the second author at AT&T Shannon Labs. Copyright ©1999, American Association for Artificial Intelligence (www.aaai.org). All rights reserved.

rarely exploited in AI applications. The first part of this paper will demonstrate how STRIPS-style planning problems extended with costs, resources, and optimality conditions can be represented as an ILP in the AMPL modeling language (Fourer, Gay, & Kernighan 1993), and solved using the branch-and-bound algorithm by a commercial mixed integer programming package (ILOG CPLEX). We will discuss various encoding schemes and their tradeoffs. We will argue that specifying a planning problem by a *combination* of STRIPS operators (to represent logical constraints between actions and their preconditions and effects) and linear inequalities (to represent resource usage and objective functions) is more elegant and natural than using *only* extend STRIPS operators or *only* linear inequalities.

2 Planning and Integer Local Search

One reason that the ILP approach has been rarely investigated in AI is that branch-and-bound is a relatively inefficient algorithm for solving problems that are mainly *logical* in nature. However, recently a new approach to integer programming has been developed by Walser (1997; 1998) based on randomized local search. This algorithm, WSAT(OIP), generalizes the Walksat algorithm for satisfiability (Selman, Kautz, & Cohen 1994) to a form of ILP's called "over-constrained integer programs (OIP)". In an OIP the objective function is represented by a set of "soft constraints" – that is, linear inequalities that may or may not hold for a feasible solution. Walser demonstrated that WSAT(OIP) is can outperform ILP branch-and-bound in a number of challenging domains, including sports scheduling and capacitated production planning (CLSP).[2]

The second part of this paper presents a case study of using WSAT(OIP) to find *better quality solutions* to a set of difficult logistics planning benchmark problems that have been frequently cited in the literature on Graphplan, SATPLAN, and other recent planning algorithms such as ASP and LRTA* (Bonet, Loerincs, & Geffner 1997). We will demonstrate that the known computational advantages of using local search on a state-based encoding (Kautz & Selman 1996) of this domain can be retained, while the integer local search framework allows us to find solutions of lower *sequential* cost. The ILP-PLAN approach improves on the best published solutions for this domain.

ILP-PLAN thus brings together work on generalizing the *expressive* power of SATPLAN with work on generalizing the Walksat *inference engine* originally employed by that system. ILP-PLAN also builds a bridge between AI or OR technology. It shows how powerful and sophisticated OR solvers can be applied to AI planning. As a contribution to OR, ILP-PLAN shows how STRIPS operators can be used to make the specification of complex optimization problems that involve action selection concise and easy to express.

---

[2]CLSP is unlike the kind of AI planning discussed in this paper in that it does not involve action selection.

3 Preliminaries

The class of planning problems considered in this paper is an extension of classical bounded-length state-space planning. States assign truth values to facts, and correspond to a bounded sequence of integers. An action is a partial function over states that can be specified by a precondition, add list, and delete list of positive facts. The parallel composition of a set of actions is defined for a state if none of the actions delete a precondition or effect of another. This core semantics underlies SATPLAN and Graphplan, and can be extended to conditional effects as described in (Koehler *et al.* 1997; Anderson, Smith, & Weld 1998).

The first extension is to introduce *resource variables* that are assigned a numeric value by each state. In general, resources may be integer or real-valued. Every resource value has a global minimum and maximum value. Actions may be extended with resource preconditions and effects. Following the framework of (Koehler 1998), a resource precondition is a simple linear inequality that must hold in any states in which the action is applicable. The effect of an action may be to *consume* (decrease), *produce* (increase), or *provide* (set) the value of a resource.[3] The parallel composition of a set of actions is defined for a state i if the following holds for every resource r:

- The set is logically conflict-free, as defined above;
- If the set contains a provider for r, it contains no other effect for r;
- The value of r at i minus the sum of the consumers of r in the set satisfies the global lower bound for r;
- The value of r at i plus the sum of the producers of r in the set satisfies the global upper bound for r;
- For any action a in the set with a resource precondition for r, the value of r at i minus the sum of the consumers of r *other than* a satisfies that precondition.

These conditions ensure that every way of sequencing a set of parallel actions is well-defined and equivalent. Note too that explicit resource preconditions on actions are redundant if they are the same as the global bounds on the resource. The second extension is addition of *optimization criteria* to the planning problems. We will want to find solutions that minimize one or more linear functions of resources, actions, and facts. Although resource consumption is a most common objective function, note that we also allow such functions as the number of actions that occur, or the number of objects for which a predicate holds.

4 Operator-based Encodings

We begin by developing encodings for STRIPS operators extended with resource effects and optimization objectives. We call these encodings "operator-based", because they are based on writing constraints between variables representing

---

[3]In this paper we only consider resource effects involving a single variable, *e.g.*, $r+=3$, not general linear equations.

actions and variables representing the preconditions and effects of those actions. In the terminology for SAT encodings from Ernst, Millstein, and Weld (1997), the encodings are an extension of "regular action representations with parallel actions and explanatory frame axioms". In the second part of the paper we will consider examples that use an alternative "state-based" encoding.

Recent work by Koehler (1998) describes an extension of the IPP/Graphplan framework to handle resource constraints via annotations on STRIPS operators. We will describe conventions for translating such annotations into ILP constraints, and present the results of applying this methodology to a transportation problem ("Airplane") and solving the instance with CPLEX, a popular branch-and-bound ILP engine. Our approach is more general than that of IPP, however, in that it allows us to include explicit optimization criteria.

4.1 Encoding Conventions

The encoding consists of three parts: constraints for the logical properties of actions; for resource usage; and for optimization objectives. The logical properties of STRIPS operators are encoded by the following kinds of axioms: (i) explanatory frame-axioms (if a state-change occurs, one action that could account for it must have taken place (Haas 1987; Schubert 1989; Kautz, McAllester, & Selman 1996)); (ii) an occurring action implies its effects and preconditions; (iii) exclusiveness of logically conflicting actions; and (iv) state invariant axioms in the style of (Kautz & Selman 1998b). See the references cited above for the details of the translation into CNF; each clause can then be easily converted into a linear inequality as described earlier.

The second set of constraints maintains the value of each resource at each point in time, and makes sure that parallel actions are free of resource conflicts, according to the rules described in section 3 above. For each resource r we introduce a set of numeric variables r_i that stand for the quantity of r at the start of step i. Let M and N be minimum and maximum bounds on r. For each ground operator a we use the variable a_i to represent the *action* of that ground operator occurring at time i. For each consumer, producer, or provider ground operator a let c_a be the amount by which the operator decreases, increases, or sets the resource. Let *Prod* and *Con* be the sets of producing and consuming ground operators respectively. For simplicity we will say there is exactly one providing ground operator, s, which resets r to its maximum N. We introduce a new set of variables k_i that stand for amount of resource created by provider s_i if it occurs. We call the k_i *provider reset* variables. Then the resource conflict constraints are:

$$r_{i+1} = r_i + k_i - \sum_{a \in Con} c_a a_i + \sum_{a \in Prod} c_a a_i \quad (1)$$

resource $0 \leq fuel \leq C$

fly(a, b: airport):
precondition: *at-plane$_a$*
effects: *at-plane$_b$*, ¬*at-plane$_a$*
  $fuel \mathrel{-}= D_{ab} \cdot F$
  ∀passenger p: *boarded$_p$*
    effects: *at$_{pb}$*, ¬*at$_{pa}$*

refuel:
effects: $fuel = C$

Figure 1: Airplane example with conditional effects. Notice that refueling fills the tank to capacity.

$$s_i \rightarrow \neg a_i \quad \forall a \in Prod \cup Con \quad (2)$$
$$s_i \rightarrow (r_{i+1} \geq N) \quad (3)$$
$$\neg s_i \rightarrow (k_i = 0) \quad (4)$$
$$M \leq r_i - \sum_{a \in Con} c_a a_i \quad (5)$$
$$N \geq r_i + \sum_{a \in Prod} c_a a_i \quad (6)$$

We have written these constraints as mixed logical / linear inequalities, but each can be converted to a linear inequality, as we will do in the example below. (1) propagates the value of the resource from one time step to the next. (2) makes providers exclusive of other actions that affect the resource, while (3) and (4) establish the amount of resource created by a providing action (if any). Finally (5) and (6) enforce the global bounds on the resource. Due to lack of space we omit the translation of resource preconditions; in fact, for all the examples considered in this paper they are redundant due to the global resource bounds. Finally, resource optimization constraints are simply arbitrary linear inequalities over all the variables described above.

Example: Resource Optimization Planning. We illustrate this translation with a a modified version of the airplane example from (Penberthy & Weld 1992) and (Koehler 1998). It simplifies the original example by ignoring timing aspects but extends it for optimization of passenger routings. The scenario is a plane that can fly between a number of different airports and consumes fuel. Passengers with checked-in status at the location of the plane can be boarded. Boarded passengers move with the plane until they are deplaned, which can occur individually in our variation. The ILP-PLAN version of the example extends the task from a decision problem (with resources) to resource optimization: An explicit optimization objective is included to minimize resource usage, in this case "fuel". Figure 1 and table 1 describe some of the operators and variables used.

Indices	Definition
i	action step (L is the last step)
a, b ; p	airports ; passenger
Constants	**Definition**
C, F	tank capacity, fuel use per dist. unit
D_{ab}	Distance from a to b
Variables	**Definition**
f_{abi}	flight from a to b occurs in step i.
$refuel_i$	refuel in step i.
$refuel\_amount_i$	provider reset variable $\in [0, C]$
$fuel_i$	plane's fuel level $\in [0, C]$

Table 1: Parameters in the ILP translation of the airplane example. All variables binary unless declared otherwise.

The following inequalities state the resource aspect of the model ($1 \leq i < L$).

$$refuel_i \rightarrow (fuel_{i+1} \geq C) \qquad (7)$$

$$\neg refuel_i \rightarrow (refuel\_amount_i = 0) \qquad (8)$$

$$fuel_{i+1} = fuel_i + refuel\_amount_i - \sum_{a,b:a \neq b} f_{abi} D_{ab} F \quad (9)$$

$$refuel_i + \sum_{a,b:a \neq b} f_{abi} \leq 1 \ \forall i \qquad (10)$$

(7) and (8) link the decision variables for refueling with the fuel and refuel amounts and (9) states the fuel balance. Note that (7)-(8) are directly translated to linear inequalities ($p \rightarrow (x \geq k)$ is translated to $x - pk \geq 0$, and $p \rightarrow (x = 0)$ yields $(1 - p)m - m \geq 0$, where p is a binary variable, variable x has bounds $0 \leq x \leq m$ and k is a constant). (10) is a compact way of making refuel (a provider) and flying (a consumer) mutually exclusive. The optimization objective is stated as

$$\text{minimize } fuel_1 - fuel_L + \sum_i refuel\_amount_i,$$

where $refuel\_amount_i$ is the provider reset variable corresponding to the *refuel* action at time i. Figure 2 shows an example problem and table 2 reports experimental results using CPLEX 5.0 with standard/auto parameters settings.

Aspects of an Automated Translation. In this work, we approach resource-optimal planning using integer programming by directly formulating state-based encodings in a high-level IP modeling language, AMPL (Fourer, Gay, & Kernighan 1993). This approach provides maximal flexibility for experimenting with various combinations of encodings and IP solvers. Nevertheless, a system that automatically translates resource-annotated STRIPS into IP would have several advantages, including an improved representation of the logical portion of the problem by the use of

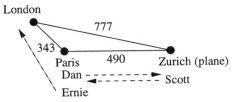

Figure 2: Scenario of initial state and travel destinations (arrows) of airplane-a. The resource-optimal plan found by CPLEX given the state-based ILP encoding has 5 steps: board Scott, fly to Paris || deplane Scott, refuel || board Dan and Ernie, fly to London || deplane Ernie, fly to Zürich || deplane Dan.

problem / steps	p/a	vars	cnstrs	min.fuel	time
airplane-a / 5	3	134	551	805	< 1s
airplane-b / 7	4	304	1774	897	54s
airplane-c / 9	5	576	4405	2096.5	895s

Table 2: Experimental results for airplane example. Columns are problem name / min. number of plan steps in a parallel plan, the number of passengers and airports (p/a), problem size in number of variables and constraints, the min. fuel consumption, and the solution time for CPLEX.

an intermediate representation such as a plan graph (Kautz & Selman 1998a), and ease in handling complex language constructs such as quantified conditional effects (Koehler *et al.* 1997; Anderson, Smith, & Weld 1998). A natural design for such a system would be a preprocessor for AMPL that handles STRIPS operators, thus allowing the user to mix the two representational levels. We are currently looking into implementation strategies.

It is important to note that many kinds of resource constraints are much more easily and naturally represented directly as linear inequalities, rather than as STRIPS annotations. For example, in the classic Missionaries and Cannibals problem, the *capacity constraint* that the cannibals never outnumber the missionaries on either shore can be written simply as

$$\sum_{m \in missionaries} at_{m,s,i} \geq \sum_{c \in cannibals} at_{c,s,i} \quad \forall i, s$$

while expressing the constraint using operator annotations is much more complex.

5 Case Study: Minimizing Plan-length

Traditionally, AI has concentrated on hard feasibility problems. In contrast, OR has put emphasis on approaches for finding near-optimal solutions to problems for which feasible solutions can be constructed easily. In both fields, there is increasing interest in finding near-optimal solutions to problems with a difficult feasibility aspect. Here, we consider a planning benchmark from the logistics domain

(Veloso 1992) that also exhibits this characteristic. The scenario is the transportation of a set of packages that involves flights and truck-drives between locations.

To model the problem, we use a variant of the state-based encodings presented in (Kautz & Selman 1996) that is extended to encode a notion of plan optimality. There are various possible criteria to optimize in this domain: (a) The total number of necessary actions, (b) the number of necessary time steps when parallel actions are allowed, (c) some function of the sequential and parallel lengths, and (d) yet more realistic measures of plan quality, *e.g.*including specific action costs for the different action types (flying an airplane is typically more expensive than driving a truck or loading a packet).

Previous approaches to the logistics domain include finding parallel optimal solutions (criterion b) using SAT-PLAN (Kautz & Selman 1996); more recently, Bonet, Loerincs and Geffner (1997) presented a method that found better serial optimal solutions (criterion a) using LRTA*, however at high computational cost for near-optimal solutions. We will concentrate on criteria (c), where our goal is find solutions of minimal sequential length *among* all solutions of minimal parallel length. This criteria allows us to directly compare the quality of our solutions to previous results in the literature. (This criteria appears to be generally useful for comparing planning systems, particularly for domains where it is easy to satisfy one of (a) or (b) alone.)

Since one of the best strategies to solve SATPLAN encodings is local search (Walksat), we employ a similar strategy for optimization encodings in ILP-PLAN. The ILP-PLAN approach to the domain casts the problem in integer constraints and solves it using integer local search, WSAT(OIP). Experimental results demonstrate that ILP-PLAN can find plans with fewer actions than SATPLAN. In comparison with LRTA* it finds plans with the same number of actions or fewer at reduced computational cost. In contrast to all previous approaches to this domain, it allows for stating planning objectives explicitly and opens up the way for even more practical criteria of plan-optimality.

5.1 Integer Local Search Encoding

The basis for the encoding developed here is the *state-based* encoding described in Kautz and Selman (1996), since it currently provides the best representation for local search algorithms in the Walksat family. State-based encodings employ axioms that directly relate changes in fluents between adjacent states without explicit reference to actions. In theory such axiomatizations could be created from operator-based encodings by resolving away all action variables (Kautz, McAllester, & Selman 1996). However, in the current version of ILP-PLAN, the encodings were created by hand in the AMPL modeling language, a widely used specification language for linear and integer optimization.

As noted earlier, the criterion of plan optimality that we will consider in this paper is to minimize sequential plan length over plans of bounded (minimal) parallel length. To formulate this, the scheme is augmented by action variables, and optimization (soft) constraints are used to formulate the objective function. However, instead of adding the full descriptive set of action variables and requiring state/action consistency, a much smaller *reduced* set of action variables is used. We will refer to this encoding scheme as an "*augmented state-based encoding*".

It is interesting to note that the obvious alternative of using an operator-based encoding of the type described in the previous section yields encodings that are much harder to solve by local search. In fact, we were surprised to discover that the conjunction of an operator-based encoding with a state-based encoding also is problematic for local search. An open question we are currently investigating is *why* the inclusion of a full (unreduced) set of action variables and corresponding axioms in this domain slows down the search; an understanding of this issue may help us devise more robust heuristics for local search that are immune to the effect. We currently hypothesize that the underlying problem is that it is costly for local search to maintain consistency between the settings of an action variable and those for its preconditions and effects (a inference step that is, by contrast, trivial for *systematic* inference engines).

Over-Constrained Integer Programs. To include optimization objectives into local search, the integer local search framework uses a representation introduced as over-constrained integer programs (OIPs) (Walser 1998). OIP formulates optimization criteria by means of soft inequality constraints over bounded integer variables and can be reduced to ILP. An OIP consists of hard and soft inequality constraints, wherein the optimization objectives are represented by the soft constraints. If all inequalities are linear, the OIP problem can be formulated in matrix notation as $Ax \geq b$, $Cx \leq d$ (*soft*), $x \in D$, where A and C are $m \times n$-matrices, b, d are m-vectors, and $x = (x_1, \dots, x_n)$ is the variable vector, ranging over positive finite domains $x_i \in D_i$. A variable assignment that satisfies all hard constraints is called a *feasible solution*. Given a tuple (A, b, C, d, D), the OIP minimization problem is

$$\min \; \{ \; \|Cx - d\| \; : \; Ax \geq b, \; x \in D\}$$

wherein the objective is to find a feasible solution with minimal soft constraint violation, $\|v\| := \sum_i \max(0, v_i)$. The contribution of each violated soft constraint to the overall objective is thus its degree of violation.

Augmented State-based OIP Encoding. The logical part of the OIP encoding for the domain is the direct translation of the CNF encoding with parallel (non-conflicting) actions used in SATPLAN. First, axioms are stated that directly relate changes in fluents between adjacent states

Indices	Definition
i, o	plan steps, objects.
a, b	locations.
v, p, t	vehicles, plane p, truck t.

Constants	Definition
c_l, c_f, c_d	cost of load/unload, flight, truck drive.

Action Variables	Definition
$load_{oi}$	load o in step i.
$unload_{oi}$	unload o in step i.
$drive\_truck_{ti}$	drive truck t in step i.
fly_plane_{pi}	fly plane p in step i.

Table 3: Parameters for the OIP encoding of 'logistics'.

without reference to action variables, as described in (Kautz & Selman 1996). An example in the logistics domain is "objects stay in place or are loaded",

$$at_{iol} \wedge \neg at_{i+1,ol} \rightarrow \bigvee_v in_{i+1,ov} \quad \forall o, l, i.$$

Further, state invariant axioms are included as in the previous example. In order to allow us to count the number of actions in a plan, we introduce a small number of reduced action variables, as mentioned above. These variables are used to help direct the search for *optimal* solutions, but not to constrain the set of *feasible* solutions. A reduced variable stands for the occurrence of any of a set of mutually exclusive actions. For example, we introduce the variable $drive\_truck_{ti}$, meaning "truck t is driven (from somewhere to somewhere else) at time i", in place of the set of variables $\{drive\_truck_{tabi}\}$ for all locations a and b. Similarly, the variable $load_{oi}$ stands for "package o is loaded (onto some vehicle)", in place of the set of actions $\{load_{ovi}\}$ for loading o onto particular vehicles, because a package can only be loaded into one vehicle at a time. Table 3 describes the indices and action variables used.

State changes are linked uni-directionally to the action variables by constraints of the type

$$at_{i,t} \wedge \neg at_{i+1,t} \rightarrow drive\_truck_{i,t} \quad \forall t, i.$$

We do not include implications in the opposite direction, that would assert that an action implies its effects and preconditions. Encoding bi-directional consistency would require full action specification and thus degrade performance for local search as mentioned above.

To optimize sequential plan length, all action variables appear in the minimization objective, weighted by cost coefficients, and formulated using soft constraints. There are many ways to write down this function; for example, one could write a *single* constraint that simply summed all the action variables. Alternatively, one could write a constraint for each time step: minimize the sum of the actions at time 1, then also at time 2, and so on. We obtained the best performance in this domain by encoding a separate soft constraint for each *object* in the domain, that is, each package,

truck, or airplane. For example, for each package o there is a soft constraint that minimizes the number of times the package is loaded or unloaded:

$$(soft) \sum_i c_l(load_{oi} + unload_{oi}) \leq c_l L_o$$

As noted in table 3, the c_l represents a cost factor for a load or unload. L_o represents a valid lower bound on the number of load/unload actions required to transport object o. L_o could be chosen as zero, but local search performance can be improved by making such bounds as tight (large) as possible (Walser 1998). It is possible to determine such tight lower bounds by *static analysis* of the problem domain. For example, in this logistics domain at least 6 load/unload actions are required for any object whose initial and goal locations are at non-airport locations in different cities.[4] In a similar fashion one can write a separate soft constraint for each truck (minimizing driving) and each airplane (minimizing flying). We did not attempt static analysis for these constraints, and simply took the right-hand sides of the soft constraints to be 0.

In summary, the representation consists of constraints for (i) state-transition consistency, (ii) state invariant axioms, (iii) implied reduced actions, and (iv) optimization criteria.

Post-optimization. To construct the full set of actions from a consistent solution encoded by fluent variables, a post-optimization stage is applied. In an AMPL control script, after a solution has been reached, all fluent variables are fixed at their current values. Subsequently, the full (bi-directional) set of state/action consistency constraints is posted, and the system is re-optimized according to the same minimization function as before, this time using ILP branch-and-bound. This post-optimization process yields the actual plan encoded by the action variables, and is a simple yet general strategy to derive valid plans.

5.2 Experimental Results

The encodings were first simplified by AMPL's presolving algorithms and subsequently solved by integer local search, WSAT(OIP). We were not able to solve the described encoding using integer programming branch-and-bound techniques, although such techniques are potentially applicable. To ensure that every ILP-PLAN solution meets the given plan length requirement, the value of the objective function was read off from the solutions and subsequently used as a lower bound on the objective function; the WSAT(OIP) search was then terminated upon reaching the bound. The SATPLAN numbers stem from evaluating the sequential plan length found in the solutions without encoding any planning objective.

---

[4] We obtained the L_o values for the problem instances in this study by simple inspection; a formal development of the static analysis necessary to derive lower bounds is beyond the scope of this paper.

problem/steps	GRAPHPLAN		SATPLAN state-based encoding			ASP functional encoding		LRTA*	ILP-PLAN augmented state-based OIP encoding			
	actions	time	m/actions	K-flips	time	actions	time	actions	actions	(f-d)	K-flips	time
log-a / 11	54	5942s	63	149	2.7s	57	34s	54	54	(6-6)	330	27s
log-a / 11									53	(5-6)	1,795	141s
log-a / 11									52	(4-6)	41,104	3,178s
log-a* / 13									51	(3-6)	4,938	401s
log-b / 13	47	2538s	68	93	0.7s	51	29s	42	42	(4-8)	3,478	340s
log-c / 13	–	–	72	161	1.4s	61	53s	52	52	(6-8)	2,466	274s
log-d / 14			86	1,425	13.3s				71	(7-15)	1,416	224s
log-d / 14									68	(7-15)	15,171	2,402s

Table 4: Performance of different planning systems. The columns are: number of sequential actions and runtime. A blank space indicates that no attempt was made at solving the problem. A dash (–) indicates that the problem could not be solved due to memory limitations. For SATPLAN, 'm/actions' reflects the mean number of actions found in 1,000 runs. The (f-d) column reflects the actual plan quality in number of required flights and truck drives. Note that the LRTA* and ASP algorithms are finding serial plans only. Solution times of LRTA* were not published. Results for SATPLAN and ILP-PLAN run on a 194 MHz R10000 SGI Challenge. ASP and LRTA* were reported for an IBM RS/6000 C10 with 100 MHz PowerPC 601 processor.

Table 4 gives the experimental results. Note that the LRTA* and ASP algorithms are finding serial plans, and their actual parallel length is unknown but could be very high. Solution times of LRTA* were not published, but it was noted that the algorithm did not converge after 500 trials (Bonet, Loerincs, & Geffner 1997). The state-based OIP encodings of ILP-PLAN were solved by WSAT(OIP) and averaged over 20 runs. Also note that SATPLAN times are for running the Walksat solver only, and do not include generating the wff (which requires approximately 1 minute on the test machines).

In addition to just sequential plan length, a more meaningful measure is given in the (f-d) column. It gives the actual number of flights and truck-drives in the solutions (all other actions are load/unload). It is clear that those numbers represent the most realistic quality measure. In general, of course one cannot infer the (f-d) value from the number of actions; however, for log-a we never observed a 54 action plan with 4 flights rather than 6. Also for log-a, we observe that it is possible to further reduce the number of actions to 51 (only 3 flights by making a circular plane trip around the airports with a single plane). This exemplifies that there is a tradeoff between short parallel and resource-optimal plans because it can be shown that a circular trip requires at least 13 steps. To compute the solution, we aided ILP-PLAN by removing one plane from the encoding labeled "log-a*/13".

Throughout the experiments, WSAT(OIP) was run with parameters $p_{hard} = 1.0$, $p_{zero} = 0.5$, $p_{noise} = 0.3$, and the following action costs were used: $c_f = 0.5$ (fly_plane), $c_d = 0.1$ (drive_truck), $c_l = 0.05$ (load/unload). We note that the computational results are relatively sensitive to the particular parameter settings. The particular setting of action costs was tuned in pre-experiments to favor short plans.

In interpreting these results it is important to note that we are comparing not just algorithms, but algorithms together with representations. Indeed, the same algorithm can yield quite different results when the same problem is encoded in different ways (Bonet, Loerincs, & Geffner 1997). In particular, only Graphplan took as input a "bare" STRIPS representation of the problem domain; for each of the others, the form of the input was tailored to the system and incorporated some degree of what is considered domain-specific knowledge. For example, SATPLAN included state-invariant axioms (e.g., a package is only at one location); ILP-PLAN added soft constraints as described above; and LRTA* included an A*-type heuristic search function.

6 Related Work

The work on ILP-PLAN was partially inspired by that of Koehler (1998) on extending Graphplan to handle resource constraints. Unlike ILP-PLAN, however, that system handled resource usage strictly by annotations on STRIPS operators, and did not include objective functions. The ZENO planner (Penberthy & Weld 1994) included a rich language that could express complex resource constraints, although it too lacked explicit optimization functions. It also differed from ILP-PLAN in that the underlying planner was a least commitment, regression planner, and the architecture involved a collection of specialized routines to handle different kinds of constraints (including a linear programming subroutine), rather than a single technique (as in ILP-PLAN) like local search or branch-and-bound. Other planners that extended nonlinear planning to include metric constraints in constraint programming type frameworks include O-PLAN (Tate 1996) and parcPLAN (El-Kholy & Richards 1996). The IxTeT planner (Laborie & Ghallab 1995) is a least-commitment planner notable for using an efficient graph-based algorithm for detecting resource conflicts between parallel actions.

Recent work by Vossen et al. (1999) describes an alternative formulation of ILP encodings for planning problems (without resources or optimality conditions) that results in stronger linear relaxations. Their techniques improve the performance of branch-and-bound solvers and are likely to be a valuable enhancement to the ILP-PLAN framework. An interesting similarity between their formulation and the one we develop for the logistics domain is that both eliminate explicit variables that represent actions (although other details differ). Independent work by Bockmayr and Dimopoulos (1998) develops ILP encodings for planning where the linear relaxation gives guidance to the branch-and-bound strategy by including (i) an objective function that maximizes the number of goals achieved, and (ii) a domain-specific strengthening of the linear relaxation which they show to be effective for the blocks world domain, but not strong enough in the logistics domain. Finally, while the ILP solvers used in our work so far (CPLEX and WSAT(OIP)) require all constraints to take the form of linear inequalities, recent work on *mixed logical/linear programming* (Hooker & Osorio 1997) may provide the underpinnings for systems that more efficiently handle ILPs that have a large logical component.

7 Conclusions

We have described ILP-PLAN, a new framework for solving AI planning problems under resource constraints and optimization objectives. By casting AI planning as integer programming, ILP-PLAN allows for constraints and objective functions over resource usage, action costs, or regular fluents. Using ILP as the base representation, it brings together threads in AI planning and integer optimization and extends previous frameworks (SATPLAN) to new practical planning *optimization* domains. The conceptual approach of ILP-PLAN integrates STRIPS style operator descriptions with linear inequality constraints. This can be seen as making ILP machinery applicable to AI planning, or conversely, as adding a new representational layer on top of linear inequalities. Like SATPLAN, ILP-PLAN is flexible with respect to inference methods and can be used in conjunction with both systematic and local search algorithms for integer optimization. We have demonstrated that two challenging planning problems can be solved effectively using a traditional ILP branch-and-bound solver and a new strategy for integer local search. For a set of hard benchmark logistics planning problems, ILP-PLAN can find better quality solutions than had been found by any earlier system.

References

Anderson, C.; Smith, D.; and Weld, D. 1998. Conditional effects in graphplan. In *Proceedings AIPS-98*.

Blum, A., and Furst, M. 1995. Fast planning through planning graph analysis. In *Proc. IJCAI-95*. Montreal, Canada.

Bonet, B.; Loerincs, G.; and Geffner, H. 1997. A robust and fast action selection mechanism for planning. In *Proc. AAAI-97*, 714–719.

Bockmayr, A., and Dimopoulos, D. 1998. Mixed integer programming models for planning problems. In *Working Notes of the CP-98 Constraint Problem Reformulation Workshop*. Pisa.

Bylander, T. 1991. Complexity results for planning. In *Proc. IJCAI-91*, 274–279. Sidney, Australia.

El-Kholy, A., and Richards, B. 1996. Temporal and resource reasoning in planning: the parcPLAN approach. In *Proc. AIPS-96*. Edinburgh.

Ernst, M.; Millstein, T.; and Weld, D. 1997. Automatic SAT-compilation of planning problems. In *Proc. IJCAI-97*. Nagoya, Japan.

Fourer, R.; Gay, D. M.; and Kernighan, B. W. 1993. *AMPL, A Modeling Language for Mathematical Programming*. Boyd & Fraser publishing Company.

Haas, A. 1987. The case for domain-specific frame axioms. In Brown, F., and Lawrence, K., eds., *The Frame Problem in Artificial Intelligence, Proceedings of the 1987 Workshop*. Morgan Kaufmann. Los Altos, CA.

Hooker, J., and Osorio, M. 1997. Mixed logical/linear programming. *Discrete Applied Mathematics*. To appear.

Hooker, J. 1988. A quantitative approach to logical inference. *Decision Support Systems* 4:45–69.

Kautz, H., and Selman, B. 1996. Pushing the envelope: Planning, propositional logic, and stochastic search. In *Proc. AAAI-96*, 1194–1201.

Kautz, H., and Selman, B. 1998a. BLACKBOX: A new approach to the application of theorem proving to problem solving. In *Working notes of the AIPS-98 Workshop on Planning as Combinatorial Search*.

Kautz, H., and Selman, B. 1998b. The role of domain-specific knowledge in the planning as satisfiability framework. In *Proceedings AIPS-98*.

Kautz, H., and Selman, B. 1999. Unifying SAT-based and graph-based planning. Under review.

Kautz, H.; McAllester, D.; and Selman, B. 1996. Encoding plans in propositional logic. In *Proc. KR-96*.

Koehler, J.; Nebel, B.; Hoffmann, J.; and Dimopoulos, Y. 1997. Extending planning graphs to an adl subset. In *Proc. 4th European Conf. on Planning*.

Koehler, J. 1998. Planning under resource constraints. In *Proceedings ECAI-98*.

Laborie, P., and Ghallab, M. 1995. Planning with sharable resource constraints. In *Proc. IJCAI-95*. Montreal, Canada.

Mali., A., and Kambhampati, S. 1998. Encoding htn planning in propositional logic. In *Proc. AIPS-98*. Pittsburgh, PA.

Penberthy, J., and Weld, D. 1992. UCPOP: A sound, complete, partial order planner for ADL. In *Proc. KR-92*, 108–114. Boston.

Penberthy, J., and Weld, D. 1994. Temporal planning with continous change. In *Proc. AAAI-94*, 1010–1015.

Schubert, L. 1989. Monotonic solution of the frame problem in the situation calculus. In Kyburg, H. *et al.* eds., *Knowledge Representation and Defeasible Reasoning*. Kluwer Academic.

Selman, B.; Kautz, H.; and Cohen, B. 1994. Noise strategies for improving local search. In *Proc. AAAI-94*, 337–343.

Tate, A. 1996. Representing plans as a set of constraints - the I-N-OVA model. In *Proc. AIPS-96*. Edinburgh.

Veloso, M. 1992. *Learning by analogical reasoning in general problem solving*. Ph.D. Dissertation, CMU.

Vossen, T.; Ball, M.; Lotem, A.; and Nau, D. 1999. On the use of Integer programming models in AI planning. In *Proc. AAAI-99*.

Walser, J. 1997. Solving linear pseudo-boolean constraint problems with local search. In *Proceedings AAAI-97*.

Walser, J. 1998. *Domain-independent Local Search for Linear Integer Optimization*. Ph.D. Dissertation, Universität des Saarlandes.

Weld, D. 1999. Recent advances in AI planning. *AI Magazine*. To appear.

Using Planning Graphs for Solving HTN Planning Problems

Amnon Lotem, Dana S. Nau, and James A. Hendler

Department of Computer Science and Institute for System Research
University of Maryland
College Park, MD 20742
{lotem, nau, hendler}@cs.umd.edu

Abstract

In this paper we present the GraphHTN algorithm, a hybrid planning algorithm that does Hierarchical Task-Network (HTN) planning using a combination of HTN-style problem reduction and Graphplan-style planning-graph generation. We also present experimental results comparing GraphHTN with ordinary HTN decomposition (as implemented in the UMCP planner) and ordinary Graphplan search (as implemented in the IPP planner). Our experimental results show that (1) the performance of HTN planning can be improved significantly by using planning graphs, and (2) that planning with planning graphs can be sped up by exploiting HTN control knowledge.

Introduction

Recent approaches to action-based planning, such as Graphplan (Blum & Furst 1995; 1997), SATPLAN (Kautz & Selman 1996), and Blackbox (Kautz & Selman 1998), achieved significant progress in the performance of action-based planning, and extended the size of problems that action-based planners can handle. In this work, we try to transfer some of that progress to hierarchical task-network (HTN) planning (Sacerdoti 75; Currie & Tate 1985)—an AI planning methodology that creates plans by *task decomposition*. Our motivation to handle HTN planning stems from the fact that applied work in AI planning has typically favored approaches based on hierarchical decomposition rather than causal chaining approach (Wilkins & Desimone 1994; Aarup *et al.* 1994; Smith *et al.*, 1998; Nau *et al.*, 1998).

We present the GraphHTN algorithm, which extends the Graphplan approach so that it can be used to solve HTN planning problems. GraphHTN compiles an HTN planning problem into two related compact data structures: a planning graph and a planning tree. The planning tree represents the HTN decomposition rules and constrains the planning graph to be consistent with the HTN constraints. The search for a plan is then performed in these two data structures.

In an initial set of experiments we compared GraphHTN with UMCP, an HTN planner which uses a classic refinement search. The planning time of GraphHTN was significantly shorter then that of UMCP, suggesting that using planning graphs is an attractive approach for HTN planning.

HTN problem specifications usually supply additional control knowledge that does not exist in the specifications for an action-based planner. For example, HTN control knowledge might include explicit specifications of the order between tasks and constraints on the possible instantiations of the tasks. The use of HTN constraints might reduce the searched space but it also introduces more nodes to the planning graph and requires additional work in handling each of these nodes. Thus, a legitimate question is whether incorporating HTN constraints in an algorithm which is based on a planning graph increases or decreases the planning time.

In order to answer that question, we did a second set of experiments that compared the time of solving HTN problems using GraphHTN with the time of solving equivalent action-based problems using IPP (Koehler *et al.*, 1997). We selected IPP for this purpose because GraphHTN uses IPP's implementation of planning graphs, augmented by code to handle HTN constraints. The results of the comparison show that for small problems, the overhead of handling HTN control knowledge leads to larger planning times of GraphHTN in comparison with IPP. However, for large problems, handling HTN constraints was cost-effective, achieving an overall better performance of GraphHTN in comparison with IPP. That means that HTN control knowledge, if available, can be exploited effectively to reduce the planning time.

Background

Planning Graphs

The *Planning graph* was introduced (Blum & Furst 1995; 1997) as a compact way for representing a STRIPS planning problem. Planning graphs are currently used in some of the fastest available action-based planners, such as IPP (an extension of Graphplan) and Blackbox (as the basis

name	specification
by_truck	transport(?p, ?o, ?d):- n1: at-truck(?t, ?o) n2: ld(?p, ?t, ?o) n3: at-truck(?t, ?d) n4: uld(?p, ?t, ?d) formula: n1 < n2 and n2 < n3 and n3 < n4 and ?o ≠d and between(at-truck(?t, ?o), n1, n2) and between(at(?p, ?t), n2, n4) and between(at-truck(?t, ?d), n3, n4)
delivery	transport(?p, ?o, ?d):- n1: pckd(?p) n2: dlvr(?p, ?o, ?d) n3: vrfy(?p, ?d) formula: n1 < n2 and n2 < n3 and initially(small(?p)) and before(at(?t, ?o), n2) and between(dlvrd(?p, ?d), n2, n3) and ?o ≠ ?d
moving_truck	at-truck(?t, ?l):- n1: mv(?t, ?o, ?l) formula: before(not at-truck(?t, ?l), n1) and before(at-truck(?t, ?o), n1)
packing	pckd(?p):- n1: pck(?p) formula: before(not pckd(?p), n1)

Table 1: The methods of the simple transportation domain.

for the SAT encoding of a planning problem). A planning graph contains alternate levels of proposition nodes and action nodes. An action appears at level i if all its preconditions appear in the i-th proposition level. A proposition appears at the first proposition level if it is a part of the initial state. A proposition appears at level $i > 1$ if it is an "add" effect of some action in the previous action level. Graphplan constructs the planning graph level by level, and searches for a plan in the current graph after each extension of the graph. During that process the algorithm identifies, propagates and makes use of certain *mutual exclusion* relations among nodes.

Recent works have extended the types of problems that can be solved using planning graphs beyond problem described as pure STRIPS-style operators, to problem descriptions that allow unified quantifiers and conditional effects (Gazen & Knoblock, 1997; Koehler *et al.*, 1997, Anderson *et al.*, 1998), simple numeric constraints (Koehler, 1998) probabilistic operators (Blum and Langford, 1998), and sensing actions in the face of uncertainty (Weld *et al.*, 1998).

mv(?t, ?o, ?d) pre: at-truck(?t, ?o) post: ~at-truck(?t, ?o), at-truck(?t, ?d)	pck(?p) pre: not pckd(?p) post: pckd(?p)
ld(?p, ?t, ?l) pre: at(?p, ?l), at-truck(?t, ?l) post: ~at(?p, ?l), at(?p, ?t)	dlvr(?p, ?o, ?d) pre: at(?p, ?o) post: ~at(?p, ?o), dlvrd(?p, ?d)
uld(?p, ?t, ?l) pre: at(?p, ?t), at-truck(?t, ?l) post: ~at(?p, ?t), at(?p, ?l)	vrfy(?p, ?l) pre: dlvrd(?p, ?l) post: ~dlvrd(?p, ?l), at(?p, ?l)

Table 2: The primitive tasks of the simple transportation domain.

HTN Planning

HTN planning is an AI planning methodology that creates plans by *task decomposition*. The planning problem is specified by an *initial task network*, which is a collection of tasks that need to be performed under specified constraints. The planning process decomposes tasks in the *initial task network* into smaller and smaller subtasks until the task network contains only *primitive tasks* (*operators*). The decomposition of a task into subtasks is performed using a *method* from the *domain description*. The *method* specifies how to decompose the task into a set of subtasks. Each *method* is associated with various constraints that limit the applicability of the method to certain conditions and define the relations between the subtasks of the method. The following constraints can be associated with a method: an *order constraint* between two subtasks $n1$ and $n2$ ($n1 < n2$), *designation* and *codesignation* constraints between two variables or between a variable and a constant ($u = v$, $u \neq v$, $u = c$, $u \neq c$) and the following *state constraints*:

- *initially*($P(?x)$) means that a specified proposition P should be true in the initial state.
- *before*($P(?x)$, n)) means that P should be true before starting subtask n of the method.
- *after*($P(?x)$, n)) means that P should be true after accomplishing subtask n of the method.
- *between*($P(?x)$, $n1$, $n2$)) means that P should be true between subtasks $n1$ and $n2$ of the method.

As an example, we will use the simple transportation domain presented in Tables 1 and 2. In this example, the *transport* compound task is responsible for transporting a package $?p$ from location $?o$ to location $?d$. It can be performed by either using a truck or a delivery service. The *by_truck* method has four subtasks: having the truck $?t$ at $?o$, loading the package into $?t$, having the truck at $?d$ and unloading the package. *at-truck* is a predicate task which is decomposed into the primitive task *mv* (move) if the truck is not yet at the desired location $?l$ or into *do-nothing* if the truck is already at $?l$. The subtasks of the method are totally ordered. *Between* constraints are used to protect the effects which are generated by one subtask and are consumed by another. The *delivery* method has three subtasks: having the package packed, delivery, and verification of the package arrival.

In general, HTN planning is strictly more expressive than STRIPS-style planning (Erol *et al.* 1994b). HTN planners traditionally use classical refinement search for finding a plan. A recent work showed how an HTN planning problem can be encoded as a propositional satisfiability problem (Mali & Kambhampati 98).

GraphHTN

GraphHTN is a novel algorithm for solving HTN planning problems based on the Graphplan approach. It gets as an input an initial task network *tn0* to be accomplished, an initial state *I*, and an HTN domain description *D* which specifies the primitive tasks (operators), compound tasks and the methods which can be used. GraphHTN produces plans in the Graphplan format: a set of actions and specified times in which each action is to be carried out. Several actions may occur at the same time if they do not interfere with each other.

Unlike Graphplan, GraphHTN has no goals that a valid plan should achieve. Instead a valid plan should be one which can be generated from the initial task network. More precisely, a plan *p* is valid iff there is a task network *tn* such that:

- *tn* can be generated from the initial task network *tn0* by a sequence of task decompositions and valid instantiation of variables.
- *tn* consists of only ground primitive tasks.
- The set of ground primitive tasks in *tn* is identical to the set of actions in *p*.

- The set of constraints associated with *tn* are satisfiable and *p* is consistent with these constraints.

The way GraphHTN finds valid plans will be illustrated using the simple transportation problem specified in Figure 1.

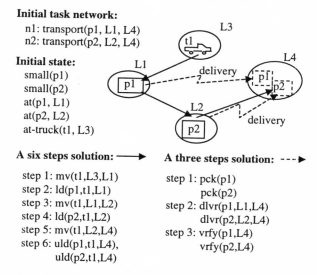

Initial task network:
n1: transport(p1, L1, L4)
n2: transport(p2, L2, L4)

Initial state:
small(p1)
small(p2)
at(p1, L1)
at(p2, L2)
at-truck(t1, L3)

A six steps solution: ⟶

step 1: mv(t1,L3,L1)
step 2: ld(p1,t1,L1)
step 3: mv(t1,L1,L2)
step 4: ld(p2,t1,L2)
step 5: mv(t1,L2,L4)
step 6: uld(p1,t1,L4),
         uld(p2,t1,L4)

A three steps solution: --->

step 1: pck(p1)
         pck(p2)
step 2: dlvr(p1,L1,L4)
         dlvr(p2,L2,L4)
step 3: vrfy(p1,L4)
         vrfy(p2,L4)

Figure 1: A simple transportation problem: two packages p1 and p2 should be transferred to L4 by either using a truck or a delivery service. Two possible solutions are presented.

The Planning Tree

A *planning tree* is an And/Or tree that represents the set of all possible decompositions of the initial task network up to a certain depth. Planning trees have two kinds of nodes: *task nodes* (the "or" nodes) and *method nodes* (the "and" nodes). The root of the planning tree is a special *method* node that is labeled *root*. The nodes immediately under the root represent the tasks in the initial task network. The

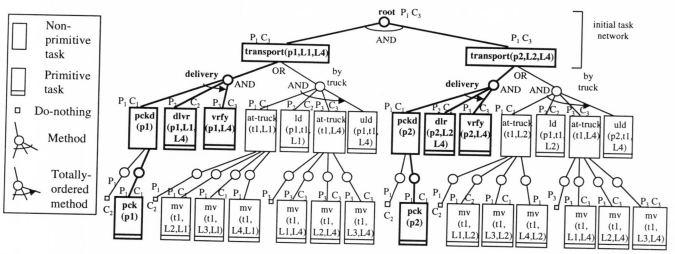

Figure 2: The planning tree for the simple transportation problems. Nodes which can generate actions for the *i*-th time step are marked by P_i. Nodes that *could be accomplished* at time *i* are marked by C_i.

children of a *task node* are all the instantiated methods that can be used for decomposing the task. The children of a *method node* are all the subtasks of the method. Figure 2 shows a planning tree for the simple transportation problem. Right under the root we have the two *transport* tasks. Both of them should be carried out in order to solve the problem. Each *transport* task can be decomposed using either the *delivery* or the *by truck* method, the *at-truck(t1, L1)* task can be decomposed to *do-nothing* or to *mv* operations from various locations, and so forth.

A specific solution for the planning problem corresponds to a subtree of the *planning tree* in which each non-primitive *task node* has exactly one *method node* as it child. For example, the subtree shown in boldface in Figure 2 represents a solution based on the *delivery* method.

The Planning Graph

GraphHTN uses a similar planning graph to the one used by Graphplan. The difference is that an action node might also represent the preconditions of a non-primitive task (as defined by *before* or *between* constraints). Such an action has no *add* or *delete* effects. Its appearance in the graph indicates that the corresponding task can start at that level.

A Description of the Algorithm

GraphHTN builds the *planning tree* and the *planning graph* synchronically and uses both of them in the search process. GraphHTN is sound and complete (Lotem and Nau 1999). However, as the HTN planning is semi-decidable (Erol 1994b), the termination of the planning process when no solution exists is not guaranteed. When no recursive method exists, the planner is guaranteed to report the *shortest* plan if a plan exists, and to halt if there is no solution.

An outline of the algorithm appears in Figure 3. GraphHTN starts with a planning tree consisting of the tasks in the *initial task network*, and a planning graph that has a single proposition level describing the *initial state*. Like Graphplan, the algorithm runs in stages. In each stage it appends to the planning graph one action level and one proposition level and searches backward for a plan in the extended graph. The HTN constraints are introduced by using the planning tree which guides both processes.

Extending the planning graph. Rather than using every applicable action for extending the graph, GraphHTN only uses actions that can be generated for the current time step by decomposing recursively the initial task network. That keeps the graph consistent with the HTN constraints (a similar idea was used (Barrett and Weld 1994) in extending UCPOP to handle tasks decomposition). Technically, this is done by extending first the prefix of the planning tree: expanding recursively the planning tree by decomposing each task t in the tree which holds the following conditions:

- Every task t_i that is ordered before t (i.e. $t_i < t$) has already been marked as *could be accomplished* in a previous

---

Algorithm GraphHTN(*tn0, I, D*)
Input: An initial task network *tn0*, an initial state *I*, and
        an HTN domain description *D*.
Output: a valid plan or "Failure".
Data Structures: A planning tree *T* and a planning graph *G*.
        Initially, *G* is empty and *T* has a single node: *root*.
Insert each $p \in I$ into the first action level of *G*.
Insert each $t \in tn0$ as a child of *T*'s root.
for *i* := 1 to max-length
        extend the prefix of the planning tree *T*;
        extend the planning graph *G*;
        if the root of the tree *could be accomplished* then
            search for plan *p* of length *i*;
            if solution was found then return "Success, plan is ", *p*;
        end;
end;
return "Failure".

Figure 3: an outline of the GraphHTN algorithm.

time step (tasks are marked as *could be accomplished* as part of extending the planning graph).

- All the preconditions of t (i.e., *before* and *between* constraints of t) are satisfied at the current proposition level.

The expansion of a task t is done by generating a child node for representing every applicable instantiation of t's methods. The instantiation of a method takes in account the current binding of free variables and the *designation*, *codesignation* and *initially* constraints of the method. For each new *method* node the algorithm creates the corresponding subtask nodes and continues to expand these new nodes recursively only if they hold the above conditions. The P_i label in Figure 2 indicates that the corresponding node was part of the prefix of the tree at time-step i.

The new actions that are created while extending the prefix of the tree are added to the *active set* of actions. Only actions from the *active set* are used (if applicable) to extend the planning graph. Including an action that represents a primitive task at level i of the graph means that the action *could be accomplished* in that time step. We extend that notion to methods and non-primitive tasks:

- A method *could be accomplished* at level i if all its subtasks *could be accomplished* at level i or earlier.

- A non-primitive task *could be accomplished* at level i if at least one of its methods *could be accomplished* at level i or earlier.

When an action is added to the planning graph the *could be accomplished* property is propagated upward in the tree. The C_i label in figure 2 indicates that the corresponding node was first marked as *could be accomplished* in step i of the algorithm.

The Search. In Graphplan a search is performed only if the last proposition level includes all the goals. In an HTN planning problem there are no goals to be achieved.

Instead, all the tasks in the initial task network should be accomplished. Therefore, the search starts when the root of the tree is marked as *could be accomplished*. Methods that could not be accomplished within the current number of time steps are filtered out of the planning tree and the planing graph (in the example: the two instances of the *by_truck* method are ignored by the search for a plan of length three). The search uses a level-by-level approach going backward from the last level of the planning graph toward its first level. However, in order to get a solution which is consistent with the HTN constraints, the search is guided top-down by the planning tree. This is done as follows:

- For each level i of the planning graph the algorithm selects the set of tasks to be *accomplished* at level i before proceeding to level i - 1. The algorithm does not decide at that point at which levels the selected tasks *start*.

- For each non-primitive task t that is selected to be accomplished at level i of the graph, the algorithm also selects a method for performing t. This is a backtracking point.

- The algorithm can select a task t to be *accomplished* at level i of the graph (i.e., t is *selectable*) only if:

  1) t is a subtask of a selected method m.

  2) Every other subtask t_i of m that is ordered after t ($t < t_i$) starts after time i.

  3) t is not mutual exclusive to any other task that has already been selected for level i.

  4) t does not delete any goals required for level $i+1$.

- The decision whether to select a selectable task t for the current level or to postpone its selection for a level smaller than i is also a backtracking point.

- Selecting a primitive task sets the *start* time of that task and possibly the start time of non-primitive tasks which are ancestors of t. The preconditions of the tasks that start at the i-th level of the graph, together with the open goals from levels greater than i, define the required goals for level $i-1$.

In the case of no recursive methods, the algorithm halts when a plan is found or when the length of the planning graph exceeds the maximum number of planning steps that can be generated by the planning tree. When the domain includes recursive methods, an *iterative deepening* approach is used in order to preserve the completeness of the algorithm. In the k-th deepening iteration, expansions are constrained to at most k recursion levels. If no solution was found in iteration k, the limit of the recursion level is increased by a predefined constant and the whole process repeats[1].

---

[1] We are currently examining an alternative approach in which the bound on the recursion level is dynamically deducted from the current length of the graph. As the length increases, nodes might be added to earlier levels of the graph. That excludes the need for

Due to space considerations, we will only mention here some of the additional extensions made to the algorithm to accommodate the requirements of HTN planning:

- mutual exclusiveness – eliminating *mutex* relations between an action and its ancestors;

- memoization – the set of tasks that can be selected for level i-1 is also recorded in the memoized configuration (in addition to the current set of goals);

- handling the *do-nothing* task;

- handling *after* and *between* constraints.

The implementation of GraphHTN consists of two major components: the HTN component, which is responsible for building and searching the planning tree, and the planning graph component. The planning graph component was adopted with some modifications from the IPP planner (Koehler *et al.*, 1997).

Experiments

Methodology

We evaluated the performance of GraphHTN by comparing it against UMCP (Erol 1994a), an HTN planner which uses a classic refinement search. We used two types of transportation problems. In problem 1, n packages in n different locations should be transferred to a common destination using a single truck. In problem 2 the packages should be transferred to n different destinations.

We used the same set of problems to assess the contribution of HTN control knowledge to the performance of the planner. We compared the time of solving the HTN problems using GraphHTN with the time of solving equivalent action-based problems using IPP (Koehler *et al.*, 1997). We chose IPP for that purpose because GraphHTN uses IPP's implementation of planning graphs, augmented by code to handle HTN constraints.

Results

The running time and the number of search nodes explored by each planner are presented in Table 3. The times were measured on Sun Ultra with 143 MHZ clock and 64 MB RAM. Figures 3 and 4 present the running times graphically using a logarithmic scale for the time.

The comparison between GraphHTN and UMCP is not absolutely fair, as UMCP is written in lisp and GraphHTN is written in C and C++. However, the performance difference between the planners is so great that re-coding UMCP in C would probably not make a big difference. We also present in Table 3 the number of search nodes explored by GraphHTN and UMCP. However, this comparison is somewhat misleading, since creating a new node in UMCP requires duplication of the whole task

---

iterations on the recursion level and assures the optimality of the extracted plan in terms of the number of time steps.

Prob lem	# of pack-ages	Plan length	Total Elapsed Time			# of Search Nodes		
			Graph HTN	UMCP	IPP	Graph HTN	UMCP	IPP
1	2	6	0.10	1.2	0.04	94	65	47
	3	8	0.26	81.1	0.09	2541	2219	1092
	4	10	1.89	> 1 h	0.64	$3.9 * 10^4$	$>2 * 10^4$	$3.8 * 10^4$
	5	12	20.29	> 1 h	25.84	$4.8 * 10^5$	-	$1.7 * 10^6$
	6	14	192	> 1 h	1501	$5.2 * 10^6$	-	$8.6 * 10^7$
	7	16	2012	> 1 h	> 1h	$4.9 * 10^7$	-	-
2	2	8	0.14	1.7	0.07	278	107	133
	3	12	0.53	327	0.31	4883	7754	10^4
	4	16	3.27	> 1 h	14.19	$4.7 * 10^4$	-	10^6
	5	20	20.22	> 1 h	1731	$3.3 * 10^5$	-	10^8
	6	24	118	> 1 h	> 1h	$2.0 * 10^6$	-	-
	7	28	1419	> 1h	> 1h	$1.0 * 20^7$	-	-

Table 3 – The total elapsed time (in seconds) and the number of searched nodes for GraphHTN, UMCP and IPP.

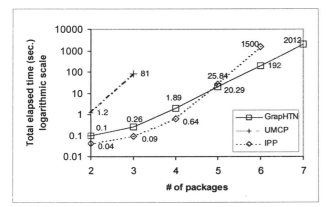

Figure 3: Total elapsed times for problem 1.

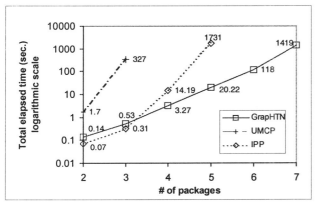

Figure 4: Total elapsed times for problem 2.

network, which involves much computation and memory. The failure of UMCP to solve the problems for more than three packages is basically due to its high consumption of memory.

The comparison with IPP shows that for small problems (up to 4 packages) the overhead of handling the HTN control knowledge led to larger planning times (using GraphHTN) than planning without it (using IPP). However, for large problems (more than 4 packages) handling HTN control knowledge was cost-effective, and led to shorter planning times than planning without it. The numbers of search nodes present a similar picture.

Discussion and Conclusions

We have presented GraphHTN—an HTN planner which compiles an HTN planning problem into a planning graph and a planning tree, and searches in this combined data structure for a plan. In our experiments, GraphHTN solved HTN planning problems significantly faster then UMCP. In addition, GraphHTN found plans that are optimal in terms of the number of time steps (this is not necessarily true for the plans found by UMCP). The primary reason for GraphHTN's fast performance relative to UMCP is somewhat similar to the reason for Graphplan's fast performance relative to UCPOP:

- The planning graph makes properties like reachability from the initial state and mutual exclusiveness explicitly available to the search phase, reducing significantly the amount of search needed.
- When failures occur for the same reason in different parts of a search space, the memoization reduces the amount of time spent in searching those different parts of the search space.

In addition, GraphHTN searches within a single (but complex) data structure, while UMCP maintains and explores hundreds of candidate task networks in its search process and thus exhausts the available memory quite fast.

We also tried to assess the value of the HTN control knowledge for reducing the planning time. There are two competing factors here:

- On one hand, there is an overhead in handling the HTN constraints: additional nodes should be introduced into the planning graph to represent preconditions of compound tasks and more time is spent in selecting a node for the solution in order to assure its consistency with the planning tree.
- On the other hand, even a small amount of HTN control knowledge might reduce the size of the searched space. For example, the *transport* method states that each package is loaded once and that this is done in the initial location of the package. In the action-based version of the problem this constraint is missing and the construction phase of the planning graph introduces for each package "load" actions that load the package at every possible location. As a result, the backward search spends extra time in eliminating these alternatives—time that is not needed in the GraphHTN algorithm.

In our experiments, for big enough problems, handling the HTN control knowledge was cost-effective and led to smaller planning times. We actually used in these experiments very limited amount of additional control knowledge—for example, we did not use GraphHTN's methods and operators as a vehicle for writing domain-specific planning algorithms, as has been done in some other HTN planners (Nau *et al.*, 1999). We believe that if we had made more control knowledge available to GraphHTN, its planning performance would have been even better.

For the future, we plan to compare GraphHTN and UMCP on a wider set of problems. We also plan to explore more systematically the value of different levels of HTN control knowledge on the performance of GraphHTN.

We intend to examine the role of propagating different HTN properties through the planning tree in limiting the search space and investigate alternative search strategies.

Another research direction is to replace GraphHTN's current search strategy by a process that encodes the planning graph and the planning tree as a propositional satisfiability problem and then uses a SAT solver for performing the search (similar to the way it is done in Blackbox for action-based planning problems).

Acknowledgments

We thank Jana Koehler for the permission to embed the code of IPP within GraphHTN. This research was supported in part by the following grants and contracts: Army Research Laboratory DAAL01-97-K0135, Naval Research Laboratory N00173981G007, Air Force Research Laboratory F306029910013, and NSF DMI-9713718.

References

Anderson, C.; Smith, D.; Weld, D. 1998. Conditional effects in Graphplan. In *Proc. AIPS-98*, 44-53.

Aarup, M. and Arentoft, M. and Parrod, Y. and Stader, J. and Stokes, I. 1994. OPTIMUM-AIV: A knowledge based planning and scheduling system for spacecraft AIV. *Intelligent Scheduling*, Morgan Kaufmann, Fox M. and Zweben M., 451-469.

Barrett, A. and Weld, D. 1994. Task decomposition via plan parsing. In *Proc. AAAI-94*, 1117-1122.

Blum, A. and Furst, M. 1995. Fast planning through planning graph analysis. In *Proc.14th Int. Joint Conf. AI*, 1636-1642.

Blum, A. and Furst, M. 1997. Fast planning through planning graph analysis. *J. Artificial Intelligence*, 90(1–2):281–300.

Blum, A. and Langford, C. 1998. Probabilistic planning in the Graphplan Framework. Working notes of the Workshop on Planning as Combinatorial Search held in conjunction with AIPS-98, Pittsburgh, PA, 1998, 8-12.

Currie, K. and Tate, A. 1985. O-Plan - control in the open planning architecture. BSC Expert Systems Conference, Cambridge University Press.

Erol, K.; Hendler, J.; and Nau, D. 1994a. UMCP: a sound and complete procedure for Hierarchical Task-Network planning, In *Proc. AIPS-94*, 249-254.

Erol, K.; Nau, D.; Hendler, J. 1994b. HTN planning: complexity and expressivity. *Proc. AAAI-94*.

Gazen, C. and Knoblock, C. 1997. Combining the expressivity of UCPOP with the efficiency of Graphplan. In *Proc. ECP-97*, Toulouse, France, 1997.

Kambhampati, S.; Knoblock, C.; and Yang, Q. 1995. Planning as refinement search: a unified framework for evaluating design tradeoffs in partial order planning. *Artificial Intelligence*, 76(1-2):167-238.

Kautz, H. and Selman, B. 1996. Pushing the envelope: Planning prepositional logic, and stochastic search. In *Proc. AAAI-96*, Portland, OR. 1996.

Kautz, H. and Selman, B. 1998. Blackbox: A new approach to the application of theorem proving to problem solving. Working notes of the Workshop on Planning as Combinatorial Search held in conjunction with AIPS-98, Pittsburgh, PA, 1998, 58-60.

Koehler, J. ; Nebel, B.; Hoffman, J; and Dimopoulus Y. 1997. Extending planning graphs to an ADL subset. In *Proc. ECP-97*, Toulouse, France, 1997.

Koehler, J. 1998. The IPP planner: exploring the possibilities of planning graphs. Working notes of the Workshop on Planning as Combinatorial Search held in conjunction with AIPS-98, Pittsburgh, PA, 1998, 71-74.

Lotem, A. and Nau., D. 1999. The Soundness and Completeness of GraphHTN. Working Paper.

Mali, A.; and Kambhampati, S. 1998. Encoding HTN planning in propositional logic. In *Proc. AIPS-98*, 190-198.

Nau, D.; Smith, S. J.; and Erol, K. 1998. Control Strategies in HTN Planning: Theory versus Practice. *AAAI-98/IAAI-98*, 1127–1133.

Nau, D.; Cao, Y.; Lotem, A.; and Muñoz-Avila, H. 1999. SHOP: Simple Hierarchical Ordered Planner. *IJCAI-99*.

Sacerdoti, E. 1975. The nonlinear nature of plans. In *Proc. IJCAI-75*, 206-214.

Smith, S. J.; Nau, D.; and Throop, T. 1998. Computer bridge: a big win for AI planning. *AI Magazine* 19(2), 93–105.

Weld, D; Anderson, C; Smith, D. 1998. Extending Graphplan to handle uncertainty & sensing actions. In *Proc. AAAI-98*, 897-904.

Wilkins, D. and Desimone R. 1994. Applying an AI planner to military operations. *Intelligent Scheduling*, Morgan Kaufmann, M. Fox and M. Zweben, 685-709.

On the Undecidability of Probabilistic Planning and Infinite-Horizon Partially Observable Markov Decision Problems

Omid Madani
Dept. of Comp. Sci. and Eng.
University of Washington, Box 352350
Seattle, WA 98195-2350 USA
madani@cs.washington.edu

Steve Hanks
Adaptive Systems Group
Harlequin Inc.
1201 Third Avenue, Suite 2380
Seattle, WA 98105 USA
hanks@harlequin.com

Anne Condon
Computer Sciences Deptartment
University of Wisconsin
Madison, WI 53706 USA
condon@cs.wisc.edu

Abstract

We investigate the computability of problems in probabilistic planning and partially observable infinite-horizon Markov decision processes. The undecidability of the *string-existence* problem for probabilistic finite automata is adapted to show that the following problem of plan existence in probabilistic planning is undecidable: *given a probabilistic planning problem, determine whether there exists a plan with success probability exceeding a desirable threshold.* Analogous policy-existence problems for partially observable infinite-horizon Markov decision processes under discounted and undiscounted total reward models, average-reward models, and state-avoidance models are all shown to be undecidable. The results apply to corresponding approximation problems as well.

1 Introduction

We show that problems in probabilistic planning (Kushmerick, Hanks, & Weld 1995; Boutilier, Dean, & Hanks 1999) and infinite-horizon partially observable Markov decision processes (POMDPs) (Lovejoy 1991; White 1993) are uncomputable. These models are central to the study of decision-theoretic planning and stochastic control problems, and no computability results have previously been established for probabilistic planning. The undecidability of finding an optimal policy for an infinite-horizon POMDP has been a matter of conjecture (Papadimitriou & Tsitsiklis 1987), (Littman 1996), (Blondel & Tsitsiklis 1998). Our results settle these open problems and complement the research on the computational complexity of finite-horizon POMDP problems (Papadimitriou & Tsitsiklis 1987; Littman 1996; Mundhenk, Goldsmith, & Allender 1997; Littman, Goldsmith, & Mundhenk 1998).

We show that the following basic *plan-existence* problem in probabilistic planning is undecidable:

Given a probabilistic planning problem:

- a set of states
- a probability distribution over the value of the initial state
- a set of goal states
- a set of operators that effect stochastic state transitions
- a rational threshold τ on the probability of plan success

determine whether there is a sequence of operators that will leave the system in a goal state with probability at least τ.

The probabilistic planning problem can be recast as an infinite-horizon undiscounted total reward POMDP problem, the problem being to determine whether there is a policy for the process with expected value at least τ (Boutilier, Dean, & Hanks 1999). Undecidability results for probabilistic planning thus have consequences for at least some POMDP problems as well. In this paper we demonstrate the undecidability of POMDPs for a variety of optimality criteria: total undiscounted and discounted reward, average reward per stage, and a state-oriented negative criterion discussed in (Puterman 1994). We also show the undecidability of several related approximation problems. An interesting consequence of our results on the impossibility of finding approximately optimal plans is that if the length of a candidate solution plan is bounded in size—even by an exponential function of the input description length—the solution found can be arbitrarily suboptimal.

Our analysis assumes incomplete information about the system state (partial observability), but does not set any *a priori* bound on the length of the solution plan. Even so, the undecidability result holds whether the set of admissible plans have finite length, infinite length, or either. Previous research had addressed either other models such as the fully observable case (Littman 1997), and bounded-length plans and finite-horizon POMDPs (see (Goldsmith & Mundhenk 1998) for a survey), or special cases, for example establishing decidability and computational complexity of goal-state reachability with either nonzero probability or probability one (Alur, Couroubetis, & Yannakakis 1995; Littman 1996).

Our undecidability results for the probabilistic planning problems are based on the *string-existence* or *emptiness* problem for probabilistic finite-state automata (PFAs). The undecidability of this problem was first established in (Paz 1971). However we use the reduction in (Condon & Lipton 1989) for our work, since properties of the reduction help establish results for several additional open problems, including the threshold-isolation problem also raised in (Paz 1971). The work in (Condon & Lipton 1989) in turn is based on an investigation of *Interactive Proof Systems* introduced in (Goldwasser, Micali, & Rackoff 1985), and an elegant technique developed in (Freivalds 1981) to show the power of randomization in two-way PFAs.

The paper is organized as follows. The next section defines PFAs and the string-existence problem, and sketches the reduction of (Condon & Lipton 1989), highlighting aspects used in subsequent proofs. The remainder of the section establishes the undecidability of related approximation problems and the threshold-isolation problem.

The following section makes the connection between PFAs and probabilistic planning, proving the undecidability of the latter problem. POMDPs are addressed next: several optimality criteria are introduced, then the policy-existence problem is defined and shown to be undecidable regardless of which optimality criterion is adopted.

2 PFAs and the String-Existence Problem

A probabilistic finite-state automaton M is defined by a quintuple $M = (Q, \Sigma, T, s, f)$ where Q is a finite set of states, Σ is the input alphabet, T is a set of $|Q| \times |Q|$ row-stochastic transition matrices[1], one for each symbol in Σ, $s \in Q$ is the initial state of the PFA, and $f \in Q$ is an *accepting* state. The automaton occupies one state from Q at any point in time, and at each stage transitions stochastically from one state to another. The state transition is determined as follows:

1. The current input symbol a determines a transition matrix M_a.

2. The current state s determines the row $M_a[s]$, a probability distribution over the possible next states.

3. The state changes according to the probability distribution $M_a[s]$.

The automaton halts when it transitions to the accepting state f. In this paper, we restrict attention to pfa's in which the accepting state f is absorbing: $M_a[f, f] = 1.0, \forall a \in \Sigma$.

---

[1]Throughout the paper, we make the standard assumption that all the numbers (e.g. transition probabilities) are rational.

We say the automaton *accepts* the string $w \in \Sigma^*$ (Σ^* denotes the set of all finite strings on Σ) if the automaton ends in the accepting state upon reading the string w, otherwise we say it *rejects* the string. We denote by $p^M(w)$ the acceptance probability of string w by PFA M. The acceptance probability $p^M(w)$ for an infinite string w is defined naturally as the limit $\lim_{i \to \infty} p^M(w_i)$, where w_i denotes the length i prefix of w.

Definition 1 *The* string-existence *problem for PFAs is the problem of deciding whether or not there is some input string $w \in \Sigma^*$ that the given PFA accepts with probability exceeding an input threshold τ.*

Both (Paz 1971) and (Condon & Lipton 1989) establish the undecidability of this problem, also known as the *emptiness problem*:

Theorem 2.1 *(Paz 1971)(Condon & Lipton 1989) The string-existence problem for PFAs is undecidable.*

In the next subsection, we describe the properties of the reduction developed in (Condon & Lipton 1989), followed by a more detailed explanation of the proof. The details of the proof are used to develop corollaries related to probabilistic planning and POMDP problems, most notably Lemma 4.3, which establishes the undecidability of optimal policy construction for discounted-total-reward infinite-horizon POMDPs.

2.1 Properties of the Reduction

In (Condon & Lipton 1989), the (undecidable) question of whether a Turing Machine (TM) accepts the empty string is reduced to the question of whether a PFA accepts any string with probability exceeding a threshold. The PFA constructed by the reduction tests whether its input is a concatenation of *accepting sequences*. An accepting sequence is a legal sequence of TM configurations beginning at the initial configuration and terminating in an accepting configuration.

The reduction has the property that if the TM is accepting, *i.e.* it accepts the empty string, then the PFA accepts sufficiently long concatenations of accepting sequences with high probability. But if the TM is *not* accepting, the PFA accepts all strings with low probability. We next formalize these properties and use them in subsequent undecidability results. The following section explains how the PFA generated by the reduction has these properties.

Theorem 2.2 *There exists an algorithm which, given a two counter TM as input and any rational $\epsilon > 0$ and integer $K \geq 1$, outputs a PFA M satisfying the following:*

1. *If the TM does not accept the empty string, the PFA M accepts no string with probability exceeding ϵ.*

2. *If the TM is accepting, then let string w represent the accepting sequence, and let w^n denote w concatenated n times. We have $\lim_{n \to \infty} p^M(w^n) = 1 - (1/2)^K$, and $\forall n, p^M(w^n) < 1 - (1/2)^K$.*

We conclude this section making two additional points about the string-existence problem.

- Due to the separation between the acceptance probability of the PFA in the two cases of the TM accepting the empty string or otherwise, the string-existence problem remains undecidable if the strict inequality in the description of the existence problem is replaced by a weak equality ($\geq$) relation.

- Although the problem is posed in terms of the existence of finite strings, the result holds even if the strings have infinite length.

2.2 Details of the Reduction

The class of TMs used in the reduction in (Condon & Lipton 1989) are *two-counter* TMs, which are as powerful as general TMs. The constructed PFA is supposed to detect whether a sequence of computations represents a valid accepting computation (accepting sequence) of the TM. This task reduces to the problem of checking the legality of each transition from one configuration of the TM to the next, which amounts to verifying that

- the first configuration has the machine in the start state

- the last configuration has the machine in the accepting state

- each transition is legal according to the TM's transition rules.

All these checks can be carried out by a deterministic finite state automaton, except the check as to whether the TM's counter contents remain valid across consecutive configurations. The PFA rejects immediately if any of the easily verifiable transition rules are violated, which leaves only the problem of validating the counters' contents across each transition.

On each computation step taken by a two-counter TM the counters' contents either stay the same, get incremented by 1, or get decremented by 1. Assuming without loss of generality that the counter contents are represented in unary, this problem reduces to checking whether two strings have the same length: given a string $a^n b^m$, does $n = m$?

Although this question cannot be answered exactly by any PFA, a *weak equality* test developed in (Condon & Lipton 1989) and inspired by (Freivalds 1981) can answer it in a strict and limited sense which is nonetheless sufficient to allow the reduction. The weak equality test works as follows. The PFA scans its input string $a^n b^m$, and with high probability enters an *indecision* state (or equivalently we say the outcome of the test is indecision). With some low probability the PFA enters a one of two "decisive" states. If the substrings have equal length the PFA either enters a *correct* state or a *suspect* state. It enters these two states equiprobably. However, suppose that the PFA enters a decisive state but the input string is composed

of *unequal*-length substrings ($m \neq n$). In this case the *suspect* outcome is k times more likely than the *correct* outcome, where the *discrimination factor* k can be made as large as desired by increasing the size of the PFA.

The PFA of the reduction carries out a *global* test of its own on a candidate accepting sequence for the TM, using the weak-equality test to check for counter increments or decrements on consecutive configurations. Given a candidate accepting sequence, if the outcome of *all* the tests are decisive and *correct*, the PFA accepts the input. If the outcome of *all* the tests are *suspect*, the PFA rejects the input. Otherwise, the PFA remains in the *global-indecision* state until it detects the start of the next candidate accepting sequence (start configuration of the TM), or until it reaches the end of the input. If it is in the global-indecision state at the end of the input, it rejects.

If the original TM accepts the empty string, observe that the probability that the PFA accepts can approach the upper limit $1/2$ on an input string consisting of a concatenation of sufficiently many accepting sequences. If the TM does not accept the empty string, it follows from the properties of the weak-equality test that the probability that the PFA accepts any string is no larger than $1/k$.

By making a minor adjustment to the PFA, the acceptance probability of the PFA when the TM accepts the empty string can be made arbitrarily close to 1: Instead of rejecting or accepting if it sees an all *suspect* or an all *correct* outcome on a single candidate accepting sequence, the PFA can instead increment an *all-decisive* counter with a finite upper limit K. The PFA accepts its input if and only if the the all-decisive counter reaches K, *and* it has seen an all *correct* on a candidate sequence. Hence, if the TM is accepting, the PFA accepts concatenation of sufficiently many accepting sequences with probability arbitrarily close to $1 - (1/2)^K$. In addition, for the cases when the TM is not accepting, the acceptance probability of the PFA can be made as small as desired for a given counter upper limit K, by choosing the discrimination factor k of the weak-equality test to be large.

2.3 Undecidability of Approximations

The question of approximability is an important one, especially when computing an optimal answer is impossible. Unfortunately, it follows from the next corollary that approximations, such as computing a string which the PFA accepts with probability within an additive constant or multiplicative factor $\epsilon < 1$ of the maximum acceptance probability of the PFA[2] are also uncomputable.

Corollary 2.3 *For any fixed $\epsilon, 0 < \epsilon < 1$, the following problem is undecidable: Given is a PFA M for*

---

[2] The maximum acceptance probability is taken as the supremum over the acceptance probability over all strings.

which one of the two cases hold:

- *The PFA accepts some string with probability greater than $1 - \epsilon$.*
- *The PFA accepts no string with probability greater than ϵ.*

Decide whether case 1 holds.

Proof. The corollary is an immediate consequence of the properties outlined in Theorem 2.2, and the fact that ϵ in the reduction can be made as small as desired. $\square$

2.4 Undecidability of the Threshold-Isolation Problem

There might be some hope for decidability of the string-existence problem for special cases: those for which the given threshold (also called a *cutpoint*) is *isolated* for the PFA:

Definition 2 *(Rabin 1963) Let M be a PFA. The threshold τ is ϵ-isolated with respect to M if $|p^M(x) - \tau| \geq \epsilon$ for all $x \in \Sigma^*$, for some $\epsilon > 0$.*

Definition 3 *The threshold-isolation problem is, given a PFA M and a threshold τ, decide whether, for some $\epsilon > 0$, the threshold τ is ϵ-isolated for the PFA M.*

Isolated thresholds are interesting because PFAs with isolated thresholds have less expressive power than general PFAs, thus the corresponding decision problems are easier. The language accepted by a PFA M given a threshold τ, denoted by $L(M, \tau)$, is the set of all strings that take the PFA to the accepting state with probability greater than τ:

$$L(M, \tau) = \{w \in \Sigma^* : p^M(w) > \tau\}.$$

General PFAs are powerful enough to accept even non-context-free languages (see (Paz 1971) for an example). However, Rabin in (Rabin 1963) showed that PFA with *isolated* thresholds accept regular languages. A natural question then is: given a PFA and a threshold, whether the threshold is isolated for the PFA. If we can compute the answer and it is positive, then we can presumably compute the regular language accepted by the PFA, and see whether it is empty or not. That would afford at least the opportunity to recognize and solve a special case of the general string-existence problem.

The decidability of the isolation problem was raised in (Paz 1971), and was heretofore an open question to the best of our knowledge. The reduction in this paper shows that recognizing an isolated threshold is hard as well:

Corollary 2.4 *The threshold-isolation problem is undecidable.*

Proof. As stated in Theorem 2.2, we can design the reduction with $\epsilon = 1/3$, and $K = 1$. It follows that if the TM is not accepting, then there is no string that the PFA accepts with probability greater than $1/3$, while

if the TM is accepting, there are (finite) strings that the PFA accepts with probability arbitrarily close to $1/2$. In other words, the threshold $1/2$ is isolated iff the TM is not accepting. $\square$

3 Undecidable Problems in Probabilistic Planning

This work was originally motivated by questions about the computability of probabilistic planning problems, e.g. the problems introduced in (Kushmerick, Hanks, & Weld 1995; Boutilier, Dean, & Hanks 1999).

The probabilistic planning problem, studied in (Kushmerick, Hanks, & Weld 1995) for example, involves a finite set of states, a finite set of actions effecting stochastic state transitions, a start state (or probability distribution over states), a goal region of the state space, and a threshold τ on the probability of plan success. The problem is to find *any* sequence of actions that would move the system from the start state to a goal state with probability at least τ.

While it had been well established that restricted versions of this problem were decidable, though intractable as a practical matter (Papadimitriou & Tsitsiklis 1987; Bylander 1994; Littman, Goldsmith, & Mundhenk 1998), the complexity of the general probabilistic planning problem (i.e. without restrictions on the nature of the transitions or the length of solution plan considered) had not been determined.

The results of the previous section establish the uncomputability of such problems in the general case—when there is no restriction imposed on the length of solution plans considered. Uncomputability follows when it is established that a sufficiently powerful probabilistic planning language can model any given PFA, so that any question about a PFA can be reformulated as a probabilistic planning problem.

This is the case for the probabilistic planning model investigated in (Kushmerick, Hanks, & Weld 1995). This model is based on STRIPS propositional planning (Fikes & Nilsson 1971) with uncertainty in the form of (conditional) probability distributions added to the action effects. It is established in (Boutilier, Dean, & Hanks 1999) that the propositional encoding of states is sufficient to represent any finite state space, and the extended probabilistic STRIPS action representation is sufficient to represent any stochastic transition matrix. Thus the string-existence problem ("is there any input string that moves the automaton from the start state to an accepting state with probability at least τ?") can be directly reformulated in the planning context ("is there any sequence of actions that moves the system from a start state to a goal state with probability at least τ?"). An algorithm that solved the planning problem would answer the question of whether or not such a plan exists by either generating the plan or terminating having failed to do so, thus solving the equivalent string-existence problem. Thus, as a corollary of the undecidability of the string-existence problem for PFAs we obtain:

Theorem 3.1 *The plan-existence problem is undecidable.*

We also note that due to the tight correspondence between PFA's and probabilistic planning problems, the other undecidability results from the previous section apply as well:

- "Approximately satisficing planning," generating a plan that is within some additive or multiplicative factor of the threshold is undecidable.

- Deciding whether the threshold for a particular planning problem represents an isolated threshold for that problem is undecidable.

Having established a connection between PFAs and probabilistic planning, we next explore the connection between PFAs (and probabilistic planning) and POMDPs.

4   Undecidable Problems for POMDPs

Markov decision processes and their partially observable variants provide a general model of control for stochastic processes (Puterman 1994). In a partially observable Markov decision process (POMDP) problem, a decision maker is faced with a dynamic system S modeled by a tuple $S = (Q, \Sigma, T, R, O, s)$, a generalization of our PFA definition with similar semantics: Q and Σ are sets of n states and m actions respectively, T is a set of $n \times n$ row-stochastic transition matrices, one for each action in Σ.

The POMDP model generalizes the PFA/Planning model in two ways: a more general model of observability, and a more general model of reward and optimality.

In the Planning/PFA model, it is assumed that the decision-making agent will not be able to observe the world as it executes its plan, thus is limited to pre-computing then blindly executing its solution. This can be viewed as a limiting case of the POMDP model: the unobservable MDP or UMDP.

In the POMDP generalization, the agent receives an *observation* from the world after every stage of execution, which might provide some information about the prevailing world state. Observation information is specified through the parameter O, which supplies probabilities of the form $P(o|s, a, s')$: the probability that observation o would have been received, given that the system was in state s, action a was performed, which effected a transition to state s'. The agent maintains a probability distribution over the prevailing world state, then updates that information every time it takes an action a and receives an observation o. The solution to a POMDP problem is a *policy*: a mapping from the actions so far taken and the observations so far received to an action. The term *plan* is often used to refer to a policy in the unobservable case, where there are no observations; thus a policy consists of a sequence of actions.

Unlike the Planning/PFA model which strives to find *any* plan that exceeds the threshold, the MDP model computes a policy that maximizes an *objective function*; a variety of objective functions are explored in the literature.

Most objective functions are based on the idea of a *reward function*, the function $R(s, a)$ which associates a reward or penalty for taking an action a while in a state s. Additional aspects of the objective function are:

- The *horizon*. The horizon determines how many actions are to be executed. Typically considered are *finite-horizon* problems where the policy is executed for a fixed number of steps, and *infinite-horizon* problems where the policy is executed for an indeterminate number of steps.

- The *discount factor*. In a *discounted* objective function, rewards gathered in earlier stages of execution are valued more highly than rewards gathered in later stages. A *discount factor* $0 \leq \beta < 1$ is provided, and the reward gathered at stage i is actually $\beta^i R(s_i, a_i)$. The *undiscounted* case—$\beta = 1$—provides the same reward for an (s, a) pair regardless of the stage at which it occurs.

- Total versus average reward. In the former case the objective is to maximize the sum of all (possibly discounted) rewards over the (possibly infinite) horizon. In the latter case the objective is to maximize the total reward divided by the number of stages (taken as a limit in the infinite-horizon case).

We will refer to the choice of a horizon, a discount factor and an aggregation operator as an *optimality criterion*. The criteria most often studied in the literature are:

- Maximizing total discounted reward over a finite or infinite horizon.

- Maximizing average reward over a finite or infinite horizon.

- Maximizing total undiscounted reward over a finite horizon.

- Maximizing total undiscounted reward over an infinite horizon under restrictions on the reward function and system dynamics that bound the total reward possible.

In this paper we are primarily interested in infinite-horizon problems, as (1) complexity results for finite-horizon problems are well established (Goldsmith & Mundhenk 1998) (Mundhenk, Goldsmith, & Allender 1997), and (2) the Planning/PFA problem maps to an infinite-horizon POMDP, but not to a finite-horizon model.

We are now in a position to define the *policy-existence* problem for POMDPs, under a given optimality criterion. The space of policies considered in the following definitions is an important consideration. All of the lemmas hold when the space of policies includes any one or more of the following sets: finite action sequences of indefinite length, infinite sequences, or algorithms that create such finite or infinite sequences.

Definition 4 *The policy-existence problem (with respect to an optimality criterion) is, given a POMDP and a threshold, whether there exists a policy with expected value greater than the threshold.*

4.1 Undecidability for Positive-Bounded Models under Total Undiscounted Reward

The most direct result involves a special case of infinite-horizon undiscounted total-reward models called *positive bounded* (Puterman 1994). The essential feature of this model is that the reward structure and system dynamics for a problem must ensure that the total reward gathered is bounded both above and below, even over an infinite horizon.

The planning problem can easily be posed as a positive-bounded POMDP:

- the same observation o is received regardless of the state and action (non-observability)

- unit reward is gathered on the execution of *any* action on the goal state (Figure 1a)

- the execution of *any* action at the goal state leads to an absorbing state: the system stays in that state and gathers no additional rewards (Figure 1a)

- all other states and actions incur no reward.

From this equivalence we can immediately establish the following lemma:

Theorem 4.1 *The policy-existence problem for positive-bounded problems under the infinite-horizon total reward criterion is undecidable.*

Proof. Since any planning problem can be posed as a positive-bounded POMDP, we can easily verify that an effective algorithm for that problem could be used to solve the plan-existence problem, and by Corollary 3.1 such an algorithm cannot exist. To see this, note that a plan, say a finite sequence of actions, exists for the planning (PFA) problem with probability of reaching the goal (success probability) exceeding τ, if and only if a finite sequence of actions exist with value exceeding τ for the corresponding UMDP model (as outlined above and in Figure 1a): Let p denote the success probability of a finite sequence of actions w in the planning problem. Then p is the expected total reward of action sequence wa (w followed by any action a) in the corresponding UMDP model. Conversely, if v is the value of a sequence w in the UMDP model, then v is the success probability of sequence w in the planning problem.

A similar equivalence holds for infinite action sequences. □

4.2 Undecidability under the Average Reward Criterion

The indirect connection to PFAs allows extension of the previous result to *all* undiscounted total-reward models, and to average-reward models as well.

Theorem 4.2 *The policy-existence problem under the infinite-horizon average reward criterion is undecidable.*

Proof. The proof is complete once we observe that questions on acceptance probability of strings for a given PFA can be readily turned to questions on the value of similar strings in a related UMDP model. This transformation is achieved by modeling the probability of reaching the accepting state f using rewards (Figure 1b). It can be verified that there is a string accepted by the PFA M with probability exceeding τ if and only if there is a string with average reward greater than τ for the corresponding UMDP model. To see this, assume for some string w, $p^M(w) > \tau$, and denote by $v(w)$ the average reward of w under the corresponding UMDP model. We must have, for any action a, $p^M(w)\frac{k+1}{k+|w|} \le v(wa^k)$ where wa^k denotes w concatenated with k repetitions of action a. The inequality follows from writing $v(w)$ in terms of the probability of reaching the goal state on each prefix of w. We thus have $\lim_{k\to\infty} v(wa^k) \ge p^M(w)$. Hence for some k, $v(wa^k) > \tau$. Conversely, we can verify that for any string w, $v(w) \le p^M(w)$, so if $v(w) > \tau$, $p^M(w) > \tau$.

A similar equivalence holds for infinite strings. □

4.3 Undecidability of the Discounted-Reward Model

We turn now to the most commonly studied model: maximizing total expected discounted reward over an infinite horizon. Here, as in the proof of Lemma 4.2, we make a small change in the PFA constructed in the emptiness reduction.

Theorem 4.3 *The policy-existence problem under the infinite-horizon discounted criterion is undecidable.*

Proof. Let us take the PFA constructed in the reduction of Section 2.2 and change it to a *leaky* PFA as follows. Let d be any rational value such that $0 < d < 1$. The leaky PFA, upon reading an input symbol, continues as the original PFA with probability $1 - d$. Otherwise, we say that it *leaks*, and in this case it makes a transition to either an absorbing rejection state or the absorbing accepting state, each with equal overall probability $d/2$. It is not hard to verify that maximizing the probability of reaching the accepting state in such a leaky PFA corresponds to maximizing the expected total discounted reward in a UMDP with a reward structure as described in the proof of Lemma 4.2 and Figure 1(a), where the discount factor is $\beta = 1 - \frac{d}{2}$. We show that if the TM is accepting (see Section 2.1), then the leaky PFA accepts some strings with probability greater than $1/2$, while if the TM is not accepting,

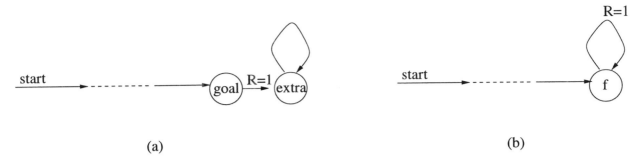

(a)   (b)

Figure 1: (a) The criterion of maximizing the probability of reaching a goal state in probabilistic planning modeled as a total reward criterion. The old absorbing goal state (labeled goal) now, on any action, has a transition to an extra absorbing state with reward of 1.0. All other rewards are zero. (b) Similarly, a PFA string-existence problem modeled as an average reward problem.

every finite string is accepted with probability less than $1/2$.

Assume the TM is accepting, and let w be an accepting sequence of the TM. Assume the original PFA accepts only after $K \geq 2$ decisive outcomes (the all-decisive counter limit K is explained in the end of the reduction subsection).

Let q denote the probability that the PFA "halts" (i.e. goes into one of the absorbing states) on reading w^j. Let p denote the probability that the PFA has leaked *given* that it halts, i.e. it halts due to the leak and not due to the remaining possibility of having K decisive outcomes (which has $1 - p$ probability). Hence, given that the PFA halts on w^j, the probability of acceptance is:

$$1/2p + (1 - p)(1 - 1/2^K) = 1/2p + (1 - p)(1/2 + \epsilon),$$

for some $\epsilon > 0$, and the overall probability of acceptance is $q[1/2p + (1 - p)(1 - 1/2^K)]$. As q approaches 1 with increasing j in w^j, we need only argue that p is bounded above by a constant strictly less than 1, for sufficiently large j, to show that acceptance probability exceeds $1/2$ for some j. We note that $p = 1$, when $j < K$. With $j \geq K$, the probability that the PFA leaks can be no larger than $1 - p(e)$, where $p(e)$ denotes the probability of event e, the event that the PFA does not leak on w^j, but halts (upon reading the last symbol, so that it has made K decisions), hence $p(e) > 0$.

Assume the TM is not accepting. A candidate (accepting) sequence refers to a sequence of TM configurations where the first one is the initial TM configuration and the last is an accepting configuration. Any input string s can be viewed as a concatenation of $j \geq 0$ candidate sequences appended with a possibly empty string u where none of the prefixes of u is a candidate sequence: $s = w_1 w_2 \cdots w_j u, j \geq 0$. If $j \leq K$, then probability of acceptance of the leaky PFA is $qp/2$, where $q < 1$ is the probability of halting on s and $p = 1$ is the probability of leaking given that the PFA halts. Here, $p = 1$ because there is no other possibil-

ity for halting, but note that $q < 1$. If $j > K$, then probability of acceptance is: $q(p/2 + (1 - p)(1/2 - \epsilon))$, where $q < 1$ is the probability of halting on s and $p < 1$ is the probability of leaking given that the PFA halts. Given that the PFA halts and does not leak, the probability of acceptance is strictly less than $1/2$, as the PFA is keeping a counter, and the probability of K suspect outcomes is more than $1/2$ (for appropriately small $K > 1$, such as $K = 2$).

A similar conversion to the one in the proof of Lemma 4.1 reduces the string-existence problem for the leaky PFA to the question of policy-existence in a UMDP under the discounted criterion, thus completing the proof. □

We note that an inapproximability result similar to the one for PFAs also holds for POMDPs under the total undiscounted reward and the average reward criteria. However, under the discounted criterion, the optimal value is approximable to within any $\epsilon > 0$, due to the presence of the discount factor.

4.4 Undecidability under a Negative Model

The optimality criteria studied to this point involve maximizing the expected benefits of executing a policy. An alternative goal would be to choose a policy likely to avoid distaster. In these cases (*state-oriented negative* models) the objective is to minimize the probability of entering one or more designated negative states over the infinite horizon. We use the reduction in the previous proof to establish the undecidability of this particular negative model; the technique should be applicable to other negative models as well.

Theorem 4.4 *Policy existence under the state-oriented negative model is undecidable.*

Proof. We reduce the string-existence question for the leaky PFA in reduction of Lemma 4.3 to this problem. Note that in the string-existence reduction for the leaky PFA, if the TM is accepting, there exist infinite (and therefore finite) sequences of symbols on which the probability of acceptance of the leaky PFA exceeds 1/2. If the TM is rejecting, the probability of acceptance of no infinite sequence is over 1/2 (an infinite sequences with acceptance equals 1/2 may exist.). Take the rejecting absorbing state of the leaky PFA to be the state to avoid and the (undecidable) question would be whether there is an infinite sequence that avoids the rejecting state with probability exceeding 1/2. □

5 Summary

This paper investigated the computability of plan existence for probabilistic planning, and policy existence for a variety of infinite-horizon POMDPs. A correspondence was established between probabilistic (non-observable) planning and probabilistic finite-state automata, and the reduction of (Condon & Lipton 1989) was exploited to show that many natural questions in this domain are undecidable. The PFA and planning problems were then viewed as a special case of infinite-horizon POMDPs, thus providing undecidability results for a variety of POMDP models, both discounted and undiscounted.

It is now well established that optimal planning without full observability is prohibitively difficult both in theory and practice (Papadimitriou & Tsitsiklis 1987; Littman 1996; Mundhenk, Goldsmith, & Allender 1997). These results suggest that it may be more promising to explore alternative problem formulations, including restrictions on the system dynamics and the agent's sensing and effecting powers that are useful for realistic problem domains yet are more amenable to exact or approximate solution algorithms.

Acknowledgements

Thanks to Bill Rounds, who first pointed out to us the connection between PFAs and probabilistic planning. Hanks and Madani were supported in part by ARPA/Rome Labs Grant F30602-95-1-0024, and in part by NSF grant IRI-9523649. Anne Condon was supported by NSF grants CCR-92-57241 HRD-627241.

References

Alur, R.; Couroubetis, C.; and Yannakakis, M. 1995. Distinguishing tests for nondeterministic and probabilistic machines. In *Proc. of 27th STOC*, 363–372.

Blondel, V. D., and Tsitsiklis, J. N. 1998. A survey of computational complexity results in systems and control. Submitted to Automatica, 1998.

Boutilier, C.; Dean, T.; and Hanks, S. 1999. Decision theoretic planning: Structural assumptions and computational leverage. *Journal of Artificial Intelligence Research* 157–171. To appear.

Bylander, T. 1994. The computational complexity of propositional STRIPS planning. *Artificial Intelligence* 69:161–204.

Condon, A., and Lipton, R. 1989. On the complexity of space bounded interactive proofs. In *30th Annual Symposium on Foundations of Computer Science.*

Fikes, R. E., and Nilsson, N. J. 1971. STRIPS: a new approach to the application of theorem proving to problem solving. *Artificial Intelligence* 2(3-4):189–208.

Freivalds, R. 1981. Probabilistic two way machines. In *Proc. International Symposium on Mathematical Foundations of Computer Science*, volume 118, 33–45. Springer-Verlag.

Goldsmith, J., and Mundhenk, M. 1998. Complexity issues in markov decision processes. In *Proc. IEEE conference on Computational Complexity.*

Goldwasser, S.; Micali, S.; and Rackoff, C. 1985. The knowledge complexity of interactive protocols. In *Proc. of 17th STOC*, 291–304.

Kushmerick, N.; Hanks, S.; and Weld, D. S. 1995. An algorithm for probabilistic planning. *Artificial Intelligence* 76(1-2):239–286.

Littman, M. L.; Goldsmith, J.; and Mundhenk, M. 1998. The computational complexity of probabilistic planning. *Artificial Intelligence Research.*

Littman, M. 1996. *Algorithms for Sequential Decision Making.* Ph.D. Dissertation, Brown.

Littman, M. L. 1997. Probabilistic propositional planning: Representaions and complexity. In *Proceedings of the 14th National Conference on AI.* AAAI Press.

Lovejoy, W. 1991. A survey of algorithmic methods for partially observable Markov decision processes. *Annals of Operations Research* 47–66.

Mundhenk, M.; Goldsmith, J.; and Allender, E. 1997. The complexity of policy existence problem for partially-observable finite-horizon Markov decision processes. In *Mathematical Foundations of Computer Science*, 129–38.

Papadimitriou, C. H., and Tsitsiklis, J. N. 1987. The complexity of Markov decision processes. *Mathematics of operations research* 12(3):441–450.

Paz, A. 1971. *Introduction to Probabilistic Automata.* Academic Press.

Puterman, M. L. 1994. *Markov Decision Processes.* Wiley Inter-science.

Rabin, M. O. 1963. Probabilistic automata. *Information and Control* 230–245.

White, D. 1993. *Markov Decision Processes.* Wiley.

Contingent Planning Under Uncertainty via Stochastic Satisfiability

Stephen M. Majercik and Michael L. Littman
Department of Computer Science
Duke University
Durham, NC 27708-0129
{majercik,mlittman}@cs.duke.edu

Abstract

We describe two new probabilistic planning techniques—C-MAXPLAN and ZANDER—that generate contingent plans in probabilistic propositional domains. Both operate by transforming the planning problem into a stochastic satisfiability problem and solving that problem instead. C-MAXPLAN encodes the problem as an E-MAJSAT instance, while ZANDER encodes the problem as an S-SAT instance. Although S-SAT problems are in a higher complexity class than E-MAJSAT problems, the problem encodings produced by ZANDER are substantially more compact and appear to be easier to solve than the corresponding E-MAJSAT encodings. Preliminary results for ZANDER indicate that it is competitive with existing planners on a variety of problems.

Introduction

When planning under uncertainty, any information about the state of the world is precious. A *contingent plan* is one that can make action choices contingent on such information. In this paper, we present an implemented framework for contingent planning under uncertainty using stochastic satisfiability.

Our general motivation for developing the probabilistic-planning-as-stochastic-satisfiability paradigm was to explore the potential for deriving performance gains in probabilistic domains similar to those provided by SATPLAN (Kautz & Selman 1996) in deterministic domains. There are a number of advantages to encoding planning problems as satisfiability problems. First, the expressivity of Boolean satisfiability allows us to construct a very general planning framework. Another advantage echoes the intuition behind reduced instruction set computers; we wish to translate planning problems into satisfiability problems for which we can develop highly optimized solution techniques using a small number of extremely efficient operations. Supporting this goal is the fact that satisfiability is a fundamental problem in computer science and, as such, has been studied intensively. Numerous techniques have been developed to solve satisfiability problems as efficiently as possible. Stochastic satisfiability is less well-studied, but many satisfiability techniques carry over to stochastic satisfiability nearly intact (Littman, Majercik, & Pitassi 1999).

There are disadvantages to this approach. Problems that can be compactly expressed in representations used by other planning techniques often suffer a significant blowup in size when encoded as Boolean satisfiability problems, degrading the planner's performance. Automatically producing maximally efficient plan encodings is a difficult problem. In addition, translating the planning problem into a satisfiability problem obscures the structure of the problem, making it difficult to use our knowledge of and intuition about the planning process to develop search control heuristics or prune plans.

Our planners solve probabilistic propositional planning problems: states are represented as an assignment to a set of Boolean state variables (fluents) and actions map states to states probabilistically. Problems are expressed using a dynamic-belief-network representation. A subset of the state variables are declared *observable*, meaning that a plan can be made contingent on any of these variables. This scheme is sufficiently expressive to allow a domain designer to make a domain fully observable, unobservable, or to have observations depend on actions and states in probabilistic ways.

We describe how to map the problem of contingent planning in a probabilistic propositional domain to two different probabilistic satisfiability problems. C-MAXPLAN, the first approach, encodes the planning problem as an E-MAJSAT instance (Majercik & Littman 1998). A set of Boolean variables (the *choice* variables) encodes the contingent plan and a second set (the *chance* variables) encodes the probabilistic outcome of the plan—the satisfiability problem is to find the setting of the choice variables that maximizes the probability of satisfaction with respect to the chance variables. The efficiency with which the resulting E-MAJSAT problem is solved, however, depends critically on the plan representation. ZANDER, the second approach, encodes the planning problem as an S-SAT instance (Papadimitriou 1985). Here, we intermingle choice variables and chance variables so that values for choice variables encoding actions can be chosen conditionally based on the values of earlier chance variables encoding observations. ZANDER encodings are substantially more compact than C-MAXPLAN encodings, and this appears to more than offset the fact that S-SAT lies in a higher complexity class than E-MAJSAT.

In the remainder of this section, we describe our domain representation and the stochastic satisfiability framework. In the following section, we describe C-MAXPLAN, providing evidence that its performance is quite sensitive to the plan representation. The next two sections introduce the S-SAT-based ZANDER encoding and an algorithm for solving S-SAT instances to find the optimal plan. The section after that reports on a set of comparative experiments; even with our preliminary S-SAT solver, ZANDER appears to be competitive with existing planners across a variety of planning problems. We conclude with some ideas for further work.

Probabilistic Planning Representation

The contingent planners we developed work on partially observable probabilistic propositional planning domains. Such a domain consists of a finite set P of n distinct *propositions*, any of which may be True or False at any (discrete) time t. A *state* is an assignment of truth values to P. A probabilistic initial state is specified by a set of decision trees, one for each proposition. A proposition p whose initial assignment is independent of all other propositions has a tree consisting of a single node labeled by the probability with which p will be True at time 0. A proposition q whose initial assignment is not independent has a decision tree whose nodes are labeled by the propositions that q depends on and whose leaves specify the probability with which q will be True at time 0. *Goal states* are specified by a partial assignment G to the set of propositions; any state that extends G is considered to be a goal state.

Each of a set A of *actions* probabilistically transforms a state at time t into a state at time $t+1$ and so induces a probability distribution over the set of all states. In this work, the effect of each action on each proposition is represented as a separate decision tree (Boutilier & Poole 1996). For a given action a, each of the decision trees for the different propositions are ordered, so the decision tree for one proposition can refer to both the new and old values of previous propositions. The leaves of a decision tree describe how the associated proposition changes as a function of the state and action.

A subset of the set of propositions is the set of *observable propositions*. Each observable proposition has, as its basis, a proposition that represents the actual status of the thing being observed. (Note that although values are assigned to observable propositions in the initial state, no action at time 1 makes use of these propositions in its decision trees, since there are no valid observations at time 0.)

The planning task is to find a plan that selects an action for each step t as a function of the value of observable propositions for steps before t. We want to find a plan that maximizes (or exceeds a user-specified threshold for) the probability of reaching a goal state.

For example, consider a simple domain based on the TIGER problem of Kaelbling, Littman, & Cassandra (1998). The domain consists of four propositions: **tiger-behind-left-door**, **dead**, **rewarded** and **hear-tiger-behind-left-door**, the last of which is observable. In the initial state, **tiger-behind-left-door** is True with

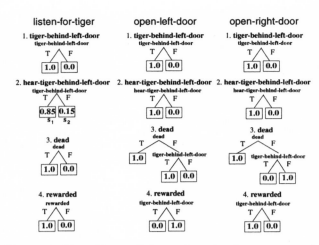

Figure 1: The effects of the actions in the TIGER problem are represented by a set of decision trees.

probability 0.5, dead is False, rewarded is False, and hear-tiger-behind-left-door is False (although irrelevant). The goal states are specified by the partial assignment (rewarded, (not dead)). The three actions are **listen-for-tiger**, **open-left-door**, and **open-right-door** (Figure 1). Actions **open-left-door** and **open-right-door** make reward True, as long as the tiger is not behind that door (we assume the tiger is behind the right door if **tiger-behind-left-door** is False). Since **tiger-behind-left-door** is not observable, the **listen** action becomes important; it causes the observable **hear-tiger-behind-left-door** proposition to become equal to **tiger-behind-left-door** with probability 0.85 (and its negation otherwise). By **listen**ing multiple times, it becomes possible to determine the likely location of the tiger.

Stochastic Satisfiability

In the deterministic satisfiability problem, or SAT, we are given a Boolean formula and wish to determine whether there is some assignment to the variables in the formula that results in the formula evaluating to True. Fixed-horizon deterministic planning problems can be encoded by SAT formulas (Kautz & Selman 1996).

A formal definition of the SAT decision problem follows. Let $\mathbf{x} = \langle x_1, x_2, \ldots, x_n \rangle$ be a collection of n Boolean variables, and $\phi(\mathbf{x})$ be a CNF Boolean formula on these variables with m clauses. For example, $(x_1 + \overline{x_2} + x_4)(x_2 + x_3 + x_4)(\overline{x_1} + \overline{x_2} + \overline{x_3})$ is a CNF formula with $n = 4$ variables and $m = 3$ clauses. This paper uses "1" and "0" for True and False, multiplication for conjunction, and addition for disjunction. Logical negation is defined as $\overline{x} = 1 - x$. With respect to a formula $\phi(\mathbf{x})$, an assignment to the Boolean variables $x_1, \ldots, x_n$ is *satisfying* if $\phi(\mathbf{x}) = 1$. In other words, a satisfying assignment makes the formula True. The decision problem SAT asks whether a given Boolean formula $\phi(\mathbf{x})$ in CNF has a satisfying assignment $(\exists x_1, \ldots, \exists x_n(\phi(\mathbf{x}) = 1))$.

Papadimitriou (1985) explored an extension of SAT in

which a random quantifier is introduced. The stochastic SAT (S-SAT) problem is to evaluate a Boolean formula in which existential and random quantifiers alternate:

$$\exists x_1, \forall x_2, \exists x_3, \ldots, \exists x_{n-1}, \forall x_n (E[\phi(\mathbf{x})] \geq \theta).$$

In words, this formula asks whether there is a value for x_1 such that, *for random* values of x_2 (choose 0 or 1 with equal probability), there exists a value of $x_3 \ldots$ such that the *expected* value of the Boolean formula $\phi(\mathbf{x})$ is at least a threshold θ. This type of satisfiability consists of alternating between making a choice of value for an odd-numbered variable with a chance selection of a value for an even-numbered variable; hence, Papadimitriou referred to S-SAT as a "game against nature." In our S-SAT problems, we will allow *blocks* of existential and random quantifiers to alternate. Furthermore, we will allow *annotated random quantifiers* such as $\forall^{0.2}$, which takes on value `True` with probability 0.2 and `False` with probability 0.8. S-SAT, like the closely related quantified Boolean formula problem, is PSPACE-complete. The specification of an S-SAT problem consists of the Boolean formula $\phi(\mathbf{x})$, the probability threshold θ, and the ordering of the quantifiers.

Different thresholds and patterns of quantifiers in S-SAT instances result in different computational problems, complete for different complexity classes. An S-SAT problem with a threshold of 1.0 and a single block of existentially quantified variables is equivalent to the NP-complete problem SAT. An S-SAT problem with an arbitrary threshold and a single block of existentially quantified variables followed by a single block of randomly quantified variables is equivalent to the NP^{PP}-complete problem E-MAJSAT. As we will describe, both E-MAJSAT formulas and S-SAT formulas can be used to encode planning problems.

Related Work

The type of partially observable planning problem we address, featuring actions with probabilistic effects and noisy observations, is a form of partially observable Markov decision process (POMDP). Algorithms that use a *flat* representation for POMDPs have been around for many years. In this section, we focus on more recent algorithms that exploit propositional state representations. Of course, any algorithm that can solve a planning problem in a flat representation can also be used to solve a problem in the propositional representation by enumerating states; in fact, this approach is often the fastest for domains with up to five or six fluents.

One of the most well-known contingent planners for probabilistic domains is C-BURIDAN (Draper, Hanks, & Weld 1994), which uses tree-based, probabilistic STRIPS operators to extend partial-order planning to stochastic domains. C-BURIDAN searches for a type of contingent plan whose probability of success meets or exceeds some prespecified threshold. As Onder & Pollack (1997) point out, however, there are some problems with C-BURIDAN, and these could prevent it from

solving arbitrary partially observable planning problems. MAHINUR (Onder & Pollack 1997) is a probabilistic partial-order planner that corrects these deficiencies by combining C-BURIDAN's probabilistic action representation and system for managing these actions with a CNLP-style approach to handling contingencies. The novel feature of MAHINUR is that it identifies those contingencies whose failure would have the greatest negative impact on the plan's success and focuses its planning efforts on generating plan branches to deal with those contingencies. Onder & Pollack (1997) identify several domain assumptions (including a type of subgoal decomposability) that underlie the design of MAHINUR, and there are no guarantees on the correctness of MAHINUR for domains in which these assumptions are violated. Our contingent planners, C-MAXPLAN and ZANDER, correct the deficiencies noted by Onder and Pollack and, in addition, avoid the assumptions made by MAHINUR, thus resulting in planners that are applicable to more general domains.

CONFORMANT GRAPHPLAN (Smith & Weld 1998) deals with uncertainty in initial conditions and action outcomes by attempting to construct a non-sensing, noncontingent plan that will succeed in all cases. PGRAPHPLAN (Blum & Langford 1998) employs forward search through the planning graph to find the contingent plan with the highest expected utility in a completely observable stochastic environment. SENSORY GRAPHPLAN (SGP) (Weld, Anderson, & Smith 1998), constructs plans with sensing actions that gather information to be used later in distinguishing between different plan branches. Thus, SGP is an approach to constructing contingent plans. However, SGP has not been extended to handle actions with uncertain effects (except in the conformant case) and imperfect observations, so it is only applicable to a subset of partially observable planning problems.

Boutilier & Poole (1996) describe an algorithm for solving partially observable planning problems based on an earlier algorithm for completely observable problems. While promising, little computational experience with this algorithm is available.

Our planners, C-MAXPLAN and ZANDER, are based on earlier work on MAXPLAN (Majercik & Littman 1998), a planner for unobservable domains. Both are based on stochastic satisfiability and can handle general (finite-horizon) partially observable planning problems. They allow both states and observations to be in a compact propositional form, and so can be used to attack large-scale planning problems.

For the partially observable planning problems they can solve, MAHINUR and SGP appear to run at state-of-the-art speeds; in the Results section, we will report favorable comparisons of ZANDER with MAHINUR and SGP, as well as an implementation of a POMDP algorithm for flat domains, on some standard test problems.

C-MAXPLAN

MAXPLAN (Majercik & Littman 1998) was initially developed to solve probabilistic planning problems in completely unobservable domains. MAXPLAN works by first converting the planning problem to an E-MAJSAT problem, which is an S-SAT problem with a single block of existential (choice) variables followed by a single block of random (chance) variables. The choice variables encode candidate plans, and the chance variables encode the probabilistic outcome of the plan. MAXPLAN solves the E-MAJSAT problem using a modified version of the Davis-Putnam-Logemann-Loveland (DPLL) procedure for determining satisfiability. Essentially, it uses DPLL to determine all possible satisfying assignments, sums the probabilities of the satisfying assignments for each possible choice-variable assignment, and then returns the choice-variable assignment (plan) with the highest probability of producing a satisfying assignment (goal satisfaction). The algorithm uses an efficient splitting heuristic (*time-ordered splitting*) and *memoization* (Majercik & Littman 1998) to accelerate this procedure. Note that in MAXPLAN an n-step plan is encoded as a selection of one action out of the $|A|$ possible actions for each of the n steps. This is shown graphically in Figure 2(a) for a 3-step plan, where action selection is indicated by bold circles.

The MAXPLAN approach can also handle contingent planning problems if given an appropriate problem encoding. A generic E-MAJSAT encoding for contingent plans follows, where c_1 is the number of choice variables needed to specify the plan, c_2 is the number of state variables (one for each proposition at each time step), and c_3 is the number of chance variables (one for each possible stochastic outcome at each time step):

$$\overbrace{\exists x_1, \ldots, \exists x_{c_1}}^{\text{the plan}} \overbrace{\exists y_1, \ldots, \exists y_{c_2}}^{\text{the state}} \overbrace{\forall^{\rho_1} z_1, \ldots, \forall^{\rho_{c_3}} z_{c_3}}^{\text{random outcomes}}$$
$$(E[(\text{initial/goal conditions } (y,z)\text{-clauses})$$
$$(\text{action exclusion } (x)\text{-clauses})$$
$$(\text{action outcome } (x,y,z)\text{-clauses})] \geq \theta).$$

The formula picks the plan and the sequence of states encountered, and then randomly selects the outcome of actions.[1] The clauses insist that initial and goal conditions are satisfied, one action is selected per time step, and that the sequence of states selected is valid given the selected actions and random outcomes.

More specifically, a contingent action in contingent MAXPLAN (C-MAXPLAN) is expressed as a group of actions, all of which execute, but only one of which has an impact on the state (the one whose set of conditions matches the set of observations generated by previous actions). Since the condition sets of the actions are mutually exclusive, the net result is that at most one action in the group will *effectively* execute (*i.e.* affect

---

[1]In fact, in our implementation, the random outcome variables precede the state variables. Although the resulting encoding isn't precisely E-MAJSAT, the values of the state variables are forced given the outcome variables, and so their quantifiers are not significant.

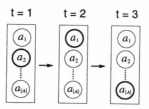

(a) 3-time-step plan in MAXPLAN

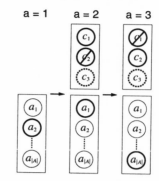

(b) 3-action-step plan in C-MAXPLAN

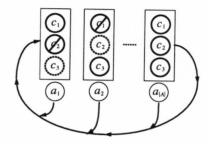

(c) Policy encoding in C-MAXPLAN

Figure 2: MAXPLAN and the two styles of encoding in C-MAXPLAN encode plans in different ways.

the state), depending on current conditions. Thus, in C-MAXPLAN, it is more appropriate to refer to *action* steps than time steps. The difference between MAXPLAN encodings and C-MAXPLAN encodings is shown graphically in Figure 2. Figure 2(a) shows a 3-step plan in MAXPLAN, where selected actions are indicated by bold circles. Figure 2(b) shows a 3-action plan in C-MAXPLAN. Actions are still selected as in MAXPLAN, but now all actions, except for Action 1, have conditions attached to them (the c variables in the boxes above the action selection boxes). These conditions specify when the action will effectively execute. In Figure 2(b), Action 2 will effectively execute if condition c_1 is True (bold circle) and condition c_2 is False (bold circle with slash). Condition c_3 is indicated to be irrelevant (it can be True *or* False) by a broken circle. Action 3 will effectively execute if condition c_1 is False and condition c_2 is True (condition c_3 is, again, irrelevant).

To encode contingent plans in this manner, we need

additional variables and clauses, and we need to alter the decision trees of the actions (which will alter some of the clauses as well). The key clauses in the contingent plan encodings are those clauses that model the satisfaction of conditions. At a high level, these clauses enforce the notion that if if condition c specifies that proposition p have truth status T and the variable indicating that our current observation of p is valid is True, and the variable indicating our perception of p has truth status T, *then* c is satisfied.

Initial tests of this technique were promising; the most basic version of C-MAXPLAN solved a contingent version of the SAND-CASTLE-67 problem, the SHIP-REJECT problem (Draper, Hanks, & Weld 1994), and the MEDICAL-1ILL problem (Weld, Anderson, & Smith 1998) in 3.5, 5.25, and 0.5 cpu seconds, respectively on a 300 MHz UltraSparcIIi. But tests on the MEDICAL-4ILL problem (Weld, Anderson, & Smith 1998) were disappointing; even accelerated versions of C-MAXPLAN had not solved the problem after several *days*.

We obtained significantly better performance by implementing three improvements. First, instead of searching for the optimal plan of a given length, we search for an optimal small *policy* to be applied for a given number of steps. In this approach, the decision trees from all actions for each proposition p are merged into a single decision tree that describes the impact of *all* the actions on p via a cascade of condition-fulfillment variables. Essentially, the decision tree says: "If the conditions specified by the policy for action a are satisfied, then decide the status of p according to a's decision tree; otherwise, if the conditions for action b are satisfied, then decide the status of p according to b's decision tree; ...; otherwise, the status of p remains the same."

In this encoding, we have a single action—*follow-the-policy*—and the choice variables are used to describe that policy. A policy is specified by describing the conditions under which each *primitive* action (an action in the original domain) should be executed. Figure 2(c) shows a policy: conditions (in the boxes) are specified for each action, and one cycle of policy execution executes the first action whose conditions match the current state. In this formulation of the problem, the algorithm searches for the setting of these policy-specification variables that maximizes the probability of satisfying the E-MAJSAT formula (achieving the goals).

The primary advantage of this approach appears to be a more compact encoding of the problem, achieved by exploiting the fact that the status of a given proposition can typically be changed by only a small percentage of the actions in the domain. (This is similar to the use of *explanatory frame axioms* by Kautz, McAllester, & Selman (1996) to reduce the size of their *linear* SAT encodings of planning problems.)

Second, we adapted the DPLL splitting heuristic described by Bayardo & Schrag (1997) for use in C-MAXPLAN. This heuristic selects an initial pool of candidates based on a score that rewards variables that appear both negated and not negated in binary clauses.

This initial pool is rescored based on the number of unit propagations that occur for each assignment to each variable, rewarding variables for which both truth values induce unit propagations. Essentially, this heuristic tries to find a variable that will induce the highest number of unit propagations, thereby maximizing pruning.

Third, we implemented a *thresholding* technique similar to that of C-BURIDAN and MAHINUR. If, instead of insisting on finding the plan with optimal probability, we supply a minimum desired probability, we can prune plans based on this threshold. For a choice variable, if the probability of success given an assignment of True is higher than our threshold, we can prune plans in which this variable would be assigned False. For a chance variable, we can perform a similar kind of pruning (although the thresholds passed down the tree must be appropriately adjusted). But, for chance variables, if the probability of success given an assignment of True is *low* enough, we can determine that the probability weighted average of both truth assignments will not meet our adjusted threshold and can return failure immediately (Littman, Majercik, & Pitassi 1999).

With these improvements, C-MAXPLAN can solve the MEDICAL-4ILL problem in approximately 100 cpu seconds. But, there are issues that make this approach problematic. First, the results described above indicate that the performance of this approach is very sensitive to the details of the plan encoding, making it less robust than desired. Second, if two actions could be triggered by the same set of conditions, only the first one in the decision-tree cascade will be triggered, so the construction of the decision tree introduces unwanted bias. Finally, plan encodings for problems in which actions need to be conditioned on an entire *history* of observations grow exponentially with the length of the history.

ZANDER

In an S-SAT formula, the value of an existential variable x can be selected on the basis of the values of all the variables to x's left in the quantifier sequence. This suggests another way of mapping contingent planning problems to stochastic satisfiability: encode the contingent plan in the variable ordering associated with the S-SAT formula. By alternating blocks of existential variables that encode actions and blocks of random variables that encode observations, we can condition the value chosen for any action variable on the possible values for all the observation variables that appear earlier in the ordering. A generic S-SAT encoding for contingent plans appears in Figure 3. This approach is agnostic as to the structure of the plan; the type of plan returned is algorithm dependent. Our S-SAT solver, described below, constructs tree-structured proofs; these correspond to tree-structured plans that contain a branch for each observable variable. Other solvers could produce DAG-structured, subroutine-structured, or value-function-based plans.

The quantifiers naturally fall into three segments: a plan-execution history, the domain uncertainty, and the

$$\overbrace{\exists x_{1,1},\ldots,\exists x_{1,c_1}}^{\text{first action}} \overbrace{\forall w_{1,1},\ldots,\forall w_{1,c_2}}^{\text{first observation}} \cdots \overbrace{\forall w_{n-1,1},\ldots,\forall w_{n-1,c_2}}^{\text{last observation}} \overbrace{\exists x_{n,1},\ldots,\exists x_{n,c_1}}^{\text{last action}} \overbrace{\forall^{\rho_1} z_1,\ldots,\forall^{\rho_{c_4}} z_{c_4}}^{\text{random outcomes}} \overbrace{\exists y_1,\ldots,\exists y_{c_3}}^{\text{the state}}$$

$$(E[(\text{initial/goal conditions } (y,z)\text{-clauses})(\text{action exclusion } (x)\text{-clauses})(\text{action outcome } (w,x,y,z)\text{-clauses})] \geq \theta).$$

c_1 is the number of variables it takes to specify a single action (the number of actions),

c_2 is the number of variables it takes to specify a single observation (the number of observable variables),

c_3 is the number of state variables (one for each proposition at each time step), and

c_4 is the number of chance variables (essentially one for each possible stochastic outcome at each time step).

Figure 3: Contingent planning problems can be encoded as an instance of S-SAT.

result of the plan-execution history given the domain uncertainty. The plan-execution-history segment is an alternating sequence of choice-variable blocks (one for each action choice) and chance-variable blocks (one for each set of possible observations at a time step).[2] In our TIGER problem, each action variable block would be composed of the three possible actions—**listen-for-tiger**, **open-left-door**, and **open-right-door**—and each observation variable block would be composed of the single variable hear-tiger-behind-left-door.

The domain uncertainty segment is a single block containing all the chance variables that modulate the impact of the actions on the observation and state variables. These variables are associated with random quantifiers; when we consider a variable that represents uncertainty in the environment, we want to take the probability weighted average of the success probabilities associated with the two possible settings of the variable. In the TIGER problem, there would be a chance variable (probability = 0.85) associated with the outcome of each **listen-for-tiger** action.

The result segment is a single block containing all the non-observation state variables. These variables are associated with existential quantifiers, indicating that we can choose the best truth setting for each variable. In reality, all such "choices" are forced by the settings of the action variables in the first segment and the chance variables in the second segment. If these forced choices are compatible, then the preceding plan-execution history is possible and has a non-zero probability of achieving the goals. Otherwise, either the plan-execution history is impossible, given the effects of the actions, or it has a zero probability of achieving the goals.

Algorithm Description

C-MAXPLAN finds the assignment to the choice variables that maximizes the probability of getting a satisfying assignment with respect to the chance variables.

ZANDER, however, must find an assignment *tree* that specifies the optimal choice-variable assignment given all possible settings of the observation variables. Note that we are no longer limiting the size of the plan to be polynomial in the size of the problem; the assignment tree can be exponential in the size of the problem.

The most basic variant of the solver follows the variable ordering exactly, constructing a binary DPLL tree of all possible assignments. Figure 4 depicts such a tree; each node contains a variable under consideration, and each path through the tree describes a plan-execution history, an instantiation of the domain uncertainty, and a possible setting of the state variables. The tree in Figure 4 shows the first seven variables in the ordering for the 2-step TIGER problem: the three choice variables encoding the action at time-step 1, the single observation chance variable, and the three choice variables encoding the action at time-step 2 (triangles indicate subtrees for which details are not shown). The observation variable is a branch point; the optimal assignment to the remaining variables will, in general, be different for different values of this variable.

This representation of the planning problem is similar to *AND/OR trees* and *MINIMAX trees* (Nilsson 1980). Choice variable nodes are analogous to OR, or MAX, nodes, and chance variable nodes are analogous to AND, or MIN, nodes. But the probabilities associated with chance variables (our opponent is nature) make the analogy somewhat inexact. Our trees are more similar to the *MINIMAX trees with chance nodes* described by Ballard (1983) but without the MIN nodes—instead of a sequence of alternating moves by opposing players mediated by random events, our trees represent a sequence of moves by a single player mediated by the randomness in the planning domain.

The solver does a depth-first search of the tree, constructing a solution subtree by calculating, for each node, the probability of a satisfying assignment given the partial assignment so far. For a choice variable, this is a maximum probability and produces no branch in the solution subtree; the solver notes which value of the variable yields this maximum. For a chance variable, the probability will be the probability weighted average of the success probabilities for that node's subtrees and will produce a branch point in the solution subtree. The solver finds the optimal plan by determining

---

[2]Although an observation is associated with a chance variable, it marks a branch point in the plan, and we want the result of an observation to be the *sum*, not the probability weighted average, of the probabilities associated with the two possible truth settings of the chance variable. We accomplish this by setting the probability associated with an observation chance variable to 0.5 and adjusting the resulting plan probability upward by the same factor.

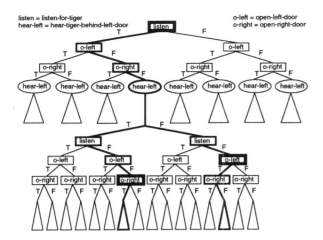

listen = listen-for-tiger
hear-left = hear-tiger-behind-left-door

o-left = open-left-door
o-right = open-right-door

Figure 4: ZANDER selects an optimal subtree.

the subtree with the highest probability of success. In Figure 4, the plan portion of this subtree appears in bold, with action choices (action variables set to True) in extra bold. The optimal plan is: **listen-for-tiger**; if hear-tiger-behind-left-door is True, **open-right-door**; if False, **open-left-door**.

We use three pruning techniques to avoid checking every possible truth assignment. Whenever a choice or chance variable appears alone in an active clause, *unit propagation* assigns the forced value to that variable. This is valid since, even if we postponed the assignment until we reached that variable in the quantifier ordering, we would still need to assign the forced value. Whenever a choice variable appears always negated or always not negated in all active clauses, *variable purification* assigns the appropriate value to that variable. This is valid since the variable would still be pure even if we postponed the assignment until we reached that variable in the quantifier ordering. *Thresholding*, as described earlier, allows us to prune plans based on a prespecified threshold probability of success, and is similar to the MINIMAX tree *cutoffs* described by Ballard (1983).

Like the solutions found by ZANDER, the solution of an AND/OR tree is a subtree satisfying certain conditions. Algorithms for solving these trees, such as AO* (Nilsson 1980), try to combine the advantages of dynamic programming (reuse of common subproblems) with advantages of branch-and-bound (use of heuristic estimates to speed up the search process). These algorithms operate by repeating a 2-phase operation: use heuristic estimates to identify the next node to expand, then use dynamic programming to re-evaluate all nodes in the current subgraph. In contrast to this approach, which must follow a prescribed variable ordering, ZAN-DER can consider variables out of the order prescribed by the problem, when this allows it to prune subtrees (as in unit propagation and variable purification). A worthwhile area of research would be to compare the performance of these two approaches and attempt to de-

Problem	Threshold Probability of Success	Solution Time (cpu seconds)		
		SPLITTING	UNITPURE	THRESH
TIGER-1	0.5	0.02	0.02	0.01
TIGER-2	0.85	0.12	0.02	0.02
TIGER-3	0.85	2.81	0.05	0.04
TIGER-4	0.93925	72.19	0.19	0.08
SHIP-REJECT	0.9215	25.40	0.06	0.06
MEDICAL-4ILL	1.0	196.40	1.77	0.25
EXTPAINT-4	0.3125	12,606.47	0.44	0.13
EXTPAINT-7	0.773437	NA	164.96	31.35
COFFEE-ROBOT	1.0	46,152.25	1,827.67	769.20

Figure 5: Unit propagation, purification, and thresholding can improve performance greatly.

velop techniques that combine the advantages of both.

Results

We tested three variants of ZANDER on problems drawn from the planning literature (see Figure 5). All tests were done on a 300 MHz UltraSparcIIi. The basic solver, which uses only variable splitting and, essentially, checks every possible assignment (SPLITTING), the basic solver augmented with unit propagation and purification (UNITPURE), and the basic solver with unit propagation, purification, and thresholding (THRESH).

The TIGER problems (with horizon increasing from one to four) contain uncertain initial conditions and a noisy observation. Note that in the 4-step TIGER problem, the agent needs the entire observation history in order to act correctly. The SHIP-REJECT problem has the same characteristics as the TIGER problem, along with a causal action (**paint**) that succeeds only part of the time. In the MEDICAL-4ILL problem, we have uncertain initial conditions, multiple perfect observations, and causal actions with no uncertainty. The EXTENDED-PAINT problems (Onder 1998) have no uncertainty in the initial conditions, but require that probabilistic actions be interleaved with perfect observations. Finally, the COFFEE-ROBOT problem, similar to a problem described by Boutilier & Poole (1996), is a larger problem (7 actions, 2 observation variables, and 8 state propositions in each of 6 time steps) with uncertain initial conditions, but perfect causal actions and observations.

As expected, the performance of SPLITTING is poor except on the simplest problems. But, the results for UNITPURE and THRESH are very encouraging; the techniques used in these variants are able to reduce solution times by as much as 5 orders of magnitude. These two variants of ZANDER appear to be quite competitive with other planners; the tests we have conducted so far, while not exhaustive, are encouraging. UNITPURE and THRESH solve the TIGER-4 problem in 0.19 and 0.08 cpu seconds respectively, compared to 0.04 cpu seconds for "Lark" pruning (Kaelbling, Littman, & Cassandra 1998) on the corresponding finite-horizon POMDP. These ZANDER variants can solve the MEDICAL-4ILL problem in 1.77 and 0.25 cpu seconds respectively, compared to 44.54 cpu seconds for SGP. And both variants can solve the SHIP-REJECT problem in 0.06 cpu seconds compared to 0.12 cpu seconds for MAHINUR.

Further Work

ZANDER's more straightforward problem encodings and better performance make it a more promising candidate for further work than C-MAXPLAN. There are a number of possibilities for improvements. Currently, ZANDER separately explores and saves two plan execution histories that diverge and remerge, constructing a plan tree when a directed acyclic graph would be more efficient. We would like to be able to memoize subplan results (a technique used by MAXPLAN) so that when we encounter previously solved subproblems, we can merge the current plan execution history with the old history.

We would like ZANDER to evaluate plans using a broader conception of *utility* than probability of success alone. For example, ZANDER sometimes returns an unnecessarily large plan; we would like the planner to discriminate between plans with equal probability of success using length as a criterion.

Better splitting heuristics could boost performance. Although we are constrained by the prescribed quantifier ordering, a splitting heuristic can be used within a block of similarly quantified variables. Early experiments indicate this can improve performance in bigger problems, where such blocks are large (Littman, Majercik, & Pitassi 1999).

We would like to create approximation techniques for solving larger planning problems. One possibility, currently being developed, uses random sampling to limit the size of the contingent plans we consider and stochastic local search to find the best size-bounded plan. This approach has the potential to quickly generate a suboptimal plan and then, in the remaining available planning time, adjust this plan to improve its probability of success. This sacrifice of optimality for "anytime" planning with performance bounds may not improve worst-case complexity, but it is likely to help for typical problems.

Finally, we would like to explore the possibility of using the approximation technique we are developing in a framework that interleaves planning and execution. This could improve efficiency greatly (at the expense of optimality) by making it unnecessary to generate a plan that considers all contingencies.

Acknowledgments: The first author acknowledges the support of a NASA GSRP Fellowship.

References

Ballard, B. W. 1983. The *-minimax search procedure for trees containing chance nodes. *Artificial Intelligence* 21(3):327—350.

Bayardo, Jr., R. J., and Schrag, R. C. 1997. Using CSP look-back techniques to solve real-world SAT instances. In *Proceedings of the Fourteenth National Conference on Artificial Intelligence*, 203–208. AAAI Press/The MIT Press.

Blum, A. L., and Langford, J. C. 1998. Probabilistic planning in the Graphplan framework. In *Working Notes of the Workshop on Planning as Combinatorial Search, held in conjunction with the Fourth International Conference on Artificial Intelligence Planning*.

Boutilier, C., and Poole, D. 1996. Computing optimal policies for partially observable decision processes using compact representations. In *Proceedings of the Thirteenth National Conference on Artificial Intelligence*, 1168–1175. AAAI Press/The MIT Press.

Draper, D.; Hanks, S.; and Weld, D. 1994. Probabilistic planning with information gathering and contingent execution. In *Proceedings of the AAAI Spring Symposium on Decision Theoretic Planning*, 76–82.

Kaelbling, L. P.; Littman, M. L.; and Cassandra, A. R. 1998. Planning and acting in partially observable stochastic domains. *Artificial Intelligence* 101(1–2):99–134.

Kautz, H., and Selman, B. 1996. Pushing the envelope: Planning, propositional logic, and stochastic search. In *Proceedings of the Thirteenth National Conference on Artificial Intelligence*, 1194–1201. AAAI Press/The MIT Press.

Kautz, H.; McAllester, D.; and Selman, B. 1996. Encoding plans in propositional logic. In *Proceedings of the Fifth International Conference on Principles of Knowledge Representation and Reasoning (KR-96)*, 374–384.

Littman, M. L.; Majercik, S. M.; and Pitassi, T. 1999. Stochastic boolean satisfiability. Submitted.

Majercik, S. M., and Littman, M. L. 1998. MAXPLAN: A new approach to probabilistic planning. In *Proceedings of the Fourth International Conference on Artificial Intelligence Planning*, 86–93. AAAI Press.

Nilsson, N. J. 1980. *Principles of Artificial Intelligence*. Palo Alto, CA: Tioga Publishing Company.

Onder, N., and Pollack, M. E. 1997. Contingency selection in plan generation. In *Proceedings of the Fourth European Conference on Planning*.

Onder, N. 1998. Personal communication.

Papadimitriou, C. H. 1985. Games against nature. *Journal of Computer Systems Science* 31:288–301.

Smith, D. E., and Weld, D. S. 1998. Conformant Graphplan. In *Proceedings of the Fifteenth National Conference on Artificial Intelligence*, 889–896. AAAI Press/The MIT Press.

Weld, D. S.; Anderson, C. R.; and Smith, D. E. 1998. Extending Graphplan to handle uncertainty and sensing actions. In *Proceedings of the Fifteenth National Conference on Artificial Intelligence*, 897–904. AAAI Press/The MIT Press.

On the utility of Plan-space (Causal) Encodings

Amol D. Mali & Subbarao Kambhampati*

Dept. of Computer Science & Engineering
Arizona State University, Tempe, AZ 85287-5406
Email: {amol.mali, rao}@asu.edu; URL: rakaposhi.eas.asu.edu/yochan.html

Abstract

Recently, casting planning as propositional satisfiability has been shown to be a very promising technique for plan synthesis. Although encodings based both on state-space planning and on plan-space (causal) planning have been proposed, most implementations and trade-off evaluations primarily use state-based encodings. This is surprising given both the prominence of plan-space planners in traditional planning, as well as the recent claim that lifted versions of causal encodings provide the smallest encodings. In this paper we attempt a systematic analytical and empirical comparison of plan-space (causal) encodings and state-space encodings. We start by pointing out the connection between the different ways of proving the correctness of a plan, and the spectrum of possible SAT encodings. We then characterize the dimensions along which causal proofs, and consequently, plan-space encodings, can vary. We provide two encodings that are much smaller than those previously proposed. We then show that the smallest causal encodings cannot be smaller in size than the smallest state-based encodings. We shall show that the "lifting" transformation does not affect this relation. Finally, we will present some empirical results that demonstrate that the relative encoding sizes are indeed correlated with the hardness of solving them. We end with a discussion on when the primacy of traditional plan-space planners over state-space planners might carry over to their respective SAT encodings.

1 Introduction

Impressive results have been obtained by casting planning problems as propositional satisfiability [Kautz & Selman 96]. The general idea of this paradigm is to construct a disjunctive structure of size k that contains all possible action sequences of length k that can potentially solve the problem. The problem of checking if there exists a sequence that actually solves the problem is posed as an instance of satisfiability checking. The encoding contains constraints that must hold for any specific sequence to be a solution. Informally, the constraints specify lines of proof that must hold for a sequence to be a solution to the given planning problem. In classical planning,

there are two general ways of "proving" that a sequence of actions solves a planning problem $[I, G]$: (i) The "state space" methods that essentially try to progress the initial state I (or regress the goal state G) through the sequence to see if the goal state (or initial state) is reached. (2) The "plan space" or "causal" methods that attempt to check if every goal and precondition of every action is effectively established (i.e., there exists some preceding action that contributes that condition, and the condition survives up to the needed step).

Although encodings based on both state space proofs and plan space proofs have been considered in the literature [Kautz et. al. 96], most implementations and trade-off studies have concentrated almost exclusively on the state-based encodings [Ernst et. al. 97; Kautz & Selman 96]. This is indeed surprising given that the only published theoretical study of causal encodings [Kautz et. al. 96] is quite supportive of the relative utility of causal encodings. That study claimed that the lifted version of causal encoding is asymptotically the smallest of all encodings including state-based encodings.

In this paper, we report on a theoretical and empirical study of the utility of causal (plan space) encodings. We make the following contributions:

- We show that there are many variations of plan space encodings that, roughly speaking, differ in the specific ways they carry out the causal proofs over action sequences. These variations are interesting as they can have significant impact on the size of the encoding.

- We analyze the sizes of our best causal encodings, and show that they have significantly better asymptotic size characteristics than the only causal encoding that has been previously described in the literature [Kautz et. al. 96].

- We compare the sizes of our causal encodings with the sizes of the best state-based encodings from the literature, and note that causal encodings are in fact never strictly smaller than best state-based encodings.

- We provide a theoretical argument as to why no type of causal encoding can be smaller than the best state-based encoding.

- We show that the "lifting" transformation *does not* change this dominance of causal encodings by the state-based encodings.

- We describe results of empirical studies that show that the hardness of solving the encodings is in fact correlated with the encoding sizes. Specifically, our studies

*Copyright(c) 1999, American Association for Artificial Intelligence (www.aaai.org). All rights reserved. This research is supported in part by NSF young investigator award (NYI) IRI-9457634, NSF grant IRI-9801676. ARPA/Rome Laboratory planning initiative grant F30602-95-C-0247, and AFOSR grant F20602-98-1-0182.

show both that our best causal encodings are better than the causal encoding previously presented in the literature, and that even our encodings are dominated by the best state-based encodings.

- We put our results in perspective by considering the reasons why plan space (or causal) approaches were found to be superior in traditional planning, and explaining why those reasons do not hold in the planning as satisfiability framework. We will also show variations to the planning as satisfiability framework where causal encodings have utility.

The paper is organized as follows. In section 2, we explain our notation used for representing the planning constraints and explain some key constraints from the state-based encoding. In section 3, we report several variants of the causal encoding of [Kautz et. al. 96] and show that some of our variants are smaller. We establish limitations on the reduction in the size of the causal encodings in section 4. In section 5, we show that the lifting transformation does not change the relationship between the sizes of the state-based and the causal encodings. Section 6 presents the results of our empirical studies on various encodings. Section 7 puts our results in perspective, and Section 8 presents the conclusions.

2 Background

As we mentioned earlier, compiling planning into satisfiability checking involves constructing a disjunctive structure of k steps, and writing down the set of constraints that must hold for any action sequence belonging to this structure to be a valid plan for the given problem. The encoding is thus specified in such a way that it has a model if and only if there exists a provably correct plan of k steps. If no model is found, it means that any plan for the problem must be longer than k steps. Accordingly, a new encoding is generated by increasing the value of k. We shall start by describing some common notation, and then go on to describe the basic ideas of the state-based encodings.

2.1 Notation

p_i denotes a step and o_j denotes a ground action. $o_j(t)$ denotes that the action o_j occurs at time t. k is the number of plan steps and U is the set of pre-condition and effect propositions u_j in the domain. $u_j(t)$ denotes that the proposition u_j is true at time t. O is the set of non-null ground actions in the domain. $(p_i = o_j)$ denotes the step→action mapping. ϕ denotes the null action (no-op) that does not cause any change to the world state. a_i denotes a fluent from the goal state (partially described) G. G is assumed to be $(a_1 \wedge a_2 \wedge a_3 ... \wedge a_h)$. F denotes the goal state step (goal state can be viewed as a step with preconditions same as the goals and no effects). I denotes the completely specified initial state and l_i denotes a fluent true in the initial state.

$\mid I \mid$ denotes the number of fluents true in I. $p_i \xrightarrow{f} p_j$ denotes a causal link where p_i adds (makes true) the condition f, p_j needs it and p_i precedes p_j. A_j, R_j, D_j denote the number of add effects, pre-conditions and delete effects of the action o_j respectively. a_{js}, r_{jt}, d_{jq} denote the individual add effects, pre-conditions and delete effects of the action o_j respectively. $Adds(p_i, u_j), Needs(p_j, u_j)$ and $Dels(p_q, u_j)$ respectively denote that the steps p_i, p_j, p_q add, need and delete u_j. $p_i \prec p_j$ denotes that the step p_i precedes the step p_j. Note that we distinguish total order on steps from contiguous order, e.g. the steps $p_1, p_2, p_3, p_1 \prec p_2, p_2 \prec p_3$ are totally ordered, but a new step p_4 can occur between them, e.g. $p_1 \prec p_4, p_4 \prec p_2$. If the steps are contiguous, no new steps can be inserted between them (although, as we shall see in Section 7, this distinction is immaterial for from-scratch planning). We denote an encoding of a planning problem P, by $E_i(P)$.

We define an encoding $E_i(P)$ to be strictly larger than an encoding $E_j(P)$ if and only if either $E_i(P)$ has higher number of variables or clauses or literals (sum of the lengths of the clauses) than $E_j(P)$, with other parameters (#variables, #clauses and #literals) being at least as high or higher.

2.2 Basics of a State-based Encoding

State-based encodings are based on the ideas of proving the correctness of a plan using progression or regression. The latter involves simulating the regression of the goal state over the last step of the plan, and regressing the resulting state over the last but one step etc. Correctness of the plan holds as long as the final state resulting from this process is subsumed by the initial state. An important notion in the state-based encodings is thus the availability of the world state at each time step. The clauses in a state-based encoding capture the following constraints: Any of the $\mid O \mid$ actions from the domain may occur at any of the k time steps from the interval $[0, k-1]$ and an action that occurs at time t implies the truth of its pre-conditions at t and the truth of its effects at $(t+1)$. The initial state is true at time 0 and the goal must be true at time k. Conflicting actions (one action deleting the pre-condition or effect of another or needing negation of pre-condition of another) cannot occur at the same time step. In addition we need frame axioms that capture the persistence of fluents. This can be done by the "classical frame" axioms that state that a fluent u_j remains unchanged in the interval $[t, t+1]$ if the action occuring at t doesn't have u_j in its add or delete list. A more efficient alternative is to use "explanatory frame axioms" which state that if the truth of a fluent u_j changes over an interval $[t, t+1]$, some action changing that truth must occur at t. We restrict our attention to the state-based encoding with explanatory frame axioms, as this encoding has been shown to have lower size, as well as faster solvability [Ernst et. al. 97]. Because of the representation of all step-action bindings, the use of explanatory frame axioms, and the fact that an action implies the truth of its pre-conditions and effects, the state-based encoding contains $O(k * (\mid O \mid + \mid U \mid))$ clauses, $O(k * (\mid O \mid + \mid U \mid))$ variables and a total of $O(k * \mid O \mid * \mid U \mid)$ literals.

3 Causal (Plan-space) Encodings

The plan space (causal) encodings are based on the ideas of proving the correctness of a plan using causal reasoning about the establishment and preservation of goals and the preconditions of individual actions. The correctness of the plan is proved by ensuring that (i) every precondition r of every step s is made true by some step s' that precedes s (establishment) and (ii) r remains true, when it is needed immediately before s (declobbering). There are several variants of "causal proof," based on how the two conditions above are guaranteed. The popular approach for establishment involves associating a "causal link" $s' \xrightarrow{r} s$, with every precondition r of s [McAllester & Rosenblitt, 91]. A problem with this approach, as we shall see below, is that encodings based on it will have a quadratic number of variables corresponding to causal links. An alternative is to dispense with causal links, and post constraints to ensure that for each precondition that there is a contributor.

To ensure that the established condition is available at the needed step, we might either require that it not be deleted by any possibly intervening step ("interval protection"), or that for every deleting step, there be a re-establishing step ("white-knight protection") [Kambhampati et. al., 95]. Finally, the specific implementations of establishment and declobbering conditions depend on the ordering between the steps in the plan. Traditionally, plan-space proofs were associated with the so-called "partial-order" planners [McAllester & Rosenblitt, 91], where the steps in the plan are partially ordered. Such an ordering was important since those planners incrementally introduced steps anywhere in the plan. As we shall see below, partial ordering is expensive to encode because of the need for encoding transitive ordering relations between the steps. This, coupled with the fact that in setting up SAT encodings, we are not interested in "inserting" new steps into an existing plan, suggests that we pursue more restrictive ordering schemes, including contiguity ordering (where the relative positions of each of the steps in the encoding are fixed *a priori*). Since all possible step→action mappings are represented in any encoding, the models of an encoding with contiguous steps are exactly same as the models of an encoding with partially ordered steps.

Given the choice in the way establishment and declobbering are realized, and the specific ordering scheme used in the encoding, we have a spectrum of possible encodings. Only one of these encodings, corresponding to casual link based establishment, interval protection based declobbering, and partially ordered steps, has been studied previously [Kautz et. al., 96]. We have studied the rest of the variations, and found that several of them have better asymptotic sizes than that in [Kautz et. al., 96]. In the following, we will present and analyze the variation corresponding to that studied in [Kautz et. al., 96], as well as two other superior variations in our spectrum.

Before we proceed however, we shall briefly describe the set of axiom schemas that are common to all the variations of causal encodings. Figure 1 lists these schemas formally. Briefly, the first two axiom schemas state that each step in the encoding must be mapped to a single domain action or a no-op. The third schema says that the facts true or false in the initial state are considered to be the effects of step I and the facts specified in the goal state are considered to be the preconditions of step F. The fourth schema says that if a step is mapped to an action, then that step inherits the preconditions and effects of that action. The fifth schema states that the only way a step can add, delete or require a condition is if the condition is added, deleted or required (respectively) by the action that the step is mapped to.

3.1 Causal links, Interval protection & Partial ordering

The first encoding we consider uses causal links for establishment, interval protection for declobbering and assumes that the steps are partially ordered. This variation corresponds to that studied in [Kautz et. al., 96]. The additional axioms (over and above the common ones already shown in Figure 1) that are needed for this encoding are shown in Figure 2. Axiom schema 6 states that each precondition must have a causal

$$\textbf{6. } \wedge_{i=1}^{k} \wedge_{j=1}^{|U|} (Needs(p_i, u_j) \Rightarrow (\vee_{q=1, q \neq i}^{k}(p_q \xrightarrow{u_j} p_i)$$
$$\vee (I \xrightarrow{u_j} p_i)))$$

$$\textbf{7. } \wedge_{i=1}^{k} \wedge_{j=1, i \neq j}^{k} \wedge_{q=1}^{|U|} (p_i \xrightarrow{u_q} p_j \Rightarrow$$
$$(Adds(p_i, u_q) \wedge Needs(p_j, u_q) \wedge (p_i \prec p_j)))$$

$$\textbf{8. } \wedge_{i=1}^{k} \wedge_{j=1, i \neq j}^{k} \wedge_{s=1, s \neq i, s \neq j}^{k} \wedge_{q=1}^{|U|} ((p_i \xrightarrow{u_q} p_j$$
$$\wedge Dels(p_s, u_q)) \Rightarrow ((p_s \prec p_i) \vee (p_j \prec p_s)))$$

$$\textbf{9. } \wedge_{i=1}^{k} \wedge_{j=1, i \neq j}^{k} \wedge_{s=1, s \neq i, s \neq j}^{k} (((p_i \prec p_j) \wedge (p_j \prec p_s))$$
$$\Rightarrow (p_i \prec p_s))$$

$$\wedge_{i=1}^{k} \wedge_{j=1}^{k} \neg((p_i \prec p_j) \wedge (p_j \prec p_i)), \wedge_{i=1}^{k} \neg(p_i \prec p_i)$$

Figure 2: Schemas for the encoding in [Kautz *et. al.*, 96]

link supporting it (with the role of contributor step played by one of the steps in the encoding). The schemas 7 and 8 ensure that the contributor step of a causal link precedes the consumer step, and that if a step is mapped to an action that deletes the condition supported by the causal link, then that step either precedes the contributor or succeeds the consumer. Finally, we also need to add a set of constraints capturing the irreflexiveness, asymmetry and the transitivity of the precedence relation (schema 9).

Since there are $O(k^2 * | U |)$ causal links each of which may be threatened by $O(k)$ steps, there are $O(k^2 * | U |)$ variables and $O(k^3 * | U |)$ clauses in the causal encoding of [Kautz et. al. 96] (for threat resolution).

3.2 Causal Links, Interval Protection & Contiguous steps

We now consider the variant that uses causal links for establishment, interval protection for declobbering but assumes that the steps are contiguous. Figure 3 shows the distinguishing schemas of this variant. Since the ordering is contiguous, we can represent it by numbering steps in the encoding successively $1 \cdots k$. There is no need to represent precedence relations, or describe their properties (including the costly transitivity relation). Schema 6 states the requirement that each precondition of each step is supported by a step whose position is before that of the consumer step. The interval protection of causal links (Schema 7) involves ensuring that no step in the positions between those of the contributor and consumer steps is mapped to an action that deletes the supported condition.

For resolving the threats to causal links $p_{i_1} \xrightarrow{f} p_{i_2}$, we need $\frac{k*(k+4)*(k-1)}{6} * | U |$ clauses. Since the encoding in [Kautz et. al., 96] uses partial ordering instead of contiguity ordering, it needs $k*(k-1)*(k-2)* | U |$ threat resolving clauses. Although both are asymptotically of the same order ($O(k^3)$), the contiguity relation allows us to achieve a percentage reduction in the number of clauses of $[1 - \frac{(k+4)}{6*(k-2)}] * 100$. As $k \to \infty$, this reduction tends to 83.33%, which is quite significant.

3.3 No Causal Links, White-knight protection & Contiguous Steps

We now consider a further departure from the encoding in [Kautz et. al., 96] by dispensing with causal links for estab-

$$1. \wedge_{i=1}^{k} \left(\vee_{j=1}^{|O|} (p_i = o_j) \vee (p_i = \phi) \right)$$

$$2. \wedge_{i=1}^{k} \wedge_{j_1=1}^{|O|} \wedge_{j_2=1, j_2 \neq j_1}^{|O|} \neg((p_i = o_{j_1}) \wedge (p_i = o_{j_2}))$$

$$\wedge_{i=1}^{k} \wedge_{j=1}^{|O|} \neg((p_i = o_j) \wedge (p_i = \phi))$$

$$3. \wedge_{s=1}^{|I|} Adds(I, l_s), \wedge_{s=1}^{|U-I|} \neg Adds(I, a_{js}), \wedge_{i=1}^{h} Needs(F, a_i)$$

$$4. \wedge_{i=1}^{k} \wedge_{j=1}^{|O|} ((p_i = o_j) \Rightarrow ((\wedge_{s=1}^{A_j} Adds(p_i, a_{js})) \wedge (\wedge_{t=1}^{R_j} Needs(p_i, r_{jt}))) \wedge (\wedge_{q=1}^{D_j} Dels(p_i, d_{jq})))$$

$$5. \wedge_{i=1}^{k} \wedge_{j=1}^{|U|} (Adds(p_i, u_j) \Rightarrow (\vee_{q=1}^{x} (p_i = o_{m_q}))), Adds(o_{m_q}, u_j)$$

$$\wedge_{i=1}^{k} \wedge_{j=1}^{|U|} (Dels(p_i, u_j) \Rightarrow (\vee_{q=1}^{x} (p_i = o_{m_q}))), Dels(o_{m_q}, u_j)$$

$$\wedge_{i=1}^{k} \wedge_{j=1}^{|U|} (Needs(p_i, u_j) \Rightarrow (\vee_{q=1}^{x} (p_i = o_{m_q}))), Needs(o_{m_q}, u_j)$$

Figure 1: The schemas common to all causal encodings.

6.
$$\wedge_{i=1}^{k} \wedge_{j=1}^{|U|} (Needs(p_i, u_j) \Rightarrow (\vee_{q=1}^{i-1} (p_q \xrightarrow{u_j} p_i) \vee (I \xrightarrow{u_j} p_i)))$$

7.
$$\wedge_{i_1=1}^{k-1} \wedge_{i_2=i_1+1}^{k} \wedge_{j=1}^{|U|} ((p_{i_1} \xrightarrow{u_j} p_{i_2}) \Rightarrow ((Needs(p_{i_2}, u_j)$$
$$\wedge Adds(p_{i_1}, u_j) \wedge (\wedge_{q=i_1+1}^{i_2-1} \neg Dels(p_q, u_j)))))$$

Figure 3: Schemas for the encoding based on causal link protection with contiguous steps

6.
$$\wedge_{i=2}^{k} \wedge_{j=1}^{|U|} (Needs(p_i, u_j) \Rightarrow$$
$$(\vee_{q=1}^{i-1} Adds(p_q, u_j) \vee Adds(I, u_j)))$$

7.
$$\wedge_{i=3}^{k} \wedge_{j=1}^{i-2} \wedge_{m=1}^{|U|} ((Needs(p_i, u_m) \wedge Dels(p_j, u_m)) \Rightarrow$$
$$(\vee_{q=j+1}^{i-1} Adds(p_q, u_m)))$$

$$\wedge_{j=1}^{k-1} \wedge_{m=1}^{h} ((Needs(F, a_m) \wedge Dels(p_j, a_m)) \Rightarrow$$
$$(\vee_{q=j+1}^{k} Adds(p_q, a_m)))$$

Figure 4: Schemas for the causal-link less encoding based white-knight protection and contiguity ordering

lishment, and using white-knight protection for declobbering. We will continue to assume that the steps in the encoding are contiguous (as in Section 3.2). This variant turns out to be the smallest (has the fewest number of clauses, variables and literals) of all the causal encodings in the spectrum of encodings we have considered.

The key schemas of this encoding are shown in Figure 4. The establishment schema 6 eliminates the causal links by only requiring only that each pre-condition of each step p_i must be added by some step whose position precedes p_i. The declobbering schema 7 says that any deleted pre-condition must be re-established. Notice that there is no reference to any particular causal link intervals. Since we are considering steps in a contiguous ordering, this schema generates only $O(k^2* \mid U \mid)$ clauses, as opposed to $O(k^3* \mid U \mid)$ in the previous two encodings. Traditional planners that use white-knight protection strategy, such as TWEAK [Chapman, 87] have been found to be inferior to the causal link-based planners because they may establish a condition multiple times [Minton *et. al.* 91]. It is thus interesting to note that the combination of white-knight protection, causal-link-less establishment and contiguous ordering leads to a very compact causal encoding (see also Section 7)!

4 Comparison with State-based Encodings

As mentioned earlier, state-based encodings with explanatory frame axioms have been shown to be smallest among state-based encodings. A comparison of the smallest vari-

ant (from section 3.3) of the causal encodings with the state-based encoding with explanatory frame axioms shows that the asymptotic number of variables in both encodings are the same ($O(k* (\mid O \mid + \mid U \mid))$). However, the state-based encoding with explanatory frame axioms has fewer (that is $O(k* (\mid U \mid + \mid O \mid))$) clauses. Hence the state-based encoding with explanatory frame axioms remains smaller than the smallest causal encoding. Indeed, we can view the white knight strategy as an *inefficient version of the explanatory frame axioms*. The regular explanatory frame axioms explain the change of truth of a world state fluent over just the unit time intervals $[t, t+1]$ (the number of these time intervals is $O(k)$), however the white-knight strategy can be seen as explaining this change over all time intervals (the number of these time intervals is $O(k^2)$).

One natural question is whether the dominance of state-based encodings holds irrespective of the specific variant of causal encodings considered. As the result below shows, the relative dominance holds irrespective of the variant of the causal encodings used. The proof is based on the observation that the causal encodings have to consider the truth of conditions over many more time intervals than state-based encodings do.

The important property of a causal proof is its ability to consider the truth of each precondition in isolation from other preconditions. This is achieved by considering all possible establishing actions and all possible ways of protecting (declobbering) those establishments. Since the precondition of an action occurring at time t could have been made true at any time $j \in [0, t]$ any causal encoding will have to refer to a quadratic number of time intervals, their lengths varying from 1 to $(k + 1)$ and resolve threats posed by steps occurring in these longer time intervals. This holds irrespective of whether the ordering between actions is partial, total or contiguous.

In contrast, in the state-based encodings, the world state at t serves as the contributor for every pre-condition of every action that occurs at t. Hence a state-based encoding need to refer to only a linear number of time intervals $((k + 1)$ for a k step plan), each of length 1.

The foregoing shows that a causal encoding will always have more clauses than a state-based encoding. It is possible to show that this dominance holds also for the number of variables and the number of literals (sum of clause lengths). Hence we have the theorem:

Theorem 1. *Causal encodings are strictly larger than the smallest state-based encoding.*

5 The effect of "lifting"

[Kautz *et. al.* 96] have argued that the smallest encoding is the "lifted" version of their causal encoding. Lifting is motivated by the fact that number of ground actions is generally combinatorially large. Lifted encodings use only the uninstantiated action schemas and leave it to the solver to decide the instantiations of arguments of the actions, by stating that each argument can be mapped to any of the elements from its domain and some other constraints. The idea is to replace the complexity of solving a larger ground encoding with the complexity of solving a smaller lifted encoding and doing unifications using the ground initial and goal state. To our knowledge, this speculation is not yet validated due to the lack of effective lifted solvers. Nevertheless, in this section, we argue that any potential size improvements from lifting will also apply to the state-based encodings. Specifically, lifted state-based encodings can be proved to be smaller than the lifted causal encodings, as shown next.

In Figure 5, we show the schemas that are required to generate a lifted version of ground state-based planning. The set of lifted actions is denoted by O'. A lifted action is denoted by o'_i, and its lifted add, delete and precondition fluents are denoted by $a'_{ij}, d'_{ij}, n'_{ij}$. U' is the set of lifted pre-conditions and effects and u'_j denotes a lifted fluent from U'. The initial and goal states are ground. Schema 3 that states the explanatory frame axioms, says that if the truth of a proposition changes, some lifted action whose ground version can cause the change must have occurred. Schema 6 states that each action argument variable x_i can take any value c_{ij} from its domain Dom_i and V denotes the set of these arguments.

It can be seen that even the lifted version of the state-based encoding with explanatory frame axioms is smaller than the lifted version of the smallest causal encoding, because the lifted state-based encoding will have $O(k * (| O' | + | U' |))$ variables and clauses, but the smallest lifted causal encoding will have $O(k^2 * | U' |)$ clauses and $O(k * (| O' | + | U' |))$ variables.

To complete the lifting transformation, we need to give the schemas for the reduction of lifted SAT to SAT. The 5 schemas in Figure 6 are same as those in [Kautz *et. al.* 96]. Here $t, u, w, f(t_1, t_2, t_3, ..., t_k), f(u_1, u_2, ..., u_k)$ denote the terms from the lifted version.

1. $\wedge_{i=0}^{k-1} \wedge_{j=1}^{|O'|} (o'_j(i) \Rightarrow (\wedge_{s=1}^{R_j} n'_{js}(i)))$

2. $\wedge_{i=0}^{k-1} \wedge_{j=1}^{|O'|} (o'_j(i) \Rightarrow$
   $((\wedge_{j_1=1}^{A_j} a'_{jj_1}(i + 1)) \wedge (\wedge_{j_2=1}^{D_j} \neg d'_{jj_2}(i + 1))))$

3. $\wedge_{i=0}^{k-1} \wedge_{j=1}^{|U'|} ((u'_j(i) \wedge \neg u'_j(i + 1)) \Rightarrow$
   $(\vee_{s=1, Can\_Del(o'_s, u'_j)}^{|O'|} o'_s(i)))$

   $\wedge_{i=0}^{k-1} \wedge_{j=1}^{|U'|} ((\neg u'_j(i) \wedge u'_j(i + 1)) \Rightarrow$
   $(\vee_{s=1, Can\_Add(o'_s, u'_j)}^{|O'|} o'_s(i)))$

4. $\wedge_{i=1}^{h} a_i(k)$

5. $(\wedge_{i=1}^{|I|} l_i(0)) \wedge (\wedge_{j=1, u_j \notin I}^{|U|} \neg u_j(0))$

6. $\wedge_{i=1}^{|V|} (\vee_{j=1}^{|Dom_i|} (x_i = c_{ij}))$

Figure 5: Lifted version of ground state-based planning

1. $t = t$
2. $(t = u) \Rightarrow (u = t)$
3. $((t = u) \wedge (u = w)) \Rightarrow (t = w)$
4. $(f(t_1, t_2, ..., t_k) = f(u_1, u_2, ..., u_k)) \Leftrightarrow$
   $((t_1 = u_1) \wedge (t_2 = u_2) \wedge .. \wedge (t_k = u_k))$
5. $\neg(t = u), t, u$ clash.

Figure 6: Additional clauses for reduction from lifted SAT to SAT

Since the lifted version of the ground state-based encoding with explanatory frame axioms is strictly smaller than the lifted version of the smallest causal encoding and since the reduction from lifted SAT to SAT in the causal encoding cannot be smaller than the corresponding size for the state-based encoding, we have the theorem:

Theorem 2. *The lifted state-based encoding with explanatory frame axioms is strictly smaller than any lifted causal encoding.*

6 Empirical Evaluation

Until now, we have shown the dominance of various types of encodings in terms of the asymptotic sizes (in terms of number of variables and clauses). Ultimately of course, we are more interested in how the encodings behave in practice. There are two possible reasons why the practice may deviate from the theory. First, the asymptotic analyses miss the constant factors, and actual encodings may in fact be larger because of the relative sizes of these ignored constants. Second, and perhaps more important, the correlation between the size of a SAT encoding and the hardness of solving it is by no means perfect. Indeed, it is known that adding certain types of constraints (including mutual exclusion constraints, domain specific constraints etc.) while increasing the encoding size, wind up facilitating simplification (through techniques such as unit propagation), making the encodings much easier to solve.

To verify if the size-based dominances that we have discussed in this paper are correlated with the hardness of solving the encodings, we conducted empirical comparisons among the causal encoding developed by [Kautz *et. al.* 96]

Domain	State-based			Our best Causal encoding (Sec. 3.3)			Kautz et. al.'s Causal encoding		
(Steps)	#Vars	#Clauses	Time	# Vars	#Clauses	Time	#Vars	#Clauses	Time
Ferry (15)	390	1519	0.23	855	4144	1.01	4714	58444	81.29
Ferry (19)	588	2436	4.17	1291	7224	125.16	8535	138172	-
Ferry (23)	826	3615	48.54	1815	11504	-	13988	280328	-
Tsp (8)	217	553	0.02	497	1661	0.07	1809	10825	2.11
Tsp(14)	631	1640	0.06	1457	6770	0.88	7785	88873	2.42
Tsp(20)	1199	3138	0.17	2779	16308	6.58	19618	335818	-
Log(19)	921	2639	0.13	2004	12120	-	13051	211696	-
Log(12)	378	1068	0.04	822	3636	0.63	3803	36611	165.97

Figure 7: Empirical results on the performance of selected encodings. Times are in CPU seconds. A "-" indicates that the encoding was not solved within 5 minutes of CPU time on a Sun Ultra with 128M RAM.

(see Section 3.1), the causal encoding that we found to be the smallest based on our analysis of the spectrum of encodings (see Section 3.3), as well as the best state-based encoding (those with explanatory frame axioms; see Section 2.2). Our experiments involved encoding a specific planning problem in each of these encodings. Following the practice of [Kautz & Selman, 96], the number of steps we used in the encodings were greater than or equal to the minimal length solution for the problem (thus eliminating the need for solving encodings of various lengths). Each of the encodings were solved with the SATZ solver[1], a state-of-the-art systematic SAT solver.

The results of our empirical study are shown in Figure 7. The descriptions of the benchmark domains we used are available at *www.cs.yale.edu/HTML/YALE/CS* in the directory *HyPlans/mcdermott.html*. "Tsp" denotes the traveling sales person domain, while "ferry" denotes the ferry domain involving transportation of objects. "Log" denotes the logistics domain. The number of steps in the encodings were same as the number of actions in the plans. Though many of the irrelevant actions were eliminated from consideration before generating the encodings, the same actions were used in all encodings of each problem.

The results show that our improved causal encoding (from section 3.3) could be solved significantly faster than the causal encoding of [Kautz *et. al.* 96]. They also show that the state-based encoding with explanatory frame axioms was still the fastest to solve. The encoding sizes, in terms of number of variables and clauses, are in accordance with the asymptotic relations. We also repeated the experiments where the encodings were first processed with traditional simplifiers (e.g. unit propagation), before being solved. The simplification did not have any appreciable effect on the relative performances of the three encodings.

7 Related Work & Discussion

As we noted, plan-space encodings are based on the ideas of proving the correctness of a plan in terms of establishment and declobbering of all goals and action preconditions in a plan. Historically, these ideas were associated with partial order planning [McAllester & Rosenblitt, 91; Penberthy & Weld, 92]. Partial order planning is known to be a more flexible and efficient form of plan synthesis [Barrett & Weld, 94],

[1]available from *aida.intellektik.informatik.th-darmstadt.de* in ~*hoos/SATLIB*

and this was to some extent the motivation for the initial interest in the causal encodings. Given this background, the results of this paper seem paradoxical, in as much as they show that causal (plan-space) encodings are dominated by the state-based encodings.

Upon closer examination however, this apparent paradox turns out to be an artifact of a misunderstanding of the relation between traditional planning algorithms, and the SAT encodings inspired by those algorithms. The primary difference between state-space and plan-space (partial-order) planners is the specific way a partial plan is extended – state space planners extend the suffix or the prefix of the plan, while partial order planners have the flexibility to insert steps anywhere in the partial plan. The specific strategies used to check if the plan under consideration constitutes a solution are in fact interchangeable [Kambhampati 97].

In contrast, as we have seen throughout this paper, the various causal encodings are distinguished by the various ways of proving the correctness of a plan. The issues of (partial) plan extension are irrelevant for SAT encodings, since SAT-based planning in essence starts with a fixed length disjunctive structure, and checks to see if some conjunctive substructure of it corresponds to a valid plan for the problem. It is only because extension is irrelevant that we were able to consider replacing partial ordering with contiguous ordering (which ultimately resulted in a better plan-space encoding).

From the above perspective, there is no reason to expect that the advantages of partial-order planners over state space planners, which are based largely on the flexibility of inserting steps anywhere in the partial plan, will transfer over to plan space (causal) encodings and state-based encodings that are distinguished by the differences in proof strategies. In fact, since causal proofs consider establishment and declobbering for each precondition of each step separately, they are an inefficient way of checking the correctness of a given action sequence. The reason they are used in partial order planners is that such planners need to interleave refinement and correctness checking of partial plans, and since plan-space refinements add actions without fixing their absolute position, causal proof strategies provide the best means of incrementalizing (finite-differencing) the proof attempts. This flexibility is clearly irrelevant in solving SAT encodings.

7.1 Two uses for Causal encodings

Although causal encodings do not have any advantages in the standard STRIPS-planning tasks, we now show that they could be advantageous in incremental planning scenarios as well as in exploiting causal domain knowledge.

Incremental planning: SAT-based planning has hither-to concentrated on "from-scratch" planning scenarios–where the planner is presented with just the specification of the planning problem. An equally important problem, that has been considered in the traditional planning scenarios, is that of "incremental planning" that arises in the context of replanning and plan-reuse. In this case, in addition to a problem specification, one is given a partial plan, with the requirement that as much of that plan as possible be reused in solving the new problem. Solving such problems could potentially benefit from the ability to insert steps flexibly into the given plan [Ihrig & Kambhampati, 94]. For example, consider a scenario where we are reusing a 2 step plan $[o_2 o_1]$ to solve a new problem, and suppose there is a solution to the new problem that involves inserting a new action o_3 at an arbitrary place in the current plan. If we solved the original problem using a causal encoding (with partial ordering), then it would be feasible to solve the new problem by incrementally extending the original encoding and re-solving it. If we want to keep the original steps as part of the new plan, we need only change their step-action mapping axiom appropriately, e.g. $(p_1 = o_1)$ (or $((p_1 = o_1) \vee (p_1 = \phi))$ if we want to allow removal of old actions.)

In contrast, if the original problem is to be solved with a state-based encoding, one has to either (i) represent a disjunction of all possible ways of respecting the the constraints from the old plan, e.g. $((o_2(0) \wedge o_1(1)) \vee (o_2(0) \wedge o_1(2)) \vee (o_2(1) \wedge o_1(2)))$ or (ii) make multiple copies of the old plan (only if the actions from the old plan may need to be reordered or removed), and reserve multiple places for the inclusion of new actions, e.g. $((o_3(0) \vee \phi(0)) \wedge o_2(1) \wedge (o_3(2) \vee \phi(2)) \wedge o_1(3) \wedge (o_3(4) \vee \phi(4)))$. In addition to increasing the size of the encodings, this approach unfortunately also opens up the possibility of having redundant occurrences of o_3 in the final plan. Indeed in the case of plan merging and reuse, it was found that the causal encodings of some problems were smaller and faster to solve than the state-based encodings [Mali 99(b)].

Using causal domain knowledge: Another scenario where the causal encodings were found to be smaller and faster to solve than the state-based encodings is the hierarchical task network planning problem cast as satisfiability [Mali 99(a)]. The causal encodings naturally capture the precedence constraints and causal links specified in the task reduction schemas. On the other hand, in the state-based encodings, these constraints need to be represented as the disjunction of all total orders on the steps that are consistent with the partial order in the constraints from the reduction schemas.

For example, in a k step encoding, the link $o_2 \xrightarrow{f} o_3$ needs to be represented as $\vee_{i=0}^{k-1} \vee_{j=i+1}^{k} (o_2(i) \wedge o_3(j) \wedge (\wedge_{q=i+1}^{j} f(q)))$. This approach significantly increases the encoding size [Mali 99(a)].

8 Conclusion

In this paper we provided a systematic analytical and empirical comparison of plan-space (causal) encodings and state-based encodings. We pointed out that the two types of encodings differ mainly in the way they attempt to prove the correctness of a plan. We then showed that there can be a large variety of causal encodings corresponding to different ways of carrying out causal proofs. The critical dimensions

are the specific ways in which establishment and declobbering of pre-conditions is ensured, and the type of ordering assumed between the steps of the encoding. We showed that the causal encoding that was previously studied in the literature corresponds to one specific variation, and presented two other variations that are significantly smaller. We went on to show that even our smallest causal encodings cannot be smaller in size than the smallest state-based encodings. We also showed that the "lifting" transformation does not affect this relation. We bolstered our claims by presenting empirical results that demonstrate that the relative encoding sizes are indeed correlated with the hardness of solving them. Finally, we discussed why it should not be surprising that the primacy of traditional plan-space planners over state-space planners does not carry over to their respective SAT encodings, and showed that causal encodings might have advantages in solving incremental planning problems.

References

[Barrett & Weld 94] Anthony Barrett and Daniel Weld, Partial order planning: Evaluating the possible efficiency gains, Artificial Intelligence 67: 71-112, May 1994.

[Chapman 87] David Chapman, Planning for conjunctive goals, Artificial Intelligence, Vol. 32, No. 3, July 1987.

[Ernst et. al. 97] Michael Ernst, Todd Millstein and Daniel Weld, Automatic SAT compilation of planning problems, Proccedings of the International Joint Conference on Artificial Intelligence (IJCAI), 1997.

[Ihrig & Kambhampati 94] Laurie Ihrig and Subbarao Kambhampati, "Derivation Replay for Partial-order Planning," Proc. 12th Natl. Conf. on Artificial Intelligence (AAAI), August 1994.

[Kambhampati et. al. 95] Subbarao Kambhampati, Craig Knoblock and Qiang Yang. Planning as Refinement Search: A unifying framework for evaluating design tradeoffs in partial order planning. Artificial Intelligence. Vol. 76. No. 1-2, September 1995. pp. 167-238.

[Kambhampati 97] Subbarao Kambhampati, Refinement planning as a unifying framework for plan synthesis, AI Magazine, 18(2): 67-97, Summer 1997.

[Kautz et. al. 96] Henry Kautz, David McAllester and Bart Selman, Encoding plans in propositional logic, Proc. of Knowledge Representation and Reasoning Conference, (KRR), 1996.

[Kautz & Selman 96] Henry Kautz and Bart Selman, Pushing the envelope: Planning, Propositional logic and Stochastic search, Proc. of the National Conference on Artificial Intelligence (AAAI), 1996.

[Mali 99(a)] Amol D. Mali, Hierarchical task network planning as satisfiability, Ph.D thesis, Dept. of computer science & engg., Arizona state university, April 1999.

[Mali 99(b)] Amol D. Mali, Plan merging and plan reuse as satisfiability, Technical report TR-99-01, Dept. of computer science & engg., Arizona state university, 1999.

[McAllester & Rosenblitt 91] David McAllester and David Rosenblitt, Systematic non-linear planning, Proceedings of the National Conference on Artificial Intelligence (AAAI), 1991.

[Minton et. al. 91] S. Minton, J. Bresina and M. Drummond, Commitment strategies in planning: a comparative analysis, Proceedings of the International Joint Conference on Artificial Intelligence (IJCAI), 1991.

[Penberthy & Weld 92] J. S. Penberthy and D. Weld, UCPOP: A sound, complete partial order planner for ADL, Proceedings of Knowledge Representation & Reasoning (KRR), 1992.

[Selman et. al. 97] Bart Selman, Henry Kautz and David McAllester, Ten challenges in propositional reasoning and search, Proceedings of the International Joint Conference on Artificial Intelligence (IJCAI), 1997.

Anytime Coordination for Progressive Planning Agents

Abdel-Illah Mouaddib

CRIL-IUT de Lens-Université d'Artois
Rue de l'université, S.P. 16
62307 Lens Cedex, France
mouaddib@cril.univ-artois.fr

Abstract

We address in this paper the problem of coordinating resource-bounded agents under time constraints in a dynamic environment. The agent society we deal with consists of coordinated agents each of which has a goal to achieve before a deadline and new agents can asynchronously appear to achieve time-constrained goals and to coordinate their plans with the already coordinated agent society. Agents use progressive planning that adapt the detail of their local plans according to local deadlines and available resources. The plan consists of a hierarchy of partial plans where each partial plan satisfies a part of the goal. In such environments, constructing a complete plan and then coordinating it with other agents doesn't guarantee that the planning and coordination operations will finish before the given deadline. What we propose is an anytime coordination that allows an agent to return a coordinated plan at any time by using series of partial planning followed by a coordination until the complete plan is constructed and coordinated or the deadline is met. This progressive plan merging operation is assessed in a resource allocation problem.

Introduction

Negotiation (Kraus, Wilkenfeld, & Zlotkin 1995) between distributed planning agents is imposed to handle potential interactions and solve conflicts. Cooperation is necessary when no agent has sufficient resources and information to solve a problem. When agents have a particular view on a problem independently of the other agents, inconsistency between local plans could arise.

Application domains concerned with such problems include the airport ground service scheduling (Neiman, Hildum, & Lesser 1994), resource allocation (Schwartz & Kraus 1997), cooperating robots (Mouaddib 1997), distributed scheduling (Sen & Durfee 1996; Mouaddib 1998) and others. Several coordination techniques (Durfee & Lesser 1987; Decker & Lesser 1992) have

been developped for such applications where it is assumed that agents are not dynamic and with unlimited rationality. It is also assumed that the coordination overhead is negligible. The system with which we work consists of a set of agents performing in a common environment with limited resources and where the coordination cost can be time consuming.

We conduct basic research in a coordination technique for a resource-bounded agent society which supports limited rationality of agents and time-consuming planning and coordination operations. This technique is a progressive planning agent-based system where each agent determines progressively its local plan (Mouaddib 1997) and reacts dynamically to local plans of other agents. This planning technique adapts dynamically the detail of the plan to the available resources. Each local plan is represented with a hierarchy of partial local plans from the mandatory one to the optional ones. The coordination is based on series of partial planning cycles followed by negotiation cycles. After each partial planning cycle a partial plan is available for a coordination with the plans of the other agents. This strategy, through an iterative coordination, allows to minimize the backtracking and to reduce the costs of planning and coordination at unnecessarily detailed levels (Mouaddib 1997). This flexible coordination can be interrupted at any time and the plan merging operation of the new agents stops by accepting only the coordinated partial local plans.

The rest of the paper presents this approach, an analysis of its performance, first experimental results and its characteristics.

Cooperative Distributed Providers

We consider the application of distributed databases (DDB) which are located in different geographical areas and time-constrained transactions conveying queries on information stored on DDB sent to distributed providers that access to DDB to construct their response. Transactions use approximate query processing where transactions are logically splitted into mandatory subtransactions that convey queries to get the mandatory information and optional subtransactions to get optional informations. Each subtransaction gets its required information from *one* database. Providers should allocate the required database in order to coordinate their access and to avoid conflicts. Providers negotiate their database access. Clients sending requests have time-bounded connection in the net to formulate their requests and receive the required information. This scenario is inspired from an electronic commercial application (Sandholm & Lesser 1995) that can be seen as a time-constrained resource allocation problem.

Providers try to maximize the overall performance of the system by providing a high quality solution. The quality improvement, achieved through the progressive satisfaction of subtransactions, is along the degree of the relevance and the level of detail. The satisfaction of each subtransaction is assigned by a monetary charge that the client is willing to pay for the information. When providers cannot construct their optimal response under time pressure and resources constraints, they negotiate to borrow resources from the least important providers (low monetary gain). The providers are cooperative because they try to maximize the overall performance by maximizing the global rewarded monetary gain.

Cooperative Progressive Planning Agents

Progressive planning agents

Progressive planning (Mouaddib 1997) consists in presenting each local plan as a hierarchy of processing levels (satisfaction of a subtransaction) $P_\alpha = \{P_\alpha^1, P_\alpha^2, \ldots, P_\alpha^{n_\alpha}\}$. The agent α starts its processing by constructing the partial local plan P_α^1 achieving the mandatory part of the goal while the other partial local plans achieve the optional parts of the goal to refine the quality resolution. We assume that the goal is logically splitted into several parts from the mandatory one to the most optional. The agent ignores the optional parts of the goal when the resources (time, servers, etc ...) are not enough large to construct a complete plan. This processing allows first an agent to adapt the detail of its local plan to its deadline and to the available resources. Agents are cooperative and try to maximize the overall performance of the system. An agent can accept to borrow resources used by an optional partial plan to another agent requiring the same resource for a more important partial plan.

We improve the expressiveness of the plan by introducing the resources used by partial local plans in order to anticipate conflicts. We assume in our environment that each partial local plan uses only one resource. The extension to several resources consists in assuming lower granularity of partial local plans. Then the local plan of an agent α can be seen as follows: $P_\alpha = \{(P_\alpha^1, r_i, I_\alpha); (P_\alpha^2, r_j, J_\alpha); \ldots; (P_\alpha^d, r_k, K_\alpha)\}$. The plan P_α is constructed through series of partial planning cycles followed by negotiation cycles. We name in the following the Partial Local Plan (PLP) an element of the plan represented by the tuple *(actions, resource, interval)*. This tuple means that the PLP (the execution of the action *actions*) will use the resource *resource* during the interval *interval*. Mandatory PLP is the tuple $(P_\alpha^1, r_i, I_\alpha)$ while optional PLPs are the tuples $(P_\alpha^k, r_i, J_\alpha)$ where $k > 1$.

The agent constructs, first, the mandatory PLP and then coordinates it with the local plans of the other agents. Afterwards, it proceeds in the same way with the optional PLPs one by one.

Stating the coordination problem

Our scenario consists of a group $A = \{\alpha, \beta, \ldots, \gamma\}$ of n agents, an environment represented with its set of resources $R = \{r_1, \ldots, r_k\}$ and a set of goals planning $\{G_1, G_2, \ldots, G_n\}$. The coordination problem in this context is summarized with the following points: (1) Each agent has a goal to achieve before a deadline. (2) Each goal can be solved at different levels of detail. (3) Each agent uses a subset of available resources. And (4) A local plan consists of a hierarchy of PLPs where each one improves the quality of the solution of its predecessor. Furthermore, agents have to coordinate their local plans to avoid conflicts on resources. The coordination of the agent society consists of two constraints:

• Each resource r_j cannot be used by more than one agent at the same time.

$$\forall (P_\alpha^i, r_j, I_\alpha) \text{ and } (P_\beta^j, r_j, I_\beta) : I_\alpha \text{ do not overlap } I_\beta \tag{1}$$

• Each agent α should respect its deadline.

$$\forall r_j \in \mathcal{R}, \ \alpha \in A : \max_{(P_\alpha^i, r_j, I_\alpha) \in P_\alpha} (end(I_\alpha)) \leq deadline(\alpha) \tag{2}$$

The strategy adopted to maintain these constraints respected, consists of an incremental merging PLP operation. The merging agent proceeds in series of partial planning cycles followed by negotiation cycles to construct and to coordinate its local plan with the other local plans of the agent society. This strategy stops as soon as the deadline of the merging agent is reached or a negotiation cycle fails (a merging current PLP operation fails). This strategy has real-time properties of anytime algorithms since it can be interrupted at any time and returns a solution consisting of the sequence of PLPs coordinated in previous cycles.

To apply to a cooperative distributed providers application, each database is a resource and a transaction is a time-bounded goal of a provider where its local plan consists of a set of tuples *(subtransaction, database, interval)* representing the subtransaction to process, the database to allocate and the interval of time during which the database will be used.

Anytime Coordination

Agent interactions: Contract-Net Protocol

The communication is based on a message-passing mechanism. A new agent, once the goal received, derives, first, the mandatory PLP. The agent broadcats, then, this plan to the other agents for coordination. These agents respond in turn only when a conflict occurs with their local plans by sending disagreement specifying the conflicts. To these disagreements, the new agent sends a resolution to the agents for avoiding conflicts. When these conflicts are solved and the PLP of the new agent is maintained, a new PLP is constructed for an optional part of the goal and a new coordination round is performed. This iterative processing is repeated until a PLP of the new agent is rejected or a deadline is met or all PLPs of the new agent are accepted.

Specifying and detecting conflicts

The merging agent receives several disagreements where each of which describes a conflict, the agent centralizes all these disagreements in order to optimally solve them.

Definition 1 *We say that the agent α is in conflict with an agent β when the merging PLP P_α^i of α shares the same resource at the same time with at least one PLP P_β^j of the agent β. Formally:*

$$\exists \, (P_\alpha^i, \, r_c, I_\alpha), \, (P_\beta^j, r_c, I_\beta) : \, I_\alpha \text{ overlaps } I_\beta \quad (3)$$

From this definition, the merging agent, that we name in the following α, classifies the collected conflicts in four categories (Mouaddib 1997). According to the category, an appropriate rule of resolution is adopted.

- **Hard critical conflict:** The mandatory PLP P_α^1 of α is in conflict with the mandatory PLP P_β^1 of an agent β.
- **Hard non-critical conflict:** The mandatory PLP P_α^1 of α is in conflict with an optional PLP P_β^i ($i > 1$) of an agent β.
- **Soft critical conflict:** An optional PLP P_α^i ($i > 1$) of α is in conflict with the mandatory PLP P_β^1 of an agent β.

- **Soft non-critical conflict:** An optional PLP P_α^i of α is in conflict with an optional PLP P_β^j of β (i and j > 1).

When the merging agent α receives disagreements from other agents, it defines for each PLP P_α^i a set of PLPs $S_{P_\alpha^i}$ with which it is in conflict. The agent α classifies $S_{P_\alpha^i}$ in four categories according to type of the conflicts:

- $S_{P_\alpha^i}$ is a **hard critical set** when P_α^i is a mandatory PLP and a hard critical conflict occurs with one element of the set $S_{P_\alpha^i}$.
- $S_{P_\alpha^i}$ is a **hard non-critical set** when P_α^i is a mandatory PLP and only hard non-critical conflicts occur with the elements of the set $S_{P_\alpha^i}$.
- $S_{P_\alpha^i}$ is a **soft critical set** when P_α^i is an optional local plan and soft critical conflicts occur with one element of the set $S_{P_\alpha^i}$.
- $S_{P_\alpha^i}$ is a **soft non-critical set** when P_α^i is an optional PLP and only soft non-critical conflicts occur with the elements of the set $S_{P_\alpha^i}$.

The detection and type of conflicts are up to the agents sending the disagreement while the agent α, receiving disagreements, is in charge of progressively resolving them. Decentralizing the detection and type of conflict can participate in reducing the time-consuming process of negotiation while centralizing their resolution can be a costly and time-consuming process. The organisation of conflicts into categories allows to define the appropriate strategy to solve them. These strategies validate progressively PLPs of merging agents as soon as the category of conflicts that they provoke are resolved.

Utility of plans

The negotiation, for resolving conflicts, uses plan's utility measure to solve these conflicts. When the utility for a plan is greater than the utility of another one, the resolution of the conflict prefers the first plan over the second. PLPs are assigned with the utility which takes two attributes into account: the *reward R* and *penalty P* values.

Definition 2 *Each PLP has a reward function $R(P_\alpha^i, \, r_j, \, duration(I_\alpha) = end(I_\alpha) - begin(I_\alpha))$ representing the value rewarded by the agent when the PLP has been executed during an amount of time by using a resource. This value can represent an amount of money to pay for delivered information.*

Definition 3 *The penalty function P evaluates the cost paid to use the resource during an amount of time*

$$P(r_j, I_\alpha) = Cost_{r_j}(duration(I_\alpha)) \quad (4)$$

Definition 4 *A time-dependent utility function, $U_{P_\alpha^i}^{r,I}$, measures the utility of executing the PLP P_α^i if it uses the resource r during the interval of time I.*

$$U_{P_\alpha^i}^{r,I} = R(P_\alpha^i, r, duration(I)) - P(r, I) \qquad (5)$$

Global strategy of resolution

The set $S_{P_\alpha^i}$ contains the PLPs in conflicts with the merging PLP P_α^i. The strategy of resolution consists of two functions: first, *Avoiding conflict* which consists in delaying, when it is possible, merging PLP of the agent α to avoid conflict and second, *non-avoided conflicts resolution* which consists in using utility of PLPs to decide whether the merging PLP should be maintained or not. We describe in the following both functions.

Avoiding conflicts This function delays the merging PLPs in conflicts rather than delaying the PLPs of the other agents that could put back in cause solved conflicts between the other agents and then other negotiation cycles should be perfomed. This solution can cause a combinatorial complexity of the strategy. The conflict avoidance function consists in making the interval I_α after the intervals I_β with which it overlaps. This means that the interval I_α should be delayed with the amount of time $end(I_\beta) - begin(I_\alpha)$. When delaying the merging PLP, the agent α verifies whether the deadline is reached or not. In order to coordinate the merging PLP P_α^i with the PLPs of P_β^j the set $S_{P_\alpha^i}$, the agent α sorts this set according to $end(I_\beta)$. Afterwards, it assesses the avoidance of conflicts between the merging PLP and the PLPs of these agents β one by one. To this end, the agent α delays progressively its merging PLP by the amount of time $end(I_\beta) - begin(I_\alpha)$ until this amount violates its deadline. By delaying the merging PLP, some conflicts in $S_{P_\alpha^i}$ disappear, but others could appear. The merging agent α sends, then, its modified PLP to the other agents that are not in negotiation to make them informed on the modification of the PLP and then to assess new conflicts. The new detected conflicts are added in the set $S_{P_\alpha^i}$. The agent α don't try to avoid them because they are later than the non-avoided ones in the set $S_{P_\alpha^i}$ and then it is not possible to avoid them. Afterwards, the set $S_{P_\alpha^i}$ contains only the conflicts that cannot be avoided and then the *conflict resolution* function is called.

Resolving non-avoided conflicts The agent α resolves conflicts according to their type. When the merging PLP is rejected, the negotiation cycle fails and the agent α stops its strategy of resolution. When a PLP P_β^j is rejected by a merging agent α, the agent β must discard all its PLPs P_β^k ($k \geq j$) due to the characteristics of the progressive planning. That's why, the resolving conflict function perfers a merging PLP P_α^i over another PLP P_β^j when its utility is higher than the cumulated utility of all P_β^k ($k \geq j$). In the following, we describe the resolving conflicts rules.

- For a hard critical set: When $U_{P_\alpha^1}^{r,I}$ is greater than $\sum_{P_\beta^j \in S_{P_\alpha^1}} \sum_{k \geq j} U_{P_\beta^k}^{r',J}$ the agent α maintains its mandatory PLP and sends back all PLPs P_β^j of $S_{P_\alpha^1}$ to their respective agents β.

When $\sum_{P_\beta^j \in S_{P_\alpha^1}} \sum_{k \geq j} U_{P_\beta^k}^{r',J}$ is greater than $U_{P_\alpha^1}^{r,I}$, the agent α accepts all the PLPs of $S_{P_\alpha^1}$ and it sends a message to the corresponding agents β. The negotiation cycle of the merging agent fails and its local plan is rejected. Consequently, the corresponding goal can not be achieved. This situation means in our application that the provider cannot deliver information, even the mandatory information.

- For a hard non-critical set: The agent α maintains its mandatory PLP P_α^1 and rejects all optional PLPs in the set $S_{P_\alpha^1}$. In this resolution, we prefer maintaining a mandatory PLP rather than several optional PLPs.
- For a soft critical set: The agent α discards its optional PLP. The negotiation cycle fails and then the incremental construction of the merging plan stops. The merging agent returns the PLPs coordinated up to this step.
- For a soft non-critical set: When the utility $U_{P_\alpha^i}^{r,I}$ is greater than $\sum_{P_\beta^j \in S_{P_\alpha^i}} \sum_{k \geq j} U_{P_\beta^k}^{r',J}$, the agent α rejects all optional PLPs of the set $S_{P_\alpha^i}$ and maintains its merging optional partial local plan. Otherwise, the agent α discards its optional PLP and negotiation cycle fails. The agent α stops its processing and returns the PLPs coordinated up to this step.

Society of new merging agents

Several new agents can proceed to a progressive plan merging opertaion. In this approach we described how a new agent progressively constructs and coordinates its plan. The same processing is repeated for each new agent one by one according to their deadline. Indeed, agents in society use two message queues where the first queue is used to store messages concerning the declaration of merging and the second queue used for messages exchanged during the coordination with the current new merging agent. As soon as the current new merging agent is coordinated, agents in society, including the new coordinated, proceed to the coordination of the next new merging agent (with the most urgent deadline). A new coalition is then created.

Analysis

The termination of the iterative processing of this approach is guaranteed because the number of rounds is bounded by the maximum number k_{max} of levels per agent. While the termination of each round is guaranteed by the number of agents in the society n. The complexity of the approach is then $O(k_{max} * n)$. In large societies (n is very large) the complexity is $O(n)$ while in small societies ($n \approx k_{max}$, $k_{max} = 5$), the complexity is equivalent to $O(n^2)$. Consequently, this approach is more suitable for the large societies. We also analyze in critical situations (where only some PLPs are accepted) and in non-critical situations (where the complete merging local plan is accepted) the cumulated cost of planning C_p and coordination C_c of our approach and a *basic approach* similar to PGP approach.

- **Our approach:** The cost of *one* round of the any-time coordination is the cost of partial plan construction C_p cycle and a coordination cycle C_c. Thus the cost of *one* round is as follows:

$$Cost_{a\ round} = C_p(P_\alpha^i) + \max_{\beta \in A}(\sum_j C_c(P_\beta^j, P_\alpha^i)) \quad (6)$$

In the most critical situation the cost of the anytime coordination is then the cost of the first round while in the other situations is the cumulated cost of *one* round: $\sum_i Cost_i$, where i is the round i of the iterative processing of the anytime coordination.

- **Basic approach:** The cost of this approach is the cost of the complete plan construction and its coordination. Thus the cost in critical and non-critical situations is the same.

$$Cost = \sum_i C_p(P_\alpha^i) + \max_{\beta \in A}(\sum_j \sum_i C_c(P_\beta^j, P_\alpha^i)) \quad (7)$$

The time consumed by our approach in non-critical situations is greater than the time consumed by the basic approach because it is trivial to prove the following:

$$\sum \max(\sum cost) > \max \sum \sum cost \quad (8)$$

In critical situations our approach is more suitable because the cost of the basic approach is the same than in non-critical situations while our approach is only the cumulated costs of performed rounds that can be in critical situations no more than $k/2$ where k is the number of partial plans of the merging agent. Finally, the approach is a greedy technique based on a local optimisation approach to a distributed allocation resource problem that is hard to optimize globally.

Experimental evaluation: First Results

This section illustrates the operation of the resulting approach and examines two fundamental questions. The first goal is to compare the performance of our approach to a basic approach similar to PGP approach (Durfee & Lesser 1987). This basic approach is based on a planning cycle to construct a complete plan followed by a negotiation cycle to coordinate the complete plan. It ignores time constraints and the overhead of construction and coordination. The second goal of the experimental evaluation is to assess the benefit of our approach in time-constrained situations.

Experiment design

A progressive planning agents language is specified allowing the system to simulate the progressive plans for the application. We have collected experimental data on the performance of our approach and the basic approach. The quality of the results for each problem instance is assessed according to two parameters: the *time consumed* in critical and non-critical situations by each approach to construct and to coordinate the plan according to the number of agents in the society, and the *cumulated utility* of coordinated partial plans according to the deadline before which the merging agent must construct and coordinate its plan. Problem instances are developed with 10 agents. This second experimental evaluation will show the benefit of our approach in time-constrained situations.

Empirical results on Consumed time

Figures 1 and 2 show that our approach is more suitable than the basic approach for critical situations while in non-critical situations it is the contrast. The theoretical explanation to that is given in equations 6, 7 and 8.

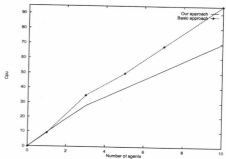

Figure 1: Time consumption in critical situations

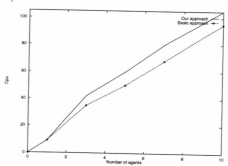

Figure 2: Time consumption in non-critical situations

Empirical results on utility

In this experiments, we measure tha value as a function of available time (deadline). This value consists of the cumulated utilities of coordinated PLPs: $\sum_i(U_i)$. Figure 3 shows the difference between the values of

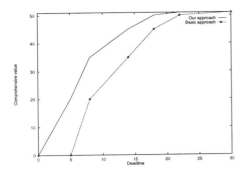

Figure 3: Comprehensive value for different deadlines

our approach and the basic approach over the deadlines. The figure confirms the fact that our approach leads to a substantial quality gain over the basic approach. The main reason to that is the basic approach can consume time for constructing partial plans that it cannot be merged in a sosciety while our approach as soon as a partial plan is constructed its coordination is immediately processed. The basic approach cannot trade-off between planning time and coordination time as it is done in our approach.

Discussion

The approach, we present, addresses a problem much more complicated than these addressed in previous works (Botti, Crespo, & Ripoll 1994; Schwartz & Kraus 1997). Our approach addresses a problem of sharing several resources while in (Botti, Crespo, & Ripoll 1994), it is proposed a mechanism of *one* resource (the blackboard). Unlike the work presented in (Schwartz & Kraus 1997) consisting of distributed servers of information negotiating to allocate each resource (dataset) to *one* server, our agents negotiate to allocate several resources. Furthermore, our approach is more suitable to dynamic and time-constrained situations through its anytime coordination. Unlike approaches described in (Sandholm 1993; Sen & Durfee 1996) which are task-based negotiation approaches, our approach can be seen as a resource-based negotiation.

PGPP approach (Mouaddib 1997) is an extension of PGP to constrained time environments. This approach progressively constructs a complete local plan and it coordinates it incrementally PLP by PLP while our new approach it constructs a PLP and it immediately coordinates it. Our new approach by stopping the incremental coordination of PLP when the merging PLP operation fails, avoids to plan at unnecessarily level of details and to predict judiciously whether more actions maximize the expected gain or not (Vidal & Durfee 1995). Furthermore, with this processing this model can take the overhead of the negotiation into consideration.

Unlike other investigators in resources allocation

domain that have proposed distributed techniques (Neiman, Hildum, & Lesser 1994; Schwartz & Kraus 1997) which can perform backtracking to coordinate activites, our approach minimize backtracking and then reduces the complexity of the algorithm. Further work will concern the application of this approach in auctions and multi-robots domains.

Acknowledgments

Support for this work was provided by the GanymedeII Project of Plan Etat/Nord-Pas-De-Calais

References

Botti, V.; Crespo, A.; and Ripoll, I. 1994. Multiple access and coherence management in a real-time temporal blackboard. In *ECAI*, 312–316.

Decker, K., and Lesser, V. 1992. Generalizing the partial global planning algorithm. *Journal on Intelligent Cooperative Information Systems* 1(2):319–346.

Durfee, E., and Lesser, V. 1987. Partial global planning: A coordination framework for distributed hypothesis formation. *IEEE Transactions on systems, Man, and Cybernetics* 21(5).

Kraus, S.; Wilkenfeld, J.; and Zlotkin, G. 1995. Multiagent negotiation under time constraints. *Artificial Intelligence* 75:297–345.

Mouaddib, A.-I. 1997. Progressive negotiation for time-constrained autonomous agents. In *First International Conference on Autonomous Agents*, 8–16.

Mouaddib, A.-I. 1998. Multistage negotiation for distributed scheduling of resource-bounded agents. In *AAAI Spring Symposium on Satisficing Models*, 54–59.

Neiman, D.; Hildum, D.; and Lesser, V. R. 1994. Exploiting meta-level information in a distributed scheduling system. In *AAAI-94*.

Sandholm, T., and Lesser, V. 1995. Issues in automated negotiation and electronic commerce: Extending the contract net framework. In *First ICMAS*, 328–335.

Sandholm, T. 1993. An implementation of the contract net protocol based on marginal cost calculations. In *AAAI*, 256–262.

Schwartz, R., and Kraus, S. 1997. Negotiation on data allocation in multi-agents environments. In *AAAI*, 29–35.

Sen, S., and Durfee, E. 1996. A contracting model for flexible distributed scheduling. *Annals of Operating Research* 65:195–222.

Vidal, J., and Durfee, E. 1995. Recursive agent modeling using limited rationality. In *ICMAS*, 126–133.

Generating Qualitatively Different Plans through Metatheoretic Biases

Karen L. Myers   Thomas J. Lee
SRI International
333 Ravenswood Ave.,
Menlo Park, CA 94025
myers@ai.sri.com   tomlee@erg.sri.com

Abstract

Current methods for generating qualitatively different plans are either based on simple randomization of planning decisions and so cannot guarantee meaningful differences among generated plans, or require extensive user involvement to drive the system into different sections of the overall plan space. This paper presents a cost-effective method for automatically generating qualitatively different plans that is rooted in the creation of *biases* that focus the planner toward solutions with certain attributes. Biases are derived from analysis of a *domain metatheory* and enforced through compilation into preferences over planning decisions. Users can optionally direct the planner into desired regions of the plan space by designating aspects of the metatheory that should be used for bias generation. Experimental results are provided that validate the effectiveness of the biasing method for reliably generating a range of plans with meaningful semantic differences.

Introduction

Automated planning tools hold much promise as decision aids for humans charged with producing plans for large-scale, demanding applications. The value of the tools lies with their ability to help humans understand the complexity of the underlying problem, providing guidance in the determination of a solution that is well-suited to their needs and concerns.

For many real-world applications, the search space is dense with solutions. Air campaign planning (Thaler & Shlapak 1995; Lee & Wilkins 1996) and travel planning (Linden, Hanks, & Lesh 1997)) provide two examples. For these applications, it is not difficult to find a solution; rather, the challenge is to produce a solution that is tailored to the preferences and needs of the user. One means by which to help users with this task is to provide a set of *qualitatively distinct* options that vary in meaningful ways. A set of solutions of this type would help the user understand the range of possibilities available to him or her.

Current automated planning tools can readily generate different plans, for example through repeated runs with randomized choices at decision points. The differences among

such plans, however, are difficult to extract and not necessarily semantically meaningful. Furthermore, different users will have different notions of what constitutes 'meaningful' differences. For example, with travel plans a budget traveler might like to see options with a range of costs while the business traveler might like to see options that maximize accumulation of frequent flier points. Ideally, a system for generating qualitatively different plans would allow the user to specify dimensions along which he or she would like to see variation.

To address the problem of meaningfulness, hill-climbing methods could be used to generate successive plans until they differed sufficiently along some defined evaluation function. Two problems arise with this approach. First, the complexity of plan generation makes it expensive to iterate through many solutions. Second, defining evaluation criteria for complex planning domains is problematic: evaluation metrics are generally difficult to elicit, multidimensional in nature, qualitative rather than quantitative, and often subjective (Gil 1998). As such, defining the ranking function required to drive a hill-climbing process will be difficult in many domains.

Recent work on mixed-initiative, interactive, and advisable planning enables users to drive the process of generating qualitatively different plans (Ferguson & Allen 1998; Tate, Dalton, & Levine 1998; Myers 1996). With these frameworks, however, the user must be involved extensively in an ongoing role to articulate desired differences and to manage the space of options.

This paper describes a framework for generating qualitatively different plans in a fully automated fashion, but that can accept user guidance to influence the types of solutions that are generated. Rather than searching through the space of plans directly, the algorithm leverages a *metatheory* of the planning domain, introduced previously to support user advisability of a planner (Myers 1996). This metatheory provides an abstracted characterization of the planning domain that highlights key semantic differences among operators, planning variables, and instances. This abstraction provides the ability to filter out irrelevant differences when generating plans, focusing instead on distinctions that are guaranteed to be semantically meaningful. Based on analysis of the metatheory, *biases* are generated that are designed to focus the planner toward solutions with certain characteristics.

These biases are enforced by imposing preferences on planning decisions. The result is plans that are guaranteed qualitatively different *by design*, rather than possibly (though not necessarily) distinct by randomization.

While the biasing approach does not require user input, it can readily accept guidance from the user to target certain subportions of the overall plan space. For example, users could indicate that they want to see plans within a range of cost and time values, while insisting on traveling by airplane (rather than train, boat, or car).

The ability to generate qualitatively different plans is essential for the effective use of generative planning technology in producing solutions that satisfy user requirements. In particular, the technology should be viewed as a tool to assist human planners rather than as a replacement for them, with the user driving the kinds of solutions that the technology produces. In particular, after requesting a set of qualitatively different plans, the user would make recommendations on how to improve them. The idea is that the generated plans act as initial seeds, which users can subsequently refine to meet their needs (using, for example, *planning advice* (Myers 1996)).

Our biasing method for generating qualitatively different plans was implemented and evaluated within SIPE–2 (Wilkins 1988), a Hierarchical Task Network (HTN) planner (Erol, Hendler, & Nau 1994). The biasing method is not specific to HTN planning but rather applies to any form of operator-based planning. Experimental evaluation was performed in a travel domain that involves selecting itineraries, schedules, accommodations, modes of travel, and carriers for business and pleasure trips. The results show that the biasing method is effective for reliably producing a range of plans with meaningful semantic differences.

Measuring Qualitative Difference

The fundamental problem that we address is to produce n solutions to a given planning problem, such that those solutions do a good job of 'covering' the set of possible solutions. We are interested in small values of n (i.e., $2 \leq n \leq 5$), since a user of an automated planning system would generally consider only a small number of options at any point in time. We consider two notions of coverage, *dispersion* and *proximity*, both of which are grounded in the notion of a measurable distance between plans.

Plan Distance

We have opted to ground plan distance in *evaluation criteria*, which have the advantage of measuring aspects of the plan that are of significance to users. This contrasts with syntactic measures of plan distance (for example, the difference in plan length), which do not necessarily correlate with semantic differences among plans.

We assume a set of k evaluation criteria that define a k-dimensional space E^K in which to situate plans. For simplicity, we assume that evaluation values are normalized to lie in the range $[0, 1]$. With these evaluation criteria, we formally define our notion of *plan distance* in terms of the Euclidean distance between the corresponding points for those plans in evaluation space.

Definition 1 (Plan Distance) *The* distance *between two plans P_1 and P_2 is defined to be*

$$Dist(P_1, P_2) = \sqrt{\sum_{i=1}^{k} \left(Eval_i(P_1) - Eval_i(P_2)\right)^2}$$

Dispersion

Dispersion is defined to be the average distance between plans in a plan set. As such, dispersion measures the degree to which solutions are spread apart from each other.

Definition 2 (Dispersion) *The* dispersion *for a plan set $\mathcal{P}$ is defined to be*

$$Disp(\mathcal{P}) = \frac{\sum_{1 \leq i < j \leq n} Dist(P_i, P_j)}{\frac{n \times (n-1)}{2}} .$$

Proximity

Proximity is defined to be the average distance for a point in the evaluation space to its closest point in the evaluation of the plan set. As such, proximity measures the degree to which the solution set is 'near' all other points in the evaluation space.

Definition 3 (Proximity) *The* proximity *of a point $e = \{e_1 \ldots e_k\} \in E^K$ to a plan set $\mathcal{P} = \{P_1 \ldots P_n\}$ is defined to be*

$$Prox(e, \mathcal{P}) = Min_{1 \leq i \leq n} \left(\sqrt{\sum_{1 \leq j \leq k} (e_j - Eval_i(P_i))^2} \right) .$$

The proximity for a plan set $\mathcal{P}$ is defined to be the average proximity to $\mathcal{P}$ from any point in E^K:

$$Prox(\mathcal{P}) = Avg_{e \in E^K} \left(Prox(e, \mathcal{P}) \right) .$$

Closed-form solutions for computing proximity are not generally available in continuous evaluation spaces. We employ sampling methods to approximate proximity measures in this paper.

Discussion

Higher dispersion values generally indicate that a plan set does a better job of covering the extremities of the plan space. As such, highly dispersed plan sets are useful when users want to investigate the limits of the solution space. In contrast, lower proximity values correlate with plan sets that are more representative of the set of possible solutions in that they are 'closer' to all points in the evaluation space. As such, low proximity plan sets are valuable for presenting users with reasonable first-cut solutions that are likely to be close to what would be the user's ideal solution.

For these reasons, we seek to generate solution sets that are highly dispersed with low proximity. These two objectives can be conflicting, depending on the distribution of plans through the evaluation space. For example, extremal points in the evaluation space will be maximally dispersed but are unlikely to yield low proximity values.

Domain Metatheory

A standard planning domain is modeled in terms of three basic types of elements: *individuals* corresponding to real or abstract objects in the domain, *relations* that describe characteristics of the world and individual world states, and *operators* that describe ways to achieve objectives.

The domain metatheory captures high-level attributes of planning operators, variables, and individuals, thus providing users with the means to describe desired solution characteristics in terms that are natural to them. The domain metatheory was developed originally to provide a language in which users could construct *advice* for a planning system (Myers 1996) but is not advice-specific: it describes general properties of elements of a planning domain and can be employed to support a variety of uses, including the generation of qualitatively different plans. The metatheory is built around three main constructs: *roles*, *features*, and *measures*.

A *feature* designates an attribute of interest for an operator that distinguishes it from other operators that could be applied to the same task. For example, among operators that can be used to refine tasks of moving from location X to location Y, there can be some that involve travel by air, land, or water; each of these media could be modeled as a feature. Because there can be multiple operators that apply to a particular task, features provide a way of abstracting from the details of an operator up to distinguishing attributes that might be of interest to users. Note that features differ from operator preconditions in that they do not directly restrict use of operators by the planner.

Related features are grouped into *feature categories*. For example, the features {Air Land Water} mentioned above define a **Transport-Media** category. Feature categories themselves can have interesting properties. Just as planning operators reflect a hierarchical structure, features and feature categories can be organized in hierarchical fashion. Certain categories may be *mutually exclusive* in that at most one feature from the category can be assigned to any given operator; this is the case for the feature category **Transit-Ownership** containing the elements {Public Private}. Other categories may support overlapping features; for example, there may be an operator that involves both Air and Land travel.

A *role* corresponds to a capacity in which an individual is to be used within an operator. For instance, a transportation activity within the travel domain could have roles such as Origin and Destination, and Carrier. Roles correspond to individual variables within a planning operator.

Feature categories can have associated *measures*. A measure corresponds to an ordering (possibly partial) of features within the category with respect to some designated criteria. For example, consider the feature category **Transit-Ownership** with features {Public Private}. For the measure COMFORT, the feature Private would rank higher than Public; for the measure AFFORDABILITY, the order would be reversed.

A single measure can be used across different feature categories. For example, AFFORDABILITY would apply to a broad range of feature categories. Thus, by expressing preferences on measure, it is possible to influence a broad range of plan generation decisions.

Vacation-Scope = {Overseas National Regional}
  AFFORDABILITY: (Overseas National Regional)
  TIME-EFFICIENCY: (Overseas National Regional)

Accommodation = {Hotel Motel Camp}
  COMFORT: (Camp Motel Hotel)
  AFFORDABILITY: (Hotel Motel Camp)

Transport-Media = {Air Land Water}
  AFFORDABILITY: (Water Air Land)
  TIME-EFFICIENCY: (Water Land Air)

Land-Transport-Mode = {Auto Bus Shuttle Taxi Train Limo}
  AFFORDABILITY: (Limo Train Auto Taxi Shuttle Bus)
  TIME-EFFICIENCY: (Bus Shuttle Auto Limo Taxi Train)
  COMFORT: (Bus Shuttle Taxi Train Auto Limo)

Transit-Ownership = {Public Private}
  COMFORT: (Public Private)
  AFFORDABILITY: (Private Public)
  TIME-EFFICIENCY: (Public Private)

Transit-Capacity = {Solo Shared}
  COMFORT: (Shared Solo)
  AFFORDABILITY: (Solo Shared)

Figure 1: Sample Feature Categories and Associated Measures from the Travel Domain

Figure 1 presents an excerpt from the metatheory for the travel domain that shows sample feature categories and associated measures. Each block defines a feature category, with the first line listing the name of the feature category followed by its constituent features. The remaining lines declare a measure associated with that feature category, and provide the ranking of the features for that measure and category. Here, we show only measures that completely order the features (although partial orders are possible).

Just as measures can be employed to rank features (and hence operators with those features), they can also be employed to rank instances. For measures on instances, an ordered set of *measure values* is defined. For each measure, a given individual can (optionally) be assigned one of these values, thus inducing a partial order over instances. In the travel domain, for example, the measure AFFORDABILITY has the values (*Extravagant Expensive Moderate Inexpensive Cheap*) in increasing order from left to right. The individual Ritz of class Hotel has the AFFORDABILITY value *Extravagant*, while the individual Motel6 of class Motel has the value *Cheap*, thus Motel6 ranks higher than Ritz with respect to AFFORDABILITY.

We define the *domain* of a measure to be the set of (partially) ordered values employed by the measure. For measures defined over feature categories, the domain is the set of features that comprise the feature category. For measures defined over instances, the domain is the set of measure values that can be assigned to instances.

Biasing Algorithm

Our approach to generating n qualitatively different plans uses the domain metatheory to establish n sets of *biases* that can direct the planner toward different sections of the overall plan space. In addition to n, our algorithm takes as input a subset of the measures provided by the domain metatheory. These measures can be selected by the user in order to influence the types of qualitative differences among the generated plans.

Bias and Region Creation

The biasing method involves partitioning the domains of the selected measures into *intervals*, and then grouping the intervals (one from each measure) into *cases* designed to force the planner into different sections of the overall plan space. We use the term *region* to refer to the collection of biases for a given case.

A bias is defined by a measure and an interval of values within the domain of the measure. To simplify manipulation and bias enforcement (described below), a proportional, order-preserving mapping from each measure domain onto the interval $[0, 1]$ is defined. For simplicity, we restrict attention to connected intervals.

Different strategies for partitioning and grouping are possible. For the results described in this paper, each measure domain is partitioned into n subintervals of equal length (relative to $[0, 1]$). A set of n regions is created by, for each measure, randomly assigning each of the n intervals for the measure to a different region.[1] This strategy provides systematic coverage of measures in that each interval appears in exactly one region. The use of random selection for region assignment is important to avoid potential problems that can arise due to correlations among measures.

Bias Enforcement

Biases are enforced in a heuristic manner: rather than imposing hard constraints, choices available to the planner are ordered to reflect the preferences inherent in the biases. Because the enforcement of biases prioritizes choices rather than filtering them, it does not restrict the set of plans that could be produced. As such, the biases can be viewed as *relaxable* constraints on plan generation.

Two types of planning decisions are influenced by biases: *operator selection* and *instance selection*.

Operator Selection Multiple operators could be used to refine a goal within a plan.

Instance Selection Instantiation of variables is performed in two situations. First, instances are selected for variables left uninstantiated after the original task has been reduced

[1]Measures with fewer than n elements are problematic in that there will be multiple intervals that contain the same domain elements. As a result, it is possible that multiple regions will contain combinations of intervals that are effectively identical. To avoid this problem, measures with fewer that n elements are combined (for region creation only) into an artificial composite measure defined by the cross-product of their domains. Partitioning and grouping are performed relative to this composite measure.

to a primitive task network. Second, certain operators dictate that variables be instantiated, although a unique value may not be determined by accumulated constraints on that variable. (Such *early commitment* is often used to reduce the complexity of constraint reasoning (Myers & Wilkins 1998).)

For each of these decision types, a scoring function defines an ordering that reflects the degree to which the choices satisfy the stated biases for the current case. Choices are made according to this order, with random selection amongst choices with equivalent scores. In particular, the most highly ranked choice will be selected first; successive choices may be made in the event that backtracking through that decision occurs.

The scoring functions take into account whether a given bias is *relevant* to a given instance or operator. We say that a bias is relevant to an instance I if the bias measure is defined for I. Similarly, a bias is relevant to an operator Opr if the operator has some feature in a feature category F for which the measure is defined.

The calculation of *bias distance* lies at the heart of the scoring mechanism. Bias distance measures the extent to which a choice satisfies a stated bias. For an instance I, the function $BDist(I, B)$ is the distance d between the interval of measure M defined by B and the measure value for I in M. If the measure is not relevant to the instance, then the distance is defined to be $\perp$; otherwise, the distance is the absolute difference between the measure-defined mapping of I and the interval onto $[0, 1]$. The function $BDist(Opr, F, B)$ for bias distance for an operator Opr and feature category F is defined similarly.

Bias distances are scored so that values in the interval are heavily rewarded while values outside the interval are penalized in proportion to the distance from it:

$$BDistScore(d) = \begin{cases} 0 & \text{if } d = \perp \\ 1 & \text{if } d = 0 \\ -d & \text{otherwise} \end{cases}$$

The score for an instance I relative to a region R is defined to be the sum of the score for I relative to each bias B in R:

$$Score(I, R) = \sum_{B \in R} InstScore(I, B)$$

$$InstScore(I, B) = BDistScore(BDist(I, B))$$

The score for an operator Opr is defined similarly. However, an operator may have features from multiple feature categories that are relevant to the stated biases. For this reason, the average score across those relevant feature categories (denoted by $\mathcal{F}_B$) is used:

$$Score(Opr, R) = \sum_{B \in R} OprScore(Opr, B)$$

$$OprScore(Opr, B) = \\ Avg_{F \in \mathcal{F}_B} BDistScore(BDist(Opr, F, B))$$

Evaluation

To evaluate our algorithm for biasing plan generation, we compared dispersion and proximity values for plan sets of varying size that were produced using biases to those generated by simply randomizing planning decisions within SIPE-2 (i.e., choice of operators and variable instances).[2] Generated plans ranged in length from 2 to 14 actions.

The evaluation space was defined by three evaluation criteria:

- the overall *cost* (measured in dollars),
- the overall *time* (measured in hours),
- the *distance* covered (measured in kms).

Evaluations for generated plans were normalized relative to assigned minimum and maximum values for each criterion. Minimal values were derived through analysis of the planning domain; maximum values were obtained by adding a small buffer (roughly 5%) to the maximum values seen throughout the course of experimentation (encompassing several thousand plans). Determining exact maximum bounds was not feasible because of the overall size of the plan space.

Figures 2 and 3 display the results for an experiment that evaluated four different generation strategies for plan sets:

- biases derived from the 2 measures {AFFORDABILITY, TIME-EFFICIENCY}.
- biases derived from the 2 measures {AFFORDABILITY, COMFORT}
- biases derived from the 3 measures {AFFORDABILITY, COMFORT, TIME-EFFICIENCY}
- randomization of planning decisions *(no biasing)*

For each strategy, 100 plan sets of sizes 2 through 9 were generated (i.e., 800 plan sets in total for each strategy).

Figure 2 plots the mean dispersion value for each trial of each method as a point, embedded in a vertical line showing the standard deviation. Figure 3 provides a similar plot for estimated proximity values, obtained by averaging proximity values for points on a uniform k-dimensional grid with 10 grid points within the evaluation space (i.e., for a total of 10^k sample points). To provide perspective for these charts, note that the maximal plan distance in the evaluation space is 1.73 while the mean plan distance is .58.[3]

The experimental results show that the two biasing methods produce solution sets with significantly better dispersion (i.e., *higher*) and proximity (i.e., *lower*) measures, from $n = 2$ through $n = 6$. Even more significant, however, are the differences in standard deviation which show that the

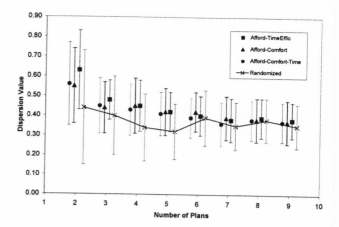

Figure 2: Plan Set Dispersion Measures for 100 Trials

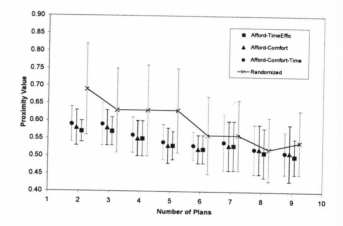

Figure 3: Plan Set Proximity Measures for 100 Trials

biasing approaches vary much less than the randomized approach. These effects are highly pronounced for $2 \leq n \leq 6$, tapering off as n increases beyond that point. As one would expect, dispersion and proximity values for all methods tend to decrease as n increases.

These experiments validate the idea that by using biases rather than randomization to direct the search process, plan sets can be generated for small values of n with significantly better coverage, and for larger values of n that are no worse. Furthermore, the *reliability* is far superior in that the user is unlikely to get bad results (i.e., low dispersion or high proximity) since the standard deviation is significantly smaller.

Future Work

As already noted, a variety of strategies is possible for constructing regions of biases. While the particular method selected worked well within our experiments, alternative approaches merit investigation. For example, the use of *dynamic feedback* among regions could lead to better results: after creating a solution for one region, its evaluation scores could lead to adaptation of other regions to promote better

---

[2]An alternative form of evaluation would be to compare the amount of time required to achieve certain levels of coverage. This definition seems less suitable: while relative comparison of dispersion and proximity values are possible, the interpretation of absolute values for these two measures is unclear.

[3]For a normalized k-dimensional space, the maximum distance between points is $\sqrt{k}$, and the expected mean distance between points is $\sqrt{\frac{k}{9}}$.

proximity or dispersion.

Additional aspects of the domain metatheory could be leveraged as well. For example, *role* information is not directly used in the current framework but could provide another input to the overall biasing algorithm. Thus, users could indicate that they want to see a range of options for air carriers, for example.

Another key area for future work is in highlighting differences among plans. Such explanatory capabilities are critical for helping users make informed choices about their options. The domain metatheory provides a means for abstracting from the details of planning decisions and could be used to concisely summarize key differences between plans. For example, summaries along the following lines could be readily extracted using the domain metatheory:

> *Accommodations* were chosen that ranked high on *affordability*, *United* was chosen as the *carrier* for air travel, and *public transit* was used whenever possible.

Discussion

Focused Biasing The experiments presented above employed biasing over the full extent of measure domains in order to provide coverage of the entire solution space. In general, users will be interested in restricting attention to subregions of the overall space (e.g., overseas vacations in the low to medium affordability range). The biasing approach presented here can readily accommodate this narrowing of the solution space by allowing the user to designate portions of the measure domains over which biases should range.

Measure-Measure Correlation Certain correlations exist among the measures defined in the metatheory for the travel domain. The measures AFFORDABILITY and COMFORT have a strong inverse correlation for feature categories and instances where they are both defined. However, there are several domains where one is defined but not the other. COMFORT and TIME-EFFICIENCY have a mild positive correlation when they overlap, but such overlaps are limited. The use of AFFORDABILITY and TIME-EFFICIENCY overlap significantly, but show a range of positive, negative, and mixed correlation,

The specific biasing method described in this paper employs random selection among measure intervals to avoid effects due to correlations among measures. However, knowledge about correlations could be used as the basis for more sophisticated biasing methods that try to leverage known correlations among measures.

Measure-Evaluation Correlation Correlations exist between certain of the metatheory measures and the evaluation criteria used to adjudicate qualitative difference. While this correlation can be strong (as between the measure AFFORDABILITY and evaluation criteria *Cost*), it is quite weak for others. Such linkage is to be expected, since the metatheoretic biases used to distinguish planning options should relate to evaluation criteria of interest to users.

Biasing Cost The cost of creating biases and regions is negligible. Similarly, enforcement of biases adds only the cost of identifying the most highly ranked choice among available options.

Related Work

Work to date on generating qualitatively different plans that is not rooted in randomization relies extensively on the user to drive the planner to different sections of the plan space. For example, TRIPS (Ferguson & Allen 1998) and O-Plan (Tate, Dalton, & Levine 1998) support mixed-initiative planning in which a user can explore different planning options by either explicitly telling the system what to do next, or imposing constraints on the plan or planning process. Similarly, the Advisable Planner (Myers 1996) provides the means to sketch desired characteristics of a single plan at high levels of abstraction.

The Automated Travel Assistant (ATA) (Linden, Hanks, & Lesh 1997) generates a sequence of plans that vary in response to user feedback on the content of earlier plans. The objective within this system is to find an acceptable solution quickly that ranks highly with respect to stated and inferred user preferences. The basic approach involves incrementally building an improved model of user preferences by analyzing user critiques of solutions that are suggested by the problem-solving system. Each generated solution reflects the evolving preference model, in a way that parallels our method of generating a single plan that reflects certain biases. However, the ATA frames planning as an *attribute selection* problem: finding values for a fixed set of variables. This problem is very different from the open-ended plan generation employed by the biasing algorithm described in this paper.

Conclusions

For many significant planning domains, users are reluctant to relinquish full control of the planning process. Rather, they would like automated planning tools that can help them understand their options. Tools that generate plans with guaranteed significant semantic differences can be of great value to these users, enabling them to make an informed selection from the space of possible solutions.

The biasing technique presented in this paper provides a simple, low-cost mechanism to reliably generate plans with meaningful semantic differences. An additional advantage of the method is that it enables the user to direct the overall process without having to be involved continuously in detailed decision-making.

Acknowledgments This research has been supported by DARPA Contract F30602-95-C-0259 as part of the ARPA/Rome Laboratory Planning Initiative.

References

Erol, K.; Hendler, J.; and Nau, D. S. 1994. Semantics for hierarchical task-network planning. Technical Report CS-TR-3239, Computer Science Department, University of Maryland.

Ferguson, G., and Allen, J. 1998. TRIPS: Towards a mixed-initiative planning assistant. In *Proceedings of the AIPS Workshop on Interactive and Collaborative Planning*.

Gil, Y. 1998. On evaluating plans. Technical report, USC/ISI Expect Project.

Lee, T. J., and Wilkins, D. E. 1996. Using SIPE-2 to integrate planning for military air campaigns. *IEEE Expert* 11(6):11–12.

Linden, G.; Hanks, S.; and Lesh, N. 1997. Interactive assessment of user preference models: The Automated Travel Assistant. In *Proceedings of the Sixth International Conference on User Modeling*.

Myers, K. L., and Wilkins, D. E. 1998. Reasoning about locations in theory and practice. *Computational Intelligence* 14(2).

Myers, K. L. 1996. Strategic advice for hierarchical planners. In Aiello, L. C.; Doyle, J.; and Shapiro, S. C., eds., *Principles of Knowledge Representation and Reasoning: Proceedings of the Fifth International Conference (KR '96)*. Morgan Kaufmann Publishers.

Tate, A.; Dalton, J.; and Levine, J. 1998. Generation of multiple qualitatively different plans. In *Proceedings of the Fourth International Conference on AI Planning Systems*.

Thaler, D. E., and Shlapak, D. A. 1995. Perspectives on theater air campaign planning. Technical report, Rand Corporation.

Wilkins, D. E. 1988. *Practical Planning: Extending the Classical AI Planning Paradigm*. Morgan Kaufmann.

Conditional, Probabilistic Planning: A Unifying Algorithm and Effective Search Control Mechanisms

Nilufer Onder
Department of Computer Science
University of Pittsburgh
Pittsburgh, PA 15260
nilufer@cs.pitt.edu

Martha E. Pollack
Department of Computer Science
and Intelligent Systems Program
University of Pittsburgh
Pittsburgh, PA 15260
pollack@cs.pitt.edu

Abstract

Several recent papers describe algorithms for generating conditional and/or probabilistic plans. In this paper, we synthesize this work, and present a unifying algorithm that incorporates and clarifies the main techniques that have been developed in the previous literature. Our algorithm decouples the search-control strategy for conditional and/or probabilistic planning from the underlying plan-refinement process. A similar decoupling has proven to be very useful in the analysis of classical planning algorithms, and we show that it can be at least as useful here, where the search-control decisions are even more crucial. Previous probabilistic/conditional planners have been severely limited by the fact that they do not know how to handle failure points to advantage. We show how a principled selection of failure points can be performed within the framework our algorithm. We also describe and show the effectiveness of additional heuristics. We describe our implemented system called Mahinur and experimentally demonstrate that our methods produce efficiency improvements of several orders of magnitude.

Introduction

Several recent papers describe algorithms for generating conditional and/or probabilistic plans. Unfortunately, these techniques have not been synthesized into a clear algorithm. In this paper, we present a unifying algorithm that incorporates and clarifies the main techniques that have been developed.

Our algorithm has three useful features. First, it decouples the search-control strategy for conditional probabilistic planning from the underlying plan-refinement process. A similar decoupling has proven to be very useful in the analysis of classical planning algorithms (Weld 1994), and we show that it can be at least as useful here, where search-control decisions are even more crucial. We achieve the decoupling by treating the possible failure points in a plan as flaws. By a *failure point*, we mean a part of the plan that (a) involves a branching action, i.e., one whose outcome is uncertain, and (b) relies on a particular outcome of that action. Where classical planning algorithms consider open conditions and

threats to be flaws, we add possible failure points into this set. Decisions about whether and when to handle each failure point can then be encoded as part of the search-control strategy.

Second, we repair plan failures in a direct way, using three logically distinct techniques: (1) *corrective repair*, originally introduced in the work on conditional planning, which involves reasoning about what to do if the desired outcome of a branching action does not occur; (2) *preventive repair*, originally introduced in the work on probabilistic planning, which involves reasoning about how to help ensure that the desired outcome of a branching action will occur; and (3) *replacement*, implemented by backtracking in the planning literature, which involves removing the branching action and replacing it with an alternative.

Finally, our planner can generate conditional plans with merged branches: if two branches involve different steps at the beginning but the final steps are the same, the final part can be shared. This way the cost of generating the same part twice can be avoided.

Previous probabilistic/conditional planners have been severely limited by the fact that they do not know how to handle failure points to advantage. For all but very small domains, the search space explodes quickly if plan failures are considered indiscriminantly. We show how a principled selection of failure points can be performed within the framework our algorithm. We also describe and show the effectiveness of a few additional heuristics. We describe our implemented system, called Mahinur, and experimentally demonstrate that our methods produce efficiency improvements of several orders of magnitude.

Background and Related Research

When a planning agent does not have complete knowledge of the environment in which its plans will be executed, it may have to create a *conditional plan*, which includes *observation steps* to ascertain the unknown conditions. Using an example from (Dearden & Boutilier 1997), imagine a robot whose goal is to deliver coffee without getting wet; imagine further that the robot does not know whether it is raining outside. A reasonable plan is to go to the window, observe whether it is dry, and if so, go to the cafe. Conditional planning systems (Warren 1976; Peot & Smith 1992; Etzioni *et al.* 1992; Goldman & Boddy 1994a; Pryor & Collins 1996) generate plans that have *branching actions*, i.e., actions with multiple possible outcomes.[1] When a branching action is initially inserted into a plan, one of its outcomes (the *desired outcome*) will be linked to a later step on the path to the goal, while the other(s) (the *undesired outcomes*) will not. We will also refer to an unlinked outcome as a *dangling edge*. In the coffee example, the knowledge that it is dry outside is the desired outcome, while knowledge that it is raining outside is the undesired outcome. The plan is guaranteed to succeed if the desired outcomes of all its observation actions occur; there is no such guarantee otherwise.

Intuitively, one way to improve such a plan is to figure out what to do if some step has an undesired outcome. We will call this a *corrective repair*, since it involves figuring out actions that can be taken to correct the situation that results after the undesired outcome occurs. For the above example, one corrective repair might be to pick up an umbrella if it is raining. In practice, conditional planners implement corrective repairs by duplicating the goal state, and attempting to find a plan that will achieve the (duplicated) goal state without relying on the assumption that the branching actions in the original plan have their desired outcomes.

A different approach is taken in probabilistic planners. Where conditional planners assume that agents have no information about the probability of alternative action outcomes but will be able to observe their environments during plan execution, probabilistic planners such as Buridan (Kushmerick, Hanks, & Weld 1995) make just the opposite assumption. They assume that planning agents have knowledge of the probabilities that their actions will have particular outcomes but that they will be unable to observe their environment. Typically, probabilistic planners model actions with a finite set of tuples $< t_i, p_{i,j}, e_{i,j} >$, where the t_i are a set of exhaustive and mutually exclusive *triggers*, and $p_{i,j}$ represents the probability that the action will have effect $e_{i,j}$ if t_i is true at the time of the action's execution. The triggers serve the role of preconditions in standard causal-link planners. Suppose that the robot's hand might get wet while closing the umbrella before entering the shop, and the coffee cup might slip if its hand is wet. In the example plan fragment shown in Fig. 1, the PICK-UP step has been inserted to achieve the goal of holding the cup. The trigger for holding-cup is hand-dry, and a DRY step has been inserted to probabilistically make that true.

As can be seen, this plan is not guaranteed to succeed. If the hand is not dry, the step will not achieve the desired outcome of holding the cup. To help prevent this undesired outcome, a planner may increase

---

[1]To simplify presentation, we will focus here on actions with two possible outcomes; generalization to a larger number of outcomes is straightforward.

Figure 1: Plan for picking up a part.

the probability that the hand is dry. One way to do this would be to add a second DRY step prior to the PICK-UP. We can call this a *preventive repair*, since it involves adding actions that help prevent the undesired outcome.

It is only natural to combine the ideas of conditional and probabilistic planning. The first combined conditional, probabilistic planning system was C-Buridan (Draper, Hanks, & Weld 1994). Interestingly, while C-Buridan uses preventive repair to increase the probability of success, it does not use corrective repair to generate conditional branches. Its branches are formed in a somewhat indirect fashion: in performing a preventive repair, it may add to the plan a step that conflicts with some other step already in the plan. To resolve this conflict, C-Buridan will split the plan into two branches, putting the conflicting steps on different branches. In effect, C-Buridan identifies a new branch only after it has been formed. Generating plans in this way has been shown to be very inefficient, involving a rapid explosion of the search space as branches are discovered haphazardly (Onder & Pollack 1997).

A more recent system that combines conditional and probabilistic planning is Weaver (Blythe & Veloso 1997) Weaver was built on top of a bidirectional planner (Prodigy 4.0), and therefore uses a different set of basic plan generation operations than those described in this paper. However, as in our approach, Weaver first reasons about which actions to choose in order to most quickly improve the likelihood of success (Blythe 1995) and then uses both preventive and corrective repair. Unlike most of the other planners, it also includes explicit mechanisms for dealing with external events. The Plinth conditional-planning system was also expanded to perform probabilistic reasoning (Goldman & Boddy 1994b). The focus of the Plinth project was on using a belief network to reason about correlated probabilities in the plan.

A different approach to planning under uncertainty is called conformant planning, and involves generating plans that achieve the goals in all the possible cases without using observation actions(Goldman & Boddy 1996). The work on Markov Decision Process (MDP) based planners focuses on finding "policies," which are functions from states to actions. To do this in an efficient way, MDP-based planners rely on dynamic programming and abstraction techniques(Dearden & Boutilier 1997). The DRIPS system (Haddawy, Doan, & Goodwin 1995) interleaves plan expansion and decision theoretic assessment but uses a previously formed

```
PLAN (init, goal, T)
plans ← { make-init-plan ( init, goal ) }
while plan-time < T and plans is not empty do
  CHOOSE (and remove) a plan P from plans
  SELECT a flaw f from P.
  add all refinements of P to plans:
    plans ← plans ∪ new-step(P, f) ∪
            step-reuse(P, f)
                        if f is an open condition,
    plans ← plans ∪ demote(P, f) ∪ promote(P, f) ∪
            confront(P, f) ∪ constrain-to-branch(P, f)
                        if f is a threat.
    plans ← plans ∪ corrective-repair(P, f) ∪
            preventive-repair (P, f)
                        if f is a dangling-edge.
return (plans)

preventive-repair (plan, f)
open-conditions-of-plan ← open-conditions-of-plan ∪
  triggers for the desired outcomes of the
  action in f.
return (plan)

corrective-repair (plan, f)
top-level-goal-nodes-of-plan ← top-level-goal-nodes-of-plan
  ∪ new-top-level-goal-node labeled not to depend
  on the desired outcomes of the action in f.
return (plan)
```

Figure 2: Conditional probabilistic planning algorithm.

plan tree (HTN-style) rather than generating plans using operator descriptions. Recent work by Weld et al. extends Graphplan to handle uncertainty (1998). The Just-In-Case scheduling algorithm (Drummond, Bresina, & Swanson 1994) involves creating an initial schedule and building contingent schedules for the points that are most likely to fail.

Algorithm

Our algorithm (Fig. 2) rests on the observation that conditional, probabilistic planning involves repairing plan flaws (closing an open precondition or resolving a threat) and repairing dangling edges (corrective repair or preventive repair). The input is a set of initial conditions, a set of goal conditions, and a time limit T. The output is a set of plans. The algorithm is a plan-space search, where, as usual, the nodes in the search space represent partial plans. We assume that actions are encoded using the probabilistic action representation described in the previous section.

Normal flaws—threats and open conditions—are repaired in the usual way. To achieve an open condition c, the planner will find an action that includes a branch $< t_i, p_{i,j}, e_{i,j} >$, such that one of the elements of $e_{i,j}$ unifies with c. The relevant trigger t_i will then become a new open condition. Note that a condition c remains "open" only so long as it has no incoming causal link; once an action α has been inserted to (probabilistically) produce c, it is no longer open, even if α

has only a small chance of actually achieving c.[2] A threat is resolved by step ordering (demote, promote), committing to desired outcomes (confront), or separating the steps into branches (constrain-to-branch). For "dangling-edge flaws", we assume that preventive repair is achieved by reintroducing the triggers for desired effects into the set of open conditions, as done in Buridan; we assume corrective repair is achieved by adding new, labeled copies of the goal node as in CNLP. Corrective repairs form new branches in the plan that indicate alternative responses to different observational results. Preventive repairs do not introduce new branches.

Consistent with the prior literature, we use SELECT to denote a non-deterministic choice that is not a backtrack point, and CHOOSE for a backtrack point. As usual, node selection, but not flaw selection, is subject to backtracking.

It is important to note that in prior algorithms such as CNLP and C-Buridan, observation actions do not differentiate between the conditions that are true in the world (state conditions) and the conditions that represent the agent's state of knowledge (information conditions). In CNLP, the outcomes of an observation action are state conditions, thus observation actions are inserted through standard backchaining. In C-Buridan, the outcomes of actions are information conditions. C-Buridan has no concept of corrective repair; instead it inserts observation actions only during threat resolution, when conflicting actions are constrained to be in different branches. During this process, C-Buridan will consider every possible observation action. It is thus complete in the sense that it will find a relevant observation action whenever one exists, even if the correlation between the observation and the condition in question has not been made explicit. However, C-Buridan's indirect method of inserting observation actions is very inefficient: it has no notion of the source and potential impact of any plan failure, and thus cannot prioritize the failures it chooses to work on (Onder & Pollack 1997).

For the sake of practicality, we have taken a middle road. We require that the connection be made explicit between an observation action and any information and state conditions it affects. Fig. 3 illustrates the act of directly observing whether it is raining outside. The observation may be inaccurate: with 0.10 probability, it will provide a false negative. The connection between the belief that it is not raining (the "report") and the fact of the matter of rain (the "subject") is explicit in the representation.

Consequently, our algorithm does need to insert observation actions by backchaining or for threat resolution. Instead, we can directly reason about which step S will have the greatest impact if it fails—i.e., does not achieve desired outcome c. Corrective repair can then be performed, directly inserting after S an observation

---

[2]A sensible heuristic is to select actions where the relevant $p_{i,j}$ is as high as possible.

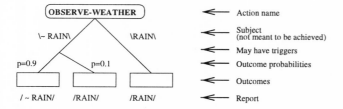

Figure 3: Observing whether it is raining.

action that reports on c, along with a *subject link* from S to the new observation action. The trade-off is that the algorithm is less complete than C-Buridan, because it will not discover observation actions whose connection to some condition are not explicitly encoded. Because the in-principle complete algorithms are too inefficient to be in-practice complete, we are willing to make this trade-off, and rely on the operator designer to encode explicitly the connections between information conditions and state conditions.

We implemented this algorithm in a planning system called Mahinur. In refining a plan, Mahinur first repairs the normal flaws until the plan is *complete*, i.e., has no open conditions or threats. It then selects a dangling edge and then works only on normal flaws until the plan is once again complete. This strategy reduces the amount of bookkeeping required to keep track of nested contexts when multiple corrective repairs are being performed. It also allows Mahinur to readily produce intermediate solutions throughout the planning process, because complete plans are potential solutions to the planning problem.

We assume that the top-level goals have additive scalar values assigned to them. Thus, the *expected value of a plan* is the sum of the products of the final probability of each top-level goal and its scalar value. We approximate the final probability of any goal by a process of simulation, in which we start with an initial state distribution, and simulate the execution of each step in the plan, updating the state distribution accordingly. We refer to the state distribution after the execution of step i as sd_i. Because the focus of our work is on search control, we finesse the issue of efficient plan assessment (i.e., calculation of the expected value) and use a random total ordering of the steps.

Efficient Corrective Repair

While the algorithm above captures the ideas inherent in the prior work on both conditional and the probabilistic planning, it also inherits a major problem: if applied without strong heuristics, it can be extremely inefficient. In particular, the time required to generate a plan with two branches can be exponentially greater than the sum of the times required to generate two separate plans, each identical to one of the branches. We illustrate this with the running example. If we ignore the possibility of rain, a simple solution is a plan with four steps, GO-CAFE;

BUY-COFFEE; GO-OFFICE; DELIVER-COFFEE, which can be generated by Mahinur in 0.24 CPU seconds using 40 plan nodes. When we re-introduce the possibility of rain, the solution has two branches because if is is raining, the robot needs to get an umbrella: SEE-IF-RAINING; if raining (GET-UMBRELLA; GO-CAFE; BUY-COFFEE; GO-OFFICE; DELIVER-COFFEE); if not raining (GO-CAFE; BUY-COFFEE; GO-OFFICE; DELIVER-COFFEE). The two branches are similar to one another, but it takes Mahinur 27.66 CPU seconds and 6902 plan nodes to generate the branching plan.[3]

The problem results from the backwards-chaining approach taken by Mahinur and other planning systems. When a new step is inserted into the plan, it is not part of any branch; it is put into a branch (by the *constrain-to-branch* procedure in Mahinur) only after a threat is detected between two steps that should be in separate branches. However, in addition to constraining, the planner needs to consider several other methods of threat resolution, resulting in exponential explosion of the search space. The intuitive solution is to prefer constraining a new step to be in a new branch when a conditional branch is being formed, i.e., corrective repairs are being performed. This can be implemented easily as a heuristic in the framework of our algorithm: while generating a new branch following observe step I, if a newly inserted step threatens a step in the first branch, prefer to resolve the threat by placing the new step into the new branch of I if it is consistent to do so.

We illustrate the proportionality of our heuristic's effect on variations of the BUY COFFEE problem. The first problem is the basic problem, including the possibility of rain; there are five steps in the new branch. In the second problem, we added a new step (GET-CREAM) to the problem, increasing the number of the steps in the new branch to 6. In the third problem, we also added the GET-SUGAR step. In Fig. 4, we tabulate the run time and the number of plans created while generating conditional plans with and without the threat resolution heuristic. (We terminated the experiment marked with "—" after 24 hours and 350000 plan nodes.) As expected, the search space is reduced significantly when the heuristic is used to control the search, and the reduction is proportional to the number of steps in the new branch. This heuristic proved to be very effective enabling us to generate plans with tens of steps and conditional branches in just a few seconds.

Selecting Contingencies

A plan is composed of many steps that establish conditions to support the goals and subgoals, but repairs for the failure of conditions are usually not expected to have equal contributions to the overall success of

---

[3]Unfortunately, benchmark problems and implemented systems for comparison of probabilistic conditional planners are not available. However, the examples given in the literature suggest that other conditional planners suffer from similar exponential explosion of the search space.

Problem	Run time (sec.) with	Run time (sec.) without	Plans created with	Plans created without
coffee	1.35	27.66	105	6902
coffee,cream	1.81	687.13	178	57912
coffee,cream,sugar	2.73	—	398	>350000

Figure 4: Effects of the threat resolution heuristic.

the plan. With the notable exception of (Feldman & Sproul 1977), the decision theoretic prioritization of repair points has not been a focus of recent systems. To identify the best repair points, we focus on two facts: first, contingencies in a plan may have unequal probability of occurrence; second, a plan may have multiple goals, each of which has some associated value. Let us leave the probability of failure aside for a moment, and consider the robot in the the previous examples and a plan involving two goals: mailing a document at the post office and delivering coffee to the user. The value of achieving the former goal may be significantly higher than the latter. Consequently, the conditions that support only the former goal (e.g., having envelopes) contribute more to the overall success of the plan than the conditions that support only the latter (e.g., having sugar). Conditions that support both goals (e.g., keeping the robot dry) will have the greatest importance. This suggests that it may be most important to have a contingency plan to handle the possibility of rain; almost as important to have a contingency plan in case there are no envelopes in the office; and less important to have a contingency plan in case there is no sugar. While performing this reasoning, we can fold the probability of failure back in as a weighing factor.

Of course, in reality the importance of having contingency plans will also depend on the likely difficulty of replanning "on-the-fly" for particular contingencies; it may be worth reasoning in advance about contingencies that are difficult to plan for. Another factor influencing the choice of a contingency is the difficulty of executing a contingent plan if not considered in advance. These types of information concern the plan that has not yet been generated, which suggests that they might have to be coded as part of the domain information, based on past experience.

Even if this type of domain information is not available, we can use the upper bound of the expected value of repairing a failure point as a good estimate for selecting contingencies. Suppose that a step S_i is used to establish a condition c, and the probability of that c will be false right after S_i is executed is $p > 0$. Then, the best the planner can do is to add a new branch that will make the top-level goals true even when c is not true. What is the value of adding such a branch? In computing this, we need to consider only the probability that immediately after executing S_i, both c and the top-level goals will be false: if a top-level goal is true anyway after executing S_i, then there is no benefit to establishing it. We also need to factor in the probabil-

ity that S_i will be executed in the first place. (If it is downstream from another branch point, it may never be executed.) The upper bound on the expected value of performing a corrective repair on S_i in the case in which desired outcome c may fail is defined as follows:

$$EVCR(S_i, c) =$$
$$\sum_{g \in G} P[\{c, \bar{g}\} \cup S_{Ci} | sd_0, < S_1, \ldots, S_i >] \times V(g),$$

where $P[\{x_1, \ldots, x_n\} | sd_0, < S_1, \ldots, S_i >]$ denotes the probability that $\{x_1, \ldots, x_n\}$ all hold in the state distribution resulting from the execution of the steps through S_i starting with the initial state distribution sd_0. S_{Ci} is the *context* of the step, i.e., the conditions under which the step will be executed.[4] That is, for each top-level goal g in G, we compute the probability that immediately after performing step S_i, c and g will both fail to hold while all the effects of S_i except c hold. We then weight the value of g ($V(g)$) by this probability, and finally sum all the weighted values. As noted, this is an upper bound; the actual value of corrective repair of s_i might be less if the repair only probabilistically establishes g, or if there are other steps in the original plan that achieve g without using c in sd_i. Our strategy for selecting contingencies is to use the formula above to compute $EVCR$ for each failure point and then to select the one with the highest value.

In order to illustrate the importance of this process, we have designed a synthetic domain with several top-level goals all of which have unit value (Fig. 5). We then ran experiments in which we started with an initial plan where each goal is achieved by a single step that has no preconditions, and achieves the goal with some probability (Fig 5a). In addition to the operators in the initial plan, we designed a set of alternative operators each of which achieves a goal with certainty. (Imagine that the probabilistic operator in the initial plan is cheaper to execute, and it is preferable to try it first and use the alternative only if it fails). In order to establish a baseline case, we designed the alternative operators to have the minimal planning effort, i.e., performing a corrective repair involves forming a branch with one step to establish the goal. This also made the corrective repair effort to be uniform for each failure point: each can be repaired by generating a one-step plan. We implemented our strategy for selecting contingencies and ran several experiments by increasing the user-specified expected value threshold. In one condition—ordered selection—we selected the contingency with the highest expected value for corrective repairs; and in another condition—random selection—we selected a contingency randomly (ordered selection always selects steps A1, B1 ... I1). In Fig. 6, we plot the time required to meet the threshold with and without ordering contingencies. As expected, by ordering

---

[4]Actually, the probability of S_{Ci} should be computed for the state that obtains just prior to the execution of S_i. However, for simplicity in the formula we compute it in the state that obtains after S_i is executed; this does not affect the result because a step cannot change its own context.

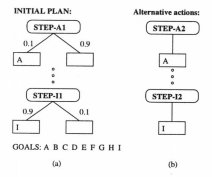

INITIAL PLAN: Alternative actions:

GOALS: A B C D E F G H I

(a)   (b)

Figure 5: A synthetic domain for experiments.

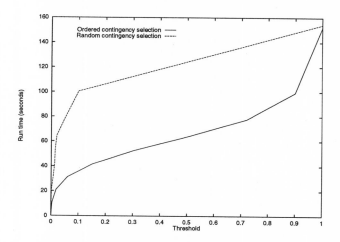

Figure 6: Time required to generate a plan that meets the threshold.

contingencies, the planner can produce better plans in shorter time. Note that, the two lines converge to the same point because once all the failures are repaired, the total expected value of the plan is the same and the total cost of repairing all the failures is the same.

A similar strategy can be used for estimating the expected value of performing preventive repairs, but we omit discussion due to space limitations.

Generating Plans with Joined Branches

The efficiency of performing corrective repairs can be further improved by sharing the final parts of two branches if they are the same. CNLP-style conditional planners cannot generate plans with joined branches because they duplicate the top-level goals and re-generate every step even if they are the same as the existing branch. However, branches can be joined by nondeterministically choosing and duplicating a subgoal rather than a top-level goal. Suppose that the delivery robot has a detailed plan to go back to the office after picking up the coffee, and is generating contingency plans for the possible failures regarding coffee pick up. In such a situation, it might be more efficient to focus on the subgoal of getting coffee rather than revising the whole

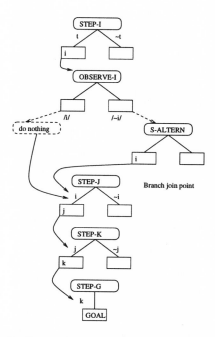

Figure 7: Corrective repairs with branch joining.

plan.

We have implemented this method in Mahinur in the following way: consider the plan in Fig. 7 and suppose that STEP-I can fail to establish i for STEP-J and this failure point has been selected for corrective repairs. Then, rather than duplicating the top level goal, the planner duplicates just STEP-J's triggers—i—and tries to find a conditional branch that establishes i without using support from STEP-I. The remainder of the plan (STEP-J and STEP-K) remains the same, and does not have to be regenerated. If the planner fails to find a plan for i, it backtracks and tries to duplicate the triggers of the next step that is connected by a causal link to the step it has just tried—the next step in the causal link path is STEP-K in this example. Imagine that the planner first tries to find alternative ways of getting coffee and then tries another beverage if this fails. Backtracking stops when a top-level goal needs to be duplicated. Note that our work focuses on generating plans with joined branches rather than merging already formed branches.

The step whose triggers are duplicated is called a *branch join point* (e.g., STEP-J in Fig. 7). No steps are necessary if STEP-I succeeds, and alternative step (S-ALTERN) will be executed if STEP-I fails. The remainder of the plan is shared by the two branches.

We conducted a set of experiments to show the possible benefits of branch joining. In these experiments, we used a set of coffee domain problems analogous to the ship-reject problem in C-Buridan (Draper, Hanks, & Weld 1994). In these problems, the robot asks whether decaffeinated coffee is available and gets it. If not available, it gets regular coffee. Both have the same price, so the steps to pay for the

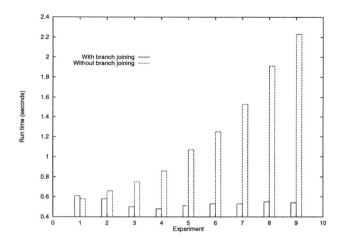

Figure 8: The CPU time required with and without branch joining to solve planning problems of increasing complexity.

coffee and to go back to the office can be shared. Without branch joining, the solution conditional plan is: `ASK; if available (GET-DECAF; PAY; GO-OFFICE; DELIVER-COFFEE); if not available (GET-REGULAR; PAY; GO-OFFICE; DELIVER-COFFEE)`. If branch joining is performed during corrective repairs, the last three steps of each branch can be shared.

If branch joining is used, the planner saves some of the effort of generating the sequence of steps after the branch join point. In order to demonstrate this, we designed a set of 9 problems based on the above problem. We made the plan generation process harder by putting more alternative steps into the domain description: In the first problem, there are no alternatives to the final three steps; in the second problem, each can be performed in two ways; and in the ninth problem, each can be performed in nine ways. For each problem, we plotted the CPU time required to generate the conditional branch with and without branch joining in Fig. 8. As expected, the planning effort does not increase when branch joining is used because the plan after the branch join point is reused while forming the new branch. When branch joining is not used, it takes the planner longer to generate the same plan because the part after the branch join point needs to be generated from scratch.

On the other hand, the planner needs to backtrack if it cannot find a plan with joined branches. In our implementation, when branch joining is enabled, the planner first duplicates the triggers of the first action that is supported by the condition which may fail. If no plan is found, it tries the next step in the path of causal links and continues until a top-level goal is reached. (We do not consider re-opening every set of possible subgoals because once the top-level goals are re-opened, an entirely new plan can be found). Obviously, if the planner spends too much time trying to find a plan with joined branches when none exists, its

performance will be worse than directly duplicating the top-level goals. As a result, domain-dependent tuning may be required to determine whether branch joining will be attempted and to select the step to be used as a branch join point. Nonetheless, the results are promising and we are optimistic about the effectiveness of our method because the savings obtained by branch joining can be significant and a strategy for branch joining can be determined by compiling typical problem instances in a domain. Branch joining is useful because it lets the planner focus on the steps that are in the vicinity of the possible failure rather than the top-level goals.

Conclusion

In real-world environments, planners must deal with the fact that actions do not always have certain outcomes, and that the state of the world will not always be completely known. Good plans can nonetheless be formed if the agent has knowledge of the probabilities of action outcomes and/or can observe the world. Intuitively, if an agent does not know what the world will be like at some point in its plan, there are two things it can do: (i) it can take steps to increase the likelihood that the world will be a certain way, and (ii) it can plan to observe the world, and then take corrective action if things are not the way the should be. These basic ideas have been included, in different ways, in the prior literature on conditional and probabilistic planning. The focus of this paper has been to synthesize this prior work in a unifying algorithm that cleanly separates the control process from the plan refinement process. Using our framework, contingencies can be handled selectively and heuristics that depend on the type of repair being performed can be used. This control is an important condition for applying conditional probabilistic planning to real world problems. We have obtained promising early results in a realistic domain(Desimone & Agosta 1994), and we will make the Mahinur system and the domain encoding publicly available.

Acknowledgments

This work has been supported by a scholarship from the Scientific and Technical Research Council of Turkey, by the Air Force Office of Scientific Research (F49620-98-1-0436), and by the National Science Foundation (IRI-9619579). We thank the anonymous reviewers for their comments.

References

Blythe, J., and Veloso, M. 1997. Analogical replay for efficient conditional planning. In *Proc. 15th Nat. Conf. on AI*, 668–673.

Blythe, J. 1995. The footprint principle for heuristics for probabilistic planners. In *Proc. European Workshop on Planning*.

Dearden, R., and Boutilier, C. 1997. Abstraction and approximate decision theoretic planning. *Artificial Intelligence* 89(1):219–283.

Desimone, R. V., and Agosta, J. M. 1994. Spill response system configuration study—final report. Technical Report ITAD-4368-FR-94-236, SRI International.

Draper, D.; Hanks, S.; and Weld, D. 1994. Probabilistic planning with information gathering and contingent execution. In *Proc. 2nd Int. Conf. on AI Planning Systems*, 31–36.

Drummond, M.; Bresina, J.; and Swanson, K. 1994. Just-in-case scheduling. In *Proc. 12th Nat. Conf. on AI*.

Etzioni, O.; Hanks, S.; Weld, D.; Draper, D.; Lesh, N.; and Williamson, M. 1992. An approach to planning with incomplete information. In *Proc. 3rd Int. Conf. on Principles of Knowledge Repr. and Reasoning*, 115–125.

Feldman, J. A., and Sproul, R. F. 1977. Decision theory and AI II: The hungry monkey. *Cognitive Science* 1:158–192.

Goldman, R. P., and Boddy, M. S. 1994a. Conditional linear planning. In *Proc. 2nd Int. Conf. on AI Planning Systems*, 80–85.

Goldman, R. P., and Boddy, M. S. 1994b. Epsilon-safe planning. In *Proc. 10th Conf. on Uncertainty in AI*, 253–261.

Goldman, R. P., and Boddy, M. S. 1996. Expressive planning and explicit knowledge. In *Proc. 3rd Int. Conf. on AI Planning Systems*, 110–117.

Haddawy, P.; Doan, A.; and Goodwin, R. 1995. Efficient decision-theoretic planning: Techniques and empirical analysis. In *Proc. 11th Conf. on Uncertainty in AI*.

Kushmerick, N.; Hanks, S.; and Weld, D. S. 1995. An algorithm for probabilistic planning. *Artificial Intelligence* 76:239–286.

Onder, N., and Pollack, M. E. 1997. Contingency selection in plan generation. In *Proc. European Conf. on Planning*, 364–376.

Peot, M. A., and Smith, D. E. 1992. Conditional nonlinear planning. In *Proc. 1st Int. Conf. on AI Planning Systems*, 189–197.

Pryor, L., and Collins, G. 1996. Planning for contingencies: A decision based approach. *Journal of AI Research* 4:287–339.

Warren, D. H. 1976. Generating conditional plans and programs. In *Proc. AISB Summer Conference*, 344–354.

Weld, D. S.; Anderson, C. R.; and Smith, D. E. 1998. Extending graphplan to handle uncertainty and sensing actions. In *Proc. 16th Nat. Conf. on AI*, 897–904.

Weld, D. S. 1994. An introduction to least commitment planning. *AI Magazine* 15(4):27–61.

CPlan: A Constraint Programming Approach to Planning

Peter van Beek and **Xinguang Chen**
Department of Computing Science
University of Alberta
Edmonton, Alberta, Canada T6G 2H1
{vanbeek,xinguang}@cs.ualberta.ca

Abstract

Constraint programming, a methodology for solving difficult combinatorial problems by representing them as constraint satisfaction problems, has shown that a general purpose search algorithm based on constraint propagation combined with an emphasis on modeling can solve large, practical scheduling problems. Given the success of constraint programming on scheduling problems and the similarity of scheduling to planning, the question arises, would a constraint programming approach work as well in planning? In this paper, we present evidence that a constraint programming approach to planning does indeed work well and has the advantage in terms of time and space efficiency over the current state-of-the-art planners.

Introduction

Constraint programming, a methodology for solving difficult combinatorial problems by representing them as constraint satisfaction problems, has shown that a general purpose search algorithm based on constraint propagation combined with an emphasis on modeling can solve large, practical scheduling problems (see, for example, (Baptiste & Le Pape 1995) and references therein). At the heart of constraint programming are constraint satisfaction problems (CSPs). A problem is represented as a set of variables, a domain of values for each variable, and a set of constraints between the variables. A solution is an instantiation of the variables that satisfies the constraints. The CSP is often solved using backtracking search and constraint programming has developed many techniques for reducing the size of the search space including adding redundant variables and redundant constraints to the CSP model .

Much work in planning, with its emphasis on a minimal domain model (just the representation of the actions) and planning specific, special purpose, search algorithms has taken an almost *opposite* approach to that of constraint programming, with its emphasis on domain knowledge and general purpose search algorithms. However, given the success of constraint programming on scheduling problems and the similarity of scheduling to planning, the question arises, would a constraint programming approach work as well in planning?

In this paper, we present evidence that a constraint programming approach to planning does indeed work well. We compare our constraint programming planner, called CPlan, to state-of-the-art planners on benchmark problems in five different domains and show that our planner has the advantage in terms of time and space efficiency and robustness. CPlan also has several other advantages which it shares with other CSP-like approaches to planning. In CPlan, the CSP model is a purely declarative representation of domain knowledge and is thus independent of any algorithm. Thus the same model can be given to a systematic solver or a solver based on local search. As well, in CPlan it is easy to represent incomplete initial states or partial information about intermediate states and to represent resource and capacity constraints. Of course, there is one important disadvantage of this approach over planners which use a minimal domain model. For each new domain, a robust CSP model must be developed. The modeling phase can require much intellectual effort and, although much of what is learned in one domain can be applied in another, each new domain does require a new model. The tradeoff is that less work needs to be done on algorithms since there are several commercial and many research constraint programming languages with general purpose constraint solvers embedded in them.

Background

We first define constraint satisfaction problems and then briefly review backtracking search (for more background on these topics see, for example, (Marriott & Stuckey 1998; Van Hentenryck 1989)).

A *constraint satisfaction problem (CSP)* consists of a set of n variables, $\{x_1, \ldots, x_n\}$; a domain D_i of possible *values* for each variable x_i, $1 \leq i \leq n$; and a collection of m constraints, $\{C_1, \ldots, C_m\}$. Each constraint C_i, $1 \leq i \leq m$, is a constraint over some set of variables called the scheme of the constraint. The size of this set is known as the *arity* of the constraint. A *solution* to a CSP is an assignment of a value $a_i \in D_i$ to x_i, $1 \leq i \leq n$, that satisfies all of the constraints.

CSPs are often solved using a backtracking algorithm. At every stage of backtracking search, there is some current partial solution which the algorithm attempts to extend to a full solution by assigning a value to an uninstantiated variable. One of the keys behind the success of constraint programming is the idea of constraint propagation. During the backtracking search when a variable is assigned a value, the constraints are used to reduce the domains of the uninstantiated variables. The algorithm we used in our experiments, which we denote as GAC+CBJ, performs generalized arc consistency propagation and conflict-directed backjumping (Prosser 1993).

Following Van Hentenryck (1989), We say that a k-ary constraint, $k \geq 2$, is *arc consistency checkable* if at least one of its variables is uninstantiated. Such a constraint is also *forward checkable* if exactly $k - 1$ of its variables have been instantiated and the remaining variable is uninstantiated. During backtracking search, the assignment of a value to a variable x_c causes some (possibly empty) set of constraints to be queued for propagation: all of the constraints that are arc consistency checkable and for which x_c is in the scheme of that constraint. For each forward checkable constraint on the queue, GAC+CBJ checks whether each value in the domain of the unassigned variable together with the values of the assigned variables satisfies the constraint, pruning those values that are inconsistent. If this process causes the unassigned variable to have all of its domain values pruned, GAC+CBJ backtracks. The arc consistency checkable constraints are processed in a similar manner: for each uninstantiated variable in the constraint, GAC+CBJ tests whether there exists values for the other variables that are consistent with the constraint, pruning those values for which this test fails and backtracking should a variable have all of its values pruned. If a variable has had its domain reduced, all of the constraints that have that variable in their scheme are added to the queue of constraints to be propagated. To backup, GAC+CBJ does not necessarily return to the chronologically most recent decision and undue that decision. Rather, it attempts to locate the source of the deadend and to jump back to that point.

Example 1 Consider the CSP with three variables x, y, and z, each with domain $\{1, 2, 3, 4\}$, and the following three constraints,

C_1: $(y \leq 3) \Rightarrow (x \geq 3)$,
C_2: $y + z \leq 6$,
C_3: alldifferent(x, y, z)

where constraint C_3 enforces that its three arguments are pair-wise different. When backtracking search starts all constraints are arc consistency checkable, but no values are pruned from the domains. Suppose backtracking search makes the assignment $x = 1$. Constraint C_1 and C_3 are queued for processing because they involve the newly instantiated variable. Processing C_1 causes the domain of y to be reduced to $\{4\}$. This causes C_2 to be added to the queue. Processing C_3 next reduces the domain of z to $\{2, 3\}$. Processing C_2 further reduces the domain of z to $\{2\}$. The rest of the search then proceeds in a backtrack-free manner.

Constraint Programming Methodology

In the constraint programming methodology we cast the problem as a CSP in terms of variables, values, and constraints. The choice of variables defines the search space and the choice of constraints defines how the search space

can be reduced so that it can be effectively searched using backtracking search. We illustrate the approach using the logistics domain. In the logistics domain, there are packages which need to be moved around between cities and between locations within cities using trucks and planes.

We model each state by a collection of variables and the constraints enforce valid transitions between states. For example, in the logistics world we have the following variables for each state S_t: $C_{i,t}$, $T_{j,t}$, and $P_{k,t}$, where i, j, k range over the number of packages, trucks, and planes, respectively and t ranges over the number of steps in the plan. The domains of the package variables are locations, trucks, and planes. Assigning a package variable a location means the package is at that location in that state and assigning a package variable a truck means the package is in that truck in that state. The common STRIPS representation of this domain has two predicates that specify whether a package is at a location or in a plane or truck, respectively and an implicit state constraint that a package is either at a location or in a vehicle, but not both. This shows how CSP variables can be more succinct than propositional variables and how some state constraints can be implicitly handled. Similarly, the domains of trucks and planes are locations.

Part of the modeling task is to specify which are the visible variables and which are the hidden variables. In the logistics domain the package variables are visible and the truck and plane variables are hidden. Thus, backtracking occurs over the package variables and once they are all instantiated, the search is guaranteed to proceed in a backtrack-free manner to find values for the hidden variables.

We now turn to specifying the constraints. Constraints are represented intensionally as functions which return true or false, given a set of assignments to the variables in the scheme of the constraint. This is a compact representation, in contrast to an extensional approach where all of the assignments of values to variables which satisfy a constraint are explicitly listed (as in the planning as satisfiability framework of Kautz and Selman).

We found the following constraint categories to be useful across the five domains to which we have applied the approach. For a minimal correct model of the domain we need the action constraints which enforce how variables can change from a state S_t to a next state S_{t+1} and the state constraints which enforce how variables within a state must be consistent. The remaining categories of constraints were found to be essential in improving the efficiency of the search for a plan. Each constraint can be classified as to whether it is redundant or non-redundant. A constraint is redundant if its removal from the CSP does not change the set of solutions. Our goal is a sound and complete planner. Thus, for each non-redundant constraint that we add, we need to provide an argument that, if the set of solutions was non-empty before the addition of the constraint, it remains non-empty after its addition. In other words, a constraint must be optimality preserving to be considered for addition to the model.

Action constraints model the effects of actions. These constraints are patterned after explanation closure axioms (Schubert 1994). For example, a package variable can only change from being at a location in S_t to being in a truck or plane in S_{t+1} (or vice-versa) and if it does change, this implies that the truck or plane must be at the same location as the package in these states.

State constraints enforce how variables within a state must be consistent.

Distance constraints are upper and lower bound constraints on how many steps are needed for a variable to change from one value to another. For example, a lower bound on the number of steps to get a package from a non-airport location in one city to a non-airport in another city is nine steps (as it needs to be loaded and unload from two trucks and one plane). These constraints were found to be among the most important for reducing the search space in the domains that we explored.

Symmetric values constraints are constraints which break symmetries on the values that variables can be assigned. For example, in the logistics domain, given two package variables, the planes in their domains are often symmetric and if there is a solution (or no solution) with a particular assignment of planes to packages, there is another solution (or no solution) with the planes swapped. With distance constraints, these constraints were found to be the most important for reducing the search space in the domains that we explored.

Action choice constraints enforce constraints on which actions can be performed in each state. Part of the explosion in the search space in planning is because a sequence of actions starting from some state can be permuted and still result in the same end state. For example, in the logistics world suppose there are two packages at an airport. A plane can either pick up both at once, or pick up one now and another later. All of these will end up being equivalent and a constraint is added which forbids all but one of the action sequences.

Capacity constraints enforce bounds on resources. In the logistics domain the trucks and planes have unlimited capacity, so these did not apply. However, in the mystery and Mprime domains (see the next section), the vehicles have capacity restrictions and there are limits on the amount of fuel available. These kinds of constraints are straightforward in the CSP approach, but difficult for traditional planners.

Domain constraints enforce restrictions on the original domains of the variables. For example, in the logistics domain, a package which is to be picked up and delivered within the same city can have its domain restricted to locations and trucks within that city.

Part of the modeling task is to specify what kind of propagation is desired for each constraint: whether a constraint should just be forward checked or arc consistency checked. Constraints of high arity are expensive to arc consistency check and may not reduce the search space enough to compensate. Experimentation is required to know whether a constraint is effective and what is the most efficient way to propagate it.

To solve an instance of a planning problem with particular initial and goal states, we start with some lower bound on the length of an optimal plan, generate a CSP model with that many steps in it, appropriately instantiate the variables in the

initial and goal state, and pass the model to the backtracking algorithm GAC+CBJ. This is repeated, each time incrementing the number of steps in the plan, until a solution is found or some upper bound on the length of an optimal plan is exceeded. The idea of incrementally finding an optimal plan is due to Kautz and Selman (1992).

GAC+CBJ uses a dynamic variable ordering that selects as the next variable to instantiate the variable with the smallest domain, breaking ties by the number of constraints that the variable participates in. Thus, planning can proceed in a forwards or backwards or middle out direction and *any* part of the plan can be worked on before other parts. The overall planning algorithm, CPlan, is sound, complete, and guaranteed to terminate (but, as with other planners, the algorithm is incomplete in any practical sense since it can run for a very long time).

Experiments

We have applied our constraint satisfaction methodology to the five test domains used in the First AI Planning Systems Competition, held in Pittsburgh, June 6–9, 1998, and compared our results to four other planners: Blackbox, HSP, IPP, and TLPlan. Blackbox, HSP, and IPP were all entered into the AIPS'98 competition and each was the best or among the best in at least one of the test domains.

Blackbox (Kautz & Selman 1998a) is based on converting planning graphs (as constructed by Graphplan (Blum & Furst 1997)) into a CNF formula, and then attempting to solve the formula using a variety of satisfiability solvers. HSP (Bonet & Geffner 1998) is a forward-chaining planner which uses hill-climbing search with an automatically generated (inadmissible) heuristic cost function to estimate the distance to the goal state. IPP (Koehler & Nebel 1998) is based on Graphplan, and like Graphplan constructs a planning graph in a forwards direction and then searches it in a backwards direction to extract a plan. IPP improves on Graphplan by having a better memoization scheme to recognize subsets of goals that have failed in the past and a richer representation language. TLPlan (Bacchus 1998) is a forward-chaining planner which allows various heuristic search algorithms to be selected and provides a temporal logic for representing declarative search control knowledge. With respect to the AIPS'98 competition benchmark problems, TLPlan only comes with domain knowledge specified for the logistics problems and so we only compared its performance to the other planners on this domains.

We used the following experimental setup. All experiments were run on 400 MHz Pentium II's with 256 Megabytes of memory. Each planner was given one hour of CPU time and 256 Megabytes of memory in which to solve a problem. If the planner solved the problem within the resource limits, the CPU time was recorded (see Tables 1–5). By solving a problem, we mean that, if a plan exists, the planner returns a plan (either optimal or non-optimal), and if a plan does not exist, the planner correctly reports this fact. For some of the planning problems in the mystery domain (see Table 3), no plan exists and, by definition, a non-systematic planner such as HSP cannot correctly solve these

Table 1: Time (seconds) to solve gripper planning problems. The absence of an entry indicates that the problem was not solved correctly within the given resource limits.

	CPlan	Blackbox	HSP	IPP
1	0.01	0.11	0.03	0.02
2	0.04	5.68	0.10	0.39
3	0.08	.	0.11	7.83
4	0.17	.	0.18	100.37
5	0.28	.	0.26	.
6	0.48	.	0.35	.
7	0.75	.	0.46	.
8	1.15	.	0.53	.
9	1.67	.	0.74	.
10	2.34	.	0.94	.
11	3.17	.	1.13	.
12	4.23	.	1.45	.
13	5.52	.	1.49	.
14	7.07	.	1.81	.
15	8.92	.	2.19	.
16	11.15	.	2.56	.
17	13.67	.	3.04	.
18	16.81	.	3.26	.
19	20.19	.	3.77	.
20	24.35	.	4.23	.

Table 2: Time (seconds) to solve logistics planning problems. The absence of an entry indicates that the problem was not solved correctly within the given resource limits.

	CPlan	Blackbox	HSP	IPP	TLPlan
1	0.05	1.48	.	0.62	0.37
2	0.06	4.29	.	552.20	1.48
3	0.94	.	.	.	15.83
4	0.17	.	.	.	44.37
5	1.73	148.01	1.17	2.52	0.28
6	18.89	.	.	.	68.80
7	0.09	.	.	3059.24	4.65
8	0.16	.	.	.	78.60
9	0.32	.	.	.	176.41
10	.	.	.	.	135.44
11	0.05	4.51	4.96	6.48	4.43
12	0.12	.	.	.	231.97
13	0.59	.	.	.	865.04
14	0.68	.	.	.	651.37
15	203.15	.	.	.	19.24
16	0.40	.	.	.	136.59
17	0.32	.	.	1935.52	74.97
18	1308.15	.	.	.	3592.67
19	1.37	.	.	.	2308.24
20	28.94	.	.	.	2897.54
21	0.72	.	.	.	1684.82
22	.	.	.	.	.
23	.	.	.	.	96.37
24	0.09	.	.	.	562.35
25	13.94	.	.	.	.
26	.	.	.	.	.
27	48.62	.	.	.	.
28	.	.	.	.	.
29	.	.	.	.	.
30	.	.	.	.	.
1	0.00	0.28	0.16	0.16	0.06
2	0.01	0.36	0.24	0.18	0.13
3	0.06	0.56	1.14	0.37	0.40
4	0.07	124.03	.	.	2.44
5	0.94	.	.	49.39	1.09

problems. As well, in the Mprime domain Blackbox sometimes incorrectly reported that no plan exists when CPlan and IPP were able to find a correct plan.

We were not able to exactly duplicate the results that the individual planners obtained in the AIPS'98 competition. To varying degrees the planners require parameter tuning on each domain they are applied to. For IPP, only the default parameters were used. For Blackbox the only parameter we needed to vary from its default setting (in order to approximately equal the performance of the planner in the AIPS'98 competition in terms of number of problems solved) was to increase the respective parameter for the maximum number of nodes at each level during the planning graph generation. For the HSP planner, more elaborate parameter tuning was required.

CPlan is guaranteed to generate optimal parallel plans. Blackbox, IPP, and TLPlan can be used as either optimal or approximate planners, whereas HSP is inherently an approximate planner. In the AIPS'98 competition, Blackbox and IPP were used as approximate planners and we did the same in our experiments. For TLPlan, we used the default settings, including using depth-first search as in (Bacchus & Kabanza 1998). Thus, TLPlan was used as an approximate planner. We found in our experiments that Blackbox and TLPlan generated high quality plans that were almost always optimal or nearly optimal. However, HSP often generated longer plans. For example, in the gripper domain, the length of the plans generated by HSP almost doubles the length of the optimal plan for each instance. For HSP, sometimes the quality of the plans can be improved with different parameter settings, but with the consequence that many fewer instances are solved.

Blackbox and IPP consume large amounts of memory and often ran out of this resource before finding a plan. Is it just a matter then of more memory and these methods could solve the problems? To examine this question, we ran the following experiments. Our machines have 256 Mb of physical memory, but processes are permitted to allocate up to 640 Mb (this is a preset limit in our configuration of Linux). The AIPS'98 competition consisted of two rounds and within a round the problems are roughly ordered by difficulty. with the easier problems coming first. For instance 3 of the logistics problems (third row of Table 2), CPlan is able to find a plan in under one second of CPU time using just under 2 Mb of memory. Blackbox on this problem exhausts the available 640 Mb quickly (in about three minutes) without finding a plan. IPP exhausts the available 640 Mb more slowly (in just over eleven hours) but also without finding a plan. For instance 6 of the mystery problems, CPlan is able to find a plan in just over three seconds of CPU time using under 2 Mb of memory. Blackbox on this problem takes 83 seconds and uses 568 Mb to find a plan. IPP on this problem takes 133 seconds and uses 107 Mb of memory to find a plan. Thus, on these smaller problems, CPlan can be one to two orders

Table 3: Time (seconds) to solve mystery planning problems. The absence of an entry indicates that the problem was not solved correctly within the given resource limits.

	CPlan	Blackbox	HSP	IPP
1	0.00	0.11	0.05	0.08
2	0.03	4.22	7.09	11.43
3	0.02	0.42	0.39	0.85
4	0.00	1.18	.	0.37
5	0.00	11.36	.	7.58
6	3.06	.	.	133.95
7	0.00	1.14	.	9.79
8	0.00	.	.	30.88
9	0.03	1.03	0.66	1.32
10	0.53	.	86.45	.
11	0.02	0.53	0.07	0.28
12	0.00	0.94	.	0.49
13	0.39	.	.	.
14	1.08	.	.	.
15	0.39	.	16.81	.
16	0.00	3.70	.	5.70
17	0.12	2.44	11.91	29.68
18	0.00	13.39	.	273.20
19	0.13	5.26	6.05	19.94
20	0.53	.	6.23	.
21	0.00	.	.	50.25
22	0.00	.	.	.
23	0.00	.	.	101.19
24	0.00	.	.	72.39
25	0.01	0.10	0.06	0.07
26	0.07	1.24	0.43	1.44
27	0.01	0.42	0.56	0.69
28	0.02	0.39	0.11	0.18
29	0.01	0.38	0.32	0.59
30	0.15	3.91	6.42	9.42

Table 4: Time (seconds) to solve Mprime planning problems. The absence of an entry indicates that the problem was not solved correctly within the given resource limits.

	CPlan	Blackbox	HSP	IPP
1	0.05	0.59	0.14	2.34
2	0.09	4.42	13.92	23.93
3	0.16	0.60	0.51	4.35
4	0.22	0.60	0.61	2.51
5	0.22	.	.	7.19
6	2.25	.	201.81	.
7	0.13	.	.	12.58
8	0.67	1.99	4.39	32.91
9	0.06	1.34	0.75	4.93
10	2.14	.	273.32	.
11	0.12	1.28	0.18	4.19
12	0.09	1.63	0.87	5.92
13	2.38	.	.	.
14	4.04	.	.	.
15	1.39	.	104.02	.
16	0.13	3.61	3.33	.
17	0.57	.	27.76	91.76
18	6.95	.	.	.
19	0.61	.	30.48	.
20	2.34	.	130.53	.
21	0.22	.	.	58.16
22	3.50	.	187.12	.
23	2.10	.	.	.
24	0.64	.	.	.
25	0.01	0.13	0.06	0.92
26	0.27	2.22	1.11	12.86
27	0.05	2.21	6.83	31.49
28	0.07	1.33	0.64	4.65
29	0.09	1.57	1.30	15.90
30	0.80	.	.	.
1	0.16	0.57	0.74	7.12
2	0.14	1.74	0.67	1.83
3	1.20	.	.	.
4	0.07	1.13	1.07	7.88
5	0.04	0.33	0.14	1.95

of magnitude more efficient in both time and space. Further, the difference between the intensional representation used by CPlan and the extensional representations used by Blackbox and IPP only grows as the problem sizes increase.

In these experiments, the planners without domain knowledge appear to be quite brittle—either solving a problem quickly or not solving it at all—and to not scale well to more difficult problems.

Related Work

In this section, we relate our work to previous work in planning. We first review previous CSP-like approaches to planning and then we review previous work on using domain specific declarative knowledge to improve planning.

The definition of a CSP is general enough that it subsumes Boolean satisfiability and integer linear programming; both of these can be viewed as particular restrictions on the domains of the variables and the forms of the constraints. The first work that we are aware of that casts planning as a CSP is the work on planning as satisfiability by Kautz and Selman (1992; 1996). Our work owes much to theirs, including the general framework of planning as satisfiability, and the idea of a state-based model with explanation closure axioms defined on state variables and no variables that explictly model

actions. More recently, Bockmayr and Dimopoulos (1998) have examined integer linear programming models of planning. They use 0-1 integer variables in their formulations in a manner similar to the satisfiability approach and examine the effect of adding redundant constraints. Their work is preliminary and it is as yet unclear whether the approach will be fruitful. (For a problem in the logistics world they report a time of 75 minutes on an unknown machine to find a plan; we are able to solve this problem in less than one minute.) As well, there has been a long history of partial order planners which are often referred to as performing constraint posting. In these approaches, constraint satisfaction techniques are added as an adjunct to the planning process, but the planning process itself is not formulated as a CSP.

There have been two streams of work on adding declarative domain knowledge to improve the performance of planners. In the first stream, the knowledge is hand-coded as in our approach. In the second, the knowledge is automatically derived. As two examples, Kautz and Selman (1998b) advocate adding domain specific knowledge in a declarative

Table 5: Time (seconds) to solve grid planning problems. The absence of an entry indicates that the problem was not solved correctly within the given resource limits.

	CPlan	Blackbox	HSP	IPP
1	0.67	8.08	1.13	3.03
2	33.36	.	4.33	9.38
3	.	.	.	.
4	1773.28	.	.	57.00
5	.	.	.	.

manner to a planner and show some limited experimentation in a satisfiability-based planner, and Bacchus and Kabanza (1998) provide a temporal language for specifying domain knowledge and show how effective it is in their TLPlan planner. For work on automatically deriving constraints from action representations and initial and goal states, HSP (1998) derives distance constraints; Fox and Long (1999), show how to identify a primitive form of symmetry and use it in a planner; Gerevini and Schubert (1998) show how to derive state constraints; and Nebel, Dimopoulos, and Koehler (1997) show how to ignore irrelevant facts and operators, all to automatically improve the performance of planners. This work may also be helpful in semi-automating the task of developing CSP models for planning.

Conclusions

We presented a constraint programming or constraint satisfaction approach to planning. The approach shares the advantages of other CSP-like approaches, including the expressiveness of the modeling language, the declarativeness of the models, and the independence of the model from the solving algorithm. We also demonstrated that a constraint programming approach has several distinct advantages over other approaches, including the succinctness of the models, and the robustness and speed with which plans can be found. Our experiments indicate that present state-of-the-art planners can be brittle, either solving the problem quickly or not at all. Our system, CPlan, can be one to two orders of magnitude more efficient in both time and space on problems which the other systems can solve and can scale to harder problems which the other systems cannot solve.

For future work, we intend to look at approximate planning, by examining whether the same declarative CSP models that we solved using a systematic search algorithm in the experiments presented in this paper can be solved effectively using local search algorithms. As Blackbox has shown, this can be an effective technique. As well, we intend to look at alternative CSP models. It is well known within the operations research and constraint programming fields that one of the keys to effectively solving difficult combinatorial problems is to find the right model of the problem. In this paper we presented results for a state-based model. The question remains if this is the best CSP model for planning.

Availability. CPlan, including source code and CSP models for the domains discussed in this paper, is available via http://www.cs.ualberta.ca/~vanbeek.

Acknowledgements. We would like to thank Fahiem Bacchus for suggesting that we evaluate our methodology on the planning problems used in the AIPS'98 competition. This work was supported in part by the Natural Sciences and Engineering Research Council of Canada.

References

Bacchus, F., and Kabanza, F. 1998. Using temporal logics to express search control knowledge for planning. Unpublished manuscript.

Bacchus, F. 1998. TLPlan (Version of September 1998). http://logos.uwaterloo.ca/~fbacchus.

Baptiste, P., and Le Pape, C. 1995. A theoretical and experimental comparison of constraint propagation techniques for disjunctive scheduling. In *IJCAI-95*, 600–606.

Blum, A. L., and Furst, M. L. 1997. Fast planning through plan graph analysis. *Artif. Intell.* 90:281–300.

Bockmayr, A., and Dimopoulos, Y. 1998. Mixed integer programming models for planning problems. In *CP98 Workshop on constraint problem reformulation*.

Bonet, B., and Geffner, H. 1998. HSP (Version of August 1998). http://www.ldc.usb.ve/~hector.

Fox, M., and Long, D. 1999. The detection and exploitation of symmetry in planning domains. Technical Report 1, Durham University, UK.

Gerevini, A., and Schubert, L. 1998. Inferring state constraints for domain-independent planning. In *AAAI-98*, 905–912.

Kautz, H., and Selman, B. 1992. Planning as satisfiability. In *ECAI-92*, 359–363.

Kautz, H., and Selman, B. 1996. Pushing the envelope: Planning, propositional logic, and stochastic search. In *AAAI-96*, 1194–1201.

Kautz, H., and Selman, B. 1998a. Blackbox (Version 3.1). http://www.research.att.com/~kautz.

Kautz, H., and Selman, B. 1998b. The role of domain-specific knowledge in the planning as satisfiability framework. In *Proc. of the 4th International Conference on AI Planning Systems (AIPS-98)*.

Koehler, J., and Nebel, B. 1998. IPP (AIPS'98 version). http://www.informatik.uni-freiburg.de/~koehler

Marriott, K., and Stuckey, P. J. 1998. *Programming with Constraints*. The MIT Press.

Nebel, B.; Dimopoulos, Y.; and Koehler, J. 1997. Ignoring irrelevant facts and operators in plan generation. In *Proc. of the European Conference on Planning (ECP-97)*, 338–350. Springer Verlag.

Prosser, P. 1993. Hybrid algorithms for the constraint satisfaction problem. *Comput. Intell.* 9:268–299.

Schubert, L. 1994. Explanation closure, action closure, and the Sandewall test suite for reasoning about change. *J. of Logic and Computation* 4:679–700.

Van Hentenryck, P. 1989. *Constraint Satisfaction in Logic Programming*. MIT Press.

Total Order Planning is More Efficient than we Thought

Vincent VIDAL, Pierre RÉGNIER

Department of "Raisonnement et décision", IRIT, Paul Sabatier University
118 route de Narbonne
31062 Toulouse cedex, FRANCE
E-mail: {vvidal, regnier}@irit.fr

Abstract

In this paper, we present VVPLAN, a planner based on a classical state space search algorithm. The language used for domain and problem representation is ADL (Pednault 1989). We have compared VVPLAN to UCPOP (Penberthy and Weld 1992)(Weld 1994), a planner that admits the same representation language. Our experiments prove that such an algorithm is often more efficient than a planner based on a search in the space of partial plans. This result is achieved as soon as we introduce in VVPLAN's algorithm a loop test relating to previously visited states. In particular domains, VVPLAN can also outperform IPP (Koehler et al. 1997), which makes a planning graph analysis as GRAPHPLAN. We present here the details of our comparison with UCPOP, the results we obtain and our conclusions.

1 Introduction

1.1 Preliminaries

Planning has represented an important part of Artificial Intelligence for almost forty years and has received numerous developments. To solve more and more difficult problems, especially in robotics and productics domains, it has improved its formalism of representation and its algorithms. So, various planners have been developed. Among them, the most recent are commonly considered as more efficient than the eldest. The most employed techniques are search in the space of states, search in the space of partial plans and planning graph analysis. The first one — the eldest, (Fikes and Nilsson 1971) — is based on backward or forward state space search and the second one — more recent, (Chapman 1987) — on refinement strategies in space of partial plans (Kambhampati and Srivastava 1995), (Kambhampati 1997). Recently, the planners GRAPHPLAN (Blum and Furst 1997), then IPP (Koehler et al. 1997) have provided excellent results analyzing planning graphs.

We detail here an experimental study about VVPLAN, a forward state space planner for the ADL language. The numerous results we have achieved allow us to discuss the common opinion of the planning community "total-order planners are less efficient than partial-order planners".

Indeed, the overwhelming majority of works that support that point of view does not take into account the knowledge about the current state of the world (which is realized planning forward). A total order planner provides good performances as soon as we use this knowledge to prune the search tree. These results complete other works as those of (Veloso and Blythe 1994), (Bacchus and Kabanza 1995) and HSP (www.ldc.usb.ve/~hector), (Bonet, Loerincs and Geffner 1997), demonstrating that state space search can be efficient in a lot of problems.

1.2 The current opinion

At present, the widespread belief in the planning community is that planning in the space of partial plans is more efficient than planning in the space of totally ordered plans or than planning in the space of states. So, in several important papers, we can quote numerous paragraphs where the authors give their opinion about total order and partial order planning according to this belief:

(Penberthy and Weld 1992): Since consensus suggests that partial order planning is preferable to total order approaches (...), we pondered the void in the space of rigorous planners.

(Kambhampati and Chen 1993): In contrast, the common wisdom in the planning community (...), has held that search in the space of plans, especially in the space of partially ordered plans provides a more flexible and efficient means of plan generation.

(Kambhampati 1995): The conventional wisdom of the planning community, supported to a large extent by the recent analytical and empirical studies (...), holds that searching in the space of plans provides a more flexible and efficient framework for planning.

(Blum and Furst 1995): It may seem puzzling that an extra level of commitment would lead to a fast planner, especially given the success enjoyed by least-commitment planners (...).

(Bacchus and Kabanza 1995): The choice between the various search spaces has been the subject of much recent inquiry (...), with current consensus seemingly converging on the space of partially ordered plans (...).

These opinions are fundamentally based on several experimental studies that conclude to the superiority of *planning in the space of partially ordered plans* on *planning in the space of totally ordered plans*: (Minton, Bresina and Drummond 1991), (Minton et al. 1992), (Minton, Bresina and Drummond 1994) and (Barrett and Weld 1994). Generally, those who quote these papers wrongly assimilate total order approaches and state space planning. In spite of this almost unanimous point of view (about the supposed efficiency of the partial order approach), two other papers — not well known and opposed to the precedent ones — really compare partial order planning and state space planning: (Veloso and Blythe 1994) demonstrate that some problems of particular domains can be solved more efficiently planning backward in the space of states than using partial order approaches. (Bacchus and Kabanza 1995) also compare, to its best advantage, the planner TLPLAN (forward state space planner, special language to express search control knowledge) to the planner SNLP (partial order planner).

Systematic comparisons between different planners begin to be dealt in controlled competitions — the first one has been organized during the last congress AIPS'98 (www.cs.yale.edu/HTML/YALE/CS/HyPlans/mcdermott.html). These experiments demonstrate the superiority of the GRAPHPLAN-like algorithms. This last generation of planners generally outperforms the conventional methods in most cases.

The experimental studies we detail here clearly demonstrate that the question is far from being solved, at least concerning the comparison between partial plans planning and planning in the space of states. First of all, we are going to sum up the papers we have quoted before: (Minton, Bresina and Drummond 1994) — revise and complete (Minton, Bresina and Drummond 1991), (Minton et al. 1992) — (Barrett and Weld 1994) which give a complementary and interesting viewpoint about the classification of planning domains, and (Veloso and Blythe 1994). Afterwards (cf. § 3), we will demonstrate that comparing UCPOP (Penberthy and Weld 1992), which is a reference for partial order planning, with VVPLAN, a forward state space planner, tests prove superior performances for the latter as soon as we prune the search tree thanks to the knowledge on already visited states. These results, which are in opposition to the common point of view, can be easily explained because most of the previous studies do not take into account this knowledge.

2 Main related works

(Minton, Bresina and Drummond 1994) compare a planner that searches in a space of partially ordered plans and a planner that searches in a space of totally ordered plans to determine the factors influencing performances and their respective importance (dimension of the search space, time cost of a refinement per plan, role of search strategies and heuristics, description language...). These algorithms are tested on a large set of randomly generated problems in the blocks world domain for various versions and heuristics. Performance criteria are the number of

developed nodes and CPU time. These works demonstrate that in the blocks world domain and with or without domain independent heuristics, the partial-order planner UA is more efficient than the total-order planner TO.

(Barrett and Weld 1994) compare three planning algorithms which are tested on several artificial domains: POCL (space of partially ordered plans), TOCL (space of totally ordered plans, pre-ordering tractability refinements) and TOPI (space of totally ordered plans, adds operators to the head of the plan and is equivalent to a backward state space planner). They propose an extension of Korf's taxonomy of subgoal collections (Korf 1987) for planning in the space of partial plans[1]. Domains are built in order to present independent, trivially serializable or laboriously serializable subgoals for the different algorithms. Performances are estimated in CPU time, according to the number of subgoals. In all the domains, POCL and TOCL perform significantly better than TOPI, POCL being itself more efficient than TOCL. Those results support the conclusions of (Minton, Bresina and Drummond 1994). Afterwards, POCL and TOCL are tested on the fairly complex "Tyre world" domain which can not be solved in its initial version neither by POCL, nor by TOCL because of the laboriously serializable subgoals. If subgoals are ordered to make them serializable, the problem is then solved by POCL and TOCL (POCL being much more efficient). TOPI always fails.

(Veloso and Blythe 1994) compare SNLP (planning in a space of partially ordered plans) with PRODIGY (planning in a space of totally ordered plans, computation of the current state of the world to control the search). They define the linkability[2] property in order to predict the more efficient algorithm for solving a particular problem. SNLP is quasi identical to POCL, and PRODIGY is based on an algorithm similar to TOPI (backward planning in a space of states with possible computation of the current state of the world to control the search). These algorithms are tested on randomly generated problems from several artificial domains specially built to present, or not, the linkability property. Performances are estimated in CPU time, according to the number of subgoals. This method is similar to those of (Barrett and Weld 1994), except for the domain property. This time, results are favorable to total order planning in accordance with the selected criteria (CPU time and algorithms linkability property for the tested domains). In all cases, PRODIGY outperforms SNLP. This conclusion is *absolutely contradictory to the two previous studies*. The main reason is the use of a simulated world state which allows a backtrack reduction on the studied domains. In all the tested domains, goals are

---

[1] For example, in a given domain, problems may have trivially serializable subgoals for an algorithm and laboriously serializable for another one.

[2] This property is related to the order employed to post interval protection constraints in partial order planning: when this order is wrongly chosen, the algorithm must backtrack and works less efficiently.

trivially linkable for PRODIGY (solved in polynomial time according to the number of subgoals) and laboriously linkable for SNLP (solved in exponential time according to the number of subgoals). This property is therefore rather favorable to total order planning. These conclusions widely moderate those of the two previous papers.

See also (Kambhampati 1994) and (Kambhampati and Srivastava 1995), (Kambhampati and al. 1996) which detail a complete comparison of different plan space planning algorithms. All these different works show the following points:

- Nor the superiority of partial order on total order planning is proved neither the contrary. We can find domains that take advantage of both techniques.

- An ambiguity remains concerning state space planning: an algorithm that searches in a space of totally ordered plans like TOPI is theoretically equivalent to a backward state space search algorithm, but it does not use the knowledge on the current state of the world to control the search. When this is done, as with PRODIGY (Veloso and Blythe 1994) or TLPLAN (Bacchus and Kabanza 1995), results are widely modified.

- Nor the linkability neither the serialization are sufficient criteria to evaluate a planner. Some other criteria should be employed and then their respective influences should be studied.

- No comparison between partial order planning and forward state space planning has been done using already produced states to prune the search tree. The main interest of (Bacchus and Kabanza 1995) is the description of a special language employed to control the search, using domain dependent knowledge.

3 Comparison UCPOP / VVPLAN

3.1 Language and equipment

We have compared the UCPOP planner (version 4.1) with VVPLAN, a planner based on a state space search algorithm. Both planners used ADL to represent problems. We performed our tests in identical conditions: same programming language (CMU Common Lisp) and same equipment (PC with linux, CPU Intel Pentium 200 Mhz). Problems we have used are the 39 classical ones supplied with UCPOP. In order to reduce the influence of the system (particularly the Lisp garbage collecting influence), each has been tested several times: 100 times concerning problems solved in less than 0,1 seconds, 10 times concerning problems solved in 1 or 2 seconds, and only one, concerning the others. These tests clearly point out the greatest efficiency of VVPLAN as soon as we introduce a test based on memoization (called state loop control).

3.2 The compared algorithms

The search algorithm of UCPOP which is our reference remains the same during all the tests: an A* algorithm in the partial plans space using a domain independent

heuristic. VVPLAN is built on a classical forward state space search algorithm. It accepts as input the current state of the world, the goal and the current plan. It begins with the initial state of the problem and the empty plan. The current plan is modified during the whole planning process. It is a totally ordered operator sequence. Three versions of this algorithm have been developed.

```
Refine-state-space (S: state, g: goal, P: plan)
1. Termination check:
   - if the goal g belongs to the state S, return
     P (P is a solution)
2. Action selection:
   - choose an action a using an operator in the
     set of operators, so that its preconditions
     belong to the state S
   - if no action can be applied to S, return fail
3. Action application:
   - apply the action a to S to reach a state S'
4. Recursive invocation:
   - Refine-state-space (S', g, P + ⟨ a ⟩ ³)
```

Figure 1: The VVPLAN algorithm.

- **VVPLAN-breadth-first without state loop control:** is a classical breadth-first search algorithm; during steps 2 and 3 of the algorithm (cf. figure 1), all the possible states are created, applying all the possible actions to the current state of the world. Afterwards, those states are placed in a FIFO list. Search is carried on using the first state of the list as current state.

- **VVPLAN-breadth-first with state loop control:** this algorithm is similar to the previous one except for the further test: when the current state has been yet visited or is already situated in the FIFO list, it is not added to the latter. Even though this test seems to be expensive (numerous states must be memorized and the more numerous the created states are, the more long the test is), our implementation (numerical encoding of the states, hash-coding tables) produces good performances.

- **VVPLAN-A*:** is a classical A* heuristic search algorithm. The difference with the previous one relies on the order used to pick up the states from the list. To order the states, we do not use a FIFO method but the minimum value of a function f = g + h which adds: the cost g (length in number of steps) of the already realized path from the initial state to the current one, and the estimated value, using a heuristic[4] function h, of the length of the remaining path (in number of steps) from the current state to the final one.

This algorithm returns the shortest plan if and only if the heuristic function h minimizes the real cost of the remaining path. When several states have the same value for f, we use the optimistic interpretation: we pick up the

---

[3] The + operation joins two operators sequences: if P = ⟨ a₁, ..., aₙ ⟩, then we have: P + ⟨ aₙ₊₁ ⟩ = ⟨ a₁, ..., aₙ, aₙ₊₁ ⟩.

[4] We use a domain independent heuristic h: the maximization of the number of solved subgoals in each state. This heuristic is generally admissible because in most of the tested domains, an action never adds at once more than one subgoal.

state with the greatest value for g i.e. both the most distant state from the initial one (g maximal) and the probably closest state to the goal (h minimal).

3.3 Description of the tests

They concern 39 different classical problems from 15 various domains, which are issued from numerous planners (STRIPS, PRODIGY, SNLP...). They have been adapted and improved thanks to the ADL language to be used by UCPOP. Those problems are performed using the three successive versions of VVPLAN. Results are estimated in CPU time and in the number of created and developed nodes. Search fails when it exceeds 100,000 created nodes.

3.4 Results

Comparison UCPOP / VVPLAN-breadth-first without state loop control. As we can see in figure 2, this first comparison gives the advantage to UCPOP. It solves 32 problems among the 39 ones (82 %) compared with only 26 for VVPLAN (66 %). Concerning these 26 problems (solved by the two planners), 12 (46 %) are performed faster by UCPOP; among the 32 problems solved by UCPOP, 18 (56 %) are solved faster by UCPOP. The difference is not so important but VVPLAN fails on 13 problems compared to 7 for UCPOP. Consequently, when VVPLAN uses the breadth-first algorithm without state loop control, these results point out UCPOP's superiority.

These results seem to confirm those of (Minton, Bresina, Drummond 1994), but 14 problems are solved faster by VVPLAN. This points out that the domains used in these studies are not different enough and are most often in favor of partial order planning.

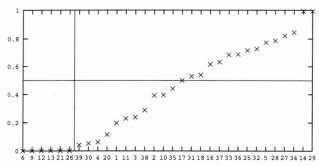

Figure 2: UCPOP / VVPLAN-breadth-first without state loop control (CPU time). *X-axis shows the tested problems (see figure 3 for the numbering of problems), and Y-axis the relative value between the CPU time of the two planners: t_{UCPOP} / $(t_{VVPLAN} + t_{UCPOP})$. Problems appear on the X-axis in the increasing order of the values, so as to obtain a usable curve. This order can vary from one curve to the other. The horizontal line (at 0.5) separates the zone in which UCPOP is more efficient (points bellow the line) from the zone in which VVPLAN is more efficient (points over the line). Problems at the left of the first vertical line (if there are some) remain unsolved by VVPLAN, and the ones at the right of the second line (if there are some) are not solved by UCPOP.*

1	fix1	11	Get-paid2	21	Monkey-test2	31	sched-test2a
2	fix2	12	get-paid3	22	monkey-test3	32	sussman-ano.
3	fix3	13	get-paid4	23	move-boxes	33	test-ferry
4	fix4	14	hanoi-3	24	prodigy-p22	34	tower-invert3
5	fix5	15	hanoi-4	25	prodigy-suss.	35	tower-invert4
6	fixa	16	mcd-suss.-an.	26	rat-insulin	36	uget-paid
7	fixb	17	mcd-sussman	27	road-test	37	uget-paid2
8	fixit	18	mcd-tower	28	r-test1	38	uget-paid3
9	fixit2	19	mcd-tower-in.	29	r-test2	39	uget-paid4
10	get-paid	20	monkey-test1	30	sched-test1a		

Figure 3: Numbering of problems.

Comparison UCPOP / VVPLAN-breadth-first with state loop control. When we add state loop control in VVPLAN's breadth-first search algorithm, results become totally different (see figure 4):

- All the 39 problems are now solved by VVPLAN, always compared with 32 (82%) problems for UCPOP. 23 problems among the 32 problems solved by the two planners are solved faster by VVPLAN (72 %, 9 more than with the first version of VVPLAN). On the average, VVPLAN solves those 32 problems 7 times faster than UCPOP (UCPOP 3.57 sec. against VVPLAN 0.48 sec.).

- VVPLAN creates far less nodes than UCPOP. Figure 5 (ratio of the created nodes: n_{UCPOP} / $(n_{UCPOP} + n_{VVPLAN})$) is similar to the CPU time graph. For 22 problems among the 32 ones solved by the two planners (69 %), UCPOP creates more nodes than VVPLAN.

- UCPOP also develops more nodes than VVPLAN in 30 of the 32 problems (93 %).

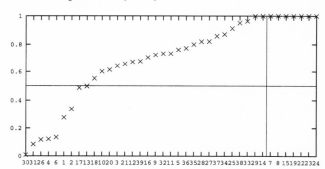

Figure 4: UCPOP vs. VVPLAN-breadth-first with state loop control (CPU time).

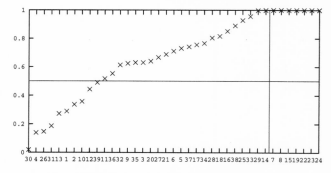

Figure 5: UCPOP vs. VVPLAN-breadth-first with state loop control (created nodes).

When these results are compared with the ones made without state loop control, we can point out that:

- On one hand, state space planning often develops a larger search space than partial order planning, which denies the current opinion.

- On the other hand, the average branching factor (number of created nodes / number of developed nodes) is higher for VVPLAN (6.38 against 1.44 for UCPOP), which confirms the established opinion.

- The difference of performance between these two versions of VVPLAN — without and with state loop control — demonstrates the interest of this test. The influence of the branching factor on the size of the search graph is minimized due to the tremendous number of pruned nodes.

Researchers using the results of (Barrett and Weld 1994) and (Minton, Bresina and Drummond 1994) to affirm that partial order planning is more efficient than state space planning make two mistakes:

- A total order planning algorithm as TOPI is not really equivalent to a state space planning algorithm. TOPI is indeed a very simple algorithm, without any improvement like state loop control. This kind of test can only be made by an algorithm which really computes states like VVPLAN. Even though this control seems to be expensive (in time and memory), it leads to really good performances thanks to the pruning of the search tree.

- (Barrett and Weld 1994) always point out that they have never obtained good performances for total order planning but only on their domains. Though they used a lot of different problems, it is not sufficient to prove that TOPI is always less efficient.

If we study the nature of the problems, we can notice:

- UCPOP's unsolved problems have a long plan-solution: on the average 12.6 actions compared with 5.2 actions for solved problems. Unsolved problems are complex ones and include a lot of operators and facts (problems "fixit", "fixb", "move-boxes"), or are problems with laboriously serializable subgoals (problem "hanoi4": the only possible serialization of subgoals is from the biggest disc to the smallest).

- The problem "fixit" is the famous one of the "Tyre World" domain (see § 2). According to (Barrett and Weld 1994), this problem can only be solved by a partial order planner like POCL or by a total order planner like TOCL (if subgoals are proposed in a serializable order) but never by a total order planner (assimilated to a state space planner) as TOPI. (Barrett and Weld 1994, p. 99) notice: "We took as our challenge, the problem of rendering this problem tractable". As it is demonstrated by our results, UCPOP does not solve this problem in its original form (without serialized subgoals) even though VVPLAN solves it in almost 6 sec, whatever is the subgoals order. VVPLAN creates 7,153 nodes to solve it, and UCPOP fails with more than 100,000 nodes.

- UCPOP's success on problems "sched-test1a", "sched-test2a" and "rat-insulin" can be explained because these problems have a lot of operators with few preconditions. This characteristic leads to an important branching factor for VVPLAN, but to a very little one for UCPOP (there are few constraints among actions). Partial plans developed by UCPOP have a lot of parallel actions. Thus, UCPOP's search space is far less important than VVPLAN's. It is typically the kind of problems that are solved faster by a partial order planner.

- Among the problems solved more efficiently by UCPOP, 4 are sub-problems of more complex ones that are not solved by UCPOP: "fix1", "fix2" and "fix4" are sub-problems of "fixit" and "fixa" is a sub-problem of "fixb". Sub-problem of a more complex one means a problem with an initial state to be reached in order to solve the complex problem, and with a goal to reach before solving the one of the complex problem. Despite the fact that UCPOP is efficient on easy problems of certain domains, it works laboriously on more complex problems in the same domains.

Comparison UCPOP / VVPLAN-A*. VVPLAN is now improved using an A* algorithm (with state loop control) and a classical domain-independent heuristic function: the maximization of the number of solved subgoals (in each state). The results we achieve are slightly better than the previous ones, even though it does not clearly appear on the figure 6 (CPU time). VVPLAN solves all the 39 problems, and UCPOP still solves 32 problems (82 %). 24 problems (one more than previously) are solved faster by VVPLAN (75 %) and the average CPU time (concerning these 32 problems) is now 0.46 sec. (against 0.48 sec. before). Furthermore, VVPLAN creates and develops slightly less nodes than in the precedent tests.

This curve does not appear to be very significant because it does not point out the improvement realized using the A* algorithm. This improvement appears if we take into account the 39 problems (cf. figure 7).

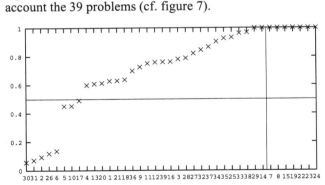

Figure 6: UCPOP / VVPLAN-A* with state loop control (CPU time).

We notice that:

- 31 problems (79 %) are solved faster by VVPLAN.

- The average CPU time (which was 2.10 sec. with VVPLAN-breadth-first) is now 1 sec. So, the time for evaluating the heuristic function does not penalize the overall performances. A* algorithm gives significantly better results on the 7 most difficult problems (which remain unsolved by UCPOP). Particularly, the CPU time needed by the two most difficult problems is now divided by 7 (problem "move-boxes") and by 6 (problem "prodigy-p22"). UCPOP's total average CPU time (109 sec.) is not really significant because it fails on 7 problems. However, this average CPU time is more than 100 times higher than VVPLAN's.

- VVPLAN-A* creates (and develops) almost 30 % less nodes than VVPLAN-breadth-first when considering the 39 problems. This difference was nearly zero when considering the only 32 problems solved by the two planners. UCPOP creates 28 times more nodes and develops 98 times more nodes than VVPLAN-A*. This clearly points out VVPLAN-A*'s superiority on the performed examples.

| | | UCPOP | VVPLAN | |
			state loop control	A*
CPU Time	32 pbs.	3.57	0.48	0.46
(sec.)	39 pbs.	> 109	2.10	1.00
Created	32 pbs.	2,286	511	494
nodes	39 pbs.	> 23,294	1,192	845
Developed	32 pbs.	1,577	80	76
nodes	39 pbs.	> 15,337	239	156

Figure 7: Results for all the problems.

5 Conclusion

In this paper, we have detailed an experimental comparison between VVPLAN, a forward state space planner, and the planner UCPOP. The results of these tests, allowed by the introduction of state loop control, show that VVPLAN outperforms UCPOP in most of the problems.

We also compared VVPLAN to IPP (results are not given here because of the lack of space). These tests demonstrate that some classes of problems can be solved more efficiently with a state space planner, giving an optimal solution. The efficiency of GRAPHPLAN-like planners is due to the internal qualities of this kind of algorithm, but this result is achieved against the quality of the solution. The latter is no more optimal in the number of actions, but in the number of time steps (a time step can hold several actions). We can suppose that problems of some domains, with no parallelism, a restricted branching factor and numerous redundant states, can be solved faster using a state space planner.

Finally, our feeling is that no planner outperforms all the others, in every domain. The differences of performance we observed seem to come essentially from some characteristics of the domains. It could be interesting to systematically try to characterize the numerous properties

of domains (serialization of subgoals, linkability, number of operators, number of preconditions, effects and interactions...) to associate to each domain the probably most efficient algorithm.

Acknowledgements

This research was greatly improved by discussions and comments by E. Jacopin and S. Souville. We also thank the anonymous reviewers of this paper.

References

Bacchus F.; Kabanza F.; 1995. "Using temporal logic to control search in a forward chaining planner". EWSP'95.

Barrett A.; Weld D.S.; 1994. "Partial-order planning: evaluating possible efficiency gains". Artificial Intelligence, 71-112.

Blum A.; Furst M.; 1995. "Fast planning through planning graph analysis". IJCAI'95.

Blum A.; Furst M.; 1997. "Fast planning through planning graph analysis". Artificial Intelligence, 281-300.

Bonet B.; Loerincs G.; Geffner H.; 1997. "A robust and fast action selection mechanism for planning". AAAI'97.

Chapman D.; 1987. "Planning for conjunctive goals". Artificial Intelligence, 333-377.

Fikes R.; Nilsson N.; 1971. "STRIPS: A new approach to the application of theorem proving to problem solving" . Artificial Intelligence, 189-208.

Kambhampati S.; 1995. "Admissible pruning strategies based on plan minimality for plan-space planning". IJCAI'95.

Kambhampati S.; Srivastava B.; 1995. "Universal Classical Planner: An algorithm for unifying State-space and Plan-space planning". ECP'95.

Kambhampati S. and al.; 1996. "A Candidate Set based analysis of subgoals interactions in conjunctive goal planning". AIPS'96.

Kambhampati S.; 1997. "Refinement planning as a unifying framework for plan synthesis". AI Magazine, 67-97.

Kambhampati S.; Chen J.; 1993. "Relative utility of EBG based plan reuse in partial ordering vs. total ordering planning". AAAI'93.

Koehler J.; Nebel B.; Hoffmann J.; Dimopoulos Y.; 1997. "Extending Planning Graphs to an ADL Subset". ECP'97.

Korf R.E.; 1987. "Planning as search: a quantitative approach". Artificial intelligence, 65-88.

Minton S.; Bresina J.; Drummond M.; 1991. "Commitment strategies in planning: a comparative analysis". IJCAI'91.

Minton S.; Bresina J.; Drummond M.; Phillips A.; 1992. "Total order vs. partial order planning: factors influencing performance". KR'92.

Minton S.; Bresina J.; Drummond M.; 1994. "Total order and partial order planning: a comparative analysis". Artificial Intelligence, 71-111.

Pednault E.; 1989. "ADL: exploring the middle ground between STRIPS and the situation calculus". KR'89.

Penberthy J.S.; Weld D.S.; 1992. "UCPOP: a sound, complete, partial order planner for ADL". KR'92.

Veloso M.; Blythe J.; 1994. "Linkability: examining causal link commitments in partial-order planning". AIPS'94.

Weld D.S.; 1994. "An introduction to least commitment planning". AI Magazine, 27-61.

Cooperative Plan Identification:
Constructing Concise and Effective Plan Descriptions

R. Michael Young
Department of Computer Science
North Carolina State University
Raleigh, NC 27695-7534
young@csc.ncsu.edu

Abstract

Intelligent agents are often called upon to form plans that direct their own or other agents' activities. For these systems, the ability to describe plans to people in natural ways is an essential aspect of their interface. In this paper, we present the Cooperative Plan Identification (CPI) architecture, a computational model that generates concise, effective textual descriptions of plan data structures. The model incorporates previous theoretical work on the comprehension of plan descriptions, using a generate-and-test approach to perform efficient search through the space of candidate descriptions.

We describe an empirical evaluation of the CPI architecture in which subjects following instructions produced by the CPI architecture performed their tasks with fewer execution errors and achieved a higher percentage of their tasks' goals than did subjects following instructions produced by alternative methods.

Introduction

Complex activities, by definition, contain a large amount of detail. When people describe activities to one another they leave out information they feel is unimportant and emphasize information they feel is essential. This economy of communication is an example of speakers obeying Grice's maxim of Quantity: say no more and no less than what is needed (Grice 1975). There is a wide range of contexts where intelligent agents that create and use plans might require the ability to generate task descriptions of similar brevity. Unfortunately, it is not a straightforward matter to produce an effective description of a given plan automatically when one or more of the intended readers or hearers are human. There is a mismatch between the amount of detail in a plan for even a simple task and the amount of detail in typical plan descriptions used and understood by people.

In this paper, we consider communication in the context called *plan identification*. In this context, a speaker describes a plan P to a hearer in order to single out P as the solution to what the speaker believes is a mutually understood planning problem. A *description* of a

plan P is a subset of the components of P used by a speaker for plan identification.

In the discussion that follows, we define a computational model of plan identification, called *cooperative plan identification* (CPI), used to generate concise descriptions of plans produced by AI planning systems. We also describe a task efficacy evaluation (Walker & Moore 1997) of the cooperative plan identification techniques where plan descriptions are used as instructions for tasks carried out by human subjects. Subjects carry out their tasks in a simulated domain and their performance on the tasks is measured to determine the effectiveness of the instructions that they follow. The experiment demonstrates that the descriptions produced by cooperative approaches are more effective than those produced by several alternative techniques.

Related Work

While several natural language systems have been developed for the generation of textual descriptions of action, these systems have been limited in the effectiveness of the descriptions they produce by the complexity of the activities that they describe. Mellish and Evans (1989) describe a system that produces textual descriptions of plans created by the NONLIN planner (Tate 1977). Their system generates text that contains reference to every component in a NONLIN plan. Consequently, as Mellish and Evans themselves point out, the resulting descriptions often contain an inappropriately large amount of detail.

Vander Linden and Martin (1995) discuss a text generation system that produces texts describing small sets of plan components, focusing on the selection of rhetorical relations that best expresses the components' procedural relationships with other actions in the same plan. The Drafter project at the University of Brighton (Hartley & Paris 1997) has developed a system to exploit a plan-based representation of activities to support multilingual instruction generation. This system represents task domains in a common action language and generates instructions based on the plans for a given task. In both these systems, plans for specific tasks are constructed by hand; because the detail present in the plans is pre-determined by human users, the systems do not need to address issues of plan size and can avoid the complexity introduced by dealing with larger, automatically generated plans.

A Cooperative Approach to Plan Description

In this research, we adopt the view that the use of plan descriptions in discourse is an instance of Gricean cooperation. A central idea in this work is that Grice's maxim of Quantity guides a speaker when he is selecting the amount and type of detail to include in a plan description. Under this interpretation, a candidate plan description contains sufficient detail precisely when a hearer can reconstruct the plan being described (or one reasonably close to it) from the content present in the candidate.

To produce cooperative plan descriptions, we use a generate-and-test architecture called *cooperative plan identification* (CPI). The process used by the architecture is divided into two functions (the overall architecture is shown in Figure 1). The first, called the *generator* function, constructs candidate descriptions; the second function, called the *evaluator*, tests descriptions against success criteria captured by the interpretation of the maxim of Quantity and described in the following section. The algorithm searches the space of descriptions of the plan that the speaker is identifying (called here the *source plan*), looking for an acceptable plan description of minimal size and structure. Searching the space of all plan descriptions is computationally expensive; rather than perform an exhaustive search for candidate descriptions, we describe two algorithms used as CPI generator functions that restrict the space they search to more tractable subsets of the full space while still producing reasonable candidates.

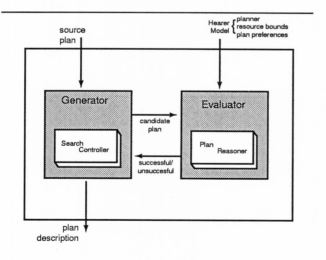

Figure 1: An Overview of the CPI Architecture.

Cooperation in Plan Description

Our previous work (Young 1996) describes a technique for characterizing the adequacy of a plan's description with repect to the amount of detail it contains. We adopt this technique as the CPI evaluator function and describe it briefly in this section. See (Young 1996) for a more complete description.

In our previous work, the plan description process is modeled as a collaboration between a speaker and a hearer. In order to understand a plan description, a hearer uses her knowledge about plans and planning to fill in any information that was missing from a speaker's description. To produce a plan description that is cooperative, a speaker uses his knowledge about the hearer's interpretation process to select a plan description that is brief but contains enough information to be understood. In this work, the hearer's interpretation process is represented by the use of a plan reasoning algorithm that takes a partial plan description and fills in its gaps, performing the same type of plan reasoning that a planning system would use to create the source plan in the first place. If the resulting complete plan (or plans) is similar enough in structure to the source plan, the algorithm characterizes the candidate as acceptable.

In this work, the interpretation of a candidate plan description is represented as search through a space of partial plans represented as a graph. The construction of the graph is controlled by a *plan-space* planning algorithm (Kambhampati, Knoblock, & Qiang 1995) that models the plan reasoning the hearer employs to reconstruct any detail missing from the candidate description. In addition to the plan reasoning algorithm, there are two other components that are central to the hearer model we use. The first is a limit on the hearer's reasoning resources — specifically, the amount of plan reasoning that she can bring to bear during the interpretation process. Clearly, the effort needed to construct a complete plan from a partial one requires the use of a hearer's reasoning resources. These resources are finite; a cooperative speaker that takes the hearer's use of these resources into account can adjust the content of his description so that the resources will not be exhausted. Here this resource limit is represented by an integer constant that places an upper bound on the number of nodes that can be searched in the plan-space graph when characterizing a candidate plan description.

The second central issue in the representation of the hearer's plan reasoning is her use of plan preferences, that is, her preferences for plans of particular structure over others. As a hearer fills in the gaps in a partial plan description, her planning activity is influenced by her preferences over aspects of the task domain. Her preferences for types of actions, for particular sequences of actions to achieve a goal, etc, all influence the structure of the complete plan that will emerge. Plan preferences are represented here by a ranking function that assigns non-negative integer rankings to plans on the fringe of the search space during construction of the graph. Regions of the graph rooted at nodes ranked most preferred will be explored before regions rooted at nodes with less preferred rankings.

The three aspects of the hearer's plan reasoning model (i.e., her planning algorithm, her resource limits and her plan preferences) operate together to construct a plan space graph representing the inferences that will be performed by the hearer when interpreting the candidate plan description. The structure of this graph determines the adequacy of the candidate to serve as the source plan's description: when all of the solution plans in the graph are reasonably similar to the source plan, then the candidate description is considered acceptable. An optimum plan description is an acceptable candidate description containing the fewest number of plan components of all similarly qualified descriptions.

While this work provided an algorithm for determining the adequacy of a given candidate description, we did not describe an algorithm for constructing candidates in an efficient manner. In the following section, we describe an architecture that combines our previously defined adequacy criteria for candidate descriptions with several related algorithms for efficiently generating candidates.

Generating Candidate Plan Descriptions

Generating an effective plan description is a difficult problem since there is no obvious technique for constructing the description directly from the source plan. While exhaustive search through the space of all the possible candidates is guaranteed to find an optimum description, the computational cost of this search is prohibitive; since every coherent subset of the source plan's components could potentially serve as the plan's description, the space of candidate descriptions is essentially the power set of the set of components in the source plan.

There is evidence, however, that optimal plan descriptions are not required for natural, concise and effective descriptions. As reported by Hull and Wright (1990), people often generate non-optimal plan descriptions and when they do so, their readers or hearers are still able to carry out the tasks at hand. A problem closely related to plan identification, the task of generating referring expressions, is similarly constrained by efficiency limitations when algorithms search for optimal descriptions. As Dale and Reiter (1995) describe in their characterization of computational models used to generate referring expressions, they adopt the strategy of restricting search to tractable subsets of the solution space in such a way that the systems generate concise (but not necessarily optimal) texts that are both natural and effective. This strategy has been adapted for use in plan identification and is discussed further below.

This section defines four implemented algorithms used to determine a set of plan components that will serve as a source plan's description. The first two are *cooperative techniques*, motivated by distinct computational interpretations of Grice's maxim of Quantity.

These two algorithms serve as generator functions in implementations of the cooperative plan identification architecture. The second pair of algorithms represent approaches that do not take a model of the hearer into account, using instead two distinct techniques that directly translate the source plan into its description. These two *direct translation techniques* are used in the evaluation described below in order to provide a basis for comparison against the two cooperative techniques. Space limitations preclude a detailed comparison of example data structures created by these algorithms; sample data structures and the texts that correspond to them are described in (Young 1997).

In this paper, we will use the DPOCL planner (Young, Pollack, & Moore 1994) as the hearer model's planning algorithm. DPOCL extends the UCPOP planner (Penberthy & Weld 1991) by incorporating hierarchical planning directly into a causal link framework. DPOCL's principal qualification for use in this work is that it is not built especially for the generation of task descriptions; rather, it is a domain-independent planning algorithm. DPOCL plans contain sufficient structure to ensure the plans' soundness and, consequently, the plans serve as strong test cases for the generation of plan descriptions. In addition, DPOCL is readily characterized as a plan-space planning algorithm.

Local Brevity: Exploiting a Plan's Structural Information. The *Local Brevity* algorithm searches for acceptable plan descriptions moving through the space of candidate descriptions from complete, detailed candidates toward partial, abstract ones. In this manner, the algorithm is similar to the Local Brevity algorithm of Dale and Reiter (1995); as in their approach, the CPI Local Brevity generator begins its search with a complete description (a complete plan) and creates new candidates by iteratively removing single components from the description based on local decisions dictated by a set of heuristics. These heuristics are based on results from studies of the comprehension of instructional and narrative texts (described below) that indicate that the presence of some plan components in a plan's description are more important to the hearer's understanding of the plan than are others. To determine the order in which components are deleted from the working description, the heuristics are used to assign a weight to each of the source plan's components. The algorithm iterates, first deleting the element in the plan that is weighted lowest, then passing the resulting working description to the evaluator function. Because the Local Brevity algorithm begins its search with a complete plan, the initial description is likely to be acceptable to the evaluator (that is, it is likely to contain sufficient information to properly identify the plan being described). The deletion process iterates until the evaluator indicates that the working plan has become too partial to be acceptable. At this point, the algorithm adds back in the last component that was deleted and uses the resulting data structure as the source plan's description.

The heuristics used to determine the order in which plan components are deleted are captured in two weighting functions, one used to rank plan steps and one used to rank causal links. These weighting functions each sum a number of terms representing the contribution of structural features of the plan to the importance of the component's appearance in the plan's description.

A plan's steps are weighted based on three factors reflected in the three terms in Equation 1 below. The equation is motivated by the following heuristics suggested by the more qualitative results described in (Trabasso & Sperry 1985; van den Broeck 1988; Graesser *et al.* 1980):

- The greater the number of causal dependencies a step has on previous steps in the plan, the more important the appearance of the step is in the plan's description.

- The greater the number of subsequent steps that depend upon a step, the more important the appearance of the step is in the plan's description.

- The deeper a step appears in the plan hierarchy, the less important the appearance of the step is in the plan's description.

For a given step s in plan P, the weight w_s assigned to s is determined by the summation of three terms:

$$w_s = (\text{In}(s, P) \times k_p) + (\text{Out}(s, P) \times k_e) + (\text{Depth}(s, P) \times k_d) \tag{1}$$

In this equation, $\text{In}(s, P)$ is a function returning the number of s's satisfied preconditions in P (i.e., the number of causal links leading in to s), k_p is a constant scaling factor for incoming causal links, $\text{Out}(s)$ is a function returning the number of causal links leading out of s, k_e is a constant scaling factor for outgoing causal links, $\text{Depth}(s)$ is a function returning the number of ancestors of s in P, and k_d is a constant scaling factor for step depth.

The values of the scaling factors are determined empirically and may vary between domains. All scaling factors in Equation 1 except k_d are constrained to be no less than 0 while the magnitude of k_d is constrained to be no greater than 0.

A single factor is used to assign weights to the causal links in a plan description: links are weighted based on their temporal duration. Results from reading comprehension and text summarization studies (Golding, Graesser, & Millis 1990; Kintsch & Van Dijk 1978; Rumelhart 1977) suggests that causal relationships between steps that are temporally close are often so readily reconstructed that references to the relationships are elided from plan descriptions. In causal link planners without an explicit representation of time (such as DPOCL), an estimate of the link's duration can be made by counting the number of steps in the plan that might possibly occur between the link's source step and its destination step. The greater the number of intervening steps, the longer the duration of the causal link. In the CPI implementation, for a given causal link l from step s_i to step s_j in plan P, the weight assigned to l is expressed by the equation

$$w_l = (\text{Inter}(l, P) \times k_l) \tag{2}$$

where $\text{Inter}(l, P)$ is the number of all steps that could possibly intervene between s_i and s_j in P and k_l is a constant scaling factor for intervening steps. k_l is restricted to be no less than 0.

To determine the sequence of components to be eliminated from the source plan, both the components' weights and their position in the plan structure are considered. In general, components with lower weights are eliminated first. However, in order to preserve the decompositional structure of the partial plan (in accordance with the constraint on referential coherence described above), steps are only eliminated from the leaves of the plan (that is, steps are only eliminated when they are either primitive steps or abstract steps whose children steps have already been eliminated). The elimination of causal links is not similarly constrained.

As steps and causal links are removed from the plan, all plan components that make reference to those steps and links are also eliminated. For instance, when a step is removed from a plan description, all causal links leading into or out of that step are removed, all ordering constraints for the step are taken out of the plan description and the step's binding constraints are also deleted.

The Plan Path Algorithm: Following the Source Planner. The *Plan Path* algorithm generates candidate descriptions following a path through the space of plans created by the source planning system as it solved the original planning problem. The Plan Path algorithm begins its search by considering the null plan at the root of this graph and moves through the graph by selecting at each choice point the child node that lies along the shortest path from the root node to the source plan. When the algorithm visits a node in this space, it sends the partial plan associated with that node to the evaluator, testing to see if the plan can serve as a description. The Plan Path algorithm halts as soon as it finds a plan that is successful (that is, a plan that contains enough information to effectively identify the plan being described).

This algorithm requires access to the list of nodes that lie along the path from root to source plan in the source planner's plan graph. In the CPI implementation, the nodes are supplied as input by the source system along with the source plan. Providing these additional data structures is a minor requirement for a refinement planning system, since the nodes are created by the source planner during the search that produces the source plan to begin with.

Two Direct Translation Algorithms. In order to provide comparisons to the cooperative plan identification algorithm, two direct translation approaches are also defined. The implementation of these approaches is described briefly below.

The Exhaustive Algorithm: The component of Mellish and Evans's system that generated the content of a plan description was relatively straightforward: the system generated a description that referred to every component of the plan being described (with the exception of certain NONLIN bookkeeping structures). The same strategy for content selection was used here in the *Exhaustive* algorithm. To generate plan descriptions, the Exhaustive algorithm takes as input the source plan and, since every element of the plan is to be included in the description, the process returns the complete source plan as its output.

The Primitive Algorithm: One possible approach to describing a plan is to describe just the lowest-level steps in the plan – those that will actually be executed. These steps correspond to the primitive steps in a DPOCL plan, the leaf node steps in the source plan data structure. The *Primitive* algorithm takes as input the source plan and selects as the plan description the primitive steps in the plan, returning those steps in a total temporal order consistent with the source plan's temporal constraints.

Empirical Evaluation

To evaluate the CPI model, we studied the empirical validity of the claim that providing conversational participants with a cooperative description of a plan increases the effectiveness of the communication. To address this claim, human subjects were presented with a series of text descriptions whose content had been automatically generated by the four algorithms described above. The subjects were asked to carry out the plan descriptions in a simulated task domain. Their actions were then analyzed along several dimensions to determine the quality of the subjects' performance. The hypothesis for the experiment stated that subjects that followed instructions produced by the cooperative techniques (i.e, the Local Brevity and Plan Path algorithms) would perform their tasks with fewer errors and achieve more of their top-level goals than subjects following instructions produced by the alternative approaches (i.e., the Exhaustive and Primitive algorithms).

The process used to produce the texts in this experiment was divided into three main components. The first module, consisting of the DPOCL planning algorithm, was used to construct solution plans for four planning problems in the task domain. The plans produced by DPOCL were then passed to the second component, a content determination module. For each input plan, this module applied each of the four approaches to content determination discussed above. The two generate-

and-test approaches and the two alternative direct-translation algorithms each generated a corresponding plan description, resulting in a total of four descriptions for each input plan. Finally, the four plan descriptions were passed to a text realization module. The realization module determined the English text used to describe the plan components included in the descriptions as well as the order that the text appeared in the text descriptions.

During the experiment, 24 human subjects [2] were individually asked to perform a series of four tasks — one for each of the four experimental source plans.[3] For each task, we provided each subject with a list of the goals for each task (taken from the goal specification of the corresponding source plan) and a set of written instructions (one of the four text descriptions that had been produced for the source plan). They were asked to carry out the task as described by the text within a computer simulation constructed using a text-based virtual reality system. The task domain simulated a college campus and subjects' tasks involved running errands across campus (e.g., checking out books from the library, registering for classes at the Registrar's Office). Subjects interacted with the simulation via a command-line interface; the simulation was designed with a one-to-one correspondence between simulation commands and the primitive actions in the operator set used by the planner when creating the source plans for the experiment.

Configuring the Experimental System

The system components described in the preceding section contain a number of user-specifiable parameters. The various settings for the parameters that were used in the experimental systems are described here.

Local Brevity Weighting Functions. The Local Brevity algorithm uses weighting functions to assign weights to each step and causal link in a plan; the weighting functions appear in Equations 1 and 2. The values of the scaling factors that were used in the experiment are as follows: for incoming causal links, $k_p = 1$, for outgoing causal links $k_e = 5$, for step depth, $k_d = 1$, for intervening steps, $k_l = 2$. These values are assigned to reflect my estimation of this relative emphasis of the factors discussed in the research by Trabasso and Sperry and by Graesser *et al* discussed above. [4]

---

[2] Subjects were solicited from the general University of Pittsburgh community and paid $9.00 per hour for their participation.

[3] Subjects were divided into four groups; each group performed the same set of tasks but was presented with the tasks in an order differing from the order used to present the tasks to the other groups.

[4] These constants are user-specifiable parameters and, short of performing extensive experiments that compare the performance of the system under various settings, no strong conclusions can be drawn about the *relative* merits of one set of values over any others.

The Hearer Model. The CPI hearer model contains three customizable parameters: the planning algorithm, the hearer's plan preferences and her plan reasoning resource limit. DPOCL, the planning algorithm used in the experiment as the model of the hearer's plan reasoning, is described in detail in (Young, Pollack, & Moore 1994). The plan ranking function used in the experiment employed a domain-independent metric, looking only at the size of the plan, preferring short, hierarchically structured plans with few top-level steps. In the absence of empirical evidence to suggest specific values for hearers' plan reasoning resource bounds, an objective method was devised to automatically generate a setting for the limit used for each plan being described. Using this method, the mid-point is found between the greatest depth bound where a complete plan description is generated and the least depth bound where an empty plan description is generated. To compute the mid-point value, each algorithm's depth bound is initially set to 0. A plan description is generated using this depth bound setting, and the depth bound value is incremented until a plan description is generated that contains less than the complete structure of the source plan. This value is taken as the lower bound of the range for the resource bound. The process continues to iterate, incrementing the depth bound and producing a new description, until the description that is produced contains no detail at all. This value is taken as the upper bound of the range for the resource bound. The mid-point between the upper and lower bounds is then used as the depth bound when generating a description for that source plan. Although the use of this technique results in the assignment of depth bounds that vary between plans, the method provides a basis for comparison by defining the same relative point in the space of all candidates that each algorithm considers.

Summary of Results

The data that was collected for each subject consisted of a series of four *executions*. Each execution represents the sequence of all commands typed by the subject. Because of the one-to-one correspondence between elements of a command (i.e., command names, argument names) and the act-types, locations and objects in the simulation domain, it was straightforward to translate each subject's exections into a sequence of fully-instantiated primitive plan steps in the language of the planner.

To measure the success of the subject's execution, we used three dependent variables:

The Step Failure Ratio (SFAIL). The percentage of the total number of steps containing preconditions that failed during the execution.

The Precondition Failure Ratio (PFAIL). The mean percentage of the number of preconditions for a failed step that were unmet when the step was executed.

The Goal Failure Ratio (GFAIL). The percentage of the plan's top-level goals that were unachieved when the execution ended.

For each dependent variable, data was averaged over items (that is, over plans) and a two-way repeated-measures ANOVA was conducted. Means and standard deviations for these variables, along with the results of the various analyses of variance, are shown in Table 1. In order to determine if the experimental source plans themselves had an effect on subjects' performance, a separate analysis was performed for each item, using a one-way, between-subjects ANOVA. Results of the second analysis are described in depth in (Young 1997) and are mentioned briefly below.

The patterns of means for each of the dependent variables clearly support the hypothesis that cooperative plan identification techniques (using the Local Brevity and Plan Path algorithms) produce more effective plan descriptions than the two alternative approaches (the Exhaustive and Primitive algorithms). In particular, the data indicate that the cooperative model has a significant effect on the number of execution errors performed by subjects during tasks ($F(3,63) = 7.06$, $p < .05$) as well as the number of goals left unachieved by subjects during tasks ($F(3,63) = 3.52$, $p < .05$); the effect on PFAIL did not reach statistical significance ($F(3,63) = 2.60$, $p < .08$). See Table 1 for relevant data.

Planned comparisons testing the specific prediction that the cooperative techniques produce more effective descriptions than the direct-translation techniques (Local Brevity and Plan Path *vs.* Exhaustive and Primitive) confirmed this hypothesis for both SFAIL and GFAIL. The comparisons also showed that the Local Brevity and Plan Path algorithms did not differ significantly from each other on any of the three dependent variables. See Table 2 for all relevant F-values. This table indicates the pairwise relationships between the means for each of the conditions of the experiment.

In order to determine if the differences in the amount of detail contained in the the plan descriptions could have accounted for these results, we performed the two-way analysis of variance for each of the dependent variables a second time, adjusting the number of errors for each subject by dividing the data by the number of components in the corresponding text description. Details of this analysis are found in (Young 1997). The results were the same as those reported for the initial analysis, with the following exceptions. The pairwise comparison between Exhaustive and Plan Path algorithms indicates that the difference between the two on the measure PFAIL and SFAIL were no longer significant ($F(3,63) = 2.44$ and $F(3,63) = 2.57$, respectively).

Discussion

The data clearly show that when subjects follow instructions produced by the cooperative techniques, they make fewer execution errors and achieve more of their

Table 1: Data for the Step Failure Ratio (SFAIL), Precondition Failure Ratio (PFAIL) and Goal Failure Ratio (GFAIL).

Exhaustive		Primitive	
M	SD	M	SD
12.8798	12.8980	7.8929	11.1346

Local Brevity		Plan Path	
M	SD	M	SD
2.3228	6.5711	2.4725	8.5909

Means and Standard Deviations for SFAIL

SOURCE	df	SS	MS	F
Algorithm	3	1846.8581	615.6194	7.06
Algorithm × Subject Grp	9	999.1757	111.0195	1.27
Error(Algorithm)	63	5751.9290	87.1504	

ANOVA Summary Table for SFAIL

Exhaustive		Primitive	
M	SD	M	SD
7.8495	7.55756	4.6242	6.92501

Local Brevity		Plan Path	
M	SD	M	SD
1.2094	3.10373	1.9524	6.02123

Means and Standard Deviations for PFAIL

SOURCE	df	SS	MS	F
Algorithm	3	258.8364	86.2788	2.60
Algorithm × Subject Grp	12	344.1140	28.6761	0.89
Error(Algorithm)	63	2023.3722	32.1170	

ANOVA Summary Table for PFAIL

Exhaustive		Primitive	
M	SD	M	SD
17.5595	22.3630	12.4999	18.1429

Local Brevity		Plan Path	
M	SD	M	SD
2.3810	9.0582	0	0

Means and Standard Deviations for GFAIL

SOURCE	df	SS	MS	F
Algorithm	3	1974.6284	658.2094	3.52
Algorithm × Subject Grp	12	4243.7423	353.6451	1.89
Error(Algorithm)	63	11765.8729	186.7598	

ANOVA Summary Table for GFAIL

Table 2: Contrast Analysis Showing Pairwise Comparison of Means

Technique	Mean	Technique	Mean	F Ratio
Exhaustive	12.880	Primitive	7.893	3.71
Exhaustive	12.880	Local Brevity	2.323	16.62*
Exhaustive	12.880	Plan Path	2.473	16.16*
Primitive	7.893	Local Brevity	2.323	4.63*
Primitive	7.893	Plan Path	2.473	4.88*
Local Brevity	2.323	Plan Path	2.473	0.00

Contrast Analysis for SFAIL

Technique	Mean	Technique	Mean	F Ratio
Exhaustive	7.849	Primitive	4.624	4.21*
Exhaustive	7.849	Local Brevity	1.209	17.85*
Exhaustive	7.849	Plan Path	1.952	14.08*
Primitive	4.624	Local Brevity	1.209	4.72*
Primitive	4.624	Plan Path	1.952	2.89
Local Brevity	1.209	Plan Path	1.952	0.22

Contrast Analysis for PFAIL

Technique	Mean	Technique	Mean	F Ratio
Exhaustive	17.559	Primitive	12.500	1.78
Exhaustive	17.559	Local Brevity	2.381	16.04*
Exhaustive	17.559	Plan Path	0.0000	21.46*
Primitive	12.500	Local Brevity	2.381	7.13*
Primitive	12.500	Plan Path	0.0000	10.88*
Local Brevity	2.381	Plan Path	0.0000	0.30

Contrast Analysis for GFAIL

* indicates significant F-value.

goals than subjects following instructions produced by the direct-translation techniques. Subjects' performance across all experimental variables shows an increase of roughly an order of magnitude, with statistically significant results obtained for both the step failure and goal failure ratios.

Since (almost all of) the results from the initial analysis are preserved when the data is adjusted to account for the length of the texts, the data suggest that the effectiveness of the cooperative techniques is not due simply to their more compact form. Not only do the cooperative approaches produce text of comparable or only slightly longer length, on average, than the Primitive algorithm (the algorithm producing the most concise texts), but the means of the Exhaustive algorithm (the algorithm producing the lengthiest texts) for all three dependent variables in the second analysis are lower than those for the Primitive algorithm. This suggests that the differences in the *content* of the descriptions produced by these techniques.

Conclusions

This paper describes the generation of textual descriptions of complex activities, specifically the generation of concise descriptions of the plans produced by computer systems. The technique, motivated by an interpretation of Grice's Maxim of Quantity, uses a generate-and-test approach to efficiently search the space of possible plan descriptions for a description that is both concise and effective.

We defined two algorithms that were used as generator functions in implementations of the CPI architecture. One, the Local Brevity algorithm, selects candidate descriptions based on the importance that the elements of a description hold for the hearer's comprehension of the description as indicated by psychological studies. The other, called the Plan Path algorithm, selects candidates based on the processing that was used to produce the source plan. For both implementations, a common evaluator function was employed that used a domain-independent planning algorithm as the hearer model's planning system and a domain-independent approach to applying the model to determine the acceptibility of candidate plan descriptions.

To characterize the efficacy of the two generator functions relative to one another and relative to two alternative direct-translation algorithms, we performed a task-efficacy evaluation. In this experiment, subjects that followed instructions produced by the CPI algorithms committed fewer execution errors and achieved more of their tasks' top-level goals than subjects following instructions produced by other techniques. The experimental results provide clear support for the greater efficacy of the cooperative techniques.

Acknowledgements

Support for this work was provided by the Office of Naval Research, Cognitive and Neural Sciences Division (Grant Number N00 014-91-J-1694) and from the DoD FY92 Augmentation of Awards for Science and Engineering Research (ASSERT). The author thanks Johanna Moore and Martha Pollack for many helpful discussions and David Allbritton for his advise on experimental design.

References

Dale, R., and Reiter, E. 1995. Computational interpretations of the Gricean Maxims in the generation of referring expressions. *Cog. Science* 19(2):233–263.

Golding, J.; Graesser, A.; and Millis, K. 1990. What makes a good answer to a question? testing a psychological model of question answering in the context of narrative text. *Discourse Processes* 13:305–326.

Graesser, A.; Roberston, S.; Lovelace, E.; and Swineheart, D. 1980. Answers to why questions expose the organization of story plot and predict recall of actions. *J. of Verb. Learning and Verb. Behavior* 19:110–119.

Grice, H. P. 1975. Logic and conversation. In Cole, P., and Morgan, J. L., eds., *Syntax and Semantics III: Speech Acts*. New York, NY: Academic Press. 41–58.

Hartley, A., and Paris, C. 1997. Multilingual document production: from support for translating to support for authoring. *Machine Translation, Special Issue on New Tools for Human Traslators* 12(1-2):109–129.

Kambhampati, S.; Knoblock, C.; and Qiang, Y. 1995. Planning as refinement search: a unified framework for evaluating design tradeoffs in partial-order planning. *Artificial Intelligence* 76:167–238.

Kintsch, W., and Van Dijk, T. A. 1978. Propositional and situational representations of text. *Psychological Review* 85:363–394.

Mellish, C., and Evans, R. 1989. Natural language generation from plans. *Computational Linguistics* 15(4):233 – 249.

Penberthy, J. S., and Weld, D. 1991. UCPOP: A sound, complete partial order planner for ADL. In *Proceedings of the Third International Conference on Knowledge Representation and Reasoning*.

Rumelhart, D. E. 1977. Understanding and summarizing brief stories. In LaBerge, D., and Samuels, S. J., eds., *Basic processes in reading: perception and comprehension*. Erlbaum.

Tate, A. 1977. Generating project networks. In *Proceedings of the International Joint Conference on Artificial Intelligence*, 888 – 893.

Trabasso, T., and Sperry, L. 1985. Causal relatedness and importance of story events. *J. of Memory and Language* 24:595–611.

van den Broeck, P. 1988. The effects of causal relations and hierarchical position on the importance of story statements. *J. of Memory and Language* 27:1–22.

Vander Linden, K., and Martin, J. H. 1995. Expressing rhetorical relations in instructional text: A case study of the purpose relation. *Computational Linguistics* 21:29–57.

Walker, M., and Moore, J. 1997. Empirical studies in discourse. *Computational Linguistics* 23(1):1–12.

Wright, D., and Hull, P. 1990. How people give verbal instructions. *J. of Appl. Cog. Psych.* 4:153–174.

Young, R. M.; Pollack, M. E.; and Moore, J. D. 1994. Decomposition and causality in partial order planning. In *Proceedings of the Second International Conference on AI and Planning Systems*, 188–193.

Young, R. M. 1996. Using plan reasoning in the generation of plan descriptions. In *Proc. of the National Conference on Artificial Intelligence*, 1075–1080.

Young, R. M. 1997. *Generating Descriptions of Complex Activities*. Ph.D. Dissertation, Intelligent Systems Program, University of Pittsburgh.

Exploiting Symmetry in the Planning graph via Explanation-Guided Search

Terry Zimmerman & Subbarao Kambhampati[*]
Department of Computer Science & Engineering
Arizona State University, Tempe AZ 85287
Email: {zim,rao}@asu.edu   URL: rakaposhi.eas.asu.edu/yochan.html

Abstract

We present a method for exploiting the symmetry in the planning graph structure and certain redundancies inherent in the Graphplan algorithm, so as to improve its backward search. The main insight underlying our method is that due to these features the backward search conducted at level k + 1 of the graph is essentially a replay of the search conducted at the previous level k with certain well-defined extensions. Our method consists of maintaining a pilot explanation structure capturing the failures encountered at previous levels of the search, and using it in an intelligent way to guide the search at the newer levels. The standard EBL and DDB techniques can be employed to control the size of the pilot explanation. The technique has been implemented in the EGBG system, and we present a preliminary empirical study.

1 Introduction

The advent of Graphplan [Blum & Furst, 95] as one of the fastest programs for solving classical planning problems, marked a significant departure from the planning algorithms studied up to that time. Recently efforts have been made to place the approach in perspective and investigate the applicability of a variety of speed-up techniques that have been proven effective in other planning and search-based problem-solving systems.

Graphplan conducts it's problem solution search by interleaving two distinct phases: a forward phase the builds a "planning graph" structure followed by a phase that conducts backward search on that structure. As it turns out, the planning graph contains a high degree of redundancy and symmetry suggesting several avenues for speeding up the search by exploiting these features.

This paper describes initial work with a novel approach that takes full advantage of the particular symmetry of the planning graph and Graphplan's backward search. During each backward search episode a concise trace structure (termed the 'pilot explanation') is generated to capture the key features of the search and this is then carried forward (assuming the search fails to find a solution) to direct subsequent search at all future levels of the planning graph. The pilot explanation thus acts a sort of memory of the previous search experience and, due to the inherent symmetry of the planning graph, closely models the search that Graphplan in fact undertakes at the next level. This trace structure prescribes the minimal set of constraints (search backtrack points) that need to be checked based on the experience at the previous level. Should all these constraints also hold at the current level the planning graph can immediately be extended to a new level. At every point where a constraint no longer holds backward search is resumed and the pilot explanation extended to reflect the experience gained

This approach, then, seeks to speedup Graphplan by avoiding all redundant search effort at each level of the planning graph at the cost of building, extending, and using the trace structure that is the pilot explanation. The idea of building an entire trace of the experience during a search process so as to later shortcut the effort needed to solve a similar problem is, of course, an old one (c.f. [Veloso, 94; Ihrig & Kambhampati, 97]). For most problems of real interest the sheer size of the trace structure makes the approach ineffective. It's the symmetry of the planning graph and the search that Graphplan conducts at each level that makes such a technique even feasible for this system. And even then, great care must be take to retain only essential search information in the trace structure and to control its growth if the "larger" planning problems of interest are to be addressed.

The rest of this paper is organized as follows. Section 2 provides a brief review of the Graphplan algorithm. Section 3 presents our approach for guiding backward search with the pilot explanation. This section first considers the sources of redundancy in the Graphplan, and explains how the representation and use of the pilot explanation is geared towards exploiting this redundancy. Section 4 describes results of preliminary experiments with EGBG, a version of Graphplan that uses the pilot explanation structure. Section 5 discusses several ways of improving the representation of the pilot explanation, by complementing the Graphplan's search algorithm with Explanation-based learning and Dependency directed backtracking. Section 6 discusses related work and Section 7 presents our conclusions.

2 Overview of Graphplan

Graphplan algorithm [Blum & Furst, 97] can be seen as a "disjunctive" version of the forward state space planners [Kambhampati et. al., 97]. It consists of two interleaved phases – a forward phase, where a data structure called "planning graph" is incrementally ex-

[*] Copyright © 1999, American Association for Artificial Intelligence (www.aaai.org). All rights reserved. This research is supported in part by NSF young investigator award (NYI) IRI-9457634, ARPA/Rome Laboratory initiative grant F30602-95-C-0247, Army AASERT grant DAAH04-96-1-0247, AFOSR grant F20602-98-1-0182 and NSF grant IRI-9801676.

tended, and a backward phase where the planning graph is searched to extract a valid plan. The planning graph (see Fig. 1) consists of two alternating structures, called proposition lists and action lists. Fig. 1 shows a partial planning graph structure. We start with the initial state as the zeroth level proposition list. Given a k level planning graph, the extension of structure to level k+1 involves introducing all actions whose preconditions are present in the kth level proposition list. In addition to the actions given in the domain model, we consider a set of dummy ``persist'' actions, one for each condition in the $k^{th}$ level proposition list. A ``persist-C'' action has C as its precondition and C as its effect. Once the actions are introduced, the proposition list at level k+1 is constructed as just the union of the effects of all the introduced actions. The planning graph maintains the dependency links between the actions at level k+1 and their preconditions in level k proposition list and their effects in level k+1 proposition list.

The planning graph construction also involves computation and propagation of ``"mutex" constraints. The propagation starts at level 1, with the actions that are statically interfering with each other (i.e., their preconditions and effects are inconsistent) labeled mutex. Mutexes are then propagated from this level forward through the use of two simple propagation rules. In Figure 1, the curved lines with x-marks denote the mutex relations: two propositions at level k are marked mutex if all actions at level k that support one proposition are mutex with all actions that support the second proposition. Two actions at level k+1 are mutex if they are statically interfering or if one of the propositions (preconditions) supporting the first action is mutually exclusive with one of the propositions supporting the second action. It should be noted that mutex checking forms an integral part of both the graph building phase and the backward search phase, and is a major contributor to the total cpu time Graphplan may spend on a problem.

The search phase on a k level planning graph involves checking to see if there is a sub-graph of the planning graph that corresponds to a valid solution to the problem. This involves starting with the propositions corresponding to goals at level k (if all the goals are not present, or if they are present but a pair of them is marked mutually exclusive, the search is abandoned right away, and planning graph is grown another level). For each of the goal propositions, we then select an action from the level k action list that supports it, such that no two actions selected for supporting two different goals are mutually exclusive (if they are, we backtrack and try to change the selection of actions). Once all goals for a level are supported, we recursively call the same search process on the k-1 level planning graph, with the preconditions of the actions selected at level k as the goals for the k-1 level search. The search succeeds when we reach level 0 (corresponding to the initial state).

A final aspect of Graphplan's search is that when a set of (sub)goals for a level k is determined to be unsolvable, they are *memoized* at that level in a hash table. Correspondingly, when the backward search process later enters level k with a set of subgoals, they are first checked against the hash table to see if they've already been proved unsolvable.

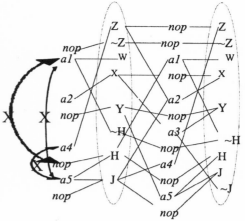

Figure 1. Example planning graph showing action and proposition levels and some of the mutex action pairs

3 Explanation-Guided Backward Search

We first describe the structural symmetry inherent in the planning graph and the use of the pilot explanation to take advantage of it during the backward search phase. The overhead entailed by such a system and the resulting tradeoffs that must be considered are then discussed.

3.1 Taking advantage of planning graph symmetry

Due to the inherent symmetry of the planning graph the backward search conducted at level k + 1 of the graph is essentially a replay of the search conducted at the previous level k *with certain well-defined extensions* [Ihrig & Kambhampati, 97]. When backward search at level k fails to find a solution the technique proposed here captures all the key features of the search episode in a special trace structure (termed the pilot explanation) which is then carried forward to direct the search at all future levels of the planning graph. At successively higher levels the trace structure prescribes the minimal set of constraints (search backtrack points) that need to be checked based on the experience at the previous level. Should all these constraints also hold at the current level the planning graph can immediately be extended to a new level. At every point where a constraint no longer holds backward search is resumed and the pilot explanation extended to reflect the experience gained

The following symmetrical or redundant features of the planning graph suggest possible shortcuts in the search process conducted at each new level:

- The proposition goal set that is to be satisfied at a new level k is exactly the same set that will be searched on at level k+1 when the planning graph is extended. That is, once the goal proposition set is present at level k it will be present at all future levels.

- The set of actions that can establish a given proposition at level k+1 always include the set establishing the proposition at level k and *may* include some newly added actions.
- The "constraints" (mutexes) that are active do not vary randomly over successive levels. A mutex that is active at level k may or may not continue to be active at level k+1, but once it becomes inactive at a level it never gets re-activated at future levels. For example, when a new action A1 is introduced at level k it's mutex status with every other action (in pair-wise fashion) at that level is determined. If it is mutex with A4 the pair may eventually become non-mutex at a future level, but thereafter they will remain non-mutex. And if A1 is initially non-mutex with A3 at level k it will never become mutex at higher levels.
- Two actions in a level that are "statically" mutex (i.e. their effects or preconditions conflict with each other) will be mutex at *all* succeeding levels

These factors, taken together, are responsible for considerable similarity (i.e. redundancy) in Graphplan's search performed at each successive planning graph level. Figure 2 illustrates the trace of such a search episode for the problem in Figure 1. The goals/subgoals to be satisfied as the backward search proceeds to each lower planning graph level are indicated within the circular nodes while the actions assigned to provide these goals are indicated by arrows. The points at which the search must backtrack (static or dynamic mutex action pairs or subgoals that are nogoods) are also shown.

The search trace in figure 2 can actually be viewed as an "explanation" for why search failed at level k or, alternately, why W X Y Z may be saved as a nogood at level k. Consider the situation once this search episode is complete and Graphplan is ready to add level k+1 to the graph and conduct backward search again at the new level. The search trace that will result from Graphplan's attempt to satisfy these goals beginning at level k+1 will closely resemble the search conducted at level k. In fact the *same search trace applies at level k+1 as long as the following 3 conditions hold*:

1. The action mutexes in the explanation for level k are *still* mutex for level k+1
2. There are no new actions establishing the goal propositions appearing in the explanation that were not also present (and explained away) at level k
3. Any nogoods appearing in the k-level failure explanation are also valid at the respective levels they map to in the search beginning at level k+1.

If these 3 conditions should happen to also hold for level k+1 we can immediately extend the graph to level k+2 because the goal set is also a nogood for level k+1. In this case the pilot explanation is carried forward to level k+2 unchanged.

A much more likely scenario will be that some number of the conditions will no longer hold when the trace is applied to level k+1. We can use the level k search trace to actually direct level k+1 search in a sound manner as long as each instance of one of these 3 conditions that appears in the trace is checked at the new level. If the constraint or condition holds no action is required. For each condition that does *not* hold the backward search

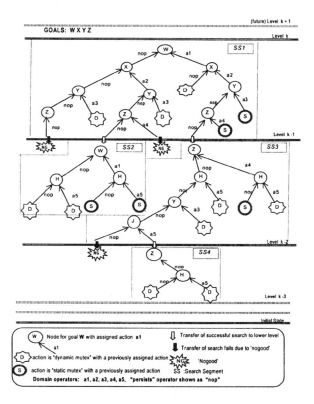

Figure 2. CSP-style trace of backward search at level k of the planning graph

must be resumed under the search parameters corresponding to the backtrack point in the search trace. Such partial search episodes will either find a solution or generate additional trace to augment the parent trace.

Because this specialized search trace can be used to direct *all* future backward search for this problem we refer to it as the ***pilot explanation (PE)***.

Note that in order to be sound the proposed system using the pilot explanation must revalidate *all* of the same constraints that standard Graphplan search would encounter at the points where it is forced to backtrack. So where is the hoped for search speedup? There are 3 primary sources:

1. *None* of the many successful action assignments made during the search that builds the PE have to be re-assigned during search at the next planning graph level. In general each of these assignments involved multiple mutex checks (with the previously assigned actions) and, as mentioned in Section 2, it is mutex checking that accounts for most of the cpu time Graphplan expends in a given search episode.
2. *None* of the many nogood checks made by Graphplan in the search embodied by the PE have to be repeated. This includes both the situations in which the subgoals were found in the memoized entries for the lower level (requiring backtracking) and situations in which the subgoals are not (initially) found to be nogood (so backward search continues at the lower level) Justification for this economy is given in the next section.

3. Having the pilot explanation available permits search at each successive level to be conducted by a variety of heuristics. That is, the search is no longer restricted to the 'top-down' serial processing dictated by standard Graphplan backward search. As long as all the constraints within the PE (as described above) are addressed before extending the planning graph, they can be processed in any desired order. For example, the approach employed in our initial experiments is to conduct search from the bottom-up during each search episode. A promising idea is to first check the PE backtrack points that lie closest to the initial state (level 0), which is the goal of the backward search. If they can be extended down to level 0 considerable search effort during that episode will be avoided.

There are of course costs incurred in building and using this potentially large search trace structure. These are addressed in section 3.3 after we first describe the algorithm for using the pilot explanation to direct all future search and planning graph extension.

3.2 Using the Pilot Explanation

EGBG (Explanation-Guided Backward-search for Graphplan) can be viewed as consisting of 3 phases. The two preliminary phases that enable the use of the PE to speed up search can be summarized as:

1. *Initial Planning graph Build Ph*ase -From the initial state build & extend the planning graph in standard Graphplan fashion until a level is reached containing the goals: separately identify/mark actions that are static and dynamic mutex
2. *First Backward Search* -Conduct the 1st backward search from the top level with goals in standard Graphplan fashion. But for *each* 'search segment', SS (see Fig. 3 for the definition of search segment):

> Save in SS, the goals addressed in that segment
> Save in SS, in the order encountered and grouped by goal: an identifier for results of each action assignment attempted
> When all segment goals have been satisfied add the list of all actions assigned & a pointer to *current* search segment to the next lower level search segment

> Insert each completed search segment into the 'pilot explanation'. If backward search reaches the initial state, return plan; else extend the planning graph one level.

When backward search fails to find a solution to satisfy the plan goals the pilot explanation acts as an explanation for this failure at the given planning graph level. An alternate view is that the PE provides an explicit guide for all future search that must be conducted (to ensure soundness) at the next planning graph level.

Let's take the trace in Fig. 2 as an example PE produced after the first attempt at backward search on the problem goals WXYZ at level k. Since a solution was not found (as evidenced by the fact that the trace does not extend down to the initial state), the planning graph is extended to level k+1 and from this point on the pilot explanation directs all search for the problem solution. There are two processes entailed that can be interleaved in *any order:*

1. Visit and check each of the backtrack points in the PE (hereafter termed 'checkpoints')
2. Resume backward search wherever a checkpoint no longer holds.

Verifying Checkpoints

Note that the trace in Fig. 2 can be viewed as four intra-level search segments; there is one search segment under level k, two under level k-1 and one under level k-2. All checkpoint verification must be done in the context of the current planning graph level that corresponds to the pilot explanation level the checkpoints appear in. Once all checkpoints in a given search segment are processed, the subgoals that were the targets of that partial search can be memoized at that level, because (assuming a solution wasn't reached) they necessarily comprise a nogood. This corresponds to the memoization performed by standard Graphplan when it backtracks out of a level during the search process.

In Fig. 2 there are 15 action mutex checkpoints and 6 nogood checkpoints to be processed. Eleven of these entail no significant processing at all:

> 5 of the mutex checkpoints are due to static mutex conditions between actions –that is the last assigned action clobbers either an effect or precondition of some action assigned higher up in that level. Such mutex conditions can never be relaxed so there is no need to check their validity on each planning graph extension. Although the relative percentages vary by problem domain, generally 20 – 50% of all mutex conditions encountered during the course of a problem search are of the static type.

> Six of the checkpoints are associated with the nogood checking that occurs when all goals in a search level are successfully assigned and the resulting subgoals are compared against the memoized nogoods for the next level. These constitute another type of redundant checking performed by Graphplan that can be avoided by using the PE. The successful transfers of subgoals to the next level in the PE (the clear arrows in Fig. 2) are guaranteed to be valid at all future levels -i.e. they

```
SEARCH-WITH-PILOT-EXPLANATION ( PE: pilot
                         explanation, PG: plan graph)
L1: Let n = number of proposition levels in plan graph
    For p = [length of pilot explanation] to 0
        (i.e. from deepest level searched previously to top level)
    For each search segment SS in level p of the pilot explanation
    Store the goal-by-goal results contained in SS-assigns in
        Gresults and clear SS-assigns
    Call Process-Assign-Level (nil, SS-goals, SS, Gresults,
                         PG, n-p )
    If no plan found, memoize SS-goals at plan graph level n-p
    PE processing complete, no soln found for n-level plan graph.
        -extend the plan graph one level
        -translate the PE up to the new top level
    Go to L1


PROCESS-ASSIGN-LEVEL (A: actions already assigned,
    G: goals left to assign,  SS: search segment, Gresults: unproc-
        essed assign results,   PG: plan graph,  k: pg level )
If G is not empty
    Select front goal g from G
    Let Ag be the set of actions from level k in PG that support g
    Add empty Newresults list to end of SS-assigns (will hold the
        results of action assigns for g)
    Select from Gresults the front set of assignment results:
        gresults (from previous search episode)
L1: Select front action act in Ag
    If Gresults is empty then act and rest of Ag are new
        establishers of g at level k:
        Call PROCESS-NEW-ACTIONS (A, G, Ag, Newresults,
                         SS, PG, k )
    else select front assign result, ares, from gresults
        If ares = 'ok' action has no conflicts, --move to next goal:
        Call PROCESS-ASSIGN-LEVEL ((A + act), (rest G), SS,
                         Gresults, PG, k)
    else if ares is an integer, act caused a dynamic mutex
        checkpoint, --it must be tested:
        If act is still dyn mutex wrt the action at position
            ares of A
            Add ares to end of Newresults
        else mutex no longer holds, resume search & extend PE
        Call ASSIGN-GOALS ((rest G), (A + act), SS, PG, k)
        (If backward search reaches the init state, returns plan)
            Add 'ok' to end of Newresults
    else ares is a checkpoint that does not need to be tested
        Add ares to end of Newresults
    If Ag is empty return, else go to L1


PROCESS-NEW-ACTIONS (A: actions already assigned,
    G: goals to assign, N: new actions for front goal,
    Newresults: list of new assign results for front goal of G,
    SS: search segment, PG: plan graph, k: pg level )
Let g be the front goal in G
L1: If N is empty, return
    else Select front action act from N
        If act is mutex with some action in A
            save the appropriate assign result ('nt' for stat mutex,
                integer for dyn mutex) in Newresults
            go to L1
        else assign act to g and resume backward search on
            remaining goals (extending the PE):
            Call ASSIGN-GOALS ((rest G), (A + act ), SS, PG, k )
            (if backward search reaches the init state, returns plan)
        go to L1.


Figure 4. Pseudo code description of EGBG's 3rd phase
```

cannot become a nogood at a higher planning graph level. The specific subgoals found to constitute a nogood (indicated by black arrows in Fig. 2) may, however, no longer be in conflict at some higher plan graph level that the PE is translated to. But since *all* search segments above and below the nogood of concern will necessarily be processed before this search episode ends the nogoods will just as necessarily be "proven" in the process -or a solution will be found making the issue moot.

Resuming Backward Search

We next describe the process entailed when a checkpoint is found to no longer hold at a new level. Amongst the checkpoints then, only dynamic mutex checkpoints must be tested. If such a mutex is found to no longer hold, the checkpoint indicates a position at which backward search must be resumed.

Invalid Mutex Conditions: If an action mutex checkpoint in the explanation is found to no longer hold at level k+1, this is indicative of a possible means of satisfying the goals that was disallowed at the previous level. Backward search therefore resumes *at the point where the mutex caused backtracking*. The action assignments for the goal propositions up to the point of the mutex failure are augmented with the action assignment that was precluded by the (no longer valid) mutex. Search continues below this point until either a solution is found or the resumption point is returned to. The PE trace is extended during this search and the mutex checkpoint is replaced by the subtrace so generated.

To ensure that the pilot explanation is complete in it's encapsulation of a Graphplan backward search episode we must also check for the presence of new actions that may be establishers of a goal at level k but not at level k-1 when the PE trace was built.

New Actions: A goal proposition 'P' at level k+1 could have more establishing actions than at level k, indicating that a new action has been added during planning graph extension. At each occurrence of unassigned proposition P in the pilot explanation search is resumed using the values of any previously assigned goal props and augmenting them with the new action assignment to P. Search continues until either a solution is found or the resumption point is returned to. In the latter case the trace for this search segment is inserted via a new establisher of P in the PE.

3.3 Costs and Tradeoffs

The overhead entailed in building the pilot explanation, storing adequate information in it, and subsequently using it is not insignificant. It's comprised primarily of:

1. PE construction time cost during backward search
2. Startup cost for backward search resumption –incurred each time a checkpoint no longer holds and the information needed to re-initiate search must be gathered.
3. Storage space required to retain the PE.

The first two of these factors will work directly to offset the three speedup factors discussed in section 3.1 The last factor impacts not only the machine storage requirements but, depending on a given platform's "garbage collection" scheme, can have a significant impact on runtime also.

For "small" problems (where the solution is found quickly by Graphplan after only a few search episodes) this approach can be expected to show little if any advantage. The overhead of constructing the pilot explanation is likely to more than offset the few search episodes in which it could be used to shortcut the search. The real speedup is likely to be seen in the larger problems involving many episodes of deep search on the planning graph. However, as we discuss in the

Problem	EGBG				Standard Graphplan			Speedup
	Total Time	Bktrks	Mutex Cheks	Size of PE	Total Time	Bktrks	Mutex Cheks	
BW-Large-B (18/18)	4.13	1100 K	3566 K	944	9.8	2823 K	8117 K	2.4x
Rocket-ext-a (7/36)	5.05	906 K	215 K	320	53.2	8128 K	2944 K	10.5x
Tower-5 (31/31)	.9	316 K	643 K	2722	21.4	7907 K	23040 K	23.8x

Table 1. Comparison of EGBG with standard Graphplan. Times given in cpu minutes on a sparc ultra 1 running Allegro common lisp. Numbers in parentheses next to the problem names list the number of time steps and number of actions respectively in the solution. A measure of the backtracks and mutex checks performed during the search are also shown. "Size of PE" gives a measure of the pilot explanation size in terms of the final number of "search segments"

Problem	EGBG with EBL/DDB				EGBG				Speed up
	Total Time	Bktrks	Mutex Cheks	Size of PE	Total Time	Bktrks	Mutex Cheks	Size of PE	
BW-Large-A (12/12)	11.9 s	2.9 K	1.1 K	47	12.5 s	3.5 K	1.4 K	75	1.05x
Rocket-3-2-5 (5/20)	12.7 s	2.0 K	1.0 K	26	24.4 s	2.0 K	1.0 K	66	1.92x
Hanoi-Tower-3	23.3 s	14.1 K	66.7 K	170	52.2 s	38.3 K	300 K	283	2.24x

Table 2. Comparison of EGBG and EGBG augmented with EBL\ DDB on 3 small problems . Times are given in cpu seconds. A measure of the backtracks and mutex checks performed during the search are also shown. "Size of PE" gives a measure of the pilot explanation size in terms of the number of "search segments" it contains in the end.

next section, these are also the kinds of problems that can generate huge pilot explanations with all the storage and garbage collection problems it entails.

4. Experimentation

The EGBG program involved a major augmentation and rewrite of a Graphplan implementation in Lisp[1]. The planning graph extension routines were augmented to discriminate between static and dynamic mutexes and to facilitate the translation of the PE across levels. The backward search routines were augmented to build the PE during search. Once the initial PE is built, search control is taken over by a separate set of routines that process any dynamic checkpoints and determine when search must be resumed.

Table 1 provides a comparison of EGBG with standard Graphplan on some "benchmark" size problems from [Kautz & Selman, 96] in three domains. The speedup advantage of EGBG is respectable on these problems, ranging from 2.4 to almost 24 times faster.

The experience to date with the EGBG system on some of the larger problems has shown it to be sensitive to space and memory management issues. While generally conducting it's level search significantly faster than Graphplan in the early to middle stages of the problem search, EGBG may eventually gets bound up by the Lisp garbage collection system before it can complete it's solution search. For example the Ferry-41 problem is solved by standard Graphplan at level 27 of the planning graph in approximately 123 minutes[2]. Up to level 18, EGBG search is 25 times faster than standard Graphplan search. However around level 19 the current implementation of EGBG suc-

cumbs to the (as yet non-optimized) garbage collection system and doesn't emerge!

There are a variety of approaches that can be pursued to enable EGBG to extend its reach to the higher levels and large search spaces. The next section explores the role of the size of the PE.

5. Minimizing the Pilot Explanation

Any reduction that can be made to the size of the pilot explanation pays off in two important ways:

- There are fewer checkpoints that need to be processed at each planning graph extension
- The storage (and garbage collection) requirements are reduced.

The blind search conducted by Graphplan travels down many fruitless search branches that are essentially redundant to other areas of its search trace. And of course EGBG builds these into the pilot explanation and retains key aspects of them, revisiting dynamic checkpoints at their leaf nodes during each backward search episode.

We are investigating two different approaches to minimizing the PE so as to extend the range of problems addressable with EGBG under our current machine limitations.

One approach that immediately presented itself was to take advantage of concurrent work being conducted in our group on improving Graphplan's memoization routines by adding dependency-directed backtracking (DDB) and explanation-based learning (EBL) capabilities [Kambhampati, 99]. The EBL and DDB strategies complement our explanation-guided backward search technique quite naturally. The presence of EBL and DDB techniques reduces the sizes of the PE's and also makes them more likely to be directly applicable in future levels (as the dynamic checkpoints embodied in the explanation are more focused). At the same time, the PE provides a more powerful way of ex-

---

[1] The original Lisp implementation of Graphplan was done by Mark Peot and subsequently improved by David Smith
[2] On an Ultra-Sparc, compiled for speed, with improved memoization based on the "UB-Tree" structures developed by Koehler and her co-workers [Koehler et. al., 97]

ploiting the past searches than EBL-based nogoods alone do.

The integration of the EBL and DDB strategies into our EGBG system significantly changes the manner in which the pilot explanation is used during each search episode. Rather than visiting and processing each checkpoint in the explanation the conflict sets generated by the mutex checks and those returned by any partial search conducted can be used to indicate *precisely which checkpoints* should be processed. This avoids visiting and possibly conducting search below checkpoints that ultimately have no possibility of leading to a solution.

Although incorporating EBL/DDB into the backward search routines in EGBG is straightforward, it is more problematic to implement efficient processing of conflict sets in the routines that search using the pilot explanation. Table 2 shows the results produced by an EBL/DDB enhanced version of EGBG on the 3 such problems. The speedup improvement is modest, as expected, since the time spent in search for these small problems is only a fraction of the total time. However, the table also shows the dramatic impact that EBL/DDB has on the size of the pilot explanation, reducing it by roughly 50%. We are currently rewriting this part of EGBG as our first version turned out to have some implementation inefficiencies that inhibited it from scaling up to larger problems.

A second promising approach is to restrict the size of the pilot explanation. EGBG currently "grows" the PE every time backward search is resumed, without regard to it's size or the possible relevance of the "explanation" it is building. However, the PE can easily be made static after a given size limit is reached and still provide, during each backward search episode, all the search shortcuts it embodies. Alternately, some type of relevance-based heuristic could be employed to determine what portions of a learned PE are mostly likely to be useful and hence should be retained. That is, the well-known EBL issue of 'how much is too much' in the way of rules (or nogoods) also applies to EGBG and it's use of the pilot explanation.

6. Related Work

Verfaillie and Schiex [94] discuss and demonstrate various EBL-type methods for improving dynamic constraint satisfaction problem (DCSP) solving, which underlies the Graphplan backward search. Our approaches, while related, are much better customized to take advantage of the particular type of DCSP structural symmetry in Graphplan backward search. As we noted earlier, our approach is also related to, and complements, the approaches to add EBL and DDB capabilities to Graphplan. In particular, EBL approaches can only help decide if all methods of making a goal-set true at a particular level are doomed to fail. The pilot explanation, on the other hand, also guides the search away from branches likely to fail, and allows the planner to capitalize on the search penetration done at previous levels. In this sense, the pilot explanations are also related to the "sticky values" approach for improving CSP [Frost & Dechter, 94]

7. Conclusion and Future Directions

We presented a method for exploiting the symmetry in the planning graph structure of Graphplan algorithm to improve its backward search. The main insight underlying our method is that due to the inherent symmetry of the planning graph the backward search conducted at level $k + 1$ of the graph is essentially a replay of the search conducted at the previous level k with certain well-defined extensions. We presented a structure called the pilot explanation, which captures the failures encountered at previous levels of the search. This structure is used in an intelligent way to guide the search at the newer levels. We implemented this approach in a system called EGBG, and presented a preliminary empirical study with the system. We also discussed the importance of minimizing the size of the pilot explanation and some relevant techniques, including a recent EBL and DDB implementation for Graphplan. Our near-term focus will be to address the problems currently limiting the size of problems that can be handled by the system. Future areas of investigation will include a study of various heuristics and methods for using the PE to direct search. These could entail jumping about to process the various checkpoints in a "best first" manner or even deliberately not processing certain unpromising checkpoints (and thereby accepting the loss of soundness) in the hopes of short-cutting the search.

References

Blum, A. and Furst, M. 1995. Fast planning through planning graph analysis. In *Proc. IJCAI-95* (Extended version appears in *Artificial Intelligence, 90(1-2)*)

Frost, D and Dechter, R. 1994. In search of best constraint satisfaction search. In Proc. AAAI-94.

Ihrig, L, and Kambhampati, S. 1997. Storing and Indexing Plan Derivations through Explanation-based Analysis of Retrieval Failures. *Journal of Artificial Intelligence.* Vol. 7. 1997.

Kambhampati, S., Parker, E., and Lambrecht, E., 1997. Understanding and Extending Graphplan. In Proceedings of 4th European Conference on Planning. Toulouse France.

Kambhampati, S. 1998. On the relations between Intelligent Backtracking and Failure-driven Explanation Based Learning in Constraint Satisfaction and Planning. *Artificial Intelligence. Vol 105.*

Kambhampati, S. 1999. Improving Graphplan's search with EBL & DDB. In *Proc. IJCAI-99.* 1999.

Koehler, J., Nebel, B., Hoffmann, J., and Dimopoulos, Y. 1997. Extending planning graphs to an ADL Subset. Technical Report No. 88. Albert Ludwigs University.

Mittal, S. and Falkenhainer, B. 1990. Dynamic Constraint Satisfaction Problems. In *Proc. AAAI-90.*

Prosser, P. 1993. Domain filtering can degrade intelligent backtracking search. In Proc. IJCAI, 1993.

Schiex, T, and G.Verfaillie. Nogood Recording for Static and Dnamic Constraint Satisfaction Problems. C.E.R.T-O.N.E.R.A.

Tsang, E. *Constraint Satisfaction.* Academic Press. 1993.

Verfaillie, G and Schiex, T. 1994. Solution Reuse in Dynamic Constraint Satisfaction Problems. In Proc. AAAI.

Veloso, M. 1994. Flexible strategy learning: Analogical replay of problem solving episodes. In Proc. AAAI.

Robotics

An Integrated System for Multi-Rover Scientific Exploration

**Tara Estlin, Alexander Gray, Tobias Mann, Gregg Rabideau, Rebecca Castaño,
Steve Chien** and **Eric Mjolsness**

Jet Propulsion Laboratory
California Institute of Technology
4800 Oak Grove Drive
Pasadena, CA 91109-8099
{firstname.lastname}@jpl.nasa.gov

Abstract

This paper describes an integrated system for co-ordinating multiple rover behavior with the overall goal of collecting planetary surface data. The Multi-Rover Integrated Science Understanding System combines concepts from machine learning with planning and scheduling to perform autonomous scientific exploration by cooperating rovers. The integrated system utilizes a novel machine learning clustering component to analyze science data and direct new science activities. A planning and scheduling system is employed to generate rover plans for achieving science goals and to coordinate activities among rovers. We describe each of these components and discuss some of the key integration issues that arose during development and influenced both system design and performance.

Introduction

Landmark events have recently taken place in the areas of space exploration and planetary rovers. The Mars Pathfinder mission was a major success, not only demonstrating the feasibility of sending rovers to other planets, but displaying the significance of such missions to the scientific community. Future missions are being planned to send additional robotic vehicles to Mars as well as to the outer planets and an asteroid (JPL 1999). In order to increase science return and enable certain types of science activities, future missions will require larger sets of rovers to gather the desired data. These rovers will need to behave in a coordinated fashion where each rover accomplishes a subset of the overall mission goals and shares any acquired information. In addition, it is desirable to have highly autonomous rovers that require little communication with scientists and engineers on Earth to perform their tasks. An autonomous rover will be able to make decisions on its own as to what exact science data should be returned and how to go about the data gathering process.

This paper presents the Multi-Rover Integrated Science Understanding System (MISUS) which provides a framework for autonomously generating and achieving planetary science goals. This system integrates

techniques from machine learning with planning and scheduling to enable autonomous multi-rover behavior for analyzing science data, evaluating what new science observations to perform, and deciding what steps should be taken to perform them. These techniques are also integrated with a simulation environment that can model different planetary terrains and science data within a terrain.

Science data analysis in MISUS is performed using machine-learning clustering methods, which use image and spectral mineralogical features to help classify different planetary rock types. These methods look for similarity classes of visible, rock image regions within individual spectral images and across multiple images. Specifically, clustering is performed by a distributed algorithm where each rover alternates between independently performing learning computations using its local data and updating the system-wide model through communication among rovers. Output clusters are used to help evaluate scientific hypotheses and also to prioritize visible surfaces for further observation based on their "scientific interest." As the system builds a model of the rock type distribution, it continuously assembles a new set of observation goals for a team of rovers to collect from different terrain locations. Thus, the clusterer drives the science process by analyzing the current data set and then deciding what new and interesting observations should be made.

A planning and scheduling component is used to determine the necessary rover activities required to achieve science goals requested by the learning system (Rabideau, Estlin, & Chien 1999). Based on an input set of goals and each rover's initial conditions, the planner generates a sequence of activities that satisfy the goals while obeying each of the rover's resource constraints and operation rules. Plans are produced by using an "iterative repair" algorithm which classifies conflicts and resolves them individually by performing one or more plan modifications. Planning is distributed among the individual rovers where each rover is responsible for planning for its own activities. A central planning system is responsible for dividing up the goals among the individual rovers in a fashion that minimizes the total traversing time of all rovers.

The components described above are also integrated with a simulation environment that models multiple-rover science operations in a Mars-like terrain. Different Martian rockscapes are created for use in the simulator by using distributions over rock types, sizes and locations. When science measurements are requested from a terrain during execution, rock and mineral spectral models are used to generate sample spectra based on the type of rock being observed.

The remainder of this paper is organized in the following manner. We begin by characterizing the cooperating rovers application domain and describing our science scenario. Next, we present the MISUS integrated system framework and describe each of its components. We then discuss design decisions and system requirements that arose during integration and any general lessons learned. In the final sections, we discuss related work, planned future work, and present our conclusions.

Cooperating Rovers for Science

Utilizing multiple rovers on planetary science missions has many advantages. First, multiple rovers can collect more data than a single rover. A team of rovers can cover a larger area in a shorter time where science gathering tasks are allocated over the team. Second, multiple rovers can perform tasks that otherwise would not be possible using a single rover. For instance, rovers landed at different locations can cover areas with impassable boundaries. Also, with several rovers, one rover can afford to take more risk and thus attempt tasks that usually might be avoided. Third, more complicated cooperative tasks can be accomplished, such as taking a wide baseline stereo image (which requires two cameras separated by a certain distance). Finally, multiple rovers can enhance mission success through increased system redundancy. If one rover fails, then its tasks could be quickly taken over by another rover. In all cases, the rovers should behave in a coordinated fashion, dividing goals appropriately among the team and sharing acquired information.

Coordinating multiple distributed agents for a mission to Mars or other planet introduces some interesting new challenges for the supporting technology. Issues arise concerning communication, control and individual on-board capabilities. Many of these design decisions are related, and all of them have an impact on any on-board technologies used for the mission. For example, for an on-board science analysis system, the amount of communication available will determine how much science data can be easily shared. This factor will also affect a planning system by determining how much each rover can coordinate with other rovers to perform tasks. The control scheme will determine which rovers execute what science gathering tasks which affects the on-board components. For instance, some rovers may be utilized only for science data gathering, while other may be used for planning and/or science analysis. Decisions on the on-board capabilities of each rover can also determine the independence of a rover.

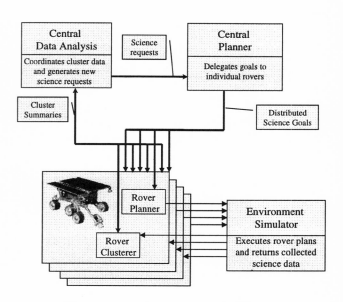

Figure 1: MISUS Architecture Diagram

For the framework presented in this paper, we have initially chosen the configuration of a team of three rovers where each rover has a planning and learning tool on-board. Each rover can thus plan for its assigned goals, collect the required data, and perform science analysis on-board which will direct its future goals. In addition, a central planner and learner are assumed to be located on either a lander or one of the rovers, which are used to coordinate science data and goals.

We evaluate our framework by testing its ability to build a model of the distribution of terrain rocks, classified according to composition as measured by a bore-sighted spectrometer. To perform testing for different planetary terrain models, different rock fields are generated by using distributions over rock types, sizes, and locations. Science goals consist of requests to take spectral measurements at certain locations or regions. These goals can be prioritized so that if necessary low priority goals can be preempted (e.g. due to resource constraints such as low battery power).

Science goals are divided among the three rovers. Each rover is identical and is assumed to have a spectrometer on-board as well as other resources including a drive motor, a solar panel that provides power for rover activities, and a battery that provides backup power when solar power is not available. The battery can also be recharged using the solar panel when possible. Collected science data is immediately transmitted to the lander where it is stored in memory. The lander can only receive transmissions from one rover at a time.

Multi-Rover Science Architecture

The overall MISUS architecture is shown in Figure 1. The system is comprised of three major components:

- **Data Analysis**: A distributed machine-learning system which performs unsupervised clustering to model the distribution of rock types observed by the rovers. This system is designed to direct rover sensing to continually improve this model of the scientific content of the planetary scene.

- **Planning**: A distributed-planning system that produces rover-operation plans to achieve input rover science goals. Planning is divided between a central planner, which efficiently divides up science goals between rovers, and a distributed set of planners which each plan for operations upon an individual rover.

- **Environment simulator**: A multiple rover simulator that models different geological environments and rover-science operations within them. The simulator manages science data for each environment, tracks rover operations within the terrain, and reflects readings by rover science instruments.

MISUS operates in a closed-loop fashion where the data analysis system can be seen to take the role of the scientist driving the exploration process. Spectra data are received by individual rover clustering algorithms, which attempt to locally model the distribution of rocks according to broad classifications of rock compositions. This information is then sent to a central clusterer which integrates all gathered data into an updated global model and broadcasts the new model back to the distributed clusterers. A prioritization algorithm uses the clustering output to generate a new set of observation goals that will further improve the accuracy of the model. These goals are passed to a central planner which assigns individual rovers to goals in a fashion that will most efficiently serve the requests. Then each rover planner produces a set of actions for that rover which will achieve as many of its assigned goals as possible. These action sequences are sent to the simulator where they are executed and any gathered data is sent back to the rover clusterers. This cycle continues until enough data is gathered to produce distinct clusters for any observed rock types.

In the next few sections, we discuss each of the MISUS system components in more detail.

Data Analysis System

To perform science analysis, we use a machine-learning system which performs unsupervised clustering to model the distribution of rock types in the observed terrain. A primary feature of the MISUS is that the separate rovers cooperate to form a joint consensus for the observed distribution of rock types. Through a learning process, the global distribution model keeps improving as more data is observed over time. For this demonstration prototype, the model used for this distribution is a simple K-means-like unsupervised clustering model, where each cluster represents a different rock type in the sensor space. In the present simulation, each sensor reading is a spectral measurement returning values at 14 wavelengths; learning takes place in the full 14-dimensional continuous space.

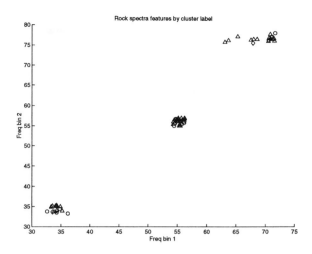

Figure 2: Example spectra feature space

Distributed Clustering At any given time, each rover has a different location on the planetary surface and is sensing different targets. So each rover has its own distinct segment of the overall dataset, stored locally in its data buffer. Over time, each rover collects a new set of data points, or 14-dimensional spectrum readings, adding it to its existing store of data points. Clustering is initiated after each rover has obtained new observations. A sample cluster model (shown for 2 of 14 dimensions) is shown in Figure 2.

Clustering based on the EM (Expectation-Maximization) algorithm, an iterative optimization procedure, normally requires several passes over the entire data. Since rovers must share information through a power-expensive communication channel. Rather than send its local dataset to one or more other rovers, the distributed clustering algorithm allows a rover to send only a small set of parameters which summarizes its local data. Each rover's model parameters are computed locally, then sent to a central clusterer which integrates them into an updated global model (which is also a small set of parameters) and broadcasts that model to all rovers in the system. Each rover takes this global model into account when making its local estimate. This process continues iteratively until convergence. This scheme trades off some accuracy in the global model in order to minimize communication. In the limit of large datasets, this scheme approximates the equivalent non-distributed clustering model (where one processor may examine all the data at once) more and more closely.

The algorithm is very homogeneous, i.e. each processor performs the same computation with the exception of the central clusterer, which performs a few additional computations to compute the global model and broadcast it to the other processors. It also tolerant to processor dropouts, i.e. a circumstance in which one or more rovers contributes zero data to the clustering, for any reason such as a rover malfunction.

$$E = \sum_r^R \sum_n^{N_r} \sum_k^K M_{nk}^r (\|\underline{x}_n - \hat{\underline{\mu}}_k^r\|^2 + \|\hat{\underline{\mu}}_k^r - \underline{\mu}_k\|^2 - \alpha_k)$$

$$+ T \sum_r^R \sum_n^{N_r} \sum_k^K M_{nk}^r (\log M_{nk}^r - 1)$$

$$+ \sum_r^R \sum_n^{N_r} \lambda_n (\sum_k^K M_{nk}^r - 1)$$

Figure 3: Clustering objective function

Model and Optimization Our clustering model is a special case of the general mixture of Gaussians studied extensively in statistics (Redner & Walker 1984). The K-means clustering model also corresponds to a special form of Gaussian mixture where a hard class membership restriction is made (Bishop 1995). Our model is similar but lifts the restriction.

Hathaway (Hathaway 1986) shows an equivalence between probabilistic and statistical mechanics-style objective functions for mixture distributions. This transformation allows us to generalize the probabilistic objective function to include a temperature variable, allowing us to use deterministic annealing to perform global optimization of the model parameters.

The distributed version of the clustering model follows a development similar to that in (Tsioutsias & Mjolsness 1994) for partitioned neural networks. The entire dataset (across all rovers) $\underline{X}$ contains N vectors $\underline{x} = (x_1, \ldots, x_D)$ indexed by n. Denoting each of the R rovers with an index r, each rover has a subset $\underline{X}_r$ of the data, containing N_r sensor readings. The global, shared clustering model consists of K centroids, $\underline{\mu}_k$. Each rover stores its own local estimates of the centroids, $\hat{\underline{\mu}}_k^r$, based on its subset of the data. M_{nk} denotes the membership of datum $\underline{x}_n$ in cluster k, where $\sum_{k=1}^K M_{nk} = 1$. Cluster membership is determined by a softmax over the distance of a datum to each cluster mean. We will write M_{nk}^r since memberships are only computed and stored locally on each rover.

The clustering algorithm adjusts the values of the centroids in order to minimize the objective function shown in Figure 3, by alternating between a centroid relaxation step, where the cluster means are re-estimated based on the current membership weights, and a membership relaxation step, where the memberships are re-estimated based on the means. α is the reward for committing to cluster k and each λ_n corresponds to a Lagrange multiplier enforcing non-negativity of memberships. T is the temperature parameter.

The first term in this objective function can be identified with minimizing the distance between centroids and the data associated with them and keeping the R estimates of the centroids close to each other. The second serves to prevent negative memberships. The third enforces that memberships sum to unity across the classes.

Goal Selection The clustering model in this initial prototype system may be viewed as the scientific end-product of the exploration. The overall purpose of the system is to increase the accuracy of the clustering model by obtaining sensor readings in regions that are likely to improve the model. An update of the clustering model determines new planetary locations to be explored by the rovers. These locations are sent as formal goals by the learner to the planner.

Recall that clusters are defined in a high-dimensional *spectra space* in which unsupervised learning will identify different rock types. Every datum also has an associated position in physical space, on the planetary surface. Assuming there is some (perhaps very noisy) correspondence between rock type and spatial location, the purpose of goal selection is to direct exploration toward certain rock types by specifying new spatial targets (coordinates in 3-space at which to take sensor readings) according to the observed rock type distribution.

A very simple heuristic for goal selection is used in the current system. A constant number G of new spatial targets will be specified for each cluster. For each cluster, two of the G spatial targets are chosen by first finding the two mutually most distant points (in physical space) of that rock type, then selecting a point in space stochastically from within a neighborhood of each of those 2 points. These goals are given high priority. The rest of the G targets are chosen from neighborhoods of randomly selected rocks in the cluster, and are given lower priority. The idea of this heuristic is to bias the system toward exploration in extremal directions, as well as to explore the rock distribution in a way which balances effort equally between rock types (thus avoiding, say, spending undue energy on a very common rock type at the expense of rare rock types).

Planning System

To produce individual rover plans, we used a distributed version of the ASPEN (Automated Scheduling and Planning Environment) system (Fukanaga *et al.* 1997). ASPEN is a configurable, generic planning/scheduling application framework that can be tailored to specific domains to create conflict-free plans or schedules. Its components include:

- An expressive modeling language to allow the user to naturally define the application domain

- A constraint management system for representing and maintaining domain operability and resource constraints, as well as activity requirements

- A set of search strategies and repair heuristics

- A temporal reasoning system for expressing and maintaining temporal constraints

- A graphical interface for visualizing plans/schedules

ASPEN employs techniques from planning and scheduling to automatically generate the necessary rover activity sequence to achieve the input goals. This sequence is produced by utilizing an iterative repair

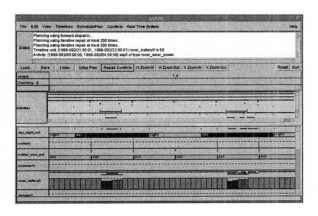

Figure 4: Example ASPEN plan

algorithm (Zweben *et al.* 1994) which classifies conflicts and attacks them each individually. Conflicts occur when a plan constraint has been violated where this constraint could be temporal or involve a resource, state or activity parameter. Conflicts are resolved by performing one or more schedule modifications such as moving, adding, or deleting activities.

A rover that is at the incorrect location for a scheduled science activity is one type of conflict. Resolving this particular conflict involves adding a traverse command to send the rover to the designated site. Other conflicts may include having more than one rover communicating with the lander at a time or having too many activities scheduled for one rover, which over subscribed its power resources. The iterative repair algorithm continues until no conflicts remain in the schedule, or a timeout has expired. Figure 4 shows an example rover-plan displayed in the ASPEN GUI interface.

Distributed Planning To support missions with multiple rovers, we developed a distributed version of ASPEN where it is assumed each rover has an onboard planner. This allows rovers to plan for themselves and/or for other rovers. If communication is slow, it may be useful to have rovers construct their own plans (and to plan dynamically when necessary, which is discussed in future work). Also, by balancing the workload, distributed planning can be helpful when individual computing resources are limited.

The approach to distributed planning utilized in MISUS is to include a planner for each rover, in addition to a central planner. The central planner develops an abstract plan for all rovers, while each rover planner develops a detailed, executable plan for its own activities. The central planner also acts as a router, taking a global set of goals and dividing it up among the rovers. For example, a science goal may request an image of a particular rock without concern for which rover acquires the image. The central planner could assign this goal to the rover that is closest to the rock in order to minimize the traversals of all rovers.

Plan Optimization One of the dominating characteristics of the multi-rover application is rover traversals

to designated waypoints. Decisions must be made not only to satisfy the requested goals, but also to provide more optimal schedules. ASPEN can consider optimization goals during the repair process. As certain types of conflicts are resolved, heuristics are used to guide the search towards making decisions that will produce higher quality schedules. In other words, when several options are available for repairing a conflict, these options are ordered based on predictions on how favorable the resulting schedule will be.

For this application, we have implemented heuristics based on techniques from the Multi-Traveling Salesmen Problem (MTSP), which is similar to the Traveling Salesman Problem (TSP) (Johnson & McGeoch 1997). For MTSP, at least one member of a sales team must visit each city such that total traveling time is minimized. Both the central and rover planners utilize the MTSP heuristics. These heuristics are used to select what rover should be assigned a particular science goal and a temporal location for the science activity. In previously reported results, they were shown to make a significant impact in reducing overall traversal distance and expected execution time (Rabideau, Estlin, & Chien 1999).

Environment Simulator

The environment simulator is designed to provide a source of data for the science analysis system by simulating the science gathering activities of the rover. Given the current science scenario, this entails the generation of an environment and the simulation of rover data gathering activities within the environment.

Generation of the environment requires producing a field of rocks for the rovers to traverse. The rock field is generated as a plane with rocks of various sizes embedded at various depths. The simulator maintains information about the mineral composition of each rock, and the spectrum that would correspond to its mineral composition. The size and spatial distributions of the rockfield were developed by examining distributions of rocks observed by the Viking Landers, Mars Lander and Mars Pathfinder. The distribution of minerals that can occur in rocks was developed in collaboration with planetary geologists at JPL, and the spectra associated with rocks are generated from the spectra of the component minerals via a linear-mixing model.

The simulation of the rover activities was done at a coarse level. Such considerations as kinematics and obstacle avoidance were not modeled in this simulation. Other considerations, such as power consumption and memory management were modeled by the planner for plan generation but not simulated by the simulator. The rovers were essentially modeled as roving spectrometers by the simulator. Figure 5 shows several rovers and their spectrometer reaches modeled in a sample rockscape. The simulation of rover activities was accomplished by executing the plan generated by the planner, consisting of a list of movement, rotation, and instrument commands. The simulator would

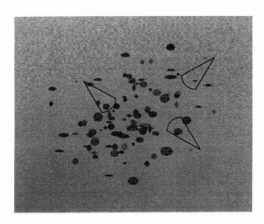

Figure 5: Overhead view of simulated rockscape. Wedges denote different rovers' spectrometers' fields of view.

then, from the location and direction specified by the movement and rotation commands, determine whether or not a rock was visible by the boresighted spectrometer. If so, the simulator would perturb the spectra in an amount proportional to the distance of the rover from the rock in order to simulate instrument noise, and store the spectrum for later communication to the relevant clusterer. After all of the activities in a plan were executed by the simulator (i.e. moves, turns, and data gathering activities), the data was communicated to each clusterer via synchronization agents. The simulator would then wait for the next plan.

Integration Issues

The integration of two AI problem solvers and a simulated environment involved a number of decisions. In this section, we review some of the interesting and challenging issues that arose in performing this integration; we particularly focus on the areas of system and interface design and system performance.

One major integration issue is interfacing between the different components. For instance, the planner was required to produce plans in a format compatible with the action representation required by the simulator. Also, the learner required the ability to ingest any science data returned from the simulator. A more complicated interface arose between the learning and planning components. Issues such as shared representation of goals and objectives had to be resolved.

When specifying a new science goal, the learning component usually requested additional measurements be taken from a particular rock. However, this general request had to be grounded in the form of terrain coordinates in order to represent the goal in the planner's modeling language. In addition, the planning and learning components had to agree on a priority representation that was expressive enough to represent the information required by the learner but that could also be easily utilized during planning to remove goals if necessary due to resource constraints. Another important issue was interfacing between science and engineering

representations. Within the planner, constraints may deal with sets of goals, resources and/or states which are primarily scientific, primarily engineering, or which form part of the interface between these two layers.

A separate design consideration was that the interactions between the modules of the integrated system be asynchronous. In other words, each module needed to signal the next module when appropriate, rather than designating one process a control process, which would then control the actions of the others. For instance, the planner would be not begin planning until receiving a new set of science requests from the science analysis module. To that end, we designed a synchronization architecture that would facilitate interprocess signaling and also communication of data. Essentially, each module acted as both a server process and a client process. A process would wait in server mode until the client initiated contact, do its processing, and then initiate contact with the server process of the next system as a client. After the process finished communicating to the next process, it would go back to server mode until it had new data to process.

One important decision is the design of the overall planner, execution, and learner feedback. How often the system loop is run is one issue. Increasing the frequency of feedback improves the responsiveness of the overall system to changes in the inputs (e.g. changes in the observed science data) but increases the computation cost of running the constituent algorithms (e.g. planner, learner). Additionally, due to the design of the algorithms, one may know how much change in information is needed to likely change the results of the computation (e.g. for the learner how much new data is likely to change the collection goals, for the planner how much of a change in execution state or goals is likely to require another plan). While not critically sensitive to the amount of new data it receives, the more data obtained by the science analysis module on a given system cycle, the more its model of the rock type distribution will improve, resulting in useful new exploration goals. If, say, the learner obtains little new information, the targets it decides upon will not be much more useful than those it produced on the last iteration.

A second issue related to system feedback is the length of the horizon (i.e. the allowed plan execution time period) that is considered by each cycle. If this horizon is short, it imposes constraints on how long the cycle must be run (e.g. if the horizon is two hours, the cycle must be run at least every two hours). If the horizon is long, the individual modules may take longer to run (e.g. a planner takes longer to plan for a longer horizon). The number of goals that are requested per iteration also (to some degree) drives the size of the planning horizon since only a certain number of goals can be solved in any set length of time.

The frequency and horizon of each cycle is not constrained by our architecture. However, for our scenario, we chose to have the cycle invoked once per local day and to include a horizon of one day. This time scale is reasonable because science activities are not possible during the night period (as the rover is mainly solar powered) but computation is possible during such periods (using the battery). Thus possible execution time is not expended during planning. However, other choices for cycle frequency and horizon are possible, and may make sense for different mission parameters.

Related Work

The idea of having a scientific discovery system direct future experiments is present in a number of other systems. Work on learning by experimentation, such as IDS (Nordhausen & Langley 1993) and ADEPT (Rajamoney 1990), varied certain quantitative and qualitative values in the domain and then measured the effects of these changes. MISUS differs from these systems in that it interacts with an environment simulator to perform experimentation and it is specialized to particular problems and scenarios in planetary science. MISUS is also integrated with a planning system which constructs the detailed activity sequence needed to perform each experiment based on a domain model.

Other work has used experimentation to learn from the environment but experiments have not been scientifically driven. EXPO (Gil 1993) integrates planning and learning methods to acquire new information by interacting with an external environment. However, while MISUS learns classification models of new geological features, EXPO tries to improve its planning-related domain knowledge.

The distributed clustering presented in this paper bears some similarity to other distributed learning methods, such as (Provost & Hennessy 1999), which are constrained by low-bandwidth communication between processors to share relatively concise data models.

There has also been a significant amount of work on cooperating robots. One related system is GRAMMPS (Bummit & Stentz 1988), which coordinates multiple mobile robots visiting locations in cluttered, partially known environments. GRAMMPS also has a low-level planner on each robot and uses a similar approach to distribute targets, however GRAMMPS does not look at multiple resources or exogenous events. Most other cooperative robotic systems utilize reactive planning techniques (Mataric 1995; Parker 1999). These systems focus on behavioral approaches and do not explicitly reason about assigning goals and planning courses of actions. Furthermore, none of these systems utilize a learning component to drive the system goals.

Future Work

A number of extensions are planned for each component of MISUS. One major extension already under way is to interface with a multiple rover execution architecture (Estlin et al. 1999) being developed at JPL that includes a number of additional components including: a real-time multi-rover hardware simulator which models rover kinematics and sensor feedback and control

software from the NASA JPL Rocky 7 rover. MISUS is intended to provide the science layer for this architecture, which will allow for more realistic testing of the MISUS framework. In the rest of this section we describe extensions planned for each MISUS component.

Future Work for the Data Analysis System

The learning component described here represents an initial model intended primarily to bring out system issues. The most straightforward of the improvements under consideration are concerned with strengthening the clustering model to include outlier handling, covariance modeling, incremental updating, model size determination, robustness to failure and missing data, and multiple parent representation.

An important area for future work is in goal selection. Combining spectral with spatial distribution models may allow for better-informed targeting. A combined clustering objective function would be more sensitive to novel data in some locations than others. The system could attempt to select target data which maximizes improvement of the data model. This is similar to the saliency measure for an attentive, relaxation-based neural network (Tsioutsias & Mjolsness 1996) To improve the system's applicability to planetary science, we are working to select targets which maximally aid discrimination between two competing hypotheses of geological processes, in collaboration with JPL geologists (Davies et al. 1999). One approach is to use stochastic parameterized grammars (Mjolsness 1997) to create a more detailed spatial-spectral model of rock distributions than a mixture of Gaussians.

Future Work for the Planning System

One improvement for the planning component is to enable dynamic planning capabilities. To accomplish this we will utilize a dynamic version of ASPEN, which monitors plan execution and allows re-planning when necessary (Chien et al. 1999). To perform autonomous rover-operations, an on-board planning system must be able to respond in a timely fashion to a dynamic, unpredictable environment. Rover plans may often need to be modified due to events such as traverses completing early and setbacks such as failure to reach an observation site.

We also intend to extend the planning model to be more robust to failure situations. For instance, if failure occurs, the planning system should recognize it (e.g. the rover has not responded for a certain amount of time), not send any new goals to that rover, and reassign any current goals assigned to that rover.

Future Work for the Simulator

We are interested in improving the environment simulator by adding different data sources, and by improving the sophistication of the hypotheses investigated.

The visual texture of a rock's surface can give clues to the composition and geological history of the rock, and is a source of information that should be used when attempting to sample from the distribution of rock compositions rather than the spatial distribution of rock locations. We intend to incorporate visual texture as a source of information for the rovers to help them choose a sampling strategy.

Modeling the distribution of rock compositions is a task that can yield useful information for geologists. Consider the scenario where an impact excavates an ancient hydrothermal system, in which there was a stable supply of hot water beneath the surface of Mars at some time in the past. It may be possible to deduce the existence of such a system from study of the impact ejecta scattered on the surface, and examination of the crater interior walls and rim deposits; hydrothermal activity would have altered the mineral characteristics of the excavated deposits.

Conclusions

This paper outlines a framework for coordinating multiple rover behavior in generating and achieving geological science goals. This system integrates techniques from machine learning and planning and scheduling to autonomously analyze and request new science data and generate the action sequences to retrieve that data. We discuss a number of integration issues including developing shared goal and plan representations, coordinating systems asynchronously, and adjusting interface parameters to best serve the overall system goal. We hope the techniques and issues presented in this paper will prove useful to other designers of integrated systems.

Acknowledgments

This work was performed by the Jet Propulsion Laboratory, California Institute of Technology, under contract with the National Aeronautics and Space Administration. This work was supported by the NASA Advanced Concept Program, Code S, managed by Neville Marzwell, and the NASA Autonomy Program, Code SM, managed by David Atkinson.

The authors acknowledge the invaluable contributions of Ashley Davies for his help in defining relevant geology scenarios for this work and for providing general knowledge of planetary geology. We also thank Padhraic Smyth for providing his environment simulation code, and Rich Maclin for leading the development of the spectra generation process.

References

Bishop, C. M. 1995. *Neural Networks for Pattern Recognition*. New York, NY: Oxford Univ. Press.

Bummit, B., and Stentz, A. 1988. GRAMMPS: A generalized mission planner for multiple mobile robots in unstructured environments. In *Proceedings of the IEEE Conference on Robots and Automation*.

Chien, S.; Knight, R.; Stechert, A.; Sherwood, R.; and Rabideau, G. 1999. Integrated planning and execution for autonomous spacecraft. In *Proceedings of the 1999 IEEE Aerospace Conference*.

Davies, A.; Mjolsness, E.; Gray, A.; Mann, T.; Castano, R.; Estlin, T.; and Saunders, R. 1999. Hypothesis-driven active data analysis of geological phenomena using semi-autonomous rovers: exploring simulations of martian hydrothermal deposits. In *American Geophysical Union Spring Meeting*.

Estlin, T.; Hayati, S.; *et al.* 1999. An integrated architecture for cooperating rovers. In *Proceedings of the 1999 International Symposium on Artficial Intelligence, Robotics and Automation for Space*.

Fukanaga, A.; Rabideau, G.; Chien, S.; and Yan, D. 1997. Towards an application framework for automated planning and scheduling. In *Proceedings of the 1997 International Symposium on Artficial Intelligence, Robotics and Automation for Space*.

Gil, Y. 1993. Efficient domain-independent experimentation. In *Proceedings of the Tenth International Conference on Machine Learning*, 128–134.

Hathaway, R. J. 1986. Another interpretation of the EM algorithm for mixture distributions. *Statistics and Probability Letters* 4:53–56.

Johnson, D., and McGeoch, L. 1997. The traveling salesman problem: A case study in local optimization. In Aarts, E. H. L., and Lenstra, J. K., eds., *Local Search in Combinatorial Optimization*. London: John Wiley and Sons. 215–310.

JPL 1999. *http://www.jpl.nasa.gov/missions/*.

Mataric, M. 1995. Designing and understanding adaptive group behavior. *Adaptive Behavior* 4(1):51–80.

Mjolsness, E. 1997. Symbolic neural networks derived from stochastic grammar domain models. In Sun, R., and Alexandre, F., eds., *Connectionist Symbolic Integration*. Lawrence Erlbaum Associates.

Nordhausen, B., and Langley, P. 1993. An integrated framework for empirical discovery. *Machine Learning* 12:17–47.

Parker, L. E. 1999. Cooperative robotics for multi-target observation. *Intelligent Automation and Soft Computing* 5(1):5–19.

Provost, F. J., and Hennessy, D. N. 1999. Scaling up: Distributed machine learning with cooperation. In *Proceedings of the Thirteenth National Conference on Ariticial Intelligence*.

Rabideau, G.; Estlin, T.; and Chien, S. 1999. Working together: Automatic generation of command sequences for multiple cooperating rovers. In *Proceedings of the 1999 IEEE Aerospace Conference*.

Rajamoney, S. 1990. A computational approach to theory revision. In Shrager, J., and Langley, P., eds., *Computational Models of Scientific Discovery and Theory Formation*. San Mateo, CA: Morgan Kaufman. 225–254.

Redner, R. A., and Walker, H. F. 1984. Mixture densities, maximum likelihood, and the EM algorithm. *SIAM Review* 26:195–239.

Tsioutsias, D., and Mjolsness, E. 1994. Optimization dynamics for partitioned neural networks. *International Journal of Neural Systems* 5(4).

Tsioutsias, D., and Mjolsness, E. 1996. A multiscale attentional framework for relaxation neural networks. *Advances in Neural Information Processing Systems* 8.

Zweben, M.; Daun, B.; Davis, E.; and Deale, M. 1994. Scheduling and rescheduling with iterative repair. In Zweben, M., and Fox, M., eds., *Intelligent Scheduling*. San Francisco, CA: Morgan Kaufmann. 241–256.

Integrated Natural Spoken Dialogue System
of Jijo-2 Mobile Robot for Office Services

Toshihiro Matsui Hideki Asoh John Fry† Youichi Motomura

Futoshi Asano Takio Kurita Isao Hara Nobuyuki Otsu

Real-World Intelligence Center
Electrotechnical Laboratory
1-1-4 Umezono, Tsukba
Ibaraki 305-8568, Japan
jijo2@etl.go.jp

† Linguistics Dept. and CSLI
Stanford University
220 Panama Street
Stanford CA94305-2150, USA
fry@csli.stanford.edu

Abstract

Our Jijo-2 robot, whose purpose is to provide office services, such as answering queries about people's location, route guidance, and delivery tasks, is expected to conduct natural spoken conversation with the office dwellers. This paper describes dialogue technologies implemented on our Jijo-2 office robot, i.e. noise-free voice acquisition system by a microphone array, inference of under-specified referents and zero pronouns using the attentional states, and context-sensitive construction of semantic frames from fragmented utterances. The behavior of the dialogue system integrated with the sound source detection, navigation, and face recognition vision is demonstrated in real dialogue examples in a real office.

Motivation

To extend applications of robots from routine tasks in traditional factories to flexible services in the offices and homes, robots are expected to have better man-machine interfaces for two reasons: (1) such settings are more dynamic and therefore require greater flexibility and adjustment to the environment on the part of the robot, and (2) the users are usually non-experts without special training in controlling or programming the robot.

We have been building a learning mobile office robot *Jijo-2* which navigates in an office, interacts with its environment and people, and provides services such as answering inquiries about people's location, route guidance, and delivery tasks. In such systems, natural man-machine interface, especially a spoken dialogue capability, plays an important role. This capability benefits not only the office users but also *Jijo-2* itself, since actions to ask nearby people for help can be taken. For example, we previously implemented a dialogue-based form of map learning and robust navigation where the robot asks a human trainer about its location when it loses its way (Asoh et al. 1996).

Our next challenge focused on realization of more natural dialogue to provide wider range of office services. For such office dialogues, we planed to add query/update to the location and schedule database of laboratory members and task commands such as Email and FAX as well as navigation dialogues for map learning. From the viewpoint of dialogue management, this extension incurs at least two problems:

Figure 1: Jijo-2 robot is talking with a human user while it is navigating in an office corridor.

A: degradation of speech recognition performance due to larger vocaburary

B: composition of semantics from many fragmented utterances, some of which are often omitted.

For **A**, we have employed the following techniques:

1. Multiple microphone array to extract clean voice signal even in noisy offices

2. Multiple voice recognizer processes employing different dictionaries and grammars to allow selection of the most plausible interpretation according to contexts.

The problem **B** is important to make Japanese conversation natural. Even a simple schedule registration can become fairly long, for example, "Matsui, a member of Jijo-2 group, will join a meeting in the main building from 3 to 5 tomorrow". We cannot expect every user to speak such a long sentence in one breath. A natural utterance is usually very short and total meaning is conveyed as a series of utterances. A shorter utterance is also preferred because of its better chances of being correctly recognized. In order to compose

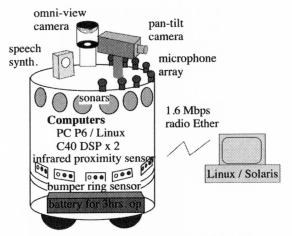

Figure 2: Hardware configuration of Jijo-2.

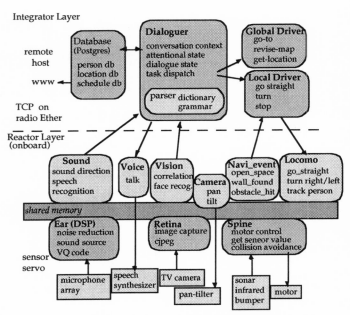

Figure 3: Organization of software modules of Jijo-2.

a complete meaning from fragmented utterances, we introduced the *dialogue context*, which is a kind of frame.

Once we allow split of a long sentence into several short utterances, another problem comes in: natural Japanese has an obvious tendency to omit subject, object, or any pronouns from an utterance whenever it is clear from context. To cope with this problem, we incorporated the *attentional state manager* to understand under-specified statements.

The major topic of this paper is the implementation of the Japanese dialogue subsystem in the *Jijo-2* office mobile robot designed to utilize robot's navigation and database connectivities. The paper is organized to reflect the order in which the dialogue components are used to recognize an underspecified human utterance in a noisy environment, assemble a semantic representation, and finally perform the required behaviors.

Overview of the Jijo-2 Architecture

Jijo-2 is based on the Nomad 200 mobile robot platform manufactured by *Nomadic Inc.* It is equipped with various sensors such as ultrasonic range sensors, infrared proximity sensors, tactile sensors, and an odometric sensor (Figure 2). The on-board computer is a PC running Linux and connected to a LAN through radio Ethernet. We added a microphone array, two CCD color cameras, digital signal processors (DSP) for processing sound signal, and a Japanese speech synthesizer "Shaberimbo".

On the robot and the remote host we have implemented several software modules for navigation and dialogue (Asoh et al. 1996; Matsui, Asoh, and Hara 1997). The overall structure of modules including *reactor modules* and *integrator modules* is depicted in Figure 3. The integrator modules are implemented in *EusLisp*, an object oriented Lisp for robot control (Matsui and Hara 1995), and reactor modules are in C for the sake of realtime control. The modules are managed in an event-driven architecture and realize both reactive and deliberative behaviors (Matsui, Asoh, and Hara 1997). Communication between modules takes place over TCP/IP connections. Major advantages of this event-driven multi-

agent architecture are implementation of concurrent behaviors (Figure 1) and plug-and-play of software modules.

Dialog System

Sound Input with Beam-Forming

In order for the *Jiio-2* to conduct smooth dialogue in real environments, dynamic noise suppression to keep a good speech recognition performance is needed. We applied a microphone array composed of eight omni-directional microphones around the top tray of the robot. Sound from a speaker arrives at each microphone with different delays. Sound signal at each microphone is digitized and fed to the first DSP (TI-C44). Based upon the delay-and-sum beam forming method (Johnson and Dungeon 1993), the direction to the sound source is computed, which is then used to form a beam to pick up the speech and reduce the ambient noises. We observe noise reduces approximately by 10dB at 3000Hz, which is crucial to the recognition of consonants. Figure 4 shows our multi-microphone system can keep relatively good performance even in noisy environments compared with a single microphone system.

Japanese Speech Recognition

The noise-clean digital sound data is sent to the second DSP through the DMA-driven communication port. The second DSP does the frequency analysis and emits the vector quantization code (VQ code) for each phonetic element every 10 ms. The VQ codes are sent to the on-board PC through a serial link.

The continuous speaker-independent Japanese speech rec-

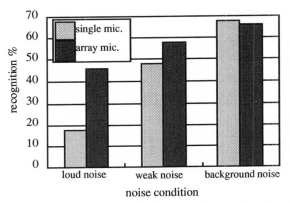

Figure 4: Speech recognition performance of multi-microphone array in various noise conditions.

ognizer, called *NINJA*, is a HMM-based system developed at our laboratory (Itou et al. 1993). Using a phonetic dictionary created by the HMM learning beforehand, the *NINJA* searches for a series of word symbols that satisfy a grammar. Thus, the speech recognition module produces a list of symbols such as, *(hello), (right to turn), (straight to go), (here is Matsui s office)*, etc., together with a recognition confidence value and a direction angle to the sound source (Note that objects precede verbs in Japanese).

Since the audio beam forming, VQ-code generation, and speech recognition are performed by the pipelined multiprocessors, the total recognition finishes almost in real-time. The greater part of a latency is brought by the pause for 0.4 second to identify the end of an utterance.

When the robot starts up, three speech recognition processes begin execution. Each recognizer handles one grammar, i.e. *reply* grammar, *location* grammar, and *full* grammar. The dialogue manager in the integrator layer chooses one grammar at a time. When a yes-or-no reply is expected, the *reply* grammar is activated. When location/person names are expected, the *location* grammar is invoked. Otherwise, the *full* grammar is used. This scheme has proven useful in raising the success rate of recognition.

Parsing

The grammar employed by the speech recognition roughly has the following descriptions:

```
sentence:       greeting
sentence:       imperative
sentence:       declarative
imperative:     action
imperative:     action please
action:         motion
action:         direction to motion
direction:      RIGHT
direction:      LEFT
     . . .
```

Phonetic representations of the terminal symbols like RIGHT and LEFT are given separately in lexicon definition descriptions. These representations can be interpreted

as not only deductive rules that expand to instances of acceptable sentences, but also as inductive rules that resolve word lists to sentences. The speech recognizer reports a list of terminal symbols that are resolved to a sentence. If we trace the resolution again, we can get intermediate symbols, namely direction, action, etc., which are used to represent meanings of word groups.

Therefore, we programmed the Lisp parser to employ the same grammar for generating semantics. This eliminated a duplicated definition of the grammar, since a single grammar representation could be used both for recognition and form semantics analysis. Since the grammar is relatively simple and a list of word tokens given to the parser has already been qualified as a sentence, the parsing finishes almost in real-time. The Lisp parser produces the semantics of the following form:

```
(greeting hello)
(imperative    :action turn
               :direction right)
(imperative    :action goto
               :destination matsui
               :via corner)
(interrogative :person matsui
               :question location)
```

Dialogue States

Jijo-2's dialogue manager traverses between several dialogue states. The state transition diagram is depicted in Figure 5. The states are used to restrict the possible utterances to which *Jijo-2* reacts. For example, to begin a conversation, a user must say "hello" before any other statements. In the confirmation state, *Jijo-2* only listens to "yes" or "no".

This state transition network is needed to eliminate spurious utterances that are often generated as noises in an office. For example, we do not want an idle robot to react suddenly in response to people's occasional laughter near the robot. This state transition is also used to choose the most appro-

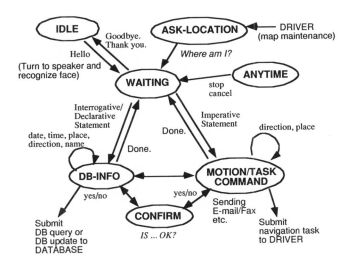

Figure 5: Dialogue states and transitions.

priate dictionary and grammar for the next speech recognition.

Commands like *stop* and *cancel* are recognized in any state. Obviously, *stop* should have the highest priority in any dialogue for safety reasons. As Bernsen (Bernsen, Dybkjoer, and Dybkjoer 1997) suggests, every practical spoken dialogue system should provide meta-commands to control conversation itself to make it robust and natural.

Dialogue Contexts

Each utterance of a human user only gives a fraction of information. For example, although "Turn" is a complete imperative sentence, the robot does not know which way to turn. In order to keep track of a series of relevant utterances and to construct semantics for a robot's behavior, we use the *dialogue context*.

Currently, we define five contexts: *query-context, update-context, identification-context, navigation-context*, and *call-context*. A context is defined to hold a number of required info and optional info as property variables of a *EusLisp* object. For example, a *query-context* that is created when an interrogative sentence is heard requires *person* property, and has *location, start-time*, and *end-time* as optional properties.

A conversation is guided to fulfill the required property by giving appropriate questions and confirmations. Optional properties may either be given in the utterance, assumed from the attentional state as described in the next section, or assumed by predefined default. For example, "a business trip" assumes the destination to be "Tokyo" unless it is explicitly spoken.

The state transition network is programmed in Prolog implemented in EusLisp.

Slot Filling by Managing Attentional States

A semantic representation of each utterance is given to the *dialogue manager* (Figure 6). The dialogue manager maintains an attentional state which indicates the relative salience of discourse referents (the individuals, objects, events, etc). Currently the attentional state is implemented as a total ordering. The function of the dialogue manager is to exploit the attentional state in order to accomplish (1) processing of under-specified input (information "unpackaging") and (2) natural-sounding language generation (information "packaging"). Though we have already shown the mechanism to control attentional states in *Jijo-2* (Fry, Asoh, and Matsui 1998), key points are summarized in the following subsections.

Japanese zero pronouns. In Japanese the problem of under-specified input is acute because in general the subject, object or any other argument to the verb is omitted from an utterance whenever it is clear from context. For example, the word "todokete" by itself is a well-formed Japanese sentence, even though its English translation "deliver!" is not. The missing arguments in Japanese are referred to as *zero pronouns* because of the analogy to the use of anaphoric pronouns in English. Thus the Japanese request *todokete*

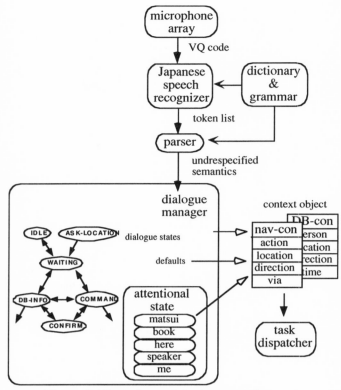

Figure 6: Flow of speech input processing.

corresponds roughly to the English request *(won't you) deliver this (to him)*.

Centering. To attack the zero pronoun ambiguity problem in a principled way we turned to the technique of *centering* (Grosz, Joshi, and Weinstein 1995). Centering is used for modeling discourse and for predicting the antecedents of pronouns based on the principle that the more salient an entity is in the discourse, the more likely it is to be pronominalized by a speaker. The centering model is broadly language-independent. The main language-dependent parameter is the criteria for ranking the salience of discourse referents.

For Japanese, we adopted the saliency ranking proposed by Walker et al. (Walker, Iida, and Cote 1994), given in Table 1. This ranking is based mainly on syntactic function, which in Japanese is indicated explicitly by post-positional particles such as *wa* and *ga* rather than by word-order position as in English. This ranking also takes into account empathy, or the perspective from which a speaker describes an event, which is an important feature of Japanese.

Language generation. In order to achieve the kind of natural-sounding dialogue, *Jijo-2* should also be able to *generate* speech output that takes into account the current dialogue context. The robot will sound awkward if it explicitly repeats the topic and subject of each sentence, or if it fails to use intonational stress to highlight newly-introduced discourse entities. For example, the highest-ranking entity in the attentional state usually does not need to be mentioned explicitly once it is established, so *Jijo-2* omits it from its spoken output.

1	Topic (marked by *wa*)
2	Empathy (marked by certain verbs)
3	Subject (marked by *ga*)
4	Indirect Object (marked by *ni*)
5	Direct Object (marked by *wo*)
6	Others (adjuncts, etc.)

Table 1: Predicted salience of entities

Integration with Database, Navigation, and Vision

Jijo-2 is an integrated robot that makes dialogue to provide services combined with its navigation and sensing capabilities. When all required slots in a context object are filled and confirmation is taken, the dialogue module tries to execute a task making use of these capabilities.

Database Behaviors

If the current context is a *query-context* or *update-context*, the task is dispatched to the *database* module. Normally, a response is immediate and the dialoguer can pronounce the result for the query or update task. If it takes long, the user may want to start another conversation, which is properly handled by the dialogue module, since the modules are all running concurrently in an event-driven manner. The database about people's schedule and location is implemented on a *postgres* server, which also provides web-based access. Therefore, once a dialogue about a user's schedule updates the database, the information is made available to public access.

Navigation Dialogue

For *navigation-* or *call-context*, the task is dispatched to the *driver* module. The map is maintained in the *driver* module, although it is learned through dialogue. Therefore, a situation where the dialogue module commands the driver to go to someone's office, but the driver does not know how to reach there, can happen. In this case, the *driver* module requests the *dialogue* module to ask for navigation instructions. During a navigation, the *driver* might encounter an unexpected landmark, which is usually a *close-to-open* event (an open space is found) from the sonar. This also leads the dialogue module to conduct a conversation to confirm the location.

Jijo-2 can continue dialogue while it navigates in a corridor. If the dialogue can be handled within the module or with the database like a query about the current date and time, it is locally processed without interfering with the navigation. But, of course, if the dialogue contains commands to stop navigation and to change destination, the dialogue module retracts the current command to the driver and restarts another behavior.

Face Recognition

Currently, the *Jijo-2's* vision system is used to look for a human user and to identify the person. When *Jijo-2* hears "hello" while it is in the waiting state, it turns to the sound source direction, and invokes the skin color detector. Moving the pan-tilter, the vision module tries to locate a human face at the center of the view. Then the face recognizer module is invoked.

The face recognizer is based upon higher order local correlation (Kurita et al. 1998). The vision module memorizes a face as a feature vector of 105 dimensions after taking at least as many shots of training images. For a particular sample image, it can tell the most plausible person name by computing distances to preobtained feature vectors in the discriminant analysis space. If the recognition succeeds, the vision module can provide the person's name to be inserted as the speaker's name in the attentional state stack of the dialogue manager.

Example Dialogue and Behavior

Figure 7 illustrates two patterns of dialogue between human users and *Jijo-2* involving several different behaviors.

Dialogue (a) is composed of simple motion commands. *Jijo-2* rotates its body by the *turn* command, and pans the camera by the *look-at* command. Though direction keyword is required for both, *Jijo-2* can assume it simply from the previous utterance.

Dialogue (b) begins with "hello", which makes *Jijo-2* turn to the person's direction. Then the robot captures the face image to recognize the person. If the recognition succeeds, the robot can know the speaker's name, which is then used to exclude misunderstandings in dialogue such as a command to send email to the speaker.

When the user asks *Asoh-san wa doko* (*Where is Mr. Asoh?*), Mr. Asoh is established as the topic of the dialogue, and therefore as the most salient entity in the attentional state. The answer given by *Jijo-2* is the under-specified response *Honkan ni imasu* (*(he) is in the main building*). Because it pronominalizes the current topic, this response is smooth and natural-sounding Japanese.

In the next sentence, the subject and indirect object of the verb *yonde* are omitted by the speaker in favor of zero pronouns. In this case, the most salient antecedent, which is Mr. Asoh, is found as the suitable referent. The *call-context* proposes sending an email message to Mr. Asoh. In the following sentences, other under-specified utterances are given appropriate antecedents or default values.

This inference for referents is not only useful to make Japanese dialogue natural and speedy, but also to attain the better speech recognition.

Performance Evaluation

Evaluating the performance and user-friendliness of integrated systems combined with human factors like Jijo-2 is a difficult problem. Except for the microphone array system,

H1(Matsui): Kon-nichiwa. (Hello.)
R: *turn to the sound's direction, locate the person's face,
      and recognize.*
      Konnichiwa, Matsui-san. (Hello, Matsui.)
H1:   Asoh-san wa doko? (Where is Asoh?)
R: Honkan ni imasu. ([He is] in the main building.)
H1:   Yonde kudasai. (Please call [him].)
R: Asoh-san ni me-ru wo okurimashouka?
      (Shall I send E-mail to him?)
H1:   Hai. (Yes.)
H1:   Motomura-san wa ? ([Where is] Motomura ?)
R: Office ni imasu. ([He is] in [his] office.)
H1:   Tsureteitte kudasai. (Please take me [to his place].)
R: Motomura-san no heya ni yukimasu.
      ([I'll] go to Motomura's office.)
      plan the path to the office, and execute the plan
R: Motomura-san no tokoro ni tsukimashita.
      ([We are] at Motomura's office.)
H2(Motomrua): Shokuji ni demasu.
      ([I'm] going out for lunch.)
R: Motomura-san wa shokuji de yoroshii desu ka?
      (Is Motomura going out for lunch ?)
H2:   Hai. (Yes.)
R: Schedule wo toroku shimasu.
      ([I'll] register [the data] to the database.)
H1:   Matsui mo. (Matsui, too.)
R: Matsui-san wa shokuji de yoroshii desu ka?
      (Is Matsui going out for lunch ?)
H1:   Hai. (Yes.)
R: schedule wo toroku shimasu.
      ([I'll] registrate [the data] to the database.)

(b) Zero pronoun filling in navigation and database tasks.
Words in brackets are assumed.

Figure 7: Sample office dialogues

quantitative evaluation has not thoroughly been done because of the difficulty of controlling environment for fair
comparisons. Here we just describe a qualitative evaluation
from our demonstrations. Detailed quantitative evaluations
should be done in the future.

Since we began building *Jijo-2*, we have demonstrated it
more than 50 times to various visitors (Matsui and Jijo-2
Group 1999). In each demonstration, we made similar conversations as shown in Figure 7, and were guided from an
office to another by the robot. Roughly speaking, 90% of
demonstrations have been successful. During a demo, 10 to
20% of utterances were misunderstood in average. How-

ever, because possible actions taken in a particular dialogue
state is limited and a confirmation is needed for a big task,
the system did not go into a disaster. When the robot made
a mistake, we could safely restart behaviors by canceling
the improper actions and repeating a desired command.

The microphone array is proven effective to eliminate ambient noises at ordinary level. The speech recognition is
confused mostly by unclear pronunciation or big noise, for
example, loud laughter of visitors.

Related Work

Dialogue with a robot is a very old topic of artificial intelligence, going back to Nilsson's classic SHAKEY robot in
the 1960s (Nilsson 1969). The influential SHRDLU system
(Winograd 1972) also took the form of a dialogue with a
robot. SHRDLU relied on syntactic analysis and was able
to overcome ambiguity and understand pronoun references.
Its success was due in large part to its restricted domain in
the blocks world. More recently, Torrance investigated natural communication with a mobile robot (Torrance 1994), and
Hashimoto et al. developed humanoid robots with dialogue
capability (Hashimoto et al. 1997). Shibata et al. (Shibata
et al. 1997) resolve ambiguities in route descriptions in natural language, using spatial relationships between the elements
of the route. Horswill(Horswill 1995) integrated a simplified SHRDLU-like language processing system with a
real-time vision system. These modern systems use language as a tool for interacting with the robot but are not
particularly concerned with the principled application of linguistic or discourse theories.

Takeda et al. (Takeda et al. 1997) are realizing a dialog
system for a mobile robot based on structured ontological
knowledge and standard multi-agent architecture. In addition to dialog with a real robot, dialog with a simulated CG
agent are also investigated recently (Hasegawa et al. 1993;
Nagao and Takeuchi 1992).

Outstanding points of our system compared with these previous works are integration with mobile robot behaviors and
a database to provide actual office services, and mechanisms
to improve the robustness and quality of natural language
spoken dialogue in real office situations.

Conclusion and Future Work

In order for a mobile robot to achieve natural Japanese conversation covering wider office task repertoire, we introduced
four elemental techniques: 1) a microphone array, 2) multiple dictionaries, 3) dialog contexts, and 4) attentional states.
1) and 2) were proven to be effective for making speech
recognition robuster in noisy environment. 3) and 4) enabled to form semantic frames for several kinds of tasks from
fragmented utterances. The latter two also contributed to
facilitate speech recognition and to make the dialog more
natural for Japanese.

Based on these techniques we could successfully implement route guidance and database query tasks as well as

dialogue-driven topological map learning. To build a truly intelligent artificial creature, one cannot rely on a single information source. By integrating the sound source detector and the face recognizer with the dialogue module, we were able to achieve a better user-friendliness (Matsui and Jijo-2 Group 1999).

An important future goal is dialogue conversed with more than one user. In such a situation, we cannot naively rely on word symbols obtained from the recognizer. Rather, we will have to incorporate capabilities to distinguish speakers using visual cues, directions of the voice, and even the difference of the voice. Such capabilities will be crucial in the next-generation office dialogue systems.

Acknowledgments

The research and development of *Jijo-2* at the RWI-Center is jointly supported by Electrotechnical Laboratory (ETL) and the Real World Computing Partnership (RWCP) of MITI, Japan.

References

Asoh, H., Motomura, Y., Matsui, T., Hayamizu, S., and Hara, I. 1996. Combining probabilistic map and dialogue for robust life-long office navigation. In *Proceedings of the 1996 IEEE/RSJ International Conference on Intelligent Rbots and Systems*, 807-812.

Bernsen, N. O., Dybkjoer, H., and Dybkjoer, L. 1997. What should your speech system say, *IEEE COMPUTER*, 30(12):25-30.

Fry, J., Asoh, H., and Matsui, T. 1998. Natural dialogue with the *Jijo-2* office robot. In *Proceedings of the 1998 IEEE/RSJ International Conference on Intelligent Robots and Systems*, 1278-1283.

Grosz, B., Joshi, A., and Weinstein, S. 1995. Centering: A framework for modelling the local coherence of discourse. *Computational Linguistics*, 21(2): 203-225.

Hasegawa, O., Itou, K., Kurita, T., Hayamizu, S., Tanaka, K., Yamamoto, K., and Otsu, N. 1993. Active agent oriented multimodal interface system, In *Proceedings of the Fourteenth International Conference on Artificial Intelligence*, 82-87.

Hashimoto, S., et al. 1997. Humanoid Robot -Development of an Information Assistant Robot Hadaly, In Proceedings of the 6th IEEE International Workshop on Robot and Human Communication, RO-MAN'97.

Horswill, I. 1995. Integrating Vision and Natural Language without Central Models, In *Proceedings of the AAAI Fall Symposium on Embodied Language and Action*, Cambridge.

Itou, K., Hayamizu, S., Tanaka, K., and Tanaka, H. 1993. System design, data collection and evaluation of a speech dialogue system. *IEICE Transactions on Information and Systems*, E76-D:121-127.

Johnson, D. H. and Dugeon, D. E. 1993. *Array Signal Processing*, Prentice Hall, Englewood Clifs, NJ.

Kurita, T., et al. 1998. Scale and rotation invariant recognition method using higher-order local autocorrelation features of log-polar images, In *Proceedings of the third Asian Conference on Computer Vision*, Vol.II, 89-96.

Matsui, T., Asoh, H., and Hara, I. 1997. An event-driven architecture for controlling behaviors of the office conversant mobile robot *Jijo-2*. In *Proceedings of the1997 IEEE International Conference on Robotics and Automation*, 3367-3371.

Matsui, T., and Hara, I. 1995. *EusLisp Reference Manual Ver.8.00*, Technical Report, ETL-TR-95-2, Electro-technical Laboratory.

Matsui, T., and *Jijo-2* Group. 1999. *Jijo-2* Project Web home pages, http://www.etl.go.jp/~7440/.

Nagao, K., Takeuchi, A. 1994. Social interaction: multimodal conversation with social agents, In *Proceedings of the Twelfth National Conference on Artificial Intelligence*, 22-28.

Nilsson, N. 1969. A mobile automaton: an application of artificial intelligence techniques. In *Proceedings of the First International Joint Conference on Artificial Intelligence*, 509-520.

Shibata, F., Ashida, M., Kakusho, K., and Kitahashi, T. 1997. Communication of a symbolic route description based on landmarks between a human and a robot. In *Proceedings of the 11th Annual Conference of Japanese Society for Artificiall Intelligence*, 429-432 (in Japanese).

Takeda, H., Kobayashi, N., Matsubara, Y., and Nishida, T. 1997. Towards ubiquitous human-robot interaction. In *Working Notes for IJCAI-97 Workshop on Intelligent Multimodal Systems*, 1-8.

Torrance, M. 1994. *Natural Communication with Robots*, Masters Thesis, Massatusetts Institute of Technology.

Walker, M., Iida, M., and Cote, S. 1994. Japanese discourse and the process of centering. *Computational Linguistics*, 20(2):193-233.

Winograd, T. 1972. *Understanding Natural Language*, Academic Press.

Gesture-Based Interaction with a Pet Robot

Milyn C. Moy

MIT Artificial Intelligence Lab / Oracle Corporation
500 Oracle Parkway
Redwood Shores, CA 94065
milyn@ai.mit.edu

Abstract

Pet robots are autonomous robots capable of exhibiting animal-like behaviors, including emotional ones, as they interact with people and objects surrounding them. As pet robots become more integrated into our lives, a more natural way of communicating with them will become necessary. Similarly, they will need to understand human gestures in order to perceive our intentions and communicate with us more effectively. In this paper, we present an extensible, real-time, vision-based communication system that interprets 2D dynamic hand gestures in complex environments. Our strategy for interpreting hand gestures consists of: hand segmentation, feature extraction, and gesture recognition. To segment the hand from the cluttered background, this system uses both motion and color information. The location of the hand is subsequently tracked as the user makes the gesture and its trajectory information is stored in a feature vector. Finally, the gesture is interpreted using this vector and translated into a command that the robot understands. We implemented our system on Yuppy, a pet robot prototype. Currently, via an external microcamera, we can navigate Yuppy in unstructured environments using hand gestures.

Introduction

As pet robots become more integrated into our everyday lives, it will become essential for them to perceive and understand our intentions and actions. We will also want to communicate with them as we do with other human beings. Yet, to communicate and interact with robots, we are still required to use specialized input devices such as keyboards, mice, trackers, or data gloves (Zimmerman & Lanier 1987). Thus, a more natural, contact-less interface would be desirable to avoid the need for external devices.

An example of such an interface is speech (Huang, Ariki, & Jack 1990). However, when we communicate with each other, we also use gestures, facial expressions, and poses as supplements or substitutes for speech.

Clearly, pet robots would perceive our intentions and communicate with us more effectively if they were able to interpret human gestures and body language.

One of the most expressive components of body language is hand gesture. We use our hands to explore objects and to express our ideas and our feelings. Thus, hand gestures provide a very natural interface for us to communicate with robots.

Recently, there has been a significant amount of research on hand gesture recognition. The two most common approaches are model-based and feature-based. Model-based approaches assume a physically valid model of the hand and attempt to recognize a gesture as a variation of the hand articulation, using techniques such as template matching (Heap & Hogg 1996; Rehg & Kanade 1994) and neural networks (Nowlan & Platt 1995). Similarly, a 3D model of a human has been used to guide stereo measurements of body parts for human-robot interaction (Kortenkamp, Huber, & Bonasso 1996). Model-based approaches generally suffer from being computationally expensive due to the need for high resolution images to ensure accurate segmentation, and the need to cope with variations in intensity, scale, orientation, and deformation.

Feature-based approaches do not assume a 3D model of the hand but instead use low-level image features. Some examples are the use of Hidden Markov Models (HMMs) (Yamato, Ohya, & Ishii 1992), a view-based approach with dynamic time warping (Darrell & Pentland 1993), and the trajectory analysis of hand gestures coupled with speech recognition for controlling a mobile robot (Perzanowski, Schultz, & Adams 1998) among others. These methods may be more suitable for real-time gesture recognition since low-level image features can be computed quickly, but they require an effective segmentation of the hand from the input images.

Accurate segmentation of the hand from the background is difficult. For this reason, some researchers have controlled the imaging conditions using special backgrounds (Darrell & Pentland 1993; Rehg & Kanade 1994), static backgrounds with background subtraction (Appenzeller, Lee, & Hashimoto 1997; Dang 1996), or special markers or colored gloves (Starner, Weaver, & Pentland 1998; Hienz, Grobel, & Offner 1996) to simplify the segmentation task. However, these systems are not flexible enough for most real world applications.

A combination of motion and color detection has been used (Appenzeller, Lee, & Hashimoto 1997; Kahn *et al.* 1996) to eliminate these constraints. Limitations still exist in the their use because they are prone to also detect shadows of moving objects and similarly colored objects. But, by using these two cues together, the false-positives are considerably reduced, making this a more flexible approach for hand segmentation.

This paper focuses on the real-time, visual interpretation of 2D dynamic hand gestures in complex environments. Our goal is to enable humans to communicate and interact with a pet robot in a more natural fashion. The scope of this work is not to create a full lexicon system that will facilitate this interaction in every possible way, but to provide an extensible mechanism to enable the recognition of new gestures.

The next section of this paper presents an overview of the system. The following sections explain the different modules of our system: hand segmentation, feature extraction, and gesture recognition. Then, the results of our experiments are discussed. Finally, the conclusion and the future work are provided in the last section.

Overview

The test bed for this system is an emotional pet robot called Yuppy (Figure 1), currently being developed at the MIT Artificial Intelligence Laboratory. This robot is built on top of a 12 inch synchrodrive base and is equipped with various sensors to increase its awareness of the environment and allow for better interaction with humans. Although this robot is meant to be fully autonomous, all perception and control code for this work temporarily run off-board on a 300 MHz Pentium Pro workstation. For development purposes an external and uncalibrated, wide-angle lens Chinon CX-062 color microcamera was used, similar to the ones on Yuppy.

Figure 1: Yuppy: An emotional pet robot

A precise "language" with a grammar is needed in human to human communication and some researchers

have worked on recognizing American Sign Languages (Starner, Weaver, & Pentland 1998; Dorner 1993). Nevertheless, a small set of gestures that is easy to use and understand will suffice to specify commands to pets. The initial goal of this system is to enable humans to direct the robot using hand gestures; thus, the lexicon chosen consists of a simple set of basic 2D gesture classes or primitive gestures (Figure 2) that can be done with a single hand in the direction of the arrow. They include linear (vertical, horizontal, and diagonal) as well as circular (clockwise and counterclockwise) gestures. Each gesture class allows for variations in the speed of the hand's motion, different ranges of hand motions, and small deviations (orientation, translation) in the trajectory of the hand's motion.

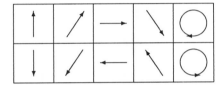

Figure 2: Primitive Gestures

Our strategy for interpreting hand gestures consists of the following three phases:

1. Segment the gesturing hand from the input images using motion and color information and track it in real-time.

2. Store the hand's trajectory information in a feature vector.

3. Interpret the user's gesture using the feature vector and issue a command for the robot to perform the desired task.

We begin with a detailed discussion of the hand segmentation, followed by the feature extraction and gesture recognition phases.

Hand Segmentation

Hand gesture recognition requires the ability to accurately segment the hand from the cluttered background. To achieve real-time performance and robustness to complex backgrounds, we use a segmentation algorithm based on motion and color information. We currently assume that users wear long-sleeved clothes and the robot is static while observing the gesture.

Motion Detection

The most common method for detecting motion is optical flow, which estimates the relative motion by means of temporal variations of the brightness pattern (Horn 1986). However, this method is slow in the absence of specialized hardware.

Another common alternative is to use image differencing. This method determines the edges of the moving components, and can be computed very fast by taking the difference between corresponding pixel values of two subsequent images and selecting the pixels that pass a certain threshold. However, it also includes in the result pixels of the background which were covered in the previous frame. To improve this method, we use the image difference of three sequential images (I_{t-2}, I_{t-1}, I_t) by taking the pixelwise difference between the RGB (Red, Green, Blue) representations of the last two and the first two images and selecting the pixels that satisfy the following condition:

$$|I_t - I_{t-1}| > \theta \text{ and } |I_{t-1} - I_{t-2}| > \theta$$

where I_t is an image frame taken at time t and θ is a threshold. This method can fail in the presence of shadows because they move with the entities that create them, but we solved this problem using color.

Color Detection

The use of color as a basis for skin segmentation has several advantages. First, human skin colors tend to cluster in color space (Yang, Lu, & Waibel 1997) due to their richness in red tones. Second, color is faster to process compared to other hand features. Third, it is orientation invariant in the 2D image plane, assuming that the image intensity is invariant between adjacent image frames. Despite these advantages, deviations in the color representation can occur due to changes in the lighting conditions, specular reflections, motion, and nonlinearities introduced by the camera and the frame grabber. However, by choosing the right color space, these deviations can be reduced.

Simple RGB and normalized RGB ($r = \frac{R}{R+G+B}$, $g = \frac{G}{R+G+B}$, $b = \frac{B}{R+G+B}$) thresholding are commonly used methods (Scheile & Waibel 1995), but they are not very robust to different skin tonalities and lighting conditions. We use the HLS (Hue, Lightness, and Saturation) color model, a linear transform of the RGB space. By disregarding the lightness component and using appropriately defined domains of hue and saturation, robustness to changes in illumination and shadows can be achieved (Saxe & Foulds 1996).

To obtain bounds for the hue and saturation of human skin color we used an a priori model of skin color. We plotted different skin tonalities under different lighting conditions in HS space. Under any given lighting condition, a skin-color distribution can be characterized by a multivariate normal distribution (Yang, Lu, & Waibel 1997). Thus, the thresholds for hue and saturations ($H_{min}, H_{max}, S_{min}, S_{max}$) were obtained by determining an area (typically two standard deviations) around the mean values of H and S. For efficiency in computation, a simple square representation in HS space is used; thus, a pixel or color pair (h, s) in this space is skin-colored if it passes the following condition:

$$(H_{min} < h < H_{max}) \text{ and } (S_{min} < s < S_{max})$$

As the gesture is made, a sequence of RGB images (100x100 pixels) is taken by the frame grabber and processed in real-time on a frame by frame basis. We currently run our algorithms in a user-specified window of attention which excludes the user's face.

In our system, motion detection is computationally less expensive than skin color detection, so it is applied to the images first, to constrain the search for skin color to moving regions only. Initially three images (I_{t-2}, I_{t-1}, I_t) are obtained from the frame grabber and processed independently by both the motion and the skin-color detectors. Motion is detected by taking the image difference of these three images. The result is stored in a binary image, I_m. To speed up the skin-color detection, we also compute a bounding box that surrounds all moving components.

The HLS representation of I_{t-1} (this image reflects the moving components as a result of the image differencing) is then used to determine the skin-colored patches inside the bounding box. The result is stored in a binary image, I_c, where 1 indicates skin color and 0 other colors. This binary image is smoothed and an 8-neighbor connected components algorithm is used to cluster each skin-colored region.

After the initial processing on the input images, the results of the motion and skin-color detection are combined by superimposing I_c on I_m. For each skin-colored region in I_c, a bounding box is placed around the moving pixels, to obtain a moving skin-colored region. The regions with very few moving pixels (noise) are discarded because they are usually similarly colored objects (e.g. a pink chair, a light-pink phone) in the image's background. The others are passed through function f which segments the hand based on the size of the skin-color region and the amount of motion within it:

$$f(moving\_pixels, skincolored\_pixels) = c_1 * moving\_pixels + c_2 * skincolored\_pixels$$

where c_1 and c_2 are constants that determine the weight each detector is given in segmenting the hand. This function allows the flexibility of adding new detectors to the system as well as using probability instead of a simple score to segment the hand.

The hand is chosen to be the region with the highest score (i.e. the skin-colored region that has the largest area and the greatest number of displaced pixels). The hand's centroid is determined and its motion is tracked in real-time as new image frames are processed. If little motion is detected or the area of the moving skin-colored region with the highest score is very small, the previously computed centroid is reused. Similarly, if the Euclidean distance between the hand's centroid of the previous image frame and the current centroid does not exceed a certain threshold, the current centroid is considered the new location of the hand; otherwise, the previous centroid is kept.

An illustration of the hand segmentation is shown in Figure 3. Image (a) shows the last image frame taken by the camera as the person makes the gesture in front of the robot. The bounding box delimits the attention window where gestures are recognized. Image (b) shows the results of the image differencing and the bounding box surrounding the moving components. Image (c) shows skin-colored areas inside the bounding box, including the pink chair in the background. Image (d) shows all the moving skin-color regions. The gesturing hand is selected from among these regions and displayed in image (e). Finally, a crosshair is drawn on the centroid of the hand in image (a).

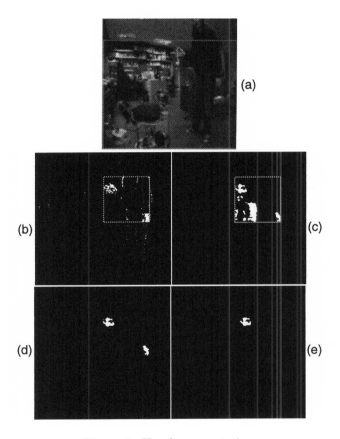

Figure 3: Hand segmentation

Feature Extraction

The information about the hand's trajectory needs to be encapsulated in a representation that can be used to identify the appropriate gesture. To achieve this, we need to first determine the beginning and the end of a gesture. The capability of determining when a gesture ends and a new one begins is called gesture segmentation and is a major problem in gesture recognition.

Different approaches have been taken by the research community to solve the segmentation problem. External devices have been used (e.g. clicking and releasing a mouse button (Rubine 1991)), but the need for these devices is cumbersome and unnatural. A fixed starting posture for each gesture (Baudel & Beaudouin-Lafon 1993) is not scalable because every gesture needs to have a different starting posture. The use of hand tension was proposed by (Harling & Edwards 1996), but it does not work on a sequence of dynamic gestures. This problem can be solved by using HMMs given that segmentation between gestures is done during the recognition process. Nevertheless, HMMs are very difficult to use because of their demanding training phase.

Our system assumes that once the hand's motion exceeds a certain velocity, the person has started a gesture. As the hand moves, the vertical and horizontal displacements (dx, dy) of the hand's centroid in the image space are calculated and stored in a feature vector until the hand stops moving for a short period of time (usually 2-3 seconds).

Gesture Recognition

In human communication, gestures are accompanied by attitudes and emotions. Thus, being able to recognize these attributes along with the type of gesture made would be desirable. We provide a gesture recognition system that is capable of interpreting a very important gesture attribute – its speed.

Gesture interpretation is achieved by analyzing the feature vector created from the hand's trajectory. In the case of linear gestures, the (dx, dy) displacements cluster around fixed axes in the dx-dy plane: vertical gestures around the dy axis, horizontal gestures around the dx axis, and diagonal gestures around the two bisecting axes (45° with respect to the dx-dy axes). The direction of motion is determined by the side of the axis (positive/negative) on which clustering occurs (e.g., vertical upward gestures have (dx, dy) clustering around the positive side of dy, and vertical downward gestures cluster around the negative side of the dy axis). Hence the (dx, dy) displacements for the 8 linear primitive gestures cluster in 8 distinct regions of the plane. The centroid of such a cluster, along with the origin of the dx-dy plane, determines a velocity vector whose magnitude indicates the speed of the gesture.

For circular gestures, however, the (dx, dy) displacements are spread in the plane. If the centroid of these displacements coincides with the origin, we conclude that the gesture is circular. The direction of motion (clockwise/counterclockwise) is deduced from the time sequence of the displacements in the feature vector.

First, the feature vector is scanned and any element that contains the same set of signs for both dx and dy as the previous element in the vector is discarded. The result of this operation is that neighboring elements in the vector have different signs for dx and dy. Second, the signs of every sequence of four (dx, dy) pairs are compared with a time-sequence model for the clockwise motion $(- +, + +, + -, - -)$ and counterclockwise motion $(+ +, - +, - -, + -)$. The sequences reflect the hand's trajectory in time on the dx-dy plane. The direction of the circular gesture results from the time-sequence model that matches the feature vector's information.

Each primitive is assigned a label that distinguishes it from other primitives. After determining the basic gesture made by the user through the analysis of the feature vector, this information is represented in a more compact way, using a descriptor. The descriptor of a gesture is an array that contains as its only element the label of the identified primitive.

Model gestures are stored in a database containing user-specified model gestures and their corresponding meanings or commands for the pet robot (e.g., a circular clockwise motion commands the robot to rotate in place clockwise). Gestures are stored as descriptors in the database. Once the descriptor produced from the user gesture is obtained, it is queried in the database. If such a gesture was found in the database, the command associated with the gesture is returned and issued to the robot; otherwise, the user gesture is ignored.

The simple gesture classes introduced above can be combined to create new ones, allowing for an extensible hand gesture recognition system. To segment these different primitives in one gesture, a hand pause is used between primitives. This pause is shorter than the one used for segmenting different gestures. When the gesture is composite, the feature vector contains the displacements of the hand's centroid for each primitive, separated by a marker. The descriptor for such a gesture will contain sequentially the different labels for each primitive in the composite gesture. This flexibility allows new gestures containing any number of primitives with new different meanings to be created and stored in the database as needed.

Experimental Results

To assess the accuracy of our system, we performed an initial experiment where 14 subjects with different skin tonalities (Asians, Caucasians, Hispanics, and Indians; Black subjects were not available) were asked to perform 5 times a sequence of 16 gestures shown in Figure 4. The environment was a crowded lab with a variety of objects spread throughout.

The accuracy rate obtained was above 90% for each primitive gesture class and slightly above 70% for composite gestures. These results demonstrate the viability of our system for unstructured environments and its robustness to different skin tonalities and varying lighting conditions. We used a commodity 300 MHz Pentium Pro system with a Matrox Meteor frame grabber, and achieved 15 frames per second (this includes processing and redrawing the frame on the computer screen). Although this speed is sufficient, higher performance can be obtained using faster hardware.

A variety of reasons explain why the obtained accuracy was not higher. First, we had slight distortions of diagonal motions due to the camera tilt, as well as tracking failures when the hand left the camera's field of view and when other bare parts of the user's body exhibited a lot of motion. Second, some subjects erred when making diagonal motions or composite gestures.

In other cases, the beginning of gestures was not detected when subjects started the motion too slowly. Third, the recognition success for composite gestures is geometrically dependent on the recognition of each one of its primitives. Lastly, the lower accuracy for composite gestures is largely due to them being less natural for humans, making it difficult for subjects to execute them correctly.

Gesture		Accuracy (%)	Gesture		Accuracy (%)
↑	front	100.0	↻	rotate-right	90.0
→	right	97.1	↺	rotate-left	95.7
↙	left-back	100.0	↑↓	calm-down	91.4
↗	right-front	98.6	↻↺	dance	80.0
↓	back	100.0	⇄	hi	82.9
↖	left-front	97.1	↻	make-square	72.9
↘	right-back	95.7	△	make-triangle	71.4
←	left	100.0	Ω	make-omega	80.0

Figure 4: Gestures accuracy $= \frac{\# \ of \ correct \ gestures}{\# \ of \ total \ gestures} = (14 \times 5) = 70$

Some of these problems are not practical concerns given that, when humans interact with a pet robot, they tend to be more cooperative. Humans position themselves close enough to the robot so that it can pay attention to them. They also make the gestures carefully, for the robot to understand them, and use the robot's behavior as feedback for improving the way they make the gestures. During the experiment, we observed how the gesture recognition's accuracy for most subjects improved as they obtained visual feedback.

Our system already allows people to interact with Yuppy in a more natural fashion. Yuppy's current interface consists of an off-board camera, via which any person can easily navigate the robot around the lab using each primitive gesture as a command (e.g., an upward hand motion commands the robot to go front, a clockwise circular motion commands the robot to rotate in place clockwise).

It is important for the robot to interpret correctly what the gestures mean and be able to respond to them accordingly, but 100% accuracy in gesture interpretation is not really necessary. Even communication between humans is sometimes ambiguous, and we expect the communication between humans and animals to be even more so. People expect objects to react immediately, predictably and consistently; however, they are more tolerant with humans and animals. Humans can accept that a pet robot might not have perceived or correctly interpreted the request; they expect and even prefer unpredictable behaviors from their pets.

Conclusion

We have presented a starting point toward understanding how vision can be used to recognize human gestures and provide a natural interface to enhance human-robot communication. Our system explored the use of fast algorithms and simple features to determine the hand's trajectory in real-time using commodity hardware.

Our system was tested on Yuppy, an emotional pet robot, and with the help of an off-board camera we were able to navigate the robot in unstructured environments using hand gestures. Initial evaluation of this system resulted in above 90% accuracy for recognition of single primitive gestures and above 70% for recognition of composite gestures, demonstrating the viability of our approach. But, we believe that better methods should be devised to further evaluate this behavioral system.

This work provides a basic interface for future behaviors implemented on Yuppy, such as approaching a person, searching for a bone, fetching the newspaper, etc. Future work will address additional competency in reliably differentiating the hand from other moving parts of the body and continuously tracking the motion of the hand, coping with simultaneous motion of both the robot and the human, and supporting simultaneous interaction of multiple people with the robot. A more general gesture recognition system would include the interpretation of hand poses and 3D gestures. We are also interested in gesture learning, the robot's reaction to both what it perceives and how it feels, and the interpretation of humans' attitudes and emotions implicit in their gestures.

Acknowledgments

Support for this research was provided by Yamaha Corporation under contract No. 65539. The author would like to thank Rodney Brooks for his continued support.

References

Appenzeller, G.; Lee, J.; and Hashimoto, H. 1997. Building topological maps by looking at people: An example of cooperation between intelligent spaces and robots. In *Proceedings of the IEEE-RSJ International Conference on Intelligent Robots and Systems*.

Baudel, T., and Beaudouin-Lafon, M. 1993. Charade: Remote control of objects using free-hand gestures. *Communications of the ACM* 36(7):28–35.

Dang, D. 1996. Template based gesture recognition. Master's thesis, MIT.

Darrell, T., and Pentland, A. 1993. Space-time gestures. In *Proceedings of the IEEE Conference on Computer Vision and Pattern Recognition*, 335–340.

Dorner, B. 1993. Hand shape identification and tracking for sign language interpretation. In *Proceedings of the IJCAI Workshop on Looking at People*, 75–88.

Harling, P., and Edwards, A. 1996. Hand tension as a gesture segmentation cue. In *Proceedings of the Progress in Gestural Interaction*.

Heap, T., and Hogg, D. 1996. Towards 3D hand tracking using a deformable model. In *Proceedings of the International Conference on Automatic Face and Gesture Recognition*, 140–145.

Hienz, H.; Grobel, K.; and Offner, G. 1996. Real-time hand-arm motion analysis using a single video camera. In *Proceedings of the International Conference on Automatic Face and Gesture Recognition*, 323–327.

Horn, B. 1986. *Robot Vision*. MIT Press.

Huang, X.; Ariki, Y.; and Jack, M. 1990. *Hidden Markov Models for Speech Recognition*. Edinburgh University Press.

Kahn, R. E.; Swain, M. J.; Prokopowicz, P. N.; and Firby, R. J. 1996. Gesture recognition using the perseus architecture. In *Proceedings of the IEEE Conference on Computer Vision and Pattern Recognition*.

Kortenkamp, D.; Huber, E.; and Bonasso, R. P. 1996. Recognizing and interpreting gestures on a mobile robot. In *Proceedings of the Thirteenth National Conference on Artificial Intelligence*, 915–921.

Nowlan, S., and Platt, J. C. 1995. A convolutional neural network hand tracker. In *Proceedings of Neural Information Processing Systems*, 901–908.

Perzanowski, D.; Schultz, A.; and Adams, W. 1998. Integrating natural language and gesture in a robotics domain. In *Proceedings of the IEEE International Symposium on Intelligent Control: ISIC/CIRA/ISIS Joint Conference*, 247–252.

Rehg, J., and Kanade, T. 1994. Visual tracking of high DOF articulated structures: An application to human hand tracking. In *Proceedings of the Third European Conference on Computer Vision*, 35–45.

Rubine, D. 1991. Specifying gestures by example. *Computer Graphics* 25(4):329–337.

Saxe, D., and Foulds, R. 1996. Toward robust skin identification in video images. In *Proceedings of the International Conference on Automatic Face and Gesture Recognition*, 379–384.

Scheile, B., and Waibel, A. 1995. Gaze tracking based on face color. In *Proceedings of the International Workshop on Automatic Face and Gesture Recognition*.

Starner, T.; Weaver, J.; and Pentland, A. 1998. A wearable computer based american sign language recognizer. In *Proceedings of the IEEE Transactions on Pattern Analysis and Machine Intelligence*.

Yamato, J.; Ohya, J.; and Ishii, K. 1992. Recognizing human action in time-sequential images using hidden markov models. In *Proceedings of the IEEE Conference on Computer Vision and Pattern Recongition*, 379–385.

Yang, J.; Lu, W.; and Waibel, A. 1997. Skin-color modeling and adaptation. Technical Report CMU-CS-97-146, Carnegie Mellon.

Zimmerman, T., and Lanier, J. 1987. A hand gesture interface device. In *ACM SIGCHI/GI*, 189–192.

Continuous Categories For a Mobile Robot

Michael T. Rosenstein and Paul R. Cohen
Department of Computer Science
University of Massachusetts
Amherst, MA 01003-4610
{mtr, cohen}@cs.umass.edu

Abstract

Autonomous agents make frequent use of knowledge in the form of categories — categories of objects, human gestures, web pages, and so on. This paper describes a way for agents to learn such categories for themselves through interaction with the environment. In particular, the learning algorithm transforms raw sensor readings into clusters of time series that have predictive value to the agent. We address several issues related to the use of an uninterpreted sensory apparatus and show specific examples where a Pioneer 1 mobile robot interacts with objects in a cluttered laboratory setting.

Introduction

"There is nothing more basic than categorization to our thought, perception, action, and speech" (Lakoff 1987). For autonomous agents, categories often appear as abstractions of raw sensor readings that provide a means for recognizing circumstances and predicting effects of actions. For example, such categories play an important role for a mobile robot that navigates around obstacles (Tani 1996), for a machine-vision system that recognizes hand gestures (Darrell, Essa, & Pentland 1996), for a simulated agent that maneuvers along a highway (McCallum 1996), and for a human-computer interface that automates repetitive tasks (Das, Caglayan, & Gonsalves 1998). Like Pierce and Kuipers (1997), Ram and Santamaria (1997) and others, e.g., (Iba 1991; Thrun 1999), we believe that sensorimotor agents can discover categories for themselves. Thus, the focus of this paper is an unsupervised method by which a mobile robot deduces meaningful categories from uninterpreted sensor readings.

Previously, we demonstrated a technique for extracting sensory concepts from time series data (Rosenstein & Cohen 1998). Our results were from a simple pursuit/avoidance game where two simulated players followed one of several deterministic movement strategies. The simulator recorded the distance between players throughout many games, and the resulting time series were transformed by an unsupervised learning algorithm into clusters of points. In effect, the algorithm

found categories of sensorimotor experience, i.e., clusters of time series with similar patterns. This paper shows that a cluster-based approach to learning such categories scales to a more complicated robot domain with diverse kinds of sensors and real-world effects such as measurement noise, wheel slippage, and sonar reflections.

The learning algorithm, which we describe in detail in the next section, returns a *prototype* (Rosch & Lloyd 1978), or best example, for each category. For this work, prototypes are time series computed by averaging the members of a category or cluster. For example, Figure 1 shows a prototype based on seven instances of a Pioneer 1 robot bumping into a wall. By recognizing that its current situation is a match to the time series in Figure 1, the robot can predict that its bump sensor will go off a short time later. Below we provide evidence that sensory categories of this sort allow an agent to carve its world in some meaningful way. Since our robot refers to its prototypes with arbitrary symbols — not words like WALL or CONTACT — the *meaning* from such categories comes from the predictions it can make about sensor readings.

From Sensors to Categories

For a mobile robot operating in an environment of even modest complexity, sensory categories supply a needed level of abstraction away from raw sensor readings (Mahadevan, Theocharous, & Khaleeli 1998; Michaud & Mataric 1998; Pierce & Kuipers 1997; Ram & Santamaria 1997). Since our objective is that agents discover such categories for themselves — without supervision — we make use of clustering techniques that offer a general, unsupervised framework for categorizing data. However, the following subproblems exist, and this section outlines our solution to each one: event detection, time series comparison, sensor comparison, and sensor weighting.

Event Detection

Agents in continuous-time settings typically generate tremendous amounts of sensor data. Temporal abstraction is needed to focus a learning algorithm on the most

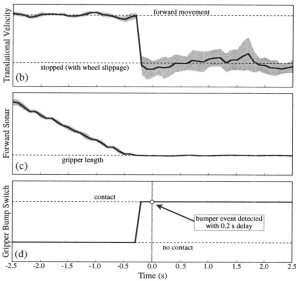

Figure 1: Prototype for seven instances of the Pioneer 1 mobile robot (a) bumping into a wall. Component time series are (b) translational velocity in mm/s, (c) forward sonar in mm, and (d) bump sensor (on or off). Gray regions indicate the level of prototype variability (one standard deviation from the mean).

pertinent parts of a robot's lifetime. For instance, a finite state machine representation can isolate key times when a robot encounters a landmark (Kuipers & Byun 1991; Mataric 1992) or branch point (Tani 1996). Another way to emphasize the most relevant parts of a long time series is to apply a suitable amount of compression and expansion along the time axis. For instance, Darrell *et al.* (1996) used a dynamic time warping (DTW) algorithm to perform this very sort of temporal abstraction when categorizing human gestures. Schmill *et al.* (1999) also utilized DTW to learn categories and operator models for a mobile robot. Dynamic time warping algorithms have the advantage of classifying time series in a velocity-independent fashion, although DTW represents a costly preprocessing step for clustering algorithms (Keogh 1997).

The alternative used here involves the real-time detection of events, i.e., key points in the sensor history.

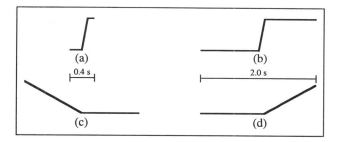

	Template			
	a	b	c	d
velocity	-0.99	-0.98	0.72	-0.70
sonar	-0.67	-0.71	0.97	-0.54
bump	1.00	1.00	-0.74	0.79

Figure 2: Event detection templates and sample correlations. The templates are (a) sharp edge, (b) long sharp edge, (c) slope-then-plateau, and (d) plateau-then-slope. The correlation values are for the data in Figure 1 where the templates were centered at the time of the rising edge for the bump switch. Shaded cells indicate values that are strong enough to trigger an event.

Our premise is that sensorimotor agents, such as infants and mobile robots, possess the innate ability to detect unexpected changes in sensor readings. A similar approach was taken by Das *et al.* (1998), who employed "triggers" as a way to isolate time series segments for a human-computer interface. In their application, a trigger such as the "Select All" command in a word processing program splits a prototype into two pieces: a prefix pattern for recognizing context and a suffix for predicting the user's next action. Our approach differs from theirs in that events act as signals for cluster analysis, rather than explicit decision points pulled out of existing clusters.

To recognize events, our learning algorithm makes use of simple rules that detect simple, conspicuous patterns such as the rising edge from a bump switch, the sudden change in wheel velocity when a robot stalls, or the jump in vision readings when an object suddenly disappears. These rules were implemented by computing the correlation of the most recent sensor readings with one of four templates (a short time series pattern) shown in Figure 2. Whenever one of the correlation values exceeds a threshold, an event signal triggers the learning algorithm to grab a five-second window of sensor readings centered on the event, and this multivariate time series then becomes a new instance for cluster analysis.

Time Series Comparison

History-based categories alleviate the real-world difficulties associated with hidden state, i.e., partially observable environments (McCallum 1996; Michaud & Mataric 1998; Ram & Santamaria 1997; Rosenstein &

Cohen 1998). One way to build such categories is to perform clustering of measurement *sequences*, although clustering algorithms originally designed for individual feature vectors must be extended to handle finite sensor histories. In other words, one must devise a means for time series comparison.

Every clustering algorithm, of which there are many (Everitt 1980), requires a measure of instance similarity, or dissimilarity, to guide its decisions about cluster membership. When designing a measure of dissimilarity for time series, one might take into account many different criteria, such as amplitude scaling, time-axis scaling, or linear drift (Keogh & Pazzani 1998). Our choice yields a very fast and simple algorithm, where we consider two time series, $\mathbf{X} = \{x_1, x_2, ..., x_m\}$ and $\mathbf{Y} = \{y_1, y_2, ..., y_m\}$, as vectors and quantify dissimilarity as the Euclidean distance[1] between them:

$$\text{dissimilarity} = \|\mathbf{X}^T - \mathbf{Y}^T\| = \sqrt{\sum_{i=1}^{m}(x_i - y_i)^2} \quad (1)$$

Our choice of Eq. (1) was motivated by our previous work with a dynamics-based simulator (Rosenstein & Cohen 1998) and with the *method of delays*, a technique based on theory about dynamics. (See (Schreiber & Schmitz 1997) and references therein for other ways to classify time series by dynamics.) The method of delays transforms part of a time series to a point in *delay-coordinate space*, where delay coordinates are just successive measurements taken at a suitable time interval (Rosenstein, Collins, & De Luca 1994). Takens (1981) proved that delay coordinates preserve certain geometric properties of a dynamical system, even when access to the underlying state space is limited to a low-dimensional projection. The relevance for cluster analysis is that nearest neighbors in state space remain near one another in delay-coordinate space.

Sensor Comparison

One difficulty in working with robots is the variety of sensors. For instance, the Pioneer 1 mobile robot used in this study has sonars that measure distance in millimeters, infrared break beams that return one of two discrete values, and a vision system that computes an object's size, among other things, in square-pixels. How should a clustering algorithm weigh the contributions of *uninterpreted* sensors with different units and different ranges of values? Furthermore, how should the algorithm deal with sensors that are both continuous and categorical, such as the sonars which normally give real-valued measurements but also return a large default value when no objects are present?

We propose a two-step solution: (1) Cluster individual sensor histories as described above, thereby creat-

---

[1]Our implementation actually makes use of the *squared* distance, which gives the same results using just m multiplications and $2m - 1$ additions or subtractions for each dissimilarity computation.

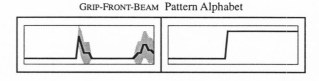

GRIP-FRONT-BEAM Pattern Alphabet

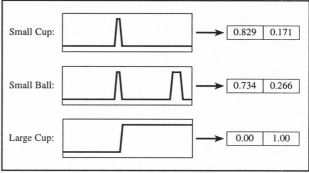

GRIP-FRONT-BEAM Signatures

Figure 3: Pattern alphabet and representative signatures from seven interactions with each of three objects. Gray regions indicate the level of pattern variability (one standard deviation from the mean). The interaction with the small cup best matches the first alphabet pattern, which accounts for 82.9% of the aggregate similarity. Comparatively, the ball exhibits an improved match with both patterns, yet the net effect is an increased emphasis in the second alphabet pattern (from 17.1% to 26.6%). Unlike the large cup, both the ball and the small cup trip the front break beam momentarily before reaching the back of the robot's gripper. The small cup and ball differ in that the ball rolls away once the robot comes to a stop (passing through the front break beam a second time).

ing a small alphabet of patterns specific to each sensor. (2) Construct a unit- and scale-independent *signature* that stores the pattern of similarity between a newly observed time series and each member of the alphabet. For robot navigation and exploration, Kuipers and Byun (1991) defined the signature of a "distinctive place" as a subset of feature values that are maximized at the place. In general, signatures can be built for sensory categories, which may or may not involve physical locations. Moreover, the feature set, i.e., the alphabet patterns, need not be specified in advance, but rather can be learned by the agent from its raw sensor readings. For instance, Thrun (1999) used artificial neural networks and Bayesian statistics to extract features from a robot's sensor/action histories.

As an example, Figure 3 shows the alphabet of patterns for the sensor GRIP-FRONT-BEAM (one of two infrared break beams between the robot's gripper paddles). With the alphabet size set to two, the first two patterns encountered make up the initial alphabet, with each subsequent pattern forcing one iteration of an agglomerative clustering algorithm (Ward 1963)

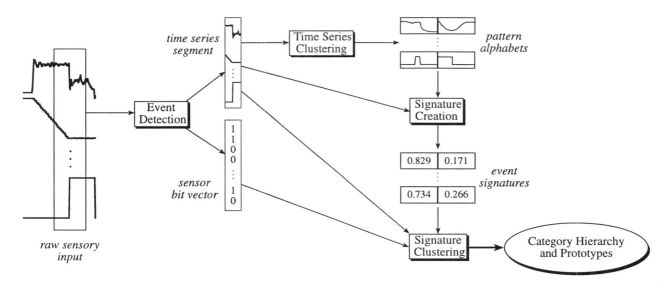

Figure 4: Schematic of the algorithm for learning time series categories from uninterpreted sensors. The first step, event detection, isolates a new segment of sensor readings and forms the input for the remaining algorithm steps. The purpose of time series clustering and signature creation is to convert each segment of sensor readings into a vector of unit- and scale-independent signatures. The final step forms clusters of signature vectors and supplies not only a category hierarchy but also a means for averaging the raw time series into a prototype for each category.

and thereby updating the alphabet to reflect the contribution of the new pattern. The signatures in Figure 3 are the result of several interactions with objects that fit the Pioneer's gripper. In each case, the slots in the signature were filled by computing the similarity (the reciprocal of dissimilarity) between the corresponding alphabet pattern and the recent history of GRIP-FRONT-BEAM. The actual values were also normalized by the total similarity for the signature. Thus, a signature is much like a unit vector in the space of alphabet patterns, with the projection onto each axis indicating the degree of match with the corresponding pattern. Notice in the figure that the small cup and the ball have similar (though consistently distinct) signatures which are vastly different from the large cup's signature. One could recognize the objects in Figure 3 based solely on the GRIP-FRONT-BEAM signature, although one must account for other sensors in more complex examples.

One limitation of the current algorithm is the need to specify the alphabet size in advance. Moreover, the same alphabet size is used for simple types of sensors (such as the break beams which show simple rising and falling edges) as for rich types of sensors (such as the sonars which respond to arbitrary movement patterns of the robot and its environment). One obvious way around this limitation is to customize each alphabet size to match the capabilities of the sensor, much like the approach taken with the event detectors. However, our previous results for a pursuit/avoidance game (Rosenstein & Cohen 1998) lead us to speculate about another alternative. We found that prediction of the game outcome was adversely affected when the number of clusters, i.e., the alphabet size, was too small, whereas little

benefit was gained by increasing the number of clusters beyond a certain point. Thus, one could initialize the alphabet size to a large, conservative value, wait until the alphabet patterns stabilize, and then gradually shrink the alphabet by combining patterns until some performance criterion degrades to an unsatisfactory level.

Sensor Weighting

For any given event, only a small subset of a robot's sensors may contribute to the time series patterns that characterize the event. More generally, a learning algorithm should weigh the importance of each sensor when deciding if two patterns belong to the same category. For example, when grasping a small object a robot should place the greatest emphasis on its gripper, with little or no attention paid to battery level. Mahadevan *et al.* (1998) solved this problem with feedforward neural networks and supervised learning, whereas Schmill *et al.* (1999) handpicked the sensors that receive the same non-zero weight before utilizing an unsupervised clustering algorithm.

The final step in our approach to learning sensory categories applies another stage of clustering, but this time with *weighted* signatures as the input rather than raw time series. Specifically, this second pass of cluster analysis computes the dissimilarity between the ith and jth event patterns by taking a weighted average of the individual signature dissimilarities:

$$\text{dissimilarity}_{ij} = \frac{\sum_{k=1}^{N}(w_{ik} + w_{jk}) \cdot \|\mathbf{S}_{ik} - \mathbf{S}_{jk}\|}{\sum_{k=1}^{N}(w_{ik} + w_{jk})}, \quad (2)$$

where N is the number of sensors and, $\mathbf{S}_{ik}$ is the ith signature for the kth sensor, with weight w_{ik}. Each

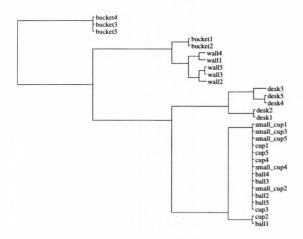

Figure 5: Category hierarchy for five interactions with each of six objects. The signature alphabet size was set to one for each sensor.

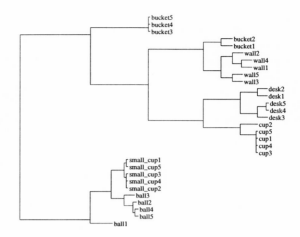

Figure 6: Category hierarchy for five interactions with each of six objects. The signature alphabet size was set to two for each sensor.

merge operation by the clustering algorithm creates another node in a cluster hierarchy, with new signatures and weights computed as an average of the constituents (adjusted for the sizes of the merged clusters). In a parallel operation, the raw time series used to create the signatures are also merged to give a prototype as in Figure 1. However, these time series play no direct role in the computation of Eq. (2).

To initialize the weights when a cluster has just one member (a new instance of sensor signatures) the learning algorithm makes use of the event detectors described previously. In particular, all the sensors that exhibit sudden changes within a 800 ms window are considered to be part of the same event and their weights are set to one; all other weights are set to zero. Essentially, the initial weights form a bit vector where 1 and 0 indicate, respectively, activity and no activity for the corresponding sensor. For example, bumping into a wall as in Figure 1 causes several sensors, like the forward sonars, the bump switch, and the velocity encoders, to have initial weights of one, but others, like the battery level and the gripper break beams, to have initial weights of zero. Although we found encouraging results with this straightforward approach that adds little computational cost, we imagine that some situations may require a more sophisticated weight initialization procedure. For instance, we make no attempt to adjust for correlated sensors such as the robot's five forward sonars. (The sonars carry, in effect, five times the influence of the bump switch which also returns information about frontward objects.)

Summary

Figure 4 is a schematic of the entire learning algorithm which runs both incrementally and in real time as the robot interacts with its environment (although the re-

sults in this paper are for post-processed data sets). On the left, raw sensor readings are made available to the robot at a rate of 10 Hz, with the event detectors continuously monitoring the time series for abrupt changes. When an event occurs, the algorithm collects a five-second segment of sensor readings and constructs a bit vector that indicates the active sensors. These data are passed to the clustering algorithms for additional analysis. First, the new time series are used to update the pattern alphabet for each sensor. Next, these same time series are converted to a set of signatures for subsequent clustering (with the bit vector acting as the initial sensor weights in Eq. (2)). On the right, the final output is a hierarchy of sensory categories with each category represented by a prototype like the one in Figure 1.

Interaction With Objects

We tested the algorithm depicted in Figure 4 by recording sensor data while the Pioneer robot interacted randomly with various objects, such as a ball, a cup, and a bucket. To control the robot we designed a simple SEEK-AND-APPROACH behavior, where the Pioneer turns a random amount, approaches the object closest to its line of sight, stops moving shortly after making contact, and then reverses direction for a randomly chosen time. Objects were recognized with the help of the robot's "blob" vision system that detects patches of red pixels in its image plane. Each object was given an otherwise indistinguishable red mark, so sensory categories were based on the nature of the interaction, not features from a detailed analysis of the visual scene. We ran the SEEK-AND-APPROACH controller repeatedly until the robot interacted at least five times with each of six objects.

Figures 5 and 6 are representative cluster hierarchies that summarize the output of the learning algorithm.

Notice that sensory experiences with the same object tend to cluster together at the lowest levels of the binary tree. Further up the hierarchy, the nodes represent abstractions of these individual experiences. For example, in Figure 5 all the graspable objects (the ball, the cups, and the leg of a desk) fall in the same branch of the tree and all the ungraspable, immovable objects (the wall) fall in another branch. Recall that labels such as "graspable" and "immovable" are meaningful to ourselves but may as well be arbitrary symbols to the robot. They symbolize prototypes, i.e., average time series.

Figures 5 and 6 differ in the size of the pattern alphabet used to construct the signatures. In Figure 5 the alphabet size was one, forcing each event's list of signatures to be equivalent to the corresponding bit vector constructed by detecting unexpected changes in sensor readings. Notice that the event detectors alone are capable of discriminating several categories of experiences. However, each bit must be expanded to a signature with at least two slots — as in Figure 6 — in order to tease apart some interactions such as those for the ball and the cups (which trigger both break beams but no other sensors). A small pattern alphabet always sufficed in our experiments, although we expect more complicated environments to require larger alphabets.

Prototypes serve not only as representatives for sensory categories, but also as state abstractions or goals. At any given time, the robot can determine its state by running a simple nearest neighbor algorithm that finds the best match between its recent sensor history and each of the prototypes. More generally, one can view the distance to the nearest neighbor as an indication of progress toward a goal state.

For example, suppose the robot's goal is to locate a small ball. Figure 7 shows the *relative* distance from the most recent sensor readings to several prototypes as the Pioneer approaches a ball. Initially, no progress is made toward each of the prospective goal states because they all involve activation of the break beams which are quiescent until about 0.5 s before the event is first detected. Moreover, the best match for the quiescent beams is the small cup since its prototype has the shortest activation time for GRIP-FRONT-BEAM. Similarly, the large cup is the worst match since its prototype has the longest activation times for both GRIP-FRONT-BEAM and GRIP-REAR-BEAM. Once the first beam breaks progress is made toward each prototype (which hurts the *relative* distance to the small cup as shown in Figure 7). At about 1.8 s after the initial event the rear break beam deactivates as the ball rolls away from the robot. Until this time, the robot's impoverished sensory apparatus is unable to distinguish the ball from the superordinate category that also includes the small cup.

Discussion

Sensory categories and their prototypes not only act as states that support recognition and prediction, but

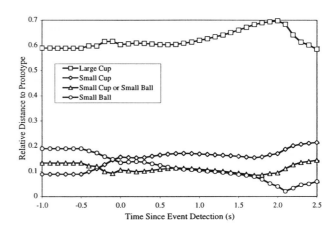

Figure 7: Relative distance to several prototypes. Shown are averages for five instances of the Pioneer robot approaching a small ball and then stopping a short time after making contact.

also serve as operator models. In this paper we took the former view and focused on prototypes as state abstractions and goals, although several researchers augmented sensory prototypes for control purposes as well. For example, Schmill *et al.* (1999) recorded a mobile robot's current activity as part of the prototype data structure. The result was an operator model for a STRIPS-like planner where the prototype was split into two parts that correspond to pre- and post-conditions for the stored activity. Similarly, Ram and Santamaria (1997) used a case-based reasoning approach to control a mobile robot for a navigation task. Their system made use of continuous cases that store time series of sensor inputs and control outputs; given a desired sensory state, a case library can be queried for the sequence of control commands most likely to achieve that state.

Whether we view them as state abstractions or operator models, sensory categories may provide the foundation upon which to form abstract, propositional concepts. Mandler postulated that to build such a foundation, humans make use of an innate mechanism for sensory analysis that searches for regularities and preserves the continuous nature of perception (Mandler 1992). The unsupervised approach proposed here performs a similar form of sensory analysis for mobile robots. In particular, our implementation finds clusters of similar time series patterns and builds prototypes that retain the characteristics of the original sensor traces. We have yet to show a path from sensory categories to highly abstract concepts, although autonomous agents can still accomplish a great deal with prototypes.

Interestingly, prototypes and categories play a crucial role in human intelligence yet the act of categorization is often automatic and unconscious (Lakoff 1987). We regularly take categories for granted until forced to reason about them explicitly, such as when designing a feature set that helps a mobile robot navigate a cluttered office environment. Then we realize how difficult it can be to list the properties, *from the robot's perspective*, of simple categories like corridors, doorways, desks, and waste buckets. Supervised learning offers one common solution, where a *person* classifies the instances for subsequent category induction by a machine learning algorithm. This research is part of an effort to push the classification process inside the machine, freeing scientists and engineers from much of the tedious work when designing autonomous agents.

Acknowledgments

This research is supported by the National Defense Science and Engineering Graduate Fellowship and by DARPA under contracts F30602-97-1-0289 and F49620-97-1-0485. The U.S. Government is authorized to reproduce and distribute reprints for governmental purposes notwithstanding any copyright notation herein. The views and conclusions contained herein are those of the authors and should not be interpreted as the official policies or endorsements, expressed or implied, of DARPA or the U.S. Government.

References

Darrell, T. J.; Essa, I. A.; and Pentland, A. P. 1996. Task-specific gesture analysis in real-time using interpolated views. *IEEE Transactions on Pattern Analysis and Machine Intelligence* 18(12):1236–1242.

Das, S.; Caglayan, A.; and Gonsalves, P. 1998. Increasing agent autonomy in dynamic environments. In *Proceedings of the Second International Conference on Autonomous Agents*. New York: ACM Press.

Everitt, B. S. 1980. *Cluster Analysis*. New York: John Wiley & Sons, Inc.

Iba, W. 1991. Learning to classify observed motor behavior. In *Proceedings of the Twelfth International Joint Conference on Artificial Intelligence*, 732–738. San Francisco, CA: Morgan Kaufmann Publishers, Inc.

Keogh, E. J., and Pazzani, M. J. 1998. An enhanced representation of time series which allows fast and accurate classification, clustering and relevance feedback. Presented at the 1998 AAAI Workshop on Predicting The Future: AI Approaches to Time Series Analysis.

Keogh, E. J. 1997. Fast similarity search in the presence of longitudinal scaling in time series databases. In *Proceedings of the Ninth International Conference on Tools with Artificial Intelligence*, 578–584. IEEE Press.

Kuipers, B., and Byun, Y.-T. 1991. A robot exploration and mapping strategy based on a semantic hierarchy of spatial representations. *Robotics and Autonomous Systems* 8:47–63.

Lakoff, G. 1987. *Women, Fire, and Dangerous Things*. Chicago: University of Chicago Press.

Mahadevan, S.; Theocharous, G.; and Khaleeli, N. 1998. Rapid concept learning for mobile robots. *Machine Learning* 31(1–3):7–27. Also published in Autonomous Robots, Volume 5, Nos. 3/4.

Mandler, J. M. 1992. How to build a baby: II. Conceptual primitives. *Psychological Review* 99(4):587–604.

Mataric, M. J. 1992. Integration of representation into goal-driven behavior-based robots. *IEEE Transactions on Robotics and Automation* 8(3):304–312.

McCallum, A. K. 1996. Learning to use selective attention and short-term memory in sequential tasks. In *From Animals to Animats: Proceedings of the Fourth International Conference on Simulation of Adaptive Behavior*, 315–324. Cambridge: MIT Press.

Michaud, F., and Mataric, M. J. 1998. Learning from history for behavior-based mobile robots in nonstationary conditions. *Machine Learning* 31(1–3):141–167. Also published in Autonomous Robots, Volume 5, Nos. 3/4.

Pierce, D., and Kuipers, B. 1997. Map learning with uninterpreted sensors and effectors. *Artificial Intelligence* 92:169–227.

Ram, A., and Santamaria, J. C. 1997. Continuous case-based reasoning. *Artificial Intelligence* 90:25–77.

Rosch, E., and Lloyd, B. B. 1978. *Cognition and Categorization*. Hillsdale, NJ: Lawrence Erlbaum Associates.

Rosenstein, M. T., and Cohen, P. R. 1998. Concepts from time series. In *Proceedings of the Fifteenth National Conference on Artificial Intelligence*, 739–745. AAAI Press.

Rosenstein, M. T.; Collins, J. J.; and De Luca, C. J. 1994. Reconstruction expansion as a geometry-based framework for choosing proper delay times. *Physica D* 73:82–98.

Schmill, M. D.; Oates, T.; and Cohen, P. R. 1999. Learned models for continuous planning. In *Proceedings of the Seventh International Workshop on Artificial Intelligence and Statistics*, 278–282. San Francisco, CA: Morgan Kaufmann Publishers, Inc.

Schreiber, T., and Schmitz, A. 1997. Classification of time series data with nonlinear similarity measures. *Physical Review Letters* 79(8):1475–1478.

Takens, F. 1981. Detecting strange attractors in turbulence. *Lecture Notes in Mathematics* 898:366–381.

Tani, J. 1996. Model-based learning for mobile robot navigation from the dynamical systems perspective. *IEEE Transactions on Systems, Man, and Cybernetics Part B* 26(3):421–436.

Thrun, S. 1999. Bayesian landmark learning for mobile robot localization. *Machine Learning*. To appear.

Ward, J. H. 1963. Hierarchical grouping to optimize an objective function. *Journal of the American Statistical Association* 58(301):236–244.

Satisfiability

DISTANCE-SAT: Complexity and Algorithms

Olivier Bailleux and **Pierre Marquis**
CRIL/Université d'Artois
rue de l'Université - S.P. 16
62307 Lens Cedex - FRANCE
e-mail: {bailleux, marquis}@cril.univ-artois.fr

Abstract

In many AI fields, the problem of finding out a solution which is as close as possible to a given configuration has to be faced. This paper addresses this problem in a propositional framework. The decision problem DISTANCE-SAT that consists in determining whether a propositional CNF formula admits a model that disagrees with a given partial interpretation on at most d variables, is introduced. The complexity of DISTANCE-SAT and of several restrictions of it are identified. Two algorithms based on the well-known Davis/Putnam search procedure are presented so as to solve DISTANCE-SAT. Their empirical evaluation enables deriving firm conclusions about their respective performances, and to relate the difficulty of DISTANCE-SAT with the difficulty of SAT from the practical side.

Introduction

In many AI fields, the problem of finding out a solution which is close as possible to a given configuration must be faced. Such a configuration typically encodes some form of preference knowledge (e.g., an expected state, or a normal state) that conflicts with the hard constraints of the problem, represented as a knowledge base. For instance, in the consistency-based diagnosis framework (Reiter 1987), the expected state of the components of a device is the one where none of them is faulty. Whenever a failure occurs, such a diagnosis no longer is possible: assuming that every component behaves as its model of correct behaviour requires it conflicts with the observations that have been made. In this situation, this assumption must be revised (some components are to be assumed faulty) so as to restore consistency. Since many fault assumptions can typically be made in order to achieve this goal, a principle of parsimony is often adopted: among the possible diagnoses, the selected ones are those including a minimal set (w.r.t. cardinality or set-inclusion) of faulty assumptions. Thus, the diagnoses that are "not so far" from the expected one are preferred to the remaining

ones: one-fault diagnoses are first considered, then two-faults diagnoses, and so on.

In this paper, this problem is addressed within a propositional framework. The knowledge base is represented as a propositional CNF formula Σ, the expected configuration as a partial interpretation PI, and we are interested in finding out a model of Σ that disagrees with PI on at most d variables. We call DISTANCE-SAT the corresponding decision problem.

In the following, the complexity of DISTANCE-SAT is identified in the general case and in some restricted cases. Like the well-known SAT problem (which can be viewed as a restriction of it), DISTANCE-SAT is NP-complete. However, DISTANCE-SAT is somewhat more difficult than SAT, in the sense that the tractable restrictions for SAT do not typically give rise to tractable restrictions for DISTANCE-SAT.

Then, two algorithms for solving DISTANCE-SAT are presented. The first one, $DP_{distance}$, is a straightforward adaptation of the Davis/Putnam search procedure. To every node of the search tree is associated a value that measures the disagreement between the given configuration and the partial interpretation that corresponds to the node (and can be read off directly by picking up the literals from the branch that ends up to the node under consideration). Whenever this value exceeds the given maximal bound d, the algorithm backtracks. Our second algorithm, $DP_{distance+lasso}$, is a variant of $DP_{distance}$. The only difference between them lies in the branching rule. While the branching rule used in $DP_{distance}$ is a standard, "efficient", branching rule for SAT, the branching rule used in $DP_{distance+lasso}$ is much more oriented towards the satisfaction of the distance constraint. The objective is to lasso in priority a model that is close to the given configuration. Thus, among the clauses that are completely falsified by the given configuration, those of minimal length are considered. Among the variables of these clauses, one of those that maximize the standard branching rule heuristic (used in $DP_{distance}$) is selected as the branching variable.

Both algorithms are empirically assessed on many random 3-CNF instances (generated using the now classical "fixed-length clauses model" (Chvátal & Szemerédi 1988)), for several values of the ratio number of clauses/number of variables, for several sizes of the given configuration, and several values of the maximal disagreement number d. When d is small, $DP_{distance+lasso}$ performs much better then $DP_{distance}$. Contrastingly, when d is large, $DP_{distance}$ is the best performer.

The rest of this paper is organized as follows. Section 2 gives some formal preliminaries. Section 3 presents DISTANCE-SAT and its computational complexity. Two algorithms for solving DISTANCE-SAT are given in Section 4. Section 5 presents an empirical evaluation of these algorithms. Section 6 concludes this paper.

Formal Preliminaries

Let $PROP_{PS}$ denote the propositional language built up from a denumerable set PS of propositional symbols (also called variables) and the connectives in the standard way. The elements of $PROP_{PS}$ are called formulas. The size of a formula Σ, noted $|\Sigma|$ is the number of signs (symbols and connectives) used to write it. $Var(\Sigma)$ is the set of propositional variables occurring in Σ.

Formulas are interpreted in the classical way. An interpretation of a formula Σ is a mapping I that associates *every* propositional variable of $Var(\Sigma)$ to one of the two truth values of $BOOL = \{true, false\}$. A partial interpretation of Σ is a mapping PI that associates *some* propositional variables of $Var(\Sigma)$ to one of the two truth values of $BOOL$. $Dom(PI) \subseteq Var(\Sigma)$ denotes the domain of PI. A complete partial interpretation is just an interpretation. In the following, (partial) interpretations are represented as sets of literals. A positive literal x (resp. a negative literal $\neg x$) appears in PI iff $PI(x) = true$ (resp. $PI(x) = false$). An interpretation I is an extension of a partial interpretation PI iff $PI \subseteq I$ holds. A clause is said completely falsified by a partial interpretation whenever every literal of the clause appears in the partial interpretation with the opposite sign.

A k-CNF of a formula is a CNF formula in which every clause contains at most k literals. A formula is Horn CNF (resp. reverse Horn CNF) iff it is a CNF formula s.t. every clause in it contains at most one positive (resp. negative) literal. A Krom formula is a 2-CNF formula, i.e., every clause in it contains at most two literals.

We assume that the reader is familiar with some basic notions of computational complexity (see e.g., (Garey & Johnson 1979)).

Definition and Complexity

Before defining DISTANCE-SAT in a formal way, we first need the definition of disagreement between two partial interpretations:

Definition 1 (disagreement)
A partial interpretation PI_1 is said to disagree with a partial interpretation PI_2 on at most d variables iff the
number of variables x of $Dom(PI_1) \cap Dom(PI_2)$ s.t. $PI_1(x) \neq PI_2(x)$ is less than or equal to d.

We are now ready to define DISTANCE-SAT.

Definition 2 (DISTANCE-SAT)
DISTANCE-SAT *is the following decision problem:*

- **Input:** *A CNF formula Σ, a partial interpretation PI, and a non-negative integer d.*
- **Question:** *Does there exist a model I of Σ s.t. I disagrees with PI on at most d variables?*

For every instance of DISTANCE-SAT, we call the constraint "I disagrees with PI on at most d variables" its *distance constraint*.

DISTANCE-SAT is closely related to the problem of repairing a supermodel (Ginsberg, Parkes, & Roy 1998). A (S_1^a, S_2^b)-supermodel of a propositional formula Σ is a model I of Σ s.t. if the variables of any subset of S_1^a of size at most a are flipped in I, a model of Σ can be obtained by flipping in I the variables of a disjoint subset of S_2^b of size at most b. Let L_1^a be a set of literals of size at most a s.t. every literal l from it is built up from a variable from S_1^a and $l \notin I$. Repairing I when it is modified as indicated by L_1^a consists in finding out a model of Σ simplified by L_1^a that disagrees on at most b variables with the restriction of I to the variables of S_2^b. Accordingly, our algorithms for DISTANCE-SAT can directly be used to determine such repairs.

Proposition 1 (complexity of DISTANCE-SAT)
The complexity of DISTANCE-SAT and of several restrictions of it obtained by considering:

- *a knowledge base Σ for which SAT is tractable,*
- *a fixed maximal distance d*

are reported in the following table.

KB	any d	a fixed d
any Σ	NP-complete	NP-complete
Σ Horn	NP-complete	in P
Σ reverse Horn	NP-complete	in P
Σ Krom	NP-complete	in P

Clearly enough, SAT, the satisfiability problem of a CNF formula is a restriction of DISTANCE-SAT (taking $PI = \emptyset$ (or $d = |Var(\Sigma)|$) so as to reduce SAT to DISTANCE-SAT is sufficient to prove the NP-hardness of DISTANCE-SAT). Hence, it is not surprising that DISTANCE-SAT is intractable in the general case, i.e., there is no known polynomial algorithm to solve it (and there can be no such algorithm unless P = NP). Nevertheless, DISTANCE-SAT is not much more difficult than SAT since it belongs to NP. Indeed, verifying that a guessed interpretation disagrees with PI on at most d variables can easily be achieved in polynomial time.

Contrastingly, focusing on the standard fragments of propositional logic where SAT is known as tractable is not sufficient to ensure the polynomiality of DISTANCE-SAT in the general case. Both NP-hardness of the restrictions where Σ is Horn, reverse Horn or Krom are consequences of the NP-hardness of DISTANCE-SAT under the restriction where Σ is a 2-CNF monotone formula, i.e., every literal of Σ has only either positive occurrences or negative occurrences in Σ. The NP-hardness of this last problem is a consequence of the fact that the well-known HITTING SET problem – that is NP-complete (Karp 1972)– can be polynomially many-one reduced to it. Thus, DISTANCE-SAT can be considered at least as difficult as SAT.

As Proposition 1 illustrates it, focusing on tractable KBs is sufficient to obtain tractable restrictions of DISTANCE-SAT as long as d is considered as a fixed constant. Some other restrictions can be considered so as to achieve tractability. Thus, while imposing PI to be a complete interpretation does not lower the complexity of DISTANCE-SAT in the general case (even when Σ is s.t. SAT is tractable), determining whether Σ has a model that disagrees with a complete interpretation I on at most d variables, where d is a constant, is in P. To be more precise, if k is the maximal length of clauses of Σ, there exists a $\mathcal{O}(|\Sigma| * k^d)$ time algorithm that solves this last problem (cf. Section 4).

Interestingly, as a by-product of Proposition 1, some new results about the complexity of the satisfiability issue for some extended propositional languages can be derived. Given a propositional language $PROP_{PS}$, let a *cardinality constraint* be an ordered pair $\langle \{l_1, ..., l_k\}, m\rangle$, where each l_i ($i \in 1 .. k$) is a literal of $PROP_{PS}$ and m is a non-negative integer that is less than or equal to k. Given an interpretation I, the semantics of such a cardinality constraint in I is *true* iff *at least m literals* from $\{l_1, ..., l_k\}$ belong to I (i.e., are interpreted as *true* in I as well). A *cardinality formula* is a (finite) conjunction of cardinality constraints (Benhamou, Saïs, & Siegel 1994) (Van Henterynck & Deville 1991).

Clearly enough, expressing that we are looking for a model of Σ that disagrees with $PI = \{l_1, ..., l_k\}$ on at most d variables amounts to look for a model of the formula obtained by adding to the clauses of Σ the single cardinality constraint $\langle \{l_1, ..., l_k\}, k - d\rangle$. Many more clauses, but a polynomial number of it, are required to reduce DISTANCE-SAT to SAT in the general case [2]. Thus, as a direct consequence of Proposition 1, checking whether a cardinality formula Σ is satisfiable is NP-complete, even when Σ contains only (classical) clauses (i.e., with $m = 1$) that form a Horn CNF formula (or a reverse Horn CNF formula or a Krom one), plus one cardinality constraint with $m \neq 1$.

Two Algorithms for DISTANCE-SAT

In this section, two algorithms for DISTANCE-SAT are presented. These algorithms are based on the standard Davis / Putnam search procedure for SAT (Davis, Logemann, & Loveland 1962). This choice is motivated by the two following facts:

---

[2]This comes from the fact that SAT is NP-complete: every problem in NP can be polynomially reduced to it.

- A naive approach that would consist in enumerating in a successive way the interpretations that do *not* disagree with PI on at most d variables is not computationally feasible in the general case, even for quite small values of n, the number of variables of Σ, and d. For instance, with $n = 100$, $d = 10$ and PI is any complete interpretation, more than 10^{13} interpretations should be considered, which makes such a naive enumerative technique far from being practical.

- The best complete algorithms for SAT that we can find in the literature are based on the Davis / Putnam search procedure, and SAT is a restriction of DISTANCE-SAT. Especially, if $\Sigma \notin$ SAT, then $\forall PI \forall d, \langle \Sigma, PI, d\rangle \notin$ DISTANCE-SAT.

Our first algorithm, $DP_{distance}$, mainly is the standard Davis/Putnam search procedure, equipped with a counter that indicates for every node of the search tree the number of variables on which the partial interpretation associated to that node disagrees with the given configuration. As soon as the value of the counter exceeds d, the algorithm backtracks.

Procedure $DP_{distance}$: $BOOLEAN$
Input : an instance $\langle \Sigma, PI, d\rangle$ of DISTANCE-SAT.
Output : *true* iff $\langle \Sigma, PI, d\rangle \in$ DISTANCE-SAT.
Begin
    unit_propagate(Σ);
    if disagree(PI_C, PI) > d then return (*false*);
    if the empty clause is generated then return (*false*);
    else if all clauses are satisfied then return (*true*)
        else begin
            $x := branching(\Sigma, PI_C)$;
            return ($DP_{distance}(\Sigma \wedge x)$ or
                $DP_{distance}(\Sigma \wedge \neg x)$);
        end;
End

In this algorithm, PI_C is the current partial interpretation, i.e., the one associated to the current node of the search tree. PI_C gathers all the variables that have been fixed from the root of the tree to the current node. *unit_propagate* is a function that performs unit-propagation through Σ. PI_C is updated by *unit_propagate*.

It is well-known that the design of a branching rule is a critical factor in the performance of any Davis/Putnam-like algorithm for SAT. Our *branching* function implements the branching rule given in (Dubois *et al.* 1996), that is one of the best performer for SAT. To be more precise, the weight of a literal l of a formula Ω is given by $w(l) = \sum_{\forall c \in \Omega, l \in c} -ln(1 - 1/(2^{|c|} - 1)^2)$ and the score of a variable x by $s(x) = w(x) + w(\neg x) + 1.5min(w(x), w(\neg x))$. A variable maximizing s is elected as the branching variable.

Clearly enough, $DP_{distance}$ is very close to the standard Davis / Putnam procedure. Actually, the unique difference between them is the additional backtrack instruction that is triggered as soon as the current partial interpretation PI_C disagrees with PI on more than d variables. Accordingly, the design of $DP_{distance}$ is mainly guided by the purpose of taking advantage of a state-of-the-art algorithm for SAT. The distance constraint is not exploited in an aggressive way, but only in a passive way.

Our second algorithm $DP_{distance+lasso}$ is a variant of $DP_{distance}$ in which the *branching* function that is used does not correspond to a standard branching rule for SAT but has been especially tailored for DISTANCE-SAT. The purpose is to take advantage of both the best branching rules that are available for SAT but also to exploit the distance constraint much more aggressively than in $DP_{distance}$. Unlike the *branching* function, all the variables occurring in Σ (simplified by PI_C) are not considered by the $branching_{lasso}$ function. Only the variables that appear in the set S_{PI_C} of the clauses of Σ simplified by PI_C that are completely falsified by PI, and are of minimal size, are taken into account. Then, the weights of these variables are computed using the same weight function as in *branching*, and a variable with a maximal weight is elected. Remark that the idea of choosing the branching variable among the variables which occur in clauses that are falsified by a reference interpretation appears in SCORE(FD/B), a local search-based complete algorithm for SAT (Chabrier, Juliard, & Chabrier 1995).

Let γ be a clause of S_{PI_C} and x a variable of γ. When x will be assigned the sign it has in γ, γ will become satisfied by the updated partial interpretation PI_C. When x will be given the opposite sign, the resulting simplified clause (i.e., γ in which the literal corresponding to x has been removed) is still completely falsified by PI, and necessarily is of minimal size. This will force the remaining variables of γ to be among the candidate variables for branching at the next choice node. Interestingly, whenever PI is a complete interpretation and the size of the longest clause of Σ is bounded by a constant k, only $\mathcal{O}(k^d)$ choice nodes are to be generated by $DP_{distance+lasso}$, provided that a variable of S_{PI_C} is always elected as the branching variable. We call such a property the *lasso effect*. When the lasso effect works, $DP_{distance+lasso}$ runs in $\mathcal{O}(|\Sigma| * k^d)$ time, i.e., the number of clauses occurring in Σ influences the computational performance of $DP_{distance+lasso}$ by only a *linear* factor. This is far from being expected for $DP_{distance}$. Though the lasso effect is not guaranteed when PI is not a complete interpretation, we will show in the following section that $DP_{distance+lasso}$ nevertheless proves "efficient" in many situations where PI is not complete.

The design of the $branching_{lasso}$ function is done so as to take advantage of both the lasso effect (considering only the variables of S_{PI_C}), and the best branching rules for SAT (the variables are ordered so as to select one that maximizes a standard weight function). In particular, since the lasso technique simply consists in filtering out some candidate variables before applying to them any *branching* function, several *branching* functions for SAT can be considered, giving rise to several $branching_{lasso}$ functions. Let us also note that the distance constraint can be exploited in a more in-

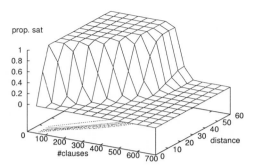

Figure 1: Proportion of satisfiable 100 variables 3-CNF instances of DISTANCE-SAT, as a function of both the number of clauses and the bound d, given a complete reference interpretation.

tegrated way within the *branching* function, especially for the propagation-based ones, like the one used in SATZ (Li & Anbulagan 1997). Propagating a literal through a CNF formula results in a partial interpretation (encoding the literals that have been fixed) and a corresponding simplified CNF formula. The value of the disagreement between such a partial interpretation and the reference one, and the tightness of the associated simplified formula are two parameters that can be used to evaluate heuristically whether propagating a literal is promising for DISTANCE-SAT.

Finally, it is worth noting that both $DP_{distance}$ and $DP_{distance+lasso}$ can be easily modified to address the function problem associated to DISTANCE-SAT, i.e., to return a model of Σ that disagrees with PI on at most d variables whenever such a model exists. Instead of returning *true* when an implicant of Σ is found, it is sufficient to return any extension of the current partial interpretation PI_C.

Empirical Evaluation

All the results presented hereafter concern random 3-CNF formulas Σ generated under the "fixed-length clauses" model (Chvátal & Szemerédi 1988): literals are drawn under uniform conditions and clauses with redundant variables are rejected. Without loss of generality, the variables of $Dom(PI)$ are the first ones w.r.t. the lexicographic order, and they are assigned to *false*. Every DISTANCE-SAT instance can be turned into an instance for which this assumption is satisfied, through a simple renaming of its literals.

The computational difficulty of a DISTANCE-SAT instance w.r.t. any of our two algorithms is quantified as the size of the corresponding search tree, where both unary and binary nodes are taken into account; in other words, it is evaluated as the number of variable assignments that are required to solve the instance. This difficulty measure does depend neither on the implementation of the algorithms nor on the computer used to perform the experiments.

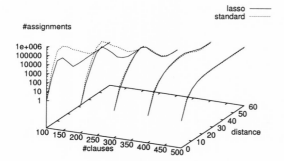

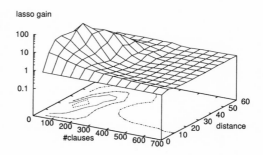

Figure 2: Average number of assignments required by $DP_{distance}$ and $DP_{distance+lasso}$ to solve random 100 variables 3-CNF instances of DISTANCE-SAT with complete reference interpretations.

Figure 1 gives the proportion of satisfiable 100 variables instances, as a function of both the number of clauses of Σ and the bound d, given a complete reference interpretation ($|Dom(PI)| = 100$). A sharp transition appears between the satisfiable and the unsatisfiable regions. When d is large, the transition appears at the well-known satisfiability threshold for SAT, i.e., when number of variables / number of clauses = 4.25 (Cheeseman, Kanefsky, & Taylor 1991) (Crawford & Auton 1996). When d decreases, less clauses are required to produce unsatisfiable instances.

Figure 2 compares the average number of variable assignments required by $DP_{distance}$ and $DP_{distance+lasso}$ to solve random 100 variables instances, for several number of clauses and several d. PI is a fixed complete interpretation ($|Dom(PI)| = 100$). Clearly enough, the lasso branching rule outperforms the standard one for many instances among the most difficult ones (100 and 200 clauses, d between 10 and 30).

This is confirmed by Figure 3, where the ratios between the number of variable assignments required by $DP_{distance}$ to the number of variable assignments required by $DP_{distance+lasso}$ are reported for the same instances as those considered in Figures 1 and 2. Contrastingly, for the largest values of d and the number of clauses, the standard branching rule is slightly better than the lasso one. As additional interesting information, Figures 1 and 2 show that the most difficult instances are near the transition from satisfiable to unsatisfiable for DISTANCE-SAT, and are much more difficult than the corresponding SAT instances (i.e., those obtained by ruling out the distance constraint).

Figure 4 gives the proportion of satisfiable 100 variables instances of DISTANCE-SAT for a fixed $d = 20$, as a function of the number of clauses and $|Dom(PI)|$. Figure 5 compares the average numbers of variable assignments needed by $DP_{distance}$ and $DP_{distance+lasso}$ to solve the instances that have been considered in Figure 4. Figure 6 gives the ratio of the number of variable assignments required by $DP_{distance}$ to the number of variable assignments required by $DP_{distance+lasso}$ for

Figure 3: Ratio between the number of assignments required by $DP_{distance}$ to the number of assignments required by $DP_{distance+lasso}$, as a function of both the number of clauses and the bound d. 100 variables 3-CNF formulas, complete reference interpretation.

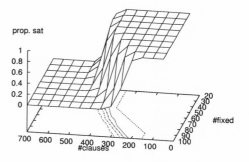

Figure 4: Proportion of satisfiable 100 variables 3-CNF instances of DISTANCE-SAT, as a function of both the number of clauses and the number of fixed variables in the reference interpretation, given $d = 20$.

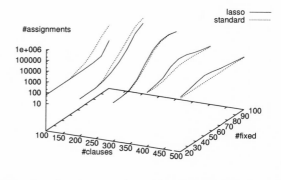

Figure 5: Average number of assignments required by $DP_{distance}$ and $DP_{distance+lasso}$ to solve 100 variables 3-CNF instances with partial reference interpretations, with $d = 20$.

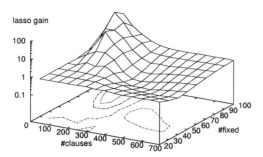

Figure 6: Ratio between the number of assignments required by $DP_{distance}$ to the number of assignments required by $DP_{distance+lasso}$, as a function of both the number of clauses and the number of fixed variables in the reference interpretation. 100 variables 3-CNF formulas, $d = 20$.

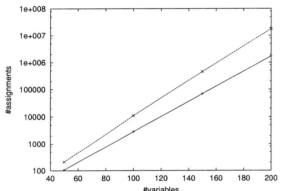

Figure 7: Performances of $DP_{distance}$ and $DP_{distance+lasso}$ in solving 3-CNF instances of DISTANCE-SAT, as a function of the number n of variables. d is fixed to $n/10$ and the number of clauses to $2n$.

solving the instances considered in Figures 4 and 5. At the light of these three figures, it appears that the most difficult instances for DISTANCE-SAT are near its transition from satisfiable to unsatisfiable. The lasso branching rule outperforms the standard one when the number of clauses is small, even when the partial interpretation PI is far from being complete (e.g., $d = 150$ and $|Dom(PI)| = 60$).

Finally, Figure 7 compares the performances of $DP_{distance}$ and $DP_{distance+lasso}$ in solving instances of DISTANCE-SAT, as a function of the number n of variables occurring in them. d is fixed to $n/10$, and the number of clauses to $2n$. These instances of DISTANCE-SAT appear as extremely difficult; in particular, they are much more difficult than their corresponding SAT instances. Clearly enough, the lasso branching rule pushed back the intractability of these instances.

Conclusion

The main contribution of this paper is the identification of the complexity of DISTANCE-SAT and of several

restrictions of it, as well as two algorithms for solving it. An empirical evaluation of these two algorithms has been conducted, allowing some conclusions about their respective applicability to be drawn.

Because instances of DISTANCE-SAT can be easily encoded as instances of the satisfiability problem for propositional cardinality formulas, it would be interesting to extend our algorithms so as to make them able to take simultaneously several distance constraints into account. This is an issue for further research.

Acknowledgements

This work has been supported in part by the Ganymède II project of the "Contrat de Plan Etat/Région Nord Pas-de-Calais" and by the IUT of Lens.

References

Benhamou, B.; Saïs, L.; and Siegel, P. 1994. Two proof procedures for a cardinality based langage in propositional calculus. In *Proc. of STACS'94*, 71–84.

Chabrier, J.; Juliard, V.; and Chabrier, J. 1995. SCORE(FD/B) an efficient complete local-based search method for satisiability problems. In *Proc. of the CP'95 Workshop on Solving Really Hard Problems*, 25–30.

Cheeseman, P.; Kanefsky, B.; and Taylor, W. 1991. Where the really hard problems are. In *Proc. of IJCAI'91*, 331–337.

Chvátal, V., and Szemerédi, E. 1988. Many hard examples for resolution. *JACM* 35(4):759–768.

Crawford, J., and Auton, L. 1996. Experimental results on the crossover point in random 3SAT. *Artificial Intelligence* 81:31–57.

Davis, M.; Logemann, G.; and Loveland, D. 1962. A machine program for theorem proving. *CACM* 5:394–397.

Dubois, O.; André, P.; Boufkhad, Y.; and Carlier, J. 1996. *SAT versus UNSAT*. Trick and Johnson. 415–436.

Garey, M., and Johnson, D. 1979. *Computers and intractability: a guide to the theory of NP-completeness*. Freeman.

Ginsberg, M.; Parkes, A.; and Roy, A. 1998. Supermodels and robustness. In *Proc. of AAAI'98*, 334–339.

Karp, R. 1972. *Reducibility among combinatorial problems*. New York: Plenum Press. chapter Complexity of Computer Computations, 85–103.

Li, C., and Anbulagan. 1997. Heuristics based on unit propagation for satisfiability problems. In *Proc. of IJCAI'97*, 366–371.

Reiter, R. 1987. A theory of diagnosis from first principles. *Artificial Intelligence* 32:57–95.

Van Henteryck, P., and Deville, Y. 1991. The cardinality operator: A new logical connective for constraint logic programming. In *Proc. of ICLP'91*, 745–749.

Beyond NP: the QSAT phase transition

Ian P. Gent and Toby Walsh *

Department of Computer Science
University of Strathclyde
Glasgow G1 1XL United Kingdom
ipg@cs.strath.ac.uk, tw@cs.strath.ac.uk

Abstract

We show that phase transition behavior similar to that observed in NP-complete problems like random 3-SAT occurs further up the polynomial hierarchy in problems like random 2-QSAT. The differences between QSAT and SAT in phase transition behavior that Cadoli et al report are largely due to the presence of trivially unsatisfiable problems. Once they are removed, we see behavior more familiar from SAT and other NP-complete domains. There are, however, some differences. Problems with short clauses show a large gap between worst case behavior and median, and the easy-hard-easy pattern is restricted to higher percentiles of search cost. We compute the "constrainedness" of k-QSAT problems for any k, and use this to predict the location of phase transitions. We conjecture that these predictions are less accurate than in NP-complete problems because of the super-exponential size of the state space, and of the weakness of first moment methods in complexity classes above NP. Finally, we predict that similar phase transition behavior will occur in other PSPACE-complete problems like planning and game playing.

Introduction

A simple generalization of propositional satisfiability (SAT) is quantified satisfiability (QSAT). This is the prototypical PSPACE-complete problem. PSPACE is the class of problems that can be solved using polynomial space. Many search problems in AI lie within this complexity class (for example, propositional reasoning in many types of non-monotonic, modal, belief, temporal, and description logics). Do we observe phase transition behavior in this complexity class similar to that seen in P and NP? Is the definition of constrainedness proposed in (Gent *et al.* 1996) again useful?

We first introduce QSAT and the random model used in (Cadoli, Giovanardi, & Schaerf 1997). We then argue

We thank Marco Cadoli for binaries for the EVALUATE algorithm. We are members of the cross-site APES Research Group, http://www.cs.strath.ac.uk/~apes, and we thank our fellow members from both Leeds and Strathclyde Universities. We thank reviewers of AAAI for helpful comments. Toby Walsh is supported by EPSRC grant GR/L24014.

that random models should avoid unary constraints like unit clauses as they are often responsible for trivially insoluble problems. We show that Cadoli et al's model suffers from this flaw and propose instead two 'flawless' models for generating random QSAT. We concern ourselves with k-QSAT, a restricted subclass of QSAT detailed below. We define the constrainedness, κ, of k-QSAT problems for all k and predict the location of the phase transition, the first time this has been done for a complexity class above NP. For 2-QSAT, we compare this prediction with empirical results. The prediction is not always as accurate as in many NP problems, and we conjecture why.

QSAT

QSAT is the problem of deciding the satisfiability of propositional formulae in which the Boolean variables are either existentially or universally quantified. For example, $\forall x \exists y \, (x \vee \neg y) \wedge (\neg x \vee y)$ evaluates to true since whatever truth value, T or F we give to x, there is a truth value for y, namely the same value as x, which satisfies the quantified formula. We can group consecutive variables sharing the same quantifier into a set bound by a single quantifier, so we assume that the quantifiers alternate, an universal following an existential and vice versa. A k-QSAT problem is a QSAT problem in which there are k alternating quantifiers applied to disjoint sets of variables, with the innermost quantifier being existential. Our example above is in 2-QSAT, while 1-QSAT is the same as SAT. Many games like generalized versions of checkers, Go, Hex, and Othello are PSPACE-complete. Indeed, we can view QSAT as a game between the existential quantifiers, which try to pick instantiations that give a satisfiable subformula, and the universal quantifiers, which try to pick instantiations that give an unsatisfiable subformula.

Whilst SAT is NP-complete, QSAT is PSPACE-complete, and k-QSAT is Σ_kP-complete (Papadimitriou 1994). Notice that the difference between QSAT and k-QSAT is that in QSAT there is no *a priori* limit on the number k of alternations. The union of the classes Σ_kP for all k defines the 'cumulative polynomial hierarchy' PH. If for some i, Σ_{i+1}P $= \Sigma_i$P then the polynomial hierarchy 'collapses' at level i and PSPACE $=$ PH $= \Sigma_i$P.

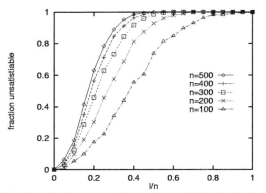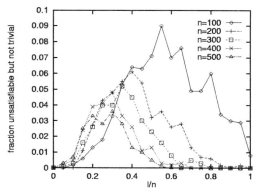

Figure 1: Random 2-QSAT problems from Cadoli *et al*'s flawed model, generated with $k = 3$ and varying n and l/n. **(left)** fraction of unsatisfiable problems; **(right)** fraction of unsatisfiable problems that are not trivial. The scale on the y-axis shows that at least 90% of all unsatisfiable problems were trivially insoluble in every case.

It is conjectured that no such collapse occurs.

In this paper, we analyse k-QSAT for all k and perform experiments on 2-QSAT. As in SAT, we can restrict the quantified formulae in a QSAT problem to conjunctive normal form (CNF). QSAT with formulae in CNF remains PSPACE-complete, and k-QSAT with formulae in 3-CNF remains Σ_kP-complete. (Cadoli, Giovanardi, & Schaerf 1998) propose an algorithm for solving QSAT problems in CNF which we use throughout this paper.

(Cadoli, Giovanardi, & Schaerf 1997) generalize the well known fixed clause model from SAT to QSAT. In this model, we fix the number of alternating quantifiers k, the cardinality of the set of variables to which each quantifier applies (typically an uniform size, n), the number of clauses l, and the size of the clauses h. Each clause is generated by choosing h distinct variables, negating each with probability $1/2$. Repeated clauses or clauses just containing universals (which are trivially unsatisfiable) are discarded.

Flawed and Flawless Problems

In SAT, empty and unit clauses are normally omitted in random generation methods where the number of literals in each clause varies. For example, in the 'constant probability' model proposed in (Mitchell, Selman, & Levesque 1992), each variable is included in a clause with some constant probability, but if only zero or one variable is included, the clause is discarded. An empty clause immediately makes a problem insoluble, but the reason for omitting unit clauses is more subtle. Suppose the model did not exclude unit clauses. Each clause generated from the n variables would have a certain probability of being unit. If the average clause size is constant, then for all n this probability is above some non-zero value q. As the l clauses are generated independently, about ql will be units. As there are only $2n$ different unit clauses, we expect to generate complementary unit clauses when $ql \approx \sqrt{2n}$, just as we expect to find two people with the same birthday in a group of about $\sqrt{365}$ people. If an instance contains complementary unit clauses it is trivially unsatisfiable. So

we expect problems to be trivially unsatisfiable when $l = O(\sqrt{n})$, but non-trivial unsatisfiability occurs at $l = O(n)$. Phase transition behavior is therefore eventually dominated by trivial insolubility. In short, a naive version of the constant probability model would be *flawed*, but Mitchell et al's version is *flawless*.

An analogous flaw was identified by (Achlioptas *et al*. 1997) in much-used random models of binary constraint satisfaction problems, although most experiments reported in the literature use parameters that are too small to be affected by flaws. (Gent *et al*. 1998) proposes a *flawless* model which eliminates the unit constraints that lead to trivially insolubility.

Cadoli et al's random QSAT model also contains a *flaw*. A QSAT instance is trivially unsatisfiable if it contains one clause with a single existential and the rest universal, and a second clause with the negation of this existential and the rest universals distinct from the first set. Such a pair of clauses is unsatisfiable since, when all the universals are F, the two units that remain after simplification are contradictory. In Cadoli et al's model with equal numbers of existential and universal variables and a fixed clause size h, the probability of each clause being unit-existential is $h/(2^h - 1)$. This is independent of n and so bounded above 0 as $n \to \infty$. As before, we expect to see two clauses with the single existential literals complementary when $l = O(\sqrt{n})$. With h fixed and $n \to \infty$, these two clauses will almost certainly have disjoint sets of universals. Unlike the constraint satisfaction models, the flaw occurs at sufficiently small problem sizes to have had a significant impact on previous experimental studies. Table 1 in (Cadoli, Giovanardi, & Schaerf 1997) appear to confirm this argument. The phase transition in solubility occurs when l is approximately proportional to $\sqrt{n}$.

To remove such trivial problems, we propose two new generation methods. We propose the name 'unit-flawless' for these methods since instances are immune from the flaws we have identified caused by unit clauses. Since it is possible that other flaws might exist the name 'flawless' is not justified, but we use it below as shorthand for 'unit-flawless' in the context of this paper. In

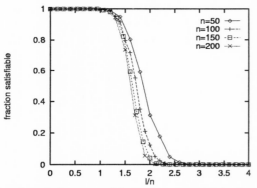
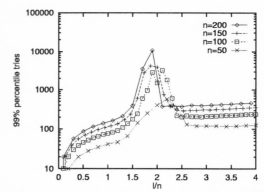

Figure 2: Random 2-QSAT problems from model A, $k = 3$, varying n and l/n. **(left)** fraction of satisfiable problems; **(right)** 99% percentile in search cost.

model A, we simply discard a clause that contains one or fewer existentials, and replace with a newly generated clause. In model B, we fix the number of existentials $e > 1$ that occur in each clause. We cannot generate a problem that is trivially unsatisfiable in either model.

Experimental verification

To show that trivially unsatisfiable problems dominate behavior in Cadoli et al's model, we ran an experiment with similar parameters to (Cadoli, Giovanardi, & Schaerf 1997). We use random 2-QSAT problems with $h = 3$. In this and subsequent experiments, we generate 1000 problems at each data point. Figure 1 shows the fraction of unsatisfiable problems and the fraction of these that are trivially unsatisfiable. We see that the phase transition is almost entirely due to trivially unsatisfiable problems. Only a few problems are unsatisfiable and not trivial, and the fraction of non-trivial ones goes down as n increases.

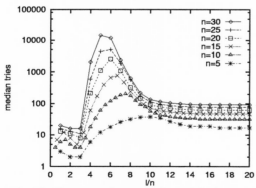

Figure 3: Median search cost of model A Random 2-QSAT problems, $h = 5$, varying n and l/n.

We next tested our proposed flawless model A, in which we discard clauses containing one or no existentials. We now observe a phase transition at an approximately fixed value of l/n. In Figure 2, we plot the fraction of satisfiable problems for random 2-QSAT

problems generated by model A, with $h = 3$. The phase transition occurs around $l/n \approx 2$. There is an easy-hard-easy pattern in search cost but only in the higher percentiles. Notice that there is an increase in search cost after the phase transition, probably associated with the overheads of dealing with more clauses. Median search cost is rather uniform across the phase transition. Model A problems are significantly harder to solve than problems from the flawed model. With the flawed model, we easily ran a phase transition experiment at $n = 500$. With model A, we were unable to run a complete phase transition experiment for $n > 200$. For problems with larger clauses, the easy-hard-easy pattern is not restricted to the higher percentiles. For example, in Figure 3 we plot the median search cost for random 2-QSAT with $h = 5$. The phase transition now occurs around $l/n \approx 6$. and we observe an easy-hard-easy pattern in median cost.

We also tested our second flawless model, model B, in which number of existentials is fixed. With two or more existentials in every clause, we again see a phase transition at an approximately fixed value of l/n. For example, in Figure 4 we plot results for random 2-QSAT problems generated by model B in which 2 out of 3 literals in each clause are existentials. The phase transition occurs around $l/n \approx 1.4$. As in Figure 2, search cost increases with l/n after the phase transition. Although these are the highest costs, we expect that the peaks in the phase transition region will dominate as n increases since they will grow faster than the overheads. The easy-hard-easy pattern in search cost is again restricted to the higher percentiles, as in model A with $h = 3$. Problems from model B are more uniform, and they tend to have less variation in problem difficulty than problems from model A. As has been seen in NP problems, more uniform models tend to lead to fewer exceptionally hard problems (Gent & Walsh 1994; Smith & Grant 1995).

State space

We can use the theory of constrainedness of search problems proposed in (Gent *et al.* 1996) to predict the location of phase transitions like this. Whilst this the-

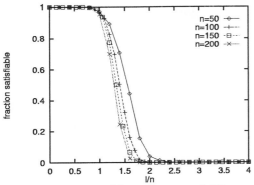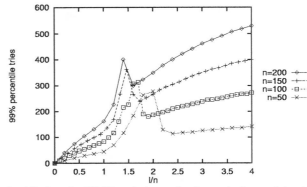

Figure 4: Random 2-QSAT problems from model B generated with 2 out of 3 literals in each clause being existentials, and varying n and l/n. (left) fraction of satisfiable problems; (right) 99% percentile in search cost.

ory was developed for NP-complete problems such as SAT, it has also been used in the complexity class P (Gent *et al.* 1997). To determine the constrainedness κ of random QSAT problems, we first identify the state space. A state is described by a set of substitutions for the existential variables. We need a set as there is a (possibly different) substitution for each set of values of the universal variables. The size of problems is equal to the number of bits needed to describe a state. For random 1-QSAT problems, we need n bits to describe a state as there are n existentials needing 1 bit each. For 2-QSAT problems, we need $n2^n$ bits to describe a state since there are 2^n different values for the universals, each of which requires n bits to specify the values for the existentials. In general, if we need s_k bits to specify a k-QSAT state for k even, we need $s_k + n$ bits for a $k+1$-QSAT state. And if we need s_k bits to specify a k-QSAT state for k odd, we need $2^n s_k$ bits to specify one k-QSAT state for each of the 2^n values of the new universal variables and hence a $k+1$-QSAT state. Thus, $2i$-QSAT problems have size $n \sum_{j=1}^{i} 2^{jn}$ and $(2i+1)$-QSAT problems have size $n \sum_{j=0}^{i} 2^{jn}$.

Constrainedness of QSAT

The informal notion of the constrainedness of a search problem has been formalised by the introduction of a constrainedness parameter, κ (Gent *et al.* 1996). Search problems with small κ values are underconstrained and almost surely soluble. Problems with large values of κ are over-constrained and almost surely insoluble. Inbetween, near $\kappa = 1$, problems are "critically constrained" and on the knife-edge between solubility and insolubility: in this region of κ we expect to see phase transition behavior and the hardest search problems. By definition (Gent *et al.* 1996) we have,

$$\kappa =_{\text{def}} -\frac{\log_2(\Pr\{\text{a state is a solution}\})}{\text{size of problem}}$$

We first derive a general formula for the constrainedness, κ, of k-QSAT problems. We will then specialize this formula for models A and B. For the general case, we assume that each of the l clauses has a probability

p_j of containing exactly j existentials but that $p_0 = 0$ to exclude clauses without any existentials. To simplify computation, we assume that clauses are generated independently of each other.

$$\begin{aligned}
&\Pr\{\text{a state is a solution}\} \\
=\ &\Pr\{\text{a state satisfies a set of } l \text{ clauses}\} \\
=\ &(\Pr\{\text{a state satisfies a clause}\})^l \\
=\ &(\sum_j p_j \Pr\{\text{a state satisfies a clause of } j \text{ existentials}\})^l
\end{aligned}$$

Given a state, and a clause with j existentials, at least one of the $h - j$ universals is true in all but 1 out of 2^{h-j} of the substitutions in the state. Hence, for random $2i$- or $2i + 1$-QSAT problems, we need not consider 2^{in} different substitutions for the existentials, but just $2^{in}/2^{h-j} = 2^{in+j-h}$, each of which is assumed to be independent[1]. One of the j existentials in a clause is true in all but 1 out of 2^j cases. Hence, $\Pr\{\text{a state satisfies a clause of } j \text{ existentials}\} = (1 - 1/2^j)^{2^{in+j-h}}$. For random $2i$-QSAT, this gives us

$$\kappa = -\frac{l}{n} \frac{1}{\sum_{j=1}^{i} 2^{jn}} \log_2(\sum_{j=1}^{h} p_j (1 - 1/2^j)^{2^{in+j-h}})$$

Similarly, for random $2i + 1$-QSAT,

$$\kappa = -\frac{l}{n} \frac{1}{\sum_{j=0}^{i} 2^{jn}} \log_2(\sum_{j=1}^{h} p_j (1 - 1/2^j)^{2^{in+j-h}})$$

Model A

As clauses containing zero or one existentials are discarded, $p_0 = p_1 = 0$ and $p_j = \binom{h}{j} / \sum_{i=2}^{h} \binom{h}{i} = \binom{h}{j} / (2^h - h - 1)$ for $j > 1$. For random 2-QSAT,

$$\kappa = -\frac{l}{n} \frac{1}{2^n} \log_2(\sum_{j=2}^{h} p_j (1 - \frac{1}{2^j})^{2^{n+j-h}})$$

---

[1] For 2-QSAT, this assumption is correct. For k-QSAT for $k > 2$, the innermost existentials can vary more than the outermost, so the assumption will start to break.

For large h, we make a mean-field approximation that each clause has $h/2$ existentials and universals. Hence,

$$
\begin{aligned}
\kappa &\approx -\frac{l}{n}\frac{1}{2^n}\log_2\left((1-\frac{1}{2^{h/2}})^{2^{n-h/2}}\right) \\
&= -\frac{l}{n}\frac{1}{2^{h/2}}\log_2(1-\frac{1}{2^{h/2}}) \\
&\approx -\frac{l}{n}\log_2(1-\frac{1}{2^h})
\end{aligned}
$$

Model B

Each of the l clauses contains exactly e existentials. That is, $p_e = 1$ and $p_j = 0$ for $j \neq e$. For random 2-QSAT, this gives,

$$
\kappa = -\frac{l}{n}2^{e-h}\log_2(1-\frac{1}{2^e})
$$

As $\log_2(1+x) \approx x/\ln(2)$ for small x, if h and e are large then,

$$
\kappa \approx \frac{l}{n}2^{e-h}\frac{1}{2^e\ln(2)} = \frac{l}{n}\frac{1}{2^h\ln(2)} \approx -\frac{l}{n}\log_2(1-\frac{1}{2^h})
$$

This is the same approximation as we derived for model A. Note that the constrainedness is independent of e, the number of existentials provided this and the clause size are large. Where there are n universal and n existential variables, the constrainedness of random 2-QSAT problems from either model is approximately *double* the constrainedness of a random SAT problem with the same number of variables, clauses, and clause size. This is perhaps not too surprising. Universally quantifying half the variables in a SAT problem is likely to give a much more constrained problem.

Location of phase transition

Constrainedness can be used to predict the location of phase transitions. In many NP-complete problems, phase transition behavior is seen at $\kappa \approx 1$ (Gent *et al.* 1996). For model B problems with 2 out of 3 literals in each clause being existential, the phase transition occurs at $\kappa \approx 0.30$, ($l/n \approx 1.4$). For model A problems with $h = 5$, the transition is at $\kappa \approx 0.28$, ($l/n \approx 6$).

To investigate why phase transitions occur earlier than predicted, we ran experiments with model B problems with $n = 25$ and $h = 5$, i.e. 5 literals in each clause, and varying numbers of existentials e in each clause. The phase transition occurs at larger values of l/n as we increase the number of existentials. With fewer, more constraining universals, we need more constraints on each of the less constraining existentials. As we move from $e = 4$ to $e = 5$, we move down a complexity class to NP. Not too surprisingly, there is a significant drop in problem hardness as we move from $e = 4$ to $e = 5$. More surprisingly, problem hardness increases as we increase the number of existentials (and reduce the number of universals) in each clause from $e = 2$ (and 3 universals in each clause) to $e = 4$ (and

just 1 universal). In Figure 5, we plot the constrainedness, κ, against the 99% percentile of search cost: as expected the peaks in search cost line up closely with the satisfiability transition. The location of the phase transition approaches $\kappa \approx 1$ as we increase the number of existentials in each clause. The rather constant shift of the phase transition as e increases may indicate a systematic error in our estimate for κ.

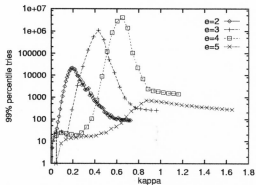

Figure 5: Model B problems with $n = 25$ and $h = 5$, varying number of existentials e, search cost *vs.* κ.

There is an alternative explanation for these errors. The prediction that the phase transition occurs around $\kappa \approx 1$ is based in part by the first moment Markov bound (that is, $prob(sol) \leq \langle Sol \rangle$). The location of phase transitions in NP problems can be predicted better by a second moment method using the variance in the number of solutions (Smith & Dyer 1996). In fact, at the SAT phase transition, an exponentially small number of problems have an exponential number of solutions (Kamath *et al.* 1995). In a PSPACE problem like QSAT, the variance in the number of solutions, and the super-exponential size of the state space, may result in the Markov bound being a less good predictor for the location of the phase transition.

Related and Further Work

This work is entirely novel in showing that the theory of constrainedness developed for NP problems (Gent *et al.* 1996) can be applied to a PSPACE problem. Since the theory has also been applied to a problem in P, that of establishing arc-consistency (Gent *et al.* 1997), constrainedness can be used both up and down the complexity hierarchy.

Phase transitions in PSPACE problems have been studied outside a general framework like the theory of constrainedness. Cadoli et al introduced an algorithm for QSAT and performed experimental evaluations (Cadoli, Giovanardi, & Schaerf 1997; 1998). As we discussed above, their randomly generated instances suffer from a flaw that can make them trivially insoluble. This may have given misleading impressions about the efficiency of their algorithm. We have introduced two new methods for generating 'flawless' random QSAT problems that are typically much harder.

The modal propositional logic K, which is PSPACE-complete, displays a phase transition and an easy-hard-easy pattern in search cost (Giunchiglia *et al.* 1998). The problem generator used in these experiments improves upon an earlier one that was criticised for giving instances that are 'trivial' as they are propositionally unsatisfiable (Hustadt & Schmidt 1997). Our use of the term 'trivial' is a complexity class lower: the unsatisfiable instances we identify in Cadoli et al's model can be found in almost linear time.

Bylander performed an average-case analysis on certain classes of problems within his model of random propositional STRIPS problems (Bylander 1996). He concluded by "suggesting that PSPACE-complete problems exhibit threshold phenomena similar to NP-complete problems." We can extend this conjecture by suggesting that the prediction of threshold phenomena using constrainedness can be extended from NP-complete problems through the polynomial hierarchy and to PSPACE-complete problems.

We have only tested our predictions experimentally for 2-QSAT. It would be interesting to investigate k-QSAT for $k > 2$, to see whether κ still makes reasonable predictions of the location of phase transitions. There are technical issues extending our definition of κ beyond k-QSAT to full QSAT (assuming the polynomial hierarchy does not collapse). Since any instance of a QSAT problem has some maximum number of alternating quantifiers, it would seem that our definition of κ for the relevant $k - $QSAT would apply. It is likely that this would work, provided that the values of p_j used in the derivation were correct. In particular, p_j would have to be the conditional probability of j existentials existing in a clause *given that* the instance contained exactly k alternating quantifiers. Even then, it is possible that technical difficulties would arise in defining κ, and we leave this question open for further investigation.

Conclusions

What general lessons can be learnt from this study? First, we can define the constrainedness of problems in PSPACE in a similar way to problems in NP. A phase transition in satisfiability and an easy-hard-easy pattern again occur at a critical value of constrainedness. However, predictions made by our theory are less accurate than in NP: we conjecture that this may be due to the huge state spaces of PSPACE-complete problems.

Second, we must take care to avoid trivially insoluble problems when generating random problems in new domains. Trivially insoluble problems have caused difficulties in propositional satisfiability, binary constraint satisfaction problems, and as we have shown here, QSAT. Since unit constraints are often the cause of trivially insolubility, we can usually generate *unflawed* problems by simply disallowing unit constraints.

Third, QSAT plays a similar role in PSPACE to the role played by SAT in NP. Because of this, we conjecture that constrainedness will be a useful theory in the study of many PSPACE problems of great interest in

AI. Outstanding examples include games playing and planning problems. While it will be interesting to see phase transitions in these problems, it will be fascinating if constrainedness can be used, as it has in NP, to suggest new search methods.

References

Achlioptas, D.; Kirousis, L.; Kranakis, E.; Krizanc, D.; Molloy, M.; and Stamatiou, Y. 1997. Random constraint satisfaction: A more accurate picture. In *Proc. CP97*, 107–120. Springer.

Bylander, T. 1996. A probabilistic analysis of propositional STRIPS planning. *Artificial Intelligence* 81:241–271.

Cadoli, M.; Giovanardi, A.; and Schaerf, M. 1997. Experimental analysis of the computational cost of evaluation quantified Boolean formulae. In *Proceedings of the AI*IA-97*, 207–218. Springer-Verlag. LNAI-1321.

Cadoli, M.; Giovanardi, A.; and Schaerf, M. 1998. An algorithm to evaluate quantified Boolean formulae. In *Proc. AAAI-98*, 262–267.

Gent, I. P., and Walsh, T. 1994. Easy problems are sometimes hard. *Artificial Intelligence* 335–345.

Gent, I.; MacIntyre, E.; Prosser, P.; and Walsh, T. 1996. The constrainedness of search. In *Proc. AAAI-96*, 246–252.

Gent, I.; MacIntyre, E.; Prosser, P.; Shaw, P.; and Walsh, T. 1997. The constrainedness of arc consistency. In *Proc. CP-97*, 327–340. Springer.

Gent, I.; MacIntyre, E.; Prosser, P.; Smith, B.; and Walsh, T. 1998. Random constraint satisfaction: Flaws and structure. Technical Report APES-08-1998, APES research group. http://www.cs.strath.ac.uk/~apes/apereports.html.

Giunchiglia, E.; Giunchiglia, F.; Sebastiani, R.; and Tacchella, A. 1998. More evaluation of decision procedures for modal logics. In *Proc. KR 98*. Morgan Kauffmann.

Hustadt, U., and Schmidt, R. 1997. On evaluating decision procedures for modal logic. In *Proc. IJCAI-97*, 202–207.

Kamath, A.; Motwani, R.; Palem, K.; and Spirakis, P. 1995. Tail bounds for occupancy and the satisfiability threshold conjecture. *Randomized Structure and Algorithms* 7:59–80.

Mitchell, D.; Selman, B.; and Levesque, H. 1992. Hard and easy distributions of SAT problems. In *Proc. AAAI-92*, 459–465.

Papadimitriou, C. 1994. *Computational Complexity*. Addison-Wesley.

Smith, B., and Dyer, M. 1996. Locating the phase transition in binary constraint satisfaction problems. *Artificial Intelligence* 81:155–181.

Smith, B., and Grant, S. 1995. Sparse constraint graphs and exceptionally hard problems. In *Proc. IJCAI-95*, 646–651.

Morphing: Combining Structure and Randomness

Ian P. Gent
Department of Computer Science
University of Strathclyde
Glasgow G1 1XL
Scotland
ipg@cs.strath.ac.uk

Holger H. Hoos
Department of Computer Science
University of British Columbia
Vancouver V6T 1Z4
Canada
hoos@cs.ubc.ca

Patrick Prosser and **Toby Walsh**
Department of Computer Science
University of Strathclyde
Glasgow G1 1XL
Scotland
{pat,tw}@cs.strath.ac.uk

Abstract

We introduce a mechanism called "morphing" for introducing structure or randomness into a wide variety of problems. We illustrate the usefulness of morphing by performing several different experimental studies. These studies identify the impact of a "small-world" topology on the cost of coloring graphs, of asymmetry on the cost of finding the optimal TSP tour, and of the dimensionality of space on the cost of finding the optimal TSP tour. We predict that morphing will find many other uses.

Introduction

Structures that occur in the real world problems tend to be neither completely regular nor completely random. Consider delivering parcels round Manhattan. One-way streets, traffic, road-works and a host of other factors make the problem more complex than navigating on a simple grid. To model the impact of one-way restrictions on such a delivery problem, we took a two-way grid and slowly introduced one-way streets into it at random (using a "morphing" process described in the next section). We did not introduce one-way streets completely at random but so that they eventually alternate in direction.

The result of this experiment was a little surprising. As expected, adding one-way streets increased the distance needed to deliver parcels to a random set of locations. However, the median cost to find the optimal route dropped. It appears to be easier to navigate in cities with one-way streets than cities with no one-way restrictions. The reason may be that one-way streets often leave few choices as to the optimal route. Whilst median cost tended to drop, higher percentiles in search cost were often larger. The reason may be that we can occasionally make a very bad choice and have to backtrack a long way.

To model structures like a Manhattan grid with a mixture of one-way and two-way streets, this paper introduces a general purpose mechanism called "morphing". We show that morphing has many other applications. It provides a simple dial with which we can introduce structure or randomness into problems. Morphing operations can be defined on almost any type of structure. For example, in our Manhattan delivery problem, we morphed directed graphs.

However, we can also morph distance matrices in traveling salesperson (TSP) problems, undirected graphs in coloring problems, clauses in satisfiability (SAT) problems, and relations in constraint satisfaction problems (CSPs). Morphing provides us with a powerful tool to study the impact of structure and randomness on these and many other types of problem.

Morphing

Given two structures, S_1 and S_2, we define either a type A, type B or type C morph from S_1 to S_2. In a type A morph, we take substructures from S_1 with probability $(1-p)$ and from S_2 with probability p. In a type B morph, we take a fraction $1-p$ of the substructures from S_1, and a fraction p of the substructures from S_2. In a type C morph, we assume the existence of suitable operations for addition and scalar multiplication, and compute $(1-p).S_1 + p.S_2$. We will often define the morphing operation so that if both structures have a substructure in common then this is also found in any morph. Here are some examples of the three types of morphs on a variety of different structures.

matrix morph (type A): the substructures are the entries; to morph between two $n \times m$ matrices we consider each entry in turn, and include the entry from the first matrix with probability $1-p$, otherwise we include that from the second matrix.

graph morph (type B): the substructures are the edges and gaps (absence of edges) between nodes; to morph between two n node graphs, G_1 and G_2, we take all edges in common, and a fraction $1-p$ of the remaining edges from the first graph, and p from the second.[1]

vector morph (type C): to morph between two vectors, $\vec{v}_1 = (x_1, y_1, \ldots)$ and $\vec{v}_2 = (x_2, y_2, \ldots)$, we construct the vector $(1-p).\vec{v}_1 + p.\vec{v}_2 = ((1-p).x_1 + p.x_2, (1-p).y_1 + p.y_2, \ldots)$.

satisfiability morph (type A): the substructures are clauses; to morph between two SAT problems, we include clauses from the first instance with probability $1-p$, and clauses from the second with probability p.

---

[1] We assume that the nodes in the two graphs share the same names.

set morph (type B): the substructures are the elements of the set; to morph between two sets, S_1 and S_2, we take all elements in common, $S_1 \cap S_2$, and a fraction $1 - p$ of the remaining elements from S_1, and p from S_2.

function morph (type C): to morph between the function $f_1(x)$ and the function $f_2(x)$, we construct the function $(1 - p).f_1(x) + p.f_2(x)$.

Two types of morph have already been studied in some detail.

random graphs: type A and B morphs between complete graphs and empty graphs give, respectively, the G_{np} and G_{nm} problem classes[2] (Bollobás 1985);

2+p-SAT problems: type B morphs between 2-SAT and 3-SAT problems give the $2 + p$-SAT problem class (Monasson *et al.* 1996), used to study changes in phase transition behavior as we move from P to NP.

In the rest of this paper, we look at four new applications: distance matrix morphs (to identify the impact of asymmetry on TSP problems); coordinate vector morphs (to study the impact of increasing the dimensionality of a TSP problem); ring lattice morphs (to model a recently identified topological structure called "small-worldiness"); and quasigroup morphs (to study in more detail the relationship between such small-worldiness and search cost).

Morphing and Small Worlds

Morphing provides us with a powerful tool to study topological structures like "small worldiness" that occur in many real-world graphs (Watts & Strogatz 1998). A small world graph has nodes that are highly clustered yet path lengths between them that are small. By comparison, random graphs with a similar number of nodes and edges have short path lengths but little clustering, whilst regular graphs like lattices tend to have high clustering but large path lengths. (Walsh 1998) shows that graphs associated with many search problems (e.g. exam timetabling, register allocation, quasigroup problems, ...) often have this topology. One reason for the occurrence of a small world topology is that it only takes a few short cuts between neighborhood cliques to turn a large world (in which the average path length between nodes is large) to a small world (in which the average path length is small). Walsh argues that a small world topology can make search problems very difficult since local decisions quickly propagate globally.

Testing for a Small World

To formalize the notion of a small world, Watts and Strogatz define the clustering coefficient and the characteristic path length. The path length is the number of edges in the shortest path between two nodes. The characteristic path length, L is the path length averaged over all pairs of nodes. The clustering coefficient is a measure of the cliqueness of the local neighborhoods. For a node with k neighbors, then at most $k(k-1)/2$ edges can exist between them (this occurs

if they form a k-clique). The clustering of a node is the fraction of these allowable edges that occur. The clustering coefficient, C is the average clustering over all the nodes in the graph. Watts and Strogatz define a small world graph as one in which $L \gtrsim L_{rand}$ and $C \gg C_{rand}$ where L_{rand} and C_{rand} are the characteristic path length and clustering coefficient of a random graph with the same number of nodes n and edges e. Walsh refines this definition, by proposing the proximity ratio μ, C/L normalized by C_{rand}/L_{rand}. Small world graphs are those in which $\mu \gg 1$.

Morphing v. Rewiring

To model small world graphs, (Watts & Strogatz 1998) and (Walsh 1998) use a rather complex method for randomly rewiring a ring lattice that circles the lattice a number of times, rewiring edges that are an increasing distance apart. This method gives graphs with a mixture of both structure and randomness. Morphing provides a much simpler and more general mechanism for constructing small world graphs. We simply morph between a clustered graph with large path lengths (e.g. a ring lattice) and a random graph (which has short path lengths but little clustering). The simplicity of the morphing process brings a variety of benefits. For example, the theoretical analysis of morphs is likely to be much easier than that of rewired graphs.

In Figure 1, we compare randomly rewiring a ring lattice with morphing between a ring lattice and a random graph. A ring lattice is a ring of n nodes, each connected to the k nearest neighbours. In this, and subsequent experiments, we use type B morphs. However, we observe very similar results with type A morphs. The characteristic path length, the clustering coefficient and proximity ratio all vary in a very similar manner, although there is a slight decrease in the maximum value of the proximity ratio, μ with morphing. At small p, we also see granularity effects. In type B graph morphs, p is the fraction of edges to include from one of the graphs. We therefore round to the nearest whole number. By comparison, p in random rewiring is a probability and so is not rounded. We also ran an experiment morphing between a ring lattice and a random graph using type A morphs. As this gave very similar results, we omit these graphs.

Local Search Procedures

To study the impact of small-worldiness on local search behavior, we encoded the problem of coloring small world graphs into SAT instances and solved these using WalkSAT, one of the most popular and efficient stochastic local search algorithms for SAT. As in the last section, we generated graphs by morphing between a ring lattice and a random graph with the same number of nodes and edges. To ensure that problems were of a manageable size for our algorithms, we used graphs with $n = 100$ and $k = 8$. Because of the regular ring lattice structure, the minimal chromatic number, c of these graphs is 5. However, some graphs with higher chromatic numbers do occur. Initial experiments indicated that the cost to color graphs with $c > 5$ is at least one order of magnitude lower than graphs with $c = 5$. To give a more homogeneous test set, we therefore filtered out the instances with $c \neq 5$ using a complete graph coloring

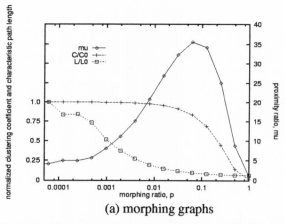

(a) morphing graphs

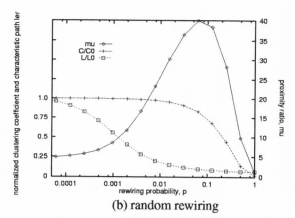

(b) random rewiring

Figure 1. Characteristic path length, clustering coefficient (left axis, normalized by the values for a regular lattice) and proximity ratio (right axis) for graphs generated (a) by morphing between a ring lattice and a random graph and (b) by random rewiring of a ring lattice. As in (Watts & Strogatz 1998), we use $n = 1000$ and $k = 10$. We vary $\log_2(p)$ from -15 to 0 in steps of 1, and generate 100 graphs at each value of p. A logarithmic horizontal scale helps to identify the interval in which the characteristic path length drops rapidly, the clustering coefficient remains almost constant, and the proximity ratio, μ peaks. To aid comparison, the same x and y scales are used in both figures.

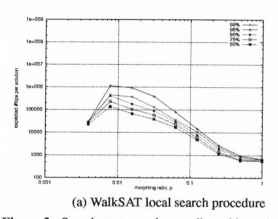

(a) WalkSAT local search procedure

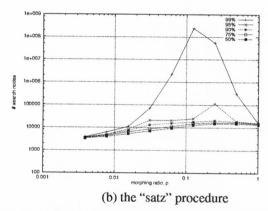

(b) the "satz" procedure

Figure 2. Search cost to color small world graphs; **(a)** percentiles of expected number of flips required by the local search procedure, WalkSAT; **(b)** percentiles of nodes visited by the complete search procedure, satz. The small world graphs are generated by morphing between a ring lattice and a random graph with $n = 100$, $k = 8$, and p varying $\log_2(p)$ from -8 to -2 in steps of 1. The proximity ratio, μ peaks around $\log_2(p) \approx -4$ similar to Figure 1. 100 5-colourable graphs were used at each value of p.

algorithm provided by Joe Culberson. We then encoded the remaining problems into SAT, with each propositional variable representing a particular color being assigned to a node. We solved each instance with WalkSAT, measuring the expected number of flips to find a solution over 100 runs of the algorithms. We set the cutoff parameter large enough that a solution was found in each run, and optimised the noise parameter for each value of p to give approximately minimal local search cost. Interestingly, the optimal noise setting appears to be positively correlated with p, i.e., the more random structure in graphs, the less greediness needed in WalkSAT to obtain optimal performance.

Figure 2 (a) shows the higher percentiles in the local search cost for varying p. All the percentiles peak at $\log_2(p) = -7$ (including the lower percentiles not shown in the graph). Near to this point, the variability in search

cost across the test set is also maximal and the variation coefficient (standard deviation/mean) = 3.05. Whilst the distribution of the expected search costs across the test set around this region, is heavy-tailed, search costs on individual instances appear to best fit an exponential distribution. This suggests that the restart mechanism does not improve performance on these problems. Note also that when decreasing $\log_2(p)$ from -7 to -8 all percentiles drop sharply, for the higher percentiles by more than an order of magnitude. This indicates that for regularly structured graphs, slightly perturbing the structure drastically increases the expected local search cost (the expected number of flips for solving the regular ring lattice graph, i.e., $p = 0$, is 19043.38). However, as we introduce more randomness into problems, the performance of local search procedures improves.

problem	n	l	density	C	C_{rand}	L	L_{rand}	μ
`hanoi4`	718	3934	1.9%	0.462	0.0187	6.713	2.796	10.278
`ssa0432-003`	435	1027	1.0%	0.445	0.0779	4.273	5.536	4.406
`bf0432-135`	424	1031	1.0%	0.442	0.0833	5.552	4.296	4.108
`par16-1-c`	317	1264	1.8%	0.364	0.0407	3.984	3.521	7.899
`aim-100-1-6-yes1-1`	100	160	7.2%	0.302	0.0747	2.740	2.534	3.745

Table 1. Characteristic path lengths, clustering coefficients and proximity ratios for satisfiability problems with n variables and l clauses from the DIMACS benchmark library. Edge density is the fraction of possible edges in the constraint graph. Problems are both satisfiable and unsatisfiable. `hanoi4` is a encoding of the Towers of Hanoi planning problem. `ssa0432-003` is an encoding of a circuit analysis problem with a "single–stuck–at" fault. `bf0432-135` is an encoding of a circuit analysis problem with a "bridge–fault". `par16-1-c` is an encoding of a problem in learning the 16 bit parity function. `aim-100-1-6-yes1-1` is an artificially generated problem with a single satisfying assignment.

Complete Methods

Comparison of our results with results reported in (Walsh 1998) for coloring randomly rewired graphs using a complete graph coloring algorithm, suggests that the performance of local and complete search methods may differ significantly on small world problems. Local and systematic search methods may therefore complement each other. With a small amount of randomness in problems, complete methods may have fewer difficulties than local search, while with more randomness, the situation seems to reverse. To test this hypothesis, we ran a second series of experiments using "satz" (Li & Anbulagan 1997), one of the best complete search algorithms for SAT.

Figure 2 (b) shows the higher percentiles of the search cost for satz. The performance of satz is clearly affected by the small-worldliness differently to WalkSAT. Median search cost increases monotonically with p up to $\log_2(p) = -1$ and then drops slightly. By comparison, there is a very distinctive peak in the 99% percentile around $p = 0.1$, in the region where the graphs have maximal small-worldliness. Around this peak, the difference between the 95% and 99% percentiles is huge (up to 4 orders of magnitude), and the distribution of search costs across the test set, as well as on individual instances, displays a heavy-tail. This suggests that a randomization and restart strategy will be effective on these problems (Gomes, Selman, & Crato 1997). Similar extremely hard instances were observed in (Walsh 1998), where a small fraction of randomly rewired graphs with high proximity ratios, μ were found to be extremely difficult for a complete graph coloring algorithm.

These results support the hypothesis that local search procedures tend to have difficulties with relatively regular instances which are easy for complete methods, while complete methods tend to have difficulties with more random instances which are easy for local search procedures. This suggests that it might pay to solve these problem by applying both algorithms simultaneously and terminating when either one finds a solution. Such "portfolios" of algorithms have been proposed in (Huberman, Lukose, & Hogg 1997; Gomes, Selman, & Kautz 1998). With such an approach, the overall performance and, perhaps even more importantly, the robustness of problem solving can be improved. The optimal mix of the algorithms in such a portfolio depends on the exact performance of each individual algorithm. The me-

dian run time (as well as the higher percentiles) for WalkSAT and satz cross over approximately where the peak in small-worldiness is located. This suggests that small-worldiness may be a structural property which tends to give *minimal* leverage for portfolio combinations of WalkSAT and satz.

Encoding Small Worlds

In recent years, there has been considerable success encoding many different search problems into SAT and using either a fast local search method like WalkSAT or an efficient complete procedure like satz. Does encoding into SAT preserve or destroy the topological structure? To measure the topology of a satisfiability problem, we construct the constraint graph, in which nodes are the propositional variables, and edges connect any variables that occur together in a clause.

We ran a test on the DIMACS satisfiability benchmark. Many of the encodings of problems in this library have a small world topology. Table 1 gives a representative sample of results. Path lengths are usually comparable to that of a random graph. However, nodes are often more clustered than in random graphs of a similar density. Other types of encoding can disguise the topological structure inherent in a problem. For example, if we encode numbers into SAT using a logarithmic representation on the binary bits (an encoding that has been used for factorization and Hamiltonian circuit problems) then the topological structures may be lost within the complexity of the encoding. However, we conjecture that encodings that are good for search will tend to preserve topological structure. Indeed, they may even emphasize it.

Morphing Quasigroups

A quasigroup is a Latin square, a m by m multiplication table in which each entry appears just once in each row or column. Quasigroups model a variety of practical problems like tournament scheduling and designing drug tests, and have been proposed as the basis of a benchmark for constraint satisfaction algorithms (Gomes & Selman 1997). The constraint graph for such problems consist of $2m$ cliques, one for each row and column, with each clique being of size m. (Walsh 1998) shows that, for large m, the constraint graph of quasigroup problems have a small world topology, with a proximity ratio $\mu \approx m/4$.

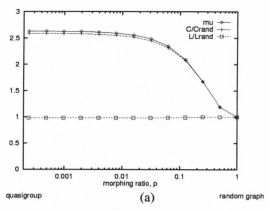
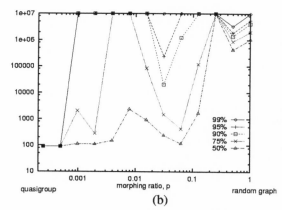

Figure 3. Morphs generated between an order 10 quasigroup and a random graph: **(a)** characteristic path length, clustering coefficient (scaled by their values for a random graph with the same number of nodes and edges) and proximity ratio, μ; **(b)** percentiles in the search cost to color these morphs.

Morphing quasigroups tends to reduce their small-worldiness as we break up the neighborhood clustering. Despite this decrease in small-worldiness, the cost to color such graphs often increases. In Figure 3, we plot the clustering coefficients, characteristic path lengths, proximity ratios and coloring cost for morphs between an order 10 quasigroup and a random graph with the same number of nodes and edges. We used a graph coloring algorithm which is based upon Brelaz's DSATUR algorithm and imposed a search cut-off at 10^7 nodes. As p increases, we break up the neighborhood structure of the quasigroup and the clustering coefficient drops. The characteristic path length is short and stays relatively constant. As a consequence, the proximity ratio, μ drops along with the clustering coefficient.

Coloring costs for these morphs are often very large. This result suggests that other factors in addition to small-worldiness contribute to the hardness of these coloring problems. Detailed analysis of the search costs shows that the heaviest-tailed distributions occur either with random graphs with a small amount of structure (e.g. $\log_2(p) = -2$) or quasigroups graphs with a small amount of randomness (e.g. $\log_2(p) = -10$ and -8). Inbetween (e.g. $\log_2(p) = -4$ and -6), we see less of a heavy-tail. We conjecture that the addition of a little randomness to structure, or a little structure to randomness can confuse search heuristics and make graphs hard to color.

Morphing TSPs

Symmetry *v.* Asymmetry

What impact does symmetry have on the TSP problem? In the Manhattan delivery example from the introduction, adding one-way streets introduces a certain amount of asymmetry into the distance matrix and usually made problems easier. Is it generally true that asymmetry will tend to make TSP problems easier? To test this, we ran an experiment morphing directly between a symmetric and an asymmetric distance matrix.

To reduce variance in inter-city distances, we took a symmetric distance matrix and made it asymmetric by permut-

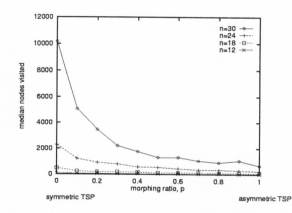

Figure 4. Median cost to find optimal tour for morphs between symmetric and asymmetric TSPs. Other percentiles and mean cost are similar. Inter-city distances are normally distributed with a mean of 10^3 and a standard deviation of 10^2. Each data point is the average of 100 problems.

ing the lower lefthand triangle. We then found the optimal tour for type B morphs between the original symmetric problem and this asymmetric problem. We generated symmetric distance matrices with between 12 and 30 cities, normally distributed with a mean inter-city distance of 10^3 and a standard deviation of 10^2. To find the optimal tour, we used a branch and bound algorithm with the Hungarian heuristic for branching.

In Figure 4, we plot the search cost to find the optimal tour. Whilst the optimal tour length decreases by just a few percent as we introduce asymmetry into the problems, the cost to find the optimal tour drops dramatically. We conjecture that asymmetry reduces search by reducing the amount of non-determinism in the problem. If the distance from A to B is significantly shorter than that from B to A, then an optimal tour that includes a leg between A and B will almost certainly visit A first. Unlike the symmetric case, we probably need not consider tours that visit B first.

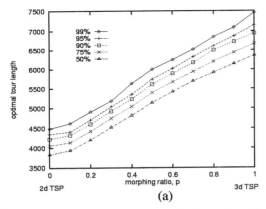
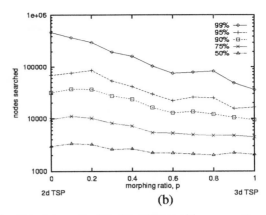

(a)   (b)

Figure 5. Percentiles in (a) optimal tour length and (b) cost to find optimal tour for 20 city TSP problems constructed by morphing between two and three dimensions. In the 3-d case, cities are distributed uniformly and at random within a cube of side 1000. In the 2-d case, we project the 3-d problems down onto the x-y plane. Each data point is the average of 1000 problems.

2-d v. 3-d

What impact does the dimensionality of a TSP problem have on optimal tour length and cost to find it? To explore this question, we ran an experiment morphing between 2-dimensional and 3-dimensional TSP problems. We took points randomly distributed in a 3-d cube and flattened them onto the x-y plane. We then constructed type C morphs between the coordinate vectors for the original 3-d problem and those for the flattened 2-d problem. As we increase the morphing ratio p, the points gradually rise off the x-y plane and the z dimension starts to contribute to the problem.

In Figure 5, we plot the optimal tour length and search cost for 20 city problems, with cities distributed uniformly and at random within a cube of side 1000. We again used a branch and bound algorithm with the Hungarian heuristic for branching. As we introduce a third dimension into the problem, cities become further apart and the optimal tour length increases. However, the cost to find the optimal tour tends to drop. For the 95% and lower percentiles, there appears to be a slight rise in cost for small p, but aside from this, search cost drops uniformly. We conjecture that a third dimension increases the variance in inter-city distances, and this makes the optimal tour more obvious.

To conclude, symmetric and 2-dimensional TSP problems appear to be harder than asymmetric and 3-dimensional problems. This is a valuable result as many TSP problems met in practice are likely to be both symmetric and 2-dimensional.

Related Work

Monasson *et al.* introduce the 2+p-SAT model to study the change from a "second order" phase transition for random 2-SAT to a "first order" transition for random 3-SAT (Monasson *et al.* 1996). In the 2+p-SAT model, problems are randomly generated with pl clauses of length 3, and $(1 - p)l$ clauses of length 2. Such problems can also be generated by morphing between random 2-SAT problems and random 3-SAT problems. They predict that for $p < 0.413\ldots$, a phase

transition in satisfiability will occur around a ratio of clauses to variables of $1/(1 - p)$. Achlioptas *et al.* prove this result for $p \leq 0.4$, and provide upper and lower bounds on the location of the phase transition for $p > 0.4$ (Achlioptas *et al.* 1997). This is a rather surprising result since it means that, for $p < 0.4$, the non-binary clauses are "irrelevant" and the binary clauses alone are enough to make problems unsatisfiable.

Gomes and Selman have proposed random quasigroup completion problems as a benchmark that combines together some of the best features of randomly generated instances and highly structured problems (Gomes & Selman 1997). Quasigroup completion is the problem of coloring a partial colored quasigroup. The preassignment of colors perturbs the problem by adding unary constraints. However, the perturbation of the binary constraints performed in morphing quasigroups appears to give more demanding problems. For example, an algorithm that maintains generalized arc-consistency can solve almost all quasigroup completion problems up to order 25 with just a few branches of search (Shaw, Stergiou, & Walsh 1998). By comparison, even with such powerful propagation techniques, quasigroup morphs of order 25 are often very hard to color.

Conclusions

We have proposed a very general mechanism called "morphing" for introducing structure or randomness into a wide variety of problems. Many different types of structures can be morphed including graphs, matrices, vectors, relations, and clauses. To illustrate the usefulness of morphing, we performed several different experimental studies. These studies identify the impact of a "small-world" topology on the cost of coloring graphs, and the benefits of a portfolio of algorithms for solving such problems; of symmetry in the cost matrix on the cost of finding the optimal TSP tour; and of the dimensionality of space on the cost of finding the optimal TSP tour.

What general lessons can be learnt from this study? First, many problems met in practice may be neither completely structured nor completely random but something inbetween. Morphing provides us with a general purpose mechanism for modelling such problems. Second, a mixture of structure and randomness can make problems very hard to solve. A little structure added to a random problem, or a little randomness added to a structured problem may be enough to mislead our search heuristics. And third, morphing provides many of the advantages of random and structured problem classes without some of the disadvantages. As in random problem classes, we can generate large, and statistically significant samples with ease. However, unlike random problems, the problems generated can contain the sort of structures met in practice.

References

Achlioptas, D.; Kirousis, L.; Kranakis, E.; and Krizanc, D. 1997. Rigorous results for random (2+p)-SAT. In *Proceedings of RALCOM-97*, 1–10.

Bollobás, B. 1985. *Random Graphs*. London: Academic Press.

Gomes, C., and Selman, B. 1997. Problem structure in the presence of perturbations. In *Proceedings of the 14th National Conference on AI*, 221–226. American Association for Artificial Intelligence.

Gomes, C.; Selman, B.; and Crato, N. 1997. Heavy-tailed distributions in combinatorial search. In Smolka, G., ed., *Proceedings of Third International Conference on Principles and Practice of Constraint Programming (CP97)*, 121–135. Springer.

Gomes, C.; Selman, B.; and Kautz, H. 1998. Boosting combinatorial search through randomization. In *Proceedings of 15th National Conference on Artificial Intelligence*, 431–437. AAAI Press/The MIT Press.

Huberman, B.A.; Lukose, R.M.; and Hogg, T. 1997. An Economics Approach to Hard Computational Problems. In *Science* 275:51–54.

Li, C., and Anbulagan. 1997. Look-ahead versus look-back for satisfiability problems. In *Proceedings of Third International Conference on Principles and Practice of Constraint Programming (CP97)*, LNCS, 341–355. Springer Verlag.

Monasson, R.; Zecchina, R.; Kirkpatrick, S.; Selman, B.; and Troyansky, L. 1996. Phase transition and search cost in the 2+p-SAT problem. In *Proceedings of 44th Workshop on Physics and Computation (PhysComp96)*. Boston University.

Shaw, P.; Stergiou, K.; and Walsh, T. 1998. Arc consistency and quasigroup completion. In *Proceedings of ECAI-98 Workshop on Non-binary Constraints, Brighton*.

Walsh, T. 1998. Search in a small world. Technical report, Department of Computer Science, University of Strathclyde, APES-07-1998. Available from http://www.cs.strath.ac.uk/ apes/reports/apes-07-1998.ps.gz.

Watts, D., and Strogatz, S. 1998. Collective dynamics of 'small-world' networks. *Nature* 393:440–442.

On the Run-time Behaviour of Stochastic Local Search Algorithms for SAT

Holger H. Hoos

University of British Columbia
Department of Computer Science
2366 Main Mall, Vancouver, B.C., Canada V6T 1Z4
hoos@cs.ubc.ca

Abstract

Stochastic local search (SLS) algorithms for the propositional
satisfiability problem (SAT) have been successfully applied
to solve suitably encoded search problems from various domains. One drawback of these algorithms is that they are
usually incomplete. We refine the notion of incompleteness
for stochastic decision algorithms by introducing the notion
of "probabilistic asymptotic completeness" (PAC) and prove
for a number of well-known SLS algorithms whether or not
they have this property. We also give evidence for the practical impact of the PAC property and show how to achieve
the PAC property and significantly improved performance in
practice for some of the most powerful SLS algorithms for
SAT, using a simple and general technique called "random
walk extension".

Introduction

Stochastic local search (SLS) algorithms for the propositional satisfiability problem (SAT) have attracted considerable attention within the AI community over the past few
years. They belong to the most powerful methods for practically solving large and hard instances of SAT, and outperform the best systematic search methods on a number
of domains. However, one of the problems with these algorithms is the fact they are usually *incomplete*, i.e., they
cannot be used to prove that a given problem instance is
unsatisfiable and — maybe worse — for soluble problem
instances, there is no guarantee that such an algorithm actually finds a solution. Early local SLS algorithms like GSAT
(Selman, Levesque, & Mitchell 1992) were mainly based on
hill-climbing and got easily trapped in local minima of the
objective function induced by the given problem instance.
These algorithms used *random restart* after a fixed number
of steps to avoid premature stagnation of the search. Later,
different strategies were used to effectively escape from local minima without using random restart; one of the most
popular of these mechanism is *random walk* (Selman, Kautz,
& Cohen 1994), which allows randomised up-hill moves
with a fixed probability. Today, the best-performing SLS algorithms for SAT use various more sophisticated strategies,
combined with random restart, to prevent early stagnation of
the search. However, although these algorithm show a very
impressive performance, there are almost no theoretical results on their concrete or asymptotic behaviour.

In this paper, we refine the notion of completeness for
the class of Las Vegas decision algorithms (a superclass of
SLS algorithms). We introduce the term "probabilistically
approximately complete" (PAC) to formalise the notion of
probabilistic algorithms which are incomplete, but find a solution of soluble instances with a probability approaching
one as the run-time approaches infinity. Next, we present
theoretical results on the PAC property for a number of popular SLS algorithms for SAT, including the recently introduced Novelty and R-Novelty variants of the WalkSAT architecture (McAllester, Selman, & Kautz 1997).

However, in practice asymptotic properties like PAC are
not always relevant. Therefore, we present some empirical results which indicate that in the cases considered here,
the theoretical results have practical consequences when applying the respective algorithms to well-known benchmark
problems. Based on these empirical results, we then show
how Novelty and R-Novelty, two of the best-performing
SLS algorithms for SAT known today, can be further improved with respect to both, their theoretical properties and
practical behaviour.

SLS Algorithms for SAT

Stochastic local search approaches for SAT became prominent in 1992, when independently Selman, Levesque, and
Mitchell (Selman, Levesque, & Mitchell 1992) as well as
Gu (Gu 1992) introduced algorithms based on stochastic local hill-climbing which could be shown to outperform state-of-the-art systematic SAT algorithms on a variety of hard subclasses of SAT (Buro & Kleine-Büning 1992;
Selman, Kautz, & Cohen 1994). The algorithms considered
here are model finding algorithms for CNF formulae. The
underlying state space is always defined as the set of all truth
assignments for the variables appearing in the given formula.
Local search steps modify at most the value assigned to one
of the propositional variables appearing in the formula; such
a move is called a *variable flip*. The objective function is
always defined as the number of clauses which are unsatisfied under a given variable assignment; thus, the models
of the given formula are always the global minima of this
function. The general idea for finding these is to perform
stochastic hill-climbing on the objective function, starting
from a randomly generated initial assignment.

The main difference between the individual algorithms
lies in the strategy used to select the variable to be flipped
next. In this paper, we focus on the well-known GSAT and

```
procedure GWSAT(F, maxTries, maxSteps, wp)
    for try := 1 to maxTries do
        a := randomly chosen assignment of the variables in formula F;
        for step := 1 to maxSteps do
            if a satisfies F then return a;
            with probability wp do
                c := randomly selected clause which is unsatisfied under a;
                v := randomly selected variable appearing in c;
            otherwise
                v := randomly selected variable the flip of which minimises
                    the number of unsatisfied clauses;
            end with;
            a := a with v flipped;
        end for;
    end for;
    return "no solution found";
end GWSAT;
```

Figure 1: The GWSAT algorithm.

```
procedure WalkSAT(F, maxTries, maxSteps, Select)
    for try := 1 to maxTries do
        a := randomly chosen assignment of the variables in F;
        for step := 1 to maxSteps do
            if a satisfies F then return a;
            c := randomly selected clause which is unsatisfied under a;
            v := variable from a selected according to a heuristic Select;
            a := a with v flipped;
        end for;
    end for;
    return "no solution found";
end WalkSAT;
```

Figure 2: The WalkSAT algorithm.

WalkSAT family of algorithms (Selman, Kautz, & Cohen 1994; Gent & Walsh 1993b; McAllester, Selman, & Kautz 1997), which provided a substantial driving force for the development of SLS algorithms for SAT and have been very successful when applied to a broad range of problems from different domains.

The GWSAT algorithm is outlined in Figure 1. Starting from a randomly chosen variable assignment, it repeatedly flips variables according to the following heuristic: With a fixed probability wp, a currently unsatisfied clause is randomly selected and one of the variables appearing in it (also randomly selected) is flipped; this is called a *random walk step*. In the remaining cases, one of the variables which, when flipped, achieve the maximal increase (or least decrease) in the total number of satisfied clauses is selected and flipped. If after *maxSteps* such flips no solution is found, the search is started from a new, randomly chosen assignment. If after *maxTries* such tries still no solution is found, the algorithm terminates unsuccessfully. GWSAT with $wp=0$ corresponds to the original GSAT algorithm.

WalkSAT algorithms (*cf.* Figure 2) also start from a randomly chosen variable assignment and repeatedly select one of the clauses which are violated by the current assignment. Then, according to some heuristic a variable occurring in this clause is flipped using a greedy bias to increase the total

number of satisfied clauses. For the original WalkSAT algorithm, in the following referred to simply as WalkSAT, the following heuristic is applied. If in the selected clause variables can be flipped without violating other clauses, one of these is randomly chosen. Otherwise, with a fixed probability p a variable is randomly chosen from the clause and with probability $1-p$ a variable is picked which minimises the number of clauses which are currently satisfied but would become violated by the variable's flip (number of breaks).

Other, more recently introduced WalkSAT algorithms (McAllester, Selman, & Kautz 1997) are given by the following heuristics for selecting the variable to be flipped within the selected clause:

WalkSAT/TABU Same as WalkSAT, but uses a tabu-list of length tl to ensure that after a variable has been flipped it cannot be flipped for the next tl steps. If within the selected clause, all variables are tabu, no variable is flipped (a so-called *null-flip*).

Novelty Considers the variables in the selected clause sorted according to their score, *i.e.*, the difference in the total number of satisfied clauses a flip would cause. If the best variable according to this ordering (*i.e.*, the one with maximal score) is not the most recently flipped one, it is flipped, otherwise, it is flipped with a fixed probability $1-p$, while in the remaining cases, the second-best variable is flipped.

R-Novelty Like Novelty, but in the case where the best variable is the most recently flipped one the decision between the best and second-best variable probabilistically depends on their score difference — the details are not important here and can be found in (McAllester, Selman, & Kautz 1997). Additionally, every 100 steps, instead of using this heuristic, the variable to be flipped is randomly picked from the selected clause.

As for GWSAT, if after *maxSteps* such flips no solution is found, the search is started from a new, randomly selected assignment; and if after *maxTries* such tries still no solution is found, the algorithm terminates unsuccessfully.

Asymptotic Behaviour of Algorithms

Las Vegas algorithms[1] are stochastic algorithms which, if they find a solution for the given problem, guarantee the correctness of this solution. This is captured by the following definition (adapted from (Hoos & Stützle 1998)):

Definition 1 *Let Π be a problem class. An algorithm A is a Las Vegas algorithm for problem class Π, if (i) whenever for a given problem instance $\pi \in \Pi$ it returns a solution s, s is guaranteed to be a valid solution of π, and (ii) on each given instance π, the run-time of A is a random variable $RT_{A,\pi}$.*

Stochastic local search algorithms are special cases of Las Vegas algorithms. According to this definition, Las Vegas algorithms are always correct, but they are not necessarily complete, *i.e.*, even if a given problem instance has a solution, a Las Vegas algorithm is generally not guaranteed to find it. However, even an incomplete Las Vegas algorithm might be asymptotically complete in the sense that by running it long enough, the probability of missing an existing

---

[1]The term was originally coined by Laszlo Babai in 1979 (personal communication).

solution can be made arbitrarily small. This property, which is often referred to as "convergence" in the literature on optimisation algorithms, is theoretically interesting (cf. (Geman & Geman 1984)) and is also potentially very relevant for practical applications. We formalise this notion for Las Vegas algorithms for decision problems in the following way.

Definition 2 *Let Π be a decision problem and A a Las Vegas Algorithm for Π. For a given problem instance $\pi \in \Pi$, let $P_s(RT_{A,\pi} \leq t)$ denote the probability that A finds a solution for π in time $\leq t$ and let $P \subseteq \Pi$. Then we call A probabilistically approximately complete (PAC) for P, if for all soluble instances $\pi \in P$, $\lim_{t \to \infty}[P_s(RT_{A,\pi} \leq t)] = 1$. Furthermore, we call A essentially incomplete for P, if it is not PAC for P, i.e., there is a soluble instance $\pi \in P$, for which $\lim_{t \to \infty}[P_s(RT_{A,\pi} \leq t)] < 1$. If A is PAC / essentially incomplete for Π, we call A probabilistically approximately complete (PAC) / essentially incomplete.*

These concepts refine the usual distinction between complete and incomplete algorithms. The simplest stochastic search algorithm which is provably PAC, is "random picking": Given a set S of candidate solutions (for SAT: all assignments for the variables appearing in the given formula), iteratively select an arbitrary element of S such that in each step, each element of S is selected with equal probability $p = 1/|S|$. Obviously this algorithm is PAC, as the probability of finding a solution in t steps, assuming that there are $k > 0$ different solutions in S, is $1 - (1 - kp)^t$. But of course, random picking is typically hopelessly inefficient in practice, in the sense that even for NP-complete problems like SAT, algorithms like GSAT or WalkSAT are orders of magnitude faster than it in finding solutions. Nevertheless, in practice, the PAC property can be important, especially with respect to the robustness of Las Vegas algorithms, as it guarantees that that the algorithm will, given sufficient time, almost certainly find a solution for a soluble problem instance.

Theoretical Results

In this section we prove a number of results regarding the PAC property of various well-known SLS algorithms for SAT. In all cases, we consider the "pure" search strategies without random restart. The rationale behind this is the following. Random restart can be easily added to any given search strategy and the resulting algorithm will always be PAC if, as the run-time increases, an arbitrarily large number of restarts can occur. However, this trivial result is practically irrelevant, as the run-times for which this asymptotic behaviour can be observed are even considerably higher than for random picking. On the other hand, as we will show later, other mechanisms, such as random walk, which achieve the PAC property are much more effective in practice.

GSAT

We start with proving that the basic GSAT algorithm is essentially incomplete. Although the fact that GSAT can get stuck in local minima of the objective function is well-known, we are not aware of a formal proof. We therefore give a proof here which also demonstrates the technique we use later to prove some previously unknown essential incompleteness results. Note that generally, to show that an

SLS algorithm for SAT is not PAC, i.e., essentially incomplete, it is sufficient to find a satisfiable problem instance and a reachable state of the algorithm from which no solution can be reached. Since all algorithms considered here start their search by randomly picking an arbitrary variable assignment, all assignments are reachable and for proving essential incompleteness we can assume any current variable assignment.

Theorem 1 *Basic GSAT, i.e., GWSAT with $wp = 0$ (without restart), is essentially incomplete.*

Proof. Let $F_1 = \bigwedge_{i=1}^{10} c_i$ be the CNF formula consisting of the clauses:

$$
\begin{aligned}
c_1 &\equiv \neg x_1 \vee x_2 \vee \neg z_1 \\
c_2 &\equiv \neg x_1 \vee x_2 \vee z_1 \\
c_3 &\equiv \neg x_1 \vee x_2 \vee \neg z_2 \\
c_4 &\equiv \neg x_1 \vee x_2 \vee z_2 \\
c_5 &\equiv x_1 \vee \neg x_2 \vee \neg z_1 \\
c_6 &\equiv x_1 \vee \neg x_2 \vee z_1 \\
c_7 &\equiv x_1 \vee \neg x_2 \vee \neg z_2 \\
c_8 &\equiv x_1 \vee \neg x_2 \vee z_2 \\
c_9 &\equiv x_1 \vee x_2 \vee \neg y \\
c_{10} &\equiv x_1 \vee x_2 \vee y
\end{aligned}
$$

F_1 is satisfiable and has 8 models ($x_1 = x_2 = \top$; y, z_1, z_2 arbitrary). Consider the 4 possible assignments for which $x_1 : \bot, x_2 : \bot, y : \bot$ and call this set A. Analogously, let B denote the set consisting of the 4 assignments with $x_1 : \bot, x_2 : \bot, y : \top$. Note that $A \cup B$ does not contain any solution. Assume that GSAT's current assignment is an element of A. Each assignment from A satisfies all clauses except c_{10} and the variables receive the following scores: $x_1, x_2 : -1, y, z_1, z_2 : 0$. Since GSAT always flips one of the variables with the highest score, z_1, z_2 or y is flipped. By flipping z_1 or z_2, another assignment in A is reached. by flipping y, depending on the values of z_1 and z_2 an assignment of B is reached. Now, all clauses except c_9 are satisfied and the variable receive the same scores as before. Again, only z_1, z_2 or y can be flipped. While in the former case, only assignments from B can reached, by flipping y always an assignment in A is obtained. Therefore, starting from an assignment in A or B, GSAT cannot reach a solution which proves the theorem. $\square$

Adding Random Walk — GWSAT

Next, we show that by adding random walk (Selman, Kautz, & Cohen 1994), basic GSAT can be made PAC. This result extends earlier work which established that satisfiable 2-SAT instances are solved by pure random walk in $O(n^2)$ time on average (Papadimitriou 1991). Using similar techniques, we first show that from an arbitrary assignment, the hamming distance to the nearest solution can always be decreased by a random walk step (flipping a variable in a randomly selected, currently unsatisfied clause).

Lemma 1 *Let a be the current (non-solution) assignment, and s the solution with minimal hamming distance h from a. For arbitrary a and s there is always a random walk step which decreases h by one.*

Proof. Assume that no such random walk step exists. Then none of the variables whose values are different in a and s can appear in an unsatisfied clause. But since a is not a solution, there has to be at least one clause c which is violated by a; now the variables appearing in c have the same value in a and s, therefore s also violates c and cannot be a solution. Thus the initial assumption has to be false, which proves the lemma. □

Based on this lemma, instead of directly showing that GWSAT is PAC, we prove a slightly more general result.

Theorem 2 *Consider the class of SLS algorithms for SAT which accept arbitrary CNF formulae as their input and search the space of assignments of the given formula. Any such algorithm which, for any current assignment, executes a random walk step with a probability of at least $p > 0$ at any given time, is PAC.*

Proof. Consider an arbitrary algorithm A satisfying the conditions from the theorem. For a given CNF formula with n variables and k clauses, we show that there exists a $p' > 0$ such that from each non-solution assignment the algorithm can reach a solution with a probability $p'' \geq p'$: Let a be the current (non-solution) assignment, and s the solution with minimal hamming distance h from a. Using Lemma 1 inductively, one can construct a sequence of h random walk steps from a to s. Next, we derive a lower bound for the probability with which A will execute this sequence.

Note first that for any assignment a', the number of unsatisfied clauses is always $\leq k$, and the number of literals occurring in unsatisfied clauses is $\leq k \cdot l$, where l is the maximal number of literals per clause for the given instance. Therefore, if A executes a random walk step, the probability to select a variable which decreases h is at least $1/(k \cdot l)$. Thus, the overall probability of executing a random walk step which decreases the hamming distance to the nearest solution is at least $p/(k \cdot l)$. Since we have a lower bound p for the probability of executing a random walk step independently from the current assignment, a lower bound for the probability of executing the correct h step sequence to reach the solution can be estimated as $[p/(k \cdot l)]^h$.

Finally, note that always $h \leq n$, and therefore the probability of reaching a solution from any given assignment a is at least $p' = [p/(k \cdot l)]^n$. Consequently, the following lower bound for the probability that A finds a solution within t steps can be easily obtained:[2]

$$1 - (1 - p')^{\lfloor t/n \rfloor}$$

For $t \to \infty$, this bound obviously converges to 1, which proves A's approximate completeness. □

Since GWSAT satisfies the conditions of Theorem 2 for arbitrary walk probabilities $wp > 0$ (let $p = wp$), we immediately get the following

Corollary 1 *GWSAT is approximately complete for all $wp > 0$.*

Note that the proof of Theorem 2 relies critically on the fact that the algorithm can decrease the hamming distance to the nearest solution in each step. Our proof shows that this is guaranteed if arbitrarily long sequences of random walk steps can be performed with a probability $p'' \geq p' > 0$ which is independent of the number of steps that have been performed in the past.

---

[2]This estimate is based on the observation that when partitioning a run of t steps into segments of n steps, the success probabilities for each of these can be independently bounded by p'.

WalkSAT Algorithms

The algorithms of the WalkSAT family, however, generally do not allow arbitrarily long sequences of random walk steps. In particular, for WalkSAT the variable selection strategy does not allow a random walk step if the selected clause contains a variable which can be flipped without breaking any currently satisfied clauses. Therefore, the PAC property cannot be proven using the scheme given above. Actually, although our empirical results suggest that WalkSAT could be PAC, a proof seems to be difficult to find. For the other members of the WalkSAT family, we can prove their essential incompleteness using a very simple example instance. The proofs for WalkSAT/TABU, Novelty, and R-Novelty are very similar; therefore we give only the proof for Novelty here and then discuss the corresponding results for the other algorithms.

Theorem 3 *Novelty (without restart) is essentially incomplete for arbitrary noise parameter settings p.*

Proof. Let $F_2 = \bigwedge_{i=1}^6 c_i$ be the CNF formula consisting of the clauses:

$$
\begin{aligned}
c_1 &\equiv \neg x_1 \vee x_2 \\
c_2 &\equiv \neg x_2 \vee x_1 \\
c_3 &\equiv \neg x_1 \vee \neg x_2 \vee \neg y \\
c_4 &\equiv x_1 \vee x_2 \\
c_5 &\equiv \neg z_1 \vee y \\
c_6 &\equiv \neg z_2 \vee y
\end{aligned}
$$

F_2 is satisfiable and has exactly one model ($x_1 = x_2 = \top, y = z_1 = z_2 = \bot$). Now assume that the algorithm's current assignment is $a_1 \equiv (x_1 = x_2 = y = z_1 = z_2 = \top)$. In this situation, all clauses except c_3 are satisfied. Applying Novelty, c_3 will be selected and the variables receive the following scores: $x_1 : 0, x_2 : 0, y : -1$. Since regardless of the noise parameter, Novelty always flips the best or second-best variable, either x_1 or x_2 will be flipped.

Because both cases are symmetric, we assume without loss of generality that x_1 is flipped. This leads to the assignment $a_2 \equiv (x_1 = \bot, x_2 = y = z_1 = z_2 = \top)$ which satisfies all clauses except c_2. The scores for x_1 and x_2 are both 0, and since x_1 is the most recently flipped variable, x_2 will be picked now. The current assignment at this point is $a_3 \equiv (x_1 = x_2 = \bot, y = z_1 = z_2 = \top)$ which satisfies all clauses except c_4. Again, x_1 and x_2 have the same score of 0, but now x_2 is the most recently flipped variable, so x_1 will be flipped. Now, the current assignment is $a_4 \equiv (x_1 = \top, x_2 = \bot, y = z_1 = z_2 = \top)$, which leaves only c_1 unsatisfied. As before, x_1 and x_2 both receive a score of 0, and x_2 will be flipped. But this leads back to the assignment $a_1 \equiv (x_1 = x_2 = y = z_1 = z_2 = \top)$; therefore, Novelty got stuck in a loop.

Therefore, we found a soluble problem instance F_2 and an initial assignment a_1 for which Novelty can never reach a solution which proves the theorem. □

Using the same formula F_2 and analogous arguments, it is now easy to prove:

Theorem 4 *WalkSAT/TABU and R-Novelty (without restart) are essentially incomplete for arbitrary tabu-list lengths and noise parameter settings, resp.*

Note that for R-Novelty, even the built-in deterministic loop breaking strategy (randomly picking a variable from the selected clause every 100th step) does not prevent the algorithm from getting stuck in loops, since these can be timed such that the loop breaker will never be activated when c_3 is violated — which would be the only way of flipping y and reaching a solution. In the case of WalkSAT/TABU, the same loop will be observed for any tabu list length $tl > 0$. For $tl \geq 2$, the reason for this is the fact that when all variables in a clause are tabu, WalkSAT/TABU will not flip any variable at all; for $tl = 1$, as for Novelty, y can never be flipped when c_3 is selected.

Practical Relevance

While the results from the last section are theoretically interesting in a similar sense as, *e.g.*, the well-known convergence result for Simulated Annealing (Geman & Geman 1984), it is not clear that they are also practically relevant. We therefore investigated the following two questions:

1. For PAC algorithms, is the convergence of the success probability fast enough to be observable when applying these algorithms to hard problem instances?

2. For essentially incomplete algorithms, is the characteristic stagnation behaviour observable for any of the usual benchmarks for SAT algorithms?

For answering these questions, we empirically analysed the behaviour of GWSAT, WalkSAT, WalkSAT/TABU, Novelty, and R-Novelty when applied to a number of benchmark problems for SAT algorithms, including hard Random-3-SAT instances like, *e.g.*, used in (Selman, Levesque, & Mitchell 1992; Parkes & Walser 1996; McAllester, Selman, & Kautz 1997), SAT-encoded graph colouring instances similar to the ones described in (Selman, Levesque, & Mitchell 1992), and SAT-encoded blocks world planning problems taken from (Kautz & Selman 1996). For our experiments, we applied each algorithm multiply to the same problem instance and measured the number of solutions found as well as the number of steps required for finding each solution. In order to observe a close-to-asymptotic runtime behaviour of the pure strategies, we used extremely high values of the *maxSteps* parameter and no random restart (*maxTries* = 1); we also made sure that between the length of the longest successful run and the cutoff (given by *maxSteps*) there was at least an additional factor of ten. Furthermore, we optimised the noise parameter settings for each benchmark problem and for each problem size such that the expected number of steps required to find a solution was minimised.

This study shows that the answers to the questions raised above are positive in both cases: PAC behaviour as well as essential incompleteness can be observed on the benchmark problems considered here. This is exemplified by the following results.[3] When applied to a set of 1,000 satisfiable, hard 3-colouring problems in random graphs (50 nodes, 239 edges), GWSAT and WalkSAT solve all instances in all runs with a mean number of less than 10,000 steps per run. When

---

[3] A complete description of the empirical study and its results can be found in (Hoos 1998) and will be presented in more detail in an extended version of this paper.

performing the same experiment for WalkSAT/TABU, Novelty, and R-Novelty, however, while still all instances were solved, 27, 9, and 6 of them, resp., were not solved in some of the runs, even when using a huge cutoff value of $maxSteps = 10^7$. Similar results could be obtained for Novelty applied to hard Random-3-SAT problems (100 variables, 430 clauses) and for large blocks world planning instances (like bw_large.c from (Kautz & Selman 1996)). In our experiments, we never observed stagnation behaviour for GWSAT or WalkSAT, while for the WalkSAT variants shown to be essentially incomplete, the typical stagnation behaviour often occurred.

Improving SLS Performance

However, consistent with (McAllester, Selman, & Kautz 1997), we generally observed significantly improved performance of WalkSAT/TABU, Novelty, and R-Novelty over WalkSAT or GWSAT in the cases where stagnation behaviour did not occur. Therefore, these algorithms seem to be superior to WalkSAT and GWSAT except for the stagnation behaviour caused by their essential incompleteness. In theory this problem can be easily solved. As mentioned before, adding random restart would make these algorithms PAC. However, in practice this approach critically relies on the use of good *maxSteps* settings. Unfortunately, in general these are extremely difficult to find *a priori* and today, to our best knowledge, there exist no theoretical results on how to determine good settings. The only empirical results we are aware of, are for GSAT when applied to hard Random-3-SAT problem distributions (Gent & Walsh 1993a); but these results are limited to Random-3-SAT and rely on properties of the respective problem distributions rather than the individual instances. On the other hand, while using inappropriately chosen *maxSteps* settings generally still eliminates essential incompleteness, in practice, it leads to extremely poor performance.

Another way of making these algorithms PAC is to extend them with random walk in such a way, that for each local search step, with a fixed probability a random walk step is performed. Random walk apparently has an advantage over random restart, since at least in GWSAT, it is more robust w.r.t. the additionally introduced parameter *wp* than random restart is w.r.t. *maxSteps* (*cf.* (Parkes & Walser 1996)). One reason for this empirically observed phenomenon is related to the inherent randomness of the random walk sequences; random restarts occur after a fixed cutoff time, whereas random walk sequences are probabilistically variable in their length and frequency of occurrence. Furthermore, when using random restart, the search process is re-initialised; consequently, a new try cannot benefit from the search effort spent in previous tries (unless information is carried from one run to the next, which is not the case for the algorithms considered here). The amount of perturbation introduced by a random walk sequence, however, probabilistically depends on the length of the sequence such that small perturbations are much more likely to occur.

Based on these considerations, we extend Novelty and R-Novelty with random walk such that in each search step, with probability *wp*, the variable to be flipped is randomly picked from the selected clause, while in the remaining cases, the variable is selected according to the heuristic for Novelty or R-Novelty, resp. For R-Novelty, we furthermore omit the deterministic loop breaking strategy which randomly flips a variable from the selected clause every 100 steps. The two algorithms thus obtained, Novelty[+] and R-Novelty[+], are obviously PAC, as they satisfy the conditions of Theorem 2; but it is not clear whether this is sufficient to overcome the stagnation behaviour observed in practice. We therefore empirically compared their behaviour to the original algorithms, using the same benchmark instances as described above. Different from the original algorithms, when using identical noise and *maxSteps* settings and a probability of $wp = 0.01$ for executing random walk steps, the modified algorithms solved all problem instances from the Random-3-SAT and graph colouring test-set in all runs. For the blocks world planning instance bw_large.c, where R-Novelty found only 28 solutions in 1,000 runs á 10^8 steps, R-Novelty[+] found 1,000 solutions with an expected local search cost of $8.09 \cdot 10^6$ steps per solution. We also compared the performance of the original and the modified algorithms when applied to instances for which no stagnation behaviour occurs. Here, no significant performance differences could be observed. This indicates that the essentially incomplete behaviour which causes the high means and standard deviations of these hardness distributions is efficiently eliminated by the random walk extension, while for instances which do not suffer from essentially incomplete behaviour, the performance remains mainly unaffected.

Conclusions

In this paper, we have shown a series of new theoretical results on the asymptotic behaviour of a number of state-of-the-art stochastic local search algorithms for SAT. As we have shown, these results are not only of theoretical interest, but their impact can also be observed when applying them to solve well-known benchmark problems. While theoretically, the standard random restart technique which is generally used with these algorithms is sufficient to make them PAC, the practical performance thus obtained is usually relatively poor, unless the cutoff parameter *maxSteps* is carefully tuned. Using a different approach, which is analogous to the random walk extension of GSAT introduced in (Selman, Kautz, & Cohen 1994), these difficulties can be avoided. By extending Novelty and R-Novelty with random walk, these essentially incomplete algorithms could be made PAC; at the same time, their empirically observed performance could be considerably improved without any additional parameter tuning.

Our results suggest that the PAC property is an important concept for the theoretical analysis as well as for the practical performance of modern SLS algorithms for SAT. Some of the best-performing algorithms, like WalkSAT/TABU, Novelty, and R-Novelty, are essentially incomplete and the corresponding stagnation behaviour can be observed when applying them to standard benchmark problems. This indicates that these algorithms, as observed for the pure R-Novelty strategy (without restart and loop-breaking) in (McAllester, Selman, & Kautz 1997), are on the verge of being too deterministic. Empirical evidence indicates that at least for the cases studied here, using a simple and generally applicable technique, the random walk extension, this problem can be overcome, resulting in hybrid algorithms which show superior performance as well as considerably increased robustness. However, although our empirical results so far are very suggestive, they are of a somewhat preliminary nature. Therefore, we feel that a considerably extended analysis should be undertaken to further investigate the practical impact of the PAC property in general, and the random walk extension in particular.

Acknowledgements

I wish to thank Joe Culberson, Ian Gent, Bart Selman, David McAllester, and Henry Kautz for their input during various discussions. Furthermore I gratefully acknowledge the comments of the anonymous referees and David Poole which helped to improve this paper. This research was partially supported IRIS Phase-III Project BOU, "Preference Elicitation and Interactive Optimization."

References

Buro, M., and Kleine-Büning, H. 1992. Report on a SAT Competition. Technical Report 110, Dept. of Mathematics and Informatics, University of Paderborn, Germany.

Geman, S., and Geman, D. 1984. Stochastic Relaxation, Gibbs Distribution, and the Bayesian Restoration of Images. *IEEE Transactions on Pattern Analysis and Machine Intelligence* 6:721–741.

Gent, I. P., and Walsh, T. 1993a. An Empirical Analysis of Search in GSAT. *(Electronic) Journal of Artificial Intelligence Research* 1:47–59.

Gent, I. P., and Walsh, T. 1993b. Towards an Understanding of Hill–Climbing Procedures for SAT. In *Proceedings of AAAI'93*, 28–33. MIT press.

Gu, J. 1992. Efficient Local Search for Very Large-Scale Satisfiability Problems. *ACM SIGART Bulletin* 3(1):8–12.

Hoos, H. H., and Stützle, T. 1998. Evaluating Las Vegas Algorithms — Pitfalls and Remedies. In *Proceedings of the Fourteenth Conference on Uncertainty in Artificial Intelligence (UAI-98)*, 238–245. Morgan Kaufmann Publishers, San Francisco, CA.

Hoos, H. H. 1998. *Stochastic Local Search — Methods, Models, Applications.* Ph.D. Dissertation, Fachbereich Informatik, Technische Universität Darmstadt.

Kautz, H., and Selman, B. 1996. Pushing the Envelope: Planning, Propositional Logic, and Stochastic Search. In *Proceedings of AAAI'96*, volume 2, 1194–1201. MIT Press.

McAllester, D.; Selman, B.; and Kautz, H. 1997. Evidence for Invariants in Local Search. In *Proceedings of AAAI'97*, 321–326.

Papadimitriou, C. 1991. On Selecting a Satisfying Truth Assignment. In *Proc. 32nd IEEE Symposium on the Foundations of Computer Science*, 163–169.

Parkes, A. J., and Walser, J. P. 1996. Tuning Local Search for Satisfiability Testing. In *Proceedings of AAAI'96*, volume 1, 356–362. MIT Press.

Selman, B.; Kautz, H. A.; and Cohen, B. 1994. Noise Strategies for Improving Local Search. In *Proceedings of AAAI'94*, 337–343. MIT Press.

Selman, B.; Levesque, H.; and Mitchell, D. 1992. A New Method for Solving Hard Satisfiability Problems. In *Proceedings of AAAI'92*, 440–446. MIT Press.

Initial Experiments in Stochastic Satisfiability

Michael L. Littman
Department of Computer Science
Duke University, Durham, NC 27708-0129
mlittman@cs.duke.edu

Abstract

This paper looks at the rich intersection between satisfiability problems and probabilistic models, opening the door for the use of satisfiability approaches in probabilistic domains. A generic stochastic satisfiability problem is examined, which can function for probabilistic domains as SAT does for deterministic domains. The paper defines a Davis-Putnam-Logemann-Loveland-style procedure for solving stochastic satisfiability problems, and reports on a preliminary empirical exploration of the complexity of the algorithm for a collection of randomly generated probabilistic problems. The results exhibit the familiar easy-hardest-hard pattern for the difficulty of random SAT formulae. Special cases of the stochastic satisfiability problem lie in different complexity classes, and one counterintuitive result is that the computational complexity and the empirical complexity of the problems examined do not track each other exactly—problems in the hardest complexity class are not the hardest to solve.

Introduction

There has been a recent focus in artificial intelligence (AI) on solving problems exhibiting various forms of uncertainty. In parallel, there is a great deal of work in AI and computer science on solving deterministic problems using techniques for testing Boolean satisfiability. Some recent work has looked at combinations of these ideas, viewing planning under uncertainty as stochastic Boolean satisfiability (Majercik & Littman 1998). This paper provides an approach for combining reasoning about uncertainty and satisfiability by exploring a framework that generalizes standard deterministic and stochastic satisfiability problems.

The remainder of this section reviews deterministic satisfiability and the following section introduces the stochastic satisfiability (SSAT) framework. The succeeding section describes the relationship between special cases of SSAT and plan-

ning and reasoning under uncertainty. The final sections describe a Davis-Putnam-Logemann-Loveland-based (DPLL) algorithm for solving SSAT problems and present empirical results applying this algorithm to randomly generated problems.

In deterministic satisfiability, or SAT, we are given a Boolean formula and wish to determine whether there is some assignment to the variables in the formula that results in the formula evaluating to "true." This problem is connected to problems throughout computer science from circuit design and complexity theory to AI. The last several years has seen tremendous progress in our ability to solve SAT problems, spurring interest in finding efficient ways to model problems such as planning (Kautz & Selman 1996) within the satisfiability framework.

Let $\mathbf{x} = \langle x_1, x_2, \ldots, x_n \rangle$ be a collection of n Boolean variables, and $\phi(\mathbf{x})$ be a k-CNF Boolean formula on these variables with m clauses. For example, $(x_1 + \overline{x_2} + x_4)(x_2 + x_3 + x_4)(\overline{x_1} + \overline{x_2} + \overline{x_3})$ is a $k = 3$-CNF formula with $n = 4$ variables and $m = 3$ clauses. This paper uses "1" and "0" for true and false, multiplication for conjunction, and addition for disjunction. Logical negation is written $\overline{x} = 1 - x$. With respect to a formula $\phi(\mathbf{x})$, an assignment to the Boolean variables $x_1, \ldots, x_n$ is *satisfying* if $\phi(\mathbf{x}) = 1$; a satisfying assignment makes the formula true. The decision problem SAT asks, given a Boolean formula $\phi(\mathbf{x})$ in 3-CNF, does it have a satisfying assignment? Or, symbolically, we want to know $\exists x_1, \ldots, \exists x_n (\phi(\mathbf{x}) = 1)$?

An interesting property of randomly generated formulae (Kirkpatrick & Selman 1994) is that when m is small relative to n, almost all formulae are satisfiable, and most algorithms find it easy to show this. When m is large relative to n, almost all formulae are unsatisfiable, and this is often relatively easy to show. For intermediate values of m (around $4.2n$), approximately half of the resulting formulae are satisfiable, and it is very difficult to show this. Thus, with respect to m, random SAT instances exhibit an "easy-hardest-hard" pattern. This pattern is consistent for various values of n, but becomes more pronounced with larger n.

Stochastic Satisfiability

Papadimitriou (1985) explored an extension of SAT in which a randomized quantifier is introduced. The stochastic SAT (SSAT) problem is to evaluate a Boolean formula with both existential and randomized quantifiers:

$$\exists x_1, \text{Я} x_2, \ldots, \exists x_{n-1}, \text{Я} x_n (E[\phi(\mathbf{x})] \geq \theta).$$

In words, this formula asks whether there is a value for x_1 such that *for random* values of x_2 (choose 0 or 1 with equal probability), there exists a value of x_3, such that... the *expected* value of the Boolean formula $\phi(\mathbf{x})$ is at least a threshold θ. This type of satisfiability consists of alternating between making assignment choices for some variables and chance selection of assignments for other variables. The specification of an SSAT problem consists of the Boolean formula $\phi(\mathbf{x})$, the probability threshold θ, and the ordering of the quantifiers.

Note that the randomized quantifier Я can be extended to allow arbitrary rational probability distributions over $\{0, 1\}$. The resulting generalization does not change any of the complexity results described in the next section, and is key to making a connection between SSAT, planning under uncertainty, and belief network inference.

Satisfiability and Uncertainty

As AI techniques are used more and more to attack real-world problems, many researchers have embraced probability theory as a way of representing the pervasive uncertainty they find. Two specific examples of this trend are the increasing use of Markov decision process models in planning and learning, and belief networks in reasoning and knowledge representation; however, the influence of probabilistic models in AI is felt quite broadly.

Whereas many basic deterministic problems are complete for the well-known complexity class NP, and are therefore formally equivalent to SAT, many planning and reasoning problems in probabilistic models lie in other complexity classes, such as #P or PP (Roth 1996; Littman, Goldsmith, & Mundhenk 1998). This means that, with respect to the current state of complexity theory, these problems cannot be reduced to SAT. However, many standard uncertain reasoning problems can be reduced to special cases of SSAT, which vary in complexity.

The NP-complete problem SAT is the SSAT problem obtained by using only existential quantifiers and setting $\theta = 1$. The problem of finding the most probable explanation (MPE) in a belief network (Dechter 1996) is equivalent to SAT. A related problem from planning under uncertainty is determining whether there is some choice of actions such that the most likely trajectory through state space to the goal exceeds a given probability threshold.

We define PP, or probabilistic polynomial time, by one of its complete problems, MAJSAT. In its standard formulation, MAJSAT asks, given a Boolean formula $\phi(\mathbf{x})$ in CNF, are at least half of its assignments satisfying? Thus, MAJSAT is concerned, not just with the existence, but the *number* of satisfying assignments.

This connects satisfiability to probability in the sense that, if we imagine that all assignments are equally likely, MAJSAT asks whether the probability of a satisfying assignment is at least $1/2$. Thus, MAJSAT can be expressed as an instance of SSAT: $\text{Я} x_1, \ldots, \text{Я} x_n (E[\phi(\mathbf{x})] \geq 1/2)$ (or θ, more generally). Thus, MAJSAT is obtained from SSAT by using only randomized quantifiers.

This "decision" form of MAJSAT is polynomially equivalent to the problem of actually computing the probability of a satisfying assignment, since we can use binary search on θ to find the exact value of θ for which the probability is at least as big, but no bigger than θ. The class PP can be viewed as the decision problem version of #P, which actually *counts* the number of satisfying assignments.

The problem of belief network inference—given a belief network, values for its evidence nodes, and the value for a query node, what is the probability that the query node takes on the given value given the evidence?—is #P-complete (Roth 1996). Any belief network (with rational conditional probability tables) can be represented as a Boolean formulae. The reduction (Littman, Majercik, & Pitassi 1999) essentially consists of creating one variable per node in the belief network and one per conditional probability table entry. Clauses in the formula select a value for each belief network node depending on its parents' values. From this, it follows that the belief network inference decision problem ("Does the query node take on the given value with probability at least θ?") can be reduced to MAJSAT and is PP-complete. A PP-complete planning problem is plan evaluation in a probabilistic domain (Littman, Goldsmith, & Mundhenk 1998).

The complexity class NP^{PP} is formed by combining NP and PP. It is the class of problems that can be solved by guessing a solution (NP) and then performing a PP calculation for verification. A satisfiability problem that is complete for this class is E-MAJSAT ("exists" MAJSAT) (Littman, Goldsmith, & Mundhenk 1998), which combines elements of SAT and MAJSAT. An E-MAJSAT instance is defined by a CNF Boolean formula $\phi(\mathbf{x})$ on n Boolean variables, a threshold value θ, and a number $0 \leq c \leq n$. The decision problem is to report whether there is an assignment to the "choice" variables $x_1, \ldots, x_c$ so that the probability that the remaining chance variables $x_{c+1}, \ldots, x_n$ constitute

class	satisfiability problem Boolean formula	belief network problem planning problem
NP	SAT $\exists x_1, \ldots, \exists x_n (E[\phi(\mathbf{x})] \geq \theta)$	most probable explanation best trajectory
PP	MAJSAT $\mathbb{Я}x_1, \ldots, \mathbb{Я}x_n (E[\phi(\mathbf{x})] \geq \theta)$	belief updating (inference) plan evaluation
NP^{PP}	E-MAJSAT $\exists x_1, \ldots, \exists x_c, \mathbb{Я}x_{c+1}, \ldots, \mathbb{Я}x_n (E[\phi(\mathbf{x})] \geq \theta)$	maximum a posteriori hypothesis best polynomial size plan
PSPACE	SSAT $\exists x_1, \mathbb{Я}x_2, \ldots, \exists x_{n-1}, \mathbb{Я}x_n (E[\phi(\mathbf{x})] \geq \theta)$	influence diagrams best polynomial horizon plan

Table 1: Different arrangements of quantifiers result in SSAT problems complete for different complexity classes and correspond to basic problems in uncertain reasoning and planning.

a satisfying assignment of $\phi(\mathbf{x})$ is at least θ. Thus, E-MAJSAT is also an SSAT problem:

$$\exists x_1, \ldots, \exists x_c, \mathbb{Я}x_{c+1}, \ldots, \mathbb{Я}x_n (E[\phi(\mathbf{x})] \geq \theta).$$

Note that, if $c = n$, E-MAJSAT is simply a version of SAT, and, if $c = 0$, E-MAJSAT is exactly MAJSAT. In terms of complexity classes, NP $\subseteq$ PP $\subseteq$ NP^{PP}; E-MAJSAT is at least as hard as MAJSAT, which is at least as hard as SAT.

Other problems are NP^{PP}-complete, such as finding small satisfactory plans in uncertain domains (Littman, Goldsmith, & Mundhenk 1998) and generating "explanations" in belief networks. The belief network problems of calculating a maximum a posteriori (MAP) hypothesis or a maximum expected utility (MEU) solution (Dechter 1996) are also complete for NP^{PP}. In these problems, the choice variables correspond to the plan or explanation and the chance variables to the uncertainty.

The class PSPACE consists of the problems solvable using a polynomial amount of space. All the previously mentioned classes (NP, PP, NP^{PP}) can be solved in polynomial space by enumerating all assignments and combining the results in the appropriate way. The SSAT problem with alternating quantifiers and QBF are satisfiability problems that are PSPACE-complete. Note that each existential quantifier in an SSAT problem can be viewed as a type of maximization operator; the problem then becomes one of maximizing the probability that $\phi(\mathbf{x})$ is satisfied, given that some of the variables are under the control of "nature." This is equivalent to solving a finite-horizon partially observable Markov decision process (Papadimitriou & Tsitsiklis 1987). The problem remains PSPACE-complete when the domain is specified compactly via probabilistic STRIPS operators or an equivalent representation. Influence diagrams are a belief-network-like representation for the same problem.

Table 1 summarizes the relations between complexity classes and the stochastic satisfiability, belief network, and planning problems discussed.

An Algorithm for SSAT

The Davis-Putnam-Logemann-Loveland (DPLL) algorithm for Boolean satisfiability (Davis, Logemann, & Loveland 1962) works by enumerating partial assignments and monitoring for opportunities to simplify the formula. The use of pruning rules makes it possible to solve problems whose set of assignments could not be fully enumerated.

DPLL is designed to solve SAT problems, and, thus, only needs to deal with existential quantifiers. The algorithm described in this section can be viewed as an extension of the DPLL algorithm to SSAT by providing pruning rules for randomized quantifiers. Cadoli, Giovanardi, & Schaerf (1998) provide a set of pruning rules for universal quantifiers (for solving QBF problems); the pruning rules described below can be combined with theirs.

Define $\phi' = \text{simplify}(\phi, x_i, b)$, where ϕ' is the $(n-1)$-variable CNF formula obtained from assigning the single variable x_i the Boolean value b in the n-variable CNF formula ϕ and simplifying the result (including any necessary variable renumbering). Variables are numbered so that x_1 corresponds to the outermost quantifier and x_n to the innermost. Let $Q(x_i)$ be the quantifier associated with variable x_i.

An SSAT formula is defined by a set of numbered variables, a CNF formula, a threshold θ, and a mapping Q from variables to quantifiers. We define the *value* of an SSAT formula to be the value of the expression obtained by taking the SSAT expression and replacing $\exists$ with max and $\mathbb{Я}$ with average. This quantity is useful because it is greater than or equal to θ if and only the SSAT formula is true and less than or equal to θ if and only if it is false.

The evalssat algorithm in Figure 1 is a generalization of DPLL. It takes formula ϕ and low and high thresholds θ_l and θ_h (both initially set equal to θ). It returns a value less than θ_l if and only if the value of the SSAT formula is less than θ_l, a value greater than θ_h if and only if the value of the SSAT formula is greater than θ_h, and otherwise the exact value of the SSAT formula. Thus, it can be evalssat$(\phi, \theta_l, \theta_h) := \{$

  if ϕ is the empty set, return 1

  if ϕ contains an empty clause, return 0

  /* *Unit Resolution* */

  if x_i is a unit variable with sign b and $Q(x_i) = \exists$,

    return evalssat$($simplify$(\phi, x_i, b), \theta_l, \theta_h)$

  if x_i is a unit variable with sign b and $Q(x_i) = \text{Я}$,

    return evalssat$($simplify$(\phi, x_i, b), 2\theta_l, 2\theta_h)/2$

  /* *Purification* */

  if x_i is a pure variable with sign b and $Q(x_i) = \exists$,

    return evalssat$($simplify$(\phi, x_i, b), \theta_l, \theta_h)$

  /* *Splitting* */

  if $Q(x_1) = \exists$, $\{$

    $v_0 =$ evalssat$($simplify$(\phi, x_1, 0), \theta_l, \theta_h)$

    if $v_0 \geq \theta_h$, return v_0

    $v_1 =$ evalssat$($simplify$(\phi, x_1, 1), \max(\theta_l, v_0), \theta_h)$

    return $\max(v_0, v_1)$

  $\}$

  if $Q(x_1) = \text{Я}$, $\{$

    $v_0 =$ evalssat$($simplify$(\phi, x_1, 0), 2\theta_l - 1, 2\theta_h)$

    if $(v_0 + 1)/2 < \theta_l$, return $v_0/2$

    if $v_0/2 \geq \theta_h$, return $v_0/2$

    $v_1 =$ evalssat$($simplify$(\phi, x_1, 1), 2\theta_l - v_0, 2\theta_h - v_0)$

    return $(v_0 + v_1)/2$

  $\}$

$\}$

Figure 1: The DPLL algorithm for satisfiability can be extended to solve SSAT problems.

used to solve the SSAT decision problem. Its basic structure is to compute the value of the SSAT formula from its definition; this takes place in the section labeled "*Splitting*", which enumerates all assignments, applying operators recursively from left to right. However, it is made more complex (and efficient) via pruning rules.

When a Boolean expression ϕ is evaluated that contains a variable x_i that appears alone in a clause in ϕ with *sign* b (0 if $\overline{x_i}$ is in the clause, 1 if x_i is in the clause), the normal right-to-left evaluation of quantifiers can be interrupted to deal with this variable. We call this case "*Unit Resolution*".

If the quantifier associated with x_i is existential, x_i can be eliminated from the formula by assigning it value b and recursing. As in DPLL, this is because assigning $x_i = 1 - b$ is guaranteed to make ϕ false, so $x_i = b$ can be no worse. If the quantifier associated with x_i is randomized, one branch of the computation will return a zero, so x_i can be eliminated from the formula by assigning it value b and recursing. The resulting value is divided by two, since it represents the value of only one branch.

The "*Purification*" pruning rule applies when there is a variable x_i that appears only with one sign b in ϕ. If $Q(x_i) = \exists$, the algorithm assigns $x_i = b$ and recurses. This is valid because any

clause satisfied by an assignment with $x_i = 1 - b$ will also be satisfied by assigning $x_i = b$. Purification pruning does not appear possible for randomized variables as both assignments give *some* contribution to the value of the SSAT formula and must be considered independently.

Another useful class of pruning rules concerns the *threshold* parameters θ_l and θ_h. While some care must be taken to pass meaningful thresholds when applying unit resolution, threshold pruning mainly comes into play when variables are split to try to prevent recursively computing the value of both assignments to x_1. If $Q(x_1) = \exists$, after the first recursive call computing v_0, it is possible that θ_h has already been exceeded. In this case, the algorithm can simply return v_0 without ever computing v_1. In particular, it is possible that $v_1 > v_0$, but all that is significant is whether the larger of the two exceeds θ_h. If v_0 exceeds θ_l but falls short of θ_h, this can be used to increase the lower threshold for the recursive computation of v_1; since only the larger of v_0 and v_1 matters, the precise value of v_1 is not crucial if it less than v_0.

Threshold pruning is not as strong for randomized variables. There are two types of threshold pruning that apply. First, if assigning 0 to x_1 is sufficient to meet the threshold θ_h, then the algorithm need not recurse on assigning 1 to the variable: if $v_0/2 \geq \theta_h$, return $v_0/2$.

If the first value v_0 is so low that, even if $v_1 = 1$, $(v_0 + v_1)/2 < \theta_l$, then again v_1 need not be computed. If both tests fail, v_1 must be computed, but the thresholds can be adjusted accordingly.

This algorithm bears a close resemblance to searching AND/OR graphs, although this similarity has not yet been exploited. Enhancements based on variable-ordering heuristics are being explored.

Empirical Results

This section presents a set of preliminary experimental results on using the DPLL-based SSAT algorithm to solve random SSAT instances.

Throughout these experiments, the same SSAT algorithm is used. A set of 1,000 formulae with $n = 20$ variables and 141 clauses were randomly generated using `makewff` from AT&T Research. Thresholds were expressed as $\theta = 1/2^{n-t}$ for integer t in the range 0 to n; this defines t so that 2^t is the required number of satisfying assignments. Formulae with m clauses were created using the first m clauses from each of the 1,000 formulae.

The first experiment compares and contrasts MAJSAT with SAT. Figure 2 illustrates the average work required to solve random MAJSAT instances, varying the number of clauses and values of the threshold parameter θ.

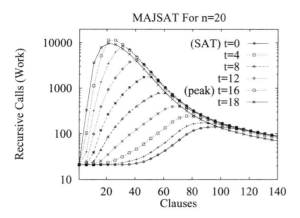

Figure 2: The difficulty of solving random MAJSAT instances varies with both the ratio of clauses to variables and with the satisfaction threshold (t).

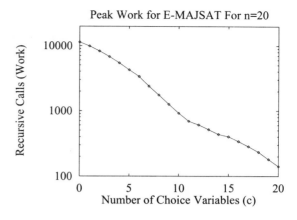

Figure 3: The difficulty of solving random E-MAJSAT instances varies with the number of choice variables c; more choice variables means easier problems.

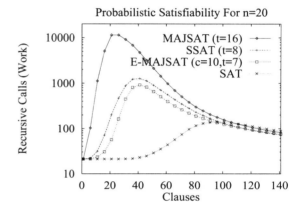

Figure 4: The peak difficulty of solving different SSAT instances varies with the structure of the operators and the number of clauses.

The line on the plot labeled $t = 0$ is the curve for SAT; this problem is asking whether the probability of satisfaction is at least $1/2^n$, which is reached as long as there is even a single satisfying assignment. The classic easy-hardest-hard pattern is visible. In fact, nearly all the threshold values produce the same basic shape.

Note that the peak difficulty over all thresholds occurs at $t = 16$; it is much higher than the peak difficulty for SAT and occurs at a much lower setting of m. Instances with high values of the threshold are difficult because the threshold pruning rules for randomized quantifiers rarely apply—it is almost always necessary to check both branches to determine whether the probability threshold can be met.

That MAJSAT is more difficult to solve than SAT is not surprising, since it belongs to a higher complexity class. A more interesting pattern occurs in E-MAJSAT formulae. As mentioned earlier, the E-MAJSAT parameter c interpolates between MAJSAT ($c = 0$) and SAT ($c = n$). In terms of complexity theory, however, intermediate values of c place E-MAJSAT in a more difficult complexity class than either endpoint. This suggests analyzing the peak difficulty of E-MAJSAT as a function of c.

The following experiment was carried out. For each value of c from 0 to $n = 20$, the formulae were solved for each clause size m from 1 to 141 by 5s and threshold parameter t from 0 to 19. Work was averaged separately for each combination of settings, and the combination of values for t and m that resulted in the maximum average work was selected for each value of c. Figure 3 summarizes the results.

The results of these experiments are somewhat counterintuitive. Instead of the peak difficulty being obtained for $c = n/2$ as might be assumed from complexity theory, the difficulty is a *logarithmic* function of the number of choice variables. It

appears that the main effect is that each randomized quantifier changed to an existential quantifier results in a constant fraction of savings of work, perhaps due to the reduction in effective branching factor (see below).

Figure 4 plots the work versus number of clauses for each of four types of SSAT problems described earlier. For each problem class, the most difficult (on average) setting of the threshold parameter observed was used. There are several things to note here. One is that all these randomized satisfiability problems exhibit the same easy-hardest-hard pattern described for SAT. However, the number of clauses corresponding to the peak work differs for each problem. Also, the higher the peak, the smaller the number of clauses at the peak.

Another observation is that the relative peak difficulty of different problems does not match what might be predicted by complexity theory. In particular, as NP $\subseteq$ PP $\subseteq$ NP^{PP} $\subseteq$ PSPACE, we might expect SAT < MAJSAT < E-MAJSAT < SSAT in terms of peak work. In fact, the experiments come out with SAT < E-MAJSAT < SSAT < MAJSAT. That is, MAJSAT comes out as the hardest instead of the second easiest. This pattern can be observed with a range of values of n and k (Littman, Majercik, & Pitassi 1999).

The facts that E-MAJSAT is easier than MAJSAT and that SAT is easier than SSAT probably stem from the fact that randomized quantifiers are harder to prune than are existential quantifiers. SSAT and E-MAJSAT ($c = n/2$) both consist of half existential and half randomized quantifiers, and have very similar curves in Figure 4.

Conclusion and Future Work

This paper described a stochastic satisfiability framework, relating it to existing problems in reasoning and planning under uncertainty. It described a DPLL-based algorithm for solving satisfiability problems in this framework and showed that the algorithm exhibits interesting empirical behavior on randomly generated formulae.

Deterministic satisfiability problems can be solved in a number of different ways, including DPLL-based algorithms, resolution-based algorithms, and stochastic search. Dechter (1996) explores resolution-based solvers for an analogous set of problems to the ones described here. The practical utility of resolution-based methods for SSAT is not clear at present; unlike DPLL-style derivations, a resolution proof does not appear to yield an efficient procedure for value calculation. An important direction for research is combining random sampling (randomized quantifiers) and stochastic search (existential quantifiers) to solve SSAT problems (Littman, Majercik, & Pitassi 1999).

Another fruitful direction for studying SSAT problems is extending existing theoretical SAT results to the probabilistic setting. This would include probing critical behavior and scaling phenomena in random formulae (Kirkpatrick & Selman 1994) and proof-size-based lower bounds for exact algorithms (Beame & Pitassi 1996). The "stochastic satisfiability" approach is already producing probabilistic planners with state-of-the-art performance (Majercik & Littman 1999). This type of research promises insight into understanding what makes many uncertain reasoning problems hard to solve and identifying faster ways to solve them.

Acknowledgments. Thanks to Judy Goldsmith, Toni Pitassi, Pankaj Agarwal, Henry Kautz, Don Loveland, Julien Basch, John Reif, Bart Selman, Moises Goldszmidt, Toby Walsh, Ian Gent, Steve Majercik, and the reviewers for feedback and suggestions.

References

Beame, P., and Pitassi, T. 1996. Simplified and improved resolution lower bounds. In *37th Annual Symposium on Foundations of Computer Science*, 274–282. IEEE.

Cadoli, M.; Giovanardi, A.; and Schaerf, M. 1998. An algorithm to evaluate quantified Boolean formulae. In *Proceedings of the Fifteenth National Conference on Artificial Intelligence (AAAI-98)*, 262–267. The AAAI Press/The MIT Press.

Davis, M.; Logemann, G.; and Loveland, D. 1962. A machine program for theorem proving. *Communications of the ACM* 5:394–397.

Dechter, R. 1996. Bucket elimination: A unifying framework for probabilistic inference. In *Proceedings of the 12th Conference on Uncertainty in Artificial Intelligence (UAI-96)*, 211–219. Morgan Kaufmann Publishers.

Kautz, H., and Selman, B. 1996. Pushing the envelope: Planning, propositional logic, and stochastic search. In *Proceedings of the Thirteenth National Conference on Artificial Intelligence*, 1194–1201. AAAI Press/The MIT Press.

Kirkpatrick, S., and Selman, B. 1994. Critical behavior in the satisfiability of random Boolean expressions. *Science* 264:1297–1301.

Littman, M. L.; Goldsmith, J.; and Mundhenk, M. 1998. The computational complexity of probabilistic plan existence and evaluation. *Journal of Artificial Intelligence Research* 9:1–36.

Littman, M. L.; Majercik, S. M.; and Pitassi, T. 1999. Stochastic Boolean satisfiability. Submitted.

Majercik, S. M., and Littman, M. L. 1998. MAXPLAN: A new approach to probabilistic planning. In Simmons, R.; Veloso, M.; and Smith, S., eds., *Proceedings of the Fourth International Conference on Artificial Intelligence Planning*, 86–93. AAAI Press.

Majercik, S. M., and Littman, M. L. 1999. Contingent planning under uncertainty via probabilistic satisfiability. In *Proceedings of the Sixteenth National Conference on Artificial Intelligence*.

Papadimitriou, C. H., and Tsitsiklis, J. N. 1987. The complexity of Markov decision processes. *Mathematics of Operations Research* 12(3):441–450.

Papadimitriou, C. H. 1985. Games against nature. *Journal of Computer Systems Science* 31:288–301.

Roth, D. 1996. On the hardness of approximate reasoning. *Artificial Intelligence* 82(1–2):273–302.

Trap Escaping Strategies in Discrete Lagrangian Methods for Solving Hard Satisfiability and Maximum Satisfiability Problems*

Zhe Wu and **Benjamin W. Wah**
Department of Electrical and Computer Engineering
and the Coordinated Science Laboratory
University of Illinois, Urbana-Champaign
Urbana, IL 61801, USA
E-mail: {zhewu, wah}@manip.crhc.uiuc.edu
URL: http://www.manip.crhc.uiuc.edu

Abstract

In this paper, we present efficient trap-escaping strategies in a search based on discrete Lagrange multipliers to solve difficult SAT problems. Although a basic discrete Lagrangian method (DLM) can solve most of the satisfiable DIMACS SAT benchmarks efficiently, a few of the large benchmarks have eluded solutions by any local-search methods today. These difficult benchmarks generally have many traps that attract local-search trajectories. To this end, we identify the existence of traps when any change to a variable will cause the resulting Lagrangian value to increase. Using the *hanoi4* and *par16-1* benchmarks, we illustrate that some unsatisfied clauses are trapped more often than others. Since it is too difficult to remember explicitly all the traps encountered, we propose to remember these traps implicitly by giving larger increases to Lagrange multipliers of unsatisfied clauses that are trapped more often. We illustrate the merit of this new update strategy by solving some of most difficult but satisfiable SAT benchmarks in the DIMACS archive (*hanoi4, hanoi4-simple, par16-1* to *par16-5, f2000,* and *par32-1-c* to *par32-3-c*). Finally, we apply the same algorithm to improve on the solutions of some benchmark MAX-SAT problems that we solved before.

Introduction

A general *satisfiability* (SAT) problem is defined as follows. Given a set of n clauses $\{C_1, C_2, \cdots, C_n\}$ on m variables $x = (x_1, x_2, \cdots, x_m)$, $x_j \in \{0, 1\}$, and a Boolean formula in conjunctive normal form:

$$C_1 \wedge C_2 \wedge \cdots \wedge C_n, \qquad (1)$$

find a truth assignment to x for (1), where a truth assignment is a combination of variable assignments that makes the Boolean formula true.

The *maximum satisfiability* (MAX-SAT) problem is a general case of SAT. In MAX-SAT, each clause C_i

Research supported by National Science Foundation Grant NSF MIP 96-32316.

Source code of DLM-98 is at http://manip.crhc.uiuc.edu.

is associated with weight w_i. The objective is to find an assignment of variables that maximizes the sum of weights of satisfied clauses.

Search methods developed previously for solving SAT can be classified into two types. Traditional approaches based on resolution, constraint satisfaction and backtracking are computationally expensive and are not suitable for solving large instances. Local-search methods (Frank 1997; Selman, Kautz, & Cohen 1994; 1993), in contrast, iteratively perturb a trajectory until a satisfiable assignment is found. These methods can solve larger instances, but may have difficulty in solving hard-to-satisfy instances.

Following the successful work of (Shang & Wah 1998), we formulate in this paper a SAT problem as a discrete, constrained optimization problem as follows:

$$\min_{x\in\{0,1\}^m} \quad N(x) = \sum_{i=1}^{n} U_i(x) \qquad (2)$$

$$\text{subject to} \quad U_i(x) = 0 \quad \forall i \in \{1, 2, \ldots, n\},$$

where $U_i(x)$ is a binary expression equal to zero when the ith clause is satisfied and to one otherwise, and $N(x)$ is the number of unsatisfied clauses. Note that in the above formulation, when all constraints are satisfied, the objective function is automatically at its minimum.

In this paper, we extend the work of (Shang & Wah 1998; Wu 1998) on discrete Lagrange-multiplier method to solve (2). After summarizing the theory of discrete Lagrange multipliers and the basic approach of (Shang & Wah 1998) for solving SAT problems, we identify traps that limit the search trajectory. Intuitively, *traps* are points in the search space that attract a search trajectory and prevent it from escaping. We present a trap escaping strategy that remembers traps implicitly by increasing the Lagrange multipliers of unsatisfied clauses found in traps, thereby forcing the search not to visit the same traps repeatedly. Finally, we show our results in solving some difficult and previously unsolved satisfiable SAT problems and some MAX-SAT benchmarks in the DIMACS archive.

Discrete Lagrangian Formulations

(Shang & Wah 1998; Wu 1998) extended the theory of Lagrange multipliers in continuous space to that of discrete space. In contrast to methods in continuous space, Lagrangian methods in discrete space do not require a continuous differentiable space to find equilibrium points. In this section, we summarize the theory of these methods for solving discrete optimization problems. Define a discrete constrained optimization problem as follows:

$$\min_{x \in E^m} \quad f(x) \tag{3}$$
$$\text{subject to} \quad g(x) \leq 0 \qquad x = (x_1, x_2, \ldots, x_m)$$
$$h(x) = 0$$

where x is a vector of m discrete variables, $f(x)$ is an objective function, $g(x) = [g_1(x), \ldots, g_k(x)]^T = 0$ is a vector of k inequality constraints, and $h(x) = [h_1(x), \ldots, h_n(x)]^T = 0$ is a vector of n equality constraints.

As discrete Lagrangian methods only handle problems with equality constraints, we first transform an inequality constraint $g_i(x) \leq 0$ into an equality constraint $\max(g_i(x), 0) = 0$. (Shang & Wah 1998) formulates the resulting discrete Lagrangian function as follows:

$$L_d(x, \lambda, \mu) = f(x) + \lambda^T h(x) + \sum_{i=1}^{k} \mu_i \max(0, g_i(x)), \quad (4)$$

where λ and μ are Lagrange multipliers that can be continuous.

The discrete Lagrangian function in (4) cannot be used to derive first-order necessary conditions similar to those in continuous space (Luenberger 1984) because there are no gradients or differentiation in discrete space. Without these concepts, none of the calculus in continuous space is applicable in discrete space.

An understanding of gradients in continuous space shows that they define directions in a small neighborhood in which function values decrease. To this end, (Wu 1998) defines in discrete space a *direction of maximum potential drop* (DMPD) for $L_d(x, \lambda, \mu)$ at point x for fixed λ and μ as a vector[1] that points from x to a neighbor of $x \in \mathcal{N}(x)$ with the minimum L_d:

$$\Delta_x L_d(x, \lambda, \mu) = \vec{\nu}_x = y \ominus x = (y_1 - x_1, \ldots, y_n - x_n) \quad (5)$$

where

$$y \in \mathcal{N}(x) \cup \{x\} \text{ and } L_d(y, \lambda, \mu) = \min_{\substack{x' \in \mathcal{N}(x) \\ \cup \{x\}}} L_d(x', \lambda, \mu). \quad (6)$$

Here, $\ominus$ is the vector-subtraction operator for changing x in discrete space to one of its "user-defined" neighborhood points $\mathcal{N}(x)$. Intuitively, $\vec{\nu}_x$ is a vector pointing from x to y, the point with the minimum L_d value

---

[1]To simplify our symbols, we represent points in the x space without the explicit vector notation.

---

among all neighboring points of x, including x itself. That is, if x itself has the minimum L_d, then $\vec{\nu}_x = \vec{0}$.

Based on DMPD, (Shang & Wah 1998; Wu 1998) define the concept of *saddle points* in discrete space similar to those in continuous space (Luenberger 1984). A point (x^*, λ^*, μ^*) is a saddle point when:

$$L(x^*, \lambda, \mu) \leq L(x^*, \lambda^*, \mu^*) \leq L(x, \lambda^*, \mu^*), \quad (7)$$

for all (x^*, λ, μ) and all (x, λ^*, μ^*) sufficiently close to (x^*, λ^*, μ^*). Starting from (7), (Wu 1998) proves stronger first-order necessary and sufficient conditions in discrete space that are satisfied by all saddle points:

$$\Delta_x L_d(x, \lambda, \mu) = 0, \quad \nabla_\lambda L_d(x, \lambda, \mu) = 0, \quad (8)$$
$$\nabla_\mu L_d(x, \lambda, \mu) = 0.$$

Note that the first condition defines the DMPD of L_d in discrete space of x for fixed λ and μ, whereas the differentiations in the last two conditions are in continuous space of λ and μ for fixed x. Readers can refer to the correctness proofs in (Wu 1998).

The first-order necessary and sufficient conditions in (8) lead to a discrete-space first-order search method that seeks discrete saddle points. The following equations are discrete approximations to implement (8).

General Discrete First-Order Search Method

$$x(k+1) = x(k) \oplus \Delta_x L_d(x(k), \lambda(k), \mu(k)) \quad (9)$$
$$\lambda(k+1) = \lambda(k) + c_1 h(x(k)) \quad (10)$$
$$\mu(k+1) = \mu(k) + c_2 \max(0, g(x(k))) \quad (11)$$

where $\oplus$ is the vector-addition operator ($x \oplus y = (x_1 + y_1, \ldots x_n + y_n)$), and c_1 and c_2 are positive real numbers controlling how fast the Lagrange multipliers change.

It is easy to see that the necessary condition for (9)-(11) to converge is when $h(x) = 0$ and $g(x) \leq 0$, implying that x is a feasible solution to the original problem. If any of the constraints is not satisfied, then λ and μ on the unsatisfied constraints will continue to evolve. Note that, as in continuous Lagrangian methods, the first-order conditions are only satisfied at saddle points, but do not imply that the time to find a saddle point is finite, even if one exists.

DLM for Solving SAT Problems
DLM-98-BASIC-SAT: A Basic DLM

The advantage of formulating the solution of SAT as discrete Lagrangian search is that the method has a solid mathematical foundation (Shang & Wah 1998; Wu 1998). The theory of discrete Lagrange multipliers also explains why other weight-update heuristics (Frank 1997; Morris 1993) work in practice, although these heuristics were developed in an ad hoc fashion.

procedure *DLM-98-BASIC-SAT*

1. Reduce original SAT problem;
2. Generate a random starting point using a fixed seed;
3. Initialize $\lambda_i \longleftarrow 0$;
4. **while** solution not found and time not used up **do**
5.   Pick $x_j \notin$ TabuList that reduces L_d the most;
6.   Maintain TabuList;
7.   Flip x_j;
8.   **if** $\#_{UpHillMoves} + \#_{FlatMoves} > \theta_1$ **then**
9. $\lambda_i \longleftarrow \lambda_i + \delta_o$;
10.   **if** $\#_{Adjust} \% \theta_2 = 0$ **then**
11. $\lambda_i \longleftarrow \lambda_i - \delta_d$ **end_if**
12.   **end_if**
13. **end_while**
end

Figure 1: *DLM-98-BASIC-SAT* (Shang & Wah 1998): An implementation of the basic discrete first-order method for solving SAT.

The Lagrangian function for the SAT problem in (2) is:

$$L_d(x, \lambda) = N(x) + \sum_{i=1}^{n} \lambda_i U_i(x) \qquad (12)$$

Figure 1 shows the basic *Discrete Lagrangian Method* (*DLM*) of (Shang & Wah 1998) for solving SAT problems. It uses two heuristics, one based on tabu lists (Glover 1989) and the other based on flat (Selman, Kautz, & Cohen 1993) and up-hill moves. We explain these steps later when we present our improved DLM.

Although quite simple, DLM-98-BASIC-SAT can find solutions to most satisfiable DIMACS benchmarks, such as all problems in the *aim-*, *ii-*, *jnh-*, *par8-*, *ssa-* classes, within seconds. However, it takes a long time to solve some DIMACS benchmarks and has difficulty in solving a few of the large ones (Shang & Wah 1998). For example, it takes a long time to solve *f2000* and *par16-1-c* to *par16-5-c* and cannot solve *hanoi4*, *hanoi4-simple*, *hanoi5*, *par16-1* to *par16-5*, and all *par32-* problems.

To improve DLM-98-BASIC-SAT, we identify in the next subsection traps that prevent DLM trajectories from moving closer to satisfiable assignments. We then propose new strategies to overcome these traps.

Traps to Local Search

By examining the output profiles when applying DLM-98-BASIC-SAT to solve hard SAT problems, we find that some clauses are frequently flipped from being satisfied to being unsatisfied. A typical scenario is as follows. A clause is initially unsatisfied but becomes satisfied after a few flips due to increases of λ for that clause. It then becomes unsatisfied again after a few more flips due to increases of λ of other unsatisfied clauses. These state changes happen repeatedly for some clauses and are tremendously inefficient because they trap the trajectory in an unsatisfiable assignment. To quantify the observations, we introduce a new concept called traps.

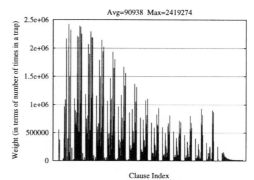

(a) *Hanoi4*: maximum $= 2.4 \times 10^6$, average $= 90,938$, total number of flips $= 1.11 \times 10^8$

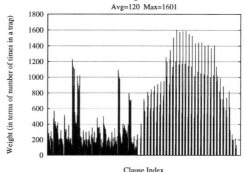

(b) *Par-16-1*: maximum $= 1.6 \times 10^3$, average $= 120$, total number of flips $= 5 \times 10^6$

Figure 2: Large disparity between the maximum and average numbers of times a clause is in traps.

A *trap* is a combination of x and λ such that a point in it has one or more unsatisfied clauses, and any change to a single variable in x will cause the associated L_d to increase. Note that a satisfiable assignment is not a trap because all its clauses are satisfied, even though its L_d may increase when x is perturbed.

To show that some clauses are more likely to be unsatisfied, we plot the number of times a clause is in a trap. This is not the same as the number of times a clause is unsatisfied because a clause may be unsatisfied when outside a trap. We do not consider the path a search takes to reach a trap, during which a clause may be unsatisfied, because the different paths to reach a trap are not crucial in determining the strategy to escape from it.

Figure 2 shows that some clauses reside in traps much more often than average when *DLM-98-BASIC-SAT* was applied to solve *hanoi4* and *par16-1*, two very hard SAT problems in the DIMACS archive. This behavior is detrimental to finding solutions because the search may be trapped at some points for a long time, and the search is restricted to a small area in the search space.

Ideally, we like a trajectory to never visit the same point twice in solving an optimization problem. This is, however, difficult to achieve in practice because it

procedure *DLM-99-SAT*
1. Reduce original SAT problem;
2. Generate a random starting point using a fixed seed;
3. Initialize $\lambda_i \longleftarrow 0$ and $t_i \longleftarrow 0$;
4. **while** solution not found and time not used up **do**
5.   Pick $x_j \notin TabuList$ that reduces L_d the most;
6.   **If** search is in a trap **then**
7.   For all unsatisfied clauses u, $t_u \longleftarrow t_u + \delta_w$ **end_if**
8.   Maintain TabuList;
9.   Flip x_j;
10.   **if** $\#_{UpHillMoves} + \#_{FlatMoves} > \theta_1$ **then**
11. $\lambda_i \longleftarrow \lambda_i + \delta_o$;
12.   **if** $\#_{Adjust}\%\theta_2 = 0$ **then**
13. $\lambda_i \longleftarrow \lambda_i - \delta_d$; **end_if**;
14.   call *SPECIAL-INCREASE*;
15   **end_if**
16. **end_while**
end
 procedure *SPECIAL-INCREASE*
17. Pick a set of clauses S;
18. **if** $\frac{\max_{i \in S} t_i}{\sum_{i \in S} t_i / n} \geq \theta_3$ **then**
19.   For clause i in S with the largest t_i, $\lambda_i \longleftarrow \lambda_i + \delta_s$;
20. **end_if**
end

Figure 3: Procedures *DLM-99-SAT*, an implementation of the discrete first-order method for solving SAT problems, and *SPECIAL-INCREASE*, special increments of λ on certain clauses when their weights are out of balance.

is impractical to keep track of the history of an entire trajectory. Alternatively, we can try not to repeat visiting the same trap many times. The design of such a strategy will depend on how we escape from traps.

There are three ways to bring a trajectory out of traps; the first two maintains history information explicitly, while the last maintains history implicitly.

a) We can perturb two or more variables at a time to see if L_d decreases, since a trap is defined with respect to the perturbation of one variable. This is not practical because there are too many combinations to enumerate when the number of variables is large.

b) We can restart the search from a random starting point in another region when it reaches a trap. This will lose valuable history information accumulated during each local search and is detrimental in solving hard SAT problems. Moreover, the history information in each local search needs to be maintained explicitly.

c) We can update λ to help escape from a trap. By placing extra penalties on all unsatisfied clauses inside a trap, unsatisfied clauses that are trapped more often will have very large Lagrange multipliers, making them less likely to be unsatisfied in the future. This strategy, therefore, implicitly reduces the probability of visiting that same trap again in the future and was used in our experiments.

DLM-99-SAT: An Improved DLM for SAT

Figure 3 outlines the new DLM for solving SAT. It defines a weight for each Lagrange multiplier and increases the weights of all unsatisfied clauses every time the search reaches a trap. This may, however, lead to an undesirable out-of-balance situation in which some clauses have much larger weights than average. To cope with this problem, when the ratio of the largest weight to the average is larger than a predefined threshold, we increase the Lagrange multipliers of clauses with the largest weight in order to force them into satisfaction. If these increases are large enough, the corresponding unsatisfied clauses are not likely to be unsatisfied again in future, thereby resolving the out-of-balance situation.

We explain next in detail each line of DLM-99-SAT.

Line 1 carries out straightforward reductions on all one-variable clauses. For all one-variable clauses, we set the value of that variable to make that clause satisfied and propagate the assignment.

Line 2 generates a random starting point using a fixed seed. This allows the experiments to be repeatable.

Line 3 initializes t_i (temporary weight for Clause i) and λ_i (Lagrange multiplier for Clause i) to zero in order to make the experiments repeatable. Note that t_i increases λ_i faster if it is larger.

Line 4 defines a loop that will stop when time (maximum number of flips) runs out or when a satisfiable assignment is found.

Line 5 chooses a variable x_j that will reduce L_d the most among all variables not in *TabuList*. If such cannot be found, then it picks x_j that will increase L_d the least. We call a flip an *up-hill move* if it causes L_d to increase, and a *flat move* (Selman, Kautz, & Cohen 1993) if it does not change L_d. We allow flat and up-hill moves to help the trajectory escape from traps.

Lines 6-7 locate a trap and increase t_u by $\delta_w (= 1)$ for all unsatisfied clauses in that trap.

Line 8 maintains *TabuList*, a first-in-first-out queue with a problem-dependent length *tabu_len* (100 for f, 10 for *par*16 and *par*32, 16 for g, and 18 for *hanoi*4).

Line 9 flips the x_j chosen (from false to true or vice versa). It also records the number of times the trajectory is doing flat and up-hill moves.

Lines 10-11 increase the Lagrange multipliers for all unsatisfied clauses by $\delta_o (= 1)$ when the sum of up-hill and flat moves exceeds a predefined threshold θ_1 (50 for f, 16 for *par*16 and *par*32, 26 for g, and 18 for *hanoi*4). Note that δ_o is the same as c_1 in (10). After increasing the Lagrange multipliers of all unsatisfied clauses, we increase a counter $\#_{Adjust}$ by one.

Lines 12-13 reduce the Lagrange multipliers of all clauses by $\delta_d (= 1)$ when $\#_{Adjust}$ reaches threshold θ_2 (12 for f, 46 for *par*16, 56 for *par*32, 6 for g, and 40 for *hanio*4). These help change the relative weights of all the clauses and may allow the trajectory to go to another region in the search space after the reduction.

Line 14 calls Procedure *SPECIAL-INCREASE* to handle the case when some clauses appear in traps more often than other clauses.

Line 17 picks a problem-dependent set S of clauses (for *par16-1* to *par16-5*, the set of all currently unsatisfied clauses; for others, the set of all clauses).

Lines 18-19 compute the ratio between the maximum weight and the average weight to see if the ratio is out of balance, where n is the number of clauses. If the ratio is larger than θ_3 (3 for *par16*, *par32*, and f, 1 for g, and 10 for *hanoi4*), then we increase the Lagrange multiplier of the clause with the largest weight by δ_s (1 for all problems).

Intuitively, increasing the Lagrange multipliers of unsatisfied clauses in traps can reduce their chance to be in traps again. Figure 4 illustrates this point by plotting the number of times that clauses appear in traps after using *SPECIAL-INCREASE*. Compared to Figure 2, we see that *SPECIAL-INCREASE* has controlled the large imbalance in the number of times that clauses are unsatisfied. For *hanoi4* (resp. *par16-1*), the maximum number of times a clause is trapped is reduced by more than 50% (resp. 35%) after the same number of flips.

Note that the balance is controlled by parameters θ_3 and δ_s. If we use smaller θ_3 and larger δ_s, then better balance can be achieved. However, better balance does not always lead to better solutions because a search may leave a trap quickly using smaller θ_3 and larger δ_s, thereby missing some solutions for hard problems.

Results on SAT and MAX-SAT

We first apply DLM-99-SAT to solve some hard but satisfiable SAT problems in the DIMACS archive. DLM-99-SAT can now solve quickly *f2000*, *par16-1-c* to *par16-5-c*, *par16-1* to *par16-5*, and *hanoi4* with a very high success ratio. These problems had not been solved well by any single method in the literature. Moreover, it can now solve *hanoi4-simple* with a very high success ratio, and *par32-1-c* to *par32-3-c*, although not with high success ratios. These problems cannot be solved by any other local search method today. For other simpler problems in the DIMACS archive, DLM-99-SAT has similar performance as the best existing method developed in the past. Due to space limitation, we will not present the details of these experiments here.

Table 1 lists the experimental results on all the hard problems solved by DLM-99-SAT and the experimental results from WalkSAT and GSAT. It lists the CPU times of our current implementation on a Pentium-Pro 200 MHz Linux computer, the number of (machine in-

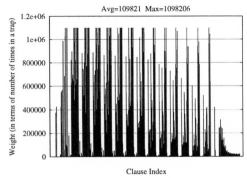

(a) *Hanoi4*: maximum $= 1.1 \times 10^6$, average $= 109,821$, total number of flips $= 1.11 \times 10^8$

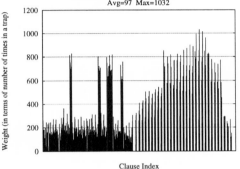

(b)
Par16-1: maximum $= 1,032$, average $= 97$, total number of flips $= 5 \times 10^6$

Figure 4: Reduced disparity between the maximum and average numbers of times a clause is in traps using *SPECIAL-INCREASE*.

dependent) flips for our algorithm to find a feasible solution, the success ratios (from multiple randomly generated starting points), and in the last two columns the success ratios (SR) and CPU times of WalkSAT/GSAT. For most problems, we tried our algorithm from 10 random starting points. For *hanoi4* and *hanoi4-simple*, we only tried 6 starting points because each run took more than 50 hours of CPU time on the average to complete. Note that *hanoi4*, *hanoi4-simple* and *par32*-problems are much harder than problems in the *par16* and f classes because the number of flips is much larger.

Table 1 also lists the results of applying DLM-99-SAT to solve the g-class problems that were not solved well by (Shang & Wah 1998). The number of flips used for solving these problems indicate that they are much easier than problems in the *par16* class.

So far, we are not able to find solutions to eight satisfiable problems in the DIMACS archive (*hanoi5*, *par32-4-c* to *par32-5-c* and *par32-1* to *par32-5*). However, we have found assignments to *hanoi5* and *par32-2-c* to *par32-5-c* with only one unsatisfied clause. These results are very encouraging from the point view of the number of unsatisfied clauses.

Next, we apply the same algorithm to improve on the solutions of some MAX-SAT benchmark problems

Table 1: Comparison of performance of DLM-99-SAT for solving some hard SAT problems and the g-class problems that (Shang & Wah 1998) did not solve well before. (All our experiments were run on a Pentinum Pro 200 computer with Linux. WalkSAT/GSAT experiments were run on an SGI Challenge with MPIS processor, model unknown. "NA" in the last two columns stands for "not available.")

Problem ID	Succ. Ratio	CPU Sec.	Num. of Flips	WalkSAT/GSAT SR	WalkSAT/GSAT Sec.
par16-1	10/10	216.5	$1.3 \cdot 10^7$	NA	NA
par16-2	10/10	406.3	$2.7 \cdot 10^7$	NA	NA
par16-3	10/10	309.2	$2.1 \cdot 10^7$	NA	NA
par16-4	10/10	174.8	$1.2 \cdot 10^7$	NA	NA
par16-5	10/10	293.6	$2.0 \cdot 10^7$	NA	NA
par16-1-c	10/10	79.9	5501464	NA	NA
par16-2-c	10/10	124.4	8362374	NA	NA
par16-3-c	10/10	116.0	7934451	NA	NA
par16-4-c	10/10	111.3	7717847	NA	NA
par16-5-c	10/10	81.9	5586538	NA	NA
f600	10/10	1.4	39935	NA	35*
f1000	10/10	8.3	217061	NA	1095*
f2000	10/10	44.3	655100	NA	3255*
hanoi4	5/6	$1.85 \cdot 10^5$	$4.7 \cdot 10^9$	NA	NA
hanoi4$_s$	5/6	$2.58 \cdot 10^5$	$9.9 \cdot 10^9$	NA	NA
par32-1-c	1/10	$5.36 \cdot 10^4$	6411650	NA	NA
par32-2-c	1/20	$2.16 \cdot 10^5$	$9.2 \cdot 10^9$	NA	NA
par32-3-c	1/30	$3.27 \cdot 10^5$	$1.4 \cdot 10^{10}$	NA	NA
g125-17	10/10	231.5	632023	7/10**	264**
g125-18	10/10	10.9	8805	10/10**	1.9**
g250-15	10/10	25.6	2384	10/10**	4.41**
g250-29	10/10	412.1	209813	9/10**	1219**

*: Results from (Selman, Kautz, & Cohen 1993) for similar but not the same problems in the DIMACS archive
**: Results from (Selman 1995)

solved by (Shang & Wah 1997) before. Recall the weight on Clause i is w_i, and the goal is to maximize the weighted sum of satisfied clauses. In solving MAX-SAT, we set initial values in DLM-99-SAT (Figure 3) to be $\theta_1 \leftarrow 20$, $\theta_2 \leftarrow 74$, $\theta_3 \leftarrow 10$ and for Clause i, $\lambda_i \leftarrow w_i + 1$, $\delta_o \leftarrow 2w_i$, $\delta_d \leftarrow w_i/4$, and $\delta_s \leftarrow 5w_i/4$.

Using these empirically set parameters, we were able to find optimal solutions to all the MAX-SAT benchmark problems within 20 runs and 10,000 flips. Table 2 presents the results with respect to the number of successes from 20 randomly generated starting points and the average CPU seconds when optimal solutions were found. For cases that did not lead to optimal solutions, we show in the third column the average deviation from the optimal solutions. The last column shows the indices of the jnh problems in the MAX-SAT benchmarks achieving the results.

Our algorithm solves MAX-SAT better than (Shang & Wah 1997) and GRASP, but our average number of successes of 14.77 is slightly worse than the average of 16.64 in (Mills & Tsang 1999). This could be due to the fact that our algorithm was originally designed for solving SAT rather than MAX-SAT.

Table 2: Performance of DLM-99-SAT in solving the 44 MAX-SAT DIMACS benchmark problems (Shang & Wah 1997). (Each problem were solved on a Sun Ultra-5 computer from 20 randomly generated starting points and with a limit of 10,000 flips. CPU sec. is the average CPU time for runs that led to the optimal solution. Deviation from optimal solution is the average deviation for runs that did not lead to the optimal solution.)

# of Succ.	CPU Sec.	Deviation from Opt.	List of $jnh-?$ Benchmark Problems Achieving Performance
2	0.06	-175.2	9
4	0.07	-33.0	18
5	0.12	-78.0	4, 5, 11, 303, 305, 307
6	0.11	-83.4	15
9	0.11	-29.4	310
10	0.13	-2.8	16
12	0.09	-47.4	19, 208
14	0.11	-49.3	302
15	0.10	-15.6	215, 216, 219, 309
16	0.11	-13.9	6, 8, 203
17	0.11	-19.3	211, 212, 308
18	0.08	-3.5	14, 207, 220
19	0.07	-1.1	301, 304
20	0.03	0.0	1, 7, 10, 12, 13, 17, 201, 202, 205, 209, 210, 214, 217, 218, 306

References

Frank, J. 1997. Learning short-term weights for GSAT. *Proc. 15'th Int'l Joint Conf. on AI* 384–391.

Glover, F. 1989. Tabu search — Part I. *ORSA J. Computing* 1(3):190–206.

Luenberger, D. G. 1984. *Linear and Nonlinear Programming*. Addison-Wesley Publishing Company.

Mills, P., and Tsang, E. 1999. Solving the MAX-SAT problem using guided local search. *Technical Report CSM-327, University of Essex, Colchester, UK.*

Morris, P. 1993. The breakout method for escaping from local minima. In *Proc. of the 11th National Conf. on Artificial Intelligence*, 40–45.

Selman, B.; Kautz, H.; and Cohen, B. 1993. Local search strategies for satisfiability testing. In *Proc. of 2nd DIMACS Challenge Workshop on Cliques, Coloring, and Satisfiability, Rutgers University*, 290–295.

Selman, B.; Kautz, H.; and Cohen, B. 1994. Noise strategies for improving local search. In *Proc. of 12th National Conf. on Artificial Intelligence*, 337–343.

Selman, B. 1995. Private communcation.

Shang, Y., and Wah, B. W. 1997. Discrete lagrangian-based search for solving MAX-SAT problems. *Proc. 15'th Int'l Joint Conf. on AI* 378–383.

Shang, Y., and Wah, B. W. 1998. A discrete Lagrangian based global search method for solving satisfiability problems. *J. Global Optimization* 12(1):61–99.

Wu, Z. 1998. *Discrete Lagrangian Methods for Solving Nonlinear Distrete Constrained Optimization Problems*. Urbana, IL: M.Sc. Thesis, Dept. of Computer Science, Univ. of Illinois.

Scheduling

Scheduling Alternative Activities

J. Christopher Beck
ILOG, S.A.
9, rue de Verdun, B.P. 85
F-94253 Gentilly Cedex FRANCE
cbeck@ilog.fr

Mark S. Fox
Department of Mechanical and Industrial Engineering
University of Toronto
Toronto, Ontario, CANADA, M5S 3G9
msf@eil.utoronto.ca

Abstract

In realistic scheduling problems, there may be choices among resources or among process plans. We formulate a constraint-based representation of alternative activities to model problems containing such choices. We extend existing constraint-directed scheduling heuristic commitment techniques and propagators to reason directly about the fact that an activity does not necessarily have to exist in a final schedule. Experimental results show that an algorithm using a novel texture-based heuristic commitment technique together with extended edge-finding propagators achieves the best overall performance of the techniques tested.

Introduction

Scheduling problems addressed in the constraint-directed scheduling literature typically have a static activity definition: each activity *must* be scheduled on its specified resource(s). It is common, however, in real-world scheduling problems to have a wider space of choices. There may be multiple process plans for the production of an inventory, or an activity may have a number of resources on which it could execute. In this paper, we show how both these alternatives (*alternative process plans* in the former case and *alternative resources* in the latter) can be addressed by explicit representation of and reasoning about *alternative activities*.

A simple example is shown in Figure 1. The activity network represents a choice of paths from activity A_1 to activity A_5: the intervening activities may be A_2, A_3, and A_4, or A_6 and A_7. We describe the "XOR" nodes in detail in the body of this paper. For now it is sufficient to understand that they represent alternative paths in the activity network and, in a final solution, only one of the alternative paths can be present. Part of the scheduling problem, then, is to decide if A_2, A_3, and A_4 will execute, or if A_6 and A_7 will execute.

The literature provides two general approaches to alternative activities. The first (Nuijten, 1994; Le Pape, 1994;

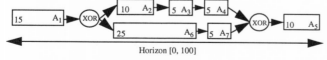

Horizon [0, 100]

Figure 1. A Process Plan with Alternatives. The duration of each activity is shown in the lower left corner of the activity.

Baptiste and Le Pape, 1995) represents alternatives with a variable in the constraint representation. While much work within this approach depends on propagation techniques to significantly prune the search space, to our knowledge, none of the sophisticated propagators developed over the past few years have been extended to directly reason about activities that may not exist in a solution. The second approach is that of multiple alternative decomposition (MAD) where the alternatives are not represented as internal variables, but rather as separate activities and process plans (Saks et al., 1993; Kott and Saks, 1998). While texture-based heuristics have been applied to such a decomposition, propagators and backtracking have not yet been integrated with the overall heuristic approach.

Our approach to scheduling alternative activities builds on the literature. We explicitly represent the alternative activities following the MAD approach, and in addition, we employ constraint mechanisms to directly reason about the relationships among activities that may not exist in a solution. This allows us to adapt existing texture-based heuristics and propagation techniques.

Probability of Existence

As may be anticipated from Figure 1, the addition of new types of temporal nodes is central to our novel techniques. Before addressing those issues, however, we turn to the representation of the fact that an activity may not exist in a final solution to a scheduling problem.

Following the knowledge-based approach to scheduling (Fox, 1983; Fox, 1986), our first task in addressing problems with alternative activities is to represent that an activity may not exist in a final solution. The *probability of existence* (PEX) of an activity, therefore, is the estimated probability at a search state that an activity will exist in a solution. The PEX value of an activity is in the range [0, 1] with 1 indicating that an activity will certainly exist and 0 indicating that it will certainly not. Returning to Figure 1, neither A_1 nor A_5 have alternatives; they must exist in a solution and so their PEX values are 1. Without additional information, each of the alternative paths between A_1 and A_5 is equally likely. The initial PEX values for all other activities, therefore, is 0.5.

With the addition of PEX variables to each activity, we face two challenges. First, we need to maintain consistent PEX values among activities related by temporal constraints. PEX propagation must ensure that if we make a PEX commitment, such as assigning the PEX value of A_3 to 1, the PEX values of the related activities would be appropriately reset. In our example, the PEX variables of A_2 and A_4 should also be set to 1 and the PEX variables of A_6 and A_7 should be set to 0. Second, we need to also maintain a consistent temporal network given that some of the activities may not execute in a solution. Returning to the original state in Figure 1 (*i.e.*, before assigning the PEX of A_3 to 1), standard temporal propagation would derive the start time window of A_1 to be [0, 45]. It is possible, however, for A_1 to start as late as time 55 if the path through A_2, A_3, and A_4 is chosen. Clearly, we need to modify the temporal propagation to account for the PEX values. In addition, we would like to be able to discover when a particular path is no longer consistent. Assume that the two alternatives in Figure 1 are still possible and that through some other scheduling decision the earliest start time of A_1 is increased to 46. In such a situation, we would like to detect that A_6 and A_7 cannot be consistently executed.

Limitations on the PEX Implementation

Each activity in the temporal graph has a PEX variable; however, the variable is not a true domain variable in the usual CSP sense. In a solution, all PEX values must be either 0 or 1, while during search each PEX variable should have a single value representing the current estimated probability of existence, rather than a domain of values. In a constructive search, if, in search state, S, a PEX variable is set to either 0 or 1, that value must be maintained in all search states below S. If a PEX variable has not been assigned to either 1 or 0, it varies during search on the domain [0,1] according to the PEX propagation algorithm.

There are a number of limitations that we have placed on the PEX representation in order to simplify the implementation. In particular, we make the following assumptions:

- The only commitments that can be made on a PEX variable are to assign it to either 0 or 1. PEX propagation will reset the PEX values of other activities appropriately.
- Each choice that remains to an alternative is equally likely: we assume that we do not have any external knowledge that biases the alternatives.

Adding PEX to the Temporal Network

Reasoning with PEX variables is achieved partly via the addition of XorNodes to the temporal network. A XorNode represents an exclusive-or constraint among a set of subgraphs which may themselves contain XorNodes. If a XorNode is present in the final solution then one and only one of the nodes directly connected upstream (resp. downstream) can be present. If a node directly connected upstream (downstream) to a XorNode exists in a solution, so must the XorNode.

As noted above, for the purposes of this paper, we further limit the XorNode behaviour by specifying that all nodes directly connected upstream (or downstream) must have equal PEX values. If a XorNode has a PEX value of x, and k upstream and l downstream links, the PEX value of each directly connected upstream node must be x/k and the PEX value of each directly connected downstream node must be x/l. The only exception to the rule of even division is when the upstream or downstream node has a PEX variable assigned to 0 or 1. If a neighboring (wolog) upstream node already has a PEX value of 0, it is not included in PEX propagation: the PEX value at the XorNode is simply divided among the upstream nodes whose previous PEX were greater than 0. If the neighboring (wolog) upstream node has a PEX value of 1, all the other directly linked upstream nodes must have a value of 0.

Propagating PEX

The basic PEX propagation is achieved through the behavior at each temporal node. At an activity, A, all the non-Xor-Nodes directly linked to A must have the same PEX value as A. For XorNodes, the sum of the PEX values for all nodes directly connected upstream must be equal to the sum of all nodes directly connected downstream which in turn must be equal to the PEX value of the XorNode.

Initial PEX propagation begins with a temporal network where PEX values are unassigned and consistently assigns the PEX variables. If a node has either no upstream or no downstream links it can not be subject to a XorNode and therefore must be present in the final solution. The initial PEX propagation algorithm begins by assigning a PEX value of 1 to all these activities. Based on a topological ordering of the activities in the graph, found with a depth-first search, these initial values are propagated throughout the graph. The complexity of the initial propagation given n nodes and m temporal constraints is $O(\max(m, n))$. Space limitations preclude presentation of the full algorithm here. See (Beck, 1999) for more details.

Incremental PEX propagation starts with a consistent network and some change to a PEX value. The change is represented by the addition of a new unary constraint assigning a PEX variable to either 0 or 1. Again, space precludes full presentation of the algorithm; however, an example serves to illustrate the process. Figure 2 presents a temporal network. Assuming X_1 and X_7 both have an initial PEX value of 1 and that, after initial propagation, we add the unary PEX constraint assigning the PEX value of activity A_1 to 1, Table 1 shows the PEX values of a subset of nodes before and after incremental PEX propagation.

As shown in Figure 2, XorNodes can be nested: the alternative represented by X_3 and X_4 is nested within the alternative represented by X_2 and X_6 which is nested within the alternative represented by X_1 and X_7. The initial step of the PEX propagation is to identify the inner-most XorNodes relevant to the node whose PEX is being assigned. Having identified these nodes (X_3 and X_4) we propagate from A_1 upstream to X_3 and downstream to X_4. This propagation assigns a PEX value of 1 to both X_3 and X_4. We then propagate downstream along all paths from X_3 to X_4 following the same rules as with initial propagation. In this case, the propagation sets the PEX of A_2 to 0.

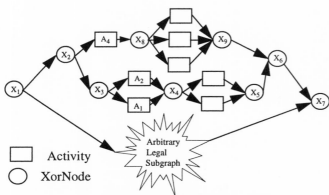

Figure 2. An Example of Cascading PEX Propagation.

The PEX values of X_3 and X_4 have been reset and therefore we continue propagation. This continuation is a *cascade* of PEX propagation. The only difference from the first round of incremental propagation is the nodes that form the starting point. Rather than starting with A_1, we now start with the inner-most XorNodes from the previous iteration. In our example, we begin with X_3 and identify the inner-most XorNode upstream (X_2). Starting from X_4, we identify the inner-most downstream XorNode (X_6). As with the initial iteration, we now reset the PEX values of the identified XorNodes (to 1 in this case) and PEX propagate downstream from X_2 to X_6. The second cascade of PEX propagation will reassign the PEX value of X_5 (to 1), the PEX values of the activities between X_4 and X_5 (to 0.5), and the PEX values of all nodes along any path from X_2 to X_9 (to 0). One more cascade assigns the PEX values of all nodes in the "Arbitrary Legal Subgraph" to 0.

At worst, PEX propagation will require $O(n)$ cascades where n is the number of temporal nodes in the graph, since, in the extreme case, there can be $O(n)$ nested alternatives. Each cascade incurs a worst-case complexity of $O(\max(n, m))$. Therefore, the overall worst-case complexity is $O(\max(n^2, nm))$.

Temporal Propagation with PEX

There are three differences in temporal propagation when XorNodes are present in the network.

Node	Initial PEX Values	PEX Values After Commitment
X_1	1.0	1.0
X_2	0.5	1.0
X_3	0.25	1.0
A_1	0.125	1.0
A_2	0.125	0
X_4	0.25	1.0
X_5	0.25	1.0
X_6	0.5	1.0
X_7	1.0	1.0

Table 1: PEX Values for a Subset of the Nodes in Figure 2.

1. Propagation through a XorNode is different than propagation through an activity.
2. When there are nodes with PEX < 1 in the graph, a state where an activity has an empty domain may not be a dead-end, but may indicate an implied PEX commitment.
3. Temporal propagation is done after PEX propagation.

Temporal Propagation through a XorNode. The temporal semantics of a XorNode require that it start at or after the finish time of at least one of its upstream neighbors and it must end at or before the start time of at least one of its downstream neighbors. During downstream propagation, therefore, the XorNode sets the lower-bound on its start time based on the minimum earliest finish time of its upstream neighbors. This start time is then propagated further downstream. During upstream propagation, the analogous process is followed.

A pair of XorNodes representing an alternative enforce an interval of time between themselves. This interval is the length of the shortest path between them (where path length is computed as the sum of the minimum durations of the temporal nodes on the path).

Deriving Implied PEX Commitments. In standard temporal propagation, if it is discovered that a variable's domain has been emptied, a dead-end is derived. When PEX variables are present, emptying a domain may indicate that a particular PEX variable must have a value of 0. When a domain is emptied in temporal propagation, the PEX value of the temporal node with the emptied domain is examined. If the PEX value is less than 1, the node is marked to indicate that the PEX value has been determined to be 0 and temporal propagation does not continue from that node. After temporal propagation, a separate algorithm asserts unary PEX commitments on the marked nodes, and then the usual PEX and temporal propagation is done.

If the domain of a temporal node with PEX of 1 is emptied, a dead-end is derived as in the standard temporal propagation. To see why this is the case, imagine emptying the start time domain of an activity, A, with a PEX value of 1. By definition, it can not have any enclosing XorNodes. Assume that the presence of some activity, B, with a PEX value of less than 1 caused the empty domain. The temporal propagation from B to A must occur through one of the XorNodes enclosing B. If that propagation empties A, then it must be that case that not only B but *all* its alternatives are inconsistent with A. Therefore, it is a true dead-end.

Temporal Propagation after PEX Propagation. After PEX propagation, temporal propagation must be performed, once for each PEX propagation cascade, to re-establish a temporally consistent network. Returning to our example in Figure 2, recall that after assigning activity A_1 a PEX value of 1, three cascades of PEX propagation were performed: X_3-X_4, X_2-X_6, and X_1-X_7. Starting from the first cascade, temporal propagation must proceed upstream from the first upstream XorNode (X_3) and downstream from the first downstream XorNode (X_4). It is then necessary to perform temporal propagation upstream from the second upstream XorNode (X_2) and downstream from the second downstream XorNode (X_6) and finally from the third pair of XorNodes (X_1 and X_7).

PEX and Heuristics

With the ability to represent and propagate the fact that some temporal nodes may not be present in a final schedule, it is necessary to extend heuristic search techniques. Here we extend three heuristics to incorporate PEX: Sum-Height, CBASlack, and LJRand.

SumHeightPEX. The SumHeight heuristic (Beck et al., 1997b) analyzes the constraint graph (via a texture measurement) to identify the critical points at which a commitment should be made. A commitment is then made to attempt to decrease the criticality. The constraint graph analysis begins a probabilistic estimate of the demand of each activity for each resource. The individual demand, $ID(A,R,t)$, is (probabilistically) the amount of resource R, required by activity A, at time t. It is found as follows, for all $est_A \leq t < lft_A$ (est_A, lft_A, dur_A, and STD_A are, respectively, the earliest possible start time, the latest possible start time, the duration, and the domain of possible start times for activity A):

$$ID(A, R, t) = \frac{min(t, lst_A) - max(t - dur_A + 1, est_A)}{|STD|} \quad (1)$$

The individual demands for each activity on a resource are then summed to give an estimate of the aggregate demand for a resource over time. The most critical resource and time point is, by definition, the one with highest aggregate demand. Given critical resource R^* and time point t^*, the SumHeight heuristic identifies the two activities that contribute the most individual demand to R^* at t^* that are not already linked by a path of temporal constraints. This activity pair is heuristically sequenced.[1]

PEX values are incorporated into the SumHeight heuristic by modifying the individual demand and by widening the commitments that can be made. The modification to incorporate PEX into the individual demand, $ID_{PEX}(A,R,t)$ multiplies by A_{PEX}, the PEX value of activity A:

$$ID_{PEX}(A, R, t) = A_{PEX} \times ID(A, R, t) \quad (2)$$

This modification has the effect of vertically scaling the individual activity demand curve. If the PEX value of A is 0.5, the individual demand at any time point t, is half what the demand would be if the PEX value were equal to 1. This modification fits with our semantic interpretation of individual demand to be the probabilistic demand of an activity at a time point. Because we interpret a PEX value as an activity's probability of existence, an activity that has only a 50% likelihood of existing has half the probabilistic demand of an identical activity that will definitely exist.[2]

---

1. See (Beck et al., 1997b) for details of the sequencing heuristics.
2. This is the same modification to individual demand used in the KBLPS scheduler to incorporate a notion similar to PEX into texture-based heuristics (Carnegie Group Inc., 1994).

Using ID_{PEX}, the individual demands are calculated and aggregated, and the resource and time point with highest criticality is identified. We, then, identify three activities:

- The activity, A, with highest individual demand for the R^* at t^* with PEX value, A_{PEX}, $0 < A_{PEX} < 1$.
- The pair of activities, B and C, that are not sequenced, with PEX values of 1, and with the highest individual demand for R^* at t^*. Assume the individual demand of activity B at t^* is greater than or equal to that of C.

A heuristic commitment is found by comparing the individual demand for A at t^* with that of B. If A is higher, it is the most critical activity and since it has a possibility of not existing, the heuristic commitment removes it from the schedule by setting its PEX value to 0. If B is of higher criticality, then it is necessary to sequence B and C to reduce criticality. We use the sequencing heuristics presented in (Beck et al., 1997b). If a PEX commitment is retracted via a complete retraction technique, we post its opposite, setting the PEX value of A to 1. Similarly, if the sequencing commitment is retracted, we post the reverse sequence.

CBASlackPEX. The CBASlack heuristic (Smith and Cheng, 1993; Cheng and Smith, 1997) identifies the pair of activities on the same resource that have the minimum biased-slack measurement, and sequences them so as to preserve the maximum amount of slack.

To adapt the CBASlack heuristic, we calculate the biased-slack only for activities with a PEX value greater than 0. The following three conditions then apply to a pair:

1. If both activities have a PEX value of 1, post the sequencing constraint that preserves the most slack.
2. If one activity, A, has a PEX value of 1 and the other, B, has a PEX value of less than 1, the greatest amount of slack is preserved by setting the PEX value of B to 0.
3. If both activities have a PEX value of less than 1, the greatest amount of slack is preserved by setting the PEX value of the activity with the longest duration to 0.

If any commitment is retracted, we post its opposite (the other sequence for case 1, or setting the PEX value to 1 in cases 2 and 3) to guarantee a complete search.

LJRandPEX. The LJRand heuristic (Nuijten, 1994) finds the smallest earliest finish time of all the unscheduled activities and identifies the set of activities which can start before this time. One activity in this set is selected randomly and scheduled at its earliest start time. When backtracking, the earliest start time of the activity is updated to the minimum earliest finish time of all other activities on that resource.

Our modification of LJRand to incorporate PEX variables, LJRandPEX, performs the following steps:

1. Find the smallest earliest finish time of all unscheduled activities with PEX greater than 0.
2. Identify the set of activities with PEX values greater than 0 that can start before the minimum earliest finish time.
3. Randomly select an activity, A, from this set.
4. Assign A to its earliest start time and assign A_{PEX} to 1.

The alternative commitment, should backtracking undo the commitment on activity A, is to update the earliest start time of A to the minimum earliest finish time of all other activities with PEX > 0 on the same resource as A. The alternative does not contain a PEX commitment: subsequent commitments can still assign A_{PEX} to either 1 or 0.

The Information Content of the Heuristics

SumHeightPEX uses the actual PEX value while LJRandPEX and CBASlackPEX only use the PEX variable as a three-value variable: 0, 1, or neither-0-nor-1. We expect that because the texture-based heuristics take into account the information represented by the value of the PEX variable, they will outperform the other heuristics. We do not incorporate the PEX value more deeply into the non-texture heuristics in order to evaluate this expectation.

PEX and Edge-Finding

Edge-finding exclusion (Nuijten, 1994) and not-first/not-last (Nuijten, 1994; Baptiste and Le Pape, 1996) are powerful propagation techniques. Based on an analysis of the time windows of activities, they are, in some situations, able to deduce constraints implied by the current search state. While the algorithms embody different implication rules and find different implied constraints, they depend on all activities having to be present in a final solution.

Edge-finding exclusion and not-first/not-last can clearly be used with activities with a PEX value of 1. Imagine the situation, however, where all activities on a resource but one, A, have a PEX value of 1. If a dead-end is found by edge-finding, we can soundly infer that activity A can not execute and set A_{PEX} to 0. If edge-finding derives new unary temporal constraints on A, they can be soundly asserted: if A is to execute, it must be consistent with the rest of the activities that must execute on the same resource. If edge-finding derives unary temporal constraints on activities other than A, they must be discarded. It is possible for A not to execute, so we can not soundly constrain the activities that have PEX values of 1.

This reasoning leads to the PEX-edge-finding algorithm that uses the usual edge-finding algorithms as sub-routines. First, the usual edge-finding is run on all activities with PEX values of 1. Then, for each activity with a PEX value between 0 and 1, its PEX value is temporarily set to 1 and the edge-finding algorithms are run again. Any new constraints are filtered as described above. Given that the standard edge-finding worst-case complexity is $O(n^2)$, the PEX-edge-finding worst-case complexity is $O(n^3)$. It is possible that this time-complexity can be improved and it is certainly the case that the average time performance can be improved by specializing the code.

Empirical Evaluation

The empirical evaluation of the PEX techniques focuses on problems with alternative process plans, and problems with both alternative process plans and alternative resources. The PEX techniques presented are applicable, without extension, to both types of problems: alternative resources are treated as a nested alternative within a process plan.[3]

The primary goal of the evaluation is to determine whether using the extra information represented by PEX values results in better heuristic commitments and overall search performance. A second goal is the evaluation of the PEX edge-finding techniques.

The six algorithms used in the experiments are summarized in Table 2. The statistical analysis[4] compares the three heuristics with each other both with and without PEX-edge-finding. We evaluate the use of PEX-edge-finding in three conditions corresponding to each of the heuristics. Each algorithm is run until it finds a solution or until a 20 minute CPU time limit has been reached in which case failure is reported. The machine used is a Sun UltraSparc-IIi, 270 Mhz, 128 M memory, running SunOS 5.6.

Experiment 1: Varying the Number of Alternatives

We constructed four problem sets with a varying maximum number of alternatives in each process plan. Each problem begins with an underlying 10×10 job shop problem. For a problem with a maximum of M alternatives per process plan, we generate $10M$ jobs. These jobs are then transformed into 10 process plans with alternatives. For each job we randomly choose the number of alternatives, k, uniformly from $[0, M]$. We then combine randomly chosen portions of the next k jobs with our original job to produce a single process plan with k alternatives. The combination process randomly chooses the to-be-combined portion and the location in the original process plan where the alternative is inserted. Each path between a pair of XorNodes representing an alternative must have the same number of activities and that number must be greater than 1.

Sets of problems with a maximum of 1, 3, 5, and 7 alternatives per process plan were generated. Each set contains

Algorithm	Heuristic	Propagators	Retraction Technique
SumHeight-PropPEX	SumHeight-PEX	All[a]	Chronological Backtracking
SumHeight-PEX	SumHeight-PEX	Non-PEX Propagators[b]	Chronological Backtracking
CBASlack-PropPEX	CBASlack-PEX	All	Chronological Backtracking
CBASlack-PEX	CBASlack-PEX	Non-PEX Propagators	Chronological Backtracking
LJRand-PropPEX	LJRandPEX	All	Chronological Backtracking
LJRandPEX	LJRandPEX	Non-PEX Propagators	Chronological Backtracking

Table 2: The Six Algorithms Used in the Experiments.

a. Temporal propagation, PEX edge-finding exclusion, PEX edge-finding not-first/not-last, and CBA.
b. Temporal propagation, edge-finding exclusion, edge-finding not-first/not-last, and CBA.

---

3. See (Davenport et al., 1999) for an application of PEX techniques to pure alternative resource problems.
4. We measure statistical significance with the bootstrap paired-t test (Cohen, 1995) with $p \leq 0.0001$ (unless otherwise noted).

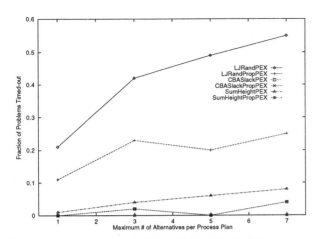

Figure 3. The Fraction of Problems in Each Problem Set for which Each Algorithm Timed-out.

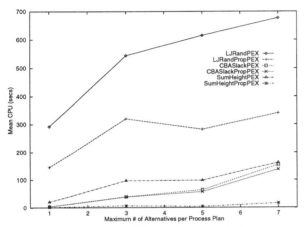

Figure 4. The Mean CPU Time in Seconds for Each Problem Set.

120 problems. The problem generation method results in problems such that a solution has exactly the same number of executing activities as the underlying job shop problem. Prior to scheduling, however, each problem has a different number of activities depending on the random generation. Table 3 shows the characteristics of the problem sets.

The proportion of the problems for which each algorithm times out is shown in Figure 3 while the mean CPU time for each algorithm is displayed in Figure 4. Statistical analysis of the number of timed-out problems indicates that there is no significant difference between SumHeightPEX and CBASlackPEX regardless of the use of PEX-edge-finding.

Problem Set (Maximum Number of Alternatives)	Activities Per Problem		
	Min	**Mean**	**Max**
1	116	131.6	156
3	142	171.8	200
5	172	204.7	251
7	167	224.2	280

Table 3: The Characteristics of the Problems in Experiment 1.

SumHeightPEX and CBASlackPEX significantly outperform LJRandPEX in both propagation conditions. In terms of the usefulness of PEX-edge-finding, SumHeightPropPEX and LJRandPropPEX time-out on significantly fewer problems than SumHeightPEX and LJRandPEX respectively. There is no significant difference in performance between CBASlackPEX and CBASlackPropPEX.

Turning to mean CPU time, SumHeightPropPEX uses significantly less mean CPU time than CBASlackPropPEX, which in turn uses significantly less than LJRandPropPEX. When PEX-edge-finding is not used, there is no difference between CBASlackPEX and SumHeightPEX while both are significantly better than LJRandPEX. Holding the heuristic component constant, we see that SumHeightPropPEX and LJRandPropPEX both incur a lower mean CPU time than their corresponding non-PEX-edge-finding algorithm, while there is no such difference for CBASlackPEX.

Other search statistics indicate that SumHeightPropPEX makes significantly fewer backtracks, commitments, and heuristic commitments than CBASlackPropPEX which makes significantly fewer backtracks, commitments, and heuristic commitments than LJRandPropPEX. Both SumHeightPEX and CBASlackPEX make significantly fewer backtracks, commitments, and heuristic commitments than LJRandPEX. The only significant difference between SumHeightPEX and CBASlackPEX is that the former makes fewer commitments ($p \leq 0.005$). With each heuristic, the use of PEX-edge-finding results in significantly fewer backtracks and heuristic commitments ($p \leq 0.005$ when CBASlackPEX is the heuristic). In terms of total commitments, LJRandPropPEX is not significantly different from LJRandPEX, while the difference is significant for the other two heuristic commitment techniques ($p \leq 0.005$ for CBASlackPropPEX versus CBASlackPEX).

Experiment 2: Adding Alternative Resources

The problems in this experiment are transformations of those in Experiment 1. Alternative resources are added to each activity by randomly generating the total number of resource alternatives following the distribution shown in Table 4. The original resource requirement and duration are preserved in the new problem. In addition, the new resource alternatives (if any) are randomly chosen with uniform probability from among the other resources in the problem. The duration of the activity on each new alternative

Alternative Resources per Activity	Probability
1	0.03125
2	0.5
3	0.25
4	0.125
5	0.0625
6	0.03125

Table 4: The Distribution of Alternative Resources for the Problems in Experiment 2.

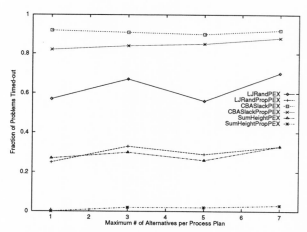

Figure 5. The Fraction of Problems in Each Problem Set for which Each Algorithm Timed-out.

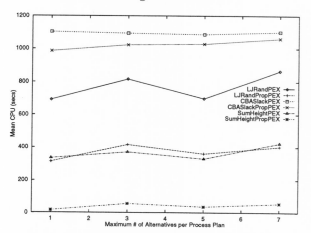

Figure 6. The Mean CPU Time in Seconds for Each Problem Set.

resource is generated by multiplying the activity's original duration by a randomly chosen factor in the domain [1.0, 1.5] and then rounding to the nearest integer value. These transformations result in problems that have widely varying PEX values: theoretically, from less than 2^{-8} to 1. Such a range should favor heuristics that reason explicitly about the PEX value (*i.e.,* SumHeightPEX).

The portion of problems in each set that each algorithm timed-out on is displayed in Figure 5. These results indicate, regardless of the use of PEX-edge-finding, that SumHeightPEX outperforms LJRandPEX which outperforms CBASlackPEX. Each heuristic times-out on significantly fewer problems when using PEX-edge-finding than without it. The mean CPU times are displayed in Figure 6. These results are consistent with the time-out results.

All the other search statistics which were evaluated (number of backtracks, number of commitments, and number of heuristic commitments) agree in the relative ranking of the performance of each heuristic: regardless of the PEX-edge-finding condition, SumHeightPEX outperforms LJRandPEX which outperforms CBASlackPEX. All heuristics exhibited significantly fewer backtracks and heuristic

commitments when used with PEX-edge-finding. Both CBASlackPEX and LJRandPEX made significantly more overall commitments when using PEX-edge-finding.

Discussion

The experiments present interesting and conflicting results. While SumHeightPEX outperforms CBASlackPEX with PEX-edge-finding, their relative performance without PEX-edge-finding is inconsistent: little difference is observed in Experiment 1, while, in Experiment 2, SumHeightPEX is significantly better. Furthermore, LJRandPEX is outperformed by both of the other heuristics (regardless of the use of PEX-edge-finding) in Experiment 1, but outperforms CBASlackPEX (again regardless of the use of PEX-edge-finding) in Experiment 2.

One explanation for the dramatic difference in the quality of heuristics between the two experiments is the fact that the non-uniformity in PEX values is much greater in the second experiment. SumHeightPEX exploits the non-uniformities among PEX values and so is able to perform better. Another, compatible, explanation for the difference is that the PEX values may be particularly damaging to the ability of CBASlackPEX to identify critical activity pairs. Recall that in the original CBASlack heuristic, the most critical activity pair is one that is not already sequenced (by the CBA propagator or previous heuristic commitments) and that has the smallest biased-slack. Because the CBA propagator cannot be used when one or both members of an activity pair have a PEX value of less than 1 (Beck, 1999), the CBASlackPEX heuristic calculates the biased-slack on such activity pairs even if their time windows do not overlap. Although activities with non-overlapping time windows do not compete with each other for a resource, their biased-slack calculation will tend to be very low. CBASlackPEX, therefore, may focus on such an activity pair even though it is not in any way critical. We hypothesize that such behavior is occurring, and at least contributing to the poor performance of CBASlackPEX. Further research is needed to confirm this behavior and, perhaps, modify CBASlackPEX to avoid it.

Through almost all experiments, PEX-edge-finding was shown to be beneficial to the overall problem solving ability. The only exception is when the CBASlackPEX heuristic is used. In general, these results are as expected. Given the significant increase in the performance of scheduling algorithms with the use of edge-finding propagators (Nuijten, 1994), we expect that some gain is likely with the PEX-edge-finding variation. Our intuitions as to why PEX-edge-finding improves search performance rests on two impacts of propagation. First, propagation techniques reduce the search space by removing alternatives that would otherwise have to be searched through. Second, propagators improve the search information upon which heuristics are based. PEX-edge-finding improves both the information represented in the PEX values and the information represented in the time windows of activities. SumHeightPEX benefits from both improvements while CBASlackPEX does not make direct use of the PEX values in forming its commitments and so does not benefit from this extra information. Another explanation for the CBASlackPEX result with PEX-edge-finding is that CBASlackPEX commitments tend to result in less propagation (Beck et al., 1997a; Beck, 1999). In Experiment 1, for example, SumHeight-PropPEX makes a significantly smaller percentage of heuristic commitments than CBASlackPropPEX. While a CBASlackPEX algorithm using PEX-edge-finding incurs the computational cost, the benefits are not apparent.

In this paper, we have not investigated the scaling behavior of our representation of alternative activities. While experiments elsewhere (Beck, 1999) indicate that the superiority of SumHeightPEX and PEX-edge-finding techniques continues with larger problems (*e.g.,* alternative process plan problems up to 20×20), the requirement to represent multiple alternatives necessarily leads to poor scaling behavior. This is empirically observed in (Davenport et al., 1999). The trade-off, of course, is that it is the representation and exploitation of the PEX information that results in both the higher quality commitments and the poor scaling behavior. Characterization of this trade-off and effort to optimize it form a central theme of our future research plans.

Conclusion

In this paper, we introduced the probability of existence (PEX) of an activity and used it to represent that an activity in the original problem definition does not necessarily have to execute in a solution. The use of PEX required extensions to the constraint representation of activities and of the temporal network, including algorithms for the propagation of PEX values among related activities and modifications to the temporal propagation. Heuristic commitment techniques and two edge-finding propagators were also extended to account for PEX values.

Experimental results indicate that incorporating PEX values into the texture-based heuristics results in significantly higher quality commitments and better overall search performance. Performance differences are especially large when there is a wide range of PEX values in a problem. Experimental results also validate the use of PEX-edge-finding which, in most cases, leads to significantly better overall search performance.

A key contribution of this work is the applicability of our representation of alternative activities to a wide variety of real-world scheduling problems. More generally, we have introduced a mechanism to explicitly reason about choosing *not* to take certain actions in order to achieve an overall goal. Such reasoning has relevance in many areas of artificial intelligence. Future research will investigate such applications.

Acknowledgements

This research was performed while the first author was a Ph.D. student at the Department of Computer Science, University of Toronto. It was funded in part by the Natural Sciences Engineering and Research Council, IRIS Research Network, Manufacturing Research Corporation of Ontario, Baan Limited, and Digital Equipment of Canada.

Thanks to Andrew Davenport and Angela Glover for discussion of and comments on previous versions of this paper.

References

Baptiste, P. and Le Pape, C. (1995). Disjunctive constraints for manufacturing scheduling: Principles and extensions. In *Proceedings of the Third International Conference on Computer Integrated Manufacturing.*

Baptiste, P. and Le Pape, C. (1996). Edge-finding constraint propagation algorithms for disjunctive and cumulative scheduling. In *Proceedings of the 15th Workshop of the UK Planning and Scheduling Special Interest Group.* Available from http://www.hds.utc.fr/ baptiste/.

Beck, J. C. (1999). *Texture measurements as a basis for heuristic commitment techniques in constraint-directed scheduling.* PhD thesis, University of Toronto. Forthcoming.

Beck, J. C., Davenport, A. J., Sitarski, E. M., and Fox, M. S. (1997a). Beyond contention: extending texture-based scheduling heuristics. In *Proceedings of AAAI-97.* AAAI Press, Menlo Park, California.

Beck, J. C., Davenport, A. J., Sitarski, E. M., and Fox, M. S. (1997b). Texture-based heuristics for scheduling revisited. In *Proceedings of AAAI-97.* AAAI Press, Menlo Park, California.

Carnegie Group Inc. (1994). Knowledge-based logistics planning system. Internal Documentation.

Cheng, C. C. and Smith, S. F. (1997). Applying constraint satisfaction techniques to job shop scheduling. *Annals of Operations Research, Special Volume on Scheduling: Theory and Practice,* 70:327–378. Forthcoming.

Cohen, P. R. (1995). *Empirical Methods for Artificial Intelligence.* The MIT Press, Cambridge, Mass.

Davenport, A. J., Beck, J. C., and Fox, M. S. (1999). An investigation into two approaches for resource allocation and scheduling. Technical report, Enterprise Integration Laboratory, Department of Mechanical and Industrial Engineering, University of Toronto.

Fox, M. (1986). Observations on the role of constraints in problem solving. In *Proceedings of the Sixth Canadian Conference on Artificial Intelligence.*

Fox, M. S. (1983). *Constraint-Directed Search: A Case Study of Job-Shop Scheduling.* PhD thesis, Carnegie Mellon University, Intelligent Systems Laboratory, The Robotics Institute, Pittsburgh, PA. CMU-RI-TR-85-7.

Kott, A. and Saks, V. (1998). A multi-decompositional approach to integration of planning and scheduling – an applied perspective. In *Proceedings of the Workshop on Integrating Planning, Scheduling and Execution in Dynamic and Uncertain Environments,* Pittsburgh, USA.

Le Pape, C. (1994). Using a constraint-based scheduling library to solve a specific scheduling problem. In *Proceedings of the AAAI-SIGMAN Workshop on Artificial Intelligence Approaches to Modelling and Scheduling Manufacturing Processes.*

Nuijten, W. P. M. (1994). *Time and resource constrained scheduling: a constraint satisfaction approach.* PhD thesis, Department of Mathematics and Computing Science, Eindhoven University of Technology.

Saks, V., Johnson, I., and Fox, M. (1993). Distribution planning: A constrained heuristic search approach. In *Proceedings of the Knowledge-based System and Robotics Workshop,* pages 13–19. Industry Canada.

Smith, S. F. and Cheng, C. C. (1993). Slack-based heuristics for constraint satisfaction scheduling. In *Proceedings AAAI-93,* pages 139–144.

Algorithm Performance and Problem Structure for Flow-shop Scheduling

Jean-Paul Watson, Laura Barbulescu, Adele E. Howe, and **L. Darrell Whitley**
Computer Science Department
Colorado State University
Fort Collins, CO 80523
e-mail: {watsonj, laura, howe, whitley}@cs.colostate.edu

Abstract

Test suites for many domains often fail to model features present in real-world problems. For the permutation flow-shop sequencing problem (PFSP), the most popular test suite consists of problems whose features are generated from a single uniform random distribution. Synthetic generation of problems with characteristics present in real-world problems is a viable alternative. We compare the performance of several competitive algorithms on problems produced with such a generator. We find that, as more realistic characteristics are introduced, the performance of a state-of-the-art algorithm degrades rapidly: faster and less complex stochastic algorithms provide superior performance. Our empirical results show that small changes in problem structure or problem size can influence algorithm performance. We hypothesize that these performance differences may be partially due to differences in search space topologies; we show that structured problems produce topologies with performance plateaus. Algorithm sensitivity to problem characteristics suggests the need to construct test suites more representative of real-world applications.

Introduction and Motivation

Algorithms for the permutation flow-shop sequencing problem (PFSP) are typically compared using problems from benchmark test suites available in the OR library (Beasley 1998). Most often, the problems in these test suites are generated by selecting job processing times from a single uniform distribution; the problems are then submitted to a search algorithm for solution. Problems are accepted as "difficult" if the search algorithm has trouble consistently finding a good solution, as measured relative either to the lower bound or to a best known solution.

An underlying assumption of these performance studies is that if an algorithm performs well on difficult synthetic problems, then it will also perform well on scheduling applications. However, real-world problems

are *not* random — they typically are characterized by some amount of structure, though it is rarely quantified and categorized. Our research addresses the issue of whether state-of-the-art algorithm performance will hold up on PFSPs that have structural features representative of those found in some real-world problems. For example, consider a circuit board manufacturing line, a real-world problem naturally expressed as a PFSP. Larger circuit boards tend to have more components, and may require longer processing times at each machine on the line. Such jobs have correlated processing times across machines. In contrast, the duration of a circuit board baking process is independent of board size. In this case, the job processing times are similar on a particular machine.

Ideally, we would like to test algorithms on real-world problems. Yet, these are difficult to obtain, incur knowledge acquisition overhead and sacrifice experimental control. Because we have not yet quantified the structure of real-world PFSP problems, we cannot control for the effects of different types and amounts of structure. Thus, test suite generation based on known characteristics of some real-world problems balances experimental control and generality of results.

The No Free Lunch (NFL) theorem for search (Wolpert & Macready 1995) informally states that the mean performance of all search algorithms is identical, independent of the chosen performance measure, when *all* possible (discrete) objective functions are considered. The NFL theorem warns us that better-than-random performance on a subset of problems may not hold for a *different* subset of problems. By relying on benchmark test suites to drive algorithm development, algorithms may be over-fit to their benchmarks.

This paper presents two major results. First, we demonstrate that superior performance on a popular synthetic benchmark test suite fails to transfer to a test suite containing problems with only modest levels of non-random features. Second, we show that the non-random flow-shop problems do not display a search space topology previously associated with difficult problems, thus partially explaining why previously successful algorithms which exploit such structure fail on non-random problems.

A Structured PFSP Generator

Our domain is the well-known n by m permutation flow-shop sequencing problem (PFSP) which Garey & Johnson (1979) showed to be NP-hard. Here, n jobs must be processed, in the same order, on each of m machines. Concurrency is not allowed: a machine can only process a single job at a time, and processing must be completed once initiated. Furthermore, machine $j+1$ cannot begin processing a job until machine j has completed processing of the same job. Each job i requires a processing time of d_{ij} on the jth machine. A candidate solution to the PFSP is simply a permutation of the n jobs, π. Given that the first job in π on the first machine begins at time step 0, the makespan of π is defined to be the finish time of the last job in π on the last machine. The objective is to find a permutation π such that the makespan is minimized.

The most commonly used PFSP benchmark problems are those introduced in Taillard (1993) and available through the OR library. In fact, the performance of many PFSP algorithms such as the Reeves/Yamada path relinking algorithm (Reeves & Yamada 1998) are compared *strictly* on these problems. Taillard generated his problems by selecting the processing times d_{ij} uniformly from the interval $[1,99]$ and then choosing a subset of problems based on several criteria, including problem difficulty as measured by a Tabu search algorithm. In expectation, and in contrast to many real-world problems, Taillard's problems contain little or no discernible structural features.

Kan (1976) introduced two methods of creating structure: job correlation and time gradients. In *job-correlated* problems, the processing times of a given job are 'correlated' in the sense that they are sampled from a relatively tight distribution specific to that job. *Time gradients* impose non-random structure by creating a trend in job processing times as a function of machine; processing times on early machines tend to be less than those of later machines. We introduce a third method to create non-random structure: *machine correlation*. In *machine-correlated* problems, the processing times of all jobs on a given machine are sampled from a relatively tight distribution specific to that machine.

We consider only job and machine-correlated PFSPs. Non-random structure is produced by drawing processing times from a number of Gaussian distributions. For job-correlated problems, we use n distributions, one for each job. For machine-correlated problems, we use m distributions, one for each machine. The generation of the x (either $x = n$ or $x = m$) distributions is a three-step process requiring four input parameters. The parameters σ_{lb} and σ_{ub} provide bounds on the distribution standard deviations, while μ_{lb} dictates a lower bound on the distribution means. Finally, α controls the expected degree of distribution overlap. Low degrees of distribution overlap yield PFSPs with more structure because processing times selected from two distributions with little overlap are typically much different. As the degree of overlap increases, the amount of structure decreases; in the limit, the distributions share the same mean, albeit with different standard deviations. Given these parameters, a PFSP is produced as follows:

Step 1: Select the Standard Deviations.
The distribution standard deviations $\sigma_i, 1 \leq i \leq x$, are selected uniformly from the interval $[\sigma_{lb}, \sigma_{ub}]$.

Step 2: Compute the Mean Interval.
The means of the x Gaussian distributions are selected uniformly from a fixed interval. The width of this interval directly influences the degree of distribution overlap. Smaller interval widths reduce the average mean separation.

Approximately 95% of the mass of a Gaussian distribution lies within $\pm 2\sigma$ of the mean. To produce x distributions with little overlap, consider placing the x Gaussian distributions side-by-side along an axis, with overlap only in the 2.5% upper and lower tails of neighboring distributions. The width of this construction is: $canonical\_Width = \sum_{i=1}^{x} 4\sigma_i$. We consider a set of distributions to exhibit minimal overlap if and only if each distribution overlaps with approximately the 2.5% upper or lower tails of neighboring distributions. Note that, in general, minimal overlap will *not* be achieved by uniform sampling of the means: an interval of width $canonical\_Width$ is the smallest interval in which it is *possible* to achieve the minimal overlap.

In expectation, selecting x distribution means uniformly from an interval of width less than $canonical\_Width$ will yield distributions with more overlap. In our generator, $canonical\_Width$ is scaled by α, where α is restricted to the interval $[0, 1]$. Lower values of α yield larger overlap in distributions, and therefore processing times.

The bounds on the distribution means are then given by $[\mu_{lb}, \mu_{ub}]$, where
$$\mu_{ub} = \mu_{lb} + \alpha \cdot canonical\_Width.$$

Step 3: Select the Distribution Means.
The means μ_i, $1 \leq i \leq x$, of the distributions are uniformly selected from the interval $[\mu_{lb}, \mu_{ub}]$.

For job-correlated PFSPs, the processing times for each job i are selected from the Gaussian distribution $\eta(\mu_i, \sigma_i)$. For machine-correlated PFSPs, the processing times for each machine j are selected from the Gaussian distribution $\eta(\mu_j, \sigma_j)$.

Finally, in contrast to Taillard (1993), we do not filter for difficult problems. Instead, we concern ourselves with algorithm performance on *classes* of problems. Taillard defines difficulty relative to a specific algorithm. Thus, any comparison of different algorithms would be biased by such filtering, as problem difficulty can only be defined relative to an algorithm.

The Algorithms

We compared the performance of algorithms based on three search methodologies: 1) path relinking, 2) incremental construction, and 3) iterative sampling. The path relinking algorithm by Reeves and Yamada (1998) was selected because it has demonstrated some of the best performance to date on the problems from Taillard's test suite. Most AI search algorithms are based on either incremental construction or iterative sampling. Incremental construction refers to algorithms that use heuristics to build up a schedule; this class was included because excellent heuristics are available for the PFSP domain. Iterative sampling refers to a class of stochastic algorithms ranging from random sampling to random-starts local search; this class was included primarily because of reported successes of such algorithms on various scheduling applications.

Path Relinking

Path relinking is a general search strategy in which the search space is explored by looking for additional optima near two known local optima. During the process of 'linking' or constructing a path between two local optima, the algorithm can check the intervening area for other optima. Path relinking is the basis for the Reeves/Yamada PFSP algorithm (Reeves & Yamada 1998), which we denote by *pathrelink*.

The search spaces for the problems in Taillard's test suite exhibit a 'big-valley' structure (Boese, Kahng, & Muddu 1994). The big-valley structure implies that the best local optima are near to the global optima. Poorer optima tend to be further away from the global optima. Path relinking has been shown to be effective on search spaces with this structure. Iterated exploration linking two highly fit local optima may be likely to expose other good local optima.

At the highest level, *pathrelink* is a steady-state genetic algorithm (Whitley 1989). A population of 15 job permutations, each representing a solution to the PFSP, is maintained; the complexity of the crossover operator forces the small population size. New candidate solutions are generated using one of two methods, each with a fixed probability. The first method uses a stochastic local search operator to improve upon an existing population member, with the goal of moving solutions toward local optima. The second method uses a form of path relinking to find new candidate solutions. First, two parent solutions are selected from the population. Starting from one parent, a path is probabilistically projected toward the other parent. A limit on the number of evaluations allocated to each projection is imposed, and the best solution along the projected path is retained. Due to the stochastic nature of the projection and the limit on the number of evaluations, complete path linking is *not* performed. Rather, search progresses toward the other parent, although not necessarily reaching it. Once a candidate solution is generated via either of these methods, it is placed into the population if the resulting makespan is better than the makespan of the worst element in the population. This process is then repeated for some fixed number of iterations.

Incremental Construction Algorithms

We studied a pure heuristic construction algorithm as well as backtracking algorithms based on this heuristic. The pure heuristic algorithm is NEH (Nawaz, Enscore, & Ham 1983), which is widely regarded as the best performing heuristic for the PFSP (Taillard 1990). The NEH algorithm can be summarized as follows:

(1) Order the n jobs by decreasing sums of total job processing times on the machines.
(2) Take the first two jobs and schedule them so as to minimize the partial makespan as if there were only two jobs.
(3) For $k=3$ to n do
  Insert the k-th job into the location in the partial schedule, among the k possible, which minimizes the partial makespan.

Despite its simplicity ($O(n^3m)$), NEH produces reasonably good solutions to Taillard's benchmark problems. However, the solutions produced by *pathrelink* are either competitive with or exceed the previously best known solutions. Yet the comparison is hardly fair: the run-time of NEH is several orders of magnitude less.

The NEH algorithm can be viewed as a greedy constructive search method, which can be extended in several ways. Backtracking mechanisms can be added to recover from poor local decisions made during step (3) of the pseudo-code. The k insertion points can be sorted in ascending order of partial makespan to provide a relative quality measure.

We implemented several systematic backtracking algorithms: Chronological Backtracking (CB), Limited Discrepancy Search (LDS), Depth-bounded Discrepancy Search (DDS), and Heuristic-Biased Stochastic Sampling (HBSS). Chronological backtracking serves as a baseline performer for the heuristic backtracking algorithms. For LDS (Harvey & Ginsberg 1995) and DDS (Walsh 1996), a discrepancy is defined as any point in the search where the advice of the heuristic is not followed. LDS iteratively increases the maximum number of discrepancies allowed on each path from the root of the search tree to any leaf. In contrast, DDS iteratively increases the depth in the search tree at which discrepancies are allowed. Both algorithms assume the availability of a good heuristic, such as NEH. DDS further assumes that discrepancies required to achieve near-optimal solutions should occur at relatively shallow depths in the search tree. As no agreed-upon convention exists, we consider *any* move other than that suggested by the heuristic as a single discrepancy. This is unlike LePape & Baptiste (1997), where $k-1$ discrepancies are counted if the kth available move is chosen.

HBSS (Bresina 1996) is an incremental construction algorithm in which multiple root-to-leaf paths are stochastically generated. Instead of randomly choosing a move, an acceptance probability is associated with each possible move. This acceptance probability is based on the rank of the move assigned by the heuristic.

A bias function is then applied to the ranks, and the resulting values are normalized. The choice of bias function "reflects the confidence one has in the heuristic's accuracy - the higher the confidence, the stronger the bias" (Bresina, 1997:271). We used a relatively strong quadratic bias function, due to the strength of the NEH heuristic: $bias(r) = r^{-2}$, where r is the rank of a move.

Iterative Sampling Algorithms

We also implemented several iterative sampling algorithms. In random sampling, a number of random permutations are generated and evaluated. Another iterative sampling algorithm can be obtained by modifying step (2) of the NEH algorithm. Instead of selecting the two largest jobs, we instead choose two jobs at random. Step (3) of the NEH is then followed, without backtracking, to produce a complete schedule. We denote this algorithm by *NEH-RS* (NEH with random-starts).

Finally, we consider iterative random sampling in which local search is applied to the randomly generated solutions; we denote this algorithm by *itsampls* (iterative random sampling with local search). Following Reeves and Yamada (1998), we use a shift local search operator coupled with a next-descent search strategy. Let π represent a permutation and π_i be the element in the ith position of the permutation. The operation $\pi_i \mapsto \pi_j$ denotes that the ith element in the original permutation is re-mapped to the jth position. Given two randomly selected positions i and j, $i < j$, the shift operator SH(i,j) transforms π as follows:

$$SH(i,j) : \pi \to \pi \begin{cases} \pi_k \mapsto \pi_{k+1} & \text{if } i \leq k < j \\ \pi_j \mapsto \pi_i & \\ \pi_k \mapsto \pi_k & \text{otherwise} \end{cases}$$

The operator is applied to all pairs of jobs in a random order, with each improving or equal move accepted. Finally, we note that because of the strong stochastic component, HBSS can be classified as either an incremental construction or iterative sampling algorithm.

Relative Algorithm Performance: Empirical Results

Algorithm performance was measured on six problem classes consisting of three sizes of both job and machine-correlated problems: 50, 100 and 200 jobs, all executed on 20 machines. For each problem class, we generated 100 problem instances with $\mu_{lb} = 35$ and α ranging from 0.1 to 1.0, in increments of 0.1 The values of σ_{lb} and σ_{ub} were set to 1 and 20, respectively. Varying the problem size allows us to assess algorithm scalability, while varying α allows us to assess the influence of structure on algorithm performance.

The process of placing a job into the best possible location of a partial schedule dominates the run-time of all NEH-based algorithms; this corresponds to the loop body in step (3) of the NEH pseudo-code. We define this computation as an evaluation and allocate 100K such evaluations to all NEH-based algorithms. For

HBSS and NEH-RS, root-to-leaf paths are repeatedly generated with the best obtained solution recorded. For the systematic heuristic backtracking algorithms (CB, LDS, and DDS), a target makespan must be specified. We begin by setting the target makespan to one less than the makespan obtained by the NEH algorithm. Once an algorithm locates a solution with a makespan equal to or better than the target makespan, a new target makespan is similarly defined, and the algorithm is restarted. For random sampling, 100K solutions are generated and evaluated, with the best retained.

For the *pathrelink* algorithm, either local search or path projection is performed at each iteration. Each local search or path projection involves 1000 steps, each requiring an evaluation. The total number of evaluations is limited to 100,000. For all *itsampls* trials, we allow two 'all-pairs' iterations and limit the total number of evaluations to 100K.

For each algorithm, we recorded the best makespan obtained on each problem. The optimal makespans for these problems are unknown; we measured individual algorithm performance by computing the *percent above the best solution found* by any of the search algorithms considered. Finally, we obtained a summary measure of algorithm performance at each level of α for each problem class by computing the average percent above best for the 100 problems.

Machine-Correlated Problems

Figures 1, 2, and 3 record algorithm performance on 50 by 20, 100 by 20, and 200 by 20 *machine-correlated* problems. All algorithms significantly outperformed random sampling. As a group, the stochastic algorithms (*itsampls*, NEH-RS, and HBSS) outperform the deterministic algorithms (NEH, LDS, and DDS). The superior performance of HBSS and NEH-RS is both sustained and magnified as problem size increases: both algorithms scale extremely well. The performance of *itsampls* fails to scale to 200 by 20 problems; for small values of α, it is outperformed by the deterministic algorithms. Interestingly, the two strongest performers, HBSS and NEH-RS, are based on a domain-specific heuristic (NEH), while *itsampls* is not.

Both LDS and DDS improve over the pure NEH algorithm and significantly outperform chronological backtracking. In comparison to LDS, the slight under-performance of DDS suggests that for machine-correlated problems it is important to consider discrepancies deep in the search tree. An analysis of LDS execution traces supports this observation and also indicates that it is often necessary to consider moves that are deemed extremely poor by the heuristic. Clearly the degradation of the NEH heuristic is not gradual.

The most striking aspect of Figures 1 - 3 is the inconsistent, and often poor, performance of the *pathrelink* algorithm. In Figure 1, *pathrelink* starts to underperform relative to both HBSS and NEH-RS between α equal to 0.1 and 0.2. At larger values of α, *pathrelink* is outperformed by many of the other, simpler algorithms.

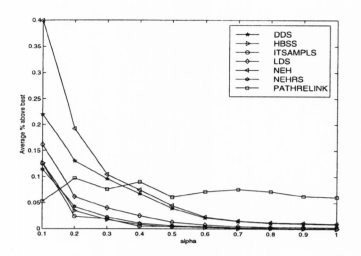

Figure 1: 50x20 machine-correlated

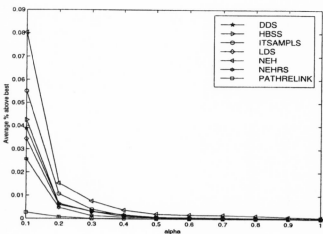

Figure 4: 50x20 job-correlated

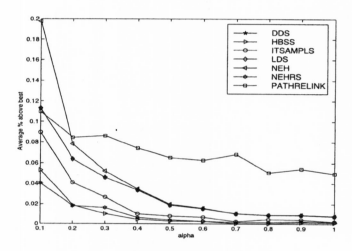

Figure 2: 100x20 machine-correlated

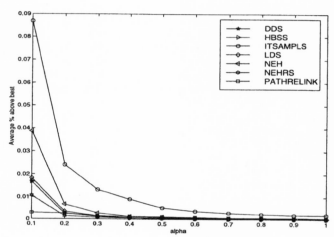

Figure 5: 100x20 job-correlated

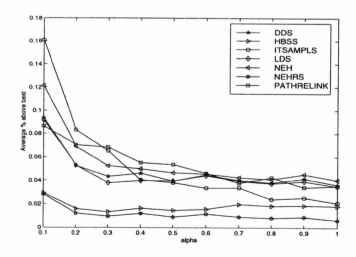

Figure 3: 200x20 machine-correlated

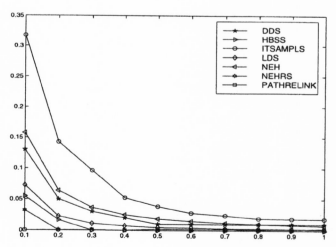

Figure 6: 200x20 job-correlated

Figures 2 and 3 show that for larger problem sizes, *pathrelink* underperforms both HBSS and NEH-RS on problems at all levels of α, including 0.1. The performance of the *pathrelink* algorithm fails in that 1) it does not scale to larger machine-correlated problems and 2) even minor amounts of structure cause it to lag the best iterative stochastic algorithms.

Job-Correlated Problems

Figures 4, 5, and 6 record algorithm performance on 50 by 20, 100 by 20, and 200 by 20 *job-correlated* problems. Again, all algorithms significantly outperformed random sampling. As was the case for machine-correlated problems, the stochastic algorithms outperform the deterministic algorithms, excepting the performance of *itsampls*, which fails to scale to larger problem sizes. Here, the performance degradation of *itsampls* is even more rapid than that exhibited on machine-correlated problems; on 100 by 20 and 200 by 20 problems, NEH obtains superior results at *all* values of α.

NEH-RS remains the strongest overall performer; it only slightly underperforms *pathrelink* when α = 0.1. HBSS, LDS, and DDS all improve over NEH and chronological backtracking, but are basically indistinguishable for larger values of α. LDS continues to perform slightly better than DDS. Finally, the move from 100 by 20 to 200 by 20 problems results in greater differences in algorithm performance, although the relative order remains stable.

The performance of *pathrelink* remains the most unexpected result of these experiments. In contrast to the machine-correlated results, *pathrelink* consistently outperforms all other algorithms, on all problem sizes, with the sole exception of NEH-RS. Even more interesting is the fact the performance *pathrelink* appears to be *independent* of α, the level of non-random problem structure.

Assessing Problem Structure

Our study of non-random PFSPs is motivated not only by the fact that they actually model real-world problem attributes, but also as an exploration of what it means to be a "hard" problem and how this influences algorithm performance. Taillard's problems have been filtered to be "hard." In other areas of AI, the phase transition regions of problems such as SAT or Hamiltonian circuits have been explored as a source of difficult test instances (Cheeseman, Kanefsky, & Taylor 1991).

Reeves and Yamada (1998) show that Taillard's difficult flow-shop problems display a *big-valley* problem structure when the *shift* local search operator is used. The notion of *big-valley* is somewhat imprecise. It suggests that 1) local optima tend to be relatively close to other local optima, 2) better local optima tend to be closer to global optima, and 3) local optima near one another have similar evaluations. To find the big-valley phenomenon, however, one must pick the "correct" local search operator. First introduced in the context of

the TSP and Graph Bipartitioning problems (Boese, Kahng, & Muddu 1994), some recent state-of-the-art algorithms are explicitly designed to exploit this structure.

We hypothesized that the poor performance of the state-of-the-art *pathrelink* on machine correlated problems algorithm might be attributable to a lack of the big-valley structure in our problems. Thus, we tested the different types of PFSPs for it. In our experimental setup, the underlying distribution (Gaussian or uniform) and the parameters defining the type of structure (correlation on jobs, machines, and α, or no correlation) are the independent variables. The dependent variables are the distance between local optima and the quality of the solutions obtained, quantifying the presence and extent of the big-valley structure.

For each problem, we generate 2000 local optima by starting with random permutations and running local search using the shift operator. The shift operator is repeatedly applied, in a next-descent strategy for all the possible pairs of jobs in the permutation, in a random order, until two passes through all the pairs does not result in any improvement. Because the global optima for our problems are unknown, we next compute for each local optimum its average distance to all the other local optima, as was done in the previous study (Reeves & Yamada 1998). We use an operator-independent precedence-based measure to compute pairwise distances. For two permutations π and π' of length n, the computation is:

$$\frac{n(n-1)}{2} - \sum_{i,j,i\neq j} preceeds(i,j,\pi) \wedge preceeds(i,j,\pi')$$

where the function $preceeds(i,j,\pi)$ returns 1 if i occurs before j in permutation π. Finally, one deficiency of this methodology is that it fails to distinguish cases where multiple local optima are equivalent, i.e., they all reside on the same plateau and can be transformed into one another by non-degrading (in terms of makespan) applications of the shift operator.

Taillard's Problems

In the top graph of Figure 7, the results for a 50x20 problem (TA052) from Taillard's test suite serve as a prototypical example of a big-valley structure. In this figure, the local optima tend to be clustered, with good local optima close to each other. We used Taillard's problem generator included with the benchmark problems in (Beasley 1998) to produce new problems. Scatterplots for these problems were similar to those of the top graph in Figure 7. Thus, *all* problems produced by this generator appear to satisfy big-valley requirements, not just the ones selected as difficult.

To determine the impact of the choice of distribution on Taillard's problem generator, we replaced the uniform distribution on the interval [1,99] with the Gaussian distribution $\eta(50, 16)$. The bottom graph in Figure 7 shows a typical example of the resulting scatterplots.

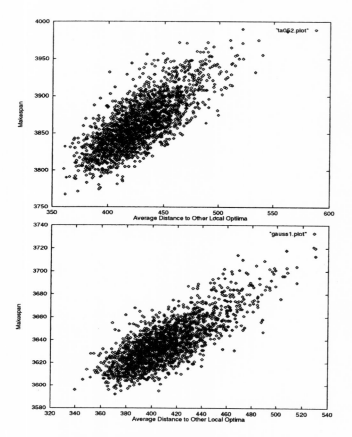

Figure 7: Taillard's TA052 50x20 Instance, uniform distribution, no correlation (top) and a Taillard-Gaussian 50x20 Instance (bottom).

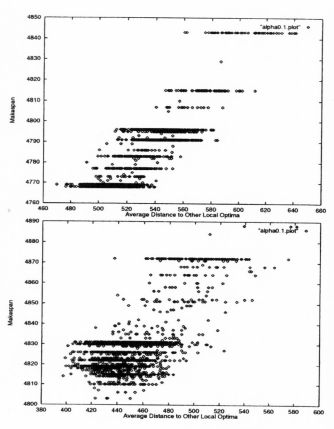

Figure 8: Machine-correlated 50x20 Instances, $\alpha=0.1$. The top graph is a uniform distribution; the bottom graph is a Gaussian distribution.

The choice of distribution appears to have no significant impact on the existence of the big-valley structure.

Correlated Problems

We next investigated the effect of correlation on the landscape generated by the shift operator, when a Gaussian distribution is used. We generated local optima and distance measures for several 50x20 instances of both job and machine-correlated problems, varying α from 0.1 to 1.0 in increments of 0.1. The bottom graph in Figure 8 shows the result for a machine-correlated problem generated with α equal to 0.1. The results for job-correlated problems were similar. Note that an α of 0.1 represents a very low level of correlation. While there is still evidence of a big-valley structure, another dominant structural feature begins to emerge: strata of local optima at specific makespan values. Further analysis indicates that many members of the same stratum actually belong to the same plateau which can be partitioned into a small number of distinct local optima.

Although not shown, we also varied the amount of problem structure as measured by α. The empirical evidence suggests that the number of plateaus gradually drops to only a few, and all local optima are gradually

absorbed into some plateau.

Finally, we checked for an interaction effect of the distribution and correlation. The question is whether the plateaus emerged due to the combined influence of correlation and Gaussian distribution. We therefore generated job and machine-correlated problems using a uniform distribution. The result from a 50x20 machine-correlated instance ($\alpha=0.1$) is shown in the top graph of Figure 8; the results for job-correlated instances were similar. As with non-correlated problems, the choice of distribution appears to have little or no impact on the results. For job and machine-correlated problems, the big-valley structure is not the dominant structural feature of the fitness landscape. As the level of structure is increased, the landscape is dominated by only a few very large plateaus of local optima.

This suggests that we still do not have a clear picture of how problem structure impacts algorithm performance. *Pathrelink* performs well on random problems and job correlated problems, but not machine correlated problems. Yet, both job correlated problems and machine correlated problems are characterized by plateaus rather than the distribution of local optima normally associated with the big-valley phenomenon.

Implications and Conclusions

PFSP test suites are developed with little regard to structural features present in real-world problems. Thus, the apparent excellent performance of particular algorithms on these problems may not generalize to superior performance on real applications.

We constructed a PFSP generator to produce problems with variable amounts of two types of structure: job and machine correlation. We then compared the performance of several algorithms on problems of various sizes, with different amounts of structure.

For both job and machine-correlated problems, a simple iterative stochastic algorithm, NEH-RS, provides the best overall performance and scalability. In comparison, the *pathrelink* algorithm, which does exceptionally well on the random Taillard PFSP test suite, fails to sustain this performance on problems with a modest amount of machine-correlated problem structure. Clearly, algorithms that work best on 'hard' problems, such as those from Taillard's test suite, may not be the best on more realistic classes of problems.

While interesting, the performance of individual algorithms was not the primary goal of these experiments. Rather, these experiments show that each of the following have a potentially significant influence on individual algorithm performance: the type of problem structure, the amount of problem structure, and the problem size.

We also compared the structure of the search spaces for Taillard's problems and problems from our generator. Previously, it had been proposed that the big-valley search space structure was characteristic of difficult flow-shop problems and that the best algorithms were designed to exploit that structure. However, we found the big-valley structure in both Taillard problems selected as difficult and in randomly generated problems. Additionally, we did not find the big-valley structure in our correlated problems; instead, we found a plateau structure. Based on this analysis, we suggest that some state-of-the-art algorithms may have been optimized for a problem structure particular to the randomly generated, uncorrelated problems. Thus, to better define algorithms for structured problems, we need measures of structure and a better understanding of the interaction of problem structure and algorithm design.

Our results reinforce the following warning: the problems found in artificial test suites provide little indication regarding the performance of algorithms on real-world problems. Furthermore, high levels of complexity may not be required to solve real-world problems: in our work, simple heuristic-based iterative sampling algorithms provided the best overall performance.

Acknowledgments

This work was sponsored by the Air Force Office of Scientific Research, Air Force Materiel Command, USAF, under grant number F49620-97-1-0271. The U.S. Government is authorized to reproduce and distribute reprints for Governmental purposes notwithstanding any copyright notation thereon. The authors would also like to thank the anonymous reviewers for their comments on an earlier version of this paper.

References

Beasley, J. E. 1998. *OR-LIBRARY*. http://www.ms.ic.ac.uk/info.html.

Boese, K. D.; Kahng, A. B.; and Muddu, S. 1994. A new adaptive multi-start technique for combinatorial global optimizations. *Operations Research Letters* 16/2:101–113.

Bresina, J. L. 1996. Heuristic-biased stochastic sampling. In *Proceedings of the Thirteenth National Conference on Artificial Intelligence.*

Cheeseman, P.; Kanefsky, B.; and Taylor, W. 1991. Where the really hard problems are. In *Proceedings of IJCAI-91.*

Garey, M. R., and Johnson, D. S. 1979. *Computers And Intractability: A Guide to the Theory of NP-Completeness.* W. H. Freemand and Company.

Harvey, W. D., and Ginsberg, M. L. 1995. Limited discrepancy search. In *Proceedings of the Fourteenth International Joint Conference on Artificial Intelligence.*

Kan, A. R. 1976. *Machine Scheduling Problems: Classification, complexity and computations.* Martinus Nijhoff, The Hague.

LePape, and Baptiste. 1997. An experimental comparison of constraint-based algorithms for the preemptive job-shop scheduling problem. In *CP97 Workshop on Industrial Constraint-Directed Scheduling.*

Nawaz, M.; Enscore, E.; and Ham, I. 1983. A heuristic algorithm for the m-machine, n-job flow-shop sequencing problem. *OMEGA, The International Journal of Management Science* 11/1:91–95.

Reeves, C. R., and Yamada, T. 1998. Genetic algorithms, path relinking, and the flowshop sequencing problem. *Evolutionary Computation* 6:45–60.

Taillard, E. 1990. Some efficient heuristic methods for the flow shop sequencing problem. *European Journal of Operations Research* 47:65–74.

Taillard, E. 1993. Benchmarks for basic scheduling problems. *European Journal of Operations Research* 64:278–285.

Walsh, T. 1996. Depth-bounded discrepancy search. In *Proceedings of the Fifteenth International Joint Conference on Artificial Intelligence.*

Whitley, L. D. 1989. The GENITOR algorithm and selective pressure: Why rank based allocation of reproductive trials is best. In *Proceedings of the Third International Conference on Genetic Algorithms.*

Wolpert, D. H., and Macready, W. G. 1995. No free lunch theorems for search. Technical Report SFI-TR-95-02-010, Santa Fe Institute.

Search

Using Probabilistic Knowledge and Simulation to Play Poker

Darse Billings, Lourdes Peña, Jonathan Schaeffer, Duane Szafron
Department of Computing Science, University of Alberta
Edmonton, Alberta Canada T6G 2H1
{darse, pena, jonathan, duane}@cs.ualberta.ca

Abstract

Until recently, artificial intelligence researchers who use games as their experimental testbed have concentrated on games of perfect information. Many of these games have been amenable to brute-force search techniques. In contrast, games of imperfect information, such as bridge and poker, contain hidden information making similar search techniques impractical. This paper describes recent progress in developing a high-performance poker-playing program. The advances come in two forms. First, we introduce a new betting strategy that returns a probabilistic betting decision, a probability triple, that gives the likelihood of a fold, call or raise occurring in a given situation. This component unifies all the expert knowledge used in the program, does a better job of representing the type of decision making needed to play strong poker, and improves the way information is propagated throughout the program. Second, real-time simulations are used to compute the expected values of betting decisions. The program generates an instance of the missing data, subject to any constraints that have been learned, and then simulates the rest of the game to determine a numerical result. By repeating this a sufficient number of times, a statistically meaningful sample is used in the program's decision–making process. Experimental results show that these enhancements each represent major advances in the strength of computer poker programs.

1. Introduction

Past research efforts in computer game-playing have concentrated on building high-performance chess programs. With the Deep Blue victory over World Chess Champion Garry Kasparov, a milestone has been achieved but, more importantly, the artificial intelligence community has been liberated from the chess "problem". The consequence is that in recent years a number of interesting games have attracted the attention of AI researchers, where the research results promise a wider range of applicability than has been seen for chess.

Computer success has been achieved in deterministic perfect information games, like chess, checkers and Othello, largely due to so-called brute-force search. The correlation of search speed to program performance gave an easy recipe to program success: build a faster search engine. The Deep Blue team took this to an extreme, analyzing roughly 250 million chess positions per second.

In contrast, until recently imperfect information games have attracted little attention in the literature. In these games, no player knows the complete state and each player has to infer the missing information to maximize the chances of success. For these games, brute-force

search is not successful since it is often impractical to search the game trees that result from all possible instances of the missing information.

Two examples of imperfect information games are bridge and poker. Recently, at least two research groups have made an effort to achieve high-performance bridge-playing programs [Ginsberg, 1999; Smith *et al.*, 1998]. The progress has been impressive, and we may not have to wait long for a world-championship caliber program.

Until now, the computing community has largely ignored poker (a recent exception being [Koller and Pfeffer, 1997]). However, poker has several attributes that make it an interesting and challenging domain for mainstream AI research [Billings *et. al.*, 1998a].

We are attempting to build a program that is capable of beating the best human poker players. We have chosen to study the game of Texas Hold'em, the poker variation used to determine the world champion in the annual World Series of Poker. Hold'em is considered the most strategically complex poker variant that is widely played.

Our program, Loki, is a reasonably strong player (as judged by its success playing on the Internet) [Billings *et. al.*, 1998a; 1998b]. The current limitation in the program's play is its betting strategy - deciding when to fold, call/check, or raise/bet. A betting strategy attempts to determine which betting action will maximize the expected winnings (or minimize the losses) for a hand. The previous version of Loki used several expert-knowledge evaluation functions to make betting decisions. These routines were rigid in the sense that they always returned a single value: the "best" betting decision. Although these evaluation functions allowed Loki to play better than average poker, it was inadequate to play at a world-class level, since continually upgrading this knowledge is difficult and error-prone.

This paper introduces two major advances in the capabilities of computer-poker-playing programs. Each is shown experimentally to result in substantial improvements in Loki's play.

First, this paper introduces a new betting strategy that returns a *probability triple* as the knowledge representation of the evaluation function. The routine returns three probabilities (one each for fold, call/check, and raise/bet). The program can then randomly select the betting decision in accordance with the probability triples. Representing decisions as a probability distribution better captures the type of information needed to perform well in a noisy environment, where randomized strategies and misinformation are important aspects of strong play. This component also allows us to unify the expert knowledge in a poker program, since the same component can be used for betting decisions, opponent modeling, and interpreting opponent actions.

Second, Loki now bases its betting strategy on a simulation-based approach; we call it *selective sampling*. It simulates the outcome of each hand, by generating opponent hands from the sample space of all *appropriate* possibilities, trying each betting alternative (call/check, bet/raise) to find the one that produces the highest expected winnings. A good definition of appropriate hands is one of the key concepts in defining selective sampling and it is one of the main topics of this paper. As with brute-force search in chess, the simulation (search) implicitly uncovers information that improves the quality of a decision. With selective sampling, the knowledge applied to a simulation *quantifies* the value of each choice, improving the chance of making a good decision.

Simulation-based approaches have been used in other games, such as backgammon [Tesauro, 1995], bridge [Ginsberg, 1999], and Scrabble[1] [Sheppard, 1998]. The simulation methods presented in this paper are quite similar to those used by Ginsberg in Gib, although there are several distinctions in the details, due to differences in the games.

For deterministic perfect information games, there is a well-known framework for constructing these applications (based on the alpha-beta algorithm). For games with imperfect information, no such framework exists. For handling this broader scope of games we propose that selective sampling simulation be such a framework.

2. Texas Hold'em

A hand of Texas Hold'em begins with the *pre-flop*, where each player is dealt two *hole cards* face down, followed by the first round of betting. Three community cards are then dealt face up on the table, called the *flop*, and the second round of betting occurs. On the *turn*, a fourth community card is dealt face up and another round of betting ensues. Finally, on the *river*, a fifth community card is dealt face up and the final round of betting occurs. All players still in the game turn over their two hidden cards for the *showdown*. The best five card poker hand formed from the two hole cards and the five community cards wins the pot. If a tie occurs, the pot is split. Typically, Texas Hold'em is played with 8 to 10 players.

Limit Texas Hold'em has a structured betting system, where the order and amount of betting is strictly controlled in each betting round.[2] There are two denominations of bets, called the small bet and the big bet ($10 and $20 in this paper). In the first two betting rounds, all bets and raises are $10, while in the last two rounds they are $20. In general, when it is a player's turn

to act, one of three betting options is available: fold, call/check, or raise/bet. There is normally a maximum of three raises allowed per betting round. The betting option rotates clockwise until each player has matched the current bet or folded. If there is only one player remaining (all others having folded) that player is the winner and is awarded the pot without having to reveal their cards.

3. Building a Poker Program

A minimal set of requirements for a strong poker-playing program includes assessing hand strength and potential, betting strategy, bluffing, unpredictability and opponent modeling. Descriptions of these as they are implemented in our program, Loki, can be found in [Billings *et. al.*, 1998a; 1998b]. There are several other identifiable characteristics that may not be necessary to play reasonably strong poker, but may eventually be required for world-class play.

The architecture of the previous version of Loki, which we now call Loki-1, is shown in Figure 1. In the diagram, rectangles are major components, rounded rectangles are major data structures, and ovals are actions. The data follows the arrows between components. An annotated arrow indicates how many times data moves between the components for each of our betting actions.

To make a betting decision, the Bettor calls the Hand Evaluator to obtain an assessment of the strength of the current cards. The Bettor uses this hand strength, the public game state data and expert-defined betting knowledge to generate an action (bet, call or raise). To evaluate a hand, the Hand Evaluator enumerates over all possible opponent hands and counts how many of them would win, lose or tie the given hand. After the flop, the probability for each possible opponent hand is different. For example, the probability that hole cards of Ace-Ace are held after the flop is much higher than 7-2, since most players will fold 7-2. Each possible hand has a weight in the Weight Table for each opponent, and these weights are modified after each opponent action. Updating the probabilities for all hands is a process called *re-weighting*. After each opponent action, the Opponent Modeler calls the Hand Evaluator once for each possible hand and increases or decreases the weight for that case to be consistent with the new information. The Hand Evaluator uses the Weight Table values to bias the calculation, giving greater weight to the more likely hands. The absolute values of the probabilities are of little consequence, since only the relative weights affect the later calculations.

Loki-1 uses expert knowledge in four places:
1. Pre-computed tables of expected income rates are used to evaluate its hand before the pre-flop, and to assign initial weight probabilities for the various possible opponent hands.
2. The Opponent Modeler applies re-weighting rules to modify the opponent hand weights based on the previous weights, new cards on the board, opponent betting actions, and other contextual information.

---

[1] ™ Milton-Bradley company.

[2] In No-limit Texas Hold'em, there are no restrictions on the size of bets.

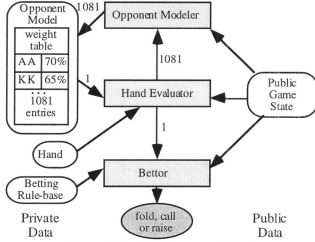

Figure 1. The architecture of Loki-1.

3. The Hand Evaluator uses enumeration techniques to compute hand strength and hand potential for any hand based on the game state and the opponent model.

4. The Bettor uses a set of expert-defined rules and a hand assessment provided by the Hand Evaluator for each betting decision: fold, call/check or raise/bet.

This design has several limitations. First, expert knowledge appears in various places in the program, making Loki difficult to maintain and improve. Second, the Bettor returns a single value (fold, call, raise), which does not reflect the probabilistic nature of betting decisions. Finally, the opponent modeler does not distinguish between the different actions that an opponent might take. A call/check versus a bet/raise gives valuable information about the opponent's cards. These issues led to a redesign of how knowledge is used in Loki.

The new version of Loki, called Loki-2 makes two fundamental changes to the architecture. First, it introduces a useful, new data object called a probability triple that is used throughout the program (Section 4). Second, simulation with selective sampling is used to refine the betting strategy (Section 5). Loki-2 can be used with or without simulation, as shown in Figure 2. With simulation, the Simulator component replaces the simpler Action Selector.

4. Probability Triples

A probability triple is an ordered triple of values, PT = $[f,c,r]$, such that $f + c + r = 1.0$, representing the probability distribution that the next betting action in a given context is a fold, call, or raise, respectively. Probability triples are used in three places in Loki-2. The Action Selector uses a probability triple to decide on a course of action (fold, call, raise). The Opponent Modeler uses an array of probability triples to update the opponent weight tables. The Simulator (see Section 5) uses probability triples to choose actions for simulated opponent hands.

Each time it is Loki-2's turn to bet, the Action Selector uses a single probability triple to decide what action to take (note that the Bettor is gone). For example, if the triple [0.0,0.8,0.2] is given, then the Action Selector would call 80% of the time, raise 20% of the time, and never fold. The choice can be made by generating a random number, allowing the program to vary its play, even in identical situations. This is analogous to a *mixed strategy* in game theory, but the probablility triple implicitly contains contextual information resulting in better informed decisions which, on average, can out-perform a game theoretic approach.

The Triple Generator is responsible for generating probability triples. As shown in Figure 2, this routine is now at the heart of Loki-2. The Triple Generator takes a two-card hand and calls the Hand Evaluator to evaluate the cards in the current context. It uses the resulting hand value, the current game state, and expert-defined betting rules to compute the triple. Note that in addition to using the Triple Generator to produce a triple for our known hand, it can also be used to assess the likely behavior of the opponent holding any possible hand.

For the Hand Evaluator to assess a hand, it compares that hand against all possible opponent holdings. To do this, it uses the opponent Weight Table. In Loki-2, the Opponent Modeler now uses probability triples to update this table after each opponent action. To accomplish this, the Triple Generator is called for each possible two-card hand. It then multiplies each weight in the Weight Table by the entry in the probability triple that corresponds to the opponent's action. For example, suppose the previous weight for Ace-Ace is 0.7 (meaning that *if* it has been dealt, there is a 70% chance the opponent would have played it in exactly the manner observed so far), and the opponent now calls. If the probability triple for the current context is [0.0, 0.2, 0.8], then the updated weight for this case would be 0.7 x 0.2 = 0.14. The relative likelihood of the opponent holding Ace-Ace has *decreased* to 14% because there was no raise. The call value of 0.2 reflects the possibility that this particular opponent might deliberately try to mislead us by calling instead of raising. Using a probability distribution allows us to account for uncertainty in our beliefs, which was not handled by the previous architecture. This process of updating the weight table is repeated for each entry.

An important advantage of the probability triple representation is that imperfect information is restricted to the Triple Generator and does not affect the rest of the algorithm. This is similar to the way that alpha-beta search restricts knowledge to the evaluation function. The probability triple framework allows the "messy" elements of the program to be amalgamated into one component, which can then be treated as a "black box" by the rest of the system. Thus, aspects like game-specific information, complex expert-defined rule systems, and knowledge of human behavior are all isolated from the engine that uses this input.

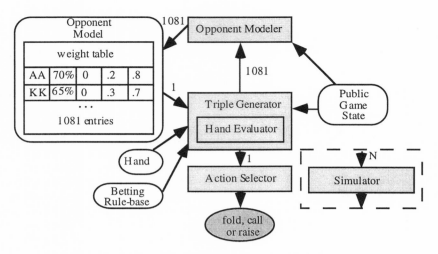

Figure 2. Using the Triple Generator in Loki-2.

The current architecture also suggests future enhancements, such as better methods for opponent modeling. For example, the cards seen at the showdown reveal clues about how that opponent perceived each decision during the hand. These hindsight observations can be used to adaptively measure important characteristics like aggressiveness, predictability, affinity for draws, and so forth. The Opponent Modeler can maintain each of these properties for use by the Triple Generator, which combines the information in proper balance with all the other factors. The knowledge is implicitly encoded in the probability distribution, and is thereby passed on to all components of the system.

Since the more objective aspects of the game could eventually be well defined, the ultimate strength of the program may depend on the success in handling imperfect information, and the more nebulous aspects of the game, such as opponent modeling.

5. Simulation-Based Betting Strategy

The original Bettor component consisted of expert-defined rules, based on hand strength, hand potential, game conditions, and probabilities. A professional poker player defined the system as a first approximation of the return on investment for each betting decision. As other aspects of Loki improved, this simplistic betting strategy became the limiting factor to the playing strength of the program. Unfortunately, any rule-based system is inherently rigid, and even simple changes were difficult to implement and verify for correctness. A more flexible, computation-based approach was needed.

In effect, a knowledge-based betting strategy is equivalent to a static evaluation function. Given the current state of the game, it attempts to determine the action that yields the best result. If we use deterministic perfect information games as a model, the obvious extension is to add search to the evaluation function. While this is easy to achieve in a perfect-information game such as chess (consider all possible moves as deeply as resources

permit), the same approach is not feasible for real imperfect information games because there are too many possibilities to consider [Koller and Pfeffer, 1997].

Consider a 10-player game of Texas Hold'em. By the time the flop cards are seen, some players may have folded. Let's assume one player bets, and it is Loki's turn to act. The program must choose between folding, calling or raising. Which one is the best decision?[1]

After the program's decision, every other active player will be faced with a similar choice. In effect, there is a branching factor of 3 possible actions for each player, and there may be several such decisions in each betting round. Further, there are still two betting rounds to come, each of which may involve several players, and one of many (45 or 44) unknown cards. Computing the complete poker decision tree in real time is in general, prohibitively expensive. Since we cannot consider all possible combinations of hands, future cards, and actions, we examine only a representative sample from the possibilities. A larger sample and more informed selection process will increase the probability that we can draw meaningful conclusions.

5.1 An Expected Value Based Betting Strategy

Loki-2's new betting strategy consists of playing out many likely scenarios to determine how much money each decision will win or lose. Every time it faces a decision, Loki-2 invokes the Simulator to get an estimate of the *expected value* (EV) of each betting action (see the dashed box in Figure 2 with the Simulator replacing the Action Selector). A simulation consists of playing out the hand a specified number of times, from the current state of the game through to the end. Folding is considered to have a zero EV, because we do not make any future profit or loss. Each trial is played out twice—once to consider the consequences of a check/call and once to consider a

---

[1] "Best" is subjective. Here we do not consider other plays, such as deliberately misrepresenting the hand to the opponents. The expected value for a whole session is more important than the expected value for a single hand.

bet/raise. In each trial the hand is simulated to the end, and the amount of money won or lost is determined. The average over all of the trials is taken as the EV of each action. In the current implementation we simply choose the action with the greatest expectation. If two actions have the same expectation, we opt for the most aggressive one (call over fold and raise over call). Against human opponents, a better strategy might be to randomize the selection of betting actions whose EVs are close in value.

Simulation is analogous to a selective expansion of some branches of a game tree. To get a good approximation of the expected value of each betting action, one must have a preference for expanding and evaluating the nodes which are most likely to occur. To obtain a correctly weighted average, all of the possibilities must be considered in proportion to the underlying probability distribution. To select the candidate hands that our opponent may have, we use *selective sampling*.

5.2 Selective Sampling

When simulating a hand, we have specific information that can be used to bias the selection of cards. For example, a player who has been raising the stakes is more likely to have a strong hand than a player who has just called every bet. For each opponent, Loki maintains a probability distribution over the entire set of possible hands (the Weight Table), and the random generation of each opponent's hole cards is based on those probabilities. Thus, we are biasing our selection of hole cards for the opponent to the ones that are most likely to occur.

At each node in the decision tree, a player must choose between one of three alternatives. Since the choice is strongly correlated to the quality of the cards that they have, we can use the Triple Generator to compute the likelihood that the player will fold, check/call, or bet/raise based on the hand that was generated for that player. The player's action is then randomly selected, based on the probability distribution defined by this triple, and the simulation proceeds. As shown in Figure 2, the Simulator calls the TripleGenerator to obtain each of our betting actions and each of our opponent actions. Where two actions are equally viable, the resulting EVs should be nearly equal, so there is little consequence if the "wrong" action is chosen.

5.3 Comments

It should be obvious that the simulation approach must be better than the static approach, since it essentially uses a selective search to augment and refine a static evaluation function. Barring a serious misconception (or bad luck on a limited sample size), playing out relevant will improve the default values obtained by heuristics, resulting in a more accurate estimate.

As has been seen in other domains, the search itself contains implicit knowledge. A simulation contains inherent information that improves the basic evaluation: hand strength (fraction of trials where our hand is better than the one assigned to the opponent), hand potential

(fraction of trials where our hand improves to the best, or is overtaken), and subtle implications not addressed in the simplistic betting strategy (e.g. "implied odds"—extra bets won after a successful draw). It also allows complex strategies to be *uncovered without providing additional expert knowledge*. For example, simulations can result in the emergence of advanced betting tactics like a check-raise, even if the basic strategy without simulation is incapable of this play

An important feature of the simulation-based framework is the notion of an obvious move cut-off. Although many alpha-beta-based programs incorporate an obvious move feature, the technique is usually *ad hoc* and the heuristic is the result of programmer experience rather than a sound analytic technique (an exception is the B* proof procedure [Berliner, 1979]). In the simulation-based framework, an obvious move is statistically well-defined. As more samples are taken, if one decision point exceeds the alternatives by a statistically significant margin, one can stop the simulation early and make an action, with full knowledge of the statistical validity of the decision.

At the heart of the simulation is an evaluation function. The better the quality of the evaluation function, the better the simulation results will be. One of the interesting results of work on alpha-beta has been that even a simple evaluation function can result in a powerful program. We see a similar situation in poker. The implicit knowledge contained in the search improves the basic evaluation, magnifying the quality of the search. As seen with alpha-beta, there are tradeoffs to be made. A more sophisticated evaluation function can reduce the size of the tree, at the cost of more time spent on each node. In simulation analysis, we can improve the accuracy of each trial, but at the expense of the number of trials performed in real-time.

Selective sampling combined with reweighting is similar to the idea of likelihood weighting in stochastic simulation [Fung and Chang, 1989; Shacter and Peot, 1989]. In our case, the goal is different because we need to differentiate between EVs (for call/check, bet/raise) instead of counting events. Also, poker complicates matters by imposing real-time constraints. This forces us to maximize the information gained from a limited number of samples. Further, the problem of handling unlikely events (which is a concern for any sampling-based result) is smoothly handled by our re-weighting system, allowing Loki-2 to dynamically adjust the likelihood of an event based on observed actions. An unlikely event with a big payoff figures naturally into the EV calculations.

6. Experiments

To obtain meaningful empirical results, it is necessary to conduct a series of experiments under different playing conditions. Each enhancement is tested against a variety of opponents having different styles (e.g. liberal or conservative, aggressive or passive, etc.). Control experiments are run at the same time to isolate the dependent variable. In some cases, experiments are designed with built-in standards for comparison, such as playing one particular version against the identical program with an enhancement.

For each test, the parameters of the experiment (number of deals, length of simulations, etc.) are assigned to produce statistically significant results. For example, 5,000 trials might be used to compare an experimental version against a homogenous field. To test the same feature against a mixed field of opponents might require a parallel control experiment and 25,000 trials to produce stable results, due to the inherently higher variance (noise) of that environment. Many experiments were performed to establish reliable results, and only a cross-section of those tests are presented here. For instance, over 30 experiments were conducted to measure the performance of the new re-weighting system.

In this paper, we study the effects of three enhancements, two of which represent improvements to a component of the previous system, and one that is a fundamental change in the way Loki makes its decisions. The features we look at are:

R: changing the re-weighting system to use probability triples (Section 4).

B: changing from a rule-based Bettor to an Action Selector that uses probability triples and incorporates a randomized action (Section 4).

S: incorporating a Simulator to compute an EV estimate, which is used to determine an action (Section 5).

It is important to note that the enhancements were not maximized for performance. The probability-triple-based betting strategy and re-weighting were implemented in only a few hours each, owing to the improved architecture.

The changes to Loki were first assessed with self-play tournaments. A tournament consisted of playing two versions of Loki against each other: a control version (8 copies) and an enhanced version (2 copies). By restricting the tournament to two different player types, we reduced the statistical variance and achieved meaningful results with fewer hands played. To further reduce variance, tournaments followed the pattern of duplicate bridge tournaments. Each hand was played ten times. Each time the seating arrangement of the players was changed so that 1) every player held every set of hidden cards once, and 2) every player was seated in a different position relative to all the opponents. A tournament consisted of 2,500 different deals (*i.e.* 25,000 games).

The number of trials per simulation was chosen to meet real-time constraints and statistical significance. In our experiments, we performed 500 trials per simulation, since the results obtained after 500 trials were quite stable. The average absolute difference in expected value after 2000 trials was small and seldom resulted in a significant change to an assessment. The difference between 100 trials and 500 trials was much more significant; the variance with 100 trials was too high.

The metric used to measure program performance is the average number of small bets won per hand (sb/hand). This is a measure sometimes used by human players. For example, in a game of $10/$20 Hold'em, an improvement of +0.10 sb/hand translates into an extra $30 per hour (based on 30 hands per hour). Anything above +0.05 small bets per hand is considered a large improvement. In play on an Internet poker server, Loki has consistently performed at or above +0.05 sb/hand.

Figure 3 shows the results of playing Loki against itself with the B and R enhancements individually and combined (B+R). Against the Loki-1 standard, B won +0.025 ± 0.007 sb/hand, R won +0.023 ± 0.0125 sb/hand and the combined B+R won +0.044 ± 0.024 sb/hand, showing that these two improvements are nearly independent of each other. Figure 3 also shows enhancement S by itself and S combined with B and R (B+R+S). Note that each feature is a win by itself and in combination with others. In general, the features are not strictly additive since there is some interdependence.

The simulation experiments generally had higher variance than those without simulation. However, all statistically significant results showed an improvement for any version of Loki augmented with selected sampling. These results are harder to accurately quantify, but an increase on the order of at least +0.05 sb/hand is evident.

These results may be slightly misleading since each experiment used two similar programs. As has been shown in chess, one has to be careful about interpreting the results of these type of experiments [Berliner *et al.*, 1990]. A second set of experiments was conducted to see how well the new features perform against a mixture of opponents with differing styles (as is typically seen in human play).

To vary the field of opponents, we defined several different playing styles to categorize players. Players vary from tight (T) to loose (L), depending on what fraction of hands they play to the flop. A style may range from aggressive (A) to conservative (C), depending on how frequently they bet and raise after the flop.

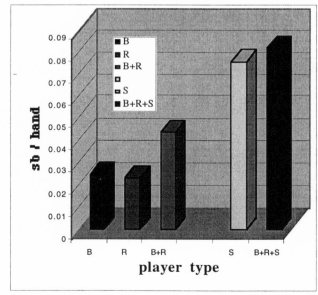

Figure 3. Experimental results of the basic Loki player versus the Loki player with enhancements.

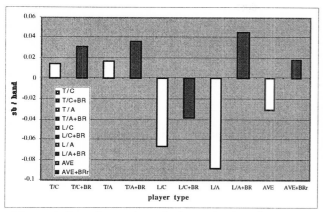

Figure 4. Experimental results in a mixed environment.

We conducted an experiment in which there was a pair of players from each of the four categories: tight/conservative, tight/aggressive, loose/conservative and loose/aggressive. In each pair, one of the players was a basic Loki-1 player and the other was a Loki-2 player with new betting strategy (B) and new re-weighting strategy (R). To fill out the field to ten players, we actually used two pairs of tight/conservative players and averaged their results. The results are shown in Figure 4. In each case, the enhanced player with BR outplayed the corresponding un-enhanced player. For example, the weakest player in the field (L/A) went from -0.088 sb/hand to +0.045 sb/hand with the B+R enhancements. There is also a data point for the average of all players. On average, an enhanced player earned +0.050 ± 0.049 sb / hand more than the corresponding un-enhanced player.

Finally, the ultimate test for Loki-2 is how it plays against human opposition. Loki-2 currently plays on an Internet Relay Chat (IRC) poker server. Interpreting the results from these games is dangerous since we have no control over the type and quality of the opponents. Nevertheless, the program is a consistent winner and appears to be better than Loki-1 in this respect. When the new features are better tuned, we expect greater success.

7. Conclusions

This paper provides two contributions to dealing with imperfect information in a poker-playing program.

First, using probability triples allows us to unify several knowledge-based components in Loki. By representing betting decisions as a probability distribution, this evaluation is better suited to representing the non-deterministic, imperfect information nature of poker. In effect, a static evaluation function now becomes a dynamic one. The added flexibility of making a probabilistic decision yields a simple Triple Generator routine that out-performs our previous best rule-based betting strategy.

Second, a simulation-based betting strategy for poker is superior to the static-evaluation-based alternative. As seen with brute-force search in games like chess, the effect of the simulation (search) magnifies the quality of the evaluation function, achieving high performance with minimal expert knowledge. Critical to this success is the notion of selective sampling; ensuring that each simulation uses data that maximizes the information gained. Selective sampling simulations are shown experimentally to significantly improve the quality of betting decisions.

We propose that the selective sampling simulation-based framework become a standard technique for games having elements of non-determinism and imperfect information. While this framework is not new to game-playing program developers, it is a technique that is repeatedly discovered and re-discovered.

Acknowledgments

This research was supported, in part, by research grants from the Natural Sciences and Engineering Research Council (NSERC) of Canada. Computation resources were provided by MACI.

References

H. Berliner, 1979. "The B* Tree Search Algorithm: A Best First proof Procedure", *Artificial Intelligence*, vol. 12, no. 1, pp. 23-40.

H. Berliner, G. Goetsch, M. Campbell and C. Ebeling, 1990. "Measuring the Performance Potential of Chess Programs", *Artificial Intelligence*, vol. 43. no. 1, pp. 7-20.

D. Billings, D. Papp, J. Schaeffer and D. Szafron, 1998a. "Poker as a Testbed for Machine Intelligence Research", in *AI'98 Advances in Artificial Intelligence* (R. Mercer and E. Neufeld, eds.), Springer Verlag, pp. 1-15.

D. Billings, D. Papp, J. Schaeffer and D. Szafron, 1998b. "Opponent Modeling in Poker", AAAI, pp. 493-499.

D. Billings, D. Papp, L. Peña, J. Schaeffer and D. Szafron, 1999. "Using Selective-Sampling Simulations in Poker", AAAI Spring Symposium.

R. Fung and K. Chang, 1989. "Weighting and Integrating Evidence for Stochastic Simulation in Bayesian Networks", *Uncertainty in Artificial Intelligence*, Morgan Kaufmann.

M. Ginsberg, 1999. "GIB: Steps Towards an Expert-Level Bridge-Playing Program", IJCAI, to appear.

D. Koller and A. Pfeffer, 1997. "Representations and Solutions for Game-Theoretic Problems," *Artificial Intelligence,* vol. 94, no. 1-2, pp. 167-215.

R. Shacter and M. Peot, 1989. "Simulation Approaches to General probabilistic Inference on Belief Networks", *Uncertainty in Artificial Intelligence*, Morgan Kaufmann.

B. Sheppard, 1998. Email communication, October 23.

S. Smith, D. Nau, and T. Throop, 1998. "Computer Bridge: A Big Win for AI Planning", *AI Magazine*, vol. 19, no. 2, pp. 93-106.

G. Tesauro, 1995. "Temporal Difference Learning and TD-Gammon", *CACM*, vol. 38, no.3, pp. 58-68.

A Space-Time Tradeoff for Memory-Based Heuristics

Robert C. Holte and **István T. Hernádvölgyi**
University of Ottawa
School of Information Technology & Engineering
Ottawa, Ontario, K1N 6N5, Canada
Email: {holte,istvan}@site.uottawa.ca

Abstract

A memory-based heuristic is a function, $h(s)$, stored in the form of a lookup table (pattern database): $h(s)$ is computed by mapping s to an index and then retrieving the appropriate entry in the table. (Korf 1997) conjectures for search using memory-based heuristics that $m \cdot t$ is a constant, where m is the size of the heuristic's lookup table and t is search time. In this paper we present a method for automatically generating memory-based heuristics and use this to test Korf's conjecture in a large-scale experiment. Our results confirm that there is a direct relationship between m and t.

Introduction

A heuristic is a function, $h(s)$, that computes an estimate of the distance from state s to a goal state. In a *memory-based heuristic* this computation consists of mapping s to an index which is then used to look up $h(s)$ in a table. Even heuristics that have a normal functional definition are often precomputed and stored in a lookup table in order to speed up search ((Prieditis 1993), (Korf 1997)). For other heuristics the tabular form is the most natural – for example, the pattern databases of (Culberson & Schaeffer 1996). Pattern databases are an important recent advance in heuristic search; they have been instrumental in efficiently solving very large problems such as Rubik's Cube (Korf 1997) and the 15-Puzzle (Culberson & Schaeffer 1996).

The attraction of memory-based heuristics is that they enable search time to be reduced by using more memory. Intuitively, a larger lookup table is capable of representing a more accurate heuristic thereby reducing search time. (Korf 1997) expresses this intuitive relationship quantitatively and conjectures that memory (m) and time (t) can be directly traded off, *i.e.*, that the product $m \cdot t$ is a constant. This conjecture is very

---

important because if it is true search time can be halved simply by doubling available memory.

In this paper we test this conjecture in a large-scale experiment in which hundreds of heuristics having a wide variety of memory requirements are evaluated; in total 236,100 problem instances are solved. For this experiment a method was required to generate a wide variety of heuristics automatically. The next two sections describe our representation for state spaces and the method used to generate memory based heuristics. Subsequent sections discuss the conjecture in more detail and present our experiment's design and results.

State Space Representation

A state space is defined by a triple $S = <s_0, O, L>$, where s_0 is a state, O is a finite set of operators, and L is a finite set of labels. The state space consists of all states reachable from s_0 by any sequence of operators.

To facilitate the automatic generation of many different abstractions of widely varying granularity, we use a simple vector notation for states and operators instead of more conventional representations such as STRIPS (Fikes & Nilsson 1971). A state is represented by a fixed length vector of labels from L. An operator is represented by a left-hand side (LHS) and right-hand side (RHS), each a vector the same length as the state vectors. Each position in the LHS and RHS vectors may be a constant (a label from L), a variable, or an underscore (_). The variables in an operator's RHS must also appear in its LHS. An operator is applicable to state s if its LHS can be unified with s. The act of unification binds each variable in LHS to the label in the corresponding position in s. RHS describes the state that results from applying the operator to s. The RHS constants and variables (now bound) specify particular labels and an underscore in a RHS position indicates that the resulting state has the same value as s in that position. For example,

$$< A, A, 1, \_, B, C > \rightarrow < 2, \_, \_, \_, C, B >$$

is an operator that can be applied to any state whose first two positions have the same value and whose third position contains 1. The effect of the operator is to set the first position to 2 and exchange the labels in the last two positions; all other positions are unchanged. We call this notation PSVN ("production system vector notation"). Although simple, it is expressive enough to specify succinctly all finite permutation groups (*e.g. Rubik's Cube*) and the common benchmark problems for heuristic search and planning (*e.g. sliding tile puzzles*).

State Space Abstraction

A *domain abstraction* is a map $\phi : L \rightarrow K$, where L and K are sets of labels and $|K| \leq |L|$. From a domain abstraction one can induce a state space abstraction, $S' = \phi(S) = \langle \phi(s_0), \phi(O), K \rangle$, by applying ϕ to each position of s_0 and to every label in the LHS and RHS of each operator in O. This definition extends the notion of "pattern" in the pattern database work (Culberson & Schaeffer 1996), which in their framework is produced by mapping several of the labels in L to a special new label ("don't care") and mapping the rest of the labels to themselves.

The key property of state space abstractions is that they are homomorphisms and therefore the distance between two states in the original space, S, is always greater than or equal to the distance between the corresponding abstract states in $\phi(S)$. Thus, abstract distances are admissible heuristics for searching in S (in fact they are monotone heuristics: for formal proofs of these assertions see (Hernádvölgyi & Holte 1999)).

The heuristic defined by an abstraction can either be computed on demand, as is done in Hierarchical A* (Holte *et al.* 1996), or, if the goal state is known in advance, the abstract distance to the goal can be precomputed for all abstract states and stored in a lookup table (pattern database) indexed by abstract states. In this paper we take the latter approach.

The memory required for a pattern database, m, is clearly just its size, $m = |\phi(S)|$, and this can vary from 1 (if ϕ maps all labels to the same value) to $n = |S| =$ the number of states in S (if ϕ is one-to-one). m can even be much larger than n. This happens if the image of S under ϕ is embedded in and connected to a larger space. We call such abstractions non-surjective and in our experiments we have intentionally avoided them since Korf's conjecture (see below) is certainly false for them. The simplest example of a non-surjective homomorphism occurs with a state space defined by $s_0 = \langle 1, 2, 3, 4 \rangle$ and one operator

$$op : \langle A, A, B, C \rangle \rightarrow \langle A, A, C, B \rangle$$

that is not applicable to s_0 because it requires the first two vector positions to be equal. S contains only one state, s_0. If $\phi(1) = \phi(2)$ and $\phi(3) \neq \phi(4)$ then $\phi(op)$ will be applicable to $\phi(s_0)$ and $\phi(S)$ will contain two states. Non-surjective abstractions do arise in practice. All our attempts to represent the Blocks World in PSVN have given rise to non-surjective homomorphisms (Hernádvölgyi & Holte 1999).

We can therefore generate a memory-based heuristic, simply by generating a domain abstraction ϕ and using it as a state space homomorphism. The memory needed for the heuristic is directly proportional to the granularity of ϕ (*i.e* K) and how many labels in L are mapped to each label in K.

Korf's Conjecture

A fundamental question about memory-based heuristics concerns the relationship between m, the size of the pattern database for a heuristic, and t, the number of nodes generated when the heuristic is used to guide search. (Korf 1997) gives an insightful, but informal, analysis of this relationship which leads to the conjecture that $t \approx n/m$. That t should be inversely proportional to m is a direct consequence of approximating t by b^{d-e} where b is the effective branching factor (the number of children of a node in the search tree), d is the average optimal solution length, and e is the average value of the heuristic being used. $b^{d-e} = b^d/b^e$ and, assuming that S and $\phi(S)$ are both tree-shaped with the same branching factor, $b^d/b^e \approx n/m$.

There are two data points of experimental evidence touching this conjecture. In (Korf 1997), the search space was Rubik's Cube and $t \cdot m$ equaled $1.4\,n$. This is in almost perfect agreement with the conjecture but it must be noted that the experiment used two independent pattern databases simultaneously whereas the analysis was based on the use of a single pattern database. In (Culberson & Schaeffer 1996) the search space was the 15-puzzle and, for the best single pattern database used, $t \cdot m$ equaled $17.3\,n$. This is in fair agreement with the conjecture , but in these experiments the Manhattan distance heuristic was used in conjunction with the pattern database and symmetries of the puzzle were used to reduce the pattern database size and increase its accuracy, so the observed performance is not attributable to the pattern database alone. Finally, both (Korf 1997) and (Culberson & Schaeffer 1996) used IDA* (Korf 1985) which produces a larger t than the search model used in the analysis.

The use of the average value of the heuristic, e, in the (Korf 1997) analysis is a weakness that is improved in (Korf & Reid 1998). There the number of nodes generated (t) in the worst case is shown to be

$$t(b, d, P) = \sum_{i=1}^{d+1} b^i P(d - i + 1) \tag{1}$$

where b and d are as above and $P(x)$ is the probability that a state $s \in S$ has a heuristic value $h(s) \leq x$. Thus

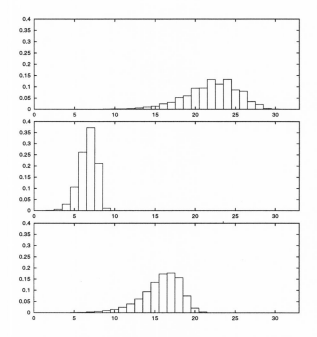

Figure 1: Solution lengths histogram for the 8-Puzzle (top), 8-Perm (middle) and (8,4)-Top-Spin (bottom).

	8-Puzzle	8-Perm	Top-Spin
n	181440	40320	40320
min m	252	56	28
max m	30240	20160	10080
b	1.667	6	2
d_{easy}	18	5	12
$d_{typical}$	22	7	16
d_{hard}	27	9	19

Table 1: Experiment Parameters

the average heuristic value is replaced by the probability distribution over the heuristic values. In a private communication, Richard Korf has suggested that equation 1 can be approximately re-expressed in terms of m as follows:

$$t \approx n \frac{log_b m}{m} \qquad (2)$$

Experiment Design

The aim of our experiments is to examine the true relationship between t and m and compare it with the relationships conjectured in (Korf 1997) and (Korf & Reid 1998). Our approach is to create abstractions with different values of m and problem instances with different values of d and measure t by running A* (not IDA*) with each abstraction on each problem instance[1]. This is repeated for different search spaces to increase confidence in the generality of our conclusions.

For a given m there can be many different abstractions. 30 are generated at random and their t values averaged[2]. t is estimated separately for "hard", "typical", and "easy" problem instances using 100 randomly selected start states of each type (the goal state is fixed for each search space). The difficulty of a problem instance is determined by how its solution length compares to the solution lengths of all other problem instances. For example, we use the median of the solution lengths to define a "typical" problem instance. Figure 1 shows the distribution of solution lengths for all problem instances in each space.

Results are presented (figure 2) as plots with m on the x-axis and t on the y-axis. Each data point represents the average of 3000 runs (30 abstractions, each applied to 100 problem instances).[3] Breadth-first search was also run on all problem instances; it represents the extreme case when $m = 1$. In total, our experiments involved solving 236,100 problem instances.

We chose state spaces large enough to be interesting but small enough that such a large-scale experiment was feasible. Table 1 gives the general characteristics and experiment parameters for each space. Note that the m values for each space range from very small to a significant fraction of n. Each state space is generated by a puzzle, which we now briefly describe.

The 8-Puzzle is composed of 8 labeled sliding tiles arranged in a 3×3 grid. There is one tile missing, so a neighboring tile can be slid into its place. In PSVN each position in the vector corresponds to a particular grid position and the label in $vector[i]$ denotes the tile in the corresponding grid position. For example, if vector position 1 corresponds to the upper left grid position, and vector position 2 corresponds to the upper middle grid position, the operator that exchanges a tile in the upper left with an empty space (λ) in the upper middle is

$$< X, \lambda, \_, \_, \_, \_, \_, \_, \_ > \to < \lambda, X, \_, \_, \_, \_, \_, \_, \_ >$$

In the N-Perm puzzle a state is a vector of length N containing N distinct labels and there are $N - 1$ operators, numbered 2 to N, with operator k reversing the order of the first k vector positions. We used $N = 8$. In PSVN operator 5, which reverses the first 5 positions, is represented

$$< A, B, C, D, E, \_, \_, \_ > \to < E, D, C, B, A, \_, \_, \_ >$$

---

[1] instead of the number of nodes *generated* we measure the number of nodes *expanded* by A*; they differ by a constant so our conclusions are not affected.

[2] for the smallest values of m for each space fewer than 30 abstractions sometimes had to be used; never were fewer than 18 abstractions used for a given m.

[3] except for the smallest values of m for which fewer than 30 abstractions had to be used.

The (N,K)-Top-Spin puzzle has N tokens arranged in a ring. The tokens can be shifted cyclically clockwise or counterclockwise. The ring of tokens intersects a region K tokens in length which can be rotated to reverse the order of the tokens currently in the region. We used $N = 8$ and $K = 4$, and three operators to define the state space

$$< I, J, K, L, M, N, O, P > \rightarrow < J, K, L, M, N, O, P, I >$$

$$< I, J, K, L, M, N, O, P > \rightarrow < P, I, J, K, L, M, N, O >$$

$$< A, B, C, D, \_, \_, \_, \_ > \rightarrow < D, C, B, A, \_, \_, \_, \_ >$$

Experimental Results

Figure 2 plots the experimental results with m on the x-axis and t on the y-axis. The scale on both axes is logarithmic but the axes are labeled with the actual m and t values. With both scales logarithmic $t \cdot m =$ constant c, the conjecture in (Korf 1997), would appear as a straight line with a slope of -1. Note that the y-axis is drawn at the smallest m value used in the experiments, not at $m = 0$.

In the top part of figure 2 a short horizontal line across each line (at around $m = 4000$) indicates the performance of the Manhattan Distance on the test problem instances. This shows that randomly generated abstractions of quite small size (5040 entries, less than 3% of the size of the state space) are as good as one of the best hand-crafted heuristics known for the 8-puzzle. The best of these randomly generated heuristics expands about 30% fewer nodes than the Manhattan distance.

A linear trend is very clear in all the curves in figure 2 The correlation between the data and the least squares regression line is 0.99 or higher in every case. However, the slope is not -1. These results therefore strongly suggest that $t \cdot m^\alpha =$ constant c for α between -0.57 and -0.8. α in this range means that doubling the amount of memory reduces the number of nodes expanded by less than a factor of 2.

Despite the very high correlation with a straight line, it appears that the top curves in each plot, and the middle curves to a lesser extent, are bowed up, *i.e.*, that for problem instances with long solutions the effect on t of increasing m depends on the value of m, with a greater reduction in t being achieved when m is large. The lowest curve for the 8-Perm puzzle appears to be bowed in the opposite direction, which would mean increases in m give diminishing returns for problem instances with short solutions in this space.

Further evidence that the curves flatten out as they approach $m = 1$ is obtained by extrapolating the regression lines to $m = 1$ and comparing them with value with the actual value at $m = 1$ (breadth-first search). In every case the extrapolated lines are much higher than the

actual value. For example, for the 8-puzzle the extrapolated lines have values at $m = 1$ of 89,322 ($d = 18$), 514,011 ($d = 22$), and 2,191,288 ($d = 27$), while the actual numbers of nodes expanded by breadth-first search are 15,725, 64,389, and 165,039 respectively. Even the regression line for the lowest curve of the 8-Perm puzzle significantly overestimates the true value at $m = 1$.

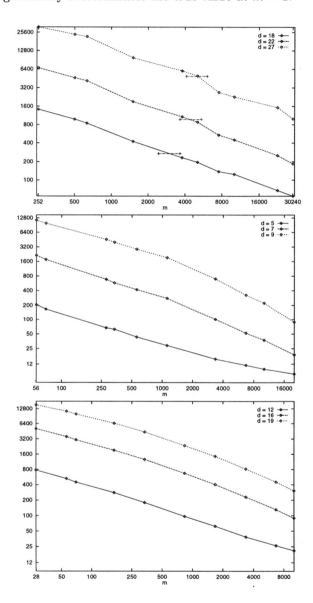

Figure 2: Number of States Expanded [t] *vs* Size of Pattern Database [m]: 8-Puzzle (top), 8-Perm (middle) and (8,4)-Top-Spin (bottom).

Similarly, the regression lines can be extrapolated to the other extreme, $m = n$, and compared to the solution length, which is the number of nodes expanded by the perfect heuristic produced when $m = n$. The lowest lines in each plot extrapolate well, giving values of 21 instead of 18 for the 8-puzzle, 4.24 instead of 5 for

8-Perm, and 8.5 instead of 12 for (8,4)-Top-Spin. The extrapolation of the middle and upper lines overestimate the value at $m = n$ significantly, the middle line's prediction being about double the true value, and the upper line's prediction being about nine times the true value. This is yet more evidence that the middle and upper curves are not strictly linear.

The more recent conjecture is that $t \cdot \frac{m}{log_b m} = $ constant c. Logarithmic scale plots of the experimental results with an x-axis of $\frac{m}{log_b m}$ instead of m produce curves that are visually indistinguishable from figure 2 but the least squares regression lines have slightly higher correlation in all cases and slopes closer to -1 (-0.67 to -0.95).

Predicting a Heuristic's Performance

One of the intuitions used in the analysis in (Korf 1997), is that the larger the average value (e) of an admissible heuristic the smaller t is expected to be. We directly tested this hypothesis for the 8-Puzzle by generating 100 random abstractions with $m = 5040$ and evaluating them on 1000 random problem instances with solution length 22 (fixed goal state, varying start state). For each of the abstractions Figure 3 shows the average heuristic value, e, on the x-axis and t, the average number of nodes expanded by A* using the heuristic on the 1000 problem instances, on the y-axis.

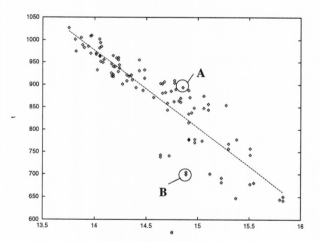

Figure 3: Number of Nodes Expanded t vs. Mean Heuristic Value e. 8-puzzle, $m = 5040$ and $d = 22$.

The first point of interest is the range of e. Although these heuristics all require the same amount of memory, there is a difference of more than 2 between the largest and smallest average heuristic values. The relationship between e and t is quite well represented by the least squares regression line (figure 3), except for the group of points with m values between 14.5 and 15.5 that lie well below the line. These points are extremely interesting because they plainly contradict the intuition that the

larger a heuristic's average value the fewer nodes A* will expand. Consider the two heuristics A and B shown on figure 3. They both have $e = 14.71$, but A expands 873 states on average, while abstraction B expands only 703. The same trends occur with the heuristics from the previous experiment with other values of m and d and for the other search spaces.

This phenomenon is partially explained by considering P, the distribution of heuristic values in S, not only e (as in (Korf & Reid 1998)). It is possible to have a different P but the same average. This is illustrated by figure 4 which plots the difference between $p_A(h)$ and

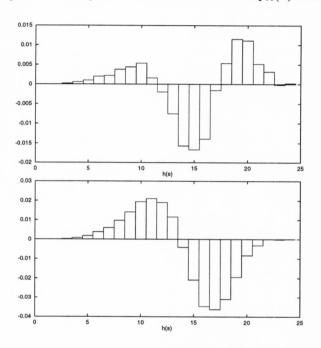

Figure 4: $p_A(h) - p_B(h)$ and $P_A(h) - P_B(h)$ vs. h

$p_B(h)$ vs. h, where h is the heuristic value provided by abstractions A and B and $p(h)$ represents the relative frequency of h within the range of heuristic values. The graph below is the cumulative difference $P_A(h) - P_B(h)$.

Although they have the same average heuristic value, abstraction B has a much higher proportion of its values near the average. By contrast abstraction A has a higher proportion of large heuristic values but also higher proportion of smaller ones. Looking at the difference in cumulative distribution, A is greater for all small values of $h(s)$. In equation 1, these values have the greatest weight, and in this case, the penalty for having more low values outweighs the savings due to having more high ones.

Conclusion

(Korf 1997) conjectured that for memory-based heuristics $t \cdot m \approx n$, where n is the size of the state space, m

is the memory needed to store the heuristic as a lookup table (pattern database) and t is the number of nodes generated by A* search using the heuristic. The main result of this paper is to provide substantial experimental evidence in favor of the slightly weaker conjecture that $\log(t)$ and $\log(m)$ are linearly related. Our experiments involved using 270 different heuristics with widely varying memory requirements and solving a total of 236,100 problem instances from three different state spaces. The results had a correlation of 0.99 or greater with the least squares regression lines. There is almost certainly a small non-linear component in the relation between $log(t)$ and $log(m)$ – especially near the extremities of m's range – but for the region of most interest the relation is essentially linear. Knowing this relationship is important because it provides an assurance that any increase in memory will produce a corresponding reduction in search time.

An important feature of our experiments is that the heuristics were generated automatically – randomly, in fact. This demonstrates that the use of memory to decrease search time does not require any form of human intervention.

There are other techniques for using memory to speed up heuristic search. (Kaindl *et al.* 1995) provides a good summary and an initial comparison of some of the techniques. These techniques can be used in combination with each other and with memory-based heuristics. The optimal allocation of memory among these techniques is an open research question. Very few previous studies investigate the space-time tradeoff in detail. Perimeter search (Dillenburg & Nelson 1994) and the related BAI algorithm (Kaindl *et al.* 1995) give significant reductions in t for small values of m. For SMA* (Russell 1992), t was found to be proportional to $m^{-1.33}$ on the "perturbed 8-puzzle".

In our experiments a single memory-based heuristic was used to guide search. This was done in order to eliminate confounding factors in interpreting the results. In practice, memory-based heuristics would be used in conjunction with other knowledge of the search space. For example, (Culberson & Schaeffer 1996) uses hand-crafted memory-based heuristics in combination with the Manhattan distance and exploits symmetries in the search space and the invertibility of the operators to decrease the size and increase the usefulness of the memory-based heuristics. (Korf 1997) uses multiple memory-based heuristics simultaneously. Our experience (not reported here) indicates that $\log(t)$ and $\log(m)$ are linearly related even when multiple memory-based heuristics are used, but for a given m, t is roughly halved if three memory-based heuristics are used together instead of using just one on its own.

In this paper we have also examined the relationship between e, the average value of a heuristic, and t. For the most part our results confirm the intuition that t

decreases as e increases, but the relationship is much closer to linear than the expected exponential. Furthermore, heuristics were found with relatively low e values that also had very good t values, due to a favorable distribution of heuristic values.

Acknowledgments

This research was supported in part by an operating grant and a postgraduate scholarship from the Natural Sciences and Engineering Research Council of Canada. Thanks to Jonathan Schaeffer and Joe Culberson for their encouragement and helpful comments and to Richard Korf for communicating his unpublished extensions of the (Korf & Reid 1998) work.

References

Culberson, J. C., and Schaeffer, J. 1996. Searching with pattern databases. *Advances in Artificial Intelligence (Lecture Notes in Artificial Intelligence 1081)* 402–416.

Dillenburg, J. F., and Nelson, P. C. 1994. Perimeter search. *Artificial Intelligence* 65:165–178.

Fikes, R., and Nilsson, N. J. 1971. STRIPS: A new approach to the application of theorem proving to problem solving. *Artificial Intelligence* 2:189–208.

Hernádvölgyi, I. T., and Holte, R. C. 1999. PSVN: A vector representation for production systems. Technical Report TR-99-04, School of Information Technology and Engineering, University of Ottawa.

Holte, R. C.; Perez, M. B.; Zimmer, R. M.; and MacDonald, A. J. 1996. Hierarchical A*: Searching abstraction hierarchies efficiently. *Proceedings of the Thirteenth National Conference on Artificial Intelligence (AAAI-96)* 530–535.

Kaindl, H.; Kainz, G.; Leeb, A.; and Smetana, H. 1995. How to use limited memory in heuristic search. *Proceedings of the Fourteenth International Joint Conference on Artificial Intelligence (IJCAI-95)* 236–242.

Korf, R. E., and Reid, M. 1998. Complexity analysis of admissible heuristic search. *Proceedings of the Fifteenth National Conference on Artificial Intelligence (AAAI-98)* 305–310.

Korf, R. E. 1985. Depth-first iterative-deepening: An optimal admissible tree search. *Artificial Intelligence* 27:97–109.

Korf, R. E. 1997. Finding optimal solutions to Rubik's cube using pattern databases. *Proceedings of the Fourteenth National Conference on Artificial Intelligence (AAAI-97)* 700–705.

Prieditis, A. E. 1993. Machine discovery of effective admissible heuristics. *Machine Learning* 12:117–141.

Russell, S. 1992. Efficient memory-bounded search methods. *Proceedings of the Tenth European Conference on Artificial Intelligence (ECAI-92)* 1–5.

PROVERB: The Probabilistic Cruciverbalist

Greg A. Keim, Noam M. Shazeer, Michael L. Littman,
Sushant Agarwal, Catherine M. Cheves, Joseph Fitzgerald,
Jason Grosland, Fan Jiang, Shannon Pollard, Karl Weinmeister
Department of Computer Science
Duke University, Durham, NC 27708-0129
contact: {keim, noam, mlittman}@cs.duke.edu

Abstract

We attacked the problem of solving crossword puzzles by computer: given a set of clues and a crossword grid, try to maximize the number of words correctly filled in. In our system, "expert modules" specialize in solving specific types of clues, drawing on ideas from information retrieval, database search, and machine learning. Each expert module generates a (possibly empty) candidate list for each clue, and the lists are merged together and placed into the grid by a centralized solver. We used a probabilistic representation throughout the system as a common interchange language between subsystems and to drive the search for an optimal solution. PROVERB, the complete system, averages 95.3% words correct and 98.1% letters correct in under 15 minutes per puzzle on a sample of 370 puzzles taken from the New York Times and several other puzzle sources. This corresponds to missing roughly 3 words or 4 letters on a daily 15 × 15 puzzle, making PROVERB a better-than-average cruciverbalist (crossword solver).

Introduction

Proverbs 022:021 *That I might make thee know the certainty of the words of truth...*

Crossword puzzles are attempted daily by millions of people, and require of the solver both an extensive knowledge of language, history and popular culture, and a search over possible answers to find a set that fits in the grid. This dual task, of answering natural language questions requiring shallow, broad knowledge, and of searching for an optimal set of answers for the grid, makes these puzzles an interesting challenge for artificial intelligence. In this paper, we describe PROVERB, the first broad-coverage computer system for solving crossword puzzles[1]. While PROVERB's performance is well below that of human champions,

[1]Crossword Maestro is a commercial solver for British-style crosswords published by Genius 2000 Software. It is intended as a solving aid, and while it appears quite good at thesaurus-type clues, in informal tests it did poorly at grid filling (under 5% words correct).

it exceeds that of casual human solvers, averaging over 95% words correct over a test set of 370 puzzles.

We will first describe the problem and some of the insights we gained from studying a large database of crossword puzzles; these motivated our design choices. We will then discuss our underlying probabilistic model and the architecture of PROVERB, including how answers to clues are suggested by expert modules, and how PROVERB searches for an optimal fit of these possible answers into the grid. Finally, we will present the system's performance on a test suite of daily crossword puzzles and on 1998 tournament puzzles.

The Crossword Solving Problem

The solution to a crossword puzzle is a set of interlocking words (*targets*) written across and down a square grid. The solver is presented with an empty grid and a set of clues; each clue suggests its corresponding target. Some clue-target pairs are relatively direct: ≺Florida fruit [6]: orange≻[2], while others are more oblique and based on word play: ≺Where to get a date [4]: palm≻. Clues are between one and a dozen or so words long, averaging about 2.5 words per clue.

To solve a crossword puzzle by computer, we assume that we have both the grid and the clues in machine readable form, ignoring the special formatting and unusual marks that sometimes appear in crosswords. The *crossword solving problem* is the task of returning a grid of letters, given the numbered clues and a labeled grid.

In this work, we focus on American-style crosswords, as opposed to British-style or cryptic crosswords. By convention, all targets are at least 3 letters in length and long targets can be constructed by stringing multiple words together: ≺Don't say another word [13]: buttonyourlip≻. Each empty square in the grid must be part of a down target and an across target.

As this is largely a new problem domain, distinct from crossword-puzzle creation (Ginsberg *et al.* 1990), we wondered how hard crossword solving really was. To

[2]Target appears in fixed-width font; all examples are taken from our crossword database (the CWDB). We will note the target length following sample clues in this paper to indicate a complete specification of the clue.

Source	Puzzles CWDB	Train	Test
New York Times (NYT)	792	10	70
Los Angeles Times (LAT)	439	10	50
USA Today (USA)	864	10	50
Creator's Syndicate (CS)	207	10	50
CrosSynergy Syndicate (CSS)	302	10	50
Universal Crossword (UNI)	262	10	50
TV Guide (TVG)	0	10	50
Dell	969	0	0
Riddler	764	0	0
Other	543	0	0
Total	**5142**	**70**	**370**

Table 1: The crossword database (CWDB) was drawn from a number of machine-readable sources. The TV Guide puzzles were added after finalizing the CWDB.

gain some insight into the problem, we studied a large corpus of existing puzzles. We collected 5142 crossword puzzles from a variety of sources, summarized in Table 1. Several are online versions of daily print newspaper puzzles (The New York Times, The Los Angeles Times, The USA Today, TV Guide), from online sites featuring puzzles (Dell, Riddler) or from syndicates specifically producing for the online medium (Creator's Syndicate, CrosSynergy Syndicate). These puzzles constitute a crossword database (the CWDB) of around 350,000 clue-target pairs (over 250,000 unique), which served as a potent knowledge source for this project.

Novelty

Human solvers improve with experience, in part because particular clues and targets tend to recur. For example, many human solvers will recognize ≺Great Lake [4]: `erie`≻ to be a common clue-target pair in many puzzles[3]. The CWDB corresponds to the number of puzzles that would be encountered over a fourteen-year period, at a rate of one puzzle a day.

What percentage of targets and clues in a new puzzle presented to our system will be in the CWDB—how novel are crossword puzzles? In Figure 1, we graph the probability of novel targets, clues, clue-target pairs, and clue words as we increase the size of the CWDB.

After randomizing, we looked at subsets of the CWDB ranging from 5,000 clues to almost 350,000. For each subset, we calculated the percentage of the item (target, clue, clue-target, clue word) that are unique. This is an estimate for the likelihood of the next item being novel. Given the complete CWDB (344,921 clues) and a new puzzle, we would expect to have seen 91% of targets, 50% of clues, and 34% of clue-target pairs. We would also expect to have seen 96% of the words appearing in the clues. The CWDB contains a tremendous amount of useful domain-specific information.

---

[3]The five most common targets in the CWDB are `era`, `ore`, `area`, `erie` and `ale`. The target `erie` appears in over 7% of puzzles.

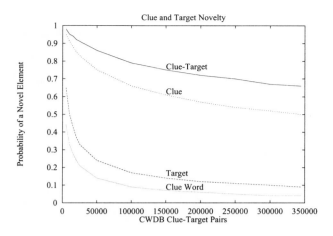

Figure 1: Clue and target novelty decreases with the size of the CWDB.

	Mon	Tue	Wed	Thu	Fri	Sat
#puz	89	92	90	91	91	87
#clues	77.3	77.2	76.7	74.7	70.0	70.2
3	16.5	18.2	17.5	18.6	17.3	16.3
4–5	64.6	61.1	62.5	54.7	44.2	40.2
6–10	15.8	17.7	16.9	23.1	35.2	41.7
11–15	3.1	2.9	3.2	3.7	3.3	1.9
Blank	8.4	8.0	6.4	6.4	5.2	4.8
Blank & " "	3.1	3.1	2.7	2.2	2.0	1.7
Single Word	15.6	14.9	16.0	17.2	16.9	20.6
(Year)	1.4	1.6	1.9	2.1	2.5	2.7
Final '?'	0.8	1.2	2.5	3.2	3.5	2.6
X, in a way	0.0	0.1	0.2	0.4	0.6	0.8

Table 2: NYT clue statistics vary by day of week.

The New York Times Crossword Puzzle

The New York Times (NYT) crossword is considered by many to be the premiere daily puzzle. NYT editors attempt to make the puzzles increase in difficulty from easy on Monday to very difficult on Saturday and Sunday. We hoped that studying the Monday-to-Saturday trends in the puzzles might provide insight into what makes a puzzle hard for humans.

In Table 2, we show how the distributions of clue types change day by day. For example, note that some "easier" clues, such as fill-in-the-blank clues ≺Mai ___ [3]: `tai`≻) get less and less common as the week goes on. In addition, clues with a trailing question mark (≺T.V. Series? [15]: `sonyrcamagnovox`≻), which is often a sign of a themed or pun clue, get more common. The distribution of target lengths also varies, with words in the 6 to 10 letter range becoming much more common from Monday to Saturday. Sunday is not included in the table as its larger (up to 23 × 23 versus 15 × 15 for the other days) makes it difficult to compare.

Categories of Clues

In the common syntactic categories shown in Table 2, such as fill-in-the-blank and quoted phrases, clue structure leads to simple ways to answer those clues. For example, given the clue ≺_____ miss [5]: hitor≻, a scan through text sources could look for all 9-letter phrases that match on word boundaries and known letters. With the clue ≺Map abbr. [3]: rte≻, a list of likely abbreviations could be returned.

In addition, a number of non-syntactic, *expert* categories stand out, such as synonyms (≺Covered [5]: awash≻), kind-of (≺Kind of duck or letter [4]: dead≻), movies (≺1954 mutant ants film [4]: them≻), geography (≺Frankfurt's river [4]: oder≻), music (≺'Upside down' singer [4]: ross≻) and literature (≺Carroll character [5]: alice≻).

There are also clues that do not fit simple patterns, but might be solved by existing information retrieval techniques (≺Nebraska tribesman [4]: otoe≻). The many different sources of information that can be brought to bear to solve clues led us to create a two-stage architecture for the solver: one consisting of a collection of general and special-purpose candidate-generation modules, and one that combines the results from these modules to generate a solution to the puzzle. This decentralized architecture allowed a relatively large group of contributors (approximately ten people) to create modules using techniques ranging from generic word lists to highly specific modules, from string matching to general-purpose information retrieval. The next section describes PROVERB's modular design.

Architecture

Figure 2 illustrates the components of PROVERB. Given a puzzle, the *Coordinator* separates the clues from the grid and sends a copy of the clue list (with target lengths) to each *Expert Module*. The expert modules generate probability-weighted candidate lists, in isolation from the grid constraints. Expert modules are free to return anything from no candidates for any clue to or 10,000 for every one. The collection of candidate lists is then reweighted by the *Merger* to compensate for differences in module weighting, and combined into a single list of candidates for each clue. Finally, the *Solver* takes these weighted lists and searches for the best solution it can find that also satisfies the grid constraints.

The *Implicit Distribution Modules* are used by the solver, and are described in a later section.

The Probabilistic Model

To unify the candidate-generation modules, it is important to first understand our underlying assumptions about the crossword-puzzle problem. First, we imagine that crossword puzzles are created by repeatedly choosing words for the slots according to a particular creator's distribution (ignore clues and crossing constraints for now). After choosing the words, if the crossing constraints are satisfied, then the creator keeps the puzzle.

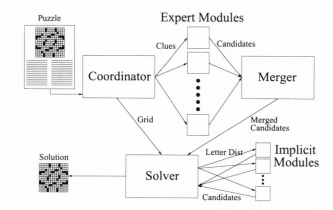

Figure 2: PROVERB consists of a set of independent communicating programs.

Otherwise, the creator draws again. Normalizing to account for all the illegal puzzles generated gives us a probability distribution over legal puzzles.

Now, suppose that for each slot in a puzzle, we had a probability distribution over possible words for the slot given the clue. Then, we could try to solve one of a number of probabilistic optimization problems to produce the "best" fill of the grid. In our work, we define "best" as the puzzle with the maximum expected number of targets in common with the creator's solution: the maximum expected overlap (Shazeer, Littman, & Keim 1999). We will discuss this optimization more in a following section, but for now it is important only to see that we would like to think of candidate generation as establishing probability distributions over possible solutions.

We will next discuss how individual modules can create approximations to these distributions, how they are combined into a unified distributions.

Candidate Generation

The first step is to have each module generate candidates for each clue, given the target length. Each module returns a confidence score (how sure it is that the answer lies in its list), and a weighted list of possible answers. For example, given the clue ≺Farrow of 'Peyton Place' [3]: mia≻, the movie module returns:

1.0: 0.909091 mia, 0.010101 tom, 0.010101 kip, ···
··· , 0.010101 ben, 0.010101 peg, 0.010101 ray .

The module returns a 1.0 confidence in its list, and gives higher weight to the person on the show with the given last name and lower weight to other cast members.

Note that most of the modules will not be able to generate actual probability distributions for the targets, and will need to make approximations. The merging step discussed next will attempt to account for the error in these estimates by testing on training data, and adjusting scaling parameters to compensate. It is important for modules to be consistent, and to give more likely candidates more weight. Also, the better control a module exerts over the overall confidence score when uncertain, the more the merger will "trust" the module's predictions.

In all, we built 30 different modules, many of which are described briefly below. To get some sense of the contribution of the major modules, Table 3 summarizes performance on 70 training puzzles, containing 5374 clues. These puzzles were drawn from the same sources as the test puzzles, ten from each. For each module, we list several measures of performance: the percentage of clues that the module guessed at (**Guess**), the percentage of the time the target was in the module's candidate list (**Acc**), the average length of the returned lists (**Len**), and the percentage of clues the module "won"— it had the correct answer weighted higher than all other modules (**Best**). This final statistic is an important measure of the module's contribution to the system. For example, the WordList-Big module generates over 100,000 words for some clues, so it often has the target in its list (97% of the time). However, since it generates so many, the individual weight given to the target is usually lower than that assigned by other modules, and, thus, it is the best predictor only 0.1% of the time.

We conducted a series of "ablation" tests in which we removed each module one at a time, rerunning the 70 training puzzles with the other $n-1$ modules. No one module's removal changed the overall percentage of words correct by more than 1%, which implies that there is considerable overlap in the coverage of the modules. We also tried removing all modules that relied in any way on the CWDB, which reduced the average percentage words correct from 94.8% to 27.1%. On the other hand, using *only* the modules that exclusively used the CWDB yielded a reduction to only 87.6% words correct. Obviously, in the current system, the CWDB plays a significant role in the generation of useful candidate lists.

Another way of looking at the contribution of the modules is to consider the probability assigned to each target given the clues. Ideally, we would like all targets to have probability 1. In general, we want to maximize the product of the probabilities assigned to the targets, since this quantity is directly related to what the solver will be maximizing. In Figure 3, the top line represents the probability assigned by the Bigram module (described later). This probability is low for all targets, but very low for the hard targets. As we add groups of modules, the effect on the probabilities assigned to targets can be seen as a lowering of the curve, which corresponds to assigning more and more probability to the target. Note the large increase due to the Exact Match module. Finally, notice that there is a segment that the modules do very poorly on—the targets that only Bigram returns. We will later describe extensions to the system that help with this range.

Word List Modules

WordList, WordList-Big ignore their clues and re-

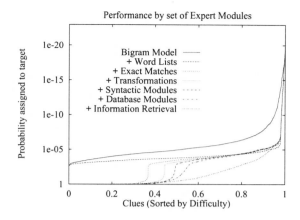

Figure 3: The cumulative probability assigned as module groups are added shows that different module types vary in contribution. Lines are sorted independently.

turn all words of the correct length from several dictionaries. WordList contains a list of 655,000 terms from sources including online texts, encyclopedias and dictionaries. WordList-Big contains everything in WordList, as well as many constructed 'terms', produced by combining related entries in databases. This includes combining first and last names, as well as merging adjacent words from clues in the CWDB. WordList-Big contains over 2.1 million terms.

WordList-CWDB contains the 58,000 unique targets in the CWDB, and returns all targets of the appropriate length, regardless of the clue. It weights them with estimates of their "prior" probabilities as targets of arbitrary clues.

CWDB-Specific Modules

Exact Match returns all targets of the correct length associated with this clue in the CWDB. Confidence is based on a Bayesian calculation involving the number of exact matches of correct and incorrect lengths.

Transformations learns a set of textual transformations which, when applied to clue-target pairs in the CWDB, generates other known clue-target pairs. When faced with a new clue, it applies all applicable transformations and returns the results, weighted based on the previous precision/recall of these transformations. Transformations include word substitution, removing one phrase from the beginning or end of a clue and adding another phrase to the beginning or end of the clue, depluralizing a word in the clue and pluralizing the associated target, and others. The following is a list of several non-trivial examples from the tens of thousands of transformations learned:

nice X $\leftrightarrow$ X in france | X starter $\leftrightarrow$ prefix with X
X for short $\leftrightarrow$ X abbr | X city $\leftrightarrow$ X capital

Information Retrieval Modules

Crossword clues present an interesting challenge to

Module	Guess	Acc	Len	Best
Bigram	100.0	100.0	-	0.1
WordList-Big	100.0	97.2	$\approx 10^5$	1.0
WordList	100.0	92.6	$\approx 10^4$	1.7
WordList-CWDB	100.0	92.3	$\approx 10^3$	2.8
ExactMatch	40.3	91.4	1.3	35.9
Transformation	32.7	79.8	1.5	8.4
KindOf	3.7	62.9	44.7	0.8
Blanks-Books	2.8	35.5	43.8	0.1
Blanks-Geo	1.8	28.1	60.3	0.1
Blanks-Movies	6.0	71.2	35.8	3.2
Blanks-Music	3.4	40.4	39.9	0.4
Blanks-Quotes	3.9	45.8	49.6	0.1
Movies	6.3	66.4	19.0	2.2
Writers	0.1	100.0	1.2	0.1
Compass	0.4	63.6	5.9	0.0
Geography	1.8	25.3	322.0	0.0
Myth	0.1	75.0	61.0	0.0
Music	0.9	11.8	49.3	0.0
WordNet	42.8	22.6	30.0	0.9
WordNetSyns	11.9	44.0	3.4	0.9
RogetSyns	9.7	42.9	8.9	0.4
MobySyns	12.0	81.6	496.0	0.4
Encyclopedia	97.9	32.2	262.0	1.3
LSI-Ency	94.7	43.8	995.0	1.0
LSI-CWDB	99.1	77.6	990.0	1.2
PartialMatch	92.6	71.0	493.0	8.1
Dijkstra1	99.7	84.8	620.0	4.6
Dijkstra2	99.7	82.2	996.0	8.7
Dijkstra3	99.5	80.4	285.0	13.3
Dijkstra4	99.5	80.8	994.0	0.1

Table 3: Performance on 70 puzzles (5374 clues) shows differences in the number of targets returned (**Len**) and contribution to the overall lists (**Best**). Also measured but not shown are the implicit modules.

traditional information retrieval (IR) techniques. While queries of similar length to clues have been studied, the "documents" to be returned are quite different (words or short sequences of words). In addition, the queries themselves are often purposely phrased to be ambiguous, and never share words with the "documents" to be returned. Despite these differences, it seemed natural to try a variety of IR techniques.

Encyclopedia searches an online encyclopedia. For each query term, the module computes a distribution of terms "close" to the query term in the text. A term is counted $10 - k$ times in this distribution for every time it appears at a distance of $k < 10$ words away from the query term. A term is also counted once if it appears in an article for which the query term is in the title, or vice versa. Terms are assigned scores proportional to their frequencies in the "close" distribution, divided by their frequency in the corpus. The distribution of scores is normalized to 1. If a query contains multiple terms, the score distributions are combined linearly according to the log inverse frequency of the query terms in the corpus with very common terms such as "as" and "and" ignored.

Partial Match uses the standard vector space model (Salton & McGill 1983), defined by a vector space with one dimension for every word in the dictionary. A clue is represented as a vector in this space. For each word w a clue contains, it gets a component in dimension w of magnitude $-\log(\text{frequency}(w))$.

For a clue c, the module find all clues in the CWDB that share words with c. The target of each such clue is given a weight based on the dot product of the clue with c. The assigned weight is geometrically interpolated between $1/\text{size(dictionary)}$ and 1 based on this dot product.

LSI, or latent semantic indexing, is an extension of the vector space model that uses singular value decomposition to identify correlations between words. LSI has been successfully applied to the related problem of synonym selection on a standardized test (Landauer & Dumais 1997). LSI modules were trained on the CWDB (all clues with the same target were treated as a document) and on an online encyclopedia.

Dijkstra Modules derive from the intuition that related words co-occur with one another or co-occur with similar words, suggesting a measure of relatedness based on graph distance. From a set of text databases, the module builds a weighted directed graph on the set of all terms. Each database d and pair of terms (t, u) that co-occur in the same document produce an edge from t to u with weight

$$-\log \left(\frac{\text{\# documents in } d \text{ containing } t \text{ and } u}{\text{\# documents in } d \text{ containing } t} \right).$$

For a one-word clue t, the modules assign a term u a score of $-\log(\text{fraction of documents containing } t) - \text{weight(minimum weight path } t \rightarrow u)$.

The module finds the highest scoring terms with a shortest-path search. Multi-word clues are scored by summing the results for their individual terms. The four Dijkstra modules use variants of this technique.

An encyclopedia index, two thesauri, a database of wordforms and the CWDB were used as databases. Littman, Keim, & Shazeer (1999) provide examples.

Database Modules

Movie uses the Internet Movie Database (www.imdb.com), an online resource with a wealth of information about all manner of movies and T.V. shows. This module looks for a number of patterns in the clue (e.g. quoted titles as in ≺'Alice' star Linda [5]: lavin≻, or Boolean operations on names as in ≺Cary or Lee [5]: grant≻), and formulates queries to a local copy of the database.

Music, Literary, Geography use simple pattern matching of the clue (looking for keywords "city", "author","band" and others as in ≺Iowa city [4]: ames≻) to formulate a query to a topical database. The literary database is culled from both online and encyclopedia resources. The geography database is from the Getty Information Institute, with additional data supplied from online lists.

Synonyms are found by four distinct modules, based on three different thesauri. Using the WordNet (Miller *et al.* 1990) database, one module looks for root forms of words in the clue, and then finds a variety of related words (e.g. ≺Stroller [6]: gocart≻). In addition, a type of relevance feedback is used to generate lists of synonyms of synonyms. Finally, if necessary, the forms of the related words are coverted back to the form of the original clue word (number, tense, etc.): ≺Contrives [7]: devises≻.

Syntactic Modules

Fill-in-the-Blanks constitute over 5% of clues in the CWDB. These modules find string patterns in music, geography, movies, literary and quotes databases: ≺'Time ____ My Side' (Stones hit) [4]: ison≻.

KindOf clues are similar to fill-in-the-blank clues in that they involve pattern matching over short phrases. We identified over 50 cues that indicate a clue of this type, for example, "starter for" (≺Starter for saxon [5]: anglo≻), and "suffix with" (≺Suffix with switch or sock [4]: eroo≻).

Merging Candidate Lists

After each expert module has generated a weighted candidate list, PROVERB must somehow merge these into a unified candidate list with a common weighting scheme for the solver. This problem is similar to the problem facing meta-crawler search engines in that separately weighted return lists must be combined in a sensible way. The crossword domain has the advantage of ready access to precise and abundant training data.

For a given clue, each expert module m returns a weighted set of candidates and a numerical level of confidence that the correct target is in this set. For each expert module m, the merger uses three real parameters: scale(m), length-scale(m) and spread(m). Each candidate is reweighted by raising its weight to the power spread(m), then normalizing the sum to 1. The confidence level is multiplied by the product of scale(m) and length-scale(m)^{targetlength}. To compute a combined probability distribution over candidates, the merger linearly combines the modified candidate sets of all the modules weighted by their modified confidence levels, and normalizes the sum to 1.

The scale, length-scale and spread parameters give the merger control over how the information returned by an expert module is incorporated into the final candidate list. Parameters are set using hill-climbing.

The objective function for optimization is the average log probability assigned to correct targets. This corresponds to maximizing the average log probability assigned by the solver to the correct puzzle fill-in, since in our model the probability of a puzzle solution is proportional to the product of the prior probabilities on the answers in each of the slots. The optimal value achieved on the 70 puzzle training set was $\log(\frac{1}{33.56})$.

Grid Filling

After realizing how much repetition occurs in crosswords, and therefore how well the CWDB covers the domain, one might wonder whether this coverage is enough to constrain solutions to such an extent that there is little left for the grid-filling algorithm to do. We did not find this to be the case. Simplistic grid filling yielded only mediocre results. As a measure of the task left to the grid-filling algorithm, on the first iteration of solving, using just the weighted candidate lists from the modules, only 40.9% of targets are in the top of the candidate list for their slot. However, the grid-filling algorithm is able to raise this to 89.4%.[4]

The algorithm employed by PROVERB (Shazeer, Littman, & Keim 1999) models grid filling as an optimization problem: find the best way of choosing a candidate for each clue, while respecting the constraints of the grid. We can define "best" in several different ways; we attempted to maximize the expected overlap with the creator's solution. Other definitions of "best" include maximizing the probability of getting the entire puzzle correct, or maximizing expected letter overlap. The decision to use expected word overlap is motivated by the scoring system used in human tournaments (see below). Finding the optimal solution to this problem is a belief net inference problem; we use a type of "turbo decoding" (Shazeer, Littman, & Keim 1999) to approximate the solutions quickly.

Implicit Distribution Modules

Our probability measure assigns probability zero to a target that is suggested by no module and probability zero to all solutions containing that target. Therefore, we need to assign non-zero probability to all letter sequences. Clearly, there are too many to list explicitly (10^{21} for a 15-letter clue). We augmented the solver to reason with probability distributions over candidate lists that are implicitly represented. These *Implicit Distribution Modules* (Figure 2) generate additional candidates once the solver can give them more information about letter probability distributions over the slot.

The most important of these is a letter Bigram module, which "generates" all possible letter sequences of a given length by returning a letter bigram distribution over all possible strings, learned from the CWDB. The bigram probabilities are used throughout the solution process, so this module is integrated into the solver.

Note in Figure 3 there are some clues for which only Bigram returns the target. In a pretest run on 70 puzzles, the clue-target with the lowest probability was ≺Honolulu wear [14]: hawaiianmuumuu≻. This target never occurs in the CWDB, although both muumuu and hawaiian occur multiple times, and it gets a particularly low probability because of the many unlikely letter

---

[4]On average, over the 70 NYT puzzles in the test suite.

pairs in the target. Once the grid-filling process is underway, estimates of probability distributions for each letter in these longer targets are available, and this can limit the search for candidates.

To address long, multiword targets, we created freestanding implicit distribution modules. Each implicit distribution module takes a letter probability distribution for each letter of the slot (computed within the solver), and returns weighted candidate lists. These lists are then added to the previous candidate lists, and the grid-filling algorithm continues. This process of getting new candidates can happen several times during the solution process.

Tetragram suggests candidates based on a letter tetragram model, built from the WordList-Big. We hoped this would provide a better model for word boundaries than the bigram model mentioned above, since this list contains many multiword terms.

Segmenter calculates the $n = 10$ most probable word sequences with respect to both the letter probabilities and word probabilities from several sources using dynamic programming. The base word probabilities are unigram word probabilities from the CWDB. In addition, the Dijkstra module (described above) suggests the best 1000 words (with weights) given the current clue. These weights and the unigram probabilities are then combined for a new distribution of word probabilities.

For example, consider the clue ≺Tall footwear for rappers? [11]: `hiphopboots`≻. Given a letter distribution and a combined word distribution, the segmenter returned the following: `tiptopboots`, `hiphoproots`, `hiphopbooks`, `hiphoptoots`, `hiphopboots`, `hiphoproofs`, `riptaproots`, `hippopboots`, `hiptaproots`, `hiptapboots`. Note that the reweighting done by the Dijkstra module by examining the clue raises the probabilites of related words like `boots`.

Results

To evaluate PROVERB's performance, we ran it on a large collection of daily puzzles, and on a set of recent tournament puzzles.

Daily Puzzles

We tested the system on puzzles from seven daily sources, listed in Table 1 (**Test**). The TV Guide puzzles go back to 1996, but the other sources were all from between August and December of 1998. We selected 70 puzzles, 10 from each source, as training puzzles for the system. The reweighting process described earlier was trained on the 5374 clues from these 70 puzzles. Additional debugging and modification of the modules was done after evaluation on these training puzzles.

Having fixed the modules and reweighting parameters, we then ran the system on the 370 puzzles in the final pool. The system acheived an average 95.3% words

correct, 98.1% letters correct, and 46.2% puzzles completely correct (94.1%, 97.6%, and 37.6% without the implicit distribution modules). The NYT puzzles were the only ones that averaged under 95% words correct. Following up on our earlier observations, we split up the NYT puzzles and found that PROVERB averaged 95.5% words correct on Monday through Wednesday puzzles and 85.0% words correct on Thursday through Sunday puzzles. As with people, the late-week NYT puzzles were more difficult for PROVERB.

Tournament Puzzles

To better gauge the system's performance against humans, we tested PROVERB using puzzles from the 1998 American Crossword Puzzle Tournament (ACPT) (Shortz 1990). The ACPT has been held annually for 20 years, and was attended in 1998 by 251 people. The scoring system for the ACPT requires that a time limit be set for each puzzle. A solver's score is then 10 times the number of words correct, plus a bonus of 150 if the puzzle is completely correct. In addition, the number of incorrect letters is subtracted from the full minutes early the solver finishes. If this number is positive, it is multiplied by 25 and added to the score.

There were seven puzzles in the offical contest, with time limits ranging from 15 to 45 minutes. We used the same version of PROVERB described in the previous section. The results over the 1998 puzzles are shown in Table 4. The best human solvers at the competition finished all puzzles correctly, and the winner was determined by finishing time (the champion averaged under seven minutes per puzzle). Thus, while not competitive with the very best human solvers, PROVERB would have placed 213 out of 251; its score on Puzzle 5 exceeded that of the median human solver at the contest.

The ACPT puzzles are very challenging, and include tricks like multiple letters or words written in a single grid cell, and targets written in the wrong slot. In spite of the fact that PROVERB could not produce answers that bend the rules in this way, it still filled in 80% of the words correctly, on average. The implicit distribution modules ("PROVERB(I)") helped improve the word score on these puzzles, but brought down the tournament score because it runs more slowly.

Conclusions

Solving crossword puzzles presents a unique artificial intelligence challenge, demanding from a competitive system broad world knowledge, powerful constraint satisfaction, and speed. Because of the widespread appeal, system designers have a large number of existing puzzles to use to test and tune their systems, and humans with whom to compare.

A successful crossword solver requires many artificial intelligence techniques; in our work, we used ideas from state-space search, probabilistic optimization, constraint satisfaction, information retrieval, machine learning and natural language processing. We

Name	Rank	Total	Avg Time
▷ Maximum	1	13140	0:59
TP (Champion)	1	12115	6:51
JJ (75%)	62	10025	-
MF (50%)	125	8575	-
MB (25%)	187	6985	-
▷ Proverb-I (24%)	190	6880	0:59
Proverb (15%)	213	6215	9:41
Proverb-I (15%)	215	6130	15:07

Table 4: PROVERB compared favorably to the 251 elite human contestants at the 1998 championship. Lines preceded by a ▷ indicate the theoretical scores if the solver did every puzzle in under a minute.

found probability theory a potent practical tool for organizing the system and improving performance.

The level of success we acheived would probably not have been possible five years ago, as we depended on extremely fast computers with vast memory and disk storage, and used tremendous amounts of data in machine readable form. Perhaps the time is ripe to use these resources to attack other problems previously deemed too challenging for AI.

Acknowledgements

We received help and guidance from other members of the Duke Community: Michael Fulkerson, Mark Peot, Robert Duvall, Fred Horch, Siddhartha Chatterjee, Geoff Cohen, Steve Ruby, Alan Biermann, Donald Loveland, Gert Webelhuth, Michail Lagoudakis, Steve Majercik, Syam Gadde. Via e-mail, Will Shortz and William Tunstall-Pedoe made considerable contributions.

References

Ginsberg, M. L.; Frank, M.; Halpin, M. P.; and Torrance, M. C. 1990. Search lessons learned from crossword puzzles. In *Proceedings of the Eighth National Conference on Artificial Intelligence*, 210–215.

Landauer, T. K., and Dumais, S. T. 1997. A solution to Plato's problem: The latent semantic analysis theory of acquisition, induction and representation of knowledge. *Psychological Review* 104(2):211–240.

Littman, M. L.; Keim, G. A.; and Shazeer, N. M. 1999. Solving crosswords with Proverb. In *Proceedings of the Sixteenth National Conference on Artificial Intelligence*.

Miller, G. R.; Beckwith, C.; Fellbaum, C.; Gross, D.; and Miller, K. 1990. Introduction to WordNet: An on-line lexical database. *International Journal of Lexicography* 3(4):235–244.

Salton, G., and McGill, M. J. 1983. *Introduction to Modern Information Retrieval*. McGraw-Hill.

Shazeer, N. M.; Littman, M. L.; and Keim, G. A. 1999. Solving crossword puzzles as probabilistic constraint satisfaction. In *Proceedings of the Sixteenth National Conference on Artificial Intelligence*.

Shortz, W., ed. 1990. *American Championship Crosswords*. Fawcett Columbine.

Value-Update Rules for Real-Time Search

Sven Koenig
College of Computing
Georgia Institute of Technology
skoenig@cc.gatech.edu

Boleslaw Szymanski
Department of Computer Science
Rensselaer Polytechnic Institute
szymansk@cs.rpi.edu

Abstract

Real-time search methods have successfully been used to solve a large variety of search problems but their properties are largely unknown. In this paper, we study how existing real-time search methods scale up. We compare two real-time search methods that have been used successfully in the literature and differ only in the update rules of their values: Node Counting, a real-time search method that always moves to the successor state that it has visited the least number of times so far, and Learning Real-Time A*, a similar real-time search method. Both real-time search methods seemed to perform equally well in many standard domains from artificial intelligence. Our formal analysis is therefore surprising. We show that the performance of Node Counting can be exponential in the number of states even in undirected domains. This solves an open problem and shows that the two real-time search methods do not always perform similarly in undirected domains since the performance of Learning Real-Time A* is known to be polynomial in the number of states at worst.

Traditional search methods from artificial intelligence, such as the A* method (Nilsson 1971), first plan and then execute the resulting plan. Real-time (heuristic) search methods (Korf 1987), on the other hand, interleave planning and plan execution, and allow for fine-grained control over how much planning to perform between plan executions. Planning is done via local searches, that is, searches that are restricted to the part of the domain around the current state of the agent. The idea behind this search methodology is not to attempt to find plans with minimal plan-execution time but rather to attempt to decrease the planning time or the sum of planning and plan-execution time over that of traditional search methods. (Ishida 1997) gives a good overview of real-time search methods. Experimental evidence indicates that real-time search methods are efficient domain-independent search methods that outperform traditional search methods on a variety of search problems. Real-time search methods have, for example, successfully been applied to traditional search problems (Korf 1990), moving-target search problems (Ishida and Korf 1991), STRIPS-type planning problems (Bonet *et al.* 1997), robot navigation and localization problems with initial pose uncertainty (Koenig and Simmons 1998), totally observable Markov decision process problems (Barto *et al.* 1995), and partially observable Markov decision process problems (Geffner and Bonet 1998), among others. Despite this success of real-time search methods, not much is known about their properties. They differ in this respect from traditional search methods, whose properties have been researched extensively. For example, real-time search methods associate values with the states that are updated as the search progresses and used to determine which actions to execute. Different real-time search methods update these values differently, and no consensus has been reached so far on which value-update rule is best. Both (Russell and Wefald 1991) and (Pemberton and Korf 1992), for example, studied several value-update rules experimentally but arrived at different conclusions about which one outperformed the others. This demonstrates the need to understand better how the value-update rules influence the behavior of real-time search methods. In this paper, we investigate how two value-update rules scale up in undirected domains: one that interprets the values as approximations of the goal distances of the states (resulting in a real-time search method called Learning Real-Time A*) and one that interprets the values as the number of times the states have been visited (resulting in a real-time search method called Node Counting). The principle behind Node Counting is simple: always move to the neighboring state that has been visited the least number of times. This appears to be an intuitive exploration principle since, when exploring unknown environments, one wants to get to states that one has visited smaller and smaller number of times with the goal to get as fast as possible to states that one has not visited yet. This explains why Node Counting has been used repeatedly in artificial intelligence. Experimental results indicate that both Node Counting and uninformed Learning Real-Time A* need about the same number of action executions on average to reach a goal state in many standard domains from artificial intelligence. However, to the best of our knowledge, our paper analyzes the performance of Node Counting in undirected domains for the first time, which is not surprising since the field of real-time search is a rather experimental one. We show that Node Counting reaches a goal state in undirected domains

Initially, the u-values $u(s)$ are zero for all $s \in S$.

1. $s := s_{start}$.
2. If $s \in G$, then stop successfully.
3. $a := $ one-of $\arg\min_{a \in A(s)} u(succ(s,a))$.
4. Update $u(s)$ using the value-update rule.
5. Execute action a and change the current state to $succ(s,a)$.
6. $s := succ(s,a)$.
7. Go to 2.

Figure 1: Real-Time Search

sometimes only after a number of action executions that is exponential in the number of states, whereas uninformed LRTA* is known to always reach a goal state after at most a polynomial number of action executions. Thus, although many standard domains from artificial intelligence (such as sliding-tile puzzles, blocksworlds, and gridworlds) are undirected, this property alone is not sufficient to explain why Node Counting performs well on them. This result solves an open problem described in (Koenig and Simmons 1996). We also describe a non-trivial domain property that guarantees a polynomial performance of Node Counting and study a probabilistic variant of Node Counting. In general, our results show that experimental comparisons of real-time search methods are often insufficient to evaluate how well they scale up because the performance of two similar real-time search methods can be very different even if experimental results seem to indicate otherwise. A formal analysis of real-time search methods can help to detect these problems and prevent surprises later on, as well as provide a solid theoretical foundation for interleaving planning and plan execution. We believe that it is important that more real-time search methods be analyzed similarly, especially since most work on real-time search has been of an experimental nature so far.

Notation

We use the following notation in this paper: S denotes the finite set of states of the domain, $s_{start} \in S$ the start state, and $\emptyset \neq G \subseteq S$ the set of goal states. The number of states is $n := |S|$. $A(s) \neq \emptyset$ is the finite, nonempty set of actions that can be executed in state $s \in S$. $succ(s,a)$ denotes the successor state that results from the execution of action $a \in A(s)$ in state $s \in S$. To simplify matters, we measure the plan-execution times and goal distances in action executions throughout this paper, which is justified if the execution times of all actions are roughly the same. We also use two operators with the following semantics: Given a set X, the expression "one-of X" returns an element of X according to an arbitrary rule. A subsequent invocation of "one-of X" can return the same or a different element. The expression "$\arg\min_{x \in X} f(x)$" returns the elements $x \in X$ that minimize $f(x)$, that is, the set $\{x \in X | f(x) = \min_{x' \in X} f(x')\}$.

Node Counting and LRTA*

We study two similar real-time search methods, namely uninformed variants of Node Counting and Learning Real-

Time A* that have a lookahead of only one action execution and fit the algorithmic skeleton shown in Figure 1. (Some researchers feel more comfortable referring to these methods as "agent-centered search methods" (Koenig 1995) and reserving the term "real-time search methods" for agent-centered search methods whose values approximate the goal-distances of the states.) We chose to study uninformed real-time search methods because one of the methods we study has traditionally been used for exploring unknown environments in the absence of heuristic information (often in the context of robot navigation). Both real-time search methods associate a *u-value* $u(s)$ with each state $s \in S$. The semantics of the u-values depend on the real-time search method but all u-values are initialized with zeroes, reflecting that the real-time search methods are initially uninformed and thus do not have any a-priori information as to where the goal states are. The search task is to find any path from the start state to a goal state, not necessarily a shortest one. Both real-time search methods first check whether they have already reached a goal state and thus can terminate successfully (Line 2). If not, they decide on which action to execute in the current state (Line 3). They look one action execution ahead and always greedily choose an action that leads to a successor state with a minimal u-value (ties are broken arbitrarily). Then, they update the u-value of their current state using a value-update rule that depends on the semantics of the u-values and thus the real-time search method (Line 4). Finally, they execute the selected action (Line 5), update the current state (Line 6), and iterate the procedure (Line 7). Many real-time search methods from the literature fit this algorithmic skeleton. We chose to compare Node Counting and Learning Real-Time A* because both of them implement simple, intuitive rules of thumb for how to interleave planning and plan execution. Node Counting can be described as follows:

Node Counting: A u-value $u(s)$ of Node Counting corresponds to the number of times Node Counting has already been in state s. Node Counting always moves to a successor state with a minimal u-value because it wants to get to states which it has visited a smaller number of times to eventually reach a state that it has not yet visited at all, that is, a potential goal state.

Value-Update Rule of Node Counting (Line 4 in Figure 1)
$$u(s) := 1 + u(s).$$

To the best of our knowledge, the term "Node Counting" was first used in (Thrun 1992b). Variants of Node Counting have been used in the literature to explore unknown grid-worlds, either on their own (Pirzadeh and Snyder 1990) or to accelerate reinforcement-learning methods (Thrun 1992b). Node Counting is also the foundation of "Avoiding the Past: A Simple but Effective Strategy for Reactive [Robot] Navigation" (Balch and Arkin 1993), except that "Avoiding the Past" is part of a schemata-based navigation architecture and thus sums over vectors that point away from adjacent locations with a magnitude that depends on how often that location has been visited. Finally, it has been suggested that variants of Node Counting approximate the exploration behavior of ants, that use pheromone traces to guide their exploration (Wagner *et al.* 1997). We compare Node Counting to Learning Real-Time A* (Korf 1990), that can be described as follows:

> **Learning Real-Time A*** (LRTA*): A u-value $u(s)$ of LRTA* approximates the goal distance of state s. LRTA* always moves to a successor state with a minimal u-value because it wants to get to states with smaller goal distances to eventually reach a state with goal distance zero, that is, a goal state.

> Value-Update Rule of LRTA* (Line 4 in Figure 1)
> $$u(s) := 1 + u(succ(s,a)).$$

LRTA* is probably the most popular real-time search method, and thus provides a good baseline for evaluating the performance of other real-time search methods.

Assumptions

We assume that one can reach a goal state from every state that can be reached from the start state. Domains with this property are called safely explorable and guarantee that real-time search methods such as Node Counting or LRTA* reach a goal state eventually. This can be shown by assuming that they cycle infinitely without reaching a goal state. The u-values of all states in the cycle then increase beyond every bound since both methods increase the smallest u-value of the states in the cycle by at least one every time the cycle is traversed. But then the u-values of all states in the cycle increase above the u-values of all states that border the cycle. Such states exist since the domain is safely explorable and one can thus reach a goal state from every state in the cycle. Then, however, Node Counting and LRTA* are forced to move to this state and leave the cycle, which is a contradiction.

Performance of Node Counting

The performance of search methods for search tasks that are to be solved only once is best measured using the sum of planning and plan-execution time. We measure the performance of real-time search methods using the number of actions that they execute until they reach a goal state. This is motived by the fact that, for sufficiently fast moving agents, the sum of planning and plan execution time is determined by the planning time, which is roughly proportional to the number of action executions since the real-time search methods perform roughly a constant amount of computations between action executions. For sufficiently slowly moving agents, on the other hand, the sum of planning and plan-execution time is determined by the plan-execution time, which is roughly proportional to the number of action executions if every action can be executed in about the same amount of time.

The performance of LRTA* is known to be at worst quadratic in the number of states in both directed and undirected domains (Koenig and Simmons 1995). The performance of Node Counting is known to be at least exponential in the number of states in directed domains (Koenig and

Simmons 1996) but many domains of artificial intelligence are undirected, including sliding-tile puzzles, blocksworlds, and gridworlds. To the best of our knowledge, the performance of Node Counting in undirected domains has not been analyzed so far. However, it has been speculated, based on the good experimental results reported by the researchers who used Node Counting, that Node Counting was efficient in undirected domains, see (Koenig and Simmons 1996) and the references contained therein for experimental results.

In the following, we present an example (our main result) that shows that the performance of Node Counting in undirected domains can be at least exponential in the number of states. Despite its elegance, this example proved to be rather difficult to construct. It refutes the hypothesis that the performance of Node Counting in undirected domains is at most polynomial in the number of states. Our examples are undirected trees (and thus planar graphs). Figure 2 shows an instance of this example. In general, the trees have $m + 1$ levels (for $m \geq 2$). The levels consist of vertices of three different kinds: g-subroots, r-subroots, and leafs that are connected to the subroots. g-subroots and r-subroots alternate. At level $i = 0$, there is one subroot, namely a g-subroot g_0. At levels $i = 1 \ldots m$, there are two subroots, namely an r-subroot r_i and a g-subroot g_i. Subroot g_i has $m + i$ leafs connected to it, and subroot r_i has one leaf connected to it. Finally, subroot g_m is connected to two additional vertices, namely the start vertex and the only goal vertex. The trees have $n = 3/2\, m^2 + 9/2\, m + 3$ vertices. Node Counting proceeds in a series of passes through the trees. Each pass traverses the subroots in the opposite order than the previous pass. We call a pass that traverses the subroots in descending order a down pass, and a pass that traverses them in ascending order an up pass. We number passes from zero on upward, so even passes are down passes and odd passes are up passes. A pass ends immediately before it switches directions. We break ties as follows: During pass zero, ties among successor states are broken in favor of leaf vertices of g-subroots (with highest priority) and then subroots. Pass zero ends when the leafs of subroot g_0 have been visited once each. As a result, at the end of pass zero the subroots g_i have been visited $m + i + 1$ times each, and their leafs have been visited once each. The subroots r_i have been visited once each, and their subroots have not been visited at all. During all subsequent passes, ties among successor states are broken in favor of subroots whenever possible. A tie between two r-subroots (when Node Counting is at a g-subroot) is resolved by continuing with the current pass. A tie between two g-subroots (when Node Counting is at an r-subroot) is resolved by terminating the current pass and starting a new one in the opposite direction. In the following, we provide a sketch of the proof that Node Counting executes (at least)

$$\Omega(n^{\sqrt{(\frac{1}{6}-\epsilon)n}})$$

actions in this case, where n is the number of states and $0 < \epsilon < 1/6$ is an arbitrarily small constant. The actual proofs are by induction, and are omitted here because they are long

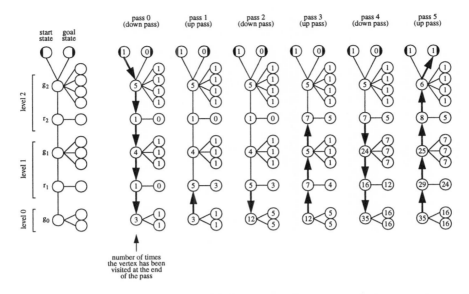

Figure 2: Node Counting has Exponential Runtime in Undirected Domains ($m = 2, n = 18$)

and tedious (Szymanski and Koenig 1998). To convince the reader of the correctness of our proofs, however, we provide experimental results from a simulation study that confirm our analytical results.

As part of the proof sketch, we study a tree with $m + 1$ levels. Let $u_{p,m}(s)$ denote the total number of times that subroot s has been entered at the end of pass p for a tree with $m+1$ levels. By definition, $u_{p,m}(s)$ is a nondecreasing function of p. Our tie breaking rules guarantee that all leafs of a subroot have been entered the same number of times at the end of each pass, so we let $w_{p,m}(s)$ denote the number of times each of the leafs of subroot s has been entered at the end of pass p for a tree with $m + 1$ levels. Finally, let $x_{p,m}(s)$ denote the total number of times subroot s has been entered from non-leafs at the end of pass p for a tree with $m + 1$ levels. These values relate as follows: The total number of times that a subroot was entered at the end of pass p is equal to the product of the number of its leafs and the total number of times that it was entered from each of its leafs at the end of pass p (which equals the total number of times that each of its leafs was entered at the end of pass p) plus the total number of times the subroot was entered from non-leafs at the end of pass p. For example, $u_{p,m}(g_i) = (m + i)w_{p,m}(g_i) + x_{p,m}(g_i)$.

Lemma 1 *Assume that Node Counting visits subroot s (with $s \neq g_m$) during pass p, where $0 < p < 2m + 2$. The values $u_{p,m}(s)$ can then be calculated as follows, for $i > 0$:*

$$u_{2k+1,m}(g_0) = m\,u_{2k,m}(r_1) + x_{2k,m}(g_0)$$
$$u_{2k,m}(g_0) = m\,u_{2k,m}(r_1) + x_{2k,m}(g_0)$$

$$u_{2k,m}(g_i) = (m + i)\min(u_{2k-1,m}(r_i), u_{2k,m}(r_{i+1})) + x_{2k,m}(g_i)$$
$$u_{2k+1,m}(g_i) = (m + i)\min(u_{2k,m}(r_{i+1}), u_{2k+1,m}(r_i)) + x_{2k+1,m}(g_i)$$
$$u_{2k,m}(r_i) = \min(u_{2k-1,m}(g_{i-1}), u_{2k,m}(g_i)) + x_{2k,m}(r_i)$$
$$u_{2k+1,m}(r_i) = \min(u_{2k,m}(g_i), u_{2k+1,m}(g_{i-1})) + x_{2k+1,m}(r_i)$$

Proof: by induction on the number of passes p. ∎

Theorem 1 *If $p = 2k$ for $0 \leq k \leq m$, then the down pass ends at subroot g_0 and it holds that*

$$u_{2k,m}(g_i) = \begin{cases} m(u_{2k-2,m}(g_i) + 2k) + k + 1 & \text{for } i = 0 < k \\ (m + i)(u_{2k-2,m}(g_i) + 2k - 2i \\ \quad +1) + 2k - 2i + 1 & \text{for } 0 < i < k \\ m + i + 1 & \text{otherwise} \end{cases}$$

$$u_{2k,m}(r_i) = \begin{cases} u_{2k-1,m}(g_{i-1}) + 2k - 2i + 2 & \text{for } 0 < i \leq k \\ 1 & \text{otherwise} \end{cases}$$

$$x_{2k,m}(g_i) = \begin{cases} k + 1 & \text{for } i = 0 \\ 2k - 2i + 1 & \text{for } 0 < i < k \\ 1 & \text{otherwise} \end{cases}$$

$$x_{2k,m}(r_i) = \begin{cases} 2k - 2i + 2 & \text{for } 0 < i \leq k \\ 1 & \text{otherwise} \end{cases}$$

$$u_{2k,m}(r_i) \geq u_{2k-1,m}(r_{i-1}) \qquad \text{for } 1 < i \leq k$$
$$u_{2k,m}(g_i) > u_{2k-1,m}(g_{i-1}) \qquad \text{for } 0 < i < k$$

If $p = 2k + 1$ for $0 \leq k \leq m$, then the up pass ends at subroot r_{k+1} (with the exception of up pass $2m + 1$ that ends at the goal state) and it holds that

$$u_{2k+1,m}(g_i) = \begin{cases} u_{2k,m}(g_i) & \text{for } i = 0 \\ (m + i)(u_{2k-1,m}(g_i) + 2k \\ \quad - 2i) + 2k - 2i + 2 & \text{for } 0 < i < k \\ m + i + 2 & \text{for } 0 < i = k \\ m + i + 1 & \text{otherwise} \end{cases}$$

$$u_{2k+1,m}(r_i) = \begin{cases} u_{2k,m}(g_i) + 2k - 2i + 3 & \text{for } 0 < i \leq k \\ u_{2k+1,m}(g_{i-1}) + 2 & \text{for } i = k + 1 \leq m \\ 1 & \text{otherwise} \end{cases}$$

$$x_{2k+1,m}(g_i) = \begin{cases} k + 1 & \text{for } i = 0 \\ 2k - 2i + 2 & \text{for } 0 < i \leq k \\ 1 & \text{otherwise} \end{cases}$$

$$x_{2k+1,m}(r_i) = \begin{cases} 2k - 2i + 3 & \text{for } 0 < i \leq k \\ 2 & \text{for } i = k + 1 \leq m \\ 1 & \text{otherwise} \end{cases}$$

$$u_{2k+1,m}(r_i) \geq u_{2k,m}(r_{i+1}) \qquad \text{for } 0 < i \leq k$$
$$u_{2k+1,m}(g_i) > u_{2k,m}(g_{i+1}) \qquad \text{for } 0 \leq i < k$$

Proof: by induction on the number of executed actions, using Lemma 1. ∎

Thus, there are $2m + 2$ passes before Node Counting reaches the goal vertex. Each down pass ends at subroot g_0. The final up pass ends at the goal state. All other up passes p end at subroot $r_{(p+1)/2}$. In the following, we need two inequalities. First, according Theorem 1, it holds for $0 \le k \le m$ that

$$u_{2k,m}(g_0) = \begin{cases} m + 1 & \text{for } k = 0 \\ m(u_{2k-2,m}(g_0) + 2k) + k + 1 & \text{otherwise.} \end{cases}$$

Solving the recursion yields

$$u_{2k,m}(g_0) = \frac{m^{k+3} + m^{k+2} + m^{k+1} - (2k+2)m^2 + (k-2)m + k + 1}{m^2 - 2m + 1}.$$

Setting $k = m$ in this formula results in

$$u_{2m,m}(g_0) = \frac{m^{m+3} + m^{m+2} + m^{m+1} - 2m^3 - m^2 - m + 1}{m^2 - 2m + 1}.$$

This implies that $u_{2m+1,m}(g_0) = u_{2m,m}(g_0) > m^m$.

Second, consider an arbitrary constant $0 < \epsilon < 1/6$ and assume that $m > \max\left(\frac{1}{\epsilon} - 4, \left(\frac{3}{2-8\epsilon}\right)^{1/\epsilon}\right) \ge 2$. Note that $n \ge m$ for our trees. Then,

$$\begin{aligned} n &= \tfrac{3}{2}m^2 + \tfrac{9}{2}m + 3 \\ &< \tfrac{3}{2}\left(1 + \tfrac{4}{m}\right)m^2 & \text{since } m > 2 \\ &< \tfrac{3}{2}\left(1 + \tfrac{4\epsilon}{1-4\epsilon}\right)m^2 & \text{since } m > \tfrac{1}{\epsilon} - 4 \\ &= \tfrac{3}{2}\tfrac{m^2}{1-4\epsilon} \end{aligned}$$

and thus $m > \sqrt{\tfrac{2}{3}n(1-4\epsilon)} > 1$ (A). In the following, we also utilize that $(an)^k > n^{(1-\epsilon)k}$ for $n > \left(\frac{1}{a}\right)^{1/\epsilon}$ and arbitrary constants $a > 0$ and $k > 0$ (B). Then,

$$\begin{aligned} m^m &> \left(\sqrt{\tfrac{2}{3}n(1-4\epsilon)}\right)^{\sqrt{\tfrac{2}{3}n(1-4\epsilon)}} & \text{since (A)} \\ &= \left(\left(\tfrac{2}{3} - \tfrac{8}{3}\epsilon\right)n\right)^{\frac{1}{2}\sqrt{\tfrac{2}{3}n(1-4\epsilon)}} \\ &> n^{(1-\epsilon)\frac{1}{2}\sqrt{\tfrac{2}{3}n(1-4\epsilon)}} & \text{since (B)} \\ &= n^{\sqrt{(1-\epsilon)^2\frac{1}{6}n(1-4\epsilon)}} \\ &> n^{\sqrt{(1-2\epsilon)\frac{1}{6}n(1-4\epsilon)}} \\ &= n^{\sqrt{\left(\frac{1}{6} - \epsilon + \frac{4}{3}\epsilon^2\right)n}} \\ &> n^{\sqrt{\left(\frac{1}{6} - \epsilon\right)n}} \end{aligned}$$

Now, let $0 < \epsilon < 1/6$ be an arbitrarily small constant. Using the two inequalities above, it holds that $u_{2m+1,m}(g_0) > m^m > n^{\sqrt{(\frac{1}{6}-\epsilon)n}}$ for $m > \max\left(\frac{1}{\epsilon} - 4, \left(\frac{3}{2-8\epsilon}\right)^{1/\epsilon}\right)$ and thus also for sufficiently large n. $u_{2m+1,m}(g_0)$ is the u-value of g_0 after Node Counting terminates on a tree with $m + 1$ levels. This value equals

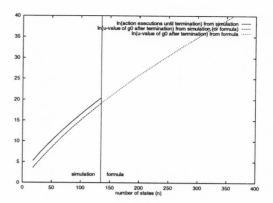

Figure 3: Results (Log Scale!)

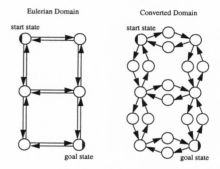

Figure 4: Sample Eulerian Domain and its Conversion

the number of times Node Counting has visited g_0, which is a lower bound on the number of actions it has executed. Consequently, Node Counting executes (at least)

$$\Omega\left(n^{\sqrt{(\frac{1}{6}-\epsilon)n}}\right)$$

actions, and the performance of Node Counting can be exponential in the number of states even in undirected domains. To confirm this analytical result, we performed a simulation study of Node Counting on our trees, see Table 1. We stopped the simulation when m reached eight because the number of action executions and thus the simulation time became large. The simulation confirmed our formulas for how the number of states n, the number of passes until termination, and the u-value of g_0 after termination depend on m. The simulation also provided us with the number of action executions until termination, for which we do not have a formula in closed form, only a lower bound in form of the u-value of g_0 after termination. How the number of action executions and its lower bound relate is shown in Figure 3, that plots the *natural logarithms* of these values.

So far, we have shown that the performance of Node Counting is not guaranteed to be polynomial in the number of states in undirected domains. We are also able to describe a domain property that guarantees a polynomial performance of Node Counting. A Eulerian graph is a directed graph, each of whose vertices have an equal number of incoming and outgoing directed edges. (Undirected domains

m	number of states n	number of passes until termination	u-value of g_0 $u_{2m+1,m}(g_0)$ after termination	$\frac{\text{u-value of } g_0}{\text{number of states}}$ after termination	action executions until termination	$\frac{\text{action executions}}{\text{number of states}}$ until termination
2	18	6	35	1.9	190	10.6
3	30	8	247	8.2	1380	46.0
4	45	10	2373	52.7	12330	274.0
5	63	12	30256	480.3	142318	2259.0
6	84	14	481471	5731.8	2063734	24568.3
7	108	16	9127581	84514.6	36135760	334590.4
8	135	18	199957001	1481163.0	740474450	5484995.9

Table 1: Simulation Results for Node Counting

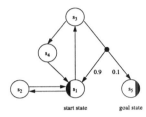

Figure 5: Node Counting does not Terminate

are a special case of Eulerian domains if one considers an undirected edge to be equivalent to a pair of directed edges with opposite directions.) Consider an arbitrary Eulerian graph whose number of edges is at most polynomial in the number of its states (for example, because no two edges connect the same states), and a graph that is derived from the Eulerian graph by replacing each of the directed edges of the Eulerian graph with two directed edges that are connected with a (unique) intermediate vertex. Figure 4 shows an example. Using results from (Koenig and Simmons 1996), we can show that the performance of Node Counting on the converted graph is guaranteed to be polynomial in its number of states. This is so because the behavior of Node Counting on the converted graph is the same as the behavior of Edge Counting on the original graph (Koenig and Simmons 1996) and the performance of Edge Counting on Eulerian graphs is polynomial in the product of the number of its edges and the number of its states (Koenig and Simmons 1996). To the best of our knowledge, this is currently the only known (non-trivial) domain property that guarantees a polynomial performance of Node Counting. We are currently investigating whether there are more realistic domain properties that also guarantee a polynomial performance of Node Counting.

Comparison of Node Counting with LRTA*

We have shown that the performance of Node Counting can be exponential in the number of states even in undirected domains. This is interesting because the value-update rule of LRTA* is similar to that of Node Counting but guarantees polynomial performance. There exist also other value-update rules that have this property in directed or undirected domains (perhaps with the restriction that every action has to result in a state change). The following table shows some

of these variants of Node Counting. The real-time search methods by (Wagner *et al.* 1997) and (Thrun 1992a) resemble Node Counting even more closely than LRTA* resembles Node Counting since their value-update rules contain the term $1 + u(s)$ just like Node Counting. While their complexity was analyzed by their authors, it has been unknown so far how their performance compares to that of Node Counting in undirected domains. Our results demonstrate that modifications of Node Counting are necessary to guarantee polynomial performance and the resulting variants of Node Counting have a huge performance advantage over Node Counting itself.

Value-Update Rules WITHOUT Polynomial Performance Guarantee

$u(s) := 1 + u(s)$.	Node Counting

Value-Update Rules WITH Polynomial Performance Guarantee

$u(s) := 1 + u(succ(s,a))$.	LRTA*
if $u(s) \leq u(succ(s,a))$ then $u(s) := 1 + u(s)$.	(Wagner *et al.* 1997)
$u(s) := \max(1 + u(s), 1 + u(succ(s,a)))$.	(Thrun 1992a)

LRTA* has other advantages over Node Counting besides a better performance guarantee, for example that it can easily be generalized to probabilistic domains. This can be done by simply replacing every occurance of the u-value of the successor state, that is, $u(succ(s,a))$, with the *expected* u-value of the successor state. (Barto *et al.* 1995) have shown that this generalization of LRTA* to probabilistic domains reaches a goal state with probability one provided that one can reach a goal state with positive probability from every state that can be reached with positive probability from the start state. (This is the probabilistic equivalent of safely explorable domains.) We show, on the other hand, that Node Counting cannot be generalized to probabilistic domains by replacing every occurance of the u-value of the successor state with the expected u-value of the successor state. Figure 5 shows a (directed) domain that contains one action with a nondeterministic effect (the other actions are deterministic). In this case, Node Counting traverses the state sequence $s_1, s_2, s_1, s_3, s_4, s_1, s_2, s_1, s_3, s_4, s_1, s_2, s_1, s_3, s_4, \ldots$ (and so forth) if ties are broken in favor of successor states with smaller indices. In particular, whenever Node Counting is in state s_3, then $u(s_1) = 2u(s_4) + 2$ and consequently $u(s_4) < 0.9u(s_1) = 0.9u(s_1) + 0.1u(s_5)$. Node Counting then moves to s_4 and never reaches the goal state although the goal state can be reached with probability one by repeatedly executing the only nondeterministic action in state s_3.

Two other advantages of LRTA* over Node Counting are that it is easy to increase its lookahead (beyond looking at only the successor states of the current state) and to make use of heuristic knowledge to bias its search towards the goal.

Conclusion

This paper showed, for the first time, that similar value-update rules of real-time search methods can result in a big difference in their performance *in undirected domains*. Moreover, we obtained this result for two value-update rules for which several experimental results in standard domains from artificial intelligence indicated that both of them performed equally well. Our main result concerned the performance of Node Counting, a real-time search method that always moves to the neighboring state that it has visited the least number of times. We showed that its performance can be exponential in the number of states even in undirected domains. In particular, we constructed an undirected tree for which Node Counting executes (at least)

$$\Omega(n^{\sqrt{(\frac{1}{6}-\epsilon)n}})$$

actions, where n is the number of states and $0 < \epsilon < 1/6$ is an arbitrarily small constant. Thus, although many standard domains from artificial intelligence (such as sliding-tile puzzles, blocksworlds, and gridworlds) are undirected, this property is not sufficient to explain why Node Counting performs well on them. Our result solved an open problem described in (Koenig and Simmons 1996) and showed that a formal analysis of search methods can help one to detect problems and prevent surprises later on, reinforcing our belief that a formal analysis of real-time search methods can be as important as experimental work. Our result suggests to either abandon Node Counting in favor of real-time search methods whose performance is guaranteed to be polynomial in the number of states (especially since experimental results only indicated that Node Counting performed as well as other real-time search methods but but did not outperform them) or study in more detail which domain properties guarantee a polynomial performance of Node Counting.

References

Balch, T. and Arkin, R. 1993. Avoiding the past: A simple, but effective strategy for reactive navigation. In *International Conference on Robotics and Automation*. 678–685.

Barto, A.; Bradtke, S.; and Singh, S. 1995. Learning to act using real-time dynamic programming. *Artificial Intelligence* 73(1):81–138.

Bonet, B.; Loerincs, G.; and Geffner, H. 1997. A robust and fast action selection mechanism. In *Proceedings of the National Conference on Artificial Intelligence*. 714–719.

Geffner, H. and Bonet, B. 1998. Solving large POMDPs by real-time dynamic programming. Technical report, Departamento de Computación, Universidad Simón Bolivar, Caracas (Venezuela).

Ishida, T. and Korf, R. 1991. Moving target search. In *Proceedings of the International Joint Conference on Artificial Intelligence*. 204–210.

Ishida, T. 1997. *Real-Time Search for Learning Autonomous Agents*. Kluwer Academic Publishers.

Koenig, S. and Simmons, R.G. 1995. Real-time search in non-deterministic domains. In *Proceedings of the International Joint Conference on Artificial Intelligence*. 1660–1667.

Koenig, S. and Simmons, R.G. 1996. Easy and hard testbeds for real-time search algorithms. In *Proceedings of the National Conference on Artificial Intelligence*. 279–285.

Koenig, S. and Simmons, R.G. 1998. Solving robot navigation problems with initial pose uncertainty using real-time heuristic search. In *Proceedings of the International Conference on Artificial Intelligence Planning Systems*. 154–153.

Koenig, S. 1995. Agent-centered search: Situated search with small look-ahead. Phd thesis proposal, School of Computer Science, Carnegie Mellon University, Pittsburgh (Pennsylvania).

Korf, R. 1987. Real-time heuristic search: First results. In *Proceedings of the National Conference on Artificial Intelligence*. 133–138.

Korf, R. 1990. Real-time heuristic search. *Artificial Intelligence* 42(2-3):189–211.

Nilsson, N. 1971. *Problem-Solving Methods in Artificial Intelligence*. McGraw-Hill.

Pemberton, J. and Korf, R. 1992. Making locally optimal decisions on graphs with cycles. Technical Report 920004, Computer Science Department, University of California at Los Angeles, Los Angeles (California).

Pirzadeh, A. and Snyder, W. 1990. A unified solution to coverage and search in explored and unexplored terrains using indirect control. In *Proceedings of the International Conference on Robotics and Automation*. 2113–2119.

Russell, S. and Wefald, E. 1991. *Do the Right Thing – Studies in Limited Rationality*. MIT Press.

Szymanski, B. and Koenig, S. 1998. The complexity of node counting on undirected graphs. Technical report, Computer Science Department, Rensselaer Polytechnic Institute, Troy (New York).

Thrun, S. 1992a. Efficient exploration in reinforcement learning. Technical Report CMU-CS-92-102, School of Computer Science, Carnegie Mellon University, Pittsburgh (Pennsylvania).

Thrun, S. 1992b. The role of exploration in learning control with neural networks. In White, D. and Sofge, D., editors 1992b, *Handbook of Intelligent Control: Neural, Fuzzy and Adaptive Approaches*. Van Nostrand Reinhold. 527–559.

Wagner, I.; Lindenbaum, M.; and Bruckstein, A. 1997. On-line graph searching by a smell-oriented vertex process. In Koenig, S.; Blum, A.; Ishida, T.; and Korf, R., editors 1997, *Proceedings of the AAAI Workshop on On-Line Search*. 122–125.

Transposition Table Driven Work Scheduling in Distributed Search

John W. Romein, Aske Plaat and **Henri E. Bal**
john@cs.vu.nl aske@cs.vu.nl bal@cs.vu.nl
Department of Computer Science,
Vrije Universiteit,
Amsterdam, The Netherlands

Jonathan Schaeffer
jonathan@cs.ualberta.ca
Department of Computing Science,
University of Alberta,
Edmonton, Canada *

Abstract

This paper introduces a new scheduling algorithm for parallel single-agent search, *transposition table driven work scheduling*, that places the transposition table at the heart of the parallel work scheduling. The scheme results in less synchronization overhead, less processor idle time, and less redundant search effort. Measurements on a 128-processor parallel machine show that the scheme achieves nearly-optimal performance and scales well. The algorithm performs a factor of 2.0 to 13.7 times better than traditional work-stealing-based schemes.

Introduction

Heuristic search is one of the cornerstones of AI. Its applications range from logic programming to pattern recognition, from theorem proving to chess playing. For many applications, such as real-time search and any-time algorithms, achieving high performance is of great importance, both for solution quality and execution speed.

Many search algorithms recursively decompose a state into successor states. If the successor states are independent of each other, then they can be searched in parallel. A typical scenario is to allocate a portion of the search space to each processor in a parallel computer. A processor is assigned a set of states to search, performs the searches, and reports back the results. During the searches, each processor maintains a list of work yet to be completed (the *work queue*). When a processor completes all its assigned work, it can be pro-active and attempt to acquire additional work from busy processors, rather than sit idle. This approach is called *work stealing*.

Often, however, application-specific heuristics and search enhancements introduce interdependencies between states, making efficient parallelization a much more challenging task. One of the most important search enhancements is the transposition table, a large cache in which newly expanded states are stored (Slate & Atkin 1977). The table has many benefits, including preventing the expansion of previously encountered states, move ordering, and tightening the search bounds. The transposition table is particularly useful when a state can have multiple predecessors (i.e., when the search

space is a graph rather than a tree). The basic tree-based recursive node expansion strategy would expand states with multiple predecessors multiple times. A transposition table can result in time savings of more than a factor 10, depending on the application (Plaat *et al.* 1996).

Unfortunately, transposition tables are difficult to implement efficiently in parallel search programs that run on distributed-memory machines. Usually, the transposition table is partitioned among the local memories of the processors (for example, (Feldmann 1993)). Before a processor expands a node, it first does a remote lookup, by sending a message to the processor that manages the entry and then waiting for the reply (see Figure 1). This can result in sending many thousands of messages per second, introducing a large communication overhead. Moreover, each processor wastes much time waiting for the results of remote lookups. The communication overhead can be reduced (e.g., by sending fewer messages), but this usually increases the size of the search tree that needs to be explored. Extensive experimentation may be required to find the "right" amount of communication to maximize performance.

In this paper, we discuss a different approach for implementing distributed transposition tables, called *transposition table driven work scheduling* (or *transposition-driven scheduling*, TDS, for short). The idea is to integrate the parallel search algorithm and the transposition table mechanism: drive the work scheduling by the transposition table accesses. The state to be expanded is migrated to the processor on which the transposition for the state is stored (see Figure 2). This processor performs the local table lookup and stores the state in its work queue. Although this approach may seem counterintuitive, it has important advantages:

1. All communication is asynchronous (nonblocking). A processor expands a state and sends its children to their home processors, where they are entered into the transposition table and in the work queue. After sending the messages the processor continues with the next piece of work. Processors never have to wait for the results of remote lookups.

2. The network latency is hidden by overlapping communication and computation. This latency hiding is effective as long as there is enough bandwidth in the network to cope with all the asynchronous messages. With modern

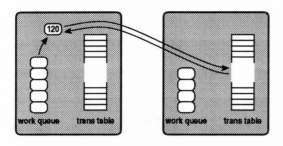

Figure 1: Work stealing with a partitioned table.

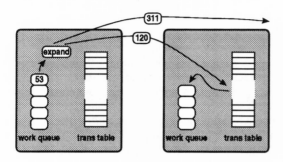

Figure 2: Transposition-driven scheduling.

high-speed networks such bandwidth usually is more than enough available.

The idea of transposition-driven scheduling can apply to a variety of search algorithms. In this paper we describe the algorithm and present performance results for single-agent search (IDA* (Korf 1985)). We have implemented TDS on a large-scale cluster computer consisting of Pentium Pro PCs connected by a Myrinet network. The performance of this algorithm is compared with the traditional work stealing scheme. Performance measurements on several applications show that TDS wins a factor of 2.0 to 13.7 at the application level and thus outperforms the work stealing scheme by a large margin. Moreover, TDS scales much better to large numbers of processors. On 128 processors, TDS is 109 to 122 times faster than on a single processor, while the work stealing algorithm obtains speedups of only 8.7 to 62.

In traditional parallel single-agent search algorithms, the algorithm revolved around the work queues, with other enhancements, such as the transposition table, added in as an afterthought. With TDS, the transposition table is at the heart of the algorithm, recognizing that the search space really is a graph, not a tree. The result is a simple parallel single-agent search algorithm that achieves high performance.

The main contribution of this paper is to show how effective the new approach is for single-agent search. We discuss in detail how TDS can be implemented efficiently and we explain why it works so well compared to work stealing. The rest of this paper is organized as follows. First, we give some background information on parallel search algorithms and related work. Then, we describe the transposition-driven scheduling approach. Next, we evaluate the performance of the new approach. The last section presents conclusions.

Background and Related Work

This paper uses IDA* (Iterative Deepening A*) as the single-agent search algorithm (Korf 1985). IDA* repeatedly performs a depth-first search, using a maximum search depth that is increased after each iteration, until a solution is found. The answer is guaranteed to be optimal, assuming that the heuristic used is admissible. We parallelize IDA* in two ways, differing in the way the search space is distributed over the processors. One uses work-stealing and the other uses TDS for distributing the work. Our analysis is facilitated by the *Multigame* environment for distributed one and two player search (Romein, Bal, & Grune 1997).

Numerous parallel single-agent search algorithms have appeared in the literature. The most popular are task distribution schemes where the search tree is partitioned among all the available processors (Rao, Kumar, & Ramesh 1987). Task distribution can be simplified by expanding the tree in a breadth-first fashion until the number of states on the search frontier matches the number of processors (Kumar & Rao 1990). This can cause load balancing problems (the search effort required for a state varies widely), implying that enhancements, such as work stealing, are necessary for high performance. A different approach is Parallel Window Search, where each processor is given a different IDA* search bound for its search (Powley & Korf 1991). All processors search the same tree, albeit to different depths. Some processors may search the tree with a search bound that is too high. Since sequential IDA* stops searching after using the right search bound, PWS results in much wasted work.

All these schemes essentially considered only the basic IDA* algorithm, without consideration of important search algorithm enhancements that can significantly reduce the search tree size (such as transposition tables).

IDA* uses less space than A*. This comes at the expense of expanding additional states. The simple formulation of IDA* does not include the detection of duplicate states (such as a cycle, or transposing into a state reached by a different sequence of state transitions). The transposition table is a convenient mechanism for using space to solve these search inefficiencies, both in single-agent (Reinefeld & Marsland 1994) and two-player (Slate & Atkin 1977) search algorithms. There are other methods, such as finite state machines (Taylor & Korf 1993), but they tend to be not as generally applicable or as powerful as transposition tables.

A transposition table (Slate & Atkin 1977) is a large (possibly set-associative) cache that stores intermediate search results. Each time a state is to be searched, the table is checked to see whether it has been searched before. If the state is in the table, then, depending on the quality of the information recorded, additional search at this node may not be needed. If the state is not in the table, then the search engine examines the successors of the state recursively, storing the search results into the transposition table.

Indexing the transposition table is usually done by hashing the state to a large number (usually 64 bits or more) called the *signature* (Zobrist 1970). The information in the table depends on the search algorithm. For the IDA* algorithm, the table contains a lower bound on the number of moves required to reach the target state. In addition, each entry may contain information used by table entry replacement algorithms, such as the effort (number of nodes searched) to compute the entry.

In parallel search programs the transposition table is typically shared among all processes, because a position analyzed by one process may later be re-searched by another process. Implementing shared transposition tables efficiently on a distributed-memory system is a challenging problem, because the table is accessed frequently. Several approaches are possible. With *partitioned* transposition tables, each processor contains part of the table. The signature is used to determine the processor that manages the table entry corresponding to a given state. To read or update a table entry, a message must be sent to that processor. Hence, most table accesses will involve communication (typically $(p-1)/p$ for p processors). Lookup operations are usually implemented using synchronous communication, where requesters wait for results. Update operations can be sent asynchronously. An advantage of partitioned tables is that the size of the table increases with the number of processors (more memory becomes available). The disadvantage is that lookup operations are expensive: the delay is at least twice the network latency (for the request and the reply messages). In theory, remote lookups could be done asynchronously, where the node expansion goes ahead speculatively before the outcome of the lookup is known. However, this approach is complicated to implement efficiently and suffers from thread-switching and speculation overhead.

Another approach is to *replicate* the transposition table entries in the local memory of each machine. This has the advantage that all lookups are local, and updates are asynchronous. The disadvantage is that updates must now be broadcast to *all* machines. Even though broadcast messages are asynchronous and multiple messages can be combined into a single physical message, the overhead of processing the broadcast messages is high and increases with the number of processors. This limits the scalability of algorithms using this technique, and replicated tables are seldom used in practice. Moreover, replicated tables have fewer entries than partitioned tables, as each entry is stored on each processor. A third approach is to let each processor maintain only a *local* transposition table, independent from the other processors (Marsland & Popowich 1985). This would eliminate communication overhead, but results in a large search overhead (different processors would search the same node). For many applications, local tables are the least efficient scheme.

Also possible are hybrid combinations of the above. For example, each processor could have a local table, but replicate the "important" parts of the table by periodically broadcasting this information to all processors (Brockington 1997). Several enhancements exist to these basic schemes. One technique for decreasing the communication overhead is to not access the distributed transposition table when searching near the leaves of the tree (Schaeffer 1989). The potential gains of finding a table entry near the root of the tree are larger because a pruned subtree rooted high in the tree can save more search effort than a small subtree rooted low in the tree. Another approach is to optimize the communication software for the transposition table operations. An example is given in (Bhoedjang, Romein, & Bal 1998), which describes software for Myrinet network interface cards that is customized for transposition tables.

Despite these optimizations, for many applications the cost of accessing and updating transposition tables is still high. In practice, this overhead can negate most of the benefits of including the tables in the search algorithm, and researchers have not stopped looking for a better solution. In the next section, we will describe an alternative approach for implementing transposition tables on distributed-memory systems: using TDS instead of work stealing. By integrating transposition table access with work scheduling, this approach makes all communication asynchronous, allowing communication and computation to be overlapped. Much other research has been done on overlapping communication and computation (von Eicken *et al.* 1992). The idea of self-scheduling work dates back to research on data flow and has been studied by several other researchers (see, for a discussion, (Culler, Schauser, & von Eicken 1993)). In the field of problem solving, there are some cases in which this idea has been applied successfully. In software verification, the parallel version of the Murphi theorem prover uses its hash function to schedule the work (Stern & Dill 1997). In game playing, a parallel generator of end-game databases (based on retrograde analysis) uses the Gödel number of states to schedule work (Bal & Allis 1995). In single agent search, a parallel version of A*, PRA*, partitions its OPEN and CLOSED lists based on the state (Evett *et al.* 1995).

Interestingly, in all three papers the data-flow-like parallelization is presented as following in a natural way from the problem at hand, and, although the authors report good speedups, they do not compare their approaches to more traditional parallelizations. The paper on PRA*, for example, does discuss differences with IDA* parallelizations, but focuses on a comparison of the *number* of node expansions, without addressing the benefit of asynchronous communication for *run times*.[1] (A factor may be that PRA* was designed for the CM-2, a SIMD machine whose architecture makes a direct comparison with recent work on parallel search difficult.)

Despite its good performance, so far no in-depth performance study between work stealing and data-flow-like approaches such as TDS has been performed for distributed search algorithms.

Transposition-Driven Work Scheduling

The problem with the traditional work stealing approach is that it is difficult to combine with shared transposition tables. To overcome this problem, we investigate a different approach, in which the work scheduling and transposition table mechanisms are integrated. The traditional approach is to move the data to where the work is located. Instead, we move the work to where the data is located. Work is sent to the processor that manages the associated transposition table entry, instead of doing a remote lookup to this processor.

---

[1] Evett et al compare PRA* against versions of IDA* that lack a transposition table. Compared to IDA* versions with a transposition table, PRA*'s node counts would have been less favorable.

```
PROCEDURE MainLoop() IS
    WHILE NOT Finished DO
        Node := GetLocalJob();
        IF Node <> NULL THEN
            Children := ExpandNode(Node);
            FOR EACH Child IN Children DO
                IF Evaluate(Child) <= Child.SearchBound THEN
                    Dest = HomeProcessor(Signature(Child));
                    SendNode(Child, Dest);
                END
            END
        ELSE
            Finished := CheckGlobalTermination();
        END
    END
END


PROCEDURE ReceiveNode(Node) IS
    Entry := TransLookup(Node);
    IF NOT Entry.Hit OR
            Entry.SearchBound <= Node.SearchBound THEN
        TransStore(Node);
        PutLocalJob(Node);
    END
END
```

Figure 3: Simplified TDS algorithm.

Once this is done, the sending processor can process additional work *without having to wait for any results to come back*. This makes all communication asynchronous, allowing the costs of communication to be hidden. Below we first describe the basic algorithm and then we look at various implementation issues.

The basic algorithm

Each state (search tree node) is assigned a *home processor*, which manages the transposition table entry for this node. The home processor is computed from the node's signature. Some of the signature bits indicate the processor number of the node's home, while some of the remaining bits are used as an index into the transposition table at that processor.

Figure 3 shows the simplified pseudo code for a transposition-driven scheduling algorithm, which is executed by every processor. The function *MainLoop* repeatedly tries to get a node from its local work queue. If the queue is not empty, it expands the node on the head of the queue by generating the children. Then it checks for each child whether the lower bound on the solution length (*Evaluate*) causes a cutoff (the lower bound exceeds the IDA* search bound). If not, the child is sent to its home processor (see also Figure 2). When the local work queue is empty, the algorithm checks whether all other processors have finished their work and no work messages are in transit. If not, it waits for new work to arrive.

The function *ReceiveNode* is invoked for each node that is received by a processor. The function first does a transposition table lookup to see whether the node has been searched before. If not, or if the node has been searched to an inadequate depth (e.g., from a previous iteration of IDA*), the node is stored into the transposition table and put into the local work queue; otherwise it is discarded because it has transposed into a state that has already been searched adequately.

The values stored in the transposition table are used differently for work stealing and TDS. With work stealing, a table entry stores a lower bound on the minimal distance to the target, derived by searching the subtree below it. Finding a transposition table hit with a suitably high table value indicates that the node has been previously searched adequately for the current iteration. With TDS, an entry contains a search *bound*. It indicates that the subtree below the node has either been previously searched adequately (as above) or is currently being searched with the given bound. Note that this latter point represents a major improvement on previous distributed transposition table mechanisms in that it prevents two processors from ever working on the same subtree concurrently.

Implementation issues

We now discuss some implementation issues of this basic algorithm. An important property in our TDS implementation of IDA* is that a child node does not report its search result to its parent. As soon as a node has forked off new work for its children, work on the node itself has completed. In some cases (for example, for two-agent search) the results of a child should be propagated to its parent. This complicates the algorithm since it requires parent nodes to leave state information behind, and may result in some work in progress having to be aborted (for example, when an alpha-beta cutoff occurs). This is the subject of ongoing research.

When no results are propagated to the parent, the TDS algorithm needs a separate mechanism to detect global termination. TDS synchronizes after each IDA* iteration, and starts a new iteration if the current iteration did not solve the problem. One of the many distributed termination detection algorithms can be used. We use the time count algorithm from (Mattern 1987). Since new iterations are started infrequently, the overhead for termination detection is negligible.

Another issue concerns the search order. It is desirable to do the parallel search in a depth-first way as much as possible, because breadth-first search will quickly run out of memory for intermediate nodes. Depth-first behavior could be achieved using priority queues, by giving work on the left-hand side of the search tree a higher priority than that on the right-hand side of the tree. However, manipulating priority queues is expensive. Instead, we implement each local work queue as a stack, at the possible expense of a larger working set. On one processor, a stack corresponds to pure depth-first search.

An interesting trade-off is when and where to invoke the node evaluation function. One option is to do the evaluation on the processor that creates a piece of work, and migrate the work to its home processor only if the evaluation did not cause a cutoff. Another option is to migrate the work immediately to its home processor, look it up in the transposition table, and then call the evaluation function only if the lookup did not cause a cutoff. The first approach will migrate less work but will always invoke the evaluation function, even if it has been searched before (on the home pro-

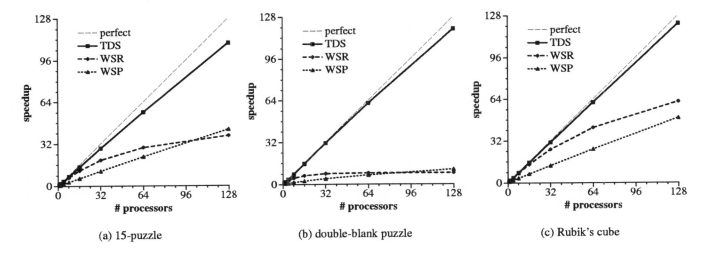

| (a) 15-puzzle | (b) double-blank puzzle | (c) Rubik's cube |

Figure 4: Average application speedups.

cessor). Whichever is more efficient depends on the relative costs for migrating and evaluating nodes. On our system, the first approach performs the best for most applications.

An important optimization performed by our implementation is message combining. To decrease the overhead per migrated state, several states that have the same source and the same destination processors are combined into one physical message. Each processor maintains a message buffer for every other processor. A message buffer is transmitted when it is full, or when the sending processor has no work to do (typically during the start and the end of each iteration, when there is little work).

Discussion

Transposition-driven scheduling has five advantages:

1. All transposition table accesses are local.

2. All communication is done asynchronously; processors do not wait for messages. As a result, the algorithm scales well to large numbers of processors. The total bandwidth requirements increase approximately linearly with the number of processors.

3. No duplicate searches are performed. With work stealing, multiple processors sometimes concurrently search a transposition because the transposition table update occurs *after* the subtree below it was searched. With the new scheme this cannot occur; all attempts to search a given subtree must go through the same home processor. Since it has a record of all completed and in-progress work (in the transposition table), it will not allow redundant effort.[2]

4. TDS produces more stable execution times for trees with many transpositions than the work stealing algorithm.

5. No separate load balancing scheme is needed. Previous algorithms require work stealing or some other mechanism to balance the work load. Load balancing in TDS is done implicitly, using the hash function. Most hash functions are uniformly distributed, causing the load to be distributed evenly over the machines. This works well as long as all processors are of the same speed. If this is not the case, then the stacks of the slow processors will grow and may exhaust memory. A flow control scheme can be added to keep processors from sending states too frequently. In our experiments, we have not found the need to implement such a mechanism.

Measurements

We compare the performance of TDS with that of work stealing, both with partitioned (WSP) and replicated (WSR) transposition tables. Our test suite consists of three games: the *15-puzzle*, the *double-blank puzzle*, and *Rubik's cube*. The double-blank puzzle is a modification to the 15-puzzle, where we removed the tile labeled '15'. By having two blanks, we create a game with many transpositions, because two consecutive moves involving both blanks can usually be interchanged.

The 15-puzzle evaluation function includes the Manhattan distance, linear conflict heuristic (Hansson, Mayer, & Yung 1992), last move heuristic (Korf & Taylor 1996), and corner conflict heuristic (Korf & Taylor 1996). The double-blank puzzle uses the same evaluation function, adapted for two blanks. The Rubik's cube evaluation is done using pattern databases (Korf 1997), one each for corners and edges.

The test positions used for the 15-puzzle are nine of the hardest positions known (Gasser 1995).[3] To avoid long

---

[2]There is one situation in which duplicate work will get done. If the transposition table is too small for the given search, some table entries will get overwritten. This loss of information can result in previously completed searches being repeated. This is a fundamental problem with fixed-size transposition tables.

[3]Most parallel 15-puzzle programs are benchmarked on the 100 test problems in (Korf 1985). Unfortunately, using a sophisticated lower bound and a fast processor means that many of these test problems are solved sequentially in a few seconds. Hence, a more challenging test suite is needed.

sequential searches, we stopped searching after a 74-ply search iteration. For the double-blank puzzle, we used the same positions with the '15'-tile removed, limited to a 66-ply search depth. Rubik's cube was tested using 5 random problems. Since a random problem requires weeks of CPU time to solve, we limited the search depth to 17. The WSP and WSR programs have been tuned to avoid remote table accesses for nodes near the leaves whenever that increases performance.

We studied the performance of each of the algorithms on a cluster of 128 Pentium Pros running at 200 MHz. Each machine has 128 Megabytes of RAM. For the 15-puzzle and the double-blank puzzle, we use 2^{22} transposition table entries per machine. For Rubik's cube we use 2^{21} entries, to leave room for pattern databases. The machines are connected through Myrinet (Boden *et al.* 1995), a 1.2 Gigabit/second switching network. Each network interface board contains a programmable network processor. WSP runs customized software on the network coprocessor to speed up remote transposition table accesses (Bhoedjang, Romein, & Bal 1998). WSR and TDS use generic network software (Bhoedjang, Rühl, & Bal 1998).

Figure 4 shows speedups with respect to TDS search on a single processor, which is virtually as fast as sequential search. TDS outperforms WSP and WSR by a factor 2.0 to 13.7 on 128 processors. TDS scales almost linearly.

Even on 128 processors, TDS only uses a small fraction of the available Myrinet bandwidth, which is about 60 MByte/s per link between user processes. The 15-puzzle requires 2.5 MByte/s, the double-blank puzzle 1.7 MByte/s, and Rubik's cube 0.38 MByte/s. Each piece of work is encoded in 32–68 bytes. For all games we combine up to 64 pieces of work into one message. The communication overhead for distributed termination detection (TDS synchronizes after each iteration) is well below 0.1% of the total communication overhead.

WSP suffers from high lookup latencies. Even with the customized network firmware, a remote lookup takes 32.5 μs. The double-blank puzzle, which does 24,000 remote lookups per second per processor, spends 78% of the time waiting for lookup replies. WSR spends most of its time handling incoming broadcast messages. For the double-blank puzzle, each processor receives and handles 11 MByte/s (680,000 updates) from all other processors. Although hard to measure exactly, each processor spends about 75–80% of the time handling broadcast messages.

	15-puzzle		double-blank puzzle		Rubik's cube	
	C_{ovh}	S_{ovh}	C_{ovh}	S_{ovh}	C_{ovh}	S_{ovh}
TDS	1.30	0.90	1.22	0.88	1.05	1.00
WSP	2.71	1.10	6.05	1.86	2.39	1.08
WSR	3.03	1.11	6.45	2.29	1.89	1.09

Table 1: Communication overheads (C_{ovh}) and search overheads (S_{ovh}) on 128 processors.

Imperfect speedups are caused by communication and search overhead. Communication overhead is due to mes-

sage creation, sending, receiving, and handling. Search overhead is the number of nodes searched during parallel search divided by the number of a sequential search. Load imbalance turned out to be negligible; the processor that does the most work, does typically less than 1% more work than the processor that does the least work.

Table 1 lists the communication and search overheads for the applications, relative to a sequential run. The overheads explain the differences in speedup. For the 15-puzzle, for example, TDS has a total overhead of $1.30 \times 0.90 = 1.17$ and WSP has an overhead of $2.71 \times 1.10 = 2.98$. The difference between the overheads is $2.98/1.17 = 2.55$, which is about the same as the difference in speedups (see Figure 4(a)).

On a large number of processors, TDS usually searches fewer nodes than on a single processor, because of the larger table. This explains the search overheads smaller than 1. WSP also benefits from this behavior, but still has search overheads greater than 1. For the 15-puzzle, this can be explained by the fact that remote lookups are skipped near the leaves since otherwise communication overhead would be too large. For the double-blank puzzle, which has many transpositions, the main reason is that transpositions may be searched by multiple processors concurrently, because a table update is done *after* the search of a node completes. This phenomenon does not occur with TDS, since the table update is done *before* the node is searched.

The speedups through 64-processors for the 15-puzzle are similar to those reported by others (e.g., (Cook & Varnell 1997) reports 58.90-fold speedups). However, previous work has only looked at parallelizing the basic IDA* algorithm, usually using the 15-puzzle with Manhattan distance as the test domain. The state of the art has progressed significantly. For the 15-puzzle, the linear conflicts heuristic reduces tree size by roughly a factor of 10, and transposition tables reduce tree size by an additional factor of 2.5. These reductions result in a less well balanced search tree, increasing the difficulty of achieving good parallel performance. Still, our performance is comparable to the results in (Cook & Varnell 1997). This is a strong result, given that the search trees are *at least* 25-fold smaller (and that does not include the benefits from the last move and corner conflict heuristics).

Conclusion

Efficient parallelization of search algorithms that use transposition tables is a challenging task, due to communication overhead and search overhead. We have described a new approach, called transposition-driven scheduling (TDS), that integrates work scheduling with the transposition table. TDS makes all communication asynchronous, overlaps communication with computation, and reduces search overhead.

We performed a detailed comparison of TDS to the conventional work stealing approach on a large-scale parallel system. TDS performs significantly better, especially for large numbers of processors. On 128 processors, TDS achieves a speedup between 109 and 122, where traditional work-stealing algorithms achieve speedups between 8.7 and 62. TDS scales well to large numbers of processors, because it effectively reduces both search overhead *and* communication overhead.

TDS represents a shift in the way one views a search algorithm. The traditional view of single-agent search is that IDA* is at the heart of the implementation, and performance enhancements, such as a transposition tables, are added in afterwards. This approach makes it hard to achieve good parallel performance when one wants to compare to the best known sequential algorithm. With TDS, the transposition table becomes the heart of the algorithm, and performance improves significantly.

Acknowledgments

We thank Andreas Junghanns, Dick Grune, and the anonymous referees for their valuable comments on earlier versions of this paper.

References

Bal, H. E., and Allis, L. V. 1995. Parallel Retrograde Analysis on a Distributed System. In *Supercomputing*.

Bhoedjang, R. A. F.; Romein, J. W.; and Bal, H. E. 1998. Optimizing Distributed Data Structures Using Application-Specific Network Interface Software. In *International Conference on Parallel Processing*, 485–492.

Bhoedjang, R. A. F.; Rühl, T.; and Bal, H. E. 1998. Efficient Multicast On Myrinet Using Link-Level Flow Control. In *International Conference on Parallel Processing*, 381–390.

Boden, N. J.; Cohen, D.; Felderman, R. E.; Kulawik, A. E.; Seitz, C. L.; Seizovic, J. N.; and Su, W. 1995. Myrinet: A Gigabit-per-second Local Area Network. *IEEE Micro* 15(1):29–36.

Brockington, M. G. 1997. *Asynchronous Parallel Game-Tree Search*. Ph.D. Dissertation, University of Alberta, Edmonton, Alberta, Canada.

Cook, D., and Varnell, R. 1997. Maximizing the Benefits of Parallel Search Using Machine Learning. In *AAAI National Conference*, 559–564.

Culler, D. E.; Schauser, K. E.; and von Eicken, T. 1993. Two Fundamental Limits on Dataflow Multiprocessing. In *Proceedings of the IFIP WG 10.3 Working Conference on Architectures and Compilation Techniques for Fine and Medium Grain Parallelism*. Orlando, FL: North-Holland.

Evett, M.; Hendler, J.; Mahanti, A.; and Nau, D. 1995. PRA*: Massively Parallel Heuristic Search. *Journal of Parallel and Distributed Computing* 25:133–143.

Feldmann, R. 1993. *Game Tree Search on Massively Parallel Systems*. Ph.D. Dissertation, University of Paderborn.

Gasser, R. 1995. *Harnessing Computational Resources for Efficient Exhaustive Search*. Ph.D. Dissertation, ETH Zürich, Switzerland.

Hansson, O.; Mayer, A.; and Yung, M. 1992. Criticizing Solutions to Relaxed Models yields Powerful Admissible Heuristics. *Information Sciences* 63(3):207–227.

Korf, R. E., and Taylor, L. A. 1996. Finding Optimal Solutions to the Twenty-Four Puzzle. In *AAAI National Conference*, 1202–1207.

Korf, R. E. 1985. Depth-first Iterative Deepening: an Optimal Admissible Tree Search. *Artificial Intelligence* 27(1):97–109.

Korf, R. E. 1997. Finding Optimal Solutions to Rubik's Cube Using Pattern Databases. In *AAAI National Conference*, 700–705.

Kumar, V., and Rao, V. 1990. Scalable Parallel Formulations of Depth-first Search. In Kumar, V.; Gopalakrishnan, P.; and Kanal, L., eds., *Parallel Algorithms for Machine Intelligence and Vision*, 1–42. Springer-Verlag.

Marsland, T. A., and Popowich, F. 1985. Parallel Game-Tree Search. *IEEE Transactions on Pattern Analysis and Machine Intelligence* 7(4):442–452.

Mattern, F. 1987. Algorithms for Distributed Termination Detection. *Distributed Computing* 2:161–175.

Plaat, A.; Schaeffer, J.; Pijls, W.; and de Bruin, A. 1996. Exploiting Graph Properties of Game Trees. *AAAI National Conference* 1:234–239.

Powley, C., and Korf, R. 1991. Single-Agent Parallel Window Search. *IEEE Transactions on Pattern Analysis and Machine Intelligence* 3(5):466–477.

Rao, V.; Kumar, V.; and Ramesh, K. 1987. A Parallel Implementation of Iterative-Deepening-A*. In *AAAI National Conference*, 178–182.

Reinefeld, A., and Marsland, T. A. 1994. Enhanced Iterative-Deepening Search. *IEEE Transactions on Pattern Analysis and Machine Intelligence* 16(7):701–710.

Romein, J. W.; Bal, H. E.; and Grune, D. 1997. An Application Domain Specific Language for Describing Board Games. In *Parallel and Distributed Processing Techniques and Applications*, volume I, 305–314. Las Vegas, NV: CSREA.

Schaeffer, J. 1989. Distributed Game-Tree Searching. *Journal of Parallel and Distributed Computing* 6:90–114.

Slate, D. J., and Atkin, L. R. 1977. CHESS 4.5 — The Northwestern University Chess Program. In Frey, P. W., ed., *Chess Skill in Man and Machine*. Springer-Verlag. 82–118.

Stern, U., and Dill, D. L. 1997. Parallelizing the Murphi Verifier. In *Ninth International Conference on Computer Aided Verification*, 256–267.

Taylor, L., and Korf, R. 1993. Pruning Duplicate Nodes in Depth-First Search. In *AAAI National Conference*, 756–761.

von Eicken, T.; Culler, D. E.; Goldstein, S.; and Schausser, K. E. 1992. Active Messages: a Mechanism for Integrated Communication and Computation. In *International Symposium on Computer Architecture*.

Zobrist, A. L. 1970. A New Hashing Method with Application for Game Playing. Technical Report 88, Computer Science Department, University of Wisconsin, Madison. Reprinted in: *ICCA Journal*, 13(2):69–73, 1990.

Tractable Reasoning

A sequential reversible belief revision method based on polynomials

Salem Benferhat and **Didier Dubois**
IRIT, université Paul Sabatier.
118 route de Narbonne. 31062 Toulouse
dubois@irit.fr and benferha@irit.fr

Odile Papini
LIM, université de la Méditerranée.
163 av. de Luminy, 13288 Marseille, cedex 09
papini@lim.univ-mrs.fr

Abstract

This paper deals with iterated belief change and proposes a drastic revision rule that modifies a plausibility ordering of interpretations in such a way that any world where the input observartion holds is more plausible that any world where it does not. This change rule makes sense in a dynamic context where observations are received, and the newer observations are considered more plausible than older ones. It is shown how to encode an epistemic state using polynomials equipped with the lexicographical ordering. This encoding makes it very easy to implement and iterate the revision rule using simple operations on these polynomials. Moreover, polynomials allow to keep track of the sequence of observations. Lastly, it is shown how to efficiently compute the revision rule at the syntactical level, when the epistemic state is concisely represented by a prioritized belief base. Our revision rule is the most drastic one can think of, in accordance with Darwiche and Pearl's principles, and thus contrasts with the minimal change rule called natural belief revision.

Introduction

One of the most fascinating problems in reasoning about knowledge is the one of belief change, and more specifically the one of iterated belief change. The most noticeable result obtained in the eighties by the AGM school is that rational revision steps require an ordering on interpretations. This ordering represents an epistemic state which distinguishes between interpretations which are more or less plausible. In the last ten years, after noticing that AGM revision could not be iterated, because it did not affect the underlying plausibility ordering, the focus point has been the construction of a rational approach to iterated belief revision. Modifying a plausibility ordering upon the arrival of a proposition μ that should be true can actually be done in several ways, called transmutations by (Williams 1994). In order to accept μ in the new epistemic state, the minimal requirement is that there are some models of μ which become more plausible than its countermodels. In natural revision, proposed by Boutilier (Boutilier 1993) but

already pointed out by Spohn (Spohn 1988), only the best models of μ are made the most plausible interpretations. Alternative plausibility ordering revision rules have been proposed by (Williams 1994), based on Spohn's ordinal conditional functions, where the plausibility of all models of μ is affected. At the opposite of Boutilier's natural revision, another possible change rule, also evoked by Spohn (Spohn 1988), where upon receiving μ, *each* model of μ becomes more plausible than *all* countermodels of μ. This rule respects Darwiche and Pearl axioms (Darwiche & Pearl 1997) since it does not affect the relative ranks of models of μ, nor the relative countermodels of μ, and if a model of μ is more plausible than a countermodel, it remains so. Such a belief change rule makes sense in a dynamic context where observations are received, and the newer observations are considered more plausible than older ones. In this context, the meaning of the input observation suggests that at the time t when the observation is received, the real situation is necessarily one of the models of μ, so that μ should remain accepted whatever additional assumption is made at time t. This paper investigates this type of revision process from a semantic and syntactic point of view. It is shown that at the semantic level, the iterated belief change is made very easy if the plausibility orderings are encoded by means of lexicographical ordering of polynomials. The dual change rule, where older observations take precedence over newly acquired information, is studied and encoded likewise. Lastly, assuming that an epistemic state is represented by a prioritized set of formulas, it is shown how to perform the belief revision rule at the syntactical level, in full agreement with plausibility ordering change studied here.

Representation of epistemic states

Let $\mathcal{W}$ be the set of interpretations of propositional calculus, denoted $\mathcal{L}_{\mathcal{PC}}$. An epistemic state, denoted Ψ, encoding a set of beliefs about the real world (based on the available information), is represented by a total pre-order on $\mathcal{W}$, denoted $\leq_\Psi$. $\omega_1 \leq_\Psi \omega_2$ (resp. $\omega_1 <_\Psi \omega_2$) means that ω_1 is preferred to (strictly preferred to) ω_2. $Bel(\Psi)$ denotes a belief set associated to $\mathcal{W}$, representing agent's current beliefs, obtained

from $\leq_\Psi$. It is a propositional formula [1] whose models are the most preferred ones w.r.t. $\leq_\Psi$, namely:
$$\mathrm{Mod}(Bel(\Psi)) = \{\omega : \nexists \omega' \text{ such that } \omega' <_\Psi \omega\}.$$

Total pre-orders have been represented according to different points of view: binary relations, kappa-rankings which associate to each world an ordinal as in (Spohn 1988), (Williams 1994), possibility distributions (Dubois & Prade 1997) which associate to each world a degree between [0,1], vectors, etc. Changing a binary relation can't be easily expressed, it requires the use of another binary relation. Possibility distributions and kappa-rankings need to verify a so-called normalization condition (the existence of a world having a rank 0 in kappa-distributions, or degree 1 in possibility distributions), after each revision operation, which makes the process more complex. Moreover, these two representations in general are not reversible, namely there is no operations to reinstall the old ranking. Vectors can't be used because after shift operations their length grows. They involve difficulties for computation and comparison.

In this paper, we propose a suitable representation of $\leq_\Psi$ based on polynomials (Papini 1999), which allow to easy formalize the change of $\leq_\Psi$ according to the incoming observation. Each interpretation is assigned a weight, defined as a polynomial. Polynomials allow to keep track of the sequence of observations, they represent the history of the observations. They easily provide the models or the countermodels of successive observations. They allow to come back to previous orders, which is not possible with the other representations and they are tailored to representing the right and left shifts which formalize the change of total pre-orders in revision operations.

Weighting

Let B be the set $\{0, 1\}$, and $B[x]$, the set of polynomials which coefficients belong to $\{0, 1\}$. Polynomials $p(x)$ in $B[x]$ have the form: $p(x) = \sum_{k=1}^{n} p_{-k} \, x^{-k} + \sum_{i=0}^{m} p_i \, x^i$. The use of negative and positive indices are necessarily to faciliting shifting steps. A right shift is simply obtained with a multiplication by x, while a left shift is obtained with a multiplication by x^{-1}. As we will see in next sections, these shift operations are the basis for the computing of the new weights in the revision process. The following definition introduces the lexicographical ordering used to compare polynomials.

Definition 1 *Let $p(x)$, $p'(x) \in B[x]$, $p(x) <_B p'(x)$ iff $\exists i \in \mathbb{Z}$ such that $\forall j, \; j < i$,$p_j = p'_j$ and $p_i < p'_i$.*

Definition 2 *A weighting distribution is a function which associates to each epistemic state Ψ and ω an interpretation, a polynomial of $B[x]$ denoted by $p^\omega(\Psi)(x)$.*

The smaller is $p^\omega(\Psi)(x)$, w.r.t $<_B$ the more plausible is ω. When the initial epistemic state Ψ has no speci-

[1]As Katsuno and Mendelzon (Katsuno & Mendelzon 1991), we use a propositional formula instead of a belief set which is a deductively closed set of formulas.

fied ranking on $\mathcal{W}$, but only the belief set $Bel(\Psi)$, the weighting distribution is defined as follows:
$\forall \omega \in \mathcal{W}$, if $\omega \in Mod(Bel(\Psi))$ then $p_0 = 0$ else $p_0 = 1$. Namely, the weight of the interpretations which are countermodels of $Bel(\Psi)$ is supposed to be lower than the weight of the interpretations which are models of $Bel(\Psi)$.

Remark 1 *If the initial epistemic state has a ranking represented by ordinals, we encode this ranking with polynomials using binary decomposition of ordinals.*

Equivalences

Iterated revision requires a carefully definition of the equivalence between two epistemic states, more formally:

Definition 3 *Let Ψ and Φ be two epistemic states. Ψ and Φ are weakly equivalent, denoted $\Psi \equiv_w \Phi$, iff $Bel(\Psi) \equiv Bel(\Phi)$, and Ψ and Φ are strongly equivalent, denoted $\Psi \equiv_s \Phi$, iff $\Psi \equiv_w \Phi$ and $\forall \omega \in \mathcal{W}$, $p^\omega(\Psi)(x) = p^\omega(\Phi)(x)$.*

The weak equivalence expresses that two beliefs sets are logically equivalent. The strong equivalence expresses that two epistemic states have equivalent associated beliefs sets and also have same weighting on $\mathcal{W}$. One of the problems arising with revision when epistemic states only consist in belief sets is that two equivalent epistemic states are revised in the same way. The definition of a weighting on $\mathcal{W}$ allows for the introduction of two kinds of equivalences, that makes it possible to solve this problem. Two weakly equivalent epistemic states shall be differently revised, on the other hand two strongly equivalent epistemic states shall be equally revised. The notion of strong equivalence is analogous to Darwiche and Pearl's equality between epistemic states (Darwiche & Pearl 1997) and to semantic equivalence in possibility logic (Dubois & Prade 1992).

Note that the function that assigns to each epistemic state Ψ the total pre-order on $\mathcal{W}$, denoted $\leq_\Psi$, defined by: $\omega_1 \leq_\Psi \omega_2$ iff $p^{\omega_1}(\Psi)(x) \leq_B p^{\omega_2}(\Psi)(x)$ is a faithful assignment, (Katsuno & Mendelzon 1991), with respect to $Bel(\Psi)$. Namely it satisfies:
(1) If $\omega_1, \omega_2 \models Bel(\Psi)$ then $\omega_1 =_\Psi \omega_2$;
(2) if $\omega_1 \models Bel(\Psi)$ and $\omega_2 \not\models Bel(\Psi)$ then $\omega_1 <_\Psi \omega_2$;
(3) $\Psi \equiv_s \Phi$ iff $\leq_\Psi = \leq_\Phi$.

In (Katsuno & Mendelzon 1991) Condition (3) only requires the logical equivalence.

Preferring newer information

The revision operation, first defined here, prefers the last item of information. The general philosophy here is that an old assertion is less reliable than a new one. We believe that in many cases it seems reasonable to decrease the confidence that one has in an item of information, as time goes by. However, this revision operation attempts to satisfy as many previous observations as possible. That is, an old observation persists until it becomes contradictory with a more recent one. The revision operation uses the history of the sequence of previous observations to perform revision.

Definition 4 *The revision of an epistemic state Ψ by a formula $\mu \in \mathcal{L}_{\mathcal{PC}}$, leads to a new epistemic state denoted $\Psi \circ_\triangleright \mu$. The modification of the weighting after revision by μ is:*

if $\omega \in Mod(\mu)$ then $p^\omega(\Psi \circ_\triangleright \mu)(x) = xp^\omega(\Psi)(x)$, otherwise $p^\omega(\Psi \circ_\triangleright \mu)(x) = xp^\omega(\Psi)(x) + 1$

The weights corresponding to the models of μ are right shifted and the weights corresponding to the counter-models of μ are right shifted and translated by 1.

Remark 2 *If $\mu = \bot$ then $Mod(Bel(\Psi \circ_\triangleright \mu)) = Mod(\Psi)$ and the total pre-order on $\mathcal{W}$ is preserved.*

Example 1 *Let Ψ be an epistemic state with a total pre-order $\leq_\Psi$ such that, $\omega_4 =_\Psi \omega_3 =_\Psi \omega_2 <_\Psi \omega_1$ and with associated belief set $Bel(\Psi) = a \vee b$. Let $\mu = \neg b$ and $\alpha = \neg a$ be propositional formulas. Let denote $r(x) = p^\omega(\Psi)(x)$, $q(x) = p^\omega(\Psi \circ_\triangleright \mu)(x)$ and $p(x) = p^\omega((\Psi \circ_\triangleright \mu) \circ_\triangleright \alpha)(x)$. The following array shows the changes of the total pre-order after a revision first by μ then by α:*

$\mathcal{W}$	a	b	$r(x)$	r_0	$q(x)$	$q_0 q_1$	$p(x)$	$p_0 p_1 p_2$
ω_1	0	0	1	1	x	01	x^2	001
ω_2	0	1	0	0	1	10	x	010
ω_3	1	0	0	0	0	00	1	100
ω_4	1	1	0	0	1	10	$1 + x$	110

In the above example, the columns $p_0 p_1 p_2$ give the total pre-order corresponding to the current epistemic state $(\Psi \circ_\triangleright \mu) \circ_\triangleright \alpha$, the columns $p_1 p_2$ give the total pre-order corresponding to the previous epistemic state $\Psi \circ_\triangleright \mu$ and the columns of p_2 gives the total pre-order corresponding to the initial epistemic state Ψ. The values of coefficients of the polynomials show whether the interpretation satisfies (value 0) or not (value 1) the successive observations. For example, ω_2 satisfies α and $Bel(\Psi)$ but does not satisfy μ. Hence, the use of polynomials allows to come back to previous epistemic states. Indeed, let Ψ' be the actual epistemic state obtained after revising Ψ by μ. Then, μ can be recovered from Ψ' by defining models of μ in the following way: $Mod(\mu) = \{\omega : p^\omega(\Psi') <_B 1\}$, and the weighting distribution associated to the previous epistemic state Ψ can be recovered from Ψ' as follows: $p^\omega(\Psi) = x^{-1} p^\omega(\Psi')$ if $p^\omega(\Psi') <_B 1$ otherwise $p^\omega(\Psi) = x^{-1}(p^\omega(\Psi') - 1)$.

In our framework, the AGM postulates for epistemic states are rephrased as follows (Alchourron, Gärdenfors, & Makinson 1985), (Katsuno & Mendelzon 1991), (Papini & Rauzy 1995):

Modified AGM postulates for epistemic states
- $(R1\triangleright)$ $Bel(\Psi \circ_\triangleright \mu) \models \mu$.
- $(R2\triangleright)$ If $Bel(\Psi) \wedge \mu$ is satisfiable, then $\Psi \circ_\triangleright \mu \equiv_w \Psi \wedge \mu$.
- $(R3\triangleright)$ If μ is satisfiable, then so is $Bel(\Psi \circ_\triangleright \mu)$.
- $(R4\triangleright)$ If $\Psi_1 \equiv_s \Psi_2$ and $\mu_1 \equiv \mu_2$ then, $\Psi_1 \circ_\triangleright \mu_1 \equiv_s \Psi_2 \circ_\triangleright \mu_2$.
- $(R5\triangleright)$ $Bel(\Psi \circ_\triangleright \mu) \wedge \phi \models Bel(\Psi \circ_\triangleright (\mu \wedge \phi))$.
- $(R6\triangleright)$ If $Bel(\Psi \circ_\triangleright \mu) \wedge \phi$ is satisfiable, then $Bel(\Psi \circ_\triangleright (\mu \wedge \phi)) \models Bel(\Psi \circ_\triangleright \mu) \wedge \phi$.

$(R1\triangleright)$, $(R2\triangleright)$, $(R3\triangleright)$, $(R5\triangleright)$ and $(R6\triangleright)$ are the straightforward translation of the corresponding original AGM postulates. For $(R5\triangleright)$ and $(R6\triangleright)$ we assume that $\not\models \neg\mu$. In contrast, $(R4\triangleright)$ is a weaker version of original AGM postulate; it requires that the epistemic states be strongly equivalent in order to be equally revised.

Theorem 1 *Let Ψ be an epistemic state, μ be a formula of $\mathcal{L}_{\mathcal{PC}}$ and let $\leq_\Psi$ be the total pre-order on $\mathcal{W}$ defined as in proposition 1. Then, the operator $\circ_\triangleright$ verifies the postulates $(R1) - (R6)$ and $Mod(Bel(\Psi \circ_\triangleright \mu)) = min(Mod(\mu), \leq_\Psi)$.* [2]

Darwiche and Pearl (Darwiche & Pearl 1997) formulated postulates which constrain the relationships between two successive epistemic states, the straightforward translation of the corresponding original DP postulates in our framework, are the following:

DP postulates for iterated revision
- $(C1\triangleright)$ If $\alpha \models \mu$ then $(\Psi \circ_\triangleright \mu) \circ_\triangleright \alpha \equiv_w \Psi \circ_\triangleright \alpha$.
- $(C2\triangleright)$ If $\alpha \models \neg\mu$ then $(\Psi \circ_\triangleright \mu) \circ_\triangleright \alpha \equiv_w \Psi \circ_\triangleright \alpha$.
- $(C3\triangleright)$ If $Bel(\Psi \circ_\triangleright \alpha) \models \mu$ then $Bel((\Psi \circ_\triangleright \mu) \circ_\triangleright \alpha) \models \mu$.
- $(C4\triangleright)$ If $Bel(\Psi \circ_\triangleright \alpha) \not\models \neg\mu$ then $Bel((\Psi \circ_\triangleright \mu) \circ_\triangleright \alpha) \not\models \neg\mu$.

The postulates $(C1\triangleright)$, $(C2\triangleright)$, $(C3\triangleright)$ and $(C4\triangleright)$ in relationship with total pre-orders associated to two successive epistemic states are the following:
- $(CR1\triangleright)$ If $\omega_1 \models \mu$ and $\omega_2 \models \mu$
  then $\omega_1 \leq_\Psi \omega_2$ iff $\omega_1 \leq_{\Psi \circ_\triangleright \mu} \omega_2$.
- $(CR2\triangleright)$ If $\omega_1 \models \neg\mu$ and $\omega_2 \models \neg\mu$
  then $\omega_1 \leq_\Psi \omega_2$ iff $\omega_1 \leq_{\Psi \circ_\triangleright \mu} \omega_2$.
- $(CR3\triangleright)$ If $\omega_1 \models \mu$ and $\omega_2 \models \neg\mu$
  then $\omega_1 <_\Psi \omega_2$ only if $\omega_1 <_{\Psi \circ_\triangleright \mu} \omega_2$.
- $(CR4\triangleright)$ If $\omega_1 \models \mu$ and $\omega_2 \models \neg\mu$
  then $\omega_1 \leq_\Psi \omega_2$ only if $\omega_1 \leq_{\Psi \circ_\triangleright \mu} \omega_2$.

Theorem 2 *The operator $\circ_\triangleright$ verifies $(C1\triangleright) - (C4\triangleright)$ and its corresponding faithful assignment verifies $(CR1\triangleright) - (CR4\triangleright)$.*

The defined $\circ_\triangleright$ revision operation preserves the relative ordering between the models of the added formula. Furthermore, the relative ordering between the countermodels of the added formula is preserved, and the ordering between models and countermodels of the added formula does not change. Moreover, this operation provides a stronger constraint because each model of the added formula is preferred to all its countermodels.

Preferring oldest information

Preferring the last item of information is not always desirable, it may, in certain cases, lead to unacceptable conclusions. We define a new revision operation which is a dual revision operation of the one previously introduced. The general philosophy here is that a new observation is less reliable than an old one. We increase the confidence that one has in an item of information, as time goes by. However, this revision operation attempt to satisfy as many new observations as possible.

---

[2] $min(Mod(\mu), \leq_\Psi)$ contains all models that are minimal in $Mod(\mu)$ according to the total pre-order $\leq_\Psi$.

Definition 5 *The revision of Ψ by a formula μ, leads to a new epistemic state denoted $\Psi \circ_{\lhd} \mu$. The modification of the weighting after revision by μ is:*

if $\omega \in Mod(\mu)$ then $p^{\omega}(\Psi \circ_{\lhd} \mu)(x) = x^{-1} p^{\omega}(\Psi)(x)$,
otherwise $p^{\omega}(\Psi \circ_{\lhd} \mu)(x) = x^{-1} p^{\omega}(\Psi)(x) + 1$

This is different from the previous revision operation, since we now use left shifts (i. e. multiplication by x^{-1}).

Theorem 3 *The operator $\circ_{\lhd}$ verifies the postulates (R2), (R4) and (R5).*

The postulates (R1), (R3) and (R6)[3] are not satisfied, because the new observation is not preferred in the next epistemic state. As older observations are preferred in the next epistemic state, the part of $Bel(\Psi)$ and the part of μ are inverted and hence new postulates can be formulated :

Proposition 1 *The operator $\circ_{\lhd}$ verifies:*

(R1 b) $Bel(\Psi \circ_{\lhd} \mu) \models Bel(\Psi)$.
(R2 b) If $Bel(\Psi) \wedge \mu$ is not satisfiable, then $\Psi \circ_{\lhd} \mu \equiv_w \Psi$.
(R3 b) $Bel(\Psi)$ is satisfiable iff $Bel(\Psi \circ_{\lhd} \mu)$ is satisfiable.

Concerning iterated revision the following result holds:

Proposition 2 *The operator $\circ_{\lhd}$ verifies (C3) and (C4), and its corresponding faithful assignment verifies (CR1), (CR2), (CR3) and (CR4).*

Although the last observations are not preferred in the next epistemic state, the postulates (C3) and (C4) are satisfied. In contrast, the postulate (C1) does not hold when $Bel(\Psi) \wedge \mu$ is satisfiable and $Bel(\Psi) \wedge \alpha$ is not satisfiable because $(\Psi \circ_{\lhd} \mu) \circ_{\lhd} \alpha \equiv_w \Psi \wedge \mu$ and $\Psi \circ_{\lhd} \alpha \equiv_w \Psi$. (C2) does not hold when $Bel(\Psi) \wedge \mu$ is satisfiable and $Bel(\Psi) \wedge \alpha$ is satisfiable because $(\Psi \circ_{\lhd} \mu) \circ_{\lhd} \alpha \equiv_w \Psi \wedge \mu$ and $\Psi \circ_{\lhd} \alpha \equiv_w \Psi \wedge \alpha$. (CR1) − (CR4) are satisfied since the defined $\circ_{\lhd}$ revision operation preserves the relative ordering between the models of the added formula.

Revision using $\circ_{\rhd}$ and $\circ_{\lhd}$ together

In certain situations it seems reasonable to prefer a new observation and in others, the oldest observation has to be preferred. In order to use the two operations together, the definition of the weights associated to countermodels of μ are slightly modified in the following way: $p^{\omega}(\Psi \circ_{\rhd} \mu)(x) = x p^{\omega}(\Psi)(x) + x^{MIN}$, and $p^{\omega}(\Psi \circ_{\lhd} \mu)(x) = x^{-1} p^{\omega}(\Psi)(x) + x^{MAX}$, where MIN and MAX are respectively the minimum and the maximum element of the set $\{i, i \in \mathbb{Z}$, such that $p_i^{\omega}(\Psi) \neq 0$, and $\omega \in \mathcal{W}\}$. When using only $\circ_{\rhd}$ (resp. $\circ_{\lhd}$) then $MIN = 0$ (resp. $MAX = 0$) then we recover the previous definitions. Using these modifications, we have:

Proposition 3 *Let Ψ be an epistemic state, and two formulas $\mu, \alpha \in \mathcal{L}_{\mathcal{PC}}$, $(\Psi \circ_{\rhd} \mu) \circ_{\lhd} \alpha \equiv_s (\Psi \circ_{\lhd} \alpha) \circ_{\rhd} \mu$.*

---

[3] (R6) requires an additional condition to be satisfied that is $Bel(\Psi \circ_{\lhd} (\mu \wedge \phi)) \models \phi$.

This result shows that the order with wich the operators are used has no importance, since the $\circ_{\rhd}$ revision operation uses right shifts and the $\circ_{\lhd}$ revision operation uses left shifts.

In previous sections we gave methods for constructing a new total pre-order on the interpretations. We now have to provide a syntactic counterpart of these semantical methods.

A syntactic representation of epistemic states

In this section, we give an alternative (but equivalent) representation of an epistemic state Ψ. Instead of explicitly specifying the total pre-order $\leq_{\Psi}$, the agent specifies a set of weighted formulas, called a weighted (or stratified) belief base and denoted by Σ_{Ψ}. Then we define a function κ which allows to recover $\leq_{\Psi}$ from Σ_{Ψ} by also associating to each interpretation ω a polynomial of B[x], that we denote by $\kappa_{\Sigma_{\Psi}}(\omega)(x)$. When this polynomial is equal to $p^{\omega}(\Psi)(x)$ for each ω we say that Σ_{Ψ} is a compact (or syntactic) representation of $\leq_{\Psi}$.

Given this compact representation, we are interested in defining syntactic counterpart of $\circ_{\rhd}$ (resp. $\circ_{\lhd}$), which syntactically transforms a weighted belief base Σ_{Ψ} and a new information μ, to a new weighted base, denoted by $\Sigma_{\Psi \circ_{\rhd} \mu}$ corresponding to the new epistemic state $\Psi \circ_{\rhd} \mu$. This new weighted base should be such that: $\forall \omega$ $p^{\omega}(\Psi \circ_{\rhd} \mu)(x) = \kappa_{\Sigma_{\Psi \circ_{\rhd} \mu}}(\omega)(x)$.

In the following, we formally define the notion of weighted belief bases, and the function κ.

Definition 6 *A weighted belief base Σ_{Ψ} is a set of pairs $\{(\phi_i, p^{\phi_i}(\Psi)(x)) : i = 1, ..., n\}$ where ϕ_i is a propositional formula, and $p^{\phi_i}(\Psi)(x)$ is a non-null polynomial of B[x] (i.e., different from the polynomial 0).*

Polynomials associated to formulas are compared according to Definition 1. When $p^{\phi}(\Psi)(x) >_B p^{\psi}(\Psi)(x)$, we say that ϕ is more important (certain, recent, has a higher priority etc) than the belief ψ. A weighted base Σ_{Ψ} is said to be consistent (resp. to entail ϕ) if its classical base (by forgetting the weights) is also consistent (resp. entails ϕ). Note that Σ_{Ψ} is not necessarily deductively closed. Moreover, nothing prevents Σ_{Ψ} from containing two weighted formulas $(\phi, p^{\phi}(\Psi)(x))$ and $(\psi, p^{\psi}(\Psi)(x))$ such that ϕ and ψ are classically equivalent, but having different weights $p^{\phi}(\Psi)(x) \neq p^{\psi}(\Psi)(x)$. In this case, we will see later that the least important belief can be removed from the weighted belief base.

Definition 7 *Let Σ_{Ψ} be a weighted belief base. The total pre-order $\leq_{\Psi}$, associated to Σ_{Ψ}, is obtained by attaching to each ω a weight $\kappa_{\Sigma_{\Psi}}(\omega)(x)$ defined by: $\kappa_{\Sigma_{\Psi}}(\omega)(x) = max\{p^{\phi_i}(\Psi)(x) : (\phi_i, p^{\phi_i}(\Psi)(x)) \in \Sigma_{\Psi}$ and $\omega \not\models \phi_i\}$, where by convention $max(\emptyset)=0$.*

This semantics is basically the same as the one used in possibilistic logic (Dubois et al., 1994), in System Z (Pearl 1995) and for generating a complete epistemic entrenchment relation from a partial one (Williams 1994). Indeed, all these approches share the same idea, where they associate to each interpretation the weight of the most important formula falsified by the interpretation. The lowest is the weight of an interpretation, the most plausible it is and the preferred it is. In particular, models of Σ_Ψ (namely those with a weight equal to 0) are the most preferred ones.

Example 2 Let: $\Sigma_\Psi = \{(\neg a \vee \neg b, \ x+1), (\neg a, \ 1), (\neg b \vee a, \ 1), (\neg a \vee \neg b, \ x), (\neg b, \ x), (a \vee b, \ x^2)\}$
Then: $\kappa_{\Sigma_\Psi}(ab) = max\{1, x, x+1, x\} = x+1$. $\kappa_{\Sigma_\Psi}(a\neg b) = max\{1\} = 1$. $\kappa_{\Sigma_\Psi}(\neg ab) = max\{x, 1\} = 1$. $\kappa_{\Sigma_\Psi}(\neg a \neg b) = max\{x^2\} = x^2$. Using Definition 1, $\neg a \neg b$ is the preferred one, then $\neg ab$ and $\neg ba$ are less preferred than $\neg a \neg b$ and lastly ab is the least preferred one. Note that there is no ω such that $\kappa_{\Sigma_\Psi}(\omega)(x) = 0$. This expresses the fact that the belief base Σ_Ψ is inconsistent.

Computing Bel(Ψ) syntactically

Given Σ_Ψ as a compact representation of $\leq_\Psi$, we propose to compute Bel(Ψ) directly from Σ_Ψ, such that:
$$Mod(Bel(\Psi)) = \{\omega : \nexists \omega' \ s.\ t.\ \kappa_\Sigma(\omega') < \kappa_\Sigma(\omega)(x)\}.$$
But first, we proceed to some pre-processing steps which make the computation easier, and which reduce the size of revised knowledge bases. These pre-processing steps consist in removing useless (or redundant) formulas. These formulas are tautologies and the so-called subsumed beliefs are defined by:

Definition 8 A formula $(\phi, \ p^\phi(\Psi)(x))$ is subsumed in Σ_Ψ if it can be classically entailed from formulas of Σ_Ψ having a weight greater than $p^\phi(\Psi)(x)$.

Theorem 4 Let Σ_Ψ be a weighted base. Let Σ'_Ψ be a new base obtained from Σ_Ψ by removing tautologies and subsumed formulas. Then Σ_Ψ and Σ'_Ψ are equivalent, in the sense that $\forall \omega$ we have: $\kappa_{\Sigma_\Psi}(\omega)(x) = \kappa_{\Sigma'_\Psi}(\omega)(x)$.

We denote by Σ_Ψ^* the weighted subbase obtained by removing tautologies and subsumed formulas from Σ_Ψ. Σ_Ψ^* is a partial epistemic entrenchment in the sense of (Williams 1995). It is easy to imagine an algorithm that computes Σ_Ψ^* from Σ_Ψ

Example 3 Let us consider the weighted belief base of the previous example. The only subsumed formulas are $(\neg a \vee \neg b, \ x)$ (which is entailed by $(\neg a \vee \neg b, \ x+1)$) and $(\neg b, \ x)$ (which is entailed by $(\neg b \vee a, \ 1)$). The previous algorithm returns the final subbase:
$\Sigma_\Psi^* = \{(\neg a \vee \neg b, \ x+1), (\neg a, \ 1), (\neg b \vee a, \ 1), (a \vee b, \ x^2)\}$.

The removing of tautologies and subsumed formulas allows us a direct computation of Bel(Ψ).

Theorem 5 If Σ_Ψ^* is consistent, then Bel(Ψ) is the classical base (i.e., without weights) associated to Σ_Ψ. If Σ_Ψ^* is not consistent, then let Minweight be the set of beliefs in Σ^* having minimal weights. Then Bel(Ψ) is the classical base of Σ_Ψ^* - Minweight.

Example 4 (continued) Since Σ_Ψ^* is inconsistent, then: Minweight $= \{(a \vee b, \ x^2)\}$. Therefore, Bel(Ψ) is the classical base (by forgetting weights) of: Σ_Ψ^* -

Minweight $= \{(\neg a \vee \neg b, \ x+1), (\neg a, \ 1), (\neg b \vee a, \ 1)\}$. Clearly, Bel($\Psi$) has exactly one model which is $\neg a \neg b$. Moreover, it is easy to check that $\neg a \neg b$ has the minimal weight in κ_{Σ_Ψ} computed previously in Example 2.

Syntactic counterpart of $\circ_\triangleright$ and $\circ_\triangleleft$

This section gives the syntactic counterpart of $\circ_\triangleright$. Let us illustrate the construction of $\Sigma_{\Psi \circ_\triangleright \mu}$ when Σ_Ψ only contains one formula $\{(\phi, \ 1)\}$ representing the initial belief set. Given a new observation μ, let the reader check that the new ordering $\leq_{\Psi \circ_\triangleright \mu}$ in the semantical construction, is encoded by: $p^\omega(\Psi \circ_\triangleright \mu)(x) = 0$ if $\omega \models \phi \wedge \mu$; $p^\omega(\Psi \circ_\triangleright \mu)(x) = x$ if $\omega \models \neg \phi \wedge \mu$; $p^\omega(\Psi \circ_\triangleright \mu)(x) = 1$ if $\omega \models \phi \wedge \neg \mu$; $p^\omega(\Psi \circ_\triangleright \mu)(x) = x+1$ if $\omega \models \neg \phi \wedge \neg \mu$. Now, let us see how to recover this ordering by building a weighted belief base $\Sigma_{\Psi \circ_\triangleright \mu}$ and using the function κ. Recall that κ is defined with respect to the strongest falsified belief. Therefore, in order to recover $\leq_{\Psi \circ_\triangleright \mu}$, one should assign to $\phi \vee \mu$ the highest weight (therefore each countermodel of $\phi \vee \mu$, namely each model of $\neg \phi \wedge \neg \mu$, gets the highest weight hence the least preferred interpretation), then $\neg \phi \vee \mu$ will get a smaller weight, which has a weight greater than $\phi \vee \neg \mu$. Therefore, we get the following weighted base:
$\Sigma_{\Psi \circ_\triangleright \mu} = \{(\phi \vee \mu, \ x+1), (\neg \phi \vee \mu, 1), (\phi \vee \neg \mu, x)\}$
It is easy, to check that: $\forall \omega, \ \kappa_{\Psi \circ_\triangleright \mu}(\omega)(x) = p^\omega(\Psi \circ_\triangleright \mu)(x)$.

Note that models of this weighted base are those which satisfy $\phi \wedge \mu$, and by definition of the function κ they get lowest rank and hence there is no need for additional beliefs. Besides, we can easily check that the above base can be simplified into an equivalent one (in the sense that they have the same κ) which is:
$\Sigma_{\Psi \circ_\triangleright \mu} = \{(\phi \vee \mu, \ x+1), (\mu, 1), (\phi \vee \neg \mu, x)\}$
Intuitively, replacing $(\neg \phi \vee \mu, 1)$ by $(\mu, 1)$ is justified by the fact that we already have $\phi \vee \mu$ with the highest rank, and from $(\phi \vee \mu, x+1)$ and $(\neg \phi \vee \mu, 1)$ we deduce $(\mu, 1)$, hence adding $(\neg \phi \vee \mu, 1)$ is equivalent to only add $(\mu, 1)$. Moreover, from $(\mu, 1)$ and $(\phi \vee \neg \mu, x)$ we also deduce (ϕ, x) To summarize, the new weighted base contains three parts: first, the old formula ϕ, with the smallest weight equal to x $p^\phi(\Psi)(x) = $ x, then the new formula μ, with a weight equal to 1, and finally, the disjunction $\phi \vee \mu$, with the highest weight equal to x $p^\phi(\Psi)(x) + 1 = x+1$.

The following definition generalizes the previous result to the case where the weighted belief base Σ_Ψ contains more than one belief.

Definition 9 The weighted base $\Sigma_{\Psi \circ_\triangleright \mu}$ associated to the epistemic state $\Psi \circ_\triangleright \mu$ is composed of:

- the new observation μ with a rank: $p^\mu(\Psi \circ_\triangleright \mu)(x) = 1$.
- all the pieces of information of Σ_Ψ however with the new rank, namely for each belief ϕ in Σ_Ψ:
  $p^\phi(\Psi \circ_\triangleright \mu)(x) = $x $p^\phi(\Psi)(x)$
- all the possible disjunctions between beliefs ϕ of Σ_Ψ and μ with the following weights:
  $p^{\phi \vee \mu}(\Psi \circ_\triangleright \mu)(x) = $x $p^\phi(\Psi)(x) + 1$

Once $\Sigma_{\Psi_{\circ_\triangleright}\mu}$ is built we remove tautologies and subsumed beliefs. The following proposition shows that $\Sigma_{\Psi_{\circ_\triangleright}\mu}$ allows us to recover the total pre-order associated to the epistemic state $\Psi \circ_\triangleright \mu$ syntactically.

Theorem 6 *Let Σ_Ψ be the weighted base associated to an epistemic state Ψ, such that $\forall \omega$, $p^\omega(\Psi)(x) = \kappa_{\Sigma_\Psi}(\omega)(x)$. Let μ be a new formula. Then for each ω:*
$$p^\omega(\Psi \circ_\triangleright \mu)(x) = \kappa_{\Sigma_{\Psi_{\circ_\triangleright}\mu}}(\omega)(x)$$

The following definition gives the syntactic counterpart of $\Psi \circ_\triangleleft \mu$ and characterizes the structure of $\Sigma_{\Psi_{\circ_\triangleleft}\mu}$, which is exactly the same as the one of $\Sigma_{\Psi_{\circ_\triangleright}\mu}$ except that the weighting is not the same.

Definition 10 *The weighted base $\Sigma_{\Psi_{\circ_\triangleleft}\mu}$ associated to the epistemic state $\Psi \circ_\triangleleft \mu$ is composed of:*

- *the new observation μ with a rank: $p^\mu(\Psi \circ_\triangleleft \mu)(x) = 1$.*
- *all the pieces of information ϕ of Σ_Ψ with the rank: $p^\phi(\Psi \circ_\triangleleft \mu)(x) = x^{-1}p^\phi(\Psi)(x)$*
- *all the possible disjunctions between beliefs ϕ of Σ_Ψ and μ with the weights: $p^{\phi \vee \mu}(\Psi \circ_\triangleleft \mu)(x) = x^{-1}p^\phi(\Psi)(x) + 1$*

The following proposition shows that $\Sigma_{\Psi_{\circ_\triangleleft}\mu}$ also allows us to recover the total pre-order associated to the epistemic state $\Psi \circ_\triangleleft \mu$ syntactically.

Theorem 7 *Let Σ_Ψ be the weighted base associated to an Ψ, and μ be a formula. Then for each ω:*
$$p^\omega(\Psi \circ_\triangleleft \mu)(x) = \kappa_{\Sigma_{\Psi_{\circ_\triangleleft}\mu}}(\omega)(x)$$

Concluding discussions

This paper proposes a revision rule, with a practical syntactic counterpart, that operates a maximal shift of all models of a new observation, while retaining their relative ordering. This type of belief change rule is the most drastic one can think of, in accordance with Darwiche and Pearl's principles, while Boutilier's natural revision is the least refined change rule, whereby only the best models of μ are made maximally plausible. Our changing rule considers that the input is strongly believed (but its strength decreases as time goes by), since each model of μ is preferred to all countermodels of μ. In contrast, Boutilier's natural revision the input is only weakly believed, since only the best models of μ are preferred to μ. Milder changing rules have been proposed by Williams (1994) and (Dubois and Prade, 1997) where they explicitly specify the level of acceptance of the input.

The proposed change rule can be viewed as based on the ceteris-paribus principle, that has been applied to representing preferences (C. Boutilier & al. 1997), whereby preferring μ means that any choice satisfying μ is better than any choice satisfying $\neg\mu$. It suggests that our revision approach might be relevant as well, not only for encoding a sequence of timed obsevations, but also for the update preference.

The use of polynomials allows to solve the drawback addressed by Spohn (Spohn 1988) concerning the reversibility of the changing rules. Indeed, we have shown that it is always possible to go back to previous epistemic states, while this is not be possible if WOP (well-ordered partitions) or ordinals have been used. It might be interesting to see if other revision tools can be efficiently encoded by means of simple operations on polynomials. Boutilier's natural belief revision can be easily encoded by shift operations on polynomials and syntactic counterpart to Boutilier's natural belief revision can be provided.

References

Alchourron, C.; Gärdenfors, P.; and Makinson, D. 1985. On the Logic of Theory Change: Partial Meet Functions for Contraction and Revision. *Journal of Symbolic Logic* 50:510–530.

Boutilier, C. 1993. Revision Sequences and Nested Conditionals. In *Proc. of the 13th Inter. Joint Conf. on Artificial Intelligence (IJCAI'93)*, 519–531.

C. Boutilier, R. B., and al. 1997. A constraint-based approach to preference elicitation and decision making. In *Working notes of the AAAI'97 Spring Symp. Series on Qualitative Preferences in Deliberation and Practical Reasoning. Stanford. Mar. 24-26*, 19–28.

Darwiche, A., and Pearl, J. 1997. On the logic of iterated revision. *Artificial Intelligence* 89:1–29.

Dubois, D., and Prade, H. 1992. Belief change and possibility theory. In Gärdenfors, P., ed., *Belief Revision*, 142–182. Cambridge University Press. U. K.

Dubois, D., and Prade, H. 1997. A synthetic view of belief revision with uncertain inputs in the framework of possibility theory. *Int. J. Approx. Reasoning* 17:295–324.

Katsuno, H., and Mendelzon, A. 1991. Propositional Knowledge Base Revision and Minimal Change. *Artificial Intelligence* 52:263–294.

Papini, O., and Rauzy, A. 1995. Revision in Extended Propositional Calculus. In Froidevaux, C., and Kholas, J., eds., *Proceedings of ECSQARU'95*, volume 946, 328–335. LNAI.

Papini, O. 1999. Iterated revision operations stemming from the history of an agent's observations. In Williams, M. A., and Rott, H., eds., *Frontiers of Belief Revision*, (to appear). Kluwer Acad. Publisher.

Pearl, J. 1995. System z: A natural ordering of defaults with tractableapplications to default reasoning. In Parikh, R., ed., *Proc. of the 3rd Conf. on Theoretical Aspects of Reasoning about Knowledge (TARK'90)*, 121–135. Morgan Kaufmann.

Spohn, W. 1988. Ordinal conditiona functions: a dynamic theory of epistemic states. In Harper, W., and Skyrms, B., eds., *Causation in Decision, Belief Change, and Statistics*, 105–134. Kluwer. Acad. Publisher.

Williams, M. A. 1994. Transmutations of Knowledge Systems. In et al., J. D., ed., *Inter. Conf. on Principles of Knowledge Representation and Reasoning (KR'94)*, 619–629. Morgan Kaufmann.

Williams, M. A. 1995. Iterated Theory Base Change:A Computational Model. In *Proc. of 14th Int. Joint Conf. on Artificial Intelligence (IJCAI'95)*, 1541–1547.

Point-Based Approaches to Qualitative Temporal Reasoning

J. Delgrande, A. Gupta,
School of Computing Science,
Simon Fraser University,
Burnaby, B.C., Canada, V5A 1S6.
E-mail: {jim, arvind}@cs.sfu.ca

T. Van Allen
Department of Computing Science,
University of Alberta,
Edmonton, Alberta, Canada T6G 2H1
E-mail: vanallen@cs.ualberta.ca

Abstract

We address the general problem of finding algorithms for efficient, qualitative, point-based temporal reasoning over a set of operations. We consider general reasoners tailored for temporal domains that exhibit a particular structure and introduce such a reasoner based on the series-parallel graph reasoner of Delgrande and Gupta; this reasoner is also an extension of the Time-Graph reasoner of Gerevini and Schubert. Test results indicate that for data with underlying structure, our reasoner performs better than other approaches. When there is no underlying structure in the data, our reasoner still performs better for query answering.

Introduction

Reasoning about temporal events is a central problem in the design of intelligent systems for such diverse areas as planning, reasoning about action and causality, and natural language understanding. Allen (All83) proposed the *interval algebra* (IA) of temporal relations wherein time intervals are taken as primitive; reasoning within this algebra is NP-complete (VK86). The *point algebra* (PA), introduced in (VK86; VKvB90), is based on time points as primitives. Many important temporal problems are expressible in the point algebra, and the existence of significantly more efficient algorithms than in the interval algebra has lead to its extensive study. Here, we are interested in the general problem of efficient, qualitative, point-based temporal reasoning.

A major problem in temporal reasoning is *scalability*. An $O(n^2)$ algorithm, while seemingly efficient, can be unacceptable for very large database. Matrix based deductive closure techniques for qualitative point based reasoning (VKvB90) require $O(n^2)$ space and $O(n^4)$ time and are only useful when data sets are small and "dense" ($O(n^2)$ assertions) and the number of queries is large. Research ((GS95; GM89)) has focused on methods which, by sacrificing query speed, achieve faster compilation and require less storage. Such approaches are appropriate for large, sparse data sets and are complementary to the matrix based approach.

Another consideration is the nature of the application domain. The underlying structure in a restricted domain may admit significantly faster algorithms. Gerevini and Schubert in their seminal work

(GS95) study reasoners where the domain is dominated by *chains* of events. Building on this, (DG96) consider a reasoner for domains that may be modelled by *series-parallel graphs*. These restricted structures may be exploited for general point-based reasoning by first decomposing a general graph into components of the restricted graphs, computing the closure of each component, and then using lookup and search to answer queries (see (GS95; GM89)).

Here we explore and compare different approaches to point-based reasoning. We first describe *point relations* and the point algebra, define entailment with respect to this algebra, and discuss operations on the language. We develop two basic reasoners, the first using standard graph operations, and a second that also uses rankings of nodes to improve query-answering times. We also consider two general reasoners tailored to temporal domains that likely exhibit a particular structure. We develop and describe an implementation of a general reasoner based on series parallel graphs, subsuming and improving on (DG96). We also reimplement the chain-based approach of Gerevini and Schubert, describing how our implementation differs from the original.

The four reasoners are tested on random data sets from different domains. The series-parallel reasoner is consistently the fastest for query answering and is faster than the Gerevini and Schubert approach for compilation even for those domains specifically tailored for this latter approach. Consequently, the series-parallel reasoner gives the best expected performance.

Preliminaries

Our results rely substantially on graph theoretic concepts (see (BM76) for terms not defined here). All graphs G are simple, finite and directed. The node and edge sets of G are denoted by $V(G)$ and $E(G)$ respectively. For $v \in V(G)$, *incoming*(G, v) (*outgoing*(G, v)) are the edges terminating (starting) at v. We use n to denote $|V(G)|$ as well as the number of points in a database of point relational constraints (these are normally the same). Similarly, e denotes the number of edges in a graph or the number of constraints in the database. For $u, v \in V(G)$, an unlabeled edge (or an edge where the label is implicit) is denoted by (u, v)

and a labeled edge by (u, m, v), where m is the label. We assume that edge labels support the standard operations of composition and summation, which we denote $\odot$ and $\oplus$ respectively (see (CLR90) for more details). Via these operations we extend the notion of edge labels to path labels. We use $u \rightsquigarrow v$ to indicate that there is a path from u to v, where a path may have length 0. A subscript will denote a path label: $u \rightsquigarrow_r v$ indicates that some edge in the path is labeled by r.

We assume that basic operations on $\log n$ bit integers are performed in constant time and the numbers require unit space. This is a standard complexity-theoretic assumption consistent with other work in the area.

Point Relations

Our primitive objects are *points* which can be viewed as "events in time" or points on the real line (but we make no such assumption). We denote the infinite set of points by P. The *point relations* are a set $R = \{\emptyset, <, >, =, <>, <=, >=, <=>\}$ where each element can be viewed as a subset of $\{<, =, >\}$, the *primitive point relations*. A point relation in R is a disjunction of primitive relations; thus $\emptyset$ is the relation that never holds and $<=>$ is the relation that always holds. The standard set operations $\cup, \cap, \subseteq, \ldots$ are defined over the point relations, with obvious interpretations. Relation r_1 is *stronger* than r_2 iff $r_1 \subseteq r_2$.

We also have two functions, $sequence: R \times R \to R$ and $inverse: R \to R$. *Sequence* is the transitive relation entailed by a sequence of two point relations. It is the composition operation for edge labels over R. *Inverse* maps a single relation onto the relation that holds in the opposite direction.

Constraints The language C is the set of all sentences $S ::= P\,R\,P$; a *constraint* is an element of C. At times we use *assertion* to mean *constraint*. For $A \subset C$, $P(A)$ is the set of all points "mentioned" in A. Entailment in C can be axiomatized as follows:

1. $\{\} \models x = x$, for all $x \in P$
2. $\{\} \models x <=> y$, for all $x, y \in P$
3. $\{x\,r\,y\} \models y\ inverse(r)\ x$
4. $\{x\,r_1\,y\} \models x\,r_1 \cup r_2\,y$, for all $r_2 \in R$
5. $\{x\,r_1\,y,\ y\,r_2\,z\} \models x\ sequence(r_1, r_2)\ z$
6. $\{x\,r_1\,y,\ x\,r_2\,y\} \models x\,r_1 \cap r_2 y$
7. $\{x <= v, x <= w, v <> w, v <= y, w <= y\} \models x < y$

Note that in Axiom 7, if $a <> b$ then either $a < b$ or $b < a$. But then, if $x <= a$ and $x <= b$, then either $x < a$ or $x < b$. This is a valid entailment in propositional logic but one which we cannot express in C. However, since $a <= y$ and $b <= y$, it follows that $x < y$. (GS95) prove completeness for this formulation. We will call *inconsistent* any set of assertions which entails $x\,\emptyset\,y$ for any $x, y \in P$.

Operations on Constraint Sets We are interested in the general problem of computing the entailments of a given set of point relational constraints. There are three basic subproblems:

1. Compilation: compile a set of constraints in C into a representation that allows efficient reasoning.
2. Querying: given such a representation, compute the strongest relation between two points.
3. Updating: change the representation to reflect the addition of a new assertion.

Generally, there is a tradeoff between compilation and query answering. In some applications it might be more efficient to precompute all strongest relations and explicitly store these; since there are $O(n^2)$ strongest relations which can be stored in a table, query answering can be performed in $O(1)$ time. However, computing deductive closure on a set of point relation constraints is not a particularly efficient process because of axiom 7 (deductive closure is not transitive closure for temporally labeled graphs). We can compute the transitive closure of the $<, <=$ labels with an $O(ne)$ algorithm, but to handle implicit $<$ relations entailed by axiom 7 we must resort to an $O(|E_{<>}| \cdot |E_{<=}|) = O(e^2)$ algorithm. The approach of (GS95) and (VKvB90) yields a $O(n^2)$ algorithm, as opposed to $O(en^2)$ by using simple search to compute all strongest relations.

For applications with static unstructured data and a large number of queries, our results suggest a "lazy" scheme which adds strongest relations to a hash table as they are computed. To maintain linear space, the table would be an $O(n)$ array with collisions resolved by overwriting previous information. With structured data however, our query answering algorithms are significantly faster than any other to date.

Temporally Labeled Graphs

Temporally labeled graphs (GS95) are used to represent "compiled" consistent sets of point relations.

Definition 1 For $A \subset C$, the *temporally labeled graph representing A* is a graph G with $V(G)$ the set of all $=$ points mentioned in A and $E(G)$ the constraints of A labeled by one of $<, <=, <>$.

Note that edges labeled $<$ or $<=$ are directed but those labeled $<>$ are undirected. $E(G)$ can be partitioned into the sets $E_<$, $E_{<=}$, and $E_{<>}$ based on edge labels. The graph composed of only edges from $E_< \cup E_{<=}$ is the $(<, <=)$-subgraph of G. Algorithms for compiling a set of assertions into such a graph and testing it for consistency are given in (GS95) and (vB92). They show that any set of constraints from C can be translated into constraints using only the relations $\{<, <=, <>\}$. The set of assertions is inconsistent iff a $<>$ or $<$ edge spans a cycle. We make G into a directed acyclic graph (DAB) by collapsing all directed cycles into single vertices.

Compilation takes $O(e)$ time using Tarjan's *strongly connected components* algorithm to isolate maximal cycles (see (CLR90)). The strongest relation between two points is found in $O(e)$ time using depth-first search to find the strongest path between the points.

For updates, suppose the assertion $x r_1 y$ is added. We compute the strongest relation, r_0, between x, and y. If r_0 is consistent with r_1 the update proceeds but any new cycle is "collapsed" to a single node of the graph; this algorithm takes $O(e)$ time.

Ranking We can speed up multiple searches in a DAG by bounding search depth. We define the *rank* of a node as the length of the longest path from the source to that node. To search all paths between two nodes we can confine our search to those nodes with intermediate ranks. We have developed both ranked and non-ranked base reasoners for comparison with other approaches.

Series Parallel Graphs

The point algebra provides a very general framework for reasoning which can be used in any domain modeled as points on a line. However, certain restricted domains lend themselves to more efficient reasoning strategies.

Consider a domain in which sets of events are related to others via some simple operations. For example, two events may occur sequentially (in *series*) or they may occur during some common time frame (in *parallel*). If the structure of our events is defined recursively by these series and parallel operations, we obtain *series parallel graph* (sp-graph) structures. We will see that more efficient, general, point-based reasoners can be constructed from this structure.

Definition 2 A *sp-graph* G with properties $source(G)$, $sink(G)$, $label(G)$, is given by:

1. (Base case) $G = edge(v, r, w)$, where:
   (a) $V(G) = \{v, w\}$, $E(G) = \{(v, r, w)\}$
   (b) $source(G) = v$, $sink(G) = w$, $label(G) = r \in \{<, \leq\}$
2. (Inductive case) $G = series(G_1, G_2)$ where:
   (a) G_1 and G_2 are sp-graphs
   (b) $V(G) = V(G_1) \cup V(G_2)$
   (c) $V(G_1) \cap V(G_2) = \{sink(G_1)\} = \{source(G_2)\}$
   (d) $E(G) = E(G_1) \cup E(G_2)$, $E(G_1) \cap E(G_2) = \{\}$
   (e) $source(G) = source(G_1)$, $sink(G) = sink(G_2)$
   (f) $label(G) = label(G_1) \odot label(G_2)$
3. (Inductive case) $G = parallel(G_1, G_2)$ where:
   (a) G_1 and G_2 are sp-graphs
   (b) $V(G) = V(G_1) \cup V(G_2)$
   (c) $V(G_1) \cap V(G_2) = \{source(G_1), sink(G_1)\}$
   (d) $E(G) = E(G_1) \cup E(G_2)$, $E(G_1) \cap E(G_2) = \{\}$
   (e) $source(G) = source(G_1) = source(G_2)$
   (f) $sink(G) = sink(G_1) = sink(G_2)$
   (g) $label(G) = label(G_1) \oplus label(G_2)$

Note that sp-graphs have a single source and sink. The label summarizes all paths from the source to the sink.

Transitive Closure

It is straightforward to compute the transitive closure of sp-graphs in $O(n^2)$ time and space when the edge labels support $O(1)$ composition and intersection. For G an edge (u, r, w), the closure is r. If G is either $series(G_1, G_2)$ or $parallel(G_1, G_2)$ we inductively compute the closure of G_1 and G_2. Additionally in the series case, for u in G_1 and v in G_2 we must compose the path from u to $sink(G_1)$ and the path from $source(G_2)$ to v.

The structure of sp-graphs allows more efficient algorithms for special cases. (DG96) show that the complexity of determining path closure is $O(n)$. This involves associating each node v with a point (x_v, y_v) in the $n \times n$ integer lattice. For $v, w \in V(G)$ there is a path from v to w iff $x_v < x_w$ and $y_v < y_w$.

Given path closure, we will compute the $<, <=$ closure in an sp-graph G in $O(n)$ time.

Definition 3 For $v \in V(G)$, let $s(v)$ be the maximum number of $<$ edges on any path from $source(G)$ to v.

Definition 4 For $v \in V(G)$, if $v = sink(G)$ or, for some w, $(v, <, w) \in E(G)$ then define $a(v) = s(v)$ otherwise define $a(v) = \min\{a(w) : (v, <=, w) \in E(G)\}$.

Lemma 1 For any $v \in V(G)$, $s(v) \leq a(v)$.

Proof: The proof is by induction. Suppose that for every child w of v, $s(w) \leq a(w)$. We show $s(v) \leq a(v)$. If $v = sink(G)$ or v has an outgoing $<$ edge, then by definition $s(v) = a(v)$. If v has no outgoing $<$ edge, then $a(v) = \min\{a(w) : (v, <=, w)\}$ and $a(v) = a(w)$ for some child w of v. Since $s(v) \leq s(w)$ and $s(w) \leq a(w) = a(v)$, the lemma follows. **QED**

Theorem 1 For $v, w \in V(G)$ such that $v \rightsquigarrow w$, $a(v) < s(w)$ iff $v \rightsquigarrow_< w$.

Proof: Suppose $v, w \in V(G)$ such that $v \rightsquigarrow w$. If $v \rightsquigarrow_< w$ there there is an edge $(x, <, y)$ such that $v \rightsquigarrow x$ and $y \rightsquigarrow w$. Since a and s are non-decreasing, $a(v) \leq a(x) = s(x) < s(y) \leq s(w)$.

Conversely assume $a(v) < s(w)$ but $v \not\rightsquigarrow_< w$. Since $s(source(G)) \leq s(v) \leq a(v) < s(w)$, $s(source(G)) < s(w)$. Then there is an edge $(x, <, y)$ such that $source(G) \rightsquigarrow x$, $y \rightsquigarrow w$ and $s(w) = s(y)$. Since $a(v) < s(w) \leq a(w) \leq a(sink(G))$, there is an edge $(u, <, z)$ such that $v \rightsquigarrow u$, $z \rightsquigarrow sink(G)$, and $a(v) = a(u)$. Since $v \not\rightsquigarrow_< w$, $z \not\rightsquigarrow w$ and $v \not\rightsquigarrow x$. Because G is a sp-graph, the three paths

1. $v \rightsquigarrow u \rightsquigarrow_< z \rightsquigarrow sink(G)$
2. $source(G) \rightsquigarrow x \rightsquigarrow_< y \rightsquigarrow w$
3. $source(G) \rightsquigarrow v \rightsquigarrow w \rightsquigarrow sink(G)$

have a common node (say j). Since $v \not\rightsquigarrow_< w$:
$$v \rightsquigarrow j \rightsquigarrow w \text{ and } y \rightsquigarrow j \rightsquigarrow u.$$
Then $a(v) \leq a(j) \leq a(u) = a(v)$ so $a(j) = a(v)$ and $s(y) \leq s(j) \leq s(w) = s(y)$ so $s(j) = s(w)$. Thus $s(j) \leq a(j) = a(v) < s(w) = s(j)$, a contradiction. **QED**

We can compute $\{s(v)\}$ using depth first search on G and compute $\{a(v)\}$ from $\{s(v)\}$ using depth first search on the transpose of G. Both these computations require $O(n)$ time. This yields the following:

Theorem 2 For G a temporally labeled sp-graph, the $<$ and $<=$ closures can be computed in $O(n)$ time with $O(n)$ bits of storage.

Notice that our technique strictly improves on that in (DG96) who also claim $O(n)$ time and space but require arbitrary real number precision ($O(n^2)$ bits of storage).

Metagraphs

We slightly generalize the terms *metagraph*, *metaedge* and *metanode* introduced in (GS95).

Definition 5 A graph G' is a *metagraph* of a DAG G iff $V(G') \subseteq V(G)$ and there is an onto function $m : E(G) \to E(G')$ such that, for $m((x,y)) = (u,v)$:

1. Either $x = u$ or for all $(w,x) \in E(G)$, $m((w,x)) = (u,v)$ (and at least one such (w,x) exists); and
2. Either $y = v$ or for all $(y,w) \in E(G)$, $m((y,w)) = (u,v)$ (and at least one such (w,x) exists).

The nodes and edges of G' are called *metanodes* and *metaedges* respectively. Metaedges correspond to (edge disjoint) single source, single sink components of G. The edge label of $(u,v) \in E(G')$ is the intersection of the labels of all paths from u to v in G.

Metagraphs are a convenient way to encapsulate subgraphs. Metaedges correspond to components. Relations between nodes inside a metaedge are determined by the subgraph corresponding to that metaedge; relations between metanodes are determined by the metagraph; while relations between nodes inside different metaedges are determined by their relationship to the sources and sinks of their metaedges, and by the relations between the source/sink metanodes.

Metagraphs are useful for representing domains where relational data is composed of "self-contained" units connected only through common sources and sinks. Using a metagraph may improve efficiency when graphs are largely composed of substructures that lend themselves to more efficient implementation of basic operations (search, closure, updates, etc.).

Series Parallel Metaedges

We present a method for partitioning the edge set of a graph into maximal series parallel metaedges. We start with a very high level algorithm that collapses all series parallel components into single edges. Let G be a DAG.

Rule A If $v \in V(G)$ has only one incoming edge (u,m,v) and only one outgoing edge (v,n,w) then remove these edges and add the edge $(u, m \odot n, v)$.

Rule B If $(u,m,v), (u,n,v) \in E(G)$ then remove these edges and add the edge $(u, m \oplus n, v)$.

These rules are iterated so that in the resulting metagraph, each metaedge represents an edge disjoint, maximal, series parallel component of the original graph. We can label metaedges with sp-graphs and define $\odot$ as a series step and $\oplus$ as a parallel step. In (VDG98) we show that this algorithm correctly reduces a graph to its maximal series parallel components.

Our Temporal Reasoner

So far we have presented a base point algebra reasoner, closure algorithms for sp-graphs, and an algorithm for transforming a graph into series parallel metaedges. Our hybrid scheme is unique in constructing a temporally labeled graph, transforming it into maximal series parallel metaedges and then computing the internal closure of the metaedges. Queries for two points in the same metaedge take constant time; for points not in the same metaedge we only search the metagraph. Updating the structure follows a similar pattern. This approach will be useful in domains where temporal information is hierarchically structured, and when queries tend to reflect that structure.

Implementation and Testing

For comparison, we implemented four temporal reasoning algorithms:

1. The simple graph-based approach.
2. The graph-based approach using ranking.
3. The TimeGraph approach of Gerevini and Schubert (GS95), updated as described below.
4. Our metagraph algorithm based on decomposing a DAG into series parallel components.

Our implementations are in Common Lisp with data structures kept consistent between the four approaches.

Reimplementing TimeGraph

The TimeGraph approach, of (GS95), is arguably the first metagraph-based approach. We implemented a revised version of TimeGraph that is significantly faster than the original but did not implement those portions of TimeGraph, dealing with disjunctive relations since they are not directly relevant to us (see (VDG98) for details.) We briefly describe our version, noting where we diverge from the original.

TimeGraph differs from the series parallel metagraph approach in several significant ways:

1. The underlying components are chains instead of series parallel graphs.
2. Entailed $<$ relations involving $<>$ are compiled out.
3. Chains may be connected via *cross-edges* (edges that originate and terminate in different chains). Computing closure within a chain involves following paths outside the chain, which takes $O(ne)$ time.

Making the Graph Explicit We must add $<$ edges so that all $<>$ relations between nodes involve a $<$ edge. For each $(u,v) \in E_{<>}$ we find the least common ancestors and descendants of u and v and add the cross product of these two sets to $E_<$. The total complexity is $O(|E_{<>}| \cdot |E_{<=}|)$. Notice that this algorithm adds at most $O(e)$ edges to the graph. Our algorithms for computing nearest common ancestors and descendants are based on an algorithm in (GS95).

Computing Closure for the Chains A chain G is a DAG such that for $v, w \in V(G)$, either $v \rightsquigarrow w$ or $w \rightsquigarrow v$. A *timechain* is an sequence of nodes, $[v_1, v_2 \ldots v_n]$, with $(v_i, <=, v_{i+1}) \in E(G)$ for $i < n$. A timechain may also contain $<$ links between any two nodes (in the consistent direction). To determine $<$ relations, each node is labeled with the index of the next $>$ node on the chain and $n+1$ if no such node exists. These labels can be determined with a single depth first search.

Since chains can be connected by cross-edges between arbitrary nodes, computing the internal closure of a chain requires searching the entire region of the graph reachable from the nodes of the chain (bounded by the rank of the last node on the chain). For c chains, this step requires $O(c(n + e))$ time; since c is $O(n)$, the complexity is $O(n(n + e))$. To compute a *nextGreater* value (ie rank of the next greater node) for each node, (GS95) use the metagraph to speed up the search. This necessitates breaking the algorithm into two parts – one to compute the *nextGreater* value based only on edges internal to the chain, and one to "refine" these *nextGreater* values by searching the graph. We use an algorithm that computes the *nextGreater* values with one depth first search for each chain.

Constructing the Metagraph The metagraph must reflect all relationships between metanodes so that any relation between two metanodes can be determined by search. (GS95) define metavertices as "cross-connected vertices" (the sources and termini of cross-edges) and the metagraph of a timegraph T as:

> ... the graph $G' = (V', E')$ where $V' = \{v : v$ is a metavertex in $T\}$ and $E' = \{(v, l, w) : (v, l, w)$ is a cross-edge in $T\} \cup \{(v, nextout(v)), (v, nextin(v))$ for all $v \in V'\}$.

where $nextout(v)$ gives the next node on v's chain with an outgoing cross-edge, and $nextin(v)$ gives the next node on v's chain with an incoming cross-edge.

However, this graph does not contain sufficient information to deduce all relations between metanodes. Consider the chains $[a, b, c, d, e]$ and $[f, g, h]$, cross-edges $(a, <=, f), (c, <=, g), (e, <=, h)$ and the transitive edge $(b, <, d)$. The metagraph in the definition above would be: $V' = \{a, c, e, f, g, h\}$ and $E' = \{(a, <=, c), (a, <=, f), (c, <=, e), (c, <=, g), (f, <=, g), (e, <=, h), (g, <=, h)\}$ In the original graph, $a < e$ and $a < h$, but the metagraph does not allow us to deduce this. To fix this, we must include b and d in V', and $(b, <, d)$ in E'. Therefore, we slightly modify the above definition to:

Definition 6 (v, r, w) is a metaedge, and v, w are metanodes, iff one of the following holds:

1. $chain(v) \neq chain(w)$.
2. w is the *nextGreater* value for v and r is $<$.
3. All of:
   (a) v, w are metanodes as defined above.
   (b) $chain(v) = chain(w)$.
   (c) No metanode lies between v and w on the chain.
   (d) r is the internal relation between v and w.

Our definition allows us to compute all relations between metanodes. We construct the metagraph by finding all edges of the first two kinds, labeling their sources and sinks as metanodes, and then adding the edges of the third kind by going through the chains and adding links between nearest metanodes.

Queries Queries in the revised TimeGraph are basically the same as in our series parallel metagraph: if the two nodes are on the same chain then their strongest

relation is computed with an $O(1)$ test; otherwise a search is conducted from the next metanode of the lowest ranked node to the previous metanode of the highest ranked node. The relation so obtained is composed with the relation each holds to the appropriate metanode to yield the strongest relation between the two nodes.

Testing

To compare approaches, we generated random sets of constraints (DAG's) and compared compile and query times. To generate a DAG over the nodes $v_1, v_2, \ldots v_n$, we let the ordering on nodes define a topological sort of the intended graph, and defined the graph by enumerating the forward edges, adding an edge with some probability. For the purpose of testing the approaches presented in this paper, we were interested only in sparse graphs, that is, when e is $O(n)$. To produce sparse graphs we add an edge with a probability of approximately k/n, for some fixed k. Then we randomly assigned labels from $\{<, <=, <>\}$ to the edges. This set of edges corresponds to a set of assertions.

Test Domains We experimented with various modifications to the basic graph generation scheme. We investigated data sets with no $<>$ assertions, data sets based on series parallel graphs with a certain amount of "noise" (random edges) introduced, and data sets based on chains where, again, a certain amount of noise was added. Here we describe three test domains:

1. Sparse graphs with all edge labels equiprobable.
2. Sparse graphs based on chains (no $<>$ edges).
3. Sparse graphs based on sp-graphs (no $<>$ edges).

Test Results Thirty data sets were generated with the average time to compile and the average time to answer 100 queries given below. Times are in milliseconds; the tests were run on a Sun UltraSparc 1 workstation.

Domain 1

	Approach	Nodes (Edges = ~ 5× nodes)				
		100	200	300	400	500
Compile Time	Base	5	9	13	17	22
	Ranked	4	10	16	21	27
	TG	304	1150	2477	4501	6857
	SP	69	138	207	286	354
Query Time	Base	38	56	69	78	91
	Ranked	19	25	28	31	35
	TG	21	25	31	35	38
	SP	18	25	30	33	35

Domain 2

	Approach	Nodes (Edges = ~ 1.2× nodes)				
		100	200	300	400	500
Compile Time	Base	3	6	10	13	15
	Ranked	3	6	10	16	20
	TG	16	41	82	133	200
	SP	17	34	52	69	86
Query Time	Base	42	61	70	77	84
	Ranked	20	26	26	27	28
	TG	10	13	14	15	17
	SP	11	12	13	14	16

Domain 3

	Approach	Nodes (Edges = ~ 1.6× nodes)				
		100	200	300	400	500
Compile Time	Base	5	6	9	12	15
	Ranked	5	7	11	16	19
	TG	31	103	214	375	557
	SP	21	42	62	83	107
Query Time	Base	45	89	133	172	225
	Ranked	21	35	44	58	65
	TG	20	34	44	55	63
	SP	13	16	21	28	30

Discussion of Test Results

The test results indicate that, as expected, the simple approaches have much lower compile times. In all domains, adding ranking ("Ranked") to brute force searching ("Base") yields significantly faster query times with little increase in compile times. When the data has no underlying structure (Domain 1), ranking and the series parallel approach perform optimally for query but because of its reduced compile time, ranking is the better approach.

The situation changes dramatically when the data has some underlying structure. When there are many chains in the database (Domain 2) both the Time-Graph approach ("TG") and the series parallel approach ("SP") yield query times that are half those of ranking. While the query times for both approaches is similar, the compile time for SP is about half that for TG. This may seem surprising but notice that when the number of edges is linear, sp-graphs effectively encompass chains. Thus the SP approach will likely have metanodes that contain many chains thus speeding up the query answering. When there are many sp-graphs in the database (Domain 3), the SP approach answers queries about twice as fast as either ranking or TG.

We conclude that, when the data exhibits no structure, ranking is a feasible approach. It is easy to implement, allows for quick compilation, and is the fastest (or near-fastest) in almost all cases. When the data exhibits chains or series parallel structures, SP is the best choice especially when a large number of queries must be performed. When query time significantly dominates compile time, the SP approach seems the best all-round approach, since it performs no worse in answering queries than other approaches, yet is able to exploit any structure in the time constraints.

Conclusion

We have addressed the general problem of qualitative, point-based temporal reasoning. To this end, we have developed two basic reasoners, one a straightforward implementation of standard graph operations, and a second that also incorporates a ranking of nodes to improve query-answering times. We also developed general reasoners tailored for temporal domains that are expected to exhibit a particular structure. This leads naturally to the notion of a *metagraph*, and metagraph

reasoners. We implemented the chain-based approach of Gerevini and Schubert and developed and implemented a *series-parallel graph* approach, roughly analogous to the Gerevini and Schubert approach but where series-parallel graphs replace chains.

Our test results indicate that when there is some underlying structure in the data, our reasoner performs better than the Gerevini and Schubert reasoner or simple search algorithms. When there is no underlying structure in the data, the series parallel reasoner still performs better for query answering than these other approaches. Hence, when there is no *known* structure in the data, we argue that our reasoner will provide the best expected performance: if the domain is indeed unstructured, our approach performs generally better than the others for the (presumably) dominant operation of query answering; if there is some structure in the date, this structure will be exploited by our reasoner for overall superior results.

References

James Allen. Maintaining knowledge about temporal intervals. *Communications of the ACM*, 26(1):832–843, 1983.

J. Bondy and U.S.R. Murty. *Graph Theory with Applications*. North-Holland, 1976.

T.H. Cormen, C.E. Leiserson, and R.L. Rivest. *Introduction to Algorithms*. The MIT Press, Cambridge, 1990.

J.P. Delgrande and A. Gupta. A representation for efficient temporal reasoning. In *Proceedings of the AAAI National Conference on Artificial Intelligence*, pages 381–388, Portland, Oregon, August 1996.

Malik Ghallab and Amine Mounir Alaoui. Managing efficiently temporal relations through indexed spanning trees. In *Proceedings of the International Joint Conference on Artificial Intelligence*, pages 1297–1303, Detroit, 1989.

Alfonso Gerevini and Lenhart Schubert. Efficient algorithms for qualitative reasoning about time. *Artificial Intelligence*, 74(2):207–248, April 1995.

Peter van Beek. Reasoning about qualitative temporal information. *Artificial Intelligence*, 58(1-3):297–326, 1992.

T. Van Allen, J. Delgrande, and A. Gupta. Point-based approaches to qualitative temporal reasoning. Technical Report CMPT TR 98-16, Simon Fraser University, 1998.

Marc Vilain and Henry Kautz. Constraint propagation algorithms for temporal reasoning. In *Proceedings of the AAAI National Conference on Artificial Intelligence*, pages 377–382, Philadelphia, PA, 1986.

Marc Vilain, Henry Kautz, and Peter van Beek. Constraint propagation algorithms for temporal reasoning: A revised report. In *Readings in Qualitative Reasoning about Physical Systems*, pages 373–381. Morgan Kaufmann Publishers, Inc., Los Altos, CA, 1990.

Querying Temporal Constraint Networks in PTIME

Manolis Koubarakis

Dept. of Informatics, University of Athens
Panepistimioupolis, TYPA Buildings
157 81 Athens, Greece
manolis@di.uoa.gr, www.di.uoa.gr/~manolis

Spiros Skiadopoulos

Dept. of Electrical and Computer Engineering
National Technical University of Athens
Zographou 157 73 Athens, Greece
spiros@dbnet.ece.ntua.gr

Abstract

We start with the assumption that temporal knowledge usually captured by constraint networks can be represented and queried more effectively by using the scheme of indefinite constraint databases proposed by Koubarakis. Although query evaluation in this scheme is in general a hard computational problem, we demonstrate that there are several interesting cases where query evaluation can be done in PTIME. These tractability results are original and subsume previous results by van Beek, Brusoni, Console and Terenziani.

Introduction

When temporal constraint networks are used in applications, their nodes represent the times when certain facts are true, or when certain events take place, or when events start or end. By labeling nodes with appropriate natural language expressions (e.g., *breakfast* or *walk*) and arcs by temporal relations, temporal constraint networks can be queried in useful ways. For example the query "Is it possible (or certain) that event *walk* happened after event *breakfast*?" or "What are the known events that come after event *breakfast*?" can be asked (Brusoni *et al.* 1994; van Beek 1991). Other kinds of knowledge cannot be queried however, although they might have been collected in the first place. For example, the query "*Who* is certainly having breakfast before taking a walk?" cannot be asked.

This situation has been understood by temporal reasoning researchers, and application-oriented systems where temporal reasoners were combined with more general knowledge representation systems have been implemented. These systems include the natural language systems EPILOG, Shocker (see `www.cs.rochester.edu/research/epilog/` and `kr-tools.html`), Telos (Mylopoulos *et al.* 1990) and TMM (Dean & McDermott 1987; Schrag, Boddy, & Carciofini 1992). EPILOG uses the temporal reasoner

Timegraph (Gerevini & Schubert 1995), Shocker uses TIMELOGIC, Telos uses a subclass of Allen's interval algebra (Allen 1983) and TMM uses networks of difference constraints (Dechter, Meiri, & Pearl 1991).

In this paper we start from the assumption that temporal knowledge usually captured by a constraint network can be represented more effectively if the network is complemented by a *database* for storing the information typically used to label the nodes of the network. The combined system can then be queried using a *first order modal query language*.

The above assumption has been made explicit in the TMM system (Dean & McDermott 1987; Schrag, Boddy, & Carciofini 1992) and the temporal relational database models of (Koubarakis 1997b; Brusoni *et al.* 1995). Of these two database proposals the most expressive one is the scheme of *indefinite constraint databases* proposed in (Koubarakis 1997b). In this paper we redefine the scheme of (Koubarakis 1997b) (using first order logic instead of relational database theory) and take it as the formalism in which we present our contributions.

We first point out that query evaluation in the presence of indefinite temporal information is a hard problem (it is NP-hard for possibility queries and co-NP-hard for certainty queries). Motivated by this negative fact, we try to discover tractable subclasses of the general query answering problem. To achieve this, we adopt the following approach. We start with the assumption that we have a class of constraints $\mathcal{C}$ with satisfiability and variable elimination problems that can be solved in PTIME. Under this assumption, we demonstrate several general classes of indefinite constraint databases and queries for which query evaluation can be done with PTIME data complexity. Then we restate these results with $\mathcal{C}$ ranging over some interesting classes of temporal constraints. The tractable query answering problems identified in this way are bound to be interesting for temporal reasoning researchers. Two of them are significant extensions of tractable problems identified previously in (Brusoni, Console, & Terenziani 1995; van Beek 1991).

The organization of this paper is as follows. The next section presents some preliminaries. Then we present the model of indefinite constraint databases. The last two sections develop our contributions.

Preliminaries

In this paper we consider first order constraint languages. For each such language $\mathcal{L}_C$, we assume an *intended structure* $\mathcal{M}_C$ which interprets formulas of $\mathcal{L}_C$. $Th(\mathcal{M}_C)$ will denote the *theory* of this structure. Finally, for each language $\mathcal{L}_C$ a class of formulas called $\mathcal{L}_C$-*constraints* will be defined.

For example let us consider $\mathcal{L}_{LIN}$: the first order language of *linear constraints over the rationals*. Its intended structure is $\mathcal{M}_{LIN} = (\mathcal{Q}, +, *, <)$ where $\mathcal{Q}$ is the set of rational numbers. We will deal with the following classes of $\mathcal{L}_{LIN}$-constraints:

- The class of *linear inequalities* LIN.

- The class of *Horn disjunctive linear constraints* HDL. An HDL constraint is a disjunction of an arbitrary number of linear disequations and *at most one* weak linear inequality.

- The class of *linear constraints with two variables per inequality and unit coefficients* UTVPI$^{\neq}$. A UTVPI$^{\neq}$ constraint is a linear constraint $ax + by \sim c$ where $a, b \in \{-1, 0, 1\}$ and $\sim$ is $\leq$ or $\neq$.

HDL constraints were defined in (Koubarakis 1996; Jonsson, P. and Bäckström, C. 1996). They subsume many interesting classes of temporal constraints. UTVPI$^{\neq}$ constraints (without disequations) have been considered in (Shostak 1981; Jaffar *et al.* 1994). UTVPI$^{\neq}$ constraints subsume the temporal constraints studied in (Koubarakis 1997a). They can also be used in spatial applications to define many kinds of polygons (e.g., arbitrary rectangles, several kinds of triangles and octagons and so on). The disequations allowed by this class give us more expressive power by allowing a limited form of negative information (e.g., they can be used to *remove* points and straight lines from polygons).

We assume that the reader is familiar with the concept of *satisfiability* of a set of constraints, and the concept of *variable elimination*.

Theorem 1 *The satisfiability of a set of HDL constraints can be decided in PTIME (Koubarakis 1996; Jonsson, P. and Bäckström, C. 1996).*

Unfortunately we do not have a nice theorem like the above concerning variable elimination for the class HDL. In fact variable elimination cannot be done in PTIME even for LIN. If we have a set C of linear inequalities, it might not be possible to describe the result of a variable elimination operation on C by a set of linear inequalities with size less than exponential in the number of eliminated variables (Yannakakis 1988).

The following result extends a similar result in (Koubarakis 1997a).

Theorem 2 *Let C be a set of UTVPI$^{\neq}$ constraints. We can eliminate any number of variables from C in $O(dn^4)$ time where d is the number of disequations and n is the number of variables in C.*

The Scheme of Indefinite Constraint Databases

In this section we present the scheme of indefinite constraint databases originally proposed in (Koubarakis 1997b). We follow the spirit (and details) of the original proposal but use first order logic instead of relational database theory.

Let $\mathcal{L}_C$ be a many-sorted first-order constraint language and $\mathcal{M}_C$ be its *intended structure*. We assume that the class of $\mathcal{L}_C$-constraints *admits variable elimination* and is *weakly closed under negation* (i.e., the negation of every $\mathcal{L}_C$-constraint is equivalent to a disjunction of $\mathcal{L}_C$-constraints). Many interesting constraint languages have this property e.g., the language $\mathcal{L}_{LIN}$ defined previously.

We start by introducing some formal tools that make our presentation easy to follow. Let $\mathcal{L}_=$ be a first order language with equality and a countably infinite set of constant symbols. The intended structure $\mathcal{M}_=$ for $\mathcal{L}_=$ interprets = as equality and constants as "themselves". $\mathcal{L}_=$-constraints or *equality constraints* are formulas of the form $x = v$ or $x \neq v$ where x is a variable, and v is a variable or a constant. In the database formalism to be developed below constants of $\mathcal{L}_=$ will be used to represent real-world entities with no special semantics e.g., *John* or *breakfast*.

Now let $\mathcal{L}_C$ be any first order constraint language. We will use $\mathcal{L}_{C,=}$ to denote the union of $\mathcal{L}_C$ and $\mathcal{L}_=$. The intended structure for $\mathcal{L}_{C,=}$ is $\mathcal{M}_C \cup \mathcal{M}_=$ and will be denoted by $\mathcal{M}_{C,=}$. Finally let us define the first order language $\mathcal{L}^*_{C,=}$. $\mathcal{L}^*_{C,=}$ is obtained by augmenting $\mathcal{L}_C$ with the *new* sort symbol $\mathcal{D}$ (for real-world entities with no special semantics), the equality symbol = for sort $\mathcal{D}$, a countably infinite set of *database predicate symbols* $p_1, p_2, \ldots$ of various arities, and a countably infinite set of variables $x_1, x_2, \ldots$ of sort $\mathcal{D}$. In other words $\mathcal{L}^*_{C,=}$ is obtained from $\mathcal{L}_{C,=}$ by introducing a countably infinite set of predicate symbols $p_1, p_2, \ldots$ of various arities.

Databases And Queries

Let $\mathcal{L}_C$ be a first order constraint language. In this section the symbols $\overline{\mathcal{T}}$ and $\overline{\mathcal{T}}_i$ will denote vectors of sorts of $\mathcal{L}_C$. The symbol $\overline{\mathcal{D}}$ will denote a vector with all its components being the sort $\mathcal{D}$.

Indefinite $\mathcal{L}_C$-constraint databases and queries are special formulas of $\mathcal{L}^*_{C,=}$ and are defined as follows.

Definition 1 *Let $\mathcal{L}_C$ be a first order constraint language. An* indefinite $\mathcal{L}_C$-constraint database *is a formula $DB(\overline{\omega})$ of $\mathcal{L}^*_{C,=}$ of the following form:*

$$ConstraintStore(\overline{\omega}) \wedge$$

$$\bigwedge_{i=1}^{m} (\forall \overline{x_i}/\overline{\mathcal{D}})(\forall \overline{t_i}/\overline{\mathcal{T}}_i)(\bigvee_{j=1}^{l} Local_j(\overline{x_i}, \overline{t_i}, \overline{\omega}) \equiv p_i(\overline{x_i}, \overline{t_i}))$$

where

- *$ConstraintStore(\overline{\omega})$ is a conjunction of $\mathcal{L}_C$-constraints in Skolem constants $\overline{\omega}$.*

- $Local_j(\overline{x_i}, \overline{t_i}, \overline{\omega})$ is a conjunction of $\mathcal{L}_C$-constraints in variables $\overline{t_i}$ and Skolem constants $\overline{\omega}$, and $\mathcal{L}_=$-constraints in variables $\overline{x_i}$.

The first part of the above formula defining a database is a *constraint store*. This store is a conjunction (or a set) of $\mathcal{L}_C$-constraints and corresponds to a constraint network. $\overline{\omega}$ is a vector of *Skolem constants* denoting entities (e.g., points and intervals in time) about which *only partial knowledge* is available. This partial knowledge has been coded in the constraint store using the language $\mathcal{L}_C$.

The second part of the database formula is a set of equivalences *defining* the database predicates p_i. These equivalences may refer to the Skolem constants of the constraint store. For temporal reasoning applications, the constraint store can be used instead of a constraint network while the predicates p_i can be used to encode the events or facts usually associated with the nodes of temporal constraint networks.

For a given database DB the first conjunct of the database formula will be denoted by $ConstraintStore(DB)$, and the second one by $EventsAndFacts(DB)$. For clarity we will sometimes write sets of conjuncts instead of conjunctions. In other words a database DB can be seen as the following pair of sets of formulas:

$$(EventsAndFacts(DB), ConstraintStore(DB)).$$

We will feel free to use whichever definition of database fits our needs in the rest of the chapter.

The new machinery in the indefinite constraint database scheme (in comparison with relational or Prolog databases) is the Skolem constants in $EventsAndFacts(DB)$ and the constraint store which is used to represent "all we know" about these Skolem constants. Essentially this proposal is a combination of constraint databases (without indefinite information) as defined in (Kanellakis, Kuper, & Revesz 1990), and the marked nulls proposal of (Imielinski & Lipski 1984; Grahne 1991).

Example 1 *The following is an indefinite $\mathcal{L}_{LIN}$-constraint database:*

$$(\{ \omega_1 < \omega_2, \ \omega_1 < \omega_3, \ \omega_3 < \omega_4 \},$$
$$\{ (\forall x/\mathcal{D})(\forall t_1, t_2/\mathcal{Q})$$
$$((x = mary \ \wedge \ t_1 = \omega_1 \ \wedge \ t_2 = \omega_2) \equiv walk(x, t_1, t_2)),$$
$$(\forall x/\mathcal{D})(\forall t_3, t_4/\mathcal{Q})$$
$$((x = mary \ \wedge \ t_3 = \omega_3 \ \wedge \ t_4 = \omega_4) \equiv paper(x, t_1, t_2)) \})$$

This database contains information about the events walk (talking a walk) and paper (reading a paper) in which Mary participates. The temporal information is indefinite since we do not know the exact constraint between Skolem constants ω_2 and ω_3.

Let us now define queries. The concept of query defined here is more expressive than the query languages for temporal constraint networks proposed in (Brusoni et al. 1994; van Beek 1991). It is very similar to the query language used in TMM (Schrag, Boddy, & Carciofini 1992).

Definition 2 *A first order modal query over an indefinite $\mathcal{L}_C$-constraint database is an expression of the form $\overline{x}/\mathcal{D}, \overline{t}/\mathcal{T} : OP \ \phi(\overline{x}, \overline{t})$ where ϕ is a formula of $\mathcal{L}_{C,=}^*$ and OP is the modal operator $\Diamond$ or $\Box$.*

Modal queries will be distinguished in *certainty* or *necessity* queries ($\Box$) and *possibility* queries ($\Diamond$).

Example 2 *The following query asks "Who is possibly having a walk before reading the paper?":*

$$x/\mathcal{D} : \ \Diamond(\exists t_1, t_2, t_3, t_4/\mathcal{Q})$$
$$(walk(x, t_1, t_2) \ \wedge \ paper(x, t_3, t_4) \ \wedge \ t_2 < t_3)$$

We now define the concept of an answer to a query.

Definition 3 *Let q be the query $\overline{x}/\overline{\mathcal{D}}, \overline{t}/\overline{\mathcal{T}} : \ \Diamond\phi(\overline{x}, \overline{t})$ over an indefinite $\mathcal{L}_C$-constraint database DB. The answer to q is a database $(\{answer(\overline{x}, \overline{t})\}, \emptyset)$ such that*

1. *$answer(\overline{x}, \overline{t})$ is a formula of the form*

$$\bigvee_{j=1}^{k} Local_j(\overline{x}, \overline{t})$$

where $Local_j(\overline{x}, \overline{t})$ is a conjunction of $\mathcal{L}_C$-constraints in variables $\overline{t}$ and $\mathcal{L}_=$-constraints in variables $\overline{x}$.

2. *Let V be a variable assignment for variables $\overline{x}$ and $\overline{t}$. If there exists a model M of DB which agrees with $\mathcal{M}_C$ on the interpretation of the symbols of $\mathcal{L}_C$, and M satisfies $\phi(\overline{x}, \overline{t})$ under V then V satisfies $answer(\overline{x}, \overline{t})$ and vice versa.*

The definition of answer in the case of certainty queries is defined accordingly. No Skolem constant (i.e., no uncertainty) is present in the answer to a modal query. Although our databases may contain uncertainty, we know for sure what is possible and what is certain.

Example 3 *The answer to the query of Example 2 is $(\{x = mary\}, \emptyset)$.*

Query evaluation over indefinite $\mathcal{L}_C$-constraint databases can be viewed as quantifier elimination in the theory $Th(\mathcal{M}_{C,=})$. $Th(\mathcal{M}_{C,=})$ admits quantifier elimination as a consequence of the assumptions given at the beginning of this section. The following theorem is essentially from (Koubarakis 1997b).

Theorem 3 *Let DB be the indefinite $\mathcal{L}_C$-constraint database*

$$ConstraintStore(\overline{\omega}) \ \wedge$$

$$\bigwedge_{i=1}^{m}(\forall \overline{x_i}/\overline{\mathcal{D}})(\forall \overline{t_i}/\overline{\mathcal{T}}_i)(\bigvee_{j=1}^{l} Local_j(\overline{x_i}, \overline{t_i}, \overline{\omega}) \equiv p_i(\overline{x_i}, \overline{t_i}))$$

and q be the query $\overline{y}/\overline{\mathcal{D}}, \overline{z}/\overline{\mathcal{T}} : \ \Diamond\phi(\overline{y}, \overline{z})$. The answer to q is $(\{answer(\overline{y}, \overline{z})\}, \emptyset)$ where $answer(\overline{y}, \overline{z})$ is a disjunction of conjunctions of $\mathcal{L}_=$-constraints in variables $\overline{y}$ and $\mathcal{L}_C$-constraints in variables $\overline{z}$ obtained by eliminating quantifiers from the following formula of $\mathcal{L}_{i,=}$:

$$(\exists \overline{\omega}/\overline{\mathcal{T}'})(ConstraintStore(\overline{\omega}) \ \wedge \ \psi(\overline{y}, \overline{z}, \overline{\omega}))$$

In this formula the vector of Skolem constants $\overline{\omega}$ has been substituted by a vector of appropriately quantified variables with the same name ($\overline{\mathcal{T}'}$ is a vector of sorts of $\mathcal{L}_C$). $\psi(\overline{y}, \overline{z}, \overline{\omega})$ is obtained from $\phi(\overline{y}, \overline{z})$ by substituting every atomic formula with database predicate p_i by an equivalent disjunction of conjunctions of $\mathcal{L}_C$-constraints. This equivalent disjunction is obtained by consulting the definition

$$\bigvee_{j=1}^{l} Local_j(\overline{x_i}, \overline{t_i}, \overline{\omega}) \equiv p_i(\overline{x_i}, \overline{t_i})$$

of predicate p_i in the database DB.

If q is a certainty query then $answer(\overline{y}, \overline{z})$ is obtained by eliminating quantifiers from the formula

$$(\forall \overline{\omega}/\overline{\mathcal{T}'})(ConstraintStore(\overline{\omega}) \supset \psi(\overline{y}, \overline{z}, \overline{\omega}))$$

where $ConstraintStore(\overline{\omega})$ and $\psi(\overline{y}, \overline{z}, \overline{\omega})$ are defined as above.

Due to lack of space we do not give any examples of this procedure. Examples can be found in (Koubarakis 1997b).

Let us close this section by pointing out that what we have defined is a *database scheme*. Given various choices of $\mathcal{L}_C$ one can use the developed formalism to study any kind of databases with indefinite information (e.g., temporal or spatial). The complexity results of the next section have been developed in a similar spirit. They talk about arbitrary constraint classes that satisfy certain properties. The instantiation of these results to classes of temporal constraints is given in the final section of the paper.

Tractable Query Evaluation in Indefinite Constraint Databases

In this paper the complexity of database query evaluation is measured using the notion of *data complexity* (Vardi 1982). When we use data complexity, we measure the complexity of query evaluation as a function of the database size only; the size of the query is considered *fixed*. This assumption has also been made in previous work on querying constraint networks (van Beek 1991). In our case we also assume that the size of any integer constant in the database is *logarithmic* in the size of the database (Kanellakis, Kuper, & Revesz 1990).

Evaluating possibility queries over indefinite constraint databases can be NP-hard even when we only have equality and inequality constraints between atomic values (Abiteboul, Kanellakis, & Grahne 1991) (similarly evaluating certainty queries is co-NP-hard). It is therefore important to seek tractable instances of query evaluation.

In this paper we start with the assumption that we have classes of constraints with some nice computational and closure properties. Under these assumptions, we show that there are several classes of indefinite constraint databases and modal queries, for which query

evaluation can be done with PTIME data complexity. We will reach tractable cases of query evaluation by restricting the classes of constraints, databases and queries we allow in our framework. We introduce the concepts of query type and database type to allow us to make these distinctions.

Query Types

A *query type* is a tuple of the following form:

$$Q(Open/Closed, Modality,$$

$$PositiveExistential/SinglePredicate, Constraints)$$

The first argument of a query type distinguishes between closed and open queries. A query is called *closed* or *yes/no* if it does not have any free variables. Queries with free variables are called *open*. The argument *Modality* can be $\diamond$ or $\square$ representing possibility or necessity queries respectively.

The third argument can be *PositiveExistential* or *SinglePredicate*. We use *PositiveExistential* to denote that the query is a *positive existential* one i.e., it is of the form $OP\ (\exists \overline{x}/\overline{s})\phi(\overline{x})$ where ϕ involves only the logical symbols $\wedge$ and $\vee$. We use *SinglePredicate* to denote that the query is of the form $\overline{u}/\overline{s}_1 : OP\ (\exists \overline{t}/\overline{s}_2)p(\overline{u}, \overline{t})$ where $\overline{u}$ and $\overline{t}$ are vectors of variables, $\overline{s}_1$, $\overline{s}_2$ are vectors of sorts, p is a database predicate symbol and OP is a modal operator.

The fourth argument *Constraints* denotes the class of constraints that is used as query conditions. For example the query

$$: \square(\exists x, y, t, u/\mathcal{Q})(r(x, t) \wedge p(y, u) \wedge 2t + 3u \leq 4)$$

is in the class $Q(Closed, \square, PositiveExistential, LIN)$.

Database Types

A *database type* is a tuple of the form

$$DB(Arity, LocalCondition, ConstraintStore)$$

where *Arity* is the arity of the database predicates, *LocalCondition* is the constraint class used in the definition of these predicates, and *ConstraintStore* is the class of constraints in the constraint store. *Arity* can have values N-*ary* and *Monadic*.

In one of our results we consider the type of a database which consists of a *single N-ary predicate* defined by constraints in some class $\mathcal{C}$, and the constraints in the constraint store belong to the same class $\mathcal{C}$. This is a special database type and is represented by

$$SinglePredDB(N\text{-}ary, Single\text{-}\mathcal{C}, \mathcal{C}).$$

Complexity Results

The following definitions are needed below.

Definition 4 *If $\mathcal{C}$ is a class of constraints then $\vee\overline{\mathcal{C}}$ is a new class of constraints defined as follows. A constraint c is in $\vee\overline{\mathcal{C}}$ iff c is a disjunction of negations of $\mathcal{C}$-constraints.*

Definition 5 *Let $\mathcal{C}$ be a class of constraints. The problem of deciding whether a given set of constraints from $\mathcal{C}$ is satisfiable will be denoted by $SAT(\mathcal{C})$. The problem of eliminating an arbitrary number of variables from a given set of constraints from class $\mathcal{C}$ will be denoted by $VAR\text{-}ELIM(\mathcal{C})$. If the number of variables is fixed then the problem will be denoted by $FVAR\text{-}ELIM(\mathcal{C})$.*

In the lemmas and theorems of this section we often assume that $SAT(\mathcal{C})$, $VAR\text{-}ELIM(\mathcal{C})$ or $FVAR\text{-}ELIM(\mathcal{C})$ can be done in PTIME. The implicit parameter of interest here is the size of the input constraint set.

Let us now present our results assuming the data complexity measure. We first consider closed queries.

Lemma 1 *Let $\mathcal{C}$ be a class of constraints. Evaluating a query of the class*

$$Q(Closed, \Diamond, PositiveExistential, \mathcal{C})$$

over an indefinite constraint database of the class $DB(N\text{-}ary, \mathcal{C}, \mathcal{C})$ is equivalent to deciding the consistency of a set of m formulas of the form

$$CS(\overline{\omega}) \wedge \theta_i(\overline{\omega}), \quad i = 1, \ldots, m$$

where CS and θ_i are conjunctions of $\mathcal{C}$-constraints.

Theorem 4 *Let $\mathcal{C}$ be a class of constraints such that $SAT(\mathcal{C})$ and $FVAR\text{-}ELIM(\mathcal{C})$ can be solved in PTIME. Let DB be an indefinite constraint database of the class $DB(N\text{-}ary, \mathcal{C}, \mathcal{C})$ and q be a query of the class $Q(Closed, \Diamond, PositiveExistential, \mathcal{C})$ The problem of deciding whether $q(DB) = yes$ can be solved with PTIME data complexity.*

Lemma 2 *Let $\mathcal{E}, \mathcal{C}$ be two classes of constraints such that $\mathcal{E} \subseteq \mathcal{C}$ and $\vee\overline{\mathcal{E}} \subseteq \mathcal{C}$. Evaluating a query of the class $Q(Closed, \Box, PositiveExistential, \mathcal{E})$ over an indefinite constraint database of the class $DB(N\text{-}ary, \mathcal{E}, \mathcal{C})$ is equivalent to deciding the consistency of a formula of the form*

$$CS(\overline{\omega}) \wedge \theta_1(\overline{\omega}) \wedge \ldots \wedge \theta_m(\overline{\omega})$$

where CS is a conjunction of $\mathcal{C}$-constraints and θ_i, $1 \le i \le m$ are $\mathcal{C}$-constraints.

Theorem 5 *Let $\mathcal{E}, \mathcal{C}$ be two classes of constraints such that $\mathcal{E} \subseteq \mathcal{C}$, $\vee\overline{\mathcal{E}} \subseteq \mathcal{C}$ and $SAT(\mathcal{C})$ and $FVAR\text{-}ELIM(\overline{\mathcal{E}})$ can be solved in PTIME. Let DB be an indefinite constraint database of the class $DB(N\text{-}ary, \mathcal{E}, \mathcal{C})$ and q be a query of the class $Q(Closed, \Box, PositiveExistential, \mathcal{E})$. The problem of deciding whether $q(DB) = yes$ can be solved with PTIME data complexity.*

We now turn our attention to tractable query evaluation for open queries.

Lemma 3 *Let $\mathcal{C}$ be a class of constraints. Evaluating a query of the class*

$$Q(Open, \Diamond, PositiveExistential, \mathcal{C})$$

over an indefinite constraint database of the class $DB(N\text{-}ary, \mathcal{C}, \mathcal{C})$ is equivalent to eliminating quantifiers from a set of m formulas of the form

$$(\exists\overline{\omega})(CS(\overline{\omega}) \wedge \theta_i(\overline{u}, \overline{\omega})), \quad i = 1, \ldots, m$$

where CS and θ_i are conjunctions of $\mathcal{C}$-constraints and $\overline{u}$ is the vector of free variables of the query.

Theorem 6 *Let $\mathcal{C}$ be a class of constraints such that $VAR\text{-}ELIM(\mathcal{C})$ can be done in PTIME. Let DB be an indefinite constraint database of the class $DB(N\text{-}ary, \mathcal{C}, \mathcal{C})$ and q be a query of the class $Q(Open, \Diamond, PositiveExistential, \mathcal{C})$. The problem of evaluating $q(DB)$ can be solved with PTIME data complexity.*

Lemma 4 *Let $\mathcal{C}$ be a class of constraints which is closed under negation. Evaluating a query of the class $Q(Open, \Box, SinglePredicate, None)$ over an indefinite constraint database of the class $SinglePredDB(N\text{-}ary, Single\text{-}\mathcal{C}, \mathcal{C})$ is equivalent to eliminating quantifiers from a formula of the form $CS(\overline{\omega}) \wedge \theta_1(\overline{u}, \overline{\omega}) \wedge \ldots \wedge \theta_l(\overline{u}, \overline{\omega})$ where CS is a conjunction of $\mathcal{C}$-constraints, θ_i, $1 \le i \le l$ are $\mathcal{C}$-constraints, $\overline{u}$ is the vector of free variables of the query and l is the number of disjuncts in the disjunction defining the single predicate referred in the query.*

Theorem 7 *Let $\mathcal{C}$ be a class of constraints such that $\mathcal{C}$ is closed under negation and $VAR\text{-}ELIM(\mathcal{C})$ can be done in PTIME. Let DB be an indefinite constraint database of the class $SinglePredDB(N\text{-}ary, Single\text{-}\mathcal{C}, \mathcal{C})$ and q be a query of the class $Q(Open, \Box, SinglePredicate, None)$. The problem of evaluating $q(DB)$ can be solved with PTIME data complexity.*

Applications to Temporal Reasoning

We will now specialize the general complexity results presented in the previous section to some interesting temporal and spatial domains. We will need the following classes of constraints:

- HDL, LIN and UTVPI$^{\neq}$ defined earlier.

- LINEQ. This is the subclass of LIN which contains only linear equalities.

- **IA.** This is the Interval Algebra of Allen (Allen 1983).

- **SIA.** This is the subalgebra of **IA** which includes only interval relations that can be translated into conjunctions of order constraints $x \le y$ or $x \ne y$ on the endpoints of intervals (van Beek & Cohen 1990).

- **ORDHorn.** This is the subalgebra of **IA** which includes only interval relations that can be translated into conjunctions of ORD-Horn constraints on the endpoints of intervals (Nebel & Bürckert 1995). An *ORD-Horn constraint* is a disjunction of weak inequalities of the form $x \le y$ and disequations of the form $x \ne y$ with the additional constraint that the number of inequalities should not exceed one (Nebel & Bürckert 1995).

- **PA** and **CPA**. **PA** is the Point Algebra of (Vilain, Kautz, & van Beek 1989). **CPA** is the subalgebra of **PA** which does not include the relation $\neq$.

- *None*. This is used when we only have the trivial constraints *true* and *false*.

Theorem 8 *Evaluation of*

1. $Q(Closed, \diamond, PositiveExistential, HDL)$ *queries over* $DB(N\text{-}ary, HDL, HDL)$ *databases,*

2. $Q(Closed, \Box, PositiveExistential, LINEQ)$ *queries over* $DB(N\text{-}ary, LINEQ, HDL)$ *databases,*

3. $Q(Open, \diamond, PositiveExistential, UTVPI^{\neq})$ *queries over* $DB(N\text{-}ary, UTVPI^{\neq}, UTVPI^{\neq})$ *databases and*

4. $Q(Open, \Box, SinglePredicate, None)$ *queries over* $SinglePredDB(N\text{-}ary, Single\text{-}UTVPI^{\neq}, UTVPI^{\neq})$ *databases*

can be performed in PTIME (using the data complexity measure).

The first part of Theorem 8 is a significant extension of the PTIME result of (Brusoni, Console, & Terenziani 1995) on possibility queries over networks of temporal constraints of the form $x - y \leq c$.

Theorem 8 does not mention constraints on higher-order objects (e.g., intervals) explicitly so one might think that it useful for temporal reasoning problems involving only points. Luckily this is not true. For example, results for interval constraint databases can be deduced immediately by taking into account the subsumption relations between classes of interval and point constraints. For example, the first part of Theorem 8 implies that evaluating

$$Q(Closed, \diamond, PositiveExistential, \mathbf{ORDHorn})$$

queries over $DB(N\text{-}ary, None, \mathbf{ORDHorn})$ databases can be done with PTIME data complexity. This is a significant extension of the PTIME result of (van Beek 1991) on possibility queries over networks of **SIA** constraints. We can also derive an extension of the PTIME results of (van Beek 1991; Brusoni, Console, & Terenziani 1995) for certainty queries with a simple modification of the definition of query (Definition 2). The details will be given in the long version of this paper.

Theorem 8 does not constrain the arity of database predicates. (van der Meyden 1992) has shown that evaluating $Q(Closed, \Box, PositiveExistential, \mathbf{CPA})$ queries over $DB(Monadic, None, \mathbf{CPA})$ databases can be done in PTIME (compare with Part 2 of Theorem 8). If we move to databases with binary predicates, the corresponding query answering problem becomes NP-complete (van der Meyden 1992). Unlike (van der Meyden 1992), we have not proven any lower bound results in this paper. More research is necessary for drawing an informative picture of tractable vs. intractable query answering problems for indefinite constraint databases.

Acknowledgements

This research has been partially supported by project CHOROCHRONOS funded by EU's 4th Framework Programme. Spiros Skiadopoulos has also been supported by a postgraduate fellowship from NATO. Most of this work was performed while both authors were with the Dept. of Computation, UMIST, U.K.

References

Abiteboul, S.; Kanellakis, P.; and Grahne, G. 1991. On the Representation and Querying of Sets of Possible Worlds. *Theoretical Computer Science* 78(1):159–187.

Allen, J. 1983. Maintaining Knowledge about Temporal Intervals. *Communications of the ACM* 26(11):832–843.

Brusoni, V.; Console, L.; Pernici, B.; and Terenziani, P. 1994. LaTeR: a general purpose manager of temporal information. In *Proceedings of the 8th ISMIS*, vol. 869 of *LNCS*. Springer-Verlag.

Brusoni, V.; Console, L.; Pernici, B.; and Terenziani, P. 1995. Extending temporal relational databases to deal with imprecise and qualitative temporal information. In Clifford, J., and Tuzhilin, A., eds., *Recent Advances in Temporal Databases*, Workshops in Computing. Springer.

Brusoni, V.; Console, L.; and Terenziani, P. 1995. On the computational complexity of querying bounds on differences constraints. *Artificial Intelligence* 74(2):367–379.

Dean, T., and McDermott, D. 1987. Temporal Data Base Management. *Artificial Intelligence* 32:1–55.

Dechter, R.; Meiri, I.; and Pearl, J. 1991. Temporal Constraint Networks. *Artificial Intelligence* 49(1-3):61–95.

Gerevini, A., and Schubert, L. 1995. Efficient Algorithms for Qualitative Reasoning about Time. *Artificial Intelligence* 74:207–248.

Grahne, G. 1991. *The Problem of Incomplete Information in Relational Databases*, vol. 554 of *LNCS*. Springer Verlag.

Imielinski, T., and Lipski, W. 1984. Incomplete Information in Relational Databases. *Journal of ACM* 31(4):761–791.

Jaffar, J.; Maher, M. J.; Stuckey, P.; and Yap, R. 1994. Beyond Finite Domains. In Borning, A., ed., *Proceedings of PPCP'94*, vol. 874 of *LNCS*, 86–94. Springer Verlag.

Jonsson, P. and Bäckström, C. 1996. A Linear Programming Approach to Temporal Reasoning. In *Proceedings of AAAI-96*.

Kanellakis, P.; Kuper, G.; and Revesz, P. 1990. Constraint Query Languages. In *Proceedings of PODS-90*, 299–313.

Koubarakis, M. 1996. Tractable Disjunctions of Linear Constraints. In *Proceedings of the 2nd International Conference on Principles and Practice of Constraint Programming (CP'96)*. 297-307.

Koubarakis, M. 1997a. From Local to Global Consistency in Temporal Constraint Networks. *Theoretical Computer Science* 173:89–112.

Koubarakis, M. 1997b. The Complexity of Query Evaluation in Indefinite Temporal Constraint Databases. *Theoretical Computer Science* 171:25–60.

Mylopoulos, J.; Borgida, A.; Jarke, M.; and Koubarakis, M. 1990. Telos: A Language for Representing Knowledge About Information Systems. *ACM Transactions on Information Systems* 8(4):325–362.

Nebel, B., and Bürckert, H.-J. 1995. Reasoning about temporal relations: A maximal tractable subclass of Allen's interval algebra. *Journal of the ACM* 42(1):43–66.

Schrag, R.; Boddy, M.; and Carciofini, J. 1992. Managing Disjunction for Practical Temporal Reasoning. In *Proceedings of KR'92*, 36–46.

Shostak, R. 1981. Deciding Linear Inequalities by Computing Loop Residues. *Journal of the ACM* 28(4):769–779.

van Beek, P. 1991. Temporal Query Processing with Indefinite Information. *Artificial Intelligence in Medicine* 3:325–339.

van Beek, P., and Cohen, R. 1990. Exact and Approximate Reasoning about Temporal Relations. *Computational Intelligence* 6:132–144.

van der Meyden, R. 1992. The Complexity of Querying Indefinite Data About Linearly Ordered Domains (Preliminary Version). In *Proceedings of PODS-92*, 331–345. Full version appears in JCSS, 54(1), pp. 113-135, 1997.

Vardi, M. 1982. The Complexity of Relational Query Languages. In *Proceedings of PODS-82*, 137–146.

Vilain, M.; Kautz, H.; and van Beek, P. 1989. Constraint Propagation Algorithms for Temporal Reasoning: A Revised Report. In Weld, D., and de Kleer, J., eds., *Readings in Qualitative Reasoning about Physical Systems*. Morgan Kaufmann. 373–381.

Yannakakis, M. 1988. Expressing Combinatorial Optimization Problems by Linear Programs. In *Proc. of STOC-88*, 223–288.

Polarity Guided Tractable Reasoning

Zbigniew Stachniak

Department of Computer Science
York University
Ontario, M3J 1P3 Canada
zbigniew@cs.yorku.ca

Abstract

Non-clausal refinement of Boolean Constraint Propagation inference procedure for classical logic, called P-BCP, is introduced within a new knowledge representational formalism of polarized formulas. P-BCP is a sound, incomplete, and linear-time inference procedure. It is shown that P-BCP can be adopted for tractable reasoning in a number of non-classical logics (including some modal and finitely-valued logics).

Introduction

The use of clausal logic for the representation of knowledge and tractable reasoning is extensive but not without its problems. Knowledge represented in clausal logic frequently results in large, difficult to handle sets of formulas. Extensions of efficient clause-based inference procedures to non-clausal theories frequently result in either intractable procedures (cf. de Kleer, 1990) or in reasoning procedures with a diminished inference power (e.g., when structure preserving CNF transformation algorithms are employed, cf. Empirical Results in (Roy-Chowdhury and Dalal, 1997)).

To find a compromise between the efficiency of reasoning and the expressive power of a knowledge representational framework one can settle for a fully non-clausal and sound reasoning system but either with significantly restricted inference power or of higher computationally complexity. Or, one can aim at the extension of the class of clauses to a class of free-form formulas that enjoy computational properties of clauses while, due to their free-form nature, they eliminate the need for a syntactic transformation into some normal form. The former approach is taken, for instance, in (Roy-Chowdhury and Dalal, 1997). The authors' Restricted Fact Propagation (RFP) is a fully non-clausal, sound, incomplete, and quadratic time inference procedure. Inferentially, RFP is equivalent to CNF-BCP, i.e., to Boolean Constraint Propagation (cf. McAllester, 1990) augmented with the standard CNF transformation of an input set into clauses. The research reported in this paper follows the latter direction. We propose a new

knowledge representational formalism of polarized formulas and refine Boolean Constraint Propagation procedure to work with theories of polarized formulas. The notion of a polarized formula is a free-form counterpart of a clause based on the notion of polarity. This notion does not rely on a specific syntactic form (polarized formulas are free-form formulas) but, instead, on polarity values of atoms that occur in such formulas. Representing knowledge using polarized formulas rather than clauses may result in an exponentially smaller theory. The proposed refinement of Boolean Constraint Propagation, named P-BCP, is a sound, incomplete, and linear time inference procedure in the domain of polarized formulas. It is inferentially equivalent to CNF-BCP, i.e., both procedures infer the same literals from the same input set of polarized formulas.

The proposed framework of polarized formulas has other unique features. It allows a universal clause-like representation of knowledge across the class of logical systems. Indeed, the definition of a polarized formula is based on the notion of polarity – the classical notion that is readily available to a variety of logical systems. As a result, P-BCP can be adopted for tractable non-classical reasoning in a number of logical systems.

This paper is organized as follows. The next section, 'Logical Preliminaries', briefly reviews the basic logical notions and notation adopted in this paper. The following two sections present the definitions of the class of polarized formulas for classical logic and of P-BCP. These sections contain the main theoretical results concerning P-BCP; the linear-time refinement of P-BCP is discussed in subsection 'Time Complexity of P-BCP'. The extension of the polarized-formula and P-BCP framework to non-classical logics is presented in section 'P-BCP for Non-Classical Logics'. We show how P-BCP algorithm can be adopted to some intensional and finitely-valued logics (e.g. the modal logic $S4$ and finitely-valued logics of Łukasiewicz). Only propositional logics are discussed.

Logical Preliminaries

Logical systems considered in this paper are pairs $\mathcal{P} = \langle L, \vdash \rangle$, where L is the (propositional) language and $\vdash$ is the inference operation of $\mathcal{P}$. We identify L with the set of all well-formed formulas which are constructed, in the usual way, from a countably infinite set of propositional variables and a finite set of logical connectives. We assume that among the connectives of $\mathcal{P}$ there are two logical constants: 1, which is a tautology of $\mathcal{P}$, and 0, which is a contradictory formula of $\mathcal{P}$. The inference relation $\vdash$ is a binary relation between sets of formulas and formulas of $\mathcal{P}$. It satisfies *inclusion* ($X \vdash \alpha$, for every $\alpha \in X$), *monotonicity* ($X \vdash \alpha$ and $X \subseteq Y$ implies $Y \vdash \alpha$), and *closure* ($Th(X) \vdash \alpha$ implies $X \vdash \alpha$, where $Th(X) = \{\beta \in L : X \vdash \beta\}$).

If $X \subseteq L$, then $Var(X)$ denotes the set of all variables that occur in formulas of X. We shall write '$\alpha(p_0, \ldots, p_k)$', or '$\alpha(p_i), i \leq k$', to indicate that $p_0, \ldots, p_k$ are among the variables of α. By '$\alpha(p/\beta)$' we denote the result of simultaneous replacement of every occurrence of p in α by a formula $\beta \in L$ (the notation '$\alpha(p_0/\beta_0, \ldots, p_k/\beta_k)$' is self-explanatory). A *tautology* is a formula α such that $\emptyset \vdash \alpha$. α is said to be a *contradictory formula* if for every $\beta \in L$, $\{\alpha\} \vdash \beta$. We call a set $X \subseteq L$ *consistent* if for some $\beta \in L, X \not\vdash \beta$. Finally, X is *inconsistent* if it is not consistent.

When semantics for $\mathcal{P}$ is provided, an *interpretation* of L is a mapping from L into a specified set of truth values TV that includes at least the truth-value 1 (true) and 0 (false). For reasons of simplicity, we identify these truth-values with the constants 0 and 1.

Polarized Formulas in Classical Logic

We begin with an example of a reasoning task that will lead us to the definition of a polarized formula – one of the central notions in this paper.

Consider the following two formulas:

$$\alpha_0 = (\neg p_1 \wedge \neg q_1) \vee \ldots \vee (\neg p_n \wedge \neg q_n)$$

$$\alpha_1 = p_1 \wedge \ldots \wedge p_{n-1},$$

$n > 1$, and the reasoning task of determining all the literals that follow from $\{\alpha_0, \alpha_1\}$ in classical propositional logic (CPL). Clearly, these literals are $p_1, \ldots p_{n-1}, \neg p_n, \neg q_n$. Clausal Boolean Constraint Propagation procedure (BCP) will infer all these literals provided that α_0 and α_1 are transformed into clauses. However, converting α_0 alone into clauses using the standard CNF transformation results in 2^n clauses, much too many for BCP to handle even for moderate values of n. On the other hand, structure preserving CNF transformation of α_0 and α_1 (cf. Tseitin, 1983) results in a set of clauses from which BCP can infer neither $\neg p_n$ nor $\neg q_n$.

The formulas α_0 and α_1 have not been selected just to score a theoretical point. In (Nayak and Williams, 1997) one can find the following small fragment of the propositional theory used for on-board real-time model-based diagnosis and recovery for the DS-1 spacecraft:

$$C_1 : \neg nc_i \vee \neg a \vee nc_0, \quad C_4 : \neg rf \vee ia, \quad C_7 : \neg ok \vee \neg uf$$
$$C_2 : \neg ia \vee nc_0, \quad\quad\quad C_5 : \neg uf \vee ia, \quad C_8 : \neg rf \vee \neg uf$$
$$C_3 : \neg ok \vee a, \quad\quad\quad\quad C_6 : \neg ok \vee \neg rf, \quad C_9 : \neg a \vee \neg ia.$$

Clauses $C_4 - C_7$ result from

$$P_2 : (\neg ok \wedge ia) \vee (\neg rf \wedge \neg uf)$$

by a standard CNF transformation. Clearly, P_2 has the same structure as α_0 ($n = 2$).

It turns out that BCP can be refined to handle explicitly such formulas as α_0 or P_2 without resorting to a CNF transformation (and, hence, without a danger of an exponential explosion or loss of inferential power). The key observation is that, from the polarity point of view, formulas like α_0, P_2, and α_1 resemble clauses: every variable in these formulas has a unique polarity value 'positive' (e.g. all the variables in α_1, or ia in P_2) or 'negative' (e.g. all the variables in α_0, or ok, rf, and uf in P_2). We shall call such formulas *polarized*. Then, in its local propagation step, BCP can make the required inferences guided by the polarity values of variables in polarized formulas.

We now describe the knowledge representational framework of polarized formulas in details. We assume that the connectives of CPL are: $\neg$ (negation), $\vee$ (disjunction), $\wedge$ (conjunction), $\rightarrow$ (implication), and the constants 0 and 1. As usual, a *literal* is either a propositional variable (a positive literal) or the negation of a propositional variable (a negative literal). A propositional *clause* is a disjunction of literals with no literal repeated and containing no complementary literals.

The positive and the negative literals in a clause C are exactly the positive and the negative variables in C under the usual polarity assignment algorithm for CPL which assigns one of the polarity values '+' ('positive'), '−' ('negative'), or 'no polarity' to every variable in every formula of CPL:

> Given a formula α and a variable $p \in Var(\{\alpha\})$ the polarity assignment algorithm first assigns a polarity value to every occurrence of p in α. It assigns '+' to an occurrence of p in α if this occurrence is in the scope of an even number of $\neg$ connectives (for the purpose of assigning polarity values to occurrences of variables we identify $\beta \rightarrow \gamma$ with $\neg\beta \vee \gamma$). Otherwise, the selected occurrence of p in α is negative. Then, p is said to be '+' ('−') in α if every occurrence of p in α is '+' (is '−'). The variable p is of no polarity if it is neither '+' nor '−' in α.

The scope of this polarity assignment algorithm is the set of all the formulas of CPL. We can therefore use the algorithm to identify the class of 'polarized' formulas which, form the polarity point of view, is a natural extension of the class of clauses.

Definition 1: *A formula α is called a polarized formula (a p-formula) if every variable of α is either positive ('+') or negative ('−').*

Example A: The fragment of the DS-1 model discussed above can be represented using fewer formulas (regardless of the intended interpretation of the variables):

$$P_1 : ((nc_i^- \wedge a^-) \vee ia^-) \rightarrow nc_0^+ \quad \text{(replaces } C_1 \text{ and } C_2\text{)}$$

$P_2 : (\neg ok^- \wedge ia^+) \vee (\neg rf^- \wedge \neg uf^-)$ (replaces $C_4 - C_7$)
$C_3 : ok^- \rightarrow a^+$, $C_8 : rf^- \rightarrow \neg uf^-$, $C_9 : a^- \rightarrow \neg ia^-$.

It can be easily verified that all these formulas are polarized. Indeed, the polarity assignment algorithm will assign the polarity values to the variables as indicated by the superscripts '+' and '−'. Henceforth we shall use this subscripting method to indicate the polarity values of variables in p-formulas. ∎

Proposition 1: *For every p-formula $\alpha(p,q)$:*

(i) $\{\alpha(p^+/0)\} \vdash \alpha(p^+)$ *and* $\{\alpha(p^+)\} \vdash \alpha(p^+/1)$;

(ii) $\{\alpha(p^-/1)\} \vdash \alpha(p^-)$ *and* $\{\alpha(p^-)\} \vdash \alpha(p^-/0)$;

(iii) *q retains its polarity value in $\alpha(p/0)$ and $\alpha(p/1)$.*

Corollary 2: *Let $\alpha(p_i^+, r_j^-)$, $i \leq k, j \leq m$, be a p-formula, where $Var(\{\alpha\}) = \{p_0, \ldots, p_k, r_0, \ldots, r_m\}$. If $\alpha(p_i^+/0, r_j^-/1)$ is a tautology, then so is α.*

P-BCP Algorithm for Classical Logic

Boolean Constraint Propagation (cf. McAllester 1990), a variant of which we describe below, is an inference procedure that accepts a finite set S of CPL formulas and returns a partial substitution h_S of constants 0 and 1 for some (possibly all or none) of the variables in $Var(S)$. In addition, BCP may declare S inconsistent.

Given S, BCP initializes h_S to 'undefined' for every variable in $Var(S)$ and, then, modifies h_S by repeating the following *local propagation step* (lp) until h_S cannot be further modified or for some formula $\beta \in S$, $h_S(\beta)$ is a contradictory formula:

(lp) a formula $\alpha \in S$ and a variable $p \in Var(S)$ are selected such that $\{h_S(\alpha)\} \vdash l$, where l is either p or $\neg p$; then $h_S(p) := 1$, if $l = p$ and $h_S(p) := 0$, if $l = \neg p$.

BCP is sound: if $h_S(p) = 1$, then $S \vdash p$; if $h_S(p) = 0$, then $S \vdash \neg p$. The local propagation step of BCP involves general entailment which is coNP-complete. However, restricted to clausal propositional theories BCP runs in linear-time in the total size of the input set (McAllester 1980). In the following subsection we adopt BCP to theories of p-formulas.

P-BCP Algorithm

To establish that $\{h_S(\alpha)\} \vdash l$ holds in the local propagation step (lp) it suffices to demonstrate that h_S cannot be extended to all the variables of α in such a way that for the resulting substitution h_S^*, $h_S^*(\alpha)$ is a tautology while $h_S^*(l)$ is a contradictory formula. If α is a p-formula, then the above property can be easily established. Indeed, suppose that l is a variable p and that $\alpha(p^+, p_i^+, r_j^-)$ is a p-formula such that $p, p_i, i \leq k$, and $r_j, j \leq m$, are all the variables of α for which h_S is undefined. By Proposition 1, if h_S^* is any extension of h_S such that $h_S^*(\alpha)$ is a tautology while $h_S^*(p) = 0$, then $h_S(\alpha(p^+/0, p_i^+/1, r_j^-/0))$ must be a tautology as

well. Conversely, if $h_S(\alpha(p^+/0, p_i^+/1, r_1^-/0))$ is a tautology, then extending h_S by making the indicated assignments, results in h_S^* such that $h_S^*(\alpha)$ is a tautology while $h_S^*(p) = 0$. We therefore conclude that for $\{h_S(\alpha)\} \vdash p$ to hold, $h_S(\alpha(p/0, p_i^+/1, r_j^-/0))$ must be a contradictory formula. A similar argument shows that for $\{h_S(\alpha)\} \vdash \neg p$ to hold, $h_S(\alpha(p^-/1, p_i^+/1, r_j^-/0))$ must be a contradictory formula (we assume that now p is '−' in α).

This observation is exactly what is needed to make BCP tractable in the domain of p-formulas. For a p-formula α and a variable p (as above), let

$$TV(\alpha, p) = \{v \in \{0,1\} : h_S(\alpha(p/v, p_i^+/1, r_j^-/0)) \text{ is a tautology}\}.$$

The new constraint propagation algorithm – BCP for p-formulas (P-BCP) – is obtained from BCP by restricting inputs to finite sets of p-formulas and by replacing (lp) with

---

(lp*) a formula $\alpha(p, p_0^+, \ldots, p_k^+, r_0^-, \ldots, r_m^-) \in S$ and a variable p are selected, where $p, p_0 \ldots, p_k, r_0, \ldots, r_m$ are all the variables of α for which h_S is undefined;

if p is '+' in α and $TV(\alpha, p) = \{1\}$, then $h_S(p) := 1$;

if p is '−' in α and $TV(\alpha, p) = \{0\}$, then $h_S(p) := 0$.

Example A (cont): Executing P-BCP on the set $S = \{P_1, P_2, C_3, C_8, C_9\}$ results in h_S being undefined for every variable in $Var(S)$. On the other hand, adding the variable ok to S results in assigning 1 to ok and to a (via C_3). Then P-BCP assigns 0 to ia (using C_9) and to rf and uf (using P_2). h_S is undefined for the remaining variables. To sum up, P-BCP infers $ok, a, \neg ia, \neg rf$, and $\neg uf$ from $S \cup \{ok\}$.

P-BCP executed on $\{\alpha_0, \alpha_1\}$ (see the previous section) infers $p_1, \ldots, p_{n-1}$ from α_1 (in $n-1$ steps) and $\neg p_n, \neg q_n$ from α_0 (in two steps). ∎

We begin the proof of the correctness of P-BCP with:

Lemma 3: *Let S be a finite set of p-formulas and let h be an interpretation of L such that $h(S) = \{1\}$. Then for every $v \in Var(S)$, if $h_S(v)$ is defined, then $h(v) = h_S(v)$.*

Proof: Let $v_0, \ldots, v_l, \ldots, v_n$ be the order in which P-BCP assigns constants 0 or 1 to propositional variables. Select $v = v_l$ and assume that for every $j < l$, $h(v_j) = h_S(v_j)$.

Suppose that $\alpha(v, p_i^+, r_j^-), i \leq k, j \leq m$, has been used by P-BCP to define $h_S(v)$. Since $h(\alpha) = 1$, $h_S(\alpha(v/h(v), p_i/h(p_i), r_j/h(r_j)))$ is a tautology. Since every p_i is '+' in α, $i \leq k$, and every r_j is '−' in α, $j \leq m$, by Proposition 1, $h_S(\alpha(v/h(v), p_i/1, r_j/0))$ is a tautology. If v is '+' in α, then $TV(\alpha, v) = \{1\}$ and we must have $h(v) = 1$. If v is '−' in α, then $TV(\alpha, v) = \{0\}$ and we have $h(v) = 0$, as required. ∎

Theorem 4 (Soundness of P-BCP): *Let S be a finite set of p-formulas, let $p \in Var(S)$, and suppose that $h_S(p)$ is defined when P-BCP is executed on S. Then:*

(i) $h_S(p) = 1$ *implies* $S \vdash p$;

(ii) $h_S(p) = 0$ *implies* $S \vdash \neg p$.

Proof: Let S and p be as stated. Let $h_S(p) = 1$. To show that $S \vdash p$, select any interpretation h of L such that $h(S) = \{1\}$. By Lemma 3, $h(p) = h_S(p) = 1$, as required by (i). The proof of (ii) is similar. $\blacksquare$

Proposition 5: *If executing P-BCP on a set S of p-formulas results in h_S such that for some $\beta \in S, h_S(\beta)$ is a contradictory formula, then S is inconsistent.*

Proof: Suppose that the execution of P-BCP on a consistent set S results in h_S that is defined for every variable of some $\beta \in S$. Let h be an interpretation of L such that $h(S) = \{1\}$. By Lemma 3, if $p \in Var(\{\beta\})$, then $h(p) = h_S(p)$. Since $h(\beta) = 1$, $h_S(\beta)$ is a tautology. $\blacksquare$

P-BCP is not deductively complete. Indeed, $\{p \to q, \neg p \to q\} \vdash q$ but after the execution of P-BCP on this set $h_S(q)$ is undefined.

Time Complexity of P-BCP

P-BCP is not a very efficient procedure when (lp*) is implemented using the naive search. A better performance can be achieved when the search for α and p in (lp*) is replaced by the deterministic choice. In this subsection we sketch one of the possible solutions that makes P-BCP a linear-time inference procedure in the total size of an input set.

To simplify the presentation, we assume that p-formulas are in *negation normal form* (NNF), i.e., they are constructed from literals using $\vee$ and $\wedge$ as the only binary connectives. (Every formula can be converted into an equivalent NNF formula in linear time.) Furthermore, since $\vee$ and $\wedge$ are associative, we assume that these connectives can conjoin an arbitrary number n of formulas, $n \geq 2$. In this representation a variable q is '$-$' in a (NNF) p-formula α, if every occurrence of q in α is negated, and is '$+$', if no occurrence of q in α is negated. Hence, similarly to clauses, polarity values of variables in a NNF p-formula are explicitly represented through syntax.

We represent every p-formula $\alpha(p_i^+, r_j^-)$ by its parse tree T_α. As usual, every node N of T_α represents a subformula of α, which we denote by α_N. We assume that leaves of T_α represent literals. Every node N of T_α has a label $\langle c_N, V_N \rangle$. c_N is the main connective of α_N; for leaves, $c_N = \alpha_N$. V_N is a subset of $Var(\{\alpha_N\})$. To explain its role and its construction, suppose that $\alpha(p_i^+, r_j^-)$ is satisfiable. By Proposition 1, $\alpha(p_i^+/1, r_j^-/0)$ is a tautology and so is every $\alpha_N(p_i^+/1, r_j^-/0)$. What we want V_N to contain are all the variables q of α_N such that flipping the truth-value

of q (from 1 to 0, if q is '$+$' in α, and from 0 to 1, otherwise) causes α_N to become a contradictory formula under the modified assignment. Hence, if N is a leaf and α_N is either q or $\neg q$, then we let $V_N = \{q\}$. To compute V_N for an internal node N, suppose that N has m children labeled with $\langle c_i, V_i \rangle, 1 \leq i \leq m$. Then

$$V_N = V_1 \cap \ldots \cap V_m$$

if the main connective of α_N is $\vee$, and

$$V_N = V_1 \cup \ldots \cup V_m$$

if the main connective of α_N is $\wedge$. Indeed, suppose that the main connective of α_N is $\vee$ and that q is a variable such that flipping the truth-value of q causes α_N to become a contradiction. So, every child (disjunct) of α_N is a contradiction under the modified assignment and, hence, q must be in every $V_i, 1 \leq i \leq m$. A similar argument can be used to justify the definition of V_N when the main connective of α_N is $\wedge$.

Example B: The parse trees of the formulas in $S = \{p^+ \wedge (q^+ \vee \neg r^-), r^+\}$ are shown in Figure 2.

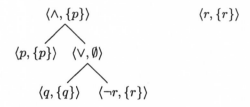

Fig. 2: Parse trees of $p \wedge (q \vee \neg r)$ and r. $\blacksquare$

Let $\langle c, V \rangle$ be the label of the root of a parse tree T_α. We call every $p \in V$ a *terminal variable* of T_α. In example B, the terminal variables are p and r. The main purpose of the construction of parse trees is to determine terminal variables – these are the variables that should be selected in (lp*) to further extend h_S.

Proposition 6: *Let α be a p-formula and let $p \in Var(\{\alpha\})$. The following conditions are equivalent:*

(i) *p is a terminal variable of T_α;*

(ii) *either $TV(\alpha, p) = \{1\}$ and p is '$+$' in α, or $TV(\alpha, p) = \{0\}$ and p is '$-$' in α.*

By Proposition 6, the local propagation step of P-BCP can be simplified to the choice of a terminal variable p of some parse tree T_α. Upon the selection, we define $h_S(p)$ guided by the polarity value of p in α: if p is '$+$', then $h_S(p) := 1$; if p is '$-$', then $h_S(p) := 0$. In other words, (lp*) can be replaced by

---

a terminal variable p of some T_α is selected; if p is '$+$' in α, then $h_S(p) := 1$, else $h_S(p) := 0$; next p is propagated through all the parse trees.

P-BCP repeats this step until h_S cannot be further extended or one of the parse trees has been reduced to the one-node tree labeled with $\langle 0, \emptyset \rangle$.

The propagation of a variable p through a parse tree T_α corresponds, roughly speaking, to the operation of substituting $h_S(p)$ for p in α and, then, simplifying $\alpha(p/h_S(p))$ using Boolean-like reduction rules (such as $(1 \wedge A) \Rightarrow A$, $(A \vee 0) \Rightarrow A$, etc.). We explain this process by continuing Example B.

Example B (cont): Suppose that P-BCP selects a terminal variable p. Since p is '+' in $p \wedge (q \vee \neg r)$, the assignment $h_S(p) := 1$ is made. To propagate p through the parse trees in Figure 2, we first relabel all the leaves that are currently labeled with $\langle p, \{p\} \rangle$. The new label is $\langle 1, \emptyset \rangle$, or to keep things simple, it is $\langle 1 \rangle$. Since there is only one such leaf, we get

$$\langle \wedge, \{p\} \rangle \qquad\qquad \langle r, \{r\} \rangle$$
$$\langle 1 \rangle \quad \langle \vee, \emptyset \rangle$$
$$\langle q, \{q\} \rangle \quad \langle \neg r, \{r\} \rangle$$

The resulting tree corresponds to $1 \wedge (q \vee \neg r)$ which clearly can be simplified to $q \vee \neg r$ using the reduction rule $(1 \wedge A) \Rightarrow A$. This simplification step performed on the trees results in the forest

$$\langle \vee, \emptyset \rangle \qquad\qquad \langle r, \{r\} \rangle$$
$$\langle q, \{q\} \rangle \quad \langle \neg r, \{r\} \rangle$$

Now, the only terminal variable left is r. Since r is '+' in itself, P-BCP makes the assignment $h_S(r) := 1$ and, then, propagates r through the forest as shown below

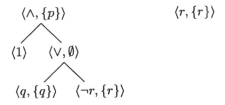

using the reduction rules: $\neg 1 \Rightarrow 0$ and $(A \vee 0) \Rightarrow A$. (Note the reduction of the one-node tree $\langle r, \{r\} \rangle$ to $\langle 1 \rangle$.) Now q becomes a terminal variable which forces P-BCP to make the assignment $h_S(q) := 1$. At the end, P-BCP infers p, r, and q from S. ∎

Let S be a finite set of p-formulas and let k be the total size of S. The creation of the forest of parse trees for formulas in S can be done in $O(k)$ steps. The total number of the simplification steps performed during the propagation of terminal variables does not exceed k. Hence, this refinement of P-BCP is linear time.

P-BCP and Definite Formulas

A *definite formula* (d-formula) is a p-formula which has at most one positive variable (Stachniak 1998). Informally speaking, d-formulas are free-form counterparts of Horn clauses. The results reported in this subsection are the refinements of Theorem 4 and Proposition 5 in the domain of d-formulas.

Theorem 7: *Suppose that S is a finite consistent set of d-formulas. Execution of P-BCP on S results in h_S such that for every $p \in Var(S)$, $S \vdash p$ iff $h_S(p) = 1$.*

Proof: In the light of Theorem 4, we only need to demonstrate the 'only if' part of the theorem. To this end, let S be as stated, let $S \vdash p$, and let h be an interpretation of L such that $h(S) = \{1\}$. Since $S \vdash p$, S contains at least one non-tautological formula. We prove the theorem by induction on the cardinality of $Var(S)$.

Let $Var(S) = \{p\}$. Note that p is '+' in every non-tautological formula of S. (Indeed, if $\beta(p^-) \in S$, then since $h(p) = 1$, $\beta(p/1)$ is a tautology; by Corollary 2, $\beta(p)$ is a tautology.) Select a non-tautological $\alpha(p^+) \in S$. By Corollary 2, if $\alpha(p/0)$ were a tautology, then so would α. So, $TV(\alpha, p) = \{1\}$ and $h_S(p) = 1$.

Next, suppose that the theorem holds for every consistent set S^* of d-formulas such that $Var(S^*)$ is of cardinality $\leq k$. Suppose that $Var(S)$ is of cardinality $k + 1$. We claim that

(a) $h_S(q)$ is defined for some $q \in Var(S)$.

If (a) were false, then we would be able to construct an interpretation h^* of L such that $h^*(S) = \{1\}$ and $h^*(p) = 0$ which, of course, would contradict $S \vdash p$. Indeed, suppose that (a) is false. For every $\alpha(q^+, r_1^-, \ldots, r_k^-) \in S$, $0 \in TV(\alpha, q)$ and $\alpha(q/0, r_1/0, \ldots, r_k/0)$ is a tautology. For every $\alpha(q^-, r_1^-, \ldots, r_k^-) \in S$, $1 \in TV(\alpha, q)$ and $\alpha(q/1, r_1/0, \ldots, r_k/0)$ is a tautology. Since q is '−' in α, by Proposition 1(ii) we conclude that also $\alpha(q/0, r_1/0, \ldots, r_k/0)$ is a tautology. So, if h^* is such that $h^*(q) = 0$, all $q \in Var(S)$, then $h^*(S) = \{1\}$ and $h^*(p) = 0$.

Let q be the first variable for which $h_S(q)$ is defined when executing P-BCP on S. If $p = q$, then by Lemma 3, $h_S(p) = h(p) = 1$. Suppose that $q \neq p$. Let S_0 be obtained from S by replacing q by $h(q)$ in all the formulas of S (and removing tautologies). Note that $h(S_0) = h(S) = \{1\}$ and $S_0 \vdash p$. By inductive hypothesis, $h_{S_0}(p) = 1$ when P-BCP is executed on S_0. When P-BCP is executed on S, $h_S(q)$ gets its value in the first place and, then, the algorithm follows the steps of P-BCP on S_0. Hence, at some point, P-BCP will assign the value to $h_S(p)$. By Lemma 3, $h_S(p) = 1$. ∎

Proposition 8: *Let S be a finite set of d-formulas. S is inconsistent iff execution of P-BCP on S results in h_S such that for some $\alpha \in S$, $h_S(\alpha)$ is a contradictory formula.*

Proof: Suppose that S is inconsistent. Let h be the interpretation of L defined as follows: $h(q) = h_S(q)$, if $h_S(q)$ is defined, and $h(q) = 0$, for the remaining variables. Since S is inconsistent, there is $\alpha \in S$ such that $h(\alpha) = 0$. We claim that h_S is defined for every $p \in Var(\{\alpha\})$. Suppose not. Let $p_0, \ldots, p_k$ be all the variables of α for which h_S is undefined. Suppose that p_0 is '+' in α. Since $0 \in TV(\alpha, p_0)$, $\alpha(p_0/0, p_1/0, \ldots, p_k/0)$ is a tautology, or $h(\alpha) = 1$ – a contradiction. If all the variables $p_0, \ldots, p_k$ are negative in α, then $1 \in TV(\alpha, p_0)$ which means that $\alpha(p_0/1, p_1/0, \ldots, p_k/0)$ is a tautology. Since p_0 is '–' in α, by Proposition 1(ii), $\alpha(p_0/0, p_1/0, \ldots, p_k/0)$ is a tautology and, again, $h(\alpha) = 1$, which is impossible.

Since h_S is defined for every variable in $Var(\{\alpha\})$, by the definition of h and the fact that $h(\alpha) = 0$ we conclude that $h_S(\alpha)$ is a contradictory formula.

For the other half of the proof see Proposition 5. ∎

P-BCP and CNF-BCP Compared

Several extensions of clausal BCP to non-clausal theories have been proposed in the literature. (McAllester, 1990) and (de Kleer, 1990) briefly review general BCP. (de Kleer, 1990) further explores CNF-BCP (we review this inference procedure below) and Prime Implicate BCP. (Dalal, 1990) and (Roy-Chowdhury and Dalal, 1997) offer two more fact propagation procedures: Fact Propagation and Restricted Fact Propagation (RFP). Of all these procedures, RFP is a reasonable compromise between efficiency and inferential power; it runs in quadratic time in the total size of an input set and is inferentially equivalent to CNF-BCP. P-BCP is a linear time procedure that operates on p-formulas. In this subsection we demonstrate that P-BCP and CNF-BCP are inferentially equivalent in the domain of p-formulas.

CNF-BCP accepts a finite set S of propositional formulas, converts S into a set S_{cnf} of clauses and, then, follows the steps of BCP on S_{cnf}. The conversion into S_{cnf} is done using the standard CNF transformation algorithm (using the laws: $\neg\neg\alpha \equiv \alpha$, $(\alpha \rightarrow \beta) \equiv (\neg\alpha \lor \beta)$, $\neg(\alpha \lor \beta) \equiv (\neg\alpha \land \neg\beta)$, $\neg(\alpha \land \beta) \equiv (\neg\alpha \lor \neg\beta)$, and $\alpha \lor (\beta \land \gamma) \equiv (\alpha \lor \beta) \land (\alpha \lor \gamma)$).

Theorem 9: *Given a finite set S of p-formulas, P-BCP and CNF-BCP infer the same literals from S.*

Proof: Let S be as stated. If $\alpha \in S$, then by α^* we denote the formula obtained from α by applying one of the laws used to convert S into S_{cnf}. Let S^* be obtained from S by replacing one of $\alpha \in S$ with α^*. We note that

(a) α and α^* are logically equivalent and have the same variables; the polarity values of the variables in α^* are the same as in α (so, α^* is a p-formula).

Hence, P-BCP executed on S and on S^* computes the same substitution, i.e., $h_S = h_{S^*}$. Repeating the process of replacement of some formula α with α^* we conclude that

(b) P-BCP infers the same literals from S as from S_{cnf}.

To conclude the proof of the theorem we need

(c) P-BCP and BCP infer the same literals from S_{cnf}.

Let $v_0, \ldots, v_i, \ldots, v_n$ be the order in which P-BCP assigns constants 0 and 1 to propositional variables. Select v_i and assume that for every $j < i$, BCP assigns $h_{S_{cnf}}(v_j)$ to v_j. If $h_{S_{cnf}}(v_i) = 1$, then there is a clause $v_i \lor C \in S$. Since $TV(\alpha, v_i) = \{1\}$, $0 \lor C$ is a contradictory formula which means that either C is the empty clause or every literal in C evaluates to 0 under $h_{S_{cnf}}$. This means that BCP must assign 1 to v_i, as required. In the same way we show that if $h_{S_{cnf}}(v_i) = 0$, then BCP assigns 0 to v_i.

To conclude the proof of (c), one needs to show that if for some $v \in Var(S_{cnf})$, BCP assigns c to v, then $h_{S_{cnf}}(v) = c$. This can be done as in the first part of the proof of (c) and is left to the reader. ∎

P-BCP for Non-classical Logics

Knowledge representation frequently resorts to non-classical logics (modal, temporal, many-valued). The Definition 1 of a polarized formula is meaningful for an arbitrary logical system $\mathcal{P}$ provided that some *polarity assignment algorithm* is specified which assigns polarity values '+', '–', or 'no polarity' to variables of $\mathcal{P}$. A number of such polarity assignment algorithms for classical as well as non-classical logics are discussed in (Manna and Waldinger, 1986) and (Stachniak, 1996). In this section we adopt the P-BCP algorithm to some non-classical logics.

Let $\mathcal{P} = \langle L, \vdash \rangle$ be an arbitrary propositional logic and let $\mathcal{A}$ be a polarity assignment algorithm which assigns the polarity values '+', '–', or 'no polarity' to variables in formulas of $\mathcal{P}$. We assume that

(i1) *the class of p-formulas determined by $\mathcal{A}$ has the properties described in Proposition 1.*

Going through the proof of Theorem 4 one realizes that P-BCP can be proved correct for a logic $\mathcal{P}$ if, roughly speaking, $\mathcal{P}$ can be defined using two-valued semantics (not necessarily truth-functional) in which interpretations are arbitrary mappings of formulas of $\mathcal{P}$ into, say, $\{0, 1\}$. In (Suszko, 1977) the author argues that 'every logic is two-valued'. Suszko shows that for every (propositional) logic $\mathcal{P} = \langle L, \vdash \rangle$ one can find a set $H_\vdash$ of functions from L into $\{0, 1\}$ (*logical interpretations*) such that for every $X \cup \{\alpha\} \subseteq L$,

$$X \vdash \alpha \text{ iff for every } h \in H_\vdash, \ h(X) \subseteq \{1\} \text{ implies } h(\alpha) = 1.$$

Indeed, the required set $H_\vdash$ can be define as follows. For every set $X \subseteq L$ consistent in $\mathcal{P}$ define $h_X : L \longrightarrow \{0, 1\}$ in the following way: $h(\alpha) = 1$ if $X \vdash \alpha$, and $h(\alpha) = 0$, if $X \nvdash \alpha$. Now, take $H_\vdash$ to be the set of all such mappings. If $\mathcal{P}$ has the property that every consistent set is included in a maximal consistent set, then it is sufficient to include in $H_\vdash$ only mappings h_X, where X is maximal consistent.

Some restrictions on $H_\vdash$ and, hence, on the logics that we shall subject to our further analysis are necessary. First, we need the proper interpretation of the constants 0 and 1:

(i2) *for every* $h \in H_\vdash, h(0) = 0$ *and* $h(1) = 1$.

Second, we need some sort of negation to allow the representation of negative information. We therefore assume that the negation connective $\neg$ is available in $\mathcal{P}$ and that it satisfies at least the following condition:

(i3) *for every p-formula* $\alpha(q)$, *if* q *is* '$+$' *(is* '$-$'*) in* α, *then* q *is* '$-$' *(is* '$+$'*) in* $\neg\alpha$; *moreover, for every* $h \in H_\vdash, h(\neg 0) = 1$ *and* $h(\neg 1) = 0$.

Finally,

(i4) *if for some* $h \in H_\vdash$, $h(\alpha(p_0, \ldots, p_k)) = 1$, *then* $\alpha(p_0/h(p_0), \ldots, p_k/h(p_k))$ *is a tautology*.

Example C: Among the logics that satisfy (i1)–(i4) there is the modal logic $S4$ (cf. Mints, 1992) over the propositional language that contains the classical connectives $\neg, \vee, \wedge, \rightarrow$, and one modal connective $\square$. For $S4$, logical interpretations in $H_\vdash$ can be defined in terms of maximal consistent sets of formulas (cf. Mints, 1992, Section 4). The class of $S4$ p-formulas is defined using the polarity assignment algorithm for CPL reviewed in section 'Polarized Formulas in Classical Logic'.

The proofs of (i1)–(i3) for $S4$ are straightforward and are omitted for reasons of space limitation. The proof of (i4) requires more work. In what follows, '$\alpha \equiv \beta$' abbreviates '$(\alpha \rightarrow \beta) \wedge (\beta \rightarrow \alpha)$'.

Lemma A: *Let* $\alpha(p)$ *be a p-formula of* $S4$. *Then:*

(i) $\{p \rightarrow 0\} \vdash_{S4} \alpha(p) \equiv \alpha(p/0)$;

(ii) $\{1 \rightarrow p\} \vdash_{S4} \alpha(p) \equiv \alpha(p/1)$.

Proof: By induction on the complexity of α. ∎

Lemma B: *Suppose that* α *is a p-formula of* $S4$ *without variables. If for some* $h_X \in H_\vdash$, $h_X(\alpha) = 1$, *then* α *is a tautology.*

Proof: Let α be as stated, let W be any maximal consistent set, and let α^* be obtained from α by removing all occurrences of $\square$. Using induction on the complexity of α one can show that

(a) $\alpha \in W$ iff $\alpha^* \in W$.

Let $h_X \in H_\vdash$ be such that $h_X(\alpha) = 1$. To show that α is a tautology we must show that for every $h_W \in H_\vdash, h_W(\alpha) = 1$ or, equivalently, that $\alpha \in W$. Select $h_W \in H_\vdash$. Since $h_X(\alpha) = 1$, $\alpha \in X$ and, by (a), $\alpha^* \in X$. Since α^* is a formula of classical logic, by the consistency of X, α^* is a tautology. Since W is maximal consistent, $\alpha^* \in W$. By (a), $\alpha \in W$. ∎

Now, we are ready to demonstrate (i4). Let $\alpha(p_0, p_1)$ be a formula of $S4$ (for simplicity, assume that α has only

two variables) and let $h_X(\alpha) = 1$, for some $h_X \in H_\vdash$. Suppose that $h_X(p_0) = 1$ and $h_X(p_1) = 0$. Since X is maximal consistent, $p_0 \in X$ and $p_1 \notin X$, which means that $1 \rightarrow p_0, p_1 \rightarrow 0 \in X$. By Lemma A, $\alpha(p_0/1, p_1/0) \in X$. Since $\alpha(p_0/1, p_1/0)$ has no variables, by Lemma B, this formula is a tautology. ∎

Soundness of Non-classical P-BCP

Let $\mathcal{P} = \langle L, \vdash \rangle$ be an arbitrary but fixed propositional logic that satisfies (i1)–(i4) with respect to some polarity assignment algorithm. Let $H_\vdash$ be a set of logical interpretations which defines $\mathcal{P}$.

Lemma 10: *Let* S *be a finite set of p-formulas of* $\mathcal{P}$ *and let* $h \in H_\vdash$ *be such that* $h(S) = \{1\}$. *Then for every* $p \in Var(S)$, *if* $h_S(p)$ *is defined when P-BCP is executed on* S, *then* $h_S(p) = h(p)$.

Proof: Let $v_0, \ldots, v_l, \ldots, v_n$ be the order in which P-BCP assigns values 0 or 1 to propositional variables. Select $v = v_l$ and assume that for every variable v_j, $j < l$, $h(v_j) = h_S(v_j)$.

Suppose that $\alpha(v, p_i^+, r_j^-)$, $i \leq k$, $j \leq m$, has been used by P-BCP to define $h_S(v)$ and that h_S is undefined for $v, p_i, i \leq k$, and $r_j, j \leq m$. Since $h(\alpha) = 1$, by (i4), $h_S(\alpha(v/h(v), p_i/h(p_i), r_j/h(r_j)))$ is a tautology. The rest of the proof is as in the proof of Lemma 3, with (i1) replacing Proposition 1. ∎

Theorem 11: *Let* S *be a finite set of p-formulas of* $\mathcal{P}$ *and let* $p \in Var(S)$ *such that* $h_S(p)$ *is defined when P-BCP is executed on* S. *Then*

(i) $h_S(p) = 1$ *implies* $S \vdash p$;

(ii) $h_S(p) = 0$ *implies* $S \vdash \neg p$.

Theorem 11 can be proved in the same way as Theorem 4, using Lemma 10 instead of Lemma 3. Following the proof of Proposition 4 (using (i4) and Lemma 10) we can prove that

Proposition 12: *If executing P-BCP on a set* S *of p-formulas of* $\mathcal{P}$ *results in* h_S *such that for some* $\beta \in S, h_S(\beta)$ *is a contradictory formula, then* S *is inconsistent.*

Example C (cont): Every formula in $S = \{\square p^+ \wedge \neg q^-, \square q^+ \vee r^+\}$ is a p-formula of $S4$. Executing P-BCP on S results in the assignments $h_S(q) := 0$ and $h_S(p) = 1$ (using $\square p \wedge \neg q$), and, then, $h_S(r) := 1$ (using $\square q \vee r$). By Theorem 11, S entails p, r, and $\neg q$ in $S4$. ∎

P-BCP and Many-Valued Logics

While the general two-valued semantics discussed above is also available to many-valued logics, these calculi frequently fail (i4) and, hence, the soundness of P-BCP may be lost. Here is an example.

Example D: The 3-valued logic of Łukasiewicz $\mathcal{P}_3 = \langle L, \vdash_3 \rangle$ is semantically defined in terms of three logical values: $0, \frac{1}{2}, 1$, where 1 is the only designated truth-value (cf. Stachniak, 1996). Logical connectives $\neg, \vee, \wedge, \rightarrow$ are interpreted as functions $1-x$, $max(x,y)$, $min(x,y)$, $min(1, 1-x+y)$, respectively, where $x, y \in \{0, \frac{1}{2}, 1\}$. It can be easily verified that $\mathcal{P}_3$ satisfies (i1)–(i3). Unfortunately, $\mathcal{P}_3$ fails (i4). Take $S = \{\neg p \rightarrow p\}$ and let $H_{\vdash_3}$ be any set of interpretations of L into $\{0,1\}$ which defines $\vdash_3$. Since $S \not\vdash_3 p$, there is $h \in H_{\vdash_3}$ such that $h(\neg p \rightarrow p) = 1$ and $h(p) = 0$. If (i4) were true, then $\neg 0 \rightarrow 0$ would be a tautology of $\mathcal{P}_3$. However, $\neg 0 \rightarrow 0$ is a contradictory formula of $\mathcal{P}_3$.

In $\mathcal{P}_3$, p is '+' in $\neg p \rightarrow p$ under the so-called vo-polarity assignment algorithm. The formal definition of this algorithm can be found in (Stachniak, 1996); the class of p-formulas of $\mathcal{P}_3$ determined by vo-polarity assignment algorithm is the same as the class of p-formulas for CPL discussed in the previous sections. Applying P-BCP to S results in the assignment $h_S(p) := 1$ in spite of the fact that $S \not\vdash_3 p$. ■

P-BCP can regain its soundness in the domain of finitely-valued logics if the definition of $TV(\alpha, p)$ in the local propagation step is adopted to a larger set of truth-values. To explain how this can be done, let us assume that a finitely-valued logic $\mathcal{P} = \langle L, \vdash \rangle$ is defined using a finite set of truth-values $TV = \{0, \frac{1}{n}, \dots, \frac{n-1}{n}, 1\}$ and that 1 is the only designated truth-value. The connectives of $\mathcal{P}$ are semantically defined by truth-tables over TV. An interpretation is a mapping that assigns a truth-value from TV to every propositional variable. Every interpretation can be extended to all the formulas of L in the usual way using the truth-tables; we shall call such an extension an interpretation of L in TV. We adopt the standard semantic definition of $\vdash$: for every $X \cup \{\alpha\} \subseteq L$,

$$X \vdash \alpha \text{ iff for every interpretation } h \text{ of } L \text{ in } TV,$$
$$h(X) \subseteq \{1\} \text{ implies } h(\alpha) = 1.$$

Let h be an interpretation, let p be a propositional variable and let $v \in TV$. By $h[p/v]$ we denote an interpretation that is defined exactly like h except that $h[p/v](p) = v$ (the notation $h[p_0/v_0, \dots, p_k/v_k]$ is self-explanatory). In the P-BCP algorithm, h_S is a partial substitution of constants 0 and 1 for propositional variables. To adopt P-BCP to a finitely-valued semantics we shall view h_S as a partial interpretation that assigns truth-values 0 and 1 to propositional variables. In the new algorithm, the set $TV(\alpha(p, p_i^+, r_j^-), p)$ is defined as

$$\{v \in TV : h_S[p/v, p_i/1, r_j/0](\alpha(p, p_i^+, r_j^-)) = 1\}.$$

Let us refer to this variant of P-BCP as MVL-BCP.

Theorem 13: *Let S be a finite set of p-formulas of a finitely-valued logic $\mathcal{P}$ which satisfies (i1)–(i3), and let p be a variable such that $h_S(p)$ is defined when MVL-BCP is executed on S. Then:*

(i) $h_S(p) = 1$ *implies* $S \vdash p$;

(ii) $h_S(p) = 0$ *implies* $S \vdash \neg p$.

The proof of this theorem is analogous to that of Theorem 3; it is based on Lemma 3 that also holds for MVL-BCP.

Example D (cont): Let us reconsider the set $S = \{\neg p \rightarrow p\}$. Executing MVL-BCP on S we get $TV(\neg p \rightarrow p, p) = \{1, \frac{1}{2}\} \neq \{1\}$. Hence, $h_S(p)$ is left undefined. On the other hand, executing P-BCP for CPL on S gives us $TV(\neg p \rightarrow p, p) = \{1\}$ and $h_S(p) = 1$. By Theorems 13 and 4, $S \not\vdash_3 p$ and $S \vdash p$ in CPL, as expected. ■

Acknowledgments

Research supported by a grant from the Natural Science and Engineering Research Council of Canada. Thanks to the anonymous reviewers for their insightful comments, and to Steven Bernstein for his work on the implementation of P-BCP.

References

de Kleer, J. 1990. Exploiting Locality in a TMS. In *Proc. of the Eighth National Conference on Artificial Intelligence*, 264–271.

Manna, Z. and Waldinger, R. 1986. Special Relations in Automated Deduction. *J. ACM* 33, 1–59.

McAllester, D. 1980. An Outlook on Truth Maintenance. Memo 551, MIT AI Laboratory, August.

McAllester, D. 1990. Truth Maintenance. In *Proc. of the Eighth National Conference on Artificial Intelligence*, 1109–1116.

Mints, G.E. 1992. Lewis' Systems and System T (1965–1973). In Minc G.E., *Selected Papers in Proof Theory*, Bibliopolis and North-Holland.

Nayak, P. and Williams, B. 1997. Fast Context Switching in Real-time Propositional Reasoning. In *Proc. of the Fourtinth National Conference on Artificial Intelligence*, 50–56.

Roy-Chowdhury, R. and Dalal, M. 1997. Model-Theoretic Semantics and Tractable Algorithm for CNF-BCP. In *Proc. of the Fourtinth National Conference on Artificial Intelligence*, 227–232.

Stachniak, Z. 1998. Non-Clausal Reasoning with Propositional Definite Theories. In *Proc. of the Int. Conf. on Artificial Intelligence and Symbolic Computation, Lecture Notes in Artificial Intelligence* 1476, 296–307, Springer-Verlag.

Stachniak, Z. 1996. *Resolution Proof Systems: An Algebraic Theory*, Kluwer Academic Publishers.

Suszko, R. 1977. The Frege Axiom and Polish Mathematical Logic in the 1920^s. *Studia Logica* 34, 377–380..

Tseitin, G.S. 1983. On the complexity of derivation in propositional calculus. *Automated Reasoning* (J. Siekmann and G. Wrightson, eds.), vol. 2, 466–483, Springer-Verlag.

Vision

Content-Based Retrieval from Medical Image Databases: A Synergy of Human Interaction, Machine Learning and Computer Vision

C. Brodley, A. Kak, C. Shyu, J. Dy
School of Electrical and
Computer Engineering
Purdue University
West Lafayette, IN 47907
brodley,kak,chiren,dy@ecn.purdue.edu

L. Broderick
Department of Radiology
University of Wisconsin Hospital
Madison, WI 53792
lsbroderick@facstaff.wisc.edu

A. M. Aisen
Department of Radiology
Indiana University Medical Center
Indianapolis, IN 46202
aaisen@iupui.edu

Abstract

Content-based image retrieval (CBIR) refers to the ability to retrieve images on the basis of image content. Given a query image, the goal of a CBIR system is to search the database and return the n most visually similar images to the query image. In this paper, we describe an approach to CBIR for medical databases that relies on human input, machine learning and computer vision. Specifically, we apply expert-level human interaction for solving that aspect of the problem which cannot yet be automated, we use computer vision for only those aspects of the problem to which it lends itself best – image characterization – and we employ machine learning algorithms to allow the system to be adapted to new clinical domains. We present empirical results for the domain of high resolution computed tomography (HRCT) of the lung. Our results illustrate the efficacy of a human-in-the-loop approach to image characterization and the ability of our approach to adapt the retrieval process to a particular clinical domain through the application of machine learning algorithms.

Introduction

Content-based image retrieval (CBIR) refers to the ability to retrieve images on the basis of image content, as opposed to on the basis of some textual description (Salton, 1986) of the images. Given a query image, the goal of a CBIR system is to search the database and return the n most visually similar images to the query image. A key element of this approach revolves around the types of patterns that can be recognized by the computer and that can serve as the indices of the image retrieval algorithm. Our research addresses the design and implementation of a CBIR system for medical image databases. The success of such an approach provides a unique opportunity to aid physicians in the process of diagnosis.

In the past decade, the field of diagnostic medical imaging has experienced rapid growth and change through both the introduction of new imaging modalities and enhancement in the capabilities of existing

techniques. The shift in technology from analog film based methodologies to computer based digital technologies is creating large digital image repositories. CBIR provides an opportunity to tap the expertise contained in these databases in the following way: observing an abnormality in a diagnostic image, the physician can query a database of known cases to retrieve images (and associated textual information) that contain regions with features similar to what is in the image of interest. With the knowledge of disease entities that match features of the selected region, the physician can be more confident of the diagnosis. In our approach to CBIR, an expert radiologist in each domain (anatomic region) selects images for the database, provides the differential diagnosis and when available, includes treatment information. As such, a less experienced practitioner can benefit from this expertise in that the retrieved images, if visually similar, provide the role of an expert consultant.

In this paper, we describe an approach to CBIR for medical databases that relies on human input, machine learning and computer vision. Fundamental to our approach is how images are characterized (indexed) such that the retrieval procedure can retrieve visually similar images within the domain of interest. To aid in the process of adding a new clinical domain, which we define to be a new image modality and anatomic region, our system adapts its image characterization procedure using machine learning algorithms.

In the remainder of this paper we first describe our human-in-the-loop approach to image characterization for medical images and explain why a totally automated approach is not possible or even desirable. We give an overview of a physician's interaction with the system and present salient aspects of the retrieval process. We then outline the steps taken when adding a new clinical domain to the system. This includes a description of the general purpose low-level image features from which our approach selects a customized set for a particular clinical domain. We present empirical results for the domain of high resolution computed tomography (HRCT) of the lung. Our results illustrate the efficacy of a human-in-the-loop approach to image characterization and the ability of our approach to adapt the

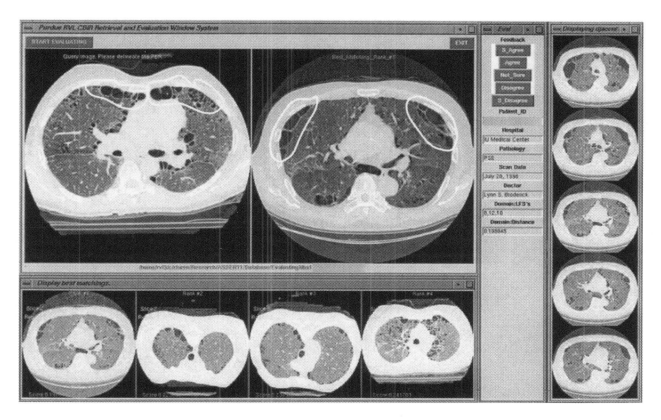

Figure 1: The User Interface

retrieval process to new clinical domains.

A Physician-in-the-Loop Approach

Given a query image, the goal of a content-based image retrieval system is to return the n most visually similar images to the query image in its database. The most common approach is to characterize the images by a global signature (Flickner, et al, 1995; Kelly, Cannon and Hush, 1995; Stone, and Li, 1996; Pentland, Picard and Sclaroff, 1994; Hou, et al. 1992). For example, the CANDID system (Kelly, Cannon and Hush, 1995) computes histograms from normalized gray levels for image characterization and the QBIC system (Flickner, et al, 1995) characterizes images by global characteristics such as color histogram, texture values and shape parameters of easily segmentable regions.

For medical images, global characterization fails to capture the relevant information (Shyu, et al, to appear). In medical radiology, the clinically useful information consists of gray level variations in highly localized regions of the image. For example, for high-resolution computed tomographic (HRCT) images of the lung, a disease such as emphysema (shown in the circled region in the image in the upper left of Figure 1) manifests itself in the form of a low-attenuation region that is textured differently from the rest of the lung. Attributes characterizing a local region are required because the ratio of pathology bearing pixels to the rest of the image is small, which means that global characteristics such as texture measures cannot capture such local variations.

A human is necessary because the *pathology bearing regions* (PBRs) in our images cannot be segmented out by any of the state-of-the-art segmentation routines due to the fact that for many diseases, these regions often do not possess sharp edges and contours. For example, the PBR's in Figure 2 lack easily discernible boundaries between the pathology bearing pixels and the rest of the lung; however, these PBR's are easily visualized by the trained eye of a physician. Our system, therefore, enlists the help of the physician. Using a graphic interface that we developed, it takes a physician only a few seconds to delineate the PBRs and any relevant anatomical landmarks. A benefit of this approach is that when a query image has more than one pathology, the physician can choose to circumscribe only one of the regions in order to focus retrieval on that pathology.

A Hierarchical Approach to Image Retrieval

In Figure 1 we show the retrieval results for a query image (shown at left in the main window). The system displays the four best matching images below the main window. For convenience, the user can click on one of these images, causing the system to display a magnified

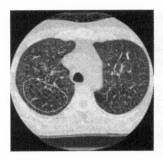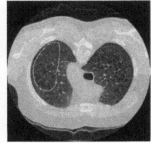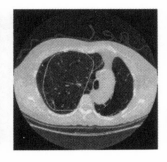

Figure 2: All three images are from patients with Centrilobular Emphysema

version of the chosen image in the window to the right of the query image. The user can provide feedback in the text window, shown on the right of the enlarged matching retrieved image. Shown in the rightmost column are the additional slices from the patient of the enlarged matching image (for each patient, an HRCT session produces on the order of 20-50 cross-section images, called slices). During image population, our expert radiologist identifies the "key" slices that we then include in the database for indexing and retrieval. Because it can be helpful to view other cross-sections, we retain the extra slices and give the user the ability to browse through them.

Given a query image with an unknown medical diagnosis, we first classify the image as one of the known disease classes. The system then uses the features associated with the predicted class to retrieve the n most similar images, as defined by Euclidean distance, to the query image. This approach is motivated by the observation that the features that are most effective in discriminating among images from different classes may not be the most effective for retrieval of visually similar images within a class. This occurs for domains in which not all pairs of images within one class have equivalent visual similarity – i.e., subclasses exists. For example, the features that we use to distinguish cats from dogs are different than those that we use to distinguish an Australian sheep dog from a collie.

Our approach, which we call *Customized Queries*, is appropriate for many clinical domains, because although each image is labeled with its disease class, within one disease class images can vary greatly with respect to visual similarity on account of the severity of disease and other such factors. Figure 2 illustrates this point. Notice that within the class Centrilobular Emphysema Figure 2c is visually dissimilar to Figures 2a and 2b. Indeed, although a given set of features may be ideal for the disease categorization of a query image, those features may not always retrieve the images that are most similar to the query image. We describe below how machine learning methods are applied to obtain the classifier and the customized feature subsets.

Handling a New Clinical Domain

Before describing each phase in detail, we give a general overview of the steps needed to add a new clinical domain to our system. The first step is to collect a database of images for which the diagnoses are known. An expert radiologist for that clinical domain provides the images and interacts with our system to delineate all of the PBRs in each image. Currently we are working with experts in the areas of pulmonary lung disease, hepatic disease (liver) and skeletal disease. Once we have collected enough images to make using the system beneficial, we apply our library of computer vision and image processing routines to extract a feature vector of the low level image characteristics for each archived image. At this point we are ready to train the system and to apply machine learning algorithms to build our hierarchical retrieval procedure.

Image Collection and Region Extraction

We rely on our medical experts to choose representative images. For a given clinical domain, our goal is to ensure a good distribution over the various diseases for two reasons. First, we would like to be able to retrieve at least four images with the same pathology for each query. Second, in order to select the features to use for classification and for retrieval in our customized queries approach we need to obtain sufficient data to make this choice accurately. The ultimate test of whether we have obtained a sufficient number of images in the database is in part measured by the accuracy of our retrieval process. This is best judged by clinicians, and therefore is an inherently subjective measure.

To archive an image into the database, a physician delineates the PBRs and any relevant anatomical landmarks. This interaction takes only a few seconds for a trained domain expert (a radiologist). The left hand image in Figure 1 shows an HRCT image with PBRs as delineated by a physician. The physician also delineates any relevant anatomical landmarks, such as the lung fissures. The information regarding the pathology of the lung resides as much in the location of each PBR with respect to the anatomical markers as it does in the characteristics of the PBRs.

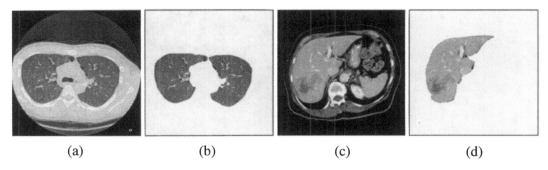

(a)   (b)   (c)   (d)

Figure 3: Region Extraction

The next step is to apply a region extraction algorithm which segments out the tissue type of interest from tissues irrelevant to the disease process. For each new clinical domain, we must write a customized region extraction algorithm. Figure 3a shows the original HRCT of a patient's lungs and 3b depicts the extracted lung region. Figure 3c shows the original CT image of a patient's liver and 3d shows the extracted liver region. Details of these algorithms can be found in (Shyu, et al, to appear).

General Purpose Image Attributes

To characterize each image, the system computes attributes that are local to the PBRs and attributes that are global to the entire anatomical region.[1] The PBRs are characterized by a set of shape, texture and other gray-level attributes. For characterizing texture within PBRs, we have implemented a statistical approach based on the notion of a gray-level co-occurrence matrix (Haralick and Shapiro, 1992). This matrix represents a spatial distribution of pairs of gray levels and has been shown to be effective for the characterization of random textures. In our implementation, the specific parameters we extract from this matrix are energy, entropy, homogeneity, contrast, correlation, and cluster tendency. In addition to the texture-related attributes, we compute three additional sets of attributes on the pixels within the PBR boundary. The first set computes measures of gray-scale of the PBR, specifically, the mean and standard deviation of the region, a histogram of the local region, and attributes of its shape (longer axis, shorter axis, orientation, shape complexity measurement using both Fourier descriptors and moments). The second set computes the edginess of the PBR using the Sobel edge operator. The extracted edges are used to obtain the distribution of the edges. We compute the ratio of the number of edge pixels to the total number of pixels in the region for different threshold channels, each channel corresponding to a different threshold for edge detection. Finally, to an-

alyze the structure of gray level variations within the PBR, we apply a region-based segmenter (Rahardja and Kosaka, 1996). From the results we compute the number of connected regions in the PBR and histograms of the regions with respect to their area and gray levels.

In addition to the texture and shape attributes, a PBR is also characterized by its average properties, such as gray scale mean and deviation, with respect to the pixels corresponding to the rest of the extracted region. The system also calculates the distance between the centroid of a marked PBR and the nearest relevant anatomical marker (e.g., the lung boundary for the domain of HRCT of the lung). For some domains, we include this anatomical information because physicians use this information to diagnose the patient.

The total number of low-level computer vision attributes is 125. While this gives us an exhaustive characterization of a PBR, for obvious reasons only a small subset of these attributes can be used for database indexing and retrieval. In the next two sections we describe how the retrieval procedure is customized for a given clinical domain.

Feature Selection for Image Classification

To select the features that will be used to classify a query image (the first level of our customized queries retrieval scheme) our goal is to determine which features provide maximal class separation. The pathology class labels are confirmed diagnoses obtained from medical records, hence we can consider these as ground truth labels.

To find the best classifier, we first extract all 125 features from each database image. We then run a series of experiments using different classifiers coupled with a forward sequential feature selection (SFS) wrapper (Kohavi and John, 1997) using MLC++.[2] SFS is a greedy search algorithm that adds one feature at a time. It adds the feature that when combined with the current chosen set of features yields the largest improvement in classification performance. Currently we are favoring forward selection over backward selection as we have found that for a given clinical domain a relatively small set is required. Note that which features are included in

---

[1]Note that the sense in which we use the word "global" is different from how it is commonly used in the literature on CBIR. Our global attributes are global only to the extent that they are based on all the pixels in the extracted region.

[2]Available at http://www.sgi.com/Technology/mlc

this subset differs from domain to domain. The resulting feature subset and classifier that perform best, as judged by a ten-fold cross-validation over the database, are used to classify the query image during retrieval. Currently we perform feature selection in conjunction with the 1-NN, 5-NN and decision tree algorithms, but there is no reason why other supervised learning algorithms could not be added to the search. Finally, it is important to note that this procedure should be periodically rerun because as we add more images and disease pathologies the set of relevant features and the best classifier may change.

Feature Selection for Retrieving Visually Similar Images within a Disease Class

After we classify the query image, the next step is to reformulate the query in terms of the feature subset customized for the predicted disease class. In the absence of subclass label information, we must simultaneously find the features that best discriminate the subclasses and at the same time find these subclasses. We resort to unsupervised clustering, which allows us to categorize data based on its structure. The clustering problem is made more difficult when we need to select the best features simultaneously. To find the features that maximize our performance criterion (e.g., retrieval precision), we need the clusters to be defined. Moreover, to perform unsupervised clustering we need the features or the variables that span the space we are trying to cluster. In addition to learning the clusters, we also need to find the optimal number of clusters, k. Hence, we have designed an algorithm that for each disease class, simultaneously finds k, the clusters and the feature set.

Our approach to feature selection is inspired by the wrapper approach for feature subset selection for supervised learning (Kohavi and John, 1997). Instead of using feature subset selection wrapped around a classifier, we wrap it around a clustering algorithm. The basic idea of our approach is to search through feature subset space, evaluating each subset, F_t, by first clustering in space F_t using the expectation maximization (EM) (Mitchell, 1997; Dempster, Laird, and Rubin, 1977) algorithm and then evaluating the resulting cluster using our chosen clustering criterion. The result of this search is the feature subset that optimizes our criterion function. Because there are 2^n feature subsets, where n is the number of available features, exhaustive search is impossible. To search the features, sequential forward, backward elimination or forward-backward search can be used (Fukunaga, 1990). Currently, our system applies sequential forward selection driven by criterion of cluster separability. Because we do not know k, the number of clusters, we adaptively search for the value of k during clustering, using Bouman et al's (1998) procedure, which applies a minimum description length penalty criterion to the ML estimates to search for k. In the remainder of this section, we provide an overview of our application of the EM algorithm and our chosen separability criterion (full details can be found in (Dy,

et al, 1999)).

We treat our data (the image vectors in our database) as a d-dimensional random vector and then model its density as a Gaussian mixture of the following form:

$$f(X_i|\Phi) = \sum_{j=1}^{k} \pi_j f_j(X_i|\theta_j)$$

where $f_j(X_i|\theta_j) = \frac{1}{(2\pi)^{\frac{d}{2}}|\Sigma_j|^{\frac{1}{2}}}e^{-\frac{1}{2}(X_i-\mu_j)^T\Sigma_j^{-1}(X_i-\mu_j)}$, is the probability density function for class j, $\theta_j = (\mu_j, \Sigma_j)$ is the set of parameters for the density function $f_j(X_i|\theta_j)$, μ_j is the mean of class j, Σ_j is the covariance matrix of class j, π_j is the mixing proportion of class j, k is the number of clusters, X_i is a d-dimensional random data vector, $\Phi = (\pi_1, \pi_2, \cdots \pi_k, \theta_1, \theta_2, \cdots \theta_k)$ is the set of all parameters, and $f(X_i|\Phi)$ is the probability density function of our observed data point X_i given the parameters Φ.

The X_i's are the data vectors we are trying to cluster. To compute the maximum likelihood estimate of $f(X_i|\Phi)$ we use the expectation-maximization (EM) algorithm. The missing data for this problem is the knowledge about to which cluster each data point belongs. In the EM algorithm, we start with an initial estimate of our parameters, Φ, and then iterate using the update equations until convergence. The exact form of the update equations can be found in (Dy, et al, 1999).

The EM algorithm can get stuck at a local maxima, hence the initialization values are important. We used $r = 10$ random restarts on k-means and pick the run with the highest maximum likelihood to initialize the parameters (Smyth, 1997). We then run EM until convergence (likelihood does not change by more than 0.0001) or up to n iterations whichever comes first for each feature selection search step. (In practice, raising n above 20, does not influence the results). We limit the number of iterations because EM converges only asymptotically, i.e., convergence is very slow when you are near the maximum. Moreover we often do not require many iterations, because initializing with k-means starts us at a high point on the hill of the space we are trying to optimize.

Fundamental to any clustering algorithm is the criterion used to evaluate the quality of the clustering assignment of the data points. We applied the $trace(S_w^{-1}S_b)$ criterion (Fukunaga, page 446, 1990). S_w is the within-class scatter matrix and measures how scattered the samples are from their cluster means and S_b is the between class scatter matrix and measures how scattered the cluster means are from the total mean. Ideally, the distance between each pair of samples in a particular cluster should be as close together as possible and the cluster means should be as far apart as possible with respect to the chosen similarity metric. We use the $trace(S_w^{-1}S_b)$ as our criterion because it is invariant under any nonsingular linear transformation, which means that once m features are chosen, any nonsingular linear transformation on these features does not change the criterion value.

The trace criterion is used to evaluate each candidate feature subset in our feature subset selection search. Note that this procedure selects features that partition the images within a disease class, but that these features do not necessarily correspond to clinically meaningful features. In other work we are investigating whether computer vision methods can capture the perceptual features that physicians say they use to discriminate among different diseases (Shyu, et al, to appear).

HRCT of the Lung: An Empirical Evaluation of the Approach

Ultimately the true test of a CBIR system is whether it is used by practitioners. To measure whether such a system would be useful, evaluation of an information retrieval system is done by measuring the recall and the precision of the queries. Recall is the proportion of relevant materials retrieved. Precision quantifies the proportion of the retrieved materials that is relevant to the query. In our approach, the precision and recall are functions of 1) the attribute vector used to characterize the images, 2) the delineation of the PBR by the physician, and 3) the retrieval scheme.

The experimental results presented in this section were designed to meet two goals. First to evaluate the contribution made by local characterization, which comes at the price of needing human interaction. Second, to evaluate the ability of the supervised and unsupervised machine learning methods to correctly identify the features used in our hierarchical retrieval scheme. In this paper, we present results using the image modality of high resolution computed tomography images and the clinical domain of pulmonary lung disease.

Our current HRCT lung database consists of 312 HRCT lung images from 62 patients. These images yield 518 PBRs. A single image may have several PBR's and these PBR's may have different diagnoses. Throughout the experiments we considered each PBR as a data point, i.e., a single image with three PBR's gives us three data points. These images were identified by radiologists during routine medical care at Indiana University Medical Center. Currently, the diseases in the database are centrilobular emphysema (CE), paraseptal emphysema (PE), sarcoid (SAR), invasive aspergillosis (ASP), broncheitasis (BR), eosinophilic granuloma(EG), and idiopathic pulmonary fibrosis (IPF). The number of PBRs of each disease is shown in the first column of Table 1.

Local versus Global Image Characterization

This experiment is designed to test the utility of characterizing medical images using local rather than global attributes. To ensure a situation that would mirror its use in a clinical setting, we omit the query-image patient's images from the database search (each patient may have more than one image in the database to

Table 1: Retrieval Accuracy of Global versus Localized Attributes.

Disease Class		Correct Retrievals		Percent of Total	
		$F_L + F_C$	F_G	$F_L + F_C$	F_G
CE	314	2.92 ± 0.18	2.12 ± 0.85	73	53
PE	54	3.04 ± 0.27	1.68 ± 1.07	76	42
IPF	51	2.88 ± 0.32	2.08 ± 0.14	72	52
EG	57	2.72 ± 0.15	1.92 ± 0.32	68	48
SAR	16	2.76 ± 0.71	1.96 ± 0.75	69	49
ASP	12	1.92 ± 0.80	1.64 ± 0.36	48	41
BR	14	3.00 ± 0.32	2.32 ± 0.55	75	58
Total	518	2.88 ± 0.23	2.03 ± 0.72	72	51

ensure a distribution over the different ways in which the disease can appear in an image). Our statistics were generated from the four highest ranking images returned by the system for each query.

Table 1 shows results for two different sets of attributes. The first is a combination of attributes extracted from the PBR region (F_L) and attributes contrasting the PBR to the rest of the lung region (F_C). The combined set $F_L + F_C$ was chosen by the SFS algorithm wrapped around a one-nearest neighbor classification algorithm. The second set of attributes F_G was customized to a global approach to image characterization. The F_G attributes were chosen by the SFS algorithm when optimizing performance for the entire lung region. For this experiment we used the nearest-neighbor retrieval method, which retrieves the four images closest to the query image as measured by the Euclidean distance of the chosen features. For each disease category in our database, we show the mean and standard deviation of the number of the four highest ranking images that shared the same diagnoses as the query image, and percentage of the four retrieved images that have the same diagnosis as the query image.

The attributes in F_L are: the gray scale deviation inside the region, gray-level histogram values inside the region, and four texture measurements (homogeneity, contrast, correlation and cluster). The attributes in set F_C contrasting the PBR to the entire lung are: the area of the PBR, the Mahalanobis distance from the centroid of PBR to the nearest lung boundary point, the difference of gray-scale mean of the PBR and the entire lung, and the difference of gray-scale deviation of the PBR and the entire lung. The attributes in set F_G are: gray scale mean and deviation, histogram distribution, histogram distribution after gamma correction, and four texture measures (cluster, contrast after gamma, cluster after gamma, and edginess of strength after gamma). From the table we see that the localized image characterization method ($F_L + F_C$) has higher precision than the global image characterization method, illustrating that local attributes significantly improve retrieval performance in the domain of HRCT of the lung.

Table 2: Retrieval Results for the Domain of HRCT of the Lung.

Disease Class	Number of Queries	k	Traditional Method					Customized Queries				
			SA	A	NS	D	SD	SA	A	NS	D	SD
CE	18	5	28	9	5	2	28	69	2	1	0	0
PE	3	4	0	0	4	0	8	10	0	1	0	1
IPF	2	3	5	0	0	0	3	3	2	2	0	1
EG	1	4	0	0	0	0	4	4	0	0	0	0
SAR	1	5	0	0	0	0	4	0	0	0	0	4
ASP	1	5	0	0	0	0	4	3	1	0	0	0
BR	1	2	0	0	0	0	4	3	1	0	0	0
total	27		33	9	9	2	55	92	6	4	0	6

One concern of a physician-in-the-loop approach is that precision is a function of PBR delineation. To address this concern, we have performed a sensitivity analysis of our ability to classify PBR to physician subjectivity. Using the same experimental setup, we compared the retrieval results of the physician marked PBRs to larger and smaller PBRs. An empirical analysis illustrated that shrinking or growing the PBR by 50% had a less than 3% impact on the classification accuracy of our method.

The Traditional Approach versus Customized Queries

This experiment illustrates that customized queries[3] results in better retrieval precision than the traditional approach to CBIR, which retrieves the n closest images in the database as measured using the Euclidean distance of the features selected to optimize the accuracy of a 1-NN classifier. In assessing the performance of customized queries we assumed an 100% accurate classifier was used to classify a query as its disease class. We did this to isolate the effect of using the appropriate customized features in retrieving the images, i.e., the utility of customizing a query. This assumption is not too limiting since the classification accuracy we obtained from a ten-fold cross-validation applied to a 1-NN classifier of the disease classes is 93.33% ± 0.70%.[4] In our conclusions we address what steps we take when unacceptable retrieval results are obtained due to an inability to classify the image correctly.

To determine which method is best, the lung specialist in our team was asked to evaluate the retrieval results of the two approaches. Throughout the test, the radiologist was not informed as to which method produced the retrieved images.[5] In Table 2 we show

the number of queries evaluated for each disease. We chose eighteen from C-Emphysema because it is the largest class in our collection (51% of our database is of class C-Emphysema). The number of clusters chosen for each class is shown in column 2. The four images ranked most similar to the query image were retrieved for each method. Note that all images of the query patient are excluded from the search. To evaluate the system, the user can choose from five responses: strongly-agree (SA), agree (A), not sure (NS), disagree (D) and strongly-disagree (SD) for each retrieved image. To measure the performance of each method, the following scoring system was used: 2 for SA, 1 for A, 0 for NS, −1 for D and −2 for SD.

The traditional approach received a total of −37 points, whereas customized queries received 178 points. If SA and A are considered as positive retrievals and the rest as negative retrievals, The traditional approach resulted in 38.89% retrieval precision and customized queries resulted in 90.74% precision. Notice that for the traditional approach precision is not the same as the accuracy obtained for the disease class classifier because there were cases for which the radiologist did not mark SA or A even though the retrieved images had the same diagnosis as the query image. From these results, we can see that customized queries dramatically improves retrieval precision compared to the traditional approach for this domain.

Conclusions and Future Work

In this paper we presented our approach to content-based image retrieval for medical images, which combines the expertise of a human, the image characterization from computer vision and image processing, and the automation made possible by machine learning techniques. We believe that our system combines the best of what can be gleaned from a physician, without burdening him or her unduly, and what can be accomplished by computer vision and machine learning.

In an empirical evaluation, we demonstrated that local attributes significantly improve retrieval performance in the domain of HRCT images of the lung over a purely global approach. A sensitivity study showed that physician subjectivity in PBR delineation impacts

---

[3]Note that for the results presented here, k was chosen using a separability criterion (Dy, et al, 1999).

[4]Note that the retrieval precision in Table 1 was not 90% because in the table we are measuring how many of the four nearest neighbors have the same disease label, whereas here the 93.33% reports the percentage of time that the nearest neighbor has the same disease label as the query image.

[5]To keep the radiologist from guessing, we randomly interleaved the two methods.

performance by only a negligible amount. In a clinical trial, we illustrated that customized queries significantly improve retrieval prevision over the traditional single vector approach to CBIR as evaluated on the domain of HRCT of the lung.

We are working on several fronts to improve our approach. In addition to the domain of HRCT of the lung, we are in the process of populating databases in the domains of CT of the liver, MRI of the knee and MRI of the brain. One potential drawback of the customized queries approach is that when the classifier misclassifies a query image, the retrieval procedure customizes the query to the wrong class. To mitigate this effect, when a physician does not enter agree (or strongly agree) for at least two of the retrieved images, we try again by resorting to the traditional method of retrieval which searches the entire database. Furthermore, although we have an overall classification accuracy of approximately 93%, this accuracy is not uniform across disease classes. For less populous disease classes, the accuracy can be far lower. One reason for this is that the supervised feature selection process does not take this uneven distribution into account. We are currently working on how to select features such that classification accuracy on the less populous classes is not sacrificed for the dominant classes. To help in this endeavor we will investigate how to combine other text-based information about the patient to aid in the initial classification of the pathology bearing region in the image, such as the results of blood tests, age, etc. Finally, we are investigating how to best use user feedback when retrieval results are judged unsatisfactory.

Acknowledgments

This work is supported by National Science Foundation under Grant No. IRI9711535 and the National Institute of Health under Grant No. 1 R01 LM06543-01A1. We would like to thank Mark Flick and Sean MacArthur for their ideas and work on system design.

References

Bouman, C., Shapiro, M. Cook, G., Atkins, C. and Cheng, H. 1998. CLUSTER: An unsupervised algorithm for modeling Gaussian mixtures, http://dynamo.ecn.purdue.edu/bouman/software/cluster

Dempster, A., Laird, N. and Rubin, D. 1977, Maximum likelihood from incomplete data via the EM algorithm, *J. Royal Statistical Society*, B, vol. 39, no. 1, pp. 1-38.

Dy, J. G., Brodley, C. E., Kak, A. Shyu, C. and Broderick, L.S., 1999. The customized-queries approach to CBIR Using EM, *Computer Vision and Pattern Recognition*, Fort Collins, CO, June 1999.

M. Flickner, et al, 1995 Query by image and video content: The QBIC system, *IEEE Computer*, pp. 23-32, September 1995.

Fukunaga, K. 1990, *Introduction to Statistical Pattern Recognition*, 2nd Edition, Academic Press.

Haralick, R. M. and Shapiro, L. G., 1992. *Computer and Robot Vision*, Addison-Wesley.

Hou, T. Y., Hsu, A., Liu, P., and Chiu, M. Y., 1992. A content-based indexing technique using relative geometry features, *Proc. SPIE Conf. on Storage and Retrieval for Image and Video Databases,* pp. 29-98.

Kohavi, R. and John, G. 1997. Wrappers for feature subset selection, *Artificial Intelligence Journal*, Vol. 97, No.s 1-2, pp. 273-324.

Kelly, P. M., Cannon, T. M., and Hush, D.R., 1995. Query by image example: The CANDID approach, in *SPIE Vol. 2420 Storage and Retrieval for Image and Video Databases III*, pp. 238-248.

Mitchell, T. 1997. *Machine Learning*, pp. 191-196, McGraw-Hill Companies Inc.

Pentland, A., Picard, R. and Sclaroff, S. 1994. Photobook: Tools for content-based manipulation of image databases, *Proc. SPIE Conf. on Storage and Retrieval for Image and Video Databases,* pp. 34-47.

Rahardja, K. and Kosaka, A. 1996. Vision-based bin-picking: Recognition and localization of multiple complex objects using simple visual cues, in *1996 IEEE/RSJ Int. Conf. on Intelligent Robots and Systems*, Osaka, Japan, November, 1996.

Salton, G. 1986. Another look at automatic text-retrieval systems. *Communications of the ACM*, 29(7), pp 648-656.

Shyu, C., Brodley, C., Kak, A., Kosaka, A., Aisen, A. and Broderick, L., to appear. ASSERT, a physician in the loop content-based image retrieval system for HRCT image databases, *Computer Vision and Image Understanding*.

Smyth, P. 1996. Clustering using Monte Carlo cross-validation, *The Second International Conference on Knowledge Discovery and Data Mining*, pp 126-133.

Stone, H. S. and Li, C. S., 1996. Image matching by means of intensity and texture matching in the Fourier domain, *Proc. SPIE Conf. in Image and Video Databases,* San Jose, CA, Jan. 1996.

Wolfe, H. H. 1970. Pattern clustering by multivariate mixture analysis, *Multivariate Behavioral Research*, vol. 5, no. 3, pp 101-116.

Using Vision to Improve Sound Source Separation

Yukiko Nakagawa [†], Hiroshi G. Okuno [†], and Hiroaki Kitano [†‡]

†Kitano Symbiotic Systems Project

ERATO, Japan Science and Technology Corp.

Mansion 31 Suite 6A, 6-31-15 Jingumae, Shibuya-ku, Tokyo 150-0001, Japan

Tel: +81-3-5468-1661, Fax: +81-3-5468-1664

‡Sony Computer Science Laboratories, Inc.

yuki@symbio.jst.go.jp, okuno@nue.org, kitano@csl.sony.co.jp

Abstract

We present a method of improving sound source separation using vision. The sound source separation is an essential function to accomplish auditory scene understanding by separating stream of sounds generated from multiple sound sources. By separating a stream of sounds, recognition process, such as speech recognition, can simply work on a single stream, not mixed sound of several speakers. The performance is known to be improved by using stereo/binaural microphone and microphone array which provides spatial information for separation. However, these methods still have more than 20 degree of positional ambiguities. In this paper, we further added visual information to provide more specific and accurate position information. As a result, separation capability was drastically improved. In addition, we found that the use of approximate direction information drastically improve object tracking accuracy of a simple vision system, which in turn improves performance of the auditory system. We claim that the integration of vision and auditory inputs improves performance of tasks in each perception, such as sound source separation and object tracking, by bootstrapping.

Introduction

When we recognize scene around us, we must be able to identify which set of perceptive input (sounds, pixels, etc) constitutes an object or an event. To understand what is in the visual scene, we (or a machine) should be able to distinguish a set of pixels which constitutes a specific object from those that are not a part of it. In auditory scene analysis, sound shall be separated into auditory streams each of which corresponds to specific auditory event (Bregman 1990; Cooke *et al.* 1993; Rosenthal & Okuno 1998).

Separation of streams from perceptive input is nontrivial task due to ambiguities of interpretation on which elements of perceptive input belong to which stream. This is particularly the case for auditory stream separation. Assume that there are two independent sound sources (this can be machines or human speakers) which create their own auditory stream, illustrated as harmonic structures shown in Fig. 1 (a). When these sound sources create sound at the

same time, two auditory streams come together to a listener, superimposed harmonic structure may look like Fig. 1 (b). In this case there are two possible ways to separate auditory streams, only one of them is correct (Fig. 1 (c)).

While many research has been carried out to accurately separate such auditory streams using heuristics, there are essential ambiguities which cannot be removed by such a method. The use of multiple microphones, such as stereo microphone, binaural microphone, and microphone array is known to improve separation accuracy (Bodden 1993; Wang *et al.* 1997). However, so far there is no research to use visual information to facilitates auditory scene analysis.

At the same time, there are many research on integration of visual, auditory, and other perceptive information. Most of these studies basically use additional perceptive input in order to provide clue to shift attention of other perceptive input. For example, research of sound-driven gaze are addressing how sound source can be used to control gaze to the object which generates sound (Ando 1995; Brooks *et al.* 1998; Wolff 1993). Similarly, integration of vision and audition to find an objects using active perception has been proposed for autonomous robot (Wang *et al.* 1997; Floreano & Mondada 1994). By the same token, touch-driven gaze is the fusion of visuo-tactile sensing in order to control gaze using tactile information (Rucci & Bajcsy 1995).

However, in these research the processing of each perceptive input is handled separately except for gaze control. Therefore, there is no effect of increased modality for each perceptive input processing.

In this paper, we argue that the use of visual information drastically improves auditory stream separation accuracy. The underlying hypothesis is that ambiguities in stream separation arise from two reasons:

- there are missing dimensions in the state-space which represents perceptive inputs, and

- some constraints are missing which can be used to eliminate spurious trajectories in the state-space.

We will demonstrate viability of the hypothesis using auditory stream separation of three-simultaneous speeches carried out by (1) a monaural microphone system, (2) a bin-

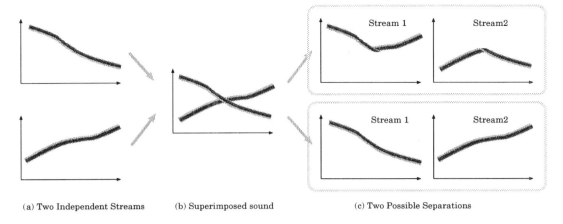

| (a) Two Independent Streams | (b) Superimposed sound | (c) Two Possible Separations |

Figure 1: Example of Overlapped Auditory Streams Separation

aural microphone system, and (3) a binaural microphone[1] system with vision.

Separation of sound source is significant challenge for auditory system for the real world. In real world environment, multiple objects create various sounds, such as human voice, door noise, automobile sounds, music, and so forth. Human being with normal hearing capability can separate these sounds even if these sounds are generated at the same time, and understand what is going on. In this paper, we focus on separation of multiple and simultaneous human speeches, where up to three persons speak simultaneously. At first glance, it may look a bit odd to assume three persons speak simultaneously. However, it turns out that this situation has many potential applications. In many voice-controlled devices, such as a voice-commanded car-navigation system, the system needs to identify and separate auditory stream of the specific speaker from environmental noise and speeches of other people. Most of commercial level speech recognition system built-in into portable devices needs identify and separate owner's voice from background noise and voices of other person happened to be talking to someone.

In addition, due to the complexity of the task, if we can succeed in separation of multiple simultaneous speeches, it would be much easier to apply the method to separate various sounds that has drastically different from human voice. "Understanding Three Simultaneous Speeches" (Okuno, Nakatani, & Kawabata 1997). is also one of the AI challenge problem chosen at IJCAI.

Needs for Visual Information

There are many candidates for clues for sound source separation; Some acoustic attributes include harmonics (fundamental frequency and its overtones), onset (starting point of sound), offset (ending point of sound), AM (Amplitude Modulation), FM (Frequency Modulation), timbre, formants, and sound source localization (horizontal and

---

[1]A binaural microphone is a pair of microphones embedded in a dummy head.

vertical directions, distance). Case-based separation with sound database may be possible.

The most important attribute is harmonics, because it is mathematically defined and thus easy to formulate the processing. Nakatani *et al.* developed Harmonic Based Stream Segregation System (HBSS) to separate harmonic streams from a mixture of sounds (Nakatani, Okuno, & Kawabata 1994). HBSS extracts harmonic stream fragments from a mixture of sounds by using multi-agent system. It uses three kinds of agent; the event detector, the generator, and tracers. The event detector subtracts predicted inputs from actual input by spectral subtraction (Boll 1979) and gives residue to the generator. The generator generates a tracer if residue contains harmonics. Each tracer extracts a harmonic stream fragment with the fundamental frequency specified by the generator and predicts the next input by consulting the actual next input. Then, extracted harmonic stream fragments are grouped according to the continuity of fundamental frequencies.

HBSS is flexible in the sense that it does not assume the number of sound sources and extracts harmonic stream fragments well. However, the grouping of harmonic stream fragments may fail in some cases. For example, consider the case that two harmonic streams cross (see Fig. 1 (b)). HBSS cannot discriminate whether two harmonic streams really cross or they come closer and then go apart, since it uses only harmonics as a clue of sound source separation.

The use of sound source direction is proposed to overcome this problem and Bi-HBSS (Binaural HBSS) is developed by Nakatani *et al.* (Nakatani, Okuno, & Kawabata 1994; Nakatani & Okuno 1999). In other words, the input is changed from monaural to binaural. Binaural input is a variation of stereo input, but a pair of microphone is embedded in a dummy head. Since the shape of a dummy head affects sounds, the interaural intensity difference is enhanced more than that for stereo microphones.

Sound source direction is determined by calculating the Interaural Time (or phase) Difference (ITD) and the Interaural Intensity Difference (IID) between the left and right channels. Usually ITD and IID are easier to calculate from

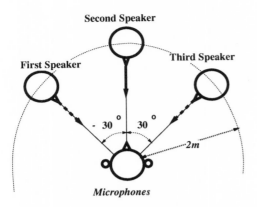

Figure 2: Position of Three Speakers for Benchmark

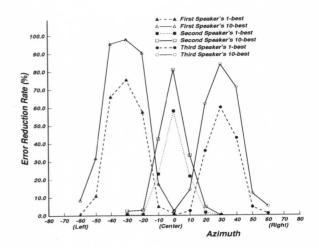

Figure 3: Error Reduction rates for the 1-best and 10-best recognition by assuming the sound source direction

binaural sounds than from stereo sounds (Bodden 1993).

Bi-HBSS uses a pair of HBSS to extract harmonic stream fragments for the left and right channels, respectively. The interaural coordinator adjusts information on harmonic structure extracted by the both HBSS. Then, sound source direction is determined by calculating ITD and IID between a pair of harmonic stream fragments. The sound source direction is fed back to the interaural coordinator to refine harmonic structure of harmonic stream fragment. Finally, harmonic stream fragments are grouped according to its sound source direction. Thus the problem depicted in Fig. 1 (b) is resolved. Speech stream is reconstructed by using harmonic streams for harmonic parts and substituting residue for non-harmonic parts (Okuno, Nakatani, & Kawabata 1996).

Preliminary Experiment

Since the direction determined above in Bi-HBSS may contain an error of $\pm 10°$, which is considered very large, its influence on the error reduction rates of recognition is investigated. For this purpose, we construct a direction-pass filter which passes only signals originating from the specified direction and cuts other signals. We measured the IID and ITD in the same anechoic room for every 5° azimuth in the horizontal plane. A rough procedure of direction-pass filter is as follows:

1. Input signal is given to a set of filter banks for the left and right channels and analyzed by discrete Fourier transformation,

2. IID and ITD for each frequency band are calculated and its direction is determined by comparing IID and ITD. This is because ITD is more reliable in lower frequency regions, while IID is more reliable in higher frequency regions.

3. Then, each auditory stream is synthesized by applying inverse Fourier transformation to the frequency components originating from the direction.

Benchmark Sounds The task is to separate simultaneous three sound sources using binaural microphone and vision. (See Fig. 2) The benchmark sound set used for the evaluation of sound source separation and recognition consists of 200 mixture of three utterances of Japanese words. The mixture of sounds are created analytically in the same manner as (Okuno, Nakatani, & Kawabata 1996). Of course, a small set of benchmarks were actually recorded in an anechoic room, and we confirmed that the synthesized and actually recorded data don't cause a significant difference in speech recognition performance.

1. All speakers are located at about 2 meters from the pair of microphones installed on a dummy head as is shown in Fig. 2.

2. The first speaker is a woman located at 30° to the left from the center.

3. The second speaker is a man located in the center.

4. The third speaker is a woman located at 30° to the right from the center.

5. The order of utterance is from left to right with about 150ms delay.
   This delay is inserted so that the mixture of sounds was to be recognized without separation.

6. The data is sampled by 12KHz and the gain of mixture of sounds is reduced if the data overflows in 16 bit. Most mixtures are reduced by 2 to 3 dB.

Evaluation Criteria The recognition performance is measured by *the error reduction rate for the 1-best and 10-best recognition*. First, *the error rate caused by interfering sounds* is defined as follows. Let the n-best recognition rate be the cumulative accuracy of recognition up to the n-th candidate, denoted by $\mathcal{CA}^{(n)}$. The suffix, *org*, *sep*, or *mix* is added to the recognition performance of the single unmixed original sounds, mixed sounds, and separated sounds, respectively. The error rate caused by interfering sounds, $\mathcal{E}^{(n)}$, is calculated as $\mathcal{E}^{(n)} = \mathcal{CA}_{org}^{(n)} - \mathcal{CA}_{mix}^{(n)}$.

Finally, the error reduction rate for the n-best recognition, $\mathcal{R}_{sep}^{(n)}$, in per cent is calculated as follows:

$$\mathcal{R}_{sep}^{(n)} = \frac{\mathcal{CA}_{sep}^{(n)} - \mathcal{CA}_{mix}^{(n)}}{\mathcal{CA}_{org}^{(n)} - \mathcal{CA}_{mix}^{(n)}} \times 100 = \frac{\mathcal{CA}_{seg}^{(n)} - \mathcal{CA}_{mix}^{(n)}}{\mathcal{E}^{(n)}} \times 100.$$

Preliminary Results 200 mixtures of three sounds are separated by using a filter bank with the IID and ITD data. We separate sounds in every 10° azimuth (direction) from 60° to the left to 60° to the right from the center. Then each separated speech stream is recognized by a Hidden Markov Model based automatic speech recognition system (Kita, Kawabata, & Shikano 1990).

The error reduction rates for the 1-best and 10-best recognition of separated sound for every 10° azimuth are shown in Fig. 3. The correct azimuth for this benchmark is 30° to the left (specified by −30° in Fig. 3), 0°, and 30° to the right. For these correct azimuths (directions), recognition errors are reduced significantly. The sensitivity of error reduction rates to the accuracy of the sound source depends on how other speakers are close to. That's why the curve of error reduction rates for the center speaker is the steepest in Fig. 3.

This experiment proves that if the correct direction of the speaker is available, separated speech is of a high quality at least from the viewpoint of automatic speech recognition. In addition, the error reduction rates is quite sensible to the accuracy of the sound source direction if speech is interfered by closer speakers.

While binaural microphone provides direction information at certain accuracy, it is not enough to separate sound source in realistic situations. There are inherent difficulties in obtaining high precision direction information by solely depending on auditory information.

The fundamental question addressed in this paper is that how the use of visual information can improve the sound source separation by providing more accurate direction information.

Integration of Visual and Auditory Stream

In order to investigate how the use of visual input can improve auditory perception, we developed a system consists of binaural microphone and CCD camera, as input devices, and sound source separation system (simply, *auditory system*) and color-based real time image processing system (simply, *vision system*), that interacts to improve accuracy of processing in both modalities. The concept of integrated system is depicted in Fig. 4.

If auditory scene analysis module detects a new sound source, it may trigger vision module to focus on it. If vision module identifies the position of the sound source, it returns the information to auditory scene analysis module and conflict resolution module checks whether the both

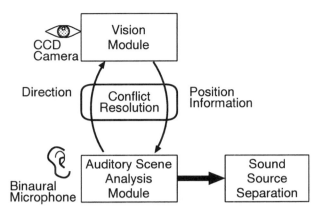

Figure 4: Concept of Integrated Vision and Auditory Systems

information specifies the same sound source. In case of the same sound source, the position information subsumes the direction information as long as the sound source exists.

While there are several ways for vision and auditory perceptions to interact, we focus on how information on position of possible sound sources derived from both vision and auditory perception interact to improve auditory stream separation. In essence, a visual input provides information on directions of possible sound sources, which can be used to better separate auditory stream. At the same time, as we will discuss in depth later, information of approximate direction of sound sources significantly improve accuracy of vision system in tracking possible sound sources by constraining possible location of target objects.

Auditory Streams

The task of audition is to understand *auditory events*, or the sound sources. An auditory event is represented by *auditory streams*, each of which is a group of acoustic components that have consistent attributes. Since acoustic events are represented hierarchically (e.g. orchestra), auditory streams have also a hierarchical structure.

Auditory system should separate auditory streams by using the sound source direction and do the separation incrementally and in real-time, but such a system has not been developed so far. Therefore, as a prototype of auditory system, we use Bi-HBSS, because it separates harmonic structures incrementally by using harmonic structure and the sound source direction.

Visual Streams

The task of vision is to identify possible sound sources. Among various methods to track moving objects, we used a simple color-based tracking. This is because we are also interested in investigating how accuracy of visual tracking can be improved using information from the auditory system, particularly sound source position.

Images are taken by a CCD camera (378K pixel 2/3" CCD) with a wide conversion lens, video capture board in a personal computer (Pentium II 450MHz, 384MB RAM), a

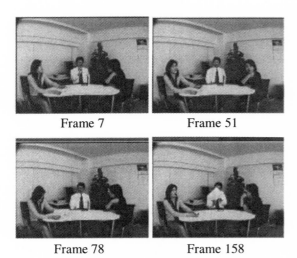

Frame 7   Frame 51

Frame 78   Frame 158

Figure 5: Some Visual Images for Tracking Experiments

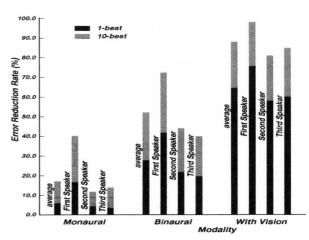

Figure 6: Experiment 1: Improvement of Error reduction rates for the 1-best/10-best recognition of each speech by incorporating more modalities

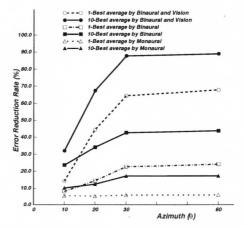

Figure 7: Experiment 2: How average of error reduction rates for the 1-best/10-best recognition of each speech by incorporating modalities vary when the position of each speaker varies.

the rate of six frames per second for forty seconds. Captured images are 640 × 480 pixels with 16 bit color. R, G and B in a pixel is represented by 5 bit, respectively. The pixel color (RGB) is translated into HSV color model to attain higher robustness against small changes in lighting condition.

In this experiment, we assume that a human face, especially mouth is a possible sound source and that the mouth is around the gravity center of face. Therefore, the vision system computes clusters of skin colors, and their center of gravity to identify the mouth.

Since there are multiple clusters of skin color, such as face, hands, and legs, clusters that are not considered as face shall be eliminated using various constraints. Such constraints includes positional information from auditory system, heights, velocity of cluster motion, etc.

Experiments

Test Data

Auditory Sounds and Criteria of Evaluation   Since the preliminary experiment is already reported in this paper, the same benchmark sounds are used and the same evaluation criteria for performance is adopted.

Visual Images   The auditory situation described above was realized in a visual image that has three people sitting around the table and discussing some business issues. Image is taken by a CCD camera positioned two meters from the speakers. Excerpts of frames from the image are shown in Fig. 5. Apart from face of each person, there are few objects that causes false tracking. One is a yellow box just left side of the person in the center, and the other is a knee (under the table) of the person in the left. In addition, hands can be mis-recognized as it has similar color with face.

Experiment 1: Effect of Modalities

In Experiment 1, we investigate the effect of three modalities. They are listed in the order of increasing modalities:

1. Speech stream separation by monaural inputs,

2. Speech stream separation by binaural inputs, and

3. Speech stream separation by binaural inputs with visual information.

We use HBSS, Bi-HBSS and simulator for integrated systems depicted in Fig. 4 for the three experiments, respectively.

Error reduction rates for the 1-best and 10-best recognition of each speech is shown in Fig. 6. As more modalities are incorporated in auditory system, error reduction rates are improved drastically.

Experiment 2: Robustness of Modality against Closer Speakers

In Experiment 2, we investigate the robustness of the three speech stream separation algorithms by changing the directions of each speakers. The azimuth between the first and second speakers and that between the second and third speakers are the same, say "θ". We measured the average error reduction rates for the 1-best and 10-best recognition for $10°$, $20°$, $30°$, and $60°$.

The result of error reduction rates by the three algorithms is shown in Fig. 7. Error reduction rates saturate around the azimuth of more than $30°$. For the azimuth of $10°$ and $20°$, error reduction rates for the second (center) speaker are quite poor compared with the other speakers (this data is not shown in Fig. 7).

Experiment 3: Accuracy of Vision System with Auditory Feedback

Experiments 1 and 2 assume that vision system provides precise direction information, and thus the auditory system can disambiguate harmonic structures without checking its validity. However, question can be raised on the accuracy of vision system. If the vision system provides wrong direction information to the auditory system, the performance of sound source separation may be drastically deteriorated, because it must operate under wrong assumptions. Therefore, Experiment 3 focuses on how the accuracy of vision system is improved as more constraints are incorporated.

We measured tracking accuracy of a simple color-based tracking system with (1) no constraints (purely rely on cluster of color), (2) presumed knowledge on human heights, (3) approximate direction information ($-40° \sim -20°$, $-10° \sim -10°$, and $20° \sim 40°$) from the auditory system, and (4) using both height and direction information. Fig. 8 shows actual tracking log for each case.

In this experimental data, speakers are sitting around the table where they can be seen at $-30°$, $0°$, and $20°$ in the visual field of the camera.

The result of tracking accuracy is shown in Fig. 8. As a reference for comparison, accurate face position is annotated manually (Fig. 8 (R)). When only color is used for tracking, there are numbers of spurious clusters that are mistakenly recognized as face (Fig. 8 (a)). Using knowledge on human height, some clusters can be ruled out when it is located at position lower than table or higher than2m. Nevertheless, many spurious clusters remains. For example, clusters at azimuth $-12°$ and $-18°$ are a yellow box at left of the person in the center. Imposing direction information from the auditory system drastically reduced spurious tracking (Fig. 8 (c)). However, there are a few remaining mis-recognition. A cluster at $-25°$ is actually a knee of the person at the left. Use of direction information cannot rule out possible cluster even if it violate height constraints, because it cannot provide position information on elevation in the current implementation. Combining direction information and height constraints drastically improve accuracy of the tracking (Fig. 8 (d)).

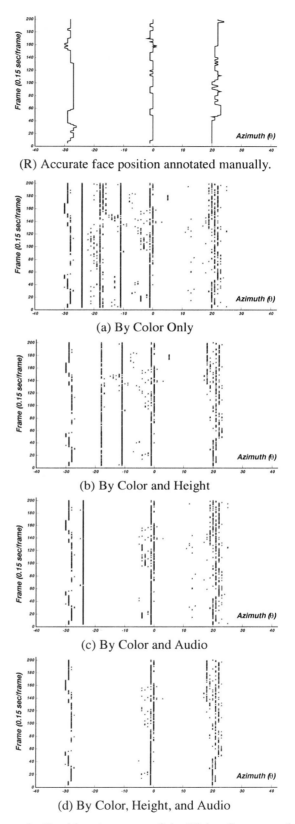

(R) Accurate face position annotated manually.

(a) By Color Only

(b) By Color and Height

(c) By Color and Audio

(d) By Color, Height, and Audio

Figure 8: Tracking Accuracy of the Vision System under various Constraints.

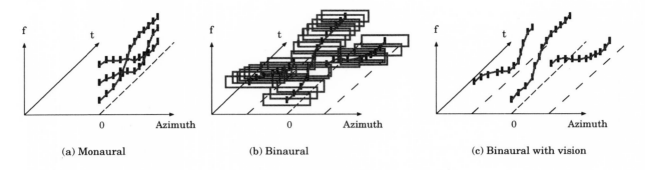

| (a) Monaural | (b) Binaural | (c) Binaural with vision |

Figure 9: Spatial Feature of Auditory Streams

Observations on Experiments

Some observations on the experiments are summarized below:

1. The error reduction rates for the 1-best and 10-best is greatly improved by fixing the direction of sound sources to the correct one. Since Bi-HBSS separates auditory streams by calculating the most plausible candidate, the direction of sound source is not stable. This is partially because some acoustic components may disappear by mixing sounds.

2. If the precise direction of visual information is available, the error reduction rates are drastically improved. Allowable margin of errors in the direction of speaker is narrower for the second (center) speaker than for the others, because he is located between them.

3. The direction of sound source can be obtained with $\pm 10°$ errors by Bi-HBSS, while our simple experiments with cameras show that error margin is about $\pm 2 \sim 3°$ even using rather simple vision system when combined with direction information from auditory system and height constraints.

   Therefore, information fusion of visual and auditory information is promising.

4. By fixing the direction supplied by vision module, precalculated IID and ITD data are required. However, this prerequisite may not be fulfilled in actual environments. Online adjustment of IID and ITD data is required to be apply to more realistic environment.

5. Another problem with Experiment 3 is that the number of auditory streams and that of visual streams differ. For example, some sound sources may be occluded by other objects. Or some possible sound source (speaker) does not speak actually but listens to other people's talk. In this paper, the latter case is excluded, but the former case remains as future work.

Discussions

The central issue addressed in this paper is that how different perceptive inputs affect recognition process of a specific perceptive input. Specifically, we focused on the issue of auditory scene analysis in the context of separating streams of multiple simultaneous speeches, and how visual inputs affects the performance of auditory perception.

As briefly discussed already, the difficulties in the auditory stream separation lies in the fact that trajectories of independent streams overlap in the state space, so that clear discrimination cannot be maintained throughout the stream. Perception based on monaural auditory input has very limited dimension as it can only use amplitude and frequency distribution. There is no spatial axis. As illustrated in Fig. 9 (a), auditory streams overlap on the same spatial plane. Using binaural inputs expands dimension as it can now use amplitude and phase difference of sound sources, which adds spatial axis to the state space.

However, spatial resolution based on sound is limited due to velocity of sounds and limitation in determining amplitude and phase differences between two microphones. This is particularly difficult in reverberant environment, where multiple paths exist between sound sources and microphone due to reflection of room walls. Thus, as illustrated in the Fig. 9 (b), there are significant overlap in the auditory streams. (Ambiguities are shown as shaded boxes.)

Introduction of visual inputs, when appropriately used, adds significantly large dimensions, such as precise position, color, object shape, motion, etc. Among these features, information on positions of objects contribute substantially to the auditory perception. With visual information, the location of sound sources can be precisely determine with an accuracy of few degrees for a point source at 2-meter distance. With this information, overlap of trajectories are significantly reduced (Fig. 9 (c)). Experimental results clearly demonstrates this is actually the case for sound source separation.

By the same token, the performance of the vision system can be improved with the information from the auditory system. As the third experiments demonstrates, even a simple color-based visual tracking system can be highly accurate if approximate position information on possible sound source were provided from the auditory system, together with other constraints such as height constraints for human face positions.

These results suggests that interaction between different

perception can bootstrap performance of each perception system. This implies that even if performance of each perception module is not highly accurate, an integrated system can exhibit much higher performance than simple combination of subsystems. It would be a major open issue for future research to identify what are conditions and principles which enables such bootstrapping.

Conclusion

The major contribution of this work is that the effect of visual information in improving auditory stream separation was made clear. While many research has been performed on integration of visual and auditory inputs, this is the first study to clearly demonstrate that information from a sensory input (e.g. vision) affects processing quality of other sensory inputs (e.g. audition). In addition, we found that accuracy of the vision system can be improved by using information derived from the auditory system. This is a clear evidence that integration of multiple modality, when designed carefully, can improve processing of other modalities, thus bootstrap the coherence and performance of the entire system.

Although this research focused on vision and audition, the same principle applies to other pairs of sensory inputs, such as tactile sensing and vision. The important research topic now is to explore possible interaction of multiple sensory inputs which affects quality (accuracy, computational costs, etc) of the process, and to identify fundamental principles for intelligence.

Acknowledgments

We thank Tomohiro Nakatani of NTT Multimedia Business Headquarter for his help with HBSS and Bi-HBSS. We also thank members of Kitano Symbiotic Systems Project, Dr. Takeshi Kawabata of NTT Cyber Space Laboratories, and Dr. Hiroshi Murase of NTT Communication Science Laboratories for their valuable discussions.

References

Ando, S. 1995. An autonomous three–dimensional vision sensor with ears. *IEICE Transactions on Information and Systems* E78–D(12):1621–1629.

Bodden, M. 1993. Modeling human sound-source localization and the cocktail-party-effect. *Acta Acustica* 1:43–55.

Boll, S. F. 1979. A spectral subtraction algorithm for suppression of acoustic noise in speech. In *Proceedings of 1979 International Conference on Acoustics, Speech, and Signal Processing (ICASSP-79)*, 200–203. IEEE.

Bregman, A. S. 1990. *Auditory Scene Analysis*. MA.: The MIT Press.

Brooks, R. A.; Breazeal, C.; Irie, R.; Kemp, C. C.; Marjanovic, M.; Scassellati, B.; and Williamson, M. M. 1998. Alternative essences of intelligence. In *Proceedings of 15th National Conference on Artificial Intelligence (AAAI-98)*, 961–968. AAAI.

Cooke, M. P.; Brown, G. J.; Crawford, M.; and Green, P. 1993. listening to several things at once. *Endeavour* 17(4):186–190.

Floreano, D., and Mondada, F. 1994. Active perception, navigation, homing, and grasping: an autonomous perspective. In *Proceedings of From Perception to Action conference*, 122–133.

Kita, K.; Kawabata, T.; and Shikano, K. 1990. HMM continuous speech recognition using generalized LR parsing. *Transactions of Information Processing Society of Japan* 31(3):472–480.

Nakatani, T., and Okuno, H. G. 1999. Harmonic sound stream segregation using localization and its application to speech stream segregation. *Speech Communication* 27(3-4). (*in print*).

Nakatani, T.; Okuno, H. G.; and Kawabata, T. 1994. Auditory stream segregation in auditory scene analysis with a multi-agent system. In *Proceedings of 12th National Conference on Artificial Intelligence (AAAI-94)*, 100–107. AAAI.

Okuno, H. G.; Nakatani, T.; and Kawabata, T. 1996. Interfacing sound stream segregation to speech recognition systems — preliminary results of listening to several things at the same time. In *Proceedings of 13th National Conference on Artificial Intelligence (AAAI-96)*, 1082–1089. AAAI.

Okuno, H. G.; Nakatani, T.; and Kawabata, T. 1997. Understanding three simultaneous speakers. In *Proceedings of 15th International Joint Conference on Artificial Intelligence (IJCAI-97)*, volume 1, 30–35. AAAI.

Rosenthal, D., and Okuno, H. G., eds. 1998. *Computational Auditory Scene Analysis*. NJ.: Lawrence Erlbaum Associates.

Rucci, M., and Bajcsy, R. 1995. Learning visuo-tactile coordination in robotic systems. In *Proceedings of 1995 IEEE International Conference on Robotics and Automation*, volume 3, 2678–2683.

Wang, F.; Takeuchi, Y.; Ohnishi, N.; and Sugie, N. 1997. A mobile robot with active localization and discrimination of a sound source. *Journal of Robotic Society of Japan* 15(2):61–67.

Wolff, G. J. 1993. Sensory fusion: integrating visual and auditory information for recognizing speech. In *Proceedings of IEEE International Conference on Neural Networks*, volume 2, 672–677.

Innovative Applications of Artificial Intelligence

Deployed Applications

Automated Instructor Assistant for Ship Damage Control

Vadim V. Bulitko & David C. Wilkins

Beckman Institute
University of Illinois at Urbana-Champaign
405 North Mathews Avenue
Urbana, IL 61801
{bulitko,dcw}@uiuc.edu

Abstract

The decision making task of ship damage control includes addressing problems such as fire spread, flooding, smoke, equipment failures, and personnel casualties. It is a challenging and highly stressful domain with a limited provision for real-life training. In response to this need, a multimedia interactive damage control simulator system, called DC-Train 2.0 was recently deployed at a Navy officer training school; it provides officers with an immersive environment for damage control training. This paper describes a component of the DC-Train 2.0 system that provides feedback to the user, called the automated instructor assistant. This assistant is based on a blackboard-based expert system called Minerva-DCA, which is capable of solving damage control scenarios at the "expert" level. Its innovative blackboard architecture facilitates various forms of user assistance, including interactive explanation, advising, and critiquing. In a large exercise involving approximately 500 ship crises scenarios, Minerva-DCA showed a 76% improvement over Navy officers by saving 89 more ships.

The Domain of Ship Damage Control

The tasks of ship damage control are vital to ship survivability, human life, and operational readiness. Most crises on military and civilian ships could be successfully addressed if handled promptly and properly. Typically the crisis management efforts on a ship are coordinated by a single person called the Damage Control Assistant (DCA). This person is in charge of maintaining situational awareness, directing crisis management crews, and managing other resources. Naturally, crisis management tasks are challenging even for seasoned Navy officers due to the inherent complexity of physical damage, limited resources, information overload, uncertainty, infrequent opportunities for realistic practice, and tremendous psychological stress. Studies have shown that the performance could be significantly improved by providing more opportunities for realistic practice (Ericsson 1993, Baumann et al. 1996). As in many other military domains, real-life training in often infeasible or inadequate due to

the high cost and a limited number of possible scenarios. The Navy has been involved in supporting the creation of various damage control simulators to compliment textbook training (Jones et al. 1998, Bulitko 1998a, Fuller 1993, Johnson 1994). One of these projects resulted in creation of DC-Train 2.0, an immersive multimedia simulator (Bulitko 1998a). The system is capable of involved simulation including physical phenomena (fire, flooding, smoke spread, equipment failures) and personnel modeling (crisis management activities, casualties, standard procedures, and communications). The physical aspects of the scenarios are simulated from first principles starting with a sophisticated scenario specification tool mapping training objectives to primary damage specifications (Grois et al. 1998). A wide range of realistic scenarios are modeled.

However, the system, as described above, still needs a human instructor to (1) demonstrate a successful scenario solution, (2) provide the student with instructional advice, (3) observe the student's problem-solving and provide a comprehensive critique, and (4) score performance on various scenarios for progress evaluation and comparative analysis purposes. While the simulator itself is implemented with numerical and knowledge-based simulation techniques, requirements of an automated instructor include, first, achievement of the level of expertise sufficient to solve arbitrary scenarios in real-time; and, second, an ability to observe the student in real-time, communicate with the student, and present intelligible feedback in a natural language format. Such functions clearly present an interesting challenge for modern AI technology.

In this paper we present an automated instructor assistant, called Minerva-DCA, that is capable of doing the aforementioned four instructor functions. Minerva-DCA has been fielded at the Navy's Surface Warfare Officer School (SWOS) in Newport, Rhode Island and has shown impressive performance.

Minerva-DCA: The Automated Instructor Assistant

AI Technology

As outlined above Minerva-DCA is a real-time problem-solver, capable of explanation, advising, critiquing, and scoring thus serving as an automated instructor for the damage control environment. These abilities result from utilizing an innovative combination of AI technology as highlighted below:

1. Minerva-DCA is based on a blackboard architecture with exhaustive deliberation on all available domain data posted on the blackboard. This approach delivers a comprehensive set of feasible actions that address the current problem state.

2. A separation and explicit representation of domain and strategy knowledge layers allows for the output of the blackboard deliberation step to be a set of dynamically constructed set of strategy networks. These facilitate explanation, advising, and critiquing.

3. An Extended Petri Net envisionment-based blackboard scheduler allows for sophisticated critiquing that accounts for creativity on the trainee's side.

In the following sections, we will go into the key details of Minerva-DCA design and implementation.

Blackboard Framework

Minerva-DCA is an extended blackboard architecture system (Hayes-Roth 1985, Carver and Lesser 1994, Bulitko and Wilkins 1998b, Nii 1989, Larsson et al. 1996, Park et al. 1994, Najem 1993, Park et al. 1991). The blackboard is accessed by a number of domain knowledge sources that constitute the domain knowledge layer. Domain knowledge sources, however, do not operate on their own but rather are used by the strategy knowledge sources. The reasoning is done via the strategy networks.

```
ccf(r1012,1,1,[alarm,fire,Where,Time],800, [fire, Where,
FireClass, discovered, Time],0.6,[]).
ccb(r1012,1,1,[alarm,fire,Where,TimeAlarm],800,[fire, Where,
FireClass, Status,Time],0.6).
```

Meaning: finding alarm indicates hypothesis fire with a confidence of 0.6.

Figure 1. Example of a domain rule that provides evidence for fire hypothesis

In the next few sections we will describe the domain and strategy level representation. This is fairly conventional in terms of second-generation expert systems (Clancey 1985, Clancey 1987, Chandrasekaran 1986); the innovative part is the way the output of the domain and strategy level unification is processed by the envisionment-based scheduler.

Domain Knowledge Layer

Each domain knowledge source contains several Horn-clause style domain rules related to a particular domain topic (e.g. handling a certain type of fire). An annotated example of an actual domain rule for the Navy damage control domain is shown in Figure 1.

Domain knowledge and domain vocabulary are conceptually organized in the domain graph (Bulitko 1998a) which is a graph with domain findings, hypotheses, and actions in the vertices. Domain rules in the presented format comprise the edges of the domain graph and thus allow movement from one domain datum to another. The entire decision process is roughly represented as traversing the domain graph starting at the vertices with known findings and eventually arriving at the vertices with domain actions.

In order to handcode the domain knowledge layer we have conducted a knowledge acquisition process involving: (1) researching the Navy damage control manuals and damage control plates (analogous to ship blueprints); (2) consulting Navy domain experts; (3) attending classes at the Surface Warfare Officer School (SWOS) in Newport, Rhode Island.

Strategy Knowledge Layer

Minerva-DCA's deliberation mechanism uses a declarative and domain-independent representation of strategy

```
Top-level goals:
        process_hypothesis(Hypothesis)
        process_finding(Finding)
        explore_hypothesis(Hypothesis)
        remove_datum(Datum)

Intermediate-level goals:
        applyrule_backward(Rule)
        applyrule_forward(Rule)
        findout(Datum)
        pursue_hypothesis(Hypothesis)
        test_hypothesis(Hypothesis)

Bottom-level goals:
        perform(Action)
        lookup(Finding)
        remove(Datum)
        conclude(Hypothesis)
```

Figure 2. Strategy goals used as nodes of the strategy networks in Minerva-DCA

knowledge. The strategy layer of Minerva-DCA knowledge is used to drive the deliberation process. Depending on the new data and other blackboard contents, Minerva performs backward or forward chaining. This makes Minerva-DCA flexible in its reasoning process. While domain knowledge sources reason over the lexicon of domain findings, hypotheses, and actions the rule-based strategy knowledge sources reason over the lexicon of domain-independent strategy goals. Strategy goals come at different levels as summarized in Figure 2.

The goals are used in building the strategy networks. A strategy network is a directed acyclic graph consisting of strategy chains. Each chain starts with a top-level goal, goes through the intermediate and top-level goals, and ends with a bottom level goal that carries a domain-level action to take. During the deliberation process the strategy knowledge sources rules are triggered by important findings and active hypotheses on the blackboard. The

```
mr(pf1,process_finding(F),applyrule_forward(Rule,Hyp)) :-
        finding(F,_),
        red-flag(F),
        ccf(Rule,N,M,F,CF,Hyp,CFC,UL),
        satisfied(F,CF).
```

Meaning: strategy goal process_finding(F) could be reduced to strategy goal applyrule_forward(Rule,Hyp) if there is a domain rule Rule with F as its condition clause and the clause is satisfied. So if we are processing finding F and there is a rule conditioned on F then try to apply that rule.

Figure 3. An example of strategy rule used for forward-chaining

triggering data is considered within the context of top-level goals. For example: fire alarm finding(fire-alarm) would lead to the top-level goal process_finding(fire-alarm). In turn, this goal will trigger other strategy rules and thus entail intermediate-level goals. This process eventually results in the strategy chain network (a strategy chain example is shown in Figure 4). Each edge in the network is labeled with the corresponding strategy operator identifier (e.g. pf5). Figure 3 shows an example of actual strategy rule. Strategy operators are also implemented as Prolog clauses. The first argument of mr is the strategy operator identifier (in this case pf1). The second argument is the higher level goal the operator applies to. Finally, the third argument is the lower-level goal. So, in a way, a strategy operator is nothing but a transition from a higher to a lower level goals. The pre-conditions of mr are various predicates that have to hold in order for the strategy operator to fire. In the example shown in Figure 3 we should apply Rule in a backward manner if:

(a) we are trying to process finding F;
(b) F is important (a "red-flag");
(c) there is (ccf) a domain rule (Rule) such that F is one of its preconditions (with the required confidence factor of CF) and Hyp is its conclusion;
(d) and finally F is known to hold with confidence factor of at least CF.

In handcoding the strategy knowledge layer we started with a strategy layer of Minerva-3 medical diagnosis expert system (Park et al. 1991, Park et al. 1994) which was a refinement of Neomycin (Clancey 1987, Wilkins 1990). The layer has then been significantly modified to

address the following major differences between damage control decision-making and medical diagnosis domains: (1) multiple simultaneous crises; (2) action generation; (3) real-time autonomous operation. Details can be found in (Bulitko 1998a).

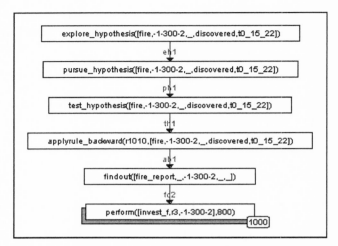

Figure 4. A Strategy Chain Example: Order Repair-3 station to investigate compartment 01-300-2 since there is a suspected fire in the compartment; a fire report would confirm/disconfirm the fire hypothesis; and a fire report could be obtained through investigation.

As we have said, for the domain and strategy knowledge layers the described knowledge representation and inference method are fairly conventional with respect to second-generation expert systems (Clancey 1987, Wilkins 1990). The innovative aspect of Minerva-DCA relates to the way the scheduler processes the output of the deliberation level created by unification of domain and strategy knowledge layers.

Scheduler Knowledge Layer

Minerva-DCA uses an innovative envisionment-based scheduler with the environment model implemented as an extended Petri Net (Bulitko 1998a). The scheduler consists of the following main parts:

1. *An Extended Petri Net (EPN) environment model* is capable of a coarse-level environment envisionment. The model takes into account the current state of the ship as well as the actions under consideration. It then predicts a sequence of ship states within the 10-minute range. Using an EPN model has a number of advantages including the following: (1) it models the ship at a coarse level of detail hence allowing for a high-speed operation (up to 600 times faster than real-time) and better noisy data handling; (2) it can model physical phenomena (fire, smoke, flooding, etc.) as well as equipment operation (overheating, failures, etc.) and personnel activities (occupation, casualties, etc.); (3) it can take proposed DCA actions as an input; (4) Petri Nets

naturally support concurrency and have a convenient graphical representation; (5) Petri Nets have a sound mathematical theory and allow for various analysis and proof methods.

2. *A static state evaluator* is used to evaluate the envisioned states with regard to the state severity from the damage control standpoint. While the EPN model describes ship states by markings of the Extended Petri Network, the state evaluator uses a vector form where each value summarizes the important parameters such as the status (engulfed, ignited, intact, etc.) and duration of the status about vital ship components. The evaluator assesses the severity of the state and outputs a single value: the estimated time to ship loss (i.e. a major disaster such as a missile magazine explosion) (Bulitko 1998a). Naturally, lower values of the time-to-ship-lost correspond to more severe states.

Having elicited domain knowledge from various sources, we handcoded the Extended Petri Net model. Automated generation of such a model is an area of current research. The state evaluator, however, has been automatically generated from the past scenarios in the following fashion. While running simulated damage control scenarios we had regularly recorded the states of the ship and time-stamped them. Complete scenario timeline available at the end of scenario was used to annotate the sequences of ship states with the time-to-ship-lost. Thus, each state annotated with

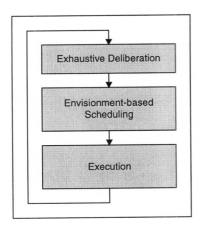

Figure 5. Minerva-DCA Operation: the blackboard problem-solving cycle stages

time-to-ship-lost constituted a single training example. A collection of such training samples has been used with well-known machine learning packages such as NeuroSolutions' back propagation learning engine (Haykin 1994) and C5.0 decision-tree/rule learner (Quinlan 1993). The output of these packages comprised the state evaluator. In the case of backpropagation learning it was an artificial neural network while C5.0 produced a decision ruleset. The decision ruleset has attained cross-validation accuracy of 80-90% (Bulitko 1998a).

The Blackboard Cycle

Minerva-DCA works in cycles (Figure 5). Each cycle consists of the following three stages:
1) Exhaustive deliberation;
2) Envisionment-Based Scheduling - qualitative prediction, state evaluation, utilities computation;
3) Execution.

The following subsections will go into details on each of the stages.

Deliberation. At the deliberation stage, the important data from the blackboard are used to trigger domain rules and build a strategy network that represents exhaustive deliberation. Each of the strategy chains starts with a top-level goal (e.g. process_hypothesis(fire)) and ends with a feasible action (e.g. perform(fight_fire)). Different networks can share different nodes. The size of the strategy network is, at most, linear in the number of important (red-flag) findings and hypotheses. Since the network is built in a depth-first manner, the deliberation time is linear in the total number of findings as well (Bulitko 1998a).

Scheduling. At the scheduling stage prediction, evaluation, and utility computation are carried out. As mentioned above, each strategy chain ends with a feasible action (either internal to the system (e.g. conclude(hypothesis)) or external or domain-level (e.g. perform(action)). While most internal actions could be executed at once, domain-level actions require scheduling due to the limited resources, different priorities, and possible inconsistencies. Scheduling stage has three substages:

(a) Envisionment-Based Scheduling: An Extended Petri Net (EPN) predictor models the environment to predict effects of a particular action or consequences of a particular finding.
(b) State evaluator evaluates the predicted states and assesses their severity levels.
(c) Utility computation module combines the outputs of the both stages above and ranks the actions by assessing their utility.

Execution. The last stage of the blackboard operating cycle is execution. There are three different execution modes: problem-solving, advising, and critiquing.

Operation Modes

The three execution modes will now be covered in detail.

In problem-solving mode, the highest-ranked domain-level (external) action is executed. All internal actions are also executed. Examples of internal actions include asserting hypotheses and removing obsolete data from the blackboard. Executing domain-level actions involves passing the appropriate messages to the actuators (either simulated or real). It is worth noticing that domain-level actions could be inconsistent with each other (e.g. one of the reasons is the existence of multiple solution paths). To avoid potential conflicts, Minerva-DCA executes the single top-ranked domain-level action at every cycle.

In advising mode, the system's external actions are not passed to the domain actuators but instead used for advising. Specifically, we present *n* top-ranked actions to the student through an Advisory Graphical User Interface (GUI). For each action the following information is available upon request:

a) Reasoning behind the action could be shown by displaying the appropriate strategy chain(s) in both graphical and textual forms. The textual form involves generating natural language output for the action and the top nodes of the chain (the short form) or possibly all

nodes of the chain (the long form). Indeed, the advantage of the explicit strategy knowledge representation and reasoning is that we can easily explain why a certain action was suggested by simply traversing the strategy chain and translating the nodes into a natural language. Figure 6 shows a screenshot of the actual GUI displaying several suggested actions and a short-form explanation for one of them.

b) Reasoning behind the action's rank could be shown by displaying the environment states predicted by the EPN prediction module and their scores computed by the state evaluator. Further details could be provided by tracking down state evaluator's reasoning if it allows for that (e.g. in case with decision trees).

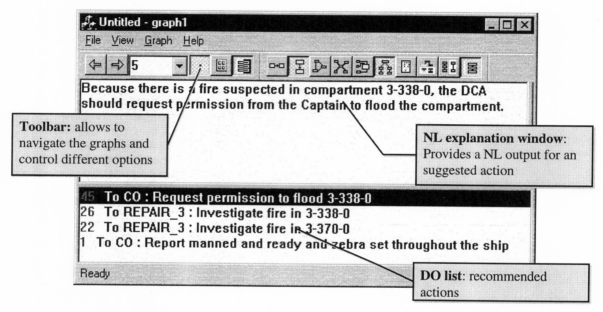

Figure 6. Minerva-DCA Advisory Graphical User Interface features natural language explanations of the advised actions

In the critiquing mode the scheduled actions are not passed to the actuators for execution but used to match against actions of the subject being critiqued. The intricate details of the approach are presented in (Bulitko 1998a) while in this section we will limit ourselves to a brief overview.

Basically, the critiques provided are of two kinds: errors of omission and errors of commission.

An *error of omission* occurs when the subject fails to take an action associated with a critical goal. This corresponds to a high-level goal remaining unaddressed on the blackboard. When displaying such an error it is easy to invoke the explanatory facilities of the shell and generate a NL explanation on why a certain action should be taken and the goal it would address.

Errors of commission are handled in two steps. First, the system tries to match a subject's action against the

actions the system has recently deliberated and scheduled for execution. If the matching succeeds and the matching action found was ranked low by the scheduler then we can critique the subject by supplying the scheduler's reasoning ("poor action" critique). If the matching action is not one of the top-ranked actions then we can critique the subject by showing a better action ("suboptimal action" critique). Finally, if there is no matching action on the system's side we feed the action to the envisionment-based scheduler. The scheduler produces a rating of the action based on the envisionment process. It may well be that the action is better than that of the Minerva-DCA problem solver, in which case no critique needs to be displayed. If the action is judged by the envisionment-based scheduler to be a poor one, then a critique is appropriate. The envisionment process outputs the deleterious consequences of the subjects action.

Figure 7 presents the Minerva's Critiquing GUI showing an error of commission critique explained. Just like with advising, the explicit strategy knowledge representation and reasoning process allow the critiquing facility to be implemented naturally without an extra dedicated critiquing expert system shell like it would with alternative critiquing approaches such as the use of a bug library.

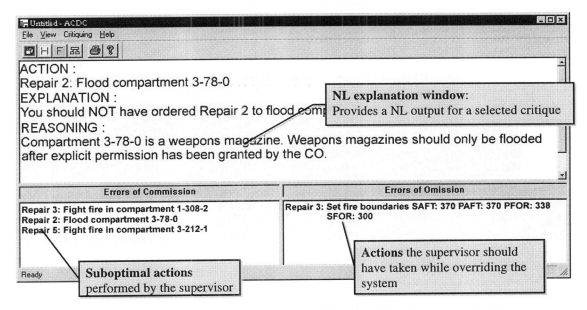

Figure 7. Minerva-DCA Critiquing Graphical User Interface features natural language explanations of the critiques

Hardware and software implementation details

Minerva-DCA is implemented in LPA Prolog and runs under Windows NT. An ODBC interface integrates it into the DC-Train simulated environment which uses Microsoft Access databases to represent the state of the ship and other dynamic and static domain information. The graphical user interfaces are implemented in Visual C++ and run as separate tasks under Windows NT. The graphical user interfaces and Minerva-DCA exchange information through ODBC interface and dedicated Access files.

In our tests Minerva-DCA has been running at 50-800 blackboard cycles per second speed on a dual-Pentium II-400MHz workstation.

Minerva-DCA Experimental Evaluation

To evaluate the performance we have run approximately 500 scenarios of the DC-Train ship damage control simulator at the Navy officer training school in Newport, Rhode Island and at our home laboratory. We have compared the problem-solving performance of Minerva-DCA to Navy officers. The results are presented in Figure 8.

Any scenario could have one of the three outcomes: "ship lost" meaning that a major disaster such as a missile magazine compartment explosion has occurred; "ship possibly saved" meaning that at 25 minutes scenario time

the ship was still alive yet there were active crises; and "ship saved" means there were no active crises at the 25-minute mark.

In the experiments Minerva-DCA has lost 21 ships. This is a 46% improvement over Navy officers where 39 ships were lost. Likewise, Minerva-DCA has shown a 76% improvement in the number of ships being saved (117 vs. 28).

Analysis of the scenarios where Minerva-DCA has failed to save the ship helped locating suboptimal components of Minerva-DCA domain knowledge layer as well as certain modeling problems of the DC-Train damage control simulator. A large-scale evaluation of the improved versions of Minerva-DCA and DC-Train is pending.

Application Use and Pay-Off

A proof-of-principle prototype, called DC-Train 1.0, was first used at the Navy officer training school in Newport, Rhode Island, in March 1997. A refinement of this system, called DC-Train 2.0, was permanently deployed at SWOS in December 1998. It is to be regularly used in the six-week damage control course, which has approximately 30-50 Navy officers every six weeks. It provides the damage control course with its first tool that can generate arbitrarily many damage control scenarios and thereby provide extensive and immersive whole-task training.

To date, the controlled evaluation has been limited to

each person solving four simulated scenarios at most, and has not involved giving the subjects feedback using the Automated Instructor Assistant. The initial limitations on the numbers of scenarios solved, and the withholding of automated feedback are necessary to establish a performance baseline. Experts have, however, validated the accuracy of the feedback generated by the Automated Instructor Assistant.

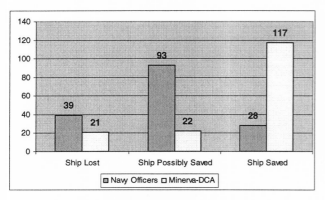

Figure 8. Minerva-DCA vs. Navy officers experimental comparison

The primary benefits of the deployed immersive simulator and trainer described in this paper include (1) decreased load on the damage control course instructors, (2) the opportunity for the students to get a comprehensive feedback on their performance anytime, and (3) uniform and standardized scoring with a graphical feedback. This is in contrast to the current practice where an instructor is always present when a student solves a scenario, which places a very large time-demand on the instructors.

Minerva-DCA deployment at SWOS

Minerva-DCA was developed in the Knowledge Based Systems Group (KBS) of Beckman Institute, University of Illinois at Urbana-Champaign. After several years of field tests the system has been permanently installed at the Navy officer training facility (SWOS) in Newport, Rhode Island. An internet link to the University of Illinois allows for real-time automated data collection and analysis.

Since the deployment of the system at SWOS, the KBS group has maintained DC-Train 2.0 and Minerva-DCA packages via a close co-operation with SWOS personnel. Maintenance has included: (1) collecting feedback from the instructors and students; (2) sending in updates and patches; and (3) discussing the new features and extensions to be implemented in the up-coming versions.

Future Work

During the remainder of 1999, a group of research psychologists will be conducting controlled experiments to measure the training effectiveness of solving large numbers of scenarios. They will also measure the impact of the feedback generated by the Automated Instructor Assistant in terms of scores, advice, and critiques. This will provide essential information for refinement of the system, and quantification of its utility.

Another near-term project goal is to install the DC-Train system aboard ships for Afloat Training. All seasoned damage control assistants aboard ships receive weeks of refresher training every year, and DC-Train will allow them for the first time to receive extensive whole-task training with an computer-based damage control simulator. This is of interest because it will be possible to explore the efficacy of a single person solving more scenarios than is possible within the context of a relatively short course.

Finally, it is planned to use Minerva-DCA as a component of a project sponsored by the Naval Research Lab on automated intelligent control for the next generation of ships to be built. It is called DC-ARM – (Damage Control: Automation for Reduced Manning). This project seeks to automated many aspects of the damage control process (Wilkins and Sniezek 1997). We will investigate the extent that Minerva-DCA can assist with the automation process, and the Intelligent Assistant can assist with providing a damage control supervisor with real-time situation awareness.

Acknowledgements

Scott Borton, Adam Boyko, Dr. Valeriy K. Bulitko, Tony Czupryna, Joel Hegg, Sebastian Magda, Arthur Menaker, and Tamar Shinar have helped with Minerva-DCA implementation and have contributed a number of valuable suggestions. We gratefully acknowledge the support of the SWOS personnel, in particular: CAPT Wittcamp, CDR Shikada, CDR Kunnert, LCDR Morrill, LT Anderson, LT Cisneros, LT Gianelli, LT Kenderick-Holmes, DCCS(SW) Ciesielczyk, and Dave Monroe. SWOS students and KBS members have been very cooperative. The research has been supported in part by ONR Grant N00014-95-1-0749, ARL Grant DAAL01-96-2-0003, and NRL Contract N00014-97-C-2061.

References

Baumann, M.R.; Sniezek, J.A.; Donovan, M.A.; Wilkins, D.C. 1996. Training effectiveness of an immersive multimedia trainer for acute stress domains: Ship damage control. University of Illinois technical report, UIUC-BI-KBS-96008.

Bulitko, V. 1998a. Minerva-5: A Multifunctional Dynamic Expert System. MS Thesis. Department of Computer Science, University of Illinois at Urbana-Champaign.

Bulitko, V.; Wilkins, D.C. 1998b. Minerva: A Blackboard Expert System for Real-Time Problem-Solving and Critiquing. Tech. Report UIUC-BI-KBS-98-003, University of Illinois at Urbana-Champaign.

Chandrasekaran, B. 1986. Generic tasks in knowledge-based reasoning: High-level building blocks for expert system design. *IEEE Expert*, 1(3):23-30.

Carver, N.; Lesser, V. 1994. The Evolution of Blackboard Control Architectures. In Expert Systems with Applications--Special Issue on the Blackboard Paradigm and Its Application, Volume 7, Number 1, pp. 1-30, Liebowitz. New York, Pergamon Press.

Clancey, W.J. 1985. Heuristic Classification. *Artificial Intelligence*, 27(3):289-350.

Clancey, W.J. 1987. Acquiring, representing, and evaluating a competence model of diagnostic strategy. In Chi, Glaser, and Farr, eds. *Contributions to the Nature of Expertise*. Lawrence Erlbaum Press.

Ericsson, K.A.; Krampe, R.T.; Tesch-Romer, C. 1993. The Role of Deliberate Practice in the Acquisition of Expert Performance. Psychological Review, 100(3): 363-407.

Feigenbaum, E.A. 1977. The Art of Artificial Intelligence: I. Themes and Case Studies of Knowledge Engineering. Proceedings of the Fifth International Joint Conference on Artificial Intelligence, 1014-1029. Cambridge, MA.

Fuller, J. V. 1993. Measuring Damage Control Assistant's (DCA) Decision-Making Proficiency in Integrated Damage Control Training Technology (IDCTT) Training Scenarios. Master's Thesis. Naval Postgraduate School: Monterey, CA.

Grois, E..; Hsu, W.H.; Voloshin, M.; Wilkins, D.C. 1998. Bayesian Network Model for Generation of Crisis Management Training Scenarios. *In The Proceedings of The Tenth IAAI conference.* 1113-1120. Menlo-Park, Calif.: AAAI Press.

Hayes-Roth, B. 1985. A blackboard architecture for control. *Artificial Intelligence*, 26(2):251-321.

Haykin, S. 1994. *Neural Networks: A Comprehensive Foundation.* Macmillan College Publishing Company.

Jones, R.M.; Laird, J.E.; Nielsen, P.E. 1998. Automated Intelligent Pilots for Combat Flight Simulation. *In The Proceedings of The Tenth IAAI conference.* 1047-1054. Menlo-Park, Calif.: AAAI Press.

Johnson, M. 1994. Validation of an active multimedia courseware package for the integrated damage control training technology (IDCTT) Trainer. Master's thesis. Naval Postgraduate School, Monterey, California.

Larsson, E.; Hayes-Roth, B.; Gaba, D. 1996. Guardian: Final Evaluation. Knowledge Systems Lab, Stanford University. TechReport KSL-96-25.

Najem, Z.H. 1993. A Hierarchical Representation of Control Knowledge For A Heuristic Classification Shell. Ph.D. Thesis. The Department of Computer Science. University of Illinois at Urbana-Champaign.1993.

Nii, H.P. 1989. Blackboard Systems. In Barr, A.; Cohen, P.R.; Feigenbaum, E.A. eds. *The Handbook of Artificial Intelligence*. Volume IV, Chapter XVI. Addison-Wesley.

Park, Y.T; Tan, K.W.; Wilkins, D.C. 1991. Minerva 3.0: A Knowledge-based Expert System Shell with Declarative Representation and Flexible Control. Tech. Report. UIUC, Department of Computer Science.

Park, Y.T.; Donoho, S.; Wilkins, D.C. 1994. "Recursive Heuristic Classification". *International Journal of Expert Systems*, Volume 7, Number 4, 329-357.

Quinlan, J.R. 1993. *C4.5: Programs for Machine Learning*, San Mateo, California: Morgan Kaufmann.

Wilkins, D.C. 1990. "Knowledge Base Refinement as Improving an Incorrect and Incomplete Domain Theory", in *Machine Learning: An Artificial Intelligence Approach, Volume III*, Y. Kondratoff and R.Michalski (eds.), Morgan Kaunfmann, 493-513.

Wilkins, D.C.; Sniezek, J.A. 1997. An Approach to Automated Situation Awareness for Ship Damage Control. KBS Tech. Report UIUC-BI-KBS-97-012. University of Illinois at Urbana-Champaign.

HKIA SAS: A Constraint-Based Airport Stand Allocation System Developed with Software Components

Andy Hon Wai Chun

City University of Hong Kong
Department of Electronic Engineering
Tat Chee Avenue, Kowloon
Hong Kong
eehwchun@cityu.edu.hk

Steve Ho Chuen Chan, Francis Ming Fai Tsang and Dennis Wai Ming Yeung

Advanced Object Technologies Limited
Unit 602A, HK Industrial Technology Centre
72 Tat Chee Avenue, Kowloon
Hong Kong
{steve, francis, dennis}@aotl.com

Abstract

SAS is an AI application developed for the Hong Kong International Airport (HKIA) at Chek Lap Kok. SAS uses constraint-programming techniques to assign parking stands to aircraft and schedules tow movements based on a set of business and operational constraints. The system provides planning, real-time operation, and problem solving capabilities. SAS generates a stand allocation plan that finely balances the objectives of the airlines/handling agents, the convenience of passengers, and the operational constraints of the airport. The system ensures a high standard of quality in customer service, airport safety, and utilization of stand resources. This paper also describes our experience in developing an AI system using standard off-the-shelf software components. SAS is an example of how development methodologies used to construct modern AI applications have become fully inline with mainstream practices.

Task Description

Costing over US$20 billion to construct, the Hong Kong International Airport (HKIA) at Chek Lap Kok replaces the old airport at Kai Tak, which was already one of the world's busiest international airports, in terms of its passenger and cargo throughput. Although there were some initial hitches when the new airport opened on 6 July 1998, operations quickly returned to normal within a week's time. Within a month, operational statistics surpassed those of the old airport – 80% of all flights were on time or within 15 minutes of schedule, all passengers cleared immigration within 15 minutes and average baggage waiting time was only 10 minutes. During 1998's Christmas holiday, HKIA serviced around 100,000 passengers daily while maintaining equally high service standards. In January 1999, Travel & Leisure Magazine awarded HKIA the Critics' Choice Award in recognition for the levels of satisfaction and praises received from travelers to Hong Kong.

The main responsibility of ensuring that the airport operates smoothly and that travellers are satisfied rests upon the shoulders of the Hong Kong Airport Authority (AA). The Airport Authority manages and controls all activities related to airport operations. It also has the responsibility of scheduling and managing all aircraft parking and ground movements at HKIA. On a daily basis, the Airport Authority assigns parking stands to aircraft based on the daily flight schedule, rotation information, and a set of operational constraints. It also schedules aircraft tows to optimise the use of inner stands. In addition, to cope with conflicts caused by changes in actual operations, AA also needs to make real-time problem solving decisions on stand reassignments.

The Stand Allocation System (SAS) was designed and developed to support AA's ramp management function. The system is installed and used in the Airport Control Center (ACC), which is located in the control tower. SAS provides planning, real-time management, and reactive scheduling capabilities for stand management. The system supports concurrent use by multiple operators in non-stop 24 hours-a-day operations, since HKIA is a 24-hour airport.

Since all stands at HKIA (passenger and cargo) are centrally allocated and managed by the Airport Authority, the main objective of SAS is to be as fair as possible to all airlines and handling agents, while making efficient and safe use of airport resources. An efficient stand allocation plan can maximize the utilization of stands and thus permit additional flights during peak traffic hours and holiday seasons. Although HKIA was designed to have more stands that the old airport, not all stands are operational yet; part of the airport terminal building is still under construction. Furthermore, air traffic will most likely increase once the second runway becomes operational. Optimization of stand assignment is still an important factor at the new airport.

Another objective is to provide better service and comfort to passengers. For example, assigning aircraft closer to proximity of the immigration counters will allow passengers to quickly exit the terminal. On the other hand, assigning flights close to airline service counters will convenience transit passengers.

Maintaining some degree of consistency or patterns in allocation, from week to week or day to day, is also very important, especially for regular flights. This will allow airlines and handling agents to perform longer term macro planning with more accuracy and a certain degree of independence.

Since the airport is a 24-hour airport, stand allocation planning will be performed at the same time as normal operations. The ability of the scheduling system to co-ordinate multiple sets of data within a multi-user environment is also very important.

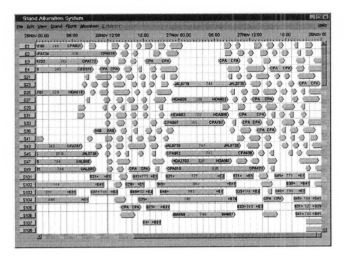

Figure 1. SAS Gantt chart with two days of assignments.

The quality of a stand allocation plan is determined by many factors – how efficient are resources being used, how convenient is it to the passengers, and most importantly, are all safety-related criteria met. Normally, a human operator must have several years of experience in order to acquire enough knowledge about airport operations before he/she can produce a "good" quality stand assignment plan. Generating an allocation plan manually not only requires a highly experienced individual but is also very time consuming since it requires balancing many objectives against many possible alternatives.

Another key problem, that is particularly difficult to perform manually, is coping with conflicts caused by operational changes. For example, flights might be delayed, aircraft might be swapped, or there might be sudden ground equipment failures. These events may invalidate previous stand assignments and affect assignments of other aircraft. In other cases, mechanical failures or other problems might occur after chocking off and the aircraft may need to return to the airport as an air return or ground return. The ability to handle changes and events like these quickly and intelligently while minimizing impact on the rest of the committed schedule is very vital to ensure airport operates smoothly.

An AI solution allows a highly optimized allocation plan to be produced in reasonable time, ensures that all operational constraints are considered all the time, and performs problem solving in real-time or close to real-time. On average, SAS produces a daily stand allocation plan in around three minutes and performs reactive problem solving in five seconds at HKIA using a Pentium II server machine.

Application Description

SAS is designed for planning, real-time operations, and data analysis. Stand assignment planning is usually performed after midnight when air traffic is light and when all the airlines have finalized their rotation changes. SAS takes the daily flight schedule for the day being plan and generates an optimized stand allocation using an algorithm for constraint-satisfaction problems (CSP). Our scheduling algorithm considers constraints related to arrival/departure times, type of flight, aircraft type/size, airline preferences, stand configurations, etc., in producing the stand allocation plan. SAS also provides a set of menus and commands to allow the operator to enter any last minutes changes before confirming and distributing the plan. The operator performing stand-planning uses a separate SAS workstation dedicated for system administrative work. Other live SAS workstations load the new plan after it is finalized.

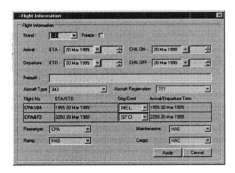

Figure 2. SAS menu to display/modify flight information.

During real-time operations, SAS operators monitor and enter up-to-date flight statuses such as estimated times of arrival/departure (ETA/ETD), actual chock on/off times, and aircraft registration. Different types of information and statuses are displayed using different icons, symbols, and color-coded shadings in SAS. SAS automatically re-evaluate all constraints whenever any new event occurs. The main screens used by operators are in the form of a Gantt chart and spreadsheets. In real-time operations, several operators and SAS workstations are involved to handle different types of information. SAS was designed for multi-user operations and ensures a consistent display on all SAS workstations. All stand-related data and information are archived for later analysis, auditing, or report generation.

Whenever an event causes a "conflict," SAS alerts the operator and highlights the conflicting assignments in red. For example, a delay in departure may prevent the next aircraft from parking, or a delay in arrival may prevent adequate time to deplane passengers before a scheduled tow. SAS has explanation generation capabilities and can give justification on assignment penalties and reasons for conflict. Once a conflict occurs, the operator may request SAS to automatically resolve the conflict using a reactive scheduling algorithm that solves conflicts while minimizing impact on current plan.

SAS was designed to supplement the centralized airport system, known as the Terminal Management System (TMS). TMS has basic stand assignment support but lacks the constraint-based intelligence and the scope of stand-related functions provided by SAS. Mission-critical AI applications, such as SAS, usually have two orthogonal sets of design criteria to satisfy – design criteria related to the AI implementation and criteria related to the IT implementation.

From the AI point-of-view, the technologies selected and used for SAS must satisfy the following criteria:

Robust – The knowledge representation used must be robust enough to capture all types of knowledge related to stand allocation. The representation must be able to capture knowledge on physical dimensions, geometry and layout, proximity, and operational requirements.

Transparent – The logic or reasoning mechanism used must be easy to understand and hence should be reasonably similar to the logic used by human operators. The system should be able to give explanation on its actions to improve transparency.

Optimizing – The reasoning mechanism must be able to optimize on a given set of potentially contradicting constraints and criteria since the airport authority needs to satisfy the needs of many different parties – airlines, handling agents, passengers, and the airport itself.

Fast – The reasoning mechanism must be highly efficient in order to be able to consider several hundred constraints for each assignment. There may be several hundred assignments per day.

Problem Solving – Since the airport is a highly dynamic environment, the AI component must be able to perform problem solving to resolve conflicts during real operations.

From the IT point-of-view, SAS was designed to operate as a mission critical application. This added additional requirements on top of those related to AI and scheduling. The following highlights some of the key IT considerations:

Real-time Performance – Mission-critical implies that SAS response time must be close to real-time and must be able to cope with real-time changes very quickly. The implementation technology selected must be highly efficient. Interpreted programming languages might perform poorly in this respect. Multi-thread support is a must.

Multi-user Support – Most mission critical operations will require several human operators co-operating together. The system architecture must support the simultaneous use by several operators and be able to synchronous all clients machines in real-time. The implementation platform must support some form of asynchronous messaging or callback.

Scalability – Although the actual number of SAS operators that will be making decisions will be limited, the number of users that need to access information from the system might eventually be large. The technology must be able to scale up to support a large number of potential users.

Fault-tolerance – Mission-critical of course implies the system must be available close to 100% of the time. The technology selected must be able to support an architecture that is fault-tolerant with hardware and software redundancy and switchover capabilities.

Load-balancing – Although not really necessary for the stand allocation problem, many mission critical systems will require some form of load balancing to improve performance.

Interoperability – Any mission critical system will need to interact with a set of other systems to exchange data or request services. This also includes the ability to easily access potentially different types of relational or object databases. The degree of interoperability will depend on the technology selected.

A Solution Based on Object Technology

Based on the AI and IT requirements, we decided to select a technology/methodology that can address all these issues at a broad level. We needed a technology that can be applied to all components within our software architecture. To meet all the rigid requirements of an intelligent AI system that is also mission critical, we finalized on a three-tiered distributed object architecture based on CORBA.

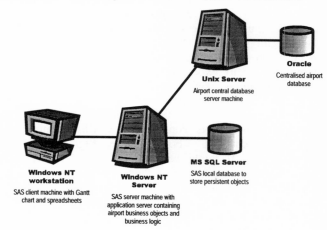

Figure 3. The SAS hardware architecture.

There is, of course, a lot of flexibility in selecting technologies if we are designing a standalone single-tiered system. There is less flexibility, but still quite a lot, if we are designing a two-tiered system. However, when it comes to developing a multi-user n-tiered architecture, the choices must be carefully made. The following highlights some of the rationale in the technologies used to construct the SAS application.

SAS was designed to operate within a Microsoft NT environment with its own NT Server and local MS SQL Server database. It interfaces to other external server machines to exchange data, such as seasonal schedules, rotation information, stand assignment, etc.

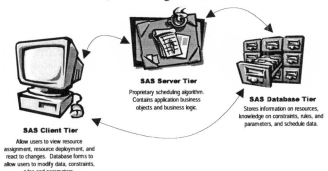

SAS Client Tier
Allow users to view resource assignment, resource deployment, and react to changes. Database forms to allow users to modify data, constraints, rules and parameters.

SAS Server Tier
Proprietary scheduling algorithm. Contains application business objects and business logic.

SAS Database Tier
Stores information on resources, knowledge on constraints, rules, and parameters, and schedule data.

Figure 4. The SAS 3-tiered software architecture .

To provide real-time performance, SAS was designed as a three-tiered architecture with an in-memory persistent business object cache within the application server. We selected an OT approach using C++ as the implementation language due to its efficiency and the availability of numerous off-the-shelf software components.

SAS uses constraint programming (CP) as the foundation for the AI component since the stand allocation problem can easily be modelled as a constraint-satisfaction problem (CSP). Constraints provided in CP were expressive enough to capture all types of knowledge required for stand allocation. Furthermore, constraint-programming capabilities were available as third-party C++ components.

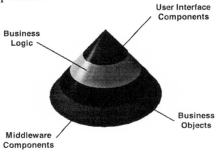

User Interface Components

Business Logic

Business Objects

Middleware Components

Figure 5. Four types of component software used by SAS.

Typical to most OT-based systems, SAS uses four main types of component software – middleware components, business objects, business logic, and graphic user interface (GUI) components. Middleware components are used in both client and server processes. The airport business

objects are implemented as CORBA objects where the implementations reside on the server and then distributed to clients as proxies. The business logic used for stand allocation is stored in the server process only. The user interface components are used mainly for the client GUI. Using an OT-approach, we were able to take advantage of commercially available best-of-breed off-the-shelf component software to support the functionality required by SAS.

The Middleware Components

SAS uses two types of middleware component – a CORBA middleware and a database middleware. We selected CORBA as the core middleware technology for SAS since it has a relatively low performance and implementation overhead. CORBA also has a broad range of services and is readily available on many platforms. To provide for multi-user support, we used push-type asynchronous messaging. For scalability, the asynchronous messaging can easily scale up to use IP Multicast. SAS uses an off-the-shelf CORBA ORB [3, 4, 5, 10] for development.

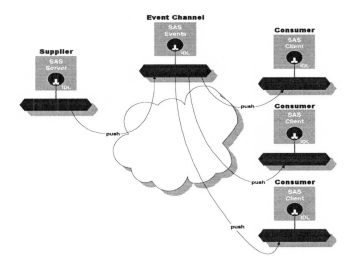

Figure 6. CORBA Event Services push updates to clients for multi-user support.

The SAS application server generates a finite set of events to notify clients of changes and updates. These events are distributed using the CORBA Event services. Incidentally, this infrastructure gives us the added advantage of potentially using same mechanism to notify other IT systems at the airport of stand-related events, such as stand/gate changes or stand closures.

Most database vendors readily support some form of fault tolerance at the third-tier. Fault tolerance in the second-tier can easily be handled by the CORBA middleware itself. Several CORBA middleware products also support loading balancing techniques.

SAS also uses a database middleware to insulate our system from the databases to communicate with. SAS uses off-the-shelf software components [10] to provide object-oriented access to relational databases.

The Business Objects

We were at an advantage in building the SAS application since most of the SAS business objects were reused from an earlier system we had built for the old Kai Tak Airport. Business objects represented entities such as flight legs, aircraft, stands, airlines, handling agents, etc. These business objects were developed on top of our proprietary **Optimiz!** scheduling framework that was implemented using off-the-shelf foundation classes [10]. The business objects are made "constraint-aware" by incorporating C++ software components that supported constraint programming [1, 6, 7, 11]. In addition, the whole system was made multithread-safe using third-party multithread components [10].

Since all key business objects in the SAS are packaged as CORBA objects, there is a great degree of interoperability with other systems using the ORB or simple bridging techniques. Although not all systems at HKIA are CORBA-based, a CORBA "wrapper" can easily be added to other IT systems to facilitate integration as illustrated in Figure 7.

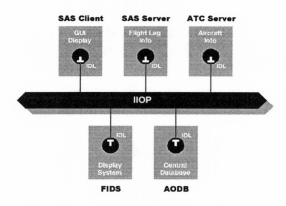

Figure 7. SAS as a CORBA-based system.

The SAS in-memory business object cache is created from a local MS SQL Server relational database using the database middleware. The database schema design is identical to that of the HKIA's Airport Operational Database (AODB). All relational tables relevant to ramp operations are mirrored and updated regularly from the AODB. Business objects are made persistent by having any changes, triggered by the SAS event mechanism, to be automatically committed to database through the database middleware.

The Business Logic

SAS business logic consists mainly of constraints defined using our pre-built C++ **Optimiz!** scheduling framework. Our framework provides a software infrastructure upon which a general class of scheduling systems can be built.

The framework contains features to facilitate problem modeling and scheduling algorithm implementation. It contains software components to represent generalized concepts such as allocatable objects, hard constraints, soft constraints, and a set of scheduling algorithms. Many generic allocation operations are built into the framework, such as freeze, move, cancel, split, swap, etc. Other facilities include reactive scheduling, what-if analysis, explanation generation, warning message generation, audit-trail logging, an event generator, and auto-testing facility.

The **Optimiz!** framework has been used for other projects and was ready off-the-shelf prior to the SAS development. As part of the actual SAS development, we defined constraints related to stand allocation using the framework and to establish a set of constraint parameters that reflected actual operations at Chek Lap Kok.

The User Interface Components

The graphic user interface for SAS client machines was developed using highly optimized C++ graphic components [2]. The user interface consists mainly of interactive Gantt charts and spreadsheets. Additional administrative user interface facilities were developed using Microsoft Visual Basic. All SAS user interface screens follow standard Windows interaction with context-sensitive menus and on-line help, thus making the system very user friendly. SAS training only takes a day's time for operators who are already familiar with airport operations.

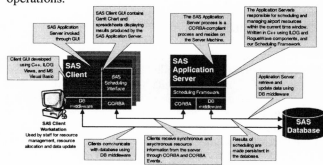

Figure 8. Distribution of software components through CORBA infrastructure.

Putting It All Together

Figure 8 documents the final system architecture once all the software components are in place and integrated into the CORBA infrastructure. This diagram represents an orchestration of many software components working efficiently in unison. As an architecture for AI applications, this is highly elegant and is made possible only through the combination of highly efficient C++, CORBA, and constraint programming.

Uses of AI Technology

The problem of stand allocation is a typical resource assignment problem that can be solved very efficiently as a constraint satisfaction problem (CSP) [1, 6, 7, 11]. CSP algorithms have been used successfully to solve a wide variety of transportation related scheduling problems [8, 9]. In general, scheduling and resource allocation problems can be formulated as a CSP that involves the assignment of values to variables subjected to a set of constraints.

For the stand allocation problem, each variable represents the stand assignment for one aircraft. Each aircraft may be associated with several variables since an aircraft may need to be towed several times during its stay at the airport. The domain of each variable will initially contain the set of all stands in the airport. The CSP constraints are restrictions on how these stands can be assigned to an aircraft. The same set of constraints might be used during reactive scheduling to solve dynamic problems.

SAS uses mainly two main types of constraints – hard constraints for domain reduction and soft constraints for value selection. These constraints are implemented using constraint components from our **Optimiz!** scheduling framework. The following highlights the key constraints for stand allocation:

No Overlap Constraint – This constraint ensures that no two aircraft will be assigned the same stand at the "same time." This time is measured between the chock-on and chock-off times, and a "clearance" to allow for aircraft movements in and out of the stand.

Stand Combination Constraint – Some stands can be combined with adjacent or nearby stands to accommodate larger aircraft or divided into several stands to accommodate smaller aircraft. This constraint ensures that these stand combinations are considered during allocation and that only one combination is active at any one time.

Passenger/Freighter Aircraft Constraint – Cargo and passenger flights have different constraints on where the aircraft can be allocated. For example, an airport may disallow any passenger flights from de-planing or boarding at cargo areas.

International/Domestic Constraint – Some stands may be dedicated to serving international or domestic flights only. In Hong Kong, despite the fact it is now SAR China, all flights are still considered as international.

Stand Closure Constraint – Stands may be closed from time to time for maintenance. This constraint ensures that no aircraft is assigned a stand when it is closed.

Stand Warning Constraint – Sometimes stands may have minor equipment failures that restrict certain types of aircraft from parking there. For example, if one of the bridges is down, a smaller aircraft type may still use the stand for de-planing and boarding.

Size Constraint – This is a physical constraint that ensures the assigned stand is large enough to fit the aircraft. In Hong Kong, most stands are large enough to fit any type of aircraft.

Adjacency Constraint – Sometimes the size of an aircraft may affect which type of aircraft can use the adjacent stands. For example, a wide-body aircraft might prohibit another wide-body from being assigned to adjacent stands. At CLK, there are no adjacency constraints for this new airport

Aircraft Type Preferences – These are soft preferences on which stands should be assigned to which aircraft types. This might be for convenience of aircraft maneuvering, convenience of passenger, or ground equipment availability.

Auto-Tow Constraint – This constraint determines when aircraft should be towed and where it should be towed. It ensures that aircraft with long ground time should be towed to temporary parking areas to optimize use of inner stands. For example, aircraft staying on ground for several hours will be towed to remote stands and then towed back for departure. Longer staying aircraft, on the other hand, will be towed to maintenance stands, which might be further away. The tow times are defined by several parameters – the minimum time needed to off-load passengers, the minimum time an aircraft should be assigned to a stand, and the minimum time needed for boarding, and the towing time from stand to stand.

Towing Preferences – This defines preferences as to where aircraft should be towed for temporary parking. For example, certain areas may be more desirable to be used as "pad" areas. On the other hand, there might be a simple preference to just tow the aircraft to the nearest outer stand, in terms of towing time.

Customary Stand Preferences – Airlines or handling agents may have preferences as to which stands their aircraft should be assigned. These preferences are usually related to the location of equipment or the transit or service counters of the airline or handling agent.

Aircraft Orientation Constraint – Aircraft assigned to remote stands may have different options as to the orientation that the aircraft be parked. This constraint may be related to convenience of aircraft maneuvering or safety of de-planing passengers at nearby stands. Unlike the old airport, at CLK all aircraft parking orientations are fixed.

Connecting Passenger Constraint – This constraint tries to optimize the allocation of aircraft such that flights with transit passengers will be assigned closer together to minimize passenger walking time.

Whenever constraint violations reach a given threshold, the flights involved will be highlighted in red. Figure 9 is an example where a flight's departure (CPA504) is delayed and causes a conflict with the next flight (CPA403) that is scheduled for the same stand (E2). There is not enough time for the departure flight to maneuver out of the stand to make room for the arrival flight. The user can invoke the SAS "Why" command to get an explanation for the constraint scoring. Figure 9 also shows how different shadings and colors are used to indicate different flight statuses, such as confirmed chock on/off and new eta/etd.

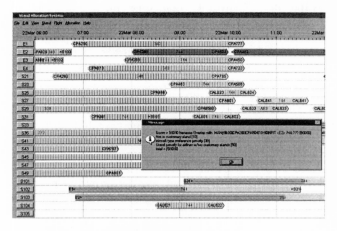

Figure 9. Explanation facility provided in SAS.

SAS automatically solves conflicts with a click of a button. It takes less than a minute to solve all conflicts for one day. The following shows the new schedule after conflict has been resolved by SAS. The conflicting flight (CPA403) has been moved to stand S105, which is a less desirable remote stand. Our reactive scheduling algorithm solves conflicts while minimizing the impact of changes to original schedule and hence minimizing the amount of inconvenience to waiting passengers.

Figure 10. Result of performing reactive scheduling.

Application Use and Payoff

SAS is used by AA airfield operation staff in the Airport Control Center (ACC) at HKIA. Roughly twenty operators, who work in shifts, were trained on the use of SAS. The system has been deployed since June 1998.

Since HKIA is a new airport, quantitative measurements on performance before and after system implementation cannot be made. However, we can still clearly identify the key benefits expected from using SAS:

A Dynamic Organization - Producing an optimized stand allocation plan manually will take at least half a day. The quality of the resulting allocation plan will vary from person to person depending on experience. SAS produces a plan in roughly three minutes and ensures that all constraints are considered, allocation plan is optimized, and high quality is maintained each time. Since scheduling time is reduced to only a few minutes, the Airport Authority becomes more dynamic as an organization and can handle last minute flight and rotation changes very quickly.

Swift Decision Making - Humans might not perform well under extreme stress and pressure such as those faced during real operations. Trying to perform problem solving under those conditions may result in less than ideal or even wrong decisions. SAS performs reactive problem solving in around five seconds and guarantees the solutions to be correct each time every time. A quick response time allows SAS operators to reply to air traffic controllers immediate while online if needed.

Guarantee Safe and Smooth Operation - Since all constraints are considered all the time, SAS guarantees that no safety-related constraints are overlooked. Over a hundred different types of aircraft lands in Hong Kong. Each aircraft has a slightly different physical dimension and equipment requirement. Bridges normally can accommodate many types of aircraft. However, certain bridge configuration or equipment failure may restrict some types of aircraft from using the bridge. There is a potential that a human operator might oversee these differences and mistakenly assign an aircraft to an improper stand. The consequence might be a disruption of aircraft ground traffic or worst, a minor collision. Even if the safety violation was identified early on, towing the aircraft to another stand will delay the plane by at least half an hour. The plan produced by SAS ensures that aircraft ground movements are safe.

Better Passenger Service – Being recognized as one of the best airports in the world, in terms of travelers' satisfaction, is not easy. Many different factors contribute to this success. Stand management also plays an important role. For example, a good allocation will allow passengers to get to their destination as quickly as possible. For arrival flights, SAS tries to assign aircraft close to immigration counters or close to unmanned transport vehicles to allow faster exit from terminal building. For transit flights, SAS tries to assign aircraft close to airline transit counters. If a stand change must be made, SAS tries to reassign aircraft to another stand in close proximity to the original assignment.

Capacity for Growth - In the long term, SAS will allow HKIA to continue to grow and accommodate more traffic in the coming years. Although HKIA is a new airport with more resources, it is still expanding. A new runaway is due to operate soon and air traffic will increase. However, the construction of the second terminal building has yet to begin. It is most likely that the airport will gradually become resource stressed in the years before the second terminal begins operation. SAS will be able to help reduce this stress by optimizing the utilization of stand resources.

Application Development and Deployment

One of the advantages of implementing an AI application using standard off-the-shelf object-oriented (OO) software components is that standard OO software engineering practices can also be followed. For SAS development, we followed an OO methodology that is based on Rational's Unified Process. User requirements were documented using Use Case Analysis and the OO design was documented using standard Unified Modeling Language (UML).

The coding of SAS was performed in iterative cycles to reduce risk. Development time allocated for SAS was extremely tight. To minimize risk, we planned the iterative cycles very carefully. The first iteration took only two weeks. The objective of the first development cycle was to implement an initial prototype that tested the integration of all the software components working together within the CORBA infrastructure. This involved hooking up software components from several third-party vendors and ensuring the whole infrastructure was solid and working from end to end.

The second iteration took another month and a half and the result was the first release of SAS with basic stand allocation capabilities. This version was used to test the completeness of the standing allocation knowledge. By integrating off-the-shelf software components we were able to dramatically shorten our development time. We were able to further shorten the development time by reusing business objects and an object-oriented scheduling framework that we had developed earlier for the old airport.

A third iteration took another month and encoded the remaining user requirements. This version was then part under extensive testing and trial use by AA operators with actual data. Since time allocated for testing was short, automatic testing software was built that automatically simulated thousands of different operational scenarios. This test suite was particularly useful early on in the project to identify coding errors that would have taken weeks to find if tested manually; some coding errors can only be revealed under very peculiar sequences of events.

The coding of SAS took roughly four months elapsed time total with a development team of ten C++ software developers who were already familiar with all the software components used in this project.

Maintenance

SAS was designed to be fully maintainable by AA's own staff members. AA senior operators maintain the knowledge base through a set of MS Visual Basic database forms. All site-specific knowledge, constraints, parameters, and data are stored in the local MS SQL Server database. Any change in domain knowledge can be performed without any SAS source code change. Knowledge related to stand operations do not really change that often. The knowledge base is usually updated only when a new stand, airline, or aircraft type is put into operation. Other routine database maintenance is performed by AA's IT staff members. In addition, we provide 24-hour technical and user support both through telephone and on-site if needed.

Conclusion

This paper provided an overview of the Stand Allocation System that we have designed and built for the new Hong Kong International Airport at Chek Lap Kok. It described the hardware and software architecture of the SAS and the constraints of the new airport. It documents our rationale in selecting the technologies we did and our experience in constructing an advanced AI application using off-the-shelf software components. Hopefully, this paper provides some insights on the design and development of mission critical component-based AI systems.

Acknowledgements

The authors would like to thank AA operations and IT staff for the tremendous co-operation, support and enthusiasm received throughout this project.

References

[1] J. Cohen, *Constraint Logic Programming,* Communications of the ACM, 33(7), pp.52-68, 1990.

[2] http://www.ilog.com

[3] http://www.iona.com

[4] http://www.inprise.com

[5] http://www.ooc.com

[6] G.L. Steele Jr., *The Definition and Implementation of a Computer Programming Language Based on Constraints,* Ph.D. Thesis, MIT, 1980.

[7] V. Kumar, "Algorithms for Constraint Satisfaction Problems: A Survey," In *AI Magazine,* 13(1), pp.32-44, 1992.

[8] J.-F. Puget, "A C++ Implementation of CLP," In *ILOG Solver Collected Papers*, ILOG SA, France, 1994.

[9] J.-F. Puget, "Object-Oriented Constraint Programming for Transportation Problems," In *ILOG Solver Collected Papers*, ILOG SA, France, 1994.

[10] http://www.roguewave.com

[11] P. Van Hentenryck, *Constraint Satisfaction in Logic Programming,* MIT Press, 1989.

Last Minute Travel Application

André Hübner, Mario Lenz, Roman Borch, and Michael Posthoff

TecInno GmbH
Sauerwiesen 2
D-67661 Kaiserslautern, Germany
{huebner,lenz}@tecinno.com

check out Touristik GmbH
Friedrichstraße 112b
D-10117 Berlin, Germany
posthoff@transmedia.de

Abstract

In this article, we present a last minute travel application as part of a complete virtual travel agency. Each year a significant amount of tour packages is sold as last minute tours in Germany. It is impossible for a travel agent to keep track of all the offered tour packages. E-Commerce applications may help to present the best possible tour package for a specific customer request. Traditional database driven applications, as used by most of the tour operators, are not sufficient enough to implement a sales process with consultation in the WWW. The last minute travel application presented here uses case-based reasoning to bridge this gap and simulate the sales assistance of a human travel agent. A *Case Retrieval Net* (CRN), as internal data structure, proofed to be efficient to handle the large amount of data. Important for the acceptance by customers is also the integration into the *Virtual Travel Agency* and the interconnections to other parts of this system, like background information or the online car rental application.

Problem Description

The biggest share of the German travel market are tour packages. A usual tour package contains the flight to the destination and back, transfers from the airport to the hotel and back, board and lodging. The market share for individual tours is much smaller than in the US and other countries.

It is common practice to offer tour packages that could not be sold until 4 weeks before departure day as *last minute tours*. Usually, a discount is given to the customer for those tour packages. Especially in recent years, the market for last minute packages grew by a vast amount and there are specific properties related to those products:

Property 1: Travel agents struggle with the *update* problem: Up to 6,000 of new packages are offered daily just by one of the major German tour providers. Traditionally, tour providers sent several dozen sheets of paper to their travel agents every day in order to inform them about available special offers.

Property 2: The above described way of informing agents via stacks of papers implies an *availability* problem: Often, the amount of places that can be booked on a specific offer is highly limited. Hence, when customers decide for one of the offers, there is a high risk that this one is no longer available. This happens because there is no feedback about offers that have been brought to the market in recent days, i.e. it is not clear whether these are still available or not.

Property 3: Thirdly, *Last minute* offers (as provided by the tour providers) are tour packages: This means that the customer may accept an offer only as it is – there are no variations of it (except if it is stored as a separate offer). Consequently, there is no negotiation during the sales process.

Property 4 Finally, although there may be a huge number of offers, it is unlikely that the desires of a customer can be fulfilled all at once. Rather, it is often the case that alternative departure dates, neighboring airports, or even other destinations need to be suggested. In contrast to people having planned and prepared their holiday carefully, customers looking for *Last Minute* vacations expect such variations.

It seems that E-Commerce would be a good way to sell these travels. Some of the tour operators are offering database driven systems in the WWW to sell their tour packages. See TUI[1] or LTU[2] for example. A shortcoming of these applications is that ordinary search requests (usually internally realized with some database query language) are not sufficient enough. Customers usually have a certain idea of what kind of tour they would like to book. They do have a preferred country, departure date and length of the tour. If the customer now specifies the request in detail, then most of the time a traditional system tells the customer "No hits found!", that means that no tour package in their database matches the request exactly (*no solution* situation). The customer himself has to widen the request by leaving some of the input fields blank. The result is that the system probably will present the customer with

---

[1] http://www.tui.com/
[2] http://www.ltu.com/

several thousand possible tour packages (*1,000 solutions* situation). These lists usually are not even ranked according to the request of the customer. So the customer himself has to look through all the presented offers to find the best matching tour package. This behavior of these conventional systems does not reflect a sales process at all. A good travel agent would never tell the customers that there is no tour package matching the request and send them away. Instead, the travel agent would propose some similar tour packages. So, an application was needed that implements a vague matching and ranks the found tour packages according to the customers request.

Application description

The last minute travel application is only one part of a complete virtual travel agency. As an E-Commerce application it is fully accessible via the WWW.

The customer usually connects to the last minute travel application by following a link from the web pages of the *Virtual Travel Agency*. The presented web page contains a form where information about the destination, the travel date, the kind of hotel room, and some other data can be entered. Note that all these input fields can also be left blank which means that the customer does not care about these features. After sending the given information to the web server of the virtual travel agency, a cgi script is started, the *retrieval client*. This retrieval client will then contact the *retrieval server* which is running in the background. The retrieval server is running 24 hours a day and can handle requests from several cgi scripts at once. The number of simultaneous retrieval clients is only limited by the systems hardware. The retrieval is performed, using case-based reasoning (CBR) (Lenz *et al.* 1998) in the server and the result, a sorted list of tour packages, is sent back to the retrieval client. The offered tour packages are ranked according to how well they fit the customers request. A template HTML page is loaded by the retrieval client and the features of the retrieved tour packages are inserted into that page before sending it back to the web browser of the customer. If exact matches are found, they will be displayed first, followed by tour packages that are most similar. The customers can decide how many offers are presented to them. Background information, like facts about the destination country, about a single tour package are provided by clicking on the appropriate link. If the customer decides to book a tour package, another form has to be filled out, and this information is then sent to the real travel agency via email. The travel agency will contact the customer to verify the booking and information given. There is no real online payment implemented yet due to security concerns. The main component of the client server system is the retrieval server which implements a case based system.

The tour package data is provided daily by the tour operator as an ASCII file. This file is automatically downloaded via FTP. The update component is now used to transfer the raw data into a more appropriate structure. Information about the offered tour packages is gathered during the updating process. This information and the tour package data are then loaded by the retrieval server. This updating process is started daily automatically via a cronjob, but can also be triggered manually if needed. The whole system was developed in the Unix environment and is now running on a linux PC. All components have been coded in C++, the entire *Virtual Travel Agency* consists of 20,000 lines of code, including all additional components. A Microsoft web server on a Win NT PC is used to connect the last minute travel application to the WWW. The user interface is completely implemented in HTML, so no plug-in or special browser is needed by the customer. Highest possible compatibility was the prime reason for this.

In order to remain flexible with respect to changes in the layout of the various pages and also to not overload the programs with too much information about the HTML layout, we implemented a strategy in which *template* HTML pages are provided by the travel agents. These are then used within the system and the data that corresponds to the current session is placed in these templates. This also made the implementation of customized releases for other partners reasonably easy.

Uses of AI Technology
Case-Based Reasoning

As already discussed, simple database approaches would not be sufficient for implementing this type of application as they cannot provide *intelligent* sales support. In particular, the following features are essential:

- Some customers enter very detailed descriptions of their intended tour packages while others only have a rough idea. Consequently, the system has to be able to deal with vague as well as highly specific queries.

- Due to Property 4, the system has to be able to suggest appropriate alternatives if no offer completely fits the customers requirements.

- The system has to present the available offers to the customer in a reasonable manner. In particular, it should definitely avoid situations in which no offer is made to the customer (*no solution* situation) as well as those where the customer is left alone with pages and pages of possible offers (*1,000 solutions* situation).

Case-Based Reasoning, in general, is a technology that satisfies at least the last two criteria:

- Alternatives are suggested by considering *similar* offers where the similarity measure takes into account information about departure dates, geographic locations of departure airports and destinations, climatic conditions etc.

- The *no solution* situation is avoided by the previous point: consideration of alternatives. The *1,000 solutions* situation, on the other hand, is avoided by

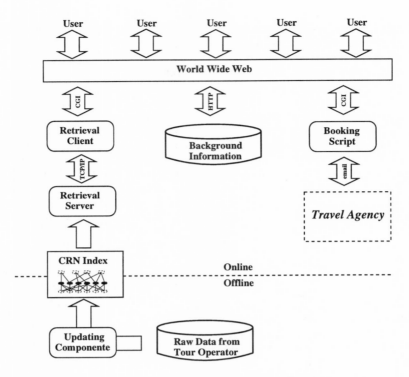

Figure 1: The last minute travel application

establishing preference orderings and presenting the best suited offers first. Hence, the result of a retrieval process is not a *set* of all applicable offers (as in databases) but a *ranking* of the most suitable offers.

Fulfillment of the first of the above criteria very much depends on the particular technique used for implementing the system. As should be clear from the description so far, a CBR system has to deal with three crucial problems in the *Virtual Travel Agency*:

Flexible Retrieval: Some customers enter very specific requests, others only express vague intentions. Hence, a CBR system needs a flexible retrieval method that can cope with both situations.

Efficient Retrieval: Customers are not willing to wait long for the result of a search request. Even the delay caused by the WWW often causes severe problems. Thus, the retrieval method has to be highly efficient due to the large amount of data that has to be managed.

Easy Updates: Since regular updates of the data are required, building the internal structures of the CBR system has to be manageable in reasonable time and possibly while the system is still running.

The model of *Case Retrieval Nets* (Burkhard & Lenz 1996) (CRNs) satisfies all three criteria. For the purpose of this paper, it suffices to think of CRNs as a specific index of the case base that can be built offline and that supports both efficient and flexible case retrieval by means of a spreading activation process in an associative memory.

A *case* is, of course, a representation of a single tour package as a vector of attribute-value pairs according to the following features:

- the `Departure Airport`,
- the `Destination` of the desired holiday trip,
- the `Departure Date`,
- the `Duration` of the trip,
- the `Type of Accommodation`
- the `Type of Catering`,
- the number of participating `Persons`,
- and, of course, the `Price`.

A *case base* is the set of all cases in a single data set.

A *query* is represented similarly to cases except that the feature `Price` has not been included as a searchable parameter. This decision was based on the observation that all offers with otherwise similar parameters will, in general, be very similar priced in *Last Minute* data sets.

Integration

As already mentioned, the last minute travel application is one part of a *Virtual Travel Agency*. A *Background Information Module* is used to display additional information about a selected tour package, such as information about the destination, the offered hotel, or the climate.

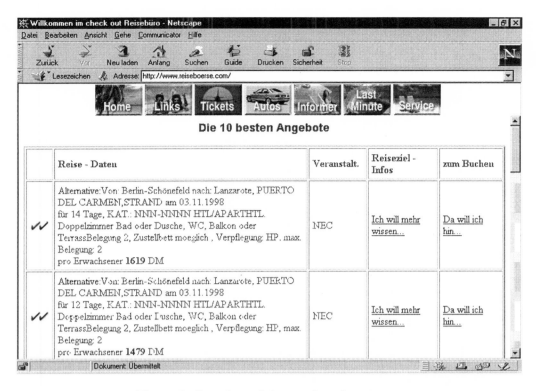

Figure 2: Snapshot of the result web page

The type of information shown depends on the data set the offer originates from. For example, there are *Last Minute* programs for which the name of the hotel is intentionally not available while for other programs this information is provided.

Another very tight connected application is called *INFORMER*. The *INFORMER* can be used as an *agent* to specify a request for a last minute tour package some time before tour packages for the desired departure time will be offered. The *INFORMER* will check each day if there is a tour package that meets the requirements of the customer, and if so it will send an email to this customer.

Insights

The last minute travel application differs from typical research applications in some important points. The model of the domain (travel) is quite simple and could be built without much effort. Much more time was required to find appropriate mechanisms to handle this huge amount of data (up to a quarter of a million). The response time of the system was crucial for the success of the last minute travel application.

Consequently, strict design decisions have been made towards a lean implementation of the system that allowed to realize a working (and profitable) tool in reasonable time. The resulting system is limited in several respects. For example, it assumes a relational data model as known from traditional database technologies and is based in fairly straight-forward similarity measures. On the other hand, the system is generic in so far as it can be used to create solutions for other E-Commerce scenarios. The system itself is based on the CBR-Sells product by TecInno

Application Use and Payoff

The first version of the last minute travel application went online in March 1997. It was considered a trial version using the environment of the university to test the system, but it was already fully integrated into the *Virtual Travel Agency*. In July 1998, it was relaunched at the commercial server of the *Virtual Travel Agency*. Since then the last minute travel application was steadily extended as much as the virtual travel agency itself. This evolutionary development will be continued in the future.

During the first year approx. 300.000 requests were measured, in peak seasons several thousands a day. The average number of requests was constantly raising during the whole year. There was no special customer group to identify, and despite the fact that the *Virtual Travel Agency* is operated by a local Berlin travel agent the requests came from all over Germany and even abroad.

During the first season almost 1.000 customer used the last minute travel application to book a tour package and an estimated turnover of 1 million German marks a year was achieved. Indirectly it was even more, because a lot customer did not use the system for buying the tour packages but for looking for the best offer and then buying it in the real travel agency, or via phone. Nevertheless so far E-Commerce is not as much deployed in Germany as it is in US. E-Commerce is still a new way of business especially for the end consumer. We expect the growth to be according growth to the whole E-Commerce market.

The system does not generate enough business yet to make a living for the operating travel agency. The traditional way of selling tour packages is still the major income source. The *Virtual Travel Agency* can be considered as an *additional* branch of the real travel agency, with its own business processes.

Application Development and Deployment

The *Virtual Travel Agency* as the overall system was first started with a flight database in 1996. From this, experiences with the WWW and cgi programming were collected and used in later applications. Travel related information was added all the time and additional applications, like renting a car online, evolved. The last minute travel application was developed by 2 people (one student, one university staff) within 3 months. The estimated effort was 2 man months.

The system was designed to be clearly subdivided into 2 parts: **the backend**, and **the frontend**.

The backend was written by the above mentioned developers in C++ and includes the cgi script, the retrieval server and the update script.

The frontend including the web pages (written in standard HTML) and therewith the layout was developed by the travel agents staff.

The overall development costs were low due to this strict separation and the university setting. This was very important because financing was a major problem, as the travel agency did not have enough money for letting such a system develop by software houses. The tour operators were not (and still aren't) interested in this system for different reasons:

1. Usually there is already a web presentation of these tour operators which they consider as sufficient enough.

2. The main business of the tour operator is generated by the travel agencies and only a small part directly via E-Commerce. The traditional travel agents are not interested in getting competitors from E-Commerce. So the tour operator can not support such a system without displeasing the travel agencies, their major business partners.

We will not go into further details about these and related problems, they are discussed more broadly in (Lenz 1998; 1999).

Maintenance

Two aspects have to be considered concerning the maintenance of the system: data update (corresponds to the case base maintenance at CBR) and model update (corresponds to similarity update at CBR).

Data update is done automatically using the update component, usually once a day, when new data from the tour provider arrives. It can also be done manually if required.

Model update is done by the travel agency staff themself and hardly ever needed. In case that a new destinations appears the system prints a log message and the travel agency staff has to insert the new destination into the similarity model. The same procedure would be done with new values at all the other features of a tour package. With the next updating process these new values are considered.

References

Burkhard, H.-D., and Lenz, M. 1996. Case Retrieval Nets: Basic ideas and extensions. Informatik-Berichte, 103–110. Berlin: Humboldt University.

Lenz, M.; Burkhard, H.-D.; Bartsch-Spörl, B.; and Wess, S. 1998. *Case-Based Reasoning Technology – From Foundations to Applications*. Lecture Notes in Artificial Intelligence 1400. Springer Verlag.

Lenz, M. 1998. Experiences from Deploying Electronic Commerce Applications. Techn. report, Humboldt University, Berlin.

Lenz, M. 1999. Experiences from deploying cbr applications in electronic commerce. In *accepted for GWCBR-99*.

A New Basis for Spreadsheet Computing:
Interval Solver™ for Microsoft® Excel

Eero Hyvönen and Stefano De Pascale

Delisoft Ltd
Urho Kekkosen katu 8 C 30, 00100 Helsinki, FINLAND
Tel. +358 9 6866550, Fax +358 9 68665544
{eero.hyvonen,stefano.depascale}@delisoft.com

Abstract

There is a fundamental mismatch between the computational basis of spreadsheets and our knowledge of the real world. In spreadsheets numerical data is represented as exact numbers and their mutual relations as functions, whose values (output) are computed from given argument values (input). However, in the real world data is often inexact and uncertain in many ways and the relationships, i.e., constraints, between input and output are far more complicated. This paper shows that Interval Constraint Solving, an emerging Artificial Intelligence based technology, provides a more versatile and useful foundation for spreadsheets. The new computational basis is 100% downward compatible with the traditional spreadsheet paradigm. The idea has been successfully integrated with Microsoft Excel as the add-in Interval Solver that seamlessly upgrades the arithmetic core of Excel into interval constraint solving. The product has been downloaded by thousands of end-users in about 70 countries around the world and has been used in various applications on business computing, engineering, education and science. There is an intriguing chance for a major breakthrough of the AI technology on the spreadsheet platform: Tens of millions of Excel users are making important decisions based on spreadsheet calculations.

1. Real world spreadsheet computing

The world is full of uncertainty and complexity. Everyday we are faced with questions like: How can I live within the given budget? Is this technical design possible, given the inaccurate component data? Uncertain data and constraints are extensively used in decision making. But spreadsheets, one of the most commonly used decision making aid of today, force us to use exact numbers for representing inexact data, thus distorting reality.

For example, consider the problem of computing the present value p of a future cash flow c that will be received after three years. If the annual future interest rates are r_1, r_2, and r_3 then p can be computed by using the (discounting) formula:

$$p = c/((1+r_1/100)\cdot(1+r_2/100)\cdot(1+r_3/100)) \qquad (1.1)$$

The problem is that future interest rates are volatile and that the value of c can be uncertain, too. The value of p is then uncertain as well. The question is: How to represent uncertain numerical values and how to compute them?

Another major limitation of spreadsheets is that the relationships between cell values can only be expressed with functions evaluating output cell values from given input cell values. In the real world things are more complicated. For example, consider the following formula for computing the y-coordinate of a projectile trajectory as a function of the x-coordinate, firing angle a and initial velocity v.

$$y = x\cdot\tan(a) + \frac{1}{2}\cdot 9.81\cdot a^2/(v^2\cdot\cos(a)^2) \qquad (1.2)$$

Assume that the target is on a 120m high hill (y) at a distance of 3200m (x). The initial speed (v) of the projectile is between 1250 m/s and 1300m/s. The task is to find out what are the possible angles (a) between 0 and 90 degrees for hitting the target. The formula and the given data clearly provide the answer but it is not clear how to back solve a from the function.

In a more general setting, the application problem may consist of a set of functions, equations, and inequalities, and the task is to solve any subset of variables involved, not only one variable. For example, what are the solutions to the equations below?

$$\begin{aligned}
\sin(x_1) + \cos(x_2) &= \ln(x_3) \\
\cos(x_1) + 2\cdot\ln(x_2) &= -\sin(x_3) + 3 \\
3\cdot\ln(x_1) &= \sin(x_2) - \cos(x_3) + 2
\end{aligned} \qquad (1.3)$$

Traditional numerical techniques may find a solution to this problem, but not necessarily. The success depends on the equations and the initial guess values used as the starting point for the iteration. At best one solution is found for one starting point. The average spreadsheet user is not interested in such hidden technical details but simply wants to find a solution or ALL solutions to his/her problem by just pushing a button! Or (s)he wants to be sure that the problem has no solutions at all.

The examples above indicate that the following two key concepts of the current numerical spreadsheet paradigm are not flexible enough:

- **Cell value.** Only exact numbers can be used as values and be evaluated by formulas. Given the widespread and diverse usage of spreadsheets, a simple way for representing uncertainty is needed.
- **Formula.** Only functions can be used as formulas that explicate the relations between cell values. Means for representing arbitrary constraints between variables involved is needed. Especially, equations and inequalities used everywhere in business, engineering, and science should be available.

The case study of this paper shows that the idea of Interval Constraint Solving developed in the fields of Artificial Intelligence and Interval Analysis provides a new practical way to overcome these limitations. By generalizing the two core concepts of the spreadsheet paradigm, "value" and "formula", a new basis for the very idea of using spreadsheets can be laid.

The new vision has been materialized as the commercial deployed add-in product Interval Solver for Microsoft Excel, the result of some 16 man-years of research and development in Finland and Japan.

From the mathematical viewpoint, the solving power of the new technology is greater than with any traditional non-interval technique: All solutions (within a given precision level) to equations and other constraints can be found if enough time and memory is available. For example, Interval Solver can actually prove that (1.3) has exactly 5 different solutions. It suffices to push a button.

This paper first explains why and when interval constraint solving and Interval Solver is of use to a spreadsheet user. The architecture of the software is then presented and application of AI techniques is discussed. In conclusion, the significance of interval constraint technology in the development of the current spreadsheet paradigm is discussed.

2. Interval Solver for Microsoft Excel

Interval Solver is an add-in that virtually extends the mathematical basis of Excel into interval constraint solving. From the user's view point this means that (s)he can make better use of imprecise real world data and constraints, and solve new kind of problems that could not be addressed with spreadsheets before. With Interval Solver one can

- **bound** worst and best cases satisfying the spreadsheet formulas,
- **solve back** argument intervals from given goals,
- **solve equations and other constraints** needed in the application, and
- **find the best solution** to a problem.

2.1. Bounding worst and best cases

Intervals are perhaps the simplest way of representing uncertain numerical data. An interval [*min*, *max*] is a continuum of values between the bounds *min* and *max*. For example, the interest rate of the next year can be estimated by interval [4.0, 5.0]% meaning any value between 4% and 5%. By using interval analysis, safe bounds for function values with interval arguments can be computed.

Figure 1 depicts the situation of formula (1.1) on an Excel sheet with Interval Solver add-in loaded. The formula for P (seen in the formula bar) has been computed with the given uncertain interest rate and cash flow intervals. All the user has to do is to write the Excel function inside the =I(*expression*) formula of Interval Solver. After this, interval arguments can be used.

	B3		=I(F3/((1+C3/100)*(1+D3/100)*(1+E3/100)))			
	A	B	C	D	E	F
1						
2		PRESENT VALUE (P)	R1 (%)	R2 (%)	R3 (%)	CASH FLOW (C)
3		[28.6, 32.8]	[4, 5]	[5, 7]	[6, 8.75]	[35, 38]
4						

Figure 1. Evaluating an Excel formula with interval arguments.

The function value was initially *free*, i.e., its value was unknown. This equals to interval (-inf, inf). Interval Solver narrowed this value to [28.6, 32.8], the interval that is *guaranteed* to bound all possible values of the function down to user-given precision. The minimum represents the *global* minimum and the maximum the global maximum of the function within the argument interval limits. Notice that a number x is actually a collapsed interval $[x, x]$ having the same lower and upper bound. This means that interval computations generalize traditional spreadsheet computations with exact values.

There are alternative approaches for representing uncertainty of numerical values, too. A simple way is to enumerate scenarios. For example, in figure 1 one could compute the formula with, e.g., all combinations of minimum and maximum values of the arguments. This simple approach is feasible only if the number of scenarios is small. In figure 1 there would be $2^4=16$ scenarios if only bounds were considered; in the general case there are infinitely many possibilities. Another problem is that usually it is very difficult to say with what argument values the formula evaluates its global minimum or maximum that is often of greatest interest to the user. In the interval approach, all infinitely many scenarios are bounded within a single interval, and the actual global minimum and maximum can always be found.

A more sophisticated approach for representing numerical uncertainty is to use probability distributions as function arguments and then evaluate the functions using Monte Carlo simulation. This is a widely used approach and there are several software add-in packages available for spreadsheets, such as Crystal Ball (Crystal Ball, 1998) and @Risk (@Risk, 1998). In the probabilistic view, an interval can be seen as a distribution whose form is completely unknown and whose definite integral over the interval is one. All variables are statistically independent from each other.

For the average spreadsheet user, probabilistic modeling may be too difficult to use. Intervals provide a simpler low-end approach for representing numerical uncertainty and have thus a better chance of being adopted by the spreadsheet users. Furthermore, intervals can be used for constraint solving as will be seen later. This is the key contribution of Interval Solver.

2.2. Solving back argument intervals

Assume that cell A1 contains the formula =A2+A3. Given argument values A2 and A3, the value of A1 is computed. The computational model of spreadsheets is a classical example of forward propagation.

However, in many problems the goal is known and the task is to back solve argument values that lead to feasible solutions. Constraint propagation is a handy classical AI technique for solving such problems. For example, if A1 and one of the arguments, say A2 are known in the above example, then the remaining argument A3 can be computed (A3=A1-A2). This value can then be propagated further to formulas in which variable A3 is used, and so on. Constraint propagation makes it possible to evaluate formulas "backwards" or "symmetrically", not only "forward" from known argument values to function value.

The idea of constraint propagation is not new in spreadsheet computing. It was actually adopted already by the early developers of the first major spreadsheet program, VisiCalc, in the late 70's. The best known result of this branch of development is TK!Solver (TK!Solver, 1998), a tool for mathematical modeling.

In interval constraint solving, the classical numerical value propagation is generalized into a still more versatile computational model: Intervals are propagated instead of exact numbers. The idea is to narrow initial variable intervals by using local consistency filtering techniques developed originally for solving discrete constraint satisfaction problems. The result of the narrowing procedure is a set of intervals that definitely bound all exact solutions to the constraints, i.e., the *solution set*.

For example, reconsider figure 1. The problem now is to determine the needed cash flow C and interest rates that would match a desired present value P. In figure 2, the user has set present value goal P=29 in the situation of figure 1. In ordinary Excel, one cannot assign to a cell a formula and a value simultaneously, but with Interval Solver this can be done by double-clicking the cell. In response, Excel has refined two interest rates and the cash flow accordingly. Modified values are shown in bold font for user's convenience. Interval Solver has bounded all possible scenarios that may lead to the goal within the given initial intervals – a useful piece of information for the decision-maker.

B3		=I(F3/((1+C3/100)*(1+D3/100)*(1+E3/100)))			
	A	B	C	D	E	F
1						
2		PRESENT VALUE (P)	R1 (%)	R2 (%)	R3 (%)	CASH FLOW (C)
3		29	[4, 5]	[6.7, 7]	[7.42, 8.75]	[35, 35.4]
4						

Figure 2. Interval goal seeking in Interval Solver.

Interval Solver is capable of determining the global value interval of function formulas, but in back solving only locally consistent (Hyvönen, 1992) bounds may be obtained. A problem of locally consistent bounds is that they may have excess width in certain situations, i.e., local narrowing does not necessarily result in the narrowest intervals bounding all solutions. Various consistency criteria can be used for filtering, such as arc-consistency, box consistency, 2B-consistency, and 3B(w)-consistency (Lebbah, Lhomme, 1998), but the problem of excess width remains in the general case. In spite of this limitation, narrowed bounds provide insight to the user regarding the safe space of possibilities available. If needed, the methods discussed below can be used for verifying the feasibility of an arbitrary point within a cell interval.

2.3. Solving equations, inequalities, and other constraints

The goal-seeking example above illustrated the idea that a spreadsheet formula is, from the mathematical viewpoint, actually a constraint *equation*. It tells how the function value and its arguments relate to each other, i.e., what value combinations are mathematically possible. In the same spirit the whole spreadsheet can be interpreted as a set of equations, inequalities, and other constraints whose variables have initial interval ranges. A spreadsheet thus formulates an Interval Constraint Satisfaction problem. The natural task then is either to

- **bound** all solutions of the constraint system or
- **find** its individual solutions.

This interpretation extends the usability of spreadsheet computing tremendously. Equations and inequalities can now be used on the sheet in addition to the traditional functions. In Interval Solver the expression inside the =I(*expression*) formula can be not only a function, but also an equation or an inequality, such as:

=I(A1^2*B2=SIN(C1)+3)
=I(LN(A1)^B1>=TAN(C1)+C1^3)

One can also use logical and numerical constraints mixed. For example:

=I(IMPLIES(A1>B1^2, AND(D2=0, A1<SIN(B1))))

Solutions to the equations and logical constraints can be generated automatically by pushing a button. The spreadsheet has become an expert for equation solving and Boolean logic.

For example, figure 3 depicts a typical problem encountered in electrical designing. The circuit to be analyzed consists of batteries and resistors whose voltages and resistances are known. The task is to solve the nine currents C13:C21 shown on the sheet. This can be done in a standard way by using Kirchoff's laws (equations) that relate resistances, voltages and currents with each other. The equations are written and shown in cells B25:B30 (for the currents) and B32:B34 (for the voltages).

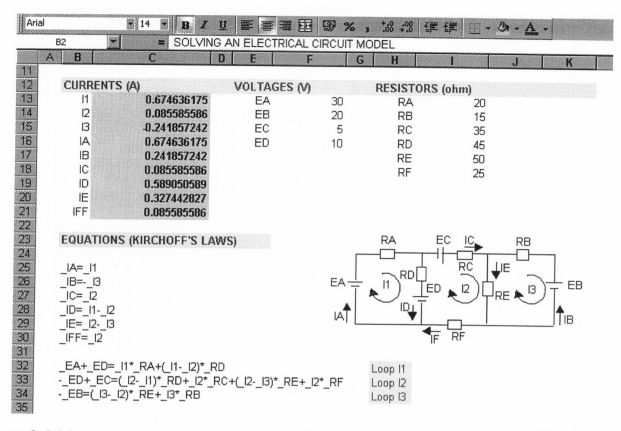

Figure 3. Solving the nine unknown currents of an electrical circuit. Cells have been given mnemonic names by using Excel's Name command on the Insert menu.

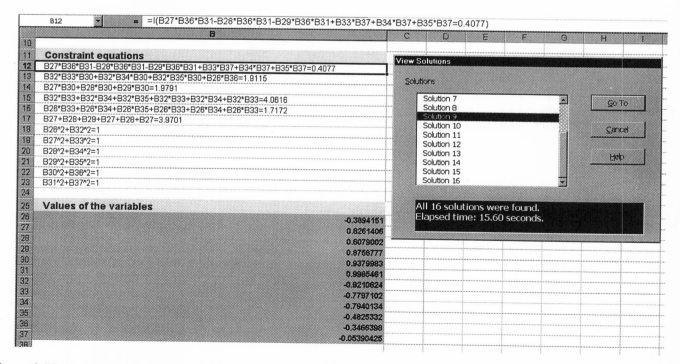

Figure 4. Finding all 16 solutions to kinematics equations describing a robot arm. The ninth solution is viewed.

Since an equation does not have a numerical value, the equation itself is shown as the value of the corresponding =I(*equation*) formula. Initially, values for the voltages and resistances were given and values for currents were unknown, i.e., they have very large interval values. The unique solution is found immediately and is shown in the figure.

Interval constraint solving techniques differ from other numerical techniques in one important way. Possible solutions are never accidentally lost. As a result, *all* solutions can always be found if enough time and memory is available. Furthermore, if a situation is found infeasible, then the problem has no solutions for sure. This guarantee holds even when rounding errors are present. In interval computations outward rounding interval arithmetic is used, and imprecise floating-point numbers are represented by tiny safe intervals bounding the actual value.

For the spreadsheet user this theoretical robustness is of great importance. Traditional numerical methods cannot in general guarantee that a solution will be found even if there were one. Convergence of iteration depends, e.g., on the gradients of the equations, initial guess values for the variables etc. It is not feasible to assume that a non-expert spreadsheet user understands the restrictions, conditions and limitations related to traditional numerical equation solving techniques. In interval solving *all* solutions can in principle *always* be found.

For example, figure 4 depicts the problem of finding the solutions to a difficult non-linear set of 12 kinematics equations. After evaluation, the View Solutions dialog box of Interval Solver has popped up and all 16 solutions to the equations can be viewed on the sheet. The user can be sure that this equation system has precisely these 16 solutions within the precision criteria used.

2.4. Finding the best solution to a problem

In figures 1 and 2, intervals were used for bounding the solution set. After the system has narrowed the intervals, the user can constrain the problem further by inserting new constraints or by modifying the intervals. For example, in figure 2 the target, present value P, was modified. After any modification, Interval Solver may be able to narrow related intervals further. The user and Interval Solver can work together in a mixed-initiative mode and the problem can be solved in a top-down fashion by refining stepwise constraints for the solutions. This is not possible in traditional spreadsheet computing.

This approach can be used for finding the best solution to the problem at hand, i.e., for solving optimization problems. The user sets desired goal values, Interval Solver narrows related cell values, the user modifies them again according to his preferences, and so on. If the situation is found at some point infeasible, special relaxation (Hyvönen, 1991) commands of Interval Solver can be applied in order to enlarge intervals and to make the bounds feasible again.

Interval Solver also contains a tool for solving traditional optimization problems directly with the help the of "Solver" add-in that comes with each Microsoft Excel copy. An interval CSP in Interval Solver consists of the interval bounds set for the cell values, their value types (real/integer), equations, inequalities, and logical constraints written on the sheet. These constructs can be transformed into a classical Excel Solver model and be solved using Excel Solver. By this way individual solutions can be found by which a given target function (cost function) gets its minimum, maximum or a preset specific value, given a set of constraints. By bounding solutions first with the interval model, the initial guess values can be selected within a reasonable range, and the optimization problem can be solved more easily. Interval Solver provides a natural way for expressing optimization problems. Any variable involved, not only the target cell value can be optimized dynamically based on the interval model.

However, since Excel Solver is a classical optimization tool, interval techniques are not used. This means that the solution found might be only a local optimum and that only at most one solution corresponding to the set of initial guess values can be found. There are in the general case no guarantees that a solution will be found even if there were one. Constrained interval optimization (Hansen, 1992) provides a remedy to this problem and will be available in future releases of Interval Solver as an alternative optimization tool.

3. Uses of AI technology

The mathematical basis of Interval Solver lays in the three InC++ interval libraries for C++, developed originally at VTT Technical Research Centre of Finland (Hyvönen, De Pascale, 1995; InC++, 1998):

Library	Purpose
LIA InC++	Overloads C++ arithmetic into extended interval arithmetic.
GIA InC++	Library for evaluating the global value range of a function with interval arguments.
ICE InC+	Interval Constraint Solving library based on LIA and GIA InC++.

Among these libraries, GIA and ICE are interesting from the AI viewpoint. Reconsider figure 1. The problem of determining the actual global minimum and maximum of P is easy in this case because the formula function happens to be monotonic. However, in the general non-monotonic case (e.g., formula (1.2)) the problem is very difficult both from the algorithmic and computational viewpoints. The global min/max is then not obtained by a combination of argument interval limits.

There is only one class of numerical techniques that is guaranteed to always find the global minimum/maximum, global interval optimization techniques (Hansen, 1992). These algorithms vary in detail but the underlying idea in all of them is to perform an exhaustive branch-and-prune search in which the initial argument intervals are split into tighter and tighter subintervals until precision conditions for the solution are satisfied. The search is accelerated by various pruning heuristics based on the best min/max candidate found thus far, on the mathematical properties of the function (such as first and second gradients), and on special narrowing operators for the arguments (such as the interval Newton operator). An indication of the implementational complexities involved is that GIA InC++ library employed in Interval Solver consists of over 50.000 lines of C++ code.

```
# include <ice.h>
// Include ICE InC++ library header
main () {
    // Construct the equation set object "I" (of class Ice)
    Ice I;
    I.SetDefaultUnknown("[-1e8,1e8]");
    // Default interval bounds for variable values
    I.InsertConstraint("x1^2+x2^2+x3^2-1=0");
    I.InsertConstraint("x1^2+x2^2+x3^2-2*x1=0");
    I.InsertConstraint("x1^2+x2^2-1=0");

    // Solve (evaluate) equation constraints
    I.SetPropagationMode(PMGlobal);
    // Set mode for finding individual solutions
    I.SetMaxSolutionNumber(1000);
    // Search for up to 1000 solutions
    ICEConsistencyType c;
    // Consistency type after evaluation
    I.Evaluate(&c);
    // Analyze and display the result
    if (c!=CTInfeasible)
        I.DisplayGlobalSolutions();
    return 0;
};
```

Figure 5. An example of programming with ICE InC++. All solutions to a set of tree equations in three variables are solved and displayed.

The key technology underlying Interval Solver is Interval Constraint Satisfaction (Davis, 1987; Cleary, 1987, Hyvönen, 1989) developed in the fields of artificial intelligence, (constraint) logic programming, and interval analysis (Interval, 1998). The interval constraint satisfaction problem (ICSP) corresponding to a sheet is represented as a C++ object of class Ice included in the ICE InC++ library. This class has a simple dynamic string-based interface by which constraints can be inserted and removed from the ICSP, interval domains set for the variables, precision criteria set for solutions etc. For an example of the programming interface, the C++ code in Figure 5 shows how to solve three equations in three variables with ICE InC++.

User operations on a sheet, such as inserting a formula, setting a cell value, etc. are mapped into sequences of member function calls of the underlying Ice object. This mapping is written in the macro language of Excel, Visual Basic. 117 different member functions of ICE InC++ library are used for the interface.

ICE InC++ library does all mathematical constraint solving regarding formulas written inside the =I(*expression*). Excel itself maintains the algebraic

formulas on the sheet mutually consistent. This makes Interval Solver invisible to the user and the integration seamless. For example, changing cell names in formulas when copying, pasting or moving cells is automatic as usual. User-defined cell names, as well as the different alias function names used in the various country versions of Excel are available with Interval Solver, too. Figure 6 illustrates the general integration architecture.

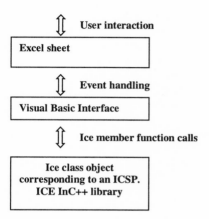

Figure 6. The interaction model of Interval Solver. Visual Basic interface layer catches user interactions (inserting data, moving cells, etc.) and commands. The Ice object, i.e., the ICSP corresponding to the sheet, is updated accordingly, or solved depending on the user interaction.

ICE InC++ library uses a large variety of interval constraint solving techniques. The constraint set is manipulated and simplified by algebraic manipulation routines in order to make it easier to solve numerically. In numerical evaluation, the tolerance propagation approach (Hyvönen, 1992) is enhanced with global interval optimization algorithms (Hansen, 1992), narrow operators (Benhamou et al., 1994; Van Hentenryck et al., 1997), conditioning matrices (Kearfott, 1996), and structure sharing techniques (Hyvönen, De Pascale, 1996).

Interval constraint solving was originally proposed as a new computational basis for spreadsheet programs in (Hyvönen, 1991; Hyvönen, De Pascale, 1996).

4. Application Use and Payoff

Interval Constraint Solving technology has recently gained more and more attention not only in AI research but in business as well. There has been a lot of development activity in the logic programming community resulting in several interval constraint extensions of Prolog, such as BNR Prolog (BNR Prolog, 1998) and Prolog IA (PrologIA, 1998). First stand-alone mathematical solvers based on the new scheme, such as Numerica (Numerica, 1998) and UniCalc (UniCalc, 1998), have been introduced in the market. These systems and tools are intended mainly for expert usage and programmers.

In contrast, Interval Solver targets (also) non-expert users of spreadsheets. With the help of the new computational basis, the usage of spreadsheets has been extended to new classes of applications that deal with uncertain data and/or involve problem solving under user-given constraints, a typical situation in business planning, technical design, science, and in many other fields.

Interval Solver is a generic tool for end-users spreadsheets. It virtually generalizes the arithmetical basis of Excel and the range of applications is therefore as wide as that of spreadsheets. Most users indicate business computations as their main area of interest. Typical applications include cash flow analysis, budgeting, and risk analysis involving uncertain future data. In engineering applications, Interval Solver provides the user with a simple tool for performing design and other calculations involving e.g. component data with tolerances, and for solving equations. The pay-off comes from getting more realistic and better results to support decision making. Non-expert users can now solve -- with little training in their customary spreadsheet environment -- new classes of mathematically complicated problems.

Together with word processing, database and Internet tools, spreadsheets have been one of the most influential software applications of information technology. According to a Gartner Group some 30 million spreadsheet programs were shipped in 1997, most of which (90%) were copies of Excel, and the market is growing rapidly. There is the intriguing possibility that interval constraint technology will eventually lead to a paradigm shift in utilizing spreadsheets.

5. Development and Deployment

In the late 80's and early 90's, research on using interval arithmetic as the basis for interval constraint satisfaction was carried at VTT Technical Research Centre of Finland, and in a joint project with Electrotechnical Laboratory, Japan. A result of this work was an interval constraint solver and an interval spreadsheet demo system implemented in Lisp. Based on the first results, it was decided to implement the technology for industrial applications in C++ and to apply it to a major commercial spreadsheet program, Excel.

It turned out, however, that the 16-bit address space provided by Excel at that time was too small for handling problems of reasonable size. Also Excel's macro language turned out to be too limited for a commercial level implementation of the new interval vision. With the new 32-bit Windows versions and the new Visual Basic macro language, the situation changed rapidly in 1996. The first implementation of interval constraints for Excel called "Range Solver" was exhibited by VTT at CeBIT 96 fair in Hannover, Germany. Interval Solver is its direct descendant commercialized by Delisoft Ltd, a spin-off of VTT.

The first version of Interval Solver 97 was finished during autumn 1997 and was released internationally in April 1998 at COMDEX Japan, Tokyo. The software evaluation kit has been available through Delisoft Web site (www.delisoft.com), Ziff-Davis Libraries, Download.com, etc., and recently also through representatives in various countries (USA, Canada, Australia, Hong Kong, Korea,...). There are currently several thousand downloaders in about 70 countries.

The software consists of over 100,000 lines of code 80% of which is mathematical routines in C++. Several people were involved with the research on interval computations, but the actual code of Interval Solver as well as the manual, setup program, and electronic tutorial were written by the authors of this paper.

The development and especially the commercialization phases of Interval Solver were far more demanding than was initially expected. In order to meet the high efficiency requirements of spreadsheet users, the software had to be geared and tuned very carefully. Tiny modifications in the algorithms easily resulted in order of magnitude differences in performance. Computational efficiency of interval constraint solving techniques is very sensitive not only to the algebraic form of the ICSP but also to the initial interval values used. Various heuristics can be used to speed up convergence, but there is no single optimal strategy that works always fine.

Besides the technical difficulties in implementing and tuning the mathematical constraint engine, lots of difficulties were encountered with the interface to Excel. A key problem there was the enormous versatility of ways in which the user may interact with Excel and potentially confuse the system by making the sheet and the underlying ICSP model mutually incoherent. Most operations in Excel such as inserting a formula can be made in several alternative ways. All of them have to be caught. An additional practical problem was that a new fundamentally different version of macro language provided by Microsoft for Excel 97 was released in the middle of the development process causing redesign needs for the interface. Fortunately, the new version was more versatile from Interval Solver viewpoint. Last but not least, several deficiencies were encountered in different Excel versions. They had to be circumscribed by special programming tricks.

6. Conclusions

Interval constraint solving and Interval Solver provide a more versatile basis for spreadsheet computing. Two key concepts of spreadsheets have been generalized:

- The idea of *cell value* is generalized from exact numbers to intervals. An exact value is a special case of the notion of interval.
- The idea of (function) *formula* is generalized into equations, inequalities, and logical constraints. A function is a special case of an equation.

From the computational viewpoint, the idea of *forward propagation* of exact values is generalized into interval constraint propagation. Again, forward propagation is a special case of the new model, interval constraint propagation.

Interval constraint solving is a conceptually simple, robust scheme for representing and solving difficult mathematical problems under uncertainty. Solutions are never lost as when using traditional numerical techniques. A price to be paid for the robustness and the ease of usage is increased computational complexity. However, results indicate that in many cases interval constraint solving methods can successfully compete with or even outperform the best traditional numerical techniques (Van Hentenryck et al., 1997).

Spreadsheet programs are among the most widely used applications of information technology. However, after the pioneering days of VisiCalc in 1979, their underlying computational idea has not changed much. Interval Solver demonstrates that artificial intelligence techniques can make a substantial contribution in the development of the spreadsheet paradigm.

Acknowledgements

Thanks to Dr. Eero Peltola, Technology Development Centre of Finland, Sitra, and VTT Information Technology for fruitful co-operation.

References

@Risk (1998) Product information of @Risk available at http://www.palisade.com.

Benhamou, F., McAllester, D., Van Hentenryck, P. (1994) CLP(Intervals) revisited. Proceedings of the International Symposium on Logic Programming (ILPS-94), Ithaca, New York, 124-138.

BNR Prolog (1998) Home page of BNR Prolog: http://www.als.com/als/clpbnr/clp_info.html.

Cleary, J. (1987) Logical Arithmetic. *Future Computing Systems* 2 (2), 1987.

Crystal Ball (1998). Product information of Crystal Ball available at http://www.decisioneering.com.

Davis, E. (1987) Constraint propagation with interval labels. *Artificial Intelligence* 8, 99-118.

Hansen, E. (1992) *Global Optimization Using Interval Analysis*, Marcel Dekker, New York.

Van Hentenryck, P., MacAllister, D., Kapur, D. (1997) Solving polynomial systems using a branch-and-prune approach. *SIAM Journal of Numerical Analysis*, 34 (2).

Van Hentenryck, P., Michel, L., Deville, Y. (1997) *Numerica. A Modeling Language for Global Optimization*. MIT Press, Cambridge.

Hyvönen, E. (1989) Constraint reasoning based on interval arithmetic. *Proceedings of IJCAI-89*, Morgan Kaufmann, Los Altos, Calif., 1193-1198..

Hyvönen, E. (1991) Interval constraint spreadsheets for financial planning. *Proceedings of the 1st International Conference on Artificial Intelligence Applications on Wall Street*. IEEE Press, New York.

Hyvönen, E. (1992) Constraint reasoning based on interval arithmetic: the tolerance propagation approach. *Artificial Intelligence* 58, 71-112.

Hyvönen, E., De Pascale, S. (1995) InC++ library family for interval computations. *Reliable Computing*, supplement, Proceedings of Applications of Interval Computations, El Paso, Texas, 1995.

Hyvönen, E., De Pascale, S. (1996) Interval Computations on the Spreadsheet. In: (Kearfott and Kreinovich, 1996), 169-210.

Hyvönen E., De Pascale, S.: Shared Computations for Efficient Interval Function Evaluation. In: G. Alefeld, E. Frommer (eds.): *Scientific Computing, Computer Arithmetic and Validated Numerics*, Akademie-Verlag, Berlin, Germany, 1996.

Interval (1998) Home page of interval computations research: http://cs.utep.edu/interval-comp/main.html.

InC++ (1998) Home page of InC++ libraries: http://www.delisoft.com/InCLibraries.

Interval Solver (1998) Interval Solver home page: http://www.delisoft.com/ExcelProducts/IntervalSolver.

Kearfott, B. (1996) *Rigorous Global Search: Continuous Problems*. Kluwer, New York.

Kearfott, B., Kreinovich, V. (eds.) (1996) *Applications of Interval Computations*. Kluwer, New York.

Lebbah, Y., Lhomme O. (1998) Acceleration methods for numeric CSPs. *Proceedings of AAAI-98*, AAAI Press, Menlo Park, Calif., 19-24.

Moore R. (1966) *Interval Analysis*. Prentice-Hall, Englewood Cliffs, N.J.

Numerica (1998) Home page of Numerica: http://www.ilog.com/html/products/optimization/numerica.htm.

Prolog IA (1998) Home page of Prolog IA software: http://prologianet.univ-mrs.fr/Us.

TK!Solver (1998) TK!Solver home page: http://www.uts.com/.

Ramp Activity Expert System for Scheduling and Co-ordination at an Airport

Geun-Sik Jo

Inha University,
Dept. of Computer Science
and Engineering
Inchon, 402-751,Korea
gsjo@dragon.inha.ac.kr

Kang-Hee Lee

Inha University,
Dept. of Computer Science
and Engineering
Inchon, 402-751,
Korea

Hwi-Yoon Lee

Korean Air
Operations Control Center
Kangseo-Ku , Seoul,
157-220
Korea

Sang-Ho Hyun

Korean Air
Information Systems Services
and Development Dept.
Kangseo-Ku, Seoul,157-220
Korea

Abstract

In this project, we have developed the Ramp Activity Coordination Expert System (RACES) in order to solve aircraft parking problems. RACES includes a knowledge-based scheduling system which assigns all daily arriving and departing flights to the gates and remote spots with domain specific knowledge and heuristics acquired from human experts. RACES processes complex scheduling problems such as dynamic inter-relations among the characteristics of remote spots/gates and aircraft with various other constraints, for example, customs and ground handling factors at an airport. By user-driven modeling for end users and near optimal knowledge-driven scheduling acquired from human experts, RACES can produce parking schedules for about 400 daily flights in approximately 20 seconds, whereas it normally takes human experts 4 to 5 hours to do the same. Scheduling results in the form of Gantt charts produced by RACES are also accepted by the domain experts. RACES is also designed to deal with the partial adjustment of the schedule when unexpected events occur. After daily scheduling is completed, the messages for aircraft changes and delay messages are reflected and updated into the schedule according to the knowledge of the domain experts. By analyzing the knowledge model of the domain expert, the reactive scheduling steps are effectively represented as the rules, and the scenarios of the Graphic User Interfaces (GUI) are designed. Since the modification of the aircraft dispositions, such as aircraft changes and cancellations of flights, are reflected in the current schedule, the modification should be sent to RACES from the mainframe for the reactive scheduling. The adjustments of the schedule are made semi-automatically by RACES since there are many irregularities in dealing with the partial rescheduling.

PROBLEM DESCRIPTION

The aircraft-parking problem is a scheduling problem which entails assigning every arriving and departing flight to in-terminal gates and remote gates satisfying various demands. It is a kind of scheduling problem which also includes job-shop scheduling if we consider the (remote)

gates as machines and incoming flights as jobs. In addition, this problem entails characteristics of temporal reasoning mechanisms. Theoretically, this problem belongs to the *NP*-class of problems in computational complexity. That is, if we try to assign m flights to n remote parking spots or gates (often referred to as bridges), then a non-polynomial number of combinations $(m!)^n$ are possible. The scheduling becomes more dynamic and difficult if the frequency of arriving and departing flights increases and unexpected events occur during the operational stage in a given time period. Increased air traffic and customs requirements also reflect difficulties in producing parking schedules. In practice, professional schedulers manually make the schedules once a day. This requires domain-specific knowledge, experience and heuristics and requires a considerable amount of time and tedious paper work to complete.

Traditionally researchers have used mathematical programming techniques to solve these kinds of problems. However, it is very difficult to model constraints and domain knowledge with only mathematical variables. In addition, there may be serious problems of remodeling and processing when unexpected events occur for large-scale practical problems. Recently, many researchers have proposed using AI techniques such as constraint directed reasoning, expert systems and Constraint Satisfaction Problem(CSP) to solve these problems (Jo, Jung, and Yang 1997, Fox 1987, Prosser 1993). AI techniques provide more flexible and expressive power than mathematical programming in modeling a complex scheduling problem. Comparison between Integer Programming and AI is well described in another work (Dhar and Ranganathan. 1990). In addition, modeling the reactive scheduling with Integer Programming is beyond our ability to formulate due to the dynamic addition of constraints and the necessity of the partial solutions.

Many expert systems have been presented in these areas. Practical expert systems have developed in the airline industry. American Airlines developed GateManager to effectively manage busy air traffic and resources (American Airlines 1993). The GATES system from Texas State University controls gate assignment and tracking in New York's JFK airport (Brazile and Swigger 1988). Knowledge Engineering, a Singapore-based company, has successfully developed a constraint-based gate allocation system using ILOG for Changi airport in Singapore (Berger 1995).

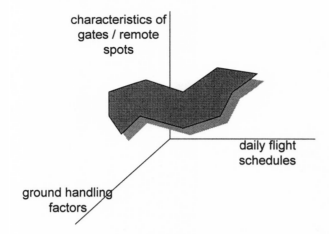

Figure 1. The feasibility region in gate allocation

DESCRIPTION OF RACES

RACES assigns daily flights to the gates and remote spots with domain specific knowledge and scheduling heuristics. Using domain filtering techniques, we can remove the inconsistency in the domain for variables and confine the search space. To find a user-driven optimal solution, RACES utilizes an efficient heuristic scheduling method to satisfy constraints. RACES produces a near optimal schedule with considerations for the flight schedules, aircraft type, characteristics of remote spots, and conditions for ground handling. Aircraft have to be assigned to adequate remote spots and gates with the satisfaction of given constraints. In addition, gates and remote spots are distinguished by size and hydrant facilities. RACES can be viewed as a three dimensional constraint solver as in figure 1, and it also maps three dimensional spaces into the two dimensional spaces which is represented in the form of a Gantt chart. RACES makes user-dependent, near-optimal schedules satisfying the given constraints with domain specific knowledge and heuristics. RACES produces the Gantt chart which represents the daily parking schedule a day beforehand.

In terms of constraint solving, there are three different types of constraints to satisfy. The first is the *strong-hard* constraint which has to be satisfied during the scheduling process. If this constraint is violated, then the solution is no longer valid. The second is the *weak-hard* constraint which can be violated in specific environments. This constraint can be violated by interacting with users, but not by RACES. The last is called a *soft-constraint* which is applied to specific flights and specific times. During scheduling, a *soft-constraint* is checked and there is an attempted to satisfy the constraint if possible. If not, this type of constraint can be relaxed by RACES. RACES can be divided into two different knowledge-based sysems. The first is to generate a one day schedule one day beforehand, which is described in the next section. The second is to adjust a schedule during an operational day. More technical details with examples for the management of constraints and the representation of domain knowledge is presented in another work (Jo, Jung, and Yang 1997).

INITIAL SCHEDULE GENERATION

After we have completed our documentation of knowledge acquired from domain experts, this knowledge is about 20 pages long, which does not include the database description. Moreover, the knowledge itself is too domain specific for the average person to understand. In this section, we describe the scheduling strategy being deployed in our system. In figure 2, RACES produces the Gantt chart which represents the daily parking schedule a day beforehand with today's schedule for co-ordination.

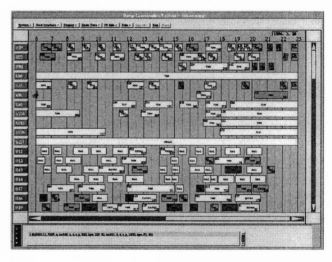

Figure 2. Generation of the initial schedule in RACES

Consistency by Domain Filtering

One scheduling procedure is responsible for binding continuous time values to the discrete time variables in order to satisfy constraints for the time restriction. To deal with the continuous time domain, we break down the continuous time values into discrete time elements. We also classify all the available remote spots and gates with *time-keys*. When the system processes scheduling, it filters domains and removes elements violating

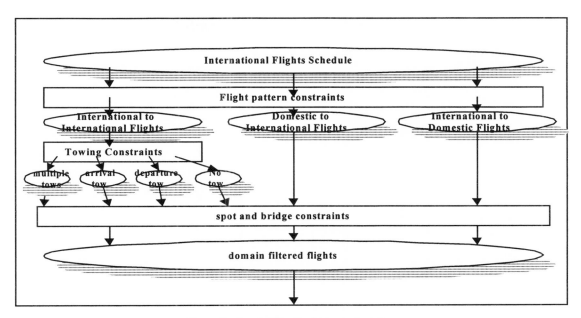

Figure 3. domain filtering before scheduling

constraints in three steps. An example of the domain filtering process for flights schedules is shown in Figure 3.

In the first step, RACES filters domains with the knowledge and constraints of various aircraft. Second, the system filters domains with the knowledge and constraints of towing. Finally, the system filters domains with the knowledge and constraints of available parking spots. As a result of the process, RACES can prune the search space significantly.

Knowledge-driven near optimal scheduling

We consider the optimal solution in terms of the user's benefit. An important factor is to minimize the number of *stand-by* flights which are not yet assigned to the gates/spots due to conjestion at the airport. During scheduling, RACES also tries to allow for the least number of towings at the airport. If the system fails to assign flights to the gates, the size of the aircraft must be taken into consideration. If *stand-by* flights involve relatively large aircraft, it is difficut for users to assign them manually after the automatic schedule is produced since the number of large spots is usally inadequate.

There are two heuristic scheduling methods in RACES. One is the time-focused method using best-fit assignment in terms of the time-span for parking. The other is the aircraft-size focused method. Each method has advantages and disadvantages in finding user-driven optimal solutions given that one method conflicts with the other method at certain points during the scheduling process. In our work, to avoid conflicts between the time-span focused method and the size-focused method, we have empirically found and exploited a trade-off point between the two. A detailed

description of these heuristic scheduling methods is presented in another work (Jo, Jung, and Yang 1997).

KNOWLEDGE-BASED REACTIVE SCHEDULING

When the real operational day is reached after the scheduling has been completed, unexpected events can occur as the environment changes. If sudden changes in schedules occur, such as the delay of an aircraft or the change of aircraft for certain flights, then schedules must be adjusted. In adjusting the daily schedules, the domain specific knowledge from domain expert is encoded into RACES.

Expert Model in Reactive Scheduling

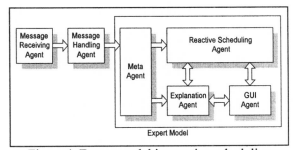

Figure 4. Expert model in reactive scheduling

The meta-agent in Figure 4 has the knowledge of which agent is activated depending on the message from the message handling agent. Although the role of each agent can not be summarized due to the page requirement, message handling agents and reactive scheduling agents are explained in brief.

The task of the message handling agent is to check sling, detect cycle and group the related messages together. The messages for AC change come into RACES in a unit of flights which are not in an ordered form, but rather in mixed forms. Therefore, the message handling agent has to rearrange them into a unit with an HL number by their scheduled time. Then the agent can check the fallacy of a sling order or an omitted sling. Generally, one aircraft makes a sequence of flight during a given day. A sling is a sequence of flights that an aircraft should make. A sling consists of flight schedule that reflects a continuous time domain.

The task of the reactive scheduling agent is to reschedule according to messages received as the environment changes during the operation. This task can be divided into two different operations: 1) Creating new standby bars. 2) Assigning these bars. The most important task of the reactive scheduling agent is to assign new standby bars to the Gantt chart. This process requires complicated and delicate domain knowledge. A variety of adjusting rules are implemented for these processes.

Interactive Graphic User Interfaces

The change of aircraft(AC) occurs in a case when an aircraft can not operate the flight that it is scheduled to run due to a delay of operations, aircraft repair, or a breakdown. In this case, the flight will be operated by another aircraft, and we call this situation an *AC change*. For an example, see Figure 5.

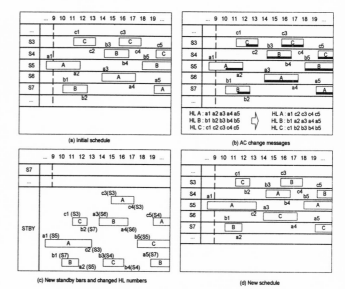

Figure 5. The steps for adjusting an initial schedule

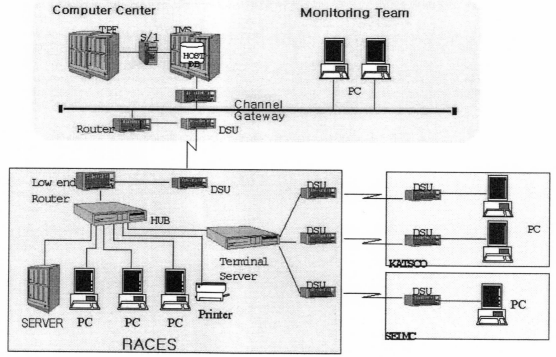

Figure 6. The relationship diagram with other systems

In Figure 5, the capital letters stand for the HL number which is the registration number for an aircraft, and the lower case letters stand for flight numbers. In the original scheduling, aircraft *A* was supposed to arrive as flight *a1* and depart as flight *a2*. Similarly, aircraft *B* was supposed to arrive as flight *b1* and depart as flight *b2*, and analogously, *C* as *c1* and *c2*. If we rotate aircraft *A* with *B*, *B* with *C* and *C* with *A* circularly, *A* will arrive as *a1* and depart as *c2*, analogously, *B* as *b1* and as *a2*, and *C* as *c1* and as *b2*. As we have shown in figure 5, each flight has a time slot for an arrival and a departure. If we change the schedule of flights for some aircraft, the length of the original solution bar may be changed. This means that we need to adjust the solution of the initial schedule. The aircraft rotation can occur not only between two aircraft but also among three, four, or more aircraft. They also occur in a cycle as we can see in Figure 5. Since the fully automatic adjustments are not consistent from time to time and they are quite complex, these are too difficult to automate. The intelligent interactive GUI is utilized for manual adjustments.

THE RELATIONSHIP BETWEEN RACES AND OTHER SYSTEMS

Figure 6 illustrates the relationship between RACES and other systems. RACES receives flight schedule data from the Computer Center in order to make an aircraft parking schedule. After RACES performs the scheduling, it transfers scheduling result into KASTCO(Korea Air Terminal Service COmpany) and SELMC(SEouL Maintenance Control department). KATSCO is responsible for performing the ground tasks of an aircraft, for example: hydrating, cleaning, and towing. With the scheduling result obtained from RACES, KATSCO can prepare their tasks efficiently. Also, SELMC is responsible for maintenance of an aircraft. They check device problems on an aircraft. They need the data from RACES to make their maintenance schedule. Actual towing of an aircraft needs cooperation between KATSCO and SELMC. The aircraft parking schedules from RACES allow them to prepare to tow an aircraft before they perform actual towing.

DEVELOPMENT HISTORY

The ramp activity coordination system for KAL(Korean Air Lines) at Kimpo Airport in Korea was managed by human experts using manual scheduling until 1995. In order to maximize the utilization of the resources of the airport, KAL and Expert Systems Lab at Inha University decided to develop the expert system with experiences and heuristics of domain experts at KAL. Three domain experts and a system engineer from KAL and five graduate students at Inha University participated in this project between 1995 and 1997 under Prof. Geun-Sik Jo's supervision. It was approximately a $ 125,000 project for Inha University, which excluded wages for three domain experts and a system engineer, and expenses for an office and other utilities, which were paid by KAL. It took 3 months to make a prototype of RACES in order to convince KAL to pilot the project. Then after about 6 months, we were able to complete the initial scheduling part of RACES. Most of the developing time was spent in reactive scheduling which took about 9 months. For another 4 months, networking routines needed for the mainframe to integrate with RACES, which in turn interacts with other computers, were added to create a real environment. To evaluate the system, two end users tested the results against real flight schedule data of the previous 120 days' data. Their test results were accepted by domain experts so that RACES could be used for real environments. For the maintenance of RACES, we explained source codes and trained a system engineer to do the maintenance job himself. At the present time, a system engineer from KAL is responsible for maintaining RACES and he is doing well. We think that the declarative features of Prolog have made it possible for only one person to do the maintenance job. In addition, at the developmental stage, we designed and implemented menus and submenus to prepare for the future extension and update of the knowledge base.

RACES was written in CHIP(Constraint Handling In Prolog) Ver 5.0 under a Unix operation system on an HP/712 machine. To retrieve and store the information on flights, bridges and remote spots, Oracle DBMS was used, where an SQL interface from the Prolog code was provided in the CHIP system.

DEPLOYMENT PROCESS

We developed RACES(Ramp Activity Coordination Expert System) in CHIP, which consists of about 50,000 lines of Prolog code with about 70 GUI menus. RACES solves the problem using methods similar to a human expert problem solving procedures. We represented and processed the domain specific knowledge and experiences. When the system processes scheduling, it can prune the search space using a domain filtering technique. RACES produces a user-driven optimal schedule using trade-off scheduling heuristics. To test accuracy of the system, we implemented RACES with the daily operational data of an actual airline company for about 120 days and the results were analyzed by domain experts. RACES has been approved by and continues to receive the approval of domain experts.

The system described in this paper was successfully deployed at Kimpo Airport in Korea. RACES has been used at Kimpo airport by KAL since 1997. The controllers at the operational control center at KAL are now using this system for monitoring and controlling the assignment of remote spots and bridges. To date, the ground controllers using this system to actually tow aircraft, assign buses and do other ground work are able to interact well with persons at the operations control center. As long as the airport is in operation, this system should run almost 24 hours a day. When the FIDS(Flight Information Display System) was connected to RACES, the time that the aircraft spent waiting to park after landing was greatly reduced.

RACES currently has the ability to reschedule in approximately 70% of the cases in a real environment situation. Reactive scheduling is one of the most important topics for researchers to use the scheduling systems in practice. However, when the system processes the rescheduling by itself, we can often find that some adjustments are not adequate. Therefore, some of the adjustments should be done in co-operation with the users by adjusting the schedule manually through GUI. Interactive GUI in RACES plays a supporting role by helping users to make the right decision.

BENEFITS OF RACES

RACES made the work paradigm-shift from manual into automatic scheduling in the ramp activity management that required domain specific human knowledge and heuristics . It is clear that the initial investment is returned within in a year after deployment. There are, however, the following benefits which are not currently measurable in terms of money:

- Time and cost involved in scheduling are drastically reduced.
- Real-time adjustment for unexpected events and weather conditions is provided for.
- Interactive GUI in RACES plays a supporting role by helping users make the right decision at the right time.
- Aircraft waiting time for parking after landing is reduced.
- High-quality passenger service is provided because RACES gives prior information about aircraft parking status, thereby, insuring the quick movement of an aircraft after landing.
- Objective verification of ramp activity management is possible.
  Finally, RACES can perform the operations necessary to maximize the utilization of ramp activity.

Acknowledgements

This project was successfully completed with the help of Korean Air and colleagues at Inha unversity who provided domain knowledge and financial support.

REFERENCES

American Airlines. 1993. GateManager, *Precision Technologies Inc.*

Berger, Rainer. 1995. Constraint-Based Gate Allocation for Airports, ILOG Solver and Schedule. *First International User's Conference proceedings*, Abbaye des Vaux de Cernay, France : 1-9.

Brazile, P., and Swigger, Kauthleen M. 1988. GATES : An Airline Gate Assignment and Tracking. *IEEE Expert* **3** : 33 - 39.

Croker, Albert E. and Dhar, Vasant. October, 1994. A Knowledge Representation for Constraint Satisfaction Problems. *IEEE transaction on Knowledge and Data Engineering* 5(5) : 740 - 752.

Dhar, Vasant and Ranganathan, Nicky. March 1990. Integer Programming vs. Expert Systems: Experimental comparison. *Communications of the ACM*, pp323-336.

Dincbas, M.; Van Hentenryck, P.; Simonis, H.; Aggoun, A.; and Graf, T.. June, 1988. Applications of CHIP to industrial and engineering problems. *In First Int. Conference on Industrial and Engineering Applications of Artificial Intelligence and Expert Systems*, Tullahoma, Tennessee.

Fox, M.S.. 1987. Constraint-Directed Search : A Case Study of Job-Shop Scheduling. Research Notes in Artificial Intelligence, *Fitman Publishing.*

Frost, Daniel and Dechter, Rinal. 1994. In search of the best constraint satisfaction search. *AAAI 94* : 301 - 306.

Jo, Geun-Sik; Jung, Jong-Jin; and Yang, Chang-Yoon. NOV, 1997. Expert System for Scheduling in an Airline Gate Allocation. *Expert Systems with Applications* 13(4) : 275-282.

Jung, Jong-Jin; Yang, Jong-Yoon; and Jo, Geun-Sik. July, 1997. RACES: Ramp Activity Coordination Expert System. *IPMM '97 Australia-Pacific Forum on Intelligent Processing and Manufacturing of Materials*, Australia.

Liu, Bing. 1994. Problem Acquisition in Scheduling Domains. *Expert System with Applications* 6 : 257 - 265.

Pierre, Baptiste; Bruno, Legeard; Marie-Ange, Manier; and Christiphe, Varnier. 1994. A scheduling Problem Optimization Solved with Constraint Logic Programming. *Artificial Intelligence* 42 : 200 - 231.

Prosser, Patrick. Domain filtering can degrade intelligent backtracking search. 1993. *International Joint Conference on Artificial Intelligence* : 262 - 267,

Using Iterative Repair to Automate Planning and Scheduling of Shuttle Payload Operations

Gregg Rabideau, Steve Chien, Jason Willis[*], and Tobias Mann

Jet Propulsion Laboratory
California Institute of Technology
4800 Oak Grove Drive, Pasadena, CA 91109-8099
firstname.lastname@jpl.nasa.gov

Abstract

This paper describes the DATA-CHASER Automated Planner/Scheduler (DCAPS) system for automated generation and repair of command sequences for the DATA-CHASER shuttle payload. DCAPS uses general Artificial Intelligence (AI) heuristic search techniques, including an iterative repair framework in which the system iteratively resolves conflicts with the state, resource, and temporal constraints of the payload activities. DCAPS was used in the operations of the shuttle payload for the STS-85 shuttle flight in August 1997 and enabled an 80% reduction in mission operations effort and a 40% increase in science return.

Introduction

Generating command sequences for spacecraft operations can be a laborious process requiring a great deal of specialized knowledge. Typically, spacecraft command sets are large, with each command performing a low-level task. There are often many interactions between the commands relating to the state of the spacecraft. In addition, due to spacecraft power and weight limitations, the resources available on-board spacecraft are often scarce. These factors in combination make manual generation of command sequences a difficult process. Because of the importance and expense of this process, tools to assist in planning and scheduling spacecraft activities are critical to reducing the effort (and hence cost) of mission operations.

This paper describes the DATA-CHASER Automated Planner/Scheduler (DCAPS) which was used to command, schedule, and reschedule the DATA-CHASER shuttle payload.

DCAPS uses search algorithms for two problems: initial schedule generation, and schedule repair/refinement. In initial schedule generation, DCAPS generates a default

schedule to perform science observations from the null schedule (i.e., an empty schedule), supporting domain specific and randomized initial schedule generation strategies. In schedule repair or refinement, DCAPS accepts an existing schedule with conflicts (i.e., resource oversubscriptions, state conflicts, etc.) and performs modifications to make the schedule consistent with the spacecraft constraints. DCAPS implements this functionality by using "iterative repair" search techniques (Zweben et al. 1994). Basically, this technique iteratively selects a schedule conflict and performs some action in an attempt to resolve the conflict. In iterative repair mode, DCAPS is well adapted for human interaction. In this mode, a user can move, add and delete activities in order to alter the schedule to their preferences. DCAPS can then be invoked to repair state, resource, and temporal constraints caused by these modifications. In this fashion, scientists who need not be spacecraft and sequence engineer experts can perform command sequence generation. This allows the scientist to become directly involved in the command sequencing process. Additionally, if there are changes in the spacecraft state (e.g., faults) or user-defined goals (e.g., science opportunities), the repair algorithm allows simple rescheduling that attempts to minimize disruption of the original schedule. Finally, the highly restrictive payload resources and constraints are constantly monitored and conflicts automatically avoided.

The sequence generation problem addressed by DCAPS includes both planning and scheduling according to typical Artificial Intelligence definitions. DCAPS performs planning in that it determines appropriate actions to achieve state and resource values required to satisfy goals. It performs scheduling in that these selected activities must be temporally placed to comply with (aggregate) resource, state, and timing constraints required by the operations constraints.

The DCAPS system was developed for operation of the DATA-CHASER shuttle payload, which was developed and managed by students and faculty of the University of Colorado at Boulder. DATA-CHASER is a science payload, with a primary focus on solar observation. The main activities for the payload involve science instrument observations, data storage, communication, and control of the power subsystem. Science activities are performed

*Work conducted while author affiliated with Colorado Space Grant, University of Colorado.
This work was performed by the Jet Propulsion Laboratory, California Institute of Technology, under contract with the National Aeronautics and Space Administration.

using three solar observing instruments: the Far Ultraviolet Spectrometer (FARUS), Soft X-ray and Extreme Ultraviolet Experiment (SXEE), and Lyman-alpha Solar Imaging Telescope (LASIT). These are imaging devices that collect data at various wavelengths.

The payload resources include power, tape storage, local memory, the three instruments, and the communication bus. DATA-CHASER is also constrained by externally driven states such as the shuttle orientation and external events such as shuttle waste material, which affect when certain science activities can be scheduled. Payload activities must be sequenced while avoiding or resolving conflicts. The DCAPS system models all of these states and resources, as well as the state and resource requirements and effects of activities. This model enables automation of command generation for the DATA-CHASER payload.

The remainder of this paper is organized as follows. First, we describe the DATA-CHASER shuttle payload and mission objectives. Next, we describe how the payload is modeled. We then describe in detail the DCAPS approach to automated command sequence generation and repair. Then, we describe how DCAPS fits in to the overall flight and ground system architecture for the DATA-CHASER mission. We then describe the experience and results from the use of DCAPS during the STS-85 flight. Finally, we discuss related work and conclusions.

DATA-CHASER Payload

DATA-CHASER consists of two synergistic projects, DATA and CHASER, which flew as a Hitchhiker (HH) payload aboard STS-85 on the International Extreme Ultraviolet Hitchhiker Bridge (IEH-2) in August 1997 (Rabideau et al. 1996). A technology experiment, DATA (Distribution and Automation Technology Advancement) demonstrated advanced semi-autonomous, supervisory operations. CHASER (Colorado Hitchhiker and Student Experiment of Solar Radiation) was a solar science experiment that served to test DATA. The DATA technologies support cooperative operations distributed between different geographic sites as well as between humans and machines, on-board autonomy, human control, and ground automation.

CHASER consists of three co-aligned instruments that take data in the far and extreme ultraviolet wavelengths. The first and oldest of these instruments (17 years old) is FARUS, which takes a continuous spectrum from 115 nm to 190 nm with a resolution of .12 nm. LASIT takes images of the full solar disk of the sun in the Lyman-alpha wavelength (121.6 nm) with a Charge Injected Device imager. The final instrument in the scientific package, SXEE, consists of four photometers, each having a different metallic coating so as to enable them to look at different wavelengths between 1 and 40 nm. The objective of these instruments is to measure the full disk solar ultraviolet irradiance and obtain images of the sun in the Lyman-alpha wavelength, providing a correlation between solar activity and radiation flux as well as an association of Lyman-alpha fluxes with individual active regions of the sun.

The flight segment of the DATA-CHASER project consists of a canister that is equipped with a Hitchhiker Motorized Door Assembly (HMDA), which houses the instruments and their support electronics. The second canister contains the flight computer for the payload as well as the 2 GB Digital Audio Tape (DAT) drive that is used to store all data that is collected during the mission. The payload data is also sent to the ground system through both low rate (available 90% of the time, at 1200 bps) and medium rate (available when scheduled, at 200 kbps). The payload is also capable of receiving commands sent from the ground system when uplink is available.

Often, DATA-CHASER was in a passive mode monitoring its state and notifying the ground of any changes. When the orbiter bay was pointed at the sun, the DATA-CHASER payload was in solar active mode where all instruments take data.

The data is both written to the DAT drive on board and downlinked to the ground system for immediate data analysis. Several times during the mission, DATA-CHASER took data while not pointing at the sun. This data is to test various portions of the DATA experiment with non-solar-pointing data in addition to being used for instrument calibration.

One of the consequences of flying on the shuttle system is that shuttle resources are shared and, hence, limited, with availability subject to change every 12 hours (the frequency at which NASA changes shuttle flight plans). These resources include access to uplink and downlink channels, and time that the payload is allowed to operate. In addition, a payload typically has thermal constraints, which would limit the duration of payload exposure to the sun (or away from the sun). Any given payload may also have environmental constraints that restrict the payload state and activities when shuttle contamination events are occurring.

In addition to modeling the internal constraints and resources of the payload, DCAPS would also search the shuttle flight plan for times when the payload was allowed to operate, downlink data, uplink new command sets, and when scientific instruments had to be protected from contamination events.

DATA-CHASER was an interesting scenario for

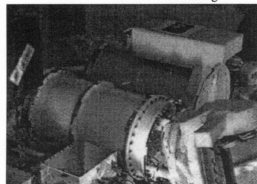

Picture 1: DATA-CHASER Payload in STS-85 Shuttle Bay

scheduling because of the complex data and power management involved in the science gathering. An automated scheduler must find an optimal "data taking" schedule, while adhering to the resource constraints. In addition, the scientists would like to perform dynamic scheduling during the mission. As an example, the summary data may indicate the presence of a solar flare. If this occurs, scientists have different requirements and goals, such as higher priorities on certain instruments or longer integration times. These new goals may require a different schedule of activities.

Modeling the Payload

In order to use the DCAPS system, the user must write a software model of the mission activities and spacecraft resources. DCAPS uses the Plan-IT II (PI2) system (Eggemeyer, 1995) to model the spacecraft activities and constraints, thus the model is expressed in the PI2 modeling language. Modeling in the PI2 language involves defining a set of objects and describing how they interact. These definitions are then used by the scheduler to create instances of the objects and reason about specific interactions (e.g., state and resource conflicts) in the schedule. The two major types of objects in the model are *activities* and *resources*.

Activities

Activities are used to model the events that affect the DATA-CHASER payload and the actions that the DATA-CHASER payload can take. All activities have a duration and a set of parameters. In addition, some activities may have a set of subactivities. For these activities, the user can also define a set of temporal constraints between the subactivities. Examples of activities in the DCAPS model include: Tracking and Data Relay Satellite System (TDRSS) contacts and turning the CHASER heater on and off (CHASER-heater-on and CHASER-heater-off). Another activity, SXEE-Scan-Step, has four sensor read steps as subactivities.

Resources

Resources define the various physical resources and the constraints they impose. There are five essential types of resources: state, concurrency, depletable, non-depletable, and simple.

State resources are used to model payload systems with discrete operating states. For each state resource, the modeler must specify the possible values for the state variable. Most of the systems have at least one state variable, which represents whether or not they are activated. Shuttle orientation is also modeled as a state variable.

Concurrency resource constraints are used to model rules that stipulate that an activity either must occur during another activity or cannot occur at the same time as another activity. One relationship that is modeled with a concurrency resource is the requirement that a downlink or uplink can only occur during contact with a TDRSS satellite. This is modeled as a resource that is present when there is TDRSS contact activity and required when there is a downlink or uplink activity.

Depletable resources are used to model aggregate resources with a fixed quantity, such as fuel or RAM. Activities can use some finite amount of a depletable resource, which may or may not be restorable. The amount used by the activity is persistent to the end of the schedule. In addition, the modeler must specify a maximum capacity for each depletable resource. In DCAPS, an onboard memory buffer is modeled as a depletable resource. Science observations produce data and use some amount of the depletable resource. Other activities, such as a transfer to permanent storage, may restore this resource.

Non-depletable resources are used to model aggregate resources with a limit to the usage at any one time, but are reset at the end of the activity that consumes the resource. Similar to depletable resources, nondepletables are assigned a maximum capacity. Power is modeled as a non-depletable resource.

Simple resources are used to model devices that can only be used by one activity at a time. For instance, each of the instruments on board DATA-CHASER (FARUS, SXEE, and LASIT) is capable of taking only one image at a time and is modeled with simple resources.

The DATA-CHASER model uses 67 resources and 58 activity types. The payload required 7 resources to model the impact of exogenous events such as shuttle contamination events, day/night cycles, shuttle maneuvers, and other external activities which impact payload operations. The payload also required 6 resources to represent possible failed states for major instruments/subsystems. For each instrument, a number of resources would be required. For example, for SXEE, there are 6 resources. One resource represents the instrument itself. Two resources are required to represent the instrument door – one for the open/closed state and another for the closing process which draws power. A SXEE-failure resource represents whether the instrument is known to have failed (and hence disables the scheduler from scheduling any SXEE activities). A SXEE-power resource tracks the power consumption of the SXEE instrument, and a SXEE-relay resource models the hardware relay used to enable/disable the SXEE instrument. In addition to the instruments, there are a number of system-wide resources to be tracked by DCAPS. Total power consumption and energy usage (for thermal considerations) are tracked for each canister. Finally, science and engineering data must be processed through a set of 3 buffers onboard the spacecraft as well as the secondary storage DAT tape drive.

The DATA-CHASER model also contained a significant number of activity types (58). Of these, the vast majority (25) were hardware control commands. Fourteen commands related to the acquisition of science and engineering data, and 6 commands controlled the downlink capability (TDRSS, medium-rate, and low-rate). Nine (9) commands were used to represent possible subsystem failures (e.g., to disable use of certain instruments and subsystems). Seven (7) activities were used to represent exogenous events (such as medium rate downlink coverage, solar pointing for the shuttle bay, etc.). The activities can also be viewed from an instrument centric perspective. From this viewpoint, the SXEE instrument has commands to: transfer SXEE data from the SXEE instrument to the general instrument buffer, open and close the SXEE instrument door, control the SXEE-relay which enables use of the instrument, take a sun scan, take a dark scan (with the instrument door closed for calibration purposes), and perform several of the typical steps to take and transfer the data to storage.

The DCAPS Automated Planner/Scheduler

The DATA-CHASER Automated Planner / Scheduler was part of the DATA-CHASER mission operations software. It was a ground-based intelligent tool used for developing a schedule of commands for uplink to the payload (Rabideau et al. 1996). The DCAPS system was used for initial schedule generation and interactive schedule repair.

During initial schedule generation, DCAPS produces a complete, valid schedule of payload operation commands from a model, initial state, and set of high-level goals. In the interactive repair phase, it takes intermediate, invalid schedules (resulting from user changes) and produces a similar, but valid schedule.

The DCAPS consists of: the Plan-IT II (PI2) sequencing tool (Eggemeyer, 1995) and the schedule reasoner. PI2 was originally designed as an "expert assistant sequencing tool." PI2 includes a GUI that allows for easy manipulation of the schedule. In addition, it serves as an activity/resource database that tracks activities and their constraints using a model of the payload in the PI2 modeling language (as described above). The schedule reasoner uses PI2 to automatically generate new schedules, repair existing faulty schedules, and optimize valid schedules. PI2 provides information about resource availability and conflicts; the scheduler must decide which activities to use to resolve the conflicts and where to place the activities temporally.

Schedule Data-Base

PI2 continually monitors activities in the sequence. As activities are added or moved, the change in resource usage is automatically updated, and the new resource profiles are displayed. With this information available, the user can immediately see the effects of a schedule change on the mission resources. For each resource, PI2 also monitors any conflicts that are occurring on the resource.

Conflicts are time intervals where the limitations of the resource have been exceeded. Finally, PI2 monitors any dependencies that have been defined between activities and resources. The values of specific parameters of activities and resources may be functionally dependent on values of other parameters. PI2 automatically keeps these parameter values consistent.

PI2 also helps out by serving as an activity and resource database, producing/accepting information to/from a sequencer. The functional interface to PI2 has been extended to better assist an automated sequencer. A basic set of "fetch" functions has been developed to quickly retrieve information about conflicts as well as the resources and activities involved in the conflict. For example, an interface function has been written to fetch the legal times where an activity can occur in the schedule. Here, "legal times" refers to positions where no conflicts are caused by any of the resources used by the given activity.

In addition to fetching information about the current state of the schedule, the user will need to be able to change the current state in attempt to fix or optimize the schedule. Some basic primitive functions are provided by PI2 to allow an external system to add and move activities, change their duration, etc. These primitives make up the set of actions that a scheduler can take when trying to resolve conflicts.

Schedule Reasoner

The second major component of DCAPS is the automated schedule reasoner. Implemented as an extension to PI2, the schedule reasoner provides three capabilities: initial schedule generation, schedule repair, and schedule optimization. In initial schedule generation, a schedule is generated from a set of user requested activities. In schedule repair, the scheduler will automatically restore the consistency of the sequence after arbitrary user interaction by rescheduling using local repair actions. The schedule repairer iteratively attempts to resolve each conflict, which involves making choices on what to repair and how to repair it. In a more advanced extension to iterative repair, schedule optimization can be performed. In this technique, portions of the schedule are examined and possibly rescheduled to improve part of the schedule that may not contain conflicts.

Initial Schedule Generator—The first step in sequencing spacecraft commands is to come up with an initial schedule of events for each phase of the mission. DCAPS supports two modes for automated initial schedule generation: a domain specific schedule generation algorithm and a randomized scheduling algorithm. The domain specific scheduling algorithm is shown in Figure 1. In this approach, the scheduler inserts necessary setup activities (powering on the payload and controlling the payload doors) and schedules an even mix of observations by sweeping forward in time. However, little effort was devoted towards optimizing this approach.

DCAPS also supports a randomized initial schedule generation algorithm. In this approach, the scheduler merely uses random placement to attempt to place science observations. As expected, this approach performs significantly worse than the domain specific approach.

Schedule Repairer—The generated initial schedule may

```
buildInitialSchedule()
    turn on the two canisters 2 hours into the mission
    and leave them on for the duration (cmds DataRelayOn,
    ChaserRelayOn)

    for each interval in which the shuttle is pointing at the sun and
    there is no contamination event
        open the hitchhiker door (HMDAOpen) at the start of the interval
        close the hitchhiker door (HMDAClose) at the end of the interval

    for each interval in which the shuttle is not in a solar pointing state for
    longer than 30 minutes
        turn on the canister heater 30 minutes after the solar pointing
        turn off the canister heater at the beginning of the next solar
        pointing interval

    loop until no legal times for a data-take (FARUS, SXEE, or LASIT)
        find legal times for the data-take  (during the solar pointing non-
        contamination events)
        place the data-take at the earliest possible start time
        place a DAT transfer after the data-take
```

Figure 1: Domain specific initial schedule generation

still violate some of the spacecraft constraints. Also, the scientists and engineers might feel that their goals were not completely satisfied or that they could be better achieved by an alternate plan. In these cases the users want to be able to interact with and modify the generated schedule. These modifications may introduce new conflicts into the schedule. The schedule repair capability can automatically repair these introduced conflicts, freeing the user from this burden and reducing overall mission operations effort. Additionally, freeing the user of the burden of low-level repair allows the user to spend more time modifying the schedule – allowing the combined user/software system to explore more of the schedule space.

Before describing the schedule repairer, we must present a few definitions. A "conflict" is a violation of one of the resource constraints. A conflict occurs over a certain time period and is caused by activities called "culprits." For example, if the power capacity is exceeded from time t_1 to time t_2, then a conflict exists from time t_1 to time t_2, and the culprits are any activities that use power and overlap the interval $[t_1, t_2]$.

There are three possible actions to take in attempt to resolve a conflict: move, add, or delete an activity. The "move" action involves moving one of the culprits of the conflict to a position that will either resolve the conflict or at least ensure that the moved activity is no longer a culprit. Some conflicts can be resolved by adding a new activity. These activities usually provide some resource that was previously not available. Finally, a conflict can also be resolved by simply deleting the culprits. This is obviously not a preferred method and is only used as a last resort.

The resolution of a conflict greatly depends on the type

of resource that is in violation. There are five different types of conflicts corresponding to the five types of resources. A *state conflict* occurs when an activity requires the resource to be in a state different from its current state. The culprits in this type of conflict are all of the activities that require the incorrect state and the activity that changed the resource to the incorrect state. Several possibilities for resolving a state conflict include moving the culprits to another interval where the required state is present or adding an activity that will change the state of the resource to the required state.

A *concurrency conflict* is when an activity requires the presence of the resource during a time for which it is absent. The culprits in this type of conflict are all of the activities that require the presence of the resource. To resolve a concurrency conflict, the scheduler can move the culprits to an interval where the resource is present or add an activity that provides the presence of the resource.

A *depletable conflict* means that the activities of the schedule have used too much of the resource. In this type of conflict, the culprits are all activities that use the resource before the point of overflow. Some depletable resources have "resetter" activities and this sort of conflict can be resolved by adding an activity that "resets" the available resource. For example, a downlink activity will free up space in the downlink buffer.

A *non-depletable conflict* occurs when activities overuse a resource during a particular time interval. The culprits in this type of conflict are all of the activities that use the resource during the conflict interval. This sort of conflict can be resolved by moving or deleting culprits. There are no activities in the DATA-CHASER model that can replenish a non-depletable resource.

Simple conflicts occur when two or more activities use the same simple resource at the same time. This type of conflict can only be resolved by moving or deleting culprits.

Given an initial schedule, the schedule repairer must find the correct activities to move, add, or delete and position them temporally in such a way that no conflicts remain. The scheduler relies on some interface functions to PI2 that describe the conflicts in the current schedule, describe the activities that could resolve a conflict, and manipulate the schedule. The schedule repair algorithm is an iterative loop with the following choice points:

1. conflict selection,
2. selection of a method to resolve the conflict from one of: move, add, or delete,
3. selection of an activity to which to apply the chosen method, and possibly
4. temporal placement of the moved or added activity (i.e., start time and duration).

In Table 1, we outline the heuristics implemented within DCAPS for each of these choice points (the heuristic method actually used is marked with an asterisk). After the chosen action is performed, the schedule repairer

Choice Point	Heuristics
Conflict Selection	Highest priority (determined by resource)
	Highest contention (oversubscription)
	Most culprits
	Largest duration
	Least culprits*
	Smallest duration
Operation selection (move, add, or delete)	Random
Activity selection for Move	Move culprit which contributes most to conflict*
	Move culprit with least temporal flexibility
	Move lowest priority
Activity selection for Add	Add activity that reduces conflict most*
	Add the activity which has the fewest legal times
	Add highest priority
Activity selection for Delete	Delete culprit that contributes most to conflict
	Delete the culprit which participates in most conflicts*
	Delete lowest priority
Time selection	Choose latest start time
	Choose earliest start time
	Choose latest start time for state conflicts and earliest start time for resource conflicts*

Table 1: Heuristics implemented for each choice point

checks to see if progress was made (defined as decreasing the number of conflicts, decreasing the number of culprits, or decreasing the duration of the conflicts). If the action did not succeed in resolving the conflict, or progress was not made, then the action is retracted. Otherwise, conflicts are recomputed and the loop counter is incremented. This process continues until all conflicts are resolved, or the loop counter exceeds a user-defined maximum bound. For every choice point in the algorithm, where a selection must be made from a list of possibilities, the schedule repairer is allowed to backtrack to that point. What this means is, that if a particular choice fails, the schedule repairer may choose another from the list before giving up. If all choices fail, then a previous decision must have been incorrect, and the repairer can backtrack to the preceding choice point. All choice points, including the decision on whether or not to backtrack, are heuristic decisions and may be customized to a particular domain.

Schedule Optimization — Often there may be many legal schedules, all of which are not equally preferred by the users. In the extreme case, the empty schedule (e.g., do nothing, or some schedule of this form) is usually a legal schedule. In the DATA-CHASER mission, the dominant quality measure is science return - which can be roughly measured by the number of science measurements taken and downlinked in the current planning cycle. In

order to improve the quality of the DCAPS-produced schedules, we implemented a simple schedule optimization algorithm that accepts as input an oversubscribed schedule. This algorithm first expands all of the activities into the lowest level (because the most detailed resource modeling may allow a more densely packed schedule). The algorithm then performs a forward sweep through the schedule in which each activity is moved to its earliest start time. This has the effect of packing the activities towards the start of the schedule potentially opening room for the extra activities towards the end. In the DATA-CHASER case, the oversubscribed activities are science data-takes and the oversubscription is due to over-use of the instrument, communications bus, and buffer resources. The schedule optimization algorithm takes an oversubscribed schedule and packs in the science observations more closely – thus allowing further science observations to fit into the schedule. This optimization algorithm can be viewed as a simplified version of the schedule packing algorithm described in (Aldas, 1997) and the doubleback algorithm described in (Crawford, 1996).

Application Development, Deployment, and System Integration

DCAPS was developed by the JPL Artificial Intelligence group as part of a set of early prototypes of automated planning and scheduling engines for use by NASA's New Millennium Program. Later, when the DATA-CHASER mission operations automation problem was studied, we determined that the iterative repair capabilities of DCAPS would be well suited for mixed-initiative partially automated, human in the loop, shuttle payload operations. At this time DCAPS was modified to meet a number of minor user interface requirements and the DATA-CHASER model was constructed over a series of software spirals with each model increasing in coverage and fidelity. The total JPL AI Group effort involved in the development of DCAPS and initial modeling was approximately 1.4 work-years. The total effort by CSGC to deploy the DCAPS system was on the order 0.4 work-years.

DCAPS was integrated into the End-to-End Mission Operations System (EEMOS) used for the DATA-CHASER portion of the STS-85 payload. This EEMOS architecture is also being evaluated as part of the Fire and Ice pre-project (Siewert & Hansen, 1996). The DATA-CHASER EEMOS consisted of seven parts: Command and Control, Fault/Event Detection Interaction Reaction (F/EDIR), DATA/IO (Data handling), the Ground Database, the Graphical User Interface, the software testbed, and finally the DCAPS planner.

The command and control language used, System Command Language (SCL, also known as Spacecraft Command Language), integrates procedural programming with a real-time, forward-chaining, rule-based system. DCAPS interfaces with SCL through DATA/IO by sending script scheduling commands to be scheduled either on the flight or ground system. This interface is implemented by mapping PI2 activities to SCL scripts that were written prior to flight and can be scheduled or event-triggered by activating rules. A list of these scheduling and rule activation commands is then sent to DATA/IO which forwards the list to the SCL Compiler. Once compiled, the list is sent to the payload through the next available uplink.

DCAPS is also interfaced with the ground EEMOS database, O2. O2 is an object-oriented database used to store all mission data and telemetry that is downlinked by the payload. O2 also stores a command history. Through DATA/IO, DCAPS requests current payload status data in the form of sensor values in the telemetry history. It also requests lists of all commands uplinked during a given time interval. These are used by DCAPS to infer command completion status as well as to get the current state of the payload so that a new schedule can be created.

During mission operations, approximately every six hours, DCAPS was asked by an operator to generate script scheduling commands and rule activations for the next six hours. This list was then reviewed by the Mission Operations staff on duty. When judged to be correct, scheduling and rule activation commands would be sent to DATA/IO during the next available uplink window. If during that six hour period there was a major change in the NASA activities, the operations staff could use DCAPS to update the schedule script on-board. If so desired, DCAPS could generate an updated command list, ask the user to verify it, and send the list to DATA/IO to be uplinked.

Impact and Results from Use During STS-85

Unfortunately, difficulties were encountered during the development and integration of the real-time DATA-CHASER flight software. Due to these difficulties and hard shuttle payload delivery constraints, the real-time onboard command execution software for the payload did not have several capabilities that were originally designed. First, the onboard software was unable to command the SXEE and LASIT instruments. Second, the onboard software did not have the capability to store and execute time-tagged command loads, thus all operations had to be carefully synchronized with real-time shuttle uplink windows. Third, the onboard tape storage device (DAT) was not functional. This meant that data storage was limited to the onboard solid state buffers. However, since the LASIT instrument was the most significant producer of data by over an order of magnitude, this was not a major problem. The first and second limitations described above meant that having an automated planning system to automatically coordinate the complex timing constraints was even more important; manually attempting to enforce such timing constraints would increase the chance of operator error causing loss of data. Likewise, being able to replan quickly and automatically when shuttle activities changed (such as downlink or uplink windows and solar view periods) was also critical.

Carrying the DATA-CHASER payload, STS-85, the Space Shuttle Discovery, launched at 7:41AM PST on Thursday August 7, 1997. Mission operations, including mission planning and scheduling were performed for the 2 week flight. During the first 5 days of DATA-CHASER operations, DCAPS was used in manual mode. In this mode, activities were placed manually and DCAPS was used to validate constraints, identify constraint violations, and generate the actual command files. During the last 7 days of the payload operation, DCAPS was used to automatically generate schedules. In this phase, the domain specific initial schedule generator was used to generate an initial schedule. Due to network lag times[1], use of the iterative repair techniques was somewhat limited. However, this did not impact operations significantly. In many cases minor conflicts were repaired manually.

The DCAPS automated scheduling capability significantly impacted DATA-CHASER mission operations. DCAPS enabled an 80% reduction in the amount of effort to produce operations plans. Manual generation of a 6-hour operations plan would require from 30 to 60 minutes in manual mode of operations and from 7 to 9 minutes using the DCAPS automated scheduling capability. This reduction in effort is because DCAPS can automatically generate an acceptable or near acceptable schedule very quickly. The number of modifications (if any) to make a DCAPS generated schedule acceptable can be made far faster than manually generating a schedule from scratch. DCAPS also enabled a 40% increase in science return. Manually generated plans had 2-3 instrument scans per viewing opportunity whereas DCAPS generated plans had 3-4 scans per viewing opportunity. This is because DCAPS could directly monitor and track all of the complex timing constraints involved in the instrument activities and pack activities more tightly than operators manually placing instrument activities. During the 7 days of DCAPS automated use, DCAPS scheduled a total of 93 science scans and 202 payload commands.

One significant feature of the DCAPS system is its declarative representation of flight rules and spacecraft constraints. This feature was tested during the STS-85 flight in the following manner. When initial command sequences were uplinked, the flight software rejected a number of commands immediately following a reset command. This was due to the fact that the initial flight rules were constructed with the assumption that payload

Picture 2: Payload Operator Jason Willis uses DCAPS to command the DATA-CHASER Payload

[1] DATA-CHASER was operated primarily from Colorado Space Grant, but because they had limited computing resources, DCAPS was run on JPL machines.

commands could be issued immediately following a reset. Actual operations showed that a delay of 30 seconds was required before the payload could accept commands. When this problem was noticed and isolated, it was a simple manner to quickly update the DCAPS model to require this delay so that future command sequences would execute without problem. This aspect of ease of modification is key in that operating procedures and constraints constantly evolve throughout the mission lifecycle as mission priorities and spacecraft characteristics evolve.

Summary and Related Work

Iterative algorithms have been applied to a wide range of computer science problems such as traveling salesman (Lin & Kernighan, 1973) as well as Artificial Intelligence Planning (Chien & DeJong, 1994, Hammond, 1989, Simmons, 1988, Sussman, 1973). Iterative repair algorithms have also been used for a number of scheduling systems. The GERRY/GPSS system (Zweben et al, 1994, Deale et al. 1994) uses iterative repair with a global evaluation function and simulated annealing to schedule space shuttle ground processing activities. The Operations Mission Planner (OMP) (Biefeld & Cooper, 1991) system used iterative repair in combination with a historical model of the scheduler actions (called chronologies) to avoid cycling and getting caught in local minima. Work by Johnston and Minton (Johnston & Minton, 1994) shows how the min-conflicts heuristic can be used not only for scheduling but for a wide range of constraint satisfaction problems. The OPIS system (Smith 1994) can also be viewed as performing iterative repair. However, OPIS is more informed in the application of its repair methods in that it applies a set of analysis measures to classify the bottleneck before selecting a repair method.

In summary, DCAPS represents a significant advance from several perspectives. First, from a mission operations perspective, DCAPS is important in that it significantly reduces the amount of effort and knowledge required to generate command sequences to achieve mission operations goals. Second, from the standpoint of Artificial Intelligence applications, DCAPS represents a significant application of planning and scheduling technology to the complex, real-world problem of spacecraft commanding. In particular, significant quantitative improvements in operations efficiency were documented during the STS-85 flight. Third, from the standpoint of Artificial Intelligence research, DCAPS mixed initiative approach to initial schedule generation, iterative repair, and schedule optimization represents a novel approach to solving complex planning and scheduling problems.

Acknowledgments

The authors also gratefully acknowledge the contributions of other participants in the DCAPS and DATA-CHASER projects who also contributed to the work described in this paper: Peter Stone, Curt Eggemeyer, and Sam Siewert.

References

A. Aldas, "A Post-process Optimization Algorithm for Resource-constrained Project Scheduling," Working Notes of the Intl. Workshop on Planning and Scheduling for Space Exploration & Science, Oxnard, CA, October 1997.

E. Biefeld and L. Cooper, "Bottleneck Identification Using Process Chronologies," Proceedings of the 1991 International Joint Conference on Artificial Intelligence, Sydney, Australia, 1991.

S. Chien and G. DeJong, "Constructing Simplified Plans via Truth Criteria Approximation," Proceedings of the Second International Conference on Artificial Intelligence Planning Systems, Chicago, IL, June 1994, pp. 19-24.

J. Crawford, "An Approach to Resource Constrained Project Scheduling," http://www.cirl.uoregon.edu /crawford/papers/albu

M. Deale, M. Yvanovich, D. Schnitzius, D. Kautz, M. Carpenter, M. Zweben, G. Davis, and B. Daun, "The Space Shuttle Ground Processing System," in Intelligent Scheduling, Morgan Kaufman, San Francisco, 1994.

W. Eggemeyer, "Plan-IT-II Bible", JPL Technical Document, 1995.

K. Hammond, "Case-based Planning: Viewing Planning as a Memory Task," Academic Press, San Diego, 1989.

M. Johnston and S. Minton, "Analyzing a Heuristic Strategy for Constraint Satisfaction and Scheduling," in Intelligent Scheduling, Morgan Kaufman, San Francisco, 1994.

S. Lin and B. Kernighan, "An Effective Heuristic for the Traveling Salesman Problem," Operations Research Vol. 21, 1973.

G. Rabideau, S. Chien, T. Mann, C. Eggemeyer, P. Stone, and J. Willis, "DCAPS User's Manual," JPL Technical Document D-13741, 1996.

S. Siewert and E. Hansen, "A Distributed Operations Automation Testbed to Evaluate System Support for Autonomy and Operator Interaction Protocols," 4th International Symposium on Space Mission Operations and Ground Data Systems, ESA, Forum der Technik, Munich, Germany, September 1996.

R. Simmons, "Combining Associational and Causal Reasoning to Solve Interpretation and Planning Problems," Technical Report, MIT Artificial Intelligence Lab., 1988.

S. Smith, "OPIS: A Methodology and Architecture for Reactive Scheduling," in Intelligent Scheduling, Morgan Kaufman, San Francisco, 1994.

G. Sussman, "A Computational Model of Skill Acquisition," Technical Report, MIT Artificial Intelligence Laboratory, 1973.

M. Zweben, B. Daun, E. Davis, and M. Deale, "Scheduling and Rescheduling with Iterative Repair," in Intelligent Scheduling, Morgan Kaufman, San Francisco, 1994.

DLMS: Ten Years of AI for Vehicle Assembly Process Planning

Nestor Rychtyckyj

Ford Motor Company
Manufacturing Quality and Business Systems, Vehicle Operations General Office
Room B154, PO Box 1586, Dearborn, MI 48121
email: nrychtyc@ford.com

Abstract

Since its presentation at the inaugural 1989 IAAI Conference (O'Brien et al. 1989), Ford's Direct Labor Management System (DLMS) has evolved from a prototype being tested at a single assembly plant to a fully-deployed application that is being utilized at Ford's assembly plants throughout the world. DLMS is Ford's automated solution to managing the automobile manufacturing process system at our vehicle assembly plants. This paper will describe our experiences and the lessons that have been learned in building and adapting an AI system to the rapidly-evolving world of automotive vehicle assembly process planning. We will cover issues such as knowledge base development and maintenance, knowledge representation, porting the system to different platforms and keeping the system viable and up-to-date through various organizational and business practice changes. We will also discuss how DLMS has become an integral part of Ford's assembly process planning business.

Problem Description

For a manufacturing company like Ford Motor Company, the assembly process planning activity is the critical link between the development and design of a product and it's final assembly and delivery to the customer. In a typical year Ford manufactures and sells over six and a half million cars and trucks all over the world. A major initiative was undertaken at Ford Vehicle Operations to improve the quality and effectiveness of the assembly process planning activity. The central theme to this project is the development of a knowledge-based system that will support the creation and manipulation of planning data in all stages of the assembly planning process, from the central office budgeting and cost estimating down to the work allocation and line balancing at the plant floor level. The result of this initiative is the Direct Labor Management System.

The development of the Direct Labor Management System (DLMS) began in 1989 at Ford's Body & Assembly Division. DLMS was designed to be an integral part of the Manufacturing Process Planning System that was being developed for the assembly plants in North America. The objectives of DLMS included standardizing the process sheet writing, creating work allocation sheets for the plant floor and estimating labor time accurately. The process sheet is the primary vehicle for conveying vehicle assembly information from the central engineering functions to the assembly plants. It contains specific information about work instructions and describes the parts and tools required for the build process. The work that is required to build the vehicle according to the process sheet instructions must then be allocated among the available personnel. Work allocation requires a precise means of measuring the labor time that is needed for any particular task.

The requirement for a system to automate process planning in automobile assembly at Ford Motor Company was very evident since the early 1980's. Previously, process sheets were written in free-form English and then sent to the assembly plants for implementation. The quality and correctness of process sheets differed greatly based upon which engineer had written a particular sheet. There was no standardization between process sheets. Industrial engineers at the assembly plants would be forced to implement work instructions based on various styles of process sheets. The process sheets could not describe the amount of labor required and the assembly plants were not able to accurately plan for labor requirements. Work usage instructions were written manually and the time required to accomplish a particular job would have to be measured manually. These manual "stopwatch" time studies suffered from several major disadvantages. A time study consisted of an industrial engineer watching an assembly line worker doing their job and measuring how long each job would take. These measurements would vary from worker to worker, so that multiple time studies were required for each particular job. Since there may be hundreds or even thousands of jobs in an assembly plant, the time studies were very expensive and time-consuming. Time studies also have a very adverse effect on worker morale and are a source of resentment among the assembly personnel. Since labor is a very significant portion of the cost of producing an automobile, there was a very strong incentive to develop a system that could both standardize the process sheet and create a tool for automatically generating work instructions and times from these process sheets. The first attempts to create DLMS were done utilizing standard third generation programming languages (COBOL) and existing IBM mainframe databases (IMS). The sheer complexity of the knowledge required to accurately generate reliable work instructions could not be represented in either a database or in a program. A database could easily store the amount of data required, but the relationships between the various components in the database could not be adequately represented. A program could be written that could explicitly list all of the inputs and desired outputs, but this program would quickly become obsolete and be impossible to maintain.

The solution to this problem was to develop a knowledge-based system that utilizes a semantic network knowledge representation scheme. DLMS utilizes techniques from natural language processing, description logics and classification-based reasoning to generate detailed plant floor assembly instructions from high-level process descriptions. This system also provides detailed estimates of the labor content that is required from these process descriptions. Techniques such as machine translation and evolutionary computation are being integrated into DLMS to support knowledge base maintenance and to deploy DLMS to Ford's assembly plants that do not use English as their main language.

The DLMS application remains a viable and integral part of vehicle assembly process planning. The writing of process sheets has been standardized through the use of Standard Language. The output of the DLMS system consists of work allocation instructions along with their associated MODAPTS codes that are converted into labor time for each operation. The following sections will describe the DLMS system in more detail and discuss the development and use of Standard Language. Other issues associated with AI systems development, such as knowledge base maintenance and the integration of DLMS with external databases and systems, will also be covered.

Application Description

The Direct Labor Management System (DLMS) is an implemented system utilized by Ford Motor Company's Vehicle Operations division to manage the use of labor on the assembly lines throughout Ford's vehicle assembly plants. DLMS was designed to improve the assembly process planning activity at Ford by achieving standardization within the vehicle process build description and to provide a tool for accurately estimating

the labor time required to perform the actual vehicle assembly. In addition, DLMS provides the framework for allocating the required work among various operators at the plant and builds a foundation for automated machine translation of the process descriptions into foreign languages.

The standard process planning document known as a process sheet is the primary vehicle for conveying the assembly information from the initial process planning activity to the assembly plant. A process sheet contains the detailed instructions needed to build a portion of a vehicle. A single vehicle may require thousands of process sheets to describe its assembly. The process sheet is written by an engineer utilizing a restricted subset of English known as SLANG (Standard LANGuage). Standard Language allows an engineer to write clear and concise assembly instructions that are machine readable.

Figure 1 shows a portion of a process sheet written in Standard Language. This process sheet is written by an engineer at the Vehicle Operations General Office; it is then sent to the DLMS system to be "validated" before it can be released to the assembly plants. Validation includes the following: checking the process sheet for errors, generating the sequence of steps that a worker at the assembly plant must perform in order to accomplish this task and calculating the length of time that this task will require. The DLMS system interprets these instructions and generates a list of detailed actions that are required to implement these instructions at the assembly plant level. These work instructions, known as "allocatable elements", are associated with MODAPTS (MODular Arrangement of Predetermined Time Standards) codes that are used to calculate the time required to perform these actions.

MODAPTS codes are widely utilized as a means of measuring the body movements that are required to perform a physical action and have been accepted as a valid work measurement system. (IES 1988). For example, the MODAPTS code for moving a small object with only a hand is M2; utilizing the arm gives a code of M3. The MODAPTS codes are then combined to describe a entire sequence of actions. MODAPTS codes are then converted into an equivalent time required to perform that action. Figure 2 shows the output generated by the DLMS system including a description of each action with its associated MODAPTS code.

The allocatable elements generated by DLMS are used by engineering personnel at the assembly plant to allocate the required work among the available personnel. DLMS is a powerful tool because it provides timely information about the amount of direct labor that is required to assemble each vehicle, as well as pointing out inefficiencies in the assembly process.

The DLMS system consists of five main subsystems:

Process Sheet Written in Standard Language
TITLE: ASSEMBLE IMMERSION HEATER TO ENGINE
10 OBTAIN ENGINE BLOCK HEATER ASSEMBLY FROM STOCK
20 LOOSEN HEATER ASSEMBLY TURNSCREW USING POWER TOOL
30 APPLY GREASE TO RUBBER O-RING AND CORE OPENING
40 INSERT HEATER ASSEMBLY INTO RIGHT REAR CORE PLUG HOSE
50 ALIGN SCREW HEAD TO TOP OF HEATER
TOOL 20 1 P AAPTCA TSEQ RT ANGLE NUTRUNNER
TOOL 30 1 C COMM TSEQ GREASE BRUSH

Figure 1.

Resulting Work Instructions Generated by DLMS For Line 20
LOOSEN HEATER ASSEMBLY TURNSCREW USING POWER TOOL
GRASP POWER TOOL (RT ANGLE NUTRUNNER) <01M4G1>
POSITION POWER TOOL (RT ANGLE NUTRUNNER) <01M4P2>
ACTIVATE POWER TOOL (RT ANGLE NUTRUNNER) <01M1P0>
REMOVE POWER TOOL (RT ANGLE NUTRUNNER) <01M4P0>
RELEASE POWER TOOL (RT ANGLE NUTRUNNER) <01M4P0>

Figure 2.

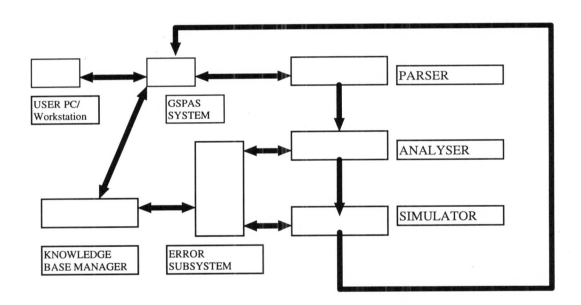

Figure 3: DLMS System Architecture

Adverb	Verb	Noun Phrase	Initial Location	Intermed Location	Final Location	Faste-ner	Tool
	Obtain	Fuel Filler Door	From Vehicle				
Auto	Load	Sub-Assembly			To Station		
	Insert	Bolt	Into slot				Using Tool
	Verify	That Bracket is in Place					

Figure 4. Template Describing A Standard Language Sentence

parser, analyzer, simulator, knowledge base manager and the error checker. The input into DLMS is a process sheet; it is initially parsed to break down the sentence into its lexical components which includes the verb, subject, modifiers, prepositional phrases and other parts of speech. Since Standard Language is a restricted subset of English, the parser has a very high rate of success in properly parsing the input from the process sheets. The parser utilizes the Augmented Transition Network (ATN) method of parsing (Charniak 1987). Any process element that is not parsed successfully will then be flagged by one of the error rules that will (hopefully) suggest to the user how to correct this element. The analyzer will then use the components of the parsed element to search the knowledge base (or taxonomy) for relevant information describing that item. For example, if the input element contained the term "HAMMER", the taxonomy will be searched for the term "HAMMER". When it is found the system will learn all of the attributes that "HAMMER" has: (it is a Tool, its size is medium, it can be used with one hand, etc.) The system performs this analysis on all of the components of the input element in order to select what work instructions are required. The work instructions are then found in the taxonomy based on all of the available input and are passed on to the simulator. The simulator uses the information found in the taxonomy to generate the allocatable elements and MODAPTS codes that describe the input element. These work instructions are then sent to the user. The knowledge base manager is used to maintain the knowledge base; this maintenance may be performed by the user community or by the system developers.

All of the associated knowledge about Standard Language, tools, parts and everything else associated with the automobile assembly process is contained in the DLMS knowledge base or taxonomy. This knowledge base structure is derived from the KL-ONE family of semantic network structures and is the integral component in the success of DLMS. DLMS also contains a rulebase of over 350 rules that are used to drive the validation process and perform error-checking on the Standard Language input. Figure 3 displays the DLMS system architecture.

The organization of the knowledge base is based on the KL-ONE model. The root of the semantic network is a concept known as THING which encompasses everything within the DLMS world. The children of the root concept describe various major classes of knowledge and include such things as TOOLS, PARTS and OPERATIONS. Each concept contains attributes or slots that describe that object. The values of these attributes are inherited from the concept's parents. Ranges of valid values can be given for any particular attribute. Any attempt to put an invalid value in that attribute will trigger an error. All of the information dealing with the organization and structure of

the taxonomy is also contained in the taxonomy itself. There are four types of links that describe the relationship between any two concepts: subsumes, specializes, immediately-subsumes and immediately-specializes. The subsumption relation describes a link between a parent concept and all of its children, including descendants of its children. The "immediately-subsumes" relation describes only the concepts that are direct children of the parent concept. The "specializes" and "immediately specializes" relations are inverses of the subsumption relation. A concept "immediately specializes" its direct parent concepts and "specializes" all of the concepts that are ancestors of its parents. These relationships are stored as attributes of any given concept and can be utilized as a tool to trace any concept through the entire taxonomy.

Uses of AI Technology

The DLMS system utilizes several different AI techniques including Description Logics, Rule-based Processing and Machine Translation. The heart of the DLMS system is the knowledge base that utilizes a semantic network model to represent all of the automobile assembly planning information. The use of a semantic network as part of knowledge representation system is also known as *Description Logics*. A Description Logic implementation known as CLASSIC has been successfully used at AT&T to develop telecommunication equipment configurators (McGuiness and Patel-Schneider 1998). Semantic networks have also been integrated into Object-Oriented Analysis (OOA) (Mylopoulos 1999). The goal of Object-Oriented Analysis is to combine ideas from object-oriented programming with semantic network modeling and knowledge representation into a powerful modeling framework. The DLMS implementation of Description Logic is based on the KL-ONE knowledge representation language.

The KL-ONE knowledge representation system (Brachman 1985) was first developed at Bolt, Baranek and Newman in the late 1970's as an outgrowth of semantic net formalisms. KL-ONE was selected for use on the DLMS project because of its adaptability for many diverse applications as well as the power of the KL-ONE classification algorithm. KL-ONE is derived from research done on semantic networks. The principal unit of information is the "concept". Each concept has a set of components or attributes that is true for each member of the set denoted by that concept. The main form of relation between concepts is called "subsumption". Subsumption is the property by which concept A subsumes concept B if, and only if, the set denoted by concept A includes the set denoted by concept B. The KL-ONE knowledge base as used in DLMS can be described as a network of concepts with the general concepts being closer to the root of the tree and the more specific concepts being the leaves of the tree. A concept in a KL-ONE knowledge base inherits attributes from the nodes that subsume it. The power of the KL-ONE system lies in the classification scheme. The system will place a new concept into its appropriate place in the taxonomy by utilizing the subsumption relation on the concept's attributes (Rychtyckyj 1994).

A strictly rule-base approach was also considered, but the complexity and future maintainability of a system containing explicit knowledge about a dynamic domain such as automobile assembly ruled this approach out. This maintainability issue was illustrated in the development of the R1 (also known as XCON) system that was utilized at Digital Equipment Corporation to assist in the configuration of DEC VAX computer systems. This equally dynamic environment showed that in any given year more than 50% of the rules were modified (Sowa 1987). Rules were later added to DLMS as part of the error checker and to control the execution of the system as this type of knowledge changes much less frequently.

A requirement for the DLMS knowledge base included the ability to make frequent and complex changes without affecting other components of the knowledge base. This required that the objects in the taxonomy be stored in classes that were analogous to the real world of automobile assembly planning. This approach led to a semantic network representation of the automobile assembly world where classes and subclasses corresponded to their appropriate equivalents in the real world. This type of semantic network representation was very similar to the KL-ONE representation language. It was decided to model the Ford automobile manufacturing knowledge base utilizing KL-ONE in order test the feasibility of this approach. This prototype proved very successful and the basic KL-ONE model proved to be both robust and flexible as the knowledge base evolved over the years. Changes were made for processing and memory efficiency (i.e. the use of a hash table to store the list of concepts), but the KL-ONE logical design has been successful in terms of our problem domain.

Since its implementation in 1990 the DLMS knowledge base has been frequently modified to keep pace with the rapidly changing automobile and truck assembly process. These changes have included the implementation of DLMS for plants outside of North America, the assembly of entirely new types of vehicles including electric and alternative fuel vehicles and the improvements in the actual assembly process. Since the complexity of the knowledge base has increased, we have become concerned about the efficiency of the subsumption and classification algorithms. One possible solution to this is to develop a tool that will assist in the re-engineering of the network to reduce complexity and increase efficiency. Currently we are utilizing an Evolutionary Computational technique, known as Cultural Algorithms (Reynolds and Chung 1996), to re-engineer the semantic network with the goal of reducing the network complexity in two ways (Rychtyckyj and Reynolds 1998). The first approach is to reduce the number of attributes that have to be compared during the classification algorithm. The second approach is to begin the classification search at a node that is lower in the network to reduce the number of nodes that have to be visited.

We are also utilizing Machine Translation software for the translation of our system output into the home languages of the countries where our plants are located in. For this approach we are working with Systran Software Inc. to customize their software to work with Standard Language and our application. One part of this involves building a lexicon of the specific Ford terminology and the required translations in each target language. Another requirement of the project is to modify the Systran software to accept the sentence structure that is utilized within Standard Language.

Application Use and Payoff

As mentioned previously, DLMS has been in use continuously within Ford Motor Company since 1990. Currently the system supports hundreds of users that are located in various Ford locations around the world including North and South America, Europe and Asia. The users are primarily engineers that are writing processes that will be used to build vehicles at Ford assembly plants. Another group of users are the engineers that are located at these assembly plants. A third group of system users are located at the central office locations and are concerned with financial planning for the labor authorizations for each assembly plant.

One of the most important tangible benefits from the utilization of DLMS has been the acceptance and use of Standard Language to describe assembly instructions throughout our engineering community. This has dramatically increased productivity by reducing ambiguity and confusion between our General Office engineers and the people at our assembly plants. Standard LANGuage (SLANG) was developed as a controlled language that would have the flexibility to describe all of the instructions required for the vehicle assembly process. SLANG needed to be both unambiguous and precise enough so that each sentence could only generate one unique set of work allocation instructions. A controlled language, such as SLANG, also needs some type of mechanism that will check the written text so ensure that it complies with the rules of that language. In DLMS this is accomplished through a parser that checks each sentence for correctness and compliance to Standard Language guidelines.

Standard Language requires that each sentence conform to a structure that can be read by the system and provides sufficient information for the AI system to generate the correct work allocation instructions for that command. In addition, each word must be found in the DLMS knowledge base and be used correctly within the Standard Language sentence. The rules for writing Standard Language can be best described by defining a template that the written text must follow. Figure 4 shows a template with examples of typical Standard Language sentences. The verb and noun phrase, which usually describes a part, are required; the other parts of the sentence are optional and used as required. The last sentence in Figure 4 ("Verify that bracket is in Place") is a special type of inspection element that can utilize a much more free-form text syntax than a regular Standard Language expression. Each sentence in Standard Language must contain a verb that describes the main action performed by the assembly operator. The Standard Language verbs have been defined by the engineering community to represent a single precise action and are not interchangeable. For example, in Standard Language the verbs "SECURE" and "TIGHTEN" describe different operations and cannot be used interchangeably. All of the lexical terms within Standard Language are defined within the DLMS knowledge base.

Standard Language provides significant benefits in reducing the ambiguity and inconsistency that is present within free-form written text. Learning to write in Standard Language incurs training costs and a learning curve for the process writers, but the benefits of Standard Language more than make up for this. DLMS has provided other benefits to Ford Motor Company, such as automatic generation of work instructions with associated times, accurate estimates of direct and indirect labor times and the ability to plan for mix/volume changes and line balancing. The work instructions that are created by DLMS are utilized by the engineers at the assembly process to allocate the work among the available personnel at the plant. The system provides a method to determine how much work each person is required to perform. This will identify any potential overwork or under-utilization for any particular operator and provide an opportunity to re-allocate the work. DLMS also distinguishes between direct and indirect labor. Direct labor describes work that is directly related to vehicle assembly. Other actions, such as walking to obtain parts or tools, are described as indirect labor. The plant engineers use DLMS to identify areas with a high proportion of indirect labor and modify that particular work area to reduce the indirect labor.

Plant engineers can also utilize the output from DLMS to simulate different scenarios on how the mix and volume

of a particular vehicle can be assembled. This is extremely useful when a new vehicle is being launched at an assembly plant. The amount of labor that is needed to build the vehicle can be calculated to produce accurate manpower estimates and tool requirements. DLMS is a tool that gives Ford the ability to manage the assembly process planning work from development to production.

Application Development and Deployment

The original DLMS prototype was developed at Ford in conjunction with Inference Corporation in 1989. It was piloted at one of our assembly plants and included knowledge about one phase of the assembly process. After this approach was validated, the DLMS system was expanded to include the entire assembly process and was deployed at other North American assembly plants. During this time period our emphasis was on building up the knowledge base and making those modifications that were necessary for the system to be accepted by our plants. This knowledge transfer consisted of working closely with assembly engineers, making periodic visits to the assembly plants and conducting monthly video conferences with the users of the system.

DLMS was originally developed using Common Lisp and the Automated Reasoning Tool (ART) from Inference Corporation. LISP is an extremely powerful symbolic programming language that includes facilities for garbage collection, symbol manipulation, rapid prototyping and object-oriented programming. ART is a LISP-based expert system shell that utilizes a forward-chaining inference engine to perform pattern-matching and rule firing. DLMS was initially deployed on the Texas Instruments Explorer platform which was a stand-alone Lisp machine that included the UNIX operating system. Communications between DLMS and the mainframe IMS database was handled using a screen emulator interface. After the initial DLMS deployment, the TI Explorer platform was discontinued and both support and maintenance for these machines became problematic. In order to ensure the future viability of DLMS the system was ported to the Hewlett Packard UNIX platform. The communications interface was rewritten utilizing the Brixton communications software through an interface with LISP. The DLMS development team usually consisted of no more than three developers at any time.

Following a major re-organization that put all the assembly plants around the world into one organization, it was decided replace the legacy mainframe Manufacturing Process Planning System(MPPS) with a new client-server application. The new Global Study Process Allocation System (GSPAS) utilizes a distributed Oracle database that needs to be accessed from DLMS. The ART software tool was not being upgraded and would not function with the latest versions of Oracle. This necessitated the conversion of DLMS from ART to another expert system shell that would preserve the functionality of the system and provide a platform for interfacing with the database. We selected the LispWorks/KnowledgeWorks tool from Harlequin Inc. due to its similarity to ART and continued support. The graphical Knowledge Base Manager facility was ported from ART to the LispWorks Common Lisp Interface Manager (CLIM) software which allows for the development of a graphical user interface from LISP. The ART rulebase was rewritten into KnowledgeWorks and DLMS was successfully deployed as part of the GSPAS system.

With the expansion of DLMS to our European assembly plants our focus shifted on expanding our knowledge base to model the assembly process in our European plants. This included modifying Standard Language and adding additional tools and parts for different vehicles. This change also produced a requirement that we translate the DLMS output into other languages.

Currently there are two versions of DLMS being utilized within Ford Vehicle Operations. The MPPS version of DLMS still utilizes ART and LISP while the GSPAS version utilizes KnowledgeWorks and LISP. Both versions run on the HP UNIX platform and share a common knowledge base. Communication to the GSPAS system is handled through the RPC protocol and the Oracle database is accessed directly from the LISP code in DLMS.

Maintenance

As mentioned previously, the DLMS taxonomy or knowledge base contains all of the relevant information that describes the vehicle assembly process at Ford Motor Company. This includes all of the lexical classes included in Standard Language such as verbs, nouns, prepositions, conjunctions and other parts of speech, various tools and parts utilized at the assembly plants, and descriptions of operations that are performed to build the vehicle. Currently the DLMS taxonomy contains over 9000 such concepts.

The DLMS Knowledge Base is maintained through the use of two different tools: the Knowledge Base Manager (KBM) and the Knowledge Base Update facility (KBU). The Knowledge Base Manager is a graphical tool that is used by the system developers to make important changes to the knowledge base that will affect the actual output generated by the system. Since this output will have a major impact on the assembly process any such change must be approved by a committee representing all of the interested parties. All changes made to the

knowledge base are logged by the system to keep a record of the system's modification history.

The Knowledge Base Update (KBU) is an automated update facility that was used by system users to make minor modifications to the knowledge base. A minor modification is a change that will not impact the output produced by the system. Examples of minor modifications include the addition of new words into the taxonomy. The KBU facility allowed users to incorporate these changes directly into the taxonomy without any kind of system developer intervention. All changes made through the KBU facility were also logged for future reference.

With the requirement that the Standard Language output be translated from English into the home languages of our assembly plants we discovered that many errors had been introduced into our system through the KBU. These consisted of simple grammatical errors such as misspellings or giving a word the incorrect part of speech, but they created serious difficulties for our translation software. Other non-technical terms that described tools or equipment at one assembly plant were not known to workers in other countries and also adversely impacted our translation. These problems have forced us to remove the Knowledge Base Utility from production and force all additions and modifications to the knowledge base to be approved by the user committee and then sent to the developers.

There have been several utilities developed that are used to validate the knowledge base and prevent any errors from being inadvertently introduced into the system. These include an automated facility that scans through the knowledge base and creates sample test cases that cover various operations within the system. These test cases are then executed and compared against a previous baseline to determine if the results have changed. There is also a suite of test cases that are manually updated to cover problems and modifications that have occurred in the system. The regression tests are also run against a similar baseline of expected results. We are also utilizing Evolutionary Computation to develop a method of automatically re-engineering the knowledge base to reduce complexity and improve efficiency of our classification algorithms.

Conclusions

DLMS has proven to be a successful implementation of AI technology that has delivered tangible benefits to Ford Motor Company. These include the following: standard and accurate process sheets through the use of Standard Language, automatic generation of work instructions with associated times, accurate estimates of direct vs. indirect labor times and the ability to plan for mix/volume changes and line balancing. Through the 10 years of work on DLMS we have validated the use of AI as a viable technology in a dynamic business environment. The use of Description Logics to model our assembly process planning environment has paid off with its flexibility and expressiveness. DLMS has provided Ford with a competitive advantage and has justified the use of AI as a tool for building and delivering systems that solve difficult business problems.

References

Brachman, R., Schmolze, J. 1985. An Overview of the KL-ONE Knowledge Representation System. *Cognitive Science* 9(2): 171-216.

Charniak, E., Riesbeck, C., McDermott, D., Meehan, J., 1987. *Artificial Intelligence Programming*, Lawrence Erlbaum Associates.

Industrial Engineering Services. 1988. *Modapts Study Notes for Certified Practitioner Training*.

McGuiness, D. and Patel-Schneider, P. 1998. Usability Issues in Knowledge Representations Systems. In *Proceedings of the Fifteenth National Conference on Artificial Intelligence*, 608-614. Menlo Park, CA: AAAI Press.

Mylopoulos, J., Chung, L., Yu, E. 1999. From Object-Oriented to Goal-Oriented Requirements Analysis. *Communications of the ACM* 42(1): 31-37.

O'Brien, J., Brice, H., Hatfield, S., Johnson, W., Woodhead, R. 1989. The Ford Motor Company Direct Labor Management System. In *Innovative Applications of Artificial Intelligence*, 331-346. MIT Press.

Reynolds, R.G. and Chung, C. 1996. A Self-adaptive Approach to Representation Shifts in Cultural Algorithms. In *Proceedings of the 1996 IEEE International Conference on Evolutionary Computing*, 94-99. Nagoya Japan: IEEE Press.

Rychtyckyj, N. 1994. Classification in DLMS Utilizing a KL-ONE Representation Language. In *Proceedings of the Sixth International Conference on Tools with Artificial Intelligence*, 339-345. IEEE Computer Science Press.

Rychtyckyj, N. 1996. DLMS: An Evaluation of KL-ONE in the Automobile Industry. In *Proceedings of the Fifth International Conference on the Principles of Knowledge Representation and Reasoning*, 588-596. Morgan Kaufmann Publishers.

Rychtyckyj, N. and Reynolds, R. G. 1998. Learning to Re-Engineer Semantic Networks Using Cultural Algorithms. In *Evolutionary Programming VII*, 181-190. Springer-Verlag.

Soloway, E., Bechant, J., Jensen, K. 1987. Assessing the Maintainability of XCON in RIME: Coping with the Problems of a Very Large Rule-Base. In *Validating and Verifying Knowledge-Based Systems*, 294-299. IEEE Press.

Using Intelligent Agents in Military Simulation
or "Using Agents Intelligently"

Gil Tidhar   Clint Heinze   Simon Goss

Graeme Murray   Dino Appla   Ian Lloyd

Defence, Science, and Technology Organisation (DSTO)
506 Lorimer Street, Fishermen's Bend,
Victoria, Australia
Firstname.Surname@dsto.defence.gov.au

Abstract

Modern defence systems include advanced aircraft, ships, radar, weapons, command and control systems, and most importantly human operators. The main objective of modelling and simulation tools is to allow operational analysts to rapidly specify and evaluate existing and proposed systems and procedures for operating these systems. Such tools are required to model all aspects of defence systems including physical systems and human operators and the reasoning processes that they adopt.

Agent-oriented technology is a natural candidate for developing a model of reasoning processes performed by human operators. It allows the operational analyst to work at a high level, formulating cognitive processes, while keeping the detailed computer programming hidden. This premise has led to the development of the Operator-Agent. The base model was completed in June 1996. The model is fully operational and is an integral part of the tools used by operational analysts from the Australian Department of Defence. It has been successfully used for operational analysis and evaluation of multi-billion dollar acquisitions.

Introduction

"Outside, it's pitch black, no moon and a heavy overcast sky has completely obliterated the meagre, night illumination.... It is not the sort of night you would like to be out driving your car, but there you are at 60 meters above the ground travelling at close to 1,000 kph. You're thinking to yourself, `the most intelligent decision I could have made was to stay at home'...."
WGCDR Rick Owen
Royal Australian Air Force

Modern defence organisations use advanced systems as part of their military operations. Defence systems are typically both expensive to purchase and operate. Furthermore the circumstances under which such systems are used are not always simple to replicate in training. Modelling and simulation is becoming the main approach used by defence organisations in support of evaluation of existing and proposed defence systems. The key

requirements are for tools that allow operational analysts to rapidly specify and evaluate defence systems and develop procedures for best use of these systems.

Human operators are an integral part of any military operation. Such operators include air-combat pilots, mission commanders, fighter controllers, ship captains, and many others. They all reason about the environment, evaluate it, make decisions about controlling defence systems, and interact with other operators.

Modelling human operators engaged in military operations is a very challenging task. This is because humans exhibit intelligent behavior that is at times difficult to understand let alone automate. Building a model of human reasoning processes that can be validated, repeated, and meets real-time performance requirements is even harder.

Development of defence systems' models has followed development of programming languages and software engineering. Current models (e.g., TAC-BRAWLER (Bent 1993) and AASPEM (Boeing 1985)) were implemented using structured or object-oriented approaches. This applies to models of physical systems and reasoning processes. In most current systems models of reasoning processes are intertwined with models of physical systems. The only exception is the TAC-Soar system developed by Tambe et al. (Tambe et al. 1994). It uses Agent-Oriented technology to model air-combat pilots.[1]

Agent-Oriented technology has focused on the development of embedded real-time software systems which also exhibits (1) autonomous behaviour; (2) both reactive-and pro-active behaviour; and (3) the ability to interact with other systems. Furthermore theoretical models of agent-oriented technology have been inspired by philosophical and psychological theories of human behaviour. One agent-oriented approach successfully used in industrial applications is the Belief-Desire-Intention (BDI) approach (Rao and Georgeff 1995). In the past decade BDI systems have matured from experimental systems to commercially developed, fully tested, and

---

[1] The TAC-Soar system is a prototype system and has not been developed for or tested under operational conditions. This primarily manifests itself in system performance.

supported systems.

The BDI approach seems a natural candidate for the development of a new model of the human operator. Seven years ago the Australian Department of Defence engaged in a project to develop Intelligent Computer Generated Forces. This included developing a model of a human operator using the BDI approach. The model is to be used for modelling human operators in large military simulations. It is referred to as the *Operator-Agent*.

Technical benefits of the Operator-Agent include the capacity of an operational analyst to work at the level of tactical representation and the general easing of the software-engineering task in developing and maintaining the knowledge base. An unexpected consequence of the adoption of agent-oriented technologies has been a change at the organisational level. Interactions between analysts and military personnel have been improved and there is now significantly greater cooperation between operational analysts and human-factors experts. These advances can be summarised as a new paradigm in knowledge representation and acquisition. It follows a more natural way of describing the decision making process of operators. This innovation has significantly reduced the time and cost of developing and maintaining a model of a human operator.

In the remainder of this paper we describe the domain of application and the requirements from the system. We also describe the underlying technology used and provide details of the implementation. Furthermore we describe the development processes that led to this implementation and the benefits obtained through the use of the system.

A Typical Simulated Scenario

Let us consider two opposing forces. Red Team is planning a strike mission to destroy a ground target within Blue Team's territory. It assembles a *package* of aircraft adopting different roles. There is a group of sweep aircraft to clear a path ahead of the strike aircraft, there are escort aircraft to accompany the strike aircraft, and there are the strike aircraft themselves. These three groups have a single goal: to attack the ground target that has been designated for them. Each has assigned responsibilities that require communication and interaction with other aircraft.

Blue Team has aircraft operating in an air defence role protecting their airspace and vital areas from the incursion by Red Team. These aircraft may either be launched from an air-base when it becomes apparent that an attack is imminent or, if hostile actions have been occurring for a number of days, the aircraft may be flying patrols over an area where an attack is expected.

The hierarchy of command within the team exists in a flexible dynamic way to allow the team to operate at several levels and to split and reform as the situation dictates (Shaw 1985). Within the operation of a standard mission there are aircraft performing different tasks. An escort aircraft may accompany a strike aircraft as its wingman. A pair of low performance fighter aircraft might accompany a pair of high performance fighter aircraft to give the illusion of four high performance fighters.

Each situation may require the use of a different command and control structure. Thus the sub-teams will, at different times, adopt various command and control roles within the team. The different mission goals adopted by the team may require the sub-teams to adopt functional responsibilities with respect to the conduct of the mission. Thus an aircraft may have both a command and control role (e.g., a leader) and a functional role (e.g., an escort).

Requirements from Reasoning Model

Tambe et al. (Tambe et al. 1994) have provided some insight into building believable agents for simulation environments. Here we provide more detailed requirements. We identify four types of requirements necessary for a model of a human involved in military scenarios: (1) ability to interact with the environment; (2) ability to exhibit rational behaviour when reasoning about the world; (3) ability to exhibit irrational behaviour; and (4) ability to provide a good simulation environment.

A basic aspect of human behaviour is the way humans interact with the environment. These interactions occur through a variety of sensors and actuators. We require that the simulation system include the following features:

1. **Sensing:** The ability to sense the world through multiple sensors, e.g., eyes, ears, etc., and create a single model of the world from multiple sensory input.

2. **Actions and Physical Capabilities:** The ability to act and affect the world, e.g., walk, talk, etc. and conform to physical limitations determined by the human body.

When reasoning about the world humans use a variety of techniques and methods. These include building and maintaining situation awareness, planning, pursuing multiple goals simultaneously, and interleaving pro-active and reactive behaviours. We thus require that the simulation system also include the following features:

3. **Building and Maintaining Situation Awareness:** The ability to analyze the model of the world and identify particular aspects that require a response.

4. **Decision Making and Reasoning:** The ability to perform complex reasoning, e.g., make decisions, plan, perform spatial and temporal reasoning, etc.

5. **Simultaneous Goals:** The ability to hold multiple goals and interleave their achievement.

6. **Proactive and Reactive:** The ability to react to the changing world and to interleave pursuing goals and reacting to the world.

Humans exhibit behaviours that are not always rational or easily explicable. Thus a model of human behaviour should be able to simulate emotions, social awareness, and innovation. We thus require that the simulation system also include the following features:

7. **Emotions:** The ability to represent and manipulate emotions and model the way these emotions affect other processes.

8. **Social Awareness:** The ability to interact with other

humans being modelled and to represent and manipulate social structures.

9. **Innovation:** The ability to adopt innovative and novel responses when faced with unfamiliar scenarios.

The above requirements relate to the fidelity of the simulation. As these models are typically used for the purpose of analysis and evaluation of military scenarios there are additional requirements from such models. These requirements refer to the simulation environment itself and include the following features:

10. **Determinism and Repeatability:** Given a particular scenario, the ability to always exhibit a predetermined behaviour and the ability to repeat the exact simulated behaviour under similar conditions.[2]

11. **High Level Specifications:** The ability to specify and modify the behaviour of the agent using a high-level and relatively appropriately abstract language.

12. **Explanations:** The ability to provide clear and high-level explanations of the way reasoning is performed.

13. **Levels of Knowledge:** The ability to model different types and levels of knowledge (e.g., knowledge about the world and about how to behave in the world).

14. **Real-Time Performance:** The ability to perform activities in a time scale comparable to human activity.

The details of the models developed depend on the required fidelity of the simulation and particular aspects of the scenario that are being investigated. For some investigations it may be sufficient to include a crude model of the behaviour or to ignore some aspects altogether.

The Underlying Technology

To model the reasoning processes performed by human operators we have adopted a Belief-Desire-Intention (BDI) agent model. In particular we have used the dMARS™ system that is an implementation of the BDI approach. We now provide a description of the underlying BDI theoretical model and the components of a dMARS agent.

The BDI Theoretical Model

The logical foundations of BDI systems are based on the philosophical concepts of intentions, plans, and practical reasoning developed by Bratman (Bratman 1987). The semantic model includes multiple possible worlds that model the uncertainty inherent in the agent's environment and the agent's limited perception of this environment.

The beliefs, goals, and intentions are represented as special modal operators. The language used is a combination of Modal Logic and Computational Tree Logic (CTL).

Beliefs represent the current state of the environment as perceived by the agent. Desires represent the states of the environment the agent would like to be in. The agent's

[2] Under probabilistic behaviour repeatability is measured statistically over repeated simulations.

*dMARS is a registered trademark of the Australian Artificial Intelligence Institute, Melbourne, Australia.

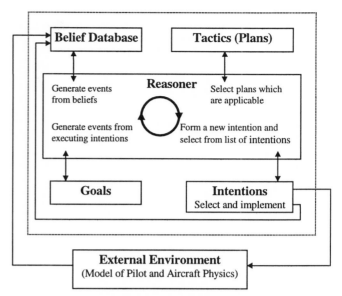

Figure 1: The Operator-Agent Control Loop

desires are limited only to those desires that are both attainable and consistent (referred to as *goals*). An intention represents the commitment of the agent to achieve a particular goal by progressing along a particular path that leads to that goal.

This logical model is augmented with plans and an operational semantics to form an abstract architecture of BDI agents (Rao and Georgeff 1995). Underlying the abstract architecture are the concepts of "bounded rationality" and "embedded systems". It is assumed that: (1) the agent has limited computational resources; (2) the agent can actually affect the world by acting; and (3) the environment is changing while the agent is reasoning.

These concepts lead to the development of a model of plans as "recipes" (Rao 1997). Plans are designed to achieve a particular goal under particular circumstances. They are supplied in advance and are not generated by the agent "on the fly". An agent can have multiple plans to achieve the same goal under the same or different circumstances.

Each plan is an abstract combination of sub-goals to be achieved or actions to be executed. Plans can be viewed as representing an abstract notion of a path that leads from the current state to the goal state. Sub-goals represent an intermediate state along the path. Plans are used in combination with a particular goal to form an intention.

Deliberation is done through the selection of goals, plans to be used to form an intention, and intentions to be executed. Decisions are based on the agent's beliefs. The process is known as *means-end reasoning*.

Intentions are executed through the achievement of sub-goals, modification of the agent's beliefs, and execution of actions. Sub-goals are achieved through the formation of sub-intentions. Sub-intentions are formed only when the achievement of the sub-goal is attempted. This is known as the *least-commitment* approach.

Components of a dMARS Agent

Each agent is composed of a set of beliefs, goals, plans, and intentions (see Figure 1). Beliefs are represented in first-order logic. For example, a belief that the range from WARLOCK1 to *BANDIT1* is 40 miles is represented as *(range WARLOCK1 BANDIT1 40)*. Goals are descriptions of desired tasks or behaviours. Plans are procedural specifications representing knowledge on ways to achieve a goal or react to a situation. Each plan includes an invocation condition, a context condition, and a body (Rao and Georgeff 1995, Rao 1997) (see Figure 2). A dMARS agent can also have meta-level plans. These plans contain information about the manipulation of the beliefs, goals, plans, and intentions of the BDI agent itself.

The invocation condition describes the event that must occur for the plan to be executed. Events may be the acquisition of a new goal (resulting in a goal-directed invocation), changes to the agent's beliefs (resulting in data-directed invocation), or messages from other agents. The context condition describes contextual information relevant for plan execution.

The body of a plan can be viewed as a procedure or a tactic. It is represented as a graph with one start node and one or more end nodes. The arcs in the graph are labeled with sub-goals to be achieved, modifications to the agent's belief database, and actions that should be performed.

In the plan language, an attempt by the team *WARLOCK* to achieve a goal to intercept *BANDIT1* is written as *(! (intercept WARLOCK12 BANDIT1))* and test for a belief that *WARLOCK1* has a control responsibility for the team *WARLOCK12* is written as *(? (role-in-team WARLOCK12 CONTROL WARLOCK1 LEADER)*. Other operators such as asserting (=>) and retracting (~>) a belief and waiting (^) for a belief to be true are also available. The character $ denotes variables in the plan language.

An intention embodies the agent's commitment to achieve a particular goal, respond to a change in its beliefs, or respond to messages from other agents, using a particular plan. It combines an event and an instantiated plan.

The agent's set of intentions contains all those tasks that the agent has chosen for execution, either immediately or at some later time. At any given moment, some of these intentions may be suspended, some may be waiting for certain conditions to hold, and some may be meta-level intentions. Only one intention can be executed at any given time. The choice of that intention depends on the agent's beliefs and the meta-level intentions. Further details on dMARS can be found elsewhere (d'Inverno et al. 1997).

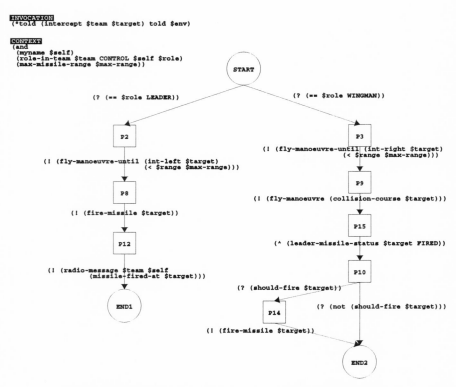

Figure 2: Team Tactics for conducting a pincer intercept

The Operator-Agent

The model of a human operator has been divided into two components: (1) the physical aspects (e.g., sensors, actuators, human body and its limitations, etc.); and (2) the reasoning and decision making performed by the human operator. The physical aspects have been implemented using standard modelling techniques.

The implementation of the BDI agent that models the reasoning of a human operator involved in military operations required the design and development of specialized features. These were done using a variety of BDI features and have resulted in a type of agent referred to as the "Operator-Agent". In the context of the Operator-Agent we refer to plans as *tactics*.

The Design of the Operator-Agent

A model of an operator that operates in highly dynamic environments has to address specific problems such as the strategies for monitoring the environment, the strategies for monitoring and adjustment of the achievement of goals and tactics, and decision making speed. The Operator-Agent includes specialized components for: (1) for dynamic monitoring of the environment; (2) monitoring and adjustment of achievement of goals and tactics; and (3) adjusting the decision making speed.

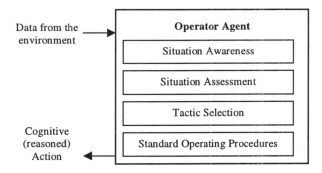

Figure 3: Agent's Architectural Design

The functional decomposition of the Operator-Agent includes the following modules (see Figure 3). **Situation Awareness** module for maintaining the agent's perceived view of the environment. **Situation Assessment** module for examining the perceived situation and producing a subjective evaluation. **Standard Operating Procedures** module containing knowledge about available tactical behaviour. **Tactics Selection** module for responding to the evaluated situation and selecting relevant tactical responses from the available Standard Operating Procedures.

Environment Monitoring

An Operator-Agent receives continuous sensory input. From this sensory input the Operator-Agent identifies an abstract situation and then re-evaluates this situation. This process is referred to as *situation assessment*. The process of situation assessment is relatively computationally intensive and is performed only as required.

Situation awareness allows the agent to determine the conditions for invoking situation assessment. This decision is itself situation specific and depends on the current activities of the agent. The processes of tactics execution and situation assessment can dynamically modify the conditions for invoking situation assessment.

Monitoring and Adjustment of Goals and Tactics

As mentioned before the Operator-Agent must exhibit a combination of reactive and goal-driven behaviour in a dynamic environment. These two features demand that the Operator-Agent continuously monitor and adjust its goals and the tactics it employs in achieving these goals. This is achieved using three specific mechanisms: (1) least commitment approach; (2) elimination of irrelevant goals; and (3) re-evaluation and re-selection of tactics.

The least commitment approach is part of the dMARS model. It allows the agent to commit to the means of achieving the sub-goal at the last possible moment. The agent can select the most appropriate plan for that time instead of committing in advance to a plan that may prove to be inappropriate when it should be executed.

In a dynamic environment it often happens that suspended intentions to achieve a previous goal or respond to a previous situation become redundant. Maintenance and housekeeping of goals and intentions are performed. In the Operator-Agent such maintenance is performed whenever a new goal is added to the Operator-Agent, a new reaction

is required, or a tactic has been completed.

When a suspended intention (or tactic) is restarted the agent re-evaluates the tactics used in achieving the goal. This evaluation involves a two step process: (1) determining what would be the best tactics to employ in the new situation; and (2) determining the exact sub-goal in the chosen tactics in which execution should proceed.

Decision Making Speed

In a real military operations there are variety of operators with varying levels of knowledge and experience. An experienced pilot may not only know more tactics but may also react faster under pressure. The agent's tactical knowledge is modelled using a variety of tactical (i.e., plan) libraries. The experience of the operator is modelled through the use of different tactical libraries and a specification of the reaction and decision making. The analyst defining the simulation can determine the time it would take the Operator-Agent to perform certain activities or make a decision. These times could be situation specific and can change dynamically.

Satisfying the Requirements

The simulation environment requirements (Requirements 10-14) state that the model used should include an explicit and well-understood formulation of the modelled behaviour. In the BDI approach specification of agent behaviour is based on the concept of a plan.

A plan is an abstract combination of sub-goals to be achieved and actions to be taken. Such plans can either be generated on the fly using a planner or can be specified in advance in plan libraries. A typical agent-oriented plan language is a high-level language (Requirement 11). This allows the analyst to gain a better understanding of the agent's behaviour (Requirement 12).

Plans are reasoned about and executed using some form of an engine that is capable of performing complex reasoning and follow some decision making procedure, e.g., means-ends analysis (Requirement 4). The nature and complexity of the reasoning is a combination of the engine itself and the plans it manipulates. These could be modified to allow for varying levels of knowledge and abilities (Requirement 13). The decision making speed depends on the complexity of the plan and reasoning. Using abstract plans provided in advance and combining them during execution allows for the real-time response (Requirement 14).

Note that the behaviour of the agent is completely dependent on the knowledge provided in the plans and the algorithm of the engine. Thus, the behaviour of the system is completely deterministic. This together with deterministic simulation of the scenario's dynamics leads to fully repeatable simulation (Requirement 10).

The explicit representation of the goals and intentions of the agent allows the agent to maintain multiple simultaneous goals (Requirement 5). This feature combined with the continuous interleaving of sensing, reasoning, and acting ensures that the agent both reacts to the changing world and interleaves goal-driven and data-driven behaviours (Requirement 6). As to situation awareness (Requirement 3) it seems that as the level of understanding of this mental process increases so does the ability to provide a formal agent-oriented model for it.

A high-level representation of beliefs and knowledge allows the agent to reason about data as well as abstract concepts (Requirement 13). Furthermore the agent can represent in some basic way social concepts such as teams, sub-teams, and roles in a team (Requirement 8). Other social phenomena such as structures for an organisation are still under investigation.

Although agents can exhibit very complex behaviour, this behaviour must be explicitly specified. It follows that they can not actually exhibit behaviour that is not well understood or follow procedures that are not clearly defined. Furthermore, such an approach does not lend itself to performing complex transformations of data (or numbers) or the filtering of such data (or numbers).

Such are the characteristics of some of the required behaviours specified above. In particular it seems that current agent-oriented systems are not very effective in performing sensing (Requirement 1) and incorporating a model of emotions (Requirement 7).

Another required behaviour which current agent-oriented systems are unable to provide is innovative behaviour (Requirement 9). This limitation goes together with the requirement for real-time performance (Requirement 14). With limitations of current technology, and our limited understanding of how humans invent novel responses, real-time simulation of such behaviour is presently impossible.

As mentioned above, the characteristics of the specification language and the reasoning engines that execute and manipulate these specifications in agent-oriented systems make them well suited for simulating human reasoning. By the same token, the characteristics of the dynamics of physical systems and the way actions taken affect the world (Requirement 2) make agent-oriented systems unsuitable for simulating them.

To overcome these limitations, both requirements 1 and 2 are currently modelled using standard modelling techniques. The information collected by the sensors is sent to the Operator-Agent and it in-turn sends high-level acting instructions to the actuators.

Implementing an Operational System

The Development Process

The initial concept of using agent-oriented technology for modelling human operators in military operations was introduced in early 1991 with a concept demonstrator (Rao et al. 1992). The development of an operational Operator-Agent, from initial specification to a fully functional operational system, took close to three years. The system has been in operational use since June 1996.

Wooldrige and Jennings (Wooldrige and Jennings 1998), note that developing agent-oriented systems is a software engineering task that includes additional risks – namely the risks associated with developing embedded real-time distributed systems. We also prescribe to this approach and have adopted state-of-the-art Software Engineering and Software Project Management techniques to mitigate these risks. The system has been developed to IEEE standards and we have adopted an iterative software development process with incremental delivery of functionality.

The behaviour of the Operator-Agent has been independently verified and validated by domain experts. This was achieved through the specification of operational scenarios and the desired behaviour. Furthermore, tracing of plan execution in the Operator-Agent has been used in validating the decision-making processes.

Given the complexity of the development and the risks involved we had to establish a specialised team. In particular we required (1) expert knowledge of the required functionality and the domain knowledge; (2) expert knowledge of the existing technology and simulation systems; (3) expert knowledge of the new technology and artificial intelligence; and (4) expert knowledge of developing advanced software systems.

The key to the successful development was the characteristics of the development team. The team included operational analysts, experts in the existing simulation systems, experts in artificial intelligence, and experts in software engineering and software project management.

The number of active team members and their expertise changed depending on the stage of the project. There were 14 people involved with an average of 8 experts actively engaged throughout the development process.

The operational analysts that use the system would typically have background in operational research, aeronautical engineering, applied mathematics, or physics. The deployment of the system to operational analysts took close to 6 months and commenced close to the completion of development. The deployment included educating operational analysts on the agent-oriented language used in developing the Operator-Agent and its tactical behaviour. Operational analysts are currently performing the maintenance, enhancement, and development of the Operator-Agent as part of their routine development of human operator models.

Occasional reviews of the Operator-Agent are performed by operational analysts and agent-oriented experts. These experts are brought in specifically for this task. To date there have not been any major design changes required.

Implementation Details

The particular implementation of the Operator-Agent involves plans, database relations, database entries, goals, and intentions. The number of plans in the agent's plan library varies from agent to agent depending on the skills and capabilities of that agent. A typical Operator-Agent has over 400 plans in its plan library.

As to the agent's database, again this number varies from agent to agent. A typical agent has close to 300 predicates defined in its database. These predicates represent the types of declarative knowledge the Operator-Agent can reason about. The amount of data stored in the agent's database depends on the size of the unfolding scenario and the information the agent has about it. A typical agent in a scenario with 32 pilots (i.e., 24 vs. 8) has approximately 800 database entries in the database.

The number of concurrent goals held by a typical agent depends on the state of the mission. The agent would typically hold around 10 concurrent goals. These goals relate to the various operations of the aircraft and achievement of the mission.

In addition to these goals the agent also has data driven behaviours in which it reacts to the various inputs from its sensors. In a typical state the agent processes, in parallel, data for as many as 8 contacts, evaluating the threat they pose to the pilot. This is done using between 10 and 14 intentions that are processed in less than 50 milliseconds. Overall, a typical Operator-Agent handles over 25 concurrent intentions on a regular basis. The overall decision making time for the Operator-Agent is modifiable to allow for modelling of pilots with a variety of decision-making capabilities. The Operator-Agent is currently running on Silicon Graphics computers running the IRIX 6.4 operating system.

Integration with Existing Simulation Systems

The approach adopted involves building a powerful operator model capable of interfacing with existing simulation systems. The key is to separate the reasoning models, physical models, and visualisation software.

From a modelling perspective, we replaced the existing reasoning processes in the existing simulation system with interfaces to the Operator-Agent. From a simulation perspective we combined time-stepped simulation of physical systems with event-based (but time dependent) operator reasoning processes. The interfacing software passes messages about the perceived physical world to the reasoning software, and transmits back instructions for continuing or changing the present action.

The existing physical models still contains routines for aircraft and systems control, such as fighter intercept and combat manoeuvres and the logic of highly dynamic one-on-one close combat counter-manoeuvring. Not transferring this to the Operator-Agent reduces the amount of information that must be passed through the interface. The reasoning system performs the role of tactician rather than that of the pilot. Tactical instructions are coded as manoeuvres to be flown or system control instructions.

Benefits and Limitations

Both technical and organisational benefits emerged from the development of the Operator-Agent. At the technical level the main benefit is that the operational analyst can now modify the knowledge base, representing the tactics and decision-making, without being concerned about the remaining physical systems modelling code. This reduced

tactical development time from 4-6 weeks to 4-6 days.

In addition this approach is eminently suited to dealing with extensive repertoires of procedural team tactics. Simulating military operations involves modelling multiple aircraft types, multiple roles, multiple weapons systems, multiple sensors, and communication systems. The accuracy of the models directly affects the fidelity of the simulation and the effectiveness of using it as a tool for understanding and analysing military operations. Incorporating intelligent agents enables higher levels of fidelity in studies of larger scenarios.

At the organisational level the main benefit is that operational analyst need only work at the high level, formulating concepts, determining mission goals, and developing pilot tactics. The use of such high level concepts has made the model easier to understand by the military personnel and hence improved the elicitation of operational knowledge and behaviour.

The operational analyst is now concerned with the explicit development of cognitive models of the human operator. This has brought the work of operational analysts and human factors experts closer together. This manifests itself in shared terminology, mutually rewarding interactions, and shared research directions.

In previous work we suggested detailed models and provided detailed analysis of the use of agent-oriented technology for tactics selection (McIlroy and Heinze 1996, Tidhar et al. 1995). These models clearly demonstrate several important technical properties:

- Agent plans are written using a graphical format that is highly recognisable as a logical flow chart. The analyst is able to concentrate on creating the logical processes rather than on the code to represent them.
- The Agent plans are easily read with only minor familiarisation with the system conventions.
- Plans are very readily edited using drag and drop tools. An edited plan can be recompiled and linked without re-compilation of remaining code.
- Plans are executed when their invocation matches the defined conditions (e.g., a radar contact) provided that their context and properties (e.g., priority) are appropriate. The analyst does not have to code the environment that calls a plan; plans invoke other plans.
- The execution of plans (i.e., intentions) is controlled through meta-level plans that resolve conflicts between plans by identification of intentions or goals. A plan can fail without affecting overall execution; alternative plans with the same invocation are used to recover. Otherwise control returns to the meta-level plans. Success or failure of a plan can be noted and used to manipulate the process.
- Intentions can be suspended until conditions are again appropriate (e.g., missile evasion suspends strike mission).
- Plan libraries can represent different types of human operators. The plans can be controlled at run time, enabling control of the representation of participants (e.g., experienced leader, rookie wingman, etc.).
- The system can be stepped or stopped for examination of the reasoning processes. Invoked plans can appear on-

screen with progressive highlighting of execution paths.
These characteristics enable educated users to rapidly develop very complex reasoning processes. The system has the high readability and traceability required for working with domain experts, such as fighter pilots and fighter controllers. This enables Air Force operational personnel to gain confidence in studies of operational effectiveness. A substantial increase in the productivity of operational analysts has been primarily gained due to:

1. The ease of implementing and modifying the behaviour of the model of human operators.
2. The increased level of abstraction in the representation of declarative and procedural knowledge in this model.
3. The improved interaction between operational analysts, human operators, and human factors experts.

The model has been successfully used for operational analysis and evaluation of multi-billion dollar acquisitions.

The main limitation of the above approach is in current state-of-the-art Agent-Oriented technology. There is still no clear and complete Agent-Oriented Analysis and Design methodology. In developing the Pilot-Agent we used a modified Object-Oriented methodology. Although this has proven useful it has been done on a relatively ad-hoc basis. This limitation is particularly significant given the background of the operational analysts. To overcome this limitation emphasis is given to reviews of the design and implementation of the Operator-Agent.

Concluding Remarks

Defence organisations are primarily interested conducting successful and efficient military operations. These operations rely on the performance of the available defence systems and the expertise of the humans operating them.
Modelling and simulation of these operations a priority for defence organisations in evaluating existing and proposed defence systems. Modelling the human operators is critical to conducting such evaluations.
Research into candidate technologies for the modelling of human decision making led to the selection of agent-oriented technology for the development of the Operator-Agent. The Operator-Agent has been integrated into existing simulation systems and has been is in use since June 1996 by DSTO for the conduct of operations research. The model is being successfully used for operational performance analysis, evaluation of multi-billion dollar acquisitions, and development of standard operating procedures with the Royal Australian Air Force. Many of the technical benefits of agent-oriented technology were expected – indeed they were the reason for the adoption of the technology. The organisational benefits were largely unforeseen during the early stages of the project. The proliferation of the technology throughout DSTO and the strength of the commitment to further research are good indicators of the magnitude of these benefits and are at the core of the way DSTO conducts business.

Acknowledgments

We thank Serena Steuart, David McIlroy, Mario Selvestrel, Arvind Chandran, Martin Cross, Anand Rao, Paolo Busetta, and Andrew Lucas for their contribution to the development of the Operator-Agent. We also thank the anonymous reviewers for their valuable comments.

References

1. Bent, N. E., 1993. The TAC BRAWLER Air Combat Analyst Manual (Rev 6.1). Decision-Science Applications Report #906.
2. Boeing, 1985. Advanced Air-to-Air System Performance Model (AASPEM) Users Manual. Boeing Document D180-28938-1.
3. Bratman, M.,1987. Intentions, Plans, and Practical Reason. Harvard University Press, Cambridge, MA.
4. d'Inverno, M., Kinny, D., Luck, M., and Wooldrige, M., 1997. A Formal Specification of dMARS. In *Proceedings of the 4th International Workshop on Theories, Architectures and Languages*.
5. McIlroy, D. and Heinze, C., 1996. Air Combat Tactics Implementation in the Smart Whole AiR Mission Model (SWARMM). In *Proceedings of the SimTecT Conference*, Melbourne, Australia.
6. Rao, A., Morley, D., Selvestrel, M., and Murray, G., 1992. Representation, Selection, and Execution of Team Tactics in Air Combat Modelling. In *Proceedings of the Australian Joint Conference on Artificial Intelligence*.
7. Rao, A. S. and Georgeff, M. P., 1995. BDI Agents: From Theory to Practice. In *Proceedings of the First International Conference on Multi-Agent Systems*.
8. Rao, A. S., 1997. A Unified View of Plans as Recipes. Contemporary Action Theory, ed. Holmstrom-Hintikka, G. and Tuomela, R., Kluwer Academic Publishers, The Netherlands.
9. Shaw, R. L., 1985. Fighter Combat Tactics and Maneuvering. US Naval Institute Press, 6th Edition.
10. Tambe, M. and Jones, R. M. and Laird, J. E. and Rosenbloom, P. S. and Schwamb, K., 1994. Building Believable Agents for Simulation Environments: Extended Abstract. In *Collected Papers of the SOAR/IFOR Project*, Information Sciences Institute, University of Southern California, pages 78-81. Marina del Ray, CA.
11. Tidhar, G., Murray, G., and Steuart S., 1995. Computer-Generated Forces and Agent-Oriented Technology. In *Proceedings of the Australian Joint Conference on Artificial Intelligence Workshop on AI in Defence*, Canberra, Australia.
12. Wooldrige, M. J. and Jennings, N. R., 1998. Pitfalls of Agent-Oriented Development. In *Proceedings of the Second International Conference on Autonomous Agents*, Minneapolis, USA.

Emerging Applications

Nurse Scheduling using Constraint Logic Programming

Slim Abdennadher
Computer Science Institute, University of Munich
Oettingenstr. 67, 80538 Munich, Germany
Slim.Abdennadher@informatik.uni-muenchen.de

Hans Schlenker
Technical University of Berlin
Franklinstr. 28/29, 10587 Berlin, Germany
hans@cs.tu-berlin.de

Abstract

The nurse scheduling problem consists of assigning working shifts to each nurse on each day of a certain period of time. A typical problem comprises 600 to 800 assignments that have to take into account several requirements such as minimal allocation of a station, legal regulations and wishes of the personnel. This planning is a difficult and time-consuming expert task and is still done manually. INTERDIP[1] is an advanced industrial prototype that supports semi-automatic creation of such rosters. Using the artificial intelligence approach, constraint reasoning and constraint programming, INTERDIP creates a roster interactively within some minutes instead of by hand some hours. Additionally, it mostly produces better results. INTERDIP was developed in collaboration with Siemens Nixdorf. It was presented at the Systems'98 Computer exhibition in Munich and several companies have inquired to market our system.

Introduction

Many real-life problems lead to combinatorial search, computationally a very intensive task. Unfortunately, no general method exists for solving this kind of problems efficiently. The automatic generation of duty rosters for hospital wards falls under this class of problems.

Since the manually generated solution of the nurse scheduling problem usually requires several hours of work, a lot of research has been done to reduce the amount of time needed in the roster development. The most popular technique is based on mathematical programming (War76). The main disadvantage of this approach is the difficulty of incorporating application-specific constraints into the problem formulation. Other methods include goal programming (AR81) and heuristic models (SWB79).

Recently, Constraint Logic Programming (JM94; FA97; MS98) (CLP) has become a promising approach for solving scheduling problems. CLP combines the advantages of two declarative paradigms: logic programming and constraint solving. In logic programming, problems are stated in a declarative way using rules to define relations (predicates). Problems are solved using chronological backtrack search to explore choices. In constraint solving, efficient special-purpose algorithms are employed to solve sub-problems involving distinguished relations referred to as constraints, which can be considered as pieces of partial information. The nurse scheduling problem can be elegantly formalized as a constraint satisfaction problem (Mac92) and implemented by means of specialized constraint solving techniques that are available in CLP languages.

In this paper, the generation of duty rosters for hospitals is tackled using the CLP framework. The System is called INTERDIP and has been successfully tested on a real ward at the "*Klinikum Innenstadt*" hospital in Munich (AS97). INTERDIP has been implemented in collaboration with Siemens-Nixdorf-Informationssysteme AG using IF/Prolog (Sie96b) which includes a constraint package (Sie96a) based on CHIP (DVS[+]88). This package includes, among others linear equations, constraints over finite domains and boolean constraints.

The nurse scheduling problem consists in assigning a working shift to each nurse on each day of a planning period (usually one month), whereby several requirements must be considered, such as minimal allocation of a ward, legal regulations and wishes of the personnel. Usually not all specified requirements can be fulfilled. The nurse scheduling problem can be modelled as a partial constraint satisfaction problem (FW92). It requires the processing of *hard* and *soft* constraints to cope with. Hard constraints are conditions that must be satisfied, soft constraints may be violated, but should be satisfied as far as possible.

Several approaches have been proposed to deal with soft constraints: Hierarchical constraint logic programming (HCLP) (BFW92) supports a hierarchical organizaton of constraints, where a constraint on some level is more important than any set of constraints from lower levels. To avoid the so called inter-hierarchy comparison in HCLP, the soft constraints are encoded in a hierarchical constraint satisfaction problem (HCSP) (Mey97). The Conplan/SIEDAplan (Mey97) considers the representation of nurse scheduling as a HCSP, where legal

---

regulations are hard constraints and wishes of nurses usually have the lowest priority level. The result is also not necessarily of a reasonable quality in respect to the nurse's wishes.

However, in practice nurses' wishes should be considered in order to support the working climate. Furthermore, some wishes of nurses are sometimes more important than some legal regulations. To deal with these requirements, INTERDIP provides a solution technique based on a variant of branch-and-bound search instead of chronological backtracking. This approach starts with a solution and requires the next solution to be better. Quality is measured by a suitable cost function. The cost function depends on the set of satisfied soft constraints.

To improve on the theoretical complexity of the problem, our system is based on an imitation of the human way of solving the problem: A roster is generated with INTERDIP through several *phases*. Additionally, several days in the roster are assigned simultaneously through user defined *patterns*. A pattern describes a preferred sequence of working days.

With INTERDIP, a user who is to some extent familiar with nurse scheduling can interactively generate a roster within minutes.

The paper is organized as follows. The next section introduces the nurse scheduling problem. Then we show how the problem can be modelled as a partial constraint satisfaction problem. In Section 4 and Section 5 we describe the implementation and the user interface. Finally, we conclude with an evaluation of our tool. Portions of this paper were taken from (AS99).

Description of the problem

In a hospital, a new duty roster must be generated for each ward monthly. A hospital ward is an organizational unit that has to fulfil some concrete tasks, and has both rooms and personnel, the nurses, at its disposal. Usually, the wards of a hospital are completely distinct: each has its own rooms and its own personnel. Therefore all rosters of a hospital can be scheduled separately. We consider in the following the scheduling problem for one ward.

A roster of one month is an assignment of the personnel of the ward to the shifts for all the days of the month. A shift is a working unit: in a common working model, each day has the units *morning shift* (e.g. 06:00 to 15:00), *evening shift* (14:00 to 23:00), and *night shift* (22:00 to 07:00) and possibly others. To each shift of every day, personnel has to be assigned.

For the generation of a roster, different kinds of constraints must be taken into account:

- *Legal regulations*, e.g. the maximum working time of a person per day or week, or time off in lieu, or maternity leave. In Germany for example the statutory monthly core working hours for a hospital with a 37.5 hour week is about 160 hours depending on the month. So, with an average shift length of 8 hours,

each nurse has to work on average 20 shifts. Another law says that between two (working-) shifts, each nurse has to have a break of at least 11 hours ("11 hours rule"). If a nurse works one day in the night shift, she must therefore not be assigned the morning or evening shift the next day. Also a morning shift must not follow an evening shift.

- *Organizational rules* are those that apply specifically to one particular hospital, a part of a hospital or even only one ward. They are given by the respective management. Those are mainly the number and kind of the shifts and – within statutory limits – the minimum personnel allocation of each ward. In the following we consider a model with three shifts: morning, evening and night shift. To morning shift and evening shift at least three nurses must be assigned, and the night shift requires at least two nurses.

- *Personnel data* define the individual frame for each person. These are mainly the contractually established monthly core working time, pending vacation and accrued hours of overtime. If, for example, a nurse has 16 hours overtime, she might be scheduled two shifts less than average.

- Finally, *wishes* are requirements given by the personnel. These are mostly wishes to have some days off, for example at weekends, holidays, birthdays, or for a vacation period.

Often, there is no duty roster that fulfills all the constraints. Therefore we distinguish two kinds of constraints. Hard constraints must always be satisfied, soft constraints may be violated. Roughly speaking, legal regulations, organizational rules and personnel data determine hard constraints, wishes may be hard or soft constraints. So for example the vacation scheduling might be done for a longer term (some months) apart from the actual roster planning. Then a wish for one day of vacation would be a hard constraint, because it was planned externally. Other wishes are mostly soft constraints. Often the nurses have the opportunity to classify their wishes into some "priority levels". If possible, the wishes in one of those levels will then be regarded as hard constraints.

A roster is correct, iff all hard constraints hold. The quality of a roster results from the number of the fulfilled soft constraints and their priorities.

Modeling the problem as PCSP

Constraint Satisfaction Problems (CSPs) have been a subject of research in artificial intelligence for many years. A CSP is a pair (V, C), where V is a finite set of variables, each associated with a finite domain, and C is a finite set of constraints. A *solution* of a CSP maps each variable to a value of its domain such that all the constraints are satisfied. A *partial constraint satisfaction problem* (PCSP) (FW92) is a triple (V, C, ω), where (V, C) is a CSP and ω maps constraints to weights. A constraint's weight expresses the importance of its fulfillment, allowing to distinguish *hard constraints*, which must not be violated, from *soft constraints*, which should not be violated, but may be violated in case this is unavoidable. Hard constraints have an infinite weight. The finite weights of soft constraints allow for the specification of priorities among constraints. A *solution* of a PCSP maps each variable to a value of its domain such that all hard constraints are satisfied and the total weight of the violated soft constraints is minimal.

In the representation of nurse scheduling as a PCSP, there is a constraint variable for each nurse on each day. The domains of the variables consist of possible shifts (also comprising vacations, recuperation of a worked public holiday, special leaves, maternity protection, unpaid leave etc.), so they usually consist of 10 values. (HW96) proposed a reduction of variable domains, based on elimination of interchangeable values introduced by Freuder (Fre91). The values of the above mentioned free shifts, e.g. vacations, can be reduced to only one value and each variable takes its values now in $\{0, 1, 2, 3\}$. For a nurse i and a day j a variable V_{ij} may have one of the following values:

- $V_{ij} = 0$: The nurse i is off-duty the day j.

- $V_{ij} = 1$: The nurse i is assigned to the "morning" shift on the day j.

- $V_{ij} = 2$: The nurse i is assigned to the "evening" shift on the day j.

- $V_{ij} = 3$: The nurse i is assigned to the "night" shift on the day j.

Reducing the variable domains from 10 values to 4 considerably improves the efficiency of the solution research. Figure 1 shows a complete schedule for 10 nurses and 14 days. Each row comprises the shifts of a certain nurse. The columns contain the shifts performed on a certain day. So, each square of the chart specifies for each nurse the working days and shifts, and days off. E.g. on the 4th day the second nurse Hilde is scheduled in shift 1, i.e. morning shift.

Now we describe how to express the most important requirements of our application in terms of IF/Prolog-Constraints (Sie96b). In the following, we use a Prolog-like notation with meta-variables. We denote the total number of nurses to be scheduled by s, the total number of days by t and a variable by V_{ij}, where i denotes the number of the nurse or the row in the roster, respectively, and j denotes the number of the day, i.e. the column in the roster. With this notation, we can write down all the variables of this modeling in a list: $[V11, V12, \ldots, Vst]$.

One requirement for a correct roster is the minimum personal allocation, i.e. the minimal number of nurses, the ward must be allocated each shift. Actually, the allocation is limited downward *and* upward. Let Min1 be the lower and Max1 be the upper allocation limit for the morning shift and Min2, Max2, Min3 and Max3 the

	1	2	3	4	5	6	7	8	9	10	11	12	13	14
KarinG			2	2	2	2	2		1	1			2	2
Hilde		1	1	1	3	3			2	2	2	3	3	
Gerda	1	3	3				2	2	2	2	2			3
Gerd		1	1	1	2	2		2	3	3			1	1
Hubert		2	2	3	3	3			1	1	1	1	1	
Anna	2	2	2		1	1				1	1	2	2	2
Norbert	2	3	3			1	1	1	1	2				
EddaA	1	2		2	2	2	3	3				1	1	1
EddaB	3			1	1	1	1	1			2	2	2	2
Ina		1	1	2					3	3	3			

File   Wishes   Ranges   Patterns   Options   Debugger   Phases

Legend: ' ' free (shift), '1' morning shift, '2' evening shift, '3' night shift

Figure 1: A nurse schedule for 10 nurses over a period of 14 days

lower and upper limits for the evening and night shifts, respectively. Therefore a correct roster must not have less than Min1 and more than Max1 times the '1' in each column and not less than Min2 and not more than Max2 the '2' and so on. So we have to state for each j $(1 \le j \le t)$ and each k $(k \in \{1, 2, 3\})$ the following constraint:

```
cardinality(Mink,Maxk,[V1j=k,V2j=k,...,Vsj=k])
```

where cardinality(Lower,Upper,Condition) is satisfied if at least *Lower* and at most *Upper* conditions in the list *Condition* are satisfied.

Another requirement a schedule has to fulfil is the compliance of the monthly core working hours of each nurse. This means that there is a lower bound and an upper bound of shifts, each nurse is to be assigned in the schedule period. This is the number of all the morning, evening and night shifts. This can be expressed simpler by the number of free shifts. Let for each nurse i $(1 \le i \le s)$ the lower bound for the working shifts be given by Min$i$ and the upper bound by Max$i$. Then we can formulate the working hours requirement using the cardinality constraint:

```
cardinality(t-Maxi,t-Mini,[Vi1=0,...,Vit=0])
```

The "11 hours rule" implies that a nurse must not work a morning shift (the day) after an evening shift and may work (the day) after a night shift only a night shift. We can express the "11 hours rule" by the following expression: If V_{ij} is assigned a specific value, the assignment of $Vi(j + 1)$ must fulfill a certain condition. This can be expressed directly by the domain_if constraint. We state for each i $(1 \le i \le s)$ and for each j $(1 \le j < t)$:

```
domain_if(Vij = 2, Vi(j + 1) \= 1) and
domain_if(Vij = 3, Vi(j + 1) in [0,3]).
```

The constraint `domain_if(Condition, ThenGoal)` is used to call a goal conditionally. If the arithmetic constraint *Condition* is satisfied, *ThenGoal* is called. If the arithmetic constraint is not satisfiable, `true` is called. The execution of the `domain_if` constraint is delayed as long as the satisfiability of *Condition* has not been determined.

Free shifts, provided they can be considered hard wishes, lead to immediate variable assignments. A wish (e.g. vacation) of nurse i at day j can then be stated as: `Vij = 0`.

Soft wishes, like all other soft conditions, can not be stated directly as (IF/Prolog-)constraints, since our constraint solver can only handle hard constraints. We only can use them for optimizing correct rosters. This will be explained in Section .

Planning in INTERDIP

The modeling just described, while being simple and straightforward, is unfortunately very costly: The search space is huge, i.e. 4^{600} for 20 nurses and a period of one month. Therefore we developed a method to prune the search tree which was inspired by the usual manual planning.

Planning by hand

Because of the huge search space a roster is usually generated by hand in two phases. In the first phase we have all liberties for assigning the cells of the roster. Therefore here we do the most complicated assignment (which is tied to most of the conditions): the allocation of the free days or shifts. Those are bound to a lot of constraints: they determine how many shifts a nurse has to work during the scheduled period, how many nurses over all shifts the ward is assigned each day, and not least most of the wishes are to be considered here: the wishes for free shifts (e.g. vacations). Closely connected with the free shifts are the night shifts: the "11 hour rule" enforces for the assignment of shifts to a nurse, that after a night shift there may follow only a night shift or a free shift (free day).

Therefore, when manually scheduling, the free and the night shifts are allocated in the first phase. In the second phase, the morning and the evening shifts are distributed among the not yet allocated cells of the roster.

The obvious advantage of the scheduling in two phases over the scheduling in one phase is the reduction of complexity: in each phase there have to be considered fewer constraints and, above all, fewer assignments[2].

---

[2]The assignment of the first phase is normally not changed within the second unless it is then impossible to get a solution and a change in the free and night shifts will probably enable one. The extent of those changes can be neglected: we never observed more than 10 changes.

Phasewise plan generation

In 1993, (van93) presented a partial automatic solution to the nurse scheduling problem that used two very different phases. It flexibly generated good rosters but did not handle night shifts. INTERDIP uses more than two phases which are performed in the same manner by one constraint solver.

We wanted to reduce the search space even further than (van93) did. The idea is to furthermore decompose the problem. We use three phases instead of two:

1st Phase Distribution of the free shifts.

2nd Phase Distribution of the night shifts.

3rd Phase Distribution of the morning and the evening shifts.

With this modeling, in each phase for every cell of the roster, only the minimal decision between two possibilities has to be made. This reduces the search space. We will see how we obtain a complete roster after the three phases.

In each phase, every variable is assigned a value out of the boolean domain $\{0, 1\}$. Depending on the phase, the values 0 and 1 have different meanings. If a variable in the first phase is assigned the value one, this means that the roster gets a free shift in the appropriate cell. The cells whose variables are bound to 0 remain undecided. The second phase only treats the undecided cells: if a variable gets the value 1, the cell is assigned a night shift. The rest remains undecided. In the third phase each still not decided cell is filled with either morning or evening shift, depending on whether the variable was assigned a 1 or a 0, respectively (see Figure 2, the meaning of the bold numbers is just as in Figure 1.). A complete roster results from all three phases.

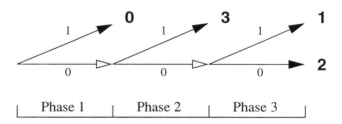

Figure 2: Allocation of the cells in three phases.

Assignment patterns

Because of the incomplete constraint propagation methods used for scheduling problems, the application programmer often has to explicitly use a labeling phase in which a backtracking search blindly tries different values for the variables. Since labeling is expensive, the programmer needs to employ techniques for reducing the search space. There is a variety of techniques to do this. For our application we add domain information about presumably good solutions by introducing *patterns*. A pattern describes a preferred sequence of working days. Coherent cells of the roster are allocated along user defined patterns.

As shown above, the variables are declared in each phase to range over the values 0 and 1 and the appropriate shifts are registered into the roster. Patterns are then meaningful combinations of roster entries, whereby a combination stands for successive days. A large number of these patterns is known. For example, we consider meaningful the combination of five days work and two days free. The appropriate pattern for the first phase, in which the working days are determined, is then: (?, ?, ?, ?, ?, 0, 0). If we assume that it is better to work on three successive days in the same shift than in different ones, we formulate for the second phase and thus for the night shifts: (3,3,3). Each phase has its own set of patterns. The patterns of a phase have an order in which they are selected: first, the ones which result in a *good* solution, since the nurses are accustomed to this pattern, and at the end trivial patterns which are necessary to generate solutions, if they exist. For filling the roster, the given patterns are translated into appropriate variable assignments which are then tried in each row from left to right.

The patterns can be considered as requirements of minor priority (soft constraints) as well as probable parts of solutions. Schedules that comply with the given patterns are explored first. Applying this specialized labeling method reorganizes the search space.

Additionally, each pattern is assigned a cost value so that for example a nurse whose wishes could not be fully fulfilled, more likely gets "better" work patterns assigned.

Optimal rosters

A roster that satisfies all hard constraints is considered feasible but this does not necessarily mean that it is sufficiently good to be used by a hospital ward.

The concept of an optimal roster is hard to define. Generally, roster quality is a subjective matter and its definition changes from problem to problem. We apply the usual measure which is common to all applications in the field of scheduling. It is given in terms of the number and the priority of soft constraints that are violated.

A popular approach consists in using a branch and bound search instead of chronological backtracking. Branch and bound starts out from a solution and requires the next solution to be better. Quality is measured by a suitable cost function. The cost function depends on the set of satisfied soft constraints. With this approach, however, soft constraints are only part of the cost function but play no role in selecting variables and values. In our multiphase method, branch and bound search is performed three times to improve the roster generated so far.

Costs arise separately for each nurse and the algorithm tries to minimize the maximum of these. This means that we have a separate cost function for each

of the nurses and the maximum value of all the functions is minimized. So, INTERDIP tries to achieve that no nurse gets a much worse allocation (e.g. no wishes satisfied) than the others.

Using the system interactively

For a nurse scheduling system to be complete, a flexible user interface should be provided, so that the specific requirements of the problem can be stated easily. INTERDIP provides such an interface.

The INTERDIP user interface has been developed using the Tcl/Tk extension of IF/Prolog. Figure 1 shows a snapshot of the top-level graphical user interface to our nurse scheduling program with a generated roster.

The interface allows the user to define the system parameters as preferred. All parameters like minimal and maximal allocation of the ward for each phase, wishes or patterns can be given graphically or in a spreadsheet.

The wishes are given in three categories: imperative, important and less important wishes. We call them *red*, *black* and *white* wishes, respectively. This naming goes back to how the wishes were actually formulated in the hospital where we tested INTERDIP: They were filled into a plan using red and black pencils. The white wishes are to some extent standard wishes, like not to work on weekends. Red wishes (like vacation) are later treated as hard constraints and all the others as soft constraints. A single wish always relates to exactly one nurse and one day.

Usually the generation of a roster runs as follows. After the user has specified all the conditions he will trigger the phases. A phase starts with generating the constraints and testing their consistency. Then, according to the above method, an optimal solution is computed. After a phase is finished, the next one is started initialized with the best result of the preceding phase, and so on. This is the automatic generation.

It may happen that there exists not even one roster that complies with all the given hard constraints. Then the problem is called *over-constrained*. INTERDIP may detect this while generating the IF/Prolog constraints and then gives the user hints which of the conditions led to the inconsistency. However, there are kinds of contradictions that are not automatically detected. Therefore we built a debugger into INTERDIP.

Being an interactive tool, INTERDIP lets the user take part in the generation in different ways. Firstly the user usually has some freedom in specifying the problem conditions. He can directly influence the planning by giving some red wishes which directly lead to variable bindings. But the user can also interfere with a concrete process of allocation: He can use the debugger to break the computation manually or to set breakpoints. At the breakpoint (a cell of the roster), he is given all the possible patterns out of which he can choose one. The computation then continues with the selected allocation. In the single-step-mode the computation is stopped after each single allocation. Additionally the user can undo allocations already made.

With the debugger, the user can manually allocate parts of the roster in order to improve automatically presented solutions on the one hand and, in case the generator did not find a solution at all, enable one on the other hand.

In addition, the user can manually alter a completely generated roster and let it check by INTERDIP. The system then tries to state all the constraints for the given variable assignments, and if one fails, it gives the user hints about the contradictions.

Conclusion

In this paper, the nurse scheduling problem is discussed and a specific system, INTERDIP, is presented, that assists a human planner in scheduling the nurse working shifts for a hospital ward. We think that our approach can be applied to many applications in the field of personnel assignment. It is quite obvious that the current implementation might even be used "as is" for every duty rota problem and therefore solves this whole problem class.

It was possible to build this planning system for nurse scheduling within a few man months using a given commercial constraint solver, IF/Prolog from Siemens Nixdorf. The CLP code is just about 4000 lines with more than half of it for user interface. INTERDIP illustrates the important potentials of constraint logic programming for the implementation of real-life applications.

INTERDIP was presented at the Systems'98 Computer exhibition in Munich and several companies are interested to market it. INTERDIP is currently tested at the "*Klinikum Innenstadt*" hospital in Munich. Typically, for 20 nurses and a period of one month, INTERDIP generates a satisfying (not optimal) schedule within a few minutes. The schedules generated by INTERDIP are comparable to those manually generated by a well experienced head nurse, sometimes even better than those. Of course this can not be guaranteed for every possible problem instance since, in general, the scheduling problem is NP-complete.

References

J. L. Arthur and A. Ravindran. A multiple objective nurse scheduling model. In *AIIE Transactions*, volume 13, 1981.

S. Abdennadher and H. Schlenker. INTERDIP – Ein Interaktiver Constraint-basierter Dienstplaner für Krankenstationen. In F. Bry, B. Freitag, and D. Seipel, editors, *12th Workshop on Logic Programming WLP'97*, September 1997.

S. Abdennadher and H. Schlenker. INTERDIP – an interactive constraint based nurse. In *Proceedings of the First International Conference and Exhibition on the Practical Application of Constraint Technologies and Logic Programming*, 1999.

A. Borning, B. N. Freeman-Benson, and M. Wilson. Constraint hierarchies. *Lisp and Symbolic Computation*, 5(3):223–270, 1992.

M. Dincbas, P. Van Hentenryck, H. Simonis, A. Aggoun, T. Graf, and F. Berthier. The Constraint Logic Programming Language CHIP. Technical Report TR-LP-37, ECRC, Munich, 1988.

T. Frühwirth and S. Abdennadher. *Constraint-Programmierung: Grundlagen und Anwendungen*. Springer-Verlag, September 1997.

E. C. Freuder. Eliminating interchangeable values in constraint satisfaction problems. In *AAAI-91 – Proceedings of the 9th national conference on artificial intelligence*, pages 227–233, 1991.

E. C. Freuder and R. J. Wallace. Partial constraint satisfaction. *Artificial Intelligence*, 58(1-3):21–70, 1992.

K. Heus and G. Weil. Constraint programming a nurse scheduling application. In *Proceedings of the Second International Conference on the Practical Application of Constraint Technology*, pages 115–127, 1996.

J. Jaffar and M. J. Maher. Constraint logic programming: A survey. *Journal of Logic Programming*, 20:503–581, 1994.

A. Mackworth. Constraint satisfaction. In Stuart C. Shapiro, editor, *Encyclopedia of Artificial Intelligence*. Wiley, 1992. Volume 1, second edition.

H. Meyer auf'm Hofe. ConPlan/SIEDAplan: Personnel assignment as a problem of hierarchical constraint satisfaction. In *Proceedings of the Third International Conference on the Practical Application of Constraint Technology*, 1997.

K. Marriott and P. Stuckey. *Programming with Constraints: An Introduction*. The MIT Press, 1998.

Siemens Nixdorf Informationssysteme AG. *IF/Prolog Constraint Problem Solver*, 1996.

Siemens Nixdorf Informationssysteme AG. *IF/Prolog Users Guide*, 1996.

L. D. Smith, A. Wiggins, and D. Bird. Post-implementation experience with computer-assisted nurse scheduling in a large hospital. In *Information Systems and Operational Research*, volume 17, 1979.

B. van den Bosch. Implementation of a CLP library and an application in nurse scheduling. Master's thesis, Katholieke Universiteit Leuven, Belgium, 1993.

D. M. Warner. Scheduling nursing personnel according to nursing preference: A mathematical programming approach. In *Operations Research*, volume 24, 1976.

The Wasabi Personal Shopper:
A Case-Based Recommender System

Robin Burke

Recommender.com, Inc.
and
University of California, Irvine
Dept. of Information and Computer Science
University of California, Irvine
Irvine, California 92697
burke@ics.uci.edu

Abstract

The Wasabi Personal Shopper (WPS) is a domain-independent database browsing tool designed for on-line information access, particularly for electronic product catalogs. Typically, web-based catalogs rely either on text search or query formulation. WPS introduces an alternative form of access via preference-based navigation. WPS is based on a line of academic research called FindMe systems. These systems were built in a variety of different languages and used custom-built ad-hoc databases. WPS is written in C++, and designed to be a commercial-grade software product, compatible with any SQL-accessible catalog. The paper describes the WPS and discusses some of the development issues involved in re-engineering our AI research system as a general-purpose commercial application.

Introduction

Although electronic commerce is clearly burgeoning, electronic product catalogs leave much to be desired. Typically implemented as a form-based front-end to an SQL database, these catalogs are frustrating to the user who does not know exactly what she is looking for. Other catalogs rely on text search. In one software catalog, entering "Windows NT Workstation" brought back over a thousand responses, since the names of compatible operating systems are often mentioned in product descriptions.

The Wasabi Personal Shopper (WPS) provides a conversational interface to a database, based on the principles of case-based reasoning. The user examines a suggestion from the system – an item from the catalog – and responds to it with a critique or *tweak*. The system uses the item and the associated tweak to formulate a new query returning a new item for consideration. The result is a natural traversal of the catalog, honing in on the product that best meets the user's needs.

Example

The Wasabi Personal Shopper (WPS) has been applied to a database of wines known as the VintageExchange <URL: http://www.vintageexchange.com>. Still in development, VintageExchange aims to be a web-based market-maker for individuals trading wines from their personal cellars. When we became involved, the site had already implemented a database of wines using descriptions and ratings licensed from the *Wine Spectator*, a well-known wine industry periodical. Consider the following hypothetical exchange between a user and WPS as implemented with the VintageExchange database:

Vintage Vinnie selects a bottle from his on-line cellar database and marks it as deleted, since he drank it last night. It was a 1994 Rochioli Russian River Pinot Noir (Three Corner Vineyard Reserve). The *Wine Spectator* describes it as follows: "Delicious Pinot Noir from the first sip. Serves up lots of complex flavors, with layers of ripe cherry, plum and raspberry and finishes with notes of tea, anise and spice. Tannins are smooth and polished and the finish goes on and on, revealing more nuances." (Rating: 94)

That was the last one in the case, so Vinnie checks to see if any similar wines are available. He selects "Find similar." The system returns with ten more Pinot Noirs, the top-most being a 1991 Williams Selyem Russian River (Rochioli Vineyard). It gets a higher rating (95) from the *Spectator*: "Rich, ripe and plummy, this is generous from start to finish, dripping with vanilla-scented fruit and spice flavors while remaining smooth and polished. The flavors linger enticingly. Delicious now."

Sounds great, but Vinnie notes the price ($45) and clicks on the "Less $$" button. The answer is a 1988 Pinot Noir Mount Harlan Jensen from California's central coast. It is still rated highly (92) and is $10 cheaper. The description says "Packs in a load of fresh, ultraripe, rich black cherry, currant, herb and spicy earth overtones. Deeply flavored and very concentrated, with smooth, supple tannins and a long, full, fruity finish. A distinctive wine. Drink now." Vinnie clicks "Buy."

This example shows how WPS allows the user to express his preferences without having to make those preferences explicit in a query. The wine that he had and liked serves as Vinnie's entry point into the system, and his preference to spend less is conveyed with a simple button click. There are about 2,400 Pinot Noirs in the system, many at the same price and rating points. All the wines found are described as having large quantities of fruit, being "smooth" and "spicy", and having long finishes. While these are qualities of many good wines, other comparable Pinot Noirs are described quite differently. For example, an otherwise similar 1989 version of the same Mount Harlan Jensen wine gets the following description:

> Broad, rich and spicy, with nice toast, coffee and brown sugar nuances to the basic plum and currant aromas and flavors that linger. The finish echoes fruit and flavor as it spreads. Approachable now, but best after 1995.

This one lacks the fresh fruit flavors found in the previous wine, and mentions burnt overtones (toast, coffee) absent in the first suggestion. Attention to such subtleties lets the WPS-enabled catalog help users find items that meet their preferences without having to make those preferences explicit.

FindMe Systems

The Wasabi Personal Shopper has its roots in a line of research known as FindMe systems.[1] See <URL: http://infolab.ils.nwu.edu/entree/> for an example of a publicly-accessible FindMe system: the Entree restaurant guide, which has been on-line since the summer of 1996.

The FindMe technique is one of knowledge-based similarity retrieval. There are two fundamental retrieval modes: similarity and tweak application. In the similarity case, the user has selected a given item from the catalog (called the *source*) and requested other items similar to it. First, a large set of candidate entities is retrieved from the database. This set is sorted based on similarity to the source and the top few candidates returned to the user.

Tweak application is essentially the same except that the candidate set is filtered prior to sorting to leave only those candidates that satisfy the tweak. For example, if a user responds to an item with the tweak "Nicer," the system determines the "niceness" value of that source item and rejects all candidates except those whose value is greater.

Our initial FindMe experiments demonstrated something that case-based reasoning researchers have always known, namely that similarity is not a simple or uniform concept.

In part, what counts as similar depends on what one's goals are: a shoe is similar to a hammer if one is looking around for something to bang with, but not if one wants to extract nails. Our similarity measures therefore have to be goal-based. We also must consider multiple goals and their tradeoffs, which are always involved in shopping. Typically, there are only a handful of standard goals in any given product domain. For each goal, we define a *similarity metric*, which measures how closely two products come to meeting the same goal. Two products with the same price would get the maximum similarity rating on the metric of price, but may differ greatly on another metric, such as quality.

We looked at the interactions between goals, and experimented with complex combinations of metrics to achieve intuitive rankings of products. We found there were well-defined priorities attached to the most important goals and that they could be treated independently. For example, in the restaurant domain, cuisine is of paramount importance. Part of the reason is that cuisine is a category that more or less defines the meaning of other features – a high-quality French restaurant is not really comparable to a high-quality burger joint, partly because of what it means to serve French cuisine.

We can think of the primary category as the most important goal that a recommendation must satisfy, but there are many other goals also. FindMe systems order these goals. For example, in the Entree restaurant recommender system, the ranking of goals was cuisine, price, quality, atmosphere, which seemed to capture our intuition about what was important about restaurants. As part of the development of WPS, we realized that different users might have different goal orderings or different goals altogether. This gave rise to the concept of the *retrieval strategy*. A retrieval strategy selects the goals to be used in comparing entities, and orders them. In VintageExchange, the standard goal ordering is wine type, price, quality, flavor, body, finish, and drinkability, but the system also has a "money no object" strategy in which price is not considered.

Given the goal ordering in the strategy, the process of finding the most similar candidate becomes an alphabetic sort. We sort the candidates into a list of buckets based on their similarity to the source along the most important goal, then sort each of these buckets based on the next most important goal, creating a new list of finer-grained buckets. (The details of the sort algorithm are discussed in [Burke, Hammond & Young, 1997].)

One benefit of this solution is that we can iteratively reduce the set of candidates under consideration as the sort proceeds. Since we are only interested in returning a small number of recommendations to the user, we need to preserve only enough buckets to ensure that we have enough candidates. Buckets farther down in the sort order can be deleted since their contents would never be presented.

---

[1] See (Burke, Hammond & Young, 1997) for a full description of the systems involved in this effort.

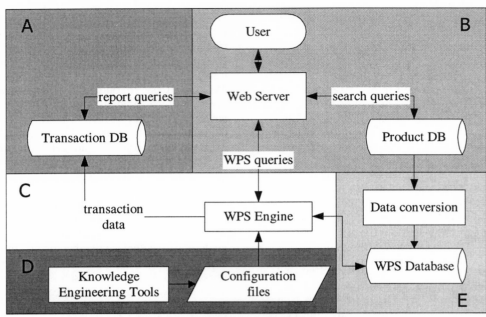

Figure 1. Wasabi Personal Shopper architecture

Architecture

Our research systems showed that the fundamental idea of FindMe worked well. In our informal evaluations, our prototypes returned products that users agreed were similar to their input entries, and the process of navigation by tweaking proved to be a natural, conversational, way to focus in on a desired item. We built enough systems to demonstrate that the idea had cross-domain applicability.

Several obstacles remained to the commercialization of FindMe. Obviously, it would be unreasonable to expect FindMe to be the only interface to a product catalog. It would have to be an add-on on to an existing product database, most likely a relational database using SQL.

Second, all of our research systems had been custom-built. The WPS had to be capable of navigating through catalogs containing any type of product. So, the system needed to be completely general and make as few assumptions about products as possible.

Finally, a truly useful catalog system needs to provide feedback to its owners. Because of the user's unique interaction with WPS, a user profile created while using the system is uniquely valuable, revealing the user's preferences with respect to specific items in the inventory, including "holes" in the product space: places where many customers attempt the same tweak, but come up empty-handed.

The WPS architecture was our response to these new requirements. It generalizes and encapsulates the previous FindMe work, making possible a commercial-grade

application. The architecture has five basic parts as shown in Figure 1:

External Information Environment (B in the diagram): We assume WPS will be running in a standard catalog serving environment where the web server will receive requests and forward them to WPS, possibly through an application server.

WPS Engine (C in the diagram): At the core of the system is the WPS Engine. It is responsible for retrieving entities, applying metrics, sorting and returning answers.

Knowledge Engineering (D in the diagram): The engine knows nothing of wines, restaurants, or any other catalogued product. It only knows entities and their features, and the metrics that operate on them. Metrics and strategies are defined as part of the configuration of the system through a knowledge engineering step.

WPS Database (E in the diagram): In the WPS Database, the system essentially has a copy of the product database in its own format. The transformation process that creates this database essentially flattens the catalog into our feature-set representation. Designing this transformation is another important knowledge engineering step involved in building a WPS system.

Profiling and Reporting (A in the diagram): As discussed above, the ability to profile users and identify patterns of catalog browsing is a crucial advantage that WPS brings. The engine creates a transaction database, recording the history of user interactions with the system, to allow for report generation.

The WPS architecture is a work in progress. As of this writing, only the WPS Engine is in its final form. Our tools for data conversion are still domain- and database-dependent. We have high-level specifications and preliminary designs for the knowledge engineering tools, but no implementations. The configuration files for existing WPS applications are created and maintained manually. We are also still implementing the transaction logging and reporting features.

Database Integration

The most significant implementation issue we faced was one of scale. Our hand-built databases or Lisp data structures could not be expected to scale to very large data sets. So it was imperative that our persistent store of entities and their features be a database. We chose relational databases instead of object-oriented ones since relational databases are the most widely-deployed systems for web applications, although OODBs would have matched our data model somewhat better.

Since we needed to be completely general, we chose a very simple database schema. Each entity has an entity ID, which serves as the primary key for accessing it in the database. The row associated with an entity ID contains two types of columns: single integer values and fixed length bit fields. The single integer columns are used for singleton features like price, where each entity has only one value. The bit field columns are used to hold multi-feature values, such as all of the flavor features of a wine.

Recall that the FindMe algorithm as originally designed took a large set of candidates and performed a series of sorting operations. We used promiscuous retrieval deliberately because other steps (such as tweaking steps) filter out many candidates and it was important not to exclude any potentially-useful entity. In our Lisp implementations, we found that applying the algorithm to a large candidate set was reasonably efficient since the candidates were already in memory. This was definitely not true in the database: queries that return large numbers of rows are highly inefficient, and each retrieved entity must be allocated on the heap. Employed against a relational store, our original algorithms yielded unacceptable response times, sometimes greater than 10 minutes.

It was necessary therefore to retrieve more precisely – to get back just those items likely to be highly rated by the sort algorithm. We needed to widen the scope of interaction between the engine and the database. We considered a fully-integrated approach: building the metrics and retrieval strategies right into the database as stored procedures. However, we opted to keep our code separate to preserve its portability.

Our solution was a natural outgrowth of the metric and strategy system that we had developed for sorting, and was inspired by the CADET system, which performs nearest-neighbor retrieval in relational databases (Shimazu, Kitano & Shibata, 1993). Each metric became responsible for generating retrieval constraints based on the source entity. These constraints could then be turned into SQL clauses when retrieval took place. This approach was especially powerful for tweaks. A properly-constrained query for a tweak such as "cheaper" will retrieve only the entities that will actually pass the "cheaper" filter, avoiding the work of reading and instantiating entities that would be immediately discarded.

The retrieval algorithm works as follows. To retrieve candidates for comparison against a source entity, each metric creates a constraint. The constraints are ordered by the priority of the metric within the current retrieval strategy. If the query is to be used for a tweak, a constraint is created that implements the tweak and is given highest priority. This constraint is considered "non-optional." An SQL query is created conjoining all the constraints and is passed to the database. If no entities (or not enough) are returned, the lowest priority constraint is dropped and the query resubmitted. This process can continue until all of the optional constraints have been dropped.

The interaction between constraint set and candidate set size is dramatic: a four-constraint query that returns nothing will often return thousands of entities when relaxed to three constraints. We are considering a more flexible constraint scheme in which each metric would propose a small set of progressively more inclusive constraints, rather than just one. Since database access time dominates all other processing time in the system, we expect that any additional computation involved would be outweighed by the efficiencies to be had in more accurate retrieval.

Similarity metrics

In general, a similarity metric can be any function that takes two entities and returns a value reflecting their similarity with respect to a given goal. Our FindMe systems implemented the similarity metric idea in many different domain-specific ways. For WPS, we have created a proprietary set of metrics general enough to cover all of the similarity computations used in our other FindMe systems and sufficient to implement the VintageExchange system. Internally, they are implemented as a single metric class with a comparison-computing "strategy" object (Gamma, et al. 1995) attached, so new metric types can be easily added if they are needed.

Natural language processing

As the example at the beginning of this paper shows, textual descriptions can be crucial discriminators in large catalogs of otherwise similar objects. We have found that many of the databases used for electronic commerce contain small amounts of descriptive data associated with each product and large chunks of human-readable text. As of this writing, the natural language component of WPS is not as well developed as the WPS Engine. We have implemented it only for the VintageExchange project, and only now beginning to explore cross-domain applications. However, the language of wine represents something of a worst case for textual description, so we are optimistic that our approach is robust.

Recall that an entity is simply a collection of features. A natural language description must therefore be transformed into atomic features. For wines, we identified four categories of descriptive information: descriptions of the flavor of the wine ("berry", "tobacco"), descriptions of the wine's body and texture ("gritty", "silky"), descriptions of the finish ("lingering", "truncated"), and descriptions of how and when the wine should be drunk ("with meat", "aperitif"), and we identified the most commonly-used terms, usually nouns, in each of these categories. We also identified modifiers both of quantity ("lots", "lacking") and quality ("lovely", "harsh").

Each description was processed as follows. First we broke the description into phrases, then we associated each phrase with a description category, since we had found that each phrase usually concentrated on one aspect of the wine. We eliminated stopwords and performed some simple stemming. At this point, we had four word groups, one for each description category, consisting of descriptive terms and modifiers, and marked with phrase boundaries. Using the phrase boundaries, we associated modifiers with each descriptive term in their scope. For example, in the description "a lovely fragrant explosion of cherry and raspberry", the "lovely fragrant explosion" refers to both of the fruit terms. This gave us a representation based on terms and modifiers.

The "term plus modifier" representation was further simplified by breaking modifiers into classes: quantity modifiers could either refer to a large quantity ("oodles"), a small quantity ("scant"), or a zero quantity ("lacking"); quality modifiers could be positive ("tasty") or negative ("stale"). Only the modifier count was retained. "A lovely fragrant explosion of cherry and raspberry" therefore became (large-quantity positive-quality*2 cherry) (large-quantity positive-quality*2 raspberry), since "lovely" and "fragrant" are both positive quality modifiers. The resulting representation loses the poetry of the original, but retains enough of its essence to enable matching.

The final step was to turn this representation into an encoding for manipulation by WPS. Recall that features in WPS are represented as integers. Treating an integer as a 32-bit vector, we used the most-significant 20 bits to represent the content term and the least-significant 12 to represent the modifiers. So, the encoding of our phrase above would ultimately come down to the following two hexadecimal integers: 803eb109, and 80388109, for cherry and raspberry, respectively. Note that the last three hex digits (12 bits) are the same, reflecting the modifier encoding, while the first 20 bits represent the particular flavor terms.[1]

Preliminary analysis of other e-commerce data sets suggests that product descriptions in general are not complex syntactically and concentrate on straightforward descriptive adjectives and nouns. Few domains have the breadth of vocabulary present in our wine descriptions. Our experience in building the next few WPS applications will reveal more about the generalizability of the natural language approach described here.

Related Work

The problem of intelligent assistance for browsing, especially web browsing, is a topic of active interest in the AI community. There are a number of lines of research directed at understanding browsing behavior in users (Konstan, et al. 1997; Perkowitz & Etzioni, 1998), extracting information from pages (Craven, et al. 1998; Knoblock et al. 1998, Cohen, 1998), and automatically locating related information (Lieberman, 1995). Because the web presents an unconstrained domain, these systems must use knowledge-poor methods, typically statistical ones.

WPS has a different niche. We expect users to have highly-focused goals, such as finding a particular kind of wine. We deal with database records, all of which describe the same kind of product. As a result, we can build detailed knowledge into our systems that enables them to compare entities in the information space, and respond to user goals. In information retrieval research, retrieval is seen as the main task in interacting with an information source, not browsing. The ability to tailor retrieval by obtaining user response to retrieved items has been implemented in some information retrieval systems through retrieval clustering (Cutting, et al., 1992) and through relevance feedback (Salton & McGill, 1983).

Schneiderman's "dynamic query" systems present another approach to database navigation (Schneiderman, 1994). These systems use two-dimensional graphical maps of a data space in which examples are typically represented by points. Queries are created by moving sliders that correspond to features, and the items retrieved by the query are shown as appropriately-colored points in the space. This technique has been very effective for two-dimensional data such as maps, when the relevant retrieval variables are scalar values. Like WPS, the dynamic query approach has the benefit of letting users discover tradeoffs in the data because users can watch the pattern of the retrieved data change as values are manipulated.

As discussed earlier, the closest precedent for our use of knowledge-based methods in retrieval comes from case-based reasoning (CBR) (Hammond, 1989; Kolodner, 1993; Riesbeck & Schank, 1989). A case-based reasoning system solves new problems by retrieving old problems likely to have similar solutions. Researchers working on the retrieval of CBR cases have concentrated on developing knowledge-based methods for precise, efficient retrieval of well-represented examples. For some tasks, such as case-based educational systems, where cases serve a variety of

---

[1] The first three digits, 803, also happen to be the same, since cherry and raspberry are both part of the "fruit" portion of the flavor hierarchy and are near each other in the configuration file. This, however, is an artifact of our numbering scheme and is not used by the metric.

purposes, CBR systems have also explored multiple goal-based retrieval strategies (Burke & Kass, 1995).

Our use of tweaks is obviously related to CBR research in case adaptation. Note however, that our use of the term is different. Tweaking in the context of CBR means to adapt a returned case to make it more closely match the problem situation in which it will be applied. The tweaks that a user invokes in WPS are applied much differently. We cannot invent a new wine, or change an existing one to match the user's desires – the best we can do is attempt a new retrieval, keeping the user's preference in mind.

Future work

A key element of future releases of Wasabi Personal Shopper will be the addition of the knowledge engineering tools. There are four major steps of the WPS knowledge engineering process: (1) identifying the anticipated goals of shoppers and their priorities, (2) mapping from these goals to entries in the appropriate columns in the appropriate database table, (3) isolating those elements of product data that will serve as features, possibly performing natural language processing, and (4) determining how similarity should be judged between the features so extracted.

We feel that step 1 will not be difficult for marketing experts, who already spend their days thinking about what motivates shoppers to buy their companies' products. Step 2, however, will present a user-interface challenge. We do not want to assume that the user has any database expertise, yet this task requires that we specify exactly what parts of a database record correspond to the price, the color, etc. The most difficult task technically is step 3. Here we are building the system's conceptual vocabulary, starting from raw database entries. Finally, our inventory of similarity metrics gives us great leverage over step 4. We have designed strategy-specific wizards that guide the user through the problem of tailoring each metric.

Many e-commerce sites use some form of collaborative filtering (Konstan et al. 1997). These systems make suggestions based on preferences of other users with similar profiles. Our profiling data could make such systems more powerful (since we get useful data from every browsing step, not just the final result). One could also imagine using collaborative filtering data to bias the browsing process, either as part of the retrieval strategy, or as a fallback when the tweaking process hits a dead end.

Acknowledgements

The FindMe research discussed in this paper was performed at the University of Chicago in collaboration with Kristian Hammond, with the assistance of Terrence Asselin, Jay Budzik, Robin Hunicke, Kass Schmitt, Robb Thomas, Benjamin Young, and others. The development of the Wasabi Personal Shopper system benefited from the insights gained during a JAD workshop with Geneer, Inc. and from the efforts of Cate Brady, Drew Scott, Jim Silverstein, Paul Steimle, and Peter Tapling. Thanks also to Mike Lyons and Stephen Schmitt of ArribaTech who made the VintageExchange database available to us.

References

Burke, R., & Kass, A. 1995. Supporting Learning through Active Retrieval of Video Stories. *Journal of Expert Systems with Applications*, 9(5).

Burke, R., Hammond, K., and Young, B. 1997. The FindMe Approach to Assisted Browsing. *IEEE Expert*, 12(4): 32-40.

Cohen, W. W. 1998. A Web-based Information System that Reasons with Structured Collections of Text. In *Proceedings of the Second International Conference on Autonomous Agents*, New York: ACM Press. pp. 400-407.

Craven, M., DiPasquo, D., Freitag, D. , McCallum, A., Mitchell, T., Nigam, K. & Slattery, S. 1998. Learning to Extract Symbolic Knowledge from the World Wide Web. In *Proceedings of the Fifteenth National Conference on Artificial Intelligence*. AAAI Press, pp. 509-516.

Cutting, D. R.; Pederson, J. O.; Karger, D.; and Tukey, J. W. 1992. Scatter/Gather: A cluster-based approach to browsing large document collections. In *Proceedings of the 15th Annual International ACM/SIGIR Conference*, pp. 318-329.

Gamma, E., Helm, R., Johnson, R. & Vlissides, J. 1995. *Design Patterns: Elements of Reusable Object-Oriented Software*. Reading, MA: Addison-Wesley.

Hammond, K. 1989. *Case-based Planning: Viewing Planning as a Memory Task*. Academic Press. Perspectives in AI Series, Boston, MA.

Knoblock C. A., Minton, S., Ambite, J. L., Ashish, N., Modi, P. J., Muslea, I., Philpot, A. G., and Tejada, S. 1998. Modeling Web Sources for Information Integration. In *Proceedings of the Fifteenth National Conference on Artificial Intelligence*. AAAI Press. pp. 211-218.

Kolodner, J. 1993. *Case-based reasoning*. San Mateo, CA: Morgan Kaufmann.

Konstan, J., Miller, B., Maltz, D., Herlocker, J., Gordon, L., and Riedl, J. 1997. GroupLens: Applying Collaborative Filtering to Usenet News. *Communications of the ACM* 40(3): 77-87.

Perkowitz, M. & Etzioni, O. 1998. Adaptive Web Sites: Automatically Synthesizing Web Pages. In *Proceedings of the Fifteenth National Conference on Artificial Intelligence*. AAAI Press. pp. 727-731.

Riesbeck, C., & Schank, R. C. 1989. *Inside Case-Based Reasoning*. Hillsdale, NJ: Lawrence Erlbaum.

Salton, G., & McGill, M. 1983. *Introduction to modern information retrieval*. New York: McGraw-Hill.

Schneiderman, B. 1994. Dynamic Queries: for visual information seeking. *IEEE Software* 11(6): 70-77.

Shimazu, H., Kitano, H. & Shibata, A. 1993. Retrieving Cases from Relational Data-Bases: Another Stride Towards Corporate-Wide Case-Base Systems. In *Proceedings of the 1993 International Joint Conference on Artificial Intelligence*, pp. 909-914.

The Use of Word Sense Disambiguation in an Information Extraction System

Joyce Yue Chai
30 Saw Mill River Rd.
IBM T. J. Watson Research Center
Hawthorne, NY 10532
jchai@us.ibm.com

Alan W. Biermann
Computer Science Department
Duke University
Durham, NC 27708
awb@cs.duke.edu

Abstract

This paper describes a rule-based methodology for word sense disambiguation and an application of the methodology to information extraction using rules generalized with the help of the WordNet system. The methodology creates word sense disambiguation rules based on user trained examples working in the domain of interest. It achieves accuracy rates comparable to the best competing methods and can be easily integrated into higher level applications.

Introduction

Most information extraction (IE) systems have used hand-crafted semantic resources for each application domain, or have employed techniques for automatically or semi-automatically constructing lexicons of annotated texts in the domain (Riloff & Lehnert 1993) (Riloff 1996) (Krupka 1995). Few examples apply general lexical semantic resources. NYU's MUC-4 system (Grishman, Macleod, & Sterling 1992) made some attempt at using WordNet for semantic classification. However, they ran into the problem of automated sense disambiguation because the WordNet hierarchy is sense dependent. Are the generic lexical semantic databases useful at all for information extraction purposes? Can we avoid the process of hand-crafting domain specific knowledge? If so, how can we effectively use the generic lexical semantics?

In order to apply generic resources effectively, sense selection among the polysemies becomes important. There is a great amount of work concerning Word Sense Disambiguation (WSD), especially various algorithms that can improve the accuracy of WSD on a predefined set of words in preannotated corpora. Some recent work on WSD includes the use of the knowledge contained in a machine-readable dictionary (Luk 1995)(Wilks *et al.* 1990), supervised learning from tagged sentences (Bruce & Wiebe 1994)(Miller 1990)(Ng & Lee 1996)(Yarowsky 1992)(Yarowsky 1994), unsupervised learning from raw

corpora (Yarowsky 1995), and hybrid methods that combine several knowledge sources, collocation and others (Bruce & Wiebe 1994) (Ng & Lee 1996). Despite the strides made in developing robust WSD algorithms, its use as a technology in higher level applications has been limited. Some work has shown WSD could help with information retrieval and machine translation. However, its role in information extraction has not been investigated. Furthermore, even with the best algorithm, the question arises as to whether that algorithm is applicable to real NLP systems, since most algorithms heavily depend on large corpora of annotated text which might not be available.

In this paper, we will describe an information extraction system that applies a generic lexical semantic resource (WordNet) and achieves competitive results. In particular, we will give a detailed description of a WSD algorithm that is integrated into the system and makes the application of generic lexical semantics possible. First, we will give a brief introduction to the system. Then we will present a rule-based WSD algorithm and its performance on a common data set. Finally, we will describe the integration of this WSD algorithm into the information extraction system and its performance.

TIMES System

The *T*rainable *Infor*Mation *E*xtraction *S*ystem (TIMES) is shown in diagram form in Figure 1 where the main processors handle Tokenization, Lexical Processing, Partial Parsing, and Rule Learning and Generalization (Chai 1998). The Tokenizer segments the input text into words and sentences. The Lexical Processing stage tags words with syntactic information from CELEX database[1] and semantic information from WordNet (Miller 1990). In particular, a Semantic Type Identifier is used to identify special semantic types such as email and web addresses, file and directory names, dates, times, and dollar amounts, telephone numbers, zip codes, cities, states, countries, names of companies, and many others. The Partial Parser uses a fi-

---

[1]CELEX was developed by several universities and institutions in the Netherlands, and is distributed by the Linguistic Data Consortium.

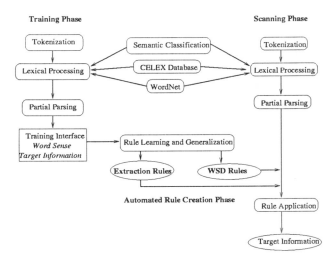

Training Phase

- Tokenization
- Lexical Processing
- Partial Parsing
- Training Interface
  Word Sense
  Target Information

- Semantic Classification
- CELEX Database
- WordNet

- Rule Learning and Generalization
- Extraction Rules
- WSD Rules

Automated Rule Creation Phase

Scanning Phase

- Tokenization
- Lexical Processing
- Partial Parsing
- Rule Application
- Target Information

Figure 1: System Overview

nite state model to discover noun phrases (NG), verb phrases (VG), and prepositions (PG). Verb phrases are further categorized as Verb Active (VG), Verb Passive (VG_ED), Verb Be (VG_BE), Verb Gerund (VG_ING), and Verb Infinitive (VG_TO). The headword of a phrase is the base form of the last word in the phrase. The Rule Learning and Generalization module constructs extraction rules based on information given by the user through the training interface and on the preprocessing of the earlier stages.

The TIMES system has three modes of operation which implement, respectively, training, rule creation, and text scanning. The first mode enables the user to move through a document and indicate desired information items in the text. All significant actions by the user are gathered by the system and used for generating rules. One of the necessary inputs by the user is a designation of the WordNet word senses for the purposes of training the system. However, the system requires only minimum linguistic and domain knowledge so that casual users should be able to use it. The rule creation phase generates rules, as described below, for information extraction and for word sense disambiguation. Finally, the scanning phase applies the created rules to any body of free text for the purposes of information extraction.

Training and Generalization for Extraction Rules

TIMES provides users a convenient interface for training. The interface shows a stack of phrases segmented from the sentence by the Partial Parser. Associated with each phrase, the syntactic category, semantic type, headword, and meanings (i.e., senses) for the headword are also given. The user is required to first define the information of interest (i.e., the target information), and then identify some phrases as one type of target information. Furthermore, the user needs to specify

the correct sense for the headword. (The training interface provides sense definitions and examples so that the user would know which sense to choose.) By default, TIMES assigns sense one, the most frequently used sense in WordNet to the headword if no specification from the user is given. In addition, if the user is experienced, he/she can assist the system to learn by specifying important phrases in the sentence that are crucial to the rule generation. However, this specification is optional. If the user does not identify the important phrases, TIMES will regard every phrase as an important phrase.

Extraction rules are generated based on the important phrases and user specified target information. For each important phrase in the training sentence, if its headword exists in WordNet, then together with its syntactic category and sense number, it can uniquely determine a concept (i.e., a synonym list) in WordNet. By following the hypernym path in WordNet, the concept becomes more and more general (Chai & Biermann 1997).

Extraction rules are pattern-action rules. The pattern, defined by the left hand side (LHS) of a rule, is a conjunction (expressed by $\wedge$) of *subsumption functions* $S(X, \alpha, target(\alpha))$. X is instantiated by a new phrase when the rule is applied; α is the concept corresponding to the headword of an important phrase in the training sentence; and $target(\alpha)$ is the type of target information identified for α. The action in the right hand side (RHS) of a rule, $FS(X, target(\alpha))$ fills a template slot, assigning the type of target information $target(\alpha)$ to the phrase X.

The subsumption function $S(X, \alpha, target(\alpha))$ looks for subsumption of concepts. It returns true if the headword of X is subsumed to the concept α. If all subsumption functions on the LHS return true, then the RHS action will take place to extract X as a type $target(\alpha)$.

The system applies a two-dimensional generalization model to learn the number of subsumption functions to be included in the LHS, the order of subsumption functions, and specification/generalization of α (from WordNet hierarchy) in the subsumption function (Chai, Biermann, & Guinn 1999). For example, the user is interested in finding out which company has what position open. Suppose the training sentence is "IBM is looking for software engineers." Through the interface, the user identifies "IBM" as the target information *COMPANY* and "software engineers" as the target information *POSITION*. Based on this input, the system can generate a set of rules. Some sample rules are shown in Figure 2. Since two types of target information are specified, two rules are necessary to capture both *COMPANY* and *POSITION* as shown in R_1 and R_2. (By our convention, each rule only captures one type of target information.) In Figure 2, R_3 is more general than R_1 since it has fewer constraints on the LHS. R_4 is more general than R_1 since the subsumed concepts in R_4 are more general than those in R_1. For each type of target

$$R_1: S(X_1, \{company\}, COMPANY) \wedge S(X_2, \{look\_for\}, none) \wedge S(X_3, \{engineer\}, POSITION)$$
$$\longrightarrow FS(X_1, COMPANY)$$
$$R_2: S(X_1, \{company\}, COMPANY) \wedge S(X_2, \{look\_for\}, none) \wedge S(X_3, \{engineer\}, POSITION)$$
$$\longrightarrow FS(X_3, POSITION)$$
$$R_3: S(X_1, \{company\}, COMPANY) \wedge S(X_2, \{look\_for\}, none) \longrightarrow FS(X_1, COMPANY)$$
$$R_4: S(X_1, \{group, ...\}, COMPANY) \wedge S(X_2, \{look\_for, \}, none) \wedge S(X_3, \{professional, ...\}, POSITION)$$
$$\longrightarrow FS(X_1, COMPANY)$$

Figure 2: Examples of Extraction Rules

information, the system will automatically determine the generalization/specification for rules.

The Semantic Tagging Approach

Successful semantic generalization by use of Word-Net conceptual hierarchy depends on the correct word senses. Semantic tagging (and the associated word sense disambiguation) has been studied in great detail. However, its use in higher level applications is limited. We have designed a WSD algorithm which can be integrated into information extraction systems, particularly IE systems which use generic lexical semantic resources. In this section, we will describe the algorithm and report on its performance on a common data set.

The Learning Model for WSD Rules

Our rule learning model follows the supervised learning paradigm. The model automatically generates useful rules from the tagged examples for WSD tasks. A *target word* is defined as the word that needs to be sense identified. The WSD rules will be generated based on the context of the target word.

Context After being processed by the Partial Parser, each pre-tagged sentence is divided into a sequence of phrases. Each phrase corresponds to a segment group $g = (phrase, head, syn\_type, sem\_type, sense)$, where *phrase* is the phrase itself; *head* is the headword of the phrase; *syn_type* is the syntactic category of the phrase; *sem_type* is the semantic type identified by the Semantic Type Identifier; *sense* is the pre-tagged sense number. If a phrase is identified as a special semantic type, then its headword is the name for that special type. Since we are only interested in nouns and verbs, the target word is always the headword of a phrase.

Within a sentence, the context of a target word is created based on the surrounding phrases. More precisely, if g_t contains a target word (where t is the position/index of the phrase in the sentence, $1 \leq t \leq n$), then the context of g_t, with contextual range d, is $(g_i, ..., g_{t-1}, g_t, g_{t+1}, ..., g_j)$, where $i = \max(t - d, 1)$, $j = \min(t+d, n)$, and each g_i corresponds to one phrase in the sentence.

For example, suppose the original sentence is: "Cray Research will retain a 10 percent interest in the new company, which will be based in Colorado Springs, CO." The sense for "interest" is pre-tagged as "5". Af-

ter applying the Partial Parser and the Semantic Type Identifier, the system will mark the sentence as: "[Cray Research/NG/Company_type] [will retain/VG] [a 10 percent/NG] [interest_5/NG] [in/PG] [the new company/NG] which [will be based/VG_ED] [in/PG] [Colorado Springs/NG/City_type] [CO./NG/State_type]." The string "A 10 percent interest" is a noun phrase parsed by the Partial Parser. However, due to the assumption that noun modifiers can be a good indicator for the sense of the target word, in our approach, the target word (if it is a noun) is separated from its noun modifiers.

Creating WSD Rules In general, rules consist of a left hand side (LHS) which defines the applicability conditions and a right hand side (RHS) which specifies the action to select senses. The LHS of a rule is a conjunction (expressed by $\wedge$) of *Match Functions*. Each Match Function corresponds to one phrase in the context of the target word. Given $g = (phrase, head, syn\_type, sem\_type, sense)$ as previously defined, the system creates a Match Function $Match(X, head, syn\_type, sense)$, where X is the variable field to be filled by a new phrase. $Match(X, head, syn\_type, sense)$ returns true if head-word of X is the same as *head* and the syntactic category of X is the same as *syn_type*. The RHS $T(X, sense)$ is the sense tagging function which identifies the sense of the headword of X as *sense*. The number of Match Functions on the LHS indicates specification/generalization of the rule. More numbers imply more constraints, and therefore, a more specific rule.

For each context of the target word, a rule with n Match Functions can be generated by simply selecting n phrases (including the one containing a target word) from the context, and creating corresponding Match Functions to make up the LHS. The RHS of the rule is generated according to the correct sense for the target word in that particular context. Some examples of WSD rules are shown in Figure 3.

The first rule in Figure 3 is very precise; however, the chance of obtaining a match in the unseen data is small. On the other hand, the fourth rule is too general. Applying this rule simply tags all words with one sense, and the highest performance would be no better than that attained by identifying all words with the most frequently used senses. Based on this scenario, we would like to generate rules with the optimum num-

1. $Match(X_1, retain, VG, 1) \wedge Match(X_2, percent, NG, 1) \wedge Match(X_3, interest, NG, 5)$
   $\wedge Match(X_4, in, PG, 1) \wedge Match(X_5, company, NG, 1) \longrightarrow T(X_3, 5)$
2. $Match(X_1, retain, VG, 1) \wedge Match(X_2, percent, NG, 1) \wedge Match(X_3, interest, NG, 5) \longrightarrow T(X_3, 5)$
3. $Match(Match(X_1, percent, NG, 1) \wedge Match(X_2, interest, NG, 5) \longrightarrow T(X_2, 5)$
4. $Match(X_1, interest, NG, 5) \longrightarrow T(X_1, 5)$

Figure 3: Examples of WSD Rules

ber of Match Functions. This process is carried out by checking the *Precision Rate* for each rule.

Suppose a rule r_i is applied to the training data, precisely, to the context of a target word. If all the entities on the LHS are satisfied, then a particular sense will be assigned to the target word. By comparing the senses identified with the original tagged senses, the Precision Rate $P(r_i)$ is derived:

$$P(r_i) = \frac{number\ of\ correct\ senses\ identified\ by\ r_i}{number\ of\ senses\ identified\ by\ r_i}$$

A threshold θ is predefined to select useful rules. If $P(r_i) > \theta$, r_i is considered a useful rule and will be applied for WSD on unseen data.

We applied a greedy covering algorithm to generate WSD rules:

1. Predefine N as the maximum number of Match Functions allowed in a rule, d as the contextual range, and θ as the threshold.

2. For each target word, based on its context with contextual range d, create all possible rules with one Match Function, two Match Functions, ..., and up to N Match Functions.

3. For each rule r_i, apply it to the training data and compute $P(r_i)$. If $P(r_i) > \theta$, put r_i in the rule base.

4. Sort the rules to ensure no repetition of rules.

Applying the Rules When useful rules are applied to new sentences, two types of match routines are used. The full match routine guarantees that only when each Match Function in the LHS of a rule returns true, does the RHS take place. The partial match routine allows a rule with N Match Functions to be activated when only $N - 1$ Match Functions are satisfied. The application of rules takes place as follows (assuming new sentences have been properly pre-processed):

- For each context of the target word, let $n = N$. Start applying rules with n Match Functions. In doing so, it first applies rules with the Precision Rate between 0.9 to 1.0. If there are matches, it selects the sense which is identified by the most of rules and proceeds to the next context. Otherwise, it applies the rules with the Precision Rate between 0.8 to 0.9. The procedure continues. If there are matches, then it assigns the sense and proceeds to the next context; otherwise it decrements the Precision Rate by 0.1 until it reaches the threshold.

- If there is no match, it applies rules with $n = n - 1$ Match Functions with the decremental Precision Rate. If there are matches, it then assigns the sense which is identified by the most of rules and proceeds to the next context; otherwise it applies rules with fewer Match Functions until n becomes 0.

- If there is no match, it operates the partial match to the rules with N entities and selects the sense which is identified by the most of those partial matches.

- If there is no match, the most frequently used sense will be assigned.

The approach for applying rules will first achieve the highest precision for a small number of identifications. Then by applying rules with decremented Precision Rate and fewer Match Functions, more identifications will take place while maintaining the overall precision.

A Test on a Common Data Set

We chose a common data set (Bruce & Wiebe 1994) involving the noun "interest" to test the performance of our WSD algorithm. This data set was extracted from Penn Treebank (Marcus, Santorini, & Marcinkiewicz 1993) and made available by Bruce and Wiebe (Bruce & Wiebe 1994). It consisted of 2369 sentences and each sentence had an occurrence of the noun "interest" tagged with a correct sense. The sense definitions used were from the Longman Dictionary of Contemporary English (LDOCE). The six senses of the noun "interest" are: 1) readiness to give attention (15% in the dataset); 2) quality of causing attention to be given (about 1%); 3) activity, subject, etc. which one gives time and attention to (3%); 4) advantage, advancement, or favor (8%); 5) a share in a company, business, etc. (21%); 6) money paid for the use of money (53%). Senses 2 and 3 are dramatically underrepresented in the data set. Before using the WSD algorithm to learn the rules, all sentences are preprocessed by the Partial Parser and the Semantic Type Identifier. In the experiment, each trial included a randomly selected 1769 sentences as training data and 600 sentences as testing data. This is the same experimental strategy as described in (Ng & Lee 1996).

We ran 100 trials. In each trial, rules were created based on contextual range 2, and threshold 0.6. The average precision for identifying all six senses was 88.2%, with a standard deviation 1.0%; the average precision for identifying sense 1, 4, 5, 6 was 89.7%, with a standard deviation of 1.0%. The average precision and the standard deviation on each sense tagging is shown in Table 1.

sense	average precision	standard deviation
1	67.8%	4.1%
2	0	0
3	52.7%	10.2%
4	70.9%	7.6%
5	88.7%	2.6%
6	99.0%	0.6%
Overall	88.2%	1.0%
1,4,5,6	89.7%	1.0%

Table 1: Performance for WSD on Individual Sense

Many research groups have investigated WSD of the word "interest." In identifying four senses of the noun "interest." Black achieved 72% (Black 1988) and Yarowsky achieved 72% (Yarowsky 1992) . However, their work was not based on the same data set. Bruce and Weibe made this common data set available (Bruce & Wiebe 1994). They developed a decomposable probabilistic model (Bruce & Wiebe 1994), which used parts of speech and morphological forms for the surrounding words. Their model achieved 78% precision on identifying all six senses, and 79% on identifying senses 1, 4 5, and 6. Based on the same data set, Ng and Lee integrated multiple knowledge sources and used exemplar learning to achieve WSD (Ng & Lee 1996). In addition to parts of speech and morphological forms, they also took local collocation (common expressions) and verb-object syntactic relationships as features. Their LEXAS system achieved 87.4% in precision on all six senses of "interest" and 89% on senses 1, 4, 5, 6. Our rule learning model achieves the comparable performance (88.2% for all senses, 89.7% for senses 1, 4, 5, 6) in this common data set. It applies limited knowledge sources (syntactic category and preliminary semantic type classification). Furthermore, the model is ready to disambiguate senses for any target word.

Experimental Results

We have conducted experiments to test the applicability of our rule-based WSD algorithm in TIMES. The working domain is the *triangle.job* newsgroup, where job advertisements are posted. The types of the target information are defined as the following: *COMPANY* (the name of the company which has job openings), *POSITION* (the name of the available position), *SALARY* (the salary, stipend, compensation information), *LOCATION* (the state/city where the job is located), *EXPERIENCE* (years of experience), *CONTACT* (the phone number or email address for contact), *SKILLS* (the specific skills required, such as programming languages, operating systems, etc), *BENEFITS* (the benefits provided by the company, such as health, dental insurance, etc). The training set consisted of 24 articles and the testing set had 40 articles. As described earlier,

in the training phase, the user is required to annotate the target information and tag the correct senses to the words which are not used as sense one. The average training time for each article was about three minutes. Based on each target word (the word which sense is not used as sense one), the system generated a set of WSD rules. In the scanning phase, WSD rules are applied to assign senses to target words. Furthermore, from the training examples, a set of extraction rules were generated to be applied in the scanning phase.

Based on the threshold 0.8 and the contextual range 2, the system generated a set of rules for the WSD task. Among those, three rules had three Match Functions, 21 rules had two Match Functions, and 10 rules had one Match Function. However, all rules with one Match Function could cover the rest of the rules since the Precision Rate for them is already very high. This observation suggested that, in a specific domain, senses of words tend to remain the same throughout the domain. For example, "position" has fifteen senses in WordNet, but in the *triangle.job* domain, every time it appears, it's always used as sense six which means a job in an organization.

The end performance of the system on extracting target information with and without WSD is shown in Table 2, The use of the WSD algorithm pushes up the overall performance in terms of F-measure by 7.5%. It is extremely helpful in enhancing recall (about 10%). This indicates that instead of building a domain specific knowledge base for information extraction, WSD can enable the use of an off-the-shelf lexical semantic resource. Our rule based WSD algorithm can be easily incorporated into such a system.

	with WSD	without WSD
precision	71.0%	67.2%
recall	67.5%	57.1%
F-measure.	69.2%	61.7%

Table 2: End Performance with and without WSD

Discussion

Since the first version of the system (Bagga, Chai, & Biermann 1997), TIMES has been upgraded in many ways. First, in the old system, the user created semantic transitions by specifying nodes and relations. The new version of the system replaces that training approach by asking users to indicate the target information and allowing the system to build rules automatically. Second, the old system only applied semantic generalization with various degrees and it didn't provide an automated mechanism to control the degree of generalization based on the training data. The new system automatically generates rules based on both syntactic generalization and semantic generalization. Furthermore the new approach determines the optimum amount of generalization for both directions. Finally, the new system provides a new framework to learn WSD rules in IE context.

By allowing the user to select the correct senses, the system can automatically generate WSD rules. Based on the assumption that most senses are used as sense one in WordNet and senses tend to remain the same for a specific domain, the sense training process is easier than the creation of a specific domain knowledge base. This process does not require the expertise in a particular domain and allows any casual user to accomplish it given a set of sense descriptions (glosses). We feel that, if possible, using generic resources is more efficient than hand-crafting domain specific knowledge with the respect to easy customization. Furthermore, in order to make the generic lexical semantic resources useful, word sense disambiguation is necessary, and moreover, an easily adaptable WSD approach is important.

In contrast with many statistically based WSD algorithms, our rule-based approach incorporates syntactic features and basic semantic knowledge. This approach has achieved comparable results on a common data set. Furthermore, the model is applicable to any target word and can be easily integrated into any system (not just information extraction systems) where large annotated corpora are not available. Finally, the rules learned can reflect the domain characteristics and allow easy interpretation.

Conclusion

In this paper, we have presented a WSD method in an information extraction system that uses WordNet for automated rule generalization. Furthermore, it demonstrates that, to successfully make use of the generic resources, WSD is very important. This calls for an adaptable WSD approach, and our rule based WSD algorithm meets this need.

Acknowledgments

We would like to thank Amit Bagga for developing the Tokenizer and the Semantic Type Identifier. We would also like to thank Jerry Hobbs for providing us with the finite state rules for the Partial Parser. This work was supported in part by an IBM Fellowship.

References

Bagga, A.; Chai, J.; and Biermann, A. 1997. The role of WordNet in the creation of a trainable message understanding system. *Proceedings of Ninth Conference on Innovative Applications of Artificial Intelligence (IAAI-97)*.

Black, E. 1988. An experiment in computational discrimination of english word senses. *IBM Journal of Research and Development* 32(2).

Bruce, R., and Wiebe, J. 1994. Word sense disambiguation using decomposable models. *Proceedings of the 32nd Annual Meeting of the Association for Computational Linguistics*.

Chai, J., and Biermann, A. 1997. Corpus based statistical generalization tree in rule optimization. *Proceedings of Fifth Workshop on Very Large Corpora (WVLC-5)*.

Chai, J.; Biermann, A.; and Guinn, C. 1999. Two dimensional generalization in information extraction. *Proceedings of Sixteenth National Conference on Artificial Intelligence*.

Chai, J. 1998. *Learning and Generalization in the Creation of Information Extraction Systems*. Ph.D. Dissertation, Department of Computer Science, Duke University.

Grishman, R.; Macleod, C.; and Sterling, J. 1992. New York University Proteus system: MUC-4 test results and analysis. *Proceedings of the Fourth Message Understanding Conference*.

Krupka, G. 1995. Description of the SRA system as used for MUC-6. *Proceedings of the Sixth Message Understanding Conference*.

Luk, A. K. 1995. Statistical sense disambiguation with relatively small corpora using dictionary definitions. *Proceedings of the 33rd Annual Meeting of the Association for Computational Linguistics*.

Marcus, M.; Santorini, B.; and Marcinkiewicz, M. 1993. Building a large annotated corpus of english: the Penn Treebank. *Computational Linguistics* 19(3).

Miller, G. 1990. WordNet: An on-line lexical database. *International Journal of Lexicography*.

Ng, H., and Lee, H. 1996. Integrating multiple knowledge sources to disambiguate word sense: An exemplar-based approach. *Proceedings of the 34th Annual Meeting of the Association for Computational Linguistics*.

Riloff, E., and Lehnert, W. 1993. Automated dictionary construction for information extraction from text. *Proceedings of Ninth IEEE Conference on Artificial Intelligence for Applications*.

Riloff, E. 1996. An empirical study of automated dictionary construction for information extraction in three domains. *AI Journal* 85.

Wilks, Y.; Fass, D.; Guo, C.; McDonald, J.; Plate, T.; and Slator, B. M. 1990. Providing machine tractable dictionary tools. *Machine Translation* 5(2).

Yarowsky, D. 1992. Word-sense disambiguation using statistical models of Roget's categories trained on large corpora. *Proceedings of the Fifteenth International Conference on Computational Linguistics*.

Yarowsky, D. 1994. Decision lists for lexical ambiguity resolution: Application to accent restoration in Spanish and French. *Proceedings of the 32nd Annual Meeting of the Association for Computational Linguistics*.

Yarowsky, D. 1995. Unsupervised word sense disambiguation rivaling supervised methods. *Proceedings of the 33rd Association of Computational Linguistics*.

Using Artificial Intelligence Planning to Generate Antenna Tracking Plans

Forest Fisher, Tara Estlin, Darren Mutz, and Steve Chien

Jet Propulsion Laboratory
California Institute of Technology
4800 Oak Grove Drive
Pasadena, CA 91109-8099
{firstname.lastname}@jpl.nasa.gov

Abstract

This paper describes the application of Artificial Intelligence planning techniques to the problem of antenna track plan generation for a NASA Deep Space Communications Station. The described system enables an antenna communications station to automatically respond to a set of tracking goals by correctly configuring the appropriate hardware and software to provide the requested communication services. To perform this task, the Automated Scheduling and Planning Environment (ASPEN) has been applied to automatically produce antenna tracking plans that are tailored to support a set of input goals. In this paper, we describe the antenna automation problem, the ASPEN planning and scheduling system, how ASPEN is used to generate antenna track plans, the results of several technology demonstrations, and future work utilizing dynamic planning technology.

INTRODUCTION

The Deep Space Network (DSN) [4] was established in 1958 and since then it has evolved into the largest and most sensitive scientific telecommunications and radio navigation network in the world. The purpose of the DSN is to support unmanned interplanetary spacecraft missions and support radio and radar astronomy observations in the exploration of the solar system and the universe. The DSN currently consists of three deep-space communications facilities placed approximately 120 degrees apart around the world: at Goldstone, in California's Mojave Desert; near Madrid, Spain; and near Canberra, Australia. This strategic placement permits constant observation of spacecraft as the Earth rotates, and helps to make the DSN the largest and most sensitive scientific telecommunications system in the world. Each DSN complex operates four deep space stations -- one 70-meter antenna, two 34-meter antennas, and one 26-meter antenna. The functions of the DSN are to receive telemetry signals from spacecraft, transmit commands that control the spacecraft operating modes, generate the radio navigation data used to locate and guide the spacecraft to its destination, and acquire flight radio science, radio and radar astronomy, very long baseline interferometry, and geodynamics measurements.

From its inception the DSN has been driven by the need to create increasingly more sensitive telecommunications devices and better techniques for navigation. The operation of the DSN communications complexes requires a high level of manual interaction with the devices in the communications link with the spacecraft. In more recent times NASA has added some new drivers to the development of the DSN: (1) reduce the cost of operating the DSN, (2) improve the operability, reliability, and maintainability of the DSN, and (3) prepare for a new era of space exploration with the New Millennium program: support small, intelligent spacecraft requiring very few mission operations personnel [8].

This paper addresses the problem of automated track plan generation for the DSN, i.e. automatically determining the necessary actions to set up a communications link between a deep space antenna and a spacecraft. Similar to many planning problems, track plan generation involves elements such as subgoaling to achieve preconditions and decomposing high-level (abstract) actions into more detailed sub-actions. However, unlike most classical planning problems, the problem of track generation is complicated by the need to reason about issues such as metric time, DSN resources and equipment states. To address this problem, we have applied the Automated Scheduling and Planning Environment (ASPEN) to generate antenna track plans on demand.

ASPEN [1,7] is a generic planning and scheduling system being developed at JPL that has been successfully applied to problems in both spacecraft commanding and maintenance scheduling and is now being adapted to generate antenna track plans. ASPEN utilizes techniques from Artificial Intelligence planning and scheduling to automatically generate the necessary antenna command sequence based on input goals. This sequence is produced by utilizing an "iterative repair" algorithm [7,9,12], which classifies conflicts and resolves them each individually by performing one or more plan modifications. This system has been adapted to input antenna tracking goals and automatically produce the required command sequence to set up the requested communications link.

This work is one element of a far-reaching effort to upgrade and automate DSN operations. The ASPEN Track Plan Generator has been demonstrated in support of the Deep Space Terminal (DS-T), which is a prototype 34-meter deep space communications station intended to be capable of fully autonomous operations [5,6].

This rest of this paper is organized in the following manner. We begin by characterizing the current mode of operations for the DSN, and then describe the track plan generation problem. Next, we introduce the ASPEN planning and scheduling system and describe its modeling language and search algorithm(s). We then present an operations example of using this system for track plan generation and discuss several successful demonstrations that were performed with Mars Global Surveyor using a 34-meter antenna station in Goldstone, CA. Finally, we discuss some related work and describe current efforts to expand this system to incorporate a dynamic planning approach which will allow for closed-loop control and automatic error recovery when executing a DSN antenna track.

HOW THE DSN OPERATES

The DSN track process occurs daily for dozens of different NASA spacecraft and projects which use the DSN to capture spacecraft data. Though the process of sending signals from a spacecraft to Earth is conceptually simple, in reality there are many earthside challenges that must be addressed before a spacecraft's signal is acquired and successfully transformed into useful information. In the remainder of this section, we outline some of the steps involved in providing tracking services and in particular discuss the problem of track plan generation.

The first step in performing a DSN track is called network preparation. Here, a project sends a request for the DSN to track a spacecraft involving specific tracking services (e.g. downlink, uplink). The DSN responds to the request by attempting to schedule the necessary resources (i.e. an antenna and other shared equipment) needed for the track. Once an equipment schedule and other necessary information has been determined, the next step is the data capture process, which is performed by operations personnel at the deep space station. During this process, operators determine the correct steps to perform the following tasks: configure the equipment for the track, perform the actual establishment of the communications link, and then perform the actual track by issuing control commands to the various subsystems comprising the link.

Throughout the track the operators continually monitor the status of the link and handle exceptions (e.g. the receiver breaks lock with the spacecraft) as they occur. All of these actions are currently performed by human operators, who manually issue tens or hundreds of commands via a computer keyboard to the link subsystems. This paper discusses the application of the ASPEN planning system to automatically generate DSN track plans (i.e. the steps necessary to set up and perform the requested track) and dramatically reduce the need for many manual steps.

TRACK PLAN GENERATION: THE PROBLEM

Generating an antenna track plan involves taking a general service request (such as telemetry - the downlink of data from a spacecraft), an antenna knowledge-base (which provides the information on the requirements of antenna operation actions), and other project specific information (such as the spacecraft sequence of events), and then generating a partially-ordered sequence of commands. This command sequence will properly configure a communications link that enables the appropriate interaction with the spacecraft. To automate this task, the ASPEN planning and scheduling system has been applied to generate antenna operation procedures on demand.

ASPEN has been adapted to use high-level antenna track information to determine the appropriate steps, parameters on these steps and ordering constraints on these steps that will achieve the input track goals. In generating the antenna track plan, the planner uses information from several sources (see Figure 1):

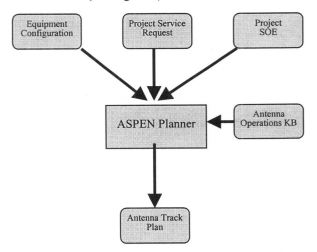

Figure 1 ASPEN Inputs and Outputs

```
1      Activity Pre_track {
2          Decompositions =
3              (Begin_pre_track, Configure_subsystems, Point_antenna, On_point_check,
4              Start_APC where ordered)
5      };
6
7       Activity Acquire_signal {
8          int way;
9          time_param bot_time;
10         Timeline_dependencies =
11             bot_time <- bot_time_sv, way <- way_sv;
12         reservations =
13             BVR,
14             Antenna_sv must_be "on_point",
15             Signal_sv change_to "acquired";
16     };
```

Figure 2 ASPEN Activity Examples

Project Service Request - The service request specifies the DSN services (e.g. downlink, uplink) requested by the project and corresponds to the goals or purpose of the track.

Project SOE - The project sequence of events (SOE) details spacecraft events occurring during the track - including the timing of the beginning and ending of the track and spacecraft data transmission bit rate changes, modulation index changes, and carrier and subcarrier frequency changes.

Antenna Operations KB - The Antenna Operations Knowledge Base (KB) stores information on available antenna operations actions/commands. This KB dictates how actions can be combined to provide essential communication services. Specifically, this includes information such as action preconditions, postconditions, and command directives and also includes any other relevant information such as resource and state descriptions.

Equipment Configuration - This configuration details the types of equipment available and includes items such as the antenna, antenna controller, the receiver, etc.

THE ASPEN MODELING LANGUAGE AND SEARCH ALGORITHM

ASPEN is a reusable, configurable, generic planning/ scheduling application framework that can be tailored to specific domains to create conflict-free plans or schedules. Its components include:
- An expressive modeling language to allow the user to naturally define the application domain
- A constraint management system for representing and maintaining antenna and/or spacecraft operability and resource constraints, as well as activity requirements
- A set of search strategies
- A temporal reasoning system for expressing and maintaining temporal constraints

- A graphical interface for visualizing plans/schedules

A brief introduction into the ASPEN modeling language is given below. For more details on ASPEN, see [1,7].

Modeling Language

The ASPEN modeling language allows the user to define activities, resources and states that describe a particular application domain. A domain model is input at run-time, so modifications can be made to the model without requiring ASPEN to be recompiled. The modeling language has a simple syntax, which can easily be used by operations personnel. Each application model is comprised of several files, which define and instantiate activities, resources and states.

The central data structure in ASPEN is an activity. An activity corresponds to the act of performing a certain function (e.g. configuring the antenna receiver) and represents an action or step in a plan/schedule. Once instantiated it has a start time, an end time, and duration. Activities can also use one or more resources and reason about domain states. Figure 2 shows several activity definitions utilized for antenna-track plan generation. Shown is a "Pre_track" activity that introduces into the plan the steps required to set up the antenna and subsystems for the actual track, and an "Acquire_signal" activity that uses the antenna receiver to acquire the spacecraft signal.

Activity parameters are used to store values in activities or reservations. Lines 8 and 9 contain parameters that specify the number of communication channels (or ways) utilized in the track and the time the track began. Parameter values can be set in an activity definition, passed in from other activities, or as in this case, determined by checking the value of a particular state (as shown on lines 10 and 11). These parameter values are then later referenced when generating the actual command that will execute this step in the final antenna track plan.

Activities can also contain decompositions, as shown in the first activity definition in Figure 2. This activity contains a decomposition into several subactivities (e.g. Configure_subsystems, Point_antenna). These subactivities are activities that can be scheduled any time within the parent activity time interval subject to any constraints within the subactivity definitions. Thus as soon as a "Pre_track" activity is instantiated in a plan, it's subactivities are also instantiated. Decompositions may also be "ordered", such as the one shown here, where all sub-activities must occur in the order specified.

Reservations are used to reserve a portion of a resource or state for the duration of an activity. The second activity in Figure 2 contains a reservation on the Block-V Receiver (BVR). There are two main types of resource reservations in ASPEN: atomic and aggregate. Line 13 of Figure 2 shows an example of an atomic reservation that reserves the BVR for the duration of the activity. No other activities can use the BVR during this time. An example of an aggregate reservation would be to use N units of power or fuel or some other depletable resource.

State reservations can be used to require a certain state be true or change the value of a state variable. Line 14 of Figure 2 requires that the antenna be "on_point" (indicating that the antenna is pointing at the correct set of coordinates) before attempting to acquire the spacecraft signal. Line 15 changes the state of the signal state variable to "acquired" indicating that the spacecraft signal has been successfully acquired by the receiver.

One other utilized feature that is not shown is temporal constraints between activities. Examples of these constraints are: starts_before, starts_after, contains, etc. These constraints can be used to specify partial ordering over certain activities. For example, in the antenna track generation model, it's specified that the activity for generating receiver predicts (where predicts dictate settings for the receiver) must be ordered before the activity which delivers the predicts to the receiver (e.g. Generate_bvr_predicts ends_before start of Deliver_bvr_predicts).

Besides activities, other defined model elements include resources and states. Resource definitions contain a profile of a physical resource over time. There are three main types of resources: atomic, depletable, and non-depletable. Atomic resources are physical devices that can only be used (reserved) by one activity at a time, such as a receiver or antenna controller. Depletable resources are resources that can be used by more than one activity at a time, but their capability is diminished after use, such as a battery or other power source. Non-depletable resources are similar to depletable resources except that their capacity does not diminish and thus they do not need to be replenished, such as memory bus. Most of the resources utilized for antenna track plan generation are atomic resources that represent different pieces of equipment.

A device or subsystem may also be represented by a state variable that gives information about its state over time. A state variable contains a state profile, which is defined as an enumerated type. Some examples of possible states are that an antenna can be "on_point", "off_point" or "stowed", a receiver can be "locked" or "unlocked" and the Conscan subsystem can be "on" or "off." States can be reserved or changed by activities and a state variable must equal some state at every time. Also, if there are several different states possible for a particular state variable, allowable state transitions can be defined where only certain transitions between those states are possible.

Conflict Detection

Conflicts arise within a plan when a constraint has been violated. This constraint could be temporal or involve a parameter, resource or state. In order to reason about temporal constraints, ASPEN utilizes a Temporal Constraint Network (TCN) that describes temporal relationships between activities. The TCN can be queried as to whether the temporal constraints currently imposed between activities are consistent. Also used is a Parameter Dependency Network (PDN) that reflects any defined dependencies between activity parameters. A dependency between two parameters is defined as a function from one parameter to another. These dependencies are maintained by the PDN which checks that at any given time all dependency relations are satisfied.

Resource timelines are used to reason about the usage of physical resources by activities. Conflicts are detected if two or more activities are utilizing an atomic resource at the same time or if the aggregate usage of a resource exceeds its capacity at any given time. State timelines represent attributes, or states, that can change over time where each state can have several possible values. As activities are placed/moved in time, the state timeline updates the values of the state, and detects possible inconsistencies or conflicts that can be introduced as a result.

Planning/Scheduling Algorithms

The search algorithms utilized in a planning/scheduling system typically search for a valid, possibly near-optimal plan/schedule. The ASPEN framework has the flexibility to support a wide-range of scheduling algorithms. For this application, we mainly utilized a repair-based algorithm [7,9,12].

An iterative repair algorithm classifies conflicts and attacks them each individually. Conflicts occur when a plan constraint has been violated, where this constraint could be temporal or involve a resource, state or activity parameter. Conflicts are resolved by performing one or more schedule modifications such as moving, adding, or deleting

```
Pre_track pre_track1{
   Start_time = 1998-213/13:32:26;
   End_time = 1998-213/13:47:26;
};

Track Track1{
   Start_time = 1998-213/13:47:26;
   End_time = 1998-213/16:40:00;
};

Post_track post_track1{
   Start_time = 1998-213/16:40:00;
   End_time = 1998-213/16:50:00;
};
```

Figure 3 Activity Instantiations

activities. The iterative repair algorithm continues until no conflicts remain in the schedule, or a timeout has expired.

For track plan generation, ASPEN begins by generating a possibly invalid complete schedule using a greedy, constructive algorithm. Then, at every iteration, the schedule is analyzed, and repair heuristics that attempt to eliminate conflicts in the schedule are applied until a valid schedule is found. Domain-dependent heuristics can also be added to direct the search towards more optimal solutions.

TRACK PLAN GENERATION: AN EXAMPLE

Given a set of tracking requests, ASPEN can generate a conflict-free track plan within the order of seconds that will correctly set up the requested communications link. In order to begin the planning process, the tracking service request, the equipment configuration, and the project SOE are parsed and relevant information is placed in a initial setup file which lists the requested track goals and any relevant initial state information. For example, Figure 3 shows three activity instantiations that request that a "Pre_track", "Track" and "Post_track" activity be placed in the final plan at specific times.

ASPEN then decomposes these activities into the necessary steps that set up the antenna and subsystems (i.e. "Pre_track"), that perform the track (i.e. "Track"), and that perform the necessary shutdown procedures once the track had ended (i.e. "Post_track"). Other initial state information is provided in a "Set_state_values" activity, which sets up the appropriate state variables. The information includes the spacecraft ID, antenna ID, the tracking goals, the carrier and sub-carrier frequency, the symbol rate, etc. ASPEN is also provided with the model files that hold the relevant activity, parameter, resource and state definitions, which were explained in the previous section.

```
Configure_equipment:

Start jsc_asn.prc(dss,sc,pass,&ret_status)
If (!ret_status) then
    Write("fatal error: cannot start pass")
    Goto fatal_err
Endif

Start ugc_hi.prc
If (!ret_status) then
    Write("fatal error: can't control UGC")
    Goto fatal_err
Endif

Start apc_hi.prc
If (!ret_status) then
    Write("fatal error: can't control APC")
    Goto fatal_err
Endif
.
.
.
Point_antenna:

Ret_status = exec("APC DCOS")
Start apc_track.prc(&ret_status)
If (!ret_status) then
    Write("fatal error: cannot point ant")
    Goto fatal_err
Endif
```

Figure 4 Antenna Control Script

Once the initial goals and state information are loaded, ASPEN utilizes its iterative repair algorithm to create a conflict-free track plan that provides the requested services. This final plan contains a large amount of information, including a list of grounded activities (where each activity has been assigned a start time and end time), and a list of constraints over those activities, including temporal, parameter, resource and state constraints. ASPEN also displays the final resource and state timelines which show the states of those entities over the course of the plan. The actual antenna control script that will be used to execute the track is output in a separate file which contains the command sequence necessary to set up, control and break down the link. In the model definition, a command (or set of commands) can be specified for each defined activity. These commands are then output in the correct sequence based on the final plan constraints. An example of this file format is shown in Figure 4. This control script is then sent to an antenna operator or execution agent where it will be used to perform the requested track.

DS-T DEMONSTRATIONS

The Deep Space Terminal (DS-T) [5,6] being developed at the NASA Jet Propulsion Laboratory is a prototype 34-meter deep space communications station intended to be

Figure 5 34m BWG Antennas at Goldstone

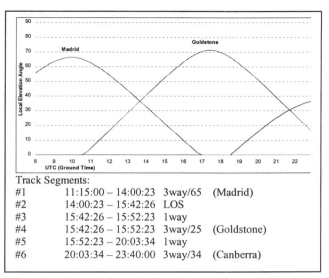

Track Segments:

#1	11:15:00 – 14:00:23	3way/65	(Madrid)
#2	14:00:23 – 15:42:26	LOS	
#3	15:42:26 – 15:52:23	1way	
#4	15:42:26 – 15:52:23	3way/25	(Goldstone)
#5	15:52:23 – 20:03:34	1way	
#6	20:03:34 – 23:40:00	3way/34	(Canberra)

Figure 6 September 16, 1998 MGS Track

capable of fully autonomous operations. When requested to perform a track, the DS-T station automatically performs a number of tasks (at appropriate times) required to execute the track. First, the Schedule Executive sets up the track schedule for execution and provides the means for automated rescheduling and/or manual schedule editing in the event of changes. The Configuration Engine is then responsible for retrieving all the necessary data needed for station operations. Next, the Script Generator (ASPEN) generates the necessary command sequence to perform the track. Finally, a Station Monitor and Control process executes the generated script and records relevant monitor data generated during the track.

The DS-T concept was validated through a number of demonstrations. The demonstrations began with the automation of partial tracks in April 1998, continued with 1-day unattended operations in May, and concluded with a 6-day autonomous *"lights-out"* demonstration in September 1998. Throughout these demonstrations ASPEN was used to automatically generate the necessary command sequences for a series of Mars Global Surveyor (MGS) downlink tracks using the equipment configuration at Deep Space Station 26 (DSS26), a 34-meter antenna located in Goldstone, CA. These command sequences were produced and executed in a fully autonomous fashion with no human intervention. During the September demonstration performed all Mars Global Surveyor coverage scheduled for the Goldstone antenna complex. This corresponded to roughly 13 hours of continuous track coverage per day.

In Figure 5, we show a picture of the three 34-meter Beam Wave Guide (BWG) antennas at the Goldstone, CA facility. In the foreground is DSS-26, which was the station selected for prototyping the DS-T.

While the overall DS-T effort consisted of a large team and a project duration of approximately 1.5 years, the DS-T automation team consisted of three team members. Of this teams work, approximately one work year was spent on the script generation effort. This effort primarily consisted of knowledge acquisition and model development, while a small effort was made in the integration of the script

generator. A key factor in the quick development was the ability to adapt a general purpose planning and scheduling system. As the domain of ground communication-station commanding shared many similarities to spacecraft commanding, ASPEN seemed like a logical choice. This was confirmed by the ease of knowledge base development and integration. Spacecraft commanding also consists of generating a sequence of commands, however it is predominately a resource-scheduling problem, whereas ground-station commanding is predominately a sequencing problem.

RESULTS

In order to provide qualitative results, we present statistical data from September 16, 1998, a representative day during our 6-day autonomous unattended demonstration, durring which we collected above 90% of the transmitted frames. This performance is on par with the operator-controlled stations, however required no support personnel (i.e. reduced operations cost).

In figure 6, the graph represents when MGS was in view of the ground stations at each of the three complexes (Madrid, Goldstone, and Canberra). DS-T, which is located at Goldstone, tracked MGS through the five track segments indicated in the figure 6.

Before continuing with the analysis of the results, let us explain the different modes indicated in figure 6 for each of the different track segments. When a spacecraft is downlinking data it is said to be in 1way mode. When an uplink and a downlink are taking place simultaneously the spacecraft is said to be in 2way mode. If a station is communicating in 2way mode with a spacecraft, and another station is listening in on the downlink of the spacecraft, the second station is said to be in 3way with the 2way station. Because DS-T is not equipped for uplink , DS-T operates in either 1way or 3way mode. Because the downlink frequency is relative to the uplink frequency, it is critical to determine the station involved in the uplink when taking part in a 3way mode of operations. In this example, during segment 4 dss25 (deep space station) was in 2way and DS-T was in 3way with 25 (3way/25).

Track segment 2, which is labeled LOS, indicates that there was a scheduled loss of signal (LOS) so during this segment no frames were collected. During each of the other respective track segment DS-T collected 75%, 91%, 96%, 90%, 23% of the broadcasted frames. As shown by the graph, during segment 1 and 6 the elevation of the dish is low in the sky. Under these circumstances there is considerably more atmospheric interference which explains the lower percent of frame collection. On the other hand, if you look at segment 4 where there is a long segment with the spacecraft high in the sky the data collection is quite high. In segment 3 and 5 the values are a little lower due to the shortness of the segments. This is explained by the fact that some data is lost during a change in mode, as in the transition from LOS to 1way and 3way/25 to 1way.

As a component of the DS-T demonstrations, the SG performed flawlessly, producing dynamically instantiated control scripts based on the desired service goals for the communications pass as specified in the service request. The use of such technology resulted in a three primary benefits:

- Autonomous operations enabled by eliminating the need for hundreds of manual inputs in the form of control directives. Currently the task of creating the communications link is a manual and time-consuming process which requires operator input of approximately 700 control directives and the constant monitoring of several dozen displays to determine the exact execution status of the system.
- Reduced the level of expertise of an operator required to perform a communication track. Currently the complex process requires a high level of expertise from the operator, but through the development of the KB by a domain expert this expertise is captured with in the system itself.
- The KB provides a declarative representation of operation procedures. Through the capture of this expertise the KB documents the procedural steps of performing antenna communication services.

RELATED WORK

There are a number of existing systems built to solve real-world planning or scheduling problems [10,11,12]. The problem of track plan generation combines elements from both these fields and thus traditional planners and schedulers cannot be directly applied. First, many classical

planning elements must be addressed in this application such as subgoaling to achieve activity preconditions (e.g. the antenna must be "on_point" to lock up the receiver) and decomposing higher-level (abstract) activities into more detailed sub-activities. In addition, many scheduling elements are presents such as handling metric time and temporal constraints, and representing and reasoning about resources (e.g. receiver, antenna controller) and states (e.g. antenna position, subcarrier frequency, etc.) over time.

One other system has been designed to generate antenna track plans, the Deep Space Network Antenna Operations Planner (DPLAN) [2]. DPLAN utilizes a combination of AI hierarchical-task network (HTN) and operator-based planning techniques. Unlike DPLAN, ASPEN has a temporal reasoning system for expressing and maintaining temporal constraints and also has the capability for representing and reasoning about different types of resources and states. ASPEN can utilize different search algorithms such as constructive and repair-based algorithms, where DPLAN uses a standard best-first based search. And, as described in the next section, ASPEN is currently being extended to perform dynamic planning for closed-loop error recovery, where DPLAN has only limited replanning capabilities.

FUTURE WORK: PROVIDING CLOSED-LOOP CONTROL THROUGH DYNAMIC PLANNING

Currently, we are working on modifying and extending the current ASPEN Track Plan Generator to provide a Closed Loop Error Recovery system (CLEaR) for DSN track automation. CLEaR is a real-time planning system built as an extension to ASPEN [3]. The approach taken is to dynamically feed monitor data (sensor updates) back into the planning system as state updates. As these dynamic updates come in, the planning system verifies the validity of the current plan. If a violation is found in the plan, the system will perform local modification to construct a new valid plan. Through this continual planning approach, the plan is disrupted as little as possible and the system is much more responsive and reactive to changes in the real (dynamic) world.

This CLEaR effort is also being integrated with a Fault Detection, Isolation and Recovery (FDIR) system. FDIR is an expert system providing monitor data analysis. As is often the case with large complex systems, monitor (sensor) data is often related in different ways that becomes difficult for a human to detect. The advantage of combining these two systems is that FDIR can first interpret the vast amount of data and summarize it into a set of meaningful values for a planning system to react to. We think of this union as intelligent analysis and intelligent response, much like a careful design and implementation; one without the other is of little use.

CONCLUSIONS

This paper has described an application of the ASPEN automated planning system for antenna track plan generation. ASPEN utilizes a knowledge base of information on tracking activity requirements and a combination of Artificial Intelligence planning and scheduling techniques to generate antenna track plans that will correctly setup a communications link with spacecraft. We also described several demonstrations that have been performed as part of the DS-T architecture where ASPEN was used to generate plans for downlink tracks with Mars Global Surveyor. Finally, we described a planned extension of this system, which will allow for closed-loop control, error recovery and fault detection using dynamic planning techniques.

ACKNOWLEDGEMENTS

This work was performed by the Jet Propulsion Laboratory, California Institute of Technology, under contract of the National Aeronautics and Space Administration. We thank members of the ASPEN scheduling team and members of the DS-T automation team for contributing to this work.

References

[1] S. Chien, D. Decoste, R. Doyle, and P. Stolorz, "Making an Impact: Artificial Intelligence at the Jet Propulsion Laboratory," AI Magazine, 18(1), 103-122, 1997.

[2] S. Chien, R. Hill Jr., A. Govindjee, X. Wang, T. Estlin, A. Griesel, R. Lam and K. Fayyad, "A Hierarchical Architecture for Resource Allocation, Plan Execution, and Revision for Operation of a Network of Communication Antennas," Proceedings of the 1997 IEEE Conference on Robotics and Automation, Albuquerque, NM, April 1997.

[3] S. Chien, R. Knight, A. Stechert, R. Sherwood, and G. Rabideau, "Integrated Planning and Execution for Autonomous Spacecraft," To appear in the Proceedings of the 1999 IEEE Aerospace Conference, Aspen, CO, March, 1999.

[4] Deep Space Network, Jet Propulsion Laboratory Publication 400-517, April 1994.

[5] F. Fisher, S. Chien, L. Paal, E. Law, N. Golshan, and M. Stockett, "An Automated Deep Space Communications Station," Proceedings of the 1998 IEEE Aerospace Conference, Aspen, CO, March 1998.

[6] F. Fisher, D. Mutz, T. Estlin, L. Paal, and S. Chien, "The Past, Present and Future of Ground Station Automation with in the DSN," To appear in the Proceedings of the 1999 IEEE Aerospace Conference, Aspen, CO, March 1999.

[7] A. Fukanaga, G. Rabideau, S. Chien, and D. Yan, "Toward an Application Framework for Automated Planning and Scheduling," Proceedings of the 1997 International Symposium of Artificial Intelligence, Robotics and Automation for Space, Tokyo, Japan, July 1997.

[8] R. W. Hill, Jr., S. A. Chien, K. V. Fayyad, C. Smyth, T. Santos, and R. Bevan, "Sequence of Events Driven Automation of the Deep Space Network," Telecommunications and Data Acquisition 42-124, October-December 1995.

[9] S. Minton and M. Johnston, "Minimizing Conflicts: A Heuristic Repair Method for Constraint Satisfaction and Scheduling Problems," Artificial Intelligence, 58:161-205, 1988.

[10] A. Tate, B. Drabble and R Kirby, "O-Plan2: An Open Architecture for Command Planning and Control," Intelligent Scheduling (Eds. M. Fox & M. Zweben), Morgan Kaufmann, 1994.

[11] D. Wilkins Practical Planning: Extending the Classical AI Planning Paradigm, Morgan Kaufmann, 1994.

[12] M. Zweben, B. Daun, E. Davis, and M. Deale, Scheduling and Rescheduling with Iterative Repair, in Intelligent Scheduling, Morgan Kaufmann, 1994.

In-Time Agent-Based Vehicle Routing with a Stochastic Improvement Heuristic

Robert Kohout and Kutluhan Erol

Intelligent Automation, Inc
2 Research Place
Rockville, Md. 20850
{kohout,kutluhan}@i-a-i.com

Abstract

Vehicle routing problems (VRP's) involve assigning a fleet of limited capacity service vehicles to service a set of customers. This paper describes an innovative, agent-based approach to solving a real-world vehicle-routing problem embedded in a highly dynamic, unpredictable domain. Most VRP research, and all commercial products for solving VRP's, make a static-world assumption, ignoring the dynamism in the real world. Our system is explicitly designed to address dynamism, and employs an *in-time* algorithm that quickly finds partial solutions to a problem, and improves these as time allows. Our fundamental innovation is a stochastic improvement mechanism that enables a distributed, agent-based system to achieve high-quality solutions in the absence of a centralized dispatcher. This solution-improvement technology overcomes inherent weaknesses in the distributed problem-solving approach that make it difficult to find high-quality solutions to complex optimization problems. In previous work on similar problems, the MARS system of Fischer and Müller, *et al.*, achieved an average route performance of roughly 124% of Solomon's algorithm for a VRP problem, which is known to achieve results that average roughly 107% of optimal. Our algorithm produces routes that average 106% those produced by an adaptation of Solomon's algorithm to a more general problem.

The Pickup and Delivery Problem with Time Windows

Vehicle routing problems (VRP's) involve assigning a fleet of limited capacity service vehicles to service a set of customers. These problems have been well studied in the Operations Research literature (e.g.,Laport 1992.) Insofar as the Travelling Salesman Problem is embedded in virtually every VRP of practical interest, this entire class of problems is intractable. The vast majority of vehicle routing research addresses a static problem in which all of the relevant data is known in advance. Typically, service vehicles are assumed to start at some initial location (the *depot*), all customer demands and constraints are known, as are the distance and travel times between each pair of customers, and between each customer and the depot. There are a number of commercial systems for solving

VRP's, and like the academic literature, all of them make a static-world assumption, ignoring the naturally occurring dynamism in the world. Customers can be late, or fail to appear. Traffic can be delayed for a variety of reasons. The time required to service a customer can be highly varying and unpredictable.

This paper describes an innovative approach to solving a vehicle routing problem embedded in a highly dynamic, unpredictable domain. It employs an *in-time* algorithm that quickly finds partial solutions to a problem, and improves these as time allows. In an online application for a dynamic environment, the problem itself may change over time, and the results need not be delivered all at once. *"In-time"* captures the essence of our algorithm in two ways: it is designed to run online in a dynamic world (i.e. in "real" time), and it returns partial results in time to execute them.

This work was conducted by the authors at Intelligent Automation, Inc. (IAI) as part of an effort to construct agent-based optimization systems for online problem solving. It was developed in collaboration with an actual airport shuttle company, and was designed to solve the Airport Shuttle Scheduling Problem, in which a fleet of limited capacity *shuttle* vehicles must be dispatched to service customers arriving at and departing from a set of regional airports. The goal of the system is to find a schedule of customer service times that minimizes the number of vehicles required to service a set of customers, with a secondary goal of minimizing the total time required to do so, while observing travel time constraints, vehicle capacity constraints and customer service time constraints. Our fundamental innovation is a stochastic improvement mechanism that enables a distributed, agent-based system to achieve high-quality solutions in the absence of a centralized dispatcher.

The airport shuttle business is highly dynamic. Customers can cancel and flights can be delayed. Traffic congestion varies routinely with the time of day, and less predictable delays due to accidents or weather are routine. Drivers get lost, and customers fail to appear as expected. Baggage delivery times vary widely by airline, time of day, and customer. Standard industry practice is to require a reservation 24 hours in advance, but this requirement is routinely waived, particularly for passengers arriving at an airport and requesting service "at the curb."

Shuttle companies typically require departing customers

to be available for shuttle pickup a minimum of two hours prior to the departure of their flight, but this time varies from company to company, and even between customers. There is generally no guarantee on how long an arriving customer's return from an airport may take, but shuttle companies have a long-term interest in ensuring that it is reasonable. The static problem, in which all of the relevant data is known is advance, is a specific instance of what the routing literature refers to as either the *Pickup and Delivery Problem With Time Windows (PDPTW)*, or sometimes as the *Dial-a-Ride Problem*. A formalization of this problem can be found in (Dumas, Desrosier and Soumis 1991).

We know of no commercially available products for solving the static PDPTW, let alone the more realistic dynamic case that an airport shuttle company would require. However, there are a number of commercial products for solving the static version of a similar, related problem: the *Vehicle Routing Problem with Time Windows (VRPTW.)* In the PDPTW, customers have two associated locations: a pickup point and a delivery point, and time windows associated with each service location. In the VRPTW, there is a single service location, and one associated time window. Unlike the PDPTW, the VRPTW has been extensively studied, and optimal solutions are known for problem instances with as many as 100 customers. Most of the commercial products for vehicle routing are based upon Solomon's insertion heuristic (Solomon, 1987), which has demonstrated the ability to find high-quality solutions in a relatively short amount of time. We will discuss this algorithm in greater detail below.

An Agent-Oriented Approach to Online Optimization

In order to address the dynamism of the airport shuttle application, we decided to design a system built around a set of cooperating software *agents,* each of which represents the interests and behavior of entities in the domain. These agents are organized into *contract nets* (Davis & Smith, 1983) that support rational, market-based assignment of resources. The use of agents for such problem-solving purposes has a number of potential advantages. Isolating system capabilities into independent processing units provides the foundation for distributing them over a large network of computers, thus allowing considerable computing power to easily be brought to bear on a given problem. Much of the promise of agent-based systems comes from the fact that software may be designed as individual capabilities and integrated into larger systems without having to reason about all of the ways in which a new capability may impact the behavior of the various other components of the system. Control is localized, and each agent can be designed to act independently, maximizing its own individual utility function without having to reason about the operation of the entire system.

While this localization of control simplifies the design of individual agents, it greatly complicates the problem of achieving high-quality global solutions. In previous work on agent-based vehicle routing systems, (Fischer, Müller, and Pischel, 1996) describe MARS (the *Modeling a Multi-Agent Scenario for Shipping Companies* system), which uses a hierarchical multi-agent system to solve the VRPTW. In OR parlance, MARS uses a heuristic local assignment procedure, followed by a 2-phase post-optimization process. Since both stages of post-optimization modify a schedule only if there is a net gain in global utility, the post-optimization (a.k.a. *local improvement*) qualifies as a hill-climbing algorithm. As noted in (Bentley, 1992) and elsewhere, such local improvement techniques are very sensitive to the quality of the initial solution, since they are only able find the local minimum of the solution space in which they begin their search. Thus, while MARS has a sophisticated market-based improvement algorithm that is well suited to agent-based routing applications, the crucial heuristic for determination of the initial solution set is less developed. (Fischer, Müller and Pischel, 1995) present a comparison of MARS with the known optimal results for 25-customer routing problems. In these cases, MARS achieves an average of roughly 133% of optimal. Solomon's algorithm is known to achieve an average of 107% of optimal prior to post-optimization, and 103% of optimal after post-optimization (Potvin and Rousseau, 1993). If we assume that the agent-based improvement mechanism is effective, MARS must be doing a poor job of initial customer insertion, and yet this is exactly the area that previous research indicates is crucial for obtaining high quality results. The significant advantages of distributed, agent-based systems for use dynamic application environments do not justify poor global performance, especially since, as we show in this paper, it is possible to obtain high-quality results in such an online control system.

Multi-Agent Architecture

The architecture of our entire system is shown in Figure 1, below. Each pending group of customers[1] is represented by a *customer agent,* and each available vehicle is represented by a vehicle agent. There is no centralized scheduler, and even the GUI's were designed to run as agents under Cybele, our software infrastructure for agent-based applications. The route/address server agent performs address lookup and verification tasks, as well as the point-to-point routing required as part of the scheduling process.

When a customer requests service, the relevant information regarding number of passengers, itineraries, service address, etc. is entered via the GUI. At this time,

---

[1] Throughout the rest of this paper, references to "customers" will refer to groups of one or more persons who have indicated a desire to travel together, and share all relevant deadlines and constraints. We assume that no such group is larger than the maximum vehicle capacity, and our algorithm makes no attempt to split groups of more than one into smaller "lots."

the customer's address is verified with the route/address server, to ensure that the routing system can find the service address in its database. Once all this information is obtained, the routing system creates a customer agent, that will be responsible for seeing that the associated customer is serviced.

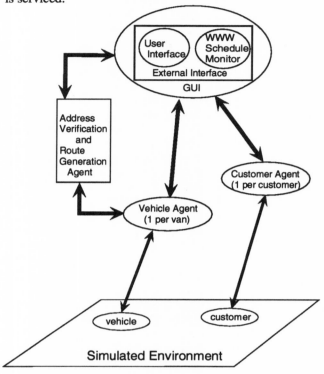

Figure 1 Routing System Architecture

The customer agent announces itself, and all vehicle agents compute the cost of carrying that customer with respect to their current schedules, and send these as quotes to the customer. Once a customer agent has received all of the expected quotes, it selects the low bidder and requests service from the associated vehicle agent. If the vehicle agent can still service the customer at the quoted price, the customer is inserted into the vehicle's schedule, and the customer agent is informed that the contract has been accepted. If the vehicle agent can no longer route the customer at the quoted price, presumably because another customer has been scheduled since the quote was sent, the vehicle agent returns a message indicating its new best price, and the customer agent repeats the process until it is scheduled.

The Algorithm

Our vehicle agents make scheduling decisions by using Solomon's insertion heuristic, adapted for the PDPTW. For this reason, and because we use a centralized implementation of this same algorithm as the basis for evaluating our improvement technique, we summarize Solomon's algorithm as Algorithm 1. If d_{ij} is the travel

time between customers i and j, and b_j is the time scheduled to begin service at customer j, then Solomon's cost heuristic defines the cost of inserting customer u between adjacent customers i and j in a route R as

$$H = (d_{iu} + d_{uj} - \mu d_{ij}) + \Delta b_j$$

Where μ is a non-negative parameter, and Δb_j is the change in service time at customer j.

```
Let L be the list of unscheduled customers
R = new vehicle route

While there are still unassigned customers in L
  Do {
    For each unassigned customer C Do
      For each potential insertion position in R
      Do {
        If C can feasibly be served in this
          route position Then
          {
            Compute H = Solomon's heuristic value
            If H is minimal Then {
            save H along with the
            corresponding position in the route
            }
          }
      }
    Assign customer with minimum H value to the
    Corresponding insertion position in R,
    and remove that customer from L.

    If NO Customer could be feasibly served in
      the current schedule Then
      { /* start a new route */
      Save R
      R = new route
      }
  }
```

Algorithm 1 - Solomon's Algorithm

Recall that this algorithm was developed to solve the VRPTW. In order to apply it to the PDPTW, our modified algorithm first locates a slot where it is feasible to insert the pickup position, and then searches forward through a vehicle's schedule for a feasible slot in which to insert the delivery point, while accounting for the implications of pickup insertion. The ultimate cost of a customer's insertion into a schedule is a weighted sum of the costs of pickup insertion and delivery insertion.

Our agent-based insertion algorithm is summarized below as Algorithm 2. This algorithm uses the exact same cost metric and low-level data structures as our implementation of Solomon's heuristic for the PDPTW. The two main differences are that it builds the routes for the various vehicle agents in parallel, and schedules each customer in the order that they are presented to the system. Solomon's heuristic builds routes one at a time. Before inserting a customer into a route, it iterates through *all* of the remaining customers, and greedily chooses the cheapest remaining customer for insertion into the current route. Only after no remaining customer can be inserted into a route does it initialize a new one.

The effect of the outer loop of Solomon's algorithm is to impose an ordering on the set of customers. If customers were presented to our agent-based system in the exact same order determined by this process, it would produce identical results. However, as we show below, in the absence of local improvement, our agent-based algorithm does quite poorly when customers are scheduled in a random order.

```
Create a vehicle route
While unscheduled customers remain Do
    Get the cost of inserting the next customer
    in each of the active vehicle routes

    If the customer cannot be inserted into any
    Vehicle Agent's Route Then
        Start a new Vehicle Agent and Route
    Else
        Insert the customer into the lowest cost
        Vehicle route
```

Algorithm 2 -Abstract Agent-Based Insertion Algorithm

We have developed a stochastic improvement heuristic that overcomes the order-sensitivity of the insertion algorithm. This improvement technique permits the system to converge to high quality solutions, in the absence of any centralized control, and without requiring any agents to maintain information about the state of any other agents in the system. A vehicle agent "sees" a customer only when the customer agent announces itself, and records information about a customer only if and when that customer is inserted into its schedule. Vehicle agents are not required or expected to cooperate with each other in any form or fashion.

The basic improvement mechanism is simple: we allow customer agents to stochastically request removal from a schedule, and go searching for a better deal by re-announcing their availability for service. In this way, we overcome the primary weakness of Algorithm 2, which is its sensitivity to the order in which customers are announced. In many cases, a customer is released from a given van only to be later rescheduled in the same vehicle, but there are enough opportunities for improvement that overall performance improves significantly.

The algorithm makes no distinction between scheduling and rescheduling. In fact "rescheduling" begins before scheduling has ever finished. The basic process can be described as follows:

1. Each vehicle agent has a "rescheduling interval", which is stochastically determined. This interval consists of some fixed period of time (the *baseline)* plus a random variable drawn from an exponential population. This period is set when a vehicle agent is initialized, and then reset to a new value at the end of each rescheduling interval. This is implemented as a timer that fires to begin a rescheduling interval.

2. During a rescheduling interval, a vehicle agent first stochastically selects an exponential random variable, which is the upper bound on the number of customers in that van that may be rescheduled, and which is bounded above by the total number of customers in the schedule.

3. Customers are selected from the vehicle, and each customer is selected for rescheduling with a probability $p_c(t)$ that goes to zero its earliest service time approaches. In the tests of the next section, $p_c(t)$ reaches zero thirty (simulated) minutes before the earliest possible time a customer could be serviced in a van.

This choice of $p_c(t)$ reflects the online application for which the algorithm was designed. In order to ensure that customers traveling early in the day are scheduled efficiently, we allow the system to run three hundred simulated minutes, plus an additional simulated minute per customer, prior to enforcing policy 3. Since customers are normally required to make reservations a day in advance, this early rescheduling is consistent with the target application.

Empirical Evaluation

We obtained a small database of typical customer information from an airport shuttle company operating in the Washington, DC metropolitan area, where there are three large regional airports. We used this information to generate distributions of relevant customer information as a function of the time of day. For the purposes of the test described in this paper, this information includes a) whether a customer is arriving or departing, and b) which airport customers are flying into or out of. We also determined the distribution of customer group sizes. To determine point-to-point travel times and distances, we used Caliper Co.'s TransCAD® system to geo-code addresses, and compute the minimum pair-wise distances and travel times for 500 addresses from this database. Note that the minimum-travel-time route is not necessarily the same as the minimum-distance route. All tests reported in this paper used the 250,000 minimum-time values obtained in this way.

This information was used to randomly generate problem sets. To create a new customer, we first randomly selected an address id in the range 0-499. We assume that these addresses are independent from the other values in the data. After selecting an address, we use a Bernoulli test to determine whether or not the customer is arriving or departing. We then select the customer's airport, based upon our distribution analysis of arriving and departing customers. To determine the airport-arrival time, we randomly select the hour of the flight based upon our distribution analysis. We then use a random number uniformly distributed between 0-59 to decide the exact minute of the flight. Finally we determine the customer group size using the empirical distribution.

This process was used to generate two different test data sets, each of one hundred problem instances. The first test set contains 100 problems of 100 customers each, and the second contains 100 problems of 200 customers each. While this data generation process is imperfect, we believe it provides an adequate model of a real-world shuttle-dispatching problem.

Recall that our system was designed to run online. In order to test this algorithm, we ran it in simulated time, as we will describe below. The results reported in this paper were run on a single 350M Hz PC with 256Mb of SDRAM, running Windows NT 4.0. Tests were run at one hundred and twenty times real time (i.e. 500 milliseconds = 1 simulated minute.) In order to prevent thrashing associated with having scores of customers simultaneously negotiating with as many as fifteen vehicle agents, we maintained a queue of unannounced customers. Every five hundred milliseconds, this queue was examined and if not empty, the customer agent at the head of the queue announced itself. Each problem was run for 1200 simulated minutes, because we observed that there was little, if any significant improvement after this cutoff.

The algorithm turns out to be very sensitive to tuning. There are a number of different tuning parameters, but for the purposes of this paper, we focused upon the two rescheduling interval parameters, and the exponentially distributed random variable that determines the maximum number of customer that will be rescheduled per van. We tuned the algorithm on ten 100-customer test problems that are not in the reported test set. The results reported in this paper use a rescheduling baseline of 5000 milliseconds, plus an exponential random variable with a mean of 5000 milliseconds. We use a value of 2.0 for the mean of the exponentially distributed number of deletions per van.

The object-oriented implementation of the algorithm makes it a simple matter to customize customer constraints. However, our tests assume a uniform set of constraints. For departing customers, we take the airport arrival time to be the latest time at which the customer can be delivered to the airport without violating a deadline. Normally, this is 30 minutes prior to flight departure. Consistent with industry practice, the earliest permissible pickup time for a departing customer is two hours prior to this time. The latest permissible pickup time is the time at which the van could arrive at the customer's site, load all passengers into the van and still be able to drive a direct path to the airport at the minimum travel time, and arrive there at the customer's airport arrival time. We allow one minute, plus one additional minute per passenger, to load and unload the van.

For arriving customers, we assume that the earliest possible pickup time is the airport arrival time, and that the customer must be picked up within two hours of this time. The earliest possible time that an arriving customer can be dropped off is in the case where the customer is picked up and loaded in to a van at the earliest possible time, and driven directly home. The latest allowable drop-off time is three hours later than this. Again, we assume one minute plus an additional minute per passenger is required to

deliver a customer to his destination, but at the airport, we allow twenty minutes, plus an additional minute per passenger. All vehicles in these experiments were given a maximum capacity of six passengers.

Results

We compare the performance of three algorithms on two sets of problems. The first algorithm is our centralized algorithm, which is an implementation of Solomon's insertion heuristic extended to the PDPTW. The second algorithm is our agent-based system in the absence of any post-optimization procedure, and corresponds to Algorithm 2 above. The third row summarizes the behavior of our agent-based scheduler with stochastic optimization.

Algorithm	Vans	Travel Time	Waiting Time	Total Time
Centralized	7.78	5291	1383	6674
Distributed / No optimization	9.77	6015	3036	9051
Distributed with optimization	7.60	4586	2545	7132

Table 1 100-Customer Routing Results

The primary optimization criteria in our target application was to minimize the number of delivery vehicles employed, with a secondary goal of minimizing the total time that vehicles were in use. Our results are presented in Tables 1 and 2. As Table 1 shows, in the 100-customer cases, our distributed algorithm uses 2.4% fewer vehicles, while producing routes that consume roughly 6.8% more time than those produced by the centralized algorithm. These differences are statistically significant. The hypothesis that the average difference in performance of these two algorithms is zero fails a paired, two-tailed T-test at the 0.04 confidence level (t = 2.07). The probability that the mean travel times found by the two algorithms are actually equal approaches zero (p = 4.11E-11, t = 7.26.) Note that the average *travel times* in the distributed routes are roughly 86.7% that of the centralized routes. The time advantage displayed by the centralized algorithm stems from the fact that the distributed algorithm finds routes with almost twice as most total *waiting time* which is essentially slack in the schedule. This is a desirable result in the highly dynamic and unpredictable application domain for which the algorithm was designed and tuned. With drivers working on commission, routes with fewer vans (and thus more customers per van), shorter total drive times and more schedule slack are ideal, in that they minimize company costs, as well as the likelihood that a service guarantee will not be met.

The total time of our solutions, with respect to the centralized algorithm, improves slightly as the number of customers increases. This is illustrated in Table 2, which presents summary results for the 200-customer problems. The distributed algorithm achieves similar vehicle savings as the 100-customer case - approximately 2.3% fewer vehicles, while coming significantly closer to the total time performance of the centralized algorithm. Again, the observed differences are statistically significant, with the difference in vehicle usage approaching the 0.001 level of confidence (t = 3.26). The difference in route distances is significant at the 0.01 confidence level (t = 2.66.)

Algorithm	Vans	Travel Time	Waiting Time	Total Time
Centralized	12.67	9129	1878	11007
Distributed / No optimization	16.6	11092	4660	15753
Distributed with Optimization	12.36	8198	3038	11236

Table 2 200-Customer Routing Results

Our distributed, asynchronous implementation platform does not permit a direct comparison of the CPU requirements of the distributed and the centralized algorithms. Instead, we present analytical evidence that suggest our approach will scale well. Asymptotically, the centralized algorithm is $O(Cn^2)$, where n is the number of customers and C is the maximum vehicle capacity. The agent-based algorithm is $O(CV)$ where V is the number of vehicles and C is as above. In addition, the number of stochastic "give backs" in the 100-customer tests averaged 611, so the cost of improvement can be viewed as a small constant multiple of the initial cost of scheduling in the distributed case. Moreover, the increase in the number of the re-insertions is less-than-linear in the increase in the number of customers. In the 200 customer tests, the total number of re-insertions averaged 782. Taken together, we have every reason to believe that the optimization technique scales well as the number of customers increases. In addition, this algorithm was explicitly designed for and implemented as a distributed application. Assuming that we assign a separate processor to each vehicle agent, the asymptotic time-to-solution is $O(C)$.

Conclusions and Future Work

The results we report in this paper were a bit of a surprise. Our goal was to design an agent-based online optimization system for vehicle routing. Like Fischer and Müller, we expected to sacrifice some level of global utility is return for the increased reactive capabilities of a distributed, agent-based system. Our hope in designing the stochastic improvement mechanism was to overcome an apparent limitation of previous approaches based upon local post-optimization, and to come relatively close to the level achieved by practical centralized heuristics. The results were surprising because they actually out-performed a centralized heuristic that is known to perform well. Note that there is nothing about our technique that explicitly precludes a market-based post-optimization mechanism such as the one used in MARS, and we hope to experiment with such a hybrid in the future.

Inasmuch as these results were unexpected, there remains a good deal to be done to prove the viability of the approach. In particular, there are no standard benchmarks for the PDPTW that we know of, but there are dozens of studies that have used Solomon's instances for the VRPTW. In addition, the nature of our implementation makes a direct analysis of the runtime performance of this algorithm impossible. From the perspective of the vehicle routing literature, a centralized implementation of this basic technique to solve the VRPTW is warranted.

The tests and results presented in this paper all address a static problem. The fact that our distributed agent-based solution to this problem performs comparably to a centralized algorithm on this problem is both surprising and noteworthy. However, our research and development focus is upon the dynamic problems associated with changes in the operating environment, such as customer cancellations and delays, that occur after the algorithm has begun to solve a problem. Evaluating the quality of performance in such dynamic systems presents a significant challenge to the research community. Our next obvious step in this direction is to introduce such dynamism into the problem, and we are already testing our system upon such problems

Acknowledgements

This work was funded in part by NASA SBIR contract NAS8-9705. We would like to thank Ben Smith and Steve Chien of NASA JPL, and James Wentworth of the US FHwA for their encouragement and support, as well as Jun Lang, Prasad Narasimhan, Angela Malais, Geoff Bernstein, and Renato Levy for their roles in the implementation.

References

Bentley,J.J. 1992. Fast algorithms for geometric travelling salesman problems. *Op. Rsrch. Soc. of America*, **4**: 387-411.

Davis,R. and Smith,R.G. 1983. Negotiation as a metaphor for distributed problem solving. Artificial Intelligence, 20:63-109.

Dumas,Y.; Desrosier,J. and Soumis,F. 1991. The pickup and delivery problem with time windows. *European Journal of Operational Research*, **54**:7-22.

Fischer,K.; Müller,J.P.; and Pischel,M. 1996. Cooperative transportation scheduling: an application domain for DAI. *Journal of Applied Artificial Intelligence. Special Issue on Intelligent Agents*, **10**.

Fischer,K;, Müller,J.P.; and Pischel,M. 1995. A model for cooperative transportation scheduling. *Proceedings of the 1st Int.l Conf. on Multiagent Systems (ICMAS'95)*, pp. 109-116.

Laporte,G. 1992. The vehicle routing problem: an overview of exact and approximate algorithms. *European Journal of Operations Research*, **59**:345-358.

Potvin,J.; and Rousseau,J. 1993. A parallel route building algorithm for the vehicle routing and scheduling problem with time windows. *European Journal of Operations Research*, **66**:331-340.

Solomon,M. 1987. Algorithms for the vehicle routing and scheduling problems with time window constraints. *Operations Research*, **35**:254-265.

HICAP: An Interactive Case-Based Planning Architecture and its Application to Noncombatant Evacuation Operations

Héctor Muñoz-Avila[†‡], David W. Aha[‡], Len Breslow[‡], & Dana Nau[†]

† Dept. of Computer Science, University of Maryland, College Park, MD 20742-3255

‡ Navy Center for Applied Research in AI, Naval Research Laboratory, Washington, DC 20375

† *lastname*@cs.umd.edu   ‡ *lastname*@aic.nrl.navy.mil

Abstract

This paper describes *HICAP*, a general purpose planning architecture that we have developed and applied to assist military commanders and their staff with planning *NEOs* (Noncombatant Evacuation Operations). HICAP integrates a hierarchical task editor, HTE, with a conversational case-based planner, NaCoDAE/HTN. In this application, HTE maintains an agenda of tactical planning tasks that, according to military doctrine, must be addressed in a NEO. Military planning personnel select a task to decompose from HTE and then use NaCoDAE/HTN to interactively refine it into an operational plan by selecting and applying cases, which represent task decompositions from previous NEO operations. Thus, HICAP helps commanders by using previous experience to formulate operational plans that are in accordance with NEO doctrine.

Introduction

NEOs (Noncombatant Evacuation Operations) are military operations that require performing hundreds of subtasks and whose primary goal is to minimize loss of life. Formulating NEO plans is a complex task because it involves considering many factors (e.g., military resources, political issues, meteorological predictions) and uncertainties (e.g., hostility levels and locations).

Flawed NEO plans could yield dire consequences. For example, doctrine states that evacuees must be inspected prior to military transport. However, Siegel (1991) reported that this task was never assigned to any ground team in Operation Eastern Exit, and one evacuee produced his weapon during a helicopter evacuation flight. Although it was immediately confiscated, this oversight could have resulted in tragedy and illustrates the difficulties with planning NEOs manually.

Our thesis is that commanders and their staff can greatly benefit from the assistance of an intelligent NEO plan formulation tool. After analyzing NEO doctrine, reviewing case study analyses, and consulting

with NEO planning experts, we concluded that commanders will not accept any assistant tool unless it exhibits the following characteristics:

- *Doctrine-driven*: Uses a doctrine task analysis to guide plan formulation.
- *Interactive*: Users control how the abstract doctrine is instantiated for a specific NEO.
- *Provide Case Access*: Indexes plan segments from previous NEOs, and retrieve them for users if warranted by the current operational environment.

Also, this tool must perform several bookkeeping tasks. Although several systems have been proposed for NEO planning, none have been deployed because they do not exhibit all of these characteristics.

This paper introduces HICAP (Hierarchical Interactive Case-based Architecture for Planning), a general-purpose plan formulation tool designed to meet these characteristics, and its application to assist NEO planners.[1] HICAP integrates a task decomposition editor, HTE, with a conversational case-based planner, NaCoDAE/HTN. The former allows users to edit doctrine tasks and select tasks to operationalize, while the latter allows users to interactively refine HTN plans. Their integration in HICAP ensures that operational plans are framed within planning doctrine or within the changes made by commanders through three mechanisms. First, it uses doctrine to guide plan formulation, as it is done in practice. Second, it supports interactive task editing. Finally, it incorporates knowledge of previous operations, represented as cases, that can be used to augment or replace doctrine-standard operational procedures.

Noncombatant Evacuation Operations

NEOs are conducted to assist the USA Department of State in evacuating endangered noncombatants (e.g., nonessential military personnel) from locations in a host foreign nation to an appropriate safe haven. They usually involve a swift insertion of a force, temporary occupation of an objective (e.g., a USA Embassy), and a planned withdrawal. NEOs are usually planned and

---

[1]A Java 2 Applet version of HICAP can be found at www.aic.nrl.navy.mil/~munoz/hicap.

operated by a Joint Task Force (JTF) and conducted under an Ambassador's authority. Force sizes can range into the hundreds with all branches of armed services involved, while the evacuees can number into the thousands. At least ten NEOs were conducted within the past decade. Unclassified publications exist that describe NEO doctrine (e.g., DoD, 1994), case studies (e.g., Stewart et al., 1994), and more general analyses (Lambert, 1992).[2]

The NEO decision making process is made at three increasingly-specific levels. First, the *strategic* level involves global and political considerations (e.g., whether to perform the NEO). Then the *tactical* level involves considerations such as determining the size and composition of the NEO force. Finally, the *operational* level is the concrete level, which assigns specific resources to specific tasks.

JTF commanders plan NEOs in the context of doctrine (DoD, 1994), which establishes a framework for designing strategic and tactical plans, but only partly addresses operational considerations. Doctrine describes general aspects that must be considered when planning a military operation (e.g., chain of command, task agenda). However, doctrine is idealized and cannot account for characteristics of specific NEOs. Thus, the JTF commander must always adapt doctrine, and does so in two ways. First, he must eliminate irrelevant planning tasks and add others, depending on the operation's needs, resource availabilities, and his experience. For example, although NEO doctrine states that a forward command element must be inserted into the evacuation area prior to the primary evacuation elements, temporal constraints sometimes prevent this insertion (e.g., Siegel, 1991). Second, he must employ experiences from previous NEOs, which complement doctrine by suggesting operational refinements suitable for the current environment. For example, previous relevant experience might dictate whether it is appropriate to concentrate the evacuees in the embassy or to plan for multiple evacuation sites. In summary, commanders and their staff use guidance from both doctrine and their operational experiences to plan NEOs.

We will describe how HICAP can assist NEO planners by interactively refining operational plans, which is the focus of the JTF's efforts. We ignore strategic issues because they involve political aspects that are challenging to model and simulate.

Knowledge Representation

We use a variant of hierarchical task networks (HTNs) (Erol et al., 1994) to represent plans in HICAP because they are expressive. We define a HTN as a set of tasks and their ordering relations, denoted as $N = \langle \{T_1, \ldots, T_m\}, \prec \rangle$ $(m \geq 0)$. The relation $\prec$ has the form $T_i \prec T_j (i \neq j)$, and expresses temporal restrictions between tasks.

---

[2]See www.aic.nrl.navy.mil/~aha/neos for more information on NEOs.

Problem solving with HTNs occurs by applying *methods* to decompose tasks into subtasks. Each method has the form $M = \langle l, T, N, P \rangle$, where l is a label, T is a task, N is a HTN, and $P = \langle p_1, \ldots, p_k \rangle$ is a set of preconditions for applying M. When P is satisfied, M can be applied to a task T to yield N.

Methods in HICAP are either *non-decomposable*, *uniquely decomposable*, or *decomposable by multiple methods*. Non-decomposable tasks are concrete actions; they can occur only at leaves of the network. Uniquely decomposable tasks correspond to those specified by doctrine, and are solved by unconditional methods (i.e., $k = 0$). In contrast, tasks that can be decomposed in multiple ways correspond to those that must be solved in a specific problem-solving context.

Methods for problem-specific tasks are represented as *cases*, which encode preconditions as a set of question-answer pairs. Cases are obtained from either operational manuals (i.e., standard operational procedures (SOP)) or reports detailing previous problem-solving episodes. When solving a task T, HICAP accesses all cases that can decompose T. If all the preconditions of a SOP case are met, then it should be used to decompose T. Otherwise, a case corresponding to the most similar problem-solving episode should instead be used. For example, one standard procedure is to concentrate all evacuees in the embassy prior to troop deployment. This is not always possible; escorted transports were organized *after* JTF deployment in Eastern Exit (Siegel, 1991) while Sharp Edge required *multiple* separate evacuations (Stewart et al., 1994).

HICAP: Interactive Case-Based Planner

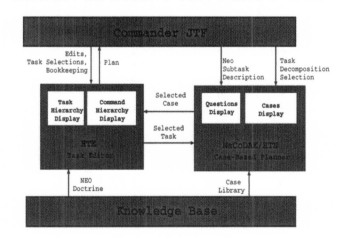

Figure 1: The HICAP architecture.

HICAP (Figure 1) integrates HTE with NaCoDAE/HTN, which are described below.

Hierarchical Task Editor

It is difficult for JTF planners to keep track of the status of NEO subtasks and JTF elements. The *Hierarchical Task Editor* (HTE) was conceived to facilitate the NEO

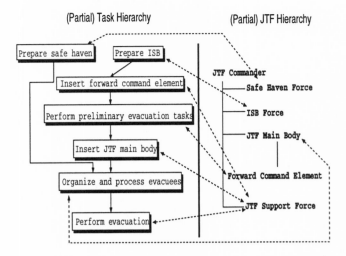

(Partial) Task Hierarchy   **(Partial) JTF Hierarchy**

Figure 2: Top level NEO tasks and their assignment to JTF command elements (double arrows denote assignments; arrows denote task orderings).

planning process. Given domain-specific knowledge for operational planning, HTE can be used to:

1. browse and edit this knowledge base's components,
2. select tasks for further decomposition,
3. edit assignments of military personnel to tasks, and
4. investigate the status of tasks.

HTE's knowledge base consists of a HTN, a command hierarchy, and an assignment of tasks to commands. For this NEO application, we encoded a HTN to capture critical planning knowledge (i.e., more than 200 tasks and their ordering relations) corresponding to NEO doctrine (DoD, 1994). Next, we elicited the JTF command hierarchy that is commonly used in NEO operations. Finally, we elicited many-to-one relations between tasks and the JTF elements responsible for them.

In addition to providing users with a visual aid for NEO doctrine, HTE can be used to edit the HTN, its ordering relations, the command hierarchy, and the task-command assignments. Thus, military planners can tailor HTE's knowledge base for a particular NEO. Figure 2 displays (left) the top level tasks that, according to doctrine, must be performed during a NEO and (right) the JTF elements responsible for them.

Conversational Task Decomposer

Doctrine describes decision-making procedures for the operational level but does not provide sufficient detail to formulate tactical plans. NaCoDAE/HTN, an extension of the NaCoDAE case retrieval tool (Breslow & Aha, 1997), helps planners to refine selected operational tasks into subtasks. Given a task T to refine, NaCoDAE/HTN conducts an interactive *conversation* that ends when the user applies a method to T.

NaCoDAE/HTN displays the labels of cases that can decompose the selected node and the questions from these cases whose answers are not yet known for the

current NEO. The user can select and answer any displayed question; $\langle q, a \rangle$ pairs are used to compute the current task's similarity with its potential decomposition methods. Cases are ranked by similarity, while questions are ranked by their frequency among the displayed cases. Answering a question modifies the case rankings and the displays. A conversation ends when the user selects a case to decompose the current task.

Some cases are SOPs; they can only be selected to decompose a task after all of their questions have been answered and match the current planning scenario (i.e., their preconditions must all match). In contrast, cases based on previous experiences can be selected even when some of their questions have not been answered, or if the user's answers differ. Thus, they support partial matching between their preconditions and the current planning scenario.

Integration

HICAP integrates HTE with NaCoDAE/HTN to formulate plans that are in accordance with both doctrine and cases. It inputs a HTN describing the doctrine for an application, along with a set of cases for each of the subtasks that can be decomposed in multiple ways. Under user control, it outputs an edited HTN whose leaves are concrete actions as specified by case applications.

Using HTE, military planners can edit the NEO knowledge base by deleting (or replacing) any task subtree, by editing the command hierarchy, and by reassigning tasks and/or command elements. HTE also allows users to select a (leaf) task T to be decomposed. This initializes a NaCoDAE/HTN conversation, using T as an index for case retrieval. A conversation yields a selected case $C = \langle l, T, N, P \rangle$, whose network N is used to decompose T. This expansion can be recursive. Eventually, non-decomposable tasks corresponding to concrete actions will be reached. Task expansions are immediately displayed by HTE.

NEO planners formulate both a main course of action (i.e., a plan) and contingency plans, such as when an element cannot accomplish a key task. Users can generate contingency plans by performing alternative task decompositions and edits to the knowledge base. Handling unforeseen contingencies that may occur during plan execution are beyond the scope of this paper.

In summary, HICAP satisfies the requirements stated in the Introduction. First, all plans obtained using HICAP are clearly circumscribed by the doctrine or by any modification introduced by the JTF commander. Second, HICAP interactively supports task editing and triggers conversations for decomposable tasks. Third, it incorporates knowledge from previous operations as cases, which serve as task decomposition alternatives. Finally, it allows the user to visually check that all tasks are assigned to JTF elements.

Example: NEO Planning

NEO planners view the top level tasks first, revising them or their assignments if necessary. They may de-

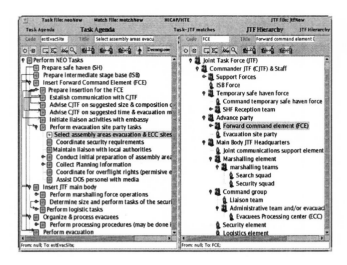

Figure 3: HICAP/HTE's snapshot displaying the doctrine tasks (left) and the JTF's hierarchical organization (right). Arrows denote ordering constraints.

compose any task and view its decomposition. Figure 3 shows an intermediate stage during this process. The user has selected the task *Select assembly areas for evacuation & ECC (Evacuation Control Center) sites*, which is highlighted together with the command element responsible for it (i.e., the FCE).

Standard procedure dictates that the embassy is the ideal assembly area. However, it is not always possible to concentrate the evacuees in the embassy. Alternative methods can be considered for decomposing this task. When the military planner selects this task, HICAP displays the alternatives and initiates a NaCoDAE/HTN conversation (see Figure 4 (left), on the following page).

If a user answers *Are there any hostiles between the embassy and the evacuees?* with "uncertain," the second displayed case (Figure 4 (right)) will become a perfect match. Figure 5 shows the decomposition when the user selects this case for decomposition; two new subtasks are displayed that correspond to its decomposition network. The *Send UAV (Unmaned Air Vehicle) to ...* task is non-decomposable; it corresponds to a concrete action. If the user tells HICAP to decompose *Determine hostile presence*, HICAP will initiate a new NaCoDAE/HTN dialogue (also in Figure 5).

Figure 6 shows a snapshot of HICAP when the user selects *The UAV detects hostiles* alternative and decides to decompose the *Handle hostile presence* subtask, which prompts a new NaCoDAE/HTN dialogue. Assuming that the user answers *Can the hostile forces ...* with "yes," this matches the situation in Operation Eastern Exit in which the evacuees were dispersed into multiple locations in Mogadishu. An escorted transport gathered all evacuees into the embassy. If the user selects this case, then its two non-decomposable subtasks, *Assign dissuasive escort* and *Escort evacuees to embassy*, will be displayed.

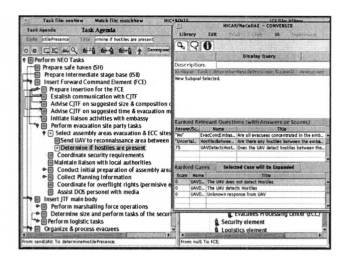

Figure 5: HICAP's interface after selecting the *Determine hostile presence* task.

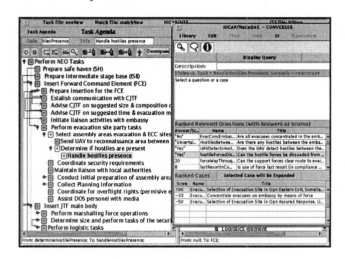

Figure 6: How to handle a hostile presence.

Related Research

At this time, there are no intelligent deployed NEO planning tools. Kostek (1988) proposed a conceptual design for predicting the force size and type required for a NEO. Chavez and Henrion (1994) described a decision-theoretic approach for instantiating a general NEO plan with specific parameters for locations, forces, and destinations, and used it to assess alternative plans. Gil et al. (1994) presented a system for predicting manning estimates for certain NEO tasks. None of these systems formulate NEO plans, although desJardins et al. (1998) recently proposed a distributed hierarchical planning approach.

Although DARPA and other agencies have sponsored several projects related to NEO planning (e.g., ARPI, Tate (1994)), HICAP is the *first* system to use a *conversational* case-based approach for plan formulation. HICAP's advantage is that it allows users to incremen-

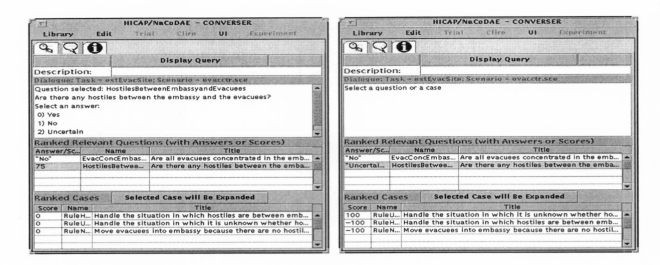

Figure 4: NaCoDAE/HTN's interface, before (left) and after (right) answering a question. The top window directs the user and lists the possible answers. The lower windows display the questions and cases, respectively.

tally elaborate a planning scenario, provides a focus of attention that guides this elaboration, and provides access to stored plan fragments for use in new NEO plans. Our approach was inspired by research on and applications of conversational case retrieval systems (Aha & Breslow, 1997), but extends them to apply to hierarchical planning tasks.

Some researchers have used case-based approaches for HTN planning tasks on military domains. For example, Mitchell (1997) used an integrated CBP (case-based planner) to select tasks for a Tactical Response Planner. NEO planning requires that each task be addressed - no choice is involved - and we use CBP to instead choose *how* to perform a task. MI-CBP (Veloso et al., 1997) uses rationale-directed CBP to suggest plan modifications, but does not perform doctrine-driven task decomposition. HICAP's interactions instead focus on retrieval rather than plan adaptation and learning. IFD4 (Bienkowski & Hoebel, 1998) automatically generates plans as guided by an editable objectives hierarchy. In contrast, HICAP's objectives are fixed, and user interaction focuses on task formulation.

Other researchers have described related crisis response systems. Ferguson and Allen (1998) described an interactive planner for military crisis response, but their system does not use cases during plan formulation and does not perform doctrine-driven task decomposition. Likewise, Wolverton and desJardins' (1998) distributed generative planner also does not use cases. Gervasio et al. (1998) described an interactive hierarchical case-based scheduler for crisis response that does not perform interactive plan formulation. Avesani et al. (1998) described a CBP for fighting forest fires that supports interactive plan adaptation, but does not use hierarchical guidelines to formulate plans (ala HICAP). Finally, Leake et al. (1996) described a CBP applied

to disaster response that focuses on learning case adaptation knowledge, but it is not doctrine-driven and focuses interaction on knowledge acquisition rather than problem elicitation.

Conclusions and Transitions

HICAP is a case-based tool that assists the military commander with formulating a plan. It is the first tool to combine a doctrine-guided task decomposition process with a case-based reasoning approach to support interactive plan formulation. Thus, it yields a plan that benefits from previous experiences and is sound according to doctrine. Furthermore, HICAP supports experience sharing, which allows planners to exploit knowledge from other planning experts. These design characteristics were chosen so as to enhance HICAP's acceptance by military planning personnel; previous approaches did not include all of these capabilities.

There is a great potential for combining HTN and case-based planning techniques in real-world applications. HICAP illustrates this by using a unified framework for a rather complex domain, noncombatant evacuation operations, that has multiple sources of information (i.e., doctrine, previous operations and standard operating procedures).

HICAP will serve as the plan formulation component for the Interactive Decision Support (IDS) system being developed at the Space and Naval Warfare Systems Command. When completed, IDS will perform distributed plan formulation, execution, monitoring, and replanning for NEO planning efforts.

We are currently integrating HICAP with SHOP (Nau et al., 1999), a simple generative HTN planner that can process numeric computations, which is particularly important for NEO planning in decisions made concerning resource capability and availability (i.e., determining whether a helicopter requires in-flight refueling for a given mission).

In an initial evaluation of HICAP using ModSAF simulations, HICAP outperformed three default planning strategies for a single planning subtask under two planning scenarios (Muñoz-Avila et al., 1999). After incorporation in IDS, HICAP will be evaluated in controlled studies by military mission planners.

Acknowledgements

Thanks to Pat Langley and Frank Weberskirch for their comments on an earlier draft. This research was supported by grants from the Naval Research Laboratory (N00173-98-1-G007), the Army Research Laboratory (DAAL01-97-K0135), and the Office of Naval Research.

References

Aha, D. W., & Breslow, L. A. (1997). Refining conversational case libraries. *Proceedings of the Second International Conference on CBR* (pp. 267–278). Providence, RI: Springer.

Aha, D.W., & Daniels, J.J. (Eds.) *CBR Integrations: Papers from the 1998 Workshop* (TR WS-98-15). Menlo Park, CA: AAAI Press.

Avesani, P., Perini, A., & Ricci, F. (1998). The twofold integration of CBR in decision support systems. In (Aha & Daniels, 1998).

Bienkowski, M.A., & Hoebel, L.J. (1998). Integrating AI components for a military planning application. *Proceedings of the Fifthteenth National Conference on AI* (pp. 561–566). Madison, WI: AAAI Press.

Breslow, L., & Aha, D. W. (1997). *NaCoDAE: Navy Conversational Decision Aids Environment* (TR AIC-97-018). Washington, DC: NRL, NCARAI.

Chavez, T., & Henrion, M. (1994). Focusing on what matters in plan evaluation: Efficiently estimating the value of information. *Proceedings of the ARPA/Rome Laboratory Knowledge-Based Planing and Scheduling Initiative* (pp. 387–399). Tuscon, AR: Morgan Kaufmann.

desJardins, M., Francis, A., & Wolverton, M. (1998). Hybrid planning: An approach to integrating generative and case-based planning. In (Aha & Daniels, 1998).

DoD (1994). *Joint tactics, techniques and procedures for noncombat evacuation operations* (Joint Publication Report 3-07.51, Second Draft). Washington, DC: Department of Defense.

Erol, K., Nau, D., & Hendler, J. HTN planning: Complexity and expressivity. *Proceedings of the Twelfth National Conference on AI* (pp. 1123–1128). Seattle, WA: AAAI Press.

Ferguson, G., & Allen, J.F. (1998). TRIPS: An integrated intelligent problem-solving assistant. *Proceedings of the Fifthteenth National Conference on AI* (pp. 567–572). Madison, WI: AAAI Press.

Gervasio, M.T., Iba, W., & Langley, P. (1998). Case-based seeding for an interactive crisis response assistant. In (Aha & Daniels, 1998).

Gil, Y., Hoffman, M. & Tate, A. (1994). Domain-specific criteria to direct and evaluate planning systems. *Proceedings of the ARPA/Rome Laboratory Knowledge-Based Planing and Scheduling Initiative* (pp. 433–444). Tuscon, AR: Morgan Kaufmann.

Kostek, S.R. (1988). *A User's Design of a Decision Support System for Noncombatant Evacuation Operations for United States Central Command.* Master's thesis, School of Engineering, Air Force Institute of Technology, Dayton, Ohio.

Lambert, Kirk S. (1992). *Noncombatant evacuation operations: Plan now or pay later* (TR). Newport, RI: Naval War College.

Leake, D. B., Kinley, A., & Wilson, D. (1996). Acquiring case adaptation knowledge: A hybrid approach. *Proceedings of the Thirteenth National Conference on AI* (pp. 684–689). Portland, OR: AAAI Press.

Mitchell, S.W. (1997). A hybrid architecture for real-time mixed-initiative planning and control. *Proceedings of the Ninth Conference on Innovative Applications of AI* (pp. 1032–1037). Providence, RI: AAAI Press.

Muñoz-Avila, H., McFarlane, D., Aha, D.W., Ballas, J., Breslow, L.A., & Nau, D. (1999). Using guidelines to constrain interactive case-based HTN planning. To appear in *Proceedings of the Third International Conference on CBR*. Munich: Springer.

Nau, D., Cao, Y., Lotem, A., & Muñoz-Avila, H. (1999). To appear in *Proceedings of the Sixteenth International Joint Conference on AI*. Stockholm: AAAI Press.

Siegel, A.B. (1991). *Eastern Exit: The noncombatant evacuation operation (NEO) from Mogadishu, Somalia, in January 1991* (TR CRM 91-221). Arlington, VA: Center for Naval Analyses.

Stewart, G., Fabbri, S.M., & Siegel, A.B. (1994). *JTF operations since 1983* (TR CRM 94-42). Arlington, VA: CNA.

Tate, A. (1994). Mixed initiative planning in O-Plan2. *Proceedings of the ARPA/Rome Laboratory Knowledge-Based Planing and Scheduling Initiative* (pp. 512–516). Tuscon, AR: Morgan Kaufmann.

Veloso, M., Mulvehill, A.M., & Cox, M.T. (1997). Rationale-supported mixed-initiative case-based planning. *Proceedings of the Ninth Conference on Innovative Applications of AI* (pp. 1072–1077). Providence, RI: AAAI Press.

Wolverton, M., & desJardins, M. (1998). Controlling communication in distributed planning using irrelevance reasoning. *Proceedings of the Fifthteenth National Conference on AI* (pp. 868–874). Madison, WI: AAAI Press.

Automated Capture of Rationale for the Detailed Design Process

Karen L. Myers   Nina B. Zumel
Artificial Intelligence Center
SRI International
333 Ravenswood Ave.
Menlo Park, CA 94025
myers@ai.sri.com   zumel@ai.sri.com

Pablo Garcia
Innovative Product Engineering and Technologies
SRI International
333 Ravenswood Ave.
Menlo Park, CA 94025
pgarcia@unix.sri.com

Abstract

The value of comprehensive rationale information for documenting a design has long been recognized. However, detailed rationale is rarely produced in practice because of the substantial time investment required. Efforts to support the acquisition of rationale have focused on languages and tools for structuring the acquisition process, but still require substantial involvement on the part of the designer. This document describes an experimental system, the Rationale Construction Framework (RCF), that acquires rationale information for the detailed design process without disrupting a designer's normal activities. The underlying approach involves monitoring designer interactions with a commercial CAD tool to produce a rich process history. This history is subsequently structured and interpreted relative to a background theory of *design metaphors* that enable explanation of certain aspects of the design process. Evaluation of RCF within a robotic arm design case has shown that the system can acquire meaningful rationale information in a time- and cost-effective manner, with minimal disruption to the designer.

Introduction

Representations of designs in current-generation computer-assisted design (CAD) frameworks consist primarily of diagrammatic specifications, possibly augmented with simple annotations and *ad hoc* documentation. Even the most sophisticated systems lack much in the way of structured *design rationale*, despite the well-accepted view within the design community that such information would be a tremendous asset. Design rationale would serve as a record of the basic structure of a design, codifying how the design satisfies specified requirements, as well as key decisions that were made during the design process. By making it easier to understand how a design works, this information would facilitate collaboration among multiple distributed designers, improve the maintainability of designs, and enable more effective reuse of designs.

Despite the many benefits that explicit design rationale would provide, it is rarely produced in practice. Tools that support the specification of structured rationale by a designer have met with limited success because they either demand substantial designer time to enter information

(Carroll & Moran 1991) or change the manner in which designers work (Conklin & Yakemovic 1991). Furthermore, there is little motivation for a designer to participate in such activities since the benefits surface downstream of his or her contribution. Recently, nonintrusive approaches have been explored that involve video or audio recording of design sessions (Chen, Dietterich, & Ullman 1991; Shipman & McCall 1997); however, a lack of structure in the produced representations hinders effective use of the results.

Given the tremendous value of structured design rationale but the unacceptable burden of constructing it manually, we were motivated to explore the use of AI methods for automatically and nonintrusively generating rationale. Our focus is on the *detailed design* phase, in which tools (*e.g.*, CAD systems, analysis packages) are used to generate a schematic for an artifact. This contrasts with the *conceptual design* phase, in which the scope and capabilities are set for the artifact to be designed. During conceptual design, the emphasis is on identifying and resolving high-level issues of functionality and requirements, with design rationale recording the justifications for the decisions that have been made. During detailed design, functionality and requirements are considered at much lower levels of abstraction. Choices and decisions are grounded primarily in physical constraints on components and the designer's insights into the composition of good designs.

The premise for our work was the observation that many of the operations that a designer can perform with modern CAD tools (*i.e.*, the *design substrate* (Fischer & Lemke 1988)) have meaningful semantic content. For example, CAD tools allow users to select objects with assigned semantic types from predefined libraries. This contrasts with most tools for designing software, where interactions are at the level of keystrokes. Noninstrusive monitoring of the actions taken by a designer with a CAD tool would thus provide a rich, semantically grounded process history for detailed design. AI techniques could be used to structure this information into representations that support improved user comprehensibility of the design process and automated inference about *designer intent*. Valuable reasoning methods would include *clustering* techniques to aggregate CAD operations into abstract summaries of designer activity, *plan recognition* to identify key episodes of activity, and *qualita-*

tive reasoning about the emerging design.

This paper describes the Rationale Construction Framework (RCF), which embodies the above ideas in a system that automatically constructs rationale information for the detailed design process. RCF records events and data of relevance to the design process, and structures them in representations that facilitate generation of explanations for designer activities. RCF operates in an opportunistic manner, extracting rationale-related information to the extent possible from observed designer operations. Within RCF, rationale is interpreted broadly to encompass any information that will further the understanding of a design and its development. This philosophy fits the *generative paradigm* (Gruber & Russell 1992) for rationale construction, which is intended to support general queries about a design and its evolution rather than answers to fixed sets of questions.

Extracted information is organized along two lines. The first is a series of hierarchical abstractions of the design history: *what* the designer did, and *when*. In addition, RCF reasons about designer intent – *why* the designer performed particular actions. Extraction of rationale related to intent is driven by a set of *design metaphors*, which describe temporally extended sets of designer operations that constitute meaningful episodes of activity. Design metaphors provide the basis for inferring intent on the part of the designer by linking observed activities to explanations for them.

Automatic generation of complete rationale for all aspects of a design is clearly infeasible. Certainly, designers make many critical decisions that are not explicit in the designs or the design process. The work reported here seeks to automate documentation of important but low-level aspects of the design process in a time- and cost-effective manner, thus freeing designers to focus their documentation efforts on the more creative and unusual aspects of the design. Ideally, the methods presented here would be complemented by interactive rationale acquisition methods that enable designers to extend and correct automatically generated information.

RCF was evaluated in a case study involving the design of a three-degree-of-freedom surgical robotic arm. The main technical challenge for this design was to provide sufficient actuation torque, while maintaining low inertia and high precision. The arm has three main subassemblies: the *base assembly*, including the actuation motors; the *arm assembly* with transmission; and the *wrist assembly*, including the end effector and tool. RCF recorded designer activity over several versions of the arm, starting from a rough initial design, through various stages of refinements and optimizations. From these recordings, RCF was able to summarize designer activity at varying levels of abstraction, to identify phases where the designer concentrated on various parts or subassemblies or where design parameters were tuned, to track the results of design tradeoffs, and to explain key design changes. The results validate the idea that meaningful rationale can be generated nonintrusively through application of appropriate AI techniques.

RCF Architecture

As depicted in Figure 1, RCF contains three main components: an enhanced CAD tool, the Monitoring module, and

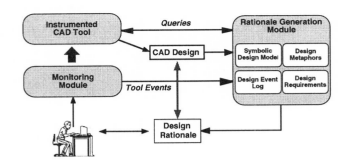

Figure 1: RCF Architecture

the Rationale Generation module (RGM).

CAD Tool

The CAD system underlying RCF is MicroStation95, a commercial product that provides sophisticated modeling capabilities sufficient for a broad range of demanding electromechanical design tasks.

To support rationale acquisition within RCF, the set of operations provided by MicroStation95 was extended to include several capabilities that raised the overall semantic content of its design substrate. One class of added operations, *annotations*, enables users to specify the *semantic type* of an object along with corresponding type-specific *semantic attributes*. For example, the designer may declare that a given solid represents a gear, as well as specifying gear-specific attributes such as number of teeth, gear ratio, or quality. Such semantic information is a by-product of the parametric design methods and part selection capabilities found in numerous state-of-the-art systems. We also augmented MicroStation with a set of analysis programs that can be linked directly to components in the CAD drawing, thus extending the limited analysis capabilities within the off-the-shelf system. This modification reflects a growing trend toward building design environments that integrate a range of design tools. Finally, the ability to select components from predefined part libraries was added, which is standard in many CAD frameworks.

Monitoring Module

Within RCF, the designer interacts with the CAD tool as if it were a stand-alone application. The operations that he performs, however, are nonintrusively tracked by the Monitoring module, generating a stream of *tool events* that are sent in real time to the RGM. The monitoring facility captures only operations that are relevant to understanding the design process. Its coverage includes the creation, deletion, modification, and annotation of design objects, the creation and importing of parts, and the invocation of built-in analysis programs. Process-level commands such as the undoing and redoing of operations are also recorded. Aspects of the design process that are ignored by the monitoring module include certain geometric information associated with the manipulation and definition of objects (*e.g.*, spatial positioning), and viewing commands.

Base-level Design Events		**Process-level Design Events**	
Create	define a new object	**Undo**	undo the previous 'undoable' operation
Copy	create a new object from an existing one	**Redo**	redo the last undone operation
Delete	delete a previously created object	**File-Open**	create or read-in a design file
Modify	change structural aspect of an object	**File-Copy**	copy a design file
Connect	create a joint between two objects	**File-Save**	save a design file
Import	read in a predefined part		
Annotate	set the semantic attributes of an object		
Analyze	invoke a tool for analyzing some design aspect		
Manipulate	reorient an object in space		

Figure 2: Design Events

Rationale Generation Module

The Rationale Generation Module (RGM), the main inferential component of the framework, is responsible for the automated generation of rationale structures. The RGM maintains an abstracted, tool-independent representation of observed CAD events, called the *design event log*. Based on the design event log, the RGM incrementally constructs a *symbolic model* of the emerging design. The design event log and symbolic design model provide the evolving information base from which rationale is generated, in conjunction with a formal specification of the *design requirements* for the given task and a set of *design metaphors*. This section describes the design events and the symbolic design model; design metaphors and requirements are discussed in subsequent sections.

Design Event Models The operations within the design event model, while not exhaustive, were chosen for their adequacy with respect to interesting design tasks. Two high-level categories of operations are defined (Figure 2). *Base-level* operations support the direct creation, modification, and manipulation of design objects. *Process-level operations* either manipulate information and metalevel structures related to the design (such as files), or impact the interpretation for previously executed operations (*e.g.*, *Undo/Redo* operations). Tracking the impact of the latter type of process-level operations requires complex bookkeeping of current and previous states to maintain an accurate characterization of the current design within the symbolic design model.

Several key properties are maintained for each design event. Type-independent properties include the corresponding tool events, timestamps, and affected objects. Type-specific properties are also stored; for example, an analysis event includes information about objects and their attributes used in the analysis, the analysis program invoked, and the results of the analysis.

Symbolic Design Model The symbolic design model provides an abstracted representation of the emerging design that supports the reasoning required by the rationale construction process. It excludes certain information stored within the CAD model (*e.g.*, geometric information plays only a limited role), but augments the CAD representation to include relevant process information for objects within the design.

Several categories of information are stored for each design object. First, there is the standard definitional information: an object's geometric category (*e.g.*, sphere, slab, line) and key *structural attributes* (*e.g.*, the diameter for a sphere). In addition, the *semantic category* and category-specific *semantic attributes* (if assigned) are stored. Because the specification of attributes can provide much insight into the evolution of a design, RCF maintains records of evolving attribute values (both structural and semantic) that enable retrieval for any stage of the design process. Several inter-object relationships are stored for use in reasoning about rationale, including *parent/child* relationships that reflect hierarchical structuring of complex objects, *copies/source* relationships, and *attachment* relationships indicating connection of two design objects through a *joint* of a designated type. We define an *assembly* to be the closure of a set of objects under the attachment relationship (*i.e.*, under joint connectivity).

On the process side, records are kept of all operations performed on an object, related analyses, time spent, origins data (*i.e.*, selected from a part library, copied from a user, created by a designer), and status information (*:alive* or *:inactive*, based on *Undo*, *Redo*, and *Delete* commands).

Rationale Extraction: Technical Approach

RCF generates two categories of rationale information: *session content* and *designer intent*. Rationale extraction is organized around a set of domain-independent *design metaphors* augmented by limited amounts of task- and domain-specific design knowledge.

Session Content RCF provides comprehensive summaries of a design session from two perspectives. The *object-centered* perspective provides historical and explanatory information for individual design objects and groups of objects that can either be explicit in the design (*e.g.*, assemblies) or *inferred* to be meaningful by RCF. The *event-centered* perspective summarizes the design session at multiple abstraction levels, using a combination of design metaphors and clustering methods to perform the abstractions.

Designer Intent A finished CAD model shows the endproduct of a designer's efforts but omits the *changes* that were made in the development of the design. Changes provide insight into the evolution of the design, showing alternative paths explored by the designer and basic strategies used. For

```
Devent 263: DELETE JOINT90          From design event 263 to design event 280
Devent 264: DELETE JOINT91              Assemblies involved:
Devent 265: CONNECT JOINT92               MAIN-ASSEMBLY
Devent 266: CONNECT JOINT93               WRIST
Devent 267: DELETE JOINT65                ARM
Devent 268: DELETE JOINT66              Parts added:
Devent 269: CONNECT JOINT94               DOBJ229 (GEAR_16_3) from assembly WRIST
Devent 270: CONNECT JOINT95               DOBJ228 (GEAR_16_3) from assembly WRIST
Devent 271: DELETE JOINT86              Parts removed:
Devent 272: DELETE JOINT87                DOBJ183 (GR_08) from assembly WRIST
Devent 273: CONNECT JOINT96             Part substitutions:
Devent 274: CONNECT JOINT97               DOBJ167 (BV_1875) was replaced by DOBJ227 (BV_1250)
Devent 275: DELETE JOINT80                DOBJ168 (BV_1875) was replaced by DOBJ226 (BV_1250)
Devent 276: CONNECT JOINT98               DOBJ212 (ARM3) was replaced by DOBJ225 (ARM4)
Devent 277: DELETE JOINT81                DOBJ213 (ARM3) was replaced by DOBJ224 (ARM4)
Devent 279: UNDO
Devent 280: DELETE JOINT82
```

Figure 3: Abstracting from Design Events to Part-level Operations

this reason, a key focus within RCF has been to identify and explain changes to a design. We have explored an approach that involves situating changes within contexts defined by *clustering* related events, and reasoning with *domain knowledge* about qualitative effects of design operations.

Design Metaphors

Design metaphors are multistep patterns of events (not necessarily contiguous) that describe episodes of coherent designer activity. They can be applied at varying scales of resolution: at the design event level, or over groupings or abstractions of events. RCF contains a suite of design metaphors whose recognition enables generation of defeasible explanations of a range of designer activity. Two example metaphors are presented here.

The *Refinement* metaphor is a cycle of *Analyze X - Revise* behavior, indicating that the designer is focusing on a particular design requirement *X*. It is reasonable to infer that intervening modifications to the design are performed with the goal of addressing *X*, although not all such revisions will have been performed with *X* in mind. Thus, while the metaphor does not definitively link action and intent, it does provide a plausible explanation for the designer's actions.

The *1:1 Part Substitution* metaphor captures the notion that the designer has swapped one functional component for another. In particular, Part *B* is considered to be substituted for Part *A* when it is observed that first, Part *A* is removed, and then some Part *B* from the same functional category is added to the assembly with the same connectivity as Part *A*. These part operations must occur within a certain window of activity but need not be consecutive.

The *Refinement* and *1:1 Part Substitution* metaphors capture general design principles and as such are applicable in most design applications. To date, all design metaphors within RCF are domain-independent. Task-specific design metaphors could readily be added to increase explanatory power, although at the cost of the knowledge engineering involved.

Task and Domain Knowledge

The use of background knowledge can greatly extend the rationale extraction capabilities. However, such knowledge can be difficult and expensive to acquire and represent. We explored a range of techniques that vary in the amount of background knowledge they require. Currently, RCF employs two kinds of optional background knowledge. First, overall *design requirements* are represented as a collection of properties, possibly with threshold constraints that must be satisfied (*e.g.*, *Arm-Inertia-I_z < 50 lb-in^2*). Nonmeasurable requirements, such as *Durability*, do not include explicit thresholds. Second, *qualitative models* of the effects of design operations can be used to generate deeper explanations of designer activity.

Event-centered Perspective

The event-centered perspective provides summarizations of a design session at varying levels of abstraction. Individual design events are grouped into *part-level operations*, which focus on design objects at the level of parts in an assembly. Next, operations are grouped into *activity phases*, which correspond to broader collections of activities with a common general design objective. Above that, phases are grouped into different *versions* for design components.

Part-level Operations The mapping from design events to part operations provides an abstracted view of the design process that is both more understandable to humans and more convenient for recognizing abstract design metaphors. Rather than examining activity on the level of features or components being modified or joined, a part-level chronology consists of parts being created, added or removed from the assembly, substituted for other parts, or modified.

Figure 3 shows a part-level abstraction produced by RCF. The excerpt from the design event log (on the left) constitutes a period of revision activity, in which the designer replaced certain components in the design. Within MicroStation95, a *joint* connects two design objects at a contact point; disconnecting a component from an assembly generally re-

```
>>>>>> Activity Phase 1: Type REVISION <<<<<<<<<
In the BEGINNING, no detected focus
In the MIDDLE, MILD focus on (WRIST)
In the END, STRONG focus on (BASE)


>>>>>>> Activity Phase 2: Type REFINEMENT <<<<<<<
In the BEGINNING, focus on (ARM-INERTIA-IZ WEIGHT)
 Refinement of ARM-INERTIA-IZ:
     (60.0 50.0) --> REDUCE
   Modifications primarily on
     DOBJ92 (BASE_GEAR) from assembly BASE
     DOBJ207 (BV_1250) from assembly WRIST

 Refinement of WEIGHT:
     (2.2 2.0) --> REDUCE
   Modifications primarily on
     DOBJ92 (BASE_GEAR) from assembly BASE
     DOBJ207 (BV_1250) from assembly WRIST

In the END, focus on (STRESS)
 Refinement of STRESS:
     (0.6 0.4) --> REDUCE
   Modifications primarily on
     DOBJ31 (BV_0625) from assembly WRIST
     DOBJ207 (BV_1250) from assembly WRIST


>>>>>> Activity Phase 3: Type CONSTRUCTION <<<<<
In the BEGINNING, STRONG focus on (GROUP4 BEAR_BR)
In the MIDDLE, STRONG focus on (GROUP4 BEAR_BR)
In the END, MILD focus on (GROUP4)
```

Figure 4: Example Activity Phases with Attention Focus

quires a series of joint deletions. The part-level description on the right abstracts the explicit joint manipulations into a summary of the parts being removed, added, or replaced.

Note that each object within RCF has a unique *design object id, e.g.,* DOBJ167. Reference to design objects that are instances of parts generally include the name of the part from which it was created. Thus, DOBJ212 and DOBJ213 are both instances of the previously created part ARM3.

Activity Phases Activity phases are groups of events that describe designer activity at the level of abstract operations on components, parts, or the design artifact itself. Four types of activity phases are extracted from the sequence of part operations, with analysis and part-level statistics kept for each:

- *Construction:* a period of interleaved part creation and part addition events
- *Revision:* a period of interleaved part revision, addition, deletion, and/or substitution events
- *Analysis:* a period of analysis events not linked to any revisions
- *Refinement:* a period of related analysis and revision events

During a given activity phase, a designer will often focus on a specific part or set of parts for some time before switching attention to another aspect of the design. RCF identifies the evolving focus of designer attention, at the level of design requirements being addressed, individual parts, subassemblies

```
---------- Design object DOBJ207 ----------

--- Source ---
is standard part BV_1250 of type GEAR
copied from file c:/models/version1/std_1250.dgn

--- Implicit Constraints ---
BV_1250 (GEAR), attributes (MATERIAL)
  constrains
BV_0625 (GEAR), attributes (MATERIAL)

--- Part Activity ---
In Version 2, Activity Phase 1, type REVISION:
 >> added to assembly as replacement for BV_1875
    --> Effects: (ARM-INERTIA-IZ DOWN)(WEIGHT DOWN)

Part modified
  Event 313: ANNOTATE MATERIAL ==> SS;
    --> Effects: (WEIGHT UP)(STRESS DOWN)
```

Figure 5: Example Part History

of parts, and *implicit groups* of parts that are identified automatically during the extraction of activity phases (discussed below). The *focus* during an interval of activity is defined as a part, a grouping of parts, or a design requirement, for which the percentage of effort devoted to it exceeds some threshold. The effort metric used to determine attention focus can be either number of operations or accumulated time per part. Figure 4 displays summaries generated by RCF for a sequence of activity phases of different types, including the detected foci within each.

Versions Versions are episodes of activity that constitute a coherent set of changes on a design or one of its components. Within RCF currently, versioning is done at fairly coarse level, with version boundaries defined by the metaphor *Create/Copy File - Activity - Save File.*

Object-centered Perspective

For each design object, a detailed history is maintained that includes the object's origins, all related design events, and effort expended for that object. Additional information is kept for parts: related part-level operations, modification histories for the part and its various attributes, whether it was replaced by another part (*i.e.,* instances of the *1:1 Part Substitution* metaphor). The context of these operations is reported: which version and what type of activity phase. Also recorded are hypothesized explanations for those actions (see next section), detected relationships between a part and any design requirements, and inferred dependencies on other parts through membership in *implicit groups*.

The aggregation of objects into logically related groups provides a powerful mechanism for improving the understandability of complex structures. Assemblies and hierarchies provide examples of groupings that a designer defines explicitly. In addition, 'hidden' relationships can be present in a design that, if made apparent, could similarly improve understanding. For example, two parts may be implicitly dependent on each other, either structurally or functionally, in

OBJECT CLASS	ATTRIBUTE	TYPE	RANK	Precision Unloaded	Precision Loaded	Torque Avail	Inertia Arm	Friction	Max Stress	Cost	Durability	Resonance Mech.	Resonance Servo	Mass
Gears	Ratio	NUMERIC		+		+				+			+	+
	Radius	NUMERIC			+		+		+	+			-	+
	Diametral Pitch	NUMERIC		+					+	+				
	Quality	NUMERIC		+			-			+				
	Width	NUMERIC				+			+		+		-	+
	Ct-Ct Tolerance	NUMERIC		+			-			+				
	Adjustable Ct-Ct Dist	BINARY	TRUE	+						+				
	Material	ENUM	Lighter				-						+	-
			Yield						+	+	+			
			Stress						+		+			

Figure 6: Excerpt from the QIC Table for the Robotic Arm Design Case

a way that would not be apparent from examination of the finished CAD model.

RCF searches for *implicit groups* of design objects that satisfy such hidden relationships. While the system may or may not be able to identify precise constraints among the parts in an implicit group, it can bring them to the attention of a designer, who may be able to identify a reason for such a dependency. RCF contains design metaphors for recognizing several types of implicit groups, including (a) parts that are consistently added, removed, or revised together during the same period of construction activity, and (b) parts that are always modified together within a single refinement phase, in connection with the same design requirement.

Figure 5 displays an object summary for the part bv_1250 (a gear), including information about its introduction into the design, subsequent modifications and their effects, and a detected implicit constraint between the material attributes of bv_1250 and part bv_0625.

Explaining Changes

A key aspect of rationale is the linking of activity with intent. RCF reasons about designer intent during refinement phases, using a set of increasingly more knowledge-intensive methods. Specifically, the system gathers *evidence* to support a range of *hypotheses* as to why particular objects were modified and the effects that those changes had on the overall design. These hypotheses postulate that the designer intended (or not) to impact some design property (*e.g.*, *Torque*), possibly to move in some specified direction (*e.g.*, *increase* or *decrease*). A calculus for combining evidence is used to infer defeasible conclusions about designer intent.

To start, *change clusters* are generated that group related events. Analysis events provide the basis for cluster generation, in accord with the metaphor *AnalysisA...AnalysisK - Activity - AnalysisL....AnalysisN*. RCF hypothesizes that events within the scope of the cluster were performed to address one or more of the design requirements linked to the cluster analyses. These basic hypotheses can be bolstered (or countered) by additional evidence, such as detection of *refinement trends* whereby an analyzed design property is observed to change monotonically within a cluster. When available, quantitative knowledge about task-specific *thresholded design requirements* can be used to weaken or strengthen cluster-based hypotheses. For example, if a

change occurs that increases the degree of satisfaction of a design requirement that is already known to be satisfied, it is less likely (but not impossible) that the designer was intentionally focusing on that design requirement.

Richer explanations of designer intent can be generated by using domain-specific background knowledge. We have developed an approach that involves reasoning qualitatively about the effects that actions have on design requirements. The possible effects are encoded in a *qualitative impact of change (QIC)* table. To date, only changes to semantic attributes are addressed, but the approach can be readily extended to handle structural changes (*e.g.*, the addition or deletion of objects). Figure 6 presents the gear portion of the QIC table for our robotic arm design case. *Numeric* attributes show positive or negative correlation with design properties. *Binary* attributes show correlation when the attribute assumes values of true or false. *Enumerated* attributes specify correlation for various ranking functions.

QIC information expands the space of both hypotheses and evidence for explaining designer activity. Figure 7 presents two example clusters. Each cluster includes (a) its key design events (here, analyses and changes to semantic attributes of objects), and (b) classification of effects of change operations within the cluster (extracted from the QIC table) as *intended* or *side* effects. Evidence to support the classification is provided: MATCHED-ANALYSES indicates multiple analyses of a particular design requirement, KNOWN-UNSAT indicates that a design requirement was known to be unsatisfied when a change was made that improved the design along that requirement, MODIFY indicates that the effect was brought about by a designated action, and MODIFY-WRONG-DIR indicates that the modification is contrary to the direction in which it should move (to satisfy some design requirement).

In the first cluster, QIC knowledge exists for only the change in material for DOBJ92 from Delrin to lighter Aluminum. RCF uses it to conclude that the possible effects are to reduce weight, decrease inertia, or increase stress. From the collected evidence, RCF's evidential reasoning calculus infers that event 312 was performed to reduce weight, but also caused an undesirable increase in stress (as indicated by the high positive and negative likelihood values, respectively). These inferences bolster the hypothesis in the second cluster that the designer

```
>>> Cluster #1  <<<                                 >>> Cluster #2  <<<
Key Design Events:                                  Key Design Events:
#306: ANALYSIS of ARM-INERTIA-IZ with result 60.0    #316: ANALYSIS of STRESS with result 0.6
#308: ANALYSIS of WEIGHT with result 2.2             #318: ANNOTATE DOBJ209 (BV_1250)
#310: ANNOTATE DOBJ209 (BV_1250)                           CAT_NUM --> BERG_M48N2A;
      CAT_NUM --> BERG_M48N2A;                            MATERIAL --> SS (was ALUMINUM);
#312: ANNOTATE DOBJ92 (BASE_GEAR)                    #321: ANNOTATE DOBJ31 (BV_0625)
      CAT_NUM --> F32-A6-96;                              CAT_NUM --> BERG_M48N3;
      MATERIAL --> DELRIN (was ALUMINUM);                MATERIAL --> SS (was ALUMINUM);
#313: ANALYSIS of ARM-INERTIA-IZ with result 50.0    #323: ANALYSIS of STRESS with result 0.4
#314: ANALYSIS of WEIGHT with result 2.0
                                                    Intended:
Intended:                                            ==> (STRESS DOWN)  Likelihood = 3
 ==> (WEIGHT DOWN) Likelihood = 3                        Evidence:
    Evidence:                                            (MATCHED-ANALYSES #318 #321)
    (MATCHED-ANALYSES #308 #314)                         (PREVIOUSLY-COUNTERED Cluster-1)
    (MODIFY #312)                                        (KNOWN-UNSAT #316)
    (KNOWN-UNSAT #308)
                                                    Side Effects:
 ==> (ARM-INERTIA-IZ DOWN)  Likelihood = 2           ==> (WEIGHT UP)  Likelihood = -5
    Evidence:                                            Evidence:
    (MATCHED-ANALYSES #306 #313)                         (MODIFY-WRONG-DIR #318 #321)
    (KNOWN-UNSAT #306)

Side Effects:
 ==> (STRESS UP)  Likelihood = -5
    Evidence:
    (MODIFY-WRONG-DIR #312)
```

Figure 7: Sample Analysis Clusters with Evidence

is attempting to reduce stress through material changes in design events 318 and 321 (reflected in the evidence PREVIOUSLY-COUNTERED), even though doing so counteracts the weight decrease of the first cluster.

Evaluation and Discussion

The motivation for building RCF was to determine whether nonintrusive methods could extract useful rationale without disrupting the design process. Although no formal evaluation has yet been undertaken, results from the application of RCF to the robotic arm design case represent a qualified success: useful rationale was extracted and represented in structures that provide ready user accessibility. However, additional mechanisms will be required to produce a deployable tool for designers.

One area in which to extend RCF is to incorporate more design metaphors, with particular focus on identifying intent. For example, an *Exploration* metaphor would track branching of a design or design component into distinct alternatives, in contrast to the linear model of versioning employed currently within RCF. Such a metaphor would enable improved understanding of the space of options that a designer had considered before settling on his or her final choice. Versioning itself could be improved by grounding it in the clustering of related changes to an object, rather than relying on file operations to mark version boundaries.

The inspiration for RCF was the observation that many of the operations that a designer can perform with a CAD tool have meaningful semantic content. As CAD tools increase in sophistication, the set of semantically meaningful operations will also increase, thus enabling additional automated rationale extraction. For example, Active Catalogs (Ling *et al.* 1997) provides a rich query interface for selecting parts from online libraries, as well as simulation capabilities to support a "try before you buy" model of interaction. Observation of the queries formulated by a designer interacting with such a tool would yield a rich data stream from which additional rationale could be inferred.

There is always a trade-off in the design of knowledge-based systems between the cost of adding more knowledge (in terms of knowledge acquisition and maintenance) and the value that the added knowledge brings to the problem-solving process. We intentionally designed RCF with an *incremental* knowledge model that enables the system to run with varying levels of domain-specific knowledge. The main categories of such knowledge within RCF are design requirements and the QIC tables. The system can operate without this information, but generates increasingly better results as more of it is provided. For domains involving many one-off designs, development of extensive background theories will not be justified. However, for domains in which designs will be repeatedly produced, the application of domain-specific knowledge could greatly increase the extent of the rationale that can be generated.

Related Work

Early work on acquisition of design rationale focused on *direct solicitation* methods, whereby users are explicitly queried or provided with structured interfaces to elicit rationale (Russell *et al.* 1990; Gruber 1991). Because these approaches impose a heavy documentation burden on designers, they have had limited success.

Several attempts have been made to ease the problem of automated rationale generation by imposing structure on the design process (Ganeshan, Garrett, & Finger 1994; Brazier, van Langen, & Treur 1997). The general idea is to model design as selection from predefined transformation rules. When a rule is selected, the choice is recorded along with rationale associated with that rule. By structuring the design process, these approaches can provide deeper explanations of designer intent than can RCF. However, they greatly constrain designer activities and are unsuitable for *ad hoc* design cases requiring novel design methods.

The Active Design Document (ADD) system (Garcia *et al.* 1997; Garcia & Howard 1992) generates rationale for *parametric design tasks*, in which the design process involves constraining or selecting values for fixed sets of parameters. This class of designs, while important, is much narrower in scope than that addressed by RCF. The early ADD system observed the designer's actions, and then attempted to generate explanations for them. If the system was unsuccessful, or predicted an action other than that taken, it would ask for explanation. In this way, a knowledge base could be built from observed cases. More recent versions of ADD can generate ranked alternatives.

The Design History Tool (Chen, Dietterich, & Ullman 1991) stores structured, hierarchical representations of a design that are extracted from manually transcribed videotapes of design sessions that include what the designer *says* as well as the operations he performs. The resultant design history is browsable with respect to structure, evolution, alternatives considered, and dependencies in the design. This system provides better coverage of designer intent than does RCF, but at the costs of intrusiveness into the design process and labor-intensive data input.

Conclusions

RCF's methods for acquiring design rationale present an innovative approach to a difficult and important problem. Previous work on rationale acquisition has focused on highly intrusive techniques that either require extensive participation by the human designer or change the underlying design process. In contrast, our idea of extracting design rationale from observations of designer activity is rooted in a philosophy of nonintrusiveness: rationale is produced as a natural by-product of the design process. The human designer will need to intervene to supply certain information of relevance to the design but should be relieved of responsibility for recording information about the noncreative aspects of a design. We have shown within RCF that this type of automation is possible by applying key AI methods: knowledge representation, knowledge-based plan recognition, clustering techniques, and basic qualitative reasoning.

Acknowledgments This research has been supported by DARPA Contract N00014-96-C-0162.

References

Brazier, F. M.; van Langen, P. H.; and Treur, J. 1997. A compositional approach to modelling design rationale. *Artificial Intelligence for Engineering Design, Analysis, and Manufacturing* 11:125–139.

Carroll, J. M., and Moran, T. P. 1991. Special issue on design rationale. *Human-Computer Interaction* 6(3-4).

Chen, A.; Dietterich, T. G.; and Ullman, D. G. 1991. A computer-based design history tool. In *NSF Design and Manufacturing Conference*, 985–994.

Conklin, E. J., and Yakemovic, K. B. 1991. A process-oriented approach to design rationale. *Human-Computer Interaction* 6:357–391.

Fischer, G., and Lemke, A. C. 1988. Construction kits and design environments: Steps toward human problem-domain communication. *Human-Computer Interaction* 3:179–192.

Ganeshan, R.; Garrett, J.; and Finger, S. 1994. A framework for representing design intent. *Design Studies* 15(1):59–84.

Garcia, A. C. B., and Howard, H. C. 1992. Acquiring design knowledge through design decision justification. *Artificial Intelligence for Engineering, Design, and Analysis in Manufacturing* 6(1):59–71.

Garcia, A. C. B.; de Andrade, J. C.; Rodrigues, R. F.; and Moura, R. 1997. ADDVAC: Applying active design documents for the capture, retrieval, and use of rationale during offshore platform VAC design. In *Proceedings of the Ninth Conference on Innovative Applications of Artificial Intelligence*, 986–991.

Gruber, T. R., and Russell, D. M. 1992. Generative design rationale: Beyond the record and replay paradigm. Technical Report KSL 92-59, Knowledge Systems Laboratory, Computer Science Department, Stanford University.

Gruber, T. R. 1991. Interactive acquisition for justifications: Learning 'why' by being told 'what'. *IEEE Expert* 6(4).

Ling, S. R.; Kim, J.; Will, P.; and Luo, P. 1997. Active catalog: Searching and using catalog information in internet-based design. In *Proceedings of the ASME Design Engineering Technical Conferences*.

Russell, D. M.; Burton, R. R.; Jordan, D. S.; Jensen, A. M.; Rogers, R. A.; and Choen, J. 1990. Creating instruction with IDE: Tools for instructional designers. *Intelligent Tutoring* 1(1):3–16.

Shipman, F. M., and McCall, R. J. 1997. Integrating different perspectives on design rationale: Supporting the emergence of design rationale from design communication. *Artificial Intelligence for Engineering Design, Analysis, and Manufacturing* 11:141–154.

A Multi-Agent System for Meting Out Influence
in an Intelligent Environment

M. V. Nagendra Prasad & **Joseph F. McCarthy**
Center for Strategic Technology Research
Andersen Consulting
3773 Willow Road
Northbrook, IL 60062 USA
+1 847 714 {2062,2260}
{nagendra,mccarthy}@cstar.ac.com

ABSTRACT

Intelligent environments are physical spaces that can sense and respond to the people and events taking place within them, providing opportunities for people to influence environmental factors that affect them, such as the lighting, temperature, décor or background music in the common areas of an office building. The designer of an environment that can be influenced by a group of collocated people rather than a single individual must decide how to accord influence among the individuals in the group. We have designed two multi-agent group preference arbitration schemes and tested them out in an intelligent environment, MUSICFX, which controls the selection of music played in a fitness center. One scheme seeks to maximize the average satisfaction of the inhabitants, the other seeks to maximize the equitable distribution of satisfaction among the inhabitants. We present the results of a series of experiments using real data collected from the deployed system, and discuss the ramifications of these two potentially conflicting goals.

Keywords

Multi-agent systems, intelligent environments, ubiquitous computing, agents[1].

INTRODUCTION

An intelligent environment can detect the people within its space and can then adapt itself to those people. Most of the research into intelligent environments and other applications of ubiquitous computing has focused on how an environment can sense and respond to a single individual [1, 2, 4, 5, 6, 7, 8, 12]. Our research, in contrast, explores the issue of how an environment can effectively adapt to a *group* of people, even when these people have a diverse set of preferences. We are interested in exploring how *background* environmental factors might be better adapted to the preferences, rather than direct commands, of

inhabitants. In this regard, our research is more akin to the ideas of calm technology [13] and ambient media [3, 14].

In this paper, we will describe the design of a multi-agent system that adapts to changes in the environment and the needs of its inhabitants. The system is set up as an artificial economy of agents serving as proxies for actual inhabitants. Within this dynamic market economy, different control strategies – implemented as simple market rules – can produce different effects on the inhabitants. The specific issue we address in this paper is the potential conflict between a strategy to maximize average inhabitant satisfaction and a strategy to maximize the equitable distribution of satisfaction among inhabitants. The former goal may lead to a "tyranny of the majority" wherein a small number of inhabitants, with preferences that vary significantly from the norm, never achieves satisfaction. The latter goal may lead to instances where the preferences of a small minority override the preferences of a large majority. One might characterize these goals as trying to please some of the people all of the time versus trying to please all of the people some of the time.

As an example, suppose an intelligent meeting room adjusts its temperature in accordance to the thermal preferences of its inhabitants. Most people prefer something close to "room temperature" (68°F/20°C), but invariably, some like it hot and some like it cold. A room that wants to maximize average satisfaction would set its temperature to the mean of the thermal preferences of its inhabitants; this would mean the outliers who like it hotter or colder would never be maximally comfortable. A room that seeks to achieve the most equitable distribution of satisfaction might often set its temperature to the average preference, but it would also occasionally set its temperature higher and occasionally set its temperature lower, so that the people on the fringes would have higher overall satisfaction over time.

Another example involves background music playing in a fitness center. An intelligent fitness center environment that seeks to maximize average satisfaction might play only the music that is most popular among the majority of its members. An environment that is more concerned with an equitable distribution of satisfaction might occasionally play music that is not the most popular with the most people, but is popular among some of members with more eclectic musical tastes.

MUSICFX [9] is a realization of such a system, having been installed in a corporate fitness center – the Fitness Xchange (FX) at Andersen Consulting Technology Park (ACTP) – where it acts as an automatic disc jockey, deciding what kind of music to play for the fitness center members working out at any given time. The system has been very popular, with over 70% of members reporting they like the MUSICFX-controlled music selection better than the previous human-controlled music selection. Although much of the discussion in this paper focuses on the MUSICFX system, we believe that the issues we are addressing are of a much more general nature, and need to be considered by the designers of any intelligent environment. MUSICFX, as a deployed system, can be regarded as an interim testbed, which provides us considerable data collected from an instantiated intelligent environment.

We begin by providing an overview of the MUSICFX system and the environment in which it operates. We then present a hypothetical scenario that highlights the tradeoffs between popularity and fairness. The next section defines our general framework for multi-agent group arbitration systems and describes two specific group preference arbitration schemes, MAX-SAT and EQUITABLE, that seek to maximize average satisfaction and maximize equitable distribution of satisfaction, respectively. We report on a series of experiments using these two schemes, and we conclude with a discussion of the ramifications this research has for the design of intelligent environments that take inhabitant preferences into account.

SYSTEM OVERVIEW

Any intelligent environment that adapts to the preferences of its inhabitants needs three main components: a mechanism for detecting inhabitants and their activities, a representation of inhabitant preferences, and an algorithm for deciding how to adapt based on those preferences.

MUSICFX detects inhabitants by requiring members to login, using a proximity badge reader and standard-issue ACTP badges, as they enter the fitness center. Rather than requiring a member to explicitly logout – for which there exists no significant incentive – we set an expiration timeout of 90 minutes after each login, after which time the system presumes the member has left.[2] MUSICFX assumes

its inhabitants' activities can be broadly classified as exercising, and doesn't require finer distinctions.

The MUSICFX preference database represents members' ratings of each of 91 genres of music, each available on a separate station from a satellite music service. Each genre is rated on a 5-point scale, from +2 through –2, interpreted as "I {love, like, don't care, dislike or hate} this kind of music." The initial set of preferences is submitted to the system remotely via an electronic enrollment form; members can update these preferences in the fitness center at any time.

When a member logs in to the system, that person's preferences are retrieved and added to the current pool of preferences. The MUSICFX Group Preference Arbitrator sorts the list of genres from most popular to least popular, and then uses a weighted random selection algorithm[3] to select one of the most popular genres to play. The Arbitrator is invoked each time a person enters or leaves the fitness center, each time a person updates his or her preferences, each time a fitness center staff member adjusts a system parameter, or after a maximum play time for a single genre has been exceeded.

A more comprehensive description of the system can be found in McCarthy & Anagnost [9].

GROUP PREFERENCES

A sample set of music preferences, for five people (Al, Barb, Carl, Deb and Ed) and ten stations, is shown in Figure 1.

i	Genre Person	A	B	C	D	E	GP_i	Pr_i
1	Alternative Rock	2	2	2	-1	-1	50	0.42
2	Hottest Hits	2	1	1	0	-2	38	0.32
3	New Music	1	1	1	-2	0	31	0.26
4	Dance	0	0	-1	2	-1	26	0.00
5	Hot Country	0	0	-2	-1	2	25	0.00
6	World Beat	0	1	-1	-1	-2	15	0.00
7	Traditional Country	-1	0	-1	1	-2	15	0.00
8	50's Oldies	0	0	-1	-1	-1	11	0.00
9	Heavy Metal	-1	-1	-1	-1	-2	4	0.00
10	Polka	-1	-1	-2	-2	-2	2	0.00

Figure 1. Sample Preferences

If we further simplify the scenario by supposing that these five people work out together all the time, then we can see that an algorithm seeking to maximize average satisfaction will always choose the top-rated station (based on simply

---

[2] For convenience, we will refer to the virtual "logout" events that occur 90 minutes after entering a fitness center as members "leaving" or "exiting" the center.

[3] Rather than always selecting the most popular station, which could result in a tyranny of the majority, an element of randomness – with probabilities distributed according to popularity – was introduced in the original algorithm in order to inject a degree of equitability.

summing the individual preferences), "Alternative Rock," even though two inhabitants (Deb and Ed) dislike this station.

Choosing the second most popular station would be an improvement for Deb, who at least doesn't mind "Hottest Hits", but Ed hates that station. Selecting the third most popular station, "New Music," is less distasteful to Ed, but anathema to Deb. In order to please Deb or Ed, an algorithm would need to play the fourth or fifth most popular stations, though these selections would not be popular among the other inhabitants.

This scenario highlights the tension between trying to achieve maximum average satisfaction and trying to achieve equitability for all inhabitants. We will return to this scenario to illustrate the behavior of the two schemes we have created in order to investigate these potentially conflicting goals.

A MULTI-AGENT GROUP ARBITRATION SYSTEM

A *multi-agent group arbitration system* consists of a set of agents (*A*), where each *agent* (*a_i*) represents a single person's preferences.[4] A market-based economy governs the arbitration process for selecting among several available *options* regarding environmental factors. The arbitration process consists of a *bid-select-redistribute* cycle, as shown in Figure 2.

Algorithm *GROUP-ARBITRATOR*

Bid:

    For each $a_i \in A$ do
        Annouce (Bid(a_i))

Select:

    Pool = For all $a_i \in A$
        (Collect (Bid(a_i)))
    Winner = Select (Pool)

Redistribute:

    For each $a_i \in A$ do
        Adjust_Influence (Bid(a_i), Pool, Winner)

Figure 2: Bid-Select-Redistribute Cycle

In the *bid* stage, each of the agents announces its bid for the different options available. The *select* stage involves the arbitration process where the bids by all agents involved are pooled and a "winning" option is chosen. The last stage is the *redistribute* stage where the future potential for an agent's capability to influence a choice may be readjusted based on the present option selected. In the case of

---

[4] We will use the terms "agent" and "person" (or "inhabitant") interchangeably in our presentation of these algorithms.

MUSICFX, an agent represents a person's preferences for different genres of music. A bid by an agent involves an announcement of an agent's strength of desire for (or aversion to) each genre. The group arbitration algorithm chooses a particular genre to be played based on the combined pool of bids by all the agents presently working out in the fitness center.

We can devise various schemes by instantiating the generic *Group Arbitrator* algorithm in different ways. Below we provide the details of two schemes we devised and studied using MUSICFX as a test-bed: MAX-SAT and EQUITABLE. MAX-SAT seeks to maximize the average satisfaction of all inhabitants. The EQUITABLE algorithm, in contrast, seeks to maximize equitability of satisfaction among all inhabitants.

Scheme *MAX-SAT*

The MAX-SAT scheme is based on the original algorithm used in MUSICFX (without the weighted random selection operator); it is designed to select the most popular station during each cycle. The popularity of a station is defined as a function of the individual preferences of all present inhabitants, but no history of past selections is maintained.

Within the framework of *Group Arbitrator*, we can specify the *bid* and *select* functions for MAX-SAT as follows:

Bid

The *Bid* function looks at the integer-valued individual preferences ($IP_{i,j}$) of agent a_i ranging from -2 to $+2$ for each of the *M* options that are rated, normalizes those preferences to non-negative integers, and squares the result to broaden the gap between stations at different levels of preference, e.g., those that are loved and those that are merely liked. This results in an *M*-component vector :

$$Bid(a_i) = \{ b_{ij} = (IP_{ij} + 2)^2 \mid j = 1 \ldots M \}$$

Select

The *Select* function takes as input a *Pool*, which is an *N* x *M* matrix where *M* is the number of categories being rated (musical genres) and *N* is the number of inhabitants (FX members who are currently working out). For each category *j*, and each agent *i*, that agent's individual preference for that category ($IP_{i,j}$) is used by the algorithm to compute the overall group preference for that category (GP_j) using the following summation formula:

$$GP_j = \sum_{i=1}^{N} b_{ij}$$

Select then chooses the winning option (*w*) that maximizes group preference (GP_j):

$$w = \arg\max\{GP_j \mid j = 1..M\}$$

Redistribute

MAX-SAT has no redistribution function, since it is explicitly not concerned with achieving equitability.

Scheme EQUITABLE

The EQUITABLE scheme takes an egalitarian approach to the choice of an option, based on *state* information stored in the agents. The state information is stored in the form of *cash*, which represents a coarse representation of the history of an agent. Each agent starts life with the same amount of cash. During each cycle, an agent's bid for a particular option is proportional to its preference for that option and the cash it has. Once an option is selected, every agent pays or receives an amount proportional to its preference for or against that option – agents that have an unfavorable option imposed on them receive payment for the inconvenience they suffer from those agents who prefer the option selected. Thus any agent that is subjected to low preference options for a long time will accumulate enough cash to dominate the bidding process at some point and thereby have one of its preferred options selected.

Instantiating this strategy within a *Group Arbitrator* framework, we have:

Bid

The *Bid* function looks at the integer-valued preferences of agent a_i ranging from -2 to $+2$, normalizes each preference rating to a non-negative integer, and multiplies this value by the amount of cash possessed by the agent. A bid factor (*bf*), a scaling constant between 0 and 1, is used to modulate the amount of cash tendered during any given cycle. This results in an *M*-component vector:

$$Bid(a_i) = \{\, b_{ij} = bf \times (IP_{i,j} + 2) \times \text{Cash}(a_i) \mid j = 1 \ldots M\}$$

Select

The *Select* function for EQUITABLE is the same as for MAX-SAT.

Redistribute

The Adjust_Influence function determines how to reallocate wealth among the agents representing the current inhabitants. The amount of compensation (C_i) paid to agents who endure unfavorable options is proportional to the difference between the maximum preference – in this case, 2 – and the agent's individual preference for the winning option (*w*), multiplied by a compensation deceleration function (cdf) of the agent's cash. This amount is adjusted by a compensation factor (*cf*), another scaling constant between 0 and 1:

$$C_i = cf \times (Max\text{-}Pref - IP_{i,w}) \times cdf(\text{Cash}(a_i))$$

The compensation deceleration function is defined as

$$cdf(\text{amount}) = 1/\,(1 + e^{2 \times (\text{amount} - \text{initial-cash})/\text{initial-cash}})$$

where *initial-cash* is a constant for all agents.

Designing general market-based multi-agent schemes involves parameterizing the system along a number of dimensions. Setting the parameters' forms and values involves a good understanding of the dynamics of the environment being modeled. The specific definition of the *cdf* function is a good example of such a parameter. Inhabitants who dislike or hate the vast majority of options are very likely to garner a huge amount of the net wealth in the system through repeated compensations. This may lead to a net drain of wealth from the rest of the system, which, in turn, may cause imbalances in the market when it starts functioning in regions of the parameter space characterized by "extreme" cash values. The *cdf* function has been designed to reduce the compensation received by agents with very high amounts of cash.

Compensatory updating of the agent cash is done as follows:

$$\text{Cash}(a_i) = \text{Cash}(a_i) + C_i$$

In order to determine how much each agent pays, we first compute the total compensation, *C*, as the sum of all individual agent compensation needs (C_i). For each agent a_i, its payment P_i is a fraction of the total compensation, based on a payment factor (*pf*), a scaling constant between 0 and 1, a payment deceleration function (*pdf*) of the agent's cash, and the agent's share of the overall group preference for the winning option selected:

$$P_i = C \times pf \times pdf(\text{Cash}(a_i)) \times (2 + IP_{i,w})/\,Total\_Pref$$

Total_Pref, the normalized total preference for *N* agents, can be defined as follows:

$$Total\_Pref = \sum_{i=1}^{N} (IP_{i,w} + 2)$$

The payment deceleration function (pdf) is defined as

$$pdf(\text{amount}) = 1/\,(1 + e^{2 \times (\text{initial-cash} - \text{amount})/\text{initial-cash}})$$

Just as the *cdf* function was designed to reduce compensation received by extremely wealthy agents, the *pdf* function was designed to reduce the compensation paid out by very poor agents.

EXPERIMENTS

Our goal is to create a multi-agent framework in which we can explore different schemes for allocating influence in an intelligent environment. In particular, we wanted to explore the tradeoff between popularity and fairness in such a setting. To this end, we ran simulations of the two algorithms described in the previous section.

The deployed MUSICFX system has extensive logs that track events that take place in the environment. In particular, we know when each person has entered and left the fitness center, what each person's preferences were at any given time, and which station has been selected at any given time. This event data can be used in our simulator, however, we wanted to first run the algorithms on smaller sets of data so that we could better understand their behavior under more tractable conditions.

We will present the behavior of our schemes using three sets of data: one corresponding to the simplified data shown in Figure 1, another using randomly generated data with a random selection of inhabitants, and a final experiment using real data from the event log from MUSICFX over a one month period.

In each experiment, we measure each inhabitant's satisfaction with the option selected. For example, using the data in Figure 1, if Deb spent four time units listening to Alternative Rock, two time units listening to Dance, and one time unit listening to Hot Country, her individual satisfaction would be $(4 \times -1) + (2 \times 2) + (1 \times -1) = -1$.

Two metrics serve as a basis for comparing the performance of the algorithms over entire populations. The first measures the total of individual satisfaction levels obtained by a scheme; the second measures the equitability of individual satisfaction levels obtained by a scheme.

Total Satisfaction. This is the sum of individual satisfaction levels for all of the inhabitants in the population.

Gini Coefficient. The Gini Coefficient is a measure of how much a given distribution of wealth (satisfaction, in this case) departs from the ideal egalitarian distribution [10]. This statistic can be explained with reference to the so-called Lorenz curve. In plotting a Lorenz curve, measures of individual wealth, or in this case, satisfaction, are sorted in an increasing order and then cumulative measures are derived. The X-axis represents the percentage of the population; the Y-axis represents the percentage of cumulative wealth. If wealth is distributed completely equitably, then the top 10% of the population owns 10% of the wealth, the top 20% owns 20% of the wealth, and so on. The ideal curve thus has a 45° slope; any deviation from this ideal curve represents a measure of the inequity across the population. The Gini Coefficient measures the difference between the Lorenz curve for a given distribution of wealth and the ideal curve representing an egalitarian distribution; thus lower values represent more egalitarian distributions than higher values. The Gini Coefficient can be defined by the following formula:

$$1 + \frac{1}{n} - \frac{2}{n \cdot Z}\left(\sum_{i=1}^{n} i \cdot z_i\right)$$

where $z_1, ..., z_n$ represent individual levels of wealth in decreasing order of size, Z is the total income, and n is the number of individuals. For our experiments, wealth is defined as satisfaction with selected options.

Experiment Set I

In the first set of experiments, we used the hypothetical data shown in Figure 1. We wanted to see whether there was any measurable difference between the behavior of the schemes when they were run with data that was constructed specifically to highlight the potential conflict between the goals of popularity and fairness. We ran each algorithm for 500 time units, tracking individual satisfaction levels.

Figure 3 shows the Lorenz curve for the performance of the two schemes on this data set, and Table 1 gives the statistics. As predicted, EQUITABLE trades off lower total satisfaction (by 17.5%) for greater equitability (by 94.2%).

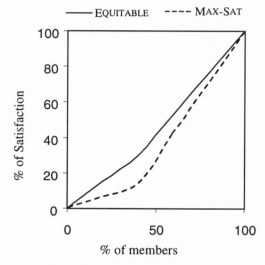

Figure 3: Lorenz curve for Experiment I

Total Satisfaction			Gini Coefficient		
Max-Sat	Equitable	% change	Max-Sat	Equitable	% change
7000	5776	-17.50%	0.26	0.01	94.20%

Table 1: Results of Experiment I

In fact, EQUITABLE nearly achieves a perfectly egalitarian distribution of satisfaction (a Gini Coefficient of 0.0 represents the ideal value).

Experiment Set II

Having convinced ourselves that the EQUITABLE scheme achieves a much more equitable distribution of satisfaction than MAX-SAT when presented with inhabitant preference data that was specially contrived to achieve this result, we next set about experimenting with randomly generated preference data. For the second set of experiments, we created a population of 15 people, each of whom were assigned randomly generated preference ratings for each of five stations. For each epoch of the experiment, we randomly selected 10 people from this population, provided them each with the same initial allocation of cash, and ran MAX-SAT for 500 time units; we then reinitialized the cash allocation for each person and ran EQUITABLE for 500 time units. We ran 10 epochs of the experiment, with the results shown in Table 2.

Epoch	Total Satisfaction			Gini Coefficient		
	Max-Sat	Equitable	% change	Max-Sat	Equitable	% change
1	14000	12521	-10.6%	0.19	0.10	50.5%
2	15500	13624	-12.1%	0.19	0.11	39.9%
3	14500	13162	-9.2%	0.22	0.13	41.8%
4	14000	12713	-9.2%	0.23	0.15	34.7%
5	12000	10825	-9.8%	0.30	0.10	68.3%
6	14500	11243	-22.5%	0.19	0.08	56.0%
7	15000	12830	-14.5%	0.16	0.15	5.4%
8	15000	12564	-16.2%	0.19	0.15	20.5%
9	14500	11939	-17.7%	0.19	0.10	49.6%
10	13000	11851	-8.8%	0.28	0.12	59.6%
Average	14200	12327	-13.1%	0.21	0.12	42.6%

Table 2: Results of Experiment II

Once again, the EQUITABLE scheme results in a lower total satisfaction than MAX-SAT (13.1% less), but achieves greater equitability of satisfaction (42.6% more). It is interesting to note that the differences in this data set are less dramatic than they are for the specially contrived data used in the first experiment.

Experiment Set III

In the final experiment, we used real event log data from the deployed MUSICFX system to test the two schemes. For each arrival event in a segment of the event log covering a period of one month, a {person id, arrival time} pair was extracted, yielding a data set that includes various groupings of 166 fitness center members. The results of this simulation are shown in Table 3.

Total Satisfaction			Gini Coefficient		
Max-Sat	Equitable	% change	Max-Sat	Equitable	% change
6767	5953	-12.0%	0.14	0.09	31.9%

Table 3: Results of Experiment III

As in the previous experiments, EQUITABLE sacrifices total satisfaction (12.0% less than MAX-SAT) for increased equitability of satisfaction (31.9% more).

Discussion

In all three experiments, EQUITABLE led to a more egalitarian distribution of satisfaction, at the cost of a lower total satisfaction among inhabitants. Although the results were most dramatic in the first experiment, using data specially constructed to highlight the conflict between popularity and fairness, there were considerable differences seen in results from the real data set.

RELATED WORK

The research described in this paper deals with the design of a multi-agent system for group preference arbitration schemes. Other researchers [8, 11] have explored applications of market-based multi-agent systems.

Huberman and Clearwater [8] created a market-based system in which a set of agents, each representing the temperature controller of an individual office within a building, bid to buy or sell thermal units. While the goal of their system – maximizing comfort – is similar to the goal of the MAX-SAT algorithm, their agents do not retain money between auctions (which are held every minute), and thus the system does not have the capability to maximize the equitability of comfort distribution over time. Another difference is that Huberman and Clearwater's agents are bidding over a variable amount (units) of a fixed resource (hot or cold air), whereas our agents are bidding over a variable amount (time) of a variable resource (91 options simultaneously available). It is interesting to note that Huberman and Clearwater also contend with the issue of people exhibiting extreme preferences, which in their case corresponds to extreme thermostat settings in individuals' offices.

Walsh and Wellman [11] present a decentralized protocol for allocating tasks among agents that contend for scarce resources. The framework described in their work is potentially applicable to a large class of multi-agent problems, including the search for information in a digital library. However, their framework does not appear to be well suited to the problem of allocating a resource (or good) that is inherently shared, such as the music played in a fitness center.

CONCLUSION

In this paper, we present a Multi-Agent Group Preference Arbitration system. At the core of this framework is a multi-agent system based on market mechanisms for resolving multiple, conflicting preferences among a group of people inhabiting a shared environment. Based on our experiences with MUSICFX, a deployed system for group preference arbitration used in the selection of music in a fitness center, we designed two distinct schemes: MAX-SAT and EQUITABLE. These schemes were tested both on artificial data and real data derived from the event logs maintained by the MUSICFX system.

The results of our experiments have provided strong empirical evidence demonstrating that we can affect the tradeoff between popularity and fairness. However, determining which of these goals should be emphasized within a given environment is a difficult policy question, the answer to which is beyond the scope of the work reported here.

One of the shortcomings of the current EQUITABLE scheme is that it does not take into account a person's overall preference distribution. Intuitively, someone who hates nearly everything should not be paid as much for his or her inconvenience as someone who has mostly positive preferences, since such a person is difficult to please anyhow. Likewise, someone who hates nearly everything should have to pay more for his or her preferred option(s), since there are so few alternatives available to that person.

Future versions of the algorithm will investigate ways to take these factors into consideration.

Another future direction involves exploring how group preference arbitration can affect other factors in a shared environment. For example, we plan to develop an application that affects visual aspects of an environment in response to the presence of different inhabitants.

One issue that arises in the deployed MUSICFX system is the requirement that a member fill out a questionnaire with 91 questions (corresponding to the different stations). This might be a disincentive for registering with the system. In addition, in a number of environments, explicit questionnaires may not be a feasible way of deriving user preferences. We are beginning to look at techniques from machine learning and collaborative filtering to induce user preferences from observation or sparse data. Another interesting direction of future work involves dealing with more than one shared resource and group arbitration in such situations. The problem here is complicated by the fact that in addition to arbitrating the users sharing a particular resource, we also have to deal with optimally partitioning users across resources.

We believe that as intelligent environments gain increasingly sophisticated ways of sensing and responding to their inhabitants, there are many important issues to explore. MUSICFX provides one environment in which to investigate some of these issues, but we look forward to a future filled with many intelligent environments in which rich and complex intra- and inter-environmental interactions can evolve.

ACKNOWLEDGMENTS

The authors wish to thank Theodore Anagnost, who has been responsible for the implementation and maintenance of the real MUSICFX system, and who has contributed many ideas to the design of both the actual algorithm used in the system and the variations described in this paper. We also wish to thank Andy Fano for helpful comments on an earlier draft of this paper.

REFERENCES

1. Michael H. Coen. 1997. Building Brains for Rooms: Designing Distributed Software Agents. In *Proceedings of the Ninth Conference on Innovative Applications of Artificial Intelligence (IAAI 97).* 971-977. Menlo Park, CA: AAAI Press..

2. Jeremy R. Cooperstock, Sidney S. Fels, William Buxton, and Kenneth K. Smith. 1997. Reactive Environments: Throwing Away Your Keyboard and Mouse. *Communications of the ACM* 40(9): 65-73.

3. Andrew Dahley, Craig Wisneski and Hiroshi Ishii. Water Lamp and Pinwheels: Ambient Projection of Digital Information into Architectural In *Proceedings of the 1998 ACM Conference on Human Factors in Computing Systems (CHI '98),* (Los Angeles, April 1998), ACM Press, pp. 269-270.

4. Scott Elrod, Gene Hall, Rick Costanza, Michael Dixon, and Jim Des Rivieres. 1993. Responsive Office Environments. *Communications of the ACM* 36(7): 84-85.

5. Jorg Geibler. Shuffle, Throw or Take It!: Working Efficiently with an Interactive Wall. In *Proceedings of the 1998 ACM Conference on Human Factors in Computing Systems (CHI 98 Summary),* (Los Angeles, April 1998), ACM Press, pp. 265-266.

6. Andy Harter and Andy Hopper. 1994. A Distributed Location System for the Active Office. *IEEE Network* 8(1): 62-70.

7. Andy Hopper, Andy Harter, and Tom Blackie. 1993. The Active Badge System. In *Proceedings of the Conference on Human Factors in Computing Systems (InterCHI 93).*

8. Bernardo A. Huberman and Scott H. Clearwater 1995. A Multi-agent System for Controlling Building Environments. In the *Proceedings of the First International Conference on Multi-Agent Systems (ICMAS 95).*

9. Joseph F. McCarthy and Theodore D. Anagnost. 1998. MUSICFX: An Arbiter of Group Preferences for Computer Supported Collaborative Workouts. In *Proceedings of the ACM 1998 Conference on Computer Supported Cooperative Work (CSCW '98),* pp. 363-372.

10. David W. Pearce (ed.), *The MIT Dictionary of Modern Economics*, 1992, MIT Press, Cambridge, MA.

11. William E. Walsh and Michael P. Wellman 1998. A Market Protocol for Decentralized Task Allocation. In the *Proceedings of the Third International Conference on Multi-agent Systems (ICMAS 98).*

12. Roy Want, Bill N. Schilit, Norman I. Adams, Rich Gold, Karin Petersen, David Goldberg, John R. Ellis, and Mark Weiser. 1995. An Overview of the PARCTAB Ubiquitous Computing Experiment. *IEEE Personal Communications* 2(6): 28-43.

13. Mark Weiser and John Seely Brown. The Coming Age of Calm Technology. In *Beyond Calculation: The Next Fifty Years of Computing.* Springer-Verlag, 1997, pp. 75-85.

14. Craig Wisneski, Hiroshi Ishii, Andrew Dahley, Matt Gorbet, Scott Brave, Brygg Ullmer and Paul Yarın. Ambient Displays: Turning Architectural Space into an Interface between People and Digital Information. In *Proceedings of the International Workshop on Cooperative Buildings (CoBuild '98).* Darmstadt, Germany, February 1998. Springer Press, pp. 22-32.

CMUnited-98: A Team of Robotic Soccer Agents

Manuela Veloso, Michael Bowling, Sorin Achim, Kwun Han, and Peter Stone

Computer Science Department
Carnegie Mellon University
Pittsburgh, PA 15213
http://www.cs.cmu.edu/~robosoccer

Abstract

In this paper, we present the main research contributions of our champion CMUnited-98 small robot team. The team is a multi-agent system in the robotic soccer entertainment application area. The robotic system has global perception and distributed cognition and action. We describe the main features of the hardware design of the physical robots, including differential drive, robust mechanical structure, and a kicking device. We briefly overview the CMUnited-98 global vision processing algorithm. We then introduce our new robot motion algorithm which reactively generates motion control to account for the target point, the desired robot orientation, and obstacle avoidance. Our robots exhibit successful collision-free motion in the highly dynamic robotic soccer environment. At the strategic and decision-making level, we present the role-based behaviors of the CMUnited-98 robotic agents. Team collaboration is remarkably achieved through a new algorithm that allows for team agents to anticipate possible collaboration opportunities. Robots position themselves strategically in open positions that increase passing opportunities. The chapter terminates with a summary of the results of the RoboCup-98 games in which the CMUnited-98 small robot team scored a total of 25 goals and suffered 6 goals in the 5 games that it played.

Introduction

The CMUnited-98 small-size robot team is a complete, autonomous architecture composed of the physical robotic agents, a global vision processing camera over-looking the playing field, and several clients as the minds of the small-size robot players.

The complete system is fully autonomous consisting of a well-defined and challenging processing cycle. The global vision algorithm perceives the dynamic environment and processes the images, giving the positions of each robot and the ball. This information is sent to an off-board controller and distributed to the different agent algorithms. Each agent evaluates the world state and uses its strategic knowledge to make decisions. Actions are motion commands that are sent by the off-board controller through radio frequency communication. Commands can be broadcast or sent directly to individual agents. Each robot has an identification binary code that is used on-board to detect commands intended for that robot. Motion is not perfectly executed due to inherent mechanical inaccuracies

and unforeseen interventions from other agents. The effects of the actions are therefore uncertain.

CMUnited-98 represents a seamless integration of reactive and strategic reasoning and real physical action in teams of robots. Robotic soccer is a growing application both in the research and in the entertainment communities (Kitano *et al.* 1997) (see http://www.robocup.org/RoboCup/).

Hardware and Vision Processing

The physical robots themselves are of size 15cm × 12cm × 10cm. Figure 1 shows our robots. A differential drive mechanism is used in all of the robots. Two motors with integrated gear boxes are used for the two wheels. Differential drive was chosen due to its simplicity and due to the size constraints. The size of our robots conforms to RoboCup Competition rules. Employing the differential drive mechanism means that the robot is non-holonomic, which makes the robot control problem considerably more challenging.

Figure 1: The CMUnited-98 robots.

The CMUnited-98 robots are entirely new constructions built upon our experience in 1997 (Veloso, Stone, & Han 1998). The new robots represent an upgrade of our own-built CMUnited-97 robots. Improvements were made in two major areas: motors and control, and the mechanical chassis, which includes a kicking device.

In designing the mechanical structure of the CMUnited-98 robots, we focused on modularity and robustness. The final design includes a battery module supplying three independent power paths (for the main-board, motors, and radio modules.) It also includes a single board containing all the required electronic circuitry, with multiple add-on capabilities. The mobile base module includes a kicking device driven by a DC motor. This motor is hardware activated by an array of four infrared sensors, which is enabled or disabled by the software control. This was all combined in a layered design within an aluminum and plastic frame. In addition, each of the modules within this design is completely interchangeable.

The CMUnited-98 vision module remains largely the same as the one used in the CMUnited-97 team (Han & Veloso 1998). The algorithm successfully detects and tracks 11 objects (5 teammates, 5 opponents and a ball) at 30 frames/s. The algorithm determines a position and orientation for the robots. In addition a Kalman-Bucy filter is used as a predictor of the ball's trajectory. This prediction is an integral factor in our robots' control and strategic decisions.

Motion Control

The goal of our low level motion control is to be as fast as possible while remaining accurate and reliable. This is challenging due to the lack of feedback from the motors, forcing all control to be done using only visual feedback. Our motion control algorithm is robust. It addresses stationary and moving targets with integrated obstacle avoidance. The algorithm makes effective use of the prediction of the ball's trajectory provided by the Kalman-Bucy filter.

We achieve this motion control functionality by a reactive control mechanism that directs a differential drive robot to a target configuration. Though based on the CMUnited-97's motion control (Veloso, Stone, & Han 1998), CMUnited-98 includes a number of major improvements. The target configuration for the motion planner has been extended. The target configuration includes: (i) the *Cartesian position*; and (ii) the *direction* that the robot is required to be facing when arriving at the target position. Obstacle avoidance is integrated into this controller. Also, the target configuration can be given as a function of time to allow for the controller to reason about intercepting the trajectory of a moving target.

Differential Drive Control for Position and Direction

CMUnited-98's basic control rules were improved from those used in CMUnited-97. The rules are a set of reactive equations for deriving the left and right wheel velocities, v_l and v_r, in order to reach a target position, (x^*, y^*):

$$\Delta = \theta - \phi \quad (1)$$
$$(t, r) = (\cos^2 \Delta \cdot \text{sgn}(\cos \Delta), \sin^2 \Delta \cdot \text{sgn}(\sin \Delta))$$
$$v_l = v(t - r)$$
$$v_r = v(t + r),$$

where θ is the direction of the target point (x^*, y^*), ϕ is the robot's orientation, and v is the desired speed (see Figure 2(a)).[1]

---

[1]All angles refer to a fixed coordinate system.

We extend these equations for target configurations of the form (x^*, y^*, ϕ^*), where the goal is for the robot to reach the specified target point (x^*, y^*) while facing the direction ϕ^*. This is achieved with the following adjustment:

$$\theta' = \theta + \min\left(\alpha, \tan^{-1}\left(\frac{c}{d}\right)\right),$$

where θ' is the new target direction, α is the difference between our angle to the target point and ϕ^*, d is the distance to the target point, and c is a clearance parameter (see Figure 2(a).) This will keep the robot a distance c from the target point while it is circling to line up with the target direction, ϕ^*. This new target direction, θ', is now substituted into equation 1 to derive wheel velocities.

In addition to our motion controller computing the desired wheel velocities, it also returns an estimate of the time to reach the target configuration, $\hat{T}(x^*, y^*, \phi^*)$. This estimate is a crucial component in our robot's strategy. It is used both in high-level decision making, and for low-level ball interception, which is described later in this section. For CMUnited-98, $\hat{T}(x^*, y^*, \phi^*)$ is computed using a hand-tuned linear function of d, α, and Δ.

Obstacle Avoidance

Obstacle avoidance was also integrated into the motion control. This is done by adjusting the target direction of the robot based on any immediate obstacles in its path. This adjustment can be seen in Figure 2(b).

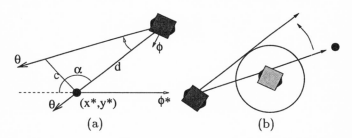

(a)   (b)

Figure 2: (a) The adjustment of θ to θ' to reach a target configuration of the form (x^*, y^*, ϕ^*); (b) The adjustment to avoid immediate obstacles.

If a target direction passes too close to an obstacle, the direction is adjusted to run tangent to the a preset allowed clearance for obstacles. Since the motion control mechanism is running continuously, the obstacle analysis is constantly replanning obstacle-free paths. This continuous replanning allows for the robot to handle the highly dynamic environment and immediately take advantage of short lived opportunities.

Moving Targets

One of the real challenges in robotic soccer is to be able to control the robots to intercept a moving ball. This capability is essential for a high-level ball passing behavior. CMUnited-98's robots successfully intercept a moving ball and several of their goals in RoboCup-98 were scored using this capability.

This interception capability is achieved as an extension of the control algorithm to aim at a stationary target. Our extension allows for the target configuration to be given as a function of time, where $t = 0$ corresponds to the present,

$$f(t) = (x^*, y^*, \phi^*).$$

At some point in the future, t_0, we can compute the target configuration, $f(t_0)$. We can also use our control rules for a stationary point to find the wheel velocities and estimated time to reach this hypothetical target as if it were stationary. The time estimate to reach the target then informs us whether it is possible to reach it within the allotted time. Our goal is to find the nearest point in the future where the target can be reached. Formally, we want to find,

$$t^* = \min\{t > 0 : \hat{T}(f(t)) \leq t\}.$$

After finding t^*, we can use our stationary control rules to reach $f(t^*)$. In addition we scale the robot speed so to cross the target point at exactly t^*.

Unfortunately, t^* cannot be easily computed within a reasonable time frame. We approximate the value t^* by discretizing time with a small time step. The algorithm finds the closest of these discretized time points that satisfies our estimate constraint. The target configuration as a function of time is computed using the ball's predicted trajectory. Our control algorithm for stationary points is then used to find a path and time estimates for each discretized point along this trajectory, and the appropriate target point is selected.

Strategy

The main focus of our research is on developing algorithms for collaboration between agents in a team. An agent, as a member of the team, needs to be capable of individual autonomous decisions while, at the same time, its decisions must contribute towards the team goals.

CMUnited-97 introduced a flexible team architecture in which agents are organized in *formations* and *units*. Each agent plays a *role* in a unit and in a formation (Stone & Veloso 1998; Veloso, Stone, & Han 1998). CMUnited-98 builds upon this team architecture by defining a set of roles for the agents. It also introduces improvements within this architecture to help address the highly dynamic environment.

CMUnited-98 uses the following roles: goalkeeper, defender, and attacker. The formation used throughout RoboCup-98 involved a single goalkeeper and defender, and three attackers.

goalkeeper

The ideal goalie behavior is to reach the expected entry point of the ball in the goal *before* the ball reaches it. Assuming that the prediction of the ball trajectory is correct and the robot has a uniform movement, we can state the ideal goalie behavior: given the predicted v_g and v_b as the velocities of the goalie and of the ball respectively, and d_g and d_b as the distances from the goalie and the ball to the predicted entry point, then, we want $\frac{d_g}{v_g} = \frac{d_b}{v_b} - \epsilon$, where ϵ is a small positive value to account for the goalie reaching the entry point slightly before the ball.

Unfortunately, the ball easily changes velocity and the movement of the robot is not uniform and is uncertain. Therefore we have followed a switching behavior for the goalie based on a threshold of the ball's estimated trajectory.

If the ball's estimated speed is higher than a preset threshold, the goalie moves directly to the ball's predicted entry goal point. Otherwise, the goalie selects the position that minimizes the largest portion of unobstructed goal area, by finding the location that bisects the angles of the ball and the goal posts, as illustrated in Figure 3.

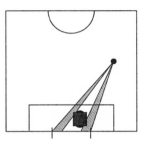

Figure 3: The goalie positions itself to minimize the unobstructed goal area.

The use of the predicted ball's velocity for the goalie's behavior was shown to be very effective in the RoboCup-98 games. It was particularly appropriate for defending a penalty shot, due to the accuracy of the predicted ball's trajectory when only one robot is pushing the ball.

Defender

The CMUnited-97's team did not have a well-specified defender's role, but our experience at RoboCup-97 made us understand that the purpose of a defending behavior is two-fold:

1. to stop the opponents from scoring in our goal; and

2. to not endanger our own goal.

The first goal is clearly a defender's role. The second goal comes as the result of the uncertain ball handling by the robots. The robots can easily push (or touch) the ball unexpectedly in the wrong direction when performing a difficult maneuver.

To achieve the two goals, we implemented three behaviors for the defender. *Blocking*, illustrated in Figure 4(a), is similar to the goalie's behavior except that the defender positions itself further away from the goal line. *Clearing*, illustrated in Figure 4(b), pushes the ball out of the defending area. It does this by finding the largest angular direction free of obstacles (opponents and teammates) that the robot can push the ball towards. *Annoying*, illustrated in Figure 4(c), is somewhat similar to the goal-keeping behavior except that the robot tries to position itself between the ball and the opponent nearest to it. This is an effort to keep the opponent from reaching the ball.

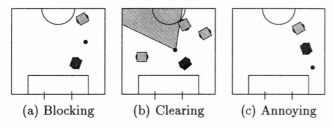

| (a) Blocking | (b) Clearing | (c) Annoying |

Figure 4: The defender's behaviors. The dark and light robots represent the defender and the opponents respectively.

Selecting when each of these behaviors is used is very important to the effectiveness of the defender. For example, clearing the ball when it is close to our own goal or when it can bounce back off another robot, can lead to scoring in our own goal. We used the decision tree in Figure 5 to select which action to perform based on the current state.

The two attributes in the tree, namely *Ball Upfield* and *Safe to Clear*, are binary. *Ball Upfield* tests whether the ball is upfield (towards the opponent's goal) of the defender. *Safe to Clear* tests whether the open area is larger than a preset angle threshold. If *Ball Upfield* is false then the ball is closer to the goal than the defender and the robot *annoys* the attacking robot. The CMUnited-98's annoying behavior needs to select one particular opponent robot to annoy. For example, when two opponent robots attack simultaneously, the current annoying behavior is able to annoy only one of them. We are planning on further improving this behavior for RoboCup-99.

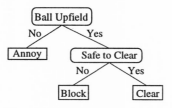

Figure 5: The decision tree for the defender's behavior.

If *Ball Upfield* is true, the defender clears or blocks, depending on the value of *Safe to Clear*. Clearing was shown to be very useful at RoboCup-98, with even a couple of our goals scored directly by a clearing action of the defender.

Attackers - Anticipation

Attacking involves one of the best opportunities for collaboration, and much of the innovation of CMUnited-98 has been developing techniques for finding and exploiting these opportunities.

In many multi-agent systems, one or a few agents are assigned, or assign themselves, the specific task to be solved at a particular moment. We view these agents as the *active* agents. Other team members are *passive* waiting to be needed to achieve another task or assist the active agent(s). This simplistic distinction between active and passive agents to capture teamwork was realized in CMUnited-97. The agent that goes to the ball is viewed as the active agent, while the other teammates are passive.

CMUnited-98 significantly extends this simplistic view in two ways: (i) we use a decision theoretic algorithm to select the active agent; and (ii) we use a technique for passive agents *to anticipate* future collaboration. Passive agents are therefore not actually "passive;" instead, they actively *anticipate* opportunities for collaboration. In CMUnited-98 this collaboration is built on robust individual behaviors.

Individual Behaviors. We first developed individual behaviors for passing and shooting. Passing and shooting in CMUnited-98 is handled effectively by the motion controller. The target configuration is specified to be the ball (using its estimated trajectory) and the target direction is either towards the goal or another teammate. This gives us robust and accurate individual behaviors that can handle obstacles as well as intercepting a moving ball.

Decision Theoretic Action Selection. Given the individual behaviors, we must select an active agent and appropriate behavior. This is done by a decision theoretic analysis using a single step look-ahead. With n agents this amounts to n^2 choices of actions involving shooting or a pass to another agent followed by that agent shooting. An estimated probability of success for each pass and shot is computed along with the time estimate to complete the action, which is provided by the motion controller. A value for each action is computed,

$$\text{Value} = \frac{\text{Pr}_{\text{pass}} \text{Pr}_{\text{shoot}}}{\text{time}}.$$

The action with the largest value is selected, which determines both the active agent and its behavior. Table 1 illustrates an example of the values for the selection considering two attackers, 1 and 2.

It is important to note that this action selection is occurring on each iteration of control, i.e., approximately 30 times per second. The probabilities of success, estimates of time, and values of actions, are being continuously recomputed. This allows for quick changes of actions if shooting opportunities become available or collaboration with another agent appears more useful.

Dynamic Positioning (SPAR). Although there is a clear action to be taken by the active agent, it is unclear what the passive agents should be doing. Al-

| Attacker | Action | Probability of Success | | Time(s) | Value |
		Pass	Shoot		
1	Shoot	–	60%	2.0	0.30
1*	Pass to 2	60%	90%	1.0	0.54
2	Shoot	–	80%	1.5	0.53
2	Pass to 1	50%	40%	0.8	0.25

Table 1: Action choices and computed values are based on the probability of success and estimate of time. The largest-valued action (marked with an *) is selected.

though, in a team multi-agent system such as robotic soccer, success and goal achievement often depends upon collaboration; so, we introduce in CMUnited-98, the concept that team agents should not actually be "passive."

CMUnited-97's team architecture allowed for the passive agents to flexibly vary their positions within their role only as a function of the position of the ball. In so doing, their goal was to *anticipate* where they would be most likely to find the ball in the near future. This is a first-level of single-agent anticipation towards a better individual goal achievement (Veloso, Stone, & Han 1998).

However, for CMUnited-98, we introduce a team-based notion of *anticipation*, which goes beyond individual single-agent anticipation. The passive team members position themselves strategically so as to optimize the chances that their teammates can successfully collaborate with them, in particular pass to them. By considering the positions of other agents and the attacking goal, in addition to that of the ball, they are able to position themselves more usefully: they *anticipate* their future contributions to the team.

This strategic position takes into account the position of the other robots (teammates and opponents), the ball, and the opponent's goal. The position is found as the solution to a multiple-objective function with repulsion and attraction points. Let's introduce the following variables:

- n - the number of agents on each team;
- O_i - the position of opponent $i = 1, ..., n$;
- T_i - the position of teammate, $i = 1, ..., n$;
- B - the position of the active teammate and ball;
- G - the position of the opponent's goal;
- P - the desired position for the passive agent in anticipation of a pass.

Given these defined variables, we can then formalize our algorithm for strategic position, which we call SPAR for *Strategic Positioning with Attraction and Repulsion.* This extends similar approaches using potential fields (Latombe 1991), to our highly dynamic, multi-agent domain. The probability of collaboration is directly related to how "open" a position is to allow

for a successful pass. SPAR maximizes the repulsion from other robots and minimizes attraction to the ball and to the goal, namely:

- *Repulsion* from opponents. Maximize the distance to each opponent: $\forall i, \max dist(P, O_i)$.
- *Repulsion* from teammates. Maximize the distance to other passive teammates: $\forall i, \max dist(P, T_i)$.
- *Attraction* to the ball: $\min dist(P, B)$.
- *Attraction* to the opponent's goal: $\min dist(P, G)$.

This is a multiple-objective function. To solve this optimization problem, we restate this function into a single-objective function. This approach has also been applied to the CMUnited-98 simulator team (Stone, Veloso, & Riley 1999).

As each term in the multiple-objective function may have a different relevance (e.g., staying close to the goal may be more important than staying away from opponents), we want to consider different functions of each term. In our CMUnited-98 team, we weight the terms differently, namely w_{O_i}, w_{T_i}, w_B, and w_G, for the weights for opponents, teammates, the ball, and the goal, respectively. For CMUnited-98, these weights were hand tuned to create a proper balance. This gives us a weighted single-objective function:

$$\max \left(\begin{array}{c} \sum_{i=1}^{n} w_{O_i} dist(P, O_i) + \sum_{i=1}^{n} w_{T_i} dist(P, T_i) - \\ -w_B dist(P, B) - w_G dist(P, G) \end{array} \right)$$

This optimization problem is then solved under a set of constraints:

- Do not block a possible direct shot from active teammate.
- Do not stand behind other robots, because these are difficult positions to receive passes from the active teammate.

The solution to this optimization problem under constraints gives us a target location for the "passive" agent. Figure 6(a) and (b) illustrate these two constraints and Figure 7 shows the combination of these two set of constraints and the resulting position returned by our algorithm for the anticipating passive teammate.

Using this anticipation algorithm, the attacking team agents behaved in an exemplary collaborative fashion. Their motion on the field was a beautiful response to the dynamically changing adversarial environment. The active and passive agents moved in great coordination using the anticipation algorithm increasing very significantly successful collaboration. The SPAR anticipation algorithm created a number of opportunities for passes and rebounds that often led to goals and other scoring chances.

In general, we believe that our approach represents a major step in team multi-agent systems in terms of incorporating *anticipation* as a key aspect of teamwork.

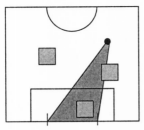 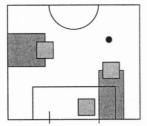

(a) Do not block goal shot   (b) Avoid difficult collaboration

Figure 6: Constraints for the anticipation algorithm for the CMUnited-98 small robot team; (a) and (b) show three opponents robots, and the position of the ball (also the active teammate's).

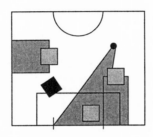

Figure 7: Position of the passive agent, dark square, as returned by SPAR, using the constraints in Figure 6.

Results

CMUnited-98 successfully defended our title of the Small Robot Champion at RoboCup-98 in Paris. The competition involved 11 teams from 7 different countries. It consisted of a preliminary round of two games, followed by the 8 advancing teams playing a 3-round playoff. CMUnited-98 won four of five games, sweeping the playoff competition, scoring a total of 25 goals scored and only 6 suffered. The individual results of these games are in Table 2.

Opponent Name	Affiliation	Score
iXS	iXs Inc.	16–2
5DPO	University of Porto	0–3
Paris-8	University of Paris-8	3–0
Cambridge	University of Cambridge	3–0
Roboroos	University of Queensland	3–1
	TOTAL	25–6

Table 2: The scores of CMUnited-98's games in the small-robot league of RoboCup-98.

There were a number of technical problems during the preliminary rounds, including outside interference with our radio communication. This problem was the worst during our game against 5DPO, in which our robots were often responding to outside commands just spinning in circles. This led to our forfeit at half time and a clear loss against 5DPO, a very good team which ended in third place at RoboCup-98. Fortunately, the communication problems were isolated and dealt with

prior to the playoff rounds.

The three playoff games were very competitive and showcased the strengths of our team. Paris-8 had a strong defense with a lot of traffic in front of the goal. Our team's obstacle avoidance still managed to find paths and to create scoring chances around their defenders. The final two games were very close against very good opponents. Our interception was tested against Cambridge, and included blocking a powerful shot by their goalie, which was deflected back into their goal. The final game against Roboroos demonstrated the dynamic positioning, especially during the final goal, which involved a pass to a strategically positioned teammate.

Conclusion

The success of CMUnited-98 at RoboCup-98 was due to several technical innovations, including robust hardware design, effective vision processing, reliable time-prediction based robot motion with obstacle avoidance, and a dynamic role-based team approach. The CMUnited-98 team demonstrated in many occasions its collaboration capabilities which resulted from the robots' behaviors. Most remarkably, CMUnited-98 introduces the concept of *anticipation*, in which passive robots (not going to the ball) strategically position themselves using attraction and repulsion (SPAR) to maximize the chances of a successful pass.

The CMUnited-98 team represents an integrated effort to combine solid research approaches to hardware design, vision processing, and individual and team robot behaviors.

Acknowledgments This research is sponsored in part by DARPA and AFRL grant F30602-97-2-0250, and in part by ONR grant N00014-95-1-0591. The views and conclusions in this document are solely those of the authors.

References

Han, K., and Veloso, M. 1998. Reactive visual control of multiple non-holonomic robotic agents. In *Proceedings of the International Conference on Robotics and Automation*.

Kitano, H.; Asada, M.; Kuniyoshi, Y.; Noda, I.; and Osawa, E. 1997. RoboCup: The robot world cup initiative. In *Proceedings of the First International Conference on Autonomous Agents*, 340–347.

Latombe, J.-C. 1991. *Robot Motion Planning*.

Stone, P., and Veloso, M. 1998. The CMUnited-97 simulator team. In Kitano, H., ed., *RoboCup-97: Robot Soccer World Cup I*. Berlin: Springer Verlag.

Stone, P.; Veloso, M.; and Riley, P. 1999. The CMUnited-98 champion simulator team. In Asada, M., and Kitano, H., eds., *RoboCup-98: Robot Soccer World Cup II*. Berlin: Springer Verlag.

Veloso, M.; Stone, P.; and Han, K. 1998. CMUnited-97: RoboCup-97 small-robot world champion team. *AI Magazine* 19(3):61–69.

Intelligent Systems Demonstrations

Sensible Agents: Demonstration of Dynamic Configuration of Agent Organizations for Responsive Planning Operations

K. S. Barber, A. Goel, D. Han, J. Kim, T. H. Liu, C. E. Martin, R. McKay

The Laboratory for Intelligent Processes and Systems
Electrical and Computer Engineering
The University of Texas
Austin, TX 78712
barber@mail.utexas.edu

Research Overview

Decisions rarely occur in isolation, and decision makers must often respond to dynamic and unexpected events. A decision-maker must consider not only its own possible actions but also the possible behaviors and the resources of others who may either assist with planning and execution, accidentally interfere, or maliciously interfere. Dynamic Adaptive Autonomy (DAA) is the fundamental technology of Sensible Agents that permits a decision-making agent (responsible for planning and execution) to react, adjust, and respond to unpredictable environments. Sensible Agents can (1) assess current and potential interaction styles for planning, and (2) optimize planning frameworks by adjusting these styles. To address these issues, dynamic configuration of decision-making agent organizations is a must. Some specific research that has contributed to flexible, adaptive multi-agent coordination includes partial global planning (Durfee and Lesser, 1987), organizational self-design (Ishida et al., 1992), STEAM flexible teamwork (Tambe, 1997), RETSINA matchmaking (Sycara and Pannu, 1998), and organizational fluidity (Glance and Huberman, 1993). However, these techniques do not specifically adapt agent planning-interaction styles.

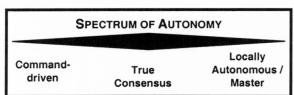

Figure 1: Spectrum of Autonomy

DAA allows agents to dynamically form, modify, and dissolve goal-oriented problem-solving agreements with other agents in a robust and flexible manner. As a member of a problem-solving organization, Sensible Agents establish their role in interacting with others by selecting an autonomy level for each goal they intend to pursue: (1) **Command driven**—agent does not plan but obeys orders given by another agent, (2) **Consensus**—agent works as a

team member to devise plans, (3) **Locally Autonomous / Master**—the agent plans alone, unconstrained by other agents, and may or may not give orders to command-driven followers.

Each Sensible Agent (Barber et al., 1999) is composed of the following components: (1) the *Action Planner*; (2) the *Perspective Modeler*; (3) the *Conflict Resolution Advisor*; and (4) the *Autonomy Reasoner*. Domain-specific information, processing rules, and state are restricted to the Action Planner module, while remaining modules are domain-independent.

Sensible Agents are capable of performing: (1) trade-off assessment regarding the impact of local decision-making and goal satisfaction on system objectives, (2) their own behaviors by planning for a goal (local or system) and/or executing actions to achieve the goal, (3) group behaviors by forming binding autonomy agreements (e.g. consensus groups, master agent planning for group of command-driven agents) (4) self-organization by determining the best problem-solving organization, autonomy level, to optimally satisfy a goal, and (5) preferential learning for associating autonomy levels to situations.

Demonstration

The Sensible Agent Testbed provides an infrastructure of well-defined, publicly available interfaces where distributed agents operate and communicate. The end-user can interact with the testbed from the viewpoint of (1) the environment, by defining scenarios and injecting contingencies, or (2) the decision maker, by participating in planning and execution and receiving assistance from other Sensible Agents.

Sensible Agent capabilities will be demonstrated in the naval radar frequency management (NRFM) domain. This domain requires maintaining a set of position and frequency relationships among geographically distributed radars such that radar interference is minimized. Radar interference occurs primarily when two or more radars are operating in close proximity at similar frequencies. For a typical group of naval ships, it may take hours or days for a human assisted by a rule-based system to determine an optimal position and frequency. Unfortunately, the environment typically changes much faster than the human can respond. Local decisions impact the entire system, requiring tradeoffs between local goal (e.g. keep my radars interference free) and system goals (e.g. keep radars in my group of ships interference free).

The NRFM Sensible Agent demonstration is used to determine the performance of Sensible Agents under different problem solving organizations. Agents monitor a naval radar for interference from external sources, and, if interference is detected, attempt to eliminate it by working alone or with others (Goel et al., 1998). Several different operating scenarios are demonstrated. Each Sensible Agent has the following capabilities:

Communication: the ability to send messages to another agent and to asynchronously respond to sent messages. Communication takes the form of (1) requesting information, (2) reporting a conflict, (3) supplying information, or (4) reporting a solution to a conflict.

Sensing: the ability to sense the position of other ships. Agents can also sense their level of interference, but cannot sense the source. If an agent detects interference it initiates problem solving to minimize the interference.

Environmental modeling: the ability to maintain an internal, local, model of the agent's world, separate from the simulation model of the world. Each agent is aware of the initial state of the system (ship positions and frequencies), however as the simulation progresses, an agent's local model may deviate from the world model. The agents use communication and sensing to update their local models.

Planning: the ability to plan at each of the autonomy levels described above. Successful planning for this problem hinges on an agent's ability to determine interference-free frequency assignments. Agents do this by modeling the spectrum of available frequencies and the necessary frequency differences (delta frequencies) for each known pair of radars. Agents then attempt to make assignments that meet all delta-frequency constraints within the restricted frequency space. Three algorithms are available to each agent's planner and are associated with the appropriate autonomy level classification.

An agent attempting to resolve interference in a locally autonomous fashion will plan alone. The agent will use its internal world model to find a frequency that is likely to be interference-free. The frequencies of other radars in the system are modeled as constraints on the search process. If no frequencies are found, searching continues at regular time intervals until one is found or a random "deadlock" time limit is reached. If the agent determines that the system is in deadlock (with respect to its interference state), it will choose a random frequency to pull the system out of deadlock.

Only the master plans in a master/command-driven relationship. If the master or its command-driven agents are experiencing interference, the master attempts to eliminate the interference through iterative assignments. First, it chooses its own frequency in the manner described above, but without considering the frequencies of its command-driven agents as constraints. It then determines an interference-free frequency for each command-driven agent, adding these frequencies as constraints, until all assignments have been made. If no set of satisfying assignments is found, the planning process is restarted. Once a solution has been found, the assignments are passed to the command-driven agents. Command-driven agents may report back to the master if they are still experiencing interference after the assignment. This may occur when the master's internal model does not match the world state.

Each agent involved in consensus interaction plays an equal part in determining frequency assignments. First, each agent independently carries out the master/command-driven planning algorithm with the other members of the consensus group treated as command-driven agents. At the conclusion of this phase, each agent proposes its solution to the rest of the consensus group during a synchronization phase. Each agent includes an estimate (based on its internal model) of the expected interference for each radar. Each consensus member deterministically selects the proposal with the least amount of estimated interference, and the agents assign frequencies accordingly.

Acknowledgements

The research was funded in part by The Texas Higher Education Coordinating Board Advanced Technology Program, The National Science Foundation and The Naval Surface Warfare Center.

References

Barber, K. S., McKay, R. M., and Liu, T. H. 1999. Group Membership Services for Dynamically Organized Sensible Agent-Based Systems. Accepted to The 12th International FLAIRS Conference (FLAIRS-99). Orlando, FL, May 1-5, 1999.

Durfee, E. H. and Lesser, V. R. 1987. Using Partial Global Plans to Coordinate Distributed Problem Solvers. In *Proceedings of the Tenth International Joint Conference on Artificial Intelligence*, 875-883. : International Joint Conferences on Artificial Intelligence, Inc.

Glance, N. S. and Huberman, B. A. 1993. Organizational Fluidity and Sustainable Cooperation. In *Proceedings of the 5th Annual Workshop on Modelling Autonomous Agents in a Multi-Agents World*, 89-103. Neuchatel, Switzerland.

Goel, A., Liu, T. H., White, E., and Barber, K. S. 1998. Implementing Sensible Agents in a Distributed Simulation Environment. In *Proceedings of the 1998 Western Multi-Conference*. San Diego, CA.

Ishida, T., Gasser, L., and Yokoo, M. 1992. Organization Self-Design of Distributed Production Systems. *IEEE Transactions on Knowledge and Data Engineering* 4(2): 123-134.

Sycara, K. P. and Pannu, A. S. 1998. The RETSINA Multiagent System: Towards Integrating Planning, Execution and Information Gathering. In *Proceedings of the Second International Conference on Autonomous Agents*, 350-351. Minneapolis/St. Paul, MN: ACM Press.

Tambe, M. 1997. Towards Flexible Teamwork. *Journal of Artificial Intelligence Research* 7: 83-124.

The Disciple Integrated Shell and Methodology for Rapid Development of Knowledge-Based Agents

Mihai Boicu, Kathryn Wright, Dorin Marcu, Seok Won Lee, Michael Bowman and Gheorghe Tecuci

Learning Agents Laboratory, Department of Computer Science, MSN 4A5, George Mason University, Fairfax, VA 22030
{mboicu, kwright, dmarcu, swlee, mbowman3, tecuci}@gmu.edu

Abstract

The Disciple Learning Agent Shell (Disciple-LAS) is an integrated set of modules for rapid development of practical end-to-end knowledge-based agents, by domain experts, with limited assistance from knowledge engineers. Disciple-LAS and its associated agent building methodology are presented in (Tecuci et al. 1999). Therefore, in this paper, we introduce two very different agents developed with Disciple-LAS, to show its applicability to a wide range of domains. Then we introduce the different modules that are part of Disciple-LAS, and present their use in the agent building process. Finally we summarize the solutions proposed by the Disciple approach to some of the issues that have been found to be limiting factors in developing knowledge-based agents.

Introduction

Disciple-LAS is an integrated set of modules for rapid development of practical end-to-end knowledge-based agents, by domain experts, with limited assistance from knowledge engineers. It consists of knowledge acquisition, learning and problem solving modules, developed to support the specific Disciple methodology for building an agent (Tecuci et al. 1999). The knowledge base of such an agent has two components: an ontology that defines the concepts from the application domain, and a set of problem solving rules expressed with these concepts. The problem solving approach of an agent built with Disciple-LAS is task reduction, where a task to be accomplished by the agent is successively reduced to simpler tasks until the initial task is reduced to a set of elementary tasks that can be immediately performed. Therefore, the rules from the KB are task reduction rules. The ontology consists of hierarchical descriptions of objects, features and tasks, represented as frames, according to the knowledge model of the Open Knowledge Base Connectivity (OKBC) protocol (Chaudhri et al. 1998).

The development of a specific Disciple agent includes the following processes: 1) the customization of the problem solver and the interfaces of Disciple-LAS for that particular domain; 2) the building of the domain ontology by ʹ importing knowledge from external repositories of knowledge and by manually defining the other components of the ontology, and 3) the teaching the agent to perform its tasks, teaching that resembles how an expert would teach a human apprentice when solving problems in cooperation.

Disciple-LAS was developed as part of the DARPA's High Performance Knowledge Bases Program (Cohen et al. 1998), and was applied to build two very different agents, a planning agent and a critiquing agent. The planning agent uses hierarchical task decomposition to generate a partially ordered plan of actions for repairing or bypassing some damage to a bridge or road. The building and evaluation of this agent is presented in (Tecuci et al., 1999). The critiquing agent analyses a military course of action (COA) to identify its strengths and weaknesses with respect to the principles of war (e.g. the principles of objective, offensive, mass, economy of force, maneuver, etc.) and the tenets of army operations (e.g. the tenets of initiative, agility, depth, etc.). The critiquing of a COA is also modeled as a task reduction process. For instance, the task of assessing a COA with respect to the principle of objective is reduced to three simpler assessment tasks: 1) assess identification of objective, 2) assess attainability of objective and 3) assess decisiveness of objective. Then each such assessment task is successively reduced to simpler assessment tasks and ultimately reduced to assertions on how the COA conforms to the principle of objective.

Disciple-LAS modules

Figure 1 presents the main modules of Disciple-LAS. They include knowledge import/export modules, ontology management modules, and problem solving and learning modules.

The problem of importing knowledge from an outside knowledge server is reduced to two simpler problems: 1) a translation problem where an external ontology is translated into a Disciple ontology, and 2) an integration problem where the translated ontological knowledge is incorporated into agent's ontology. For the first process one uses either the OKBC protocol to extract knowledge from an OKBC sever, or a translator from KIF (Genesereth and Fikes, 1992) into Disciple. For the second process one uses the ontology management tools of Disciple.

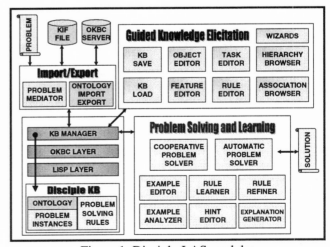

Figure 1: Disciple-LAS modules.

The ontology management tools include a specialized editor for each type of knowledge element to facilitate the interaction with the users. For instance, there is an Object Editor, a Feature Editor, and a Task Editor. We attempt to provide each module with a certain degree of "intelligence", based on "wizards". An important wizard is the Delete Wizard that is automatically invoked whenever the user attempts to delete an element from the KB. This wizard guides the user through a sequence of modifications of the KB that are necessary in order to maintain the consistency of the KB.

The problem solving and learning modules include a Cooperative Step-by-step Problem Solver and an Autonomous Problem Solver, a Rule Learner, and a Rule Refiner, an Example Editor, an Example Analyzer, a Hint Editor, and an Explanation Generator. Their interactions are presented in the following section.

Cooperative problem solving and learning

After an initial ontology has been created, the subject matter expert may start to teach the Disciple agent how solve problems, by following an interaction pattern shown in Figure 2.

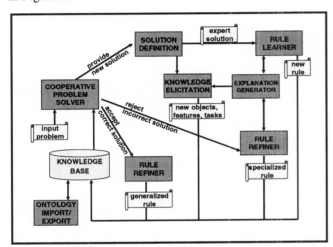

Figure 2: Expert-agent interactions.

The expert invokes the Cooperative Problem Solver, selects or defines an initial task and asks the Disciple agent to reduce it. Disciple uses its task reduction rules to reduce the current task to simpler tasks, showing the expert the reductions found. The expert may accept a reduction proposed by the agent, may reject it or may decide to define himself or herself a new reduction.

To define a new reduction the expert uses the Example Editor. This, in turn, may invoke the Object Editor, the Feature Editor or Task Editor, if the specification of the example involves new knowledge elements that are not present in the current ontology. Once the reduction has been defined the Rule Learner is invoked to generalize the example to a task reduction rule. The Rule Learner automatically invokes the Explanation Generator that tries to find the explanation of why the reduction indicated by the expert is correct. The Explanation Generator proposes several plausible explanations from which the expert has to select the correct one. The expert may help the agent to

find the correct explanation by providing a hint defined with the Hint Editor. This may again lead to the invocation of the ontology management modules to define any new knowledge base element that is included in the hint.

If the expert accepts a reduction proposed the agent then the Rule Refiner is invoked and may generalize the rule that has led to this reduction.

If the expert rejects a reduction proposed by the agent then the agent attempts to find an explanation of why the reduction is not correct, the Explanation Generator and the Hint Editor being invoked, as described above. The explanation found is used by the Rule Refiner to specialize the rule.

After a new rule is learned or an existing rule is refined, the Cooperative Problem Solver resumes the task reduction process until a solution of the initial problem is found.

Final Remarks

Disciple-LAS provides solutions to some of the issues that have been found to be limiting factors in developing knowledge-based agents. Through ontology import it can reuse previously developed knowledge. The knowledge acquisition and adaptation bottlenecks are alleviated through the use of apprenticeship multistrategy learning methods and a synergistic interaction between the expert and the agent where each does what it can do best, and receives help from the other party. Disciple-LAS contains many general modules that will be part of any Disciple agent, but it also allows for the customization of some of its modules, trying to achieve a suitable balance between reusing general modules and developing domain specific ones. Finally, Disciple-LAS and the Disciple agents are portable, being implemented in JAVA and Common LISP.

Acknowledgments. This research was supported by the AFOSR grant F49620-97-1-0188, as part of the DARPA's High Performance Knowledge Bases Program.

References

Chaudhri, V. K., Farquhar, A., Fikes, R., Park, P. D., and Rice, J. P. 1998. OKBC: A Programmatic Foundation for Knowledge Base Interoperability. In *Proc. AAAI-98*, pp. 600 – 607, Menlo Park, CA: AAAI Press.

Cohen P., Schrag R., Jones E., Pease A., Lin A., Starr B., Gunning D., and Burke M. 1998. The DARPA High-Performance Knowledge Bases Project, *AI Magazine*, 19(4),25-49.

Genesereth M.R. and Fikes R.E. 1992. Knowledge Interchange Format, Version 3.0 Reference Manual. KSL-92-86, Knowledge Systems Laboratory, Stanford University.

Tecuci, G. 1998. *Building Intelligent Agents: An Apprenticeship Multistrategy Learning Theory, Methodology, Tool and Case Studies*. London, England: Academic Press.

Tecuci G., Boicu M., Wright K., Lee S.W., Marcu D., and Bowman M., *An Integrated Shell and Methodology for Rapid Development of Knowledge-Based Agents*, In *Proc. AAAI-99*, Menlo Park, CA: AAAI Press.

SMILE©: Structural Modeling, Inference, and Learning Engine and GeNIe: A Development Environment for Graphical Decision-Theoretic Models

Marek J. Druzdzel

Decision Systems Laboratory
School of Information Sciences, Intelligent Systems Program,
and Center for Biomedical Informatics, University of Pittsburgh
Pittsburgh, PA 15260

marek@sis.pitt.edu, http://www.pitt.edu/~druzdzel

Abstract

SMILE© (Structural Modeling, Inference, and Learning Engine) is a fully portable library of C++ classes implementing graphical decision-theoretic methods, such as Bayesian networks and influence diagrams, directly amenable to inclusion in intelligent systems. Its Windows user interface, **GeNIe** is a versatile and user-friendly development environment for graphical decision-theoretic models. Both modules, developed at the Decision Systems Laboratory, University of Pittsburgh, have been made available to the community in July 1998 at http://www2.sis.pitt.edu/~genie and have over 1,200 users worldwide (as of April 1999). This document summarizes the basic features of **GeNIe** and **SMILE**©.

Decision-theoretic systems

Decision-theoretic systems are increasingly applied in various domains because of their sound foundations, ability to combine existing data with expert knowledge, and intuitive framework of directed graphical models, such as Bayesian networks and influence diagrams. Some of the applications of decision-theoretic systems are: medical diagnosis and therapy planning, machine diagnosis, natural language processing, vision, robotics, planning, fraud detection, processing of military intelligence data in the context of battle damage assessment, and many others (March 1995 issue of *Communications of the ACM* lists several practical applications of Bayesian networks; others can be found in the proceedings of the Annual Conference on Uncertainty in Artificial Intelligence, available on-line in electronic format at http://www.sis.pitt.edu/~dsl/uai.html). Given the current interests in the application of decision-theoretic methods and the speed with which they are applied in practice, it can be expected that they will remain to be core modeling tools in intelligent systems.

GeNIe and SMILE©

The Decision Systems Laboratory at the University of Pittsburgh (http://www.sis.pitt.edu/~dsl) has been working in the domain of decision-theoretic decision support systems for

almost six years. Our theoretical and technical contributions have found their way into a general-purpose decision modeling environment, **SMILE**© (Structural Modeling, Inference, and Learning Engine) and its Windows user interface, **GeNIe**. We have made both programs available for non-commercial research, teaching, and personal use since July 1998 at http://www2.sis.pitt.edu/~genie and as of February 1999 have more than 1,200 users from over 80 countries. Some of the applications, built using **GeNIe** or **SMILE**©, are: battle damage assessment (Rockwell International and U.S. Air Force Rome Laboratory), group decision support models for regional conflict detection (Decision Support Department, U.S. Naval War College) intelligent tutoring systems (Learning and Development Research Center, University of Pittsburgh), medical therapy planning (National University of Singapore), medical diagnosis (Medical Informatics Training Program, University of Pittsburgh; Technical University of Bialystok, Poland). **GeNIe** and **SMILE**© have been also used in teaching statistics and decision-theoretic methods at several universities.

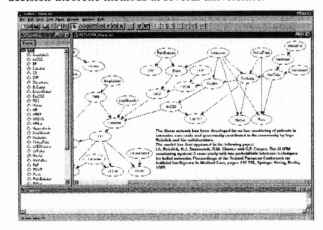

Figure 1: A schematic view of the **GeNIe** window

In the development of **GeNIe**, we stressed accessibility and friendliness of the user interface (see Figure 1 for a snapshot of the program interface). The architecture of the system

(Figure 2) is flexible: **SMILE**© is the core reasoning engine that can be embedded in dedicated user interfaces (**GeNIe** is in fact one such interface!). An example of a dedicated user interface to **SMILE**©, a medical system for diagnosis of liver disorders developed at the Technical University of Bialystok, is shown in Figure 3. The interface shows on the left hand side a list of risk factors and symptoms that a physician can enter and on the right hand side a list of possible disorders according to their likelihood as computed by the program.

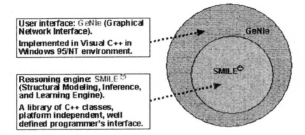

Figure 2: The architecture of **GeNIe** and **SMILE**©

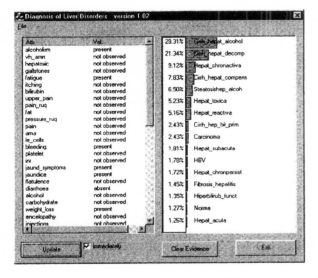

Figure 3: A dedicated interface to a **SMILE**© model.

Some features of **GeNIe** and **SMILE**©

GeNIe and **SMILE**© implement Bayesian networks and influence diagrams with a robust and reliable user interface both in terms of the development environment (**GeNIe**) and the programmer's interface to the library classes (**SMILE**©). The modeling language includes hierarchical sub-models, Noisy-OR nodes, deterministic nodes, multiple decision nodes, multiple utility nodes, linearly additive Multi-Attribute utility nodes (we will have generalized MAU nodes in the future). The development environment includes a pleasant graphical interface with aid in model navigation, such as hierarchical sub-models, a Windows-style tree view, on-screen comments, a comprehensive HTML-based help system, and many other useful features that one would want from a development environment for graphical models. The help system is fully integrated with the World Wide Web and has many useful links to web resources. We use **Ge-NIe** in teaching and the help system includes many useful documents and tutorials. We believe that it is basically a standalone guide to decision-theoretic modeling. **SMILE**© algorithms include relevance reasoning that includes designating nodes as targets, value of information computation, and several Bayesian network algorithms to choose from. **GeNIe** is the Decision Systems Laboratory's research and teaching vehicle, so naturally it will evolve as time goes.

One feature that may contribute to sharing research and development results in the community is that **GeNIe** and **SMILE**© are able to read and write several popular Bayesian network and influence diagram file formats, including the most recent version of the Bayesian network interchange format. It can thus be used as a conversion program.

GeNIe runs on Windows 95/98/NT computers. **SMILE**© is a fully portable library of classes accessible from C++. We have also developed **SmileX**, an ActiveX Windows component that allows **SMILE**© to be accessed from any Windows programming environment, including World Wide Web pages.

Acknowledgments

Support for the development of **GeNIe** and **SMILE**© has been provided in part by the Air Force Office of Scientific Research under grant F49620-97-1-0225 and by the National Science Foundation under Faculty Early Career Development (CAREER) Program, grant IRI-9624629. The past and present principal developers **GeNIe** and **SMILE**© (listed alphabetically) are: Steve Birnie, Jeroen J.J. Bogers, Jian Cheng, Denver H. Dash, Marek J. Druzdzel, Daniel Garcia Sanchez, Nancy Jackson, Hans van Leijen, Yan Lin, Tsai-Ching Lu, Agnieszka Onisko, Hans Ove Ringstad, Jiwu Tao, Carl P.R. Thijssen, Daniel Tomalesky and Haiqin Wang.

Knowledge Base Discovery Tool*

Erik Eilerts, Kathleen Lossau, Christopher York

Austin Info Systems, Inc.
303 Camp Craft Road
Austin, TX 78746
{eilerts, lossau, yorkc}@ausinfo.com

Abstract

The Knowledge Base Discovery Tool (KBDT) is a suite of tools and components to improve the indexing of and search for documents. KBDT extracts and displays content from documents and builds knowledge indexes based on meaning, rather than keywords. KBDT uses the indexes to perform more intelligent searches. It also includes visualization technology to display relevant results using multi-media, rather than plain text. This paper describes prototypes of two tools in this suite that use components for searching, extraction, and display of requested information. The tools are the Knowledge Base Editor and the Intelligent Information Retrieval Engine.

Overview

KBDT is a suite of tools and components under development by Austin Info Systems, Inc. (AIS) to improve the indexing of and search for on-line documents. This suite consists of the following components:

✦ **Extraction tool** - extracts content (not keywords) from documents in multiple formats (e.g. HTML, PDF, Microsoft Word)
✦ **Knowledge base** - contains an ontology that is used for content extraction and stores content-based indexes to documents processed by the extraction tool
✦ **Search portal** - provides a single interface for searching distributed information sources (world-wide web, ODBC databases, etc.) using multiple search strategies (including existing search engines)
✦ **Results engine** – organizes search results based on the document's content
✦ **Rendering engine** - converts search results into various multi-media formats, including tables, maps, charts, video, HTML, as well as plain text.

Knowledge Base Editor

The Knowledge Base Editor is used by humans to browse the ontology in the knowledge base and by other KBDT components to find content. The ontology is the core of the knowledge base. It is used for parsing and storing

content-based indexes. The initial ontology was derived from the WordNet database (Fellbaum 1998). The primary component of the ontology is a "concept."

In the knowledge base, a concept denotes a collection of synonyms plus a description that indicates the concept's usage. One definition for "concept" is:

something that exists or that can be thought about.

The following example best illustrates this:

✦ *tank, army tank - a military tank*
✦ *tank, storage tank - container holding gases or liquids*

The word tank has at least two different meanings or *senses*, making it impossible to specify its usage using the word tank alone. By combining the word tank with its synonyms and a description, a common meaning can be determined. Information in the knowledge base is stored based on the synonym collections or *senses*, rather than as single words. The synonym collections are called Concepts and are organized into the following part of speech categories: Noun, Verb, Adverb, and Adjective. Concepts greatly improve the representative power of the knowledge base by allowing information to be attached to a words' usage, rather than just to the individual word.

The job of the KB Editor is to enable browsing of the Concepts, their parts of speech, and the synonyms that make up each one. The specific functionality that is demonstrated by the Knowledge Base Editor includes:

✦ Finding a Concept
✦ Selecting a Concept with multiple senses
✦ Moving between Concepts by following links.

Finding a Concept

The tool starts by asking for a word that is related to the Concept being searched for (Concept To View). Selecting one of the part of speech buttons or "All" to view Concepts in all parts of speech categories begins the search for the Concepts related to this word. Three possible results are displayed:

✦ A list of Concepts that make use of the word entered, including each Concept's parts of speech
✦ Information related to the Concept, if the word entered is only used in one Concept
✦ An error message indicating that no Concept in the knowledge base corresponds to the word that was entered.

---

* This work is supported in part by a CECOM C2SID Phase II SBIR
Contract number: DAAB07-98-C-D027.

Selecting a Concept with Multiple Senses

If multiple Concepts are related to an individual word, a list of the Concepts is displayed, including the part of speech, synonyms, and a description of each concept. The purpose of this step is to help the user select the appropriate Concept based on usage. Based on the previous example, the user has to decide whether they are interested in the Noun-category Concept for an army tank or a tank of water.

Moving between Concepts by following Links

Once a concept has been selected, the user is presented with the following information:

✦ **Name** - a concatenation of the concept's synonyms and its part of speech
✦ **Description** - a textual description of the concept, potentially including some sample sentences showing its usage
✦ **Connections** - a list of connections between the concept and other related concepts

To view one of the connections, the user selects its hyperlink. All connections are links to other concepts, except for the Synonym connections. When a synonym is selected, the knowledge base is searched for all Concepts that use the selected synonym word. The result of the search is displayed according to the options in "*Finding A Concept.*"

Intelligent Information Retrieval Engine

This Intelligent Information Retrieval Engine provides the capability for the user to discover information relevant to a given Concept or set of Concepts. It makes extensive use of the Concepts that are stored in the knowledge base for both query preparation and post-processing of query results.

The specific functionality that is demonstrated by the Intelligent Information Retrieval Engine includes:

✦ Entering A Query
✦ Providing Semantic Contexts for a Query's Terms
✦ Conducting a Search using Semantic Contexts

These tasks provide further details about how the concepts are used.

Entering A Query

The tool starts by asking for a short description of the item to search for. At this point, a typical search engine extracts keywords from this description and then runs the query. Instead, the IIR engine retrieves Concepts related to the words in the description. This allows documents to be located based on the meanings of the words, rather than just the words themselves.

Providing Semantic Contexts for a Query's Terms

The tool next asks for a clarification of the search terms, if multiple Concepts are found for individual words. This is the step where the quality of the search is significantly improved, since the search is now focused on Concepts, not just words. For example, if *tank* was entered, the user must now decide whether they are interested in an army tank or a tank of water. The Concepts used at this step are extracted from the knowledge base.

Conducting a Search using Semantic Contexts

After the user has selected meanings for each of the query's terms, this tool conducts a search of the world-wide web to find documents related to the search topic. The search is focused on documents that contain the selected concepts and do not contain the discarded concepts. For example, if the user had selected *army tank*, then the documents must contain the phrase *tank* or *army tank*. Documents that contain the phrase *storage tank* are discarded.

The quality of the results provided by semantic-context information retrieval depend on the amount and kind of information in the knowledge base related to the user's topic of interest.

Conclusion

The demonstration covers early prototypes of two tools that are part of a larger project devoted to knowledge discovery and intelligent information retrieval. The early prototypes indicate that Concepts provide a useful foundation for discovering relevant information from a wide variety of sources, and encourage future project development in this area.

Future

The next set of tools to be developed include a parsing engine for extracting concepts form documents and a concept builder to help average users expand the contents of the knowledge base. The concept builder presents the user with a list of words extracted from a document that are not yet in the knowledge base and helps the user to create a definition for the new terms. Prototypes of these tools should be available by mid-year 1999.

Demo URL

The demonstration can be viewed via the Internet by accessing the following URL:

http://www.ausinfo.com/kbdt/aaai99.html

References

Fellbaum, C. ed. *1998 WordNet: An Electronic Lexical Database.* Cambridge, Mass.: MIT Press.

Mayk, et.al. 1998 *A Knowledge Based Doctrine Tool for Command and Control,* Proceedings of the Command and Control Research and Technology Symposium.

TRIPS: The Rochester Interactive Planning System

George Ferguson and **James F. Allen**
Department of Computer Science
University of Rochester
Rochester, NY 14627-0226
{ferguson,james}@cs.rochester.edu
http://www.cs.rochester.edu/research/trips/

Abstract

This demonstration showcases TRIPS, The Rochester Interactive Planning System, an intelligent, collaborative, conversational planning assistant. TRIPS collaborates with the user using both spoken dialogue and graphical displays to solve problems in a transportation logistics domain. In our demonstrations, users are encouraged to sit down and try the system, with only rudimentary guidance from us. For further information, including QuickTime movies of the system in action, please visit our website at the URL listed above.

Introduction

TRIPS, The Rochester Interactive Planning System (Ferguson & Allen 1998), is the latest in a series of prototype collaborative planning assistants developed at the University of Rochester's Department of Computer Science (Allen *et al.* 1995; Ferguson *et al.* 1996; Ferguson, Allen, & Miller 1996). The goal of the project is an intelligent planning assistant that interacts with its human manager using a combination of natural language and graphical displays. The two of them collaborate to construct plans in crisis situations. The system understands the interaction as a *dialogue* between it and the human. The dialogue provides the context for interpreting human utterances and actions, and provides the structure for deciding what to do in response. With the human in the loop, they and the system together can solve harder problems faster than either could solve alone.

TRIPS operates in a simplified logistics and transportation world, with cargos being delivered using a variety of vehicles. One example scenario involves evacuating the island of Pacifica ahead of an approaching hurricane. The manager's task is to plan the evacuation, using a variety of vehicles (with varying capabilities) at his or her disposal. There may be a variety of constraints placed on the final plans, such as time, cost, weather effects, and so on.

TRIPS Architecture

TRIPS is designed as a set of loosely-coupled modules that exchange information by passing KQML messages. A schematic description of the system is shown in Figure 1. At the top of the schematic are modality processing modules, such speech recognition and generation, keyboard input and output, and interactive graphical displays. Input from these modules is parsed into a uniform representation of the user's input as one or more communicative acts.

The middle layer in the TRIPS architecture contains the core modules of the system, responsible for mantaining the conversation with the user and helping them achieve their (and the system's) objectives. The Conversational Agent combines the interpreted communicative acts from the input with the discourse context in order to determine the intended speech acts, which might be either indirect ("Do you know the time?") or ambiguous ("Send the truck to Delta" when there are two trucks). The Problem-Solving Manager plays two roles in maintaining the dialogue. First, it helps resolve ambiguities by applying plan recognition techniques. In the previous example of an ambiguous reference to "the truck," for example, the PSM might infer that only one truck is not already at Delta, and so the user must be referring to it. Second, it coordinates the invocation of the specialized reasoners that provide solutions in service of user and system objectives.

These specialized reasoners form the bottom layer of the TRIPS architecture, and currently include a powerful but incomplete temporal logic-based planner, router, scheduler, temporal knowledge base, and a fast simulator with data mining capabilities for detecting (and hopefully correcting) problems with planned activities. The Problem-Solving Manager invokes these reasoners as appropriate, and integrates their responses into the problem-solving context.

Finally, the Conversational Agent uses the results of task-specific problem-solving (*e.g.*, a new part of a plan, or an answer to a query) together with general dialogue principles to determine appropriate responses. Both spoken language and graphical displays can be generated from the intended communicative acts specified by the Conversational Agent.

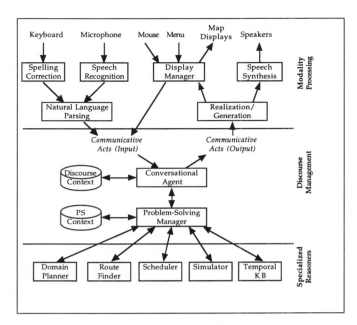

Figure 1: TRIPS System Architecture

Key Features

Space precludes a detailed discussion of TRIPS capabilities and shortcomings, so what follows is a just a quick summary of some of the main features.

- **Intuitive Interaction**: The goal of the project is to make interaction with intelligent systems like TRIPS as natural as human conversation. The representation based on communicative acts and the structuring of the interaction as a dialogue provide the structure for intelligent interaction.

- **Robust Understanding**: One of the main thrusts of our work on TRAINS and now on TRIPS has been making the system robust. This includes handling speech recognition errors, handling ungrammatical or partial utterances, dealing with the system's own shortcomings gracefully, and, hopefully, even handling system errors and continuing the conversation.

- **Recognition of User Intention**: TRIPS explicitly attempts to understand the intentions of the user in understanding their utterances. This is used both to resolve ambiguities and to provide useful or helpful responses. It can also drive the system into sub-dialogues to resolve problems.

- **Intelligent Plan Revision**: We have found that planning from scratch for goals is not the most important part of TRIPS. In the first place, it is impossible in practice for the user to fully specify their goals in any reasonably complex domain. Thus they will need to refine their plans as they discover new constraints, add new objectives, and so on. Even if the users knew exactly what they wanted, planning is so hard that it is unlikely that we will be able to do the planning in a reasonable amount time. The

best we could hope for would be approximate solutions that the user and the system can collaboratively refine. Thus while we have developed some sophisticated planning techniques, they are incomplete compared to traditional planning algorithms but are also much more flexible, in order to accomodate human guidance and incremental refinement.

- **Simulation and Evaluation**: We are investigating the use of simulation to detect problems in plans, to repair problems, to help monitor plan execution, and to generate visualizations essential to human understanding and evaluation of plans.

- **Experimental Infrastructure**: TRIPS is designed to be an experimental testbed. To this end, we have built up a significant infrastructure to support repeated experimentation, evelution, and analysis. This includes, for example, the ability to replay sessions in real time, and to construct new, repeatable scenarios for use in controlled experiments.

Acknowledgements

The TRIPS development team includes Donna Byron, Amanda Stent, Lucian Galescu, and Myroslava Dzikovska, in addition to the authors. Further thanks are due to Len Schubert, and to the members of the original TRAINS group from which TRIPS emerged.

TRIPS is funded in part by DARPA research grant no. F30602-98-2-0133, USAF/Rome Laboratory research grant no. F30602-97-1-0348, ONR research grant no. N00014-95-I-1088, and NSF research grant no. IRI-9711009.

References

Allen, J. F.; Schubert, L. K.; Ferguson, G.; Heeman, P.; Hwang, C. H.; Kato, T.; Light, M.; Martin, N. G.; Miller, B. W.; Poesio, M.; and Traum, D. R. 1995. The TRAINS project: A case study in defining a conversational planning agent. *Journal of Experimental and Theoretical AI* 7:7–48.

Ferguson, G., and Allen, J. F. 1998. TRIPS: An integrated intelligent problem-solving assistant. In *Proceedings of the Fifteenth National Conference on AI (AAAI-98)*, 567–573.

Ferguson, G.; Allen, J.; and Miller, B. 1996. TRAINS-95: Towards a mixed-initiative planning assistant. In Drabble, B., ed., *Proceedings of the Third Conference on Artificial Intelligence Planning Systems (AIPS-96)*, 70–77.

Ferguson, G.; Allen, J. F.; Miller, B. W.; and Ringer, E. K. 1996. The design and implementation of the TRAINS-96 system: A prototype mixed-initiative planning assistant. TRAINS Technical Note 96-5, Department of Computer Science, University of Rochester, Rochester, NY.

A Natural-Language Speech Interface Constructed Entirely as a Set of Executable Specifications

R. A. Frost

Department of Computer Science
University of Windsor, Windsor
Ontario, Canada N9B 3P4
richard@uwindsor.ca

Abstract

SpeechNet is a collection of speech-accessible hyper-linked objects called sihlos. Sihlos are deployed over the Internet and are accessed by remote speech browsers. When a speech browser accesses a sihlo, it begins by download-ing a grammar file which is used to configure the browser in order to achieve high recognition accuracy. Sihlos are hy-perlinked in a manner that is similar to the linking of html pages. SpeechNet provides non-visual access to knowledge which is analogous to visual access provided by the web. One of the sihlos can answer thousands of spoken pseudo-natural-language questions about the solar system. This sihlo has been constructed entirely as a set of executable specifications of the language that it can process.

SpeechNet

The world-wide web is primarily based on visual brows-ing of hyperlinked text and graphical objects. The huge knowledge base available on the web is largely inacces-sible to visually-challenged users. The SpeechNet project at the University of Windsor (Frost 1999b) overcomes this problem by augmenting the web with a network of speech-accessible hyperlinked objects called sihlos.

Each sihlo consists of a language processor and a gram-mar defining the syntax of the input language. When a remote speech browser contacts a sihlo, it downloads the grammar in order to configure the speech recognizer. This alleviates a major difficulty in building accurate speech interfaces to large knowledge bases. Sihlos enable the knowledge to be divided into small modules each having a "small" language associated with it. This allows highly accurate user-independent continuous-speech recognition. Hyperlinking sihlos allows the user to navigate through a complex interrelated body of knowledge using spoken prompts in a way that is analogous to the way in which the web is navigated using visual prompts.

Although sihlos can alleviate the problem of building so-phisticated speech interfaces, their design and construction can be quite difficult. The task of building the language processors is compounded by the concurrent task of de-signing a grammar which has high recognition accuracy. It has been shown (Frost 1995) that this process can be facilitated if the interpreter and speech recognizer are con-structed as executable specifications. In the following, we describe an example of applying this approach.

The Natural-Language Query Interpreter

The `solar man` sihlo is a natural-language interface to a database containing information about the planets, moons and people who discovered them. This sihlo is constructed as an 800–line executable specification of an attribute grammar defining the syntax and semantics of the input language. The specification is written in a language called W/AGE developed at the University of Windsor. (Frost 1994). The specification includes:

- A dictionary, where meanings of words are defined directly in terms of database constructs, or indirectly as being equivalent to the meaning of other phrases.
- A set of production rules (syntax rules) augmented with semantic actions which define how attributes of a compound expression are computed from the attributes of its component expressions.
- A set of Chomsky-like syntactic re-write rules.
- A set of equations defining the semantic model on which the processor is based.

The semantic theory underlying `solar man` is loosely based on Montague's approach to semantics (Dowty, Wall and Peters 1981). The processor can answer several thou-sand well-formed queries expressed in a sub-set of English. For example:

```
who discovered a moon that orbits mars
did Hall discover every moon
how many moons were discovered by
                    Hall or Kuiper
was every moon discovered by a man
```

```
which planets are orbited by a moon that
                was discovered by Galileo
which moons were discovered by nobody
is every planet orbited by a moon
which planets are orbited by two moons
who was the discoverer of phobos
Hall discovered a moon that orbits mars
does every moon orbit every planet
does phobos orbit mars
```

In addition to access trhough a speech browser, `solar man` can also be accessed through an html web page, which contains a full listing of the executable specification and a paper describing the W/AGE executable specification language.

```
www.cs.uwindsor.ca/users/r/
    richard/miranda/wage_demo.html
```

W/AGE and Executable Grammar Objects

W/AGE allows language processors to be constructed by defining the syntax and semantics of the language to be processed. The notation is a variant of standard textbook notation for attribute grammars. Advantages of the "attribute-grammar programming paradigm" are discussed in (Paaki 1995). W/AGE has been used in the construction of various types of language processor including VLSI design transformers, theorem provers, as well as the natural-language speech interface discussed here.

Current work includes the implementation of W/AGE in Java. This involves the development of *executable grammar objects* which allow object-oriented language processors to be built with structures that are closely related to the grammars defining the language to be processed (Frost 1999a).

The Speech Browser

The prototype speech browser is written in Java. It uses the IBM Via Voice speech-recognition engine and IBM's implementation of the Java speech APIs. The browser runs on regular PCs, needs no training (is user-independent), and accepts continuous-speech input. Speech-recognition accuracy is very high for the `solar man` example. Response from the browser is in real-time and the downloading of the grammar and reconfiguration of the speech recognizer (when sihlos are changed) is not noticeable.

Concluding Comments

The real potential of SpeechNet will only be attained if tools are developed to assist people with the task of designing grammars, constructing language processors, and deploying sihlos in an appropriate manner over the Internet. The approach described in this paper goes some way towards achieving the second of these goals.

Current work is investigating the use of the Common Object Request Broker Architecture in the deployment of sihlos. This will facilitate resource sharing, openness, and scalability. It will also enable sihlos to have "sessions" with end users thereby supporting human/computer speech dialogue.

If tools are available to facilitate the construction and deployment of sihlos, it may be possible to create a huge hyperlinked body of knowledge that is accessible through remote speech interfaces anywhere that has access to the Internet.

Acknowledgments

Many people at the University of Windsor have contribute to SpeechNet and to the construction of the solar interface. In particular, the author would like to thank Sanjay Chitte, who wrote the Java code for the prototype speech browser and Barbara Szydlowski who built the web interface to the solar man interpreter. The author acknowledges the support provided by NSERC in the form of an individual research grant.

References

Frost, R. A. 1999a. Improving the efficiency of executable grammar objects. University of Windsor, Department of Computer Science Technical Report CS1999–01.

Frost, R. A. 1999b. SpeechNet: A network of hyperlinked speech-accessible objects. Proc. WECWIS '99: *International Workshop on Advanced Issues of E-Commerce and Web-Based Information Systems*. Santa Clara, CA. Apr. 1999.

Frost, R. A. 1995. Use of executable specifications in the construction of speech interfaces. *Proc. IJCAI Workshop on Developing AI Applications for the Disabled*, Montreal 1995.

Frost, R. A. 1994. W/AGE The Windsor Attribute Grammar Programming Environment. *Schloss Dagstuhl International Workshop on Functional programming in the Real World*.

Paaki, J. 1995. Attribute grammar paradigms — a high-level methodology in language implementation, *ACM Computing Surveys* 27(2) 196–255.

Dowty, D. R., Wall, R. E. and Peters, S. 1981. *Introduction to Montague Semantics*. D. Reidel Publishing Company, Dordrecht, Boston, Lancaster, Tokyo.

A System for the Semantic Interpretation of Unrestricted Domains using WordNet

Fernando Gomez
School of Computer Science
University of Central Florida, Orlando, FL 32816
gomez@cs.ucf.edu

Carlos Segami
Dept. of Mathematics and Computer Science
Barry University, Miami Shores, Fl 33161
segami@euclid.barry.edu

In this demonstration, we show an algorithm for the semantic interpretation of unrestricted texts. The algorithm presents a solution for the following interpretation problems: determination of the meaning of the verb, identification of thematic roles and adjuncts, and attachments of prepositional phrases (PPs). An interesting aspect of the algorithm is that the solution of all these problems is interdependent. The interpretation algorithm uses WordNet (Miller *et al.* 1993) as its lexical knowledge-base. Predicates, or verbal concepts, have been defined for WordNet verb classes (Fellbaum 1993), which have been reorganized considerably following the criteria imposed by the interpretation algorithm. The WordNet ontology for nouns has also undergone some reorganization and redefinition to conform with the entries in the thematic roles of the predicates. We have taken a top-down approach that defines generic abstract predicates subsuming semantically and syntactically a large class of verbs. WordNet verb classes have been mapped into these generic predicates. Some of this mapping has required us to define new classes and to reclassify and/or redefine some WordNet classes and subclasses (Gomez 1998a). The predicates form a hierarchy in which thematic roles and inferences are inherited by subpredicates from their superpredicates. Two major consequences derive from anchoring verb classes in abstract semantic predicates: coalescing several WordNet senses into a predicate, which reduces the systemic polysemy in some WordNet senses, and mapping the same WordNet synset into distinct predicates. For instance, all the 5 synsets listed by WordNet for "travel": "travel1, go, move, locomote;" "travel2, journey;" "travel3, take a trip, make a trip;" "travel4, journey;" and "travel5 (undergo transportation, as in a vehicle)" are coalesced into the abstract semantic predicate *change-of-location-by-animate*. This predicate defines a class of verbs containing the most generic properties shared by all members of the class. The *differentia* between this predicate and its subpredicates are given by one or more of the following: a) specific selectional restrictions for the thematic roles, b) different syntactic

realizations of the thematic roles, and c) specific sets of inferences associated with the subpredicates. For instance, the *instrument* of *drive* is always a vehicle, while the *instrument* of *change-of-location-by-animate* can be an animate, an animate body part, etc. The *instrument* of *drive* is never realized by a subject, but the *instrument* of the generic predicate can be realized by a subject, e.g., "This bus goes to Cambridge every Wednesday." On the other hand, *migrate* differs from *change-of-location-by-animate* only by the specific inferences associated with this predicate. Subpredicates inherit all the thematic roles not listed in their definitions from their parent predicates. The entry for the predicate *change-of-location-by-animate* is listed on the next column. The *wn-map* entry means that all the five senses of "travel" and all the verb forms under them are, in principle, coalesced into the concept *change-of-location-by-animate*. These synsets group under them about 1,200 verb forms. However, subpredicates of this predicate will be recognized. Any WordNet synset that satisfies any of the *differentia* given above is mapped into a subpredicate of *change-of-location-by-animate*. In fact, we have defined 48 subpredicates of *change-of-location-by-animate*. But, if they were not recognized, then any form that is mapped by WordNet into any of the five senses of "travel" would be mapped into the predicate *change-of-location-by-animate*. Of course, if the form is also mapped by WordNet to another sense besides any of the senses of "travel," then it will be mapped into whatever predicate we identify for that sense. The generic meaning expressed by all these verbs is that of the change of location by an animate being, in which the *agent* and the *theme* are the same. The entry *agent* indicates that the agents of this predicate are entities belonging to the classes *animal* or *social-group* (a group of humans or animals). It also expresses that the agent is realized syntactically by the subject of the sentence. The *theme* is also realized by the subject. The selectional restrictions for the role *to-loc* are, in order of preference, *location* and *physical-thing*. This role is realized syntactically by a PP containing any of the prepositions listed. The different ways of expressing a path, namely *toward-loc*, *near-loc*, etc. have been collapsed here into *to-loc* for space reasons.

```
[change-of-location-by-animate(is-a (action))
(wn-map (travel1) (travel2) (travel3)
        (travel4) (travel5))
(agent(animal social-group) (subj))
(theme(animal social-group) (subj))
(to-loc
 (location physical-thing) ((prep towards
    toward around through into back-to along
    over beside above by under below throughout
    beyond past across near up down))
 (location -social-group -animal
        physical-thing)       ((prep to))
 (location) ((prep for)))
(from-loc (location -animal -social-group
        physical-thing) ((prep from out-of))
        (location) (obj))
(instrument
  (conveyance)(subj obj (prep with in on))
  (animal)   ((prep on))
  (extremity1) ((prep on with)))
(medium (road-or-path)((prep on)))
(distance(distance linear-measure)
        (obj(prep for)))]
```

The sign "-" preceding a selectional restriction means that any noun sense that is subsumed by the semantic category preceded by "-" does not realize that thematic role. The *to-loc* can also be realized by the preposition "to" and the semantic category *location*, but not by *social-group* nor *animal*, and yes by *physical-thing*. This is a way of saying that it is realized by *location* and *physical-thing* excluding *social-group* and *animal* from *physical-thing*. The *from-loc* role contains two pairs of lists. The first pair expresses this role when it is realized by a PP, and the second pair when it is realized by obj. The reason for using two pairs of lists is that "from" expresses a *from-loc* role in most cases. Hence, if the object of the PP is not classified as a *location* in the ontology but just as a *physical-thing*, one can assume, quite safely, that the PP expresses a *from-loc*. However, in the case of obj, one needs to be certain that the head noun of the NP is a location; otherwise one may incorrectly identify a thematic role and, possibly, a predicate. Similar explanations apply to the remainder of the thematic roles. As of this writing, 1198 predicates have been defined for 70% of WordNet verb forms.

The semantic interpretation algorithm (Gomez 1998b) is activated by the parser after parsing a clause. The parser recognizes clausal and NP complements, relative clauses, resolves gaps resulting from questions and relativization, and handles coordination and subordination. It does not resolve structural ambiguity, which is delayed until semantic interpretation. Our mapping of WordNet verb synsets to predicates provides a list containing the predicates for the verb of the clause. The goals of the algorithm are to select one predicate from that list, attach PPs and identify thematic roles and adjuncts. All these tasks are simultaneously achieved. For each syntactic relation (SR) in the clause (starting with the NP complements) and for every predicate in

the list of predicates, the algorithm checks if the predicate explains the SR. A predicate *explains* an SR if there is a thematic role in the predicate realized by the SR and the selectional restrictions of the thematic role subsume the ontological category of the head noun of the syntactic relation. This process is repeated for each SR in the clause and each predicate in the list of predicates. Then, the predicate that explains the most SRs is selected as the meaning of the verb. The thematic roles of the predicate have been identified as a result of this process. In case of ties, the predicate that has the greatest number of thematic roles realized is selected. Every syntactic relation that has not been mapped to a thematic role must be an adjunct or an NP modifier. The entries for adjuncts are stored in the root node *action* and are inherited by all predicates. Adjuncts are identified *after the meaning of the verb has been determined* because adjuncts are not part of the argument structure of the predicate. We have integrated the semantic interpreter into SNOWY and begun to look into the task of acquiring biographic knowledge from the *The World Book Encyclopedia*.

The system has been implemented in Franz Common Lisp and runs on Sun Sparc workstations. The WordNet lexicon for nouns and verbs has been converted into a Lisp-based representation. The semantic interpreter takes 0.96 MB, the parser 0.48 MB, the WordNet lexicon in the Lisp representation 35.00 MB, the parser lexicon 4.40 MB and the verbal predicates that we have defined for the WordNet verb class 0.25 MB. In the demo, we will type some sentences in order to illustrate the organization of the lexical knowledge, the predicates and the different aspects of the algorithm. Then, we will let the audience actively participate by forming their own sentences and trying them in the system.

Acknowledgements. We want to thank Bruce Martin for creating the database for the WordNet lexicon in Lisp.

References

Fellbaum, C. 1993. English verbs as a semantic net. Technical report, Princeton. CSL Report 43, revised March 1993.

Gomez, F.; Segami, C.; and Hull, R. 1997. Determining prepositional attachment, prepositional meaning, verb meaning and thematic roles. *Computational Intelligence* 13(1):1–31.

Gomez, F. 1998a. Linking wordnet verb classes to semantic interpretation. In *COLING-ACL Workshop on Usage of WordNet in NLP Systems*, 58–64.

Gomez, F. 1998b. Semantic interpretation of unrestricted domains using wordnet. Technical report, University of Central Florida, Department of Computer Science. CS-TR-98-2, Jan. 1998.

Miller, G.; Beckwith, R.; Fellbaum, C.; Gross, D.; and Miller, K. 1993. Introduction to WordNet: An on-line lexical database. Technical report, Princeton. CSL Report 43, revised March 1993.

DIPLOMAT: Compiling Prioritized Default Rules into Ordinary Logic Programs, for E-Commerce Applications

Benjamin N. Grosof*
IBM T.J. Watson Research Center
30 Saw Mill River Rd., Hawthorne, NY 10532, USA
grosof@us.ibm.com (alt.: grosof@cs.stanford.edu)
http://www.research.ibm.com/people/g/grosof

Abstract

Rules promise to be widely useful in Internet electronic commerce. Declarative prioritized default rule knowledge representations offer the advantage of handling conflicts that arise in updating rule sets, but have as yet had little practical deployment. DIPLOMAT is a Java library that embodies a new approach to the implementation of such prioritized default rules: to compile them into ordinary logic programs (LP's) cf. pure Prolog. We apply the approach to a newly generalized version of courteous LP's, a semantically attractive and computationally tractable form of prioritized default rules. Compilation enables courteous LP's functionality to be added modularly to ordinary LP rule engines, via a preprocessor, with tractable computational overhead. This takes a long step towards actual deployment of prioritized-default knowledge representation in commercially fielded technology and applications.

We give in the demo storyboard an automated example e-commerce application scenario: inferencing in a 70-rule courteous LP that represents personalized pricing and promotions on a bookstore's Web storefront.

The extended version of this paper, available as an IBM Research Report, contains the demo storyboard and technical details.

Rules in E-Commerce, Challenge of Prioritized Default Rules

Rules[1] promise to be widely useful in Internet electronic commerce as an automatically executable specification language / programming mechanism. Rules are useful, for example, to represent: seller offerings of products and services, buyer requirements, contractual agreements, authorization policies, and more generally, many e-business policies and processes. A characteristic of this realm is that, often, rules need to be modified frequently and by multiple players. Conflicts between rules often arise during updating and merging.

In e-commerce applications, rules are specified by business-domain experts such as marketing managers and are modified frequently, including by merging rules specified by different people in different organizations.

Another characteristic of this realm is that it is desirable for the rules knowledge representation (KR) to be highly declarative: to have a semantics, independent of inferencing algorithm details, that specifies which set of conclusions are entailed by a given set of premise rules. Declarativeness aids exchange of rules between heterogeneous applications or enterprises, modification of rules, understandability of rules by humans.

We are attracted by some virtues of prioritized default rules (in declarative KR): they handle conflicts, including during updating of rule sets, using partially-ordered prioritization info that is naturally available based on relative specificity, recency, and authority.

In Internet e-commerce, the prioritized default expressive features are valuable especially because they greatly facilitate incremental specification, by often eliminating the need to explicitly modify previous rules when updating or merging.

The **overall problem we address** is: how to enable prioritized default rules to be used as a widely practical knowledge representation for specification and execution of rule-based software, especially in e-commerce.

Prioritized default rules are of long-standing interest in the knowledge representation (KR) community, and have received much study. However, they have as yet had little impact on practical rule-based systems and software engineering generally, and had very few deployed serious applications.

One difficulty is getting the semantics right, including intuitively simple enough that non-experts in KR can feel comfortable specifying, and often repeatedly modifying, rule sets. Another difficulty is the complexity of implementing inferencing in a new KR. A third difficulty is facilitating a transition, which is best made incrementally, by builders and users of previous rule-based technology, to a new representation.

We take a new overall approach to remedy these three difficulties, especially the third.

[1](in the sense of knowledge representation and rule-based systems)

DIPLOMAT, Compilation Approach, Generalized Courteous Logic Programs

The DIPLOMAT system is a Java library that embodies our new approach to the implementation of prioritized default rules: to **compile** them into ordinary logic programs (OLP's). ("Logic program" here means in the sense of declarative knowledge representation (Baral & Gelfond 1994), not just Prolog). DIPLOMAT currently implements such compiling for one particular prioritized default rule KR: **courteous logic programs**. The compiler is run as a pre-processor, then its output is fed to an OLP inferencing engine, which may be forward-chaining or backward-chaining.

Besides the compiler, DIPLOMAT includes the **interlingua** capability to translate ordinary LP's (e.g., the results of its compilation) to and fro multiple other pre-existing ordinary-LP inferencing engines, e.g., Prolog systems and intelligent agent systems. DIPLOMAT currently implements such compiling for 3 such OLP engines.

As a target KR, OLP's are very attractive. They are computationally tractable[2], unlike even the propositional case of classical logic, yet represent basic non-monotonicity via the negation-as-failure expressive feature. They are in widespread deployment and application, including by many programmers who know and care very little about KR generally. There are a number of highly efficient and sophisticated OLP rule systems / inferencing engines available. OLP's are also closely related to derived relations in SQL relational databases, and to several other varieties of rule-based systems.

Courteous logic programs (Grosof 1997) are our favorite previous prioritized default rule KR. Courteous LP's include ordinary LP's as a special case but further feature classical negation and prioritized conflict handling. Courteous LP's have a number of attractive properties. They have a unique consistent conclusion set, and are computationally tractable[3], with relatively modest extra computational cost compared to OLP's. Their behavior captures many examples of prioritized default reasoning in a graceful, concise, and intuitive manner. They have a number of established well-behavior properties, including under merging.

DIPLOMAT implements a version of courteous LP's that is expressively generalized in several aspects from the previous version of courteous LP's in (Grosof 1997) but retains the previous version's above attractive properties. First, it enables recursion, i.e., cyclic dependence of a predicate through rules upon itself. Second, it enables reasoning about the prioritization, i.e., inferencing to conclude that one rule has higher priority than another. Third, it enables the scope of conflict to be specified not just in terms of classical negation (a proposition p versus its classical negation), but more generally as a set of **pairwise mutual exclusion constraints** (mutex's). It then enforces these mutex's and ensures consistency with respect to them. Mutex's are practically extremely useful even for otherwise relatively expressively simple rule sets, to represent reasoning about k-valued properties for k greater than 2. E.g., in a mail agent, one might wish that a message's urgency level should be inferred to be at most one of 4 levels: emergency, high, medium, or low. This can be specified via mutex's pairwise: e.g., urgency must not be both high and medium, nor both high and low, etc..

Demo Storyboard

We give in the demo storyboard an automated example e-commerce application scenario: inferencing in a courteous LP that represents personalized pricing and promotions on a bookstore's Web storefront. The example courteous LP contains about 70 rules and facts. Conclusions are drawn about what price discounts to offer and what targeted ads to show, for a given shopper.

Here, rules are specified by business-domain experts such as marketing managers and are modified frequently, including by merging rules specified by different people in different organizations. The prioritized conflict handling facilitates representing a sequence of such modifications as a simple accumulation of rules (and facts) — without necessitating explicit revision of previous rules.

The demo storyboard illustrates running the compiler, then (via the interlingua) using a pre-existing OLP engine (developed by others) to perform inferencing on the post-compilation OLP.

Acknowledgements

Hoi Chan, Michael Travers, and Xiaocheng Luan have also contributed to the DIPLOMAT implementation, especially the interlingua. Manoj Kumar contributed early concept work to the storyboard example.

References

Baral, C., and Gelfond, M. 1994. Logic programming and knowledge representation. *Journal of Logic Programming* 19,20:73–148. Includes extensive review of literature.

Grosof, B. N. 1997. Prioritized conflict handling for logic programs. In Maluszynski, J., ed., *Logic Programming: Proceedings of the International Symposium (ILPS-97)*, 197–211. Cambridge, MA, USA: MIT Press. Held Port Jefferson, NY, USA, Oct. 12-17, 1997. http://www.ida.liu.se/~ilps97. Extended version available as IBM Research Report RC 20836 at http://www.research.ibm.com .

---

[2]Inferencing is worst-case polynomial-time for the propositional case; or, more generally, given the commonly-met restrictions of (1) Datalog (no logical functions with non-zero arity) and (2) bounded number of logical variables appearing per rule.

[3]under the same restrictions mentioned earlier

Solving Crosswords with PROVERB

Michael L. Littman, Greg A. Keim, Noam M. Shazeer
Department of Computer Science
Duke University, Durham, NC 27708-0129
{mlittman, keim, noam}@cs.duke.edu

Abstract

We attacked the problem of solving crossword puzzles by computer: Given a set of clues and a crossword grid, try to maximize the number of words correctly filled in. PROVERB, the probabilistic cruciverbalist, separates the problem into two, more familiar subproblems: candidate generation and grid filling. In candidate generation, each clue is treated as a type of query to an information retrieval system, and relevant words of the correct length are returned along with confidence scores. In grid filling, the candidate words are fit into the puzzle grid to maximize an overall confidence score using a combination of ideas from belief network inference and constraint satisfaction. For our demonstration, we will have an interactive version of the candidate-generation process available via the web, and will also give people an opportunity to go head-to-head against PROVERB in solving complete puzzles.

Crossword puzzles have been an AI staple for many years, both as an example of the constraint satisfaction paradigm (Mackworth 1977) and as a testbed for search (Ginsberg *et al.* 1990). However, we are aware of no attempts to create a broad-coverage crossword puzzle solver—one that solves crosswords based on their clues. PROVERB was developed by a group at Duke University to solve American-style crossword puzzles.

The architecture of the system consists primarily of a set of 30 "Expert Modules" responsible for suggesting solutions to the clues, and a "Solver" responsible for selecting candidate answers for each clue that fit together in the grid.

To illustrate the candidate-generation process, we took the 70 clues from the crossword puzzle published in the New York Times, Thursday, October 10th, 1998. These clues were run through the expert modules and approximately 33 were solved with high confidence (in the top 10). After grid filling (combining crossing constraints with information from the clue), 62 clues were answered correctly. We examined the 33 well-solved clues to determine which expert modules contributed to the solution. These are described below.

Modules come in several different types:

- *Word list modules* ignore their clues and return all words of the correct length from a dictionary.

- *CWDB-specific modules* make use of a crossword database (CWDB) of over 350,000 crossword clues with their solutions.

- *Information retrieval modules* retrieve answers from full text sources such as online encyclopedias.

- *Database modules* create domain-specific queries for focused databases of authors, songwriters, actors, etc.

- *Syntactic modules* solve fill-in-the-blank-type clues.

Exact Match

This CWDB-specific module returns all targets of the correct length associated with this clue in the CWDB. Confidence is based on a Bayesian calculation.

Of the 70 clues in the puzzle, 18 clues (25.7%) appeared before in the CWDB. Of these, 11 (15.7%) appeared with targets of the correct length. This is actually fairly low—average puzzles tend to have closer to 30% of their clues in the database. Of these, six appear with the correct answer, shown in bold:

clue	found
Cut off: `isolated`	amputate
Pal of Pooh: `tigger`	eeyore
Fruitless: `arid`	vain (2)
Corporate image: `logo`	**logo**
Highball ingredient: `rye`	**rye**, ice
Transfix: `impale`	**impale**
Tortellini topping: `marinara`	parmesan
"Rouen Cathedral" painter: `monet`	**monet**
Nothing _____: `less`	toit
Key material: `ebony`	**ebony**, ivory
Like mud: `oozy`	**oozy**

Transformations

Another CWDB-specific module learns a set of textual transformations which, when applied to clue-target pairs in the CWDB, generates other clue-target pairs in the database. When faced with a new clue, it applies all applicable transformations and returns the results, weighted based on the previous precision/recall of these transformations. For example, from pairs of clues like Nymph pursuer: `satyr` and Nymph chaser: `satyr`, the module learns that clues with the word "pursuer" can be often be changed to "chaser" without affecting the meaning. For example:

clue	found
Bugs chaser: `elmer`	Bugs pursuer
Rushes: `hies`	Hurries
Pickle: `jam`	Predicament
Statue base: `plinth`	Statue stand

Partial Match

This module combines the vector space model of information retrieval with the data in the CWDB:

clue	found
Monk's head: `abbot`	Monk's superior
Playwright/novelist Capek: `karel`	Playwright Capek
Bad atmosphere: `miasma`	Poisonous atmosphere
The end of Plato?: `omega`	The end in Athens
TV captain: `kirk`	Spock's captain

Dijkstra Modules

The Dijkstra modules were inspired by the intuition that related words either co-occur with one another or co-occur with similar words. This suggests a measure of relatedness based on graph distance. From a selected set of text databases, the module builds a weighted directed graph on the set of all terms. For databases, we used an encyclopedia index, two thesauri, a database of wordforms and the CWDB. Example clues:

clue	path to target
Trigger, for one: `palomino`	trigger $\rightarrow$ palominos
Ace place?: `sleeve`	ace
Deadly desire: `envy`	deadly $\rightarrow$ deadlies, desire
4:00 service: `teaset`	service
Warner of Hollywood: `oland`	warner
Onetime electronics giant: `itt`	electronics, giant
Kind of coal or coat: `pea`	coal, coat
Meadowsweet: `spiraea`	meadowsweet

Movie

The Internet Movie Database (`www.imdb.com`) is an online resource with a wealth of information about all manner of movies and T.V. shows. This module looks for a number of patterns in the clue. Two clues in the example puzzle could have been answered by the movie module: Princess in Woolf's "Orlando": `sasha`, and "The Thief of Baghdad" role: `abu`.

Synonyms

Using Roget's thesaurus and the online thesaurus wordnet, PROVERB solves "synonym" type clues: Fruitless: `arid`, Now and again: `attimes`, Chop-chop: `APACE`.

Fill-in-the-Blanks

Over five percent of all clues in CWDB have a blank in them. We searched a variety of databases to find clue patterns with a missing word (music, geography, movies, literary and quotes). For example: "Heavens _____!": `above`.

Acknowledgements

PROVERB was developed by the Duke Crossword Team: Sushant Agarwal, Catherine M. Cheves, Joseph Fitzgerald, Jason Grosland, Fan Jiang, Shannon Pollard, Karl Weinmeister, and the authors. We received help and guidance from other members of the Duke Community: Michael Fulkerson, Mark Peot, Robert Duvall, Fred Horch, Siddhartha Chatterjee, Geoff Cohen, Steve Ruby, Nabil H. Mustafa, Alan Biermann, Donald Loveland, Gert Webelhuth, Robert Vila, Sam Dwarakanath, Will Portnoy, Michail Lagoudakis, Steve Majercik, Syam Gadde. Via e-mail, Will Shortz and William Tunstall-Pedoe made considerable contributions.

References

Ginsberg, M. L.; Frank, M.; Halpin, M. P.; and Torrance, M. C. 1990. Search lessons learned from crossword puzzles. In *Proceedings of the Eighth National Conference on Artificial Intelligence*, 210–215.

Mackworth, A. K. 1977. Consistency in networks of relations. *Artificial Intelligence* 8(1):99–118.

Shortz, W., ed. 1990. *American Championship Crosswords*. Fawcett Columbine.

Worldwide Aeronautical Route Planner

Charles B. McVey   **David P. Clements**   **Barton C. Massey**   **Andrew J. Parkes**

Computational Intelligence Research Laboratory
University of Oregon
Eugene, OR 97403-1269
{mcvey, clements, bart, parkes}@cirl.uoregon.edu

Introduction

We consider the common problem of calculating routes from a starting point to a destination through a given space. This process typically involves discretizing the navigational space into a graph of intermediate waypoints linked together through transitions. A search for a solution that fits desired criteria can then be performed. Typical criteria include: minimum distance, minimum transit time, minimum fuel use, and maximum agent safety.

Our work in this area focuses on the rapid determination of minimal fuel routes for aircraft to fly from any source point to any destination point on the earth. The Worldwide Aeronautical Route Planner (WARP) is our prototype demonstration of technology developed to perform optimal real-time (under one minute per route) flight planning. WARP uses high-fidelity aircraft flight models, standard rules of flight operation, actual time-dependent worldwide weather data, and a variant of A* (Multi-Pass A*) which retains A*'s completeness and optimality properties. WARP discovers the flight plan that guarantees minimal use of fuel. Typical routes are generated by WARP in under thirty seconds, with fuel savings on the order of one to eight percent compared to great circle (minimum distance) routes.

Modeling

WARP's model of airspace represents aircraft position (in time, altitude, and latitude/longitude coordinates) as well as weather. In direct flight, with no zones of avoidance or predefined airways which must be followed, the USAF Air Mobility Command's (AMC) standard operating procedure (SOP) allows aircraft to change heading only when over integral latitude/longitude points in which either the latitude is evenly divisible by five or the longitude is evenly divisible by ten. The route generated by WARP must conform to this restriction, leading to a waypoint discretization of five degree by ten degree zones upon the surface of the earth. On the borders of these sections, every integral degree point is a potential waypoint for

WARP to consider during its search. Depending upon whether a waypoint is located on a five degree latitude line, ten degree longitude line, or an intersection of the two, the number of two dimensional neighbors for that waypoint will be forty, fifty, or sixty respectively.

Transitions in altitude are allowed among eighteen discrete levels, and are subject to another SOP rule: an aircraft may only change its altitude if it has flown at least 400 miles since its last altitude change. This has the benefit of restricting the search space. The aircraft performance models also restrict altitude changes by not allowing the aircraft to ascend or descend at a rate which is not physically possible, or to ascend to an altitude which the aircraft at current weight is not capable of reaching.

Weather representation within WARP is discretized into cells. Each cell is 2.5 degrees in latitude by 2.5 degrees in longitude, and contains the temperature, wind direction, and wind speed for a specific altitude at a specific point in time. Forecast data are available covering fifteen different altitude ranges at ten different times over a three day period. Since the weather cells are of different size than, and offset from, the latitude/longitude and altitude discretized grid, weather effects are calculated using a weighted interpolation scheme during the search.

Multi-Pass A*

A* is a well-known and well-studied best-first search algorithm (Hart, Nilsson, and Raphael 1968). It typically searches outward from the starting node until it reaches the goal node. At each step the current fringe node with the minimum combined actual cost from the start to the fringe node plus expected remaining cost (the heuristic cost) to get from the fringe node to the goal node is expanded. If the heuristic always underestimates the cost from any node to the goal, then it is said to be admissible, and A* will find the optimal solution. However, if the heuristic is too optimistic then A* will expand too many nodes and may run out of time before a solution is found. If the heuristic is pessimistic then a solution will likely be found quickly, but it will almost certainly be suboptimal. In this work, we must generate optimal routes as quickly as possible, so our heuristic function must be optimistic, but as close to the real cost to the goal as possible.

Most A* work has assumed that the cost of evaluating an edge in the search graph is minimal, and that the primary goal is to expand as few nodes as possible. However, in realistically modeled flight planning problems, the number of nodes is relatively small (on the order of one quarter million), but the cost of evaluating edges is extremely expensive. We therefore seek to keep the number of expensive edge evaluations done to a minimum. This is related, but not identical, to minimizing the number of nodes expanded.

Fortunately, a "cheap" heuristic is available to guide the search; it assumes that the remaining distance from a node to the goal will be flown under the best weather conditions that can possibly be reached on the current flight. The heuristic is admissible, but is typically optimistic by approximately twenty percent. While the heuristic successfully prunes much of the search space, using it with A* and the exact flight performance models still requires excessive computation time; it needs to be less optimistic.

To overcome this problem, we developed and implemented a two-pass version of A* (Multi-Pass A*) which uses approximate, cached "cheap heuristic" flight performance values during an initial *backward* pass (it searches from the destination to the point of departure), and exact values during a final *forward* pass. We determine the initial time and fuel weight for the backward search by first "flying" a great circle route from the origin to destination and using the resulting time and weight at arrival.

During the backwards search, we *decrement* time and *increment* fuel in the aircraft. The cost of flying backwards from the destination to each waypoint is recorded as the new heuristic estimate for the cost to reach the destination from that particular waypoint. Nodes are expanded in minimum cost order, with the total great-circle-route cost serving as a bound to prune those nodes with a larger cost plus heuristic estimate (Dijkstra 1959). The results of this initial backward pass then guide a second, much tighter, forward pass. In this forward search, we utilize the expensive exact flight-model equations. However, far fewer nodes are explored since the heuristic values were well tightened by the backward seeding.

This approach does not decrease the number of edges evaluated, but it greatly reduces the average cost of edge evaluation. The majority (typically over eighty percent) of nodes expanded during the entire search process are expanded during the backward pass in which cheaper approximate values are used. As a result, the forward search runs in a fraction of the time taken by the backward search, despite its use of expensive performance models.

The existing system for route planning in use by the AMC employs search that is bounded by a narrow window around the great circle route. This approach can obviously never guarantee to find optimal solutions. In comparisons with WARP in which the optimal route was near the great circle, both systems produce similar results. However, in many cases WARP finds optimal routes that deviate enough from the great circle that the existing system's search method never discovered them. The improvements in these cases translate into enormous savings when one considers the amount of fuel used by the AMC annually.

The Demonstration

WARP's user interface displays a plot of the earth's surface, allowing the user point-and-click selection of source and destination coordinates, as well as straightforward specification of departure time, starting fuel (or ending fuel), and payload weight. The user may also pick a variety of different search strategies, including multi-pass A* or single pass A*, and use of approximate or exact aircraft modeling values. During route generation, the display first shows the nodes expanded by the backward bounded Dijkstra pass, followed by the nodes expanded by the highly optimized forward A* search.

After route generation, the solution is displayed along with the great-circle-route from source to destination, allowing easy visual comparison. Statistics are also presented, including the fuel usage and distance traveled along both the optimal and the great-circle routes, the CPU time required to generate the solution, and the number of nodes and edges expanded during each phase of the search.

The route consists of a list of waypoints and headings to follow during the flight, along with information such as time, altitude, and fuel load at each waypoint. A list of waypoints is shown in a list panel on the display, and an altitude profile for the flight is shown in the bottom panel of the interface. The user may click on various parts of the display to solicit detailed information about the solution.

Acknowledgments

We wish to thank the members of CIRL for their suggestions and support. We also thank Majors Adrian Hayes and Mark Weiser (USAF) and John Will (NCI) for sharing expertise in this domain. Efforts sponsored by DARPA and AFRL, Air Force Materiel Command, USAF, under agreement number F30602-95-1-0294. The U.S. Government is authorized to reproduce and distribute reprints for Governmental purposes notwithstanding any copyright annotation thereon. The views and conclusions contained herein are those of the authors and should not be interpreted as necessarily representing the official policies or endorsements, either expressed or implied, of DARPA, AFRL, or the U.S. Government.

References

Dijkstra, E. 1959. A note on two problems in connection with graphs. *Numerische Mathematik* 1:269-271.

Hart, P., Nilsson, N., and Raphael, B. 1968. A formal basis for the heuristic determination of minimum cost paths. *IEEE Transactions on SCC* 4:100-107.

Authoring New Material in a Reading Tutor that Listens

Jack Mostow and Gregory Aist

Project LISTEN
4910 Forbes Ave., LTI
Carnegie Mellon University
Pittsburgh, Pennsylvania 15213
mostow@cs.cmu.edu

Abstract

Project LISTEN's Reading Tutor helps children learn to read by providing assisted practice in reading connected text. A key goal is to provide assistance for reading any English text entered by students or adults. This live demonstration shows how the Reading Tutor helps users enter and narrate stories, and then helps children read them.

Areas: intelligent interfaces, computer-aided instruction, dialog, speech recognition

Why Authoring?

Project LISTEN's Reading Tutor listens to children read aloud. In an intelligent tutor for reading, why should students write? Writing as a part of intensive reading interventions such as Reading Recovery (Clay 1985) is believed to help students succeed at reading (Pinnell et al. 1994) and learning vocabulary (Gipe & Arnold 1978). Writing stories for other students to read can be motivational as well. In addition, students may more easily learn to read from stories written in familiar language styles (Serwer 1969), such as stories written by older schoolmates. Finally, allowing teachers to enter instructional material would allow the Reading Tutor to be more tightly integrated into the classroom.

Why narrate stories? The Reading Tutor eschews synthesized speech – used in Kurzweil's (1999) reading system – in favor of recorded human voices, which are much more expressive. Martin Luther King's stirring delivery of his "I Have a Dream" speech – an oft-chosen Reading Tutor selection – conveys this point dramatically. This preference induces a requirement to capture human narrations, especially in the author's own voice.

Writing a New Story

Adding a story starts with an Edit window (Figure 1) with initial text "My Story, by <FirstName> <LastInitial>." This box is a standard Windows editor, into which the user can type, or paste copied text.

The Edit window also gives young writers rudimentary spoken help. When the user types a letter, the Reading Tutor speaks it. When the user ends a word with a space or other punctuation, the Reading Tutor speaks the word. To accommodate variations in typing ability, the "talking typewriter" is speed sensitive. A letter or word is spoken only if the user hesitates before typing more. Thus only very slow typing (such as a child's) elicits letter names. Fluent typing with pauses between words speaks just the words. Rapid typing suppresses speech output.

Narrating the New Story

When the user leaves Edit after typing in or editing a story, the Reading Tutor enters narration mode (Figure 2). This mode differs from normal tutoring mode because its goal is to capture a fluent reading of the sentence, without substitutions, deletions, long hesitations, self-corrections, or other insertions. If the output of the speech recognizer matches the sentence perfectly, the Reading Tutor echoes the reading and goes on to display the next sentence. Otherwise, the Reading Tutor asks the user to read it again. This cycle repeats until the Reading Tutor accepts the sentence or the reader clicks *Go* (Figure 2) to proceed without narrating the sentence. At any time, the user can click *Back* to return to a previous sentence and re-record it.

Besides capturing sentence narrations, the Reading Tutor needs to capture individual words not previously recorded. The Reading Tutor uses the time alignment output by the speech recognizer to excerpt the segment of the recording corresponding to each unrecorded word. The time alignment is not always correct. Fortunately, the Reading Tutor already has high-quality recordings of hundreds of the most common words. Thus the remaining unrecorded words tend to be longer content words that get aligned more accurately than shorter words. To further reduce the effect of poor alignment, the Reading Tutor uses such captured word recordings only for the story where they are recorded, and not in other stories.

The *Edit Text* button displayed during narration mode lets the user return to the Edit window to modify the text. When the user leaves Edit, the Reading Tutor returns to narration mode, starting at the first unnarrated sentence.

Figure 1. Write (Edit).   **Figure 2. Narrate.**   **Figure 3. Read.**

The *Edit Media* button lets the user find a picture (using a standard file browser) to illustrate the current sentence.

When the user reaches the end of the story, the Reading Tutor leaves narration mode and returns to its menu of stories, which now include the narrated story.

Reading the New Story

The new story is now available for children to select and read. The Reading Tutor presents one sentence at a time, graying out earlier text (Figure 3). Listening with continuous, open-mike speech recognition, the Reading Tutor visibly shadows the word it expects to hear next, and tracks student performance, turning words green that it accepts as read correctly.

The Reading Tutor gives help on a word or sentence when the student clicks for help, gets stuck, makes a mistake, or is considered likely to misread a difficult word [Aist & Mostow, CALL97; Mostow & Aist, CALICO99]. The Reading Tutor may also backchannel after a brief silence, give praise for good or improved reading, go on to the next sentence when appropriate, or suggest what to click.

The Reading Tutor is designed to help the student read any input English text, making use of resources when they are available, and fallbacks when they are not. The narrated sentences and words are key resources.

For example, the Reading Tutor's most common intervention is to read a sentence aloud by playing its recorded narration. This intervention exploits the expressiveness of the human narration.

The time alignment captured in the narration process has several uses. The alignment lets the Reading Tutor highlight successive words as it reads a sentence. The alignment also allows the Reading Tutor to "recue" a word by rereading the words that lead up to it, and then underlining the word to prompt the student to reread it. The alignment lets the Reading Tutor extract in-context recordings of individual words from the sentence. This capability is especially useful when the Reading Tutor has no recording of the word in isolation. It also addresses the issue of homonyms (different words spelled the same) by providing the context-appropriate pronunciation to use.

If a sentence was not narrated, the Reading Tutor falls back on reading the sentence word by word. This intervention lacks expressiveness, but retains the quality of human speech. Finally, if a word is not recorded, the Reading Tutor uses a synthesizer to speak it. The Reading Tutor also uses a synthesizer to guess a pronunciation to listen for in the speech recognizer if a word is not in the pronunciation dictionary.

Word help may include saying the word, recuing the word, sounding or spelling it out, splitting it (visibly and audibly) into syllables, giving a rhyming hint, or (if available) displaying a picture or playing a sound effect.

Acknowledgements

This research is supported in part by the National Science Foundation (NSF) under Grants No. IRI-9505156 and CDA-9616546 and by the second author's NSF and Harvey Fellowships. Any opinions, findings, conclusions, or recommendations expressed in this publication are those of the author(s) and do not necessarily reflect the views of NSF or the official policies, either expressed or implied, of the sponsors or of the United States Government.

References

(For Project LISTEN publication references, please see the list of publications at http://www.cs.cmu.edu/~listen.)

Clay, M. 1985. *The Early Detection of Reading Difficulties.* (Third ed.) Portsmouth, NH: Heinemann.

Gipe, J.P., and Arnold, R.D.. 1978. Teaching vocabulary through familiar associations and contexts. Journal of Reading Behavior 11(3): 281-285.

Kurzweil Educational Systems, Inc. 1999. Kurzweil 3000. http://www.kurzweiledu.com/kurzweil3000.html

Pinnell, G. S., Lyons, C. A., DeFord, D. E., Bryk, A. S., and Seltzer, M. 1994. Comparing instructional models for the literacy education of high-risk first graders. Reading Research Quarterly 29(1), pp. 8-39.

Serwer, B. L. 1969. Linguistic support for a method of teaching beginning reading to black children. Reading Research Quarterly 4(4): 449-467, Summer 1969.

Demonstration of Rational Communicative Behavior in Coordinated Defense

Sanguk Noh and **Piotr J. Gmytrasiewicz**
Department of Computer Science and Engineering
University of Texas at Arlington
{noh, piotr}@cse.uta.edu

Introduction

The primary goal of our demonstration is to show results we obtained on communication among artificial and human agents interacting in a simulated air defense domain. For artificial agents, we advocate a decision-theoretic message selection mechanism which maximizes the expected utility of the communicative actions. Thus, the agents compute the expected utility of alternative communicative behaviors, and execute the one with the highest value (Noh & Gmytrasiewicz 1999). Following the principle of maximizing the expected utility, our agents are intended to be rational in their communicative behavior; they send only the most valuable messages, and never send messages they consider to be damaging given the circumstances at hand.

In the anti-air defense the agents, human or artificial, are coordinating their defense actions, in this case interception of threats, with other defense agents. The goal of defending agents is to minimize damages to their territory. To fulfill their mission, the agents need to coordinate and, sometimes, to communicate with other agents. However, since the communication bandwidth is usually limited in a battlefield environment, it is more valuable for a defending agent to be selective as to what messages should be sent to other agents. Endowing the agents with a decision-theoretic method to choose their own communicative behavior given a situation at hand frees our agents from depending on communication protocols, frequently advocated in other work. We feel that relying on protocols drawn up beforehand could lock the agents into suboptimal behavior in unpredictable domain like the battlefield, in which situations that were not foreseen by the designer are likely to occur.

Our approach uses the Recursive Modeling Method proposed before in (Gmytrasiewicz & Durfee 1995). RMM endows an agent with a compact specialized representation of other agents' beliefs, abilities, and intentions. As such, it allows the agent to predict the message's decision-theoretic (DT) pragmatics, i.e., how a particular message will change the decision-making situation of the agents, and how the other agents are

likely to react to it. We propose that modeling other agents while communicating is crucial; clearly, without a model of the other agents' states of beliefs it would be impossible to properly assess the impact of the communicative act on these beliefs (Cohen & Levesque 1990). Based on the message's DT pragmatics, our method quantifies the gain obtained due to the message as the increase in expected utility obtained as a result of the interaction.

Our demonstration consists of our RMM and human agents interacting in two different air defense scenarios in cases when communication is, and is not, available. We will show how communication can benefit the agents in coordination tasks, and compare performance of RMM and human agents.

Demonstration Settings

In our implementation, the anti-air defense simulator with communication was written in Common LISP and built on top of the MICE simulator. Our demonstration is intended to compare the performance achieved by RMM team with that of human team, with and without communication, in two different scenarios.

In the anti-air defense domain, two defense units are faced with an attack by seven incoming missiles, as depicted in Figure 1. The warhead sizes of missiles are 470, 410, 350, 370, 420, 450, and 430 unit for missiles A through G, respectively. The positions of defense units are fixed and those of missiles are randomly generated. Each of two defense units is assumed to be equipped with three interceptors, if they are not incapacitated. Thus, they can launch one interceptor at a given state, and do it three times during a course of one defense episode.

For all settings, each defense unit is initially assumed to have the following uncertainties (beliefs) in its knowledge base:

- The other battery is fully functional and has both long- and short-range interceptors with probability 60%;

- The other battery is operational and has only long-range interceptors with probability 20% (In this case,

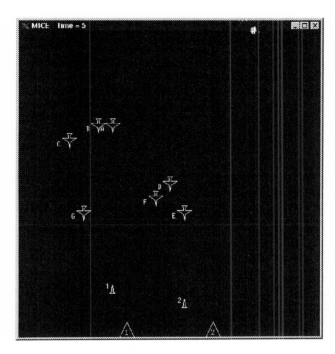

Figure 1: A complex air defense scenario.

it can shoot down only distant missiles, which are higher than a specific altitude.);

- The other battery has been incapacitated by enemy fire with probability 10%;

- The other battery is unknown with probability 10%.

In each demonstrated scenario we allow for one-way communication at a time between defense units. Thus, if both agents want to send messages, the speaker is randomly picked in the RMM team, and the human team flips a coin to determine who will be allowed to talk. The listener is silent and can only receive messages. Each of human subjects is presented with the scenarios, and is given a description of what is known and what is uncertain in each case. They are then asked to indicate which of the 11 messages is the most appropriate in each case. In all of the anti-air defense scenarios, each battery is assumed to have a choice of the following communicative behaviors:

- "No communication."
- "I'll intercept missile *A*."
...
- "I'll intercept missile *G*."
- "I have both long- and short-range interceptors."
- "I have only long-range interceptors."
- "I'm incapacitated."

Given the uncertainties and the communicative behaviors, we set up two different scenarios. For each scenario, RMM and human agents intercept incoming targets with and without communication, respectively.

We demonstrate their target selection sequences in all settings by retrieving them from http://dali.uta.edu.

To evaluate the quality of the agents' performance, we express the results in terms of (1) the number of selected targets, i.e., targets the defense units attempted to intercept, and (2) the total expected damage to friendly forces after all six interceptors were launched. The total expected damage is defined as a sum of the residual warhead sizes of the attacking missiles. Thus, if a missile was targeted for interception, then it contributed $\{(1 - probability\_of\_hit) \times warhead\_size\}$ to the total damage. If a missile was not targeted, it contributed all of its warhead size value to the damage.

Conclusion

Our demonstration presents the implementation and evaluation of the decision-theoretic message selection used by automated agents coordinating in an anti-air defense domain. When the communication requires valuable bandwidth resources, our message prioritization method can be useful for agents coordinating in a military situation by allowing them to determine the expected utility value for each possible communicative act.

We measure the increase in performance achieved by rational communicative behavior in the RMM team, and compare it to the performance of the human-controlled defense batteries. The results are intuitive: as expected, communication improves the coordinated performance achieved by the teams. An interesting aspect of the demonstration is that it shows the differences between the communicative behaviors exhibited by RMM and human agents. While human communicative behaviors are often similar to those selected by the RMM agents, there are telling differences that, in our experimental runs, allow the RMM team to achieve a slightly better performance. It may be that the differences in processing of probabilistic information about the uncertainties involved explain why decision making achieved by artificial agents tends to be somewhat superior to that of human agents.

References

Cohen, P. R., and Levesque, H. J. 1990. Rational interaction as the basis for communication. In Cohen, P. R.; Morgan, J.; and Pollack, M. E., eds., *Intentions in Communication*. MIT Press.

Gmytrasiewicz, P. J., and Durfee, E. H. 1995. A rigorous, operational formalization of recursive modeling. In *Proceedings of the First International Conference on Multi-Agent Systems*, 125–132. Menlo Park: AAAI Press/The MIT Press.

Noh, S., and Gmytrasiewicz, P. J. 1999. Implementation and evaluation of rational communicative behavior in coordinated defense. To appear in *Proceedings of the Third International Conference on Autonomous Agents*, Seattle, Washington.

Automated Team Analysis

Taylor Raines, Milind Tambe, Stacy Marsella

Information Sciences Institute and University of Southern California
4676 Admiralty Way, Suite 1001
Marina del Rey, CA 90292, USA
{Raines, Tambe, Marsella}@isi.edu

An interesting problem that AI researchers face today is that of constructing experts that can recognize and analyze team behavior and provide advice to improve it. Team analysis is critical to many areas of research, such as the evaluation of human teams as well as evaluation of alternative designs of synthetic agent teams. In particular, evaluation of synthetic agent teamwork is a critical requirement as agent teams are employed across an increasing range of multi-agent synthetic environments, including such diverse application areas as virtual environments for training, interactive entertainment, multi-robotic space missions, and simulated synthetic air combat. In the RoboCup synthetic agent environment, a research environment based on the team sport of soccer, teamwork among the synthetic player agents is clearly fundamental, and as such makes an excellent test bed for our research.

We have created an agent for analyzing and improving synthetic teams. The agent is built in a bottom-up fashion using little specific domain knowledge. In lieu of extensive domain knowledge, data mining and inductive learning techniques are used in an attempt to isolate the key issues determining the successes or failures of these teams. This approach has been applied to the RoboCup domain, with a current focus on analyzing shots on goal and with future plans for assists, passing, and general teamwork.

Figure 1: ISAAC online at http://coach.isi.edu

ISAAC is our web-based off-line soccer expert that uses automated analysis to aid in improving a team's behavior (See Figure 1). ISAAC approaches the analysis problem by investigating actions that did not produce the desired result and then classifying the contexts in which failures occurred. Based on that classification, ISAAC recommends changes in behavior to avoid the failures: either the team should perform a different action in that context or should perform the action in a modified context. More specifically, ISAAC's analysis starts with logs of a particular team's games. From the logs, ISAAC extracts interesting behaviors and the outcomes of those behaviors. For instance, shots on goal are interesting behaviors, so ISAAC gathers data on such shots, and whether they succeed. ISAAC then classifies these successes and failures into subclasses with similar contexts. An example subclass might be all shots on goal that fail when an opponent is nearby. Currently, C4.5 is used to induce these subclasses by generating rules that classify the successes and failures of the shooting team.

ISAAC's next step is to formulate suggestions that may improve the team's performance, once again using a knowledge-lean approach. To that end, ISAAC formulates and analyzes perturbations of the rules. Each rule consists of a number of conditions that must be satisfied for the rule to be valid. We define a perturbation to be the rule that results from reversing one condition. The successes and failures governed by the perturbations of a rule are examined to determine which conditions have the most effect in changing the outcome of the original rule, turning a failure into a success.

More recently, ISAAC has been extended to analyze sequences of behaviors, such as sequences of actions (e.g., passes) that lead up to successes or failures. This analysis has revealed that out of the top four teams of RoboCup'97, ISIS is at one extreme with little or no emergent pattern of assists, while CMUnited shows deeper patterns of assists and passing. In analyzing agent behavior in complex multi-agent dynamic environments, the approach of using knowledge poor data-driven analysis techniques combined with human oversight has shown considerable promise.

eMediator: a Next Generation Electronic Commerce Server

Tuomas Sandholm[*]
sandholm@cs.wustl.edu
Department of Computer Science
Washington University
St. Louis, MO 63130

Abstract

eMediator, a next generation electronic commerce server, demonstrates ways in which AI, algorithmic support, game theoretic incentive engineering, and GUI design can jointly improve the efficiency of ecommerce.

The first component, *eAuctionHouse*, is a configurable auction house that supports a large variety of parameterizable auction types. It supports generalized combinatorial auctions with new algorithms for winner determination. It also allows bidding via graphically drawn price-quantity graphs. It has an expert system for helping the user decide which auction type to use. Finally, it supports mobile software agents that bid optimally on the user's behalf based on game theoretic analyses.

The second component, *eCommitter*, is a leveled commitment contract optimizer. In automated negotiation systems consisting of self-interested agents, contracts have traditionally been binding. Leveled commitment contracts—i.e. contracts where each party can decommit by paying a predetermined penalty—were recently shown to improve Pareto efficiency even if agents rationally decommit in Nash equilibrium using inflated thresholds on how good their outside offers must be before they decommit. *eCommitter* solves the Nash equilibrium thresholds. Furthermore, it optimizes the contract price and decommitment penalties themselves.

1 Introduction

Electronic commerce is taking off rapidly, but the full power of AI, algorithmic support, and game theoretic tools has not been harnessed to improve its efficiency. This paper presents *eMediator*, a next generation electronic commerce server that demonstrates ways in which these techniques can improve ecommerce both in terms of processes and outcomes. The result of our 2-year implementation effort is now available for use on the web at http://ecommerce.cs.wustl.edu/emediator/, see also (Sandholm 1999b). The components of *eMediator* include an auction house and a leveled commitment contract optimizer.

2 *eAuctionHouse*: A configurable auction

Several successful Internet auction sites exist such as eBay and OnSale. Our motivation to develop an auction server, *eAuctionHouse*, was to prototype next generation features, and to test their feasibility computationally and in terms of user comfort. *eAuctionHouse* allows users across the Internet to buy and sell goods as well as to set up auctions. It is a third party site, so both sellers and buyers can trust that it executes the

auction protocols as stated. To our knowledge, it is the first—and currently only—Internet auction that supports combinatorial auctions, bidding via graphically drawn price-quantity graphs, and by mobile agents.

2.1 Combinatorial auctions

Usually, items are auctioned independently. If a bidder has preferences over combinations of items (as is common e.g. in electricity markets, equities trading, bandwidth auctions, and transportation exchanges (Sandholm 1993)), bidding is difficult. To determine how to bid on an item, the bidder needs to speculate which other items she will receive in other auctions. This introduces counterspeculation cost, and often leads to inefficient allocations where bidders fail to get the combinations they want and get ones they do not.

Combinatorial auctions can be used to overcome the need for lookahead and the inefficiencies, see e.g. (Sandholm 1993). In a combinatorial auction, bidders may place bids on combinations of items. This allows the bidders to express complementarities between items instead of having to speculate into an item's valuation the impact of possibly getting other items. *eAuctionHouse* supports a variety of combinatorial auctions:

OR-bids In the most commonly discussed combinatorial auction protocol, each bidder can bid on combinations of items, and her bids are joined with OR, i.e. any number of her bids can be accepted. Determining the winners so as to maximize the auctioneer's revenue is $\mathcal{NP}$-complete and inapproximable. *eAuctionHouse* tackles this via an optimal search algorithm that capitalizes on the fact that the space of bids is necessarily sparsely populated in practice (Sandholm 1999a).

XOR-bids OR-bids are based on the common assumption that the bids are superadditive: $b_i(S \cup S') \geq b_i(S) + b_i(S')$. But what happens if agent 1 bids $b_1(\{1\}) = 5$, $b_1(\{2\}) = 4$, and $b_1(\{1,2\}) = 7$, and there are no other bidders? The auctioneer could allocate items 1 and 2 to agent 1 separately, and that agent's bid for the combination would value at $5+4 = 9$ instead of 7. So, OR-bids focus on situations where combinational bids are introduced to capture positive complementarities among items. In many real world settings local subadditivities can occur as well. To address this, the bidders in *eAuctionHouse* can submit *XOR-bids*, i.e. bids on combinations such that only one of the combinations can get accepted. This allows the bidders to express general preferences with both positive and negative complementarities.

OR-XOR-bids While XOR-bids allow the bidder to express general preferences, in the worst case this would

---

[*]This material is based upon work supported by the National Science Foundation under CAREER Award IRI-9703122, Grant IRI-9610122, and Grant IIS-9800994.

involve placing a bid for each of the $2^{\#items} - 1$ possible combinations. *eAuctionHouse* allows the user to submit multiple XOR-bids. We do this in table form, where each row is a combinational bid, and the rows are combined with XOR. These multiple bids are combined together with a non-exclusive OR. We do this by allowing the user to submit multiple tables. This method maintains full expressive capability, is a more natural way to input preferences, and leads to shorter input descriptions than XOR-bids only.

Other generalizations of combinatorial auctions *eAuctionHouse* also allows combinatorial double auctions, and combinatorial auctions where the agents can bid for multiple units of each item in a combination.

2.2 Bidding via price-quantity graphs
Price-quantity graphs are supported so bidders can express continuous preferences. E.g. when bidding for a larger quantity, one might only accept a lower unit price.

2.3 Support for choosing an auction type
eAuctionHouse supports a wide variety of auction types and helps the user choose an appropriate one. First, only auction types that are sensible based on game theoretic analyses or economics experiments are offered. Second, there is an expert system that restricts the choice of auction types given the auction setting. For any given auction setting, it tells the user what bid types should be acceptable, what price determination schemes should be chosen among, etc. The auction setting differs based on whether it is a single or double auction, whether there is one or multiple items, and whether there is one or multiple units of each item. Furthermore, the units can be divisible or indivisible. The bid types include a regular price bid, a price-quantity graph bid, an OR-bid, and an OR-XOR-bid. The pricing schemes include first-price, Vickrey, multi-unit Vickrey, Groves, and middle-price. The auctions in *eAuctionHouse* also have several other parameters.

2.4 *NOMAD*: Mobile agents in auctions
Our auction house supports mobile agents so that a user can have her agent actively participating in the auction while she is disconnected. Mobile agents that execute on the agent dock which is on (or near) the host machine of the auction server also reduce the network latency—a key advantage in time-critical bidding. Our auction server uses the Concordia agent dock to provide mobile agents a safe execution platform from where they can monitor the auctions, bid, set up auctions, move to other hosts, etc. The user has the full flexibility of Java programming at her disposal when designing her agent. We also provide an HTML interface for non-programmers where the user can specify what she wants her agent to do, and the system automatically generates the Java code for the corresponding mobile agent, and launches it. Some of these predesigned agents are alerting tools, others bid optimally on the user's behalf based on game theoretic analyses. This helps put novice bidders on an equal footing with experts.

3 *eCommitter*
Normal full commitment contracts are unable to take advantage of the possibilities that future events provide. Although a contract may be profitable to an agent when viewed *ex ante*, it need not be profitable when viewed after some future events have occurred. Similarly, a contract may have too low expected payoff, but in some realizations of the future events it may be desirable.

Leveled commitment contracts are a method for capitalizing on uncertain future events. Instead of conditioning the contract on future events, the level of commitment is controlled by decommitment penalties, one for each agent. If an agent wants to decommit—i.e. to be freed from the contract obligations—it can do so by paying the penalty to the other party.

Rational agents are reluctant in decommitting because there is a chance that the other party will decommit, in which case the former agent gets freed from the contract, does not have to pay a penalty, and collects a penalty from the breacher. (Sandholm & Lesser 1996) showed that despite such insincere decommitting, leveled commitment increases each contract party's expected payoff, and enables contracts in settings where no full commitment contract is beneficial to all parties. Given a contract and the probability distributions of the agent's outside offers (or analogously of the agents' future valuations of the contract), our *eCommitter* system computes the Nash equilibria, i.e. decommitting threshold pairs such that neither agent wants to change its decommitting strategy given that the other party does not change. The algorithm is conceptually highly nontrivial, but fast (Sandholm, Sikka, & Norden 1999). *eCommitter* also computes each agent's decommitting probability and expected payoff.

Furthermore, given no contract, but only the distributions of outside offers, *eCommitter* computes the welfare maximizing contracts (price and penalties). It gives a range of optimal contracts that are individually rational for both parties, and suggests the fair contract.

References
Sandholm, T., and Lesser, V. 1996. Advantages of a leveled commitment contracting protocol. In *AAAI*, 126–133.

Sandholm, T.; Sikka, S.; and Norden, S. 1999. Algorithms for optimizing leveled commitment contracts. In *IJCAI*. Extended version: Washington University, Dept. of Computer Science WUCS-99-02.

Sandholm, T. 1993. An implementation of the contract net protocol based on marginal cost calculations. In *AAAI*, 256–262.

Sandholm, T. 1999a. An algorithm for optimal winner determination in combinatorial auctions. In *IJCAI*. Extended version: Washington University, Dept. of Computer Science WUCS-99-01.

Sandholm, T. 1999b. *eMediator*: A next generation electronic commerce server. WUCS-99-02, Washington University, Dept. of Computer Science.

MailCat: An Intelligent Assistant for Organizing E-Mail

Richard B. Segal and Jeffrey O. Kephart

IBM Thomas J. Watson Research Center
Yorktown Heights, NY 10598
rsegal@watson.ibm.com, kephart@watson.ibm.com

Abstract

MailCat is an intelligent assistant that helps users organize their e-mail into folders. It uses a text classifier to learn each user's mail-filing habits. MailCat uses what it learns to predict the three folders in which the user is most likely to place each incoming message. It then provides shortcut buttons to file each message into one of these three folders. When one of MailCat's predictions is correct, the effort required to file a message is reduced to a single button click.

Introduction

Most mail readers allow users to organize their messages into folders to ease later retrieval. One might suppose that the effort required to file a message using these programs would be negligible. In practice, however, many users find the cognitive burden of deciding where to file a message plus the time spent interacting with the user interface to be a substantial barrier. This barrier is significant enough that many users quickly fall behind and let unfiled messages pile up in their mailboxes.

MailCat is an intelligent personal assistant that reduces the cognitive burden and the time required for organizing e-mail into folders (Segal and Kephart 1999). Using a text classifier that adapts dynamically to a user's mail-filing habits, it predicts the three folders that are most likely to be appropriate for a given message and provides shortcut buttons that facilitate filing that message into one of its predicted folders. When one of the folders predicted by MailCat is correct, the user's task is greatly simplified. Rather than having to derive a best choice from a large set of folders, the user can merely confirm one of MailCat's suggested choices using a single mouse click. Given that MailCat's prediction accuracy is roughly 80% to 90% even for users with as many as 60 folders, MailCat offers a qualitative enhancement that is likely to encourage users to file their mail.

MailCat offers these advantages without demanding anything in return. Users have nothing new to learn or do. When a user first installs MailCat, it analyzes their existing folders and constructs a text classifier that is tuned to that user's mail-filing behavior. Thereafter, the user may use the shortcut buttons, or may opt to use the standard message-filing interface if none of the suggested folders are appropriate. Regardless of whether its suggestions are accepted, MailCat updates its classifier promptly as each new message is filed.

MailCat

Figure 1 shows how MailCat simplifies the task of organizing messages. MailCat places three buttons above each message that allow the user to quickly file each message into one of the three folders it suggests. When one of the three buttons is clicked, the message is immediately moved to the indicated folder.

MailCat uses a text classifier to predict the likely destination folders for each message. MailCat builds its text classifier by learning from user actions. Maes (Maes 1994) suggests that it can take some time for a user to file enough messages for an e-mail assistant to learn a good classifier. Maes proposes collaborative learning as a solution to this problem in which each e-mail agent learns from other e-mail agents whose users have similar mail-filing habits. While this works well if one can find a user with similar mail-filing habits, finding such a user seems unlikely in practice given the diversity of mail-filing schemes.

An alternative solution is to learn from messages previously filed by the user. Most e-mail users already have a large database of previously-filed messages which can be used to bootstrap the text classifier — the messages currently stored in their folders. This database provides ample training data to get the classifier quickly up to speed. When MailCat is first installed, it reads the user's database of previously-filed messages and uses this information to train a TF-IDF text classifier. After this initial training, MailCat can immediately begin making useful predictions.

The initial training of the classifier is only half the battle. Users are constantly creating, deleting and reorganizing their folders. Even if the folders remain the same, the type of messages placed in a folder changes over time. MailCat adapts to changing conditions by using a classifier that supports incremental learning.

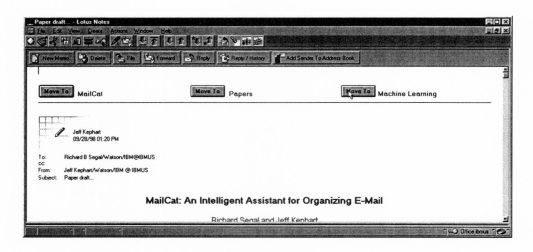

Figure 1: MailCat creates shortcut buttons for the three folders in which it predicts the user is most likely to place each message. When its predictions are correct, the user can file each message using a single button click.

Once the classifier has been trained, the classifier's model can be updated by presenting to it the messages that have been added or deleted from each folder. After updating, the classifier's predictions are indistinguishable from what they would have been had the classifier been trained from scratch on the entire mail database.

The low cost of incremental learning allows MailCat to update the classifier as the user interacts with their mail client. If the user creates a new folder and adds a few messages, MailCat instantly learns about the folder and can start predicting which messages are likely to be placed in the new folder.

While MailCat's use of three buttons rather than one may seem trivial, it is in fact quite significant because it substantially improves MailCat's usefulness. Our experimental results show that the use of three buttons cuts MailCat's failure rate in half without introducing any adverse side-effects. MailCat's use of three buttons is a direct result of our decision to provide an assistant that *facilitates* rather than *automates* message filing — a choice that itself arose from our emphasis on avoiding negative impacts on users. Since a message can be automatically filed in only one folder, automatic categorization systems have to rely solely on the accuracy of their first prediction.

Experiments

We evaluated MailCat by simulating its performance on the mailboxes of six real users. Table 1 shows the accuracy of MailCat for each user when providing from one to three shortcut buttons. The table also lists the number of folders in each user's mailbox because, as the number of folders increases, so does the difficulty of the classification problem. The accuracy of MailCat with N buttons is the frequency that one of the first N buttons it provides will move the message into the correct folder.

The results show that MailCat is fairly accurate with

User	# Folders	1	2	3
R. Segal	66	77.8	88.5	91.8
J. Kephart	56	59.8	72.8	80.2
User #3	43	64.9	78.1	84.8
User #4	34	65.9	75.7	81.1
User #5	15	70.1	88.1	93.6
User #6	14	81.1	94.4	98.1

Table 1: MailCat simulation results for six users.

just one button, achieving between 59.8% and 81.1% accuracy. MailCat improves its performance by simply providing more than one shortcut button. By using three buttons, MailCat improves its accuracy to 80.2% to 98.1% — a factor of two reduction in its error rate.

Conclusions

MailCat simplifies the task of filing messages by analyzing the user's mail-filing habits to predict the three most-likely folders for each message and then providing shortcut buttons to quickly file each message into one of its predicted folders. Since its predictions are accurate 80% to 90% of the time, MailCat substantially reduces the effort required to file messages.

While MailCat was developed for electronic mail, it can easily be used to organize other types of electronic documents. The concepts behind MailCat can be applied to organizing bookmarks, files, audio recordings, and other text-based documents that are placed into a hierarchy of folders.

References

P. Maes. Agents that reduce work and information overload. *CACM*, 37(7):31–40, July 1994.

R. Segal and J. Kephart. MailCat: An intelligent assistant for organizing e-mail. In *Proceedings of Agents'99*, May 1999.

HIKE (HPKB Integrated Knowledge Environment) – A Query Interface and Integrated Knowledge Environment for HPKB

Barbara H. Starr
Science Applications International Corporation
4035 Hancock Street, MS T1, San Diego, CA 92130
Barbara.H.Starr@cpmx.saic.com

Vinay K. Chaudhri
Artificial Intelligence Center, SRI International
333 Ravenswood Avenue, Menlo Park, CA 94025-3493
Vinay@ai.sri.com

Boris Katz
Massachussetts Institute of Technology, Artificial Intelligence Laboratory
545 Technology Square #824 , Cambridge, MA 02139
Boris@ai.mit.edu

Benjamin Good
Science Applications International Corporation
4035 Hancock Street, MS T1, San Diego, CA 92130
Benjamin.M.Good@cpmx.saic.com

Jerome Thomere
Artificial Intelligence Center, SRI International
333 Ravenswood Avenue, Menlo Park, CA 94025-3493
thomere@ai.sri.com

Abstract

This demonstration is based upon the results of a research project sponsored by the Defense Advance Research Projects Agency (DARPA), called High Performance Knowledge Bases (HPKB). The demonstrated portion of HPKB follows a question-answering paradigm. The integrated architecture developed at Science Applications International Corporation (SAIC), called the HPKB Integrated Knowledge Environment (HIKE) is introduced. Following this, the components involved in the demonstration, which include a natural language understanding system, a first order theorem prover, and a knowledge server are briefly described. The demonstration effectively illustrates the use of both a graphical user interface and a natural language interface to query a first order theorem prover with similar results.

Introduction

This demonstration displays the integration of multiple technology components brought together to achieve the goals set out for the HPKB Crisis Management Challenge Problem. For this experiment, a participant contractor in the HPKB program provides a set of queries and knowledge sources. In order to answer these queries, knowledge bases are constructed manually from the provided sources, and semi-automatically from other non-restricted sources. First order theorem provers are then applied to these knowledge bases to generate answers to queries. This demonstration focuses on the integration of the varying technology components required to accomplish this process.

System Architecture

Different research groups have developed the various components of the HIKE system. Because of this, these components clearly have different integration needs and application programming interfaces. An architecture diagram is provided in figure 1 below. Central to the system architecture is an Open Knowledge Base Connectivity (OKBC) bus [1].

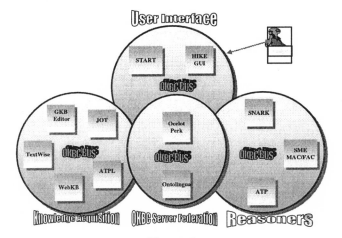

Figure 1

The system components are divided into four categories: user interface, OKBC server federation, knowledge acquisition and reasoners. It also needs to be noted that this classification is not absolute, and some of the systems overlap in the roles they perform

The user interface category contains components that allow two types of interfaces. HIKE provides a form-based GUI. Users can construct queries using pull down menus. Query construction templates are defined according to the templates defined in the Crisis Management specification. Questions can also be entered in natural language. MIT's component, Syntactic Analysis using Reversible Transformations (START) [3] accepts natural language queries and then attempts to answer the questions. For answering questions that involve more complex types of reasoning, START generates a formal representation of the query and passes it to one of the theorem provers.

The OKBC server federation category, within the SAIC Crisis Management portion of the HPKB program makes use of KSL's Ontolingua [5], as well as SRI International's Ocelot and Perk systems. Providing a federation of OKBC servers facilitates the development of a distributed heterogeneous environment.

The knowledge acquisition category includes all those components used for both manual and semi-automatic knowledge acquisition. SRI International's Generic Knowledge Base (GKB) editor [6] is a graphical tool for browsing and editing large knowledge bases, used primarily for manual knowledge acquisition. WebKB supports semi-automatic knowledge acquisition [7]. Given some training data and an ontology as input, a web spider searches in a directed manner and populates instances of classes and relations defined in the ontology. TextWise extracts data from text and newswire feeds, converting them into KIF [4] triples (concept-relation-concept), which are then loaded into the knowledge servers. JOT is a web-based editor developed by Stanford KSL that is used with Ontolingua. ATPL (Abstract Theorem Prover Listener) allows the user easy access to theorem prover usage and knowledge acquisition.

The reasoners category supports multiple reasoning methods. SRI International's SNARK (SRI's New Automated Reasoning Kit) is a first order theorem prover [8]. Stanford KSL's ATP (Abstract Theorem Prover) is also a first order theorem Prover. SME and MAC/FAC developed by NWU provide the capability for analogical reasoning.

Question Answering Protocol

Consider an example of a question being answered by the system. The system was developed to answer questions about international crises, so a sample question would be, "What risks would Kuwait face in attacking targets in Iran with chemical weapons?" [10]. The user enters a query

by either selecting parameters on HIKE or typing in natural language to START. In either situation, the query is converted to a formal representation in a standardized grammar. This formalized query is then converted into a representation unique to the theorem prover that will answer it (such as SNARK or ATP). This query is then sent to the theorem prover which, in turn, sends the answer to the query back to HIKE where it is displayed for the user. Thus, HIKE creates an integrated knowledge environment by providing connectivity between an array of complimentary technology components.

References

[1] Vinay K. Chaudhri, Adam Farquhar, Richard Fikes, Peter D. Karp, and James P. Rice. OKBC: A Foundation for Knowledge Base Interoperability. In *Proceedings of the National Conference on Artificial Intelligence,* July 1998.

[2] Michael R. Genesereth and Richard E. Fikes. Knowledge Interchange Format, Version 3.0 Reference Manual. Technical Report Logic-92-1, Computer Science Department, Stanford University, Stanford, CA, 1992.

[3] Boris Katz. From Sentence Processing to Information Access on the World Wide Web. *In AAAI Spring Symposium on Natural Language Processing for the World Wide Web*, Stanford, CA, 1997.

[4] Michael R. Genesereth and Richard E. Fikes. Knowledge Interchange Format, version 3.0 Reference Manual. Technical Report Logoc-92-1, Computer Science Department, Stanford University, Stanford, CA, 1992.

[5] Adam Farquhar, Richard Fikes, and James P. Rice. A Collaborative Tool for Ontology Construction. *International Journal of Human Computer Studies*, 46:707-727, 1997.

[6] Peter D. Karp, Vinay K. Chaudhri, and Suzanne M. Paley. A Collaborative Environment for Authoring Large Knowledge Bases. Journal of Intelligent Information Systems, 1998. To appear.

[7] M. Craven, D. DiPasquo, D. Freitag, A. McCallum, T. Mitchell, K. Nigam, and S. Slattery. Learning to Extract Symbolic Knowledge from the World Wide Web. In *Proceedings of the National Conference on Artificial Intelligence*, July 1998.

[8] M. Stickel, R. Waldinger, M. Lowry, T. Pressburger, and I. Underwood. Deductive Composition of Astronomical Software from Subroutine Libraries. In *Proceedings of the Twelfth International Conference on Automated Deduction (CADE-12),* pages 341-355, June 1994.

[9] M. Veloso, J. Carbonell, A. Perez, D. Borrajo, E. Fink, and J. Blythe. Integrating Planning and Learning: The Prodigy Architecture. *Journal of Experimental and Theoretical AI, Vol 7,* 1995.

[10] Paul Cohen, Robert Schrag, Eric Jones, Adam Pease, Albert Lin, Barbara Starr, David Gunning, and Murray Burke. The DARPA High Performance Knowledge Bases Project. *AI Magazine, Winter, 1998. pp. 25-49*

Intelligent Agents in Computer Games

Michael van Lent, John Laird, Josh Buckman, Joe Hartford,
Steve Houchard, Kurt Steinkraus, Russ Tedrake

Artificial Intelligence Lab
University of Michigan
1101 Beal Ave.
Ann Arbor, MI 48109
vanlent@umich.edu

As computer games become more complex and consumers demand more sophisticated computer controlled opponents, game developers are required to place a greater emphasis on the artificial intelligence aspects of their games. Our experience developing intelligent air combat agents for DARPA (Laird and Jones 1998, Jones at al. 1999) has suggested a number of areas of AI research that are applicable to computer games. Research in areas such as intelligent agent architectures, knowledge representation, goal-directed behavior and knowledge reusability are all directly relevant to improving the intelligent agents in computer games. The Soar/Games project (van Lent and Laird 1999) at the University of Michigan Artificial Intelligence Lab has developed an interface between Soar (Laird, Newell, and Rosenbloom 1987) and the commercial computer games Quake II and Descent 3. Techniques from each of the research areas mentioned above have been used in developing intelligent opponents in these two games.

The Soar/Games project has a number of goals from both the research and game development perspective. From the research perspective, computer games provide domains for exploring topics such as machine learning, intelligent architectures and interface design. The Soar/Games project has suggested new research problems relating to knowledge representation, agent navigation and human-computer interaction. From a game development perspective, the main goal of the Soar/Games project is to make games more fun by making the agents in games more intelligent. If done correctly, playing with or against these AI agents will more closely capture the challenge of playing online against other people. A flexible AI architecture, such as Soar, will also make the development of intelligent agents for games easier by providing a common inference engine and reusable knowledge base that can be easily applied to many different games.

Quake II and Descent 3, both popular first person perspective action games, include software hooks allowing programmers to write C code that can access the game's internal data structures and agent controls. This has allowed us to extract symbolic information from the games without interpreting the image displayed on the computer screen. A common approach to building intelligent agents in computer games is to use C code and these programming hooks to control agents via a large number of nested if and switch statements. As the agents get more complex, the C code becomes difficult to debug, maintain and improve. A more constrained language that better organizes the conditional statements could be developed but we believe that language would be similar to the Soar architecture. By using the Soar architecture, we are taking advantage of the Soar group's 15 years of research into agent architectures.

Soar serves as the inference engine for the intelligent agent (see figure 1). The job of the inference engine is to apply knowledge to the current situation and decide on internal and external actions. The agent's current situation is represented by data structures representing the states of simulated sensors implemented in the interface and contextual information stored in Soar's internal memory. Soar allows easy decomposition of the agent's actions through a hierarchy of operators. Operators at the higher levels of the hierarchy explicitly represent the agent's goals, while the lower level operators represent sub-steps and atomic actions used to achieve these goals. Representing goals explicitly in internal memory encourages agent developers to create goal directed agents. Soar selects and executes the operators relevant to the current situation that specify external actions, the agent's moves in the game, and internal actions, such as changes to the agent's internal goals. Soar constantly cycles through a perceive, think, act loop, which is called the decision cycle.

1. Perceive: Accept sensor information from the game
2. Think: Select and execute relevant knowledge
3. Act: Execute internal and external actions

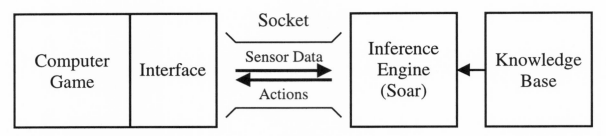

Figure 1: Soar is attached to the computer game through a socket connection to an interface that is compiled into the computer game.

One of the lessons learned, as a result of the DARPA project and the Soar/Games project, is the importance of carefully designing the interface between the inference engine and the simulated environment. The interface extracts the necessary information from the game and encodes it into the format required by Soar. Each game requires a custom interface because the details of the interaction and the content of the knowledge extracted vary from game to game. For example, Descent 3 agent's, flying in a spaceship without gravity, must have the ability to move and rotate in all six degrees of freedom. Quake II agents, running normally with gravity, require only four degrees of freedom. However, basing each interface on a common template allows much of the knowledge developed for one game to be reused in other games.

The Soar/Games project uses the standard Soar knowledge representation of a hierarchy of operators each implemented by multiple production rules. The operators at the top level of the hierarchy represent the agent's general goals or modes of behavior. For example, the top-level operators in a Quake II or Descent 3 agent might include attack, explore, retreat and wander. The lower levels of the hierarchy represent successively more specific representations of the agent's behavior. Sub-operators of the top-level attack operator could include different styles of attacking, such as pop-out-attack or circle-strafe, or steps followed to implement an attack, like select-attack-type and face-enemy. The operators at the bottom of the hierarchy are atomic steps and actions that implement the operators above, such as shoot, move-to-door and stop-moving. The Quake II agent currently under development consists of a five level operator hierarchy containing 57 different operators implemented with more than 400 production rules. Our hope is that many of these rules can be reused in the development of a Descent 3 agent. Because Quake II and Descent 3 are the same genre of games, they share many similarities at the strategic and tactical levels. We hope to take advantage of this by creating a game independent, genre specific knowledge base used by both games.

The game portion of our demonstration consists of six workstations (200MHz or faster Pentium machines), three for the Quake II demonstration and three for Descent 3.

For each game one workstation runs the game server and AI system, a second displays the ongoing game from the agent's perspective and audience members can play the game against the AI agent on the third. In addition to understanding how the research has resulted in valuable concepts and how those concepts are used, the audience will also be able to evaluate the effectiveness of the concepts by playing the games. Both games are easily understood, action oriented and visually impressive, which leads to an accessible, exciting demonstration of applied artificial intelligence research.

Acknowledgements

The authors would like to thank Outrage Entertainment Inc. for allowing us to work with Descent 3 while in development and Intel for the donation of machines.

References

Laird, J. E. and Jones, R. M. 1998. Building Advanced Autonomous AI systems for Large Scale Real Time Simulations. In *Proceedings of the 1998 Computer Game Developers' Conference*, 365-378. Long Beach, Calif.: Miller Freeman.

Laird, J. E., Newell, A. and Rosenbloom, P.S. 1987. Soar: An architecture for general intelligence. Artificial Intelligence 33:1-64.

Jones, Randolph M., Laird, John E., Nielsen, Paul E., Coulter, Karen J., Kenny, Patrick. and Koss, Frank V. 1999. Automated Intelligent Pilots for Combat Flight Simulation. AI Magazine, 20(1):27-41.

van Lent, M. C. and Laird, J. E. 1999. Developing an Artificial Intelligence Engine. In *Proceedings of the 1999 Game Developers' Conference*, 577-587. San Jose, Calif.

Robot Competition &
Exhibition

Sensor Based Coverage of Unknown Environments for Land Mine Detection

Ercan Acar, Morgan Simmons, Michael Rosenblatt, Maayan Roth,
Mary Berna, Yonatan Mittlefehldt, Howie Choset

Carnegie Mellon University
Pittsburgh, PA15213
eua@andrew.cmu.edu

Abstract

This paper introduces a sensor based coverage algorithm and an overview of a mobile robot system for demining. The algorithm is formulated in terms of *critical points* which are the points where the topology of an environment changes. We developed a provably complete coverage algorithm which makes a robot pass over all possible points of an unknown environment.

Overview of The Coverage Algorithm

Conventional path planning determines a path between two points. This type of planning is suitable for guidance, pick and place operations etc.. Applications such as vacuum cleaning, floor scrubbing, area surveying, demining (Land & Choset 1998) and harvesting (Ollis & Stentz 1996) require more than point to point planning. They require a coverage algorithm which determines a path that passes the robot over all possible points in an environment.

In many scenarios, the robot may not know its environment a priori, and thus a sensor based coverage algorithm is necessary. Sensor based coverage determines a path for a robot such that it passes over all possible points in an unknown environment. Completeness of such a coverage algorithm is of utmost importance. As an example, all possible points of a minefield should be covered to guarantee not to miss a single mine.

Different types of coverage algorithms were developed by several researchers. Some of the algorithms are grid based (Zelinsky *et al.* 1993), (Pirzadeh & Snyder 1990) and some of them are cellular decomposition based (Cao, Huang, & Hall 1988), (Vladimir J. Lumelsky & Sun 1990), (Hert, Tiwari, & Lumelsky 1996). Behavior based algorithms for coverage are also considered (MacKenzie & Balch 1996). However all these algorithms either work only in certain types of environments, make unrealistic assumptions about the sensors, or completeness of the algorithm is not shown.

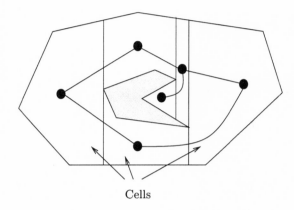

Cells

Figure 1: Cellular Decomposition

We developed a provably complete coverage algorithm and implemented it on a mobile platform.

Our method is based on a geometric structure called cellular decomposition (Latombe 1991), which is the union of non-overlapping subregions of the free space, called *cells*. An adjacency graph encodes the topology of the cells in the environment where nodes are cells and edges connect nodes of adjacent cells (Fig. 1). Since simple back and forth motions cover each cell, *complete* coverage is reduced to finding an exhaustive walk through the adjacency graph (Choset & Pignon 1997).

The cellular decomposition defines its cells in terms of critical points. If the robot knows the critical points, then it effectively knows the decomposition. When the environment is not known, neither are the critical points. Therefore sensor based coverage is covering the environment while determining the locations of critical points.

We developed methods to sense critical points in unknown environments. The notion of critical point sensing was first introduced in (Rimon & Canny 1994) and it was called the critical point sensor.

Generically each cell is characterized by two critical points. Instead of forming an adjacency graph with nodes as cells, we form a dual graph where nodes are

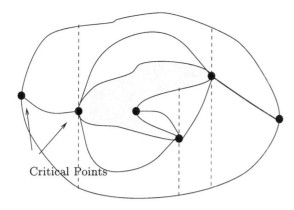

Figure 2: Dual adjacency graph representation of the environment. Nodes represent critical points, branches represent cells.

critical points and edges are the cells. Each time the robot encounters a new critical point, a new node is created, the edge corresponding to the current cell is terminated at the new node and depending on the type of the critical point two more edges are instantiated or no edge is created. If the robot encounters an already discovered critical point, then the edge corresponding to the current cell is terminated at the critical point and the "dangling" edge (*i.e.* it only has one node) of the already discovered critical point is deleted. When all the nodes have edges ending with another node, coverage is completed.

An essential part of the complete coverage is developing an algorithm which guarantees to see all the critical points. Such an algorithm was developed and its completeness was proved.

Overview of the Demining Robot

It is estimated that there are over 120 million active land mines in the world which cause the deaths of over 25,000 people each year. Many of these casualties are civilians, many of which are children. Current removal methods involve trained technicians searching with hand held electronic instruments (often metal detectors), while working on their hands and knees. Not only is this dangerous, but it is also very difficult for a person to reliably cover an entire area. Autonomous robotic coverage provides a solution which helps to remove people from this dangerous occupation, as well as to enable more reliable and efficient coverage strategies.

The testing vehicle that we are using in the implementation of our project is an original design which provides ruggedness and flexibility for an outdoor environment. The welded aluminum structure has a payload space of 13 × 8 × 20 inches, and is impact resistant in all directions. Four ten-inch pneumatic wheels are driven in a differential drive configuration by twin variable-speed electric motors (one for each side, front,

and rear wheels will be chained together). A removable fiberglass cradle is attached to the front of the vehicle and houses an array of four metal detecting sensors.

The vehicle's on board computer is currently a HandyBoard robot controller which is powered by Motorola 68HC11 micro-processor. The Motorola 68HC11 can control external devices, read input information, and communicate with a personal computer. A Pentium based computer can be easily added to the system whenever the processing power of the 68HC11 becomes insufficient. The vehicle is equipped with numerous sensing systems. Attached to the drive train are shaft encoders that monitor the displacement and velocity of the wheel. Also on board is a digital compass which uses coils (no moving parts) to detect the earth's magnetic field and returns a compass heading in degrees. The shaft encoders and digital compass are used to enable the vehicle to position and direct itself through the environment. The metal detection sensors cover the entire front of the vehicle and are used to detect simulated land mines.

References

Cao, Z. L.; Huang, Y.; and Hall, E. 1988. Region filling operations with random obstacle avoidance for mobile robots. *Journal of Robotic systems* 87–102.

Choset, H., and Pignon, P. 1997. Coverage path planning: The boustrophedon decomposition. In *Proceedings of the International Conference on Field and Service Robotics.*

Hert, S.; Tiwari, S.; and Lumelsky, V. 1996. A Terrain-Covering Algorithm for an AUV. *Autonomous Robots* 3:91–119.

Land, S., and Choset, H. 1998. Coverage path planning for landmine location. In *Third International Symposium on Technology and the Mine Problem.*

Latombe, J. 1991. *Robot Motion Planning.* Boston, MA: Kluwer Academic Publishers.

MacKenzie, D., and Balch, T. 1996. Making a Clean Sweep: Bahavior Based Vacuuming. In *AAAI Fall Symposium, Instationating Real-World Agents.*

Ollis, M., and Stentz, A. 1996. First Results in Vision-Based Crop Line Tracking. In *IEEE International Conference on Robotics and Automation.*

Pirzadeh, A., and Snyder, W. 1990. A unified solution to coverage and search in explored and unexplored terrains using indirect control. In *Proc. of IEEE Int'l. Conference on Robotics and Automation*, 2113–2119.

Rimon, E., and Canny, J. 1994. Construction of C-space Roadmaps Using Local Sensory Data — What Should the Sensors Look For? In *Proc. IEEE Int. Conf. on Robotics and Automation*, 117–124.

Vladimir J. Lumelsky, S. M., and Sun, K. 1990. Dynamic path planning in sensor-based terrain acquisition. *IEEE Transactions on Robotics and Automation* 6(4):462–472.

Zelinsky, A.; Jarvis, R.; Byrne, J.; and Yuta, S. 1993. Planning Paths of Complete Coverage of an Unstructured Environment by a Mobile Robot. In *Proceedings of International Conference on Advanced Robotics*, pp533–538.

A Natural Interface and Unified Skills for a Mobile Robot *

William Adams, Dennis Perzanowski, and Alan C. Schultz

Navy Center for Applied Research in Artificial Intelligence
Naval Research Laboratory
Washington, DC 20375-5337, U.S.A.
adams,dennisp,schultz@aic.nrl.navy.mil

Our research is aimed at developing an independent, cooperative, autonomous agent. Toward this end, we are working on two areas: a natural interface for interacting with the robot, and the basic underlying skills for navigating in previously unknown environments.

The interface we are developing combines natural language and gestures [1]. While human communication between individuals occurs on many channels, two of them, natural language and gesture, complement each other fairly regularly in daily communication. Since people interweave them freely during their interations, we assume they might readily do so in their interactions with a mobile robot.

Our interface allows the processing of complete or incomplete (fragmentary) commands. To process these types of commands, we keep track of the various goals during human-robot interactions by instantiating "context predicates," which are basically lists of the verbal predicates and their arguments expressed in logical form.

By utilizing context predicates, a discourse component of the interface tracks exactly which and to what extent each goal was achieved. With this information and by tracking goal achievement, the robot can continue to achieve unaccomplished goals on its own, no matter at what point or in what state the system is currently. Thus, context predicates permit the system to work independently on achieving previously stated, but as yet uncompleted, goals. This capability ultimately allows the user greater freedom to interact naturally without having to explicitly state or re-state each expected or desired action when an interruption occurs. We hope to extend goal tracking so that the mobile robot can complete semantically related goals which are not initially specified or which are unknown to the human at the time when the initial goal is instantiated.

This natural interface is currently in use with a mobile robot. Navigation goals and locations are specified by speech and/or with natural gestures. Commands can be interrupted and subsequently completed with fragmentary utterances.

To provide the basic underlying skills for navigating in previously unknown environments, we are working to create a mobile robot system that is robust and adaptive in rapidly changing environments. We view integration of these skills as a basic research issue, studying the combination of different, complementary capabilities. One principle that aids integration is the use of unifying representations which allow better communication and interaction among different components.

Our most recent work uses evidence grids as a common representation to integrate mobile robot exploration, localization, navigation, and planning [?]. In addition, this integrated system includes methods for adapting maps to allow for robust navigation in dynamic environments. As a result, a robot can enter an unknown environment, map it while remaining confident of its position, and robustly plan and navigate within the environment in real time.

We create two types of representations with the evidence grids: short-term perception maps, and long-term metric maps. The short-term maps store very recent sensor data that does not contain significant odometry error, and these maps can be used for obstacle avoidance and for localization. The long-term maps represent the environment over time, and can be used for navigation and path-planning.

The use of evidence grids requires that the robot be localized within its environment. To overcome odometric drift and errors, we have developed a method for *continuous localization*, in which the robot continually corrects its position estimates. Continuous localization builds the short-term perception maps, and at frequent intervals registers the oldest short-term map against the long-term map, locating the robot within

---
*This work was sponsored by the Office of Naval Research.

the environment.

In order for mobile robots to operate in unknown environments, they need the ability to explore and build maps that can be used for navigation. We have developed the *frontier-based exploration* strategy based on the concept of frontiers, regions on the boundary between open space and unexplored space. When a robot moves to a frontier, about half of its sensors can still see the old, known environment, which can be used by continuous localization to maintain accurate odometry. Its other sensors see into unexplored space and expand the map. By moving to successive frontiers, the robot can constantly increase its knowledge of the world. The new, expanded maps produced by the exploration are passed to continuous localization as its new long-term map.

After exploration is complete, changes in the world (blocked passages, moved obstacles, etc) must also be modeled. We have added a learning component to the continuous localization algorithm to allow the long-term map to be updated with recent sensor data from the short-term perception maps, making the long-term map adaptive to the environment.

In order to provide robust navigation, we have incorporated Trulla, a propagation-based path planner which uses a navigability grid to describe which areas in the environment are navigable (considering floor properties, obstacles, etc). In our system, we have integrated Trulla by replacing its navigability grid with our long-term metric map. As our long-term map adapts to changes in the environment, Trulla can replan using the robot's current knowledge about the world.

Continuous localization's long-term map update method can adapt to somewhat rapid and persistent changes in the environment, but not to very fast changes, such as a person walking through the room. Accordingly, paths generated by Trulla are not sufficient to prevent collisions with transient obstacles.

We have integrated the Vector Field Histogram (VFH) reactive navigation method to avoid transient obstacles that are not yet represented in the evidence grid. VFH uses an HIMM occupancy grid to model the robot's immediate surroundings. In our integration, we replace the HIMM occupancy grid with the short-term perception map produced by continuous localization. The short-term perception map allows VFH to consider all sensors, and yields a less noisy picture of the robot's immediate environment. Fig. 1 illustrates the complete architecture.

When heading into an unknown environment, the robot autonomously maps the environment while maintaining accurate odometry, producing the initial

long-term map. Each new short-term perception map long-term map is sent to a Map Server process which in turn makes the sensor-fused perceptions of the environment available to the various processes.

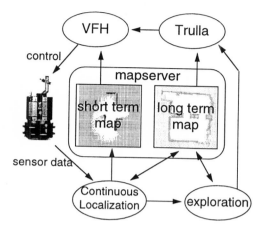

Figure 1: Architecture of integrated system

After exploration, the user specifies a navigation goal to Trulla, which consults the Map Server for the current long-term map and computes the vector field describing the best path from each cell to the goal. Trulla sends the vector field to VFH, which uses the robot's current position to index the vector field and get the direction to the goal. VFH retrieves the short-term map from the Map Server, and steers the robot in the direction closest to that which was planned by Trulla.

While VFH is steering the robot, continuous localization continues to correct odometry and produce short-term and adapted long-term maps. With each new long-term map, Trulla replans and sends a new vector field to VFH which uses it for subsequent navigation.

References

[1] Perzanowski, D., Schultz, A., and Adams, W. (1998). "Integrating natural language and gesture in a robotics domain," In Proc. of the IEEE International Symposium on Intelligent Control: ISIC/CIRA/ISIS Joint Conference, Gaithersburg, MD, 247-252.

[2] Schultz, A. and Adams, W. (1998). "Continuous localization using evidence grids," In Proc. of the 1998 IEEE International Conference on Robotics and Automation, Leuven, Belgium, 2833-2839.

Kansas State Robotics

Frank Blecha, Tim Beese, Damon Kuntz, Jonathan Cameron,
David Sexton, and Dr. David Gustafson

Computing and Information Sciences Department,
Kansas State University
Manhattan, KS 66506
dag@cis.ksu.edu

The Computing and Information Sciences Department at Kansas State University has developed a software control laboratory for the purpose of exposing undergraduate students to the problems of developing software on real, moving equipment. The equipment in the laboratory consists of two Nomad200 robots and two Scout robots from Nomadic Technology, Inc. The main use of the equipment is in a capstone, two-semester software engineering sequence. In this course, selected teams of students develop software to control the robot in tasks such as maze running, object identification or environment mapping. In the last few AAAI robotic contests, the tasks have been similar to projects in the course.

Introduction

The mobile robotics team from Kansas State University presently consists of five undergraduate students and a faculty advisor from the Department of Computing and Information Sciences. The group intends to compete in the Scavenger Hunt' event at this year's AAAI 99 Mobile Robotics Competition. Kansas State University has participated in five of the last six robotics competitions, placing teams in first, second and third place in events.

This year's team has two principal goals: to win the 'Scavenger Hunt' event and to extend the foundation on which future teams may build.

Hardware

The group's test platform is a Nomad 200 mobile robot, a commercial system designed and built by Nomadic Technologies Inc. (Mountain View, CA). The Nomad consists of a base unit, capable of translation and steering motions, and a moveable turret, also capable of rotation, on which all sensors are mounted. An array of sixteen

ultrasonic range sensors are mounted along the turret's circumference, and provide information about the distance to any obstacles in the robot's vicinity. There are three CCD cameras mounted on top of the robot's turret; one is color, the other two are monochrome. A microphone is available for sensing sound. All processing is carried out on an Intel-based Pentium 233MHz single board computer, which is equipped with 128 megabytes of main memory, and a wireless Ethernet interface.

Software

This year's team is using a model-based approach to object recognition, while using a simple reactive navigation scheme to guide the robot around obstacles and through the environment. One of the more difficult challenges is the efficient use of limited hardware resources, while successfully dealing with constraints imposed by the event rules. Machine vision requires a significant amount of processing power and is confined to object recognition and path planning. Most navigational activities can be adequately handled with information from the ultrasonic sensors; the reduced computational requirements will allow for quick reaction to obstacles, and a faster movement from one destination to another.

Future Work

As was mentioned earlier, a second, and equally important goal of the group is to provide a solid base of reusable software on which future teams may build. To this end, object-oriented design techniques are being used to build classes that encapsulate not only the functionality of various hardware items (such as cameras, sonar sensors, and the robot itself), but also of behaviors (both low-level reactive, and higher-level deliberative), and more abstract concepts (for example, images and topological maps).

Web-Based Mobile Robot Simulator

Dan Stormont

Utah State University
9590 Old Main Hill
Logan UT 84322-9590
stormont@hass.usu.edu

Many roboticists rely on simulation during the early phases of developing navigation algorithms for their autonomous mobile robots. While many commercial robots now come with robust development environments that include visual simulators, these tools aren't available to robotics researchers who are working with a custom-built robot or who have not yet determined which commercial robot will satisfy their requirements. Even researchers using one of the commercial development environments will have difficulty sharing their simulation results with colleagues or others who do not have access to the commercial development tools. Believing that the ability to share simulation results visually with the greatest number of people would be an important capability to have led to the development of the web-based simulation approach described in this paper.

First Generation

The "first generation" of this web-based simulation began with a text file full of waypoints. The text file was being generated by a probability grid-based navigation scheme being investigated for implementation on the mobile robot LOBOtomous at the University of New Mexico. Realizing that this cryptic output file would be incomprehensible to most viewers motivated the initial experimentation with a web-based simulation.

The most important consideration in this initial experiment was making the simulation results accessible to the largest possible audience. This motivated the decision to use the World Wide Web to distribute the visual results and the search for a format that would be platform (and web browser) independent. A number of different visualization tools were evaluated, including Chrome, Live 3D, QuickTime VR, Real-Time Authoring for Virtual Environments (RAVE), and the Virtual Reality Modeling Language (VRML). Of these, only VRML was an open standard that was supported on a large number of platforms with a number of freely distributed VRML browsers and plug-ins. Also, with the release of VRML 2.0, a number of the shortcomings in VRML that had prevented it from

being used for anything more than static visualization of three dimensional objects were addressed. It was now possible to have an animated object move through a virtual environment, while providing the user with a nearly limitless number of viewpoints. Additional flexibility was provided by the ability to run active elements (like Java applets) from the VRML browser.

Having selected the tool to be used, the next step was to build a VRML model of the robot to be simulated, in this case, the robot LOBOtomous. LOBOtomous is a custom built robot with two driving wheels and two castors centered around a central pivot point. The wider base contains the motors and drive circuitry, while the narrower cylindrical body contains the PC-104 control computer, the ultrasonic sensors and their circuitry, in addition to any circuitry added to increase LOBOtomous' capabilities. The VRML model was built to have the minimal detail while still being recognizable as LOBOtomous. A screen shot of the LOBOtomous model is shown in Figure 1.

Figure 1. VRML model of the robot LOBOtomous

Figure 2 shows LOBOtomous in a simulated lab environment. The lab environment is very simplistic, since the furniture is not detailed (the lab benches and other obstacles are nothing more than solid blocks in the model), but the model does allow the visualization of the robot's motion through this environment from starting point to goal.

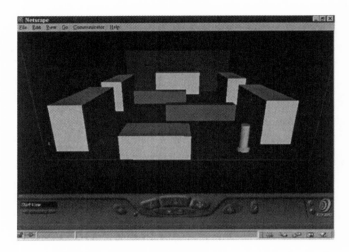

Figure 2. VRML model of lab.

The drawback to the first implementation is that it is not very flexible. The animation of the robot's path through the lab was hand coded in VRML using the text output of a simulated run of the robot through the lab. Changes in the algorithm, environment, or even start and goal positions requires recoding the animation. This lack of flexibility motivated the next generation of the VRML simulation.

Next Generation

As stated earlier, VRML 2.0 greatly enhanced the capabilities of VRML as a modeling tool. Events can be triggered by sensing actions, such as movement of the mouse, a mouse click, or collision with an object. Additionally, the ability to incorporate active code (such as a Java applet) opens the possibility of running the navigation algorithm within the VRML viewer. These untapped capabilities of VRML are the basis for the ongoing work with the VRML simulator.

Specifically, some of the potential enhancements being worked on now will provide the user of the simulation with the following capabilities:

- Use the mouse to select the start and goal locations;
- Navigate through a more realistic environment, with furniture that is recognizable as furniture and possibly varying sensor effects based on the furniture style;
- Select the navigation algorithm to be used from a list of Java applets;
- Select the type of robot simulated, with the appropriate motion model for the drive wheel configuration; and

- Build a map to be navigated through by providing a grid full of cubes and allowing the user to make selected cubes "disappear" by clicking on them with the mouse.

As enhancements become available, they will be posted on the Utah State University web server at http://www.usu.edu/~afrotc/cadre/stormont/vrml.html. The first generation of simulations are already available on the web site.

SIGART / AAAI
Doctoral Consortium

Elaboration Tolerance of Logical Theories

Eyal Amir
Department of Computer Science,
Gates Building, 2A wing
Stanford University, Stanford, CA 94305-9020, USA
eyala@cs.stanford.edu

We consider the development and modification of logical theories (e.g., commonsense theories). During development of such knowledge bases (KBs) a knowledge engineer makes some design and modeling choices. These decisions may later force the KB to undergo some redesign and rewriting when new knowledge needs to be integrated. We then say that the KB lacks *Elaboration Tolerance*. (McCarthy 1998) illustrated this problem using example elaborations for the toy problem of the Missionaries and Cannibals.

The influence of representation on elaboration tolerance is not well understood at present (see (Gogic *et al.* 1995)). In fact, unlike many other development tasks, there is no model for the development of logical theories in general and commonsense theories in particular.

We investigate elaboration tolerance in two complementary directions: (1) We model the development of logical theories, and explore the theoretical properties of change in our model; and (2) We develop a knowledge representation system that follows the intuitions arising from knowledge and software engineering.

On the theoretical front, we have defined a measure of syntactic distance between formal systems (Amir 1998). This measure counts the number of the operations of *add axiom* and *remove axiom* that one must do to transform one knowledge base to be logically equivalent to another. Comparing various reformulations of KBs, we found that (1) some reformulations can make a knowledge base have a shorter syntactic distance to all theories, but in the extreme a price must be paid in terms of the size of the resulting theory and language; and (2) changing the entailment relation does not have such a drastic impact on syntactic distance.

Currently, we are working on expanding our theoretical model to an Oracle-based search (somewhat similar to some Inductive Logic Programming models). In this model, the Oracle is expected to answer whether the current node is the goal node and, if not, what sentence should hold that does not (or vice versa). Consider a typical situation in which our advisor asks us to expand our KB T to accommodate the fact φ. As we try to comply with our supervisor's request, we look for theories under our representational constraints/biases. First, we look for what we believe our supervisor is asking for ($T \circ \varphi$). Many times she will tell us that it is not good enough because it satisfies another condition ψ that it should not (or vice-versa). The process continues until a satisfying theory is found. In the future, we intend to apply this model to the examples given by McCarthy and use it to learn commonsense theories.

On the pragmatic front, we defined two variants of an Object-Oriented First Order Logic (OOFOL): monotonic and nonmonotonic. In these logics, an object is a theory with an internal language and an interface language. These objects are connected by links to form complex theories (directional links in the nonmonotonic case). Inheritance was also defined to facilitate knowledge engineering. OOFOL theories support inference that is local to each object and incremental compilation of an object to its interface language.

An application that uses a variant of the nonmonotonic OOFOL is the Logic-based Subsumption Architecture (LSA) (Amir & Maynard-Reid 1999). LSA is built along lines similar to Brooks' Subsumption Architecture but having a logical theory for each layer. The subsumption is carried out by sending logical sentences from one layer to the next, having the lower layer ignore some of its default assumptions if needed.

In the future we will implement our OOFOL for Frame Systems, expand the application of the LSA to *synthetic agents* and evaluate the success of these object-oriented structures using our theoretical model.

References

Amir, E., and Maynard-Reid, P. 1999. Logic-based subsumption architecture. In *Proc. IJCAI-99*.

Amir, E. 1998. Towards a Formalization of Elaboration Tolerance: Adding and Removing Axioms. In *Frontiers of Belief Revision*. Kluwer.

Gogic, G.; Kautz, H.; Papadimitriou, C.; and Selman, B. 1995. The comparative linguistics of knowledge representation. In *Proc. IJCAI-95*, 862–869.

McCarthy, J. 1998. Elaboration Tolerance. Common-Sense '98.

Approximation Algorithms for Solving
Cost Observable Markov Decision Processes

Valentina Bayer
Department of Computer Science
Oregon State University
Corvallis, OR 97331
bayer@cs.orst.edu

Partial observability is a result of noisy or imperfect sensors that are not able to reveal the real state of the world. Problems that suffer from partial observability have been modelled as Partially Observable Markov Decision Processes (POMDPs). They have been studied by researchers in Operations Research and Artificial Intelligence for the past 30 years. Nevertheless, solving for the optimal solution or for close approximations to the optimal solution is known to be NP-hard. Current algorithms are very expensive and do not scale well. Many applications can be modelled as POMDPs: quality control, autonomous robots, weapon allocation, medical diagnosis.

Designing approximation algorithms to solve problems that have partial observability is the focus of this research. The model we propose (Cost Observable Markov Decision Processes or COMDPs) associates costs with obtaining information about the current state (Bayer 1998). The COMDP's actions are of two kinds: world actions and observation actions. World actions change the state of the world, but return no observation information. Observation actions return observation information, but the state of the world does not change while performing them.

COMDPs are intended to model situations that arise in diagnosis and active vision where there are many observation actions that do not change the world and relatively few world-changing actions. We are particularly interested in problems where there are many alternative sensing actions (including, especially, no sensing at all) and where, if all observation actions are performed, the entire state of the world is observable (but presumably at very great cost). Hence, COMDPs can also be viewed as a form of fully observable Markov Decision Processes (MDPs) where the agent must pay to receive state information (they are "cost-observable").

Any POMDP can be modeled as a COMDP and vice versa. We want to approximately solve COMDPs and determine what POMDP classes these approximations are good for.

There are two fundamental problems that any POMDP approximation algorithm must address: how to act when "lost" and how to avoid getting "lost".

All current POMDP approximation algorithms address only the first of these two problems. In a situation where the agent is uncertain about the state of the world, they choose an action based on a heuristic such as performing the action whose one-step value-of-information is highest.

We are experimenting with an approximation algorithm for COMDPs that addresses both fundamental problems. Given the underlying fully-observable MDP, the algorithm constructs a new MDP whose reward function incorporates the cost of making observations. Then, by computing the value function of this modified MDP, the "costs of getting unlost" (i.e., the costs of observations) are propagated backward along action trajectories. This allows the agent to choose actions to avoid getting lost. A sequence of MDPs is constructed iteratively, each MDP introducing observation costs based on the preceding MDP. If this sequence of MDPs converges, our method will predict when and how much it is necessary to observe at execution time. We are currently comparing the performance of this algorithm (and variations of it) to optimal policies computed by exact POMDP solution methods and to policies computed by policy-space search. We want to extend this off-line approximation algorithm to an on-line version.

Our long term goal is to apply the COMDP approximation algorithms to the problem of active visual perception in real-time problem-solving tasks such as air traffic control. We also want to look at reinforcement learning algorithms for learning the COMDPs.

Acknowledgements

I want to thank my advisor, Prof. Tom Dietterich, for his continuous guidance and support. This work was supported by NSF grant 9626584-IRI, ONR grant N00014-95-1-0557, and AFOSR Grant F49620-98-1-0375.

References

Bayer, V. 1998. Approximation Algorithms for Solving Cost Observable Markov Decision Processes. Technical Report 99-50-01, Oregon State University, Dept. of Computer Science.

Using Formal Meta-Data Descriptions for Automated Ecological Modeling

Virgínia V. B. Biris Brilhante

School of Artificial Intelligence - Division of Informatics - University of Edinburgh
80 South Bridge
Edinburgh EH1 1HN, UK
virginia@dai.ed.ac.uk

System dynamics is a mathematical modeling approach widely used in environmental studies for representing and simulating ecological systems, giving support to prediction and decision making. The knowledge sources for model design are, essentially, human expertise and ecological data at various levels of abstraction. We observe that property descriptions of ecological data (ecological meta-data), such as functional, temporal and spatial relations between variables, seem to be cognitively close to the concepts and reasoning used by model designers. Can the process of linking ecological meta-data to model design be automated?

We aim to answer this question by: *(1)* developing a formal language for expressing ecological meta-data; *(2)* building a logic-based formalisation of connections between the meta-data descriptions and model design; and *(3)* semi-automating model design endorsed by meta-data descriptions.

Logic-based approaches for ecological modeling have been proposed in (Robertson *et al.* 1991). Emphasis is placed on the use of domain knowledge to support modeling automation, making model assumptions explicit to enable more informed model analysis. Our work evolves from these ideas, adding to them by investigating how ecological meta-data (which play a part in domain knowledge) can be conducive to model construction.

Automated modeling based on meta-data can only be attractive if the mechanisms supporting it are not restrictive to specific datasets. Pre-defining a detailed knowledge representation system still general enough to express properties of every ecological dataset is infeasible. Thus, what is needed is a general framework for meta-data description which can be instantiated to specific datasets and model purposes. We have a prototype ontology, named *Ecolingua*, for such a framework, providing a vocabulary and axioms for ecological meta-data description.

Ecolingua has been designed by trying and describing a diverse dataset generated by a tropical forest logging experiment in the Amazon, Brazil (Biot 1995). As design tool we have been using the www-based Ontolingua Server (Farquhar, Fikes, & Rice 1996) for ontology construction and sharing, which provides an extensive library of sharable ontologies. Ontolingua, the representation language used by the server, was created as an attempt to solve the ontologies' portability problem. It provides a standard representation with translations to the syntax of specific target languages. Our target language is Prolog, which we use to connect meta-data descriptions to endorsements of model structure. The server automatically translates *Ecolingua* plus all the ontologies it refers to, into a file containing a very large (5.3Mb) ill-structured knowledge base in a Prolog-readable version of the Ontolingua syntax. To extract a manageable knowledge base from this file we built tools for syntactic correction, consistency checking, pruning and mapping of logical sentences into more elegantly constructed Horn clauses. The outcome is a knowledge base providing a logical foundation for inference connecting meta-data descriptions to model design. This includes definitions inherited from the other ontologies used to build *Ecolingua* on the Ontolingua server.

Features of the meta-data description (instantiated to a particular dataset) are used to reconstruct semi-automatically steps taken in performing parameter estimation, a basic task of model construction. The ultimate goal is to build a system that semi-automates a range of system dynamics modeling tasks (parameter estimation, model structuring, equation design) and is able to furnish the user with the underlying meta-data support rationale. The system will infer prototypical models (or parts of them) to be interactively further refined by human modelers.

Acknowledgments. To D. Robertson, R. Muetzelfeldt, and CAPES - Brazil, grant BEX1498/96-7.

References

Biot, Y. 1995. Data survey report - BIONTE Project. Technical report, INPA - Brazil and ODA - UK, Manaus, Brazil.

Farquhar, A.; Fikes, R.; and Rice, J. 1996. The ontolingua server: a tool for collaborative ontology construction. Technical Report KSL-96-26, Computer Science Department, Stanford University.

Robertson, D.; Bundy, A.; Muetzelfeldt, R.; Haggith, M.; and Uschold, M. 1991. *Eco-Logic: logic-based approaches to ecological modelling*. The MIT Press.

Modelling Higher Cognitive Functions with Hebbian Cell Assemblies

Marcin Chady

The University of Birmingham
Edgbaston, Birmingham B15 2TT
United Kingdom
M.Chady@cs.bham.ac.uk

Problem Outline

The objective of this work is to develop a model of higher cognitive behaviour using the connectionist paradigm. Examples of such work within the field of artificial neural networks are exceptionally scarce, mainly due to the difficulty of implementing symbol processing in neural hardware. Problems like compositionality and variable binding, as well as the selection of a suitable representation scheme, are a major obstacle to achieving the kind of intelligent behaviour which would extend beyond simple pattern recognition.

This is demonstrated by the following inference example: *if X loves Y, and Y loves Z, and Z is different than X, then X is jealous of Z.* A connectionist system, in order to perform such inference, needs to be able to: i) bind the symbol representations of instances of *X*, *Y* and *Z* to their roles, either by moving them around or by assigning tags; ii) maintain that binding between the stages of stating the proposition and producing the result.

This is inherently hard for connectionist systems due to the locality of their processing. A pattern presented to one set of synapses will be interpreted differently than when it is presented to another set. Although there are connectionist systems which are capable of advanced inferencing (cf. Shastri and Ajjanagadde 1993, or Barnden 1991), they always compromise their flexibility and, most importantly, their capability to learn. All connections in such systems are fixed, having been carefully prearranged by the designer.

What we want to achieve is a self-organising system which is able to learn from a continuous stream of input data and make generalising predictions based on its previous experience.

Our Approach

The approach suggested here is based on the properties of Hebbian cell assemblies, particularly the associative memory and attractor dynamics. Hebbian cell assemblies are clusters of neurons with reciprocal connections between each other. A very simple and biologically plausible local

learning rule governs the updating of synaptic efficacies: $\Delta w_{ij} = \eta \xi_i \xi_j$, where $\xi_i \in \{0, 1\}$ represents the state of neuron i (*off* or *on*) and η is a learning rate factor. Such a network tends to prefer states which persistently occurred during its previous history. If just a portion of the original pattern of activity is given, the network will complete it. A preferred state of the network is called an *attractor*.

Inspired by these properties, this study investigates connectionist systems consisting of multiple cell assemblies. Assemblies can be either isolated, overlapping, or connected by long-distance axons. It is expected that activity induced by the input signal in one part of the network will propagate to other parts and, after a while, the network will settle in a global attractor (i.e. the preferred state of the system) representing a balance between all the local attractors. This global attractor may represent the current state of the "working memory", e.g. the proposition "John loves Mary". The next input, say "Mary loves Mark", could then affect the current attractor in such a way that the resulting state will be the one corresponding to "John is jealous of Mark".

Obviously, this general scenario does not answer the question how the variables are bound and transferred from one proposition to another. Some mechanism for "buffering" the variables is required. This can by accommodated e.g. by varying the learning rate. Assemblies with a high learning rate would accept, and sustain for a short time, a wide range of patterns, which makes them a good candidate for a "variable buffer". However, there are many other issues involved. Hopefully they will be addressed in the course of the study.

References

Shastri, L., and Ajjanagadde, V. 1993. From simple associations to systematic reasoning: A connectionist representation of rules, variables and dynamic bindings using temporal synchrony, *Behavioral and Brain Sciences* 16:417-494.

Barnden, J. A. 1991. Encoding complex symbolic data structures with some unusual connectionist techniques. In Barnden, J. A., Pollack, J. B. eds. 1991. *Advances in Connectionist and Neural Computation Theory, Vol. 1: High-level Connectionist Models.* Norwood, New Jersey.: Ablex Publishing Corporation.

Learning form-meaning mappings for language

Nancy Chang

University of California, Berkeley and International Computer Science Institute
1947 Center Street, Suite 600
Berkeley, CA 94704
nchang@cs.berkeley.edu

The proposed thesis research addresses two of the main obstacles to building agents that communicate using natural language: the need for richer representations of linguistic constructions that incorporate aspects of conceptual knowledge, context and goals; and the need for a principled approach to the automatic acquisition of such structures from examples. More generally, it explores the idea that patterns that arise in language are inextricably linked with and motivated by patterns of meaning and experience. This view, along with empirical evidence suggesting that linguistic knowledge at all levels can be characterized as mappings between form and meaning, serves as the basis for a computational model of the acquisition of simple phrasal and clausal constructions.

The idea that language involves associations between sounds (form) and relatively richer sets of stimuli (meaning) is neither new nor surprising. Indeed, such an assumption is made without controversy in some recent models of the acquisition of individual words, including those for objects, spatial relations, and actions (Regier 1996; Bailey 1997; Siskind 1997; Roy & Pentland 1998). Thus far, however, models of the learning of larger phrasal and clausal structures have been oriented toward the problem of acquiring symbolic syntactic patterns, usually based around verbal argument structure (e.g., Brent 1994). The meaning of these larger structures is typically assumed to be predictable from the meaning of its constituents.

The current work adopts the less strictly compositional framework of Construction Grammar (Goldberg 1994). On this view, although phrasal and clausal constructions require more complex structural description of the relations between their constituents, they can still be described, like words, as mappings between form and meaning. Parameters of form consist primarily of phonological cues, such as features of intonation, words and their inflections, and word order. Parameters of meaning encompass a much larger set of possibilities, including event structure, sensorimotor control, force dynamics, attentional state, perspective-switching ability, and communicative and social goals. These features, while complex, play an important role in both cognitively motivated linguistic theories and cross-linguistic evidence from the study of early child language (Slobin 1985).

The model described here assumes some initial set of constructions corresponding to already learned individual words or unanalyzed phonological units, where constructions are mappings or associations between hierarchically structured sets of features corresponding to phonological input (form) and a simple event (meaning). The learning problem is to hypothesize, based on the current inventory of constructions and new input, the best new set of constructions to fit the data and generalize to future input. We extend previous work using Bayesian model merging as the basis for generalization (Stolcke 1994; Bailey 1997) to include composition, subset selection, and extension as possible operations on the set of existing constructions. Since these operations are not sufficient for expressing constructions that include binding *relations* between entities, we propose additional operations that allow a constrained form of unification in which relations detectable from the form representation can be associated with relations over corresponding entities in the meaning representation.

Besides addressing an instance of the general problem of learning relations and correlations over previously learned associations, this approach to grammar learning is also intended as a cognitive model that can make tractable the modeling of empirical data, such as that in the CHILDES corpus of parent-child interactions (MacWhinney 1991). The use of relatively rich cognitive structures for meaning places most of the generalization power in the semantic domain, creating a tradeoff between the (mostly semantic) drive to generalize and the map-enforced need to adhere to specific form-based correlates. The resulting learning behavior accords well with the observation that children acquire constructions on a verb-specific basis before generalizing to more abstract constructions (Tomasello 1992), demonstrating how a richer approach to meaning representation can facilitate the acquisition of natural language for both human and artificial agents.

Full references available upon request.

Development of a Methodology and Software Shell for the Automatic Generation of Intelligent Tutoring Systems from Existing Generic Task-based Expert Systems

Eman M. El-Sheikh

Computer Science and Engineering Department
Michigan State University
3115 Engineering Building
East Lansing, MI 48824
elsheikh@cse.msu.edu

There is a growing demand for a wide array of principled and useful instructional software applications, in both academic and industrial settings. The need for effective tutoring and training is increasingly important in industry and engineering fields, which demand the learning of complex tasks with the use of large knowledge stores. In the last two decades, intelligent tutoring systems (ITSs) were proven to be highly effective as learning aides (Shute and Psotka, 1996), and numerous ITS research and development efforts were initiated. However, few tutoring systems have made the transition to the commercial market thus far. The main reasons for this failure to deliver are that the development of ITSs is difficult, time-consuming, and costly (Murray, 1998). Thus, there is a need for easier, more cost-effective means of developing tutoring systems.

My doctoral research proposes a novel approach to developing an intelligent tutoring system shell that will generate tutoring systems for a wide range of domains. The goal is to develop an ITS authoring environment that interacts with any generic task-based (GT) expert system (Chandrasekaran, 1986), and to produce a tutoring system for the domain knowledge represented in that system. The focus is on the issue of reusability. The knowledge-rich structure of generic tasks can be reused for instructional purposes, allowing the tutoring of domain knowledge embedded within the expert system and of problem solving skills utilized by the expert system. By integrating this reusable knowledge with other reusable ITS components, a powerful authoring environment is created for the generation of tutoring systems for various domains. In effect, such an authoring environment can be linked to any generic task-based expert system, allowing the same tutoring components to be coupled with different knowledge bases.

The proposed solution adopts a task-specific approach to ITS generation, allowing the development of ITSs for a specific class of tasks. There are several benefits to such an approach. First, a task-specific ITS shell is more reusable than domain-specific or individual component approaches, yet is easier to use and more useful than general-purpose approaches. Moreover, the shell can be grounded in a task-specific model of learning. Overall, a task-specific approach offers flexibility and power as an ITS authoring methodology. The AI objectives of my doctoral research include the generation of tutoring systems from GT components, knowledge representation and reuse, reuse of tutoring components, support for rapid prototyping of tutoring systems, and development of an ontology for task-specific tutoring. The education objectives include grounding the ITS shell in a model of learning and using it as an evaluation tool for various learning scenarios.

References

Chandrasekaran, B. 1986. Generic tasks in knowledge-based reasoning: high-level building blocks for expert system design. *IEEE Expert* 1(3):23-30.

Murray, T. 1998. Authoring Knowledge-Based Tutors: Tools for Content, Instructional Strategy, Student Model, and Interface Design. *The Journal of the Learning Sciences* 7(1):5-64.

Shute, V., and Psotka, J. 1996. Intelligent Tutoring Systems: Past, Present, and Future. *Handbook of Research for Educational Communications and Technology*. D. Jonassen, ed. New York, NY: Macmillan.

Towards Bounded Optimal Meta-Level Control: A Case Study

Daishi Harada
UC Berkeley
daishi@cs.berkeley.edu

The Idea

In this thesis abstract, due to space limitations, we omit references and assume that the reader is familiar with the basic ideas and terminology from the fields of reinforcement learning, search, and rationality. In this first section, we motivate our idea using MDPs.

Let $\langle X, U, T, R \rangle$ be a MDP of $\langle$states, controls, transitions, rewards$\rangle$. Assume that we have an estimate of the value function $\hat{V}$. The standard method of obtaining a policy π from this estimate is to define $\pi_{\hat{V}}(x) = \mathrm{argmax}_{u \in U} E\left[R(x, u) + \gamma \hat{V}(Y)\right]$. It is clear that this may be interpreted as the controller performing a depth 1 search/lookahead.

Now suppose we instead allow the controller to perform arbitrary search, and to base its control on the backed up information. To do this, we need to make decisions about the following: the order in which search nodes are expanded, and when to stop searching and actually "commit" to a control. The approach that we take is to view these decisions as the meta-level control problem. With some care in the formulation, it can be seen that a solution to this meta-level control problem will provide us with a bounded optimal controller. We would like to solve this problem by using algorithms from reinforcement learning.

Some Discussion

Let us now consider the issues and problems presented by this approach. First, we would certainly like a formalism which allows us to express the joint system of the domain and the controller as an asynchronous, "actively" interacting pair of systems. This is difficult because the standard formulation of MDPs does not include a notion of time. Although SMDPs address the issue of time, it does not easily express the idea of strongly coupled subsystems. Currently the most promising approach seems to be that of merging the formalisms considered by the two communities of reinforcement learning and concurrent systems.

Given a formalism, the theoretical results which we would like to show concern whether it is possible to find the optimal policy. It is fairly clear that given the "more sophisticated" formalism posited above it will be necessary to similarly extend the canonical "learning algorithms" from reinforcement learning. In particular, it will be necessary to integrate the techniques explored by the hierarchical/modular architecture subcommunity with that of the function approximation subcommunity. That the latter is relevant follows directly from the assumption that we have an estimate of the value function. The former also follows since we have a system with subcomponents (the domain and the controller); indeed, even stronger connections follow from the fact that we are considering a controller based on search.

Setting theoretical concerns aside, it still seems plausible that intuition can be used to guide us towards building a system that is at least useful in practice. Unfortunately, this is also non-trivial. Returning to the idea presented in the previous section, note that since we have assumed that having the controller search ahead to improve its performance is reasonable, the problem which remains is to construct an architecture for the meta-level controller which guides the search.

The search community has been exploring this issue soley within the context of search for quite some time. In general, the underlying intuition has been to formulate the "value" of searching further along a particular path in terms of the volatility of the search nodes. There is not, however, a foundation to motivate the idea of "value". Our perspective is an attempt to address this. In principle, the problem of real time control provides a framework within which one can formulate a coherent notion of the value of computation.

Based on the practical successes of the intuitions from the search community, it seems reasonable to use some measure of volatility as a relevant feature for the meta-level controller. Using this information to obtain a meta-level decision efficiently returns to the hierarchical framework alluded to above. In particular, the sequence of decisions from the root concerning which branch to expand next has a nice interpretation within this framework.

Execution Monitoring and Diagnosis in Multi-Agent Environments

Gal A. Kaminka

Computer Science Department and Information Sciences Institute
University of Southern California
4676 Admiralty Way, Marina del Rey, CA 90292
galk@isi.edu

Agents in complex, dynamic, multi-agent environments face uncertainty in the execution of their tasks, as their sensors, plans, and actions may fail unexpectedly, e.g., the weather may render a robot's camera useless, its grip too slippery, etc. The explosive number of states in such environments prohibits any resource-bounded designer from predicting all failures at design time. This situation is exacerbated in multi-agent settings, where interactions between agents increase the complexity. For instance, it is difficult to predict an opponent's behavior.

Agents in such environments must therefore rely on run-time execution monitoring and diagnosis to detect a failure, diagnose it, and recover. Previous approaches have focused on supplying the agent with *goal-attentive* knowledge of the ideal behavior expected of the agent with respect to its goals. These approaches encounter key pitfalls and fail to exploit key opportunities in multi-agent settings: (a) only a subset of the sensors (those that measure achievement of goals) are used, despite other agents' sensed behavior that can be used to indirectly sense the environment or complete the agent's knowledge; (b) there is no monitoring of social relationships that must be maintained between the agents regardless of achievement of the goal (e.g., teamwork); and (c) there is no recognition of *failures in others*, though these change the ideal behavior expected of an agent (for instance, assisting a failing teammate).

To address these problems, we investigate a novel complementary paradigm for multi-agent monitoring and diagnosis. *Socially-Attentive Monitoring* (SAM) focuses on monitoring the social relationships between the agents as they are executing their tasks, and uses models of multiple agents and their relationships in monitoring and diagnosis. We hypothesize that failures to maintain relationships would be indicative of failures in behavior, and diagnosis of relationships can be used to complement goal-attentive methods. In particular, SAM addresses the weaknesses listed above: (a) it allows inference of missing knowledge and sensor readings through other agents' sensed behavior; (b) it directly monitors social relationships, with no attention to the goals; and (c) it allows recognition of failures in others (even if they are not using SAM!).

SAM uses the STEAM teamwork model, and a role-similarity relationship model to monitor agents. It relies on plan-recognition to infer agents' reactive-plan hierarchies from their observed actions. These hierarchies are compared in a top-down fashion to find relationship violations, e.g., cases where two agents selected different plans despite their being on the same team. These trigger diagnosis that uses the relationship models to facilitate recovery. For example, in teamwork, a commitment to joint selection of plans further mandates mutual belief in preconditions. Thus a difference in selected plans may be explained by a difference in preconditions, and can lead to recovery using negotiations.

We empirically and analytically investigate SAM in two dynamic, complex, multi-agent domains: the ModSAF battlefield simulation, where SAM is employed by helicopter pilot agents; and the RoboCup soccer simulation where SAM is used by a coach agent to monitor teams' behavior. We show that SAM can capture failures that are otherwise undetectable, and that distributed monitoring is better and simpler (sound and complete detection, no representation of ambiguity) than a centralized scheme (complete and unsound, requiring representation of ambiguity). Key contributions and novelties include: (i) a general framework for socially-attentive monitoring, and a deployed implementation for monitoring teamwork; (ii) rigorously proven guarantees on the applicability and results of practical socially-attentive monitoring of teamwork under conditions of uncertainty; (iii) procedures for diagnosis based on a teamwork relationship model. Future work includes the use of additional relationship models and formalization of social diagnosis capabilities.

An example. Three helicopters (using SAM) were to fly to a specified land-mark, and switch to a scouting plan in which two of them land. One pilot did not see the land mark, while its team-mate detected it and landed. Using SAM, the agents involved detected that the team is no longer in agreement on the plan being executed. Diagnosis lead them to realize that the landmark was seen only by some pilots, and the failure was recovered from.

References

Kaminka, G. A., and Tambe, M. 1999. I'm OK, You're OK, We're OK: Experiments in Distributed and Centralized Relational Execution Monitoring. In *Proc. of the 3rd International Conf. on Autonomous Agents (Agents-99)*.

Corpus-Based Induction of Lexical Representation and Meaning

Maria Lapata
School of Cognitive Science, University of Edinburgh
2 Buccleuch Place
Edinburgh EH8 9LW, UK
mlap@cogsci.ed.ac.uk

Motivation

The acquisition of linguistic knowledge, i.e., the identification, extraction, and encoding of linguistic information in a corpus, has been one of the main motivations for data-driven approaches to natural language. Methods have been developed for the acquisition of, for instance, parts of speech, noun compounds, collocations, support verbs, subcategorization frames, phrase structure rules, selectional restrictions and sense induction (cf. Armstrong (1993) for an overview).

Drawing on this body of research, I am investigating the acquisition of lexical semantic knowledge from corpora, thereby addressing the logical problem of language acquisition, one of the fundamental issues in linguistics and cognitive science. My guiding assumption is that syntactic as well as semantic representations are projected from information in the lexicon, and that a crucial part of the relevant lexical information is the result of language experience, and hence can be induced from corpora.

The proposed research includes three main subtasks: (a) induction of different types of ("low-level") lexical semantic information (i.e., subcategorization frames, selectional restrictions, semantic classes), using established corpus-based methods; (b) combination of the induced types of lexical semantic information into ("high-level") semantic representations, based on existing theories of the lexicon; (c) evaluation of the resulting model against human intuitions.

By applying corpus-based techniques to lexical semantics, i.e., a classical representational problem in linguistics, I hope to contribute to bridging the gap between current data-driven approaches to language and the knowledge-driven methods of traditional linguistics.

Results

I carried out work on automatically acquiring subcategorization frames from the British National Corpus (BNC) and showing that subcategorization preferences can be modeled as differences in frame frequencies derived from corpora. A high correlation was obtained

between frequencies acquired by the subcategorization learning model and frequencies reported in psycholinguistic studies (Lapata & Keller 1998).

I also examined the extent to which diathesis alternations (changes in the realization of the argument structure of a verb accompanied by changes in meaning) are empirically attested in corpus data. The research focuses on the automatic acquisition of alternating verbs from the BNC by using partial-parsing methods and taxonomic information (i.e., WordNet) and demonstrates how type and token frequencies acquired from corpus data can be used to quantify linguistic generalizations such as the productivity of an alternation and the typicality of its members (Lapata 1999).

Finally, I carried out some preliminary work on using subcategorization information to disambiguate verb semantic classes. This work casts the task of verb class disambiguation in a probabilistic framework which exploits Levin's (1993) taxonomy of verbs and frame frequencies acquired from the BNC (Lapata & Brew 1999).

These three studies support the following claims:

- lexical preferences can be reliably acquired from corpora and shown to correspond to human intuitions as measured by psycholinguistic experiments;

- corpus frequencies can be used to quantify lexical generalizations such as Levin's semantic classification;

- the framework of a semantic theory (i.e., Levin) allows for the acquisition of refined semantic features that do not emerge from purely corpus-based collocational analysis.

References

Armstrong, S., ed. 1993. *Using Large Corpora*. Cambridge, MA: MIT Press.

Lapata, M., and Brew, C. 1999. Using subcategorization to resolve verb class ambiguity. Unpubl. ms., U. of Edinburgh.

Lapata, M., and Keller, F. 1998. Corpus frequency as a predictor of verb bias. Presented at *AMLAP-98*, Freiburg.

Lapata, M. 1999. Acquiring lexical generalizations from corpora: A case study for diathesis alternations. *Proceedings of ACL-99*, College Park, MD.

Levin, B. 1993. *English Verb Classes and Alternations: A Preliminary Investigation*. Chicago: U. of Chicago Press.

Data Driven Profiling of Dynamic System Behavior using Hidden Markov Model based Combined Unsupervised and Supervised Classification

Cen Li

Department of Computer Science
Vanderbilt University
Nashville, TN 37235
cen.li@vanderbilt.edu

Dynamic systems are often best characterized by a combination of static and temporal features, with the static features describing time-invariant properties of the system, and the temporal features capturing dynamic aspects of the system. Our goal is to construct context based temporal behavior models of dynamic systems using information from both types of features.

Our dynamic system profiling framework consists of three main steps: (i) model generation, (ii) model validation, and (iii) model interpretation. Model generation step can be further decomposed into two components: (ia) temporal model generation, and (ib) context generation.

Based on temporal feature values of the systems, temporal model generation step constructs K models to account for dynamic behavior patterns. We choose Hidden Markov Model(HMM)(Rabiner 1989) representation for temporal models. One important and desirable characteristic of HMM is that the hidden states of a HMM can effectively be used to model the set of potentially valid stages going through by a dynamic system and the directed probabilistic links between states be used to model its transition patterns among the set of stages. Our HMM clustering scheme tries to improve upon existing methods in two ways: First, existing HMM clustering systems assume fixed, pre-specified HMM topology. To obtain better fit models, we propose a dynamic and automatic HMM refinement procedure that interleaves with the clustering process and constructs HMMs of appropriate topologies for individual clusters. Bayesian model selection criteria(Chichering & Heckerman 1997) are employed in this process. Second, existing HMM clustering systems rely on predefined threshold values to determine number of clusters, i.e., the value of K, in the final partition. We take a model based approach(Cheeseman & Stutz 1996) Our clustering model is composed of clusters in the current partition and one hidden state that assigns cluster membership for each object. Given this clustering model structure, the number of clusters in the final partition is one that gives the highest model posterior probability.

The K clusters derived from temporal model generation step provide class labels for data objects. Supervised classification can then be applied to induce contexts, or pre-conditions, of each temporal model based on information from static features. We plan to use C4.5(Quinlan 1993), a decision-tree based classifier, for this process. Given a set of labeled static data, C4.5 generates a classification tree and a set of decision rules characterizing each class. The end result of this two-step model generation procedure is K context based dynamic behavior models.

The models will be validated through likelihood tests. Given an object from test data, we first determine its most probable temporal model based on its static feature values and the context definitions of the set of models. Then we compare the likelihood of its temporal data given its appointed model against the likelihood of the data given the other models. If the percentage of all test cases that obtain higher likelihood from their appointed model is greater than certain confidence level, then we accept the set of models as validated.

Once validated, we then incorporate domain knowledge to interpret the context-based models. Based on HMM state emission probabilities, characterized by multi-variant normal distributions associated with individual states of a HMM, state definitions may be assigned in a domain and task specific manner. Dynamic behavior of the system can be interpreted in terms of the probabilistic transitions between pairwise states.

References

Cheeseman, P., and Stutz, J. 1996. Bayesian classification(autoclass): Theory and results. In Fayyad, U. M.; Piatetsky-Shapiro, G.; Smyth, P.; and Uthurusamy, R., eds., *Advances in Knowledge Discovery and Data Mining*. AAAI-MIT press. chapter 6, 153–180.

Chichering, D. M., and Heckerman, D. 1997. Efficient approximations for the marginal likelihood of bayesian networks with hidden variables. *Machine Learning* 29:181–212.

Quinlan, J. R. 1993. *C4.5: Programs for Machine Learning*. Morgan Kaufmann.

Rabiner, L. R. 1989. A tutorial on hidden markov models and selected applications in speech recognition. *Proceedings of the IEEE* 77(2):257–285.

Planning Under Uncertainty via Stochastic Satisfiability

Stephen M. Majercik

Department of Computer Science
Duke University
Durham, NC 27708-0129
majercik@cs.duke.edu

A probabilistic propositional planning problem can be solved by converting it to a stochastic satisfiability problem and solving that problem instead. I have developed three planners that use this approach: MAX-PLAN, C-MAXPLAN, and ZANDER. MAXPLAN, which assumes complete unobservability, converts a dynamic belief network representation of the planning problem to an instance of a stochastic satisfiability problem called E-MAJSAT. MAXPLAN then solves that problem using a modified version of the Davis-Putnam-Logemann-Loveland (DPLL) procedure for determining satisfiability along with *time-ordered splitting* and *memoization* (Majercik & Littman 1998).

C-MAXPLAN and ZANDER extend this paradigm to contingent planning in stochastic domains with partial observability. Like MAXPLAN, C-MAXPLAN maps the problem to an E-MAJSAT instance. By using 1) a compact problem encoding, which encodes a *policy* rather than a plan, 2) a more sophisticated splitting heuristic, and 3) a technique that prunes plans based on a specified probability threshold, C-MAXPLAN is competitive with SENSORY GRAPHPLAN on some problems (Majercik & Littman 1999). ZANDER encodes the contingent planning problem as an S-SAT problem in which the values chosen for blocks of existentially quantified variables that encode actions can be conditioned on the values of all preceding blocks of randomly quantified variables that encode observations. Rather than finding a single best assignment, ZANDER finds an assignment *tree* that specifies the optimal action variable assignment given all possible settings of the observation variables. Initial tests of ZANDER have been very encouraging; on a range of problems, ZANDER is competitive with both SENSORY GRAPHPLAN and MAHINUR (Majercik & Littman 1999).

Both C-MAXPLAN and ZANDER could benefit from more sophisticated data structures to store the plan encodings, better splitting heuristics, and static state-analysis techniques that improve performance by making structural features of the domain explicit and, thus, more readily available for exploitation. ZANDER can be improved in a number of additional ways. Currently, ZANDER separately explores and saves two plan execu-tion histories that diverge and remerge, constructing a plan *tree* when a *directed acyclic graph* would be more efficient. I would like to be able to memoize subplan results (a technique used by MAXPLAN) so that when we encounter previously solved subproblems, we can merge the current plan execution history with the old history. I would like to augment ZANDER so that it can distinguish between two plans that have the same probability of success but that differ with respect to a secondary criterion, such as length.

I will also create approximation techniques for solving larger planning problems. One possibility, currently being developed, uses random sampling to limit the size of the contingent plans we consider and stochastic local search to find the best size-bounded plan. Another possibility is to convert the probabilistic planning problem into a deterministic planning problem, solve that problem efficiently, and then gradually reintroduce uncertainty—and increase solution difficulty—only where it is necessary to achieve a specified probability of success. Both of these approaches have the potential to quickly generate a suboptimal plan and then, in the remaining available planning time, adjust this plan to improve its probability of success. This sacrifice of optimality for "anytime" planning with performance bounds may not improve worst-case complexity, but it is likely to help for typical problems. Finally, I would like to explore the possibility of using the approximation techniques I will develop in a framework that interleaves planning and execution.

Acknowledgments: This work is supported by a NASA GSRP Fellowship.

References

Majercik, S. M., and Littman, M. L. 1998. MAX-PLAN: A new approach to probabilistic planning. In *Proceedings of the Fourth International Conference on Artificial Intelligence Planning*, 86–93. AAAI Press.

Majercik, S. M., and Littman, M. L. 1999. Contingent planning under uncertainty via stochastic satisfiability. In *Proceedings of the Sixteenth National Conference on Artificial Intelligence*. The AAAI Press/The MIT Press. To appear.

Applying Supervised Learning to Real-World Problems

Dragos D. Margineantu
Oregon State University
Department of Computer Science
303 Dearborn Hall
Corvallis, Oregon 97331-3202
margindr@cs.orst.edu

The last years have seen machine learning methods applied to an increasing variety of application problems such as: language, handwriting and speech processing, document classification, knowledge discovery in databases, industrial process control and diagnosis, fraud and intrusion detection, image analysis and many others.

Our work starts from the realization that most of these problems require significant reformulation before learning algorithms can be applied, and in many cases, existing algorithms require modifications before being applied to a problem.

The problems mentioned above differ in many aspects but, if subdivided into smaller problems (and this is the approach commonly taken), the sub-problems can often be formulated and approached by employing similar, unified supervised learning techniques. However, this divide-and-conquer process creates dependencies in the data that violate the assumption that the data are independent and identically distributed (iid) and that all errors are of equal cost, issues that involve making changes to existing learning algorithms.

Our purpose is to identify some procedural steps that are shared among the learning approaches to complex real-world problems, and to develop robust general purpose techniques and tools to replace ad-hoc decisions that are currently made during an application effort. The main topics of my thesis are described as follows.

Learning with misclassification costs. Most classification algorithms assume uniform class distribution and try to minimize the misclassification error. However, many applications require classifiers that minimize an asymmetric loss function rather than the raw misclassification rate. In general, the cost of a wrong prediction depends both on the actual class and on the predicted class. One way to incorporate loss information into classifiers is to alter the priors based on labels of the training examples. For 2-class problems, this can be easily accomplished for any loss matrix, but for $k > 2$ classes, it is not sufficient. We have studied methods for setting the priors to best approximate an arbitrary $k \times k$

loss matrix in decision tree learners. We are currently studying alternative methods to incorporate loss information into decision trees, neural networks and other supervised learning algorithms.

Incorporating prior and common sense knowledge and learning with non-independent data examples. Generally, besides the data available, there is simple, common sense knowledge about the data that is not made explicit in the dataset or database. One question is whether this knowledge is useful, and, if so, how it can be represented and communicated to a learning tool. Another question is what independence assumptions are made by the learning algorithm. The standard learning models and algorithms assume that the data is drawn independently and that it is identically distributed. How is it possible to apply a learning method when this assumption is violated? One result that we have in this direction is that, if the data has a significant number of non-independent examples, ensemble learning methods do not improve performance (as expected) over single learners.

Determination of the granularity of the examples. As described in the previous section, the granularity of the examples is a common problem for supervised learning approaches to different tasks. We believe that there are two distinct granularity problems to be solved for each general learning task: the granularity of the features (e.g. how large is the sliding window in a text-to-speech learning task?) and the granularity of the target labels (what do we want to predict, e.g. phonemes, stresses, or both?). Our work on this topic includes only some experiments on a manufacturing dataset.

Examples with multiple labels. The vast majority of the research in supervised learning assumes that the labels of the examples are single values. However, there are cases when each example belongs to multiple classes. The training examples may be labeled either with single values or with a set of values. Possible approaches to multiple label problems include: using learning algorithms to output multiple values by exploiting the probability distributions, and using neural networks and to change the error function that is propagated back.

Modeling Prosody Automatically in Concept-to-Speech Generation

Shimei Pan
Department of Computer Science
Columbia University
1214 Amsterdam Ave, Mail code 0401
New York, NY 10027
pan@cs.columbia.edu

A Concept-to-Speech (CTS) Generator is a system which integrates language generation with speech synthesis and produces speech from semantic representations. This is in contrast to Text-to-Speech (TTS) systems where speech is produced from text. CTS systems have an advantage over TTS because of the availability of semantic and pragmatic information, which are considered crucial for prosody generation, a process which models the variations in pitch, tempo and rhythm. My goal is to build a CTS system which produces more natural and intelligible speech than TTS. The CTS system is being developed as part of MAGIC (Dalal *et al.* 1996), a multimedia presentation generation system for health-care domain.

My thesis emphasizes investigation and establishment of systematic methodologies for automatic prosody modeling using corpus analysis. Prosody modeling in most previous CTS systems employs hand-crafted rules, with little evaluation of the overall performance of the rules. By systematically employing different machine learning techniques on a speech corpus, I am able to automatically model prosody for a given domain. Another focus of my thesis is on system architecture. There are two concerns when designing a CTS system: modularity and extensibility. The goal is to design a flexible CTS system so that new prosody generators, natural language generators and speech realization systems can be incorporated without requiring major changes to the existing system. Designing a CTS system to facilitate multimedia synchronization is another focus of this research.

I have conducted initial investigations on different prosody models using a speech corpus collected from a medical domain. Different machine learning techniques were explored. For example, a classification based rule induction system and a generalized linear model are used in identifying and combining salient prosody indicators. Hidden Markov Models are also used to automatically derive probability models to predict a sequence of prosodic features from a sequence of language features. Preliminary results (Pan and McKeown 1998)

show that the output features of a general-purpose natural language generator, FUF/SERGE, are useful in improving the performance of prosody models. Recent results also indicate that the semantic informativeness of a word is an effective predictor of pitch accent assignment. In the future, I plan to investigate the effects of more discourse and semantic features, such as given/new, semantic focus, rhetorical relations, and build a more comprehensive prosody model. Both subjective and objective evaluations will be provided for the final comprehensive prosody models.

In order to design a flexible CTS architecture, I employ a SGML-based markup language as a standard interface between CTS components. The elements defined in the markup language are typical language and speech features. As a result, different prosody generators, natural language generators and speech synthesizers can be integrated in the CTS system through this interface.

In order to design a CTS system in a multimedia context, I have modified the sentence planner to produce different paraphrases to facilitate the coordination with spatial constraints from graphics. Similarly, in the lexical selection and prosody generation module, special considerations are incorporated to facilitate temporal coordination with other media.

Acknowledgments

This work has been advised by Kathleen McKeown and Julia Hirschberg and is supported by NSF under Grant NO. IRI 9528998 and the New York State Science and Technology Foundation under Grant No. NYSSTF CAT 97013 SC1.

References

M. Dalal, S. Feiner, K. McKeown, S. Pan, M. Zhou, T. Höellerer, J. Shaw, Y. Feng, and J. Fromer. Negotiation for automated generation of temporal multimedia presentations. In *Proceedings of ACM Multimedia'96*, pages 55–64, 1996.

S. Pan and K. McKeown. Learning intonation rules for Concept-to-Speech generation. In *Proceedings of COLING/ACL'98*, Montreal, Canada, 1998.

A Bayesian approach to object identification

Hanna Pasula
pasula@cs.berkeley.edu
Computer Science Division
University of California, Berkeley

There are many real world domains where an agent can observe the world state only partially and intermittently, using noisy sensors. Merely keeping track of the objects present in such a system is non-trivial. The problem may be complicated further if the system dynamics are not fully known or unpredictable, so that some on-line learning is necessary. I have been working on a principled approach to state estimation and prediction under these realistic conditions. So far, I have focused mostly on *object identification*, deciding if some newly observed object is the same as a previously observed one. The work has been applied to the surveillance of a large metropolitan freeway system. The vehicles are observed through scattered cameras, and both the viewing and traffic conditions are highly variable.

The general approach is based on a probabilistic formulation of the domain. The conditional independence and variable density distribution assumptions are made explicit, so the domain can be expressed as a *dynamic probabilistic network* (DPN). The right assumptions can simplify the problem considerably, although care must be taken to make them realistic. As an example, consider the traffic surveillance domain. There, we can assume that certain observations are dependent on the sensor where they are made, and the object generating them, but not directly dependent on what happens at other sensors. Color, for example, is constant for each vehicle, and the way it appears at each observation site depends on the characteristics of that site. The introduction of hidden variables representing such features of objects in the system enables us to remove many inter-sensor dependencies. As a result, we can use small, local probability models. We learn model parameters using the *Expectation Maximazation* (EM) algorithm.

Unfortunately, inference in large, complex problems will remain intractable even if the probabilistic network is simplified. The correspondence between observations and objects is unknown, and so inference in the system should involve summing over all the possibilities. Since the number of possible observation-object assignments is exponential in the number of objects, solving such a summation exactly is a $\#P$ problem. Our solu-

tion has been to depend on an approximation method based on *Monte Carlo Markov Chain* (MCMC) sampling. We define a Markov chain over the space of all observation-object assignments. Then, we define the probabilistic transitions in the chain so that the stationary distribution is equivalent to the probability distribution over these assignments, given all the observations. The chain is run to convergence, and then the samples it generates are used to approximate this distribution. Jerrum and Sinclair [1997] have shown that this method is a tractable and efficient approximation to an explicit summation. Constructing the chain is not difficult, and running it involves some specialized DPN inference, which can be made very efficient. One important application of this method is the approximation of the hidden variable values called for by the EM algorithm.

Interacting with the world in a real-time manner is a further problem. For one, we have to be able to keep up with changing parameter values. This can be done by calling EM at intervals, but, if every EM iteration depends on a full MCMC run, this may be slow. We are currently experimenting with on-line EM, where each call involves only a single iteration. Then, there is the question of how to run MCMC on a changing state space. This space will expand as new observations are made, and we need a principled way of cutting out old observations. At the same time, we may want to keep the old information around for as long as it may help us improve our models. A simple answer might be to simply incorporate the information from dropped observations into the parameter priors. It might, however, prove more useful to add a meta-level which would reason about issues such as the information content of old data, and the long-term changes of the models. This level could also be helpful when the approach is extended to predict, as well as estimate, the world state.

The system has been tested extensively on simulated data, as well as on small quantities of real data. It has been shown to outperform existing approaches, such as that of Huang and Russell [1998].

To conserve space, full citations are available upon request.

Over-Constrained Systems

Hana Rudová [1]

Faculty of Informatics, Masaryk University
Botanická 68a
Brno 602 00, Czech Republic
hanka@fi.muni.cz

Over-constrained systems are unsolvable by traditional methods with respect to the existing contradictory constraints in a problem definition. Solutions of such systems are defined and computed by giving some preferences or weights to the individual constraints and minimizing the violations of constraints using these preferences. The complexity and size of solved problem is often very large and computing of optimal solution requires use of sophisticated methods.

Standard methods for solving over-constrained problems apply constraint preferences for definition of optimal solution. There are, however, over-constrained problems with partially or even completely ordered variables and this ordering creates natural preferences for given problem. I developed a new constraint solving environment, where these preferences (variables' annotations) dependent on variable occurence in constraint are applied (Rudová 1998b).

The proposed solution allows to define mapping of variable's annotations to existing over-constrained systems – constraint hierarchies (Rudová 1998a) and to possibilistic CSPs. With that an algorithm for solving constraints with annotations through mapping to constraint hierarchy was described. This algorithm for acyclic set of inequality constraints was implemented in SICStus Prolog. This part of thesis will conclude with description of some examples demonstrating advantages and scope of annotations and implemented algorithm.

The properties of variables' annotations were still explored on the small or artificial (toy) examples. Currently I try to apply variables' annotations for solving timetabling problem in our faculty. The working with timetabling problem is a bit more complex than usual, because I would like to create individual timetable for every student – as (s)he registers for a set of courses. Also the number of required courses is small, majority of courses are optional and so the sets of registered courses for each student can be very different. Preferences of variables express how important are given

teachers and their requirements (professors, assistants, ...), lecture halls (small or large, with special equipment), and which courses are (not) allowed to overlap in dependency on the type and the number of students registered for the course. I would like to compare through this timetabling application variables' annotations with standard constraint preferences in constraint hierarchies, possibilistic CSPs, and weighted CSPs.

Based on a precise definition of our timetabling problem and comparisons of different approaches I should obtain basic interpretation of annotations (not depending on a constraint preferences) as a theoretical background for system design issued from annotations. At this point I should also consider possible combination of annotations with constraint preferences. This part will be concluded by implementation of proposed system.

Variables' annotations seem to be interesting framework for expressing preferences of global constraints as for example all-different. Trivially the annotations of global constraints can be combined with standard constraint preferences. Their broader application depends on a proposed interpretation of annotations. When the global soft constraints are applied in target application solution, I should seriously consider complexity of an algorithm to provide an implementation – research in the area of global constraints offering partial solutions is still very narrow in scope.

Properties and scope of proposed system will be verified by realization of original timetabling problem and also by other selected problems within the area of digital typesetting and natural language processing. As a consequence of these realizations I will try to define classes of problems which can be successfully solved by annotations.

---

[1]This work is supported by the Universities Development Fund of the Czech Republic under the contract #0407/1999.

References

Rudová, H. 1998a. Constraints with variables' annotations and constraint hierarchies. In Rovan, B., ed., *SOFSEM'98: Theory and Practice of Informatics*, 409–418. Springer-Verlag LNCS 1521.

Rudová, H. 1998b. Constraints with variables' annotations. In Prade, H., ed., *13th European Conference on Artificial Intelligence Proceedings*, 261–262. John Wiley & Sons, Ltd.

Reasoning about Sensing Actions and Reactivity

Son Cao Tran

Computer Science Department
University of Texas at El Paso
El Paso, Texas 79968
Email: tson@cs.utep.edu

Advisor: Dr. Chitta Baral

This thesis focuses on the problem of reasoning about sensing actions and the relationship between action theory and reactive control. The first approach to reasoning about sensing actions is due to Moore[1]. He used the possible world semantics to represent knowledge and treated the accessible relation between world models as a fluent. Later, Hass proposed another way of formulating sensing actions using first order logic. Moore's formulation was then adapted to reasoning about sensing actions in situation calculus by Scherl and Levesque.

In 1997, Lobo, Taylor, and Mendez extended the language $\mathcal{A}$, a high-level action description language of Gelfond and Lifschitz, to allow sensing actions and called the new language $\mathcal{A}_K$. Lobo et al. defined the semantics of $\mathcal{A}_K$, which will be denoted by $\models_{LTM}$ hereafter, by situation transition functions, which are extensions of the state transition functions of $\mathcal{A}$. Baral and Son proposed different approximations for the semantics of $\mathcal{A}_K$, denoted by $\models_a$ [2]. However, it was not clear whether there is a situation calculus counterpart of $\mathcal{A}_K$, as Kartha proved for $\mathcal{A}$, or not. Another question was to prove the soundness of $\models_a$ with respect to $\models_{LTM}$.

We will present a new approach to reasoning about sensing actions in $\mathcal{A}_K$, in which transition functions are defined over *knowledge states* (or *k-states*). A k-state is a pair $\langle s, \Sigma \rangle$ where s is a state and Σ is a set of states. Intuitively, s represents the real state of the world and Σ represents the possible states of the world in which an agent thinks it may be in. We denote the new semantics by $\models_{\mathcal{A}_K}$ and prove that Kartha's results can be extended to domains with sensing actions. More importantly, we prove the soundness of the different approximations of $\mathcal{A}_K$, $\models_a$, with respect to $\models_{\mathcal{A}_K}$ and $\models_{LTM}$. To compute $\models_{\mathcal{A}_K}$, we translate domain descriptions in $\mathcal{A}_K$ into extended logic programs where the answer set semantics of the latter coincides with $\models_{\mathcal{A}_K}$. It is also expected that our formalism corresponds to POMDP (Partial Observable Markov Decision Process), a well-known statistical approach to reasoning about sensing actions.

Theories of actions can be used to model deliberate agents which achieve their goals by repeatedly (a) making observa- tions, (b) creating a plan, and (c) executing the plan. Since planning in general is NP-complete, deliberate agents cannot react effectively to changes caused by exogenous actions. Reactive agents have been proposed to overcome this weakness of deliberate agents.

There have been many formalisms for reactive agents, for example, Schopper's universal planner or Kaelbling and Rosenschein's situated agent architecture. However, the re- lationship between reactive control and theories of actions has not been well established. Brooks even argued that per- haps reactive behaviors do not need reasoning and knowl- edge representation at all.

We define a control module as a set of *condition-action rules* of the form "**if** α **then** γ" where α is a condition and γ is a sequence of actions. Intuitively, a control module could be viewed as a case statement which tells the agent what it needs to do in a given state. We formalize precisely what it means for a control module to achieve a goal with respect to a set of initial states. We also give sufficient conditions for such control modules to achieve (or maintain) a goal with respect to a set of states and a theory of action. More impor- tantly, we develop algorithms that automatically construct a control module that achieves a goal given an action theory, a set of initial states, and the goal. These algorithms are not planners, rather they are built upon planners.

We expect to have an implemenation of the aforemen- tioned algorithms when the thesis is done. Also, we would like to improve our robot control software[3] by develop- ing new planning and scheduling modules which will allow users to specify dynamic domains in a high-level action de- scription language and write robot programs. To achieve a goal means then to ask the robot to execute a corresponding program. For this purpose, we intend to use ConGolog, a logic programming language[4] that offers a number of desir- able features for modeling dynamic domains such as reac- tivity, concurrency, and non-determinism. We will add to ConGolog a new construct which can simplify ConGolog- programming in domains where partial order between ac- tions and temporal constraints are important.

---

[1]Precise references are omitted due to space constraint.

[2]a is 0, 1, or ∞.

[3]We participated in the *"Scheduling a meeting"* and *"Tidy Up"* in AAAI'96 and AAAI'97 robot competitions and won the third and first prize respectively.

[4]Developed by the Cognitive Robotics group at the University of Toronto

Student Abstracts

Applying Genetic Algorithms to Pronoun Resolution*

Donna K. Byron and James F. Allen
University of Rochester Department of Computer Science
P.O. Box 270226, Rochester NY 14627, U.S.A.
dbyron/james@cs.rochester.edu

Introduction

Many pronoun resolution algorithms work by calculating the most salient candidate antecedent. However, many factors affect salience, for example being the syntactic subject or the most frequently mentioned item, and these factors must be combined into an aggregate salience score. One technique is to assign weights for each factor representing the amount by which that factor impacts the overall salience, and the candidate antecedent which accumulates the most weight is selected. Previous authors assigned weights heuristically (cf. Mitkov 1998). By using a genetic algorithm to select the weights, our program beats baseline techniques, and can be customized for each language domain.[1]

General outline of the algorithm

For this study, each salience factor was implemented as an independent module. The modules developed at this time were inspired by a number of previous studies:

- Increase salience of candidate selected by Hobbs' naive algorithm (Hobbs 1986)[2]
- Decrease salience of quoted speech (Kameyama 1998)
- Decrease salience of indefinite NPs (Mitkov 1998)
- Increase salience of first NP in sentence (Mitkov 1998)
- Decrease if in relative clause (Kennedy & Boguraev 1996)
- Decrease if in prepositional phrase (Mitkov 1998)
- Increase salience of subjects
- Increase salience of most recent candidate

Input to the program is:

- $\vec{W} \mid 0 \leq W_i \leq 15$ is the weight assigned to $module_i$
- $\vec{C}$ is the vector of candidate antecedents

$\vec{W}$ is generated by the genetic algorithm using random numbers for the first generation, then standard mutate, crossover, and replicate operations for subsequent generations. Each individual's fitness is the percent of pronouns resolved correctly. The initial population size is fifteen, and after each generation the five most fit individuals are allowed to reproduce, halting after twenty generations.

[1] A more detailed version of this paper is available as URCS-TR 713, from http://www.cs.rochester.edu/trs/ai-trs.html

[2] Hobbs' algorithm was slightly modified to allow for the syntactic structure of Treebank trees (see Ge, Hale, & Charniak 1998).

Most-recent	Modified Hobbs	Genetic
47%	67.8%	69.1%

Table 1: Pronoun resolution accuracy on the test corpus

Experimental Results

Our evaluation corpus is 3900 sentences of Treebank text (Marcus, Santorini, & Marcinkiewicz 1993) for which antecedents of definite pronouns were annotated (Ge, Hale, & Charniak 1998). 70% of the corpus was used to train the genetic algorithm, the remaining 30% was the test corpus.

Table 1 shows pronoun resolution accuracy for our three experiments. The 'most-recent-candidate' module on its own correctly resolved only 47%. Hobbs' algorithm, which uses syntactic structure, improved to 67.8%. Hobbs' algorithm performed best of all the modules when run in isolation. The genetic algorithm correctly resolved 69.1%, a slight improvement over Hobbs.

Using the same evaluation corpus, Ge *et al* (1998) developed a probabilistic model that resolved 84.2% of singular, third-person pronouns correctly. Two powerful predictors from their study, mention counts and selectional restrictions, were not included in our system. We plan to integrate those factors as well as additional salience modules and calculations of non-coreference in future experiments. We also plan to use a more sophisticated method of combining salience weights into an overall score, using one of the many techniques available in the machine learning literature.

References

Ge, N.; Hale, J.; and Charniak, E. 1998. A statistical approach to anaphora resolution. In *Proceedings of the Sixth Workshop on Very Large Corpora*.

Hobbs, J. 1986. Resolving pronoun reference. In *Readings in Natural Language Processing*. Morgan Kaufmann.

Kameyama, M. 1998. Intrasentential centering: A case study. In Walker, M.; Joshi, A.; and Prince, E., eds., *Centering Theory in Discourse*, 89–112. Clarendon, Oxford.

Kennedy, C., and Boguraev, B. 1996. Anaphora in a wider context: Tracking discourse referents. In *ECAI-96*.

Marcus, M.; Santorini, B.; and Marcinkiewicz, M. 1993. Building a large annotated corpus of english: The Penn Treebank. *Computational Linguistics* 19(2):313–330.

Mitkov, R. 1998. Robust pronoun resolution with limited knowledge. In *Proceedings of ACL '98*, 869–875.

Automatic Sample-by-sample Model Selection Between Two Off-the-shelf Classifiers

Steve P. Chadwick

University of Texas at Dallas
P.O. Box 830688, EC3.1
Richardson, Texas 75083
chadwick@utdallas.edu

If one could predict which of two classifiers will correctly classify a particular sample, then one could use the better classifier. Continuing this selection process throughout the data set should result in improved accuracy over either classifier alone. Fortunately, scalar measures which relate to the degree of confidence that we have in a classification can be computed for most common classifiers (Hastie & Tibshirani 1996). Some examples of confidence measures are distance from a linear discriminant separating plane (Duda & Hart 1973), distance to the nearest neighbor, distance to the nearest unlike neighbor, and distance to the center of correctly classified training data. We propose to apply discriminant analysis to the confidence measures, producing a rule which determines when one classifier is expected to be more accurate than the other.

Let $q_1(x)$ and $q_2(x)$ be scalar functions for the confidence measures of two off-the-shelf classifiers. Each sample, x_i, is mapped to $(q_1(x_i), q_2(x_i))$ in the decision space for selecting a classifier, thus the decision space has only two dimensions. Observe that the sample space has d-dimensions where d is the number of features in the sample. In this respect the dimensionality of selecting the classifier is reduced from d to 2.

In order to select the better classifier, we need an estimate of where each classifier succeeds or fails. Both classifiers are applied to each training sample to create this estimate. Classifiers which never misclassify a training sample, such as nearest neighbors, are evaluated by leave-one-out runs. Each training sample now has two confidence values, one from each confidence function. It is also known whether each classifier has correctly classified each of the training samples. This classification information is used to associate a value selected from $\{-1, 0, 1\}$ with each training sample. This value is termed *correctness*.

$$correctness = \begin{cases} 1, & \text{if first is best;} \\ 0, & \text{if both the same;} \\ -1, & \text{if second is best.} \end{cases}$$

If the first classifier is correct and the second classifier is incorrect, the correctness value is 1. Conversely,

if the first classifier is incorrect and the second classifier is correct, the correctness value is -1. If both classifiers perform the same, the correctness value is 0. The confidence values with non-zero correctness are treated as two-dimensional coordinates and class so a linear discriminant can be applied to the correctness data.

This linear discriminant is the rule used to select the classifier for each testing sample. The linear discriminant provides weights w_1 and w_2 and threshold t. For testing sample x_i and confidence functions q_1 and q_2, the second classifier is used if $w_1 q_1(x_i) + w_2 q_2(x_i) \leq t$, otherwise the first classifier is used.

While Arcing (Breiman 1996) also uses misclassification, it produces many classifiers and uses voting to classify a sample. Our technique uses an additional classifier to select which original classifier is used to classify a sample. In this respect our technique is similar to Stacked Generalization (Wolpert 1992).

Our technique can improve upon dissimilar classifiers, such as Nearest Unlike Neighbor and Fisher's linear discriminant, as seen in Table 1 which shows the performance of our technique on the breast cancer data from the University Medical Centre, Institute of Oncology, Ljubljana, Slovenia. Our technique is also able to use off-the-shelf classifiers.

Percent misclassified		
Fisher	NUN	Selected
29.58	36.08	29.30

Table 1: Ljubljana Breast Cancer

References

Breiman, L. 1996. Bias, variance, and arcing clasifiers. Technical Report 460, Department of Statistics, University of California, Berkeley, CA 94720.

Duda, R. O., and Hart, P. E. 1973. *Pattern Classification and Scene Analysis*. John Wiley and Sons.

Hastie, T., and Tibshirani, R. 1996. Classification by pairwise coupling. Technical report, Stanford Department of Statistics.

Wolpert, D. H. 1992. Stacked generalization. *Neural Networks* 5(2):241–259.

Structural Knowledge Discovery in Chemical and Spatio-Temporal Databases

Ravindra N. Chittimoori, Jesus A. Gonzalez and Lawrence B. Holder
Department of Computer Science and Engineering
University of Texas at Arlington
Box 19015, Arlington, TX 76019-0015
{chittimo,gonzalez,holder}@cse.uta.edu

Most current knowledge discovery systems use only attribute-value information. But relational information between objects is also important to the knowledge hidden in today's databases. Two such domains are chemical structures and domains where objects are related in space and time. Inductive Logic Programming (ILP) discovery systems handle relational data, but require data to be expressed as a subset of first-order logic. We are investigating the application of the graph-based relational discovery system SUBDUE (Cook, Holder, & Djoko 1996) in structural domains. Input to SUBDUE is a graph with labeled vertices and directed or undirected labeled edges. SUBDUE performs a beam search of the space of all possible subgraphs of the input graph. The search is guided by the minimum description length (MDL) principle, looking for subgraphs (substructures) with many instances that can be used to compress the original data and represent structural knowledge.

We applied SUBDUE to the task of identifying structural patterns that distinguish carcinogenic and non-carcinogenic chemical compounds available from the National Toxicology Program (ntp-server.niehs.nih.gov). Each atom in a compound is represented as a vertex with directed edges to other vertices, where the edge labels specify whether the vertex is the atom name, type or partial charge. Bonds between atoms are represented as undirected edges between the vertices. We divided the data into a training set (268 compounds) and a testing set (30 compounds).

SUBDUE found a substructure containing a bromine atom that occurred in 134 of the 143 carcinogenic training compounds and in only 24 of the 125 noncarcinogenic training compounds. This same substructure was found in 15 of the 19 carcinogenic testing compounds and in only 4 of the 11 noncarcinogenic testing compounds. The results are similar to those of ILP systems like PROGOL (Srinivasan et al. 1997). We are experimenting with a new concept-learning version of SUBDUE that finds substructures compressing the positive data without compressing the negative data. Preliminary results show that the new version is competitive with the predominantly concept-learning ILP systems.

We have applied SUBDUE to two spatio-temporal domains: the Aviation Safety Reporting System (ASRS) database (olias.arc.nasa.gov/ASRS) and the Earthquake database (wwwneic.cr.usgs.gov). The ASRS database consists of a set of reports containing 74 fields describing an incident that might affect aviation safety. Each record in the earthquake database consists of 35 fields describing the seismic event. In both databases an event is represented by a vertex with attribute-labeled directed edges to vertices labeled with that attribute's value. The data was augmented with *near_in_distance* and *near_in_time* relational edges between such events. We empirically selected the distance and time thresholds to not overload the graph with spatio-temporal information, but to still bias SUBDUE during the search.

In the ASRS domain SUBDUE found a substructure relating similar events of type *damage* using the *near_in_distance* relation, suggesting that such incidents are localized and recommending further investigation in that region. In the earthquake database SUBDUE found a substructure relating two earthquakes, whose epicenters were at the same depth of 33km, using a *near_in_distance* relation. Our collaborator, Dr. Burke Burkart of the UT Arlington geology department, says this pattern suggests a fault in the area.

Experimental results show that SUBDUE is able to discovery relevant structural knowledge in a graphical representation of real-world structural domains like chemical toxicity and in databases augmented with spatio-temporal relations like the ASRS and earthquake databases. We will continue analysis of these and other structural domains, comparing performance to competing ILP systems and domain-specific approaches. Source code for the SUBDUE system is available at http://cygnus.uta.edu/subdue.

References

Cook, D. J.; Holder, L. B.; and Djoko, S. 1996. Scalable discovery of informative structural concepts using domain knowledge. *IEEE Expert* 11(5).

Srinivasan, A.; King, R. D.; Muggleton, S. H.; and Sternberg, M. J. E. 1997. Carcinogenesis predictions using ILP. In *Proceedings of the Seventh International Conference on Inductive Logic Programming*, 273–288.

Learning Design Guidelines by Theory Refinement

Jacob Eisenstein

Stanford University
549 Lasuen Mall
Stanford, California 94305
jacob@redwhale.com

The automation of design decisions can be seen as a problem of generating mappings between elements in an abstract specification of the object to be designed and the concrete parts of the object itself (Puerta and Eisenstein 1999). In some cases, it is difficult to discover a formalism that takes all relevant variables into account: human designers proceed by "intuition." Individual designers may have stylistic preferences that are purely idiosyncratic or are common only to one particular "school." By ignoring such preferences, automatic design forfeits the flexibility, creativity, and vitality of human design.

In short, automatic design algorithms suffer from a lack of flexibility. Adaptation is offered as a solution to this problem. By making automatic design algorithms adaptive, we can begin to do automation without a complete knowledge base—it can be developed and refined along the way. Stylistic preferences can likewise be accommodated if an automatic design algorithm can adapt to the user.

We add adaptation to an existing piece of automatic design software: the TIMM module of the MOBI-D user-interface design environment (Puerta 1997). MOBI-D maintains explicit, formal representations of the abstract and concrete sides of the interface. TIMM automates the mappings between the abstract domain objects and concrete presentation elements, using a decision tree. Although there exists a body of work on using decision trees to automate selection of interactors (Vanderdonckt and Bodart 1996), most theory-refinement algorithms involve neural nets (Maclin and Shavlik 1996). A theory-refinement algorithm for decision trees is presented below.

An error occurs when the user disagrees with one of TIMM's design decisions. The system then searches for a set of operations that can be performed on the decision tree so as to yield the least number of errors, when applied over the entire history of user interactions.

When multiple solutions produce the same number of errors, operations that are reversible and do not affect the structure of the decision tree are preferred. The most preferred operation is to change the output of the leaf that produced the error. Suppose that the decision tree dictates that boolean domain elements are best treated by a checkbox, but the user selects radio buttons instead. This stylistic preference can be satisfied by changing the output of the leaf for boolean domain variables to radio buttons.

An alteration of the boundary conditions is the next most preferred operation, because it can be reversed by altering the boundary conditions again. Suppose that the decision-tree selects radio buttons for variables with less than four allowed values, and list boxes when there are four or more allowed values. If the user rejects the selection of list boxes in cases where there are four allowed values, then a shift in the boundary condition will produce more agreeable output.

There is no facility for removing branches. Thus, the addition of a new branch is the least preferred operation, as it is irreversible. It is necessary to add a branch when there is a relevant piece of information that the decision tree did not consider. The designer's selection of certain interactors might be influenced by the size of their parent dialog window. Adding a new discriminant to take that information into account is the only way to properly correct the decision tree.

Preliminary testing has shown that all of these operations are useful. Local minima have not appeared, so the fact that our search is a greedy hill-climb does not pose a problem. Earlier, three advantages of adaptation were cited: acquisition of new design knowledge, accommodation of user preferences, and update of the automation algorithm in response to changing technology. Testing has shown that the theory-refinement algorithm described here can deliver all three of those advantages.

Acknowledgements

I thank my advisor, Angel Puerta, for the direction and support. This work is supported by RedWhale Software.

References

Maclin, R. and Shavlik, J. 1996. Creating Advice-Taking Reinforcement Learners. *Machine Learning*, 22:251-281.

Puerta, A.R. and Eisenstein, J. 1999. Towards a General Computational Framework for Model-Based Interface Development Systems. In Proc. of IUI'99, pp. 171-178. Los Angeles: ACM Press.

Puerta, A.R. 1997. A Model-Based Interface Development Environment. *IEEE Software*, 14(4): 41-47.

Vanderdonckt, J. and Bodart, F. 1996. The "Corpus Ergonomicus": a Comprehensive and Unique Source for Human-Machine Interface Guidelines, in "Advances in Applied Ergonomics." In ICAE'96, p. 162-169. Istanbul – West Lafayette: USA Publishing.

Using Neural Networks in Agent Teams to Speed Up Solution Discovery for Hard Multi-Criteria Problems

Shaun Gittens
Dept. of Computer Science
AV Williams Bldg.
Univ of Maryland
College Park, MD 20782
sgittens@cs.umd.edu

Richard Goodwin
Jayant Kalagnanam
Sesh Murthy
IBM TJ Watson Research Center
Route 134 and Taconic Hwy
Yorktown Heights, NY 10598
(rgoodwin,jayant,smurthy)us.ibm.com

Hard multi-criteria (MC) problems are computationally intractable problems requiring optimization of more than one criterion. However, the optimization of two or more criteria tends to yield not just one optimal solution, but rather a set of non-dominated solutions. As a result, the evolution of a Pareto-Optimal set of non-dominated solutions from some population of candidate solutions is often the most appropriate course of action. The non-dominated set of a population of solutions is comprised of those solutions whose criteria cannot all be dominated by those of at least one other solution in the current population.

The framework we use, called the Asynchronous Team (A-Team) architecture (Talukdar, Souza, & Murthy 1993), deploys teams of optimizing agents to evolve population(s) of candidate solutions to instances of hard MC problems in order to develop very good solutions. In this framework, agents embody specific heuristics geared to create, modify, or destroy any of a number of possible solutions to a problem instance. These agents are capable of choosing when and on which potential solutions they would like to work on. As a result, as the system progresses in iterations, the population of possible solutions as a whole tends to improve towards a Pareto-Optimal frontier of solutions. The Pareto Optimal frontier would consist of solutions whose individual criteria cannot be further optimized without resulting in a decline in other criteria.

Currently, the method by which each agent chooses to work on particular solutions must be hand coded into the system. It can be very difficult to accomplish this since one would have to determine ahead of time which agents work best on which solutions, requiring much time and effort. In addition, the developer may introduce a 'teacher's bias' to the agent, hand coding incorrect decision-making based on the developer's incorrect analysis of the agents improvement capability. Furthermore, this approach is inflexible as the hand coding done for one problem will not likely be applicable to other problems.

Without hand coding this feature, agents are deployed at random with an equal likelihood. This random deployment, however, often results in CPU cycles being wasted as some agents may be invoked at times when they are unlikely to yield improvements. This problem is significant in that improved decision making by agents should result in the evolution of very good solutions in less time than was previously required.

Thus far we have attempted to remedy this shortcoming by implementing neural network (NN) error back propagation learning techniques (Mehrotra, K. Mohan, & Ranka 1997) to allow individual agents to learn when and on what solutions they work well. We investigate neural network strategies here since they can be trained to approximate smooth functions which output, in constant time, the likely improvement the agent can have on each criterion of a problem instance. One way we implement this is to assign one NN per agent and train it based on the successes and failures that agent achieved over many past runs. The agent's neural network is trained to report a +1 if some preset percentage of improvement (say 10%) in at least one important parameter is expected in the event that the agent is applied to a particular solution in the population. A second, and seemingly more effective, method we use is to train each agent NN until it can estimate the expected improvement the agent could make on a particular solution.

Initial results obtained from testing on tough instances of the Bicriteria Sparse Multiple Knapsack Problem did indeed demonstrate that improved decision making on the part of agents using well-trained neural nets often resulted in significant speedup and overall improved solution quality over the population. More work is being done to overcome drawbacks inherent to neural network solutions such as generalization, input parameter selection, etc. Further study should reveal how solving problems in this fashion fares against the performance of other multiple objective optimization approaches.

References

Mehrotra, K.; K. Mohan, C.; and Ranka, S. 1997. *Elements of Artificial Neural Networks.* MIT Press.

Talukdar, S. N.; Souza, P. d.; and Murthy, S. 1993. Organization for computer-based agents. *Engineering Intelligent Systems.*

OBDD-Based Planning with Real-Valued Variables in Non-Deterministic Environments

A. Goel and K.S. Barber

The University of Texas at Austin
Department of Electrical and Computer Engineering
24th and Speedway, ENS 240
Austin, TX 78712-1084
{agoel, barber}@mail.utexas.edu

Planning for highly dynamic and uncertain real-world domains is difficult using current planning tools. These domains may be characterized by non-deterministic actions and the need to represent large real-valued state spaces. Classical planning considers only deterministic domains and sidesteps the issue of non-determinism. Real-valued variables are handled by requiring domains to either represent real variables as relative booleans (e.g. using *on-table* or *on-block* in the classical blocks world), or to explicitly enumerate each possible value for a real variable (e.g. using *at11*, *at12*, *at21*, *at22* for block position in a 2x2 blocks world). The former approach is a lossy transformation where positioning information is lost while the latter is subject to state explosion for large domains.

We are developing a planner that can efficiently handle non-determinism and real variables using neither relative values nor explicit enumeration. In doing so, we are leveraging tools and representations from *(i)* planning and *(ii)* logic synthesis for computer-aided verification.

We propose the use of OBDDs (Ordered Binary Decision Diagrams) to deal with the large amounts of space required to represent domains and plans. OBDDs have recently been shown to be effective in modeling non-deterministic domains and provide a concise representation for state diagrams because their size (number of nodes) is not necessarily related to the size of the state space (Cimatti et al., 1998). OBDDs are currently used to represent gate-level logic for logic synthesis and computer-verification problems and have a wealth of prior research and tools available for manipulation and searching (Goel et al., 1998). These tools can be extended to handle non-determinism and real-variable based plan generation.

Recent work in the use of un-interpreted functions with OBDDs has outlined a method for modeling and interpreting real variables (Goel et al., 1998). A full explanation of this technique is beyond the scope of this abstract. However, this methodology allows real variables to be used without requiring relative boolean values or explicit enumeration. The real variables are directly represented and used to calculate the satsifiability of the

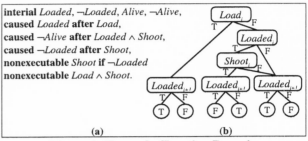

Figure 1: Example Shooting Domain

OBDDs. A satisfiable path through an OBDD represents a statement supported by the information in the OBDD.

This method can be used as a tool to analyze OBDD-based domain and plan characterizations. This will allow us to provide mappings between various domain and action representation languages. Among those being considered are: *(i)* the Planning Domain Definition Language (PDDL) and *(ii)* **C**, a new causal representation language (McCain and Hudson, 1997). An example specification in **C** and one sample OBDD is shown in Figure 1. In Figure 1.b, $Load_i \wedge Loaded_{i+1}$ is a satisfying path. Thus, finding and executing a plan is equivalent to finding a set of satisfiable paths that is consistent across all the OBDDs representing a domain and achieves the desired goal state.

Acknowledgements

The authors would like to thank Drs. Adnan Aziz and Vladimir Lifschitz at UT Austin for their support regarding logic synthesis and causal planning languages.

References

Cimatti, A., Roveri, M., and Traverso, P. 1998. Automatic OBDD-based Generation of Universal Plans in Non-Deterministic Domains. In *Proceedings of the 15th National Conference on Artificial Intelligence (AAAI-98)*, 875-881. Madison, WI: AAAI Press/ The MIT Press.

Goel, A., Sajid, K., Zhou, H., Aziz, A., and Singhal, V. 1998. BDD Based Procedures for a Theory of Equality With Uninterpreted Functions. In *Proceedings of the 10th International Conference on Computer Aided Verification (CAV'98)*, 244-255. Vancouver, BC, Canada: Springer-Verlag.

McCain, N. and Hudson, T. 1997. Causal Theories of Action and Change. In *Proceedings of the 14th National Conference on Artificial Intelligence (AAAI-97)*, 460-465. Providence, Rhode Island: AAAI Press/ The MIT Press.

This research is sponsored in part by the Texas Higher Education Coordinating Board #003658-415

Expectation-based Learning in Design

Dan L. Grecu, David C. Brown

Department of Computer Science
Worcester Polytechnic Institute
Worcester, MA 01609, USA
dgrecu, dcb@cs.wpi.edu

Design problems typically have a very large number of problem states, many of which cannot be anticipated at the onset of the design. Some design problem states are characterized by as many as hundreds of parameters. Given these amounts of uncertainty and information, AI design systems faced with learning tasks cannot know from the beginning what needs to be learned, and whether these needs will remain the same. In this abstract we describe how LEAD (Learning Expectations in Agent-based Design), a multi-agent system for parametric and configuration design, addresses these challenges in design learning.

LEAD design agents are *specialized* problem-solvers, having knowledge about a specific facet of a design domain. Each design agent also has a *partial* view of what the other agents are doing. As a consequence, during learning agents have to deal with a limited access to relevant information, because they either do not understand all the information, and/or because that information resides in other agents. An agent compensates for these limitations by using 'expectations.' An expectation is an assumption that a *fact* will be true under given *conditions*. For example, the price of a spring can be expected to be in the range (p_1, p_2), if it is made of material m, if its diameter is smaller than d, and if it is manufactured using technology t. In this case the expectation fact is the range of the price, while the material and diameter values, and the manufacturing technology are the conditions for the expectation. Expectations represent empirical knowledge that cannot be inferred in a deductive manner due to limited resources, such as time, or information. Expectations have been used with different meanings in other contexts, such as conditioned learning (Catania 1998), and language understanding (Schank 1982).

Since design problems have large number of constraints that agents are likely to violate, LEAD agents use expectations to evaluate the consequences of possible decisions before committing to one of them. This strategy aims to reduce backtracking and conflicts with other agents, and helps an agent find out whether its decisions will satisfy the design goals. To evaluate the consequences of a decision an agent inferences from facts that describe current values and events in the design system. The values may refer to properties in the design domain, such as material selections, or component dimensions, but they may also refer to what other agents are doing, e.g., whether agent A has made a decision before or after agent B. In this inferencing process, the agent evaluating decision consequences may also use expectation facts in addition to the facts that are currently true in the system. An expectation fact can be used in inferencing only if the expectation is active, that is, if its conditions are satisfied by facts or other active expectations. Expectations together with the existing facts determine how far ahead an agent can predict the results of its actions, i.e., how informed its decisions are.

In LEAD, expectations are learned when an agent decides that their associated facts would allow the agent to extend the evaluation of decision consequences further into the future. When designing, an agent keeps track of the missing pieces of information that prevent it from adding further conclusions to the chain of consequences of a decision. A design or design process property that has been repeatedly identified as potentially useful in evaluating decision consequences, and which is not available, initiates a learning process to acquire an expectation description. Expectation descriptions are learned as concepts. The concept features are represented by the expectation conditions, and the concept values (i.e. the expectations facts) are derived from the observed values for the piece of information that is needed.

Consider an agent building an expectation for the values of a parameter P. Once the agent detects the need for an expectation, the learning follows three phases. The agent first *collects information to be used in describing the expectation*. Based on its knowledge about P, such as dependencies and constraints in which the parameter P is involved, the agent sets up a set of *candidate* design and design process properties that might influence the values of P. During subsequent design sessions the values of these properties are recorded whenever the agent needs P for evaluation purposes. The value of P resulting from the design process is associated with the values of the candidate properties, and represents a training instance. The agent then *builds the description of the expectation*, by identifying which of the candidate properties that were selected in the first phase are relevant conditions for the expectation-concept. LEAD uses wrappers (Kohavi & John 1998) to determine relevant subsets of features for a concept and to generate a concept description. Finally, once an agent has acquired an expectation description, *the description remains open to revision*. Whenever the agent uses the expectation, it verifies whether the value predicted by the expectation matches the value that results in the design process. Mismatches are recorded, and used for retraining and updating of the expectation description.

References

Catania, A.C. *Learning*, Prentice Hall, Upper River Springs, NJ, 1998.

Kohavi, R., and John, G.H. 1998. "Wrappers for Feature Subset Selection," *Artificial Intelligence*, 97: 273-324.

Schank, R. 1982. *Dynamic memory*, Cambridge University Press, Cambridge, England.

A Framework for Problem Solving Activities in Multi-Agent Systems

D. C. Han, T. H. Liu, K. S. Barber

The Laboratory for Intelligent Processes and Systems
Department of Electrical and Computer Engineering, ENS 240
University of Texas at Austin
Austin, TX 78712-1084
{dhan, thliu, barber}@lips.utexas.edu

The basic research issues in multi-agent systems (MAS) include problem decomposition, task distribution, communication, plan synthesis, coordination, conflict resolution, and organization design. For practical implementation, there is a need for an integrated framework that can help MAS designers to select appropriate techniques for building their specific systems. Difficulties in the integration of techniques for each of these issues is due to the interdependencies among the issues themselves. We propose a framework that describes the activities that occur during problem solving. This framework is based upon the premise that meta-level reasoning about the agents' activities adds flexibility to each agent, allowing them to adjust to changes in their environments or operating conditions.

Generally speaking, to accomplish a specific goal, agents must perform a sequence of actions that trigger events and change certain states. A strategy is a decision-making mechanism that provides long-term consideration for selecting actions toward specific goals which can help agents to observe the environment, evaluate alternatives, and prescribe and schedule actions. Since different strategies may be more or less appropriate in different situations and within different agent organizations, meta-level reasoning is required for strategy selection.

Problem solving activities can be decomposed into three phases: organization design, coordinated planning, and plan execution. Strategies have been developed to address the problems posed by each of these phases. Allowing the agent to select the strategy to apply towards a problem increases flexibility and responsiveness to new situations. For this purpose, each phase can follows the three levels of reasoning described above; reasoning on actions, strategies, and strategic decision making. Coordination during each phase occurs through communication.

Upon considering goals the agent wishes to achieve, the agent (or the system designers) must decide the manner in which it will interact with other agents. The result could be static or dynamic organizational structures that are designed for each goal or all goals the agents consider. Organization design may result in an agent being the master of other agents, a peer of other agents, command driven by other agents, or independent.

The coordinated planning phase is composed of three tasks: (1) *Plan Generation*: The agents must select the actions that must be taken to achieve the goal. This may take the form of any planning algorithm. (2) *Task Allocation*: The agents must allocate responsibility for tasks to individual agents. (3) *Plan Integration*: The agents must coordinate the solutions to each agent's subtasks in order to prevent conflicts. This involves the integration of partial plans while preventing "clobbering", scheduling each agent's actions to avoid resource conflicts, and so on.

During the plan execution phase, agents must monitor (1) the execution of their chosen actions to insure that the intended effects are achieved, and (2) the states of the environment (as well as behaviors of other agents) to insure that resources are available and cooperation (if there is any) is still working. If agents realize certain planned actions are not available or the plan is not achievable, the agent may restart planning at an earlier phase.

The problem-solving framework proposed here is aids in the design of MAS, such as Sensible Agents (SA) (Barber, 1996). SA use Dynamic Adaptive Autonomy (DAA) for organization design. SA have the ability to choose between and use both hierarchical planning strategies and operator search based strategies for plan generation (Barber and Han, 1998). Conflicts may be resolved using multiple strategies such as negotiation, arbitration, or self modification. Continuing development of the SA capabilities are currently being implemented and tested in the Sensible Agent Testbed.

References

Barber, K. S. 1996. The Architecture for Sensible Agents. In *Proceedings of the International Multidisciplinary Conference, Intelligent Systems: A Semiotic Perspective*, 49-54. Gaithersburg, MD: National Institute of Standards and Technology.

Barber, K. S. and Han, D. C. 1998. Multi-Agent Planning under Dynamic Adaptive Autonomy. In *Proceedings of the IEEE International Conference on Systems, Man, and Cybernetics*, 399-404. San Diego, CA, USA: IEEE.

This research is sponsored in part by the Texas Higher Education Coordinating Board #003658-415

Robot Navigation with a Polar Neural Map

Michail G. Lagoudakis[*]
Department of Computer Science
Duke University
Durham, NC 27708
mgl@cs.duke.edu

Anthony S. Maida
Center for Advanced Computer Studies
University of Southwestern Louisiana
Lafayette, LA 70504
maida@cacs.usl.edu

Neural maps have been recently proposed as an alternative method for mobile robot path planning (Glasius, Komoda, and Gielen 1995). However, these proposals are mostly theoretical and are primarily concerned with biological plausibility. Our purpose is to investigate their applicability on real robots.

Information about the environment is mapped on a topologically ordered neural population. The diffusion dynamics force the network into a unique equilibrium state that defines the navigation landscape for the given target. A path from any initial position to the target (corresponding to the peak of the activation surface) is derived by a steepest ascent procedure. The figures below show an example on a 50×50 rectangular map (a. Environment, b. Contours of activation, c. Path).

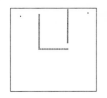 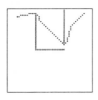

We attempted to implement the approach on a Nomad 200 mobile robot for sonar-based navigation. However, we found that the neural map requires reorganization in a polar topology that reflects the distribution of the sonar data points, the only source of information about the environment. The polar map covers the local circular area around at the robot. Sonar data points are mapped scaled to the physical robot size. At each step of the control loop, the dynamics of the map is used to derive the angular and radial displacement required to reach the target from the current configuration. A simplified example is shown below (bird's eye view). Sensor uncertainty and noise is handled by a sonar short-term memory and appropriate coordinate mapping for reuse. Motion control is based on an optimization procedure that combines ideas from Fox, Burgard, and Thrun (1997) and Hong et al (1996), and takes into account the kinematic and dynamic constraints of the robot. The complete architecture of the resulting local (sensor-based) navigation system is shown below.

* Partially supported by the Lilian-Boudouri Foundation in Greece.

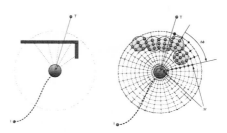

The system was tested in both simulated and real world (office) environments (see figure). It was able to successfully navigate avoiding static and dynamic obstacles. Complete description of the system as well as information on how it can be used for global navigation can be found in (Lagoudakis 1998).

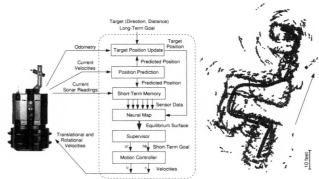

References

Fox, D.; Burgard, W.; and Thrun, S. 1997. The Dynamic Window Approach to Collision Avoidance. *IEEE Journal of Robotics and Automation* 4(1):23–33.

Glasius, R.; Komoda, A.; and Gielen, S. 1995. Neural Network Dynamics for Path Planning and Obstacle Avoidance. *Neural Networks* 8(1):125–133.

Hong, S.; Kim, S.; Park, K.; and Lee, J. 1996. Local Motion Planner for Nonholonomic Mobile Robots in the Presence of the Unknown Obstacles. In *Proc. IEEE Intl. Conf. on Robotics and Automation*, 1212–1217.

Lagoudakis, M. 1998. Mobile Robot Local Navigation with a Polar Neural Map. M.Sc. thesis, Center for Advanced Computer Studies, University of Southwestern Louisiana. Available online at http://www.cs.duke.edu/~mgl/acadpape.html.

Comparison of Clustering Metrics and Unsupervised Learning Algorithms on Genome-Wide Gene Expression Level Data

Sonia Leach†   Lawrence Hunter‡   David Landsman§

†Brown University
Box 1910
Providence RI 02912
sml@cs.brown.edu

‡National Cancer Institute, MS-9105
7550 Wisconsin Ave., Room 3C06
Bethesda, MD 20892-9015
hunter@msb.nci.nih.gov

§National Center for Biotechnology Information
National Library of Medicine
Bethesda MD 20894
landsman@ncbi.nlm.nih.gov

With the recent availability of genome-wide DNA sequence information, biologists are left with the overwhelming task of identifying the biological role of every gene in an organism. Technological advances now provide fast and efficient methods to monitor, on a genomic scale, the patterns of gene expression in response to a stimulus, lending key insight about a gene's function. With this wealth of information comes the need to organize and analyze the data.

One natural approach is to group together genes with similar patterns of expression. Several alternatives have been proposed for both the similarity metric and the clustering algorithm (Wen *et al.* 1998; Eisen *et al.* 1998). However, these studies used a specific metric-clustering algorithm pair. In our work, we aim to provide a more systematic investigation into the various metric and clustering algorithm alternatives. We also offer two methods to handle missing data.

The data sets include a single time course of rat spinal cord development, a single time course of a human cell growth model, and an aggregation of data from the yeast *S. cervisiae* under several experimental conditions. The data contains missing datapoints in cases of measurement error or inconclusive signal. We consider two techniques for handling missing datapoints, namely weighting by the number of valid points, and linear interpolation.

For similarity metrics, we compare a euclidean distance metric, a correlation metric, and a mutual information-based metric. The euclidean metric is commonly used due to its spatially intuitive interpretation of distance and ease of calculation. However, it might fail to recognize negative correlation, thus we use sample correlation to capture both positive and negative correlation. Not all the significant relationships between genes are modelled under either metric. In particular, both summarize the contributions along the whole trajectory, assuming that the type of correlation is constant throughout time. Two genes might be correlated positively within a certain range of their values and negatively related in another range. To capture this type of dependence, we consider a third metric based on mutual information.

We combine the metrics with unsupervised learning algorithms. We consider *k*-means, hierarchical agglomerative clustering and AutoClass (Cheeseman *et al.* 1988). The advantage of *k*-means is its simplicity. However, many iterations may be required and the number of clusters must be specified *a priori*. The hierarchical clustering algorithm attempts to cluster all elements (pairwise) into a single tree. The algorithm is fast and requires no *a priori* knowledge of the number of clusters. However, the cluster boundaries are usually manually extracted based on other known information, such as gene function. AutoClass (Cheeseman *et al.* 1988) can be viewed as a stochastic version of *k*-means which models the means as gaussians. AutoClass automatically searches for the number of clusters. However, as an approximation to the full-Bayesian classification, AutoClass can be slow on large problems.

We address questions like how different are the results using a particular combination of metric, clustering algorithm and missing value compensation? Which one is the best for this important application? How stable and reliable are the clusters? How well do the clusters match known functional classes? How sensitive are the methods to missing values?

The work by Sonia Leach was funded by a fellowship from the Rhode Island Space Grant Program under the National Space Grant College and Fellowship Program.

References

Cheeseman, P.; Kelly, J.; Self, M.; Stutz, J.; Taylor, W.; and Freeman, D. 1988. AutoClass: A Bayesian classification system. In *Proceedings of the Fifth International Conference on Machine Learning*, 54–64.

Eisen, M. B.; Spellman, P. T.; Brown, P. O.; and Botstein, D. 1998. Cluster analysis and display of genome-wide expression patterns. *Proceedings of the National Academy of Sciences USA* 95:14863–14868.

Wen, X.; Fuhrman, S.; Michaels, G. S.; Carr, D. B.; Smith, S.; Barker, J. L.; and Somogyi, R. 1998. Large-scale temporal gene expression mapping of central nervous system development. *Proceedings of the National Academy of Sciences* 95(1):334–339.

Knowledge Base Revision through
Exception-driven Discovery and Learning

Seok Won Lee and Gheorghe Tecuci

Learning Agents Laboratory, Computer Science Department, MSN 4A5, George Mason University, Fairfax, VA 22030-4444, USA
{swlee, tecuci}@gmu.edu

We are currently witnessing a trend toward an architectural separation of a knowledge base (KB) into an ontology and a set of rules. The ontology is a description of the concepts and relationships from the application domain; the rules are problem solving procedures expressed with the terms from the ontology. Moreover, terminological standardization taking place in more and more domains has led to the development of domain ontologies. These two developments raise the prospect of reusing existing ontologies when building a new knowledge based system. For instance, the Disciple approach for building a knowledge based agent relies on importing ontologies from existing repositories of knowledge, and on teaching the agent how to perform various tasks, in a way that resembles how an expert would teach a human apprentice when solving problems in cooperation (Tecuci, 1998; Tecuci et al. 1999). In Disciple, the ontology serves as the generalization hierarchy for learning, an example being basically generalized to a rule by replacing its objects with more general objects from the ontology. However, the learning works well only if the ontology contains all the concepts needed to represent the application domain. We make the assumption that an ontology built from previously developed KBs will contain useful concepts, but it is incomplete and will not contain the more subtle distinctions needed for competent and efficient problem solving in a particular domain. These missing concepts will manifest themselves as *exceptions* to the learned problem solving rules. A negative exception of the rule is a negative example that is covered by the rule and any specialization (within the current ontology) of the rule that would uncover the exception would result also in uncovering of positive examples of the rule. Similarly, a positive exception of the rule is a positive example that is not covered by the rule and any generalization of the rule that would cover the exception would also result in covering of negative examples of the rule.

We are enhancing Disciple by developing a mixed-initiative multistrategy approach to KB revision that will result in an extended and domain-adapted ontology, as well as a set of rules with fewer (if any) exceptions. We are developing two classes of KB revision methods, a class of local methods and a class of global methods. The local methods focus on one rule with its exceptions at a time, in conjunction with the current ontology. Some of the local methods use analogical transfer of discriminating features from some objects to other objects in the positive examples of a rule, by considering the similarities between the positive examples and their dissimilarities with the negative exceptions. Other local methods use explanation-based techniques, and similarities between the current rule and other rules, to discover or elicit from the expert discriminating features in the form of explanations of why a negative exception of a rule is not a correct problem solving episode. These local methods work well when the ontology already contains the definitions of the discriminating features, but the descriptions of some of the objects from the ontology are incomplete with respect to those features. The methods perform a local extension of the ontology that leads to a refinement of a rule and a removal of some of its exceptions.

Other local methods do not immediately extend the ontology, but suggest characterizations of new concepts that would remove the exceptions. An example of such a characterization is the following: a concept that covers the maximum number of objects from a set of objects and the minimum number of objects from another set of objects. The global methods analyze the alternative concept characterizations suggested by the local methods and attempt to discover a reduced set of concept characterizations that would remove exceptions from a set of rules. In this process, they use various specialization and generalization operators that combine the concept characterizations into a reduced set. They then interact with the domain expert to identify which of the most useful characterizations correspond to meaningful concepts or features in the application domain. The global methods lead to the extension of the ontology with definitions of new objects and features.

A significant part of our research effort is also devoted to the evaluation of the developed approach by measuring the effectiveness of the exception-driven discovery and learning with respect to the number of exceptions removed, the impact of the discovered knowledge on the remaining rules, the knowledge acquisition effort required from the domain expert, and the effect of the discovered knowledge on the agent's performance on a set of tasks.

In conclusion, we are developing a suite of methods that continuously extend the ontology and revise the rules in the KB through discovery, learning and an interaction with a domain expert in order to achieve competent and efficient problem solving in a particular domain.

Acknowledgments This work is supported by AFOSR grant F49620-97-1-0188, as part of DARPA's HPKB program.

References

Tecuci, G. 1998. *Building Intelligent Agents: An Apprenticeship Multistrategy Learning Theory, Methodology, Tool and Case Studies.* Academic Press.

Tecuci, G., Boicu, M., Wright, K., Lee, S.W., Marcu, D., and Bowman, M. 1999. An Integrated Shell and Methodology for Rapid Development of Knowledge-Based Agents. In *Proc. AAAI-99*, Menlo Park, CA: AAAI Press.

Autonomous Discovery In Empirical Domains

Gary Livingston

University of Pittsburgh
Room 202 Mineral Industries Building
Pittsburgh, PA 15260
Email: gary@cs.pitt.edu; WWW: www.cs.pitt.edu/~gary

Bruce G. Buchanan

University of Pittsburgh

We have tested a hypothesis that the agenda-based architecture used in AM (Lenat 1982) can be adapted to perform autonomous discovery in empirical domains. Our preliminary evaluation of our adaptation, HAMB (Heuristic, Autonomous Model Builder), suggests that the architecture is practical and sufficient for empirical discovery. HAMB was able to make many discoveries and rediscoveries from the domain of macromolecule crystal-growing experiments (Gililand 1987).

Adapting AM to Empirical Discovery

We made three types of changes to AM's basic structure:

- **New concept-space.** Instead of AM's concept-space of set- and number-theoretic concepts, we substituted concepts encountered while performing rule-induction: attributes, rules, conjuncts, example-sets, rule-sets, and example-classes.
- **New operation-types.** Because we changed the fundamental discovery-type and concept-space, we provided new operation-types.
- **New heuristics.** Because we changed the operation-types, we also changed the heuristics performing them.

HAMB's basic operation is identical to AM's: (1) select and remove the most "plausible" task from an agenda of tasks, (2) perform the task using heuristics provided for performing tasks, and (3) repeat steps (1) and (2) until a set of stopping criteria are satisfied. Tasks are put onto the agenda during initialization and while executing heuristics when performing tasks.

Calculating Plausibility: Reasons and Ratings

When putting a task onto the agenda, a heuristic provides *reasons*, text justifications, for performing the task, and corresponding *ratings*, numeric values indicating the relative strengths of the reasons. No task is allowed on the agenda without a reason for performing it. If a task is suggested that is already on the agenda, any new reasons and corresponding ratings are associated with the existing task, increasing its plausibility (see below).

A task's *plausibility* is calculated from the *ratings* of its reasons and the *worths* (interestingnesses) of the items in the task. *We feel that this use of a task's reasons and ratings as well as the worths of its items to calculate its plausibility makes the architecture particularly well suited for empirical discovery and discovery in general.*

The architecture's use of reasons and ratings has the following properties (ceteris paribus):

- No task is performed without a reason for performing it.
- A task with more or stronger reasons is more plausible.
- A task with more interesting items is more plausible.
- As additional reasons are identified for performing a task, the task's plausibility increases.

The reasons and ratings also provide two additional benefits. Because they are intuitive and heuristic in nature, they aid the creation of heuristics and task-types and increase the expressiveness of the task-types. And, reasons and ratings provide documentation for HAMB's choices of tasks, facilitating comprehension of its actions.

Conclusion

We have adapted Lenat's AM to autonomous empirical discovery. Our tests indicate that our adaptation, HAMB, is practical and sufficient for empirical discovery, making several significant discoveries and rediscoveries in the domain of macromolecule crystal-growing.

Bibliography

Gililand, G. C. 1987. A Biological Macromolecule Crystallization Database: A Basis for a Crystallization Strategy. In *Proceedings of the Second International Conference on Protein Crystal Growth.* Bischenberg, Strasbourg, France, North Holland.

Lenat, D. 1982. "AM: Discovery in Mathematics as Heuristic Search." In Lenat, D., and Davis, R., Eds., *Knowledge-Based Systems in Artificial Intelligence.* New York, New York, McGraw-Hill: 3-225.

Learning in Broker Agent

Xiaocheng Luan, Yun Peng, and Timothy Finin

Department of Computer Science and Electrical Engineering, University of Maryland Baltimore County
1000 Hilltop Circle
Baltimore, MD 21250
{xluan1, ypeng, finin}@cs.umbc.edu

One of the common ways to achieve interoperability among the autonomous agents is to use a broker agent (or a facilitator). The idea is, on the one hand, individual agents can advertise their capabilities to the broker agent; on the other hand, an agent can also ask the broker agent which agent(s) has certain capabilities (ask for recommendation). Simple broker agents provide match-making services based on the capability information volunteered by individual agents and the (recommendation) request. The problem is, even with a very good agent capability description language and a powerful match-making mechanism (such as LARKS), if the actual capability information volunteered by each individual agent is not accurate, it won't be of much help. Given that the autonomous agents might be written by different people, at different time, and for different purpose, this is likely to occur. For example, two Toyota car dealers (A and B) might give the same advertisement "We sell all models of Toyota cars, lowest price guaranteed". The fact might be that at dealer A, you have fewer or no choice of colors on popular models as you can at the other dealer. The service quality is different.

This work is an attempt to solve such problems by incorporating learning into broker agents so that the broker agents can capture more accurate information about the capabilities of individual agents. This is a result of an intuitive observation in the real world: don't be fooled by the beautiful words and colorful pictures in the commercials, consult a consumer report. In analogy, the broker tries to build agent consumer reports through learning. One of the learning methods we propose is based on concept-generalization and concept-specialization. In this learning method, we assume that the broker agent has limited domain knowledge, in the form of domain ontology, which is organized into tree-like class hierarchy. Based on this domain hierarchy, the broker agent can build service information trees. The capability information of an agent is associated with the appropriate nodes of the trees. Then, the broker agent continuously refines its knowledge about these agents through the interactions with them, and possibly by observing the interactions among the agents. The broker can learn the capability information from the following channels: advertisements from individual agents, interrogating/testing an agent about its capabilities, feedback for previous recommendations (volunteered or requested), and possibly the "past experience" of some agents and the (recommendation) requests from individual agents. One of the insights behind this learning method is the law of locality. The more frequently an aspect of an agent's capability is referenced, the more accurately the capability information around this aspect will be captured by the broker (through learning), and thus better overall system performance could be achieved.

We are also exploring the collaboration of multiple brokers. This includes the distribution of agent capability information over the brokers, collaborative learning, and knowledge sharing. With collaborative brokering, the bottle neck problem and the single point of failure problem could be avoided.

By incorporating learning techniques, a broker agent would be able to capture more accurate capability information of individual agents, build "agent consumer reports", and can thus help achieve more effective cooperation among agents.

References

Gruber, T. R. 1991. The Role of Common Ontology in Achieving Sharable, Reusable Knowledge Bases. In Allen, J. A., Fikes, R., and Sandewall, E. (Eds). Principles of Knowledge Representation and Reasoning: *Proceedings of the Second International Conference.* San Mateo, CA: Morgan KaufMann.

Lenzmann, B. and Wachsmuth, I. 1997. Contract Net Based Learning in a User-Adaptive Interface Agency. In Weiss, G., editor (*LNAI* 1221), *Distributed Artificial Intelligence Meets Machine Learning*, pages 223-241. Springer Verlag.

Weiss, G. 1995. Adaptation and Learning in Multi-Agent Systems: Some Remarks and a Bibliography. In Weiss, G. and Sen, S. editors (*LNAI* 1042), *Adaptation and Learning in Multi-Agent Systems*, pages 1-21. Springer Verlag.

http://www.cs.cmu.edu/~softagents/interop/matchmaking.html

Text Compression as a Test for Artificial Intelligence

Matthew V. Mahoney

Florida Institute of Technology
150 W. University Blvd.
Melbourne FL 32901
matmahoney@aol.com

It is shown that optimal text compression is a harder problem than artificial intelligence as defined by Turing's (1950) imitation game; thus compression ratio on a standard benchmark corpus could be used as an objective and quantitative alternative test for AI (Mahoney, 1999). Specifically, let L, M, and J be the probability distributions of responses chosen by a human, machine, and human judge respectively to the judge's questions in the imitation game. The goal of AI is $M = L$, the machine is indistinguishable from human. But the machine wins (the judge guesses that it is human) when $H_J(M) < H_J(L)$, where $H_Q(P) \equiv -\Sigma_x P(x) \log Q(x)$ is the cross entropy of Q with respect to P. This happens when J is a poor estimate of L, meaning that the interrogator fails to anticipate the human's responses, but even in the worst case when $J = L$, the machine can still win with a suboptimal solution ($M \neq L$) by deterministically favoring the most likely responses over the true distribution. In contrast, optimal compression of a probabilistic language L with unknown distribution (such as English) using an estimated distribution M (an encoding of length $-\log_2 M(x)$ bits for each string x) is $M = L$, by the discrete channel capacity theorem (Shannon, 1949).

Answering questions in the Turing test (*What are roses?*) seems to require the same type of real-world knowledge that people use in predicting characters in a stream of natural language text (*Roses are ___?*), or equivalently, estimating $L(x)$ for compression. Shannon (1951), and Cover and King (1978) established an upper bound of 1.3 bits per character (bpc) for the entropy (information content) of English narrative in a 27-character alphabet (A-Z and space) using human prediction tests.

No compression program has achieved this. Seven programs, including those top-rated by Gilchrist (1998) and Bell (1998) were used to compress English narrative, *Alice in Wonderland* (*alice30.txt* from the Gutenberg press, minus header) and *Far from the Madding Crowd* by Thomas Hardy (*book1* from the Calgary corpus), after reducing both to 27 characters. The best compression was achieved by *rkive 1.91b1*: 1.86 bpc on *alice* and 1.94 on *book1*. Others tested (from worst to best) were *compress 4.3d, pkzip 2.04e, gzip 1.2.4, ha 0.98, szip 1.05x,* and *boa 0.58b*. All program options were set for maximum compression.

Better compressors "learn", using prior input to improve compression on subsequent input. *szip* was the best learner, compressing *book1* to about 95% of the size of the two halves compressed separately. The first figure below shows the correlation between compression and learning. Similar results were obtained for *alice*.

It was also found that better compressors make greater use of the syntactic and semantic constraints of English. Lexical,

syntactic, and semantic constraints were selectively broken by swapping pairs of letters within words, pairs of words, or pairs of phrases respectively. Results for the original text of *book1* are shown in the second figure, with similar results for *alice*. The swapping transforms are reversible and do not change file size or information content.

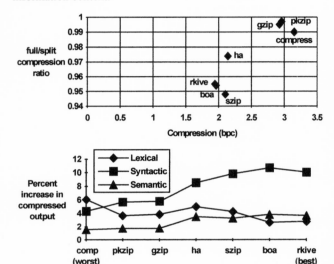

Acknowledgments. I would like to thank Dr. Phil Chan for guidance in developing this paper.

References

Bell, T., 1998. Canterbury Corpus, http://corpus.canterbury.ac.nz/

Cover, T. M., and King, R. C., 1978. A Convergent Gambling Estimate of the Entropy of English. *IEEE Transactions on Information Theory* 24:413-421.

Gilchrist, J. 1998. Archive Comparison Test, http://www.geocities.com/SiliconValley/Park/4264/act-mcal.html

Mahoney, M., 1999. Text Compression as a Test for Artificial Intelligence, http://www.he.net/~mmahoney/paper4.ps.Z

Shannon, C., and Weaver W., 1949. *The Mathematical Theory of Communication*. Urbana: University of Illinois Press.

Shannon, C. 1951. Prediction and Entropy in Printed English. *Bell Sys. Tech. J.* 3:50-64.

Turing, A. M., 1950. Computing Machinery and Intelligence. *Mind* 59:433-460.

Externalizing Internal State

Amol D. Mali
Dept. of computer science & Engg.
Arizona state university, Tempe, AZ 85287-5406
amol.mali@asu.edu

Current autonomous robots that are highly reactive are not significantly intelligent and the robots that are significantly intelligent are not highly reactive. The previous research has concentrated on modifications to internal computational structures of robots, ignoring the modifications to external environments (which can preserve both intelligence and reactivity). This work is the first to formalize the modification of an environment that externalizes the internal states. Since some reactive robots exhibited problems like deadlocks and myopic functionality, hybrid architectures with modules like planners began to be explored. In this transition, the potential of reactivity went largely unexamined. Making a robot more reactive means transforming its internal state into an external state that can be extracted through perception (we do not use response time to measure the degree of reactivity, though the response time is important). Some internal states have to be updated whenever external world changes and externalizing these states eliminates such updates, since the most recent information is available in the world itself. Hence there are reasons for robots to be more reactive.

In the mobile robot competitions of the American Association of Artificial Intelligence, the rocks in the event of finding life on Mars were painted black to aid in visual recognition. However this kind of environmental modification has not been formally incorporated into the architectures of autonomous robots. As a result, it has been viewed more as a low level fix rather than as a paradigm that deserves a separate investigation. Our work bridges this gap.

The states are externalized through environment modifiers called "markers". These markers are semantically equivalent to the internal states that they externalize, e.g. a blue strip of paper (a marker) on the door of a refrigerator can be used to recognize the refrigerator and thus the presence of the blue strip is equivalent to the presence of the refrigerator (when these strips are put only on the refrigerators). An introduction of markers requires a modification to the behaviors' stimuli, so that the markers can play an active role in the functionality of a robot. Markers can be kept only on certain ob-

jects that meet a criterion (local externalization) or on all objects that meet the criterion (global externalization). Markers can also be used to specialize stimuli of behaviors (to avoid triggering of the behaviors on unwanted occasions). In [1], we have handled these technical challenges in formalizing the state externalization and defined various metrics to capture properties of the markers. The "strength" of a marker captures the extent to which one can exploit the marker in externalizing state. The time required to recognize a marker is a measure of its "efficiency". The relationships between logical formulae describing the markers can be used to test the "redundancy" of a set of markers. Though externalizing internal state can be seen as replacing the complexity of state update by the complexity of sensing, there will be a net benefit if the markers are "efficient".

We have also addressed [1] the problem of automated synthesis of markers. It may be desirable for certain chains of behaviors to execute after certain other chains of behaviors, since this fulfills some goals of interest to a user. Since there is no explicit representation of goals in a purely reactive robot, such an ordering of behaviors is hard to guarantee. The chains of behaviors may not execute in the desired order, either because the relevant stimuli are absent or are not strong enough to be detected. Given two chains of behaviors, what marker should be introduced in the environment to join these chains? We have proposed a procedure to compute markers that concatenate the chains of behaviors *through the external world*, rather than generating them through internal reasoning, as in the classical planners. This illustrates the utility of markers in the composition of more complex reactive behavior. One may be concerned that a frequent change in the tasks of a user will require a significant user intervention for a frequent introduction and removal of markers or a change in the definitions of the robot's behaviors. To prevent this, we have shown how the markers can be automatically introduced and removed, with the help of a marker management module. We intend to test the formalization [1] through simulation in future.

[1] **Mali A. D.**, Externalizing Internal State, Technical Report TR-98-016, Dept. of Computer Science, Arizona state university, 1998.

Hybrid Propositional Encodings of Planning

Amol D. Mali

Dept. of computer science & Engg.
Arizona state university, Tempe, AZ 85287-5406
amol.mali@asu.edu

Casting planning as propositional satisfiability has been recently shown to be a very promising technique of plan synthesis. Some challenges, one of which is the development of hybrid propositional encodings (that combine the important notions from the existing encodings) have also been posed to the community [1]. The existing encodings [3] are either entirely based only on the plan space planning (also known as "causal" or "least commitment" or "partial order" planning) or only on the state space planning. To answer this challenge, we have developed several hybrid encodings.

A key difference between state space planning and plan space planning is that state of the world is represented at each time step during the state space planning process and it is never available during the partial order planning process. This also holds for the corresponding propositional encodings. We bridge these extremes of not representing the state at all and maintaining the state at each time step, by controlling the number of time steps at which the state is represented. Our hybrid *unifying encoding* (Fig. 1) not only represents the world states, but also allows partial order on the plan steps that are "sandwiched" in the "regions" between the consecutive world states. We also developed several other hybrid encodings shown in Fig. 2. Since the hardness of solving an encoding is generally correlated with its size (especially in domain independent planning), we computed the number of clauses and variables in each of these hybrid encodings and theoretically proved [2] that no hybrid encoding can have fewer clauses or fewer variables than the currently smallest encoding (state space encoding with explanatory frame axioms [3]). Our future work involves an empirical evaluation of these hybrid encodings as well as their integer linear programming formulations.

[1] **Subbarao Kambhampati**, Challenges in bridging the plan synthesis paradigms, Proceedings of the International Joint Conference on Artificial Intelligence (IJCAI), 1997.
[2] **Amol D. Mali**, On the hybrid propositional encodings of planning, Technical Report TR-98-019, Dept. of computer science & engg., Arizona state university, 1998.
[3] **Henry Kautz, David McAllester and Bart Selman**, Encoding plans in propositional logic, Proceedings of the Knowledge Representation & Reasoning (KRR) conference, 1996.

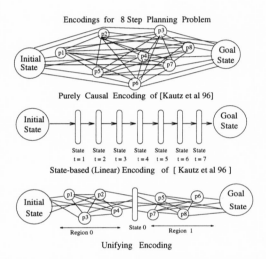

Figure 1: Propositional Encodings of Classical Planning Problems.

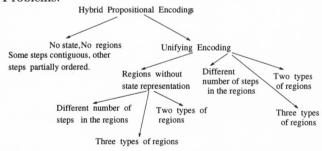

Figure 2: Hybrid Encodings of Classical Planning Problems. A region can be of one of the three types, based on the ordering of the steps in the region - 1. All steps are contiguous, 2. All steps are partially ordered, 3. Some steps are partially ordered, others are contiguous.

Causal Discovery
from Population-Based Infant Birth and Death Records

Subramani Mani and **Gregory F. Cooper**
Center for Biomedical Informatics, Suite 8084, Forbes Tower, 200 Lothrop Street,
University of Pittsburgh, Pittsburgh PA 15213, Ph: 412-647-7113; Fax: 412-647-7190
{mani,gfc}@cbmi.upmc.edu

Introduction

The most useful explanation of a phenomenon is often a description of the underlying causal processes (Salmon 1998). This is particularly true in the domain of medicine where identification of the causal factors of a disease influence treatment planning and development of intervention strategies for disease prevention and control. The study described here focuses on causal discovery from observational data related to infant mortality in the United States.

Methods

Infant Birth and Death Dataset

We used the U.S. Linked Birth/Infant Death dataset for 1991. This consists of information on all the live births in the United States for the year 1991. It also has linked data for infants who died within one year of birth. We selected a random subset of 41,155 cases (1% of the total sample) for use in the current study.

An Algorithm for Causal Discovery

In this section, we introduce a causal discovery algorithm called LCD2. LCD2 assumes the following:

Assumption 1: Causal relationships are represented using Bayesian Networks.

Assumption 2: Variables W and Y test as being independent given variable X, if and only if W and Y are d-separated (Pearl 1991) given X.

Assumption 3: There is a variable W that is not caused by any other measured variable in the dataset.

Given Assumptions 1–3 above and using a set of *independence* and *dependence* tests detailed in (Cooper 1997), the LCD2 algorithm explores a database for possible causal relationships of the following form $W \rightarrow X \rightarrow Y$. This is a causal model in which W causes X, and X causes Y. If the data suggests the presence of such causal relationships, LCD2 outputs that X causally influences Y, and it displays the probability distribution of Y given X. The time complexity of LCD2 is $O(mn^2)$, where m is the number of records in the database and n is the number of variables. We implemented LCD2 in the PERL programming language. For W we used *Race of the mother*.

Results

When applied to the infant birth and death dataset, LCD2 output nine purported causal relationships. Table 1 shows the probability distributions associated with one of the relationships: *Birth-weight* → *Infant Outcome*.

Table 1: Conditional Probability Table of Infant Outcome At One Year given Infant Birth Weight

Birth Weight	Infant outcome at one year	
	Survived	Died
<1500 gms.	0.713*	0.287
1500–2499 gms.	0.977	0.023
≥ 2500 gms.	0.997	0.003

*The probability that Infant outcome at one year equals Survived *given* that Infant Birth Weight *is* <1500 grams.

Discussion and Conclusion

Out of the nine causes discovered in the infant birth and death dataset, eight appear plausible. Due to space limitations we showed only one of them here. From Table 1 we can see that as the birth weight increases from less than 1500 grams to 1500–2499 grams and then to 2500 or more grams, the probability of survival increases from 0.713 to 0.977 and further to 0.997.

In summary, for this dataset, the LCD2 algorithm appears to be outputting relationships that on the whole are plausibly causal.

References

Cooper, G. F. 1997. A Simple Constraint-Based Algorithm for Efficiently Mining Observational Databases for Causal Relationships. *Data Mining and Knowledge Discovery* 1:203–224.

Pearl, J. 1991. *Probabilistic Reasoning in Intelligent Systems*. San Francisco, California: Morgan Kaufmann.

Salmon, W. C. 1998. *Causality and Explanation*. New York: Oxford University Press.

Interacting with a Pet Robot using Hand Gestures

Milyn C. Moy

MIT Artificial Intelligence Lab / Oracle Corporation
500 Oracle Parkway
Redwood Shores, CA 94065
milyn@ai.mit.edu

Pet robots are autonomous robots capable of exhibiting animal-like behaviors, including emotional ones. As they become more integrated into our lives, we will need a more natural way of communicating with them. Similarly, to perceive our intentions more effectively, they will need to understand human gestures.

This work focuses on the real-time, visual interpretation of 2D dynamic hand gestures in complex environments. Our goal is to enable humans to communicate and interact with Yuppy, a pet robot being developed at the MIT AI Lab. The gesture lexicon consists of a set of 2D gesture classes (primitives) that include linear (vertical, horizontal, and diagonal) as well as circular (clockwise and counterclockwise) gestures.

As the user makes the gesture, images taken by the robot's camera are processed on a frame by frame basis. We assume that the user wears long-sleeved clothes and the robot is static while observing the gesture. Our strategy for interpreting hand gestures consists of: hand segmentation, feature extraction, and gesture recognition. Currently, our algorithms run in a user-specified window of attention which excludes the user's face.

We use both motion and color information to segment the hand from the cluttered background. Motion is detected by taking the image difference of three sequential RGB images. The skin-colored regions are computed by comparing the HLS representation of an input image with an a priori model of skin color in HS space. The results of these two modules are combined and the hand is chosen to be the skin-colored region with the largest area and the greatest number of displaced pixels. The motion of the hand's centroid is tracked in real-time as new image frames are processed.

Our system assumes that once the hand's velocity exceeds a certain threshold, the user has started a gesture. As the hand moves, the horizontal and vertical displacements (dx, dy) of the hand's centroid are stored in a feature vector until the hand pauses for 2-3 seconds.

To recognize a gesture, we analyze the feature vector. For linear gestures, the (dx, dy) displacements cluster around fixed axes in the dx-dy plane: vertical gestures around the dy axis, horizontal gestures around the dx axis, and diagonal gestures around the two bisecting axes (45° with respect to the dx-dy axes). The direction of motion is determined by the side of the axis (positive/negative) on which clustering occurs. For circular gestures, the centroid of these displacements coincides with the origin, and the direction of motion is deduced from the time sequence of (dx, dy) in the feature vector.

Once the gesture is identified, it is queried in a database of user-specified gestures. If found, the command associated with the gesture is issued to the robot; otherwise, the gesture is ignored. Composite gestures can also be recognized by combining these primitives.

We performed an initial experiment where 14 subjects were asked to perform 5 times a sequence of 16 gestures. We achieved above 15 frames per second using a 300 MHz Pentium Pro system. The accuracy rate is over 90% for primitive gestures and slightly above 70% for composite gestures. These results demonstrate the viability of our system for unstructured environments and its robustness to different skin tonalities and varying lighting conditions. Some reasons for which the obtained accuracy was not higher include problems in reliably tracking the hand and detecting the beginning of gestures, distortions caused by the camera's tilt, and errors made by the subjects while gesturing.

Despite these problems, via an off-board color microcamera, any person can easily navigate the robot around the lab using each primitive gesture as a command. New behaviors such as approaching a person and searching for a bone can be implemented on Yuppy using this interface. Future work will address additional competency in tracking the hand's motion, coping with simultaneous motion of both the robot and the human, and supporting simultaneous interaction of multiple people with the robot. We are also interested in gesture learning, the robot's reaction to both what it perceives and how it feels, and the interpretation of humans' emotions implicit in their gestures. See (Moy 1999) for a more detailed description of this work.

References

Moy, M. C. 1999. Gesture-based interaction with a pet robot. In *Proceedings of the Sixteenth National Conference on Artificial Intelligence*.

Active Learning for Hierarchical Wrapper Induction

Ion Muslea, Steve Minton, and Craig Knoblock
Information Sciences Institute / University of Southern California
4676 Admiralty Way
Marina del Rey, CA 90230, USA
{muslea, minton, knoblock}@isi.edu

Information mediators that allow users to integrate data from several Web sources rely on *wrappers* that extract the relevant data from the Web documents. Wrappers turn collections of Web pages into database-like tables by applying a set of extraction rules to each individual document. Even though the extraction rules can be written by humans, this is undesirable because the process is tedious, time consuming, and requires a high level of expertise.

As an alternative to manually writing extraction rules, we created STALKER (Muslea, Minton, & Knoblock 1999), which is a wrapper induction algorithm that learns high-accuracy extraction rules. The major novelty introduced by STALKER is the concept of *hierarchical* wrapper induction: the extraction of the relevant data is performed in a hierarchical manner based on the embedded catalog tree (ECT), which is a user-provided description of the information to be extracted. Consider the sample document

<html> Name: Joe's <p>
Cuisine: American <p>
Menu: Salad $2, Soup $1.5, Steak $4.25. </html>

It is easy to see that the document above has a hierarchical structure: at the top level, the whole page can be seen as a 3-tuple that contains the name, cuisine, and menu. The name and cuisine are atomic items (i.e., strings), while the menu is an *embedded list* of 2-tuples that contain the course name and the price. Consequently, the relevant data in the document can be seen as the leaves of a tree-like structure in which the root represents the whole page, and all internal nodes are embedded lists. STALKER generates one extraction rule for each node in the tree, together with an additional list iteration rule for each internal node.

Given the learned rules and the ECT of the documents, the extraction is performed in a hierarchical manner. A straightforward example would be to extract the restaurant name from the page above: we can use the rule SkipTo(Name:) to ignore everything until "Name:", which immediately precedes the restaurant name; then we can apply SkipUntil(<p>) to extract all characters until we find "<p>". In order to perform a more complicated task, say to extract the names of all the courses in the menu, STALKER first extracts the whole menu, and then it applies the corresponding list iteration rule to obtain the individual 2-tuples

that describe each course. Finally, the rule for the course name is applied to each 2-tuple obtained during the previous step.

Our approach has two main advantages. First, it can be applied to sources that contain arbitrarily many sibling and embedded lists. For instance, the pages might also include a list of accepted credit cards, and each 2-tuple in the menu might also include an embedded list of actual dishes (e.g., "Soup (bean, beef, chicken) $1.5"). Second, as sibling nodes are extracted independently of each other, the learning process is not affected by the various orders in which the items may appear in the pages.

As labeling the training data is the major bottleneck in all inductive approaches to information extraction, researchers have tried to reduce the burden by using active learning (see (Califf 1998) and (Soderland 1999)). We created SGAL, which is a committee-based active learning algorithm that uses STALKER to generate 2-member committees of extraction rules. Our approach is similar to *active learning with committees* (Liere & Tadepalli 1997), except that our committee members are not chosen randomly: the two extraction rules in the committee belong to the most specific and most general borders of the version space (Mitchell 1977).

In this abstract we relate the idea of active learning with committees to version space, and we apply it to hierarchical wrapper induction. The initial results are promising: we compared SGAL and STALKER on 14 extraction tasks, and the former always does at least as well as the latter. More important, SGAL learns 100% accurate rules on four out of the five tasks on which STALKER fails to do so.

References

Califf, M. 1998. Relational learning techniques for natural language information extraction. *PhD Thesis, U. Texas.*

Liere, R., and Tadepalli, P. 1997. Active learning with committees for text categorization. *AAAI-97.*

Mitchell, T. 1977. Version spaces: a candidate elimination approach to rule learning. *IJCAI-77.*

Muslea, I.; Minton, S.; and Knoblock, C. 1999. A hierarchical approach to wrapper induction. *Auton. Agents-99.*

Soderland, S. 1999. Learning information extraction rules for semi-structured and free text. *J. of Machine Learning.*

Decision-Theoretic Layered Robotic Control Architecture

Gilbert Peterson and Diane J. Cook

University of Texas at Arlington
Computer Science and Engineering
Planning and Learning Laboratory
Box 19015, Arlington, TX 76019-015
{gpeterson, cook}@cse.uta.edu

One of the current methods for developing task control software for robots is a layering approach. This approach generally consists of a symbolic planner, a task sequencer, and a behavioral robotic controller. The task sequencer is responsible for taking a command from an abstract plan and selecting which robot level actions and behaviors to execute. This representation leads to a robust functioning software control for a robot and a single task [Bonnasso and Kortenkamp, 1996]. When the robot must be reconfigured for a new task, elements must be added to the sequencer, and behaviors to the behavioral controller.

We are currently developing a decision-theoretic planner to function as the planning and sequencing layers for the architecture. It is our expectation that using a decision-theoretic planner as the sequencer will reduce the amount of work to reconfigure for a new task. We will verify the reconfigurability of our system by creating one set of behavior controllers for our robots and demonstrating the effectiveness of the controllers on multiple diverse plans. Nourbakhsh has implemented a similar system using a symbolic planner in which all planning was abstracted into three levels [Nourbakhsh, 1997]. We choose to incorporate a decision-theoretic planner instead of a symbolic one to make tradeoffs between risk and desire. In addition, this representation allows us to formally reason about the uncertainty that is inherent with robot tasks.

Our planner, DT-Graphplan, adds decision theory into the Graphplan algorithm, extending the domain to handle contingent and probabilistic actions as well as utility driven search. This is an extension of the recent work conducted on extending Graphplan to handle probabilities [Weld et al. 1998]. We incorporate utility reasoning into the existing multiple world approach that represents the effect of each action in all possible worlds. Instead of specifying a goal criterion, a minimum acceptable utility threshold is set for the planner. The planner searches for a plan that meets this minimum threshold, pruning world state with low utility values. Requests made to the robot are not represented as goals, but receive a utility commensurate with their value, and instigate replanning.

Certain elements in a robotic domain are best represented with decision-theoretic methods. One such element is resource manipulations associated with actions. For example, for a time-constrained task, the robot should perform actions to reach a goal, trading off taking great risks, or postponing a less important task to save time. The comparison between the risk of an action and its chance of success is another example. The utility of a risky move with low probability of success but great potential rewards will be compared with the utility of a conservative move with high probability of success and moderate potential rewards.

One issue that must be addressed regarding the decision-theoretic approach specific to robotic domains is associated with action looping. An example of the problem arises with sonar sensors. A percentage of error in sonar readings comes from specular reflections. If the robot remains in the same location and continues to read the sonar, this error may never resolve itself. However, each time the sonar is read, the belief in the validity of the reading increases to the point that an incorrect reading is accepted as valid. The sonar should instead be represented as two types of probability, an intermittent failure probability, and a non-looping failure. The non-looping failure prevents the probability of success from increasing each time the same action is immediately repeated.

Through decision-theoretic reasoning, our system can act as both the planner and sequencer in a robust, reconfigurable layered robot control architecture. The end goals are the creation of a decision-theoretic version of Graphplan, and a three layered robot control system where the planner handles each finer level of plan detail. Resulting in a system that can switch tasks with less programming, and plan in a resource dictated manner.

References

Bonasso, R.P. and Kortenkamp, D. 1996. Using a layered control architecture to alleviate planning with incomplete information. In Proceedings of the AAAI Spring Symposium, "Planning with Incomplete Information for Robot Problems". 1-4.

Nourbakhsh, I. 1997. Interleaving Planning and Execution for Autonomous Robots. Ph.D. thesis. Department of Computer Science, Stanford University.

Weld, D., Anderson, C., and Smith, D. 1998. Extending Graphplan to Handle Uncertainty & Sensing Actions. AAAI-98. 897-904.

Learning of Compositional Hierarchies
By Data-Driven Chunking

Karl Pfleger
Computer Science Department
Stanford University
Stanford, CA 94305
kpfleger@cs.stanford.edu

Compositional hierarchies (CHs), layered structures of *part-of* relationships, underlie many forms of data, and representations involving these structures lie at the heart of much of AI. Despite this importance, methods for learning CHs from data are scarce. We present an unsupervised technique for learning CHs by an on-line, bottom-up *chunking* process. At any point, the induced structure can make predictions about new data.

Currently we work with with 1-dimensional, discrete-position data (sequential data but not necessarily directional), where each position is occupied by a symbol from a discrete, finite alphabet, and where the data is potentially unbounded in both directions, not organized into a set of strings with definite beginnings and ends. Unlike some chunking systems, our chunking is purely data-driven in the sense that only the data, and its underlying statistical regularities, are used to construct the hierarchy. Abstractly, we proceed by repeatedly identifying frequently occurring substructures and forming new nodes for them in the hierarchy.

We have developed two systems, both implemented as symmetric, recurrent neural networks. Both can be viewed as follow-ups to the successful interactive activation model (IAM) (McClelland & Rumelhart 1981), extending it in a number of ways, primarily to incorporate learning. The first system and more details on CH learning in general are described in (Pfleger 1998).

The second system uses a Boltzmann machine, extended to handle categorical values and weight sharing. As with IAM, the network encodes a CH directly using a localist representation. Weight sharing and "hardware" duplication (unrolling) are used to model atomic symbols and chunks at different positions. Atomic symbols (the data) are visible variables and the chunks are hidden variables. Chunking is accomplished as an on-line structure modification rule. Specifically, new chunks are created when the weights between existing atoms or chunks show strong positive co-occurrence. Somewhat like a reverse-decimation, the original direct weight is removed and a new node representing the aggregation is created with links to its two constituents.

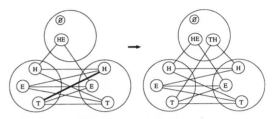

A novel use of Hebbian weight dynamics is the key to triggering chunking. The now 50-year-old Hebb rule says that the weight between two nodes should increase when the nodes are simultaneously active. Thus, the magnitude of the weight measures co-occurrences and can be used to directly signal chunking. This can be seen as automatically promoting 2nd-order correlations to become themselves first-class entities, allowing the subsequent detection of higher and higher order relationships, specifically higher order relationships that correspond to compositional structure.

The ability to grow the width of interactions captured by the model provides clear advantages over applying standard ML models in a fixed-width, sliding window fashion. Also, the ability to make predictions about any position provides more flexibility than predict-the-next-symbol paradigms. Space prevents discussion of the relations with HMMs and grammar induction methods.

In summary, this work can be seen as a long overdue continuation of work that makes predictions using hand-crafted CHs, such as early blackboard systems and IAM. We believe that compositional aggregation is one of the keys for bridging the gap between low-level, fine-grained representations and high level concepts, and that this is extremely important for long-lived autonomous systems in complex environments.

References

McClelland, J. L., and Rumelhart, D. E. 1981. An interactive activation model of context effects in letter perception: Part 1. an account of basic findings. *Psychological Review* 88:375–407.

Pfleger, K. 1998. Learning of compositional hierarchies for the modeling of context effects. Technical Report KSL–98–04, Stanford. See www-ksl.stanford.edu/publications/.

A representation reducing approach to scientific discovery

Joseph Phillips

University of Michigan
1101 Beal Ave., Ann Arbor, MI 48109-2110, USA
josephp@eecs.umich.edu

The proliferation of sensors and the ease of large dataset maintenance have given many scientists more data than can be analyzed by traditional means. Computers have long been used to help scientists calculate. Science, however, is more than calculating. Science at least also involves hypothesis generation and testing, planning, and integrating prior knowledge with new ideas. Artificial intelligence (AI) and database (DB) technologies have grown to the point where they may be able to help scientists in more meaningful ways. We investigate a principled approach to semi-automated knowledge discovery in databases (KDD) for integrated scientific discovery and the rationale for this approach.

Nordhausen and Langley developed perhaps the first system for integrated automated scientific discovery (Nordhausen & Langley 1990). IDS (for Integrated Discovery System) takes an initial **is-a** hierarchy and a sequential list of "histories" (qualitative states) and produces a fuller, richer hierarchy of classified history abstractions with associated state and transition laws. The system can learn taxonomic, qualitative and numeric relations and can make predictions.

Unfortunately, IDS' hierarchy imposes a scientifically irrelevant bias. Operations are limited to local tree manipulations. This constrains search by limiting operator applicability. However, it also limits the resulting knowledge to be obtainable by local comparison.

Some sort of bias is needed to control search. We suggest replacing this external bias with one that many believe is already employed in scientific discovery: Occam's Razor. Occam's razor has the advantage of having a history in both machine learning (Briscoe & Caelli 1996) and scientific discovery (Mach 1895). Our approach is to try to minimize the combined size of a stylized Prolog program that can predict the data with some degree of accuracy, and, a correcting string composed of the errors (*i.e* observed value minus predicted). The method is motivated by Minimum Description Length encoding (Rissanen 1983). Prolog programs are chosen from a restricted class that have some of the computational machinery of modern science. Like IDS, these programs can represent and use taxonomies, equa-tions and symbolic knowledge. Correcting strings have a field for each observed value. The length of each field increases monotonically with the magnitude of the error. Unless we want to compress the table without loss, it suffices to estimate a correcting string's length rather than actually identify it.

Just because we change the bias to the "tried-and-true" Occam's razor does not make the problem simpler, however. One problem is that we do not know *a priori* which operators are best. This may be cast as a multi-armed bandit problem where a discovery operator instance's probability of success depends on its type. Operator instance types group instances by the operator, the kind of data that the operator is applied to, the results of prior operator instances, *etc*. Our research investigates a method of intelligently estimating the operator instance's probability of success from estimates generated by its and similar types. Success estimates generated at different levels of type specificity are combined so that more specific information is relied upon more heavily as it becomes more statistically significant. The main responsibility for estimating success probability smoothly transitions from very general to very specific estimators for as many levels of specificity as desired.

I present criteria for KDD specific to scientific discovery that allow me to characterize how well my approach does when compared with IDS and other KDD methods. Seismology is used as a test domain.

References

Briscoe, G., Caelli, T., 1996. *A Compendium of Machine Learning, Volume 1: Symbolic Machine Learning.* Norwood, New Jersey: Ablex.

Mach, E. 1895. The Economical Nature of Physics in *Popular scientific lectures.* tr. by T. J. McCormack, Chicago: The Open Court Publishing Company, 1895.

Nordhausen, B., Langley, P., 1990. An Integrated Approach to Empirical Discovery. In J. Shrager and P. Langley (Eds.) *Computational Models of Scientific Discovery and Theory Formation*, San Mateo, CA: Morgan Kaufmann, 1990.

Rissanen, J., 1983. A Universal Prior For Integers And Estimation By Minimum Description Length, *The Annals of Statistics*, Vol 11, No. 2, p. 416-431.

Minimal Cost Complexity Pruning of Meta-Classifiers

Andreas L. Prodromidis and **Salvatore J. Stolfo**
Department of Computer Science
Columbia University
New York, NY 10027
{andreas,sal}@cs.columbia.edu

Integrating multiple learned classification models (classifiers) computed over large and (physically) distributed data sets has been demonstrated as an effective approach to scaling inductive learning techniques, while also boosting the accuracy of individual classifiers. These gains, however, come at the expense of an increased demand for run-time system resources. The final ensemble meta-classifier may consist of a large collection of base classifiers that require increased memory resources while also slowing down classification throughput. To classify unlabeled instances, predictions need to be generated from all base-classifiers before the meta-classifier can produce its final classification. The throughput (prediction rate) of a meta-classifier is of significant importance in real-time systems, such as in e-commerce or intrusion detection.

This extended abstract describes a *pruning* algorithm that is independent of the combining scheme and is used for discarding redundant classifiers without degrading the overall predictive performance of the pruned meta-classifier. To determine the most effective base classifiers, the algorithm takes advantage of the *minimal cost-complexity pruning* method of the CART learning algorithm (Breiman *et al.* 1984) which guarantees to find the best (with respect to misclassification cost) pruned tree of a specific size (number of terminal nodes) of an initial unpruned decision tree. An alternative pruning method using Rissanen's minimum description length is described in (Quinlan & Rivest 1989).

Minimal cost complexity pruning associates a complexity parameter with the number of terminal nodes of a decision tree. It prunes decision trees by minimizing the linear combination of the complexity (size) of the tree and its misclassification cost estimate (error rate). The degree of pruning is controlled by adjusting the weight of the complexity parameter, i.e. an increase of this weight parameter results in heavier pruning.

Pruning an arbitrary meta-classifier consists of three stages. First we construct a decision tree model (e.g. CART) of the original meta-classifier, by learning its input/output behavior. This new model (a decision tree with base classifiers as nodes) reveals and prunes the base classifiers that do not participate in the splitting criteria and hence are redundant. The next stage aims to further reduce, if necessary, the number of selected classifiers. The algorithm applies the minimal cost-complexity pruning method to reduce the size of the decision tree model and thus prune away additional base classifiers. The degree of pruning is dictated by the system requirements and is controlled by the complexity parameter. In the final stage, the pruning algorithm re-applies the original combining technique over the remaining base-classifiers (those that were not discarded during the first two phases) to compute the new final pruned meta-classifier.

To evaluate these techniques, we applied 5 inductive learning algorithms on 12 disjoint subsets of 2 data sets of real credit card transactions, provided by Chase and First Union bank. We combined (using the weighted voting and stacking (Wolpert 1992) combining schemes) the 60 base classifiers in a 6-fold cross validation manner.

The measurements show that using decision trees to prune meta-classifiers is remarkably successful. The pruned meta-classifiers computed over the Chase data retain their performance levels to 100% of the original meta-classifier even with as much as 60% of the base classifiers pruned or within 60% of the original with 90% pruning. At the same time, the pruned meta-classifiers exhibit 230% and 638% higher throughput respectively. For the First Union base classifiers, the results are even better. With 80% pruning, there is no appreciable reduction in accuracy, while with 90% pruning they are within 80% of the performance of the unpruned meta-classifier. The throughput improvements in this case is 5.08 and 9.92 times better, respectively.

References

Breiman, L.; Friedman, J. H.; Olshen, R. A.; and Stone, C. J. 1984. *Classification and Regression Trees.* Belmont, CA: Wadsworth.

Quinlan, R., and Rivest, R. 1989. Inferring decision trees using the minimum description length princliple. *Information and Computation* 80:227–248.

Wolpert, D. 1992. Stacked generalization. *Neural Networks* 5:241–259.

Comparison of Second-order Polynomial Model Selection Methods: an Experimental Survey

Grace W Rumantir
School of Computer Science and Software Engineering
Monash University – Clayton Vic 3168 Australia
gwr@csse.monash.edu.au

This abstract gives an overview of the work described in (Rumantir 1999). The paper compares some of the most commonly cited model selection criteria that claim to have the mechanism to balance between model complexity and goodness of fit. The model chosen by any of the methods is claimed to be a parsimonious description of the data at hand, therefore has predictive power for future data.

This work tests the robustness of each method in support of the above claim in performing two tasks. First, to recover models from artificial data generated from known true models. Second, to parsimoniously select models from real data for the purpose of forecasting hurricane intensity change. The models selected are then compared with the benchmark models being used in operation.

In addition to polynomials with single independent variables, the products of variables up to the second order are also considered. A method based on the Minimum Message Length (MML) principle has been formulated and is compared with the methods found in the literature. A common gradient descent search strategy has been developed and is used with all of the model selection criteria. The summary of the methods examined is given in the table below.

Method		Reference
Minimum Message Length	MML	Wallace 1987
Minimum Description Length	MDL	Rissanen 1978
Stochastic Complexity	SC	Rissanen 1987
Akaike's Information Criterion	AIC	Akaike 1973
Corrected AIC	CAICF	Bozdogan 1987
Bayesian Information Criterion	BIC	Schwarz 1978
Structured Risk Minimisation	SRM	Vapnik 1995
Mallows' C_p	C_p	Mallows 1973
F-to-enter & F-to-exit	F-test	in Miller 1990
Adjusted Coeff. of Determination	adjR^2	Ezekiel 1930
Generalized Cross Validation	GCV	Wahba 1979
Predictive sum of squares	PRESS	Allen 1974

Based on the experiments with artificial data and real atmospheric data for hurricane intensity change forecasting, it is shown that MML, MDL, CAICF, SRM

and SC methods are good candidates for fully automated model selection tasks. Given a noisy data set, the methods can reliably converge to a true model (if one exists) or to a reasonably parsimonious model.

AIC, BIC, C_p, F-test and adjR^2 have overfitted the training data which suggests that when comparing two models with different complexity, the increase in the penalty terms for model complexity is not sufficient compared to the decrease in the terms for goodness of fit. This prompted the doubt that the balancing mechanism of the methods might not be robust enough for automated model selection task.

PRESS and GCV have overfitted the test data which not only suggests that their performance on test data cannot guarantee convergence into parsimonious models, but also necessitates the availability of a third independent data set for validation of model selection.

For the task of building models for hurricane intensity change forecasting, the methods MML, MDL, CAICF, SRM and SC come up with models with superior predictive performance than the standard benchmark models used in operation. The results emphasize two things. First, the importance of having homogenous data for training and test data sets for a model selection method to pick up regularities in the training data that can be extrapolated into the test data set and beyond. Second, that the unavoidable practice of using non-exhaustive search strategy on large search space pronounces the influence of selection bias in determining to which local minimum a model selection method would converge.

Acknowledgments

The atmospheric data discussed in the paper was generously supplied by Chris Landsea of the Hurricane Research Centre NOAA, Miami Florida. The author is grateful to Chris Wallace for guidance in the development of the MML method. The author is a recipient of the Australian Postgraduate Award (Industry).

References

Rumantir, G. W. 1999. Comparison of second-order polynomial model selection methods: an experimental survey. Technical report, School of Computer Science and Software Engineering, Monash University.

Learning State Features from Policies
to Bias Exploration in Reinforcement Learning

Bryan Singer and **Manuela Veloso**
Computer Science Department
Carnegie Mellon University
Pittsburgh, PA 15213
Email: {bsinger+, mmv+}@cs.cmu.edu

When given several problems to solve in some domain, a standard reinforcement learner learns an optimal policy from scratch for each problem. This seems rather unfortunate in that one might expect some domain-specific information to be present in the solution to one problem for solving the next problem. Using this information would improve the reinforcement learner's performance. However, policies learned by standard reinforcement learning techniques are often very dependent on the exact states, rewards, and state transitions in the particular problem. Therefore, it is infeasible to directly apply a learned policy to new problems, and so several approaches have been and are being investigated to find structure, abstraction, generalization, and/or policy reuse in reinforcement learning (e.g., as overviewed in (Sutton & Barto 1998)). Within our line of research, we describe each state in terms of local features, assuming that these state features together with the learned policies can be used to abstract out the domain characteristics from the specific layout of states and rewards of a particular problem. When given a new problem to solve, this abstraction is used as an exploration bias to improve the rate of convergence of a reinforcement learner.

There are two assumptions required by our learning approach: (i) a domain with local state features predefined for each state, and (ii) a set of sufficiently simple Markov Decision Problems (MDPs) within the domain. Our approach consists of the following procedure:

1. Using a Q-learner, we solve a set of training problems, saving the Q-tables.

2. We generate training examples from the Q-tables by describing states by their local state features and labeling the examples as either positive or negative for taking a particular action. Specifically, the action that has the maximum Q-value out of a state is used as a positive example, as it is viewed as one that may be worth exploring in other similar states. Likewise, an action that has a Q-value indicating that this action never led to the goal state is one that may not be worth exploring in other similar states and is labeled as a negative example.

3. We train a set of classifiers on the examples to map local state features to successful actions. Each classifier in the set learns whether a particular action will or will not be successful.

4. In new problems, we bias the reinforcement learner's exploration by the trained classifiers. This bias allows the reinforcement learner to solve other, potentially more difficult, problems within the domain more effectively than a reinforcement learner would if starting from scratch.

We have empirically validated this algorithm in grid-like domains, and in particular, in the complex domain of Sokoban (Wilfong 1988). Sokoban is an interesting domain of puzzles requiring an agent to push a set of balls to a set of destination locations without getting the balls stuck in various locations such as corners. From a set of training puzzles, we trained a neural network to map from features describing the locations a small radius around the agent to successful actions. As an example of our results, the figure shows the average number of steps required to reach the goal in a new puzzle during learning for both a Q-learner biased with the learned neural network and an unbiased Q-learner. We found that by utilizing solutions to previous problems, our algorithm significantly reduces learning time in new problems.

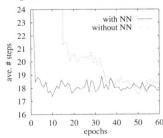

Acknowledgements Special thanks to Sebastian Thrun for several initial discussions. This work is sponsored in part by DARPA and AFRL under agreement number F30602-97-2-0250 and by a NSF Graduate Fellowship.

References

Sutton, R. S., and Barto, A. G. 1998. *Reinforcement Learning: An Introduction.* MIT Press.

Wilfong, G. 1988. Motion planning in the presence of moving obstacles. In *Proceedings of the Fourth Annual ACM Symposium on Computational Geometry.*

Investigating the Effect of Relevance and Reachability Constraints on SAT Encodings of Planning*

Biplav Srivastava (biplav@asu.edu)
Advisor: Subbarao Kambhampati (rao@asu.edu)
Department of Computer Science and Engineering
Arizona State University, Tempe, AZ 85287-5406.

Recently, satisfiability (SAT) techniques have been shown to be more efficient at extracting solutions from a planning graph in Graphplan (Blum & Furst 1995) than the standard backward search(Kautz & Selman 1998). Graphplan gains efficiency from forward propagation and backward use of mutual exclusion constraints. The utility of SAT techniques for solution extraction raises two important questions: (a) Are the mutual exclusion constraints equally useful for solution extraction with SAT encodings? (b) If so, are there additional types of propagated constraints that can benefit them even more? Our ongoing research investigates these two questions.

The mutual exclusion relations (mutex) used in the standard Graphplan, that we shall refer to as *fmutex* constraints, are propagated by the following rules: Two facts P and Q are fmutex if all actions supporting P are pair-wise fmutex with all actions supporting Q. Two actions are fmutex if action A_1 deletes another action A_2's preconditions or effects, or if preconditions of A_1 are pairwise fmutex with preconditions of A_2. Fmutex relations propagate forward from the initial state to provide "reachability" information to the backward search. Though they increase the size of the SAT encoding with a quadratic number of additional clauses, the overall encoding is simplified through unit-propagation based methods. E.g., fmutexes helps an 11 step/73 action logistics problem that takes 6 min 30 sec on Blackbox to solve in 7sec (60x speedup). It is also possible to propagate "relevance" relations starting from the goals. Such constraints would not be useful for standard Graphplan, unless it conducts the search in the forward direction.

In contrast, the search in SAT encodings is "directionless" in that it neither goes exclusively backward from goals nor exclusively forward from the initial state. Any variable that has the best heuristic properties (smallest live domain (Tsang 1993), maximum unit propagation (Li & Anbulagan 1997)) is selected, irrespective of its position in the corresponding planning graph. This means that the solver can potentially exploit mutex relations based on reachability as well as relevance. With this insight, we developed two types of constraints that can be propagated in backward direction, and carry relevance information:

Backward mutex (bmutex): Bmutex constraints attempt to capture the idea that two actions (or propositions) are never relevant together. Facts in the goal level are not bmutex. If actions A_1 and A_2 give the same set of facts at the next level, then A_1 is bmutex with A_2. Moreover, if all the facts that A_1 supports are pairwise bmutex with all the effects that A_2 supports, then A_1 is bmutex with A_2. Given two facts P and Q, if all the actions that consume P are pairwise bmutex with all the actions that consume Q, then P and Q are bmutex.

Inseparability relations (insep): Inseparability constraints capture the relation that a set of actions (propositions) must be either relevant all together, or none of them are relevant. The top level goals are inseparable in the goal level. If facts G_1 and G_2 are inseparable, let $A(G_1)$ be set of actions supporting G_1 and $A(G_2)$ be the set of actions supporting G_2. If the actions in $A(G_1)$ do not support any other relevant fact and so is also the case with $A(G_2)$, then the actions in $A(G_1)$ are pair-wise inseparable with those in $A(G_2)$. A proposition P_1 is inseparable from proposition P_2 if every action that P_1 supports is pairwise inseparable from every action that P_2 supports. An action is inseparable with itself while a proposition is not so. If an action A_1 is being considered to support proposition P, and Q is a proposition that is inseparable with P, then A_1 cannot delete Q.

Our experience in adding these propagated constraints to SAT encodings has been somewhat mixed to-date. The bmutex constraints, as stated, do not seem to propagate well and taper off after some levels. This is largely due to the requirement that for any two actions to be bmutex, they must have exactly the same set of useful effects. In the case of inseparability relations, pair-wise relations miss the case where even if $A(G_1)$ supports facts other than G_1, those facts may be inseparable with G_2 (and vice-versa) making $A(G_1)$ and $A(G_2)$ inseparable. At present we are looking into variations of these constraints that have better propagation capabilities.

In summary, we have found that reachability based mutex propagation does improve the solvability of SAT encodings. Motivated by this, and the fact that SAT searchers are direction-less, we are investigating the utility of additional mutex relations based on relevance.

References

Blum, A., and Furst, M. 1995. Fast planning through planning graph analysis. *Proc IJCAI-95* 1636–1642.

Kautz, H., and Selman, B. 1998. Blackbox: A New Appr. Applic. of Theorem Proving to Problem Solv.. *Wksp Plan. Comb. Search, AIPS-98, Pittsburgh, PA, 1998.*.

Li, C.M., and Anbulagan. Heuristics based on unit propagation for satisfiability problems. Proc. 15th IJCAI. 1997.

Tsang, E. *Foundations of Constraint Satisfaction*. Acad. Press. San Diego. CA. 1993

Learning to Handle Inconsistency for Multi-Source Integration

Sheila Tejada   Craig A. Knoblock Steven Minton

University of Southern California/ISI

4676 Admiralty Way, Marina del Rey, California 90292

{tejada,knoblock,minton}@isi.edu,

(310) 822-1511 x799

Abstract

Many problems arise when trying to integrate information from multiple sources on the web. One of these problems is that data instances can exist in inconsistent formats across several sources. An example application of information integration is trying to integrate all the reviews of Los Angeles restaurants from Yahoo's Restaurants webpage with the current health rating for each restaurant from the LA County Department of Health's website. Integrating these sources requires determining if they share any of the same restaurants by comparing the data instances from both sources (**Figure 1**). Because the instances can be in different formats, e.g. the restaurant "Jerry's Famous Deli" from Yahoo's webpage can appear as "Jerry's Famous Delicatessen" in the Dept. of Health's source, they can not be compared using equality; but must be judged according to similarity.

Name	Address	Phone
1. Jerry's Famous Deli, 342 Beverly Blvd, (310)302-5319		
Jerry's Famous Delicatessen,342 Beverly Boulevard,310-302-5319		
2. CPK, 65 La Cienga Blvd, 310-987-8923		
California Pizza Kitchen,65 La Cienga Blvd,310-987-8923		
3. The Beverly, 302 MLK Blvd, 213-643-2154		
Cafe Beverly, 302 Martin Luther King Jr. Boulevard,645-4278		

Figure 1: *Matched Restaurant*

Once the matching objects have been determined, this information about which objects are mapped together can be stored in the form of a mapping table, or as a mapping function, so that these sources can be properly integrated in the future. The goal of this research [1] is to be able to create these mapping constructs so that an information broker, like Ariadne [2], can use it to properly integrate data from inconsistent sources in an intelligent and efficient manner.

We have currently developed a semi-automated tool that is able to create these mapping constructs. This tool is composed of three main components (**Figure 2**). The first component, the match generator, compares all of the shared attributes of the sources in order to determine which objects are matched, (**Name** with **Name**, **Address** with **Address, Phone** with **Phone**). To determine the similarity

between the instances we have developed general domain independent transformation rules to recognize transformations like substring, acronym, and abbreviation. For example, "Deli" is a substring transformation of "Delicatessen." This component computes the set of possible matched pairs using these general transformation rules and calculates a similarity score for each of the attributes of each matched pair.

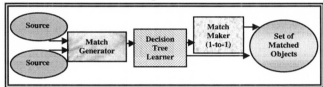

Figure 2: *Mapping Tool Components*

The second component is a decision tree learner which takes, as input, a subset of the possible matched pairs that have been labeled as matched or not matched by the user. From this training set the learner can discover which attribute or combination of attributes are most important for matching objects by determining the thresholds for the probabilistic score of these attributes. For this restaurant example, the learner could discover that in order for two objects to be matched, the similarity score for the attribute **Name** must be greater than 0.8. The learned decision tree is then used to classify the remaining set of possible matched pairs. The third component is a one-to-one match maker which enforces the one-to-one relationship that might exist in the application domain. For our future work we are adding an active learning or query by committee technique in order to reduce the size of the training set [3].

References

[1] **Tejada, et. al.** Handling Inconsistencies for Multi-Source Integration. Proceedings of the 15th National Conference on Artificial Intelligence, Madison, WI, 1998.

[2] **Knoblock, et. al.** Modeling Web Sources for Information Integration. Proceedings of the 15th National Conference on Artificial Intelligence, Madison, WI, 1998.

[3] **Naoki Abe and Hiroshi Mamitsuka.** Query Learning Strategies Using Boosting and Bagging. Proc. of the 15th International Conference on Machine Learning, July 1998.

Learning rewrite rules to improve plan quality

Muhammad Afzal Upal
Department of Computing Science
University of Alberta
upal@cs.ualberta.ca

Considerable planning and learning research has been devoted to the problem of learning domain specific search control rules to improve planning efficiency. There have also been a few attempts to learn search control rules that improve plan quality but such efforts have been limited to state-space planners. The reason being that most of the newer planning approaches are based on plan refinement. In such planners, information about the current state of the world that is required to evaluate a complex quality metric is simply not available during planning. An alternative technique is *planning by rewriting* that suggests first generating an initial plan using a refinement planner and then using a set of rewrite-rules to transform it into a higher quality plan (Ambite & Knoblock 1997). Unlike the search control rules that are defined on the space of partial plans, rewrite rules are defined on the space of complete plans. This paper presents a system called REWRITE that automatically learns rewrite rules and uses them to produce higher quality plans.

REWRITE has three main components. The first is a partial-order causal-link planner (POP). The second component does the analytic work of identifying the *replacing* and *to-be-replaced* action sequences. The third component is a case library of plan-rewrite rules.

The input to REWRITE's analytic component is (a) a problem described by an initial state and goals (b) the plan and planning trace produced by the partial order planner for this problem, and (c) a "better plan" for the same problem. The better plan is the one that has a higher quality rating than the one produced by the underlying partial-order planner, as per the quality function that assesses how resources are impacted by each plan. This better plan might be provided by some oracle, by a user, or by some other planner.

REWRITE's analytic component first reconstructs a set of causal link relationships between the steps in the better plan and a set of required ordering constraints. The second step is to retrace POP's planning-trace, looking for plan-refinement decisions that added a constraint that is not present in the better plan's constraint set. We call such a decision point a *conflicting choice point*. Each conflicting choice point indicates a gap in REWRITE's knowledge and hence a possible opportunity to learn. For any conflicting choice point, there are two different plan-refinement decision sequences that can be applied to a partial plan: the one added by the default POP algorithm, and the other inferred from the better-quality plan. The application of one set of plan-refinement decisions leads to a higher quality plan and the other to a lower quality plan. However, all of the *downstream* planning decisions may not be relevant to resolving the flaw at the conflicting choice point. The rest of the better-plan's trace and the rest of the worse-plan's trace are then examined, with the goal of labeling a subsequent plan-refinement decision q relevant if (a) there exists a causal-link $q \xrightarrow{c} p$ such that p is a relevant action, or (b) q binds an uninstantiated variable of a relevant open-condition.

Once both the better plan's relevant decisions and the worse plan's relevant decisions have been identified, REWRITE computes (a) the actions that are added by the worse plan's relevant decision sequence. These become the action sequence to-be-replaced; (b) The actions that are added by the better plan's relevant decision sequence. These become the replacing action sequence; (c) The preconditions and effects of the replacing and the to-be-replaced action sequence. REWRITE then stores this information as a rule. Currently, REWRITE uses a speed-up partial order planning system DerPOP to generate an initial plan P along with the casual-link and ordering constraints (Upal & Elio 1999). All rules whose to-be-replaced action sequence S_1 is a subset of P are then retrieved and applied and the highest quality plan thus produced is returned.

Preliminary evaluation results indicate that the overhead for applying these techniques to identify, store and then use planning-rewrite rules is not large. The benefit is that rewrite rules do not have to be hand-coded.

References

Ambite, J., and Knoblock, C. 1997. Planning by rewriting. In *Proc. of AAAI-97*.

Upal, M. A., and Elio, R. 1999. Learning rationales to improve plan quality. In *Proc. of FLAIRS-99*.

Word Sense Disambiguation for Information Retrieval

Ozlem Uzuner, Boris Katz, Deniz Yuret

MIT Artificial Intelligence Laboratory
545 Technology Sq Cambridge MA 02139
{ozlem,boris,deniz}@ai.mit.edu

Despite their increasing importance as data retrieval tools, most Information Retrieval (IR) systems do not have high precision and recall. Lack of disambiguation power is one reason for the poor performance of these systems. Correctly disambiguating and expanding a query only with intended synonyms before retrieval may improve their performance.

We use the local context[1] of a word to identify its sense. Words used in the same context (called selectors) often have related senses. So, *an occurrence of a word and its synonym belong to the same sense if they have similar local contexts*.

We use WordNet (Miller 1990) and selectors extracted from Associated Press articles (Yuret 1998) for disambiguation. Selectors help us find the right WordNet synset (synonyms of only one sense) of a word in its context.

Figure 1 shows the process of extracting selectors of *charge* in a given sentence. The final tally of identified selectors is shown in Table 1.

Selector	Appointed	Assigned	Established	Hired
Frequency	52	28	20	16

Table 1: **Final tally of selector frequencies for Figure 1.**

Once the selectors are extracted, the appropriate WordNet synset is selected by comparing the selectors against the ambiguous word's WordNet synsets.

Semcor, a subset of Brown corpus, is commonly used for disambiguation evaluation. In Semcor, each word is tagged with its correct part of speech and sense number taken from WordNet.

The "most frequent heuristic" is accepted as the baseline for measuring performance of WSD algorithms. When tested only on words with more than one sense, the accuracy of the "most frequent" heuristic on Semcor was approximately 54%. In comparison, our algorithm achieved an accuracy of 45%.

To evaluate the effect of disambiguation on IR, we tested the performance of Smart (Buckley et. al., 1995). These tests were done in two ways: In the first, the original queries were expanded with the identified potential synonyms. In the second test, the queries were replicated by replacing only the target word with one of its identified synonyms. This was done for all content words in the query. Retrieval tests were done on CACM, CISI and CRAN collections. In all cases, the performance of the system became worse.

Figure 1: Identification of selectors in a given context

Low disambiguation performance is probably the main cause of poor IR performance (Voorhees 1993, Sanderson 1994). Improving disambiguation performance through use of a different lexical source, or through use of different context definitions can improve IR performance as well.

References

Buckley C., Singhal A., Mitra M., Salton G., 1995. New Retrieval Approaches Using SMART: TREC 4. *Proceedings of the 3rd Text Retrieval Conference,* NIST Special Publ.

Miller, G. A. 1990. WordNet: An online lexical database. *Int'l Journal of Lexicography,* 3(4):235-312.

Sanderson, M. 1994. Word disambiguation and information retrieval. *Proceedings of ACM SIGIR Conference.*

Uzuner, O. 1998. Word-sense Disambiguation Applied to Information Retrieval. M.Eng Thesis, Dept. of EECS, MIT.

Voorhees, E. M. 1993. Using WordNet to Disambiguate Word Senses for Text Retrieval. *Proceedings of ACM SIGIR Conference.,* pages 171-180.

Yuret, D. 1998. Discovery of Linguistic Relations Using Lexical Attraction. Ph.D. , Dept. of Comp. Sci., MIT.

---

[1] Local context of a word is the ordered list of words from the closest content word on each side up to the target word expressed as a placeholder. For example, in "the jury had been charged to investigate reports of irregularities in the primary..." the right-side local context of "charged" is "X to investigate".

Invited Talk

Game Playing: The Next Moves

Susan L. Epstein

Department of Computer Science
Hunter College and The Graduate School of The City University of New York
695 Park Avenue, New York, NY 10021
epstein@roz.hunter.cuny.edu

Abstract

Computer programs now play many board games as well or better than the most expert humans. Human players, however, learn, plan, allocate resources, and integrate multiple streams of knowledge. This paper highlights recent achievements in game playing, describes some cognitively-oriented work, and poses three related challenge problems for the AI community.

Game Playing as a Domain

Work on games has had several traditional justifications. Given unambiguous rules, playing a game to win is a well-defined problem. A game's rules create artificial world states whose granularity is explicit. There is an initial state, a state space with clear transitions, and a set of readily describable goal states. Without intervening instrumentation, games are also noise-free. For these reasons, as well as for their ability to amuse, games have often been referred to as "toy domains." To play the most difficult games well, however, a program must contend with fundamental issues in AI: knowledge representation, search, learning, and planning.

There are two principal reasons to continue to do research on games, despite Deep Blue's triumph (Hamilton and Hedberg 1997). First, human fascination with game playing is long-standing and pervasive. Anthropologists have catalogued popular games in almost every culture. Indeed, the same game, under various names, often appears on many continents (Bell 1969; Zaslavsky 1982). Games intrigue us because they address important cognitive functions. In particular, the games humans like to play are probably the ones we are good at, the ones that capitalize on our intellectual strengths and forgive our weaknesses. A program that plays many games well must simulate important cognitive skills. The second reason to continue game-playing research is that some difficult games remain to be won, games that people play very well but computers do not. These games clarify what our current approach lacks. They set challenges for us to meet, and they promise ample rewards.

This paper summarizes the role of search and knowledge in game playing, the state of the art, and recent relevant data on expert human game players. It then shows how cognitive skills can enhance a game-playing program, and poses three new challenge problems for the

AI community. Although rooted in game playing, these challenges could enhance performance in many domains.

Search and Knowledge

In this paper, a *game* is a multi-agent, noise-free, discrete space with a finite set of objects (the *playing pieces*) and a finite, static set of rules for *play* (agents' serial behavior). The rules delineate where playing pieces can reside in the space, and when and how *contestants* (the agents) can *move* (transform one state into another). A *position* is a world state in a game; it specifies the location of the playing pieces and the agent permitted to act (the *mover*). The rules specify time limits for computation, a set of initial states, and a set of *terminal* states in which no agent is the mover. The rules assign to each terminal state a game-theoretic value, which can be thought of as a numerical score for each agent. The goal of each agent is to reach a terminal state that optimizes the game-theoretic value from its perspective. This definition includes finite-board games (e.g., tic-tac-toe and chess), games with imperfect information (e.g., poker and backgammon), and games with sequential team play (e.g., bridge), but excludes parallel activities (e.g., tennis and soccer).

A game may be represented by a *game tree*, in which each node represents a position and each link represents one action by one agent (called a *ply*). A *contest* at a game is a finite path through a game tree from an initial state. A contest ends at the first terminal state it reaches; it may also be terminated by the rules because a resource limit has been exceeded or because a position has repeatedly occurred. The *outcome* of a contest is the value of its terminal state, or the value (typically a draw) that the rules assign to a terminated contest.

An *optimal move* from position *p* is an action that creates a position with maximal value for the mover in *p*. In a terminal state, that value is determined by the rules; in a non-terminal state, it is the best result the mover can achieve if subsequent play to the end of the contest is always optimal. An *evaluation function* maps positions to scores for each agent. A *perfect* evaluation function preserves order among all positions' game-theoretic values; a *heuristic* one attempts to approximate them.

Given a subtree whose leaves are labeled by an evaluation function, a *minimax* algorithm backs those values up, one ply at a time, selecting the optimal move at each node

(Shannon 1950). With a small game tree, prior to any play one can minimax the values of all terminal nodes to compute the game-theoretic value of every node (*full retrograde analysis*) and cache those values with the optimal moves. The resultant table is a perfect evaluation function that can eliminate search during competition.

In a challenging game, a perfect evaluation function is unknown to human experts, and full retrograde analysis is intractable, as the search space sizes in Table 1 indicate. During play, *exhaustive search* (from the current position to only terminal states) followed by minimax could theoretically identify the correct move. The number of nodes visited during such search is dependent both on the game's *branch factor* (average number of legal moves from each position) and the depth of the subtree. Unless a contest is near completion or few pieces remain on the board, such a search is likely to be intractable.

Table 1: Estimated average branch factor and search space size for some challenging board games.

Game	Board	Pieces	Branch factor	Space
Checkers	8×8	32	$8 - 20$	$5 \cdot 10^{20}$
Chess	8×8	32	35	10^{120}
Shogi	9×9	40	$80 - 150$	10^{226}
Go	19×19	381	250	10^{360}

Resource conservation during game tree search has been attempted in both hardware and software. Hardware designed for a particular evaluation function can speed computation. Deep Blue's custom chess-searching chips, for example, enabled it to evaluate 50 to 100 billion moves in three minutes, sometimes to depths over 30 ply. Search algorithms can also improve efficiency. Some variations preserve exhaustive search's correctness: saving previously evaluated positions in a transposition table, the α-β algorithm (Slate and Atkin 1977), extensions along promising lines of play, and extensions that include forced moves (Anantharaman, Campbell, and Hsu 1990). Other search algorithms take conservative risks, pruning unpromising lines early (Berliner 1987) or seeking a stable heuristic evaluation (Beal 1990). Still others grow a best-first tree, guided by values estimated for the current leaves (Baum and Smith 1997; McAllester 1988; Palay 1985; Rivest 1987). Whatever its search mechanisms, however, a powerful game playing program typically plays only a single game, because it also relies on knowledge.

Knowledge can be incorporated into a game-playing program in three standard ways. First, formulaic behavior early in play (*openings*) is prerecorded in an *opening book*. Early in a contest, the program identifies the current opening and continues it. Second, knowledge about important principles in a game (e.g., control of the center) is embedded in a heuristic evaluation function. During play, the typical program searches to generate a subtree rooted at the current node, applies its heuristic evaluation function to the leaves of that subtree, and minimaxes those values to estimate the correct move. Finally, partial retrograde analysis may be performed offline, to calculate and

store some true game-theoretic values and optimal moves. For nodes several ply from a terminal node, this is called a *closing book*. Because a heuristic evaluation function always returns any available closing book values, the larger the closing book, the more accurate the evaluation and the better a search engine is likely to perform. The best programs use both search and knowledge to win at difficult games.

The State of the Art

Checkers and chess

In 1994, Chinook became the world's champion checker player (Schaeffer 1997). Its opening book had 80,000 positions, and its 10-gigabyte closing book had some 443 billion positions, every position in which no more than eight checkers remain on the board. In the course of its development, it became clear that Chinook's ultimate prowess would be its knowledge base. As its closing book grew, Chinook improved. Eventually, with only the last 8 ply solved completely, Chinook defeated Marion Tinsley, long the human world champion.

In 1996, Garry Kasparov defeated Deep Blue, but in 1997 he lost to a program that used the same special-purpose hardware. In the intervening year, the program had received a substantial infusion of grandmaster-level knowledge. Its evaluation function had been strengthened, and its opening book had "a few thousand [items] chosen to match [its] style" plus statistics on grandmasters' opening play in 600,000 contests. Its closing book included all chess positions with five or fewer pieces, as well as number of moves to completion.

Chinook and Deep Blue are examples of *brute force*, the exploitation of search and knowledge on a heretofore-unprecedented scale. Each of them had a search engine that explored enormous subtrees, and supported that search with extensive opening and closing books. Each also had a carefully tuned, human-constructed, heuristic evaluation function, with features whose relative importance was well understood in the human expert community. There are, however, games whose large branch factors preclude deep search, games where human experts cannot provide all the knowledge computers need to win. Programs that play such games well have learned offline.

Backgammon, Othello, and Scrabble®

In 1997 Logistello defeated Takeshi Murakami, the human world Othello champion (Buro 1998), winning all 6 contests in the match. Logistello's heuristic evaluation function is primarily a weighted combination of simple patterns that appear on the board, such as horizontal or diagonal lines. (Parity and *stage,* how far a contest has progressed, are also included.) To produce this evaluation function, 1.5 million weights for conjunctions of these features were calculated with gradient descent during offline training, from analysis of 11 million positions. Although it uses a sophisticated search algorithm and a large opening book, Logistello's evaluation function is the key to its prowess. No more than 22 moves before the end of a contest, Logistello correctly computes the outcome.

TD-gammon, the best backgammon program by far, also relies on an evaluation function that was learned offline. TD-gammon narrowly lost at the AAAI-98 Hall of Champions to world champion Malcolm Davis by eight points over 100 contests. In backgammon, the dice introduce a branch factor of 400, rendering extensive, Deep-Blue-style search impossible. Instead, TD-gammon models decision making with a neural network pretrained by temporal difference learning on millions of offline contests between two copies of the program. During competition, TD-gammon uses its model to select a move after a 2-to-3-ply search. Since a reworking of its doubling algorithm, Tesauro estimates that TD-gammon has a slight advantage over the best human experts.

In the 1998 AAAI Hall of Champions, Maven defeated grandmaster Adam Logan 9 contests to 5 at Scrabble®, a game in which contestants place one-letter tiles into a crossword format. Maven is the best Scrabble® program, and among the top players of the game (Sheppard 1999). Scrabble® is subject to chance (tiles are chosen at random) and includes imperfect information (unplayed tiles are concealed). Maven uses a standard, game-specific move generator (Appel and Jacobson 1988) and the B* search algorithm (Berliner 1979); what distinguishes it from other programs is its learned evaluation function. Indeed, since their 1992 announcement, Maven's weights have become the standard for human and machine players. The current version also includes a probabilistic simulation of tile selection with 3-ply lookahead.

Although these three programs search and employ extensive knowledge, the changes that made them champions were ultimately changes to their learned evaluation functions. The creators of these programs gave learning a headstart: the right raw material from which to construct a powerful evaluation function. If the branch factor is too large, however, even a good evaluation function may be not be enough.

Current targets

Research on bridge and poker, card games of imperfect information, is ongoing. One program found five errors in the Official Encyclopedia of Bridge with a new heuristic technique (Frank, Basin, and Matsubara 1998). Loki now plays poker "better than the average club player" (Schaeffer 1999). At the same time, work on two perfect information games indicates that neither brute force nor offline learning will suffice.

Shogi is a chess-like game, with generals and lances instead of queens. In addition, most shogi pieces can be promoted to other pieces with more varied legal moves. Further complexity is introduced by the ability to *drop* (add to one's own forces any piece previously captured from the opposition) anywhere on the board. Shogi has a much larger branch factor than chess and, because of

dropping, rarely ends in a draw. Positions are rarely *quiet* (having a relatively stable heuristic evaluation in a small subtree). Shogi has its own annual computer tournament, but no entry has yet played as well as a strong amateur.

Go presents an even greater challenge. Professional Go players develop slowly, typically after 10 years of full time study. Amateur Go players are ranked from 30 kyu to 1 kyu, and then from 1 dan to 6 dan. Professional players are ranked above that, from 1 to 9 dan. The Ing Cup, established in 1986, promises approximately $1.8 million for the first program to defeat Taiwan's three best 14-to-16 year-old players before 2000. Such a program would be ranked about 3 dan professional, a level hundreds of people attain. The best Go-playing program, however, now ranks only about 4 kyu. The Go-programming community generally acknowledges that the Ing Cup will expire without being won.

Heuristics are essential for games of incomplete information, which are NP-hard (Blair, Mutchler, and Liu 1993). They are also necessary to play shogi and Go well, but the requisite knowledge is inaccessible. Because their endgames are likely to have a larger branch factor and at least as many playing pieces, the generation of a useful closing book is intractable. Knowledge for a heuristic evaluation function is also problematic. In shogi, unlike chess, there is not even human consensus on the relative strength of the individual pieces (Beal and Smith 1998). In Go, the rules distinguish no *stone* (playing piece) from any other of the same color; a stone's significance is determined by the position. There are, moreover, thousands of possible Go features whose interactions are not well understood. To excel at their current targets, game playing programs will need something more.

Cognitive Science and Game Playing

Cognitive scientists seeking the source of human prowess have studied expert game players for more than a century. They take *protocols,* transcripts of peoples' verbal commentary during and after play. Cognitive scientists also use highly accurate devices to track experts' eye movements. Together, protocols and eye movement data suggest how experts play.

Perception and cognition

Neuroscientists have identified distinct regions in the human brain for visual perception and for high-level reasoning. In people, there is evidence that perceptual salience cues functional significance, thereby directing human attention (Tversky 1989). This is corroborated by timed images of a chess player's brain during decision making (Nichelli, Grafman, Pietrini, Alway, Carton, and Miletich 1994). Perception appears to begin first, followed somewhat later (and then in parallel with) reasoning and their integration. Indeed, protocols on game players regularly highlight *spatial cognition*, a process whereby people attend to visual features, determine their significance, and then value them accordingly. This is why people play better without blindfolds — vision not only focuses their attention, but is also an integral part of decision making.

Given the link between them, attention to perceptually salient features could cue learning about function (Tversky 1990). When a person needs to learn an evaluation function for playing the games considered here, she receives strong visual cues for the important features: the location of playing pieces and the shapes they form on the board. How might these cues be integrated with high-level reasoning?

A position can be described in terms of *patterns*, relations between playing pieces. When early results found no measurable difference in experts' and amateurs' search (de Groot 1965), Chase and Simon proposed that chess expertise lay in the acquisition and application of unordered spatial patterns they called *chunks*. Expert game players, they theorized, knew many important patterns, recognized them quickly, and associated a move selection mechanism with them. Better players would simply know more chunks, and propose moves appropriate to them.

Discrete chunks were not detected in Go (Reitman 1976), however, nor was pattern recognition alone able to account for differences detected more recently in the way better chess players search (Gobet 1998). Moreover, extensive studies indicate that expert Go players use not only static patterns but also dynamic ones (Yoshikawa and Saito 1997). With only one kind of piece for each contestant, Go appears to require a different kind of looking, one that dynamically invests stones with multiple roles, interleaving perception with cognition (Burmeister, Saito, Yoshikawa, and Wiles 1997). Professional Go players focused on lookahead and "good shape," an abstract image of certain parts of the current position, an image that lookahead manipulates and reformulates (Yoshikawa and Saito 1997). Go experts in those experiments looked at only a small part of the board, between stones, as if narrowing their options, and on recall often attributed a plausible meaning to a move. In response, several theories that annotate patterns have been proposed, including larger, frame-like structures called *templates* (Gobet and Simon 1996) and more flexible, more elaborate structures called *hybrid patterns* (Yoshikawa and Saito 1997). Whichever theory proves correct, vision is certain to play an integral role.

Less search and knowledge

Expert human game players have fast access to large stores of carefully organized, game-specific knowledge which they use both to focus their attention and to guide search. Compared to champion programs, however, human experts have far smaller opening and closing books. Their pattern-oriented representation for this data appears to be adapted to a specific game (Eisenstadt and Kareev 1975) and tailored only to positions that can arise during play (Chase and Simon 1973).

Compared to champion programs, human experts also consider fewer alternatives and search less deeply. Chess experts consider only a few moves, and rarely search more than 8 or 9 ply (Gobet 1998). Go experts perform relatively small searches, with average depth 4 and maximum branch factor 3 (Yoshikawa and Saito 1997). Human experts focus their attention on *candidate moves* (those worthy of search to evaluate them further) more quickly than novices. Eye movement studies confirm this in both chess and Go: experts look at very few points when they solve a test problem (de Groot 1965; Gobet 1998; Yoshikawa and Saito 1997). The Go players' speed is particularly remarkable: in 0.2—0.3 seconds the expert's eye fixates on the correct move. Accompanying protocols suggest that the selection of candidate moves involves both inference and pattern recognition.

Alternative cognitive mechanisms

There is increasing evidence, from a variety of domains, that people *satisfice*, that is, make a decision that is good enough. Satisficing often integrates a variety of strategies to accomplish problem solving (Biswas, Goldman, Fisher, Bhuva, and Glewwe 1995; Crowley and Siegler 1993; Ratterman and Epstein 1995). Satisficing may also include the ability to reason from incomplete or inconsistent information.

People develop expertise over time, through study and competition; they do not begin a new game as experts (Ericsson, Krampe, and Tesch-Römer 1993; Holding 1985). During development, people learn, particularly from their mistakes, whereas a deterministic program makes the same error repeatedly. Although TD-gammon, Logistello, and Maven have learned evaluation functions, they do not learn from their mistakes during competition, the way people would. Nor do people require millions of contests to achieve expert status. The initial learning curve in Go, for example, can be very rapid — a 5 kyu rank can be reached in several months (Saito and Yoshikawa 1997). In addition, as people have more experience with a task, their speed at it generally improves. In contrast, programs whose evaluation function functions rely upon more knowledge typically require more time at each search node, resulting in shallower search that can degrade performance (Anantharaman, Campbell, and Hsu 1990; Buro 1998).

Protocols also provide extensive evidence of high-level language concepts used to formulate subgoals, and of planning to reach those subgoals. Game playing experts summarize some of their knowledge this way. They use *tactics* (short-term plans) and *strategies* (long-term plans) to make decisions and to explain their behavior to each other. This is particularly accessible from protocols on masters playing Soudan Go, where each side is played in a separate room by a freely communicating team of two players (Yoshikawa, Kojima, and Saito 1998). The protocols demonstrate that "both sides clearly understand their opponent's intention and their understandings agree completely" (Saito and Yoshikawa 1997). Such evidence motivated the annotation of templates and hybrid patterns with variabilized plans and strategies.

Learning to Satisfice

Hoyle is a program whose cognitive orientation enables it to play a broad variety of games surprisingly well. Like people, but unlike the programs described thus far, Hoyle can play any two-person, perfect information, finite-board game, given the rules (Epstein, Gelfand, and Lock 1998). To date it has learned online, during competition, to play 18 games expertly in real time. The games, on two- and three-dimensional boards of various shapes, are drawn from anthropology texts, and are intended to capture problems that intrigue people. Although their game trees are relatively small (the largest has only several billion states), the speed with which Hoyle masters them, and its transparency, make the approach of interest here.

Hoyle begins any new game as a novice, but it knows what to learn. As it plays, it gradually acquires *useful knowledge*, probably correct and possibly applicable information from the contests it has experienced. Each kind of useful knowledge is prespecified, with its own representation and a procedure to learn it. An opening, for example, might be learned as a tree by rote.

Hoyle also begins with a set of move-selection rationales called *Advisors*. Given the acquired useful knowledge for a game and a position from it, an Advisor can recommend or caution against any number of moves by generating *comments*. Advisors are subject to resource limits, but not to any uniform decision process or representation.

Advisors are categorized into three tiers. Those in tier 1 rely on shallow search and learned game-theoretic values

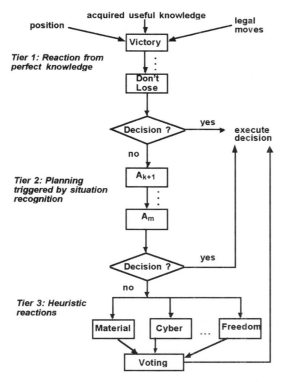

Figure 1: A schematic for Hoyle's move selection.

to provide perfect guidance on a single move, mandating its selection or avoidance. Tier-1 Advisors make easy decisions quickly, and prevent obvious blunders. Victory, for example, makes an immediately winning move. All other Advisors are heuristic, either because they depend upon induced useful knowledge or because their reasoning method is approximately correct. Material, for example, encourages piece capture in tier 3. Tier-2 Advisors advocate a sequence of moves (a *plan*), while tier-3 Advisors advocate a single move.

Comments are combined to select a move, as shown in Figure 1. Advisors are consulted serially in tiers 1 and 2, where the first Advisor able to determine the next move does so. In tier 3 Advisors are consulted in parallel, and a weighted combination of their comment strengths selects the best move. Weights are both game-dependent and stage-dependent, and are learned.

On a few simple games, Hoyle has been cognitively validated, that is, its learning and decision making have been shown similar to that of people (Ratterman and Epstein 1995). Indeed, the program intentionally has many of the hallmarks of human expert play:

• Hoyle satisfices. While it decides in real time, it tolerates incomplete and incorrect information, entertains a variety of conflicting rationales simultaneously, and degrades gracefully in unfamiliar situations.

• Hoyle learns quickly. It usually achieves its expertise in less than 100 contests.

• Hoyle is transparent. It can explain its moves through a natural language interpretation of its Advisors' comments.

• Hoyle integrates visual perception with high-level reasoning. Its allowance for multiple representations, in useful knowledge and in Advisors, supports this. The current position, for example, can be simultaneously represented as a list, an array, a bipartite graph, a set of fixed-shape patterns, and a set of piece-delineated territories.

• Hoyle links perception with function. It learns visually-based, high-level, game-dependent concepts as game-specific Advisors for tier 3. For example, it can learn that the consolidation of territory is advisable in a game, determine how that territory should be demarcated, and create and use an Advisor to encourage that behavior.

• Hoyle plans. It acquires both specific and tactical move sequences as tier-2 Advisors.

• Hoyle uses high-level concepts. Some, such as blocking a winning move, are game-independent, and prespecified in tier 1. Other, game-dependent ones are learned from perceptual cues, as described above.

New Game Playing Challenges

Results with Hoyle suggest ways in which a program might be more like a human champion. Hoyle's penchant for useful knowledge and multiple heuristic opinions is likely to prove helpful in addressing the following challenge problems. Each increases with difficulty, of course, according to the target game.

Problem 1: Model a contestant

Strategic and tactical decisions are often affected by the nature of one's problem solving environment. An important factor in game playing decisions, for example, should be the nature of one's opponent. The first challenge problem is to construct a model of a particular contestant in a two-person game. Given a suite of contests played by a single person or program against various competitors, the program should produce natural language that characterizes the opponent's current play in a contest (e.g., "Black isn't interested in cashing in his initiative with 19...Bxd4? 20 cxd4 Qxd4 when White has excellent play for the pawn"). It should also identify general strengths, weaknesses, and predilections, such as "In the opening, Kasparov plays black like white," "Karpov strives to improve his position little by little, maneuvering subtly, making his threats," "He is *always* attacking, often from directions his opponents hadn't considered, playing moves that have subtle multiple threats," and "You can tell from [his opponents'] moves they are scared. Their attacks are wild and hopeless or else very timid." (Waitzkin 1990).

Some groundbreaking work on this has been done in poker (Billings, Papp, Schaeffer, and Szafron 1998) and Go (Isozaki and Katsuno 1996). The generation and analysis of summary statistics would be a reasonable way to continue. Plan detection is required, as well as some representation for volition, aggression, and risk. Knowledge about emotions and the ability to generate metaphors should prove helpful.

Problem 2: Annotate a contest

People annotate a chess contest both move by move (e.g., "Far from losing a tempo, Black has really gained time since the knight stood better on d4 than b3") and with tactics and strategy (e.g., "try to play d2-d4, bring the knight on b1 to e2, and follow up with Nf3-e5, playing on the dark squares.") Annotations contain commentary and often diagrams. Since 1993, the International Computer Chess Association has awarded an annual prize to the program that best annotates an input chess contest in real time, but entries are few and quite machine-like (Bjornsson and Marsland 1998). Programs are encouraged to propose variations, include written comments, and provide explanatory diagrams.

The second challenge problem is to annotate a contest so well that people cannot distinguish it from a human-generated, popularly published annotation, say from *The New York Times*. A solution must generate both natural language and appropriate diagrams. It will also require high-level concepts appropriate to the game, context-sensitive perspectives, and the induction of a model for each contestant as an agent with intentions and the ability to deceive.

Problem 3: Teach a game

One measure of human expertise is the ability to convey knowledge. The third challenge problem is to have an expert game playing program (the *instructor*) teach its skill to a person or another program (the *student*). To do this well, the instructor must first analyze and represent its own knowledge. Next, the instructor would model the student's knowledge, diagnose its weaknesses, and formulate a curriculum. Instruction could be presented as positions, lines of play, or entire contests, all couched in appropriate natural language. An analysis of the student's learning style is likely to prove helpful. Once the student consistently plays as well as the teacher, the problem will be solved.

Conclusion

Champion programs thus far lack cognitive features often cited as hallmarks of human intelligence: online learning, planning, and the ability to communicate knowledge. There is a growing interest, however, in reactive, hierarchical satisficers like Hoyle, and in the kind of agent interaction and modeling targeted by the challenge problems posed here (Dobson and Forbus 1999). We can look forward, therefore, to programs that narrow their options, learn from their mistakes, model other agents, explain their rationales, and teach us to play better.

Acknowledgments

This work was supported in part by NSF grant #9423085. Thanks to Michael Buro, Murray Campbell, Takuya Kojima, Jonathan Schaeffer, Brian Sheppard, Gerry Tesauro, and Atsushi Yoshikawa for generously sharing their substantial expertise. Discussions with Hans Berliner, Ian Frank, Jack Gelfand, Esther Lock, and Donald Michie have inspired and informed much of this work.

References

Anantharaman, T., Campbell, M. S. and Hsu, F.-h. 1990. Singular Extensions: Adding Selectivity to Brute-Force Searching. *Artificial Intelligence*, 43(1): 99-110.

Appel, A. W. and Jacobson, G. J. 1988. The World's Fastest Scrabble Program. *Communications of the ACM*, 31(5): 572-578.

Baum, E. B. and Smith, W. D. 1997. A Bayesian Approach to Relevance in Game Playing. *Artificial Intelligence*, 97: 195-242.

Beal, D. and Smith, M. 1998. First results from Using Temporal Difference learning in Shogi. In *Proceedings of the First International Conference on Computers and Games*. Tsukuba, Japan.

Beal, D. F. 1990. A Generalised Quiescence Search Algorithm. *Artificial Intelligence*, 43(1): 85-98.

Bell, R. C. 1969. *Board and Table Games from Many Civilizations*. London: Oxford University Press.

Berliner, H. J. 1979. The B*Tree Search Algorithm: A Best-First Proof Procedure. *Artificial Intelligence*, 12(1): 23-40.

Berliner, H. J. 1987. Some Innovations Introduced by

HITECH. *ICAA Journal*, 18(2): 71-76.

Billings, D., Papp, D., Schaeffer, J. and Szafron, D. 1998. Opponent Modeling in Poker. In *Proceedings of the Fifteenth National Conference on Artificial Intelligence*, 493-499. Madison: AAAI Press.

Biswas, G., Goldman, S., Fisher, D., Bhuva, B. and Glewwe, G. 1995. Assessing Design Activity in Complex CMOS Circuit Design. In P. Nichols, S. Chipman, & R. Brennan (Ed.), *Cognitively Diagnostic Assessment*, Hillsdale, NJ: Lawrence Erlbaum.

Bjornsson, Y. and Marsland, T. 1998. Fritz 5.0 Wins the 1997 Herschberg Best-Annotation Award. *ICCA Journal*, 20(1): 65-66.

Blair, J., Mutchler, D. and Liu, C. 1993. Games with Imperfect Information. In *Proceedings of the Fall Symposium on Games: Planning and Learning*, 59-67.

Burmeister, J., Saito, Y., Yoshikawa, A. and Wiles, J. 1997. Memory Performance of Master Go Players. In *Proceedings of the IJCAI Workshop on Using Games as an Experimental Testbed for AI Research*.

Buro, M. 1998. From Simple Features to Sophisticated Evaluation Functions. In *Proceedings of the 1st International Conference on Computers and Games*. Tsukuba.

Chase, W. G. and Simon, H. A. 1973. The Mind's Eye in Chess. In W. G. Chase (Ed.), *Visual Information Processing*, 215-281. New York: Academic Press.

Crowley, K. and Siegler, R. S. 1993. Flexible Strategy Use in Young Children's Tic-Tac-Toe. *Cognitive Science*, 17(4): 531-561.

de Groot, A. 1965. *Thought and Choice in Chess*. The Hague: Mouton.

Dobson, D. and Forbus, K. (1999). *Proceedings of the AAAI 1999 Spring Symposium on Artificial Intelligence and Computer Games*.

Eisenstadt, M. and Kareev, Y. 1975. Aspects of Human Problem Solving: The Use of Internal Representations. In D. A. Norman, & D. E. Rumelhart (Ed.), *Explorations in Cognition*, 308-346. San Francisco: Freeman.

Epstein, S. L., Gelfand, J. and Lock, E. T. 1998. Learning Game-Specific Spatially-Oriented Heuristics. *Constraints*, 3(2-3): 239-253.

Ericsson, K. A., Krampe, R. T. and Tesch-Römer, C. 1993. The Role of Deliberate Practice in the Acquisition of Expert Performance. *Psychological Review*, 100(3): 363-406.

Frank, I., Basin, D. and Matsubara, H. 1998. Finding Optimal Strategies for Incomplete Information Games. In *Proceedings of the Fifteenth National Conference on Artificial Intelligence*, 500-507. Madison: AAAI Press.

Gobet, F. 1998. Chess Players' Thinking Revisited. *Swiss Journal of Psychology*, 57(1): 18-32.

Gobet, F. and Simon, H. 1996. Templates in Chess memory: A Mechanism for Recalling Several Boards. *Cognitive Psychology*, 31: 1-40.

Hamilton, C. M. and Hedberg, S. 1997. Modern Masters of an Ancient Game. *AI Magazine*, 18(4): 11-12.

Holding, D. 1985. *The Psychology of Chess Skill*. Hillsdale, NJ: Lawrence Erlbaum.

Isozaki, H. and Katsuno, J. 1996. A Semantic Characterization of an Algorithm for Estimating Others' Beliefs from Observation. In *Proceedings of the Thirteenth National Conference on Artificial Intelligence*, 543-549. MIT Press.

McAllester, D. A. 1988. Conspiracy Numbers for Min-Max Search. *Artificial Intelligence*, 35(3): 287-310.

Nichelli, P., Grafman, J., Pietrini, P., Alway, D., Carton, J. and Miletich, R. 1994. Brain Activity in Chess Playing. *Nature*, 369: 191.

Palay, A. J. 1985. *Searching with Probabilities*. Pitman.

Ratterman, M. J. and Epstein, S. L. 1995. Skilled like a Person: A Comparison of Human and Computer Game Playing. In *Proceedings of the Seventeenth Annual Conference of the Cognitive Science Society*, 709-714. Pittsburgh: Lawrence Erlbaum Associates.

Reitman, J. S. 1976. Skilled Perception in Go: Deducing Memory Structures from Inter-Response Times. *Cognitive Psychology*, 8: 36-356.

Rivest, R. L. 1987. Game Tree Searching by Min/Max Approximation. *Artificial Intelligence*, 34(1): 77-96.

Saito, Y. and Yoshikawa, A. 1997. Go as a Testbed for Cognitive Science Studies. In *Proceedings of the IJCAI-97 Workshop on Using Games as an Experimental Testbed for AI Research*.

Schaeffer, J. 1997. *One Jump Ahead: Challenging Human Supremacy in Checkers*. New York: Springer-Verlag.

Schaeffer, J. (1999). Personal communication.

Shannon, C. E. 1950. Programming a Computer for Playing Chess. 41(256): 275.

Sheppard, B. (1999). Personal communication.

Slate, D. J. and Atkin, L. R. 1977. CHESS 4.5 - The Northwestern University Chess Program. In P. Frey (Ed.), *Chess Skill in Man and Machine*, Berlin: Springer.

Tesauro, G. 1995. Temporal Difference Learning and TD-Gammon. *CACM*, 38(3): 58-68.

Tversky, B. 1989. Parts, Partonomies, and Taxonomies. *Developmental Psychology*, 25(6): 983-995.

Tversky, B. 1990. Where Partonomies and Taxonomies Meet. In S. L. Tsohatzidis (Ed.), *Meanings and Prototypes - Studies in Linguistic Categorization*, 334-344. London: Routledge.

Waitzkin, F. (1990). *Kasparov*. The New York Times Magazine: 28-30, 60-64, 86-87.

Yoshikawa, A., Kojima, T. and Saito, Y. 1998. Relation between the Way of Using Terms and the Skill - from Analysis of Protocols of the Game of Go. In *Proceedings of the First International Conference on Computers and Games*, 211-227. Tsukuba.

Yoshikawa, A. and Saito, Y. 1997. Hybrid Pattern Knowledge: Go Players' Knowledge Representation for Solving Tsume-Go Problems. In *Proceedings of the South Korean International Conference on Cognitive Science*.

Zaslavsky, C. 1982. *Tic Tac Toe and Other Three-in-a-Row Games, from Ancient Egypt to the Modern Computer*. New York: Crowell.

Index